OAS-L	OAS's definition of Latin America (*see* p. x and SALA, 24-1000)		P10I	per ten thousand inhabitants
OECD	Organization for Economic Cooperation and Development		PTP	percent of total population
			R-GAP	relative gap
OECS	Organization of Eastern Caribbean States (*see* SALA, 24-1000)		SDRs	Special Drawing Rights (IMF's currency)
			SNA	system of national accounts
OPEC	Organization of Petroleum Exporting Countries		T	Thousand (i.e., 000 omitted)
p (pp)	page(s)		TJ	Terajoules
PC	percentage change		U	unit
PHI	per hundred inhabitants		UN	United Nations
PHTI	per hundred thousand inhabitants		US	U.S. currency
PI	per inhabitant		U.S. or USA	United States of America
PIB	*producto interno bruto* (English = GDP)		WDC	Washington, D.C.
PMI	per million inhabitants		YA	yearly arithmetic mean
PTI	per thousand inhabitants		YE	year end

Sources

Sources frequently cited (abbreviation generally shows agency followed by title of publication or series).
Other sources appear in tables throughout.

ADEMA	*See* ECLA		IASI-C	*Características de la Estructura Demográfica*
AE	Anuario Estadístico		IBRD	International Bank for Reconstruction and Development. (*see* WB)
AR	Annual Report			
BDM	Banco de México		ICAO	International Civil Aviation Organization
BID	Banco Interamericano de Desarrollo (*see* IDB)		ICAO-DS-B	Digest of Statistics, *Bulletin*
C/CAA	Caribbean/Central American Action, *Caribbean Data Book*		ICAO-DS-T	Digest of Statistics, *Traffic: Commercial Air Carriers*
CELADE	Centro Latinoamericano de Demografía (Santiago)		ICAO-DS-AT	Digest of Statistics, *Airport Traffic*
			IDA	International Development Association
CELADE-BD	*Boletín Demográfico*		IDB	Inter-American Development Bank (WDC)
CEPAL	Comisión Económica para América Latina (*see* ECLA)		IDB-AR	*Annual Report*
			IDB-SPTF	Social Progress Trust Fund, *Socio-Economic Progress in Latin America* (1961-71)
COHA	Council on Hemispheric Affairs, *Washington Report on the Hemisphere*			
			IDB-ESPLA	*Economic and Social Progress in Latin America* (1972)
Colombia-DANE	Departamento Administrativo Nacional			
Cuba-CEE	Comité Estatal de Estadística		ILO	International Labour Office (Geneva)
DGE	Dirección General de Estadística		ILO-YLS	*Yearbook of Labor Statistics*
DGEC	Dirección General de Estadística y Censos		IMF	International Monetary Fund (WDC)
ECLA	Economic Commission for Latin America (Santiago)		IMF-BPS	*Balance of Payment Statistics*
			IMF-BPS-Y	*Balance of Payment Statistics Yearbook*
ECLA-ADEMA	*Agua, Desarrollo y Medio Ambiente* (1977)		IMF-DOT	*Direction of Trade Statistics*
ECLA-AE	*Anuario Estadístico de América Latina*		IMF-DOT-Y	*Yearbook*
ECLA-BPAL	*Balance de Pagos 1950-77*		IMF-GFSY	*Government Finance Statistics Yearbook*
ECLA-CC	Cuadernos de la CEPAL		IMF-IFS	*International Financial Statistics*
ECLA-CEC	Cuadernos Estadísticos de la CEPAL		IMF-IFS-S	*IFS Supplement* (No. 1, 1981–). (*See also* IFS-Y)
ECLA-D	Document			
ECLA-EIC	*Estudios e Informes de la CEPAL*		IMF-IFS-Y	*Yearbook* (entitled IFS-S from 1961 through 1978)
ECLA-N	*Notas sobre la Economía y el Desarrollo*			
ECLA-S	*Economic Survey of Latin America*		INE	Instituto Nacional de Estadística
ECLA-SHCAL	*Series Históricas del Crecimiento 1900-76* (1978)		INEC	Instituto Nacional de Estadística y Censos
			JLP	José López Portillo (Mexico City)
ECLA-SP	Preliminary version of ECLA-S		JLP-AE-H	*Anexo Estadístico Histórico*
ECLA-SY	*Statistical Yearbook* (*see* ECLA-AE)		JLP-AP-E	*Anexo de Política Económica*
EYB	*Europa Year Book*		Mexico-	
FAO	UN, Food and Agriculture Organization (Rome)		BANAMEX	Banco Nacional de México
			BANAMEX-	
FAO-FY	*Fertilizer Yearbook*		RESM	Review of the Economic Situation of Mexico
FAO-PY	*Production Yearbook* (1958-)		Mexico-BDM	Banco de México
FAO-SFA	*State of Food and Agriculture*		BDM-IE	*Indicadores Económicos*
FAO-TY	*Trade Yearbook* (1958-)		BDM-IE-AH	*Indicadores Económicos, Acervo Histórico*
FAO-YFP	*Yearbook of Forestry Products*		Mexico-BNCE	Banco Nacional de Comercio Exterior
FAO-YFS	*Yearbook of Fishery Statistics*		BNCE-CE	*Comercio Exterior*
FAO-YFSCL	*Catches and Landings*		Mexico-INEGI	Instituto Nacional de Estadística, Geografía e Informática
FAO-YFSFC	*Fishery Commodities*			
IASI	OAS, Inter-American Statistical Institute		INEGI-EHM	Estadísticas Históricas de México
IASI-AC	*América en Cifras*		Mexico-NAFINSA	Nacional Financiera, S.A.
IASI-BE	*Boletín Estadístico*		NAFINSA-EMC	*La Economía Mexicana en Cifras*

Continued on back endsheet.

STATISTICAL ABSTRACT OF LATIN AMERICA

Series Editor

JAMES W. WILKIE

SALA PUBLICATION HISTORY

Edition	Editors	Year of Publication
1 (1955)	[Robert N. Burr and Russell H. Fitzgibbon], 8 tables	1956
2 (1956)	[John D. Rees], 10 tables	1957
3 (1957)	[Berl Golomb], 18 tables	1959
4 (1960)	[Berl Golomb], 20 tables	1960
5 (1961)	[Berl Golomb], 23 tables	1961
6 (1962)	Berl Golomb and Ronald H. Dolkart, 51 tables	1963
7 (1963)	Donald S. Castro, Berl Golomb, and C. Breyer, 59 tables	1963
8 (1964)	Juan Gómez-Quiñones, 78 tables	1965
9 (1965)	Norris B. Lyle and Richard A. Calman, 102 tables	1966
10 (1966)	C. Paul Roberts and Takako Kohda, 81 tables	1967
11 (1967)	C. Paul Roberts and Takako Kohda, 95 tables	1968
12 (1968)	C. Paul Roberts and Takako Kohda Karplus, 102 tables	1969
13 (1969)	Kenneth Ruddle and Mukhtar Hamour, 131 tables	1970
14 (1970)	Kenneth Ruddle and Mukhtar Hamour, 200 tables	1971
15 (1971)	Kenneth Ruddle and Donald Odermann, 195 tables	1973
16 (1972)	Kenneth Ruddle and Kathleen Barrows, 282 tables	1974
17*	James W. Wilkie and Paul Turovsky, 303 tables	1976
18	James W. Wilkie and Peter Reich, 415 tables	1977
19	James W. Wilkie and Peter Reich, 439 tables	1978
20	James W. Wilkie and Peter Reich, 684 tables	1980
21	James W. Wilkie and Stephen Haber, 666 tables	1981
22	James W. Wilkie and Stephen Haber, 752 tables	1983
23	James W. Wilkie and Adam Perkal, 892 tables	1984
24	James W. Wilkie and Adam Perkal, 982 tables	1985
25	James W. Wilkie and David E. Lorey, 1063 tables	1987
26	James W. Wilkie, David E. Lorey, and Enrique Ochoa, 1077 tables	1988
27	James W. Wilkie and Enrique Ochoa, 1259 tables	1989
28	James W. Wilkie, Enrique C. Ochoa, and David E. Lorey, 1353 tables	1990

*Beginning with volume 17, designation by volume number rather than year of edition.

STATISTICAL ABSTRACT OF LATIN AMERICA

Volume 28

JAMES W. WILKIE
Editor

ENRIQUE C. OCHOA
and
DAVID E. LOREY
Co-Editors

UCLA Latin American Center Publications
University of California ● Los Angeles

Citation

James W. Wilkie, Enrique C. Ochoa, and David E. Lorey, eds., *Statistical Abstract of Latin America*, Volume 28 (Los Angeles: UCLA Latin American Center Publications, University of California, 1990).

Other Library Entries

1. Statistical Abstract of Latin America.

2. California. University, Los Angeles. Latin American Center. Statistical Abstract of Latin America.

3. [Earlier name]. California. Univeristy, Los Angeles. Committee on Latin American Studies. Statistical Abstract of Latin America.

4. University of California. Los Angeles. Latin American Center. *Statistical Abstract of Latin America.*

Statistical Abstract of Latin America Volume 28
UCLA Latin American Center Publications
Los Angeles, California 90024-1447

Copyright © 1990 by The Regents of the University of California

ISBN (cloth): 0-87903-252-9

Library of Congress Card Number: 56-63569

Printed in the United States of America

Contents

PART VIII. FOREIGN TRADE

PART IX. FINANCIAL FLOWS

PART X. NATIONAL ACCOUNTS, GOVERNMENT POLICY AND FINANCE, AND PRICES

PART XI. DEVELOPMENT OF DATA

Preface

Goals of the Statistical Abstract

The goals of the *Statistical Abstract of Latin America* (SALA) are ten:

1. To provide a yearly one-volume selection of important statistics culled from more than 200 sources.
2. To offer the latest figures available on a timely basis for the 20 countries of Latin America, defined below.
3. To provide a context for present and future-oriented statistics by presenting whenever possible the data in series covering several decades or years.
4. To generate through research new data not published elsewhere.
5. To develop new types of data and/or to provide new analytical treatment of statistical series through SALA-sponsored research.
6. To guide the user of this volume to the wide variety of statistical material and sources available.
7. To suggest kinds of data that may be found in other sources as well as where to look for more complete coverage than can be abstracted here.
8. To present maps and graphs so that statistics take on greater meaning than would otherwise be possible to achieve.
9. To provide a SALA Supplement Series which offers interpretation, longitudinal data, and cartographic analysis of statistics on Latin America.
10. To coordinate presentation of statistics in SALA with the theory and model presented in James W. Wilkie, *Statistics and National Policy*, Statistical Abstract of Latin America, Supplement 3 (1974).

Organization

In order to accomplish these goals, SALA is organized in the following ways:

1. Historical statistics are presented across time. As new statistics become available, they can be traced back in time from volume to volume generating a long-term profile of Latin America's past and present as well as providing baselines for projecting into the future.
2. Explicit sources and qualifying notes are given for all data presented. Sources are given at the end of each table, not at the end of chapters where difficulty of use would be increased manyfold.
3. Source abbreviations and symbols are standardized. A key to sources is included for convenient reference.

4. A section on "Explanation of Terms" lists the abbreviations used. This information is repeated in the front endsheets for easy use.
5. The "Note on Statistical Definitions" gives weight and measure equivalencies and explains alternative methods for calculating rate of change over time.
6. Data are cross-referenced from one table to another throughout the volume.
7. Each volume is fully indexed to help readers find topics and related subjects.
8. A "Guide to Data" section in some volumes leads the user to additional sources and supplemental bibliographic aids.
9. The "Development of Data" section contains analysis of concepts, problems, and methods in organizing new topics or chapters included in SALA.
10. A carefully selected international advisory board guides the research and compilation for SALA and its Supplements.

Thus, SALA is intended to be the standard source for statistical information on Latin America and to encourage the use of data by scholars, researchers, business, and governments.

Cautions in Use of Statistics

Readers are cautioned that all data for any topic vary according to definition, parameters, methods of compilation and calculation, and completeness of coverage as well as data gathered, and/or date adjusted. Indeed, readers are reminded that statistics do not reveal "truth," but rather serve as proxy to interpret reality, and alternative statistics are available for most data series. Although such data as import statistics are often suspect because they do not take into account the extensive smuggling of goods, such figures are important because national and international policy decisions are made on the basis of the data recorded, data which interact with events to help change the course of "history." In this manner, "statistical reality" becomes quite as important as "reality" itself.

Presentation of Data

To help make the SALA series more useful to readers, beginning with Volume 24, we have included alternative data in the form of partial tables from previous issues going back to Volume 17. Previously we included in a cumulative index references to tables not reprinted from volume to volume. Such an index, however, created a problem for investigators who had to consult each back issue in order to determine whether or not (regardless of title) the table format carried the information (or additional data) actually sought.

For example, the method of presenting a partial table showing subheadings and data for one country among the twenty permits the reader to see at a glance the relevance of the type of information given, hence eliminating searches in earlier issues.

Elimination of the cumulative index also has two added advantages:

1. Data and references (to full data in the partial tables) on similar topics are now grouped together and not separated between the chapters and the index.
2. No cumulative index is necessary—the cumulative index often led readers to the same table (with no new information) reprinted in more than one volume for persons who might not have a complete set of SALA.

Latin America Defined

The concept of Latin America used in SALA utilizes the standard definition involving 20 countries. This standard definition is used for two reasons. First, Latin America's own self-identification of the 20 countries is critical, as discussed below. Second, data are not consistently available for the various other definitions of Latin America, some of which include units (such as Martinique and French Guiana) that are not independent bodies but rather colonies of Europe, legally as well as in economic and financial flows. Although SALA focuses on the standard list of 20 countries of Latin America, at times comparative data are given for bodies considered part of the region when it is defined in extended terms, that is, as Extended Latin America (ELA).

The 20 countries of Latin America (coded A through T) are presented in table 1, which presents Latin America as perceived by itself. According to Latin America's self-identification, the region is traditionally united by core language, religion, culture, bureaucratic outlook, and timing of the post-independence experience based upon nineteenth-century liberalism and free trade. Haiti is included not because of its Latin-based French language but because of its interaction with the Dominican Republic (which it ruled between 1822 and 1844) and its historic identification with Latin American affairs. Former non-Spanish colonies of the Caribbean and South America are excluded because they have had little or no interaction in dialogue and events in Latin America. Puerto Rico is excluded from Latin America, of course, because it has never been independent, belonging until 1898 to Spain and subsequently to the United States.

Problems in the definition of Latin America have come from several directions. After 1910 the 20 traditional Latin American republics (plus the United States) made up the Pan

Table 1

THE 20 COUNTRIES OF LATIN AMERICA

A. ARGENTINA	K. GUATEMALA
B. BOLIVIA	L. HAITI
C. BRAZIL	M. HONDURAS
D. CHILE	N. MEXICO
E. COLOMBIA	O. NICARAGUA
F. COSTA RICA	P. PANAMA
G. CUBA	Q. PARAGUAY
H. DOMINICAN REPUBLIC	R. PERU
I. ECUADOR	S. URUGUAY
J. EL SALVADOR	T. VENEZUELA

Source: See table 1001.

American Union, known since 1948 as the Organization of American States (OAS). Cuba was expelled from the OAS in 1962, reducing the number of Latin American members to 19. In 1967 the former English colonies of Barbados and Trinidad-Tobago joined the OAS as did Jamaica in 1969; and thus, in the minds of those who equate the Latin American region with the OAS, the number of countries south of the U.S. border rose to 22. Canada joined the OAS in 1990, further complicating the relationship of the OAS and nontraditionally defined Latin America. Statistical publications of the OAS in the 1970s began to compare total figures for the 22 countries with data for the United States, with the total reaching 31 in the 1980s. Additional problems of definition come from some geographically minded observers who have sought to delimit the world neatly into physical regions regardless of cultural ties and other historical patterns. For those observers "Latin America" includes all of the islands of the Caribbean and the three South American mainland Guianas (see table 3) even though they are oriented toward Europe. Latin America sees its own regional groupings in table 2.

With regard to cartographic representation, which shows the size of countries according to population rather than according to geographical area, several views help in understanding the relationships of Latin America's 20 countries. The situation in 1980 is shown in figure 6:1 (see Chapter 6). The cartographic view in 1972 of Latin America's 20 countries (figure 1) is compared to that view for Extended Latin America (ELA) based on 30 political units (figure 2). In 1972 Latin America had an estimated population of 283,822,140 compared with ELA's 291,646,708. The difference of 7.8 million meant that Latin America had 97 percent of ELA's population. Of ELA's 19 metropolitan areas of one million persons or more in 1972, 18 were in Latin America. San Juan, Puerto Rico, was the only major city in ELA outside of Latin America proper.

Various definitions of Extended Latin America are given in table 3, with concepts differing according to agency. ELA contains up to 25 more bodies than the 20 standard Latin

Table 2

REGIONAL GROUPINGS IN LATIN AMERICA

LAIA   *Latin American Integration Association*
(Latin American Free Trade Association [LAFTA]
from 1960–80)

Member	Date of Entry
ARGENTINA	Jan. 1981
BOLIVIA	Mar. 1982
BRAZIL	Nov. 1981
CHILE	May 1981
COLOMBIA	May 1981
ECUADOR	Mar. 1982
MEXICO	Feb. 1981
PARAGUAY	Dec. 1980
PERU	Nov. 1981
URUGUAY	Mar. 1981
VENEZUELA	Mar. 1982

AG   *Cartagena Agreement, Andean Group*

Member	Date of Entry
BOLIVIA	Nov. 1969
CHILE	Sept. 1969[a]
COLOMBIA	Sept. 1969
ECUADOR	Nov. 1969
PERU	Oct. 1969
VENEZUELA	Nov. 1973

CACM   *Central American Common Market*

Member	Date of Entry
COSTA RICA	Sept. 1963
EL SALVADOR	May 1961
GUATEMALA	May 1961
HONDURAS	Apr. 1962[b]
NICARAGUA	May 1961

a. Withdrew Oct. 1976.
b. Withdrew Jan. 1971.

American countries. Table 3 expands Latin America to ELA on the basis of the "Caribbean" units defined by the Caribbean/Central American Action (C/CAA). Because C/CAA is oriented toward the U.S. legislative concept called the Caribbean Basin Initiative, C/CAA considers as belonging to the Caribbean 25 political units in addition to the Central American countries (including even El Salvador, which borders the Pacific Ocean, not the Caribbean). The FAO definition is almost as inclusive as that of the C/CAA, omitting only Bermuda. The OAS has 31 members, the Latin American countries plus the 11 included in table 3. (Since 1962 Cuba has been suspended from activities but not membership; Guyana has observer status but not membership.)

Figures 3 and 4 present a geographical view and a political view of ELA, respectively. Some small Caribbean islands appear as dots on these maps, but are better represented in figure 2 which portrays the population relationship.

The comparative land area of Latin America proper is detailed in table 4. Comparisons are made not only among the 20 countries but with states in the United States and with three small countries which have achieved major roles on the world stage—Israel, Japan, and Switzerland. Comparisons of the size of Latin American countries vary according to observers; for example, in England Guatemala is often compared to Greece but in Guatemala the comparison is to Holland, Belgium, and Switzerland. Latin America constitutes 97 percent of ELA, as can be calculated from table 6.

Rankings of the 20 Latin American countries are given in table 5. The countries with the first and third largest land area (Brazil and Mexico) contain 52.4 percent of the region's territory (see table 4). The countries with the first and second largest populations (Brazil and Mexico) contained 53.4 percent of the region's population in 1972—see figure 1. (In 1980 these two countries reached 54.3 percent of the total Latin American population, as can be calculated from figure 6:1.) The country with the smallest land area (El Salvador) was the highest in density even though it ranked 14 in population size. The country with the smallest population (Panama) ranked 16 in area and 11 in density. The country of median rank (10) in area is Ecuador, which in the 1970s ranked 9 in population and 13 in density.

For expanded discussion defining Latin America, see the Preface to SALA 23 and SALA 25.

Analysis of New Trends in Latin America or in Meaning of Statistical Data

In addition to organizing and presenting data, SALA often seeks through its Preface to assess new trends in the Latin American situation as well as types of data becoming available (or decreasing in availability). Previous issues of SALA contain discussion of the following topics:

"On the Accuracy of Statistics and Development of Time-Series Data" (vol. 19)
"On Defining the Concepts of Latin America, the Caribbean, and Economically Questionable Nations (EQNs)" (vol. 23)
"Views of Latin America's Reality," (vol. 25).

Development of Data

To develop new statistical series on Latin America, SALA and the SALA Supplement Series carry articles analyzing sources, methods, and findings. Articles appearing to date in SALA and Supplement 6 (*Quantitative Latin American Studies*, 1977), Supplement 7 (*Money and Politics in Latin America*, 1977), and Supplement 10 (*Society and Economy in Mexico*, 1990) include the following (arranged by area and topic):

Figure 1

POPULATION CARTOGRAM OF LATIN AMERICA

(1972)

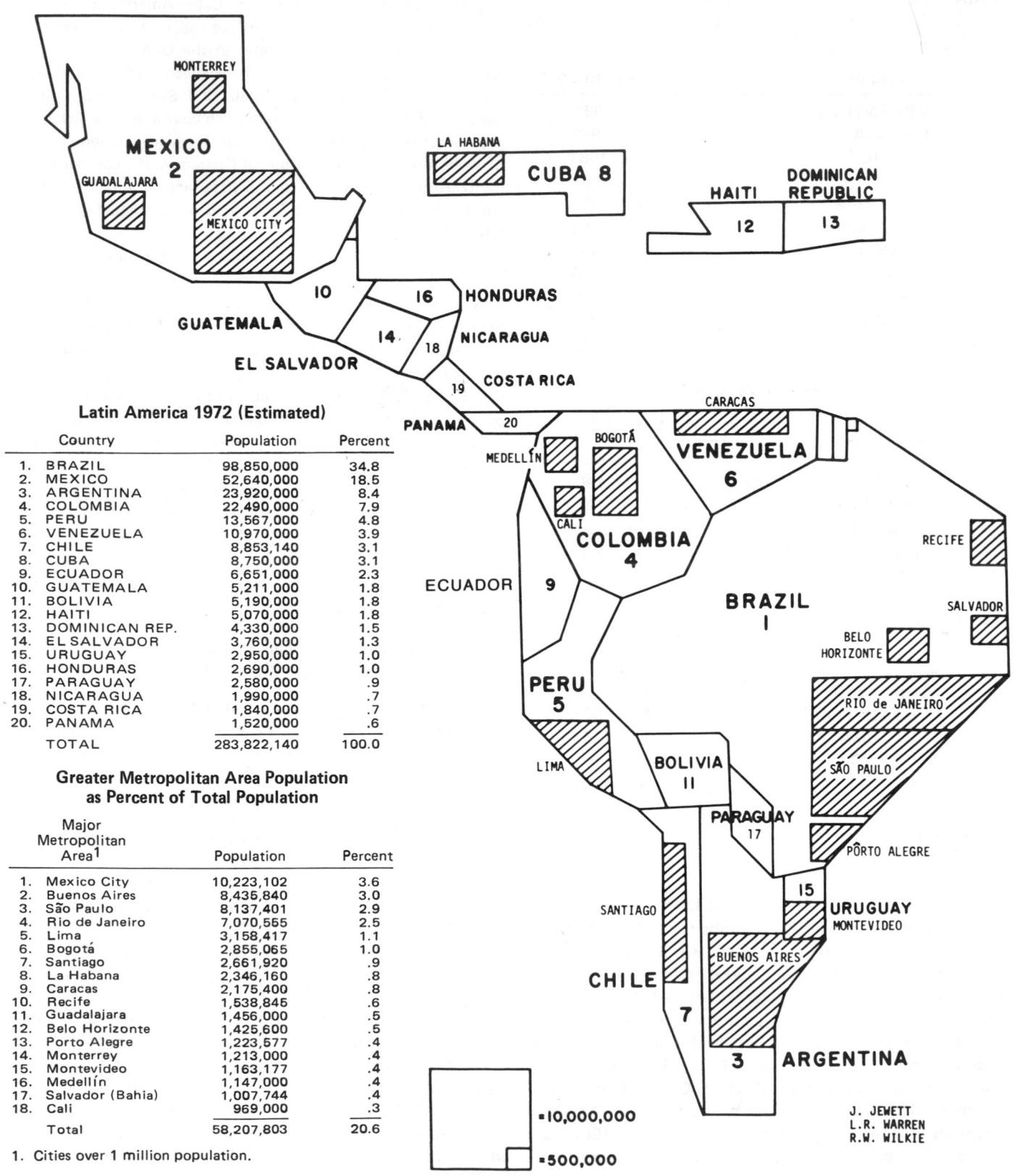

Latin America 1972 (Estimated)

	Country	Population	Percent
1.	BRAZIL	98,850,000	34.8
2.	MEXICO	52,640,000	18.5
3.	ARGENTINA	23,920,000	8.4
4.	COLOMBIA	22,490,000	7.9
5.	PERU	13,567,000	4.8
6.	VENEZUELA	10,970,000	3.9
7.	CHILE	8,853,140	3.1
8.	CUBA	8,750,000	3.1
9.	ECUADOR	6,651,000	2.3
10.	GUATEMALA	5,211,000	1.8
11.	BOLIVIA	5,190,000	1.8
12.	HAITI	5,070,000	1.8
13.	DOMINICAN REP.	4,330,000	1.5
14.	EL SALVADOR	3,760,000	1.3
15.	URUGUAY	2,950,000	1.0
16.	HONDURAS	2,690,000	1.0
17.	PARAGUAY	2,580,000	.9
18.	NICARAGUA	1,990,000	.7
19.	COSTA RICA	1,840,000	.7
20.	PANAMA	1,520,000	.6
	TOTAL	283,822,140	100.0

Greater Metropolitan Area Population as Percent of Total Population

	Major Metropolitan Area[1]	Population	Percent
1.	Mexico City	10,223,102	3.6
2.	Buenos Aires	8,435,840	3.0
3.	São Paulo	8,137,401	2.9
4.	Rio de Janeiro	7,070,555	2.5
5.	Lima	3,158,417	1.1
6.	Bogotá	2,855,065	1.0
7.	Santiago	2,661,920	.9
8.	La Habana	2,346,160	.8
9.	Caracas	2,175,400	.8
10.	Recife	1,538,845	.6
11.	Guadalajara	1,456,000	.5
12.	Belo Horizonte	1,425,600	.5
13.	Porto Alegre	1,223,577	.4
14.	Monterrey	1,213,000	.4
15.	Montevideo	1,163,177	.4
16.	Medellín	1,147,000	.4
17.	Salvador (Bahia)	1,007,744	.4
18.	Cali	969,000	.3
	Total	58,207,803	20.6

1. Cities over 1 million population.

J. JEWETT
L.R. WARREN
R.W. WILKIE

Figure 2

CARTOGRAM OF EXTENDED LATIN AMERICA (ELA)

(1972)

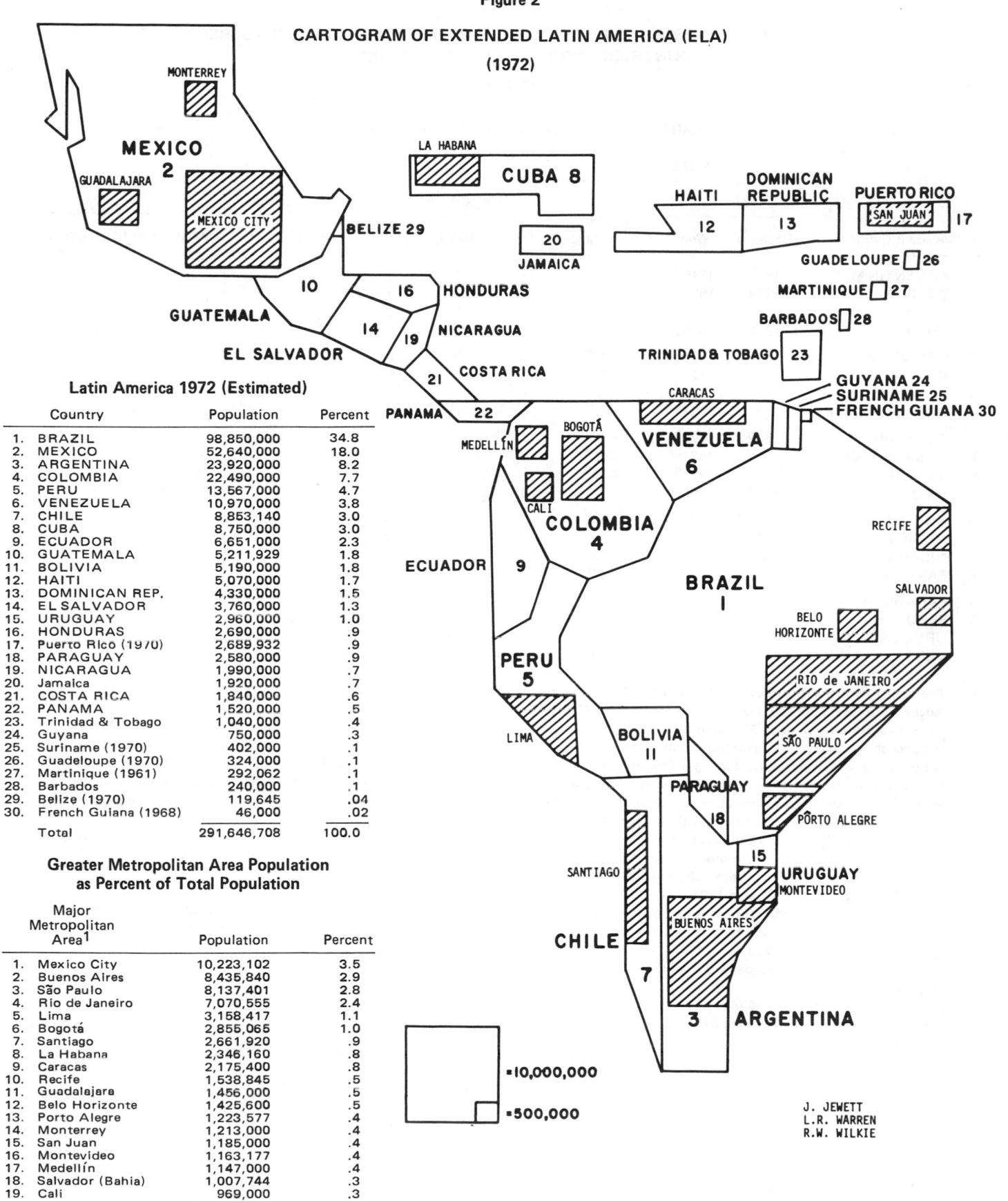

Latin America 1972 (Estimated)

	Country	Population	Percent
1.	BRAZIL	98,850,000	34.8
2.	MEXICO	52,640,000	18.0
3.	ARGENTINA	23,920,000	8.2
4.	COLOMBIA	22,490,000	7.7
5.	PERU	13,567,000	4.7
6.	VENEZUELA	10,970,000	3.8
7.	CHILE	8,853,140	3.0
8.	CUBA	8,750,000	3.0
9.	ECUADOR	6,651,000	2.3
10.	GUATEMALA	5,211,929	1.8
11.	BOLIVIA	5,190,000	1.8
12.	HAITI	5,070,000	1.7
13.	DOMINICAN REP.	4,330,000	1.5
14.	EL SALVADOR	3,760,000	1.3
15.	URUGUAY	2,960,000	1.0
16.	HONDURAS	2,690,000	.9
17.	Puerto Rico (1970)	2,689,932	.9
18.	PARAGUAY	2,580,000	.9
19.	NICARAGUA	1,990,000	.7
20.	Jamaica	1,920,000	.7
21.	COSTA RICA	1,840,000	.6
22.	PANAMA	1,520,000	.5
23.	Trinidad & Tobago	1,040,000	.4
24.	Guyana	750,000	.3
25.	Suriname (1970)	402,000	.1
26.	Guadeloupe (1970)	324,000	.1
27.	Martinique (1961)	292,062	.1
28.	Barbados	240,000	.1
29.	Belize (1970)	119,645	.04
30.	French Guiana (1968)	46,000	.02
	Total	291,646,708	100.0

Greater Metropolitan Area Population as Percent of Total Population

	Major Metropolitan Area[1]	Population	Percent
1.	Mexico City	10,223,102	3.5
2.	Buenos Aires	8,435,840	2.9
3.	São Paulo	8,137,401	2.8
4.	Rio de Janeiro	7,070,555	2.4
5.	Lima	3,158,417	1.1
6.	Bogotá	2,855,065	1.0
7.	Santiago	2,661,920	.9
8.	La Habana	2,346,160	.8
9.	Caracas	2,175,400	.8
10.	Recife	1,538,845	.5
11.	Guadalajara	1,456,000	.5
12.	Belo Horizonte	1,425,600	.5
13.	Porto Alegre	1,223,577	.4
14.	Monterrey	1,213,000	.4
15.	San Juan	1,185,000	.4
16.	Montevideo	1,163,177	.4
17.	Medellín	1,147,000	.4
18.	Salvador (Bahia)	1,007,744	.3
19.	Cali	969,000	.3
	Total	59,079,038	20.3

1. Cities over 1 million population.

J. JEWETT
L.R. WARREN
R.W. WILKIE

Table 3

POLITICAL DEPENDENCE, INDEPENDENCE, AND INTERNATIONAL MEMBERSHIPS OF COUNTRIES AND TERRITORIES, 20 L AND 45 ELA

(1983)

PART I. TRADITIONALLY DEFINED LATIN AMERICA

	As Result of			Memberships							
	War[2]		Special								
Independent Countries[1]	Declared	Won	Circumstances	OAS	IDB:L	ECLA:L	ALADI	AG	CACM	CBI-IB	SELA
A. ARGENTINA	1810	1816[a]		A	A	A	A				A
B. BOLIVIA	1809	1825[a]		B	B	B	B	B			B
C. BRAZIL			1822[b]	C	C	C	C				C
D. CHILE	1810	1818[a]		D	D	D	D	D[5]			D
E. COLOMBIA	1810	1824[a]	1830[e]	E	E	E	E	E			E
F. COSTA RICA		1821[c]	1838[d]	F	F	F			F	F	F
G. CUBA		1898[a]	1902[i]	G[4]		G					G
H. DOMINICAN REP.[3]		1821[a]	1844[h]	H	H	H				H	H
I. ECUADOR[7]	1809	1822[a]	1830[e]	I	I	I	I	I			I
J. EL SALVADOR		1821[c]	1841[d]	J	J	J			J	J	J
K. GUATEMALA		1821[c]	1839[d]	K	K	K			K	K	K
L. HAITI	1791	1804[k]		L	L	L				L	L
M. HONDURAS		1821[c]	1838[d]	M	M	M			M[6]	M	M
N. MEXICO	1810	1821[a]		N	N	N	N				N
O. NICARAGUA		1821[c]	1838[d]	O	O	O			O	O	O
P. PANAMA			1903[j]	P	P	P				P	P
Q. PARAGUAY			1811[a]	Q	Q	Q	Q				Q
R. PERU	1821	1824[a,f]		R	R	R	R	I			R
S. URUGUAY	1811	1814[a]	1828[l]	S	S	S	S				S
T. VENEZUELA[7]	1810	1821[a,g]	1829[e]	T	T	T	T	T			T

1. The three events that provided the immediate stimulation for independence were the U.S. War for Independence (1776-81); the French Revolution of 1789 proclaiming the Rights of Man and abolishing slavery for France but not its colonies—the most prosperous of which was Saint Domingue (the future Haiti); and the capture of the Spanish monarch by Napoleon Bonaparte, Spain's "ally," who placed his brother Joseph on the throne of Spain in 1808, thus breaking strong allegiances between Spain and its colonies. (The latter event occurred after France had passed through Spain, driving the monarchy of Portugal to Brazil in 1807, laying the basis for Brazil's independence once the monarchy returned to Portugal in 1821.)
2. Excludes precursor movements such as that by Tiradentes in 1788 (Brazil) or by Miranda in 1806 (Venezuela).
3. France ceded to Spain in 1795.
4. Since 1962 Cuba has been suspended from OAS activities but not membership.
5. Chile withdrew from AG in 1976.
6. Honduras partially withdrew from CACM in 1971.
7. Member of OPEC.

a. Won from Spain.
b. Won from Portugal.
c. Won from Spain and became part of Mexico in 1822-23.
d. Breakup of United Provinces of Central America, which existed to unite Costa Rica, El Salvador, Guatemala, Honduras, and Nicaragua from 1823 to 1841. For all practical purposes the breakup came by 1838 and attempts to revive union were militarily defeated by 1842.
e. Breakup of Gran Colombia, which existed to unite Colombia, Ecuador, and Venezuela from 1819 to 1830.
f. Last Spanish troops left Peru in 1826.
g. Last Spanish troops left Venezuela in 1823.
h. Won from Haiti, which governed Hispaniola or Santo Domingo (future Dominican Republic) from 1822 to 1844. Spain reoccupied from 1861 to 1865.
i. Won from the United States.
j. Won from Colombia.
k. Won from France.
l. Won from Brazil.

SOURCE: SALA, 23-1.

Table 3 (Continued)

POLITICAL DEPENDENCE, INDEPENDENCE, AND INTERNATIONAL MEMBERSHIPS
OF COUNTRIES AND TERRITORIES, 20 L AND 45 ELA

(1983)

PART II. NON-TRADITIONALLY DEFINED LATIN AMERICA ADDS:

Independent Countries	Year of Independence	From	Organization by Country								
			OAS	IDB:L	ECLA:L	CARICOM[1]	ECCM	OECS	CBI-IB	FAO[4]	SELA[5]
1. Antigua-Barbuda	1981	Gr. Britain	1			1	1	1	1	1	
2. Bahamas	1973	Gr. Britain	2	2	2				2	2	
3. Barbados	1966	Gr. Britain	3	3	3	3			3	3	3
4. Belize	1981	Gr. Britain				4			4	4	
5. Dominica	1978	Gr. Britain	5			5	5	5	5	5	
6. Grenada	1974	Gr. Britain	6		6	6	6	6	6	6	6
7. Guyana	1966	Gr. Britain		7	7	7			7	7	7
8. Jamaica	1962	Gr. Britain	8	8	8	8			8	8	8
9. St. Kitts-Nevis[2]	1983	Gr. Britain	9			9	9	9	9	9	
10. St. Lucia	1977	Gr. Britain	10			10	10	10	10	10	
11. St. Vincent-Grenadines	1979	Gr. Britain	11			11	11	11	11	11	
12. Suriname	1975	Netherlands	12	12	12				12	12	12
13. Trinidad and Tobago	1962	Gr. Britain	13	13	13	13					13

Dependent Countries	Belonging to	OAS	IDB:L	ICLA:L	CARICOM[1]	ECCM	OECS	CBI-IB	FAO
T1. Anguilla	Great Britain					T1			T1
T2. Bermuda	Great Britain[3]								
T3. British Virgin Islands	Great Britain							T3	T3
T4. Cayman Islands	Great Britain							T4	T4
T5. French Guiana	France								T5
T6. Guadeloupe	France								T6
T7. Martinique	France								T7
T8. Montserrat	Great Britain				T8	T8	T8	T8	T8
T9. Netherlands Antilles	Netherlands							T9	T9
T10. Puerto Rico	United States								T10
T11. Turks and Caicos	Great Britain							T11	T11
T12. U.S. Virgin Islands	United States								T12

1. The Caribbean Community and Common Market (CARICOM)
   was established in 1973 to replace the Caribbean Free Trade
   Association (CARIFTA), founded in 1967.
2. St. Kitts is officially known as St. Christopher.
3. Bermuda has been self-governing since 1968. Although under
   Great Britain, it claims Bermudian nationality.
4. Includes Falkland Islands.
5. The Sistema Económico para Latinoamérica was established in
   October 1975.

SOURCE: Various, including especially C/CAA, 1983; COHA, May 4,
1982, p. 4; WA, 1987, p. 640.

Table 4

LAND AREA OF LATIN AMERICA, 20 LRC

Country	% of Latin America	Sq Mi. (T)	Equals Approximate Foreign Area as Coded	
Latin American Total	100.0	7.686	ASA	2 X the 50 U.S. States[6]
A. ARGENTINA[1,2]	14.0	1,072	ASA	4 X Texas
B. BOLIVIA[4]	5.5	423	SLT	California and Texas
C. BRAZIL[2]	42.5	3,265	ASA	9% larger than continental U.S.[7]
D. CHILE[1,2]	3.8	292	SLT	2 X California
E. COLOMBIA[2]	5.7	440	SLT	California, Texas, Maryland and Connecticut
F. COSTA RICA	.3	20	ASA	5 X Los Angeles County
G. CUBA	.6	44	SLT	Pennsylvania
H. DOMINICAN REP.	.2	19	ASA	Vermant and New Hampshire
I. ECUADOR[2]	1.4	104	ASA	Colorado
J. EL SALVADOR	.1	8	ASA	2 X Los Angeles County
K. GUATEMALA	.5	42	ASA	Tennessee
L. HAITI	.1	11	ASA	Maryland
M. HONDURAS	.6	43	MT	Tennessee
N. MEXICO[3]	9.9	760	SLT	3 X Texas
O. NICARAGUA[8]	.6	46	SLT	Mississippi
P. PANAMA[5]	.4	30	SLT	South Carolina
Q. PARAGUAY	2.0	157	SLT	California
R. PERU[2,9]	6.4	494	SLT	2 X Texas
S. URUGUAY	.9	69	MT	Washington State
T. VENEZUELA[2,10]	4.5	347	MT	2 X California
Israel	**	8	ASA	2 X Los Angeles County
Japan	**	144	SLT	California
Switzerland	**	16	ASA	4 X Los Angeles County

Code: ASA = about same as . . .
MT = more than . . .
SLT = slightly less than . . .

1. Excludes Argentina's South Atlantic islands and Antarctica (482,000 sq. mi.) and Chile's Antarctica (483,000 sq. mi.).
2. Excludes areas in litigation.
3. Excludes islands.
4. Excludes 1,424 sq. mi. of Bolivia's part of Lake Titicaca.
5. Includes Panama Canal Zone (568 sq. mi).
6. Fifty U.S. states = 3,540 sq. mi., excluding lakes.
7. Forty-eight continental states = 2,968 sq. mi., excluding lakes.
8. Excludes 3,474 sq. mi. of Nicaragua's lakes.
9. Excludes 1,917 sq. mi. of Peru's part of Lake Titicaca.
10. Excludes 5,113 sq. mi. of Venezuela's Lake Maracaibo and Lake Valencia.

SOURCE: Calculated from SALA, 21–300 and 21–301; IASI-AC, 1972, table 101–04 and IASC-AC, 1974, table 201–01. Bolivia is from Jorge Muñoz Reyes, *Geografía de Bolivia* (La Paz: Academia Nacional de Ciencias de Bolivia, 1977), p. 2; United States is from USBC-SA, 1978, p. 6. Israel, Japan, and Switzerland is from WA, 1984, pp. 509, 512, 541. For area in square kilometers, including each country's lakes and inland waters, see table 100, below.

Table 5

LATIN AMERICAN COUNTRIES RANKED ACCORDING TO AREA, POPULATION SIZE, AND DENSITY[1]

Country (Largest Area to Smallest)	Area (Excluding Lakes)[2]	Population (Highest = 1) (1972)	Density[3] (Lowest = 1) (1970s)[4]
BRAZIL	1	1	5
ARGENTINA	2	3	3
MEXICO	3	2	14
PERU	4	5	4
COLOMBIA	5	4	10
BOLIVIA	6	11	1
VENEZUELA	7	6	8
CHILE	8	7	7
PARAGUAY	9	17	2
ECUADOR	10	9	13
URUGUAY	11	15	9
NICARAGUA	12	18	6
CUBA	13	8	17
HONDURAS	14	16	12
GUATEMALA	15	10	16
PANAMA	16	20	11
COSTA RICA	17	19	15
DOMINICAN REP.	18	13	18
HAITI	19	12	19
EL SALVADOR	20	14	20

1. For discussion, see SALA 25, pp. xxii–xxvi.
2. Excluding lakes and inland waters; for these inclusions, see table 100 below.
3. Persons per km^2 (population divided by area).
4. Varying years from 1971 to 1982; according to data in tables 627–648.

SOURCE: SALA 25, p. xxiii.

Table 6

LATIN AMERICA LAND AREA IN ELA AND THE WORLD

Category	Area (k^2)	Explanation
World	132,495,836	
A. ELA[1]	20,447,284	A = B + G
B. Latin America	19,907,626	Included in A
C. CACM[2]	411,170	Included in B
D. ALADI[3]	19,228,658	Included in B
E. Andean Group	5,443,818	Included in D
F. CLA[4]	267,798	Included in B
G. CNLA[5]	539,658	Included in A
H. CARICOM[6]	257,384	Included in G

1. Extended Latin America.
2. Central American Common Market.
3. Latin American Integration Association.
4. Caribbean Latin America.
5. Caribbean Not Latin America.
6. Caribbean Community and Common Market.

SOURCE: Adapted in summary form from SALA, 23-2.

Figure 3

MAP OF EXTENDED LATIN AMERICA (ELA)

(Mercator Projection)

SOURCE: SALA-SNP, p. xxvi.

Figure 4

POLITICAL MAP OF EXTENDED LATIN AMERICA (ELA)

Latin America

"Announced U.S. Assistance to Latin America, 1946–88: Who Gets It? How Much? And When?," by Christof Anders Weber (vol. 28)

"U.S.–Latin American Senior-Level Exchanges, 1953–88," by John L. Martin (vol. 28)

"The People Speak: A Database and Sample Analysis of Latin American Public Opinion Polls, 1947–86," by Louise Harris Berlin (vol. 28)

"Comparative Analysis of Human Rights Violations under Military Rule in Argentina, Brazil, Chile, and Uruguay," by Peter John King (vol. 27)

"Soviet Economic Relations with Latin America: Trade and Economic Assistance since 1964," by Charles N. Grimes (vol. 27)

"The Rapid Expansion of Voter Participation in Latin America: Presidential Elections, 1845–1986," by Enrique C. Ochoa (vol. 25)

"On Measuring Political Conflict in Latin America, 1948–1967," by Manual Moreno-Ibáñez (vol. 20)

"Survey Research in Authoritarian Regimes: Brazil and the Southern Cone of Latin America Since 1970," by Brian H. Smith and Frederick C. Turner (vol. 23)

"Democratic versus Dictatorial Budgeting: The Case of Cuba with Reference to Venezuela and Mexico," by Enrique A. Baloyra (Supp. 7)

"Measuring the Scholarly Image of Latin American Democracy, 1945–1970," by Kenneth F. Johnson (vol. 17)

"Research Perspectives on the Revised Fitzgibbon-Johnson Index of the Image of Political Democracy in Latin America, 1945–1975," by Kenneth F. Johnson (Supp. 6)

"Measuring U.S. Government Perception of the 'Communist Menace' in Latin America, 1947–1976," by Peter Reich (vol. 19)

"Alternative Interpretations of Time-Series Data on the Growth of the Latin American Film Industry, 1926–1970," by Daniel I. Geffner (vol. 19)

"Religious Data History, [1956–1974]," by Peter Reich (vol. 18)

"Protestant Church Growth in Twentieth-Century Central America and the Caribbean," by T. D. Proffitt III (vol. 22)

"Exchange Rate History, 1937–1974," by Bridget Reynolds (vol. 17)

"Labor's Real Wages in Latin America Since 1940," by John L. Martin (vol. 18)

"Problems of Measuring Housing and Shelter in Latin America, 1940–1980," by Manual Moreno-Ibáñez (vol. 22)

"Projecting the HEC (Health, Education, and Communication) Index for Latin America Back to 1940," by James W. Wilkie and Maj-Britt Nilsson (Supp. 6)

"Educational Enrollment History, [1880–1929]," by José Casimiro Ortal (vol. 18)

"Food Production in Latin America Since 1942," by James W. Wilkie and Manual Moreno-Ibáñez (vol. 23)

"Latin American Fisheries: National Resources and Expanded Jurisdiction, 1938–1978," by Manual Moreno-Ibáñez (vol. 21)

"Problems in Comparative Crime Statistics for Latin America and the English-Speaking Caribbean, 1973–1978," by Luis P. Salas and Raymond Surette (vol. 23)

"Determining the Population in the Largest City of Each Latin American Country, 1900–1970," by Marshall C. Eakin (vol. 19)

"The Populations of Mexico and Argentina in 1980: Preliminary Data and Some Comparisons," by Richard W. Wilkie (vol. 21)

Argentina

"The Rural Population of Argentina to 1970," by Richard W. Wilkie (vol. 20)

"Losses and Lessons of the 1982 War for the Falklands," by Adam Perkal (vol. 23)

"Financing Argentine Industrial Corporate Development in the Aftermath of the First Perón Period," by David K. Eiteman (Supp. 7)

Bolivia

"Bolivia: Ironies in the National Revolutionary Process," by James W. Wilkie (vol. 25)

"U.S. Foreign Policy and Economic Assistance in Bolivia, 1948–1976," by James W. Wilkie (vol. 22)

"Bolivian Public Expenditure and the Role of Decentralized Agencies: A Test of the Wilkie View," by Thomas M. Millington (vol. 21)

Cuba

"An Index of Cuban Industrial Output, 1930–1958," By Jorge F. Pérez-López (Supp. 6)

El Salvador

"The Demographics of Land Reform in El Salvador Since 1980," by Roy L. Prosterman (vol. 22)

Mexico

"Monterrey, Mexico, during the Porfiriato and the Revolution: Population and Migration Trends in Regional Evolution," by David E. Lorey (vol. 28)

"The Six Ideological Phases of Mexico's 'Permanent Revolution' since 1910," by James W. Wilkie (Supp. 10)

"The Mexican Financial Imbroglio: Debt, Public Expenditure, and Nationalized Banking," by James W. Wilkie (vol. 27)

"From Economic Growth to Economic Stagnation in Mexico: Statistical Series for Understanding Pre- and Post-1982 Change," by James W. Wilkie (vol. 26)

"The Development of Engineering Expertise for Social and Economic Modernization in Mexico since 1929," by David E. Lorey (Supp. 10)

"Professional Expertise and Mexican Modernization: Sources, Methods, and Preliminary Findings," by David E. Lorey (vol. 26)

"Complexities of Measuring the Food Situation in Mexico: Supply versus Self-Sufficiency of Basic Grains, 1925–1986," by Aída Mostkoff and Enrique Ochoa (Supp. 10)

"Mexican Community Studies in a Historical Framework, 1930–1970," by Stephen Haber (vol. 21)

"Modernization and Change in Mexican Communities, 1930–1970," by Stephen Haber (vol. 22)

"Changes in Mexico Since 1895: Central Government Revenue, Public Expenditure, and National Economic Growth," by James W. Wilkie (vol. 24)

"Mexico's 'New' Financial Crisis of 1982 in Historical Perspective," by James W. Wilkie (vol. 22)

"The Dramatic Growth of Mexico's Economy and the Rise of Statist Government Budgetary Power, 1910–82," by James W. Wilkie (Supp. 10)

"Borrowing as Revenue: The Case of Mexico, 1935–82," by James W. Wilkie (Supp. 10)

"Sources of Investment Capital in Twentieth-Century Mexico," by Dale Story (vol. 23)

"Las Distintas Caras de la Deuda del Sector Público Mexicano, 1970–1976," by Samuel Schmidt (vol. 22)

"Revisando la Deuda Pública en México, 1970–1982," by Samuel Schmidt (vol. 23)

"Quantifying the Class Structure of Mexico, 1895–1970," by James W. Wilkie and Paul D. Wilkins (vol. 21)

"The Class Structure of Mexico, 1895–1980," by Stephanie Granato and Aída Mostkoff (Supp. 10)

"Mexican Demographic History of the Nineteenth Century: Evidence and Approaches," by John E. Kicza (vol. 21)

"Employment and Lack of Employment in Mexico, 1900–1970," by Donald B. Keesing (Supp. 6)

"Losers in Mexican Politics: A Comparative Study of Official Party Precandidates for Gubernatorial Elections, 1970–1975," by Roderic A. Camp (Supp. 6)

"Mexican Military Leadership in Statistical Perspective Since the 1930s," by Roderic A. Camp (vol. 20)

"Federal Expenditures and 'Personalism' in the Mexican 'Institutional' Revolution," by James A. Hanson (Supp. 7)

"Mexico in the U.S. Press: A Quantitative Study, 1972–1978," by Thomas Michael Laichas (vol. 20)

Venezuela

"Sowing the Petroleum" in Higher Education: Venezuela's Development of Professional Expertise for Social Modernization, 1900–86," by David Lorey (vol. 27)

Guides to Statistical Data for Research

To assess research on Latin American statistics, SALA and the SALA Supplement Series publish articles on issues and publications. Articles to date include the following:

"The Development of Quantitative History in Mexico since 1940: Socioeconomic Change, Income Distribution, and Wages," by Jeffrey Bortz (vol. 27)

"A Guide to Quantitative Research on Nicaragua since Independence," by Enrique C. Ochoa (vol. 27)

"The Management and Mismanagement of National and International Statistics," by James W. Wilkie (vol. 22)

"The Status of Quantitative Research on Latin America," by James W. Wilkie (vol. 19)

"A Social Census Questionnaire for Latin American Countries," by James W. Wilkie, John C. Super, and Edna Monzón de Wilkie (vol. 18)

"Quantitative Research on Latin America: An Inventory of Data Sets," by Carl W. Deal (vol. 17)

"Quantitative Data Sets on Latin America: The Second Survey by the Latin American Studies Association," by Carl W. Deal (vol. 21)

"File Inventory of the Latin American Data Bank, University of Florida, Gainesville," by M. J. Carvajal and J. E. Uquillas (vol. 17)

"Latin American Official Statistical Series on Microfiche, 1860–1974," compiled by Valerie Bloomfield (vol. 20)

Special SALA Supplements

In addition to the above listed 58 articles on development of statistical series and 9 articles on guides to data (all published in SALA and SALA Supplements 6, 7, and 10), 8 supplements have been published to treat specially focused topics.

Urbanization

Latin American Population and Urbanization Analysis: Maps and Statistics, 1950–1982, No. 8 (1984; reprint 1990), by Richard W. Wilkie

Urbanization in 19th Century Latin America: Statistics and Sources, No. 4 (1973), by Richard E. Boyer and Keith A. Davies

Society and Economy

United States–Mexico Border Statistics since 1900, No. 11 (1990), edited by David E. Lorey

Statistical Abstract of the United States–Mexico Borderlands, No. 9 (1984), edited by Peter L. Reich

Measuring Land Reform: Bolivia, Venezuela, and Latin America, No. 5 (1974), by James W. Wilkie

Cuba 1968, No. 1 (1970), edited by C. Paul Roberts and Mukhtar Hamour

Policy and Politics

Statistics and National Policy, No. 3 (1974), by James W. Wilkie

Latin American Political Statistics, No. 2 (1972), edited by Kenneth Ruddle and Philip Gillette

SALA Supplements are published periodically, and are not correlated with any particular edition of SALA.

Request for User Assistance

SALA welcomes comments and suggestions for improvement in presentation of statistics as well as notice of clarifications and corrections needed. We would very much like to receive statistics that we might publish in SALA and will give appropriate credit.

Fira Town, Santorini   J.W.W.
Cyclades Islands, Greece
September 1989

Tables

Detailed data in tables may not equal totals because of rounding

PART I. GEOGRAPHY AND LAND TENURE

PART II. TRANSPORTATION AND COMMUNICATION

PART III. POPULATION, HEALTH, AND EDUCATION

PART IV. CHURCH, STATE, AND CRIME

Chapter 12 The Military, Drugs, and Crime

PART V. WORKING CONDITIONS, MIGRATION, AND HOUSING

PART VI. INDUSTRY, MINING, AND ENERGY

PART VIII. FOREIGN TRADE

Chapter 24 Selected Commodities in Foreign Trade

PART IX. FINANCIAL FLOWS

PART X. NATIONAL ACCOUNTS, GOVERNMENT POLICY AND FINANCE, AND PRICES

PART XI. DEVELOPMENT OF DATA

Figures

Explanation of Terms

Cautions

1. All data for any topic vary according to definition, parameters, methods of compilation and calculation, and completeness of coverage as well as date gathered, date prepared, and/or date adjusted.

2. Totals for the "Latin American region" and for the "world" vary according to the definition used by the different international statistical agencies.

Symbols

‡	Preliminary, provisional, or unofficial	**	Data not applicable
0 or #	Zero or negligible (less than half of unit employed, e.g., less than .05 or 500,000)	$	U.S. dollars
~	Data not available in source	† or x	Estimate by or in source
- -	Source does not specify whether data are recorded separately, not applicable, zero or negligible	@	Estimate made herein
		***	Obviously erroneous data
		*	Link (splice) in series or technical change
1965/66	Split year, e.g., fiscal or crop year	( )	Subtotal within tabular data

Abbreviations

A	arithmetic mean	EQN	Economically Questionable Nation
AA	average annual change	EVN	Economically Viable Nation
AA-EC	AA, exponential (see p. xxxvi)	FAO	UN, Food and Agriculture Organization
AA-GA	AA, geometric approximation (see p. lx)	FOB or fob	free on board
AA-GR	AA, Growth rate in source	FY	fiscal year
AAPC	average annual percentage change	G	grams
ADCs	advanced developing countries	GA	Grupo Andino (see p. xi and SALA 24-1000)
AG	Andean Group (see p. xi and SALA, 24-1000)	GDP	gross domestic product (Spanish = PIB)
A-GAP	absolute gap	GDP/C	GDP per capita
ALALC	Asociación Latinoamericano de Libre Comercio (see p. xi and SALA, 24-1000)	GNP	gross national product
		H	hundred
ALADI	Latin American Integration Association (see p. xi)	Ha	hectare(s)
		IDB	Inter-American Development Bank
APGR	average of PC (see p. lx)	IDB-L	IDB's definition of Latin America (see SALA, 24-1000)
B	billion (i.e., 000,000,000 omitted)		
BDM-DGE	Banco de México-Dirección General de Estadística	kg	kilogram(s)
C	per capita (e.g., GDP/C)	km, km²	kilometer(s), square kilometers
ca.	about	Kw	kilowatt(s)
CA	Central America	KWH	kilowatt hours
CACM	Central American Common Market (see p. xi and SALA, 24-1000)	L or LA	Latin American countries (cf. EL; see SALA, 23, pp. vii-xxv)
CARICOM	Caribbean Common Market (see SALA, 24-1000)	LAFTA	Latin American Free Trade Association (see p. xi)
CARIFTA	Caribbean Free Trade Association (see SALA, 24-1000)	LAIA	Latin American Integration Association (see p. xi and SALA, 24-1000)
CBI	Caribbean Basin Initiative (U.S. legislation) (see SALA, 23, pp. vii-xxv)	LC	Latin American countries and comparisons (e.g., to USA)
CBI-IB	Caribbean Basin Initiative—Intended Beneficiaries (see SALA, 24-1000 and SALA, 23, pp. vii-xxv)	LDCs	Less Developed Countries
		LR	Latin American countries and their regional totals
CIF or cif	cost, insurance, and freight	LRC	20 Latin American countries, regional total, and comparison (e.g., USA)
CLA	Caribbean Latin America (cf. CNLA, ECR; see SALA, 23, pp. vii-xxv)		
CNLA	Caribbean Not Latin America (e.g., Grenada; cf. CLA). See SALA, 23, pp. vii-xxv	M	million (i.e., 000,000 omitted)
		M₁	currency outside of banks plus private sector demand deposits
CSOR	Caribbean Sea Oriented Region (includes CBI-IB and Cuba; cf. ECR; see SALA, 23, pp. vii-xxv)	M₂	M₁ plus time, savings, and foreign currency deposits
		Me²	square meters
EAP	economically active population	Me³	cubic meters
ECCM	Eastern Caribbean Common Market (see SALA 24-1000)	MERCOMUN	Mercado Común Centroamericano (see p. xxxv and SALA, 24-1000)
ECLA	Economic Commission for Latin America	MET	metric tons
ECLA-L	ECLA definition of L (see SALA 24-1000)	Mw	megawatts
ECR	Extended Caribbean Region (cf. CSOR; see SALA, 23, pp. vii-xxv)	N	number
		NC	national currency
EEC	European Economic Community	nes	not elsewhere shown
EFTA	European Free Trade Area	NIC	newly industrializing country
EL or ELA	Extended Latin America (cf. L; see SALA, 23, pp. vii-xxv)	nie	not included elsewhere
		NYC	New York City
EPI	export price index	OAS	Organization of American States (see SALA, 24-1000)

OAS-L	OAS's definition of Latin America (*see* p. x and SALA, 24-1000)	P10I	per ten thousand inhabitants
OECD	Organization for Economic Cooperation and Development	PTP	percent of total population
		R-GAP	relative gap
OECS	Organization of Eastern Caribbean States (*see* SALA, 24-1000)	SDRs	Special Drawing Rights (IMF's currency)
		SNA	system of national accounts
OPEC	Organization of Petroleum Exporting Countries	T	Thousand (i.e., 000 omitted)
p (pp)	page(s)	TJ	Terajoules
PC	percentage change	U	unit
PHI	per hundred inhabitants	UN	United Nations
PHTI	per hundred thousand inhabitants	US	U.S. currency
PI	per inhabitant	U.S. or USA	United States of America
PIB	*producto interno bruto* (English = GDP)	WDC	Washington, D.C.
PMI	per million inhabitants	YA	yearly arithmetic mean
PTI	per thousand inhabitants	YE	year end

Sources

Sources frequently cited (abbreviation generally shows agency followed by title of publication or series).
Other sources appear in tables throughout.

ADEMA	*See* ECLA	IASI-C	*Características de la Estructura Demográfica*
AE	*Anuario Estadístico*	IBRD	International Bank for Reconstruction and Development. (*see* WB)
AR	*Annual Report*		
BDM	*Banco de México*	ICAO	International Civil Aviation Organization
BID	*Banco Interamericano de Desarrollo* (*see* IDB)	ICAO-DS-B	Digest of Statistics, *Bulletin*
C/CAA	Caribbean/Central American Action, *Caribbean Data Book*	ICAO-DS-T	Digest of Statistics, *Traffic: Commercial Air Carriers*
CELADE	Centro Latinoamericano de Demografía (Santiago)	ICAO-DS-AT	Digest of Statistics, *Airport Traffic*
		IDA	International Development Association
CELADE-BD	*Boletín Demográfico*	IDB	Inter-American Development Bank (WDC)
CEPAL	Comisión Económica para América Latina (*see* ECLA)	IDB-AR	*Annual Report*
		IDB-SPTF	Social Progress Trust Fund, *Socio-Economic Progress in Latin America* (1961-71)
COHA	Council on Hemispheric Affairs, *Washington Report on the Hemisphere*	IDB-ESPLA	*Economic and Social Progress in Latin America* (1972)
Colombia-DANE	Departamento Administrativo Nacional		
Cuba-CEE	Comité Estatal de Estadística	ILO	International Labour Office (Geneva)
DGE	Dirección General de Estadística	ILO-YLS	*Yearbook of Labor Statistics*
DGEC	Dirección General de Estadística y Censos	IMF	International Monetary Fund (WDC)
ECLA	Economic Commission for Latin America (Santiago)	IMF-BPS	*Balance of Payment Statistics*
		IMF-BPS-Y	*Balance of Payment Statistics Yearbook*
ECLA-ADEMA	*Agua, Desarrollo y Medio Ambiente* (1977)	IMF-DOT	*Direction of Trade Statistics*
ECLA-AE	*Anuario Estadístico de América Latina*	IMF-DOT-Y	*Yearbook*
ECLA-BPAL	*Balance de Pagos 1950-77*	IMF-GFSY	*Government Finance Statistics Yearbook*
ECLA-CC	*Cuadernos de la CEPAL*	IMF-IFS	*International Financial Statistics*
ECLA-CEC	*Cuadernos Estadísticos de la CEPAL*	IMF-IFS-S	*IFS Supplement* (No. 1, 1981-). (*See also* IFS-Y)
ECLA-D	Document	IMF-IFS-Y	*Yearbook* (entitled IFS-S from 1961 through 1978)
ECLA-EIC	*Estudios e Informes de la CEPAL*		
ECLA-N	*Notas sobre la Economía y el Desarrollo*	INE	Instituto Nacional de Estadística
ECLA-S	*Economic Survey of Latin America*	INEC	Instituto Nacional de Estadística y Censos
ECLA-SHCAL	*Series Históricas del Crecimiento 1900-76* (1978)	JLP	José López Portillo (Mexico City)
		JLP-AE-H	*Anexo Estadístico Histórico*
ECLA-SP	Preliminary version of ECLA-S	JLP-AP-E	*Anexo de Política Económica*
ECLA-SY	*Statistical Yearbook* (*see* ECLA-AE)	Mexico-	
EYB	*Europa Year Book*	BANAMEX	Banco Nacional de México
FAO	UN, Food and Agriculture Organization (Rome)	BANAMEX-	
FAO-FY	*Fertilizer Yearbook*	RESM	Review of the Economic Situation of Mexico
FAO-PY	*Production Yearbook* (1958-)	Mexico-BDM	Banco de México
FAO-SFA	*State of Food and Agriculture*	BDM-IE	*Indicadores Económicos*
FAO-TY	*Trade Yearbook* (1958-)	BDM-IE-AH	*Indicadores Económicos, Acervo Histórico*
FAO-YFP	*Yearbook of Forestry Products*	Mexico-BNCE	Banco Nacional de Comercio Exterior
FAO-YFS	*Yearbook of Fishery Statistics*	BNCE-CE	*Comercio Exterior*
FAO-YFSCL	*Catches and Landings*	Mexico-INEGI	Instituto Nacional de Estadística, Geografía e Informática
FAO-YFSFC	*Fishery Commodities*		
IASI	OAS, Inter-American Statistical Institute	INEGI-EHM	Estadísticas Históricas de México
IASI-AC	*América en Cifras*	Mexico-NAFINSA	Nacional Financiera, S.A.
IASI-BE	*Boletín Estadístico*	NAFINSA-EMC	*La Economía Mexicana en Cifras*

NAFINSA-MV	*Mercado de Valores*
OAS	Organization of American States (WDC)
OAS-A	*Latin America's Development and the Alliance for Progress* (1973)
OAS-DB	*Datos Básicos de Población*
OASL	OAS's definition of L (*see* SALA, 24-1000)
OAS-SB	*Statistical Bulletin*
PAHO	Pan American Health Organization (WDC)
PAHO-F	*Facts on Health Progress*
PAHO-HC	*Health Conditions in the Americas*
PC	Population Council (NYC)
PC-PFP	*Population and Family Planning*
PC-RPFP	*Report on Population/Family Planning*
SA	*South American Handbook*
SALA	*Statistical Abstract of Latin America*
SALA, 23:1	Volume 23, figure 1 (sample reference)
SALA, 23-100	Volume 23, table 100 (sample reference)
SALA-Cuba	Supplement 1: *Cuba 1968*
SALA LAPUA	Supplement 8: *Latin American Population and Urbanization Analysis*
SALA-MB	Supplement 9: *Statistical Abstract of the United States—Mexico Borderlands*
SALA-MLR	Supplement 5: *Measuring Land Reform*
SALA-SEM	Supplement 10: *Society and Economy in Mexico*
SALA-SNP	Supplement 3: *Statistics and National Policy*
SALA-TNG	Supplement forthcoming: *The Narrowing Gap*
Schroeder	Susan Schroeder, *Cuba: A Handbook of Historical Statistics* (Boston: G. K. Hall, 1982)
SELA	Sistema Económico para Latinoamérica
SIPRI-Y	Stockholm International Peace Research Institute, *Yearbook*
SY	*Statistical Yearbook*
UN	United Nations (NYC)
UN-CSS	*Compendium of Social Statistics*
UN-DY	*Demographic Yearbook*
UN-MB	*Monthly Bulletin of Statistics*
UN-SP	*Statistical Papers*
UN-SP-A	*Series A, Population and Vital Statistics*
UN-SP-J	*Series J, World Energy Supplies*
UN-SP:T	*Series T, Direction of International Trade*
UN-SY	*Statistical Yearbook*
UN-YCS	*Yearbook of Construction Statistics*
UN-YIS	*Yearbook of Industrial Statistics*
UN-YITS	*Yearbook of International Trade Statistics*
UN-YNAS	*Yearbook of National Account Statistics*
UN-YWES	*Yearbook of World Energy Statistics*
UNESCO	UN Educational and Scientific Organization (NYC)
UNESCO-SY	*Statistical Yearbook*
U.S.	United States (WDC)
USAID	U.S. Agency for International Development
USAID-OLG	*U.S. Overseas Loans and Grants and Assistance from International Organizations*
USBC	U.S. Bureau of the Census
USBC-HS	*Historical Statistics of the United States*
USBC-SA	*Statistical Abstract of the United States*
USBG	U.S. Board of Governors, Federal Reserve System
USBG-FRB	*Federal Reserve Bulletin*
USBOM	U.S. Bureau of the Mines
USBOM-MCP	*Mineral Commodity Profiles*
USBOM-MIS	*Mineral Industry Surveys*
USBOM-MY	*Minerals Yearbook*
USCIA	U.S. Central Intelligence Agency
USDA	U.S. Department of Agriculture
USDA-AT	*Agricultural Trade of the Western Hemisphere*
USDA-ERS	Economic Research Service
USDA-FAT	*Foreign Agricultural Trade*
USDC-SCB	U.S. Dept. of Commerce, *Survey of Current Business*
USDOD	U.S. Department of Defense
USDOD-FMSA	*Foreign Military Sales Assistance*
USEX-IM	U.S. Export-Import Bank
USINS	U.S. Immigration and Naturalization Service
USINS-AR	*Annual Report*
USINS-SY	*Statistical Yearbook*
USNCC	U.S. National Climatic Center
USNCC-MCDW	*Monthly Climatic Data of the World*
WA	*World Almanac*
WB	World Bank (formerly IBRD)
WB-AR	*Annual Report*
WB-EDC	*Energy in Developing Countries*
WB-WDR	*World Development Report*
WB-WT	*World Bank Tables*, published by Johns Hopkins University Press, 1976, 1980
WCE	*World Christian Encyclopedia*
WHO	World Health Organization
WHO-WHSA	*World Health Statistics Annual*
Wilkie	*See* SALA
WTO	World Tourism Organization (Madrid)
WTO-WTS	*World Tourism Statistics*
YC	Yearbook Compendium

Note on Statistical Definitions

Weights and Measures

Length		
	1 kilometer	.6213712 mile
	1.609344 kilometers	1 mile
	1 yard	.914 meter
	1 meter	1.093 yard
	1 foot	.3048 meters
	1 meter	3.2808 feet
	1 inch	25.4 millimeter
	1 inch	2.54 centimeter
	1 millimeter	.03937 inch
	1 centimeter	.3937 inch

Area		
	1 Hectare (10,000 sq. meters)	2.471054 acres
	.4046856 hectares	1 acre
	1 square kilometer	.3861022 square mile
	2.589988 square kilometers	1 square mile

Volume		
	1 cubic meter	35.31467 cubic feet
		1.307951 cubic yards
	.02831685 cubic meter	1 cubic foot

Liquid measure		
	1 liter	1.056688 U.S. quarts
		.26417200 U.S. gallon
	1 U.S. quart	.9463529 liter
	1 U.S. gallon	3.785412 liters

Weight		
	1 kilogram	35.27396 avoirdupois ounces
		32.15075 troy ounces
	.45359237 kilogram	1 avoirdupois pound
	1 metric ton	1.1023113 short tons
		.9842065 long ton
	.9071847 metric ton	1 short ton (2,000 pounds)
	1.0160469 metric tons	1 long ton (2,240 pounds)

Ship tonnage		
	1 register ton (110 cubic feet)	2.83 cubic meters
	1 deadweight ton (1 long ton)	1.016047 metric tons

Rail traffic		
	1 metric ton-kilometer	.684945 short ton-mile
		.611558 long ton-mile
	1 short ton-mile	1.459972 ton-kilometers
	1 long ton-mile	1.635169 ton-kilometers

Lumber		
	1 cubic meter	220.75 board feet
	1,000 board feet	4.53 cubic meters

Agricultural products		Bales per metric ton
Wheat, pulses, and root crops	Bushel (60 lbs.)	36.744
Maize	Bushel (56 lbs.)	39.638
Coffee	Bags (132.28 lbs.)	16.67
Coffee (El Salvador)	Bags (152.12 lbs.)	14.493
Cotton	Gross Bales (500 lbs.)	4.409
	Net Bales (480 lbs.)	4.593

Coal equivalence	Metric tons of coal equivalent
Bituminous coal briquettes (1 metric ton)	1.00
Lignite briquettes (1 metric ton)	.67
Pitch coal and black lignite (1 metric ton)	.67
Lignite and brown coal (1 metric ton)	.33
Coke (1 metric ton)	.90
Crude petroleum and shale oil (1 metric ton)	1.30
Gasoline and fuel oil (1 metric ton)	1.50
Natural gas (1,000 cubic meters)	1.33
Manufactured gas (1,000 cubic meters)	.60
Refinery gas (1,000 cubic meters)	1.67
Electric energy (1,000 kilowatt hours)	.125

Energy equivalence

Terajoule $\quad$ 1 TJ = 7 x 10^6/.0293076 Kilo. calories

Temperature Equivalence

See table 305

Other conversions

For other conversions used to obtain standard measures of international comparability, see appendices to U.N., *Statistical Yearbook*; F.A.O., *Production Yearbook*; F.A.O., *World Forestry Inventory 1963*; and especially, U.N., Statistical Papers, Series M, No. 21, *World Weights and Measures*, 1955.

Mathematical Calculation of "Average" Rates of Change Over Time

Example data for calculating rate of change in a country according to four methods

Elapsed Time	Date	Absolute Data
0.00	March 26, 1937	15,920,694
10.00	March 26, 1947	18,966,767
13.49	Sept. 20, 1960	26,085,326

Methods of Calculating Average Annual (AA) Change[1] in Example Data

Category	Linear	Non-Linear		
	1. APGR Average of Percent Change	2. AA-EC Exponential Change	3. AA-GA Geometric Approximation	4. Geometric Change
Formula[2]	$r = \dfrac{\left(\dfrac{P_n}{P_o}\right) - 1}{n}$	$r = \dfrac{\log \dfrac{P_n}{P_o}}{n \log e}$	$r = \dfrac{2(P_n - P_o)}{n(P_n + P_o)}$	$r = \dfrac{\log\left(\dfrac{P_n}{P_o}\right)}{n}$
Rate 1937-47	1.91	1.75	1.75	1.77
Rate 1947-60	2.78	2.36	2.34	2.39
Analysis	$\dfrac{PC}{n}$	Continuous compounding	Annual compounding; adequate for periods of 5 years or longer	Annual compounding
Short-cut Method	**	Calculate P_n/P_o and look up corresponding value of x in U.S. National Bureau of Standards, *Tables of the Exponential Function e^x*, Applied Mathematics Series 14 (1951), "values of the ascending exponential," pp. 18 and 32. Divide result by elapsed time in example data (10.00 and 13.49).	**	**

[1] For further analysis of methodology, see U.S. Bureau of the Census, *The Methods and Materials of Demography*, 2 vols. (Washington, D.C.: Government Printing Office, 1971), II, pp. 377-380, from which the presentation of methods 2, 3, and 4 is adapted. Cf. *SNP*, p. 184.

[2] P_o the initial population

P_n the population at the end of period (in years)

n, the time in years

b, the annual amount of change

e, a mathematical constant (logarithm to the base 10 = .4342945)

PC, percentage change

Part I
Geography and
Land Tenure

Note: This volume contains statistics from numerous sources. Alternative data on many topics are presented. Variations in statistics can be attributed to differences in definition, parameters, coverage, methodology, as well as date gathered, prepared, or adjusted. See also Editor's Note on Methodology.

1
Geography

Figure 1:1

POLITICAL MAP OF EXTENDED LATIN AMERICA (ELA)

NOTE: See SALA 23, pp. vii-xxv, for additional maps and analysis.

Figure 1:2

POLITICAL MAP OF EXTENDED CARIBBEAN REGION (ECR)

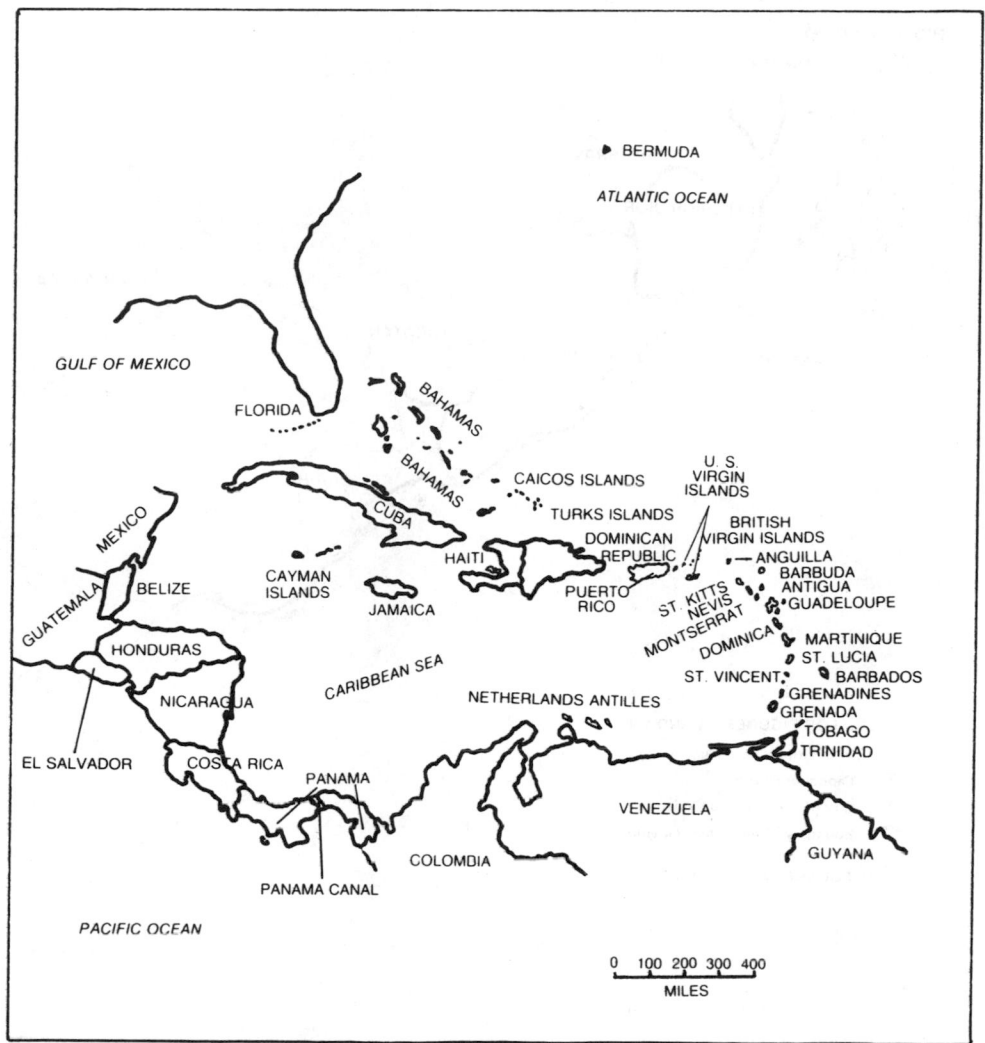

NOTE: See SALA 23, pp. vii-xxv, for additional maps and analysis.

Figure 1:3

CENTRAL AMERICA AND THE CARIBBEAN: HYDROGRAPHIC REGIONS

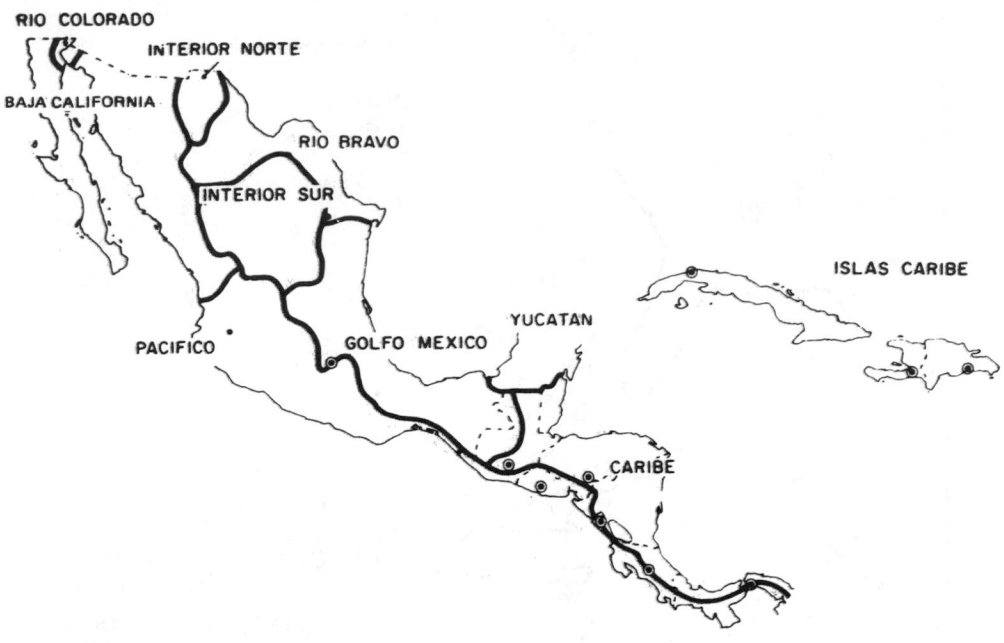

LEGEND FOR FIGURES 1:3 AND 1:4

- - -   International boundary

⊙   Capital of country

•   City of over 1 million inhabitants

〜   Boundary of major hydrographic regions

SOURCE: ADEMA, 1977.

Figure 1:4

SOUTH AMERICA: HYDROGRAPHIC REGIONS

NOTE: See SALA 19, pp. 6-10, for maps of River Usage, Reservoir Capacity, and Major Irrigated Areas.

Figure 1:5

RIVER SYSTEMS AND ELECTRIC PLANT LOCATIONS, SOUTH AMERICA

(ca. 1977)

LEGEND

- ● Thermal plants
- ▲ Hydroelectric plants
- - - - International boundary
- ⊙ Capital of country
- ▬▬ Navigable rivers for ocean-going vessels
- ▬ Navigable rivers except for ocean-going vessels
- R River

Table 100

ECONOMIC REGIONS: AREA, POPULATION, AND DENSITY, 20 LRC

Country	Area (km²)	Population 1986 M	%ᵃ	Densityᵇ
A. World				
Total	135,747,000	4,902	100.0	36
Africa	30,313,000	572	11.6	19
Asia‡	27,572,000	2,854	58.2	104
Europe	4,937,000ᶜ	494	10.0	100
Oceania	8,509,000	25	.5	3
USSR	22,402,200	280.14	5.7	13
Americas	42,078,000	677	13.8	16
B. Americas				
Total	42,078,000	677	100.0	16
United States	9,372,614	241.6	35.6	26
Latin America	20,548,000	410	60.56	20
Canada	9,976,139	25.6	3.78	3
Other	2,176,247	~	~	~
C. Latin American Economic Regional Groupings				
CACM	422,718	23.6	100.0	56
Costa Rica	50,700	2.67	11.3	53
El Salvador	21,041	4.91	20.8	233
Guatemala	108,889	8.19	34.7	75
Honduras	112,088	4.51	19.1	40
Nicaragua	130,000	3.38	14.3	26
ALADI	19,309,635	351.59	100.0	18
Argentina	2,766,889	31.03	8.8	11
Bolivia	1,098,581	6.55	1.8	6
Brazil	8,511,965	138.49	39.3	16
Chile	756,945	12.33	3.5	16
Colombia	1,138,914	29.19	8.3	26
Ecuador	283,561	9.65	2.7	34
Mexico	1,972,547	79.56	22.6	40
Paraguay	406,762	3.81	1.08	9
Peru	1,285,216	20.21	5.7	16
Uruguay	176,215	2.98	.84	17
Venezuela	912,050	17.79	5.05	20
AG	4,718,322	82.92	100.0	18
Bolivia	1,098,581	6.55	7.8	6
Colombia	1,138,914	29.19	35.2	26
Ecuador	283,561	9.65	11.6	34
Peru	1,285,216	20.21	24.3	16
Venezuela	912,050	17.32	20.8	20
Other				
Total	263,417	24.08	100.0	91
Cuba	110,861	10.25	42.5	92
Dominican Rep.	48,734	6.24	26.9	132
Haiti	27,750	5.36	22.2	193
Panama	77,082	2.23	9.2	29

a. Percentages are calculated and may not add up to 100 percent due to rounding.
b. Population divided by area.
c. Area calculated.
d. Density for region calculated.

SOURCE: UNESCO-SY, 1986, table 1.1; 1988, table 1.1.

Table 101

ARGENTINA MAJOR CIVIL DIVISIONS: AREA AND PERCENTAGE
(1980)

Division[1]	Area[2]	
	km^2	%
Total	2,780,092[a,b]	100.0
Federal District	200	#
Provinces		
Buenos Aires	307,571	11.1
Catamarca	100,967	3.6
Chaco	99,633	3.6
Chubut	224,686	8.1
Córdoba	168,766	6.1
Corrientes	88,199	3.2
Entre Ríos	78,781	2.8
Formosa	72,066	2.6
Jujuy	53,219	1.9
La Pampa	143,440	5.2
La Rioja	89,680	3.2
Mendoza	148,827	5.4
Misiones	29,801	1.1
Neuquén	94,078	3.4
Río Negro	203,013	7.3
Salta	154,775	5.6
San Juan	89,651	3.2
San Luis	76,748	2.8
Santa Cruz	243,943	8.8
Santa Fe	133,007	4.8
Santiago del Estero	135,254	4.9
Tucumán	22,524	.8
National territory		
Tierra del Fuego	21,263	.8

1. For number of civil subdivisions during previous years, see SALA, 23-310.
2. Totals may not add up due to rounding.

a. Excludes the Antarctic sector (964,250 km^2), the South Atlantic Islands (5,214 km^2), and the claimed Islas Malvinas (11,718 km^2).
b. Includes inland water (estimated at 30,2000 km^2).

SOURCE: Argentina AE, 1981–82, p. 7; *The Statesman's Yearbook*, 1987–88, pp. 88–89; 1988–89, pp. 88–89; *The World Factbook, 1988*, p. 11; *South America, Central America, and the Caribbean*, 1988, p. 121.

Table 102

BOLIVIA MAJOR CIVIL DIVISIONS: AREA AND PERCENTAGE
(1985)

Division[1]	Area[2]	
	km^2	%
Total	1,098,581[a,b]	100.0
Departments		
Bení	213,564	19.4
Chuquisaca	51,524	4.7
Cochabamba	55,631	5.1
La Paz	133,985	12.2
Oruro	53,588	4.9
Pando	63,827	5.8
Potosí	118,218	10.8
Santa Cruz	370,621	33.7
Tarija	37,623	3.4

1. For number of civil subdivisions during previous years, see SALA, 23-301.
2. Totals may not add up due to rounding.

a. Includes 14,190 km^2 of inland water.

SOURCE: *Bolivia en Cifras 1985*, p. 3; *The Statesman's Yearbook*, 1987–88, p. 217; 1988–89, p. 217; *South America, Central America, and the Caribbean 1988* (Europa Publications, 1987), p. 181; 1988, p. 181.

Table 103

BRAZIL MAJOR CIVIL DIVISIONS: AREA AND PERCENTAGE
(1986[†])

Division[1]	Area[2]	
	km[2]	%
Total	8,511,965[a]	100.0
Federal District	5,814	#
States		
Acre	152,589	1.8
Alagoas	27,731	.3
Amazonas	1,564,445	18.4
Bahía	561,026	6.6
Ceará	148,016	1.7
Espírito Santo[5]	45,597	.5
Goiás	642,092	7.5
Maranhão	328,663	3.9
Mato Grosso[3]	881,001	10.4
Mato Grosso do Sul[3]	350,548	4.1
Minas Gerais	587,172	6.9
Pará	1,248,042	14.7
Paraíba	56,372	.7
Paraná	199,554	2.3
Pernambuco	98,281	1.2
Piauí	250,934	2.9
Rio de Janeiro[4]	44,268	.5
Rio Grande do Norte	53,015	.6
Rio Grande do Sul	282,184	3.3
Rondônia	243,044	2.9
Santa Catarina	95,985	1.1
São Paulo	247,898	2.9
Sergipe	21,994	2.7
Territories		
Amapa	140,276	1.6
Fernando de Noronha[6]	26	#
Roraima	230,104	2.7

1. For number of civil subdivisions during previous years, see SALA, 23-301.
2. Totals may not add up due to rounding.
3. Mato Grosso and Mato Grosso do Sul are new states created by dividing the old state of Mato Grosso.
4. Guanabara and Rio de Janeiro states were combined to create the new state of Rio de Janeiro.
5. Includes the islands of Trindade and Martin Uaz.
6. The archipelago comprises the main island, of the same name, and about twenty small islands. Territory created in 1942.

a. Includes 55,467 km[2] of inland water, and two litigious areas: one between Amazonas and Pará (2,680 km[2]), and another between Piauí and Ceará (2,614 km[2]). The areas given for these states exclude the litigious areas.

SOURCE: *Brazil, AE, 1985*, 1986, pp. 18 and 22; *The Statesman's Yearbook*, 1987–88, p. 227; 1988–89, p. 227; and *The World Factbook 1988*, p. 31; *South America, Central America, and the Caribbean*, 1988, p. 201.

Table 104

CHILE MAJOR CIVIL DIVISIONS: AREA
AND PERCENTAGE
(1987)

Division[1]	Area[2]	
	km^2	%
Total	757,940[‡]	100.0
Regions		
Aysén del General Carlos Ibáñez del Campo	109,025	14.4
Antofagasta	126,444	16.7
Araucanía	31,858	4.2
Atacama	75,573	10.0
Bío-Bío	36,929	4.9
Coquimbo	40,656	5.4
Libertador General Bernardo O'Higgins	16,365	2.2
Los Lagos	66,997	8.8
Magallanes y Antártida Chilena	132,034	17.4
Maule	30,302	4.0
Metropolitan (Santiago)	15,349	2.0
Tarapacá	58,698	7.7
Valparaíso	16,396	2.2

1. For number of civil subdivisions during previous years, see SALA, 23-301.
2. Totals may not add up due to rounding.

a. Excluding the Chilean Antarctic Territory, which has an area of 1,269,723 km^2 and has been administered by Magallanes since July 21,1955. Includes an estimated 8,150 km^2 of inland water.

SOURCE: *The Statesman's Yearbook*, 1987–88, p. 344; 1988–89, p. 346; and *The World Factbook 1988*, p. 46; *South America, Central America, and the Caribbean*, 1988, p. 234.

Table 105

COLOMBIA MAJOR CIVIL DIVISIONS: AREA AND PERCENTAGE
(1985)

Division[1]	Area[2]	
	km^2	%
Total	1,141,748[a]	100.0
Special District (Bogotá)	1,587[b]	.2
Departments		
Antioquia	63,612	5.6
Atlántico	3,388	.3
Bolívar	25,978	2.3
Boyacá	23,189	2.0
Caldas	7,888	.7
Caquetá[3]	88,965	7.8
Cauca	29,308	2.6
Cesar	22,905	2.0
Chocó	46,530	4.1
Córdoba	25,020	2.2
Cundinamarca (excludes Bogotá, D.E.)	22,478‡	2.0
Huila	19,890	1.7
La Guajira	20,848	1.8
Magdalena	23,188	2.0
Meta	85,635	7.5
Nariño	33,268	2.9
Norte de Santander	21,658	1.9
Quindío	1,845	.2
Risaralda	4,140	.4
Santander	30,537	2.7
Sucre	10,917	1.0
Tolima	23,562	2.1
Valle del Cauca	22,140	1.9
Intendencias		
Arauca	23,818	2.1
Casanare	44,640	3.9
Putumayo	24,885	2.2
San Andrés y Providencia Islands	44	#
Comisarías		
Amazonas	109,665	9.6
Guainía	72,238	6.3
Guaviare[4]	53,460‡	4.7
Vaupés	54,135‡	4.7
Vichada	100,242	8.8

1. For number of civil subdivisions during previous years, see SALA, 23-301.
2. Totals may not add up due to rounding.
3. Formerly an intendencia. Became a department in 1981.
4. Created in 1977 by dividing Vaupés.

a. Includes an estimated 100,210 km^2 of inland water.
b. Municipality of Bogotá only.

SOURCE: *The Statesman's Yearbook*, 1987–88, pp. 368–369; 1988–89, p. 370; *División Político Administrativa de Colombia 1985*, July, 1985, p. 23; and *The World Factbook 1988*, p. 51; *South America, Central America, and the Caribbean*, 1988, p. 257.

Table 106

COSTA RICA MAJOR CIVIL DIVISIONS: AREA AND PERCENTAGE

(1984)

Division[1]	Area[2]	
	km^2	%
Total	51,000[a],‡	100.0
Provinces		
Alajuela	9,753	19.1
Cartago	3,125	6.1
Guanacaste	10,141	19.8
Heredia	2,657	5.2
Limón	9,189	18.0
Puntarenas	11,277	22.1
San José	4,960	9.7

1. For number of civil subdivisions during previous years, see SALA, 23-301.
2. Totals may not add up due to rounding.

a. Includes an estimated 240 km^2 of inland water.

SOURCE: *The Statesman's Yearbook*, 1987–88, p. 381; 1988–89, p. 383; and *The World Factbook 1988*, p. 56; *South America, Central America, and the Caribbean*, 1988, p. 278.

Table 107

CUBA MAJOR CIVIL DIVISIONS: AREA AND PERCENTAGE

(1987)

Division[1]	Area[2]	
	km^2	%
Total	110,860[a]	100.0
City		
La Habana	727	.6
Provinces		
Camagüey	14,134	12.7
Ciego de Avila	6,485	5.8
Cienfuegos	4,149	37.1
Granma	8,452	7.5
Guantánamo	6,366	5.6
Holguín	9,105	8.2
La Habana	5,671	5.1
Las Tunas	6,373	5.7
Matanzas	11,669	10.5
Pinar del Río	10,860	9.8
Sancti Spíritus	6,737	6.1
Santiago de Cuba	6,343	5.7
Villa Clara	8,069	7.3
Special Municipality		
Isla de la Juventud	2,199	1.9
Offshore Islets and Keys	3,036	2.7

1. For number of civil subdivisions during previous years, see SALA, 23-301.
2. Totals may not add up due to rounding.

a. Land area only.

SOURCE: *The Statesman's Yearbook*, 1988–89, p. 392; *South America, Central America, and the Caribbean*, 1988, p. 298.

Table 108

DOMINICAN REPUBLIC MAJOR CIVIL DIVISIONS: AREA AND PERCENTAGE
(1981)

Division[1]	Area[2] km^2	Area[2] %
Total	48,442[a]	100.0
National District (Santo Domingo)	1,477	3.0
Provinces[3]		
Azua	2,430	5.0
Bahoruco	1,376	2.8
Barahona	2,528	5.2
Dajabón	890	1.8
Duarte	1,292	2.7
Elías Piña	1,788	3.7
El Seibo	2,989	6.2
Espaillat	1,000	2.1
Independencia	1,861	3.8
La Altagracia	3,084	6.4
La Romana	541	1.1
La Vega	3,377	7.0
María Trinidad Sánchez	1,310	2.7
Monte Cristi	1,989	4.1
Pedernales	967	2.0
Peravia	1,622	3.3
Puerto Plata	1,881	3.9
Salcedo	533	1.1
Samaná	989	2.0
Sánchez Ramírez	1,174	2.4
San Cristóbal	3,743	7.7
San Juan	3,561	7.4
San Pedro de Macorís	1,166	2.4
Santiago	3,122	6.4
Santiago Rodríguez	1,020	2.1
Valverde	570	1.2

1. For number of civil subdivisions during previous years, see SALA, 23-301.
2. Totals may not add up due to rounding.
3. In February 1986 it was decided to increase the number of provinces to 29: Hato Major, Monseñor Nouel, and Monte Plata were to be created.

a. The total area, including 350 km^2 of inland water, is estimated at 48,730 km^2 by *The World Factbook 1988*.

SOURCE: *The World Factbook 1988*, May 1988, p. 65; and *República Dominicana en Cifras 1987*, vol. 14, Oct. 1987, pp. 3 and 61; *The Statesman's Yearbook*, 1988–89; *South America, Central America, and the Caribbean*, 1988, p. 318.

Table 109

ECUADOR MAJOR CIVIL DIVISIONS: AREA AND PERCENTAGE

(1982)

| Division[1] | Area[2] | |
	km[2]	%
Total	270,670[a],[‡]	100.0
Provinces		
Azuay	8,092	3.0
Bolívar	4,142	1.5
Cañar	3,481	1.3
Carchi	3,744	1.4
Chimborazo	6,056	2.2
Colón (Galápagos)[3]	7,994	3.0
Cotopaxi	5,198	1.9
El Oro	5,908	2.2
Esmeraldas	15,162	5.6
Guayas	21,382	7.9
Imbabura	4,976	1.8
Loja	11,472[b]	4.2
Los Ríos	6,370	2.4
Manabí	18,105	6.7
Morona-Santiago	26,418[b]	9.8
Napo	52,318[b]	19.3
Pastaza	30,269[b]	11.2
Pichincha	16,587	6.1
Tungurahua	3,110	1.1
Zamora-Chinchipe	18,394[b]	6.8

1. For number of civil subdivisions during previous years, see SALA, 23-301.
2. Totals may not add up due to rounding.
3. Includes the Galápagos Islands (7,844 km[2]).

a. Excludes litigation zone between Peru and Ecuador, which is 190,807 km[2]. Includes 6,720 km[2] of inland water.
b. Excluding Peru-Ecuador litigation zone.

SOURCE: *The Statesman's Yearbook*, 1987–88, p. 436; and *South America, Central America, and the Caribbean 1988* (Europa Publications, 1987), p. 337; *The Statesman's Yearbook, 1988–89*, p. 438; *South America, Central America, and the Caribbean*, 1988, p. 337.

Table 110

EL SALVADOR MAJOR CIVIL DIVISIONS: AREA AND PERCENTAGE

(1981)

| Division[1] | Area[2] | |
	km[2]	%
Total	21,393[a],[‡]	100.0
Departments		
Ahuachapán	1,281	6.0
Cabañas	1,075	5.0
Chalatenango	2,507	11.7
Cuscatlán	766	3.6
La Libertad	1,650	7.7
La Paz	1,155	5.4
La Unión	1,738	8.1
Morazán	1,364	6.4
San Miguel	2,532	11.8
San Salvador	892	4.2
Santa Ana	1,829	8.6
San Vicente	1,175	5.5
Sonsonate	1,133	5.3
Usulután	1,780	8.3

1. For number of civil subdivisions during previous years, see SALA, 23-301.
2. Totals may not add up due to rounding.

a. Includes 320 km[2] of inland water.

SOURCE: *The Statesman's Yearbook*, 1987–88, p. 449; 1988–89, p. 451; and *South America, Central America, and the Caribbean 1988* (Europa Publications, 1987), p. 358; 1988, p. 358.

Table 111

GUATEMALA MAJOR CIVIL DIVISIONS: AREA AND PERCENTAGE
(1987)

Division[1]	Area[2] km^2	%
Total	108,889[a]	100.0
Departments		
Alta Verapaz	8,686	8.0
Baja Verapaz	3,124	2.9
Chimaltenango	1,979	1.8
Chiquimula	2,376	2.2
El Progreso	1,922	1.8
Escuintla	4,384	4.0
Guatemala	2,126	2.0
Huehuetenango	7,403	6.8
Izabal	9,038	8.3
Jalapa	2,063	1.9
Jutiapa	3,219	3.0
Petén	35,854	32.9
Quezaltenango	1,951	1.8
Quiché	8,378	7.7
Retalhuleu	1,858	1.7
Sacatepéquez	465	.4
San Marcos	3,791	3.5
Santa Rosa	2,955	2.7
Sololá	1,061	1.0
Suchitepéquez	2,510	2.3
Totonicapán	1,061	1.0
Zacapa	2,690	2.5

1. For number of civil subdivisions during previous years, see SALA, 23-301.
2. Totals may not add up due to rounding.

a. Includes 460 km^2 of inland water.

SOURCE: *The Statesman's Yearbook*, 1987–88, p. 574; 1988–89, p. 576; and *South America, Central America, and the Caribbean 1988* (Europa Publications, 1987), p. 389; 1988, p. 389.

Table 112

HAITI MAJOR CIVIL DIVISIONS: AREA AND PERCENTAGE
(1985)

Division[1]	Area[2] km^2	%
Total	27,750[a]	100.0
Departments		
Artibonite	4,895	17.6
Centre	3,597	13.0
Grande Anse	3,100	11.2
Nord	2,175	7.8
Nord-Est	1,698	6.1
Nord-Ouest	2,094	7.5
Ouest	4,595	16.6
Sud	2,602	9.4
Sud-Est	2,077	7.5

1. For number of civil subdivisions during previous years, see SALA, 23-301.
2. Totals may not add up due to rounding.

a. Land area: 27,560 km^2.

SOURCE: *The Statesman's Yearbook*, 1987–88, p. 530; 1988–89, p. 592; and *The World Factbook 1988*, p. 101; *South America, Central America, and the Caribbean, 1988*, p. 417.

Table 113

HONDURAS MAJOR CIVIL DIVISIONS: AREA AND PERCENTAGE
(1986)

Division[1]	Area[2]	
	km^2	%
Total	112,088[a]	100.0
Federal District	1,648	1.5
Departments		
Atlántida	4,251	3.8
Choluteca	4,211	3.8
Colón	8,875	7.9
Comayagua	5,196	4.6
Copán	3,203	2.9
Cortés	3,954	3.5
El Paraíso	7,218	6.4
Francisco Morazán	6,298	5.6
Gracias a Dios	16,630	14.8
Intibucá	3,072	2.7
Islas de la Bahía	261	.2
La Paz	2,331	2.1
Lempira	4,290	3.8
Ocotepeque	1,680	1.5
Olancho	24,350	21.7
Santa Bárbara	5,115	4.6
Valle	1,565	1.4
Yoro	7,939	7.1

1. For number of civil subdivisions during previous years, see SALA, 23-301.
2. Totals may not add up due to rounding.

a. Includes 200 km^2 of inland water.

SOURCE: *The Statesman's Yearbook*, 1987–88, p. 595; 1988–89, p. 597; and *South America, Central America, and the Caribbean 1988* (Europa Publications, 1987), p. 430; 1988, p. 430.

Table 114

MEXICO MAJOR CIVIL DIVISIONS: AREA AND PERCENTAGE
(1983)

Division[1]	Area[2]	
	km^2	%
Total	1,958,201[a]	100.0
Federal District	1,479	#
States		
Aguascalientes	5,471	.3
Baja California	69,921	3.6
Baja California Sur	73,475	3.8
Campeche	50,812	2.6
Chiapas	74,211	3.8
Chihuahua	244,938	12.5
Coahuila	149,982	7.8
Colima	5,191	.3
Durango	123,181	6.3
Guanajuato	30,491	1.6
Guerrero	64,281	3.3
Hidalgo	20,813	1.1
Jalisco	80,836	4.1
México	21,355	1.1
Michoacán	59,928	3.1
Morelos	4,950	.3
Nayarit	26,979	1.4
Nuevo León	64,924	3.3
Oaxaca	93,952	4.8
Puebla	33,902	1.7
Querétaro	11,449	.6
Quintana Roo	50,212	2.6
San Luis Potosí	63,068	3.2
Sinaloa	58,328	3.0
Sonora	182,052	9.3
Tabasco	25,267	1.3
Tamaulipas	79,384	4.1
Tlaxcala	4,016	.2
Veracruz	71,699	3.7
Yucatán	38,402	2.0
Zacatecas	73,252	3.7

1. For number of civil subdivisions during previous years, see SALA, 23-301.
2. Totals may not add up due to rounding.

a. Includes 49,510 km^2 of inland water.

SOURCE: *The Statesman's Yearbook*, 1987–88, p. 851; 1988–89, p. 853; *Anuario de Estadísticas Estatales*, 1985, p. 7; and *South America, Central America, and the Caribbean 1988* (Europa Publications, 1987), p. 475; 1988, p. 475.

Table 115

NICARAGUA MAJOR CIVIL DIVISIONS: AREA AND PERCENTAGE

(1985)

Division[1]	Area[2]	
	km^2	%
Total	120,349[a,b]	100.0
Departments		
Boaco	4,271	3.5
Carazo	1,097	.9
Chinandega	4,789	4.0
Chontales	6,324	5.3
Estelí	2,173	1.8
Granada	992	.8
Jinotega	9,640	8.0
León	5,243	4.4
Madriz	1,612	1.3
Managua	3,368	2.8
Masaya	690	.6
Matagalpa	6,929	5.8
Nueva Segovia	3,594	3.0
Río San Juan	7,402	6.2
Rivas	2,190	1.8
Zelaya[3]	60,035	49.9

1. For number of civil subdivisions during previous years, see SALA, 23-301.
2. Totals may not add up due to rounding.
3. Land area only.

a. Includes 11,250 km^2 of inland water.
b. The total area has been estimated at 129,494 km^2 (120,254 km^2 for land area only) by *The World Factbook*, 1988, p. 172.

SOURCE: *Nicaragua AE, 1985*, 1986, pp. 6–8; and *South America, Central America, and the Caribbean 1988* (Europa Publications, 1987), p. 518; 1988, p. 518; *The Statesman's Yearbook*, 1988–89, p. 922.

Table 116

PANAMA MAJOR CIVIL DIVISIONS: AREA AND PERCENTAGE

(1985)

Division[1]	Area[2]	
	km^2	%
Total	78,046[a,‡]	100.0
Provinces		
Bocas del Toro	5,711	7.4
Chiriquí	8,758	6.5
Coclé	5,035	11.4
Colón	8,167	10.6
Darién	16,803	21.8
Herrera	2,427	3.1
Los Santos	3,867	5.0
Panamá	12,022	15.6
Veraguas	11,086	14.4
Special Territory		
San Blas	3,206	4.2

1. For number of civil subdivisions during previous years, see SALA, 23-301.
2. Totals may not add up due to rounding.

a. Includes the Canal zone (1,432 km^2), and inland water (total: 1,090 km^2).

SOURCE: *The Statesman's Yearbook*, 1987–88, p. 964; 1988–89, p. 966; and *South America, Central America, and the Caribbean 1988* (Europa Publications, 1987), p. 538; 1988, p. 538.

Table 117

**PARAGUAY MAJOR CIVIL DIVISIONS: AREA
AND PERCENTAGE**

(1986)

Division[1]	Area[2]	
	km²	%
Total	406,752[a]	100.0
Capital District: Asunción	117	#
Departments		
Alto Paraguay	45,982	11.3
Alto Paraná	14,895	3.7
Amambay	12,933	3.2
Boquerón	46,708	11.5
Caaquazú	12,298	3.0
Caazapá	9,496	2.3
Canendiyú	14,667	3.6
Central	2,465	.6
Chaco	36,367	8.9
Concepción	18,051	4.4
Cordillera	4,948	1.2
Guairá	3,022	.7
Itapúa	16,525	4.1
Misiones	9,556	2.3
Ñeembucú	12,147	3.0
Nueva Asunción	44,961	11.1
Paraguarí	8,705	2.1
Presidente Hayes	72,907	17.9
San Pedro	20,002	4.9

1. For number of civil subdivisions during previous years, see SALA, 23-301.
2. Totals may not add up due to rounding.

a. Includes an estimated 9,452 km² of inland water.

SOURCE: *Paraguay AE 1979*, Nov. 1980, pp. 15–16; and *The World Factbook 1988*,
    p. 187; *The Statesman's Yearbook*, 1988–89, p. 978; *South America, Central America,
    and the Caribbean, 1988*, p. 551.

Table 118

PERU MAJOR CIVIL DIVISIONS: AREA AND PERCENTAGE
(1987)

Division[1]	Area[2]	
	km^2	%
Total	1,285,216[a]	100.0
Departments		
Amazonas	41,297	3.2
Ancash	36,669	2.8
Apurímac	20,550	1.6
Arequipa	63,528	4.9
Ayacucho	44,181	3.4
Cajamarca	34,930	2.7
Cuzco	76,329	5.9
Huancavelica	21,079	1.6
Huánuco	34,094	2.7
Ica	21,251	1.7
Junín	41,296	3.2
La Libertad	23,241	1.8
Lambayeque	13,737	1.0
Lima	33,821	2.6
Loreto	379,025	29.4
Madre de Dios	78,403	6.1
Moquegua	15,709	1.2
Pasco	24,035	1.9
Piura	36,403	2.8
Puno[4]	72,382	5.6
San Martín	52,309	4.0
Tacna	15,232	1.2
Tumbes	4,732	.4
Ucayali[3]	100,831	7.8
Constitutional Province		
Callao	148	#

1. For number of civil subdivisions during previous years, see SALA, 23-301.
2. Totals may not add up due to rounding.
3. The department of Ucayali was created on June 18, 1980, and is formed by the provinces of Ucayali and Coronel Portillo.
4. Includes the Peruvian sector of Lake Titicaca (4,996 km^2).

a. Includes 5,216 km^2 of inland water.

SOURCE: *Peru Compendio Estadístico 1987*, May 1988, p. 26; and *South America, Central America, and the Caribbean 1988* (Europa Publications, 1987), p. 577; 1988, p. 577; *The Statesman's Yearbook*, 1988–89, p. 984.

Table 119

URUGUAY MAJOR CIVIL DIVISIONS: AREA
AND PERCENTAGE
(1985)

Division[1]	Area[2]	
	km^2	%
Total	176,215[a]	100.0
Departments		
Artigas	11,928	6.8
Canelones	4,536	2.6
Cerro Largo	13,648	7.7
Colonia	6,106	3.5
Durazno	11,643	6.6
Flores	5,144	2.9
Florida	10,417	5.9
Lavalleja	10,016	5.7
Maldonado	4,793	2.7
Montevideo	530	.3
Paysandú	13,922	7.9
Río Negro	9,282	5.3
Rivera	9,370	5.3
Rocha	10,551	6.0
Salto	14,163	8.0
San José	4,992	2.8
Soriano	9,008	5.1
Tacuarembó	15,438	8.8
Treinta y Tres	9,529	5.4

1. For number of civil subdivisions during previous years, see SALA, 23-301.
2. Totals may not add up due to rounding.

a. Excludes 142,177 km^2, consisting of the insular area in the Uruguay River (105 km^2); the Rincón de Artigas (237 km^2); the Mar Territorial (125,057 km^2); and the territorial waters of Río de la Plata (15,240 km^2), Laguna Merín (1,031 km^2), and Río Uruguay (528 km^2). Includes 2,600 km^2 of inland water.

SOURCE: *Uruguay AE, 1986*; *Resultados de 1985*, pp. 4, and 11; and *The World Factbook 1988*, p. 247; *The Statesman's Yearbook*, 1988–89, p. 1569; *South America, Central America, and the Caribbean*, 1988, p. 645.

Table 120

VENEZUELA MAJOR CIVIL DIVISIONS: AREA AND PERCENTAGE

(1985)

Division[1]	Area[2] km²	Area[2] %
Total	912,050[a]	100.0
Federal District	1,930	.2
States		
Anzoátegui	43,300	4.8
Apure	76,500	8.4
Aragua	7,014	.8
Barinas	35,200	3.9
Bolívar	238,000	26.1
Carabobo	4,650	.5
Cojedes	14,800	1.6
Falcón	24,800	2.7
Guárico	64,986	7.1
Lara	19,800	2.2
Mérida	11,300	1.2
Miranda	7,950	.9
Monagas	28,900	3.2
Nueva Esparta	1,150	.1
Portuguesa	15,200	1.7
Sucre	11,800	1.3
Táchira	11,100	1.2
Trujillo	7,400	.8
Yaracuy	7,100	.8
Zulia	63,100	6.9
Federal Territory		
Amazonas	175,750	19.3
Delta Amacuro	40,200	4.4
Federal Dependencies	120	#

1. For number of civil subdivisions during previous years, see SALA, 23-301.
2. Totals may not add up due to rounding.

a. Land area is 882,050 km².

SOURCE: *Venezuela AE 1985*, p. 18; and *The World Factbook 1988*, p. 250; *The Statesman's Yearbook, 1988–89*, p. 1580; *South America, Central America, and the Caribbean*, 1988, p. 659.

Table 121

ALTITUDE OF PRINCIPAL MOUNTAINS, 20 L

	Country	Peak or Volcano	Cordillera	Major Political Division	Altitude Above Sea Level Meters	Altitude Above Sea Level Feet
A.	ARGENTINA	Aconcagua	Andes	Mendoza	6,960[a]	22,835

Continued in SALA, 23-302.

Table 122

HIGH PEAKS OF LATIN AMERICA

(In Descending Order of Altitude)

Peak	Mountain Range	Country	Meters	Peak	Mountain Range	Country	Meters
Aconcagua	Andes	Argentina-Chile	7,040[a]	Huila	Andes	Colombia	5,750

Continued in SALA, 23-303.

Table 123

VOLCANOES OF LATIN AMERICA

(In Descending Order of Altitude)

Volcano (Last Eruption)	Place	Meters
North America		
Colima (1982)	Mexico	4,268
El Chichoń (1983)	Mexico	2,225
Citlaltepec (Orizaba)	Mexico	5,676
Popocatépetl (1920)	Mexico	5,452
Colima (1975)	Mexico	3,960
Paricutín (1952)	Mexico	3,170
Central America—Carribean		
Tajumulco	Guatemala	4,220
Tacana	Guatemala	4,092
Acatenango (1972)	Guatemala	3,976
Santiaguito (Santa María) (1982)	Guatemala	3,772
Fuego (1980)	Guatemala	3,736
Atitlán	Guatemala	3,537
Irazú (1967)	Costa Rica	3,432
Poás (1982)	Costa Rica	2,704
Pacaya (1983)	Guatemala	2,552
San Miguel (1976)	El Salvador	2,130
Izalco (1966)	El Salvador	1,965
Rincon de la Vieja (1968)	Costa Rica	1,806
El Viejo (San Cristóbal) (1981)	Nicaragua	1,745
Ometepe (Concepcion) (1982)	Nicaragua	1,610
Arenal (1982)	Costa Rica	1,552
Conchagua (1947)	El Salvador	1,250
Momotombo (1982)	Nicaragua	1,191
Telica (1982)	Nicaragua	1,010
Masaya (1978)	Nicaragua	635
South America		
Guallatiri (1960)	Chile	6,060
Cotopaxi (1975)	Ecuador	5,897
El Misti	Peru	5,825
Ubinas (1969)	Peru	5,672
Lascar (1968)	Chile	5,641
Tupungatito (1980)	Chile	5,640
Tolima (1943)	Colombia	5,525
Sangay (1976)	Ecuador	5,230
Tungurahua (1944)	Ecuador	5,016
Pichincha (1982)	Ecuador	4,787
Nevada del Ruiz (1985)	Colombia	4,724
Purace (1977)	Colombia	4,600
Reventador (1976)	Ecuador	3,485
Lautaro (1960)	Chile	3,380
Llaima (1979)	Chile	3,124
Villarrica (1980)	Chile	2,840
Hudson (1973)	Chile	2,600
Rinihue	Chile	2,430
Puyhue (1960)	Chile	2,240
Calbuco (1961)	Chile	2,015
Fernandina (1977)	Galapagos Is.	1,546
Alcedo (1970)	Galapagos Is.	1,127

SOURCE: WA, 1980, p. 437; *National Geographic Magazine*, Jan. 1981, pp. 7ff; WA, 1980, p. 437; WA, 1984, p. 593; 1989, pp. 512–513.

Table 124

MAJOR EARTHQUAKES WORLDWIDE
(20th Century)

Date	Country	Deaths	Magnitude
1933 March 2	Japan	2,990	8.9
1950 Aug 15	India	1,530	8.7
1920 Dec 16	China	100,000	8.6
1906 Aug 16	Chile	20,000	8.6
1964 Mar 27	USA (Alaska)	114	8.5
1946 Dec 21	Japan	2,000	8.4
1934 Jan 15	India	10,700	8.4
1960 May 21–30	Chile	5,000	8.3
1939 Jan 24	Chile	28,000	8.3
1927 May 22	China	200,000	8.3
1923 Sept 1	Japan	100,000	8.3
1906 April 18–19	USA (San Francisco)	452	8.3
1977 Nov 23	Argentina	100	8.2
1985 Sept 19	Mexico	9,500	8.1
1979 Dec 12	Colombia and Ecuador	800	7.9
1976 Nov 24	Eastern Turkey	4,000	7.9
1939 Dec 26	Turkey	30,000	7.9
1976 July 28	China	242,000	7.8 to 8.2
1988 Dec 7	USSR (Armenia)	55,000	6.9

SOURCE: *Los Angeles Times*, December 13, 1988.

Table 125

MAJOR EARTHQUAKES IN LATIN AMERICA, 1797–1988

Date	Place	Deaths	Magnitude[a]
1797 Feb 4	Quito, Ecuador	41,000	~
1868 Aug 13–15	Peru and Ecuador	40,000	~
1875 May 16	Venezuela and Colombia	16,000	~
1906 Aug 16	Valparaiso, Chile	20,000	8.6
1939 Jan 24	Chillan, Chile	28,000	8.3
1949 Aug 5	Pelileo, Ecuador	6,000	6.8
1960 May 21–30	Southern Chile	5,000	8.3
1970 May 31	Northern Peru	66,794	7.7
1972 Dec 23	Nicaragua	5,000	6.2
1976 Feb 4	Guatemala	22,778	7.5
1979 Dec 12	Colombia and Ecuador	800	7.9
1983 Mar 31	Southern Colombia	250	5.5
1983 Apr 3	Southwest Costa Rica	~	7.2
1983 June 7	Southern Mexico	~	7.0, 6.7
1983 June 19	El Salvador	~	7.0
1983 Nov 19	Central Peru	~	6.5
1983 Dec 16	Western Cuba	~	4.4
1985 Mar 3	Chile	146	7.8
1985 Sept 19	Central Mexico	10,000[b]	7.8
1986 June 11	Venezuela	~	~
1986 Oct 10	El Salvador	890[c]	5.4
1987 Mar 5–6	Northeast Ecuador	4,000[†]	7.3
1988 April 12	Arequipa, Peru	~	7.0
1988 Feb 5	North Chile	~	6.7
1988 Jan 19	Taltal, Chile	~	6.8
1988 Aug 8	North Chile	~	7.0

a. Each higher number represents a tenfold increase in energy measured in ground motion.
b. Mexican government estimate.
c. El Salvador government estimate.

SOURCE: WA, 1984, pp. 593, 698; 1988, p. 524; 1989, p. 524.

Table 126

RIVERS

Part I: Principal Rivers of the World

River	Continent	Length (Miles)	Drainage Area (T Sq. Mi.)	Flow[1]
Nile	Africa	4,145	1,082	110
Amazon	South America	4,000	2,375	6,180
Mississippi-Missouri	North America	3,740	1,247	640,300
Yangtze	Asia	3,720	705	770
Congo	Africa	2,880	1,476	1,377
Amur–Argun	Asia	3,590	792	390
Lena	Asia	2,730	961	569
Yenisei	Asia	3,650	1,011	636
La Plata-Paraná	South America	3,030	1,197	809
Ob–Irtysh	Asia	3,360	1,154	441

Part II: Principal Rivers of Latin America

River	Continent	Length (Miles)	Drainage Area (T Sq. Mi.)	Flow[1]
Amazon	South America	4,000	2,375	6,180
Araguaia	South America	1,367	~	~
La Plata-Paraná	South America	2,450	1,198	2,800
Madeira	South America	2,013	463	770
Orinoco	South America	1,600	1,340	890
Paraguay	South America	1,610	425	155
Paraná	South America	3,030	1,197	809
Purus	South America	1,860	~	~
Río Grande	North America	1,885	172	3
São Francisco	South America	1,988	236	120
Tocantins	South America	1,677	~	~

1. Thousands of cubic feet per second.

SOURCE: U. S. National Oceanic and Atmospheric Administration, *Principal Rivers and Lakes of the World* (Rockville, Md.: U.S. Department of Commerce), 1971, 1982.

Table 127

PRINCIPAL NATURAL LAKES OF LATIN AMERICA

Lake	Continent	Depth (Feet)	Sq. Mile Area	Length (Miles)
Maracaibo	South America	197	5,200	115
Nicaragua	North America	230	3,150	102
Titicaca	South America	990	3,200	122

SOURCE: U.S. National Oceanic and Atmospheric Administration, *Principal Rivers and Lakes of the World* (Rockville, Md.: U.S. Department of Commerce, 1982).

Table 128

PRINCIPAL DESERTS OF LATIN AMERICA

Desert	Place	Sq. Mile Area
Atacama	Northern Chile	70,000
Bolsón de Mapimi	North Central Mexico	50,000
Olmos	Northwestern Peru	1,000
Morrope	Northwestern Peru	1,500
Sechura	Northwestern Peru	2,000
Vizcaino	Northwestern Mexico	6,000

Source: See table 127.

Table 129

TEMPERATURE AND RAINFALL BY GEOGRAPHIC LOCATION, 20 L

$$\left(\frac{\text{Temp., }^\circ\text{F}}{\text{Rain, inches}}\right)$$

Station	Years Covered	Elev.	Lat.	Long.	Jan.	Feb.	Mar.	Apr.	May	June	July	Aug.	Sept.	Oct.	Nov.	Dec.	Annual
A. ARGENTINA					58.5	57.2	53.1	48.0	42.1	38.1	36.7	37.0	41.0	46.4	50.4	54.3	46.9
SAN CARLOS DE BARILOCHE	30	2,798	41.09	71.18	1.16	1.42	2.40	2.97	5.66	7.95	6.65	5.17	3.08	1.75	1.82	1.75	41.78

Continued in SALA, 23-309 to 23-328. For centigrade conversions, see SALA, 22-305.

Table 130

HIGH AND LOW TEMPERATURE — MONTHLY AVERAGES IN CAPITAL CITY,[1] 20 L

(Fahrenheit)[2]

Country		Jan.	Feb.	March	Apr.	May	June	July	Aug.	Sept.	Oct.	Nov.	Dec.
A. ARGENTINA	High	83	83	79	72	64	57	57	60	64	69	76	82
	Low	63	63	60	53	47	41	42	43	46	50	56	61

Continued in SALA, 23-329. For centigrade conversions, see SALA, 22-305.

Table 131

AVERAGE NUMBER OF DAYS WITHOUT RAIN EACH MONTH, 20 L

(Capital Cities)

Country	Jan.	Feb.	March	April	May	June	July	Aug.	Sept.	Oct.	Nov.	Dec.
A. ARGENTINA	24	22	24	22	24	23	23	22	22	22	21	23

Continued in SALA, 23-330.

2
Land Use

Table 200

EXTENT OF MAJOR SOIL UNITS, 2 LR

Soil Unit	Andean	C. BRAZIL	Caribbean	Central America	N. MEXICO	Southern Cone	Latin American Countries
Yermosol							
T Ha	3,362	0	0	0	20,436	52,873	76,671
%	.7	0	0	0	10.2	11.9	3.5
Acrisol							
T Ha	94,838	197,174	12,553	9,926	3,071	7,427	324,989
%	20.7	20.8	17.3	20.3	1.5	1.7	15.0
Andosol							
T Ha	19,604	0	112	3,313	10,149	10,817	43,995
%	4.3	0	.2	6.8	5.1	2.4	2.0
Arenosol							
T Ha	5,384	85,415	1,963	0	0	879	93,641
%	1.2	9.0	2.7	0	0	.2	4.3
Cambisol							
T Ha	28,319	14,359	3,068	5,685	7,404	3,352	62,187
%	6.2	1.5	4.2	11.6	3.7	.8	2.9
Ferralsol							
T Ha	76,105	365,324	17,454	324	0	5,453	464,660
%	16.6	38.6	24.1	.7	0	1.2	21.4
Fluvisol							
T Ha	19,136	8,463	3,066	1,963	2,391	37,805	72,824
%	4.2	.9	4.2	4.0	1.2	8.5	3.4
Gleysol							
T Ha	45,272	67,391	5,694	5,179	8,968	22,143	154,647
%	9.9	7.1	7.9	10.6	4.5	5.0	7.1
Histosol							
T Ha	2,547	259	1,500	1,152	524	3,465	9,447
%	.6	0	2.1	2.4	.3	.8	.4
Kastanozem							
T Ha	9,662	0	12	0	30,854	40,641	81,169
%	2.1	0	0	0	15.5	9.1	3.7
Lithosol							
T Ha	81,446	51,435	6,868	4,164	37,263	55,575	236,751
%	17.8	5.4	9.5	8.5	18.7	12.5	10.9
Luvisol							
T Ha	16,752	66,030	3,130	5,791	23,247	5,193	120,143
%	3.65	6.97	4.32	11.85	11.65	1.16	5.53
Nitosol							
T Ha	11,623	22,266	8,725	4,439	3,907	8,943	59,903
%	2.5	2.4	12.0	9.1	2.0	2.0	2.8
Phaeozem							
T Ha	2,802	13,061	3	0	1,421	38,083	55,370
%	.6	1.4	0	0	.7	8.5	2.5
Planosol							
T Ha	8,876	25,686	242	1,332	372	32,820	69,328
%	1.9	2.7	.3	2.7	.2	7.4	3.2
Podzol							
T Ha	383	1,109	1,036	17	458	3,855	6,858
%	.1	.1	1.4	0	.2	.9	.3
Ranker							
T Ha	0	2,268	0	0	0	5,370	7,638
%	0	.2	0	0	0	1.2	.4
Regosol							
T Ha	9,623	6,680	2,247	2,059	12,497	22,423	55,529
%	2.1	.7	3.1	4.2	6.3	5.0	2.6
Rendzina							
T Ha	251	564	2,244	1,610	13,315	170	18,154
%	.1	.1	3.1	3.3	6.7	0	.8
Solonchack							
T Ha	2,663	3,237	207	0	436	18,204	24,747
%	.6	.3	.3	0	.2	4.1	1.1
Solonetz							
T Ha	2,971	5,692	286	235	1,413	26,487	37,084
%	.6	.6	.4	.5	.7	5.9	1.7
Vertisol							
T Ha	6,351	10,373	1,762	1,661	10,110	10,252	40,509
%	1.4	1.1	2.4	3.4	5.1	2.3	1.9
Xerosol							
T Ha	9,045	0	30	0	11,390	28,658	49,123
%	2.0	0	0	0	5.7	6.4	2.3
Miscellaneous							
T Ha	1,796	0	245	0	0	4,917	6,958
%	.39	0	.34	0	0	1.10	.32

SOURCE: FAO ANNEX IV, Natural Resources and the Environment, 1988, table II.2, p. 13.

Table 201

DISTRIBUTION OF ARABLE LAND IN USE BY
LAND-WATER CLASSES, 2 LR, 1982–84

Region/Country	Low Rainfall	Uncertain Rainfall	Good Rainfall	Problem Land	Flooded Land	Desert Land	Total Land
Andean							
Arable Land (T Ha)	1,671	3,621	4,999	7,654	1,263	906	20,114
% of Class in Total Land	8.3	18.0	24.9	38.1	6.3	4.5	100
C. BRAZIL							
Arable Land (T Ha)	2,456	6,546	34,889	32,593	6,025	0	82,509
% of Class in Total Land	3.0	7.9	42.3	39.5	7.3	0	100
Caribbean[1]							
Arable Land (T Ha)	81	1,339	1,474	2,710	431	0	6,035
% of Class in Total Land	1.3	22.2	24.4	44.9	7.1	0	100
Central America							
Arable Land (T Ha)	0	0	2,882	2,995	220	0	6.098
% of Class in Total Land	0	0	47.3	49.1	3.6	0	100
N. MEXICO							
Arable Land (T Ha)	1,079	6,092	9,316	4,376	181	2,690	23,734
% of Class in Total Land	4.5	25.7	39.3	18.4	.8	11.3	100
Southern Cone							
Arable Land (T Ha)	4,082	5,325	34,708	10,498	551	1,253	56,417
% of Class in Total Land	7.2	9.4	61.5	18.6	1.0	2.2	100
Total Latin America							
Arable Land (T Ha)	9,369	22,923	88,268	60,826	8,671	4,849	194,907
% of Class in Total Land	4.8	11.8	45.3	31.2	4.4	2.5	100

1. Cuba, Dominican Republic, Guyana, Haiti, Jamaica, Suriname, and Trinidad and Tobago.

SOURCE: FAO ANNEX IV, Natural Resources and the Environment, 1988, table IV.2, p. 32.

Table 202

FAO LAND USE DATA, 20 LRC
(T Ha 1986[a])

		Surface		Agricultural			Nonagricultural	
	Country	Total Area[1]	Land Area[2]	Arable Land[3]	Land Under Permanent Crops[4]	Permanent Meadows and Pastures[5]	Forests and Woodlands[6]	Other Uses
A.	ARGENTINA[7]	276,689	273,669	26,300[t]	9,750[t]	142,600[t]	59,600[t]	35,419
B.	BOLIVIA	109,858	108,439	3,270[t]	128[t]	26,800[t]	55,830[t]	22,411
C.	BRAZIL	851,197	845,651	65,000[t]	11,780[t]	167,000[t]	560,420[t]	41,451
D.	CHILE	75,695	74,880	5,350[t]	200[t]	11,900[t]	8,680[t]	48,750
E.	COLOMBIA	113,891	103,870	3,805[t]	1,493[t]	39,800[t]	51,500[t]	7,272
F.	COSTA RICA	5,070	5,066	285[t]	241[t]	2,300[t]	1,640[t]	600
G.	CUBA	11,086	11,086	2,600[t]	718[t]	2,654[t]	2,731[t]	2,383
H.	DOMINICAN REP.	4,873	4,838	1,120[t]	355[t]	2,092[t]	623[t]	648
I.	ECUADOR	28,356	27,684	1,650[t]	946	4,900[t]	12,093	8,095
J.	EL SALVADOR	2,104	2,072	565[t]	168[t]	610[t]	104[t]	625
K.	GUATEMALA	10,889	10,843	1,360[t]	485[t]	1,334[t]	4,070[t]	3,594
L.	HAITI	2,775	2,756	555[t]	350[t]	496[t]	52[t]	1,303
M.	HONDURAS	11,209	11,189	1,575[t]	210[t]	3,400[t]	3,580[t]	2,424
N.	MEXICO	197,255	192,304	23,200[t]	1,555[t]	74,499[t]	44,620[t]	48,430
O.	NICARAGUA	13,000	11,875	1,095[t]	173[t]	5,200[t]	3,820[t]	1,587
P.	PANAMA[8]	7,708	7,599	438[t]	135[t]	1,161[t]	3,990[t]	1,875
Q.	PARAGUAY	40,675	39,730	2,060[t]	116[t]	15,400[t]	20,300[t]	1,854
R.	PERU	128,522	128,000	3,385[t]	325[t]	27,120[t]	69,400[t]	27,770
S.	URUGUAY	17,622	17,362	1,400[t]	46[t]	13,551	630[t]	1,735
T.	VENEZUELA	91,205	88,205	3,130[t]	680[t]	17,500[t]	31,335[t]	35,560
	LATIN AMERICA	2,054,852	2,019,684	148,143	29,854	560,317	935,018	312,232
	UNITED STATES	937,261	916,660	187,881	2,034	241,467	265,188	220,090

1. Refers to total area of country, including area under inland water bodies. Definition of such bodies usually embraces major rivers and lakes.
2. Refers to total area excluding that beneath water bodies.
3. Land under temporary crops, temporary meadows for mowing or pasture, truck gardens or temporarily fallow or idle. Areas double cropped are counted only once.
4. Refers to long-lived perennial crops. Trees for timber production are excluded.
5. Land under permanent (5 or more years) herbaceous forage crops, both cultivated and natural.
6. Land under natural or planted stand of trees, whether productive or not.
7. Continental sector only.
8. Excludes Canal Zone.

a. For previous years see SALA, 18-400; SALA, 19-400; SALA, 20-400; SALA, 21,400; SALA, 22-400; SALA, 23-400; SALA, 24-200; SALA, 26-200; SALA, 27-200.

SOURCE: FAO-PY, 1987, table 1, p. 47.

Table 203

IDB LAND USE DATA BY REGION
(km^2 1977)

Region	Arable Land Area	%	Pastures Area	%	Forests Area	%	Other Area	%
Mexico	232,200	12.1	744,990	38.7	707,000	36.8	238.850	12.4
Central America[1]	60,580	11.9	96.140	18.9	271,130	53.3	80,850	15.0
Caribbean[2]	60,620	25.9	54,030	23.1	47,220	20.2	71,700	30.7
South America								
Andean[3]	226,690	5.0	908,000	19.9	2,700,100	59.2	728,270	15.9
Atlantic[4]	740,369	7.9	1,821,140	19.6	5,373,382	57.8	1,358,550	14.6
Southern Cone[5]	427,380	11.6	1,700,500	46.3	809,068	22.0	734,340	20.0
Latin America and the Caribbean	1,747,839	8.5	5,324,800	26.3	9,907,900	49.1	3,212,560	15.9

1. Belize, Costa Rica, El Salvador, Guatemala, Honduras, Nicaragua, and Panama.
2. Cuba, Haiti, and the Dominican Republic plus thirteen smaller island republics and possessions.
3. Bolivia, Colombia, Ecuador, Peru, and Venezuela.
4. Brazil, French Guiana, Guyana, Paraguay, and Suriname.
5. Argentina, Chile, and Uruguay.

SOURCE: IDB-SPTF, 1983, table II-1.

Table 204

IDB AGRICULTURAL LAND USE DATA BY REGION
(km^2 1977)

Region	Arable	Cultivated	Irrigated Area	Irrigated % of Cultivated Land
Mexico	232,200	151,900	50,000	32.9
Central America	60,580	43,979	3,210	7.3
Caribbean	60,620	55,175	10,070	18.3
South America				
Andean	226,690	108,850	24,500	22.5
Atlantic	740,369	471,590	12,070	2.6
Southern Cone	427,380	310.360	28,700	9.2
Latin America and the Caribbean	1,747,839	1,141,854	128,550	11.3

SOURCE: IDB-SPTF, 1983, table II-2.

Table 205

CULTIVATED LAND, 20 LR, 1959–74

		T Ha.					Indexes (1959-61 = 100)			
	Country	1959-1961	1964-1966	1970	1973	1974	1964-1966	1970	1973	1974
A.	ARGENTINA	14,498	14,745	15,232	15,687	15,655	101.7	106.1	108.2	108.0
B.	BOLIVIA	613	680	771	771	888	110.9	125.8	125.8	144.9
C.	BRAZIL	25,152	29,441	33,906	36,662	40,971	117.1	134.8	145.8	162.9
D.	CHILE	1,544	1,424	1,425	1,200	1,312	92.2	92.3	77.7	85.0
E.	COLOMBIA	3,192	3,546	3,580	3,804	3,997	111.1	112.2	119.2	125.2
F.	COSTA RICA	321	401	352	351	358	124.9	109.7	109.3	111.5
G.	CUBA	1,710	1,679	2,026	1,810	1,817	98.2	118.5	105.8	106.3
H.	DOMINICAN REP.	625	618	667	671	676	98.9	106.7	107.4	108.2
I.	ECUADOR	1,024	1,425	1,678	1,662	1,644	139.2	163.9	162.3	160.5
J.	EL SALVADOR	585	708	614	709	689	121.0	105.0	121.2	117.8
K.	GUATEMALA	1,257	1,523	1,491	1,759	1,809	121.2	118.6	139.9	143.9
L.	HAITI	867	917	931	956	957	105.8	107.4	110.3	110.4
M.	HONDURAS	618	617	599	660	682	99.8	96.9	106.8	110.4
N.	MEXICO	11,458	14,225	13,971	14,570	14,632	124.1	121.9	127.2	127.7
O.	NICARAGUA	518	819	705	708	715	158.1	136.1	136.7	138.0
P.	PANAMA	371	332	449	458	478	89.5	121.0	123.5	128.8
Q.	PARAGUAY	336	497	622	618	742	147.9	185.1	183.9	220.8
R.	PERU	1,612	1,727	1,894	1,749	1,809	107.1	117.5	108.5	112.2
S.	URUGUAY	1,415	1,231	1,035	989	1,073	87.0	73.1	69.9	75.8
T.	VENEZUELA	1,250	1,332	1,727	1,534	1,659	106.6	138.2	122.7	132.7
	LATIN AMERICA[1]	69,257	78,292	84,023	87,677	92,913	111.9	121.3	126.6	134.2

1. Includes Barbados, Guyana, Jamaica, Trinidad and Tobago.

SOURCE: ECLA, *El Desarrollo Latinoamericano y la Coyuntura Económica Internacional,* *Tercera Parte*, 1975, p. 253.

Table 206

FAO IRRIGATED LAND DATA, 20 LRC, 1961–86
(T Ha)

	Country	1961-65	1966	1970	1975	1977	1978	1979[†]	1980	1982	1984	1985	1986
A.	ARGENTINA	1,046[†]	1,650[†]	1,700[†]	1,800[†]	1,510[†]	1,540[†]	1,560	1,580	1,620[†]	1,660[†]	1,680[†]	1,700[†]
B.	BOLIVIA	74[†]	75[†]	80[‡]	120[†]	120[†]	125[†]	125	140	150[†]	155[†]	160[†]	160[†]
C.	BRAZIL	546[†]	640[†]	796	950[†]	1,000[†]	1,050[†]	1,700	1,800[†]	2,000[†]	2,200[†]	2,300[†]	2 400[†]
D.	CHILE	1,084	1,100[†]	1,180[†]	1,260[†]	1,300[†]	1,320[†]	1,252	1,255[†]	1,259[†]	1,257	1,257[†]	1,257[†]
E.	COLOMBIA	231	240[†]	250[†]	280[†]	290[†]	295[†]	305	310[†]	318[†]	322[†]	324[†]	470[†]
F.	COSTA RICA	26	26[‡]	26[‡]	26[‡]	26[‡]	26[‡]	26	61[†]	74	84[†]	110[†]	110[†]
G.	CUBA	280	500[†]	520[†]	535[†]	700	720[†]	900	962	1,000[†]	1,030[†]	865	870[†]
H.	DOMINICAN REP.	113	120[†]	125	135	140[†]	140[†]	145	145[†]	176	180[†]	198	200[†]
I.	ECUADOR	446[†]	463[‡]	470[†]	500[†]	510[†]	520[†]	520	520[†]	530[†]	537[†]	540[†]	542[†]
J.	EL SALVADOR	18	20[‡]	20[‡]	33	50	50	102	110[†]	110	110[†]	110[†]	112[†]
K.	GUATEMALA	38	45[†]	56	60[‡]	64[†]	64[†]	66	68[†]	72[†]	75[†]	75[†]	77[†]
L.	HAITI	38[†]	42	60[†]	70	70[‡]	70[‡]	70	70[‡]	70[†]	70[†]	70[†]	70[†]
M.	HONDURAS	60	66[‡]	70[†]	80[†]	80[†]	80[†]	80	82[†]	84[†]	85[†]	85[†]	87[†]
N.	MEXICO	2,900[†]	3,750[†]	3,950[†]	4,479	5,000[†]	5,000[†]	5,100	5,100[†]	5,053	5,100[†]	4,890[†]	4,900[†]
O.	NICARAGUA	18	18[‡]	29[‡]	32	74	76[†]	78	80[†]	82[†]	83[†]	83[†]	83[†]
P.	PANAMA	15	18[†]	20[†]	23[†]	25[†]	26[†]	28	28[†]	28[†]	30[†]	30[†]	30[†]
Q.	PARAGUAY	30[†]	40[†]	40[†]	55[†]	55[†]	55[†]	55	60[†]	62[†]	62[†]	65[†]	65[†]
R.	PERU	1,041	1,078	1,106	1,130[†]	1,180[†]	1,180[†]	1,180	1,190[†]	1,180[†]	1,200[†]	1,210[†]	1,220[†]
S.	URUGUAY	32	42	52	57[†]	60[†]	64[†]	70	80[†]	88[†]	92[†]	94[†]	96[†]
T.	VENEZUELA	218	255[‡]	284[‡]	314[‡]	350[†]	360[†]	310	315[†]	317[†]	322[†]	324[†]	326[†]
	LATIN AMERICA	8,254	9,725[@]	10,364[@]	11,439[@]	12,604[@]	12,761[@]	13,672[@]	13,921[@]	14,273[@]	14,654[@]	14,470	14,775
	UNITED STATES	14,659	15,300[†]	15,900[†]	16,500[†]	17,200[†]	16,700[†]	16,697	20,582	19,831	19,831[†]	18,102	18,102

SOURCE: FAO-PY, 1976-81, table 2; 1983, table 2; 1985, table 2; 1986, table 2; 1987, table 2.

Table 207

IDB ARABLE AND IRRIGATED LAND DATA
(T Ha, ca. 1978)

Country	Land Arable[1]	Under Irrigation[2]	Under Irrigation/Arable (%)
A. ARGENTINA	34,420	1,400	4.1
B. BOLIVIA	1,100	100	9.1
C. BRAZIL	38,803	851	2.2
D. CHILE	5,742	1,244	21.7
E. COLOMBIA	5,090	270	5.3
F. COSTA RICA	622	66	10.6
H. DOMINICAN REP.	995	130	13.1
I. ECUADOR	4,324	190	4.4
J. EL SALVADOR	733	26	3.5
K. GUATEMALA	1,700	60	3.5
L. HAITI	908	70	7.7
M. HONDURAS	870	44	5.1
N. MEXICO	27,390	5,000	18.3
O. NICARAGUA	960	29	3.0
P. PANAMA	555	30	5.4
Q. PARAGUAY	970	50	5.2
R. PERU	2,880	1,120	38.9
S. URUGUAY	2,252	45	2.0
T. VENEZUELA	5,214	235	4.5
LATIN AMERICA[3]	135,528	10,960	8.1

1. Includes annual and perennial crops, cultivated prairies, and fallow lands.
2. Includes all land irrigated by means of canals, deposits, common and artesian wells, and machinery for drip irrigation, whether it is subject to irrigation all year or only during the dry season.
3. Includes Guyana, Jamaica, Trinidad and Tobago.

SOURCE: IDB-SPTF, 1983, table III-4.

Table 208

U.N. ARABLE LAND AND CROPLAND, 20 LC
(Ha per Capita and per Person Agriculturally Employed, 1970)

Country	Arable Land PI	Cropland PI	Cropland Agricultural Population
A. ARGENTINA	1.43	1.07	7.03
B. BOLIVIA	.47	.63	1.08
C. BRAZIL	.36	.32	.73
D. CHILE	.55	.47	1.86
E. COLOMBIA	.23	.25	.55
F. COSTA RICA	.28	~	~
G. CUBA	.42	.43	1.30
H. DOMINICAN REP.	.23	~	~
I. ECUADOR	.63	~	~
J. EL SALVADOR	.18	~	~
K. GUATEMALA	.30	.29	.46
L. HAITI	.21	.08	.10
M. HONDURAS	.33	~	~
N. MEXICO	.55	.47	1.01
O. NICARAGUA	.46	~	~
P. PANAMA	.37	~	~
Q. PARAGUAY	.43	~	~
R. PERU	.21	.21	.46
S. URUGUAY	.63	.67	4.04
T. VENEZUELA	.48	.47	1.81
UNITED STATES	.94	.86	21.48

SOURCE: UN-CSS, 1977, pp. 150-152, 1157.

Table 209

TROPICAL LAND DEVELOPMENT PROJECTS, 8 L

Level of Government Participation and Project	Country	Date of Project Initiation	Gross Area (Ha)[1]	No. of Farms[1]	Rural and Urban Population in Project Area[1]	Ecological Zone[2]
Directed Colonization						
Nuevo Ixcatlán	Mexico	1955	13,400	703	3,000	Sw
Cihualtepec	Mexico	1957	18,600	476	1,700	Sm
La Joya	Mexico	1956	8,000	285	1,400	Sm
La Chontalpa	Mexico	1965	83,000	4,900	22,000	Tm
Bataan	Costa Rica	1964	10,500	265	1,300	Tw
Alto Beni I	Bolivia	1959	7,000	520	2,500	Tm
Alto Beni II	Bolivia	1963	36,000	1,400	6,500	Tm
Chimoré	Bolivia	1963	120,000	700	3,400	Tr
Yacapani	Bolivia	1963	110,000	1,900	9,500	Sm
Semidirected Colonization[3]						
Santo Domingo de los Colorados	Ecuador	1964	210,000	5,200	40,000	S/Tm
Valle del Upano	Ecuador	1964	170,000	1,400	7,150	Sr
Tingo María-Tocache	Peru	1966	127,500	2,150	30,000	Sw
Puerto Presidente Stroessner	Paraguay	1963	45,000	900	4,500	Sm
Spontaneous Colonization[3]						
Caranavi	Bolivia	1945	500,000	8,250	39,000	Sm
Chapare	Bolivia	1920	185,000	5,460	18,600	Tr
Caquetá	Colombia	1932	1,050,000	22,000	175,000	Tw
Puyo-Tena	Ecuador	1940	220,000	4,000	30,000	Sr
Private Subdivision and Development						
Ivinheima (SOMECO)	Brazil	1958	1,000,000	1,800	28,000	Sm
Cia. Melhoramentos Norte do Paraná	Brazil	1930	1,250,000	39,000	1,700,000	Sm
Gleba Arinos (CONOMALI)	Brazil	1954	200,000	120	600	Tw
Tournavista	Peru	1954	410,000	100	600	Tw
Foreign Colonization						
San Juan	Bolivia	1957	35,000	280	1,580	Sm
Okinawa	Bolivia	1957	55,000	600	4,000	Sm
Filadelfia	Paraguay	1927	500,000	1,500	20,000	Sd

1. Data are for 1967–68.
2. T = tropical, S = subtropical, r = rainy, w = wet, m = moist, d = dry.
3. Projects involving provision of services in areas already occupied by spontaneous settlers.

SOURCE: IDB-SPTF, 1985.

Table 210

HUMID TROPICAL LAND RESOURCES OF SOUTH AMERICA, 8 LR

(M Ha)

				Soil Areas According to Suitability						
		Cropping								
Country	Alluvial[1]	Hydromorphic[2]	Good Upland[3]	Marginal-low Fertility[4]	Marginal-shallow or Steep[5]	Total	Pasture or Plantations[6]	Forestry or Reserve	Total
A. ARGENTINA	2.7	2.3	3.1	5.7	1.7	15.5	15.2	6.5	37.2
B. BOLIVIA	.7	10.8	.6	12.3	2.2	26.6	52.2 ←	→	78.8
C. BRAZIL	3.2	25.4	21.8	174.4	18.5	243.3	333.3	170.1	746.7
E. COLOMBIA	3.6	6.3	1.5	20.2	.4	32.0	69.4 ←	→	101.4
I. ECUADOR	.1	.6	.4	4.8	.1	6.0	15.3 ←	→	21.3
Q. PARAGUAY	.7	2.8	4.2	7.1	.7	15.5	14.8	10.4	40.7
R. PERU	.1	2.7	1.6	17.2	.4	22.0	55.1 ←	→	77.1
T. VENEZUELA	.2	5.7	2.3	17.1	5.0	30.3	6.1	18.7	55.1
Total	11.3	56.6	35.5	258.8	29.0	391.2	767.1 ←	→	1,158.3

1. Soils developed from recent deposits and located in floodplains or deltas. Characteristics of the soils depend on their parent material.
2. These soils are found on flat or depressed landscapes with little or no runoff where drainage presents a problem.
3. These soils occur on undulating or level topography, are well drained, are not susceptible to serious erosion, and have medium-high natural fertility.
4. These soils are of the upland type but with very low natural fertility. With appropriate crops and fertilizer, reasonable yields may be expected.

5. These soils pose special problems for agricultural use due to shallowness or slope, heavy texture or sandiness. They occur primarily in highland areas and are susceptible to severe erosion.
6. These soils are unsuited to normal crop production because of major limiting factors such as steep topography, poor drainage, low fertility, sandiness, heavy texture, and rock outcrops or stones.

SOURCE: Adapted from Michael Nelson, *The Development of Tropical Lands: Policy Issues in Latin America* (Baltimore: Johns Hopkins University Press, 1973), table 2.

Table 211

PROJECTED NEW LAND DEVELOPMENT AND INVESTMENTS IN SOUTH AMERICA, 7 LR, 1962–85

(M Ha)

			Dry and Irrigated Cropland[1]					
Country	Irrigated	Dry Land	From Pasture[2]	From Forest	Total	Pasture From Forest	Total Forest Clearing	Total Investment[3]
B. BOLIVIA	.3	#	.15	.15	.3[a]	4.15	4.3	120
C. BRAZIL	.4	9.4	4.9	4.9	9.8	12.2	17.1	2,120
E. COLOMBIA	.3	1.7	1.0	1.0	2.0[a]	6.6	7.6	440
I. ECUADOR	.1	.6	.35	.35	.7	.85	1.2	93
Q. PARAGUAY	#	.4	.2	.2	.4	3.7	3.9	147
R. PERU	.3[b]	.8	.4	.4	.8	.7	1.1	70
T. VENEZUELA	.3	.1	.2	.2	.4[a]	3.8	4.0	270
TOTAL	1.7	13.0	7.2	7.2	14.4	31.7	39.2[c]	3,260

1. Irrigated land derived 50 percent from pasture and 50 percent from dryland crop area. For table on humid land tropical resources, see SALA, 18-403.
2. Assumption that 50 percent of new cropland will be derived from existing pasture.
3. Investment in development of new lands not associated with irrigation, drainage, or flood control, at 1962 prices.

a. Total area in nonirrigated crops in Colombia is projected to increase by 1.7 million ha. The additional .3 million compensate for projected irrigation of currently nonirrigated pasture and croplands. Increases of .3 million ha. are made for both Bolivia and Venezuela in similar compensation.
b. Irrigated land derived from desert.
c. Annual rate of forest clearing would be 1.75 million ha.

SOURCE: FAO, *Indicative World Plan for Agricultural Development to 1975 and 1985, South America*, vol. 1 (Rome, 1968). Cf. table 2300.

Table 212
FERTILIZER CONSUMPTION,[1] 20 LRC, 1970–86[a]
(T MET)

Country	1970	1974	1975	1976	1977	1978	1979	1980	1981	1982	1983	1984	1985	1986
A. ARGENTINA	87	75‡	60‡	78	74	107	130	113	96	113	131‡	148‡	155	155
B. BOLIVIA	2	6‡	3‡	3‡	4	5	3	3	7	3‡	8	5	6‡	7‡
C. BRAZIL	1,002	1,825	1,978	2,528	3,209	3,222	3,567	4,201	2,753	2,729	2,272	3,364	3,223	3,946‡
D. CHILE	153	167	99	121	103	129	121	132	113	105	137	180	216	222‡
E. COLOMBIA	144	250	215	246	292‡	291	312	312‡	280‡	325‡	318‡	363‡	366‡	408
F. COSTA RICA	49	73‡	66‡	56	67‡	80‡	79‡	74‡	72‡	72‡	88‡	96‡	81‡	85‡
G. CUBA	396	302	331	356	418‡	451	464	530	607	554	528	580	585	663
H. DOMINICAN REP.	38	98	73‡	76‡	50‡	57	72	52‡	58‡	51‡	42‡	59‡	61‡	61‡
I. ECUADOR	34	41	33	81	86	71	79	73	70‡	72	74‡	73	72	106‡
J. EL SALVADOR	65	99‡	94‡	102	106	112	75‡	60	88	60	82	55	85	66
K. GUATEMALA	46	65	55‡	95	103	95	100‡	86‡	89	89	68	90‡	95	115‡
L. HAITI	~	2	2‡	~	3‡	4‡	4‡	~	6‡	5‡	3‡	4‡	3‡	2‡
M. HONDURAS	24‡	19‡	20‡	25‡	28‡	23‡	20‡	29‡	28‡	24	28	36	23	39
N. MEXICO	538	864	1,073	1,120	1,068	1,067	1,134	1,238	1,561	1,825	1,486‡	1,661‡	1,714	1,826
O. NICARAGUA	26	35‡	19‡	48	48	48	23‡	54	60‡	23‡	71	49	63	68
P. PANAMA	21	28	25	23‡	23	23‡	30‡	31‡	30‡	27‡	23‡	28‡	26‡	35‡
Q. PARAGUAY	9	2	1	1‡	1‡	3‡	11	6	14	10	10	15	12	12‡
R. PERU	84‡	142	104	129	139	137	117	118	132	93	79	78	74	116
S. URUGUAY	69	68	47	74	63	58	92	81	64‡	49‡	42‡	53‡	55‡	68‡
T. VENEZUELA	59	129	140	161	176	197	222	241	146	153‡	154‡	268‡	408‡	535‡
LATIN AMERICA	2,846@	4,290@	4,438@	5,323@	6,061@	6,180@	6,655@	7,434@	6,274@	6,832@	5,644@	7,205@	7,306@	8,535@
UNITED STATES	15,535	15,941	18,914	20,059	18,676	20,471	20,941	21,480	19,439	16,416	19,768	19,688	17,804	17,431
WORLD	69,068	82,041	90,423	95,489	100,391	108,140	112,248	116,559	114,815	114,500	125,237	139,356	128,672	133,176

1. Includes nitrogenous, phosphate, and potash fertilizers.

a. For 1961–70 data, see SALA, 23-1519.

SOURCE: FAO-FY, 1979 and 1981, table 33; 1983, table 32; 1986, table 32; 1987, table 32.

Table 213
FERTILIZER CONSUMPTION[1] PER HECTARE OF ARABLE
LAND AND PER INHABITANT, 20 LC, 1970–86[a]
(H G)

Country	Per Ha Arable Land and Permanent Crops							PI						
	1970	1975	1980	1982	1984	1985	1986	1970	1975	1980	1982	1984	1985	1986
A. ARGENTINA	26	17	33	31	37	43	43	36	23	41	41	44	51	50
B. BOLIVIA	7	10	9	8	25	17	20	3	7	5	5	14	9	10
C. BRAZIL	186	328	591	365	304	425	514	105	183	346	213	175	238	285
D. CHILE	313	188	239	189	249	391	400	162	96	119	91	118	180	182
E. COLOMBIA	286	405	553	538	558	643	770	69	93	121	113	115	127	139
F. COSTA RICA	1,001	1,301	1,229	1,134	1,391	1,332	1,616	285	336	323	310	357	310	319
G. CUBA	1,517	1,064	1,655	1,726	1,642	1,809	1,998	462	365	544	564	533	583	654
H. DOMINICAN REP.	334	582	363	353	288	415	414	88	148	93	82	70	98	96
I. ECUADOR	133	127	295	277	297	285	409	56	47	89	85	83	77	110
J. EL SALVADOR	1,043	1,442	832	830	1,132	1,156	906	181	227	126	118	157	152	116
K. GUATEMALA	298	336	489	498	375	518	621	88	91	124	115	90	119	140
L. HAITI	4	24	4	51	36	35	23	1	4	1	8	5	5	3
M. HONDURAS	156	122	162	137	159	128	220	91	65	77	61	69	52	87
N. MEXICO	232	450	505	778	602	693	737	105	178	178	247	198	217	226
O. NICARAGUA	215	157	435	186	557	360	536	126	80	196	80	231	139	201
P. PANAMA	387	467	551	469	411	452	616	137	146	156	135	111	118	159
Q. PARAGUAY	98	10	36	39	46	52	57	39	4	20	23	26	31	33
R. PERU	300	327	336	266	224	201	314	64	69	68	50	42	38	58
S. URUGUAY	485	330	558	376	292	378	471	247	168	278	184	142	182	224
T. VENEZUELA	170	391	642	408	411	108	1,405	56	111	160	92	94	236	301
LATIN AMERICA[2]	149	223	353	270	234	328	397	87	126	199	150	127	172	205
UNITED STATES	816	1,005	1,127	867	1,041	937	918	758	876	943	712	843	745	724
WORLD	226	305	417	779	853	474	904	86	107	137	250	268	145	271

1. Includes nitrogenous, phosphate, and potash fertilizers.
2. Does not include Mexico, Central America, and the Caribbean.

a. For earlier years see previous issues of SALA.

SOURCE: FAO, Annual Fertilizer Review, 1976, table 12; FAO-FY, 1979-81, table 11; 1983, table 10; 1985–86, table 10; 1987, table 10.

Table 214

TRACTORS IN USE, 20 LRC, 1961–86

(N)

	Country	1961–65	1969–71	1974	1977	1979[†]	1980[†]	1981	1982	1983	1984	1985	1986
A.	ARGENTINA	139,000	171,450	184,000	195,000[†]	171,400	166,700	158,900	203,700	201,800	203,700	204,000	206,000[†]
B.	BOLIVIA	220	355	720[†]	665	750	750	740[†]	750[†]	760[†]	770[†]	780[†]	790[†]
C.	BRAZIL	97,200	168,257	236,000[†]	280,000[†]	320,000	330,000	340,000[†]	655,000[†]	710,000[†]	765,000[†]	770,000[†]	775,000[†]
D.	CHILE	21,061	21,523	28,000[†]	20,700[†]	34,550	34,600	34,650[†]	34,700[†]	34,360[†]	34,350[†]	34,340	37,920
E.	COLOMBIA	24,290	22,780	31,000[†]	25,594	27,500	28,423	28,500[†]	28,600[†]	28,700[†]	28,800[†]	28,900[†]	33,757[†]
F.	COSTA RICA	4,311	5,100	5,500[†]	5,750[†]	5,900	5,950	6,000[†]	6,050[†]	6,100[†]	6,150[†]	6,200[†]	6,250[†]
G.	CUBA	19,800	48,434	52,700	64,423	70,374	68,300	64,500	66,509	66,262	65,900[†]	68,585	68,500[†]
H.	DOMINIAN REP.	2,330	2,510	5,500[†]	2,930[†]	3,050	3,150	3,220[†]	3,250[†]	2,210[†]	2,230[†]	2,250[†]	2,270[†]
I.	ECUADOR	1,689	3,133	3,400[†]	5,440	5,650	5,750	6,844	7,186	7,400[†]	7,600[†]	7,800[†]	8,000[†]
J.	EL SALVADOR	1,800	2,514	2,850[†]	3,050[†]	3,250	3,300	3,320[†]	3,340[†]	3,360[†]	3,380[†]	3,390[†]	3,400[†]
K.	GUATEMALA	2,250	3,167	3,600[†]	3,800[†]	3,950	4,000	4,020[†]	4,040[†]	4,060[†]	4,080[†]	4,100[†]	4,120[†]
L.	HAITI	271	363	420[†]	460[†]	500	520	530[†]	540[†]	550[†]	560[†]	565[†]	570[†]
M.	HONDURAS	331	1,693	950[†]	3,100[†]	3,160	3,250	3,280[†]	3,300[†]	3,310[†]	3,330[†]	3,350[†]	3,370[†]
N.	MEXICO	72,000	91,318	135,000[†]	101,611	114,000	120,000	143,078	146,083	152,319[†]	155,000[†]	157,000[†]	160,000[†]
O.	NICARAGUA	450	500	768	1,636	2,100	2,200	2,250[†]	2,300[†]	2,350[†]	2,400[†]	2,430[†]	2,450[†]
P.	PANAMA	789	2,414	3,500[†]	3,850[†]	3,950	4,000	4,050[†]	4,100[†]	4,150[†]	4,180[†]	4,200[†]	6,400[†]
Q.	PARAGUAY	1,500	2,200	2,600[†]	2,900[†]	3,100	3,200	3,300[†]	8,000[†]	8,500[†]	9,000[†]	9,500[†]	9,900[†]
R.	PERU	7,707	10,902	12,000[†]	13,000[†]	13,600	13,900	14,300[†]	16,500[†]	17,300[†]	17,800[†]	18,300[†]	18,600[†]
S.	URUGUAY	23,812	26,659	27,400[†]	27,700[†]	28,000	28,200	33,470[†]	33,550[†]	33,490[†]	33,500[†]	33,520[†]	33,550[†]
T.	VENEZUELA	13,086	19,200	23,460	33,888	37,000	38,000	39,000[†]	40,000[†]	41,500[†]	42,500[†]	43,500[†]	44,500[†]
	LATIN AMERICA	433,447	604,472	765,200[@]	795,497[@]	851,784[@]	864,193[@]	893,952[@]	1,267,498[@]	1,328,481[@]	1,390,210[@]	1,402,710[@]	1,425,347[@]
	UNITED STATES	4,751,600	4,584,000	4,273,000	4,370,000	4,810,000	4,775,000	4,655,000	4,669,000	4,671,000	4,657,000[†]	4,676,000	4,676,000[†]

SOURCE: FAO-PY, 1976–81, table 109; 1983, table 117; 1985, table 117; 1986, table 118; 1987, table 118.

Table 215

AGRICULTURAL TECHNOLOGY, 8 LR

(1980)

			Cereals			Fertilizers		Tractor (units)	
		Cereal Yield/ Hectare	Agricultural EAP	Tractors	% Irrigated Area	Tons/1,000 Arable Hectares	1,000 Agricultural EAP	1,000/Arable Hectares	1,000 Agricultural EAP
	UNITED STATES	4,162	135.6	.06	10.8	54.2	4,639.5	25.0	2,142.0
	BULGARIA	3,854	5.3	.13	28.6	100.6	272.0	14.8	40.0
	JAPAN	5,272	2.2	.01	66.6	159.2	117.5	224.5	165.7
	NETHERLANDS	5,688	4.4	.01	31.9	504.6	1,659.1	206.7	607.5
A.	ARGENTINA	2,204	13.0	.09	4.5	1.7	43.4	5.8	150.0
C.	BRAZIL	1,329	1.8	.08	2.9	12.7	52.0	5.2	21.2
E.	COLOMBIA	2,390	1.3	.11	5.5	26.9	68.4	4.9	18.0
F.	COSTA RICA	2,207	1.0	.04	~	80.4	152.7	9.9	22.0
J.	EL SALVADOR	1,737	.8	.18	~	71.3	68.3	4.6	4.4
K.	GUATEMALA	1,524	.9	.26	3.8	32.1	48.8	2.2	3.3
N.	MEXICO	1,918	1.6	.10	22.0	35.6	114.6	4.9	15.8
T.	VENEZUELA	1,882	1.8	.04	8.5	26.1	118.3	6.3	4.0
	LATIN AMERICA		1.8	.09	8.3	15.0	61.6	5.1	21.0

SOURCE: CEPAL Review 24 (1984).

3

Land Tenure

Table 300
SYSTEMS OF LAND TENURE, ABSOLUTE DATA, 18 LC
(N and Ha.)

				Operated Under Single Tenurial Systems		Rented from Others								
Country	Year	N/Ha	Total	Total	Operated by Owner	Total	Payment in Cash/Kind	Partnerships or Similar Forms	Payment by Services	Other Arrangements	Occupied Without Title	Operated Under Collective System	Operated Under Other Simple Systems	Operated Under Mixed Systems
A. ARGENTINA[1,2]	1960	N	457,173	~	~	~	~	~	#	~	#	#	~	#
		Ha.	175,142,497	~	103,219,103	29,592,386	22,679,273	2,095,770[a]	#	4,817,343[b]	#	#	42,331,008[c]	#
B. BOLIVIA[3]	1950[v]	N	86,377	~	64,396[d]	17,248	13,598	3,033	617[e]	#	#	3,779[f]	954[g]	#
		Ha.	32,749,850	~	22,227,498[d]	2,471,306	1,983,765	382,115	105,426[e]	#	#	7,178,448[f]	872,598[g]	#
C. BRAZIL	1970	N	4,924,019	4,793,215	2,975,572	1,006,505	~	~	~	~	811,338	~	~	130,804
		Ha.	294,145,466	252,020,808	242,873,710	17,949,833	~	~	~	~	21,197,265	~	~	12,124,658
D. CHILE[6]	1965	N	253,532	225,572	119,704	99,746	12,312	18,009	53,922	15,503[n]	6,122	#	#	27,960
		Ha.	30,644,131	27,513,587	22,669,238	4,354,313	3,523,319	261,673	94,607	474,714[n]	490,037	#	#	3,130,543
E. COLOMBIA[4]	1960	N	1,209,672	1,110,316	755,318	282,347	~	~	~	~	46,961	#	25,690	99,356
		Ha.	27,337,826	25,660,351	19,779,585	2,009,274	~	~	~	~	3,314,076	#	557,416	1,677,475
F. COSTA RICA	1973	N	81,562	81,562	69,660	3,821[b]	1,474	359	~	244	—[o]	7,909	172	:
		Ha.	3,122,457	3,122,457	2,836,060	37,993[b]	24,926	3,563	~	2,712	—[o]	243,495	4,909	:
H. DOMINICAN REP.	1960	N	447,098	~	262,979	137,865	16,474	30,782	8,716[r]	81,893[pp]	39,596[j]	~	6,658	~
		Ha.	2,069,166[t]	~	1,512,375	427,241	92,549	86,561	35,840[r]	212,291[pp]	109,281[j]	~	20,259	~
I. ECUADOR	1954	N	344,234	313,582	233,900	50,121	17,038	13,336[o]	19,747[p]	#	#	5,778[f]	23,783[q]	30,652
		Ha.	5,999,700	5,668,800	4,889,400	551,700	426,200	64,700[o]	60,800[p]	#	#	25,700[f]	202,000[q]	330,900
J. EL SALVADOR	1961	N	226,896	197,091	89,918	99,226	43,457	~	55,769[r]	~	#	#	7,947	29,805[i]
		Ha.	1,581,428	1,458,110	1,225,221	122,954	78,877	~	44,077[r]	~	#	#	109,935	123,900[i]
EL SALVADOR	1971	N	272,432	233,999	107,450	126,549	80,547	~	~	~	#	#	46,002[s]	38,433[i]
		Ha.	1,463,859	1,326,162	1,118,080	208,082	108,841	~	~	~	#	#	99,241[s]	137,697[i]
K. GUATEMALA	1964	N	417,344	371,039	241,541	95,631	47,026	~[w]	48,605[f]	~	~[q]	20,593[f]	13,274[y]	46,305
		Ha.	3,448,736	2,983,292	2,670,962	195,380	106,712	~[w]	88,668[f]	~	~[q]	59,328[f]	57,622[y]	465,445
M. HONDURAS	1966	N	178,361	148,564	39,991	60,142	40,053	~	~	20,089[z]	4,308	44,123[aa]	#	29,797
		Ha.	2,417,053	1,869,402	1,106,907	363,710	122,760	~	~	240,950[z]	30,114	368,671[aa]	#	547,651
N. MEXICO[7]	1970	N	1,020,016	997,324	931,476	52,433	27,277	25,156[bb]	~	~[cc]	20,375[dd]	~[ee]	38,324	22,692
		Ha.	139,868,191	70,144,089	62,243,958	3,669,841	3,047,110	622,731[bb]	~	~[cc]	1,747,805[dd]	~[ee]	2,482,486	69,724,102
O. NICARAGUA	1963	N	102,201	88,223	39,445	12,872	4,799	2,906	1,215	3,952	16,049	8,170[aa]	11,687[ff]	13,978
		Ha.	3,822,813	3,822,813	2,550,113	98,300	53,135	13,542	4,354	27,269	735,846	311,343[aa]	127,211[ff]	~99
P. PANAMA	1971	N	105,272	92,971	12,906	4,671	~	~	~	~	75,394	:	:	12,301
		Ha.	2,098,062	1,552,489	545,414	73,961	~	~	~	~	933,144	:	:	545,573

Table 300 (Continued)
SYSTEMS OF LAND TENURE, ABSOLUTE DATA, 18 LC
(N and Ha.)

Country	Year	Total	Operated by Owner	Rented from Others — Total	Payment in Cash/Kind	Partnerships or Similar Forms	Payment by Services	Other Arrangements	Occupied Without Title	Operated Under Single Tenurial Systems — Operated Under Collective System	Operated Under Other Simple Systems	Operated Under Mixed Systems
Q. PARAGUAY[5]	1961											
N		160,777	59,994	12,000	12,000	#	#	#	66,653	#	#	22,130
Ha.		17,473,474	14,200,935	726,799	726,799	#	#	#	1,235,656	#	#	1,310,084
R. PERU	1961											
N		869,945[hh]	574,560	132,647	84,139	48,508[ii]	#	#	#	45,235[jj]	28,678	88,825
Ha.		17,722,044	11,875,859	2,465,253	2,256,939	2,208,314[ii]	#	#	#	1,933,939[jj]	540,887	906,106
S. URUGUAY[8]	1966											
N		79,193	43,656	22,068	19,201	2,867[k]	#	#	4,147	#	2,090	7,232
Ha.		16,533,556	8,198,667	3,845,625	3,688,187	157,438[k]	#	#	167,936	#	503,314	3,818,014
URUGUAY[8]	1970											
N		77,163	45,205	17,398	15,086	2,312[k]	#	#	4,233	#	2,662	7,665
Ha.		16,517,730	8,700,215	3,081,084	2,933,699	147,385[k]	#	#	174,984	#	606,670	3,954,777
T. VENEZUELA	1961[n]											
N		320,094[m]	125,627	41,189	25,966	15,223	#	#	124,119	#	#	24,542
Ha.		26,004,862[x]	21,187,669	613,631	494,950	118,681	#	#	2,832,834	#	#	1,370,728
UNITED STATES	1959											
N		2,730,250	1,705,720	352,923	~	~[u]	~	~	..	~	~[h]	671,607[i]
Ha.		430,336,324	151,799,714	55,688,760	~	~[u]	~	~	..	~	~[h]	222,847,850[i]

1. Details on the number of holdings were not obtained.
2. Excluding 14,583 holdings, the area of which is unknown.
3. For data on Bolivian and Venezuelan land reform, see James W. Wilkie, *Measuring Land Reform, Supplement 5 (1974).*
4. Excluding *Intendencias* and *Comisarías.*
5. Data obtained by sampling.
6. Excluding 5,125 properties without lands.
7. The data refer to the type of producer for 997,324 of total number.
8. Excluding holdings with an area of less than 1 ha.

a. "Medieros y Tanteros."
b. Free occupancy.
c. Comprises 29,477,389 ha. operated in the *Tierras Fiscales* and 12,883,619 ha. operated under "Other Forms of Tenancy."
d. Comprises holdings worked by proprietors alone, properties with settlers, day laborers, etc.
e. "Tolerados."
f. Communal lands.
g. Comprises 818 properties (439,264 ha.) operated by possessors of *Tierras Fiscales* and 136 properties (433,334 ha.) operated by *Granjas Cooperativas y Sociedades Agrícolas.*
h. Holdings operated by administrators.
i. Holdings operated by proprietors lessees.
j. Concessionaire.
k. Holdings operated by "Medianeros."
ℓ. Holdings operated illegally.
m. Including 4,617 holdings without agricultural land.

r. For data on Venezuelan land reform, see Wilkie, *Measuring Land Reform.*
c. Holdings operated by "Partidarios."
f. Holdings operated by "Huasipungueros."
c. Data obtained by sampling.
r. Properties operated by settlers.
s. Holdings operated by "Colonos."
t. Excluding 188,544 ha. in sugar cane.
u. Holdings operated by sharecroppers and livestock sharers.
v. See note 3.
w. Excluding 14,583 holdings, the area of which is unknown.
x. See note 3.
y. Comprises those lands not included in preceding categories. Such lands include those in legal usufruct at time of census; those continuously and pacifically occupied without owners' permission by squatters who do not pay rent; lands in judicial process of transfer.
z. Agricultural holdings in National Lands.
aa. Agricultural holdings in Ejidal Lands.
bb. "Aparcero" only.
cc. "Arrendatario."
dd. "Ocupantes."
ee. Property overseen by ejidal president.
ff. Including 7,543 properties (93,716 ha.) operated by usufructuaries.
gg. Farms operated under mixed tenure systems are included in the category of those operated under single systems.
hh. Including 26,663 holdings without land.
ii. Comprises partnership and bound-service by Amerinds (*Yanaconaje*).
jj. Including communal lands.

SOURCE: IASI-AC, 1974, table 311-03; IASI-AC, 1977, table 311-03.

Table 301
SYSTEMS OF LAND TENURE, PERCENTAGE DATA, 18 LC
(N and Ha.)

Country	Year	Total	Operated Under Single Tenurial Systems			Rented from Others				Occupied Without Title	Operated Under Collective System	Operated Under Other Simple Systems	Operated Under Mixed Systems
			Total	Operated by Owner	Total	Payment in Cash/Kind	Partnerships or Similar Forms	Payment by Services	Other Arrangements				
A. ARGENTINA[1,2] 1960													
N		100.0	100.0	~	~	~	~	#	~	#	#	~	#
Ha.		100.0	100.0	58.9	16.9	12.9	1.2[a]	#	2.8[b]	#	#	24.2[c]	#
B. BOLIVIA[3] 1950[u]													
N		100.0	100.0	74.6[d]	20.0	15.8	3.5	.7[e]	#	#	4.4[f]	1.1[g]	#
Ha.		100.0	100.0	67.9[d]	7.5	6.0	1.2	.3[e]	#	#	21.9[f]	2.7[g]	#
C. BRAZIL 1970													
N		100.0	97.3	60.4	20.4	~	~	~	~	16.5	~	~	2.7
Ha.		100.0	95.9	82.6	6.1	~	~	~	~	7.2	~	~	4.1
D. CHILE[6] 1965													
N		100.0	89.0	47.2	41.8	4.9	7.1	21.3	6.1	2.4	#	#	11.0
Ha.		100.0	89.8	74.0	14.2	11.5	.9	.3	1.5	1.6	#	#	10.2
E. COLOMBIA[4] 1960													
N		100.0	91.8	62.4	23.3	~	~	~	~	3.9	#	2.1	8.2
Ha.		100.0	93.9	72.4	7.3	~	~	~	~	12.1	#	2.0	6.1
F. COSTA RICA[5] 1973													
N		100.0	90.1	85.4	4.7[b]	1.8	.4[j]	..	.3[k]	..[l]	9.7	.2	..
Ha.		100.0	92.0	90.8	1.2[b]	.8	.1[j]	..	.1[k]	..[l]	7.8	.2	..
H. DOMINICAN REP. 1960													
N		100.0	~	58.8	30.8	3.7	6.9	1.9[r]	18.3[jj]	8.9[jj]	~	1.5	~
Ha.		100.0[ii]	~	73.1	20.6	4.5	4.2	1.7[r]	10.3[jj]	5.3[jj]	~	1.0	~
I. ECUADOR 1954													
N		100.0	91.1	67.9	14.6	5.0	3.9[n]	5.7[o]	#	#	1.7[f]	6.9[p]	8.9
Ha.		100.0	94.5	81.5	9.2	7.1	1.1[n]	1.0[o]	#	#	.4[f]	3.4[p]	5.5
J. EL SALVADOR 1961													
N		100.0	86.9	39.6	43.7	19.2	~	24.6[q]	~	#	#	3.5	13.1[i]
Ha.		100.0	92.2	77.5	7.8	5.0	~	2.8[q]	~	#	#	7.0	7.8[i]
EL SALVADOR 1971													
N		100.0	85.9	39.4	46.5	29.6	~	~	~	#	#	16.9[r]	14.1[i]
Ha.		100.0	90.6	76.4	14.2	7.4	~	~	~	#	#	6.8[r]	9.4[i]
K. GUATEMALA 1964													
N		100.0	88.9	57.9	22.9	11.3	~[v]	11.6[q]	#	~	4.9[f]	3.2[x]	11.1
Ha.		100.0	86.5	77.4	5.7	3.1	~[v]	2.6[q]	#	~	1.7[f]	1.7[x]	13.5
M. HONDURAS 1966													
N		100.0	83.3	22.4	33.8	22.5	~	~	11.3[y]	2.4	24.7[aa]	#	16.7
Ha.		100.0	77.3	45.8	15.0	5.1	~	~	10.0[y]	1.2	15.3[aa]	#	22.7
N. MEXICO[7] 1970													
N		100.0	97.8	~	~	~	~[bb]	~	~[cc]	~[dd]	~	~	2.2
Ha.		100.0	50.2	44.5	2.6	2.2	.4[bb]	~	~[cc]	1.2[dd]	~	1.8	49.8
O. NICARAGUA 1963													
N		100.0	86.3	38.6	12.6	4.7	2.8	1.2	3.9	15.7	8.0[aa]	11.4[ee]	13.7
Ha.		100.0	100.0	66.7	2.6	1.4	.4	.1	.7	19.2	8.1[aa]	3.3[ee]	~[ff]
P. PANAMA[8] 1971													
N		100.0	88.3	12.3	4.4	~	~[j]	~	~	71.6	..	..	11.7
Ha.		100.0	74.0	26.0	3.5	~	~	~	~	44.5	..	..	26.0
Q. PARAGUAY[9] 1961													
N		100.0	86.2	37.3	7.5	7.5	#	#	#	41.5	#	#	13.8
Ha.		100.0	92.5	81.3	4.2	4.2	#	#	#	7.1	#	#	7.5
R. PERU 1961													
N		100.0[ii]	89.8	66.0	15.2	9.7	5.6[gg]	#	#	#	5.2[hh]	3.3	10.2
Ha.		100.0	94.9	67.0	13.9	12.7	1.2[gg]	#	#	#	10.9[hh]	3.1	5.1
S. URUGUAY[8] 1966													
N		100.0	90.9	55.1	27.9	24.2	3.6[2]	#	#	5.2	#	2.6	9.1
Ha.		100.0	76.9	49.6	23.3	22.3	1.0[2]	#	#	1.0	#	3.0	23.1
URUGUAY[8] 1970													
N		100.0	90.1	58.6	22.6	19.6	3.0[2]	#	#	5.5	#	3.4	9.9
Ha.		100.0	76.1	52.7	18.6	17.7	.9[2]	#	#	1.1	#	3.7	23.9
T. VENEZUELA 1961[w]													
N		100.0[s]	90.9	39.2	12.9	8.1	4.8	#	#	38.8	#	#	7.7
Ha.		100.0[m]	94.7	81.5	2.4	1.9	.5	#	#	10.9	#	#	5.3
UNITED STATES 1969													
N		100.0	75.4	62.5	12.9	~	~[t]	~	~	..	..	..[h]	24.6[i]
Ha.		100.0	48.2	35.3	12.9	~	~[t]	~	~	..	..	..[h]	51.8[i]

Table 301 (Continued)

SYSTEMS OF LAND TENURE, PERCENTAGE DATA, 18 LC

(N and Ha.)

1. Details on the number of holdings were not obtained.
2. Excluding 14,583 holdings, the area of which is unknown.
3. For data on Bolivian and Venezuelan land reform, see James W. Wilkie, *Measuring Land Reform*, Supplement 5 (1974).
4. Excluding *Intendencias and Comisarías*.
5. Data obtained by sampling.
6. Excluding 5,125 properties without lands.
7. The data refer to the type of producer.
8. Excluding holdings with an area of less than 1 ha.

a. *"Medieros y Tanteros."*
b. Free occupancy.
c. Comprises 29,477,389 ha. operated in the *Tierras Fiscales* and 12,833,619 ha. operated under "Other Forms of Tenancy."
d. Comprises holdings worked by proprietors alone, properties with settlers, day laborers, etc.
e. *"Tolerados."*
f. Communal lands.
g. Comprises 818 properties (439,264 ha.) operated by possessors of *Tierras Fiscales* and 136 properties (433,334 ha.) operated by *Granjas Cooperativas y Sociedades Agrícolas.*
h. Holdings operated by administrators.
i. Holdings operated by proprietors lessees.
j. Product-sharing arrangements.
k. Holdings operated without payment.
l. Holdings operated illegally.
m. For data on Venezuelan land reform, see Wilkie, *Measuring Land Reform.*
n. Holdings operated by *"Partidarios."*
o. Holdings operated by *"Huasipungueros."*

p. Data obtained by sampling.
q. Properties operated by settlers.
r. Holdings operated by *"Colonos."*
s. Including 4,617 holdings without agricultural land.
t. Holdings operated by sharecroppers and livestock-sharers.
u. See note 3.
v. Excluding 14,583 holdings, the area of which is unknown.
w. See note 3.
x. Comprises those lands not included in preceding categories. Such lands include those in legal usufruct at time of census; those continuously and pacifically occupied without owner's permission by squatters who do not pay rent; lands in judicial process of transfer.
y. Agricultural holdings in National Lands.
z. Holdings operated by *"Medianeros."*
aa. Agricultural holdings in Ejidal Lands.
bb. *"Aparcero"* only.
cc. *"Arrendatario."*
dd. *"Ocupantes."*
ee. Including 7,543 properties (93,716 ha.) operated by usufructuaries.
ff. Farms operated under mixed tenure systems are included in the category of those operated under single systems.
gg. Comprises partnership and bound-service by Amerinds (*Yanaconaje*).
hh. Including communal lands.
ii. Excluding 188,544 ha. in sugar cane.
jj. Concessionaire.

SOURCE: IASI-AC, 1974, table 311-03; IASI-AC, 1977, table 311-03.

Table 302

AGRICULTURAL LANDHOLDINGS:[1] NUMBER AND AREA BY SIZE AND CLASS, 20 L

(T Ha.)

Country	Row	Total	Under 1 Ha. N	%	1 to 5 Ha. N	%	5 to 10 Ha. N	%	10 to 20 Ha. N	%	20 to 50 Ha. N	%	50 to 100 Ha. N	%	100 to 200 Ha. N	%	200 to 500 Ha. N	%	500 to 1,000 Ha. N	%	1,000 to 2,500 Ha. N	%	Over 2,500 Ha. N	%
A. ARGENTINA (1960)[2,3]	N	457,173	71,814	15.7	→		109,590	24.0	→		127,463	27.9	→		58,795	12.9	38,277	8.4	24,876	5.4	14,889	3.3	11,459	2.5
	Ha.	175,142	201	.1	→		1,559	.9	→		7,710	4.4	→		8,778	5.0	10,290	6.2	15,625	8.9	25,774	14.7	104,576	59.7
B. BOLIVIA (1950)[4]	N	86,377	24,756	28.7	26,472	30.6	8,760	10.1	5,881	6.8	4,837	5.6	2,776	3.2	2,239	2.6	2,443	2.8	1,540	1.8	2,140	2.5	3,272	3.8
	Ha.	32,750	11	#	63	.2	63	.2	82	.3	142	.4	183	.6	295	.9	756	2.3	1,051	3.2	3,295	10.1	26,803	81.8
C. BRAZIL (1970)[5,10]	N	4,905,642	396,846	8.1	1,403,397	18.7	719,387	14.7	768,448	15.7	824,090	16.7	341,854	7.0	215,329	4.4	151,514	3.1	47,903	1.0	36,847	.8	↑	
	Ha.	294,145	236	.1	3,661	1.2	5,186	1.8	10,743	3.7	25,425	8.6	23,902	8.1	29,700	10.1	45,958	15.6	33,084	11.3	116,250	29.5	↑	
D. CHILE (1965)[6,7]	N	253,532	45,233	17.8	78,460	30.9	33,076	13.0	29,976	11.8	29,360	11.6	14,785	5.8	9,164	3.6	6,998	2.8	3,156	1.2	3,324	1.3	↑	
	Ha.	30,644	22	.1	184	.6	230	.8	414	1.4	912	3.0	1,023	3.3	1,262	4.1	2,168	7.1	2,144	7.0	22,285	72.7	↑	
E. COLOMBIA (1971)[10]	N	1,176,811	268,705	22.9	431,520	36.7	159,659	13.6	117,863	10.0	100,010	8.5	47,763	4.1	26,553	2.2	16,344	1.4	4,927	.4	3,467	.3	↑	
	Ha.	30,993	127	.4	1,020	3.3	1,088	3.5	1,599	5.2	3,054	9.9	3,198	10.3	3,552	11.4	4,700	15.2	3,229	10.4	9,426	30.4	↑	
F. COSTA RICA (1973)[8,9,10]	N	81,562	14,413	17.1	20,830	25.7	9,095	11.0	8,777	11.0	12,436	14.6	5,801	7.3	2,922	3.7	1,929	2.5	495	.6	300	.4	↑	
	Ha.	3,123	6	.2	53	1.7	65	2.1	123	3.9	387	12.4	396	12.7	392	12.6	577	18.4	339	10.9	785	25.1	↑	
G. CUBA (1952)	N	100,965	2,912	2.9	11,146	11.0	12,480	12.4	30,045	29.8	20,427	20.2	11,282	11.2	10,158	10.1	→		1,638	1.6	877	.9	↑	
	Ha.	7,790	~	~	~	~	~	~	~	~	~	~	~	~	~	~	→		~	~	~	~	↑	
H. DOMINICAN REP. (1971)[10]	N	304,820	97,981	32.1	136,962	44.9	33,803	11.1	16,909	5.6	12,078	3.9	3,974	1.3	1,791	.7	884	.3	222	.1	216	.1	↑	#
	Ha.	2,736	41	1.5	311	11.3	231	8.4	231	8.5	357	13.1	268	9.8	249	9.1	268	9.8	148	5.4	632	23.1	↑	
I. ECUADOR (1974)[9,10]	N	519,111	134,684	26.0	201,297	38.7	54,935	10.6	41,425	7.9	42,537	8.1	22,276	4.2	5,760	1.2	3,897	.8	825	.2	609	.2	↑	
	Ha.	7,949	63	.8	476	6.0	378	4.8	558	7.0	1,312	16.5	1,353	17.0	682	8.6	994	12.5	544	6.8	1,589	20.0	↑	
J. EL SALVADOR (1971)[9,10]	N	318,041	132,464	41.8	102,477	32.1	15,598	5.0	9,164	2.8	6,986	2.2	2,238	.6	1,103	.3	636	.2	139	.1	63	.1	↑	
	Ha.	1,452	70	4.8	213	14.7	111	7.6	127	8.8	215	14.8	154	10.6	152	10.5	191	13.2	95	6.5	124	8.5	↑	
K. GUATEMALA (1964)[8]	N	417,344	364,879	87.4	→		37,025	8.9	→		6,631	1.6	7,859	1.9	→		→		561	.1	294	.1	95	#
	Ha.	3,449	642	18.7	→		447	13.0	→		204	5.9	915	26.5	→		→		346	10.0	387	11.2	509	14.8
L. HAITI (1971)[10]	N	616,710	361,985	58.7	231,340	37.4	18,550	3.1	3,945	.6	890		→		→		→		→		→		→	.2
	Ha.	864	185	21.4	485	56.1	121	14.0	49	5.7	24		→		→		→		→		→		→	2.8
M. HONDURAS (1974)[10]	N	195,341	33,771	17.5	91,010	46.7	28,264	14.4	19,220	9.7	15,170	7.7	4,433	2.1	1,971	1.0	1,057	.5	276	.2	169	.1	↑	
	Ha.	2,630	22	.8	218	8.3	201	7.6	268	10.2	461	17.5	301	11.5	267	10.2	313	11.9	184	7.0	395	15.0	↑	
N. MEXICO (1970)[9,10]	N	1,020,016	255,020	25.0	266,757	26.2	101,922	10.0	78,984	7.8	83,232	8.1	49,119	4.8	33,530	3.3	28,036	2.7	13,780	1.4	22,479	2.2	↑	
	Ha.	139,868	145	.1	736	.5	778	.6	1,198	.9	2,783	2.0	3,714	2.6	4,916	3.5	9,148	6.5	10,023	7.2	106,427	76.1	↑	
O. NICARAGUA (1963)[8,11]	N	102,201	51,936	50.8	→		13,273	13.0	25,652	25.1	→		6,291	6.2	3,554	3.5	→		920	.9	405	.4	170	.2
	Ha.	3,823	133	3.5	→		122	3.2	783	20.5	→		538	14.1	673	17.6	→		409	10.7	394	10.3	771	20.2

Table 302 (Continued)

AGRICULTURAL LANDHOLDINGS:[1] NUMBER AND AREA BY SIZE AND CLASS, 20 L

(T Ha.)

Country		Total	Under 1 Ha. N	%	1 to 5 Ha. N	%	5 to 10 Ha. N	%	10 to 20 Ha. N	%	20 to 50 Ha. N	%	50 to 100 Ha. N	%	100 to 200 Ha. N	%	200 to 500 Ha. N	%	500 to 1,000 Ha. N	%	1,000 to 2,500 Ha. N	%	Over 2,500 Ha. N	%
P. PANAMA (1971)[9,10]	N	115,364	20,032	17.4	34,368	29.5	13,937	12.2	14,179	12.2	14,138	12.2	5,526	5.2	1,920	1.7	853	.9	211	.2	108⌐		#	↑ 16.3
	Ha.	2,098	5	.3	72	3.4	90	2.6	183	4.3	415	19.8	363	17.3	252	12.0	238	11.3	139	6.6	341⌐			
Q. PARAGUAY (1961)[12]	N	160,777	7,937	4.9	66,622	41.4	37,735	23.5	26,451	16.5	13,700	8.5	3,053	1.9	1,699	1.1	1,310	.8	641	.4	720	~	909	.6
	Ha.	17,473	~		~		~		~		~		~		~		~		~		~		~	
R. PERU (1972)[10]	N	1,390,877	483,939	33.1	600,425	43.2	153,141	11.0	78,699	5.7	46,648	3.3	12,944	.9	7,034	.5	4,245	.3	1,615	.1	2,187⌐		.1	↑ 61.7
	Ha.	23,545	185	.8	1,375	5.8	1,011	4.3	1,026	4.3	1,339	5.7	843	3.6	908	3.9	1,243	5.3	1,087	4.6	14,528⌐			
S. URUGUAY (1970)[13]	N	77,163	22,982⌐		←		↑	29.8	12,259	15.9	13,071	16.9	7,927	10.3	6,603	8.6	6,734	8.7	3,626	4.7	2,784	3.6	1,177	1.5
	Ha.	16,518	110⌐		←		↑	1.7	169	1.0	411	2.5	559	3.4	931	5.6	2,133	12.9	2,561	15.5	4,305	26.1	5,339	32.3
T. VENEZUELA (1971)[9,10]	N	287,919	13,134	4.5	108,644	37.9	49,345	17.0	41,358	14.2	32,414	11.4	14,308	4.9	8,340	2.8	7,903	2.8	3,883	1.4	4,904⌐			↑ 1.7
	Ha.	26,470	6	#	246	.9	315	1.2	512	1.9	918	3.5	920	3.5	1,051	4.0	2,291	8.7	2,534	9.6	17,667⌐			↑ 66.7

1. Economic units of land used for the production of agricultural crops or of livestock. These units are worked or administered by one person, with or without the aid of others; they may consist of either one or of several parcels of land separated one from another so long as they form part of the same economic or management unit.
2. Excluding 14,583 holdings for unknown areas.
3. Actual sizes are: 5–25; 200–400; 400–1,000
4. Including 1,127 (1.4%) holdings (8,747 equals .03% ha.) not distributed for extension.
5. Excluding 18,377 holdings of size not reported.
6. Excluding 5,162 holdings without area.
7. Actual sizes are: 1,000–2,000; 2,000 and over.
8. Original figures presented in manzanas. A manzana is equal to .7 ha. Sixty-four manzanas equal one caballeria.
9. Total number of holdings includes holdings without land.
10. Actual sizes are: 1–2; 2–5; 1,000 and over.
11. Actual sizes are: 0–6.99; 7.00–13.99; 14.00–69.99; 70.00–139.99; 140.00–349.99; 350.00–699.99; 700.00–1,749.99; 1,750.00 and over.
12. Data obtained by sampling.
13. Excluding holdings less than 1 ha.

SOURCE: Adapted from IASI-AC, 1972, table 311-04. FAO Preliminary Results of the 1960 World Census of Agriculture, 5th, 19th and 21st Issues. IASI-AC, 1974, table 311-04; FAO 1970 World Census of Agriculture, tables 2.2, 2.3, 3.2, and 3.3.

Table 303

SIZE OF AGRICULTURAL HOLDINGS, 15 LC, 1950-70
(Area in T Ha.)

Size of Holding	Number 1970	Number 1960	Number 1950	Area 1970	Area 1960	Area 1950
A. ARGENTINA[1]						
Total	527,314‡	457,173	441,431	142,445‡	175,142	173,448
To 5.0	—	71,814	59,616	—	201	—
5.1-25.0	—	109,590	101,836	—	1,559	—
25.1-100.0	—	127,463	128,285	—	7,710	—
100.1-200.0	—	58,795	63,025	—	8,778	—
200.1-400.0	—	38,277	62,976	—	10,920	—
400.1-1,000.0	—	24,876		—	15,625	—
1,000.1-2,500.0	—	14,899	20,151	—	25,774	—
2,500.1-5,000.0	—	5,798		—	22,240	—
5,000.1-10,000.0	—	3,110	3,393	—	23,929	—
10,000.1+	—	2,551	2,149	—	58,407	—
C. BRAZIL[2]						
Total	4,905,642	3,333,746	2,064,278	294,145	249,862	232,211
To 10	2,519,630	1,495,020	710,934	9,083	5,952	3,025
10 to less than 100	1,934,392	1,491,415	1,052,557	60,070	47,566	35,563
100 to less than 1,000	414,746	314,831	268,159	108,742	86,029	75,521
1,000 to less than 10,000	36,847	30,883	31,017	116,250	71,421	73,093
10,000+		1,597	1,611		38,893	45,009
D. CHILE[3]						
Total	258,657	253,532	159,959	30,644	30,644	27,712
Less than 1.0	—	45,233	28,246	—	22	8
1.0-4.9	—	78,460	27,515	—	184	70
5.0-9.9	—	33,076	19,866	—	230	139
10.0-19.9	—	29,976	19,225	—	414	272
50.0-99.9	—	14,785	12,346	—	1,023	857
100.0-199.9	—	9,164	8,474	—	1,262	1,164
200.0-499.9	—	6,998	6,766	—	2,168	2,100
500.0-999.9	—	3,156	3,076	—	2,144	2,101
1,000.0-1,999.9	—	1,533	1,555	—	2,115	2,112
2,000-4,999.9	—	1,061	999	—	3,315	3,020
5,000.0+	—	730	696	—	16,855	15,165
E. COLOMBIA[4]						
Total	1,176,811	1,209,672	919,000	30,993	27,338	27,748
Less than .5	268,705	165,652	161,778	127	38	84
.5 to less than 1		132,419			94	
1 to less than 2		191,347			270	
2 to less than 3	431,550	117,005	342,788a	1,020	276	843a
3 to less than 4		92,001			309	
4 to less than 5		58,181			252	
5 to less than 10	159,659	169,145	143,549	1,088	1,165	983
10 to less than 20	117,863	114,231	101,275	1,599	1,572	1,376
20 to less than 30		44,049			1,044	
30 to less than 40	100,010	26,500	85,371b	3,054	890	2,594b
40 to less than 50		16,240			705	
50 to less than 100	47,763	39,990	37,814	3,198	2,680	2,586
100 to less than 200	26,553	22,317	22,969	3,552	2,996	3,432
200 to less than 500	16,344	13,693	15,366	4,700	3,994	4,686
500 to less than 1,000	4,927	4,141	4,912	3,229	2,731	3,749
1,000 to less than 2,500	3,467	1,975	2,541	9,426	2,808	4,037
2,500+		786	637		5,513	3,378

Size of Holding	Number 1970	Number 1960	Number 1950	Area 1970	Area 1960	Area 1950
F. COSTA RICA[5]						
Total	81,562	64,621	47,286	3,123	2,671	1,854
0.70-1.04	—	3,661	2,940	—	3	2
1.05-4.89	—	19,572	10,693	—	49	21
4.90-6.99	—	4,692	7,362	—	26	35
7.00-10.49	—	6,113	4,580	—	51	38
10.50-13.99	—	3,429	2,468	—	40	29
14.00-20.99	—	5,732	4,231	—	95	70
21.00-34.99	—	7,435	5,614	—	195	147
35.00-69.99	—	7,240	5,061	—	342	238
70.00-101.49	—	2,522	1,725	—	205	139
101.50-121.49	—	745	480	—	82	52
122.50-174.99	—	1,174	704	—	169	101
175.00-199.49	—	318	183	—	58	34
199.50-349.99	—	973	634	—	247	160
350.00-699.99	—	596	359	—	276	164
700.00-1,000.99	—	177	92	—	144	74
1,001.00-1,049.99	—	14	13	—	14	14
1,050.00-2,449.99	—	169	97	—	244	147
2,450.00+	—	59	50	—	431	388
J. EL SALVADOR[6]						
Total	318,041	226,896	174,204	1,452	1,581	1,530
To .99	132,464	107,054	70,416	70	61	35
1.00-1.99		48,501	35,189		68	48
2.00-2.99		22,038	19,882		54	48
3.00-3.99	102,477	8,527	7,760	213	31	27
4.00-4.99		7,178	7,226		33	32
5.00-9.99	15,598	14,001	14,064	111	99	99
10.00-19.99	9,164	8,824	8,874	127	117	122
20.00-49.99	6,986	6,711	6,660	215	209	206
50.00-99.99	2,238	2,214	2,107	154	155	148
100.00-199.99	1,103	1,121	1,059	152	158	146
200.00-499.99	636	713	654	191	219	198
500.00-999.99	139	189	168	95	128	115
1,000.00-2,499.99	63	91	110	124	132	172
2,500.00+		34	35		117	133
K. GUATEMALA[7]						
Total	—	417,344	348,687	—	3,449	3,721
To .69	—	85,083	74,289	—	33	29
0.70-1.39	—	98,658	91,581	—	95	95
1.40-3.49	—	129,116	99,779	—	271	212
3.50-6.99	—	52,023	42,444	—	243	198
7.00-22.39	—	37,025	26,916	—	447	311
22.40-44.71	—	6,631	6,125	—	204	190
44.72-447.19	—	7,859	6,488	—	915	813
447.20-894.39	—	561	569	—	346	354
894.40-2,235.99	—	293	358	—	387	496
2,236.00-4,471.99	—	56	104	—	170	328
4,472.00-8,943.99	—	30	32	—	178	196
8,944.00+	—	9	22	—	161	500

Table 303 (Continued)

SIZE OF AGRICULTURAL HOLDINGS, 15 LC, 1950-70

(Area in T Ha.)

Size of Holding	Number 1970	Number 1960	Number 1950	Area 1970	Area 1960	Area 1950
L. HAITI[8]						
Total	616,710	?	?	864	?	?
To .10	16,820	?	?	1	?	?
.11-.20	36,050	?	?	6	?	?
.20-.32	107,480	?	?	35	?	?
.33-.49	28,485	?	?	13	?	?
.50-.64	104,890	?	?	66	?	?
.65-1.00	68,260	?	?	64	?	?
1.01-1.29	76,010	?	?	96	?	?
1.30-1.99	65,920	?	?	116	?	?
2.00-2.58	44,340	?	?	110	?	?
2.59-3.00	9,260	?	?	27	?	?
3.01-3.87	27,370	?	?	97	?	?
3.88-4.99	8,440	?	?	39	?	?
5.00-5.16	4,300	?	?	22	?	?
5.17-6.45	7,810	?	?	48	?	?
6.46-9.99	6,440	?	?	51	?	?
10.00-12.90	2,660	?	?	29	?	?
12.91-19.99	1,285	?	?	20	?	?
20.00-25.80	590	?	?	13	?	?
25.81+	300	?	?	11	?	?
M. HONDURAS[9]						
Total	195,341	178,361	156,135	2,630	2,417	2,507
To .69	?	26,719	?	?	19	?
.70-3.49	?	57,409	?	?	113	?
3.50-6.99	?	36,313	?	?	163	?
7.00-13.99	?	27,112	?	?	252	?
14.00-34.99	?	19,977	?	?	412	?
35.00-69.99	?	6,429	?	?	298	?
70.00-139.99	?	2,449	?	?	226	?
140.00-349.99	?	1,286	?	?	265	?
350.00-699.99	?	398	?	?	190	?
700.00-1,749.99	?	196	?	?	202	?
1.750.00+	?	73	?	?	272	?
N. MEXICO[10]						
Total	1,020,016	1,365,141	1,383,212	139,868	169,084	145,517
Less than 1	255,020	} 899,108	499,399	145	} 1,328	182
1-5	266,757		506,440	736		1,180
5-10	101,922	94,319	101,143	778	679	703
10-25	162,216	132,335	59,605	3,981	2,105	1,708
25-50	49,119	70,250	43,568	3,714	2,490	2,237
50-100	33,530	59,091	28,585	4,916	4,169	3,304
100-200	28,036	42,264	24,247	9,148	5,846	4,212
200-500	13,780	30,382	11,469	10,023	9,492	8,057
500-1,000	} 22,479	14,749	14,802	} 106,427	10,436	8,359
1,000-5,000		} 17,036	2,564		} 39,905	33,757
5,000-10,000			2,174			18,110
10,000+		5,564			92,635	63,706

Size of Holding	Number 1970	Number 1960	Number 1950	Area 1970	Area 1960	Area 1950
O. NICARAGUA[11]						
Total	?	102,201	51,581	?	3,823	2,372
To .69	?	2,258	~	?	1	~
.70-3.49	?	33,948	10,214	?	58	18
3.50-6.99	?	15,730	7,729	?	74	36
7.00-13.99	?	13,273	8,621	?	122	79
14.00-34.99	?	14,703	10,687	?	308	224
35.00-69.99	?	10,949	7,829	?	475	344
70.00-139.99	?	6,291	3,782	?	538	321
140.00-349.99	?	3,554	1,874	?	673	366
350.00-699.99	?	920	483	?	409	215
700.00-1,749.99	?	405	256	?	394	249
1.750.00+	?	170	106	?	771	529
P. PANAMA[12]						
Total	115,364	95,505	85,473	2,098	1,806	1,159
.5 to less than 1	20,032	} 4,969	} 44,442	5	} 3	} 96
1-5	34,368	38,733		72	93	
5-10	13,937	18,086	16,847	90	118	106
10-20	14,179	14,897	12,235	183	192	153
20-50	14,138	12,038	8,231	415	355	237
50-100	5,526	4,329	2,407	363	284	156
100-200	1,920	1,574	809	250	201	103
200-500	853	665	348	238	189	100
500-1,000	211	133	96	139	87	67
1,000+	108	91	58	341	284	141
Q. PARAGUAY[13]						
Total	?	160,777	149,614	?	17,473	16,817
.1-.4	?	2,192	1,593	?	?	?
.5-.9	?	5,745	4,829	?	?	3
1.0-1.9	?	18,870	17,549	?	?	22
2.0-2.9	?	18,977	17,793	?	?	40
3.0-3.9	?	15,575	15,253	?	?	49
4.0-4.9	?	13,200	11,697	?	?	49
5.0-9.9	?	37,735	34,949	?	?	230
10.0-19.9	?	26,451	25,192	?	?	317
20.0-49.9	?	13,700	12,982	?	?	183
50.0-99.9	?	3,053	2,837	?	?	224
100.0-199.9	?	1,699	1,568	?	?	375
200.0-499.9	?	1,310	1,234	?	?	399
500.0-999.9	?	641	589	?	?	?
1,000-1,999.9	?	} 720	} 1,015	?	?	} 2,220
2,000-4,999.9	?	361		?	?	
5,000-9,999.9	?	270	259	?	?	1,795
10,000-19,999.9	?	132	130	?	?	1,787
20,000+	?	146	145	?	?	8,783

Table 303 (Continued)

SIZE OF AGRICULTURAL HOLDINGS, 15 LC, 1950-70
(Area in T Ha.)

Size of Holding	Number			Area		
	1970	1960	1950	1970	1960	1950
S. URUGUAY[14]						
Total	77,163	86,928	85,258	16,518	16,988	16,974
1-4	11,085	12,769	10,953	30	34	29
5-9	11,897	13,028	11,117	80	89	77
10-19	12,259	14,032	13,771	169	197	193
20-49	13,071	15,715	16,910	411	495	535
50-99	7,927	9,490	10,375	559	674	732
100-199	6,603	7,387	7,814	931	1,042	1,104
200-499	6,734	6,986	7,241	2,133	2,174	2,272
500-999	3,626	3,712	3,475	2,561	2,609	2,444
1,000-2,499	2,784	2,587	2,452	4,305	3,994	3,810
2,500-4,999	869	891	763	2,963	3,043	2,584
5,000-9,999	253	280	316	1,644	1,857	2,065
10,000+	55	51	71	732	780	1,130
T. VENEZUELA[15]						
Total	287,910	315,477	234,730	26,470	26,005	22,127
Less than .5	13,134	5,068	14,274	6	1	7
.5-.9		12,666			8	
1.0-1.9		40,920			49	
2.0-2.9	108,644	42,449	111,716	246	94	260
3.0-3.9		29,899			98	
4.0-4.9		24,615			107	
5.0-5.9		19,083			103	
6.0-6.9	49,395	14,703	42,014	315	95	276
7.0-7.9		8,874			65	
8.0-8.9		10,392			88	
9.0-9.9		4,750			45	

Size of Holding	Number			Area		
	1970	1960	1950	1970	1960	1950
T. VENEZUELA (Cont'd)						
10.0-14.9	41,358	29,535	27,551	512	316	363
15.0-19.9		11,852			191	
20.0-29.9		15,920			345	
30.0-39.9	32,414	7,646	18,900	918	251	546
40.0-49.9		5,034			220	
50.0-99.9	14,308	11,567	7,123	920	719	464
100.0-199.9	8,340	7,332	4,284	1,051	943	541
200.0-499.9	7,903	6,147	3,582	2,291	1,766	1,044
500.0-999.9	3,883	2,802	1,864	2,534	1,844	1,221
1,000-2,499.9	4,904	2,335	1,669	17,667	3,456	2,468
2,500.0 +		1,888	1,753		15,199	14,936
UNITED STATES[16]						
Total	2,730,250	3,157,857	3,710,503	430,321	449,293	454,631
to 4.04	?	182,581	244,328	?	315	431
4.05-20.23	?	637,434	813,216	?	7,012	8,896
20.24-40.46	?	542,430	657,990	?	16,022	19,397
40.47-56.65	?	324,652	394,505	?	15,333	18,624
56.66-72.84	?	308,288	378,003	?	19,711	24,155
72.85-89.02	?	191,254	225,576	?	15,299	18,035
89.03-105.21	?	164,188	188,899	?	15,805	18,166
105.22-202.34	?	451,301	471,547	?	64,589	67,051
202.35-404.69	?	210,437	200,012	?	58,519	55,444
404.70 +	?	145,292	136,427	?	236,688	224,432

1. 1960 = Census of September, 1960; 1950 = Census of April, 1947.
2. 1970 = Census of December, 1970; 1960 = Census of September, 1960; 1950 = Census of July, 1950.
3. 1960 = Census of April, 1965; 1950 = Census of April 1955.
4. 1960 - Census of 1960; 1950 = Census of June, 1954; 1970 = Census of 1971.
5. 1960 = Census of April, 1963; 1950 = Census of March, 1955.
6. 1970 = Census of July 1971; 1960 = Census of June, 1961; 1960 = Census of October, 1950.
7. 1960 = Census of April, 1964; 1950 = Census of April, 1950.
8. 1970 = Census of September, 1971.
9. 1960 = Census of March, 1966; 1950 = Census of March, 1952.
10. 1960 = Census of May, 1960; 1950 = Census of May, 1950; 1970 = Census of 1970.

11. 1960 = Census of May, 1963; 1950 = Census of May, 1952.
12. 1970 = Census of May, 1971; 1960 = Census of April, 1961; 1950 = Census of December, 1950.
13. 1960 = Census of August, 1961; 1950 = Census of September, 1956.
14. 1970 = Census of 1970; 1960 = Census of May, 1961; 1950 = Census of May, 1951.
15. 1960 = Census of February, 1961; 1950 = Census of November, 1950; 1970 = Census of 1971.
16. 1960 = Census of October, 1964; 1950 = Census of October, 1959.

a. 1-5 Ha.
b. 21-50 Ha.

SOURCE: IASI-AC, 1974, table 311-04; FAO-PY, 1975, table 3; FAO 1970 World Census of Agriculture, tables 2.2 and 3.2.

Table 304

NUMBER AND AVERAGE SIZE OF SMALL FARMS, 19 L, 1914–83

	Country	Year	Maximum Farm Size (Ha)	Number of Farms	% of Farms	% of Area	Average Farm Size (Ha)
A.	ARGENTINA	1914	25	100,836	33.0	1.0	9.6
		1947		161,452	34.3	1.0	10.9
		1952		235,953	41.8	1.1	9.2
		1960		181,404	38.5	1.0	9.7
		1969		226,065	42.0	.9	8.9
B.	BOLIVIA	1950	5		59.3	.2	
C.	BRAZIL	1940	5		21.8	.5	
		1950		458,676	22.2	.5	2.6
		1960		1,029,336	30.8	1.0	2.5
		1970		1,800,243	36.6	1.3	2.2
		1975		1,911,730	38.3	1.2	2.1
		1980		1,888,196	36.6	1.1	2.1
		1950	10	710,934	34.4	1.3	4.3
		1960		1,495,020	44.4	2.3	4.0
		1970		2,519,630	51.2	3.1	3.6
		1975		2,601,860	52.1	2.8	3.5
		1980		2,598,019	50.4	2.5	3.5
D.	CHILE	1955	10	75,627	61.0	.8	2.9
		1965		156,769	62.0	1.4	2.8
		1965	5 BIH[1]	189,529	81.0	9.7	
		1972			79.0	9.7	
		1976			71.0	9.7	
		1979	5.1 BIH[1]	254,925	75.0	14.6	
E.	COLOMBIA	1954	10	648,115	71.0	6.9	2.9
		1960		925,750	77.0	8.8	2.6
		1970		859,884	73.0	7.2	2.6
F.	COSTA RICA	1955	10.5	25,575	54.0	5.2	3.8
		1963		34,038	53.0	4.8	3.8
		1963	10	30,377	50.0	5.0	4.1
		1973		29,927	48.0	4.0	3.9
H.	DOMINICAN REP.	1971	5	235,000	77.1	12.9	1.5
		1981		314,700	81.7	12.2	1.0
I.	ECUADOR Sierra	1954	10	234,596	90.0	16.0	2.1
		1974		280,974	87.0	18.0	1.9
J.	EL SALVADOR	1950	5	140,473	80.7	17.4	1.4
		1961		193,298	85.3	14.5	1.3
		1971		234,941	86.9	19.6	1.2
K.	GUATEMALA	1950	7	308,000	88.0	14.0	2.4
		1964		364,879	88.0	19.0	2.5
		1979		547,574	90.0	16.0	1.8
L.	HAITI	1971	5	593,325	96.0	78.0	1.1
M.	HONDURAS	1952	5	88,997	57.0	8.0	2.3
		1966			47.0	6.0	
		1974		124,781	64.0	9.0	1.9
N.	MEXICO	1950	5 private	1,020,747	39.2	7.6	1.5
		1960		928,717	34.2	6.1	1.6
		1970		678,214	25.2	5.0	1.7
		1950	4 ejido	569,866	21.9	6.1	2.1
		1960		668,162	24.6	5.9	2.1
		1970		951,878	35.6	8.6	2.1
O.	NICARAGUA	1952	7	17,943	34.8	2.3	3.0
		1963		51,936	50.0	3.5	2.6
		1971		37,500	43.8	2.2	3.5
		1978				2.0	
		1983				5.4	
P.	PANAMA	1950	5	44,442	52.0	8.3	2.2
		1961		43,692	45.7	5.3	2.2
		1971		41,307	45.3	3.7	1.8
Q.	PARAGUAY	1943	6	45,426	48.1	8.0	2.7
		1956		68,716	45.9	1.0	2.4
		1961		74,559	46.4		
R.	PERU	1961	5	699,427	82.9	5.2	1.3
		1972		1,083,775	77.9	6.6	1.4
S.	URUGUAY	1951	20	35,841	42.0	1.8	8.3
		1961		38,829	45.8	1.9	8.0

Table 304 (Continued)

NUMBER AND AVERAGE SIZE OF SMALL FARMS, 19 L, 1914–83

Country	Year	Maximum Farm Size (Ha)	Number of Farms	% of Farms	% of Area	Average Farm Size (Ha)
T. VENEZUELA	1950	5	125,990	54.7	1.2	2.1
	1961		155,617	49.3	1.4	2.3
	1971		121,778	42.3	1.0	2.2
LATIN AMERICA	1950	Small Farms	4,134,000			2.4
	1980		7,949,000			2.1

1. Basic irrigated hectare: an index used to convert physical hectare to a common pattern of similar productive potential.

SOURCE: FAO, ANNEX II, Rural Poverty, 1988, table 3.6, pp. 46–47.

Table 305

AGRICULTURAL LAND AVAILABILITY, 2 LRC, 1983–85
(Ha/PI)

	Crop Land/C[1]		Crop and Pasture Land/C[2]	
	Total Population	EAP in Agriculture	Total Population	EAP in Agriculture
Andean	.23	2.5	1.5	16.1
C. BRAZIL	.55	5.5	1.8	17.5
Caribbean	.21	1.7	.4	3.4
CARICOM	.25	2.0	.6	4.9
Islands	.20	1.6	.4	3.0
Central America	.26	1.9	.8	5.7
N. MEXICO	.31	2.9	1.3	11.5
Southern Cone	.91	17.1	4.7	87.4
Total Latin America	.44	4.4	1.8	18.0

1. Arable plus permanent crops lands.
2. Arable plus permanent crops plus permanent pasture lands.

SOURCE: FAO, ANNEX IV, Natural Resources and the Environment, 1988, table IV, p. 28.

Table 306

INDEX OF LAND CONCENTRATION, 13 L, 1960–80

	Country	Gini Coefficient		
		1960	1970	1980
C.	BRAZIL	.85 (1960)	.84 (1970)	.86 (1980)
E.	COLOMBIA	.87 (1960)	.86 (1970–71)	~
F.	COSTA RICA	~	.83 (1973)	~
H.	DOMINICAN REP.	~	.79 (1971)	~
J.	EL SALVADOR	.84 (1961)	.81 (1971)	~
K.	GUATEMALA	~	.85 (1979)	~
L.	HAITI	~	.50 (1971)	~
M.	HONDURAS	~	.78 (1974)	~
P.	PANAMA	~	.78 (1971)	.84 (1981)
Q.	PARAGUAY	~	~	.94 (1981)
R.	PERU	.95 (1961)	~	~
S.	URUGUAY	.83 (1966)	.82 (1970)	.84 (1980)
T.	VENEZUELA	.94 (1961)	.92 (1971)	~

SOURCE: FAO, ANNEX II, Rural Poverty, 1988, table 3.7, p. 49.

Table 307

AGRICULTURAL INPUT USE, 20 L, 1970–85

	Country	Fertilizer (kgs/Ha)				Tractors/T Ha			
		1970	1975	1980	1985	1970	1975	1980	1985
A.	ARGENTINA	2.62	1.75	3.28	4.49	5.07	5.21	4.74	5.66
B.	BOLIVIA	.69	.99	.88	1.71	.16	.23	.22	.23
C.	BRAZIL	18.56	32.75	59.06	45.54	3.07	4.21	7.67	10.16
D.	CHILE	31.25	18.81	23.90	39.13	6.95	6.52	6.22	6.21
E.	COLOMBIA	28.57	40.54	55.27	64.27	4.49	4.55	5.03	5.07
F.	COSTA RICA	100.13	130.12	122.91	133.22	10.34	11.12	9.95	10.27
G.	CUBA	151.71	106.40	165.47	180.87	19.75	17.64	21.34	21.19
H.	DOMINICAN REP.	33.38	58.17	36.34	41.50	1.72	1.63	1.51	1.53
I.	ECUADOR	13.35	12.66	29.48	28.48	1.21	1.97	2.52	3.07
J.	EL SALVADOR	104.31	144.24	83.24	115.62	4.01	4.45	4.55	4.63
K.	GUATEMALA	29.78	33.58	48.86	~	2.03	2.26	2.29	~
L.	HAITI	44	2.44	.45	3.54	.44	.51	.58	.62
M.	HONDURAS	15.58	12.23	16.22	12.76	1.10	1.73	1.85	1.88
N.	MEXICO	23.24	45.03	50.47	69.26	3.96	4.14	4.69	6.34
O.	NICARAGUA	21.47	15.69	43.50	35.96	.41	.86	1.77	1.92
P.	PANAMA	38.67	45.55	55.14	45.25	4.42	6.78	7.21	7.39
Q.	PARAGUAY	9.82	.98	3.64	5.18	2.40	2.86	3.92	4.37
R.	PERU	29.97	32.67	33.56	20.06	3.90	3.91	4.03	4.96
S.	URUGUAY	48.51	32.99	55.83	37.83	18.68	20.72	22.69	23.18
T.	VENEZUELA	16.98	39.13	64.21	108.22	5.48	7.98	10.12	11.54

SOURCE: FAO, ANNEX II, Rural Poverty, 1988, table 3.8, p. 52.

Table 308

CUMULATIVE LAND REFORM DATA[1], 15 L
(Through 1969)

	Country	Initiation of Program	Number of Families Benefitted	Number of Hectares Distributed or Confirmed
B.	BOLIVIA	1955	208,181	9,740,681
C.	BRAZIL	1964	46,457	957,106
D.	CHILE	1965	15,800	2,093,300
E.	COLOMBIA	1961	91,937	2,832,312
F.	COSTA RICA	1963	3,889	60,055
H.	DOMINICAN REPUBLIC	1963	9,717	46,082
I.	ECUADOR	1964	27,857	152,115
K.	GUATEMALA	1955	26,500	166,734
M.	HONDURAS	1963	5,843	90,642
N.	MEXICO	1916	2,525,811	59,413,656
O.	NICARAGUA	1964	8,117	357,989
P.	PANAMA	1963	2,594	37,339
Q.	PARAGUAY	1963	#	#
R.	PERU	1961	31,600	850,522
T.	VENEZUELA	1959	117,286	4,605,594

1. Excludes colonization and land settlement.

SOURCE: James W. Wilkie, *Measuring Land Reform*, Statistical Abstract of Latin America, Supplement 5 (Los Angeles: UCLA Latin American Center Publications, University of California, 1974), p. 3, from which this table is adapted.

Table 309

LAND REFORM AND NUMBER OF PEASANT FAMILIES BENEFITED, 9 L

(Through 1982)

Country	Agriculture and Forest Surface Distributed[1] (T Ha)			Number of Recipients		
	Total	Assigned	%	Total[2]	Benefited	%
B. BOLIVIA	3,275.0[a]	2,740.0[d]	83.4	516,200	384,560[d]	74.5
D. CHILE	28,759.0[j]	2,940.0[e]	10.2	412,000	38,000[e]	9.2
F. COSTA RICA	3,122.4[b]	221.6[b]	7.1	155,200	8,349[b]	5.4
H. DOMINICAN REP.	2,676.7[c]	374.6[c]	14.0	697,800	59,411[c]	8.5
I. ECUADOR	7,949.0[j]	718.1[l]	9.0	749,000	78,088[l]	10.4
N. MEXICO	139,868.0[j]	60,724.0[f]	43.4	4,629,000	1,986,000[f]	42.9
P. PANAMA	2,253.9[k]	493.2[g]	21.9	132,800	17,703[g]	13.3
R. PERU	23,545.0[j]	9,255.6[h]	39.3	1,419,400	431,982[h]	30.4
T. VENEZUELA	26,470.0[j]	5,118.7[i]	19.3	561,800	171,861[i]	30.6

1. Total surface of exploitations.
2. Based on FAO data.

a. 1950 data.
b. Corresponds to the peasant settlements created by the Instituto de Tierras y Colonización through 1980.
c. 1983 data.
d. Through 1976.
e. Through 1981.
f. 1970 data.
g. 1977 data.
h. Through 1981.
i. Through 1978.
j. As of 1981.
k. Undated.
l. Through 1982.

SOURCE: IDB-SPTF, 1986, p. 130.

Table 310

WOMEN IN THE LATIN AMERICAN LAND REFORMS, 13 L

Country	% Women Beneficiaries	Beneficiary Criteria
B. BOLIVIA	~	Individuals over 18 if *feudatario*; over 14 if married; widows with children may receive land
D. CHILE	~	18 years and married or effective heads of household; point system, favored "aptitude" for agriculture
E. COLOMBIA	~	Individuals; point system favored farming experience, education
F. COSTA RICA	~	Individuals over 18; preference to household heads with most dependents and farming experience
G. CUBA[1]	26	Individuals; state policy goal to incorporate women
H. DOMINICAN REP.	~	Heads of household
I. ECUADOR	~	Individuals
J. EL SALVADOR	~	Individuals
M. HONDURAS[2]	3.8	16 years if single male; any age if married male; single or widowed women with children may apply
N. MEXICO	~	Individuals over 16; any age if have dependent; men or women farmers
O. NICARAGUA[3]	6	Individual; an objective of agrarian reform to incorporate women
R. PERU	~	18 years, heads of household with dependent children, agriculturalists
T. VENEZUELA	~	Individuals over 18; preference to household heads with most dependents and most efficient farmers

1. 1983.
2. 1979.
3. 1982.

SOURCE: Carmen D. Deeve, *Rural Women and State Policy: The Latin American Agrarian Reform Experiences*, Michigan State University Working Paper No. 81, 1985, p. 26.

Table 311

BOLIVIA BENEFICIARIES OF LAND REFORM BY DEPARTMENT, 1975–78

Department	1975	1976	1977	1978
Total	208,944	224,772	235,683	239,668
Chuquisaca	31,949	32,839	33,381	33,754
La Paz	67,605	70,150	72,645	73,792
Cochabamba	48,281	53,252	56,319	56,656
Oruro	1,096	1,200	1,464	1,490
Potosí	28,092	29,103	31,818	32,859
Tarija	9,143	9,544	9,940	10,079
Santa Cruz	20,153	24,800	26,046	26,827
Beni	2,420	3,638	3,819	3,963
Pando	205	246	251	268

SOURCE: *Bolivia en Cifras*, 1980 (La Paz: Instituto Nacional de Estadística, 1981), table 55, p. 108.

Table 312

BOLIVIA ENTITLED LAND DISTRIBUTED THROUGH LAND REFORM, 1975–78

(Ha)

Department	1975	1976	1977	1978
Total	22,458,438.87	26,397,419.48	28,818,705.88	28,929,370.92
Chuquisaca	2,244,140.76	2,474,209.50	2,659,893.18	2,775,939.75
La Paz	3,128,543.00	3,730,828.52	4,654,845.33	4,738,297.41
Cochabamba	1,758,732.85	1,972,706.29	2,046,156.79	2,067,307.95
Oruro	581,700.25	617,712.86	729,126.55	790,520.53
Potosí	1,634,990.26	1,674,940.82	1,943,738.29	1,491,697.35
Tarija	1,000,432.06	1,162,861.90	1,240,901.99	1,253,797.32
Santa Cruz	7,122,500.91	8,421,256.73	8,948,816.70	9,119,443.13
Beni	4,916,475.14	6,267,386.18	6,518,156.16	6,612,411.61
Pando	70,923.64	75,516.68	77,070.89	79,955.87

SOURCE: *Bolivia en Cifras*, 1980 (La Paz: Instituto Nacional de Estadística, 1981),
table 54, p. 107.

Table 313

BRAZIL AGRICULTURAL LANDHOLDINGS BY NUMBER AND AREA, 1920–75

PART I. N

Size (Ha)	1920 N	1920 %	1940 N	1940 %	1950 N	1950 %	1960 N	1960 %	1970 N	1970 %	1975 N	1975 %
0–100	463,879	72	1,629,995	86	1,763,491	85	2,986,435	89	4,454,022	90	4,500,809	90
100–1000	157,959	24	243,818	13	268,159	13	314,831	10	414,746	9	446,170	9
1000 or more	26,315	4	27,812	1	32,628	2	32,480	1	36,874	1	41,468	1
Undeclared	#	#	2,964	#	364	#	4,023	#	18,377	#	4,805	#
TOTAL	648,153	100	1,904,589	100	2,064,642	100	3,337,769	100	4,924,019	100	4,993,252	100

PART II. Ha

Size (Ha)	1920 N	1920 %	1940 N	1940 %	1950 N	1950 %	1960 N	1960 %	1970 N	1970 %	1975 N	1975 %
0–100	15,708,314	9	36,005,599	18	38,588,119	17	53,518,671	21	69,153,199	23	69,154,283	21
100–1000	48,415,737	28	66,184,999	34	75,520,717	32	86,029,455	34	108,742,676	37	115,923,043	36
1000 or more	110,980,624	63	95,529,649	48	118,102,270	51	110,314,016	44	116,249,591	40	138,818,756	43
TOTAL	175,104,675	100	197,720,247	100	232,211,106	100	249,862,142	100	294,145,466	100	323,896,082	100

SOURCE: "Alguns Dados Sobre o Solo Agrario no Brasil," by C. E. Guanziroli and
E. Bohadano, in *Donos da Terra e a Luta pela Reforma Agraria* (Rio de Janeiro:
IBASE, 1984), table 7, p. 79.

Table 314

BRAZIL RELATIONSHIP TO AGRICULTURAL LAND BY NUMBER OF ESTABLISHMENTS AND AREA, 1920–75

PART I. N

Relationship	1920 N	%	1940 N	%	1950 N	%	1960 N	%	1970 N	%	1975 N	%
Owner	577,210	89	1,376,602	72	1,553,349	75	2,553,349	67	2,932,245	60	3,077,561	62
Tenant	23,371	4	221,505	12	186,949	9	579,969	17	993,167	20	863,978	17
Occupant	#	#	109,016	6	208,657	10	356,502	11	792,972	16	917,271	18
Administrator	47,572	7	178,376	9	115,512	6	116,236	5	205,635	4	134,442	3
No Data	#	#	19,090	1	175	#	102	#	#	#	#	#
TOTAL	648,153	100	1,904,589	100	2,064,642	100	3,337,764	100	4,924,019	100	4,993,252	100

PART II. Ha

Relationship	1920 N	%	1940 N	%	1950 N	%	1960 N	%	1970 N	%	1975 N	%
Owner	126,787,281	72	127,276,879	64	154,460,678	66	161,102,822	64	178,292,474	62	210,606,530	65
Tenant	8,575,917	5	19,117,981	10	12,946,538	6	18,109,824	7	16,195,544	5	11,222,459	4
Occupant	#	#	5,278,125	3	9,947,607	4	9,087,028	4	18,955,220	6	20,259,138	6
Administrator	39,741,477	23	44,832,481	23	54,837,701	24	61,548,812	25	80,702,228	27	81,807,956	25
No Data	#	#	1,214,781	#	18,582	#	13,656	#	#	#	#	#
TOTAL	175,104,675	100	197,720,247	100	232,211,106	100	249,862,142	100	294,145,466	100	323,896,082	100

SOURCE: "Alguns Dados Sobre o Solo Agrario no Brasil," by C. E. Guanziroli and E. Bohadano, in *Donos da Terra e a Luta pela Reforma Agraria* (Rio de Janeiro: IBASE, 1984), table 7, p. 79.

Table 315

BRAZIL LANDHOLDINGS BY REGION
(%, 1975)

Region	Under 10 Ha Holdings	Area	10 to 100 Ha Holdings	Area	100 to 1,000 Ha Holdings	Area	1,000 to 10,000 Ha Holdings	Area	Over 10,000 Ha Holdings	Area
North	44.7	1.8	40.0	14.7	14.5	28.9	.7	21.8	.1	32.8
Northeast	70.0	5.4	24.0	22.8	5.6	41.6	.4	23.3	#	6.9
Southeast	31.8	1.9	52.2	22.6	15.0	47.1	1.0	24.8	#	3.6
South	40.0	5.2	54.5	36.0	5.1	33.8	.4	22.8	#	2.2
Center-West	26.6	.4	39.4	4.6	28.1	25.8	5.5	40.0	.4	29.2
C. BRAZIL	52.3	2.8	37.9	18.6	8.9	35.9	.9	28.3	#	14.4

SOURCE: *Brazil, a Country Study*, Richard F. Nyrop, ed., Area Handbook Studies, U.S. Government, Secretary of the Army, 1983, table 9, p. 345.

Table 316

BRAZIL LANDHOLDINGS, SELECTED YEARS, 1920–75
(%)

Size (Ha)	1920 Holdings	Area	1940 Holdings	Area	1950 Holdings	Area	1960 Holdings	Area	1970 Holdings	Area	1975 Holdings	Area
Under 10			34.4	1.7	34.4	2.3	44.8	2.4	51.2	3.1	52.2	2.8
10 to 20			16.6	2.3	16.7	2.1	16.4	3.1	15.7	3.7	14.8	3.2
20 to 50	71.6	9.0	23.9	7.2	23.7	6.5	20.2	8.3	16.8	8.6	16.3	7.8
50 to 100			10.8	7.2	10.6	6.6	8.2	7.6	6.9	8.1	6.9	7.6
100 to 1,000	24.4	27.6	12.8	33.5	13.0	32.5	9.4	34.4	8.5	37.0	8.9	35.8
1,000 to 10,000	3.8	37.4	1.4	31.4	1.5	30.7	.9	28.6	.8	27.2	.9	27.7
Over 10,000	.2	26.0	.1	17.0	.1	19.3	.1	15.6	.1	12.3	#	15.1
Total	100.0	100.0	100.0	100.0	100.0	100.0	100.0	100.0	100.0	100.0	100.0	100.0

SOURCE: *Brazil, a Country Study*, Richard F. Nyrop, ed., Area Handbook Studies, U.S. Government, Secretary of the Army, 1983, table 10, p. 345.

Table 317

BRAZIL AVERAGE SIZE OF LANDHOLDINGS, SELECTED YEARS, 1920–75

(Ha)

Size	1920	1940	1950	1960	1970	1975
Under 10		4.4	4.2	4.0	3.6	3.5
10 to 20		14	15	14	14	14
20 to 50	34	31	31	31	31	31
50 to 100		70	70	70	70	70
100 to 1,000	307	271	282	273	262	260
1,000 to 10,000	2,657	2,337	2,357	2,313	2,260	2,267
Over 10,000	27,274	26,320	27,938	24,354	24,976	26,897
Average	270	104	112	75	60	65

SOURCE: *Brazil, a Country Study*, Richard F. Nyrop, ed., Area Handbook Studies,
U.S. Government, Secretary of the Army, 1983, table 11, p. 346.

Table 318

BRAZIL LANDHOLDINGS BY FORM OF TENANCY, BY REGION, 1975

(%)

Region	Owners		Renters		Sharecroppers		Squatters	
	Holdings	Area	Holdings	Area	Holdings	Area	Holdings	Area
North	36.6	58.8	6.0	5.7	1.3	1.0	56.1	34.5
Northeast	53.8	90.9	17.2	2.3	4.4	1.0	24.6	5.8
Southeast	80.6	92.7	6.5	3.6	6.2	1.1	6.7	2.6
South	71.5	87.1	7.6	6.0	11.9	3.5	9.0	3.4
Center-West	61.4	89.2	11.8	2.3	4.8	.5	22.0	8.0
C. BRAZIL	61.8	87.4	12.1	3.4	6.3	1.2	19.8	8.0

SOURCE: *Brazil, a Country Study*, Richard F. Nyrop, ed., Area Handbook Studies,
U.S. Government, Secretary of the Army, 1983, table 12, p. 346.

Table 319

BRAZIL LAND DISTRIBUTION BY TENANCY

(%, 1975)

Size (Ha)	Owners		Renters		Sharecroppers		Squatters	
	Holdings	Area	Holdings	Area	Holdings	Area	Holdings	Area
Under 1 hectare	3.6	#	26.3	.9	7.4	.4	17.3	.4
1 to 5	18.6	.6	47.4	5.8	44.7	9.9	46.4	4.3
5 to 10	13.8	1.1	10.2	3.9	24.7	13.9	12.4	3.2
10 to 20	18.4	2.8	6.0	4.5	14.5	15.3	8.3	4.3
20 to 50	22.2	7.6	4.3	7.3	6.3	14.2	7.8	8.9
50 to 100	9.9	7.5	2.1	8.0	1.3	6.7	3.2	8.5
100 to 1,000	12.3	35.7	3.5	41.8	1.0	19.4	4.3	39.2
1,000 to 10,000	1.2	29.5	.2	20.0	.1	13.2	.3	21.3
Over 10,000	#	15.2	#	7.8	#	7.0	#	9.9
Total	100.0	100.0	100.0	100.0	100.0	100.0	100.0	100.0

SOURCE: *Brazil, a Country Study*, Richard F. Nyrop, ed., Area Handbook Studies,
U.S. Government, Secretary of the Army, 1983, table 13, p. 346.

Table 320

CHILE REDISTRIBUTION OF LAND OF THE REFORMED SECTOR[1]
(SEPTEMBER 1973–APRIL 1979)

Farm Category	Number of Farms	Average Size (bih)[2]	% Land Area (bih)[2]
Total of Reformed Sector (September 1973)	5,809	154.2	100.0
Total of Returned Farms	3,809	66.0	28.1
Fully Returned Farms	1,638	86.5	15.8
Partially Returned Farms	2,171	50.5	12.3
Assignment of Family Units (parcelas)	36,673	10.1	41.5
Garden Plots (sitios)	6,185	.27	.2
Sold by Tender	1,587	50.1	8.9
State Owned	1,155	83.0	10.7
Retained by Reformed Sector as Cooperatives	265	361.8	10.7

1. The Reformed Sector refers to agricultural lands affected by the agrarian reforms of Eduardo Frei and Salvador Allende.
2. Basic irrigated hectare.

SOURCE: Cristóbal Kay, "The Monetorist Experiment in the Chilean Countryside," in *El Sector Agrario en América Latina*, Mauricio Díaz, ed. (Instituto de Estudios Latino-americanos de Estocolmo, 1979), p. 309.

Table 321

CHILE DISTRIBUTION OF LAND BY SIZE, 1965, 1973, AND 1977

Size (Standardized Irrigated Hectares)	Holdings (N)			Amount of Land			% Holdings			% Land		
	1965	1973	1977	1965	1973	1977	1965	1973	1977	1965	1973	1977
Less than 5	189,539	190,000	190,000	199,796	200,000	200,000	81.4	79.3	70.1	9.7	9.67	9.6
5–20	26,877	27,000	58,266	263,377	270,000	557,458	11.5	11.2	21.5	12.7	13.05	26.8
20–40	6,959	8,000	8,000	195,015	240,000	240,000	3.0	3.4	2.9	9.4	11.60	11.5
40–60	2,989	6,000	8,160	146,063	300,000	408,700	1.3	2.5	3.0	7.1	14.50	19.6
60–80	1,715	2,909	2,909	118,553	217,833	217,800	.7	1.2	1.1	5.7	10.53	10.5
Over 80	4,876	~	1,612	1,144,994	~	127,000	2.1	~	.6	55.4	~	6.1
Subtotal		233,909			1,227,833			97.6			59.43	
Reformed sector		5,655	2,343[a]		839,983	331,621[a]		2.4	.9		40.57	15.9
Total	232,955	239,564	271,190	2,067,798	2,067,816	2,082,579						

a. The "reformed sector" in 1977 consisted of land still in CORA hands due to be "assigned" to beneficiaries or sold off to private purchasers.

SOURCE: L. Castillo and D. Lehmann, "Agrarian Reform and Structural Change in Chile," in *Agrarian Reform in Developing Countries*, Ajit Kumar Ghoss, ed. (New York: St. Martin's Press, 1983), p. 264.

Table 322

COLOMBIA LAND ENTITLEMENT, 1962–83

Year	Titles (N)	Ha	Average Size of Grant (Ha)
1962	1,272	104,539	82.2
1963	2,842	146,368	51.5
1964	6,011	233,492	38.8
1965	9,726	281,648	29.0
1966	12,895	331,701	25.7
1967	13,402	453,052	33.8
1968	15,072	375,225	24.9
1969	16,599	320,602	19.3
1970	15,335	419,728	27.4
1971	14,467	327,985	22.7
1972	14,601	351,640	24.1
1973	11,278	236,484	21.0
1974	9,830	182,599	18.6
1975	9,212	315,492	34.2
1976	9,073	282,206	31.1
1977	9,707	313,392	32.3
1978	10,087	318,635	31.6
1979	9,093	326,381	35.9
1980	9,398	321,688	34.2
1981	14,845	526,011	35.4
1982	10,380	365,604	35.2
1983	11,020	335,100	30.4

SOURCE: *Estructura Económica Colombiana*, Gilberto Arango Londoño, ed. (Bogotá: Editorial Norma, 1985), table 3.2, p. 52.

Table 323

COLOMBIA LAND DISTRIBUTION BY SIZE OF GRANT,[1] 1960 AND 1970

	Grants			
	1960		1970	
Size (Ha)	N	%	N	%
-----------	-----	-----	-----	-----
Less than 5	756,605	62.6	700,225	59.5
5.0–9.9	169,145	14.0	156,659	13.6
10.0–49.9	201,020	16.6	217,873	18.5
50.0–99.9	39,990	3.3	47,763	4.1
100.0–499.9	36,010	3.0	42,897	3.6
500.0–999.9	4,141	.3	4,927	.4
Greater than 1,000	2,761	3.2	3,467	.3
Total	1,209,672	100.0	1,176,811	100.0

	Size			
	1960		1970	
Size (Ha)	T Ha	%	T Ha	%
-----------	------	-----	------	-----
Less than 5	1,239	4.5	1,146	3.7
5.0–9.9	1,165	4.3	1,088	3.5
10.0–49.9	4,211	15.4	4,653	15.0
50.0–99.9	2,680	9.8	3,198	10.3
100.0–499.9	6,990	25.6	8,253	26.6
500.0–999.9	2,731	10.0	3,229	10.4
Greater than 1,000	8,322	30.4	9,426	30.5
Total	27,338	100.0	30,993	100.0

1. Excludes Chocó and Guajira.

SOURCE: *Estructura Económica Colombiana*, Gilberto Arango Londoño, ed. (Bogotá: Editorial Norma, 1985), table 3.1, p. 48.

Table 324

ECUADOR BENEFICIARIES OF LAND REFORM, 1964–79

Region	1964–71	1972	1973	1974	1975	1976	1977	1978[‡]	1979[‡]	1964–79
National Total	31,460	1,838	1,932	2,930	3,413	5,430	4,621	5,275	2,762	59,661
Mountains	29,120	1,601	1,844	809	2,510	4,365	3,132	2,833	1,458	47,672
Azuay	1,448	7	131	65	- -	23	32	258	106	2,070
Bolívar	245	1	- -	- -	11	110	22	131	- -	520
Cañar	1,993	73	180	119	239	21	60	- -	- -	2,685
Carchi	1,734	268	9	240	129	115	126	- -	97	2,718
Cotopaxi	4,722	209	306	20	3	122	86	75	- -	5,543
Chimborazo	6,290	9	111	119	696	2,287	502	942	314	11,270
Imbabura	1,665	45	3	1	3	9	136	69	2	1,933
Loja	3,810	671	918	133	195	909	1,798	981	495	9,910
Pichincha	6,653	305	179	112	1,234	716	369	377	443	10,388
Tungurahua	560	13	7	- -	- -	53	1	- -	1	635
Coast	2,340	237	88	2,121	903	1,062	1,485	2,442	1,303	11,981
El Oro	207	28	1	61	- -	1	20	219	65	602
Esmeraldas	1	- -	- -	- -	- -	- -	- -	- -	4	5
Guyas	1,775	184	7	1,328	853	950	1,043	1,027	955	8,122
Los Rios	354	4	80	732	50	88	381	1,130	274	3,093
Managi	3	21	- -	- -	- -	23	41	66	5	159
East						3	4	- -	1	8
Morona Santiago	- -	- -	- -	- -	- -	- -	- -	- -	- -	- -
Napo	- -	- -	- -	- -	- -	- -	- -	- -	1	1
Pastaza	- -	- -	- -	- -	- -	- -	- -	- -	- -	- -
Zamora Chinchipe	- -	- -	- -	- -	- -	3	4	- -	- -	7

SOURCE: *La Economía Ecuatoriana en la Década de los Años 70 y Perspectivas Futuras*,
Nestor Vega Moreno, ed. (Quito, 1980), table 8.1, p. 204.

Table 325

ECUADOR WORKERS ACCORDING TO LAND OWNERSHIP
(1975)

Size (Ha)	Farms		Area		Workers		Workers by Farm	Workers by Ha
	N	%	Ha	%	N	%		
Fewer than 5	469,378	75.2	706,231	10.8	535,448	59.7	1.14	.76
5–10	67,387	10.8	458,532	7.0	113,009	12.6	1.68	.25
10–50	64,497	10.3	1,389,595	21.3	134,534	15.0	2.09	.10
Greater than 50	22,776	3.7	3,987,775	60.9	113,906	12.7	5.00	.03
Total	624,038	100.0	6,542,133	100.0	896,897	100.0	1.44	.14

SOURCE: *La Economía Ecuatoriana en la Década de los Años 70 y Perspectivas Futuras*,
Nestor Vega Moreno, ed. (Quito, 1980), table 8.5, p. 208.

Table 326

HONDURAS LAND REFORM, 1962–84

Year	Families Benefited	Ha
1962–68[a]	129	786
1969	1,738	5,735
1970	1,236	6,386
1971	1,871	7,751
1972	3,331	10,585
1973	8,674	32,454
1974	9,828	47,098
1975	6,751	37,252
1976	6,274	26,913
1977	3,381	15,985
1978	1,745	5,415
1979	2,442	9,005
1980	2,577	16,713
1981	2,475	8,145
1982	3,506	16,847
1983	4,930	19,016
1984	4,805	22,907

a. Annual average over seven years.

SOURCE: J. Mark Ruhl, "The Honduran Agrarian Reform under Suazo Córdova, 1982–85: An Assessment," *Inter-American Economic Affairs*, 39:2 (Autumn), 63–80.

Table 327

MEXICO SUMMARY OF SELECTED LAND TITLE RESOLUTIONS, 1916–76

Year	Provisional Grants	Positive Definitive Grants	Beneficiaries	Derechos a Salvo	Types of Land Granted (Ha) Total	Irrigated	Rainfed	Pasture	Mountain	Desert	Undefined
1916	2	1	182	0	773	0	0	0	0	0	773
1917	90	50	6,137	5,601	60,119	341	5,448	115	153	0	54,062
1918	143	76	11,288	7,974	77,861	91	6,737	5,551	400	0	65,083
1919	226	85	16,771	5,967	61,811	966	10,917	1,241	67	0	48,619
1920	203	105	18,441	3,155	162,040	5,220	32,356	1,371	12,781	0	110,365
1921	298	205	39,538	2,027	551,831	2,069	55,497	20,943	28,889	1,325	443,108
1922	89	56	10,327	2,693	117,298	3,592	14,316	3,759	686	0	94,946
1923	234	151	34,042	5,392	373,978	8,624	44,808	49,614	2,513	0	268,419
1924	457	322	59,543	5,394	595,565	8,689	68,404	57,323	12,211	0	448,938
1925	577	424	78,423	4,049	939,454	5,546	66,652	28,743	13,426	2,116	822,970
1926	522	290	52,944	2,598	684,582	10,132	34,203	120,020	17,647	0	502,581
1927	774	485	80,765	4,100	1,015,153	14,322	83,706	63,793	61,960	170	791,202
1928	501	341	48,648	4,499	591,599	9,612	68,178	63,750	79,180	478	368,399
1929	706	507	70,015	7,294	720,296	24,587	116,934	103,479	112,829	3,564	358,903
1930	1,137	906	104,858	13,681	1,850,882	35,362	215,232	318,723	263,204	11,635	1,006,734
1931	571	428	43,437	2,898	732,059	16,974	97,715	159,697	130,386	33,158	294,136
1932	323	203	18,754	1,334	292,288	7,272	36,403	110,712	84,158	23,563	30,181
1933	478	340	32,619	4,962	499,938	35,685	74,541	247,935	71,500	9,184	61,096
1934	1,314	1,206	102,592	15,477	1,540,113	52,654	354,095	558,916	321,079	88,689	164,689
1935	1,235	1,106	91,660	26,607	1,598,554	134,919	396,756	766,440	277,282	3,702	19,462
1936	2,480	2,218	157,237	79,463	3,571,549	205,562	771,614	1,449,927	562,477	32,511	549,507
1937	2,524	2,295	148,410	80,929	4,212,035	127,677	764,453	2,719,506	385,743	131,229	83,445
1938	1,332	1,224	77,101	35,475	2,161,399	76,345	424,782	1,350,432	226,889	9,622	73,345
1939	2,624	2,032	140,193	64,655	3,488,852	191,343	542,205	1,802,615	421,725	28,694	502,301
1940	2,470	1,716	101,448	52,513	3,539,986	209,365	437,811	1,261,579	1,443,882	94,140	93,226
1941	1,654	832	34,576	26,247	1,625,467	17,991	220,512	894,709	370,016	4,077	118,165
1942	1,655	792	35,045	20,353	1,824,507	24,285	197,424	932,230	392,392	2,530	275,646
1943	1,051	436	22,265	10,366	875,691	17,096	106,425	535,657	190,015	59	24,448
1944	1,140	538	22,250	13,890	858,070	19,764	157,926	530,554	136,710	608	12,521
1945	955	387	15,001	11,037	676,159	9,466	119,964	397,246	73,320	1	76,161
1946	1,177	285	10,938	6,890	427,746	5,267	93,475	246,948	77,660	2,208	2,195
1947	1,325	466	15,665	17,184	764,794	12,430	135,967	491,987	64,838	35,353	24,228
1948	1,242	261	8,861	8,163	503,085	8,055	69,246	388,596	29,418	1,821	5,952
1949	1,525	171	4,401	7,019	378,115	18,452	47,834	268,757	37,052	235	5,792
1950	1,326	164	6,118	5,023	296,804	5,122	49,950	217,224	14,797	0	9,718
1951	1,839	433	15,945	14,500	968,677	10,521	171,691	726,212	41,878	1,500	16,885
1952	1,759	252	11,127	6,162	487,950	14,708	108,977	320,107	32,739	0	11,416
1953	1,472	340	12,696	12,012	964,978	13,589	142,089	740,210	43,867	4,750	20,488
1954	1,644	343	13,738	11,788	717,796	18,860	152,761	417,469	99,130	23,273	6,318
1955	1,903	281	10,528	6,751	681,359	6,739	122,933	488,903	43,516	0	19,267

Table 327 (Continued)

MEXICO SUMMARY OF SELECTED LAND TITLE RESOLUTIONS, 1916–76

Year	Provisional Grants	Positive Definitive Grants	Beneficiaries	Derechos a Salvo	Types of Land Granted (Ha)						
					Total	Irrigated	Rainfed	Pasture	Mountain	Desert	Undefined
1956	1,737	229	9,878	4,235	404,754	6,992	125,941	222,241	39,706	0	9,874
1957	1,371	207	7,875	5,406	392,076	4,426	105,143	241,580	38,747	0	2,189
1958	1,972	217	9,442	5,079	572,028	5,551	123,224	378,157	33,545	0	31,559
1959	1,652	192	10,119	5,874	839,897	22,609	91,307	696,977	27,188	0	1,817
1960	1,667	344	23,909	7,855	1,474,042	35,071	265,849	1,088,174	59,946	3,736	21,267
1961	1,048	441	22,069	13,705	1,013,767	11,382	237,868	596,377	114,736	6,100	47,329
1962	1,142	395	17,750	10,499	1,411,601	23,118	201,842	1,106,035	68,943	0	11,667
1963	928	311	14,119	10,073	983,181	4,951	191,968	632,367	42,223	0	111,672
1964	2,141	495	28,900	17,290	1,872,567	52,075	301,972	1,296,344	141,680	7,777	72,723
1965	1,146	497	19,507	18,759	1,586,224	12,646	282,933	1,171,164	110,306	166	9,016
1966	1,589	624	16,804	29,042	2,026,059	9,604	281,533	1,451,409	223,632	1,253	58,632
1967	2,347	629	28,477	20,056	2,861,835	4,456	375,297	2,033,904	392,367	0	55,820
1968	1,920	789	31,507	27,496	3,392,561	18,398	453,603	2,607,729	262,113	0	50,731
1969	1,613	587	21,394	19,916	3,588,630	6,487	311,383	3,011,442	155,556	80,867	22,905
1970	2,564	767	33,006	20,609	6,566,476	22,101	274,474	5,692,766	556,697	0	22,450
1971	1,776	309	19,871	1,938	2,005,953	11,305	125,147	1,587,076	25,154	5	257,272
1972	2,162	234	16,366	486	1,764,052	5,857	98,526	1,549,654	55,979	0	54,035
1973	1,608	299	22,631	589	1,848,401	5,059	113,765	1,597,843	47,512	2,941	81,283
1974	3,616	234	16,991	1,007	540,725	7,126	93,152	379,195	53,410	1,852	5,992
1975	5,672	303	24,116	178	1,607,211	19,919	94,222	902,233	70,984	84	519,771
1976	5,575	314	18,911	2,739	841,463	8,376	90,130	656,096	65,904	1,756	19,205
Unknown	209	119	10,309	1,830	173,785	28,025	14,839	53,677	24,173	16,545	36,529
	88,423	31,289	2,208,478	840,783	79,258,501	1,714,828	10,875,055	47,817,379	8,788,916	673,277	9,389,428

SOURCE: Susan R. Walsh Sanderson, *Land Reform in Mexico: 1910–1980* (Orlando: Academic Press, 1984), Appendix E, pp. 164–165.

Table 328

NICARAGUA LAND REFORM, BY REGION,[1] 1981–86

Region	1981–86	1986
Region 1		
Co-ops[2]	102,391	5,489
Individuals[3]	24,153	18,132
Families[4]	598	470
Region 2		
Co-ops	165,891	31,065
Individuals	28,832	24,720
Families	8,179	1,071
Region 3		
Co-ops	59,839	9,312
Individuals	5,123	1,481
Families	205	152
Region 4		
Co-ops	154,291	35,633
Individuals	7,793	15,158
Families	1,310	1,200
Region 5		
Co-ops	148,826	80,379
Individuals	46,543	15,311
Families	793	~
Region 6		
Co-ops	132,205	24,329
Individuals	42,960	30,420
Families	2,316	2,187
Special Zone 1		
Co-ops	22,767	0
Individuals	0	0
Families	~	0
Special Zone 2		
Co-ops	24,411	6,800
Individuals	14,350	14,350
Families	91	91
Special Zone 3		
Co-ops	73,164	6,250
Individuals	34,178	18,726
Families	552	~
Total		
Co-ops	899,137	199,207
Individuals	203,932	138,298
Total land	1,103,069	337,505
Total families	60,282	14,276

1. As of 1982, Nicaragua was divided into the following regions:
   Region 1, Departments of Esteli and Nueva Segovia
   Region 2, Department of León
   Region 3, Department of Managua
   Region 4, Departments of Granada, Masaya, and Rivas
   Region 5, Departments of Chontales, Boaco, and Zelaya
   Region 6, Departments of Matagalpa and Jinotega
   Special Zone 1, Northern Zelaya
   Special Zone 2, Southern Zelaya
   Special Zone 3, Department of Rio San Juan.
2. Co-ops: Amount of land distributed to Sandinista Agricultural Cooperatives in hectares.
3. Individuals: Amount of land distributed to individual farmers, in hectares.
4. Families: Number of families benefiting under land reform.

SOURCE: *Central American Report*, April 10, 1987.

Table 329

PARAGUAY LAND REFORM, 1956–86

Category	1956–85	1979	1980	1981	1982	1983	1984	1985	1986
Number of Lots Distributed	111,506	2,506	3,931	4,316	3,036	2,604	5,026	4,966	4,536
Amount of Land Distributed (T Ha)	9,957	422	717	473	598	302	816	310	253
Average (Ha)	89	168	182	110	197	116	162	63	56
Definite Title									
Number of Beneficiaries	110,331	3,814	3,836	4,054	4,224	4,093	5,090	6,068	4,824
Amount Given (T Ha)	7,600	284	719	729	460	410	500	437	404
Average (Ha)	69	74	187	180	109	100	98	72	84

SOURCE: ECLA-S, 1986, p. 570.

Table 330

PARAGUAY PROPERTY REGISTERED WITH
PROPERTY TAX OFFICE, 1920–84

Year	N	Increment
1920	90,967	
1921	93,533	2,586
1922	96,213	2,660
1923	98,948	2,725
1924	101,718	2,770
1925	104,616	2,898
1926	107,590	2,974
1927	110,650	3,060
1928	113,195	3,145
1929	117,030	3,235
1930	120,360	3,330
1931	123,783	3,423
1932	127,297	3,514
1933	130,918	3,621
1934	134,640	3,722
1935	138,470	3,830
1936	142,409	3,939
1937	146,459	4,050
1938	150,625	4,166
1939	154,910	4,285
1940	159,319	4,409
1941	163,852	4,533
1942	168,514	4,662
1943	173,312	4,798
1944	208,876	35,564
1945	253,524	44,648
1946	256,774	3,250
1947	257,098	324
1948	258,063	965
1949	259,778	1,615
1950	261,525	1,847
1951	263,597	2,072
1952	265,141	2,144
1953	267,958	2,217
1954	271,039	3,081
1955	275,897	4,858
1956	280,215	4,318
1957	284,216	4,046
1958	289,590	5,329
1959	297,419	7,829
1960	306,994	9,575
1961	324,424	17,430
1962	347,203	22,779
1963	359,540	12,337
1964	375,563	16,023
1965	392,163	16,600
1966	404,125	11,962
1967	416,457	12,332
1968	426,201	9,744
1969	440,068	13,867
1970	451,309	11,241
1971	461,565	10,256
1972	471,302	9,737
1973	483,131	11,829
1974	493,913	10,782
1975	504,853	10,940
1976	516,225	11,372
1977	528,652	12,427
1978	542,284	13,632
1979	582,890	40,606
1980	635,341	52,451
1981	672,007	36,666
1982	737,541	65,534
1983	772,389	34,848
1084	855,982	83,573

SOURCE: Juan Manuel Frutos, *Un Millón de Propiedades para Un Millón de Felices Propietarios* (Asunción: Editorial El Foro, 1985), pp. 108–109.

Table 331

PARAGUAY LAND ENTITLEMENT TO ORGANIZATIONS, BY INSTITUTO DE BIENESTAR RURAL, 1970–85
(Ha)

Organization	1970	1971	1972	1973	1974	1975	1976	1977	1978	1979	1980	1981	1982	1983	1984	1985	Total
Military	1	--	--	--	--	--	227	--	--	1	--	--	1,846	251	375	10,046	13,343
Religious	2	--	2	--	4	--	22	1	--	3	--	1	2	11	18	58	151
Social and Sports Clubs	1	--	1	50	--	2	--	11	1	--	1	--	29	--	2	32	105
Municipalities	68	--	--	1,117	--	--	16	400	--	81	--	936	577	6	471	355	4,025

SOURCE: Adapted from Juan Manuel Frutos, *Un Millón de Propiedades para un Millón de Felices Propietarios* (Asunción: Editorial El Foro, 1985), pp. 102–104.

Table 332

PERU SIZE AND TYPE OF PRODUCTION UNITS AT END OF LAND REFORM
(1977)[‡]

Size and Type of Production Units	Total		Coast		Mountains		Jungle	
	N	Ha	N	Ha[2]	N	Ha[2]	N	Ha[2]
Smaller than 20 Ha[1]	1,459.0	3,956	167.0	446	1,174.0	2,843	118.0	667
Ex-tenants	197.0	74	10.0	36[a]	177.0	64[a]	10.0	36[a]
Small Producers	1,262.0	3,242	157.0	410	997.0	2,201	108.0	631
From 20 to 100 Ha	57.6	2,022	4.6	182	32.0	1,126	21.0	714
Ex-tenants	2.0	46	--	2[a]	2.0	42[a]	--	2[a]
Middle Producers	55.6	1,976	4.6	180	30.0	1,084	21.0	712
Larger than 100 Ha	8.1	17,931	.6	1,237	7.2	15,708	.3	986
Individual Producers	2.3	350	--	--	2.3	350	--	--
Associations	5.8	17,581	.6	1,237	4.9	15,367	.3	986
Cooperatives	1.8	9,390	.4	1,106[b]	1.3	7,380[b]	.1	904[b]
Communities	4.0	8,191	.2	131[c]	3.6	7,987	.2	82[c]
Total	1,524.7[d]	23,909	172.2	1,865	1,213.2	19,677	139.3	2,367
Individual Producers	1,535.9	6,328	171.6	628	1,208.3	4,310	.3	1,381
Associations	5.8	17,581	.6	1,237	4.9	15,367	139.0	986

1. Includes some families for whom agriculture is not the principal source of income. The number of independent producers in 1972 was 987 and in 1981 was 1,183.
2. Calculated on the basis of 1972 census data with adjustments.

a. Distribution of tenants assumes (arbitrarily) 90% Mountains, 5% Coast, and 5% Jungle.
b. Regional distribution of associations based on data from Dirección General de Reforma Agraria.
c. Based on data from census of 1972.
d. Includes lands once worked by tenants who joined associations following the Agrarian Reform.

SOURCE: *Peru: El Agro en Cifras*, Hector Maletta, ed. (Lima: Universidad del Pacífico, 1983), table 2.7, p. 62.

Table 333

PARAGUAY TYPES OF LAND OWNERSHIP BY REGION
(%, 1984)

Region and Department	Entitled		Leased		Occupied	
	N	Area	N	Area	N	Area
North						
Concepción	56.0	94.1	8.5	3.3	35.3	2.6
San Pedro	13.4	89.2	9.2	2.3	35.7	7.3
Central						
Cordillera	61.3	88.2	15.1	3.6	21.8	7.5
Guairá	44.2	77.6	15.1	4.8	37.9	16.4
Caazapá	46.4	89.0	19.7	4.1	33.7	6.8
Paraguarí	50.0	88.7	16.8	2.9	31.7	7.5
Central	78.5	95.1	9.3	2.3	9.7	2.0
Misiones						
Misiones	53.9	94.7	14.4	2.5	31.0	2.6
Ñeembucú	47.0	91.0	14.4	3.7	35.9	4.0
Canendiyu						
Caaguazú	51.1	80.5	11.2	3.0	35.8	14.0
Alto Paraná	57.8	86.3	16.2	5.3	25.6	8.1
Amambay	69.0	94.0	10.9	4.5	18.6	1.5
Canendiyú	60.0	90.9	14.9	2.5	24.9	6.5
Itapua						
Itapua	60.1	85.3	11.5	13.1	27.4	10.5
Chaco Paraguayo						
Pdte. Hayes	74.0	98.0	7.3	.8	12.2	.5
Alto Paraguay	80.0	96.9	2.9	.6	14.5	2.4
Chaco	97.0	99.1	- -	- -	3.3	.9
Nueva Asunción	96.0	78.8	- -	- -	14.3	21.2
Boquerón	94.2	90.6	.4	.4	4.8	8.7

SOURCE: *Tierra y Sociedad: Problemática de la Tierra Urbana, Rural e Indígena en el Paraguay* (Conferencia Episcopal Paraguaya, 1984), p. 324.

Table 334

PERU ADJUDICATION OF LAND BY DECREE AND UNIT
(1983)

Decree	Unit	Enterprises (N)	Beneficiary Families (N)	Land (Ha)
No. 15037	Cooperatives	12	424	134,799
	Communities	24	5,045	146,611
	Peasant Groups	3	82	30,010
	Individual	#	9,054	87,420
Subtotal		39	14,605	398,840
No. 17716	Cooperatives	552	99,473	2,146,575
	Communities	652	157,629	1,368,569
	Peasant Groups	997	53,009	1,890,290
	S.A.I.C.	58	48,879	2,702,411
	Individual	#	42,023	475,112
	FONAPS (Transfers)	10	1,507	228,665
	Government Agencies	#	#	125,853
Subtotal		2,269	402,520	8,937,475
No. 20653 and	Cooperatives	32	1,051	68,943
No. 22175	Peasant Groups	24	525	11,117
	Individuals	#	22,196	490,267
Subtotal		56	23,776	570,327
No. 20653 and No. 22175	Entitlement to Indigenous Groups	390	12,836	1,352,714
Total		2,754	453,737	11,259,356

SOURCE: *Información Estadística Básica del Sector Agropecuario Peruano, 1960–82*, Custodio Arias Nieto, ed. (Lima: Universidad Nacional Mayor de San Marcos, 1983), table 29.

Table 335

PERU LAND TENURE, 1961 AND 1972

| | Production Units | | | | Area Covered | | | |
| | 1961 | | 1972 | | 1961 | | 1972 | |
Size (Ha)	N	%	N	%	Ha	%	Ha	%
Less than 1	292,920	34.7	483,350	34.8	129,092	.7	185,132	.8
1–5	406,507	48.2	600,425	43.2	907,096	5.1	1,375,316	5.8
5–20	107,853	12.8	231,840	16.7	887,574	5.0	2,036,421	8.6
20–100	24,638	2.9	59,592	4.3	953,307	5.4	2,182,599	9.3
100–500	7,684	.9	11,279	.8	1,551,039	8.8	2,150,668	9.1
500–2,500	2,612	.3	2,785	.2	2,642,106	14.9	2,824,225	12.0
More than 2,500	1,026	.1	1,017	.1	10,651,831	60.1	12,790,788	54.3
Total	843,240	99.9	1,390,288	100.1	17,722,045	100.0	23,545,149	99.9

SOURCE: Tom Alberts, *Agrarian Reform and Rural Poverty: A Case Study of Peru* (Boulder, Colo.: Westview Press, 1983), table 5.1, p. 137.

Table 336

PERU ADJUDICATION OF LAND REFORM, 1967–79

| | Total | | Type of Adjudication | | | | | | | | | | | | | | | | |
| | | | Individual | | | Cooperatives | | | Groups | | | Communities | | | SAIS | | |
Year	Ha	Families	Enterprises	Ha	Families	N	Ha	Families	N	Ha	Families	N	Ha	Families	N	Ha	Families
1967	140,219	3,593	11	17,071	2,877	6	97,964	249	2	24,805	55	3	379	412	..	..	..
1968	182,236	7,812	25	18,887	3,525	6	36,505	160	..	..	..	19	126,414	4,127	..	..	..
1969	256,774	7,355	34	37,545	3,313	7	35,520	368	43	103,129	679	14	74,282	2,967	..	6,298	28
1970	691,697	42,343	114	26,517	4,223	81	225,054	29,030	14	28,221	971	14	90,381	4,716	5	321,524	3,403
1971	538,083	18,671	35	6,690	766	16	99,627	7,903	7	27,565	594	8	14,924	2,580	4	389,276	6,828
1972	1,119,223	38,976	111	12,154	1,629	37	526,316	20,067	53	61,055	2,391	9	28,713	3,642	12	490,985	11,247
1973	1,336,692	56,496	259	1,860	393	139	461,083	20,193	75	130,940	5,585	27	50,953	11,916	18	691,856	18,409
1974	865,938	42,065	219	6,011	737	65	243,115	9,084	107	196,163	8,530	38	83,974	9,068	9	336,675	14,646
1975	1,083,471	36,686	287	9,131	1,260	96	342,222	11,453	135	377,341	7,682	48	96,964	11,642	8	257,813	4,649
1976	640,253	40,550	278	7,503	676	38	106,088	4,001	148	292,655	9,025	92	124,147	26,268	..	109,860	580
1977	566,080	29,406	229	33,151	1,337	13	40,082	1,240	144	270,907	8,459	69	78,741	11,881	3	143,199	923
1978	320,059	23,119	163	45,633	1,650	16	74,741	931	79	145,274	3,905	68	46,767	16,588	..	7,644	45
1979†	210,426	10,369	104	37,685	1,307	10	13,588	528	68	111,731	3,168	26	42,529	5,247	..	4,893	39
Total	7,837,933	349,669	1,827	254,613	23,438	530	2,300,761	104,928	822	1,709,579	49,598	416	825,811	111,054	59	2,732,830	60,533

SOURCE:: *Información Estadística Básica del Sector Agropecuario Peruano, 1960–1982*, Custodio Arias Nieto, ed. (Lima: Universidad Nacional Mayor de San Marcos, 1983), table 25.

Part II

Transportation and Communication

Note: This volume contains statistics from numerous sources. Alternative data on many topics are presented. Variations in statistics can be attributed to differences in definition, parameters, coverage, methodology, as well as date gathered, prepared, or adjusted. See also Editor's Note on Methodology.

4
Transportation

Figure 4:1

MAJOR HIGHWAYS OF SOUTH AMERICA

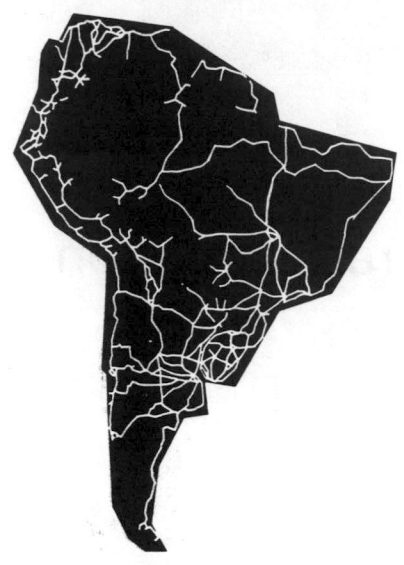

Source: IDB-SPTF, 1984, p. 82.

Table 400

CITY TO CITY DISTANCES BY NONSTOP AIR SERVICE
(Miles)

From/To	Country[1]	City Code/ Miles	From/To	Country[1]	City Code/ Miles	From/To	Country[1]	City Code/ Miles
ACAPULCO	**MEX**	**ACA**	SANTA MARTA	COL	42	MANAUS	BRAZ	1,119
			SANTO DOMINGO	D R	619	MANIZALES	COL	109
ATLANTA GA	USA	1,507	VALLEDUPAR	COL	109	MARACAIBO	VEN	447
CHICAGO ILL	USA	1,879				MEDELLIN	COL	145
DALLAS TEX	USA	1,124	**BELEM**	**BRAZ**	**BEL**	MEXICO CITY	MEX	1,961
GUADALAJARA	MEX	346	BELO HORIZONTE	BRAZ	1,382	MIAMI FLA	USA	1,513
HOUSTON TEX	USA	934	BRASILIA	BRAZ	1,001	NEIVA	COL	145
LIMA	PERU	2,527	CAMPO GRANDE	BRAZ	1,545	NEW YORK NY	USA	2,487
LOS ANGELES CAL	USA	1,654	CAYENNE	F GU	506	OCANA	COL	250
MEXICO CITY	MEX	191	CONCEICAO	BRAZ	480	PANAMA CITY	PAN	470
MONTREAL QUE	CAN	2,487	CUIABA	BRAZ	1,567	PEREIRA	COL	112
NEW YORK NY	USA	2,260	CURITIBA	BRAZ	1,674	POINTE A PITRE	GUAD	1,171
OAXACA	MEX	204	FLORIANOPOLIS	BRAZ	1,828	QUITO	ECUA	450
PAPEETE	F POL	4,138	FORTALEZA	BRAZ	710	RIO DE JANEIRO	BRAZ	2,827
PUERTO VALLARTA	MEX	448	GOIANIA	BRAZ	1,102	SAN ANDRES	COL	749
SAN ANTONIO TEX	USA	886	IMPERATRIZ	BRAZ	400	SAN JUAN	P R	1,096
TORONTO ONT	CAN	2,202	LISBON	PORT	3,733	SANTA MARTA	COL	444

Continued in SALA, 23-308.

Table 401

AIR PASSENGER KILOMETERS OF SCHEDULED SERVICE,[1] 20 LC, 1985–87[a]

(M)

Country	Total[3]			International Flights[4]		
	1985	1986	1987	1985	1986	1987
A. ARGENTINA	7,531	7,942	8,652	3,774	4,087	4,423
B. BOLIVIA	894‡	884	912	513‡	531‡	583
C. BRAZIL	18,494	23,471	22,613	7,370	8,540	8,138
D. CHILE	1,772	1,961	2,117‡	1,167	1,351	1,433
E. COLOMBIA	4,242‡	4,260‡	4,230‡	1,959	1,934	1,995
F. COSTA RICA	570	560‡	610‡	567	554	604
G. CUBA	1,801‡	1,856	1,997	1,459‡	1,511	1,661
H. DOMINICAN REP.	606‡	542	213	606‡	542	213
I. ECUADOR	969‡	1,073‡	1,013‡	754	853‡	853‡
J. EL SALVADOR	575‡	517	489‡	575‡	517	489‡
K. GUATEMALA	156‡	137	165	150‡	132	160
L. HAITI‡	~	~	~	~	~	~
M. HONDURAS	391	377‡	495‡	368	377‡	469‡
N. MEXICO	17,773‡	16,885	17,649‡	7,853	7,755	9,696
Q. NICARAGUA	115‡	85‡	90‡	115‡	85‡	90‡
P. PANAMA	534	505	491‡	534	505	491‡
Q. PARAGUAY	635‡	987‡	1,083‡	620‡	970‡	1,065‡
R. PERU	1,598	2,110	2,670‡	704	865	857‡
S. URUGUAY	389	459	454‡	373	459	454‡
T. VENEZUELA	4,370	4,339‡	2,446	2,139	2,213‡	72
UNITED STATES[2]	531,739	582,863	642,121	107,478	106,587	130,695

1. Regularly scheduled domestic and international services of the registered airlines, including flights occasioned by excess traffic. Air passenger kilometers obtained by multiplying number of passengers by number of kilometers traveled.
2. Since 1965 flights to U.S. territories have been considered domestic.
3. Includes scheduled domestic and international services of the registered domestic and international airlines.
4. Includes international flights from international scheduled, registered airlines.

a. For earlier years, see previous issues of SALA.

SOURCE: Calculated from ICAO-DS-T, 1969–73, no. 33, vol. 2, tables 9 and 14; ICAO-DS-T, 1975–79, no. 39, parts B and C; ICAO-DS-T, 1978–82, parts A, B, and C; ICAO Bulletin, July 1984; ICAO, Advance 1983 Statistics for Scheduled Services; data for 1984 from ICAO Bulletin, July 1985; UN-SY, 1983/84, table 176; *Civil Aviation Statistics of the World, 1985*; ICAO-Y, 1986, 1987, 1988.

Table 402

KILOMETERS[1] FLOWN OF SCHEDULED SERVICE,[2] 20 LC, 1985–87[a]

(T)

Country	1985	1986	1987
A. ARGENTINA	79,300	76,700	84,000
B. BOLIVIA	11,300[‡]	11,500[‡]	11,300
C. BRAZIL	228,100	255,400	266,600
D. CHILE	24,400	27,500	32,500[‡]
E. COLOMBIA	61,300	63,700	65,600[‡]
F. COSTA RICA	7,100	6,900[‡]	7,900[‡]
G. CUBA	18,200[‡]	19,600	20,800
H. DOMINICAN REP.	4,900[‡]	4,500	3,000[‡]
I. ECUADOR	16,900[‡]	18,700[‡]	19,700[‡]
J. EL SALVADOR	7,100[‡]	5,200	5,100[‡]
K. GUATEMALA	2,600[‡]	2,100	2,700
L. HAITI	700[‡]	700[‡]	700[‡]
M. HONDURAS	6,000	5,200[‡]	6,100[‡]
N. MEXICO	185,900[‡]	175,800	180,200[‡]
O. NICARAGUA	1,700[‡]	1,200[‡]	1,200
P. PANAMA	6,300	6,500	6,700[‡]
Q. PARAGUAY	7,900[‡]	9,700[‡]	10,700[‡]
R. PERU	22,500	26,400	29,900[‡]
S. URUGUAY	5,300	4,800	4,800[‡]
T. VENEZUELA	43,300	44,500	30,900
UNITED STATES	5,177,300	5,806,600	6,249,100

1. Some figures may be rounded.
2. Regularly scheduled domestic and international services of the registered airlines, including flights occasioned by excess traffic.

a. For earlier years, see previous issues of SALA.

SOURCE: ICAO-DS-T, 1969–73, no. 33, vol. 2, table 4; ICAO-DS-T, 1975–79, no. 39, parts B and C; ICAO-DS-T, 1978–82, parts A, B, and C; ICAO-DST, Advance 1983 Statistics for Scheduled Services at International Airlines; UN-SY, 1983/84, 1986, table 176; *Civil Aviation Statistics of the World, 1985*; ICAO-Y, 1986, 1987, 1988.

Table 403

AIR PASSENGERS TRANSPORTED,[1] 19 LRC, 1986–87

(T)

	Country	1986			1987		
		Total	Domestic	International	Total	Domestic	International
A.	ARGENTINA	5,035	4,081	954	5,406	4,315	1,091
B.	BOLIVIA	1,301‡	1,014‡	287	1,233	916	317
C.	BRAZIL	17,195	15,682	1,513	17,069	15,684	1,385
D.	CHILE	875	565	310	992‡	647‡	345
E.	COLOMBIA	5,729‡	5,112‡	617	5,599‡	4,974‡	625
F.	COSTA RICA	335	44	291	348‡	46‡	302
G.	CUBA	913	677	236	889	650‡	239
H.	DOMINICAN REP.	615	0	615	300	0	300
I.	ECUADOR	697‡	465‡	232‡	692‡	465‡	227‡
J.	EL SALVADOR	468	0	468	465‡	0	465‡
K.	GUATEMALA	103	20	83	115	18‡	97
M.	HONDURAS	320‡	0	320‡	512‡	167‡	345‡
N.	MEXICO	13,825	10,403	3,422	13,505‡	9,199‡	4,306
O.	NICARAGUA	81‡	0	81‡	85‡	0	85‡
P.	PANAMA	364	0	364	621‡	0	621‡
Q.	PARAGUAY	184‡	24‡	160‡	205‡	30‡	175‡
R.	PERU	2,153	1,891	262	3,009‡	2,767‡	252‡
S.	URUGUAY	341	0	341	348‡	0	348‡
T.	VENEZUELA	5,791	5,209‡	582‡	5,913	5,767‡	146
	LATIN AMERICA	51,780	36,533	15,247	62,829[a]	46,986[a]	15,843[a]
	UNITED STATES	408,472‡	378,080‡	30,392	439,732	402,861	36,871

1. Regularly scheduled domestic and international services of the airlines registered in each country, including flights occasioned by excess traffic.

a. Includes Caribbean.

SOURCE: 1970–82 calculated from ICAO-DS-t, 1969–73, no. 33, vol. 2, tables 4, 9, and 14; ICAO-DS-T, 1975–79, no. 39, parts B and C; ICAO-DS-T, 1978–82, parts A, B, and C; ICAO-DS-T, Advance 1983 Statistics for Scheduled Services of International Airlines; UN-SY, 1983/84, 1986, table 176; *Civil Aviation Statistics of the World, 1985*; ACAO-Y, 1986, 1987, 1988.

Table 404

UTILIZATION OF AIRLINE CAPACITY, PASSENGER
LOAD FACTOR,[1] 20 LC, 1970–87[a]

(%)

	Country	1970	1980	1986	1987
A.	ARGENTINA	53	60	63	60
B.	BOLIVIA	43[†]	61	63	64
C.	BRAZIL	59	63	71	65
D.	CHILE	55	64	61	61
E.	COLOMBIA	54	63	64	65
F.	COSTA RICA	61	69[b]	61	59
G.	CUBA	86	69[b]	74	77
H.	DOMINICAN REP.	48[†]	78[b]	68	61
I.	ECUADOR	57	62	60	57
J.	EL SALVADOR	52[†]	70	65	61
K.	GUATEMALA	53[†]	41	59	60
L.	HAITI	54[†]	~	~	~
M.	HONDURAS	49	57	63	65
N.	MEXICO	51	66[b]	59	61
O.	NICARAGUA	49[†]	~	58	60
P.	PANAMA	52[†]	57	63	56
Q.	PARAGUAY	54[†]	~	66	66
R.	PERU	52	61	66	72
S.	URUGUAY	39	~	69	67
T.	VENEZUELA	44	46	57	60
	UNITED STATES	49	59[b]	60	62

1. Obtained by dividing actual passengers/km by available seats/km of the regularly
   scheduled domestic and international services of the registered airlines, including
   flights occasioned by excess traffic.

a. Data for the years 1972-77 are from SALA, 22-2103.

b. Data for one or more months missing.

SOURCE: ICAO-DS-T, 1969-73, no. 33, vol. 2, table 4; ICAO-DS-T, 1975-79, vol. 39;
1980-82 calculated from ICAO-DS-T, 1978-82, parts B and C; ICAO-DS-T, Advance
1983 Statistics for Scheduled Services of International Airlines, *Civil Aviation
Statistics of the World, 1985*; ICAO-Y, 1986, 1987, 1988.

Table 405

AIR TRANSPORT IN TON KILOMETERS,[1] 19 LC, 1970–87[a]

(M)

Country	Total[3]				International Flights[4]			
	1970	1985	1986	1987	1970	1985	1986	1987
A. ARGENTINA								
Freight	47.9	187.1	192.0	197.5	35.9	147.2	146.2	157.9
Mail	6.0	~	~	~	4.5	~	~	~
Total[2]	277.0	858.0	913.0	978.0	177.0	517.0	545.0	590.0
B. BOLIVIA								
Freight	1.5	41.5‡	27.8‡	25.5	.6	38.0‡	24.7‡	23.3
Mail	~	~	~	~	~	~	~	~
Total[2]	12.0	120.0‡	107.0	107.0	5.0	86.0‡	75.0‡	79.0
C. BRAZIL								
Freight	164.1	909.2	1,013.7	1,014.4	129.8	513.1	552.2	610.5
Mail	9.3	~	~	~	6.2	~	~	~
Total[2]	538.0	2,547.0	3,074.0	3,006.0	340.0	1,233.0	1,379.0	1,411.0
D. CHILE								
Freight	41.1	114.2	137.2	186.4‡	18.6	101.1	123.0	172.2
Mail	1.1	~	~	~	.8	~	~	~
Total[2]	117.0	276.0	316.0	380.0	59.0	208.0	247.0	303.0
E. COLOMBIA								
Freight	74.7	375.7‡	398.8‡	398.3	31.0	329.9	348.4‡	351.3
Mail	4.1	~	~	~	3.2	~	~	~
Total[2]	260.0	757.0‡	391.6‡	398.3‡	116.0	519.0	537.0	547.0
F. COSTA RICA								
Freight	9.3	25.3	24.8‡	30.0‡	7.8	25.3	24.8	30.0
Mail	.2	~	~	~	~	~	~	~
Total[2]	25.0	90.0	87.0‡	99.0‡	21.0	89.0	87.0	98.0
G. CUBA								
Freight	9.1	17.1	22.0	25.5	5.7	14.9‡	19.9	23.2
Mail	2.1	~	~	~	1.8	~	~	~
Total[2]	53.0	179.0‡	199.0	209.0	24.0	150.0‡	169.0	181.0
H. DOMINICAN REP.								
Freight	~	8.5‡	5.6	3.0	~	8.5‡	5.6	3.0
Mail	~	~	~	~	~	~	~	~
Total[2]	~	63.0‡	54.0	22.0	~	63.0‡	54.0	22.0
I. ECUADOR								
Freight	9.3	50.7‡	58.6‡	70.0‡	1.7	42.7	50.6‡	62.0‡
Mail	.3	~	~	~	.3	~	~	~
Total[2]	34.0	147.0‡	166.0‡	176.0‡	19.0	120.0	138.0‡	148.0‡
J. EL SALVADOR								
Freight	11.4	~	2.6	2.5‡	11.4	~	2.6	2.5‡
Mail	#	~	~	~	#	~	~	~
Total[2]	26.0	49.0‡	49.0	47.0‡	26.0	49.0‡	49.0	47.0‡
K. GUATEMALA								
Freight	6.3	9.0‡	7.2	11.4	5.5	8.9‡	7.0	11.3
Mail	.2	~	~	~	.1	~	~	~
Total[2]	16.0	23.0‡	20.0	26.0	14.0	22.0‡	19.0	26.0
M. HONDURAS‡								
Freight	3.6	2.0	2.2‡	2.2‡	2.7	2.0	2.2‡	2.2‡
Mail	~	~	~	~	~	~	~	~
Total[2]	18.0	41.0	40.0‡	64.0‡	15.0	39.0	40.0‡	62.0‡
N. MEXICO								
Freight	36.7	170.0‡	155.1	169.0	17.1	92.9	81.2	95.6
Mail	3.7	~	~	~	1.9	~	~	~
Total[2]	288.0	1,699.0‡	1,609.0	1,634.0‡	138.0	773.0	762.0	92.90
O. NICARAGUA‡								
Freight	.8	1.4‡	1.0‡	1.1‡	.5	1.4‡	1.0‡	1.1‡
Mail	.1	~	~	~	.1	~	~	~
Total[2]	8.0	12.0‡	9.0‡	9.0‡	7.0	12.0‡	9.0‡	9.0‡
P. PANAMA								
Freight	4.2	4.3	9.4	14.8‡	3.9	4.3	9.3	14.8‡
Mail	~	~	~	~	~	~	~	~
Total[2]	16.0	54.0	56.0	60.0‡	13.0	54.0	56.0	60.0‡
Q. PARAGUAY								
Freight	.7	3.1‡	13.7‡	15.1‡	.1	2.4‡	12.9‡	14.3‡
Mail	#	~	~	~	#	~	~	~
Total[2]	8.0	60.0‡	103.0‡	113.0‡	6.0	58.0‡	101.0‡	111.0‡
R. PERU								
Freight	22.4	47.4‡	70.6‡	78.7‡	16.1	18.2‡	46.4‡	34.4‡
Mail	2.2	~	~	~	2.1	~	~	~
Total[2]	99.0	192.0	261.0	320.0‡	83.0	82.0	124.0	112.0‡

Table 405 (Continued)

AIR TRANSPORT IN TON KILOMETERS,[1] 19 LC, 1970–87[a]

(M)

Country	Total[3]				International Flights[4]			
	1970	1985	1986	1987	1970	1985	1986	1987
S. URUGUAY								
Freight	.3	1.9	2.6	2.1[‡]	.3	1.8	2.6	2.1[‡]
Mail	~	~	~	~	~	~	~	~
Total[2]	5.0	37.0	43.0	43.0[‡]	5.0	36.0	43.0	43.0[‡]
T. VENEZUELA								
Freight	58.6	83.1	98.9[‡]	2.1	54.1	81.8	97.3[‡]	.2
Mail	2.1	~	~	~	2.0	~	~	~
Total[2]	166.0	476.0	486.0[‡]	210.0[‡]	132.0	282.0	302.0[‡]	6.0
UNITED STATES								
Freight	5,151.2	9,648.0	10,712.6[‡]	11,924.1	7,714.3	4,163.6	4,797.0	5,654.8
Mail	2,154.8	~	~	~	990.1	~	~	~
Total[2]	26,537.0	60,285.0	66,018.0[‡]	72.697.0	6,198.0	14,550	15,091.0	18,148.0

1. To convert to long ton miles, multiply by coefficient of .6611558. Ton kilometers
    obtained by multiplying the number of tons of freight transported by number of
    kilometers traveled.
2. Includes freight, mail, and passengers.
3. Includes domestic and international scheduled, registered airlines.
4. International flights from international scheduled, registered airlines.

a. For intervening years see previous issues of SALA.

SOURCE: UN-SY, 1979/80, table 151; UN-SY, 1983/84, 1986, table 176; *Civil Aviation
Statistics of the World, 1985*; ICAO-Y, 1986, 1987, 1988.

Table 406

LENGTH OF RAILWAY NETWORK, 17 LR, 1970–86[a]

(km)

Country	1970	1980	1984	1985	1986
A. ARGENTINA	39,905	34,077	34,345	34,447	34,428
B. BOLIVIA	3,284	3,328	3,628	3,628	3,628
C. BRAZIL	30,445[b]	28,671	27,983	28,684	29,465
D. CHILE	6,475	6,302	6,858	6,740	6,551
E. COLOMBIA	3,436	3,403	3,255	3,255	3,257
G. CUBA	5,286	4,382	4,909	4,889	4,881
I. ECUADOR	~	965	966	966	966
J. EL SALVADOR	620	602	674	674	674
K. GUATEMALA	~	927	927	927	927
M. HONDURAS	~	205	205	205	205
N. MEXICO	19,868	20,058	20,015	15,591	20,312
O. NICARAGUA	318	345	331	331	331
P. PANAMA	- -	118	109	109	109
Q. PARAGUAY[1]	441	441	441	441	441
R. PERU	2,242	2,099	2,159	2,159	2,159
S. URUGUAY	2,975	3,005	3,001	2,991	2,991
T. VENEZUELA[2]	226	268	280	280	445
LATIN AMERICA[3]	115,521	109,496	110,846	107,017	112,470

1. President Carlos A. López railway only.
2. Excluding the 145 km Orinoco Mining Company railway.
3. Does not include Costa Rica, Dominican Republic, Haiti.

a. For intervening years see SALA, 27-406.
b. 1969. -

SOURCE: ECLA-AE, 1984, table 343; 1985, table 343; 1988, table 361.

Table 407

RAILWAY ROLLING STOCK, 20 LC[a]

	Country	Year	Rolling Stock		
			Locomotives	Coaches	Cars
A.	ARGENTINA	1976[‡]	3,104	3,837	60,275
B.	BOLIVIA	1972	156	236	2,005
C.	BRAZIL	1976[‡]	1,970	3,042	63,770
D.	CHILE	1976[‡]	672	709	10,046
E.	COLOMBIA	1975[‡]	208	316	5,719
F.	COSTA RICA	1975[‡]	94	225	2,821
G.	CUBA	~	~	~	~
H.	DOMINICAN REP.	1973[‡]	2	2	15
I.	ECUADOR[1]	1971	60	50	518
J.	EL SALVADOR	1971	55	96	747
K.	GUATEMALA	1972	92	106	2,121
L.	HAITI	~	~	~	~
M.	HONDURAS	1972	66	90	2,846
N.	MEXICO	1976[‡]	1,293	1,634	39,240
O.	NICARAGUA	1972	8	35	231
P.	PANAMA	1972	42	70	1,473
Q.	PARAGUAY[2]	1973	17	9	151
R.	PERU[3]	1972	158	233	4,806
S.	URUGUAY[4]	1976[†]	157	117	2,438
T.	VENEZUELA[5]	1972	13	19	265
	UNITED STATES	1976[‡]	27,573	5,478	1,269,602

1. Data for Empresa de Ferrocarriles del Estado.
2. Data for Ferrocarril Central del Paraguay.
3. Including 286 km of lines used exclusively for industrial and agricultural purposes.
4. Data for Los Ferrocarriles del Estado only.
5. Data for El Instituto Autónomo de Administración de Ferrocarriles del Estado only.

a. Only government railroads.

SOURCE: IASI-AC, 1970, 1972 and 1974, tables 333-01-03; UN-SY, 1977, table 158.

Table 408

RAILROAD PASSENGER KILOMETERS,[1] 18 LC, 1970–87

(M)

Country	1970	1980	1983	1984	1985	1986[c]	1987[b]
A. ARGENTINA	12,828	12,706	10,260	10,464	10,470	13,225	11,246
B. BOLIVIA	271	529	771[a]	684[c]	748[c]	657	~
C. BRAZIL	12,070	12,376	13,797	17,444[c]	17,669[c]	18,433	~
D. CHILE	2,338	1,431	1,575	1,424	1,524	1,275	1,176
E. COLOMBIA	249	315	175	193	228	181	168
F. COSTA RICA[5]	55	~	152	152[a]	79[c]	79[c]	~
G. CUBA	1,130	1,802	2,144	2,352	2,256	2,200	2,184
I. ECUADOR	85	70	~	36[c]	40[c]	29	~
J. EL SALVADOR	33	25	4	5	5[c]	5	~
K. GUATEMALA	106	~	~	~	~	~	~
M. HONDURAS	- -	8	8[a]	8[c]	8[c]	8	~
N. MEXICO	4,534	5,296	5,630	5,950	5,940	5,245	5,952
O. NICARAGUA	30	19	45	60	26[c]	26	~
P. PANAMA	544	38	22[a]	22[c]	22[c]	22	~
Q. PARAGUAY[2]	24	22[c]	20[c]	22[c]	26[c]	26	~
R. PERU	248	586	454	486	486[c]	491	~
S. URUGUAY	529	418	312[a]	331[c]	241[c]	196	~
T. VENEZUELA[3]	36	28	381[d]	547[d]	641[d]	791[d]	~
UNITED STATES[4]	17,284	17,695	28,807	29,773	~	~	~

1. To convert to passenger miles, multiply by coefficient .62137. Passenger kilometers obtained by multiplying the number of passengers by the number of kilometers traveled. For intervening years, see previous issues of SALA.
2. Presidente Carlos A. López railway only.
3. Excluding the 145 km Orinoco Mining Company railway.
4. Beginning 1967, Class 1 railway only.
5. Incomplete coverage.

a. Data from ECLA-AE, 1985, table 344.
b. Calculated from monthly averages.
c. Data from ECLA-AE, 1988, table 362.
d. Includes Metro de Caracas (joint stock company).

SOURCE: IASI-AC, 1970 and 1972, tables 333-01-03; ECLA-AE, 1983, table 349.
U.S. data: UN-SY, 1981, table 189; U.S. data: UN-SY, 1982, table 174; UN-SY,
1983/84, table 171; ECLA-SY, 1985, table 344; UN-MB, August 1987, table 52;
UN-MB, January 1988, table 52; UN-MB, February 1989, table 49.

Table 409

RAILROAD FREIGHT IN TON KILOMETERS,[1] 18 LC, 1965–87

(M)

Country	1965	1980	1983[g]	1984[j]	1985[j]	1986[j]	1987[i]
A. ARGENTINA	14,027	9,492	13,391	11,235	9,530	8,793	8,016
B. BOLIVIA	301	658	590	559	458	458	~
C. BRAZIL	18,815[a]	40,603	36,187	38,680	44,529	64,232	~
D. CHILE	2,621	1,445	1,792	1,667	1,805	1,814	2,748
E. COLOMBIA	934	862	642	726	777	694	564[a]
F. COSTA RICA[4]	31	~	~	~	~	~	~
G. CUBA	1,326	2,358[h]	2,724[h]	2,809	2,935	2,460	2,100
I. ECUADOR	84[b]	32	7,440	~	7,473	6,787	~
J. EL SALVADOR	72	55	31[h]	25	25	25	~
K. GUATEMALA	129	91	565	565	565	565	~
M. HONDURAS	~	29	386	386	386	385	~
N. MEXICO	18,332	41,831	42,586	44,815	37,689	40,608	40,812
O. NICARAGUA	13	6	2[h]	68	68	68	~
P. PANAMA	19,070	10	~	~	~	~	~
Q. PARAGUAY[2]	19[c]	29	19	16	13	17	~
R. PERU	464[d]	742	529	736	744	732	~
S. URUGUAY	332[e]	253	220	273	185	203	~
T. VENEZUELA[3]	32[f]	21	22[h]	247	247	12	~
UNITED STATES[5]	1,029,585	1,341,717	1,237,428[h]	1,377,264	1,310,388	~	~

1. To convert to long ton miles, multiply by coefficient of .6611558. Ton kilometers obtained by multiplying the number of tons of freight transported by the number of kilometers traveled. For intervening years see previous issues of SALA.
2. Presidente Carlos A. López railway only.
3. Excluding the 145 km Orinoco Mining Company railway.
4. Incomplete coverage.
5. Class 1 railways only.

a. Including service traffic.
b. Data for Empresa de Ferrocarriles del Estado.
c. Data for Ferrocarril Central del Paraguay.
d. Including 286 km of lines used exclusively for industrial and agricultural purposes.
e. Data for Los Ferrocarriles del Estado only.
f. Data for El Instituto Autoónomo de Administración de Ferrocarriles del Estado only.
g. Data from ECLA-AE, 1985, table 344, unless otherwise noted.
h. Data from UN-SY, 1985, table 171.
i. Calculated from monthly averages in UN-MB.
j. Data from ECLA-AE, 1988, table 362.

SOURCE: IASI-AC, 1970 and 1972, tables 333-01-03; ECLA-AE, 1983, table 349; U.S. data; UN-SY, 1981, table 189; ECLA-AE, 1984, table 344; U.S. data; UN-SY, 1982, table 174; UN-SY, 1983/84, table 176, ECLA-AE, 1985, table 344; UN-MB, August 1987, table 52; UN-MB, January 1988; UN-MB, February 1989; ECLA-AE, 1988, table 362.

Table 410

LENGTH OF ROADS, 20 LR

(ca. 1985)

	Country	Year	Total (km)	Percentage Paved
A.	ARGENTINA	1985	211,341	27
B.	BOLIVIA	1983	40,969	4
C.	BRAZIL	1985	1,583,172	7
D.	CHILE	1984	79,224	12
E.	COLOMBIA	1981	74,735	13
F.	COSTA RICA	1985	35,267	13
G.	CUBA	1987	13,079[b]	~
H.	DOMINICAN REP.	1982	17,362	29
I.	ECUADOR	1985	36,187	28
J.	EL SALVADOR	1985	12,164	14
K.	GUATEMALA	1980	26,429	11
L.	HAITI	1985	3,700	17
M.	HONDURAS	1984	12,058	16
N.	MEXICO	1982	214,403	46
O.	NICARAGUA	1985	14,651	11
P.	PANAMA	1980	11,110	37
Q.	PARAGUAY	1983	11,320	19
R.	PERU	1979	56,642	~
S.	URUGUAY	1981	49,813	20
T.	VENEZUELA	1985	75,772	32
	LATIN AMERICA	1983[a]	143,166	20

a. Ca. 1983
b. Paved only.

SOURCE: ECLA-AE, 1984, table 342; 1986, table 335; 1988, table 360.

Table 411

COMMERCIAL MOTOR VEHICLE REGISTRATION,[1] 20 LC, 1960–85[a]

(T)

	Country	1960	1978	1980	1982	1983	1984	1985
A.	ARGENTINA	389.7	1,203.4	1,333.4	~	~	1,388.0	~
B.	BOLIVIA	~	29.4	32.5	59.1	63.5	~	~
C.	BRAZIL	~	1,574.6	1,569.8	1,758.9	1,825.7	1,796.4	~
D.	CHILE[2,3]	68.8	191.2	219.6	256.5	248.8	237.2	257.6
E.	COLOMBIA[4]	82.9	256.3	294.9	353.9	368.3	~	~
F.	COSTA RICA[2]	9.7	58.9	65.9	65.9	65.7	~	~
G.	CUBA	65.3[‡]	107.2	132.6	152.4	158.9	164.5	172.8
H.	DOMINICAN REP[5]	6.3	46.2	46.9	60.6	62.3	59.1	52.0
I.	ECUADOR	19.0	114.9	112.2	~	~	~	~
J.	EL SALVADOR	9.0	46.4	71.4	67.8	60.8	65.2	~
K.	GUATEMALA	14.7	56.0	81.5	~	~	~	~
L.	HAITI	3.7	6.5	11.2	~	~	~	~
M.	HONDURAS[2,7]	5.2	33.5	45.4	49.9	49.0	~	~
N.	MEXICO	315.0	1,352.2	1,574.8	1,872.6	2,038.2	~	~
O.	NICARAGUA	5.5	25.5	27.7	~	~	~	~
P.	PANAMA	6.6	24.7	32.5	38.3	39.8	41.8	~
Q.	PARAGUAY	2.5	30.8	17.7	12.6	23.6	~	~
R.	PERU	65.2	167.2	176.6	204.6	212.9	217.0	220.3
S.	URUGUAY	76.0	41.0	42.7	52.5	49.3	45.1	46.5
T.	VENEZUELA	100.7	560.8	718.3	891.1	951.4	1,019.0	1,094.0
	UNITED STATES[6]	11,466.9	32,203.0	33,410.6	35,852.0	37,133.0	~	~

1. Including trucks, buses, tractor and semitractor combinations; but excluding trailers
   and farm tractors.
2. Including vehicles operated by police and government security organizations.
3. Including special-purpose vehicles.
4. Including vehicles no longer in circulation.
5. Excluding jeeps beginning 1978.
6. Excluding Alaska and Hawaii.
7. Excluding tractors and semi-trailer combinations.

a. For intervening years see previous issues of SALA.

SOURCE: UN-SY, 1972, table 150; 1974, table 153; 1981, table 190; 1982, table 175;
1983/84, table 172; 1985/86, table 145.

Table 412

PASSENGER MOTOR VEHICLE REGISTRATION,[1,4] 20 LC, 1960–85[a]

(T)

Country	1960	1978	1980	1982	1983	1984	1985
A. ARGENTINA	473.5	2,683.7	3,024.4	~	~	3,685.0	~
B. BOLIVIA	9.7	38.6	50.2	66.6	72.6	~	~
C. BRAZIL	~	7,123.9	8,004.6	8,909.5	9,378.9	9,293.3	~
D. CHILE	57.6	335.8	448.5	605.6	618.7	629.3	624.9
E. COLOMBIA[2]	89.6	434.7	522.7	669.9	723.4	~	~
F. COSTA RICA[3]	16.0	79.6	88.1	91.4	101.3	~	~
G. CUBA	179.6‡	160.4	159.4	182.2	190.4	200.1	206.3
H. DOMINICAN REP.	11.0	90.6	94.4	97.2	87.6	116.2	101.5
I. ECUADOR	9.3	61.0	65.1	~	~	~	~
J. EL SALVADOR	20.2	69.9	72.5	82.7	88.0	85.3	~
K. GUATEMALA	26.1	156.4	166.9	~	~	~	~
L. HAITI	8.2	24.3	21.8	~	~	~	~
M. HONDURAS[3]	5.5	24.1	25.6	28.9	28.7	28.5	34.2
N. MEXICO	476.4	3,359.9	4,241.4	4,759.8	4,853.9	~	~
O. NICARAGUA	8.6	41.0	37.8	~	~	~	~
P. PANAMA	17.6	75.4	98.0	110.2	115.9	121.0	~
Q. PARAGUAY	3.8	24.8	58.5	62.9	78.7	~	~
R. PERU	79.4	302.0	309.5	359.7	371.7	374.1	376.0
S. URUGUAY	99.8	207.7	220.4	298.4	291.8	292.4	306.3
T. VENEZUELA	268.7	1,277.3	1,501.8	1,814.0	1,955.4	2,115.0	2,289.0
UNITED STATES	61,430.9	116,575.0	118,458.7	123,698.0	126,728.0	~	~

1. Motor cars seating less than eight persons, including taxis, jeeps, and station-wagons.
2. Including vehicles no longer in circulation.
3. Including vehicles operated by police and government security organizations.
4. Official estimates of vehicles in use. Unless otherwise stated, special-purpose vehicles are not included.

a. For intervening years see previous issues of SALA.

SOURCE: UN-SY, 1972, table 153; 1974, table 153; 1981, table 190; 1982, table 175; 1983/84, table 172; 1985/86, table 146.

Table 413

MERCHANT FLEETS,[1] 16 L, 1982–87

(Tons)

		Overseas					Coastal				
Country	Year	Cargo Vessels	Bulk Carriers	Refrigerated Vessels	Tankers	Others	Cargo Vessels	Bulk Carriers	Tankers	Others	Inland Waterways
A. ARGENTINA	1982	626,554	434,465	43,754	~	~	29,454	~	709,847	13,779	172,374
	1984	608,598	485,126	43,754	11,773	~	29,454	~	656,797	~	164,661
	1985	595,510	348,090	43,754	3,567	~	29,454	~	654,064	~	162,619
	1986	518,201	456,607	38,510	3,567	~	27,855	14,306	583,371	~	163,796
	1987	502,940	399,278	38,510	3,567	~	29,863	4,571	575,058	~	163,896
B. BOLIVIA	1982	10,915	~	~	~	~	~	~	~	~	~
	1984	10,915	~	~	~	~	~	~	~	~	~
	1985	10,915	~	~	~	~	~	~	~	~	~
	1986	9,610	~	~	~	~	~	~	~	~	~
	1987	9,610	~	~	~	~	~	~	~	~	~
C. BRAZIL	1982	803,638	1,135,788	13,478	2,304,159	~	190,527	~	437,277	178,005	86,256
	1984	816,021	1,329,043	13,478	2,305,937	~	209,691	~	444,570	16,929	91,323
	1985	814,339	1,473,316	13,478	2,317,470	~	204,813	~	616,952	16,929	88,608
	1986	1,032,389	2,381,202	13,478	1,228,239	~	397,295	201,651	776,727	16,929	96,825
	1987	899,487	2,295,445	13,478	1,164,836	~	413,265	229,702	785,233	16,929	104,794
D. CHILE	1982	99,354	87,853	~	204,434	~	17,693	~	26,966	10,842	~
	1984	122,391	70,889	~	204,434	~	4,950	~	41,245	13,959	~
	1985	117,492	109,985	~	129,000	~	2,700	~	104,226	9,306	~
	1986	158,980	174,279	16,104	~	10,491	9,363	82,436	28,792	9,306	~
	1987	155,723	179,547	8,069	~	10,491	13,345	95,781	32,608	9,306	~
E. COLOMBIA	1982	270,123	36,056	~	~	~	1,544	~	25,271	11,234	~
	1984	253,107	36,056	~	~	~	1,544	~	25,271	11,234	~
	1985	247,955	18,028	~	4,225	~	~	~	26,283	11,234	~
	1986	262,834	18,020	~	4,225	~	18,176	~	25,148	11,234	~
	1987	232,228	80,593	~	4,225	~	14,112	5,942	1,090	11,234	~
F. COSTA RICA	1982	~	5,940	~	~	~	~	~	~	2,509	~
	1984	5,940	~	~	~	~	~	~	~	2,509	~
	1985	~	~	~	~	~	~	~	~	2,509	~
	1986	~	~	~	~	~	~	~	~	2,509	~
	1987	6,712	~	~	~	~	~	~	~	2,509	~
G. CUBA	1982	463,907	62,576	71,472	3,600	2,333	52,376	~	62,217	21,658	~
	1984	464,147	62,576	71,472	3,600	2,333	59,124	~	62,217	21,658	~
	1985	440,856	62,576	78,385	3,600	2,333	65,955	~	62,217	11,009	~
	1986	516,957	62,576	78,385	3,600	2,333	50,047	~	60,981	22,118	~
	1987	592,327	165,768	12,464	~	~	44,980	9,746	70,416	3,902	~
H. DOMINICAN REP.	1982	18,462	12,002	~	~	~	~	~	~	~	~
	1984	24,217	1,599	~	~	~	~	~	~	~	~
	1985	19,104	14,084	~	~	~	~	~	~	~	~
	1986	14,344	14,084	1,399	~	~	~	~	~	~	~
	1987	14,344	23,676	1,399	~	~	~	~	~	~	~
I. ECUADOR	1982	113,964	11,153	81,031	82,613	~	1,132	~	83,684	3,845	~
	1984	99,484	11,153	109,916	82,613	~	1,132	~	83,684	3,845	~
	1985	99,484	15,772	126,195	82,613	~	1,132	~	78,766	3,845	~
	1986	93,158	4,619	126,195	84,445	~	1,132	~	78,044	3,845	~
	1987	82,677	26,767	121,535	84,445	~	1,132	~	78,044	6,049	~
J. EL SALVADOR	1982	~	~	~	~	~	~	~	~	~	~
	1984	~	~	~	~	~	~	~	~	~	~
	1985	~	~	~	~	~	~	~	~	~	~
	1986	~	~	~	~	~	~	~	~	~	~
	1987	~	~	~	~	~	~	~	~	~	~
K. GUATEMALA	1982	12,091	3,527	~	~	~	~	~	~	~	~
	1984	12,179	3,527	~	~	~	~	~	~	~	~
	1985	4,217	~	~	~	~	~	~	~	~	~
	1986	7,900	~	~	~	~	~	~	~	~	~
	1987	4,217	~	~	~	~	~	~	~	~	~
L. HAITI	1982	~	~	~	~	~	~	~	~	~	~
	1984	~	~	~	~	~	~	~	~	~	~
	1985	~	~	~	~	~	~	~	~	~	~
	1986	~	~	~	~	~	~	~	~	~	~
	1987	~	~	~	~	~	~	~	~	~	~
M. HONDURAS	1982	- -	- -	- -	- -	- -	~	~	~	~	~
	1984	~	~	~	~	~	~	~	~	~	~
	1985	~	~	~	~	~	~	~	~	~	~
	1986	~	~	~	~	~	~	~	~	~	~
	1987	~	~	~	~	~	~	~	~	~	~
N. MEXICO	1982	- -	- -	- -	- -	- -	8.432	4,695	266,082	84,854	~
	1984	125,351	209,830	~	647,616	~	18,531	~	266,082	72,746	~
	1985	116,403	276,766	~	561,784	~	23,546	~	263,643	72,746	~
	1986	144,187	194,512	~	611,367	~	24,675	~	164,346	76,083	~
	1987	161,452	176,615	5,950	579,418	~	17,367	14,319	142,301	79,636	~

Table 413 (Continued)

MERCHANT FLEETS,[1] 16 L, 1982–87

(Tons)

		Overseas					Coastal				
Country	Year	Cargo Vessels	Bulk Carriers	Refrigerated Vessels	Tankers	Others	Cargo Vessels	Bulk Carriers	Tankers	Others	Inland Waterways
O. NICARAGUA	1982	9,650	2,353	~	~	~	~	~	~	~	~
	1984	12,003	~	~	~	~	~	~	~	~	~
	1985	18,922	~	~	~	~	~	~	~	~	~
	1986	9,272	~	~	~	~	~	~	~	~	~
	1987	9,272	~	~	~	~	~	~	~	~	~
P. PANAMA	1982	~	~	~	~	~	~	~	~	~	~
	1984	~	~	~	~	~	~	~	~	~	~
	1985	~	~	~	~	~	~	~	~	~	~
	1986	~	~	~	~	~	~	~	~	~	~
	1987	~	~	~	~	~	~	~	~	~	~
Q. PARAGUAY	1982	12,714	~	~	~	~	~	~	~	~	17,857
	1984	19,726	~	~	~	~	~	~	~	~	~
	1985	18,836	~	~	~	~	~	~	~	~	17,856
	1986	17,933	~	~	~	~	~	~	~	~	15,922
	1987	14,338	~	~	~	~	~	~	~	~	15,922
R. PERU	1982	279,982	201,057	1,544	35,823	~	~	~	119,184	~	10,955
	1984	270,374	159,883	1,544	35,823	~	~	~	135,817	~	10,955
	1985	~	~	~	~	~	~	~	135,817	~	10,955
	1986	213,309	145,710	1,544	1,450	~	~	~	139,327	~	10,955
	1987	193,203	122,951	1,544	38,001	~	~	~	131,951	~	10,955
S. URUGUAY	1982	54,708	13,203	4,172	88,617	~	1,110	~	2,516	~	3,749
	1984	47,790	13,203	4,172	88,617	~	1,110	~	3,956	~	3,749
	1985	37,172	~	~	68,617	~	1,110	~	3,956	~	3,749
	1986	33,610	~	6,738	68,931	~	1,110	~	3,956	~	7,887
	1987	19,762	~	6,738	68,931	~	1,110	~	2,516	~	7,887
T. VENEZUELA	1982	208,701	56,784	6,682	11,065	~	4,896	~	443,666	91,629	1,325
	1984	216,465	57,400	~	15,870	~	1,355	~	499,905	67,671	1,325
	1985	249,704	79,684	~	277,790	~	18,961	~	237,985	38,130	1,325
	1986	235,170	88,300	~	278,135	12,555	2,542	~	237,985	48,009	1,324
	1987	224,594	135,862	~	278,135	14,069	2,542	~	237,985	41,842	1,342

1. Gross registered tons for vessels of 1,000 tons and over.

SOURCE: ECLA-AE, 1984, table 345; 1985, table 345; 1986, table 338; 1987, table 340; 1988, table 363.

Table 414

NATIONAL MERCHANT MARINES, 16 L
(1986)

	State Sector					Private Sector					Total				
Country	Units	Gross Registered Tons	Gross Freight Tons	Average Age	% According to Gross Freight Tons	Units	Gross Registered Tons	Gross Freight Tons	Average Age	% According to Gross Freight Tons	Units	Gross Registered Tons	Gross Freight Tons	Average Age	% According to Gross Freight Tons
A. ARGENTINA	70	806,000	1,202,000	9.3	5.9	76	1,001,000	1,611,000	16.4	8.0	146	1,806,000	2,814,000	13.3	13.9
B. BOLIVIA	1	10,000	16,000	10.0	.1	~			~	~	3	8,000	12,000	18.4	.1
C. BRAZIL	147	4,433,000	7,673,000	9.2	38.0	209	1,711,000	2,479,000	8.5	12.3	356	6,145,000	10,152,000	9.0	50.2
D. CHILE	5	96,000	180,000	12.3	.9	33	394,000	604,000	15.7	3.0	38	490,000	784,000	15.0	3.9
E. COLOMBIA	5	11,000	11,000	16.6	.1	30	328,000	428,000	12.7	2.1	35	340,000	434,000	12.8	2.1
F. COSTA RICA	2	3,000	1,000	28.5	0	~	~	~	~	~	2	3,000	1,000	28.5	~
G. CUBA	104	797,000	1,124,000	11.6	5.6	~			~	~	104	797,000	1,124,000	11.6	5.6
H. DOMINICAN REP.	~	~	~	~	~	7	30,000	49,000	18.2	.2	7	30,000	49,000	18.2	.2
I. ECUADOR	18	227,000	357,000	8.3	1.8	33	165,000	199,000	19.7	1.0	51	391,000	555,000	13.1	2.7
K. GUATEMALA	~	~	~	~	~	3	8,000	12,000	18.4	.1	1	10,000	16,000	10.0	.1
N. MEXICO	60	776,000	1,144,000	11.7	5.7	29	440,000	734,000	10.6	3.6	89	1,215,000	1,878,000	11.3	9.3
O. NICARAGUA	2	9,000	14,000	23.5	.1	~	~	~	~	~	2	9,000	14,000	23.5	.1
Q. PARAGUAY	16	24,000	25,000	16.8	.1	6	10,000	14,000	18.0	.1	22	34,000	39,000	17.2	.2
R. PERU	27	296,000	473,000	11.3	2.3	21	217,000	333,000	16.9	1.6	48	512,000	805,000	13.7	4.0
S. URUGUAY	3	74,000	137,000	12.4	.7	10	49,000	61,000	21.8	.3	13	122,000	199,000	16.1	1.0
T. VENEZUELA	34	692,000	1,051,000	7.6	5.2	44	212,000	282,000	16.2	1.4	78	904,000	1,333,000	9.6	6.6
TOTAL	494	8,252,000	13,406,000	9.7	66.3	501	4,568,000	6,802,000	12.8	33.7	995	12,815,000	20,208,000	10.8	100.0

SOURCE: *Los Conceptos Básicos del Transporte Marítimo y la Situación de la Actividad en América Latina* (Santiago: Cuadernos de la CEPAL, 1987, table 11).

Table 415

PRINCIPAL MERCHANT MARINES OF THE WORLD,[1] 6 LC, 1985
(T Tons)

Country	World Rank	Number of Vessels	Gross Registered Tons	Gross Freight Tons	% of Gross Freight Tons
A. ARGENTINA	35	198	1,930.5	3,022.4	.5
C. BRAZIL	17	407	6,118.6	10,217.3	1.7
G. CUBA	51	126	825.0	1,157.8	.2
N. MEXICO	101	101	1,203.7	1,857.8	.3
P. PANAMA[2]	2	3,960	40,660.3	67,444.6	11.0
T. VENEZUELA	50	109	896.2	1,348.0	.2
WORLD	**	34,068	372,274.5	613,141.5	100.0

1. Vessels of 300 or more gross registered tons.
2. Pavillion of open registration or flag of convenience.

SOURCE: *Los Conceptos Básicos del Transporte Marítimo y la Situación de la Actividad en América Latina* (Santiago: Cuadernos de la CEPAL, 1981), pp. 32–33.

Table 416

INTERNATIONAL SEABORNE SHIPPING,[1] 20 LC, 1975–87

(Vessels in T Net Registered Tons; Goods in T MET)

Country		1865	1980	1986	1987
A. ARGENTINA[12]					
Vessels:[2]	entered	12,859	16,560	~	~
	cleared	~	~	~	~
Goods:[3,5,15]	loaded	11,770	20,000	29,160	22,320
	unloaded	12,220	10,568	7,140	9,144
B. BOLIVIA		~	~	~	~
C. BRAZIL					
Vessels:[2,4]	entered	143,172	178,791	~	~
	cleared	~	~	~	~
Goods[5,6,15]	loaded	92,985	107,596	142,764	142,380
	unloaded	55,605	71,855	58,248	61,872
D. CHILE					
Vessels:	entered	~	~	~	~
	cleared	~	~	~	~
Goods[3,5,7,15,17]	loaded	12,361	12,590	13,452	15,144
	unloaded	5,925	8,792	4,800	5,952
E. COLOMBIA					
Vessels:[2]	entered	10,943	11,200	~	~
	cleared	~	~	~	~
Goods:[5,15]	loaded	3,374	6,038‡	11,196	17,544
	unloaded	2,101	7,276	5,628	6,096
F. COSTA RICA					
Vessels:	entered	3,736	~	~	~
	cleared	~	~	~	~
Goods:[15]	loaded	1,448	1,284	~	~
	unloaded	1,216	1,862	~	~
G. CUBA					
Vessels:	entered	~	~	~	~
	cleared	~	~	~	~
Goods:[15]	loaded	5,943	7,500	2,208	2,196
	unloaded	13,302	16,900	2,364	2,232
H. DOMINICAN REP.					
Vessles:[2]	entered	~	8,904	~	~
	cleared:	~	~	~	~
Goods:[13,15]	loaded	2,596	2,411	~	~
	unloaded	3,065	1,457‡	~	~
I. ECUADOR					
Vessels:	entered	13,244	11,491	~	~
	cleared	~	~	~	~
Goods:[8,15]	loaded	9,557	8,371	~	~
	unloaded	3,140	2,282	~	~
J. EL SALVADOR					
Vessels:	entered	2,291	2,741	~	~
	cleared	~	~	~	~
Goods:[15]	loaded	490	361	288	~
	unloaded	1,281	1,482	1,920	~
K. GUATEMALA					
Vessels:[2]	entered	~	~	~	~
	cleared	~	~	~	~
Goods:[15]	loaded	771	1,022	~	~
	unloaded	1,201	2,405	~	~
L. HAITI					
Vessels:[2]	entered	~	~	~	~
	cleared	~	~	~	~
Goods:[15]	loaded	632	620‡	~	~
	unloaded	461	521‡	~	~
M. HONDURAS					
Vessels:[2]	entered	~	~	~	~
	cleared	~	~	~	~
Goods:[5,15]	loaded	1,256	1,597‡	~	~
	unloaded	1,163	1,252‡	~	~
N. MEXICO					
Vessels:	entered	10,102	13,190	~	~
	cleared	12,058	27,582	~	~
Goods:[15]	loaded	13,980	50,430	82,800	89,580
	unloaded	9,300	14,557	9,012	11,244
O. NICARAGUA					
Vessels:[2]	entered	~	~	~	~
	cleared	~	~	~	~
Goods:[5]	loaded	765‡	382	~	~
	unloaded	1,475‡	1,283	~	~

Table 416 (Continued)

INTERNATIONAL SEABORNE SHIPPING,[1] 20 LC, 1975–87

(Vessels in T Net Registered Tons; Goods in T MET)

Country			1865	1980	1986	1987
P. PANAMA						
	Vessels:	entered	~	~	~	~
		cleared	~	~	~	~
	Goods:	loaded	1,770	977	~	~
		unloaded	4,793	2,647	~	~
	(FORMER) CANAL ZONE					
	Vessels:	entered	~	~	~	~
		cleared	~	~	~	~
	Goods:[12,15]	loaded	85,440[a]	90,756	88,404	96,332
		unloaded	56,904[b]	83,220	62,676	61,668
Q. PARAGUAY			~	~	~	~
R. PERU						
	Vessels:[2]	entered	19,982	~	~	~
		cleared	~	~	~	~
	Goods:[9]	loaded	9,173	9,277	~	~
		unloaded	8,043	3,831	~	~
S. URUGUAY						
	Vessels:	entered	~	~	~	~
		cleared	~	~	~	~
	Goods:[14]	loaded	947	457	~	~
		unloaded	2,595	888	~	~
T. VENEZUELA						
	Vessels:	entered	~	~	~	~
		cleared	~	~	~	~
	Goods:[5,10]	loaded	~	110,452[‡]	~	~
		unloaded	6,707	11,966	~	~
	UNITED STATES						
	Vessels:[10,15]	entered	254,346	320,684	~	~
		cleared	188,845	269,660	~	~
	Goods:[11,16]	loaded	246,311[‡]	366,348	297,936	324,132
		unloaded	435,970[‡]	468,909	408,432	424,668

1. Vessels: Unless otherwise stated, the data for vessels entered and cleared represent the sum of the net registered tonnage of sea-going foreign and domestic merchant vessels entered with cargo, from or cleared with cargo to a foreign port. They refer to only one entrance of clearance for each foreign voyage. Where possible the data exclude vessels "in ballast."
   Goods: The data for goods loaded and unloaded represent the weight of goods (including packaging) in external trade loaded onto and unloaded from sea-going vessels of all flags at the ports of the country in question. Goods excluded are: bunker, ships' stores, ballast, and transshipment.
2. Includes vessels in ballast.
3. Excluding packing and reexports before 1979; after 1983, except for Chile.
4. All entrances counted.
5. Excluding transit traffic and packing until 1978; Colombia, transit traffic only.
6. Including mail, passengers' baggage until 1979, and a small amount of goods imported and exported other than by sea before 1979 and after 1983.
7. Including mail, passengers' baggage, bullion, and bunkers before 1979.
8. Excluding transit traffic, packing, and certain government goods; including goods imported and exported other than by sea until 1978.
9. Excluding transit traffic, packing, reexports, and certain government goods until 1978.
10. Including Great Lakes International traffic. For goods 1965 and after 1983.
11. Including transshipments until 1978.
12. Data are for former Canal Zone only. Prior to 1977, 12 months ending June 30. From 1977, 12 months beginning October 1. Goods in transit for 1965, 1970, and 1973–78.
13. Including goods imported and exported other than by sea until 1978.
14. Port of Montevideo only after 1978.
15. Calculated from monthly averages, for goods only.
16. Including Puerto Rico and the Virgin Islands, except for 1965 for the Virgin Islands.
17. Including ships' stores until 1978.

a. Traffic from Atlantic to Pacific.
b. Traffic from Pacific to Atlantic.

SOURCE: UN-SY, 1974, table 157; 1977, table 162; 1979, table 150; 1982, tables 177 and 178; 1983/84, tables 174 and 175; UN-MB, August 1987, table 53; UN-MB, January 1988, table 53; UN-MB, February 1989, table 50.

Table 417

INTERNATIONAL SEABORNE GOODS LOADED AND UNLOADED, 18 LC, 1979–85[a]
(T MET)

| | | Goods Loaded | | | | Goods Unloaded | | | |
| | | | Petroleum | | | | Petroleum | | |
Country	Year	Total	Crude	Products	Dry Cargo	Total	Crude	Products	Dry Cargo
A. ARGENTINA	1979	28,500[‡]	~	500	28,000[‡]	12,616[‡]	341[‡]	3,475[‡]	8,800[‡]
	1980	20,500	~	1,373[‡]	19,127[‡]	10,568	2,255[‡]	481[‡]	7,832[‡]
	1981	30,047	~	2,777[‡]	27,270[‡]	8,816	1,622[‡]	522[‡]	6,672[‡]
	1982	26,490	~	2,616	23,874	6,599	667[‡]	1,842	7,090
	1983	35,201	~	1,731	33,470	5,579	~	1,768	3,811
	1984	31,610	~	1,603	30,007	6,280	~	1,785	4,495
	1985	37,724	407	2,971	34,346	5,375	~	1,755	3,620

Continued in SALA, 27-415.

Table 418

EVOLUTION OF ALADI MERCHANT MARINES, 11 LR, 1961–87[a]

Country	Year	Units	Gross Registered Tons (T)	% Variation 1961-85	Gross Freight Tons (T)	Average Age
A. ARGENTINA	1961	151	664		1,274	20.0
	1970	185	1,090		1,425	19.5
	1987	146	1,806	121	2,814	13.3

Continued in SALA, 27-418.

5
Communication

Table 500

DAILY NEWSPAPERS, CIRCULATION, AND NEWSPRINT CONSUMPTION PER INHABITANT, 20 LC, 1965-85

Country	Newspapers Published[1] (N)							Circulation (PTI)							Newsprint, Consumption[2] (kg/PI)								
	1965	1970	1975	1979	1982	1984	1985	1965	1970	1975	1979	1982	1984	1985	1965	1970	1975	1979	1980	1982	1983	1984	1985
A. ARGENTINA	171	179	164	133	191	188	?	149	?	?	?	?	?	?	10.1	11.6	5.7	7.9	9.6	5.0	6.3	6.9	6.7
B. BOLIVIA	9	21	14	14	12	13	?	22	?	41	39	46	50	?	.7	1.1	1.0	1.3	1.1	1.2	1.1	.6	.5
C. BRAZIL	?	?	299	328	?	314	?	?	?	47	44	?	57	?	2.1	2.2	2.2	1.9	2.2	2.4	2.0	2.0	2.2
D. CHILE	?	?	47	37	37	38	?	?	?	89	86	?	96	?	4.8	4.9	4.0	5.4	6.1	6.0	5.4	5.0	4.7
E. COLOMBIA	39	?	40	38	28	31	?	?	?	?	48b	?	?	?	2.4	2.8	1.9	2.6	2.8	3.5	2.8	2.7	2.7
F. COSTA RICA	?	8	6	4	4	5	?	?	102	89	70	77	72	?	4.1	6.4	5.7	6.9	5.3	3.0	4.6	4.5	4.2
G. CUBA	?	16	15	9	17	18	?	?	?	6	92	118	144	?	2.4	2.7	2.9	3.3	3.3	3.4	3.9	3.9	4.3
H. DOMINICAN REP.	7	?	10	7	9	7	?	28	?	42	40	?	30	?	.2	1.0	1.3	1.8	2.2	2.4	2.4	2.0	1.2
I. ECUADOR	23	25	29	38	18	16	?	47	41	49	51	64	?	?	2.6	2.3	1.5	3.9	4.0	3.7	3.6	3.5	4.2
J. EL SALVADOR	?	13	12	12	6	6	?	?	?	?	?	?	?	?	3.0	3.6	2.5	3.0	3.1	2.6	2.4	2.4	2.3
K. GUATEMALA	?	8	10	9	9	5	?	?	28	41	?	?	?	?	1.2	1.6	1.3	1.7	2.5	1.5	1.4	1.7	.9
L. HAITI	6	7	?	4	4	4	?	6	17	18	6	4	?	?	.1	.2	.2	.1	.1	.1	.1	.1	.1
M. HONDURAS	?	?	8	7	6	6	?	?	?	32	63	61	?	?	.7	1.0	.7	1.3	1.8	1.5	1.0	1.1	1.5
N. MEXICO	220	200	256	?	374	312	?	116	?	?	?	?	120	?	2.6	3.1	3.6	3.0	3.3	6.4	3.0	3.0	3.8
O. NICARAGUA	6	?	7	8	3	3	?	50	?	?	63	50	47	?	1.7	1.8	1.7	1.0	1.1	1.4	1.2	1.2	1.5
P. PANAMA	10	7	6	6	5	6	?	82	85	75	78	61	?	?	2.8	3.9	1.9	2.4	1.3	1.4	2.7	2.7	2.9
Q. PARAGUAY	?	11	8	5	5	5	?	?	?	?	?	?	?	?	.7	1.8	1.2	2.1	2.5	1.5	.1	1.7	2.2
R. PERU	69	85	49	59	68	60	?	?	?	91	?	?	?	?	3.5	3.7	3.4	.1	2.1	8.0	2.6	3.0	1.6
S. URUGUAY	?	?	30	28	24	21	?	?	?	?	?	?	?	?	6.4	7.4	3.7	4.7	5.2	7.4	2.9	2.9	2.5
T. VENEZUELA	33	?	49	69	36	61	?	70	?	89	164	?	186	?	4.8	7.9	6.8	9.4	9.4	8.4	10.1	9.3	7.9
UNITED STATES	1,751a	1,763a	1,775a	1,787a	1,710	1,687	?	311	303	281	276	269	268	?	39.3	44.0	39.4	45.1	46.9	44.1	45.7	50.3	51.8

1. A daily newspaper is defined as a publication devoted primarily to recording news of current events in public affairs, international affairs, politics, etc., and which is published at least four times a week.

2. Newsprint consumption represents apparent consumption (i.e., domestic production plus imports, minus exports, or simply annual imports). For a few countries, where information is available, fluctuation in stocks has been taken into account, and this is indicated in a footnote. Data cover newsprint for both daily and non-daily newspapers.

a. English-language papers only.

b. Circulation figures refer to 33 dailies only.

SOURCE: UNESCO-SY, 1977, tables 12.1, 13.1; UNESCO-SY, 1981, tables 8.16, 8.19; UNESCO-SY, 1982, tables 8.16, 8.19; UNESCO-SY, 1984, tables 7.20, 7.23; UNESCO-SY, 1986, table 7.22; UNESCO-SY, 1987, tables 7.19, 7.22; UNESCO-SY, 1988, tables 7.17, 7.19.

Table 501

NEWSPRINT: VOLUME OF IMPORTS, 20 LC, 1965–86
(T MET)

Country	1965	1970	1975	1980	1981	1982	1983	1984	1985	1986
A. ARGENTINA	220	274	149	174	137	49	28	18	11‡	11†
B. BOLIVIA	3‡	5	5	6‡	7‡	7‡	7‡	4‡	3‡	3†
C. BRAZIL	54	149	116‡	167‡	170‡	161	158‡	164	95	218
D. CHILE	5	1	#	#	#	#	~	~	~	~
E. COLOMBIA	45	59	44	71‡	95‡	95	78	76‡	78‡	73‡
F. COSTA RICA	6	11	11	12‡	8‡	7	11	11	11‡	11†
G. CUBA	19	23‡	27‡	32	32	32	39	39	43	43†
H. DOMINICAN REP.	1	4	7	12	15	14	14	12	8	8†
I. ECUADOR	13	14	11	33	37‡	28	32	32	40	23
J. EL SALVADOR	9	13	10	15‡	15	12‡	13	13†	13	14
K. GUATEMALA	6	8	8	17	10	11	11	13	7	8
L. HAITI	~	1†	1‡	~	1‡	1‡	1†	1†	1†	~
M. HONDURAS	2	3	2	7‡	6‡	4	4	5†	5†	6†
N. MEXICO	91	119	186	110‡	230‡	148	67	26‡	38	38†
O. NICARAGUA	3	4	4	3‡	5‡	4	4†	4†	4†	5†
P. PANAMA	4	6	3	3	5	3	6	6	6†	6†
Q. PARAGUAY	1	4	3†	8	5	10	3‡	6	8	6
R. PERU	40	49	51	7	32	48‡	38‡	35‡	32‡	43†
S. URUGUAY	18	21	11	15	22	13	9	10†	8‡	8†
T. VENEZUELA	43	84	86	141‡	168‡	151	167	156‡	136‡	150‡
UNITED STATES	5,736	6,019	5,305	6,594	6,330	5,924	6,277	7,161	7,686	7,791

SOURCE: FAO-YFP, 1973, p. 275; FAO-YFP, 1975, p. 264; FAO-YFP, 1976, p. 264; FAO-YFP, 1980, p. 324; FAO-YFP, 1981, p. 317; FAO-YFP, 1982, p. 317; FAO-YFP, 1983, p. 316, FAO-YFP, 1984, p. 309, FAO-YFP, 1985, p. 256; FAO-YFP, 1986, p. 257.

Table 502

NEWSPRINT: VALUE OF IMPORTS, 20 LC, 1965–86
(T US)

Country	1965	1970	1975	1980	1981	1982	1983	1984	1985	1986
A. ARGENTINA	36,345‡	47,870	73,990	98,724	83,637	30,843	16,019	10,902	7,000†	7,000†
B. BOLIVIA	319‡	950	950†	2,200	3,000†	2,900†	2,900†	1,900†	1,400†	1,400†
C. BRAZIL	10,259	27,950	40,252†	98,000†	106,400†	98,938†	68,800	67,354	45,210	92,034
D. CHILE	872	88	#	#	#	#	#	#	#	~
E. COLOMBIA	7,349	9,947	16,608	26,379	48,567	58,530	45,205	46,900	44,700†	42,200†
F. COSTA RICA	843	1,918	4,262	5,400†	4,600†	4,294	6,454	6,419	5,700†	5,700†
G. CUBA	3,015	3,370‡	4,500†	11,679	11,300†	11,727	15,926	16,855	18,072	18,072†
H. DOMINICAN REP.	100	607	2,100‡	4,957	7,168	6,606	6,901	5,400	4,700	4,700
I. ECUADOR	1,867	2,306	7,600	17,227	19,000‡	12,605	17,965	16,877	20,988	12,504
J. EL SALVADOR	1,360	2,171	4,000	6,900	7,200	6,800	6,970	6,970†	7,040	4,117
K. GUATEMALA	888	1,352	2,722	9,016	5,609	6,447	5,601	6,543†	3,591	3,485
L. HAITI	80‡	123†	190†	139†	373†	285†	285†	285†	194†	194†
M. HONDURAS	280	472	801	2,595	3,400†	3,186	2,376	2,500†	3,600†	3,600†
N. MEXICO	13,644	19,016	59,687	64,200†	144,200†	89,000†	31,667	12,300†	17,700†	17,700†
O. NICARAGUA	443	635	1,607†	1,600†	2,600	2,331	1,600†	3,200†	3,300†	3,300†
P. PANAMA	457	818	1,130	1,079	2,388	1,385	2,739	2,887	3,383	3,383†
Q. PARAGUAY	199	636	1,366†	3,877	2,624	5,400†	1,315	2,106	3,304	2,362
R. PERU	5,940	7,171	18,182	3,450	20,281	30,400†	24,000†	16,500†	16,000†	20,000†
S. URUGUAY	3,213	3,347	4,805	8,635	11,686	8,484	4,603	5,000†	4,000†	4,000†
T. VENEZUELA	6,008	12,180	25,284†	54,000†	65,200†	94,561	87,749	81,900†	72,000†	79,300†
UNITED STATES	789,604	929,626	1,456,915	2,637,857	2,824,777	3,748,652	2,817,193	3,369,904†	3,720,143	3,682,352

SOURCE: FAO-YFP, 1973, p. 277; FAO-YFP, 1977; FAO-YFP, 1980, p. 326; FAO-YFP, 1981, p. 319; FAO-YFP, 1982, p. 319; FAO-YFP, 1983, p. 319; FAO-YFP, 1984, p. 311; FAO-YFP, 1985, p. 258; FAO-YFP, 1986, p. 259.

Table 503

BOOK PRODUCTION: TITLES BY SUBJECT, 11 L, 1982–86

Country/Year

Subject	A. ARGENTINA (1983)	(1986)	B. BOLIVIA (1982)	C. BRAZIL (1984)	D. CHILE (1985)	(1986)	E. COLOMBIA (1984)	F. COSTA RICA (1984)	(1986)[e]
1. Generalities	189	262	8	2,598	34	50	1,078	38	8
2. Philosophy, Psychology	536	226	1	773	31	22	239	47	5
3. Religion, Theology	~b	302	13	1,870	126	102	352	82	12
4. Sociology, Statistics	337	103	14	911	39	66	205	89	7
5. Political Science	~c	293	15	391	138	144	413	197	41
6. Law, Public Administration	342	484	23	1,661	111	90	1,025	191	19
7. Military Art	#	7	2	6	9	13	89	1	8
8. Education, Leisure	243	798	16	3,504	137	150	517	88	39
9. Trade, Transport	#	17	2	94	8	8	340	3	2
10. Ethnography, Folklore	#	31	21	504	13	10	195	7	0
11. Linguistics, Philology	~a	24	11	487	31	30	290	69	1
12. Mathematics	179	52	1	577	13	16	530	77	6
13. Natural Sciences	20	99	10	1,117	53	75	568	77	2
14. Medical Sciences	131	213	3	892	35	39	4,787	18	13
15. Engineering, Crafts	492	81	2	924	38	31	365	60	0
16. Agriculture	36	80	3	236	29	42	570	185	2
17. Domestic Science	#	44	#	107	12	15	150	4	0
18. Management, Administration	#	42	4	259	15	14	195	24	8
19. Planning, Architecture	7	32	1	115	10	11	135	20	4
20. Plastic Arts	639	35	9	502	11	6	205	6	0
21. Performing Arts	~d	34	13	185	17	10	332	3	3
22. Games, Sports	56	58	4	616	19	6	325	3	3
23. Literature									
(A) History and Criticism	58	605	64	2,588	12	8	340	150	6
(B) Literary Texts	934	606	~a	2,074	498	295	1,161	190	20
24. Geography, Travel	17	34	14	355	28	19	290	49	1
25. History, Biography	a	256	47	426	181	99	345	81	12
26. Total	4,216	4,818	301	21,184	1,638	1,499	15,041	1,759	807

Country/Year

Subject	G. CUBA (1985)	(1986)	N. MEXICO (1985)	O. NICARAGUA (1984)	R. PERU (1985)	(1986)	S. URUGUAY (1984)	(1986)
1. Generalities	256	270	776	4	12	15	21	1
2. Philosophy, Psychology	30	32	216	1	8	6	22	10
3. Religion, Theology	1	~	125	2	19	15	42	21
4. Sociology, Statistics	25	22	156	#	31	25	46	40
5. Political Science	83	69	454	1	93	88	69	120
6. Law, Public Administration	26	59	301	#	62	84	112	101
7. Military Art	3	4	13	#	1	1	11	13
8. Education, Leisure	338	284	453	#	17	33	76	38
9. Trade, Transport	21	5	65	#	3	14	84	29
10. Ethnography, Folklore	10	8	12	1	7	4	3	2
11. Linguistics, Philology	151	104	198	#	2	9	6	17
12. Mathematics	64	149	168	#	8	17	50	30
13. Natural Sciences	101	65	328	#	6	13	27	46
14. Medical Sciences	250	166	315	#	15	41	52	56
15. Engineering, Crafts	163	255	249	#	15	13	79	21
16. Agriculture	23	41	48	#	6	8	59	77
17. Domestic Science	3	9	10	#	3	2	4	0
18. Management, Administration	15	27	66	#	20	7	37	4
19. Planning, Architecture	6	11	24	#	1	24	24	10
20. Plastic Arts	19	16	70	#	2	4	15	5
21. Performing Arts	29	41	49	#	7	6	21	10
22. Games, Sports	39	66	28	#	2	1	16	3
23. Literature								
(A) History and Criticism	81	45	224	1	19	22	36	29
(B) Literary Texts	317	324	813	14	79	122	169	146
24. Geography, Travel	34	35	64	#	25	24	45	12
25. History, Biography	80	67	269	2	55	37	80	100
26. Total	2,168	2,174	5,482	26	518	635	1,206	941

a. Included in History Criticism.
b. Included in Philosophy, Psychology.
c. Included in Sociology, Statistics.
d. Included in Plastic Arts.
e. Included in the total are 585 university theses, but not distributed in the 25 groups.

SOURCE: UNESCO-SY, 1987, table 7.8; 1988, table 7.6.

Table 504

LATIN AMERICA SCIENTIFIC ARTICLES PUBLISHED IN INTERNATIONAL JOURNALS, 20 LRC, 1973–84

	Country of Origin	1973	1974	1975	1976	1977	1978	1979	1980	1981	1982	1983	1984	Total[a]
A.	ARGENTINA	832	709	611	612	614	590	597	706	747	870	855	770	8,511
	Barbados	3	3	6	5	7	3	4	3	4	2	6	4	51
B.	BOLIVIA	6	7	7	2	6	7	5	4	4	2	6	5	62
C.	BRAZIL	619	645	739	835	844	869	975	1,004	1,088	981	994	953	10,545
D.	CHILE	355	313	316	332	296	326	378	374	418	476	478	386	4,448
E.	COLOMBIA	46	47	51	50	65	65	51	56	53	56	46	38	625
F.	COSTA RICA	38	24	39	40	33	31	19	41	29	33	28	22	378
G.	CUBA	19	14	17	30	23	18	27	28	39	51	50	33	351
H.	DOMINICAN REP.	2	1	1	2	3	2	4	2	5	5	1	2	30
I.	ECUADOR	6	5	6	10	3	8	4	4	6	8	13	7	81
J.	EL SALVADOR	3	7	12	7	9	6	2	6	5	0	2	0	59
K.	GUATEMALA	18	29	38	19	21	10	20	19	24	17	9	8	232
	Guyana	8	3	2	2	6	1	2	4	9	5	10	6	59
L.	HAITI	0	1	4	1	1	1	0	1	2	1	4	2	19
M.	HONDURAS	5	9	3	5	8	6	3	5	2	2	2	2	53
	Jamaica	70	68	44	56	56	66	56	47	56	45	34	30	627
N.	MEXICO	381	370	374	362	370	392	413	476	489	541	527	435	5,131
O.	NICARAGUA	4	1	1	2	3	1	0	0	1	0	0	0	15
P.	PANAMA	13	9	10	7	4	3	7	8	15	9	13	14	114
Q.	PARAGUAY	3	2	2	2	6	0	5	2	1	1	1	2	29
R.	PERU	38	34	37	41	28	30	26	33	27	29	23	21	366
	Suriname	0	0	1	3	4	3	4	1	2	1	2	2	24
	Trinidad and Tobago	39	43	25	37	17	37	24	22	27	29	33	34	367
S.	URUGUAY	29	27	29	19	27	16	26	14	20	26	28	26	286
T.	VENEZUELA	161	159	144	214	229	263	265	268	229	220	202	197	2,549
	Western Hemisphere	2,700	2,532	2,521	2,698	2,684	2,754	2,919	3,134	3,307	3,412	3,369	3,001	35,031
	World	279,570	272,807	274,707	276,738	282,720	276,244	277,106	280,305	287,761	288,128	291,262	263,072	3,350,421

a. Totals may not add up because of rounding.

SOURCE: IDB-SPTF, 1988, table IX-3.

Table 505

RANKING OF COUNTRIES WITH THE LARGEST NUMBER OF SCIENTIFIC ARTICLES PUBLISHED, 10 LRC, 1973 AND 1984

		1973				1984	
	Country	Articles (N)	% of Total		Country	Articles (N)	% of Total
A.	ARGENTINA	832	30.8	C.	BRAZIL	953	31.7
C.	BRAZIL	619	22.9	A.	ARGENTINA	770	25.7
N.	MEXICO	381	14.1	N.	MEXICO	435	14.5
D.	CHILE	355	13.1	D.	CHILE	386	12.8
T.	VENEZUELA	161	6.0	T.	VENEZUELA	197	6.6
	Jamaica	70	2.6	E.	COLOMBIA	38	1.3
E.	COLOMBIA	46	1.7		Trinidad and Tobago	34	1.1
	Trinidad and Tobago	39	1.5	G.	CUBA	33	1.1
F.	COSTA RICA	38	1.4		Jamaica	30	1.0
R.	PERU	38	1.4	S.	URUGUAY	26	0.9
	Other	121	4.5		Other	99	3.3
	Western Hemisphere Total	2,700	100.0		Western Hemisphere Total	3,001	100.0

SOURCE: IDB-SPTF, 1988, table IX-2.

Table 506

MAIL TRAFFIC,[1] 16 LC, 1970–78

(M items sent or received)

Country	Code[2]	1970	1971	1972	1973	1974	1975	1976	1977	1978
A. ARGENTINA	A	833	903	885	960	870	737	620	~	~
	B	124	103	87	88	89	79	70	~	~
	C	55	61	55	54	58	56	50	~	~

Continued in SALA, 23-1205.

1. The figure covers letters (airmail, ordinary mail, and registered), postcards, printed
   matter, merchandise samples, small packets, and phonopost packets. Includes mail
   carried without charge, but excludes ordinary parcels, and insured letters and boxes.
2. Code: A = Domestic: items mailed for distribution within the national territory.
           B = Foreign-received: items received from or mail from places outside the
                national territory. Mail in transit is not included.
           C = Foreign-sent: items sent or mailed for distribution outside the national
                territory. Mail in transit is not included.

Table 507

TELEGRAPH SERVICE, BY NUMBER OF TELEGRAMS, 12 L, 1970–81[a]

(T)

Country		1970	1973	1975	1976	1977	1978	1979	1980	1981
A. ARGENTINA	Domestic	14,645	17,409	14,340	12,400	12,710	11,193	12,255	13,435	15,509
	Foreign	689	564	515	342	364	376	382	421	420

Continued in SALA, 25-506.

Table 508

U.N. DATA ON TELEPHONES, 19 L, 1975–84[a]

	Country	T								PHI							
		1975	1978	1979	1980	1981	1982	1983	1984	1975	1978	1979	1980	1981	1982	1983	1984
A.	ARGENTINA	1,996	2,404	2,491	2,588	2,767	3,235	3,108	~	7.8	9.1	9.2	9.3	9.8	11.2	10.4	~
C.	BRAZIL	3,372	5,525	6,494	7,496	8,536	9,126	9,856	10,570	3.0	4.5	5.1	6.3	7.2	7.3	7.7	8.0
D.	CHILE	434	514	536	551	595	584	629	680	4.1	4.8	4.8	5.0	5.2	5.2	5.4	5.7
E.	COLOMBIA	1,227	1,493	1,587	1,718	1,842	1,866	1,894	1,978	5.2	5.8	6.0	6.4	6.5	6.5	6.5	6.6
F.	COSTA RICA	122	185	200	236	256	283	292	304	6.3	8.8	9.3	10.7	10.9	11.8	11.8	12.1
G.	CUBA	~	341	362	~	406	~	~	493	~	3.5	3.7	~	4.2	~	~	4.9
H.	DOMINICAN REP.	108	~	155	165	175	~	~	~	2.4	~	2.9	2.9	3.0	~	~	~
I.	ECUADOR	182	240	260	272	290	312	318	332	2.7	3.0	3.2	3.3	3.3	3.9	4.0	3.6
J.	EL SALVADOR	60	80	83	86	100	100	116	124	1.5	1.8	1.9	1.9	2.2	2.1	2.3	2.4
K.	GUATEMALA	~	~	~	~	~	~	~	~	~	~	~	~	~	~	~	~
L.	HAITI	~	~	~	~	~	~	~	~	~	~	~	~	~	~	~	~
M.	HONDURAS	20	21	27	~	~	~	35	46	.7	.7	.8	~	~	~	.9	1.1
N.	MEXICO	2,915	4,140	4,533	4,992	5,511	5,961	6,414	6,796	5.0	6.4	6.8	7.2	7.7	8.1	8.9	9.1
O.	NICARAGUA	36	~	58	~	33	~	~	50	1.6	~	2.2	~	1.1	~	~	1.6
P.	PANAMA	142	152	164	173	185	213	220	227	8.4	8.3	8.7	9.5	9.5	10.7	10.5	10.4
Q.	PARAGUAY	37	48	55	59	64	71	78	83	1.4	1.6	1.8	1.8	1.9	2.3	2.2	2.6
R.	PERU	369	420	437	475	~	520	543	571	2.5	2.5	2.5	2.7	~	3.0	2.9	3.1
S.	URUGUAY	250	270	279	287	294	~	332	338	9.0	9.6	9.9	9.9	10.1	~	10.3	11.3
T.	VENEZUELA	660	678	789	~	~	1,378	1,021	1,311	5.3	5.1	5.8	~	~	9.4	6.7	7.8

a. For pre-1975 data see SALA, 21-1207.

SOURCE: UN-SY, 1977, p. 620; UN-SY, 1978, p. 628; UN-SY, 1979, table 154; UN-SY,
    1981, table 188; UN-SY, 1982, table 181; UN-SY, 1983, table 117; UN-SY, 1984, table 117.

Table 509

AMERICAN TELEPHONE AND TELEGRAPH DATA ON TELEPHONES, 20 LC, 1960–81

Country	T Telephones[1]						PHI[1]					
	1960	1970	1975	1979	1980	1981	1960	1970	1975	1979	1980	1981
A. ARGENTINA	1,244	1,668	2,374	2,660	2,760	2,881	6.0	6.9	9.4	10.1	10.3[†]	10.4
B. BOLIVIA	21	38	~	126	~	135	.6	.8	~	2.6	~	2.6

Continued in SALA, 24-508.

Table 510

TELEPHONES BY CONTINENTAL AREA, 1960–81

Category	1960	1965	1970	1975	1979	1980	1981
Absolute Total (Million)	133.6	182.5	255.2	358.6	448.3	472.1	508.3
Percentage Total	100.0	100.0	100.0	100.0	100.0	100.0	100.0
Latin America[1]	3.1	3.0	3.1	3.5	5.0	4.0	3.9
North America	56.9	52.3	48.6	43.5	41.1	40.5	41.0
Europe	30.2	31.5	32.8	34.6	37.2	37.6	37.4
Africa	1.4	1.3	1.2	1.2	1.1	1.0	1.0
Asia	6.1	9.7	12.2	15.2	14.8	14.9	14.7
Oceania	2.3	2.2	2.1	2.0	1.8	2.0	2.0

1. Includes non-Latin American Caribbean and mainland countries and dependencies.

SOURCE: American Telephone and Telegraph Overseas Administration, *World's Telephones*, 1960, 1965, 1969, 1970, 1971, 1974, 1977, 1978, 1979, 1980, and 1981.

Table 511

RADIO AND TELEVISION TRANSMITTERS, 20 LC

	Country	Radio[1]					Television[2]				
		Year	Total	Governmental	Public	Commercial	Year	Total	Governmental	Public	Commercial
A.	ARGENTINA	1985	175	40	8	127	1985	~	~	~	183
B.	BOLIVIA	1981	184	5	25	154	1985	~	42	~	~
		1985	191	~	~	~					
C.	BRAZIL	1983	1,818	27	15	1,776	1983	137	2	12	123
		1985	1,729	~	~	~					
D.	CHILE	1980	295	13	18	264	1985	131	~	~	~
		1985	302	~	~	~					
E.	COLOMBIA	1985	439	~	~	439	1983	49	#	49	#
F.	COSTA RICA	1981	123	3	17	103	1981	14	~	4	10
		1985	80	1	14	65	1985	12	#	1	11
G.	CUBA	1985	160	160	#	#	1985	~	78	~	~
H.	DOMINICAN REP.	1985	126	#	#	126	1985	~	~	~	19
I.	ECUADOR	1985	370	~	~	~	1985	~	~	14	~
J.	EL SALVADOR	1985	79	#	#	79	1985	5	2	~	3
K.	GUATEMALA	1985	104	#	#	104	1985	24	1	~	23
L.	HAITI	1985	35	1	#	34	1985	~	~	4	~
M.	HONDURAS	1985	209	6	6	198	1985	~	~	~	39
N.	MEXICO	1985	887	47	#	840	1985	430	226	27	177
O.	NICARAGUA	1979	87	#	5	82	1985	7	7	~	~
		1985	44	~	~	~					
P.	PANAMA	1985	85	#	#	85	1985	14	~	1	13
Q.	PARAGUAY	1985	48	#	#	48	1985	~	~	~	5
R.	PERU	1985	413	#	#	413	1985	138	~	~	~
S.	URUGUAY	1981	94	4	~	90	1983	33	12	#	21
		1983	115	~	~	~					
T.	VENEZUELA	1985	221	13	3	205	1985	63	28	1	34
	UNITED STATES	1977	8,359	414	531	7,414	1977	972[a]	184	71	717

1. Figures relate to low-, medium-, high-, super-high frequency transmitters in service used for domestic radio broadcasts to the general public.
2. Figures relate to very-high and ultra-high frequency transmitters operating on a regular basis and used for broadcasting to the general public.

a. Does not include relay transmitters.

SOURCE: UNESCO-SY, 1987, tables 10.1, 10.3; UNESCO-SY, 1988, tables 10.1, 10.3.

Table 512

RADIO RECEIVERS,[1] 20 LC, 1965–86

	Country	T						PTI					
		1965	1970	1975	1980	1985	1986	1965	1970	1975	1980	1985	1986
A.	ARGENTINA	6,600	9,000	9,890	12,000	20,000	20,000	296	376	380	425	654	645
B.	BOLIVIA	~	402	1,150	2,800	3,000	3,850	~	93	235	503	581	587
C.	BRAZIL	~	11,800	16,980	35,000	53,000	50,540	~	123	157	289	391	365
D.	CHILE	~	1,400	1,700	3,250	4,000	4,100	~	148	164	292	332	335
E.	COLOMBIA	1,600	2,217	2,808	3,250	4,000	4,500	88	107	121	126	139	153
F.	COSTA RICA	~	130	151	180	220	700	~	75	77	79	85	263
G.	CUBA	~	1,330	1,805	2,914	3,282	3,400	~	155	193	299	327	335
H.	DOMNICAN REP.	~	164	160	900	1,000	1,050	~	~	160	81	160	164
I.	ECUADOR	540	1,700	~	2,350	2,750	2,850	105	281	~	289	293	295
J.	EL SALVADOR	396	583	1,100	1,550	1,900	2,000	132	163	266	323	342	349
K.	GUATEMALA	~	220	262	310	350	500	~	42	44	45	44	61
L.	HAITI	63	76	93	101	140	200	15	17	18	17	21	30
M.	HONDURAS	135	108	142	176	1,600	1,700	~	41	46	48	366	377
N.	MEXICO	8,600	14,005	~	19,000	15,000	16,000	208	~	~	130	190	197
O.	NICARAGUA	100	137	~	700	800	870	57	67	~	256	244	257
P.	PANAMA	~	215	260	300	400	410	~	140	149	153	183	184
Q.	PARAGUAY	~	~	180	224	600	624	~	~	67	71	163	165
R.	PERU	~	1,748	2,050	2,750	4,000	5,000	~	132	135	169	203	247
S.	URUGUAY	900	1,000	1,500	1,630	1,800	1,800	334	356	530	561	598	592
T.	VENEZUELA	~	~	4,775	5,600	7,300	7,550	~	~	377	373	422	425
	UNITED STATES	240,000	290,000	401,000	453,000	500,000	510,000	1,235	1,414	1,857	1,989	2,101	2,126

1. Estimated number of receivers in use.

SOURCE: UNESCO-SY, 1983, table 9.2; UNESCO-SY, 1984, table 9.2; UNESCO-SY, 1986, table 10.2; UNESCO-SY, 1987, table 10.2; UNESCO-SY, 1988, table 10.2.

Table 513

TELEVISION SETS,[1] 20 LC, 1965–86

	Country	T						PTI					
		1965	1970	1975	1980	1985	1986	1965	1970	1975	1980	1985	1986
A.	ARGENTINA	1,600	3,500	4,000	5,140	6,500	6,650	72	146	154	182	213	214
B.	BOLIVIA	~	~	45	300	420	500	~	~	9	54	66	76
C.	BRAZIL	~	6,100	~	15,000	25,000	26,000	~	64	~	124	184	188
D.	CHILE	~	500	700	1,225	1,750	2,000	~	53	68	110	145	164
E.	COLOMBIA	350	810	1,600	2,250	2,750	3,000	19	39	69	87	96	102
F.	COSTA RICA	50	100	128	162	200	210	34	58	65	106	77	79
G.	CUBA	~	~	595	1,273	1,977	2,050	~	~	64	131	197	202
H.	DOMINICAN REP.	50	100	180	400	500	515	13	23	36	72	80	81
I.	ECUADOR	42	150	252	500	600	700	8	25	36	62	64	73
J.	EL SALVADOR	35	92	135	300	350	400	12	26	33	63	63	70
K.	GUATEMALA	55	72	110	175	207	300	12	14	18	25	26	37
L.	HAITI	~	11	13	16	20	25	~	2.4	2.6	2.8	3	4
M.	HONDURAS	2.2	22	34	49	280	300	1	8.3	11	13	64	67
N.	MEXICO	1,200	3,000	~	3,820	8,500	9,490	28	59	~	55	108	117
O.	NICARAGUA	16	55	83	175	190	200	9	27	34	63	58	59
P.	PANAMA	70	~	185	220	350	360	53	~	106	112	160	161
Q.	PARAGUAY	~	~	54	68	85	88	~	~	20	21	23	23
R.	PERU	210	395	610	850	1,500	1,701	18	30	40	49	76	84
S.	URUGUAY	200	~	351	363	500	520	74	~	124	125	166	171
T.	VENEZUELA	650	~	1,284	1,710	2,250	2,500	72	~	101	114	130	141
	UNITED STATES	70,350	84,600	121,000	155,800	190,000	195,000	362	413	560	684	798	813

1. Estimated number of television sets in use.

SOURCE: UNESCO-SY, 1983, table 9.4; UNESCO-SY, 1984, table 9.4; UNESCO-SY, 1985, table 10; UNESCO-SY, 1987, table 10.4; UNESCO-SY, 1988, table 10.4.

Table 514

CINEMA ATTENDANCE, 20 LC, 1955–85

Country	1955 Attendance (M)	1955 Per Capita Visits	1960 Attendance (M)	1960 Per Capita Visits	1965 Attendance (M)	1965 Per Capita Visits	1970 Attendance (M)	1970 Per Capita Visits	1975 Attendance (M)	1975 Per Capita Visits	1980 Attendance (M)	1980 Per Capita Visits	1985 Attendance (M)	1985 Per Capita Visits
A. ARGENTINA	120[a]	6.3[a]	145	7.0	344[b]	15.5[b]	53	2.2	82	3.2	44[m]	.2[m]	49.9[u]	1.7[u]
B. BOLIVIA	~	~	~	~	3[c]	7[c]	~	~	~	~	31[n]	5.7[n]	~	~
C. BRAZIL	312[d]	5.0[d]	316	4.5	314[e]	3.8[e]	234[b]	2.5[b]	276	2.6	138[m]	1.3[m]	91.0	.7
D. CHILE	28	4.2	~	~	61	7.1	47[f]	4.8[f]	23	2.3	15[m]	~	12.6	1.0
E. COLOMBIA	56[g]	4.1[g]	67[h]	5.8[h]	80	4.3	92[j]	4.2[j]	96	4.1	68[m]	2.4[m]	56.1	2.0
F. COSTA RICA	~	~	~	~	~	~	~	~	~	~	~	~	73.5	.1*
G. CUBA	~	~	49[j]	8.4[j]	~	~	~	~	124[q]	14.2[q]	50[m]	9.2[m]	38.2	7.6
H. DOMINICAN REP.	4	1.5	~	~	~	~	~	~	~	~	~	~	~	~
I. ECUADOR	8	2.2	~	~	15	2.9	22	3.7	39	5.6	~	~	~	~
J. EL SALVADOR	9	4.1	15	8.1	~	~	10[f]	2.9[f]	14[r]	3.5[r]	16[t]	1.4[n]	7.9[v]	1.0[v]
K. GUATEMALA	9	2.6	10	3.6	~	~	9[f]	1.7[f]	15[s]	2.8[t,s]	10[n]	1.3[m]	2.1[m]	.4[m]
L. HAITI	1	—	1[k]	1.3[k]	1[c]	—	~	~	6[o]	1.3[o]	6[o]	~	~	~
M. HONDURAS	2	1.2	~	~	~	~	~	~	~	~	~	~	~	~
N. MEXICO	362	11.7	374[j]	10.7[j]	346	8.0	251	4.9	251	4.2	264[p]	3.7[p]	~	~
O. NICARAGUA	5[i]	3.9[i]	6	5.7	7	4.1	5[j]	3.6[j]	.3[r]	6.5[r]	5[m]	1.9[m]	~	~
P. PANAMA	~	~	~	~	~	~	~	~	~	~	~	~	~	~
Q. PARAGUAY	~	~	~	~	~	~	~	~	~	~	~	~	~	~
R. PERU	~	~	67[j]	6.7[j]	~	~	~	~	~	~	33[p]	1.9[p]	~	~
S. URUGUAY	~	~	25[h]	9.8[h]	16[e]	5.7[e]	~	~	~	~	6.2[m]	2.1[m]	~	~
T. VENEZUELA	42	7.0	60[h]	7.8[h]	~	~	37[f]	3.5[f]	33[o]	2.6[o]	67.6[m]	4.7[m]	13.2	.8
UNITED STATES	2,000	12.1	2,165[j]	12.0[j]	2,288	11.8	920	4.5	1,565[t,o]	7.2[o]	1,067[m]	4.6[m]	1,053.3[u]	5.1[u]

a. 1953.
b. 1967.
c. 1964.
d. 1954.
e. 1963.
f. 1971.
g. 1956.
h. 1959.
i. 1968.
j. 1961.
k. 1958.
l. 1952.
m. 1981.
n. 1979.
o. 1977.
p. 1980.
q. 1972.
r. 1974.
s. 1973.
t. 1976.
u. 1983.
v. 1982.

SOURCE: For years 1955-70, Daniel I. Geffner, "Alternative Interpretations of Time-Series Data on the Growth of Latin American Film Industry, 1926-1970," SALA, 19-3601. For subsequent years see UNESCO-SY, 1977, table 14.3; UNESCO-SY, 1980, table 9.3; UNESCO-SY, 1983, table 8.3; UNESCO-SY, 1984, table 8.3; UNESCO-SY, 1986; UNESCO-SY, 1987, table 9.3; UNESCO-SY, 1988, table 9.3.

Table 515

MOTION PICTURE THEATERS,[1] 20 LC, 1926–85

(N)

Country	1926	1930	1940	1950	1960	1965	1970	1975	1980	1983	1985
A. ARGENTINA	200	975	1,208	1,881	2,228	1,587[a,b]	1,637[c]	1,420	1,018[n]	921	~
B. BOLIVIA	16	20	38	60	82	120[d]	~	~	226[q]	225[q]	~
C. BRAZIL	200	1,600	1,300	1,736	3,284	3,261[e]	3,194[a]	2,910	2,264[n]	2,237[n]	1,410
D. CHILE	200	221	263	300	336	336	368[f]	291	172[n]	161	177
E. COLOMBIA	200	218	274	500	819[g]	895	726[h]	700	393[n]	323	586
F. COSTA RICA	8	21	42	100	136[i]	~	~	~	~	~	104
G. CUBA	350	457	375	516	481[i,k]	~	439[l,c]	888[s]	1,322[n]	1,405	510
H. DOMINICAN REP.	~	31	28	55	84	~	80[f,c]	~	~	~	~
I. ECUADOR	25	25	37	71	122	164	164	255[t]	~	~	~
J. EL SALVADOR	33	~	41	32	55[i]	~	57[f]	72[t]	~	~	79
K. GUATEMALA	20	39	28	25	105	~	105[f,c]	131[u]	126[q]	140[v]	~
L. HAITI	6	9	7	24	26[m,i]	20[d,b]	~	~	23[p]	~	~
M. HONDURAS	6	27	23	28	60[i]	~	~	~	~	~	~
N. MEXICO	700	701	829	1,726	2,000[i,k]	1,555[b]	1,765[c]	2,505	2,831[o]	3,026	2,241
O. NICARAGUA	11	24	27	~	98	104[e,i]	~	~	128[n]	127[n]	~
P. PANAMA	30	38	54	60	62	~	23[h,c]	6[t]	~	~	~
Q. PARAGUAY	~	9	8	~	55	~	~	~	~	~	~
R. PERU	60	70	212	~	319[j]	~	276[l,c]	388[p]	425[o]	425[o]	~
S. URUGUAY	101	125	181	177	223[g,i]	386[e]	180[a]	~	120[n]	120[n]	~
T. VENEZUELA	18	123	177	350	744[g,k]	~	436[f,c]	588[p]	555[n]	535[n]	437
LATIN AMERICA	~	~	5,162	~	11,319	~	~	~	9,603[r]	~	~
UNITED STATES	~	23,000	17,003	20,239	15,105[j,k]	9,805[b]	10,520[c]	15,000	18,040[n]	16,032	~

1. Includes mobile and fixed units.

a. 1967.
b. Does not include drive-in cinemas or their capacity (in parentheses) for cars: Argentina 1; Haiti, 1 (450); Mexico, 5 (3,200); United States, 3,600.
c. Does not include drive-in cinemas or their capacity (in parentheses) for cars: Argentina, 8 (5,150); Cuba, 1 (550); Dominican Republic, 2 (420); Guatemala, 1 (544); Mexico, 3 (1,970); Panama, 1 (330); Peru, 1 (100); Venezuela, 20 (4,030); United States, 3,900.
d. 1964.
e. 1963.
f. 1971.
g. 1959.
h. 1968.
i. It was not indicated if the cinemas concerned were equipped to exhibit 35 mm or 16 mm films.
j. 1961.

k. Does not include drive-in cinemas or their capacity (in parentheses) for cars: Cuba, 2 (1,366); Mexico, 5 (2,500); Venezuela, 3 (900); United States, 6,000 (2,400,000).
l. 1972.
m. 1958.
n. 1981.
o. 1980.
p. 1977.
q. 1979.
r. Indicates the number of fixed cinemas for 1981.
s. 1972.
t. 1974.
u. 1976.
v. 1982.

SOURCE: For years 1926-70, same as table 513. For subsequent years see UNESCO-SY, 1977, table 14.3; UNESCO-SY, 1978-79, table 17.3; UNESCO-SY, 1983, table 8.3; UNESCO-SY, 1984, table 8.3; UNESCO-SY, 1986, table 9.3; UNESCO-SY, 1987, table 9.3.

Table 516

ADVERTISING EXPENDITURES, 6 LC

(1977 M US)

Country	Total	Print	Television	Radio
A. ARGENTINA	382.2	181.6	120.9	51.3
C. BRAZIL	1610.9	483.8	697.1	337.6
E. COLOMBIA[1]	167.8	36.4	91.0	29.0
H. DOMINICAN REP.	41.1	12.3	18.8	6.3
N. MEXICO	298.3	37.3	202.0	46.6
T. VENEZUELA	280.2	108.7	92.7	48.8
UNITED STATES[2]	25,269.0	14,605.0	7,612.0	2,634.0

1. Data are for 1978.
2. Expenditure for cinema not reported.

SOURCE: World Press Encyclopedia, 1984.

Table 517

COMPUTER FACILITIES IN LATIN AMERICA, 11 L

(N)

		Computer Class					
Country	Mini/Micro	Small	Medium	Large	Total	Total P 10 I	Total per B GNP
A. ARGENTINA							
1973	~	~	~	~	446	.19	12
1982	7,664	~	3,909	~	11,575	4.11	161
B. BOLIVIA[†]							
1980	~	~	~	~	85	.15	25
C. BRAZIL							
1973	~	~	~	~	754	.08	10
1982	15,037	3,107	301	148	18,593	1.54	69
D. CHILE							
1973	~	~	~	~	52	.05	8
1981	907	209	51	28	1,195	1.06	41
E. COLOMBIA							
1973	~	~	~	~	86	.04	8
1983	~	~	~	~	2,381	.90	65
F. COSTA RICA							
1973	~	~	~	~	29	.16	19
1981	91	118	30	9	248	1.06	74
M. HONDURAS							
1981	~	~	~	~	100	.26	44
N. MEXICO[†]							
1973	~	~	~	~	573	.11	12
1982	7,300	2,195	499	62	10,056	1.41	63
Q. PARAGUAY							
1973	~	~	~	~	6	.02	6
1983	~	~	~	~	350	1.14	70
S. URUGUAY							
1973	~		~	~	34	.11	12
1983	699	331	25	18	1,073	3.66	130
T. VENEZUELA							
1973	~	~	~	~	302	9.29	17
1983	5,500	1,700	165	70	7,435	4.82	114

SOURCE: SELA, "Trade and Foreign Direct Investment in Data Services," August 20,
1985.

Table 518

GENERAL PURPOSE COMPUTERS, STOCK BY REGION OF ORIGIN,
BEGINNING OF 1981, 2 LRC

(M US AND N)

	United States					
Country	IBM	Other	Total United States	Western Europe	Japan	Total
C. BRAZIL						
Value	1,089	431	1,520	5	44	1,569
Number	1,698	704	2,402	21	59	2,482
N. MEXICO						
Value	320	205	525	1	~	526
Number	779	385	1,164	10	~	1,174
Caribbean						
Value	110	56	166	17	~	183
Number	275	93	368	68	~	436
Other Latin America						
Value	585	241	826	4	~	830
Number	925	427	1,352	9	~	1,361
Total Latin America						
Value	2,104	933	3,037	27	44	3,108
Number	3,677	1,609	5,286	108	59	5,453
Total Developing Countries						
Value	3,661	1,646	5,307	287	113	5,721
Number	5,951	2,559	8,510	734	125	9,398

SOURCE: SELA, "Trade and Foreign Direct Investment in Data Services," August 20,
1985.

Table 519

INSTALLED COMPUTERS IN BRAZIL, 1970–81

Class[1]	1970	1973	1975	1977	1979	1981	Growth Rates 1970–75	1977–81	1973–81
Micro	~	586	2,143	3,846	4,791	8,576	~	20.1	33.5
Mini	~	19	173	356	1,015	2,719	~	50.8	62.1
Small	378	639	1,057	1,296	1,494	1,858	25.7	9.0	15.9
Medium	122	250	327	353	377	408	24.7	3.6	12.1
Large	2	45	82	122	226	374	92.8	28.0	52.3
Very Large	4	33	61	87	97	134	68.1	10.8	35.1
Total	506	1,572	3,843	6,060	8,000	14,069	50.7	21.1	33.8

1. The class sizes are generally based on the size of the equipment, as well as upon prices and technical parameters (CPU speed, memory, and input/output capacity).

SOURCE: Alexandra Pou, "The Brazilian Informática Sector." Master's Thesis, University of California, Los Angeles, 1985.

Table 520

BRAZIL ELECTRONIC EQUIPMENT MARKET, 1981 AND 1986
(M US)

Product	1981	1986[†]
Computer Equipment	1,008	3,200
Consumer Goods	1,845	2,900
Telecommunications Equipment	749	1,200
Instrumentation and Control Equipment	64	200
Other[1]	69	500
Total	3,735	8,000

1. Includes defense, medicine, and the motor vehicle sector.

SOURCE: IDB-SPTF, 1988, table VII-4.

Table 521

BRAZIL INFORMATION TECHNOLOGY EQUIPMENT SOLD, 1986 AND 1987

Product	1986	1987[a]
Superminis	86	91
Minis	1,370	621
Supermicros	1,240	1,273
Personal Micros	32,814	28,995
Professional Micros — 8 bits	49,261	6,762
Professional Micros — 16 bits	56,636	58,139
Serial Printers	60,857	88,242
Line Printers	1,890	1,499
Communication Terminals	32,940	27,913
Financial Terminals	18,134	8,932
Point of Sale Terminals	1,223	2,519
Videotext Terminals	3,621	4,875
Telex Terminals	**	2,261
Terminal Concentrators	2,587	1,085
Video Monitors	7,886	18,439
Process Control Equipment	332	351
Magnetic Tape Unit (reel)	1,110	941
Magnetic Tape Unit (cartridge)	7,360	5,804
Winchester Disk Unit	26,374	44,370
Floppy Disk Unit 5-1/4"	118,902	76,355
Multiplexers	816	570
Modems	33,840	37,615
Local Networks	**	1,190

a. The data for 1987 include figures of sales actually made for the first semester of the year and estimates for the second.

SOURCE: IDB-SPTF, 1988, table VII-9.

Part III
Population, Health, and Education

6

Demography

Figure 6:1

POPULATION CARTOGRAM OF LATIN AMERICA, 1980

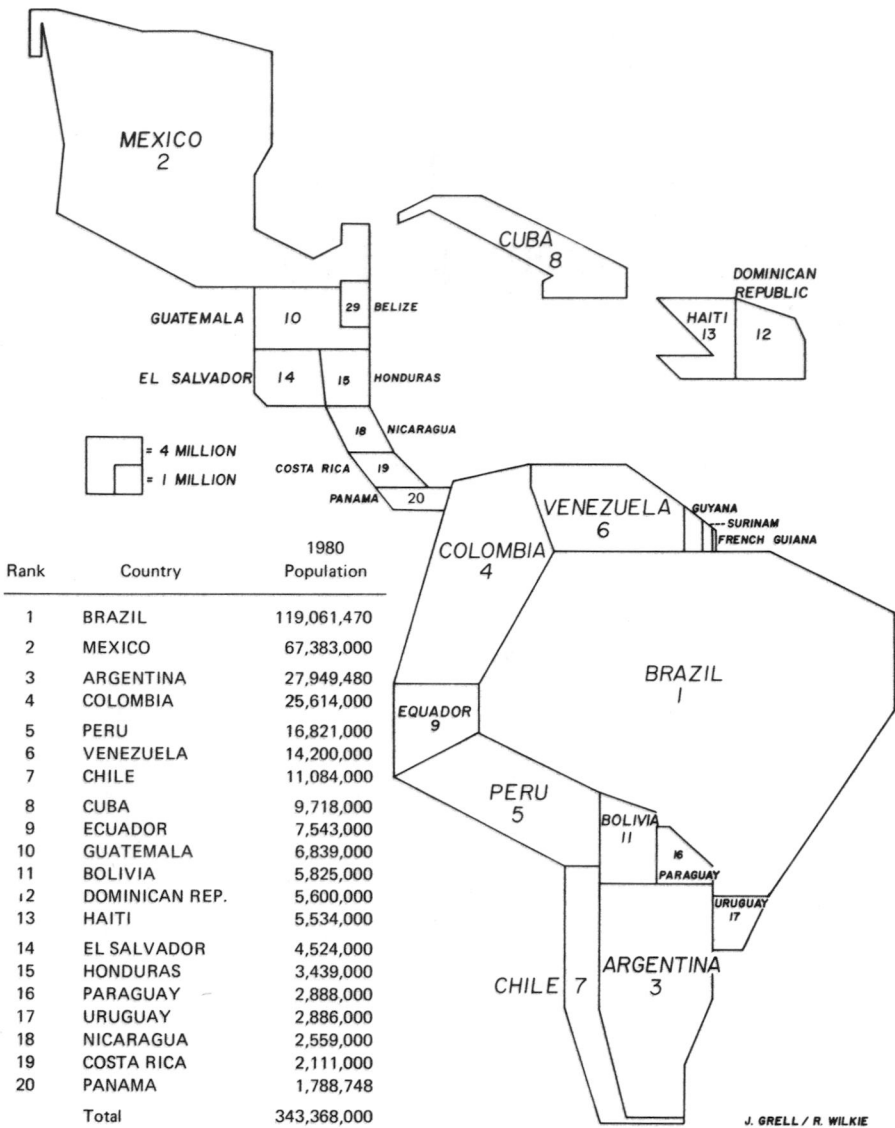

Rank	Country	1980 Population
1	BRAZIL	119,061,470
2	MEXICO	67,383,000
3	ARGENTINA	27,949,480
4	COLOMBIA	25,614,000
5	PERU	16,821,000
6	VENEZUELA	14,200,000
7	CHILE	11,084,000
8	CUBA	9,718,000
9	ECUADOR	7,543,000
10	GUATEMALA	6,839,000
11	BOLIVIA	5,825,000
12	DOMINICAN REP.	5,600,000
13	HAITI	5,534,000
14	EL SALVADOR	4,524,000
15	HONDURAS	3,439,000
16	PARAGUAY	2,888,000
17	URUGUAY	2,886,000
18	NICARAGUA	2,559,000
19	COSTA RICA	2,111,000
20	PANAMA	1,788,748
	Total	343,368,000

J. GRELL / R. WILKIE
S 81

SOURCE: SALA LAPUA, pp. 30, 33.

Table 600

WORLD POPULATION (MID-1987) AND AVERAGE ANNUAL GROWTH
RATES AND RANKS, 20 LRC, 1960–87
(130 Countries with Populations of 1 Million or More)

Population Rank	Country	Population (T)		AA–GR %		
		1986	1987	1960–73	1973–86	1980–87
1	China	1,054,041	1,068,734	1.7[a]	1.4	1.2
2	India	781,367	797,060	2.3	2.2	2.1
3	USSR	281,123	283,555	1.0	.9	1.0
4	United States[1]	241,596	243,381	1.0	1.0	1.0
5	Indonesia	166,627	169,735	2.1	2.2	2.2
6	**Brazil**	138,370	141,235	2.9	2.3	2.2
7	Japan	121,492	122,129	1.2	.8	.6
8	Nigeria	103,147	106,736	2.5	2.9	3.3
9	Bangladesh	103,213	105,868	2.4	2.5	2.6
10	Pakistan	99,215	102,474	2.9	3.1	3.1
11	**Mexico**	80,247	81,950	3.5	2.8	2.2
12	Vietnam	63,341	65,001	2.6	2.6	2.6
13	Germany, Federal Republic of	60,909	60,824	.6	#	.2
14	Philippines	57,036	58,279	3.0	2.7	2.4
15	Italy	57,240	57,317	.7	.3	.2
16	United Kingdom[2]	56,734	56,851	.4[b]	0	.1
17	France[3]	55,389	55,609	.8	.5	.5
18	Thailand	52,642	53,535	3.0	2.2	2.0
19	Turkey	51,550	52,850	2.4	2.3	2.5
20	Egypt, Arab Republic of	49,739	50,954	2.5	2.7	2.7
21	Iran, Islamic Republic of	45,582	47,007	3.2	3.0	2.8
22	Ethiopia	43,498	44,788	2.4	2.6	2.4
23	Korea, Republic of	41,467	42,031	1.9	1.5	1.4
24	Spain	38,699	38,866	1.1	.9	.5
25	Burma	37,670	38,410	2.2	2.0	1.9
26	Poland	37,503	37,786	.8	.9	.9
27	South Africa	32,436	33,285	3.2	2.4	2.3
28	Zaire	31,672	32,655	2.7	3.0	3.1
29	**Argentina**	31,030	31,436	1.5	1.6	1.6
30	**Colombia**	28,961	29,498	1.8	1.9	1.9
31	Canada	25,612	25,861	1.4	1.2	1.0
32	Tanzania[c]	23,049	23,884	2.8	3.4	3.5
33	Yugoslavia	23,280	23,413	.9	.8	.7
34	Sudan	22,567	23,214	2.8	2.9	2.8
35	Algeria	22,520	23,060	3.4	3.2	3.2
36	Morocco	22,466	22,968	2.4	2.4	2.5
37	Romania[d]	22,850	22,946	1.2	.7	.5
38	Kenya	21,221	22,097	3.2	4.0	4.2
39	Korea, Democratic Republic	20,862	21,330	2.8	2.6	2.4
40	**Peru**	20,210	20,730	2.9	2.3	2.6
41	**Venezuela**	17,791	18,271	3.4	2.6	2.8
42	Nepal	17,038	17,444	1.9	2.6	2.5
43	Iraq[d]	16,492	17,105	3.2	3.7	3.6
44	Germany, Democratic Republic	16,624	16,625	#	.1	.1
45	Sri Lanka	16,101	16,362	2.3	1.6	1.5
46	Malaysia	16,110	16,560	2.6	2.4	2.7
47	Australia	15,974	16,180	1.9	1.3	1.4
48	Afghanistan[f]	~	~	2.2	~	~
49	Uganda[e]	15,160	15,655	2.8	2.8	3.1
50	Czechoslovakia	15,534	15,578	.3	.5	.3
51	Netherlands[4]	14,563	14,616	1.1	.6	2.5
52	Mozambique	14,186	14,591	2.0	2.7	2.7
53	Ghana	13,163	13,599	2.6	2.7	3.4
54	**Chile**	12,327	12,537	2.2	1.7	1.8
55	Saudi Arabia	11,976	12,459	1.7	4.8	4.1
56	Syrian Arab Republic	10,846	11,248	3.3	3.5	3.6
57	Cameroon	10,548	10,927	2.0	3.2	3.3
58	Madagascar	10,551	10,894	2.7	3.0	3.3
59	Hungary	10,628	10,617	.3	.1	.1
60	**Cuba**	10,194	10,270	2.0	.8	.9

Table 600 (Continued)

WORLD POPULATION (MID–1987) AND AVERAGE ANNUAL GROWTH RATES AND RANKS, 20 LRC, 1960–87

(130 Countries with Populations of 1 Million or More)

Population Rank	Country	Population (T) 1986	1987	AA–GR % 1960–73	1973–86	1980–87
61	Portugal[5]	10,187	10,212	#	1.0	.4
62	Greece	9,966	10,002	.5	.9	.5
63	**Ecuador**	9,638	9,898	3.4	2.9	2.9
64	Belgium	9,859	9,860	.5	.1	0
65	Angola	8,999	9,243	1.3	3.0	2.6
66	Bulgaria	8,985	9,004	.7	.3	.2
67	Zimbabwe	8,705	9,001	3.3	3.3	3.7
68	Sweden	8,354	8,357	.7	.2	.1
69	Ivory Coast[f]	~	~	3.8	~	~
70	**Guatemala**	8,195	8,438	2.4	2.8	2.9
71	Yemen Arab Republic	8,191	8,430	2.4	2.8	2.5
72	Mali	7,575	7,768	2.1	2.5	2.4
73	Malawi	7,380	7,629	2.6	3.1	3.3
74	Austria	7,565	7,557	.5	0	0
75	Tunisia	7,311	7,481	2.1	2.4	2.3
76	Zambia	6,946	7,196	2.9	3.3	3.5
77	Kampuchea, Democratic	~	~	~	~	~
78	Senegal	6,770	6,969	2.1	2.8	2.9
79	Niger	6,592	6,798	2.7	3.0	3.0
80	**Bolivia**	6,611	6,796	2.6	2.7	2.9
81	**Dominican Republic**	6,568	6,716	2.9	2.4	2.9
82	Switzerland	6,504	6,501	1.3	.1	.3
83	Guinea	6,322	6,470	2.8	2.2	2.4
84	Rwanda	6,236	6,454	3.4	3.3	3.3
85	Upper Volta[f]	~	~	2.1	~	~
86	**Haiti**	6,050	6,164	1.7	1.8	1.9
87	Somalia	5,547	5,712	2.4	2.8	2.9
88	Hong Kong	5,410	5,429	3.3	2.3	1.2
89	Chad[e]	5,146	5,273	1.8	2.2	2.4
90	Denmark	5,121	5,105	.7	.1	0
91	Burundi	4,834	4,978	2.0	2.3	2.7
92	**El Salvador**	4,876	4,973	3.5	1.7	1.3
93	Finland	4,929	4,947	.3	.4	.5
94	**Honduras**	4,528	4,677	3.2	3.5	3.6
95	Israel	4,304	4,374	3.1	2.1	1.7
96	Benin	4,177	4,315	2.7	2.9	3.2
97	Norway	4,169	4,175	.8	.4	.3
98	Libya	3,908	4,057	3.7	4.3	3.9
99	**Paraguay**	3,808	3,922	2.6	3.2	3.2
100	Sierra Leone	3,752	3,845	2.2	1.9	2.4
101	Lao, People's Democratic Republic	3,684	3,774	2.4	1.6	2.1
102	Jordan[f]	3,620	3,752	3.3	3.0	3.7
103	Ireland	3,582	3,611	.5	1.0	.8
104	**Nicaragua**	3,388	3,501	2.6	3.1	3.4
105	Papua New Guinea	3,411	3,494	2.4	2.6	2.1
106	Puerto Rico	3,312	3,346	1.0	1.1	.5
107	New Zealand	3,277	3,298	1.6	.6	.9
108	Togo	3,144	3,254	2.7	2.9	3.4
109	**Uruguay**	2,982	3,014	1.3	.6	.4
110	Albania	3,022	3,087	2.8	2.0	2.1
111	Central African Republic	2,654	2,727	2.2	2.4	2.5
112	Lebanon	~	~	2.6	~	~
113	**Costa Rica**	2,640	2,710	3.1	2.8	2.9
114	Singapore	2,585	2,610	2.1	1.3	1.1
115	Liberia	2,253	2,327	3.3	3.4	3.3
116	Jamaica	2,336	2,351	1.6	1.2	1.5
117	Yemen, People's Democratic Republic of	2,205	2,276	3.1	2.3	3.2
118	**Panama**	2,227	2,272	3.1	2.3	2.2
119	Congo, People's Republic of the	1,950	2,020	2.7	3.1	2.9
120	Mongolia	1,960	2,011	2.7	2.7	2.8

Table 600 (Continued)

**WORLD POPULATION (MID–1987) AND AVERAGE ANNUAL GROWTH
RATES AND RANKS, 20 LRC, 1960–87**

(130 Countries with Populations of 1 Million or More)

Population Rank	Country	Population (T)		AA–GR %		
		1986	1987	1960–73	1973–86	1980–87
121	Mauritania	1,809	1,858	2.1	1.4	2.6
122	Kuwait	1,775	1,837	~	5.5	4.2
123	Lesotho	1,586	1,629	2.2	2.6	2.7
124	United Arab Emirates	1,403	1,456	~	7.9	5.3
125	Oman	1,294	1,345	8.1	4.8	4.5
126	Bhutan	1,313	1,345	2.3	2.0	2.1
127	Nambia	1,179	1,218	3.7	2.7	3.1
128	Trinidad and Tobago	1,199	1,217	1.7	1.6	1.5
129	Botswana	1,107	1,146	11.0	4.2	3.5
130	Mauritius	1,029	1,042	3.3	2.8	1.0
	Latin American 20-Country Average[8]	19,991	20,050	2.7	2.3	~

1. Excluding data for Puerto Rico, the Trust Territory of the Pacific Islands, and its unorganized and unincorporated territories.
2. Excluding data for its colonies, dependencies, and associated states.
3. Excluding data for its overseas departments and territories.
4. Exluding data for the overseas portion of the Netherlands realm.
5. Excluding data for its overseas administered territory.
6. Excluding data for the overseas integral ports with home rule of the Danish realm.
7. Excluding data for its overseas territory and self-governing associated states.
8. Regardless of size.

a. Includes data for Taiwan, China, which are as follows: population, mid–1979: 17,307,000; growth rate, 1970–79; 2.0%
b. Excludes Puerto Rico, the Trust Territory of the Pacific Islands, and its unorganized and unincorporated territories.
c. Mainland Tanzania.
d. GNP per capita estimated to be more than $1,726.
e. GNP per capita estimated to be less than $425.
f. Data based on 1980 population figures.

SOURCE: Adapted from the following: World Bank, *Atlas*, 1975, 1980, 1981, 1983, 1987, 1988.

Table 601

ARGENTINA POPULATION ESTIMATE AND INDEX, 1900–88[a]

Year	M	1970 = 100	Year	M	1970 = 100
1900	4.61	19	1950	17.07	72
1901	4.74	20	1951	17.48	74
1902	4.87	21	1952*	17.70	75
1903	4.98	21	1953	17.96	76
1904	5.10	22	1954	18.24	77
1905	5.29	22	1955	18.53	78
1906	5.52	23	1956	18.80	79
1907	5.82	25	1957	19.10	80
1908	6.15	26	1958	19.38	82
1909	6.43	27	1959	19.66	83
1910	6.80	29	1960	19.92	84
1911	7.07	30	1961	20.24	85
1912	7.47	31	1962	20.54	86
1913	7.84	33	1963	20.85	88
1914	8.00	34	1964	21.17	89
1915	8.15	34	1965	22.18	93
1916	8.30	35	1966	22.49	95
1917	8.45	36	1967	22.80	96
1918	8.60	36	1968	23.11	97
1919	8.75	37	1969	23.43	99
1920	8.97	38	1970	23.75	100
1921	9.22	39	1971	24.07	101
1922	9.52	40	1972	24.39	103
1923	9.89	42	1973	24.82	105
1924	10.22	43	1974	25.22	106
1925	10.50	44	1975	26.05	110
1926	10.80	45	1976	26.48	112
1927	11.13	47	1977	26.91	113
1928	11.44	48	1978	27.35	115
1929	11.75	49	1979	27.79	117
1930	12.05	51	1980	28.24	119
1931	12.29	52	1981	28.69	121
1932	12.52	53	1982	29.16	123
1933	12.73	54	1983	29.63	125
1934	12.94	54	1984	30.10	127
1935	13.15	55	1985	30.56‡	129
1936	13.37	56	1986	31.03	131
1937	13.61	57	1987	31.50	133
1938	13.84	58	1988	31.96	134
1939	14.06	59			
1940	14.17	60			
1941	14.40	62			
1942	14.64	62			
1943	14.88	63			
1944	15.13	64			
1945	15.40	65			
1946	15.65	66			
1947	15.93	67			
1948	16.27	69			
1949	16.66	70			

a. Mid-year estimates.

SOURCE: 1900-51 data from SALA-SNP, pp. 173–183; since 1952, data from IMF-IFS-Y, 1980, 1986, 1988, 1989; UN-MB, June 1987; cf. SALA, 26–600, 624, and 626.

Table 602

BOLIVIA POPULATION ESTIMATE AND INDEX, 1900–88[a]

Year	M	1970 = 100	Year	M	1970 = 100
1900	1.77	39	1950	3.01	66
1901	1.79	39	1951	3.07	67
1902	1.80	39	1952*	3.13	68
1903	1.82	40	1953	3.19	70
1904	1.84	40	1954	3.26	71
1905	1.86	41	1955	3.34	73
1906	1.88	41	1956	3.42	75
1907	1.90	41	1957	3.50	76
1908	1.91	42	1958	3.59	78
1909	1.93	42	1959	3.70	81
1910	1.95	43	1960	3.82	83
1911	1.97	43	1961	3.92	86
1912	1.98	43	1962	4.02	88
1913	2.01	44	1963	4.12	90
1914	2.03	44	1964	4.23	92
1915	2.04	45	1965	4.33	95
1916	2.06	45	1966	4.45	97
1917	2.08	45	1967	4.48‡	98
1918	2.10	46	1968	4.51‡	98
1919	2.12	46	1969	4.55‡	99
1920	2.14	47	1970	4.58‡	100
1921	2.16	47	1971	4.62‡	101
1922	2.19	48	1972	4.64‡	101
1923	2.21	48	1973	4.67‡	102
1924	2.24	49	1974	4.75‡	104
1925	2.26	49	1975*	4.89	107
1926	2.29	50	1976	5.03	110
1927	2.32	51	1977	5.16	113
1928	2.34	51	1978	5.30	116
1929	2.37	52	1979	5.45	119
1930	2.40	52	1980	5.60	122
1931	2.43	53	1981	5.76	126
1932	2.45	53	1982	5.92	129
1933	2.48	54	1983	6.08	133
1934	2.51	55	1984	6.25	136
1935	2.54	55	1985	6.43‡	140
1936	2.57	56	1986	6.55	143
1937	2.60	57	1987	6.80	148
1938	2.63	57	1988	6.99	152
1939	2.66	58			
1940	2.70	59			
1941	2.72	59			
1942	2.75	60			
1943	2.79	61			
1944	2.82	62			
1945	2.85	62			
1946	2.88	63			
1947	2.92	64			
1948	2.95	64			
1949	2.96	65			

a. Mid-year estimates.

SOURCE: 1900-51 data from SALA-SNP, pp. 173–183; since 1952, data from IMF-IFS-Y, 1980, 1986, 1988, 1989; UN-MB, June 1987; cf. SALA, 26–600, 624, and 626.

Table 603

BRAZIL POPULATION ESTIMATE AND INDEX, 1900-88[a]

Year	M	1970 = 100	Year	M	1970 = 100
1900	17.98	19	1950	52.18	56
1901	18.39	20	1951	53.68	58
1902	18.78	22	1952	55.10	60
1903	19.18	21	1953	56.74	61
1904	19.58	21	1954	58.44	63
1905	20.00	22	1955	60.18	65
1906	20.43	22	1956	61.98	67
1907	20.86	23	1957	63.83	69
1908	21.30	23	1958	65.74	71
1909	21.75	24	1959	67.70	73
1910	22.22	24	1960*	69.72	75
1911	22.69	25	1961	71.94	78
1912	23.17	25	1962	74.17	80
1913	23.66	26	1963	76.53	83
1914	24.16	26	1964	78.73	85
1915	24.67	27	1965	81.01	88
1916	25.20	27	1966	82.93	90
1917	25.73	28	1967	85.24	92
1918	26.28	28	1968	87.62	95
1919	26.84	29	1969	90.07	97
1920	27.40	30	1970	92.52	100
1921	27.97	30	1971	95.17	103
1922	28.54	31	1972	97.85	106
1923	29.13	31	1973	99.92	108
1924	29.72	32	1974	102.40	111
1925	30.33	33	1975	104.94	113
1926	30.95	33	1976	107.54	116
1927	31.59	34	1977	110.21	119
1928	32.23	35	1978	112.94	122
1929	32.90	36	1979*	115.74	125
1930	33.57	36	1980	121.27	131
1931	34.26	37	1981	124.02	134
1932	34.96	38	1982	126.81	137
1933	35.67	39	1983	129.66	140
1934	36.40	39	1984	132.58	143
1935	37.15	40	1985	135.56[‡]	146
1936	37.91	41	1986	138.49	150
1937	38.69	42	1987	141.45	153
1938	39.48	43	1988	144.43	156
1939	40.29	44			
1940	41.11	44			
1941	42.07	45			
1942	43.06	47			
1943	43.99	48			
1944	44.84	48			
1945	45.86	50			
1946	46.97	51			
1947	48.16	52			
1948	49.42	53			
1949	50.76	55			

a. Mid-year estimates.

SOURCE: 1900-51 data from SALA-SNP, pp. 173-183; since 1952, data from IMF-IFS-Y, 1980, 1986, 1988, 1989; UN-MB, June 1987; cf. SALA, 26–600, 624 and 626.

Table 604

CHILE POPULATION ESTIMATE AND INDEX, 1900–88[a]

Year	M	1970 = 100	Year	M	1970 = 100
1900	2.96	32	1950	6.07	65
1901	2.99	32	1951	6.21	65
1902	3.03	32	1952*	6.30*	67
1903	3.07	33	1953	6.46	69
1904	3.10	33	1954	6.62	71
1905	3.14	34	1955	6.79	72
1906	3.18	34	1956	6.96	74
1907	3.21	34	1957	7.14	76
1908	3.25	35	1958	7.32	78
1909	3.29	35	1959	7.49	80
1910	3.34	36	1960	7.58	81
1911	3.38	36	1961	7.76	83
1912	3.42	36	1962	7.95	85
1913	3.47	37	1963	8.14	87
1914	3.51	37	1964	8.33	89
1915	3.55	38	1965	8.51	91
1916	3.60	38	1966	8.68	93
1917	3.64	39	1967	8.85	94
1918	3.69	39	1968	9.03	96
1919	3.74	40	1969	9.20	98
1920	3.79	40	1970	9.37	100
1921	3.85	41	1971	9.53	102
1922	3.91	42	1972	9.70	104
1923	3.96	42	1973	9.86	105
1924	4.02	43	1974	10.03	107
1925	4.07	43	1975	10.20	109
1926	4.13	44	1976	10.37	111
1927	4.19	45	1977	10.55	113
1928	4.25	45	1978	10.73	115
1929	4.31	46	1979	10.92	117
1930	4.37	47	1980	11.10	118
1931	4.43	47	1981	11.29	120
1932	4.50	48	1982	11.49	123
1933	4.56	49	1983	11.68	125
1934	4.63	49	1984	11.88	127
1935	4.70	50	1985	12.07[‡]	129
1936	4.77	51	1986	12.33	132
1937	4.84	52	1987	12.54	134
1938	4.91	52	1988	12.75	136
1939	4.99	53			
1940	5.06	54			
1941	5.15	55			
1942	5.24	56			
1943	5.34	57			
1944	5.44	58			
1945	5.54	59			
1946	5.64	60			
1947	5.75	61			
1948	5.85	62			
1949	5.96	64			

a. Mid-year estimates.

SOURCE: 1900-51 data from SALA-SNP, pp. 173-183; since 1952, data from IMF-IFS-Y, 1980, 1986, 1988, 1989; UN-MB, June 1987; cf. SALA, 26–600, 624, and 626.

Table 605

COLOMBIA POPULATION ESTIMATE AND INDEX, 1900–88[a]

Year	M	1970 = 100	Year	M	1970 = 100
1900	3.89	19	1950	11.33	56
1901	3.94	19	1951	11.62	57
1902	3.99	19	1952*	11.81	58
1903	4.04	20	1953	12.07	59
1904	4.09	20	1954	12.34	61
1905	4.14	20	1955	12.97	64
1906	4.28	21	1956	13.59	67
1907	4.41	21	1957	14.03	69
1908	4.54	22	1958	14.48	71
1909	4.67	23	1959	14.94	73
1910	4.81	23	1960	15.42	76
1911	4.94	24	1961	15.91	78
1912	5.07	25	1962	16.42	80
1913	5.19	25	1963	16.94	83
1914	5.32	26	1964	17.48	86
1915	5.45	27	1965	18.04	88
1916	5.58	27	1966	18.47	90
1917	5.72	28	1967	18.96	93
1918	5.86	29	1968	19.46	95
1919	6.03	29	1969	19.98	98
1920	6.09	30	1970	20.53	100
1921	6.21	30	1971	21.09	103
1922	6.37	31	1972	21.67	106
1923	6.46	31	1973	22.34	109
1924	6.59	32	1974	22.98	112
1925	6.72	33	1975	23.64	115
1926	6.86	33	1976	24.33	119
1927	7.00	34	1977	25.05	122
1928	7.14	35	1978	25.64	125
1929	7.28	35	1979	26.36	128
1930	7.43	36	1980	27.09	132
1931	7.57	37	1981	26.73*	130
1932	7.73	38	1982	27.19‡	132
1933	7.88	38	1983	27.52‡	134
1934	8.03	39	1984	28.22‡	137
1935	8.20	40	1985	28.62‡	139
1936	8.36	41	1986	29.19	142
1937	8.53	42	1987	29.73	145
1938	8.70	42	1988	30.24	147
1939	8.90	43			
1940	9.10	44			
1941	9.32	45			
1942	9.54	47			
1943	9.77	48			
1944	10.02	49			
1945	10.27	50			
1946	10.53	52			
1947	10.80	53			
1948*	10.85	53			
1949	11.09	54			

a. Mid-year estimates.

SOURCE: 1900-51 data from SALA-SNP, pp. 173-183; since 1952, data from IMF-IFS-Y, 1980, 1986, 1988, 1989; UN-MB, June 1987; cf. SALA, 26–600, 624, and 626.

Table 606

COSTA RICA POPULATION ESTIMATE AND INDEX, 1900–88[a]

Year	M	1970 = 100	Year	M	1970 = 100
1900	.31	18	1950	.80	47
1901	.31	18	1951	.83	48
1902	.32	19	1952*	.92	54
1903	.32	19	1953	.95	55
1904	.33	19	1954	.99	58
1905	.34	20	1955	1.03	60
1906	.34	20	1956	1.07	62
1907	.35	21	1957	1.11	65
1908	.35	21	1958	1.15	67
1909	.36	21	1959	1.19	69
1910	.36	21	1960	1.25	75
1911	.37	22	1961	1.30	76
1912	.38	22	1962	1.35	78
1913	.38	22	1963	1.39	81
1914	.39	23	1964	1.44	84
1915	.39	23	1965	1.49	87
1916	.40	24	1966	1.54	89
1917	.40	24	1967	1.59	92
1918	.41	24	1968	1.63	95
1919	.42	25	1969	1.69	98
1920	.42	25	1970	1.73	100
1921	.43	25	1971	1.80	104
1922	.43	25	1972	1.84	107
1923	.44	26	1973	1.87	108
1924	.45	26	1974	1.92	111
1925	.46	27	1975	1.96	113
1926	.47	28	1976	2.01	116
1927	.47	28	1977	2.07	120
1928	.48	28	1978	2.12	123
1929	.49	29	1979	2.17	125
1930	.50	29	1980	2.25	130
1931	.51	30	1981	2.27	131
1932	.52	30	1982	2.32	134
1933	.53	31	1983	2.38	138
1934	.54	32	1984*	2.42	140
1935	.55	32	1985	2.49	144
1936	.56	33	1986	2.67*	154
1937	.58	34	1987	2.78	161
1938	.59	35	1988	~	~
1939	.61	36			
1940	.62	36			
1941	.63	36			
1942	.65	37			
1943	.66	39			
1944	.68	40			
1945	.70	41			
1946	.71	41			
1947	.73	43			
1948	.75	44			
1949	.77	45			

a. Mid-year estimates.

SOURCE: 1900-51 data from SALA-SNP, pp. 173-183; since 1952, data from IMF-IFS-Y, 1980, 1986, 1988, 1989; UN-MB, June 1987; cf. SALA, 26–600, 624 and 626.

Table 607

CUBA POPULATION ESTIMATE AND INDEX, 1900–88[a]

Year	M	1970 = 100	Year	M	1970 = 100
1900	1.60	19	1950	5.51	65
1901	1.68	20	1951	5.62	66
1902	1.76	21	1952	5.73	67
1903	1.84	22	1953*	6.04	71
1904	1.88	22	1954	6.16	72
1905	1.93	23	1955	6.28	73
1906	1.98	24	1956	6.41	75
1907	2.03	24	1957	6.54	76
1908	2.09	25	1958	6.76	79
1909	2.15	20	1959	6.90	81
1910	2.22	20	1960	7.03	83
1911	2.29	27	1961	7.13	84
1912	2.36	40	1962	7.25	85
1913	2.41	29	1963	7.41	87
1914	2.51	30	1964	7.61	89
1915	2.59	31	1965	7.81	92
1916	2.66	32	1966	7.99	94
1917	2.75	33	1967	8.14	96
1918	2.83	45	1968	8.28	97
1919	2.91	34	1969	8.42	99
1920	3.00	35	1970	8.55	100
1921	3.08	36	1971	8.69	102
1922	3.17	37	1972	8.86	104
1923	3.26	39	1973	9.04	106
1924	3.35	40	1974	9.19	108
1925	3.43	41	1975*	8.55	100
1926	3.52	42	1976	9.43	110
1927	3.61	43	1977	9.55	112
1928	3.51	41	1978	9.64	113
1929	3.58	42	1979	9.72	114
1930	3.65	43	1980	9.72	114
1931	3.96	47	1981	9.72	114
1932	3.96	47	1982	9.80	115
1933	3.96	47	1983	9.90	116
1934	4.04	48	1984	9.99	117
1935	4.07	48	1985	10.10	118
1936	4.11	48	1986	10.19	119
1937	4.17	49	1987	10.29	120
1938	4.23	50	1988	10.38	121
1939	4.25	50			
1940	4.29	51			
1941	4.33	51			
1942	4.37	52			
1943	4.78	56			
1944	4.85	57			
1945	4.93	58			
1946	5.04	59			
1947	5.15	61			
1948	5.27	62			
1949	5.39	63			

a. Mid-year estimates.

SOURCE: 1900-52 data from SALA–SNP, p. 176; 1953-74 data from Cuba, JUCEPLAN, AE, 1972, 1974, and 1975; since 1975, data from UN-MB, March 1985 , June 1987, and October 1988.

Table 608

DOMINICAN REPUBLIC POPULATION ESTIMATE AND INDEX, 1900–88[a]

Year	M	1970 = 100	Year	M	1970 = 100
1900	.60	15	1950	2.24	55
1901	.61	15	1951	2.31	57
1902	.63	16	1952*	2.29	56
1903	.64	16	1953	2.37	58
1904	.66	17	1954	2.45	60
1905	.67	17	1955	2.54	63
1906	.68	17	1956	2.63	65
1907	.70	18	1957	2.73	67
1908	.71	18	1958	2.83	70
1909	.73	18	1959	2.93	72
1910	.74	19	1960	3.04	75
1911	.75	19	1961	3.12	77
1912	.77	19	1962	3.21	79
1913	.78	20	1963	3.31	82
1914	.80	20	1964	3.41	84
1915	.81	20	1965	3.51	87
1916	.82	21	1966	3.62	90
1917	.84	21	1967	3.72	92
1918	.85	21	1968	3.83	95
1919	.87	22	1969	3.95	98
1920	.88	22	1970	4.06	100
1921	.91	23	1971	4.18	103
1922	.95	24	1972	4.30	106
1923	.98	25	1973	4.43	110
1924	1.02	26	1974	4.56	113
1925	1.05	26	1975	4.70	116
1926	1.09	27	1976	4.89	120
1927	1.13	28	1977	5.03	124
1928	1.17	29	1978	5.17	127
1929	1.21	30	1979	5.30	131
1930	1.26	31	1980	5.44	134
1931	1.30	32	1981	5.58	137
1932	1.35	34	1982	5.74	141
1933	1.39	35	1983	5.96	147
1934	1.44	36	1984	6.10	150
1935	1.48	37	1985	6.24	154
1936	1.52	38	1986	6.42	158
1937	1.56	39	1987	6.72	166
1938	1.60	40	1988	6.87	169
1939	1.63	41			
1940	1.76	44			
1941	1.80	45			
1942	1.84	46			
1943	1.89	47			
1944	1.93	48			
1945	1.98	49			
1946	2.03	50			
1947	2.08	52			
1948	2.13	53			
1949	2.19	54			

a. Mid-year estimates.

SOURCE: 1900-51 data from SALA-SNP, pp. 173-183; since 1952, data from IMF-IFS-Y, 1980, 1986, 1988, 1989; UN-MB, June 1987; cf. SALA, 26–600, 624, and 626.

Table 609

ECUADOR POPULATION ESTIMATE AND INDEX, 1900–88[a]

Year	M	1970 = 100	Year	M	1970 = 100
1900	1.30	22	1950	3.20	54
1901	1.31	22	1951	3.25	55
1902	1.32	22	1952*	3.43	58
1903	1.34	22	1953	3.53	59
1904	1.35	23	1954	3.64	61
1905	1.36	23	1955	3.75	63
1906	1.37	23	1956	3.87	65
1907	1.38	23	1957	3.98	67
1908	1.40	23	1958	4.11	69
1909	1.41	24	1959	4.23	71
1910	1.42	24	1960	4.36	73
1911	1.43	24	1961	4.50	76
1912	1.45	24	1962*	4.65	78
1913	1.46	24	1963	4.78	80
1914	1.47	25	1964	4.93	83
1915	1.48	25	1965	5.07	85
1916	1.49	25	1966	5.22	88
1917	1.51	25	1967	5.40	91
1918	1.52	26	1968	5.58	94
1919	1.53	26	1969	5.77	97
1920	1.54	26	1970	5.96	100
1921	1.57	26	1971	6.17	104
1922	1.61	27	1972	6.38	107
1923	1.65	28	1973	6.60	111
1924	1.69	28	1974	6.83	115
1925	1.72	29	1975	7.03‡	118
1926	1.76	30	1976	7.24	121
1927	1.80	30	1977	7.45	125
1928	1.84	31	1978	7.67	129
1929	1.90	32	1979	7.89	132
1930	1.94	33	1980	8.12	136
1931	2.00	34	1981	8.36	140
1932	2.05	34	1982	8.61	144
1933	2.10	35	1983	8.86	149
1934	2.14	36	1984	9.11	153
1935	2.20	37	1985	9.38	157
1936	2.25	38	1986	9.65	162
1937	2.30	39	1987	9.92	166
1938	2.36	40	1988	10.20	171
1939	2.41	40			
1940	2.47	41			
1941	2.52	42			
1942	2.58	43			
1943	2.64	44			
1944	2.71	45			
1945	2.78	47			
1946	2.85	48			
1947	2.94	49			
1948	3.02	51			
1949	3.10	52			

a. Mid-year estimates.

SOURCE: 1900-51 data from SALA-SNP, pp. 173-183; since 1952, data from IMF-IFS-Y, 1980, 1986, 1988, 1989; UN-MB, June 1987; cf. SALA, 26–600, 624, and 626.

Table 610

EL SALVADOR POPULATION ESTIMATE AND INDEX, 1900–88[a]

Year	M	1970 = 100	Year	M	1970 = 100
1900	.80	24	1950	1.86	54
1901	.82	24	1951	1.90	56
1902	.84	25	1952*	1.97*	58
1903	.86	25	1953	2.02	59
1904	.87	26	1954	2.08	61
1905	.89	26	1955	2.14	63
1906	.91	27	1956	2.20	64
1907	.93	27	1957	2.26	66
1908	.95	28	1958	2.32	68
1909	.97	29	1959	2.39	70
1910	.99	29	1960	2.45	72
1911	1.00	29	1961*	2.51	73
1912	1.02	30	1962†	2.63	77
1913	1.04	31	1963†	2.72	79
1914	1.06	31	1964†	2.82	82
1915	1.07	32	1965†	2.93	86
1916	1.10	32	1966†	3.04	89
1917	1.11	33	1967†	3.15	92
1918	1.13	33	1968†	3.27	95
1919	1.15	34	1969†	3.36	98
1920	1.17	34	1970†	3.44	100
1921	1.19	35	1971†	3.55	104
1922	1.22	36	1972*	3.67	107
1923	1.24	36	1973	3.77	107
1924	1.27	37	1974	3.89	113
1925	1.30	38	1975	4.01	117
1926	1.33	39	1976	4.12	120
1927	1.35	40	1977	4.26	124
1928	1.39	41	1978	4.35	126
1929	1.41	41	1979	4.44	129
1930	1.44	42	1980	4.75	138
1931	1.46	43	1981	4.87	142
1932	1.47	43	1982	5.00	145
1933	1.49	44	1983	5.23‡	152
1934	1.51	44	1984	4.78	140
1935	1.53	45	1985	4.82	140
1936	1.55	45	1986	4.91	143
1937	1.57	46	1987	5.01	146
1938	1.59	47	1988	5.11	148
1939	1.61	47			
1940	1.63	48			
1941	1.65	48			
1942	1.68	48			
1943	1.69	50			
1944	1.72	50			
1945	1.74	51			
1946	1.76	52			
1947	1.78	52			
1948	1.81	53			
1949	1.84	54			

a. Mid-year estimates.

SOURCE: 1900-51 data from SALA-SNP, pp. 173-183; since 1952, data from IMF-IFS-Y, 1980, 1986, 1988, 1989; UN-MB, June 1987; cf. SALA, 26–600, 624, and 626.

Table 611

GUATEMALA POPULATION ESTIMATE AND INDEX, 1900–88[a]

Year	M	1970 = 100	Year	M	1970 = 100
1900	.89	19	1950*	2.81	58
1901	.91	19	1951	2.89	60
1902	.94	20	1952	2.98	61
1903	.96	21	1953	3.07	63
1904	.99	21	1954	3.18	66
1905	1.01	21	1955	3.29	68
1906	1.03	22	1956	3.39	70
1907	1.05	22	1957	3.49	72
1908	1.06	22	1958	3.61	74
1909	1.08	23	1959	3.72	77
1910	1.10	23	1960	3.83	79
1911	1.12	23	1961	3.95	81
1912	1.14	24	1962	4.06	84
1913	1.17	24	1963	4.19	86
1914	1.18	25	1964*	4.31	89
1915	1.20	25	1965†	4.41	91
1916	1.21	25	1966†	4.50	93
1917	1.23	26	1967†	4.70	95
1918	1.24	26	1968†	4.84	97
1919	1.26	26	1969	5.02	99
1920	1.27	26	1970	5.27	100
1921	1.32	27	1971	5.42	102
1922	1.37	28	1972	5.58	106
1923	1.42	29	1973	5.74	109
1924	1.47	31	1974*	6.05	115
1925	1.51	31	1975	6.24	118
1926	1.56	32	1976	6.43	122
1927	1.60	33	1977	6.63	126
1928	1.66	34	1978	6.84	130
1929	1.71	35	1979	7.05	134
1930	1.76	36	1980	7.26	138
1931	1.81	37	1981	7.48	142
1932	1.86	39	1982	7.70	146
1933	1.91	40	1983	7.46*	142
1934	1.94	40	1984	7.60	144
1935	1.98	40	1985	7.96	151
1936	2.02	42	1986	8.19	155
1937	2.07	43	1987	8.44	160
1938	2.11	44	1988	8.68	165
1939	2.15	44			
1940	2.20	45			
1941	2.25	47			
1942	2.30	47			
1943	2.34	48			
1944	2.39	49			
1945	2.44	50			
1946	2.50	52			
1947	2.57	53			
1948	2.64	54			
1949	2.72	56			

a. Mid-year estimates.

SOURCE: 1900-51 data from SALA-SNP, pp. 173-183; since 1952, data from IMF-IFS-Y, 1980, 1986, 1988, 1989; UN-MB, June 1987; cf. SALA, 26–600, 624, and 626.

Table 612

HAITI POPULATION ESTIMATE AND INDEX, 1900–88[a]

Year	M	1970 = 100	Year	M	1970 = 100
1900	1.25	30	1950	3.39	80
1901	1.29	31	1951	3.44	82
1902	1.34	32	1952	3.61	83
1903	1.38	33	1953	3.58	84
1904	1.43	34	1954	3.65	86
1905	1.47	35	1955	3.72	88
1906	1.51	36	1956	3.80	90
1907	1.56	37	1957*,[a]	3.75	88
1908	1.56	37	1958[a]	3.70	87
1909	1.64	39	1959[a]	3.67	87
1910	1.69	40	1960*	3.62	85
1911	1.73	41	1961	3.68	87
1912	1.77	42	1962	3.74	88
1913	1.82	43	1963	3.79	89
1914	1.86	44	1964	3.85	91
1915	1.91	45	1965	3.91	92
1916	1.95	46	1966	3.97	94
1917	1.99	47	1967	4.03	95
1918	2.04	49	1968	4.10	97
1919	2.08	49	1969	4.16	99
1920	2.12	50	1970	4.24	100
1921	2.15	51	1971	4.31	103
1922	2.18	52	1972	4.37	103
1923	2.21	53	1973	4.44	105
1924	2.23	53	1974	4.51	107
1925	2.26	54	1975	4.58	108
1926	2.29	54	1976	4.67	110
1927	2.33	55	1977	4.75	112
1928	2.36	56	1978	4.83	114
1929	2.39	57	1979	4.92	116
1930	2.42	58	1980	5.01	118
1931	2.46	58	1981	5.10	120
1932	2.50	59	1982	5.05*	119
1933	2.54	60	1983	5.12‡	121
1934	2.57	61	1984	5.18‡	122
1935	2.61	62	1985	5.27‡	124
1936	2.65	63	1986	5.36	126
1937	2.70	64	1987	5.44	128
1938	2.74	65	1988	5.52	130
1939	2.79	66			
1940	2.83	67			
1941	2.88	68			
1942	2.94	70			
1943	2.98	71			
1944	3.03	72			
1945	3.09	73			
1946	3.14	74			
1947	3.20	76			
1948	3.26	77			
1949	3.32	79			

a. Mid-year estimates.

SOURCE: 1900-56 data from SALA-SNP, p. 179; 157–59, estimated by SALA with assumed impact of Duvalier's rise to power; since 1960, data from IMF-IFS-Y, 1986, 1988, 1989, and UN-MB, June 1987; cf. SALA, 26–600, 624, and 626.

Table 613

HONDURAS POPULATION ESTIMATE AND INDEX, 1900-88[a]

Year	M	1970 = 100	Year	M	1970 = 100
1900	.42	16	1950	1.43	54
1901	.44	17	1951	1.47	56
1902	.45	17	1952*	1.53*	58
1903	.47	18	1953	1.57	59
1904	.48	18	1954	1.62	61
1905	.50	19	1955	1.65	63
1906	.51	19	1956	1.68	64
1907	.52	20	1957	1.71	65
1908	.53	20	1958	1.75	66
1909	.54	20	1959	1.80	68
1910	.55	21	1960	1.85	70
1911	.56	21	1961	1.91	72
1912	.57	22	1962	1.97	75
1913	.58	22	1963	2.04	77
1914	.59	22	1964	2.11	80
1915	.60	23	1965	2.18	83
1916	.61	23	1966	2.26	86
1917	.63	24	1967	2.28	86
1918	.66	25	1968	2.31	88
1919	.69	26	1969	2.45	93
1920	.72	27	1970	2.64	100
1921	.74	28	1971	2.72	103
1922	.77	29	1972	2.81	106
1923	.80	30	1973	2.90	110
1924	.82	31	1974	2.99	113
1925	.85	32	1975	3.09	117
1926	.88	33	1976	3.20	121
1927	.89	34	1977	3.32	126
1928	.91	34	1978	3.44	130
1929	.93	35	1979	3.56	135
1930	.95	36	1980	3.69	140
1931	.97	37	1981	3.83	145
1932	.99	38	1982	3.96	150
1933	1.01	38	1983	4.09	155
1934	1.02	39	1984	4.23	160
1935	1.04	39	1985	4.37	165
1936	1.06	40	1986	4.51	171
1937	1.08	41	1987	4.66	177
1938	1.10	42	1988	4.80	182
1939	1.12	42			
1940	1.15	44			
1941	1.17	44			
1942	1.20	45			
1943	1.21	46			
1944	1.24	47			
1945	1.26	48			
1946	1.29	49			
1947	1.32	50			
1948	1.35	51			
1949	1.39	53			

a. Mid-year estimates.

SOURCE: 1900-51 data from SALA-SNP, pp. 173-183; since 1952, data from IMF-IFS-Y, 1980, 1986, 1988, 1989; UN-MB, June 1987; cf. SALA, 26–600, 624 and 626.

Table 614

MEXICO POPULATION ESTIMATE AND INDEX, 1900-88[a]

Year	M	1970 = 100	Year	M	1970 = 100
1900	13.61	27	1950	25.79	51
1901	13.76	27	1951	25.59	50
1902	13.91	27	1952	27.85*	55
1903	14.07	28	1953	28.70	57
1904	14.21	28	1954	29.61	58
1905	14.36	28	1955	30.56	60
1906	14.52	29	1956	31.56	62
1907	14.68	29	1957	32.61	64
1908	14.84	29	1958	33.70	66
1909	15.00	30	1959	34.86	69
1910	15.16	30	1960	36.05	71
1911	15.33	30	1961	37.27	74
1912	15.51	31	1962	38.54	76
1913	15.37	30	1963	39.87	79
1914	15.09	30	1964	41.25	81
1915	14.64	29	1965	42.69	84
1916	14.03	28	1966	44.14	87
1917	13.90	27	1967	45.67	90
1918	14.00	28	1968	47.27	93
1919	14.15	28	1969	48.93	97
1920	14.15	28	1970	50.69	100
1921	14.34	28	1971	52.45	103
1922	14.44	28	1972	54.27	107
1923	14.69	29	1973	56.16	111
1924	14.95	29	1974	58.12	115
1925	15.20	30	1975	60.15	119
1926	15.47	31	1976	62.33	123
1927	15.74	31	1977	64.59	127
1928	16.01	32	1978*	65.43	129
1929	16.93	33	1979	67.42	133
1930	16.55	33	1980	69.35	137
1931	16.88	33	1981	71.19	140
1932	17.17	34	1982	73.01	144
1933	17.47	34	1983	75.10‡	148
1934	17.78	35	1984	76.79‡	151
1935	18.09	36	1985	78.52‡	155
1936	18.41	36	1986	79.56	157
1937	18.76	37	1987	81.16	160
1938	19.07	38	1988	82.73	163
1939	19.41	38			
1940	19.65	39			
1941	20.21	40			
1942	20.66	41			
1943	21.17	42			
1944	21.67	43			
1945	22.23	44			
1946	22.78	45			
1947	23.44	46			
1948	24.13	48			
1949	24.83	49			

a. Mid-year estimates.

SOURCE: 1900-51 data from SALA-SNP, pp. 173-183; since 1952, data from IMF-IFS-Y, 1980, 1986, 1988, 1989; UN-MB, June 1987; cf. SALA, 26–600, 624, and 626.

Table 615

NICARAGUA POPULATION ESTIMATE AND INDEX, 1900–88[a]

Year	M	1970 = 100	Year	M	1970 = 100
1900	.42	23	1950	1.06	58
1901	.43	24	1951	1.09	60
1902	.45	25	1952*	1.12*	62
1903	.46	26	1953	1.15	63
1904	.48	27	1954	1.18	65
1905	.49	27	1955	1.22	67
1906	.51	28	1956	1.26	69
1907	.52	29	1957	1.29	71
1908	.52	29	1958	1.33	73
1909	.53	29	1959	1.37	75
1910	.54	30	1960	1.41	77
1911	.55	30	1961	1.45	80
1912	.56	31	1962	1.50	82
1913	.57	32	1963	1.54	85
1914	.58	32	1964	1.58	87
1915	.59	33	1965	1.62	89
1916	.60	33	1966	1.66	91
1917	.61	34	1967	1.70	93
1918	.62	34	1968	1.74	95
1919	.63	35	1969	1.79	98
1920	.64	35	1970	1.83	100
1921	.64	35	1971	1.89	104
1922	.65	36	1972	1.95	107
1923	.65	36	1973	2.01	110
1924	66	36	1974	2.08	114
1925	.66	36	1975	2.16	118
1926	.67	37	1976	2.24	122
1927	.67	37	1977	2.32	127
1928	.67	37	1978	2.41	132
1929	.68	38	1979	2.54	144
1930	.68	38	1980	2.73	149
1931	.69	38	1981	2.86	156
1932	.69	38	1982	2.96	162
1933	.70	39	1983	3.06	167
1934	.71	39	1984	3.16‡	173
1935	.73	40	1985	3.27‡	177
1936	.75	41	1986	3.38	185
1937	.77	42	1987	3.50	191
1938	.78	43	1988	~	~
1939	.81	45			
1940	.83	46			
1941	.84	46			
1942	.86	47			
1943	.88	48			
1944	.90	50			
1945	.92	51			
1946	.95	52			
1947	.98	54			
1948	1.00	55			
1949	1.03	57			

a. Mid-year estimates.

SOURCE: 1900-51 data from SALA-SNP, pp. 173-183; since 1952, data from IMF-IFS-Y, 1980, 1986, 1988, 1989; UN-MB, June 1987; cf. SALA, 26–600, 624, and 626.

Table 616

PANAMA POPULATION ESTIMATE AND INDEX, 1900–88[a]

Year	M	1970 = 100	Year	M	1970 = 100
1900	.26	19	1950	.80	56
1901	.27	19	1951	.82	58
1902	.28	20	1952*	.84*	59
1903	.28	20	1953	.87	61
1904	.29	21	1954	.89	63
1905	.30	21	1955	.92	65
1906	.30	21	1956	.95	67
1907	.31	22	1957	.97	68
1908	.32	23	1958	1.00	70
1909	.33	23	1959	1.03	72
1910	.33	23	1960	1.06	75
1911	.34	24	1961	1.09	77
1912	.35	25	1962	1.13	79
1913	.36	26	1963	1.17	82
1914	.38	27	1964	1.20	84
1915	.39	28	1965	1.24	87
1916	.40	28	1966	1.27	89
1917	.41	29	1967	1.31	92
1918	.43	30	1968	1.35	95
1919	.44	31	1969	1.39	98
1920	.45	32	1970	1.43	100
1921	.45	32	1971	1.48	104
1922	.45	32	1972	1.52	107
1923	.45	32	1973	1.57	110
1924	.46	33	1974	1.62	114
1925	.46	33	1975	1.68	117
1926	.46	33	1976	1.72	120
1927	.46	33	1977	1.77	124
1928	.46	33	1978	1.81	127
1929	.47	33	1979	1.85	129
1930	.47	33	1980	1.90	133
1931	.49	35	1981	1.94	136
1932	.50	35	1982	2.04	143
1933	.52	37	1983	2.09	146
1934	.53	37	1984	2.13	149
1935	.55	39	1985	2.18	152
1936	.56	40	1986	2.23	156
1937	.58	41	1987	2.27	159
1938	.59	42	1988	2.32	162
1939	.61	43			
1940	.62	44			
1941	.64	45			
1942	.65	46			
1943	.67	47			
1944	.69	49			
1945	.70	49			
1946	.72	51			
1947	.74	52			
1948	.76	54			
1949	.78	55			

a. Mid-year estimates.

SOURCE: 1900-51 data from SALA-SNP, pp. 173-183; since 1952, data from IMF-IFS-Y, 1980, 1986, 1988, 1989; UN-MB, June 1987; cf. SALA, 26–600, 624, and 626.

Table 617

PARAGUAY POPULATION ESTIMATE AND INDEX, 1900-88[a]

Year	M	1970 = 100	Year	M	1970 = 100
1900	.49	22	1950	1.40	61
1901	.51	23	1951	1.43	63
1902	.52	23	1952*	1.46	64
1903	.54	24	1953	1.50	66
1904	.56	25	1954	1.53	67
1905	.57	25	1955	1.57	69
1906	.58	26	1956	1.61	70
1907	.59	26	1957	1.68‡	73
1908	.60	26	1958	1.68‡	73
1909	.61	27	1959	1.71‡	74
1910	.62	27	1960	1.75	76
1911	.63	28	1961	1.80	78
1912	.64	28	1962	1.85	80
1913	.65	29	1963	1.91	83
1914	.66	29	1964	1.97	86
1915	.66	29	1965	2.03	88
1916	.67	30	1966	2.07	90
1917	.68	30	1967	2.13	93
1918	.69	30	1968	2.18	95
1919	.69	30	1969	2.24	97
1920	.70	31	1970	2.30	100
1921	.72	32	1971	2.36	103
1922	.73	32	1972	2.43	106
1923	.75	33	1973*	2.50	109
1924	.77	34	1974	2.57	112
1925	.79	35	1975	2.69	117
1926	.80	35	1976	2.78	121
1927	.82	36	1977	2.87	125
1928	.84	37	1978	2.97	129
1929	.86	38	1979	3.07	133
1930	.88	39	1980	3.17	138
1931	.90	40	1981	3.27	142
1932	.92	40	1982	3.37	147
1933	.94	41	1983	3.47	151
1934	.97	43	1984	3.28*	143
1935	.99	43	1985	3.68*	160
1936	1.01	44	1986	3.81	166
1937	1.04	46	1987	3.92	170
1938	1.06	46	1988	4.04	176
1939	1.09	48			
1940	1.11	49			
1941	1.14	50			
1942	1.16	51			
1943	1.19	52			
1944	1.22	53			
1945	1.25	55			
1946	1.28	56			
1947	1.31	57			
1948	1.34	59			
1949	1.37	60			

a. Mid-year estimates.

SOURCE: 1900–51 data from SALA-SNP, pp. 173–183; since 1952 data from IMF-IFS-Y, 1980, 1986, 1988, 1989; UN-MB, June 1987; cf. SALA, 26–600, 624, and 626.

Table 618

PERU POPULATION ESTIMATE AND INDEX, 1900-88[a]

Year	M	1970 = 100	Year	M	1970 = 100
1900	3.00	23	1950	7.97	60
1901	3.10	23	1951	8.12	61
1902	3.20	24	1952*	8.27	62
1903	3.30	25	1953	8.43	63
1904	3.40	26	1954	8.60	64
1905	3.50	26	1955	8.79	65
1906	3.60	27	1956	9.00	67
1907	3.70	28	1957	9.23	69
1908	3.80	29	1958	9.48	70
1909	3.90	29	1959	9.75	72
1910	4.00	30	1960	10.02	74
1911	4.10	31	1961	10.32	77
1912	4.19	32	1962	10.63	79
1913	4.27	32	1963	10.96	82
1914	4.35	33	1964	11.30	84
1915	4.43	33	1965	11.65	87
1916	4.51	34	1966	12.01	90
1917	4.59	35	1967	12.31	92
1918	4.67	35	1968	12.67	94
1919	4.75	36	1969	13.05	97
1920	4.83	36	1970	13.45	100
1921	4.91	37	1971	13.59	101
1922	4.99	38	1972	13.95	104
1923	5.07	38	1973	14.35	107
1924	5.15	39	1974	15.16	113
1925	5.23	39	1975	15.47	115
1926	5.31	40	1976	15.57	116
1927	5.40	41	1977	15.99	119
1928	5.48	41	1978	16.41	122
1929	5.57	42	1979	16.85	125
1930	5.65	42	1980	17.30	129
1931	5.74	43	1981	17.75	132
1932	5.84	44	1982	18.23	136
1933	5.94	45	1983	18.71	139
1934	6.04	45	1984	19.20	143
1935	6.13	46	1985	19.70‡	146
1936	6.24	47	1986	20.21	150
1937	6.35	48	1987	20.73	154
1938	6.46	48	1988	21.26	158
1939	6.57	49			
1940	6.68	50			
1941	6.80	51			
1942	6.92	52			
1943	7.04	53			
1944	7.16	54			
1945	7.29	55			
1946	7.42	56			
1947	7.55	57			
1948	7.68	58			
1949	7.82	59			

a. Mid-year estimates.

SOURCE: 1900–51 data from SALA-SNP, pp. 173–183; since 1952, data from IMF-IFS-Y, 1980, 1986, 1988, 1989; UN-MB, June 1987; cf. SALA, 26–600, 624, and 626.

Table 619

URUGUAY POPULATION ESTIMATE AND INDEX, 1900–88[a]

Year	M	1970 = 100	Year	M	1970 = 100
1900	.96	35	1950	2.20	81
1901	.97	36	1951	2.22	81
1902	.90	33	1952*	2.26*	83
1903	1.02	37	1953	2.30	84
1904	1.04	38	1954	2.33	85
1905	1.07	39	1955	2.36	86
1906	1.10	40	1956	2.40	88
1907	1.14	42	1957	2.43	89
1908	1.05	38	1958	2.46	90
1909	1.10	40	1959	2.50	92
1910	1.13	41	1960	2.54	93
1911	1.18	43	1961	2.58	95
1912	1.23	45	1962	2.61	96
1913	1.28	47	1963	2.65	97
1914	1.32	48	1964	2.68	98
1915	1.35	49	1965	2.71	99
1916	1.38	51	1966	2.75	101
1917	1.41	52	1967	2.69‡	99
1918	1.43	52	1968	2.70‡	99
1919	1.46	53	1969	2.71‡	99
1920	1.48	54	1970	2.73‡	100
1921	1.50	55	1971	2.74‡	100
1922	1.52	56	1972	2.75‡	101
1923	1.54	56	1973	2.76‡	101
1924	1.55	57	1974	2.77‡	101
1925	1.57	58	1975*	2.83	104
1926	1.60	59	1976	2.85	104
1927	1.63	60	1977	2.86	105
1928	1.67	61	1978	2.88	105
1929	1.70	62	1979	2.89	106
1930	1.73	63	1980	2.91	107
1931	1.76	64	1981	2.93	107
1932	1.79	66	1982	2.95	108
1933	1.82	67	1983	2.97	109
1934	1.84	67	1984	2.99	109
1935	1.87	68	1985	3.01‡	110
1936	1.89	69	1986	2.98	109
1937	1.91	70	1987	3.04	111
1938	1.93	71	1988	3.06	112
1939	1.95	71			
1940	1.97	72			
1941	1.99	73			
1942	2.01	74			
1943	2.03	74			
1944	2.06	75			
1945	2.08	76			
1946	2.10	77			
1947	2.12	78			
1948	2.14	78			
1949	2.17	79			

a. Mid-year estimates.

SOURCE: 1900–51 data from SALA-PNP, pp. 173–183; since 1952, dated from IMF-IFS-Y, 1980, 1986, 1988, 1989; UN-MB, June 1987; cf. SALA, 26–600, 624, and 626.

Table 620

VENEZUELA POPULATION ESTIMATE AND INDEX, 1900–88[a]

Year	M	1970 = 100	Year	M	1970 = 100
1900	2.45	24	1950	4.97	48
1901	2.45	24	1951	5.14	50
1902	2.46	24	1952*	5.39	52
1903	2.47	24	1953	5.62	55
1904	2.47	24	1954	5.85	57
1905	2.49	24	1955	6.09	59
1906	2.51	24	1956	6.33	62
1907	2.53	25	1957	6.57	64
1908	2.55	25	1958	6.83	66
1909	2.57	25	1959	7.09	69
1910	2.60	25	1960	7.35	71
1911	2.61	25	1961	7.61	74
1912	2.64	26	1962	7.86‡	76
1913	2.66	26	1963	8.12	79
1914	2.68	26	1964	8.40	82
1915	2.71	26	1965	8.71	85
1916	2.73	27	1966	9.03	88
1917	2.75	27	1967	9.31	91
1918	2.77	27	1968	9.62	94
1919	2.79	27	1969	9.94	97
1920	2.82	27	1970	10.28	100
1921	2.84	28	1971	10.61	103
1922	2.87	28	1972	10.94	106
1923	2.90	28	1973	11.28	110
1924	2.93	29	1974	11.63	113
1925	2.95	29	1975*	12.67	123
1926	2.98	29	1976	13.12	128
1927	3.01	29	1977	13.59	132
1928	3.04	30	1978	14.07	137
1929	3.08	30	1979	14.55	142
1930	3.12	30	1980	15.02	146
1931	3.15	31	1981	15.48	151
1932	3.19	31	1982	15.94	155
1933	3.23	31	1983	16.39	159
1934	3.26	32	1984	16.85	164
1935	3.30	32	1985	17.32	168
1936	3.38	33	1986	17.79	173
1937	3.46	34	1987	18.27	178
1938	3.55	35	1988	18.75	182
1939	3.63	35			
1940	3.71	36			
1941	3.80	37			
1942	3.91	38			
1943	4.03	39			
1944	4.15	40			
1945	4.27	42			
1946	4.39	43			
1947	4.55	44			
1948	4.69	46			
1949	4.83	47			

a. Mid-year estimates.

SOURCE: 1900–51 data from SALA-PNP, pp. 173–183; since 1952, data from IMF-IFS-Y, 1980, 1986, 1988, 1989; UN-MB, June 1987; cf. SALA, 26–600, 624, and 626.

Table 621

UNITED STATES POPULATION ESTIMATE
AND INDEX, 1900-88[a]

Year	M	1970 = 100	Year	M	1970 = 100
1900	76.09	37	1950	152.27	74
1901	77.59	38	1951	154.88	76
1902	79.16	39	1952*	157.55	77
1903	80.63	39	1953	160.18	78
1904	82.17	40	1954	163.03	80
1905	83.82	41	1955	165.93	81
1906	84.44	41	1956	168.90	82
1907	87.00	42	1957	171.98	84
1908	88.71	43	1958	174.88	85
1909	90.49	44	1959	177.83	87
1910	92.40	45	1960*	180.68	88
1911	93.87	46	1961	183.69	90
1912	95.33	46	1962	186.54	91
1913	97.23	47	1963	189.24	92
1914	99.12	48	1964	191.89	94
1915	100.55	49	1965	194.30	95
1916	101.97	50	1966	196.56	96
1917	103.27	50	1967	198.71	97
1918	103.20	50	1968	200.71	98
1919	104.51	51	1969	202.68	99
1920	106.47	52	1970	205.05	100
1921	108.54	53	1971	207.66	101
1922	110.95	54	1972	209.90	102
1923	111.95	55	1973	211.91	103
1924	114.11	56	1974	213.85	104
1925	115.83	56	1975	215.97	105
1926	117.40	57	1976	218.04	106
1927	119.04	58	1977	220.24	107
1928	120.50	59	1978	222.59	109
1929	121.77	59	1979	225.06	110
1930	123.07	60	1980	227.66	111
1931	124.84	61	1981	229.81	112
1932	124.84	61	1982	232.06	113
1933	125.58	61	1983	234.50	114
1934	126.37	62	1984	236.68	115
1935	127.25	62	1985	239.28	117
1936	128.05	62	1986	241.60	118
1937	128.83	63	1987	243.77	119
1938	129.83	63	1988	246.33	120
1939	130.88	64			
1940	132.59	65			
1941	133.89	65			
1942	135.36	66			
1943	137.25	67			
1944	138.92	68			
1945	140.47	69			
1946	141.94	69			
1947	144.70	71			
1948	147.21	72			
1949	149.77	73			

a. Mid-year estimates.

SOURCE: 1900-51 data from SALA-SNP, pp. 173-183; since 1952, data from
    IMF-IFS-Y, 1980, 1986, 1988, 1989; UN-MB, June 1987; cf. SALA, 26-600,
    624, and 626.

Table 622

INDEX OF ESTIMATED POPULATION, 20 LRC, 1900-80
(1970 = 100)

	Country	1900	1910	1920	1930	1940	1950	1960	1970	1980
A.	ARGENTINA	19	29	38	51	60	72	84	100	119
B.	BOLIVIA	39	43	47	52	59	66	83	100	122
C.	BRAZIL	19	24	30	36	44	56	75	100	131
D.	CHILE	32	36	40	47	54	65	81	100	118
E.	COLOMBIA	19	23	30	36	44	56	76	100	132
F.	COSTA RICA	18	21	25	29	36	47	75	100	130
G.	CUBA	19	20	35	43	51	65	83	100	114
H.	DOMINICAN REP.	15	19	22	31	44	56	75	100	134
I.	ECUADOR	22	24	26	33	41	54	73	100	140
J.	EL SALVADOR	24	29	34	42	48	54	72	100	138
K.	GUATEMALA	19	23	26	36	45	58	79	100	149
L.	HAITI	30	40	50	58	67	80	85	100	118
M.	HONDURAS	16	21	27	36	44	54	70	100	140
N.	MEXICO	27	30	28	33	39	51	71	100	137
O.	NICARAGUA	23	30	35	38	46	58	77	100	149
P.	PANAMA	19	23	32	33	44	56	75	100	133
Q.	PARAGUAY	22	27	31	39	49	61	76	100	138
R.	PERU	23	30	36	42	50	60	74	100	129
S.	URUGUAY	35	41	54	63	72	81	93	100	107
T.	VENEZUELA	24	25	27	30	36	48	71	100	146
	LATIN AMERICA	24	28	34	40	49	60	77	100	131
	UNITED STATES	37	45	52	60	65	74	88	100	111

SOURCE: SALA, 26-601 through 621; cf. SALA, 26-600, 624, and 626.

Table 623

POPULATION ESTIMATES BY DECADE, 20 LRC, 1900-80
(M)

	Country	1900	1910	1920	1930	1940	1950	1960	1970	1980
A.	ARGENTINA	4.61	6.80	8.97	12.05	14.17	17.07	19.92	23.75	28.24
B.	BOLIVIA	1.77	1.95	2.14	2.40	2.70	3.01	3.82	4.58	5.60
C.	BRAZIL	17.98	22.22	27.40	33.57	41.11	52.18	69.72	92.52	121.27
D.	CHILE	2.96	3.34	3.79	4.37	5.06	6.07	7.58	9.37	11.10
E.	COLOMBIA	3.89	4.81	6.09	7.43	9.10	11.33	15.42	20.53	27.09
F.	COSTA RICA	.31	.36	.42	.50	.62	.80	1.25	1.73	2.25
G.	CUBA	1.60	2.22	3.00	3.65	4.29	5.51	7.03	8.55	9.72
H.	DOMINICAN REP.	.60	.74	.88	1.26	1.76	2.24	3.04	4.06	5.44
I.	ECUADOR	1.30	1.42	1.54	1.94	2.47	3.20	4.36	5.96	8.35
J.	EL SALVADOR	.80	.99	1.17	1.44	1.63	1.86	2.45	3.44	4.75
K.	GUATEMALA	.89	1.10	1.27	1.76	2.20	2.81	3.83	4.88	7.26
L.	HAITI	1.25	1.69	2.12	2.42	2.83	3.39	3.62	4.24	5.01
M.	HONDURAS	.42	.55	.72	.95	1.15	1.43	1.85	2.64	3.69
N.	MEXICO	13.61	15.16	14.15	16.55	19.65	25.79	36.05	50.69	69.35
O.	NICARAGUA	.42	.54	.64	.68	.83	1.06	1.41	1.83	2.73
P.	PANAMA	.26	.33	.45	.47	.62	.80	1.06	1.43	1.90
Q.	PARAGUAY	.49	.62	.70	.88	1.11	1.40	1.75	2.30	3.17
R.	PERU	3.00	4.00	4.83	5.65	6.68	7.97	10.02	13.45	17.30
S.	URUGUAY	.96	1.13	1.48	1.73	1.97	2.20	2.54	2.73	2.91
T.	VENEZUELA	2.45	2.60	2.82	3.12	3.71	4.97	7.35	10.28	15.02
	LATIN AMERICA	59.56	72.56	84.58	102.82	123.66	155.09	204.07	268.96	352.15
	UNITED STATES	76.09	92.40	106.47	123.07	132.59	152.27	180.68	205.05	227.66

SOURCE: SALA, 26-601 through 621; cf. SALA, 26-600, 624, and 626.

Table 624

CELADE POPULATION ESTIMATES AND PROJECTIONS BY DECADE, 20 LRC, 1920–2025

(T)

Country	1920	1930	1940	1950	1960	1970	1980	1990	2000	2010	2020	2025
A. ARGENTINA	8,861	11,896	14,169	17,150	20,616	23,962	28,237	32,322	36,238	40,193	43,837	45,505
B. BOLIVIA	1,918	2,153	2,508	2,766	3,428	4,325	5,570	7,314	9,724	12,820	16,401	18,294
C. BRAZIL	27,404	33,568	41,233	53,444	72,594	95,847	121,286	150,368	179,487	207,454	233,817	245,809
D. CHILE	3,783	4,424	5,147	6,082	7,614	9,504	11,145	13,173	15,272	17,182	18,973	19,774
E. COLOMBIA	6,057	7,350	9,077	11,597	15,538	20,803	25,794	31,820	37,999	43,840	49,259	51,718
F. COSTA RICA	421	499	619	862	1,236	1,731	2,284	3,015	3,711	4,366	4,977	5,250
G. CUBA	2,950	3,837	4,566	5,858	7,029	8,572	9,732	10,540	11,718	12,584	13,307	13,575
H. DOMINICAN REP.	1,140	1,400	1,759	2,353	3,231	4,423	5,697	7,170	8,621	9,903	11,001	11,447
I. ECUADOR	1,898	2,160	2,586	3,310	4,413	6,051	8,123	10,782	13,939	17,403	21,064	22,910
J. EL SALVADOR	1,168	1,443	1,633	1,940	2,570	3,588	4,525	5,252	6,739	8,491	10,348	11,299
K. GUATEMALA	1,450	1,771	2,201	2,969	3,964	5,246	6,917	9,197	12,222	15,827	19,706	21,668
L. HAITI	2,124	2,422	2,825	3,097	3,675	4,500	5,413	6,504	7,838	9,293	10,785	11,534
M. HONDURAS	783	948	1,119	1,401	1,935	2,627	3,662	5,138	6,846	8,668	10,558	11,510
N. MEXICO	14,500	16,589	19,815	28,012	38,020	52,771	70,416	88,598	107,233	125,166	142,135	150,062
O. NICARAGUA	639	742	893	1,098	1,493	2,053	2,771	3,871	5,261	6,824	8,435	9,219
P. PANAMA	429	502	595	839	1,105	1,487	1,956	2,418	2,893	3,324	3,701	3,862
Q. PARAGUAY	699	880	1,111	1,351	1,774	2,351	3,147	4,277	5,538	6,928	8,423	9,182
R. PERU	4,862	5,651	6,681	7,632	9,931	13,193	17,295	22,332	27,952	33,479	38,647	41,006
S. URUGUAY	1,391	1,704	1,947	2,239	2,538	2,808	2,908	3,128	3,364	3,581	3,782	3,875
T. VENEZUELA	2,408	2,950	3,710	5,009	7,502	10,604	15,024	19,735	24,715	30,006	35,394	37,999
LATIN AMERICA	84,885	102,889	124,194	159,009	210,206	276,446	351,902	436,954	527,310	617,332	704,550	745,498
UNITED STATES[1]	106,470	123,070	132,590	152,270	180,680	205,050	227,660	249,657	267,955	283,238	296,597	301,394

1. U.S. data from 1990 are middle series projections.

SOURCE: CELADE-BD, 23 (1979); and CELADE-BD, 35 (1985). For higher range
estimates, see CELADE data quoted in SALA, 22–624 and 625. U.S. data are from
SALA, 26–621 through 1980, then from USBC-SA, 1987, p. 15; CELADE-BD,
42 (1988).

Table 625

IDB TOTAL POPULATION AND AVERAGE ANNUAL GROWTH RATES, 19 LR, 1960–87

	Country	Population (T)					AA–GR (%)		
		1960	1970	1980	1986	1987[‡]	1960–70	1971–80	1981–87
A.	ARGENTINA	20,616	23,062	28,237	30,737	31,137	1.5	1.7	1.4
B.	BOLIVIA	3,428	4,325	5,570	6,548	6,730	2.4	2.6	2.7
C.	BRAZIL	72,594	95,847	121,286	138,493	141,452	2.8	2.4	2.2
D.	CHILE	7,614	9,504	11,145	12,327	12,536	2.2	1.6	1.7
E.	COLOMBIA	15,538	20,803	25,794	29,323	29,942	3.0	2.2	2.2
F.	COSTA RICA	1,236	1,731	2,284	2,716	2,791	3.4	2.8	2.9
H.	DOMINICAN REP.	3,231	4,423	5,697	6,565	6,716	3.2	2.6	2.4
I.	ECUADOR	4,413	6,051	8,123	9,647	9,923	3.2	3.0	2.9
J.	EL SALVADOR	2,570	3,588	4,525	4,846	4,934	3.4	2.3	1.2
K.	GUATEMALA	3,964	5,246	6,917	8,195	8,434	2.8	2.8	2.9
L.	HAITI	3,675	4,500	5,413	6,033	6,147	2.0	1.9	1.8
M.	HONDURAS	1,935	2,627	3,662	4,531	4,679	3.1	3.4	3.6
N.	MEXICO	38,020	52,771	70,416	81,201	83,039	3.3	2.9	2.4
O.	NICARAGUA	1,493	2,053	2,771	3,384	3,501	3.2	3.0	3.4
P.	PANAMA[1]	1,105	1,487	1,956	2,227	2,274	3.0	2.8	2.2
Q.	PARAGUAY	1,773	2,351	3,147	3,807	3,922	2.9	3.0	3.2
R.	PERU	9,931	13,193	17,295	20,208	20,727	2.9	2.7	2.6
S.	URUGUAY	2,538	2,808	2,908	3,034	3,057	1.0	.4	.7
T.	VENEZUELA	7,502	10,604	15,024	17,792	18,272	3.5	3.5	2.8
	LATIN AMERICA	206,851	272,261	347,089	396,922	405,594	2.8	2.5	2.3

1. Population for former Canal Zone included from 1980. Growth rate for 1971–80 will
   be slightly higher than for comparable populations.

SOURCE: Adapted from IDB-SPTF, 1986, table 1, p. 389; 1988, table A-1.

Table 626

CELADE POPULATION GROWTH RATES, 1985–2025

(PTI)

	Country	1985–90	1990–95	1995–2000	2000–05	2005–10	2010–15	2015–20	2020–25
A.	ARGENTINA	12.71	11.67	11.20	10.73	9.98	9.10	8.26	7.47
B.	BOLIVIA	27.57	28.16	28.72	28.12	27.07	25.49	23.72	21.82
C.	BRAZIL	20.71	18.66	16.72	15.13	13.81	12.61	11.31	10.00
D.	CHILE	16.63	15.53	14.03	12.36	11.21	10.41	9.42	8.26
E.	COLOMBIA	20.52	18.70	16.78	15.01	13.58	12.29	11.01	9.74
F.	COSTA RICA	26.34	22.50	19.01	17.03	15.49	13.90	12.28	10.67
G.	CUBA	9.76	11.29	9.91	7.63	6.62	6.01	5.17	3.99
H.	DOMINICAN REP.	22.19	19.77	17.07	14.77	12.95	11.34	9.69	7.96
I.	ECUADOR	27.85	26.54	24.76	23.00	21.33	19.83	18.33	16.79
J.	EL SALVADOR	19.33	24.71	25.11	24.01	22.15	20.51	19.03	17.57
K.	GUATEMALA	28.76	28.74	28.03	26.72	24.91	22.93	20.86	18.97
L.	HAITI	18.75	18.87	18.39	17.57	16.46	15.40	14.38	13.42
M.	HONDURAS	31.73	29.90	27.40	24.71	22.42	20.54	18.87	17.27
N.	MEXICO	21.96	20.09	18.06	16.23	14.68	13.34	12.08	10.85
O.	NICARAGUA	33.53	31.80	29.46	27.18	24.74	22.34	20.03	17.77
P.	PANAMA	20.66	19.00	16.87	14.80	12.96	11.43	10.01	8.53
Q.	PARAGUAY	29.28	26.87	24.73	23.05	21.72	20.23	18.81	17.25
R.	PERU	25.07	23.52	21.32	19.04	17.02	15.20	13.50	11.85
S.	URUGUAY	7.55	7.43	7.11	6.50	6.02	5.63	5.28	4.87
T.	VENEZUELA	26.11	23.63	21.33	20.03	18.73	17.26	15.75	14.20
	LATIN AMERICA	21.10	19.62	17.95	16.42	15.09	13.84	12.58	11.30

SOURCE: CELADE-BD, 42 (1988).

Table 627

U.N. AND WB POPULATION PROJECTIONS, BY MAJOR REGIONS
OF THE WORLD, 1985–2025

(M)

	United Nations			World Bank		
	1985	2000	2025	1985	2000	2025
World	4,837	6,122	8,206	4,840	6,176	8,188
Less Developed	3,663	4,845	6,809	3,663	4,913	6,850
Africa	555	872	1,617	560	871	1,495
Latin America	405	546	779	398	529	715
Asia and Oceania	2,703	3,427	4,414	2,704	3,513	4,639
More Developed[1]	1,174	1,277	1,396	1,177	1,263	1,338
USSR and Eastern Europe	391	435	499	389	426	469
Other Developed	783	842	897	788	837	869

1. More developed countries comprise all of North America, Europe, the USSR, Japan in
   Asia, and Australia and New Zealand in Oceania. Yugoslavia is included in other developed
   countries.

SOURCE: *Population Bulletin*, vol. 43, no. 2, April 1988.

Table 628

BOLIVIA POPULATION PROJECTIONS, BY SEX, 1990–2000

(T)

Year	Total	%	Male	%	Female	%
1990	7,322	100	3,609	49.3	3,713	50.7
1991	7,528	100	3,712	49.3	3,817	50.7
1992	7,739	100	3,817	49.3	3,923	50.7
1993	7,957	100	3,925	49.3	4,032	50.7
1994	8,181	100	4,037	49.3	4,144	50.7
1995	8,411	100	4,152	49.4	4,260	50.6
1996	8,649	100	4,271	49.4	4,378	50.6
1997	8,893	100	4,393	49.4	4,500	50.6
1998	9,144	100	4,518	49.4	4,626	50.6
1999	9,402	100	4,647	49.4	4,755	50.6
2000	9,668	100	4,780	49.4	4,888	50.6

SOURCE: *Hoy Internacional* (La Paz), February 21, 1989.

Table 629

NATIONAL POPULATION CENSUS SERIES, 20 L, 1774–1985[a]

A. ARGENTINA		G. CUBA		N. MEXICO	
1869	1,737,076	1774	171,620	1895	12,632,427
1895	3,954,911	1792	272,300	1900	13,607,259
1914	7,885,237	1817	572,363	1910	15,160,369
1947	15,897,127	1827	704,487	1921	14,334,780
1960	20,010,539	1841	1,007,624	1930	16,552,722
1970	23,362,204[‡]	1861	1,396,530	1940	19,653,552
1980	27,947,446	1877	1,509,291	1950	25,791,017
		1887	1,631,687	1960	34,923,129
B. BOLIVIA[1]		1899	1,572,797	1970	48,225,238
1831	1,018,900	1907	2,048,980	1980	66,846,833
1835	992,700	1919	2,889,004		
1845	1,031,500	1931	3,962,344	O. NICARAGUA	
1854	1,544,300	1943	4,778,583	1778	106,926
1882	1,097,600	1953	5,829,029	1867	257,000
1900	1,696,400	1970	8,569,121[e]	1906	505,377
1950	3,019,031	1981	9,723,605	1920	638,119
1976	4,613,486			1940	983,000
		H. DOMINICAN REP.		1950	1,057,023
C. BRAZIL		1920	894,665	1963	1,535,588
1872	10,112,061	1935	1,479,417	1971	1,877,952[e]
1890	14,333,915	1950	2,135,872		
1900	17,318,556	1960	3,047,070	P. PANAMA[2]	
1920	30,635,605	1970	4,006,405	1911	336,742
1940	41,236,315	1981	5,647,977[‡]	1920	446,098
1950	51,944,397			1930	467,459
1960	70,119,071	I. ECUADOR		1940	622,576
1970	92,341,556[a]	1950	3,202,757	1950	805,285
1980	118,674,604	1962	4,476,000	1960	1,075,541
		1974	6,521,710	1970	1,428,082[d]
D. CHILE		1982	8,050,630[f]	1980	1,824,796[i]
1835	1,010,336				
1843	1,083,801	J. EL SALVADOR		Q. PARAGUAY	
1854	1,439,120	1930	1,434,361	1936	931,799
1865	1,819,223	1950	1,855,917	1950	1,328,452
1875	2,075,971	1961	2,510,984	1962	1,819,103
1885	2,507,005	1971	3,554,648	1972	2,357,955
1895	2,695,625			1982	3,029,830
1907	3,231,022	K. GUATEMALA			
1920	3,730,235	1880	1,224,602	R. PERU	
1930	4,287,445	1893	1,364,678	1836	1,373,736
1940	5,023,539	1921	2,004,900 ***	1850	2,001,203
1952	5,932,995	1930	1,771,000	1862	2,460,684[c]
1960	7,374,115	1935	1,996,000	1876	2,651,840[c]
1970	8,884,768	1940	2,222,000	1940	6,208,000
1982	11,275,440	1950	2,790,686	1961	9,906,746
		1964	4,284,473	1972	14,121,564[h,]
E. COLOMBIA		1973	5,160,221[e]	1981	17,005,210[g]
1825	1,223,598	1981	6,054,227[‡,e]		
1835	1,686,038			S. URUGUAY	
1843	1,955,264	L. HAITI		1852	131,969
1851	2,243,730	1918	1,631,260	1860	229,480
1864	2,694,487	1950	3,097,220	1908	1,042,686
1870	2,391,984	1971	4,329,991	1963	2,595,510
1905	4,143,632	1982	5,053,792[‡,e]	1975	2,788,429
1912	5,072,604			1985	2,934,564
1918	5,855,077	M. HONDURAS			
1928	7,851,000[b]	1791	93,505	T. VENEZUELA	
1938	8,701,816	1801	130,000	1873	1,784,194
1964	17,484,508	1881	307,289	1881	2,075,545
1973	22,551,811	1887	331,917	1891	2,323,527
1985	27,837,932	1905	500,136	1920	2,365,098
		1910	553,446	1926	2,890,631
F. COSTA RICA		1916	605,997	1936	3,491,159
1864	120,499	1926	700,811	1941	3,850,771
1883	182,073	1930	854,184	1950	5,034,838
1892	243,205	1935	962,000	1961	7,523,999
1927	471,524	1940	1,107,859	1971	10,721,522
1950	800,875	1945	1,200,542	1981	14,516,735
1963	1,336,274	1950	1,368,605		
1973	1,871,780[e]	1961	1,884,765		
1984	2,416,809[e]	1974	2,656,948[e]		

1. Territorial variations have been taken into account — the figures refer to the population within the present boundaries of the country.
2. Includes the indigenous population.

a. Territorial changes have not necessarily been taken into account.
b. This census was not accepted by the National Congress because it was believed that the figures for certain civil divisions were inflated.
c. Excludes the population of the province of Arica and the department of Tarapaca.
d. Excludes former U.S. Canal Zone.
e. De jure population.
f. Excluding nomadic Indian tribes.

g. Excluding Indian jungle population.
h. Adjusted census total.
i. Excluding Indian jungle population estimated at 39,800 in 1972.
j. Census data have not been adjusted for underenumeration estimated at 6.6%.

SOURCE: Since 1900, SALA-SNP, table VIII-1; BE, 96, 109, 114, 122; IASI-AC, 1974; Cuban, El Salvadoran, Guatemalan, Mexican, and Venezuelan statistical agencies. Before 1900, IASI, Noticiero, January 3, 1965. Data for the 1970s and 1980s revised with figures from UN-DY, 1979–1985, table 3, except Chile from SALA-LAPUA, p. 178 and p. 430; Mexico data from Instituto Nacional de Estadística, Resumen General Abreviado (1984); and Peru data from SALA, 25–645.

Table 630

POPULATION CENSUS AND DENSITY OF
MAJOR CIVIL DIVISIONS, 20 L

A. ARGENTINA

Division	Population	%	Density Per km^2
Total	27,949,480	100.0	10
Capital Federal	2,922,829	10.4	14,614
Provinces			
Buenos Aires	10,865,408	38.9	35
Catamarca	207,717	.7	2

Continued in SALA, 23-626.

Table 631

EXTENDED CARIBBEAN REGION (ECR) POPULATION, 28 CSOR, 6 CA,
AND 3 TANGENTIAL COUNTRIES, 1960-79

Category	T		Change	PC
	1960	1979		
I. Caribbean Sea Oriented Region (CSOR)				
Anguilla	6[@]	6[@]	0	0
Antigua-Barbuda[1]	55	74	19	34.5
Bahamas[1]	112	236	124	110.7
Barbados[1]	232	279	47	20.3
Belize[1]	92	152	60	65.2
Bermuda	45	72	27	60.0
British Virgin Islands[1]	7	12	5	71.4
Cayman Islands[1]	8	17	9	112.5
G. Cuba	7,027	9,824	2,797	39.6
Dominica[1]	60	78	18	30.0
H. Dominican Republic[1]	3,159	5,551	2,392	75.7
French Guiana	32	63	31	96.9
Grenada[1]	90	106	16	17.8
Guadeloupe	273	312	39	14.3
Guyana[1]	571	832	261	45.7
L. Haiti[1]	3,723	5,670	1,947	52.3
Jamaica[1]	1,632	2,215	583	35.7
Martinique	283	310	27	9.5
Montserrat[1]	12	11	-1	-.8
Netherlands Antilles[1]	194	240	46	23.7
Puerto Rico	2,358	3,395	1,037	44.0
St. Kitts-Nevis[1]	51	51	0	0
St. Lucia[1]	88	121	33	37.5
St. Vincent and Grenadines[1]	81	111	30	37.0
Suriname[1]	285	404	119	41.8
Trinidad and Tobago[1]	840	1,150	310	36.9
Turks and Caicos[1]	6	7	1	16.7
U.S. Virgin Islands	33	99	66	200.0
Total CSOR	(21,355)	(31,398)	(10,043)	(47.0)
II. Central America (CA)				
F. Costa Rica[1]	1,248	2,184	936	75.0
J. El Salvador[1]	2,574	4,662	2,088	81.1
K. Guatemala[1]	3,969	6,849	2,880	72.5
M. Honduras[1]	1,952	3,645	1,693	86.7
O. Nicaragua[1]	1,438	2,365	927	64.5
P. Panama[1]	1,112	1,876	764	68.7
Total CA	(12,293)	(21,581)	(9,288)	75.6
III. Mainland Tangential Countries				
E. Colombia	15,953	26,205	10,252	64.3
N. Mexico	36,182	65,770	29,588	81.8
T. Venezuela	7,632	14,539	6,907	90.5
Total Tangential	(59,767)	(106,514)	(46,747)	78.2
Total ECR	93,415	159,493	66,078	70.7
Subtotal CBI-IB[2]	(23,591)	(38,898)	(15,307)	(64.9)

1. CBI-IB.
2. CBI-IB includes CA and CSOR, except Anguilla, Bermuda, Cuba, French Guiana,
   Guadeloupe, Martinique, Puerto Rico, U.S. Virgin Islands.

SOURCE: James W. Wilkie, "On Defining the Concepts of Latin America, the Caribbean,
and Economically Questionable Nations (EQNs)," SALA, vol. 23, Preface.

Table 632

POPULATION OF LARGEST CITY, 20 L, 1900–85

(T)

Country/Largest City	1900	1920	1930	1940	1950	1960	1970	Ca. 1984	1985
A. ARGENTINA (Buenos Aires)[1]	756	1,576	~	2,410	5,213	7,000	9,400	9,928	10,728[t,z]
B. BOLIVIA (La Paz)[1]	54	~	~	~	300	400	500	881[t,l,n]	993[t,l,n,u]
C. BRAZIL (Rio de Janeiro except Sao Paulo in 1970 and 1984)[1]	683	1,158	~	1,519	3,025	4,692	8,213	10,099[‡,p]	10,099[t,‡,p,y]
D. CHILE (Santiago)[1]	307	507	713	952	1,275	1,907	2,600	4,067[t,l]	4,100[t,l,v]
E. COLOMBIA (Bogotá)	101	144[a]	260	356[b]	607	1,241	2,500	4,169[t,l]	3,975[z]
F. COSTA RICA (San José)[1]	28	39	89[c]	~	140	257	435	395[m,p,o]	275[t,p,l,w]
G. CUBA (Havana)[1]	209	466[d]	721[e]	936[f]	1,081	1,549	1,700	1,992[t]	2,015[t,l]
H. DOMINICAN REP. (Santo Domingo)	15	31	~	71[g]	182	367	650	818	~
I. ECUADOR (Guayaquil)	79	~	~	~	259	450	800	1,388[t,l]	~
J. EL SALVADOR (San Salvador)[1]	49	81	89	103	162	239	375	336[l]	~
K. GUATEMALA (Guatemala City)[1]	41	112[h]	~	186	294	474	770	754[p,l]	~
L. HAITI (Port-au-Prince)	56	~	~	~	134	240	400	738[t,p,z]	~
M. HONDURAS (Tegucigalpa)[1]	12	~	~	56[i]	72	159	281	539[t,l]	598[t,x,l]
N. MEXICO (Mexico City)[2]	381	615	1,049	1,560	2,872	4,910	8,567	14,750[t,z]	~
O. NICARAGUA (Managua)[1]	24	28	~	63	109	197	350	608[t,l]	~
P. PANAMA (Panama City)[1]	--	~	74	112	128	273	440	424[t,q]	~
Q. PARAGUAY (Asunción)[1]	42	~	~	~	219	311	445	719[t]	~
R. PERU (Lima-Callao)[1]	78	255	~	~	947	1,519	2,500	5,008[‡,r]	5,008[t,l]
S. URUGUAY (Montevideo)	290	393	482	537	609	962	1,530	1,173[l]	1,248[l]
T. VENEZUELA (Caracas)[1]	80	92	259[j]	354[k]	694	1,280	2,147	2,944[s]	3,185[t,s,z]

1. Beginning in 1950, figures are for city proper and adjacent urban area.
2. All figures are for city proper and adjacent urban area.

a. 1918.
b. 1938.
c. 1927.
d. 1919, Greater Havana.
e. 1931, Greater Havana.
f. 1943.
g. 1935.
h. 1921.
i. 1945.
j. 1936, metropolitan area.
k. 1941, metropolitan area.
l. For city proper area only.
m. Metropolitan area.
n. La Paz is the actual capital and the seat of the government, but Sucre is the legal capital and the seat of the judiciary.
o. For July 1, 1970.
p. De jure population.
q. Including corregimientos of Bella Vista, Betania, Calidonia, Curundú, El Chorillo, Juan Díaz, Parque Lefevre, Pedregal, Pueblo Nuevo, Río Abajo, San Felipe, San Francisco, and Santa Ana.
r. "Metropolitan Area" (Gran Lima).
s. For June 30, 1986. "Metropolitan Area" comprising Caracas proper (the urban parishes of Department of Libertador) and a part of district of Sucre in state of Miranda.
t. "Metropolitan Area," comprising Asunción proper and localities of Trinidad, Zeballos Cué, Campo Grande, and Lambaré.
u. "Metropolitan Area," comprising central San José (including San José city), cantones Corridabat, Escazu, Montes de Oca, and Tibas, and parts of cantones of Alajuelita, Desamparados, Goicoechea, and Moravia.
v. "Metropolitan Area" (Gran Santiago).
w. For July 1, 1983.
x. For June 30, 1986.
y. For "municipios" which may contain rural areas as well as urban centers.
z. Urban agglomeration. Urban agglomeration has been defined as comprising the city or town proper and also the suburban fringe or thickly settled territory lying outside of, but adjacent to, the city boundaries.

SOURCE: 1900–1970: Marshal C. Eakin, "Determining the Population in the Largest City of Each Latin American Country, 1920–1970," SALA, 19–3500 and 19–3503; 1984 data from UN-DY, 1985, table 8; 1985 data from UN-DY, 1986, table 8.

Table 633

PERCENTAGE OF POPULATION OF LARGEST CITY, 20 L, 1900-85

Country/Largest City	1900	1920	1930	1940	1950	1960	1970	Ca. 1984	1985
A. ARGENTINA (Buenos Aires)	16.4	17.6	~	17.0	30.5	35.1	39.6	32.9	35.1
B. BOLIVIA (La Paz)	3.1	~	~	8.5	10.0	10.8	10.7	14.6	15.4
C. BRAZIL (Rio de Janeiro except São Paulo for 1970 and 1984)	3.8	4.2	~	3.7	5.8	6.7	8.9	7.4	7.4
D. CHILE (Santiago)	10.4	13.4	16.3	18.8	21.0	25.2	27.7	34.2	40.0
E. COLOMBIA (Bogotá)	2.6	2.5[a]	3.5	4.1[b]	5.4	8.0	12.2	14.8	13.8
F. COSTA RICA (San José)	9.3	9.3	18.9[c]	10.6	17.5	20.6	25.1	19.5	11.0
G. CUBA (Havana)	13.1	16.0[d]	18.2[e]	19.6[f]	19.6	22.0	19.9	19.9	20.0
H. DOMINICAN REP. (Santo Domingo)	2.5	3.5	~	4.8[g]	8.1	12.1	16.0	13.6	~
I. ECUADOR (Quito, except Guayaquil since 1940)	6.1	~	~	5.2	8.1	10.3	13.7	15.2	~
J. EL SALVADOR (San Salvador)	6.2	6.9	6.2	6.3	8.7	9.8	10.9	6.8	~
K. GUATEMALA (Guatemala City)	4.7	8.5[h]	~	8.5	10.5	12.4	15.8	9.8	~
L. HAITI (Port-au-Prince)	4.5	~	~	4.0	4.0	6.2	9.4	18.0	~
M. HONDURAS (Tegucigalpa)	3.0	~	~	4.4[i]	5.0	8.6	11.2	12.3	13.7
N. MEXICO (Mexico City)	2.8	4.3	6.3	7.9	11.1	14.1	17.8	20.1	~
O. NICARAGUA (Managua)	5.9	4.4	~	7.6	10.3	14.0	19.1	20.0	~
P. PANAMA (Panama City)	~	14.4[j]	15.7	18.1	16.0	25.8	30.8	19.9	~
Q. PARAGUAY (Asunción)	8.7	~	~	8.7	15.6	17.6	19.3	15.3	~
R. PERU (Lima-Callao)	2.6	5.3	~	7.4	11.9	15.1	18.6	26.1	25.4
S. URUGUAY (Montevideo)	30.3	26.6	27.9	27.3	27.7	37.9	52.9	40.0	41.5
T. VENEZUELA (Caracas)	3.3	3.3	7.7[k]	9.3[l]	14.0	17.4	20.6	18.1	17.4

a. 1918.   g. 1935.
b. 1938.   h. 1921.
c. 1927.   i. 1945.
d. 1919.   j. 1919.
e. 1931.   k. 1936.
f. 1943.   l. 1941.

SOURCE: 1900–70 data from SALA, 19–3501; 1983 data calculated from SALA, 27–601
    through 620 and 630.

Table 634

CITIES WITH POPULATIONS OVER 500,000, 1950-80

(T)

Ranking	City	Country	1950	1960	1970	1980
1	Mexico City Metro Area	Mexico	3,198	5,380	8,592	13,734
2	São Paulo Metro Area	Brazil	2,584	4,579	8,206	12,706
3	Greater Buenos Aires	Argentina	5,131	6,761	8,433	9,927
4	Rio de Janeiro Metro Area	Brazil	3,287	5,019	7,174	9,154
5	Lima-Callao	Peru	1,176	1,725	2,990	4,419
6	Greater Santiago	Chile	1,350	1,907	2,819	4,039
7	Caracas Metro Region	Venezuela	986	1,750	2,716	3,492
8	Bogotá, Special District	Colombia	670	1,290	2,380	3,462
9	Belo Horizonte Metro Area	Brazil	475	885	1,628	2,584
10	Recife Metro Area	Brazil	819	1,240	1,824	2,399
11	Porto Alegre Metro Area	Brazil	592	1,039	1,554	2,284
12	Guadalajara Metro Area	Mexico	452	867	1,480	2,245
13	Monterrey Metro Area	Mexico	380	716	1,250	2,000
14	Salvador Metro Area	Brazil	464	740	1,170	1,795
15	Medellín Metro Area	Colombia	374	720	1,214	1,703
16	Fortaleza Metro Area	Brazil	388	654	1,053	1,615
17	Curitiba Metro Area	Brazil	314	524	838	1,471
18	Guatemala City	Guatemala	336	528	898	1,430
19	Montevideo	Uruguay	1,086	1,231	1,297	1,373
20	Santo Domingo	Dominican Rep.	181	370	668	1,254
21	Brazilia Metro Area	Brazil	0	141	538	1,177
22	Cali Metro Area	Colombia	228	469	812	1,163
23	Guayaquil	Ecuador	259	468	720	1,105
24	Puebla Metro Area	Mexico	351	449	680	1,056
25	Belém Metro Area	Brazil	264	417	665	1,016
26	Greater Córdoba	Argentina	418	577	792	982
27	Goainia Metro Area	Brazil	97	228	512	975
28	Campinas Agglomeration	Brazil	162	262	498	955
29	Greater Rosario	Argentina	513	666	813	954
30	Maracaibo Metro Area	Venezuela	250	454	685	935
31	Baranquilla Metro Area	Colombia	284	441	652	930
32	Santos Agglomeration	Brazil	260	409	634	919
33	San Salvador Metro Area	El Salvador	213	328	534	857
34	Quito	Ecuador	209	330	518	799
35	Asunción	Paraguay	271	409	579	797
36	Panama City	Panama	216	331	519	794
37	Valencia Metro Area	Venezuela	106	200	455	786
38	Port-au-Prince	Haiti	134	289	458	684
39	Vina-Valparaíso	Chile	338	410	499	668
40	Managua	Nicaragua	109	194	357	661
41	Manaus	Brazil	95	163	300	639
42	La Paz	Bolivia	321	441	563	635
43	León Metro Area	Mexico	140	231	392	633
44	Maracay Metro Area	Venezuela	91	186	374	615
45	Vitoria Agglomeration	Brazil	95	181	363	614
46	Greater Mendoza	Argentina	166	395	477	596
47	Concepción	Chile	265	357	445	594
48	Greater La Plata	Argentina	252	406	486	560
49	Barquisimeto Metro Area	Venezuela	108	204	345	548
50	Juárez	Mexico	122	262	407	544
51	São Luis Agglomeration	Brazil	88	139	308	510
52	San José	Costa Rica	146	225	347	507

SOURCE: Adopted from preliminary data supplied by Robert Fox.

Table 635

POPULATION OF PRINCIPAL CITIES, ACCORDING TO RECENT CENSUSES,[1] 20 L

A. ARGENTINA (Estimated VII–I, 1985)

Buenos Aires	10,728,000
Rosario, Santa Fé	1,016,000
Córdoba, Córdoba	1,055,000
Mendoza, Mendoza	668,000
La Plata, Buenos Aires	611,000
Mar del Plata, Buenos Aires	448,000
San Miguel de Tucumán, Tucumán	394,117
San Juan, San Juan	324,000
Santa Fé, Santa Fé	310,000
Salta	302,000[f]
Bahía Blanca	242,000
Corrientes	197,000[f]
Paraná	178,000[f]
Santiago del Estero	172,000[f]

B. BOLIVIA (Estimated VII-I, 1985)[f]

La Paz, La Paz[2]	992,592[a]
Santa Cruz, Santa Cruz	441,717[a]
Cochabamba, Cochabamba	317,251[a]
Oruro, Oruro	178,693[a]
Potosí, Potosí	113,380[a]
Sucre, Chuquisaca[2]	86,609[a]

C. BRAZIL (Estimated VII-1, 1985)[‡,o]

São Paulo, São Paulo	10,099,086
Rio de Janeiro, Guanabara	5,615,149
Belo Horizonte, Minas Gerais	2,122,073
Recife, Pernambuco	1,289,627
Salvador, Bahia	1,811,367
Porto Alegre, Rio Grande do Sul	1,275,483
Belém, Pará	1,120,777
Fortaleza, Ceará	1,588,709
Curitiba, Paraná	1,285,027
Santo André, São Paulo	637,010
Gioania, Goiás	928,046
Nova Iguacú, Rio de Janeiro	1,324,639
Campinas, São Paulo	845,057
Santos, São Paulo	461,096
Niterói, Rio de Janeiro	442,706
Manaus, Amazonas	834,541
Osasco, São Paulo	594,249
Brasília, Distrito Federal	1,576,657
Duque de Caxias, Rio de Janeiro	666,128
Natal, Rio Grande do Notre	512,241
Maceló, Alagoas	484,094
Guarulhos, São Paulo	717,723
Juiz de Fora, Minas Gerais	350,687
João Pessoa, Paraíba	397,715
Ribeirão Prêto, São Paulo	384,604
Olinda, Pernambuco	335,889
Teresina, Pisuí	476,102
Aracaju, Sergipe	361,544
São Luis, Maranhão	564,434
Sorocaba, São Paulo	328,787
São João de Meriti, Rio de Janeiro	459,103
Campina Grande, Paraíba	280,665
São Gonçalo, Rio de Janeiro	731,061
Londrina, Paraná	347,707
Campos, Rio de Janeiro	367,134
Ponta Grossa, Paraná	223,989
Pelotas, Rio Grande do Sul	278,427
São Caetano do Sul	171,187
Canoas, Rio Grande do Sul	262,156
Jundiaí, São Paulo	314,909
Campo Grande, Mato Grosso	386,520
Nilópolis, Rio de Janeiro	166,324
Feira de Santana, Bahia	356,660
Piracicaba, São Paulo	252,945

C.[a] BRAZIL (Continued)

Governado Valadares, Espírito Santo	217,434
Vitória, Espírito Santo	325,448
Montes Claros, Minas Gerais	215,323
Santa María, Rio Grande do Sul	197,177
Volta Redonda, Rio de Janeiro	220,084
Bauru, São Paulo	220,871
Rio Grande, Rio Grande do Sul	164,636
Petrópolis, Rio de Janeiro	275,076
Florianópolis, Santa Catarina	218,853
Maringá, Paraná	197,527
Santarém, Pará	227,412
Mogi das Cruzes, São Paulo	234,937
Caxias do Sul, Rio Grande do Sul	267,869
Marília, São Paulo	136,518
Caruaru, Pernambuco	136,212

D. CHILE (Estimated XII-31, 1985)[‡,f]

Santiago, Santiago[3]	4,099,714
Concepción, Concepción	280,713
Valparaíso, Valparaíso	273,213
Vina del Mar Valparaíso	261,118
Talcahuano	217,660
Antofagasta	203,067
Temuco	168,120
Arica	158,422
Rancagua	157,209
Talca	137,621
Chillán	126,581
Valdivia	104,910

E. COLOMBIA

	(Census of X-24-1973)	Estimated 1985
Bogotá D.E., Cundinamarca	2,855,065	4,208,000
Medellín, Antioquia	1,159,194	2,069,000
Cali, Valle de Cauca	990,304	1,654,000
Barranquilla, Atlántico	691,728	1,120,000
Bucaramanga, Santander	322,883	545,000
Cartegena, Bolívar	354,735	530,000[f]
Cúcuta, Norte de Santander	278,933	441,000
Pereira, Risaralda	226,888	390,000
Manizales, Caldas	231,888	328,000[f,d]
Ibagué, Tolima	233,112	285,000[f]
Bello, Antioquia	122,780	~
Montería, Córdoba	172,407	~
Armenia, Quinidio	160,345	239,000[f]
Valledupar, Magdalena	160,654	301,000
Palmirá Valle del Cauca	184,970	~
Pasto, Narino	158,533	245,000[f]
Buenaventura, Valle del Cauca	136,308	193,000[f]
Neiva, Huila	128,784	193,000[f]
Santa Marta, Magdalena	150,987	216,000[f]

F. COSTA RICA (Estimate of VII-1-1983)

San José, San José	395,401[c,j,m]
Limón, Limón	35,000[p]
Puntarenas, Punterenas	30,000[p]
Alajuela, Alajuela	28,000[p]
Heredia, Heredia	22,000[p]
Cartago, Cartago	21,000[p]

G. CUBA (Estimate of XI1-31-1985)[f]

La Habana, Habana	2,014,806
Santiago de Cuba, Oriente	358,764
Camagüey, Carnagüey	260,782
Santa Clara, Las Villas	178,278
Guantánamo, Oriente	174,383
Matanzas, Matanzas	105,382
Holquín	194,728
Cienfuegos	109,304
Bayamo	105,302

Table 635 (Continued)
POPULATION OF PRINCIPAL CITIES, ACCORDING TO RECENT CENSUSES,[1] 20 L

H. DOMINICAN REP. (XII-12-1981)[f]

Santo Domingo, Distrito Nacional	1,313,172
Santo de los Caballers, Santiago	278,638
La Romana, La Romana	91,571
San Pedro de Macorís, San Pedro de Macorís	78,562
San Francisco de Macorís, Duarte	64,906
Concepción de la Vega	52,432

I. ECUADOR (Estimate of VI-30-1984)[f]

Guayaquil, Guayas	1,387,819
Quito, Pichincha	1,003,875
Machaía	123,966
Portoviejo	120,896
Cuenca	176,865
Manta	117,461
Ambato	114,493
Esmeraldas	105,153

J. EL SALVADOR (Census of VI-28-1971)

San Salvador, San Salvador	335,930[f]
Santa Ana, Santa Ana	168,047[l]
San Miguel, San Miguel	107,658[l]
Nueva San Salvador, La Libertad	36,000[k]
Villa Delgado, San Salvador	30,000[k]

K. GUATEMALA (Census of 1981)

Ciudad de Guatemala, Guatemala	754,243
Escuintla, Escuintla	75,442
Quezaltenango, Quezaltenango	72,922
Puerto Barrios, Izabel	46,882
Retalhulev	46,652

L. HAITI (Estimate of VII-I-1984)[c]

Port-au-Prince, Ouest	738,342[a]
Cap-Haitien, Nord	46,000[q]
Gonaives, Artibonite	29,000[q]
Les Cayes, Sud	22,000[q]

M. HONDURAS (Estimate of VI-30-1986)

Tegucigalpa, D.C., Francisco Morazán	597,512[f]
San Pedro Sula, Cortés	397,201[f]
La Ceiba, Atlántida	103,600[f,r]
Choluteca	50,700
El Progreso, Yoro	50,000

N. MEXICO (Estimate of VI-30-1979)[a,g]

Ciudad de México, Distrito Federal	14,750,182
Guadalajara, Jalisco	2,467,657
Monterrey, Nuevo León	2,018,625
León, Guanajuato	624,816
Puebla de Zaragoza, Puebla	710,833
Ciudad Juárez, Chihuahua	625,040
Mexicali, Baja California	348,528
Chihuahua, Chihuahua	385,953
Culiacán, Sinoloa	324,292
Tijuana, Baja California	566,344
San Luis Potosí, San Luis Potosí	327,333
Terreón, Coahuila	407,271

N. MEXICO (Continued)

Mérida, Yucatán	269,582
Veracruz, Veracruz	306,843
Aguascalientes, Aguascalientes	257,179
Morelia, Michoacán	251,011
Hermosillo, Sonora	319,257
Tampico, Tamaulipas	389,940
Durango, Durango	228,686
Saltillo, Coahuila	258,492
Matamoros, Tamaulipas	193,305
Villa de Guadalupe, Hidalgo (part of Federal District)	124,573[b]
Nuevo Laredo, Tamaulipas	223,606

O. NICARAGUA (Estimate of VII-1-1979)

Managua, D.N., Managua	608,020[f]
León, León	58,000[f]
Granada, Granada	36,000[f]
Masaya, Masaya	30,000[f]
Chinandega, Chinandega	30,000[f]

P. PANAMA (Estimate of VII-1-1984)[f]

Panamá, Panamá	424,204[i]
San Miguelito	200,584

Q. PARAGUAY (Census of 1982)

Asunción	457,210[f]
San Lorenzo	74,359
Fernando de la Mora	66,810
Lambaré	65,145

R. PERU (Estimate of XII-30-1985)[f,f]

Lima, Lima	5,008,400[h]
Callao, Provincia Constitucional de Callao	515,200
Arequipa, Arequipa	545,165
Trujillo, La Libertad	421,345
Chiclayo, Lemayeque	349,249
Cuzco, Cuzco	235,857
Chimbote	255,078
Huancayo	190,226
Iquitos	229,557
Piura	265,866
Tacna	125,848

S. URUGUAY (Census of 1975)

Montevideo	1,229,748
Salto	71,000
Pay Sandú	61,000
Las Piedras	53,000

T. VENEZUELA A (Census of X-20-1981)

Caracas, Distrito Federal	2,944,000[a,e]
Maracaibo, Zulia	888,824
Valencia, Carabobo	616,037
Barquismeto, Lara	496,684
Maracay, Araqua	440,098
San Cristóbal, Táchira	198,578
Cabimas, Zulia	138,529
Ciudad Bolívar, Bolívar	181,864

1. Unless otherwise indicated, data refer to "Urban Agglomeration." Each city is followed by the name of the major territorial division (department, state, province, etc.) to which it belongs.
2. La Paz is the actual capital and seat of government, but Sucre is the legal capital and seat of the judiciary.
3. "Metropolitan Area" (Gran Santiago).
a. Estimate of questionable reliability.
b. Villa de Guadalupe, 1973.
c. De jure population.
d. Includes population of Villamaría.
e. "Metropolitan Area," comprising Caracas proper (the urban parishes of the department of Libertador) and a part of the district of Sucre in the state of Miranda.
f. Data refer to city proper.
g. Data refer to city proper with the exception of Mexico City, Guadalajara, Monterrey, Tampico, and Torreón.

h. Data refer to "Metropolitan Area" (Gran Lima).
i. Data refer to city proper and include the *corregimientos* of Bella Vista, Betania, Calidonia, Curundo, El Chorillo, Juan Diaz, Parque Lefevre, Pedregal, Pueblo Nuevo, Río Abajo, San Felipe, San Francisco, and Santa Ana.
j. "Metropolitan area" comprising *cantón central* of San José (including San José city), cantones Curridabat, Escazú, Montes de Oca, and Tibá, and parts of cantones of Alajuelita, Desamparados, Goicoechea, and Moravia.
k. 1961 estimate.
l. 1969 estimate.
m. For July 1, 1970.
n. For September 29, 1976.
o. Data refer to "urban agglomeration" and "city proper."
p. 1973 estimate.
q. 1971 estimate.
r. 1985 estimate.

SOURCE: Colombia estimates from *Colombia Today, 21:3* (1986); Dominican Rep., Guatemala, Paraguay, and Uruguay estimates from *South America, Central America, and the Caribbean* (London: Europa Publications Limited, 1986); Costa Rica, El Salvador, Haiti and Nicaragua estimates from IASI-AC, 1970 and 1973, table 201–07 and UN-DY, 1984, table 8; and UN-DY, 1985 and 1986, table 8.

Table 636

POPULATION PROJECTIONS AND RANKS FOR THE LARGEST METROPOLITAN AREAS, 7 L, 1950–2000

(T)

		1950	Population Rank	1985	Population Rank	2000	Population Rank
A.	ARGENTINA						
	Buenos Aires	5,250	1	10,880	3	13,180	4
C.	BRAZIL						
	Belo Horizonte	480	10	3,250	9	5,110	8
	Porto Alegre	670	9	2,740	11	4,020	11
	Rio de Janeiro	3,480	2	10,370	4	13,260	3
	São Paulo	2,760	4	15,880	2	23,970	2
D.	CHILE						
	Santiago	1,430	5	4,160	7	5,260	7
E.	COLOMBIA						
	Bogotá	700	7	4,490	6	6,530	6
N.	MEXICO						
	Guadalajara	430	11	2,770	10	4,110	10
	Mexico City	3,050	3	17,300	1	25,820	1
	Monterrey	380	12	2,530	12	3,970	12
R.	PERU						
	Lima	1,050	6	5,680	5	9,140	5
T.	VENEZUELA						
	Caracas	680	8	3,740	8	5,030	9

SOURCE: Adapted from *Population Bulletin*, vol. 41, no. 3, July 1986, p. 25.

Table 637

CELADE URBAN POPULATION PERCENTAGES, NON-STANDARD TERMS,[1] 20 LR, 1970–2025

(%)

Country	1970	1975	1980	1985	1990	1995	2000	2005	2010	2015	2020	2025
A. ARGENTINA	78.48	80.16	81.62	82.96	84.10	85.15	86.05	86.85	87.55	88.20	88.70	89.14
B. BOLIVIA	38.19	41.30	44.68	50.54	51.45	54.28	56.58	58.15	60.53	62.85	65.30	67.65

Continued in SALA 24, 653.

Table 638

POPULATION OF CAPITAL CITY URBAN AREAS, ACCORDING TO RECENT CENSUSES,[1] 20 LC

	Country	Date of Estimate	Date of Census[2]	Capital City	City Proper	Urban Agglomeration
A.	ARGENTINA	VII-I-1985	X-22-1980	Buenos Aires	2,922,829	10,728,000[b]
B.	BOLIVIA	VII-I-1985	**	LaPaz[6]	922,592	~
C.	BRAZIL[‡]	VII-I-1985	**	Brasilia, D.F.	1,576,657[f]	~
D.	CHILE[‡]	VII-I-1985	**	Santiago	4,067,047[g]	~
E.	COLOMBIA	**	X-15-1985	Bogota	3,974,812	~
F.	COSTA RICA[3]	VII-I-1983	**	San José	274,832	395,401[a,e]
G.	CUBA	XII-31-1985	**	La Habana	2,014,806	~
H.	DOMINICAN REP.	**	I-9-1970	Santo Domingo	673,470	817,645
I.	ECUADOR	VI-30-1984	**	Quito	1,003,875	~
J.	EL SALVADOR	**	VI-28-1971	San Salvador	335,930	~
K.	GUATEMALA	III-23-1981	**	Guatemala, Ciudad de	754,243	~
L.	HAITI[‡,3]	VII-I-1984	**	Port-Au-Prince	461,464[b]	738,342
M.	HONDURAS	VII-I-1986	**	Tegucigalpa	597,512	485,049
N.	MEXICO	VI-30-1979	VI-IV-1980	México, Ciudad de	8,831,079	14,750,182[b]
O.	NICARAGUA	VII-I-1979	**	Managua	608,020	~
P.	PANAMA	VII-I-1984	**	Panamá	424,204[c]	~
Q.	PARAGUAY	**	VII-II-1982	Asunción	457,210	718,690[d]
R.	PERU[‡]	VI-30-1985	**	Lima	5,008,400	~
S.	URUGUAY	**	X-23-1985	Montevideo	1,247,920	~
T.	VENEZUELA	**	VI-30-1986	Caracas	1,232,254	3,184,958
	UNITED STATES[4,5]	VII-I-1984	**	Washington, D.C.	622,800	3,369,600

1. Definition of cities varies from country to country. Urban agglomeration includes the suburban fringe or thickly settled territory lying outside of, but adjacent to, the city boundaries.
2. Data are the result of a national or municipal census.
3. Based on de jure population.
4. De jure population, but excluding armed forces overseas and civilian citizens absent from the country for an extended period of time.
5. Urban agglomeration data refer to "Standard Metropolitan Statistical Area."
6. La Paz is the actual capital and seat of government, but Sucre is the legal capital and the seat of the judiciary.

a. "Metropolitan Area," comprising *canto central* of San José (including San José city), *cantones* Curridabat, Escazú, Montes de Oca, and Tibás, and parts of *cantones* of Alajuelita, Desamparados, Goicoechea, and Moravia.
b. Estimate of questionable reliability.
c. Including *corregimientos* of Bella Vista, Betania, Calidonia, Curundú, El Chorillo, Juan Díaz, Parque Levevre, Pedregal, Pueblo Nuevo, Río Abajo, San Felipe, San Francisco, and Santa Ana.
d. "Metropolitan Area," comprising Asuncíon proper and localities of Trinidad, Zeballos, Cué, Campo Grande, and Lambaré.
e. For VII-I-1970.
f. Includes urban population.
g. "Metropolitan Area" (Gran Santiago).

SOURCE: UN-DY, 1984, 1985 and 1986, table 8.

Table 639

PERSONS BY AGE UP TO 15 YEARS, 20 LC

(N)

	Country	Year	Code	Age			
				Under 1 Year	1-4 Years	5-9 Years	10-14 Years
A.	ARGENTINA[‡,4]	1985	E	3,472,635[a]	~[a]	3,223,845	2,776,709
B.	BOLIVIA[3]	1985	E	250,252	845,292	897,974	769,922
C.	BRAZIL[‡,2]	1985	E	18,072,000[a]	~[a]	16,368,000	14,926,000
D.	CHILE[3,‡]	1985	E	1,393,890[a]	~[a]	1,221,864	1,232,665
E.	COLOMBIA[‡,4]	1985	C	612,050	2,757,872	3,444,848	3,226,267
F.	COSTA RICA[‡,1,11]	1984	E	~[b]	~[b]	701,566[b]	193,881[c]
G.	CUBA	1985	E	179,506	612,885	753,256	1,081,829
H.	DOMINICAN REP.[9]	1980	E	183,719	736,468	890,819	774,522
I.	ECUADOR[4,5,9]	1984	E	1,444,948	~[a]	1,255,783	1,135,082
J.	EL SALVADOR[‡]	1985	E	789,501	~[a]	755,434	652,566
K.	GUATEMALA[‡]	1985	E	1,433,545	~[a]	1,213,313	1,008,947
L.	HAITI[‡,9,10]	1985	E	159,057	623,371	703,660	598,636
M.	HONDURAS[‡,9]	1985	E	169,918	630,851	680,714	569,777
N.	MEXICO[‡,1,4,9]	1985	E	11,280,453[a]	~[a]	11,037,365	10,541,500
O.	NICARAGUA[9]	1980	E	466,640[a]	~[a]	455,852	387,061
P.	PANAMA[9]	1984	E	57,435	222,011	270,343	264,083
Q.	PARAGUAY[‡]	1982	C	105,317	358,663	396,065	376,179
R.	PERU[3,6,9]	1985	E	2,999,691[a]	~[a]	2,602,421	2,368,746
S.	URUGUAY[9]	1980	E	274,427[a]	~[a]	267,110	245,206
T.	VENEZUELA[‡,7,9]	1986	E	2,601,325	~[a]	2,328,199	2,050,643
	UNITED STATES[‡,4,8,10]	1985	E	3,742,000	14,295,000	16,822,000	17,103,000

Code: C = census data; E = estimate.

1. De jure population.
2. Excluding Indian jungle population.
3. Data have been adjusted for underenumeration at latest census.
4. Because of rounding, totals are not in all cases the sum of the parts.
5. Excluding nomadic Indian tribes.
6. Excluding Indian jungle population estimated at 39,800 in 1972.
7. Excluding Indian jungle population estimated at 31,800 in 1961.
8. De jure population, but excluding civilian citizens absent from country for extended period of time.
9. Estimates are unreliable.
10. Excluding armed forces overseas.
11. Excluding transients afloat and non-locally domiciled military and civilian services personnel and their dependents and visitors, numbering 5,553, 5,187, and 8,985 respectively at 1980 census.

a. Figures for under one year category include 1-4 years population.
b. Figures for 5 to 9 years of age include persons under 12 years of age.
c. Includes persons 12 to 14 years of age.

SOURCE: Adapted from UN-DY, 1986, table 7.

Table 640

POPULATION BULLETIN POPULATION (AGE 15–24) PROJECTIONS, 20 L, 1985–2025
(T)

	Country	Population Age 15–24		
		1985	2000	2025
A.	ARGENTINA	4,770	6,635	7,395
B.	BOLIVIA	1,207	1,890	3,686
C.	BRAZIL	27,566	33,671	38,854
D.	CHILE	2,455	2,380	2,639
E.	COLOMBIA	6,261	7,192	8,259
F.	COSTA RICA	561	676	812
G.	CUBA	2,251	1,555	1,750
H.	DOMINICAN REP.	1,388	1,621	1,957
I.	ECUADOR	1,913	2,695	4,017
J.	EL SALVADOR	1,105	1,738	2,799
K.	GUATEMALA	1,541	2,479	4,228
L.	HAITI	1,293	1,929	3,677
M.	HONDURAS	864	1,433	2,680
N.	MEXICO	16,552	22,095	24,666
O.	NICARAGUA	656	1,066	1,752
P.	PANAMA	460	536	593
Q.	PARAGUAY	750	1,074	1,519
R.	PERU	3,989	5,454	6,828
S.	URUGUAY	486	536	563
T.	VENEZUELA	3,550	4,794	6,407

SOURCE: *Population Bulletin*, vol. 41, no. 3, July 1986, p. 45.

Table 641

CELADE MALE AND FEMALE POPULATION PROJECTIONS, 20 LR, 1970–2000
(T)

PART I. TOTALS

	Country	1970			1980			1990			2000		
		Total	Male	Female	Total	Male	Female	Total	Male	Female	Total	Male	Female
A.	ARGENTINA	23,962	12,019	11,943	28,237	14,045	14,192	32,879	16,285	16,594	37,197	18,391	18,806
B.	BOLIVIA	4,325	2,134	2,191	5,570	2,744	2,826	7,314	3,605	3,709	9,724	4,800	4,924
C.	BRAZIL	95,847	47,984	47,863	121,286	60,607	60,679	150,368	74,992	75,376	179,487	89,323	90,164

Continued in SALA, 25-655.

Table 642

POPULATION PERCENTAGE UNDER 15 YEARS,
20 LRC, 1950–2010
(%)

	Country	1950	1960	1970	1980	1990	2000	2010
A.	ARGENTINA	30.6	30.7	29.2	28.2	27.3	25.0	27.2
B.	BOLIVIA	42.5	41.9	43.7	43.8	42.5	41.2	42.6
C.	BRAZIL	42.4	43.5	42.7	41.5	39.9	37.3	28.7
D.	CHILE	38.2	39.1	38.1	32.5	30.6	28.1	26.0
E.	COLOMBIA	43.3	46.8	46.1	40.4	38.4	35.2	28.9
F.	COSTA RICA	43.5	47.5	46.1	37.9	34.1	31.7	28.1
G.	CUBA	36.2	34.4	37.1	32.0	25.9	25.1	21.3
H.	DOMINICAN REP.	44.8	47.8	49.0	44.8	38.8	35.5	28.9
I.	ECUADOR	41.7	44.4	45.3	44.4	43.9	41.3	37.8
J.	EL SALVADOR	42.2	45.1	46.1	45.1	43.4	40.6	37.3
K.	GUATEMALA	44.3	46.2	45.7	44.1	41.8	39.5	36.6
L.	HAITI	39.5	40.9	42.9	43.6	43.6	43.4	42.4
M.	HONDURAS	44.7	45.7	47.5	47.8	45.2	42.3	41.4
N.	MEXICO	42.9	45.6	46.5	45.3	44.8	42.3	30.0
O.	NICARAGUA	44.1	47.8	48.5	48.0	46.5	44.0	38.4
P.	PANAMA	41.6	44.0	43.3	39.8	34.7	31.5	27.8
Q.	PARAGUAY	42.4	45.9	46.0	44.3	42.7	39.7	34.2
R.	PERU	41.1	43.6	44.3	42.5	40.8	38.0	31.1
S.	URUGUAY	28.2	28.5	28.2	27.2	26.7	26.1	24.5
T.	VENEZUELA	42.3	46.2	46.4	41.6	39.9	35.6	32.4
	LATIN AMERICA[1]	40.6	42.5	42.7	40.9	39.5	37.1	30.5
	Caribbean	39.1	40.2	41.7	37.5	33.3	31.7	30.3[a]
	Continental Middle America	43.0	45.8	46.4	45.2	44.1	41.7	36.7[b]
	Temperate South America	32.2	32.7	31.4	29.4	28.1	26.0	28.5[c]
	Tropical South America	42.4	44.3	43.7	41.7	40.1	37.3	31.9[d]
	UNITED STATES	26.9	31.1	28.3	22.5	22.7	21.9	~

1. Includes Barbados, Guadeloupe, Guyana, Jamaica, Martinique, Puerto Rico, Suriname, Trinidad and Tobago, and the Windward Islands for decades 1950 to 2010.

a. Includes Mexico, Cuba, Dominican Republic, and Haiti.
b. Includes Costa Rica, El Salvador, Guatemala, Honduras, Nicaragua, and Panama.
c. Includes Argentina, Brazil, Paraguay, and Uruguay.
d. Includes Bolivia, Chile, Colombia, Ecuador, Peru, and Venezuela.

SOURCE: PAHO-HC, table 1-5; 2010 data calculated from CELADE-BD, 32 (1983).

Table 643

ESTIMATES OF FEMALE POPULATION 15–49 YEARS OF AGE, 20 LRC, 1950–2010

(%)

Country	1950	1960	1970	1980	1990	2000	2010
A. ARGENTINA	54.1	51.2	49.8	48.3	48.4	49.6	49.2
B. BOLIVIA	46.8	47.4	45.8	45.4	46.4	47.6	47.7
C. BRAZIL	47.9	46.2	46.5	47.1	48.2	49.7	52.9

Continued in SALA, 25-656.

Table 644

SALA RURAL POPULATION PERCENTAGES ACCORDING TO NATIONAL SELF-PERCEPTION, 20 LRC, 1940–80[a]

(Non-Standard Definition)

Country	Data Years	ca. 1940	ca. 1950	ca. 1960	ca. 1970	ca. 1980	Rural Defined as Population Clusters Which Are:
A. ARGENTINA	1947, 1960, 1970, 1980	~	38	26	21	17	Less than 2,000 persons
B. BOLIVIA	1950, 1960, 1970, 1980	~	74	76	72	67	Less than 2,000 persons
C. BRAZIL	1940, 1950, 1960, 1970, 1980	69	64	54	44	36	Non-administrative centers
D. CHILE	1940, 1952, 1960, 1970, 1980	48	40	32	24	19	Lack of certain public services
E. COLOMBIA	1938, 1951, 1964, 1973, 1980	71	61	47	40	32	Less than 1,500 persons
F. COSTA RICA	1950, 1963, 1973, 1980	~	67	65	59	54	Non-administrative centers
G. CUBA	1943, 1953, 1960, 1970, 1980	54	49	45	40	35	Less than 2,000 persons (adjusted by source)
H. DOMINICAN REP.	1935, 1950, 1960, 1970, 1980	82	76	70	60	53	Non-administrative centers
I. ECUADOR	1950, 1962, 1974, 1980	·	72	64	59	50	Non-administrative centers
J. EL SALVADOR	1930, 1950, 1961, 1971, 1980	62	64	61	60	56	Lightly populated
K. GUATEMALA	1940, 1950, 1964, 1973, 1980	74	75	66	66	62	Varies[1]
L. HAITI	1950, 1960, 1971, 1980	~	88	85[†]	80	75	Non-administrative centers
M. HONDURAS	1950, 1960, 1974, 1980	~	82[†]	77	69	51	Less than 1,000-2,000 persons
N. MEXICO	1940, 1950, 1960, 1970, 1980	65	57	49	42	34	Less than 2,500 persons
O. NICARAGUA	1950, 1963, 1971, 1980	~	65	59	52	46	Non-administrative centers
P. PANAMA	1940, 1950, 1960, 1970, 1980	63	64	58	52	46	Less than 1,500 persons
Q. PARAGUAY	1950, 1962, 1972, 1980	~	65	64	62	58	Non-administrative centers
R. PERU	1940, 1950, 1961, 1972, 1980	65	59[†]	53	40	35	Non-administrative centers and/or lack of certain public services
S. URUGUAY	1950, 1960, 1970, 1980	~	43[†]	28[†]	16[†]	15	Not cities[2]
T. VENEZUELA	1941, 1950, 1961, 1971, 1980	69	52	37	25	21	Less than 2,500 persons
LATIN AMERICA	20 countries	67[b]	63	56	42	36	Average of above, weighted by population
UNITED STATES	1940, 1950, 1960, 1970, 1980	39	36	30	27	23	"Current Definition"[3]

1. In 1940: hamlets, small settlements, and farms; since 1950: less than 2,000 except 1,500 if running water.

2. In 1963 census definition gave 19%.
3. Less than 2,500 persons except for urbanized unincorporated areas; data for 1940 adjusted for consistency.

a. Self-definitions vary according to national circumstances.
b. Calculated from population-weighted data for 11 countries which had 80% of Latin America's population.

SOURCE: See SALA, 24–658.

Table 645

SALA URBAN POPULATION PERCENTAGES ACCORDING TO
NATIONAL SELF-PERCEPTION, 20 LRC, 1940–80
(Non-Standard Definition)[1]

	Country	%				
		Ca. 1940	Ca. 1950	Ca. 1960	Ca. 1970	Ca. 1980
A.	ARGENTINA	~	62	74	79	83
B.	BOLIVIA	~	26	24	28	33
C.	BRAZIL	31	36	46	56	64
D.	CHILE	52	60	68	76	81
E.	COLOMBIA	29	39	53	60	68
F.	COSTA RICA	~	33	35	41	46
G.	CUBA	46	51	55	60	65
H.	DOMINICAN REP.	18	24	30	40	47
I.	ECUADOR	~	28	36	41	44
J.	EL SALVADOR	38	36	39	40	44
K.	GUATEMALA	26	25	34	34	38
L.	HAITI	~	12	15	20	25
M.	HONDURAS	~	18	23	31	49
N.	MEXICO	35	43	51	58	66
O.	NICARAGUA	~	35	41	48	54
P.	PANAMA	37	36	42	48	54
Q.	PARAGUAY	~	35	36	38	42
R.	PERU	35	41	47	60	65
S.	URUGUAY	~	57	72	84	85
T.	VENEZUELA	31	48	63	75	79
	LATIN AMERICA	33	37	44	58	64
	UNITED STATES	61	64	70	73	77

1. For national definitions, cf. SALA, 25–657.

SOURCE:
 1940: U.N., *Demographic Yearbook* (1948), pp. 213-216.
 1950: SALA, 3-2.
 1960: IASI-AC, 1970, table 201-08.
 1970: IASI-AC, 1977, table 201-08.
 1980: ECLA, *Latin American Development Projections for the 1980s* (Santiago, 1982)
    p. 19. Exceptions: Data for Haiti in 1960, Peru for 1950, and Uruguay for
    1950-1960 are from Kingsley Davis, *World Urbanization, 1950-1970*; 2 vols.
    (Berkeley: Population Monograph Series, University of California, 1969), 1,
    pp. 54-68. Figure for Colombia in 1950 is from AC, 1977, table 201-08.
    Bolivian data for 1950 are from *Human Resources in Bolivia* (Columbus: Center
    for Human Resource Research, Ohio State University, 1971), p. 55 and for
    1960 and 1970 from WB-WBT, 1980, p. 439. Mexican data are from the Mexi-
    can Statistical Agency. Cuban data for 1943 and 1953 are from UCLA-Cuba,
    p. 24 and 1960 from WB-BDR, 1982, p. 149. Venezuelan data are from DGE,
    Censo de Población, 1961, A, p. 11; and *idem, Censo General de Población y
    Vivienda*, 1971: *Resultados Comparativos*, table 2. U.S. Data are from
    USBC-SA, p. 17, the figure for 1940 being adjusted here (splice of "previous"
    and "current" series). Bolivia, Cuba, and United States for 1980 are from
    WB-WDR, 1982, pp. 148-149. Cf. SALA-SNP, p. 483.

Table 646

CELADE URBAN AND RURAL POPULATION ESTIMATES, NON-STANDARD TERMS,[1] 20 LR, 1970–2020

(T)

Country	1970	1980	1990	2000	2010	2020
A. ARGENTINA						
Total	23,748	27,036	30,277	33,222	35,843	38,101
Urban	18,637	22,066	25,463	28,586	31,380	33,795
Rural	5,111	4,970	4,814	4,636	4,463	4,306

1. For each of the countries involved, the definition adopted for an urban population is the one appearing in the last population census of the corresponding country. Cf. SALA, 25–657.

Continued in SALA, 23–654.

Table 647

ECLA URBAN AND RURAL POPULATION ESTIMATES, BY AGE GROUP, NON-STANDARD DEFINITION,[1] 20 L, 1975–2025

(% and T)

Country/Age Group	1975		1980		2000		2025	
	Urban	Rural	Urban	Rural	Urban	Rural	Urban	Rural
A. ARGENTINA								
0-14 (%)	26.38	36.42	26.05	36.12	24.07	33.95	20.96	30.46
15-59	60.85	54.87	60.45	54.67	60.65	55.52	61.02	56.74
60-	12.77	8.71	13.50	9.21	15.28	10.53	18.02	12.80
Total (T)	20,343	5,035	22,066	4,970	28,586	4,636	34,816	4,241

1. Rural and urban defined according to national self-perception as defined in SALA, 25–657.

Continued in SALA, 23-656.

Table 648

URBAN POPULATION IN NON-STANDARD AND STANDARD TERMS, 20 LR, 1960-80

	Country	Density Per km[2]			Non-Standard Terms[1] T			Non-Standard Terms[1] %			Standard Terms % over 20,000			Standard Terms % over 100,000		
		1960	1970	1980	1960	1970	1980	1960	1970	1980	1960	1970	1980	1960	1970	1980
A.	ARGENTINA	7.4	8.6	10.2	15,112	18,810	23,041	73.3	78.5	81.6	59.0	66.3	70.2	50.6	55.6	57.7
B.	BOLIVIA	3.1	3.9	5.1	1,035	1,652	2,490	30.2	38.2	44.7	22.9	27.2	34.0	15.3	20.9	29.2
C.	BRAZIL	8.6	11.3	14.3	33,538	53,483	76,168	46.2	55.8	62.8	27.0	36.2	45.7	25.2	32.5	38.0
D.	CHILE	10.1	12.5	14.7	5,144	7,111	8,756	67.6	75.2	78.7	50.6	60.6	67.9	32.9	41.7	52.0
E.	COLOMBIA	13.6	18.3	22.6	7,551	12,336	17,101	48.6	59.3	66.3	33.5	43.9	54.3	27.5	35.7	42.5
F.	COSTA RICA	24.3	34.0	44.8	421	672	1,042	34.1	38.8	45.7	18.5	26.0	30.1	18.5	20.9	22.2
G.	CUBA	63.4	77.2	87.7	3,803	5,109	6,520	54.1	59.6	67.0	38.9	43.4	47.5	24.5	30.8	33.2
H.	DOMINICAN REP.	66.6	89.4	114.7	935	1,690	2,601	29.0	19.4	45.8	18.7	30.2	40.8	12.1	20.7	27.5
I.	ECUADOR	17.0	22.9	30.8	1,406	2,359	3,585	31.8	39.6	44.7	26.5	33.0	39.5	18.6	22.0	28.7
J.	EL SALVADOR	123.0	170.6	229.1	808	1,415	2,120	31.4	39.5	44.2	17.7	20.5	24.9	13.3	15.7	17.8
K.	GUATEMALA	36.4	49.1	66.7	1,214	1,841	2,651	30.6	34.4	36.5	14.5	15.9	18.9	13.2	13.7	14.3
L.	HAITI	134.6	164.5	209.9	484	912	1,342	13.0	19.8	23.1	9.5	13.4	16.5	7.9	11.1	14.7
M.	HONDURAS	17.3	23.6	32.9	464	876	1,432	23.9	33.2	38.8	11.1	17.7	23.8	6.9	13.3	17.9
N.	MEXICO	18.8	26.0	35.3	19,204	30,143	45,452	51.8	58.9	65.5	29.6	34.8	42.5	13.6	23.3	29.8
O.	NICARAGUA	12.6	17.4	23.4	596	965	1,491	39.9	47.0	53.8	20.3	30.5	36.9	14.1	20.5	24.4
P.	PANAMA	14.6	19.6	25.9	454	711	1,082	41.1	47.8	55.3	33.1	39.4	40.9	25.4	30.3	30.6
Q.	PARAGUAY	4.4	5.6	7.8	558	847	1,223	31.4	37.0	38.6	22.1	27.3	32.2	22.1	24.2	25.9
R.	PERU	7.7	10.3	13.5	4,419	7,652	10,965	44.5	58.0	63.4	27.4	38.5	47.2	18.3	28.0	38.0
S.	URUGUAY	13.6	15.0	15.6	1,972	2,303	2,437	77.7	82.0	83.8	60.0	63.3	66.1	40.4	44.7	41.5
T.	VENEZUELA	8.4	11.8	16.7	4,719	7,645	11,448	62.9	72.1	76.2	47.0	59.4	67.0	25.8	38.0	52.7
	LATIN AMERICA	10.5	13.8	17.6	103,837	158,532	222,947	49.6	57.7	63.3	32.4	39.9	47.3	25.3	31.5	36.4

1. Urban defined according to national definitions; Cf. SALA, 25-657.

SOURCE: ECLA-N, No. 397/8 (July, 1984), p. 5.

Table 649

NUMBER AND POPULATION OF PLACES WITH 20,000 INHABITANTS AND OVER, ACCORDING TO CENSUSES, 20 L, ca. 1950, 1960, 1970

	Country	Number of Inhabitants	1950 Number of Localities	1950 Population	1960 Number of Localities	1960 Population	1970 Number of Localities	1970 Population
A.	ARGENTINA	Total 20,000+	42	7,934,082	57	11,804,276	79	15,479,372
		1,000,000 and more	1	4,927,919	1	6,807,236	1	8,435,840
		500,000 — 999,999	=	=	2	1,260,736	2	1,597,450
		100,000 — 499,999	7	1,694,032	10	2,059,161	12	2,951,313
		50,000 — 99,999	8	552,643	7	475,009	16	1,057,550
		20,000 — 49,999	26	759,488	37	1,202,134	48	1,437,219

Continued in SALA, 24-658.

Table 650

INDICES OF URBANIZATION AND URBAN CONCENTRATION,[1] 20 LR, 1950 AND 1975

	Country	Year	% Total Population in Urban Areas of 20,000 Inhabitants or More	% Total Population in Urban Areas of 100,000 Inhabitants or More	% Total Population in Urban Areas of Most Populated City[2]	% Urban Population in Urban Areas of 100,000 Inhabitants or More	% Urban Population in Urban Areas of Most Populated City[3]
A.	ARGENTINA	1950	52.4	44.0	32.0	84.0	61.1
		1975	69.8	57.9	37.0	83.0	53.0

Continued in SALA, 21-635.

Table 651

VANHANEN URBAN AND RURAL POPULATION PERCENTAGE ESTIMATES, 20 LRC, 1900–70
(Urban = Clusters of Population 20,000 and Over)

PART I. URBAN

(%)

Country	1900	1910	1920	1930	1940	1950	1960	1970
A. ARGENTINA	24.9	28.4	37.0	38.0	41.0	49.91	58.98	66.25
B. BOLIVIA	6.6	9.2	9.4[a]	13.1[b]	18.7[c]	19.36	22.93	27.22

PART II. RURAL

(%)

Country	1900	1910	1920	1930	1940	1950	1960	1970
A. ARGENTINA	75.1	71.6	63.0	62.0	59.0	50.1	41.0	33.8
B. BOLIVIA	93.4	90.8	90.6[a]	86.9[b]	81.3[c]	80.1	77.1	72.8

Continued in SALA, 24–657.

Table 652

AGE STRUCTURE, 20 LC, 1960–80
(%)

Country	0-14 Years			15-64 Years			65 Years and Over		
	1960	1970	1980	1960	1970	1980	1960	1970	1980
A. ARGENTINA	31.0	29.0	28.1	63.0	63.0	63.2	6.0	8.0	8.6
B. BOLIVIA	42.0	42.0	43.9	54.0	55.0	52.7	4.0	3.0	3.4

Continued in SALA, 24–661.

Table 653

DISTRIBUTION OF POPULATION BY SEX AND AGE, 18 LC
(%, 1980)

Country	All Ages		Under 5 Years		5-14 Years		15-24 Years		25-44 Years		45-64 Years		65 Years and Over	
	M	F	M	F	M	F	M	F	M	F	M	F	M	F
A. ARGENTINA	49.9	50.1	5.1	4.9	9.2	8.9	8.5	8.2	13.5	13.2	9.7	10.1	3.8	4.8
B. BOLIVIA	49.3	50.7	8.5	8.4	13.5	13.5	9.4	9.6	11.0	11.5	5.3	5.9	1.5	1.9

Continued in SALA, 24–662.

Table 654

U. S. POPULATION CENSUS DATA ON HISPANICS
(1980)

PART I. STATE

Rank	State	Hispanic Population	Hispanic Percentage of Population	Percentage of U.S. Hispanic State Population	Hispanics in State Elected Offices
1	California	4,543,770	19.2	31.1	10/120[a]
2	Texas	2,985,643	21.0	20.4	22/181[b]
3	New York	1,659,245	9.5	11.4	7/210
4	Florida	857,898	8.8	5.9	1/170
5	Illinois	635,525	5.6	4.4	0/236
6	New Jersey	491,867	6.7	3.4	0/120
7	New Mexico	476,089	36.6	3.3	33/112**
8	Arizona	440,915	16.2	3.0	12/90
9	Colorado	339,300	11.7	2.3	9/100
10	Michigan	162,388	1.8	1.1	2/148
11	Pennsylvania	154,004	1.3	1.1	0/252
12	Massachusetts	141,043	2.5	1.0	0/199
13	Connecticut	124,499	4.0	.9	0/187
14	Washington	119,986	2.9	.8	0/147
15	Ohio	119,880	1.1	.8	0/132

PART II. CITY

Rank	City	Hispanic Population	Percentage of Total Population	Hispanics on Elected Council[1]
1	New York City	1,405,957	19.9	3/43
2	Los Angeles	815,989	27.5	1/15[c]
3	Chicago	422,061	14.0	1/50
4	San Antonio[2]	421,774	53.7	4/9
5	Houston	281,224	17.6	1/14
6	El Paso	265,819	62.5	2/6
7	Miami[2]	194,087	55.8	2/4
8	San Jose	140,574	22.1	1/6
9	San Diego	130,610	14.9	1/8
10	Phoenix	115,572	15.1	0/6
11	Albuquerque	112,084	33.8	3/9
12	Dallas	111,082	12.3	1/10
13	Corpus Christi	108,175	46.6	0/6
14	Hialeah[2]	107,908	74.3	2/7
15	Denver	91,937	18.7	2/13
16	Santa Ana	90,646	39.3	2/7
17	Laredo[2]	85,076	93.0	8/8
18	San Francisco	83,373	12.3	0/11
19	Tucson	82,189	24.9	2/6
20	Brownsville[2]	71,139	83.7	3/4

1. Column shows the number of Hispanics and the total membership of the city council or comparable elected body. For example, of New York City's 43 council members, 3 are Hispanic.
2. City has a Hispanic mayor.

a. These figures include both houses of state legislatures.
b. Figures adjusted after November 1982 elections.
c. As of 1985.

SOURCE: *Los Angeles Herald Examiner,* Nov. 21, 1982. See also table 1500.

Table 655

CELADE RATES OF DEMOGRAPHIC GROWTH, 20 LR, 1920-2000[a]

(AA-GR)

Country	1920-25	1925-30	1930-35	1935-40	1940-45	1945-50	1950-55	1955-60	1960-65	1965-70
A. ARGENTINA	3.17	2.81	1.86	1.67	1.67	2.11	2.05	1.98	1.58	1.56
B. BOLIVIA	1.06	1.26	1.45	1.62	1.78	1.92	1.97	2.16	2.29	2.41
C. BRAZIL	2.05	2.05	2.05	2.11	2.27	2.55	2.97	3.03	2.86	2.87
D. CHILE	1.54	1.61	1.55	1.50	1.54	1.74	2.41	2.40	2.50	2.26
E. COLOMBIA	1.94	1.96	2.03	2.19	2.36	2.65	3.05	3.27	3.32	3.46
F. COSTA RICA	1.61	1.82	2.00	2.35	2.98	3.44	3.74	4.13	3.65	3.05
G. CUBA	2.66	2.67	1.93	1.58	1.55	2.28	2.13	2.14	2.07	2.00
H. DOMINICAN REP.	1.99	2.16	2.28	2.34	2.62	2.84	3.02	3.20	3.25	3.44
I. ECUADOR	1.14	1.46	1.71	1.91	2.06	2.41	2.83	3.11	3.35	3.41
J. EL SALVADOR	2.18	2.09	1.19	1.30	1.23	2.05	2.51	2.90	3.04	3.36
K. GUATEMALA	1.11	2.94	2.42	1.97	3.36	3.10	2.67	2.82	2.98	2.89
L. HAITI	1.25	1.39	1.51	1.60	1.78	1.84	1.95	2.15	2.28	2.45
M. HONDURAS	1.94	1.92	1.61	1.73	2.01	2.36	2.62	3.18	3.37	3.43
N. MEXICO	.95	1.76	1.75	1.84	2.88	3.12	2.94	3.20	3.45	3.50
O. NICARAGUA	1.46	1.55	1.74	2.00	2.27	2.55	2.66	3.04	3.06	2.98
P. PANAMA	1.58	1.59	.86	2.57	2.55	2.53	2.89	2.97	3.23	3.27
Q. PARAGUAY	2.35	2.31	2.34	2.37	1.82	2.01	2.60	2.78	3.24	3.46
R. PERU	1.47	1.56	1.65	1.72	1.75	1.81	1.98	2.66	3.05	3.12
S. URUGUAY	2.06	2.04	1.50	1.18	1.13	1.30	1.48	1.44	1.35	1.23
T. VENEZUELA	1.93	2.17	2.27	2.37	2.84	3.11	3.99	3.92	3.31	3.37
LATIN AMERICA	1.86	2.03	1.89	1.91	2.22	2.54	2.73	2.85	2.85	2.91

Country	1970-75	1975-80	1980-85	1985-90	1990-95	1995-2000
A. ARGENTINA	1.3	1.3	1.2	1.1	9.7***	8.8***
B. BOLIVIA	2.5	2.6	2.7	2.8	2.8	2.9
C. BRAZIL	2.6	2.4	2.3	2.2	2.1	2.0
D. CHILE	1.7	1.7	1.7	1.6	1.4	1.3
E. COLOMBIA	2.2	2.1	2.1	2.1	1.9	1.7
F. COSTA RICA	2.5	2.4	2.3	2.2	2.1	1.9
G. CUBA	1.7	.8	.6	1.0	1.1	1.0
H. DOMINICAN REP.	2.0	2.6	2.4	2.3	2.2	2.1
I. ECUADOR	2.9	3.0	3.1	3.1	3.0	2.8
J. EL SALVADOR	2.9	2.9	2.9	3.1	3.0	2.9
K. GUATEMALA	3.1	3.0	2.9	2.8	2.8	2.7
L. HAITI	2.3	2.4	2.5	2.6	2.7	2.7
M. HONDURAS	3.2	3.5	3.4	3.1	3.1	3.2
N. MEXICO	3.2	3.0	2.9	2.7	2.4	2.2
O. NICARAGUA	3.3	3.3	3.3	3.2	3.1	3.1
P. PANAMA	2.7	2.5	2.2	2.1	1.9	1.8
Q. PARAGUAY	3.2	3.3	3.0	2.8	2.6	2.3
R. PERU	2.7	2.7	2.8	2.8	2.8	2.7
S. URUGUAY	.1	.5	.7	.7	.7	.7
T. VENEZUELA	3.6	3.5	3.3	2.9	2.6	2.3
LATIN AMERICA	2.6	2.5	2.4	2.3	2.2	2.0

a. 1920-70 estimated in 1972; 1970-80 estimated in 1981.

SOURCE: CELADE-BD, 10 (1972); CELADE-BD, 28 (1981); CELADE-BD, 30 (1982).

Table 656

CELADE GROWTH RATES FOR TOTAL, URBAN, AND RURAL POPULATION, 20 LR, 1970-2000

(AA-GR for Non-Standard Definition)[1]

Country	Period					
	1970-75	1975-80	1980-85	1985-90	1990-95	1995-2000
A. ARGENTINA						
Total	1.3	1.3	1.2	1.1	9.7	8.8
Urban	1.8	1.6	1.5	1.4	1.2	1.1
Rural	-.3	-.3	-.3	-.3	-.4	-.4

Continued in SALA, 23-655 (based upon CELADE-BD, 30 [1982]).

Table 657

ESTIMATED AMERIND POPULATION, 16 L, MID-1950s

Country	Date	Total Population	Amerind Population	%	Geographic Distribution of Principal Amerind Groups
A. ARGENTINA	1960	20,956,039	130,000	.6	a. Northern or Chaqueña region (30,000). Chulupíes, Chorotes, Matacos, Tobas, Pilagas. b. Northwest or Andean regions and Central (18,000). Coyas, Tobas, Mocobies. c. Pampeana region and South (18,000). Araucanos, Onas, Yaganes, Alacalufes.

Continued in SALA, 17-610.

Table 658

AMERIND POPULATION ESTIMATES,[1] 16 LC, LATE 1970s

(1978)

Category	Indigenous Population (T)	% of National Population
Countries with High Percentage of Indigenous Peasant Population		
B. BOLIVIA	3,526	59.2
I. ECUADOR	2,564	33.9
K. GUATEMALA	3,739	59.7
N. MEXICO	8,042	12.4
R. PERU	6,025	36.8
Countries with Principally Tribal Indigenous Population		
C. BRAZIL	243	.2
E. COLOMBIA	547	2.2
P. PANAMA	121	6.8
Q. PARAGUAY	67	2.3
T. VENEZUELA	202	1.5
Countries with Indigenous Minorities		
A. ARGENTINA	398	1.5
D. CHILE	616	5.7
F. COSTA RICA	10	.6
J. EL SALVADOR[2]	100	2.3
M. HONDURAS[2]	107	3.2
O. NICARAGUA[2]	43	1.8
UNITED STATES[3]	1,568	.7
TOTAL	27,927	

1. Indigenous peoples are those who still maintain specific social ties that give them an identity of their own as indigenous in the local context and are, in turn, recognized as such by the nonindigenous people of the countries, although they might have undergone substantial changes since their first contacts with the European colonizers.
2. Unreliable information.
3. The 1980 census gave a total of 1,418,195 who identified themselves as Indian, including American Indians, Eskimos, and Aleuts.

SOURCE: Inter-American Indian Institute, "La Población Indígena en América en 1978," *América Indígena* 39:2 (1979), quoted in *Intercom*, The International Population News Magazine of the Population Reference Bureau 9:6(1981), 4.

7

Vital Statistics and Disease

Table 700

LIFE EXPECTANCY,[1] 20 LC

PART I. AGES 0-80

Country	Years[2]	0 Male	0 Female	1 Male	1 Female	5 Male	5 Female	10 Male	10 Female	15 Male	15 Female	20 Male	20 Female	25 Male	25 Female	30 Male	30 Female
A. ARGENTINA	1975-80	65.4	72.1	67.5	73.9	64.0	70.4	59.2	65.6	54.3	60.7	49.6	55.9	45.1	51.2	40.5	46.5
B. BOLIVIA	1975-80	48.6a	53.0a	53.5	57.3	55.7	58.6	52.0	54.7	47.7	50.3	43.6	46.1	39.8	42.1	36.0	38.1
C. BRAZIL	1975-80	60.9a	66.0a	64.5	67.7	62.9	65.4	58.5	60.8	53.8	56.1	49.3	51.4	44.9	46.9	40.7	42.5
D. CHILE	1985	65.0	71.7	67.9	72.5	64.3	69.7	59.5	64.9	54.6	60.0	49.9	55.2	45.3	50.3	40.7	45.6
E. COLOMBIA	1975-80	61.4a	66.0a	63.2	67.0	61.8	65.1	57.4	60.7	52.9	56.1	48.4	51.6	44.2	47.2	39.8	43.8
F. COSTA RICA	1975-80	70.5a	75.7a	70.4	74.9	66.8	71.4	62.0	66.5	57.2	61.6	52.5	56.8	48.0	52.0	43.4	47.2
G. CUBA	1983-84	72.7	76.1	73.0	76.2	69.3	72.4	64.5	67.5	59.6	62.6	54.9	57.9	50.2	53.2	45.6	48.4
H. DOMINICAN REP.	1975-80	60.7a	64.6a	62.3	65.4	60.7	63.7	56.4	59.4	51.9	54.8	47.5	50.5	43.3	46.2	39.1	42.0
I. ECUADOR	1975-80	58.0	62.0	62.9	65.8	61.7	64.0	57.3	59.5	52.8	54.8	48.5	50.4	44.4	46.1	40.2	41.8
J. EL SALVADOR	1975-80	62.6a	64.6a	64.7	68.8	63.2	67.0	59.2	63.0	54.5	58.2	50.0	53.7	45.6	49.1	41.3	44.8
K. GUATEMALA	1975-80	56.9	58.8	61.2	62.2	60.9	62.3	57.0	58.3	52.5	53.9	48.0	49.4	43.8	45.1	39.7	40.9
L. HAITI	1975-80	51.2a	54.4a	55.5	57.7	55.4	57.0	51.3	52.8	47.0	48.4	43.0	44.3	39.2	40.4	35.4	36.5
M. HONDURAS	1975-80	55.4	58.9	61.2	62.9	61.0	62.5	57.0	58.3	52.5	53.8	48.1	49.3	43.9	45.0	39.8	40.7
N. MEXICO	1975-80	62.1a	66.0a	65.3	69.2	63.2	67.1	58.7	62.6	54.0	57.8	49.5	53.2	45.0	48.6	40.7	44.2
O. NICARAGUA	1975-80	58.7a	61.0	60.3	61.7	59.7	60.8	55.4	56.6	51.3	52.1	46.9	47.8	42.9	43.8	38.9	39.8
P. PANAMA	1975-80	69.2a	72.85a	69.0	72.0	66.1	69.1	61.5	64.5	56.8	59.7	52.3	55.0	47.8	50.3	43.4	45.7
Q. PARAGUAY	1975-80	62.8a	67.5a	64.5	68.3	62.5	65.9	58.0	61.3	53.3	56.5	48.9	51.8	44.6	47.4	40.3	42.9
R. PERU	1975-80	56.8a	60.5a	61.0	64.2	60.7	63.8	56.4	59.5	51.9	55.0	47.4	50.5	43.2	46.2	39.0	41.9
S. URUGUAY	1975-80	66.4	73.0	68.7	74.7	65.0	71.0	60.2	66.1	55.3	61.2	50.6	56.4	45.9	51.6	41.3	46.8
T. VENEZUELA	1985	66.7	72.8	68.5	74.2	65.0	70.7	60.3	65.9	55.5	61.0	50.9	56.2	46.4	51.4	41.9	46.7
UNITED STATES‡	1984	71.2	78.2	71.1	78.0	67.2	74.1	62.3	69.2	57.4	64.2	52.7	59.4	48.2	54.5	43.5	49.7

Country	Years[2]	35 Male	35 Female	40 Male	40 Female	45 Male	45 Female	50 Male	50 Female	55 Male	55 Female	60 Male	60 Female	65 Male	65 Female	70 Male	70 Female	75 Male	75 Female	80 Male	80 Female
A. ARGENTINA	1975-80	35.9	41.8	31.5	37.3	27.3	32.8	23.3	28.4	19.6	24.2	16.2	20.0	13.1	16.1	10.3	12.6	7.8	9.3	5.4	6.6
B. BOLIVIA	1975-80	32.1	34.1	28.3	30.1	24.5	26.1	20.8	22.3	17.2	18.5	13.9	15.0	10.9	11.8	8.3	9.0	6.2	6.7	4.7	5.0
C. BRAZIL	1975-80	36.5	38.1	32.5	33.9	28.5	29.8	24.7	25.8	21.0	22.0	17.5	18.3	14.3	14.9	11.3	11.8	8.6	9.0	6.3	6.6
D. CHILE	1985	36.3	40.9	31.9	36.3	27.7	31.9	23.8	27.6	20.0	23.5	16.6	19.6	13.4	15.0	10.8	12.9	8.5	10.0	6.4	7.5
E. COLOMBIA	1975-80	35.5	38.5	31.3	34.1	27.1	29.8	23.1	25.6	19.3	21.4	15.7	17.4	12.3	13.8	9.4	10.5	6.9	7.7	5.0	5.7
F. COSTA RICA	1975-80	38.8	42.4	34.3	37.7	29.9	33.1	25.6	28.6	21.5	24.2	17.5	19.9	14.0	16.0	10.8	12.4	8.0	9.2	5.6	6.5
G. CUBA	1983-84	41.0	43.7	36.4	39.0	31.9	34.4	27.6	29.9	23.4	25.5	19.3	21.3	15.6	17.3	12.2	13.7	9.4	10.6	7.1	8.0
H. DOMINICAN REP.	1975-80	35.0	37.8	30.9	33.7	27.0	29.6	23.2	25.6	19.6	21.8	16.3	18.2	13.4	14.9	10.6	11.8	8.5	9.3	6.3	6.9
I. ECUADOR	1975-80	36.0	37.5	31.9	33.3	27.9	29.1	24.0	25.1	20.2	21.2	16.7	17.5	13.4	14.0	10.4	10.9	7.9	8.2	5.8	6.0
J. EL SALVADOR	1975-80	37.1	40.5	32.8	36.2	28.7	32.0	24.7	27.8	21.0	23.8	17.4	19.9	14.2	16.0	11.3	12.4	8.9	9.5	6.9	7.0
K. GUATEMALA	1975-80	35.6	36.8	31.6	32.7	27.6	28.7	23.8	24.7	20.2	20.9	16.8	17.2	13.6	14.0	11.0	11.0	8.3	8.5	6.1	6.1
L. HAITI	1975-80	31.6	32.5	27.9	28.7	24.2	24.9	20.7	21.3	17.4	17.9	14.3	14.7	11.5	11.8	9.0	9.2	7.0	7.1	5.5	5.5
M. HONDURAS	1975-80	35.7	36.6	31.7	32.5	27.7	28.5	23.8	24.5	20.0	20.6	16.5	17.0	13.4	13.8	10.5	10.8	7.9	8.1	5.3	5.5
N. MEXICO	1975-80	36.5	39.8	32.4	35.4	28.4	31.2	24.6	27.0	21.0	23.0	17.6	19.2	14.4	15.7	11.6	12.6	9.1	9.9	6.8	7.4
O. NICARAGUA	1975-80	34.9	35.7	30.9	31.6	26.9	27.5	23.1	23.6	19.4	19.8	15.9	16.2	12.7	13.0	9.8	10.0	7.5	7.7	5.7	5.8
P. PANAMA	1975-80	38.9	41.1	34.4	36.6	30.1	32.2	25.9	27.8	21.9	23.6	18.1	19.6	14.7	15.9	11.7	12.6	8.9	9.7	6.7	7.2
Q. PARAGUAY	1975-80	36.0	38.4	31.8	34.1	27.7	29.9	23.7	25.7	19.9	21.7	16.2	17.9	13.0	14.3	10.0	11.1	7.7	8.4	5.9	6.4
R. PERU	1975-80	34.7	37.6	30.5	33.3	26.4	29.0	22.5	24.8	18.7	20.7	15.2	16.7	11.9	13.1	9.0	9.9	6.6	7.3	4.8	5.2
S. URUGUAY	1975-80	36.6	42.0	32.1	37.4	27.7	32.8	23.6	28.4	19.7	24.1	16.2	20.1	13.0	16.3	10.3	12.8	7.9	9.8	6.0	7.3
T. VENEZUELA	1985	37.4	41.0	33.1	37.3	28.9	32.8	24.8	28.4	20.9	24.2	17.3	20.3	14.2	16.7	11.4	13.5	9.1	10.7	7.2	8.3
UNITED STATES‡	1984	38.9	44.9	34.3	40.1	29.9	35.5	25.4	30.9	21.5	26.6	17.9	22.5	14.6	18.6	11.6	15.0	9.0	11.8	6.9	8.9

1. The life expectancy represents average number of years of life remaining to persons surviving to exact age specified if subject to mortality conditions of period indicated, i.e., the average number of years a person of the age specified may be expected to live if the age specific mortality rates of the indicated period do not change in the future.

2. For previous years, see SALA, 23-700.

a. Estimates prepared in the Population Division of the United Nations in 1980-85.

SOURCE: CELADE-BD, 33, 1984, tables 2-21, except data for U.S. from UN-DY, 1985, table 34; 1986, table 16.;

Table 700 (Continued)

LIFE EXPECTANCY,[1] 20 LC

PART II. ESTIMATES AND PROJECTIONS, 1950–2000

Country	1950-55			1980-85			1995-2000			2020-25		
	M	F	T	M	F	T	M	F	T	M	F	T
A. ARGENTINA	60.4	65.1	62.7	66.7	73.3	69.9	68.1	74.5	71.2	68.6	75.5	72.0
B. BOLIVIA	38.5	42.5	40.4	48.6	53.0	50.7	57.0	62.0	59.4	64.5	70.0	67.2

Continued in SALA, 27-700.

Table 701

LIVE BIRTHS BY AGE OF MOTHER, 20 L
(N)

Country	Year	Total Births	Age of Mother									
			Under 15	15–19	20–24	25–29	30–34	35–39	40–44	45–49	50+	Unknown
A. ARGENTINA	1982	663,429	2,652	83,311	179,410	180,090	123,285	61,306	18,360	2,192	860	11,963
B. BOLIVIA	1977	142,277	106	14,779	39,220	36,251	24,989	16,778	6,804	2,443	907	- -

Continued in SALA, 27-701.

Table 702

FETAL DEATHS BY AGE OF MOTHER, 10 LC, 1977–85

Country	All Ages	−15	15–19	20–24	25–29	30–34	35–39	40–44	45–49	50+	Unknown
C. BRAZIL											
1977	70,471	139	8,432	17,105	14,523	9,651	7,199	3,251	528	34	9,609
1978	69,472	148	8,222	17,194	14,404	9,682	6,966	3,098	548	28	9,182
1979	69,450	146	8,327	17,204	14,602	9,632	6,774	3,063	482	24	9,196
1980	67,377	166	8,150	16,700	14,544	9,530	6,591	3,067	443	24	8,162
1981	68,654	176	8,272	17,321	14,752	9,736	6,483	2,994	441	26	8,453
1982	65,994	188	8,146	16,807	14,472	9,213	6,017	2,787	441	25	7,898
1983	61,246	168	8,008	15,806	13,500	8,600	5,576	2,540	392	19	6,637
1984	34,742	84	4,156	8,718	7,913	5,178	3,290	1,576	212	15	3,600
1985	33,707	100	4,005	8,707	7,597	5,019	3,271	1,359	196	12	3,441
D. CHILE											
1977	2,909	13	445	841	607	433	369	168	32	1	#
1978	2,534	11	436	673	526	416	306	136	30	#	#
1979	2,361	6	381	657	501	401	273	115	26	1	#
1980	2,257	6	349	678	491	339	268	111	14	1	#
1981	2,032	5	323	539	469	362	218	101	15	#	#
1982	2,003	9	308	564	454	333	226	97	11	1	#
1983	1,542	18	231	474	334	259	154	64	8	#	#
1984	1,612	28	211	471	370	241	194	85	12	#	#
1985	1,522	23	185	460	337	256	177	76	8	#	#
G. CUBA											
1977	1,981	31	579	556	391	233	121	42	7	21	#
1978	1,709	23	531	498	321	195	91	36	6	8	#
1979	1,880	15	542	461	405	241	146	57	3	10	#
1980	1,704	17	468	459	371	224	114	36	5	10	#
1981	1,652	13	426	510	346	211	121	22	2	1	#
1982	1,879	15	484	581	393	240	138	26	1	1	#
1983	1,913	15	493	592	401	244	140	25	2	1	#
1984	1,933	17	468	646	394	264	110	30	2	#	2
1985	2,059	13	437	694	458	277	154	24	2	#	#
I. ECUADOR											
1977	5,571	19	810	1,390	1,062	758	659	310	79·	484	#
1978	5,890	12	886	1,400	1,104	790	660	327	60	651	#
1979	5,586	22	797	1,293	1,071	735	618	272	60	718	#
1980	4,997	13	661	1,163	911	718	540	250	53	688	#
J. EL SALVADOR											
1977	1,324	#	259	368	241	169	159	70	20	#	38
1978	1,145	#	246	311	229	156	112	44	7	#	40
1979	1,149	#	243	287	198	128	124	56	12	#	101
1980	1,047	#	249	252	182	103	85	61	14	3	98
1981	844	3	188	233	139	81	67	31	7	1	94
1982	780	3	166	204	131	79	77	30	9	#	81
1983	961	7	202	252	154	105	88	28	3	#	122
1984	864	7	163	222	129	106	92	27	5	1	112
K. GUATEMALA											
1977	6,739	14	1,204	1,842	1,350	939	788	336	65	9	192
1978	6,825	17	1,160	1,865	1,401	1,013	843	328	66	10	122
1979	6,866	16	1,230	1,874	1,378	949	780	355	75	11	198
1981	6,709	23	1,167	1,831	1,367	1,036	809	321	69	12	74
1982	6,173	20	1,097	1,651	1,235	902	713	318	69	168	#
1983	6,316	18	1,021	1,617	1,191	979	746	325	44	8	367
1984	6,363	27	1,004	1,552	1,163	981	733	305	52	4	542
1985	6,796	52	1,075	1.615	1,328	996	816	305	60	8	541
N. MEXICO											
1977	40,876	89	4,855	8,455	7,076	4,990	4,162	1,786	272	13	9,178
1978	34,694	70	4,211	7,638	5,988	4,408	3,662	1,507	254	14	6,942
1979	34,708	65	4,149	7,434	5,990	4,233	3,381	1,429	256	21	7,750
1980	32,464	62	3,763	6,985	5,774	4,023	3,069	1,260	229	39	7,280
1981	31,583	52	3,573	6,703	5,696	3,887	2,962	1,198	235	· #	7,277
1982	28,792	42	3,161	6,036	4,864	3,409	2,477	1,042	141	12	7,608
P. PANAMA											
FORMER CANAL ZONE											
1977	7	#	1	4	2	#	#	#	#	#	#
1978	4	#	#	1	2	1	#	#	#	#	#
S. URUGUAY											
1981	776	7	78	175	153	135	120	69	#	#	21
T. VENEZUELA											
1977	8,213	51	1,371	2,168	1,797	1,285	1,038	411	67	8	17
1980	7,665	152	1,247	2,080	1,701	1,255	847	337	41	5	#
1981	7,307	137	1,171	1,966	1,613	1,247	773	342	56	2	#
1982	6,790	158	1,099	1,806	1,468	1,141	744	319	53	2	#
1983	6,850	275	1,103	1,809	1,418	1,140	735	324	46	#	#

SOURCE: UN-DY, 1986, table 39.

Table 703

CRUDE BIRTH RATES, 20 LC, 1960-86[a]
(PTI)[1]

	Country	Code	1960	1965	1970	1975	1980	1981	1982	1983	1984	1985	1986
A.	ARGENTINA	C	22.8[‡]	21.7	22.7	~	24.7	23.7	22.8	23.9	~	~	~
B.	BOLIVIA[9,10]	U	25.6[‡,c]	46.1	45.6	46.6	44.8	~	~	~	~	~	~
C.	BRAZIL[10]	U	~	42.1	38.8	35.8	33.3	30.6[‡]	30.6[‡]	30.6[‡]	30.6[‡]	30.6	~
D.	CHILE[8]	C	35.7	33.2	27.6	24.2	22.2	23.4	23.8	22.2	22.2	21.6	~
E.	COLOMBIA[10]	U	42.4[c,d]	44.6	39.6	33.3	32.0	31.0[‡]	31.0[‡]	31.0[‡]	31.0[‡]	31.0[‡]	~
F.	COSTA RICA	C	48.4	42.3	33.4	29.5	29.4	29.8	30.7	30.0	32.7	33.9	~
G.	CUBA[2,4,11]	C	29.8	33.8	27.6	20.7	14.1	14.0	16.3	16.7	16.6	18.0	16.2[‡]
H.	DOMINICAN REP.[2,10]	C	36.8[c]	42.7	35.8	22.9	24.7	21.8	22.1	22.9	20.8	~	~
I.	ECUADOR[3,10]	U	47.7[c]	46.1	44.2	42.2	41.6	36.8[‡]	36.8[‡]	36.8[‡]	36.8[‡]	36.8[‡]	~
J.	EL SALVADOR	C	46.5	46.9	40.0	39.9	24.7	21.8	22.1	22.9	20.8	~	~
K.	GUATEMALA	C	49.5	45.3	40.3	41.4	43.9	43.4	42.7	40.8	40.3	41.0	~
L.	HAITI[10]	U	~	44.4	43.7	42.7	41.8	41.3[‡]	41.3[‡]	41.3[‡]	41.3[‡]	41.3[‡]	~
M.	HONDURAS[2,10]	U	44.7[c,d]	50.9	50.0	48.6	47.1	43.9[‡]	43.9[‡]	43.9[‡]	43.9[‡]	43.9[‡]	~
N.	MEXICO[2,10]	U	46.0[b,d]	44.6	43.9	41.8	37.6	33.9[‡]	33.9[‡]	33.9[‡]	33.9[‡]	33.9[‡]	~
O.	NICARAGUA[2,10]	U	45.2[c,d]	50.0	48.6	48.3	46.6	44.2[‡]	44.2[‡]	44.2[‡]	44.2[‡]	44.2[‡]	~
P.	PANAMA[6]	C	40.8	38.4	36.4	33.2	26.9	26.9	26.7	26.4	26.5	26.6	~
Q.	PARAGUAY[3,10]	U	~	42.2	40.4	37.5	36.7	36.0[‡]	36.0[‡]	36.0[‡]	36.0[‡]	36.0[‡]	~
R.	PERU[2,7,10]	U	38.9[c,d]	46.4	44.5	40.0	40.0	41.5	35.7	36.8	36.4	35.5	~
S.	URUGUAY[2]	C	21.4[‡,c,d]	22.4	19.5	20.9	18.5	18.4	18.5	18.0	17.7	~	~
T.	VENEZUELA[5,10]	U	45.9[c,d]	45.2	37.0	35.2	32.8	32.1	32.0	31.4	29.9	29.0	~
	UNITED STATES	C	23.7	19.4	18.2	14.6	15.9	15.8	15.8	15.5	15.5	15.7[‡]	15.4[‡]

Code: C = Data estimated to be virtually complete, representing at least 90% of the events occurring each year.

U = Data estimated to be incomplete, representing less than 90% of the events occurring each year.

1. Crude birth rates are determined by the number of live births per thousand, mid-year population.
2. Data tabulated by year of registration rather than year of occurrence.
3. Excluding nomadic Amerind tribes.
4. For 1960, data estimates based on analysis of 1943 and 1953 census returns plus an assumed rate of growth.
5. Excluding Indian jungle population estimated at 31,800 in 1961.
6. Excluding Canal Zone.
7. Excluding Indian jungle population.
8. For 1960, data are births tabulated by year of occurrence.
9. Data for 1975 were based on a national sample survey.
10. U.N. Population Division estimate for years 1965-86.
11. Based on births registered in National Consumer Register.

a. For 1930-59 data, see SALA, 21-705.
b. Data considered complete.
c. Data considered incomplete.
d. Data tabulated by year of registration.

SOURCE: UN-DY, 1964, 1981 and 1985, tables 16, Special Topic Table 21, and 9 respectively; 1986, Table 21.

Table 704

AGE-SPECIFIC FERTILITY RATES, CRUDE BIRTH RATE (CBR), TOTAL FERTILITY RATE (TFR), AND GROSS REPRODUCTION RATE (GRR), 20 LC, 1975-80

		Age of Mother									
	Country	15-19	20-24	25-29	30-34	35-39	40-44	45-49	CBR	TFR	GRR
A.	ARGENTINA	57.2	149.1	158.5	115.4	66.8	21.9	5.4	21.24	2.87	1.40

Continued in SALA, 23-702.

Table 705

TOTAL FERTILITY RATES,[1] 20 L, 1950–85

| | | Period | | | % Change | |
| | | | | | 1950–55 to 1960–65 | 1960–65 to 1980–85 |
	Country	1950–55	1960–65	1980–85		
A.	ARGENTINA	3.2	3.1	3.4	–2.6	9.9
B.	BOLIVIA	6.7	6.6	6.3	–1.8	–5.6
C.	BRAZIL	6.2	6.2	3.8	0	–38.0
D.	CHILE	4.9	5.1	2.6	4.2	–49.4
E.	COLOMBIA	6.7	6.7	3.9	0	–41.5
F.	COSTA RICA	6.7	6.9	3.5	3.4	–49.6
G.	CUBA	4.0	4.7	2.0	16.4	–57.7
H.	DOMINICAN REP.	7.5	7.3	4.2	–2.5	–42.9
I.	ECUADOR	6.9	6.9	5.0	0	–27.6
J.	EL SALVADOR	6.5	6.8	5.6	6.0	–18.9
K.	GUATEMALA	7.1	6.8	6.1	–3.5	–10.5
L.	HAITI	6.2	6.2	5.7	0	–6.7
M.	HONDURAS	7.1	7.4	6.5	4.4	–11.7
N.	MEXICO	6.7	6.7	4.6	0	–31.6
O.	NICARAGUA	7.3	7.3	5.9	0	–19.0
P.	PANAMA	5.7	5.9	3.5	4.3	–41.5
Q.	PARAGUAY	6.6	6.6	4.9	0	–26.6
R.	PERU	6.9	6.9	5.0	0	–27.2
S.	URUGUAY	2.7	2.9	2.8	6.0	–4.3
T.	VENEZUELA	6.5	6.5	4.1	0	–36.5

1.   Average number of lifetime births per woman at current age-specific fertility rates.

SOURCE: *Population Bulletin* (July 1986), vol. 41, no. 3, p. 16.

Table 706

TOTAL FERTILITY RATES,[1] 4 L, 1970–2000

(N)

	Country	1970	1975	1980	1985	1990	1995	2000
C.	BRAZIL	5.33	4.54	4.42	4.06	3.74	3.45	3.20
E.	COLOMBIA	~	4.44	3.60	3.22	2.90	2.57	2.25
N.	MEXICO	6.83	~	4.57	4.05	3.59	3.20	2.85
R.	PERU	6.28	5.69	5.19	4.74	4.23	3.74	3.30

1.   Average number of children born per woman.

SOURCE: Adapted from USBC, *World Population Profile: 1985* (Washington, D.C.: U.S. Government Printing Office, 1986), p. 47.

Table 707

FERTILITY RATES, BY AGE OF MOTHER, 4 LC, 1985
(Births per 1,000 Women)

	Country	Under 20	20–24	25–29	30–34	35–39	40–44	45+
					Age of Mother			
C.	BRAZIL	74.7	198.8	210.8	160.5	108.3	48.8	10.0
E.	COLOMBIA	52.8	168.3	158.4	124.4	85.9	46.5	7.2
M.	HONDURAS	121.2	281.8	255.7	225.1	158.8	77.5	21.9
N.	MEXICO	93.8	205.4	194.4	162.1	105.4	42.6	7.0
	UNITED STATES	53.3	115.3	115.4	66.2	20.9	4.0	.2

SOURCE: Adapted from USBC, *World Population Profile: 1985* (Washington D.C.:
U.S. Government Printing Office, 1986), p. 48.

Figure 7:1

FERTILITY RATES,[1] BY AGE OF MOTHER, 4 LC, 1985
(Births per 1,000 Women)

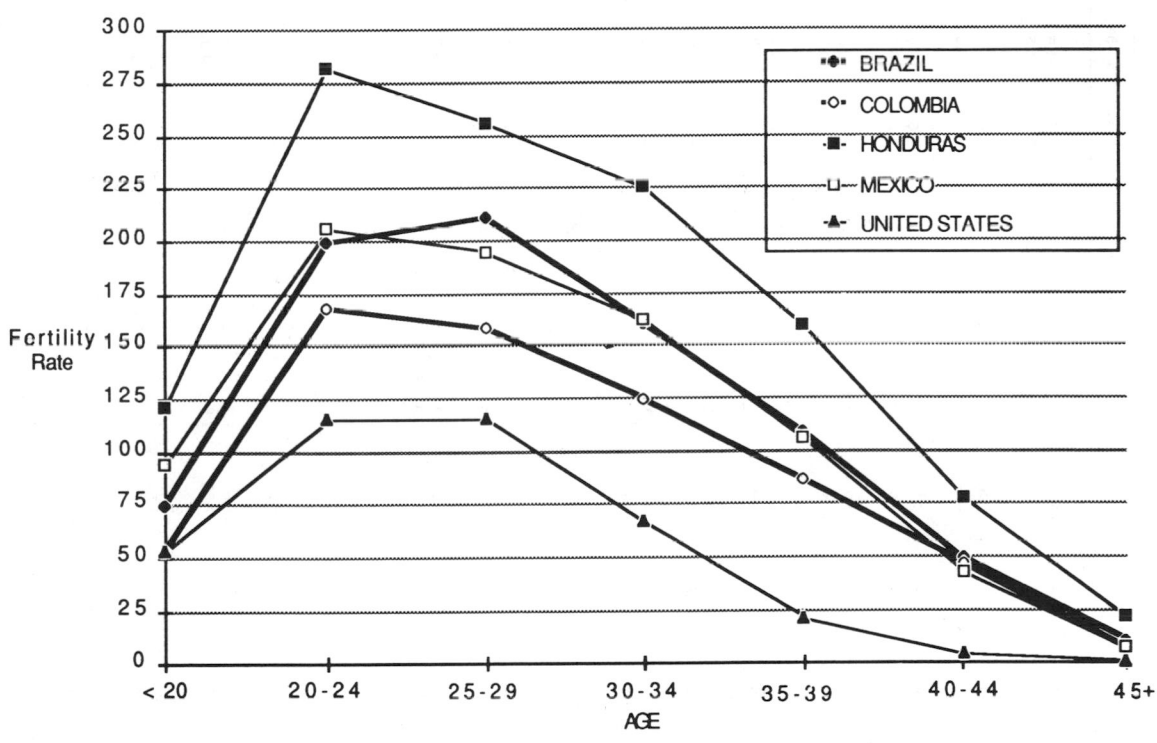

SOURCE: Table 706, above.

Table 708

DEATH RATES, BY AGE AND SEX, 15 L[1]

Age (in Years)

Country	5-9	10-14	15-19	20-24	25-29	30-34	35-39	40-44	45-49	50-54	55-59	60-64	65-69	70-74	75-79	80-84	85 Plus
A. ARGENTINA (1980)																	
Male	.5	.5	1.1	1.4	1.6	2.0	2.9	4.7	7.7	11.4	17.2	24.4	37.4	55.2	82.6	181.8	↑
Female	.4	.4	.7	.8	1.0	1.4	2.0	2.7	3.7	5.5	8.0	11.4	18.5	30.9	54.8	158.4	↑
B. BOLIVIA (1976)																	
Male	1.2	.8	1.3	2.1	2.5	3.2	3.9	5.0	6.9	8.2	11.2	15.2	32.7	↑	↑	↑	↑
Female	1.1	.8	1.1	1.8	2.4	3.1	3.2	3.8	4.6	5.6	6.9	10.0	31.2	↑	↑	↑	↑
C. BRAZIL (1985)																	
Male	.7	.7	1.5	2.3	2.8	3.4	4.5	6.2	8.6	12.0	16.1	22.5	33.3	77.7	↑	↑	↑
Female	.4	.4	.7	.8	1.0	1.4	2.1	3.1	4.4	6.2	8.9	13.1	21.2	65.1	↑	↑	↑
D. CHILE (1986)[a]																	
Male	.5	.4	1.0	1.6	1.7	2.1	2.6	4.1	6.3	9.5	15.5	21.5	33.5	55.5	86.2	148.3	↑
Female	.3	.3	.4	.5	.6	.9	1.3	2.1	3.2	4.8	8.2	11.3	18.8	32.4	52.6	125.2	↑
F. COSTA RICA (1984)																	
Male	.3	.5	.7	1.4	1.7	1.5	2.0	2.5	4.2	6.1	10.5	14.3	24.9	36.2	55.5	92.4	156.1
Female	.2	.3	.3	.6	.6	.9	1.4	1.8	2.7	3.9	6.8	10.0	16.2	27.0	48.2	72.8	144.2
G. CUBA (1986)[a]																	
Male	.5	.6	1.0	1.4	1.6	1.9	2.2	3.1	4.6	6.6	9.8	16.0	50.8	↑	↑	↑	↑
Female	.4	.4	.9	.9	1.0	1.2	1.5	2.0	3.3	4.9	7.4	11.0	41.1	↑	↑	↑	↑
I. ECUADOR (1984)[c]																	
Male	1.1	.9	1.4	2.3	2.6	2.9	3.8	4.2	6.2	8.1	10.9	16.4	21.2	40.0	61.2	186.8	↑
Female	1.0	.7	1.0	1.4	1.5	1.7	2.3	2.8	3.2	5.6	6.9	11.3	15.7	28.1	40.1	165.0	↑
K. GUATEMALA (1985)[a]																	
Male	2.0	1.3	1.9	3.3	4.0	4.8	6.4	6.6	8.2	11.4	14.8	22.8	35.8	58.4	88.1	170.7	↑
Female	2.0	1.1	1.4	2.2	2.6	3.1	4.6	4.7	5.8	7.7	11.2	17.9	25.0	49.1	75.5	163.8	↑
M. HONDURAS (1981)[b]																	
Male	1.1	.8	1.4	2.3	2.7	3.1	3.4	4.6	5.7	6.2	8.4	12.3	18.5	32.1	45.0	367.8	↑
Female	1.0	.6	.9	1.4	1.3	1.6	2.1	3.0	3.7	4.5	6.3	10.0	13.8	24.7	37.0	265.4	↑
N. MEXICO (1980)[a]																	
Male	1.0	.9	1.9	3.3	3.8	4.4	6.0	7.1	9.2	12.0	15.7	21.0	29.9	46.0	70.6	156.5	↑
Female	.7	.6	.9	1.3	1.5	1.9	2.8	3.5	4.7	6.9	9.0	13.8	20.5	33.1	52.7	153.2	↑
P. PANAMA (1986)[a]																	
Male	.5	.4	1.1	1.3	1.6	1.6	2.2	2.5	4.0	5.6	8.5	14.1	23.1	38.3	55.9	118.9	↑
Female	.5	.3	.6	.6	.7	1.2	1.4	1.6	2.2	3.5	5.2	8.5	15.6	27.2	41.7	106.4	↑
Q. PARAGUAY (1985)[a,b]																	
Male	.6	.4	.7	1.0	1.1	1.2	1.5	2.9	3.3	6.4	9.8	13.4	20.9	42.0	110.7	↑	↑
Female	.4	.4	.6	.8	1.0	1.0	1.6	2.5	3.1	5.1	5.5	8.7	14.1	27.3	102.8	↑	↑
R. PERU (1981)[b,d]																	
Male	.9	.7	1.0	1.5	1.6	1.7	2.1	2.8	3.9	5.2	7.0	11.2	16.2	25.9	77.5	↑	↑
Female	.9	.5	.8	1.2	1.3	1.5	2.1	2.4	3.1	4.0	5.5	8.1	13.1	19.8	81.9	↑	↑
S. URUGUAY (1975)[b]																	
Male	.5	.5	1.1	1.5	1.7	1.9	2.6	4.2	6.8	10.9	17.3	25.7	38.4	57.4	82.0	119.0	↑
Female	.4	.4	.6	.7	.9	1.0	1.7	2.4	3.2	5.3	8.6	12.1	20.0	33.3	53.6	93.8	↑
T. VENEZUELA (1986)[e]																	
Male	.5	.6	1.3	2.1	2.2	2.3	2.4	3.5	5.4	7.9	12.6	18.9	28.2	47.7	99.3	181.8	↑
Female	.4	.4	.6	.7	.9	1.2	1.5	2.2	3.4	5.1	7.6	12.8	19.6	34.4	86.0	175.3	↑

1. Data are for latest year available. Data exclude fetal deaths. Rates are the number of deaths by age and sex per 1,000 corresponding population.
a. Urban and Rural classification data available in source.
b. Data tabulated by date of registration rather than occurrence.
c. Excluding nomadic Indian tribes.
d. Excluding Indian jungle population, estimated at 39,800 in 1972.
e. Excluding Indian jungle population, estimated at 31,800 in 1961.
SOURCE: UN-DY, 1987, table 20.

Table 709

PERCENT OF MARRIED WOMEN[1] USING CONTRACEPTION, 18 LC, 1977–86
(%)

	Country	Year	% of Women
A.	ARGENTINA	1977	2
B.	BOLIVIA	1983	24
C.	BRAZIL	1986	65
D.	CHILE	1978	43
E.	COLOMBIA	1986	63
F.	COSTA RICA	1986	69
H.	DOMINICAN REP.	1986	50
I.	ECUADOR	1982	40
J.	EL SALVADOR	1985	48
K.	GUATEMALA	1983	25
L.	HAITI	1977	19
M.	HONDURAS	1981	27
N.	MEXICO	1982	48
O.	NICARAGUA	1977	9
P.	PANAMA	1984	58
Q.	PARAGUAY	1979	39
R.	PERU	1986	46
T.	VENEZUELA	1977	60
	UNITED STATES	1982	68

1. Ages 15 to 44.

SOURCE: Adapted from USBC, *World Population Profile: 1985* (Washington, D.C.: U.S. Government Printing Office, 1986), p. 46; 1987, pp. 51–52.

Table 710

ANNUAL BIRTH AND DEATH RATES, 20 L, 1930–85
(AA, PTI)

	Country	1930–35		1945–49		1960–65		1980–85	
		Birth	Death	Birth	Death	Birth	Death	Birth	Death
A.	ARGENTINA	28.9	11.6	25.2	9.6	23.2	8.8	24.6	8.7
B.	BOLIVIA	~	~	47.1[a]	24.1[a]	46.1	21.5	44.0	13.9
C.	BRAZIL	~	~	44.6[a]	15.1[a]	42.1	12.3	30.6	8.4
D.	CHILE	40.2	24.5	37.0	17.5	36.4	11.8	22.7	6.7
E.	COLOMBIA	43.3	22.5	43.4	20.8	44.6	12.2	31.0	7.7
F.	COSTA RICA	44.6	21.5	42.7	13.2	45.3	9.1	30.5	4.2
G.	CUBA	31.3	13.3	30.0	8.7	35.3	8.8	16.9	6.4
H.	DOMINICAN REP.	~	~	49.1[a]	21.8[a]	47.7	15.4	33.1	8.0
I.	ECUADOR	48.5	25.7	45.9	20.0	45.6	14.3	36.8	8.1
J.	EL SALVADOR	46.5	32.7	44.8	22.8	47.4	15.3	40.2	8.1
K.	GUATEMALA	46.2	31.7	49.1	26.5	47.8	18.3	42.7	10.5
L.	HAITI	~	~	45.5[a]	26.8[a]	44.4	21.6	41.3	14.2
M.	HONDURAS	42.0	21.7	44.5	19.0	50.9	17.7	43.9	10.1
N.	MEXICO	44.1	26.7	44.5	17.8	44.9	11.3	33.9	7.1
O.	NICARAGUA	~	~	54.1[a]	22.7[a]	50.3	17.1	44.2	9.7
P.	PANAMA	37.4	15.1	38.3	10.8	40.8	9.6	28.0	5.4
Q.	PARAGUAY	~	~	45.5[a]	15.5[a]	42.2	11.9	36.0	7.2
R.	PERU	~	~	44.9	24.7	46.3	17.6	36.7	10.7
S.	URUGUAY	22.3	11.6	19.7	9.1	21.9	9.6	19.5	10.2
T.	VENEZUELA	39.9	21.9	43.6	16.1	44.2	9.1	33.0	5.5

a. Data are for 1950–55 from UN, 1984 Assessment.

SOURCE: *Population Bulletin* (July 1986), vol. 41, no. 3, p. 8.

Table 711

FETAL MORTALITY RATES,[1] 16 LC, 1960-83[a]

(Deaths per 1,000 Live Births)

Country	1960	1965	1970	1975	1977	1978	1979	1980	1981	1982	1983
A. ARGENTINA	24.3	23.9	20.6	~	~	~	17.8	12.7	12.3	~	~
C. BRAZIL[2]	28.5	~	~	~	29.4	19.0	18.5	17.2	17.0	16.0	16.1

Continued in SALA, 27-709.

Table 712

INFANT MORTALITY RATES, 19 LC, 1960-85[a]

(Deaths per 1,000 Live Births)[1]

Country	Code	1960	1965	1970	1975	1980	1981	1982	1983	1984	1985
A. ARGENTINA[11]	C	62.4	56.9	58.9	~	33.2	33.6	~	35.3	~	~
B. BOLIVIA[11]	**	~	76.5	~	~	138.2[‡]	124.4[‡]	124.4[‡]	124.4[‡]	124.4[‡]	124.4[‡]
C. BRAZIL[2,11]	U	~	~	~	~	78.8[‡]	70.6[‡]	70.6[‡]	70.6[‡]	70.6[‡]	70.6[‡]
D. CHILE[6,11]	C	125.1	107.1	78.8	56.4	33.0	27.0	23.6	21.9	19.6	~
E. COLOMBIA[2,3,7,11]		99.8	82.4	~	46.7	55.0[‡]	50.0[‡]	50.0[‡]	50.0[‡]	50.0[‡]	50.0[‡]
F. COSTA RICA[12]	C	70.8	71.8	61.5	38.2	20.2	19.1	19.3	18.6	~	~
G. CUBA[2,5,9]	C	35.4[c]	38.4	35.9	27.3[‡]	19.6	18.5	17.3	16.8	15.0[‡]	16.5[‡]
H. DOMINICAN REP.[11]	U	100.6[d]	72.7	50.1	43.5	84.3[‡]	74.5[‡]	74.5[‡]	74.5[‡]	74.5[‡]	74.5[‡]
I. ECUADOR[8,11,12]	U	100.0	93.0	76.6	65.8	82.4[‡]	69.5[‡]	69.5[‡]	69.5[‡]	69.5[‡]	69.5[‡]
J. EL SALVADOR	C	76.3	70.6	66.6	58.1	42.0	44.0	42.2	~	35.1	~
K. GUATEMALA	C	91.9	92.6	87.1	81.4	65.5	63.9	62.5	71.5	~	~
M. HONDURAS[2,11]	U	52.0	41.2	33.2	33.7	94.7[‡]	81.5[‡]	81.5[‡]	81.5[‡]	81.5[‡]	81.5[‡]
N. MEXICO[2,11,13]	U	74.2[b]	60.7	68.5	52.8	60.0[‡]	53.0[‡]	53.0[‡]	53.0[‡]	53.0[‡]	53.0[‡]
O. NICARAGUA[2,11]	U	70.2	51.6[d]	~	~	93.0[‡]	76.4[‡]	76.4[‡]	76.4[‡]	76.4[‡]	76.4[‡]
P. PANAMA[4,11]	U	56.9	44.7	40.5	31.6	31.6[‡]	25.6[‡]	25.6[‡]	25.6[‡]	25.6[‡]	25.6[‡]
Q. PARAGUAY[2,11]	U	~	41.5	33.3	~	48.6[‡]	45.0[‡]	45.0[‡]	45.0[‡]	45.0[‡]	45.0[‡]
R. PERU[10,11,2]	U	92.1	90.7	~	~	104.9[‡]	98.6[‡]	98.6[‡]	98.6[‡]	98.6[‡]	98.6[‡]
S. URUGUAY[2]	C	47.4[‡,c]	49.8	42.6	48.8[d]	37.6	33.4	29.4	30.0	~	~
T. VENEZUELA[8,11]	U	53.9	47.7	49.3	43.7[d]	43.3[‡]	27.7[‡]	27.7[‡]	27.7[‡]	27.7[‡]	27.7[‡]
UNITED STATES	C	26.0	24.7	20.0	16.1	12.6	11.9	11.5	10.9[‡]	10.6[‡]	10.5[‡]

Code: C = Data estimated to be virtually complete, representing at least 90% of the
          events occurring each year.
       U = Data estimated to be virtually incomplete, representing less than 90% of the
          events occurring each year.

1. Number of deaths of infants of less than 1 year, per 1,000 live births.
2. Data tabulated by year of registration rather than of occurrence.
3. Prior to 1951 tabulated by year of registration rather than of occurrence.
4. Excluding the former Canal Zone.
5. Prior to 1957 rates excluded those dying within 24 hours of birth. Beginning in
   1957 rates computed on births which are in turn estimates based on analysis of
   1943 and 1953 census and the application of an assumed rate of growth.
6. Prior to 1968 rates computed on live births with an upward adjustment for
   undernumeration.
7. Rates computed on number of baptisms recorded in Roman Catholic Church
   registers, for years 1960, 1965, and 1970 while 1975 data are based on burial
   permits.
8. Excluding tropical forest Amerinds.
9. Rates for 1965-85 computed on live births recorded in the National Register of
   Consumers established December 31, 1964.
10. Excluding Indian jungle population estimated at 100,830 in 1961.
11. Estimate for 1975-85 prepared by the Population Division of the United Nations.
12. Rates for 1960 and 1965 were computed on live births registered during the period
    1951-65 tabulated by year of occurrence.
13. Rates computed by date of occurrence for years 1975-85.

a. For 1930-59, see SALA, 23-705.
b. Data considered complete.
c. Data considered incomplete.
d. Data tabulated by year of occurrence.

SOURCE: UN-DY, 1966, 1974, tables 14 and 20 respectively; 1979 and 1983, table 15;
   1985, table 20.

Table 713

DEATHS OF CHILDREN UNDER 5 YEARS BY PRINCIPAL CAUSE,[1] 20 LC
(N, PHTI, and %)

	Country	Date	Total		Childhood Diseases[8]			Gastritis, Enteritis, etc.[9]			Influenza, and Pneumonia		
			Number	Rate	Number	Rate	%	Number	Rate	%	Number	Rate	%
A.	ARGENTINA	1981	26,904	3,588.2	4,516	400.9	16.7	1,812	236.2	6.7	2,012	260.7	7.4
B.	BOLIVIA	1965	14,706	~	4,451	~	30.3	798	~	5.4	315	~	2.1
C.	BRAZIL	1962	45,134	2,219.0	12,344	606.9	27.3	7,885	387.6	17.5	5,351	263.1	11.9
D.	CHILE[2]	1983	6,963	2,331.8	776	267.5	11.1	338	115.9	-4.7	903	303.4	12.9
E.	COLOMBIA[6]	1967	83,935	2,398.2	17,752	507.2	21.1	18,930	540.9	22.6	9,177	262.2	10.9
F.	COSTA RICA	1983	1,624	2,226.1	255	349.5	15.7	199	272.8	12.3	111	152.2	6.8
G.	CUBA	1983	3,248	1,960.8	525	316.9	16.2	212	127.9	6.5	293	176.9	9.0
H.	DOMINICAN REP.[2]	1982	8,256	3,468.1	2,621	1,001.9	31.7	1,190	497.0	19.6	415	153.1	5.0
I.	ECUADOR[7]	1980	22,464	1,005.8	8,939	4,002.2	39.8	5,589	2,502.3	24.9	2,341	1,048.1	10.4
J.	EL SALVADOR[3]	1984	7,031	4,944.4	1,996	1,403.6	28.4	1,229	864.3	17.5	288	202.5	4.1
K.	GUATEMALA[2]	1981	28,436	6,634.9	14,377	2,946.9	50.5	7,115	1,520.4	25.0	5,002	1,158.6	17.5
L.	HAITI	~	~	~	~	~	~	~	~	~	~	~	~
M.	HONDURAS[4]	1981	6,226	3,866.6	2,601	1,615.3	41.8	1,501	932.2	24.1	374	232.3	6.0
N.	MEXICO	1982	100,278	4,190.8	31,693	1,324.5	31.6	24,328	1,016.7	24.3	16,442	687.1	16.4
O.	NICARAGUA[2]	1966	5,405	1,753.9	1,370	444.6	25.3	1,267	411.1	23.4	318	103.2	5.9
P.	PANAMA[2,5]	1984	1,473	2,599.7	238	420.0	16.2	112	197.7	7.6	95	167.7	6.4
Q.	PARAGUAY	1984	3,928	6,966.3	1,230	2,181.4	31.3	678	1,202.4	17.3	511	906.3	13.0
R.	PERU	1982	32,462	4,780.8	11,215	1,651.7	34.5	5,674	835.6	17.5	6,685	984.5	20.6
S.	URUGUAY	1984	1,805	3,014.5	332	554.5	18.4	148	247.2	8.2	73	121.9	4.0
T.	VENEZUELA[7]	1983	17,544	3,410.7	5,418	1,053.3	30.9	3,338	648.9	19.0	1,484	288.5	8.5
	UNITED STATES	1983	48,428	1,340.1	1,550	42.9	3.2	1,011	27.9	2.1	1,001	27.7	2.1

1. Unless otherwise stated, the causes of death have been classified according to the ninth revision of the International Classification of Diseases. The data refer to the number of deaths of children under 5 years of age with the national boundaries indicated. Fetal deaths are excluded as, in some cases, are those which occurred before the respective births or within 24 hours of birth.
2. Causes of death classified according to the eighth revision of the International Classification of Diseases.
3. Includes deaths of residents living abroad.

4. Data tabulated by year of record and not of death.
5. Excluding Canal Zone.
6. Data based on burial permits.
7. Excluding Selvatic Amerinds.
8. Includes infectious and parasitic diseases, measles, protein-caloric malnutrition, and meningitis except in the cases of Bolivia, Brazil, Colombia, Haiti, and Nicaragua.
9. Corresponds to the classification: Other intestinal infectious diseases.

SOURCE: AC, 1974, table 207-28; adapted from WHO-WHSA, 1985 and 1986, tables 13 and 11 respectively.

Table 714

MATERNAL DEATH RATES,[1] 14 LC, 1970–85

(Deaths PHT Live Births)

Country	1970	1975	1977	1978	1979	1980	1981	1982	1983	1984	1985
A. ARGENTINA[10]	~	~	91.5	84.5	84.6*	69.5	69.4	~	~	~	~
C. BRAZIL[3,4]	~	~	~	~	96.8	92.1	88.6	77.1	78.1	~	~
D. CHILE[10]	125.7	122.2	107.8	94.7	74.9	74.9*	43.8	52.5	41.0	35.5	~
E. COLOMBIA[2,4]	~	~	133.5[b]	~	~	~	~	~	~	~	~
F. COSTA RICA[9,10]	105.6	70.5	53.0	39.5[a]	44.3[a]	24.2*,[a]	38.4[3]	29.5[a]	26.0[a]	22.4	~
G. CUBA[10]	48.0[c]	38.9[c]	49.1[c]	45.2[c]	~	59.9*	51.4	55.7	45.4	46.3	~
I. ECUADOR[2,4,5]	220.3	231.9	198.5	216.3	~	~	185.9	~	~	~	~
J. EL SALVADOR[3]	~	~	~	~	~	70.6	61.8	84.8	74.2	69.6	~
K. GUATEMALA[10]	142.8	~	120.8	119.8	150.3*	91.0	105.7	~	~	75.6	~
N. MEXICO[10]	135.3	113.5	~	100.4	108.3*	93.9	86.9	90.5	~	~	~
P. PANAMA[4,6,9,10]	118.2	94.7	68.3	90.5	69.9*	72.2	61.3	89.9	59.8	49.4[a]	56.9
R. PERU[4,7,10]	198.5[c]	~	171.5[c]	148.2	69.9*	108.2	91.9	88.4	~	~	~
S. URUGUAY[2]	44.8[a]	69.3	58.6	55.9	~	~	59.3	36.6	39.3	37.8	~
T. VENEZUELA[4,8,10]	~	68.4	74.8	65.2	~	64.7	53.3	~	58.9	~	~
UNITED STATES[10]	18.1	12.9	11.2	9.6	9.6*	9.2	8.5	7.9	8.0	~	~

1. Deaths due to complications of pregnancy, childbirth, and the puerperium. For an alternative series, 1965–75, see SALA, 21-711.
2. All data classified by 1965 Revision.
3. All data classified by 1975 Revision.
4. Data from incomplete civil registers.
5. Excluding nomadic Indian tribes.
6. Prior to 1980, excluding former Canal Zone.
7. Excluding Indian jungle population estimated at 100,831 in 1961 and 39,800 in 1972.
8. Excluding Indian jungle population estimated at 31,800 in 1961.
9. Data for 1970 were classified by 1965 Revision.
10. Separates data classified by 8th and 9th Revisions of the Abbreviated List of Causes for Tabulation of Mortality in the International Classification of Diseases.

a. Rates based on 30 or fewer maternal deaths.
b. Based on burial permits.
c. Data tabulated by date of registration rather than date of occurrence.

SOURCE: UN-DY, 1979 and 1985, tables 17 and 24, respectively; 1986, table 11.

Table 715

FIRST FIVE PRINCIPAL CAUSES OF DEATH AND RATE BY SEX, 18 LC

(All Ages)

Principal Cause of Death	Total				Male				Female			
	Rank Order	N	Rate PHTI	%	Rank Order	N	Rate PHTI	%	Rank Order	N	Rate PHTI	%
A. ARGENTINA (1981)												
All causes	**	241,904	843.2	100.0	**	138,504	802.2	100.0	**	103,400	905.0	100.0
Diseases of the heart[2]	1	77,483	269.2	31.9	1	43,194	250.0	31.3	1	34,115	300.0	33.1
Malignant neoplasms	2	42,700	148.8	17.6	2	24,693	143.0	17.8	2	18,007	157.6	17.5
Cerebrovascular disease	3	23,044	80.3	9.5	3	11,981	69.4	8.7	3	11,063	96.8	10.7
Accidents and adverse effects	4	12,293	42.8	5.1	4	8,767	50.8	6.3	5	3,526	30.9	3.4
Causes of perinatal mortality	5	10,348	36.1	4.3	5	5,926	34.3	4.3	4	4,422	38.7	4.3

Continued in SALA, 26-713.

Table 716

ARGENTINA FIVE PRINCIPAL CAUSES OF DEATH, BY AGE AND SEX
(1981)

Principal Causes of Death, All Ages	Total				Male				Female			
	Rank	N	Rate	%	Rank	N	Rate	%	Rank	N	Rate	%
All Deaths		241,904	843.0	100.0		138,504	971.0	100.0		103,400	716.6	100.0
Diseases of the Heart	1	70,246	244.8	29.0	1	40,241	282.1	29.0	1	30,005	207.9	29.0
Malignant Neoplasms	2	41,885	146.0	17.3	2	24,016	168.4	17.3	2	17,869	123.8	17.3
Cerebrovascular Disease	3	23,045	80.3	9.5	3	11,932	84.0	8.6	3	11,063	76.7	10.7
Accidents	4	12,293	42.8	5.1	4	8,767	61.5	6.3	- -	3,526	24.4	3.4
Atherosclerosis	5	11,584	40.4	4.8	- -	5,231	36.7	3.8	4	6,353	44.0	6.1
Certain Conditions Originating in the Perinatal Period	- -	10,653	37.1	4.4	5	6,113	42.9	4.4	5	4,540	31.5	4.4

SOURCE: PAHO-HC, 1981–84.

Table 717

CHILE TEN PRINCIPAL CAUSES OF DEATH, 1981–84

Cause	1981		1982		1983		1984	
	N	%	N	%	N	%	N	%
Total	69,871	100.0	69,999	100.0	74,428	100.0	74,455	100.0
Diseases of the Circulatory System	19,040	27.3	19,312	27.6	20,555	27.6	21,101	28.3
Malignant Neoplasms	11,476	16.4	11,772	16.8	11,969	16.1	11,987	16.1
Injury and Poisoning	8,839	12.6	8,576	12.2	9,130	12.3	9,104	12.2
Diseases of the Respiratory System	6,563	9.4	5,931	8.5	7,413	10.0	7,821	10.5
Symptoms, Signs, and Ill-Defined Conditions	5,898	8.4	6,058	8.6	6,733	9.0	6,544	8.8
Diseases of the Digestive System	5,788	8.3	6,003	8.6	6,612	8.9	6,489	8.8
Infectious and Parasitic Diseases	2,856	4.1	2,678	3.8	2,694	3.6	2,662	3.6
Causes of Perinatal Mortality	2,642	3.8	2,542	3.6	2,218	3.0	1,814	2.4
Endocrine, Nutritional, and Metabolic Diseases and Immunity Disorders	1,697	2.4	1,987	2.8	1,845	2.5	1,745	2.3
Diseases of the Genitourinary System	1,562	2.2	1,445	2.1	1,573	2.1	1,671	2.2
Other	3,510	5.1	3,737	5.4	3,686	4.9	3,517	4.8

SOURCE: PAHO-HC, 1981–84.

Table 718

HONDURAS TEN PRINCIPAL CAUSES OF DEATH
AND RATE, 1979 AND 1983

Rank	Cause (1983)	Rate PHTI	
		1979	1983
1	Ill-Defined Intestinal Infections	56.5	33.5
2	Cardiac Dysrhythmias	17.5	16.2
3	Ill-Defined Descriptions and Complications of Heart Disease	15.4	12.6
4	Pneumonia, Organism Unspecified	11.7	9.5
5	Assault by Other and Unspecified Means	9.5	8.7
6	Other and Unspecified Environmental and Accidental Causes	8.8	8.4
7	Other and Ill-Defined Cerebrovascular Disease	~	8.3
8	Malignant Neoplasm without Specification of Site	9.6	6.8
9	Assault by Firearms and Explosives	~	6.6
10	Other and Ill-Defined Conditions Originating in the Perinatal Period	~	6.4

SOURCE: PAHO-HC, 1981–84.

Table 719

VENEZUELA POPULATION, DEATHS BY AGE GROUP, AND RATE, 1978 AND 1982

Age Group (Year)	Population		Deaths		Rates PTI	
	1978	1982	1978	1982	1978	1982
Total	14,070,880	15,939,738	72,470	78,329	5.2	4.9
Under 1	492,200	528,217	16,325	15,231	34.3[a]	29.9[a]
1–4	1,745,070	1,883,736	4,021	3,657	2.3	1.9
5–14	3,925,775	4,017,101	2,294	2,196	.6	.5
15–24	2,856,389	3,320,019	4,405	4,949	1.5	1.5
25–44	3,180,019	3,958,604	7,714	8,714	2.4	2.2
45–64	1,477,442	1,709,916	14,589	15,959	9.9	9.3
65 and Over	393,985	522,147	23,122	27,627	58.7	52.9

a. Rates per 1,000 live births.

SOURCE: PAHO-HC, 1981–84.

Table 720

ARGENTINA MORTALITY RATE BY SEX AND AGE, AND MORTALITY RATIO BY SEX, 1960 AND 1980

Age Group (Year)	Rate (1960)			Ratio Male/Female (1960)	Rate (1980)			Ratio Male/Female (1980)
	Total	Male	Female		Total	Male	Female	
Under 1	62.37	67.06	57.47	1.17	33.22	36.71	29.65	1.24
1–4	4.54	4.54	4.54	1.00	1.55	1.62	1.48	1.09
5–9	.89	.95	.81	1.17	.47	.54	.40	1.35
10–14	.71	.80	.62	1.29	.45	.52	.38	1.37
15–19	1.34	1.61	1.08	1.49	.88	1.08	.67	1.61
20–24	1.83	2.20	1.48	1.49	1.14	1.47	.82	1.79
25–29	2.12	2.49	1.76	1.41	1.35	1.65	1.05	1.57
30–34	2.32	2.66	1.98	1.34	1.70	2.01	1.38	1.46
35–39	3.01	3.68	2.34	1.57	2.47	3.02	1.93	1.57
40–44	4.30	5.35	3.25	1.65	3.81	4.84	2.78	1.74
45–49	6.49	8.33	4.65	1.79	5.81	7.82	3.81	2.05
50–54	10.41	13.72	6.96	1.97	8.46	11.61	5.49	2.11
55–59	15.82	20.88	10.40	2.01	12.49	17.25	8.01	2.15
60–64	24.46	32.39	16.41	1.97	18.72	26.22	12.09	2.17
65–69	35.09	44.73	25.40	1.76	27.62	38.21	18.78	2.03
70 and Over	80.36	92.02	70.45	1.31	77.27	84.85	66.43	1.28
Total	8.96	10.46	7.38	1.42	8.63	9.98	7.32	1.36

SOURCE: PAHO-HC, 1981–84.

Table 721

MEXICO DEATHS, BY AGE GROUP
(1981)

Age Group (Years)	Deaths	Rate[1]
Total	424,274	5.95
Infants (Under 1)	87,358	34,52
Preschool (1–4)	24,820	2.74
School Age (5–14)	14,856	.74
15–24	25,927	1.79
25–34	26,307	2.75
35–44	28,703	4.67
45–54	33,195	7.78
55–64	39,829	14.31
65 and Over	134,846	53.22
Unspecified Age	8,433	- -

1. Infant mortality is calculated per 1,000 registered live births. The crude death rate and death rates by age group are per 1,000 persons.

SOURCE: PAHO-HC, 1981–84.

Table 722

PARAGUAY DEATHS, BY AGE GROUP, 1981–84

Age Group (Years)	Deaths				%				Rate PTI			
	1981	1982	1983	1984	1981	1982	1983	1984	1981	1982	1983	1984
Total	12,603	12,308	13,507	14,106	100	100	100	100	6.3	6.4	6.7	6.6
Under 1	2.688	2,570	2,688	2,808	21.3	20.9	19.9	19.9	59.0	51.2	51.0	49.8
1–4	948	937	985	1,120	7.5	7.6	7.3	7.9	4.2	3.8	3.8	4.1
5–14	336	351	366	395	2.7	2.8	2.7	2.8	.6	.7	.7	.7
15 and Over	8,631	8,450	9,468	9,783	68.7	68.7	70.1	69.4	7.5	7.7	8.1	8.0

SOURCE: PAHO-HC, 1981–84.

Table 723

GUATEMALA GENERAL, MATERNAL, AND INFANT MORTALITY RATE, 1970–84

Category	1970	1982	1983	1984
General Mortality (PTI)	14.7	9.5	10.1	8.6
Maternal Mortality (Per 1,000 live births)	1.6	1.3	1.2	.8
Infant Mortality (Per 1,000 live births)	80.5	48.3	81.1	68.5

SOURCE: PAHO-HC, 1981–84.

Table 724

REPORTED CASES AND DEATHS FROM DIPHTHERIA, 20 LC, 1973–76

| | Cases | | | | | | | | Deaths | | | | | | | |
| | N | | | | PHTI | | | | N | | | | PHTI | | | |
Country	1973	1974	1975	1976	1973	1974	1975	1976	1973	1974	1975	1976	1973	1974	1975	1976
A. ARGENTINA	325	290	148	183	1.3	1.2	.6	.7	~	~	~	~	~	~	~	~

Continued in SALA, 24-709.

Table 725

REPORTED CASES AND RATES OF AMEBIASIS AND BACILLARY DYSENTERY, 17 LC, 1973–76

| | Amebiasis | | | | | | | | Bacillary Dysentery | | | | | | | |
| | N | | | | PHTI | | | | N | | | | PHTI | | | |
Country	1973	1974	1975	1976	1973	1974	1975	1976	1973	1974	1975	1976	1973	1974	1975	1976
A. ARGENTINA[a]	~	~	~	~	~	~	~	~	139,439	144,811	~	~	564.1	578.1	~	~

Continued in SALA, 24-710.

Table 726

WESTERN HEMISPHERE RANKING OF TOTAL CONFIRMED CASES OF AIDS, 19 LC

(December 31, 1986)

Ranking	Country	Cases	Deaths
1	UNITED STATES	29,003	16,301
2	Canada	926	436
3	BRAZIL[a]	921	497
4	HAITI[b]	507	111
5	MEXICO[c]	316	100
6	Trinidad and Tobago	134	93
7	DOMINICAN REP.	96	35
8	Bahamas	85	29
9	VENEZUELA	69	54
9	ARGENTINA	69	37
11	French Guiana	58	41
12	Bermuda	48	29
13	Guadeloupe	40	23
14	COLOMBIA	30	15
15	CHILE	22	14
16	Martinique	16	10
16	COSTA RICA	16	11
18	GUATEMALA	15	8
18	Barbados	15	9
20	HONDURAS	13	7
21	PANAMA[d]	12	9
22	PERU[b]	9	6
23	URUGUAY	8	5
24	ECUADOR[b]	7	4
25	Jamaica	6	6
25	EL SALVADOR	6	3
27	St. Lucia[b]	3	2
27	St. Vincent[b]	3	2
27	Grenada	3	3
30	Suriname[b]	2	2
30	Antigua and Barbuda	2	2
30	Turks and Caicos	2	2
33	PARAGUAY	1	1
33	BOLIVIA[b]	1	1
33	CUBA[b]	1	1
33	Caymans	1	1
33	St. Chris/Nevis[b]	1	0
33	Belize	1	0

a. As of November 20, 1986.
b. As of June 31, 1986.
c. As of January 15, 1987.
d. As of September 30, 1986.

SOURCE: *Times of the Americas*, May 6, 1987.

Table 727

RANKING OF AMERICAN COUNTRIES
BY CASES OF AIDS, 19 LC
(PHTI, December 31, 1986)

Ranking	Country	Number
I	BERMUDA	84.73
2	FRENCH GUIANA	79.43
3	BAHAMAS	37.28
4	TURKS AND CAICOS	26.90
5	GUADELOUPE	12.82
6	TRINIDAD AND TOBAGO	12.42
7	UNITED STATES	12.08
8	HAITI[a]	8.83
9	Barbados	5.98
10	Caymans	5.33
11	Martinique	5.28
12	Canada	3.69
13	Grenada	3.26
14	Antigua and Barbuda	2.52
15	St. Lucia[a]	2.42
16	St. Vincent[a]	2.35
17	St. Chris/Nevis[a]	2.25
18	DOMINICAN REP.	1.71
19	BRAZIL[b]	.65
19	Belize	.65
21	COSTA RICA	.62
22	PANAMA[c]	.60
23	Suriname[a]	.50
24	VENEZUELA	.47
25	MEXICO[d]	.40
26	HONDURAS	.30
27	URUGUAY	.27
28	Jamaica	.26
29	ARGENTINA	.23
30	GUATEMALA	.19
31	CHILE	.18
32	EL SALVADOR	.12
33	COLOMBIA	.11
34	ECUADOR[a]	.8
35	PERU[a]	.5
36	PARAGUAY	.3
37	BOLIVIA[a]	.2
38	CUBA[a]	.1

a. As of June 31, 1986.
b. As of November 20, 1986.
c. As of September 30, 1986.
d. As of January 15, 1987.

SOURCE: *Times of the Americas*, May 6, 1987.

Table 728

CUMULATIVE KNOWN AIDS CASES AND DEATHS, 20 LC

(1987)

Subregion and County	Cases	Deaths	Date of First Report	Date of Last Report
LATIN AMERICA	4,338	1,392		
Southern Cone[2]	181	95		
A. ARGENTINA	112	56	31 Dec 83	18 Sep 87
D. CHILE	42	22	31 Dec 84	30 Jun 87
Q. PARAGUAY	14	9	31 Dec 86	30 Jun 87
S. URUGUAY	13	8	31 Dec 83	30 Jun 87
C. BRAZIL	2,013	734	31 Dec 82	15 Sep 87
Andean Area	352	140		
B. BOLIVIA	2	1	31 Dec 85	18 Sep 87
E. COLOMBIA	153	53	31 Dec 86	1 Sep 87
I. ECUADOR	52	6	31 Dec 85	15 Sep 87
R. PERU	44	6	30 Jun 82	15 Sep 87
T. VENEZUELA	101	74	31 Dec 84	18 Sep 87
Central America	142	84		
F. COSTA RICA	31	18	31 Dec 83	30 Jun 87
J. EL SALVADOR	12	6	31 Dec 85	30 Jun 87
K. GUATEMALA	27	27	30 Sep 86	30 Jun 87
M. HONDURAS	29	13	30 Jun 85	30 Jun 87
O. NICARAGUA	19	0	18 Sep 87	18 Sep 87
P. PANAMA	22	18	31 Dec 84	18 Sep 87
M. MEXICO	534	177	30 Jun 81	30 Jun 87
Latin Caribbean	1,116	162		
G. CUBA	4	3	31 Dec 86	30 Jun 87
H. DOMINICAN REP.	200	35	31 Dec 85	31 Mar 87
L. HAITI	912	124	31 Dec 84	18 Sep 87
OTHER CARRIBBEAN[3]	628	350		
NORTH AMERICA	43,138	24,770		
Bermuda	62	43	31 Dec 84	30 Jun 87
Canada	1,258	657	31 Dec 79	14 Sep 87
UNITED STATES[4]	41,818	24,070	30 Jun 81	14 Sep 87
Total	48,104	26,512		

1. As of September 1987.
2. Includes Falkland Islands.
3. Includes French Guiana, Guyana, and Suriname.
4. Includes Puerto Rico.

SOURCE: "PAHO Bulletin," vol. 21, No. 4, 1987, p. 423.

Table 729

MARRIAGES, 19 LC, 1965-85

N

Country	Code	1965	1970	1975	1980	1982	1983	1984	1985	1986
A. ARGENTINA	C	152,625	174,137	~	~	~	177,010‡	~	~	~
B. BOLIVIA	U	20,838	~	24,315	26,990	~	~	~	~	~
C. BRAZIL6	U	~	109,027	840,614	948,164	994,246	866,190	936,070	~	~
D. CHILE1	C	64,922	71,631	76,205	86,001	80,115	82,483	87,261	91,099	~
E. COLOMBIA1,4	U	86,722	110,704	72,370	~	~	~	~	~	~
F. COSTA RICA	C	8,562	11,024	14,683	17,527	18,542	19,171	20,558	~	~
G. CUBA	C	67,323	110,982	65,416‡	68,941	80,295	75,920	75,524	80,407	82,815‡
H. DOMINICAN REP.1	C	12,712	16,987	20,411	26,862	28,874	~	~	~	~
I. ECUADOR5	U	30,362	35,558	37,858	48,305	~	49,571	54,038	56,560	~
J. EL SALVADOR	C	10,315	11,763	16,628	22,763	20,387	~	16,727	~	~
K. GUATEMALA	C	15,112	18,150	24,354	29,519	31,233	30,422	33,415	38,489	~
M. HONDURAS1	C	7,611	9,704	11,254	~	16,051	19,875	~	~	~
N. MEXICO1	C	293,227	356,658	472,091	495,996	528,963	~	~	~	~
O. NICARAGUA1	C	6,224	~	~	17,174	~	~	~	~	~
P. PANAMA2	C	4,710	7,324	8,042	10,252	11,321	11,346	12,253	12,430	~
Q. PARAGUAY1	U	8,065	13,103	14,313	17,259	13,053	~	16,354	~	~
R. PERU1,7	C	45,160	50,810	~	~	109,200	~	~	~	~
S. URUGUAY3	C	20,976	23,668	24,404	22,448	20,068	19,168	~	~	~
T. VENEZUELA8	~	49,523	60,128	85,662	92,608	90,977	93,452	92,137	93,939	~
UNITED STATES	C	1,800,207	2,158,802	2,127,000	2,390,252	2,495,000‡	2,445,604	2,477,192	2,425,000	2,430,000‡

Rate PTI

Country	1965	1970	1975	1980	1982	1983	1984	1985	1986
A. ARGENTINA	6.8	7.3	~	~	~	6.0	~	~	~
B. BOLIVIA	4.8	~	4.3	4.8	~	~	~	~	~
C. BRAZIL	~	1.2	~	7.8	7.8	6.7	7.1	~	~
D. CHILE	7.5	7.7	7.4	7.7	7.0	7.0	7.3	7.5	~
E. COLOMBIA	4.8	5.2	3.1	~	~	~	~	~	~
F. COSTA RICA	5.7	6.4	7.5	7.8	8.0	7.9	3.5	~	~
G. CUBA	8.8	13.1	7.0	7.1	8.2	7.7	7.6	8.0	8.1‡
H. DOMINICAN REP.	3.5	4.2	4.4	4.9	5.0	~	~	~	~
I. ECUADOR	5.9	5.8	5.4	5.8	~	5.6	5.9	6.0	~
J. EL SALVADOR	3.5	3.3	4.2	4.8	4.4	~	3.5	~	~
K. GUATEMALA	3.4	3.6	4.0	4.1	4.3	4.0	4.3	4.8	~
M. HONDURAS	3.5	3.9	3.6	~	4.1	4.9	~	~	~
N. MEXICO	6.9	7.0	7.8	7.2	7.2	~	~	~	~
O. NICARAGUA	3.8	~	~	6.3	~	~	~	~	~
P. PANAMA	4.0	5.1	4.8	5.2	5.5	5.4	5.7	5.7	~
Q. PARAGUAY	4.0	5.7	5.4	5.4	4.3	~	4.6	~	~
R. PERU	3.9	3.7	~	2.7	6.0	6.5	~	~	~
S. URUGUAY	7.7	8.2	8.7	7.7	6.8	5.7	5.5	5.4	~
T. VENEZUELA	5.7	5.9	7.1	6.7	5.7	~	5.5	5.4	~
UNITED STATES	9.3	10.5	10.0	10.5	10.7‡	10.4	10.5	10.1‡	9.9‡

Code: C = Data estimated to be virtually complete, representing at least 90% of the events occurring each year.

U = Data estimated to be incomplete, representing less than 90% of the events occurring each year.

1. Data tabulated according to year of registration rather than year of marriage.
2. Excludes marriages in Canal Zone and indigenous villages.
3. Data for years 1965 and 1970 are considered incomplete.
4. Except for Bogotá, data are only for marriages recorded in Roman Catholic Church registers.
5. Excludes marriages in indigenous jungle population.
6. For state capitals only except for the 1965 data.
7. Excludes marriages in indigenous jungle population, estimated at 39,800 in 1972.
8. Excludes marriages in indigenous jungle population, estimated at 31,800 in 1961.

SOURCE: UN-DY, 1969, 1974, tables 47 and 11 respectively; 1979 and 1983, table 23; 1985, table 12; 1986, table 17.

Table 730

DIVORCES, 19 LC, 1965–85

N

Country	Code	1965	1970	1975	1980	1981	1982	1983	1984	1985
A. ARGENTINA[1]	~	**	**	**	**	**	**	**	**	**
B. BOLIVIA[1]	~	**	**	**	**	**	**	**	**	**
C. BRAZIL[10]	~	**	**	**	**	~	27,266	31,521	30,847	~
D. CHILE[1]	~	**	**	**	**	**	**	**	**	**
E. COLOMBIA[1]	~	**	**	**	**	**	**	**	**	**
F. COSTA RICA	C	181	226	318	1,733	2,010	2,371	~	~	~
G. CUBA[7]	C	8,937	24,813	22,819[‡]	24,487	28,091	31,343	29,931	28,310	29,297
H. DOMINICAN REP.[2]	C	1,199	3,754	9,292	~	~	~	~	~	~
I. ECUADOR[6]	~	1,300	1,291	1,679	2,737	3,010	2,967	3,133	3,546	~
J. EL SALVADOR	C	671	847	1,286	1,549	1,589	1,738	~	1,549	~
K. GUATEMALA[2]	C	436	674	912	~	1,368[‡]	1,126[‡]	1,328[‡]	1,302[‡]	1,435[‡]
M. HONDURAS[2]	C	363	454	672	~	885	970	1,520	~	~
N. MEXICO[2]	C	24,705	28,779	16,791	21,674	22,989	25,901	~	~	~
O. NICARAGUA[1]	~	292	~	~	759	~	~	~	~	~
P. PANAMA[3]	C	579	574	949	1,116	1,039	1,156	1,172	1,361	1,476
Q. PARAGUAY[1]	~	**	**	**	**	**	**	**	**	**
R. PERU[4]	~	1,803	~	~	~	~	~	~	~	~
S. URUGUAY[2,8,9]	C	2,500	2,927	3,430	4,298	4,297	3,706	3,023	~	~
T. VENEZUELA[4]	~	2,292	2,467	4,377	~	5,653	5,371	5,740	~	~
UNITED STATES[5]	U	479,000	708,000	1,026,000	1,189,000	1,213,000	1,170,000	1,158,000	1,169,000	1,187,000

Rate PTI

Country	Code	1965	1970	1975	1980	1981	1982	1983	1984	1985
A. ARGENTINA[1]	~	**	**	**	**	**	**	**	**	**
B. BOLIVIA[1]	~	**	**	**	**	**	**	**	**	**
C. BRAZIL[10]	~	**	**	**	**	~	.21	.24	.23	~
D. CHILE[1]	~	**	**	**	**	**	**	**	**	**
E. COLOMBIA[1]	~	**	**	**	**	**	**	**	**	**
F. COSTA RICA	C	.12	.13	.16	.77	.88	1.02	~	~	~
G. CUBA[7]	C	1.17	2.92	2.45[‡]	2.52	2.89	3.20	3.02	2.83	2.90
H. DOMINICAN REP.[2]	C	.33	.92	1.98	~	~	~	~	~	~
I. ECUADOR[6]	~	.25	.21	.24	.33	.36	.34	.35	.39	~
J. EL SALVADOR	C	.23	.24	.32	.33	.35	.37	~	.32	~
K. GUATEMALA[2]	C	.10	.13	.15	~	.19[‡]	.15[‡]	.18[‡]	17[‡]	18[‡]
M. HONDURAS[2]	C	.17	.18	.24	~	.23	.24	.37	~	~
N. MEXICO[2]	C	.58	.57	.28	.31	.32	.35	~	~	~
O. NICARAGUA[1]	~	.18	**	**	.28	~	~	~	~	~
P. PANAMA[3]	C	.49	.40	.57	.57	.52	.56	.56	.64	.68
Q. PARAGUAY[1]	~	**	**	**	**	**	**	**	**	**
R. PERU[4]	~	.15	~	~	~	~	~	~	~	~
S. URUGUAY[2,8,9]	C	.92	1.01	1.22	1.48	1.44	1.26	1.02	~	~
T. VENEZUELA[4]	~	.26	.24	.37	~	.36	.34	.35	~	~
UNITED STATES[5]	U	2.47	3.47	4.82	5.22	5.27	5.03	4.94	4.93	4.96

Code: C = Data estimated to be virtually complete, representing at least 90% of the events
    occurring each year.
    U = Data estimated to be incomplete, representing less than 90% of the events
    occurring each year.

1. There are no legal provisions for "divorce."
2. Data tabulated according to year of registration and not year of divorce.
3. Excludes divorces in the Canal Zone and among indigenous tribal Indian population
   numbering 62,187 in 1960.
4. Excludes indigenous jungle population.
5. Estimates based on incomplete data for some states; includes annulments.
6. Excludes nomadic Indian tribes.
7. Data for years 1965 and 1970 are considered incomplete.
8. Includes annulments since 1970.
9. Data for 1965 are considered incomplete.
10. Divorce legal in Brazil since 1981.

SOURCE: UN-DY, 1969, 1974, tables 49 and 13 respectively; 1979 and 1983, table 25;
    1985, table 14; 1986, table 19.

8

Health, Nutrition, Family Planning and Welfare

Table 800

SUMMARY OF HEALTH, EDUCATION, AND COMMUNICATION (HEC) INDICATORS, 1940–80

PART I: HEC COMPONENTS

Health (H), 5 items

    Life expectancy at birth—LIFE
    Infant mortality rate (deaths under one year of age per 1,000 live births)—INFANT
    Persons per hospital bed—BEDS
    Population per physician—DOCTORS
    Persons per dentist—DENTISTS

Education (E), 4 items

    Literacy percentage for population age 15 and over—Literate
    Percentage of school-age population 7-14 enrolled in primary school—Primary
    Students enrolled in secondary school as a percentage of school-age population 13-18—Secondary
    College enrollment (including, professional, technical, and vocational schools) as a percentage of
        primary school enrollment—College

Communication (C), 3 items

    Newspaper circulation, copies per 1,000 persons—News
    Number of telephones per 100 persons—Telephone
    Number of persons per motor vehicle (autos, buses, trucks) in use—Motor

PART II: HEC INDEXES[1] AND INDEX REDUCTION RATES (IRR) FOR LATIN AMERICA
(0% = EQUALITY)

Health Indexes

Year	LIFE	INFANT	BEDS	DOCTORS	DENTISTS	Subtotals and Total Indexes[2]	IRR[3]
1940	39.5	67.8	81.5	73.0	81.9	68.7	- -
1950	26.5	73.6	82.8	77.4	82.7	68.6	−.1
1960	18.6	70.5	79.1	73.5	80.6	64.5	−6.0
1970	14.1	74.4	70.7	69.6	69.9	59.7	−7.4
1980	12.2	80.3	64.3	64.1	64.0	57.0	−4.5

Education Indexes

Year	LITERATE	PRIMARY	SECONDARY	COLLEGE		
1940	48.5	44.4	89.0	90.7	68.2	- -
1950	43.3	49.0	90.4	85.0	66.9	−1.9
1960	32.7	36.0	83.3	80.9	58.2	−13.0
1970	26.3	22.2	69.9	82.2	50.2	−13.7
1980	19.2	16.2	58.8	82.5	44.2	−12.0

Communication Indexes

Year	NEWS	TELEPHONE	MOTOR		
1940	78.4	93.7	98.4	90.2	- -
1950	82.2	95.0	97.9	91.7	1.7
1960	76.4	95.0	97.1	89.5	−2.4
1970	74.3	94.9	95.6	88.3	−1.3
1980	70.2	92.7	91.7	84.9	−3.6

Total Index

Year		IRR
1940	73.9	- -
1950	73.8	−.1
1960	68.6	−7.0
1970	63.7	−7.1
1980	59.7	−6.3

1. The indexes (weighted by population in each Latin American country) presented here are calculated as the scaled percentage decrease necessary in each year to bring the United States and Latin America to equality. (The scale occurs in the process of calculating the percentage decrease between high and low absolute numbers because there is a ceiling of 100% on possible changes.) At .0 equality will exist. In 1940 the total index was 73.9, closing to 63.7 in 1970. If during the 1970s to 1990s the Index Reduction Rate (IRR) closes linearly at the same rate as during the 1950s and 1960s, the index will stand at about 59.2 by 1980 and 51.1 by the year 2000.
2. Arithmetic mean for 5 Health items, 4 Education items, 3 Communication items, and 12 HEC items in each decade. Each item is equally weighted, thus giving Health an implicit weight of 42% in the total index, Education 33%, and Communication 25%.
3. The IRR is calculated here as the rate of change in the subtotals and totals, summary index scores from decade to decade. A minus sign (−) indicates that the index is improving, i.e., the gap is narrowing between Latin America and United States.

SOURCE: James W. Wilkie, *The Narrowing Gap: Primary Social Change in the Americas since 1940.* Statistical Abstract of Latin America Supplement Series (Los Angeles: UCLA Latin American Center Publications, forthcoming).

Table 801

HEC TOTAL INDEX BY COUNTRY,[1] 20 LRC, 1940–80

(Average for 12 indicators; 0 = U.S. Equality with Latin America)

	Country	1940	1950	1960	1970	1980
A.	ARGENTINA	46.1	46.4	39.9	34.0	38.2
B.	BOLIVIA	83.9	79.8	76.1	70.6	67.8
C.	BRAZIL	74.7	73.9	68.5	61.5	56.4
D.	CHILE	63.5	61.8	57.9	54.1	55.1
E.	COLOMBIA	77.3	73.8	69.7	65.6	61.7
F.	COSTA RICA	69.3	65.8	60.9	57.2	49.9
G.	CUBA	58.7	57.5	55.2	54.3	40.3
H.	DOMINICAN REP.	80.4	77.5	70.2	66.7	67.2
I.	ECUADOR	80.2	76.3	71.2	67.7	60.6
J.	EL SALVADOR	79.9	78.8	74.1	69.7	69.9
K.	GUATEMALA	83.8	81.2	79.1	77.0	76.1
L.	HAITI	88.3	89.7	86.7	86.2	83.9
M.	HONDURAS	82.9	81.0	77.2	71.7	73.1
N.	MEXICO	74.1	75.5	70.1	63.8	54.9
O.	NICARAGUA	80.3	76.9	73.3	68.9	66.8
P.	PANAMA	66.9	61.9	60.3	56.6	48.0
Q.	PARAGUAY	77.0	71.8	67.9	67.3	63.8
R.	PERU	77.5	75.5	67.6	61.2	56.8
S.	URUGUAY	44.2	42.3	40.6	40.4	34.9
T.	VENEZUELA	75.2	69.9	61.2	55.8	49.2
	LATIN AMERICA[2]	73.9	73.8	68.6	63.7	59.7

1. The index presented here is calculated as the scaled percentage decrease necessary to bring the United States and Latin America to equality. (The scale occurs in the process of calculating the percentage decrease between high and low absolute numbers because there is a ceiling of 100% on possible changes.) At .0 no index gap will exist. In 1940 the 12-item average was 73.9 closing to 63.7 in 1970.
2. Data are weighted by the population of each Latin American country.

SOURCE: See table 800.

Table 802

ADJUSTED PHYSICAL QUALITY OF LIFE INDEX (PQLI),[1] 20 LRC, 1950 TO MID 1970s

(Zero = No Gap with U.S. Best Performance Expected by the Year 2000 for Arithmetic Average of Three Equally Weighted Items)[2]

	Country	1950	1960	1970[a]	Mid-1970s
A.	ARGENTINA	12	9	8	10
B.	BOLIVIA	~	~	~	56
C.	BRAZIL	36	28	27	29
D.	CHILE	27	26	16	16
E.	COLOMBIA	42	27[g]	20	23
F.	COSTA RICA	22	13[f]	7[j]	10
G.	CUBA	~	~	~	10
H.	DOMINICAN REP.	42[k]	29	30	31
I.	ECUADOR	41[b]	31[c]	26	26
J.	EL SALVADOR	38	30[e]	29[i]	31
K.	GUATEMALA	53	47[e]	41	41
L.	HAITI	~	68	56	55
M.	HONDURAS	~	~	~	42
N.	MEXICO	34[k]	26[d]	22	20
O.	NICARAGUA	47	38[f]	~	40
P.	PANAMA	21	18	12[i]	16
Q.	PARAGUAY	~	~	~	20
R.	PERU	~	33[e]	27	30
S.	URUGUAY	~	6[h]	~	9
T.	VENEZUELA	31	22[e]	14[i]	16
	LATIN AMERICA[3]	~	~	~	25

1. Converted here from "100 = no gap" to "0 = no gap" according to the following formula: (100) minus (unadjusted PQLI) minus (U.S. figure).
2. The PQLI includes 3 items: life expectancy at age 1, infant mortality, literacy of persons age 15 and over.

   a. Compared to United States in 1971.
   b. 1952.   d. 1959.   f. 1963.   h. 1966.   j. 1973.
   c. 1962.   e. 1961.   g. 1964.   i. 1971.   k. 1951.
3. Data are weighted by the population of each Latin American country.

SOURCE: 1950-70 data adapted from Morris David Morris, *Measuring the Condition of the World's Poor: The Physical Quality of Life Index* (New York: Pergamon, 1979), pp. 150-152; and *The United States and World Development: Agenda 1979* (New York: Praeger, 1979), pp. 169-171. Mid-1970s data adapted from *Agenda 1979*, pp. 158-166, except total here calculated with population weights for each country.

Table 803

FOOD, HEALTH, AND NUTRITION, 19 L, 1965–87

Country	1965	1975	1980–87[a]
A. ARGENTINA			
Index of Food Production/C (1979–81 = 100)	86	94	98
Per Capita Supply of:			
Calories (per Day)	3,209	3,287	3,216
Proteins (Grams per Day)	101	107	107
Population per Physician (T)	.6	.5	~
Population per Nurse (T)	.6	1.0	~
Population per Hospital Bed (T)	~	~	~
Access to Safe Water (% of Population):			
Total	~	66	67
Urban	~	76	72
Rural	~	26	19
B. BOLIVIA			
Index of Food Production/C (1979–81 = 100)	89	109	89
Per Capita Supply of:			
Calories (per Day)	1,868	2,017	2,171
Proteins (Grams per Day)	50	53	57
Population per Physician (T)	3.3	2.1	4.8
Population per Nurse (T)	4.0	3.1	2.5
Population per Hospital Bed (T)	~	.5	~
Access to Safe Water (% of Population):			
Total	~	34	43
Urban	~	81	78
Rural	~	6	12
C. BRAZIL			
Index of Food Production/C (1979–81 = 100)	86	94	103
Per Capita Supply of:			
Calories (per Day)	2,405	2,490	2,657
Proteins (Grams per Day)	60	60	60
Population per Physician (T)	2.5	1.6	1.3
Population per Nurse (T)	1.5	2.3	1.1
Population per Hospital Bed (T)	~	.2	~
Access to Safe Water (% of Population):			
Total	~	77	75
Urban	~	87	80
Rural	~	57	52
D. CHILE			
Index of Food Production/C (1979–81 = 100)	97	96	105
Per Capita Supply of:			
Calories (per Day)	2,591	2,530	2,544
Proteins (Grams per Day)	70	69	65
Population per Physician (T)	2.1	~	~
Population per Nurse (T)	.6	.5	~
Population per Hospital Bed (T)	~	~	.3
Access to Safe Water (% of Population):			
Total	~	70	85
Urban	~	78	100
Rural	~	14	18
E. COLOMBIA			
Index of Food Production/C (1979–81 = 100)	83	92	97
Per Capita Supply of:			
Calories (per Day)	2,174	2,325	2,588
Proteins (Grams per Day)	51	49	57
Population per Physician (T)	2.5	1.9	~
Population per Nurse (T)	.9	7.5	~
Population per Hospital Bed (T)	~	~	.6
Access to Safe Water (% of Population):			
Total	~	64	70
Urban	~	86	89
Rural	~	33	30
F. COSTA RICA			
Index of Food Production/C (1979–81 = 100)	76	107	92
Per Capita Supply of:			
Calories (per Day)	2,366	2,575	2,807
Proteins (Grams per Day)	58	60	64
Population per Physician (T)	2.0	~	~
Population per Nurse (T)	.6	.5	~
Population per Hospital Bed (T)	~	~	.3
Access to Safe Water (% of Population):			
Total	59	72	88
Urban	85	100	93
Rural	44	56	86

Table 803 (Continued)

FOOD, HEALTH, AND NUTRITION, 19 L, 1965–87

Country	1965	1975	1980–87[a]
H. DOMINICAN REP.			
Index of Food Production/C (1979–81 = 100)	95	101	97
Per Capita Supply of:			
Calories (per Day)	1,870	2,198	2,530
Proteins (Grams per Day)	41	46	51
Population per Physician (T)	1.7	2.3	1.4
Population per Nurse (T)	1.6	2.2	1.2
Population per Hospital Bed (T)	~	.4	~
Access to Safe Water (% of Population):			
Total	~	55	62
Urban	~	88	85
Rural	~	27	33
I. ECUADOR			
Index of Food Production/C (1979–81 = 100)	118	106	105
Per Capita Supply of:			
Calories (per Day)	1,942	2,042	2,005
Proteins (Grams per Day)	51	48	43
Population per Physician (T)	3.0	2.9	~
Population per Nurse (T)	2.3	6.3	~
Population per Hospital Bed (T)	~	.4	~
Access to Safe Water (% of Population):			
Total	12	36	59
Urban	33	67	98
Rural	2	8	21
J. EL SALVADOR			
Index of Food Production/C (1979–81 = 100)	95	106	89
Per Capita Supply of:			
Calories (per Day)	1,859	2,061	2,155
Proteins (Grams per Day)	50	53	52
Population per Physician (T)	~	4.1	2.6
Population per Nurse (T)	1.3	.9	~
Population per Hospital Bed (T)	~	.5	~
Access to Safe Water (% of Population):			
Total	~	53	55
Urban	~	89	71
Rural	~	28	43
K. GUATEMALA			
Index of Food Production/C (1979–81 = 100)	87	102	94
Per Capita Supply of:			
Calories (per Day)	2,028	2,184	2,345
Proteins (Grams per Day)	57	57	61
Population per Physician (T)	3.7	~	~
Population per Nurse (T)	8.2	~	1.4
Population per Hospital Bed (T)	~	.5	.6
Access to Safe Water (% of Population):			
Total	11	39	51
Urban	30	85	90
Rural	2	14	26
L. HAITI			
Index of Food Production/C (1979–81 = 100)	106	105	95
Per Capita Supply of:			
Calories (per Day)	2,007	1,926	1,784
Proteins (Grams per Day)	46	45	42
Population per Physician (T)	14.0	12.5	8.2
Population per Nurse (T)	12.9	7.4	~
Population per Hospital Bed (T)	~	1.3	1.4
Access to Safe Water (% of Population):			
Total	~	12	33
Urban	~	46	73
Rural	~	3	25
M. HONDURAS			
Index of Food Production/C (1979–81 = 100)	92	89	88
Per Capita Supply of:			
Calories (per Day)	1,963	2,112	2,224
Proteins (Grams per Day)	51	52	55
Population per Physician (T)	5.4	3.8	3.1
Population per Nurse (T)	1.5	1.5	~
Population per Hospital Bed (T)	~	.6	.8
Access to Safe Water (% of Population):			
Total	~	41	69
Urban	~	99	91
Rural	~	13	55

Table 803 (Continued)

FOOD, HEALTH, AND NUTRITION, 19 L, 1965–87

Country	1965	1975	1980–87[a]
N. MEXICO			
Index of Food Production/C (1979–81 = 100)	90	92	95
Per Capita Supply of:			
Calories (per Day)	2,643	2,860	3,126
Proteins (Grams per Day)	67	72	79
Population per Physician (T)	2.1	1.5	1.2
Population per Nurse (T)	1.0	1.4	~
Population per Hospital Bed (T)	~	.8	~
Access to Safe Water (% of Population):			
Total	~	62	74
Urban	~	70	90
Rural	~	49	40
O. NICARAGUA			
Index of Food Production/C (1979–81 = 100)	97	113	73
Per Capita Supply of:			
Calories (per Day)	2,398	2,378	2,464
Proteins (Grams per Day)	69	69	64
Population per Physician (T)	2.6	2.1	2.3
Population per Nurse (T)	1.4	~	.6
Population per Hospital Bed (T)	~	.4	.4
Access to Safe Water (% of Population):			
Total	13	56	56
Urban	29	100	98
Rural	0	14	9
P. PANAMA			
Index of Food Production/C (1979–81 = 100)	91	99	95
Per Capita Supply of:			
Calories (per Day)	2,255	2,312	2,423
Proteins (Grams per Day)	57	63	59
Population per Physician (T)	2.1	1.7	1.0
Population per Nurse (T)	.7	1.6	~
Population per Hospital Bed (T)	~	.3	.3
Access to Safe Water (% of Population):			
Total	~	77	62
Urban	~	100	97
Rural	~	54	26
Q. PARAGUAY			
Index of Food Production/C (1979–81 = 100)	95	89	100
Per Capita Supply of:			
Calories (per Day)	2,627	2,686	2,873
Proteins (Grams per Day)	70	72	81
Population per Physician (T)	1.9	2.3	1.8
Population per Nurse (T)	1.6	2.2	.7
Population per Hospital Bed (T)	~	.6	~
Access to Safe Water (% of Population):			
Total	6	13	25
Urban	15	25	46
Rural	0	5	10
R. PERU			
Index of Food Production/C (1979–81 = 100)	132	119	96
Per Capita Supply of:			
Calories (per Day)	2,324	2,272	2,120
Proteins (Grams per Day)	62	59	52
Population per Physician (T)	1.7	1.9	1.5
Population per Nurse (T)	.9	~	~
Population per Hospital Bed (T)	~	.4	.6
Access to Safe Water (% of Population):			
Total	~	47	52
Urban	~	72	73
Rural	~	15	18
S. URUGUAY			
Index of Food Production/C (1979–81 = 100)	95	100	97
Per Capita Supply of:			
Calories (per Day)	2,811	2,907	2,791
Proteins (Grams per Day)	85	88	79
Population per Physician (T)	.9	.9	.5
Population per Nurse (T)	.6	~	~
Population per Hospital Bed (T)	~	.2	.3
Access to Safe Water (% of Population):			
Total	~	76	83
Urban	~	97	95
Rural	~	25	27

Table 803 (Continued)

FOOD, HEALTH, AND NUTRITION, 19 L, 1965–87

Country	1965	1975	1980–87[a]
T. VENEZUELA			
Index of Food Production/C (1979–81 = 100)	103	109	98
Per Capita Supply of:			
Calories (per Day)	2,321	2,475	2,485
Proteins (Grams per Day)	59	65	66
Population per Physician (T)	1.2	1.1	1.2
Population per Nurse (T)	.6	2.6	3.2
Population per Hospital Bed (T)	~	3.0	2.7
Access to Safe Water (% of Population):			
Total	~	74	80
Urban	~	79	80
Rural	~	59	79

a. Refers to most recent estimates of population between 1980 and 1987.

SOURCE: WB, *Health Indicators* (1988).

Table 804

PHYSICIANS, NURSES, AND NURSING AUXILIARIES, 20 LRC

(Ca. 1979)

		Physicians				Nursing Personnel			
						Nurses		Nursing Auxiliaries	
Country	Year	N	PTI	Year		N	PTI	N	PTI
A. ARGENTINA	1979	71,253	26.7	1977		18,658	7.2	22,153	8.5
B. BOLIVIA	1974	2,583	4.7	1980		955	1.7	2,498	4.5

Continued in SALA, 27-803.

Table 805

POPULATION PER PHYSICIAN 20 L, 1960–80

Country	1960	1969	1970	1971	1972	1973	1974	1975	1976	1977	1978	1979	1980
A. ARGENTINA	680	518	~	~	495	~	~	521	~	~	~	383	~
B. BOLIVIA	5,756	~	2,231	~	2,342	~	2,117	~	~	~	~	~	~

Continued in SALA, 28-804.

Table 806

PROFESSIONAL AND AUXILIARY HEALTH PERSONNEL, 20 LC

(Ca. 1979)

PART I.

Country	Year	Pharmacy		Radiology		Midwifery			Community Health	
		Pharma-cists	Auxil-iaries	Radiol-ogists	X-Ray Techni-cians[1]	Nurse Midwives	Assistant Midwives	Tradition-al Birth Attendants	Health Educa-tors	Health Promo-ters
A. ARGENTINA	1979	919	692	~	3,447	~	~	~	25	1,789

PART II.

Country	Year	Environmental Health		Nutrition	Data Management		Rehabilitation	Health Institution Support Personnel		Animal Health
		Sanitary Engineers	Sanitary Inspectors	Nutritionists and Dieticians	Statistical Personnel	Medical Re-cord Personnel	Therapy Personnel	Health Admin-istrators[1]	Laboratory Personnel	Veterinarians
A. ARGENTINA	1979	~	61	508	1,283	~	~	~	3,142	~

Continued in SALA, 24-805.

Table 807

DENTISTS AND DENTAL AUXILIARIES, 20 LC

(Ca. 1979)

Country	Year	Dentists		Dental Auxiliaries[1]
		N	PTI	N
A. ARGENTINA	1979	7,415	2.8	1,068

Continued in SALA, 24-806.

Table 808

NURSES BY MAJOR FUNCTION, 18 LC

(Ca. 1980)

Country	Practicing Nurses	Hospital Nurses	Nursing Faculty	Providers of Direct Com-munity Care	Community Health Supervisors	Trainers of Community Health Workers	Private Sector	Other
A. ARGENTINA	18,658	12,607	310	~	~	380	5,361	#

Continued in SALA, 23-809.

Table 809

HOSPITALS BY TYPE, 20 LRC

			Short-Stay Hospitals				Other Hospitals					
Country	Year	Total	Total	General[2]	Maternity	Pediatrics	Total	Tuberculosis	Mental Diseases	Leprosy	Cancer	Other[3]
A. ARGENTINA	1973	2,864	2,733	2,486	216	31	131	31	57	7	6	30

Continued in SALA, 24-808.

Table 810

HOSPITALS: NUMBER, PERCENTAGE, AND OWNERSHIP, 20 LRC

			Government		Private Non-Profit		Private Profit	
Country	Year	Total	N	%	N	%	N	%
A. ARGENTINA	1969	2,864	1.294[c]	45.2[c]	~	~	1,570	54.8

Continued in SALA, 24-809

Table 811

**SHORT-STAY HOSPITALS[1]: INDICES OF UTILIZATION
BY ALL TYPES OF OWNERSHIP, 19 LRC**

(Ca. 1978)

Country	Year	Beds	Discharges	Patient Days	Turnover Rate	Average Days of Stay	Occupancy Rate (%)
A. ARGENTINA	1973	72,221	1,174,415	18,314,265	16.3	15.6	69.5

Continued in SALA, 24-810.

Table 812

**HOSPITAL BEDS AND RATE, IN THE CAPITAL
AND REST OF COUNTRY, 20 LC**

		Total	Capital and Major Cities		Rest of Country	
Country	Year	Hospital/ Beds	Beds	Rate PTI	Beds	Rate PTI
A. ARGENTINA	1971	46,149	32,129[g]	2.5[g]	14,020	1.3

Continued in SALA, 20-810.

Table 813

HOSPITAL BEDS: NUMBER, PERCENTAGE, AND OWNERSHIP, 20 LRC

(Ca. 1978)

Country	Year	Total	Government		Private Non-Profit		Private Profit	
			N	%	N	%	N	%
A. ARGENTINA	1969	133,847	103,752[a]	77.5[a]	~	~	30,095	22.5

Continued in SALA, 24-812.

Table 814

HEALTH ESTABLISHMENTS WITH OUTPATIENT SERVICES, 15 L

(Ca. 1979)

Country	Year	Total	Health Centers	Clinics and Dispensaries	Other
C. BRAZIL	1980	8,646	4,370	4,276	#

Continued in SALA, 23-804.

Table 815

URBAN AND RURAL HEALTH ESTABLISHMENTS WITH OUTPATIENT SERVICES, 8 L

(Ca. 1979)

Country	Year	Total	Localities of 20,000 or More				Localities of 19,999 or Less			
			Total		Hospitals	Other	Total		Hospitals	Other
			N	%			N	%		
J. EL SALVADOR	1979	330	125	37.9	25	100	205	62.1	7	198

Continued in SALA, 23-805.

Table 816

MENTAL HEALTH CLINICS, REHABILITATION CENTERS, AND DENTAL CLINICS, 11 LC
(Ca. 1972 and 1978)

Country	Mental Health Clinics 1972	1978	Rehabilitation Centers 1972	1978	Dental Clinics 1972	1978
D. CHILE	2	4	24	~	1	50

Continued in SALA, 23-806.

Table 817

CHILD HEALTH SERVICES, 8 L
(Ca. 1979)

Country	Year	Children Attended Centers with Information	Under 1 Year	Per 100 Live Births	1-4 Years	Ratio[1]	Visits Centers with Information	Under 1 Year	1-4 Years
E. COLOMBIA	1976	~	502,431	68.7	703,915	20.6	~	1,011,195	1,373,960

Continued in SALA, 23-812.

Table 818

CHILDREN UNDER ONE YEAR RECEIVING BCG, DPT, MEASLES, AND POLIOMYELITIS VACCINES, 20 L
(%)

Country	BCG	DPT First Dose	Third Dose	Measles	Polio First Dose	Third Dose
A. ARGENTINA	64	67	42	60	100	96

Continued in SALA, 23-813.

Figure 8:1

A. ARGENTINA 1955-BASED INDEX OF FOOD/C PRODUCTION, 20 LRC, 1952–81

(1955 = 100)

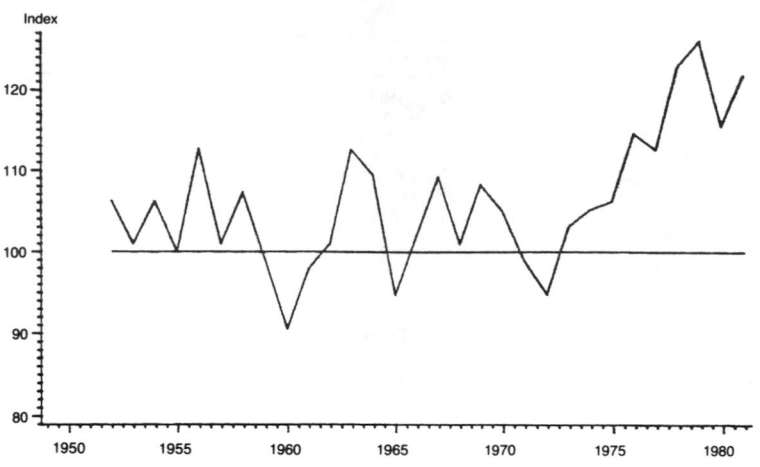

Continued in James W. Wilkie and Manuel Moreno–Ibáñez "Food Production in Latin
America Since 1952," SALA 23-35:23 through 35:44.

Figure 8:2

A. ARGENTINA PC IN FOOD/C PRODUCTION, 20 LRC, 1953–81

(0 = Equilibrium between Food Production and Population)

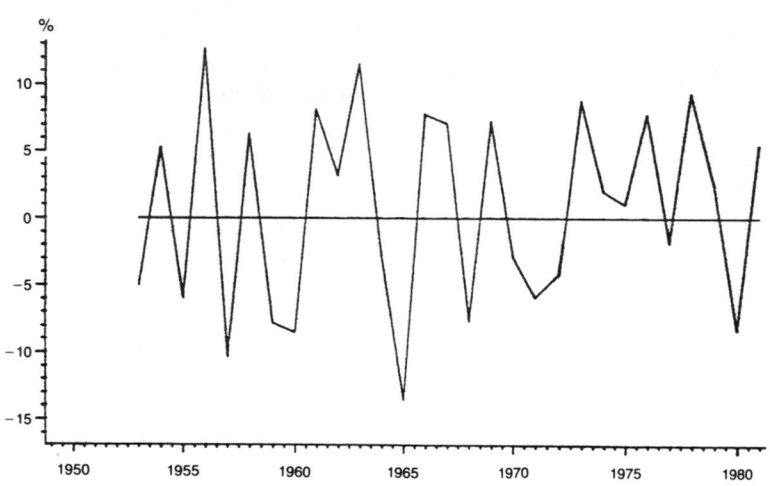

Continued in James W. Wilkie and Manuel Moreno–Ibáñez "Food Production in Latin
America Since 1952," SALA 23-35:1 through 35:22.

Table 819

TOTAL FOOD PRODUCTION INDEX,[1] 20 LC, 1974–87
(1979–81 = 100)

Country	1974	1975	1976	1977	1978	1979	1980	1981	1982	1983	1984	1985	1986	1987
A. ARGENTINA	87.71	86.79	93.88	93.00	98.23	102.09	95.88	102.33	107.47	104.44	107.60	105.50	108.72	107.18
B. BOLIVIA	88.05	95.41	98.77	93.09	93.58	94.12	99.44	106.44	111.88	83.86	107.30	115.40	112.46	112.71
C. BRAZIL	80.10	83.73	89.09	93.21	88.55	92.62	103.03	104.35	112.81	108.20	114.48	124.33	116.95	127.83
D. CHILE	87.07	88.70	87.26	95.54	89.58	96.50	97.29	106.21	104.60	99.08	104.47	107.29	116.07	118.00
E. COLOMBIA	76.20	82.27	89.00	88.72	94.09	99.01	98.87	102.12	100.54	99.07	103.35	104.95	112.81	116.42
F. COSTA RICA	84.48	92.43	95.79	97.64	98.99	102.11	98.67	99.22	94.22	96.66	106.31	104.53	108.22	104.50
G. CUBA	79.04	78.47	81.96	89.05	96.74	101.91	93.84	104.25	108.50	105.87	114.75	110.89	113.82	106.22
H. DOMINICAN REP.	94.36	90.21	95.82	98.05	101.19	100.80	98.89	100.61	105.16	110.54	115.00	112.14	111.26	112.11
I. ECUADOR	88.45	91.86	93.35	95.04	92.86	95.13	101.19	103.68	107.69	91.91	102.32	119.95	119.43	117.97
J. EL SALVADOR	80.61	91.35	90.66	91.91	104.12	106.33	100.41	93.26	86.42	91.12	103.86	99.11	104.08	101.01
K. GUATEMALA	79.18	88.99	92.91	95.12	96.10	96.04	99.82	104.44	112.03	111.79	111.73	110.53	114.30	107.02
L. HAITI	92.85	93.37	96.15	91.92	98.12	101.37	98.94	99.69	99.87	104.18	106.73	109.29	110.88	114.37
M. HONDURAS	80.96	74.28	80.35	87.64	95.73	90.22	100.89	108.89	101.19	94.81	95.52	94.71	95.01	95.41
N. MEXICO	78.68	80.07	81.56	88.85	97.22	93.57	100.07	106.36	102.68	109.39	109.82	110.10	109.82	110.81
O. NICARAGUA	87.77	98.50	103.78	106.59	116.14	124.58	86.49	88.93	94.48	94.57	90.35	92.19	91.61	85.00
P. PANAMA	85.50	88.17	87.03	93.97	96.93	98.06	97.76	104.18	102.04	107.15	106.85	110.15	113.85	107.06
Q. PARAGUAY	77.97	76.24	80.58	86.98	87.60	95.98	98.16	105.86	107.84	112.66	121.23	128.99	119.55	134.05
R. PERU	105.98	104.24	106.59	107.00	104.39	104.72	93.34	101.95	111.68	103.08	115.46	113.34	112.24	115.35
S. URUGUAY	98.39	97.06	109.46	91.50	89.65	89.52	95.64	114.84	111.97	114.81	104.66	106.06	105.83	107.67
T. VENEZUELA	81.69	92.43	87.07	89.46	96.36	100.38	99.84	99.78	99.22	107.53	104.04	102.95	116.19	109.73
UNITED STATES	83.38	90.01	92.36	95.92	94.64	99.00	95.78	105.22	104.76	89.65	102.22	107.81	102.36	98.96

1. Food Production Index is included in Index of Total Agricultural Production, table 2100.

SOURCE: FAO-PY, 1985, table 4; 1986, table 4; 1987, table 4.

Table 820

PER CAPITA FOOD PRODUCTION INDEX,[1] 20 LC, 1976–87

(1979–81 = 100)[a],[b]

Country	1976	1977	1978	1979	1980	1981	1982	1983	1984	1985	1986	1987
A. ARGENTINA	100.09	97.56	101.42	103.73	95.57	100.70	104.07	99.54	100.95	97.47	98.98	96.17
B. BOLIVIA	109.70	100.76	98.71	96.71	99.54	103.75	106.19	77.49	96.49	100.99	95.74	93.33
C. BRAZIL	97.77	99.93	92.77	94.83	103.10	102.07	107.90	101.20	104.74	111.31	102.55	109.80
D. CHILE	92.63	99.93	92.33	98.01	97.37	104.63	101.43	94.59	98.17	99.25	105.75	105.89
E. COLOMBIA	96.98	94.64	98.24	101.17	98.88	99.95	96.31	92.88	94.84	94.29	99.28	100.38
F. COSTA RICA	107.85	106.70	104.91	105.04	98.56	96.40	89.14	89.09	95.51	91.52	92.47	87.14
G. CUBA	84.49	90.94	98.02	102.55	93.83	103.62	107.23	104.02	112.04	107.50	109.27	100.98
H. DOMINICAN REP.	105.03	104.96	105.88	103.12	98.58	98.30	100.36	103.06	104.75	99.82	96.88	95.48
I. ECUADOR	104.80	103.66	98.41	97.95	101.25	100.79	101.74	84.37	91.26	103.95	100.66	96.69
J. EL SALVADOR	101.81	100.22	110.23	109.30	100.25	90.45	81.44	83.40	92.32	85.49	87.04	81.88
K. GUATEMALA	103.86	103.42	101.65	98.81	99.59	101.61	105.97	102.80	99.89	96.08	96.53	87.82
L. HAITI	105.77	98.77	102.95	103.84	98.92	97.24	95.04	96.68	96.56	96.39	95.26	95.71
M. HONDURAS	92.78	97.65	102.94	93.62	101.05	105.33	94.55	85.64	83.44	80.08	77.89	75.82
N. MEXICO	91.37	96.67	102.81	96.23	100.15	103.62	97.44	101.14	99.00	96.79	94.26	92.87
O. NICARAGUA	115.71	115.61	122.61	127.90	86.20	85.90	88.30	85.46	78.91	77.81	74.77	67.07
P. PANAMA	95.15	100.44	101.33	100.26	97.80	101.94	97.69	100.38	97.98	98.87	100.09	92.22
Q. PARAGUAY	91.93	95.99	93.52	99.15	98.21	102.64	101.42	102.85	107.45	111.07	100.11	109.17
R. PERU	118.32	115.68	109.93	107.44	93.30	99.26	105.94	95.27	103.97	99.46	96.06	96.28
S. URUGUAY	112.19	93.33	90.89	90.16	95.70	114.13	110.52	112.53	101.86	102.47	101.46	102.46
T. VENEZUELA	99.59	98.89	102.93	103.63	99.61	96.76	93.52	98.52	92.65	89.11	97.98	90.14
UNITED STATES	96.43	99.14	96.79	100.13	95.74	104.12	102.64	87.01	98.32	102.77	96.74	92.73

1. Per Capita Food Production Index is included in Index of Per Capita Agricultural Production, table 2101. For a long-term data, cf. SALA, 23, Ch. 35.

a. These index numbers are calculated by FAO on a uniform basis employing regionally constant weights. They differ from national index numbers produced by the countries themselves because of differences in concepts of production, coverage, weights, time reference of the production data, and method of calculation. They are not substitutes for National Index numbers. Whenever revised basic data are reported, the index numbers previously published are revised accordingly.

b. For previous years, see SALA, 24-819, and SALA, 25-819.

SOURCE: FAO-PY, 1988, table 9.

Table 821

DAILY CALORIC INTAKE, 20 LRC, 1961-86

(PI)

YA

Country	1961-63	1965	1966-68	1969-71	1975-77	1978-80	1979-81	1980-82	1981-83	1983-85	1984-86
A. ARGENTINA	3,135	2,868	3,252	3,318	3,362	3,386	3,239	3,368	3,195	3,195	3,191
B. BOLIVIA	1,794	1,731	1,915	1,948	2,041	2,086	2,097	2,116	2,061	2,114	2,127
C. BRAZIL	2,311	2,541	2,487	2,469	2,493	2,517	2,621	2,574	2,564	2,629	2,643
D. CHILE	2,562	2,523	2,742	2,675	2,616	2,738	2,637	2,706	2,662	2,589	2,574
E. COLOMBIA	2,231	2,220	~	2,158	~	2,473	2,499	2,536	2,543	2,578	2,550
F. COSTA RICA	2,196	2,223	2,313	2,404	2,480	2,635	2,615	2,638	2,548	2,772	2,781
G. CUBA	2,274	2,665	2,381	2,582	2,678	2,717	2,839	2,917	2,874	3,094	3,107
H. DOMINICAN REP.	1,872	2,004	1,919	2,085	2,117	2,133	2,323	2,147	2,330	2,468	2,464
I. ECUADOR	1,817	1,848	1,924	1,955	2,087	2,092	2,059	2,081	2,052	2,031	2,058
J. EL SALVADOR	~	1,877	1,840	~	2,076	2,163	~	~	~	~	~
K. GUATEMALA	1,946	1,952	1,971	2,098	2,035	2,064	2,194	2,111	2,189	2,298	2,296
L. HAITI	1,993	1,904	1,855	1,913	1,793	1,882	1,887	1,906	1,901	1,843	1,902
M. HONDURAS	1,924	1,930	2,059	2,151	2,081	2,175	2,176	2,170	2,143	2,208	2,078
N. MEXICO	2,559	2,623	2,685	2,704	2,756	2,803	3,051	2,930	2,966	3,147	2,925
O. NICARAGUA	~	2,253	2,523	~	2,445	2,284	~	~	~	~	~
P. PANAMA	2,243	2,317	2,425	2,344	2,398	2,290	2,338	2,388	2,305	2,420	2,439
Q. PARAGUAY	2,427	2,732	2,658	2,754	2,774	2,902	2,770	2,824	2,817	2,813	2,843
R. PERU	2,227	2,255	2,225	2,289	2,209	2,166	2,166	2,141	2,150	2,144	2,192
S. URUGUAY	2,783	3,039	2,837	3,003	2,918	2,868	2,793	2,809	2,706	2,721	2,676
T. VENEZUELA	2,221	2,392	2,316	2,412	2,538	2,649	2,662	2,557	2,664	2,550	2,532
LATIN AMERICA[1]	2,251	2,295	2,333	2,403	2,416	2,449	2,498	2,467	2,481	2,534	2,521
UNITED STATES	3,189	3,393[a]	3,380	3,392	3,552	3,652	3,529	3,630	3,647	3,652	3,642

1. Unweighted average.

a. 1966-68.

SOURCE: Derived from Mexico — BNCE — CE, March 1981; FAO-PY, 1982, table 103; 1984, table 105; 1985, table 105; 1986, table 106; 1987, table 106.

Table 822

PERCENT OF MINIMUM DAILY CALORIC REQUIREMENTS, 19 LR, 1961-77

Country	1961-63	1975-77
A. ARGENTINA	137.9	143.1

Continued in SALA, 23-108.

Table 823

FISH CONSUMPTION,[1] 11 LC, 1949-74
(kg PI)

Country	1949-51	1970	1974
A. ARGENTINA	4.0	4.8	6.9

Continued in SALA, 23-3510.

Table 824

FATS CONSUMED DAILY,[1] 20 LRC, 1961-86
(PI)

Country		YA (G)						
	1961-63	1966-68	1969-71	1975-77	1978-80	1979-81	1981-83	1983-85	1984-86
A. ARGENTINA	100.2	111.7	112.1	117.2	119.1	113.9	112.2	108.7	111.8
B. BOLIVIA	34.4	36.8	37.8	42.1	44.6	43.1	44.3	45.0	42.8
C. BRAZIL	41.4	48.4	47.8	50.9	51.5	53.3	51.1	56.8	57.5
D. CHILE	55.1	58.4	59.3	51.7	55.7	55.7	58.0	55.3	55.5
E. COLOMBIA	41.6	~	42.5	~	~	47.4	~	~	54.5
F. COSTA RICA	53.7	53.7	57.1	62.1	65.8	65.5	58.6	66.2	70.3
G. CUBA	47.7	52.6	56.3	56.3	58.8	59.4	62.4	68.2	66.1
H. DOMINICAN REP.	37.3	45.9	50.2	50.3	49.9	58.8	58.1	62.5	61.7
I. ECUADOR	39.2	43.5	44.3	50.3	54.1	50.5	53.1	53.6	54.8
J. EL SALVADOR	~	40.0	~	46.0	46.7	~	~	~	~
K. GUATEMALA	35.1	35.5	38.0	37.6	39.3	41.0	41.3	44.8	42.6
L. HAITI	26.9	28.1	26.9	28.0	30.2	31.4	30.5	30.3	34.4
M. HONDURAS	34.5	38.4	41.0	39.3	41.6	43.4	45.3	45.4	42.7
N. MEXICO	59.3	55.6	60.5	59.7	62.7	82.9	74.5	88.7	87.1
O. NICARAGUA	~	51.6	~	56.2	51.5	~	~	~	~
P. PANAMA	45.9	51.1	52.1	55.5	55.7	58.0	59.0	65.0	66.2
Q. PARAGUAY	64.5	72.8	74.2	73.5	78.9	77.0	73.8	72.8	74.6
R. PERU	42.0	45.8	43.0	44.3	44.0	39.9	40.6	39.1	39.5
S. URUGUAY	106.4	104.7	111.2	108.4	104.7	102.2	101.9	95.8	95.6
T. VENEZUELA	57.6	57.6	59.2	66.5	69.4	70.0	72.8	71.3	72.4
LATIN AMERICA[2]	51.3	54.3	56.3	57.7	59.1	60.7	57.6	62.9	62.8
UNITED STATES	138.8	154.8	152.1	161.5	169.2	159.5	167.3	167.2	164.4

1. Total grams per day includes vegetable and animal products.
2. Unweighted average.

SOURCE: FAO-PY, 1982, table 105; 1983, table 107; 1985, table 107; 1986, table 108;
    1987, table 108.

Table 825

ANNUAL AVERAGE APPARENT CONSUMPTION OF
FRESH COW'S MILK, 20 L, 1964-66 AND 1975-77
(Kilograms/C)

Country	1964–66	1975–77
A. ARGENTINA	75.5	67.9
B. BOLIVIA	2.9	6.7

Continued in SALA, 26-2207.

Table 826

PER CAPITA PRIVATE FOOD CONSUMPTION CHANGE, 19 LR, 1960-75
(AAGR)

Country	Previous Decade		1970	1971	1972	1973	1974	1975
	Decade	Second Half of Decade						
A. ARGENTINA	3.1	2.4	2.8	2.0	1.4	2.8	6.3	1.9

Continued in SALA, 21-107.

Table 827

PROTEIN CONSUMPTION, 20 LRC, 1961–86

Country	Total Proteins Daily G PI									Vegetable Proteins Daily G PI								
	1961–63	1965	1969–71	1975–77	1979–81	1980–82	1981–83	1983–85	1984–86	1961–63	1965	1969–71	1975–77	1979–81	1980–82	1981–83	1983–85	1984–86
A. ARGENTINA	106.0	88.5	105.0	109.8	107.7	112.8	103.4	104.4	105.7	40.0	36.8	38.9	37.5	35.9	37.7	37.6	38.5	36.5
B. BOLIVIA	49.1	45.1	49.4	52.5	54.9	56.1	54.2	54.9	56.2	35.7	33.0	35.6	36.7	37.1	38.5	37.2	36.8	38.0
C. BRAZIL	57.2	63.9	61.0	60.0	61.0	60.4	60.6	60.6	61.1	39.2	41.5	41.1	37.1	38.3	39.0	38.2	39.7	39.5
D. CHILE	67.6	65.3	70.3	70.0	72.3	73.1	73.1	69.4	68.2	43.8	40.2	44.7	46.3	44.8	45.8	45.4	45.1	44.3
E. COLOMBIA	51.6	53.2	49.1	51.1	54.4	56.1	56.4	56.7	56.2	28.0	30.5	26.9	28.6	31.2	32.3	32.5	33.1	32.4
F. COSTA RICA	52.5	56.7	57.0	57.4	63.6	62.2	60.4	64.4	66.6	30.9	32.1	33.9	30.7	32.9	32.5	33.8	37.9	37.1
G. CUBA	55.2	62.5	68.7	71.2	74.0	77.8	75.7	76.2	78.9	32.5	35.2	34.8	37.4	38.7	40.3	38.6	40.1	40.5
H. DOMINICAN REP.	40.6	44.8	45.1	44.0	50.5	46.3	50.4	51.9	52.5	26.1	27.5	28.2	28.7	30.8	28.8	31.4	33.1	32.4
I. ECUADOR	48.6	46.7	48.9	48.1	46.8	47.3	46.9	45.0	48.3	29.8	30.5	29.8	27.5	30.8	24.4	23.8	24.0	24.3
J. EL SALVADOR	~	62.9	~	54.3	~	~	~	~	~	~	32.9	~	37.6	~	~	~	~	~
K. GUATEMALA	55.3	49.2	57.1	53.7	57.0	57.1	58.1	60.4	60.2	42.1	37.3	44.6	41.3	44.6	43.1	44.7	47.7	47.8
L. HAITI	45.3	46.8	44.0	41.8	44.4	44.9	45.4	44.0	45.4	39.3	42.1	37.4	34.0	37.1	38.0	38.4	37.0	37.5
M. HONDURAS	50.7	48.6	54.8	50.3	53.7	55.1	52.8	54.0	52.3	38.0	35.5	40.2	38.0	38.3	38.8	38.1	40.3	36.8
N. MEXICO	65.0	66.5	69.2	69.7	78.8	76.6	76.2	81.3	82.0	47.6	52.3	49.9	49.0	49.8	51.9	51.8	52.4	52.6
O. NICARAGUA	~	60.7	~	69.9	~	~	~	~	~	~	40.9	~	39.7	~	~	~	~	~
P. PANAMA	57.8	62.5	57.2	58.6	59.4	63.1	60.6	60.7	60.2	34.8	37.6	33.3	31.9	29.1	29.9	29.2	31.1	31.0
Q. PARAGUAY	68.9	68.1	74.4	76.1	78.1	79.4	78.6	78.6	79.0	33.9	38.3	41.1	46.0	45.2	47.3	48.2	49.4	47.7
R. PERU	60.9	58.5	61.1	56.7	57.2	58.6	58.2	56.8	58.3	40.0	38.3	40.2	37.2	37.1	36.6	36.9	37.2	37.9
S. URUGUAY	86.2	105.4	90.9	86.7	84.7	84.5	83.5	79.1	79.8	28.6	33.7	32.0	31.3	30.9	29.7	29.2	30.9	30.0
T. VENEZUELA	57.2	61.1	61.8	66.7	71.7	69.6	73.0	69.0	68.5	31.1	34.5	34.3	34.4	35.3	33.7	36.0	35.0	34.8
LATIN AMERICA[1]	59.8	60.8	62.5	63.0	65.0	65.6	64.9	64.9	65.5	35.6	36.5	37.1	37.0	35.4	37.1	37.3	38.3	37.8
UNITED STATES	98.5	104.1[a]	103.2	106.7	102.3	105.4	105.8	104.4	106.5	32.8	33.0[a]	32.7	34.5	33.6	34.1	34.9	35.1	35.6

Table 827 (Continued)

PROTEIN CONSUMPTION, 20 LRC, 1961–86

	Country	Animal Proteins Daily G PI								
		1961–63	1965	1969–71	1975–77	1979–81	1980–82	1981–83	1983–85	1984–86
A.	ARGENTINA	66.0	51.7	66.7	72.2	71.7	75.1	65.9	65.9	69.2
B.	BOLIVIA	13.8	12.1	13.8	15.8	17.8	17.6	17.1	18.1	18.1
C.	BRAZIL	17.9	22.4	19.9	22.8	22.7	21.4	22.4	20.9	21.7
D.	CHILE	23.8	25.1	25.6	23.5	27.5	27.2	27.7	24.4	23.9
E.	COLOMBIA	23.6	22.7	22.2	22.4	23.2	23.9	23.9	23.6	23.7
F.	COSTA RICA	21.7	24.6	23.4	26.6	30.7	28.8	26.6	26.4	29.5
G.	CUBA	22.7	27.3	33.9	33.9	35.3	37.6	37.1	36.1	38.4
H.	DOMINICAN REP.	14.5	17.3	16.9	15.3	19.7	17.4	19.0	18.8	20.1
I.	ECUADOR	19.1	16.2	19.1	20.7	22.5	22.9	23.0	21.0	24.0
J.	EL SALVADOR	~	30.0	~	16.8	~	~	~	~	~
K.	GUATEMALA	13.2	11.9	12.5	12.4	12.4	14.0	13.5	12.7	12.3
L.	HAITI	5.9	4.7	6.6	7.9	7.3	6.9	7.0	7.0	7.9
M.	HONDURAS	12.7	13.1	14.5	12.3	15.4	16.3	14.6	13.6	15.5
N.	MEXICO	17.4	14.2	19.3	20.7	29.0	24.7	24.4	28.9	29.4
O.	NICARAGUA	~	19.8	~	30.1	~	~	~	~	~
P.	PANAMA	23.0	24.9	23.9	26.6	30.3	33.2	31.4	29.5	29.2
Q.	PARAGUAY	35.1	29.8	33.3	30.1	32.9	32.2	30.5	29.3	31.2
R.	PERU	20.9	20.2	20.9	19.5	20.0	22.0	21.3	19.6	20.4
S.	URUGUAY	57.6	71.7	58.9	55.4	53.8	54.8	54.3	48.3	49.8
T.	VENEZUELA	26.1	26.6	27.5	32.3	36.5	35.9	36.9	34.0	33.8
	LATIN AMERICA[1]	24.2	24.3	25.5	26.1	28.3	25.6	27.6	26.6	27.7
	UNITED STATES	65.7	71.1[a]	70.6	72.2	68.7	71.3	70.9	69.3	70.4

1. Unweighted average.

a. 1966–68.

SOURCE: Derived from Mexico-BNCE-CE, March 1981; FAO-PY, 1982, table 104; 1984, table 104; 1985, table 106; 1986, table 107; 1987, table 107.

Table 828

AVERAGE YEARLY PC IN FOOD/C PRODUCTION
BY PERIOD, 20 LRC, 1953–81

	Country	1953–59 (7 years)	1960–69 (10 years)	1970–79 (10 years)	1980–81 (2 years)	Total (29 years)
A.	ARGENTINA	−.7	1.3	1.7	−1.5	.7
B.	BOLIVIA	4.8	1.1	.7	−1.9	1.7
C.	BRAZIL	2.0	1.3	2.2	3.8	1.9
D.	CHILE	.4	−.4	.1	1.1	.1
E.	COLOMBIA	−.8	−.4	2.5	.5	.6
F.	COSTA RICA	−1.5	.8	1.9	−3.1	.4
G.	CUBA	−2.8	−1.1	4.6	−3.8	.3
H.	DOMINICAN REP.	−.1	−1.5	.2	1.0	−.4
I.	ECUADOR	6.9	−.1	−.7	3.8	1.6
J.	EL SALVADOR	−3.7[a]	−.4	1.2	−6.9	−.6[b]
K.	GUATEMALA	−.1	.8	1.7	0	.8
L.	HAITI	−2.0[a]	0	−.9	−3.8	−1.0[b]
M.	HONDURAS	−.3	1.7	−2.0	0	−.2
N.	MEXICO	3.4	1.0	.4	3.4	1.5
O.	NICARAGUA	1.1[a]	1.7	.7	−12.9	−.1[b]
P.	PANAMA	1.7	2.0	−.5	2.5	1.1
Q.	PARAGUAY	−.1	−.4	1.6	.2	.4
R.	PERU	.1	.8	−1.2	1.1	0
S.	URUGUAY	−3.7	2.6	−.4	11.2	.6
T.	VENEZUELA	1.3	3.1	1.0	−5.2	1.4
	LATIN AMERICA[1]	.2	.2	.9	1.0	.5
	UNITED STATES	.2	.5	1.7	1.9	.9

1. ELA.

a. 1955–59.
b. 27 years.

SOURCE: SALA, 23-3502.

Table 829

ACCEPTORS OF GOVERNMENT FAMILY PLANNING SERVICES BY METHOD AND
YEAR OF ACCEPTANCE,[1] 12 L, 1971 AND 1975

(T)

	Country	All Program Methods		IUD		Oral Contraceptives		Sterilization		Other Program Methods	
		1971	1975	1971	1975	1971	1975	1971	1975	1971	1975
B.	BOLIVIA	~	7.6	~	5.6	~	1.2	~	- -	~	.8

Continued in SALA, 20-802.

Table 830

ACCEPTORS OF GOVERNMENT FAMILY PLANNING SERVICES BY METHOD
AND AGE OF WIFE,[1] 7 L

	Country	Year	Method	N (T)	% in Wife's Age Group							Wife's Median Age
					Under 20	20-24	25-29	30-34	35-39	40+	Unknown	
C.	BRAZIL	1974	All	15.4	13.1	32.0	25.6	15.6	9.1	4.1	.5	25.9
			IUD	1.0	3.6	22.5	31.5	22.5	12.6	6.8	.5	28.7
			Oral	13.6	14.0	32.8	25.3	15.0	8.8	3.7	.4	25.5

Continued in SALA, 20-803.

Table 831

ACCEPTORS OF GOVERNMENT FAMILY PLANNING SERVICES BY METHOD AND NUMBER OF LIVING CHILDREN,[1] 7 L

Country	Year	Method	N (T)	% by Number of Living Children							Median Number of Living Children
				0-1	2	3	4	5	6+	Unknown	
C. BRAZIL	1974	All	15.4	33.5	21.3	13.4	27.2 ←		→	4.6	2.2
		IUD	1.0	19.7	23.3	17.9	37.2 ←		→	1.9	2.8
		Oral	13.6	34.4	21.5	13.2	26.5 ←		→	4.4	2.1

Continued in SALA, 20-804.

Table 832

USERS OF BIRTH CONTROL METHODS BY PUBLIC AND PRIVATE SOURCE,[1] 6 L

Country	Year[2]	Method	All Sources		National Program Supplies and Services		Private Sector Supplies and Services	
			N (T)	Users as % of Married Women Age 15-44	N (T)	Users as % of Married Women Age 15-44	N (T)	Users as % of Married Women Age 15-44
F. COSTA RICA	1976	All	78.8	33.7	~	~	~	~
		IUD	8.1	3.5	~	~	~	~
		Oral	53.7	23.0	~	~	~	~
		Condoms	9.0	3.8	~	~	~	~
		Other	8.1	3.4	~	~	~	~

Continued in SALA, 20-805.

Table 833

RELATIVE AGE DISTRIBUTION OF FAMILY PLANNING PARTICIPANTS AT ENTRY INTO PROGRAM, 14 L

Country	Year	Relative Age Distribution						Median Age
		15-19	20-24	25-29	30-34	35-39	40+	
B. BOLIVIA	1973	5.5	26.5	32.0	23.1	11.6	1.3	28.1

Continued in SALA, 20-807.

Table 834

WOMEN PARTICIPATING IN FAMILY PLANNING PROGRAMS, BY BIRTH CONTROL METHOD, 19 LR, 1970–73

Country and Years	Total		IUD		Oral		Sterilization		Other		Not Specified	
	N	%	N	%	N	%	N	%	N	%	N	%
A. ARGENTINA	27,003	100.0	7,627	28.2	18,187	67.4	–	–	1,189	4.4	–	–
1970	11,162	100.0	2,582	23.1	8,209	73.6	–	–	371	3.3	–	–

Continued in SALA, 20-808.

Table 835

HEALTH AS SHARE OF TOTAL CENTRAL GOVERNMENT PUBLIC EXPENDITURE, 19 L, 1970–87

(%)

Country	1970	1971	1972	1973	1974	1975	1976	1977	1978	1979	1980	1981	1982	1983	1984	1985	1986	1987
A. ARGENTINA	3.7	4.2	4.1	3.8	2.7	3.2	3.9	5.3	3.7	3.4	3.3	2.5	2.1	2.1	3.3	2.4	3.2	3.3
B. BOLIVIA	9.1	9.7	6.8	8.8	11.1	8.3	8.0	7.9	8.7	9.1	12.4	7.8	1.9	3.8	1.6	3.1	~	~
C. BRAZIL	12.5	10.9	10.6	10.4	11.3	5.8	6.6	5.5	5.8	5.7	5.2	5.5	5.8	4.8	5.3	3.3	2.9	~
D. CHILE	4.3	6.0	6.8	5.9	4.7	5.5	5.2	6.4	6.3	5.8	6.6	9.0	9.2	8.8	8.6	8.2	~	~
E. COLOMBIA	~	7.9	6.4	8.0	8.4	7.6	7.8	6.9	8.9	9.5	7.6	7.9	6.4	6.7	5.7	~	~	~
F. COSTA RICA	3.1	8.1	6.2	9.5	7.2	6.7	6.2	5.5	6.7	5.7	7.9	5.9	6.2	5.0	6.3	2.6	2.4	~
H. DOMINICAN REP.	~	10.6	10.3	10.1	10.0	8.8	11.1	10.9	11.5	11.4	11.5	14.5	9.5	8.5	9.6	7.6	6.9	~
I. ECUADOR	~	~	~	~	~	~	11.4	11.1	16.0	15.6	12.8	13.2	13.9	15.0	14.7	7.3	7.2	~
J. EL SALVADOR	10.5	10.9	10.1	10.6	10.6	10.6	9.4	9.2	8.4	8.6	8.3	7.7	7.2	6.6	7.5	6.8	~	~
K. GUATEMALA	~	~	8.1	8.7	8.3	8.3	6.3	7.1	8.5	8.7	11.2	7.1	10.8	6.3	7.1	7.4	9.4	~
L. HAITI	7.9	6.7	6.2	6.6	10.0	7.7	6.2	4.3	4.3	6.9	5.5	4.5	5.1	4.3	4.3	4.2	~	~
M. HONDURAS	9.1	9.1	8.9	10.6	10.3	7.3	10.1	8.0	6.4	6.7	6.0	7.3	6.7	6.7	5.7	8.1	11.0	9.2
N. MEXICO	~	3.1	3.3	3.0	2.8	2.7	2.7	3.2	3.4	3.1	2.4	2.2	1.1	.6	1.1	1.1	~	~
O. NICARAGUA	5.9	7.1	4.2	5.1	6.0	8.1	6.9	5.3	4.3	10.7	13.4	12.7	10.6	7.5	7.3	9.1	13.3	~
P. PANAMA	9.3	9.2	8.9	8.6	8.9	8.4	7.5	7.3	6.6	5.4	6.1	6.0	6.0	6.9	6.9	8.0	5.8	5.3
Q. PARAGUAY	3.4	3.3	3.0	3.8	3.2	3.1	3.1	3.1	3.2	4.1	3.9	4.3	7.2	7.8	8.4	7.8	~	~
R. PERU	6.3	5.7	5.9	5.3	5.3	5.2	5.9	4.6	5.5	6.0	5.6	6.0	5.2	5.4	5.8	6.0	~	~
S. URUGUAY	~	~	3.3	6.9	8.5	5.5	5.8	5.6	7.2	6.2	6.7	5.4	4.1	5.4	4.3	5.3	~	~
T. VENEZUELA	7.6	7.1	7.3	7.2	3.3	4.1	5.2	4.8	5.1	5.8	4.7	5.0	5.1	5.2	4.7	4.8	5.2	~

SOURCE: IDB-SPTF, 1988, table IV-9.

Table 836

PUBLIC EXPENDITURE ON HEALTH AS PERCENT OF GROSS DOMESTIC PRODUCT, 19 L, 1970–87

(%)

Country	1970	1971	1972	1973	1974	1975	1976	1977	1978	1979	1980	1981	1982	1983	1984	1985	1986	1987
A. ARGENTINA	.3	.4	.4	.5	.3	.4	.4	.8	.6	.4	.5	.4	.3	.4	.4	.5	.6	.6
B. BOLIVIA	.9	1.1	1.0	1.2	1.2	1.0	1.0	1.0	1.1	1.1	1.7	1.0	.4	.4	.5	.4	~	~
C. BRAZIL	1.3	1.2	1.1	1.1	1.1	1.2	1.3	1.3	1.4	1.3	1.3	1.5	1.7	1.5	1.5	~	~	~
D. CHILE	1.7	3.0	3.4	2.8	2.5	2.4	2.1	2.2	2.2	1.9	2.1	2.9	3.6	3.0	3.0	2.7	~	~
E. COLOMBIA	~	.8	.7	.8	.8	.7	.7	.6	.8	.9	.8	.9	.7	.8	.7	.5	~	~
F. COSTA RICA	.4	1.3	1.0	1.6	1.1	1.0	1.1	.9	1.2	1.1	1.6	1.1	1.1	1.0	1.2	.5	.4	~
H. DOMINICAN REP.	~	1.9	1.7	1.6	1.7	1.6	1.8	1.6	1.9	2.2	2.0	2.1	1.2	1.1	1.2	1.0	1.0	~
I. ECUADOR	.5	.4	.3	.6	.9	.8	1.4	1.5	1.8	1.6	1.8	2.1	2.2	2.0	1.9	1.1	1.1	~
J. EL SALVADOR	1.3	1.4	1.3	1.3	1.3	1.5	1.4	1.4	1.3	1.3	1.5	1.6	1.4	1.4	1.4	1.2	1.0	~
K. GUATEMALA	~	~	.9	.9	.8	.8	.8	.8	1.0	1.1	1.6	1.1	1.4	.7	.8	.7	~	~
L. HAITI	1.1	1.0	1.0	.8	1.4	1.2	1.0	.7	.8	1.2	.8	.8	1.3	1.0	1.0	.9	~	~
M. HONDURAS	1.5	1.4	1.3	1.4	1.6	1.4	1.9	1.5	1.3	1.2	1.4	1.5	1.6	1.6	1.5	2.0	2.6	2.2
N. MEXICO	~	.3	.4	.4	.4	.4	.4	.5	.5	.5	.4	.5	.3	.1	.3	.3	~	~
O. NICARAGUA	.7	1.0	.6	.7	1.0	1.5	1.2	.9	.9	2.1	4.4	4.6	4.4	4.8	4.3	5.0	6.6	~
P. PANAMA	1.9	1.7	1.9	1.7	1.8	1.9	1.7	1.7	1.6	1.7	1.6	1.5	1.6	1.8	1.8	1.8	.4	.4
Q. PARAGUAY	.4	.4	.3	.3	.3	.3	.3	.3	.3	.4	.4	.5	.8	.8	.9	.7	~	~
R. PERU	.9	.9	1.0	.9	.8	.9	1.1	.9	1.0	1.0	1.1	1.1	.9	1.0	1.0	1.0	~	~
S. URUGUAY	~	~	.5	1.1	1.5	.9	.9	.9	1.1	.9	1.1	.9	1.0	1.1	.8	.9	~	~
T. VENEZUELA	1.5	1.4	1.5	1.4	1.1	1.4	1.4	1.5	1.4	1.2	1.1	1.5	1.4	1.3	1.2	1.3	1.3	~

SOURCE: IDB-SPTF, 1988, table IV-8.

Table 837

COST OF SOCIAL SECURITY, 18 L, 1965 and 1977

	Revenue and Expenditure as % of GDP					
	Revenue		Expenditure			
			Total		Benefits	
Country	1965	1977	1965	1977	1965	1977
A. ARGENTINA	3.8	8.0[a]	3.2	7.3[a]	~	7.0[a]
B. BOLIVIA	4.3[b]	3.5[c]	3.6[b]	3.1[c]	3.0[b]	2.8[c]

Continued in SALA, 27-836.

Table 838

FINANCING OF SOCIAL SECURITY, BY SOURCE, 20 L, LATE 1970s

| | Legal Contribution as % of Salary (Ca. 1980) | | | Distribution of Benefits of Social Security | | | | |
Country	Insured	Employer	Government	Insured	Employer	Government	Investment	Other
A. ARGENTINA	14.0–15.0	21.5	15.3	27.3	57.2	6.8	6.8	1.9
B. BOLIVIA	3.5	20.0	1.5	28.5	47.6	11.8	0	12.1

Continued in SALA, 27-837.

Table 839

TOTAL POPULATION AND EAP COVERED BY SOCIAL SECURITY, 20 LR, 1980

Country	Total Population (T)	Total Insured[1] (T)	Coverage (%)	Distribution (%)	EAP	Active Insured[2] (T)	Coverage (%)	Distribution (%)
A. ARGENTINA	28,237	22,278	78.9	10.3	10,690	7,391	69.1	10.5
B. BOLIVIA	5,570	1,412	25.4	.7	1,754	324	18.5	.5

Continued in SALA, 27-838.

Table 840

CHILE REAL VALUE OF ANNUAL PENSIONS, 1964–80[a]

| Year | Pensions (M Pesos) | Persons with Pension (T) | Average Pension PI (Pesos) | Index (1970 = 100) | | |
				Nominal Pension	Inflation[1]	Real Pension
1964	.5	380	1.4	16	24	66.7
1965	.8	436	1.9	23	31	74.2

Continued in SALA, 27-839.

Table 841

HEALTH SERVICES AND INDICATORS, 20 L, 1980–85

	Country	Hospital Beds (PTI) (1980–85)	Doctors (P1OI) (1980–85)	Infant Mortality (1985)	Life Expectancy (1985)
A.	ARGENTINA	5.4	25.7	34	70
B.	BOLIVIA	1.8	5.1	117	53
C.	BRAZIL	4.2	7.8	67	65
D.	CHILE	3.5	9.7	20	69
E.	COLOMBIA	1.7	5.8	55	65
F.	COSTA RICA	3.3	10.0	18	74
G.	CUBA	4.6	20.8	17	74
H.	DOMINICAN REP.	2.6[b]	4.1	70	64
I.	ECUADOR	1.7	8.8	54[c]	63
J.	EL SALVADOR	1.2	3.2	65	64
K.	GUATEMALA	1.6	4.1	65	60
L.	HAITI	.9[a]	1.2	123	54
M.	HONDURAS	1.3	4.0	76	62
N.	MEXICO	1.2	9.0	39[c]	67
O.	NICARAGUA	1.6	6.7	69	59
P.	PANAMA	3.2	10.3	25	72
Q.	PARAGUAY	1.0	6.2	43	66
R.	PERU	1.7	8.7	95	60[c]
S.	URUGUAY	6.0	19.9	30[c]	72
T.	VENEZUELA	2.7	12.0	37	70

a. Only.
b. 1975.
c. 1984.

SOURCE: Carmelo Mesa-Lago, "Aspectos Económico-Financieros de la Seguridad Social en
    América Latina y el Caribe: Tendencias, Problemas y Alternativas para el Año 2000,"
    an Unpublished World Bank Study (Washington, D.C., June 30, 1989).

Table 842

INTRODUCTION OF SOCIAL INSURANCE PENSION PROGRAMS BY WORLD REGION, 1889–1985

Year of Introduction	Industrialized[1]			Latin America and Caribbean			Asia, Oceania, Middle East			Africa		
	N	Cumulative	%	N	Cumulative	%	N	Cumulative	%	N	Cumulative	%
1889–1920	15	15	52	0	0	0	0	0	0	0	0	0
1921–30	6	21	72	4	4	12	0	0	0	1	1	3
1931–40	6	27	93	3	7	20	0	0	0	0	1	3
1941–50	2	29	100	6	13	38	2	2	8	2	3	8
1951–60	0	29	100	2	15	44	11	13	52	10	13	34
1961–70	0	29	100	14	29	85	3	16	64	15	28	74
1971–80	0	29	100	5	34	100	5	21	84	4	32	84
1981–85	0	29	100	0	34	100	0	21	84	0	32	84
Without	0	29	100	0	34	100	4	21	84	6	32	84
Total	29	29	100	34	34	100	25	21	84	38	32	84

1. Includes seven European countries not considered fully industrialized according to the
    World Bank classification.

SOURCE: Carmelo Mesa-Lago, "Investment Portfolio of Social Insurance/Pension Funds
    in Latin America and the Caribbean: Significance, Composition and Performance," an
    Unpublished World Bank Study (Washington, D.C., June 13, 1989).

Table 843

COSTA RICA SOCIAL SECURITY LEGISLATION, BY
RISKS PROTECTED AND GROUPS COVERED,
1886–1983

Year[1]	Risks Protected[2]	Groups Covered
1886, 1958	VIS	Education
1918	VIS	Communication

Continued in SALA, 27-840.

Table 844

COSTA RICA COST OF SOCIAL SECURITY, 1960–80

(M Colones and %)

			Expenditure on Social Security[1]		
		Total		% of	
Year	GNP	Expenditure of the Central Government	Total	GNP	Government Expenditure
1961	2,929	419	56	1.9	13.4
1965	3,928	649	90	2.3	13.9
1970	6,524	1,192	349	5.3	29.3
1975	16,805	3,544	1,104	6.6	31.2
1979	34,584	8,658	2,764	8.0	31.9
1980	41,405	10,436	3,716	9.0	35.6

1. Includes expenditure of CCSS and the Ministry of Health; excludes expenditure on occupational hazards.

SOURCE: Carmelo Mesa-Lago, *El Desarrollo de la Seguridad Social en América Latina* (Santiago, 1985).

Table 845

CUBA SOCIAL SECURITY LEGISLATION, BY RISKS PROTECTED
AND GROUPS COVERED, 1913–83

Year[1]	Risks Protected[2]	Groups Covered
1913, 1934	VIS	Armed Forces
1915	VIS	Communications
1916, 1933	RP	Salaried Employees of Public and Private Sectors
1917, 1927	VIS	Judicial Powers

Continued in SALA, 27-842.

Table 846

CUBA REAL VALUE OF ANNUAL PENSIONS, 1962–81[a]

Year	Pensions (M Pesos)	Persons with Pensions (T)	Average Pension PI (Pesos)	Index (1970 = 100)		
				Nominal Pension	Inflation	Real Pension
1962	152	213	713	90.2	79.2	114.0
1965	208	298	699	88.4	93.4	94.6

Continued in SALA, 26-840.

Table 847

CUBA DIFFERENCES IN LOANS AND HEALTH SERVICES, BY PROVINCE, 1982

Province	Expenditure of Monetary Loans (Pesos) (PI)	Doctors (P10I)	Hospital Beds (PTI)
Pinar del Río	66.81	11.8	4.6
La Habana	99.85	14.0	2.6

Continued in SALA, 26-841

Table 848

PERU ESTIMATED POPULATION COVERED BY SOCIAL SECURITY MEDICAL CARE PROGRAM, 1975–85

T

Year	Contributing Insured				Dependents			Total A + B	Total Population
	Salaried[1]	Self-employed	Pensioners[2]	Subtotal (A)	Spouses[3]	Children[4]	Subtotal (B)		
1975	1,562	17	146	1,725	507[a]	~	507	2,232	15,161
1980	2,014	39	211	2,264	546	66	612	2,876	17,295
1981	2,093	50	230	2,373	554	68	622	2,995	17,755
1982	2,167	61	243	2,471	572	70	642	3,113	18,226
1983	2,243	74	256	2,573	705	102	807	3,380	18,707
1984	2,321	87	270	2,678	734	105	839	3,517	19,198
1985	2,403	101	283	2,787	765	109	874	3,661	19,698

PTI

Year	Salaried[1]	Self-employed	Pensioners[2]	Subtotal (A)	Spouses[3]	Children[4]	Subtotal (B)	Total A + B	Total Population
1975	10.3	.1	1.0	11.4	3.3[a]	~	3.3	14.7	100
1980	11.6	.2	1.2	13.1	3.2	.4	3.5	16.6	100
1981	11.8	.3	1.3	13.4	3.1	.4	3.5	16.9	100
1982	11.9	.3	1.3	13.6	3.1	.4	3.5	17.1	100
1983	12.0	.4	1.4	13.8	3.8	.5	4.3	18.1	100
1984	12.1	.5	1.4	13.9	3.8	.5	4.4	18.3	100
1985	12.2	.5	1.4	14.1	3.9	.6	4.4	18.6	100

1. Includes domestic workers. Excludes independently covered armed forces, police, fishermen, and jockeys.
2. Includes old age disability-survivor and occupational-risk pensioners in private and public sectors. Excludes pensioners from armed forces, police, fishing, and racetracks.
3. Spouses of active and passive insured entitled only to maternity care.
4. Children under one year old entitled to out-patient care; 1984 extension to age 14. not yet widely implemented.

a. Includes children.

SOURCE: Dieter K. Zschock, ed., *Health Care in Peru: Resources and Policy* (Boulder, Colo.: Westview Press, 1987), p. 247.

Table 849

URUGUAY COST OF SOCIAL SECURITY, 1965–82
(M New Pesos and %)[1]

| | | Total Expenditure of Central Government | Expenditure on Social Security | | |
| | | | | % of | |
Year	GNP		Total	GNP	Federal Expenditure
1965	52	13	8	14.5	61.5
1969	499	118	70	14.2	59.3
1975	7,108	1,878	872	12.3	46.4
1980	81,429	20,812	6,797	8.3	32.6
1981	106,384	30,969	12,192	11.4	39.4
1982	112,564	41,274	14,398	12.8	34.9

1. Billions of old pesos in 1965 and 1969; new peso = 1,000 old pesos.
2. Excludes expenditure on occupational hazards and lesser programs.

SOURCE: Carmelo Mesa-Lago, *El Desarrollo de la Seguridad Social en América Latina* (Santiago, 1985).

Table 850

URUGUAY REAL VALUE OF ANNUAL PENSIONS, 1963–82[a]

| Year | Pensions (M New Pesos)[1] | Persons with Pension (T) | Average Pension PI (New Pesos)[2] | Index (1970 = 100)[2] | | |
				Nominal Pension	Inflation[3]	Real Pension
1963	2.1	328	6.4	7.0	5.4	129.6
1964	2.7	346	7.9	8.7	7.5	116.0

Continued in SALA, 27-847.

Table 851

SOCIAL SECURITY: PERCENT SERVED OF ECONOMICALLY ACTIVE POPULATION, 20 LR, 1960 and 1970

Country	1960	1970
A. ARGENTINA	53.8	67.4

Continued in SALA, 17-810.

Table 852

INSURED POPULATION IN RELATION TO TOTAL AND ECONOMICALLY ACTIVE POPULATION, 5 L, 1960–71

A. ARGENTINA

Year	Total Population[1] (T) (1)	Economically Active Population[1,2] (T) (2)	Insured Population[3]				Percent of EAP Insured (3)/(2)	Percent of Total Population Insured (6)/(1)	Ratio of Active to Passive (3)/(4)
			Active[4] (3)	Passive[5] (4)	Dependents (5)	Total (6)			
1960	20,850	7,270	4,011	745	4,412	9,168	55.2	44.0	5.4
1961	21,203	7,334	4,031	812	4,407	9,250	55.0	43.6	5.0

Continued in SALA, 24-834 through 24-838.

Table 853

VENEZUELA EVOLUTION OF THE COMPOSITION OF GOVERNMENT SOCIAL EXPENDITURE, 1972–82

Year	Social Expenditure		Composition of Social Expenditure				
	Total (MNC of 1968)	% of Total Expenditure	Education (%)	Health (%)	Social Security and Assistance (%)	Housing (%)	Other Social Services (%)
1972	5,808	44.0	42.8	19.0	23.8	11.4	3.0
1973	5,904	43.4	42.9	19.5	22.2	12.5	2.9

Continued in SALA, 27-850.

Table 854

INDEX OF GOVERNMENT PER CAPITA EXPENDITURE ON HEALTH, 18 L, 1981–85
(1980 = 100)

	Country	1981	1982	1983	1984	1985
A.	ARGENTINA	75.2	53.0	72.7	86.1	81.1
B.	BOLIVIA	54.0	22.3	31.2	45.8	~
C.	BRAZIL	100.8	114.4	126.8	40.6	~
D.	CHILE	105.2	96.0	78.0	76.2	117.4
F.	COSTA RICA	62.0	57.5	54.2	83.5	27.7
H.	DOMINICAN REP.	105.7	58.5	57.1	53.5	48.2
I.	ECUADOR	126.6	115.8	94.2	103.7	60.3
J.	EL SALVADOR	98.4	83.8	71.5	67.6	62.5
K.	GUATEMALA	69.9	81.6	39.6	41.7	35.9
L.	HAITI	97.0	141.1	110.4	~	~
M.	HONDURAS	98.9	101.9	103.6	84.8	124.4
N.	MEXICO	100.0	73.8	49.2	36.4	57.4
O.	NICARAGUA	113.6	96.0	99.9	~	~
P.	PANAMA	98.2	104.5	112.7	~	~
Q.	PARAGUAY	135.7	212.4	212.6	170.3	169.4
R.	PERU	119.3	118.5	169.5	160.4	80.3
S.	URUGUAY	87.5	83.8	86.6	103.0	66.7
T.	VENEZUELA	108.6	96.2	88.8	78.0	93.2

SOURCE: FAO, Annex III, Food Systems and Securities, 1988, table 21, p. 62, on the basis of P. Musgrove, "The Economic Crisis and Its Impact on Health and Health Care in Latin America and the Caribbean," *International Journal of Health Services*, 17:3 (1987).

Table 855

ESTIMATED IMMUNIZATION COVERAGE WITH BCG, DPT, POLIOMYELITIS, MEASLES, AND TETANUS VACCINES, 4 L

(December 1987)

Country	Newborns Surviving to 1 Year of Age (M)	Cumulative % of Surviving Infants	Specific Vaccine Coverage (%)				
			Children Less Than 1 Year of Age Given:				Pregnant Women Given Tetanus-2
			BCG	DPT-3	Polio-3	Measles	
A. ARGENTINA (1986)	.72	78	89	67	79	87	~
C. BRAZIL (1986)	2.49	52	56	52	89	55	~
E. COLOMBIA (1986)	.86	76	69	57	65	56	~
N. MEXICO (1986)	2.55	49	54	34	96	60	~

SOURCE: *Who Bulletin* 66:5 (February 15, 1989).

Table 856

HEALTH AND MILITARY EXPENDITURE, 4 L, Ca. 1980

Country	% of Overall Health Expenditure Coming from Government	Government Expenditure/C (US)	
		Health	Military
A. ARGENTINA	31	22	58
E. COLOMBIA	67	16	12
N. MEXICO	69	11	11

SOURCE: *World Health Forum* 9·4 (March 2, 1989).

Table 857

MANDATORY AIDS AND SEROPOSITIVITY REPORTING, 9 LC

Country	AIDS (All States and Territories)	Seropositivity (All States and Territories)
C. BRAZIL	X	#
D. CHILE	X	#
F. COSTA RICA	X	X
K. GUATEMALA	X	#
N. MEXICO	X	X
P. PANAMA	X	#
Q. PARAGUAY	X	#
R. PERU	X	#
T. VENEZUELA	X	X
UNITED STATES	X	X

SOURCE: *World Health Forum* 9:3 (November 21, 1988).

9

Education and Science

Table 900

ILLITERACY, BY URBAN AND RURAL AREAS, AGE GROUP, AND SEX, 20 L

Country	Year	Age Group	Illiterate Population			% of Total Population		
			Total	Male	Female	Total	Male	Female
A. ARGENTINA								
Total Population	1970	15+	1,225,850	532,350	693,500	7.4	6.5	8.3
Total Population	1971	18+	1,177,400	~	~	8.4	~	~
Total Population	1980	15+	1,184,964	543,174	641,790	6.1	5.7	6.4
Urban Population	1980	10+	747,233	315,215	432,018	4.1	3.6	4.5
Rural Population	1980	10+	517,417	273,641	243,776	14.6	14.2	15.1
B. BOLIVIA								
Total Population	1976	15+	993,437	315,460	667,977	36.8	24.2	48.6
Urban Population	1976	15+	176,748	34,393	142,355	15.2	6.2	23.2
Rural Population	1976	15+	816,689	281,067	535,622	53.2	37.3	68.5
C. BRAZIL[1]								
Total Population	1970	15+	18,146,977	8,109,291	10,037,686	33.8	30.6	36.9
Urban Population	1970	15+	6,381,253	2,378,134	4,003,119	20.0	15.8	24.0
Rural Population	1970	15+	11,765,724	5,731,157	6,034,567	53.6	50.2	57.3
Total Population	1976	15+	15,644,700	6,916,600	8,728,100	24.3	22.0	26.5
Total Population	1976	10+	18,171,552	8,315,449	9,856,103	23.2	21.7	24.8
Urban Population	1976	10+	7,427,313	2,972,258	4,455,055	14.4	12.0	16.6
Rural Population	1976	10+	10,744,239	5,343,191	5,401,048	40.6	39.4	41.9
Total Population	1978	15+	16,223,404	7,308,436	8,914,965	23.9	22.0	25.7
Urban Population	1978	15+	7,308,975	2,870,786	4,438,189	15.6	12.8	18.1
Rural Population	1978	15+	8,914,429	4,437,653	4,476,776	42.4	40.9	43.9
Total Population	1980	15+	18,716,847	8,560,176	10,156,671	25.5	23.7	27.2
Urban Population	1980	15+	8,743,376	3,540,018	5,203,358	16.8	14.2	19.2
Rural Population	1980	15+	9,973,471	5,020,158	4,953,313	46.3	44.7	48.0
Total Population	1985	15+	~	~	~	22.2	20.9	23.4
D. CHILE								
Total Population	1970	15+	594,749	262,937	331,812	11.0	10.1	11.8
Urban Population	1970	15+	276,270	103,183	173,087	6.6	5.4	7.7
Rural Population	1970	15+	318,479	159,754	158,725	25.6	23.6	27.9
Total Population	1982	15+	681,039	315,538	365,501	8.9	8.5	9.2
Urban Population	1982	15+	397,557	165,546	232,011	6.2	5.5	6.8
Rural Population	1982	15+	283,482	149,992	133,490	21.9	20.9	23.2
E. COLOMBIA								
Total Population	1973	15+	2,110,850	933,027	1,177,823	19.2	18.0	20.2
Urban Population	1973	15+	814,945	288,686	526,259	11.2	9.0	13.0
Rural Population	1973	15+	1,295,905	644,341	651,564	34.7	32.8	36.8
Total Population	1981	15+	2,407,458	1,091,407	1,316,051	14.8	13.6	16.1
Urban Population	1981	15+	923,430	~	~	9.0	~	~
Rural Population	1981	15+	1,484,028	~	~	24.8	~	~
F. COSTA RICA[2]								
Total Population	1973	15+	121,312	59,084	62,228	11.6	11.4	11.8
Urban Population	1973	15+	23,177	8,522	14,655	4.9	4.0	5.7
Rural Population	1973	15+	98,135	50,562	47,573	17.0	16.6	17.5
Total Population	1984	15+	112,946	55,432	57,515	7.4	7.3	7.4
G. CUBA[3]								
Total Population	1979	15–49	218,358	101,119	117,239	4.6	4.3	4.9
Total Population	1981	15–49	105,901	~	~	2.2	~	~
	1981	10+	~	~	~	3.8	3.8	3.8
H. DOMINICAN REP.								
Total Population	1970	15+	683,637	322,402	361,235	33.0	31.4	34.6
Urban Population	1970	15+	165,841	~	~	19.0	~	~
Rural Population	1970	15+	517,796	~	~	43.4	~	~
Total Population	1981	5+	1,519,198	770,758	748,440	31.4	31.8	30.9
Urban Population	1981	5+	532,695	242,984	289,711	20.9	20.0	21.6
Rural Population	1981	5+	986,503	527,774	458,729	43.0	43.5	42.5
I. ECUADOR[4]								
Total Population	1974	15+	932,723	390,435	542,288	25.8	21.8	29.6
Urban Population	1974	15+	153,280	50,615	102,665	9.7	6.9	12.2
Rural Population	1974	15+	779,443	339,820	439,623	38.2	32.3	44.4
Total Population	1982	15+	758,272	298,018	460,254	19.8	15.8	23.8
Urban Population	1982	15+	154,736	51,134	103,602	6.2	4.3	8.0
Rural Population	1982	15+	603,536	246,884	356,652	27.3	21.7	33.1

Table 900 (Continued)

ILLITERACY, BY URBAN AND RURAL AREAS, AGE GROUP, AND SEX, 20 L

Country	Year	Age Group	Illiterate Population			% of Total Population		
			Total	Male	Female	Total	Male	Female
J. EL SALVADOR								
Total Population	1971	5+	816,631	362,556	454,075	42.9	39.2	46.4
Urban Population	1971	5+	180,204	59,466	120,738	21.8	15.9	26.7
Rural Population	1971	5+	636,427	303,090	333,337	59.0	55.1	63.1
Total Population	1975	10+	1,064,159	462,705	601,454	38.0	34.5	41.1
Urban Population	1975	10+	216,593	67,830	148,763	18.0	12.7	22.2
Rural Population	1975	10+	847,566	394,875	452,691	53.0	48.9	57.2
Total Population	1980	15+	818,100	~	~	32.7	~	~
Total Population	1980	10+	946,000	403,300	542,700	30.2	26.9	33.2
Urban Population	1980	10+	217,200	64,900	152,300	15.5	10.3	19.6
Rural Population	1980	10+	728,800	338,400	390,400	42.2	39.0	45.5
K. GUATEMALA[5]								
Total Population	1973	15+	1,528,732	651,915	876,817	54.0	46.4	61.5
Urban Population	1973	15+	291,380	97,460	193,920	28.2	20.0	35.5
Rural Population	1973	15+	1,235,220	549,980	685,240	68.6	59.9	77.6
Total Population	1985	15+	2,519,543	1,070,325	1,449,218	45.0	37.4	52.9
L. HAITI[6]								
Total Population	1970	ALL	3,435,504	1,585,529	1,849,975	80.4	77.1	83.6
Urban Population	1970	ALL	472,419	175,973	296,446	51.8	45.3	56.7
Rural Population	1970	ALL	2,963,085	1,409,556	1,553,529	88.2	84.5	91.9
Total Population	1971	15+	2,005,052	884,678	1,120,374	78.7	73.8	83.1
Urban Population	1971	15+	240,922	68,808	172,114	45.2	32.3	53.8
Rural Population	1971	15+	1,764,130	815,870	948,260	87.6	82.8	92.2
Total Population	1982	15+	2,004,791	926,751	1,078,040	66.2	62.7	67.5
M. HONDURAS[7]								
Total Population	1974	15+	594,194	274,815	319,379	43.1	41.1	44.9
Urban Population	1974	15+	99,015	37,523	61,492	21.1	17.6	24.0
Rural Population	1974	15+	495,179	237,292	257,887	54.4	52.1	56.8
Total Population	1985	15+	~	~	~	40.5	39.3	41.0
N. MEXICO[8]								
Total Population	1970	15+	6,693,706	2,772,999	3,920,707	25.8	21.8	29.8
Urban Population	1970	15+	2,621,751	979,296	1,642,455	16.7	13.1	20.0
Rural Population	1970	15+	4,071,955	1,793,703	2,278,252	39.7	34.3	45.3
Total Population	1980	15+	6,451,750	2,545,171	3,906,569	17.0	13.8	20.1
Total Population	1985	15+	4,400,000	1,700,000	2,700,000	9.7	7.7	11.7
O. NICARAGUA[9]								
Total Population	1971	15+	410,755	193,475	217,277	42.5	42.0	42.9
Urban Population	1971	15+	94,319	33,873	60,446	19.5	16.1	22.1
Rural Population	1971	15+	316,436	159,605	156,831	65.4	63.8	67.0
P. PANAMA[10]								
Total Population	1970	15+	175,152	86,388	88,764	21.7	21.0	22.2
Urban Population	1970	15+	26,221	10,985	15,236	6.3	5.6	7.0
Rural Population	1970	15+	149,162	75,687	73,475	38.1	35.5	41.1
Total Population	1980	15+	156,531	74,737	81,794	14.4	13.7	15.1
Urban Population	1980	15+	26,727	11,373	15,354	4.5	4.1	4.9
Rural Population	1980	15+	129,804	63,364	66,440	26.0	23.6	28.9
Total Population	1985	15+	~	~	~	11.8	11.0	12.3
Q. PARAGUAY								
Total Population	1972	15+	256,690	93,150	163,540	19.9	14.9	24.5
Urban Population	1972	15+	61,570	18,240	43,330	11.4	7.4	14.7
Rural Population	1972	15+	195,120	74,910	120,210	25.9	19.7	32.3
Total Population	1982	15+	219,120	84,340	134,780	12.5	9.7	15.2
R. PERU[11]								
Total Population	1972	15+	2,062,870	624,018	1,438,852	27.5	16.7	38.2
Urban Population	1972	15+	581,194	137,018	444,176	12.4	5.9	18.9
Rural Population	1972	15+	1,481,676	487,000	994,676	51.1	33.9	68.0
Total Population	1981	15+	1,799,458	485,486	1,313,972	18.1	9.9	26.1
S. URUGUAY[12]								
Total Population	1975	15+	124,664	65,007	59,657	6.1	6.6	5.7
Urban Population	1975	15+	87,500	40,200	47,300	5.2	5.1	5.2
Rural Population	1975	15+	37,000	24,900	12,100	11.0	12.6	8.5

Table 900 (Continued)

ILLITERACY, BY URBAN AND RURAL AREAS, AGE GROUP, AND SEX, 20 L

Country	Year	Age Group	Illiterate Population			% of Total Population		
			Total	Male	Female	Total	Male	Female
T. VENEZUELA[13]								
Total Population	1971	15+	1,373,561	585,928	787,633	23.5	20.3	26.6
Total Population	1981	15+	1,319,265	579,180	740,085	15.3	13.5	17.0

1. For 1976, de jure population. For 1985, estimates made by national authorities.
2. For 1973, de jure population.
3. For 1981, not including functionally and physically handicapped.
4. Including nomadic Indian tribes.
5. For 1973, de jure population, based on a 5% sample. For 1985, estimates made by national authorities.
6. For 1971, de jure population.
7. For 1974, de jure population. For 1985, estimates made by national authorities.
8. For 1970, de jure population. For 1985, estimates made by national authorities.
9. De jure population. In 1980, after the National Literacy Campaign, the Ministry of Education estimated that of the 722,431 illiterates identified in the census of October 1979, 130,372 were *analfabetos inaptos*, and 406,056 were made literate, leaving only 186,003 *analfabetos aptos* (or 12.96% of the population of 10 years and over.)
10. For 1985, estimates made by national authorities.
11. Excluding Indian jungle population.
12. Based on a sample tabulation of census returns.
13. For 1971, excluding Indian jungle population.

SOURCE: UNESCO-SY, 1988, table 1.3.

Table 901

ILLITERACY AND HIGHER EDUCATION, 20 L

Country	Gross Rate of Schooling (to 1980)		Illiterates Age 15 and Over (%)		Illiterates Age 15-24
	Universities and Similar Institutions	Tertiary Level	1950	1980	1970
Rapid Modernization Countries					
A. ARGENTINA	18.0	22.2	13.6	6.7	4.2
D. CHILE	10.9	13.2	19.8	7.5	4.7
F. COSTA RICA	21.5	25.8	20.6	7.0	5.2
G. CUBA	19.5	19.5	22.1	3.9	~
P. PANAMA	22.2	22.2	30.0	15.3	12.4
S. URUGUAY	16.1	16.1[b]	9.5	6.1	~
T. VENEZUELA	17.9	20.2	50.5	17.7	12.0
TOTAL	17.1	19.7[c]	26.1	9.7	7.7
Big Countries with Rapid Unbalanced Modernization					
C. BRAZIL	11.7	11.7	50.5	26.0	24.5
E. COLOMBIA	10.5	10.9	37.7	13.7	11.5
N. MEXICO	12.2	14.0	43.2	16.0	16.4
TOTAL	11.7	12.3[c]	43.8	18.6	17.5
Medium-Sized and Small Countries with Partial Modernization					
H. DOMINICAN REP.	7.5	7.5	57.1	26.4	21.1
I. ECUADOR	36.6	36.6	44.3	18.7	14.2
Q. PARAGUAY	6.7	6.8	34.2	14.3	9.6
R. PERU	15.4	19.2[b]	38.9	18.5	13.5
TOTAL	18.0	10.0	46.2	10.8	14.6
Countries with Incipient Modernization					
B. BOLIVIA	9.3	9.3	67.9	36.7	17.3
J. EL SALVADOR	2.9	3.9[d]	60.6	35.3	28.8
K. GUATEMALA	6.7	7.2	70.7	47.3	45.4
L. HAITI	.8	.8[b]	89.5	71.3	~
M. HONDURAS	7.6	8.2	64.8	31.4	27.1
O. NICARAGUA	13.7	14.1	61.6	33.5	35.1
TOTAL	6.2	6.6[c]	65.1	36.8	30.7

a. Calculated as the ratio of graduates to the population aged 20 to 24.
b. These countries were excluded to establish the averages of the country categories.
c. Arithmetical averages.
d. In 1979 the figures for El Salvador were 7.4 and 8.1 respectively.

SOURCE: Henry Kirsch, "University Youth As Social Protagonist in Latin America," *Cepal Review* No. 29 (Santiago, 1986).

Table 902

DROPOUT AND GRADE REPETITION AT THE PRIMARY LEVEL, 8 LR, 1970-84

(%)

Country	1970 Repeat	1970 Dropout	1979 Repeat	1979 Dropout	1980 Repeat	1980 Dropout	1981 Repeat	1981 Dropout	1982 Repeat	1982 Dropout	1983 Repeat	1983 Dropout	1984 Repeat	1984 Dropout
F. COSTA RICA	10.3	4.4	7.6	4.2	7.9	4.2	7.4	3.8	7.1	4.2	11.6	3.0	11.2	2.0
H. DOMINICAN REP.	12.7	9.8	13.7	8.5	11.9	5.9	11.1	4.8	10.4	4.2	9.7	4.1	9.0	3.0
J. EL SALVADOR	16.6	~	7.6	8.6	10.6	10.5	8.9	8.7	~	~	~	~	~	~
K. GUATEMALA	15.8	10.6	11.1	12.4	12.7	11.9	10.0	17.4	14.8	8.7	15.4	8.3	~	8.4
L. HAITI	~	~	~	~	~	~	31.0[†]	13.0[†]	~	~	~	~	~	~
M. HONDURAS	~	15.0	17.0	5.0	17.0	4.0	16.0	5.0	16.0	6.0	~	5.2	~	4.8
O. NICARAGUA	12.8	~	~	~	16.6	23.3	16.6	23.3	15.3	15.1	~	~	~	~
P. PANAMA	15.4	1.9	12.9	3.5	13.0	2.3	12.8	3.7	12.6	2.9	12.0	2.5	~	3.2
LATIN AMERICA AND CARIBBEAN	15.5	~	~	~	14.7	~	~	~	~	~	~	~	~	~

SOURCE: *Educación en América e Informaciones Estadísticas: Centroamérica, República Dominicana y Haiti* (Washington, D.C.: Departamento de Asuntos Educativos, Organización de los Estados Americanos, 1986).

Table 903

STUDENTS ENROLLED AS SHARE OF ELIGIBLE AGES, 20 LR, 1960 AND 1980

(%)

	Country	6 to 11 Years		12 to 17 Years		18 to 23 Years	
		1960	1980	1960	1980	1960	1980
A.	ARGENTINA	91.2	99.9	48.1	72.7	13.2	36.7
B.	BOLIVIA	45.1	76.6	29.0	54.2	5.0	17.1
C.	BRAZIL	47.7	76.2	29.6	58.6	4.7	32.0
D.	CHILE	76.4	100.0	54.7	86.5	7.2	22.2
E.	COLOMBIA	47.9	70.0	28.8	63.8	4.4	32.9
F.	COSTA RICA	74.4	97.5	35.7	54.7	8.0	21.4
G.	CUBA	77.7	100.0	43.0	83.4	6.6	29.9
H.	DOMINICAN REP.	66.8	82.2	39.4	64.4	3.7	20.6
I.	ECUADOR	66.3	80.0	30.3	60.8	5.1	28.5
J.	EL SALVADOR	48.7	69.2	40.3	58.1	8.5	18.9
K.	GUATEMALA	32.0	53.3	17.7	33.8	3.6	10.1
L.	HAITI	33.6	41.4	16.4	21.9	1.9	4.3
M.	HONDURAS	49.5	71.3	24.6	44.7	3.2	14.8
N.	MEXICO	58.4	94.2	37.4	67.3	4.7	18.2
O.	NICARAGUA	42.9	60.8	29.7	53.7	3.6	18.6
P.	PANAMA	68.3	95.7	50.3	83.2	12.7	43.3
Q.	PARAGUAY	69.7	80.0	44.8	51.9	5.8	13.3
R.	PERU	56.7	83.9	43.2	84.0	13.0	32.6
S.	URUGUAY	89.9	~	53.2	67.2	14.1	24.3
T.	VENEZUELA	68.8	83.2	49.0	60.9	8.6	24.0
	LATIN AMERICA[1]	57.3	82.3	35.4	63.3	6.3	26.1

1. Includes Barbados, Guyana, Jamaica, and Trinidad and Tobago.

SOURCE: ECLA-D, "Informe del Secretario Ejecutivo al Décimonoveno Período de Sesiones de la Comisión," July 27, 1981.

Table 904

ENROLLMENT RATIOS FOR THE FIRST, SECOND, AND THIRD LEVELS OF EDUCATION, 20 LC

Country	Year	Sex	First Level Gross	First Level Net	Second Level Gross	Second Level Net	First and Second Levels	Third Level
A. ARGENTINA	1975	MF	106	96	54	42	85	27.2
		M	106	96	51	39	84	28.1
		F	106	97	57	45	86	26.2
	1980	MF	106	~	~	~	~	21.6
		M	106	~	~	~	~	21.2
		F	106	~	~	~	~	22.1
	1983	MF	107	~	60	~	89	25.2
		M	107	~	57	~	89	23.1
		F	107	~	62	~	90	27.4
	1984	MF	107	~	65	~	91	29.3
		M	107	~	62	~	90	27.1
		F	107	~	69	~	93	31.6
	1985	MF	108	~	70	~	94	36.4
		M	107	~	66	~	92	34.2
		F	108	~	75	~	96	28.8
	1986	MF	109	~	74	~	96	38.7
		M	109	~	68	~	94	35.9
		F	109	~	79	~	98	41.5
B. BOLIVIA	1975	MF	85	73	31	21	69	11.7
		M	94	~	~	~	~	~
		F	76	~	~	~	~	~
	1980	MF	84	77	36	16	70	16.5
		M	90	82	41	18	76	~
		F	78	72	31	14	64	~
	1983	MF	87	~	35	~	72	20.6
		M	94	~	38	~	78	~
		F	81	~	32	~	67	~
	1984	MF	91	81	37	25	76	19.5
		M	96	86	40	27	80	~
		F	85	77	34	23	70	~
	1985	MF	~	~	~	~	~	19.0
	1986	MF	87	79	37	26	73	~
		M	93	83	40	28	77	~
		F	82	75	34	24	68	~
C. BRAZIL	1975	MF	88	71	26	9	72	10.7
		M	89	~	24	8	73	~
		F	87	~	28	10	72	~
	1980	MF	99	81	34	14	81	11.9
		M	101	~	31	13	82	12.3
		F	97	~	36	16	80	11.6
	1983	MF	103	83	35	14	86	11.3
		M	108	~	~	~	~	11.3
		F	99	~	~	~	~	11.4
	1984	MF	103	83	35	15	85	~
	1985	MF	101	82	36	15	84	~
	1986	MF	105	~	~	~	~	~
D. CHILE	1975	MF	115	96	47	33	93	16.2
		M	115	95	44	31	92	17.6
		F	115	97	51	36	94	14.7
	1980	MF	112	~	53	~	92	13.0
		M	113	~	50	~	91	14.7
		F	111	~	57	~	93	11.3
	1983	MF	108	92	63	46	93	14.7
		M	109	92	60	44	93	16.8
		F	107	93	66	48	93	12.5
	1984	MF	107	92	66	~	93	15.3
		M	108	~	63	~	93	17.3
		F	106	~	69	~	94	13.2
	1985	MF	109	~	69	~	95	15.9
		M	110	~	66	~	95	17.8
		F	108	~	72	~	96	13.9
	1986	MF	110	~	70	~	96	~
		M	110	~	67	~	95	~
		F	109	~	63	~	96	~

Table 904 (Continued)

ENROLLMENT RATIOS FOR THE FIRST, SECOND, AND
THIRD LEVELS OF EDUCATION, 20 LC

			Enrollment Ratios					
			First Level		Second Level		First and Second Levels	Third Level
Country	Year	Sex	Gross	Net	Gross	Net		
E. COLOMBIA	1975	MF	118	~	39	~	77	8.0
		M	116	~	39	~	76	10.1
		F	120	~	39	~	79	5.8
	1980	MF	128	~	44	~	82	10.6
		M	127	~	43	~	81	11.7
		F	130	~	45	~	83	9.5
	1983	MF	121	~	46	~	80	12.4
		M	120	~	43	~	78	~
		F	122	~	50	~	83	~
	1984	MF	119	76	49	~	81	12.8
		M	119	~	48	~	81	13.3
		F	119	~	49	~	82	12.4
	1985	MF	117	75	50	~	82	13.0
		M	116	~	50	~	81	13.3
		F	119	~	51	~	83	12.7
	1986	MF	114	73	56	~	83	13.1
		M	112	72	55	~	82	13.6
		F	115	74	56	~	84	12.6
F. COSTA RICA	1975	MF	107	92	42	35	79	17.5
		M	108	92	40	33	78	~
		F	106	92	45	37	79	~
	1980	MF	106	90	47	39	79	23.0
		M	107	89	44	36	77	~
		F	105	91	51	43	80	~
	1983	MF	102	~	44	~	75	22.1
		M	103	~	41	~	75	~
		F	100	~	46	~	76	~
	1984	MF	101	~	42	~	75	22.1
		M	102	~	40	~	75	~
		F	100	~	45	~	75	~
	1985	MF	101	87	41	35	75	23.0
		M	101	86	39	33	75	~
		F	100	87	43	37	75	~
	1986	MF	102	88	42	36	77	23.8
		M	103	87	41	34	77	~
		F	101	88	44	37	77	~
G. CUBA	1975	MF	124	~	48	~	88	11.0
		M	126	~	44	~	87	~
		F	122	~	52	~	89	~
	1980	MF	108	98	80	~	94	19.5
		M	111	98	78	~	94	19.8
		F	105	97	83	~	94	19.3
	1983	MF	108	97	82	~	94	19.6
		M	111	97	80	~	94	18.0
		F	105	97	84	~	94	21.2
	1984	MF	106	95	82	~	93	20.1
		M	110	95	81	~	94	18.1
		F	102	94	86	~	93	22.2
	1985	MF	105	94	85	69	94	21.4
		M	108	94	82	65	93	19.2
		F	101	94	88	73	94	23.8
	1986	MF	105	95	86	69	94	22.5
		M	108	95	84	66	94	20.1
		F	101	94	89	72	94	25.0

Table 904 (Continued)

ENROLLMENT RATIOS FOR THE FIRST, SECOND, AND
THIRD LEVELS OF EDUCATION, 20 LC

Country	Year	Sex	Enrollment Ratios					
			First Level		Second Level		First and Second Levels	Third Level
			Gross	Net	Gross	Net		
H. DOMINICAN REP.	1975	MF	104	~	36	~	74	10.1
		M	~	~	~	~	~	11.3
		F	~	~	~	~	~	8.9
	1980	MF	114	~	43	~	81	~
	1983	MF	112	73	50	~	83	~
		M	107	74	~	~	~	~
		F	117	72	~	~	~	~
	1984	MF	121	69	50	~	87	~
		M	119	~	44	~	83	~
		F	123	~	57	~	91	~
	1985	MF	124	68	50	~	88	19.3
		M	121	69	44	~	83	~
		F	126	68	56	~	92	~
	1986	MF	133	79	47	~	91	~
		M	131	80	~	~	~	~
		F	135	78	~	~	~	~
I. ECUADOR	1975	MF	101	78	39	28	73	26.9
		M	103	78	41	28	75	~
		F	99	78	38	27	72	~
	1980	MF	113	~	51	~	85	36.5
		M	115	~	51	~	85	45.2
		F	112	~	51	~	84	27.5
	1981	MF	115	~	53	~	86	34.1
		M	~	~	53	~	~	42.2
		F	~	~	53	~	~	25.9
	1982	MF	116	~	55	~	87	32.1
		M	~	~	54	~	~	~
		F	~	~	56	~	~	~
	1983	MF	117	~	52	~	86	32.5
		M	117	~	51	~	86	39.4
		F	117	~	53	~	87	25.5
	1984	MF	114	~	55	~	86	33.1
J. EL SALVADOR	1975	MF	75	~	19	~	63	7.9
		M	76	~	21	~	64	10.4
		F	74	~	17	~	62	5.4
	1980	MF	74	~	23	~	63	3.9
		M	74	~	24	~	63	5.3
		F	74	~	23	~	63	2.4
	1983	MF	69	64	24	~	60	11.9
		M	69	64	23	~	59	13.5
		F	69	63	25	~	60	10.3
	1984	MF	70	62	24	14	60	12.8
		M	69	61	23	12	59	14.2
		F	70	62	26	16	61	11.3
	1985	MF	~	~	~	~	~	13.8
		M	~	~	~	~	~	15.4
		F	~	~	~	~	~	12.2
	1986	MF	~	~	~	~	~	14.1
		M	~	~	~	~	~	15.9
		F	~	~	~	~	~	12.3
K. GUATEMALA	1975	MF	63	53	12	10	40	4.3
		M	69	57	13	10	43	6.5
		F	57	49	11	9	37	2.0
	1980	MF	71	58	18	13	47	8.4
		M	77	~	20	~	51	~
		F	65	~	17	~	43	~
	1984	MF	76	~	19	~	51	8.2
	1985	MF	76	~	19	~	51	8.4
		M	83	~	~	~	~	~
		F	70	~	~	~	~	~
	1986	MF	76	~	20	~	51	8.6
		M	82	~	~	~	~	~
		F	70	~	~	~	~	~
	1987	MF	77	~	21	~	52	~

Table 904 (Continued)

ENROLLMENT RATIOS FOR THE FIRST, SECOND, AND
THIRD LEVELS OF EDUCATION, 20 LC

Country	Year	Sex	Enrollment Ratios					
			First Level		Second Level		First and Second Levels	Third Level
			Gross	Net	Gross	Net		
L. HAITI	1975	MF	60	~	8	~	34	.7
		M	~	~	8	~	~	1.0
		F	~	~	7	~	~	.3
	1980	MF	67	33	12	~	42	.9
		M	72	34	13	~	45	1.3
		F	62	33	12	~	39	.5
	1981	MF	67	38	12	~	42	~
		M	72	39	13	~	45	~
		F	63	37	12	~	39	~
	1982	MF	72	42	14	~	46	1.0
		M	77	42	14	~	48	~
		F	68	41	14	~	43	~
	1983	MF	76	39	16	~	49	1.1
		M	81	40	16	~	51	1.5
		F	72	38	16	~	46	.8
	1984	MF	78	44	18	~	50	1.1
		M	83	45	19	~	54	1.5
		F	72	42	17	~	47	.8
M. HONDURAS	1975	MF	88	~	16	~	59	4.6
		M	89	~	16	~	60	6.0
		F	86	~	17	~	59	3.2
	1980	MF	95	76	30	~	69	8.2
		M	96	76	29	~	69	10.2
		F	95	75	30	~	69	6.2
	1982	MF	99	85	32	~	72	9.7
		M	100	85	30	~	72	11.1
		F	98	84	34	~	72	8.3
	1983	MF	101	86	33	24	73	9.7
		M	101	86	31	23	73	11.1
		F	100	86	34	26	73	8.3
	1984	MF	102	87	33	20	74	9.6
		M	102	86	31	18	73	~
		F	101	87	36	22	75	~
	1985	MF	102	~	36	~	75	9.5
		M	103	~	~	~	~	11.0
		F	102	~	~	~	~	7.9
N. MEXICO	1975	MF	109	~	34	~	76	10.6
		M	112	~	41	~	80	~
		F	106	~	28	~	71	~
	1980	MF	120	~	47	~	87	14.6
		M	121	~	50	~	89	19.5
		F	119	~	45	~	85	9.7
	1983	MF	119	~	55	~	89	15.7
		M	120	~	56	~	91	20.0
		F	117	~	53	~	87	11.3
	1984	MF	116	97	55	~	88	~
		M	118	~	57	~	89	~
		F	115	~	52	~	86	~
	1985	MF	115	98	55	45	87	16.0
		M	116	~	56	~	88	19.8
		F	114	~	54	~	86	12.2
	1986	MF	114	97	55	46	86	15.7
		M	115	~	56	~	87	19.0
		F	113	~	54	~	85	12.3

Table 904 (Continued)

ENROLLMENT RATIOS FOR THE FIRST, SECOND, AND THIRD LEVELS OF EDUCATION, 20 LC

Country	Year	Sex	First Level Gross	First Level Net	Second Level Gross	Second Level Net	First and Second Levels	Third Level
O. NICARAGUA	1975	MF	82	65	24	~	56	8.3
		M	80	~	23	~	54	11.0
		F	85	~	24	~	58	5.7
	1980	MF	99	74	43	23	76	14.1
		M	96	73	40	21	73	~
		F	102	75	45	25	79	~
	1983	MF	103	73	44	21	79	12.8
		M	100	72	39	16	75	14.1
		F	106	75	48	27	82	11.5
	1984	MF	99	72	43	20	76	11.0
		M	97	71	34	17	71	11.6
		F	102	73	53	23	82	10.5
	1985	MF	101	76	39	~	76	9.8
		M	96	74	23	~	66	8.5
		F	107	79	55	~	86	11.0
	1986	MF	98	75	42	~	75	8.7
		M	93	72	27	~	66	7.5
		F	103	77	57	~	84	9.9
P. PANAMA	1975	MF	114	87	55	39	87	17.3
		M	116	87	52	37	87	17.1
		F	111	88	57	41	87	17.5
	1980	MF	106	88	61	46	85	22.0
		M	108	88	57	43	84	19.3
		F	104	89	65	49	86	24.8
	1983	MF	104	87	59	46	82	22.0
		M	106	87	55	43	82	17.9
		F	101	87	62	49	82	26.3
	1984	MF	105	87	59	47	83	25.1
		M	107	87	56	44	82	21.8
		F	102	87	63	50	83	28.5
	1985	MF	105	89	59	47	83	25.9
		M	107	88	56	44	82	21.7
		F	102	89	63	50	83	30.2
	1986	MF	106	89	59	48	83	28.2
		M	109	90	56	44	83	~
		F	104	89	63	51	84	~
Q. PARAGUAY	1975	MF	102	85	20	16	64	7.0
		M	106	87	20	16	66	~
		F	97	83	20	16	61	~
	1980	MF	103	87	27	~	68	8.8
		M	107	88	~	~	~	~
		F	99	85	~	~	~	~
	1983	MF	102	86	30	~	69	10.3
		M	106	87	~	~	~	~
		F	99	85	~	~	~	~
	1984	MF	101	85	31	~	69	9.7
		M	105	87	~	~	~	~
		F	98	84	~	~	~	~
	1985	MF	101	86	31	~	68	~
		M	104	87	31	~	70	~
		F	98	85	30	~	66	~
	1986	MF	99	85	30	25	67	~
		M	102	86	30	25	69	~
		F	97	84	29	24	65	~

Table 904 (Continued)

ENROLLMENT RATIOS FOR THE FIRST, SECOND, AND THIRD LEVELS OF EDUCATION, 20 LC

			Enrollment Ratios					
			First Level		Second Level		First and Second Levels	Third Level
Country	Year	Sex	Gross	Net	Gross	Net		
R. PERU	1975	MF	113	~	46	~	85	14.6
		M	~	~	50	~	~	19.6
		F	~	~	41	~	~	9.5
	1980	MF	114	86	59	~	91	19.4
		M	117	~	63	~	94	24.8
		F	111	~	54	~	87	13.9
	1982	MF	118	92	61	~	94	21.5
		M	122	~	64	~	98	27.4
		F	115	~	57	~	90	15.6
	1984	MF	~	~	~	~	~	23.8
	1985	MF	122	97	65	~	98	23.8
		M	125	~	68	~	101	~
		F	120	~	61	~	95	~
	1986	MF	~	~	~	~	~	24.6
S. URUGUAY	1975	MF	107	~	60	~	84	16.0
		M	107	~	~	~	~	17.8
		F	106	~	~	~	~	14.2
	1980	MF	106	~	60	~	84	17.3
		M	107	~	59	~	84	15.8
		F	106	~	61	~	84	18.8
	1983	MF	109	88	67	~	89	23.7
		M	110	~	~	~	~	20.9
		F	107	~	~	~	~	26.6
	1984	MF	108	89	70	55	90	30.0
		M	110	90	~	~	~	~
		F	107	88	~	~	~	~
	1985	MF	110	91	71	~	91	35.8
		M	111	~	~	~	~	~
		F	109	~	~	~	~	~
	1986	MF	110	92	~	~	~	41.6
		M	111	~	~	~	~	~
		F	109	~	~	~	~	~
T. VENEZUELA	1975	MF	100	81	45	35	77	18.1
		M	99	~	42	33	75	~
		F	100	~	48	37	79	~
	1980	MF	109	86	41	34	76	21.4
		M	~	~	36	~	~	~
		F	~	~	45	~	~	~
	1983	MF	108	86	43	36	77	23.8
		M	108	~	39	33	75	~
		F	108	~	48	40	79	~
	1984	MF	109	86	45	38	78	23.4
		M	109	~	40	34	76	~
		F	108	~	49	41	80	~
	1985	MF	108	86	45	38	79	26.4
		M	109	~	41	35	77	30.6
		F	108	~	50	42	81	22.2
	1986	MF	110	~	46	~	80	~
		M	110	~	41	~	78	~
		F	110	~	50	~	82	~

SOURCE: UNESCO-SY, 1988, table 3.2.

Table 905

COMPULSORY EDUCATION, ENTRANCE AGES, AND DURATION OF SCHOOLING AT FIRST AND SECOND LEVELS, 20 LC

	Country	Compulsory Education		Pre-Primary Entrance Age	First Level		Second Level	
		Age Limits	Duration (Years)		Entrance Age	Duration (Years)	Entrance Age	Duration (Years)
A.	ARGENTINA	6-14	7	3	6	7	13	3 + 2
B.	BOLIVIA	6-13	8	4	6	8	14	4
C.	BRAZIL	7-14	8	4	7	8	15	3
D.	CHILE	6-13	8	5	6	8	14	2 + 2
E.	COLOMBIA	6-14	5	5	6	5	11	4 + 2
F.	COSTA RICA	6-15	9	5.5	6	6	12	3 + 2
G.	CUBA	6-11	6	5	6	6	12	3 + 3
H.	DOMINICAN REP.	7-14	8	3	7	8	15	4
I.	ECUADOR	6-14	6	4	6	6	12	3 + 3
J.	EL SALVADOR	7-15	9	4	7	9	16	3
K.	GUATEMALA	7-14	6	4	7	6	13	3 + 3
L.	HAITI	6-12	6	4	7	6	12	3 + 3
M.	HONDURAS	7-13	6	4	7	6	12	3 + 2
N.	MEXICO	6-14	6	4	6	6	12	3 + 3
O.	NICARAGUA	7 12	6	3	7	6	13	3 + 2
P.	PANAMA	6-15	9	5	6	6	12	3 + 3
Q.	PARAGUAY	7-13	6	6	7	6	13	3 + 3
R.	PERU	6-12	6	3	6	6	12	3 + 2
S.	URUGUAY	6-15	9	3	6	6	12	3 + 3
T.	VENEZUELA	7-15	9	3	7	6	13	3 + 3
	UNITED STATES	6-16	11	3	6	8	14	4

SOURCE: UNESCO–SY, 1986, table 3.1; 1987, table 3.1; 1988, table 3.

Table 906

EDUCATIONAL ATTAINMENT, BY URBAN AND RURAL AREAS, AGE, AND SEX, 20 LC

Highest Level Attained[1] (%)

Country and Category	Year	Sex	Age Group	Total Population	No Schooling	First Level Incompleted	First Level Completed	Entered Second Level First Cycle	Entered Second Level Second Cycle	Post-Secondary
A. ARGENTINA										
Total Population	1980	MF	25+	14,913,575	7.1	33.4	33.0	24.5 →		6.1
		F	25+	7,711,356	6.7	32.1	35.2	20.1 →		5.8
B. BOLIVIA										
Total Population	1976	MF	25+	1,759,432	48.6	28.5 →		10.8	7.1	5.0
		F	25+	918,709	62.2	20.7 →		8.2	5.6	3.3
Urban Population		MF	25†	690,374	23.2	30.6 →		19.7	15.6	10.9
		F	25†	368,977	34.3	28.6 →		17.0	13.0	7.2
Rural Population		MF	25†	1,069,058	65.0	27.2 →		5.1	1.5	1.3
		F	25†	549,732	80.8	15.4 →		2.3	.7	.7
C. BRAZIL										
Total Population	1980	MF	25+	48,310,722	32.9	50.4	4.3	6.9 →		5.0
		F	25+	24,576,023	35.2	48.8	4.6	7.2 →		4.1
Urban Population		MF	25†	34,355,258	22.8	54.7	6.5	9.2 →		6.8
		F	25†	17,928,564	25.9	53.1	6.0	9.4 →		5.6
Rural Population		MF	25†	13,955,464	57.7	40.0	.9	1.0 →		.4
		F	25†	6,647,459	60.5	37.3	.9	1.1 →		.3
D. CHILE										
Total Population	1982	MF	25+	5,204,698	9.4	56.6 →		26.9 →		7.2
		F	25+	2,724,739	10.0	56.9 →		27.1 →		5.9
Urban Population	1970	MF	25+	2,712,020	8.3	34.1	26.0	27.0 →		4.8
Rural Population	1970	MF	25+	792,400	29.8	54.2	10.0	5.4 →		.6
E. COLOMBIA										
Total Population	1973	MF	20+	8,478,100	22.4	55.9 →		18.4 →		3.3
		F	20+	4,483,086	23.7	56.0 →		18.5 →		1.8
Urban Population		MF	20+	5,593,002	14.2	54.8 →		26.1 →		4.9
		F	20+	3,108,408	16.1	56.2 →		25.1 →		2.6
Rural Population		MF	20+	2,885,098	38.4	58.0 →		3.5 →		.2
		F	20+	1,374,677	40.8	55.6 →		3.5 →		.1
F. COSTA RICA										
Total Population	1973	MF	25+	657,543	16.1	49.1	17.8	6.3	4.9	5.8
		F	25+	331,240	16.0	49.8	17.7	6.5	4.5	5.4
Urban Population		MF	25+	297,887	7.2	37.4	24.8	10.9	90	10.6
		F	25+	161,996	8.1	39.3	24.4	10.9	8.1	9.3
Rural Population		MF	25+	359,656	23.6	58.8	12.1	2.4	1.4	1.8
		F	25+	169,244	23.6	59.8	11.4	2.3	1.1	1.7
G. CUBA										
Total Population	1981	MF	25+a	3,013,315	3.7	22.6	27.6	40.2 →		5.9
		F	25+a	1,511,380	4.1	27.0	28.4	35.9 →		4.5
Urban Population		MF	25+a	2,165,853	2.0	16.8	26.0	47.4 →		7.8
Rural Population		MF	25+a	847,462	8.1	37.5	31.6	21.9 →		1.0
H. DOMINICAN REP.										
Total Population	1970	MF	25+	1,145,090	40.1	41.6	4.3	9.6	2.5	1.9
		F	25+	563,150	42.8	40.9	3.9	8.7	2.4	1.3
Urban Population		MF	25+	487,675	22.9	42.1	7.4	18.3	5.2	4.1
Rural Population		MF	25+	657,415	52.8	41.2	2.0	3.2	.5	.3
I. ECUADOR										
Total Population	1982	MF	25+	2,887,330	25.4	17.0	34.1	8.1	7.9	7.6
		F	25+	1,457,435	29.6	16.8	31.1	8.3	8.7	5.6
Urban Population	1974	MF	25+	958,110	13.0	56.7 →		12.1	11.2	7.0
		F	25+	508,630	16.4	56.3 →		11.9	11.9	3.5
Rural Population	1974	MF	25+	1,338,172	45.4	51.5 →		1.5	1.1	.4
		F	25+	652,265	52.8	44.7 →		1.3	1.1	.2
J. EL SALVADOR										
Total Population	1980	MF	10†	3,132,400	30.2	60.7 →		6.9 →		2.3
		F	10†	1,635,100	33.1	58.3		6.6		1.9
Urban Population		MF	10†	1,405,000	15.5	66.2 →		13.5 →		4.8
		F	10†	776,200	19.6	64.0 →		12.5 →		3.9
Rural Population		MF	10†	1,727,400	42.2	56.2 →		1.4 →		.2
		F	10†	858,900	45.4	53.7 →		1.3 →		.2
K. GUATEMALA										
Total Population	1973	MF	25+	1,785,720	93.9 →	→		4.9 →		1.2
		F	25+	897,960	94.7 →	→		4.8 →		.5
Urban Population		MF	25+	639,780	85.2 →	→		11.8 →		2.9
Rural Population		MF	25+	1,145,940	98.7 →	→		1.1 →		.2
L. HAITI[2]										
Total Population	1982	MF	25+	2,103,124	77.0	15.2 →		7.2 →		.7
		F	25+	1,093,992	81.3	12.3 →		5.9 →		.4
Urban Population	1971	MF	25+	325,778	50.3	24.5	6.5	7.8	9.4	1.5
		F	25+	192,574	59.2	22.0	6.0	6.0	5.9	.9
Rural Population	1971	MF	25+	1,400,330	91.2	7.4	.7	.4	.3	.0
		F	25+	723,070	95.7	3.7	.3	.2	.1	.0

Table 906 (Continued)

EDUCATIONAL ATTAINMENT, BY URBAN AND RURAL AREAS, AGE, AND SEX, 20 LC

Country and Category	Year	Sex	Age Group	Total Population	No Schooling	First Level — Incompleted	First Level — Completed	Entered Second Level — First Cycle	Entered Second Level — Second Cycle	Post-Secondary
M. HONDURAS										
Total Population	1983	MF	25+	858,459[b]	33.5	51.3 →		4.3	7.6	3.3
		F	25+	440,453[b]	34.1	51.1 →		4.4	8.3	2.2
Urban Population		MF	25+	279,554[b]	17.3	51.8 →		8.2	15.4	7.4
		F	25+	152,135[b]	19.4	51.8 →		8.4	15.8	4.6
Rural Population		MF	25+	578,905[b]	46.1	51.0 →		1.2	1.6	.1
		F	25+	288,318[b]	46.9	50.3 →		1.0	1.7	.1
N. MEXICO										
Total Population	1980	MF	25+	24,116,344	38.1	31.7	17.3	6.4	1.7	4.9
O. NICARAGUA										
Total Population	1971	MF	25+	593,100	53.9	41.8 →	→		4.4 →	
P. PANAMA										
Total Population	1980	MF	25+	718,509	17.4	27.3	23.4	11.7	11.8	8.4
		F	25[†]	355,390	18.3	26.5	23.3	11.7	12.3	7.8
Q. PARAGUAY										
Total Population	1972	MF	25+	842,223	19.6	57.7	10.3	5.9	4.6	2.0
		F	25+	438,419	25.4	53.8	10.6	5.1	4.0	1.2
Urban Population		MF	25+	346,870	11.3	46.8	16.5	11.0	9.8	4.6
		F	25+	192,086	15.4	47.0	17.5	9.5	8.0	2.5
Rural Population		MF	25+	495,353	25.5	65.3	5.9	2.2	.9	.2
		F	25+	246,333	33.2	59.1	5.1	1.6	.8	.1
R. PERU[3]										
Total Population	1981	MF	25+	6,532,002	21.6	27.3	17.4	33.7	~	~
		F	25+	3,322,482	30.6	25.2	15.9	28.3	~	~
Urban Population		MF	5+	7,073,800	23.7	31.1	17.6	12.8	10.1	4.8
		F	5+	3,545,100	28.4	31.2	16.8	11.0	9.0	3.6
Rural Population		MF	5+	4,689,400	57.7	32.8	6.3	2.0	.9	.3
		F	5+	2,334,600	70.3	24.3	3.6	1.1	.5	.2
S. URUGUAY										
Total Population	1975	MF	25+	1,590,200	9.9	36.7	29.6	17.4 →		6.3
		F	25+	824,700	10.4	34.9	31.2	16.6 →		6.8
T. VENEZUELA[4]										
Total Population	1981	MF	25+	5,542,852	23.5	47.2 →		22.3 →		7.0
		F	25+	2,802,602	26.4	46.2 →		21.9 →		5.5
UNITED STATES										
Total Population	1981	MF	25+	132,899,000	3.3 →		64.6	→		32.2
		F	25+	70,390,000	3.1 →		68.8	→		28.0

1. For definition of levels, see table 1003, above.
2. "No Schooling" includes illiteracy data.
3. "No Schooling" includes persons who did not state their level of education.
4. The number and percentage within the total population of persons whose educational level is unknown was: MF 25+ 426,614 (15.3%); F 25+ 194,484 (14.2%).

a. Cuba, 25-49.
b. Population data for 1974.

SOURCE: UNESCO-SY, 1986, table 1.4; 1987, table 1.4; 1988, table 1.4.

Table 907

TEACHERS PER 10,000 PERSONS AGES 7–14, 20 LR, 1960–75

Country	1960	1965	1970	1975
A. ARGENTINA	343.4	388.4	470.1	525.3
B. BOLIVIA	145.8	164.8	187.7	239.9
C. BRAZIL	125.8	170.3	220.4	288.4

Continued in SALA, 26-907.

Table 908

TEACHERS AND ENROLLMENT, BY LEVEL AND TYPE, 20 L

Country	Level and Type of Education	Year	Teaching Staff		Students Enrolled	
			Total	Females	Total	Females
A. ARGENTINA	Pre-primary	1986	39,842	39,665	719,928	360,504
	Primary	1986	238,818	221,079	4,778,264	2,346,724
	Intermediate	1986	238,211	158,468	1,929,570	1,021,419
	Higher	1986	69,985	33,101	902,882	479,172
B. BOLIVIA	Pre-Primary	1986	6,941	~	133,677	65,713
	Primary	1986	47,363	~	1,204,534	575,319
	Intermediate	1986	~	~	209,293	96,960
	Higher	1985	~	~	~	~
C. BRAZIL	Pre-Primary	1986	118,336	~	2,699,287	~
	Primary	1986	1,055,170	~	26,225,857	~
	Intermediate	1985	206,124	~	3,016,175	~
	Higher	1983	122,697[†]	52,935	1,479,397[†]	740,327[†]
D. CHILE	Pre-Primary	1986	~	~	209,970	103,365
	Primary	1986	~	~	2,048,107	995,605
	Intermediate	1986	~	~	680,038	349,996
	Higher	1985	~	~	197,437	85,600
E. COLOMBIA	Pre-Primary	1986	11,485	~	276,476	~
	Primary	1986	135,924	107,380	4,002,543	2,000,871
	Intermediate	1986	107,084	~	2,136,239	1,067,794
	Higher	1986	43,279	10,217	417,654	203,384
F. COSTA RICA	Pre-Primary	1986	1,184	~	38,705	19,032
	Primary	1986	11,785	~	380,384	184,130
	Intermediate	1986	6,469	~	114,655	58,512
	Higher	1986	~	~	66,550	~
G. CUBA	Pre-Primary	1986	5,772	~	111,582	~
	Primary	1986	75,723	58,342	1,000,971	472,460
	Intermediate	1986	101,022	51,537	1,153,659	583,507
	Higher	1986	21,573	9,346	256,619	141,697
H. DOMINICAN REP.	Pre-Primary	1986	~	~	125,780	~
	Primary[1]	1986	31,275	~	1,296,366	649,201
	Intermediate	1986	~	~	~	~
	Higher	1985	6,539	~	123,748	~
I. ECUADOR	Pre-Primary	1983	2,777	2,645	80,079	40,280
	Primary	1984	51,300	~	1,672,608	~
	Intermediate	1984	~	~	~	~
	Higher	1984	~	~	280,594	~
J. EL SALVADOR	Pre-Primary	1984	1,144	1,112	61,223	31,672
	Primary	1984	21,145	14,018	883,329	438,883
	Intermediate	1984	3,590	1,097	85,081	44,968
	Higher	1986	4,789	1,642	74,024	31,921
K. GUATEMALA	Pre-Primary	1987	5,029	~	144,312	~
	Primary	1987	31,441	~	1,097,851[†]	~
	Intermediate	1987	16,332[†]	~	241,053[†]	~
	Higher	1986	~	~	51,860	~
L. HAITI	Pre-Primary	1984	956	956	21,000	~
	Primary	1984	20,331	~	819,565	378,721
	Intermediate	1984	~	~	~	~
	Higher	1983	~	~	6,289	2,119
M. HONDURAS	Pre-Primary	1985	~	~	48,610	~
	Primary	1985	~	~	765,809	380,074
	Intermediate	1985	~	~	184,112	~
	Higher	1985	2,662	917	36,620	~
N. MEXICO	Pre-Primary	1986	88,988	88,988	2,547,358	1,271,587
	Primary	1986	456,919	~	14,994,642	7,292,379
	Intermediate	1986	388,876	~	6,702,732	3,258,108
	Higher	1986	115,902	~	1,222,046	~
O. NICARAGUA	Pre-Primary	1986	2,254	2,192	72,569	37,107
	Primary	1986	17,199	14,445	556,684	287,854
	Intermediate	1986	~	~	167,024	112,708
	Higher	1987	1,410	~	26,878	14,759
P. PANAMA	Pre-Primary	1986	1,217	1,202	29,481	14,582
	Primary	1986	15,446	11,937	343,616	164,242
	Intermediate	1986	9,873	5,244	187,312	97,514
	Higher	1986	3,581	~	62,143	31,856
Q. PARAGUAY	Pre-Primary	1986	~	~	21,942	11,095
	Primary	1986	23,407	~	579,687	277,858
	Intermediate	1986	~	~	150,207	~
	Higher	1984	~	~	33,203	~
R. PERU	Pre-Primary	1985	11,206	11,059	342,779	172,141
	Primary	1985	106,600	64,036	3,711,592	1,787,244
	Intermediate	1985	~	~	~	~
	Higher	1986	~	~	472,600	~

Table 908 (Continued)

TEACHERS AND ENROLLMENT, BY LEVEL AND TYPE, 20 L

Country	Level and Type of Education	Year	Teaching Staff		Students Enrolled	
			Total	Females	Total	Females
S URUGUAY	Pre-Primary	1986	1,878	~	55,524	27,588
	Primary	1986	16,212	~	354,883	173,188
	Intermediate	1985	~	~	213,774	~
	Higher	1985	~	~	87,707	~
T. VENEZUELA	Pre-Primary	1986	23,178	22,825	549,376	272,510
	Primary	1986	112,157	93,361	2,880,333	1,409,171
	Intermediate	1986	61,671	~	1,058,058	575,385
	Higher	1985	30,844	~	443,064	182,455

1. Data include intermediate education (grades 7 and 8 of traditional education).

SOURCE: UNESCO-SY, 1988, tables 3.3, 3.4, 3.5, and 3.7.

Table 909

PRE-PRIMARY SCHOOLS, TEACHERS, AND PUPILS, 20 LC

	Country	School Year Beginning	Number of Institutions	Teaching Staff			Pupils Enrolled			
				Total	Female	%	Total	Female	%	% Private
A.	ARGENTINA	1986	8,294	39,842	39,665	100	719,928	360,504	50	31
B.	BOLIVIA	1986	2,038	6,941	~	~	133,677	65,713	49	11
C.	BRAZIL	1986	35,146[†]	118,336[†]	~	~	2,699,287[†]	~	~	37[†]
D.	CHILE	1986	~	~	~	~	209,970	103,365	49	45
E.	COLOMBIA	1986	5,669	11,485	~	~	276,476	~	~	55
F.	COSTA RICA	1986	568	1,184	~	~	38,705	19,032	49	12
G.	CUBA	1986	~	57,772	~	~	111,582	~	~	#
H.	DOMINICAN REP.	1986	~	~	~	~	125,780	~	~	63
I.	ECUADOR	1983	1,235	2,777	2,645	95	80,079	40,280	50	44
J.	EL SALVADOR	1984	770	1,144	1,112	97	61,223	31,672	52	26
K.	GUATEMALA	1987	2,992	5,029[†]	~	~	144,312[†]	~	~	27[†]
L.	HAITI	1984	360	956	956	100	21,000	~	~	63
M.	HONDURAS	1985	~	~	~	~	48,610[†]	~	~	~
N.	MEXICO	1986	40,843	88,988	88,988	100	2,547,358	1,271,587	50	6
O.	NICARAGUA	1986	853	2,254	2,192	97	72,569	37,107	51	25
P.	PANAMA	1986	675	1,217	1,202	99	29,481	14,582	49	26
Q.	PARAGUAY	1986	~	~	~	~	21,942	11,095	51	56
R.	PERU	1985	5,268	11,206	11,059	99	342,779	172,141	50	23
S.	URUGUAY	1986	983	1,878	~	~	55,524	27,588	50	26
T.	VENEZUELA	1986	~	23,178	22,825	98	549,376	272,510	50	16
	UNITED STATES	1986	~	~	~	~	6,515,000	3,120,000	48	36

SOURCE: UNESCO-SY, 1984, 1986, 1987, 1988, table 3.3.

Table 910

PRIMARY SCHOOLS, TEACHERS, AND PUPILS, 20 LC

	Country	School Year Beginning	Number of Institutions (A)	Teaching Staff			Pupils Enrolled			Pupil/Teacher Ratio (H)
				. Total (B)	Female (C)	% Female (D)	Total (E)	Female (F)	% Female (G)	
A.	ARGENTINA	1986	20,865	238,818	221,079	93	4,778,264	2,346,724	49	20
B.	BOLIVIA	1986	12,451	47,363	~	~	1,204,534	565,319	47	25
C.	BRAZIL	1986	209,248	1,055,170	~	~	26,225,857	~	~	25
D.	CHILE	1986	9,036	~	~	~	2,048,107	995,605	49	~
E.	COLOMBIA	1986	36,979	135,924	107,380	79	4,002,543	2,000,871	50	29
F.	COSTA RICA	1986	3,107	11,785	~	~	380,384	184,130	48	32
G.	CUBA	1986	9,837	75,273	58,342	78	1,000,971	472,460	47	13
H.	DOMINICAN REP.[1]	1986	~	31,275	~	~	1,296,366	649,201	50	41
I.	ECUADOR	1984	~	51,300	~	~	1,672,608	~	~	33
J.	EL SALVADOR	1984	2,631	21,145	14,018	66	883,329	438,883	50	42
K.	GUATEMALA	1987	8,481	31,441	~	~	1,097,851†	~	~	35†
L.	HAITI	1984	3,677	20,311	~	~	819,565	378,721	46	40
M.	HONDURAS	1985	~	~	~	~	765,809	380,074	50	~
N.	MEXICO	1986	80,045	456,919	~	~	4,994,642	7,292,379	49	33
O.	NICARAGUA	1986	4,526	17,199	14,445	84	556,684	287,854	52	32
P.	PANAMA	1986	2,571	15,446	11,937	77	343,616	164,242	48	22
Q.	PARAGUAY	1986	4,101	23,407	~	~	579,687	277,858	48	25
R.	PERU	1985	24,327	106,600	64,036	60	3,711,592	1,787,244	48	35
S.	URUGUAY	1986	2,613	16,212	~	~	354,883	173,188	49	22
T.	VENEZUELA	1986	13,262	112,157	93,361	83	2,880,333	1,409,171	49	26
	UNITED STATES[2]	1986	~	~	~	~	27,117,000	13,127,000	48	~

1. Data include intermediate education (grades 7 and 8 of traditional education).
2. Data on pupils refer to grades 1 to 8, while data on teaching staff refer to kindergarten and elementary schools; whole duration is six or eight grades depending on the state.

SOURCE: UNESCO-SY, 1984, 1986, 1987, 1988, table 3.4.

Table 911

HIGHER EDUCATION:[1] TEACHERS AND STUDENTS, BY TYPE OF INSTITUTION, 20 LC

Country	School Year Beginning	All Institutions		Universities and Equivalent Institutions		Other Non-University Institutions	
		Total	Female	Total	Female	Total	Female
A. ARGENTINA							
Teachers	1986	69,985	33,101	41,804	13,691	28,181	19,410
Students	1986	902,882	479,172	707,016	326,716	195,866	152,456
B. BOLIVIA							
Teachers	1985	~	~	4,924	~	~	~
Students	1985	~	~	95,052	~	~	~
C. BRAZIL							
Teachers	1983	122,697	52,935	122,697	52,935	#	#
Students	1983	1,479,397	740,327	1,479,397	740,327	#	#
D. CHILE							
Teachers	1984	15,131	3,350	11,603	2,209	3,528	1,141
Students	1984	197,437	85,600	132,254	52,565	56,411	28,087
E. COLOMBIA							
Teachers	1986	43,279	10,217	36,443	8,285	6,497	1,816
Students	1986	417,654	203,384	320,371	149,375	49,738	28,804
F. COSTA RICA							
Teachers	1986	~	~	5,211	1,697	~	~
Students	1986	66,550	~	50,033	~	6,294	~
G. CUBA							
Teachers	1986	21,573	9,346	21,573	9,346	#	#
Students	1986	256,619	141,697	256,619	141,697	#	#
H. DOMINICAN REP.							
Teachers	1985	6,539	~	~	~	~	~
Students	1985	123,748	~	~	~	~	~
I. ECUADOR							
Teachers	1987	~	~	12,278	~	~	~
Students	1987	280,594	~	264,941	103,815	~	~
J. EL SALVADOR							
Teachers	1986	4,789	1,642	3,821	1,361	705	215
Students	1986	28,281	31,921	61,323	25,612	8,429	4,398
K. GUATEMALA[2]							
Teachers	1984	3,043	~	3,043	~	~	~
Students	1986	51,860	~	51,860	~	~	~
L. HAITI							
Teachers	1982	817	104	~	~	~	~
Students	1984	~	~	4,513	1,432	~	~
M. HONDURAS							
Teachers	1985	2,662	917	2,274	762	388	155
Students	1985	36,620	~	30,623	12,721	5,997	~
N. MEXICO							
Teachers	1986	115,902	~	115,902	~	#	#
Students	1986	1,222,046	~	191,997	473,074	#	#
O. NICARAGUA							
Teachers	1987	1,410	~	1,252	~	158	~
Students	1987	26,878	14,759	23,873	12,653	3,005	2,106
P. PANAMA							
Teachers	1986	3,581	~	3,581	~	#	#
Students	1986	62,143	~	62,143	~	#	#
Q. PARAGUAY							
Teachers	1984	~	~	2,694	~	~	~
Students	1984	33,203	~	30,222	~	2,981	~
R. PERU							
Teachers	1984	24,793	~	19,408	~	5,385	~
Students	1986	472,600	~	373,500	~	99,100	~
S. URUGUAY							
Teachers	1984	4,561	~	4,537	~	24	#
Students	1986	~	~	91,580	~	10,227	~
T. VENEZUELA							
Teachers	1985	30,844	~	23,951	~	6,460	~
Students	1985	443,064	182,455	347,618	~	74,757	~
UNITED STATES							
Teachers	1986	701,000	~	492,000	~	209,000	~
Students	1986	1,239,800	6,558,000	7,754,000	3,949,000	4,644,000	2,609,000

1. For pre-higher education levels, see table 903.
2. University of San Carlos only.

SOURCE: UNESCO-SY, 1984, 1986, 1987, 1988, table 3.7.

Table 912

HIGHER EDUCATION:[1] DISTRIBUTION OF STUDENTS, BY SEX AND FIELD OF STUDY, 17 L, 1980–86

Country and Field of Study	1980		1985		1986	
	MF	F	MF	F	MF	F
A. ARGENTINA[2]						
Total	491,473	247,656	~	~	~	~
Education Science and Teacher Training	84,727	74,588	~	~	~	~
Humanities, Religion, and Theology	24,738	18,746	~	~	~	~
Fine and Applied Arts	7,214	5,372	~	~	~	~
Law	60,981	28,416	~	~	~	~
Social and Behavioral Science	10,749	7,690	~	~	~	~
Commercial and Business Administration	74,963	25,606	~	~	~	~
Mass Communication and Documentation	1,788	1,062	~	~	~	~
Home Economics (Domestic Science)	#	#	~	~	~	~
Service Trades	#	#	~	~	~	~
Natural Science	18,877	11,473	~	~	~	~
Mathematics and Computer Science	20,022	13,874	~	~	~	~
Medical Science and Health-Related	57,460	31,583	~	~	~	~
Engineering	68,861	8,235	~	~	~	~
Architecture and Town Planning	29,920	12,206	~	~	~	~
Trade, Craft, and Industrial Programs	6,139	2,028	~	~	~	~
Transport and Communications	#	#	~	~	~	~
Agriculture, Forestry, and Fishery	25,034	6,777	~	~	~	~
Other and Not Specified	#	#	~	~	~	~
B. BOLIVIA[3,4]						
Total	~	~	~	~	~	~
Education Science and Teacher Training	~	~	~	~	~	~
Humanities, Religion, and Theology	~	~	~	~	~	~
Fine and Applied Arts	~	~	~	~	~	~
Law	~	~	~	~	~	~
Social and Behavioral Science	~	~	~	~	~	~
Commercial and Business Administration	~	~	~	~	~	~
Mass Communication and Documentation	~	~	~	~	~	~
Home Economics (Domestic Science)	~	~	~	~	~	~
Service Trades	~	~	~	~	~	~
Natural Science	~	~	~	~	~	~
Mathematics and Computer Science	~	~	~	~	~	~
Medical Science and Health-Related	~	~	~	~	~	~
Engineering	~	~	~	~	~	~
Architecture and Town Planning	~	~	~	~	~	~
Trade, Craft, and Industrial Programs	~	~	~	~	~	~
Transport and Communications	~	~	~	~	~	~
Agriculture, Forestry, and Fishery	~	~	~	~	~	~
Other and Not Specified	~	~	~	~	~	~
C. BRAZIL[5]						
Total	1,409,243	~	~	~	~	~
Education Science and Teacher Training	403,949	~	~	~	~	~
Humanities, Religion, and Theology	77,696	~	~	~	~	~
Fine and Applied Arts	13,849	~	~	~	~	~
Law	137,373	~	~	~	~	~
Social and Behavioral Science	87,696	~	~	~	~	~
Commercial and Business Administration	208,620	~	~	~	~	~
Mass Communication and Documentation	34,486	~	~	~	~	~
Home Economics (Domestic Science)	1,956	~	~	~	~	~
Service Trades	6,331	~	~	~	~	~
Natural Science	51,374	~	~	~	~	~
Mathematics and Computer Science	12,710	~	~	~	~	~
Medical Science and Health-Related	110,123	~	~	~	~	~
Engineering	156,726	~	~	~	~	~
Architecture and Town Planning	24,287	~	~	~	~	~
Trade, Craft, and Industrial Programs	13,891	~	~	~	~	~
Transport and Communications	#	#	~	~	~	~
Agriculture, Forestry, and Fishery	33,162	~	~	~	~	~
Other and Not Specified	35,014	~	~	~	~	~

Table 912 (Continued)

HIGHER EDUCATION:[1] DISTRIBUTION OF STUDENTS, BY SEX AND FIELD OF STUDY, 17 L, 1980–86

Country and Field of Study	1980		1985		1986	
	MF	F	MF	F	MF	F
D. CHILE						
Total	145,497	62,804	~	~	~	~
Education Science and Teacher Training	11,732	9,538	~	~	~	~
Humanities, Religion, and Theology	12,097	7,361	~	~	~	~
Fine and Applied Arts	5,738	3,176	~	~	~	~
Law	2,757	838	~	~	~	~
Social and Behavioral Science	1,743	916	~	~	~	~
Commercial and Business Administration	17,188	5,929	~	~	~	~
Mass Communication and Documentation	2,825	1,996	~	~	~	~
Home Economics (Domestic Science)	756	573	~	~	~	~
Service Trades	7,176	4,468	~	~	~	~
Natural Science	9,015	4,335	~	~	~	~
Mathematics and Computer Science	8,674	3,793	~	~	~	~
Medical Science and Health-Related	14,531	8,701	~	~	~	~
Engineering	33,508	4,175	~	~	~	~
Architecture and Town Planning	2,797	737	~	~	~	~
Trade, Craft, and Industrial Programs	3,391	938	~	~	~	~
Transport and Communications	1,594	901	~	~	~	~
Agriculture, Forestry, and Fishery	3,023	1,090	~	~	~	~
Other and Not Specified	6,952	3,339	~	~	~	~
E. COLOMBIA[6,11]						
Total	271,630	~	391,490	189,937	417,654	203,384
Education Science and Teacher Training	44,379	~	74,783	50,866	84,779	58,241
Humanities, Religion, and Theology	2,755	~	2,677	1,334	2,351	1,323
Fine and Applied Arts	~	~	8,765	5,324	9,514	5,782
Law	25,646	~	48,405	27,373	46,885	27,185
Social and Behavioral Science	14,069	~	~	~	~	~
Commercial and Business Administration	88,192	~	104,334	51,967	106,035	54,219
Mass Communication and Documentation	~	~	~	~	~	~
Home Economics (Domestic Science)	~	~	~	~	~	~
Service Trades	~	~	~	~	~	~
Natural Science	5,830	~	6,477	2,439	6,512	2,465
Mathematics and Computer Science	~	~	~	~	~	~
Medical Science and Health-Related	25,934	~	39,904	22,589	40,784	24,198
Engineering	36,657	~	95,280	25,212	109,550	27,018
Architecture and Town Planning	17,805	~	~	~	~	~
Trade, Craft, and Industrial Programs	~	~	~	~	~	~
Transport and Communications	~	~	~	~	~	~
Agriculture, Forestry, and Fishery	10,363	~	10,865	2,833	11,244	2,953
Other and Not Specified	#	#	#	#	#	#
F. COSTA RICA[7]						
Total	50,812	~	58,393	~	~	~
Education Science and Teacher Training	6,838	~	6,209	~	~	~
Humanities, Religion, and Theology	7,947	~	11,421	~	~	~
Fine and Applied Arts	924	~	1,323	~	~	~
Law	2,428	~	3,884	~	~	~
Social and Behavioral Science	4,622	~	6,162	~	~	~
Commercial and Business Administration	5,778	~	6,815	~	~	~
Mass Communication and Documentation	636	~	1,314	~	~	~
Home Economics (Domestic Science)	#	#	#	#	~	~
Service Trades	#	#	264	~	~	~
Natural Science	1,952	~	1,604	~	~	~
Mathematics and Computer Science	2,065	~	2,354	~	~	~
Medical Science and Health-Related	2,824	~	3,130	~	~	~
Engineering	4,319	~	4,962	~	~	~
Architecture and Town Planning	1,161	~	947	~	~	~
Trade, Craft, and Industrial Programs	- -	#	#	#	~	~
Transport and Communications	- -	#	#	#	~	~
Agriculture, Forestry, and Fishery	3,169	~	2,058	~	~	~
Other and Not Specified	6,149	~	5,946	~	~	~

Table 912 (Continued)

HIGHER EDUCATION:[1] DISTRIBUTION OF STUDENTS, BY SEX AND FIELD OF STUDY, 17 L, 1980–86

Country and Field of Study	1980 MF	1980 F	1985 MF	1985 F	1986 MF	1986 F
G. CUBA[8]						
Total	151,733	~	235,224	127,054	256,619	141,697
Education Science and Teacher Training	60,942	~	107,399	67,572	123,423	79,917
Humanities, Religion, and Theology	2,795	~	1,966	1,383	3,190	2,291
Fine and Applied Arts	902	~	952	400	1,491	883
Law	3,175	~	1,803	1,171	2,789	1,894
Social and Behavioral Science	1,727	~	24,012	14,120	17,853	8,515
Commercial and Business Administration	15,340	~	5,376	3,517	8,414	5,524
Mass Communication and Documentation	1,222	~	678	228	1,452	826
Home Economics (Domestic Science)	#	#	#	#	#	#
Service Trades	#	#	#	#	#	#
Natural Science	3,791	~	2,090	1,078	2,966	1,999
Mathematics and Computer Science	1,475	~	1,474	756	1,791	1,001
Medical Science and Health-Related	15,559	~	28,101	16,424	31,540	18,400
Engineering	18,893	~	25,398	8,115	25,434	8,176
Architecture and Town Planning	4,876	~	7,104	3,213	6,984	3,065
Trade, Craft, and Industrial Programs	~	~	#	#	411	306
Transport and Communications	1,987	~	3,130	408	3,130	358
Agriculture, Forestry, and Fishery	14,538	~	15,718	6,426	14,970	6,084
Other and Not Specified	4,511	~	10,023	2,243	10,781	2,458
I. ECUADOR[9]						
Total	269,775	97,350	~	~	~	~
Education Science and Teacher Training	59,426	30,497	~	~	~	~
Humanities, Religion, and Theology	13,379	8,210	~	~	~	~
Fine and Applied Arts	1,394	406	~	~	~	~
Law	13,394	4,004	~	~	~	~
Social and Behavioral Science	21,219	8,526	~	~	~	~
Commercial and Business Administration	35,307	15,791	~	~	~	~
Mass Communication and Documentation	1,377	523	~	~	~	~
Home Economics (Domestic Science)	225	223	~	~	~	~
Service Trades	357	221	~	~	~	~
Natural Science	6,194	2,270	~	~	~	~
Mathematics and Computer Science	4,679	409	~	~	~	~
Medical Science and Health-Related	30,233	12,556	~	~	~	~
Engineering	47,244	5,194	~	~	~	~
Architecture and Town Planning	10,456	2,527	~	~	~	~
Trade, Craft, and Industrial Programs	1,800	483	~	~	~	~
Transport and Communications	#	#	~	~	~	~
Agriculture, Forestry, and Fishery	16,584	2,898	~	~	~	~
Other and Not Specified	6,507	2,612	~	~	~	~
J. EL SALVADOR[10]						
Total	16,838	5,202	70,499	20,058	74,024	19,878
Education Science and Teacher Training	698	236	12,009	5,799	12,120	5,316
Humanities, Religion, and Theology	158	44	1,654	299	1,847	396
Fine and Applied Arts	339	240	197	132	169	146
Law	592	250	4,735	647	5,259	703
Social and Behavioral Science	1,959	952	5,883	1,706	5,905	1,545
Commercial and Business Administration	4,198	1,277	16,715	5,730	17,472	5,873
Mass Communication and Documentation	#	#	951	331	1,350	644
Home Economics (Domestic Science)	#	#	#	#	#	#
Service Trades	99	75	69	50	246	142
Natural Science	29	8	1,887	191	2,219	155
Mathematics and Computer Science	#	#	295	#	313	3
Medical Science and Health-Related	479	479	7,118	1,617	8,307	1,628
Engineering	6,308	1,156	10,851	1,042	11,311	1,024
Architecture and Town Planning	945	398	2,723	1,129	2,679	1,028
Trade, Craft, and Industrial Programs	551	87	319	73	174	10
Transport and Communications	#	#	#	#	#	#
Agriculture, Forestry, and Fishery	483	#	3,045	150	2,710	111
Other and Not Specified	#	#	2,048	1,212	1,946	1,154

Table 912 (Continued)

HIGHER EDUCATION:[1] DISTRIBUTION OF STUDENTS, BY SEX AND FIELD OF STUDY, 17 L, 1980–86

Country and Field of Study	1980 MF	1980 F	1985 MF	1985 F	1986 MF	1986 F
L. HAITI[11],[3]						
Total	4,671	1,410	~	~	~	~
Education Science and Teacher Training	324	79	~	~	~	~
Humanities, Religion, and Theology	~	~	~	~	~	~
Fine and Applied Arts	#	#	~	~	~	~
Law	1,039	432	~	~	~	~
Social and Behavioral Science	769	209	~	~	~	~
Commercial and Business Administration	#	#	~	~	~	~
Mass Communication and Documentation	#	#	~	~	~	~
Home Economics (Domestic Science)	#	#	~	~	~	~
Service Trades	#	#	~	~	~	~
Natural Science	175	20	~	~	~	~
Mathematics and Computer Science	~	~	~	~	~	~
Medical Science and Health-Related	1,112	506	~	~	~	~
Engineering	908	68	~	~	~	~
Architecture and Town Planning	#	#	~	~	~	~
Trade, Craft, and Industrial Programs	#	#	~	~	~	~
Transport and Communications	#	#	~	~	~	~
Agriculture, Forestry, and Fishery	174	24	~	~	~	~
Other and Not Specified	170	72	~	~	~	~
M. HONDURAS						
Total	25,825	9,736	36,620	~	~	~
Education Science and Teacher Training	491	343	6,234	~	~	~
Humanities, Religion, and Theology	204	114	244	114	~	~
Fine and Applied Arts	16	3	23	8	~	~
Law	2,222	766	3,546	1,435	~	~
Social and Behavioral Science	3,345	1,575	2,354	1,163	~	~
Commercial and Business Administration	6,171	2,626	6,277	2,822	~	~
Mass Communication and Documentation	147	56	449	195	~	~
Home Economics (Domestic Science)	61	61	#	#	~	~
Service Trades	#	#	#	#	~	~
Natural Science	232	120	1,677	1,209	~	~
Mathematics and Computer Science	215	107	196	79	~	~
Medical Science and Health-Related	4,432	2,300	4,349	2,352	~	~
Engineering	6,389	1,009	6,904	1,364	~	~
Architecture and Town Planning	#	#	444	196	~	~
Trade, Craft, and Industrial Programs	#	#	#	#	~	~
Transport and Communications	#	#	#	#	~	~
Agriculture, Forestry, and Fishery	707	#	2,885	~	~	~
Other and Not Specified	1,193	656	1,038	642	~	~
N. MEXICO[3]						
Total	785,419	239,791	1,199,120	454,366	1,191,997	473,074
Education Science and Teacher Training	10,528	5,308	156,168	91,099	141,776	85,564
Humanities, Religion, and Theology	9,894	5,115	22,298	11,510	14,541	8,331
Fine and Applied Arts	5,825	2,922	1,236	645	2,321	1,177
Law	65,726	19,892	112,295	38,146	110,542	39,844
Social and Behavioral Science	55,600	29,026	81,278	48,486	83,412	48,867
Commercial and Business Administration	162,402	61,600	218,150	96,783	234,399	111,132
Mass Communication and Documentation	13,188	7,270	23,472	14,906	24,887	16,613
Home Economics (Domestic Science)	#	#	#	#	#	#
Service Trades	7,394	4,712	#	#	#	#
Natural Science	21,024	7,095	26,836	10,325	29,895	12,695
Mathematics and Computer Science	7,855	1,871	34,342	11,862	25,167	10,198
Medical Science and Health-Related	155,100	66,839	148,709	70,978	136,635	68,990
Engineering	160,522	14,586	209,357	24,267	281,767	36,696
Architecture and Town Planning	31,409	5,735	55,106	14,658	55,330	15,997
Trade, Craft, and Industrial Programs	2,268	818	#	#	#	#
Transport and Communications	467	33	#	#	#	#
Agriculture, Forestry, and Fishery	75,038	6,763	97,639	12,762	34,059	6,246
Other and Not Specified	1,179	206	12,234	7,939	17,266	10,746

Table 912 (Continued)

HIGHER EDUCATION:[1] DISTRIBUTION OF STUDENTS, BY SEX AND FIELD OF STUDY, 17 L, 1980–86

Country and Field of Study	1980		1985		1986	
	MF	F	MF	F	MF	F
O. NICARAGUA						
Total	35,268	~	~	~	26,878	14,759
Education Science and Teacher Training	2,253	~	~	~	4,617	3,010
Humanities, Religion, and Theology	675	~	~	~	168	137
Fine and Applied Arts	#	#	~	~	152	109
Law	1,145	~	~	~	948	461
Social and Behavioral Science	2,957	~	~	~	2,443	1,263
Commercial and Business Administration	3,871	~	~	~	3,242	1,869
Mass Communication and Documentation	346	~	~	~	388	343
Home Economics (Domestic Science)	129	~	~	~	360	329
Service Trades	#	#	~	~	#	#
Natural Science	1,239	~	~	~	415	297
Mathematics and Computer Science	759	~	~	~	1,005	702
Medical Science and Health-Related	1,987	~	~	~	3,634	2,388
Engineering	3,538	~	~	~	3,432	911
Architecture and Town Planning	497	~	~	~	332	209
Trade, Craft, and Industrial Programs	66	~	~	~	241	165
Transport and Communications	#	#	~	~	#	#
Agriculture, Forestry, and Fishery	933	~	~	~	4,065	2,245
Other and Not Specified	14,873	~	~	~	1,436	321
P. PANAMA[12]						
Total	31,277	16,852	55,303	31,856	~	~
Education Science and Teacher Training	1,210	996	3,567	2,756	~	~
Humanities, Religion, and Theology	1,293	966	2,082	1,531	~	~
Fine and Applied Arts	553	257	498	286	~	~
Law	1,739	641	2,439	1,043	~	~
Social and Behavioral Science	3,156	1,653	3,987	2,152	~	~
Commercial and Business Administration	8,968	5,368	17,620	11,692	~	~
Mass Communication and Documentation	968	620	2,854	1,977	~	~
Home Economics (Domestic Science)	319	319	217	217	~	~
Service Trades	#	#	7	4	~	~
Natural Science	2,278	914	1,737	8⌐5	~	~
Mathematics and Computer Science	284	141	794	394	~	~
Medical Science and Health-Related	3,200	2,296	3,855	3,057	~	~
Engineering	1,747	401	10,195	2,675	~	~
Architecture and Town Planning	764	205	787	235	~	~
Trade, Craft, and Industrial Programs	1,984	326	585	279	~	~
Transport and Communications	#	#	#	#	~	~
Agriculture, Forestry, and Fishery	457	110	245	51	~	~
Other and Not Specified	2,357	1,639	3,834	2,642	~	~
R. PERU[13]						
Total	306,353	~	~	~	~	~
Education Science and Teacher Training	23,314	~	~	~	~	~
Humanities, Religion, and Theology	3,513	~	~	~	~	~
Fine and Applied Arts	441	~	~	~	~	~
Law	14,534	~	~	~	~	~
Social and Behavioral Science	37,388	~	~	~	~	~
Commercial and Business Administration	76,026	~	~	~	~	~
Mass Communication and Documentation	5,670	~	~	~	~	~
Home Economics (Domestic Science)	1,425	~	~	~	~	~
Service Trades	403	~	~	~	~	~
Natural Science	8,373	~	~	~	~	~
Mathematics and Computer Science	4,201	~	~	~	~	~
Medical Science and Health-Related	23,781	~	~	~	~	~
Engineering	53,338	~	~	~	~	~
Architecture and Town Planning	5,049	~	~	~	~	~
Trade, Craft, and Industrial Programs	10,523	~	~	~	~	~
Transport and Communications	#	#	~	~	~	~
Agriculture, Forestry, and Fishery	24,018	~	~	~	~	~
Other and Not Specified	14,356	~	~	~	~	~

Table 912 (Continued)

HIGHER EDUCATION:[1] DISTRIBUTION OF STUDENTS, BY SEX AND FIELD OF STUDY, 17 L, 1980–86

Country and Field of Study	1980		1985		1986	
	MF	F	MF	F	MF	F
S. URUGUAY[6,14]						
Total	36,298	19,236	91.580	~	91,580	~
Education Science and Teacher Training	253	199	1,561	~	1,561	~
Humanities, Religion, and Theology	582	435	3,675	~	3,675	~
Fine and Applied Arts	312	175	3,008	~	3,008	~
Law	10,812	6,641	17,805	~	17,805	~
Social and Behavioral Science	1,310	1,018	10,014	~	10,014	~
Commercial and Business Administration	4,183	2,055	14,078	~	14,078	~
Mass Communication and Documentation	156	145	1,217	~	1,217	~
Home Economics (Domestic Science)	#	#	160	146	160	146
Service Trades	#	#	#	#	#	#
Natural Science	627	348	1,937	~	1,937	~
Mathematics and Computer Science	496	178	5,190	~	5,190	~
Medical Science and Health-Related	10,324	5,788	18,613	11,816	18,613	11,816
Engineering	1,303	116	4,367	~	4,367	~
Architecture and Town Planning	1,850	712	3,714	~	3,714	~
Trade, Craft, and Industrial Programs	74	#	480	~	480	~
Transport and Communications	#	#	#	#	#	#
Agriculture, Forestry, and Fishery	3,600	1,042	4,849	1,583	4,849	1,583
Other and Not Specified	416	384	912	832	912	832
T. VENEZUELA						
Total	307,133	~	443,064	~	~	~
Education Science and Teacher Training	44,875	~	82,550	~	~	~
Humanities, Religion, and Theology	3,478	~	4,830	~	~	~
Fine and Applied Arts	410	~	651	~	~	~
Law	18,975	~	37,456	~	~	~
Social and Behavioral Science	21,699	~	44,213	~	~	~
Commercial and Business Administration	42,286	.	70,015	. .	. .	. .
Mass Communication and Documentation	3,667	~	6,539	~	~	~
Home Economics (Domestic Science)	#	#	#	#	~	~
Service Trades	1,419	~	393	~	~	~
Natural Science	5,912	~	7,300	~	~	~
Mathematics and Computer Science	6,221	~	8,623	~	~	~
Medical Science and Health-Related	35,650	~	46,465	~	~	~
Engineering	51,306	~	78,271	~	~	~
Architecture and Town Planning	5,858	~	6,424	~	~	~
Trade, Craft, and Industrial Programs	1,175	~	#	#	~	~
Transport and Communications	#	#	220	~	~	~
Agriculture, Forestry, and Fishery	12,813	~	11,539	~	~	~
Other and Not Specified	51,389	~	30,775	~	~	~

1. Includes awards not equivalent to a first university degree, first university degrees, and post-graduate university degrees.
2. Data for 1983 refer to 1981 and to universities and equivalent degree-granting institutions.
3. Data refer to universities and degree-granting institutions only.
4. Excludes Universidad Católica Boliviano.
5. For 1980 data on education science and teacher training include part of natural science, and of humanities, religion, and theology.
6. Data for 1983 and 1984 refer respectively to 1984 and 1985.
7. Data refer to universities only.
8. For 1980 engineering includes trade, craft, and industrial programs.
9. For 1980 data on female students refer to universities and equivalent degree-granting institutions only.
10. 1980 data exclude figures for the National University which was closed in 1979.
11. Natural science includes mathematics and computer science. Law includes economics. In 1980 education science and teacher training includes humanities, religion, and theology.
12. For 1980 data exclude regional centers.
13. For 1982 data refer to universities only.
14. For 1986 data refer to universities only.

SOURCE: UNESCO-SY, 1987, table 3.12; 1988, table 3.9.

Table 913

HIGHER EDUCATION: GRADUATES, BY LEVEL[1] AND FIELD OF STUDY, 16 LC

Country and Field of Study	All Levels		Level 5		Level 6		Level 7	
	MF	F	MF	F	MF	F	MF	F
B. BOLIVIA (1981)[2,3]								
Total	1,272	~	~	~	~	~	~	~
Education Science and Teacher Training	~	~	~	~	~	~	~	~
Humanities, Religion, and Theology	139	~	~	~	~	~	~	~
Fine and Applied Arts	#	#	~	~	~	~	~	~
Law	192	~	~	~	~	~	~	~
Social and Behavioral Science	222	~	~	~	~	~	~	~
Commercial and Business Administration	#	#	~	~	~	~	~	~
Mass Communication and Documentation	#	#	~	~	~	~	~	~
Home Economics (Domestic Science)	#	#	~	~	~	~	~	~
Service Trades	#	#	~	~	~	~	~	~
Natural Science	51	~	~	~	~	~	~	~
Mathematics and Computer Science	#	#	~	~	~	~	~	~
Medical Science and Health-Related	359	~	~	~	~	~	~	~
Engineering	235	~	~	~	~	~	~	~
Architecture and Town Planning	23	~	~	~	~	~	~	~
Trade, Craft, and Industrial Programs	13	~	~	~	~	~	~	~
Transport and Communications	#	#	~	~	~	~	~	~
Agriculture, Forestry, and Fishery	38	~	~	~	~	~	~	~
Other and Not Specified	#	#	~	~	~	~	~	~
C. BRAZIL (1982)								
Total	253,553	151,391	#	#	244,639	147,501	8,914	3,890
Education Science and Teacher Training	48,932	41,170	#	#	48,208	40,632	724	538
Humanities, Religion, and Theology	20,621	17,944	#	#	19,865	16,993	756	951
Fine and Applied Arts	6,890	5,567	#	#	6,871	5,556	19	11
Law	21,983	8,723	#	#	21,287	8,470	696	253
Social and Behavioral Science	34,499	24,314	#	#	33,598	24,188	901	126
Commercial and Business Administration	32,596	12,087	#	#	32,322	12,035	274	52
Mass Communication and Documentation	7,173	5,015	#	#	7,033	4,958	140	57
Home Economics (Domestic Science)	253	246	#	#	253	246	#	#
Service Trades	624	504	#	#	624	504	#	#
Natural Science	7,726	4,127	#	#	5,927	3,376	1,799	751
Mathematics and Computer Science	4,369	2,311	#	#	4,020	2,192	349	119
Medical Science and Health-Related	23,528	14,470	#	#	22,222	13,895	1,306	575
Engineering	21,025	2,678	#	#	19,992	2,498	1,033	180
Architecture and Town Planning	2,954	1,695	#	#	2,873	1,661	81	34
Trade, Craft, and Industrial Programs	1,716	225	#	#	1,716	225	#	#
Transport and Communications	#	#	#	#	#	#	#	#
Agriculture, Forestry, and Fishery	6,832	1,374	#	#	6,033	1,142	799	232
Other and Not Specified	11,832	8,941	#	#	11,795	8,930	37	11
D. CHILE (1984)								
Total	20,256	9,945	1,462	350	18,581	9,505	213	90
Education Science and Teacher Training	4,391	3,238	#	#	4,367	3,225	24	13
Humanities, Religion, and Theology	2,038	1,314	34	30	1,996	1,280	8	4
Fine and Applied Arts	770	437	#	#	770	437	#	#
Law	377	149	1	1	360	144	16	4
Social and Behavioral Science	591	298	#	#	580	294	11	4
Commercial and Business Administration	1,897	506	92	42	1,803	463	2	1
Mass Communication and Documentation	153	79	38	14	115	65	#	#
Home Economics (Domestic Science)	142	111	#	#	109	86	33	25
Service Trades	36	29	36	29	#	#	#	#
Natural Science	1,197	605	38	22	1,127	577	32	6
Mathematics and Computer Science	625	271	41	17	565	249	19	5
Medical Science and Health-Related	2,704	1,602	#	#	2,668	1,579	36	23
Engineering	3,580	612	779	88	2,790	522	11	2
Architecture and Town Planning	330	83	12	3	312	79	6	1
Trade, Craft, and Industrial Programs	330	94	330	94	#	#	#	#
Transport and Communications	#	#	#	#	#	#	#	#
Agriculture, Forestry, and Fishery	357	105	61	10	282	93	14	2
Other and Not Specified	738	412	#	#	737	412	1	#

Table 913 (Continued)

HIGHER EDUCATION: GRADUATES, BY LEVEL[1] AND FIELD OF STUDY, 16 LC

Country and Field of Study	All Levels		Level 5		Level 6		Level 7	
	MF	F	MF	F	MF	F	MF	F
E. COLOMBIA (1986)[4]								
Total	56,052	29,779	15,420	9,811	37,729	18,775	2,903	1,193
Education Science and Teacher Training	10,694	7,840	2,337	2,247	7,769	5,221	589	372
Humanities, Religion, and Theology	563	259	65	57	396	151	102	51
Fine and Applied Arts	1,627	1,115	1,281	920	346	195	#	#
Law	7,462	4,337	395	253	6,407	3,773	660	311
Social and Behavioral Science	~	~	~	~	~	~	~	~
Commercial and Business Administration	15,690	8,073	6,109	3,781	8,895	4,084	686	208
Mass Communication and Documentation	~	~	~	~	~	~	~	~
Home Economics (Domestic Science)	~	~	~	~	~	~	~	~
Service Trades	~	~	~	~	~	~	~	~
Natural Science	747	300	267	131	372	146	108	23
Mathematics and Computer Science	~	~	~	~	~	~	~	~
Medical Science and Health-Related	6,837	4,105	678	649	5,567	3,284	592	172
Engineering	11,363	3,489	4,027	1,707	7,192	1,741	144	41
Architecture and Town Planning	~	~	~	~	~	~	~	~
Trade, Craft, and Industrial Programs	~	~	~	~	~	~	~	~
Transport and Communications	~	~	~	~	~	~	~	~
Agriculture, Forestry, and Fishery	1,069	261	261	66	786	180	22	15
Other and Not Specified	~	#	#	#	#	#	#	#
F. COSTA RICA (1985)[5,6]								
Total	4,908	~	711	~	4,012	~	185	~
Education Science and Teacher Training	1,057	~	226	~	823	~	8	~
Humanities, Religion, and Theology	305	~	34	~	265	~	6	~
Fine and Applied Arts	70	~	19	~	51	~	#	#
Law	621	~	#	#	610	~	11	~
Social and Behavioral Science	533	~	165	~	356	~	12	~
Commercial and Business Administration	400	~	49	~	351	~	#	#
Mass Communication and Documentation	154	~	#	#	154	~	#	#
Home Economics (Domestic Science)	#	#	#	#	#	#	#	#
Service Trades	#	#	#	#	#	#	#	#
Natural Science	181	~	34	~	139	~	8	~
Mathematics and Computer Science	139	~	4	~	134	~	1	~
Medical Science and Health-Related	674	~	104	~	450	~	120	~
Engineering	411	~	63	~	348	~	#	#
Architecture and Town Planning	54	~	#	#	54	~	#	#
Trade, Craft, and Industrial Programs	#	#	#	#	#	#	#	#
Transport and Communications	#	#	#	#	#	#	#	#
Agriculture, Forestry, and Fishery	303	~	12	~	272	~	19	~
Other and Not Specified	6	~	1	~	5	~	#	#
G. CUBA (1986)								
Total	27,513	15,551	#	#	27,513	15,551	#	#
Education Science and Teacher Training	11,137	7,457	#	#	11,137	7,457	#	#
Humanities, Religion, and Theology	400	303	#	#	400	303	#	#
Fine and Applied Arts	178	82	#	#	178	82	#	#
Law	357	272	#	#	357	272	#	#
Social and Behavioral Science	1,637	859	#	#	1,637	859	#	#
Commercial and Business Administration	1,106	750	#	#	1,106	750	#	#
Mass Communication and Documentation	228	121	#	#	228	121	#	#
Home Economics (Domestic Science)	#	#	#	#	#	#	#	#
Service Trades	#	#	#	#	#	#	#	#
Natural Science	332	208	#	#	332	208	#	#
Mathematics and Computer Science	224	136	#	#	224	136	#	#
Medical Science and Health-Related	3,536	2,399	#	#	3,536	2,399	#	#
Engineering	3,326	1,190	#	#	3,326	1,190	#	#
Architecture and Town Planning	905	442	#	#	905	442	#	#
Trade, Craft, and Industrial Programs	50	38	#	#	50	38	#	#
Transport and Communications	409	60	#	#	409	60	#	#
Agriculture, Forestry, and Fishery	2,313	931	#	#	2,313	931	#	#
Other and Not Specified	1,375	303	#	#	1,375	303	#	#

Table 913 (Continued)

HIGHER EDUCATION: GRADUATES, BY LEVEL[1] AND FIELD OF STUDY, 16 LC

Country and Field of Study	All Levels		Level 5		Level 6		Level 7	
	MF	F	MF	F	MF	F	MF	F
I. ECUADOR (1981)								
Total	15,441	6,262	~	~	~	~	~	~
Education Science and Teacher Training	6,892	3,603	~	~	~	~	~	~
Humanities, Religion, and Theology	179	92	~	~	~	~	~	~
Fine and Applied Arts	86	43	~	~	~	~	~	~
Law	858	225	~	~	~	~	~	~
Social and Behavioral Science	1,445	603	~	~	~	~	~	~
Commercial and Business Administration	991	350	~	~	~	~	~	~
Mass Communication and Documentation	93	32	~	~	~	~	~	~
Home Economics (Domestic Science)	61	61	~	~	~	~	~	~
Service Trades	#	#	~	~	~	~	~	~
Natural Science	#	#	~	~	~	~	~	~
Mathematics and Computer Science	#	#	~	~	~	~	~	~
Medical Science and Health-Related	2,077	883	~	~	~	~	~	~
Engineering	1,074	100	~	~	~	~	~	~
Architecture and Town Planning	397	71	~	~	~	~	~	~
Trade, Craft, and Industrial Programs	~	~	~	~	~	~	~	~
Transport and Communications	#	#	~	~	~	~	~	~
Agriculture, Forestry, and Fishery	1,252	187	~	~	~	~	~	~
Other and Not Specified	36	12	~	~	~	~	~	~
J. EL SALVADOR (1986)								
Total	5,634	2,921	3,051	1,755	2,583	1,166	#	#
Education Science and Teacher Training	2,448	1,630	1,692	1,193	756	437	#	#
Humanities, Religion, and Theology	33	20	#	#	33	20	#	#
Fine and Applied Arts	5	4	#	#	5	4	#	#
Law	46	14	#	#	46	14	#	#
Social and Behavioral Science	158	78	#	#	156	78	#	#
Commercial and Business Administration	802	327	273	150	429	177	#	#
Mass Communication and Documentation	14	13	#	#	14	13	#	#
Home Economics (Domestic Science)	#	#	#	#	#	#	#	#
Service Trades	20	15	20	15	#	#	#	#
Natural Science	61	41	14	8	47	33	#	#
Mathematics and Computer Science	#	#	#	#	#	#	#	#
Medical Science and Health-Related	449	230	76	76	373	154	#	#
Engineering	822	102	374	28	448	74	#	#
Architecture and Town Planning	186	119	17	3	169	116	#	#
Trade, Craft, and Industrial Programs	54	29	51	27	3	2	#	#
Transport and Communications	#	#	#	#	#	#	#	#
Agriculture, Forestry, and Fishery	322	34	245	13	77	21	#	#
Other and Not Specified	316	263	289	242	27	21	#	#
L. HAITI (1982)								
Total	831	276	~	~	~	~	~	~
Education Science and Teacher Training	68	20	~	~	~	~	~	~
Humanities, Religion, and Theology	~	~	~	~	~	~	~	~
Fine and Applied Arts	#	#	~	~	~	~	~	~
Law	108	25	~	~	~	~	~	~
Social and Behavioral Science	116	34	~	~	~	~	~	~
Commercial and Business Administration	#	#	~	~	~	~	~	~
Mass Communication and Documentation	#	#	~	~	~	~	~	~
Home Economics (Domestic Science)	#	#	~	~	~	~	~	~
Service Trades	#	#	~	~	~	~	~	~
Natural Science	33	10	~	~	~	~	~	~
Mathematics and Computer Science	~	~	~	~	~	~	~	~
Medical Science and Health-Related	264	166	~	~	~	~	~	~
Engineering	200	13	~	~	~	~	~	~
Architecture and Town Planning	#	#	~	~	~	~	~	~
Trade, Craft, and Industrial Programs	#	#	~	~	~	~	~	~
Transport and Communications	#	#	~	~	~	~	~	~
Agriculture, Forestry, and Fishery	42	8	~	~	~	~	~	~
Other and Not Specified	#	#	~	~	~	~	~	~

Table 913 (Continued)

HIGHER EDUCATION: GRADUATES, BY LEVEL[1] AND FIELD OF STUDY, 16 LC

Country and Field of Study	All Levels		Level 5		Level 6		Level 7	
	MF	F	MF	F	MF	F	MF	F
M. HONDURAS (1985)								
Total	1,430	~	~	~	~	~	~	~
Education Science and Teacher Training	36	~	~	~	~	~	~	~
Humanities, Religion, and Theology	27	~	~	~	~	~	~	~
Fine and Applied Arts	1	~	~	~	~	~	~	~
Law	118	~	~	~	~	~	~	~
Social and Behavioral Science	178	~	~	~	~	~	~	~
Commercial and Business Administration	164	~	~	~	~	~	~	~
Mass Communication and Documentation	4	~	~	~	~	~	~	~
Home Economics (Domestic Science)	#	#	~	~	~	~	~	~
Service Trades	#	#	~	~	~	~	~	~
Natural Science	5	~	~	~	~	~	~	~
Mathematics and Computer Science	5	~	~	~	~	~	~	~
Medical Science and Health-Related	357	~	~	~	~	~	~	~
Engineering	241	~	~	~	~	~	~	~
Architecture and Town Planning	26	~	~	~	~	~	~	~
Trade, Craft, and Industrial Programs	#	#	~	~	~	~	~	~
Transport and Communications	#	#	~	~	~	~	~	~
Agriculture, Forestry, and Fishery	168	~	~	~	~	~	~	~
Other and Not Specified	#	#	~	~	~	~	~	~
N. MEXICO (1986)[2]								
Total	120,829	~	#	#	112,810	~	8,019	~
Education Science and Teacher Training	16,059	~	#	#	15,409	~	650	~
Humanities, Religion, and Theology	1,133	~	#	#	1,029	~	104	~
Fine and Applied Arts	163	~	#	#	163	~	#	#
Law	9,657	~	#	#	9,053	~	605	~
Social and Behavioral Science	8,854	~	#	#	8,106	~	748	~
Commercial and Business Administration	24,264	~	#	#	22,465	~	1,799	~
Mass Communication and Documentation	2,402	~	#	#	2,314	~	88	~
Home Economics (Domestic Science)	#	#	#	#	#	~	#	#
Service Trades	#	#	#	#	#	~	#	#
Natural Science	3,102	~	#	#	2,724	~	378	~
Mathematics and Computer Science	1,445	~	#	#	1,151	~	294	~
Medical Science and Health-Related	18,669	~	#	#	16,494	~	2,175	~
Engineering	26,013	~	#	#	25,272	~	741	~
Architecture and Town Planning	4,120	~	#	#	3,995	~	125	~
Trade, Craft, and Industrial Programs	#	#	#	#	#	~	#	#
Transport and Communications	#	#	#	#	#	~	#	#
Agriculture, Forestry, and Fishery	2,875	~	#	#	2,563	~	312	~
Other and Not Specified	2,073	~	#	#	2,073	~	#	#
O. NICARAGUA (1987)								
Total	2,087	~	407	~	1,680	~	#	#
Education Science and Teacher Training	358	~	9	~	349	~	#	#
Humanities, Religion, and Theology	#	#	#	#	#	#	#	#
Fine and Applied Arts	#	#	#	#	#	#	#	#
Law	31	~	#	#	31	~	#	#
Social and Behavioral Science	121	~	#	#	121	~	#	#
Commercial and Business Administration	180	~	58	~	122	~	#	#
Mass Communication and Documentation	41	~	#	#	41	~	#	#
Home Economics (Domestic Science)	31	~	#	#	31	~	#	#
Service Trades	#	#	#	#	#	#	#	#
Natural Science	61	~	#	#	61	~	#	#
Mathematics and Computer Science	52	~	32	~	20	~	#	#
Medical Science and Health-Related	493	~	140	~	353	~	#	#
Engineering	185	~	#	#	185	~	#	#
Architecture and Town Planning	36	~	#	#	36	~	#	#
Trade, Craft, and Industrial Programs	26	~	26	~	#	#	#	#
Transport and Communications	#	#	#	#	#	#	#	#
Agriculture, Forestry, and Fishery	366	~	142	~	224	~	#	#
Other and Not Specified	106	~	#	#	106	~	#	#

Table 913 (Continued)

HIGHER EDUCATION: GRADUATES, BY LEVEL[1] AND FIELD OF STUDY, 16 LC

Country and Field of Study	All Levels		Level 5		Level 6		Level 7	
	MF	F	MF	F	MF	F	MF	F
P. PANAMA (1986)								
Total	3,717	2,354	1,332	924	1,980	1,185	405	245
Education Science and Teacher Training	838	614	315	286	150	113	373	215
Humanities, Religion, and Theology	198	140	2	1	196	139	#	#
Fine and Applied Arts	58	34	23	10	35	24	#	#
Law	130	50	#	#	130	50	#	#
Social and Behavioral Science	217	139	#	#	217	139	#	#
Commercial and Business Administration	829	566	271	235	558	331	#	#
Mass Communication and Documentation	101	56	18	6	83	50	#	#
Home Economics (Domestic Science)	11	11	#	#	11	11	#	#
Service Trades	32	18	32	18	#	#	#	#
Natural Science	76	43	6	5	70	38	#	#
Mathematics and Computer Science	34	19	#	#	34	19	#	#
Medical Science and Health-Related	482	433	235	231	216	172	31	30
Engineering	501	156	388	114	113	42	#	#
Architecture and Town Planning	43	17	10	4	33	13	#	#
Trade, Craft, and Industrial Programs	28	16	20	9	8	7	#	#
Transport and Communications	#	#	#	#	#	#	#	#
Agriculture, Forestry, and Fishery	115	20	12	5	103	15	#	#
Other and Not Specified	24	22	#	#	23	22	1	#
R. PERU (1985)[2]								
Total	9,706	~	~	~	~	~	~	~
Education Science and Teacher Training	1,720	~	~	~	~	~	~	~
Humanities, Religion, and Theology	43	~	~	~	~	~	~	~
Fine and Applied Arts	7	~	~	~	~	~	~	~
Law	684	~	~	~	~	~	~	~
Social and Behavioral Science	867	~	~	~	~	~	~	~
Commercial and Business Administration	1,804	~	~	~	~	~	~	~
Mass Communication and Documentation	69	~	~	~	~	~	~	~
Home Economics (Domestic Science)	120	~	~	~	~	~	~	~
Service Trades	#	#	~	~	~	~	~	~
Natural Science	229	~	~	~	~	~	~	~
Mathematics and Computer Science	56	~	~	~	~	~	~	~
Medical Science and Health-Related	1,611	~	~	~	~	~	~	~
Engineering	1,162	~	~	~	~	~	~	~
Architecture and Town Planning	156	~	~	~	~	~	~	~
Trade, Craft, and Industrial Programs	#	#	~	~	~	~	~	~
Transport and Communications	#	#	~	~	~	~	~	~
Agriculture, Forestry, and Fishery	748	~	~	~	~	~	~	~
Other and Not Specified	530	~	~	~	~	~	~	~
S. URUGUAY (1986)[2]								
Total	3,488	2,121	1,182	932	2,306	1,189	#	#
Education Science and Teacher Training	18	15	#	#	18	15	#	#
Humanities, Religion, and Theology	85	82	72	71	13	11	#	#
Fine and Applied Arts	5	4	#	#	5	4	#	#
Law	856	559	#	#	856	559	#	#
Social and Behavioral Science	242	199	239	197	3	2	#	#
Commercial and Business Administration	418	237	118	95	300	142	#	#
Mass Communication and Documentation	33	32	33	32	#	#	#	#
Home Economics (Domestic Science)	#	#	#	#	#	#	#	#
Service Trades	#	#	#	#	#	#	#	#
Natural Science	23	17	#	#	23	17	#	#
Mathematics and Computer Science	167	72	167	72	#	#	#	#
Medical Science and Health-Related	1,005	711	489	410	516	301	#	#
Engineering	174	27	#	#	174	27	#	#
Architecture and Town Planning	69	20	#	#	69	20	#	#
Trade, Craft, and Industrial Programs	14	0	14	0	#	#	#	#
Transport and Communications	#	#	#	#	#	#	#	#
Agriculture, Forestry, and Fishery	320	89	#	#	320	89	#	#
Other and Not Specified	59	57	59	57	#	#	#	#

Table 913 (Continued)

HIGHER EDUCATION: GRADUATES, BY LEVEL[1] AND FIELD OF STUDY, 16 LC

Country and Field of Study	All Levels		Level 5		Level 6		Level 7	
	MF	F	MF	F	MF	F	MF	F
T. VENEZUELA (1985)[6]								
Total	29,406	#	7,490	#	21,916	#	~	~
Education Science and Teacher Training	6,432	#	521	#	5,911	#	~	~
Humanities, Religion, and Theology	200	#	~	~	200	#	~	~
Fine and Applied Arts	56	#	~	~	56	#	~	~
Law	1,623	#	~	~	1,623	#	~	~
Social and Behavioral Science	3,610	#	1,676	#	1,934	#	~	~
Commercial and Business Administration	4,185	#	2,621	#	1,564	#	~	~
Mass Communication and Documentation	672	#	85	#	587	#	~	~
Home Economics (Domestic Science)	~	~	~	~	~	~	~	~
Service Trades	38	#	27	#	11	#	~	~
Natural Science	592	#	217	#	375	#	~	~
Mathematics and Computer Science	508	#	221	#	287	#	~	~
Medical Science and Health-Related	3,797	#	99	#	3,698	#	~	~
Engineering	5,615	#	1,233	#	4,382	#	~	~
Architecture and Town Planning	788	#	~	~	788	#	~	~
Trade, Craft, and Industrial Programs	~	~	~	~	~	~	~	~
Transport and Communications	14	#	14	#	~	~	~	~
Agriculture, Forestry, and Fishery	1,209	#	776	#	433	#	~	~
Other and Not Specified	67	#	~	~	67	#	~	~
UNITED STATES (1985)								
Total	1,830,284	928,911	456,550	253,250	979,477	496,949	394,257	178,712
Education Science and Teacher Training	179,214	131,217	7,765	5,396	88,161	66,897	83,288	58,924
Humanities, Religion, and Theology	82,010	43,931	1,844	950	56,484	33,524	23,682	9,457
Fine and Applied Arts	61,085	34,223	13,742	5,690	37,936	23,430	9,407	5,103
Law	42,609	17,314	2,060	1,749	1,157	708	39,392	14,857
Social and Behavioral Science	163,366	83,526	3,664	2,208	134,139	69,174	25,563	12,144
Commercial and Business Administration	423,735	207,007	121,991	80,637	233,351	105,319	68,390	21,051
Mass Communication and Documentation	54,473	32,166	4,305	1,778	42,285	25,021	7,883	5,367
Home Economics (Domestic Science)	27,834	23,839	9,620	6,998	15,555	14,539	2,659	2,302
Service Trades	~	~	~	~	~	~	~	~
Natural Science	83,829	31,956	3,462	1,505	62,177	25,018	17,690	5,433
Mathematics and Computer Science	78,633	31,011	13,679	6,551	54,024	21,281	10,930	3,179
Medical Science and Health-Related	182,519	138,337	19,158	60,911	64,513	54,727	48,848	22,699
Engineering	101,301	13,644	~	~	77,154	11,195	24,147	2,449
Architecture and Town Planning	14,179	5,672	1,490	1,216	9,325	3,306	3,364	1,150
Trade, Craft, and Industrial Programs	83,824	7,043	64,233	5,519	18,951	1,457	640	67
Transport and Communications	~	~	~	~	~	~	~	~
Agriculture, Forestry, and Fishery	29,832	8,989	6,584	2,100	18,107	5,630	5,141	1,259
Other and Not Specified	222,341	119,036	132,953	70,042	66,158	35,723	23,230	13,271

1. Level 5: Programs leading to an award not equivalent to a first university degree. Programs of this type are usually vocational.
   Level 6: Programs leading to a first university degree or equivalent qualification. These include bachelor's degrees and doctorates awarded after completion of studies in medicine, engineering, law, etc.
   Level 7: Programs leading to a post-graduate university degree or equivalent qualification.
2. Data refer to universities and equivalent degree-granting institutes only.
3. Data exclude Universidad Católica Boliviana.
4. Law includes Social and Behavioral Science. Commercial and Business Administration includes Mass Communication and Documentation, Home Economics, and Service Trades. Natural Science includes Mathematics and Computer Science. Engineering includes Architecture and Town Planning, Trade, Craft, and Industrial Programs, and Transport and Communications.
5. Data refer to universities only.
6. Programs of level 5 and 6 are combined.

SOURCE: UNESCO-SY, 1986, table 3.13; 1987, table 3.14; 1988, table 3.10.

Table 914

PERCENTAGE OF "LEFTIST" STUDENTS IN SAMPLE[1] BY FATHER'S RELIGION AND UNIVERSITY, 4 L

	Father's Religion		
Country	Practicing Catholic	Non-practicing Catholic	Non-Catholic, Atheist, Agnostic
E. COLOMBIA Los Andes[2]	9	21	13

Continued in SALA, 24-913.

Table 915

ACADEMIC STUDENTS STUDYING IN COMMUNIST COUNTRIES, 10 L

(December 1978)

Country	Total	USSR	Eastern Europe
B. BOLIVIA	170	110	60

Continued in SALA, 24-914.

Table 916

SCHOOL ENROLLMENT, 20 L, 1880–1929

A. ARGENTINA

Year	Total	Primary	Secondary	Higher	Year	Total	Primary	Secondary	Higher
1880	~	~	~	~	1905	~	543,881[†]	~	~
1881	~	~	1,616	~	1906	~	659,460[†]	16,852[†,i]	~
1882	101,027	97,756[a]	2,270	1,001	1907	~	~	~	~
1883	~	107,961	~	~	1908	~	~	~	~
1884	~	~	5,198[†,b]	904[c]	1909	~	668,534	~	10,289

Continued in SALA, 18-1024 through 1043.

Table 917

ADULT EDUCATION: TEACHERS AND STUDENT ENROLLMENT, 20 L

Country	Number of Teachers				Number of Students Enrolled				Ratio of Students to Teachers
	Year	Total	Male	Female	Year	Total	Male	Female	
A. ARGENTINA[1]	1973[‡]	19,204	~	~	1973[‡]	518,752	~	~	27.0

Continued in SALA, 18-1022.

Table 918

SPECIAL EDUCATION: ESTABLISHMENTS, TEACHERS, AND STUDENT ENROLLMENT, 20 L

Country	Year	Type of Establishment (N)					Teachers	Students Enrolled		
		Total	Blind	Deaf and Dumb	Mentally Retarded	Others		Total	Male	Female
A. ARGENTINA	1971	316	17	16	283	- -	5,675	22,668	14,043	8,625

Continued in SALA, 18-1023.

Table 919

UNIVERSITY LIBRARY COLLECTIONS, BORROWERS, WORKS LOANED, CURRENT EXPENDITURE, AND PERSONNEL, 13 LC

Country	Year	Number of Administrative Units	Number of Service Units	Meters of Shelving	Number of Volumes (T)	Annual Additions (Volumes)	Number of Registered Borrowers	Works Loaned (Volumes)	Amount (T)	Staff (%)	Total	Holding a Diploma	Trained on the Job
					Collections				Current Expenditures		Library Employees		
A. ARGENTINA	1977	1,528	1,528	317,723	9,532	~	4,201,244	9,552,904	~	~	~	~	~
B. BOLIVIA	1980	~	99	33,622	125	599	1,119,618	~	9,664	~	110	~	54
C. BRAZIL	1982	3,600	~	~	18,106	~	2,919,155	7,728,684	~	~	10,533	~	~

Continued in SALA, 26-919

Table 920

LIBRARIES BY CATEGORY, 17 LC

Country	Year	Category of Libraries	Number of Libraries	Collections		Annual Additions (Volumes)	Number of Registered Borrowers
				Number of Volumes (T)	Meters of Shelving		
A. ARGENTINA	1984	Special	63	1,645	~	~	654,288
B. BOLIVIA	1980	National	2	135	1,200	600	~
	1980	Public	~	125	~	599	119,618
	1983	Higher Education	17	220	~	3,000	~
	1982	Non-Specialized	13	220	6,220	1,890	~
C. BRAZIL[1]	1984	National	1	1,993	~	~	94,690
	1982	Public	3,600	18,106	~	~	2,919,155
	1984	Higher Education	981	8,570	~	~	1,425,220
	1984	School	14,334	20,762	~	~	~
	1982	Special	1,494	12,854	~	~	424,425
	1982	Non-Specialized	763	2,175	~	~	276,169
D. CHILE	1984	National	1	2,766	~	8,380	1,694
	1983	Public	179	783	~	~	18,345
	1981	School	~	551	1,458	~	~
	1985	Special	4	86	2,510	1,813	**
E. COLOMBIA[2]	1980	National	1	540	18,000	26,027	~
	1985	Public	974	2,381	~	~	~
	1985	Higher Education	225	1,143	~	69,472	~
F. COSTA RICA[3]	1983	National	1	1,000	~	40,828	~
	1983	Higher Education	1	227	6,826	10,687	17,000
G. CUBA	1984	National	1	1,396	~	~	~
	1984	Public	295	3,711	~	~	~
	1984	Higher Education	70	2,484	~	153,530	56,706
	1984	School	3,261	13,855	~	517,393	1,255,778
	1985	Special	6	225	~	~	**
H. DOMINICAN REP.	1980	Public	68	~	~	~	532,852
I. ECUADOR	1983	Special	1	2	60	330	230
J. EL SALVADOR	1980	National	1	80	2,442	1,000	22,780
K. GUATEMALA	1983	National	~	1,824	~	30,377	~
	1981	Higher Education	1	120	818	~	45,000
	1986	Special	16	500	~	1,416	**
M. HONDURAS	1984	Higher Education	7	145	~	5,814	12,957
	1985	Special	1	1	~	600	**
N. MEXICO	1983	National	2	1,548	~	~	~
	1983	Public	557	3,720	~	~	~
	1981	Higher Education	329	3,243	~	~	~
	1981	School	1,880	5,403	~	~	~
	1983	Special	171	2,300	~	~	~
P. PANAMA	1980	National	~	221	6,784	13,572	49,794
	1980	Public	18	26	~	450	~
	1985	Special	1	57	~	1,500	**
R. PERU	1983	National	1	2,690	19,507	69,155	39,672
	1980	Public	520	4,102	~	~	~
	1984	Higher Education	2	295	9,957	4,000	10,200
	1981	School	292	516	~	102,500	447,000
S. URUGUAY	1983	National	1	879	25,356	19,109	~
	1984	Higher Education	2	152	3,080	838	20,434
	1985	Special	15	863	18,398	~	**
	1984	Non-Specialized	1	115	2,700	~	~
T. VENEZUELA[4]	1980	National	1	765	3,830	7,077	~
	1980	Public	23	977	31,315	87,120	66,250
	1984	School	155	254	~	566,472	~
UNITED STATES	1978	National	3	20,799	~	359,656	~
	1978	Public	8,456	439,486	5,679,317	26,007,296	~
	1979	Higher Education	3,122	519,895	~	21,608,010	~
	1978	School	85,096	591,261	24,646,328	32,717,838	~
	1978	Non-Specialized	1,877	36,348	~	1,591,752	~

1. Data on libraries of institutions of higher education refer only to libraries which are not part of a university and data on number of volumes refer to university libraries only.
2. Data on libraries of institutions of higher education refer to 109 central or main libraries.
3. Data on libraries of institutions of higher education refer to the University of 'Maria Aurora Zamora Gonzalez' only.
4. Data on school libraries refer to 155 of the total of 332 libraries.

SOURCE: UNESCO-SY, 1986, 1987, 1988, table 7.1.

Table 921

SCHOOL AND FINANCIAL YEARS, 20 LC

	Country	School Year Beginning	School Year End	Financial Year Beginning
A.	ARGENTINA	March	November	January
B.	BOLIVIA	February	October	January
C.	BRAZIL	February	December	January
D.	CHILE	March	December	January
E.	COLOMBIA	February	November	January
F.	COSTA RICA	March	November	January
G.	CUBA	September	June	January
H.	DOMINICAN REP.	September	June	January
I.	ECUADOR	October	July	January
J.	EL SALVADOR	January	November	January
K.	GUATEMALA	January	October	January
L.	HAITI	October	June	October
M.	HONDURAS	February	November	January
N.	MEXICO	September	June	January
O.	NICARAGUA	March	November	January
P.	PANAMA	April	December	January
Q.	PARAGUAY	February	November	January
R.	PERU	April	December	January
S.	URUGUAY	March	December	January
T.	VENEZUELA	October	July	January
	UNITED STATES	September	May	October

SOURCE: UNESCO-SY, 1986 and 1988, Appendix B.

Table 922

TOTAL PUBLIC EDUCATIONAL EXPENDITURE, 20 LC
(Current and Capital Funds)

	Country	Year	Total Educational Expenditure Amount (T NC)	As % of Gross National Product	As % of Total Government Expenditure	Current Educational Expenditure Amount (T NC)	As % of Total	As % of Gross National Product	As % of Total Government Expenditure	Capital Expenditure (T NC)
A.	ARGENTINA	1986	1,286,675	1.8	7.5	1,127,774	87.7	1.6	7.5	158,901
B.	BOLIVIA[1]	1984	79,678,156	.5	~	79,398,676	99.6	.5	~	288,480
C.	BRAZIL[2]	1985	44,519,421,000	3.3	17.2	~	~	~	~	~
D.	CHILE	1985	101,492,580	4.5	15.3	101,092,833	99.6	4.5	17.3	399,747
E.	COLOMBIA[3]	1986	178,919,000	2.9	24.7	167,154,000	93.4	2.8	33.2	11,765,000
F.	COSTA RICA	1986	10,992,893	5.2	20.4	10,052,674	91.4	4.8	25.7	940,219
G.	CUBA[4]	1985	1,690,400	6.3	~	1,587,800	93.9	5.9	~	102,600
H.	DOMINICAN REP[5]	1986	227,701	1.6	10.0	219,417	~	~	~	4,535
I.	ECUADOR	1986	45,253,822	3.4	~	41,054,062	90.7	3.1	~	4,199,760
J.	EL SALVADOR	1984	335,535	3.0	~	292,928	87.3	2.6	~	42,607
K.	GUATEMALA	1984	163,367	1.8	12.4	159,778	97.8	1.7	23.1	3,589
L.	HAITI	1985	117,557	1.2	16.5	117,314	99.8	1.2	16.7	243
M.	HONDURAS	1986	340,672	5.0	16.4	332,927	97.7	4.9	~	7,745
N.	MEXICO[6]	1986	1,551,300,000	2.1	~	1,438,152,000	92.7	1.9	~	113,148,000
O.	NICARAGUA[3,4]	1986	26,557,400	6.6	12.6	26,368,700	99.3	6.5	15.5	188,700
P.	PANAMA	1986	238,788	5.0	14.3	233,170	97.6	4.8	15.4	5,618
Q.	PARAGUAY[5]	1985	20,662,000	1.5	16.7	16,822,000	81.4	1.2	18.8	3,840,000
R.	PERU[3]	1986	5,870,500	1.7	15.7	~	~	~	~	~
S.	URUGUAY	1986	28,135,168	3.1	14.5	26,615,304	94.6	2.9	14.9	1,519,864
T.	VENEZUELA	1985	24,113,381	6.8	21.3	~	~	~	~	~
	UNITED STATES	1983	226,500,000	6.7	~	~	~	~	~	~

1. Expenditure on universities is not included.
2. Expenditures of municipalities are not included.
3. Data refer to expenditure of the Ministry of Education only.
4. Expenditure on education is calculated as percentage of global social product.
5. Data on current and capital expenditure refer to the Ministry of Education only.
6. Data on current, capital, and total expenditures refer to the Ministry of Education only. Percentages shown have therefore been calculated using expenditure of the central government only.

SOURCE: UNESCO-SY, 1984, 1985, 1987, 1988, table 4.1.

Table 923

PUBLIC CURRENT EDUCATIONAL EXPENDITURE, BY LEVEL, 20 LC

	Country	Year	Total Expenditure (T NC)	Total = 100%					
				Pre-school	First Level	Second Level	Third Level	Other Types of Education	Expenditure Not Allocated by Level
A.	ARGENTINA	1984	180,530	..[a]	37.7	27.4	19.2	.7	15.0
B.	BOLIVIA[1]	1982	10,211,808	..[a]	71.9	13.0	3.2	3.3	8.5
C.	BRAZIL[2,3]	1985	44,519,421,000	..[a]	45.9	7.7	19.6	.9	25.9
D.	CHILE	1985	101,092,833	6.0	51.0	19.5	20.3	#	3.2
E.	COLOMBIA[2,4]	1985	136,570,000	..[a]	39.2	30.8	22.2	3.4	4.3
F.	COSTA RICA	1986	10,052,674	..[a]	37.8	21.6	39.7	.9	#
G.	CUBA	1985	1,587,800	5.6	20.7	42.0	12.9	10.2	8.7
H.	DOMINICAN REP.[2]	1986	223,952	.7	44.4	18.4	19.7	7.1	9.7
I.	ECUADOR	1986	41,054,062	5.9	42.6	33.6	15.2	2.6	0
J.	EL SALVADOR	1981	321,814	#	60.3	6.0	15.7	1.9	16.2
K.	GUATEMALA	1976	67,193	2.5	51.3	15.5	19.9	3.3	7.5
L.	HAITI	1985	117,314	#	51.0	18.1	10.8	7.7	12.4
M.	HONDURAS	1986	332,927	..[a]	48.5	17.1	20.7	.6	13.1
N.	MEXICO[4]	1986	1,438,152,000	4.9	27.4	16.2	31.8	4.7	15.0
O.	NICARAGUA[4]	1986	26,368,700	2.8	37.8	18.3	21.2	7.4	12.5
P.	PANAMA	1986	233,170	#	40.7	25.3	21.6	4.9	7.5
Q.	PARAGUAY	1985	16,822,000	#	36.6	29.7	23.8	2.8	7.1
R.	PERU	1985	4,854,900	4.0	35.6	20.5	2.7	5.0	32.2
S.	URUGUAY	1986	26,615,304	..[a]	36.5	27.8	24.2	1.9	9.5
T.	VENEZUELA[5]	1984	16,750,700	3.7	24.5	6.5	43.4	3.2	18.8
	UNITED STATES	1982	215,400,000	..[a]	61.7	..[a]	38.3	#	#

1. Expenditure on universities not included.
2. Data include capital expenditure.
3. Expenditure of the municipalities is not included.
4. Expenditure of the Ministry of Education only.
5. Expenditure of Central Government only.

a. Included in First Level.

SOURCE: UNESCO-SY, 1984, 1986, 1987, 1988, table 4.3.

Table 924

SCIENTISTS AND ENGINEERS ENGAGED IN RESEARCH AND DEVELOPMENT (R AND D), BY FIELD OF SCIENCE, 15 L

| | | | | | Scientists and Engineers | | | | | |
| | | | | | Field of Science | | | | | |
Country	Year	Sex	Code[1]	Total	Natural Sciences	Engineering and Technology	Medical Sciences	Agriculture	Social Sciences and Humanities	Other
A. ARGENTINA	1982	MF	FT	10,486	4,024	1,971	856	1,835	1,076	724
		F	FPT	6,705	3,107	452	797	645	1,275	429
C. BRAZIL[2]	1977	MF	FTE	13,678	4,363	2,581	1,817	2,693	2,224	#
D. CHILE	1984	MF	FT	466	123	218	31	66	24	4
		MF	PT	3,844	988	838	1,061	155	758	44
		MF	FTE	1,587	485	474	284	110	220	14
E. COLOMBIA[3]	1982	MF	FT	831	288	49	21	334	139	#
		MF	PT	3,939	1,238	544	1,088	358	710	#
		MF	FTE	1,083	341	150	299	98	195	#
G. CUBA	1985	MF	FT	8,919	774	2,191	1,417	2,230	1,744	563
		MF	PT	6,889	29	1,131	1,205	720	419	3,385
		MF	FTE	10,305	789	2,407	1,601	2,395	1,849	1,264
I. ECUADOR[4]	1976	MF	FT	378	88	33	#	242	15	#
		MF	PT	239	26	26	#	180	7	#
		MF	FTE	469	100	45	#	304	20	#
J. EL SALVADOR[5]	1974	MF	FT	674	190	71	153	78	182	#
		MF	PT	255	#	98	60	14	83	#
		MF	FTE	802	190	120	183	85	224	#
K. GUATEMALA	1974	MF	FT	250	34	79	16	49	72	#
		MF	PT	134	18	42	9	27	38	#
		MF	FTE	310	43	98	20	61	88	#
M. HONDURAS[6]	1974	MF	FT	5	#	5	#	#	#	#
N. MEXICO	1984	MF	FTE	16,679	3,786	2,690	3,866	2,385	3,952	#
		F	FTE	4,319	980	697	1,001	618	1,023	#
O. NICARAGUA	1986	MF	FPT	502	144	60	26	163	109	#
P. PANAMA[7]	1975	MF	FT	193	39	41	31	33	28	21
		MF	PT	34	1	2	21	#	#	10
		MF	FTE	204	39	41	40	33	28	23
		F	FTE	67	19	9	23	3	8	5
R. PERU[8,9]	1970	MF	FT	1,522	445	76	267	494	151	#
		MF	PT	318	100	13	125	24	54	#
		MF	FTE	1,686	496	83	330	507	180	#
S. URUGUAY[8,10]	1971	MF	FPT‡	1,537‡	184‡	356‡	359‡	253‡	160‡	#
		MF	FTE‡	1,150‡	142‡	285‡	239‡	253‡	109‡	#
T. VENEZUELA	1983	MF	FPT	4,568	1,457	727	558	874	802	150
		MF	FTE	2,175	786	300	204	437	388	60
		F	FPT	1,478	438	134	302	171	375	59

1. FT = Full-Time; PT = Part-time; FPT = Full-time plus part-time; FTE = Full-time equivalent.
2. Data refer to post-graduate fundamental research and post-graduate teaching in the higher education sector only.
3. Not including data for the productive sector (non-integrated R&D).
4. Data refer to research and development in the agricultural sciences only.
5. Data refer to 28 institutions out of a total of 41 which perform research and development.
6. Data relate to one research institute only.
7. Data also include scientific and technological services (SIS).
8. Total data include scientists and engineers for whom a distribution by field of science is unknown.
9. Excludes humanities and education.
10. Data refer to the year 1971–72.

SOURCE: UNESCO-SY, 1977, table 7.3; 1978, table 7.3; 1980, table 5.3; 1984, table 5.3; 1986, table 5.5; 1987, table 5.6; 1988, table 5.5.

Table 925

RESEARCH AND DEVELOPMENT (R AND D) PERSONNEL, BY SECTOR OF PERFORMANCE, 15 LC

	Country	Year	Type of Personnel[1]	(A) All Sectors	(B) Integrated R&D	(C) Non-integrated R&D	(D) Higher Education	(E) General Service
A.	ARGENTINA	1982	% by Sector	100	4.5	23.5	33.3	38.6
			Scientists & Engineers	10,486	476	2,466	3,497	4,047
C.	BRAZIL	1978	Total in R&D	~	43,056	⟶	~	~
			Scientists & Engineers	~	8,497	⟶	15,518	~
			Technicians	~	5,392	⟶	~	~
			Auxiliary	~	29,167	⟶	~	~
D.	CHILE[1]	1984	% by Sector	100	1.5	30.2	65.8	2.5
			Total in R&D	1,691	26	510	1,112	43
			Scientists & Engineers	1,587	23	432	1,094	38
			Technicians	104	3	78	18	5
E.	COLOMBIA[2]	1982	Total in R&D	3,709	91	~	1,474	2,144
			% by Sector	100	2.5	~	39.7	57.8
			Scientists & Engineers	1,083	33	~	687	363
			Technicians	1,024	34	~	388	602
			Auxiliary	1,602	24	~	399	1,179
G.	CUBA[3]	1986	Total in R&D	32,192	1,204	16,945	3,292	10,751
			% by Sector	100	3.7	52.6	10.2	33.4
			Scientists & Engineers	10,068	557	4,071	1,929	3,511
			Technicians	8,687	342	4,649	527	3,169
			Auxiliary	13,437	305	8,225	836	4,071
I.	ECUADOR[4,5]	1979	Total in R&D	5,297	270	⟶	1,202	3,825
			% by Sector	100	5.1	⟶	22.7	72.2
			Scientists & Engineers	2,049	52	⟶	599	1,398
			Technicians	1,252	44	⟶	283	925
			Auxiliary	1,996	174	⟶	320	1,502
J.	EL SALVADOR	1981	Total in R&D	2,535	1,656	~	454	425
			% by Sector	100	65.3	~	17.9	16.8
			Scientists & Engineers	564	42.1	~	115	28
			Technicians	1,971	1,235	~	339	397
K.	GUATEMALA[1]	1974	Total in R&D	749	#	290	113	346
			% by Sector	* *	#	38.7	15.1	46.2
			Scientists & Engineers	310	#	166	43	101
			Technicians	439	#	124	70	245
M.	HONDURAS[6]	1974	Total in R&D	7	#	#	#	7
			% by Sector	* *	#	#	#	100
			Scientists & Engineers	5	#	#	#	5
			Technicians	1	#	#	#	1
			Auxiliary	1	#	#	#	1
N.	MEXICO	1984	Total in R&D	68,972	24,283	⟶	26,628	18,061
			% by Sector	100	35.2	⟶	38.6	26.2
			Scientists & Engineers	16,679	5,268	⟶	7,979	3,432
			Technicians	29,467	12,535	⟶	11,151	5,781
			Auxiliary	22,826	6,480	⟶	7,498	8,848
P.	PANAMA[4]	1975	Total in R&D	982	#	600	249	133
			% by Sector	100	#	61.1	25.4	13.5
			Scientists & Engineers	204	#	116	62	26
			Technicians	301	#	194	80	27
			Auxiliary	477	#	290	107	80
Q.	PARAGUAY	1971	% by Sector	* *	28.4	⟶	36.6	35.1
			Scientists & Engineers	134	38	⟶	49	47
R.	PERU[1]	1981	Total in R&D	18,596	1,811	⟶	5,767	11,018
			% by Sector	100	9.7	⟶	31.0	59.2
			Scientists & Engineers	7,464	896	⟶	3,600	2,968
			Technicians	5,064	373	⟶	1,153	3,538
			Auxiliary	~	~	~	~	~
S.	URUGUAY[7]	1971	Total in R&D	3,033‡	385‡	758‡	1,068‡	822‡
			% by Sector	* *	12.7‡	25.0‡	35.2‡	27.1‡
			Scientists & Engineers	1,150‡	114‡	280‡	537‡	219‡
			Technicians	1,087‡	138‡	241‡	336‡	372‡
			Auxiliary	796‡	133‡	237‡	195‡	231‡

Table 925 (Continued)

RESEARCH AND DEVELOPMENT (R AND D) PERSONNEL, BY SECTOR OF PERFORMANCE, 15 LC

Country	Year	Type of Personnel[1]	(A) All Sectors	(B) Integrated R&D	(C) Non-integrated R&D	(D) Higher Education	(E) General Service
T. VENEZUELA[3,5]	1983	Total in R&D	10,687	903	337	5,913	3,534
		% by Sector	100	8.4	3.2	55.3	33.1
		Scientists & Engineers	4,568	347	117	2,921	1,183
		Technicians	2,692	97	126	1,297	1,172
		Auxiliary	3,427	459	94	1,695	1,179
UNITED STATES	1986	% by Sector	100	73.7	⟶	14.4	11.9
		Scientists & Engineers	787,400	580,300	⟶	113,300	93,800

1. Excludes auxiliary personnel.
2. Not including data for the productive sector (non-integrated R&D).
3. Not including military and defense R&D.
4. Data also include scientific and technological services (STS).
5. Data refer to the number of full-time plus part-time scientists and engineers and technicians.
6. Data relate to one research institute only.
7. Data refer to full-time scientists and engineers and technicians engaged in scientific and technological activities (STA).
8. Data refer to 1971–72.

SOURCE: UNESCO-SY, 1984, table 5.4; 1986, table 5.6; 1987, table 5.; 1988, table 5.6.

Table 926

INDICATORS OF SCIENTIFIC AND TECHNOLOGICAL DEVELOPMENT, 17 LC

	Country	Year	Qualified Manpower — Scientists and Engineers (PMI)	Qualified Manpower — Technicians (PMI)	Personnel Engaged in R&D — Scientists and Engineers (FTE)[1] (PMI)	Personnel Engaged in R&D — Technicians (PMI)	Number of Technicians per Scientists and Engineers	Expenditure for R&D — % of GNP	Expenditure for R&D — Per Capita (NC)	Expenditure for R&D — Annual Average per R&D Scientists and Engineers (NC)
A.	ARGENTINA[2,3]	1982	18,970	60,077	360	~	~	.4	80,959.4	221,431,600
B.	BOLIVIA	1976	11,563	~	~	~	~	~	~	~
C.	BRAZIL[3]	1982	11,231	25,348	256	~	~	~	2,407.1‡	9,397,700‡
D.	CHILE	1985	~	~	442	⟶	··	.4	419.3	~
E.	COLOMBIA	1982	~	~	40	38	.9	.1	102.1	2,543,200
F.	COSTA RICA	1982	~	~	171	~	~	.1	33.8	197,900
G.	CUBA[4]	1986	14,172	~	991	855	.9	.8	20.2	20,300
I.	ECUADOR	1979	~	~	259	158	.6	.4	108.3	417,800
J.	EL SALVADOR	1986	~	~	807	⟶	~	1.7	58.5	~
K.	GUATEMALA[5]	1984	~	~	348	⟶	~	.5	5.9	~
M.	HONDURAS	1974	22.5ᵃ	10.6ᵃ	.02ᵃ	~	.2	~	~	~
N.	MEXICO[6]	1984	~	~	216	382	1.8	.6	2,066.7	9,522,800
O.	NICARAGUA	1985	~	~	199	65	.3	.3	90.1	453,600
P.	PANAMA[7,8]	1976	3,150	8,058	121	179	1.5	.2	1.9	16,200
Q.	PARAGUAY	1981	~	~	247	⟶	~	.2	70.7	1,248,200
R.	PERU[9]	1981	16,426	78,691	273	~	~	.3	8,282.2	~
S.	URUGUAY[10]	1975	19,939‡	~	~	~	~	.2	.6	1,620‡
T.	VENEZUELA[9,11]	1983	21,818	96,454	279	165	.6	.4	80.9	298,100‡
	UNITED STATES[11]	1986	14,777	~	3,282	~	~	2.8	494.3	150,600

1. Code: FTE = Full-time equivalent.
2. Data for Expenditure for R & D refer to 1981.
3. Data for Qualified Manpower refer to 1980.
4. Data for Qualified Manpower refer to 1981.
5. Data for Expenditure for R & D refer to 1983.
6. Data for Qualified Manpower refer to 1969. Expenditure for R & D refer to 1973.
7. Data for Personnel Engaged in R & D refer to 1975.
8. Data for Expenditure for R & D refer to 1975.
9. Data for Expenditure for R & D refer to 1984.
10. Data for Expenditure for R & D refer to 1972.
11. Data for Qualified Manpower refer to 1982.

a. Data expressed in P10TI.

SOURCE: UNEXCO-SY, 1984, table 5.14 and table 5.15; 1986, table 5.18 and 5.19; 1987, tables 5.19, 5.20; 1988, tables 5.18 and 5.19.

Table 927

CUBA SECONDARY, TECHNICAL, AND UNIVERSITY ENROLLMENT, 1970–85

School Year	Secondary Technical Schools			Universities		
	Total	Machinery Construction	Electronics, Automation, and Communications	Total	Machinery Construction	Electronics, Automation, and Communications
1970/71	27,566	~	~	35,137	~	~
1971/72	30,429	~	~	36,877	~	~
1972/73	41,940	~	~	48,735	~	~
1973/74	56,959	~	~	55,635	~	~
1974/75	94,634	~	~	68,451	~	~
1975/76	114,653	~	~	84,750	~	~
1976/77	159,440	7,207	3,059	107,091	2,945	2,710
1977/78	194,034	27,243	5,757	122,597	3,376	3,000
1978/79	198,261	25,259	5,464	133,014	3,643	3,164
1979/80	214,615	27,099	4,577	146,240	4,469	3,331
1980/81	228,487	25,466	4,986	151,733	4,821	3,293
1981/82	263,981	29,964	6,131	165,496	4,817	3,372
1982/83	285,765	32,177	6,057	173,403	5,188	3,396
1983/84	312,867	36,106	7,718	192,958	5,588	3,837
1984/85	305,556	34,116	9,330	212,155	6,147	4,186

SOURCE: Claes Brundenius, "Development and Prospects of Capital Goods Production in Revolutionary Cuba," in Andrew Zimbalist, ed., *Cuba's Socialist Economy Toward the 1990's* (Lynne Rienner Publishers: Boulder & London, 1987).

Part IV
Church, State, and Crime

10
Political Statistics

Table 1000

POLITICAL DEPENDENCE, INDEPENDENCE, AND INTERNATIONAL MEMBERSHIPS OF COUNTRIES AND TERRITORIES, 20 L AND 45 ELA

(1983)

PART I. TRADITIONALLY DEFINED LATIN AMERICA

Independent Countries[1]	As Result of			Memberships						
	War[2]		Special Circumstances	OAS	IDB:L	ECLA:L	ALADI	AG	CACM	CBI-IB
	Declared	Won								
A. ARGENTINA	1810	1816[a]		A	A	A	A			
B. BOLIVIA	1809	1825[a]		B	B	B	B	B		
C. BRAZIL			1822[b]	C	C	C	C			
D. CHILE	1810	1818[a]		D	D	D	D	D[5]		
E. COLOMBIA	1810	1824[a]	1830[e]	E	E	E	E	E		
F. COSTA RICA		1821[c]	1838[d]	F	F	F			F	F
G. CUBA		1898[a]	1902[i]	G[4]		G				
H. DOMINICAN REP.[3]		1821[a]	1844[h]	H	H	H				H
I. ECUADOR[7]	1809	1822[a]	1830[e]	I	I	I	I	I		
J. EL SALVADOR		1821[c]	1841[d]	J	J	J			J	J
K. GUATEMALA		1821[c]	1839[d]	K	K	K			K	K
L. HAITI	1791	1804[k]		L	L	L				L
M. HONDURAS		1821[c]	1838[d]	M	M	M			M[6]	M
N. MEXICO	1810	1821[a]		N	N	N	N			
O. NICARAGUA		1821[c]	1838[d]	O	O	O			O	O
P. PANAMA			1903[j]	P	P	P				P
Q. PARAGUAY			1811[a]	Q	Q	Q	Q			
R. PERU	1821	1824[a,f]		R	R	R	R	I		
S. URUGUAY	1811	1814[a]	1828[l]	S	S	S	S			
T. VENEZUELA[7]	1810	1821[a,g]	1829[e]	T	T	T	T	T		

1. The three events that provided the immediate stimulation for independence were the U.S. War for Independence (1776-81); the French Revolution of 1789 proclaiming the Rights of Man and abolishing slavery for France but not its colonies—the most prosperous of which was Saint Domingue (the future Haiti); and the capture of the Spanish monarch by Napoleon Bonaparte, Spain's "ally," who placed his brother Joseph on the throne of Spain in 1808, thus breaking strong allegiances between Spain and its colonies. (The latter event occurred after France had passed through Spain, driving the monarchy of Portugal to Brazil in 1807, laying the basis for Brazil's independence once the monarchy returned to Portugal in 1821.)
2. Excludes precursor movements such as that by Tiradentes in 1788 (Brazil) or by Miranda in 1806 (Venezuela).
3. France ceded to Spain in 1795.
4. Since 1962 Cuba has been suspended from OAS activities but not membership.
5. Chile withdrew from AG in 1976.
6. Honduras partially withdrew from CACM in 1971.
7. Member of OPEC.

a. Won from Spain.
b. Won from Portugal.
c. Won from Spain and became part of Mexico in 1822-23.
d. Breakup of United Provinces of Central America, which existed to unite Costa Rica, El Salvador, Guatemala, Honduras, and Nicaragua from 1823 to 1841. For all practical purposes the breakup came by 1838 and attempts to revive union were militarily defeated by 1842.
e. Breakup of Gran Colombia, which existed to unite Colombia, Ecuador, and Venezuela from 1819 to 1830.
f. Last Spanish troops left Peru in 1826.
g. Last Spanish troops left Venezuela in 1823.
h. Won from Haiti, which governed Hispaniola or Santo Domingo (future Dominican Republic) from 1822 to 1844. Spain reoccupied from 1861 to 1865.
i. Won from the United States.
j. Won from Colombia.
k. Won from France.
l. Won from Brazil.

SOURCE: SALA, 23-1.

Table 1000 (Continued)

POLITICAL DEPENDENCE, INDEPENDENCE, AND INTERNATIONAL MEMBERSHIPS OF COUNTRIES AND TERRITORIES, 20 L AND 45 ELA

(1983)

PART II. NON-TRADITIONALLY DEFINED LATIN AMERICA ADDS:

Independent Countries	Year of Independence	From	Organization by Country							
			OAS	IDB:L	ECLA:L	CARICOM[1]	ECCM	OECS	CIB-IB	FAO[4]
1. Antigua-Barbuda	1981	Gr. Britain	1			1	1	1	1	1
2. Bahamas	1973	Gr. Britain	2	2	2				2	2
3. Barbados	1966	Gr. Britain	3	3	3	3			3	3
4. Belize	1981	Gr. Britain				4			4	4
5. Dominica	1978	Gr. Britain	5			5	5	5	5	5
6. Grenada	1974	Gr. Britain	6		6	6	6	6	6	6
7. Guyana	1966	Gr. Britain		7	7	7			7	7
8. Jamaica	1962	Gr. Britain	8	8	8	8			8	8
9. St. Kitts-Nevis[2]	1983	Gr. Britain	9			9	9	9	9	9
10. St. Lucia	1977	Gr. Britain	10			10	10	10	10	10
11. St. Vincent-Grenadines	1979	Gr. Britain	11			11	11	11	11	11
12. Suriname	1975	Netherlands	12	12	12				12	12
13. Trinidad and Tobago	1962	Gr. Britain	13	13	13	13				

Dependent Countries	Belonging to	OAS	IDB:L	ICLA:L	CARICOM[1]	ECCM	OECS	CIB-IB	FAO
T1. Anguilla	Great Britain					T1			T1
T2. Bermuda	Great Britain[3]								
T3. British Virgin Islands	Great Britain							T3	T3
T4. Cayman Islands	Great Britain							T4	T4
T5. French Guiana	France								T5
T6. Guadeloupe	France								T6
T7. Martinique	France								T7
T8. Montserrat	Great Britain				T8	T8	T8	T8	T8
T9. Netherlands Antilles	Netherlands							T9	T9
T10. Puerto Rico	United States								T10
T11. Turks and Caicos	Great Britain							T11	T11
T12. U.S. Virgin Islands	United States								T12

1. The Caribbean Community and Common Market (CARICOM) was established in 1973 to replace the Caribbean Free Trade Association (CARIFTA), founded in 1967.
2. St. Kitts is officially known as St. Christopher.
3. Bermuda has been self-governing since 1968. Although under Great Britain, it claims Bermudian nationality.
4. Includes Falkland Islands.

SOURCE: SALA, 23-1; and WA, 1987, p. 640.

Table 1001

POLITICAL STATUS, 9 LC, 1964–84

Country Ruled by Military	Years	Country in Which Electoral Process Remained Intact	Country with "Rigged" Elections
A. ARGENTINA	1966–1973 1976–1983	E. COLOMBIA F. COSTA RICA	K. GUATEMALA[2] L. HAITI[2]

Continued in SALA, 27-1001.

Table 1002

LOS ANGELES TIMES VIEW OF EMERGING DEMOCRACY IN LATIN AMERICA, 20 L
(1986)

Country	Type of Rule	Year of Newly Established Democracy[2]	Year of Previous Military Rule
A. ARGENTINA	Democratic	1983	7
B. BOLIVIA	Democratic	1982	18

Continued in SALA, 27-1002.

Table 1003

STATUS OF PRESIDENTIAL TERMS, 20 L
(As of September 1, 1989)

Country	Most Recent Military Seizure of Power	Most Recent Military Relinquishes Presidency	Most Recent Civilian President Takes Office	President Taking Office	Next Civilian Presidency Scheduled to Begin
A. ARGENTINA	1976	1983	1989	Carlos Menem	1995
B. BOLIVIA	1980	1982	1989	Jaime Paz Zamora	1993
C. BRAZIL	1964	1985	1985	José Sarney	1989
D. CHILE	1973		1970	Augusto Pinochet	1990
E. COLOMBIA	1953	1958	1986	Virgilio Barco	1990
F. COSTA RICA	1944[a]	1948	1986	Oscar Arias Sánchez	1990
G. CUBA	1959				
H. DOMINICAN REP.	1965	1965	1986	Joaquín Balaguer	1990
I. ECUADOR	1968	1979	1988		
J. EL SALVADOR	1977	1980	1989	Alfredo Christiani	1992
K. GUATEMALA	1970	1986	1986	Vinicio Cerezo	1994
L. HAITI	1988		1988		1990
M. HONDURAS	1972	1982	1986	José Azcuna Hoya	1990
N. MEXICO	1919	1920	1988	Carlos Salinas de Gortari	1994
O. NICARAGUA	1936		1984	Daniel Ortega	1990
P. PANAMA	1968[b]		1984[b]	Andrés Rodríguez	1994
Q. PARAGUAY	1954[c]		1989		
R. PERU	1963	1980	1985	Alan García	1990
S. URUGUAY	1976[d]	1985	1985	José Maria Sanguinetti	1990
T. VENEZUELA	1948	1959	1989	Carlos Andrés Pérez	1994

a. President Teodoro Picado (1944–48) shared power with Manuel Mora (founder and leader of the Costa Rican communist party, the labor squads of which oppressed opposition groups); this situation caused José Figueres to launch the civil war of 1948 to restore democracy.

b. The National Guard has controlled the presidency since 1968, in spite of the rigged 1984 election of "President" Nicolás Ardito Bartletta, who was dismissed by the Guard before he could complete one year in office.

c. General Adolfo Stroessner was "reelected" in 1958, 1963, 1968, 1973, 1978, 1983, 1988. He was overthrown Feb. 3, 1989, by General Andrés Rodríguez, who called for elections within 90 days.

d. President Juan María Bordaberry effectively turned over power to the military in 1973, the military taking full power in 1976.

SOURCE: Assembled by SALA staff.

Table 1004

FREEDOM HOUSE RANKING OF POLITICAL AND CIVIL RIGHTS,[1] 20 LC, 1972–89

(1+ = Best Score; 7– = Worst Score)

Country	Year	Political Rights[2]	Civil Rights[3]	Country	Year	Political Rights[2]	Civil Rights[3]
A. ARGENTINA	1972	6	3	E. COLOMBIA	1972	2	2
	1973	2	2		1973	2	2
	1974	2	4–		1974	2	2
	1975	2	4		1975	2	3–
	1976	6–	5–		1976	2	3
	1977	6	6–[a]		1977	2	3
	1978	6	5+		1978	2	3
	1979	6	5		1979	2	3
	1980	6	5		1980	2	3
	1981	6	5		1981	2	3
	1982	6	5		1982	2	3
	1983	3+	3+		1983	2	3
	1984	2+	2+		1984	2	3
	1985	2	2		1985	2	3
	1986	2	1+		1986	2	3
	1987	2	1		1987	2	3
	1988	2	1		1988	2	3
	1989	2	1		1989	2	3
B. BOLIVIA	1972	5	4	F. COSTA RICA	1972	1	1
	1973	5	4		1973	1	2
	1974	6–	5–		1974	1	1
	1975	6	5		1975	1	1
	1976	6	4[a]		1976	1	1
	1977	6	4		1977	1	1
	1978	5+	3+		1978	1	1
	1979	3+	3		1979	1	1
	1980	7–	5–		1980	1	1
	1981	7	5		1981	1	1
	1982	2+	3+		1982	1	1
	1983	2	3		1983	1	1
	1984	2	3		1984	1	1
	1985	2	3		1985	1	1
	1986	2	3		1986	1	1
	1987	2	3		1987	1	1
	1988	2	3		1988	1	1
	1989	2	3		1989	1	1
C. BRAZIL	1972	5	5	G. CUBA	1972	7	7
	1973	5	5		1973	7	7
	1974	4+	4+		1974	7	7
	1975	4	5–		1975	7	7
	1976	4	5		1976	7	6[a]
	1977	4	5		1977	7	6
	1978	4	4+		1978	6[a]	6
	1979	4	3+		1979	6	6
	1980	4	3		1980	6	6
	1981	4	3		1981	6	6
	1982	3+	3		1982	6	6
	1983	3	3		1983	6	6
	1984	3	3		1984	6	6
	1985	3	2+		1985	6	6
	1986	2+	2		1986	6	6
	1987	2	2		1987	6	6
	1988	2	2		1988	6	6
	1989	2	3[a]		1989	7[a]	6
D. CHILE	1972	1	2	H. DOMINICAN REP.	1972	3	2
	1973	7[b]	5[b]		1973	3	2
	1974	7	5		1974	4	2
	1975	7	5		1975	4	2
	1976	7	5		1976	4	3[a]
	1977	7	5		1977	4	2+[a]
	1978	6+	5		1978	2+	2
	1979	6	5		1979	2	3–
	1980	6	5		1980	2	3
	1981	6	5		1981	2	3
	1982	6	5		1982	1+	2+
	1983	6	5		1983	1	2
	1984	6	5		1984	1	3–
	1985	6	5		1985	1	3
	1986	6	5		1986	1	3
	1987	6	5		1987	1	3
	1988	6	5		1988	1	3
	1989	5[b]	4[b]		1989	1	3

Table 1004 (Continued)

FREEDOM HOUSE RANKING OF POLITICAL AND CIVIL RIGHTS,[1] 20 LC, 1972–89
(1+ = Best Score; 7– = Worst Score)

Country	Year	Political Rights[2]	Civil Rights[3]	Country	Year	Political Rights[2]	Civil Rights[3]
I. ECUADOR	1972	7	3	M. HONDURAS	1972	7	3
	1973	7	4a		1973	6	3
	1974	7	4		1974	6	3
	1975	7	4		1975	6	3
	1976	6a	4		1976	6	3
	1977	6	4		1977	6	3
	1978	5+	3+		1978	6	3
	1979	2+	2+		1979	6	3
	1980	2	2		1980	4+	3
	1981	2	2		1981	3+	3
	1982	2	2		1982	2+	3
	1983	2	2		1983	3–	3
	1984	2	2		1984	2+	3
	1985	2	3		1985	2	3
	1986	2	3		1986	2	3
	1987	2	3		1987	2	3
	1988	2	3		1988	2	3
	1989	2	2b		1989	2	3
J. EL SALVADOR	1972	2	3	N. MEXICO	1972	5	3
	1973	2	3		1973	4b	3
	1974	2	3		1974	4	3
	1975	2	3		1975	4	3
	1976	3–	3		1976	4	4–
	1977	3	3		1977	4	4
	1978	4–	4–		1978	4	4
	1979	5a	3+		1979	3+	3+
	1980	6–	4–		1980	3	4
	1981	5	5–		1981	3	4
	1982	4+	5		1982	3	4
	1983	4	5		1983	3	4
	1984	3+	5		1984	3	4
	1985	2+	4+		1985	4–	4
	1986	3	4		1986	4	4
	1987	3	4		1987	4	4
	1988	3	4		1988	4	4
	1989	3	3b		1989	3b	4
K. GUATEMALA	1972	2	3	O. NICARAGUA	1972	4	3
	1973	2	2		1973	5	4b
	1974	4	3		1974	5	4
	1975	4	3		1975	5	4
	1976	4	3		1976	5	5a
	1977	4	4a		1977	5	5
	1978	3+	4		1978	5	5
	1979	3	5a		1979	5	5
	1980	5–	6–		1980	5	5
	1981	6–	6		1981	6–	5
	1982	6	6		1982	6	5
	1983	6	6		1983	6	5
	1984	5+	6		1984	5+	5
	1985	4+	4+		1985	5	5
	1986	3+	3+		1986	5	6–
	1987	3	3		1987	5	5+
	1988	3	3		1988	5	5+
	1989	3	3		1989	5	4a
L. HAITI	1972	7	6	P. PANAMA	1972	7	6
	1973	6	6		1973	7	6
	1974	6	6		1974	7	6
	1975	6	6		1975	7	6
	1976	6	6		1976	7	6
	1977	7a	6		1977	6+	5+
	1978	7	6		1978	5+	5
	1979	6+	5+		1979	5	5
	1980	6	6–		1980	4+	4+
	1981	7–	6		1981	4	4
	1982	7	6		1982	5–	5–
	1983	7	6		1983	5	4+
	1984	7	6		1984	4+	3+
	1985	7	6		1985	6–	3
	1986	5+	4+		1986	6	3
	1987	6–	5–		1987	5	5–
	1988	6–	5–		1988	5a	5–
	1989	7b	5		1989	6	5

Table 1004 (Continued)

FREEDOM HOUSE RANKING OF POLITICAL AND CIVIL RIGHTS,[1] 20 LC, 1972–89

(1+ = Best Score; 7– = Worst Score)

Country	Year	Political Rights[2]	Civil Rights[3]	Country	Year	Political Rights[2]	Civil Rights[3]
Q. PARAGUAY	1972	4	6	T. VENEZUELA	1972	2	2
	1973	5	5		1973	2	2
	1974	5	5		1974	2	2
	1975	5	5		1975	2	2
	1976	5	6–		1976	1[a]	2
	1977	5	6		1977	1	2
	1978	5+	5		1978	1	2
	1979	5	5		1979	1	2
	1980	5	5		1980	1	2
	1981	5	5		1981	1	2
	1982	5	5		1982	1	2
	1983	5	5		1983	1	2
	1984	5	5		1984	1	2
	1985	5	5		1985	1	2
	1986	5	6–		1986	1	2
	1987	5	6		1987	1	2
	1988	5	6		1988	1	2
	1989	6[a]	6		1989	1	2
R. PERU	1972	7	5	UNITED STATES	1972	1	1
	1973	7	5		1973	1	1
	1974	6[a]	6–		1974	1	1
	1975	6	4+		1975	1	1
	1976	6	4		1976	1	1
	1977	6	4		1977	1	1
	1978	5+	4		1978	1	1
	1979	6	4		1979	1	1
	1980	2+	3+		1980	1	1
	1981	2	3		1981	1	1
	1982	2	3		1982	1	1
	1983	2	3		1983	1	1
	1984	2	3		1984	1	1
	1985	2	3		1985	1	1
	1986	2	3		1986	1	1
	1987	2	3		1987	1	1
	1988	2	3		1988	1	1
	1989	2	3		1989	1	1
S. URUGUAY	1972	3	4				
	1973	5[b]	5[b]				
	1974	5	5				
	1975	5	5				
	1976	6–	6–[a]				
	1977	6	6				
	1978	6	6				
	1979	6	6				
	1980	5+	5+				
	1981	5	5				
	1982	5	4+				
	1983	5	4				
	1984	5	4				
	1985	2+	2+				
	1986	2	2				
	1987	2	2				
	1988	2	2				
	1989	2	2				

1. This "freedom" survey, conducted annually by Freedom House, defines freedom in terms of both civil and political freedoms as these have been traditionally understood in the constitutional democratic states.
2. The score for *political rights* is determined by the degree to which a given country satisfies the following requirements: (a) that leaders are chosen in decisions made on the basis of an open voting process, (b) that significant opposition is allowed to compete in this process, (c) that there are multiple political parties and candidates not selected by the government, (d) that polling and counting of votes is conducted without coercion or fraud, (e) that a significant share of political power is exercised by elected representatives, (f) that all regions, even the most remote, are included in the political process, and (g) that the country is free of foreign or military control or influence. Countries assigned a rank of 1 most closely satisfy these requirements and those assigned a rank of 7 most seriously violate them.

3. The score for *civil rights* is determined by the degree of liberty a given country grants its news media and individual citizens, primarily as it applies to political expression. The survey looks at censorship applied to the press or radio. It also assesses the rights granted any individual to openly express ideas, to belong to an organization free of government supervision, and the individual's right to a free trial, i.e., the degree to which the judiciary is independent of administrative control. Also important is the number of political prisoners held in a country, the use of torture or brutality, and the degree to which the state security forces respect individual rights. Countries assigned the rank of 1 grant the greatest degree of civil liberties and those assigned the rank of 7 most seriously violate them.

a. Change in status since the previous year owing to reevaluation by the author. This does not imply any change in the country.
b. Change in status since the previous year owing to events in the country.

SOURCE: Freedom House — *Freedom at Issue*, Jan.–Feb., 1973–89.

Table 1005

REVISED FITZGIBBON-JOHNSON INDEX RANKINGS: U.S. VIEW OF POLITICAL DEMOCRACY, FIVE KEY CRITERIA,[1] 20 L, 1945-85

(Most Democratic = 1)

	Country	1945	1950	1955	1960	1965	1970	1975	1980	1985
A.	ARGENTINA	9	15[a]	15	4	7	14	5	15	4
B.	BOLIVIA	16	13	12	15	16	15	15	17	15
C.	BRAZIL	12[a]	5	4	6	10	17	16	11	12
D.	CHILE	3[a]	2	3	3	2[a]	2	18	18	19
E.	COLOMBIA	3[a]	6	9	5	5	5	3	3	3
F.	COSTA RICA	2	4	2	2	1	1	1	1	1
G.	CUBA	5	3	10	16	19	19	14	12	16
H.	DOMINICAN REP.	20	20	20	20	14[a]	10	6	6	8
I.	ECUADOR	12[a]	7	6	9	12	7	10	7	7
J.	EL SALVADOR	14	14	8	13	11	8	8	14[c]	14
K.	GUATEMALA	11	11	13	12	13	9	9	13	17
L.	HAITI	19	17	14	18	20	20	20	20	20
M.	HONDURAS	17	8	11	14	14[a]	12	12	10	13
N.	MEXICO	7	9	5	7	6	6	4	4	5
O.	NICARAGUA	15	18	19	17	17	16	17	8	11
P.	PANAMA	6	10	7	11	9	11	11	9[b]	10
Q.	PARAGUAY	18	19	18	19	18	18	19	19	18
R.	PERU	8	15[a]	17	10	8	13	13	5	6
S.	URUGUAY	1	1	1	1	2[a]	3	7	16	9
T.	VENEZUELA	10	12	10	8	4	4	2	2	2

1. The five criteria are:
   1. Free speech
   2. Free elections
   3. Free party organization
   4. Independent judiciary
   5. Civilian supremacy

a. Tie ranking.
b. Johnson reports that corrected raw score is 992.
c. Corrected raw score is 688.

SOURCE: Kenneth F. Johnson, "Research Perspectives on the Revised Fitzgibbon-Johnson Index of the Image of Political Democracy in Latin America, 1945-75," in James W. Wilkie and Kenneth Ruddle, eds. *Quantitative Latin American Studies*, Statistical Abstract of Latin America Supplement 6 (Los Angeles: UCLA Latin American Center Publications, 1977), pp. 87-91; table is from p. 89. Data for 1980 are from *Latin American Research Review* 17:3 (1982), p. 198. Unpublished 1985 data provided by Kenneth F. Johnson and Philip L. Kelly, "Political Democracy in Latin America 1985: Partial Results of the Image-Index Survey," Emporia State University, Emporia, Kansas, 1985.

Table 1006

U.S. GOVERNMENT ESTIMATES OF COMMUNIST PARTY MEMBERSHIP, 20 LR, 1947–88

(T)

Country	1947	1952	1956	1957	1958	1959	1960	1961	1962	1963	1964	1965
A. ARGENTINA	30.00	30.00	50.00	80.00	80.00	80.00	80.00	50.00	50.00	45.00	65.00	65.00
B. BOLIVIA	:	2.00	2.00	4.00	4.00	4.30	4.00	5.00	5.00	6.50	4.50	4.50
C. BRAZIL	150.00	60.00	100.00	50.00	50.00	25.00	50.00	40.00	35.00	31.00	31.00	23.00
D. CHILE	50.00	35.00	40.00	25.00	25.00	~e	25.00	20.00	25.00	25.00	27.50	30.00
E. COLOMBIA	5.00	3.00	5.00	5.00	5.00	5.00	5.00	8.00	10.00	11.00	13.00	12.00
F. COSTA RICA	3.00	2.00	1.00	.30	.30	.30	.30	.30	.30	.30	.30	.40
G. CUBA	50.00	25.00	30.00	12.00	12.00	27.00	27.00	27.00	60.00	28.00	35.00	50.00
H. DOMINICAN REP.	.50	~	~	~	~	~	~	~	~	~	~	1.70
I. ECUADOR	2.50	2.00	5.00	1.00	1.00	1.00	1.00	3.00	3.00	2.50	2.50	2.50
J. EL SALVADOR	:	.50	1.00	.50	.50	1.00	1.00	.50	.50	.50	.20	.20
K. GUATEMALA	:	1.00	1.00	1.00	1.00	1.20	1.20	1.00	1.10	1.30	1.30	1.00
L. HAITI	.50	:	~	~	~	~	~	~	~	~	~	~
M. HONDURAS	:	:	.50	.50	.50	.40	.40	2.00	2.00	2.40	2.40	1.30
N. MEXICO	10.00	5.00	5.00	5.00	5.00	5.00	5.00	6.00	6.00	50.00	50.00	5.25
O. NICARAGUA	.50	.50	.50	.20	.20	.20	.20	.30	.30	.25	.25	.20
P. PANAMA	.50	.50	.50	~	~	~	.30	.15	.15	.40	.40	.50
Q. PARAGUAY	8.00	1.00	2.00	.50	.50	.50	.50	5.00	4.00	3.50	5.00	5.00
R. PERU	30.00	10.00	5.00	6.00	6.00	6.00	7.00	7.00	10.00	8.50	8.50	5.00
S. URUGUAY	15.00	10.00	5.00	3.00	3.00	5.00	4.00	3.00	5.00	10.00	10.00	10.00
T. VENEZUELA	20.00	10.00	10.00	9.00	35.00	40.00	40.00	20.00	30.00	30.00	30.00	20.00
LATIN AMERICA	375.50	197.50	263.50	203.00	229.00	~e	251.90	198.25	247.35	256.15	286.85	237.55

(T)

Country	1966	1967	1968	1969	1970	1971	1972	1973	1974	1975	1976
A. ARGENTINA	60.00	60.00	60.00	55.00	60.00	60.00	70.00	75.00	126.00	147.00	100.00
B. BOLIVIA	5.50	6.00	6.00	5.00	4.50	2.80	3.20	2.60	.45	.45	.50
C. BRAZIL	20.00	20.00	15.75	16.00	14.00	13.00	13.00	6.00	6.00	7.00	6.00
D. CHILE	30.00	32.50	45.00	45.00	45.00	90.00	120.00	~e	~e	100.00	~e
E. COLOMBIA	10.00	9.00	9.00	9.00	9.00	11.00	11.00	11.00	11.00	12.00	11.00†
F. COSTA RICA	.45	.55	.60	.60	1.00	1.00	1.00	1.00	1.00	1.50	3.20
G. CUBA	60.00	60.00	60.00	120.00	125.00	125.00	125.00	153.00	200.00	200.00	200.00
H. DOMINICAN REP.	1.30	1.30	1.10	1.10	1.68	1.40	1.40	1.40	1.40	1.50	1.65
I. ECUADOR	1.50	1.50	1.65	1.65	1.25	1.20	1.20	.75	.75	.60	.80
J. EL SALVADOR	.20	.20	.20	.20	.10	.10	.13	.15	.20	.18	.15
K. GUATEMALA	1.00	.75	.75	.75	.75	.75	.75	.75	.75	.75	.75†
L. HAITI	~	~	~	~	~	~	~	~	~	.15	~
M. HONDURAS	1.30	.65	.30	.30	.30	.30	.30	.30	.35	.75	.65
N. MEXICO	5.25	5.25	5.25	5.00	5.00	5.00	5.00	5.00	5.00	5.00	5.00
O. NICARAGUA	.20	.20	.20	.20	.10	.10	.10	.10	.15	.15	.10
P. PANAMA	.50	.25	.25	.25	.13	.25	.50	.50	.50	.50	.60
Q. PARAGUAY	5.00	5.00	5.00	4.50	4.50	4.50	3.50	3.50	3.50	3.50	3.50
R. PERU	5.00	5.00	5.00	5.00	3.20	3.20	3.20	3.20	3.20	3.20	3.20
S. URUGUAY	15.00	21.00	21.00	20.00	20.00	20.00	22.00	30.00	30.00	30.00	6.00†
T. VENEZUELA	10.00	5.00	5.00	8.00	8.00	8.00	8.00	7.50	6.00	6.00	6.00
LATIN AMERICA	232.20	234.15	242.05	297.55	303.51	347.60	389.28	~e	~e	520.23	~e

Table 1006 (Continued)

U. S. GOVERNMENT ESTIMATES OF COMMUNIST PARTY MEMBERSHIP, 20 LR, 1947-88

(T)

	Country	1977	1978	1979	1980	1981	1982	1983	1984	1985	1986	1987	1988
A.	ARGENTINA	70.00†,d	3.90†,d	70.00†,d	70.00†,d	70.00†,d	70.00†,d	70.00†,d	70.00†,d	70.00†,d	70.00†,d	70.00†,d	70.00†,d
B.	BOLIVIA	.50†	.50†,d	.50†,d	.50†,d	.50†,d	.50†,d	.50†,d	~	~	~	~	~
C.	BRAZIL	6.00	6.00	6.00	6.00	6.00	6.00	6.00	6.00	6.00	6.00	30.00†	30.00
D.	CHILE	200.00	20.00†,a	20.00†,a	20.00†,a	20.00†,a	20.00†,a	20.00†,a	20.00†,a	20.00†,a	50.00†,a	50.00†,a	50.00†,a
E.	COLOMBIA	12.00†,d	12.00†,d	12.00†,d	12.00†,d	12.00†,d	12.00†,d	12.00†,d	12.00†,d	12.00†,d	18.00†,c,d	18.00†,c,d	18.00†,c,d
F.	COSTA RICA	3.20†	3.20d	3.20d	3.20d	3.20d	10.00†,b	10.00†,b	10.00†,b	10.00b	7.50b	7.50b	7.50b
G.	CUBA	200.00†,d	200.00†,d	200.00†,d	200.00†,d	200.00†,d	400.00†,d	400.00†,d	400.00†,d	400.00†,d	400.00†,d	500.00d	500.00d
H.	DOMINICAN REP.	1.80†,d	1.80†,d	1.80†,d	1.80†,d	1.80†,d	9.00†,d	9.00†,d	9.00†,d	9.00†,d	10.00†,d	10.00†,d	10.00†,d
I.	ECUADOR	.80†,d	.80†,d	.80†,d	.80†,d	.80†,d	.80†,d	.80†,d	17.10†,b	17.10†,b	17.10†,b	17.10†,b	17.10†,b
J.	EL SALVADOR	.20†,a	.20†,a	.53†,a	2.23†,a	~	~	~	~	~	~	~	~
K.	GUATEMALA	.75†,d	.75†,d	.75†,d	1.00†,d	~	~	~	~	~	~	~	~
L.	HAITI	~	~	~	~	~	~	~	~	~	~	2.00†	2.00†
M.	HONDURAS	.65†	.65†	.65†	1.50†	1.50†	1.50†	1.50†	1.50†	1.50†	1.50†	1.50†	1.50†
N.	MEXICO	5.00†,d	5.00†,d	25.00†,d	~	~	~	~	~	~	~	~	~
O.	NICARAGUA	.25†,d	.25†,d	1.30d	~	~	~	~	~	~	~	~	~
P.	PANAMA	.60†,a	1.40†,d	1.40†,d	1.40†,d	1.40†,d	2.30†,b	2.30†,b	36.50†	36.50†	~	3.00†	3.00†
Q.	PARAGUAY	4.00†,b	4.00†,b	4.00†,b	4.00†,b	4.00†,b	4.00†,b	4.00†,b	4.00†,b	4.00†,b	4.00†,b	4.00†,b	4.00†,b
R.	PERU	3.20†	3.20†	3.20†	3.20†	3.20†	3.20†	3.20†	3.20†	3.20†	3.20†	2.00†	2.00†
S.	URUGUAY	40.00b,c	40.00b,c	10.00b,c	10.00†,b	10.00†,b	10.00†,b	10.00†,b	10.00†,b	10.00†,b	18.00†	30.00	30.00
T.	VENEZUELA	6.00†,d	6.00†,d	6.00†,d	5.00†,d	5.00†,d	5.00†,d	5.00†,d	5.00†,d	5.00†,d	10.00†,d	10.00†,d	10.00†,d
	LATIN AMERICA	554.95	309.65	367.13	~f	~f	~f	~f	~f	~f	~f	~f	~f

a. Active militants only.
b. Includes sympathizers.
c. Includes Communist Party youth organization members.
d. Communist Party members.
e. The unavailability of Chilean data renders total figures for 1959, 1973, 1974, and 1976 invalid for comparison with other years.
f. The unavailability of data renders total figures for 1980-88 invalid for comparison with other years.

SOURCE: Peter Reich, "Measuring U. S. Government Perception of the 'Communist Menace' in Latin America, 1947-1976," SALA, 19, chapter 34; Central Intelligence Agency, *National Basic Intelligence Factbook* (Washington, D. C.: U. S. Government Printing Office, 1977-1980); and *The World Factbook* (Washington, D. C.: U. S. Government Printing Office, 1981-88).

Table 1007

U. N. SUPPORT FOR U. S. POLICY, 20 L, 1981–88[a]

(%)

	Country	1981–82	1983–84	1984–85	1985–86	Sept.–Dec. 1988[b]
A.	ARGENTINA	30	19	14	16	~
B.	BOLIVIA	42	23	20	19	10.91
C.	BRAZIL	28	24	15	16	~
D.	CHILE	44	33	29	31	~
E.	COLOMBIA	41	25	25	28	13.21
F.	COSTA RICA	41	31	26	29	18.56
G.	CUBA	12	10	4	6	~
H.	DOMINICAN REP.	39	24	27	25	17.31
I.	ECUADOR	28	25	26	25	11.71
J.	EL SALVADOR	36	30	30	30	17.53
K.	GUATEMALA	52	41	33	25	14.29
L.	HAITI	36	32	24	24	13.59
M.	HONDURAS	45	30	29	30	20.00
N.	MEXICO	26	20	9	15	~
O.	NICARAGUA	19	14	7	8	~
P.	PANAMA	27	22	22	20	~
Q.	PARAGUAY	59	45	36	35	~
R.	PERU	31	24	17	18	11.61
S.	URUGUAY	41	29	31	18	~
T.	VENEZUELA	29	22	14	19	~

a. Percent voting with U. S. each General Session.
b. Based on 166 votes, 43rd General Assembly.

SOURCE: *Inter-American Economic Affairs*, Summer 1983, Summer 1984, and Autumn
1985; *New York Times*, July 4, 1986; *Wall Street Journal*, June 2, 1989.

Table 1008

SHARE OF ADULT POPULATION VOTING, 12 LC

	Country	Year	Type of Election[1]	Total Vote (T)	% Adult Population Voting[2]
A.	ARGENTINA	1983	P, L	15,180	89
C.	BRAZIL	1982	L	48,440	81
E.	COLOMBIA	1982	P	6,816	68
F.	COSTA RICA	1982	P, L	992	87
I.	ECUADOR	1984	L	2,204	53
J.	EL SALVADOR	1984	P	1,524	69
K.	GUATEMALA	1984	CA	1,856	57
M.	HONDURAS	1981	P, L	1,171	79
N.	MEXICO	1982	P, L	22,523	75
O.	NICARAGUA	1984	P, CA	1,170	91
R.	PERU	1980	P, L	4,030	49
T.	VENEZUELA	1983	P, L	6,741	90
	UNITED STATES	1984	P, L	92,000	53

1. P = Presidential, L = Legislative, CA = Constituent Assembly.
2. Estimates based on votes cast as a percentage of total population age 20 or over.

SOURCE: *LASA Forum* (Latin American Studies Association), Winter, 1985, p. 25.

Table 1009

U.N. VOTING PATTERNS OF LEADING U.S. AID RECIPIENTS, 10 LC
(September through December 1988)[a]

	Country	% Agreement with U.S.	% Agreement with U.S.S.R.	Total U.S. Aid in 1987 (T US)		Country	% Agreement with U.S.	% Agreement with U.S.S.R.	Total U.S. Aid in 1987 (T US)
	Israel	89.74	25.27	3,000,000	H.	DOMINICAN REP.	17.31	95.52	56,931
	Egypt	8.62	98.64	2,309,731	R.	PERU	11.61	98.62	56,531
	Pakistan	8.94	99.35	646,047		Sri Lanka	9.76	98.06	51,473
	Turkey	26.83	89.62	594,215		Somalia	9.92	99.35	49,978
J.	EL SALVADOR	17.53	94.62	507,764	I.	ECUADOR	11.71	98.61	49,112
	Philippines	12.28	98.64	393,524		Senegal	8.77	99.32	47,086
	Greece	31.71	87.74	344,250		Yemen Arab Republic	5.93	100.00	41,483
M.	HONDURAS	20.00	94.49	254,928		Liberia	12.38	98.51	41,001
K.	GUATEMALA	14.29	97.83	181,240		Mozambique	5.17	100.00	38,629
F.	COSTA RICA	18.56	95.97	179,448		Ireland	42.86	79.21	35,002
	Bangladesh	8.47	99.32	164,996		Cameroon	12.00	98.44	33,811
	Jordan	11.76	97.96	152,941		Niger	8.55	99.33	26,385
	Portugal	68.35	55.67	147,364		Lebanon	9.65	100.00	22,778
	Indonesia	8.06	99.36	140,255		Zambia	8.33	98.68	22,292
	India	6.67	100.00	138,023		Chad	11.71	98.60	19,517
	Morocco	7.83	98.64	134,929		Tanzania	6.90	100.00	18,836
	Spain	52.00	72.92	113,000		Burma	10.09	97.89	17,761
L.	HAITI	13.59	98.51	98,827		Nepal	10.81	98.61	17,539
	Jamaica	13.33	98.35	87,801		Ghana	8.94	99.37	17,289
	Thailand	11.65	98.53	81,699	E.	COLOMBIA	13.21	98.57	16,604
	Sudan	7.26	99.34	81,663		Madagascar	7.44	100.00	16,466
	Tunisia	8.40	99.34	78,265		Botswana	11.71	98.63	16,029
B.	BOLIVIA	10.91	98.61	72,174		Belize	17.17	95.08	15,884
	Zaire	13.13	97.69	60,551		Lesotho	12.50	97.06	15,309
	Kenya	10.74	98.70	59,892		Oman	8.04	98.58	15,017

a. Based on 166 votes, 43rd General Assembly.

SOURCE: *Wall Street Journal*, June 2, 1989.

Table 1010

IMPACT OF WOMEN'S SUFFRAGE ON VOTER PARTICIPATION, 20 LC

	Country	Year of Women's Suffrage A	PC in Voter Participation After Women's Suffrage B
A.	ARGENTINA	1947	+146.0
B.	BOLIVIA	1952	+705.0
C.	BRAZIL	1932	+509.0[a]
D.	CHILE	1949	+77.6
E.	COLOMBIA	1957	+108.7
F.	COSTA RICA	1949	+63.1
G.	CUBA	1934	+126.3
H.	DOMINICAN REP.	1942	+63.1
I.	ECAUDOR	1929	−50.0[a]
J.	EL SALVADOR	1939	+258.0
K.	GUATEMALA	1945	+31.1
L.	HAITI	1950	+443.5
M.	HONDURAS	1955	+46.1[a]
N.	MEXICO	1953	+69.5
O.	NICARAGUA	1955	+61.8
P.	PANAMA	1945	+29.5[a]
Q.	PARAGUAY	1961	−9.3
R.	PERU	1955	+113.0
S.	URUGUAY	1932	−73.9
T.	VENEZUELA	1947	+53.8[a]
	Latin America Average[b]		+138.6
	UNITED STATES	1920	+36.4

a. Elections where zero percent of the population voted were not used; the next election in which at least 1 percent voted, was used.
b. Unweighted by population.

SOURCE: Enrique C. Ochoa, "The Rapid Expansion of Voter Participation in Latin America: Presidential Elections, 1845–1986," SALA, 25-3423.

Table 1011

LATIN AMERICA PRESIDENTIAL ELECTIONS, BY DECADE, 1840–1986

Decade	Number of Elections
1841–1850	12
1851–1860	39
1861–1870	35
1871–1880	45
1881–1890	40
1891–1900	42
1901–1910	40
1911–1920	45
1921–1930	41
1931–1940	43
1941–1950	39
1951–1960	38
1961–1970	35[a]
1971–1980	14[a]
1981–1986	21[a]

a. Brazilian elections are not included from 1964 through 1984, because the president was chosen by congress.

SOURCE: Enrique C. Ochoa, "The Rapid Expansion of Voter Participation in Latin America: Presidential Elections, 1845–1986," SALA, 25-3424.

Table 1012

LOCAL GOVERNMENTS, 17 L

	Country	Number of Regional Governments	Number of Local Governments	Grants from Other Levels of Government as Percent of Total Local Government Revenue and Grants in Year Indicated	Outlays of Local Government as Percent of Total General Government Outlays in Year Indicated	
A.	ARGENTINA	23	1,617	~	~	~
B.	BOLIVIA	9	~	47.8	1.8	1984
C.	BRAZIL	25	3,991	72.2	6.3	1985
D.	CHILE	~	317	~	8.0	1986
E.	COLOMBIA	24	967	41.5	9.1	1983
F.	COSTA RICA	~	85	14.3	3.9	1985
H.	DOMINICAN REP.	~	126	73.3	5.0	1985
I.	ECUADOR	19	136	6.3	12.4[a]	1980
J.	EL SALVADOR	~	262	~	5.8[b]	1978
K.	GUATEMALA	~	328	8.3	4.6	1983
M.	HONDURAS	~	281	7.4	7.5	1976
N.	MEXICO	32	2,376	1.5	2.9	1984
O.	NICARAGUA	~	135	~	~	~
P.	PANAMA	~	66	2.4	2.0	1985
Q.	PARAGUAY	~	193	5.2	4.6	1984
R.	PERU	180	1,578	~	~	~
S.	URUGUAY	~	19	8.4	8.2	1984
T.	VENEZUELA	22	189	61.4	2.4	1979

a. As percent of central, regional, and local government expenditure.
b. As percent of central and local government expenditure.

SOURCE: *IMF Survey*, May 16, 1988.

Table 1013

RANKING OF LEGAL RESTRICTIONS ON SOCIETY, 1974–85

(1 = Most Restrictive)

	Country	A.[1]	B.	C.	D.	E.	F.	Total	Relative Position
A.	ARGENTINA	.33	.5	.67	1	.5	.5	3.5	4
C.	BRAZIL	1	.33	.5	.5	.83	1	4.16	2
D.	CHILE	.16	.16	.16	.33	.16	0	.97	6
N.	MEXICO	.83	.67	.33	.83	.33	0	2.99	5
R.	PERU	.5	.83	.83	.67	.67	.67	4.14	3
T.	VENEZUELA	.67	1	1	1	1	.83	5.5	1

1. Key: A. Restrictions on property.
           B. Restrictions on credit and interchange.
           C. Restrictions on utility companies and renationalization of capital.
           D. Restrictions on the employment of foreign labor.
           E. Restrictions on local content of labor.
           F. Other restrictions.

SOURCE: *Economía y Administración* (Universidad de Chile), no. 54, April 1987, p. 14.

Table 1014

ARGENTINA PRESIDENTIAL AND CONGRESSIONAL FINAL ELECTION RESULTS, BY POLITICAL PARTY

(October 30, 1983)

Party	Presidential/Vice Presidential			Congressional		
	Votes	As % of Total Votes Received	Electoral Votes	Votes	As % of Total Votes Received	Electoral Votes
Alianza Demócrata Socialista	47,736	.32	0	121,889	.82	0
Demócrata Progresista	2,183	.01	0	2,907	.02	0
Socialista Democrático	269	.00	0	293	#	0

Table 1015

POPULATION VOTING IN PRESIDENTIAL ELECTIONS, 20 LC, 1853–1983

(%)

A. ARGENTINA

Year	A Number of Voters (A)	B Total Population (T) (B)	C Percentage of Population Voting (A/B)	D Person Elected President
1853[a]	106	640	1.0	Justo José de Urquiza
1859	~	1,280	1.0	Santiago Derqui
1862	133	1,400	1.0	Bartolomé Mitre
1868	127	1,688	1.0	Domingo Faustino Sarmiento
1874	224	2,154	1.2	Nicolás Avellaneda
1880	225	2,640	2.0	Julio A. Roca
1886	213	3,094	2.0	Miguel Juárez Celman
1892	215	3,858	2.0	Luis Sáenz Peña
1898	256	4,462	2.0	Julio A. Roca
1904	295	5,716	2.5	Manual Quintana
1910	265	7,092	2.8	Roque Sáenz Peña
1916	723,909	8,300	8.8	Hipólito Irigoyen
1922	823,380	9,368	8.8	Marcelo T. de Alvear
1928	1,461,671	11,282	12.9	Hipólito Irigoyen
1931	1,355,954	12,167	11.1	Agustín P. Justo
1937	1,913,164	13,490	14.2	Roberto M. Ortiz
1946	2,690,333	15,654	17.2	Juan Domingo Perón
1951	7,461,555	17,635	42.3	Juan Domingo Perón
1958	9,063,498	19,250	47.1	Arturo Frondizi
1963	9,325,997	21,688	43.0	Arturo Illía
1973	12,077,422	24,820	48.6	Juan Domingo Perón
1983	15,374,769	29,630	52.0	Raul Alfonsín

a. For 1853 through 1910 the number of electors is given. The percentage is equal to the
    number of people who voted for the electors.

Continued in Enrique C. Ochoa, "The Rapid Expansion of Voter Participation in Latin
   America: Presidential Elections, 1845–1986," SALA, 25-3400 through 3420.

Figure 10:1

POPULATION VOTING IN PRESIDENTIAL ELECTIONS, 20 LC, 1853–1983

(%)

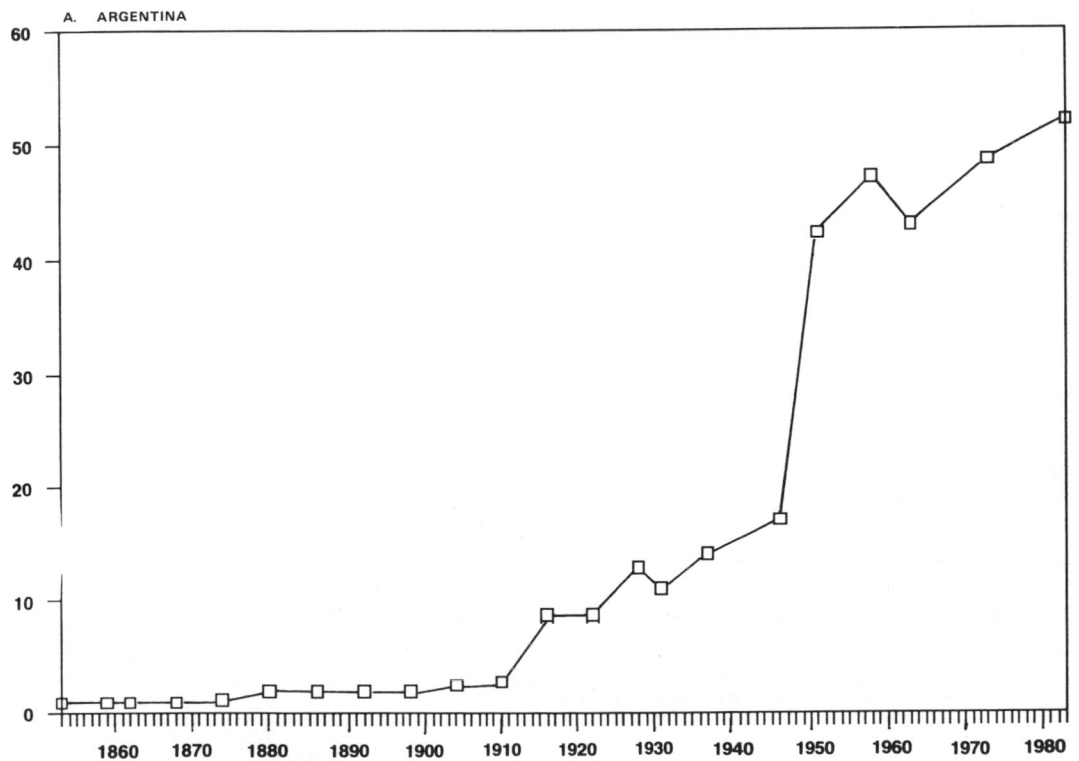

A. ARGENTINA

Continued in Enrique C. Ochoa, "The Rapid Expansion of Voter Participation in Latin
   America: Presidential Elections, 1845–1986," SALA, 25-34:1 through 34:19.

Table 1016

REGISTERED VOTERS VOTING IN PRESIDENTIAL ELECTIONS, 4 L

A.   ARGENTINA

Year	Number of Voters A	Number Registered B	Percentage of Registered Who Voted[1] A/B
1916	723,909	1,189,254	60.9
1922	823,380	1,586,366	52.0
1928	1,461,671	1,807,566	80.9
1931	1,355,954	2,116,552	64.1
1937	1,913,154	2,672,750	71.6
1946	2,690,333	3,405,173	79.0
1951	7,461,555	8,623,998	86.5
1958	9,063,498	10,002,327	90.6
1963	9,325,997	11,356,240	82.1
1973	12,077,422	14,334,253	84.3
1983	15,374,769	17,890,000	85.9

1. After 1951 null and blank votes included.

Continued in Enrique C. Ochoa, "The Rapid Expansion of Voter Participation in Latin
America: Presidential Elections, 1845–1986," in SALA, 25-3427 through 3430.

Figure 10:2

REGISTERED VOTERS VOTING IN PRESIDENTIAL ELECTIONS, 4 L

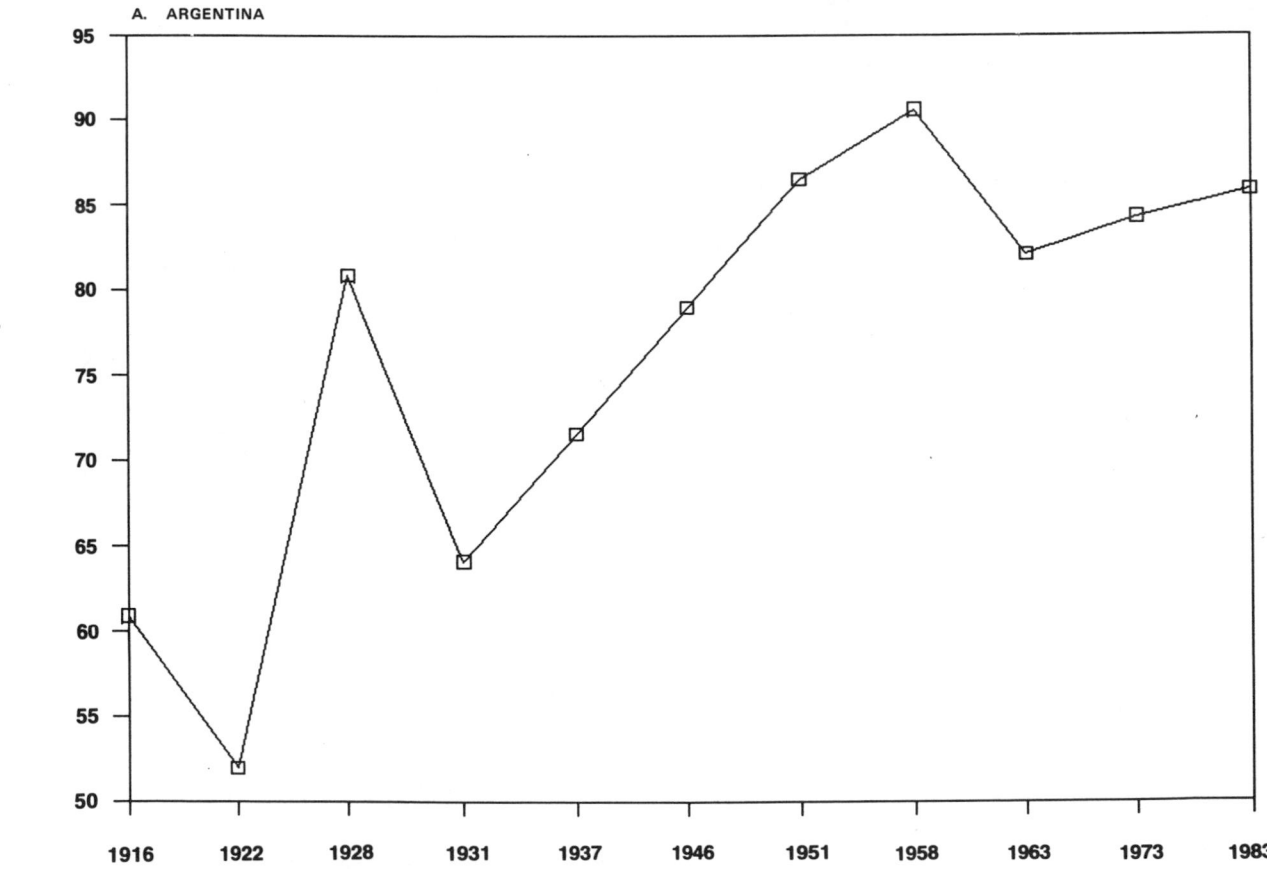

Continued in Enrique C. Cchoa, "The Rapid Expansion of Voter Participation in Latin
America: Presidential Elections, 1845–1986," in SALA, 25-34:24 through 34:27.

Table 1017

ARGENTINA PRESIDENTIAL ELECTION RESULTS, BY POLITICAL PARTY AND PROVINCE
(October 30, 1983)

Political Party
(% of Total Vote)

Province	Alianza Demócrata Socialista	Alianza Federal	Comunista	Demócrata Cristiano	Frente de Izquierda Popular	Intransigente	Justicialista	Movimiento al Socialismo	Movimiento de Integración y Desarrollo	Obrero	Socialista Popular	Unión Cívica Radical	Unión del Centro Democrático	Positive Votes	Null Votes	Blank Votes	Participation as % of Eligible Voters
Federal Capital	.32	.72	#	.18	.05	4.48	27.36	.40	.73	.13	.09	64.26	1.28	98.34	.62	1.05	85.78
Buenos Aires	.25	.59	#	.23	.07	3.24	42.23	.44	.84	.11	.09	51.41	.44	97.23	.38	2.39	87.69
Catamarca	**	**	#	.47	.11	.58	43.50	.09	.77	~	.13	46.73	**	95.00	.95	4.06	82.90
Córdoba	.19	**	#	.37	.08	.87	39.92	.17	.93	.05	.18	56.22	**	97.68	.33	1.99	88.35

Continued in SALA, 24-1005.

Table 1018

ARGENTINA PRESIDENTIAL ELECTION RESULTS, BY POLITICAL PARTY[1] AND DEPARTMENT

(1989)

District	UCR %	UCR N Votes	Al. Centro %	Al. Centro N Votes	Frejupo %	Frejupo N Votes	Al. Izq. Unida %	Al. Izq. Unida N Votes	Fte. Hum-Verde %	Fte. Hum-Verde N Votes	Obrero %	Obrero N Votes	CFI %	CFI N Votes	Bl. Jubilados %	Bl. Jubilados N Votes	Al. Un. Social. %	Al. Un. Social. N Votes	Small and Regional Parties %	Small and Regional Parties N Votes
Buenos Aires	28.97	1,822,311	6.80	428,275	49.97	3,144,072	3.29	207,177	.21	12,978	.28	17,301	4.27	268,602	4.60	288,912	1.49	93,714	.04	8,399
Capital Federal	36.31	730,823	12.35	248,455	36.64	737,761	3.38	68,056	.21	4,173	.27	5,438	8.75	176,153	.29	5,768	1.71	34,375	.10	2,056
Santa Fe	33.80	523,230	5.94	91,885	51.56	798,137	2.03	31,468	.25	3,796	.27	4,196	1.60	24,824	.80	12,824	3.42	52,982	.1	3,122
Córdoba	42.32	650,541	3.76	57,829	44.65	686,415	1.52	23,300	.28	4,331	.40	6,165	5.95	91,524	#		1.12	17,196	#	
Mendoza	32.92	226,967	16.70	115,104	42.17	290,689	3.99	27,497	.51	3,490	.50	3,461	.67	4,630	#		1.71	11,804	.3	2,709
Tucumán	17.95	97,873	1.14	6,234	41.34	225,281	.97	5,290	.18	969	.19	1,018	9.25	50,446	.14	737	.55	2,975	28.1	154,203
Entre Rios	39.06	220,857	5.99	33,872	51.64	291,979	1.13	6,396	.46	2,579	.26	1,482	#		#		1.45	8,206	#	
Chaco	38.28	146,614	1.91	7,383	51.80	197,860	.67	2,594	.39	1,485	.24	940	.59	2,269	#		#		6.0	23,100
Corrientes	26.57	100,310	1.22	4,628	42.03	158,797	.55	2,892	.15	579	.15	577	1.28	4,854	#		.24	892	28.8	104,219
Salta	28.25	92,635	3.25	10,725	41.28	135,434	1.25	4,142	.41	1,354	.79	2,617	21.01	69,250	#		.32	1,045	3.3	11,276
Santiago del Estero	28.96	88,449	.65	1,998	27.29	83,349	.74	2,267	.14	422	#		1.19	3,638	1.18	3,615	.55	1,682	39.1	119,981
Misiones	38.41	119,467	4.60	14,292	52.78	164,126	.53	1,660	.43	1,325	.24	733	2.43	7,558	#		.59	1,830	#	
San Juan	28.94	72,849	6.21	15,632	46.39	116,798	1.83	4,610	.32	795	#		#		.58	1,459	.62	1,551	15.0	38,067
Jujuy	17.74	36,243	1.35	2,695	43.15	88,302	1.79	3,676	.32	651	.41	834	18.73	38,425	#		.57	1,159	15.7	32,655
Rio Negro	41.83	85,038	6.71	13,634	47.21	95,980	2.30	4,685	.46	933	.62	1,270	#		#		.87	1,760	#	
Formosa	39.98	59,407	.67	1,332	58.26	85,847	.39	574	.12	168	#		#		#		.25	361	.1	176
Chubut	33.47	48,452	6.99	10,119	42.65	61,739	1.89	2,731	.22	323	.43	626	12.55	18,171	#		.97	1,398	.8	1,211
San Luis	41.02	58,684	3.88	5,555	48.47	69,347	2.05	2,931	.48	681	#		1.46	2,087	.54	773	.44	625	1.6	2,395
Neuquén	29.30	43,070	3.80	5,582	39.26	57,706	2.02	2,972	.53	775	.34	505	#		#		.72	1,052	24.0	35,329
La Pampa	38.35	55,377	4.51	6,508	51.56	74,451	1.92	2,776	.37	537	#		1.93	2,786	#		1.37	1,973	#	
Catamarca	39.51	48,096	.92	1,135	55.98	68,163	1.08	1,336	.37	458	#		#		1.36	1,689	.36	449	.3	527
La Rioja	28.40	29,990	.38	1,532	66.68	70,406	.82	870	.19	202	#		.22	235	1.79	1,891	#		#	
Santa Cruz	38.22	24,233	3.90	2,474	54.77	34,727	1.65	1,046	.21	133	.76	485	2.09	595	#		.48	303	#	
Tierra del Fuego	36.65	10,428	8.34	2,374	42.76	12,167	5.39	1,533	.46	132	.84	238	#		#		.92	261	2.4	728
Total Argentina	32.49	5,523,320	6.27	1,065,900	47.36	8,051,230	2.48	421,602	.26	44,200	.29	49,300	4.55	773,503	1.91	324,701	1.31	222,701	3.08	523,602

1. UCR, Unión Cívica Radical
Al. Centro, Alianza de Centro: Ucede y Demócrata Progresista
Frejupo, Frente Justicialista Popular
Al. Izq. Unida, Alianza Izquierda Unida
Fte. Hum-Verde, Frente Humanista Verde
CFI, Confederación Federalista Independiente
Bl. Jubilados, Partido Blanco de Jubilados
Al. Un. Social., Alianza de Unidad Socialista

SOURCE: *Clarín* (Buenos Aires), May 16 and 17, 1989.

Table 1019

ARGENTINA ELECTION RESULTS, BY POLITICAL PARTY, FEDERAL CAPITAL

(1989)

Party	President/Vice President	%	National Senators	%	National Deputies	%	Council Members	%
Frejupo	737,761	36.65	654,161	32.61	631,905	31.53	640,617	32.14
UCR	730,823	36.30	663,221	33.06	570,138	28.45	614,017	30.81
Alianza de Centro	248,455	12.34	393,062	19.59	442,027	22.06	402,701	20.21
Alianza Federal-CFI	176,153	8.75	135,802	6.77	144,114	7.19	109,927	5.52
Alianza Izquierda Unida	68,056	3.38	89,848	4.48	108,523	5.42	110,385	5.54
Alianza Unidad Socialista	34,375	1.71	50,701	2.53	86,817	4.33	90,836	4.56
Blanco Jubilados	5,768	.29	6,366	.32	6,769	.34	7,930	.40
Obrero	5,438	.27	5,808	.29	6,097	.30	6,741	.34
Frente Humanista-Verde	4,173	.21	5,100	.25	5,812	.29	7,674	.39
Alianza Popular	2,056	.10	1,980	.10	1,882	.09	2,112	.11
Blank Votes	18,940	.93	26,102	1.28	27,213	1.33	39,959	1.96

SOURCE: *Clarín* (Buenos Aires), May 16, 1989, p. 9.

Table 1020

ARGENTINA CONGRESSIONAL ELECTION RESULTS
BY POLITICAL PARTY

(November 3, 1985)

	Chamber of Deputies		
	1983	1985	
Party	Seats Won	Seats Won	Votes Cast
Unión Cívica Radical	129	130	43.5
Movimiento Nacionalista Justicialista	111	103	34.5
Partido Intransigenta	3	6	6.0
Uníon del Centro Democrática	2	3	3.0
Partido Demócrata Cristiano	1	~	~
Other	8	12	13.0
Total	254	254	100.0

SOURCE: *Keesing's Contemporary Archives: Record of World Events* (Oct. 1986), vol. 32, p. 34666.

Table 1021

BOLIVIA CONGRESSIONAL ELECTION RESULTS, BY
POLITICAL PARTY AND CANDIDATE

(June 29, 1980)

Party	Candidate	Seats Won
Unión Democrática Popular[1]	Hernán Siles Zuazo	57
Movimiento Nacionalista Revolucionario Histórico	Víctor Paz Estenssoro	44
Acción Democrática Nacionalista	Hugo Bánzer Suárez	30
Partido Socialista–Uno	Marcelo Quiroga Santa Cruz	11
Others	— —	15
Total	**	157[a]

1. Alliance with Movimiento Nacionalista Revolucionario de Izquierda, Movimiento de la Izquierda Revolucionario, and Partido.

a. Comprising 27 senators and 130 members of the Chamber of Deputies.

SOURCE: *South America, Central America and the Caribbean* (London: Europa Publications Limited 1986), p. 152.

Table 1022

BOLIVIA ELECTION RESULTS, BY POLITICAL PARTY AND DEPARTMENT
(1989)

Department	FSB[1]	MRTKL	FULKA	ADN	CONDEPA	MIR	MIN	PS-1	IU	MNR	Valid	Blank	Null	Total
Chuquisaca														
Votes	542	734	1,037	17,420	684	19,279	875	2,996	15,618	16,559	75,744	4,862	4,647	85,253
%	.64	.86	1.22	20.43	.80	22.61	1.03	3.51	18.32	19.42	88.85	5.70	5.45	
Congress. Seats	0	0	0	4	0	6	0	0	3	3				
La Paz														
Votes	3,455	14,595	11,002	110,341	158,742	92,143	2,672	13,465	22,087	99,222	527,724	22,830	37,807	588,361
%	.59	2.48	1.87	18.75	26.98	15.66	.45	2.29	3.75	16.86	89.69	3.88	6.43	
Congress. Seats	0	0	0	8	11	5	0	0	1	6				
Cochabamba														
Votes	1,182	1,755	1,293	56,326	5,519	56,335	1,752	8,259	31,030	57,908	221,359	12,898	12,102	246,359
%	.48	.71	.52	22.86	2.24	22.87	.71	3.35	12.60	23.51	89.85	5.24	4.91	
Congress. Seats	0	0	0	5	0	6	0	0	3	7				
Oruro														
Votes	517	2,536	1,060	23,933	2,744	27,627	550	3,744	7,395	23,892	93,998	5,184	7,419	106,601
%	.48	2.38	.99	22.45	2.57	25.92	.52	3.51	6.94	22.41	88.18	4.86	6.96	
Congress. Seats	0	0	0	4	0	6	0	0	0	3				
Potosi														
Votes	1,111	2,356	1,278	28,642	2,126	32,502	1,790	4,578	19,281	30,274	123,938	12,093	11,475	147,506
%	.75	1.60	.87	19.42	1.44	22.03	1.21	3.10	13.07	20.52	84.02	8.20	7.78	
Congress. Seats	0	0	0	5	0	8	0	0	3	6				
Tarija														
Votes	247	328	208	16,048	545	16,124	367	565	5,185	27,664	67,281	2,571	3,297	73,149
%	.34	.45	.28	21.94	.75	22.04	.50	.77	7.09	37.82	91.98	3.51	4.51	
Congress. Seats	0	0	0	2	0	4	0	0	0	6				
Santa Cruz														
Votes	2,624	592	479	85,724	2,488	57,482	1,566	5,718	9,869	89,775	256,317	6,544	7,316	270,177
%	.97	.22	.18	31.73	.92	21.26	.58	2.12	3.65	33.23	94.87	2.42	2.71	
Congress. Seats	0	0	0	7	0	4	0	0	0	9				
Beni														
Votes	836	77	52	15,583	542	6,251	96	337	2,572	14,667	41,013	1,460	4,829	47,302
%	1.77	.16	.11	32.94	1.15	13.22	.20	.71	5.44	31.01	86.70	3.09	10.21	
Congress. Seats	0	0	0	6	0	1	0	0	0	5				
Pando														
Votes	94	10	7	3,281	69	1,290	19	101	472	3,152	8,495	184	403	9,082
%	1.04	.11	.08	36.13	.76	14.20	.21	1.11	5.20	34.71	93.54	2.03	4.44	
Congress. Seats	0	0	0	5	0	1	0	0	0	4				
Total														
Votes	10,608	22,983	16,416	357,298	173,459	309,033	9,687	39,763	113,509	363,113	1,415,869	68,626	89,295	1,573,790
%	.67	1.46	1.04	22.70	11.02	19.64	.62	2.53	7.21	23.07	89.97	4.36	5.67	
Congress. Seats	0	0	0	46	11	41	0	0	10	49				
Percent	.67	1.46	1.04	22.7	11.02	19.4	.62	2.53	7.21	23.07		4.36	5.67	100

1. FSB, Falange Socialista Boliviana
   MRTKL, Movimiento Revolucionario Tupac-Katari Liberación
   ADN, Acción Democrática Nacionalista
   MIR, Movimiento de Izquierda Revolucionaria
   MIN, Movimiento de Izquierda Nacional
   PS-1, Partido Socialista-1
   IU, Izquierda Unida
   MNR, Movimiento Nacionalista Revolucionario

SOURCE: U.S. Embassy, La Paz, Political Section, June 20, 1989.

Table 1023

BOLIVIA PRESIDENTIAL AND CONGRESSIONAL ELECTION RESULTS, BY POLITICAL PARTY AND CANDIDATE
(July 14, 1985)

Party	Candidate	As % of Total Votes Cost	Votes Received	Congressional Seats Won
Acción Democrática Nacionalista	Hugo Bánzer Suárez	28.6	493,735	51
Movimiento Nacionalista Revolucionario Histórico	Víctor Paz Estenssoro[1]	26.4	456,704	59
Movimiento de la Izquierda Revolucionaria	Jaime Paz Zamora	8.8	153,143	16
Movimiento Nacionalista Revolucionario de la Izquierda	Roberto Jordán Pando	4.8	82,418	8
Movimiento Nacionalista Revolucionario de Vanguardia	Carlos Serrate Reich	4.2	72,197	6
Portido Socialista–Uno	Ramiro Velasco	2.2	38,782	5
Frente Pueblo Unido	Antonio Araníbar Quiroga	2.2	38,124	4
Movimiento Revolucionario Tupaj Katari–Liberación	Flores Santos	1.8	31,678	2
Partido Demócrata Cristiana	Luis Ossio Sanjines	1.4	24,079	3
Falange Socialista Boliviana	David Añez Pedraza	1.2	19,985	3
	Total	81.6	1,410,845	157[a]

1. Since no candidate attained absolute majority, as required by the constitution, Victor Paz Estenssoro was finally elected president after winning a clear majority vote from the new congress.

a. Consists of 130 deputies and 27 senators.

SOURCE: *Keesing's Contemporary Archives: Record of World Events* (Oct. 1985), vol. 31, p. 33905.

Table 1024

BOLIVIA OFFICIAL RESULTS OF MUNICIPAL ELECTIONS, BY DEPARTMENT AND POLITICAL PARTY
(December 7, 1987)

Party	Abbreviation	Chuquisaca	La Paz	Cochabamba	Oruro	Potosí	Tarija	Santa Cruz	Beni	Pando	Total Votes
Acción Democrática Nacionalista	ADN	12,733	124,314	65,700	19,714	16,445	8,469	69,521	17,547	2,269	336,712
Movimiento de Izquierda Revolucionaria	MIR	13,681	156,004	20,684	20,587	34,073	10,378	46,215	6,303	733	308,668
Movimiento Nacionalista Revolucionario	MNR	7,052	33,921	16,635	10,447	17,157	14,632	47,070	10,470	1,486	158,870
Movimiento Bolivia Líbre	MBL	17,671	12,131	35,298	1,419	16,338	1,085	4,808	452	45	89,247
Vanguardia Revolucionaria 9 de Abril	VR-9	1,690	55,769	3,064	3,494	5,439	1,225	1,817	476	~a	72,974
Alianza Patriótica	AP	3,143	32,329	2,097	16,685	6,267	2,433	4,664	2,371	264	70,253
Partido Socialista Uno	PS-1	2,414	13,074	4,756	2,662	3,869	648	18,178	1,186	110	46,897
Frente Revolucionario de Izquierda	FRI	~a	~a	5,021	2,048	5,667	9,696	2,257	~a	~a	24,689
Falange Socialista Boliviana	FSB	1,307	9,350	~a	1,060	1,929	525	5,978	3,121	378	23,648
Movimiento Federalista Democrático	MFD	777	3,079	497	576	~a	544	13,783	220	16	19,492
Movimiento de Izquierda Nacional	MIN	~a	6,528	2,436	~a	~a	~a	9,270	~a	~a	18,234
Partido Demócrata Cristiano	PDC	731	~a	6,799	~a	2,043	~a	~a	400	64	10,037
Izquierda Democrática	ID	~a	7,547	~a	~a	2,346	~a	~a	~a	~a	9,893
Valid Votes		61,199	454,046	162,987	78,702	111,573	49,635	223,561	42,546	5,365	1,189,614
Blank Votes		6,020	30,586	10,723	7,673	11,770	3,285	8,621	1,680	165	80,523
Null Votes		3,932	40,039	9,725	6,725	9,553	2,470	5,643	1,341	111	79,539
Total Votes		71,151	524,671	183,435	93,100	132,896	55,390	237,825	45,567	5,641	1,349,675

a. Did not present a candidate.

SOURCE: *Hoy Internacional* (La Paz), Jan. 3, 1988, p. 6.

Table 1025

BOLIVIA REGISTERED CITIZENS AND VOTES, BY DEPARTMENT, 1985–89

Department	1985 Registered Citizens	1985 Votes	1987 Registered Citizens	1987 Votes	Feb. 17, 1989 Registered Citizens[1]	1985–89 Registered Citizens %	1987–89 Registered Citizens %	1985 Contribution to Elections %	1989 Contribution to Elections %
Chuquisaca	123,845	99,369	92,224	71,479	116,173	93.81	125.97	5.87	5.67
Capital	42,218	36,548	41,560	34,668	48,416	114.68	116.50	2.00	2.36
Provinces	81,627	62,821	50,664	36,811	67,757	83.01	133.74	3.87	3.31
La Paz	718,091	606,207	646,909	525,472	728,087	101.39	112.55	34.06	35.53
Capital	415,378	341,032	423,422	348,511	462,375	111.31	109.20	19.70	22.56
Provinces	302,713	265,175	223,487	176,961	265,712	87.78	118.89	14.36	12.97
Cochabamba	355,596	267,655	306,000	183,100	355,964	100.10	116.33	16.87	17.37
Capital	134,893	100,442	133,500	97,688	149,784	111.04	112.20	6.40	7.31
Provinces	220,703	167,213	172,500	85,412	206,180	93.42	119.52	10.47	10.08
Oruro	136,905	117,735	126,335	84,281	122,276	89.31	96.79	6.49	5.97
Capital	72,239	64,438	78,635	53,368	77,668	107.52	98.77	3.43	3.79
Provinces	64,666	53,297	47,700	30,913	44,608	68.98	93.52	3.07	2.18
Potosí	254,637	200,846	154,201	113,962	187,806	73.75	121.79	12.08	9.16
Capital	55,799	40,801	36,350	30,184	44,655	80.03	122.85	2.65	2.18
Provinces	198,838	160,045	117,851	83,778	143,151	71.99	121.47	9.43	6.99
Tarija	86,786	74,856	67,164	54,615	86,996	100.24	129.53	4.12	4.25
Capital	25,282	22,349	26,494	22,478	29,852	118.08	112.67	1.20	1.46
Provinces	61,504	52,507	40,670	32,137	57,144	92.91	140.51	2.92	2.79
Santa Cruz	357,722	299,542	351,839	205,791	372,203	104.05	105.79	16.97	18.16
Capital	184,020	156,235	196,839	133,381	204,449	111.10	103.87	8.73	9.98
Provinces	173,702	143,307	155,000	72,410	167,754	96.58	108.23	8.24	8.19
Beni	64,509	53,406	60,991	44,537	68,821	106.68	112.84	3.06	3.36
Capital	18,067	13,655	18,497	14,551	19,263	106.62	104.14	.86	.94
Provinces	46,442	39,751	42,494	29,986	49,558	106.71	116.62	2.20	2.42
Pando	10,367	8,767	6,625	5,641	10,900	105.14	164.53	.49	.53
Capital	2,959	2,640	3,199	2,861	3,673	124.13	114.82	.14	.18
Provinces	7,408	6,127	3,426	2,780	7,227	97.56	210.95	.35	.35
Total Electors	2,108,458	1,728,383	1,812,288	1,288,878	2,049,226	97.19	113.07		
Total Capitals	950,855	778,140	958,496	737,690	1,040,135	109.39	108.52		
Total Provinces	1,157,603	950,243	853,792	551,188	1,009,091	87.17	118.19		

1. Data for 1989 are unofficial, taken from votes and registered citizens up to February 17, 1989. Official elections were held May 7, 1989.

SOURCE: *Hoy Internacional* (La Paz), February 17, 1989.

Table 1026

BOLIVIA UNOFFICIAL VOTES, BY POLITICAL PARTY

(1989)

Parties, Fronts, and Coalitions	Abbreviations	Country Valid Votes	Country %	Department of La Paz Valid Votes	Department of La Paz %
Acción Democrática Nacionalista	ADN	326,855	25.36	124,376	23.67
Movimiento de Izquierda Revolucionaria	MIR	298,439	23.15	156,075	29.70
Movimiento Nacionalista Revolucionario	MNR	146,627	11.38	33,992	6.47
Movimiento Bolivia Libre	MBL	86,485	6.71	12,160	2.31
Vanguardia Revolucionaria 9 de Abril	VR-9	71,458	5.54	55,970	10.65
Alianza Patriótica	AP	68,193	5.29	32,464	6.18
Partido Socialista-1	PS-1	45,313	3.52	13,079	2.49
Falange Socialista Boliviana	FSB	22,824	1.77	9,369	1.78
Frente Revolucionario de Izquierda	FRI	22,770	1.77		
Movimiento Federalista Democrático	MFD	18,985	1.47	3,085	.59
Movimiento de Izquierda Nacional	MIN	16,584	1.29	6,539	1.24
Izquierda Democrática	ID	9,582	.74	7,550	1.44
Partido Demócrata Cristiano	PDC	9,511	.74		
Total Valid Votes		1,143,699	88.73	454,659	86.52
Blank Votes		72,224	5.60	30,729	5.85
Null Votes		73,031	5.67	40,084	7.63
Total Votes		1,288,933	100.00		

SOURCE: *Hoy Internacional* (La Paz), February 21, 1989.

Table 1027

BOLIVIA MUNICIPAL ELECTION RESULTS, BY POLITICAL PARTY, 1979–89

Party[a]	1979	1980	1985	1987	1989
ADN	218,597	220,309	493,375	336,684	326,855
MNR	527,184	263,309	455,754	158,906	146,627
UDP	528,969	507,173	~	~	~
MIR	~	~	153,143	308,714	298,439
PS-1	70,657	113,959	38,786	46,897	45,313
FSB	~	21,372	19,985	23,654	22,824
FPU	~	~	38,124	~	~
MBL	~	~	~	89,247	86,485
AP	~	~	~	70,264	68,193
VR-9	~	~	72,197	72,974	71,458
FRI	~	~	~	~	22,770
MFD	~	~	~	~	18,985
MIN	~	~	~	~	16,584
ID	~	~	~	~	9,582
PDC	~	~	~	~	9,511
Other	124,415	133,261	231,472	72,236	~
Blank	54,986	239,882[b]	126,800	80,513	72,224
Null	168,960	~	97,509	79,561	73,031
Valid Votes	1,469,287	1,259,383	1,503,856	1,179,676	1,143,678
Total	1,693,233	1,499,265	1,728,145	1,349,797	1,288,933

a. For complete name of party see table 1024.
b. Null and blank votes in 1980 are combined.

SOURCE: *Hoy Internacional* (La Paz), Jan. 11–17, 1988, p. 6; Feb. 21, 1989.

Table 1028

BOLIVIA NUMBER OF VOTERS, BY DEPARTMENT, 1985–89

Department	1985	1987	1989
La Paz	606,207	525,472	588,361
Santa Cruz	299,542	205,791	270,177
Cochabamba	267,655	183,100	246,359
Oruro	117,735	84,281	106,601
Potosí	200,846	113,962	147,506
Chuquisaca	99,369	71,479	85,253
Tarija	74,856	54,615	73,149
Beni	54,406	44,537	47,302
Pando	8,767	5,641	9,082

SOURCE: *Hoy Internacional* (La Paz), Jan. 11–17, 1988, p. 6.

Table 1029

CHILE ELECTORAL INTENTIONS IN SANTIAGO PLEBISCITE (%, September 1980)

Response	Aug. 25	Aug. 29	Sept. 3	Sept. 5	Sept. 7	Sept. 9
Yes	50.0	45.3	51.0	52.4	58.7	58.4
No	32.1	31.4	32.5	28.4	19.5	19.4
No answer	18.9	23.3	16.5	19.2	21.8	22.2
	(483)	(468)	(433)	(487)	(491)	(448)

SOURCE: SALA, 23-3701.

Table 1030

CHILE COMPARISON OF GALLUP PREDICTIONS WITH ACTUAL VOTE IN SANTIAGO PLEBISCITE
(%, September 1980)

Response	Gallup Forecast	Official Vote in Santiago	Difference
Yes	61.5	62.1	-.6
No	34.8	35.6	-.8
Null	3.6	2.2	+1.4

SOURCE: SALA, 23-3702.

Table 1031

CHILE RESULTS OF PRESIDENTIAL PLEBISCITE
(October 1988)

Response	Votes	%
Yes	2,290,972	44.34
No	2,754,805	53.31
Null	68,108	1.31
Blank	53,292	1.03
Total	5,167,177	100

SOURCE: *El Mercurio*, Edición Internacional, September 29–October 6, 1988.

Table 1032

COLOMBIA PRESIDENTS, 1930–86

Year	President	Political Orientation
1930	Enrique Olaya-Herrera	Liberal
1934	Alfonso López-Pumarejo	Liberal
1938	Eduardo Santos	Liberal
1942	Alfonso López-Pumarejo[1]	Liberal
1945	Alberto Lleras-Camargo	Liberal
1946	Mariano Ospina-Pérez	Conservative
1950	Laureano Gómez[2]	Conservative
1953	Roberto Urdaneta-Arbeláez	Conservative
1953	Gustavo Rojas-Pinilla	Military
1957	Military Junta[3]	Military
1958	Alberto Lleras Camargo	Liberal
1962	Guillermo León-Valencia	Conservative
1966	Carlos Lleras Restrepo	Liberal
1970	Misael Pastrana-Borrero	Conservative
1974	Alfonso López-Michelsen	Liberal
1978	Julio Cesar Turbay-Ayala	Liberal
1982	Belisano Betancur	Conservative
1986	Virgilio Barco-Vargas	Liberal

1. Resigned and was succeeded by Vice President, Alberto Lleras Camargo.
2. Resigned and was succeeded by Vice President, Roberto Urdaneta-Arbeláez.
3. Functioned as interim government following the overthrow of Rojas-Pínilla.

SOURCE: 1930–82 data from *Colombia Today*, 21:3 (1986); and 1986 data from *El Espectador* (Bogotá), May 27, 1986.

Table 1033

COLOMBIA PRESIDENTIAL ELECTION RESULTS,[‡] BY DEPARTMENT AND POLITICAL PARTY CANDIDATE
(1986)

Department	PC[1] Alvaro Laureano Gómez Hurtado	PDC[2,7] Luis Enrique Agudelo-Pino	PH[3] Juan David Pérez-Gracía	PL[4] Virgilio Barco-Vargos	MM[5] Regina Betancourt-de-Liska	UP[6] Jaime Pardo-Leal	Total Voting Tables	Tables Tabulated	% of Tabulated Tables	Non-Registered Candidates	Blank Votes	Null Votes	Total Votes
Antioquia	321,185	890	29	441,271	9,298	32,097	5,194	5,003	99.3	205	5,826	729	811,530
Atlántico	87,066	71	14	185,362	495	9,003	2,033	2,013	99.0	3	1,603	266	283,883

Continued in SALA, 25-1014.

Table 1034

COLOMBIA PRESIDENTIAL WINNING PERCENTAGES, BY POLITICAL PARTY AND CANDIDATE
(1986)

Party	Candidate	Votes Cast[‡]	As % of Total Votes Cast
Partido Conservador	Alvaro Laureano Gómez-Hurtado	2,535,953	35.84
Partido Demócrata Cristiano	Luis Enrique Agudelo-Pino[1]	1,027	#
Partido Humanista	Juan David Pérez–Garciá	438	#
Partido Liberal	Virgilio Barco-Vargas	4,123,716	58.29
Movimiento Metapolítico	Regina Bentancourt-de-Liska	49,745	.70
Unión Patriótica	Jaime Pardo–Leal	312,494	4.42
Blank and Null Votes[2]	~	51,353	.73
Total	**	7,074,726[a]	100.00

1. Withdrew before elections.
2. Includes votes from non-registered candidates and abroad.

a. There were 13 million eligible voters.

SOURCE: Adapted from *El Espectador* (Bogotá), May 22 and 27, 1986.

Table 1035

COLOMBIA PRESIDENTIAL ELECTION RESULTS, 1978 AND 1982[a]
(T)

Regions and Departments	Conservatives		Liberals		"New Liberalism"
	1978	1982	1978	1982	1982
Total	2,357	3,155	2,504	2,749	751
Eastern Region[1]	590	703	564	582	144

Continued in SALA, 24–1009.

Table 1036

COSTA RICA PRESIDENTIAL WINNING PERCENTAGES, 1953–86[a]

Year	President	%
1953	José Figueres	64.70
1958	Mario Echandi	46.42
1962	Francisco J. Orlich	50.29
1966	José Joaquín Trejos	50.47
1970	José Figueres	54.78
1974	Daniel Oduber	43.44
1978	Rodrigo Carazo	50.51
1982	Luis Alberto Monge	58.60
1986	Oscar Arias Sánchez	52.33[a]

a. Refers to valid votes.

SOURCE: Adapted from the following: *La Nación* (San José), Feb. 9, 1982, p. 12A; and *La Nación* (San José), Feb. 13, 1986.

Table 1037

COSTA RICA COMPARATIVE PRESIDENTIAL WINNING PERCENTAGES BETWEEN MAJOR POLITICAL PARTIES, 1982 AND 1986

	Liberación Nacionál				Unidad Social Christiana			
	1982		1986		1982		1986	
Province	Valid Votes	%	Valid Votes	%	Valid Votes	%	Valid Votes	%
San José	230,958	58.3	256,781	54.4	128,623	32.5	207,615	43.8
Alajuela	102,324	59.5	112,298	53.0	61,026	35.5	97,560	45.7
Cartago	65,676	61.9	71,977	54.1	34,806	32.8	58,969	44.3
Heredia	45,976	57.0	53,687	52.8	29,288	36.3	45,972	45.2
Guanacaste	50,215	60.7	46,301	50.0	27,202	34.6	45,011	48.7
Puntarenas	50,215	58.3	51,200	48.2	28,208	32.8	52,319	49.2
Limón	25,526	53.9	27,440	42.4	16,034	33.8	34,988	54.0
Total	568,374	58.8	620,314	52.3	325,187	33.6	542,434	45.8

SOURCE: *La Nación* (San José), Feb. 2, 1986.

Table 1038

COSTA RICA PRESIDENTIAL ELECTION RESULTS, BY PROVINCE AND POLITICAL PARTY
(February 2, 1986)

Province	Registered Voters	Partido Alianza Nacional Cristiana	Partido Inde-pendiente	Partido Liberación Nacional[1]	Partido Unidad Social Cristiana[2]	Alianza Popular (Coalición)	Pueblo Unido (Coalición)	Valid Votes
San José	590,640	2,407	477	256,781	207,615	3,943	2,640	473,863
Alajuela	257,699	721	123	112,928	97,560	1,044	850	213,226
Cartago	161,467	695	140	71,977	58,969	667	538	132,986
Heredia	122,123	503	74	53,687	45,972	778	644	101,658
Guanacaste	114,457	289	117	46,301	45,011	304	440	92,462
Puntarenas	145,609	583	125	51,200	52,319	1,294	757	106,278
Limón	94,479	449	73	27,440	34,988	1,069	730	64,749
Total	1,486,474	5,647	1,129	620,314	542,434	9,099	6,599	1,185,222[a]

1. Oscar Arias Sánchez was the candidate.
2. Rafael Angel Calderón was the candidate.

a. Excludes 26,090 null votes as reported by the U.S. Embassy, Costa Rica.

SOURCE: Adapted from *La Nación* (San José), February 2, 1986.

Table 1039

COSTA RICA PRESIDENTIAL WINNING PERCENTAGES, BY POLITICAL PARTY

(February 2, 1986)

Party	Valid Votes	As % of Registered Voters[1]	As % of Total Valid Votes[2]
Partido Alianza Nacional Cristiana	5,647	.37	.48
Partido Independiente	1,129	.08	.10
Partido Liberación Nacional	620,314	41.73	52.33
Partido Unidad Social Cristiana	542,434	36.49	45.76
Alianza Popular (Coalición)	9,099	.60	.77
Pueblo Unido (Coalición)	6,599	.44	.56
Total	1,185,222	79.71[a]	100.00

1. There were 1,486,474 registered voters.
2. Excludes blank and null votes.

a. This implies an abstention rate, including blank and null ballots, of approximately 20.29%.

SOURCE: Derived from table 1018.

Table 1040

DOMINICAN REPUBLIC PRESIDENTIAL AND CONGRESSIONAL ELECTION RESULTS, BY POLITICAL PARTY AND CANDIDATE

(May 16, 1982)

Party	Candidate	Votes	As % of Total Votes	Congressional Seats Won Senate	Chamber of Deputies
Partido Revolucionario Dominicano	Salvador Jorge Blanco	854,868	50.17	17	62

Continued in SALA, 26-1027.

Table 1041

DOMINICAN REPUBLIC PRESIDENTIAL ELECTION RESULTS, BY POLITICAL PARTY

(May 16, 1986)

Party	Votes	As % of Valid Votes	As % of Registered Votes
Partido Reformista Social Cristiano	855,565	40.51	28.15

Continued in SALA, 25-1021.

Table 1042

ECUADOR PRESIDENTIAL ELECTIONS, FINAL RESULTS, BY PROVINCE AND POLITICAL PARTY

(June 1984)

Province	FRN[1]		CID[2]		Null Votes		Blank Votes		Total		
	Votes	%	Votes	%	Votes	%	Votes	%	Votes	Voters	%
Azuay	47,662	31.97	87,596	58.76	10,809	7.25	2,998	2.01	149,065	191,995	77.64

Continued in SALA, 24-1010.

Table 1043

ECUADOR ABSENTEEISM IN ELECTIONS, BY PROVINCE, 1978 AND 1984

Province	1978				1984			
	Registered N	Participated N	Absentee		Registered[1] N	Participated N	Absentee	
			N	%			N	%
Carchi	43,117	36,501	6,616	15.34	63,981	47,748	16,233	25.37

Continued in SALA, 24-1011.

Table 1044

ECUADOR CONGRESSIONAL ELECTION RESULTS
BY POLITICAL PARTY, 1979–86

(N)

Party	April 1979 (69 seats)	January 1984 (71 seats)	June 1986 (71 seats)
Izquierda Democrática (ID)	15	24	17
Democracia Popular (DP)	0	4	8
Partido Roldocista Ecuatoriano (PRE)	0	3	5
Movimiento Popular Democrático (MPD)	1	3	4
Frente Amplio de Izquierda	0	2	3
Partido Socialista (PSE)	0	1	6
Partido Social Cristiano (PSC)	3	9	15
Partido Demócrata (PD)	0	5	1
Concentración de Fuerzas Populares (CFP)	29	7	4
Frente Radical Alfarista (FRA)	0	6	3
Partido Liberal Radical (PLR)	4	4	3
Partido Conservador (PC)	10	2	1
Partido Nacional Revolucionario (PNR)	2	1	0
Partido Nacional Velasquista	1	0	0
Coalición Institucionalista Democrática	3	0	0
Pueblo, Cambio y Democracia (PCD)	0	0	1

SOURCE: David Corkill and David Cubitt, *Ecuador: Fragile Democracy* (London: Latin America Bureau, 1988).

Table 1045
ECUADOR ELECTIONS FOR PROVINCIAL DEPUTIES, BY POLITICAL PARTY
(June 1984)

Province	PCE[1]	LRE[2]	PD[3]	CFP[4]	DP[5]	SC[6]	PCD[7]	CID[8]	FADI[c]	PRE[10]	FNR[11]	ID[12]	APRE[13]	FRA[14]	MPD[15]	Nacional Velazquista	Socialista Ecuatoriano	Valid Votes	Null Votes	Blank Votes	Total
Pichincha	14,158	44,809	70,661	10,127	20,221	71,820	6,521	5,588	27,869	11,333	3,958	108,950	210	24,166	30,576	1,611	5,133	457,521	45,700	48,963	530,184

Continued in SALA, 24-1012.

Table 1046
ECUADOR PRESIDENTIAL ELECTION RESULTS, CANDIDATES, AND RUNNING MATES[1]
(January 1988)[a]

	Candidate and Running Mate	Party[2]	First Round Vote	% of Valid Vote
1.	Rodrigo Borja / Luis Parodi	ID	506,574	24.1
2.	Sixto Durán / Pablo Baquerizo	PSC	313,990	15.2
3.	Angel Duarte / Teresa Minuche	CFP	154,979	7.4
4.	Abdalá Bucaram / Hugo Caicedo	PRE	368,900	17.6
5.	Frank Vargas / Enrique Ayala	APRE	280,562	13.4
6.	Jamil Mahaud / Juan José Pons	DP	243,002	11.6
7.	Jaime Hurtado / Ernesto Alvarez	MPD FADI	97,767	4.6
8.	Carlos Julio Emanuel / Pedro José Arteta	FRA	66,888	3.2
9.	Miguel Albornez / Roberto Goldblum	PL	29,326	1.4
10.	Guillermo Sotomayor	PR[3]	23,974	1.1

1. First round of elections.
2. See table 1038 for complete names of parties.
3. Newly formed Partido Republicano.
a. Provisional results based on figures from El Comercio 2:2 (1988).

SOURCE: David Corkill and David Cubitt, Ecuador: Fragile Democracy (London: Latin America Bureau, 1988).

Table 1047

ECUADOR PRESIDENTIAL ELECTION RESULTS,
BY PROVINCE AND CANDIDATE[1]

(May 8, 1988)

Province	Rodrigo Borja	Abdalá Bucaram	Null Votes	Blank Votes	Total Votes
Azuay	115,647	40,525	16,561	2,285	175,018
Bolívar	28,048	17,192	8,756	1,015	55,011
Cañar	35,784	19,452	7,936	1,234	64,406
Carchi	29,234	20,509	6,162	661	56,566
Cotopaxi	54,729	35,069	19,203	3,297	112,298
Chimborazo	78,621	34,260	24,334	4,528	141,743
El Oro	67,035	67,597	11,695	1,046	147,373
Esmeraldas	37,900	50,895	10,305	1,106	100,206
Guayas	280,327	575,154	127,689	7,470	990,640
Imbabura	60,348	30,289	16,497	1,796	108,930
Loja	74,469	50,524	14,217	2,044	141,254
Los Ríos	52,050	102,104	23,141	1,739	179,034
Manabí	133,309	171,877	30,417	2,722	338,325
Morona Santiago	15,462	6,591	1,964	279	24,296
Napo	24,297	15,342	5,074	699	45,412
Pastaza	8,121	3,653	1,173	125	13,072
Pichincha	514,417	144,584	71,838	6,594	737,423
Tungurahua	79,710	55,995	23,091	2,514	161,310
Zamora Chinchipe	9,796	5,781	1,792	237	17,606
Galápagos	1,354	1,105	235	18	2,712
Total	1,700,648	1,448,498	422,080	41,409	3,612,635

1. Results refer to second round of voting.

SOURCE: El Comercio (Quito), June 3, 1988.

Table 1048

EL SALVADOR FIRST ROUND PROVISIONAL ELECTION RESULTS,
BY DEPARTMENT AND POLITICAL PARTY

(March 25, 1984)

	Party								Factors						
Department	Arena[1]	PDC[2]	PCN[3]	Mercen[4]	PAISA[5]	PPS[6]	AD[7]	POP[8]	Valid Votes	Null Votes	Abstentions	Contested Votes	Not Used	Lost Ballots	Total
San Salvador	101,834	205,381	44,701	3,066	4,239	6,237	19,196	1,677	386,331	29,606	3,261	1,506	363,536	1,760	791,000

Continued in SALA, 24-1013.

Table 1049

EL SALVADOR ELECTION RESULTS FOR PRESIDENT AND VICE PRESIDENT
(March 1989)

PART I. BY POLITICAL PARTY[1] AND DEPARTMENT

Department	Number of Municipalities	PDC	%	ARENA	%	PCN	%	MAC	%	CD	%	UP	%	AD	%	PAR	%	Total Valid Votes
San Salvador	19	97,252	35.34	147,691	53.67	5,962	2.17	1,590	.58	18,205	6.62	2,036	.74	1,468	.53	962	.35	275,166
Santa Ana	13	35,050	37.32	47,136	50.19	5,512	5.87	775	.83	4,016	4.28	469	.50	603	.64	350	.37	93,911
San Miguel	15	22,917	39.21	30,913	52.89	2,451	4.19	514	.88	1,070	1.83	145	.25	270	.46	169	.29	58,449
La Libertad	22	35,320	33.73	58,776	56.13	3,789	3.62	789	.75	4,532	4.33	549	.52	567	.54	384	.37	104,706
Usulutan	20	14,953	32.82	26,469	58.09	2,165	4.75	709	1.56	806	1.77	152	.33	163	.36	150	.33	45,567
Sonsonate	16	37,525	41.25	46,340	50.94	3,644	4.01	718	.79	1,792	1.97	272	.30	377	.41	295	.32	90,963
La Unión	18	16,286	46.82	16,114	46.33	1,416	4.07	398	1.14	284	.82	90	.26	70	.20	124	.36	34,782
La Paz	20	13,836	32.42	25,125	58.87	1,782	4.18	453	1.06	964	2.26	205	.48	173	.41	139	.33	42,677
Chalatenango	33	10,852	38.35	14,058	49.68	1,765	6.24	896	3.17	376	1.33	174	.61	79	.28	97	.34	28,297
Cuscatlan	16	8,266	23.04	24,280	67.69	1,443	4.02	452	1.26	1,078	3.01	98	.27	145	.40	108	.30	35,870
Ahuchapan	12	20,645	36.49	28,882	51.06	4,022	7.11	970	1.71	1,527	2.70	187	.33	150	.27	187	.33	56,570
Morazan	26	8,244	36.96	10,804	48.44	2,222	9.96	551	2.47	262	1.17	50	.22	77	.35	93	.42	22,303
San Vicente	13	11,579	40.08	15,518	53.71	864	2.99	164	.57	454	1.57	123	.43	115	.40	76	.26	28,893
Cabañas	9	5,644	26.97	13,264	63.39	1,181	5.64	321	1.53	276	1.32	59	.28	106	.51	73	.35	20,924
Total	252	338,369	36.03	505,370	53.82	38,218	4.07	9,300	.99	35,642	3.80	4,509	.49	4,363	.46	3,207	.34	939,078

PART II. BY POLITICAL PARTY[1]

Political Party	Votes	%
PDC	338,369	36.03
ARENA	505,370	53.82
PCN	38,218	4.07
MAC	9,300	.99
CD	35,642	3.80
UP	4,609	.49
AD	4,363	.46
PAR	3,207	.34
Total	939,078	100.00

1. ARENA, Alianza Republicana Nacionalista
PDC, Partido Democrático Cristiano
CD, Convergencia Democrática
PCN, Partido de Conciliación Nacional
UP, Unión Popular
AD, Acción Democrática

SOURCE: U.S. Embassy, San Salvador, Political Section.

Table 1050

EL SALVADOR ELECTION RESULTS, BY POLITICAL PARTY,[1] 1982–89[a]

Political Party	1982	1984	1985	1988	1989
PDC	546,218 (40.1)	549,727 (43.4)	505,338 (52.35)	326,716 (35.1)	338,369 (36.03)
ARENA	402,304 (29.53)	376,917 (29.76)	286,665 (29.7)	447,696 (48.1)	505,370 (53.82)
PCN	261,153 (19.17)	244,556 (19.31)	80,730 (8.36)	78,756 (8.5)	38,218 (4.07)
CD	#	#	#	#	35,642 (3.8)
AD	100,586 (7.38)	43,929 (3.46)	35,565 (3.68)	16,211 (1.7)	4,363 (.46)
MERECEN	#	6,645 (.52)	689 (.071)	#	#
MAC	#	#	#	#	93,000 (.99)
POP	12,574 (.92)	4,677 (.36)	836 (.087)	1,752 (.19)	#
PAISA	#	15,430 (1.21)	33,101 (3.430)	19,609 (2.1)	#
PPS	39,504 (2.9)	24,395 (1.92)	16,344 (1.69)	#	#
Liberación	#	#	#	34,960 (3.8)	#
UP	#	#	#	#	4,609 (.49)
PAR	#	#	2,963 (.31)	5,059 (.54)	3,207 (.34)

1. For names of parties, see table 1049.

a. The data in parentheses refer to the percent of total valid votes received by each party.

SOURCE: *Central America Bulletin*, vol. 8, no. 6, May 1989, p. 6.

Table 1051

EL SALVADOR PRESIDENTIAL ELECTION RESULTS
(March 19, 1989)

Party[1]	Votes	%
ARENA	510,126	53.82
PDC	340,664	36.03
CD	35,794	3.20
MAC	9,151	.94
UP	4,363	.5
AD	4,440	.5
PAR	3,247	.5
Votes in Dispute	5,375	
Unmarked Ballots	7,226	
Annuled Ballots	48,843	
Total Votes	1,008,130	
Total Valid Votes	946,686	
Eligible Voters	3,100,000	
Registered Voters	2,200,000	
Registered Voters Who Received Registration Cards	1,834,000	
Voters	1,008,130	
Valid Votes	946,686	

1. For names of parties, see table 1049.

SOURCE: *Central America Bulletin*, vol. 8, no. 6, May 1989, p. 3.

Table 1052

EL SALVADOR VOTER ABSENTEEISM, 1982–89

Year	Election	Participation (N)	Absenteeism (%)
1982	Constituent Assembly	1,362,339	26.5
1984	President (First Round)	1,419,000	43.1
1984	President (Second Round)	1,520,000	31.5
1985	Assembly and Municipal	1,100,000	52.0
1988	Assembly and Municipal	941,179	60.3
1989	Presidential	946,686	67.4

SOURCE: *Central America Bulletin*, vol. 8, no. 6, May 1989, p. 3.

Table 1053

EL SALVADOR ELECTION RESULTS, BY DEPARTMENT AND MUNICIPALITY
(March 1989)

Department/Municipality	PDC[1]	ARENA	PCN	MAC	CD	UP	AD	PAR	Null Votes	Abstentions	Disputed Votes	Invalid Votes	Left Over	Missing
El Salvador														
San Salvador	36,308	66,279	1,426	524	7,035	753	525	275	2,773	218	48	0	0	0
Ciudad Delgado	6,506	8,572	433	134	1,530	144	130	76	905	75	47	0	0	0
Mejicanos	8,749	10,999	400	178	1,886	159	118	90	964	81	47	0	0	0
Soyapango	11,439	15,124	602	154	2,153	265	202	115	1,113	64	129	0	0	0
Cuscatancingo	2,677	2,390	158	44	498	73	30	32	365	29	35	0	0	0
San Marcos	4,346	5,076	254	121	907	92	65	60	544	71	77	0	0	0
Ilopango	5,364	7,509	274	65	1,122	136	66	67	520	48	68	0	0	0
Nejapa	1,465	1,266	274	42	225	48	36	55	382	57	105	0	0	0
Apopa	5,531	6,675	320	95	1,036	65	83	47	606	154	112	0	0	0
San Martín	3,030	5,665	375	46	372	66	44	27	535	79	131	0	0	0
Panchimalco	1,216	2,781	278	33	144	31	29	14	414	48	66	0	0	0
Aguilares	2,321	3,065	354	31	122	16	34	20	294	46	42	0	0	0
Tonacatepeque	1,239	2,416	158	29	116	33	17	16	219	80	14	0	0	0
Santo Tomás	1,407	2,511	153	20	213	30	23	15	275	147	28	0	0	0
Santiago Texacuangos	650	1,621	115	10	73	25	10	11	171	29	5	0	0	0
El Paisnal	410	300	52	3	6	3	3	2	63	9	2	0	0	0
Guazapa	1,786	1,563	104	23	75	12	9	12	243	62	2	0	0	0
Ayutuxtepeque	2,385	3,060	143	30	651	70	40	25	272	24	10	0	0	0
Rosario de Mora	423	819	89	8	41	15	4	3	97	15	0	0	0	0
Department Total	97,252	147,691	5,962	1,590	18,205	2,036	1,468	962	10,755	1,336	968	0	0	0
Santa Ana														
Santa Ana	16,758	23,410	2,322	445	2,722	251	305	194	2,198	436	344	0	0	0
Chalchuapa	4,781	6,430	860	146	745	167	106	60	1,086	209	83	0	0	0
Metapan	4,812	4,910	495	36	198	15	121	15	448	53	37	0	0	0
Coatepeque	1,389	1,876	372	31	72	7	18	20	366	48	12	0	0	0
El Congo	1,560	2,629	305	30	67	8	13	13	356	61	92	0	0	0
Texistepeque	1,738	1,649	197	22	61	4	16	12	286	39	37	0	0	0
Candelaria de la Frontera	1,901	2,893	350	16	59	5	8	19	377	68	63	0	0	0
San Sebastián Salitrillo	393	554	155	20	33	5	5	3	130	23	0	0	0	0
Santa Rosa Guachipilín	224	546	64	4	5	4	2	3	35	12	0	0	0	0
Santiago de la Frontera	503	929	107	7	12	0	2	2	102	19	0	0	0	0
El Porvenir	423	494	111	7	20	2	1	1	77	32	31	0	0	0
Masahuat	171	370	63	8	22	3	2	5	83	14	1	0	0	0
San Antonio Pajonal	397	446	111	3	0	0	4	3	49	6	14	0	0	0
Department Total	35,050	47,136	5,512	775	4,016	469	603	350	5,593	1,020	714	0	0	0
San Miguel														
San Miguel	15,981	18,604	1,303	280	792	77	209	80	1,379	96	77	0	0	0
Chinameca	826	1,556	68	17	105	7	7	10	207	29	31	0	0	0
El Tránsito	798	2,774	203	31	29	8	9	13	269	42	22	0	0	0
Ciudad Barrios	981	1,188	231	19	22	4	10	10	130	22	48	0	0	0
Chirilagua	689	428	104	8	7	1	2	13	95	1	4	0	0	0
Sesori	144	262	43	5	6	0	3	3	26	9	6	0	0	0
Moncagua	1,081	1,819	187	16	25	7	8	14	180	17	35	0	0	0
Lolotique	599	877	79	30	16	17	5	11	152	6	5	0	0	0
San Jorge	241	741	59	47	12	1	3	5	98	6	37	0	0	0
Chapeltique	271	392	52	6	9	0	1	2	45	0	15	0	0	0
Quelepa	241	734	60	39	5	2	6	2	61	9	0	0	0	0
Nueva Guadalupe	524	717	20	8	36	19	4	3	74	13	23	0	0	0
Uluazapa	259	492	20	6	4	2	1	0	52	8	0	0	0	0
Comacaran	212	259	20	1	2	0	2	1	15	3	0	0	0	0
San Antonio del Mosco	70	70	2	1	0	0	0	2	8	18	0	0	0	0
Department Total	22,917	30,913	2,451	514	1,070	145	270	169	2,791	273	303	0	0	0

Table 1053 (Continued)

EL SALVADOR ELECTION RESULTS, BY DEPARTMENT AND MUNICIPALITY
(March 1989)

Department/Municipality	PDC[1]	ARENA	PCN	MAC	CD	UP	AD	PAR	Null Votes	Abstentions	Disputed Votes	Invalid Votes	Left Over	Missing
La Libertad														
Nueva San Salvador	7,808	15,832	614	173	1,845	195	140	82	1,096	114	42	722	17,416	16
Quezaltepeque	3,614	5,048	461	66	717	45	81	61	863	173	111	4	10,055	1
Ciudad Arce	3,491	3,674	409	52	251	43	42	44	0	0	0	0	0	0
San Juan Opico	3,671	4,936	285	113	169	38	56	33	501	49	74	1,618	5,860	2
Colón	2,950	5,288	349	64	366	35	83	34	747	130	41	6	6,391	8
La Libertad	3,100	3,230	253	42	189	59	39	16	412	55	100	37	7,551	0
Antiguo Cuscatlan	2,416	5,040	100	51	502	65	30	22	200	23	1	321	4,429	1
Comasagua	727	1,553	152	41	22	4	9	9	205	51	13	3	2,010	1
San Pablo Tacachico	1,171	1,273	211	12	67	2	7	13	198	40	67	9	4,127	2
Jayaque	531	1,737	79	14	88	6	20	9	195	25	0	1	1,794	0
Huizucar	418	1,067	91	5	21	7	1	6	202	17	22	7	836	0
Tepecoyo	614	1,389	91	12	24	14	6	8	164	37	0	0	1,241	0
Teotepeque	535	1,053	79	11	16	5	3	7	137	15	6	3	2,030	0
Chiltiupan	607	1,270	82	29	15	1	3	1	124	6	14	1	1,146	1
Nuevo Cuscatlan	471	985	44	15	31	6	6	6	119	39	9	1	967	2
Tamanique	347	747	53	2	16	2	2	2	140	44	0	0	1,342	3
Sacacoyo	606	959	67	9	26	1	4	5	122	20	12	12	1,148	3
San José Villanueva	365	815	77	18	36	1	8	4	122	10	18	7	1,218	1
Zaragoza	811	1,368	203	28	109	16	14	9	257	29	9	4	2,540	2
Talnique	389	668	35	11	7	3	5	3	64	2	0	3	895	0
San Matías	477	487	34	18	14	1	7	8	85	2	12	0	921	0
Jicalapa	201	357	20	3	1	1	1	2	40	2	6	1	565	0
Department Total	35,320	58,776	3,789	789	4,532	549	567	384	5,993	898	557	2,760	74,482	43
San Vicente														
San Vicente	5,100	7,868	315	64	253	55	53	25	593	91	77	23	7,357	17
Tecoluca	291	493	34	5	13	4	4	7	77	17	4	158	372	1
San Sebastián	1,042	1,397	69	39	41	21	12	7	90	27	33	2	2,920	0
Apastepeque	1,571	1,104	100	20	53	8	15	12	133	53	25	1	3,503	1
San Esteban Catarina	324	291	51	1	12	1	1	1	37	13	3	0	465	0
San Ildefonso	529	494	60	7	8	1	5	3	85	18	3	165	1,766	0
Santa Clara	242	206	8	7	4	1	1	4	16	1	4	4	806	0
San Lorenzo	315	402	30	3	1	1	0	0	43	3	20	9	672	0
Verapaz	442	852	43	5	15	20	9	3	83	29	17	0	881	2
Guadalupe	303	1,139	31	4	7	3	4	5	65	17	0	3	821	0
Santo Domingo	751	591	33	4	20	2	7	7	77	19	23	4	1,163	0
San Cayetano Istepeque	300	396	32	3	22	1	2	0	41	3	6	3	691	0
Tepetitan	369	285	38	7	5	5	2	2	32	12	0	9	720	1
Department Total	11,579	15,518	864	164	454	123	115	76	1,372	303	215	381	22,137	22
Cabañas														
Sensuntepeque	1,952	4,975	325	109	129	31	33	33	463	50	17	0	0	0
Ilobasco	2,324	5,556	568	159	109	12	60	23	394	52	105	0	0	0
Victoria	284	870	58	24	20	2	3	6	116	13	2	0	0	0
San Isidro	548	899	25	15	6	6	6	5	84	9	8	0	0	0
Jutiapa	9	15	2	0	0	0	0	0	1	0	1	0	0	0
Tejutepeque	171	204	83	3	6	1	2	3	100	31	3	0	0	0
Dolores	177	389	49	1	2	3	0	3	37	6	14	0	0	0
Cinquera	7	16	2	1	0	0	0	0	0	0	0	0	0	0
Guacotecti	172	340	69	9	4	4	1	0	23	5	4	0	0	0
Department Total	5,644	13,264	1,181	321	276	59	106	73	1,218	166	154	0	0	0

Table 1053 (Continued)

EL SALVADOR ELECTION RESULTS, BY DEPARTMENT AND MUNICIPALITY
(March 1989)

Department/Municipality	PDC[1]	ARENA	PCN	MAC	CD	UP	AD	PAR	Null Votes	Abstentions	Disputed Votes	Invalid Votes	Left Over	Missing
Usulutan														
Usulutan	3,630	8,499	633	163	313	33	62	46	729	78	59	0	0	0
Jiquilisco	1,733	2,021	183	240	77	15	14	15	321	27	51	0	0	0
Berlin	1,511	1,569	144	38	67	12	12	6	176	33	15	0	0	0
Santiago de María	1,585	2,455	149	38	69	18	15	10	237	32	26	0	0	0
Jucuapa	708	1,882	115	38	100	10	6	10	168	30	47	0	0	0
Santa Elena	452	1,338	137	30	12	6	4	3	172	22	10	0	0	0
Ozatlan	680	707	58	26	8	6	2	11	132	6	0	0	0	0
Estanzuelas	325	796	57	6	16	2	2	4	57	14	12	0	0	0
Mercedes UMA#A	604	884	133	12	22	0	5	0	135	26	0	0	0	0
Alegría	274	320	97	20	7	4	5	4	50	11	13	0	0	0
Concepción Batres	409	811	61	16	16	2	7	5	84	5	0	0	0	0
Puerto El Triunfo	1,398	1,413	100	12	21	30	10	6	177	13	2	0	0	0
Tecapan	412	538	47	20	21	0	0	6	76	6	14	0	0	0
San Dionisio	98	122	49	1	1	0	1	1	14	0	3	0	0	0
Ereguayquin	229	715	42	18	7	5	3	5	49	8	26	0	0	0
Santa María	235	722	47	14	14	2	5	4	94	12	0	0	0	0
Nueva Granada	63	369	36	0	2	2	2	1	47	6	0	0	0	0
El Triunfo	220	589	40	0	15	1	1	7	49	18	16	0	0	0
San Buenaventura	249	271	11	3	10	1	0	3	31	3	0	0	0	0
California	138	348	26	14	8	7	2	3	39	7	0	0	0	0
Department Total	14,953	26,469	2,165	709	806	152	163	150	2,837	357	296	0	0	0
Sonsonate														
Sonsonate	10,439	11,396	684	204	735	96	130	89	1,276	123	64	0	0	0
Izalco	4,207	7,388	417	69	153	36	41	40	1,051	103	64	4	6,907	21
Acajutla	6,387	3,592	431	89	164	18	44	36	618	88	106	12	6,748	13
Armenia	2,722	4,483	440	89	204	32	48	35	655	83	52	3	1,653	0
Nahuizalco	3,246	4,083	275	46	130	15	24	14	612	83	95	5	3,672	0
Juayua	1,761	3,314	340	32	119	23	21	21	421	64	57	5	0	0
San Julian	1,849	1,787	147	21	51	6	14	15	228	28	17	1	2,136	0
Sonzacate	980	1,556	189	42	71	17	22	10	251	32	0	0	1,329	0
San Antonio del Monte	1,056	1,327	126	17	82	16	11	7	243	28	12	1	1,275	0
Nahulingo	988	853	122	38	31	6	0	3	175	20	41	4	1,019	0
Cuisnahuat	900	1,205	117	6	4	2	4	6	78	24	30	0	1,224	0
Santa Catarina Masahuat	825	841	70	20	12	1	6	5	85	11	1	5	805	1
Caluco	751	592	94	4	7	0	5	5	118	12	0	0	811	1
Santa Isabel Ishuatan	697	630	70	11	10	2	2	2	72	8	20	0	866	0
Salcoatitan	280	1,033	83	17	8	2	2	3	68	16	4	3	581	0
Santo Domingo de Guzmán	437	760	39	13	11	0	3	4	82	2	6	2	740	1
Department Total	37,525	46,340	3,644	718	1,792	272	377	295	6,033	725	569	40	29,766	37
La Unión														
La Unión	6,039	3,947	273	81	134	18	19	16	608	125	95	3	9,628	14
Santa Rosa de Lima	2,406	2,313	190	47	35	31	11	17	226	16	20	3	5,480	5
Pasaquina	1,260	1,142	72	15	12	1	3	11	141	10	23	2	3,894	14
San Alejo	696	1,118	90	24	12	2	5	11	92	22	36	4	2,987	2
Anamoros	267	744	59	9	18	1	4	7	60	18	2	4	5,400	7
El Carmen	913	975	107	51	9	2	5	10	105	8	23	14	2,576	2
Conchagua	1,080	830	75	7	23	24	4	5	147	12	27	0	1,965	1
El Sauce	352	792	32	5	5	0	4	2	114	7	11	11	1,970	2
Lislique	36	81	15	1	2	0	1	2	30	7	1	0	1,026	1
Yucuaiquin	360	525	44	52	3	1	2	3	108	4	1	0	1,591	2
Nueva Esparta	460	472	75	8	6	1	4	15	94	8	1	0	1,852	0
Poloros	117	410	91	3	2	1	3	1	32	12	98	0	1,936	2
Bolivar	481	702	10	26	2	0	0	3	26	6	2	0	826	19
Concepción de Oriente	289	422	37	6	9	0	0	9	62	3	51	9	2,077	3
Intipuca	679	591	94	38	7	2	2	6	51	27	37	0	1,482	3
San José las Fuentes	298	409	13	2	2	0	0	1	38	8	0	0	431	3
Yayantique	447	403	49	22	3	1	3	0	57	3	6	1	1,086	2
Meanguera del Golfo	106	238	90	1	0	3	1	6	47	21	0	0	701	0
Department Total	16,286	16,114	1,416	398	284	90	70	124	2,038	316	426	51	46,908	79

Table 1053 (Continued)

EL SALVADOR ELECTION RESULTS, BY DEPARTMENT AND MUNICIPALITY

(March 1989)

Department/Municipality	PDC[1]	ARENA	PCN	MAC	CD	UP	AD	PAR	Null Votes	Abstentions	Disputed Votes	Invalid Votes	Left Over	Missing
La Paz														
Zacatecoluca	5,021	7,317	441	235	653	74	92	57	926	106	144	0	0	0
Santiago Nonualco	1,390	3,496	209	44	39	17	14	19	221	33	67	0	0	0
San Pedro Masahuat	380	755	17	10	7	1	2	0	52	8	0	0	0	0
Olocuilta	737	1,949	174	13	70	10	13	9	192	33	7	0	0	0
San Francisco Chinameca	111	629	47	8	8	2	3	2	25	5	3	0	0	0
San Juan Talpa	343	841	76	8	7	6	2	2	71	11	2	0	0	0
El Rosario	686	1,274	84	10	42	7	13	11	108	19	29	0	0	0
San Rafael Obrajuelo	635	1,176	58	11	21	14	9	1	61	14	8	0	0	0
Santa María Ostuma	116	876	133	4	15	18	2	2	95	18	8	0	0	0
San Luis Talpa	1,081	1,397	76	11	25	6	5	10	186	24	6	0	0	0
San Antonio Masahuat	204	488	14	33	2	6	1	1	25	9	4	0	0	0
San Miguel Tepezontes	141	1,056	60	4	5	19	0	3	45	11	1	0	0	0
San Juan Tepezontes	128	440	49	3	4	2	2	0	44	15	0	0	0	0
Tapalhuaca	111	431	97	8	8	1	3	3	38	7	0	0	0	0
Cuyultitan	334	564	34	15	17	5	2	2	34	16	10	0	0	0
Paraíso de Osorio	74	511	8	7	8	4	2	1	28	5	0	0	0	0
San Emigdio	59	461	16	4	5	1	0	2	20	13	0	0	0	0
Jerusalén	77	286	58	3	2	3	1	5	32	7	0	0	0	0
Mercedes la Ceiba	80	40	29	3	6	1	1	0	6	5	0	0	0	0
San Luis La Herradura	2,128	1,138	102	19	24	8	6	9	177	27	18	0	0	0
Department Total	13,836	25,125	1,782	453	964	205	173	139	2,386	386	299	0	0	0
Chalatenango														
Chalatenango	2,114	3,038	264	70	124	46	20	14	431	58	25	6	4,587	3
Nueva Concepción	2,166	2,237	436	444	75	42	7	21	265	31	62	17	7,397	0
La Palma	796	870	116	48	33	2	4	3	136	0	8	1	3,367	0
Tejutla	308	630	51	126	7	12	2	2	57	11	0	582	2,392	0
La Reina	200	654	138	13	14	5	4	4	0	0	0	0	1,975	0
Arcatao	31	99	11	0	0	0	1	0	13	2	0	0	443	1
San Ignacio	350	439	72	33	4	1	0	3	60	5	0	0	2,032	0
Dulce Nombre de María	124	93	31	0	2	1	1	1	22	1	50	0	275	0
Citala	430	774	20	3	5	1	0	2	74	16	5	1	1,065	1
Agua Caliente	202	202	55	8	16	2	4	11	77	20	25	0	1,176	0
Concepción Quezaltepeque	634	765	70	18	5	8	6	9	69	21	0	3	1,593	0
Nueva Trinidad	148	160	17	3	3	4	1	2	36	6	7	11	499	0
Las Vueltas	41	106	0	2	1	1	0	1	5	6	0	0	123	7
Comalapa	397	180	47	11	8	10	9	1	26	18	17	0	769	7
San Rafael	295	411	60	9	8	0	1	2	36	11	20	0	947	0
Las Flores	81	138	10	1	2	0	0	0	15	1	3	0	349	0
Ojos de Agua	22	84	1	1	0	1	0	0	6	0	0	0	785	0
Nombre de Jesús	81	57	30	1	11	0	0	2	11	2	8	9	1,007	5
Potonico	51	46	3	0	1	0	0	0	4	1	0	5	489	0
San Francisco Morazan	89	182	26	7	2	2	4	1	6	0	2	0	279	0
Santa Rita	353	462	14	2	5	0	4	1	49	7	20	0	583	0
La Laguna	267	245	85	11	7	1	3	4	71	17	0	0	789	0
San Isidro Labrador	24	34	5	1	0	0	0	0	9	0	0	0	227	0
San Antonio de la Cruz	140	42	9	1	2	0	1	1	5	23	12	0	387	0
El Paraíso	858	944	148	62	27	16	8	8	142	0	11	0	2,256	2
San Miguel de Mercedes	268	353	11	2	11	4	5	1	20	6	1	0	516	2
San Luis del Carmen	70	239	4	4	0	1	0	0	21	0	0	0	261	0
Cancasque	20	14	4	12	0	0	0	0	1	0	0	0	549	0
San Antonio los Ranchos	14	31	6	0	2	2	0	1	5	1	0	0	237	0
El Carrizal	19	22	5	1	0	0	0	0	2	0	0	0	851	0
San Fernando	4	4	2	0	0	0	0	0	0	0	0	0	289	0
Azacualpa	128	323	11	0	0	4	0	0	33	4	0	0	396	1
San Francisco Lempa	127	180	3	1	1	9	0	1	10	0	4	0	263	1
Department Total	10,852	14,058	1,765	896	376	174	79	97	1,717	268	280	635	39,153	22

Table 1053 (Continued)

EL SALVADOR ELECTION RESULTS, BY DEPARTMENT AND MUNICIPALITY
(March 1989)

Department/Municipality	PDC[1]	ARENA	PCN	MAC	CD	UP	AD	PAR	Null Votes	Abstentions	Disputed Votes	Invalid Votes	Left Over	Missing
Cuscatlan														
Cojutepeque	3,287	8,511	404	209	606	48	63	38	722	84	51	0	9,697	10
Suchitoto	526	786	59	22	21	3	4	2	124	46	1	0	1,106	0
San Pedro Perulapan	604	2,636	97	11	44	1	4	8	248	52	32	3	4,359	2
San José Guayabal	435	955	83	7	30	1	3	11	134	49	7	15	1,570	2
Tenancingo	64	116	28	0	7	0	2	2	26	7	0	0	588	0
San Rafael Arcangel o Cedros	899	1,788	196	10	72	7	11	9	166	21	30	2	2,489	0
Candelaria	236	1,474	71	5	20	0	4	4	80	18	0	2	1,089	2
El Carmen	247	1,233	110	12	21	2	6	3	99	24	1	1	1,215	0
Monte San Juan	74	1,354	81	6	16	1	4	5	64	9	27	1	1,086	0
San Cristóbal	358	1,144	36	38	34	2	6	3	68	15	0	0	995	3
Santa Cruz Michapa	296	1,019	86	21	30	3	9	6	119	11	19	0	1,381	2
San Bartolome Perulapia	504	921	55	58	97	11	24	7	130	26	6	354	1,106	1
San Ramón	287	732	28	19	55	3	1	2	35	9	14	0	911	0
El Rosario	82	711	56	25	10	1	2	4	56	14	0	0	609	0
Oratorio de Concepción	215	502	21	0	9	0	5	0	57	14	0	0	377	0
Santa Cruz Analquito	152	398	32	9	6	17	0	4	27	7	0	2	520	0
Department Total	8,266	24,280	1,443	452	1,078	98	145	108	2,155	406	187	378	29,098	20
Ahuachapan														
Ahuachapan	6,023	10,008	1,702	556	837	114	77	69	1,438	223	125	0	0	0
Atiquizaya	2,047	3,689	596	95	402	14	20	28	606	120	19	0	0	0
San Francisco Menendez	2,564	3,390	152	22	43	15	11	20	231	39	34	0	0	0
Tacuba	2,546	1,845	390	24	55	11	3	9	343	94	70	0	0	0
Concepción de Ateco	1,287	1,985	352	36	53	6	9	19	305	62	22	0	0	0
Jujutla	1,378	1,115	114	21	19	5	3	4	165	13	1	0	0	0
Guaymango	1,851	1,521	126	27	23	1	8	6	297	25	0	0	0	0
Apaneca	673	1,536	232	53	27	5	5	6	244	61	5	0	0	0
San Pedro Puxtla	926	954	116	22	17	6	5	7	113	16	25	0	0	0
San Lorenzo	602	852	47	8	8	0	3	6	52	8	2	0	0	0
Turin	454	981	113	97	29	5	4	8	112	30	14	0	0	0
El Refugio	294	1,006	82	9	14	5	5	5	76	18	10	0	0	0
Department Total	20,645	28,882	4,022	970	1,527	187	150	187	3,982	709	327	0	0	0
Morazan														
San Francisco Gotera	1,066	2,208	358	91	77	7	16	8	251	80	37	834	4,406	4
Jocoro	1,254	934	154	72	31	3	4	4	110	25	21	31	2,757	0
Corinto	1,049	950	209	14	9	3	5	6	296	41	4	0	5,219	0
Sociedad	593	678	101	8	16	3	8	3	316	17	0	0	2,310	0
Cacaopera	385	448	360	17	20	4	8	16	243	9	0	0	2,100	0
Guatajiagua	154	136	22	4	0	4	2	2	63	10	5	0	2,013	7
El Divisadero	600	468	104	4	13	2	3	2	89	3	5	3	1,590	7
Jocoaitique	96	101	16	19	2	1	2	2	17	5	0	0		0
Osicala	354	1,390	203	74	16	4	8	10	185	11	44	1	2,287	1
Chilanga	567	508	137	39	21	4	8	9	193	5	1	0	2,064	2
Meanguera	48	61	10	1	1	0	0	0	17	11	0	0	162	0
Torola	45	43	12	1	0	0	0	0	5	2	0	0	492	0
San Simón	244	488	73	45	8	2	0	8	81	0	3	0	0	0
Delicias de Concepción	370	627	92	30	8	7	2	5	111	10	53	0	882	0
Joateca	19	77	6	2	0	0	0	0	5	2	1	0	0	0
Arambala	47	82	5	4	1	0	0	1	11	2	1	0	0	0
Lolotiquillo	423	216	40	6	5	0	0	3	73	6	0	0	0	0
Yamabal	23	138	7	0	2	1	0	1	0	3	11	18	718	7
Yoloaiquin	271	204	45	68	1	1	0	3	71	0	0	0	0	0
San Carlos	231	416	40	28	13	2	4	0	64	9	2	166	218	7
El Rosario	23	25	3	4	1	0	0	0	2	0	0	0	244	0

Table 1053 (Continued)

EL SALVADOR ELECTION RESULTS, BY DEPARTMENT AND MUNICIPALITY
(March 1989)

Department/Municipality	PDC[1]	ARENA	PCN	MAC	CD	UP	AD	PAR	Null Votes	Abstentions	Disputed Votes	Invalid Votes	Left Over	Missing
Morazan (Continued)														
Perquin	35	65	7	2	0	0	0	0	7	0	0	0	784	0
Sensembra	57	151	53	8	11	2	2	3	26	0	5	0	382	0
Gualococti	238	252	153	6	6	1	6	6	67	8	0	0	153	2
San Fernando	18	32	8	3	0	0	0	0	7	1	0	0	231	2
San Isidro	34	106	4	1	0	0	0	0	2	0	0	0	0	0
Department Total	8,244	10,804	2,222	551	262	50	77	93	2,312	246	189	1,053	29,012	23

1. For names of parties, see table 1049.

SOURCE: U.S. Embassy, San Salvador.

Table 1054

EL SALVADOR ELECTION RESULTS FOR THE CONSTITUENT ASSEMBLY, BY POLITICAL PARTY
(March 31, 1985)[a]

Party	Seats Won
Partido Demócrata Cristiano	33

Continued in SALA, 26-1033.

Table 1055

EL SALVADOR SECOND ROUND PROVISIONAL ELECTION RESULTS, BY DEPARTMENT AND POLITICAL PARTY
(May 6, 1984)

Department	Arena[1]	PDC[2]	Valid Votes	Null Votes	Abstentions	Contested Votes	Not Used	Lost Ballots	Total
San Salvador	156,460	278,786	435,246	25,678	6,840	1,917	319,312	1,513	790,506

Continued in SALA, 24-1014.

Table 1056

GUATEMALA PRESIDENTIAL ELECTION RESULTS,[1] BY POLITICAL PARTY AND CANDIDATE

(March 7, 1982)

Candidate	Political Party	Votes Received	As % of Total Votes
Angel Aníbal Guevara	Coalition with Partido Institucional, Partido Revolucionario, and Frente de Unidad Nacional	379,051	38.9

Continued in SALA, 26-1035.

Table 1057

GUATEMALA CONGRESSIONAL ELECTION RESULTS, BY POLITICAL PARTY

(July 1, 1984)

Party	Seats Won
Movimiento de Liberación Nacional and Central Auténtica Nacionalista Coalition	23

Continued in SALA, 27-1046.

Table 1058

GUATEMALA PRESIDENTIAL AND CONGRESSIONAL ELECTION RESULTS, BY POLITICAL PARTY AND CANDIDATE

(November 3, 1985)

Party	Candidate	As % of Total Votes Cast[1]	Congressional Seats Won
Partido Democracia Cristiana Guatemalteca	Vinicio Cerezo[a]	38.7	51

Continued in SALA, 27-1047.

Table 1059

GUATEMALA MUNICIPAL ELECTION RESULTS, BY POLITICAL PARTY

(April 24, 1988)

Party	Political Orientation	Number of Mayoral Posts Won
Democracia Cristiana Guatemalteca (DCG)	Center	140
Unión del Centro Nacional (UCN)	Center	56
Movimiento de Liberación Nacional (MLN)	Right	12
Partido Revolucionario (PR)	Center-Right	9
Partido de Cooperación Nacional (PDCN)	Right	3
Movimiento de Acción Solidario (MAS)	Right	2
La Central Auténtica Nacional (CAN)	Right	1
Partido Institucional Democrático (PID)	Right	1
Partido Socialista Democrático (PSD)	Left	1
Frente de Unidad Nacional (FUN)	Right	0
Partido Nacional Revolucionario (PNR)	Right	0
Movimiento Emergente de Concordancia (MEC)	Right	0
Right-Wing Coalition		34
Civil Committees		12
Total		271

SOURCE: *Inforpress Centroamericana*, April 28, 1988.

Table 1060

HAITI PRESIDENTIAL ELECTION RESULTS, BY POLITICAL PARTY AND CANDIDATE

(January 1988)

Party and Candidate	Votes	%
Social Christian Party		
Grégoire Eugène	97,556	9.19
National Democratic Progressive Party		
Leslie Manigat	534,080	50.29
Movement for National Organization		
Gérard Philippe-August	151,391	14.25
Other Parties	68,447	6.45
Hubert de Ronceray	210,526	19.82
Total	1,062,000	100.00

SOURCE: *Keesing's Contemporary Archives*, February 1988.

Table 1061

HONDURAS PRESIDENTIAL ELECTION RESULTS

(1981)

Department	PDCH[1]	PINU[2]	PL[3]	PN[4]	Total Valid Votes	Blank Votes	Null Votes	Total Votes
Atlántida	701	2,031	33,900	21,879	58,511	885	1,102	60,498

Continued in SALA, 23–3411.

Table 1062

HONDURAS REGISTERED POLITICAL PARTIES
(November 1985)

Party	Leader	Political Inclination
Partido Demócrata Cristiano	Efrain Díaz Arrivillaga	Moderate left

Continued in SALA, 26-1039.

Table 1063

HONDURAS CURRENT AND AMENDED CONGRESSIONAL APPORTIONMENT, BY DEPARTMENT AND POLITICAL PARTY, 1981–85
(N)

Department	PDCH[1]	PINU[2]	PL[3]	PN[4]	1981 Total	1985 Total
Atlántida	--	--	2	3	4	8
Colón	--	--	1	1	2	4

Continued in SALA, 26-1040.

Table 1064

HONDURAS PRESIDENTIAL WINNING PERCENTAGES, BY POLITICAL PARTY AND CANDIDATE
(1985)

Party	Candidate	Valid Votes	As % of Total Valid Votes
Partido Demócrata Cristiano de Honduras	Hernán Corrales Padilla	30,173	1.9

Continued in SALA, 26-1041.

Table 1065

HONDURAS PRESIDENTIAL ELECTION RESULTS, BY DEPARTMENT AND CANDIDATE

(1985)

Department	PDCH[1]	PINU[2]	PL[3]				PN[4]		
	Hernán Corrales Padilla	Enrique Aguilar Paz	Oscar Mejía Arellano	Efraín By Girón	José Azcona del Hoyo	Carlos Roberto Reina	Rafael Leonardo Callejas	Fernando Lardizábal	Juan Pablo Urrutia
Atlántida	1,110	1,273	6,633	3,876	27,825	2,869	31,102	886	1,498
Colón	1,032	587	9,861	1,103	11,391	1,212	16,441	431	178

Continued in SALA, 26-1042.

Table 1066

HONDURAS PRESIDENTIAL ELECTION RESULTS, BY DEPARTMENT AND POLITICAL PARTY

(1985)

Department	PDCH[1]	PINU[2]	PL[3]	PN[4]	Blank Votes	Null Votes	Total Valid Votes[5]	Other[6]	Total Votes[7]
Atlántida	1,110	1,273	41,499	33,595	1,394	1,279	80,150	7,526	98,579
Colón	1,032	587	23,719	17,147	921	911	44,317	~	55,818

Continued in SALA, 26-1043.

Table 1067

MEXICO GUBERNATORIAL ELECTIONS IN BAJA CALIFORNIA, 1953-89

Year	Candidate (Party)[1]	Votes
1953	Lic. Braulio Maldonado (PRI)[1]	60,006
	Dr. Francisco Cañedo (PAN)	4,864
1959	Ing. Eligio Esquivel Méndez (PRI)	89,558
	Lic. Salvador Rosas Magallón (PAN)	46,570
1965	Ing. Raúl Sánchez Díaz (PRI)	102,719
	Norberto Corella Gil (PAN)	37,373
1971	Lic. Milton Castellanos Everardo (PRI)	148,495
	Lic. Salvador Rosas Magallón (PAN)	82,291
1977	Roberto de la Madrid Romandia (PRI)	181,760
	Lic. Héctor Terán Terán	89,574
	Prof. Pánfilo Orozco (PPS)	5,641
	Sr. Blas Manrique (PCM)	2,169
1983	Lic. Xicotencati Leyva (PRI-PST)	268,929
	Lic. Héctor Terán Terán	121,818
	Sr. José Luis Alonso (PDM-PSUM)	10,215
	Prof. Sergio Quiroz Miranda (PPS)	5,510
	Sr. Roberto Mota Fabela (PRT)	2,235
1989	Lic. Ernesto Ruffo Appel (PAN)	204,507
	Lic. Margarita Ortega (PRI)	163,245

1. PRI, Partido Revolucionario Institucional
PAN, Partido de Acción Nacional
PPS, Partido Popular Socialista
PCM, Partido Comunista Mexicana
PDM-PSUM, Partido Demócrata Mexicana-Partido Socialista
    Unificada Mexicana
PRT, Partido Revolucionario Trabajadora

SOURCE: *Zeta* (Tijuana), July 14-21, 1989.

Table 1068

MEXICO PRESIDENTIAL ELECTION RESULTS, BY CANDIDATE, 1910–88

Year	Candidate	Number of Valid Votes	%
1910	Porfirio Díaz	18,625	98.93
	Francisco I. Madero	196	1.04
	José Ives Limantour	1	.00
1911	Francisco I. Madero	19,997	99.26
	Francisco León de la Barra	87	.40
	Francisco Vazquez Gómez	16	.07
	Other	45	.12
1917	Venustiano Carranza	797,305	98.07
	Pablo González	11,615	1.43
	Alvaro Obregón	4,008	.49
1920	Alvaro Obregón	1,131,751	95.78
	Alfredo Robles Domínguez	47,442	4.01
	Other	2,357	.19
1924	Plutarco E. Calles	1,340,634	84.14
	Angel Flores	252,599	15.86
	Other	24	.00
1928	Alvaro Obregón	1,670,453	100.00
1929	Pascual Ortiz Rubio	1,947,848	93.55
	José Vasconcelos	110,979	5.32
	Other	23,279	.11
1934	Lázaro Cárdenas	2,225,000	98.19
	Antonio Villarreal	24,395	1.07
	Adalberto Tejeda	16,037	.70
1940	Manuel Avila Camacho	2,476,641	93.89
	Juan A. Almazán	151,101	5.72
	Rafael Sánchez Tapia	9,840	.37
1946	Miguel Alemán	1,786,901	77.90
	Ezequiel Padilla	443,357	19.33
	Enrique Calderón	33,952	1.48
	Other	29,337	1.27
1952	Adolfo Ruiz Cortines	2,713,419	74.31
	Miguel Henríquez Guzmán	579,745	15.87
	Efraín González Luna	285,555	7.82
	Vicente Lombardo Toledano	72,482	1.98
1958	Adolfo López Mateos	6,767,754	90.43
	Luis H. Alvarez	705,303	9.42
	Other	10,346	.13
1964	Gustavo Díaz Ordaz	8,368,446	88.82
	José González Torres	1,034,337	10.98
	Other	19,402	.20
1970	Luis Echeverría Alvarez	11,970,893	86.02
	Efraín González Morfín	1,945,070	13.98
1976	José López Portillo	16,727,993	100.00
1982	Miguel de la Madrid	16,748,006	70.9
	Pablo Emilio Madero	3,700,045	15.7
	Arnoldo Martínez Verdugo	821,995	3.5
	Ignacio González Gollaz	433,886	1.8
	Cándido Díaz Cerecero	342,005	1.5
	Rosario Ibarra de la Piedra	416,448	1.8
1988	Carlos Salinas de Gortari	9,604,905	50.36
	Cuauhtémoc Cárdenas	5,376,946	31.12
	Manuel J. Clouthier	3,288,523	17.07
	Gumersindo Magaña	198,854	1.04
	Rosario Ibarra de la Piedra	79,294	.42

SOURCE: 1910–1982, *La Jornada*, July 6, 1988; 1988, El Día, July 16, 1988.

Table 1069

MEXICO REGISTERED VOTERS VOTING, BY POLITICAL PARTY, 1985–86

(% of Registered Voters)

	Type of Election							
	Governor		Congress				Local Officials	
			Relative Majority		Proportional Representation			
Political Party	1985	1986	1985	1986	1985	1986	1985	1986
Registered Voters	100.0	100.0	100.0	100.0	100.0	100.0	100.0	100.0

Continued in SALA, 27-1057.

Table 1070

MEXICO NATIONAL ELECTION RESULTS FOR THE CHAMBER OF DEPUTIES, BY POLITICAL PARTY, 1961–85

| | As % of Votes Case | | | | | | | | | Seats Won[‡] | | | |
| | | | | | | | | | | 1982 | | 1985 | |
Party	1961	1964	1967	1970	1973	1976	1979	1982	1985	First Allotment[1]	Second Allotment[2]	First Allotment[1]	Second Allotment[2]
Partido Acción Nacional	7.6	11.5	12.4	13.9	14.7	8.5	10.8	17.5	15.5	1	50	8	32

Continued in SALA, 27-1058.

Table 1071

MEXICO PRESIDENTIAL ELECTION RESULTS, BY POLITICAL PARTY AND STATE
(July 4, 1982)

State	PAN[1]	PRI[2]	PPS[3]	PARM[4]	PDM[5]	PSUM[6]	PST[7]	PRT[8]	PSD[9]	Other[10]	Total[11]	Null
Aguascalientes	31,576	137,847	1,379	770	3,112	1,879	4,809	1,306	345	38	200,023	16,967
Baja California Norte	147,092	271,899	12,264	3,510	6,298	16,456	11,047	12,403	1,149	385	533,499	50,996
Baja California Sur	13,852	64,573	996	479	537	2,336	763	3,444	124	23	90,744	3,617
Campeche	8,052	103,193	993	230	401	898	419	333	52	29	124,231	9,631
Coahuila	86,155	224,753	2,499	1,435	996	4,770	6,581	2,334	351	292	334,972	4,805
Colima	7,126	136,139	965	267	2,009	1,331	1,788	737	82	15	153,993	3,534
Chiapas	21,103	679,429	6,691	5,863	1,463	7,745	8,848	4,998	1,109	762	753,144	15,200
Chihuahua	153,709	362,027	7,184	3,062	4,729	13,139	5,683	2,811	739	67	600,770	47,620
Distrito Federal	906,753	1,796,431	71,798	33,097	86,929	284,796	72,639	195,348	17,369	2,836	3,759,299	291,303
Durango	67,159	280,606	4,620	3,584	2,732	7,619	2,453	2,080	413	13	379,331	8,052
Guanajuato	178,468	518,412	8,232	6,039	61,135	10,755	12,194	3,053	1,154	76	887,274	27,756
Guerrero	22,392	422,905	3,516	4,419	5,667	20,798	15,583	6,522	594	17	517,563	15,155
Hidalgo	50,641	487,739	8,977	2,407	2,998	8,876	10,289	4,806	537	107	595,775	18,398
Jalisco	360,192	814,470	15,354	11,863	49,243	89,842	12,208	8,694	2,301	115	1,438,001	75,519
Mexico	606,871	1,490,682	58,957	25,067	67,432	140,745	40,001	91,490	7,669	383	2,710,762	180,965
Michoacán	88,330	599,255	7,563	4,280	35,121	16,771	7,825	5,078	692	63	794,567	29,585
Morelos	33,673	249,765	3,968	2,326	4,754	8,587	6,514	15,142	644	44	337,447	12,026
Nayarit	6,883	157,242	3,184	1,135	2,013	22,577	1,106	708	160	48	205,159	10,103
Nuevo León	213,919	635,010	4,128	4,696	2,460	4,447	3,633	3,975	843	12	888,019	14,896
Oaxaca	46,185	638,965	27,896	14,549	2,296	20,908	4,467	4,948	580	64	766,915	11,057
Puebla	135,372	1,050,921	13,346	5,837	8,443	25,393	9,061	10,714	1,172	98	1,303,271	42,919
Querétaro	40,518	197,152	1,350	1,616	4,543	3,439	1,429	1,267	467	18	263,021	11,222
Quintana Roo	3,513	87,798	1,344	221	247	896	845	300	65	15	96,587	1,343
San Luis Potosí	41,171	411,796	2,020	2,035	21,249	3,909	4,139	2,391	710	49	499,790	10,321
Sinaloa	65,035	475,275	9,267	4,739	2,713	31,947	4,596	5,374	827	142	615,027	15,112
Sonora	113,166	422,712	2,686	1,250	1,688	6,759	1,215	4,759	742	152	576,464	21,335
Tabasco	11,706	309,194	5,186	960	645	2,129	2,921	1,045	207	9	339,082	5,080
Tamaulipas	60,620	463,612	5,011	45,579	6,234	8,255	3,986	3,319	961	2,695	620,648	20,376
Tlaxcala	23,890	187,790	2,001	963	10,035	3,897	836	1,028	139	35	236,372	5,758
Veracruz	70,630	1,705,902	71,740	45,103	29,185	43,783	73,689	13,995	4,565	14,217	2,116,943	44,564
Yucatán	59,275	270,002	1,352	490	389	3,022	411	536	141	19	347,499	11,862
Zacatecas	39,859	347,836	1,958	1,192	2,707	6,903	1,587	1,435	176	25	412,196	8,518
Total	3,714,886	16,061,340	363,025	239,063	430,376	825,607	333,565	414,333	47,079	23,388	23,498,393	1,045,731

1. Partido Acción National (Pablo Emilio Madero).
2. Partido Revolucionario Institucional (Miguel de la Madrid).
3. Partido Popular Socialista (Miguel de la Madrid).
4. Partido Auténtico de la Revolución Mexicana (Miguel de la Madrid).
5. Partido Demócrata Mexicano (Ignacio González Gollaz).
6. Partido Socialista Unificado de México (Arnoldo Martínez Verdugo).
7. Partido Socialista de los Trabajadores (Cándido Díaz Cerecedo).
8. Partido Revolucionario de los Trabajadores (Rosario Ibarra de la Piedra).
9. Partido Social Demócrata (Manuel Moreno Sánchez).
10. Unregistered.
11. Includes null votes.

SOURCE: Secretaría General y Presidencia del Comité Técnico y de Vigilancia del Registro Nacional de Electores. México, D.F., August 18, 1982.

Table 1072

MEXICO PRELIMINARY PRESIDENTIAL ELECTION RESULTS, BY CANDIDATE AND STATE

(July 6, 1988)

State	Cuauhtémoc Cárdenas	Manuel J. Clouthier	Rosario Ibarra	Gumersindo Magaña	Carlos Salinas de Gortari
Aguascalientes	31,541	47,987	488	4,073	84,800
Baja California	153,949	100,961	3,949	3,365	151,739
Baja California Sur	22,028	16,273	536	410	46,267
Campeche	18,920	14,364	163	367	82,293
Coahuila	98,320	50,349	464	920	178,147
Colima	34,778	14,404	565	1,020	46,549
Chiapas	42,326	23,319	719	889	581,786
Chihuahua	35,340	199,334	1,034	1,391	284,896
Distrito Federal	1,429,312	639,081	21,390	22,855	791,531
Durango	67,081	60,546	1,184	813	236,822
Guanajuato	159,831	217,420	1,660	27,603	319,798
Guerrero	129,417	12,450	1,887	4,384	309,202
Hidalgo	119,214	24,638	1,170	3,830	273,041
Jalisco	285,060	367,350	3,583	29,857	508,407
México	694,451	390,784	17,511	36,054	694,451
Michoacán	394,534	63,188	1,506	12,972	142,700
Morelos	160,379	20,699	1,407	1,854	93,869
Nayosít	58,975	19,364	288	945	90,529
Nuevo León	26,941	169,915	1,265	1,511	507,524
Oaxaca	189,919	29,111	5,205	2,977	400,833
Puebla	193,142	107,718	3,631	6,082	781,085
Querétaso	37,633	46,251	632	2,759	150,783
Quintana Roo	22,682	9,138	141	298	61,973
San Luis Patosí	33,457	80,473	672	6,120	250,625
Sinaloa	104,531	200,063	1,008	1,270	317,028
Sonora	40,937	85,579	1,289	1,117	281,464
Tabasco	53,449	14,078	252	1,126	199,166
Tamaulipas	141,793	46,589	836	2,050	279,041
Tlaxcala	57,034	10,818	715	4,653	110,730
Veracruz	469,503	78,716	4,185	13,290	948,148
Yucatán	4,964	95,950	192	176	206,375
Zacatecas	65,507	31,613	399	1,823	193,303
Total	5,376,946	3,288,523	79,294	198,854	9,604,905

SOURCE: *El Día*, July 16, 1988.

Table 1073

MEXICO LEGITIMIZATION OF THE PRI[1] IN THE 1982 AND 1988 ELECTIONS

Category	MMH[b] 1982	%	CSG[c] 1982	%
PRI Votes[a]	16,748.0		9,641.3	
Voting Age Population	35,715.5	46.9	52,207.8	18.5
Registered Population	31,526.6	53.1	38,074.9	25.3
Population Voting	23,593.2	71.0	19.145.0	50.4

1. PRI (Partido Revolucionario Institucional).

a. Includes the votes of the PPS and of the PARM in 1982.
b. MMH (Miguel de la Madrid Hurtado).
c. CSG (Carlos Salinas de Gortari).

SOURCE: *El Cotidiano: Revista de la Realidad Mexicana Actual*, 25 (September–October 1988), p. 15.

Table 1074

MEXICO ELECTORAL ABSTENTION, 1982–88

	Abstention (T)		Population Over 18 Years of Age (T)		Registered Voters (T)		Unregistered Voters (%)		Registered Voters Not Voting (%)	
	1982	1988	1982	1988	1982	1988	1982	1988	1982	1988
Aguascalientes	61.1	166.0	268.0	355.4	260.9	334.9	23.4	46.71	23.4	49.57
Baja California	152.4	403.5	660.0	962.0	685.9	817.5	22.1	41.94	22.2	49.36
Baja California Sur	25.7	64.7	119.9	168.3	116.4	150.3	22.1	38.44	22.1	43.05
Campeche	44.1	113.8	220.0	317.5	168.3	229.9	26.2	35.84	26.2	49.50
Coahuila	346.6	538.0	804.1	1,044.7	681.6	866.2	50.9	51.50	50.9	62.11
Colima	16.8	120.7	182.5	232.9	170.6	218.0	9.8	51.82	9.8	55.37
Chiapas	170.0	530.8	1,093.8	1,315.9	923.1	1,189.0	18.4	40.34	18.4	44.64
Chihuahua	363.6	773.1	1,029.6	1,311.0	963.9	1,295.1	37.7	58.97	37.7	59.69
Distrito Federal	962.6	2,191.3	5,570.1	6,208.8	4,780.0	5,095.5	20.1	35.29	20.1	43.00
Durango	225.5	325.8	578.3	714.2	603.0	682.3	37.4	45.62	37.4	47.75
Guanajuato	509.6	846.4	1,513.4	1,877.0	1,398.8	1,572.8	36.4	45.09	36.4	53.81
Guerrero	467.0	690.0	1,099.4	1,311.2	984.3	1,200.8	47.4	52.62	47.4	57.46
Hidalgo	171.5	390.3	754.6	954.8	748.9	812.2	22.9	40.88	22.9	48.05
Jalisco	594.7	1,320.5	2,220.7	2,809.9	2,031.5	2,514.8	29.3	46.99	29.3	52.51
México	388.1	1,858.7	3,984.6	6,409.9	3,102.1	4,190.2	12.5	29.00	12.5	44.36
Michoacán	563.2	915.5	1,517.1	1,735.3	1,359.2	1,530.4	41.4	52.76	41.4	59.82
Morelos	55.1	305.4	551.0	681.4	392.6	583.6	14.0	44.82	14.0	52.33
Nayarít	127.3	200.1	362.9	456.9	332.5	405.3	38.3	43.80	38.3	49.37
Nuevo León	275.0	805.4	1,331.0	1,754.6	1,155.7	1,509.6	23.8	45.90	23.8	53.35
Oaxaca	364.6	736.8	1,320.8	1,414.7	1,131.5	1,364.5	32.2	52.08	32.2	54.00
Puebla	173.2	603.7	1,648.4	2,104.0	1,591.9	1,695.4	10.9	28.69	10.9	35.61
Querétaro	84.1	171.3	356.0	483.8	347.1	409.4	24.2	35.41	24.2	41.84
Quintana Roo	11.5	93.9	129.5	205.3	108.1	188.2	10.6	45.74	10.6	49.89
San Luis Potosí	228.1	487.9	847.2	1,037.5	728.0	868.3	31.3	47.03	31.3	56.19
Sinaloa	249.7	490.1	958.3	1,237.7	864.6	1,114.0	20.9	39.60	28.9	43.99
Sonora	157.3	488.9	824.0	1,033.3	727.8	899.2	21.6	47.31	21.6	54.37
Tabasco	107.3	366.6	535.1	668.9	446.4	634.7	24.0	54.81	24.0	57.76
Tamaulipas	267.4	649.9	1,048.6	1,283.3	887.2	1,120.3	30.1	50.64	30.1	58.01
Tlaxcala	24.6	147.9	283.8	331.2	261.0	331.9	9.4	44.66	9.4	44.56
Veracruz	437.0	1,529.5	2,806.1	3,692.9	2,517.9	3,045.7	17.4	41.42	17.4	50.22
Yucatán	176.6	294.4	573.8	7,447.7	511.3	602.0	34.5	3.95	34.5	48.90
Zacatecas	132.1	309.1	523.4	645.6	544.3	602.8	24.3	47.88	24.3	51.28
Total	7,933.4	18,930.0	35,715.5	52,207.6	31,526.4	38,074.9	22.2	36.26	25.2	49.72

SOURCE: *El Cotidiano: Revista de la Realidad Mexicana Actual*, 25 (September–October 1988), p. 12.

Table 1075

MEXICO FINAL ELECTION RESULTS BY FEDERAL ENTITY

(July 6, 1988)

Federal Entity	%					Total	Total Registered Voters Voting	
	MJC[a]	CSG[b]	CCS[c]	GMN[d]	RIP[e]		N	%
Total	17.07	50.36	31.12	1.04	.42	19,145,012	38,074,926	50.28
Aguascalientes	28.42	50.21	18.67	2.41	.29	168,899	334,920	50.43
Baja California	24.39	36.66	37.19	.81	.95	413,953	817,466	50.64
Baja California Sur	19.00	54.02	25.87	.48	.63	85,643	150,348	56.96
Campeche	12.37	70.88	16.30	.32	.14	116,107	229,954	50.49
Coahuila	15.34	54.27	29.95	.29	.14	328,239	866,211	37.89
Colima	14.80	47.83	35.74	1.05	.58	97,316	218,028	44.63
Chiapas	3.39	89.91	6.45	.14	.11	658,195	1,189,034	55.36
Chihuahua	38.19	54.58	6.77	.27	.20	521,995	1,295,067	40.31
Distrito Federal	22.01	27.25	49.22	.79	.74	2,904,169	5,095,462	57.00
Durango	16.99	63.63	18.82	.23	.33	356,446	682,290	52.24
Guanajuato	29.93	44.03	22.01	3.80	.23	726,312	1,572,760	46.18
Guerrero	2.44	60.53	35.80	.86	.37	510,797	1,200,804	42.54
Hidalgo	5.84	64.72	28.26	.91	.28	421,893	812,252	51.94
Jalisco	30.76	42.57	23.87	2.50	.30	1,194,247	2,514,777	47.49
México	16.33	29.79	51.58	1.55	.75	2,331,479	4,190,232	55.64
Michoacán	10.28	23.21	64.16	2.11	.24	614,899	1,530,443	40.18
Morelos	7.44	33.74	57.65	.67	.51	278,208	583,597	47.67
Nayarít	5.72	56.56	36.80	.71	.20	205,214	405,300	50.63
Nuevo León	23.70	72.08	3.83	.21	.18	704,156	1,509,564	46.65
Oaxaca	4.63	63.81	30.25	.47	.83	628,155	1,364,539	46.03
Puebla	9.87	71.55	17.69	.56	.33	1,091,658	1,695,380	64.39
Querétaro	19.43	63.34	15.81	1.16	.27	238,058	409,408	58.15
Quintana Roo	9.69	65.70	24.14	.32	.15	94,322	188,191	50.12
San Luis Potosí	21.15	68.25	8.81	1.61	.18	380,418	868,279	43.81
Sinaloa	32.07	50.81	16.75	.20	.16	623,904	1,113,969	56.01
Sonora	20.85	68.59	9.98	.27	.31	410,386	899,250	45.64
Tabasco	5.25	74.30	19.94	.42	.09	268,071	634,687	42.24
Tamaulipas	9.91	59.33	30.15	.44	.18	470,309	1,120,265	41.98
Tlaxcala	5.88	60.21	31.00	2.53	.39	184,000	331,907	55.44
Veracruz	5.21	62.59	31.05	.88	.28	1,516,257	3,045,721	49.78
Yucatán	31.19	67.08	1.61	.06	.06	307,657	602,041	51.10
Zacatecas	10.77	66.17	22.31	.62	.14	293,650	602,780	48.72

a. MJC (Manual J. Clouthier for Partido de Acción Nacional).
b. CSG (Carlos Salinas de Gortari for Partido Revolucionario Institucional).
c. CCS (Cuauhtémoc Cárdenas Solórzano for a coalition of parties).
d. GMN (Gumersindo Magaña Negrete for Partido Demócrata Mexicano).
e. RIP (Rosario Ibarra de la Piedra for Partido Revolucionario de los Trabajadores).

SOURCE: *El Cotidiano: Revista de la Realidad Mexicana Actual*, 25 (September–
October 1988), p. 16.

Table 1076

MEXICO ELECTORAL POLLS, 1988

Results %

Author	Date of Report	Geographic Coverage	PRI[1]	CSG[2]	PAN[3]	MJC[4]	FDN[5]	CC[6]	PMS[7]	HC[8]	PDM[9]	GM[10]	PRT[11]	PRI	Others — Party	Others — Candidate	Annuled Votes
La Jornada[12]	February 8 and 9, 1988	Federal District	--	37.8	--	15.2	--	15.7	--	11.2	--	.2	--	2.0	--	17.1[a]	--
Aurora Berdejo[13]	February 1988	Coahuila	54.3	46.7	23.1	19.4	14.4	17.2	1.2	--	.6	.6	--	--	15.7[c]	13.4[b]	--
PEAC[14]	April 8–13, 1988	Z. M. Valle Méx.	44.4	45.4	17.3	9.9	17.1	26.3	3.2	2.3	.6	.6	--	2.1	--	5.2	--
UNAM/Faculty of Political and Social Science[15]	May 1988	National and Federal District	--	42.0	--	15.7 / 22.6	--	15.2[d] / 21.8[d]	--	--	--	1.9 / 2.2	--	--	--	9.8	--
Project Datavox-Punto[16]	May 4 and 5, 1988	Federal District	41.8	41.8	23.1	23.1	27.9[e]	32.8	4.8	--	1.0	1.0	1.2	1.6	--	1.0	--
El Universal[12]	May 5, 1988	National	--	57.1	--	17.0	20.8	--	--	--	--	2.2	--	--	--	--	--
UAEM/Faculty of Political Science[15]	Without a date	State of Mexico	40.0	--	17.0	--	24.5	--	4.2	--	2.1	--	2.3	--	--	--	--
UAM[17]	May 28 to June 4, 1988	Federal District	--	14.8	--	15.8	--	43.4	--	--	--	--	--	--	--	--	--
El Colegio de México[18]	Without a date	National	--	61.4	--	21.0	--	17.5	--	--	--	--	--	--	--	--	--
El Universal[12]	May 12, 1988	National	--	56.2	--	18.1	--	21.6	--	--	--	.48	--	2.2	--	--	--
The Gallup Organization, Inc.[19]	May 12 to June 1, 1988	National	--	56.0	--	19.0	--	23.0	--	--	--	1.0	--	1.0	--	--	--
El Universal[12]	June 26, 1988	National	--	54.1	--	22.0	--	19.1	--	--	--	--	--	--	--	--	--
Faculty of Social Science U. A. Zacatecas[17]	May 16–31, 1988	Zacatecas, Zac. y Munic. de Gpe.	41.1	--	11.9	--	23.8	--	5.5	--	1.8	--	1.7	--	--	--	2.4
PIECE/FPSS/UNAM[20]	June 27 and 28, 1988	Federal District	--	18.9	--	10.2	52.5	--	--	--	--	.2	--	1.2	--	--	--
El Universal[12]	July 3, 1988	National	--	57.2	--	21.0	--	18.0	--	--	--	.7	--	2.1	--	--	--
Project Datavox-Punto[16]	July 24–26, 1988	Federal District	36.9	36.9	23.4	23.4	26.1	37.3	8.0	~	1.1	.5	1.3	.7	--	8.7[f]	--
PEAC[14]	July 6–17, 1988	National	--	43.6	--	17.4	--	29.1	--	--	--	.9	--	1.3	--	13.2[f]	--
COMECSO[21]	July 17–26, 1988	Federal District	--	34.6	--	12.2	37.8	32.4	--	~	--	.5	--	.4	--	3.0	18.4[g]
Bendixen & Law[17]	July 11–19, 1988	National	36.0	38.0	26.0	26.0	22.0	29.0	5.0	~	~	~	2	2.0	~	--	5.0[h]
Mario Ramírez Rancaño/ Alvaro Arreola[22]	May 15 to July 20, 1988	Federal District	--	14.7	--	16.7	--	42.7	--	4.7	--	.0	--	1.2	--	1.2	18.5[i]

1. PRI (Partido Revolucionario Institucional).
2. CSG (Carlos Salinas de Gortari, PRI presidential candidate).
3. PAN (Partido de Acción Nacional).
4. MJC (Manual J. Clouthier, PAN presidential candidate).
5. FDN (Frente Democrático Nacional).
6. CC (Cuauhtémoc Cárdenas, FDN presidential candidate).
7. PMS (Partido Mexicano Socialista).
8. HC (Heberto Castillo, PMS presidential candidate).
9. PDM (Partido Demócrata Mexicano).
10. GM (Gumersindo Magaña, PDM presidential candidate).
11. PRT (Partido Revolucionario de los Trabajadores)
12. Newspaper.
13. Inquest mentioned in "Frentes Políticos" by Aurora Berdejo in *Excélsior* newspaper.
14. Centro de Prospectiva Estrategia Inquest, *La Jornada* newspaper.
15. Published in *Excélsior* newspaper.
16. Published in *Punto* newspaper.
17. Published in *La Jornada* newspaper.
18. Published in *Uno Más Uno* newspaper.
19. Inquest by the Gallup Organization, Inc., published in *La Jornada* newspaper.
20. PIECE (Proyecto Interdisciplirario para el Estudio del Cambio Estructural) of the Faculty of Political and Social Science/UNAM.
21. Inquest by Estudios Electorales del Consejo Mexicano de Ciencias Sociales, published in *La Jornada* newspaper.
22. Inquest of the IIS (Instituto de Investigación Social)/UNAM denominated "Cultura Política en al Distrito Federal."

a. Others include: those who registered but did not vote: 6.2; anyone not of the PRI (Partido Revolucionario Institucional): 3.9; undecided: 5.5; those who consider their decision secret and those who tore up their ballot: 1.5.
b. Without a candidate: 9.10%; other candidates: 4.3%.
c. Without a party: 9.29%; none: 6.49%.
d. Includes voting of the PMS (Partido Mexicano Socialista). Without it the results of the FDN (Frente Democrático Nacional) would be 11.8% national and 16% in the Federal District.
e. PFCRN (Partido del Frente de Reconstrucción Nacional): 11.9%; PPS (Partido Popular Socialista): 11.1%; and PAFM (Partido Auténtico de la Revolución Mexicana): 4.9%.
f. None.
g. Composed of: "Undecided," 7.2%; "No reply," 11.2%.
h. "Blank vote" 4.0% and "Annuled vote" 1.0%.
i. "None" 8.75%; "Do not know" 3.25%; "No reply" 6.5%.

SOURCE: *El Cotidiaro: Revista de la Realidad Mexicana Actual*, 25 (September–October 1988), p. 34.

Table 1077

MEXICO PRELIMINARY FDN[1] TABULATION
OF PRESIDENTIAL ELECTION RESULTS[2]
(July 6, 1988)

Candidate	Votes	%
Cuauhtémoc Cárdenas	4,079,692	39.40
Carlos Salinas de Gortari	3,703,527	35.76
Manuel Clouthier	2,214,387	21.38
Other	357,687	3.46
Votes Tabulated	10,355,293[a]	

1. Frente Democrática Nacional.
2. As of July 12, 1988.

a. 54.09 percent of total votes tabulated.

SOURCE: Provided by FDN Electoral Committee.

Table 1078

NICARAGUA ELECTION RESULTS
(1984)

Party	Presidential Votes	% of Valid Votes Cast	Seats Won in Assembly
FSLN[1]	735,967	67.0***	61
PCD[2]	154,327	14.0	14
PLI[3]	105,560	9.6	9
PPSC[4]	61,199	5.6	6
PCdeN[5]	16,034	1.5	2
PSN[6]	14,494	1.3	2
MAP–ML[7]	11,352	1.0	2
Null	71,209	- -	- -
Total	1,170,142	100.0	96

1. Frente Sandinista de Liberación Nacional.
2. Partido Conservador Demócrata de Nicaragua.
3. Partido Liberal Independiente.
4. Partido Popular Social Cristiano.
5. Partido Comunista de Nicaragua.
6. Partido Socialista Nicaragüense.
7. Movimiento de Acción Popular Marxista Leninista.

SOURCE: *LASA Forum* (Latin American Studies Association), Winter, 1985, p. 24.

Table 1079

PANAMA PRESIDENTIAL ELECTION RESULTS,
BY POLITICAL PARTY
(May 20, 1984)

Party	Votes
Unión Nacional Democrática[1]	266,533
Alianza de Oposición[2]	299,035[a]
Partido del Pueblo	4,598
Acción Popular	13,782
Partido Nacionalista Popular	15,976
Partido Socialista de los Trabajadores	2,085
Partido Revolucionario de los Trabajadores	3,969

1. Formed by the Partido Liberal (28,568 votes), Partido Revolucionario Democrático (175,722 votes), Frampo (5,280 votes), Partido Laborista (45,384 votes), and Partido Panameñista (11,579 votes), led by Nicolás Ardito Barletta.
2. Formed by Partido Demócrata Cristiano (46,963 votes), Molinena (30,737 votes), and Partido Panameñista Auténtico (221,335 votes), led by Arnulfo Arias.

a. The military did not allow Arias to take office; Barletta assumed the office.

SOURCE: Information provided by the U.S. Embassy, Panama.

Table 1080

PARAGUAY PRESIDENTIAL AND CONGRESSIONAL ELECTION RESULTS, BY POLITICAL PARTY AND CANDIDATE

(February 6, 1983)

Party	Candidate	Votes	% As of Total Votes	Congressional Seats Won	
				Senate	Chamber of Deputies
Partido Colorado	Alfredo Stroessner	919,533	90.0***	20	40
Partido Liberal Radical	Enzo Doldán	58,076	5.7	6	13
Partido Liberal	Hugo Fulvio Celaudro	32,935	3.2	4	7
Null Votes	**	11,053	1.1	**	**
Total	**	1,021,597	100.0	30	60

SOURCE: Adapted from *South America, Central America and the Caribbean* (London: Europa Publications Limited, 1986), p. 484.

Table 1081

PARAGUAY PRESIDENTIAL ELECTION RESULTS, BY CANDIDATE AND POLITICAL PARTY

(1988)

Candidate	Party	Votes	%
Alfredo Stroessner[a]	Partido Colorado	982,316	89
Luis María Vega	Partido Liberal Radical	78,141	7
Carlos Ferreira Ibarra	Partido Liberal	32,403	3

a. Eighth time to be reelected. In 1983 Stroessner was reelected with 90% of the vote. Has been in office since 1954.

SOURCE: *La Opinión* (Los Angeles), Feb. 2, 1988, p. I, 11.

Table 1082

PERU PRESIDENTIAL AND CONGRESSIONAL ELECTION RESULTS, BY POLITICAL PARTY AND CANDIDATE

(April 14, 1985)

Party	Candidate	Votes	% As of Total Votes	Congressional Seats Won	
				Senate	Chamber of Deputies[1]
Alianza Popular Revolucionaria Americana	Alan García Pérez	3,457,030	45.7	32	107
Izquierda Unida	Alfonso Barrantes Lingán	1,606,914	21.3	15	48
Convergencia Democrática[2]	Luis Bedoya Reyes	773,705	10.2	7	12
Acción Popular	Javier Alva Orlandini	472,627	6.3	5	10
Izquierda Nacionalista	--	--	--	1	1
Others[2]	--	1,246,906[a]	16.5	--	2
Total	**	7,557,182	100.0	60	180

1. Elections were held on May 18, 1980.
2. An alliance between the Partido Popular Cristiano and Movimiento Bases Hayistas.
3. Includes Independents.

a. Includes invalid votes.

SOURCE: Adapted from *South America, Central America and the Caribbean* (London: Europa Publications Limited, 1986), pp. 501-502.

Table 1083

PERU PRESIDENTIAL ELECTION RESULTS, BY POLITICAL PARTY

(1985)

Party[1]	Number of Votes	Party[1]	Number of Votes
APRA	3,457,030	FDUN	54,560

Continued in SALA, 27-1071.

Table 1084

PERU PRESIDENTIAL ELECTION RESULTS, BY DEPARTMENT AND POLITICAL PARTY

(1985)

Department	Party[1] (%)					Null Votes	Blank Votes (%)	Abstentions
	APRA	IU	AP	CODE	Other			
Amazonas	57.14	16.62	18.67	5.57	2.00	10.64	8.44	9.28

Continued in SALA, 27-1072.

Table 1085

PERU LEGISLATIVE SEATS WON, BY POLITICAL PARTY[1]

PART I. SENATE

Party	Number of Seats	Party	Number of Seats
APRA	32	CODE	6
IU	18	AP	4
		Total	60

PART II. CHAMBER OF DEPUTIES

Department	Party (Number of Seats)				
	APRA	IU	CODE	AP	Ind.
Amazonas	3				
Ancash	7	1			
Apurimac	2	1			
Arequipa	3	3	1	1	1
Ayacucho	2	2			
Cajamarca	7	2		1	
Callao	5	1	1		
Cuzco	4	4			
Huancavelica	1	2			
Huanuco	3	1			
Ica	4	1	1		
Junín	4	4	1	1	
La Libertad	10	1			
Lambayeque	6	2			
Lima (Metro)	21	10	7	2	
Lima (Provincial)	5	2	1	1	
Loreto	3	1		1	
Madre de Dios					1
Moquegua		1			
Pasco	1	1			
Piura	7	3	1		
Puno	3	3	1	1	
San Martín	2	1			
Tacna	1	1			
Tumbes	1				
Ucayali	2				

1. For political party names, see table 1051, note.

SOURCE: U.S. Embassy, Lima (May 1987).

Table 1086

URUGUAY PRESIDENTIAL AND CONGRESSIONAL ELECTION RESULTS, BY POLITICAL PARTY AND CANDIDATE
(November 25, 1984)

Party	Candidate	Votes	% As of Total Votes	Congressional Seats Won	
				Senate	Chamber of Deputies
Partido Colorado	Julio María Sornguinetti	744,999	38.63	13	41
Partido Nacional	Alberto Sáenz de Zumarán	634,166	32.88	11	35
Frente Amplio	Juan José Crottogini	393,949	20.43	6	21
Unión Cívica	--	--	--	--	2
Others	--	~	8.06	--	--
Total		1,773,114	100.00	30	99

SOURCE: Adapted from *South America, Central America and the Caribbean* (London: Europa Publications Limited, 1986), p. 553.

Table 1087

VENEZUELAN PRESIDENTIAL ELECTION RESULTS, 1947-88

Year	Candidate	Votes	%	Year	Candidate	Votes	%
1947	Rómulo Gallegos	871,752	74.34	1983	Jaime Lusinchi	3,733,220	57.17
	Rafael Caldera	262,204	22.36		Rafael Caldera Rodríguez	2,271,269	34.78
	Gustavo Machado	38,587	3.29		Teodoro Petkoff	274,197	4.19
	Total	1,172,543			José Vicente Rangel	219,368	3.35
1958	Rómulo Betancourt	1,284,092	49.18		Jorge Olavarria	31,099	.47
	Wolfgang Larrazábal	903,479	34.60		Total	6,529,153[a]	
	Rafael Caldera	423,262	16.21	1988	Carlos Andrés Pérez	3,884,202	54.56
	Total	2,610,833			Eduardo Fernández	2,971,677	41.74
1963	Raúl Leoni	957,574	32.84		Teodoro Petkoff	193,975	2.72
	Rafael Caldera	589,177	20.21		Gastón Guisandes	10,550	.15
	Jóvito Villalba	510,975	17.50		Edmundo Chirinos	59,470	.84
	Arturo Uslar Pietri	469,363	16.08		Ismenia Villalba	62,286	.87
	Wolfgang Larrazábal	275,325	9.43		Leopoldo Díaz Bruzual	2,440	.03
	Raúl Ramos Giménez	66,880	2.29		David Nieves	9,858	.14
	Germán Borregeles	9,292	.31		Andrés Velásquez	26,257	.37
	Total	2,878,586			Alberto Martini Urdaneta	5,679	.08
1968	Rafael Caldera	1,083,712	29.13		Vladimir Gessen	27,678	.39
	Gonzalo Barrios	1,050,806	28.24		José Rojas Contreras	1,642	.02
	Miguel Angel Burelli	826,758	22.22		Alberto Solano	773	.01
	Luis Beltrán Prieto	719,461	19.34		Luis Hernández Campos	2,509	.04
	Alejandro Hernández	27,336	.73		Godofredo Marín	62,623	.88
	Germán Borregales	12,587	.34		Napoleón Barrios	592	.01
	Total	3,720,660			Jorge Olavarria	9,997	.14
1973	Carlos Andrés Pérez	2,130,743	48.70		Rómulo Abreu Duarte	1,478	.02
	Lorenzo Fernández	1,605,628	36.70		Arévalo Tovar Yajure	402	.01
	Jesús A. Paz Galarraga	221,827	5.07		Hermann Escarra Quintana	1,429	.02
	José Vicente Rangel	186,255	4.26		Rómulo Yordi Carvajal	369	.01
	Jóvito Villalba	134,478	3.07		Juan Pablo Bront	307	.00
	Miguel Angel Burelli	33,977	.77		Alejandro Peña Esclusa	2,203	.03
	Pedro Tinoco	29,399	.66		Luis Alfonso Godoy	2,885	.04
	Martín Garcia Villasmil	11,965	.27		Total	9,185,647	
	Germán Borregales	9,331	.21				
	Pedro Segnini La Cruz	6,176	.14				
	Raimundo Verde Rojas	3,754	.08				
	Alberto Solano	1,736	.03				
	Total	4,375,269					
1978	Luis Herrera Campíns	2,469,042	46.63				
	Luis Piñerua Ordaz	2,295,052	43.34				
	José Vicente Rangel	272,595	5.15				
	Diego Arria	90,379	1.71				
	Luis Alberto Prieto	58,723	1.11				
	Américo Martin	51,972	.98				
	Héctor Mújica	28,835	.54				
	Leonardo Montiel Ortega	13,754	.26				
	Alejandro Gómez Silva	8,583	.16				
	Pablo Salas Castillo	5,990	.11				
	Total	5,294,925					

a. There were eight other candidates.

SOURCE: Armando Veloz Mancera, *Manual Electoral: 1946, 1947, 1952, 1957, 1958, 1963, 1968, 1973, 1978,* 2nd ed. [Caracas: COPEI[?], 1978], pp. 69, 89; *El Nacional* (Caracas), Dec. 11, 1979; and *South America, Central America and the Caribbean* (London: Europa Publications Limited, 1986), p. 572; *Boletín Extra Oficial*, no. 6, Consejo Supremo Electoral, Sistema de Totalización de Votos, 1988, Caracas.

Table 1088

VENEZUELA VALID VOTES FOR PRESIDENTIAL CANDIDATES, BY DEPARTMENT

(1988 Elections)

PART I. ABSOLUTE DATA

Candidate	Amacuro	Amazonas	Zulia	Yaracuy	Trujillo	Tachira	Sucre	Portuguesa	Monagas	Nueva Esparta	Miranda	Mérida
Carlos Andrés Pérez	16,183	9,955	426,090	70,293	108,972	175,581	147,730	111,146	108,777	61,038	397,799	110,954
Eduardo Fernández	11,704	9,212	373,849	74,079	90,851	1'3,246	97,654	86,964	75,959	41,359	291,662	103,541
Teodoro Petkoff	717	281	16,647	4,415	2,130	5,243	3,513	5,055	1,944	1,575	27,462	3,661
Gastón Guisandes	15	10	3,327	107	97	114	127	102	37	184	1,560	132
Edmundo Chirinos	129	62	7,782	1,120	1,624	1,016	1,830	3,197	943	845	6,209	1,330
Ismenia Villalba	144	156	4,415	970	909	892	2,593	1,475	1,467	2,503	9,912	1,107
Leopoldo Díaz Bruzual	1	1	99	22	27	31	18	48	26	15	894	65
David Nieves	33	3	767	104	156	54	590	175	187	117	1,069	297
Andrés Velásquez	22	6	596	221	174	213	367	258	248	162	4,792	568
Alberto Martini Urdaneta	6	4	256	81	98	162	67	123	36	46	1,334	118
Vladimir Gessen	5	16	1,920	304	291	373	237	330	188	153	5,710	398
José Rojas Contreras	0	2	385	41	65	23	38	44	17	9	221	48
Alberto Solano	1	2	55	16	16	8	13	24	7	3	104	18
Luis Hernández Campos	3	3	60	19	29	106	13	51	7	13	526	89
Godofredo Marín	317	687	8,356	976	1,302	1,572	3,467	4,853	1,667	644	4,768	1,177
Napoleón Barrios	0	0	14	6	6	12	139	9	11	12	79	6
Jorge Olavarria	1	3	900	91	89	323	87	110	47	79	2,386	179
Rómulo Abreu Duarte	2	1	76	27	25	17	19	25	11	18	404	34
Arévalo Tovar Yajure	1	0	30	20	13	10	14	20	5	1	63	10
Hermann Escarra Quintana	1	1	50	15	12	15	33	23	12	8	485	18
Rómulo Yordi Carvajal	3	0	25	5	4	11	8	7	1	3	69	8
Juan Pablo Bront	2	0	25	2	4	4	7	3	7	0	62	2
Alejandro Peña Esclusa	2	5	188	41	65	56	51	88	31	18	359	54
Luis Alfonso Godoy	1	3	88	52	43	37	25	34	18	27	572	67

Candidate	Lara	Guarico	Falcón	Cajedes	Carababa	Barinas	Aragua	Apure	Anzoategui	Distrto Federal	Bolívar
Carlos Andrés Pérez	220,842	109,096	138,947	41,082	281,511	82,432	237,111	52,929	198,985	563,802	212,947
Eduardo Fernández	221,787	74,235	113,481	32,111	246,930	63,503	197,069	36,947	125,278	388,428	101,828
Teodoro Petkoff	23,274	3,306	4,846	1,109	15,691	2,052	20,342	579	6,155	39,687	4,291
Gastón Guisandes	317	81	215	58	589	48	610	33	228	2,314	245
Edmundo Chirinos	4,124	701	2,739	418	4,750	828	3,375	449	3,211	10,970	1,818
Ismenia Villalba	2,934	1,615	2,793	700	4,661	662	3,548	523	3,640	12,525	2,142
Leopoldo Díaz Bruzual	97	20	39	2	118	21	116	6	44	692	38
David Nieves	917	176	146	20	465	72	620	11	782	2,629	467
Andrés Velásquez	1,148	177	559	83	2,878	187	1,284	83	974	7,506	3,751
Alberto Martini Urdaneta	201	101	79	25	365	59	418	24	117	1,864	95
Vladimir Gessen	962	243	567	114	3,628	119	1,857	20	1,191	8,461	591
José Rojas Contreras	73	27	35	20	106	33	106	16	44	247	42
Alberto Solano	35	9	21	6	72	10	164	3	27	136	18
Luis Hernández Campos	67	97	28	17	188	59	378	18	45	644	49
Godofredo Marín	3,510	2,009	1,753	334	2,485	2,651	2,987	1,543	2,989	6,605	5,991
Napoleón Barrios	18	6	12	4	25	12	35	2	27	147	10
Jorge Olavarria	486	74	253	47	836	44	972	15	276	2,492	207
Rómulo Abreu Duarte	54	23	18	14	68	10	87	6	39	474	26
Arévalo Tovar Yajure	26	15	12	1	27	9	39	12	12	61	11
Hermann Escarra Quintana	66	25	25	6	55	20	50	5	22	467	15
Rómulo Yordi Carvajal	20	12	8	4	34	5	30	2	13	91	6
Juan Pablo Bront	24	7	27	2	26	2	23	1	9	59	9
Alejandro Peña Esclusa	213	57	79	22	192	34	180	13	59	345	51
Luis Alfonso Godoy	132	22	41	9	133	23	242	9	54	1,215	38

Table 1088 (Continued)

VENEZUELA VALID VOTES FOR PRESIDENTIAL CANDIDATES, BY DEPARTMENT

(1988 Elections)

PART II. PERCENTAGE DATA

Candidate	Amacuro	Amazonas	Zulia	Yaracuy	Trujillo	Tachira	Sucre	Portusuesa	Monagas	Nueva Esparta	Miranda	Mérida
Carlos Andrés Pérez	55.50	54.20	51.73	47.36	54.05	59.73	58.84	53.36	57.59	58.02	54.48	51.12
Eduardo Fernández	40.14	50.16	45.39	49.92	45.06	38.52	38.90	41.75	40.22	39.32	40.02	47.71
Teodoro Petkoff	2.46	1.53	2.02	2.97	1.06	1.78	1.40	2.43	1.03	1.50	3.77	1.69
Gastón Guisandes	.05	.05	.40	.07	.05	.04	.05	.05	.02	.17	.21	.06
Edmundo Chirinos	.44	.34	.94	.75	.81	.35	.73	1.53	.50	.80	.85	.61
Ismenia Villalba	.49	.85	.54	.65	.45	.30	1.03	.71	.78	2.38	1.36	.51
Leopoldo Díaz Bruzual	0	.01	.01	.01	.01	.01	.01	.02	.01	.01	.12	.03
David Nieves	.11	.02	.09	.07	.08	.02	.23	.08	.10	.11	.15	.14
Andrés Velásquez	.08	.03	.07	.15	.09	.07	.15	.12	.13	.15	.66	.26
Alberto Martini Urdaneta	.02	.02	.03	.05	.05	.06	.03	.06	.02	.04	.18	.05
Vladimir Gessen	.02	.09	.23	.20	.14	.13	.09	.16	.10	.15	.78	.18
José Rojas Contreras	0	.01	.05	.03	.03	.01	.02	.02	.01	.01	.03	.02
Alberto Solano	0	.01	.01	.01	.01	0	.01	.01	.02	.01	.01	.01
Luis Hernández Campos	.01	.02	.01	.01	.01	.04	.01	.02	0	.01	.07	.04
Godofredo Marín	1.09	3.74	1.01	.66	.65	.53	1.38	2.33	.88	.61	.65	.54
Napoleón Barrios	0	0	0	0	0	0	.06	0	.01	.01	.01	0
Jorge Olavarria	0	.02	.11	.06	.04	.11	.03	.05	.02	.08	.33	.08
Rómulo Abreu Duarte	.01	.01	.01	.02	.01	.01	.01	.01	.01	.02	.06	.02
Arévalo Tovar Yajure	0	0	0	.01	.01	0	.01	.01	0	0	.01	0
Hermann Escarra Quintana	0	.01	.01	.01	.01	.01	.01	.01	.01	.01	.07	.01
Rómulo Yordi Carvajal	.01	0	0	0	0	0	0	0	0	0	.01	0
Juan Pablo Bront	.01	0	0	0	0	0	0	0	0	0	.01	0
Alejandro Peña Esclusa	.01	.03	.02	.03	.03	.02	.02	.04	.02	.02	.05	.02
Luis Alfonso Godoy	0	.02	.01	.04	.02	.01	.01	.02	.01	.03	.08	.03

Candidate	Lara	Guarico	Falcón	Cajedes	Carababa	Barinas	Aragua	Apure	Anzoategui	Distrito Federal	Bolivar
Carlos Andrés Pérez	46.63	58.17	54.01	55.44	51.11	54.90	52.45	58.05	59.48	55.59	66.61
Eduardo Fernández	46.83	39.58	44.11	43.33	44.83	42.29	43.59	40.52	37.45	38.30	31.85
Teodoro Petkoff	4.91	1.76	1.88	1.50	2.85	1.37	4.50	.64	1.84	3.91	1.34
Gastón Guisandes	.07	.04	.08	.08	.11	.03	.13	.04	.07	.23	.08
Edmundo Chirinos	.87	.37	1.06	.56	.86	.55	.75	.49	.96	1.08	.57
Ismenia Villalba	.62	.86	1.09	.94	.85	.44	.73	.57	1.09	1.23	.67
Leopoldo Díaz Bruzual	.02	.01	.02	0	.02	.01	.03	.01	.01	.07	.01
David Nieves	.19	.09	.06	.03	.08	.05	.14	.01	.23	.26	.15
Andrés Velásquez	.24	.09	.22	.11	.52	.12	.28	.09	.29	.74	1.17
Alberto Martini Urdaneta	.04	.05	.03	.03	.07	.04	.09	.03	.03	.18	.03
Vladimir Gessen	.20	.13	.22	.15	.66	.08	.41	.02	.36	.83	.18
José Rojas Contreras	.02	.01	.01	.03	.02	.02	.02	.02	.01	.02	.01
Alberto Solano	.01	0	.01	.01	.01	.01	.04	0	.01	.01	.01
Luis Hernández Campos	.01	.05	.01	.02	.03	.04	.03	.02	.02	.06	.02
Godofredo Marín	.74	1.07	.67	.45	.45	1.77	.66	1.69	.89	.65	.87
Napoleón Barrios	0	0	0	.01	0	.01	.01	0	.01	.01	0
Jorge Olavarria	.10	.04	.10	.06	.15	.03	.22	.02	.08	.25	.06
Rómulo Abreu Duarte	.01	.05	.02	.02	.01	.01	.02	.01	.02	.05	.02
Arévalo Tovar Yajure	.01	.01	0	0	0	.01	.01	0	0	.01	0
Hermann Escarra Quintana	.01	.01	.01	.01	.01	.01	.01	.01	.01	.05	0
Rómulo Yordi Carvajal	0	.01	0	.01	.01	0	.01	0	0	.01	0
Juan Pablo Bront	.01	0	.01	0	0	0	.01	0	0	.01	0
Alejandro Peña Esclusa	.04	.03	.03	.03	.03	.02	.04	.01	.02	.03	.02
Luis Alfonso Godoy	.03	.01	.02	.01	.02	.02	.05	.01	.02	.12	.01

SOURCE: *Boletín Extra Oficial*, no. 6, Consejo Supremo Electoral, Sistema de Totalización de Votos, 1988, Caracas.

Table 1089

VENEZUELA CONGRESSIONAL ELECTION RESULTS, BY POLITICAL PARTY
(December 4, 1983)

	Seats Won	
Party	Senate	Chamber of Deputies
Acción Democrática	27	109
Partido Social-Cristiano	16	60
Movimiento al Socialismo	2	10
Unión Republicana Democrática	2	8
Opinión Nacional	--	3
Movimiento de Izquierda Revolucionaria	--	2
Partido Comunista de Venezuela	--	2
Movimiento de Integración Nacional	--	1
Nueva Alternativa	--	1
Total	47	196

SOURCE: Adapted from *South America, Central America and the Caribbean* (London: Europa Publications Limited, 1986), pp. 572–573.

Table 1090

COST OF THE "CONTRA" WAR TO NICARAGUAN GOVERNMENT, 1980–87

Year	Deaths	Direct Economic Losses[1] (US $)	Defense Expenditures[2] (%)	Exports[1] (US $)
1980	4	1.5	20.4	450.0
1981	134	15.6	22.0	499.0
1982	864	70.5	18.9	406.0
1983	5,053	240.	18.2	420.0
1984	8,324	305.	24.1	385.1
1985	10,529	268.	34.	301.5
1986	12,194	275.	38.5	229.8
1987[a]	6,000	52.6	46.3	280.0

1. In millions of dollars. (Does not include indirect losses such as blocked multilateral loans, lost trade opportunities, etc.)
2. As a percentage of total government spending.

a. Based on information available as of June 30, 1987.

SOURCE: Central American Research Institute, *Central American Bulleton*, Sept. 1987, p. 3.

Table 1091

USSR MILITARY AID TO NICARAGUA, 1979–87

Year	Arms Shipments (N)	Metric-Tons (T)	Value, (M US)	As of	Troop Strength, Nicaraguan Army
				19 July 79	6,000
1979	~	~	~	1 Jan 80	16,000
1980	~	1.6	10	1 Jan 81	24,000
1981	2	9.1	160	1 Jan 82	39,000
1982	6	11.2	140	1 Jan 83	41,000[b]
1983	25	13.9	250	1 Jan 84	46,000
1984	37	20.0	370	1 Jan 85	67,000
1985	35	19.4	280	1 Jan 86	74,850
1986	50	22.0	600	1 Jan 87	74,850
1987[a]	8	5.7	140	1 Apr 87	74,850
Total	163	102.9	$1.95 billion		

a. Through April 1, 1987.
b. This nearly seven-fold increase in the size of the Nicaraguan military was achieved before there was any significant armed resistance to the Sandinistas. The "contras" were not a significant factor until 1983.

SOURCE: Council for Inter American Security, *West Watch*, July 1987, p. 5.

11
Religion

Table 1100

CATHOLIC CHURCH HIERARCHY AND INSTITUTIONS, 20 L, 1981–88[a]

Country	Year	Cardinals	Archbishops	Bishops	Priests	Seminarians	Brothers	Sisters	Missionary Personnel[1]	Pontifical Universities	Catholic % of Total Population
A. ARGENTINA	1981	3	10	66	5,450	1,373	1,179	12,446	~	1	92.1
	1982	3	10	65	5,482	1,655	1,188	12,552	~	1	92.8
	1984	3	14	69	5,496	1,940	1,159	12,709	~	1	92.8
	1985	3	14	74	5,446	2,231	1,138	11,497	~	1	93.0
	1988	3	14	77	5,572	2,104	1,148	1,678	~	1	93.0
B. BOLIVIA	1981	1	4	19	929	167	233	1,682	236	~	93.7
	1982	1	5	17	872	165	232	1,680	229	~	94.0
	1984	1	7	20	828	176	200	1,732	217	~	94.6
	1985	1	7	20	823	282	179	1,693	~	~	94.0
	1988	1	7	23	833	313	180	1,694	197	~	93.6
C. BRAZIL	1981	7	37	239	13,169	4,283	2,701	37,024	457	4	90.1
	1982	6	35	237	13,443	4,606	2,638	36,983	454	4	90.1
	1984	6	47	305	~	5,661	2,339	36,772	456	5	90.1
	1985	5	48	305	13,764	5,912	2,579	37,546	~	6	88.6
	1988	7	48	309	13,832	6,049	2,476	37,647	410	6	90.0
D. CHILE	1981	1	4	24	2,020	663	467	5,088	175	2	85.5
	1982	1	3	24	2,046	895	445	5,091	178	2	85.5
	1984	1	4	29	2,163	999	446	4,994	173	2	85.0
	1985	2	4	29	2,199	910	396	4,455	~	2	85.0
	1988	2	6	33	2,192	870	385	4,454	190	2	85.0
E. COLOMBIA	1981	1	11	49	5,254	1,857	1,025	17,654	~	2	95.5
	1982	2	12	49	5,196	2,174	939	18,304	~	2	95.5
	1984	2	15	57	5,355	2,443	889	18,171	~	2	94.8
	1985	1	15	57	5,482	2,673	802	18,339	~	2	95.0
	1988	2	14	65	5,568	2,908	873	18,469	~	2	95.0
F. COSTA RICA	1981	0	1	5	434	189	31	867	~	~	93.5
	1982	0	1	5	452	226	29	1,001	~	~	92.7
	1984	0	2	5	461	294	48	898	~	~	92.3
	1985	0	2	5	475	338	42	865	~	~	89.3
	1988	0	1	6	479	368	47	886	~	~	88.5
G. CUBA	1981	0	2	5	200	50	22	214	~	1	41.2
	1982	0	2	5	221	47	20	218	~	1	41.2
	1984	0	2	6	205	47	25	240	~	1	41.0
	1985	0	2	6	200	29	23	247	~	1	41.2
	1988	0	2	6	208	29	21	251	~	1	41.2
H. DOMINICAN REP.	1981	1	2	8	505	286	90	1,496	~	~	94.8
	1982	1	2	8	550	283	82	1,320	~	~	94.8
	1984	1	1	9	484	263	84	1,322	~	~	93.7
	1985	1	1	9	524	398	87	1,384	~	~	92.0
	1988	1	1	9	539	380	70	1,414	50	1	91.9
I. ECUADOR	1981	1	3	19	1,513	185	367	4,151	~	1	90.2
	1982	1	3	18	1,524	180	367	4,133	~	1	91.0
	1984	1	3	24	1,537	293	329	4,112	~	1	92.0
	1985	1	3	27	1,517	401	361	4,320	~	1	94.5
	1988	1	3	27	1,564	427	361	4,011	~	1	93.5
J. EL SALVADOR	1981	0	0	5	361	105	88	836	~	~	90.4
	1982	0	1	6	347	110	76	852	~	~	90.9
	1984	0	1	6	391	129	60	890	~	~	91.7
	1985	0	~	~	365	191	73	1,026	~	~	90.9
	1988	0	1	10	378	214	104	1,011	~	~	92.6
K. GUATEMALA	1981	1	0	14	699	244	136	1,191	179	1	83.6
	1982	0	0	13	652	251	124	1,181	169	1	83.3
	1984	0	0	15	655	310	127	1,094	159	1	84.0
	1985	0	1	14	648	452	187	1,281	~	1	88.5
	1988	0	1	14	670	460	189	1,290	215	1	86.4
L. HAITI	1981	0	1	6	405	139	239	900	43	~	83.4
	1982	0	1	6	420	149	218	917	45	~	86.5
	1984	0	1	6	427	165	205	905	42	~	86.0
	1985	0	1	7	438	177	234	913	~	~	89.5
	1988	0	2	9	453	219	253	895	44	~	89.5
M. HONDURAS	1981	0	1	6	236	26	22	359	~	~	95.8
	1982	0	1	7	249	29	16	341	~	~	96.0
	1984	0	1	7	240	46	12	308	~	~	96.0
	1985	0	1	8	242	95	13	331	~	~	95.1
	1988	0	1	9	258	105	23	364	~	~	94.5
N. MEXICO	1981	3	10	74	10,087	2,947	1,127	25,598	215	~	92.8
	1982	3	10	74	10,235	3,385	1,155	25,468	212	~	96.4
	1984	3	10	75	10,110	4,217	1,423	24,207	211	~	95.0
	1985	2	10	80	10,298	4,923	1,363	24,450	~	~	96.0
	1988	2	11	77	10,653	4,960	1,271	24,906	259	~	96.1

Table 1100 (Continued)

CATHOLIC CHURCH HIERARCHY AND INSTITUTIONS, 20 L, 1981–88[a]

Country	Year	Cardinals	Archbishops	Bishops	Priests	Seminarians	Brothers	Sisters	Missionary Personnel[1]	Pontifical Universities	Catholic % of Total Population
O. NICARAGUA	1981	0	1	7	340	49	100	692	~	~	91.6
	1982	0	1	7	341	52	95	701	~	~	90.7
	1984	1	0	9	327	46	61	651	~	~	86.8
	1985	1	0	9	345	96	53	648	~	~	87.0
	1988	0	1	9	347	114	71	584	~	~	88.3
P. PANAMA	1981	0	1	6	290	52	46	457	~	1	88.8
	1982	0	1	6	302	105	39	490	~	1	89.0
	1984	0	1	6	280	130	39	454	~	1	88.1
	1985	0	1	6	291	123	38	455	~	1	86.6
	1988	0	1	5	290	108	49	469	~	1	86.7
Q. PARAGUAY	1981	0	1	15	543	151	106	932	~	1	91.2
	1982	0	1	14	554	172	96	977	~	1	91.4
	1984	0	1	15	536	249	103	997	~	1	91.9
	1985	0	1	15	570	307	82	1025	~	1	92.3
	1988	0	1	14	557	323	88	1,114	~	1	92.0
R. PERU	1981	1	6	42	2,233	693	443	4,732	438	1	92.1
	1982	1	5	44	2,198	787	427	4,944	429	1	92.4
	1984	1	6	44	2,258	895	461	4,910	459	1	92.4
	1985	1	6	41	2,276	1,034	444	4,874	~	1	92.3
	1988	1	6	44	2,378	1,062	450	4,716	459	1	92.0
S. URUGUAY	1981	0	1	10	587	67	149	1,621	~	~	78.6
	1982	0	1	11	586	89	148	1,595	~	~	78.6
	1984	0	1	11	552	124	148	1,641	~	~	79.0
	1985	0	1	11	548	121	119	1,769	~	1	78.9
	1988	0	1	12	703	81	144	2,029	~	1	78.9
T. VENEZUELA	1981	1	6	29	1,995	371	326	4,345	~	1	92.2
	1982	2	5	31	2,022	383	229	4,270	~	1	92.4
	1984	2	4	33	1,975	496	234	3,862	~	1	91.0
	1985	2	4	33	2,008	663	270	3,876	~	~	91.5
	1988	2	4	33	2,005	700	285	3,930	~	1	91.7

1. Field distribution.

a. The source supplies 1984 data that are identical to those for 1983, 1987 identical
   to 1985, and data for 1986 identical to 1984. For years 1956–80, see SALA, 23-1100.

SOURCE: *Catholic Almanac*, 1982–88, pp. 332–364; 1989, pp. 333–368.

Table 1101

INHABITANTS PER CATHOLIC PRIEST, 20 L, 1912–88[a]

(T)

	Country	1912	1945	1950	1955	1960	1966	1970	1975	1980	1982	1984	1985[a]	1986	1987	1988
A.	ARGENTINA	4.5	5.1	4.3	4.3	4.3	4.3	4.2	5.0	5.5	5.3	5.4	5.6	5.4	5.6	5.6
B.	BOLIVIA	2.8	5.8	6.1	5.1	4.9	4.8	4.3	6.9	6.8	6.9	7.3	7.8	7.3	7.8	7.9
C.	BRAZIL	5.7	6.8	6.9	6.8	6.4	7.1	7.8	8.6	8.5	9.4	9.7	9.8	9.7	9.8	10.0
D.	CHILE	2.1	3.2	3.3	3.5	3.1	3.6	3.6	4.7	5.7	5.6	5.4	5.5	5.4	5.5	5.6
E.	COLOMBIA	3.8	3.8	3.7	3.7	3.6	3.3	3.6	5.0	5.4	5.2	5.1	5.2	5.1	5.2	5.2
F.	COSTA RICA	2.5	4.7	4.8	4.1	4.6	4.2	3.7	5.4	5.7	5.1	5.0	5.5	5.2	5.5	5.6
G.	CUBA	6.1	9.5	10.8	8.8	9.4	34.4	39.8	48.4	50.1	49.7	48.3	50.5	48.2	50.5	49.3
H.	DOMINICAN REP.	10.0	17.3	13.5	10.5	11.0	9.7	9.0	10.7	11.4	11.8	12.3	11.9	12.3	11.9	11.9
I.	ECUADOR	2.2	3.1	3.2	3.3	3.3	3.4	4.2	5.3	6.2	5.6	5.8	6.2	6.0	6.2	6.2
J.	EL SALVADOR	7.0	8.7	8.7	9.1	9.2	8.4	9.0	10.2	13.8	14.4	13.4	13.2	13.4	13.2	13.0
K.	GUATEMALA	9.4	20.7	21.2	13.5	12.3	9.5	10.2	9.3	10.8	11.8	11.4	12.3	12.1	12.3	12.2
L.	HAITI	10.5	12.5	9.3	8.4	7.8	10.7	10.5	15.0	13.1	12.5	11.9	12.0	12.4	12.0	11.8
M.	HONDURAS	5.0	12.3	11.9	13.0	11.5	12.0	10.6	14.9	9.7	15.9	17.0	18.1	17.0	18.1	17.5
N.	MEXICO	2.6	5.3	5.8	5.3	5.3	5.8	5.7	6.4	6.9	7.1	7.4	7.6	7.4	7.6	7.5
O.	NICARAGUA	~	~	~	~	~	~	6.3	7.2	8.5	9.5	9.4	9.5	9.4	9.5	9.7
P.	PANAMA	6.4	7.8	6.7	6.2	6.2	6.0	5.6	6.0	6.5	6.8	7.5	7.5	7.5	7.5	7.7
Q.	PARAGUAY	7.2	6.1	6.3	5.7	4.9	4.5	6.6	5.7	6.2	6.1	6.5	6.5	6.5	6.5	6.8
R.	PERU	3.6	5.8	6.0	5.9	5.7	5.3	5.9	6.8	7.8	8.3	8.3	8.7	8.3	8.7	8.5
S.	URUGUAY	4.8	3.6	3.7	4.3	4.1	4.2	4.1	5.0	5.2	5.0	5.4	5.5	5.4	5.5	4.2
T.	VENEZUELA	4.4	6.4	6.4	5.3	5.2	5.1	5.5	5.7	7.0	7.9	8.3	8.6	8.3	8.6	8.9

a. The source supplies 1984 data that are identical to those of 1983.

SOURCE: Data 1912–60 from Yvan Labelle and Adriana Estrada (Comp.), *Latin America in Maps, Charts, Tables: No. 2: Socio-Religious Data (Catholicism)* (Mexico, D.F.: Center of Intercultural Formation, 1964); data for 1966 from *Atlas Hier-archicus*, 1968; and data for 1970–85 calculated from number of priests in *Catholic Almanac*, 1973–88 and SALA, 25–601 through 621; 1989.

Table 1102

CATHOLICS PER CATHOLIC PRIEST, 20 L, 1986–88

(T)

	Country	1986	1987	1988
A.	ARGENTINA	5.4	5.2	5.2
B.	BOLIVIA	7.0	7.3	7.4
C.	BRAZIL	8.7	8.7	8.9
D.	CHILE	4.6	4.7	4.8
E.	COLOMBIA	4.9	5.0	5.0
F.	COSTA RICA	4.8	4.9	4.9
G.	CUBA	19.8	20.8	20.3
H.	DOMINICAN REP.	11.5	11.0	11.0
I.	ECUADOR	5.5	5.8	5.8
J.	EL SALVADOR	12.3	12.0	12.0
K.	GUATEMALA	10.2	10.9	10.6
L.	HAITI	10.7	10.7	10.6
M.	HONDURAS	10.7	17.2	16.5
N.	MEXICO	7.1	7.3	7.2
O.	NICARAGUA	8.1	8.2	8.6
P.	PANAMA	6.6	6.5	6.7
Q.	PARAGUAY	6.0	6.0	6.3
R.	PERU	7.7	8.0	7.8
S.	URUGUAY	4.3	4.3	3.4
T.	VENEZUELA	7.5	7.9	8.1

SOURCE: *Catholic Almanac*, 1987–89.

Table 1103

JEHOVAH'S WITNESSES PUBLISHERS AND MEMBERS, 20 LC, 1986–88[a]

Country	Year	Publishers[1] (N)	Population per Publisher	Persons Baptized (N)	Congregations (N)	Memorial Attendance (N)
A. ARGENTINA	1986	59,348	505	5,587	877	149,905
	1987	64,862	469	5,779	988	170,120
	1988	69,794	446	5,756	1,104	187,510
B. BOLIVIA	1986	4,467	1,455	642	86	21,674
	1987	4,979	1,206	681	96	21,778
	1988	5,604	1,136	744	98	25,237
C. BRAZIL	1986	196,948	748	19,878	3,056	533,400
	1987	203,405	654	18,467	3,326	657,784
	1988	228,802	586	23,556	3,626	718,414
D. CHILE	1986	27,585	445	3,052	316	90,290
	1987	29,346	405	2,457	327	95,664
	1988	31,082	390	2,730	339	107,264
E. COLOMBIA	1986	27,587	1,010	3,831	365	121,358
	1987	30,857	861	3,381	508	144,449
	1988	34,910	753	3,112	602	169,432
F. COSTA RICA	1986	9,433	273	641	178	25,990
	1987	10,067	246	597	193	30,534
	1988	10,801	248	858	223	33,060
G. CUBA	1986	~	~	~	~	~
	1987	~	~	~	~	~
	1988	~	~	~	~	~
H. DOMINICAN REP.	1986	9,307	607	718	143	35,374
	1987	9,929	543	884	151	39,108
	1988	10,519	580	840	159	39,079
I. ECUADOR	1986	10,013	909	1,011	147	49,967
	1987	11,195	851	1,011	160	58,043
	1988	12,682	753	893	188	66,519
J. EL SALVADOR	1986	14,546	361	1,363	281	51,151
	1987	15,232	337	1,251	295	58,933
	1988	16,159	331	1,481	310	61,409
K. GUATEMALA	1986	8,401	923	811	130	29,720
	1987	9,200	834	812	153	36,907
	1988	10,018	794	754	163	37,220
L. HAITI	1986	4,220	1,422	699	79	22,530
	1987	4,598	1,226	417	83	29,598
	1988	5,011	1,143	549	100	34,047
M. HONDURAS	1986	4,161	1,054	370	73	20,080
	1987	4,565	935	341	82	23,160
	1988	4,929	921	433	86	25,944
N. MEXICO	1986	186,291	428	22,054	5,878	838,467
	1987	210,536	365	31,703	6,482	957,081
	1988	235,870	332	23,888	7,343	1,004,062
O. NICARAGUA	1986	~	~	~	~	~
	1987	~	~	~	~	~
	1988	~	~	~	~	~
P. PANAMA	1986	4,480	497	384	96	17,466
	1987	4,755	452	258	100	18,888
	1988	5,233	425	236	116	22,966
Q. PARAGUAY	1986	2,251	1,496	157	35	5,696
	1987	2,379	1,400	109	36	6,040
	1988	2,511	1,244	186	38	6,262
R. PERU	1986	21,471	931	2,580	432	95,062
	1987	24,121	773	2,571	486	104,684
	1988	26,844	715	2,921	560	110,782
S. URUGUAY	1986	5,596	522	654	92	16,828
	1987	5,956	470	534	94	18,220
	1988	6,469	429	516	96	19,053
T. VENEZUELA	1986	31,691	584	4,008	307	128,627
	1987	36,035	495	4,050	375	148,843
	1988	40,328	447	4,133	438	154,881
UNITED STATES	1986	710,344	334	41,697	8,336	1,691,297
	1987	734,378	312	39,189	8,547	1,778,066
	1988	762,960	305	43,415	8,754	1,822,607

1. Local printers or distributors who are Jehovah's Witnesses.

a. Average for year.

SOURCE: *Yearbook of Jehovah's Witnesses*, 1987 and 1988; 1989, pp. 34–41.

Table 1104

ESTIMATED JEWISH POPULATION,[1] 20 LC, 1965–86

(N)

Country	1965	1970	1975	1979	1980	1982	1984	1986
A. ARGENTINA[2]	450,000	500,000	300,000	300,000	242,000	233,000	228,000	224,000
B. BOLIVIA	4,000	2,000	2,000	750	1,000	1,000	600	600
C. BRAZIL	130,000	150,000	165,000	150,000[b]	110,000	100,000	100,000	100,000
D. CHILE	30,000	35,000	27,000	30,000[b]	25,000	20,000	17,000	17,000
E. COLOMBIA	10,000	10,000	12,000[c]	12,000	7,000	7,000	7,000	6,500
F. COSTA RICA	1,500	1,500	1,500	2,500	2,500	2,200	2,500	2,000
G. CUBA	2,400	1,700	1,500	1,500	1,000	700	700	700
H. DOMINICAN REP.	400	350	200[c]	200	200	100	100	100
I. ECUADOR	2,000	2,000	1,000	1,000	1,000	1,000	1,000	1,000
J. EL SALVADOR	300	300	310[c]	350	350	~	~	~
K. GUATEMALA	1,200	1,900	1,900	2,000	1,100	900	800	800
L. HAITI	150	150	150	150	200	100	100	~
M. HONDURAS	150	150	200[c]	200[b]	~	~	~	~
N. MEXICO	30,000	35,000[a]	37,500[c]	37,500	35,000	35,000	35,000	35,000
O. NICARAGUA	200	200	200	200	~	~	~	~
P. PANAMA	2,000	2,000	2,000	2,000	2,000	3,500	3,800	3,800
Q. PARAGUAY	1,200	1,200	1,200	1,200	700	700	900	900
R. PERU	4,000	5,300	6,000	5,200	5,000	5,000	5,000	4,000
S. URUGUAY	50,000	50,000	50,000	50,000[b]	40,000	30,000	27,000	25,000
T. VENEZUELA	85,000	12,000	15,000	15,000	17,000	20,000	20,000	20,000
UNITED STATES	5,720,000	5,870,000	5,840,000	5,920,890	5,690,000	5,705,000	5,705,000	5,700,000

1. Prepared by AJY staff from questionnaires sent to local Jewish community leaders.
2. Decline after 1972 reflects revision of estimate rather than mass exodus.

a. 49,181 according to 1970 Mexican census.
b. Reply to 1980 inquiry.
c. Reply to 1974 inquiry.

SOURCE: *American Jewish Year Book*, 1966, 1971, 1977, 1978, 1980, 1981, 1983, 1984, 1987; 1989, p. 420.

Table 1105

WORLD CHRISTIAN ENCYCLOPEDIA (WCE) SCHEME[1] FOR CATEGORIZING RELIGIOUS (INCLUDING PROTESTANT) AND NON-RELIGIOUS PERSONS, 1900–80

(Guide to table 1106)

Category[2] (A + G = 100.0%)	Definition
A. Christians	Total of all Christian adherents of all kinds (professing and crypto-Christians, which is by definition equal to nominal plus affiliated).
B. Professing (C + D)	Those publicly professing (declaring, stating, confessing, self-identifying) their preference or adherence in a government census or public opinion poll, hence known to the state or society or the public.
(Crypto-Christians)	Secret believers in Christ not professing publicly nor enumerated or known in government census or public opinion poll, hence known to the state or the public or society (but usually affiliated and known to churches), of the following seven varieties: (1) unorganized individuals in legal churches, (2) political prisoners or exiles, (3) organized believers in unregistered denominations or congregations, (4) members of deliberately clandestine illegal underground churches, (5) members of anti-state minority churches or sects, (6) organized believers in Christ rejecting the label Christian (anti-church believers), and (7) isolated radio or radiophonic or correspondence-course believers in small groups or cells in non-Christian or anti-Christian areas.

Continued in SALA, 25-1104.

Table 1106

RELIGIOUS (INCLUDING PROTESTANT)
AND NON-RELIGIOUS PERSONS, 20 LC, 1900–80
(A + G = 100.0%)

A. ARGENTINA	1900		1970		AA–GR	1980	
Category	N	%	N	%	1970-80	N	%
A. Christians	4,126,500	98.3	22,757,300	95.8	1.28	25,871,100	95.6
B. Professing (C + D)	4,126,500	98.3	22,757,300	95.8	1.28	25,871,100	95.6
C. Roman Catholics	4,092,100	97.4	21,962,300	92.5	1.21	24,802,600	91.6
Christo-pagans	50,000	(1.2)	200,000	(.8)	(1.31)	228,000	(.8)
D. Protestants	29,000	.7	500,000	2.1	3.03	676,600	2.5
Argentinian indigenous	0	.0	120,000	.5	4.56	189,500	.7
Orthodox	3,000	.1	100,000	.4	1.31	114,000	.4
Marginal Protestants	1,000	.0	45,000	.2	1.84	54,000	.2
Catholics (non-Roman)	0	.0	20,000	.1	1.40	23,000	.1
Anglicans	1,000	.0	10,000	.0	1.31	11,400	.0
E. Nominal	21,000	.5	337,000	1.4	2.46	430,940	1.6
F. Affiliated (B – E) = (1 to 8)	4,105,000	97.8	22,419,000	94.4	1.26	25,440,160	94.0
1. Doubly-affiliated	–72,000	–1.7	–975,000	–4.1	2.86	–1,291,380	–4.8
2. Roman Catholics	4,132,000	98.4	22,301,530	93.9	1.26	25,304,840	93.5
3. Protestants	40,000	1.0	593,007	2.5	2.80	784,900	2.9
4. Argentinian Indigenous	0	.0	251,400	.9	3.60	351,800	1.3
5. Orthodox	3,000	.1	122,000	.5	1.23	138,000	.5
6. Marginal Protestants	1,000	.0	63,774	.3	2.25	80,000	.4
7. Catholics (non-Roman)	0	.0	50,000	.2	1.32	57,000	.2
8. Anglicans	1,000	.0	13,200	.1	1.28	15,000	.1
G. Jews	6,500	.2	475,000	2.0	1.28	540,000	2.0
Non-religious	5,000	.1	210,000	.9	3.20	290,000	1.1
Atheists	5,000	.1	140,000	.6	1.94	170,000	.6
Muslims	4,000	.1	50,000	.2	1.31	57,000	.2
Spiritists[1]	1,000	.0	50,000	.2	1.48	58,000	.2
Tribal religionists[2]	50,000	1.2	30,000	.1	–4.00	20,000	.1
Buddhists	1,000	.0	10,000	.0	.95	11,000	.0
Baha'is	0	.0	5,700	.0	1.90	6,900	.0
Other religionists	1,000	.0	20,000	.1	6.67	40,000	.1
Country Population	4,200,000	100.0	23,748,000	100.0	1.31	27,064,000	100.0

1. Spiritists: Organized under the Confederación Espiritista Argentina. A number of lapsed Catholics and Protestants become spiritists each year, and by 1976 spiritism was recognized as a growing phenomenon.
2. Tribal Religionists: Of the 170,000 tribal lowland Amerindians (or Aborigines) in 1970, mostly along the Paraguayan border, a proportion are still shamanists or animists, including a majority of the 20,000 Chiriguano (Guarani) and the other 8 Aboriginal groups: Chane (Guana), Chorote, Chulupi, Mataco (population 12,000), Mbya, Mocovi, Pilaca and some Toba (17,060). Guarani shamans in particular occupy a respected healing role in society, and Guarani mysticism remains the main agent for social cohesion.

DEFINITIONS: See table 1104.

Continued in SALA, 23-1115 through 1134.

Table 1107

PRACTICING AND NON-PRACTICING CHRISTIANS, 20 LC, 1900-80
(Total = 100.0%)

	Country	Practicing[1]			Non-Practicing[2]		
		1900	1970	1980	1900	1970	1980
A.	ARGENTINA	90	70	70	10	30	30
B.	BOLIVIA	85	71	69	15	29	31
C.	BRAZIL	80	62	60	20	38	40
D.	CHILE	80	75	65	20	25	35
E.	COLOMBIA	96	92	92	4	8	8
F.	COSTA RICA	95	85	85	5	15	15
G.	CUBA	90	40	60	10	60	40
H.	DOMINICAN REP.	90	70	70	10	30	30
I.	ECUADOR	90	80	80	10	20	20
J.	EL SALVADOR	95	85	85	5	15	15
K.	GUATEMALA	90	75	75	10	25	25
I.	HAITI	95	85	85	5	15	15
M.	HONDURAS	90	80	80	10	20	20
N.	MEXICO	80	65	65	20	35	35
O.	NICARAGUA	95	85	85	5	15	15
P.	PANAMA	90	80	80	10	20	20
Q.	PARAGUAY	70	45	45	30	55	55
R.	PERU	95	80	80	5	20	20
S.	URUGUAY	80	70	70	20	30	30
T.	VENEZUELA	85	70	70	15	30	30
	UNITED STATES	95	90	88	5	10	12

1. Practicing: Total affiliated of all denominations who attend public worship at least once a year, or who fulfill their churches' minimum annual attendance requirements, or who are radio/TV-service listeners (% here = % of affiliated, not % of total population); church attenders (daily, weekly, fortnightly, monthly, occasional, on festivals only, or annual), excluding civic attenders, private attenders, attending non-members, and attending non-Christians; active Christians, committed Christians, militant Christians.

2. Non-Practicing: Affiliated but inactive, non-attending (dominant Christians) (% = % of affiliated).

SOURCE: See table 1105.

Table 1108

ORGANIZED BIBLE DISTRIBUTION PER YEAR, 20 LC, 1900-75
(N)

	Country	Free					Subsidized					Commercial
		1900	1950	1960	1970	1975	1900	1950	1960	1970	1975	1975
A.	ARGENTINA	0	0	0	0	0	13,000	37,579	73,640	67,191	44,159	60.000
B.	BOLIVIA	0	0	0	0	0	0	8,016	10,434	15,894	39,401	10,000
C.	BRAZIL	0	0	0	260	0	17,782	77,387	297,546	204,943	189,005	486,975

Continued in SALA, 26-1109.

Table 1109

CATHOLIC BAPTISMS PER 1,000 CATHOLICS, 20 L, 1972–88[a]

Country	1972	1975	1980	1984	1985	1986	1987	1988
A. ARGENTINA	21.7	21.7	24.8	22.1	21.5	22.1	21.5	21.2
B. BOLIVIA	25.7	25.5	31.0	33.6	31.4	33.6	31.2	31.3
C. BRAZIL	27.8	26.1	25.1	24.3	22.1	21.9	22.1	22.1
D. CHILE	17.9	18.0	19.4	19.5	17.5	19.5	17.5	16.6
E. COLOMBIA	32.1	18.0	27.7	29.2	27.4	29.2	27.4	28.2
F. COSTA RICA	31.6	27.9	25.8	30.6	31.2	30.6	31.2	31.2
G. CUBA	16.5	10.2	4.9	5.4	6.4	5.4	6.4	7.6
H. DOMINICAN REP.	21.1	18.9	18.3	15.9	18.2	15.9	18.2	17.6
I. ECUADOR	30.2	32.8	27.3	23.7	24.8	23.7	24.8	23.1
J. EL SALVADOR	30.0	28.8	17.9	17.4	21.4	17.4	21.4	21.3
K. GUATEMALA	30.9	35.9	29.6	26.8	30.5	26.8	30.5	33.1
L. HAITI	23.7	21.8	21.0	21.7	21.4	21.7	21.2	20.8
M. HONDURAS	32.4	27.5	30.7	23.6	18.1	23.6	18.1	18.1
N. MEXICO	37.0	35.6	30.4	28.6	28.1	28.6	28.1	27.2
O. NICARAGUA	31.6	31.8	27.5	27.2	28.4	27.2	28.4	27.9
P. PANAMA	26.3	25.3	20.7	~	18.5	~	18.5	18.7
Q. PARAGUAY	27.2	28.6	32.1	31.7	29.1	31.7	29.1	29.1
R. PERU	26.9	23.5	25.8	24.9	25.1	24.9	25.1	25.4
S. URUGUAY	15.2	14.6	18.3	17.1	18.2	17.1	18.2	18.3
T. VENEZUELA	27.1	25.8	27.2	21.7	22.2	21.7	22.2	22.8

a. The source supplies 1984 data that are identical to those for 1983. Data for 1980–83 represent figures as of December 31 for each corresponding year.

SOURCE: Data from 1972–75 from Consejo Episcopal Latinoamericano (CELAM), *Iglesia y América Latina Cifras,* 1978, p. 6; and 1980–83 data adapted from *Catholic Almanac,* 1983–88; 1989.

Table 1110

PROTESTANT SECTS AND MISSIONARIES,[1] 20 LC

(1968)

Country	Places of Worship	Protestant Population	Native Personnel		Foreign Missionaries		Seminaries and Bible Schools
			Ordained	Laymen	Ordained	Laymen	
A. ARGENTINA	2,412	529,657	695	506	401	112	15

Continued in SALA, 21-1108.

Table 1111

CHURCH OF JESUS CHRIST OF LATTER-DAY SAINTS, 20 L, 1987

Country	Stakes	Wards	Stake Branches	Missions	Districts	Mission Branches	Membership	% of Total Population
A. ARGENTINA	26	148	81	6	13	118	114,000	.37
B. BOLIVIA	9	55	20	2	7	43	40,000	.05
C. BRAZIL	57	331	101	10	16	85	249,000	.17
D. CHILE	48	293	139	6	18	112	196,000	1.60
E. COLOMBIA	9	45	20	3	17	65	60,000	.20
F. COSTA RICA	2	12	12	1	2	7	8,900	.27
G. CUBA	- -	- -	- -	- -	- -	1	100[a]	- -
H. DOMINICAN REP.	1	5	8	2	7	47	15,000	.22
I. ECUADOR	- -	- -	- -	- -	- -	4	100	- -
J. EL SALVADOR	6	41	26	1	- -	- -	24,000	.35
K. GUATEMALA	13	86	51	3	12	78	63,000	.86
L. HAITI	- -	- -	- -	1	1	15	2,000	.04
M. HONDURAS	5	24	22	1	7	27	23,000	.45
N. MEXICO	92	531	249	14	35	209	360,000	.44
O. NICARAGUA	1	4	5	- -	- -	- -	3,900	.10
P. PANAMA	3	15	10	- -	3	12	12,000	.49
Q. PARAGUAY	2	10	9	1	5	22	8,000	.19
R. PERU	31	181	55	5	16	110	125,000	.62
S. URUGUAY	13	61	37	1	- -	- -	42,000	1.43
T. VENEZUELA	5	35	13	2	12	54	35,000	.20

a. Fewer than 100.

SOURCE: *Deseret News 1989–90 Church Almanac.*

Table 1112

CHURCH OF JESUS CHRIST OF LATTER-DAY SAINTS, FIRST STAKES[1] ORGANIZED IN LATIN AMERICA, 20 L

Country	Date Organized
A. ARGENTINA	Nov. 20, 1966
B. BOLIVIA	Jan. 14, 1979
C. BRAZIL	May 1, 1966
D. CHILE	Nov. 19, 1972
E. COLOMBIA	Jan. 23, 1977
F. COSTA RICA	Jan. 20, 1977
G. CUBA	- -
H. DOMINICAN REP.	Mar. 23, 1986
I. ECUADOR	Jun. 11, 1978
J. EL SALVADOR	Jun. 3, 1973
K. GUATEMALA	May 21, 1967
L. HAITI	- -
M. HONDURAS	Apr. 10, 1977
N. MEXICO	Dec. 9, 1895
O. NICARAGUA	Mar. 22, 1981
P. PANAMA	Nov. 11, 1979
Q. PARAGUAY	Feb. 25, 1979
R. PERU	Feb. 22, 1970
S. URUGUAY	Nov. 12, 1967
T. VENEZUELA	May 15, 1977

1. A stake is a jurisdictional body equivalent to a diocese or a parish.

SOURCE: *Deseret News 1989–90 Church Almanac.*

Table 1113

CHURCH OF JESUS CHRIST OF LATTER-DAY SAINTS, FULL-TIME MISSIONS IN LATIN AMERICA[1]

Name	Date Organized	First President
Mexican	Nov. 16, 1879	Moses Thatcher
Discontinued June 1889		
Reopened June 8, 1901		
June 10, 1970, MEXICO[2]		
June 20, 1974, MEXICO MEXICO CITY[2]		
July 1, 1978, MEXICO MEXICO CITY SOUTH[2]		
Brazilian	May 25, 1925	Rulon S. Howells
June 10, 1970, BRAZIL CENTRAL[2]		
Discontinued Oct. 17, 1972, transferred to Brazil North Central and Brazil South Central		
Argentina	Aug. 14, 1935	W. Ernest Young
June 10, 1970, ARGENTINA SOUTH[2]		
June 20, 1974, ARGENTINA BUENOS AIRES NORTH[2]		
Uruguay	Aug. 31, 1947	Frederick S. Williams
June 10, 1970, URUGUAY-PARAGUAY[2]		
June 20, 1974, URUGUAY MONTEVIDEO[2]		
Northern Mexican	June. 10, 1956	Joseph T. Bentley
June 10, 1970, MEXICO NORTH[2]		
June 20, 1974, MEXICO MONTEREY[2]		
Brazilian South	Sep. 20, 1959	Asael T. Sorensen
June 10, 1970, BRAZIL SOUTH[2]		
June 20, 1974, BRAZIL PORTO ALEGRE[2]		
Andes	Nov. 1, 1959	J. Vernon Sharp
June 10, 1970, PERU-ECUADOR[2]		
Aug. 1, 1970, PERU[2]		
Feb. 1971, PERU ANDES[2]		
Apr. 1971, ANDES PERU[2]		
June 20, 1974, PERU LIMA[2]		
Jan. 1, 1977, PERU LIMA SOUTH[2]		
West Mexican	Nov. 1, 1960	Harold E. Turley
June 10, 1970, MEXICO WEST[2]		
June 20, 1974, MEXICO HERMOSILLO[2]		
Chilean	Oct. 8, 1961	A. Delbert Palmer
June 10, 1970, CHILE[2]		
June 20, 1974, CHILE SANTIAGO[2]		
Jan. 1, 1977, CHILE SANTIAGO SOUTH[2]		
North Argentine	Sep. 16, 1962	Ronald V. Stone
June 10, 1970, ARGENTINA NORTH[2]		
June 20, 1974, ARGENTINA CORDOBA[2]		
Southeast Mexican	Mar. 27, 1963	Carl J. Beecroft
June 10, 1970, MEXICO SOUTHEAST[2]		
June 20, 1974, MEXICO VERACRUZ[2]		
Guatemala-El Salvador	Aug. 1, 1965	Terrance L. Hansen
June 20, 1974, GUATEMALA GUATEMALA CITY[2]		
Mar. 29, 1988, GUATEMALA GUATEMALA CITY SOUTH[2]		
Andes South	Nov. 14, 1966	Franklin Kay Gibson
1969 BOLIVIA[2]		
June 20, 1974, BOLIVIA LA PAZ[2]		
Colombia-Venezuela	Jul. 1, 1968	Stephen L. Brower
July 1, 1971, COLOMBIA[2]		
June 20, 1974, COLOMBIA BOGOTA[2]		
Brazilian North	Jul. 7, 1968	Hal Roscoe Johnson
June 10, 1970, BRAZIL NORTH[2]		
June 20, 1974, BRAZIL RIO DE JANEIRO[2]		
Mexico North Central	Aug. 5, 1968	Arturo R. Martínez
June 20, 1974, MEXICO TORREON[2]		
Ecuador	Aug. 1, 1970	Louis W. Latimer
June 20, 1974, ECUADOR QUITO[2]		
Venezuela	Jul. 1, 1971	Clark D. Webb
June 20, 1974, VENEZUELA CARACAS[2]		
Argentine East	Jul. 30, 1972	Joseph T. Bentley
June 20, 1974, ARGENTINA ROSARIO[2]		
Brazil North Central	Oct. 17, 1972	Leroy A. Drechsel
June 20, 1974, BRAZIL SAO PAULO NORTH[2]		
Brazil South Central	Oct. 17, 1972	Owen Nelson Baker
June 20, 1974, BRAZIL SAO PAULO SOUTH[2]		

Table 1113 (Continued)

**CHURCH OF JESUS CHRIST OF LATTER-DAY SAINTS,
FULL-TIME MISSIONS IN LATIN AMERICA[1]**

Name	Date Organized	First President
Argentina Buenos Aires South	Jul. 23, 1974	Juan Carlos Avila
Chile Concepción	Jul. 1, 1975	Lester D. Haymore
Colombia Cali	Jul. 1, 1975	Jay E. Benson
Mexico Guadalajara	Jul. 1, 1975	Isauro Gutierres
Mexico Villahermosa	Jul. 1, 1975	Abraham Lozano
El Salvador San Salvador	Jul. 1, 1976	Eddy L. Barillas
Chile Santiago North	Jan. 1, 1977	Berkely A. Spencer
Peru Lima North	Jan. 1, 1977	Jose A. Sousa
Bolivia Santa Cruz	Jul. 1, 1977	DeVere R. McAllister
Chile Osorno	Jul. 1, 1977	Lester D. Haymore
Guatemala Quezaltenango	Jul. 1, 1977	John F. O'Donnal
Paraguay Asunción	Jul. 1, 1977	Mearl K. Bair
Ecuador Guayaquil	Jul. 1, 1978	William J. Mitchell
Mexico Mexico City North	Jul. 1, 1978	John B. Dickson
Peru Arequipa	Jul. 1, 1978	Norval C. Jesperson
Brazil Recife	Jul. 1, 1979	Harry Eduardo Klien
Chile Viña Del Mar	Jul. 1, 1979	Gerald J. Day
Venezuela Maracaibo	Jul. 1, 1979	Alejandro Portal
Honduras Tegucigalpa	Feb. 1, 1980	Samuel Flores
Argentina Bahia Blanca	Jul. 1, 1980	Allen B. Oliver
Brazil Curitiba	Jul. 1, 1980	Dixon D. Cowley
Dominican Republic Santo Domingo	Jan. 1, 1981	John A. Davis
Haiti Port-Au-Prince	Aug. 1, 1984	James S. Arrigona
El Salvador San Salvador	Oct. 1, 1984	Manuel Antonio Díaz
Peru Trujillo	Jul. 1, 1985	Roberto Vidal
Brazil Brasília	Jul. 1, 1985	Demar Staniscia
Brazil Campinas	Jul. 1, 1986	Sheldon R. Murphy
Mexico Mexico City East	Jan. 1, 1987	Enrique Moreno
Dominican Republic Santiago	Jul. 1, 1987	Michael D. Stirling
Brazil Fortaleza	Jul. 1, 1987	Helvecio Martins
Mexico Mazatlán	Jul. 1, 1987	Samuel Lara M.
Guatemala Guatemala City North	Jan. 1, 1988	Gordon W. Romney
Argentina Salta	Jan. 8, 1988	Francisco José Vinas
Mexico Chihuahua	Jan. 8, 1988	Victor M. Cerda
Mexico Tuxtla-Gutiérrez	Jan. 8, 1988	Alberto de la O
Peru Lima East	Jan. 8, 1988	Douglas K. Earl
Brazil Belo Horizonte	Jul. 1, 1988	Nivio Varella Alcover
Chile Antofagasta	Jul. 1, 1988	Carlos Ramon Espinola
Colombia Barranquilla	Jul. 1, 1988	Frank Berrett
Mexico Puebla	Jul. 1, 1988	George G. Sloan
Mexico Tampico	Jul. 1, 1988	Hector Ceballos

1. Missions are listed in chronological order and according to the name under which they were originally organized. On June 20, 1974, most of the mission names were changed under the Church's new naming system. These and other name changes are indicated on the lines beneath the "Name" column.
2. Denotes name change. Capital letters indicate mission's new name.

SOURCE: *Deseret News 1989–90 Church Almanac,* pp. 260–276.

Table 1114

ROMAN CATHOLIC WELFARE INSTITUTIONS, 20 LRC, 1982–86

Country	1982	1983	1984	1985	1986
A. ARGENTINA					
Hospitals	115	115	103	96	91
Dispensaries	53	85	85	77	86
Leprosaria	4	2	2	2	2
Homes[1]	130	141	144	150	158
Orphanages	159	157	166	143	144
Nurseries	211	234	236	257	303
Others[2]	138	164	223	300	358
Total	810	898	959	1,025	1,142
B. BOLIVIA					
Hospitals	37	35	36	39	34
Dispensaries	222	216	261	164	184
Leprosaria	2	2	2	2	2
Homes[1]	10	10	11	14	9
Orphanages	18	18	23	82	103
Nurseries	8	4	3	6	17
Others[2]	181	175	204	206	141
Total	478	460	540	513	490
C. BRAZIL					
Hospitals	711	726	726	670	687
Dispensaries	928	851	881	853	922
Leprosaria	30	31	35	35	30
Homes[1]	523	582	626	731	727
Orphanages	383	403	458	564	506
Nurseries	494	596	717	799	823
Others[2]	2,241	2,669	3,710	4,114	3,944
Total	5,290	5,858	7,153	7,766	7,650
D. CHILE					
Hospitals	41	48	43	42	41
Dispensaries	61	146	141	182	242
Leprosaria	1	~	~	~	~
Homes[1]	546	123	120	125	132
Orphanages	117	109	109	116	82
Nurseries	54	57	77	140	138
Others[2]	856	1,050	953	1,178	1,591
Total	1,676	1,533	1,443	1,783	2,196
E. COLOMBIA					
Hospitals	171	165	180	184	179
Dispensaries	273	200	222	336	326
Leprosaria	2	2	2	2	2
Homes[1]	169	160	167	176	195
Orphanages	170	156	169	194	178
Nurseries	118	104	109	161	135
Others[2]	462	565	833	808	1,057
Total	1,365	1,352	1,682	1,861	2,072
F. COSTA RICA					
Hospitals	1	1	1	~	~
Dispensaries	18	15	18	18	18
Leprosaria	~	~	~	~	~
Homes[1]	31	30	30	32	32
Orphanages	4	5	5	7	8
Nurseries	20	19	18	25	27
Others[2]	59	57	59	61	62
Total	133	130	131	143	147
G. CUBA					
Hospitals	1	1	1	1	1
Dispensaries	~	~	~	~	~
Leprosaria	~	~	~	~	~
Homes[1]	7	7	7	7	7
Orphanages	~	~	~	~	~
Nurseries	~	~	~	~	~
Others[2]	~	~	1	~	~
Total	8	8	9	8	8
H. DOMINICAN REP.					
Hospitals	14	14	14	16	15
Dispensaries	82	89	89	90	95
Leprosaria	5	5	1	1	5
Homes[1]	11	11	11	15	13
Orphanages	9	12	13	13	9
Nurseries	6	7	7	7	8
Others[2]	198	235	239	215	230
Total	325	373	374	357	375

Table 1114 (Continued)

ROMAN CATHOLIC WELFARE INSTITUTIONS, 20 LRC, 1982–86

Country	1982	1983	1984	1985	1986
I. ECUADOR					
Hospitals	41	38	37	34	34
Dispensaries	233	204	203	217	219
Leprosaria	2	2	2	3	3
Homes[1]	20	22	29	34	31
Orphanages	24	24	25	25	29
Nurseries	15	14	14	22	24
Others[2]	150	278	365	469	536
Total	485	580	675	805	879
J. EL SALVADOR					
Hospitals	10	15	27	14	15
Dispensaries	7	9	50	77	91
Leprosaria	~	~	~	~	~
Homes[1]	9	5	5	8	11
Orphanages	7	4	4	6	7
Nurseries	5	5	5	5	5
Others[2]	30	37	31	39	46
Total	68	75	122	149	175
K. GUATEMALA					
Hospitals	21	32	29	15	30
Dispensaries	410	398	404	455	106
Leprosaria	1	1	1	2	2
Homes[1]	6	7	9	10	13
Orphanages	12	15	14	17	22
Nurseries	5	2	3	2	2
Others[2]	251	317	103	373	687
Total	706	772	563	874	862
L. HAITI					
Hospitals	17	18	14	17	18
Dispensaries	203	196	192	194	193
Leprosaria	2	1	2	2	2
Homes[1]	15	15	14	16	21
Orphanages	33	33	35	38	35
Nurseries	2	4	3	4	4
Others[2]	88	110	140	151	158
Total	360	377	403	422	431
M. HONDURAS					
Hospitals	4	4	4	3	4
Dispensaries	25	22	26	34	91
Leprosaria	~	~	~	~	~
Homes[1]	5	5	5	5	4
Orphanages	3	3	4	4	5
Nurseries	34	27	34	37	38
Others[2]	20	32	28	25	58
Total	91	93	101	108	200
N. MEXICO					
Hospitals	185	175	166	233	237
Dispensaries	525	602	558	881	961
Leprosaria	1	1	2	1	1
Homes[1]	164	168	175	239	269
Orphanages	121	131	139	177	177
Nurseries	29	36	32	113	106
Others[2]	520	735	772	1,325	1,408
Total	1,545	1,848	1,844	2,969	3,159
O. NICARAGUA					
Hospitals	4	5	5	5	4
Dispensaries	52	24	30	26	30
Leprosaria	1	1	~	5	~
Homes[1]	9	9	10	9	8
Orphanages	9	6	9	10	10
Nurseries	3	4	4	4	3
Others[2]	5	6	18	29	29
Total	83	55	76	88	84
P. PANAMA					
Hospitals	1	1	~	~	~
Dispensaries	3	3	4	4	3
Leprosaria	2	1	~	~	~
Homes[1]	6	7	6	6	6
Orphanages	5	4	4	4	6
Nurseries	~	15	15	15	15
Others[2]	11	23	30	27	31
Total	28	54	59	56	61

Table 1114 (Continued)

ROMAN CATHOLIC WELFARE INSTITUTIONS, 20 LRC, 1982–86

Country	1982	1983	1984	1985	1986
Q. PARAGUAY					
Hospitals	10	9	15	16	16
Dispensaries	155	71	102	107	111
Leprosaria	1	1	1	1	1
Homes[1]	4	4	5	7	5
Orphanages	7	5	5	5	3
Nurseries	10	8	9	8	18
Others[2]	158	222	293	391	409
Total	345	320	430	535	563
R. PERU					
Hospitals	34	30	32	33	31
Dispensaries	315	166	203	237	250
Leprosaria	1	1	3	3	3
Homes[1]	34	33	33	34	28
Orphanages	41	38	31	32	73
Nurseries	14	16	32	33	1,066
Others[2]	318	561	634	758	780
Total	757	845	968	1,130	2,231
S. URUGUAY					
Hospitals	27	30	22	22	22
Dispensaries	46	50	58	59	63
Leprosaria	1	1	1	1	1
Homes[1]	18	17	17	19	19
Orphanages	25	26	26	25	26
Nurseries	39	39	39	40	43
Others[2]	195	203	196	225	219
Total	351	366	359	391	393
T. VENEZUELA					
Hospitals	13	14	14	11	11
Dispensaries	67	67	69	46	46
Leprosaria	~	~	~	~	~
Homes[1]	42	43	44	46	47
Orphanages	43	35	38	40	47
Nurseries	15	15	16	17	18
Others[2]	84	96	139	147	157
Total	264	270	320	307	326
LATIN AMERICA[3]					
Hospitals	1,431	1,449	1,446	1,423	1,446
Dispensaries	3,402	3,139	3,319	3,777	3,734
Leprosaria	49	46	52	58	60
Homes[1]	1,735	1,374	1,445	1,654	1,703
Orphanages	1,132	2,517	1,233	1,455	1,429
Nurseries	1,086	1,206	1,373	1,692	2,788
Others[2]	5,695	7,202	8,602	10,488	11,530
Total	14,530	15,559	17,470	20,547	22,678
UNITED STATES					
Hospitals	650	660	656	656	640
Dispensaries	40	50	37	61	88
Leprosaria	1	2	2	2	1
Homes[1]	611	630	668	688	680
Orphanages	227	212	223	215	293
Nurseries	135	147	183	207	298
Others[2]	1,147	1,397	1,443	1,419	1,812
Total	2,811	3,098	3,212	3,248	3,722

1. Homes for the old, the chronically ill, invalids, and the handicapped.
2. Combines three categories in source comprising Matrimonial Advice Centers, Special
   Centers for Social Education or Re-education, and Other Institutions.
3. Includes Belize; does not include the Caribbean.

SOURCE: SYC, 1982–86, table 32.

Table 1115

ROMAN CATHOLIC EDUCATIONAL INSTITUTIONS, 20 LRC, 1982–86

Country	1982	1983	1984	1985	1986
A. ARGENTINA					
Kindergartens	1,173	1,204	1,197	1,132	1,157
Kindergarten Students	106,257	121,874	128,062	135,116	138,130
Primary Schools	1,474	1,434	1,426	1,552	1,564
Primary School Students	560,643	587,070	586,860	629,091	630,336
Secondary Schools	1,073	1,085	1,086	1,144	1,169
Secondary School Students	263,071	276,696	275,184	297,639	312,705
Higher Institute Students	19,404	25,704	29,977	43,763	34,853
University (Eccles.) Students	350	418	495	530	3,082
University (Other) Students	34,687	34,336	34,024	31,922	23,261
B. BOLIVIA					
Kindergartens	69	75	77	80	83
Kindergarten Students	10,472	11,362	13,061	12,676	7,718
Primary Schools	651	347	336	342	296
Primary School Students	93,741	86,060	88,433	85,886	76,236
Secondary Schools	314	308	190	189	201
Secondary School Students	51,140	53,618	55,590	57,314	59,811
Higher Institute Students	1,555	1,135	1,086	1,046	621
University (Eccles.) Students	170	126	2,126	2,276	2,182
University (Other) Students	180	3,080	30,180	30,781	163
C. BRAZIL					
Kindergartens	1,361	1,474	1,519	1,466	1,591
Kindergarten Students	155,273	184,825	190,252	197,580	259,329
Primary Schools	2,316	2,436	2,274	2,254	2,166
Primary School Students	997,388	1,059,496	1,088,659	1,065,696	1,139,915
Secondary Schools	1,211	1,179	1,168	1,252	1,079
Secondary School Students	623,191	634,026	645,268	661,150	511,274
Higher Institute Students	8,039	3,041	8,005	9,395	13,526
University (Eccles.) Students	1,499	1,572	1,295	1,704	1,783
University (Other) Students	212,599	235,723	223,669	230,485	218,560
D. CHILE					
Kindergartens	288	177	196	211	358
Kindergarten Students	18,360	19,127	21,532	22,150	24,215
Primary Schools	546	552	559	571	632
Primary School Students	249,146	251,874	251,705	256,544	286,056
Secondary Schools	275	283	287	286	324
Secondary School Students	91,716	92,570	97,373	92,307	103,041
Higher Institute Students	9,127	9,241	9,217	1,910	9,774
University (Eccles.) Students	9,516	9,584	9,574	7,293	230
University (Other) Students	9,594	9,594	10,458	22,110	22,122
E. COLOMBIA					
Kindergartens	343	316	345	357	402
Kindergarten Students	29,050	30,768	32,281	47,506	50,787
Primary Schools	1,533	1,600	1,515	1,730	1,571
Primary School Students	473,438	470,847	508,663	550,742	587,415
Secondary Schools	890	924	913	1,155	961
Secondary School Students	387,525	420,662	449,468	455,425	501,056
Higher Institute Students	4,101	4,214	4,960	15,776	16,957
University (Eccles.) Students	5,743	1,013	989	2,799	2,964
University (Other) Students	37,114	46,721	48,616	56,020	67,177
F. COSTA RICA					
Kindergartens	19	20	~	25	25
Kindergarten Students	1,040	1,177	~	1,454	1,432
Primary Schools	27	28	~	28	28
Primary School Students	8,694	9,402	~	8,283	8,682
Secondary Schools	35	34	~	27	27
Secondary School Students	14,902	14,559	~	11,177	11,251
Higher Institute Students	88	90	~	~	~
University (Eccles.) Students	~	~	~	~	~
University (Other) Students	~	~	~	~	~
G. CUBA					
Kindergartens	~	~	~	~	~
Kindergarten Students	~	~	~	~	~
Primary Schools	~	1	~	1	~
Primary School Students	~	200	~	1,800	~
Secondary Schools	~	~	~	~	~
Secondary School Students	~	~	~	~	~
Higher Institute Students	~	~	~	~	~
University (Eccles.) Students	~	~	~	~	~
University (Other) Students	~	~	~	~	~
H. DOMINICAN REP.					
Kindergartens	30	21	~	18	65
Kindergarten Students	4,208	1,000	~	835	6,026
Primary Schools	127	5	~	5	125
Primary School Students	63,473	3,247	~	3,163	63,913
Secondary Schools	153	2	~	2	115
Secondary School Students	38,779	1,109	~	1,058	41,619
Higher Institute Students	174	~	~	~	1,088
University (Eccles.) Students	~	~	~	~	~
University (Other) Students	7,950	~	~	~	7,214

Table 1115 (Continued)

ROMAN CATHOLIC EDUCATIONAL INSTITUTIONS, 20 LRC, 1982-86

Country	1982	1983	1984	1985	1986
I. ECUADOR					
Kindergartens	134	170	180	207	713
Kindergarten Students	11,520	14,121	14,640	16,923	17,657
Primary Schools	788	764	767	726	643
Primary School Students	183,614	190,675	194,407	197,067	193,232
Secondary Schools	276	322	326	324	330
Secondary School Students	99,502	103,239	107,621	114,627	113,370
Higher Institute Students	941	930	1,231	1,618	1,118
University (Eccles.) Students	207	~	~	~	~
University (Other) Students	23,203	20,812	23,987	33,618	33,073
J. EL SALVADOR					
Kindergartens	49	51	~	59	64
Kindergarten Students	6,408	6,451	~	6,233	6,439
Primary Schools	101	101	~	106	114
Primary School Students	34,860	37,269	~	46,989	61,151
Secondary Schools	63	63	~	50	54
Secondary School Students	20,277	20,948	~	12,549	14,810
Higher Institute Students	~	~	~	~	~
University (Eccles.) Students	~	~	~	~	~
University (Other) Students	5,890	5,890	~	6,244	5,777
K. GUATEMALA					
Kindergartens	35	26	~	38	34
Kindergarten Students	1,620	1,370	~	1,959	1,955
Primary Schools	175	173	~	164	190
Primary School Students	86,818	85,354	~	96,711	97,432
Secondary Schools	71	67	~	99	94
Secondary School Students	61,789	61,100	~	59,904	59,588
Higher Institute Students	35	35	~	683	100
University (Eccles.) Students	156	156	~	300	300
University (Other) Students	19,528	19,424	~	26,450	26,850
L. HAITI					
Kindergartens	93	91	~	92	110
Kindergarten Students	3,346	3,342	~	2,685	3,662
Primary Schools	609	626	~	728	755
Primary School Students	151,851	266,339	~	291,736	294,736
Secondary Schools	81	79	~	85	88
Secondary School Students	13,336	13,818	~	16,071	33,842
Higher Institute Students	110	120	~	120	120
University (Eccles.) Students	100	~	~	~	~
University (Other) Students	550	~	~	56	96
M. HONDURAS					
Kindergartens	6	19	~	11	13
Kindergarten Students	229	780	~	566	1,067
Primary Schools	24	26	~	24	25
Primary School Students	7,204	7,348	~	7,213	7,657
Secondary Schools	24	24	~	21	21
Secondary School Students	13,670	14,163	~	11,565	11,689
Higher Institute Students	~	~	~	~	~
University (Eccles.) Students	~	~	~	~	~
University (Other) Students	~	~	~	~	~
N. MEXICO					
Kindergartens	669	679	~	712	746
Kindergarten Students	61,753	67,499	~	75,840	77,187
Primary Schools	1,699	1,673	~	1,632	1,671
Primary School Students	635,847	642,207	~	562,270	591,610
Secondary Schools	1,014	1,038	~	1,102	1,088
Secondary School Students	248,300	265,429	~	255,078	288,095
Higher Institute Students	19,759	23,979	~	22,212	30,935
University (Eccles.) Students	408	378	~	2,975	231
University (Other) Students	52,566	56,000	~	55,426	59,113
O. NICARAGUA					
Kindergartens	22	21	~	32	32
Kindergarten Students	5,603	1,086	~	3,421	3,869
Primary Schools	124	64	~	66	66
Primary School Students	77,531	81,371	~	85,227	86,057
Secondary Schools	93	49	~	46	46
Secondary School Students	37,065	39,878	~	38,121	38,818
Higher Institute Students	13,520	13,888	~	1,337	1,334
University (Eccles.) Students	~	~	~	~	~
University (Other) Students	31,200	31,200	~	31,200	31,200
P. PANAMA					
Kindergartens	203	113	~	144	125
Kindergarten Students	5,591	3,226	~	2,835	2,593
Primary Schools	63	28	~	28	29
Primary School Students	21,125	12,370	~	13,025	12,598
Secondary Schools	92	78	~	80	80
Secondary School Students	25,751	18,986	~	20,085	18,760
Higher Institute Students	212	210	~	26	16
University (Eccles.) Students	~	~	~	~	~
University (Other) Students	5,280	6,196	~	4,884	4,590

Table 1115 (Continued)

ROMAN CATHOLIC EDUCATIONAL INSTITUTIONS, 20 LRC, 1982–86

Country	1982	1983	1984	1985	1986
Q. PARAGUAY					
Kindergartens	64	59	62	73	74
Kindergarten Students	3,875	3,876	3,015	4,879	4,567
Primary Schools	177	172	184	180	181
Primary School Students	58,709	58,464	50,249	57,150	56,610
Secondary Schools	111	122	123	121	114
Secondary School Students	28,809	25,325	23,276	25,957	27,022
Higher Institute Students	727	582	606	524	522
University (Eccles.) Students	500	~	~	~	295
University (Other) Students	10,871	9,629	11,051	13,635	14,049
R. PERU					
Kindergartens	971	435	443	457	113
Kindergarten Students	28,188	26,498	29,091	29,592	18,467
Primary Schools	394	362	300	354	373
Primary School Students	178,607	197,020	214,613	214,161	225,191
Secondary Schools	284	317	345	358	371
Secondary School Students	147,579	188,991	208,468	196,387	211,729
Higher Institute Students	8,323	7,983	9,114	21,612	23,126
University (Eccles.) Students	312	353	407	407	452
University (Other) Students	31,753	23,521	55,121	62,763	58,028
S. URUGUAY					
Kindergartens	188	97	103	97	101
Kindergarten Students	9,421	4,211	4,227	3,972	4,256
Primary Schools	192	191	180	176	177
Primary School Students	53,494	51,394	50,595	52,546	54,519
Secondary Schools	87	91	89	92	92
Secondary School Students	22,567	20,191	20,302	21,220	21,360
Higher Institute Students	800	785	785	846	841
University (Eccles.) Students	~	~	~	~	127
University (Other) Students	~	~	~	~	~
T. VENEZUELA					
Kindergartens	288	286	298	265	304
Kindergarten Students	28,181	27,429	29,281	27,413	28,863
Primary Schools	535	538	547	528	503
Primary School Students	191,998	199,438	202,762	204,397	205,145
Secondary Schools	287	309	321	271	248
Secondary School Students	84,735	92,385	105,165	99,174	102,849
Higher Institute Students	330	370	803	810	885
University (Eccles.) Students	~	~	~	74	143
University (Other) Students	11,326	11,387	19,446	13,400	14,200
LATIN AMERICA[1]					
Kindergartens	5,940	5,279	5,438	5,432	6,000
Kindergarten Students	487,150	529,999	558,405	594,521	653,102
Primary Schools	11,005	10,975	10,353	10,642	10,420
Primary School Students	3,958,000	4,078,000	4,065,879	4,177,476	4,355,182
Secondary Schools	6,221	6,312	6,290	6,635	6,316
Secondary School Students	2,228,000	2,349,000	2,398,075	2,436,754	2,414,520
Higher Institute Students	86,961	92,187	92,911	121,558	134,611
University (Eccles.) Students	18,861	13,600	15,602	18,358	11,789
University (Other) Students	485,791	513,513	581,541	618,938	578,163
UNITED STATES					
Kindergartens	3,973	4,297	~	4,690	5,026
Kindergarten Students	133,048	144,955	~	165,049	167,706
Primary Schools	7,976	7,954	~	7,764	7,691
Primary School Students	2,203,000	2,124,000	~	2,005,211	1,946,200
Secondary Schools	1,500	1,488	~	1,425	1,429
Secondary School Students	826,978	792,978	~	774,218	731,578
Higher Institute Students	255,872	273,592	~	230,005	214,836
University (Eccles.) Students	3,731	6,463	~	3,442	3,634
University (Other) Students	304,445	308,294	~	351,037	422,454

1. Includes Belize; does not include the Caribbean.

SOURCE: SYC, 1982–86, table 25.

12

The Military, Drugs, and Crime

Table 1200

U.S. DATA ON MILITARY EXPENDITURES, ARMED FORCES, GNP, AND CENTRAL
GOVERNMENT EXPENDITURES, 20 LRC, 1977–87[a]

Year	Military Expenditures (ME) (M US) Current	Constant 1987	Armed Forces (T)	GNP (M US) Current	Constant 1987	Central Government Expenditures (CGE) (M US) Constant 1987	People (M)	ME/GNP (%)	ME/CGE (%)	ME Per Capita (Constant 1987 Dollars)	Armed Forces (PTI) (Soldiers)	GNP Per Capita (Constant 1987 Dollars)
A. ARGENTINA												
1977	1,467	2,566	155	45,650	79,830	13,640	26.9	3.2	18.8	95	5.8	2,968
1978	1,416	2,307	155	47,270	77,020	14,930	27.3	3.0	15.5	84	5.7	2,817
1979	1,743	2,610	155	54,900	82,220	15,820	27.8	3.2	16.5	94	5.6	2,959
1980	2,141	2,939	155	60,270	82,730	17,370	28.2	3.6	16.9	104	5.5	2,930
1981	2,263	2,834	155	59,590	74,620	19,180	28.7	3.8	14.8	99	5.4	2,602
1982	3,837	4,515	175	59,190	69,650	17,430	29.1	6.5	25.9	155	6.0	2,393
1983	2,902	3,288	175	62,820	71,170	21,990	29.5	4.6	14.9	111	5.9	2,410
1984	2,473[†]	2,701[†]	174	66,870	73,040	15,660	29.9	3.7	17.2	90	5.8	2,439
1985	2,203[†]	2,336[†]	129	66,610	70,650	21,760	30.4	3.3	10.7	77	4.3	2,328
1986	1,503[†]	1,552[†]	104	73,390	75,790	18,520	30.8	2.0	8.4	50	3.4	2,465
1987	1,100[†]	1,100[†]	118	76,850	76,850	9,168	31.1	1.4	12.0	35	3.8	2,467
B. BOLIVIA[1]												
1977	55	96	20	2,813	4,919	651	5.0	2.0	14.7	19	4.0	976
1978	69	113	20	3,106	5,061	699	5.2	2.2	16.1	22	3.9	981
1979	77	115	20	3,332	4,991	688	5.3	2.3	16.6	22	3.8	946
1980	97	133	24	3,538	4,857	742	5.4	2.7	18.0	25	4.4	900
1981	125	157	26	3,856	4,829	692	5.5	3.3	22.7	28	4.7	875
1982	69	81	26	3,881	4,567	~	5.6	1.8	~	14	4.6	809
1983	47	53	27	3,769	4,270	496	5.8	1.2	10.7	9	4.7	739
1984	67	74	28	3,906	4,266	~	5.9	1.7	~	12	4.7	722
1985	~	~	28	3,888	4,124	~	6.0	~	~	~	4.6	683
1986	121[†]	125[†]	30	3,914	4,043	~	6.2	3.1	~	20	4.9	655
1987	127[†]	127[†]	30	4,160	4,160	762[†]	6.3	3.0	16.6	20	4.8	659
C. BRAZIL												
1977	1,085	1,897	450	113,900	199,300	47,540	114.1	1.0	4.0	17	3.9	1,746
1978	1,112	1,812	450	127,300	207,400	52,500	117.0	.9	3.5	15	3.8	1,772
1979	1,117	1,673	450	147,900	221,500	52,750	120.0	.8	3.2	14	3.7	1,845
1980	1,253	1,720	450	175,200	240,500	60,900	123.2	.7	2.8	14	3.7	1,952
1981	1,326	1,661	450	183,800	230,200	64,760	126.4	.7	2.6	13	3.6	1,821
1982	1,933	2,274	460	194,800	229,200	70,740	129.7	1.0	3.2	18	3.5	1,767
1983	1,756	1,990	460	196,400	222,500	70,810	133.1	.9	2.8	15	3.5	1,671
1984	1,801	1,967	459	215,600	235,500	69,320	136.5	.8	2.8	14	3.4	1,725
1985	2,446	2,595	496	241,500	256,100	72,210	140.0	1.0	3.6	19	3.5	1,829
1986	3,860[†]	3,986[†]	527	272,400	281,400	65,010	143.5	1.4	6.1	28	3.7	1,960
1987	2,200[†]	2,200[†]	541	291,300	291,300	35,490	147.1	.8	6.2	15	3.7	1,980
D. CHILE												
1977	313[a]	547[a]	111	7,748	13,550	4,582	10.6	4.0	11.9	52	10.5	1,278
1978	378[a]	616[a]	111	8,992	14,650	4,880	10.8	4.2	12.6	57	10.3	1,362
1979	383[a]	574[a]	111	10,540	15,790	4,779	10.9	3.6	12.0	53	10.2	1,445
1980	443[a]	608[a]	116	12,350	16,950	5,040	11.1	3.6	12.1	55	10.5	1,528
1981	532[a]	666[a]	116	14,110	17,680	5,615	11.3	3.8	11.9	59	10.3	1,567
1982	526[a]	618[a]	116	12,410	14,600	4,935	11.5	4.2	12.5	54	10.1	1,271
1983	541[a]	613[a]	126	12,860	14,570	4,842	11.7	4.2	12.7	52	10.8	1,247
1984	584[a]	638[a]	123	13,880	15,160	5,380	11.9	4.2	11.9	54	10.4	1,276
1985	611[a]	648[a]	124	14,910	15,810	5,659	12.1	4.1	11.4	54	10.3	1,310
1986	567[a]	586[a]	127	15,720	16,230	5,364	12.3	3.6	10.9	48	10.3	1,324
1987	683[†,a]	683[†,a]	127	17,110	17,110	5,400	12.4	4.0	12.7	55	10.2	1,375
E. COLOMBIA												
1977	99	173	60	13,610	23,800	2,683	25.1	.7	6.5	7	2.4	949
1978	116	190	60	15,870	25,850	3,015	25.5	.7	6.3	7	2.4	1,013
1979	177	265	60	18,260	27,350	3,442	26.0	1.0	7.7	10	2.3	1,052
1980	223	306	60	20,810	28,560	3,955	26.5	1.1	7.7	12	2.3	1,077
1981	236	296	65	23,200	29,050	4,296	27.1	1.0	6.9	11	2.4	1,073
1982	370	435	70	24,700	29,060	4,768	27.6	1.5	9.1	16	2.5	1,052
1983	346	393	70	25,960	29,410	4,694	28.2	1.3	8.4	14	2.5	1,042
1984	393	429	70	27,560	30,100	4,802	28.8	1.4	8.9	15	2.4	1,045
1985	362[†]	384[†]	66	29,190	30,960	4,845	29.4	1.2	7.9	13	2.2	1,053
1986	330[†]	341[†]	76	31,130	32,150	4,699	30.0	1.1	7.3	11	2.5	1,070
1987	371[†]	371[†]	86	33,870	33,870	4,995	30.7	1.1	7.4	12	2.8	1,105
F. COSTA RICA												
1977	17	29	5	2,076	3,631	736	2.1	.8	3.9	14	2.4	1,719
1978	16	26	5	2,349	3,828	948	2.2	.7	2.8	12	2.3	1,742
1979	19	28	6	2,660	3,984	1,036	2.3	.7	2.7	12	2.6	1,758
1980	19	27	6	2,886	3,962	1,049	2.3	.7	2.5	12	2.6	1,718
1981	19	24	6	3,025	3,788	885	2.4	.6	2.7	10	2.5	1,601
1982	19	22	6	2,863	3,369	740	2.4	.6	3.0	9	2.5	1,384
1983	25	28	7	3,129	3,545	941	2.5	.8	3.0	11	2.8	1,414
1984	27	30	8	3,548	3,875	976	2.6	.8	3.0	11	3.1	1,501
1985	24	26	8	3,705	3,930	930	2.7	.7	2.8	10	3.0	1,479
1986	25	25	8	4,031	4,164	1,173	2.7	.6	2.2	9	2.9	1,522
1987	26[†]	26[†]	8	4,288	4,288	~	2.8	.6	~	9	2.8	1,525

Table 1200 (Continued)

U.S. DATA ON MILITARY EXPENDITURES, ARMED FORCES, GNP, AND CENTRAL GOVERNMENT EXPENDITURES, 20 LRC, 1977–87[a]

Year	Military Expenditures (ME) (M US) Current	Constant 1987	Armed Forces (T)	GNP (M US) Current	Constant 1987	Central Government Expenditures (CGE) (M US) Constant 1987	People (M)	ME / GNP (%)	ME / CGE (%)	ME Per Capita (Constant 1987 Dollars)	Armed Forces (PTI) (Soldiers)	GNP Per Capita (Constant 1987 Dollars)
G.	**CUBA**											
1977	~	~	200	12,960[†]	22,670[†]	~	9.5	~	~	~	21.0	2,376
1978	1,040[a]	1,695[a]	210	14,830[†]	24,160[†]	~	9.6	7.0	~	176	21.8	2,508
1979	1,160[a]	1,737[a]	210	16,600[†]	24,860[†]	~	9.7	7.0	~	179	21.6	2,560
1980	1,140[a]	1,565[a]	220	17,630[†]	24,200[†]	~	9.7	6.5	~	162	22.8	2,507
1981	1,200[a]	1,503[a]	225	20,840[†]	26,100[†]	~	9.7	5.8	~	155	23.2	2,687
1982	1,330[a]	1,565[a]	230	22,770[†]	26,790[†]	~	9.8	5.8	~	160	23.5	2,737
1983	1,470[a]	1,665[a]	250	25,230[†]	28,580[†]	~	9.9	5.8	~	168	25.3	2,892
1984	1,586[a]	1,732[a]	297	26,990[†]	29,480[†]	~	10.0	5.9	~	174	29.8	2,953
1985	1,600[a]	1,697[a]	297	29,500[†]	31,290[†]	~	10.1	5.4	~	168	29.5	3,104
1986	~	~	297	33,140[†]	34,230[†]	~	10.2	~	~	~	29.2	3,366
1987	~	~	297	26,420[†]	26,420[†]	~	10.3	~	~	~	28.9	2,576
H.	**DOMINICAN REP.**											
1977	37	65	19	2,113	3,695	606	5.4	1.7	10.7	12	3.5	688
1978	47	77	19	2,321	3,782	680	5.5	2.0	11.3	14	3.4	685
1979	54	81	19	2,626	3,933	846	5.7	2.1	9.5	14	3.3	693
1980	44	61	24	3,009	4,131	782	5.8	1.5	7.8	10	4.1	709
1981	54	68	24	3,393	4,249	770	6.0	1.6	8.9	11	4.0	710
1982	54	64	25	3,704	4,358	649	6.1	1.5	9.8	10	4.1	710
1983	55	62	23	4,016	4,550	715	6.3	1.4	8.7	10	3.7	722
1984	49	53	22	4,106	4,485	640	6.5	1.2	8.3	8	3.4	694
1985	50	53	22	4,036	4,280	661	6.6	1.2	8.0	8	3.3	646
1986	58	60	21	4,168	4,304	670[†]	6.8	1.4	8.9	9	3.1	634
1987	64	64	21	4,631	4,631	585[†]	7.0	1.4	10.9	9	3.0	665
I.	**ECUADOR**											
1977	107[a]	180[a]	30	4,634	8,104	1,114	7.5	2.3	16.7	25	4.0	1,087
1978	150[a]	245[a]	35	5,291	8,621	991	7.7	2.8	24.7	32	4.6	1,124
1979	142[a]	213[a]	35	5,976	8,951	983	7.9	2.4	21.6	27	4.4	1,134
1980	152[a]	209[a]	35	6,790	9,321	1,393	8.1	2.2	15.0	26	4.3	1,147
1981	173[a]	216[a]	34	7,712	9,658	1,641	8.4	2.2	13.2	26	4.1	1,155
1982	164[a]	194[a]	36	8,114	9,548	1,600	8.6	2.0	12.1	22	4.2	1,109
1983	139[a]	158[a]	39	8,183	9,271	1,327	8.9	1.7	11.9	18	4.4	1,045
1984	141[a]	154[a]	39	8,662	9,460	1,363	9.1	1.6	11.3	17	4.3	1,035
1985	180[a]	191[a]	43	9,347	9,913	1,618	9.4	1.9	11.8	20	4.6	1,054
1986	237[a]	245[a]	44	9,942	10,270	1,798	9.7	2.4	13.6	25	4.5	1,061
1987	250[a]	250[a]	44	9,715	9,715	1,634	10.0	2.6	15.3	25	4.4	976
J.	**EL SALVADOR**											
1977	35	61	8	2,960	5,177	790	4.4	1.2	7.7	14	1.8	1,188
1978	55	89	11	3,362	5,477	809	4.5	1.6	11.0	20	2.3	1,223
1979	79	118	14	3,632	5,439	811	4.6	2.2	14.5	26	3.0	1,182
1980	97	133	16	3,592	4,931	858	4.7	2.7	15.5	28	3.4	1,054
1981	127	159	23	3,575	4,477	921	4.7	3.6	17.3	34	4.9	961
1982	148	174	28	3,561	4,190	854	4.7	4.2	20.4	37	6.0	896
1983	152	172	32	3,725	4,220	757	4.8	4.1	22.8	36	6.7	881
1984	~	~	45	3,953	4,317	853	4.9	~	~	~	9.2	880
1985	~	~	48	4,152	4,403	810	5.0	~	~	~	9.6	877
1986	~	~	48	4,287	4,428	634	5.1	~	~	~	9.3	862
1987	178	178	49	4,546	4,546	587	5.3	3.9	30.3	34	9.3	864
K.	**GUATEMALA**											
1977	45	78	14	3,568	6,240	734	6.5	1.2	10.6	12	2.2	965
1978	49	79	14	4,020	6,551	794	6.7	1.2	10.0	12	2.1	980
1979	55	82	21	4,582	6,862	314	6.9	1.2	26.0	12	3.0	994
1980	72	98	21	5,153	7,073	919	7.1	1.4	10.7	14	2.9	992
1981	76	95	27	5,666	7,096	1,013	7.4	1.3	9.4	13	3.6	959
1982	111[†]	130[†]	30	5,805	6,831	879	7.6	1.9	14.8	17	3.9	896
1983	121[†]	138[†]	40	5,879	6,661	756	7.8	2.1	18.2	18	5.1	854
1984	118[†]	129[†]	40	6,070	6,630	734	8.0	1.9	17.5	16	5.0	829
1985	114[†]	120[†]	43	6,208	6,584	646	8.2	1.8	18.6	15	5.2	802
1986	~	~	43	6,371	6,579	667	8.4	~	~	~	5.1	782
1987	104[†]	104[†]	43	6,768	6,768	794	8.6	1.5	13.1	12	5.0	785
L.	**HAITI**											
1977	13	23	7	1,090	1,907	386	5.2	1.2	5.9	4	1.3	366
1978	16	25	7	1,223	1,993	373	5.3	1.3	6.8	5	1.3	376
1979	18	27	7	1,433	2,147	407	5.4	1.2	6.6	5	1.3	398
1980	27	38	7	1,683	2,310	405	5.5	1.6	9.3	7	1.3	422
1981	34	43	8	1,796	2,249	455	5.6	1.9	9.4	8	1.4	405
1982	33	39	8	1,843	2,169	541	5.7	1.8	7.3	7	1.4	384
1983	30	34	8	1,922	2,177	565	5.8	1.6	6.1	6	1.4	378
1984	32	35	6	2,008	2,193	436	5.9	1.6	8.1	6	1.0	374
1985	32	34	6	2,079	2,205	450	6.0	1.5	7.5	6	1.0	370
1986	~	~	8	2,148	2,219	392	6.1	~	~	~	1.2	365
1987	40[†]	40[†]	8	2,231	2,231	415	6.2	1.8	9.6	6	1.2	361

Table 1200 (Continued)

U.S. DATA ON MILITARY EXPENDITURES, ARMED FORCES, GNP, AND CENTRAL GOVERNMENT EXPENDITURES, 20 LRC, 1977–87[a]

Year	Military Expenditures (ME) (M US) Current	Constant 1987	Armed Forces (T)	GNP (M US) Current	Constant 1987	Central Government Expenditures (CGE) (M US) Constant 1987	People (M)	ME/GNP (%)	ME/CGE (%)	ME Per Capita (Constant 1987 Dollars)	Armed Forces (PTI) (Soldiers)	GNP Per Capita (Constant 1987 Dollars)
H. HONDURAS												
1977	32	55	12	1,584	2,771	510	3.4	2.0	10.9	16	3.5	816
1978	43	70	14	1,819	2,965	627	3.5	2.4	11.2	20	3.8	842
1979	50	75	14	2,105	3,152	661	3.6	2.4	11.4	21	3.8	865
1980	52[t,b]	71[t,b]	14	2,339	3,211	790[t]	3.8	2.2	9.0	19	3.7	850
1981	47[t,b]	59[t,b]	17	2,606	3,264	755[t]	3.9	1.8	7.8	15	4.3	830
1982	57[t,b]	67[t,b]	17	2,680	3,154	814[t]	4.1	2.1	8.2	16	4.2	775
1983	76[t,b]	86[t,b]	19	2,826	3,201	693[t]	4.2	2.7	12.4	20	4.5	761
1984	121[t,b]	132[t,b]	20	2,999	3,275	840[t]	4.4	4.0	15.7	30	4.6	753
1985	121[t,b]	128[t,b]	21	3,181	3,374	988[t]	4.5	3.8	12.9	28	4.7	749
1986	128[t,b]	132[t,b]	22	3,361	3,472	936[t]	4.7	3.8	14.1	28	4.6	745
1987	133[t,b]	133[t,b]	22	3,624	3,624	998[t]	4.8	3.7	13.3	28	4.5	752
N. MEXICO												
1977	358	625	100	58,260	101,900	16,220	64.9	.6	3.9	10	1.5	1,570
1978	309	504	120	67,680	110,300	17,720	66.6	.5	2.8	8	1.8	1,655
1979	368	552	120	80,070	119,900	20,640	68.4	.5	2.7	8	1.8	1,754
1980	373	513	120	93,510	128,400	23,920	70.1	.4	2.1	7	1.7	1,831
1981	550	688	125	110,600	138,500	30,190	71.9	.5	2.3	10	1.7	1,928
1982	562	661	130	114,500	134,700	43,340	73.6	.5	1.5	9	1.8	1,831
1983	585	663	130	112,900	127,900	34,860	75.3	.5	1.9	9	1.7	1,700
1984	795	868	129	122,100	133,400	32,880	76.9	.7	2.6	11	1.7	1,733
1985	860	912	140	131,300	139,200	36,250	78.6	.7	2.5	12	1.8	1,772
1986	795	821	141	128,200	132,400	40,690	80.2	.6	2.0	10	1.8	1,650
1987	726[t]	726[t]	141	139,200	139,200	31,750	81.9	.5	2.3	9	1.7	1,701
O. NICARAGUA[2]												
1977	647	1,131	6	25,380	44,390	9,539	2.6	2.5	11.9	444	2.4	17,410
1978	857	1,397	6	24,970	40,690	8,312	2.6	3.4	16.8	537	2.3	15,640
1979	668	1,000	6	20,480	30,670	6,852	2.7	3.3	14.6	373	2.2	11,450
1980	1,447[t]	1,986[t]	24	24,770	34,000	10,580	2.8	5.8	18.8	711	8.6	12,170
1981	2,018[t]	2,528[t]	39	27,380	34,290	14,340	2.9	7.4	17.6	876	13.5	11,880
1982	3,255[t]	3,830[t]	41	28,810	33,900	17,870	3.0	11.3	21.4	1,293	13.8	11,440
1983	3,552[t]	4,024[t]	46	31,560	35,750	25,610	3.0	11.3	15.7	1,328	15.2	11,800
1984	4,519[t]	4,935[t]	67	30,910	33,760	23,670	3.1	14.6	20.9	1,593	21.6	10,900
1985	5,225[t]	5,541[t]	74	30,320	32,160	21,160	3.2	17.2	26.2	1,751	23.4	10,160
1986	~	~	75	31,140	32,160	16,930	3.2	~	~	~	23.1	9,934
1987	~	~	80	33,170	33,170	~	3.3	~	~	~	24.1	9,994
P. PANAMA												
1977	14	25	8	1,915	3,348	1,109	1.8	.7	2.3	14	4.3	1,820
1978	26[t]	43[t]	8	2,275	3,706	1,167	1.9	1.2	3.7	23	4.3	1,979
1979	28[t]	42[t]	8	2,574	3,854	1,513	1.9	1.1	2.8	22	4.2	2,013
1980	~	~	8	3,099	4,254	1,486	2.0	~	~	~	4.1	2,174
1981	42[t]	52[t]	9	3,565	4,464	1,665	2.0	1.2	3.2	26	4.5	2,234
1982	60[t]	71[t]	10	3,963	4,663	1,984	2.0	1.5	3.6	35	4.9	2,283
1983	88[t]	99[t]	10	4,103	4,648	1,799	2.1	2.1	5.5	48	4.8	2,227
1984	99[t]	108[t]	11	4,284	4,679	1,870	2.1	2.3	5.8	51	5.2	2,194
1985	101[t]	107[t]	12	4,576	4,853	1,654	2.2	2.2	6.5	49	5.5	2,227
1986	106[t]	110[t]	12	4,862	5,021	1,723	2.2	2.2	6.4	49	5.4	2,255
1987	105[t]	105[t]	12	5,160	5,160	~	2.3	2.0	~	46	5.4	2,268
P. PARAGUAY												
1977	28	50	15	1,630	2,851	324	3.1	1.7	15.3	16	4.9	934
1978	31	51	15	1,917	3,124	370	3.2	1.6	13.7	16	4.8	990
1979	34	52	15	2,340	3,504	384	3.3	1.5	13.4	16	4.6	1,073
1980	41	56	15	2,941	4,037	419	3.4	1.4	13.3	17	4.4	1,195
1981	53	66	15	3,512	4,398	498	3.5	1.5	13.2	19	4.3	1,259
1982	64[t]	75[t]	16	3,673	4,322	470	3.6	1.7	16.0	21	4.4	1,197
1983	90[t]	102[t]	16	3,657	4,143	455	3.7	2.5	22.4	27	4.3	1,109
1984	63[t]	68[t]	17	3,886	4,244	472	3.9	1.6	14.5	18	4.4	1,099
1985	47[t]	49[t]	14	4,095	4,343	~	4.0	1.1	~	12	3.5	1,088
1986	~	~	16	4,239	4,378	359	4.1	~	~	~	3.9	1,063
1987	47[t]	47[t]	16	4,566	4,566	417[t]	4.3	1.0	11.2	11	3.8	1,074
R. PERU												
1977	1,318	2,306	125	19,630	34,330	5,863	16.0	6.7	39.3	144	7.8	2,147
1978	1,059	1,725	125	20,750	33,820	5,386	16.4	5.1	32.0	105	7.6	2,060
1979	868	1,300	125	23,530	35,240	5,236	16.8	3.7	24.8	77	7.4	2,092
1980	1,354	1,858	151	27,220	37,370	6,874	17.3	5.0	27.0	107	8.7	2,161
1981	1,331	1,666	157	31,410	39,330	7,029	17.8	4.2	23.7	94	8.8	2,215
1982	1,554	1,828	164	33,550	39,480	6,060	18.2	4.6	30.2	100	9.0	2,166
1983	1,462	1,657	167	30,020	34,010	5,521	18.7	4.9	30.0	89	8.9	1,817
1984	1,835[t]	2,004[t]	135	32,620	35,620	5,215	19.2	5.6	38.4	104	7.0	1,855
1985	2,166[t]	2,297[t]	128	34,510	36,600	5,393	19.7	6.3	42.6	117	6.5	1,857
1986	2,565[t]	2,649[t]	127	39,750	41,050	6,432	20.2	6.5	41.2	131	6.3	2,031
1987	2,198[t]	2,198[t]	127	44,580	44,580	8,875	20.7	4.9	24.8	106	6.1	2,150

Table 1200 (Continued)

U.S. DATA ON MILITARY EXPENDITURES, ARMED FORCES, GNP, AND CENTRAL GOVERNMENT EXPENDITURES, 20 LRC, 1977–87[a]

Year	Military Expenditures (ME) (M US) Current	Constant 1987	Armed Forces (T)	GNP (M US) Current	Constant 1987	Central Government Expenditures (CGE) (M US) Constant 1987	People (M)	ME/GNP (%)	ME/CGE (%)	ME Per Capita (Constant 1987 Dollars)	Armed Forces (PTI) (Soldiers)	GNP Per Capita (Constant 1987 Dollars)
S. URUGUAY												
1977	88	154	28	3,714	6,496	1,592	2.9	2.4	9.7	54	9.8	2,271
1978	96	156	28	4,193	6,832	1,615	2.9	2.3	9.7	54	9.8	2,380
1979	116	174	28	4,874	7,300	1,556	2.9	2.4	11.2	60	9.7	2,535
1980	166	228	28	5,623	7,719	1,733	2.9	2.9	13.1	79	9.7	2,671
1981	247	309	28	6,300	7,890	2,005	2.9	3.9	15.4	107	9.7	2,720
1982	245	288	29	5,977	7,033	2,181	2.9	4.1	13.2	99	10.0	2,417
1983	190	216	30	5,669	6,422	1,739	2.9	3.4	12.4	74	10.3	2,199
1984	160	175	30	5,701	6,227	1,609	2.9	2.8	10.9	60	10.2	2,124
1985	154	163	30	5,897	6,255	1,536	2.9	2.6	10.6	55	10.2	2,126
1986	163	168	30	6,626	6,843	1,667	3.0	2.5	10.1	57	10.2	2,318
1987	~	~	28	7,222	7,222	1,299	3.0	~	~	~	9.4	2,437
T. VENEZUELA												
1977	345	603	55	22,100	38,650	12,380	13.6	1.6	4.9	44	4.0	2,844
1978	384	626	55	24,200	39,440	11,660	14.1	1.6	5.4	44	3.9	2,803
1979	386	578	55	26,680	39,960	9,102	14.6	1.4	6.3	40	3.8	2,746
1980	365	501	55	28,780	39,510	10,320	15.0	1.3	4.9	33	3.7	2,630
1981	359	449	55	31,590	39,560	14,000	15.5	1.1	3.2	29	3.6	2,555
1982	563	663	56	32,570	38,330	13,020	15.9	1.7	5.1	42	3.5	2,405
1983	731	828	56	31,460	35,640	10,460	16.4	2.3	7.9	51	3.4	2,174
1984	677	740	64	32,680	35,690	9,636	16.9	2.1	7.7	44	3.8	2,117
1985	433	460	71	33,160	35,170	10,240	17.3	1.3	4.5	27	4.1	2,029
1986	580	599	66	37,200	38,420	11,650	17.8	1.6	5.1	34	3.7	2,157
1987	1,379[†]	1,379[†]	69	38,370	38,370	12,900[†]	18.3	3.6	10.7	75	3.8	2,098
UNITED STATES												
1977	100,900	170,500	2,000	1,991,000	3,481,000	741,100	220.2	5.1	23.8	801	9.4	15,810
1978	109,200	178,000	2,033	2,250,000	3,666,000	775,000	222.6	4.9	23.0	800	9.1	16,470
1979	122,300	183,100	2,050	2,508,000	3,756,000	785,800	225.1	4.9	23.3	814	9.1	16,690
1980	144,000	197,600	2,101	2,732,000	3,750,000	854,200	227.8	5.3	23.1	868	9.2	16,470
1981	169,900	212,800	2,168	3,053,000	3,823,000	899,900	230.1	5.6	23.6	924	9.4	16,610
1982	196,400	231,100	2,201	3,166,000	3,725,000	924,400	232.5	6.2	25.0	994	9.5	16,020
1983	217,200	246,000	2,201	3,406,000	3,858,000	969,800	234.8	6.4	25.4	1,048	9.4	16,430
1984	237,100	258,900	2,222	3,772,000	4,120,000	979,500	237.0	6.3	26.4	1,092	9.4	17,380
1985	266,800	281,900	2,244	4,015,000	4,258,000	1,065,000	239.3	6.6	26.5	1,178	9.4	17,800
1986	280,900	290,100	2,269	4,240,000	4,379,000	1,070,000	241.6	6.6	27.1	1,201	9.4	18,130
1987	296,200	296,200	2,279	4,527,000	4,527,000	1,057,000	243.8	6.5	28.0	1,215	9.3	18,570
LATIN AMERICA[3,4]												
1977	7.0	12.3	1,438	353	617	138.4	335.0	2.0	8.9	37	4.3	1,842
1978	7.3	11.9	1,478	390	635	145.6	343.0	1.9	8.2	35	4.3	1,853
1979	7.6	11.4	1,491	442	662	146.0	351.2	1.7	7.8	32	4.2	1,884
1980	9.6	13.2	1,561	509	698	167.9	359.5	1.9	7.9	37	4.3	1,942
1981	10.9	13.7	1,617	556	697	189.4	368.0	2.0	7.2	37	4.4	1,893
1982	15.1	17.8	1,687	579	681	208.8	376.6	2.6	8.5	47	4.5	1,808
1983	14.6	16.5	1,746	585	663	209.1	385.4	2.5	7.9	43	4.5	1,721
1984	15.9	17.4	1,798	627	685	196.1	394.2	2.5	8.9	44	4.6	1,737
1985	17.2	18.2	1,814	671	711	205.8	403.2	2.6	8.9	45	4.5	1,765
1986	17.6	18.1	1,835	725	749	196.4	412.2	2.4	9.2	44	4.5	1,817
1987	15.2	15.2	1,879	767	767	145.5	421.3	2.0	10.4	36	4.5	1,821
WORLD[4,5]												
1977	457.4	800.0	25,830	8,379	14,650	3,975.7	4,233.5	5.5	20.1	189	6.1	3,461
1978	502.8	819.3	26,530	9,332	15,210	4,160.2	4,306.6	5.4	19.7	190	6.2	3,531
1979	550.9	825.1	26,820	10,500	15,730	4,348.5	4,382.4	5.2	19.0	188	6.1	3,590
1980	627.4	861.2	26,970	11,710	16,070	4,639.0	4,458.9	5.4	18.6	193	6.0	3,604
1981	710.3	889.6	27,670	13,000	16,280	4,802.0	4,536.6	5.5	18.5	196	6.1	3,589
1982	795.1	935.5	27,560	13,860	16,310	4,959.1	4,617.3	5.7	18.9	203	6.0	3,532
1983	848.8	961.7	27,850	14,730	16,690	5,071.8	4,698.2	5.8	19.0	205	5.9	3,553
1984	901.5	984.6	28,710	15,860	17,320	5,134.2	4,780.1	5.7	19.2	206	6.0	3,624
1985	956.0	1,013.9	28,950	16,810	17,830	5,306.5	4,862.6	5.7	19.1	209	6.0	3,667
1986	983.8	1,016.1	29,350	17,780	18,360	5,385.6	4,947.5	5.5	18.9	205	5.9	3,711
1987	1,016.4	1,016.4	29,150	18,870	18,870	5,344.6	5,035.0	5.4	19.0	202	5.8	3,748

Table 1200 (Continued)

U.S. DATA ON MILITARY EXPENDITURES, ARMED FORCES, GNP, AND CENTRAL GOVERNMENT EXPENDITURES, 20 LRC, 1977–87[a]

1. Devaluation (i.e., increase in the national–currency–units per dollar exchange rate) between edition base years 1984 and 1987 substantially exceeded the national currency inflation rate, causing their national expenditures in 1987 dollars to be more than 50% lower than in 1984 dollars.

2. As with most non–communist countries, Nicaraguan national currency amounts (in base–year prices) are converted to dollars at the IMF/World Bank–reported average exchange rate for the base year of this edition (1987). For Nicaragua, the resulting dollar values are inordinately higher than the dollar amounts obtaining in the previous edition (conversion base year = 1984) and substantially overstate the relative purchasing power of Nicaraguan expenditures (after allowing for the 9.2% U.S. dollar inflation in 1984–87). This is due to the fact that the extremely high (58–fold) inflation rate experienced by Nicaragua in 1984–87 was not matched by the seven–fold change in the average exchange rate. A number of other countries, particularly developed ones, experienced substantial increases on the order of 50–80% in values in 1987 dollars over those in 1984 dollars, due to the general devaluation of the U.S. dollar in this period.

3. In order to reduce distortions in grouped data trends caused by data gaps for individual countries and years, the totals for the world, regions, and organizations include rough approximations for the gaps.

4. Billions of dollars.

5. This ratio is calculated from the two variables as expressed in dollar terms. Since in this case the two variables are converted to, or estimated in, dollars in differing ways, the ratio in dollars differs from what it would be in national currency terms.

a. For previous years, see SALA, 17–2300, 26–1200, and 27–1200.

b. This series probably omits a major share of total military expenditures, probably including most arms acquisitions. Table 1201 shows estimated annual arms imports; it should be kept in mind, however, that data in Table 1201 represent the estimated value of arms delivered in a given year, not actual expenditures on those arms.

c. Estimated by adding arms imports to data on military expenditures, which are believed to exclude arms purchases. However, it should be noted that the value of arms deliveries in a given year, as show in Table 1201 (converted at current exchange rates), may differ significantly from actual expenditures on arms imports in that year.

SOURCE: U.S. Arms Control and Disarmament Agency, *World Military Expenditures and Arms Transfers, 1975–1985* (Washington, D.C., 1988) Table I.

Table 1201

U.S. DATA ON VALUE OF ARMS TRANSFERS AND TOTAL IMPORTS AND EXPORTS, BY REGION, ORGANIZATION, AND COUNTRY, 20 LRC, 1977–87[a]

Year	Arms Imports[1] (M US) Current	Arms Imports[1] (M US) Constant 1987	Arms Exports[1] (M US) Current	Arms Exports[1] (M US) Constant 1987	Total Imports[2] (M US) Current	Total Imports[2] (M US) Constant 1987	Total Exports[2] (M US) Current	Total Exports[2] (M US) Constant 1987	Arms Imports[3] Total Imports (%)	Arms Exports[3] Total Exports (%)
A. ARGENTINA										
1977	40	70	5	9	4,162	7,279	5,652	9,885	1.0	.1
1978	370	603	#	#	3,834	6,247	6,400	10,430	9.7	#
1979	500	749	10	15	6,700	10,030	7,810	11,700	7.5	.1
1980	210	288	5	7	10,540	14,470	8,021	11,010	2.0	.1
1981	500	626	10	13	9,430	11,810	9,143	11,450	5.3	.1
1982	290	341	#	#	5,337	6,280	7,625	8,972	5.4	#
1983	975	1,105	20	23	4,504	5,103	7,836	8,878	21.6	.3
1984	450	491	120	131	4,585	5,008	8,107	8,855	9.8	1.5
1985	180	191	60	64	3,814	4,045	8,396	8,905	4.7	.7
1986	30	31	5	5	4,724	4,879	6,852	7,077	.6	.1
1987	30	30	20	20	6,119	6,119	6,360	6,360	.5	.3
B. BOLIVIA										
1977	10	17	#	#	591	1,034	632	1,105	1.7	#
1978	20	33	#	#	769	1,253	629	1,025	2.6	#
1979	80	120	#	#	980	1,468	760	1,138	8.2	#
1980	40	55	#	#	678	931	942	1,293	5.9	#
1981	70	88	#	#	975	1,221	912	1,142	7.2	#
1982	#	#	#	#	578	680	828	974	#	#
1983	#	#	#	#	589	667	755	855	#	#
1984	10	11	#	#	492	537	725	792	2.0	#
1985	#	#	#	#	552	585	623	661	#	#
1986	20	21	#	#	716	739	564	582	2.8	#
1987	#	#	#	#	761	761	566	566	#	#
C. BRAZIL										
1977	90	157	80	140	13,260	23,190	12,120	21,200	.7	.7
1978	200	326	100	163	15,050	24,530	12,660	20,630	1.3	.8
1979	240	359	110	165	19,800	29,660	15,240	22,830	1.2	.7
1980	130	178	140	192	24,960	34,260	20,130	27,640	.6	.7
1981	60	75	170	213	24,080	30,150	23,290	29,170	.2	.7
1982	30	35	675	794	21,070	24,790	20,170	23,740	.1	3.3
1983	40	45	130	147	16,800	19,030	21,900	24,810	.2	.6
1984	150	164	625	683	15,210	16,610	27,000	29,500	1.0	2.3
1985	50	53	350	371	14,330	15,200	25,640	27,190	.3	1.4
1986	120	124	220	227	15,560	16,070	22,350	23,080	.8	1.0
1987	100	100	600	600	16,580	16,580	26,220	26,220	.6	2.3
D. CHILE										
1977	60	105	#	#	2,259	3,951	2,190	3,830	2.7	#
1978	60	98	#	#	3,002	4,891	2,478	4,038	2.0	#
1979	180	270	#	#	4,218	6,317	3,894	5,832	4.3	#
1980	250	343	#	#	5,124	7,034	4,671	6,412	4.9	#
1981	310	388	5	6	6,364	7,970	3,906	4,892	4.9	.1
1982	280	329	#	#	3,528	4,151	3,710	4,365	7.9	#
1983	90	102	#	#	2,969	3,364	3,836	4,346	3.0	#
1984	160	175	20	22	3,191	3,485	3,657	3,994	5.0	.5
1985	20	21	80	85	2,743	2,909	3,823	4,055	.7	2.1
1986	10	10	10	10	2,914	3,009	4,222	4,360	.3	.2
1987	30	30	170	170	3,793	3,793	5,091	5,091	.8	3.3
E. COLOMBIA										
1977	10	17	#	#	2,028	3,547	2,443	4,273	.5	#
1978	10	16	#	#	2,836	4,621	3,003	4,893	.4	#
1979	20	30	#	#	3,233	4,842	3,300	4,942	.6	#
1980	70	96	#	#	4,663	6,401	3,945	5,415	1.5	#
1981	40	50	#	#	5,199	6,511	2,956	3,702	.8	#
1982	130	153	#	#	5,478	6,446	3,095	3,642	2.4	#
1983	30	34	#	#	4,968	5,628	3,081	3,491	.6	#
1984	700	765	#	#	4,498	4,913	3,462	3,781	15.6	#
1985	20	21	#	#	4,141	4,392	3,552	3,767	.5	#
1986	30	31	#	#	3,862	3,989	5,102	5,269	.8	#
1987	10	10	#	#	4,322	4,322	1,158	1,158	.2	#
F. COSTA RICA										
1977	#	#	#	#	1,021	1,786	828	1,448	#	#
1978	#	#	#	#	1,166	1,900	865	1,409	#	#
1979	#	#	#	#	1,397	2,092	934	1,399	#	#
1980	#	#	#	#	1,540	2,114	1,002	1,375	#	#
1981	#	#	#	#	1,209	1,514	1,008	1,262	#	#
1982	#	#	#	#	889	1,046	870	1,024	#	#
1983	#	#	#	#	988	1,119	873	989	#	#
1984	5	5	#	#	1,094	1,195	1,006	1,099	.5	#
1985	20	21	#	#	1,098	1,165	976	1,035	1.8	#
1986	10	10	#	#	1,148	1,186	1,121	1,158	.9	#
1987	#	#	#	#	1,383	1,383	1,158	1,158	#	#

Table 1201 (Continued)

U.S. DATA ON VALUE OF ARMS TRANSFERS AND TOTAL IMPORTS AND EXPORTS, BY REGION, ORGANIZATION, AND COUNTRY, 20 LRC, 1977–87[a]

Year	Arms Imports[1] (M US) Current	Arms Imports[1] Constant 1987	Arms Exports[1] (M US) Current	Arms Exports[1] Constant 1987	Total Imports[2] (M US) Current	Total Imports[2] Constant 1987	Total Exports[2] (M US) Current	Total Exports[2] Constant 1987	Arms Imports[3] Total Imports (%)	Arms Exports[3] Total Exports (%)
G. CUBA										
1977	450	787	10	17	4,362	7,629	3,669	6,417	10.3	.3
1978	800	1,303	#	#	4,751	7,741	4,575	7,454	16.8	#
1979	700	1,048	#	#	5,089	7,622	4,829	7,232	13.8	#
1980	480	659	#	#	6,409	8,798	5,593	7,677	7.5	#
1981	1,500	1,878	10	13	6,546	8,198	5,406	6,770	22.9	.2
1982	1,700	2,000	20	24	6,645	7,819	5,928	6,975	25.6	.3
1983	1,300	1,473	40	45	7,235	8,197	6,416	7,269	18.0	.6
1984	1,400	1,529	20	22	8,213	8,970	6,174	6,743	17.0	.3
1985	2,400	2,545	5	5	8,677	9,203	6,502	6,896	27.7	.1
1986	1,600	1,652	#	#	9,158	9,458	6,290	6,496	17.5	#
1987	1,800	1,800	#	#	7,236	7,236	7,236	7,236	24.9	#
H. DOMINICAN REP.										
1977	#	#	#	#	975	1,705	780	1,364	#	#
1978	#	#	#	#	987	1,608	676	1,101	#	#
1979	#	#	#	#	1,213	1,817	869	1,301	#	#
1980	10	14	#	#	1,640	2,251	962	1,321	.6	#
1981	#	#	#	#	1,668	2,089	1,188	1,488	#	#
1982	10	12	#	#	1,444	1,699	768	904	.7	#
1983	5	6	#	#	1,471	1,667	785	889	.3	#
1984	10	11	#	#	1,446	1,579	868	948	.7	#
1985	5	5	#	#	1,487	1,577	735	780	.3	#
1986	5	5	#	#	1,433	1,480	718	742	.3	#
1987	5	5	#	#	1,783	1,783	711	711	.3	#
I. ECUADOR										
1977	160	280	#	#	1,189	2,080	1,436	2,512	13.5	#
1978	90	147	#	#	1,505	2,452	1,558	2,539	6.0	#
1979	170	255	#	#	1,600	2,396	2,104	3,151	10.6	#
1980	180	247	#	#	2,253	3,093	2,481	3,406	8.0	#
1981	100	125	#	#	2,246	2,813	2,542	3,183	4.5	#
1982	280	329	#	#	2,169	2,552	2,327	2,738	12.9	#
1983	180	204	#	#	1,487	1,685	2,348	2,660	12.1	#
1984	140	153	#	#	1,616	1,765	2,620	2,862	8.7	#
1985	50	53	#	#	1,767	1,874	2,905	3,081	2.8	#
1986	30	31	#	#	1,810	1,869	2,172	2,243	1.7	#
1987	70	70	#	#	2,052	2,052	2,021	2,021	3.4	#
J. EL SALVADOR										
1977	#	#	#	#	929	1,625	972	1,700	#	#
1978	5	8	#	#	1,027	1,673	801	1,305	.5	#
1979	30	45	#	#	1,039	1,556	1,131	1,694	2.9	#
1980	#	#	#	#	962	1,321	1,074	1,474	#	#
1981	10	13	#	#	985	1,234	797	998	1.0	#
1982	40	47	#	#	857	1,008	699	823	4.7	#
1983	50	57	#	#	891	1,009	735	833	5.6	#
1984	80	87	#	#	977	1,067	725	792	8.2	#
1985	90	95	#	#	961	1019	679	720	9.4	#
1986	80	83	#	#	902	932	757	782	8.9	#
1987	50	50	#	#	~	~	~	~	~	~
K. GUATEMALA										
1977	5	9	#	#	1,053	1,842	1,182	2,067	.5	#
1978	10	16	#	#	1,286	2,095	1,113	1,813	.8	#
1979	10	15	#	#	1,504	2,252	1,270	1,902	.7	#
1980	10	14	#	#	1,598	2,194	1,557	2,137	.6	#
1981	#	#	#	#	1,674	2,096	1,254	1,570	#	#
1982	10	12	#	#	1,388	1,633	1,153	1,357	.7	#
1983	5	6	#	#	1,126	1,276	1,190	1,348	.4	#
1984	40	44	#	#	1,279	1,397	1,137	1,242	3.1	#
1985	30	32	#	#	1,175	1,246	1,054	1,118	2.6	#
1986	#	#	#	#	960	991	1,103	1,139	#	#
1987	5	5	#	#	1,479	1,479	1,084	1,084	.3	#
L. HAITI										
1977	#	#	#	#	213	373	149	261	#	#
1978	#	#	#	#	233	380	155	253	#	#
1979	#	#	#	#	272	407	185	277	#	#
1980	#	#	#	#	375	515	226	310	#	#
1981	10	13	#	#	461	577	152	190	2.2	#
1982	#	#	#	#	387	455	163	192	#	#
1983	5	6	#	#	441	500	154	174	1.1	#
1984	#	#	#	#	450	491	179	196	#	#
1985	10	11	#	#	442	469	174	185	2.3	#
1986	#	#	#	#	~	~	186	192	~	#
1987	#	#	#	#	~	~	166	166	~	#

Table 1201 (Continued)

U.S. DATA ON VALUE OF ARMS TRANSFERS AND TOTAL IMPORTS AND EXPORTS, BY REGION, ORGANIZATION, AND COUNTRY, 20 LRC, 1977–87[a]

Year	Arms Imports[1] (M US) Current	Constant 1987	Arms Exports[1] (M US) Current	Constant 1987	Total Imports[2] (M US) Current	Constant 1987	Total Exports[2] (M US) Current	Constant 1987	Arms Imports[3] Total Imports (%)	Arms Exports[3] Total Exports (%)
M. HONDURAS										
1977	5	9	#	#	579	1,013	519	908	.9	#
1978	5	8	#	#	699	1,139	613	999	.7	#
1979	10	15	#	#	826	1,237	734	1,099	1.2	#
1980	#	#	#	#	1,009	1,385	830	1,139	#	#
1981	10	13	#	#	945	1,183	729	913	1.1	#
1982	#	#	#	#	692	814	668	786	#	#
1983	10	11	#	#	823	932	671	760	1.2	#
1984	80	87	#	#	954	1,042	746	815	8.4	#
1985	20	21	#	#	890	944	765	811	2.2	#
1986	60	62	#	#	875	904	854	882	6.9	#
1987	60	60	#	#	~	~	~	~	~	~
N. MEXICO										
1977	10	17	#	#	5,883	10,290	4,518	7,902	.2	#
1978	10	16	#	#	7,555	12,310	5,958	9,708	.1	#
1979	10	15	#	#	12,090	18,100	8,982	13,450	.1	#
1980	20	27	#	#	19,460	26,710	15,570	21,370	.1	#
1981	50	63	#	#	24,070	30,140	19,650	24,600	.2	#
1982	200	235	#	#	15,130	17,800	21,210	24,960	1.3	#
1983	40	45	#	#	8,023	9,090	21,820	24,720	.5	#
1984	20	22	#	#	11,790	12,870	24,410	26,660	.2	#
1985	30	32	#	#	13,990	14,840	22,110	23,450	.2	#
1986	100	103	#	#	12,030	12,430	16,240	16,770	.8	#
1987	240	240	#	#	12,730	12,730	20,890	20,890	1.9	#
Q. NICARAGUA										
1977	10	17	#	#	762	1,333	637	1,114	1.3	#
1978	10	16	#	#	596	971	646	1,053	1.7	#
1979	5	7	#	#	360	539	567	849	1.4	#
1980	10	14	#	#	887	1,218	451	619	1.1	#
1981	160	200	#	#	999	1,251	508	636	16.0	#
1982	150	177	#	#	776	913	406	478	19.3	#
1983	280	317	#	#	807	914	429	486	34.7	#
1984	350	382	#	#	826	902	386	422	42.4	#
1985	270	286	#	#	892	946	302	320	30.3	#
1986	575	594	#	#	770	795	247	255	74.7	#
1987	500	500	#	#	923	923	300	300	54.2	#
P. PANAMA										
1977	5	9	#	#	861	1,506	251	439	.6	#
1978	#	#	#	#	942	1,535	256	417	#	#
1979	#	#	#	#	1,184	1,773	303	454	#	#
1980	30	41	#	#	1,449	1,989	360	494	2.1	#
1981	5	6	#	#	1,540	1,929	328	411	.3	#
1982	10	12	#	#	1,569	1,846	375	441	.6	#
1983	#	#	#	#	1,412	1,600	321	364	#	#
1984	10	11	#	#	1,423	1,554	276	301	.7	#
1985	10	11	#	#	1,392	1,476	335	355	.7	#
1986	10	10	#	#	1,229	1,269	341	352	.8	#
1987	5	5	#	#	1,270	1,270	357	357	.4	#
Q. PARAGUAY										
1977	#	#	#	#	308	539	279	488	#	#
1978	10	16	#	#	383	624	257	419	2.6	#
1979	10	15	#	#	521	780	305	457	1.9	#
1980	40	55	#	#	615	844	310	426	6.5	#
1981	5	6	#	#	600	751	296	371	.8	#
1982	#	#	#	#	672	791	330	388	#	#
1983	#	#	#	#	546	619	269	305	#	#
1984	20	22	#	#	586	640	335	366	3.4	#
1985	10	11	#	#	502	532	304	322	2.0	#
1986	10	10	#	#	577	596	234	242	1.7	#
1987	#	#	#	#	595	595	353	353	#	#
R. PERU										
1977	460	805	#	#	1,911	3,342	1,726	3,019	24.1	#
1978	370	603	#	#	1,959	3,192	1,941	3,163	18.9	#
1979	90	135	#	#	1,820	2,726	3,491	5,228	4.9	#
1980	280	394	#	#	2,500	3,432	3,898	5,351	11.2	#
1981	300	376	#	#	4,258	5,332	3,802	4,761	7.0	#
1982	240	282	60	71	4,168	4,904	3,721	4,378	5.8	1.6
1983	230	261	#	#	3,049	3,454	2,722	3,084	7.5	#
1984	140	153	#	#	2,212	2,416	3,147	3,437	6.3	#
1985	80	85	#	#	2,023	2,146	2,979	3,159	4.0	#
1986	170	176	#	#	2,909	3,004	2,531	2,614	5.8	#
1987	430	430	#	#	3,435	3,435	2,605	2,605	12.5	#

Table 1201 (Continued)

U.S. DATA ON VALUE OF ARMS TRANSFERS AND TOTAL IMPORTS AND EXPORTS, BY REGION, ORGANIZATION, AND COUNTRY, 20 LRC, 1977–87[a]

Year	Arms Imports[1] (M US) Current	Arms Imports[1] (M US) Constant 1987	Arms Exports[1] (M US) Current	Arms Exports[1] (M US) Constant 1987	Total Imports[2] (M US) Current	Total Imports[2] (M US) Constant 1987	Total Exports[2] (M US) Current	Total Exports[2] (M US) Constant 1987	Arms Imports[3] Total Imports (%)	Arms Exports[3] Total Exports (%)
S. URUGUAY										
1977	20	35	#	#	730	1,277	608	1,063	2.7	#
1978	5	8	#	#	757	1,233	686	1,118	.7	#
1979	5	7	#	#	1,206	1,806	788	1,180	.4	#
1980	40	55	#	#	1,680	2,306	1,059	1,454	2.4	#
1981	60	75	#	#	1,641	2,055	1,215	1,522	3.7	#
1982	20	24	#	#	1,110	1,306	1,023	1,204	1.8	#
1983	10	11	#	#	788	893	1,045	1,184	1.3	#
1984	#	#	#	#	777	849	925	1,010	#	#
1985	#	#	#	#	708	751	909	964	#	#
1986	#	#	#	#	870	899	1,088	1,124	#	#
1987	#	#	#	#	1,142	1,142	1,189	1,189	#	#
T. VENEZUELA										
1977	100	175	#	#	10,940	19,130	9,551	16,700	.9	#
1978	30	49	#	#	11,770	19,170	9,187	14,970	.3	#
1979	40	60	#	#	10,670	15,980	14,320	21,440	.4	#
1980	130	178	#	#	11,830	16,230	19,220	26,380	1.1	#
1981	290	363	#	#	13,110	16,410	20,980	26,270	2.2	#
1982	250	294	#	#	12,940	15,230	16,500	19,410	1.9	#
1983	90	102	#	#	8,710	9,868	15,050	17,050	1.0	#
1984	370	404	#	#	7,594	8,294	13,970	15,260	4.9	#
1985	440	467	#	#	8,234	8,733	12,270	13,020	5.3	#
1986	100	103	#	#	9,565	9,878	10,050	10,380	1.0	#
1987	90	90	#	#	8,725	8,725	8,402	8,402	1.0	#
UNITED STATES										
1977	120	210	6,700	11,720	160,400	280,600	121,200	212,000	.1	5.5
1978	120	196	6,400	10,430	186,000	303,100	143,800	234,200	.1	4.5
1979	130	195	5,900	8,836	222,200	332,800	182,000	272,600	.1	3.2
1980	140	192	6,400	8,785	257,000	352,800	220,800	303,100	.1	2.9
1981	210	263	8,500	10,640	273,400	342,300	233,700	292,700	.1	3.6
1982	430	506	9,200	10,830	254,900	299,900	212,300	249,800	.2	4.3
1983	500	566	11,600	13,140	269,900	305,800	200,500	227,200	.2	5.8
1984	470	513	10,600	11,580	341,200	372,600	217,900	238,000	.1	4.9
1985	600	636	11,100	11,770	361,600	383,500	213,100	226,100	.2	5.2
1986	430	444	9,100	9,398	387,100	399,800	217,300	224,400	.1	4.2
1987	625	625	12,600	12,600	424,100	424,100	250,400	250,400	.1	5.0
LATIN AMERICA[4]										
1977	1,435	2,510	95	166	58	101	54	94	2.5	.2
1978	2,005	3,267	100	163	65	106	58	95	3.1	.2
1979	2,100	3,145	120	180	80	120	76	114	2.6	.2
1980	1,960	2,690	145	199	106	145	98	135	1.9	.1
1981	3,490	4,371	195	244	114	143	106	133	3.1	.2
1982	3,650	4,295	755	888	93	110	96	113	3.9	.8
1983	3,350	3,795	190	215	73	83	96	109	4.6	.2
1984	4,155	4,538	785	857	74	80	104	113	5.7	.8
1985	3,755	3,982	495	525	74	78	99	105	5.1	.5
1986	2,970	3,067	235	243	76	78	86	89	3.9	.3
1987	3,455	3,455	790	790	80	80	90	90	4.3	.9
WORLD[4]										
1977	22,390[a]	39,170[a]	22,460	39,290	1,147	2,006	1,122	1,963	2.0	2.0
1978	26,850[a]	43,750[a]	26,850	43,760	1,333	2,172	1,296	2,112	2.0	2.1
1979	31,180[a]	46,700[a]	31,140	46,640	1,663	2,491	1,628	2,439	1.9	1.9
1980	34,810[a]	47,790[a]	34,780	47,750	2,033	2,791	1,983	2,722	1.7	1.8
1981	42,290[a]	52,960[a]	42,490	53,220	2,015	2,523	1,957	2,451	2.1	2.2
1982	47,150[a]	55,480[a]	47,260	55,620	1,906	2,243	1,849	2,175	2.5	2.6
1983	49,310[a]	55,870[a]	49,570	56,170	1,860	2,107	1,808	2,048	2.7	2.7
1984	52,250[a]	57,070[a]	52,170	56,990	1,966	2,147	1,905	2,081	2.7	2.7
1985	45,550[a]	48,310[a]	45,960	48,740	2,001	2,122	1,927	2,044	2.3	2.4
1986	42,960[a]	44,370[a]	43,150	44,560	2,201	2,273	2,139	2,209	2.0	2.0
1987	47,410[a]	47,410[a]	47,380	47,380	2,541	2,541	2,484	2,484	1.9	1.9

1. To avoid the appearance of excessive accuracy, arms transfer data have been independently rounded, with greater severity for large numbers. Because of this rounding and the fact that they are obtained from different sources, world arms exports do not equal world arms imports.
2. Total imports and exports usually are as reported by individual countries and the extent to which arms transfers are included is often uncertain. Imports are reported "cif" (including cost of shipping, insurance, and freight) and exports are reported "fob" (excluding these costs). For these reasons and because of divergent sources, world totals for imports and exports are not equal.

3. Because some countries exclude arms imports or exports from their trade statistics and their "total" imports and exports are therefore understated and because arms transfers may be estimated independently of trade data, the resulting ratios of arms to total imports or exports may be overstated and may even exceed 100 percent.
4. In order to reduce distortions in grouped data trends caused by data gaps for individual countries and years (shown as "NAs"), the totals for the world, regions, and organizations include rough approximations for the gaps.

a. Includes transfers to NATO agencies as such, which are not attributable to individual recipient countries.

SOURCE: U.S. Arms Control and Disarmament Agency, *World Military Expenditures and Arms Transfers, 1973–1984* (Washington, D.C., 1988), Table II.

Table 1202

U.S. DATA ON WORLD ARMS TRADE: RECIPIENT COUNTRIES BY MAJOR SUPPLIERS, 20 LR, CUMULATIVE 1983–87[a]

(M US)

	Recipient	Total[1]	Soviet Union[2]	United States	France	United Kingdom	West Germany	China	Poland	Czecho-slovakia	Italy	Bulgaria	Other
A.	ARGENTINA	1,700	0	60	10	0	1,400	0	0	0	10	0	220
B.	BOLIVIA	25	0	10	5	0	0	0	0	0	0	0	10
C.	BRAZIL	460	0	170	130	10	0	0	0	0	60	0	90
D.	CHILE	315	0	5	70	60	130	0	0	0	0	0	50
E.	COLOMBIA	785	0	100	0	5	650	0	0	10	10	0	10
F.	COSTA RICA	30	0	30	0	0	0	0	0	0	0	0	0
G.	CUBA	8,380	7,000	0	0	0	0	0	130	350	0	250	650
H.	DOMINICAN REP.	20	0	10	10	0	0	0	0	0	0	0	0
I.	ECUADOR	460	0	70	80	30	0	0	0	0	220	0	60
J.	EL SALVADOR	340	0	310	0	0	0	0	0	0	0	0	30
K.	GUATEMALA	75	0	5	0	0	0	0	0	0	0	0	70
L.	HAITI	20	0	5	0	0	0	0	0	0	10	0	5
M.	HONDURAS	230	0	160	0	0	0	0	0	0	0	0	70
N.	MEXICO	430	0	300	20	0	10	0	0	0	0	0	100
O.	NICARAGUA	1,970	1,800	0	10	0	0	0	5	5	0	10	140
P.	PANAMA	45	0	30	10	0	0	0	0	0	0	0	5
Q.	PARAGUAY	50	0	0	0	0	0	0	0	0	0	0	50
R.	PERU	1,060	430	130	340	0	60	0	0	0	30	0	70
S.	URUGUAY	10	0	5	5	0	0	0	0	0	0	0	0
T.	VENEZUELA	1,090	0	550	30	0	40	0	0	0	60	0	410
	LATIN AMERICA	17,575	9,240	1,980	720	105	2,290	0	135	365	400	260	2,080

1. Comparable totals in Tables III and IV do not agree precisely due to the fact that rounding was done at different stages of aggregation.
2. Estimates of the Soviet Union's arms exports in value terms in this and the previous edition are revised and substantially larger than those shown in earlier editions. See Statistical Notes, Arms Transfers.

a. For previous years, see SALA, 18-2802 and 18-1202; 27-1202.

SOURCE: U.S. Arms Control and Disarmament, *World Military Expenditures and Arms Transfers, 1975–1985* (Washington, D.C.), 1986, pp. 145–146; 1987, p. 129; 1980, p. 113.

Table 1203

IISS DATA ON ARMED FORCES EXPENDITURE, PERSONNEL, VESSELS, AND AIRCRAFT, 20 L

(1987)

	Country	Defense Expenditure (MUS)	Total Armed Forces (N)	Army (N)	Army Reserves (N)	Navy (N)	Naval[1] Vessels (N)	Air Force (N)	Combat Aircraft (N)	Para-Military (N)
A.	ARGENTINA	891.86	95,000	55,000	~	25,000	90	15,000	155	18,000
B.	BOLIVIA	93.91[i]	27,600	20,000	~	3,600[a]	11	4,000	45	21,000
C.	BRAZIL	2.58	319,200	218,000	~	50,500[b]	90	50,700	215	243,000
D.	CHILE	790.59[c]	101,000	57,000	100,000	29,000[b]	33	15,000	96	27,000
E.	COLOMBIA	272.99[c]	86,300	69,000	110,900	10,600[a]	30	6,700	43	92,500
F.	COSTA RICA	30.91[d]	~	~	~	~	~	~	~	9,500
G.	CUBA	1.66[c]	180,500	145,000	130,000	13,500	84	22,000	220	1,409,000
H.	DOMINICAN REP.	50.99[f]	20,800	13,000	~	4,000	23	3,765	8	1,000
I.	ECUADOR	188.00[c]	40,000	33,000	~	4,000[a]	24	3,000	52	200[e]
J.	EL SALVADOR	177.00[c]	55,000	39,000	~	1,000	5	2,000	88	24,600[g]
K.	GUATEMALA	265.80[c]	42,000	40,000	5,000	1,200	4	850	25	736,600[g]
L.	HAITI	30.54[f]	7,600	7,000	~	300	4	300	10	~
M.	HONDURAS	75.00	18,700	15,400	50,000	1,200[a]	13	2,200	27	5,000
N.	MEXICO	612.46[i]	254,500	105,000	300,000	26,000	119	7,000	103	120,000
O.	NICARAGUA	436.09[c]	77,000[h]	70,000	50,000	4,000	26	3,000	19	2,000
P.	PANAMA	104.60[i]	7,300	6,000	~	400	11	400	0	12,300
Q.	PARAGUAY	70.50[c]	16,000	12,500	36,300	2,500	10	1,000	16	7,500
R.	PERU	702.61[i]	118,000	80,000	188,000	23,000[a]	55	15,000	141	42,000
S.	URUGUAY	150.19[i]	24,000	17,200	~	4,200	18	3,000	12	2,670
T.	VENEZUELA	817.22[i]	69,000[a,g]	34,000	~	10,000[b]	34	5,000	104	20,000

1. Naval vessels may include submarines, aircraft carriers, destroyers, corvettes, patrol ships, patrol vessels, fast attack craft, anti-mine vessels, frigates, river ships, tankers, amphibious craft, hospital ships, oceanographic vessels, submarine support vessels, gunboats, landing craft, intelligence collectors, replenishment ships, minesweepers, cargo.

a. Includes marines.
b. Includes naval air force and marines.
c. Defense budget 1987.
d. Figures for public security and civil guard.
e. Coast guard.
f. Defense budget 1985.
g. Includes national guard, national police, treasury police.
h. Includes active duty reserves and militia.
i. Defense budget 1986.

SOURCE: International Institute for Strategic Studies (IISS), *The Military Balance*, 1986–1987, pp. 174–197; 1987–1988, pp. 177–200; 1988–1989, pp. 183–207.

Table 1204

IISS DATA ON DEFENSE EXPENDITURE PER MILITARY MAN AND AS PERCENTAGE OF TOTAL GOVERNMENT SPENDING PER MILITARY MAN, 20 LC, 1975–87

(T)

Country	Per Military Man (US)							% of Government Spending						
	1975	1978	1983	1984	1985	1986	1987	1975	1978	1983	1984	1985	1986	1987
A. ARGENTINA	41	102	81	77	89	37	31	9.7	16.8	16.5	17.1	17.1	7.7	7.4
B. BOLIVIA	~	20	34	37	36	21	68	~	16.5	28.2	21.7	~	13.5	~
C. BRAZIL	12	16	10	8	12	11	8	9.3	9.3	2.1	5.8	3.8	3.3	7.4
D. CHILE	~	94	141	135	149	60	63	~	25.2	26.1	25.2	24.7	14.9	9.4
E. COLOMBIA	~	11	17	15	15	14	9	~	7.0	10.4	10.0	9.1	8.3	~
F. COSTA RICA	~	~	11	8	8	12	~	~	~	3.7	3.6	2.9	3.7	~
G. CUBA	~	120	134	134	136	145	162	~	5.6	10.1	10.3	~	10.9	~
H. DOMINICAN REP.	~	20	22	26	26	11	14	~	10.7	10.6	12.2	12.2	9.0	10.9
I. ECUADOR	~	23	25	35	22	16	17	~	15.8	10.3	13.1	13.1	10.3	~
J. EL SALVADOR	~	15	32	39	35	29	31	~	10.3	22.3	23.1	17.9	23.0	~
K. GUATEMALA	~	15	22	22	21	29	30	~	13.4	14.2	15.0	15.9	14.5	12.9
L. HAITI	~	~	5	6	5	~	~	~	~	9.9	8.9	~	~	~
M. HONDURAS	~	~	17	21	21	~	14	~	~	5.6	6.6	6.2	~	~
N. MEXICO	10	9	8	7	7	8	~	2.4	2.2	1.6	1.3	1.4	1.2	~
O. NICARAGUA	~	~	112	195	199	131	~	~	~	16.6	23.3	24.0	13.9	~
P. PANAMA	~	~	32	42	42	45	10	~	~	5.7	7.7	~	5.9	1.1
Q. PARAGUAY	~	15	34	23	23	22	20	~	17.4	16.1	17.1	10.0	27.3	~
R. PERU	24	31	74	67	67	35	~	5.3	20.6	29.9	27.0	27.3	10.0	~
S. URUGUAY	~	64	63	51	52	52	~	~	17.6	16.9	12.0	12.0	12.0	~
T. VENEZUELA	41	52	58	63	58	43	~	5.4	5.6	5.3	8.7	8.7	5.4	~
UNITED STATES	417	491	926	1,001	978	1,167	1,185	23.8	23.7	26.9	27.8	27.2	28.4	28.7

SOURCE: International Institute for Strategic Studies (IISS), *The Military Balance*, 1978–79, pp. 88–89; 1983–84, pp. 126–127; 1984–85, pp. 140–142; 1985–86, pp. 170–173; 1986–87, pp. 214–215; 1988–89, pp. 224–227.

Table 1205

MILITARY EXPENDITURE AS PERCENTAGE OF GDP, 20 LC, 1962–87ᵃ

Country	1962	1964	1965	1966	1967	1969	1970	1971	1972	1973	1974	1975	1976	1977	1978	1979	1980	1981	1982	1983	1984	1985	1986	1987
A. ARGENTINA	2.2	1.7	1.8	2.1	2.3	1.9	1.9	1.7	1.6	1.8	1.7	2.0	2.4	2.4	2.7	2.5	2.6	2.9	5.9†	3.9†	3.3	3.9	3.7	~
B. BOLIVIA	1.1	2.3	2.5	2.2	2.0	1.3	1.6	1.4	1.6	1.6	1.8	2.4	3.8	3.3	3.5	3.5	3.7†	4.9†	4.8†	4.4	4.0†	~	~	~
C. BRAZIL	1.7	1.7	2.5	2.2	2.9	2.6	1.9	1.5	1.4	2.1	1.3	1.3	1.3	1.1	.9	.8	.5	.7	.6	.8†	.7†	.8†	~	~
D. CHILE	2.4	1.9	1.9	2.1	2.0	2.0	2.5	2.3	2.5	5.9	6.7	5.7	6.7	6.9	6.4	6.5	6.3	.7	8.9	8.0	8.8†	6.8	6.9	~
E. COLOMBIA	1.9	2.0	2.0	2.0	2.0	1.3	1.4	2.5	1.2	1.0	.9	1.0	1.2†	~	~	1.7	1.8	1.8	1.8	2.3	2.0	2.3	~	~
F. COSTA RICA	1.1	.9	.9	1.0	.9	1.1	.5	.6	.5	.5	.6	.6	.7	.8	.7	.7	.7	.6	.7	.7	.7	.7	.7	~
G. CUBA	6.6	5.3	5.1	5.3	6.1	6.0	6.9	4.9	4.1	3.7	3.6	3.7†	3.7†	~	8.3	8.5	7.8	8.0	9.2	8.6	9.7	~	~	~
H. DOMINICAN REP.	3.7	3.4	3.7	3.1	2.8	2.3	2.1	1.9	1.7	1.6	1.6	1.6	1.7	1.7	1.8	2.0	1.5	1.7†	1.6†	1.5	1.5	1.4		~
I. ECUADOR	2.0	1.9	1.9	1.7	1.7	2.2	2.2	1.8	2.0	2.0	1.9	2.3	2.2	3.1	2.1	2.0	1.9	1.9†	1.7	1.7†	1.8†	~	~	~
J. EL SALVADOR	1.4	1.2	1.2	1.1	1.1	3.0	1.0	1.1	1.1	1.5	1.7	1.6	1.7	2.0	2.1	2.0	2.8	3.7	4.4	4.4	.5	6.4	5.5	~
K. GUATEMALA	.8	1.0	1.1	1.1	1.1	.9	1.5	.9	1.1	.8	.9	1.2	1.5	1.5	1.7	1.7	1.8	1.9	2.4	2.6	2.9	3.6	~	~
L. HAITI	2.6	2.3	2.1	1.9	1.9	1.8	1.7	1.6	1.6	1.2	1.4	1.7	1.2	1.2	1.3	1.4	1.4	1.4	1.3	1.2	1.1	~		~
M. HONDURAS	1.9	1.3	1.2	1.3	1.3	2.2	1.2	1.5	1.8	1.7	1.6	1.9	1.8	1.9	2.3	2.3	3.2	3.7†	3.9	4.1	5.1	4.7	~	~
N. MEXICO	.7	.7	.7	.7	.7	.7	.7	.6	.6	.5	.5	.5	.6	.6	.5	.6	.6	.6	.6	.7†	.6†	.6	.7	~
O. NICARAGUA	1.9	1.5	1.4	1.6	1.6	1.4	1.6	1.5	1.8	1.4	1.5	1.7	2.1	2.5	3.2	3.1†	4.4†	5.0†	5.9†	9.6†	11.7†	12.0	~	~
P. PANAMA	.5	.4	.5	.4	.5	.7	.8	1.2	.7	.7	.7	.8	1.7	1.5†	1.5†	1.5†	1.2†	1.2†	1.3†	1.4†	1.9	1.9	1.9	~
Q. PARAGUAY	1.7†	1.6†	1.7†	1.9	2.0	2.0	2.0	2.2	2.0	1.7	1.5	1.7	1.7	1.6	1.5	1.3	1.4	1.5	1.6†	1.8	.9	1.1	~	~
R. PERU	2.4†	2.9	2.9	2.6	3.2	3.2	3.7	3.6	3.2	3.8	3.5	4.6	5.0	7.3	5.5	3.9	5.7†	7.2†	7.1	8.6†	8.0	7.7	6.2	~
S. URUGUAY	1.2	1.6	1.7	1.5	1.9	1.8	1.9	2.6	2.5	2.4	2.8	2.6	2.2	2.3	2.3	2.4	2.9	3.9	4.0	~	~	4.4	~	~
T. VENEZUELA	1.7	1.8	2.0	2.0	2.1	1.9	1.7	1.9	2.1	1.7	1.5	1.5	2.2	2.2	2.1	2.4	2.7	3.1	3.4	2.9	2.8	3.0	3.0	~
UNITED STATES	9.2	8.0	7.5	8.4	9.4	8.7	8.0	7.1	6.6	6.0	6.1	5.9	5.4	5.3	5.1	5.1	5.6	5.8	6.5	6.7	6.5	6.6	6.6	6.4

a. For previous years, see SALA, 25-1205.

SOURCE: SIPRI-Y, 1977, pp. 222–225, 242–246; 1979, pp. 36–37, 54–57; 1980, pp. 29–33; 1981, pp. 166–169; 1982, pp. 150–153; 1983, pp. 171–174; 1984, pp. 127–131; 1986, pp. 243–246; 1987; 1988, pp. 176–177; 1988, pp. 168–172.

Table 1206

USDOD DATA ON U.S. MILITARY SALES AGREEMENTS, 20 LR, FY 1978-88[a]

(T US)

	Country	1978	1979	1980	1981	1983	1984	1985	1986	1987	1988
A.	ARGENTINA	5,061	#	#	#	#	54	4,020	219	2,974	5,590
B.	BOLIVIA	#	42	19	#	#	4	2,945	444	1,643	12,135
C.	BRAZIL	10,549	311	2,506	3,535	31,142	8,339	17,812	5,906	18,419	130,480
D.	CHILE	#	#	#	#	#	#	#	673	694	744
E.	COLOMBIA	6,927	4,332	8,876	8,435	15,230	2	767	6,254	43,177	10,105
F.	COSTA RICA	#	316	#	#	4,012	2,551	15,606	5,978	893	1,422
G.	CUBA	#	#	#	#	#	#	#	#	#	#
H.	DOMINICAN REP.	#	112	*	3	586	6,721	3,865	6,796	4,917	2,469
I.	ECUADOR	29,980	13,155	2,137	10,856	1,667	25,885	1,397	5,306	847	7,347
J.	EL SALVADOR	9	*	2,291	9,842	65,154	121,146	138,923	115,017	104,926	102,420
K.	GUATEMALA	3,618	1,903	10	4	71	2,851	1,786	5,079	4,134	8,320
L.	HAITI	#	241	12	#	#	71	8	1,175	1,667	63
M.	HONDURAS	639	203	2,262	4,181	24,508	33,654	91,608	75,689	101,017	32,246
N.	MEXICO	1,973	90	17	91,462	1,884	2,929	5,970	5,583	20,974	6,065
O.	NICARAGUA	2	#	1	#	#	#	#	#	#	#
P.	PANAMA	116	123	244	382	178	809	17,355	3,124	1,700	#
Q.	PARAGUAY	40	9	90	23	7	#	#	#	#	#
R.	PERU	10,578	4,947	3,778	5,201	2,049	2,846	668	8,745	4,302	4,805
S.	URUGUAY	44	2	624	626	434	346	123	1,090	601	907
T.	VENEZUELA	3,807	1,437	2,818	54,170	3,463	4,123	10,549	42,877	13,731	63,839
	LATIN AMERICA	73,343	27,223	25,685	188,720	150,385	212,329	310,896	289,953	323,642	388,957

a. For 1950–74, see SALA, 23-1103; for 1975–76, see SALA, 24-1206.

SOURCE: USDOD-FMSA, Sept. 1983, pp. 5-7; Sept. 1985, pp. 6-7; Sept. 1986, pp. 6-7; Sept. 1987, pp. 6-7; Sept. 1988, pp. 6-7.

Table 1207

USDOD DATA ON U.S. MILITARY SALES DELIVERIES, 20 LR, 1977-88[a]

(T US)

	Country	1977	1978	1979	1980	1981	1983	1984	1985	1986	1987	1988
A.	ARGENTINA	6,815	9,426	6,635	14,423	6,426	1,769	1,195	633	720	2,523	3,046
B.	BOLIVIA	24	90	23	186	- -	- -	- -	10	2,557	1,683	1,267
C.	BRAZIL	8,531	6,324	7,591	7,213	5,032	8,924	9,748	10,269	25,275	13,505	14,155
D.	CHILE	56,026	10,993	5,127	4,797	- -	- -	- -	- -	- -	78	186
E.	COLOMBIA	944	1,917	5,018	3,689	8,959	6,994	10,575	2,425	3,808	4,456	36,640
F.	COSTA RICA	- -	21	266	123	- -	814	2,712	8,305	8,338	2,449	2,012
G.	CUBA	- -	- -	- -	- -	- -	- -	- -	- -	- -	- -	- -
H.	DOMINICAN REP.	2	71	8	137	- -	329	3,598	2,104	2,860	3,209	4,367
I.	ECUADOR	9,051	7,798	5,990	9,951	5,832	28,317	5,152	2,856	8,742	13,012	5,216
J.	EL SALVADOR	257	594	21	1,109	1,953	28,096	77,045	112,149	103,125	74,231	81,175
K.	GUATEMALA	2,167	2,410	3,374	1,884	462	668	546	969	916	1,861	4,010
L.	HAITI	102	314	251	79	12	5	- -	35	457	718	404
M.	HONDURAS	384	461	899	581	1,319	12,106	19,488	26,412	58,820	65,546	50,713
N.	MEXICO	3,612	467	362	2,015	1,325	15,601	2,842	3,513	5,408	4,114	9,596
O.	NICARAGUA	354	768	43	18	- -	- -	- -	- -	- -	- -	- -
P.	PANAMA	243	148	246	187	154	481	546	2,124	12,304	3,729	435
Q.	PARAGUAY	219	43	2	48	41	9	- -	1	2	- -	- -
R.	PERU	25,911	13,345	10,442	13,951	5,907	3,195	2,432	1,608	3,513	5,703	3,148
S.	URUGUAY	5,088	1,171	202	717	689	679	295	664	753	310	861
T.	VENEZUELA	42,451	3,894	4,767	5,838	13,809	32,753	136,473	243,241	80,336	51,148	31,478
	LATIN AMERICA	162,179	60,263	51,267	67,078	51,920	140,740	272,647	417,318	317,934	248,275	248,709

a. For 1950–74, see SALA, 23-1104; for 1975–76, see SALA, 24-1207.

SOURCE: USDOD-FMSA, Sept. 1983, pp. 13-15; Sept. 1985, pp. 14-15; Sept. 1986, pp. 14-15; Sept. 1987, pp. 16-17; Sept. 1988, pp. 20-21.

Table 1208

USDOD DATA ON STUDENTS TRAINED UNDER U.S. INTERNATIONAL MILITARY EDUCATION AND TRAINING PROGRAM, 20 LR, FY 1978–88[a]

(N)

Country	1978	1979	1980	1981	1982	1983	1984	1985	1986	1987	1988
A. ARGENTINA	#	#	#	#	#	#	#	#	#	#	13
B. BOLIVIA	227	211	36	#	#	#	29	70	21	43	67
C. BRAZIL	#	#	#	#	#	#	#	#	#	#	9
D. CHILE	#	#	#	#	#	#	#	#	#	#	#
E. COLOMBIA	257	408	444	539	642	910	665	720	813	867	889
F. COSTA RICA	#	#	#	37	55	79	36	71	71	68	70
G. CUBA	#	#	#	#	#	#	#	#	#	#	#
H. DOMINICAN REP.	90	113	47	163	129	153	168	168	130	133	83
I. ECUADOR	421	451	385	217	252	381	146	168	143	159	54
J. EL SALVADOR	#	#	125	256	736	1,223	104	276	371	315	356
K. GUATEMALA	#	#	#	#	#	#	#	123	95	113	68
L. HAITI	14	17	10	27	25	29	64	45	20	13	#
M. HONDURAS	219	226	166	261	328	332	326	321	349	321	361
N. MEXICO	39	54	43	107	63	28	33	76	19	98	71
O. NICARAGUA	275	6	#	#	#	#	#	#	#	#	#
P. PANAMA	83	219	202	293	219	301	260	183	166	116	#
Q. PARAGUAY	145	#	#	#	8	14	16	19	19	23	20
R. PERU	56	72	195	178	369	284	88	160	53	2	45
S. URUGUAY	#	#	#	#	1	15	45	18	19	20	34
T. VENEZUELA	30	#	#	18	22	52	46	49	61	82	79
LATIN AMERICA	1,856	1,777	1,653	2,096	2,849	3,801	2,026	2,467	2,350	2,373	2,219

a. For 1950–74, see SALA, 23-1108; for 1975–76, see SALA, 24-1208.

SOURCE: USDOD-FMSA, Sept. 1983, pp. 92–93; Sept. 1985, pp. 88–91; Sept. 1986, pp. 88–91; Sept. 1987, pp. 88–91; Sept. 1988, pp. 96–99.

Table 1209

USDOD DATA ON U.S. EXPENDITURE FOR INTERNATIONAL MILITARY EDUCATION AND TRAINING PROGRAM, 20 LR, FY 1978–88[a]

(T US)

Country	1978	1979	1980	1981	1982	1983	1984	1985	1986	1987	1988
A. ARGENTINA	#	#	#	#	#	#	#	#	#	#	36
B. BOLIVIA	628	367	144	#	#	#	125	348	141	196	400
C. BRAZIL	#	#	#	#	#	#	#	#	#	#	43
D. CHILE	#	#	#	#	#	#	#	#	#	#	#
E. COLOMBIA	1,122	455	258	246	345	597	751	788	998	1,465	1,243
F. COSTA RICA	#	#	#	31	46	123	134	230	215	218	239
G. CUBA	#	#	#	#	#	#	#	#	#	#	#
H. DOMINICAN REP.	610	443	239	345	430	572	678	705	686	832	682
I. ECUADOR	703	453	222	296	477	527	698	677	669	537	678
J. EL SALVADOR	#	#	244	1,157	5,250	4,984	3,590	1,474	1,440	1,455	1,444
K. GUATEMALA	#	#	#	#	#	#	#	451	357	494	475
L. HAITI	130	173	116	110	212	339	699	388	232	275	#
M. HONDURAS	692	240	435	537	1,223	782	910	1,095	1,050	1,197	1,185
N. MEXICO	115	173	121	101	82	61	160	216	190	241	223
O. NICARAGUA	384	7	#	#	#	#	#	#	#	#	#
P. PANAMA	439	392	270	328	359	466	453	570	516	591	#
Q. PARAGUAY	587	#	#	#	8	55	75	97	100	125	136
R. PERU	779	398	289	278	453	486	685	526	555	147	394
S. URUGUAY	#	#	#	#	5	58	98	81	104	197	167
T. VENEZUELA	101	#	#	8	23	42	45	94	99	137	139
LATIN AMERICA	6,290	3,101	2,338	3,437	8,913	9,092	9,101	7,740	7,352	8,107	7,484

a. For 1950–74, see SALA, 23-1106; for 1975–76, see SALA, 24-1209.

SOURCE: USDOD-FMSA, Sept. 1983, pp. 86–87; Sept. 1985, pp. 80–83; Sept. 1986, pp. 80–83; Sept. 1987, pp. 80–83; Sept. 1988, pp. 88–91.

Table 1210

USDOD DATA ON TOTAL VALUE OF U.S. ARMS TRANSFERS,[1]
20 L, FY 1970–88
(T US)

	Country	1970[a]	1977	1978	1979	1980	1981	1982	1984	1985	1986	1987	1988
A.	ARGENTINA	10,730	13,129	22,684	36,131	21,746	10,979	9,227	9,037	21,187	8,866	8,269	12,531
B.	BOLIVIA	345	732	884	1,427	386	9	700	29	154	2,931	1,845	2,063
C.	BRAZIL	2,458	14,586	11,117	15,765	14,788	14,933	14,269	30,708	36,721	44,231	34,364	46,439
D.	CHILE	6,982	57,383	10,993	5,127	3,774	- -	- -	11	1,104	1,117	1,138	1,336
E.	COLOMBIA	1,317	8,015	4,500	7,099	5,108	11,664	19,435	14,362	13,091	16,843	5,852	38,939
F.	COSTA RICA	#	132	187	470	325	57	159	2,957	17,691	8,457	2,743	2,170
G.	CUBA	#	- -	- -	- -	- -	- -	- -	- -	- -	- -	- -	- -
H.	DOMINICAN REP.	222	841	891	204	443	101	4,176	4,893	2,368	2,987	3,536	5.108
I.	ECUADOR	770	9,694	24,356	8,580	10,286	7,242	12,697	9,469	7,691	11,413	27,822	8,703
J.	EL SALVADOR	35	486	864	172	1,316	1,970	17,015	78,737	114,510	104,688	74,552	81,429
K.	GUATEMALA	701	3,189	2,960	4,242	2,301	469	1,381	583	1,251	997	2,127	4,372
L.	HAITI	#	553	710	268	79	18	200	290	3,261	460	738	404
M.	HONDURAS	26	486	1,563	2,758	1,247	2,242	1,926	22,965	27,924	61,911	65,422	52,369
N.	MEXICO	12	5,998	3,077	1,746	3,750	4,928	72,855	7,753	19,082	27,749	211,645	41,564
O.	NICARAGUA	423	1,960	1,359	44	18	5	50	1	1	4	2	1
P.	PANAMA	206	2,823	1,124	1,074	29,428	906	1,360	2,346	2,971	12,991	4,141	485
Q.	PARAGUAY	151	672	255	279	688	218	482	63	61	87	35	21,597
R.	PERU	2,185	31,279	17,714	12,025	14,794	9,259	10,573	5,858	9,527	5,719	8,914	6,969
S.	URUGUAY	2,375	5,483	1,238	316	976	1,280	695	454	1,019	900	767	1,253
T.	VENEZUELA	738	51,433	9,784	13,394	19,280	21,809	29,036	147,452	330,139	91,146	82,796	39,174

1. Includes foreign military sales deliveries, commercial exports licensed under arms export control act, and military assistance program excess defense articles program acquisition act.

a. Data on commercial export licensed under arms control act not available prior to 1971.

SOURCE: USDOD-FMSA, Dec. 1979, pp. 2, 3, 16, 22; 2; Sept. 1983, pp. 12–13, 42–43, 66–67; Sept. 1985, pp. 14–15, 42–45, 68–69; Sept. 1987, pp. 16–17, 43–44, 73; Sept. 1988, pp. 20–21, 48–51, 70–71.

Table 1211

ARGENTINA AND GREAT BRITAIN (GB) HUMAN LOSSES IN THE 1982 FALKLANDS WAR

PART I. ARGENTINA

Category	Freedman			GB Official	Gaceta Marinera			Press[1]	
	Engaged	Killed	Injured	Prisoners	Engaged	Killed	Injured	Killed	Prisoners
Navy									
Regular	~	~	~	~	~	244[a]	~	**	~
Conscripted	~	~	~	~	~	124[a]	~	**	~
Total	~	~	~	~	~	368[a]	~	**	~
Air Force	~	~	~	~	~	~	~	**	~
Army	~	50	~	~	~	~	~	**	~
Belgrano Incident	~	360	~	~	1,042	321	~	**	~
Total	12,000	800-1,000	~	11,400	~	~	~	1,000	11,845

PART II. GREAT BRITAIN

Category	Freedman			GB Official			Gaceta Marinera			Press[1]	
	Engaged	Killed	Injured	Engaged	Killed	Injured	Engaged	Killed	Injured	Killed	Injured
Marines	3,000	~	~	~	~	~	~	~	~	**	**
Air Force	~	~	~	~	~	~	~	~	~	**	**
Army	6,000	~	~	~	~	~	~	~	~	**	**
Total	~	~	~	28,000	255	777	~	~	~	250+	**
Remaining Garrison	~	**	**	3,000-4,000[b]	**	**	~	**	**	**	**

1. Ongoing casualty reports by the press are not considered applicable since they were often drastically inaccurate. The totals cited are from "Surrender in the Falklands," *Newsweek*, June 28, 1982, pp. 33-37.

a. To date there have been no official reports on Argentine war losses. The data presented are for those men given distinction and honors by the Argentine navy for death in combat. It appears that none of these medals were given to victims of the *General Belgrano* sinking.

b. Based upon press reports outlined by the British Consul General (letter to the author, January 14, 1983).

SOURCE: Adam Perkal, "Losses and Lessons of the 1982 War for the Falklands," SALA, 23, Chapter 38.

Table 1212

COCAINE BASES AND SALTS SEIZED, 15 LRC, 1983–85

(kg)

	Country	1983	1984	1985
A.	ARGENTINA	73.59	141.78	160.06
B.	BOLIVIA	1,035.82	972.12	3,261.57
C.	BRAZIL	599.61	551.11	160.06
D.	CHILE	64.88	32.53	29.59
E.	COLOMBIA	18,769.44	37,559.40	8,100.12
F.	COSTA RICA	.05	~	~
I.	ECUADOR	85.26	84.79	697.91
K.	GUATEMALA	5.00	6.92	~
L.	HAITI	1.00	~	700.00
M.	HONDURAS	612.00	1,084.00	1.02
N.	MEXICO	324.00	458.00	2,562.70
P.	PANAMA	57.83	33.54	106.27
Q.	PARAGUAY	~	~	46.10
R.	PERU	7,184.60	1,972.69	3,223.08
T.	VENEZUELA	733.00	1,665.63	1,029.75
	United States	8,901.73	11,495.10	25,776.01
	Western Hemisphere	39,814.85	58,221.74	52,934.11

SOURCE: U.N. Commission on Narcotic Drugs (Thirty-Second Session), January 23, 1987.

Table 1213

LSD SEIZED, 4 LRC, 1983–85

(Units)

	Country	1983	1984	1985
A.	ARGENTINA	1,406	26	5,607
C.	BRAZIL	~	33	27
D.	CHILE	64	13	21
N.	MEXICO	~	1,383	~
	United States	2,951,059	299,527	14,608,679
	Western Hemisphere	3,102,440	460,658	14,736,336

SOURCE: U.N. Commission on Narcotic Drugs (Thirty-Second Session), January 23, 1987.

Table 1214

CANNABIS PLANTS SEIZED, 17 LC, 1983–85

(kg)

	Country	1983	1984	1985
A.	ARGENTINA	470.65	745.69	27.19
B.	BOLIVIA	22.66	102.82	~
C.	BRAZIL	1,037,097.10	2,650,776.11	27.19
D.	CHILE	8,325.00	8,007.84	10,021.03
E.	COLOMBIA	7,940,451.84	7,194,968.45	1,066,778.20
F.	COSTA RICA	98.87	~	~
G.	CUBA	~	33,977.82	16,980.13
I.	ECUADOR	112.95	67.68	146.92
K.	GUATEMALA	~	3,000.00	~
L.	HAITI			
M.	HONDURAS	20,865.00	1,068,228.00	120.00
N.	MEXICO	68,052.00	8,560,018.00	173,448.50
O.	NICARAGUA	.-	61.01	~
P.	PANAMA	402.27	322,639.23	1,074.11
Q.	PARAGUAY	~	~	1,349,248.12
R.	PERU	518.22	450.70	149.48
T.	VENEZUELA	18.29	17,844.01	48,377.09
	United States	814,608.93	1,319,700.05	854,050.74

SOURCE: U.N. Commission on Narcotic Drugs (Thirty-Second Session), January 23, 1987.

Table 1215

COCA LEAF SEIZED, 7 LR, 1983–85

(kg)

	Country	1983	1984	1985
A.	ARGENTINA	11,774.25	13,132.06	13,661.21
B.	BOLIVIA	~	~	4,468.00
C.	BRAZIL	154,616.03	4,395,625.00	13,661.21
D.	CHILE	16.56	~	103.63
E.	COLOMBIA	~	~	152,295.03
M.	HONDURAS	~	~	4.00
R.	PERU	~	~	165.00
	Western Hemisphere	166,406.84	4,408.06	184,358.07

SOURCE: U.N. Commission on Narcotic Drugs (Thirty-Second Session), January 23, 1987.

Table 1216

HEROIN SEIZED, 2 LRC, 1983–85

(kg)

	Country	1983	1984	1985
C.	BRAZIL	~	.002	~
N.	MEXICO	11	25	8.8
	United States	300.372	385.043	419.097
	Western Hemisphere	343.475	449.75	491.119

SOURCE: U.N. Commission on Narcotic Drugs (Thirty-Second Session), January 23, 1987.

Table 1217

ILLICIT DRUG PRICES, 4 L, 1980–84[a]

(US per Ounce)

	Country	1980[b]	1982	1984
E.	COLOMBIA			
	Santa Marta Golds, Reds	10–15	10–15	15–20
	Commercial Domestic	2–5	2–5	5–10
	Mushrooms	40–75	40–75	40–75
	Cocaine	175–225	175–225	175–225
I.	ECUADOR			
	Commercial Colombian	7–10	7–10	7–10
	Cocaine[1]	25–40	25–40	25–40
	LSD[2] (Imported)	5	5	5
N.	MEXICO			
	Oaxacan Tops	7–12	12–15	10
	Acapulco Gold	10–20	10–20	20
	Guerrero Gold	7–12	7–12	25
	Cocaine[1]	30–50	30–50	30–50
	Opium	50–100	~	~
P.	PANAMA			
	Red Sinsemilla	~	160	160
	Panama Red	~	50–65	50–65
	Seeded Redhair	~	150	150

1. Unit is gram.
2. Unit is individual capsule.

a. Prices are for the beginning of each year.
b. Year end.

SOURCE: *High Times*, various volumes.

Table 1218

DRUG OFFENSES, 6 L, 1979–84

Country	1979	1980	1981	1982	1983	1984
D. CHILE						
Reported Cases	1,472	1,296	1,432	1,621	1,138	1,345
PTI	13.48	11.57	12.57	14.11	974	11.32
F. COSTA RICA						
Reported Cases	105	95	~	~	~	~
PTI	4.81	4.23	~	~	~	~
H. DOMINICAN REP.						
Reported Cases	~	~	~	~	438	547
PTI	~	~	~	~	7.35	8.76
I. ECUADOR						
Reported Cases	~	~	~	~	103	184
PTI	~	~	~	~	1.20	2.09
R. PERU						
Reported Cases	1,652	2,552	~	~	~	~
PTI	9.55	14.35	~	~	~	~
T. VENEZUELA						
Reported Cases	2,849	4,038	4,296	4,378	4,371	5,212
PTI	21.08	29.02	27.74	27.47	26.66	30.93

SOURCE: International Criminal Police Organization (INTERPOL), *International Crime Statistics*, 1979–84.

Table 1219

AVAILABILITY OF CRIMINAL STATISTICS FOR
LATIN AMERICA AND THE ENGLISH-SPEAKING
CARIBBEAN

Country	Data Year Utilized In 1978 Survey			
	Crimes	Arrests	Sentenced	Inmates
A. ARGENTINA	~	1975	1976	1975
Bahamas	1973	~	1973	1973
Barbados	1973	~	1973	1973

Continued in SALA, 24-1333.

Table 1220

PERSONS ARRESTED, 5 L, 1965–70

Country	1965	1966	1967	1968	1969	1970
C. BRAZIL	47,094	49,606	50,323	62,721	69,809	~
D. CHILE	548,944	610,729	614,049	647,048	~	~
J. EL SALVADOR	47,599	55,999	54,875	50,817	46,892	43,550
K. GUATEMALA	85,609	69,566	~	~	~	~
P. PANAMA	27,584	28,440	33,671	35,926	36,320	36,206

SOURCE: IASI-AC, 1967 and 1972, table 603-01.

Table 1221

PRISON POPULATION, 4 L, 1965–70

Country	1965	1966	1967	1968	1969	1970
C. BRAZIL	23,385	24,219	22,534	24,767	27,521	28,538
E. COLOMBIA	32,088	31,816	~	~	~	~
J. EL SALVADOR	11,043	5,148	5,541	5,745	5,729	5,425
T. VENEZUELA	9,025	10,519	10,858	11,492	11,278	11,144

SOURCE: IASI-AC, 1967 and 1972, table 603-01.

Table 1222

MURDERS, 6 LC, 1979–84

Country	1979	1980	1981	1982	1983	1984
D. CHILE						
Reported Cases	685	686	804	729	644	744
PTI	6.27	6.13	7.06	6.35	5.51	6.26
F. COSTA RICA						
Reported Cases	125	145	~	~	~	~
PTI	5.72	6.46	~	~	~	~
H. DOMINICAN REP.						
Reported Cases	~	~	~	~	505	582
PTI	~	~	~	~	8.47	9.32
I. ECUADOR						
Reported Cases	~	~	16	133	200	400
PTI	~	~	.25	1.50	2.33	4.53
R. PERU						
Reported Cases	313	392	~	~	~	~
PTI	1.81	2.20	~	~	~	~
T. VENEZUELA						
Reported Cases	1,959	1,881	1,697	1,747	2,043	1,673
PTI	14.49	13.52	10.96	10.96	12.46	9.93
UNITED STATES						
Reported Cases	21,456	23,044	~	~	19,310	18,690
PTI	10	10	~	~	8.25	7.91

SOURCE: International Criminal Police Organization (INTERPOL), *International Crime Statistics*, 1979–84.

Table 1223

RAPES, 6 LC, 1979–84

Country	1979	1980	1981	1982	1983	1984
D. CHILE						
Reported Cases	1,249	1,355	1,345	1,200	1,264	1,257
PTI	11.44	12.10	11.81	10.45	10.82	10.58
F. COSTA RICA						
Reported Cases	202	222	~	~	~	~
PTI	9.25	9.88	~	~	~	~
H. DOMINICAN REP.						
Reported Cases	~	~	~	~	214	235
PTI	~	~	~	~	3.59	3.76
I. ECUADOR						
Reported Cases	~	~	37	199	480	520
PTI	~	~	.57	2.38	5.58	5.89
R. PERU						
Reported Cases	1,330	2,185	~	~	~	~
PTI	7.69	12.29	~	~	~	~
T. VENEZUELA						
Reported Cases	2,031	2,169	2,562	2,651	2,812	2,928
PTI	15.03	15.59	16.55	16.63	17.15	17.38
UNITED STATES						
Reported Cases	75,989	82,088	~	~	78,920	84,230
PTI	35	36	~	~	33.73	35.67

SOURCE: International Criminal Police Organization (INTERPOL), *International Crime Statistics*, 1979–84.

Table 1224

AUTO THEFTS, 6 LC, 1979–84

Country	1979	1980	1981	1982	1983	1984
D. CHILE						
Reported Cases	721	851	910	1,089	1,383	901
PTI	6.60	7.60	7.99	9.48	11.84	7.59
F. COSTA RICA						
Reported Cases	~	~	~	~	~	~
PTI	~	~	~	~	~	~
H. DOMINICAN REP.						
Reported Cases	~	~	~	~	180	638
PTI	~	~	~	~	3.02	10.22
I. ECUADOR						
Reported Cases	~	~	723	160	280	684
PTI	~	~	11.09	1.91	3.26	7.75
R. PERU						
Reported Cases	1,031	2,119	~	~	~	~
PTI	5.96	11.92	~	~	~	~
T. VENEZUELA						
Reported Cases	22,796	23,413	20,036	20,613	18,931	14,482
PTI	168.67	168.28	129.39	129.32	115.48	85.94
UNITED STATES						
Reported Cases	1,097,189	1,114,651	~	~	1,007,900	1,032,200
PTI	499	495	~	~	430.76	437.08

SOURCE: International Criminal Police Organization (INTERPOL), *International Crime Statistics*, 1979–84.

Table 1225

RANKING[1] OF DEATHS BY MOTOR VEHICLE ACCIDENTS, 17 LC
(PHTI)

Ranking	Country	Year	Deaths by Motor Vehicle Accidents
	Latin America		
1	HONDURAS	1978	.5
2	PERU	1978	5.4
3	NICARAGUA	1978	7.0
4	URUGUAY	1980	7.2
5	DOMINICAN REP.	1980	7.8
6	CHILE	1979	12.9
7	PARAGUAY	1977	13.7
8	ARGENTINA	1978	14.4
9	COLOMBIA	1980	14.7
10	CUBA	1978	15.5
11	MEXICO	1980	18.2
12	COSTA RICA	1978	18.7
13	PANAMA	1978	19.1
14	GUATEMALA	1979	19.3
15	BRAZIL	1976	21.1
16	ECUADOR	1977	23.0
17	VENEZUELA	1979	36.7
	Other		
	England	1981	8.2
	Greece	1981	15.2
	Spain	1980	17.7
	West Germany	1979	18.2
	Switzerland	1981	18.2
	France	1981	20.5
	Canada	1978	22.0
	United States	1979	23.3

1. Low ranking is favorable.

SOURCE: Banamex, *Estudios Sociales, México Social 1984: Indicadores Seleccionados*, 1984, p. 378.

Table 1226

RANKING[1] OF HOMICIDES WITH MOTOR VEHICLES, 17 LC
(PHTI)

Ranking	Country	Year	Homicides
	Latin America		
1	HONDURAS	1978	1.2
2	PERU	1978	1.5
3	URUGUAY	1978	2.0
4	PANAMA	1980	2.2
5	CHILE	1980	2.6
6	ARGENTINA	1979	3.7
7	CUBA	1977	3.9
8	DOMINICAN REP.	1978	4.6
9	COSTA RICA	1980	5.8
10	ECUADOR	1978	6.1
11	PARAGUAY	1980	9.1
12	VENEZUELA	1978	9.1
13	NICARAGUA	1978	10.7
14	BRAZIL	1979	11.3
15	MEXICO	1976	16.4
16	COLOMBIA	1977	21.7
17	GUATEMALA	1979	22.3
	Other		
	England	1981	.4
	Greece	1981	.8
	France	1980	1.0
	Spain	1979	1.1
	Switzerland	1981	1.2
	West Germany	1981	1.3
	Canada	1978	2.5
	United States	1979	9.9

1. Low ranking is favorable.

SOURCE: Banamex, *Estudios Sociales, México Social 1984: Indicadores Seleccionados,*
1984, p. 378.

Table 1227

RANKING OF SUICIDES WITH MOTOR VEHICLES, 17 LC
(PHTI Low Rank being favorable)

Ranking	Country	Year	Suicides
	Latin America		
1	NICARAGUA	1978	.2
2	GUATEMALA	1978	1.3
3	PERU	1978	1.4
4	MEXICO	1980	1.7
5	DOMINICAN REP.	1980	2.0
6	PANAMA	1979	2.1
7	ECUADOR	1977	2.7
8	COLOMBIA	1978	2.9
9	PARAGUAY	1980	3.1
10	BRAZIL	1978	3.5
11	VENEZUELA	1980	4.6
12	CHILE	1978	4.9
13	COSTA RICA	1978	5.4
14	ARGENTINA	1979	6.7
15	URUGUAY	1976	10.5
16	CUBA	1977	17.7
17	HONDURAS	1979	~
	Other		
	Greece	1981	3.3
	Spain	1981	4.1
	England	1980	8.9
	United States	1979	12.1
	Canada	1981	14.8
	France	1981	19.4
	West Germany	1978	21.7
	Switzerland	1979	23.8

SOURCE: Banamex, *Estudios Sociales, México Social 1984: Indicadores Seleccionados,*
1984, p. 378.

Table 1228

MEXICO DRUG SEIZURES AND AREA DESTROYED, 1982–88[a]

Category	1982–88	1988[b]
Fields Destroyed		
Opium Poppy	158,840	17,210
Marijuana	122,052	10,073
Area Destroyed (H$_a$)		
Opium Poppy	14,606	1,480
Marijuana	16,420	1,377
Seizures (kg)		
Cocaine[1]	22,109	4,137
Marijuana	9,586,689	179,621
Opium Derivatives	667[c]	164[d]

1. Does not include seizures by the Mexican army.

a. Data are for actions taken by the U.S. Attorney General and do not include those by Mexican armed forces.
b. Jan. 1–July 31, 1988.
c. Does not include 978 kg of poppy seeds.
d. Does not include 160 kg of poppy seeds.

SOURCE: *U.S.-Mexico Report*, Sept. 1988.

Table 1229

MEXICO DRUG SEIZURES ALONG THE MEXICAN–U.S. BORDER, 1987–88[a]
(kg)

State	Marijuana[1]	Opium and Heroin	Cocaine
Baja California	26,900	31	3,866
Sonora	91,573	77	1,789
Chihuahua	1,140	11	109
Coahuila	3,931	240[b]	869
Nuevo León	18,782	550	36
Tamaulipas	40,423	2	60
Total	205,139	122	7,336

1. Dried and packaged.

a. Jan. 1, 1987–July 31, 1988.
b. Grams.

SOURCE: *U.S.-Mexico Report*, Sept. 1988.

Table 1230

MEXICO DRUG CONSUMPTION AMONG STUDENTS, BY REGION AND DRUG, 1976–86

Drug	Northern Region[1] 1976 (n = 3,247)	1986 (n = 2,568)	PC	Central Region[2] 1976 (n = 5,643)	1986 (n = 6,751)	PC	Southern Region[3] 1976 (n = 1,010)	1986 (n = 596)	PC
Marijuana	1.9	3.7	+1.8	.95	3.1	+2.2	.89	1.6	+.71
Inhalants	.8	4.2	+3.4	1.0	4.5	+3.5	.79	4.1	+3.31
Amphetamines	2.8	3.5	+.7	2.0	3.4	+1.4	1.7	2.6	.9
Tranquilizers	1.9	2.6	+.7	2.9	2.4	−.5	3.1	3.6	−.1
Sedatives	1.2	.7	−.5	1.4	1.0	−.4	.6	.5	−.1
Hallucinogens	.7	.42	−.3	.83	.7	−.13	.5	.1	−.4
Cocaine	.6	1.3	+.7	.5	.9	+.4	.5	.6	+.1
Heroin	.2	.54	+.34	.4	.5	+.1	.009	0	0

1. Baja California, Baja California Sur, Sinaloa, Sonora, Coahuila, Chihuahua, Tamaulipas, and Nuevo León.
2. Durango, San Luis Potosí, Nayarit, Aguascalientes, Jalisco, Michoacán, Guanajuato, Hidalgo, Estado de México, Distrito Federal, Puebla, Veracruz, and Guerrero.
3. Campeche, Tabasco, Yucatan, Chiapas, and Oaxaca.

SOURCE: *El Día*, July 16, 1988, p. 24.

Table 1231

MEXICO SUSPECTS AND SENTENCED DELINQUENTS, 1976–81

Jurisdiction	1976	1977	1978	1979	1980	1981
Federal Court						
Suspects	7,597	8,272	5,799	7,507	6,418	7,952
Male	7,113	7,739	5,441	7,075	6,018	7,503
Female	483	531	352	411	395	449
Not Specified	1	2	6	21	5	~
Sentenced	6,621	7,204	5,245	7,448	7,117	7,853
Male	6,228	6,782	4,903	7,043	6,756	7,409
Female	393	419	336	387	350	444
Not Specified	~	3	6	18	11	~
Other Courts						
Suspects	62,471	72,196	69,227	67,184	69,748	68,232
Male	57,095	65,680	62,990	61,498	63,752	62,211
Female	5,376	6,515	6,198	5,636	5,965	5,968
Not Specified	~	1	39	50	31	53
Sentenced	46,982	50,870	53,847	53,989	56,939	57,603
Male	43,037	46,290	48,654	49,008	51,891	52,323
Female	3,943	4,573	5,095	4,920	5,011	5,234
Not Specified	2	7	98	61	37	46

SOURCE: Banamex, *Estudios Sociales, México Social 1984: Indicadores Seleccionados,* 1984, p. 369.

Table 1232

MEXICO ATTEMPTED SUICIDES, 1980-83

Attempted Suicides	1980			1981			1982			1983		
	Total	Male	Female	Total	Male	Female	Total	Male	Female	Total	Male	Female
Place	42	18	24	52	23	29	66	32	34	56	29	27
Home	36	13	23	44	15	29	50	19	31	43	22	21
Hotel or Bordinghouse	1	~	1	1	1	~	1	~	1	3	3	~
Public Road	3	3	~	1	~	~	6	6	~	2	1	1
Countryside	~	~	~	2	2	~	~	~	~	1	~	1
Jail	1	1	~	1	1	~	5	5	~	1	1	~
Public Building	~	~	~	1	1	~	~	~	~	1	~	1
Bar, Restaurant, Café or Cabaret	1	1	~	1	1	~	3	2	1	1	1	1
Hospital, Sanitarium or Clinic	~	~	~	~	~	~	~	~	~	1	~	1
Factory or Workshop	~	~	~	~	~	~	~	~	~	1	1	~
Other	~	~	~	2	2	~	1	~	1	2	1	1
Means Employed												
Firearm	9	7	2	10	6	4	12	5	7	9	7	2
Sword or Knife	8	5	3	11	4	7	14	9	5	10	9	1
Strangulation	3	3	~	6	5	1	4	2	2	1	1	~
Precipitation[1]	~	~	~	2	~	2	3	2	1	1	1	~
Poisoning	9	1	8	8	2	6	8	2	6	13	2	11
Burns	~	~	~	1	1	~	~	~	~	~	~	~
Drowning	~	~	~	~	~	~	1	~	1	1	~	1
Other Means	12	2	10	14	5	9	21	9	12	19	8	11
Unknown	1	~	1	~	~	~	3	3	~	2	1	1
Cause												
Love Related	7	4	3	4	4	~	7	~	7	7	4	3
Economic	1	1	~	3	1	2	1	1	~	4	2	2
Family Problems	12	3	9	22	5	17	24	9	15	19	7	12
Grave and Incurable Illnesses	3	1	2	6	1	5	4	1	3	1	1	~
Mental Disorder	~	~	~	6	3	2	7	6	1	~	~	1
Alcohol Intoxication	2	1	1	2	2	~	~	~	~	3	3	~
Drug Overdose	1	~	1	~	~	~	~	~	~	1	~	1
Remorse	~	~	~	2	2	~	~	~	~	~	~	~
Other Cause	4	2	2	2	~	2	4	4	~	14	8	6
Unknown	12	6	6	6	5	1	19	11	8	7	4	3
Age Groups (Years)												
Under 15	2	~	2	2	1	1	~	~	~	~	~	~
From 15 to 19	6	2	4	8	2	6	11	~	11	10	4	6
From 20 to 24	10	4	6	9	3	6	14	8	6	10	2	8
From 25 to 29	8	3	5	9	5	4	5	2	3	5	5	~
From 30 to 34	3	3	~	9	3	6	4	2	2	11	7	4
From 35 to 39	4	2	2	3	2	1	2	2	~	1	1	~
From 40 to 49	~	~	~	2	2	~	1	1	~	4	2	2
From 50 to 59	1	1	~	1	1	~	8	5	3	1	1	~
From 60 and Above	~	~	~	2	1	1	2	2	~	1	~	1
Not Specified	8	3	5	7	3	4	19	10	9	13	7	6
Civil Status												
Single	16	7	9	21	8	13	29	11	18	20	12	8
Married	14	5	9	17	8	9	23	12	11	24	10	14
Widowed	2	1	1	2	~	2	5	2	3	~	~	~
Divorced	2	2	~	2	1	1	1	1	~	~	~	~
Free Union	3	~	3	5	3	2	~	~	~	1	~	1
Not Specified	5	3	2	5	3	2	8	6	2	11	7	4

1. Jumping off a precipice.

SOURCE: Banamex, *Estudios Sociales, México Social 1984: Indicadores Seleccionados,*
1984, p. 375.

Table 1233

MEXICO SUICIDES, 1980-83

Suicides	1980			1981			1982			1983		
	Total	Male	Female	Total	Male	Female	Total	Male	Female	Total	Male	Female
Place	672	558	114	951	774	177	1,042	835	207	648	543	105
Home	478	381	97	650	495	155	764	591	173	444	360	84
Hotel or Bordinghouse	11	9	2	24	22	2	24	18	6	19	16	3
Public Road	60	55	5	97	87	10	79	72	7	54	48	6
Countryside	44	42	2	60	59	1	66	65	1	50	46	4
Jail	14	14	~	33	31	2	25	23	2	18	18	~
Public Building	12	11	1	15	14	1	16	11	5	10	10	~
Bar, Restaurant, Café or Cabaret	2	2	~	4	4	~	3	2	1	9	6	3
Hospital, Sanitarium or Clinic	11	7	4	9	7	2	16	12	4	3	2	1
Factory or Workshop	1	1	~	7	7	~	10	9	1	4	3	1
Other	32	29	3	45	44	1	35	29	6	37	34	3
Not Specified	7	7	~	7	4	3	4	3	1	~	~	~
Means Employed												
Firearm	213	195	18	336	287	49	343	287	56	221	196	25
Sword or Knife	11	11	~	23	19	4	13	12	1	16	15	1
Strangulation	263	234	29	367	328	39	393	355	38	236	220	16
Hacking	4	4	~	2	1	1	3	3	~	1	1	~
Precipitation[1]	26	16	10	19	16	3	29	26	3	18	15	3
Poisoning	98	53	45	117	55	62	145	71	74	98	57	41
Poisonous Gas	3	3	~	4	2	2	5	2	3	5	1	4
Burns	1	~	1	6	6	~	4	2	2	5	2	3
Drowning	3	3	~	15	14	1	9	5	4	3	2	1
Other Means	43	33	10	37	28	9	69	47	22	41	32	9
Unknown	7	6	1	25	18	7	29	25	4	4	2	2
Cause												
Love Related	53	37	16	56	40	16	94	76	18	39	31	8
Economic	14	12	2	22	21	1	21	16	5	16	15	1
Family Problems	57	39	18	79	48	31	89	55	34	49	36	13
Grave and Incurable Illnesses	53	49	4	67	52	15	86	74	12	50	44	6
Mental Disorder	40	34	6	54	45	9	58	45	13	19	16	3
Alcohol Intoxication	34	32	2	66	58	8	68	64	4	42	41	1
Drug Overdose	8	8	~	12	12	~	8	6	2	3	1	2
Remorse	6	6	~	7	7	~	13	10	3	8	6	2
Other Cause	24	20	4	36	33	3	36	27	9	371	311	60
Unknown	383	321	62	552	458	94	569	462	107	51	42	9
Age Groups (Years)												
Under 15	17	15	2	16	12	4	40	25	15	16	11	5
From 15 to 19	86	63	23	143	101	42	121	84	37	78	57	21
From 20 to 24	130	106	24	186	159	27	180	145	35	117	97	20
From 25 to 29	89	77	12	129	106	23	110	89	21	93	84	9
From 30 to 34	51	44	7	66	49	17	105	87	18	53	44	9
From 35 to 39	38	34	4	64	53	11	67	49	18	58	52	6
From 40 to 49	58	52	6	76	65	11	90	79	11	57	48	9
From 50 to 59	53	45	8	64	58	6	68	59	9	43	34	9
From 60 and Above	63	55	8	58	55	3	103	98	5	61	56	5
Not Specified	87	67	20	149	116	33	158	120	38	72	60	12
Civil Status												
Single	284	240	44	425	368	57	421	330	91	260	223	37
Married	281	234	47	372	284	88	427	358	69	264	223	41
Widowed	21	16	5	25	23	2	32	26	6	19	14	5
Divorced	12	11	1	12	8	4	13	9	4	12	8	4
Free Union	37	25	12	68	50	18	77	51	26	59	45	14
Not Specified	37	32	5	49	41	8	72	61	11	34	30	4

1. Jumping off a precipice.

SOURCE: Banamex, *Estudios Sociales, México Social 1984: Indicadores Seleccionados*, 1984, p. 375.

Part V
Working Conditions, Migration, and Housing

13

Labor Force, EAP, Unemployment, and Class Structure

Table 1300

TOTAL PARTICIPATION RATES,[1] 9 L, 1970–86

(AA)

Country	1970	1976	1980	1981	1982	1983	1984	1985	1986[‡]
B. BOLIVIA[10]	47.3	48.1	49.6	49.2	49.1	49.0	48.9	48.7	~

Continued in SALA, 27-1300.

Table 1301

LABOR FORCE PARTICIPATION BY SEX, 17 L, 1950–80

(%)

Country	1950			1960			1970			1980		
	Total	M	F	Total	M	F	Total	M	F	Total	M	F
A. ARGENTINA	51.36	79.14	21.71	50.18	77.69	21.78	48.36	72.59	23.98	48.16	71.28	25.30

Continued in SALA, 27-1301.

Table 1302

ESTIMATED GROWTH OF LABOR FORCE BY SEX, 19 L, 1975–2000

(AA-GR)

	Country	1975-80			1980-85			1985-90			1990-95			1995-2000		
		Total	M	F	Total	M	F	Total	M	F	Total	M	F	Total	M	F
A.	ARGENTINA	1.10	.87	1.76	1.09	.89	1.65	1.08	.87	1.66	1.12	.95	1.54	1.08	.94	1.42
B.	BOLIVIA	2.40	2.19	3.20	2.54	2.25	3.60	2.63	2.32	3.69	2.84	2.42	4.16	2.84	2.42	4.06
C.	BRAZIL	2.81	2.50	3.91	2.93	2.54	4.20	2.92	2.52	4.13	3.03	2.59	4.26	2.96	2.55	4.03
D.	CHILE	2.66	2.28	3.84	2.48	2.19	3.34	2.13	1.89	2.81	1.93	1.73	2.46	1.88	1.67	2.41
E.	COLOMBIA	3.25	3.25	3.24	3.40	3.31	3.67	3.28	3.20	3.52	3.33	3.17	3.80	3.17	3.01	3.61
F.	COSTA RICA	3.59	3.26	4.91	3.27	2.92	4.55	2.86	2.56	3.91	2.79	2.44	3.93	2.67	2.32	3.73
H.	DOMINICAN REP.	3.27	3.12	4.35	3.42	3.24	4.68	3.50	3.32	4.67	3.61	3.38	5.00	3.62	3.39	4.89
I.	ECUADOR	3.34	3.07	4.37	3.46	3.12	4.67	3.38	3.05	4.52	3.39	3.00	4.63	3.28	2.88	4.43
J.	EL SALVADOR	3.38	3.12	4.44	3.36	3.06	4.53	3.25	2.96	4.30	3.33	2.95	4.60	3.31	2.93	4.52
K.	GUATEMALA	2.87	2.74	3.73	2.90	2.72	3.95	2.90	2.71	3.98	2.95	2.71	4.24	2.91	2.66	4.13
L.	HAITI	1.49	1.62	1.34	1.51	1.71	1.27	1.54	1.77	1.28	1.72	1.98	1.40	1.80	2.08	1.46
M.	HONDURAS	3.19	3.07	3.91	3.36	3.20	4.37	3.42	3.24	4.47	3.40	3.19	4.54	3.34	3.14	4.35
N.	MEXICO	3.39	3.13	4.49	3.49	3.18	4.71	3.43	3.12	4.59	3.58	3.21	4.86	3.59	3.21	4.78
O.	NICARAGUA	3.26	3.00	4.23	3.44	3.10	4.61	3.54	3.18	4.65	3.72	3.27	5.02	3.67	3.24	4.83
P.	PANAMA	2.78	2.77	2.82	2.82	2.75	3.03	2.66	2.62	2.78	2.78	2.61	3.26	2.73	2.55	3.21
Q.	PARAGUAY	3.12	2.86	4.01	3.18	2.83	4.28	3.15	2.79	4.22	3.23	2.78	4.45	3.91	2.76	4.30
R.	PERU	3.12	2.82	4.14	3.28	2.91	4.48	3.31	2.94	4.42	3.35	2.96	4.44	3.27	2.89	4.26
S.	URUGUAY	1.00	.75	1.61	1.19	.97	1.73	1.03	.81	1.54	1.05	.88	1.42	.97	.80	1.32
T.	VENEZUELA	3.73	3.34	5.02	3.59	3.24	4.67	3.25	2.93	4.17	3.08	2.84	3.72	3.02	2.78	3.63

SOURCE: ILO, *Labor Force Estimates and Projections, 1950-2000*, 1977.

Table 1303

CHILDREN IN THE LABOR FORCE,[1] 20 LC, 1960–2000

	T				PTI			
Country	1960	1970	1975	2000	1960	1970	1975	2000
A. ARGENTINA	211	192	167	107	10.2	8.1	6.6	3.3

Continued in SALA, 21-1310.

Table 1304

COMPOSITION OF LABOR FORCE, 20 LC, 1965–2000

(%)

	Working Age Population (15–64 Years)		Labor Force						AA–GR of Labor Force		
			Agriculture		Industry		Services				
Country	1965	1985	1965	1980	1965	1980	1965	1980	1965–80	1980–85	1985–2000
A. ARGENTINA	63	60	18	13	34	34	48	53	1.1	1.1	1.5
B. BOLIVIA	53	53	54	46	20	20	26	34	2.0	2.7	2.7
C. BRAZIL	53	59	49	31	20	27	31	42	3.3	2.3	2.1
D. CHILE	56	63	27	17	29	25	44	58	2.2	2.6	1.7
E. COLOMBIA	49	59	45	34	21	24	34	42	2.6	2.8	2.3
F. COSTA RICA	49	59	47	31	19	23	34	46	3.8	3.1	2.4
G. CUBA	~	~	~	~	~	~	~	~	~	~	~
H. DOMINICAN REP.	47	53	59	46	14	15	27	39	2.8	3.5	2.9
I. ECUADOR	50	53	55	39	19	20	26	42	2.7	3.1	2.9
J. EL SALVADOR	50	60	50	43	10	19	20	37	3.3	2.9	3.3
K. GUATEMALA	50	53	64	57	15	17	21	26	2.3	2.8	3.3
L. HAITI	52	51	77	70	7	8	16	22	1.0	2.0	2.2
M. HONDURAS	50	50	68	61	12	16	20	23	2.8	3.9	3.9
N. MEXICO	49	54	50	37	22	29	29	35	3.9	3.2	3.0
O. NICARAGUA	48	50	57	47	16	16	28	38	2.9	3.8	3.9
P. PANAMA	51	58	46	32	16	18	38	50	2.7	3.0	2.6
Q. PARAGUAY	49	51	55	49	20	21	26	31	3.2	3.1	2.8
R. PERU	51	56	50	40	19	18	32	42	2.9	2.9	2.8
S. URUGUAY	63	63	20	16	29	29	51	55	.4	.6	.9
T. VENEZUELA	49	56	30	16	24	28	47	56	4.2	3.5	3.0
UNITED STATES	60	66	5	4	35	31	60	66	2.2	1.2	.8

SOURCE: *World Development Report*, 1987, table 32.

Table 1305

LABOR FORCE STRUCTURE, 20 LC, 1960–2000

	Country	% of Population of Working Age (15–64 Years)				% Agriculture				% Industry				% Services				AA–GR			
		1960	1965	1982	1984	1960	1965	1980	1981	1960	1965	1980	1981	1960	1965	1980	1981	1960–70	1965–73	1973–84	1980–2000
A.	ARGENTINA	64	63	63	61	44	18	13	13	29	34	34	28	27	48	53	59	.4	1.4	1.1	1.5
B.	BOLIVIA	55	53	53	53	61	54	46	50	18	20	20	24	21	26	34	26	1.7	1.8	2.5	2.9
C.	BRAZIL	54	53	55	58	52	48	31	30	15	20	27	24	33	31	42	46	2.7	2.5	3.0	2.3
D.	CHILE	57	56	62	63	31	27	16	19	20	29	25	19	50	44	58	62	1.4	1.3	2.5	2.1
E.	COLOMBIA	50	49	60	59	51	45	34	26	19	21	24	21	29	34	42	53	3.0	3.1	2.8	2.5
F.	COSTA RICA	50	49	59	59	51	47	31	29	19	19	23	23	30	34	46	48	3.5	3.7	3.8	2.8
G.	CUBA	61	59	61	65	39	33	24	23	22	25	29	31	39	41	48	46	.8	1.0	2.2	1.7
H.	DOMINICAN REP.	49	48	53	55	67	59	46	49	12	13	16	18	21	27	39	33	2.2	2.7	3.3	3.0
I.	ECUADOR	52	50	52	53	57	55	39	52	19	19	20	17	23	26	42	31	2.9	3.1	2.9	3.0
J.	EL SALVADOR	52	50	52	51	62	59	56	50	17	16	14	22	21	25	30	28	2.6	3.2	2.9	3.4
K.	GUATEMALA	51	50	54	53	67	64	57	55	14	15	17	21	19	21	25	24	2.8	2.7	2.8	2.9
L.	HAITI	55	54	53	55	80	77	70	74	6	7	8	7	14	16	22	19	.6	.7	1.6	2.0
M.	HONDURAS	52	50	50	50	70	68	61	63	11	12	16	20	19	20	23	17	2.5	2.4	3.3	3.4
N.	MEXICO	51	49	52	53	55	50	37	36	20	22	29	26	25	29	34	38	2.8	3.1	3.2	3.2
O.	NICARAGUA	50	48	50	50	62	57	47	39	16	16	16	14	22	27	38	47	2.3	3.0	3.2	3.7
P.	PANAMA	52	51	56	57	51	46	32	33	14	16	18	18	35	38	50	49	3.4	3.3	2.6	2.2
Q.	PARAGUAY	51	50	53	55	56	55	49	49	19	20	21	19	25	26	31	32	2.3	2.5	3.3	3.0
R.	PERU	52	51	54	56	52	50	40	40	20	19	18	19	28	31	42	41	2.1	2.4	2.9	2.9
S.	URUGUAY	64	63	63	63	21	20	16	11	30	29	29	32	50	51	55	57	.8	.3	.5	.9
T.	VENEZUELA	51	49	55	55	35	30	16	18	22	24	28	27	43	47	56	55	2.8	3.5	3.9	3.4
	UNITED STATES	60	60	66	66	7	5	4	2	36	35	31	32	57	60	66	66	1.8	1.9	1.6	.9

SOURCE: WB-WDR, 1984 and 1986, table 30.

Table 1306

SECTORAL DISTRIBUTION OF THE LABOR FORCE,[1]
19 LC, 1960–80
(%)

	Country	Agriculture 1960	Agriculture 1980	Industry 1960	Industry 1980	Services 1960	Services 1980
1.	Capitalist industrial countries	18	6	38	38	44	56
2.	Socialist industrial countries	41	16	31	45	28	39
3.	Latin American countries	47	31	20	24	33	45
N.	MEXICO	55	36	20	26	25	38
K.	GUATEMALA	67	55	14	21	19	24
J.	EL SALVADOR	65	58	17	22	21	27
M.	HONDURAS	70	63	11	15	19	22
O.	NICARAGUA	62	39	16	14	22	47
F.	COSTA RICA	51	29	19	23	30	48
P.	PANAMA	51	27	14	18	35	55
T.	VENEZUELA	35	18	22	27	43	55
E.	COLOMBIA	51	26	19	21	30	53
I.	ECUADOR	58	52	19	17	23	31
R.	PERU	52	40	20	19	28	41
B.	BOLIVIA	61	50	18	24	21	26
Q.	PARAGUAY	56	49	19	19	25	32
D.	CHILE	30	19	20	19	50	62
A.	ARGENTINA	20	13	36	28	44	59
S.	URUGUAY	21	11	29	32	50	57
C.	BRAZIL	52	30	15	24	33	46
G.	CUBA	39	23	22	31	39	46
H.	DOMINICAN REP.	67	49	12	18	21	33

1. Order corresponds to that in Figure 13:1, above.
2. The Agricultural sector includes crop and stock farming, forestry, hunting and fishing.
   The Industrial sector includes mining, manufacturing, construction and public utilities
   (electricity, water, and gas). All other branches of economic activity are included in the
   Services category.

SOURCE: Aníbal Pinto, "Metropolization and Tertiarization," *Cepal Review* 24,
(Santiago, 1984).

Table 1307

AGRICULTURAL LABOR FORCE,[1] 26 ECLA:L,[2] 1950–75

Country	1950	1955	1960	1965	1970	1975*	1950–60	1960–70	1970–75	1950–75
				T				AA–GR		
A. ARGENTINA	4,318	4,270	4,118	4,023	3,883	3,142	−.5	−.6	−.7	−.6
Bahamas	23	26	30	33	35	34	2.7	1.6	−.6	1.5
Barbados	61	62	62	54	47	41	.2	−2.7	−2.7	−1.5
B. BOLIVIA	1,855	2,067	2,307	2,470	2,655	2,869	2.2	1.4	1.6	1.8

Continued in SALA, 24–1305.

Table 1308

AGRICULTURAL POPULATION AS SHARE
OF TOTAL POPULATION,[1]
26 ECLA:L,[2] 1950–75

	Country	1950	1960	1970	1975*
A.	ARGENTINA	25.2	20.0	16.4	14.7
	Bahamas	28.9	26.8	19.7	16.7
	Barbados	28.9	26.8	19.7	16.7
B.	BOLIVIA	61.4	61.0	55.5	53.0

Continued in SALA, 24–1306.

Table 1309

AGRICULTURAL POPULATION AND ECONOMICALLY ACTIVE POPULATION IN AGRICULTURE, 20 LC, 1980–87[a]

	1980					1987				
Country	Total Population (T)	Agricultural Population (T)	EAP Total (T)	EAP In Agriculture (T)	% Agriculture	Total Population (T)	Agricultural Population (T)	EAP Total (T)	EAP In Agriculture (T)	% Agriculture
A. ARGENTINA	28,237	3,660	10,792	1,399	13.0	31,470	3,497	11,145	1,238	11.1
B. BOLIVIA	5,570	2,784	1,819	909	50.0	6,733	2,893	2,100	902	42.9
C. BRAZIL	121,286	46,319	38,157	14,572	38.2	141,302	37,056	51,729	13,566	26.2
D. CHILE	11,104	2,099	3,673	678	18.4	12,409	1,732	4,461	607	13.6
E. COLOMBIA	25,794	7,062	2,692	2,106	27.4	29,918	8,824	9,657	2,848	29.5
F. COSTA RICA	2,279	799	764	268	35.1	2,730	713	950	245	257
G. CUBA	9,732	2,267	2,971	692	23.3	10,236	2,103	4,170	857	20.5
H. DOMINICAN REP.	5,558	3,118	1,461	820	56.1	6,525	2,514	1,985	765	38.5
I. ECUADOR	8,021	3,565	2,553	1,135	44.4	9,916	3,260	3,010	983	32.7
J. EL SALVADOR	4,797	2,465	1,495	754	50.4	5,908	2,351	1,955	764	39.1
K. GUATEMALA	7,262	3,985	2,207	1,211	54.9	8,435	4,462	2,401	1,270	52.9
L. HAITI	5,809	3,870	2,902	1,933	66.6	6,940	4,299	2,941	1,932	65.7
M. HONDURAS	3,691	2,310	1,087	680	62.6	4,652	2,722	1,405	796	56.7
N. MEXICO	69,393	24,995	19,999	7,204	36.0	82,860	26,411	27,761	8,849	31.9
O. NICARAGUA	3,056	1,199	911	366	42.8	3,500	1,419	1,073	437	40.8
P. PANAMA	1,956	674	657	226	34.5	2,272	603	803	216	26.9
Q. PARAGUAY	3,168	1,549	1,019	498	48.9	3,892	1,883	1,295	605	46.7
R. PERU	17,625	6,976	5,189	1,937	37.3	20,712	7,924	6,562	2,378	36.2
S. URUGUAY	2,908	345	1,151	126	11.9	3,058	435	1,189	169	14.2
T. VENEZUELA	15,620	2,804	4,166	857	18.0	18,246	2,147	6,248	769	12.3
UNITED STATES	227,700	4,896	103,672	2,229	2.2	243,565	7,211	119,559	3,143	2.6

a. For 1965, 1981, and 1983, see SALA, 24-1307; for 1970 and 1975, see SALA, 25-1307; for 1986, see SALA, 27-1309.

SOURCE: FAO-PY, 1985, table 3; 1986, table 3; 1987, table 3.

Table 1310

ECONOMICALLY ACTIVE POPULATION (EAP),[1] 20 LC

Country	Year[4]	Code[2]	Total Population	Economically Active Population N	Economically Active Population %	Males	Active Males As % of Total Male Population	Females	Active Females As % of Total Female Population
A. ARGENTINA[3]	1987	F	31,497,000	11,793,000	37.4	8,609,000	55.1	3,184,000	20.0
B. BOLIVIA[†]	1987	F	6,729,620	2,101,052	31.2	1,605,647	48.4	495,405	14.5
C. BRAZIL	1986	E	135,608,433	56,816,215	41.9	37,596,569	56.3	19,219,646	27.9
D. CHILE[6]	1986	D	12,161,400	4,269,000	35.1	2,988,600	50.2	1,280,400	20.6
E. COLOMBIA[‡]	1987	E	8,992,473	3,959,596	44.0	2,314,064	55.1	1,645,532	34.3
F. COSTA RICA[5]	1987	E	2,606,374	977,847	37.5	707,898	54.0	269,949	20.8
G. CUBA[‡]	1986	D	10,245,913	4,342,280	42.4	2,786,597	54.0	1,555,683	30.6
H. DOMINICAN REP.[‡]	1981	A	5,647,977	1,915,388	33.9	1,361,109	48.1	554,279	19.7
I. ECUADOR[5,‡]	1988	A	10,203,723	3,444,368	33.8	2,409,125	46.9	1,035,243	20.4
J. EL SALVADOR	1980	E	4,592,546	1,622,217	35.3	1,056,652	47.9	565,565	23.7
K. GUATEMALA[12]	1986–87	F	8,162,529	2,740,061	33.6	2,069,076	51.3	670,985	16.2
L. HAITI[‡]	1988	F	5,566,743	2,350,302	42.2	1,388,436	51.4	961,866	33.6
M. HONDURAS[10]	1984	F	3,955,116[a]	1,256,349	~	1,046,415	~	209,934	~
N. MEXICO	1930	A	66,846,833	22,066,084	33.0	15,924,806	48.2	6,141,278	18.2
O. NICARAGUA[9]	1930	F	2,703,147	863,925	32.0	681,089	51.4	182,836	13.3
P. PANAMA[7]	1986	D	~	719,574	~	492,806	~	226,768	~
Q. PARAGUAY[5]	1982	A	3,029,830	1,039,258	34.3	834,308	54.8	204,950	13.6
R. PERU[13]	1987	E	5,202,888	2,164,604	41.6	1,281,899	49.8	882,705	33.6
S. URUGUAY[3]	1985	A	2,940,000	1,172,300	39.9	784,200	54.8	388,100	25.7
T. VENEZUELA	1987	E	18,388,817	6,321,566	34.4	4,568,451	49.2	1,753,115	19.3
UNITED STATES[8,11]	1987	D	243,400,000	121,602,000	50.0	67,784,000	57.2	53,818,000	43.1

1. "Economically active" includes all persons engaged or seeking to be engaged in productive work in some branch of economic activity. Comparability of data is limited by the various differing minimum age limits, seasonal fluctuations in some economies, and international differences in the concepts and definitions of the term "labor force."

2. Codes: A, complete count, final data;
   B, sample tabulation, size not specified;
   C, sample tabulation, size specified;
   D, labor force sample survey;
   E, household survey;
   F, official estimates.

3. Economically active population figures relate to persons 14 years of age and over.

4. May or may not coincide with year of population census.

5. Economically active population figures relate to persons 12 years of age and over.

6. Figures rounded to the nearest hundred.

7. Includes 12,796 male and 3,093 female workers in the Canal Zone.

8. Economically active population figures relate to persons 16 years of age and over.

9. Excludes unemployed.

10. Data exclude unemployed persons not previously employed.

11. Economically active population figures include 1,737,000 resident members of the armed forces. Figures are rounded to the nearest thousand.

12. Excludes institutional households.

13. Economically active population figures relate to persons 6 years of age and over.

a. 1982 estimate.

SOURCE: ILO-YLS, 1983–87, table 1; 1988, table 1.

Table 1311

EAP BY INDUSTRY, 20 LC

Country	Year	Code[1]	EAP	Agriculture Forestry, Hunting, and Fishing		Mining and Quarrying		Manufacturing		Construction		Electricity Gas, and Water		Wholesale/Retail Trade, Restaurants, and Hotels	
				N	%	N	%	N	%	N	%	N	%	N	%
A. ARGENTINA[2]	1980	A	10,033,798	1,200,992	12.0	47,171	.4	1,985,995	19.8	1,003,175	10.0	103.256	1.1	1,702,080	16.9
B. BOLIVIA	1976	A	1,501,391	693,049	46.2	60,599	4.0	145,404	9.7	82,447	5.5	2,143	.1	106,862	7.1
C. BRAZIL[3]	1986	E	56,816,215	14,330,630	25.2	8,986,445	15.8	~f		3,588,651	6.3	820,609	1.5	6,252,111	11.0
D. CHILE[10],‡	1987	D	4,352,600	862,700	19.8	87,000	2.0	660,500	15.2	244,200	5.6	27,000	.6	737,700	17.0
E. COLOMBIA‡	1987	E	3,959,596	49,606	1.3	14,734	.3	821,687	20.8	230,603	5.8	19,682	.5	939,765	23.7
F. COSTA RICA[4]	1987	E	977,847	268,653	27.5	2,596	.2	167,641	17.2	58,665	6.0	11,599	1.2	154,362	15.8
G. CUBA	1981	A	3,540,692	790,869	22.3	668,340 h	18.9 h	~f		313,240	8.9	~f		305,630	8.6
H. DOMINICAN REP.‡	1981	A	1,915,388	420,463	22.0	4,743	.2	224,437	11.7	80,850	4.3	13,891	.7	192,181	10.0
I. ECUADOR[4]	1982	A	2,346,063	786,972	33.5	7,406	.4	286,530	12.2	158,009	6.8	13,183	.5	271,914	11.6
J. EL SALVADOR	1980	E	1,593,353	636,617	40.0	4,394	.2	247,621	15.6	80,089	5.0	9,681	.6	256,086	16.1
K. GUATEMALA[5],‡	1986–87	A	2,740,061	1,365,251	49.8	2,735	.1	334,107	12.2	94,672	3.5	10,556	.4	357,279	13.0
L. HAITI[9],‡	1988	F	2,350,302	1,184,804	50.4	17,635	.8	115,498	4.9	22,423	1.0	2,912	.1	260,708	11.0
M. HONDURAS[6]	1984	F	1,256,349	718,505	57.2	3,895	.3	167,597	13.3	43,470	3.5	5,151	.4	107,292	8.5
N. MEXICO‡	1987	F	27,324,000	7,060,500	25.8	636,600	2.4	3,194,200	11.7	1,620,300	5.9	144,800	.5	2,166,800	7.9
O. NICARAGUA[7]	1980	F	863,925	391,963	45.4	6,566	.7	91,403	10.6	37,322	4.3	6,652	.8	105,053	12.2
P. PANAMA	1986	D	719,574	188,217	26.2	420	~	70,026	9.7	40,134	5.6	9,067	1.3	104,427	14.5
Q. PARAGUAY[4]	1982	A	1,039,258	445,518	42.9	1,406	.1	124,658	12.0	69,900	6.8	2,605	.2	85,956	8.2
R. PERU[11],‡	1981	A	5,309,215	1,864,008	35.1	96,692	1.8	556,430	10.5	197,211	3.8	17,764	.3	632,506	11.9
S. URUGUAY‡	1985	A	1,172,300	179,200	15.3	1,900	.1	211,600	18.1	63,300	5.4	17,100	1.5	136,800	11.6
T. VENEZUELA	1987	E	6,321,566	857,141	13.6	62,126	.9	1,072,785	17.0	589,928	9.4	70,489	1.1	1,210,416	19.1
UNITED STATES[8,12]	1987	D	121,602,000	3,622,000	3.0	906,000	.7	22,250,000	18.3	8,256,000	6.8	1,572,000	1.3	25,021,000	20.6

Table 1311 (Continued)
EAP BY INDUSTRY, 20 LC

Country	Year	Code[1]	Transport, Storage, and Communication		Financing, Insurance Real Estate, and Business Services		Community, Social, and Personal Services		Activities Not Adequately Defined		Other[13]	
			N	%	N	%	N	%	N	%	N	%
A. ARGENTINA[2]	1980	A	460,476	4.6	395,704	4.0	2,399,039	23.9	691,302	6.9	44,608	.4
B. BOLIVIA	1976	A	55,972	3.8	12,941	.8	281,911	18.8	53,600	3.6	6,463	.4
C. BRAZIL[3]	1986	E	1,988,692	3.5	1,569,188	2.8	16,337,526	28.7	1,562,121	2.8	1,380,242	2.4
D. CHILE[10],‡	1987	D	273,500	6.3	188,700	4.3	1,204,600	27.7	1,200	#	65,500	1.5
E. COLOMBIA‡	1987	E	215,216	5.5	260,586	6.5	1,006,548	25.5	1,044	#	400,125	10.1
F. COSTA RICA[4]	1987	E	39,667	4.0	27,649	2.8	226,229	23.2	8,887	.9	11,899	1.2
G. CUBA	1981	A	248,644	7.0	~[k]	~[k]	1,086,052[a]	30.7[a]	127,917[d]	3.6[d]	~	~
H. DOMINICAN REP.‡	1980	A	40,470	2.1	22,369	1.2	363,125	18.9	421,628	22.0	131,231	6.9
I. ECUADOR[4]	1982	A	101,321	4.3	44,116	1.9	554,915	23.6	38,594	1.7	83,103	3.5
J. EL SALVADOR	1980	E	65,593	4.1	15,863	1.0	250,158	15.7	224	#	27,027	1.7
K. GUATEMALA[5]	1986–87	A	51,904	1.9	30,699	1.1	394,807	14.4	68,036	2.5	30,015	1.1
L. HAITI[9]	1988	F	16,599	.8	3,577	.1	115,453	4.9	48,909	2.1	561,784	23.9
M. HONDURAS[6]	1984	F	37,565	3.0	12,438	1.0	160,436	12.8	~	~	~	~
N. MEXICO‡	1987	F	847,000	3.1	511,000	1.9	3,035,700	11.1	7,954,100	29.1	153,000	.6
O. NICARAGUA[7]	1980	F	30,064	3.4	16,761	2.0	158,789	18.4	19,352	2.2	~	~
P. PANAMA	1986	D	40,498	5.6	28,519	4.0	192,643	26.8	15,316	2.1	30,307	4.2
Q. PARAGUAY[4]	1982	A	30,524	3.0	18,019	1.7	174,228	16.8	79,568	7.6	6,876	.7
R. PERU[11],‡	1981	A	210,007	3.9	121,606	2.3	1,067,754	20.1	271,455	5.1	119,555	2.3
S. URUGUAY	1985	A	59,100	5.1	42,100	3.6	361,800	30.8	80,500	6.9	18,900	1.6
T. VENEZUELA	1987	E	396,204	6.3	320,712	5.0	1,646,928	26.1	28,786	.5	66,051	1.0
UNITED STATES[8],[12]	1987	D	6,641,000	5.4	13,039,000	10.8	37,600,000	30.9	1,775,000[b]	1.4	921,000	.8

1. Code: A, complete count, final data;
   B, sample tabulation, size not specified.
   C, sample tabulation, size specified;
   D, labor force sample survey;
   E, household survey;
   F, official estimates.

2. Figures relate to persons 14 years of age and over.
3. Figures based on 1% sample of census returns.
4. Figures relate to persons 12 years of age and over.
5. Excludes institutional households.
6. Data exclude unemployed persons not previously employed.
7. Excludes unemployed.
8. Economically active population figures refer to persons 16 years of age and over.
9. Figures based on a 2.5% sample tabulation of census returns.

10. Figures rounded to the nearest hundred.
11. Economically active population figures relate to persons 10 to 69 years of age.
12. Figures rounded to the nearest thousand.
13. Data refer to persons seeking first job.

a. Includes financing, insurance, real estate, and business services.
b. Includes 1,737,000 members of the armed forces.
c. Includes electricity, gas, water, and sanitary services.
d. Data refer to members of producers' co-operatives.
e. Includes persons seeking first job.
f. Included in mining and quarrying industries.
g. Included in transport, storage, and communication.
h. Includes manufacturing, electricity, gas, and water.
i. Not recommended separately.

SOURCE: ILO-YLS, 1977 and 1981–87, table 2A; 1988, table 2A.

Table 1312

EAP BY MAJOR OCCUPATIONS, 20 LC

Country	Year	Code[1]	Total EAP	Professional, Technical, and Related Workers (0-1)		Administrative and Managerial Workers (2)		Clerical and Related Workers (3)		Sales Workers (4)		Service Workers (5)		Agriculture, Animal Husbandry, and Forestry Workers, Fishermen and Hunters (6)		Production and Related Workers, Transport Equipment Operators and Laborers (7-9)		Workers Not Classifiable by Occupation (X)		Person Seeking First Job	
				N	%	N	%	N	%	N	%	N	%	N	%	N	%	N	%	N	%
A. ARGENTINA	1970	B	9,011,450	677,500	7.5	137,850	1.5	1,025,400	11.4	1,072,800	11.9	1,136,550b	12.6b	1,296,100	14.4	3,091,350	34.3	573,900	6.4	~	~
B. BOLIVIA	1976	A	1,501,391	85,500	5.7	9,092	.6	59,609	4.0	91,385	6.1	128,595h	8.5h	1,067,675c	71.1c	~	~	53,072	3.6	6,463	.4
C. BRAZIL[4]	1970	C	29,557,224	1,410,746	4.8	497,079	1.7	1,561,678	5.3	2,193,661	7.4	3,404,014h	11.6h	13,039,149	44.0	6,263,571	21.2	1,187,308	4.0	~	~
D. CHILE[6],‡	1970	D	4,353,100	320,000	7.4	125,200	2.8	505,800	11.6	472,800	10.9	563,900	13.0	866,200	19.9	1,390,200	31.9	43,500	1.0	65,500	1.5
E. COLOMBIA[5,16]	1987	E	3,959,596	383,222	9.7	57,764	1.4	434,833	11.0	733,754	18.5	659,746	16.7	51,538	1.3	1,238,428	31.3	186	#	~d	~d
F. COSTA RICA[12]	1987	E	977,847	83,993	8.6	31,844	3.2	75,042	7.7	99,419	10.2	133,047	13.6	261,642	26.8	272,902	27.9	8,059	.8	11,899	1.2
G. CUBA[10,7]	1970	~	2,633,309	220,298	8.4	112,745	4.3	136,185	5.2	564,403e	21.4e	~e	~e	708,165	26.9	857,089	32.5	34,424	1.3	~	~
H. DOMINICAN REP.‡	1981	A	1,915,388	77,573	4.0	20,364	1.1	96,592	5.1	133,153	6.9	207,645	10.8	428,045	22.4	345,525	18.0	475,260	24.8	131,231	6.9
I. ECUADOR[12]	1982	A	2,346,063	183,579	7.8	11,123	.5	131,925	5.6	209,380	8.9	179,444	7.7	784,767	33.4	601,374	25.7	161,368i	6.9i	83,103	3.5
J. EL SALVADOR	1980	E	1,593,353	67,411	4.2	8,476	.6	85,929	5.4	225,438	14.1	128,413	8.1	629,345	39.5	421,090	26.4	224	#	27,027	1.7
K. GUATEMALA[13]	1981	A	1,696,464	81,237	4.8	20,117	1.2	56,568	3.3	99,516	5.9	109,848	6.5	911,256	53.7	349,943	20.6	55,342	3.3	12,636	.7
L. HAITI‡	1988	F	2,350,302	41,136	1.8	12,519	.5	8,943	.4	189,581	8.0	44,713	1.9	1,015,877	43.3	135,928	5.7	339,821	14.5	561,784	23.9
M. HONDURAS	1974	~	762,795	30,982	4.1	7,012	.9	31,784	4.2	43,907	5.8	49,674	6.5	453,113	59.4	131,408	17.2	7,744	1.0	7,171	.9
N. MEXICO[6,9],‡	1987	F	27,324,000	1,981,000	7.3	297,800	1.0	2,497,400	9.2	1,997,400	7.3	2,262,400	8.3	6,852,900	25.6	6,981,300	25.6	4,300,800	15.7	153,000	.5
O. NICARAGUA	1971	~	504,240	26,040	5.2	4,750	.9	21,080	4.2	35,840	7.1	55,130	10.9	235,120	46.7	110,500	21.9	15,780	3.1	~	~
P. PANAMA[3,13]	1986	D	719,574	73,663	10.2	35,145	4.9	74,602	10.4	59,300	8.2	105,423	14.7	179,594	24.9	161,165	22.4	375	.1	30,307	4.2
Q. PARAGUAY[12]	1982	A	1,039,258	53,820	5.2	53,720a	5.1a	~f	~f	66,690	6.5	87,710	8.5	445,650	43.3	246,970	24.0	66,770	6.5	6,130	.6
R. PERU[15],‡	1981	A	5,281,734	392,593	7.4	24,329	.5	514,363	9.7	523,921	10.0	375,804	7.1	1,817,407	34.4	992,653	18.8	284,963	5.4	355,701	6.7
S. URUGUAY[2]	1985	A	1,172,300	97,900	8.4	31,600	2.6	139,300	11.9	117,400	10.0	173,300	14.8	171,700	14.7	302,400	25.8	119,800	10.2	18,900	1.6
T. VENEZUELA[7]	1987	E	6,321,566	695,146	11.0	233,675	3.7	606,095	9.6	853,254	13.5	848,104	13.4	848,014	13.4	2,116,850	33.5	54,373	.9	66,051	1.0
UNITED STATES[8,11,14]	1987	D	121,602,000	18,176,000	14.9	13,666,000	11.3	19,056,000	15.7	14,171,000	11.6	16,313,000	13.4	3,775,000	3.1	33,749,000	27.8	1,775,000g	1.4	421,000	.8

1. Code: A, Complete count, final data;
   B, Sample tabulation, size not specified;
   C, Sample tabulation, size specified;
   D, Labor force sample survey;
   E, Household survey;
   F, Official estimates.

2. Includes persons 14 years of age and over.
3. Excludes persons working in the Canal Zone.
4. De jure population. EAP figures based on a 25% sample tabulation of census returns.
5. Figures include persons seeking work for the first time.
6. Figures rounded to nearest hundred.
7. Figures related to persons 15 years of age and over.
8. Beginning 1983, data based on revised occupational classification system and are not comparable with those for previous years.
9. De jure population. Includes persons 12 years of age and over.
10. Does not include domestic servants.
11. Includes persons 16 years of age and over.

12. Figures related to persons 12 years of age and over.
13. Figures exclude institutional household, ds.
14. Figures rounded to nearest thousand.
15. Economically active population figures relate to persons 10 to 69 years of age.
16. Data relate to Bogotá, Barranquilla, Medellín, Cali, Bucaramanga, Manizales, and Pasto.

a. Figures include clerical and related workers.
b. Figures include members of the armed forces.
c. Figures include miners and quarrymen.
d. Not recorded separately.
e. Figures for service workers are included under sales workers.
f. Included in category 2.
g. Figures in Category 6 include workers from Categories 7-9.
h. Service workers includes sport and recreation workers.
i. Includes 39,363 unemployed persons previously employed.

SOURCE: ILO-YLS, 1977, 1980, and 1982–88, table 2B.

Table 1313

OCCUPATIONAL CATEGORIES, BY SEX, 20 LC
(% of Sex)

	Country	Year	Code[1]	N (M) M	N (M) F	Professional, Technical, and Related Workers (0-1) M	F	Administrative and Managerial Workers (2) M	F	Clerical and Related Workers (3) M	F	Sales Workers (4) M	F	Service Workers (5) M	F	Agriculture, Animal Husbandry, and Forestry Workers, Fishermen and Hunters (6) M	F	Production and Related Workers, Transport Equipment Operators and Laborers (7-9) M	F	Workers Not Classifiable by Occupation (X) M	F	Person Seeking First Job M	F
A.	ARGENTINA	1970	~	6.7	2.3	4.5	1.6	1.9	.4	9.8	15.9	12.1	11.2	6.7	30.0	18.1	3.4	41.0	15.2	5.9	7.6	~	~
B.	BOLIVIA	1976	A	1.2	.3	4.3	10.5	.6	.4	3.5	3.5	3.5	14.9	4.9a	21.2a	52.2	26.5	26.6b	18.0b	3.8	2.6	.6	.4
C.	BRAZIL	1970	~	23.4	6.2	2.5	13.5	1.9	1.0	4.4	6.5	8.0	5.2	3.7	35.6	50.4	20.4	23.7	11.4	3.9	4.4	1.5a	#
D.	CHILE[2]	1987	D	3.0	1.3	5.0	12.8	3.4	1.7	9.7	16.1	9.0	15.2	5.1	31.4	26.2	5.1	39.1	15.0	1.4	.1	1.1	2.5
E.	COLOMBIA[8]	1987	E	2.3	1.6	9.7	9.7	.2	.7	8.3	14.8	19.7	16.9	8.5	28.1	1.8	.5	42.6	15.4	#	**	7.5c	13.7c
F.	COSTA RICA[9]	1987	E	.7	.3	6.4	14.4	3.5	2.6	5.3	13.9	9.7	11.3	7.2	30.4	35.2	4.5	30.9	20.0	.8	.8	.9	2.0
G.	CUBA[8]	1970	~	2.2	.5	8.4	6.9	4.3	.8	5.2	7.9	21.4e	6.4	..e	↓	26.9	↓	32.5	↓	1.3	↓	~	~
H.	DOMINICAN REP.‡	1981	A	1.4	.5	2.9	6.9	1.2	.8	3.9	7.9	7.2	6.4	4.2	27.3	28.4	7.4	21.8	8.8	23.5	28.2	7.1d	6.3d
I.	ECUADOR[9]	1982	A	1.9	.5	4.5	3.3	.4	#	3.1	2.5	6.3	2.8	3.0	4.6	30.9	2.5	22.8	2.9	5.8	1.1	2.7d	.9d
J.	EL SALVADOR	1980	E	1.0	.6	3.6	5.4	.7	.2	4.8	6.5	6.3	28.9	3.6	16.5	49.5	20.8	30.7	18.4	.0	.0	.8	.3
K.	GUATEMALA[3,10]	1981	A	1.4	.3	3.4	12.9	1.2	1.3	2.3	9.5	4.6	13.5	2.6	29.3	61.9	8.4	21.3	17.7	2.6	7.3	~	~
L.	HAITI[11]	1982	B	1.3	.8	2.1	1.9	.6	.4	.3	.5	1.6	20.5	1.3	3.6	63.0	30.9	7.8	5.2	12.1	23.2	11.2c	13.6c
M.	HONDURAS	1974	~	.6	.1	2.6	12.2	.8	1.3	3.5	7.8	4.3	13.5	2.1	30.3	69.6	5.0	15.2	28.0	1.0	1.0	.9d	.9d
N.	MEXICO	1980	A	15.9	6.1	5.4	9.7	.1	.1	8.1	14.8	6.8	8.4	6.6	14.4	30.5	11.0	25.1	13.2	16.8	27.9	.5d	.6d
O.	NICARAGUA	1971	~	.4	.1	3.7	10.2	1.0	.5	3.4	7.0	4.5	16.3	3.0	39.1	57.8	6.4	23.6	15.7	2.7	4.6	~	~
P.	PANAMA[4,14]	1986	D	.5	.2	6.9	17.4	5.1	3.1	4.6	24.3	5.8	7.8	8.9	28.7	34.4	2.5	29.1	6.8	2.8	2.6	2.8	5.9
Q.	PARAGUAY[7]	1982	A	.8	.2	2.9	2.3	3.3f	1.9f	~g	~g	4.0	2.5	4.0	5.3	40.7	2.1	20.0	4.2	5.0	1.3	.6	.1
R.	PERU[12],‡	1981	A	3.9	1.3	6.3	10.8	.6	.1	8.5	13.4	8.7	13.6	4.6	14.5	39.6	19.1	22.4	8.3	4.0	9.5	5.4c	10.7c
S.	URUGUAY[13]	1985	A	.8	.4	3.3	5.0	2.0	.7	6.5	5.4	6.6	3.5	4.4	10.4	13.8	.9	21.2	4.6	8.3	2.0	1.0	.7
T.	VENEZUELA	1987	E	4.6	1.8	7.0	21.4	4.4	1.9	5.3	20.8	13.1	14.6	8.6	25.6	17.9	1.7	41.7	12.1	1.1	2.5	.8	1.6
	UNITED STATES[5,6]	1987	D	67.8	53.8	13.5	16.8	12.5	9.7	5.6	28.3	10.7	12.8	9.5	18.4	4.7	1.1	40.6	11.6	2.4h	.3h	.6	.9

1. Code: A, Complete count, final data;
   B, Sample tabulation, size not specified;
   C, Sample tabulation size specified;
   D, Labor force sample survey;
   E, Household survey;
   F, Official estimates.
2. Figures rounded to the nearest hundred.
3. Excludes institutional households.
4. Excludes persons working in the Canal Zone.
5. Economically active population figures relate to persons 16 years of age and over.
6. All figures rounded to nearest thousand; consequently, the totals shown may differ from the sum of the component parts.
7. Based on a 10% sample tabulation.
8. Data relate to Bogotá, Barranquilla, Medellín, Cali, Bucaramanga, Manizales and Pasto.
9. Figures relate to persons 12 years of age and over.

10. Figures relate to persons 10 to 79 years of age and over.
11. Figures based on a 2.5% sample tabulation of census returns.
12. Figures relate to persons 10 to 69 years of age.
13. Persons aged 14 years and over.
14. Figures exclude institutional households.

a. Includes members of the armed forces.
b. Figures include miners, quarrymen, and related workers.
c. Figures refer to the unemployed.
d. Figures refer to persons seeking work for the first time.
e. Figures for service workers are included in sales workers.
f. Includes clerical and related workers.
g. Included in administrative and managerial workers.
h. Includes Armed Forces.

SOURCE: ILO-YLS, 1976, 1977, 1979–82, 1984–88, table 2B.

Table 1314

OCCUPATIONAL STRATA,[1] 9 L, 1960–73

(%)

Category	A. ARGENTINA 1960	A. ARGENTINA 1970	C. BRAZIL 1960	C. BRAZIL 1972	D. CHILE 1960	D. CHILE 1970	F. COSTA RICA 1963	F. COSTA RICA 1970
1. Medium and High Strata (except the occupations of the primary sector)	31.4	32.2	15.0	23.3	20.3	27.8	33.6	46.2
a. Employees	8.2	4.3	1.9	4.1	1.5	2.4	3.0	6.0
b. Self-Employed, Owners of Commercial Establishments	2.4	4.4	.2	1.6	3.7	4.9	4.4	3.1

	J. ECUADOR 1962	J. ECUADOR 1968	P. PANAMA 1960	P. PANAMA 1970	Q. PARAGUAY 1962	Q. PARAGUAY 1972	S. URUGUAY 1963	S. URUGUAY 1970	T. VENEZUELA 1960	T. VENEZUELA 1973
	25.0	39.8	16.4	21.8	11.8	13.9	50.9	45.8	23.9	36.8
	1.7	4.1	1.3	1.0	1.2	1.4	8.4	5.6	1.8	3.6
	9.1	12.1	.9	1.3	2.7	3.1	3.0	3.8	5.4	7.0

Continued in SALA, 21-1304.

Table 1315

ECONOMICALLY ACTIVE POPULATION ESTIMATED BY AGE GROUP, 20 LR, 1970–2000

Country	Age Groups	1970	1975	1980	1985	1990	1995	2000
A. ARGENTINA	Total	9,429,603	10,139,106	10,726,912	11,452,423	12,304,794	13,363,746	14,611,885
	10-14	203,219	191,983	181,811	194,872	214,161	217,129	210,275
	15-19	1,082,636	1,068,007	1,006,875	1,031,474	1,141,226	1,291,981	1,354,283
	20-24	1,286,940	1,431,032	1,477,305	1,554,659	1,679,103	1,955,616	2,331,904
	25-29	1,163,412	1,329,935	1,462,758	1,554,482	1,630,617	1,754,440	2,036,065
	30-34	1,058,637	1,162,099	1,321,442	1,474,883	1,556,897	1,621,853	1,733,485
	35-39	1,015,080	1,056,883	1,157,263	1,310,830	1,448,328	1,513,083	1,560,043
	40-44	968,658	1,005,217	1,043,096	1,125,520	1,271,948	1,401,679	1,460,507
	45-49	850,743	935,959	960,269	978,816	1,058,121	1,197,551	1,321,603

Continued in SALA, 25-1313.

Table 1316

EAP BY ACTIVITY,[1] 14 L, 1950–80

(%)

Country	Year	Urban Formal (1)	Urban Informal[a] (2)	Urban Total (3)	Agricultural Modern (4)	Agricultural Traditional (5)	Agricultural Total (6)	Mining (7)	Coverage of the Underemployed (2+5) (8)
A. ARGENTINA	1950	56.8	15.2	72.0	19.9	7.6	27.5	.5	22.8
	1970	66.0	15.6	81.6	11.2	6.7	17.9	.5	22.3
	1980[b]	65.0	19.4	84.4	8.8	6.3	15.1	.5	25.7

Continued in SALA, 24–1314.

Table 1317

POPULATION EMPLOYED BY SECTOR, 13 L, 1960 AND 1970

(N)

Country	Agricultural Sector 1960	Agricultural Sector 1970	Basic Services 1960	Basic Services 1970	And Other Services 1960	And Other Services 1970
A. ARGENTINA	19.1	15.2	38.0	37.0	42.9	47.8

Continued in SALA, 21-1305.

Table 1318

EMPLOYMENT IN MANUFACTURING, 18 LC, 1970-87[a]

(T)

Country	Code[1]	1970	1972	1973	1974	1975	1976	1977	1978	1979	1980	1981	1982	1983	1984	1985	1986	1987
A. ARGENTINA[12,15,18,20]	C	**	**	**	**	**	223.1	217.6	199.7	193.8	180.6	160.9	143.8	149.3	156.9	151.2	~	~
B. BOLIVIA[12,15,23]	D	103.9	112.6	117.1	121.8	**	152.3	160.5	166.1	172.7	177.7	168.4	155.5	150.2	149.3	147.1	117.1	118.1
C. BRAZIL[2,15,23]	A[19]	2,499b	2,830b	3,230b	3,720b	**	6,266	6,510	7,099	7,288	~	7,562	7,790	~	~	7,847	8,986	~
D. CHILE[2,28]	A	**	**	~	~	**	~	~	486.1	496.1	524.1	516.2	373.9j	405.9	463.4	494.7k	531.3	607.3
E. COLOMBIA[4]	C	100.0	106.2	111.7	116.4	117.9	120.6	122.3	124.5	127.2	100.0	95.4	90.5	84.5	83.6	82.3	82.4	84.9
F. COSTA RICA[5,14,15,24]	A	**	**	**	**	**	78.4	85.8	87.9	94.5	95.9	88.1	89.5	98.3	101.7d	100.0	112.5	112.4
G. CUBA[6,26,27]	C[25]	**	438.5	453.2	466.7	472.2	514.1	550.5	558.7	559.9	565.7	564.9	596.6	639.2	674.8	695.1	711.9i	~
H. DOMINICAN REP.	C	110.7	124.2	137.7	139.4	122.3	110.8	112.6	113.3	~	~	~	~	~	~	~	~	~
I. ECUADOR[7]	C	--	125.4	132.1	139.2	147.6	158.7	154.1	165.3	173.2	174.5	177.4	189.4	181.0	~	~	~	~
J. EL SALVADOR[16]	C	**	**	**	**	49.5	54.2	56.4	57.7	58.8	54.3	50.6	47.8	50.6	49.9	48.9‡	~	~
K. GUATEMALA[3]	C	**	40.9	41.6	37.4	32.8	32.4	36.8	38.6	46.5	41.3	40.3	35.9	32.9	46.2	48.3	50.4	~
L. HAITI[2,8]	D	118.7	121.6	120.9	121.5	122.3	115.9	116.6	117.2	117.8	132.2	134.2	121.2	121.7	~	~	~	~
M. HONDURAS	D	~	--	--	--	**	98.3	103.7	109.4	115.5	121.9	128.6	~	~	~	~	~	~
N. MEXICO[12,17,22]	C	~	346.2	362.2	403.2e	413.5	491.2f	487.2	510.1	547.6	587.2	619.3	605.1	548.2	537.9	554.3	532.8	515.7
O. NICARAGUA[10,12]	B	22.2	23.6	22.4	25.0	26.6	28.2	30.5	29.2	24.8	27.9	~	~	~	~	~	~	~
P. PANAMA[11,14,28]	A	**	**	~	37.4c	33.7c	34.2	37.9c	39.9	42.7	~	~	44.8	49.6	47.4	51.0	~	~
R. PERU[2]	D	574.0	627.4	658.4	694.7	727.9	744.0	741.2	772.3	803.9	812.5	808.4	~	~	~	~	~	~
S. URUGUAY[9,29]	A	--	--	--	--	~	130.2	139.6	139.9	140.7	130.7a	145.5	120.7	110.5a	115.6	123.0	111.3	116.7
T. VENEZUELA[13,16,21]	C	61.4	62.9	65.5	70.1	289.7	392.8	419.6	455.2	404.6	477.1	412.5	449.4	453.5	468.4	~	~	~
U. UNITED STATES[21]	C	19,367	19,151	20,154	20,077	18,323	18,997	19,682	20,505	21,040	20,285	20,170	18,781	18,434	19,378	19,260	18,994	19,065

1. The series refer, in general, to salaried employees and wage earners in manufacturing (excluding public utilities, building, and other construction). Workers on paid or unpaid holiday or vacation are generally included, but employers, self-employed, and workers on strike, or temporary military leave or temporarily laid off are generally excluded. Code A, Labor force sample surveys, B, Social insurance statistics; C, Statistics of establishments; D, Official estimates.
2. Civilian labor force employed.
3. Wage earners after 1974.
4. Base: 1980 = 100, prior to 1980: July 1970 — June 1971 = 100.
5. July of each year after 1974.
6. Prior to 1977. Includes mining and quarrying, electricity, gas, and water; state sector.
7. Base: 1965 = 100.
8. Year beginning in July of each year indicated.
9. Montevideo.
10. Eight main cities of the country.
11. August of each year.
12. Employees after 1974.
13. Second semester of each year, prior to 1975.
14. Wage earners and salaried employees.
15. Includes mining and quarrying after 1974.
16. After 1974, includes establishments with five or more persons employed.
17. Last week of October of each year.
18. July 1st of each year after 1975.

19. Prior to 1975, statistics of establishments.
20. Prior to 1975, civilian labor force employed.
21. Registered employees prior to 1975.
22. Prior to 1975, include 57 industrial groups of the national classification.
23. Persons 10 years and over.
24. Persons 12 years and over.
25. Prior to 1976, official estimates.
26. State sector employees.
27. Includes fishing, gas, mining and quarrying, and water.
28. After 1975, persons 15 years and over.
29. Includes professional army and excludes compulsory military service.

a. For employment indices data, 1964-79, see SALA, 22-1304.
b. December.
c. October.
d. November.
e. Not strictly comparable.
f. Prior to 1975: 54 industrial groups.
g. Prior to 1983: First semester of each year.
h. Excludes the rural population of the northern region.
i. Prior to 1986, includes water.
j. Prior to 1982: persons aged 12 years and over.
k. Beginning fourth quarter 1985: sample design revised; 1985: quarter Nov. 1985-Jan. 1986.

SOURCE: Data for 1970-74 from ILO-YLS, 1980, table 6A; 1975-85 data from ILO-YLS, 1985 and 1987, table 5A 1988, table 5A.

Table 1319

EMPLOYMENT INDEX FOR MANUFACTURING, 9 L, 1977-83[a]

(1980 = 100)

Country	1977	1978	1979	1980	1981	1982	1983	% Change[3] 1977	1978	1979	1980	1981	1982	1983
A. ARGENTINA[1]	109.7	99.3	97.2	100.0	78.4	74.2	76.7	-6.2	-9.7	-2.1	2.9	-21.6	-5.4	3.3
C. BRAZIL[1]	91.8	93.7	96.9	100.0	92.6	86.5	80.1	1.0	2.1	3.4	3.2	-7.4	-6.7	-7.4
D. CHILE[2]	91.4	92.7	93.1	100.0	102.2	80.9	78.8	2.2	1.4	.5	7.4	2.2	-20.8	-2.6
E. COLOMBIA[1]	96.9	98.6	100.8	100.0	95.5	90.7	85.1	1.5	1.8	2.2	-.8	-4.5	-5.0	-7.2
F. COSTA RICA[2]	98.7	99.2	99.5	100.0	100.4	102.1	101.8	7.0	.5	.4	.5	.4	1.7	-2.0
I. ECUADOR[1]	89.2	94.5	97.3	100.0	107.1	109.6	104.0	6.0	6.0	2.9	2.8	7.1	2.3	-3.4
N. MEXICO[1]	82.5	86.6	93.2	100.0	105.6	103.0	94.4	.9	4.9	7.6	7.3	5.6	-2.4	-8.3
R. PERU[1]	98.6	97.9	97.9	100.0	101.1	94.7	94.3	.7	.7	#	2.1	1.1	-1.4	-5.4
T. VENEZUELA[2]	91.7	99.6	99.1	100.0	101.8	100.8	94.5	6.2	8.6	-.5	1.0	1.8	-1.0	-6.1

1. Personnel employed in manufacturing, according to periodic sample surveys of enterprises.
2. Personnel employed in manufacturing, according to household surveys.
3. In relation to the same period in the preceding year.

a. For ILO-YLS employment indices data, 1964-79, see SALA, 22-1304.

SOURCE: ECLA-CC, 1985, vol. 49, table 7.

Table 1320

HOURS OF WORK IN MANUFACTURING, 12 LC, 1964–87
(Actual Hours of Work per Week per Worker)[1]

Country	1964	1970	1975	1976	1977	1978	1979	1980	1981	1982	1983	1984	1985	1986	1987
A. ARGENTINA[8,9]	..	..	**	**	**	**	191.4	186.7	180.4	181.3	177.9	178.4	179.7	188.4[b]	~
B. BOLIVIA[7]	..	..	43.1	46.1	46.9	47.7	~	46.8	46.3	~	~	~	44.9	~	~
D. CHILE	~	~	~	~	~	**	**	**	**	43.3	43.2	43.6	43.1[d]	44.3	44.1
E. COLOMBIA	50.0	..	..	..	..	..	..	..	..	..	..	..	..	..	~
F. COSTA RICA[10,11,12]	**	..	**	**	48.9	48.3	49.5	49.8	48.5	48.0	49.3	42.5[a]	43.0	~	~
G. CUBA[13,14,4,15]	**	**	**	**	**	43.1	42.1	42.4	42.2	41.8	43.1	43.2	43.4	43.4[c]	~
I. ECUADOR	45.0	48.0	51.0	50.0	51.0	53.0	47.0	45.0	45.0	45.0	44.0	44.0	~	~	~
J. EL SALVADOR[2,3]	49.5	48.0	44.3	44.3	44.3	44.6	44.6	44.6	44.5	44.2	44.0	44.0	44.0	~	~
K. GUATEMALA[4]	45.7	45.9	47.2	47.3	48.5	47.5	47.4	45.1	46.1	45.7	46.5	48.7	48.6	~	~
N. MEXICO[5]	45.6	44.9	45.6	45.6	45.5	46.4	46.5	46.6	46.0	45.6	45.8	46.4	~	~	~
P. PANAMA	44.6	42.3	45.5	45.9	45.9	45.4	46.0	~	45.5	45.8	46.1	43.1	~	~	~
R. PERU[5,6]	47.3	**	46.1	48.1	45.4	45.8	45.7	45.6*	45.0	45.4	47.8	45.9	44.8	48.5	47.4
T. VENEZUELA	~	44.4	42.3	43.1	43.7	43.9	44.9	44.2	45.4	~	43.3	40.1	40.6	40.7	40.2
UNITED STATES[16]	40.7	39.8	39.5	40.1	40.3	40.4	40.2	39.7	39.8	38.9	40.1	40.7	40.5	40.7	41.0

1. The series generally represent the average hours actually worked by wage earners. In a few cases the data refer to hours paid for, or to normal hours, rather than to actual hours worked. Where possible, annual data are averages of twelve monthly figures.
2. San Salvador.
3. Males only.
4. Prior to 1974, Guatemala City.
5. October of each year.
6. Lima, May of each year; prior to 1980, June of each year.
7. Employees.
8. Per month.
9. Averages: April and October of each year.
10. Includes mining and quarrying.

11. July of each year.
12. Civilian labor force employed.
13. Includes fishing, mining and quarrying, water, and gas.
14. State sector.
15. Wage earners.
16. Hours paid for.

a. November figures.
b. April.
c. Prior to 1986, incluces water.
d. Beginning fourth quarter 1985: sample design revised; 1985: quarter Nov. 1985– Jan. 1986.

SOURCE I.O-YLS 1974, 1980, table 13A; and 1985, 1986, and 1987, table 12A: 1988, table 12A.

Table 1321

GOVERNMENT EMPLOYEES BY LEVEL, 6 LC

Country	Year	Central Government T	Central Government PHI	State and Local Government T	State and Local Government PHI	Nonfinancial Public Enterprises T	Nonfinancial Public Enterprises PHI	General Government T	General Government PHI	Public Sector T	Public Sector PHI
A. ARGENTINA	1981	573.5	2.12	703.0	2.60	313.8	1.16	1,276.5	4.72	1,590.3	5.88
I. ECUADOR	1980	163.3	1.96	~	~	~	~	~	~	~	~
J. EL SALVADOR	1982	111.5	2.32	~	~	13.9	.29	~	~	13.1	1.81
K. GUATEMALA	1981	105.0	1.45	18.8	.26	7.3	.10	123.8	1.71		
M. HONDURAS	1981	27.0	.73	~	~	~	~	~	~	~	~
P. PANAMA	1979	63.7	3.39	4.1	.22	38.5	2.05	71.7	3.81	110.2	5.86

SOURCE: IMF, Occasional Paper 24, October 1983, tables 20 and 21.

Table 1322

UNDERUTILIZATION OF LABOR, 6L
(Ca. 1970)

Country	EAP N	EAP Agricultural	EAP Nonagricultural	Open Unemployment Thousands	Open Unemployment Rate[3]	Equivalent Unemployment in Agriculture[1] Thousands	Equivalent Unemployment in Agriculture[1] Rate[3]	Nonagricultural Underemployment[2] Thousands	Nonagricultural Underemployment[2] Rate[3]	Equivalent Nonagricultural Employment Thousands	Equivalent Nonagricultural Employment Rate[3]	Total Underutilization of Labor Thousands	Total Underutilization of Labor Rate[3]
A. ARGENTINA	8,823	1,318	7,505	168	1.9	132	10	2,086	27.8	901	12.0	1,201	13.6

Continued in SALA, 21-1309.

Table 1323

UNDEREMPLOYMENT TOPICS COVERED IN HOUSEHOLD SURVEYS, 13 L

Country	Hours Worked	Average Workday	Reasons for Not Working Longer Hours	Desire to Work Longer Hours	Job Stability	Method of Payment	Reasons for Not Having Worked	Job Search	Reasons for Search
A. ARGENTINA	Yes	No	No	Yes	Yes	No	Yes	Yes	Yes

Continued in SALA, 23-1310.

Table 1324

UNEMPLOYMENT TOPICS COVERED IN HOUSEHOLD SURVEYS, 13 L

Country	Length of Search for Employment	Means of Search	Part-time or Full-time Search	Type of Employment Sought	Characteristics of Last Employment					
					Date of Last Employment	Occupation	Economic Activity	Employment Category	Size of Establishment	Reasons for Leaving
A. ARGENTINA	Yes	No	No	Yes	Yes	Yes	Yes	Yes	Yes	Yes

Continued in SALA, 23-1311.

Table 1325

MINIMUM AGE FROM WHICH ECONOMIC CHARACTERISTICS
WERE INVESTIGATED IN POPULATION CENSUSES AND
NATIONAL HOUSEHOLD SURVEYS IN THE 1970s, 20 L

	Country	Population Censuses	Household Surveys
A.	ARGENTINA	10 years and over	- -
B.	BOLIVIA	7 years and over	- -
C.	BRAZIL	10 years and over	10 years and over
D.	CHILE	12 years and over	12 years and over
E.	COLOMBIA	10 years and over	12 years and over
F.	COSTA RICA	12 years and over	12 years and over
G.	CUBA	10 years and over	- -
H.	DOMINICAN REP.	10 years and over	- -
I.	ECUADOR	12 years and over	- -
J.	EL SALVADOR	10 years and over	10 years and over
K.	GUATEMALA	10 years and over	- -
L.	HAITI	5 years and over	- -
M.	HONDURAS	10 years and over	- -
N.	MEXICO	12 years and over	12 years and over
O.	NICARAGUA	10 years and over	- -
P.	PANAMA	10 years and over	15 years and over
Q.	PARAGUAY	12 years and over	- -
R.	PERU	6 years and over	14 years and over
S.	URUGUAY	12 years and over	14 years and over
T.	VENEZUELA	15 years and over	10 years and over

SOURCE: ECLA-CC, Nov. 1983, table III.3, p. 157.

Table 1326

DECLARATION PERIOD AND MINIMUM TIME OF EMPLOYMENT FOR
DETERMINING ACTIVITY STATUS, POPULATION CENSUS 1970, 20 L

Country	Criteria Used in Determining Activity Status (type)		Additional Criteria Concerning Minimum Time of Employment Required for Inclusion in the Category of:	
	Period of Declaration	Minimum Time Employed	Work	Unpaid Family Worker
A. ARGENTINA	Preceding week	Majority of week, i.e. 4 normal working days	Not specified	Not specified
B. BOLIVIA	Preceding week	Majority of week	Not specified	Not specified

Continued in SALA, 27-1328.

Table 1327

OPEN UNEMPLOYMENT,[1] 14 LC, 1980–87

		1980		1981		1982		1983		1984		1985		1986		1987	
Country	Code[2]	T	%	T	%	T	%	T	%	T	%	T	%	T	%	T	%
A. ARGENTINA[3,11]	A	82.2	2.3	174.8	4.5	183.6	4.8	159.4	4.2	152.1	3.8	216.2	5.2	177.8[d]	4.4[d]	230.5	5.2
B. BOLIVIA	C	105.9	5.8	180.5	9.7	200.7	10.5	277.6	14.2	303.2	15.1	370.9	18.0	415.4	20.0	430.7	20.5
C. BRAZIL[4]	A		~	2,023.0	4.3	2,533.0	~		~		~	1,862.0	15.3		~		~
D. CHILE[5,12]	A	152.4	12.0	121.3	9.0	272.1	20.0	248.9	17.1	281.8	18.5	241.4	15.3		~		~
E. COLOMBIA[6,13,14]	A	320.8	9.1	266.2	8.1	311.6	9.2	406.5	11.2	503.5	13.0	499.9	14.0	482.8	13.0	400.1	10.2
F. COSTA RICA[14,15]	A	45.6	5.9	69.6	8.7	78.6	9.4	76.2	9.0	44.4[a]	5.0[a]	60.8	6.8	56.7	6.2	54.5	5.6
K. GUATEMALA[7]	B	.2	~	.3	~	.3	~	.3	~	.4	~	.2	~	.3	~		~
M. HONDURAS	C	117.0	~	113.5	~	128.3	~	254.2	~		~		~		~		~
N. MEXICO[10]	A	~	4.5	~	4.2	~	4.2	~	6.7	~	6.0	~	4.8	~	4.9	~	~
O. NICARAGUA	~	~	~	~	~	~	~	~	~	~	~	~	~	~	~	~	~
P. PANAMA[12]	A	~	~	~	~	51.5[b]	8.4[b]	64.2[b]	9.7[b]	68.8[b]	10.1[b]	88.3	12.3	75.8	10.5	89.3[‡]	11.6[‡]
R. PERU[8]	A	394.5	7.0	392.0	6.8	417.1	7.0	564.6	9.2	691.4	10.9	773.2	11.8	554.1	8.2		~
S. URUGUAY[9,16]	A	40.0	7.3	37.0	6.6	60.9[c]	11.0[c]	89.7	15.4	83.7	13.9	77.9	13.0	64.2[c]	11.4[c]	48.4	9.3
T. VENEZUELA[12]	A	263.4	6.0	287.7	6.2	333.3[c]	7.1[c]	469.0[c]	9.8[c]	706.3[c]	13.4[c]	767.1	13.1	668.1	11.0	573.4	9.1
UNITED STATES[17]	A	7,637.0	7.0	8,273.0	7.5	10,678.0	9.5	10,717.0	9.5	8,539.0	7.4	8,312.0	7.1	8,237.0	6.9		

1. The series generally represent the total number of persons wholly unemployed and temporarily laid off. The nature of Latin American economies makes gathering, reporting, and interpretation of unemployment somewhat difficult. Thus cautious use of the few data available is recommended.
2. Code: A, Labor force sample surveys and general household sample surveys; B, Employment office statistics; C, Office estimates.
3. Greater Buenos Aires.
4. Data for 1965 relate to Rio de Janeiro, São Paulo, and other areas varying according to the surveys. Data exclude rural areas of Rondaná, Acre, Amazonas, Roraima, Pará, Amapá, Mato Grosso, and Goiás.
5. Greater Santiago.
6. Bogotá, Barranquilla, Bucaramanga, Cali, Manizales, Medellín, and Pasto for September of each year.
7. Guatemala City, Quetzaltenango, Escuintla, and Puerto Barrios; prior to 1973 Guatemala City only.
8. Urban areas, for 1965 data.
9. Montevideo.
10. Metropolitan areas of Mexico City, Monterrey, and Guadalajara.
11. After 1975, averages: April and Oct. of each year.
12. Persons 15 years and over.
13. After 1975, Sept. of each year.
14. Persons 12 years and over.
15. After 1975, July of each year.
16. Persons 14 years and over.
17. Persons 16 years and over.

a. Nov.
b. August.
c. First semester.
d. October.

SOURCE: ILO-YLS, 1975, 1980, table 10; 1985, 1986, and 1987, table 9A. For 1963, 1968, and 1971–77 data, see SALA, 24-1326; for 1965–78 data, see SALA, 25-1327; ILO-YLS, 1988, table 9A.

Table 1328

UNEMPLOYMENT ACCORDING TO PREVIOUS JOB EXPERIENCE, 8 LC, 1975–87

(T)

Country	Category[1]		1975	1978	1979	1980	1981	1982	1983	1984	1985	1986	1987
A. ARGENTINA[2,3]	A. Total		75.8	82.3	57.9	68.4	145.4	150.9	119.5	117.3	185.8	150.2[a]	190.3
	B. Total		21.2	19.3	11.5	10.3	22.3	29.6	32.2	23.9	30.4	27.6[a]	40.1
D. CHILE[3,8]	A. Total		308.2	343.5	336.1	273.9	321.3	563.7	437.2	411.1	404.1*	297.7	278.0
	B. Total		159.4	151.8	138.1	104.4	95.7	153.9	114.8	119.3	112.6*	76.3	65.3
E. COLOMBIA[3,4]	A. Total		161.95	157.59	194.33	217.78	187.80	221.43	292.68	358.77	354.5	334.4	273.2
		Male	95.09	89.35	106.24	122.76	~	~	~	~	~	~	~
		Female	66.86	68.24	88.09	95.01	~	~	~	~	~	~	~
	B. Total		91.17	86.05	98.56	103.02	78.41	90.17	113.84	144.71	145.4	148.5	126.9
		Male	41.97	37.10	38.53	39.01	~	~	~	~	~	~	~
		Female	49.21	48.95	60.03	64.01	~	~	~	~	~	~	~
F. COSTA RICA[3,5]	A. Total		~	23.64	25.60	35.35	58.54	62.66	59.80	34.89[b]	49.23	46.4	42.6
	B. Total		~	9.55	11.27	10.21	11.08	15.91	16.64	9.49[b]	11.53	10.4	11.9
P. PANAMA[3,9,11]	A. Total		24.40[b]	21.17	30.12	~	~	29.06	39.63	39.22	51.39	43.6	57.1‡
		Male	13.70[b]	12.21	17.36	~	~	16.19	23.11	23.79	29.10	26.2	32.7‡
		Female	10.70[b]	8.96	12.76	~	~	12.87	16.53	15.43	22.29	17.4	24.5‡
	B. Total		7.20[b]	22.61	20.61	~	~	22.44	20.49	29.57	33.16	30.1	32.2‡
		Male	3.50[b]	11.20	9.56	~	~	10.49	12.51	15.13	15.62	15.8	14.7‡
		Female	3.70[b]	11.41	11.50	~	~	11.95	12.08	14.44	17.54	14.3	17.5‡
R. PERU[3]	A. Total		~	~	~	~	~	~	~	~	~	~	~
	B. Total		~	~	~	~	~	~	~	~	~	~	~
S. URUGUAY[3,6,12]	A. Total		~	32.2	29.0	27.3[c]	24.5	48.7	73.0	61.7	56.8	47.5[c]	34.5
	B. Total		~	17.8	13.4	12.7[c]	12.5	12.2	16.7	22.0	21.1	16.7[c]	13.9
T. VENEZUELA[3,7,10,11,13]	A. Total		207.84	151.57	207.85	239.56[c]	280.78*	321.70	454.23	599.76	672.5	588.6	504.6
		Male	~	125.78	170.34	196.74[c]	230.12*	269.60	373.34	483.67	528.4	460.6	409.4
		Female	~	25.78	37.41	42.81[c]	50.66*	52.10	80.89	116.09	144.2	128.0	95.2
	B. Total		33.91	28.79	36.79	32.80[c]	44.14*	52.53	82.03	106.50	94.6	79.5	68.9
		Male	~	16.09	20.42	19.29[c]	24.37*	30.62	48.18	61.09	49.2	41.7	39.5
		Female	~	12.70	16.38	13.51[c]	19.77*	21.91	33.85	45.41	45.4	37.8	29.4
UNITED STATES[3,14]	A. Total		7,101	6,316	6,310	6,764	7,201	9,488	9,498	7,425	7,271	7,200	6,504
		Male	4,063	2,748	2,767	3,861	4,105	5,612	5,670	4,215	4,033	4,049	3,687
		Female	3,037	2,569	2,553	2,903	3,186	3,876	3,828	3,210	3,238	3,157	2,817
	B. Total		828	886	818	873	982	1,190	1,219	1,114	1,041	1,031	921
		Male	379	394	353	406	472	567	590	529	488	481	414
		Female	449	492	465	467	510	623	629	585	553	550	507

1. Category A refers to those with previous job experience. Category B refers to those seeking their first job.
2. Greater Buenos Aires.
3. Labor force sample survey or general household sample survey.
4. September of each year and includes seven main cities.
5. July of each year.
6. Montevideo.
7. Second semester.
8. Prior to 1982: persons 12 years and over, while 1982 figures and beyond relate to persons 15 years and over.

9. Data for 1976, 1978, 1979, and 1982–84 represent August figures.
10. Data for 1980–83 represent first semester figures.
11. Persons 15 years and over.
12. Persons 14 years and over.
13. Data for 1982–85 represent first semester figures.
14. Persons 16 years and over.

a. October
b. November.
c. First semester.

SOURCE: ILO-YLS, 1981, 1985, 1986, and 1987, table 10A; 1988, table 10A.

Table 1329

EVOLUTION OF URBAN UNEMPLOYMENT, 16 L, 1975-88
(AA)

Country	1975	1977	1978	1979	1980	1981	1982	1983	1984	1985	1986	1987	1988
A. ARGENTINA[1]	3.7	2.8	2.8	2.0	2.3	4.5	4.7	4.2	4.6	6.1	5.2a	5.9	6.5
B. BOLIVIA[2]	~	~	~	~	7.1	5.9	8.2	8.5	6.9	5.8	7.0	5.2	11.7
C. BRAZIL[3]	~	~	6.8	6.4	6.3d	7.9	6.3	6.7	7.1	5.3	3.6	3.8	4.0b
D. CHILE[6]	15.0	13.9	13.7	13.4	11.8	9.0	20.0	18.9c	18.5	17.2	13.1	11.9	11.2
E. COLOMBIA[4]	11.0	9.0	9.0	8.9	9.7	8.2	9.3	11.8	13.5	14.1k	13.8e	11.8	11.4j
F. COSTA RICA[5]	~	5.1	5.8	5.3	6.0	9.1	9.9	8.6	6.6f	6.7	6.7f	5.6	5.2
I. ECUADOR[8,†]	**	~	~	5.4	5.7	6.0	6.3	6.7	10.6	10.4	12.0	12.0	13.0
K. GUATEMALA[8,†]	**	~	~	~	2.2	2.7	6.0	9.9	9.1	12.0	14.2	12.6	12.0
M. HONDURAS[8,†]	**	~	~	~	8.8	9.0	9.2	9.5	10.7	11.7	12.1	13.0	13.1
N. MEXICO[7]	7.2	8.3	6.9	5.7	4.5	4.2	4.1	6.7	6.0	4.4	4.3	3.9	3.6g
O. NICARAGUA[8]	~	~	~	~	22.4	19.0	19.9	18.9	21.1	22.3	21.7	~	~
P. PANAMA[12]	8.6	~	10.4	11.9	10.4	10.7	10.1	11.7	12.4	15.6	12.6	14.1	20.8
Q. PARAGUAY[8,9]	~	3.7	4.1	5.9	3.9	2.2	5.6	8.3	7.3	5.2	6.1	5.6	~
R. PERU[13]	~	9.4	8.0	6.5	7.1	6.8	6.6	9.0	8.9	10.1	5.3	4.8	~
S. URUGUAY[10]	~	11.8	10.1	8.3	7.4	6.7i	11.9i	15.5i	14.0i	13.1i	10.7i	9.3i	9.2
T. VENEZUELA[11]	8.3	5.5	5.1	5.8	6.6	6.8	7.8	10.5	14.3	14.3	12.1	9.8	~

1. Includes Federal Capital and Greater Buenos Aires and the average for April and October.
2. National data, not comparable over time due to changes in geographical coverage.
3. Metropolitan areas of Rio de Janeiro, Sao Paulo, Belo Horizonte, Porto Alegre, Salvador, and Recife.
4. Data for March, June, September, and December for the areas of Bogotá, Barranquilla, Medellín, and Cali.
5. Includes urban data for March, July, and November. After 1987, changes in methodology.
6. Greater Santiago data for four quarters. Since 1985 changes in design and size of sample.
7. Data for four quarters in metropolitan areas of Mexico City, Guadalajara, and Monterrey.
8. National averages.
9. Data for areas of Asunción, Fernando de la Mora, Lambaré, Lugue, and San Lorenzo.
10. Montevideo data for two quarters.
11. Data for two semesters.
12. August of each year. From 1978 refer to Metropolitan region.
13. Metropolitan Lima.

a. October.
b. January through September.
c. Metropolitan region of Santiago.
d. June through December.
e. April, June, September and December.
f. March, and July.
g. January through September.
h. January through November.
i. Average for four quarters.
j. Average for March, June, and September.
k. Average for March, July, and December.

SOURCE: ECLA-N, Dec. 1985, 1986, 1987, 1988, pp. 12, 15, and 16, respectively.

Table 1330

EVOLUTION OF UNEMPLOYMENT RATE IN PRINCIPAL CITIES, 11 L, 1979–1987

(%)

Country/City	1979	1980	1981	1982	1983	1984	1985	1986	1987[‡]
A. ARGENTINA[1]									
Buenos Aires	2.0	2.3	4.5	4.7	4.2	3.8	5.3	4.6	5.3
Córdoba	2.2	2.4	3.8	4.4	5.0	4.8	5.0	5.8	5.2
Mendoza	3.1	2.3	4.8	4.1	4.5	3.5	3.7	4.2	3.4
Rosario	2.9	3.4	5.8	8.4	6.3	6.5	10.7	7.0	7.8
B. BOLIVIA									
La Paz	7.6[a]	7.5[b]	~	9.4[c]	12.8[c]	12.6	~	~	~
C. BRAZIL[2]									
Rio de Janeiro	~	7.5	8.6	6.6	6.2	6.8	4.9	3.7	3.2
Sao Paulo	~	5.6	7.3	6.0	6.8	6.8	5.0	3.3	3.8
Recife	~	6.8	8.6	7.5	8.0	9.0	7.2	4.6	5.2
Porto Alegre	~	4.6	5.8	5.2	6.7	7.0	5.4	4.4	3.9
D. CHILE[4]									
Santiago	13.6	11.8	11.1	22.1	22.2	19.3	16.3	13.5	12.3
E. COLOMBIA[4]									
Bogotá	6.6	7.9	5.5	7.4	9.4	12.2	12.8	13.2	11.1
Barranquilla	6.3	8.1	11.1	10.4	13.8	13.0	15.7	16.4	13.0
Medellín	14.3	14.7	~	13.3	17.0	16.4	16.0	15.2	12.2
Cali	10.7	10.0	~	9.6	11.6	13.3	14.0	12.7	12.4
F. COSTA RICA[5]									
San José	4.5	5.6	9.3	10.5	8.5	6.6	6.5	6.8	5.4
N. MEXICO[3]									
Mexico City	5.7	4.3	3.9	4.0	6.3	5.8	4.9	5.1	~
Guadalajara	5.7	5.0	5.8	5.0	7.4	6.1	3.4	3.2	~
Monterrey	5.9	5.2	4.2	4.9	9.8	7.5	5.4	5.4	~
Q. PARAGUAY[6]									
Asunción	5.9	3.9	2.2	5.6	8.4	7.4	5.2	6.1[e]	5.6
R. PERU									
Lima	6.5[d]	7.1	6.8	6.6	9.0	8.9	10.4	5.4	4.8[f]
S. URUGUAY									
Montevideo	8.4	7.4[a]	6.6	11.9	15.5	14.0	13.1	10.7	9.4[g]
T. VENEZUELA[7]									
Caracas	~	6.7	5.7	7.0	10.5	11.3[d]	13.2	9.6	7.9

1. April and October figures.
2. Twelve-month average; 1980, June-December average.
3. Quarter averages.
4. March, June, September, and December figures.
5. March, July, and November figures, metropolitan area.
6. Including Fernando de la Mora, Lambaré, and the urban areas of Luque and San Lorenzo.
7. Metropolitan area, two-semester averages; 1985, first semester.

a. Two semesters.
b. May through October.
c. June and December.
d. September.
e. Averages for the months of June, July, and August.
f. Excludes household workers.
g. Average based on data for months of March, June, September, and December.

SOURCE: Adapted from ECLA-S, 1984 and 1985, vol. 1, p. 24; 1986, p. 25; 1987, p. 46.

Table 1331

EVOLUTION OF URBAN UNEMPLOYMENT IN SECTORS OF ECONOMIC ACTIVITY, 6 L, 1982–87

(AA)

Country	Business						Manufacturing						Construction					
	1982	1983	1984	1985	1986	1987	1982	1983	1984	1985	1986	1987	1982	1983	1984	1985	1986	1987
A. ARGENTINA[1]	3.2	3.3	3.2	~	~	~	4.6	2.8	3.2	~	~	~	11.2	9.3	10.1	~	~	~
C. BRAZIL[2]	~	6.8	6.5	5.6	~	~	~	6.4	7.1	5.2	~	~	~	11.7	12.8	7.7	~	~
D. CHILE[3]	14.5	16.0	13.1	11.1	9.7	9.5	26.7	25.9	19.5	14.9	12.9	11.0	49.4	49.0	34.9	27.9	25.1	19.3
F. COSTA RICA[4]	8.8	~	6.6	6.3	~	~	10.0	~	6.4	4.7	~	~	15.0	~	14.0	8.4	~	~
S. URUGUAY[5]	7.7	13.3	11.3	11.1	9.6	9.2	13.0	16.6	13.3	12.3	10.1	8.2	9.7	16.6	17.5	13.3	12.4	9.3
T. VENEZUELA[6]	5.1	7.8	10.3	10.7	9.1	7.6	7.8	11.7	13.0	13.2	10.9	8.0	13.3	21.4	29.3	30.2	23.3	19.5

1. Greater Buenos Aires for April through October.
2. Metropolitan areas of Rio de Janeiro, Sao Paulo, Belo Horizonte, Porto Alegre, Salvador, and Recife.
3. Greater Santiago for March, June, September, and December.
4. San José metropolitan area data for March.
5. Data for Montevideo for four quarters.
6. Data for two quarters.

SOURCE: ECLA-S, 1984 and 1985, vol. 1, pp. 28 and 27, respectively; 1987.

Table 1332

URBAN OPEN UNEMPLOYMENT, 12 LR, 1970–82
(%)

Country	1970	1978	1979	1980	1981	1982
A. ARGENTINA	4.9	2.8	2.0	2.3	4.5	5.7

Continued in SALA, 23-1315.

Table 1333

MIDDLE AND UPPER CLASSES, 18 L, 1950–70
(%)

	Country	1950	1960	1970
A.	ARGENTINA	35.9	36.6	38.2
B.	BOLIVIA	~	~	~
C.	BRAZIL	15.2	15.3	18.6
D.	CHILE	21.4	22.1	29.0
E.	COLOMBIA	21.9	23.6	26.8
F.	COSTA RICA	22.3	22.1	24.1
H.	DOMINICAN REP.	~	13.6	18.2
I.	ECUADOR	10.5	15.0	18.7
J.	EL SALVADOR	10.5	12.2	13.6
K.	GUATEMALA	7.7	12.3	11.8
M.	HONDURAS	5.1	10.9	20.6
N.	MEXICO	~	21.1	24.4
O.	NICARAGUA	~	14.7	19.2
P.	PANAMA	15.2	20.4	23.4
Q.	PARAGUAY	14.2	14.3	15.7
R.	PERU	~	18.1	23.2
S.	URUGUAY	~	35.8	35.0
T.	VENEZUELA	18.2	24.8	31.3

SOURCE: Carlos Filgueira and Carlo Genelitti, *Estratificación y Movilidad Ocupacional en América Latina*, ECLA-CC, E/CEPAL/G, 1122, Oct. 1981, p. 53.

Figure 13:1

AGRICULTURAL SECTOR SHARE IN PRODUCT
AND EMPLOYMENT, 17 LR, 1980

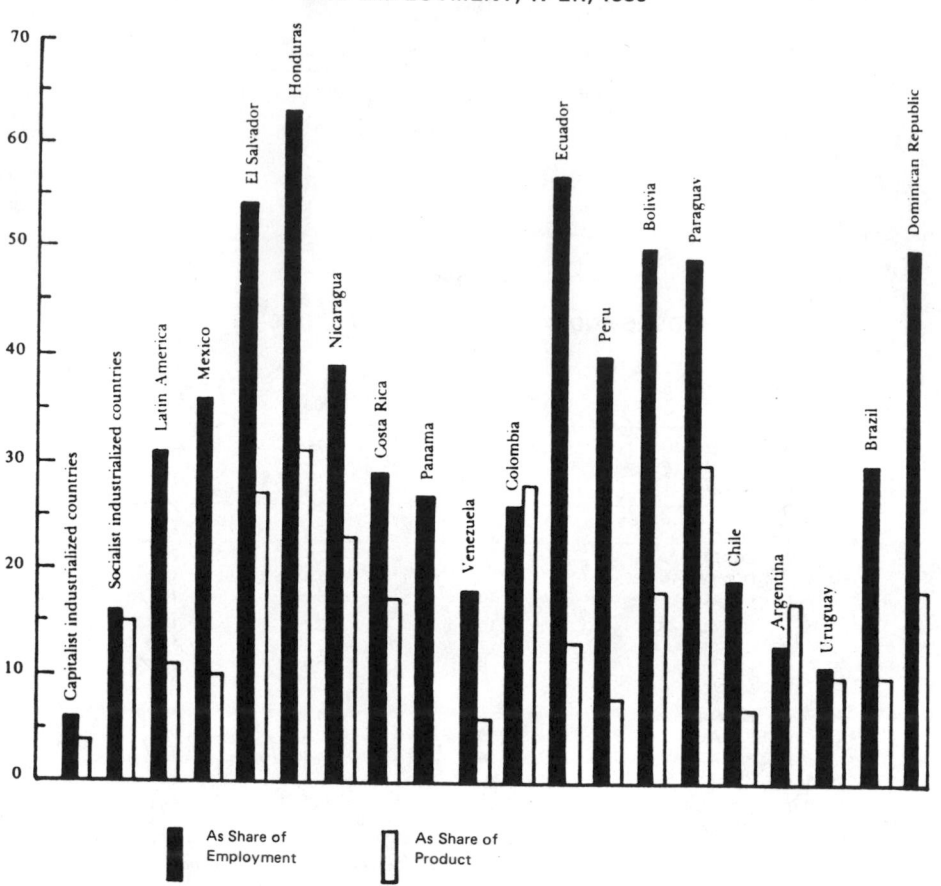

As Share of
Employment

As Share of
Product

SOURCE: *Cepal Review* 24 (Santiago, 1984).

Figure 13:2

EVOLUTION OF URBAN UNEMPLOYMENT, 15 L, 1976–88[a]

(AA)

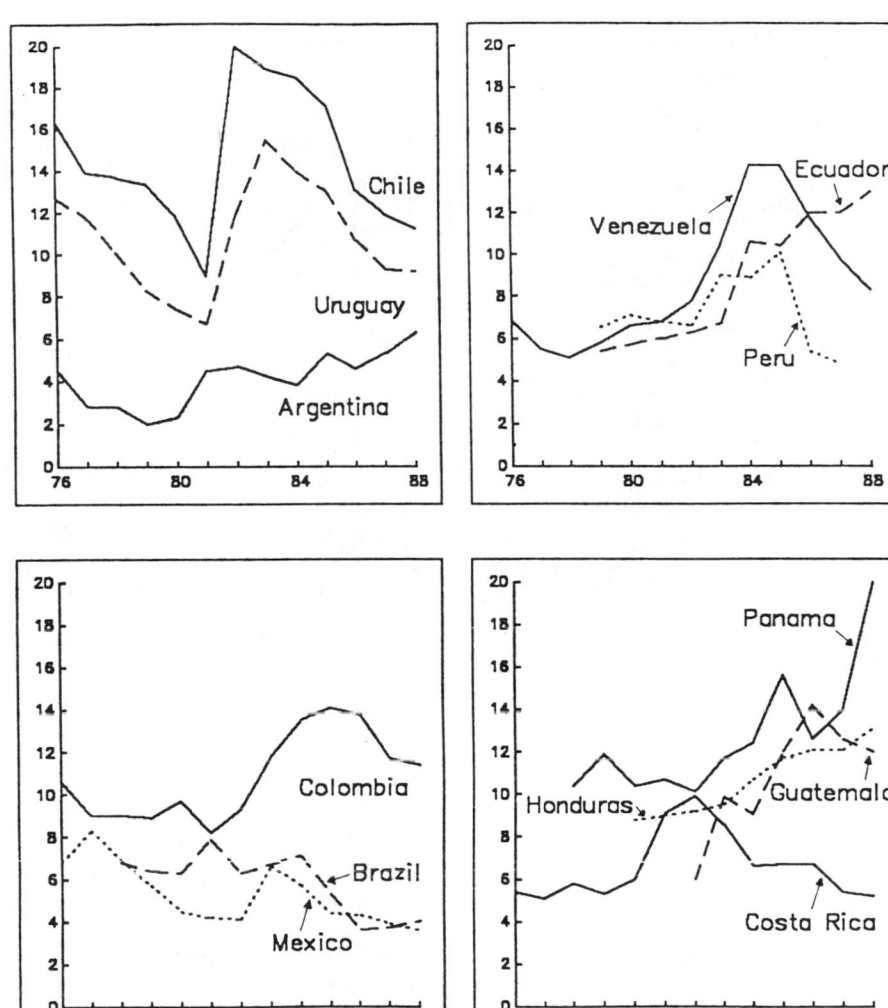

a. For 1976–87, see SALA 27, 13:2.
b. Estimates.

SOURCE: ECLA-N, Dec. 1988, p. 28.

Figure 13:3

EVOLUTION OF URBAN EMPLOYMENT IN PRINCIPAL CITIES,
8 L, 1983–88[a]

(AA)

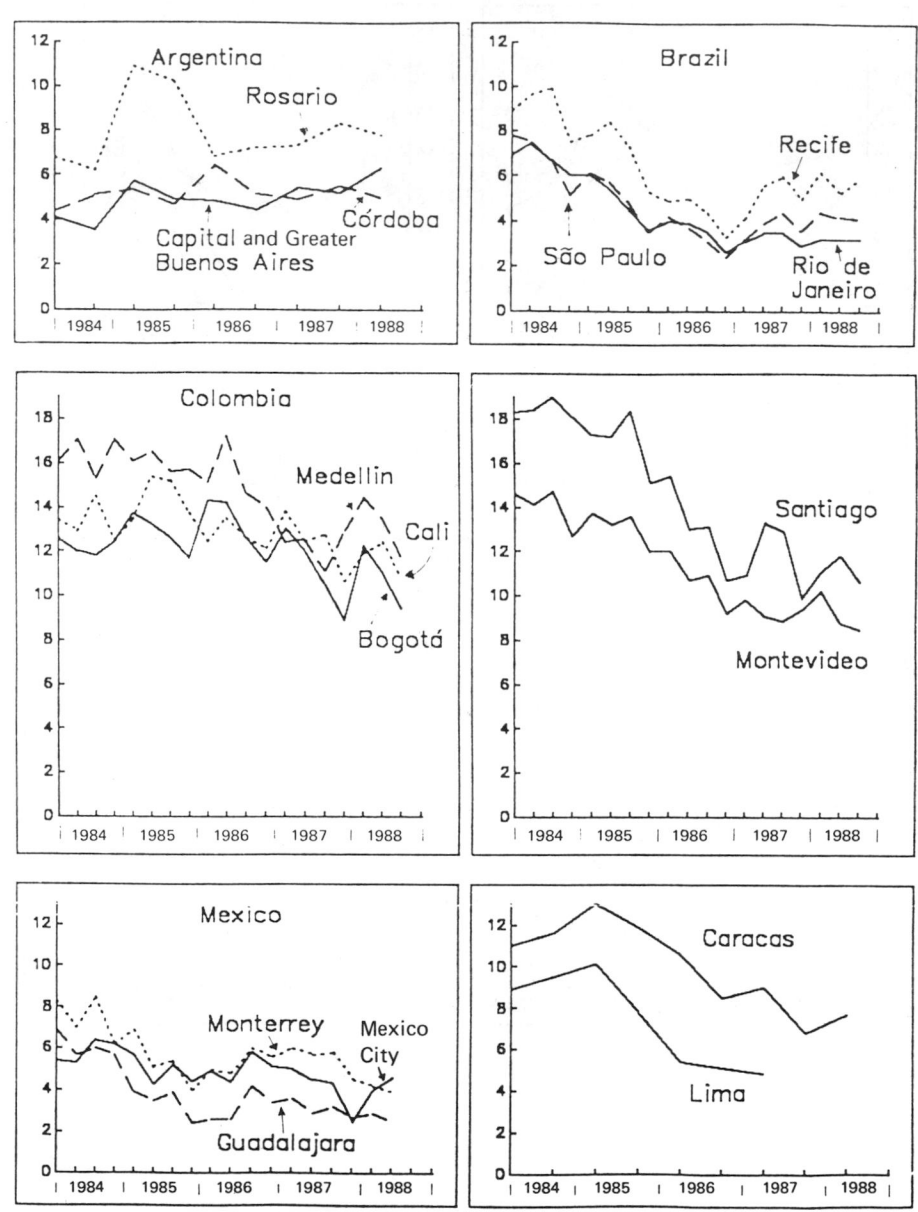

a. For 1982–87, see SALA 27, 13:3.

SOURCE: ECLA-N, Dec. 1988, p. 29.

Figure 13:4

THE MIDDLE CLASS, 17 L, 1950–70
(% of EAP)

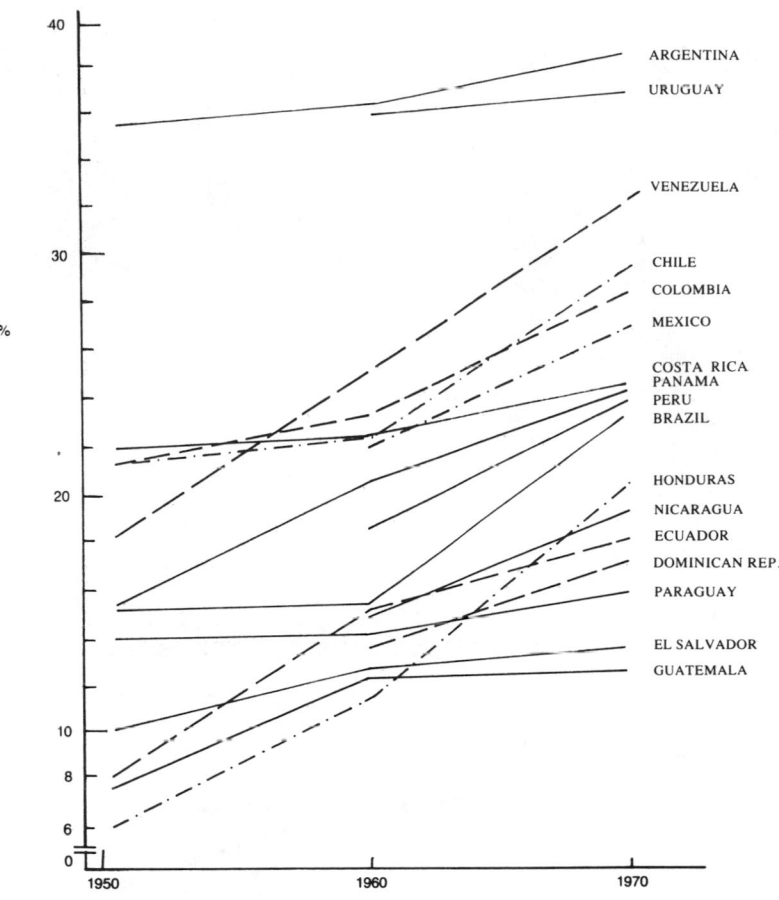

SOURCE: Table 1333, above.

Table 1334

MEXICO CLASS STRUCTURE, REVISED, 1950–80

(%)

Class and Subclass	1950			1960			1970			1980		
	Income[1]	Occupation	Combined[1]	Income[1]	Occupation	Combined[1]	Income	Occupation	Combined[1]	Income	Occupation	Combined[1]
Upper	1.8	1.6	1.7	5.6	2.0	3.8	7.0	4.4	5.7	6.7	3.6	6.2
Leisure	.2	.8	.5	1.0	.8	.9	1.5	2.5	2.0	2.4	1.2	1.8
Semi-leisure	1.6	.8	1.2	4.6	1.2	2.9	5.9	1.9	3.7	4.3	2.4	3.4
Middle	19.4	16.6	18.0	21.8	20.2	21.0	32.5	23.4	27.9	36.3	25.9	31.1
Stable	3.2	6.6	4.9	4.8	8.5	6.6	7.9	10.0	8.9	11.1	11.7	11.4
Marginal	16.2	10.0	13.1	17.0	11.7	14.4	24.6	13.4	19.0	25.2	14.2	19.7
Lower	78.8	81.8	80.3	72.6	77.8	75.2	60.5	72.2	66.4	67.0	70.5	63.7
Transitional	25.4	20.0	22.7	15.8	20.9	18.4	12.4	24.8	18.6	12.0	24.7	18.3
Popular	53.4	61.8	57.6	56.8	56.9	56.8	48.1	47.4	47.8	45.0	45.8	45.4
Total	100.0	100.0	100.0	100.0	100.0	100.0	100.0	100.0	100.0	100.0	100.0	100.0

1. Arithmetic average of the data for incomes and occupations.

SOURCE: Stephanie Granato and Aída Mostkoff, "The Class Structure of Mexico, 1895–1980," in James W. Wilkie, ed., *Society and Economy in Mexico*, Statistical Abstract of Latin America Supplement 10 (Los Angeles: UCLA Latin American Center Publications, forthcoming).

Figure 13:5

CHANGES IN MEXICAN CLASS STRUCTURE, 1895–1980

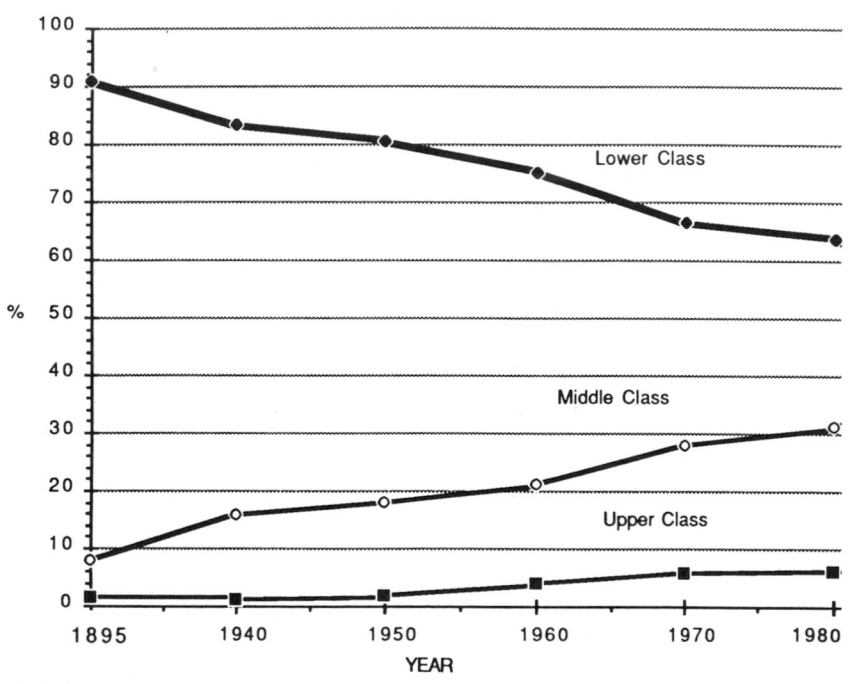

SOURCE: Stephanie Granato and Aida Mostkoff, "The Class Structure of Mexico, 1895–1980," in James W. Wilkie, ed., *Society and Economy in Mexico*, Statistical Abstract of Latin America Supplement 10 (Los Angeles: UCLA Latin American Center Publications, forthcoming).

Table 1335

MEXICO SOCIAL MODERNIZATION INDEX (SMI),[1] 1930–70
(Zero Indicates Complete Modernization)[2]

Category[3]	1930[e]	1940	1950	1960	1970
Selected Rural[a]	69.1	67.7	61.1	54.6	46.2
Selected Semiurban[b]	34.0	30.8	25.6	20.7	16.5
Selected Urban[c]	10.5	7.2	5.9	6.1	5.2
National Average[d]	52.6	48.6	40.7	33.5	24.1

1. Nonmodern persons live in social isolation (are [1] illiterate, [2] speak Indian and Spanish, or [3] do not speak Spanish) and geographic isolation (definition as [4] living in localities of less than 2,500 persons), eat a nonmodern diet (measured by [5] share of persons who habitually consume tortillas instead of wheat bread), and have traditional dress patterns (those who [6] go barefoot or who [7] wear sandals instead of shoes). These seven items in the SMI are averaged with equal weight because there is no theoretical reason to assume that any one component is more important than the others as a measure of modernization.
2. The SMI divides the total of seven components by five values instead of seven because non-Spanish speakers and bilingual persons are both part of a larger category of Indian speakers, and barefoot persons and sandal-wearers are subcategories of the larger category of shoeless persons.
3. Represents 103 sample municipios from the 2,367 Mexican municipios including the municipio in each state which had the highest percentage of illiterates in 1940, the capital of each of the 32 Mexican states, and 40 municipios represented in the community-study literature.
a. Municipios which in 1930 had more than 50% of the population living in localities of less than 2,500 persons.
b. Municipios not included in "Rural" or "Urban."
c. Mexico City, Guadalajara, and Monterrey.
d. Includes all of Mexico's population in 2,367 municipios.
e. Variance between seven-item average (seven items, five values) and four-item average (four items, three values) in 1940 is used to link the 1930 index to make it comparable to the post-1940 index.

SOURCE: Stephen Haber, "Modernization and Change in Mexican Communities, 1930–1970," SALA, 22, ch. 40.

Figure 13:6

MEXICO SMI FOR RURAL, SEMIURBAN, AND URBAN CATEGORIES, 1930–70
(100 = Nonmodern Characteristics)

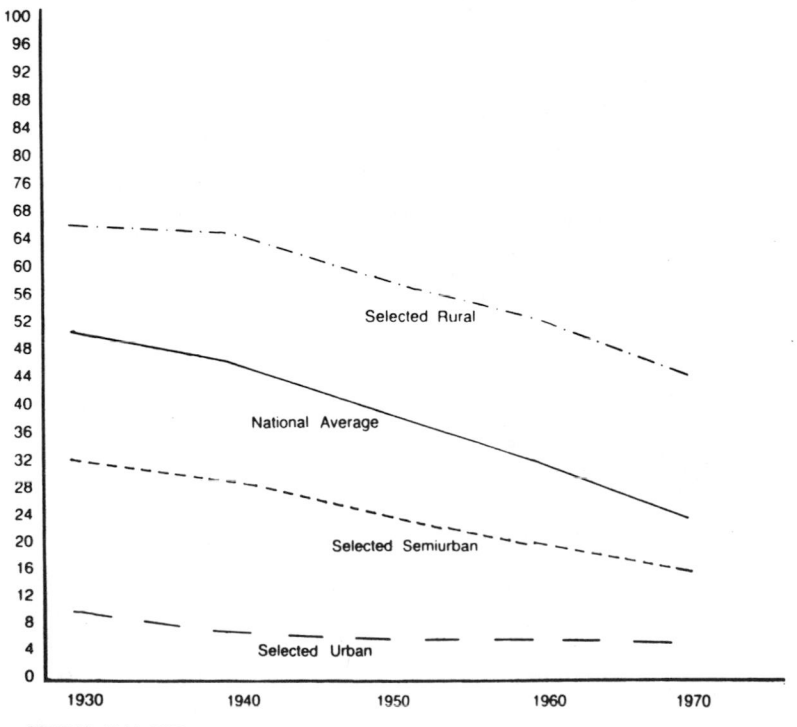

SOURCE: Table 1335.

Figure 13:7

SOCIAL POVERTY INDEX FOR MEXICO, 1910–70

(%)

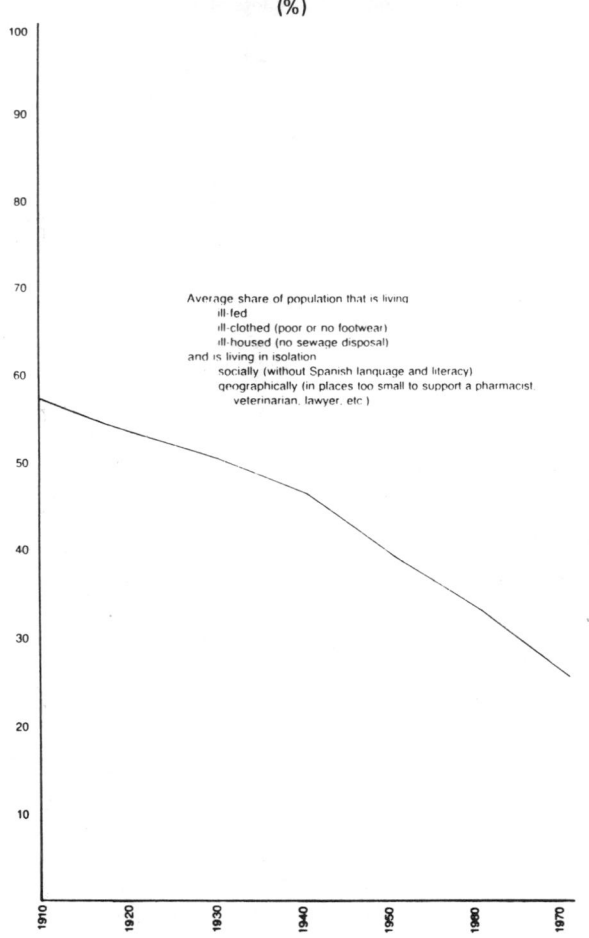

Average share of population that is living
   ill-fed
   ill-clothed (poor or no footwear)
   ill-housed (no sewage disposal)
and is living in isolation
   socially (without Spanish language and literacy)
   geographically (in places too small to support a pharmacist,
      veterinarian, lawyer, etc.)

SOURCE: James W. Wilkie, *La Revolución Mexicana (1910-1976): Gasto Público y Cambio Social* (México, D.F.: Fondo de Cultura Económica, 1978), p. 384.

Table 1336

UNITED STATES INCOME INEQUALITY, 1969–86

(% of Money Income Received by Each Quintile)

Year	Lowest	2nd	Middle	4th	Highest
1969	5.6	12.4	17.7	23.7	40.6
1974	5.5	12.0	17.5	24.0	41.0
1979	5.2	11.6	17.5	24.1	41.7
1980	5.1	11.6	17.5	24.3	41.6
1981	5.0	11.3	17.4	24.4	41.9
1982	4.7	11.2	17.1	24.3	42.7
1983	4.7	11.1	17.1	24.3	42.8
1984	4.7	11.0	17.0	24.4	42.9
1985	4.6	10.9	16.9	24.2	43.5
1986	4.6	10.8	16.8	24.0	43.7

SOURCE: *Wall Street Journal*, March 21, 1988.

Table 1337

CALCULATIONS OF POVERTY, 20 LR, 1970–80

| | Country | % Undernourished | | | Rural % of Under-nourished | Life Expectancy at Birth 1970 | Infant Mortality 1980 | GDP/C 1980 | % Under-employed 1980 | % Employed in Agriculture 1980 | % Rural Population 1980 | Share of Poorest 40% | Productivity of Agricultural Labor 1980 |
		Total	Rural	Urban									
A.	ARGENTINA	8	19	5	51	70	45	2,390	27.7	13	18	14.1	7,343
B.	BOLIVIA	~	~	~	~	50	131	570	74.1	50	67	~	730
C.	BRAZIL	49	73	35	59	63	77	2,050	44.5	30	32	7.0	1,172
D.	CHILE	17	25	12	59	67	43	2,150	28.9	19	29	13.4	1,512
E.	COLOMBIA	45	54	38	49	63	56	1,180	41.0	26	30	~	1,971
F.	COSTA RICA	24	34	14	83	70	24	1,730	27.2	29	57	12.0	2,060
G.	CUBA	~	~	~	~	73	21	~	~	23	27	~	~
H.	DOMINICAN REP.	~	~	~	~	61	68	1,160	~	49	49	~	916
I.	ECUADOR	~	~	~	~	61	82	1,270	63.3	52	55	~	672
J.	EL SALVADOR	68	76	61	66	63	78	660	49.0	50	59	~	832
K.	GUATEMALA	79	82	75	67	59[1]	70	1,080	50.9	55	61	~	1,047
L.	HAITI	90	4	71	68	53	115	270	~	74	72	~	312
M.	HONDURAS	61	75	40	80	58	88	560	~	63	64	~	628
N.	MEXICO	34	45	20	69	65	56	2,090	40.4	36	33	9.9	1,302
O.	NICARAGUA	64	80	50	67	56	91	740	~	39	47	~	975
P.	PANAMA	35	~	~	~	70	22	1,730	46.6	27	46	~	1,807
Q.	PARAGUAY	~	~	~	~	65	47	1,300	~	49	61	7.2	1,669
R.	PERU	50	61	35	67	58	88	930	55.8	40	33	7.0	405
S.	URUGUAY	~	~	10	~	71	40	2,810	27.0	11	16	~	4,215
T.	VENEZUELA	25	36	20	56	67	42	3,630	31.5	18	17	~	2,401
	LATIN AMERICA	40	62	26	60	64	~	2,174	42.0	35	41	~	1,417

SOURCE: Alberto Couriel, "Poverty and Underemployment in Latin America," *Cepal Review* 24 (Santiago, 1984).

Table 1338

ABSOLUTE POVERTY ESTIMATES, 10 LR
(%, Ca. 1970)

| | Households Below the Poverty Line | | | Households Below the Extreme Poverty Line | | |
Country	Urban	Rural	National	Urban	Rural	National
A. ARGENTINA	5	19	8	1	1	1
C. BRAZIL	35	73	49	15	42	25

Continued in SALA, 24–1332.

14

Wages and Income Distribution

Table 1400

COMPENSATION OF EMPLOYEES AND NATIONAL INCOME,[1] 15 LC, 1962–75

(M of NC)

Country	Code[2]	1962	1965	1967	1968	1969	1970	1971	1972	1973	1974	1975
A. ARGENTINA	A	~	~	58,700	67,900	79,600	93,800	124,451	209,460	350,376	469,022	1,289,312
	B	~	~	24,200	27,300	31,500	38,500	55,928	85,813	156,638	208,963	579 370
	C	~	~	41.2	40.2	39.6	41.0	44.9	41.0	44.7	44.6	44.9

Continued in SALA, 21–1404.

Table 1401

WAGES IN NONAGRICULTURAL ACTIVITIES,[1] 8 LC, 1965–87

Country	1965	1970	1975	1980	1981	1982	1983	1984	1985	1986	1987
B. BOLIVIA[2,3]	~	1,015	2,171	5,540	6,681	14,714	61,089	501,964[†]	~	~	~
F. COSTA RICA[4]	~	~	1,339	2,728	3,293	4,995	7,337	8,813	11,090	12,409	14,922
G. CUBA[3,4,15,16]	~	~	~	154	172	179	183	188	190	189	~
M. HONDURAS[3,5,6]	~	~	43.21	93.52	130.28	197.84	139.79	167.92	227.80	~	~
O. NICARAGUA[3,7,8]	~	3.55	5.92	11.23	~	~	~	~	~	~	~
R. PERU[9,10]	72.60	115.12	260	1.432[a]	2.428	3.979	6.837	12.134	25.16	75.34	154.89
S. URUGUAY[11,12,13]	~	100	1,593	9,860	14,424	17,054	20,361	29,880	169.2	322.5	572.8
T. VENEZUELA[4,14]	~	1,201	1,523	2,733	2,956	~	~	~	~	5,819	6,982
UNITED STATES[7]	2.45	3.23	4.53	6.66	7.25	7.68	8.02	8.32	8.57	8.76	8.98

1. The wage series shown in this table cover the following divisions of economic activity: mining and quarrying; manufacturing; electricity, gas, and water; construction; wholesale and retail trade, restaurants, and hotels; transports, storage, and communication; financing, insurance, real estate, and business services; community, social, and personal services. In some cases, however, these divisions are only represented by certain of the groups composing them.
2. Rates per month.
3. Includes salaried employees.
4. Earnings per month.
5. Establishments with ten or more persons employed.
6. Earnings per week.
7. Earnings per hour.
8. Excluding electricity, gas, water, wholesale and retail trade, restaurants, hotels, financing, insurance, real estate, business services, and community, social, and personal services.
9. Excluding mining, quarrying, electricity, gas and water.
10. Earnings per day for Lima only during May of each year.
11. For Montevideo only.
12. Excluding mining and quarrying.
13. For private sector employees with an index of average monthly earnings (1968 = 100).
14. Excluding construction and transport.
15. Including fishing.
16. State sector (civilian).

a.   Prior to 1980, data were taken at June of each year.

SOURCE: ILO-YLS, 1975 and 1980, tables 18 and 17 respectively; 1985, 1986, 1987, and 1988, table 16.

Table 1402

WAGES IN MANUFACTURING,[1] 18 LC, 1965–87

(NC)

	Total	Specification	1965	1970	1975	1980	1982	1983	1984	1985	1986	1987
A.	ARGENTINA[2,16]	Australes/hour	69.30	1.65[a]	20	20	1.27	7.68	62.36	.40	.83	1.69
B.	BOLIVIA[3]	Pesos/month	~	902	1,709	5,182	9,984	50,328	399,353[†]	~	~	~
C.	BRAZIL[3,4]	Cruzeiros/month	~	535	1,938	~	~	~	~	~	~	~
D.	CHILE[10,11]	Pesos/month	212.14	1,041.63	206	10,890	16,432	31,717	38,867	48,089	58,703	70,529
E.	COLOMBIA[3]	Index: 1980 = 100	3.65	* *	13.18	100.0	167.9	212.9	262.7	317.9	393.6	483.1
F.	COSTA RICA[13,17]	Colones/month	~	~	1,123	2,335	4,450	6,634	6,920	9,038	11,583	13,211
G.	CUBA[3,14]	Pesos/month	~	~	141	156	183	188	192	193	189	~
H.	DOMINICAN REP.[3]	Pesos/month	76.59	72.06	120.25	155.62	185.85	190.75	208[†]	~	~	~
I.	ECUADOR	Sucres/hour	3.22	6.10	13.20	35.8	43.1	55.4	72.0	~	~	~
J.	EL SALVADOR[5]	Colones/hour	.81	.94	1.14	2.61	2.81	3.27	3.31	3.56	~	~
K.	GUATEMALA	Quetzales/hour	37.3	43.30	.46	.91	1.07	1.17	.87	.89	~	~
M.	HONDURAS[3,15]	Lempiras/week	~	* *	41.30	70.35	174.42	272.29	97.00	107.10	~	~
N.	MEXICO	Pesos/month	1,324	1,703	3,412	9,147	18,792	27,853	44,277	70,253	117,279	272,369[†]
O.	NICARAGUA[3]	Córdobas/hour	2.08	3.24	5.54	10.90	~	~	~	~	~	~
P.	PANAMA	Balboas/hour	.65	.80	1.07	~	1.53	1.69	1.81	1.82	~	~
R.	PERU[6,7,12]	Intis/day	~	~	~	1.48	4.11	7.10	12.56	26.72	70.64	144.21
S.	URUGUAY[8,9,18]	Index: 1968 = 100	~	100	1,492	8,844	14,604	17,286	26,203	54,945	321.8	~
T.	VENEZUELA	Bolívares/month	793.0	960	1,473	4,184	~	~	~	~	5,084	7,440
	UNITED STATES	Dollars/hours	2.61	3.35	4.83	7.27	8.49	8.83	9.19	9.54	9.73	9.91

1. The figures generally relate to average earnings of all wage-earners. They normally include bonuses, cost of living allowances, taxes, social insurance contributions payable by the employed person and, in some cases, payment in kind. They normally exclude social insurance contributions payable by the employers, family allowances, and other social security benefits. Unless otherwise indicated, figures relate to earnings of both male and female wage-earners.
2. Minimum earnings; unskilled workers.
3. Including salaried employees.
4. 1964-65, production workers.
5. Metropolitan area. Figures are for male wage-earners only. Data for female wage-earners are as follows: 1965 — .57; 1970 — .77; 1975 — 1.03; 1976 — 1.25; 1977 — 1.20; 1978 — 1.39, 1979 — 1.50, 1980 — 2.12, 1981 — 2.37; 1982 — 2.51; 1983 — 2.51; 1984 — 2.77; 1985 — 2.90; 1986 — ~.
6. Lima and Callao.
7. May of each year, from 1980 — 1985.
8. Montevideo only.
9. Private sector; employees; index of average monthly earnings.
10. Including the value of payments in kind.
11. April of each year.
12. June of 1986.
13. Insured persons since 1975.
14. Including mining and quarrying, electricity, gas, and water for the years 1975-77.
15. Includes establishments with ten or more persons employed.
16. Prior to 1985; pesos: 1 Austral = 1,000 pesos.
17. Including electricity, gas, and water.
18. In 1986, Index = 1984 = 100.

a. New currency introduced in January 1970: 1 new peso = 100 old pesos.

SOURCE: ILO-YLS 1975 and 1980, tables 19 and 18A respectively; 1985, 1986, 1987, and 1988, table 17A.

Table 1403

WAGES IN CONSTRUCTION,[1] 15 LC 1965–87

(NC)

	Country	Specification	1965	1970	1975	1980	1982	1983	1984	1985	1986	1987
A.	ARGENTINA[2,3,4]	Pesos/hour	76.44	1.79	~	~	~	~	~	~	~	~
B.	BOLIVIA[6]	Pesos/month	~	775	1,609	5,476	7,513	25,887	230,671‡	~	~	~
C.	BRAZIL	Cruzeiros/hour	~	~	~	~	~	~	~	~	~	~
F.	COSTA RICA[12]	Colones/month	~	~	883	1,857	3,362	5,452	6,466	8,210	9,971	13,440
G.	CUBA[6]	Pesos/month	~	~	157	164	186	195	205	202	200	~
J.	EL SALVADOR[7]	Colones/hour	.70	.69	~	~	~	~	~	~	~	~
K.	GUATEMALA	Quetzales/week	~	~	~	~	~	~	~	~	~	~
M.	HONDURAS[5,6]	Lempiras/week	~	~	36.52	77.59	241.50	256.44	126.00	135.00	~	~
N.	MEXICO[8]	Pesos/hour	3.40	5.31	11.51	29.13	66.32	92.92	158.95	~	~	~
O.	NICARAGUA[6]	Córdobas/hour	~	3.39	5.40	9.94	~	~	~	~	~	~
P.	PANAMA	Balboas/week	~	~	~	~	~	~	~	~	~	~
Q.	PARAGUAY	Guaraníes/month	~	~	~	~	~	~	~	~	~	~
R.	PERU[9,13,14]	Intis/day	~	~	~	1.41	4.21	7.06	11.95	23.17	97.0	140.10
S.	URUGUAY[10,15]	1970 = 100	~	100.0	2,064	12,320	21,404	24,538	100.0	154.3	293.8	566.3
T.	VENEZUELA[11]	Bolívares/day	~	~	~	~	~	~	~	~	~	~
	UNITED STATES	Dollars/hour	3.55	5.24	7.31	9.94	11.63	11.94	12.13	12.32	12.48	12.69

1. Unless otherwise indicated the data pertain to the average nominal gross wages (i.e., before tax deductions and the workers' social security contribution) of construction workers.
2. Minimum earnings.
3. Unskilled workers.
4. To make the series uniform, wages to 1969 were converted to new pesos which equal 100 of the former pesos.
5. Establishments with ten or more persons employed.
6. Including salaried employees.
7. Males only: metropolitan area of San Salvador.
8. October of each year.
9. Lima, mean of the observation: May of each year; prior to 1980, June of each year.
10. Montevideo; private sector only and including salaried employees; index of average monthly wage rates.
11. The data refer to the average nominal wages of electricians in Caracas during the fourth trimester of the year indicated.
12. Insured persons.
13. May of each year, from 1980–85.
14. June of 1986.
15. 1984 = 100, from 1984–86.

SOURCE: ILO-YLS, 1975 and 1980, tables 21 and 20 respectively; 1985, 1986, 1987, and 1988, table 19.

Table 1404

WAGES IN TRANSPORT, STORAGE, AND COMMUNICATION,[1] 13 LC, 1965–87

(NC)

	Country	Specification	1965	1970	1975	1980	1982	1983	1984	1985	1986	1987
A.	ARGENTINA[2,3]	Road Haulage/hour	58.88	1.67[a]	~	~	~	~	~	~	~	~
B.	BOLIVIA[5]	Transports/month	~	982	1,717	6,947	16,031	59,303	531,966[†]	~	~	~
C.	BRAZIL[4]	Per month	~	~	~	~	~	~	~	~	~	~
F.	COSTA RICA[10]	Per month	~	~	1,289	2,320	4,414	6,861	9,098	10,390	12,548	15,834
G.	CUBA[5]	Transports/month	~	~	162	177	202	208	212	211	213	~
M.	HONDURAS[5,9]	Per week	~	~	109.10	74.30	253.26	176.32	139.00	154.50	~	~
N.	MEXICO[6]	Transports/hour	8.00	8.09	~	~	~	~	~	~	~	~
O.	NICARAGUA[5]	Per hour	~	3.80	5.60	11.17	~	~	~	~	~	~
P.	PANAMA	Per week	~	~	~	~	~	~	~	~	~	~
Q.	PARAGUAY	Per month	~	~	~	~	~	~	~	~	~	~
R.	PERU[7]	Intis/day	~	~	~	1.79	5.06	9.02	17.05	34.25	99.75	240.15
S.	URUGUAY[5,8,11]	Index: 1970 = 100	~	100	1,333	8,030	14,909	17,837	100.0	168.4	343.6	588.5
T.	VENEZUELA	Bus Drivers/day	~	~	~	~	~	~	~	~	~	~
	UNITED STATES	Principal Railways/hour	3.00	3.89	6.05	9.92	11.50	12.84	13.33	13.64	13.89	14.29

1. Unless otherwise indicated, the data pertain to the average nominal gross wages (i.e., before income tax deduction and the workers' social security contribution) in national currency of workers in transport, storage, and communications. Details concerning the type of work and earnings are included under the column "specifications." Due to the use of different data sources, not all specifications are equally detailed for every country.
2. Minimum earnings: unskilled workers.
3. To make the series uniform wages for 1963 to 1969 were converted to new pesos which equal 100 of the former pesos.
4. Includes workers in maritime transport.
5. Data include salaried employees.
6. October of each year.
7. Lima area; May of each year from 1980–85; June of each year from 1986 onward.
8. Montevideo; private sector only.
9. Establishments with ten or more persons employed.
10. Insured persons.
11. 1984 = 100, from 1984–86.

a. New currency Jan. 1970; 1 new peso = 100 old pesos.

SOURCE: ILO-YLS, 1975 and 1980, tables 22 and 21 respectively; 1985, 1986, 1987, and 1988, table 20.

Table 1405

WAGES IN AGRICULTURE,[1] 15 LC, 1965–87

(NC)

Country/Specification	Code	1965	1970	1975	1977	1980	1982	1983	1984	1984	1986	1987
A. ARGENTINA[2]												
Unskilled Workers	M-I-H	43.99	1.14c	16.83	106.32	~	~	~	~	~	~	~
C. BRAZIL[3]												
Workers in Rice Production	H	~	~	~	~	~	~	~	~	~	~	~
D. CHILE[3,4]	M-I-D	3.26	12.00	4.35b	41.44	108.25	207.43	212.61	217.80	270.0	311.78	~
E. COLOMBIA	M-I-D	11.95	19.30	~	~	~	~	~	~	~	~	~
	F-I-D	9.55	14.75	~	~	~	~	~	~	~	~	~
	MF-I-D	~	~	~	92.13	181.50	~	~	~	~	~	~
F. COSTA RICA[3]												
General Farm Hands:												
Coffee Plantations[9]	MF-III-H	1.28	1.34	2.52	3.39	5.27	12.00	18.42	~	~	~	~
Agriculture and Livestock	MF-III-H	1.15	1.21	~	~	~	~	~	~	~	~	~
G. CUBA[5]	MF-I-Mo	~	**	**	112	127	167	167	175	179	181	~
J. EL SALVADOR[6]	M-I-D	~	2.25	3.10	3.75	5.20	~	~	~	~	~	~
Permanent Workers	F-I-D	~	1.75	2.50	3.15	4.60	~	~	~	~	~	~
M. HONDURAS[7]												
Establishments with Ten or												
More Persons Employed	W	~	~	**	30.69	108.72	91.83	~	157.89	224.94	~	~
N. MEXICO[3,10]												
Regular Day Laborers	M-II-D	13.47	21.20	46.10	76.48	134.16	251.63	421.05	650.14	1,036.4	1,769.1	3,855.1
O. NICARAGUA	W	~	~	238	310	593	~	~	~	~	~	~
P. PANAMA												
Agriculture, Silviculture,												
Hunting and Fishing	W	~	~	~	~	~	~	~	~	~	~	~
Q. PARAGUAY	Mo	~	~	~	~	~	~	~	~	~	~	~
R. PERU												
General Farm Hands	MF-I-D	~	~	~	~	~	~	~	~	~	46.85	91.88
S. URUGUAY[8]												
General Farm Hands	MF-I-Mo	920	17,315	206a	460	1,500	2.015	2,787	5,425	9,586	16,177	~
	MF-II-Mo	530	12,070	140a	260	848	1,139	1,575	3,250	5,685	9,696	~
T. VENEZUELA												
Agricultural Workers	D	~	~	~	~	~	~	~	~	~	~	~
General Farm Hands	D	~	~	~	~	~	~	~	~	~	~	~
UNITED STATES	MF-I-H	~	~	2.60	3.06	3.82	~	~	~	~	~	~
	MF-I+III-H	~	~	2.43	2.87	3.66	~	~	~	~	~	~

1. The statistics of agricultural wages presented in this table refer in most cases to wages paid in national currency to general farm laborers. A distinction is made between permanent workers, seasonal workers, and day workers; in the last mentioned group, regular day laborers and casual day laborers are distinguished. These distinctions as well as any further details are included under Specifications. The methods of payment and the types of labor contracts and arrangements in agriculture are often quite different from those in other activities. To indicate the sex of the laborer and the nature of the wage statistics, special notations have been adopted under Code. The key to this Code is as follows:

    M — Male laborer
    F — Female laborer
    MF — Both male and female
    I — Complete Wage — workers remunerated wholly in cash
    II — Cash part only of remuneration — where received partly in cash and partly in kind.
    III — Cash part of remuneration — where received partly in cash and partly in kind — as well as the estimated value of payments in kind for board and lodging.
    H — Hourly earnings
    D — Daily earnings

    W — Weekly earnings
    Mo — Monthly earnings

Owing to the use of different data sources, not all details of labor arrangements are available in every country.

2. To make the series uniform, wages from 1963 to 1969 were converted to new pesos which equal 100 of the former pesos.
3. Minimum wages.
4. Adults only.
5. Excludes fishing.
6. Department of San Salvador.
7. Includes salaried employees.
8. December of each year.
9. Includes livestock beginning with 1975 data.
10. January of each year figures.

a. New currency July 1975: 1 peso = 1,000 old pesos.
b. New currency September 1975: 1 peso = 1,000 old escudos.
c. New currency January 1970: 1 new peso = 100 old pesos.

SOURCE: ILO-YLS, 1975 and 1980, tables 23 and 23 respectively; 1985, 1986, 1987, and 1988, table 21.

Table 1406

MINIMUM URBAN WAGES AND AGRICULTURAL, INDUSTRIAL, AND CONSTRUCTION WAGES, 18 L, 1965-80
(NC, Monthly)

A. ARGENTINA

| | Nominal Wages | | | | | | Real Wages (1970 Prices) | | | | |
| | Manufacturing | | Construction (Laborer) | Agriculture (Laborer) | Urban Minimum | Consumer Price Index (1970=100) | Manufacturing | | Construction (Laborer) | Agriculture (Laborer) | Urban Minimum |
Year	Base MA[1]	Paid NA[2]	MA	NA	MA	MA	Base MA[1]	Paid NA[2]	MA	NA	MA
1965	139	#	153	88	116	41	339	#	373	215	283
1966	189	#	201	117	158	55	344	#	365	213	287
1967	245	#	262	153	158	70	350	#	374	219	226

Continued in SALA, 23-1406 through 1423.

Table 1407

METROPOLITAN LEGAL MINIMUM WAGES, 18 L, 1965-80
(NC, Monthly)

Year	A. ARGENTINA	B. BOLIVIA	C. BRAZIL	D. COLOMBIA	E. CHILE	F. COSTA RICA	H. DOMINICAN REP.	I ECUADOR	J. EL SALVADOR
1965	116	#	62	364	.21	310	55.1	#	~
1966	158	#	81	364	.26	310	55.1	#	~

Continued in SALA, 24-1411.

Table 1408

EVOLUTION OF URBAN REAL MINIMUM WAGE, 18 L, 1978–88[a]

(1980 = 100)

PART I. INDEXES

Country	1978	1980	1981	1982	1983	1984	1985	1986	1987	1988[‡]
A. ARGENTINA[1]	81.0	100.0	95.8	97.6	137.7	173.5	117.1	111.1	122.3	95.8
C. BRAZIL[2]	97.7	100.0	104.4	104.6	93.8	85.6	87.0	87.1	71.2	67.1
D. CHILE[16]	100.7	100.0	115.7	117.2	94.2	80.7	76.4	73.6	69.1	73.4
E. COLOMBIA[3]	89.5	100.0	98.9	103.6	107.9	113.5	109.4	114.2	113.0	111.3
F. COSTA RICA[1]	96.0	100.0	90.4	85.9	99.3	104.4	112.2	118.7	118.6	116.5
H. DOMINICAN REP.[1]	94.7	100.0	93.0	86.4	80.8	82.0	80.2	~	~	~
I. ECUADOR[4]	48.1	100.0	86.2	75.9	63.6	62.8	60.4	65.0	61.4	53.6
J. EL SALVADOR[5]	90.3	100.0	96.8	86.6	76.5	76.8	66.3	~	~	~
K. GUATEMALA[1]	70.0	100.0	107.5	107.5	102.5	99.1	83.6	~	~	~
L. HAITI[6]	94.1	100.0	93.5	99.3	91.5	86.0	88.3	85.4	~	~
M. HONDURAS[7]	100.0	100.0	105.6	104.5	96.6	92.1	88.8	85.1	~	~
N. MEXICO[8]	108.6	100.0	101.9	92.7	76.6	72.3	71.1	64.9	60.6	53.6
O. NICARAGUA[9]	119.8	100.0	90.2	74.4	56.7	63.6	45.1	~	~	~
P. PANAMA[10]	115.7	100.0	93.3	89.4	102.1	100.8	99.7	99.9	~	~
Q. PARAGUAY[11]	94.8	100.0	103.6	101.4	93.9	93.7	99.6	108.3	122.6	134.2
R. PERU[12]	72.3	100.0	84.2	77.8	89.2	69.0	60.3	62.5	64.0	60.1
S. URUGUAY[13]	113.6	100.0	103.4	104.6	89.6	89.9	94.1	88.3	91.1	85.6
T. VENEZUELA[14]	69.3	100.0	86.2	78.5	73.9	66.5	96.8	92.3	95.3	76.2

PART II. % VARIATION[15]

Country	1978	1980	1981	1982	1983	1984	1985	1986	1987	1988
A. ARGENTINA[1]	−18.8	17.3	−4.8	1.8	41.1	26.0	−32.5	−5.1	10.1	−21.8
C. BRAZIL[2]	~	2.6	6.1	.7	−10.2	−8.8	1.7	4.4	−18.3	−7.4
D. CHILE[16]	26.5	.2	15.9	.6	−19.5	−14.5	−5.2	−3.3	−6.0	6.1
E. COLOMBIA[3]	13.1	2.5	−1.1	4.3	4.1	5.2	−3.6	4.4	−.1	−3.0
F. COSTA RICA[1]	11.4	1.4	−9.6	−5.1	15.7	5.2	7.4	5.8	0	−2.5
H. DOMINICAN REP.[1]	~	−4.8	−7.0	−7.1	−6.5	1.5	−2.2	~	~	~
I. ECUADOR[4]	−10.6	65.5	−13.8	−11.9	−16.2	−1.3	−3.2	7.5	−5.5	−12.6
J. EL SALVADOR[5]	#	8.6	−3.2	−10.5	−11.7	.4	−13.6	~	~	~
K. GUATEMALA[1]	−9.7	59.9	7.5	~	−4.7	−3.3	−15.6	~	~	~
L. HAITI[6]	26.6	16.5	−6.5	6.2	−7.9	6.0	2.7	−3.2	~	~
M. HONDURAS[7]	−4.4	−8.3	5.0	−.5	−7.7	−4.5	−3.3	−4.2	~	~
N. MEXICO[8]	−3.4	−6.7	1.9	−9.0	−17.4	−5.6	−1.7	−8.8	−6.6	−11.6
O. NICARAGUA[9]	~	−11.3	−9.8	−17.5	−23.8	12.1	−29.1	~	~	~
P. PANAMA[10]	−4.0	−12.0	−6.7	−4.2	14.2	−1.3	−1.1	.1	~	~
Q. PARAGUAY[11]	3.1	8.0	3.6	−2.0	−7.5	−.2	6.2	8.7	13.2	9.5
R. PERU[12]	−23.2	27.5	−15.8	−7.6	2.4	−22.7	−12.6	3.6	2.5	−3.1
S. URUGUAY[13]	−.5	−4.6	3.4	1.2	−14.3	.3	4.7	−6.2	3.2	−6.0
T. VENEZUELA[14]	−6.8	62.8	−14.1	−8.9	−5.9	−10.0	45.5	−4.7	3.4	−22.2

1. National figures.
2. Rio de Janeiro, deflated by the corresponding consumer price index.
3. For upper urban sectors.
4. Includes legal supplementary benefits.
5. Non-agricultural sectors in San Salvador.
6. Industry in general.
7. Central Disctrict and San Pedro Sula for manufacturing.
8. Mexico City, deflated by the corresponding consumer price index.
9. Department of Managua industry.
10. Excluding construction.
11. Asunción and Puerto Stroesner.
12. Lima for non-agricultural activities.
13. National figures for workers over 18 years of age.
14. National figures excluding agricultural and cattle-raising activities.
15. Compared with the same period in the preceding year.
16. Minimum Income.

a. For earlier and intervening years, see previous issues of SALA.

SOURCE: ECLA-S, 1985, Vol. 1, p. 34; ECLA-S, 1986, p. 40; ECLA-N, 1987, p. 18;
ECLA-N, 1988, p. 20.

Table 1409

EVOLUTION OF REAL WAGES, BY SECTOR, 10 LR, 1978-82

(1970 = 100)

Country	Minimum Real Salaries					Real Industrial Salaries					Real Construction Salaries				
	1978	1979	1980	1981	1982	1978	1979	1980	1981	1982	1978	1979	1980	1981	1982
A. ARGENTINA[1]	50.5	46.8	55.0	53.6	49.1	72.3	83.1	92.9	82.9	73.8	60.6	59.2	63.7	58.7	~

Continued in SALA, 24–1406.

Table 1410

REAL WAGE INDEXES,[1] 18 L, 1965-80

(1970 = 100)

Country	Code	1965	1966	1967	1968	1969	1970	1971	1972	1973	1974	1975	1976	1977	1978	1979	1980
A. ARGENTINA	Sm	128.6	130.5	102.7	87.7	103.2	100.0	106.8	95.0	111.3	136.4	101.8	52.7	50.9	50.5	46.8	55.0
	Si(1)	102.7	104.2	106.1	93.9	96.4	100.0	101.8	94.2	103.0	106.7	104.8	60.3	54.5	47.3	47.9	56.7
	Si(2)	#	#	#	#	#	100.0	103.4	98.3	104.4	117.9	111.7	74.2	81.4	79.7	90.4	~
	Sc(m)	104.2	102.0	104.5	95.3	97.2	100.0	101.1	93.0	103.1	110.1	137.4	73.2	72.1	60.6	~	~
	Sa(m)	94.3	93.4	96.1	87.3	90.8	100.0	113.6	103.1	115.4	132.5	122.8	67.5	61.8	54.4	~	~

Continued in SALA, 24–1407.

Table 1411

EVOLUTION OF REAL AVERAGE WAGES, 11 L, 1981–88[a]

(1980 = 100)

PART I. INDEXES

	Country	1981	1982	1983	1984	1985	1986	1987	1988[‡]
A.	ARGENTINA[1]	89.4	80.1	100.5	127.1	107.8	109.5	103.0	97.9
C.	BRAZIL[2]								
	Rio de Janeiro	108.5	121.6	112.7	105.1	112.7	121.8	102.4	99.8
	São Paulo	104.7	107.2	94.0	97.9	120.4	150.7	143.2	147.5
D.	CHILE[3]	108.9	108.6	97.1	97.2	93.5	95.1	94.7	100.9
E.	COLOMBIA[1]	101.4	105.2	110.4	118.7	114.9	120.2	119.7	119.0
F.	COSTA RICA[4]	88.3	70.8	78.5	84.7	92.2	97.8	~	~
N.	MEXICO[1]	103.6	104.4	80.7	75.7	76.6	72.3	72.8	~
O.	NICARAGUA[4]	91.2	81.0	69.8	66.6	52.5	~	~	~
P.	PANAMA[9]	98.7	94.1	98.2	105.8	107.0	110.0	~	~
Q.	PARAGUAY[5]	105.3	102.4	95.2	91.8	89.9	86.2	~	~
R.	PERU[6]	98.3	100.5	83.7	71.0	59.6	75.5	80.0	52.7
S.	URUGUAY[7]	107.5	107.1	84.9	77.1	88.0	94.0	98.5	100.8

PART II. % VARIATION[8]

	Country	1981	1982	1983	1984	1985	1986	1987	1988
A.	ARGENTINA[1]	−10.6	−10.4	25.5	26.4	−15.2	1.6	−5.9	−5.0
C.	BRAZIL[2]								
	Rio de Janeiro	8.5	12.1	−7.3	−6.7	7.2	8.1	−16.0	−12.8
	São Paulo	4.7	2.4	−12.3	4.1	23.0	25.2	−5.0	4.6
D.	CHILE[3]	9.1	−.2	−10.7	.1	−3.8	1.7	−.3	6.7
E.	COLOMBIA[1]	1.4	3.7	5.0	7.3	−3.0	4.9	−.4	−.6
F.	COSTA RICA[4]	−11.7	−19.8	10.9	7.8	8.9	6.1	~	~
N.	MEXICO[1]	3.5	.9	−22.7	−6.6	1.6	−5.6	.7	~
O.	NICARAGUA[4]	−8.8	−11.2	−13.8	−4.5	−21.2	~	~	~
P.	PANAMA[9]	−1.3	−4.7	4.4	7.7	1.1	2.8	~	~
Q.	PARAGUAY[5]	5.3	−2.7	−7.1	−3.5	−2.1	−4.1	~	~
R.	PERU[6]	−1.7	2.3	−16.8	−15.2	−15.0	26.7	6.0	−34.5
S.	URUGUAY[7]	7.5	−.3	−20.7	−9.2	14.1	6.7	4.8	2.3

1. Manufacturing.
2. Industry in general.
3. Non-agricultural sectors, excluding large-scale copper mining and pulp and paper industries.
4. Affiliates of the Social Security System.
5. General wages for Asunción.
6. Private sector in the metropolitan area of Lima.
7. Private and public sectors in Montevideo and the interior.
8. Compared with the same period of the preceding year.
9. Mean industrial wages in Panamá City and Colón.

a. For earlier years, see previous issues of SALA.

SOURCE: ECLA-S, 1985, Vol. 1, p. 39; 1986, p. 34; ECLA-N, 1988, p. 19.

Table 1412

REAL AVERAGE HOURLY WAGES, SELECTED LATIN AMERICAN COUNTRIES AND PACIFIC RIM COMPETITORS, 1975–85[a]

(US 1980)

	Country	1975	1976	1977	1978	1979	1980	1981	1982	1983	1984	1985
A.	ARGENTINA	1.1	.8	.8	.7	.9	1.0	.9	.7	.7	.9	1.1
C.	BRAZIL	.8	.8	.8	.8	.9	.9	1.0	1.1	1.0	1.0	1.1
F.	COSTA RICA	.9	.9	.9	.9	1.0	1.0	1.0	1.1	1.2	1.4	.6
N.	MEXICO	1.7	1.8	1.9	1.8	1.8	1.7	1.7	1.9	1.5	1.1	.7
R.	PERU	1.2	1.3	1.1	1.0	.9	1.0	.9	.9	1.8	.6	.3
	JAPAN	4.5	4.7	4.7	4.8	5.0	4.9	5.0	5.1	5.1	5.3	~
	KOREA	.6	.7	.9	1.1	1.2	1.1	.9	1.2	1.3	1.3	~
	UNITED STATES	7.4	7.5	7.7	7.8	7.6	7.3	7.2	7.3	7.3	7.3	7.3

a. Manufacturing.

SOURCE: El Cotidiano 3(12):61.

Figure 14:1

EVOLUTION OF REAL AVERAGE WAGES, 12 L, 1970-86[a]

(AA, 1980 = 100)

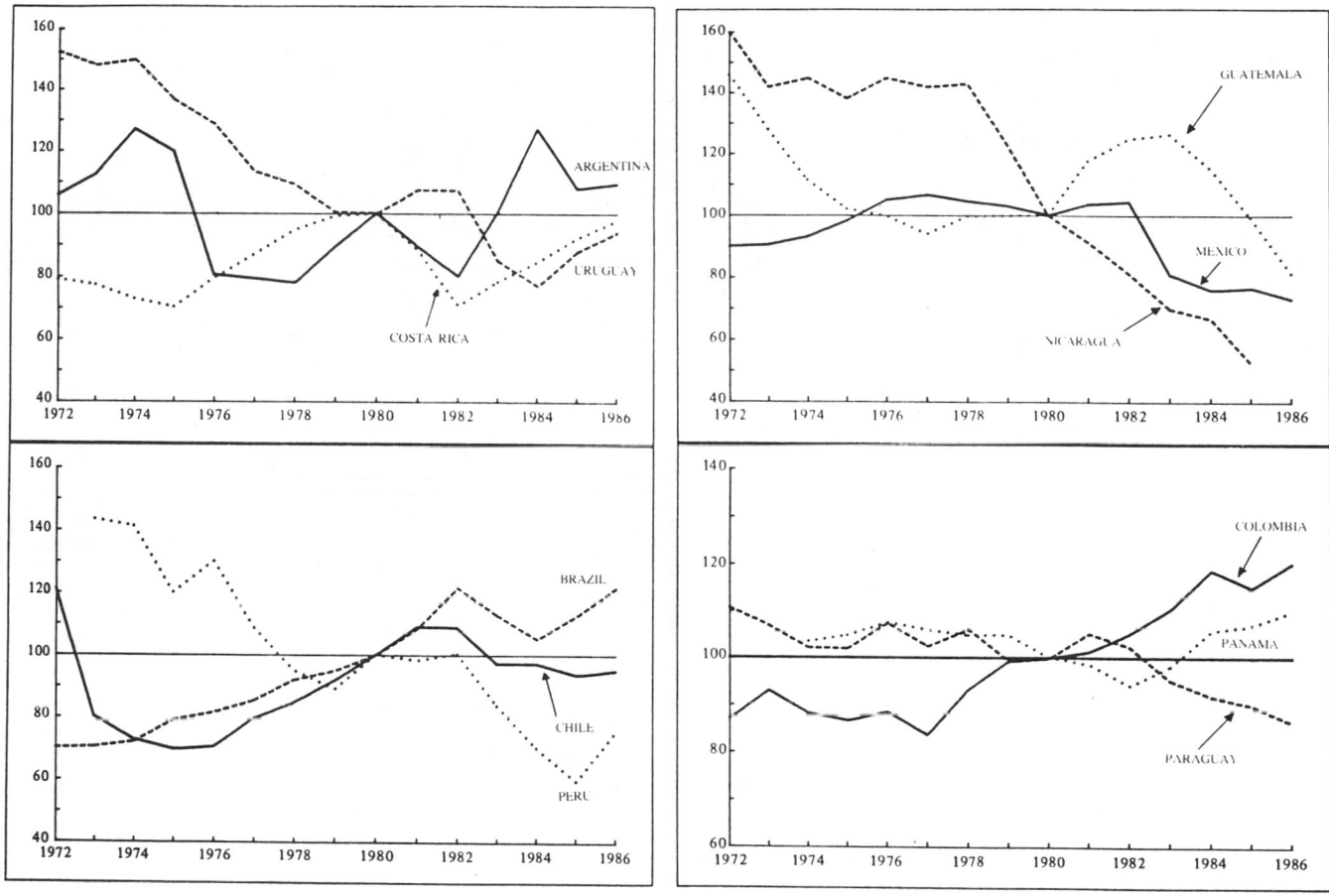

a. See SALA, 26-1411.

SOURCE: ECLA-S, 1986, vol. 1, pp. 37–38.

Figure 14:2

VARIATION IN REAL AVERAGE WAGES, 6 L, 1981–86[a]

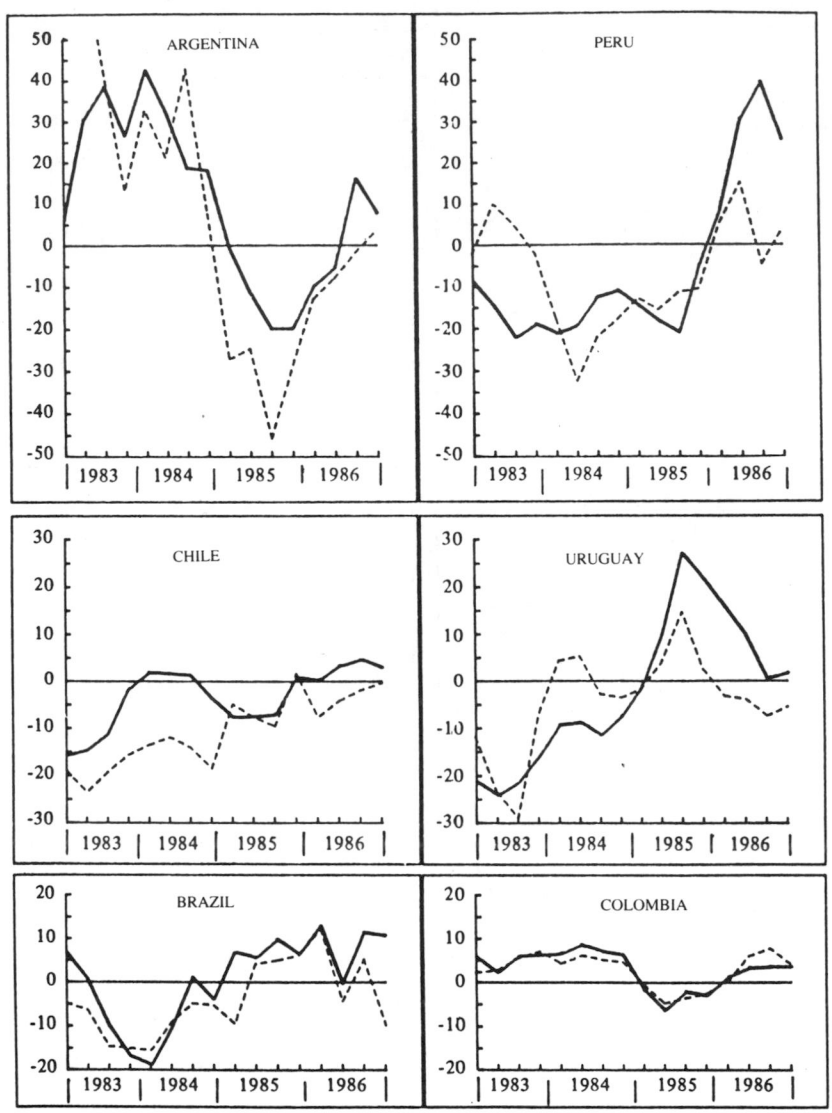

————— Average wage in the manufacturing sector

– – – – – Minimum urban wage

a. See SALA, 26-1411, Part II.

SOURCE: ECLA-S, 1986, vol. 1, p. 42.

Table 1413

REAL INDUSTRIAL WAGE INDEX (RIWI) FOR MEXICO CITY, 1934–76

Year	(A) Worker Cost of Living[1] Index (WCL)	(B) Annual Average Percentage Change	(C) New WCL (BXC)[2]	(D) Industrial Wage Index (IWI)	(E) Annual Average Percentage Change	(F) New IWI (FXF)[2]	(G) RIWI (F/C)	(H) Annual Average Percentage Change
1934	100	**	63.7	.28	**	44.5	70	**
1935	108	8.0	68.8	.30[a]	7.1	47.6	69	−1.4
1936	114	5.6	72.6	.33	10.0	52.4	72	4.3

Continued in SALA, 21-1405.

Table 1414

REAL INDUSTRIAL WAGE INDEX, 18 LC, 1940–73

A. ARGENTINA

Year	(A) Consumer Price Index (CPI)	(B) Percentage Change	(C) New CPI (A x B)	(D) Industrial Wage Index (IWI)	(E) Percentage Change	(F) New IWI (D x E)	(G) RIWI (F/C)	(H) Percentage Change
1940	91.2	~	100	88	~	100	100	~
1941	93.6	2.6	103	91	3.4	103	101	1.0
1942	98.9	5.7	108	96	5.5	109	101	#

Continued in SALA, 18-1411 through 1429.

Table 1415

REAL WAGES AND URBAN UNEMPLOYMENT, 7 L, 1981–84

(PC)

		Real Wages (AA-GR)				Urban Unemployment (% of Labor Force)			
	Country	1981	1982	1983	1984	1981	1982	1983	1984
A.	ARGENTINA	-10.3	-10.5	19.1	5.3	4.5	4.7	4.0	3.8
C.	BRAZIL	-3.9	1.7	-16.1	-5.2	7.9	6.3	6.7	7.5
D.	CHILE	8.9	-.2	-10.7	-6.5	9.0	20.0	19.0	18.5
E.	COLOMBIA	-.2	4.9	6.5	3.1	8.2	9.3	11.8	13.5
N.	MEXICO	4.9	-4.1	-20.0	-9.8	4.2	4.1	6.9	6.3
R.	PERU	-4.1	.1	-6.6	-2.9	6.8	7.0	8.8	10.0
T.	VENEZUELA	-3.1	-2.8	-.5	.5	6.8	7.8	9.8	11.0

SOURCE: U.N., *Food and Nutrition Bulletin*, Vol. 9, No. 1, March 1987.

Table 1416

GUATEMALA AVERAGE REAL ANNUAL SALARIES, 1980–86[1]

(Quetzales)

Year	Total	Agriculture	Mining	Industry	Construction	Essential Services	Commerce	Transportation	Services
1980	1,389	619	4,006	2,108	1,889	1,889	2,870	1,788	1,974
1981	1,636	833	3,966	2,348	2,308	2,853	2,788	1,700	1,825
1982	1,734	844	4,047	2,415	2,299	1,585	3,026	1,891	1,937
1983	1,754	894	4,193	2,349	2,142	1,948	2,844	2,430	1,888
1984	1,596	773	4,086	2,479	1,478	1,840	2,799	1,675	1,727
1985	1,377	717	3,142	2,232	1,277	1,604	2,590	1,567	1,413
1986	1,127	611	1,942	1,815	996	1,301	2,073	1,233	1,157

1. For workers registered with the Guatemalan Social Security Institute.

SOURCE: *Central American Report*, January 29, 1988, p. 32.

Table 1417

GUATEMALA MINIMUM WAGES, 1980–88

(Quetzales per Day)

Activity	1980	1988	Increase
Agriculture	3.20	4.50	1.30
Mining	3.72	5.00	1.28
Industry[1]	3.84	5.80	1.96
Services[1]	3.63	6.66	3.03
Construction[2]	~	16.00	~
		10.00	~
		8.00	~
Commerce	3.48	7.04	3.56
Average	3.57	5.80	2.23
Real Value (Based on 1980 levels)	3.57	2.64	1.01

1. Averages.
2. Wages for various categories.

SOURCE: *Central American Report*, January 29, 1988, p. 32.

Table 1418

INDUSTRIAL DISPUTES,[1] 16 LC, 1970–87[a]

Country	Code[2]	1970	1980	1981	1982	1983	1984	1985	1986	1987
A. ARGENTINA[6]	A[4,5]	5	~	~	~	~	~	~	~	~
	B[3]	2,912	~	~	~	~	~	~	~	~
	C	32,849	~	~	~	~	~	~	~	~
B. BOLIVIA	A	**	**	31	301	261	500	319	188	207
	C	**	162	45	~	744	2,573	1,624	897	1,246
C. BRAZIL	A	**	81	79	126	312	534	843	1,493	~
D. CHILE	A[4]	1,819	89[b]	~	~	41	38	42	41	~
	B	656,170	29,730	24,882	2,367	4,373	3,595	8,532	3,900	~
	C	2,814,517	428,300	676,290	51,644	58,492	41,980	131,630	60,730	~
E. COLOMBIA	A	~	261	219	149	146	147	87	15	17
	B	~	30,915	22,560	60,119	54,391	30,624	10,481	3,758	6,663
	C	~	~	~	~	2,305	925	461	728	432
F. COSTA RICA	A	~	61	6	14	15	15	10	23	7
	B	~	24,750	7,380	13,387	8,248	13,780	10,915	37,928	5,250[†]
	C	~	427,350	166,580	285,930	34,049	265,090	239,010	40,250	909[†]
I. ECUADOR	A	~	75	99	86	97	96	72	78	74
	B	~	16,065	12,255	15,776	13,913	13,866	9,248	11,963	13,904
	C	~	508,170	368,910	431,980	467,540	372,730	266,860	432,500	333,610
J. EL SALVADOR	A	~	42[c]	15	4	15	36	54	~	~
	B	~	12,110[c]	5,324	373	2,680	26,311	30,336	~	~
	C	~	44,217[c]	138,490	4,975	92,732	233,490	350,680	~	~
K. GUATEMALA	A	36	51	3	#	#	**	**	33	12[†]
	B[3]	27,067	68,683	1,350	#	#	**	**	~	~
	C	50,934	817,300	37,070	#	#	**	**	~	390[†]
L. HAITI	A	~	2,946	2,728	2,642	2,161	1,845	1,653	1,767	~
	B	~	3,688	3,686	3,464	2,808	2,644	3,030	3,777	~
	C	~	21,954	21,565	24,074	~	~	2,094,200	644,740	~
M. HONDURAS	A	~	37	49	~	~	28	14	46	28
	B	~	34,431	9,273	13,387	~	3,643	744	~	~
N. MEXICO	A[4]	206	1,339	1,066	1,925	216	427	159	312	174
	B[3]	14,329	42,774	31,512	25,173	45,949	65,359	57,354	82,833	9,540
	C	~	~	~	1,363,200	775,100	238,000	333,600	121,100	81,700
P. PANAMA	A	6	18	16	7	9[d]	12[d]	7	13	7
	B	17,510	2,438	7,835	1,333	6,677	755	795	8,057	1,727
	C[7]	13,148	158,740	248,280	5,463	635,660	15,942	19,867[‡]	316,500	450,250
Q. PARAGUAY	A	~	~	~	~	~	~	~	~	~
	B	~	~	~	~	~	~	~	~	~
	C	~	~	~	~	~	~	~	~	~
R. PERU	A	345	739	871	809	643	509	566	642	726
	B	110,990	481,480	856,910	572,260	785,540	696,820	235,340	239,270	311,540
	C[7]	722,732	2,239,900	2,496,700	2,843,900	2,537,500	1,712,200	1,528,500	2,108,400	1,147,500
T. VENEZUELA	A	64	195	129	102	67	73	99	~	~
	B	23,934	67,960	29,560	14,870	17,420	12,130	12,945	~	~
	C[7]	234,349	315,310	255,920	329,600	418,170	108,300	95,800	~	~
UNITED STATES[5,8]	A	5,716	187	145	96	81	62	54	69	46
	B	3,305,200	795,300	728,900	855,800	909,400	376,000	323,900	533,200	174,300
	C	66,413,800	20,844,000	16,908,000	9,061,200	17,461,000	8,498,800	7,079,100	11,861	4,455,600

1. This table shows the total number of industrial disputes which resulted in a stoppage of
   work, and the numbers of workers involved and working days lost. No differentiation
   between strikes and lockouts has been possible, since in most countries the distinction
   is not observed in the compilations. In a few cases, however, the data relate to strikes
   only. Disputes of small importance and political strikes are frequently not included in
   the statistics. In some cases the data do not cover workers "indirectly affected," i.e.,
   workers who, though not parties in the dispute, are thrown out of work within the
   establishment directly affected by the stoppage of work. As far as possible such cases
   are indicated by footnotes. Various methods are used for calculating the number of
   working days lost, and these data, as well as the statistics of workers involved, are often
   approximations only. Nevertheless, the statistics indicate in a general way the extent
   of industrial disputes in the different countries.
2. Code: A — number of disputes;
        B — number of workers involved;
        C — number of working days lost.
3. Excluding workers indirectly affected.
4. Strikes only.
5. Excluding disputes involving less than 1,000 workers and those lasting less than
   a full day or shift.
6. Buenos Aires.
7. Computed on the basis of eight-hour working days.
8. Disputes can extend to many divisions.

a. For earlier and intervening years, see previous issues of SALA.
b. Includes data from Sept. 1979 to Dec. 1980.
c. Includes data from Jan. to June.
d. Excluding illegal strikes.

SOURCE: ILO-YLS, 1975, table 27; 1985, 1986, 1987, and 1988, table 30A.

Table 1419

INCOME DISTRIBUTION AMONG INCOME GROUPS AND INDICATORS IN INEQUALITY, 13 L

| | | | | | Percentiles of Recipients (%) | | | | | | | |
	Country	Year	Incomes Recipient Unit	Q_1 0–20	Q_2 21–40	Q_3 41–60	Q_4 61–80	D_9 81–90	D_{10} 91–95	D_{10} 96–100	Gini Coefficient	Theil Index
A.	ARGENTINA	1961	Economically active person	5.2	8.3	13.1	18.3	13.2	10.7	31.2	.478	.475
		1961	Household	7.0	10.3	13.1	17.6	12.9	9.7	29.4	.425	.398
C.	BRAZIL	1960	Economically active person	4.0	7.0	10.0	20.4	18.0	11.6	29.0	.520	.510
		1970	Household	4.0	8.0	12.0	18.0	18.0	13.0	27.0	.500	.467
D.	CHILE	1968	Household	4.0	8.0	13.0	17.5	15.0	12.1	30.4	.503	.499
E.	COLOMBIA	1964	Economically active person	2.9	6.0	10.2	18.3	14.8	12.0	35.8	.572	.655
		1974	Household	4.0	6.5	13.0	18.0	15.0	12.0	31.5	.520	.533
F.	COSTA RICA	1971	Household	6.0	8.5	12.0	18.4	15.1	11.0	29.0	.466	.437
I.	ECUADOR	1970	Economically active person	2.9	4.7	6.4	16.5	18.0	14.0	37.5	.625	.777
J.	EL SALVADOR	1961	Economically active person	5.5	6.5	8.8	17.8	15.8	12.6	33.0	.532	.574
M.	HONDURAS	1967–68	Household	3.2	4.1	7.7	17.5	16.9	14.6	36.0	.612	.735
N.	MEXICO	1969	Household	4.0	6.5	9.5	16.0	13.0	15.0	36.0	.567	.666
P.	PANAMA	1970	Economically active person	2.5	5.7	12.3	18.9	15.4	11.8	33.4	.558	.608
R.	PERU	1961	Economically active person	2.5	5.5	10.2	17.4	15.2	10.2	39.0	.591	.712
S.	URUGUAY	1967	Household	3.8	9.0	14.0	23.0	17.0	11.0	22.5	.449	.363
T.	VENEZUELA	1962	Household	3.3	6.3	11.2	20.2	17.8	14.0	27.2	.531	.512
		1976	Economically active person	3.5	6.0	11.0	20.0	17.0	13.0	29.5	.540	.539

SOURCE: Jacques Lecaillon et al., *Income Distribution and Economic Development*
(Geneva: International Labour Office, 1984).

Table 1420

INCOME DISTRIBUTION,[1] 9 LC

(% Share of Household Income by Percentile
Groups of Households[2])

	Country	Year	Lowest 20%	Second Quintile	Third Quintile	Fourth Quintile	Highest 20%	Highest 10%
A.	ARGENTINA	1970	4.4	9.7	14.1	21.5	50.3	35.2
C.	BRAZIL	1972	2.0	5.0	9.4	17.0	66.6	50.6
D.	CHILE	1968	4.4	9.0	13.8	21.4	51.4	34.8
E.	COSTA RICA	1971	3.3	8.7	13.3	19.9	54.8	39.5
J.	EL SALVADOR	1976–77	5.5	10.0	14.8	22.4	47.3	29.5
N.	MEXICO	1977	2.9	7.0	12.0	20.4	57.7	40.6
P.	PANAMA	1973	2.0	5.2	11.0	20.0	61.8	44.2
R.	PERU	1972	1.9	5.1	11.0	21.0	61.0	42.9
T.	VENEZUELA	1970	3.0	7.3	12.9	22.8	54.0	35.7
	UNITED STATES	1980	5.3	11.9	17.9	25.0	39.9	23.3

1. These estimates should be treated with caution because the collection of data on
   income distribution has not been systematically organized and integrated with the
   official statistical system in many countries; estimates were typically derived from
   surveys designed for other purposes, most often consumer expenditure surveys, which
   also collect some information or income. These surveys use a variety of income
   concepts and sample designs. Furthermore, the coverage of many of these surveys
   is too limited to provide reliable nationwide estimates of income distribution. Thus,
   although the estimates shown are considered the best available, they do not avoid all
   these problems and should be interpreted with extreme caution.
   The scope of the indicator is similarly limited. Because households vary in size, a
   distribution in which households are ranked according to per capita household income,
   not according to their total household income, is superior for many purposes. The
   distinction is important because households with low per capita incomes frequently
   are large households, whose total income may be relatively high.
2. Data refer to distribution of total disposable household income accruing to percentile
   groups of households ranked by total household income. The distributions cover rural
   and urban areas.

SOURCE: WB-WDR, 1986, table 24; 1987, table 26; 1988, table 26.

Table 1421

INCOME DISTRIBUTION: LATIN AMERICA AVERAGE,[1] 1960 AND 1970

Stratum	Share of Each Stratum in the Total Income		Per Capita Income in 1960 Dollars[a]		Increase in Per Capita Income		Total Increase	Percentage of the Total Increase Represented by the Increase in Each Stratum
	1960	1970	1960	1970	Percentage	1960 Dollars		
20% poorest	3.1	2.5	53	55	3.8	2	107.6	.4
30% following	10.3	11.4	118	167	41.5	49	3,919	15.4
20% following	14.1	13.9	243	306	25.9	63	3,359	13.2
20% before the highest 10%	24.6	28.0	424	616	45.3	192	10,237	40.3
10% highest	47.9	44.2	1,643	1,945	17.7	292	7,785	30.7
(5% highest)[b]	(33.4)	(29.9)	(2,305)	(2,630)	(14.1)	(325)	(4,332)	(17.1)
Total	100.0	100.0	345	440	27.5	95	25,406	100.0

1. The average distribution in Latin America in 1970 has been estimated on the basis of information provided by Argentina, Brazil, Chile, Colombia, Mexico, Paraguay, Honduras, and Venezuela.

a. Corresponds to the concept of personal per capita income.
b. Subtotal within 10% highest.

SOURCE: ECLA, *Long-Term Trends and Projections of Economic Development of Latin America*, Spanish edition, 1977, table 1.

Table 1422

DISTRIBUTION OF INCOME: CHRONOLOGICAL SERIES, 3 LC, 1953–62

	Country	Year	Unit[1]	Income PI, (US)[2]	Coefficients		D.S. Log
					Gini	Variation	
A.	ARGENTINA	1953	H	786	.41	1.09	.64
		1959	H	832	.45	1.29	.70
		1961	H	927	.42	1.18	.67

Continued in SALA, 25-1418.

Table 1423

DISTRIBUTION OF AVERAGE PER INHABITANT INCOME, BY INCOME GROUPS, 5 L, 1965

	Country	Average PI Personal Income[1]	Average Income by Group				
			Poorest 20%	30% Below the Median	30% Above the Median	15% Below the Top	Top 5%
C.	BRAZIL	260	45	100	200	380	2,055
	Rio de Janeiro	805	200	405	780	1,425	3,880
	São Paulo	775	225	390	675	1,280	4,340

Continued in SALA, 25-1419.

Table 1424

INCOME GROUPS, PERCENTAGE SHARES, 5 L, 1965

	Country	Lowest 20%	30% Below the Median	30% Above the Median	15% Below the Median	Top 5%
A.	ARGENTINA	5.2	15.3	25.4	22.9	31.2
F.	COSTA RICA	5.5	12.5	22.0	25.0	35.0
J.	EL SALVADOR	5.5	10.5	22.2	28.4	32.9
N.	MEXICO	3.6	11.8	26.1	29.5	29.0
T.	VENEZUELA	3.0	11.3	27.7	31.5	26.5

SOURCE: SALA, 16-16 (p. 26).

Table 1425

NATIONAL DISTRIBUTION OF TOTAL HOUSEHOLD INCOME, BY INCOME GROUPS, 10 L

Country	Year	Per Capita GDP (Dollars at 1970 Prices)	Household Percentile Groups (Percentage Shares in Total Income)						Coefficients of Concentration	
			0-20	21-40	41-60	61-80	81-90	91-100	Gini	Theil
A. ARGENTINA	1970	1,208	4.4	9.7	14.1	21.5	15.1	35.2	.44	.15

Continued in SALA 24, 1418.

Table 1426

URBAN DISTRIBUTION OF HOUSEHOLD INCOME, BY INCOME GROUPS, 11 L

Country	Year	Non-Agricultural GDP (Dollars at 1970 Prices)	Household Percentile Groups (Percentage Shares in Total Income)						Coefficients of Concentration	
			0-20	21-40	41-60	61-80	81-90	91-100	Gini	Theil
A. ARGENTINA	1970	1,254	4.3	9.3	14.2	21.3	15.1	35.8	.45	.15

Continued in SALA 24, 1419.

Table 1427

NUMBER OF COOPERATIVES AND MEMBERSHIP, 20 L, 1962 AND 1969

Country	Cooperatives			Membership		
	1962	1969	PC	1962	1969	PC
A. ARGENTINA	3,220	3,654	13	2,088,000	3,453,947	65

Continued in SALA 24, 1420.

15

Migration and Tourism

Table 1500

POPULATION IN UNITED STATES REPORTING LATIN AMERICAN ANCESTRY[1]
(Number of Persons Reporting in 1980)

PART I. TOTAL NUMBER OF PERSONS REPORTING

Nation of Ancestry	Type of Ancestry				Location in the U.S.			
	Single[2] Ancestry	Multiple[3] Ancestry	Reported[4] Ancestry	Percent of[5] Total	Northeast	North Central	South	West
A. ARGENTINA	28,109	9,800	37,909	.02	15,357	2,439	7,915	12,198
B. BOLIVIA	12,585	3,463	16,048	.01	3,516	1,853	5,402	5,277
C. BRAZIL	18,750	8,890	27,640	.01	12,035	3,128	6,387	6,090
D. CHILE	24,410	7,433	31,843	.02	10,711	2,829	7,678	10,625
E. COLOMBIA	137,162	19,114	156,276	.08	84,307	10,793	40,214	20,962
F. COSTA RICA	21,121	5,871	26,992	.01	9,623	1,828	5,009	10,532
G. CUBA	500,564	97,138	597,702	.32	143,036	24,625	373,695	56,346
H. DOMINICAN REP.	155,930	14,768	170,698	.09	156,053	2,054	9,939	2,652
I. ECUADOR	77,247	10,726	87,973	.05	56,392	5,961	9,804	15,816
J. EL SALVADOR	77,384	7,373	84,757	.05	10,992	2,286	7,917	63,562
K. GUATEMALA	54,674	7,424	62,098	.03	10,508	7,507	7,897	36,186
L. HAITI	81,509	8,714	90,223	.05	65,246	3,505	19,346	2,126
M. HONDURAS	45,294	10,271	55,565	.03	19,986	4,297	18,568	12,714
N. MEXICO	6,992,476	700,143	7,692,619	4.09	62,116	705,349	2,663,868	4,261,286
O. NICARAGUA	37,845	7,232	45,077	.02	6,239	1,543	12,257	25,038
P. PANAMA	33,546	11,208	44,754	.02	21,557	3,376	10,669	9,152
R. PERU	44,884	13,054	57,938	.03	24,360	4,538	11,237	17,803
S. URUGUAY	7,240	1,350	8,590	#	4,876	543	1,842	1,329
T. VENEZUELA	25,548	7,481	33,029	.02	10,355	3,536	14,031	5,107
PUERTO RICO	1,270,420	173,442	1,443,862	.77	1,057,461	157,857	120,394	108,150
SPANISH/ HISPANIC[6]	1,685,151	1,001,529	2,686,680	1.43	613,844	205,758	705,594	1,161,484
OTHER SPANISH[7]	52,774	12,421	65,195	.03	14,992	4,887	27,199	18,117

1. The source provides "ethnic data on persons regardless of the number of generations removed from their country of origin." The ancestry question was based on self-identification. About 83% of the population reported at least one specific ancestry.
2. Persons reporting only one ancestry group.
3. Persons reporting more than one ancestry group. Double origin ancestry reports were coded; 17 triple-origin ancestries expected to be frequently reported were also coded. A person reporting double origin will appear twice in the table.
4. Reported at least one specific ancestry. Sum of single and multiple ancestry. The total of the column will add to more than the total reporting a Latin American ancestry due to double counting (see note 3 above).
5. Percent of total population reporting at least one specific ancestry. Numbers and percents by ancestry group do not add to totals due to persons with multiple ancestry being included in more than one group.
6. This category represents a general type of response, which may encompass several ancestry groups.
7. Other Spanish not elsewhere considered. Since the "Spaniard" entry excludes Basques they may appear here. However, Latin America appears under the general heading "Spanish" so a clear distinction is lacking.

SOURCE: US–BC, 1980 Supplementary Report, PC 80-SI-10, April 1983, table 3.

Table 1500 (Continued)

POPULATION IN UNITED STATES REPORTING LATIN AMERICAN ANCESTRY[1]
(Number of Persons Reporting in 1980)

PART II. NUMBER OF PERSONS REPORTING AT LEAST ONE SPECIFIC ANCESTRY GROUP

	Nation of Ancestry	New England	Middle Atlantic	East North Central	West North Central	South Atlantic	East South Central	West South Central	Mountain	Pacific
A.	ARGENTINA	1,629	13,728	1,990	449	6,254	242	1,419	1,027	11,171
B.	BOLIVIA	412	3,104	1,442	411	4,041	152	1,209	630	4,647
C.	BRAZIL	2,683	9,352	2,549	579	4,677	426	1,284	1,020	5,070
D.	CHILE	1,306	9,405	2,209	620	6,171	213	1,294	1,186	9,439
E.	COLOMBIA	7,961	76,346	9,104	1,689	33,072	635	6,507	1,732	19,230
F.	COSTA RICA	1,829	7,794	1,600	228	3,189	197	1,623	533	9,999
G.	CUBA	10,603	132,433	21,965	2,660	355,950	2,123	15,622	5,972	50,374
H.	DOMINICAN REP.	7,360	148,493	1,861	193	8,747	172	1,020	590	2,062
I.	ECUADOR	2,102	54,290	5,336	625	7,899	154	1,751	668	15,148
J.	EL SALVADOR	874	10,118	1,948	338	5,371	253	2,293	947	62,615
K.	GUATEMALA	2,028	8,480	7,127	380	4,984	217	2,696	862	35,324
L.	HAITI	6,004	59,242	3,132	373	18,446	184	716	198	1,928
M.	HONDURAS	1,919	18,067	3,638	659	8,499	775	9,294	690	12,024
N.	MEXICO	10,849	51,267	579,234	126,115	98,860	17,891	2,547,117	781,190	3,480,096
O.	NICARAGUA	312	5,927	1,150	393	8,945	252	3,060	421	24,617
P.	PANAMA	1,129	20,428	2,570	806	6,886	670	3,113	1,102	8,050
R.	PERU	2,538	21,822	3,904	634	8,349	342	2,546	1,274	16,529
S.	URUGUAY	469	4,407	471	72	1,452	48	342	109	1,220
T.	VENEZUELA	2,209	8,146	2,574	962	9,131	823	4,077	1,020	4,087
	PUERTO RICO	118,833	938,628	151,896	5,961	92,515	5,493	22,386	11,018	97,132
	SPANISH/HISPANIC[2]	81,970	531,060	158,210	47,630	362,633	32,078	320,983	548,787	612,697
	OTHER SPANISH[3]	1,065	13,927	4,382	505	6,245	456	20,498	1,272	16,845

1. The source provides "ethnic data on persons regardless of the number of generations removed from their country of origin." The ancestry question was based on self-identification. About 83% of the population reported at least one specific ancestry. Some individuals reported a single ancestry group; others reported more than one group. All single- and double-ancestry responses were coded. In addition, 17 triple-origin ancestries expected to be frequently reported were coded; only the first two ancestries were coded for all other responses of three or more ancestries. Since persons who reported multiple ancestries were included in more than one group, the sum of persons reporting the ancestry group is greater than the total.
2. This category represents a general type of response, which may encompass several ancestry groups.
3. Other Spanish not elsewhere considered. Since the "Spaniard" entry excludes Basques they may appear here. However, Latin America appears under the general heading "Spanish" so a clear distinction is lacking.

SOURCE: US-BC, 1980 Supplementary Report, PC 80-SI-10, April 1983, table 3.

Table 1501

IMMIGRATION TO UNITED STATES, BY COUNTRY OF LAST RESIDENCE, 14 LR, 1820–1987

(T)

	Country	Total 1820–1987	Total 1961–70	Total 1971–80	1982	1983	1984	1985	1986	1987
	Americas	11,049	1,716.4	1,982.5	193.5	204.6	208.1	225.5	254.1	265.0
A.	ARGENTINA	114	49.7	29.9	2.1	2.0	2.3	1.9	2.3	2.2
C.	BRAZIL	76	29.3	17.8	1.5	1.5	2.2	2.6	2.7	2.7
	Canada	4,237	413.3	169.9	10.8	11.4	15.7	16.4	16.1	16.7
E.	COLOMBIA	241	72.0	77.3	8.6	9.7	10.9	11.8	11.2	11.5
G.	CUBA	661	208.5	264.9	8.2	9.0	5.7	17.1	30.8	27.4
H.	DOMINICAN REP.	407	93.3	148.1	17.5	22.1	23.2	23.9	26.2	24.9
I.	ECUADOR	129	36.8	50.1	4.1	4.2	4.2	4.6	4.5	4.7
J.	EL SALVADOR	120	15.0	34.4	7.1	8.6	8.8	10.1	10.9	10.6
K.	GUATEMALA	77	15.9	25.9	3.6	4.1	4.0	4.4	5.3	5.8
L.	HAITI	166	34.5	56.3	8.8	8.4	9.6	9.9	12.4	14.6
M.	HONDURAS	66	15.7	17.4	3.2	3.6	3.4	3.7	4.6	4.8
N.	MEXICO	2,710	453.9	640.3	56.1	59.1	57.8	61.3	66.8	72.5
P.	PANAMA	77	19.4	23.5	3.3	2.5	3.2	3.2	3.1	2.8
R.	PERU	88	19.1	29.2	4.2	4.4	4.3	4.1	4.8	5.8
	West Indies	1,172	133.9	271.8	32.9	33.8	29.9	28.5	29.2	48.3
	Other Americas	703	106.1	125.7	21.5	20.2	22.9	22.0	23.2	9.7

SOURCE: USINS-SY, 1988 (Preliminary), p. 591.

Table 1502

IMMIGRANTS ADMITTED TO UNITED STATES,[1] 20 LC, 1976–86[a]

(N)

	Country	1976	1978	1979	1980	1981	1982	1983	1984	1985	1986
A.	ARGENTINA	2,267	3,732	2,856	2,815	2,236	2,065	2,029	2,141	1,844	2,187
B.	BOLIVIA	522	1,030	751	730	820	750	823	918	1,006	1,079
C.	BRAZIL	1,038	1,923	1,450	1,570	1,616	1,475	1,503	1,847	2,272	2,332
D.	CHILE	1,266	3,122	2,289	2,569	2,048	1,911	1,970	1,912	1,992	2,243
E.	COLOMBIA	5,742	11,032	10,637	11,289	10,335	8,608	9,658	11,020	11,982	11,408
F.	COSTA RICA	1,137	1,575	1,467	1,535	1,359	1,272	1,182	1,473	1,281	1,356
G.	CUBA	29,233	29,754	15,585	15,054	10,858	8,209	8,978	10,599	20,334	33,114
H.	DOMINICAN REP.	12,526	19,458	17,519	17,245	18,220	17,451	22,058	23,147	23,787	26,175
I.	ECUADOR	4,504	5,732	4,383	6,133	5,129	4,127	4,243	4,164	4,482	4,516
J.	EL SALVADOR	2,363	5,826	4,479	6,101	8,210	7,107	8,596	8,787	10,156	10,929
K.	GUATEMALA	1,970	3,996	2,583	3,751	3,928	3,633	4,090	3,937	4,389	5,158
L.	HAITI	5,410	6,470	6,433	6,540	6,683	8,779	8,424	9,839	10,165	12,666
M.	HONDURAS	1,310	2,727	2,545	2,552	2,358	3,186	3,619	3,405	3,726	4,532
N.	MEXICO	57,863	92,367	52,096	56,680	101,268	56,106	59,079	57,557	61,077	66,533
O.	NICARAGUA	934	1,888	1,938	2,337	2,752	3,077	2,983	2,718	2,786	2,826
P.	PANAMA[4]	1,699	3,108	3,472	3,572	4,613	3,320	2,546	2,276	2,611	2,194
Q.	PARAGUAY	110	202	175	181	153	161	187	167	170	~
R.	PERU	2,640	5,243	4,135	4,021	4,664	4,151	4,384	4,368	4,181	4,895
S.	URUGUAY	676	1,052	754	887	972	707	681	712	790	699
T.	VENEZUELA	191	990	841	1,010	1,104	1,336	1,508	1,721	1,714	1,854
	LATIN AMERICA[2]	133,000	200,000	125,700	~	182,643	137,431	~	~	~	~
	ALL COUNTRIES[3]	398,613	601,442	460,348	530,639	596,600	594,131	559,763	543,903	570,009	~

1. Countries indicated are those of birth rather than those of last permanent residence.
2. Excludes Bolivia and Paraguay. In addition, the total figures for 1951–60, 1961–70, and 1971–80 exclude Chile, Costa Rica, Honduras, Nicaragua, Uruguay, and Venezuela.
3. Includes Latin America.
4. Historical data for the Canal Zone are included in Panama.

a. For prior years since 1951, see SALA, 25–1501.

SOURCE: USBC-SA, 1984, table 126; USINS-SY, 1979/80, table 13; USINS-SY, 1982, IMM 1.3; USINS-SY, 1983/84; USINS-SY, 1984/85, table IMM 1.3; USINS-SY, 1986–87, table 18, pp. 36–37.

Table 1503

IMMIGRANTS ADMITTED TO UNITED STATES, BY OCCUPATION, 10 L

(1986)[a]

Country of Birth	Total	Occupation									
		Total	Professional Specialty	Executive, Administrative, and Managerial	Sales	Administrative Support	Precision Production, Craft, and Repair	Operator, Fabricator, and Laborer	Farming, Forestry, Fishing	Service	No Occupation
A. ARGENTINA	2,187	870	260	99	59	70	141	77	9	155	1317
B. BOLIVIA	1,079	427	103	30	14	54	45	35	3	143	652
C. BRAZIL	2,332	852	248	90	49	95	65	75	3	227	1,480
D. CHILE	2,243	837	199	90	59	100	99	113	4	173	1,406
E. COLOMBIA	11,408	3,361	445	253	245	292	507	807	35	777	8,047
I. ECUADOR	4,516	1,723	162	95	141	175	345	446	20	339	2,793
Q. PARAGUAY[1]	~	~	~	~	~	~	~	~	~	~	~
R. PERU	4,895	1,950	240	170	95	329	225	424	13	454	2,945
S. URUGUAY	699	336	38	35	17	20	62	75	3	86	363
T. VENEZUELA	1,854	527	206	87	31	66	29	32	~	76	1,327

1. Data not available.

a. For prior years, 1973–78, see SALA, 25–1502.

SOURCE: USINS-SY, 1985, table IMM 6.1; USINS-SY, 1986-87, table 18, pp. 36-37.

Table 1504

IMMIGRANTS ADMITTED TO UNITED STATES, BY OCCUPATION, 20 LRC (FY 1988)

Country of Birth	Total	Total	Occupation								
			Professional Specialty and Technical	Executive, Administrative, and Managerial	Sales	Administrative Support	Precision Production, Craft and Repair	Operator, Fabricator, and Laborer	Farming, Forestry, and Fishing	Service	No Occupation or Not Reported
A. ARGENTINA	2,371	1,028	277	134	59	111	135	112	7	193	1,343
B. BOLIVIA	1,038	430	78	30	16	60	39	49	2	156	608
C. BRAZIL	2,699	1,006	262	86	74	123	73	81	10	297	1,693
D. CHILE	2,137	835	176	78	57	133	96	88	3	204	1,302
E. COLOMBIA	10,322	3,594	432	182	194	312	351	1,309	25	789	6,728
F. COSTA RICA	1,351	523	60	34	24	62	58	148	10	127	828
G. CUBA	17,558	9,297	536	184	413	774	1,854	3,037	111	2,388	8,261
H. DOMINICAN REP.	27,189	8,605	938	467	424	640	1,514	2,285	489	1,848	18,584
I. ECUADOR	4,716	2,038	130	93	121	267	313	560	18	536	2,678
J. EL SALVADOR	12,045	6,565	206	130	214	444	778	1,677	72	3,044	5,480
K. GUATEMALA	5,723	2,801	194	139	95	280	334	764	52	943	2,922
L. HAITI	34,806	24,828	696	149	310	511	3,120	5,788	2,758	11,496	9,978
M. HONDURAS	4,302	1,781	127	87	53	152	221	680	30	431	2,521
N. MEXICO	95,039	56,713	1,666	1,279	1,589	3,018	6,247	28,734	3,135	11,045	38,326
O. NICARAGUA	3,311	1,360	141	114	114	240	141	271	18	321	1,951
P. PANAMA	2,486	863	169	84	34	224	85	84	3	180	1,623
Q. PARAGUAY	483	81	17	5	3	12	10	10	4	20	402
R. PERU	5,936	2,618	340	184	140	367	224	701	28	634	3,318
S. URUGUAY	612	321	59	25	11	27	41	67	4	87	291
T. VENEZUELA	1,791	617	215	74	57	85	36	33	4	113	1,174
LATIN AMERICA	235,917	125,944	6,719	3,558	4,002	7,842	15,670	46,478	6,783	34,852	110,011
WORLD	643,025	280,081	45,188	20,014	12,027	25,452	28,460	68,269	15,513	65,158	362,944

SOURCE: USINS-SY, 1988 (Preliminary), table 20.

Table 1505

IMMIGRANTS ADMITTED TO UNITED STATES, BY COUNTRY OF BIRTH, 19 LR, 1978–88
(FY)

Country of Birth	1978	1979	1980	1981	1982	1983	1984	1985	1986	1987	1988
A. ARGENTINA	3,732	2,856	2,816	2,236	2,065	2,029	2,141	1,844	2,187	2,106	2,371
B. BOLIVIA	1,030	751	730	820	750	823	918	1,006	1,079	1,170	1,038
C. BRAZIL	1,923	1,450	1,570	1,616	1,475	1,503	1,847	2,272	2,332	2,505	2,699
D. CHILE	3,122	2,289	2,569	2,048	1,911	1,970	1,912	1,992	2,243	2,140	2,137
E. COLOMBIA	11,032	10,637	11,289	10,335	8,608	9,658	11,020	11,982	11,408	11,700	10,322
F. COSTA RICA	1,575	1,467	1,535	1,359	1,272	1,182	1,473	1,281	1,356	1,391	1,351
G. CUBA	29,754	15,585	15,054	10,858	8,209	8,978	10,599	20,334	33,114	28,916	17,558
H. DOMINICAN REP.	19,458	17,519	17,245	18,220	17,451	22,058	23,147	23,787	26,175	24,858	27,189
I. ECUADOR	5,732	4,383	6,133	5,129	4,127	4,243	4,164	4,482	4,516	4,641	4,716
J. EL SALVADOR	5,826	4,479	6,101	8,210	7,107	8,596	8,787	10,156	10,929	10,693	12,045
K. GUATEMALA	3,996	2,583	3,751	3,928	3,633	4,090	3,937	4,389	5,158	5,729	5,723
L. HAITI	6,470	6,433	6,540	6,683	8,779	8,424	9,839	10,165	12,666	14,819	34,806
M. HONDURAS	2,727	2,545	2,552	2,358	3,186	3,619	3,405	3,726	4,532	4,751	4,302
N. MEXICO	92,367	52,096	56,680	101,268	56,106	59,079	57,557	61,077	66,533	72,351	95,039
O. NICARAGUA	1,888	1,938	2,337	2,752	3,077	2,983	2,718	2,786	2,826	3,294	3,311
P. PANAMA	3,108	3,472	3,572	4,613	3,320	2,546	2,276	2,611	2,194	2,084	2,486
R. PERU	5,243	4,135	4,021	4,664	4,151	4,384	4,368	4,181	4,895	5,901	5,936
S. URUGUAY	1,052	754	887	972	707	681	712	790	699	709	612
T. VENEZUELA	990	841	1,010	1,104	1,336	1,508	1,721	1,714	1,854	1,694	1,791
Other Latin America	294	247	312	246	259	308	245	264	294	435	638
LATIN AMERICA	201,319	136,460	146,703	186,419	137,529	148,662	189,786	171,629	197,500	211,887	236,070

SOURCE: USINS-SY, 1988 (Preliminary), table 3.

Table 1506

STATUS OF PERMANENT IMMIGRANTS TO UNITED STATES, 19 LR
(FY 1988)

Country of Birth	Total	Visitors for Business	Visitors for Pleasure	Treaty Traders and Investors[1]	Students[1]	Temporary Workers[1]	Exchange Visitors[1]	Fiances-(ees)[2]	Intracompany Transferees[1]	Refugees and Parolees	Other
A. ARGENTINA	1,094	27	701	23	55	84	17	21	106	29	31
B. BOLIVIA	371	10	242	#	85	1	1	1	2	7	22
C. BRAZIL	1,402	36	928	3	131	70	28	52	80	19	55
D. CHILE	898	31	546	#	85	55	15	29	39	36	62
E. COLOMBIA	2,498	83	1,701	30	275	68	12	73	97	104	55
F. COSTA RICA	417	6	313	1	30	2	2	15	4	30	14
G. CUBA	13,851	4	1,527	#	15	7	5	5	4	12,271	13
H. DOMINICAN REP.	1,906	128	1,543	2	65	51	#	23	3	56	35
I. ECUADOR	1,141	29	970	1	61	10	1	13	6	26	24
J. EL SALVADOR	1,349	12	1,141	1	78	9	5	10	10	57	26
K. GUATEMALA	1,295	21	1,134	1	43	21	1	7	10	38	19
L. HAITI	26,886	101	19,584	#	56	17	3	6	2	6,975	142
M. HONDURAS	857	29	625	1	71	7	1	19	4	85	15
N. MEXICO	42,271	155	40,145	4	474	306	32	489	95	359	212
O. NICARAGUA	1,521	17	1,144	10	99	14	#	4	22	189	22
P. PANAMA	573	13	421	1	70	5	#	15	9	23	16
R. PERU	2,200	70	1,672	2	160	50	18	31	60	80	57
S. URUGUAY	255	6	179	1	8	22	6	5	4	6	18
T. VENEZUELA	1,023	23	409	3	349	55	10	22	67	65	20
LATIN AMERICA	74,922	803	74,925	102	2,210	854	157	840	624	20,455	858

1. Includes spouses and children.
2. Includes children.

SOURCE: USINS-SY, 1988 (Preliminary), table 9.

Table 1507

U.S. NATURALIZATION, BY YEAR OF ENTRY AND COUNTRY OF BIRTH, 19 LRC, 1976-88 (FY)

Country of Birth	Total	1988 and 1987	1986	1985	1984	1983	1982	1981	1980	1979	1978	1977	1976	Before 1976	Unknown or Not Reported
A. ARGENTINA	1,289	3	2	9	32	50	109	110	109	80	92	79	48	565	1
B. BOLIVIA	449	3	6	13	14	23	55	61	34	32	35	30	11	130	2
C. BRAZIL	550	17	17	16	30	18	50	36	32	26	29	25	13	241	0
D. CHILE	1,043	6	43	35	44	42	126	109	81	65	86	85	65	256	0
E. COLOMBIA	5,014	35	50	75	134	188	348	501	406	336	334	311	148	2,143	5
F. COSTA RICA	728	7	4	9	15	19	42	66	68	25	30	40	21	382	0
G. CUBA	11,255	12	24	19	45	78	257	528	2,512	384	155	195	227	6,817	2
H. DOMINICAN REP.	5,776	9	9	23	69	150	505	517	489	353	357	231	189	2,874	1
I. ECUADOR	1,783	9	6	6	29	41	104	141	160	93	82	107	85	920	0
J. EL SALVADOR	2,291	16	20	29	62	126	311	318	292	135	167	167	61	586	1
K. GUATEMALA	1,362	25	26	22	36	42	107	140	132	80	94	107	59	492	0
L. HAITI	2,359	5	6	3	61	57	360	361	257	162	113	116	81	773	4
M. HONDURAS	1,227	15	22	27	40	66	140	158	106	95	84	62	26	386	0
N. MEXICO	22,134	60	70	80	347	524	993	1,604	1,217	810	1,333	759	925	13,391	21
O. NICARAGUA	1,365	9	6	10	30	68	215	269	116	93	81	69	34	365	0
P. PANAMA	1,570	65	14	25	57	70	160	226	160	117	112	60	60	442	2
R. PERU	2,247	15	9	28	148	135	312	330	194	166	176	157	83	493	1
S. URUGUAY	408	--	--	6	10	6	44	68	43	27	32	33	19	120	0
T. VENEZUELA	468	--	3	12	27	26	60	61	39	28	27	13	7	164	1
LATIN AMERICA	29,419	311	337	447	1,230	1,729	4,298	5,604	6,447	3,107	3,419	2,646	2,162	31,540	41
WORLD	242,063	1,279	1,801	2,799	8,063	10,735	41,456	35,874	27,965	17,596	12,142	8,803	7,041	66,339	170

SOURCE: USINS-SY, 1988 (Preliminary), table 57.

Table 1508

U.S. NATURALIZATION, BY MAJOR OCCUPATION AND COUNTRY OF ORIGIN, 19 LR

(FY)

Country of Origin	Total	Occupation									
		Total	Professional Specialty	Executive, Administrative, and Managerial	Sales	Administrative Support	Precision Production, Craft and Repair	Operator, Fabricator, and Laborer	Farming, Forestry, and Fishing	Service	No Occupation or Not Reported
A. ARGENTINA	1,288	871	145	88	71	171	93	128	4	171	417
B. BOLIVIA	448	310	61	34	25	59	23	24	1	83	138
C. BRAZIL	553	333	70	29	32	71	23	47	3	58	220
D. CHILE	1,040	662	103	56	48	126	70	96	4	159	378
E. COLOMBIA	5,021	3,250	395	219	270	808	292	645	7	614	1,771
F. COSTA RICA	726	451	64	24	28	102	50	72	2	109	275
G. CUBA	11,228	7,418	653	416	802	2,236	930	1,314	47	1,020	3,810
H. DOMINICAN REP.	5,842	3,349	221	159	268	721	378	982	3	617	2,493
I. ECUADOR	1,774	1,219	113	98	91	324	125	264	2	202	555
J. EL SALVADOR	2,291	1,547	176	94	75	413	149	228	7	405	744
K. GUATEMALA	1,358	891	94	59	42	197	98	164	4	233	467
L. HAITI	2,350	1,816	244	55	93	396	143	335	2	548	534
M. HONDURAS	1,229	732	70	36	60	177	65	139	3	182	497
N. MEXICO	22,085	13,426	1,084	820	914	2,412	1,669	3,083	550	2,894	8,659
O. NICARAGUA	1,363	929	124	60	101	272	77	100	2	193	434
P. PANAMA	1,561	1,011	141	51	81	291	148	74	4	221	550
R. PERU	2,255	1,574	242	117	97	349	150	303	2	314	681
S. URUGUAY	406	299	35	17	18	58	42	76	2	51	107
T. VENEZUELA	490	321	75	38	37	71	32	28	--	40	169
LATIN AMERICA	63,308	40,409	4,110	2,470	3,105	9,254	4,557	8,102	651	8,114	22,899

SOURCE: USINS-SY, 1988 (Preliminary), table 56.

Table 1509

IMMIGRANTS ADMITTED TO THE UNITED STATES, BY CLASSIFICATION, 20 L

(1980)

Country	Total Admitted (1+2)	Immigrants Subject to Numerical Limitation (1)	Immigrants Admitted Without Numerical Limitation (2=3+4+5+6+7+8+9+10)	Parents of U.S. Citizens (3)	Spouses of U.S. Citizens (4)	Children of U.S. Citizens[1] (5)	Special Immigrants (6)	Spouse Child[2] (7)	Children Born Abroad to Aliens[3] (8)	Refugee and Exile (9)	Other (10)
A. ARGENTINA	2,815	1,824	891	150	566	74	33	28	14	25	1

Continued in SALA, 24-1503.

Table 1510

U.S. NATURALIZATION, BY COUNTRY OF ORIGIN AND YEAR OF ENTRY, 20 L, 1965-80

(N)

Country	1965	1970	1971	1972	1973	1974	1975	1976	1977	1978	1979	1980[a]
A. ARGENTINA	151	85	51	91	103	117	28	26	8	3	3	~

Continued in SALA, 24-1504.

Table 1511

"DEPORTABLE ALIENS" LOCATED IN THE UNITED STATES, FY 1966-86

(N)

Year	Total	Mexican	Mexicans as % of Total
1966	138,520[a]	89,751	65
1967	161,608[a]	108,327	67
1968	212,057[a]	151,705	72
1969	283,557[a]	201,636	71
1970	231,116*	219,254*	94*
1971	302,517	290,152	95
1972	369,495	355,099	96
1973	498,123	480,588	96
1974	634,777	616,630	97
1975	596,796	579,448	97
1976	871,189	848,130	97
1977	812,541	792,613	97
1978	862,217	841,525	97
1979	888,729	866,761	97
1980[b]	910,361	817,479	90
1981	975,780	874,433	90
1982	970,246	887,481	91
1983	1,246,491	1,172,297	94
1984	1,246,977	1,170,769	94
1985	1,348,749	1,266,999	94
1986	1,767,400	1,671,458	95

a. Includes "involuntary" deportation given in table 1509.
b. Year ended Sept. 30, 1980.

SOURCE: USINS-AR, various years; USINS-SY, 1984/85, p. 177; USINS-SY, 1985/86, p. 96.

Table 1512
IMMIGRANTS ADMITTED TO UNITED STATES, BY CLASS OF ADMISSION AND COUNTRY OF BIRTH, 20 LRC
(FY 1988)

Country of Birth	Total	Subject to Numerical Limitations	Immigrants Exempt from Numerical Limitations								
			Total	Immediate Relatives[1]	Parents of Adult U.S. Citizens	Spouses of U.S. Citizens[2]	Children of U.S. Citizens[3]	Refugee and Asylee Adjustments	Special Immigrants	1972 Registry Provision[4]	Other
A. ARGENTINA	2,371	1,184	1,187	929	168	655	106	20	36	193	9
B. BOLIVIA	1,038	485	553	457	123	258	76	6	13	68	9
C. BRAZIL	2,699	840	1,859	1,734	77	1,308	349	8	63	41	13
D. CHILE	2,137	734	1,403	1,118	220	539	359	26	57	200	2
E. COLOMBIA	10,322	5,103	5,219	4,714	830	2,576	1,308	66	35	341	63
F. COSTA RICA	1,351	502	842	748	68	458	222	24	14	57	6
G. CUBA	17,558	3,136	14,422	689	452	147	90	13,612	22	99	0
H. DOMINICAN REP.	27,189	19,080	8,109	7,562	1,150	4,345	2,067	17	22	264	244
I. ECUADOR	4,716	2,724	1,992	1,580	358	884	318	16	21	353	42
J. EL SALVADOR	12,045	7,788	4,257	3,433	765	1,914	754	170	24	614	16
K. GUATEMALA	5,723	2,995	2,728	2,066	433	1,079	554	37	23	587	15
L. HAITI	34,806	6,787	28,019	2,184	563	1,070	531	25,481	47	303	24
M. HONDURAS	4,302	2,093	2,209	1,985	230	1,087	668	72	9	135	8
N. MEXICO	95,039	20,341	74,698	42,689	3,857	30,755	8,077	33	186	30,319	1,471
O. NICARAGUA	3,311	1,456	1,855	1,079	361	487	231	647	19	110	0
P. PANAMA	2,486	845	1,641	1,403	156	833	414	17	155	49	17
Q. PARAGUAY	483	81	402	394	20	66	308	0	5	3	0
R. PERU	5,936	2,448	3,488	2,999	675	1,827	497	59	30	390	10
S. URUGUAY	612	284	328	247	49	169	29	5	20	51	5
T. VENEZUELA	1,791	638	1,153	1,034	44	783	207	58	17	31	13
LATIN AMERICA	233,465	79,544	156,362	79,004	10,599	51,240	17,165	40,374	818	34,208	1,952
WORLD	643,025	264,148	378,877	219,340	47,500	130,977	40,863	110,721	5,120	39,999	3,697

1. Includes parents, spouses, and children of U.S. citizens.
2. Includes persons who entered as fiances(ees) and have married U.S. citizens.
3. Includes children whose parents entered as fiances(ees) and have married U.S. citizens.
4. Prior to fiscal year 1987 aliens must have entered before 6/30/48 to be eligible for the registry provisions.

SOURCE: USINS-SY, 1988 (Preliminary), table 7.

Table 1513

ALIENS REQUIRED TO DEPART UNITED STATES, BY CAUSE AND COUNTRY OF NATIONALITY, 12 LR

(FY 1988)

Country of Nationality	Total	Criminal	Violation of Narcotic Law	Previously Excluded or Deported	Mental or Physical Defect	Entered without Proper Documents	Failed to Maintain or Comply with Conditions of Nonimmigrant Status	Entered without Inspection or by False Statements	Miscellaneous	Not Reported
C. BRAZIL	61	0	0	0	0	3	47	11	0	0
E. COLOMBIA	595	1	24	0	0	4	128	437	0	1
F. COSTA RICA	46	0	0	0	0	3	20	23	0	0
H. DOMINICAN REP.	321	0	6	0	0	10	71	234	0	0
I. ECUADOR	144	0	1	0	0	3	51	89	0	0
J. EL SALVADOR	1,828	2	1	0	1	6	61	1,756	0	1
K. GUATEMALA	813	1	1	1	0	5	47	758	0	0
L. HAITI	437	0	0	0	0	5	239	191	0	2
M. HONDURAS	218	0	1	0	0	1	45	171	0	0
N. MEXICO	4,741	57	136	20	0	128	335	4,052	4	9
O. NICARAGUA	173	0	0	0	0	1	32	140	0	0
R. PERU	176	0	3	0	1	1	57	111	0	3

SOURCE: USINS-SY, 1988 (Preliminary), table 65.

Table 1514

APPLICATIONS FOR REFUGEE STATUS, 1980–88[a]

Year	Applications Pending Beginning of Year	Applications Filed During Year	Applications Approved During Year	Applications Denied During Year	Applications Otherwise Closed During Year	Applications Pending End of Year
1980 (April–September)	16,642	111,883	89,580	6,149	1,197	14,957
1981	14,957	193,230	155,291	15,322	3,998	18,619
1982	18,619	94,769	61,527	14,943	6,631	11,668
1983	11,668	104,190	73,645	20,255	2,489	7,801
1984	7,801	107,437	77,932	16,220	604	12,681
1985	12,681	93,415	59,436	18,430	1,842	13,707
1986	13,707	81,017	52,081	9,679	3,362	15,895
1987	15,895	101,718	61,529	13,911	6,126	20,152
1988	20,152	125,176	80,282	11,821	5,632	27,441

a. The Refugee Act of 1980 went into effect on April 1, 1980.

SOURCE: USINS-SY, 1988 (Preliminary), table 23.

Table 1515

APPLICATIONS FOR REFUGEE STATUS, BY GEOGRAPHIC AREA AND COUNTRY OF CHARGEABILITY, 3 LR

(FY 1988)

Geographic Area and Country of Chargeability	Applications Pending Beginning of Year	Applications Filed During Year	Applications Approved During Year	Applications Denied During Year	Applications Otherwise Closed During Year	Applications Pending End of Year
G. CUBA	6	2,976	2,277	171	477	51
J. EL SALVADOR	0	14	11	2	1	0
O. NICARAGUA	6	429	164	153	109	3
Other Latin America	0	11	0	3	8	0
LATIN AMERICA	12	3,430	2,452	329	595	54

SOURCE: USINS-SY, 1988 (Preliminary), table 24.

Table 1516

DEPORTABLE ALIENS LOCATED, BY STATUS AT ENTRY, 12 LR
(FY 1988)

Country of Nationality	All Located	Visitor	Crewman	Student	Temporary Worker Agriculture	Temporary Worker Other	Immigrant	Stowaway	TWOV	Entry Without Inspection	Other
C. BRAZIL	618	174	5	4	0	2	7	3	0	410	13
E. COLOMBIA	2,869	499	27	32	1	3	312	107	1	1,808	79
G. CUBA	912	17	0	4	0	0	135	5	0	402	349
H. DOMINICAN REP.	3,883	127	38	3	1	3	515	102	3	3,029	62
I. ECUADOR	897	59	3	4	0	1	44	4	0	775	7
J. EL SALVADOR	14,322	110	4	8	1	0	37	1	21	14,110	30
K. GUATEMALA	9,246	211	11	3	0	0	27	11	2	8,951	30
L. HAITI	402	88	27	1	2	0	76	7	2	141	58
M. HONDURAS	3,943	88	40	7	0	0	20	7	5	3,723	53
N. MEXICO	949,722	3,615	1	101	26	19	1,800	0	1	943,147	1,012
O. NICARAGUA	3,280	86	9	7	0	0	26	2	2	3,136	12
R. PERU	646	115	9	5	1	1	21	0	0	488	6

SOURCE: USINS-SY, 1988 (Preliminary), table 61.

Table 1517

U.S. NATURALIZATION, BY COUNTRY OF FORMER ALLEGIANCE, 19 LR
(FY 1979–88)

Country of Former Allegiance	1979	1980	1981	1982	1983	1984	1985	1986	1987	1988
A. ARGENTINA	1,350	1,183	1,025	1,021	1,006	1,235	1,456	1,593	1,194	1,288
B. BOLIVIA	237	276	251	237	298	319	484	514	401	448
C. BRAZIL	612	453	407	461	409	488	655	615	466	553
D. CHILE	551	586	549	529	760	915	1,213	1,242	955	1,040
E. COLOMBIA	2,923	2,940	3,203	3,161	2,952	3,543	4,136	5,156	4,006	5,021
F. COSTA RICA	435	417	451	442	438	663	819	968	658	726
G. CUBA	13,317	12,717	11,329	9,551	10,365	15,756	10,487	13,818	6,738	11,228
H. DOMINICAN REP.	3,350	3,392	5,720	5,369	4,828	4,875	5,887	5,980	4,257	5,842
I. ECUADOR	1,187	1,189	1,290	1,219	1,177	1,458	1,739	1,870	1,519	1,774
J. EL SALVADOR	770	988	1,252	1,187	1,126	1,380	2,119	2,628	2,428	2,291
K. GUATEMALA	525	652	636	785	952	968	1,408	1,841	1,490	1,358
L. HAITI	2,567	1,748	1,990	2,083	2,169	2,592	2,545	2,608	1,936	2,350
M. HONDURAS	698	619	756	728	768	1,063	1,219	1,400	964	1,229
N. MEXICO	8,046	9,341	9,545	11,423	12,594	14,575	23,042	27,807	21,999	22,085
O. NICARAGUA	483	724	656	664	616	762	965	1,343	1,118	1,363
P. PANAMA	1,001	795	1,004	1,034	853	1,023	1,201	1,317	1,151	1,561
R. PERU	1,533	1,369	1,193	1,184	1,217	1,451	1,969	2,180	1,844	2,255
S. URUGUAY	363	332	313	286	328	406	458	337	379	406
T. VENEZUELA	203	212	225	259	234	326	348	468	373	490
LATIN AMERICA	40,151	39,933	41,795	41,623	43,088	53,798	62,150	73,685	53,876	63,308

SOURCE: USINS-SY, 1988 (Preliminary), table 55.

Table 1518

TEMPORARY WORKERS ADMITTED TO THE UNITED STATES, 19 L, 1985–86

(N)

	Country	Total	Workers of Distinguished Merit and Ability	Other Temporary Workers	Industrial Trainees	Total	Workers of Distinguished Merit and Ability	Other Temporary Workers	Industrial Trainees
			1985				1986		
A.	ARGENTINA	2,554	660	29	20	2,844	755	27	28
B.	BOLIVIA	379	29	1	#	439	51	3	1
C.	BRAZIL	3,837	554	24	100	4,035	556	25	85
D.	CHILE	1,148	171	40	3	1,381	249	43	12
E.	COLOMBIA	1,963	416	36	24	2,318	637	45	24
F.	COSTA RICA	743	110	51	11	1,215	185	21	13
H.	DOMINICAN REP.	1,828	977	338	18	1,267	614	277	11
I.	ECUADOR	454	36	#	9	497	56	#	11
J.	EL SALVADOR	1,199	118	21	6	1,215	185	21	13
K.	GUATEMALA	1,030	126	14	2	1,696	160	93	5
L.	HAITI	210	88	21	3	259	103	8	3
M.	HONDURAS	628	45	12	2	769	33	9	1
N.	MEXICO	10,081	2,761	2,212	80	12,029	3,217	3,913	104
O.	NICARAGUA	262	73	1	1	310	75	9	2
P.	PANAMA	711	63	42	3	1,005	64	42	1
Q.	PARAGUAY	117	1	#	#	125	4	#	#
R.	PERU	1,199	200	186	10	1,341	260	164	1
S.	URUGUAY	390	46	8	9	387	55	4	3
T.	VENEZUELA	2,851	480	97	25	2,771	627	100	27

SOURCE: USINS-SY, 1984, p. 140; 1985, p. 136; 1985/86, p. 48.

Table 1519

MEXICAN IMMIGRATION TO THE UNITED STATES,[1,2] 1900–88

(N)

Year	N	Year	N	Year	N	Year	N
1900	237	1924	89,336	1948	8,384	1972	64,040
1901	347	1925	32,964	1949	8,803	1973	70,141
1902	709	1926	43,316	1950	6,744	1974	71,586
1903	528	1927	67,721	1951	6,153	1975	62,205
1904	1,009	1928	59,016	1952	9,079	1976	57,863
1905	2,637	1929	40,154	1953	17,183	1977	44,079
1906	1,997	1930	12,703	1954	30,645	1978	92,400
1907	1,406	1931	3,333	1955	43,702	1979	52,100
1908	6,067	1932	2,171	1956	61,320	1980[a]	56,680
1909	16,251	1933	1,936	1957	49,321	1981	101,268
1910	18,691	1934	1,801	1958	26,791	1982	56,106
1911	19,889	1935	1,560	1959	22,909	1983	59,079
1912	23,238	1936	1,716	1960	32,708	1984	57,557
1913	11,926	1937	2,347	1961	41,476	1985	61,077
1914	14,614	1938	2,502	1962	55,805	1986	66,533
1915	12,340	1939	2,640	1963	55,986	1987	~
1916	18,425	1940	2,313	1964	34,448	1988	95,039
1917	17,869	1941	2,824	1965*	37,969		
1918	18,524	1942	2,378	1966	45,163		
1919	29,818	1943	4,172	1967	42,371		
1920	52,361	1944	6,598	1968	43,563		
1921	30,758	1945	6,702	1969	44,623		
1922	19,551	1946	7,146	1970	44,469		
1923	63,768	1947	7,558	1971	50,103		

1. Immigration data to 1907 refer only to seaport arrivals.
2. Excludes undocumented or illegal immigrants.

a. Year ended Sept. 30, 1980.

SOURCE: 1900–64: USBC-HS, 1976; 1965–77: USINS-AR, 1965–77, yearly. USINS-AR,
    1966–77, yearly: USINS-SY, 1977/80; 1983/84; 1984/85, table IMM 1.3; 1985/86;
    table 7; 1988.

Table 1520

MEXICAN "ILLEGAL" ALIENS REPORTED,[1] 1924–86

(N)

Year	Total	Year	Total	Year	Total
1924	4,614	1945	63,602	1966	89,751
1925	2,961	1946	91,456	1967	108,327
1926	4,047	1947	182,986	1968	151,705
1927	4,495	1948	179,385	1969	201,636
1928	5,529	1949	278,538	1970	277,377
1929	8,538	1950	458,215	1971	348,178
1930	18,319	1951	500,000	1972	430,213
1931	8,409	1952	543,538	1973	576,823
1932	7,116	1953	865,318	1974	709,959
1933	15,875	1954	1,075,168	1975	680,392
1934	8,910	1955	242,608	1976	781,474
1935	9,139	1956	72,442	1977	954,778
1936	9,534	1957	44,451	1978	976,667
1937	9,535	1958	37,242	1979	866,761
1938	8,684	1959	30,196	1980	817,479
1939	9,376	1960	29,651	1981	874,433
1940	8,051	1961	29,817	1982	887,481
1941	6,082	1962	30,272	1983	1,172,297
1942	~	1963	39,124	1984	1,170,769
1943	8,189	1964	43,844	1985	1,266,999
1944	26,689	1965	55,349	1986	1,671,458

1. Includes deportations, voluntary departures, and forced departures.

SOURCE: Julian Samora, *Los Mojados: The Wetbacks* (South Bend, Ind.: University of Notre Dame Press, 1971); USINS-AR, 1966-78, yearly; USINS-SY, various years.

Table 1521

U.S. IMMIGRATION AND NATURALIZATION SERVICE MAN-HOURS PER DEPORTABLE UNDOCUMENTEDS LOCATED, 1978-82[a]

(N)

Year	Border Patrol[1] Mexican Undocumenteds	All Undocumenteds	Investigations[2] Mexican Undocumenteds	All Undocumenteds
1978	7.03	6.86	21.38	15.58
1979	7.22	7.04	22.17	16.20
1980	8.26	7.99	33.70	19.53
1981	7.94	7.68	34.62	20.60
1982	8.12	7.88	25.48	16.44

1. Includes line watch, patrol, farm-ranch check, traffic check, city patrol, boat patrol, crewman-stowaway, aircraft operations, liaison, intelligence, litigation, identification, special programs, and headquarters staff sections.
2. Includes subversive, criminal, fraud, general, and area control sections.

a. Productive and support hours divided by number of undocumenteds located inside the United States.

SOURCE: SALA-MB, table 404.

Table 1522

MEXICAN UNDOCUMENTED ALIENS COUNTED[†] IN THE 1980 U.S. CENSUS, BY PERIOD OF ENTRY, 1960–80[a]

Period of Entry	Mexican Undocumenteds (T)	As % of Western Hemisphere Undocumenteds in U.S.	As % of Total Undocumenteds in U.S.
Total Entered Since 1960[1]	931	64.1	45.5
Entered 1960-69	138	42.3	24.2
Entered 1970-74	280	64.7	50.8
Entered 1975-80	292	72.3	53.5

1. Includes 36,000 Mexican undocumenteds who entered before 1960 (only figure available for pre-1960 undocumenteds).

a. Estimates based on differences between 1980 census alien population as modified and 1980 alien registration (I-53) data adjusted for underregistration.

SOURCE: SALA-MB, table 405.

Table 1523

U. S. BORDER PATROL APPREHENSIONS ALONG U. S.–MEXICAN BORDER, 1981–85

(N)

Year	Number
1981	750,559
1982	743,830
1983	1,034,142
1984	1,056,907
1985	1,185,795

SOURCE: USINS.

Table 1524

"ILLEGAL" ALIENS APPREHENDED IN THE UNITED STATES, 1951–86

(N)

Year	Number	Year	Number
1951	509,040	1969	283,557
1952	543,535	1970	345,353
1953	885,587	1971	420,126
1954	1,089,583	1972	505,949
1955	254,096	1973	655,968
1956	87,696	1974	788,145
1957	59,918	1975	766,600
1958	53,474	1976	875,915
1959	45,336	1977	1,042,215
1960	70,684	1978	1,057,977
1961	88,823	1979	1,076,418
1962	92,758	1980	910,361
1963	88,712	1981	975,780
1964	86,597	1982	970,246
1965	110,371	1983	1,251,357
1966	138,520	1984	1,246,981
1967	161,608	1985	1,348,749
1968	212,057	1986	1,767,400

SOURCE: USINS-SY, 1985/86, p. 95.

Table 1525

KNOWN EXCLUDABLE HAITIAN ARRIVALS
MIAMI, FLORIDA,[1] 1979-82
(N)

1979	1080	1981	1982
2,522	15,093	8,069	~

1. Low illegal entry figures for the period beginning October 1981 and ending June 1982 are the result of an Interdiction Program jointly conducted by the INS and the Coast Guard. Initiated in October 1981, after a joint U.S.–Haitian deportation agreement was signed, the program proved to be a deterrent to unauthorized traffic to U.S. shores.

SOURCE: USINS-AR, 1982, p. 8.

Table 1526

KNOWN IMMIGRANTS TO AND EMIGRANTS FROM CUBA,
1959-77
(N)

Year	Immigrants	Emigrants	Balance
1959	86,069	73,724	12,345
1960	56,557	118,936	−62,379

Continued in SALA, 25–1512.

Table 1527

REFUGEES "IN NEED'" 18 L, 1983–87

(N)

Country of Asylum	Source Country/Area	1983	1984	1985	1986	1987
A. ARGENTINA	Europe, Latin America, Southeast Asia	12,300	12,300	11,500‡	12,000‡	6,800^{a}
B. BOLIVIA	Guatemala, Chile	220	~	~	220^{b}	220^{b}
C. BRAZIL	Europe, other	5,400	5,000	5,300‡	450^{c}	450^{c}
D. CHILE	Europe	1,500	3,000	2,500	500^{c}	450^{c}
E. COLOMBIA	Europe, other	~	~	~	410^{h}	410^{h}
F. COSTA RICA	Latin America	15,000^{t}	17,000^{t}	18,800	30,000^{d}	32,000^{d}
G. CUBA	Haiti, other	~	~	~	2,000	2,000^{e}
H. DOMINICAN REP.	Haiti	5,000	5,000	6,000‡	5,500‡	6,000^{‡,f}
I. ECUADOR	Chile, other	~	~	~	800^{g}	800^{g}
J. EL SALVADOR	Europe, other	~	~	~	200	200
K. GUATEMALA	El Salvador, Nicaragua	70,000	70,000	70,000‡	12,000^{‡,i}	400^{j}
M. HONDURAS	Latin America	33,000^{u}	38,000^{x}	62,500^{‡,z}	62,450^{l}	52,500^{k}
N. MEXICO	Latin America	175,000^{v}	170,000^{y}	175,000^{‡,y}	175,000^{‡,m}	165,000^{m}
O. NICARAGUA	Latin America	~	~	~	3,300^{n}	8,200^{o}
P. PANAMA	Latin America	1,000^{w}	2,000^{w}	4,700^{w}	1,000^{p}	1,000^{p}
R. PERU	Europe, Latin America	500	500	600	700^{q}	700^{q}
S. URUGUAY	Latin America	~	~	~	160^{r}	160^{r}
T. VENEZUELA	Europe, Latin America	500	1,000	1,400	500^{s}	500^{s}

a. 5,500 from Chile, 1,000 from Southeast Asia, 300 from Latin America.
b. 120 from Guatemala, 100 from Chile.
c. 450 from Europe.
d. 22,000 from Nicaragua, 6,100 from El Salvador, 2,500 from Cuba, 300 from other.
e. 2,000 from Haiti.
f. 6,000 from Haiti.
g. 480 from Chile, 320 various countries.
h. 200 from Europe, 210 from various Latin America countries.
i. 10,000 from El Salvador, 2,000 from Nicaragua.
j. 300 from Nicaragua, 100 from El Salvador.
k. 32,000 from Nicaragua, 200 from El Salvador, 500 from Guatemala.
l. 35,000 from El Salvador, 26,450 from Nicaragua, 1,000 from Guatemala.
m. 120,000 from El Salvador, 45,000 from Guatemala.
n. 2,300 from El Salvador, 500 from Guatemala, 500 from other Latin American
   countries.
o. 7,800 from El Salvador, 400 from Guatemala.
p. 800 from El Salvador, 200 from other Latin American countries.
q. 700 from various countries.
r. 160 from various countries.
s. 400 from Latin America and the Caribbean, 100 from various countries.
t. 10,000 from El Salvador.
u. 20,000 from El Salvador, 12,000 from Nicaragua.
v. 120,000 from El Salvador, 20,000 from Guatemala.
w. 1,000 from El Salvador.
x. 19,000 from Nicaragua, 18,000 from El Salvador.
y. 120,000 from El Salvador, 40,000 from Guatemala.
z. 32,000 from Nicaragua, 30,000 from El Salvador.

SOURCE: USCR-WRS, 1983, 1984, 1985, 1986, 1987.

Table 1528

PERSONS INTERNALLY DISPLACED, 6 L, 1984–87^{a}

(T)

Country	1984	1985	1986	1987
D. CHILE	~	~	20	20
J. EL SALVADOR	400–700	500–525	500	450
K. GUATEMALA	35–500	250	300	300
M. HONDURAS	~	~	12	12
O. NICARAGUA	100	120–170	350	250
R. PERU	~	~	350	350

a. People are displaced internally within their homelands as a result of civil strife, persecu-
   tion, or drought and other natural disasters. Although they share many characteristics
   with refugees who cross international borders, they are generally not eligible for
   international refugee assistance. No agency has the capacity or responsibility for keep-
   ing track of all displaced people. Since information is generally less specific than for
   refugees, only reported estimates or ranges are presented. Because the figures are not
   comprehensive, no total is provided.

SOURCE: VSCR-WRS, 1984, 1985, 1986, 1987.

Table 1529

REFUGEES AND ASYLEES GRANTED LAWFUL PERMANENT RESIDENT STATUS IN UNITED STATES, BY REGION AND COUNTRY OF BIRTH

(FY 1979–88)

Region and Country of Birth	1979	1980	1981	1982	1983	1984	1985	1986	1987	1988
North America	12,240	10,247	5,030	4,125	4,547	5,146	15,667	31,086	32,303	40,886
Caribbean	12,143	10,141	4,844	3,917	4,142	4,599	15,090	30,356	31,474	39,873
G. CUBA	12,130	10,056	4,815	3,885	4,118	4,560	15,080	30,333	26,952	13,612
L. HAITI	0	63	16	22	10	22	5	7	4,429	25,481
Other Caribbean	13	22	13	10	14	17	5	16	93	780
Central America	28	67	163	192	386	512	556	682	787	967
J. EL SALVADOR	5	4	9	0	22	112	166	289	172	170
O. NICARAGUA	5	1	136	178	317	319	347	324	555	647
Other Central America	18	62	18	14	47	81	43	69	60	150
Other North America	69	39	23	16	19	35	21	48	42	46
South America	50	423	227	242	156	178	124	195	160	265

SOURCE: USINS-SY, 1988 (Preliminary), table 39.

Table 1530

ASYLUM CASES FILED WITH INS DISTRICT DIRECTORS[1]

(FY 1973–88)

Year	Cases Received	Cases Completed	Cases Approved	Cases Denied	Cases Adjudicated	% Approved
1973	1,913	1,510	380	1,130	1,510	25.2
1974	2,716	2,769	294	2,475	2,769	10.6
1975	2,432	1,664	562	1,102	1,664	33.8
1976	2,733	1,914	590	1,324	1,914	30.8
1976	896	370	97	273	370	26.2
1977	2,529	1,939	754	1,185	1,939	38.9
1978	3,702	2,312	1,218	1,094	2,312	52.7
1979	5,801	2,312	1,227	1,085	2,312	53.1
1980	26,512	2,000	1,104	896	2,000	55.2
1981	61,568	4,521	1,175	3,346	4,521	26.0
1982	33,296	11,326	3,909	7,255	11,164	35.0
1983	26,091	25,447	7,215	16,811	24,026	30.0
1984	24,295	54,320	8,278	32,344	40,622	20.4
1985	16,622	28,528	4,585	14,172	18,757	24.4
1986	18,889	45,792	3,350	7,882	11,241	29.9
1987	26,107	44,785	4,062	3,454	7,516	54.0
1988	60,736	68,357	5,531	8,582	14,113	39.2

1. The Refugee Act of 1980 went into effect on April 1, 1980. Data for fiscal years 1982 and 1983 have been estimated due to changes in the reporting procedures during those two periods. Cases completed cover approvals, denials, and cases otherwise closed. Cases otherwise closed are those in which the applicant withdrew the case from consideration, never acknowledged a request for an interview with the INS, or died. Cases adjudicated cover approvals and denials.

SOURCE: USINS-SY, 1988 (Preliminary), table 30.

Table 1531

INDIVIDUALS GRANTED ASYLUM, BY NATIONALITY, 2 LR
(FY 1984–88)

Nationality	1984	1985	1986	1987	1988
All Nationalities	11,627	6,514	4,284	5,093	7,340
G. CUBA	18	65	17	73	36
J. EL SALVADOR	503	129	90	39	149

SOURCE: USINS-SY, 1988 (Preliminary), table 31.

Table 1532

ALIENS DEPORTED, BY NATIONALITY, 20 LR, 1980–88

Country of Nationality	1980	1981	1982	1983	1984	1985	1986	1987	1988
A. ARGENTINA	32	20	28	25	34	36	41	24	25
B. BOLIVIA	5	15	22	32	51	52	65	34	17
C. BRAZIL	9	21	33	30	36	35	87	64	45
D. CHILE	62	35	28	33	30	30	29	21	14
E. COLOMBIA	358	406	442	521	677	953	1,084	909	572
F. COSTA RICA	18	27	31	88	47	50	63	30	38
G. CUBA	7	4	6	28	15	14	6	3	4
H. DOMINICAN REP.	255	261	169	176	310	192	183	335	430
I. ECUADOR	134	116	154	125	132	152	167	91	63
J. EL SALVADOR	1,774	2,723	2,066	3,398	2,615	3,346	3,643	2,114	2,112
K. GUATEMALA	448	637	640	1,000	907	1,960	2,478	1,568	1,596
L. HAITI	25	18	22	26	41	88	118	127	108
M. HONDURAS	119	503	264	533	467	918	1,087	927	1,083
N. MEXICO	9,612	10,276	8,440	10,940	10,714	11,095	11,123	13,033	9,485
O. NICARAGUA	27	50	54	59	64	163	153	59	19
P. PANAMA	32	42	39	46	49	42	46	45	47
Q. PARAGUAY	3	0	4	11	4	6	5	7	15
R. PERU	76	106	100	89	80	146	118	93	68
S. URUGUAY	18	19	13	17	4	17	29	13	7
T. VENEZUELA	17	12	22	33	51	41	44	37	35
LATIN AMERICA	13,031	15,291	12,577	17,210	16,328	19,336	20,569	19,534	15,783

SOURCE: USINS-SY, 1988 (Preliminary), table 68.

Table 1533

NONIMMIGRANTS ADMITTED TO UNITED STATES, BY CLASS OF ADMISSION AND COUNTRY OF CITIZENSHIP, 19 LR
(FY 1988)

Country of Citizenship	All Classes	Foreign Government Officials	Temporary Visitors for Business	Temporary Visitors for Pleasure	Transit Aliens	Treaty Traders and Investors	Students	Spouses and Children of Students	Temporary Workers and Trainees	Spouses and Children of Temporary Trainees
A. ARGENTINA	133,948	1,909	21,746	99,048	1,993	752	1,825	168	1,085	313
B. BOLIVIA	21,724	231	3,856	14,300	994	158	1,055	19	77	23
C. BRAZIL	289,629	2,851	45,729	224,086	2,573	85	4,324	510	945	288
D. CHILE	66,109	959	12,272	45,702	2,302	28	775	134	410	86
E. COLOMBIA	165,303	1,440	27,898	120,579	5,196	944	4,239	184	978	159
F. COSTA RICA	59,513	396	10,064	42,929	3,104	214	818	40	228	24
H. DOMINICAN REP.	65,560	258	14,133	42,625	6,609	10	528	14	734	50
I. ECUADOR	58,840	1,190	7,529	43,800	3,247	10	1,594	46	198	32
J. EL SALVADOR	60,362	1,101	8,668	41,912	5,990	9	1,114	30	295	40
K. GUATEMALA	102,799	556	19,953	75,454	3,293	6	1,045	35	250	29
L. HAITI	94,819	165	17,717	70,640	4,735	1	986	9	175	3
M. HONDURAS	68,583	761	11,059	45,153	8,442	104	1,628	48	98	12
N. MEXICO	992,039	2,158	160,253	785,517	11,662	106	10,234	620	12,045	583
O. NICARAGUA	25,770	71	1,306	20,216	3,335	4	201	9	44	4
P. PANAMA	56,772	499	7,567	41,215	3,276	24	2,698	47	147	51
Q. PARAGUAY	7,670	180	907	5,551	394	76	229	18	18	2
R. PERU	86,315	1,274	11,720	64,263	2,498	15	2,493	109	688	104
S. URUGUAY	18,827	209	3,188	13,439	513	11	194	11	79	19
T. VENEZUELA	176,879	1,680	32,744	127,380	3,766	121	5,242	443	1,134	350
LATIN AMERICA	2,551,461	17,888	418,309	2,307,335	73,920	2,668	40,447	2,494	19,628	2,172

SOURCE: USINS-SY, 1938 (Preliminary), table 43.

Table 1534

TOTAL CHILEAN POPULATION IN PATAGONIA,[1] 1914–80

Population	1914	1947	1960	1970	1980
Total Population	7,903,662	15,893,811	20,013,793	23,364,431	27,949,480
Total Population in Patagonia	106,625	361,553	506,457	705,000	1,032,619
Total Chileans	34,568	51,563	118,165	142,300	215,623
Chileans in Patagonia	21,867	33,137	68,918	83,450	111,552

1. Patagonia comprises the provinces of Neuquén, Río Negro, Chubut, Santa Cruz, and the
    territory of Tierra del Fuego in Argentina.

SOURCE: *International Migration Review*, vol. 27, no. 2, June 1989, p. 245.

Table 1535

CHILEAN POPULATION IN PATAGONIA,[1]
BY ADMINISTRATIVE UNIT
(1988)

District	Number of Chileans	% of Chileans in Total Population	Relative % of Chileans in the District
Patagonia	111,552	10.8	100.0
Neuquén	19,345	7.9	17.3
Chubut	22,554	8.6	20.2
Río Negro	40,739	10.6	36.6
Santa Cruz	21,859	19.0	19.6
Tierra del Fuego	7,055	25.8	6.3

1. Patagonia comprises the provinces of Neuquén, Río Negro, Chubut, Santa Cruz, and
    the territory of Tierra del Fuego in Argentina.

SOURCE: *International Migration Review*, vol. 27, no. 2, June 1989, p. 245.

Table 1536

APPLICATIONS FOR REFUGEE STATUS IN THE UNITED STATES,[1] BY GEOGRAPHIC AREA AND COUNTRY OF CHARGEABILITY,[2] 6 LC, FY 1982–86

Country of Chargeability	Applications Pending Beginning of FY	Applications Filed During FY	Applications Approved During FY	Applications Denied During FY	Applications Otherwise Closed During FY	Applications Pending End of FY
N FY 1982						
D. CHILE	6	7	- -	7	- -	- -
G. CUBA	49	984	580	311	67	26
J. EL SALVADOR	16	16	- -	- -	- -	16
L. HAITI	- -	2	- -	- -	- -	2
M. HONDURAS	- -	2	- -	- -	- -	2
O. NICARAGUA	8	15	- -	7	- -	8
LATIN AMERICA	79	1,026	580	325	67	54
N FY 1983						
A. ARGENTINA	- -	1	- -	1	- -	- -
D. CHILE	- -	4	- -	4	- -	- -
G. CUBA	26	944	710	206	5	23
J. EL SALVADOR	16	20	- -	- -	10	10
L. HAITI	2	2	- -	- -	2	- -
M. HONDURAS	2	3	- -	1	2	- -
O. NICARAGUA	8	11	- -	2	6	3
LATIN AMERICA	54	965	710	214	25	36
N FY 1984						
E. COLOMBIA	- -	3	- -	3	- -	- -
G. CUBA	23	140	57	49	- -	34
J. EL SALVADOR	10	129	96	21	- -	12
N. MEXICO	- -	2	- -	2	- -	- -
O. NICARAGUA	3	58	3	55	- -	- -
LATIN AMERICA	36	332	156	130	- -	46
N FY 1985						
D. CHILE	- -	4	- -	- -	- -	4
G. CUBA	34	2,104	1,865	149	38	54
J. EL SALVADOR	12	12	- -	11	- -	1
O. NICARAGUA	- -	11	3	8	- -	
LATIN AMERICA	46	2,131	1,868	168	36	59
N FY 1986						
G. CUBA	54	105	47	7	49	0
LATIN AMERICA	59	111	47	7	55	2

1. Refers to applications under U.S. Code, Section 207, PL96–212.
2. Refers to refugees "charged" to a country's quota.

SOURCE: USINS-SY, 1982, Ref. 1.3; 1983, p. 73; 1984, p. 71; 1985/86, p. 41.

Table 1537

APPLICATIONS RECEIVED FOR LEGALIZATION AND FARM WORKER PROGRAMS IN THE UNITED STATES
(1987)[a]

Country[1]	%
E. COLOMBIA	1.1
J. EL SALVADOR	6.1
K. GUATEMALA	2.0
L. HAITI	4.9
N. MEXICO	68.9
O. NICARAGUA	1.1

1. Applies to Latin American countries only.

a. Number of applications received between May 5 and Oct. 31, 1987; total number of applications received was 935,547.

SOURCE: *Los Angeles Times*, Nov. 15, 1987.

Table 1538

ALIENS DEPORTED, BY COUNTRY AND CAUSE, 20 LC, FY 1981-88

(N)

Country to Which Deported	Total					Criminal					Violation of Narcotics Laws				
	1981	1984	1985	1986	1988	1981	1984	1985	1986	1988	1981	1984	1985	1986	1988
A. ARGENTINA	28	43	27	50	29	1	2	2	?	1	2	4	3	6	2
B. BOLIVIA	13	48	55	52	23	?	?	1	1	?	3	18	22	16	13
C. BRAZIL	15	36	21	88	71	1	?	1	1	2	?	3	3	15	10
D. CHILE	30	25	21	40	20	?	?	?	?	5	?	2	?	1	3
E. COLOMBIA	368	624	817	1,112	842	1	2	10	14	25	11	115	111	126	221
F. COSTA RICA	23	53	49	54	49	?	1	1	1	1	1	?	2	2	5
G. CUBA	?	2	18	?	?	?	1	1	?	?	?	?	2	?	?
H. DOMINICAN REP.	307	300	184	197	546	8	11	10	14	35	1	9	18	18	164
I. ECUADOR	96	150	139	167	87	?	4	?	3	10	?	7	4	9	20
J. EL SALVADOR	2,333	2,585	3,078	3,690	2,711	2	15	23	53	56	?	5	22	30	146
K. GUATEMALA	557	880	1,649	2,369	2,049	2	2	6	21	19	?	3	8	6	61
L. HAITI	12	35	60	141	151	?	1	1	2	14	1	?	1	4	53
M. HONDURAS	487	469	771	1,074	1,312	?	4	2	9	14	?	4	2	2	17
N. MEXICO	10,452	10,510	11,284	11,384	12,945	96	388	527	842	1,241	70	204	339	523	2,809
O. NICARAGUA	40	41	134	174	36	?	2	?	7	5	?	3	1	1	1
P. PANAMA	44	25	33	51	57	1	1	1	7	?	4	3	5	11	17
Q. PARAGUAY	1	3	8	?	19	?	?	?	?	?	?	?	?	?	7
R. PERU	87	81	118	137	92	?	21	3	3	6	5	12	10	15	12
S. URUGUAY	17	7	18	?	?	?	?	?	?	?	?	?	?	?	?
T. VENEZUELA	18	41	40	46	47	?	1	?	1	?	4	7	?	10	20

Country to Which Deported	Previously Excluded or Deported					Entered Without Proper Documents					Failed to Comply with Conditions of Nonimmigrant Status				
	1981	1984	1985	1986	1988	1981	1984	1985	1986	1988	1981	1984	1985	1986	1988
A. ARGENTINA	?	?	?	?	?	1	1	?	?	2	17	24	11	24	11
B. BOLIVIA	1	?	?	?	?	?	1	?	1	?	7	18	22	7	4
C. BRAZIL	1	?	?	?	1	?	1	?	1	1	8	23	13	30	12
D. CHILE	3	?	?	?	1	1	?	1	1	1	14	12	9	22	?
E. COLOMBIA	5	3	3	11	12	8	7	7	7	4	72	136	149	127	94
F. COSTA RICA	?	1	?	1	2	?	1	1	2	?	10	13	13	9	8
G. CUBA	?	?	?	?	?	?	?	1	?	?	?	?	1	?	?
H. DOMINICAN REP.	9	4	6	3	4	14	14	8	7	14	32	37	40	35	32
I. ECUADOR	?	3	?	?	2	?	4	?	2	?	33	53	35	23	8
J. EL SALVADOR	4	4	8	14	19	24	7	14	11	4	29	17	18	33	9
K. GUATEMALA	3	4	3	11	5	10	6	3	7	8	25	24	36	36	10
L. HAITI	?	?	1	?	?	1	5	1	1	19	9	13	14	19	16
M. HONDURAS	?	2	4	5	7	3	3	?	5	7	369	30	51	8	21
N. MEXICO	55	68	96	133	317	318	246	301	242	238	138	194	231	276	135
O. NICARAGUA	?	?	?	?	?	3	?	?	1	?	3	7	11	8	?
P. PANAMA	6	?	?	1	2	6	?	3	?	2	11	9	19	14	11
Q. PARAGUAY	?	?	?	?	?	?	?	?	?	?	1	2	?	?	1
R. PERU	4	1	?	1	2	4	3	1	1	?	37	25	38	35	13
S. URUGUAY	?	?	1	?	?	?	?	?	?	?	4	5	8	?	?
T. VENEZUELA	?	?	1	?	?	?	?	?	1	?	10	25	14	18	11

Table 1538 (Continued)

ALIENS DEPORTED, BY COUNTRY AND CAUSE, 20 LC, FY 1981–88

(N)

Country to Which Deported	Entered Without Inspection or by False Statements				
	1981	1984	1985	1986	1988
A. ARGENTINA	8	12	11	20	13
B. BOLIVIA	2	11	10	27	6
C. BRAZIL	5	9	4	42	45
D. CHILE	11	11	11	15	10
E. COLOMBIA	270	361	537	824	483
F. COSTA RICA	12	37	33	39	33
G. CUBA	~	1	13	~	~
H. DOMINICAN REP.	243	225	102	117	296
I. ECUADOR	63	79	35	130	47
J. EL SALVADOR	2,274	2,536	2,992	3,546	2,476
K. GUATEMALA	517	841	1,592	2,284	1,946
L. HAITI	1	16	41	114	47
M. HONDURAS	114	425	712	1,017	1,244
N. MEXICO	9,765	9,362	9,782	9,308	8,140
O. NICARAGUA	34	32	122	163	34
P. PANAMA	19	12	25	18	20
Q. PARAGUAY	~	1	8	~	11
R. PERU	41	37	65	82	58
S. URUGUAY	13	2	8	~	~
T. VENEZUELA	4	8	11	17	16

SOURCE: USINS unpublished data; USINS-SY, 1985, p. 198; 1986-87, p. 110; 1988 (Preliminary), table 69.

Table 1539

EXIT OF NATIONAL TOURISTS, 14 LC, 1970–76

(N)

Country	1970	1971	1972	1973	1974	1975	1976
B. BOLIVIA	42,948	55,022	68,261	76,859	87,220	~	~

Continued in SALA, 20-3209.

Table 1540

RECEIPTS FROM TOURISM,[1] 19 LC, 1965-85

(M US)

	Country	1965	1970	1975	1979	1980	1981	1982	1983	1984	1985
A.	ARGENTINA	~	74.0	154	279	345	510	516	651[‡]	~	673[*]
B.	BOLIVIA	2	2.6	19	37	40	36	30	35[‡]	~	36
C.	BRAZIL	30	30.0	72	132	1,794	1,727	1,608[a]	1,533	1,512	1,739
D.	CHILE	45	50.0	83	127	166	192	118	85	104	112[*]
E.	COLOMBIA	28	54.0	164	358	357	384	231	235	209	229[*]
F.	COSTA RICA	~	22.1	52	71	87	94	131	131	117	118
H.	DOMINICAN REP.	3	16.4	61	131	168	~	~	260	277	297
I.	ECUADOR	7	8.5	29	80	91	~	~	120	120	130
J.	EL SALVADOR	~	8.5	18	14	7	4	7	4	5	10
K.	GUATEMALA	6	12.1	78	201	183	131	87	62	57	67
L.	HAITI[3]	1	8.7	22	63	65	~	~	~	~	69
M.	HONDURAS	~	4.1	11	29	27[†]	~	~	45	~	24[*]
N.	MEXICO	782	1,454.0	2,171	1,443	1,671	1,760	1,406	1,625	3,282	2,900
O.	NICARAGUA	~	13.2	26	18	22	23	20	5	~	5[*]
P.	PANAMA	~	78.1	133	164	167	171	169	171	186	200
Q.	PARAGUAY	~	14.2	10	69	91	80	54	49	96	80
R.	PERU	25	52.0	91	202	334	257	257	253	258	278[*]
S.	URUGUAY	~	40.8	57	223	298	283[b]	149[b]	47	107	129
T.	VENEZUELA	15	50.0	180	265	246	251	264[‡]	257[‡]	~	367
	UNITED STATES[2]	1,380	2,330.0	4,842	8,335	10,058	12,163	11,293	11,187	11,386	~

1. Travel receipts are defined by the International Monetary Fund to include receipts for
   goods and services provided to foreigners visiting the reporting country, including
   transportation within that country. Includes funds spent by tourists, business
   travelers, students, patients undergoing medical treatment, military personnel on
   leave, and traveling government officials. In many cases, comparable data for a
   national series are not available throughout the period covered by the table, and
   also close comparisons between countries are often rendered difficult by the lack
   of uniformity in definitions and scope.
2. For all countries figures cover the following categories of travelers who are formally
   admitted into the United States as non-immigrant aliens: temporary visitors for
   pleasure, students, temporary visitors for business, foreign government officials and
   their employees and families, treaty traders and investors, representatives to
   international organizations, and miscellaneous minor groups. These figures do not
   include less formally admitted visitors arriving from Mexico for less than three days.
3. Fiscal year ending September 30.

a. International tourism receipts for 1982 have been estimated by EMBRATUR through
   sample survey based parameters.
b. Calculated on the basis of the average rate of the dollar in Dec. 1982.

SOURCE: UN-SY, 1972 and 1973, table 153; UN-SY, 1975, table 164; UN-SY, 1976,
   table 161; UN-SY, 1977, table 163; UN-SY, 1978, table 162; WTO-WTS, 1978/79,
   table 20; WTO-WTS, 1979/80, payments section. WTO-WTS, 1981/82, table 15;
   World Travel and Tourism Statistics, Vol. 38, 1983–84; UN-SY, 1983/84, table 169;
   World Travel and Tourism Statistics, Vol. 39, 1985–86.

Table 1541

TOURIST ARRIVALS, 19 L, 1970–87

					Tourist Arrivals[1]					
	Country	1970	1975	1980	1981	1982	1983	1984	1985	1986	1987
A.	ARGENTINA	694,940	1,200,000	~	~	1,296,244	1,312,952	1,608,207	1,503,099	727,723	~
B.	BOLIVIA	22,248	72,943	155,412	155,602	150,142	175,903	163,183	127,027	133,169	~
C.	BRAZIL	244,900	517,967	1,625,422	1,357,879	1,146,881	1,420,481	1,595,726	1,735,982	1,934,091	~
D.	CHILE	198,824	235,624	493,328	401,708	276,658	284,653	362,416	418,050	581,117	575,221
E.	COLOMBIA	161,668	443,264	1,227,666	1,059,630	1,127,662	506,883	715,277	784,028	732,200	~
F.	COSTA RICA	154,867	297,207	345,470	333,102	371,582	325,593	273,901	261,552	260,840	~
H.	DOMINICAN REP.	~	16,918	17,406	17,438	18,775	21,180	22,256	20,433	~	~
I.	ECUADOR	57,548	172,945	244,485	226,297	217,008	192,921	219,232	238,105	266,761	~
J.	EL SALVADOR	137,804	266,016	118,700	82,500	98,800	106,100	104,477	133,206	~	~
K.	GUATEMALA	173,652	454,436	466,041	328,878	233,881	235,166	191,934	251,946	287,460	~
L.	HAITI	62,304	79,150	136,056	139,235	135,000	144,646	141,379	~	~	~
M.	HONDURAS[2]	145,800	164,462	145,955	230,678	183,037	165,153	~	~	~	~
N.	MEXICO	2,250,000	3,218,000	4,144,249	4,038,000	3,767,600	4,749,000	4,655,000	4,207,000	4,625,000	~
O.	NICARAGUA	132,000	189,100	~	~	~	~	~	~	~	~
P.	PANAMA[3]	~	283,983	377,629	346,709	336,301	298,912	304,576	314,902	318,489	282,516
Q.	PARAGUAY	119,239	81,113	281,372	241,132	150,542	116,466	239,348	211,732	298,039	240,654
R.	PERU	133,546	256,210	372,390	334,819	316,873	273,324	278,783	299,958	303,279	330,110
S.	URUGUAY	567,300	593,515	1,066,694	927,666	621,732	614,332	855,407	902,100	994,739	~
T.	VENEZUELA	116,962	292,384	215,042	200,035	196,779	199,962	233,202	268,735	527,179	614,813
	Total	5,373,602	18,484,762	12,799,027	10,421,308	6,917,897	12,191,627	11,870,304	16,289,921	11,409,550	1,468,668

		% of Total				AA–GR			
	Country	1970	1975	1980	1987	1970–75	1980–85	1985–86	1986–87
A.	ARGENTINA	9.87	11.08	~	~	11.54	~	−51.59	~
B.	BOLIVIA	.32	.67	1.03	~	26.81	−3.95	4.48	~
C.	BRAZIL	3.48	4.78	10.81	~	16.16	1.32	11.41	~
D.	CHILE	2.82	2.18	3.28	~	3.45	−3.26	−99.86	−1.01
E.	COLOMBIA	2.30	4.09	8.17	~	22.35	−8.58	−6.61	~
F.	COSTA RICA	2.20	2.74	2.30	~	13.93	−5.41	−.27	~
H.	DOMINICAN REP.	~	.16	.12	~	~	3.26	~	~
I.	ECUADOR	.82	1.60	1.63	~	24.62	−.53	12.04	~
J.	EL SALVADOR	1.96	2.46	.79	~	14.06	2.33	~	~
K.	GUATEMALA	2.47	4.20	3.10	~	21.22	−11.57	14.10	~
L.	HAITI	.88	.73	.91	~	4.90	~	~	~
M.	HONDURAS[2]	2.07	1.52	.97	~	2.44	~	~	~
N.	MEXICO	31.94	29.72	27.57	~	7.42	.30	9.94	~
O.	NICARAGUA	1.87	1.75	~	~	7.45	~	~	~
P.	PANAMA[3]	0	2.62	2.51	~	~	−3.57	1.14	−11.29
Q.	PARAGUAY	1.69	.75	1.87	~	−7.42	−5.53	40.76	−19.25
R.	PERU	1.90	2.37	2.48	~	13.92	~	1.11	~
S.	URUGUAY	8.05	5.48	7.10	~	.91	−3.30	10.27	~
T.	VENEZUELA	1.66	2.70	1.43	~	20.11	4.56	96.17	16.62
	Total	76.3	70.52	76.07	~	203.87	−33.93	246.63	−14.93

1. Tourist arrivals by air and sea.
2. Includes excursionists.
3. Includes passengers in transit with one– and two–day stays.

SOURCE: OAS-SB, July–December, 1987, pp. 86–87, table A-21.

Table 1542

TOURIST ENTRY,[1] BY MEANS OF TRANSPORTATION, 18 LC, 1970–83

(%)

	Recipient Country	Means	1970	1975	1977	1978	1979	1980	1981	1982	1983
A.	ARGENTINA	Air	45.0	40.9[†]	69.0[†]	68.3[†]	69.8	~	~	40.4	27.69
		Land	15.4	17.3[†]	~[†]	~	~	~	~	38.8	33.07
		Sea	1.3	.7[†]	24.9[†]	25.4	24.1	~	~	20.8	39.24
		Other	38.4[b]	41.1[b,†]	6.1	6.3[†]	6.1	~	~	#	#

Continued in SALA, 25–1522.

Table 1543

VISITOR GROSS EXPENDITURES, 19 L, 1970–87

(M US)

	Country	Visitor Gross Expenditures									
		1970	1975	1980	1981	1982	1983	1984	1985	1986	1987
A.	ARGENTINA	73.50	154.40	344.80	510.00	610.30	434.00	602.00	522.00	~	~
B.	BOLIVIA	~	~	~	~	30.00	47.00	32.00	30.00	30.00	~
C.	BRAZIL	~	571.80	1,794.36	1,726.73	1,607.74	1,532.65	1,511.51	1,492.64	1,527.22	~
D.	CHILE	49.50	76.30	344.80	510.00	610.30	434.00	602.40	522.00	~	~
E.	COLOMBIA	~	~	672.86	760.26	231.09	234.98	209.13	286.46	220.67	~
F.	COSTA RICA	~	~	81.00	93.70	123.00	114.00	119.00	113.60	132.70	~
H.	DOMINICAN REP.	~	~	2.92	3.17	4.03	4.50	4.50	4.50	~	~
I.	ECUADOR	~	28.80	~	~	~	~	120.00	120.00	~	~
J.	EL SALVADOR	~	17.08	6.83	4.37	5.81	4.00	5.00	~	~	~
K.	GUATEMALA	21.70	85.90	183.50	131.20	87.00	62.00	57.00	~	~	~
L.	HAITI	~	~	~	~	~	~	~	~	~	~
M.	HONDURAS[2]	~	10.70	24.50	30.50	~	45.00	~	~	~	~
N.	MEXICO	1,465.10	2,724.80	5,393.40	6,530.00	3,682.10	3,251.30	1,952.70	1,719.70	1,791.70	~
O.	NICARAGUA	~	~	~	~	~	~	~	~	~	~
P.	PANAMA[3]	40.88	93.37	171.15	174.89	173.69	171.81	188.60	207.88	204.69	187 85
Q.	PARAGUAY	14.23	12.38	90.67	80.15	58.91	48.78	96.34	105.07	148.00	102.00
R.	PERU	44.03	97.25	292.00	262.00	251.00	210.00	125.00	231.00	301.86	393.16
S.	URUGUAY	42.60	98.10	297.60	283.40	106.00	89.70	210.00	235.20	257.80	~
T.	VENEZUELA	~	~	243.00	251.00	299.00	~	~	~	~	~
	Total	1,751.24	3,872.28	9,943.30	11,351.37	7,879.97	6,756.72	5,835.18	5,469.41	9,118.62	1,366.02

	Country	% of Total				AA–GR[1]			
		1975	1980	1986	1987	1970–75	1980–85	1985–86	1986–87
A.	ARGENTINA	3.31	3.01	~	~	16.00	~	~	~
B.	BOLIVIA	~	~	.59	~	~	~	0	~
C.	BRAZIL	12.27	15.67	30.19	~	~	–3.62	2.32	~
D.	CHILE	1.64	3.01	~	~	9.04	~	~	~
E.	COLOMBIA	~	5.88	~	~	~	–15.70	~	~
F.	COSTA RICA	~	~	2.62	~	~	7.00	16.81	~
H.	DOMINICAN REP.	~	.03	~	~	~	9.04	~	~
I.	ECUADOR	.62	~	~	~	~	~	~	~
J.	EL SALVADOR	.37	.06	~	~	~	~	~	~
K.	GUATEMALA	1.84	1.60	~	~	31.68	~	~	~
L.	HAITI	~	~	~	~	~	~	~	~
M.	HONDURAS[2]	.23	.21	~	~	~	~	~	~
N.	MEXICO	58.46	47.10	35.42	~	13.21	–20.44	4.19	~
O.	NICARAGUA	~	~	~	~	~	~	~	~
P.	PANAMA[3]	2.00	1.49	4.05	~	17.96	3.97	–1.53	–8.23
Q.	PARAGUAY	.27	.79	2.93	~	–2.75	2.99	40.86	–31.08
R.	PERU	2.09	2.55	5.97	~	~	–4.58	30.67	30.25
S.	URUGUAY	2.10	2.60	5.10	~	18.15	–4.60	9.61	~
T.	VENEZUELA	~	2.12	~	~	~	~	~	~
	Total	99.73	86.12	86.87	~	103.29	–25.94	102.93	–9.06

1. Tourist arrivals by air and sea.
2. Includes excursionists.
3. Includes passengers in transit with one– and two–day stays.

SOURCE: OAS-SB, July–December, 1987, pp. 90–91, table A-23.

Table 1544

TOURIST AVERAGE LENGTH OF STAY, 1980–85

	Country	1980	1981	1982	1983	1984	1985
A.	ARGENTINA	~	~	~	~	~	~
B.	BOLIVIA	~	~	3	3	3	3
C.	BRAZIL	15	15	16	14	14	14
D.	CHILE	3	3	3	3	3	3
E.	COLOMBIA	8	~	~	~	~	~
F.	COSTA RICA	~	~	~	~	~	~
H.	DOMINICAN REP.	3	3	3	3	3	3
I.	ECUADOR	2	2	3	3	~	~
J.	EL SALVADOR	3	3	3	~	~	~
K.	GUATEMALA	10	10	6	6	~	~
L.	HAITI	~	~	~	~	~	~
M.	HONDURAS	~	~	3	4	~	~
N.	MEXICO	10	10	10	9	10	9
O.	NICARAGUA	~	~	~	~	~	~
P.	PANAMA	~	~	~	~	~	~
Q.	PARAGUAY	3	3	3	3	3	3
R.	PERU	14	14	14	~	~	~
S.	URUGUAY	18	15	18	18	18	18
T.	VENEZUELA	~	~	9	~	~	~
	TOTAL	89	78	94	66	54	53

SOURCE: OAS-SB, July-December, 1986, p. 94, table A-24.

Table 1545

HOTELS, ROOMS, AND BEDS, 12 L, 1980–87

(N)

Country	Number							
	1980	1981	1982	1983	1984	1985	1986	1987
A. ARGENTINA								
Hotels, Motels	~	~	~	4,440	~	~	~	~
Rooms	~	~	~	109,269	~	~	~	~
Beds	~	~	~	256,670	~	~	~	~
B. BOLIVIA								
Hotels, Motels	341	336	348	344	352	357	364	~
Rooms	8,220	8,315	8,539	8,561	8,576	8,600	8,768	~
Beds	14,943	15,515	15,809	15,845	16,005	16,049	16,296	~
C. BRAZIL								
Hotels, Motels	1,255	1,482	1,611	1,707	1,810	1,937	2,018	~
Rooms	80,481	93,062	99,854	105,342	110,872	116,702	120,550	~
Beds	160,962	186,124	199,708	210,684	221,744	233,404	241,100	~
D. CHILE								
Hotels, Motels	576	685	634	622	609	599	618	~
Rooms	15,164	17,599	152,670	160,466	157,749	157,749	159,364	~
Beds	34,399	38,458	319,553	336,914	331,401	331,401	339,581	~
I. ECUADOR								
Hotels, Motels	~	~	~	~	~	1,052	~	~
Rooms	~	~	~	23,585	22,795	23,291	~	~
Beds	~	~	~	41,795	40,639	42,079	~	~
K. GUATEMALA								
Hotels, Motels	303	297	307	292	~	~	~	~
Rooms	7,513	7,337	7,514	7,615	7,871	7,751	~	~
Beds	~	~	~	15,742	15,230	~	~	~
M. HONDURAS								
Hotels, Motels	~	~	~	160	~	~	~	~
Rooms	~	~	~	4,441	~	~	~	~
Beds	~	~	~	8,077	~	~	~	~
N. MEXICO								
Hotels, Motels	7,838	8,028	8,268	8,293	5,310	6,761	6,822	~
Rooms	237,564	246,356	257,221	263,231	262,475	300,500	305,543	~
Beds	~	~	~	~	~	~	~	~
P. PANAMA								
Hotels, Motels	~	~	21	19	20	23	23	24
Rooms	~	~	2,888	2,791	2,849	3,006	2,909	3,119
Beds	~	~	~	5,586	5,684	~	~	~
Q. PARAGUAY								
Hotels, Motels	~	~	107	105	105	112	139	145
Rooms	~	~	3,076	3,177	3,280	3,420	3,892	4,159
Beds	~	~	6,806	6,985	6,938	3,892	8,206	9,219
R. PERU								
Hotels, Motels	~	~	1,569	1,523	1,627	1,666	1,703	~
Rooms	~	~	41,301	40,573	42,231	43,021	43,969	~
Beds	~	~	70,822	71,685	74,504	76,494	78,314	~
S. URUGUAY								
Hotels, Motels	286	286	286	286	232	232	287	~
Rooms	11,293	11,293	11,293	11,293	9,166	9,166	~	~
Beds	25,104	25,104	25,104	24,937	22,131	22,131	24,327	~

SOURCE: OAS-SB, July–December, 1986, pp. 95–97, table A-25; July–December, 1987, pp. 93–95, table A-25.

Table 1546

LODGING ESTABLISHMENTS CAPACITY,[1] 16 LC, 1982–84

(N)

		1982		1983		1984	
	Country	Rooms	Beds	Rooms	Beds	Rooms	Beds
A.	ARGENTINA	~	~	109,269	256,670	~	~
B.	BOLIVIA	~	~	3,424	6,300	3,405	6,437
C.	BRAZIL[2]	99,854	199,708	105,342	210,684	110,872	221,744
D.	CHILE	14,293	31,913	14,494	15,010	32,450	32,595
E.	COLOMBIA[2]	15,439	41,840	13,922	30,869	14,230	31,512
F.	COSTA RICA	3,804	7,608	~	~	~	~
G.	CUBA	~	~	14,061	27,422	13,335	29,359
I.	ECUADOR	~	~	23,585	41,795	22,793	40,639
J.	EL SALVADOR	1,740	2,585	1,701	2,597	1,742	2,678
K.	GUATEMALA[2]	7,514	15,028	7,615	15,742	7,871	15,230
M.	HONDURAS	~	~	~	~	4,441	8,077
N.	MEXICO	~	~	216,831	~	~	~
P.	PANAMA[2]	2,916	5,213	2,793	5,586	2,842	5,684
Q.	PARAGUAY	2,786	6,135	2,899	6,460	3,005	6,271
R.	PERU	~	~	40,573	71,595	42,316	74,512
S.	URUGUAY[2]	11,293	25,114	11,293	25,104	9,166	22,131
	UNITED STATES[2]	~	~	2,500,000	~	5,000,000	~

1. Unless otherwise indicated, figures refer to lodging establishments called hotels and motels.
2. Hotels only.

SOURCE: *World Travel and Tourism Statistics*, Vol. 38, 1983–84.

Table 1547

COLOMBIA FIRST CLASS HOTELS, BY REGION, 1986

Region	Hotels (N)	%	Rooms (N)	%
North Coast				
Cartagena	7		1,220	
San Andrés Island	6		651	
Barranquilla	4		513	
Santa Marta	2		266	
Guajira (Riohacha)	1		99	
Cordoba (Monteria)	1		66	
Cesar (Valledupar)	1		54	
Total	22	34.4	2,869	32.5
Central				
Bogotá	10		2,148	
Boyacá Province	3		205	
Giradot	2		181	
Ibague	1		136	
Neiva	1		70	
Meta (Villavicencio)	1		117	
Total	18	28.1	2,857	32.3
Western				
Medellín	6		923	
Cali	5		742	
Pereira	1		240	
Manizales	1		100	
Pasto	2		128	
Buenaventura	1		76	
Buga	1		64	
Popayan	1		50	
Total	18	28.1	2,323	26.3
Northeastern				
Cucuta	4		511	
Bucaramanga	1		200	
San Gil	1		73	
Total	6	9.4	784	8.9
Total	64	100.0	8,833	100.0

SOURCE: *Colombia Today*, vol. 22, no. 10, 1987.

Table 1548

COLOMBIA TOURISM EARNINGS, 1986

Region of Origin	M US	%
South America	97.8	44.3
North America	60.0	27.2
Europe	44.2	20.0
Central America	12.5	5.7
Caribbean Islands	1.5	.7
Rest of the World (Asia, Africa and Oceania)	4.6	2.1
Total	220.6	100.0

SOURCE: *Colombia Today*, vol. 22, no. 10, 1987.

Table 1549

TOURIST ARRIVALS TO CUBA, 1950–76[a]
(T)

Year	N	Year	N
1950	168.0	1957	272.3

Continued in SALA, 23-3315.

Table 1550

PARAGUAY TOURISTS, BY COUNTRY OF ORIGIN, 1980–87

Category	1980	1981	1982	1983	1984	1985	1986	1987[†]
Total Tourists	302.1	267.1	178.4	147.8	292.0	262.7	370.7	303.2
Argentina	132.6	122.5	56.9	47.1	141.3	107.2	155.7	116.2
Brazil	104.8	92.1	93.8	70.3	97.6	93.4	124.5	67.0
United States	3.3	4.3	3.9	3.5	7.5	6.2	7.8	10.1
Japan	3.9	2.5	1.0	1.9	2.7	2.8	3.4	4.9
Uruguay	3.9	7.5	5.4	3.1	10.2	4.6	18.4	25.3
Other Countries	53.6	38.2	17.9	22.1	32.7	40.9	60.9	79.7
Average Stay (Days)	3.3	3.3	3.3	3.3	3.0	3.0	3.0	4.7
Total Sales (M US)	300	300	330	332	330	399	400	400

SOURCE: ECLA-S, 1987, p. 552.

16

Construction, Housing, and Utilities

DEFINITIONS OF TERMS

STAGES OF CONSTRUCTION
Construction Authorized. Building projects for the carrying out of which a permit has been issued.
Construction Completed. It is considered that the work is completed when the building or other structure is physically ready to be occupied or to be put into use.

TYPE OF BUILDING ACTIVITY
Building. A building is any independent structure comprising one or more rooms or other spaces, covered by a roof, enclosed with external walls or dividing walls, which extend from the foundation to the roof and intended for residential, industrial, commercial, educational, or other purposes.
Residential building. A building should be regarded as residential when the major part of the building (i.e., more than half of its floor area) is used for dwelling purposes.
One- or two-dwelling buildings. Detached, semi-detached, row, and terraced buildings with one or two dwellings on one or more floors.
Multi-dwelling buildings. All residential buildings other than one- or two-dwelling buildings.
Non-residential buildings. A building should be regarded as non-residential when less than half of its floor area is used for dwelling purposes.
    Industrial buildings. All buildings which are used to house the production, assembly, and warehousing activities of industrial establishments, i.e., factories, plants, workshops, etc.
    Commercial buildings. Office buildings and all buildings which are intended for use primarily in wholesale, retail, and service trades, i.e., hotels, restaurants, shops, warehouses, public garages, etc.
    Educational buildings. All buildings which are intended for use directly in instructional activities, furnishing academic and technical courses, i.e., schools, universities, etc., as well as museums, art galleries, libraries, etc.
    Health buildings. All buildings which are primarily engaged in providing hospital and institutional care, i.e., hospitals, infirmaries, sanitariums, etc.
Other Buildings. Buildings which are not included in any of the above classifications, i.e., non-residential farm buildings, stadiums, recreational buildings, etc.

FLOOR AREA OF BUILDINGS
The sum of the area of each floor of the building measured to the outer surface of the outer walls including the area of lobbies, cellars, elevator shafts, and in multi-dwelling buildings all the common spaces. Areas of balconies are excluded.

DWELLING
A dwelling is a room or a suite of rooms and its accessories in a permanent building or a structurally separated part which is intended for private habitation. It should have a separate access to a street or to a common space within the buildings. Detached rooms for habitation which are clearly built to be used as a part of the dwelling should be counted as part of the dwelling.

Table 1600

NEW BUILDING CONSTRUCTION AUTHORIZED AND COMPLETED, 17 LC, 1973–85

(N)

Country	Code[1]	1973	1975	1977	1979	1980	1981	1982	1983	1984	1985
A. ARGENTINA	I[a]	101,593	143,483	54,198	95,811	102,842	92,635	80,879	80,783	81,323	~
	II	~	~	~	~	~	~	~	~	~	~
C. BRAZIL	I[b,c]	108,154	112,169	116,555	137,615	162,217	132,222	170,716	122,036	101,710	82,268
	II[b]	60,019	63,086	64,479	89,567	90,026	88,910	107,590	98,135	74,812	67,181
D. CHILE	I	~	~	~	~	~	~	~	~	~	~
	II	~	~	~	~	~	~	~	~	~	~
E. COLOMBIA	I[c]	17,706	13,768	16,040	14,984	15,194	16,183	16,585	16,872	16,614	17,133
	II	~	~	~	~	~	~	~	~	~	~
F. COSTA RICA	I[d,e]	11,027	14,316	13,878	15,269	15,958	11,385	11,614	11,334	5,311	12,338
	II	~	~	~	~	~	~	~	~	~	~
G. CUBA	I[z]	~	~	~	1,558	1,568	28,112	27,784	27,917	31,027	32,952
	II	~	~	~	~	~	~	~	~	~	~
H. DOMINICAN REP.	I[f]	3,059	5,331	4,656	8,286	9,577	12,940	10,583	8,085	6,287	4,429
	II	~	~	~	~	~	~	~	~	~	~
I. ECUADOR	I[c,g]	5,869	7,699	8,824	9,726	9,612	10,494	11,585	11,978	18,103	25,589
	II	~	~	~	~	~	~	~	~	~	~
J. EL SALVADOR	I[c,h]	2,016	2,463	1,521	4,124	5,290	10,957	17,337	12,672	4,267	6,486
	II[i]	2,851	2,744	4,203	5,264	3,183	3,031	7,227	8,649	9,091	7,943
K. GUATEMALA	I[e,u]	1,618	1,701	2,432	1,904	1,529	1,222	1,793	1,734	1,509	3,989[c,k]
	II[e,v]	975	1,034	950	1,008	750	877	851	674	500	~
L. HAITI	I[c,j,x]	369	320	445	428	364	310	250	117	156	161[k]
	II[e,j]	408	398	527	553	620	597	358	449	479	464
M. HONDURAS[1,2]	I[k,y]	1,143	1,683	1,727	1,593	2,271	2,858	5,122	1,773	1,773	1,242
	II[k,y]	1,219	1,683	1,727	1,593	2,271	~	~	~	~	~
O. NICARAGUA	I[t]	478	1,789	1,162	168	356	1,017	1,259	419	870	~
	II	~	~	~	~	~	~	~	~	~	~
P. PANAMA	I[l,s]	1,621	506	872	1,184	952	878	1,094	841	1,743	1,278
	II[l,s]	~	~	~	3,426	2,948	2,830	3,207	3,060	4,081	2,954
Q. PARAGUAY	I	~	~	~	~	~	~	~	~	~	~
	II	~	~	~	~	~	~	~	~	~	~
S. URUGUAY	I[m]	514	515	1,120	~	1,629	1,900	1,565	1,124	1,320	1,439
	II	~	~	~	~	~	~	~	~	~	2,283[y]

Table 1600 (Continued)

NEW BUILDING CONSTRUCTION AUTHORIZED AND COMPLETED, 17 LC, 1973–85

(N)

Country	Code[1]	1973	1975	1977	1979	1980	1981	1982	1983	1984	1985
T. VENEZUELA	I[c,n]	5,229	5,512	5,778	4,495	5,661	4,687	3,678	2,807	2,860	2,811
	II	~	~	~	~	~	~	~	~	~	~
UNITED STATES	I[o,p,q]	1,402.4[r]	1,052.9[r]	1,602.1[r]	1,494.4[r]	1,137.3[r]	986.5[r]	979.8[r]	1,402.7[r]	1,475.3[r]	1,504.3
	II	~	~	~	~	~	~	~	~	~	~

1. Code: I = New building construction authorized.
   II = New buildings completed.
2. Data on construction authorized and completed refer to private construction in Tegucigalpa, San Pedro Sola, and La Ceiba.

a. For 1977 and 1978 data refer to the capital and Greater Buenos Aires.
b. Including reconstruction and alterations.
c. Data refer to buildings for which a building permit has been issued.
d. Data based on building permits issued by the municipalities.
e. Number of works.
f. Data cover only the urban areas of the country.
g. Including reconstructions.
h. Permits issued by the municipalities to private enterprises and individuals. Construction work done by the Instituto de Vivienda Urbana and the Instituto de Colonización Rural are excluded.
i. Data provided by the Dirección General de Servicios Eléctricos.
j. Data relating to construction authorized and completed cover the municipalities of Port-au-Prince and Petion Ville.
k. Year ending 30 September of the year stated.
l. New construction excluding extensions.
m. Data obtained from the Intendencia Municipal de Montevideo and refer to new construction, restoration, and conversion in the capital.
n. Data refer to private building construction.

o. Data do not include buildings constructed in areas not requiring building permits and represent, therefore, only about 92% of the actual number of all buildings stated. Prior to 1978, construction authorized in building permit–issuing places were based on a universe of 14,000 places. In 1978, the universe was increased to 16,000, accounting for an increase of about 7% in total new building construction authorized. In 1984, it was increased to 17,000, accounting for an increase of about 1%.
p. Excluding publicly owned structures.
q. Excluding extensions.
r. Thousands.
s. Data for construction authorized are based on permits supplied by the Oficina de Seguridad and refer to new private construction in Panama City. Data for construction completed refer to new private construction authorized in 21 districts of Panama, including the districts of Panamá and Colón.
t. Data on construction authorized refer to building activity in Managua only.
u. Beginning in 1981, data refer to private building activity in the Greater Metropolitan Area of Guatemala City. Prior to 1981, data refer to Guatemala City only.
v. Data refer to private building activity in Guatemala City.
w. Residential buildings only.
x. Data are for October 1–August 31.
y. Data for 1985 exclude Montevideo and Maldonado.
z. Beginning 1981, including own account construction by individuals.

SOURCE: UN-YCS, 1973–85. For earlier years see previous issues of SALA.

Table 1601

ARGENTINA NEW BUILDING CONSTRUCTION AUTHORIZED, 1982–85[a]

Category	Unit	1982	1983	1984	1985
All Buildings					
Number	N	80,879	80,783	81,223	~
Floor Area	T Me[2]	10,369	10,118.5	10,606.8	~

a. For earlier years see previous issues of SALA.

SOURCE: UN-YCS, 1973–85.

Table 1602

BRAZIL NEW BUILDING CONSTRUCTION AUTHORIZED AND NEW BUILDINGS COMPLETED, 1982–85[a]

Category	Unit	1982	1983	1984	1985
I. New Building Construction Authorized[1,2]					
All Buildings					
Number	N	170,716	122,036	101,710	82,268
Floor Area	T Me^2	39,254	30,754	23,487	23,430
Tender Value	T NC	~	~	~	~
Residential					
Number	N	163,584	114,453	94,492	74,402
Floor Area	T Me^2	33,155	24,836	18,191	18,051
Non-Residential					
Number	N	7,132	7,583	7,218	7,866
Floor Area	T Me^2	6,099	5,918	5,296	5,379
Industrial					
Number	N	720	669	589	6,33
Floor Area	T Me^2	897	813	806	759
Commercial					
Number	N	5,065	5,444	5,145	5,528
Floor Area	T Me^2	3,920	3,903	3,478	3,362
Educational					
Number	N	173	180	172	197
Floor Area	T Me^2	217	220	200	296
Health					
Number	N	55	54	50	73
Floor Area	T Me^2	130	75	72	85
Other					
Number	N	1,119	1,236	1,262	1,435
Floor Area	T Me^2	935	907	740	877
II. New Buildings Completed[1,3]					
All Buildings					
Number	N	107,590	98,135	74,812	67,181
Floor Area	T Me^2	23,917	20,993	18,002	15,840
Value	T NC	~	~	~	~
Residential					
Number	N	103,469	93,936	70,217	62,164
Floor Area	T Me^2	20,404	17,628	14,304	12,069
Non-Residential					
Number	N	4,121	4,199	4,595	5,017
Floor Area	T Me^2	3,513	3,365	3,698	3,771
Industrial					
Number	N	507	444	466	475
Floor Area	T Me^2	678	584	704	793
Commercial					
Number	N	2,978	3,035	3,334	3,681
Floor Area	T Me^2	2,350	2,225	2,293	2,203
Educational					
Number	N	97	134	137	112
Floor Area	T Me^2	140	192	174	149
Health					
Number	N	36	31	28	45
Floor Area	T Me^2	40	32	58	90
Other					
Number	N	503	555	630	704
Floor Area	T Me^2	305	332	469	536

1. Including reconstruction and alterations.
2. Data for construction authorized refer to buildings for which a building permit has been issued.
3. Information covers buildings for which occupancy permits have been issued, although in some cities occupancy permits are not required after completion.

a. For earlier years see previous issues of SALA.

SOURCE: UN-YCS, 1973–85.

Table 1603

CHILE NEW BUILDING CONSTRUCTION AUTHORIZED AND NEW BUILDINGS COMPLETED, 1982–85[a]

Category	Unit	1982	1983	1984	1985
I. New Building Construction Authorized[1,2]					
All Buildings					
Floor Area	T Me^2	1,941.2	2,292.5	2,656.5	3,707.3
Tender Value	M NC	14,518.8	19,504	25,165	43,629
Residential					
Floor Area	T Me^2	1,308.9	1,770.3	2,105.3	2,953
Tender Value	M NC	9,810.1	15,570	19,703	34,727
Non-Residential					
Floor Area	T Me^2	632.3	522.2	551.2	754.3
Tender Value	M NC	4,708.7	3,934	5,462	8,902
Industrial[3]					
Floor Area	T Me^2	453.9	363.4	424	462.7
Tender Value	M NC	3,033.5	2,387	3,876	4,370
Other[4]					
Floor Area	T Me^2	178.4	158.8	127.2	291.1
Tender Value	M NC	1,675.2	1,547	1,586	4,532
II. New Buildings Completed[5]					
All Buildings					
Floor Area	T Me^2	186.6	155.3	136	123.7
Value	M NC	2,185.8	1,725	1,968	2,117
Residential					
Floor Area	T Me^2	25.4	62.0	23	29.9
Value	M NC	234.1	615	303	463
Non-Residential					
Floor Area	T Me^2	161.2	93.3	113	93.8
Value	M NC	1,951.7	1,110	1,665	1,654
Industrial[3]					
Floor Area	T Me^2	11.7	2.6	4.7	5.2
Value	M NC	92.0	27	58	63
Other[4]					
Floor Area	T Me^2	149.5	90.7	108.3	88.6
Value	M NC	1,859.7	1,083	1,607	1,591

1. Private new construction projects, excluding extensions.
2. Data refer to private building projects in 80 communes, approved by the Dirección de Obras Municipales.
3. Including commercial buildings.
4. Including educational and health buildings.
5. Construction started by government institutions in the public sector, throughout the country.

a. For earlier years see previous issues of SALA.

SOURCE: UN-YCS, 1973–85.

Table 1604

COLOMBIA NEW BUILDING CONSTRUCTION AUTHORIZED,[1] 1982–85[a]

Category	Unit	1982	1983	1984	1985
All Buildings					
Number of Permits	N	15,575	16,872	16,614	17,133
Floor Area	T Me^2	6,327.9	8,572.5	7,711.2	8.628.3
Tender Value	M NC	43,836.3	56,764	52,057	72,546
Residential					
Number of Permits	N	14,403	15,649	15,435	15,691
Floor Area	T Me^2	4,929.9	7,293.6	6,808.3	7,403.8
Tender Value	M NC	32,614.7	44,974.5	43,992	59,770
One, Two-Dwelling					
Number of Permits	N	8,879	7,480	5,300	7,739
Multi-Dwelling					
Number of Permits	N	5,524	8,169	10,135	7,952
Non-Residential					
Number of Permits	N	1,172	1,223	1,179	1,442
Floor Area	T Me^2	1,398.0	1,278.9	902.9	1,225
Tender Value	M NC	11,221.6	11,789.5	8,065	12,776
Industrial					
Number of Permits	N	106	107	87	104
Floor Area	T Me^2	175.4	129.9	86.6	116.6
Tender Value	M NC	1,176.4	1,085.5	631.9	1,184
Commercial					
Number of Permits	N	792	794	801	941
Floor Area	T Me^2	769	754.8	546.9	699
Tender Value	M NC	6,983.4	7,610.8	5,410.8	8,091.9
Educational					
Number of Permits	N	52	74	63	74
Floor Area	T Me^2	72.7	122.0	72.1	90.8
Tender Value	M NC	473.0	862.0	550	731.1
Health					
Number of Permits	N	40	16	28	40
Floor Area	T Me^2	98.9	30.6	42	102.3
Tender Value	M NC	1,192.4	142.3	443.5	836
Other					
Number of Permits	N	181	232	200	283
Floor Area	T Me^2	177.5	241.6	155.3	215.8
Tender Value	M NC	1,300.0	2,088	1,028.8	1,932.8

1. Data are derived from information supplied to local authorities by enterprises and collected by the Departamento Administrativo Nacional de Estadística, and cover 56 urban centers (51 were selected for their large population, and 5 for their location).

a. For earlier years see previous issues of SALA.

SOURCE: UN-YCS, 1973–85.

Table 1605

COSTA RICA NEW BUILDING CONSTRUCTION AUTHORIZED,[1] 1982–85[a]

Category	Unit	1982	1983	1984	1985
All Buildings					
Number of Works	N	11,614	11,334	5,311	12,338
Floor Area	T Me^2	875	792	372	938
Tender Value	M NC	1,534.9	4,286.6	1,972	6,313.9
Residential					
Number of Works	N	8,317	8,180	4,004	9,470
Floor Area	T Me^2	702	664	304	760
Tender Value	M NC	1,022.4	3,068.8	1,559	5,019.2
Non-Residential					
Number of Works	N	3,297	3,154	1,307	2,868
Floor Area	T Me^2	173	128	68	178
Tender Value	M NC	512.5	1,217.8	413	1,294.7
Industrial					
Number of Works	N	75	82	~	124
Floor Area	T Me^2	23	21	~	40
Tender Value	M NC	53.6	79.1	~	209.2
Commercial					
Number of Works	N	335	412	~	664
Floor Area	T Me^2	68	86	~	106
Tender Value	M NC	202.9	550.2	~	826
Educational					
Number of Works	N	14	19	~	10
Floor Area	T Me^2	4	10	~	3
Tender Value	M NC	15.6	82.8	~	24.7
Health					
Number of Works	N	#	#	~	~
Floor Area	T Me^2	#	#	~	~
Tender Value	M NC	#	#		~
Other^2					
Number of Works	N	2,873	2,641	~	2,070
Floor Area	T Me^2	78	11	~	29
Tender Value	M NC	240.4	505.7	~	234.8

1. Based on building permits issued by the municipalities.
2. Including health buildings for 1985.

a. For earlier years see previous issues of SALA.

SOURCE: UN-YCS, 1973–85.

Table 1606
CUBA NEW BUILDINGS COMPLETED,[1] 1982-85[a]

Category	Unit	1982	1983	1984	1985
All Buildings					
Number	N	27,784	27,917	31,027	32,952
Floor Area	T ME^2	4,957.4	5,450.9	4,492.5	6,622.4
Tender Value	M NC	531	581.1	540.6	589.4
Residential					
Number	N	27,555	27,661	30,519	32,483
Floor Area	T ME^2	2,859	4,061.4	3,347.4	4,819.1
Tender Value	M NC	258.1	287.4	308.7	353.2
Non-Residential					
Number	N	225	256	508	469
Floor Area	T ME^2	2,098.4	1,389.5	1,145.1	1,803.3
Tender Value	M NC	272.9	293.7	231.9	236.2
Industrial					
Number	N	106	133	101	75
Floor Area	T ME^2	1,774	1,173	977	1,057.1
Tender Value	M NC	157.6	176	83.9	78.1
Commercial					
Number	N	15	7	12	10
Floor Area	T ME^2	9.8	9.8	5.6	34.1
Tender Value	M NC	2.1	4.4	1.2	15.4
Educational					
Number	N	26	24	11	22
Floor Area	T ME^2	64.3	93.7	76	62.6
Tender Value	M NC	15.1	27.7	14.6	26.4
Health					
Number	N	22	21	15	21
Floor Area	T ME^2	147.6	34.6	26.4	116
Tender Value	M NC	46.3	7.9	7.5	53.3
Other					
Number	N	60	71	369	341
Floor Area	T ME^2	102.8	78.3	60.1	533.5
Tender Value	M NC	51.8	77.7	124.7	63

1. Data refer to the activities of the construction sector, local administrations, cooperatives, and own account construction by individuals.

a. For earlier years see previous issues of SALA.

SOURCE: UN-YCS, 1983-85.

Table 1607
DOMINICAN REPUBLIC NEW BUILDING CONSTRUCTION AUTHORIZED,[1] 1982-85[a]

Category	Unit	1982	1983	1984	1985
All Buildings					
Number	N	10,583	8,085	6,287	4,429
Floor Area	T Me^2	968	1,175	1,004	870
Tender Value	M NC	216.4	234.1	229.2	302.3
Residential					
Number	N	10,088	7,438	5,857	3,958
Floor Area	T Me^2	727	777	692	641
Tender Value	M NC	164.2	169.4	162.5	229.3
One, Two-Dwelling					
Number	N	9,949	7,050	5,371	2,899
Multi-Dwelling					
Number	N	139	388	486	1,059
Non-Residential					
Number	N	495	647	430	471
Floor Area	T Me^2	241	398	312	229
Tender Value	M NC	52.2	64.7	66.7	73.0
Industrial					
Number	N	9	15	25	26
Floor Area	T Me^2	5	12	39	32
Tender Value	M NC	1.1	2	6.4	8.8
Commercial					
Number	N	132	106	79	71
Floor Area	T Me^2	39	56	98	32
Tender Value	M NC	7.6	8.4	19.2	9.9
Educational					
Number	N	5	17	6	4
Floor Area	T Me^2	5	16	3	5
Tender Value	M NC	1.6	3.1	1	1.5
Health					
Number	N	3	7	8	3
Floor Area	T Me^2	3	9	31	1
Tender Value	M NC	1.0	1.9	7.7	.4
Other					
Number	N	346	502	312	367
Floor Area	T Me^2	189	305	141	159
Tender Value	M NC	40.9	49.3	32.4	52.4

1. Data do not include work under contract by the Instituto Nacional de la Vivienda.

a. For earlier years see previous issues of SALA.

SOURCE: UN-YCS, 1973-85.

Table 1608

ECUADOR NEW BUILDING CONSTRUCTION AUTHORIZED,[1] 1982–85[a]

Category	Unit	1982	1983	1984	1985
All Buildings					
Number of Permits	N	11,585	11,978	18,103	25,589
Floor Area	T Me^2	2,671.3	2,628	2,913.5	4,238
Tender Value	M NC	12,228.1	14,155.3	20,179	34,308
Residential					
Number of Permits	N	10,945	11,439	16,989	24,993
Floor Area	T Me^2	2,077.5	2,110.1	2,451.4	3,825.3
Tender Value	M NC	10,233.3	12,235.3	17,268.9	31,391.9
One, Two-Dwelling					
Number of Permits	N	7,190	7,563	13,323	18,609
Multi-Dwelling					
Number of Permits	N	3,755	3,876	3,666	6,384
Non-Residential					
Number of Permits	N	640	539	1,114	596
Floor Area	T Me^2	443.8	373.1	433.1	412.7
Tender Value	M NC	1,994.8	1,920	2,910.1	2,916.1
Industrial					
Number of Permits	N	95	64	65	67
Floor Area	T Me^2	116.7	73.4	102.1	74
Tender Value	M NC	408	250.5	530	426.8
Commercial					
Number of Permits	N	417	358	925	369
Floor Area	T Me^2	252.2	214.6	246.2	227.2
Tender Value	M NC	1,179.6	1,157.6	1,665.4	1,488.1
Educational					
Number of Permits	N	34	25	37	26
Floor Area	T Me^2	22.7	22.2	29	23.4
Tender Value	M NC	108.5	103.3	219.6	205.4
Health					
Number of Permits	N	8	16	10	21
Floor Area	T Me^2	9.1	7.5	12.2	9.7
Tender Value	M NC	39	41.3	141.5	86.4
Other					
Number of Permits	N	86	76	77	113
Floor Area	T Me^2	43.1	55.4	43.6	78.4
Tender Value	M NC	259.7	367.3	353.6	709.4

1. Includes reconstructions, and is based on municipality permits for private construction in the urban areas.

a. For earlier years see previous issues of SALA.

SOURCE: UN-YCS, 1973–85.

Table 1609

EL SALVADOR NEW BUILDING CONSTRUCTION AUTHORIZED AND COMPLETED, 1982–85[a]

Category	Unit	1982	1983	1984	1985
I. New Building Construction Authorized[1]					
All Buildings					
Number of Permits	N	17,337	12,672	4,267	6,486
Floor Area	T Me^2	706.6	588.2	223.3	433
Tender Value	M NC	265.6	204.6	105.5	197.1
Residential					
Number of Permits	N	17,256	12,620	4,232	6,405
Floor Area	T Me^2	684.3	566	200.3	374.8
Tender Value	M NC	255.8	196.6	84.1	168.3
One, Two-Dwelling					
Number of Permits	N	17,112	12,482	4,232	6,405
Multi-Dwelling					
Number of Permits	N	144	138	~	~
Non-Residential					
Number of Permits	N	81	52	35	81
Floor Area	T Me^2	22.3	22.2	23	58.2
Tender Value	M NC	9.8	8	21.4	28.8
Industrial					
Number of Permits	N	2	6	2	6
Floor Area	T Me^2	.9	4.9	2.2	7.0
Tender Value	M NC	.3	1.5	1.1	3.5
Commercial[2]					
Number of Permits	N	79	46	33	75
Floor Area	T Me^2	21.4	17.3	20.8	51.2
Tender Value	M NC	9.5	6.5	20.3	25.3
II. New Buildings Completed[3]					
All Buildings					
Number	N	7,227	8,649	9,091	7,943
Floor Area	T Me^2	290.3	348.2	384.3	341.4
Value	M NC	107.2	134.5	155.7	146.5
Residential					
Number	N	7,227	8,647	9,081	7,935
Floor Area	T Me^2	290.3	348.2	383.6	340.7
Value	M NC	107.2	134.5	155.1	146.1
One, Two-Dwelling					
Number	N	7,187	8,628	8,963	7,626
Multi-Dwelling					
Number	N	40	19	118	309
Non-Residential					
Number	N	#	2	10	8
Floor Area	T Me^2	#	#	.7	.7
Value	M NC	#	#	.6	.4
Industrial					
Number	N	#	#	#	~
Floor Area	T Me^2	#	#	#	~
Value	M NC	#	#	#	~
Commercial[2]					
Number	N	#	2	~	~
Floor Area	T ME^2	#	#	~	~
Value	M NC	#	#	~	~

1. Permits issued by the municipalities to private enterprises and individuals. Construction work done by the Instituto de Vivienda Urbana and the Instituto de Colonización Rural is excluded.
2. Including educational, health, and other buildings.
3. Data provided by the Dirección General de Servicios Eléctricos.

a. For earlier years see previous issues of SALA.

SOURCE: UN-YCS, 1973–85.

Table 1610

GUATEMALA NEW BUILDING CONSTRUCTION AUTHORIZED AND COMPLETED, 1982–85[a]

Category	Unit	1982	1983	1984	1985
I. New Building Construction Authorized[1]					
All Buildings					
Number of Construction Works	N	1,793	1,734	1,509	3,969
Floor Area[3]	T Me^2	377.7	343.5	227.5	413
Tender Value	M NC	42.5	41.4	30	51.4
Residential					
Floor Area[3]	T Me^2	268.7	222.7	128.7	269
Tender Value	M NC	33.2	29.4	17.3	37.6
Non-Residential					
Floor Area[3]	T Me^2	109.0	120.8	98.8	144
Tender Value	M NC	9.3	12.0	12.7	13.8
Industrial					
Floor Area[3]	T Me^2	14.0	15.2	25.2	30.5
Tender Value	M NC	1.7	1.8	3.0	3.6
Commercial					
Floor Area[3]	T Me^2	21.7	37.7	45.8	36.9
Tender Value	M NC	3.0	5.7	7.4	5.7
Other[4]					
Floor Area[3]	T Me^2	73.3	67.9	27.8	76.6
Tender Value	M NC	4.6	4.5	2.3	4.5
II. New Buildings Completed[2]					
All Buildings					
Number of Construction Works	N	851	674	500	~
Floor Area[3]	T Me^2	170.2	131.3	100.6	~
Value	M NC	21.4	16.3	12.8	~

1. Beginning 1981, construction authorized refers to private building in the Greater Metropolitan Area of Guatemala City.
2. Refers to private building activity in Guatemala City.
3. Area covered by the building.
4. Including educational and health buildings.

a. For earlier years see previous issues of SALA.

SOURCE: UN-YCS, 1973–85.

Table 1611

HAITI NEW BUILDING CONSTRUCTION AUTHORIZED AND COMPLETED,[1] 1982–85[a]

Category	Unit	1982	1983	1984	1985
I. New Building Construction Authorized					
Residential					
Number of Permits	N	250	117	156	161
II. New Buildings Completed					
All Buildings					
Number of Works	N	358	449	479	464

1. Data cover the municipalities of Port-au-Price and Petion-Ville. Completed buildings include those constructed without a permit.

a. For earlier years see previous issues of SALA.

SOURCE: UN-YCS, 1973–85.

Table 1612

HONDURAS NEW BUILDING CONSTRUCTION AUTHORIZED AND COMPLETED,[1] 1982–85[a]

Category	Unit	1982	1983	1984	1985
I. New Building Construction Authorized[2]					
All Buildings					
Number	N	~	~	~	~
Floor Area	T Me^2	~	~	~	~
Tender Value	M NC	~	~	~	~
Residential[3]					
Number	N	~	~	~	~
Floor Area	T Me^2	~	~	~	~
Tender Value	M NC	~	~	~	~
Non-Residential					
Number	N	~	~	~	~
Floor Area	T Me^2	~	~	~	~
Tender Value	M NC	~	~	~	~
Industrial					
Number	N	~	~	~	~
Floor Area	T Me^2	~	~	~	~
Tender Value	M NC	~	~	~	~
Commercial					
Number	N	~	~	~	~
Floor Area	T Me^2	~	~	~	~
Tender Value	M NC	~	~	~	~
Other[4]					
Number	N	~	~	~	~
Floor Area	T Me^2	~	~	~	~
Tender Value	M NC	~	~	~	~
II. New Buildings Completed[2]					
All Buildings					
Number	N	5,122	1,773	1,773	1,742
Floor Area	T Me^2	332	198	257.1	236
Value	M NC	79.9	60.1	73.9	79.5
Residential[3]					
Number	N	5,004	1,679	1,691	1,130
Floor Area	T Me^2	268.2	154.2	181.1	149.9
Value	M NC	63.8	50.4	55.6	53.7
Non-Residential					
Number	N	118	94	82	112
Floor Area	T Me^2	63.8	43.8	76	86.1
Value	M NC	16.1	9.7	18.3	25.8
Industrial					
Number	N	10	8	7	11
Floor Area	T Me^2	11.8	12.3	13.3	16
Value	M NC	1.9	2.1	2.2	3.9
Commercial					
Number	N	90	74	47	83
Floor Area	T Me^2	46.5	23.5	47.6	61.1
Value	M NC	12.8	5	11.4	18.9
Other[4]					
Number	N	18	12	28	18
Floor Area	T Me^2	5.5	8	15.1	9
Value	M NC	1.4	2.6	4.7	3

1. Data on construction authorized and completed refer to private construction in Tegucigalpa, San Pedro, Sula and La Ceiba.
2. 1984: 11 months ending Aug. 31. All other years: Fiscal year ending Sept. 30 of the year stated; except 1985, October 1 through July 31.
3. Dwellings or one-family houses.
4. Includes educational and health buildings.

a. For earlier years see previous issues of SALA.

SOURCE: UN-YCS, 1973–85.

Table 1613

NICARAGUA NEW BUILDING CONSTRUCTION AUTHORIZED,[1] 1982–85[a]

Category	Unit	1982	1983	1984	1985
All Buildings					
Number	N	1,259	419	870	~
Floor Area	T Me^2	62.5	47.1	62.8	~
Tender Value	M NC	60.6	77.9	157.7	~
Residential					
Number	N	1,234	366	842	~
Floor Area	T Me^2	57.3	20.3	43.2	~
Tender Value	M NC	49.7	18.5	64.1	~
Non-Residential					
Number	N	25	53	28	~
Floor Area	T Me^2	5.2	26.8	19.6	~
Tender Value	M NC	10.9	59.4	93.6	~
Industrial[2]					
Number	N	8	7	2	~
Floor Area	T Me^2	2.4	7.1	.3	~
Tender Value	M NC	7.2	25.3	1.4	~
Commercial[2]					
Number	N	6	10	4	~
Floor Area	T Me^2	.9	3.1	1.9	~
Tender Value	M NC	1.2	3.4	18.6	~
Educational[2]					
Number	N	3	5	#	~
Floor Area	T Me^2	1.1	5.3	#	~
Tender Value	M NC	1.6	3.8	#	~
Other[2,3]					
Number	N	8	31	22	~
Floor Area	T Me^2	.8	11.3	17.4	~
Tender Value	M NC	.9	26.9	73.6	~

1. Data refer to building activity in Managua only.
2. Extensions to all non-residential buildings are included in other buildings.
3. Includes health buildings.

a. For earlier years see previous issues of SALA.

SOURCE: UN-YCS, 1973-85.

Table 1614

PANAMA NEW BUILDING CONSTRUCTION AUTHORIZED AND COMPLETED, 1982–85[a]

I. New Building Construction Authorized[1,2]

Category	Unit	1982	1983	1984	1985
All Buildings					
Number	N	1,094	841	1,743	1,278
Floor Area	T Me^2	574.4	323.1	378	483.9
Tender Value	M NC	112.4	65.0	78.3	89.9
Residential					
Number	N	964	762	1,668	1,188
Floor Area	T Me^2	304.4	175.2	302	341.4
Tender Value	M NC	67.3	37.9	67.3	71
One, Two-Dwelling[3]					
Number	N	879	667	1,504	991
Multi-Dwelling[3]					
Number	N	85	95	164	197
Non-Residential					
Number	N	130	79	75	90
Floor Area	T Me^2	270	147.9	76	142.5
Tender Value	M NC	45.1	27.1	11	18.9
Industrial					
Number	N	18	7	8	17
Floor Area	T Me^2	19.6	8.1	5.4	30.4
Tender Value	M NC	2	.6	.4	3.3
Commercial					
Number	N	93	63	56	66
Floor Area	T Me^2	226.3	128.5	64.4	103.8
Tender Value	M NC	40.4	24.2	9.6	15.2
Educational					
Number	N	2	·	~	~
Floor Area	T Me^2	2.2	~	~	~
Tender Value	M NC	.3	~	~	~
Other[4]					
Number	N	15	9	11	7
Floor Area	T Me^2	16.6	11.3	6.2	8.3
Tender Value	M NC	1.8	2.3	1	.4

II. New Buildings Completed[5]

Category	Unit	1982	1983	1984	1985
All Buildings					
Number	N	3,207	3,060	4,081	2,954
Value	M NC	135.5	84.9	97.7	106.2
Residential					
Number	N	2,795	2,736	3,753	2,715
Value	M NC	78.8	52	82.7	82.6
Non-Residential					
Number	N	412	324	328	239
Value	M NC	56.7	32.9	15	23.6
Industrial					
Number	N	39	21	19	32
Value	M NC	3	1.3	.7	3.9
Commercial					
Number	N	331	272	280	184
Value	M NC	47.1	28.2	13.2	18.2
Other					
Number	N	42	31	29	23
Value	M NC	6.6	3.4	1.1	1.5

1. Data based on permits supplied by the Oficina de Seguridad and refer to new private construction in Panama City.
2. New construction excluding extensions.
3. Buildings with two dwellings are included with multi-dwelling buildings; prior to 1982 data include health buildings.
4. Including health buildings prior to 1983. Beginning in 1983, includes educational and health buildings.
5. Data refer to private construction authorized, excluding extensions, in 21 districts of Panama, including the districts of Panamá and Colón.

a. For earlier years see previous issues of SALA.

SOURCE: UN-YCS, 1973–85.

Table 1615

PARAGUAY NEW BUILDINGS COMPLETED,[1] 1982-85[a]

Category	Unit	1982	1983	1984	1985
All Buildings					
Number	N	1,565	1,124	1,320	1,439
Floor Area[2]	T Me[2]	327	248.7	216.5	224
Value	M NC	6,693.1	4,976.8	4,295	5,509.3
Residential Buildings					
Number	N	451	214	210	218
Floor Area[2]	T Me[2]	117	74	55.4	60.8
Value	M NC	2,751.2	1,817.2	1,346.2	1,559
One, Two Dwelling Buildings[3]	N	418	194	204	208
Multi-Dwelling Buildings[3]	N	33	20	6	10
Non-Residential Buildings					
Number	N	1,114	910	1,110	1,221
Floor Area[2]	T Me[2]	210.6	174.7	161.1	163.2
Value	M NC	3,941.9	3,159.6	2,948.8	3,950.3
Industrial					
Number	N	31	0	0	1
Floor Area[2]	T ME[2]	17	0	0	.3
Value	M NC	98.3	0	0	5.9
Commercial					
Number	N	123	116	64	59
Floor Area[2]	T Me[2]	74	48	31.6	31.5
Value	M NC	1,517.7	824.4	603	765
Educational					
Number	N	5	4	0	1
Floor Area[2]	T Me[2]	3	4.8	0	2.0
Value	M NC	33.3	37.5	0	51.5
Health					
Number	N	4	2	0	0
Floor Area[2]	T Me[2]	4	1.6	0	0
Value	M NC	212.9	65.1	0	0
Other[4]					
Number	N	951	788	1,046	1,160
Floor Area[2]	T Me[2]	112.3	120.3	129.5	129.7
Value	M NC	2,079.7	2,232.6	2,345.8	3,127.9

1. Data are from the Dirección de Obras Particulares de la Municipalidad de la Capital and refer to private building activity in the municipality of Asuncion.
2. Area occupied by the buildings.
3. Two-dwelling buildings are included with multi-dwelling buildings.
4. Extensions and reconstruction of all types of buildings are included with other buildings.

a. For earlier years see previous issues of SALA.

SOURCE: UN-YCS, 1982; 1985.

Table 1616

PERU NEW BUILDING CONSTRUCTION AUTHORIZED AND COMPLETED, 1982-85[a]

Category	Unit	1982	1983	1984	1985
I. New Building Construction Authorized[1,4]					
All Buildings					
Tender Value	M NC	271.1	328.2	652.5	677
Residential					
Tender Value	M NC	60.6	82.1	56.2	20.4
Non-Residential					
Tender Value	M NC	188.5	272.1	592.3	656.6
II. New Buildings Completed[2,4]					
Residential Buildings					
Floor Area	T Me[2]	1,276.9	1,011.8	910.2	951.5
Value[3]	M NC	3	2.4	2.2	1.7

1. Public construction.
2. Private construction.
3. In constant prices of 1973.
4. According to the Cámara Peruana de la Construcción.

a. For earlier years see previous issues of SALA.

SOURCE: UN-YCS, 1982-85.

Table 1617

URUGUAY NEW BUILDING CONSTRUCTION AUTHORIZED AND COMPLETED, 1982–85[a]

Category	Unit	1982	1983	1984	1985
I. New Building Construction Authorized[1,5,6]					
All Buildings					
Number	N	~	~	~	2,283
Floor Area	T Me^2	574.5	202.4	378	181.7
Tender Value	M NC	~	~	~	~
Residential					
Number	N	~	~	~	2,168
Floor Area[3]	T Me^2	427.1	126.8	238.8	160.1
Non-Residential					
Number	N	~	~	~	105
Floor Area[4]	T Me^2	147.4	75.6	139.2	21.4
II. New Buildings Completed[1,2]					
All Buildings					
Floor Area	T Me^2	1,198.5	866.2	705.2	516.2
Value	M NC	4,833.3	5,217.2	4,704.6	~
Residential					
Floor Area	T Me^2	932.5	725.8	615.4	~
Value	M NC	4,078.4	4,632.9	4,285.2	~
Non-Residential					
Floor Area	T Me^2	266	140.4	89.7	~
Value	M NC	754.9	584.3	419.4	~

1. Construction in Montevideo only, prior to 1984.
2. Private construction only. Data from the Banco Central del Uruguay.
3. Residential area of all buildings, prior to 1979.
4. Non-residential area of all buildings, prior to 1979.
5. Data from the Cámara de la Construcción del Uruguay. Data cover both private and public sectors.
6. Data for 1985 exclude Montevideo and Maldonado.

a. For earlier years see previous issues of SALA.

SOURCE: UN-YCS, 1973–85.

Table 1618

VENEZUELA NEW BUILDING CONSTRUCTION AUTHORIZED,[1] 1982–85[a]

Category	Unit	1982	1983	1984	1985
All Buildings					
Number of Permits	N	3,678	2,807	2,860	2,811
Floor Area	T Me^2	6,473.0	3,677.1	3,073.5	3,106.7
Tender Value	M NC	9,594.4	5,350.1	5,990.6	6,918
Residential					
Number of Permits	N	2,875	2,172	2,251	2,264
Floor Area	T Me^2	5,083.1	2,574.5	2,173.6	2,318.9
Tender Value	M NC	8,072.1	4,076.0	4,743.6	5,815.2
One, Two-Dwelling					
Number of Permits	N	2.375	1,826	1,883	1,930
Multi-Dwelling					
Number of Permits	N	500	346	368	334
Non-Residential					
Number of Permits	N	803	635	609	547
Floor Area	T Me^2	1,389.9	1,102.6	899.9	787.8
Tender Value	M NC	1,522.4	1,274.1	1,247	1,102.8
Industrial					
Number of Permits	N	196	114	99	109
Floor Area	T Me^2	511.3	362.1	207.3	268.9
Tender Value	M NC	373.5	295.0	194	237.2
Commercial					
Number of Permits	N	558	470	456	391
Floor Area	T Me^2	781.5	633.1	544.1	441.3
Tender Value	M NC	1,041.3	833	838.5	750.7
Educational					
Number of Permits	N	19	13	16	10
Floor Area	T Me^2	25.9	28	51	12.2
Tender Value	M NC	31.9	35.6	76.6	21.9
Health					
Number of Permits	N	4	6	5	6
Floor Area	T Me^2	19.2	35.5	4.4	14.6
Tender Value	M NC	31.6	57.5	13.7	42.6
Other					
Number of Permits	N	26	32	33	31
Floor Area	T Me^2	39.6	43.9	93.1	50.8
Tender Value	M NC	44.1	53.0	124.2	50.4

1. Data refer to private building construction, and are obtained from Funda Construcción.

a. For earlier years see previous issues of SALA.

SOURCE: UN-YCS, 1973–85.

Table 1619

INDEX OF CONSTRUCTION ACTIVITY, 20 LC, 1975–85[a]

(1980 = 100)

	Country	1975	1976	1977	1978	1979	1980	1981	1982	1983	1984	1985
A.	ARGENTINA	72	93	104	99	99	100	86	69	64	52	43
B.	BOLIVIA	96	100	111	114	113	100	65	39	39	77	79
C.	BRAZIL	~	78	84	90	93	100	96	96	82	83	~
D.	CHILE	72	61	60	65	81	100	121	92	88	91	106
E.	COLOMBIA	98	83	90	88	87	100	107	111	126	128	
F.	COSTA RICA	64	77	80	85	101	100	78	53	56	68	~
G.	CUBA	80	84	92	99	100	100	114	115	127	147	152
H.	DOMINICAN REP.	77	78	85	88	93	100	99	96	105	108	96
I.	ECUADOR	86	93	95	100	99	100	105	106	96	94	94
J.	EL SALVADOR	131	104	141	132	130	100	85	81	83	78	82
K.	GUATEMALA	45	78	88	90	96	100	118	105	77	54	50
L.	HAITI[b]	73	78	81	88	97	100	104	94	99	101	114
M.	HONDURAS	70	73	86	90	97	100	96	100	101	105	105
N.	MEXICO	71	74	70	79	89	100	112	106	87	90	~
O.	NICARAGUA	44	44	46	49	76	100	114	126	155	202	~
P.	PANAMA	77	80	59	82	82	100	103	124	86	76	70
Q.	PARAGUAY	30	35	46	61	79	100	117	110	103	101	~
R.	PERU	101	105	88	82	82	100	112	112	88	88	82
S.	URUGUAY	57	64	66	86	96	100	103	100	69	54	42
T.	VENEZUELA	79	96	120	133	120	100	98	90	78	51	48
	UNITED STATES	62	64	70	79	90	100	106	108	110	114	122

a. For earlier years see SALA, 21-901.
b. Year ending Sept. 30.

SOURCE: UN-YCS, 1974–82, pp. 234–236; 1982, pp. 234–235; 1983, p. 239; 1984,
pp. 237–241; 1985, p. 232.

Table 1620

POPULATION WITH WATER SUPPLY AND SEWERAGE SERVICES, 19 L

(As of December 31, 1980)

	Country	Total					Urban					Rural				
		Total	With Water (T)	(%)	With Sewerage (T)	(%)	Total	With Water (T)	(%)	With Sewerage (T)	(%)	Total	With Water (T)	(%)	With Sewerage (T)	(%)
A.	ARGENTINA	27,863	16,141	58	12,560	45	22,359	14,636	65	8,060	36	5,504	1,505	27	4,500[b]	82

Table 1621

WATER SERVICES IN 26 CITIES, 13 L, 1975

	Drinking Water		Sewerage	Recipient Water Body			Flow Me³/sec.		Estimated Outflow of Sewage Me³/sec.
City	Coverage[1] (%)	Quantity[1] (L/I/D)[2]	Coverage[1] (%)	Name (R = Rio)	Type[3]		Annual minimum	Annual average	
A. ARGENTINA									
Buenos Aires	885-91	852[a]	52.4	R. de la Plata and Affluents	II		~	20,425	96
Córdova	65	460	~	R. Primero	I		2.52	9.44	4

Continued in SALA, 20-910.

Table 1622

HOUSING ACCESS TO WATER SUPPLY, 18 L

(%)

			Piped System					Self-Supply				
Country	Area	Year	Inside House	Within Lot but Outside House	Less than 100 Meters from House	More than 100 Meters from House	Subtotal[a]	Well	Rainwater	River	Other Means	Subtotal[a]
A. ARGENTINA	Total	1960	43.5	3.6	4.4	~	51.5	41.8	~	~	6.7	48.5
	Urban	1960	54.5	3.9	4.5	←———┤	62.9	33.5	~	~	3.6	37.1
	Rural	1960	7.4	2.3	4.4	←———┤	14.1	68.9	~	~	16.9	85.9

Continued in SALA, 24 1610.

Table 1623

HOUSING SANITARY FACILITIES, 18 LC

(%)

			Water Closet				
County	Area	Year	Sewerage	Septic Tank	Subtotal[a]	Latrine[a]	None or Unknown[a]
A. ARGENTINA	Total	1960	~	~	61.5	25.2	13.3
	Urban	1960	~	~	73.8	19.3	6.9
	Rural	1960	~	~	21.1	44.7	34.2

Continued in SALA, 24-1620.

Table 1624

ESTIMATED PROVISION OF WATER SUPPLY
AND EXCRETA DISPOSAL,[1] 20 LC

(Late 1970s, % of Population)

	Country	Water Supply[2]		Sewerage[2]		Other Excreta[2] Disposal Devices[2]
		Urban	Rural	Urban	Rural	Rural
A.	ARGENTINA[a]	70	14	33	~	66
B.	BOLIVIA[b]	30	2	31	#	4
C.	BRAZIL[c]	66	10	65	9	31
D.	CHILE[b]	92	13	69	9	81
E.	COLOMBIA[b]	80	29	76	7	81
F.	COSTA RICA[d]	95	60	42	4	79
G.	CUBA[d,e]	91	10	46	6	~
H.	DOMINICAN REP.[d]	66	12	27	~	40
I.	ECUADOR[b]	73	6	63	3	7
J.	EL SALVADOR[d]	54	3	34	~	21
K.	GUATEMALA[b]	58	6	40	~	17
L.	HAITI[d]	17	#	#	#	5
M.	HONDURAS[b]	75	13	43	1	10
N.	MEXICO[d]	70	32	41	#	35
O.	NICARAGUA[d]	65	9	38	#	18
P.	PANAMA[b]	92	12	74	6	41
Q.	PARAGUAY[b]	27	#	38	#	92
R.	PERU[b]	55	3	42	1	1
S.	URUGUAY[b]	75	24	54	21	55
T.	VENEZUELA[b]	65	31	65	15	73

1. This table is based upon various sources including censuses and PAHO Surveys. The most significant source is indicated for each country and entry.
2. Water supply is taken to be a connection to a centralized piped system either in the house or lot. Sewerage is connection to a sewerage system or a septic tank. Other excreta disposal devices are mainly latrines.

a. Argentina, Secretaría de Estado de Transporte y Obras Públicas, Subsecretaría de Recursos Hídricos, Instituto Nacional de Ciencia y Técnica Hídricas, *La demanda de agua en la República Argentina* (Mendoza, 1976).
b. Most recent census of population or housing.
c. IBRD, Brazil, *Human Resources Special Report.*
d. Pan American Health Organization, *Health Conditions in the Americas,* 1977.
e. In the case of Cuba, the government has adopted a policy of concentration of the rural population and the provision of sewerage. In consequence, the use of other sanitary devices is not relevant to future policies and no estimate of the population currently so served has been made.

SOURCE: U.N., CEPAL, *Drinking Water Supply and Sanitation in Latin America 1981–1990* (Santaigo, 1983), p. 81.

Table 1625

ELECTRICALLY LIGHTED OCCUPIED HOUSING UNITS, 13 LC

	Country	Year	Area	Number of Occupied Housing Units				
				Total	With Electric Lighting	Lacking Electric Lighting		
						Total	Kerosene	Other
B.	BOLIVIA[1]	1976[†]	Total	989,055	326,287	662,768	~	~

Continued in SALA, 20-907.

Table 1626

POPULATION WITH ELECTRIC LIGHTING, 20 LR, 1960–73

(%)

Country	1960	1970	1973
A. ARGENTINA	69.0	76.0	78.5

Continued in SALA, 21-902.

Table 1627

HOUSING DEFICIT, 20 L, 1960–69

(N)

	Housing Unit Deficit			Housing Units Constructed by Public Sector			
Country	Ca. 1960	Ca. 1965	Ca. 1969	1960-69	Annual Average 1960-65	Annual Average 1960-69	% Increase in Average
A. ARGENTINA	1,500,000	2,000,000	2,630,000	240,323	21,187	28,300	33.6

Continued in SALA, 18-903.

Table 1628

OCCUPIED HOUSING UNITS BY NUMBER OF ROOMS, 15 LC

				Room					
Country	Year	Area	Total	1	2	3	4	5	6 and Over
B. BOLIVIA	1976[1,2]	Total	989,055[a]	441,388	115,458	41,066	12,425	4,414	2,132

Continued in SALA, 20-904.

Table 1629

TENANCY OF OCCUPIED HOUSING UNITS, 19 LC, 1970–76

			Total		Urban Areas		Rural Areas	
Country	Year	Code	N	%	N	%	N	%
A. ARGENTINA	1970	A[1]	6,056,100	100.0	~	~	~	~
		B	3,553,250	58.7	~	~	~	~
		C	1,380,950	22.8	~	~	~	~
		D	1,121,900	18.5	~	~	~	~

Continued in SALA, 20-905.

Table 1630

INHABITANTS BY SIZE OF HOUSEHOLD,[1] 20 LC

Country	Year	Total	Size of Household				
			1 Person	2 Persons	3-4 Persons	5-8 Persons	9 and Over
A. ARGENTINA[2],[‡]	1970	22,961,500	615,900	2,250,500	8,711,800	9,661,100	1,722,200

Continued in SALA, 20-903.

Table 1631

STATUS OF PERSONS RESIDING IN PRIVATE HOUSEHOLDS, 14 L

Country	Year of Census	Total	Heads of Household	Spouses	Children	Other Relatives	Guests	Servants	Other Persons
A. ARGENTINA	1960	19,227,447	4,418,791	3,252,791	7,820,735	2,325,279	772,271	239,576	398,776

Continued in SALA, 18-902.

Table 1632

MEXICO: GEOGRAPHIC DISTRIBUTION OF CONSTRUCTION ACCORDING TO THE INTERNAL CONSUMPTION OF CEMENT, 1970–79
(Each Year = 100.0%)

State	1970	1971	1972	1973	1974	1975	1976	1977	1978	1979
Aguascalientes	1.0	1.0	.8	.8	.9	.9	.9	.9	1.0	.9

Continued in SALA, 23-904.

Part VI
Industry, Mining, and Energy

17

Industrial Production

Table 1700

INDUSTRIAL PRODUCTION INDEX, 18 LC, 1970–83

(1975 = 100)

Country	1970	1975	1976	1977	1978	1979	1980	1981	1982	1983
A. ARGENTINA										
General[†]	79	100	96	100	91	100	97	83	79	87
Mining	100	100	102	111	114	121	125	126	128	130
Manufacturing	78	100	96	100	89	98	94	79	76	83
Electricity, gas, and water	67	100	103	109	114	130	141	138	142	153
Construction	~	100	112	128	128	131	139	128	86	80

Continued in SALA, 24-1700.

Table 1701

AUTOMOBILE PRODUCTION, ALADI COUNTRIES,[1] 10 LR, 1977-82

(N)

Country	1977	1978	1979	1980	1981	1982[‡]
A. ARGENTINA	235,350	179,160	253,217	281,793	172,363	132,116

Continued in SALA, 24-1701.

Table 1702

BUTTER PRODUCTION, 20 LC, 1959–86

(T MET)

Country	1959	1970	1975	1979	1980	1981	1982	1983	1984	1985	1986
A. ARGENTINA[a]	61	28	40	33	29	32	37	34	31	33	33
B. BOLIVIA	~	#	#	#	1[†]	1[†]	~	~	~	~	~
C. BRAZIL	29	45[†]	63[‡]	90[‡]	90[‡]	95[‡]	70[‡]	70[‡]	70	70	65
D. CHILE[1]	7	8[‡]	7	4	4[‡]	5	3	4	3	5	6
E. COLOMBIA	~	11[†]	11[†]	12[†]	12[†]	12[†]	13	13[†]	13	14	14
F. COSTA RICA	~	3[†]	3[†]	3[†]	3[†]	3[†]	4	4[†]	4	3	3
G. CUBA	~	#	8	11	10	9	10	10	11	10	10
H. DOMINICAN REP.	~	#	1	1	1	1	1	1	1	2	2
I. ECUADOR	~	4[†]	5[†]	4[†]	4[†]	4	4	4[†]	4	4	4
J. EL SALVADOR	~	5[†]	5[†]	6[†]	6[†]	6	6	6[†]	6	5	5
K. GUATEMALA	~	4[†]	4[†]	4[†]	4[†]	5	5	5[†]	4	5	5
L. HAITI	~	~	~	~	~	~	~	~	~	~	~
M. HONDURAS	~	4[†]	4[†]	4[†]	4[†]	4	4	4	4	4	4
N. MEXICO	~	18[†]	23[†]	24[‡]	21[‡]	21[‡]	23	24	25	25	25
O. NICARAGUA	~	3[†]	4[†]	4[†]	2[†]	2[†]	2[†]	2[†]	2	2	2
P. PANAMA	~	#[†]	#[†]	#[†]	#[†]	#[†]	~	~	~	~	~
Q. PARAGUAY	~	~	~	~	~	~	~	~	~	~	~
R. PERU	3	5	6	5[‡]	5[‡]	4	4	3	3	2	2
S. URUGUAY	5	7	6[‡]	6	8[‡]	8	8	12	12	12	12
T. VENEZUELA	4	5	6	10[‡]	10[‡]	10	10	8	10	5	6
UNITED STATES	640	518	446	447	519	557	570	589	508	566	548

1. Twelve months beginning in April of year stated.

SOURCE: SALA, 22–1904; UN-SY, 1982, table 116; UN-SY, 1983–84, table 110;
   UN-SY, 1985–86, table 100.

Table 1703

CEMENT PRODUCTION,[1] 20 LC, 1953–86

(T MET)

	Country	1953	1970	1976	1980	1981	1982	1983	1984	1985	1986
A.	ARGENTINA	1,655	4,770	5,707	7,280	6,913	5,818	5,882	5,220	4,795	5,558
B.	BOLIVIA	34	116	220	318	388	325‡	327‡	220	145‡	294‡
C.	BRAZIL	1,655	9,002	18,675	25,880	24,886	25,440	20,586	19,497	20,635	25,260
D.	CHILE	762	1,349	968	1,583	1,863	1,131	1,255	1,390	1,430	1,441
E.	COLOMBIA	875	1,757	3,612	4,356	4,610	4,572	4,740	5,280	5,412	5,916
F.	COSTA RICA	~	187	362	554	460	424	386	350	460‡	454‡
G.	CUBA	405	742	2,501	2,831	3,292	3,163	3,231	3,347	3,182	3,305
H.	DOMINICAN REP.	130	493	654	928	960	959	1,047	1,109	1,001	952
I.	ECUADOR	91	458	608	1,389	1,451	1,400	1,420	1,730	1,281	1,397‡
J.	EL SALVADOR	30	167	322	519	459	276	320	407‡	446‡	440‡
K.	GUATEMALA	67[a]	231	445	569	568‡	613	491	786‡	988‡	988‡
L.	HAITI	26[b]	65	246	243	241‡	213	216	248	263	248
M.	HONDURAS	~	161	234	232	184	165	300	368	378	360
N.	MEXICO	1,754	7,267	12,691	16,398	18,173	19,343	17,363	18,702	20,255	19,825
O.	NICARAGUA	24	98	226	154‡	100‡	100‡	298	280	100	100‡
P.	PANAMA	80	181	282	565	520	350	350	304	305	336
Q.	PARAGUAY	3	63	155	177	156	111	155	109	46	50‡
R.	PERU	449	1,144	1,966	2,758	3,080‡	2,477	1,972‡	1,939	1,780	2,205
S.	URUGUAY	297	497	676	684	604	550	401	347‡	317	329
T.	VENEZUELA	982	2,318	3,538	4,842	4,900	5,594	4,147	4,783	5,121	5,875‡
	UNITED STATES	45,001	67,682	67,581	68,241	65,054	57,475	63,883	70,450	70,284	71,112

1. The figures cover, as far as possible, all hydraulic cements used for construction
(portland, metallurgic, aluminous, natural, etc.).

a. Refers to volume of sales only.
b. 1954.

SOURCE: UN-SY, 1967, table 125; UN-SY, 1978, table 124; UN-SY, 1979/80, table 112;
UN-SY, 1981, table 152; UN-SY, 1982, table 140; UN-SY, 1983–84, table 134;
UN-SY, 1985–86.

Table 1704

CHEESE PRODUCTION, 20 LC, 1959–86

(T MET)

	Country	1959	1970	1975	1980	1981	1982	1983	1984	1985	1986
A.	ARGENTINA	116	167	226	248	229	232	248	210	215	245
B.	BOLIVIA[1]	~	6†	7†	7†	7†	7†	8†	8	7	8
C.	BRAZIL[2,3]	31	50†	53†	58†	58†	59†	59†	59	59	59
D.	CHILE[1]	~	23	14	18	19	22	19	18	19	24
E.	COLOMBIA[1]	~	39†	38†	44†	45†	47†	47†	48	50	50
F.	COSTA RICA[1]	~	4	5†	6	5	6†	6†	6	5	5
G.	CUBA[1]	~	1	7	11	12	10	11	14	14	16
H.	DOMINICAN REP.[1]	1	1	1	2	2	3	3	3	3	3
I.	ECUADOR[1,2]	~	10†	13†	12†	12†	13†	13†	13	14	14
J.	EL SALVADOR[1]	~	15†	16†	18†	18†	18†	18†	18	15	15
K.	GUATEMALA[1]	~	12†	13†	14†	15†	15†	15†	15	16	16
L.	HAITI[3]	~	1†	2†	2†	2†	2†	2†	2	~	~
M.	HONDURAS[1]	~	7†	8†	8†	8†	8†	8†	8	8	8
N.	MEXICO[1,3]	~	78†	89	97†	99†	101†	100†	100	100	100
O.	NICARAGUA[1]	~	14†	16†	7†	8†	8†	8†	8	8	8
P.	PANAMA	~	1	#	#†	#†	~	~	~	~	~
Q.	PARAGUAY	~	~	~	~	~	~	~	~	~	~
R.	PERU[1,3]	9	35	37	34	33	33	25	29	15	16
S.	URUGUAY[1]	7	9	8†	12	12	15	10‡	10	11	15
T.	VENEZUELA[1]	15	27	39	28‡	28‡	28‡	29‡	29	33	35
	UNITED STATES[1]	~	1,330	1,593	2,109	2,234	2,345	2,471	2,402	2,714	2,809

1. Cheese from whole and partly skimmed milk of cows or buffalo.
2. Cheese from sheep milk.
3. Cheese from goat milk.

SOURCE: SALA, 22-1904; UN-SY, 1981, table 126; UN-SY, 1982, table 117; UN-SY,
1983–84, table 111; UN-SY, 1985–86, table 101.

Table 1705

CIGARETTE PRODUCTION, 20 LC, 1953-86

(M)[1]

	Country	1953	1963	1970	1975	1980	1983	1984	1985	1986
A.	ARGENTINA	21,675	24,619	30,220	38,621	34,680	28,241	30,843	31,092	45,400
B.	BOLIVIA	443	496	730	1,500	1,265	1,200[‡]	368	1,200[‡]	1,200[‡]
C.	BRAZIL[3]	41,599	59,964	70,703	101,741	142,300[‡]	129,200[‡]	127,800	146,300	168[‡]
D.	CHILE	5,382	6,315	6,590	8,149	10,510	7,680	8,107	8,053	8,269
E.	COLOMBIA	12,089	17,753	19,080	16,972	21,200	21,700[‡]	23,400	24,050[‡]	24,200[‡]
F.	COSTA RICA	~	1,265	1,420	2,154	2,252	2,200	2,200	2,200	~
G.	CUBA	7,743	15,346	19,806	15,366	15,109	16,802	18,697	17,761	16,841
H.	DOMINICAN REP.	896	1,722	2,125	3,023	3,375	3,604	3,696	3,826	4,164
I.	ECUADOR	743	729	1,295	2,085	3,858	5,000	5,000	4,800	4,600[‡]
J.	EL SALVADOR	799	1,076	1,441	1,779	2,570	2,500[‡]	2,500[‡]	2,300[‡]	2,100[‡]
K.	GUATEMALA	1,550	1,997	2,986	2,360	2,699	2,156	2,700[‡]	2,400[‡]	1,300[‡]
L.	HAITI	259	336	421	674	1,094	909	886	806	829
M.	HONDURAS	801	1,214	1,266	1,804	2,475	2,300[‡]	2,145	2,311	2,300[‡]
N.	MEXICO	26,434	33,659	40,633	46,763	54,520	46,798	51,666	54,332	49,898
O.	NICARAGUA	654	891	1,260	1,588	2,228	1,919	2,318	2,440	2,400[‡]
P.	PANAMA	~	742	1,011	1,045	1,083	981	911	873	873
Q.	PARAGUAY	660	528	458	834	648	931	878	834	~
R.	PERU	2,280	1,938	2,904	3,722	4,034	3,181	3,489	3,102	3,741
S.	URUGUAY	~	2,455	3,121	3,349[‡]	3,914	3,750[‡]	3,800[‡]	3,098	3,583
T.	VENEZUELA	2,725	8,256	10,463	16,486	21,300	20,200[‡]	20,643	19,760[‡]	18,000[‡]
	UNITED STATES[2]	423,070	543,687	562,153	626,760	697,000	710,565	668,800	655,300	652,000

1. Where production of cigarettes was reported by weight, a conversion rate of one million cigarettes per metric ton has been used.
2. Twelve months ending June 30 of year stated.
3. Production by main establishments only.

SOURCE: UN-SY, 1968, table 95; UN-SY, 1978, table 92; UN-SY, 1979/80, table 86; UN-SY, 1981, table 132; UN-SY, 1982, table 123; UN-SY, 1983-84, table 117; UN-SY, 1985-86.

Table 1706

COPPER (REFINED) PRODUCTION, 4 LC, 1970-83

(T MET)

	Country	1970	1975	1980	1981	1982	1983
C.	BRAZIL	18.6[a]	74.8	63.0	45.0	61.8	103.0
D.	CHILE	461.3	535.2	810.7	775.5	729.1	692.7
N.	MEXICO	53.9	73.6	85.6	61.3	61.3	80.9
R.	PERU	36.2	53.8	230.6	209.1	224.9	190.6
	UNITED STATES	2,065.7	1,621.9	1,725.9	2,037.6	1,694.6	1,583.7

a. Primary metal only.

SOURCE: UN-SY, 1977, table 129; UN-SY, 1982, table 143; UN-SY, 1983-84, table 137.

Table 1707

COTTON (WOVEN) FABRIC PRODUCTION,[1] 16 LC, 1953-86
(Measure Varies)[3,4,7]

Country	Code[2]	1953	1963	1970	1975	1980	1982	1983	1984	1985	1986
A. ARGENTINA[3]	A + B	72	63	76	70	~	~	~	~	~	~
B. BOLIVIA[7]	A	6	10	12	10	13	5‡	8‡	7	~	~
C. BRAZIL[4]	A + B	~	231	784ª	864ª	1,253	1,018	~	~	~	~
D. CHILE[4,5]	A + B	81	89	100	53	53	27	28	48	54	62
E. COLOMBIA[4,6]	A	181	299	~	~	~	~	~	~	~	~
G. CUBA[7]	A + B	~	91	76	138	157	138	156	156	177	183
H. DOMINICAN REP.[4,8]	A + B	2	8	7	8	15	8	10	13	13	~
I. ECUADOR[4,9]	A + B	17	31	29	28	9	2	~	~	~	~
J. EL SALVADOR[4,6]	A	13	36	37	23	16	~	~	~	~	~
L. HAITI[4]	A	2	3	3	1	1	1	1	1	1	1
M. HONDURAS[4,6]	A	1	2	11	15	8	8‡	9	11	10	~
N. MEXICO[3]	A + B	36	99	119	123	67	66	66	460	511	504
O. NICARAGUA[4]	A	4	11	16	~	7.4	14	16	31	~	~
Q. PARAGUAY[4]	A	2	15	20	16	17	9	6	7	11‡	~
R. PERU[4]	A	~	85	~	126	~	~	~	~	~	~
T. VENEZUELA[4,6]	A + B	18	59	80	~	~	~	~	~	~	~
UNITED STATES[4]	A + B	9,330	8,009	5,711	3,744	3,310	2,668	2,940‡	3,346	3,278	5,219

1. The data refer, in general, to the total production of woven cotton fabrics (including mixed fabrics where indicated) before undergoing finishing processes such as bleaching, dyeing, printing, mercerizing, glazing, etc.
2. Code: A = pure; B = mixed.
3. Thousand metric tons.
4. Million meters.
5. Incomplete coverage.
6. Including finished fabrics.
7. Million square meters.
8. Including a small amount of rayon fabrics.
9. After undergoing finishing processes.

a. Incomplete coverage.

SOURCE: UN-SY, 1968, table 99; UN-SY, 1978, table 94; UN-SY, 1979/80, table 88; UN-SY, 1981, table 133; UN-SY, 1982, table 124; UN-SY, 1983–84, table 118; UN-SY, 1985-86.

Table 1708

COTTON (YARN) FABRIC PRODUCTION,[1] 13 LC, 1953-86
(T MET)

Country	Code[4]	1953	1963	1970	1980	1982	1983	1984	1985	1986
A. ARGENTINA	A	76.2	72.8	89.6	74.9	68.4	8.3	~	~	~
B. BOLIVIA	A	.2	.3	1.2	.8	4.5‡	~	~	~	~
C. BRAZIL[2]	A + B	71.1	110.9	118.0	~	~	~	~	~	~
D. CHILE[3]	A	3.9	23.4	26.8	4.8	4.6	3.6	~	~	~
E. COLOMBIA	A + B	.6	5.4	1.3	~	15.0‡	2.5ª	2.5ª	2.8ª	~
G. CUBA	A	~	14.2	11.8	25.0	23.9	26.4	26.7	30.8	34.1
H. DOMINICAN REP.	B	.2	~	#	.7	.5	.5	.7	.8	~
I. ECUADOR	A + B	.3	.9	1.7	2.2	1.5	~	~	~	~
J. EL SALVADOR	A	.7	3.1	3.7	3.9	3.0	~	~	~	~
N. MEXICO	A	~	103.7	132.0	~	~	~	~	~	~
Q. PARAGUAY	A	12.0	12.9	11.6	74.9	90.8	77.2	~	~	~
R. PERU	A + B	~	17.5	~	~	~	~	~	~	~
T. VENEZUELA	A + B	4.2	13.6	13.0	~	~	~	~	~	~
UNITED STATES	A + B	1,695.0	1,761.4	1,525	1,114.0	932.0	1,063.8	125.0ª	136.8ª	189.2ª

1. The data refer to the total weight of pure cotton yarn spun (including mixed yarns where indicated), whether for sale, on commission, or for further processing. Yarn spun from cotton waste is included. Unless otherwise stated, tire cord yarn is excluded.
2. Production in Sao Paulo only.
3. Estimated on the basis of mill consumption data supplied by the international Cotton Advisory Committee, allowing an average waste rate of about 8%.
4. Code: A = pure; B = mixed.

a. Mixed only.

SOURCE: UN-SY, 1968, table 98; UN-SY, 1978, table 93; UN-SY, 1979/80, table 87; UN-SY, 1981, table 134; UN-SY, 1982, table 125; UN-SY, 1983–84, table 119; UN-SY, 1985–86.

Table 1709

MEAT PRODUCTION,[1] 19 LC, 1961–86

(T MET)

Country	1961–65	1970	1975	1980	1981	1982	1983	1984	1985	1986
A. ARGENTINA	2,569	3,021	2,825	3,220	3,353	2,977	2,764	2,919	3,104	3,136
B. BOLIVIA	70	90	113	145	147	150	153	155	179	172
C. BRAZIL	2,026	2,669	2,981	3,115	3,147	3,418	3,362	3,205	3,021	3,029
D. CHILE	202	249	273	232	261	272	285	275	255	266
E. COLOMBIA	447	495	577	698	747	709	742	754	738	798
F. COSTA RICA	36	52	74	86	90	77	65	70	106	121
G. CUBA	190	237	171	206	222	225	225	235	246	252
H. DOMINICAN REP.	33	43	57	61	47	55	59	63	88	115
I. ECUADOR	81	99	115	164	158	161	161	181	159	170
K. GUATEMALA	55	72	75	99	115	95	83	85	74	63
L. HAITI	33	47	56	51	47	43	45	46	43	47
M. HONDURAS	27	40	48	65	64	80	77	76	78	80
N. MEXICO	705	708	923	2,014	1,151	1,172	2,453	2,401	2,256	2,369
O. NICARAGUA	40	76	82	66	56	74	75	74	57	59
P. PANAMA	29	39	50	48	57	60	60	59	71	68
Q. PARAGUAY	139	172	156	198	202	187	180	178	224	231
R. PERU	175	190	188	185	194	199	216	203	187	188
S. URUGUAY	381	488	407	384	471	449	490	414	394	355
T. VENEZUELA	182	253	357	435	434	430	436	446	443	473
UNITED STATES	13,826	16,448	16,675	17,680	17,707	17,045	17,812	17,818	17,874	17,831

1. Beef, veal, pork, mutton, and lamb.

SOURCE: UN-SY, 1976, table 80; UN-SY, 1978, table 80; UN-SY, 1979/80, table 75;
   UN-SY, 1981, table 124; UN-SY, 1982, table 115; UN-SY, 1983–84, table 109;
   UN-SY, 1985–86, table 99.

Table 1710

METAL (SHEET) PRODUCTION, ALADI COUNTRIES,
9 LR, 1977–85

(T MET)

Country	1977	1980	1982	1983	1984	1985
A. ARGENTINA	2,282	2,127	2,345	2,492	2,365	1,054
C. BRAZIL	8,815	12,850	11,462	12,457	14,705	7,835
D. CHILE	383	571	390	~	~	~
E. COLOMBIA	295	320	314	377	408	250
I. ECUADOR	74	116	127	~	~	~
N. MEXICO	4,151	5,876	5,568	5,364	5,950	3,446
R. PERU	312	285	218	~	~	~
S. URUGUAY	15	34	40	~	~	~
T. VENEZUELA	1,140	1,698	2,061	2,030	2,236	1,452
ANDEAN GROUP	~	2,418	2,718	2,709	2,994	1,928
LATIN AMERICA	17,467	23,877	22,525	25,429	28,658	15,965

SOURCE: Mexico-NAFINSA-MV, May 9, 1983; Mexico-NAFINSA-MV, Jan. 13, 1986.

Table 1711

SHIPS (MERCHANT VESSELS) UNDER CONSTRUCTION IN ARGENTINA, 1975-83

(T Gross Tons Registered)

Year	Amount
1975	97
1976	136
1977	117
1978	170
1979	143
1980	127
1981	155
1982	78
1983	82

SOURCE: UN-MB, Jan. 1983, special table A, p. xv; Oct. 1984, special table A, p. xiv.

Table 1712

STEEL (CRUDE) PRODUCTION, 9 LR, 1950-86[a]

(T MET)

PART I. MV SERIES

	Country	1950	1965	1977	1978	1979	1980	1981	1982	1983	1984	1985	1986[‡]
A.	ARGENTINA	100	1,300	2,684	2,782	3,199	2,687	2,541	2,913	2,943	2,622	2,941	3,243
C.	BRAZIL	800	3,000	11,253	12,205	13,893	15,309	13,213	12,995	14,671	18,386	20,457	21,236
D.	CHILE	100	500	559	616	642	746	657	492	618	688	681	703
E.	COLOMBIA	#	200	330	390	361	402	396	422	482	507	530	602
G.	CUBA[†]	~	~	302	300	300	300	300	300	300	300	300	300
N.	MEXICO	400	2,500	5,601	6,775	7,117	7,156	7,663	7,056	6,978	7,560	7,367	7,170
R.	PERU	~	~	379	377	436	470	360	272	299	342	411	487
S.	URUGUAY	~	~	19	9	14	16	14	28	46	41	39	31
T.	VENEZUELA	#	600	803	860	1,506	1,820	2,030	2,225	2,367	2,770	3,060	3,467
	LATIN AMERICA[1]	1,400	8,100	21,992	24,378	27,566	29,028	27,400	27,042	28,996	33,522	36,070	37,722

1. Total from above.

a. Steel and hot sheet metal production

SOURCE: Mexico-NAFINSA-MV, May 9, 1983; for 1950 and 1965 data, Jan. 7, 1985; NAFINSA-MV, Jan. 13, 1986; NAFINSA-MV, Aug. 7, 1987.

PART II. UN-SY SERIES

	Country	1969	1970	1975	1980	1982	1983	1984	1985	1986
A.	ARGENTINA	1,720	1,859	2,043	2,556	2,752	2,828	2,483	2,748	3,116
C.	BRAZIL	4,925	5,390	7,829	10,232	7,660	8,166	10,707	11,399	11,341
D.	CHILE	601	547	458	695	429	618	692[‡]	689	708
E.	COLOMBIA	206	239	266	263	215	272	257	274	~
G.	CUBA	119	140	298	304	301	364	325	401	412
N.	MEXICO	3,470	3,846	5,196	7,003	6,926	6,747	7,279	7,162	6,949
R.	PERU	194	94	432	447	274	289	342	411	484
T.	VENEZUELA	840	927	919	1,784	2,296	2,246	2,770	3,061	3,402
	UNITED STATES	128,152	119,309	105,817	101,456	67,656	76,762	83,940	80,067	74,032

SOURCE: UN-SY, 1979-80, table 114; UN-SY, 1981, table 153; UN-SY, 1982, table 141; UN-SY, 1983-84, table 135; UN-SY, 1985-86.

Table 1713

SUGAR (RAW) PRODUCTION,
20 LC, 1950–85
(M MET)

Part I. 1950–85

| Year | World[1] | Cuba | |
		Plan	Actual
1950	29.2		5.6
1951	33.6		5.8
1952	36.1		7.3
1953	35.0		5.2
1954	38.8		5.0
1955	38.4		4.6
1956	39.7		4.8
1957	41.6		5.7
1958	44.4		5.9
1959	49.6		6.0
1960	52.1		5.9
1961	54.7		6.9
1962	51.6		4.9
1963	52.6		3.9
1964	60.1		4.5
1965	65.1	6.0[b]	6.2
1966	64.2	6.5	4.5
1967	66.7	7.5	6.2
1968	66.9	8.0	5.2
1969	70.0	9.0	4.5
1970	71.1	10.0	7.6
1971	74.0	7.0	5.9
1972	75.7	- -	4.3
1973	75.8	5.5	5.3
1974	76.4	- -	5.9
1975	78.8	- -	6.3
1976	82.4	- -	6.2
1977	90.4	- -	6.5
1978	90.6	7.3	7.4
1979	89.2	- -	8.0
1980	84.6	- -	6.7
1981	92.6	- -	7.4
1982[‡]	100.7	- -	8.0
1983	96.9	- -	7.4
1984	99.2	- -	7.8
1985	99.1	- -	7.9

1. Cane and beet.

a. Excludes India and some Far Eastern production prior to 1900.

b. No plan prior to 1965.

SOURCE: 1950-69, compiled from *Los Angeles Times, New York Times, Wall Street Journal*, USDA, FAO, and ECLA sources. World data are from Deere, *History of Sugar*.
1970-81, UN-SY, 1981, table 128, and Cuba, CEE, *Anuario Estadístico*, 1983, p. 109; UN-SY, 1982, table 119; UN-SY, 1983–84, table 113; UN-SY, 1985–86, table 103.

Table 1713 (Continued)

SUGAR (RAW) PRODUCTION, 20 LC, 1950–87

(T MET)

PART II. 19 LC[1]

Country	1953	1970	1975	1979	1980	1981	1982	1983	1984	1985	1986	1987
A. ARGENTINA	740	976	1,353	1,411	1,716	1,624	1,623	1,624	1,545	1,188	1,120	1,063
B. BOLIVIA	3	131	213	288	262	260	228	197	198	175‡	180‡	200‡
C. BRAZIL[2]	2,002	5,019ª	6,299	7,362	8,270	8,726	8,941	9,555	9,259	8,455	7,999	9,266
D. CHILE	~	228	219	97	60	235	132	229	360	351	481	437
E. COLOMBIA	190	676	970	1,107	1,247	1,212	1,318	1,340	1,177	1,367	1,272	1,293
F. COSTA RICA	31	150	205	204	220	190	194	206	245‡	230‡	220	230‡
H. DOMINICAN REP.	552	1,014	1,170	1,200	1,013	1,108	1,285	1,209	1,133	921	895	816
I. ECUADOR[3]	61	235‡	292	355	368	330	246	164	329	300	286	341
J. EL SALVADOR	30	117	244	274	217	182	199	259	242	279	292	262
K. GUATEMALA	37	185	384	415	452	474	580	614	555	583‡	651	639
L. HAITI	55	66	69	60	65	50	55	43	41	50	40	35
M. HONDURAS	8	53‡	75‡	164	191	196	217	221	207	235	227	190‡
N. MEXICO	868	2,402	2,636	3,095	2,719	2,642	2,739	3,076	3,308	3,492	4,068	4,061
O. NICARAGUA	33	141	210‡	202	190	214	247	249	267	240‡	256	199
P. PANAMA	17	76	135‡	226	200	186	239	215‡	176	160	139	100‡
Q. PARAGUAY	14	52	59	76	89	77	85	92	92‡	80‡	75‡	75‡
R. PERU	602	771	964ª	715	553	492	623	452	645‡	710‡	585	560
S. URUGUAY	21	53	95‡	84	102	97	103	104	100‡	90‡	98	103
T. VENEZUELA	78	455	508	347	358	303	382	377	390‡	470‡	650‡	655
UNITED STATES	3,148	5,327	5,680	5,435ᵇ	5,313ᵇ	5,789ᵇ	5,418ᵇ	5,215ᵇ	5,342ᵇ	5,415ᵇ	5,676	6,603

1. Covers the production of centrifugal sugar from both beet and cane, and the figures are expressed, as far as possible, in terms of raw sugar. Where exact information about polarization or grades is lacking, qualities are expressed in terms of sugar "Tel quel".
2. "Tel quel" sugar indicates lack of exact information about polarization of grades.
3. Crop year, except 1967.

a. "Tel quel" (see note 2).
b. Includes data for Puerto Rico.

SOURCE: UN-SY, 1968, table 89; UN-SY, 1978, table 86; UN-SY, 1979–80, table 81; UN-SY, 1981, table 128; UN-SY, 1982, table 119; UN-SY, 1983–84, table 113; UN-SY, 1985–86, table 103; UN-SY, 1987, table 103.

Table 1714

CUBA SUGAR INDUSTRY INDICATORS, 1960–87

Year	Production (T MET)[1]		Industrial Output (%)	Days		Cane Ground Per Day (MET)	
	Ground Cane	Raw Sugar (Base 96°)		Crop	Effective	Crop	Effective
1960	47,492	5,943	12.51	103	88	466,289	542,344
1965	56,687	6,156	10.86	130	105	388,449	482,050
1970	79,678	8,538	10.71	217	143	367,442	557,818
1975	50,770	6,314	12.44	123	99	413,747	513,521
1976	51,999	6,156	11.84	130	99	399,088	526,922
1977	56,149	6,485	11.55	142	104	395,774	542,951
1978	67,043	7,351	10.96	168	119	400,087	563,198
1979	73,050	7,992	10.94	182	128	402,320	571,424
1980	61,600	6,665	10.82	149	109	412,663	565,775
1981	66,408	7,359	11.08	136	114	489,100	580,300
1982	73,500	8,210	11.17	152	124	484,600	594,100
1983	68,687	7,109	10.35	160	113	429,600	608,900
1984	78,358	8,207	10.47	166	126	471,101	620,218
1985	66,756	8,004	11.99	135	103	495,228	646,498
1986	68,300	7,255	10.62	137	104	497,800	656,600
1987‡	66,892	7,117	10.64	141	99	473,300	673,900

1. Crop years.

SOURCE: ECLA-S, 1987, p. 249.

Table 1715

WHEAT FLOUR PRODUCTION,[1] 19 LC, 1953–86

(T MET)

Country	1953	1963	1967	1970	1975	1980	1983	1984	1985	1986
A. ARGENTINA	2,013	2,163	2,161	2,347	2,483	2,438	2,678	2,754	2,801	2,762
B. BOLIVIA	~	10	20	39	60	225	200[‡]	209	~	~
C. BRAZIL	1,475	1,607	1,865	2,393	2,053[a]	5,154	4,540	4,812	4,722	~
D. CHILE	585	653	762	808	479	874	913	911	919	941
E. COLOMBIA	56	170	180	231	215	329	376	520[‡]	399	~
G. CUBA	~	133	131	160	176	271	428	422	442	443
H. DOMINICAN REP.	~	44	53	55	85	115	127	108	139	141
I. ECUADOR[3,4]	31	64	68	91	156	164	185	278	~	~
J. EL SALVADOR	~	27	41	43	56	82	84[‡]	97	103[‡]	~
K. GUATEMALA	15	58	71	72	86	~	97	~	~	~
L. HAITI	~	44	42	28	67	117	139	111	132	142
M. HONDURAS	5	15	23	33	35	40	75[‡]	41[‡]	68[‡]	75[‡]
N. MEXICO	368	1,040	1,142	1,331	1,580	2,147	2,544	2,630	2,523	2,263
O. NICARAGUA	~	~	24	29	~	40	47	43	~	~
P. PANAMA[5]	~	~	~	32	38	45	61	48	52	~
Q. PARAGUAY	34	85	60	70	38	82	100	90	99	~
R. PERU[2]	265	364	417	500	587	733	761	788[‡]	694	875
S. URUGUAY	~	239	249	251	~	240	260[‡]	200[‡]	153	~
T. VENEZUELA	~	257	322	388	457	540	600	~	~	~
UNITED STATES	10,078	11,794	11,124	11,504	11,747	12,821	14,133	13,584	14,232	15,472

1. Sifted (bolted) flours from soft and hard wheat and from spelt. Bran and offal, wheat
   groats, meal, and flour obtained by milling cereals other than wheat are excluded.
2. Incomplete coverage. Data for main establishments only.
3. Twelve months ending June 30.
4. Including flour from other grains.
5. Including groats.

a. Incomplete coverage. Data for main establishments only.

SOURCE: IASI-AC, 1970, table 323-05; UN-SY, 1968, table 88; UN-SY, 1978, table 85;
UN-SY, 1979–80, table 80; UN-SY, 1981, table 127; UN-SY, 1982, table 118; UN-SY,
1983–84, table 112; UN-SY 1985–86.

Table 1716

MEXICO MAQUILADORA EMPLOYMENT, 1965–86

Year	Total Plants (N)	Plants Located in Interior (%)	Total Employees (YA)	Foreign Exchange Earnings (M US)
1965	~	~	3,000	~
1966	57	- -	4,257	- -
1967	72	- -	17,936	- -
1968	79	- -	17,000	- -
1969	108	- -	15,858	- -
1970	120	- -	20,327	81
1971	209	- -	20,000	102
1972	339	- -	48,060	165
1973	357	3.9	64,330	278
1974	455	5.7	75,974	444
1975	454	7.9	67,214	454
1976	448	9.4	74,796	536
1977	443	10.1	78,433	525
1978	457	8.1	90,704	714
1979	540	11.1	111,365	638
1980	620	11.3	119,546	773
1981	605	11.2	130,973	976
1982	585	11.7	127,048	851
1983	629	12.2	150,867	829
1984	685	12.0	203,000	1,200
1985	780	12.0	230,000	1,450
1986[a]	1,034	~	270,000	~

a. Estimate January–November 1986 from U.S. Chamber of Commerce in Mexico City.

SOURCE: Ellwyn R. Sloddard, *Maquila: Assembly Plants in Northern Mexico* (El Paso,
1987), p. 24.

Table 1717

PLANNED STRIKES AND ACTUAL STRIKES IN MAQUILADORA INDUSTRY, MEXICO, 1967–83

(N)

	Planned Strikes			Actual Strikes		
Year	Tijuana	Ciudad Juárez	Matamoros	Tijuana	Ciudad Juárez	Matamoros
1967	3	- -	- -	- -	- -	- -
1968	- -	- -	- -	- -	- -	- -
1969	- -	1	- -	- -	- -	- -
1970	2	- -	- -	- -	- -	- -
1971	- -	- -	- -	- -	- -	- -
1972	4	5	- -	- -	- -	- -
1973	10	14	11	5	1	- -
1974	7	10	13	1	1	- -
1975	7	8	17	1	1	1
1976	5	10	18	- -	- -	- -
1977	3	8	26	- -	- -	- -
1978	9	15	12	1	1	- -
1979	16	14	12	1	1	- -
1980	11	12	17	- -	2	- -
1981	14	14	16	- -	2	- -
1982	24	38	53	- -	- -	1
1983	20	21	25	1	1	- -

SOURCE: MEXICO-BNCE-CE, Jan. 1986.

Table 1718

ARGENTINA MANUFACTURING PRODUCTION INDICATORS, 1980–87

Category	1980	1984	1985	1986	1987[‡]
Value of Manufacturing at Factor Cost[1]	2,464.9	2,252.8	2,020.1	2,280.2	2,267.3
Food	535.9	529.3	529.4	576.0	553.3
Textiles	246.0	224.3	174.4	212.7	196.7
Lumber	44.6	29.4	25.2	29.9	30.2
Paper	122.4	114.3	110.5	115.9	111.1
Chemical Products	364.9	387.0	364.8	398.2	388.7
Non-Metallic Minerals	132.9	102.9	80.0	98.0	107.3
Basic Metal Industries	136.8	137.6	128.4	144.6	164.6
Machinery and Equipment	711.3	572.5	468.0	547.6	599.1
Other Industries	170.2	155.5	139.4	157.3	156.4
Production of Selected Industries[2]					
Finished Hot Rolling[3]	2,653	2,441	2,057	2,479	2,805
Cold Rolled Sheet	732	818	574	828	917
Automobile Engines (T Units)	282	167	138	171	193
Tractors (Units)	3,481	12,322	6,377	8,056	3,153

1. Australs at 1970 prices.
2. T MET.
3. Includes production employed in cold rolling.

SOURCE: ECLA-S, 1987, p. 97.

Table 1719

BRAZIL MANUFACTURING PRODUCTION INDICATORS, 1983–87
(Average 1981 = 100)[a]

Category	1983	1984	1985	1986	1987[‡]
Manufacturing Production	93.6	99.3	107.6	120.0	121.6
Capital Goods	68.7	78.8	88.5	108.3	106.0
Intermediate Goods[1]	99.7	109.9	117.8	128.3	130.4
Consumer Durables	107.1	99.1	114.1	137.5	130.4
Non-Durable Consumer Goods	97.4	99.3	107.1	116.2	117.9
Industrial Sectors					
Food	104.4	103.5	103.5	104.0	111.3
Beverages	92.5	92.0	102.1	126.1	120.3
Tobacco	102.5	105.9	117.0	127.6	129.4
Textiles	93.8	90.5	102.7	116.3	115.9
Clothing	91.1	92.8	99.8	104.6	95.8
Paper Products	109.0	116.5	123.9	137.0	142.0
Petroleum Derivatives	98.7	106.1	106.2	125.3	132.8
Other Chemical Products	107.9	118.9	131.0	125.3	132.8
Pharmaceuticals	93.3	101.4	106.7	130.8	133.4
Perfume, Soap, and Candles	104.8	103.6	116.9	143.2	167.7
Rubber	94.7	103.1	111.5	130.0	135.1
Plastic Products	97.1	100.9	112.2	136.9	131.9
Non-Metallic Minerals	81.2	81.1	87.2	103.2	106.8
Metallurgy	94.0	107.0	114.5	127.9	128.9
Machinery	71.6	84.9	93.5	113.9	120.0
Electronics	91.9	94.4	112.6	141.3	133.5
Transport Material	90.6	94.6	105.7	118.8	106.8

1. Includes mining.

a. At constant 1980 prices.

SOURCE: ECLA-S, 1987, p. 160.

Table 1720

BRAZIL AUTOMOTIVE INDUSTRY PRODUCTION, 1982–87

Category	T Units						Growth Rates					
	1982	1983	1984	1985	1986	1987	1982	1983	1984	1985	1986	1987
Motor Vehicles	860.0	896.0	865.0	967.0	1,057.0	920.2	10.1	4.2	−3.5	11.8	9.3	−12.9
Automobiles	475.1	576.0	538.0	759.0	816.0	684.0	16.9	21.2	−6.6	41.1	7.5	−16.2
Pickup Trucks and Other												
Transport Vehicles	328.0	278.0	272.0	134.0	146.0	148.5	15.9	−15.2	−2.2	−50.7	9.0	1.7
Trucks	47.0	36.0	49.0	65.0	83.8	74.1	−38.2	−23.4	36.1	32.7	28.9	−11.6
Buses	10.0	6.0	7.0	8.0	11.2	13.6	−26.2	−40.0	16.7	14.3	40.0	21.4
Alcohol-Driven Vehicles[1]	238.0	592.0	561.0	642.0	699.0	458.7	80.6	148.7	−5.2	14.4	8.9	−34.4
Exports[2]	173.0	169.0	196.0	208.0	183.0	344.7	−18.5	−2.3	16.0	6.1	−12.0	88.4

1. Included in the total number of vehicles.
2. Includes exports of completely unassembled components (CKD).

SOURCE: ECLA-S, 1987, p. 161.

Table 1721

CHILE MANUFACTURING PRODUCTION INDICATORS, 1983–87

(1980 = 100)

Category	1983	1984	1985	1986	1987[‡]
Industrial Product[1]	1,942	2,131	2,159	2,332	2,460
Industrial Production					
INE[2]	94.5	103.9	104.0	112.6	117.3
SOFOFA[3]	89.5	98.7	98.8	106.3	113.1
Non-Durable Consumer Goods	92.5	100.3	98.3	108.6	114.0
Consumer Durables	40.7	54.3	48.7	69.4	79.2
Transport Material	35.8	52.5	53.3	48.6	65.3
Capital Goods	62.2	72.7	84.1	95.4	95.7
Intermediate Goods for:					
Industry	105.1	114.0	116.0	121.8	125.8
Construction	79.4	95.2	92.8	104.3	124.8
Mining	91.7	98.7	100.8	116.3	122.2
Forestry	142.6	178.6	182.1	219.1	198.3
Packing and Accessories	95.5	106.1	106.4	111.7	124.0
Energy, Fuels, and Lubricants	84.1	84.4	84.5	88.8	94.9
Furniture	79.2	104.3	93.0	83.0	96.5
Industrial Sales					
INE	94.2	101.1	104.3	111.4	116.3
SOSOFA	90.7	98.8	100.9	107.7	114.7

1. M 1970 dollars.
2. Instituto Naciónal de Estadísticas (1979 = 100).
3. Sociedad de Fomento Fabril.

SOURCE: ECLA-S, 1987, p. 286.

Table 1722

COLOMBIA MANUFACTURING PRODUCTION INDICATORS, 1981–87

(Rates of Growth)

Category	1981	1982	1983	1984	1985	1986	1987[‡]
Total	-2.7	-3.3	-.5	9.9	2.7	7.1	7.1
Consumer Goods	-2.9	-4.8	1.1	9.1	4.9	3.4	4.4
Food	-6.4	-1.6	3.1	12.3	8.0	.9	2.1
Beverages	-2.6	-6.1	6.1	4.4	6.0	2.9	7.2
Tobacco	4.9	-1.5	9.4	13.8	6.6	.9	-8.7
Textiles	2.3	-6.6	-7.6	12.6	4.6	10.1	8.8
Clothing	1.1	-7.8	-9.4	9.3	-12.2	3.0	9.5
Footwear	2.7	-10.0	1.6	-14.9	-.3	6.1	-6.5
Furniture	-8.5	-22.3	-14.6	4.6	3.9	-8.4	.8
Printed Material	-4.6	2.3	-1.4	-10.3	-6.6	6.3	3.6
Various Industries	-6.6	-26.1	12.3	23.4	5.2	6.5	8.2
Intermediate Goods	-2.4	.6	1.8	7.6	7.7	9.6	8.1
Lumber	6.0	6.7	-3.8	1.3	2.4	3.3	23.1
Paper Products	-2.1	-4.1	-1.7	12.1	7.5	4.3	11.1
Industrial Chemicals	-12.4	.9	14.3	23.3	9.3	10.9	8.8
Other Chemical Products	-5.3	6.7	-3.7	7.4	13.6	12.5	6.1
Petroleum Derivatives	12.8	.1	10.0	1.4	5.6	14.4	8.2
Other Petroleum and Coal Derivatives	1.4	5.5	6.5	-.5	20.6	-1.9	5.4
Rubber Products	5.5	-10.1	-6.1	8.6	6.1	-1.2	-6.1
Plastic Products	-6.2	-.1	7.1	-7.1	-3.3	18.1	.4
Glass Products	-3.0	-.8	-3.5	-4.2	21.2	1.3	17.9
Other Non-metallic Mineral Products	-2.1	4.0	-2.7	14.8	-2.6	6.6	3.6
Basic Iron and Steel Industries	3.9	5.5	8.9	-7.8	- -	7.7	12.9
Basic Non-Ferrous Metal Industries	.2	-9.6	.4	-8.9	-.4	19.8	28.0
Clay, Porcelain, and China Products	-4.0	-3.4	-9.3	5.2	13.8	15.4	15.7
Leather Products	2.9	-7.1	-19.2	2.2	.4	19.2	5.4
Capital Goods	-2.9	-7.3	-9.3	17.1	-13.2	11.6	11.6
Metallic Products Excluding Machinery	-4.5	-7.4	-.1	7.0	-2.1	13.1	2.3
Machinery, Excluding Electronics	-1.1	-2.6	-9.7	-2.2	-26.2	16.1	13.8
Electronic Products and Machinery	7.2	-2.5	-15.7	.8	-1.6	5.3	3.7
Transport Material and Equipment	-10.9	16.4	-13.6	55.6	-21.1	12.4	21.5
Professional and Scientific Equipment	19.3	1.3	-.7	28.4	9.5	6.2	14.3

SOURCE: ECLA-S, 1987, p. 194.

Table 1723

COSTA RICA MANUFACTURING PRODUCTION INDICATORS, 1980–87

Category	1980	1984	1985	1986	1987[‡]
Value Added Index (1977 = 100)	112.0	110.9	113.1	121.2	127.9
Consumer Goods					
Food, Beverages, and Tobacco	116.3	129.8	134.8	138.3	146.3
Coffee	134.2	173.0	156.6	146.7	~
Meat	128.2	135.7	170.3	186.5	~
Sugar	104.2	132.2	132.9	125.7	~
Other Foods	117.0	119.5	126.2	133.3	~
Textiles, Leather, and Footwear	105.7	108.1	105.8	101.2	96.0
Lumber and Furniture	118.2	77.4	84.5	83.8	95.3
Printing and Publishing	121.6	132.5	144.9	158.1	168.2
Others	80.7	72.2	77.7	73.0	83.0
Intermediate Goods					
Paper and Paper Products	145.0	163.5	163.0	165.0	175.6
Chemical and Rubber Products	123.8	98.4	99.2	103.0	102.4
Petroleum Refining	210.2	182.9	183.8	278.1	~
Non-Metallic Minerals	128.1	124.0	128.0	136.7	154.1
Metallurgy	138.7	72.4	77.6	88.6	96.0

SOURCE: ECLA-S, 1987, p. 222.

Table 1724

CUBA MANUFACTURING PRODUCTION INDICATORS, 1980–87[a]
Index of Material Product (1975 = 100)

Category	1980	1984	1985	1986	1987[‡]
Total	110.5	156.7	168.9	169.7	162.7
Non-Durable Goods	104.2	150.1	161.7	160.2	151.8
Food (Excludes Sugar)	115.5	148.4	156.8	159.0	158.4
Sugar and Derivatives	112.6	137.1	139.2	132.3	121.1
Beverages and Tobacco	84.0	160.5	182.0	178.5	159.7
Confections	115.9	159.6	172.4	188.1	208.4
Printed Material	128.8	162.2	182.3	197.8	229.6
Intermediate Goods	107.1	122.2	131.4	133.9	135.9
Textiles	115.0	140.2	175.6	192.7	217.7
Chemicals	109.8	128.8	141.3	142.7	137.2
Fuels	97.8	106.9	107.4	106.7	106.8
Construction Material	137.6	129.0	136.2	139.6	148.0
Consumer Goods and Capital Goods	164.3	303.3	336.9	342.0	304.2
Non-Electric Machinery	175.5	332.3	360.4	351.4	312.4
Electronics	148.7	286.6	351.1	401.0	319.6
Metallic Products[1]	140.3	228.4	260.1	280.6	271.6
Other Manufacturers[2]	127.0	187.3	196.7	207.3	209.8

1. Excludes basic metals.
2. Includes, among others, leather, glass and ceramics, paper and cellulose, forestry and wood products industries.

a. At constant 1981 prices.

SOURCE: ECLA-S, 1987, p. 247.

Table 1725

CUBA PRODUCTION OF SELECTED INDUSTRIES, 1980–87

Category	T MET					Rates of Growth					
	1980	1984	1985	1986	1987‡	1982	1983	1984	1985	1986	1987‡
Non-Durable Consumer Goods (Excludes Sugar)											
Meat	35	62	64	66	64	17.6	13.3	12.7	4.4	3.1	–3.5
Flour	269	422	442	443	454	9.0	11.0	–1.4	4.7	.4	2.4
Fruit and Vegetable Preserves	122	162	182	173	165	–7.9	12.6	9.5	12.3	–5.3	–4.6
Alcoholic Beverages[1]	396	656	618	577	606	48.2	2.7	11.9	–5.7	–6.7	5.0
Tobacco	167	302	366	340	279	55.6	–7.1	–9.4	21.2	–7.1	–18.1
Fishing Industry											
Gross Catch	186	200	220	245	214	18.7	1.6	1.0	10.0	11.2	–12.4
Unloaded Total	153	171	183	193	182	21.4	8.0	3.5	7.1	5.5	–5.6
Clothing[2]	44	51	52	58	61	10.7	2.4	–2.3	2.0	11.0	6.2
Intermediate Goods											
Textiles[3]	160	172	205	221	258	–10.8	11.1	1.2	19.3	7.5	16.9
Cement	2,831	3,347	3,182	3,305	3,535	–3.9	2.1	3.6	–4.9	3.9	7.0
Paints, Enamels, and Varnishes	158	236	241	222	191	–53.4	140.4	45.8	2.1	–7.8	–14.2
Sulphuric Acid (98%)	399	336	374	396	377	–19.4	7.0	–5.7	11.3	5.9	–5.0
Sodium Hydroxide	3	18	14	21	18	–39.3	46.5	12.5	–22.2	51.8	–14.5
Phosphate	18	10	15	3	9	–22.8	–60.6	11.1	50.0	–78.8	168.8
Ammonium Nitrates	312	336	328	330	296	–42.0	–15.1	90.9	–2.4	.7	–10.3
Complete Fertilizers	1,060	1,036	1,160	1,045	996	–3.8	5.4	–4.2	12.0	–9.9	–4.7
Urea	16	65	81	75	68	–43.0	13.8	103.1	25.2	–7.5	–8.7
Bottles[3]	176	265	264	308	339	47.9	–19.5	41.7	–.4	16.5	10.0
Cardboard	22	19	16	21	19	4.4	–19.0	–9.5	–15.8	30.7	–9.2
Capital and Durable Consumer Goods											
Refrigerators[4]	26	24	28	18	6	–56.5	–11.4	50.0	16.7	–33.8	–67.9
Radios[4]	200	253	236	237	227	–6.6	14.3	–7.3	–6.7	.3	–4.0
Televisions[4]	40	92	94	102	56	–36.2	80.4	1.1	2.2	8.5	–55.6
Cane Transport Vehicles	501	631	606	613	620	–.5	8.0	–2.9	–4.0	1.2	1.1
Buses[5]	1,846	2,219	2,393	2,351	2,341	–3.8	16.2	19.2	7.8	–1.8	–.4
Cables and Electrical Wiring											
Uncovered[6]	2,547	2,069	2,785	3,002	2,600	–41.5	42.8	1.8	34.6	7.8	–13.3
Covered[7]	38	52	64	77	53	–37.4	24.5	23.8	23.1	19.6	–31.1
Bathroom Fixtures[4]	298	336	338	371	387	12.8	–2.4	–3.9	.6	9.7	4.3

1. T Hectoliters.
2. M units.
3. M Me^2.
4. T units.
5. Units.
6. MET.
7. T km.

SOURCE: ECLA-S, 1987, p. 248.

Table 1726

ECUADOR VALUE OF MANUFACTURING PRODUCTION, 1984–87
(M 1975 Sucres)

Category	1984	1985	1986	1987‡
Total[1]	28,643	28,741	28,615	28,781
Food, Beverages, and Tobacco	11,335	11,381	11,425	11,590
Textiles, Clothing, and Leather	6,659	6,639	6,282	6,188
Lumber	1,575	1,583	1,622	1,736
Paper	1,767	1,811	1,971	2,050
Chemicals and Plastics	1,726	1,564	1,656	1,623
Non-Metallic Minerals and Basic Metals	3,473	3,662	3,498	3,411
Machinery, Equipment, and Others	2,108	2,101	2,161	2,183

1. Excludes the refinement of petroleum.

SOURCE: ECLA-S, 1987, p. 319.

Table 1727

EL SALVADOR MANUFACTURING PRODUCTION INDICATORS, 1975–87

Category	1975	1984	1985	1986	1987[‡]
Value Added Indices (1980 = 100)	98.6	84.8	87.9	90.1	92.8
Food, Beverages, and Tobacco	88.5	90.6	96.6	98.2	100.4
Textiles, Clothing, and Leather Articles	118.9	63.3	58.1	61.1	61.7
Textiles	116.8	55.1	46.9	56.4	58.6
Clothing, Footwear, and Other Leather Articles	121.0	71.2	69.0	65.5	64.4
Lumber and Paper	76.3	82.4	81.4	79.1	82.6
Lumber	69.4	114.8	117.7	124.6	132.0
Paper and Paper Products	81.4	57.9	53.9	44.8	45.4
Chemicals, Petroleum Derivatives, and Rubber	137.6	87.2	82.6	84.0	86.8
Chemical Products	211.6	108.3	96.1	99.6	102.1
Petroleum Derivatives and Rubber	106.2	77.9	76.6	77.1	80.1
Non-Metallic Mineral Products	97.6	80.6	84.6	89.0	102.3
Machinery and Metallic Products	118.6	67.5	72.7	80.8	82.9
Metallic Products	135.8	80.6	90.4	99.1	101.4
Machinery	110.6	61.4	64.5	72.4	74.4
Others	154.4	68.7	63.2	74.1	76.4

SOURCE: ECLA-S, 1987, p. 344.

Table 1728

GUATEMALA MANUFACTURING PRODUCTION INDICATORS, 1983–87[a]

Category	1983	1984	1985	1986	1987[‡]
Manufacturing Production Index (1980 = 100)	90.1	90.5	89.9	90.5	91.9
Food	104.1	105.0	105.3	106.7	~
Textiles	96.7	95.5	95.7	96.1	~
Clothing	99.7	100.2	100.6	101.2	~
Chemicals	110.5	109.8	106.0	102.6	~
Other	114.5	115.0	114.5	115.2	~

a. At 1958 prices.

SOURCE: ECLA-S, 1987, p. 366.

Table 1729

HAITI MANUFACTURING PRODUCTION INDICATORS, 1980–87

Category	1980	1985	1986	1987[‡]
Value Added Indices (1976 = 100)	147	122	118	114
Food	135	133	130	~
Beverages	143	137	133	~
Tobacco	152	109	106	~
Textiles, Clothing, and Leather Articles	99	87	85	~
Chemicals	187	50	49	~
Non-Metallic Minerals	110	125	121	~
Metallurgy	268	212	206	~
Others	126	108	105	~
Production of Selected Industries (T MET)				
Flour	85	113	128	92
Sugar	54	58	41	33
Lard	3	6	7	7
Edible Oils	19	38	40	24
Carbonated Beverages[1]	74	61	65	~
Beer	5	4	4	4
Cigarettes[2]	1,064	786	846	888
Soap	13	29	31	40
Detergents[3]	579	1,302	1,373	1,916
Essential Oils[3]	242	154	153	167
Cement	243	263	221	~
Other Manufacturing Production Indicators				
Commercial and Industrial Consumption of Electricity[4]	156	174	160	154
Sugar Industry	18	10	9	6
Cement Industry	21	22	20	~

1. M bottles.
2. M units.
3. MET.
4. M kw.

SOURCE: ECLA-S, 1987, p. 390.

Table 1730

HONDURAS PRODUCTION OF SELECTED INDUSTRIES, 1984–87

Category	1984	1985	1986	1987[‡]
Cement[1]	534	348	360	451
Fibrous Cement Sheets[2]	2,090	2,470	2,294	3,204
Iron Rods[3]	8,647	16,371	11,846	16,598
Cloth[4]	16	14	12	18
Vegetable Oils[5]	7	5	6	15
Flour[6]	63	67	74	75
Pasteurized Milk[7]	43	46	49	53
Cane Sugar[6]	218	213	222	187
Cigarettes[8]	107	116	107	105
Matches[9]	60	65	68	62
Beer[10]	142	132	145	153
Carbonated Soft Drinks[10]	516	533	510	588
Cane Alcohol[11]	1,546	1,555	1,693	1,683
Liquor[11]	4,483	4,272	4,484	4,220
Industrial Consumption of Electricity[12]	170.0	169.2	146.0	132.8

1. M MET.
2. T ME[2].
3. T kg.
4. M yards.
5. M lbs.
6. T MET.
7. M liters.
8. M packs.
9. M 50 count boxes.
10. M 12 oz. bottles.
11. T liters.
12. M kw.

SOURCE: ECLA-S, 1987, p. 413.

Table 1731

MEXICO MANUFACTURING PRODUCTION INDICATORS, 1980–87

Category	1980	1985	1986	1987[‡]
Index of Manufacturing Production (1970 = 100)	198.8	212.0	203.4	207.7
Food, Beverages, and Tobacco	166.6	192.7	192.2	193.3
Textiles and Clothing	168.6	167.8	161.0	160.9
Lumber	180.0	202.4	191.9	187.8
Paper and Printing	192.2	226.4	219.9	218.3
Chemicals, Rubber, and Plastics	242.7	293.4	293.4	307.7
Non-Metallic Minerals	193.4	185.5	158.5	179.2
Basic Metals	202.1	196.5	178.9	198.8
Metallic Products and Machinery	242.8	215.7	192.7	189.6
Production of Selected Industries				
Beer	187.2	199.6	204.8	222.9
Basic Petrochemicals	325.3	555.9	658.6	763.7
Fertilizers	313.4	359.1	337.9	336.4
Iron Casting	227.7	214.9	218.3	226.4
Automotive	300.3	248.0	178.9	198.5

SOURCE: ECLA-S, 1987, p. 443.

Table 1732

PANAMA MANUFACTURING PRODUCTION INDICATORS, 1984–87

Category	1984	1985	1986	1987[‡]
Index of Manufacturing Production (1981 = 100)	98.6	99.8	102.7	106.1
Food, Beverages, and Tobacco	99.5	103.8	108.4	107.2
Textiles, Clothing, and Leather Products	92.1	99.1	98.9	97.3
Lumber, Furniture, and Accessories	107.5	104.2	101.1	91.8
Paper, Printing, and Publishing	95.6	96.0	91.6	93.6
Chemicals and Petroleum Derivatives	111.7	107.6	105.3	123.2
Non-Metallic Minerals	77.9	75.5	91.7	98.6
Basic Metallic Industries	63.4	66.9	76.0	101.0
Metallic Products	103.6	92.9	93.3	107.2
Other Industries	92.7	92.1	106.1	98.7
Production of Selected Industries				
Fish Oil[1]	7.5	33.7	14.5	13.8
Fish Meal[1]	22.5	45.7	17.1	31.4
Sugar[1]	167.0	151.0	131.0	115.1
Beer[2]	73.4	79.7	92.5	101.4
Carbonated Beverages[2]	77.4	79.4	90.6	98.6
Evaporated, Condensed, and Powdered Milk[1]	17.8	19.2	22.2	20.8
Cigarettes[3]	911.3	873.0	872.8	825.6
Footwear[4]	1,617.6	1,794.3	2,050.4	1,957.8

1. T MET.
2. M liters.
3. M units.
4. T pairs.

SOURCE: ECLA-S, 1987, p. 512.

Table 1733

PARAGUAY MANUFACTURING PRODUCTION INDICATORS, 1984–87

(1982 = 100)

Category	1984	1985	1986	1987[‡]
Total	101.1	105.1	103.6	107.2
Food	109.2	111.9	122.2	125.6
Beverages	110.2	112.5	113.4	117.6
Tobacco	119.2	121.4	109.7	153.7
Textiles	106.1	157.0	107.0	61.1
Confections	112.4	128.6	105.8	116.5
Footwear	106.1	100.8	103.8	111.4
Lumber	92.0	83.1	85.1	95.3
Furniture	125.8	128.4	131.2	136.3
Paper and Paper Products	94.3	98.1	112.4	121.2
Publishing and Printing	69.2	70.4	64.5	65.6
Leather	78.9	70.8	90.2	92.9
Chemicals	134.0	149.1	116.8	146.8
Other Chemical Products	127.5	153.9	124.2	126.8
Petroleum Derivatives	74.5	84.8	83.2	104.6
Plastics	116.2	117.5	102.4	108.0
Non-Metallic Minerals	100.6	88.4	116.2	134.0
Iron and Non-Ferrous Metals	116.4	123.3	124.0	294.7
Metallic Products Excluding Machinery	113.1	128.4	114.9	118.2
Machinery, Appliances, and Transport Equipment	139.1	204.9	172.3	162.0
Others	124.6	139.7	117.4	120.8
Crafts	88.0	96.0	81.4	~
Production of Selected Industries (M MET)				
Cotton Fabrics	6.1	9.2	11.8	6.2
Cotton Fibers[1]	105.3	160.0	99.9	52.4
Tannins	11.2	10.9	5.7	13.9
Almond Paste	8.2	4.7	4.9	3.6
Tung	9.0	9.4	7.2	8.1
Cement	109.0	45.6	178.7	269.2
Cigarettes[2]	43.9	41.7	37.5	56.7
Carbonated Beverages[3]	137.3	138.7	124.8	129.2
Flour	89.9	99.5	107.8	115.4
Sugar	85.2	73.1	68.7	104.2
Leather	8.3	7.7	10.1	10.4
Pure Alcohol[4]	11.0	15.0	~	~

1. T Me^3.
2. T packs.
3. T liters.
4. M liters.

SOURCE: ECLA-S, 1987, p. 544.

Table 1734

URUGUAY MANUFACTURING PRODUCTION
INDICATORS, 1985–87

(1982 = 100)

Category	1985	1986	1987
Manufacturing Production Index	94.3	105.7	117.4
Food	89.0	91.2	87.0
Other Food Industries	86.4	88.5	100.7
Beverages	79.9	90.4	98.0
Tobacco	81.7	81.6	90.6
Textiles	132.8	155.0	156.5
Clothing	117.1	131.8	141.8
Leather	85.2	91.7	95.8
Footwear	89.5	107.0	119.6
Paper	117.5	145.7	150.4
Printed Material	99.5	102.6	117.2
Industrial Chemicals	103.1	142.2	172.3
Other Chemical Products	92.2	110.2	108.8
Petroleum Refineries	78.2	70.6	81.7
Rubber	124.2	155.7	176.6
Plastics	106.1	123.8	142.2
Clay, Porcelain, and China Products	113.0	175.7	233.2
Glass	108.1	141.9	176.2
Other Non-Metallic Mineral Products	49.8	57.3	77.8
Basic Ferrous Metals	94.9	100.0	118.8
Basic Non-Ferrous Metals	128.9	134.8	145.1
Metallic Products	91.4	112.7	134.7
Electronic Equipment and Machinery	85.5	107.3	123.9
Transport Material	94.0	126.5	195.1
Professional and Scientific Equipment	75.4	103.4	108.8
Other Manufacturing Industries	107.4	132.6	154.5

SOURCE: ECLA-S, 1987, p. 641.

Table 1735

VENEZUELA MANUFACTURING PRODUCTION INDICATORS, 1980–87

Category	1980	1984	1985	1986	1987[‡]
Manufacturing Production Index (1980 = 100)[1]	100.0	99.5	99.9	107.5	106.7
Food, Beverages, and Tobacco	100.0	108.2	105.8	106.7	108.1
Textiles, Clothing, and Leather	100.0	110.7	110.2	117.0	115.7
Lumber and Furniture	100.0	69.9	69.5	79.6	73.8
Paper and Publishing	100.0	134.1	126.5	139.2	148.1
Chemicals	100.0	94.1	103.0	108.8	121.8
Non-Metallic Minerals	100.0	101.4	111.0	130.7	124.8
Basic Metals	100.0	68.1	58.7	76.5	80.7
Metallic Products, Machinery, and Equipment	100.0	85.9	87.3	102.4	91.1
Other Manufacturing Industries	100.0	79.8	70.7	73.5	52.9
Production of Selected Industrial Products[2]					
State Enterprises					
Iron	~	13,053	14,737	16,851	17,111
Steel	1,784	2,523	2,785	3,402	3,307[a]
Aluminum	156	385	405	428	442[b]
Ammonia	439	572	490	655	~
Sulphuric Acid	114	158	156	179	~
Urea	276	460	315	542	~
Fertilizers	441	759	649	904	1,016
Private Sector					
Sugar	323	389	457	538	588
Cement[3]	4,842	4,783	5,121	5,875	~
Automobile Tires[4]	3,483	2,985	4,518	5,017	5,447
Passenger Vehicles[4]	155	110	116	133	~
Employment[5]	752	743	790	878	978

1. Excludes state enterprises.
2. T MET.
3. B sacks.
4. T units.
5. T people.

a. January–October.
b. January–August.

SOURCE: ECLA-S, 1987, p. 678.

18
Mining Production

Table 1800

ANTIMONY MINE PRODUCTION, 7 LC, 1977–87

(Short Tons)

	Country	1977	1979	1980[‡]	1981	1982	1983	1984	1985	1986[‡]	1987[†]
B.	BOLIVIA	18,012	14,351	17,047	16,866	15,408	10,969	10,231	9,838	11,291	9,000
C.	BRAZIL	289	80	51	297	298	330	~	~	~	~
K.	GUATEMALA	1,010	728	613	563	550	500	100[†]	1,165	2,092	2,100
M.	HONDURAS[‡]	77	51	25	22[†]	11[†]	11	120	100	110	110
N.	MEXICO[1]	2,974	3,166	2,399	1,984	1,725	2,777	3,377	4,702	3,678	3,300
R.	PERU[3]	903	602	379	755	814	786	741	655	740[†]	720
	UNITED STATES[2]	610	722	343	646	503	838	557	~	~	~

1. Antimony content of ores for export plus antimony content of antimonial lead
   and other smelter products produced.
2. Production from antimony mines; excludes a small amount produced as a byproduct
   of domestic lead ores; 1986 data withheld to avoid disclosing company proprietary data.
3. Recoverable.

SOURCE: USBOM-MY, 1981, Volume I; USBOM-MIS, *Antimony in 1982*, p. 3; 1983, p. 3;
   USBOM-MY, 1983, Volume 1; USBOM-MY, 1984, Volume 1; USBOM-MY, 1985, Volume 1;
   USBOM-MY, 1986, Volume 1, pp. 122 and 123; USBOM-MY, 1987, Volume 1, p. 111.

Table 1801

BAUXITE MINE PRODUCTION, 3 LC, 1977–87[a]

(T MET)

	Country	1977	1979	1980	1981	1982	1983	1984	1985	1986[‡]	1987[†]
C.	BRAZIL	1,120[†]	2,388	5,538	5,770	6,289	7,199	6,433	5,846	6,544	7,250
H.	DOMINICAN REP.[1]	576	635	606	457	141	~	~	~	~	211[b]
L.	HAITI[1,2]	588	584	312	427	377	~	~	~	~	~
	UNITED STATES[1]	2,013	1,821	1,559	1,510	732	679	856	674	510	576[b]

1. Dry Bauxite equivalent of Crude Ore.
2. Shipment.

a. Data available through July 8, 1988.
b. Reported figure.

SOURCE: USBOM-MY, 1981, Volume I; USBOM-MIS, *Bauxite in 1982*, p. 5; 1983, p.3;
   USBOM-MY, 1984, Volume 1; USBOM-MY, 1985, Volume 1; USBOM-MY, 1986, Volume 1,
   p. 154; USBOM-MY, 1987, Volume 1, p. 142.

Table 1802

CHROMITE MINE PRODUCTION, 3 L, 1977–87[a]

(T Short Tons)

	Country	1977	1979	1980	1981	1982	1983	1984	1985	1986[‡]	1987
C.	BRAZIL[1]	342	375	345	261	304	171	282	209	220[†]	250
E.	COLOMBIA[†]	6	6	6	6	~	~	~	~	~	~
G.	CUBA[2]	22	31	35	23	30	37	41	40[†]	120[†]	135

1. Figures are sum of (1) crude ore sold directly for use and (2) concentrate output, both
   as reported in Brazilian sources. Data for 1979 and 1980 may include 45,000 to 55,000
   short tons annually of run-of-mine ore that required benefication. Total run-of-mine crude
   ore production (not comparable to data for other countries) was as follows, in thousand
   short tons: 1979–983; 1981–1,021; 1982–736, and 1983–740 (estimated).
2. Production of marketable product (direct-shipping lump ore plus concentrates and
   foundry sand).

a. Date available through May 6, 1988.

SOURCE: USBOM-MY, 1981, Volume I; 1983, p. 3; USBOM-MY, 1984, Volume 1;
   USBOM-MY, 1985, Volume 1; USBOM-MY, 1986, Volume 1, p. 239; USBOM-MY,
   1987, Volume 1, p. 230.

Table 1803

COPPER MINE PRODUCTION, 12 LC, 1977–87
(T MET)

Country	1977	1978	1979	1980	1981	1982	1983	1984	1985	1986[‡]	1987[†]
A. ARGENTINA	.2	.3	.1	.2	.1	.3	.3	.3	.4	.3	.3
B. BOLIVIA	3.2	2.9	1.8	1.9	2.6	2.3	2.0	1.6	1.7	.3	#[a]
C. BRAZIL	#	#	5.3	1.4	11.8	24.4	32.1	35.2	41.0	36.2	37.8
D. CHILE[3]	1,056.2	1,035.5	1,062.7	1,067.9	1,081.1	1,242.2	1,257.5	1,290.7	1,359.8	1,399.4	1,417.8
E. COLOMBIA	#	.1	.1	.1	.5	.1	.2	.2	#	~	~
G. CUBA	2.6	2.8	2.8	3.3	2.9	2.6	2.7	2.7	3.1	3.3[†]	3.0
I. ECUADOR	1.0	.8	.7	.9	.8	#[a]	#[a]	.2[†]	.1	.1	.1
K. GUATEMALA	2.5	2.1	1.8	.8	.7	.7[†]	#	#	4.5	4.2[†]	4.2
M. HONDURAS	.5	.6	1.4	.3	.5	.5	.6	.7[†]	5.1	5.0[†]	5.0
N. MEXICO[3]	89.7	87.2	107.1	175.4	232.9	229.2	196.0	303.5	276.1	285.0[†]	300.0
O. NICARAGUA[1]	3	.1[†]	- -	- -	- -	~	~	~	~[b]	~	~
R. PERU[3]	338.1	366.4	390.7	366.8	342.1	353.8	318.8	353.9	391.3	397.4	392.3
UNITED STATES[2,4]	1,364.4	1,357.6	1,446.6	1,281.1	1,538.2	1,147.0	1,038.1	1,102.6	1,105.8	1,147.3	1,255.9[b]

1. Copper content of concentrates produced.
2. Recoverable.
3. Copper content by analysis of concentrates for export plus nonduplicative total of copper content of all metal and metal products produced indigenously from domestic ores and concentrates.
4. By concentration, and leaching (electrowon).

a. Less than 50 tons.
b. Reported figure.

SOURCE: USBOM-MY, 1981, Volume I; USBOM-MIS, *Copper in 1982*, p. 3; 1983, p. 3; USBOM-MY, 1984, Volume 1; USBOM-MY, 1985, Volume 1; USBOM-MY, 1986, Volume 1, pp. 353 and 354; USBOM-MY, 1987, Volume I, p. 334.

Table 1804

FLUORSPAR PRODUCTION,[1,2] 5 LC, 1977–87
(Short Tons)

Country	1977	1979	1980	1981	1982	1983	1984	1985	1986[‡]	1987[†]
A. ARGENTINA	48,272	41,972	17,050	22,878	26,155	31,950	25,526	35,100	26,500	26,500
B. BOLIVIA	75,598	57,866	61,144	66,000	~	~	~	~	~	~
C. BRAZIL[4]	127,824	57,760	61,034	59,116	56,303	77,854	83,456	79,802	93,228	99,500
N. MEXICO	727,621	964,759	1,219,155	1,230,177	810,198	666,897	770,989	803,156	845,277	908,184[a]
S. URUGUAY[†]	83	85[†]	89	#	#	#	#	~	~	~
UNITED STATES[3]	169,489	109,299	92,635	115,404	77,017[‡]	61,000	72,000	66,000	78,000	70,000

1. Data available through May 13, 1988.
2. Total for all grades.
3. Shipments.
4. Series revised. Data presented are marketable concentrates (1979–83).

a. Reported figure.

SOURCE: USBOM-MY, 1981, Volume I; USBOM-MIS, *Fluorspar in 1982*, p. 3; USBOM-MCP, *Fluorspar, 1982*, p. 5; 1983, p. 3; USBOM-MY, 1984, Volume 1; USBOM-MY, 1985, Volume 1; USBOM-MY, 1986, Volume 1, pp. 402 and 403; USBOM-MY, 1987, Volume 1, pp. 378–379.

Table 1805

GOLD MINE PRODUCTION, 14 LC, 1977–87

(Troy Ounces)

	Country	1977	1979	1980	1981	1982	1983	1984	1985‡	1986‡	1987†
A.	ARGENTINA	5,509	10,140	10,622	14,757	22,248	24,660	22,120	28,357	26,700	30,000
B.	BOLIVIA	24,293	30,319	52,075	66,372	40,146	49,217	40,827	30,000†	30,000	39,000
C.	BRAZIL[1,†]	279,520	319,258	1,300,000	1,200,000	1,500,000	1,750,000	1,750,000	2,000,000	2,000,000	2,300,000
D.	CHILE	116,376	111,405	219,773	400,478	543,569	570,971	541,051	554,281	576,719	530,000
E.	COLOMBIA	257,070	269,369	510,439	529,214	472,674	438,579	799,889	1,142,830	1,400,000	850,711[a]
F.	COSTA RICA[†]	12,200	16,700	18,000	20,000	27,000	30,000	35,000	15,997[a]	11,600	13,000
H.	DOMINICAN REP.	342,755	352,982	369,603	407,813	386,309	354,023	338,272	328,046	282,990	246,000
I.	ECUADOR	8,124	2,251	225	2,347	1,601	608	1,000†	1,000†	2,000	320,000
J.	EL SALVADOR	2,156	2,720	2,492	3,883	3,300	650	285	- -	- -	- -
M.	HONDURAS	2,481	1,501	2,027	1,579	1,711	2,151	2,784	5,023	5,000	2,500
N.	MEXICO[2]	212,709	190,364	176,089	198,594	214,349	198,177	270,998	265,693	280,000	250,000
O.	NICARAGUA	65,764	61,086	59,984	61,913	54,384	46,428	35,000†	24,491	24,000	31,628
R.	PERU	104,393	141,656	142,041	161,590	134,647	168,534	187,406	212,870	215,862	215,000
T.	VENEZUELA	17,403	14,989	13,565	27,810	27,993	33,200†	50,885†	74,180	82,800	86,000
	UNITED STATES	1,100,347	964,390	969,782	1,379,161	1,465,686	1,002,526	2,084,615	2,427,232	3,739,015	4,966,382

1. All figures except those for 1978 differ substantially from those appearing in latest available official Brazilian sources owing to the inclusion here of estimates for unreported production by small mines (garimpos).
2. Production series for Mexico revised since 1980 to reflect mine output data published for each state and municipality.

a. Reported figure.

SOURCE: USBOM-MY, 1981, Volume 3; USBOM-MIS, *Gold in 1982*, p. 3; USBOM-MCP, *Gold*, 1982, p. 4; 1983, p. 3; USBOM-MY, 1984, Volume 1; USBOM-MY, 1985, Volume 1; USBOM-MY, 1986, Volume 1, pp. 455 and 456; USBOM-MY, 1987, Volume 1.

Table 1806

GYPSUM MINE PRODUCTION, 17 LC, 1977–87

(T Short Tons)

	Country	1977	1978	1979	1980	1981	1982	1983	1984	1985	1986‡	1987†
A.	ARGENTINA	603	674	648	1,028	739	679	637	625	508	509	507
B.	BOLIVIA	1†	1†	1†	1	1	1	1	1	1	1	1
C.	BRAZIL[1]	599	523	512	668	659	750	613	544	617	777	960
D.	CHILE	162	192	179	300	262	99	73	185	216	213	258[a]
E.	COLOMBIA	231	281	283	289	328	309	262	287	276	325	330
G.	CUBA[†]	100	105	100	134	143	140	145	145	145	145	145
H.	DOMINICAN REP.	249	190	193	259	225[a]	230†	230†	230†	342	146	65[a]
I.	ECUADOR	46	38	7	7	2[a]	2†	2†	2†	2	2	2
J.	EL SALVADOR	8	8	8	10	7†	6†	5†	5†	4	4	4
K.	GUATEMALA	35	42	28	37	32	31	43	28	19	31	26[a]
M.	HONDURAS[†]	20	25	25	25	22	22	25	25	25	25	25
N.	MEXICO	1,649	1,938	2,228	2,393	2,635	2,251	3,261	3,247	2,608	2,894	2,708
O.	NICARAGUA	40	40	40	44	33†	22	13	10†	9	9†	9
Q.	PARAGUAY	15	10	12†	13	11	7	4	7	3	3	3
R.	PERU	157	186	240	309	386[a]	400†	85	74	32	190	165
S.	URUGUAY	~	~	~	~	~	135	167	82	110†	110†	110
T.	VENEZUELA	184	206	287	129	241	175	226	158	147	275†	275
	UNITED STATES[2]	13,390	14,891	14,630	12,376	11,497	10,538	12,884	14,319	14,414	15,403	15,612[a]

1. Series revised to represent sum of (1) mine product sold without benefication and (2) output of concentrates.
2. Excludes byproduct gypsum.

a. Reported figure.

SOURCE: USBOM-MY, 1981, Volume I; USBOM-MIS, *Gypsum in 1982*, p. 3; 1983, p. 3; USBOM-MY, 1984, Volume 1; USBOM-MY, 1985, Volume 1; USBOM-MY, 1986, Volume 1, pp. 478 and 479; USBOM-MY, 1987, Volume 1, pp. 454–455.

Table 1807

IRON ORE PRODUCTION,[1,2] 8 LC, 1977–87

(T Long Tons)

	Country	1977	1979	1980	1981	1982	1983	1984	1985[‡]	1986[†]	1987
A.	ARGENTINA	1,014	601	430	392	1,140	581	563	629	797	750
B.	BOLIVIA	7	25	6	6	8	11	- -	- -	- -	- -
C.	BRAZIL	80,706	102,440	112,920	97,928	91,687	87,315	110,361	126,225	130,199	129,500
D.	CHILE	7,535	7,006	8,451	8,380	6,368	5,717	6,579	6,431	6,871	6,580
E.	COLOMBIA	497	391	498	426	463	449	434	440	643	605[a]
N.	MEXICO[3]	5,296	5,965	7,510	8,573	8,026	7,913	8,186	7,696	7,183	7,400
R.	PERU	6,184	5,358	5,614	5,973	5,683	4,219	3,916	4,815	4,956	4,770
T.	VENEZUELA	13,467	15,019	15,848	15,286	11,023	9,562	12,848	15,972	18,823	17,500
	UNITED STATES[4]	55,750	85,716	69,613	73,174	35,433	37,562	51,269	48,751	38,862	46,817[a]

1. Data available through July 22, 1988.
2. Gross weight: insofar as availability of sources permits, gross weight data represent the nonduplicative sum of marketable direct-shipping iron ores, iron ore concentrates, and iron ore agglomerates produced by each of the listed countries. Concentrates and agglomerates produced from imported iron ores have been excluded, under the assumption that the ore from which such materials are produced has been credited as marketable ore in the country where it was mined.
3. Gross weight calculated from reported iron content based on grade of 66% Fe.
4. Includes byproduct ore.

a. Reported figure.

SOURCE: USBOM-MY, 1981, Volume I; USBOM-MIS, *Iron in 1982*, p. 3; 1983, p. 3; USBOM-MY, 1984, Volume 1; USBOM-MY, 1985, Volume 1; USBOM-MY, 1986, Volume 1, pp. 527 and 528; USBOM-MY, 1987, Volume 1, pp. 493–494.

Table 1808

LEAD MINE PRODUCTION,[1] 11 LC, 1977–87

(T MET)

	Country	1977	1978	1979	1980	1981	1982	1983	1984	1985	1986[‡]	1987[†]
A.	ARGENTINA	33.6	30.3	31.8	32.6	32.7	32.8	31.7	28.5	28.6	28.9	28.8
B.	BOLIVIA	18.9	18.0	15.4	17.7	16.8	12.4	11.8	7.4	6.2	3.1	0.2
C.	BRAZIL	24.0	31.2	27.9	21.8	21.7	19.4	18.8	16.7	19.2	19.5[†]	14.9
D.	CHILE	.1	.4	.3	.3	.2	1.6	1.7	4.3	2.5	1.5	.9
E.	COLOMBIA	.2	.1	.2	.3	.2	.2	.2	.1	.1	.2	.2[b]
I.	ECUADOR	.2	.2	.2	.2	.2	.2	.2	.2	.2[†]	.2[†]	.2
K.	GUATEMALA[†]	.1	.1	.1	.1	#[a]	#[a]	~	~	~	~	~
M.	HONDURAS	20.6	21.8	16.4	13.3	12.6	15.1	19.3	20.5	21.2	12.6	20.0
N.	MEXICO[2,4]	163.5	170.6	173.5	147.2	148.9	170.2	184.3	202.6	197.5	207.0	200.0
O.	NICARAGUA	1.0	.4	- -	- -	- -	- -	~	~	~	~	~
R.	PERU[3]	175.7	182.7	174.0	189.1	192.7	197.6	207.4	193.7	201.5	194.4	204.0
	UNITED STATES	537.5	529.7	525.6	573.1	459.0	530.3	465.6	334.5	424.4	353.1	318.7

1. Data available through June 24, 1988.
2. Recoverable metal content of lead in concentrates for export plus lead content of domestic smelter products (refined lead, antimonial lead, mixed bars, and other unspecified items).
3. Recoverable metal content of lead in concentrates for export plus lead content of domestic smelter products (refined lead, antimonial lead, and bizmuth-lead bars).
4. Production series modified according to data on mine output per municipality and state.

a. Revised to zero.
b. Reported figure.

SOURCE: USBOM-MY, 1981, Volume I; USBOM-MIS, *Lead in 1982*, p. 3; 1983, p. 3; USBOM-MY, 1984, Volume 1; USBOM-MY, 1985, Volume 1; USBOM-MY, 1986, Volume 1, p. 601; USBOM-MY, 1987, Volume 1, p. 561.

Table 1809

MANGANESE ORE PRODUCTION, 4 L, 1980–87

(T Short Tons Unless Otherwise Specified)

	Country	1980	1981	1982	1983	1984	1985	1986[‡]	1987[†]
B.	BOLIVIA[1,2]	5[‡]	- -	- -	- -	- -	~	~	~
C.	BRAZIL[1,2]	2,515[a]	2,251[a]	2,580[b]	2,306	2,969	2,781	2,866	2,650
D.	CHILE	31	30[†]	~	~	~	~	~	~
N.	MEXICO	493[†]	637[†]	561[†]	386[†]	525[†]	437[†]	506[†]	425

1. Gross weight reported; metal content estimated.
2. Calculated metal content includes allowance for assumed moisture content.

a. Figures are the sum of (1) sales of direct-shipping manganese ore and (2) productioned
   beneficiated ore, both as reported in Anuário Mineral Brasiliero.
b. Reported Figure.

SOURCE: USBOM-MY, 1985, Volume 1; USBOM-MY, 1986, Volume 4, p. 655. For
   years 1977, 1978, 1079, see SALA, 24-1809; USBOM-MY, 1987, Volume 1, p. 613.

Table 1810

MERCURY MINE PRODUCTION, 3 LC, 1977–87

(Flasks)

	Country	1977	1979	1980	1981	1982	1983	1984	1985[‡]	1986[†]	1987[†]
D.	CHILE	20	- -	- -	- -	~	~	~	~	~	~
H.	DOMINICAN REP.	495	128	159	77	49	60	80	121[a]	120	100
N.	MEXICO	9,660	1,973	4,206	6,962	8,558	6,411	11,140	11,430	10,008	10,000
	UNITED STATES	28,244	29,519	30,657	27,904	25,760	25,070	19,048	16,530	~	~

a. Reported figure.

SOURCE: USBOM-MY, 1981, Volume I; USBOM-MIS, *Mercury in 1982*, p. 3; 1983, p. 3;
   USBOM-MY, 1984, Volume 1; USBOM-MY, 1985, Volume 1; USBOM-MY, 1986,
   Volume 1, p. 665; USBOM-MY, 1987, Volume 1, p. 623.

Table 1811

MOLYBDENUM MINE PRODUCTION, 3 LC, 1977–87

(T Pounds Contained Molybdenum)

	Country	1977	1979	1980	1981	1982	1983	1984	1985	1986[‡]	1987[†]
D.	CHILE	24,112	29,895	30,133	33,863	44,198	33,651	37,172	40,541	36,555	36,800
N.	MEXICO	2	105	163	994	11,442	12,932	8,938	8,292	7,385	8,000
R.	PERU	1,005	2,637	5,926	5,485	6,427	5,825	6,557	8,898	7,681	7,700
	UNITED STATES	122,408	143,967	150,686	139,900	84,381	33,593	103,664	108,409	93,976	75,117[a]

a. Reported figure.

SOURCE: USBOM-MY, 1981, Volume I; USBOM-MIS, *Molybdenum in 1982*, p. 3; 1983, p. 3;
   USBOM-MY, 1984, Volume 1; USBOM-MY, 1985, Volume 1; USBOM-MY, 1986, Volume 1,
   p. 684; USBOM-MY, 1987, Volume 1, p. 640.

Table 1812

NICKEL MINE PRODUCTION,[1] 5 LC, 1977–87

(Short Tons)

	Country	1977	1979	1980	1981	1982	1983	1984	1985	1986[‡]	1987[†]
C.	BRAZIL[2]	4,675	3,267	2,504	7,239	15,929	17,153	25,940	22,377	14,843	14,700
E.	COLOMBIA[3]	~	~	~	~	~	19,243	24,124	17,013	20,500[†]	22,800
G.	CUBA[4]	40,510	34,275	40,338	42,489	39,790	41,487	35,087	35,458	36,000[†]	37,500
H.	DOMINICAN REP.	27,446	27,680	18,019	20,601	5,926	21,552	26,371	28,450	24,239	24,500
K.	GUATEMALA	328	6,833	7,434	~	~	~	~	~	~	~
N.	MEXICO[2]	37	1	- -	- -	~	~	~	~	~	~
	UNITED STATES[5]	14,347	15,065	14,653	12,099	3,203	- -	14,540	6,127	1,175	- -

1. Data available through June 24, 1988.
2. Content of ore.
3. Content of ferroalloys.
4. Content of oxide, sinter, and sulfide.
5. Content of ore shipped.

SOURCE: USBOM-MY, 1981, Volume I; USBOM-MIS, *Nickel in 1982*, p. 3; USBOM-MCP,
Nickel, 1982, p. 6; 1983, p. 6; USBOM-MY, 1984, Volume 1, USBOM-MY, 1985,
Volume 1; USBOM-MY, 1986, Volume 1, p. 698; USBOM-MY, 1987, Volume 1, p. 649.

Table 1813

PHOSPHATE ROCK MINE PRODUCTION,[1] 5 LC, 1977–87

(T MET)

	Country	1977	1979	1980	1981	1982	1983	1984	1985	1986[‡]	1987[†]
C.	BRAZIL[2]	676	1,628	2,612	3,238	2,732	3,208	3,855	4,214	4,509	4,777
D.	CHILE	~	~	~	~	~	1	5	7	7	7
E.	COLOMBIA	6	6	6	17	20	17	11	24	27	34
N.	MEXICO	285	274	397	252	379	389	375	550	600	640
R.	PERU	~	5	14	12	29	3	13	12	30	90
T.	VENEZUELA	139	- -	- -	- -	~	~	~	~	~	~
	UNITED STATES	47,256	51,611	54,415	53,624	37,414	42,573	49,197	50,835	38,710	40,954

1. Data derived from International Fertilizer Industry Association and official sources
   where available.
2. Figure represents total of direct sales of run-of-mine product plus output of marketable
   concentrate. Direct sales of run-of-mine product were as follows, in thousand metric
   tons: 1977, 26; 1978, 27; 1979, 39; 1980, 40; 1981, 40 (estimated). Total output of
   crude ore reported in Brazilian sources is far higher than figures presented here, but
   such figures are not equivalent to data shown for other countries.

SOURCE: USBOM-MY, 1981, Volume I; USBOM-MY, 1984, Volume 1, USBOM-MY, 1985,
Volume 1; USBOM-MY, 1986, pp. 737 and 738; USBOM-MY, 1987, Volume 1, p. 686.

Table 1814

SALT PRODUCTION,[1] 15 LC, 1977–87

(T Short Tons)

	Country	1977	1979	1980	1981	1982	1983	1984	1985	1986[‡]	1987[†]
A.	ARGENTINA[2]	2	1	1	1,034	656	747	1,033	1,596	1,343	1,301
C.	BRAZIL[3]	323	759	877	3,974	4,105	4,615	4,990	3,008	3,900[†]	3,900
D.	CHILE	467	650	486	320	743	788	690	831	1,138	960
E.	COLOMBIA[3]	383	422	383	789	554	765	1,031	805	802	722[a]
F.	COSTA RICA[4]	30	51	44	43	121	120	120	33[a]	33	33
G.	CUBA	142	134	144	177	218	198	204	244	254	250
H.	DOMINICAN REP.[†]	38	42	61	70	70	70	70	52[a]	60	60
J.	EL SALVADOR[†]	30[‡]	30[‡]	2	2	2	2	3	3	3	3
K.	GUATEMALA	12	16	11	15	15[†]	17	18[†]	19	43	41[a]
M.	HONDURAS[†]	35	35	35	35	35	35	35	35	35	35
N.	MEXICO	5,400[†]	6,800	7,248	8,767	6,130	6,287	6,798	7,129	6,533	6,600
O.	NICARAGUA[†]	18[†]	20	22	20	20	20	17	17	17	17
P.	PANAMA[5]	23	21	20	35	27	94	20	18	11	11
R.	PERU	350	440	504	558	535[†,a]	165	279	226	440	440
T.	VENEZUELA	266	170[†]	268	275[†]	375	342[a]	360	390	463	440
	UNITED STATES[2,6]	43,412	45,793	40,351	38,915	37,910	34,605	39,256	40,102	36,703	36,532

1. Data available through July July 8, 1988.
2. Rock salt plus other salt.
3. Rock salt plus marine salt.
4. Marine salt.
5. Crude.
6. Including Puerto Rico (sold or used by producers).

a. Reported figure.

SOURCE: USBOM-MY, 1981, Volume I; USBOM-MIS, *Salt in 1982*, p. 3; 1983, p. 3;
USBOM-MY, 1984, Volume 1; USBOM-MY, 1985, Volume 1; USBOM-MY, 1986,
Volume 1, pp. 796–798; USBOM-MY, 1987, Volume 1, pp. 741–743.

Table 1815

SILVER MINE PRODUCTION,[1] 14 LC, 1977–87

(T Troy Ounces)

	Country	1977	1979	1980	1981	1982	1983	1984	1985	1986	1987[†]
A.	ARGENTINA	2,450	2,209	2,357	2,518	2,684	2,500	1,984	2,170	2,134	2,000
B.	BOLIVIA	5,813	5,742	5,099	6,394	5,472	6,025	4,560	3,580	3,058	3,800
C.	BRAZIL[3]	372	1,065	784	765	760	486	829	1,013[†]	1,490[†]	1,610
D.	CHILE	8,461	8,740	9,598	11,610	12,288	15,055	15,766	16,633	16,078	15,800
E.	COLOMBIA[2]	91	99	152	143	136	99	130	153	168[†]	144
F.	COSTA RICA[†]	1	2	2	2	2	2	2	2	2	2
H.	DOMINICAN REP.	1,852	2,276	1,623	2,034	2,198	1,329	1,207	1,581	1,356	1,150
I.	ECUADOR	57	44	29	32	10	3	2	2[†]	2[†]	2
J.	EL SALVADOR	112	152	146	137	86	22	22	~	~	~
K.	GUATEMALA[†]	~	10	10	8	3	~	~	~	~	~
M.	HONDURAS	2,819	2,434	1,766	1,823	2,100	2,587	2,697	2,765	1,745	2,000
N.	MEXICO	47,030	49,408	50,052	52,916	59,175	63,607	75,340	73,167	75,200[†]	75,000
O.	NICARAGUA	167	389	164	140	76	63	50[†]	30	25[†]	25
R.	PERU	39,731	29,248	44,419	46,940	41,957	50,477	53,080	58,230	61,916	66,000
	UNITED STATES	38,166	37,896	32,329	40,683	40,248	43,431	44,592	39,433	34,524	39,790[a]

1. Data available through July 1, 1988.
2. Smelter and/or refinery production.
3. Partially revised officially reported output; of total production, the following
quantities in thousand troy ounces, are identified as placer silter (the balance
being silver content of other ores and concentrates); 1980–47; 1981–144;
1982–123; 1983–247; and 1984– not available.

a. Reported figure.

SOURCE: USBOM-MY, 1981, Volume 1; USBOM-MIS, *Gold and Silter in 1982*, p. 5; 1983, p. 5;
USBOM-MY, 1984, Volume 1; USBOM-MY, 1985, Volume 1; USBOM-MY, 1986, Volume 1, p. 856;
USBOM-MY, 1987, Volume 1, p. 782.

Table 1816

SULFUR PRODUCTION,[1,2] 11 LC, 1977–87
(T MET)

Country	1977	1979	1980	1981	1982	1983	1984	1985	1986[‡]	1987[†]
A. ARGENTINA[†]	47	20	~	10	~	~	#	~	~	~
B. BOLIVIA[3]	6[a]	15[a]	11	10	6	3	2	3	5	10
C. BRAZIL[4]	44	92	156	163	184	188	216	229	272	288
D. CHILE[3]	61	104	115	143	137	131	86	109	98	97
E. COLOMBIA[10]	29	18	27	28	36	37	46	51	46[†]	50
G. CUBA[5,†]	42[†]	20[†]	30	22	28	13	8	8	8	8
I. ECUADOR[3,†]	13[†]	15[†]	14	12	15	15	15	14	14	15
N. MEXICO[6,†]	1,936[†]	2,125[†]	2,217	2,178	1,916	1,702	1,985	2,180	2,220	2,399
R. PERU[11]	20	20	20	20	73	65	64	68	66[†]	66
S. URUGUAY[7,†]	2	2	2	2	2	2	2	2	2	2
T. VENEZUELA[8,†]	95	85	85	85	85	85	86	88	90	92
UNITED STATES[9]	10,727	12,101	11,866	12,145	9,787	9,290	10,652	11,609	11,087	10,539

1. Data available through June 3, 1988.
2. In all forms.
3. Data are for native sulfur. May, however, produce limited quantities of byproduct sulfur from crude oil and natural gas and/or from petroleum refining. May also produce limited quantities of byproduct sulfur from metallurgical operations and/or coal processing.
4. By product, petroleum, metallurgy.
5. Pyrites, By product, petroleum.
6. Frasch, By product, metallurgy, petroleum.
7. By product, petroleum.
8. By product, petroleum and natural gas.
9. Frasch, pyrites, By product, metallurgy, natural gas, petroleum and unspecified.
10. Data are for native sulfur plus by-product petroleum.
11. Data are for native sulfur plus by-product, all sources.

a. Exports regarded as tantamount to production, owing to minimal domestic consumption levels.

SOURCE: USBOM-MY, 1981, Volume I; USBOM-MY, 1984, Volume 1; USBOM MY, 1985, Volume 1; USBOM-MY, 1986, Volume 1, pp. 910–915; USBOM-MY, 1987, Volume 1, pp. 853–857.

Table 1817

TIN MINE PRODUCTION,[1,2] 5 L, 1977–87
(MET)

Country	1977	1979	1980	1981	1982	1983	1984	1985	1986[‡]	1987[†]
A. ARGENTINA	537	386	351	413	342	291	274	451	379	300
B. BOLIVIA	33,740	27,648	27,291	29,830	26,773	25,278	19,911	16,136	10,479	7,000
C. BRAZIL	6,287	7,005	6,377	8,297	8,218	13,275	19,957	26,514	25,200	28,900
N. MEXICO	220	23	60	28	27	334	416	380	585	372[a]
R. PERU	329	870	1,077	1,519	1,672	2,808	3,314	3,779	4,817	5,000

1. Data available through June 17, 1988.
2. Data derived in part from the monthly Statistical Bulletin of the International Tin Council.

a. Reported figure.

SOURCE: USBOM-MY, 1981, Volume I; USBOM MIS, *Tin in 1982*, p. 3; 1983, p. 3, USBOM-MY, 1984, Volume 1; USBOM-MY, 1985, Volume 1; USBOM-MY, 1986, Volume 1, pp. 942 and 943; USBOM-MY, 1987, Volume 1, p. 883.

Table 1818

TUNGSTEN CONCENTRATE PRODUCTION,[1] 6 LC, 1977–87

(T Pounds of Contained Tungsten)

	Country	1977	1979	1980[a]	1981	1982	1983	1984	1985	1986[‡]	1987[†]
A.	ARGENTINA	154	130	44	11	17	41	37	17	25[†]	25
B.	BOLIVIA	5,355	5,445	2,732	2,779	2,534	2,449	1,893	1,643	1,095	500
C.	BRAZIL	2,672	2,595	1,116	1,576	1,524	1,026	1,037	1,090	800	672[b]
K.	GUATEMALA	~	~	~	~	40	~	~	6	9	10
N.	MEXICO	421	556	266	263	194	186	274	282	294	213[b]
R.	PERU	1,160	1,243	581	521	682	762	699	723	593	600
	UNITED STATES	6,008	6,643	2,754	3,605	1,521	980	1,203	996	780	34[b]

1. Data available through May 20, 1988.

a. 1980 and subsequent years measured in metric tons of tungsten content.
b. Reported figure.

SOURCE: USBOM-MY, 1981, Volume I; USBOM-MIS, *Tungsten in 1982*, p. 3; 1983, p. 3;
    USBOM-MY, 1984, Volume 1; USBOM-MY, 1985, Volume 1; USBOM-MY, 1986,
    Volume 1, p. 977; USBOM-MY, 1987, Volume 1, p. 914.

Table 1819

ZINC MINE PRODUCTION,[1] 11 LC, 1977–87

(T MET)

	Country	1977	1979	1980	1981	1982	1983	1984	1985	1986[‡]	1987[†]
A.	ARGENTINA	39.2	37.5	33.4	35.2	36.6	36.6	34.9	35.7	39.5	37.0
B.	BOLIVIA	61.4	51.6	50.3	47.0	45.7	47.1	37.8	37.1	33.5	36.3
C.	BRAZIL	57.6	89.9	67.0	95.2	110.6	118.6	113.7	123.8	123.9	119.4
D.	CHILE	3.9	1.8	1.1	1.5	5.7	6.0	19.2	22.3	10.5	19.6
E.	COLOMBIA	- -	- -	.3	.3	#	~	~	2.0	11.0	~
I.	ECUADOR	2.0	1.6	.6	.7	#	#	#	#	#	#
K.	GUATEMALA	1.0	1.0[†]	~	3.0	#	~	~	~	~	~
M.	HONDURAS	26.5	22.0	16.0	16.2	24.6	38.0	41.5	44.0	25.4[a]	10.0
N.	MEXICO	265.5	245.5	235.8	206.6	242.3	266.3	303.6	291.9	271.4	304.0
O.	NICARAGUA	11.2	- -	- -	- -	~	~	~	~	~	~
R.	PERU	405.3	432	487.6	498.9	507.1	576.4	558.5	588.6	597.6	592.3[a]
	UNITED STATES	407.9	267.3	348.0	343.0	326.5	296.7	277.5	251.9	216.0	232.9[a]

1. Data available through July 15, 1988.

a. Reported figure.

SOURCE: USBOM-MY, 1981, Volume I; USBOM-MIS, *Zinc in 1982*, p. 3; 1983, p. 3;
    USBOM-MY, 1984, Volume 1; USBOM-MY, 1985, Volume 1; USBOM-MY, 1986,
    Volume 1, pp. 1022–1023; USBOM-MY, 1987, Volume 1, p. 954.

Table 1820

INDICATORS FOR THE ECONOMIC CONTRIBUTION OF MINING
(%)

| | | | Share of the Mining Sector in: | | |
| | | | Exports | | |
Country	GDP 1981	Employment Various, 1970-76	Non-Fuel Minerals[1]	Petroleum[2]	Public Revenues Year Varies
Mining Economies			Average, 1978-80		
B. BOLIVIA	6.8	3.9	41.2	3.4	90.0

Continued in SALA, 24–1820.

Table 1821

PRODUCTION AND RESERVES OF NON-FUEL MINERALS BY MAJOR PRODUCERS
(%, 1982)

| | Share of Major Producers In | |
Mineral and Major Producer	World Production	World Reserves[1]
Ferrous Metals		
Colombium (Brazil)	85.8[a]	93.4[a]

Continued in SALA, 24–1821.

19

Energy Resources: Production, Consumption, and Reserves

Table 1900

ANNUAL GROWTH IN COMMERCIAL ENERGY PRODUCTION AND CONSUMPTION, 20 LC, 1965–86

| | | Average Annual Energy Growth Rate % | | | | Energy Consumption/C (kg) | | Energy Imports as % of Merchandise Imports | |
| | | Production | | Consumption | | | | | |
	Country	1965–80	1980–86	1965–80	1980–86	1965	1986	1965	1986
A.	ARGENTINA	4.5	2.5	4.3	1.4	975	1,427	8	3
B.	BOLIVIA	9.5	–.6	7.7	–2.0	155	255	1	2
C.	BRAZIL	8.6	11.7	9.9	4.2	286	830	14	19
D.	CHILE	1.8	3.7	3.0	1.2	657	812	5	7
E.	COLOMBIA	1	9.4	6.0	2.1	413	728	1	4
F.	COSTA RICA	8.2	5.7	8.8	2.3	267	565	8	8
G.	CUBA	~	~	~	~	~	~	~	~
H.	DOMINICAN REP.	10.9	7.3	11.5	2.6	127	337	8	28
I.	ECUADOR	35	7.7	11.9	2.6	162	575	11	2
J.	EL SALVADOR	9	3.6	7	1.5	140	216	5	8
K.	GUATEMALA	12.5	6.7	6.8	–1.3	150	171	9	10
L.	HAITI	~	5.3	8.4	1.6	24	50	6	4
M.	HONDURAS	14	1.7	7.6	1.5	111	192	5	10
N.	MEXICO	9.7	2.6	7.9	.5	604	1,235	4	1
O.	NICARAGUA	2.6	2.7	6.5	1.7	172	259	6	20
P.	PANAMA	6.9	12.9	5.8	4.9	576	653	~	~
Q.	PARAGUAY	~	15.9	9.7	5.1	84	224	17	32
R.	PERU	6.6	–.1	5.0	–.3	395	478	3	1
S.	URUGUAY	4.7	13.7	1.3	–2.8	765	742	13	13
T.	VENEZUELA	–3.1	–2.3	4.6	2.4	2,319	2,502	#	#
	UNITED STATES	1.1	.2	2.3	–.1	6,535	7,193	8	19

SOURCE: *World Development Report 1988*, table 10.

Table 1901

TOTAL COMMERCIAL ENERGY PRODUCTION,[1] 20 LC, 1950–86

(M MET Coal Equivalent)

	Country	1950	1960	1970	1980	1982	1983	1984	1985	1986
A.	ARGENTINA	5.00	15.22	37.29	51.13	53.54	56.12	56.50	56.20	55.85
B.	BOLIVIA	.14	.74	1.76	4.66	5.26	4.99	4.76	4.65	4.83
C.	BRAZIL	2.60	9.02	18.69	34.50	42.18	49.62	62.13	71.17	73.43
D.	CHILE	2.10	3.20	6.11	5.77	6.60	6.69	6.93	6.72	6.93
E.	COLOMBIA	8.72	14.55	21.81	21.90	23.31	25.29	26.45	29.99	41.06
F.	COSTA RICA	.02	.05	.12	.26	.29	.35	.37	.34	.35
G.	CUBA	.03	.02	.24	.43	.80	1.10	1.11	1.26	1.35
H.	DOMINICAN REP.	~	.01	.01	.07	.10	.10	.06	.13	.11
I.	ECUADOR	.54	.57	.38	15.32	15.61	17.67	19.31	21.03	21.59
J.	EL SALVADOR	.01	.03	.06	.18	.17	.18	.19	.21	.21
K.	GUATEMALA	.01	.02	.04	.33	.50	.60	.41	.35	.60
L.	HAITI	~	~	~	.03	.03	.03	.03	.03	.04
M.	HONDURAS	#	#	.02	.10	.11	.11	11	.11	.11
N.	MEXICO	16.18	29.04	53.81	198.10	262.74	259.10	256.72	249.72	234.31
O.	NICARAGUA	#	#	.04	.06	.05	.04	.06	.07	.07
P.	PANAMA	#	#	.01	.15	.13	.11	.18	.24	.26
Q.	PARAGUAY	~	~	.02	.07	.08	.10	.11	.16	.20
R.	PERU	3.43	4.34	6.43	16.57	16.38	14.03	15.44	15.49	14.77
S.	URUGUAY	.07	.08	.15	.43	.62	.88	.87	.79	.90
T.	VENEZUELA	114.88	224.94	298.49	193.94	172.02	163.08	166.33	157.12	170.16
	UNITED STATES	1,156.42	1,414.50	2,103.70	2,045.68	1,993,45	1,897.81	2,048.32	2,019.21	1,993.40

1. Based on the production of coal, lignite, crude petroleum, natural gas, and hydro and nuclear electricity. Where peat used as fuel is important, it is included with coal and lignite.

SOURCE: UN-SP: J, 19 (1976), tables 1 and 2; UN-YWES, 1979–86, table 1.

Table 1902

PC OF TOTAL COMMERCIAL ENERGY PRODUCTION, 20 LC, 1955–86
(APGR)

	Country	1955	1960	1970	1975	1980	1982	1983	1984	1985	1986
A.	ARGENTINA	80.0	24.56	10.9	2.1	5.2	2.1	4.8	.7	–.5	–.6
B.	BOLIVIA	50.0	10.2	28.2	35.3	.4	5.6	–5.1	–4.6	–2.3	3.9
C.	BRAZIL	7.4	26.3	11.9	6.2	11.6	13.3	17.6	25.2	14.6	3.2
D.	CHILE	8.5	8.5	–1.5	–.6	8.1	–.3	1.4	3.6	–3.0	3.1
E.	COLOMBIA	3.3	11.5	4.2	–2.3	8.5	1.4	8.5	4.6	13.4	36.9
F.	COSTA RICA	10.0	13.3	14.3	6.7	30.0	3.6	20.7	5.7	–8.1	2.9
G.	CUBA	26.7	–14.3	40.0	10.0	–6.5	105.1	37.5	.9	13.5	7.1
H.	DOMINICAN REP.	~	~	0	0	600.0	0	0	–40.0	116.7	–15.4
I.	ECUADOR	3.7	–2.2	–5.9	612.6	–4.8	–1.4	13.2	9.3	8.9	2.7
J.	EL SALVADOR	20.0	10.0	4.0	0	0	6.3	5.9	5.6	10.5	0
K.	GUATEMALA	20.0	0	60.0	5.0	120.0	42.9	20.0	–31.7	–14.6	71.4
L.	HAITI	~	~	~	~	0	0	0	0	0	33.3
M.	HONDURAS	~	~	20.0	30.0	42.9	10.0	0	0	0	0
N.	MEXICO	4.5	8.8	5.6	10.5	30.5	13.2	–1.4	–.9	–2.7	–6.2
O.	NICARAGUA	~	~	6.7	5.0	20.0	–16.7	–20.0	50.0	16.7	0
P.	PANAMA	~	~	~	0	50.0	–18.8	–15.4	63.6	13.3	8.3
Q.	PARAGUAY	~	~	~	50.0	–22.2	–11.1	25.0	10.0	45.5	25.0
R.	PERU	–2.5	8.3	4.8	1.4	5.7	1.3	–14.3	10.0	.3	–4.6
S.	URUGUAY	2.9	0	17.5	–1.3	230.8	100.0	41.2	–1.1	–9.2	13.9
T.	VENEZUELA	6.5	9.4	4.2	–6.6	–5.9	–9.2	–5.2	2.0	–5.5	8.3
	UNITED STATES	1.8	2.6	5.8	–1.3	–1.4	–1.9	–5.0	7.9	–1.4	–1.3

SOURCE: SALA calculations from table 1901.

Table 1903

INDEX OF TOTAL PRODUCTION OF COMMERCIAL ENERGY,[1] 20 LC, 1970–86
(1975 = 100)

	Country	1970	1980	1982	1983	1984	1985	1986
A.	ARGENTINA	91	124	130	136	137	137	136
B.	BOLIVIA	36	101	110	102	98	95	99
C.	BRAZIL	76	141	172	203	254	291	300
D.	CHILE	103	97	111	113	117	113	117
E.	COLOMBIA	113	109	121	131	137	155	213
F.	COSTA RICA	72	164	181	219	231	213	219
G.	CUBA	68	121	222	306	308	350	375
H.	DOMINICAN REP.	157	89	1,000	1,000	600	1,300	1,100
I.	ECUADOR	3	128	130	147	161	175	112
J.	EL SALVADOR	100	302	283	300	317	350	350
K.	GUATEMALA	86	723	1,000	1,200	820	700	1,200
L.	HAITI	~	179	150	150	150	150	200
M.	HONDURAS	47	152	220	220	220	220	220
N.	MEXICO	66	228	320	316	313	304	286
O.	NICARAGUA	86	139	100	80	120	140	140
P.	PANAMA	84	1,265	1,300	1,100	1,800	2,400	2,600
Q.	PARAGUAY	29	161	114	143	157	229	286
R.	PERU	93	233	238	204	224	225	214
S.	URUGUAY	110	201	443	629	621	564	643
T.	VENEZUELA	150	97	86	82	83	78	85
	UNITED STATES	107	107	102	97	104	103	102

1. Includes all types of solid, liquid, and gaseous fuels, plus electricity production.

SOURCE: SALA calculations from table 1901.

Table 1904

COMMERCIAL ENERGY PRODUCTION, BY RESOURCE CLASSIFICATION, 20 LC, 1980–86

Country/Year	Coal Equivalent (T MET)					%				
	Total	Solids[1]	Liquids[2]	Gas[3]	Electricity[4]	Total[5]	Solids	Liquids	Gas	Electricity
A. ARGENTINA										
1980	51,534	329	37,499	11,555	2,151	100.0	.6	72.8	22.4	4.2
1981	52,405	420	38,229	11,606	2,150	100.0	.8	72.9	22.1	4.1
1982	53,535	434	37,308	13,403	2,390	100.0	.8	69.7	25.0	4.5
1983	56,123	410	37,456	15,577	2,681	100.0	.7	66.7	27.8	4.8
1984	56,504	429	36,749	16,315	3,011	100.0	.8	65.0	28.9	5.3
1985	56,203	337	35,261	17,360	3,245	100.0	.6	62.7	30.9	5.8
1986	55,846	308	33,399	18,857	3,283	100.0	.5	59.8	33.8	5.9
B. BOLIVIA										
1980	4,662	**	1,805	2,724	133	100.0	0	38.7	58.4	2.9
1981	4,885	**	1,763	2,980	142	100.0	0	36.1	61.0	2.9
1982	5,263	**	1,930	3,185	148	100.0	0	36.7	60.5	2.8
1983	4,990	**	1,786	3,060	144	100.0	0	35.8	61.3	2.9
1984	4,756	**	1,666	2,944	146	100.0	0	35.0	61.9	3.1
1985	4,647	**	1,589	2,916	142	100.0	0	34.2	62.8	3.0
1986	4,825	**	1,711	2,970	144	100.0	0	35.5	61.6	2.0
C. BRAZIL										
1980	34,500	3,744	13,494	1,406	15,856	100.0	10.9	39.1	4.1	46.0
1981	37,220	4,003	15,868	1,265	16,084	100.0	10.8	42.6	3.4	43.2
1982	42,177	4,424	18,953	1,464	17,336	100.0	10.5	44.9	3.5	41.1
1983	49,615	4,684	24,173	2,151	18,606	100.0	9.4	48.7	4.3	37.5
1984	62,126	5,226	33,805	2,632	20,463	100.0	8.4	54.5	4.2	32.9
1985	71,168	5,384	40,157	3,301	22,326	100.0	7.6	56.4	4.6	31.4
1986	73,432	5,154	42,071	3,758	22,449	100.0	7.0	57.3	5.1	30.6
D. CHILE										
1980	5,765	978	2,960	924	903	100.0	17.0	51.3	16.0	15.7
1981	6,619	1,104	3,443	1,139	933	100.0	16.7	52.0	17.2	14.1
1982	6,602	994	3,392	1,177	1,039	100.0	15.1	51.4	17.8	15.7
1983	6,691	999	3,344	1,251	1,097	100.0	14.9	50.0	18.7	16.4
1984	6,930	1,191	3,338	1,256	1,146	100.0	17.2	48.2	18.1	16.5
1985	6,719	1,293	2,874	1,280	1,272	100.0	19.2	42.8	19.1	18.9
1986	6,930	1,630	2,741	1,170	1,389	100.0	23.5	39.6	16.9	20.0
E. COLOMBIA										
1980	21,901	4,947	9,761	5,137	2,056	100.0	22.6	44.6	23.5	9.4
1981	22,997	4,870	10,357	5,600	2,170	100.0	21.2	45.0	24.4	9.4
1982	23,311	4,875	10,725	5,432	2,279	100.0	20.9	46.0	23.3	9.8
1983	25,294	5,810	11,522	5,640	2,322	100.0	23.2	45.0	22.5	9.3
1984	26,447	5,810	12,637	5,630	2,371	100.0	22.0	47.6	21.5	9.0
1985	29,986	8,690	13,253	5,647	2,396	100.0	22.6	47.5	21.3	8.6
1986	41,061	10,361	22,623	5,657	2,420	100.0	25.2	55.1	13.8	5.9
F. COSTA RICA										
1980	262	**	**	**	262	100.0	0	0	0	100.0
1981	277	**	**	**	277	100.0	0	0	0	100.0
1982	292	**	**	**	292	100.0	0	0	0	100.0
1983	348	**	**	**	348	100.0	0	0	0	100.0
1984	369	**	**	**	369	100.0	0	0	0	100.0
1985	340	**	**	**	340	100.0	0	0	0	100.0
1986	353	**	**	**	353	100.0	0	0	0	100.0
G. CUBA										
1980	434	**	398	24	12	100.0	0	91.7	5.5	2.8
1981	387	**	368	12	7	100.0	0	95.1	3.1	1.8
1982	791	**	773	13	5	100.0	0	97.7	1.6	.6
1983	1,078	**	1,060	10	8	100.0	0	98.3	.9	.7
1984	1,113	**	1,100	4	9	100.0	0	98.8	.4	.8
1985	1,255	**	1,240	9	7	100.0	0	98.7	.7	.6
1986	1,354	**	1,340	7	7	100.0	0	99.0	.5	.5
H. DOMINICAN REP.										
1980	71	**	**	**	71	100.0	0	0	0	100.0
1981	101	**	**	**	101	100.0	0	0	0	100.0
1982	93	**	**	**	93	100.0	0	0	0	100.0
1983	96	**	**	**	96	100.0	0	0	0	100.0
1984	63	**	**	**	63	100.0	0	0	0	100.0
1985	127	**	**	**	127	100.0	0	0	0	100.0
1986	111	**	**	**	111	100.0	0	0	0	100.0

Table 1904 (Continued)

COMMERCIAL ENERGY PRODUCTION, BY RESOURCE CLASSIFICATION, 20 LC, 1980–86

Country/Year	Coal Equivalent (T MET) Total	Solids[1]	Liquids[2]	Gas[3]	Electricity[4]	% Total[5]	Solids	Liquids	Gas	Electricity
I. ECUADOR										
1980	15,322	**	15,162	51	109	100.0	0	99.0	.3	.7
1981	15,828	**	15,640	91	97	100.0	0	98.8	.6	.6
1982	15,607	**	15,376	121	110	100.0	0	98.5	.8	.7
1983	17,674	**	17,321	140	213	100.0	0	98.0	.8	1.2
1984	19,315	**	18,788	134	393	100.0	0	97.3	.7	2.0
1985	21,132	**	20,502	232	398	100.0	0	97.0	1.1	1.9
1986										
J. EL SALVADOR										
1980	177	**	**	**	177	100.0	0	0	0	100.0
1981	164	**	**	**	164	100.0	0	0	0	100.0
1982	171	**	**	**	171	100.0	0	0	0	100.0
1983	183	**	**	**	183	100.0	0	0	0	100.0
1984	192	**	**	**	192	100.0	0	0	0	100.0
1985	205	**	**	**	205	100.0	0	0	0	100.0
1986	205	**	**	**	205	100.0	0	0	0	100.0
K. GUATEMALA										
1980	335	**	301	**	34	100.0	0	89.9	0	10.1
1981	344	**	302	**	42	100.0	0	87.8	0	12.2
1982	512	**	453	**	59	100.0	0	88.5	0	11.5
1983	599	**	500	**	99	100.0	0	83.5	0	16.5
1984	413	**	339	**	74	100.0	0	82.1	0	17.9
1985	346	**	263	**	83	100.0	0	76.0	0	24.0
1986	496	**	413	**	84	100.0	0	83.0	0	17.0
L. HAITI										
1980	27	**	**	**	27	100.0	0	0	0	100.0
1981	28	**	**	**	28	100.0	0	0	0	100.0
1982	31	**	**	**	31	100.0	0	0	0	100.0
1983	32	**	**	**	32	100.0	0	0	0	100.0
1984	32	**	**	**	32	100.0	0	0	0	100.0
1985	32	**	**	**	32	100.0	0	0	0	100.0
1986	39	**	**	**	39	100.0	0	0	0	100.0
M. HONDURAS										
1980	96	**	**	**	96	100.0	0	0	0	100.0
1981	101	**	**	**	101	100.0	0	0	0	100.0
1982	107	**	**	**	107	100.0	0	0	0	100.0
1983	111	**	**	**	111	100.0	0	0	0	100.0
1984	107	**	**	**	107	100.0	0	0	0	100.0
1985	107	**	**	**	107	100.0	0	0	0	100.0
1986	108	**	**	**	108	100.0	0	0	0	100.0
N. MEXICO										
1980	198,099	5,007	155,561	35,339	2,192	100.0	2.5	78.5	17.8	1.1
1981	232,017	5,776	187,847	35,247	3,147	100.0	2.5	81.0	15.2	1.4
1982	262,737	5,453	217,624	36,687	2,973	100.0	2.1	82.8	14.0	1.1
1983	259,104	6,394	217,258	32,739	2,714	100.0	2.5	83.8	12.6	1.1
1984	256,720	5,991	223,582	24,073	3,074	100.0	2.3	87.1	9.4	1.2
1985	249,722	6,000	218,217	22,080	3,425	100.0	2.4	87.4	8.8	1.4
1986	234,305	6,036	203,745	20,939	3,585	100.0	2.6	87.0	8.9	1.5
O. NICARAGUA										
1980	63	**	**	**	63	100.0	0	0	0	100.0
1981	61	**	**	**	61	100.0	0	0	0	100.0
1982	52	**	**	**	52	100.0	0	0	0	100.0
1983	39	**	**	**	39	100.0	0	0	0	100.0
1984	62	**	**	**	62	100.0	0	0	0	100.0
1985	69	**	**	**	69	100.0	0	0	0	100.0
1986	70	**	**	**	70	100.0	0	0	0	100.0
P. PANAMA										
1980	145	**	**	**	145	100.0	0	0	0	100.0
1981	164	**	**	**	164	100.0	0	0	0	100.0
1982	132	**	**	**	132	100.0	0	0	0	100.0
1983	106	**	**	**	106	100.0	0	0	0	100.0
1984	183	**	**	**	183	100.0	0	0	0	100.0
1985	237	**	**	**	237	100.0	0	0	0	100.0
1986	257	**	**	**	257	100.0	0	0	0	100.0

Table 1904 (Continued)

COMMERCIAL ENERGY PRODUCTION, BY RESOURCE CLASSIFICATION, 20 LC, 1980–86

Country/Year	Coal Equivalent (T MET)					%				
	Total	Solids[1]	Liquids[2]	Gas[3]	Electricity[4]	Total[5]	Solids	Liquids	Gas	Electricity
Q. PARAGUAY										
1980	71	**	**	**	71	100.0	0	0	0	100.0
1981	87	**	**	**	87	100.0	0	0	0	100.0
1982	79	**	**	**	79	100.0	0	0	0	100.0
1983	96	**	**	**	96	100.0	0	0	0	100.0
1984	109	**	**	**	109	100.0	0	0	0	100.0
1985	155	**	**	**	155	100.0	0	0	0	100.0
1986	201	**	**	**	201	100.0	0	0	0	100.0
R. PERU										
1980	16,566	56	14,081	1,491	938	100.0	.3	85.0	9.0	5.7
1981	16,612	69	13,899	1,660	984	100.0	.4	83.7	10.0	5.9
1982	16,382	47	13,803	1,500	1,032	100.0	.2	84.3	9.2	6.3
1983	14,029	89	12,288	656	996	100.0	.6	87.6	4.7	7.1
1984	15,437	103	13,476	805	1,053	100.0	.7	87.3	5.2	6.8
1985	15,486	122	13,397	823	1,144	100.0	.8	86.5	5.3	7.4
1986	14,768	147	12,613	785	1,224	100.0	1.0	85.4	5.3	8.3
S. URUGUAY										
1980	428	**	**	**	428	100.0	0	0	0	100.0
1981	313	**	**	**	313	100.0	0	0	0	100.0
1982	615	**	**	**	615	100.0	0	0	0	100.0
1983	883	**	**	**	883	100.0	0	0	0	100.0
1984	873	**	**	**	873	100.0	0	0	0	100.0
1985	792	**	**	**	792	100.0	0	0	0	100.0
1986	896	**	**	**	896	100.0	0	0	0	100.0
T. VENEZUELA										
1980	193,939	44	170,194	21,938	1,763	100.0	#	87.8	11.3	.9
1981	189,477	46	165,505	22,070	1,856	100.0	#	87.3	11.6	1.0
1982	172,020	47	146,722	23,286	1,965	100.0	#	85.3	13.5	1.1
1983	163,078	39	138,083	22,782	2,174	100.0	#	84.7	14.0	1.3
1984	166,334	51	138,597	25,270	2,416	100.0	#	83.3	15.2	1.5
1985	157,116	41	129,589	24,944	2,543	100.0	#	82.5	15.9	1.6
1986	170,158	57	137,888	29,597	2,616	100.0	#	81.0	17.4	1.5
UNITED STATES										
1980	2,045,683	626,451	696,522	657,039	65,671	100.0	30.6	34.0	32.1	3.2
1981	2,032,150	621,064	694,353	650,233	66,500	100.0	30.6	34.2	32.0	3.3
1982	1,993,451	631,957	685,577	602,418	73,499	100.0	31.7	34.4	30.2	3.7
1983	1,897,809	586,244	688,269	545,440	77,857	100.0	33.0	35.2	27.7	4.1
1984	2,048,316	668,387	707,189	591,691	81,049	100.0	32.6	34.5	28.9	4.0
1985	2,019,211	666,401	710,914	558,390	83,506	100.0	33.0	35.2	27.7	4.1
1986	1,993,398	669,509	688,739	546,597	88,553	100.0	33.6	34.6	27.4	4.4

1. Comprised of hard coal, lignite-brown coal, peat, and oil shale.
2. Comprised of crude petroleum and natural gas liquids.
3. Comprised of natural gas.
4. Comprised of electricity generation from hydro, nuclear, and geothermal sources.
5. May not total due to rounding.

SOURCE: UN-YWES, 1984–86, table 1; percentages calculated by SALA.

Table 1905

TOTAL COMMERCIAL ENERGY CONSUMPTION,[1] 20 LC, 1929-86[a,b,c,d]
(M MET Coal Equivalent and Kg PI)

Year	A. ARGENTINA Total	Per Capita	B. BOLIVIA Total	Per Capita	C. BRAZIL Total	Per Capita	D. CHILE Total	Per Capita	E. COLOMBIA Total	Per Capita	F. COSTA RICA Total	Per Capita	G. CUBA Total	Per Capita	H. DOMINICAN REP. Total	Per Capita	I. ECUADOR Total	Per Capita	J. EL SALVADOR Total	Per Capita	K. GUATEMALA Total	Per Capita
1929	7.58	680	.10	30	4.13	100	3.09	740	.60	70	.08	150	2.11	590	.10	40	.04	20	.08	40	.13	60
1937	9.22	650	.13	40	5.02	130	3.21	670	1.18	140	.09	150	1.49	340	.07	40	.11	40	.06	40	.12	60
1950	12.52	730	.25	89	9.60	180	3.64	597	3.04	264	.16	182	2.51	429	.15	61	.34	103	.13	68	.30	97
1960	22.3	1,057	.5	150	22.16	305	5.29	697	7.6*	487	.3	222	6.06	862	.5	142	.8	186	.3	117	.63	158
1970	37.9	1,581	1.0	225	41.7	435	10.8	1,152	12.7	609	.7	374	8.5	997	1.4	318	1.7	282	.7	192	1.0	191
1971	40.4	1,678	.01	230	46.4	488	11.8	1,239	13.0	617	.8	437	9.1	1,046	1.7	396	1.9	301	.7	197	1.1	204
1972	41.4	1,698	.2	251	52.0	532	11.5	1,187	13.3	615	.9	469	9.4	1,059	2.2	509	1.9	299	.7	199	1.2	217
1973	44.3	1,793	1.2	259	59.5	591	11.6	1,177	14.6	655	1.0	534	10.0	1,102	2.7	566	2.1	313	.9	241	1.3	228
1974	44.0	1,756	.4	298	66.7	649	11.3	1,124	15.2	660	1.0	500	10.1	1,096	2.8	622	2.4	355	.9	234	1.4	233
1975	43.1	1,654	1.6	333	71.2	659	9.8	956	16.0	688	1.0	524	11.8	1,261	2.7	549	2.8	409	1.0	230	1.5	239
1976	44.2	1,720	1.8	357	77.7	712	9.6	933	16.6	684	1.0	483	10.7	1,126	2.6	537	3.2	433	1.0	251	1.4	217
1977	46.1	1,769	2.1	410	82.0	731	10.1	956	17.9	713	1.2	582	12.4	1,297	2.6	520	3.2	418	1.1	259	1.6	226
1978	44.9	1,746	2.2	427	87.8	777	10.4	972	19.3	754	1.4	645	12.7	1,312	2.4	465	4.3	543	1.1	260	1.8	263
1979	48.6	1,831	2.3	430	91.2	788	10.9	1,002	19.8	749	1.2	572	13.2	1,346	2.2	410	5.0	621	1.2	261	2.1	291
1980	49.3	1,746	2.1	383	92.5	763	11.4	1,025	23.8	923	1.2	547	13.6	1,394	2.8	501	5.6	708	1.0	199	1.9	267
1981	47.7	1,663	2.4	412	86.8	700	11.4	1,006	22.1	840	1.2	523	14.0	1,436	2.7	474	6.0	728	.9	186	1.7	226
1982	48.8	1,673	2.4	410	87.4	689	10.5	913	22.0	815	1.1	463	15.0	1,521	2.6	443	6.2	719	.9	177	1.6	212
1983	51.6	1,743	2.4	398	87.1	671	10.7	914	23.7	862	1.1	458	13.8	1,395	3.5	585	6.0	669	1.0	185	1.4	190
1984	52.2	1,736	2.1	346	90.0	679	10.9	922	23.1	820	1.2	463	14.7	1,475	3.0	490	6.1	666	1.0	179	1.6	204
1985	50.0	1,636	2.1	323	96.2	709	10.8	895	23.6	820	1.3	485	13.9	1,383	2.7	428	6.0	640	1.0	175	1.6	198
1986	53.9	1,737	2.2	335	105.4	761	11.3	921	22.8	779	1.3	470	14.4	1,424	2.9	448	6.3	656	1.0	166	1.5	186

Table 1905 (Continued)

TOTAL COMMERCIAL ENERGY CONSUMPTION,[1] 20 LC, 1929–86[a,b,c,d]
(M MET Coal Equivalent and Kg PI)

Year	L. HAITI Total	Per Capita	M. HONDURAS Total	Per Capita	N. MEXICO Total	Per Capita	O. NICARAGUA Total	Per Capita	P. PANAMA Total	Per Capita	Q. PARAGUAY Total	Per Capita	R. PERU Total	Per Capita	S. URUGUAY Total	Per Capita	T. VENEZUELA Total	Per Capita	UNITED STATES Total	Per Capita	WORLD Total	Per Capita
1929	.02	10	.22	236	4.82	300	.03	40	--	--	--	--	.86	140	.82	440	.70	230	803.40	6,570	1,857.4	975
1937	.02	10	.18	167	8.19	440	.05	60	--	--	.01	10	.85	130	.83	400	1.04	300	759.30	5,890	2,002.2	1,001
1950	.06	17	.14	102	13.2	481	.09	81	.24	300	.03	22	2.05	268	1.0	445	5.0	953	1,138.07	7,474	2,391.9	955
1960	.1	34	.3	147	26.6	717	.25	165	.5	493	.14	80	4.0	396	2.1	788	13.8	1,824	1,454.0	8,047	3,924.2	1,302
1970	.2	37	.6	227	53.1	1,038	.7	320	.9	629	.3	142	8.0	608	2.5	887	24.6	2,242	2,216.9	10,811	6,439.6	1,748
1971	.2	42	.6	207	57.6	1,098	.7	366	1.1	768	.3	130	8.3	600	2.6	889	25.1	2,369	2,258.8	10,909	6,770.8	1,817
1972	.2	41	.6	226	61.2	1,128	.8	397	1.2	818	.3	134	8.3	583	2.8	944	27.1	2,478	2,376.6	11,380	7,078.7	1,868
1973	.2	42	.7	230	65.9	1,174	.8	415	1.3	846	.4	154	8.6	589	2.7	955	31.8	2,817	2,437.7	11,504	7,438.1	1,923
1974	.2	36	.7	223	71.9	1,238	.9	429	1.3	799	.4	162	9.0	596	2.6	947	32.1	2,760	2,345.6	11,070	7,471.3	1,899
1975	.2	40	.7	232	73.7	1,226	.9	375	1.4	856	.4	149	10.2	674	2.6	931	33.5	2,558	2,260.8	10,468	7,439.7	1,825
1976	.2	40	.8	247	77.6	1,247	1.0	442	1.4	842	.5	169	10.1	634	2.9	1,030	35.8	2,975	2,378.3	11,054	7,872.2	1,930
1977	.2	48	.9	275	84.3	1,290	1.2	505	1.4	809	.6	198	10.1	619	2.8	946	37.9	2,952	2,406.2	11,095	8,075.5	1,946
1978	.3	67	.8	229	93.5	1,397	1.1	456	1.4	760	.7	233	10.2	612	2.7	931	40.0	3,046	2,489.8	11,186	8,369.7	1,967
1979	.3	67	.8	231	106.6	1,536	.8	296	1.5	817	.6	210	10.8	626	2.8	981	45.6	3,372	2,502.5	11,120	8,653.5	2,000
1980	.3	56	.8	245	118.6	1,709	.9	330	1.6	849	.7	233	12.0	693	2.8	957	49.0	3,140	2,364.5	10,386	8,544.3	1,919
1981	.3	56	.9	218	129.8	1,821	1.0	359	1.6	763	.7	225	12.4	697	2.6	878	50.2	3,109	2,302.0	10,018	8,457.4	1,867
1982	.3	53	.9	219	129.3	1,766	1.0	345	1.4	703	.7	212	12.1	662	2.4	825	51.8	3,248	2,196.3	9,468	8,436.7	1,831
1983	.3	54	.9	223	128.4	1,710	1.0	330	1.5	723	.8	218	10.2	543	2.1	699	53.0	3,232	2,177.4	9,305	8,590.3	1,834
1984	.3	53	1.0	225	129.2	1,678	1.0	304	1.4	672	.8	231	10.5	546	1.9	647	56.0	3,321	2,262.3	9,586	8,906.1	1,871
1985	.3	51	1.0	220	132.8	1,681	1.0	307	1.4	661	.9	239	10.4	529	1.8	608	56.3	3,252	2,282.8	9,591	9,142.3	1,890
1986	.3	49	.9	204	129.8	1,604	1.0	307	1.4	636	1.0	252	10.6	524	1.9	610	60.1	3,380	2,278.1	9,489	9,321.9	1,896

1. Includes solid and liquid fuels; natural and imported gas, hydro, nuclear, and imported electricity.

a. Change in terminology: "gross commercial consumption" through 1950; "gross consumption" through 1954; "aggregate consumption" since 1955.

b. Prior to 1960 total data given to two decimal places, and per capita data for 1951-54 calculated with population statistics in SALA-SNP, chapter VIII. Per capita data for 1929 and 1937 calculated with population statistics in WA, 1929 and 1937.

c. For yearly data in 1940s and 1950s, see SALA, 24-1906.

d. Kilograms per capita (1982-85).

SOURCE: SALA-SNP, XI-1; UN-SP: J, 1 (1952); J, 17 (1974); J, 19 (1976), table 2; WA, 1929 and 1973; UN-SP: J, 20 (1977), table J, 21 (1978), table 2: UN-YWES, yearly, 1979-86, table 1.

Table 1906

INDEX OF TOTAL CONSUMPTION OF COMMERCIAL ENERGY,[1] 20 LC, 1970–86

(1975 = 100)

	Country	1970	1972	1974	1976	1978	1980	1981	1982	1983	1984	1985	1986
A.	ARGENTINA	88	96	102	103	107	115	111	113	120	121	116	125
B.	BOLIVIA	60	70	87	110	139	131	150	150	150	131	131	138
C.	BRAZIL	59	73	94	110	123	132	122	123	122	126	135	148
D.	CHILE	109	118	116	99	105	116	116	107	109	111	110	115
E.	COLOMBIA	77	86	98	107	124	133	138	138	148	144	148	143
F.	COSTA RICA	65	88	98	99	132	120	120	110	110	120	130	130
G.	CUBA	73	89	96	101	108	117	119	127	117	125	118	122
H.	DOMINICAN REP.	50	~	~	~	~	102	100	96	130	111	100	107
I.	ECUADOR	60	67	86	112	152	198	214	221	214	218	214	225
J.	EL SALVADOR	72	~	~	~	~	100	90	90	100	100	100	100
K.	GUATEMALA	69	80	91	95	120	130	113	107	93	107	107	100
L.	HAITI	82	~	~	~	~	158	150	150	150	150	150	150
M.	HONDURAS	83	88	93	110	110	116	129	129	129	143	143	129
N.	MEXICO	73	83	97	105	128	160	176	175	174	175	180	176
O.	NICARAGUA	73	86	99	110	122	97	111	111	111	111	111	111
P.	PANAMA	64	87	90	101	96	132	114	100	107	100	100	100
Q.	PARAGUAY	81	82	104	115	103	148	175	175	200	200	225	250
R.	PERU	78	81	88	99	101	109	122	119	100	103	102	104
S.	URUGUAY	95	102	96	107	101	105	100	92	81	73	69	73
T.	VENEZUELA	73	83	99	110	119	146	150	155	158	168	168	179
	UNITED STATES	98	104	103	105	110	107	102	97	96	101	101	101
	WORLD	~	~	~	~	~	~	114	113	115	120	123	125

1. Includes all types of solid, liquid, and gaseous fuels, plus electricity production.

SOURCE: UN-YWES, 1979, table 7; 1981, table 2; 1983, table 2; 1984, table 2; 1985,
   table 2; 1986, table 2.

Table 1907

CRUDE OIL PRODUCTION, 11 LC AND 10 L, 1955-87

PART I: M MET

	Country	1955	1960	1965	1970	1973	1975	1978	1979	1980	1981	1982	1983	1984	1985	1986
A.	ARGENTINA	4.37	9.17	13.81	20.02	21.48	20.77	23.24	24.28	25.28	25.53	25.28	25.20	24.64	23.61	22.28
B.	BOLIVIA	.35	.41	.44	1.12	2.20	1.87	1.51	1.29	1.11	1.03	1.13	1.03	.97	.92	1.02
C.	BRAZIL	.28	3.87	4.49	7.98	8.28	8.35	7.79	8.04	9.08	10.66	12.98	16.60	23.22	27.49	28.78
D.	CHILE	.35	.96	1.71	1.47	1.28	.99	.78	1.01	1.60	1.95	2.00	1.92	1.88	1.59	1.49
E.	COLOMBIA	5.49	7.71	10.17	11.33	9.49	8.10	6.76	6.41	6.50	6.97	7.33	7.85	8.66	9.11	15.67
G.	CUBA	.05	.01	.06	.16	.14	.23	.29	.29	.27	.25	.54	.74	.77	.87	.94
I.	ECUADOR	.48	.38	.39	.19	10.62	8.16	10.22	10.87	10.42	10.75	10.75	12.09	13.09	14.24	14.55
K.	GUATEMALA	~	~	~	~	~	~	~	~	.21	.21	.32	.35	.24	.18	.29
N.	MEXICO	13.02	15.75	18.54	21.51	23.26	36.89	63.33	75.48	96.85	115.41	142.78	139.76	139.95	135.67	126.23†
R.	PERU	2.41	2.64	3.19	3.55	3.48	3.55	7.44	9.45	9.65	9.52	9.62	8.59	9.36	9.30	8.76
T.	VENEZUELA	115.54	152.86	182.84	194.31	175.78	122.40	113.63	124.03	114.79	111.69	100.39	94.47	94.85	88.19	93.98
	UNITED STATES	352.12	364.34	405.36	475.29	454.19	413.09	428.49	420.82	424.20	421.80	425.59	427.52	438.13	441.48	428.15
	WORLD	791.65	1,076.29	1,539.04	2,275.0	2,779.94	2,643.66	3,010.12	3,126.08	2,978.66	2,794.85	2,674.40	2,648.46	2,679.24	2,655.02	2,800.08

SOURCE: SALA-SNP, p. 223; UN-SP: J, 17 (1974); UN-SP: J, 19 (1976); J 20 (1977),
p. 64; J 21 (1978), table 6; J, 22 (1979), table 10; UN-YWES, yearly, 1978-81,
table 16; 1983, table 14; 1984, table 14; 1985, table 14; 1986, table 14.

PART II: T BARRELS

	Country	1960	1973	1975	1978	1979	1980	1981	1982	1983	1984	1985	1986	1987†
A.	ARGENTINA	63,860	153,537	144,465	165,119	172,354	179,680	181,316	179,071	179,120	175,102	167,848	151,182	152,935
B.	BOLIVIA	3,111	17,261	14,732	11,845	10,200	8,704	8,091	8,918	8,100	7,624	7,248	7,100	6,752
C.	BRAZIL	29,614	62,397	62,700	58,528	60,434	66,435	80,321	91,980	114,975	173,010	205,495	208,829	215,166
D.	CHILE	7,231	11,430	8,946	6,291	7,572	12,140	15,104	14,965	14,365	14,069	13,048	12,205	10,922
E.	COLOMBIA	55,770	66,657	57,318	47,245	44,979	45,629	48,819	51,779	55,488	61,153	64,352	110,318	141,547
I.	ECUADOR	2,807	76,358	58,753	73,896	78,320	74,769	77,028	77,090	86,691	93,880	102,416	106,755	63,671
K.	GUATEMALA	#	#	#	221	571	1,513	1,494	2,292	2,549	1,715	1,068	1,803	1,423
N.	MEXICO	99,049	164,909	294,254	442,607	536,926	708,593	844,241	1,003,084	981,222	1,024,341	986,697	912,390	926,297
R.	PERU	19,272	25,767	26,294	55,071	69,952	71,356	70,431	71,197	62,454	67,374	68,788	64,799	60,846
T.	VENEZUELA	1,041,675	1,228,594	856,364	790,590	863,590	793,488	769,055	691,687	657,365	656,635	612,105	607,689	581,044

SOURCE: IDB-SPTF, yearly, 1978-86, table 66; 1987, table 69; 1988, table G-1.

Table 1908

PC OF CRUDE OIL PRODUCTION, 11 LC, 1973–86

	Country	1973	1975	1976	1978	1979	1980	1981	1982	1983	1984	1985	1986
A.	ARGENTINA	-2.9	-1.8	.2	4.8	4.5	4.1	1.0	-1.3	#	-2.2	-4.2	-5.6
B.	BOLIVIA	8.4	-11.4	1.1	-6.2	-14.6	-14.0	-7.2	9.7	-9.7	-5.8	-5.2	10.9
C.	BRAZIL	1.7	-3.1	-2.8	-.3	3.2	9.9	17.3	21.8	21.8	39.9	18.4	4.7
D.	CHILE	-9.9	-10.8	-5.1	-16.1	38.4	58.4	16.9	2.6	-4.0	-2.1	-15.4	-6.3
E.	COLOMBIA	-6.3	-6.8	-6.8	-4.9	-5.1	1.4	6.6	6.1	7.1	10.3	5.2	72.0
G.	CUBA	27.3	35.3	0	20.8	0	-6.9	3.7	116.0	27.0	4.1	13.0	8.0
I.	ECUADOR	164.8	-9.3	16.3	10.1	6.4	-4.1	3.0	#	12.5	8.3	8.8	2.2
K.	GUATEMALA	~	~	~	~	~	~	~	52.4	8.6	-31.4	-25.0	61.1
N.	MEXICO	5.0	24.7	12.1	28.5	19.2	28.3	19.2	23.7	-2.2	.1	-3.1	-7.0[†]
R.	PERU	9.1	-7.1	6.5	65.3	27.0	2.1	-1.0	-10.1	-10.7	9.0	-.6	-5.8
T.	VENEZUELA	4.6	-21.6	-1.8	-2.9	9.2	-7.2	-3.1	-10.1	-6.3	.4	-7.0	6.6
	UNITED STATES	-2.7	-4.6	-2.9	5.6	-1.8	.2	#	.9	.5	2.5	.8	-3.0
	WORLD	9.1	-5.2	8.6	.8	3.9	-4.8	-6.2	-4.3	-.9	1.2	-.9	5.5

SOURCE: SALA calculations from table 1907, part I.

Table 1909

OFFSHORE PRODUCTION OF CRUDE PETROLEUM, 6 LC, 1970–86

(T MET)

	Country	1970	1973	1975	1976	1978	1979	1980	1981	1982	1983	1984	1985	1986
A.	ARGENTINA	95[†]	90[†]	90[†]	90[†]	90[†]	90[†]	95[†]	95[†]	95[†]	95[†]	95[†]	0	0
C.	BRAZIL	396	661	1,340	1,584	2,104	2,763	3,738	5,009	6,854	9,919	15,926	19,000[†]	19,750[†]
D.	CHILE	~	~	~	~	~	~	~	1,511	1,610	1,300	1,200[†]	1,044	1,059
N	MEXICO	1,001	1,777	2,005	2,242	2,199	4,914	34,669	56,277	84,085	85,533	89,050	90,667	81,740[†]
R.	PERU	1,000[†]	1,544	1,500[†]	1,600	1,427[†]	1,437[†]	1,380	1,320	1,363	1,204	1,325	1,359	1,275[†]
T.	VENEZUELA	128,050	140,543	85,000[†]	85,000[†]	56,852[†]	55,302[†]	58,013[†]	56,000[†]	50,300[I]	47,700[†]	48,002[†]	44,500[†]	47,425[†]
	UNITED STATES	77,786	79,690	67,200	62,351	55,914	52,500	51,033	50,895	54,640	58,848	63,295	61,492	61,843

SOURCE: UN-YWES, yearly, 1979–81, table 16; 1983, table 14; 1984, table 14; 1985, table 14; 1986, table 14.

Table 1910

PROVEN CRUDE OIL RESERVES, 6 LRC, 1983–87

(M Barrels)

Country	1983	1984	1985	1986	1987	PC 1987 over 1986
North America	34,170	34,418	33,472	31,695	30,076	–5.1
Canada	6,435	5,972	5,056	4,806	4,806	#
United States	27,735	28,446	28,416	26,889	25,270	–6.0
Extended Latin America	83,859	84,830	112,637	112,623	114,491	1.7
A. ARGENTINA	2,429	2,266	2,300	2,270	2,270	#
C. BRAZIL	1,850	1,976	2,070	2,250	2,340	4.0
E. COLOMBIA	560	624	1,224	1,291	1,590	23.2
I. ECUADOR	860	1,181	1,181	1,672	1,615	–3.4
N. MEXICO	49,911	48,600	49,300	48,000	47,000	–2.1
T. VENEZUELA	25,887	28,028	54,454	55,521	58,079	4.6
Other	2,362	2,155	2,107	1,620	1,597	–1.4
Western Europe	17,445	17,124	19,358	18,511	22,648	22.4
Denmark	324	400	465	440	440	#
Italy	800	800	740	722	739	2.4
Norway	7,660	8,300	10,900	10,500	14,800	41.0
United Kingdom	6,960	6,015	5,663	5,310	5,138	–3.2
Other	1,701	1,609	1,591	1,539	1,532	–.5
Middle East	392,175	430,400	431,641	536,838	567,028	5.6
I.R. Iran	51,000	58,874	59,000	92,860	92,860	#
Iraq	65,000	65,000	65,000	72,000	100,000	38.9
Kuwait	67,000	92,710	92,464	94,522	94,525	#
Oman	2,982	3,495	4,000	4,032	4,012	–.5
Qatar	3,330	4,500	4,500	4,500	4,500	#
Saudi Arabia	168,848	171,710	171,490	169,180	169,585	.2
Syrian Arab Republic	1,490	1,450	1,541	1,400	1,750	25.0
United Arab Emirates	32,340	32,490	32,990	97,203	98,105	.9
Other	186	171	656	1,141	1,691	48.3
Africa	56,964	56,249	57,707	57,602	57,958	.6
Algeria	9,220	9,000	8,820	8,800	8,500	–3.4
Egypt	3,450	3,200	3,850	3,600	4,300	19.4
Gabon	547	518	678	733	733	#
S.P. Libyan A.J.	21,270	21,100	21,300	22,800	22,800	#
Nigeria	16,550	16,650	16,600	16,000	15,980	–.1
Tunisia	1,820	1,514	1,800	1,800	1,800	#
Other	4,107	4,267	4,659	3,869	3,845	–.6
Asia and Far East	16,842	16,872	17,238	17,849	18,103	1.4
Brunei	1,390	1,400	1,480	1,421	1,421	#
India	3,485	3,500	3,735	4,203	4,250	1.1
Indonesia	9,100	8,650	8,500	9,000	9,000	#
Malaysia	2,600	2,900	3,100	2,821	2,900	2.8
Other	267	422	423	405	532	31.4
Oceania	1,756	1,586	1,625	1,880	1,852	–1.5
Australia	1,586	1,431	1,449	1,713	1,692	–1.2
Other	170	155	176	167	160	–4.2
Centralized Planned Economies (CPEs)	105,301	100,960	82,805	80,700	78,950	–2.2
China	18,200	18,200	18,420	18,400	18,400	#
USSR	84,846	81,000	62,685	60,700	59,000	–2.8
Other	2,255	1,760	1,700	1,600	1,550	–3.1
Total World	708,512	742,438	756,482	857,697	891,106	3.9
OPEC	470,952	510,411	536,977	644,791	676,282	4.9
OPEC Percentage	66.5	68.7	71.0	75.2	75.9	~
Total World Excluding CPEs	603,211	641,478	673,677	776,997	812,156	4.5
OPEC Percentage	78.1	79.6	79.7	83.0	83.3	~

SOURCE: OPEC-SB, 1986, 1988.

Table 1911

REFINED OIL PRODUCTION, 18 L, 1973–87

(T Barrels)

	Country	1973	1975	1978	1979	1980	1981	1982	1983	1984	1985[‡]	1986	1987[‡]
A.	ARGENTINA	162,548	157,931	117,283	182,400	189,624	189,771	183,217	175,857	170,441	164,990	146,841	148,309
B.	BOLIVIA	9,308	7,365	8,400	10,044	9,618	8,651	8,810	7,925	7,898	7,847	6,800	6,800
C.	BRAZIL	205,100	336,150	385,577	401,931	405,101	397,922	394,958	386,462	408,070	404,420	421,640	433,295
D.	CHILE	36,559	31,783	34,442	37,278	35,805	35,455	27,729	30,583	31,046	30,918	31,622	31,788
E.	COLOMBIA	59,713	57,685	57,461	59,247	58,699	62,343	63,291	69,199	69,063	69,279	79,897	83,892
F.	COSTA RICA	3,358	1,941	3,054	2,981	3,690	3,488	2,923	2,412	2,709	3,077	2,800	2,800
H.	DOMINICAN REP.	5,465	8,545	9,422	9,147	9,384	9,447	8,804	9,679	10,413	9,345	10,373	10,373
I.	ECUADOR	11,023	14,643	30,063	31,931	34,122	32,562	34,009	27,493	32,498	31,438	34,496	36,227
J.	EL SALVADOR	4,199	4,491	5,254	5,288	4,588	4,304	3,994	4,220	4,420	4,491[†]	4,400	4,400
K.	GUATEMALA	7,132	4,855	5,959	5,767	5,381	5,345	4,508	4,306	5,009	5,017	3,821	3,700
M.	HONDURAS	3,439	3,459	3,107	3,383	3,639	1,900	678	2,329	2,973	2,569	1,437	1,400
N.	MEXICO	206,108	232,839	320,220	349,926	417,114	459,990	451,458	455,683	485,182	504,141	534,210	544,800
O.	NICARAGUA	3,869	4,728	4,459	1,364	4,709	4,621	4,237	3,911	3,097	3,518	3,734	3,700
P.	PANAMA	25,974	~	17,013	15,731	13,653	10,543	11,807	11,720	10,653	8,919	8,500	8,000
Q.	PARAGUAY	1,480	1,662	2,278	2,186	1,960	1,913	1,610	1,583	1,116	1,570	1,400	1,420
R.	PERU	36,624	41,157	44,399	53,282	53,692	56,281	57,801	54,864	60,871	61,763	61,293	60,065
S.	URUGUAY	11,667	12,465	13,490	12,964	12,377	11,603	12,031	9,179	9,173	8,266	7,692	7,700
T.	VENEZUELA	376,836	317,044	358,940	360,255	377,452	313,535	316,090	327,770	303,315	331,785	329,595	329,000

SOURCE: IDB-SPTF, 1978, p. 470; 1979, p. 455; 1980, p. 451; 1983, p. 395; 1985, table 66,
p. 437; 1986, table 66, p. 443; 1987, table 69, p. 497; 1988, table G-1, p. 596.

Table 1912

PC OF REFINED OIL PRODUCTION, 18 L, 1974–87

	Country	1974	1975	1976	1978	1979	1980	1981	1982	1983	1984	1985	1986	1987
A.	ARGENTINA	-3.7	.9	5.0	1.2	2.8	4.0	.1	-3.5	-4.0	-3.1	-3.2	11	1.0
B.	BOLIVIA	7.2	24.2	16.3	-9.5	19.6	-4.2	-10.1	1.8	-10.0	-.3	-.6	-13.3	0
C.	BRAZIL	49.9	9.4	2.4	12.1	4.2	.8	-1.8	-.7	-2.2	5.6	-.9	4.3	2.8
D.	CHILE	4.8	-17.0	7.6	-2.1	8.2	-4.0	-1.0	-21.8	10.3	1.5	-.4	2.3	.5
E.	COLOMBIA	1.5	-4.8	2.5	-4.5	3.1	-9.2	6.2	1.5	9.3	-.2	.3	15.3	5.0
F.	COSTA RICA	-18.5	-29.1	-2.0	20.4	-2.4	23.8	-5.5	-16.2	-17.5	11.9	14.0	-9.0	0
H.	DOMINICAN REP.	21.1	29.1	4.0	4.6	-2.9	2.6	1.0	-7.1	9.9	7.6	-2.3	11.0	0
I.	ECUADOR	15.7	14.8	6.3	-5.2	6.2	6.9	4.6	4.4	-19.2	18.2	-3.3	9.7	5.0
J.	EL SALVADOR	-4.5	11.9	4.2	5.9	.6	-13.2	-6.2	-7.2	5.7	4.7	1.6	-2.0	0
K.	GUATEMALA	-8.4	-25.7	-8.5	29.1	-3.2	-6.7	-.7	-15.7	-4.5	16.3	.2	-23.8	-3.2
M.	HONDURAS	-3.8	4.5	-13.2	.6	8.9	7.6	-47.8	-64.3	243.5	27.7	-13.6	-44.1	-2.6
N.	MEXICO	8.4	4.3	10.9	6.5	9.3	19.2	10.3	-1.8	.9	1.4	-.1	6.0	2.0
O.	NICARAGUA	14.5	6.7	5.9	-17.1	-69.4	245.2	-1.9	-8.3	-7.7	-20.8	15.9	6.1	-.9
P.	PANAMA	~	~	~	-16.8	-7.5	-13.2	-22.8	12.0	-.7	-9.1	-16.3	-4.7	-5.9
Q.	PARAGUAY	13.5	-1.1	27.6	22.3	-4.0	-10.3	-2.4	-15.8	-1.7	-29.5	40.7	-10.1	1.4
R.	PERU	8.5	3.6	.9	2.5	20.0	.1	4.8	2.7	-5.1	10.9	1.4	-.8	-2.0
S.	URUGUAY	-2.5	7.3	-.1	5.7	-3.9	-4.5	-6.3	3.7	-23.7	-.1	-9.9	-6.9	.1
T.	VENEZUELA	15.8	-27.4	13.8	1.7	.4	-6.0	-16.9	.8	3.7	-7.5	9.4	-.7	-.2

SOURCE: SALA calculations from table 1911.

Table 1913

PETROLEUM REFINERY DISTILLATION CAPACITY, 19 LC, 1970–86

(T MET)

	Country	1970	1975	1978	1979	1980	1981	1982	1983	1984	1985	1986
A.	ARGENTINA	23,980	31,310	33,786	34,235	34,500[†]	34,604	34,600	34,600	34,600	34,600	34,600
B.	BOLIVIA	1,180	1,290	1,955	3,715[†]	3,725	2,800[†]	2,800[†]	3,000[†]	3,000[†]	3,000[†]	2,179
C.	BRAZIL	27,300	51,700	62,300	62,300[†]	72,200	72,260	76,350	76,780	76,780[†]	75,000[†]	66,500
D.	CHILE	3,850	6,000	6,000	6,000[†]	6,000[†]	6,000[†]	6,000[†]	6,000	6,000	6,000[†]	6,000[†]
E.	COLOMBIA	7,000[†]	8,670	8,670	8,670[†]	9,680	10,250	10,675	10,810	10,810[†]	10,900[†]	11,672
F.	COSTA RICA	470	470	470[†]	470[†]	550	678	678	678	678	678[†]	680
G.	CUBA	4,340	6,000[†]	6,450[†]	6,450[†]	7,970	7,970	7,970	7,970	7,970	7,970[†]	7,970[†]
H.	DOMINICAN REP.	~	1,500	2,350[†]	2,350[†]	2,350[†]	2,350[†]	2,350[†]	2,350[†]	2,350[†]	2,350[†]	2,350[†]
I.	ECUADOR	1,740	2,190	5,040	4,800	4,800[†]	4,800[†]	4,800	4,800	4,800[†]	4,950[†]	5,043
J.	EL SALVADOR	650	750	800[†]	800[†]	800[†]	800[†]	800[†]	800[†]	800[†]	800[†]	800[†]
K.	GUATEMALA	1,250	1,250	1,250[†]	1,250[†]	1,250[†]	1,250[†]	1,250[†]	1,250[†]	1,250[†]	1,250[†]	1,250[†]
M.	HONDURAS	700	700	700[†]	700[†]	700[†]	700[†]	700[†]	700[†]	700[†]	700[†]	700[†]
N.	MEXICO	29,600	39,250	49,322	66,910	66,025[†]	66,025[†]	66,025[†]	72,500[†]	72,500[†]	72,500[†]	70,134[†]
O.	NICARAGUA	650	750	750[†]	750[†]	750[†]	750[†]	750[†]	750[†]	750[†]	750[†]	750[†]
P.	PANAMA	4,000	5,000	5,000[†]	5,000[†]	5,000[†]	5,000[†]	5,000[†]	5,000[†]	5,000[†]	5,000[†]	5,000[†]
Q.	PARAGUAY	500[†]	500[†]	500[†]	500[†]	500[†]	350[†]	375[†]	375[†]	375[†]	375[†]	375[†]
R.	PERU	4,680	5,540	9,060	9,060[†]	8,900	8,000[†]	8,400[†]	9,200[†]	9,200[†]	9,200[†]	8,660[†]
S.	URUGUAY	2,250	2,450	2,232	2,232	2,232	2,408	2,408	2,408	2,408	2,408	2,408
T.	VENEZUELA	68,200	77,750	75,500	75,500	71,645	71,456	70,090	69,407	64,418	64,483	64,483[†]
	UNITED STATES	643,000	760,000	839,700	885,200	890,730	792,450	829,642	804,184	770,563	760,730	767,780

SOURCE: UN-YWES, 1979, table 26; 1981, table 21; 1983; table 16; 1984, table 16; 1985, table 16; 1986, table 16.

Table 1914

PRODUCING OIL WELLS, OPEC MEMBER COUNTRIES, 2 LC, 1981–87

(YE)

Country	1981	1982	1983	1984	1985	1986	1987
Algeria							
Flowing	785	720	630	640	635	640	675
Artificial Lift	115	140	170	191	200	205	215
Total	900	860	800	831	835	845	890
I. ECUADOR							
Flowing	276	96	95	68	79	87	90
Artificial Lift	577	794	510	516	197	802	819
Total	853	890	605	584	276	898	909
Gabon							
Flowing	129	120	142	154	110	134	151
Artificial Lift	70	83	89	91	140	* 156	170
Total	199	203	231	245	250	290	321
Indonesia							
Flowing	~	707	672	995	726	676	690
Artificial Lift	~	3,695	3,898	4,587	4,911	5,145	5,255
Total	4,565	4,402	4,570	5,582	5,637	5,821	5,945
I.R. Iran							
Flowing	~	~	~	~	237	92	90
Artificial Lift	~	~	~	~	0	0	0
Total	~	530	~	230	237	92	90
Iraq							
Flowing	280	~	~	~	~	~	~
Artificial Lift	~	~	~	~	~	~	~
Total	280	280	~	~	~	~	~
Kuwait							
Flowing	550	461	315	429	353	380	380
Artificial Lift	~	~	14	4	18	20	0
Total	550	461	329	433	371	400	380
Libya							
Flowing	~	438	406	415	430	428	438
Artificial Lift	~	484	555	586	594	592	593
Total	1,000	922	961	1,001	1,024	1,020	1,031
Nigeria							
Flowing	1,158	906	897	969	302	310	312
Artificial Lift	123	136	129	143	811	830	1,500
Total	1,281	1,042	1,026	1,112	1,113	1,140	1,812
Qatar							
Flowing	141	160	169	179	184	165	194
Artificial Lift	~	~	0	0	0	2	3
Total	141	160	169	179	184	167	197
Saudi Arabia							
Flowing	646	510	391	370	731	588	580
Artificial Lift	~	~	~	~	314	0	0
Total	646	510	391	370	1,045	588	580
Saudi Arabian-Kuwaiti Divided Zone							
Flowing	150	158	153	158	156	157	161
Artificial Lift	256	303	306	300	290	280	280
Total	406	461	459	458	446	437	441
United Arab Emirates							
Flowing	~	331	349	389	419	678	614
Artificial Lift	~	121	180	184	213	223	205
Total	412	452	529	573	632	901	819
T. VENEZUELA							
Flowing	1,884	1,997	1,330	1,716	1,886	1,538	1,475
Artificial Lift	10,765	12,770	12,075	8,160	8,973	8,517	10,499
Total	12,649	14,767	13,405	9,876	10,859	10,055	11,974
Total OPEC							
Flowing	5,999	6,604	5,549	6,482	6,248	5,873	5,850
Artificial Lift	11,906	18,526	17,926	14,762	16,661	16,772	19,539
Total[a]	23,882	25,940	23,475	21,474	22,909	22,645	25,389

a. Summation of wells by category may not equal total due to unavailable breakdown for some countries.

SOURCE: OPEC-SB, 1986, 1988.

Table 1915

WORLD REFINERY CAPACITY, 6 LRC, 1983–87

(T Barrels/Calendar Day)

Country	1983	1984	1985	1986	1987	PC 1987 over 1986
North America	18,031.2	17,589.3	17,382.6	17,325.2	17,565.9	1.4
Canada	1,834.1	1,868.5	1,855.8	1,759.7	1,868.9	6.2
United States	16,197.1	15,720.8	15,526.8	15,565.5	15,697.0	.8
Extended Latin America	7,969.3	7,286.5	7,221.4	7,030.6	7,222.0	2.7
A. ARGENTINA	678.4	678.4	667.2	669.8	689.5	2.9
Bahamas	500.0	350.0	350.0	~	~	~
C. BRAZIL	1,301.4	1,305.1	1,305.1	1,321.1	1,407.3	6.5
E. COLOMBIA	211.0	211.0	211.0	226.0	226.0	0
I. ECUADOR	94.6	94.6	94.6	94.6	139.0	46.9
N. MEXICO	1,269.0	1,269.0	1,269.0	1,349.0	1,354.0	.4
Netherlands Antilles	740.0	320.0	320.0	320.0	320.0	0
Puerto Rico	121.0	121.0	123.0	123.0	123.0	0
Trinidad and Tobago	375.0	320.0	260.0	300.0	300.0	0
T. VENEZUELA	1,323.1	1,224.2	1,229.2	1,224.2	1,258.3	2.8
US Virgin Islands	515.0	545.0	545.0	545.0	545.0	0
Other	840.8	848.2	847.3	857.9	859.9	.2
Western Europe	16,862.2	16,285.9	14,833.7	14,411.9	14,735.2	2.2
Belguim	694.1	692.5	652.1	647.5	630.5	−2.6
France	2,531.4	2,386.0	1,946.9	1,834.1	1,940.6	5.8
Germany	2.386.3	2,171.6	1,932.8	1,719.8	1,647.8	−4.2
Italy	3,050.1	2,969.3	2,738.1	2,678.7	2,563.1	−4.3
Netherlands	1,551.5	1,498.5	1,468.4	1,400.8	1,381.0	−1.4
Spain	1,493.0	1,493.0	1,367.0	1,305.0	1,305.0	0
United Kingdom	2,091.5	2,007.7	1,791.7	1,779.7	1,802.7	1.3
Other	3,064.2	3,067.3	2,936.7	3,046.3	3,464.5	13.7
Middle East	3,808.9	4,026.4	4,259.9	4,439.4	4,468.2	.6
I.R. Iran	670.0	615.0	615.0	615.0	615.0	0
Iraq	365.5	365.5	365.5	365.5	365.5	0
Kuwait	614.0	614.0	614.0	720.0	720.0	0
Qatar	63.0	63.0	63.0	63.0	63.0	0
Saudi Arabia	935.0	1,100.0	1,440.0	1,490.0	1,490.0	0
United Arab Emirates	175.5	162.0	162.0	162.0	162.0	0
Other	985.9	1,016.9	1,000.4	1,023.9	1,052.7	2.8
Africa	2,235.6	2,456.4	2,521.8	2,540.7	2,637.4	3.8
Algeria	471.2	471.2	471.2	471.2	471.2	0
Egypt	369.3	369.3	434.2	452.1	452.1	0
Gabon	44.0	44.0	44.0	21.0	21.0	0
Libya	117.0	315.0	333.0	342.0	342.0	0
Nigeria	234.0	234.0	234.0	243.0	243.0	0
Other	1,000.1	1,022.9	1,028.5	1,011.4	1,108.1	9.6
Asia and Far East	9,633.9	9,574.1	9,646.9	9,660.5	9,473.9	−1.9
India	778.7	704.8	866.7	991.1	1,058.7	6.8
Indonesia	837.0	837.0	837.0	738.7	738.7	0
Japan	4,724.0	4,724.0	4,724.0	4,618.5	4,460.8	−3.4
Korea (Rep. of)	775.9	776.0	782.0	862.0	820.0	−4.9
Singapore	1,101.0	1,081.0	1,027.0	970.0	858.0	−11.5
Taiwan	515.4	542.5	542.5	542.5	600.0	10.6
Other	901.9	908.3	867.6	937.7	937.7	0
Oceania	840.0	793.8	719.5	680.1	718.8	5.7
Australia	722.1	696.9	622.6	626.1	637.1	1.8
Other	117.9	96.9	96.9	54.0	81.7	51.3
Centralized Planned Economies (CPEs)	16,670.5	16,600.5	16,600.5	17,010.5	16,989.0	−.1
China	2,050.0	2,050.0	2,050.0	2,200.0	2,200.0	0
USSR	12,000.0	12,000.0	12,000.0	12,260.0	12,260.0	0
Other	2,620.5	2,550.5	2,550.5	2,550.5	2,529.0	−.8
Total World	76,051.5	74,612.8	73,186.0	73,098.7	73,810.5	1.0
OPEC	5,943.9	6,229.5	6,479.5	6,550.2	6,628.7	1.2
OPEC Percentage	8.0	8.5	9.0	9.0	9.0	0
Total World Excluding CPEs	59,494.1	58,120.4	56,781.8	56,088.2	56,821.5	1.3
OPEC Percentage	10.2	10.9	11.6	11.7	11.7	0

SOURCE: OPEC-SB, 1986, 1988.

Table 1916

REFINERY CAPACITY, OPEC MEMBER COUNTRIES, 2 LC, 1965–87

(T Barrels/Calendar Day)

	Country	1965	1970	1975	1980	1983	1984	1985	1986	1987
	Algeria	43.7	57.5	115.8	471.2	471.2	471.2	471.2	471.2	471.2
I.	ECUADOR	18.2	34.5	43.9	94.5	94.6	94.6	94.6	94.6	139.0
	Gabon	~	16.0	20.0	44.0	44.0	44.0	21.0	21.0	21.0
	Indonesia	236.9	283.5	361.3	473.4	837.0	837.0	837.0	738.7	738.7
	I.R. Iran	466.5	594.0	810.0	1,320.0	670.0	615.0	615.0	615.0	615.0
	Iraq	81.7	115.7	253.5	305.5	365.5	365.5	365.5	365.5	365.5
	Kuwait	342.0	437.0	609.0	594.0	614.0	614.0	614.0	720.0	720.0
	Libya	9.0	9.0	63.0	117.0	117.0	315.0	333.0	342.0	342.0
	Nigeria	30.3	52.1	54.0	234.0	234.0	234.0	234.0	243.0	243.0
	Qatar	.6	.7	.7	10.5	63.0	63.0	63.0	63.0	63.0
	Saudi Arabia	302.5	676.0	703.0	878.0	935.0	1,190.0	1,440.0	1,490.0	1,490.0
	United Arab Emirates	~	~	~	13.5	175.5	162.0	162.0	162.0	162.0
T.	VENEZUELA	1,119.8	1,289.4	1,444.9	1,444.9	1,323.1	1,224.2	1,229.2	1,224.2	1,258.3
	Total OPEC	2,651.2	3,565.4	4,488.1	6,000.5	5,943.9	6,229.5	6,479.5	6,550.2	6,628.7

SOURCE: OPEC-SB, 1986, 1988.

Table 1917

INDEX OF TOTAL PRODUCTION OF CRUDE PETROLEUM, 10 LC, 1970–86

(1975 = 100)

	Country	1970	1974	1978	1981	1982	1983	1984	1985	1986
A.	ARGENTINA	96	102	112	123	121	121	119	114	107
B.	BOLIVIA	60	113	80	55	61	55	52	49	55
C.	BRAZIL	96	103	93	128	155	199	278	329	345
D.	CHILE	148	112	78	196	202	194	189	161	151
E.	COLOMBIA	140	107	83	85	90	97	107	112	193
G.	CUBA	70	74	127	112	239	328	341	378	409
I.	ECUADOR	~	~	~	132	132	148	160	175	178
N.	MEXICO	58	80	172	326	387	379	379	368	342
R.	PERU	100	107	209	268	271	243	264	262	247
T.	VENEZUELA	159	128	93	91	82	77	77	72	77
	UNITED STATES	115	105	104	102	103	103	106	107	104
	WORLD	86	105	114	106	101	100	101	100	106

SOURCE: UN-YWES, 1979, table 23; 1981, table 18; 1983, table 14; 1984, table 14;
    1985, calculated from UN-YWES, 1985, table 14; 1986, table 14.

Table 1918

INDEX OF TOTAL CONSUMPTION OF CRUDE PETROLEUM, 19 LC, 1970–86

(1975 = 100)

	Country	1970	1974	1978	1979	1980	1981	1982	1983	1984	1985	1986
A.	ARGENTINA	96	105	113	115	122	119	115	110	108	104	97
B.	BOLIVIA	62	107	133	149	133	109	111	101	104	104	114
C.	BRAZIL	59	100	122	128	121	121	120	123	129	128	136
D.	CHILE	92	125	121	140	127	117	88	97	98	95	104
E.	COLOMBIA	88	107	98	96	94	99	104	115	120	124	134
F.	COSTA RICA	113	147	148	144	194	175	153	118	147	146	158
G.	CUBA	72	93	108	107	105	111	114	115	116	115	118
H.	DOMINICAN REP.	~	76	112	105	115	119	108	137	127	120	120
I.	ECUADOR	54	83	195	206	221	249	285	268	324	280	226
J.	EL SALVADOR	27	87	118	116	107	92	88	95	97	89	89
K.	GUATEMALA	78	98	87	89	90	87	75	66	79	78	79
M.	HONDURAS	112	97	65	78	78	36	15	42	41	42	43
N.	MEXICO	72	98	131	139	187	207	208	195	206	201	195
O.	NICARAGUA	70	92	99	75	93	102	95	85	68	79	78
P.	PANAMA	94	92	61	54	49	44	46	44	47	32	33
Q.	PARAGUAY	91	112	156	139	155	132	114	105	73	87	105
R.	PERU	72	~	~	~	129	136	142	134	142	146	144
S.	URUGUAY	97	93	100	98	99	92	88	69	67	59	57
T.	VENEZUELA	149	141	109	110	103	98	99	97	96	97	98
	UNITED STATES	88	98	119	118	108	100	95	94	96	96	102
	WORLD	86	104	115	118	113	107	104	103	105	104	106

SOURCE: UN-YWES, 1979, table 23; 1981, table 18; 1983, table 14; 1984, table 14; 1985, 1986 calculated from UN-YWES, 1985, 1986, table 14.

Table 1919

ARGENTINA OIL INDUSTRY BASIC STATISTICS, 1910–80

(M Barrels/Year)

Year	Production	Exports	Consumption	Refinery Capacity	Imports
1910	0	~	1.0	~	1.0
1911	0	~	1.1	~	1.1
1912	0	~	1.3	~	1.3
1913	.1	~	1.9	~	1.8
1914	.3	~	1.8	~	1.5
1915	.5	~	3.4	~	2.9
1916	.9	~	3.2	~	2.3
1917	1.2	~	3.4	~	2.2
1918	1.4	~	2.5	~	1.2
1919	1.3	~	4.7	~	3.4
1920	1.7	~	6.7	~	5.0
1921	2.1	~	8.2	~	6.1
1922	2.9	~	9.4	~	6.6
1923	3.3	~	10.8	~	7.5
1924	4.7	~	12.8	~	8.1
1925	6.0	~	11.4	~	5.3
1926	7.9	~	14.8	~	6.9
1927	8.6	~	17.5	~	8.8
1928	9.1	~	19.8	~	10.7
1929	9.4	~	21.4	~	12.0
1930	9.0	~	21.6	~	12.6
1931	11.7	~	21.6	~	9.9
1932	13.2	~	20.2	~	7.1
1933	13.7	~	20.4	~	6.7
1934	14.0	~	21.9	~	7.8
1935	14.3	~	24.1	~	9.8
1936	15.5	~	25.6	~	10.1
1937	16.4	~	28.1	~	11.7
1938	17.1	~	31.9	~	14.8
1939	18.6	~	32.8	~	14.2
1940	20.6	~	33.7	37.6	13.1
1941	21.7	~	35.3	~	13.6
1942	23.7	~	31.1	~	7.4
1943	24.9	~	~	~	~
1944	24.3	~	~	~	~
1945	22.9	~	~	~	~
1946	20.8	~	~	~	~
1947	21.9	~	~	~	~
1948	23.3	~	~	~	~
1949	22.6	~	~	~	~
1950	23.5	~	56.7	55.5	33.2
1951	24.5	~	~	~	~
1952	24.9	~	~	~	~
1953	28.5	~	~	~	~
1954	29.7	~	~	~	~
1955	30.6	~	70.1	~	39.6
1956	31.1	~	71.1	~	40.0
1957	34.0	~	75.5	~	41.5
1958	35.7	~	80.5	~	44.8
1959	44.6	~	76.1	~	31.4
1960	64.0	~	90.3	86.9	26.3
1961	84.6	~	110.4	~	25.8
1962	98.4	~	117.9	~	19.5
1963	97.3	~	108.0	~	10.7
1964	100.4	~	114.3	~	13.9
1965	98.4	~	130.6	~	32.1
1966	104.9	~	139.0	~	34.0
1967	114.9	~	137.2	~	22.4
1968	125.7	~	139.4	~	13.7
1969	130.1	~	145.3	~	15.0
1970	143.6	~	164.2	183.2	20.6
1971	154.8	~	173.7	~	19.0
1972	158.7	~	170.0	229.9	11.3
1973	153.7	~	175.1	219.7	21.4
1974	150.7	~	172.2	227.8	21.6

Table 1919 (Continued)

ARGENTINA OIL INDUSTRY BASIC STATISTICS, 1910-80
(M Barrels/Year)

Year	Production	Exports	Consumption	Refinery Capacity	Imports
1975	144.5	~	160.1	263.2	15.6
1976	145.6	~	167.8	249.7	22.2
1977	157.5	~	179.0	256.6	21.5
1978	165.2	~	180.0	239.1	15.6
1979	~	~	~	239.1	~
1980	~	~	~	246.7	~

SOURCE: John D. Wirth, ed., *Latin American Oil Companies and the Politics of Energy* (Lincoln: University of Nebraska Press, 1985), pp. 267–268.

Table 1920

BRAZIL OIL INDUSTRY BASIC STATISTICS, 1920–83

(M Barrels/day)

Year	Production	Exports	Consumption	Refinery Capacity	Imports
1920	~	~	6.6	~	6.6
1921	~	~	7.8	~	7.8
1922	~	~	5.9	~	5.9
1923	~	~	6.6	~	6.6
1924	~	~	8.9	~	8.9
1925	~	~	10.7	~	10.7
1926	~	~	10.0	~	10.0
1927	~	~	14	~	14
1928	~	~	12	~	12
1929	~	~	16	~	16
1930	~	~	15	~	15
1931	~	~	14	~	14
1932	~	~	12	~	12
1933	~	~	15	~	15
1934	~	~	16	~	16
1935	~	~	17	~	17
1936	~	~	19	~	19
1937	~	~	22	~	22
1938	~	~	23	~	23
1939	~	~	25	4	25
1940	~	~	25	~	25
1941	~	~	21	~	21
1942	.1	~	15.1	~	15
1943	.1	~	15.1	~	15
1944	.2	~	15.2	--	15
1945	.2	~	19.2	~	19
1946	.2	~	32.2	~	32
1947	.3	~	48.3	~	48
1948	.4	~	61.4	~	61
1949	.3	~	69.3	~	69
1950	1	~	85	12	84
1951	2	~	104	~	102
1952	2	~	121	~	119
1953	3	~	130	~	127
1954	3	~	154	~	151
1955	7	~	178	106	171
1956	11	~	197	~	186
1957	28	~	198	~	170
1958	52	~	247	~	195
1959	65	~	250	~	185
1960	81	~	270	208	194
1961	95	~	280	~	210
1962	91	~	310	~	223
1963	98	~	340	~	231
1964	91	~	350	~	235
1965	94	~	330	364	221
1966	116	~	380	~	243
1967	147	1.6	380	380	226
1968	164	.3	460	~	286
1969	175	.5	480	501	281
1970	165	17	510	500	329
1971	170	30	560	565	398
1972	165	42	650	795	474
1973	165	71	770	795	663
1974	175	40	830	1,020	681
1975	170	30	870	1,020	706
1976	170	56	970	1,020	827
1977	165	40	1,010	1,175	827
1978	165	28	1,050	1,230	910
1979	170	~	1,180	1,230	~
1980	185	~	~	1,375	999
1981	213	~	~	~	812
1982	268	~	1,020	~	696
1983	~	~	950	~	

SOURCE: John D. Wirth, ed., *Latin American Oil Companies and the Politics of Energy* (Lincoln: University of Nebraska Press, 1985), pp. 271–272.

Table 1921

COLOMBIA PROJECTIONS OF CRUDE PETROLEUM OUTPUT AND SURPLUS, 1985–92
(Barrels per Day)

Year	Output of Crude Petroleum	Export Surplus of Crude
1985	176,400	~
1986	302,139	85,781
1987	405,050	137,146
1988	461,080	245,080
1989	532,920	316,920
1990	570,510	345,510
1991	575,080	359,080
1992	586,740	280,740

SOURCE: *Colombia Today*, vol. 22, No. 9, 1987.

Table 1922

ECUADOR CRUDE OIL PRODUCTION, 1918–87
(T Barrels)

Year	Daily Average	Cumulative	Annual PC in Daily Production	Year	Daily Average	Cumulative	Annual PC in Daily Production
1918–	~	1,398	~	1958	8.5	74,024	-2.3
1927				1959	7.6	76,783	-10.6
1928	3.0	2,482	~	1960	7.5	79,513	-1.3
1929	3.8	3,863	26.7	1961	8.0	82,439	6.7
1930	4.3	5,416	13.2	1962	7.0	85,012	-12.5
1931	4.8	7,178	11.6	1963	6.8	87,477	-2.9
1932	4.4	8,775	-8.3	1964	7.6	90,273	11.8
1933	4.4	10,395	0	1965	7.8	93,122	2.6
1934	4.5	12,032	2.3	1966	7.3	95,782	-6.4
1935	4.7	13,764	4.4	1967	6.2	98,054	-15.1
1936	5.3	15,706	12.8	1968	5.0	99,869	-19.4
1937	5.9	17,867	11.3	1969	4.4	101,477	-12.0
1938	6.2	20,113	5.1	1970	4.1	102,957	-6.8
1939	6.3	22,426	1.6	1971	3.7	104,311	-9.8
1940	6.4	24,775	1.6	1972	78.1	132,890	2,010.8
1941	4.3	26,332	-32.8	1973	208.8	209,111	167.3
1942	6.2	28,610	44.2	1974	177.0	273,716	-15.2
1943	6.3	30,925	1.6	1975	160.9	332,437	-9.1
1944	8.1	33,892	28.6	1976	187.8	401,187	16.7
1945	7.3	36,556	-9.9	1977	183.4	468,128	-2.3
1946	6.4	38,879	-12.3	1978	201.8	541,796	10.0
1947	6.3	41,161	-1.6	1979	214.2	619,965	6.1
1948	7.0	43,724	11.1	1980	204.9	694,958	-4.3
1949	7.2	46,341	2.9	1981	211.0	771,973	3.0
1950	7.2	48,973	0	1982	198.3	844,353	-6.0
1951	7.4	51,681	2.8	1983	237.5	931,087	19.8
1952	7.8	54,520	5.4	1984	256.1	1,024,820	7.8
1953	8.3	57,560	6.4	1985	280.6	1,127,239	9.6
1954	8.6	60,706	3.6	1986	256.5	1,220,869	-8.6
1955	9.9	64,305	15.1	1987	180.9	1,286,883	-29.5
1956	9.3	67,725	-6.1				
1957	8.7	70,916	-6.5				

SOURCE: OPEC-SB, 1987, 1988.

Table 1923

VENEZUELA CRUDE OIL PRODUCTION, 1917–87
(T Barrels)

Year	Daily Average	Cumulative	Annual PC in Daily Production	Year	Daily Average	Cumulative	Annual PC in Daily Production
1917	.3	121	~	1953	1,765.0	7,468,892	−2.2
1918	.9	442	200.0	1954	1,895.3	8,160,680	7.4
1919	.8	747	−11.1	1955	2,157.2	8,948,064	13.8
1920	1.3	1,209	62.5	1956	2,456.8	9,847,247	13.9
1921	4.0	2,658	207.7	1957	2,779.2	10,861,671	13.1
1922	6.1	4,893	52.5	1958	2,604.8	11,812,438	−6.3
1923	11.9	9,220	95.1	1959	2,771.0	12,823,857	6.4
1924	24.9	18,349	109.2	1960	2,846.1	13,865,532	2.7
1925	54.6	38,282	119.3	1961	2,919.9	14,931,289	2.6
1926	97.7	73,936	78.9	1962	3,199.8	16,099,205	9.6
1927	165.5	134,355	69.4	1963	3,247.9	17,284,688	1.5
1928	289.5	240,312	74.9	1964	3,392.8	18,526,470	4.5
1929	372.8	376,386	28.8	1965	3,472.9	19,794,072	2.4
1930	370.5	511,632	−.6	1966	3,371.1	21,024,536	−2.9
1931	320.2	628,505	−13.6	1967	3,542.1	22,317,410	5.1
1932	319.0	745,242	−.4	1968	3,604.8	23,636,767	1.8
1933	323.8	863,441	1.5	1969	3,594.1	24,948,604	−.3
1934	373.4	999,728	15.3	1970	3,708.0	26,302,024	3.2
1935	406.9	1,148,244	9.0	1971	3,549.1	27,597,446	−4.3
1936	422.5	1,302,883	3.8	1972	3,219.9	28,775,929	−9.3
1937	508.9	1,488,637	20.4	1973	3,366.0	30,004,519	4.5
1938	515.2	1,676,677	1.2	1974	2,976.3	31,090,869	−11.6
1939	560.4	1,881,211	8.8	1975	2,346.2	31,947,232	−21.2
1940	502.3	2,065,042	−10.4	1976	2,294.4	32,786,969	−2.2
1941	621.3	2,291,823	23.7	1977	2,237.9	33,603,786	−2.5
1942	405.9	2,439,978	−34.7	1978	2,165.5	34,394,194	−3.2
1943	491.5	2,619,362	21.1	1979	2,356.4	35,254,269	8.8
1944	702.3	2,876,399	42.9	1980	2,165.0	36,046,659	−8.1
1945	866.0	3,199,803	26.2	1981	2,108.3	36,816,189	−2.6
1946	1,064.3	3,588,282	20.1	1982	1,895.0	37,507,877	−10.1
1947	1,191.5	4,023,173	12.0	1983	1,800.8	38,165,169	−5.0
1948	1,338.8	4,513,173	12.4	1984	1,695.5	38,785,722	−5.8
1949	1,321.4	4,995,474	−1.3	1985	1,564.0	39,356,573	−7.8
1950	1,498.0	5,542,240	13.4	1986	1,648.5	39,958,275	5.4
1951	1,704.6	6,164,436	13.8	1987	1,575.5	40,533,333	−4.4
1952	1,803.9	6,824,669	5.8				

SOURCE: OPEC-SB, 1987, 1988.

Table 1924

MEXICO OIL INDUSTRY BASIC STATISTICS, 1910–81

(M Barrels/Year)

Year	Production	Exports	Consumption	Refinery Capacity	Imports
1910	3.6	.7	~	~	~
1911	12.5	.9	~	~	~
1912	16.5	8	~	~	~
1913	25.7	21	~	~	~
1914	26.2	23	~	~	~
1915	32.9	25	~	~	~
1916	40.6	27	~	~	~
1917	55.2	46	~	~	~
1918	63.8	52	~	~	~
1919	87.1	76	~	~	~
1920	157.1	146	~	~	~
1921	193.4	172	~	~	~
1922	182.3	181	~	~	~
1923	149.6	136	~	~	~
1924	139.7	130	~	~	~
1925	115.5	99	~	~	~
1926	90.4	81	~	~	~
1927	64.1	53	~	~	~
1928	50.1	33	~	~	~
1929	44.7	27	~	~	~
1930	39.5	27	~	~	~
1931	33.0	23	~	~	~
1932	32.8	23	~	~	~
1933	34.0	22	~	~	~
1934	38.2	25	~	~	~
1935	40.2	25	~	~	~
1936	41.0	25	~	~	~
1937	46.1	15	~	~	~
1938	38.8	4	28.2	33.7	1.7
1939	43.3	9	24.6	31.9	1.3
1940	44.4	9	28.0	32.1	2.2
1941	43.4	8	25.5	34.9	2.2
1942	35.1	1	27.0	33.2	2.4
1943	35.5	1	29.6	34.5	2.8
1944	38.5	1	31.3	36.5	3.3
1945	43.9	2	32.9	43.1	4.1
1946	49.5	3	38.2	51.3	4.5
1947	57.1	7	46.3	51.3	5.6
1948	59.8	7	45.7	49.8	5.3
1949	62.2	7	52.2	54.7	5.6
1950	73.9	12	58.0	55.9	7.3
1951	78.8	14	63.9	61.3	8.3
1952	78.9	9	65.2	65.1	7.7
1953	74.1	3	66.4	71.5	8.9
1954	85.2	5	68.2	77.1	11.5
1955	91.4	6	73.9	81.0	15.0
1956	94.1	7	80.8	80.8	18.0
1957	92.2	4	89.0	85.2	17.1
1958	100.6	1	94.4	94.3	12.4
1959	105.8	.1	93.4	101.7	8.4
1960	108.8	1.1	101.4	102.4	7.9
1961	116.8	6.7	109.1	115.8	6.9
1962	121.6	7.1	105.3	116.8	6.0
1963	125.8	7.1	108.4	117.8	7.5
1964	129.5	7.6	117.5	127.0	9.6
1965	132.1	4.8	118.1	127.2	9.4
1966	135.0	~	121.1	129.5	12.8
1967	149.9	~	146.8	146.8	11.9
1968	160.5	~	143.9	155.9	11.8
1969	168.4	~	154.1	161.3	16.8
1870	177.6	~	162.7	175.6	17.3
1971	177.3	~	176.2	177.7	24.9
1972	185.0	~	200.5	193.4	25.5
1973	191.5	~	221.1	106.1	33.1
1974	238.3	6	240.4	234.3	23.6
1975	294.3	34	255.3	240.9	25.0
1976	327.3	34	272.9	268.3	15.7
1977	396.2	74	290.5	300.6	8.5
1978	485.3	194	320.8	320.2	13.6
1979	590.6	303	341.4	349.9	10.0
1980	709.0	401	~	~	~
1981	844.0	~	~	~	~

SOURCE: John D. Wirth, ed., *Latin American Oil Companies and the Politics of Energy*
(Lincoln: University of Nebraska Press, 1985), pp. 263–264.

Table 1925

MEXICO OIL EARNINGS, AMOUNT AND USES, 1980–81

	1980		1981	
Category	M Pesos	%	M Pesos	%
Income from Oil	211.6	100.0	417.8	100.0
PEMEX Savings	55.3	26.1	151.3	36.2
Export Tax[1]	156.3	73.9	266.5	63.8
Allocation	211.6	100.0	417.8	100.0
PEMEX Investment[2]	55.3	26.1	151.3	36.2
Expenditure Other Sectors	156.3	79.3	266.5	63.8
Agriculture	38.2	18.1	66.6	15.9
Communications and Transport	31.2	14.7	53.3	12.8
Social Welfare	37.5	17.7	64.0	15.3
Industry, Except PEMEX	23.9	11.3	42.6	10.2
States and Municipalities	25.5	12.1	40.0	9.6

1. In addition, PEMEX paid domestic taxes totaling 29.7 and 41.0 billion Mexican pesos in 1980 and 1981, respectively.
2. Constitutes 44.5% and 97.2% of the total PEMEX Investment Program for 1980 and 1981, respectively.

SOURCE: *Mexico's Energy Resources: Toward a Policy of Diversification* (Boulder, Colo.: Westview Press, 1985), p. 42.

Table 1926

MEXICO PROVEN OIL RESERVES AND PRODUCTION, 1971–79

(M Barrels)

Category	1971	1972	1973	1974	1975	1976	1977	1978	1979
Total Hydrocarbons Reserves	5,428	5,388	5,432	5,773	6,338	11,160	16,002	40,194	45,803
Production	306	326	335	402	464	500	545	672	803
Total Hydrocarbons Production per Year	18	16	16	14	14	22	25	60	67

SOURCE: *Mexico's Energy Resources: Toward a Policy of Diversification* (Boulder, Colo.: Westview Press, 1985), p. 32.

Table 1927

MEXICO ENERGY RESERVES

Category	Crude Oil	Natural Gas[1]	Subtotal	Coal[2]	Hydraulic[3]	Uranium[4]	Geothermal[5]	Total
M Tons of Oil Equivalent								
Proven	6,808	3,387	10,195	856	638	130	74	11,893
Probable	~	~	18,500	1,000	1,356	260	484	21,600
Potential	~	~	35,397	1,419	3,988	1,300	7,440	49,544
As Percent of Total Reserves								
Proven	66.8[a]	33.2[a]	85.7	7.2	5.4	1.1	.6	100
Probable	~	~	85.7	4.6	6.3	1.3	2.2	100
Potential	~	~	71.4	3.0	8.0	3.1	15.0	100

1. Natural gas includes nonassociated gas and gas liquids.
2. Coal: figures given are for in situ reserves, evaluated according to the caloric content of coal.
3. Hydraulic: reserves estimated in accordance with the consumption of oil products by an equivalent thermal power station operating for thirty years.
4. Uranium: the energy that could be generated per unit of uranium consumed was calculated and then the consumption of oil products by an equivalent thermal power station was estimated.
5. Geothermal: power includes high enthalpy, water, and steam reserves: probable includes high, medium, and low enthalpy reserves; potential includes super hot water, steam geopressurized, and lava reserves.

a. Percentage of subtotal.

SOURCE: *Mexico's Energy Resources: Toward a Policy of Diversification* (Boulder, Colo.: Westview Press, 1985), p. 40.

Table 1928

VENEZUELA OIL INDUSTRY BASIC STATISTICS, 1920–82
(M Barrels/Day)

Year	Production	Exports	Consumption	Refinery Capacity	Imports
1920	1	2	1	1	
1921	4	3	1	1	
1922	6	5	1	1	
1923	12	9	1	2	
1924	25	23	1	2	
1925	55	50	1	3	
1926	98	90	1	4	
1927	166	156	1	7	
1928	290	275	1	14	
1929	373	358	1	13	
1930	371	367	1	14	
1931	320	307	1	17	
1932	319	302	1	18	
1933	324	310	1	20	
1934	373	357	1	22	
1935	407	380	1	25	
1936	423	411	1	23	
1937	509	460	1	24	
1938	515	489	5	26	
1939	560	518	6	37	
1940	512	429	7	73	
1941	621	611	8	87	
1942	416	386	8	63	
1943	409	477	8	61	
1944	702	682	11	72	
1945	886	870	12	89	
1946	1,064	1,082	16	96	
1947	1,191	1,161	25	101	
1948	1,342	1,282	29	119	
1949	1,321	1,260	40	145	
1950	1,494	1,424	52	250	
1951	1,705	1,612	57	315	
1952	1,809	1,715	62	348	
1953	1,765	1,662	75	413	
1954	1,890	1,789	90	443	
1955	2,157	2,024	106	537	
1956	2,464	2,312	123	624	
1957	2,779	2,576	142	689	
1958	2,605	2,437	131	732	
1959	2,771	2,578	134	824	
1960	2,846	2,685	128	882	
1961	2,920	2,764	122	923	
1962	3,200	3,018	151	1,025	
1963	3,248	3,074	152	1,042	
1964	3,393	3,213	166	1,092	
1965	3,473	3,253	176	1,175	
1966	3,371	3,182	180	1,174	
1967	3,542	3,362	183	1,221	
1968	3,615	3,369	194	1,186	
1969	3,594	3,411	192	1,156	
1970	3,708	3,470	201	1,292	
1971	3,549	3,282	211	1,245	
1972	3,220	3,065	228	1,125	
1973	3,366	3,150	254	1,303	
1974	2,976	2,752	249	1,196	
1975	2,346	2,086	244	886	
1976	2,294	2,156	244	987	
1977	2,238	1,987	254	967	
1978	2,166	1,963	283	983	
1979	2,356	2,099	317	987	
1980	2,168	1,864	355	922	
1981	2,107	1,759	369	859	
1982	1,893	1,554	381	866	

SOURCE: John D. Wirth, ed., *Latin American Oil Companies and the Politics of Energy*
(Lincoln: University of Nebraska Press, 1985), pp. 366–367.

Table 1929

REFINED PETROLEUM PRODUCTS PRODUCTION,[1] 20 LC, 1950–86
(T MET)

Country	1950	1955	1960	1965	1970	1975	1979	1980	1981	1982	1983	1984	1985	1986
A. ARGENTINA														
Liquefied Petrol. Gas	30	51	74	323	548	677	718	765	883	1,025	1,173	1,203	1,138	1,138
Motor Spirit	1,525	1,681	1,951	32,000	3,978	3,841	4,621	5,157	5,121	5,146	5,137	4,971	4,681	4,721
Kerosene	586	844	1,124	1,057	886	853	524	591	425	437	527	457	419	417
Jet Fuel	3†	4	19	122	301	463	625	782	786	661	608	662	690	696
Distillate Fuel Oils	763	1,170	1,623	3,092	4,829	5,512	6,775	7,621	7,778	7,752	7,793	7,921	7,897	7,675
Residual Fuel Oils	2,573	3,716	6,264	7,990	8,502	7,749	8,421	8,134	8,129	7,231	6,539	6,113	5,312	5,317
Lubricating Oils	85	109	145	140	144	244	307	277	268	282	282	258	274	284
Bitumen (Asphalt)	~	~	263	374	695	429	677	640†	623	487	393	367	381	412
Petroleum Coke	~	~	84	356	663	666	810	710†	869	970	983	944	1,072	963
B. BOLIVIA														
Liquefied Petrol. Gas	~	6	6	~	3	27	84	103	148	183	172	162	159	151
Motor Spirit	39	108	106	139	220	377	526	406	324	385	332	342	343	462
Kerosene	9	19	52	66	103	143	133	129	92	90	83	87	89	56
Jet Fuel	~	~	~	2	13	43	70	92	91	68	73	76	82	93
Distillate Fuel Oils	6	32	48	73	89	159	253	261	272	235	214	230	229	276
Residual Fuel Oils	25	113	82	124	143	191	210	151	124	128	140	101	80	46
Lubricating Oils	~	~	~	~	7	14	22	25	19	21	15	16	15†	9
C. BRAZIL														
Liquefied Petrol. Gas	~	47	242	562	972	1,940	2,274	2,342	2,432	2,291	2,588	2,839	2,983	3,097
Motor Spirit	19	1,323	2,514	4,310	7,067	10,472	9,959	10,419	10,531	11,533	11,712	13,875	14,894	17,243
Kerosene	7	12	519	531	629	830	700	530	510	518	576	495	412	402
Jet Fuel	~	~	~	~	663	1,413	1,911	2,170	2,503	2,573	2,260	2,884	2,749	2,522
Distillate Fuel Oils	24	298	1,378	3,831	5,766	10,316	15,350	16,986	16,013	16,889	16,817	17,734	17,756	19,640
Residual Fuel Oils	14	1,560	3,561	5,282	8,439	14,762	17,100	16,515	15,517	13,644	12,238	12,499	11,808	12,699
Lubricating Oils	~	~	~	5	11	218	485	556	546	659	675†	700	659	707
Bitumen (Asphalt)	3†	40†	207	300	702	807	1,316	1,028	888	973	800†	740	1,020	1,419
Petroleum Coke	~	~	~	~	#	116	~	182	212	210	225†	278	291	390
D. CHILE														
Liquefied Petrol. Gas	7	7	29	46	226	457	481	479	483	403	443	448	425	442
Motor Spirit	~	213	527	751	1,137	899	1,010	990	1,052	856	947	956	960	907
Kerosene	~	15	142	240	354	322	260	227	215	164	172	111	97	125
Jet Fuel	~	~	~	~	62	95	165	158	195	147	145	164	156	177
Distillate Fuel Oils	~	99	264	418	607	824	1,207	1,211	1,089	850	1,048	1,107	1,193	1,313
Residual Fuel Oils	~	251	378	679a	1,090	1,332	1,645	1,629	1,430	1,008	1,065	1,005	958	1,085
Lubricating Oils	~	~	~	~	~	~	~	~	62	51	47	59	55	57
Bitumen (Asphalt)	~	~	~	~	7	6	~	6†	31	23	8	7	4	12
E. COLOMBIA														
Liquefied Petrol. Gas	~	~	46	95	292	320	285	260	281	263	411	423	408	415
Motor Spirit	227	556	1,022	1,410	1,810	2,311	1,797	2,138	2,438	2,434	2,489	2,696	2,521	2,893
Kerosene	50	145	232	250	457	432	413	352	336	291	289	260	278	276
Jet Fuel	~	~	6	31	167	315	453	453	502	539	533	449	470	493
Distillate Fuel Oils	76	201	460	636	920	916	1,074	1,187	1,337	1,335	1,434	1,453	1,542	1,543
Residual Fuel Oils	926	834	1,450	1,515	2,470	2,643	2,304	2,566	2,462	2,691	3,060	3,025	2,994	3,174
Lubricating Oils	11	9	10	60	68	9	10†	10†	6†	5†	5†	6†	6†	6†
Bitumen (Asphalt)	~	~	28	30	116	92	117	156	187	184	162	160	153	161
Petroleum Coke	~	~	98	109	158	148	175†	150†	140†	90†	100†	175†	150†	200†
F. COSTA RICA														
Liquefied Petrol. Gas	~	~	~	~	1	5	8	8	7	7	3	4	5	5
Motor Spirit	~	~	~	~	57	60	70	87	85	87	69	74	77	77
Kerosene	~	~	~	~	18	22	24	20	12	11	10	12	15	15
Jet Fuel	~	~	~	~	~	~	~	~	14	14	11	13	13	12
Distillate Fuel Oils	~	~	~	~	116	63	85	151	143	116	75	104	88	85
Residual Fuel Oils	~	~	~	~	112	113	181	216	212	176	144	183	202	200
Bitumen (Asphalt)	~	~	~	~	~	5	~	12†	11	9	12	12	12†	10†

Table 1929 (Continued)

REFINED PETROLEUM PRODUCTS PRODUCTION,[1] 20 LC, 1950-86

(T MET)

Country	1950	1955	1960	1965	1970	1975	1979	1980	1981	1982	1983	1984	1985	1986
G. CUBA														
Liquefied Petrol. Gas	~	~	~	52	57	83	92	106	104	112	106	116	125	116
Motor Spirit	84	118	710	810	745	947	872	1,898	2,143	918	961	1,057	1,029	1,058
Kerosene	59	107	130	202	401	447	415	438	429	456	494	506	528	568
Jet Fuel	~	~	~	~	~	~	~	39	57	76	66	89	81	69
Distillate Fuel Oils	54	129	606	643	583	1,084	1,094	1,098	1,118	1,117	1,060	1,020	979	992
Residual Fuel Oils	38	81	1,654	1,899	2,367	2,821	3,213	3,026	3,130	3,198	3,414	3,340	3,318	3,314
Lubricating Oils	~	~	~	67	95	151	133	130	115	137	135	130	123	117
Bitumen (Asphalt)	~	~	~	10	63	148	173	196	210	198	223	234	238	245
Petroleum Coke	~	~	~	~	9	17	~	20	18	18	20	24	26	25
H. DOMINICAN REP.														
Liquefied Petrol. Gas	~	~	~	~	~	47	67	53	42	45	45	43	38	24
Motor Spirit	~	~	~	~	~	322	301	289	267	240	260	295	291	344
Kerosene	~	~	~	~	~	17	27	69	71	72	81	93	72	107
Jet Fuel	~	~	~	~	~	34	40	42	45	17	19	21	20	20
Distillate Fuel Oils	~	~	~	~	~	370	347	393	374	351	476	407	344	441
Residual Fuel Oils	~	~	~	~	~	369	353	536	659	457	815	537	512	528
I. ECUADOR														
Liquefied Petrol. Gas	1	1	1	1	5	5	70	75	65	78	55	94	95	140
Motor Spirit	62	78	204	254	365	668	958	968	918	890	720	922	913	1,030
Kerosene	16	25	39	57	65	184	322	292	284	325	265	293	274	287
Jet Fuel	~	~	4	23	79	60	146	139	148	137	117	135	145	135
Distillate Fuel Oils	33	47	96	133	255	436	711	785	694	723	605	749	748	842
Residual Fuel Oils	104	117	194	224	352	541	2,096	2,260	2,163	2,189	1,886	2,131	1,865	2,087
Lubricating Oils	1	1	13	16	9	19	37	42	43	46	32	39	40	41
Bitumen (Asphalt)	~	~	~	~	#	#	~	52	48	49	42	66	75†	97
J. EL SALVADOR														
Liquefied Petrol. Gas	~	~	~	3	4	18	28	26	24	22	25	27	28	25
Motor Spirit	~	~	~	104	36	115	153	128	115	107	120	127	130	125
Kerosene	~	~	~	52	15	32	42	27	23	27	27	26	28	27
Jet Fuel	~	~	~	27	6	14	9	17	17	17	20	18	18	17
Distillate Fuel Oils	~	~	~	140	43	206	240	194	182	171	185	181	180	175
Residual Fuel Oils	~	~	~	105	68	220	213	191	193	182	190	196	190	180
Bitumen (Asphalt)	~	~	~	~	~	21	18	16	20†	20†	22†	21†	21†	20†
K. GUATEMALA														
Liquefied Petrol. Gas	~	~	~	3	9	6	3	2	2	2	3	5	5	5
Motor Spirit	~	~	~	105	163	209	132	108	109	100	104	122	120	115
Kerosene	~	~	~	27	49	51	35	37	35	29	32	33	30	28
Jet Fuel	~	~	~	16	31	39	46	32	27	25	28	29	30	28
Distillate Fuel Oils	~	~	~	98	215	225	259	242	222	204	200	232	230	225
Residual Fuel Oils	~	~	~	155	257	360	307	313	334	246	209	251	250	245
L. HAITI	~	~	~	~	~	~	~	~	~	~	~	~	~	~
M. HONDURAS														
Liquefied Petrol. Gas	~	~	~	~	4	8	3	3	4	3	4	4	4	4
Motor Spirit	~	~	~	~	106	84	86	81	42	26	50	55	60	58
Kerosene	~	~	~	~	30	32	40	40	8	0	5	8	8	9
Jet Fuel	~	~	~	~	6	11	19	20	18	10	10	12	12	10
Distillate Fuel Oils	~	~	~	~	214	172	190	202	58	12	89	90	90	85
Residual Fuel Oils	~	~	~	~	348	313	118	141	56	32	87	90	90	85

Table 1929 (Continued)

REFINED PETROLEUM PRODUCTS PRODUCTION,[1] 20 LC, 1950–86
(T MET)

Country	1950	1955	1960	1965	1970	1975	1979	1980	1981	1982	1983	1984	1985	1986
N. MEXICO[2]														
Liquefied Petrol. Gas	50	101	334	503	1,134	1,620	2,838	3,763	4,258	4,726	4,854	4,903	5,236	5,150
Motor Spirit	1,298	1,831	3,090	4,514	5,913	7,839	11,878	13,983	15,360	14,736	14,708	15,057	14,891	14,150
Kerosene	547	888	1,413	1,567	1,461	1,666	1,893	1,953	1,938	2,130	1,813	1,477	1,456	1,385
Jet Fuel	~	~	23	138	397	718	1,179	1,299	1,360	1,439	1,272	1,573	1,547	1,545
Distillate Fuel Oils	735	680	1,649	2,908	4,206	7,626	10,619	12,364	13,629	11,652	11,309	11,792	12,376	11,950
Residual Fuel Oils	4,883	7,221	6,354	6,325	7,195	9,853	13,143	17,053	19,131	19,279	19,306	20,724	21,810	22,165
Lubricating Oils	27	81	151	195	276	423	400	404	494	408	344	358	348	345†
Bitumen (Asphalt)	32	178	299	249	1,076	342	351	1,017	1,100	1,205	1,023	1,371	1,382	1,350†
Petroleum Coke	~	~	~	~	54	71	89	30	46	93	68	29	23	20†
O. NICARAGUA														
Liquefied Petrol. Gas	~	~	~	2	9	13	13	16	17	16	16	14	18	15
Motor Spirit	~	~	~	79	109	141	121	134	133	107	90	61	72	70
Kerosene[3]	~	~	~	25	27	17	13	14	17	19	20	27	21	20
Jet Fuel	~	~	~	~	~	~	~	~	~	21	15	16	15	15
Distillate Fuel Oils	~	~	~	65	129	159	131	174	198	168	160	127	129	125
Residual Fuel Oils	~	~	~	47	158	243	117	160	217	228	221	180	222	215
Bitumen (Asphalt)	~	~	~	~	~	31	15†	15†	13	6	4	3	6	5†
P. PANAMA														
Liquefied Petrol. Gas	~	~	~	~	19	35	23	22	20	25	20	20	20	20
Motor Spirit	~	~	~	314	386	342	277	240	220	210	200	190	170	165
Kerosene	~	~	~	95	54	16	10	10	12	15	16	15	10	10
Jet Fuel	~	~	~	44	318	337	135	125	100	100	100	75	60	55
Distillate Fuel Oils	~	~	~	702	725	662	576	462	400	400	400	350	300	275
Residual Fuel Oils	~	~	~	1,210	2,048	2,366	1,021	1,001	900	940	875	775	640	625
Bitumen (Asphalt)	~	~	~	~	90	10†	20†	18†	20†	25†	20†	20†	15†	12†
Q. PARAGUAY														
Liquefied Petrol. Gas	~	~	~	~	3	3	4	2	3	6	7	3	4	3
Motor Spirit	~	~	~	~	77	51	85	106	63	64	58	47	68	79
Kerosene	~	~	~	~	19	14	20	16	12	8	10	11	7	3
Jet Fuel	~	~	~	~	5	6	10	13	14	13	11	2	15	21
Distillate Fuel Oils	~	~	~	~	34	80	95	115	112	99	97	71	86	88
Residual Fuel Oils	~	~	~	~	33	41	50	56	59	35	30	22	28	33
Bitumen (Asphalt)	~	~	~	~	3	4†	2†	2†	2†	2†	1†	~	~	~
R. PERU														
Liquefied Petrol. Gas	4	6	7	22[d]	27	167	122	106	129	137	102	129	130	120
Motor Spirit	454	551	576	711	1,116	1,525	1,540	1,533	1,642	1,600	1,256	1,348	1,359	1,275
Kerosene	153	327	470	423	510	605	793	368	902	916	775	801	871	820
Jet Fuel	~	~	32	102	198	238	342	387	425	371	350	342	252	235
Distillate Fuel Oils	194	547	705	865	929	1,006	1,653	1,712	1,801	1,676	1,333	1,647	1,670	1,570
Residual Fuel Oils	832	473	372	820	1,231	1,931	2,335	2,511	2,564	2,848	3,498	4,076	3,906	3,675
Lubricating Oils	11	12	10	12[c]	11	12	20	12	15†	21	26†	17†	19†	17†
Bitumen (Asphalt)	11	30	9	33	47	38	30	39	42	52	28†	35†	35†	30†
S. URUGUAY														
Liquefied Petrol. Gas	~	~	~	17	31	29	37	40	36	44	41	47	47	44
Motor Spirit	173	239	243	268	244	268	225	207	185	204	164	173	162	174
Kerosene	153	327	470	166	168	160	133	24	96	88	80	66	49	49
Jet Fuel	~	~	7	14	23	23	41	28	26	28	19	9	22	22
Distillate Fuel Oils	63	167	205	307	361	423	460	473	468	492	432	444	388	315
Residual Fuel Oils	376	581	651	751	785	816	788	845	788	701	437	392	310	346
Lubricating Oils	~	~	2	1	8	8	8	7	6	6	7	6†	7	7
Bitumen (Asphalt)	~	~	11	19	41†	39†	59	51	37	54	40	37	27	32
Petroleum Coke	~	~	~	~	11	9	~	15	12	12	12	11	11	17

Table 1929 (Continued)

REFINED PETROLEUM PRODUCTS PRODUCTION,[1] 20 LC, 1950–86

(T MET)

Country	1950	1955	1960	1965	1970	1975	1979	1980	1981	1982	1983	1984	1985	1986
VENEZUELA														
Liquefied Petrol. Gas	111	316	640	489	1,295	1,842	1,957	1,647	1,429	1,505	1,298	1,551	1,578	1,529
Motor Spirit[4]	620†	1,215†	1,755†	2,247	3,138	4,674	6,774	6,772	7,009	8,095	9,200	9,196	9,200	10,402
Kerosene	282	984	1,223	1,038	554	421	482	560	678	473	572	552	436	411
Jet Fuel	~	~	473	2,206	3,494	1,062	1,391	1,498	1,457	1,850	2,486	1,866	2,352	2,675
Distillate Fuel Oils	2,378	5,727	7,671	9,584	7,628	6,908	7,737	8,809	8,562	8,679	9,338	10,127	12,845	12,059
Residual Fuel Oils	7,879	15,832	28,613	40,917	44,939	26,953	30,764	25,663	22,220	21,153	17,485	17,742	16,310	14,433
Lubricating Oils	523	143	209	527	551	497	439	469	392	355	343	335	335	374
Bitumen (Asphalt)	109	163	1,047	912	849	564	1,219	1,135	1,531	1,540	1,432	1,479	1,689	1,982
Petroleum Coke	#	~	#	~	160	120†	~	125†	149†	99†	132†	126†	239†	200†
UNITED STATES														
Liquefied Petrol. Gas	7,530	13,015	20,045	26,433	45,123	47,859	48,765	48,229	49,225	47,865	51,442	53,310	53,397	53,104
Motor Spirit	108,835	143,274	166,192	193,554	245,377	279,999	294,223	280,194	275,053	272,153	272,257	277,887	275,654	289,962
Kerosene	15,262	15,085	13,504†	11,996	12,321	7,170	8,601	6,447	5,613	5,406	5,153	5,385	4,441	4,204
Jet Fuel	~	7,169	15,150†	27,516	38,883	40,950	47,548	47,081	45,487	45,974	48,055	53,356	55,876	60,779
Distillate Fuel Oils	55,177	83,344	92,266	105,824	124,085	133,983	159,173	134,743	131,932	131,579	124,006	135,722	135,682	138,008
Residual Fuel Oils	64,224	63,486	50,167	40,564	38,894	68,113	92,976	87,364	82,814	58,962	46,952	49,267	48,634	48,989
Lubricating Oils	7,403	7,990	8,498	9,004	9,470	8,045	10,157	9,318	8,666	8,335	7,699	7,595	7,595	8,323
Bitumen (Asphalt)	10,698	15,051	17,236	21,449	24,190	23,744	27,908	23,339	20,412	19,743	22,431	23,370	24,195	24,759
Petroleum Coke	3,122	5,141	10,877	15,594	19,551	23,449	24,907	24,580	25,842	27,132	27,816	29,118	30,090	33,442
WORLD														
Liquefied Petrol. Gas	8,072	15,321	26,182	45,029	81,477	99,925	119,926	118,931	120,488	125,720	134,056	141,087	142,059	143,257
Motor Spirit	148,543	213,861	273,626	365,848	478,095	585,457	655,723	650,077	643,643	641,240	652,023	667,110	670,123	695,629
Kerosene	30,937	41,421	55,921	64,546	91,796	104,865	129,077	110,491	108,634	109,321	110,008	111,712	109,070	110,260
Jet Fuel	472	12,414	25,338	50,700	81,373	89,900	105,789	106,422	104,894	106,394	109,140	116,561	119,056	127,600
Distillate Fuel Oils	94,942	157,588	219,722	322,560	482,643	589,398	727,867	722,837	695,204	692,597	689,440	715,737	723,894	740,831
Residual Fuel Oils	175,429	235,150	330,798	513,241	798,319	880,417	974,154	904,535	829,239	769,888	758,214	745,580	699,564	712,989
Lubricating Oils	10,016	12,181	14,631	18,335	28,721	31,228	39,469	41,241	39,282	37,703	36,617	38,145	36,664	37,981
Bitumen (Asphalt)	13,654	21,833	30,668	42,688	75,457	85,721	102,009	100,389	95,854	95,522	97,112	97,482	99,114	101,047
Petroleum Coke	3,142	5,535	12,017	17,186	22,534	27,052	31,449	31,458	32,636	35,422	36,724	38,277	39,790	43,181

1. The figures in this table refer to the liquid fuels, lubricant oils, and solid and semisolid products obtained by distillation of domestic and imported crude petroleum, shale oil, or unfinished petroleum products. So far as possible, the figures include fuels consumed in refining petroleum products obtained from natural gas, coal, lignite, and their derivatives.

Liquefied petroleum gas. A hydrocarbon fraction of the paraffin series lighter than gasoline derived from the distillation of crude petroleum only (excluding LPG from natural gas or liquefied natural gas and also unique-fied gases). It is presented in the liquid state by compression or absorption process to facilitate storage, transport, and handling. It mainly consists of butanes (normal butane and isobutane) and propane or a mixture of them, and is used in domestic heating, as fuel and as solvent.

Motor spirit. Blended light petroleum fuel. Commonly known as petrol or gasoline, suitable as a fuel in spark-ignition internal-combustion engines.

Aviation gasoline. Any of the specially blended grades of gasoline, with high antiknock value, high stability, a high volatility, and low freezing point, intended for use in aviation piston power unit only.

Kerosene. A refined crude petroleum fuel, in volatility between motor spirit and gas oil, free of gasolines and heavy hydrocarbons such as gas oil and lubricating oil. It is used as an illuminant and as a fuel in certain types of spark-ignition engines such as those used for agricultural tractors and stationary engines. The data cover those products commonly termed as burning oil, vaporizing oil, power kerosene illuminating oil, and also white spirit (used commonly as a paint thinner).

Jet fuels. Fuel meeting the required properties for use in jet engines and aircraft turbine engines, mainly refined from kerosene; gasoline-type jet fuel is included.

Distillate fuel oils. A fuel oil which is a crude petroleum distillate, having a viscosity and distillation range between those of kerosene and lubricating oil; used as a fuel for internal combustion in diesel engines, as a burner fuel in heating installations such as furnaces, and for enriching water gas to increase its luminosity. The data cover those products commonly termed as diesel fuel (diesel oil) or gas oil, solar oil, etc.

Residual fuel oil. A fuel oil which is crude petroleum residues, such as viscous residuum, obtained by the refinery opeations of crude petroleum after gasoline, kerosene, and sometimes heavier distillates (such as gas oil or diesel oil) have been removed. It is commonly used by ships and industrial, large-scale heating installations as a fuel in furnace or boilers firing to produce heat and power (known as mazout).

Lubricating oils. A heavy liquid disilate obtained by refining crude petro-leum, used for lubricating purposes. It may be produced either from petroleum distillates or residues at refineries. Solid lubricants (e.g., grease) are excluded.

Bitumen. Brown or black solid or semisolid material, obtained as a residue in the distillation of crude petroleum; used mainly for asphalt paving in road construction. Excluding that which may be obtained from natural occurrence.

Petroleum coke. A solid residue consisting mainly of carbon, obtained by the distillation of heavier petroleum oils, used mainly in metallurgical processes (excluding those solid residues obtained from carbonization of coal).

2. Including aviation spirit.
3. Including jet fuel. Except 1982–85.
4. Including naphtha prior to 1968.
a. Excluding quantities used at refineries and lost.
b. Data not strictly comparable with those of previous years.
c. Including grease.
d. Including liquefied petroleum gas made from natural gas.
e. Including aviation spirit.

SOURCE: SALA, 16-226; UN-SP: J, 14-16 (1970-1973), tables 9, 11, 12, 13, 14, J, 19 (1976), tables 9, 11, 12, 13, 14; J, 20 (1977), tables 9, 11, 12, 13, 14; J, 21 (1978), tables 9, 11, 12, 13, 14; J, 22 (1979), tables 13, 15, 16, 17, 18; UN-YWES, 1979, tables 28 and 30; UN-SP: J, 19 (1950-74), tables 9, 11, 12, 13 and 14; UN-YWES, 1981, tables 22 through 28 and 30; 1982, tables 19, 21, 22–25, 27; 1983, 1984, 1985, 1986, tables 17, 19, 20–23, 25.

Table 1930

CONSUMPTION OF PETROLEUM AND DERIVATIVES, 19 L, 1960–84

(T Barrels)

	Country	1960	1973	1978	1979	1980	1981	1982	1983	1984[‡]
A.	ARGENTINA	95,285	167,766	138,113	177,285	168,266	173,777	168,240	142,465	139,095
B.	BOLIVIA	1,819	4,526	7,625	7,261	8,690	8,689	9,720	8,445	~
C.	BRAZIL	96,106	281,654	385,368	411,237	413,882	372,715	373,709	350,927	363,279
D.	CHILE	16,179	37,376	36,736	37,258	36,941	39,057	36,376	34,562	34,718
E.	COLOMBIA	21,179	47,270	53,206	59,814	60,375	56,420	56,474	60,890	61,897
F.	COSTA RICA	1,304	3,797	6,927	5,957	5,343	4,549	3,789	3,810	3,962
H.	DOMINICAN REP.	2,835	12,331	14,879	15,879	15,123	14,892	14,277	16,256	17,667
I.	ECUADOR	3,806	10,795	22,786	25,526	28,020	30,194	30,322	27,741	29,337
J.	EL SALVADOR	1,588	3,972	5,067	4,761	3,909	3,572	3,971	3,987	4,004
K.	GUATEMALA	3,523	7,014	10,702	11,575	11,422	10,177	9,199	8,308	9,023
L.	HAITI	620	971	1,697	1,775	1,674	1,670	1,528	~	~
M.	HONDURAS	1,495	3,283	3,792	4,711	5,019	3,723	4,000[†]	2,945	3,043
N.	MEXICO	104,100	175,930	334,340	376,315	455,520	531,440	523,775	520,125	544,215
O.	NICARAGUA	1,418	4,107	6,226	4,302	5,000	4,730	4,649	4,652	4,573
P.	PANAMA	2,845	6,405	7,266	7,098	7,200[†]	~	~	~	6,249
Q.	PARAGUAY	673	1,750	3,100	3,032	3,215	3,107	3,553	3,300	3,712
R.	PERU	18,514	39,085	43,300	44,700	48,253	48,180	46,927	40,626	41,623
S.	URUGUAY	9,888	12,509	12,850	12,052	13,597	12,245	11,981	9,161	8,605
T.	VENEZUELA	46,683	92,548	109,183	120,251	133,900	142,100	143,100	143,300	131,600

SOURCE: IDB-SPTF, yearly, 1978–85, table 69.

Table 1931

ACTUAL AND POTENTIAL PROVEN RESERVES AND PRODUCTION OF CRUDE PETROLEUM
AND NATURAL GAS, 19 L, 1960–82

PART I: 1960 AND 1975

		Crude Petroleum						Natural Gas					
		Reserves (M Barrels)		Production (M Barrels)		Production Potential[1] (Years)		Reserves (B Cubic Feet)		Production (B Cubic Feet)		Production Potential[1] (Years)	
	Country	1960	1975	1960	1975	1960	1975	1961	1975	1961	1975	1961	1975
A.	ARGENTINA	1,550	2,465	63.9	144.4	24.2	17.1	6,004	7,200	156.3	276.0	38.4	26.1
B.	BOLIVIA	125	235	3.1	14.7	40.1	16.0	250	10,800	5.8	137.4	53.1	78.6

Continued in SALA, 24–1918.

Table 1932

WORLD MARKETED PRODUCTION OF NATURAL GAS, 6 LRC, 1981–87

(M Me^3)

Country	1981	1982	1983	1984	1985	1986	1987	PC 1987 over 1986
North America	613,645	577,303	525,428	570,679	548,019	531,449	546,320	2.8
Canada	70,525	74,420	71,450	78,190	84,130	78,660	84,960	8.0
United States	543,120	502,883	453,978	492,489	463,889	452,789	461,360	1.9
Extended Latin America	65,129	70,988	75,865	76,961	74,024	76,554	76,269	−.4
A. ARGENTINA	8,735	9,790	13,140	13,480	13,890	15,510	15,410	−.6
B. BOLIVIA	2,464	2,620	2,600	2,560	2,710	2,670	2,810	5.2
D. COLOMBIA	3,242	2,960	4,140	4,080	4,110	4,150	4,060	−2.2
I. ECUADOR	55	73	85	81	78	80	40	−50.0
N. MEXICO	30,250	31,640	31,110	29,350	26,990	26,080	26,360	1.1
Trinidad and Tobago	3,197	2,900	5,060	5,540	4,140	4,280	4,050	−5.4
T. VENEZUELA	14,459	17,005	15,640	17,300	17,326	19,074	18,589	−2.5
Other	2,727	4,000	4,090	4,570	4,780	4,710	4,950	5.1
Western Europe	187,820	176,354	183,071	186,550	194,686	190,305	199,395	4.8
France	6,125	6,586	6,580	6,260	5,350	4,160	3,800	−8.7
Germany	17,460	16,606	17,730	18,336	17,210	15,460	17,680	14.4
Ireland	1,340	2,050	2,460	2,340	2,400	1,680	1,670	−.6
Italy	13,770	14,590	13,070	13,840	14,250	15,960	16,300	2.1
Netherlands	81,526	69,730	74,700	75,140	80,640	74,080	75,280	1.6
Norway	26,470	24,890	25,660	28,330	26,550	27,100	29,420	8.6
United Kingdom	37,390	38,280	39,530	38,530	42,950	45,310	47,640	5.1
Yugoslavia	2,187	2,190	1,950	1,880	2,490	2,500	2,890	15.6
Other	1,552	1,432	1,391	1,894	2,846	4,055	4,715	16.3
Middle East	52,806	40,750	37,770	58,656	63,860	76,070	85,840	12.8
Bahrain	3,538	3,760	3,680	3,790	4,540	5,100	6,130	20.2
I.R. Iran	5,950	7,200	11,000	13,500	14,600	15,200	16,000	5.3
Iraq	620	680	470	590	850	1,550	3,750	141.9
Kuwait	4,684	3,675	4,035	4,376	4,200	5,730	5,300	−7.5
Oman	1,950	2,700	460	1,000	2,000	2,010	2,260	12.4
Qatar	4,323	5,055	5,235	5,930	5,460	5,800	5,610	−3.3
Saudi Arabia	22,245	8,950	4,380	18,200	18,800	25,200	26,800	6.3
United Arab Emirates	9,075	8,320	8,400	11,060	13,210	15,220	19,310	26.9
Other	421	410	110	210	200	260	680	161.5
Africa	29,489	35,060	46,344	46,632	50,361	53,140	59,156	11.3
Algeria	21,862	26,686	36,267	35,039	36,470	37,560	43,170	14.9
Egypt	1,580	2,670	3,130	4,020	4,930	5,680	6,280	10.6
Gabon	143	150	118	71	80	90	115	27.8
Libya	3,150	3,350	3,710	4,600	5,200	5,600	5,000	−10.7
Nigeria	2,155	1,413	2,298	2,051	2,800	3,299	3,700	12.2
Other	599	791	821	851	881	911	891	−2.2
Asia and Far East	46,279	52,146	59,662	76,349	82,335	89,174	94,580	6.1
Afghanistan	2,689	2,800	2,850	2,900	2,900	2,900	2,800	−3.4
Bangladesh	1,570	1,940	3,300	2,540	2,840	3,240	3,720	14.8
Brunei	8,427	9,210	8,620	8,570	8,350	8,290	8,710	5.1
India	1,753	2,520	2,990	3,240	3,780	5,890	6,420	9.0
Indonesia	18,775	19,076	21,992	32,969	33,905	35,374	36,550	3.3
Japan	2,463	2,050	2,310	2,370	2,230	2,110	2,100	−.5
Malaysia	1,328	1,580	4,200	9,200	12,380	14,950	15,600	4.3
Pakistan	7,504	9,740	9,720	10,040	10,370	11,100	11,880	7.0
Other	1,770	3,230	3,680	4,520	5,580	5,320	6,800	27.8
Oceania	12,330	13,900	13,030	14,070	16,060	17,690	17,620	−.4
Australia	10,600	10,970	10,980	11,420	12,670	13,650	13,870	1.6
New Zealand	1,730	2,930	2,050	2,650	3,390	4,040	3,750	−7.2
CPEs	543,010	579,990	616,070	665,180	727,740	770,050	811,080	5.3
China	19,450	17,650	18,700	18,000	19,700	20,550	20,700	.7
German Dem. Rep.	8,500	8,100	11,100	12,370	11,430	11,430	13,000	13.7
Hungary	6,632	6,630	6,500	6,900	7,440	7,100	7,000	−1.4
Poland	4,784	5,530	5,470	6,070	6,370	5,820	5,750	−1.2
Romania	38,954	39,050	37,600	33,300	38,770	38,020	36,300	−4.5
USSR	463,619	502,000	535,700	587,400	643,000	685,850	727,000	6.0
Other	1,071	1,030	1,000	1,140	1,030	1,280	1,330	3.9
Total World	1,550,508	1,546,491	1,557,240	1,695,077	1,757,085	1,804,432	1,890,260	4.8
OPEC	107,496	101,633	113,630	145,767	152,979	169,777	183,934	8.3
OPEC Percentage	6.9	6.6	7.3	8.6	8.7	9.4	9.7	
Total World Excluding CPEs	1,007,498	966,501	941,170	1,029,897	1,029,345	1,034,382	1,079,180	4.3
OPEC Percentage	10.7	10.5	12.1	14.2	14.9	16.4	17.0	

SOURCE: OPEC-SB, 1986, 1988.

Table 1933

NATURAL GAS PRODUCTION,[1] 20 LC, 1970–86

(T TJ)

	Country	1970	1975	1980	1981	1982	1983	1984	1985	1986
A.	ARGENTINA	209.0	265.5	326.9	340.2	392.8	456.5	478.2	508.8	552.6
B.	BOLIVIA	1.3	59.1	79.8	90.0	93.3	89.7	86.3	85.5	87.0
C.	BRAZIL	3.3	24.6	41.2	37.1	42.9	63.0	77.1	96.7	110.2
D.	CHILE	48.1	45.8	27.1	33.4	34.5	36.7	36.8	37.5	34.3
E.	COLOMBIA	55.2	73.2	150.6	164.1	159.2	165.3	165.0	165.5	165.8
F.	COSTA RICA	#	#	#	#	#	#	#	#	#
G.	CUBA	~	.7	.7	.4	.4	.3	.1	.3	.2
H.	DOMINICAN REP.	#	#	#	#	#	#	#	#	#
I.	ECUADOR	.7	1.5	1.5	2.6	3.5	4.1	3.9	3.8	4.2
J.	EL SALVADOR	#	#	#	#	#	#	#	#	#
K.	GUATEMALA	#	#	#	#	#	#	#	#	#
L.	HAITI	#	#	#	#	#	#	#	#	#
M.	HONDURAS	#	#	#	#	#	#	#	#	#
N.	MEXICO	450.9	523.5	1,036	1,033	1,075	959.5	705.5	647.1	613.7
O.	NICARAGUA	#	#	#	#	#	#	#	#	#
P.	PANAMA	#	#	#	#	#	#	#	#	#
Q.	PARAGUAY	#	#	#	#	#	#	#	#	#
R.	PERU	16.0	27.4	43.7	48.6	44.0	19.2	23.6	24.1	23.0
S.	URUGUAY	#	#	#	#	#	#	#	#	#
T.	VENEZUELA	381.9	480.4	643.0	646.8	682.4	667.7	740.6	731.0	867.4
	UNITED STATES	22,860	20,723	19,256	19,057	17,655	15,986	17,341	16,365	16,019
	WORLD	38,440	46,232	53,938	54,471	54,150	54,383	53,309	60,141	61,625

1. Natural gas comprises any combustible gas of natural origin from underground sources consisting primarily of hydrocarbons.

SOURCE: UN-YWES, 1981, table 35; 1983, table 28; 1984, table 28; 1985, table 28; 1986, table 28.

Table 1934

WORLD PROVEN NATURAL GAS RESERVES, 4 LRC, 1981–87

(B Me^3)

Country	1981	1982	1983	1984	1985	1986	1987	PC 1987 over 1986
North America	8,258.4	8,310.9	8,296.3	8,414.4	8,259.6	8,171.1	8,040.0	−1.6
Canada	2,546.0	2,604.7	2,625.9	2,822.8	2,784.0	2,746.0	2,725.0	−.8
United States	5,712.4	5,706.2	5,670.4	5,591.6	5,475.6	5,425.1	5,315.0	−2.0
Extended Latin America	5,094.2	5,260.4	5,330.3	5,441.0	5,662.3	6,564.4	7,038.8	7.2
A. ARGENTINA	662.7	692.0	679.0	667.9	681.0	671.0	758.0	13.0
I. ECUADOR	121.8	116.1	116.0	115.0	115.0	114.0	114.0	#
N. MEXICO	2,134.0	2,148.1	2,181.0	2,172.0	2,167.0	2,146.0	2,119.0	−1.3
Trinidad and Tobago	305.9	311.5	305.0	350.0	487.0	462.0	460.0	−.4
T. VENEZUELA	1,365.1	1,471.2	1,562.3	1,666.3	1,734.8	2,649.5	2,765.2	4.4
Other	504.7	521.5	487.0	469.8	477.6	521.9	822.6	57.6
Western Europe	4,269.0	4,252.1	5,463.4	5,637.3	5,551.1	5,586.1	5,529.1	−1.0
France	55.0	47.0	44.0	41.0	36.0	33.0	34.0	3.0
Germany	175.0	186.0	192.6	191.1	191.9	182.0	179.0	−1.6
Italy	175.0	186.0	245.0	250.0	292.0	290.0	290.0	#
Netherlands	1,577.5	1,515.0	1,940.0	1,900.0	1,855.0	1,815.0	1,770.0	−2.5
Norway	1,398.2	1,440.0	2,039.0	2,236.0	2,228.0	2,296.0	2,285.0	−.5
United Kingdom	664.0	633.0	712.0	725.0	648.0	634.0	644.0	1.6
Other	224.3	245.1	290.8	294.1	300.1	336.1	327.1	−2.7
Middle East	24,579.9	25,410.6	25,889.9	27,120.9	27,559.7	30,316.4	31,170.9	2.8
I.R. Iran	13,707.2	13,667.5	13,592.2	13,774.6	13,860.0	13,860.0	14,000.0	1.0
Iraq	773.2	815.6	821.2	815.5	821.2	821.2	1,000.0	21.8
Kuwait	981.3	965.4	995.6	1,037.8	1,036.5	1,167.0	1,205.0	3.3
Qatar	2,830.0	3,145.0	3,400.0	4,280.0	4,440.0	4,440.0	4,440.0	#
Saudi Arabia	3,346.1	3,432.2	3,544.0	3,608.0	3,687.0	4,021.0	4,135.7	2.9
United Arab Emirates	2,529.0	2,973.0	3,049.0	3,108.0	3,148.0	5,414.2	5,414.2	#
Other	413.1	411.9	488.0	497.0	567.0	593.0	976.0	64.6
Africa	5,944.6	6,427.1	5,932.3	5,920.6	5,948.3	7,163.0	7,195.0	.4
Algeria	3,707.2	3,681.2	3,120.0	3,089.4	3,032.2	3,000.0	2,950.0	−1.7
Egypt	83.8	203.3	201.1	235.0	254.9	290.0	325.0	12.1
Gabon	15.0	15.0	15.0	15.6	18.5	17.0	18.0	5.9
Libya	657.0	608.8	604.6	600.3	626.0	728.0	727.0	−.1
Nigeria	1,147.0	1,385.0	1,345.0	1,330.0	1,340.0	2,400.0	2,407.0	.3
Tanzania	27.0	118.0	115.0	115.0	115.0	118.0	118.0	#
Other	307.6	415.8	531.7	535.4	561.9	610.0	650.0	6.6
Asia and Far East	4,157.3	4,366.9	4,675.3	5,226.1	5,742.5	6,592.3	6,754.3	2.5
India	352.0	410.9	459.7	478.0	480.0	906.0	1,005.0	10.9
Indonesia	863.7	960.0	1,189.3	1,699.0	1,982.2	2,265.0	2,367.0	4.5
Malaysia	1,370.0	1,385.0	1,400.0	1,390.0	1,494.0	1,501.0	1,487.0	−.9
Pakistan	464.5	481.0	510.0	520.0	623.0	635.0	626.0	−1.4
Other	1,107.1	1,130.0	1,116.3	1,139.1	1,163.3	1,285.3	1,269.3	−1.2
Oceania	1,050.4	1,065.0	1,183.7	1,611.0	1,697.2	2,278.0	2,516.0	10.4
Australia	880.0	908.0	1,027.0	1,457.0	1,522.0	1,089.0	2,282.0	9.2
New Zealand	170.4	157.0	156.7	154.0	175.2	189.0	234.0	23.8
CPEs	34,227.7	36,523.5	37,413.0	38,909.0	41,468.0	42,618.0	43,301.0	1.6
China	736.0	765.0	800.0	850.0	865.0	870.0	900.0	3.4
USSR	32,851.9	35,117.5	36,000.0	37,500.0	40,000.0	41,000.0	41,700.0	1.7
Other	639.8	641.0	613.0	559.0	603.0	748.0	701.0	−6.3
Total World	87,581.5	91,616.5	94,184.2	98,280.2	101,888.7	109,289.3	111,545.1	2.1
OPEC	32,043.5	33,236.1	33,354.2	35,139.5	35,841.3	40,896.9	41,543.1	1.6
OPEC Percentage	36.6	36.3	35.4	35.8	35.2	37.4	37.2	
Total World Excluding CPEs	53,353.8	55,093.0	56,771.2	59,371.2	60,420.7	66,671.3	68,244.1	2.4
OPEC Percentage	60.1	60.3	58.8	59.2	59.3	61.3	60.9	

SOURCE: OPEC-SB, 1986, 1988.

Table 1935

HARD COAL PRODUCTION,[1] 20 LC, 1970-86
(T MET)

	Country	1970	1975	1980	1982	1983	1984	1985	1986
A.	ARGENTINA	616	502	390	515	486	509	400	365
B.	BOLIVIA	#	#	#	#	#	#	#	#
C.	BRAZIL	2,361	2,817	5,240	6,346	6,737	7,519	7,712	7,391
D.	CHILE	1,351	1,461	968	985	990	1,184	1,291	1,633
E.	COLOMBIA	2,268	3,447	4,947	5,035[†]	6,000[†]	6,000[†]	8,475[†]	10,700[†]
F.	COSTA RICA	#	#	#	#	#	#	#	~
G.	CUBA	#	#	#	#	#	#	#	#
H.	DOMINICAN REP.	#	#	#	#	#	#	#	~
I.	ECUADOR	#	#	#	#	#	#	#	~
J.	EL SALVADOR	#	#	#	#	#	#	#	~
K.	GUATEMALA	#	#	#	#	#	#	#	~
L.	HAITI	#	#	#	#	#	#	#	~
M.	HONDURAS	#	#	#	#	#	#	#	~
N.	MEXICO	2,959	5,193	7,010	7,634	8,951	8,387	8,400[†]	8,450[†]
O.	NICARAGUA	#	#	#	#	#	#	#	~
P.	PANAMA	#	#	#	#	#	#	#	#
Q.	PARAGUAY	#	#	#	#	#	#	#	~
R.	PERU	156	23	56[†]	73	92	105	125	150[†]
S.	URUGUAY	#	#	#	#	#	#	#	~
T.	VENEZUELA	40	60	44	47	39	51	41	57
	UNITED STATES	550,388	575,901	710,384	712,777	656,568	750,262	735,923	738,927
	WORLD	824,911	992,116	2,728,475	2,828,344	2,830,685	2,967,066	3,097,398	3,194,528

1. Hard coal comprises all grades of anthracite and bituminous coal with a gross calorific value over 5,700 calories per gram. Includes lignite, brown coal, and peat.

SOURCE: UN-YWES, 1981, table 7; 1983, table 6; 1984, table 6; 1985, 1986, table 6.

Table 1936

BITUMINOUS COAL/ANTHRACITE RESOURCES, 6 LC
(M MET)

	Country	Year	Total	Proven Reserves In Place	Proven Reserves Recoverable	Additional Resources
C.	BRAZIL	1978	1,717	270	189	1,447
D.	CHILE	1979	522	231	27	291
E.	COLOMBIA	1979	9,225	2,025	1,010	7,200
N.	MEXICO	1981	2,800[b]	1,623	1,295	1,960
R.	PERU	1981	960[b]	28	~	856
T.	VENEZUELA	1981	4,861[b]	161[b]	275	1,000
	UNITED STATES	1979	1,286,366[a]	223,725	125,353	472,103

a. 1974 estimate.
b. 1979 estimate.

SOURCE: UN-YWES, 1979 and 1980, table 56; UN-YES, 1983, table 38.

Table 1937

SUB-BITUMINOUS COAL/LIGNITE RESOURCES, 10 LC
(M MET)

	Country	Year	Total	Proven Reserves		Additional Resources
				In Place	Recoverable	
A.	ARGENTINA	1981	9,900[b]	195	130	7,735
C.	BRAZIL	1981	14,090[b]	23,000	13,000	12,770
D.	CHILE	1979	5,285	1,150	1,150	4,135
E.	COLOMBIA	1979	~	48	25	790
I.	ECUADOR	1981	36[c]	#	18	6
L.	HAITI	1979	40	13	~	27
M.	HONDURAS	1979	21	~	~	~
N.	MEXICO	1981	980[c]	620	496	400
R.	PERU	1979	~	~	~	100
T.	VENEZUELA	1981	4,317[c]	17[c]	34	14,058
	UNITED STATES	1979	2,313,291[a]	205,113	131,750	669,321

a. 1974 estimate.
b. 1978 estimate.
c. 1979 estimate.

SOURCE: UN-YWES, 1979 and 1980, table 56; UN-YES, 1983, table 38.

Table 1938

GEOTHERMAL ENERGY INSTALLED
CAPACITY, 5 LC, 1980–2000
(T Kw)

	Country	1980	1985	1990	1995	2000
D.	CHILE	#	#	15	15[a]	15[a]
F.	COSTA RICA	#	#	80	380	380
J.	EL SALVADOR	95	150	260	425	535
N.	MEXICO	150	620	1,000	2,000	4,000
O.	NICARAGUA	#	#	35	35	100
	UNITED STATES	923	1,674	4,374	4,974	5,284

a. Minimum estimate.

SOURCE: Mexico-NAFINSA-MV, August 17, 1981, p. 863.

Table 1939

ELECTRICAL ENERGY PRODUCTION,[1] [2] LC, 1975-86[a]
(M KWH)

Country	1975 Total	1975 Hydro-Electric	1980 Total	1980 Hydro-Electric	1982 Total	1982 Hydro-Electric	1984 Total	1984 Hydro-Electric	1985 Total	1985 Hydro-Electric	1986 Total	1986 Hydro-Electric
A. ARGENTINA	29,468	5,197	39,676	15,148	39,804	17,586	44,914	19,874	45,265	20,649	48,984	21,015
B. BOLIVIA	1,057	800	1,564	1,080	1,677	1,205	1,636	1,188	1,610	1,160	1,625	1,170
C. BRAZIL[2]	78,936	72,287	139,485	128,907	151,999	141,132	178,532	166,593	192,731	178,375	201,618	182,615
D. CHILE	8,732	6,135	11,751	7,343	11,872	8,459	13,498	9,332	14,040	10,358	14,820	11,307
E. COLOMBIA	14,025	9,851	22,935	16,717	25,605	18,553	26,500	19,300	26,800	19,505	27,000	19,700
F. COSTA RICA	1,531	1,301	2,227	2,130	2,457	2,376	3,069	3,008	2,826	2,767	2,918	2,875
G. CUBA	6,583	62	9,896	97	11,070	43	12,292	70	12,199	54	13,167	59
H. DOMINICAN REP.[2]	2,556	54	3,317	578	3,206	757	4,009	514	4,229	1,036	4,614	900
I. ECUADOR	1,650	647	3,352	887	4,118	899	4,207	3,196	4,750	3,730	5,301	4,315
J. EL SALVADOR	1,059	404	1,544	1,078	1,489	800	1,684	890	1,785	935	1,790	940
K. GUATEMALA	1,167	382	1,617	278	1,623	481	1,690	605	1,755	678	1,760	680
L. HAITI	158	123	315	220	360	250	375	260	375	260	438	318
M. HONDURAS	545	419	928	783	1,090	870	1,060	874	1,065	875	1,075	880
N. MEXICO	43,329	15,140	66,954	16,910	80,589	22,924	86,971	23,603	93,405	26,241	97,518	27,473
O. NICARAGUA	932	371	1,049	515	1,054	425	973	235	1,059	264	1,063	268
P. PANAMA	1,447	98	2,454	1,182	2,238	1,074	2,360	1,491	2,570	1,929	2,736	2,096
Q. PARAGUAY	598	538	700	575	681	647	920	886	1,262	1,258	1,644	1,640
R. PERU	7,486	5,470	9,805	7,622	11,350	8,401	11,717	8,571	12,115	9,316	12,818	9,961
S. URUGUAY	2,444	1,132	4,559	3,477	6,156	5,009	7,244	7,107	6,602	6,451	7,429	7,293
T. VENEZUELA	19,591	8,898	35,932	14,337	39,964	16,000	44,300	19,665	45,400	20,700	46,724	21,300
UNITED STATES[2]	2,003,002	303,153	2,354,384	277,721	2,302,287	310,759	2,479,304	323,550	2,564,766	284,846	2,582,510	294,594
WORLD	6,518,535	1,456,368	8,247,331	1,755,010	8,476,214	1,823,056	9,310,069	1,972,525	9,711,734	1,998,770	9,962,264	2,027,100

1. Unless otherwise indicated, the data refer to the production of generating centers and therefore include station use and transmission loss. "Total" refers to all. "Total" minus "Hydroelectric" production generally equals "Thermal" (not given), except for data on the United States. Unless stated otherwise, production includes electrical energy produced for both public and industrial purposes.

2. Production of industrial establishments nil or negligible.

a. For data prior to 1975 see SALA, 21–2008.

SOURCE: UN-YWES, 1979, tables 49 and 50; 1981, table 42; 1983, table 34; 1984, table 34; 1985, 1986, table 34.

Table 1940

ELECTRICITY CONSUMPTION,[1] 20 LC, 1929–86[a]

(Total = B Kw, Per Capita = KWH)

Year	A. ARGENTINA Total	Per Capita	B. BOLIVIA Total	Per Capita	C. BRAZIL Total	Per Capita	D. CHILE Total	Per Capita	E. COLOMBIA Total	Per Capita	F. COSTA RICA Total	Per Capita	G. CUBA Total	Per Capita	H. DOMINICAN REP. Total	Per Capita	I. ECUADOR Total	Per Capita	J. EL SALVADOR Total	Per Capita	K. GUATEMALA Total	Per Capita
1929	1.67	143	.02	8	.74	22	.68	158	.15	21	.03	61	.20	56	.01	8	.04	21	.02	14	.02	12
1937	2.20	162	.05	19	2.03	52	1.45	302	.29	34	.06	104	.26	62	.02	13	.05	22	.03	19	.03	14
1950	4.43	259	.20	67	4.70	90	3.00	492	.71	61	.10	125	.76	138	.08	36	.13	41	.08	42	.07	25
1960	10.5	510	.5	135	22.9	328	4.6	597	3.8	265	.4	374	2.7	399	.4	116	.4	90	.3	103	.3	75
1970	21.7	915	.8	184	45.4	491	7.6	806	8.8	426	1.0	595	4.9	570	1.0	247	.9	159	.7	190	.8	144
1972	25.3	1,037	.9	193	64.7	582	8.9	919	11.0	508	1.3	687	5.3	594	1.2	279	1.1	175	.8	228	.9	169
1973	26.7	1,081	.9	198	64.8	664	8.8	889	12.6	564	1.3	719	5.7	631	2.3	509	1.3	190	.9	242	1.0	178
1974	28.0	1,119	1.0	208	80.3	701	9.3	923	13.2	575	1.4	764	6.0	655	2.4	527	1.4	209	1.0	254	1.1	187
1975	29.5	1,164	1.1	216	79.0	744	8.7	857	14.0	594	1.5	778	6.6	705	2.6	544	1.7	234	1.1	264	1.2	187
1976	30.4	1,184	1.1	225	90.1	812	9.3	888	15.5	637	1.6	818	7.2	761	2.6	534	1.9	258	1.2	291	1.3	198
1977	32.6	1,249	1.3	244	100.9	890	9.8	918	16.1	643	1.7	850	7.7	802	3.1	615	2.2	299	1.4	318	1.6	236
1978	33.5	1,270	1.4	256	112.4	995	10.4	965	18.1	707	1.9	911	8.5	875	3.2	629	2.6	326	1.5	342	1.7	252
1979	37.7	1,406	1.4	264	126.0	1,089	11.1	1,020	19.9	754	2.0	917	9.4	962	3.1	590	2.7	331	1.6	358	1.9	272
1980	39.7	1,467	1.6	281	139.2	1,148	11.8	1,058	22.9	890	2.2	977	9.9	1,017	3.4	597	3.4	420	1.5	325	1.6	223
1981	39.0	1,361	1.7	294	142.0	1,144	12.0	1,061	24.3	921	2.4	1,055	10.6	1,079	3.6	630	3.7	452	1.5	299	1.6	213
1982	39.8	1,367	1.7	286	153.8	1,212	11.9	1,034	25.6	950	2.4	977	11.1	1,124	3.2	551	4.1	482	1.5	293	1.6	222
1983	42.9	1,451	1.7	277	165.0	1,272	12.6	1,082	26.1	947	2.4	984	11.6	1,166	3.4	570	4.3	486	1.6	306	1.6	215
1984	44.9	1,492	1.6	264	181.4	1,368	13.5	1,139	26.5	942	2.6	1,036	12.3	1,233	4.0	657	4.2	463	1.7	313	1.7	218
1985	45.3	1,481	1.6	253	195.6	1,442	14.0	1,166	26.8	933	2.8	1,068	12.2	1,215	4.2	677	4.8	508	1.8	322	1.8	220
1986	48.9	1,578	1.6	249	212.2	1,532	14.8	1,212	26.9	921	2.9	1,123	13.2	1,301	4.6	723	5.3	551	1.8	313	1.8	215

Year	L. HAITI Total	Per Capita	M. HONDURAS Total	Per Capita	N. MEXICO Total	Per Capita	O. NICARAGUA Total	Per Capita	P. PANAMA Total	Per Capita	Q. PARAGUAY Total	Per Capita	R. PERU Total	Per Capita	S. URUGUAY Total	Per Capita	T. VENEZUELA Total	Per Capita	UNITED STATES Total	Per Capita	WORLD Total	Per Capita
1929	.01	4	.01	11	1.46	86	.01	15	.02	43	.01	1	.20	36	.13	76	.10	32	92.18	756	255.9	134
1937	.01	4	.02	18	2.48	132	.01	13	.03	52	.01	10	.32	50	.20	105	.07	20	118.91	922	411.4	205
1950	.02	6	.05	36	4.42	171	.03	27	.09	113	.03	21	.80	100	.60	273	.52	104	329.14	2,164	959.2	386
1960	.1	23	.1	48	11.2	320	.2	131	.2	223	.1	55	2.7	268	1.2	512	4.7	632	848.8	4,698	2,300.9	772
1970	.1	28	.3	119	28.9	569	.6	342	.8	573	.2	95	5.5	411	2.2	811	12.7	1,237	1,642.0	8,008	4,953.8	1,393
1972	.1	30	.3	146	34.7	640	.8	386	1.1	724	.3	112	6.3	442	2.4	825	14.8	1,356	1,861.1	8,911	5,398.7	1,501
1973	.1	32	.4	151	37.4	667	.7	354	1.3	811	.3	120	6.7	455	2.5	913	16.1	1,425	1,979.1	9,339	6,127.7	1,584
1974	.1	32	.5	183	41.1	707	.9	419	1.4	877	.3	133	7.3	484	2.4	860	18.2	1,567	1,980.0	9,344	6,313.8	1,604
1975	.2	34	.5	176	43.6	725	.9	432	1.5	868	.4	163	7.5	484	2.5	875	19.6	1,632	2,009.2	9,303	6,516.7	1,626
1976	.2	45	.6	187	46.5	747	1.1	476	1.5	898	.4	143	7.9	497	2.6	973	21.0	1,701	2,417.4	9,901	6,983.4	1,711
1977	.2	45	.7	209	50.7	784	1.2	516	1.5	864	.5	170	8.6	527	2.8	1,001	23.0	1,808	2,528.2	10,299	7,296.0	1,759
1978	.2	51	.8	226	57.3	855	1.2	489	1.6	876	.5	178	8.8	521	3.1	1,074	25.6	1,951	2,305.2	10,357	7,686.8	1,806
1979	.3	57	.9	240	62.9	906	1.0	373	1.8	961	.6	211	9.3	535	2.7	955	28.4	2,100	2,348.4	10,435	7,998.0	1,848
1980	.3	54	.9	250	67.0	972	1.1	380	2.5	1,255	.7	213	9.8	567	4.6	1,182	35.9	2,298	2,354.4	10,459	8,247.3	1,851
1981	.3	55	1.0	264	73.8	1,036	1.1	388	2.0	1,019	1.0	304	10.8	606	3.6	1,238	37.5	2,319	2,392.9	10,414	8,384.2	1,851
1982	.4	59	1.1	274	80.5	1,100	1.2	391	2.2	1,095	.9	279	11.4	623	3.7	1,262	40.0	2,507	2,333.0	10,057	8,475.5	1,836
1983	.4	60	1.1	280	82.3	1,095	1.3	416	2.4	1,144	1.0	294	10.7	571	3.7	1,249	42.0	2,562	2,402.8	10,269	8,823.2	1,884
1984	.4	58	1.2	290	87.0	1,128	1.2	392	2.4	1,106	1.1	312	11.8	610	4.0	1,340	44.3	2,630	2,518.9	10,674	9,309.2	1,956
1985	.4	57	1.2	282	93.4	1,182	1.2	381	2.6	1,178	1.2	337	12.1	615	3.9	1,303	45.4	2,621	2,605.7	10,947	9,710.7	2,008
1986	.4	65	1.2	273	96.2	1,188	1.3	370	2.7	1,229	1.6	421	12.8	634	4.3	1,410	46.7	2,626	2,618.4	10,906	9,969.1	2,028

1. Prior to 1950 data are for production, in Latin America essentially the same as consumption. For further notes and methods, see SALA-SNP, especially with regard to calculation per capita data through 1954 and rounding of data after 1960.

a. For yearly data in 1950s and 1960s, see SALA, 24-1926.

SOURCE: SALA-SNP, XI-9, updated with WA, 1929, 1937, and 1949; UN-SP: J, 17 (1974); J, 19 (1976), table 21; J, 20 (1977), table 21; J, 21 (1978), table 21; J, 22 (1979), table 25; UN-YWES, 1979, table 50; 1981, table 43; 1983, table 35; 1984, table 35; 1985, table 35; 1986, table 35.

Table 1941

INDEX OF TOTAL PRODUCTION OF ELECTRICITY, 20 LC, 1970–86

(1975 = 100)

	Country	1970	1976	1979	1980	1981	1982	1983	1984	1985	1986
A.	ARGENTINA	74	103	128	135	132	135	146	152	154	166
B.	BOLIVIA	74	107	135	148	159	159	161	155	152	154
C.	BRAZIL	58	114	160	177	180	193	205	222	244	255
D.	CHILE	86	106	127	135	137	136	145	154	161	170
E.	COLOMBIA	62	110	142	172	181	192	186	189	191	193
F.	COSTA RICA	67	108	130	202	154	160	191	200	185	191
G.	CUBA	74	109	143	150	160	168	175	187	185	200
H.	DOMINICAN REP.	39	101	122	107	140	125	133	157	165	181
I.	ECUADOR	58	114	162	187	226	250	260	267	288	321
J.	EL SALVADOR	63	93	141	146	139	141	151	159	169	169
K.	GUATEMALA	65	109	164	139	137	139	139	145	150	151
L.	HAITI	75	132	177	199	206	228	236	237	237	277
M.	HONDURAS	58	110	158	170	186	200	211	194	195	197
N.	MEXICO	66	107	145	155	170	186	190	201	216	225
O.	NICARAGUA	67	114	106	113	119	113	101	104	114	114
P.	PANAMA	66	106	131	170	141	155	165	163	178	189
Q.	PARAGUAY	36	89	129	156	131	114	137	154	211	275
R.	PERU	74	106	124	131	144	152	143	157	162	171
S.	URUGUAY	90	108	111	187	147	252	300	296	270	304
T.	VENEZUELA	65	107	145	183	192	204	214	226	232	238
	UNITED STATES	82	106	116	118	118	115	118	124	128	129
	WORLD	76	107	123	126	128	130	135	143	149	153

SOURCE: UN-YWES, 1979, table 51; 1981, table 44; 1983; table 35; 1984, table 35;
1985, table 35; 1986, table 35.

Table 1942

INDEX OF TOTAL CONSUMPTION OF ELECTRICITY, 20 LC, 1970–86

(1975 = 100)

	Country	1970	1976	1979	1980	1981	1982	1983	1984	1985	1986
A.	ARGENTINA	74	103	128	134	132	135	146	152	154	166
B.	BOLIVIA	74	107	135	148	159	159	155	146	146	146
C.	BRAZIL	58	114	160	176	180	192	205	222	246	269
D.	CHILE	86	106	127	135	137	136	145	154	161	170
E.	COLOMBIA	62	110	142	172	182	191	203	208	201	192
F.	COSTA RICA	67	108	130	145	154	161	156	173	187	193
G.	CUBA	74	109	143	150	160	168	175	187	185	200
H.	DOMINICAN REP.	39	101	122	107	140	125	133	157	162	177
I.	ECUADOR	58	114	162	188	227	250	261	268	282	312
J.	EL SALVADOR	63	113	150	146	139	141	151	159	164	164
K.	GUATEMALA	65	109	164	139	137	133	134	142	150	150
L.	HAITI	75	132	177	199	206	228	200	200	200	200
M.	HONDURAS	58	110	157	170	185	199	220	240	240	240
N.	MEXICO	66	107	144	155	169	185	189	199	214	221
O.	NICARAGUA	67	114	106	113	119	124	136	133	134	144
P.	PANAMA	58	106	122	169	140	154	164	162	177	180
Q.	PARAGUAY	50	89	148	194	227	258	274	295	300	400
R.	PERU	74	106	124	131	144	152	143	157	162	171
S.	URUGUAY	90	108	111	186	147	146	150	148	159	172
T.	VENEZUELA	65	107	145	183	191	204	215	226	232	238
	UNITED STATES	82	106	117	119	119	116	120	125	130	130
	WORLD	76	107	123	128	128	130	135	143	149	153

SOURCE: UN-YWES, 1979, table 51; 1981, table 44; 1983, table 35; 1984, table 35;
1985, table 35; 1986, table 35.

Table 1943

CUBA GENERATING CAPACITY OF ELECTRICAL SYSTEM[1]
(Mw)

Year	Total	Thermal	Hydro	Diesel
1980	2,210.9	1,956.2	46.0	67.1
1981	2,215.3	1,956.2	46.0	71.5
1982	2,417.0	2,156.2	46.0	73.2
1983	2,415.2	2,156.2	46.0	71.4
1984	2,496.0	2,260.3	45.0	70.7
1985[2]	2,608.8	2,375.3	45.0	68.5

1. Public service only. In addition, some industries (e.g., sugar, nickel) also generate their own electricity. Data on generating capacity outside of the public service system are not available.
2. In 1985, the public service system accounted for 85% of gross electricity generation.

SOURCE: Jorge Pérez-López, "Nuclear Power in Cuba after Chernobyl," *Journal of Inter-American Studies and World Affairs* (Summer 1987), p. 85.

Table 1944

CUBA PROJECTIONS OF GENERATING CAPACITY OF ELECTRICAL SYSTEM BY FUEL MIX[1]
(Mw)

Fuel Mix	Actual[2] 1985	1990	1995	2000
Non-nuclear	2,609	3,739	4,189	4,689
Nuclear	0	440	1,320	3,520
Total	2,609	4,179	5,509	8,209
Percent Nuclear	0	10.5	24.0	42.9

1. Public service only. In addition, some industries (e.g., sugar, nickel) also generate their own electricity. Data on generating capacity outside of the public service system are not available.
2. In 1985, the public service system accounted for 85% of gross electricity generation.

SOURCE: Jorge Pérez-López, "Nuclear Power in Cuba after Chernobyl," *Journal of Inter-American Studies and World Affairs* (Summer 1987), p. 85.

Table 1945

URANIUM PRODUCTION,[1] 3 LC, 1970–86

(MET)

	Country	1970	1973	1975	1978	1979	1980	1981	1982	1983	1984	1985	1986
A.	ARGENTINA	45	24	22	126	134	187	187	155	179	129	126	173
C.	BRAZIL	#	#	#	#	103	#	#	242	189	117	115	115
N.	MEXICO	~	~	#	#	90[†]	~	~	~	~	~	~	~
	UNITED STATES	9,900	10,200	8,900	14,200	14,400	16,800	16,800	10,331	8,135	5,722	4,400	5,200
	WORLD	18,289	19,773	19,068	33,891	38,303	43,093	43,093	41,256	36,696	36,696	38,713	35,025

1. Uranium content.

SOURCE: UN-YWES, 1981, table 46; 1983, table 37; 1984, table 37; 1985, table 37; 1986,
   table 37.

Table 1946

NUCLEAR REACTORS,[1] 4 L

(1989)

	Country	Installed Capacity (MW)	% of Total Electricity	Under Construction (MW)	Current Plans (MW)	Previous Plans		Obstacles
						Units/MW by 2000	Status	
A.	ARGENTINA	968	13.4	745	~	2	Suspended	Fin/env
C.	BRAZIL	626	.5	2,490	~	8	Cancelled	Fin/env
G.	CUBA	~	~	1,760	~	~	~	~
N.	MEXICO	~	~	1,290	2	20	Cancelled	Fin/env

1. Fin = financial; env = environmental.

SOURCE: *South*, April 1989.

Part VII
Sea and Land Harvests

20

Fisheries Production

STATISTICAL NOTES

This chapter presents annual time-series statistics on Latin American fisheries production. The data include statistics on the nominal catches of fish, crustaceans, molluscs, and other types of acquatic animals and plants which have been killed, caught, trapped, collected, bred, or cultivated for all kinds of commercial, industrial, and subsistence purposes. The nominal catch data include quantities taken by all types and classes of fishing units operating in both fresh and marine fishing areas, with the exception of quantities taken in recreational facilities by sports fishermen.

The statistical category *nominal catches* refers to the landings converted to a live weight basis. The term *landings* refers to the weight of fish and fish products brought ashore, i.e., the actual weight of the quantities landed. The nominal catch data include quantities caught during the calendar year (January–December) although landed in the subsequent year. Nominal catch data for Argentina, Chile, Mexico, Peru, Uruguay, and the United States exclude the production of acquatic plants.

For a related discussion of Latin American fisheries resources and fishery statistics between 1938 and 1970 see, M. Moreno Ibáñez, "Latin American Fisheries: Natural Resources and Expanded Jurisdiction, 1938–1978," SALA, 21.

Figure 20:1

FAO FISHING AREA CODES

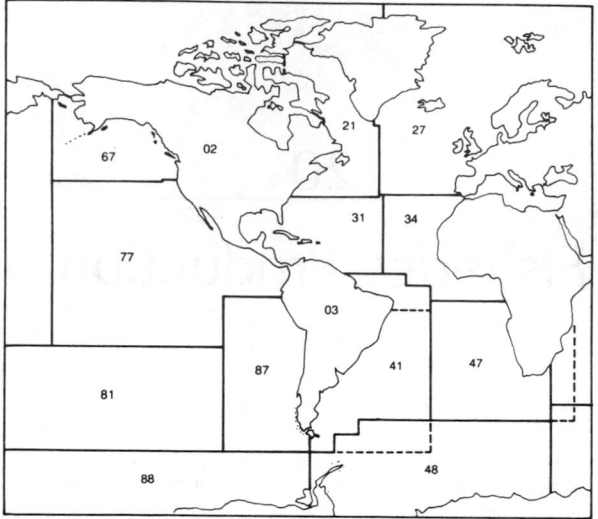

FAO fishing areas. 02, America, North—Inland Waters; 03, America, South—Inland Waters; 21, Atlantic, Northwest; 27, Atlantic, Northeast; 31, Atlantic, Western Central; 34, Atlantic, Eastern Central; 41, Atlantic, Southwest; 47, Atlantic, Southeast; 48, Atlantic, Antarctic; 67, Pacific Northeast; 77, Pacific, Eastern Central; 81, Pacific Southwest; 87, Pacific, Southeast; 88, Pacific, Antarctic.

SOURCE: Adapted from FAO map of major fishing areas for statistical purposes.

Table 2000

TOTAL NOMINAL CATCHES BY MAJOR FISHING AREA,[1] 20 LC, 1970-86[a]
(MET)

Country	Code[2]	1970	1975	1977	1978	1979	1980	1981	1982	1983	1984	1985	1986
A. ARGENTINA	03	5,400	15,068	10,436	15,077	16,082	8,407	9,689	15,395	14,594	9,286	9,565	8,539
	34	600	#	#	~	#	#	#	#	#	#	#	#
	41	208,800	213,830	359,281	504,138	550,266	376,865	351,857	459,648	401,771	305,484	396,826	411,767
	Total	214,800	228,898	369,717	519,215	566,348	385,272	361,546	475,043	416,365	314,770	406,391	420,306
B. BOLIVIA	03	1,600	1,800	2,300	1,550	3,650	4,379	5,617	4,375	4,405	4,435	4,731	4,800†
	Total	1,600	1,800	2,300	1,550	3,650	4,379	5,617	4,375	4,405	4,435	4,731	4,800†
C. BRAZIL	03	93,500	173,455	168,444	170,645	126,701	187,594	97,340	207,919	205,345	211,502	211,078	215,000†
	41	434,800	598,691	580,031	631,983	728,418	632,239	631,316	622,720	549,366	624,995	628,146	632,889†
	Total	528,300	772,146	748,475	802,628	855,119	819,833	828,656	830,639	754,711	836,497	839,224	847,889†
D. CHILE	03	#	~	#	~	35	92	52	257	253	386	619	1,007
	48									4,880	1,649	2,598	3,264
	87	1,181,400	929,464	1,318,950	1,929,091	2,632,216	2.8·6,614	3,385,346	3,672,740	3,972,922	4,497,227	4,801,213	5,567,367
	Total	1,181,400	929,464	1,318,950	1,929,091	2,632,251	2.8·6,706	3,385,398	3,672,997	3,978,055	4,499,262	4,804,430	5,571,638
E. COLOMBIA	03	33,200	42,075	42,174	56,612	48,535	46,903	47,719	49,000	45,343	53,354	47,368	54,876
	31	13,600	11,600	7,621	5,837	5,320	5,155	9,363	6,367	3,058	7,491	9,924	10,364
	77	7,700	12,900	14,170	17,129	9,538	24,139	37,608	16,014	9,136	17,669	12,444	15,205
	Total	54,500	66,575	63,965	79,578	63,393	76,197	94,690	71,381	57,537	78,514	69,736	80,445
F. COSTA RICA	02	#	50	61	61	100	350	400	455	523	213	300	300
	31	100	423	254	342	110	132	141	228	255	562	402	298
	77	7,000	13,591	12,781	16,919	20,649	14,405	14,482	10,219	9,789	13,659	18,284	20,301
	Tota	7,100	14,064	13,096	17,322	20,859	14,887	15,023	10,902	10,567	14,434	18,986	20,899
G. CUBA	02	500	1,700	1,900	3,200	5,400	6,339	10,314	13,629	14,121	16,199	16,881	16,100
	21	#	7,495	18,282	13,124	12,482	9,255	6,668	18,565	14,786	20,521	23,509	24,806
	31	61,800	58,900	72,300	71,077	66,100	68,424	59,846	68,718	74,374	76,818	79,651	98,123†
	34	22,100	6,600	20,700	7,200	7,500	9,258	9,016	6,874	6,670	17,685	12,732	17,207†
	41	~								0	56	4,557	46†
	47	21,400	44,630	29,300	63,569	42,917	4,555	#	689	32,741	34,162	35,634	24,980
	87	#	24,000	42,700	55,000	19,400	88,650	78,791	86,771	55,639	34,131	46,867	63,338†
	Total	105,800	143,325	185,182	213,170	153,799	186,481	164,815	195,246	198,331	199,572	219,831	244,600
H. DOMINICAN REP.	02	200	585	359	513	1,040	2,459	2,836	1,721	4,338	1,769	2,524	846
	31	5,000	6,467	4,235	4,573	6,845	8,199	9,167	11,448	10,951	12,845	15,814	16,336
	Total	5,200	7,052	4,594	5,086	7,885	10,658	12,003	13,169	15,289	14,614	18,338	17,182
I. ECUADOR	03	91,400	263,400	433,950	616,550	607,835	671,310†	731,024	665,471	323,612	844,818	946,132	1,018,404
	77	#				#				845	994	867	900
	Total	91,400	263,400	433,950	616,550	607,835	671,310†	731,024	665,471	324,457	845,812	946,999	1,019,304
J. EL SALVADOR	02	800	2,689	1,624	1,512	1,719	1,818	983	551	795	1,705	1,700†	1,700†
	77	10,300	7,861	4,744	8,028	11,019	12,140	19,271	12,966	6,808	10,484	10,400†	10,800†
	Total	11,100	10,550	6,368	9,540	12,738	13,958	20,254	13,517	7,603	12,189	12,100†	12,500†
K. GUATEMALA	02	1,400	550	600	580	615	400	410	721	40	54	47	120
	31	100	100	100	100	100	50	50	150	150	150	150	150
	77	3,500	3,880	2,374	4,824	4,183	3,057	3,805	3,413	2,186	2,759	2,510	1,849
	Total	5,000	4,530	3,074	5,504	4,898	3,507	4,265	4,284	2,376	2,963	2,707	2,119
L. HAITI	02	300†	300†	300†	300†	300†	300†	300†	300†	200†	300†	300†	300†
	31	2,200†	3,700†	3,700†	3,700†	3,700†	3,700†	3,700†	3,900†	6,200†	6,700†	7,200†	7,700†
	Total	2,500†	4,000†	4,000†	4,000†	4,000†	4,000†	4,000†	4,200†	6,500†	7,000†	7,500†	8,000†
M. HONDURAS	02	100	170	97	114	110	83	238	74	65	113	120	180
	31	3,700	3,066	4,953	5,478	6,333	5,031	4,550	3,906	7,621	6,113	7,426	9,479
	77	#	26	782	783	859	1,295	1,512	1,043	746	2,155	2,046	3,749
	Total	3,800	3,262	5,832	6,375	7,302	6,409	6,300	5,023	8,432	8,381	9,592	13,408

Table 2000 (Continued)
TOTAL NOMINAL CATCHES BY MAJOR FISHING AREA,[1] 20 LC, 1970–86[a]
(MET)

Country	Code[2]	1970	1975	1977	1978	1979	1980	1981	1982	1983	1984	1985	1986
N. MEXICO	02	7,500	17,826	18,971	18,865	28,653	9,809	19,614	12,473	100,527	116,922	113,028	92,959
	21	1,400	#	#	3,954	8,085	4,697	#	6,584	13,321	9,037	6,000	7,997
	31	114,200	117,454	124,886	147,499	163,687	222,330	290,377	282,835	288,690	294,871	265,154	290,244
	77	267,700	364,064	466,909	532,315	676,554	985,614	1,226,199	1,018,866	661,754	682,827	842,062	912,520
	Total	390,800	499,344	610,766	702,633	876,979	1,222,450	1,536,190	1,321,028	1,064,292	1,103,657	1,226,244	1,303,720
O. NICARAGUA	02	1,300	3,500	4,043	178	126	79	193	486	378	118	84	55
	31	6,200	9,900	12,889	7,676	5,637	5,025	3,385	2,701	3,018	2,767	2,179	1,540
	77	2,300	5,000	5,429	2,306	1,478	1,892	2,366	1,813	1,152	1,454	1,901	826
	Total	9,800	18,400	22,361	10,160	7,241	6,996	5,944	5,000	4,548	4,339	4,164	2,421
P. PANAMA	02	#	#	#	#	#	#	#	#	#	#	#	#
	31	~	~	~	~	~	3,558†	1,445	4,972	547	2,995	601	696
	34	~	~	~	~	~	7,392†	3,323	4,163	6,587	4,010	2,814	3,520†
	77	53,200	81,085	207,798	109,958	147,072	205,418†	144,700	107,416†	162,265	131,235	276,666	124,770†
	Total	53,200	81,055	207,798	109,958	147,072	216,368†	149,468	116,551†	169,399	138,240	280,081	128,986†
Q. PARAGUAY	03	1,800†	2,700†	2,700†	2,700†	2,700†	3,300†	3,350†	3,400†	3,500	5,000	7,500	13,000
	Total	1,800†	2,700†	2,700†	2,700†	2,700†	3,300†	3,350†	3,400†	3,500	5,000	7,500	13,000
R. PERU	03	2,000†	6,777	9,015	14,064	15,217	12,538	16,077	17,358	33,019	29,732	27,583	28,200
	87	12,532,900	3,440,713	2,525,388	3,458,341	3,666,969	2,722,356	2,725,104	3,511,252	1,536,477	3,287,767	4,108,135	5,581,388
	Total	12,534,900	3,447,490	2,534,403	3,472,405	3,682,186	2,734,894	2,741,181	3,528,610	1,569,496	3,317,499	4,135,718	5,609,588
S. URUGUAY	03	#	245	321	472	578	312	321	186	57	435	660	750
	41	13,200	26,088	47,953	73,751	107,555	120,087	146,652	119,015	144,064	133,592	138,418	140,538
	Total	13,200	26,333	48,274	74,223	108,133	120,399	146,973	119,201	144,121	134,027	139,078	141,288
T. VENEZUELA	03	12,300	7,657	8,021	11,260	12,456	15,933	13,346	14,998	20,009	21,073	15,258	16,000†
	31	114,100	145,750	137,898	154,858	113,573	161,640	161,687	188,257	197,913	219,045	219,529	225,766†
	77	~	~	~	~	~	9,000	16,898	18,000	7,540	16,070	22,250	38,570
	87	~	~	~	~	~	~	~	~	5,250	3,210	7,730	3,300
	Total	126,400	153,407	145,919	166,118	126,029	186,573	191,931	221,255	230,712	259,398	264,767	283,636†
UNITED STATES	02	78,000	77,267	71,831	80,416	65,684	69,572	65,197	73,433	74,190	73,213	72,782	72,005
	21	972,500	930,879	1,076,037	1,117,140	1,196,504	1,298,798	1,236,253	1,205,930	1,236,464	1,251,780	1,215,789	1,131,517
	27								1,067	#	#	#	#
	31	1,016,300	1,024,947	940,874	1,332,572	1,281,468	1,216,251	1,259,201	1,490,374	1,556,757	1,846,681	1,521,052	1,333,280
	34	~	~	10,616	5,789	2,764	2,650	3,904	~	19	#	#	#
	47							498					
	67	397,200	352,602	477,662	516,175	593,307	653,674	806,594	845,010	1,017,703	1,270,603	1,614,024	2,035,720
	71	~	~	~	~	~	3,759	26,728	41,264	152,390	155,733	114,479	134,600
	77	312,400	533,071	398,536	364,107	367,883	369,493	353,945	325,251	215,312	209,553	227,177	234,313
	81	~	~	~	~	~	7,218	3,529	1,857	4,044	#	#	#
	87	#	1,172	4,740	1,360	3,244	13,111	11,584	4,118	#	5,313	#	1,778
	Total	2,776,400	2,919,938	2,980,296	3,417,559	3,510,854	3,634,526	3,767,433	3,988,304	4,256,879	4,812,876	4,766,805	4,943,213

1. Includes marine and inland catches.
2. Code: 02, America, North–Inland Waters; 03, American, South–Inland Waters; 21, Atlantic, Northwest; 31, Atlantic, Western Central; 34, Atlantic, Eastern Central; 41, Atlantic, Southwest; 47, Atlantic, Southeast; 48, Atlantic, Antarctic; 67, Pacific, Northeast; 77, Pacific, Eastern Central; 87, Pacific, Southeast. See map of FAO fishing areas on following page.

a. For 1964–69 and 1971–73 data see SALA, 21-3815.

SOURCE: FAO-YFSCL, 1976–84, tables A-2, D-2, and D-3: 1985, D-2, D-3; 1986, D-2, D-3.

Table 2001

NOMINAL CATCHES, MARINE AREAS, 18 LRC, 1971–86

(MET)

	Country	1971	1974	1975	1976	1977	1978	1979
A.	ARGENTINA	201,400	266,380	199,068	256,672	370,419	504,033	551,594
C.	BRAZIL	493,800	557,775	579,536	507,834	562,321	581,556	652,331
D.	CHILE	1,491,600	1,127,772	899,458	1,378,600	1,316,936	1,927,040	2,630,264
E.	COLOMBIA	18,400	25,184	24,500	23,670	21,791	22,966	14,858
F.	COSTA RICA	7,200	13,450	14,052	12,832	14,167	18,457	22,203
G.	CUBA	125,400	162,779	141,625	192,690	180,182	209,756	147,799
H.	DOMINICAN REP.	4,100	8,025	5,309	6,435	4,235	4,573	6,845
I.	ECUADOR	106,700	174,400	223,738	299,668	433,050	616,550	609,101
J.	EL SALVADOR	9,900	8,110	7,861	6,058	4,744	8,028	11,019
K.	GUATEMALA	2,800	3,353	3,980	3,079	2,474	4,924	4,283
L.	HAITI	2,500[†]	3,700[†]	3,700[†]	3,700[†]	3,850	4,000[†]	4,200[†]
M.	HONDURAS	6,600	3,403	4,484	4,290	5,735	6,261	7,192
N.	MEXICO	390,200	387,506	449,677	476,465	511,783	775,301	948,371
O.	NICARAGUA	8,100	8,229	10,419	10,161	10,161	9,982	7,115
P.	PANAMA	72,500	89,392[†]	117,071[†]	184,196[†]	239,526	139,470	165,069
R.	PERU	10,526,100	4,139,395	3,439,804	4,336,816	2,490,560	3,428,765	3,637,670
S.	URUGUAY	14,400	15,700	26,003	33,425	47,953	73,751	107,555
T.	VENEZUELA	133,400	135,774	145,176	139,184	143,033	154,858	162,076
	LATIN AMERICA	13,615,100	7,130,327	6,294,827	7,874,819	6,362,920	8,490,271	9,689,545
	UNITED STATES	2,797,700	2,762,078	2,764,803	2,974,100	2,910,157	3,337,144	3,445,170
	WORLD	59,678,800	59,103,900	58,752,300	62,156,900	60,905,600	63,049,100	63,805,200

	Country	1980	1981	1982	1983	1984	1985	1986
A.	ARGENTINA	376,865	351,857	459,648	401,771	305,484	396,826	411,767
C.	BRAZIL	547,397	557,662	524,882	549,366	624,995	628,146	632,889[†]
D.	CHILE	2,815,081	3,385,091	3,672,415	3,977,802	4,498,876	4,803,811	5,570,631
E.	COLOMBIA	29,294	46,971	22,381	12,194	25,160	22,368	25,569
F.	COSTA RICA	19,673	16,944	12,709	10,044	14,221	18,686	20,599
G.	CUBA	180,097	154,452	180,986	184,210	183,373	202,950	228,500
H.	DOMINICAN REP.	8,199	9,167	11,448	10,951	12,845	15,814	16,336
I.	ECUADOR	643,476	484,523	666,491	323,612	844,818	946,132	1,018,404
J.	EL SALVADOR	12,140	19,271	12,966	6,808	10,484	10,400[†]	10,800[†]
K.	GUATEMALA	3,107	3,855	3,563	2,336	2,909	2,660	1,999
L.	HAITI	4,700[†]	5,200[†]	5,700[†]	6,200[†]	6,700[†]	7,200[†]	7,700[†]
M.	HONDURAS	6,326	6,062	4,949	8,367	8,268	9,472	13,228
N.	MEXICO	1,212,625	1,516,574	1,308,283	963,765	986,735	1,113,216	1,210,761
O.	NICARAGUA	6,917	5,751	4,514	4,170	4,221	4,080	2,366
P.	PANAMA	216,368	149,468	116,551	169,399	138,240	280,081	128,986[†]
R.	PERU	2,696,074	2,700,186	3,495,888	1,536,477	3,287,767	4,108,135	5,581,388
S.	URUGUAY	120,087	146,653	119,015	144,064	133,592	138,418	140,538
T.	VENEZUELA	169,352	172,091	206,257	210,703	238,325	249,509	267,636[†]
	LATIN AMERICA[1]	9,067,778	9,731,778	10,828,646	8,522,239	11,327,013	12,957,904	15,290,097
	UNITED STATES	3,564,950	3,702,236	3,914,871	4,182,689	4,739,663	4,692,521	4,871,208
	WORLD	64,459,600	66,596,200	68,298,200	68,151,900	73,688,700	75,138,000	80,345,000

1. Latin American total computed by SALA.

SOURCE: FAO-YFSCL, 1979–86, table A-4.

Table 2002

DISTRIBUTION OF MARINE AREA NOMINAL CATCHES, 18 LR, 1971–86

(%)

	Country	1971	1973	1975	1977	1978	1979	1980	1981	1982	1983	1984	1985	1986
A.	ARGENTINA	1.5	5.4	3.1	5.8	5.9	5.7	4.2	3.6	4.2	4.7	2.7	3.1	2.7
C.	BRAZIL	3.6	12.4	9.2	8.8	6.8	6.7	6.0	5.7	4.8	6.4	5.5	4.8	4.1
D.	CHILE	11.0	13.5	14.3	20.6	22.7	27.1	31.0	34.8	33.9	46.7	39.7	37.0	36.4
E.	COLOMBIA	.1	.6	.3	.3	.3	.2	.3	.5	.2	.1	.2	.2	.2
F.	COSTA RICA	.1	.2	.2	.2	.2	.2	.2	.2	.1	.1	.1	.1	.1
G.	CUBA	.9	3.0	2.2	2.8	2.4	1.5	2.0	1.6	1.7	2.2	1.6	1.6	1.5
H.	DOMINICAN REP.	0	.2	0	.1	.1	.1	.1	.1	.1	.1	.1	.1	.1
I.	ECUADOR	.8	3.1	3.6	6.8	7.3	6.3	7.0	5.0	6.2	3.8	7.5	7.3	6.7
J.	EL SALVADOR	.1	.2	.1	.1	.1	.1	.1	.2	.1	.1	.1	.1	.1
K.	GUATEMALA	0	.1	0	0	.1	0	0	0	0	0	0	0	0
L.	HAITI	0	.1	0	.1	0	0	0	.1	.1	.1	.1	.1	.1
M.	HONDURAS	0	.1	0	.1	.1	.1	.1	.1	0	.1	.1	.1	.1
N.	MEXICO	2.9	8.7	7.1	8.0	9.1	9.8	13.4	15.6	12.1	11.3	8.7	8.6	7.9
O.	NICARAGUA	.1	.2	.1	.2	.1	.1	.1	.1	0	0	0	0	0
P.	PANAMA	.5	1.9	2.8†	3.8	1.6	1.7	2.4	1.5	1.1	2.0	1.2	2.2	1.0
R.	PERU	77.8	46.8	56.4	39.1	40.4	37.5	29.7	27.8	32.3	18.0	29.0	31.7	36.5
S.	URUGUAY	.1	.4	.4	.8	.9	1.1	1.3	1.5	1.1	1.7	1.2	1.1	1.0
T.	VENEZUELA	1.0	3.2	2.3	2.2	1.8	1.7	1.9	1.8	1.9	2.5	2.1	1.9	1.8
	LATIN AMERICA	100.0	100.0	100.0	100.0	100.0	100.0	100.0	100.0	100.0	100.0	100.0	100.0	100.0

SOURCE: Calculated from table 2001.

Table 2003

PC OF NOMINAL CATCHES IN MARINE AREAS, 18 LRC, 1971–86

	Country	1971	1973	1975	1977	1978	1979	1980	1981	1982	1983	1984	1985	1986
A.	ARGENTINA	8.2	27.9	−25.3	44.3	36.1	9.4	−31.7	−6.6	30.6	−12.6	−24.0	29.9	37.7
C.	BRAZIL	14.1	17.3	3.9	10.7	3.4	12.2	−16.1	1.9	5.9	4.7	13.8	.5	.8†
D.	CHILE	24.3	−16.0	−25.4	−4.4	46.3	36.5	7.0	20.2	8.5	8.3	13.1	6.8	16.0
E.	COLOMBIA	−13.6	15.4	−2.7	−7.9	5.4	−35.3	97.2	60.4	−52.4	−45.5	106.3	−11.1	14.3
F.	COSTA RICA	2.9	−.9	4.5	10.4	30.3	20.3	−11.4	−13.9	−25.0	−21.0	41.6	31.4	10.2
G.	CUBA	19.1	7.4	−13.0	−6.5	16.4	29.5	21.9	−14.2	17.2	1.8	−.5	10.7	12.6
H.	DOMINICAN REP.	−18.0	93.5	−51.2	−34.2	8.0	49.7	19.8	11.8	24.9	−4.3	17.3	23.1	3.3
I.	ECUADOR	16.7	42.2	22.1	30.8	42.4	−1.2	5.6	−24.7	37.6	−51.4	161.1	12.0	7.6
J.	EL SALVADOR	−3.9	14.6	−3.1	−21.7	69.2	37.3	10.2	58.7	−32.7	−47.5	54.0	−.8†	3.8†
K.	GUATEMALA	−6.7	18.5	18.7	−19.6	99.0	−13.0	−27.5	24.1	−7.6	−34.4	24.5	−8.6	−24.8
L.	HAITI	13.6	13.8	0	3.9	3.9	5.0	11.9†	10.6†	9.6†	8.8†	8.1†	−7.5†	−6.9†
M.	HONDURAS	78.4	−27.5	31.8	33.7	9.2	14.9	−12.0	−4.2	−18.4	69.1	−1.2	14.6	39.7
N.	MEXICO	13.4	4.5	16.0	7.4	51.5	22.3	27.9	25.1	−13.7†	−26.3	2.4	12.8	8.8
O.	NICARAGUA	−4.7	13.0	26.6	10.4	−1.8	−28.7	−2.8	−16.9	−21.5	−7.6	1.2	−3.3	−42.0
P.	PANAMA	0	45.6	31.0†	30.0†	−41.8†	18.4	31.1	−30.9	−22.0	45.3	−18.4	102.6	−53.9†
R.	PERU	−16.0	−50.8	−16.9	−42.6	37.7	6.1	−25.9	.2	29.5	−56.0	114.0	25.0	35.9
S.	URUGUAY	9.1	−15.0	65.6	43.5	53.8	45.8	11.7	22.1	−18.8	21.0	−7.3	3.6	1.5
T.	VENEZUELA	8.8	5.5	6.5	2.8	8.3	4.7	4.5	1.6	19.9	2.2	13.1	4.7	7.3†
	LATIN AMERICA	90.2	−15.0	−11.7	−19.2	33.4	14.1	−6.4	7.3	11.3	21.3	32.9	14.4	18.0
	UNITED STATES	2.5	1.0	.1	−2.1	14.7	3.2	34.8	3.9	5.7	6.8	13.3	−1.0	3.8
	WORLD	.3	.8	5.8	−2.0	3.5	1.2	1.0	3.3	2.6	−.2	8.1	2.0	6.9

SOURCE: Calculated from table 2001.

Table 2004

NOMINAL CATCHES, INLAND WATERS, 18 LRC, 1971-86

(MET)

	Country	1971	1975	1976	1977	1978	1979	1980	1981	1982	1983	1984	1985	1986
A.	ARGENTINA	5,700	15,068	9,846	10,436	15,077	16,082	8,407	9,689	15,395	14,594	9,286	9,565	8,539
B.	BOLIVIA	1,900	1,050	1,250	1,550	1,550	3,650	4,379	5,617	4,375	4,405	4,435	4,731	4,800†
C.	BRAZIL	87,900	173,455	144,829	168,444	170,645	126,701	87,594	197,340	207,919	205,345	211,502	211,078	215,000†
D.	CHILE	#	#	#	#	#	35	92	52	257	253	386	619	1,007
E.	COLOMBIA	19,300	42,075	51,437	42,174	56,612	48,535	46,903	47,719	49,000	45,343	53,354	47,368	54,876
F.	COSTA RICA	..	50	60	61	61	100	350	400	455	523	213	300	300
G.	CUBA	600	1,700	1,800	1,900	3,200	5,400	6,339	10,314	13,629	14,121	16,199	16,881	16,100
H.	DOMINICAN REP.	500	585	618	359	513	1,040	2,459	2,836	1,721	4,338	1,769	2,524	846
J.	EL SALVADOR	800	869	1,143	1,624	1,512	1,719	1,818	983	551	795	1,705	1,700†	1,700†
K.	GUATEMALA	500	550	574	600	580	615	400	410	721	40	54	47	120
L.	HAITI	300†	300†	300†	300†	300†	300†	300†	300†	300†	300†	300†	300†	300†
M.	HONDURAS	100	170	170	97	114	110	83	238	74	65	113	120	180
N.	MEXICO	7,900	17,826	2,277	2,699	6,253	6,464	9,809	19,614	12,743	100,527	116,992	113,028	92,959
O.	NICARAGUA	1,300	359	458	393	178	126	79	193	486	378	118	84	55
Q.	PARAGUAY	2,200†	2,800†	2,900†	3,000†	3,100†	3,200†	3,300†	3,350†	3,400†	3,500	5,000	7,500	13,000
R.	PERU	2,500	6,671	6,280	12,597	14,064	14,426	12,538	16,974	17,357	33,019	29,732	27,583	28,200
S.	URUGUAY	..	245	179	321	472	578	312	321	186	57	435	660	750
T.	VENEZUELA	5,700	7,657	6,626	8,021	11,260	6,934	15,933	13,346	14,998	20,009	21,073	15,258	16,000†
	LATIN AMERICA	137,200	278,160	230,747	254,576	285,491	236,015	300,815	329,696	343,561	447,612	472,666	459,346	454,732
	UNITED STATES	77,500	77,267	76,368	70,281	78,817	63,914	68,194	63,840	72,140	74,190	73,213	72,782	72,005
	WORLD	6,382,000	6,961,000	6,904,300	7,170,600	7,098,100	7,270,300	7,668,300	8,146,900	8,483,600	9,236,500	9,794,700	10,488,200	11,111,800

SOURCE: FAO-YFSCL, 1979-86, table A-3.

Table 2005

DISTRIBUTION OF NOMINAL CATCHES IN INLAND WATERS, 18 LR, 1971–86

(%)

	Country	1971	1975	1976	1977	1978	1979	1980	1981	1982	1983	1984	1985	1986
A.	ARGENTINA	4.2	5.6	4.0	3.9	5.0	6.1	2.7	2.9	4.5	3.3	2.0	2.1	1.9
B.	BOLIVIA	1.4	.4	.5	.6	.5	1.4	1.4	1.7	1.8	1.0	.9	1.0	1.1[†]
C.	BRAZIL	64.1	63.9	58.8	63.1	57.3	48.0	62.4	59.8	60.5	45.9	44.7	46.0	47.3[†]
D.	CHILE	0	0	0	0	0	0	0	0	.1	.1	.1	.1	.2
E.	COLOMBIA	14.1	15.5	20.9	15.8	19.0	18.4	15.1	14.5	14.3	10.1	11.3	10.3	12.1
F.	COSTA RICA	0	0	0	0	0	0	.1	.1	.1	.1	0	.1	.1
G.	CUBA	.4	.6	.7	.7	1.1	2.0	2.0	3.1	4.0	3.2	3.4	3.7	3.5
H.	DOMINICAN REP.	.4	.2	.2	.1	.2	.4	.8	.9	.5	1.0	.4	.5	.2
J.	EL SALVADOR	.6	1.0	1.2	1.1	.5	.7	.6	.3	.2	.2	.4	.4[†]	.4[†]
K.	GUATEMALA	.4	.2	.2	.2	.2	.2	.1	.1	.2[†]	0	0	0	0
L.	HAITI	.2	.1	.1	.1	.1	.1	0	0	.1[†]	.1[†]	.1[†]	.1[†]	.1[†]
M.	HONDURAS	.1	.1	.1	0	0	0	0	0	0	0	0	0	0
N.	MEXICO	5.8	6.4	1.0	1.1	2.2	2.7	3.3	5.9	3.7	22.5	24.8	24.6	20.4
O.	NICARAGUA	.9	.1	.2	.1	.1	0	0	0	.2	.1	0	0	0
Q.	PARAGUAY	1.6	1.0[†]	1.3[†]	1.2[†]	1.1[†]	1.4[†]	1.1[†]	1.0[†]	1.0[†]	.8	1.1	1.6	2.9
R.	PERU	1.8	2.4	2.5	5.0	4.7	6.1	4.2	5.1	5.1	7.4	6.3	6.0	6.2
S.	URUGUAY	0	.1	.1	.1	.2	.2	.1	.1	.1	0	.1	.1	.2
T.	VENEZUELA	4.2	2.8	2.6	2.9	3.8	2.9	5.3	4.0	4.4	4.5	4.5	3.3	3.5[†]
	LATIN AMERICA	100.0	100.0	100.0	100.0	100.0	100.0	100.0	100.0	100.0	100.0	100.0	100.0	100.0

SOURCE: Calculated from table 2004.

Table 2006

PC OF NOMINAL CATCHES IN INLAND WATERS, 18 LRC, 1971–86

	Country	1971	1975	1976	1977	1978	1979	1980	1981	1982	1983	1984	1985	1986
A.	ARGENTINA	5.6	48.0	−34.7	6.0	44.5	6.7	−47.7	15.3	58.2	−5.0	−36.4	3.0	−10.7
B.	BOLIVIA	18.8	0	19.0	24.0	0	135.5	20.0	28.3	−22.1	.7	.7	6.7	1.5
C.	BRAZIL	−6.0	3.2	−16.5	16.3	1.3	−25.8	48.0	5.2	5.3	−4.5[†]	3.0	0	1.9
D.	CHILE	0	0	0	0	0	**	162.9	−43.5	39.4	−1.6	52.6	60.4	62.7
E.	COLOMBIA	−41.9	13.0	22.3	−18.0	34.2	−14.3	−3.7	1.7	2.7	−7.5	−11.2	15.9	
F.	COSTA RICA	~	25.0	20.0	1.7	0	63.9	25.0	14.3	13.8	0[†]	−59.3	40.8	0
G.	CUBA	50.0	−22.7	5.9	5.6	68.4	68.8	17.3	62.7	32.1	3.6	14.7	4.2	−4.6
H.	DOMINICAN REP.	150.0	59.4	5.6	−41.9	42.9	102.7	136.4	15.3	−39.3	152.1	−59.2	42.7	−66.5
J.	EL SALVADOR	0	−42.6	31.5	42.1	−6.9	13.7	5.8	−45.9	−43.9	44.3	114.5	.3[†]	0[†]
K.	GUATEMALA	25.0	4.2	4.4	4.5	−3.3	6.0	−35.0	2.5	75.9	0[†]	35.0	−13.0	155.3
L.	HAITI	0[†]	0[†]	0[†]	0[†]	0[†]	0[†]	0[†]	0[†]	0[†]	0[†]	0[†]	0[†]	0[†]
M.	HONDURAS	0	−1.2	0	−42.9	17.5	−3.5	−24.5	186.7	−68.9	−12.1	73.8	6.2	50.0
N.	MEXICO	9.7	25.9	−87.2	18.5	131.7	3.4	51.8	100.0	−35.0	62.4[†]	10.9	−3.4	−17.8
O.	NICARAGUA	0	−22.0	27.6	−14.2	−54.7	−29.2	−37.3	144.3	151.8	−22.2	−68.8	−28.8	−34.5
Q.	PARAGUAY	22.2	3.7	3.6	3.4	3.3	3.2	3.1	1.5	1.5	2.9	42.9	50.0	73.3
R.	PERU	25.0	22.9	−7.3	100.6	56.0	2.6	−13.1	35.4	2.3	90.2	−10.0	−7.2	2.2
S.	URUGUAY	~	−18.3	−26.9	79.3	47.0	22.5	−46.0	2.9	−42.1	−69.3	663.2	51.7	13.6
T.	VENEZUELA	50.0	−16.8	−13.5	21.1	40.4	−38.4	129.8	−15.9	12.4	33.4	5.3	−27.6	4.9[†]
	LATIN AMERICA	−9.7	9.5	−17.0	10.3	12.1	−17.3	27.5	9.6	4.2	30.3	5.6	−2.8	−1.0
	UNITED STATES	−4.0	−8.6	−1.2	−5.9	12.0	−18.3	5.9	−6.3	12.6	3.2	−1.5	−.5	−1.1
	WORLD	4.8	2.1	−.8	3.1	−.9	2.9	5.0	7.1	3.9	8.1	3.6	6.6	5.9

SOURCE: Calculated from table 2004.

Table 2007

PRODUCTION OF SEAWEEDS,[1] 5 LC, 1970–86[a]
(MET)

	Country	1970	1975	1977	1979	1980	1982	1984	1985	1986
A.	ARGENTINA	23,300	18,073	22,856	15,299	14,739	13,072	7,522	12,879	5,987
D.	CHILE	28,000	30,000	30,000	65,000	74,523	173,375	174,756	182,410	123,899
N.	MEXICO	35,200	31,841	45,553	48,039	34.698	35,277	30,934	39,643	50,713
R.	PERU	#	193	265	286	361	136	144	245	437
S.	URUGUAY	#	85	100	37	#	#	#	#	#
	UNITED STATES	117,100	157,853	160,810	160,624	162,809	78,475	39,000	81,239	55,496
	WORLD	1,633,400	2,480,500	3,083,100	3,192,700	3,354,300	3,125,600	3,605,000	3,719,600	3,470,700

1. Includes production of seaweeds and other aquatic plants through both culture and harvesting of wild stocks.

a. For intervening years see previous issues of SALA.

SOURCE: FAO-YFSCL, 1979–86, table A-6.

Table 2008

CHILE SALMON PRODUCTION, 1981–87
(Tons)

Year	Output
1981	70
1982	80
1983	94
1984	104
1985/6	1,300
1986/87	1,600

SOURCE: *Chile Economic Report* (February 1988).

21
Agricultural Production

Table 2100

INDEX OF TOTAL AGRICULTURAL PRODUCTION,[1] 20 LC, 1975–87

(1979–81 = 100)[a]

	Country	1975	1977	1978	1979	1980	1981	1982	1983	1984	1985	1986	1987
A.	ARGENTINA	87.76	94.23	98.96	102.57	95.77	101.66	107.53	104.30	107.69	105.22	108.19	106.63
B.	BOLIVIA	96.62	93.80	94.74	95.15	99.17	105.69	110.36	84.17	105.87	114.02	111.38	111.90
C.	BRAZIL	84.53	91.41	88.55	92.72	100.21	107.07	108.48	108.01	112.99	125.37	112.61	127.72
D.	CHILE	88.60	95.32	89.69	96.42	97.39	106.19	104.62	99.22	104.56	107.22	115.87	117.70
E.	COLOMBIA	81.81	90.13	94.05	98.43	98.93	102.65	101.13	100.02	101.14	102.61	109.71	111.48
F.	COSTA RICA	87.75	94.62	97.27	99.72	99.01	101.27	97.59	101.21	111.43	114.51	110.51	110.08
G.	CUBA	79.81	89.89	96.98	101.99	92.54	105.47	109.39	105.56	115.14	111.50	114.21	107.06
H.	DOMINICAN REP.	89.91	98.50	98.46	101.61	99.20	99.19	105.21	110.73	114.89	112.79	110.15	106.19
I.	ECUADOR	91.55	95.23	92.57	96.04	100.14	103.81	106.73	91.58	103.21	120.87	120.89	119.55
J.	EL SALVADOR	93.89	86.74	95.53	103.75	100.95	95.31	90.78	86.42	92.24	76.56	83.52	82.38
K.	GUATEMALA	86.43	96.28	98.06	98.03	99.91	102.06	107.63	103.30	104.73	102.43	102.76	97.26
L.	HAITI	95.01	91.00	96.18	101.19	100.16	98.65	98.77	103.96	105.85	107.79	109.35	112.37
M.	HONDURAS	72.15	83.31	93.79	94.16	98.21	107.64	101.21	98.74	96.55	96.55	96.59	94.32
N.	MEXICO	80.39	89.43	97.69	93.85	100.27	105.88	102.31	108.70	108.59	109.04	109.30	109.46
O.	NICARAGUA	103.73	110.58	121.27	122.26	83.30	94.44	100.00	95.25	93.65	92.01	85.74	80.91
P.	PANAMA	87.24	93.37	96.58	97.69	97.96	104.35	102.52	107.66	108.45	110.91	115.13	110.98
Q.	PARAGUAY	73.74	89.06	90.57	95.48	96.99	107.53	107.01	110.08	122.28	136.11	121.52	134.90
R.	PERU	99.92	103.42	102.48	104.55	94.12	101.32	105.39	100.83	112.66	111.36	108.90	112.62
S.	URUGUAY	96.12	91.77	89.32	89.81	96.35	113.85	111.42	114.84	106.02	107.30	108.03	111.06
T.	VENEZUELA	94.57	90.56	97.00	100.78	99.76	99.46	98.91	106.92	104.07	103.96	116.25	109.86
	UNITED STATES	89.75	96.54	94.52	98.93	95.32	105.75	104.24	88.16	101.75	106.80	100.23	98.47

1. The index numbers of total agricultural production cover all of the items included in
food production (cereals, starchy roots, sugar, pulses, edible oil crops, nuts, fruit,
vegetables, wine, cocoa, livestock and livestock products) and, in addition, industrial
oilseeds, tobacco, fibres (vegetable and animal), rubber, coffee and tea. Agricultural
commodities used in the agricultural production process are deducted from total production. The deduction items include amounts used for seed (or, in the case of eggs,
used for hatching), and for livestock feed, i.e., agricultural products fed as such and
semi-processed feed such as oilcakes and grain as well as imported feed, to the extent
that adequate estimates are possible.

a. For subindex of food production, see SALA, 26-818.

SOURCE: FAO-PY, 1985, 1986, 1987, table 5.

Table 2101

INDEX OF PER CAPITA AGRICULTURAL PRODUCTION,[1] 20 LC, 1975–87

(1979–81 = 100)[a]

	Country	1975	1977	1978	1979	1980	1981	1982	1983	1984	1985	1986	1987
A.	ARGENTINA	95.11	98.82	102.17	104.23	95.75	100.02	104.24	99.47	101.13	96.04	96.22	95.67
B.	BOLIVIA	110.04	101.92	100.37	98.28	99.25	102.47	104.09	77.87	91.26	95.69	87.39	92.65
C.	BRAZIL	94.98	98.31	93.01	95.09	100.30	104.61	103.55	100.53	103.70	111.02	100.50	109.72
D.	CHILE	95.45	98.97	92.01	97.76	97.81	104.42	100.69	94.93	98.18	99.52	105.76	105.62
E.	COLOMBIA	91.07	96.20	98.15	100.53	98.94	100.54	96.92	94.03	94.44	92.80	94.13	96.13
F.	COSTA RICA	101.70	103.27	102.91	102.66	98.95	98.39	91.91	93.01	97.17	100.56	94.68	91.83
G.	CUBA	83.22	87.90	96.11	101.99	93.94	104.07	107.61	103.18	111.74	108.91	108.64	101.77
H.	DOMINICAN REP.	101.03	105.50	103.22	103.98	99.11	96.91	100.57	103.52	104.82	99.04	92.22	90.42
I.	ECUADOR	105.76	104.23	98.88	99.07	100.14	100.79	100.61	84.35	92.89	102.77	102.80	97.98
J.	EL SALVADOR	108.50	97.03	103.73	109.30	103.12	87.59	79.41	81.41	83.35	81.10	70.86	66.81
K.	GUATEMALA	99.29	104.81	103.73	101.00	99.84	99.16	101.39	94.28	93.40	88.83	85.36	79.78
L.	HAITI	106.99	98.55	101.84	104.51	98.22	97.27	95.02	97.08	96.68	93.71	94.41	94.03
M.	HONDURAS	86.17	94.07	101.16	98.21	98.82	102.97	95.23	89.72	85.25	86.30	88.45	74.91
N.	MEXICO	92.80	97.34	103.20	96.51	100.29	103.20	96.88	100.37	98.48	95.94	95.12	91.73
O.	NICARAGUA	119.08	119.77	128.07	125.04	82.37	92.59	91.88	82.97	80.39	76.66	70.00	63.89
P.	PANAMA	97.67	99.99	101.16	100.08	98.20	101.72	98.16	101.96	99.80	101.09	97.02	95.59
Q.	PARAGUAY	87.00	99.54	96.46	98.53	100.68	100.79	101.54	100.29	97.05	111.09	100.67	109.89
R.	PERU	113.43	111.55	107.86	107.02	94.30	98.68	99.82	93.74	101.44	97.62	94.24	93.99
S.	URUGUAY	98.86	93.55	90.54	90.43	96.33	113.24	110.12	112.72	103.24	105.40	102.59	105.68
T.	VENEZUELA	111.92	100.09	103.50	103.95	99.58	96.47	95.91	95.91	91.60	93.05	93.90	90.25
	UNITED STATES	94.60	99.70	96.63	100.12	95.29	104.60	102.17	85.43	97.64	101.83	96.01	92.27

1. For alternative data from 1971 to 1977, see SALA, 21–1517.

a. For subindex of per capita food production, see SALA, 26–819.

SOURCE: FAO-PY, 1986, 1987, table 10.

Table 2102

BARLEY PRODUCTION, 10 LC, 1982–87[a]

(Area = T Ha.; Production = T MET; Yield = kg/Ha.)

	Country	1982 Area[1]	1982 Production	1982 Yield[2]	1985 Area[1]	1985 Production	1985 Yield[2]	1986 Area[1]	1986 Production	1986 Yield[2]	1987 Area[1]	1987 Production	1987 Yield[2]
A.	ARGENTINA	119	211	11,778	76	118	1,559	135[‡]	190[‡]	1,407	135[†]	150[†]	1,111
B.	BOLIVIA	84	61	726	94	75	800	95	78	823	83	67	807
C.	BRAZIL	167	99	590	110	165	1,493	102	180	1,766	103	193	1,876
D.	CHILE	57	118	2,050	35	85	2,425	23	68	2,996	16	48	2,952
E.	COLOMBIA	35	56	1,593	31	60	1,980	38	73	1,952	47	85	1,790
I.	ECUADOR	34	35	1,045	29	27	908	36	41	1,158	40[‡]	43[‡]	1,075
K.	GUATEMALA	~	1[†]	1,486	~	1[†]	1,481	~	~	1,481	~	~	1,481
N.	MEXICO	281	396	1,407	282	544	1,927	280	415[‡]	1,482	350	592	1,691
R.	PERU	90	100	1,112	95	108	1,133	98	116	1,186	116	119	1,026
S.	URUGUAY	26	45	1,741	64	80	1,239	51	77	1,518	60	90	1,500
	UNITED STATES	3,647	11,233	3,080	4,696	12,876	2,742	4,859	13,292	2,736	4,058	11,474	2,828

1. Area harvested.
2. Yield may not equal kg/Ha. due to rounding of area and production data.

a. For prior years see previous issues of SALA.

SOURCE: FAO-PY, 1980–81, table 12; 1985, table 18; 1986, 1987, table 19.

Table 2103

BANANA PRODUCTION, 17 LC, 1970–87[a]

(T MET)

	Country	1970	1975	1980	1981	1982	1983	1984	1985	1986	1987
A.	ARGENTINA	223	374	146	180[†]	89	126	161	163	165[†]	165[†]
B.	BOLIVIA	212	252	216	220[†]	152	154	160[†]	210[‡]	290[‡]	350[‡]
C.	BRAZIL	6,408[†]	5,311	6,736	6,696	6,818	6,566	7,062	4,815	5,042	5,188
E.	COLOMBIA	780	1,050[†]	1,030[‡]	1,155[‡]	1,147	1,173	1,450[‡]	1,200[‡]	1,300[†]	1,340[†]
F.	COSTA RICA	1,146[‡]	1,121	1,092	1,144	1,136	1,153	1,169	1,008	1,000[†]	925
G.	CUBA	47	92[‡]	145	155	192	200	221	201	147	160[†]
H.	DOMINICAN REP.	275	318	301	320[‡]	320[‡]	320[‡]	330[‡]	314[‡]	422[‡]	400[†]
I.	ECUADOR	2,700[‡]	2,544	2,269	2,275[‡]	1,999	1,642	1,678	1,970	2,316	1,962[‡]
J.	EL SALVADOR	45	53[†]	52[†]	53[†]	54[†]	54[†]	55[†]	33	36	36
K.	GUATEMALA	487	520[†]	650[†]	650[†]	655[†]	675[†]	680[†]	690[†]	690[†]	709[†]
L.	HAITI	176[†]	51[†]	200[†]	210[†]	230[†]	230[†]	235[†]	235[‡]	250[‡]	256[†]
M.	HONDURAS	1,200[†]	852	1,330[†]	1,330[†]	1,425	1,186	992	1,091	1,020	1,020[†]
N.	MEXICO	1,136	1,194	1,515	1,562[†]	1,572	1,640	2,093	1,151	1,473	1,489[†]
O.	NICARAGUA[1]	217	153	171[†]	170[†]	157[‡]	128	116	127	101	119
P.	PANAMA	947	989	1,050[†]	1,082[†]	1,057	1,045	1,056	1,067	907	907[†]
Q.	PARAGUAY	249	260	300[†]	305[†]	314[‡]	315[†]	325[†]	325[†]	325[†]	333[†]
T.	VENEZUELA	968	860	983	980	917	934	965	989	1,007[‡]	1,000[†]
	UNITED STATES	3	3	2	3	3	2	4	4	4	5

1. Refers to exports.

a. For prior years see previous issues of SALA.

SOURCE: FAO-PY, 1972, table 76; 1976–77 and 1979–81, table 65; 1985, table 73; 1986, 1987, table 74.

Table 2104

BEAN PRODUCTION,[1] 20 LC, 1982–87[a]

(Area = T Ha.; Production = T MET; Yield = kg/Ha.)

	Country	1982			1985			1986			1987		
		Area[2]	Production	Yield[3]	Area[2]	Production	Yield[3]	Area[2]	Production	Yield[3]	Area[2]	Production	Yield[3]
A.	ARGENTINA	230	254	1,106	225‡	240‡	1,067	240‡	240‡	1,000	243†	200‡	823
B.	BOLIVIA	4†	4†	1,053	9	13	1,388	10†	14†	1,438	8	11	1,313
C.	BRAZIL	5,926	2,903	490	5,317	2,548	479	5,484	2,221	405	5,217	2,026	388
D.	CHILE	122	162	1,337	83	101	1,212	90	89	993	98	81‡	828
E.	COLOMBIA	112	73	650	132	100	755	135	111	822	120	90	748
F.	COSTA RICA	38	16	424	44	26	606	58	31	540	56	31	557
G.	CUBA	35†	27†	757	35†	27†	771	35†	27†	780	35†	28†	786
H.	DOMINICAN REP.	55‡	58	1,056	53	40	761	42	28	671	47	38	806
I.	ECUADOR	51	29	560	40	26	644	58‡	34‡	580	58‡	38‡	665
J.	EL SALVADOR	56	38	687	58	35	593	61	50	820	59	24	415
K.	GUATEMALA	97‡	84‡	866	167†	113†	677	167†	113†	677	170†	115†	676
L.	HAITI	90†	50†	556	85†	48	565	85†	48†	565	90†	50†	556
M.	HONDURAS	51	31	600	66	48	730	75	40	537	22	22	1,000
N.	MEXICO	1,712	1,093	638	1,769	905	512	1,850	1,089	589	2,316	1,026	443
O.	NICARAGUA	68	47	684	86	57	662	104	71	680	50†	34	680
P.	PANAMA	9	3	358	11	4	394	10†	3†	300	11‡	4‡	336
Q.	PARAGUAY	80	60	750	57	49	860	41	28	684	59	48	807
R.	PERU	50	43	868	57	46	814	75†	54	719	75†	54†	720
S.	URUGUAY	5†	3†	587	5†	3†	617	5†	3†	617	5†	3†	638
T.	VENEZUELA	63	30	477	73‡	37‡	507	81‡	46‡	568	94‡	49‡	521
	UNITED STATES	719	1,160	1,612	600	1,006	1,678	605	1,039	1,717	691	1,193	1,725

1. Includes *Phaseolus vulgaris, P. lunatus, P. aureus,* and *p. mungo.*
2. Area harvested.
3. Yield may not equal kg/Ha. due to rounding of area and production data.

a. For prior years see previous issues of SALA.

SOURCE: FAO-PY, 1984 and 1985, table 31; 1986, 1987, table 32.

Table 2105

CASSAVA PRODUCTION, 18 L, 1982–87[a]

(Area = T Ha.; Production = T MET; Yield = kg/Ha.)

	Country	1982			1985			1986			1987		
		Area[1]	Production	Yield[2]	Area[1]	Production	Yield[2]	Area[1]	Production	Yield[2]	Area[1]	Production	Yield[2]
A.	ARGENTINA	24	216	9,076	16†	140†	8,750	16†	140†	8,750	16†	140†	8,750
B.	BOLIVIA	21	271	12,868	41	376	9,142	40	420	10,500	41	425	10,366
C.	BRAZIL	2,122	24,072	11,344	1,867	23,111	12,376	2,049	25,542	12,464	2,033	24,704	12,150
E.	COLOMBIA	207	2,000	9,662	154	1,367	8,868	150	1,338	8,930	161	1,408	8,722
F.	COSTA RICA	5	17	3,131	5†	15	2,907	5†	15†	3,000	5†	16†	3,200
G.	CUBA	49†	330‡	6,735	46†	300†	6,522	47†	304†	6,527	47†	310†	6,596
H.	DOMINICAN REP.	13	68	5,105	19	114	6,044	25	107	4,296	17	103‡	5,909
I.	ECUADOR	20	184	9,231	22	229	10,301	28‡	252‡	9,000	27‡	240‡	8,889
J.	EL SALVADOR	2	23	11,829	2†	28	14,785	2‡	27‡	14,670	2‡	30‡	15,000
K.	GUATEMALA	3†	9†	3,600	3†	9†	3,760	3‡	10†	3,800	3†	10†	3,800
L.	HAITI	64†	260‡	4,063	65†	270†	4,154	65‡	270†	4,154	68†	290†	4,265
M.	HONDURAS	2†	8†	5,000	~	7†	17,500	~	7†	17,500	~	7†	17,500
N.	MEXICO	2‡	43‡	17,660	2†	43†	17,551	2†	43†	17,551	~	1†	10,000
O.	NICARAGUA	7†	27†	4,015	7†	27†	4,030	7†	27†	4,029	6†	65†	11,404
P.	PANAMA	5†	35	7,277	5†	35	7,112	5†	35†	7,143	5†	35†	7,224
Q.	PARAGUAY	141‡	2,111‡	14,972	186	2,861	15,347	200	2,875	14,405	222	3,389	15,268
R.	PERU	30	324	10,997	32	337	10,489	31†	340†	10,968	37†	400†	10,811
T.	VENEZUELA	39	301	7,701	39‡	310‡	7,949	39†	312†	8,023	41†	315†	7,778

1. Area harvested.
2. Yield may not equal kg/Ha. due to rounding of area and production data.

a. For prior years see previous issues of SALA.

SOURCE: FAO-PY, 1984 and 1985, table 27; 1986, 1987, table 28.

Table 2106

COCOA BEAN PRODUCTION, 16 L, 1982–87[a]

(Area = T Ha.; Production = T MET; Yield = kg/Ha.)

	Country	1982 Area[1]	1982 Production	1982 Yield[2]	1985 Area[1]	1985 Production	1985 Yield[2]	1986 Area[1]	1986 Production	1986 Yield[2]	1987 Area[1]	1987 Production	1987 Yield[2]
B.	BOLIVIA	5[†]	3[‡]	556	5[†]	3[†]	667	5[†]	3[‡]	667	5[†]	3[†]	667
C.	BRAZIL	533	351	658	640	420	655	658	459	698	651	405	622
E.	COLOMBIA	77	39	510	87	43	497	96[‡]	46[‡]	479	102	51	500
F.	COSTA RICA	12	5	453	12	4	360	10	5	481	21[‡]	4[‡]	195
G.	CUBA	2	2	708	3[†]	2	701	3[†]	2[‡]	750	11[†]	2[‡]	220
H.	DOMINICAN REP.	135[†]	43	321	119[†]	35	290	119[‡]	37[‡]	311	129[‡]	39[‡]	302
I.	ECUADOR	277	97	350	287	131	456	263	100	380	294[‡]	85[‡]	289
J.	EL SALVADOR	~	~	1,000	~	~	1,000	~	~	1,000	~	~	1,000
K.	GUATEMALA	3[†]	2[†]	500	4[†]	2[†]	500	4[†]	2[‡]	500	4[†]	2[†]	500
L.	HAITI	2	3[‡]	2,000	3[†]	5	2,022	3[†]	5[†]	2,000	3[†]	5[†]	1,800
M.	HONDURAS	1[†]	1[†]	1,000	2[†]	2[‡]	1,000	2[†]	2[‡]	1,000	2[†]	2[†]	1,000
N.	MEXICO	82	38	466	82[†]	41[‡]	500	82[†]	43[‡]	518	80[†]	45[†]	563
O.	NICARAGUA	3[†]	~	143	2[†]	~	150	1[†]	~	154	2[†]	~	150
P.	PANAMA	6[†]	2	311	3[†]	1[‡]	294	2[†]	1[‡]	294	4[†]	2[†]	341
R.	PERU	15[†]	9[‡]	600	11[†]	6	543	11[†]	7[†]	591	11[†]	7[†]	591
T.	VENEZUELA	64	13	208	62[‡]	11[‡]	177	61[‡]	12[‡]	189	62[‡]	14[‡]	218

1. Area harvested.
2. Yield may not equal kg/Ha. due to rounding of area and production data.

a. For prior years see previous issues of SALA.

SOURCE: FAO-PY, 1984 and 1985, table 78; 1986, 1987, table 79.

Table 2107

COFFEE PRODUCTION, 17 LC, 1982–87[a]

(Area = T Ha.; Production = T MET; Yield = kg/Ha.)

	Country	1982 Area[1]	1982 Production	1982 Yield[2]	1985 Area[1]	1985 Production	1985 Yield[2]	1986 Area[1]	1986 Production	1986 Yield[2]	1987 Area[1]	1987 Production	1987 Yield[2]
B.	BOLIVIA	24	21	900	22[‡]	19[†]	868	22[‡]	19[†]	864	28	25	900
C.	BRAZIL	1,895	958	505	2,483	1,877	756	2,259	1,004	444	2,461	2,112[‡]	812
E.	COLOMBIA	1,087[‡]	861[‡]	792	930[‡]	676	726	945[‡]	708	749	925[‡]	654[‡]	659
F.	COSTA RICA	85[‡]	115	1,354	90	155	1,727	111	128	1,155	110[†]	138	1,255
G.	CUBA	50[†]	29	574	50[†]	24	480	50[†]	21[†]	420	130[†]	21[‡]	162
H.	DOMINICAN REP.	160[†]	63	397	162[†]	72	444	165[†]	55[‡]	331	100	47[‡]	472
I.	ECUADOR	322	84	261	427	121	283	390	131	336	347[‡]	118[‡]	340
J.	EL SALVADOR	161[‡]	146	908	185	161[‡]	868	180[‡]	141	781	160[‡]	881	141[‡]
K.	GUATEMALA	257[‡]	159[‡]	619	260[‡]	152[‡]	585	260[‡]	156[‡]	600	260[‡]	159[‡]	612
L.	HAITI	35[†]	39[‡]	1,114	33[†]	37	1,118	33[†]	38[†]	1,152	34[†]	37[‡]	1,088
M.	HONDURAS	123	85	688	124	78	630	126[‡]	78[‡]	619	126[‡]	70[‡]	556
N.	MEXICO	420	231	550	415[‡]	269[‡]	648	415[‡]	278[‡]	670	415[‡]	315[‡]	759
O.	NICARAGUA	100	71	713	93	50	538	77	44	567	77	41	538
P.	PANAMA	24	8	339	30[†]	9	313	38[†]	16[‡]	411	38[†]	15[‡]	395
Q.	PARAGUAY	16[‡]	16[‡]	1,016	21[‡]	17[‡]	786	12	18	1,493	19[‡]	19[‡]	1,027
R.	PERU	142[†]	90	633	140[‡]	91	647	140[‡]	97	692	142[‡]	97[†]	683
T.	VENEZUELA	254	58	229	265[‡]	73[‡]	275	270[‡]	69[‡]	256	276[‡]	66[‡]	239
	UNITED STATES	1	~	468	1	1	974	1	1	1,304	1	1	725

1. Area harvested.
2. Yield may not equal kg/Ha. due to rounding of area and production data.

a. For prior years see previous issues of SALA.

SOURCE: FAO-PY, 1984 and 1985, table 77; 1986, 1987, table 78.

Table 2108

COPRA PRODUCTION, 11 L, 1970–87[a]

(T MET)

	Country	1970	1975	1980	1984	1985	1986	1987
C.	BRAZIL	2.2	2[†]	2[†]	3[†]	3[†]	3[†]	3[†]
E.	COLOMBIA	2.2[†]	~	~	~	~	~	~
F.	COSTA RICA	1.2	2[†]	2[†]	2[†]	2[†]	2[†]	2[†]
H.	DOMINICAN REP.	7.5	9[†]	12[†]	14[‡]	14[‡]	15[‡]	16[‡]
I.	ECUADOR	2.2[†]	4[†]	14[†]	13[†]	14[†]	9[†]	9[‡]
J.	EL SALVADOR	3.0[†]	5[‡]	3[‡]	3[†]	3[‡]	3[‡]	3[‡]
M.	HONDURAS	2.4[†]	3[†]	3[†]	2[†]	2[†]	1[†]	1[†]
N.	MEXICO	137.4	145[‡]	140[‡]	120	120	196	175[†]
O.	NICARAGUA	.2[†]	~	~	~	~	~	~
P.	PANAMA	.6	1[†]	1[†]	1[†]	~	~	~
T.	VENEZUELA	16.9	18	12	12[‡]	9[‡]	9[‡]	11[‡]

a. For prior years see previous issues of SALA.

SOURCE: FAO-PY, 1974, table 57; 1977–81, table 38; 1985, table 46; 1986, 1987,
    table 47.

Table 2109

COTTON LINT PRODUCTION, 18 LC, 1970–87[a]

(T MET)

	Country	1970	1975	1980	1984	1985	1986	1987
A.	ARGENTINA	145	171	146	180	171	120	105[‡]
B.	BOLIVIA	5	22	7	1	2	5	6
C.	BRAZIL	672	515	572[‡]	723[‡]	926[‡]	735[‡]	529[‡]
E.	COLOMBIA	128	121	116[‡]	126[‡]	114[‡]	119	114
F.	COSTA RICA	1[†]	1	4[‡]	2	2	1	1[‡]
G.	CUBA	1[†]	1[‡]	1[‡]	1[‡]	1[‡]	1[‡]	~
H.	DOMINICAN REP.	1[†]	1[†]	2[‡]	2[‡]	1[‡]	2[‡]	2[†]
I.	ECUADOR	4[‡]	11	15[‡]	3[‡]	7[‡]	13[‡]	13[‡]
J.	EL SALVADOR	46	78	65	30	31	18	11
K.	GUATEMALA	57	105[‡]	156	59	68[‡]	41[‡]	30[‡]
L.	HAITI	1[†]	1[†]	1[†]	2[†]	2[†]	2[†]	2[†]
M.	HONDURAS	3	5[‡]	7[‡]	6[‡]	5[‡]	3[‡]	3[†]
N.	MEXICO	312	197	329[‡]	300	209[‡]	144	153[‡]
O.	NICARAGUA	67	123	21[‡]	85	69	49	49
Q.	PARAGUAY	13	33[‡]	75	105	160[‡]	107	114[‡]
R.	PERU	92	60[‡]	90[‡]	94[‡]	93[‡]	71[‡]	87[‡]
S.	URUGUAY	- -	1	~	~	~	~	~
T.	VENEZUELA	13	31	18	15[‡]	27[‡]	24[‡]	18[‡]
	UNITED STATES	2,213	1,807	2,422	2,827	2,924	2,119	3,206

a. For prior years see previous issues of SALA.

SOURCE: FAO-PY, 1971, table 96; 1976–81, table 78; 1985, table 86; 1986, 1987,
    table 87.

Table 2110

COTTONSEED PRODUCTION, 18 LC, 1970–87[a]

(T MET)

	Country	1970	1975	1980	1984	1985	1986	1987
A.	ARGENTINA	249	541	276	326	293	218[‡]	175[†]
B.	BOLIVIA	10	61[‡]	12[‡]	2[‡]	3[‡]	9[‡]	10[‡]
C.	BRAZIL	1,227	1,751	1,125[‡]	1,380	1,810	1,466	1,020[‡]
E.	COLOMBIA	231	385	216[‡]	243	220[‡]	184	175
F.	COSTA RICA	2	2[‡]	8[†]	4[†]	3[‡]	1[†]	1[†]
G.	CUBA	2[†]	3[†]	2[‡]	2[‡]	2[†]	2[†]	~
H.	DOMINICAN REP.	3	2[†]	4[‡]	4[‡]	2[†]	4[†]	4[†]
I.	ECUADOR	10[‡]	30	24[‡]	5[‡]	11[‡]	17	18[†]
J.	EL SALVADOR	76	210	109	45[†]	45[‡]	26	15
K.	GUATEMALA	92	280[‡]	251	92	105[†]	74[‡]	44
L.	HAITI	1[†]	3[†]	2[†]	4[†]	4[†]	4[†]	4[†]
M.	HONDURAS	6	15[‡]	15[‡]	11[†]	9[†]	6	6[†]
N.	MEXICO	550	544	538	436	310[‡]	226	250
O.	NICARAGUA	112	330[†]	37[‡]	126	98	77[‡]	93[‡]
Q.	PARAGUAY	25	94[‡]	146[‡]	198[‡]	300[‡]	232[‡]	240[‡]
R.	PERU	153	180[‡]	172[‡]	178[‡]	175[†]	140[†]	165[†]
S.	URUGUAY	#	2	~	~	~	~	~
T.	VENEZUELA	23	88	32[‡]	25[‡]	40[+]	38[+]	30[+]
	UNITED STATES	3,690	4,556	4,056	4,671	4,789	3,448	5,263

a. For prior years see previous issues of SALA.

SOURCE: FAO-PY, 1971, table 80; 1976–81, table 37; 1984 and 1985, table 45; 1986, 1987, table 46.

Table 2111

MAIZE PRODUCTION, 20 LC, 1982–87[a]

(Area = T Ha.; Production = T MET; Yield = kg/Ha.)

	Country	1982 Area[1]	1982 Production	1982 Yield[2]	1985 Area[1]	1985 Production	1985 Yield[2]	1986 Area[1]	1986 Production	1986 Yield[2]	1987 Area[1]	1987 Production	1987 Yield[2]
A.	ARGENTINA	3,170	9,600	3,028	3,190	11,530	3,614	3,351	12,400	3,700	2,900[‡]	9,250	3,190
B.	BOLIVIA	286	450	1,572	349	554	1,588	294	457	1,555	329	543	1,651
C.	BRAZIL	12,620	21,842	1,731	11,802	22,020	1,866	12,465	20,510	1,645	13,511	26,824	1,985
D.	CHILE	115	425	3,696	131	772	5,913	105	721	6,886	87	617	7,121
E.	COLOMBIA	636	899	1,413	541	763	1,411	592	788	1,332	626	888	1,418
F.	COSTA RICA	54	85	1,579	69	125	1,802	62	104[‡]	1,691	75	113	1,518
G.	CUBA	77[†]	96[†]	1,247	77[†]	95[‡]	1,234	77[‡]	95[‡]	1,234	77[†]	95[†]	1,234
H.	DOMINICAN REP.	21	28	1,299	38	62	1,628	32	47	1,487	31	52	1,709
I.	ECUADOR	217	324	1,496	255	381	1,490	250[‡]	309	1,235	203[‡]	330[‡]	1,625
J.	EL SALVADOR	239	414	1,734	253	495	1,954	257	391	1,519	279	572	2,051
K.	GUATEMALA	669	1,100	1,645	660	1,073	1,627	687[‡]	1,106	1,610	610[‡]	920[‡]	1,508
L.	HAITI	186	176[‡]	945	100[‡]	110[‡]	1,100	175[‡]	160[‡]	914	200[‡]	190[‡]	950
M.	HONDURAS	272	366	1,345	285	424	1,487	345	484	1,402	284	438	1,543
N.	MEXICO	5,704	10,030	1,759	7,498	13,957	1,861	6,818	12,154	1,783	8,387	10,988	1,310
O.	NICARAGUA	164	164	997	161	234	1,452	211	264	1,250	191	277	1,448
P.	PANAMA	69	62	900	79	96	1,210	70[‡]	75[‡]	1,071	94[‡]	90[‡]	957
Q.	PARAGUAY	420	510	1,214	470	801	1,702	376	469	1,245	547	917	1,677
R.	PERU	218	631	2,900	365	698	1,912	418	864	2,066	460	919	1,998
S.	URUGUAY	95	97	1,025	89	108	1,207	76	92	1,200	88	104	1,185
T.	VENEZUELA	305	501	1,643	467	868	1,861	510[‡]	1,300[‡]	2,549	660[†]	1,200[‡]	1,818
	UNITED STATES	29,428	209,180	7,108	30,442	225,478	7,407	28,000	209,632	7,487	23,944	179,437	7,494

1. Area harvested.
2. Yield may not equal kg/Ha. due to rounding of area and production data.

a. For prior years see previous issues of SALA.

SOURCE: FAO-PY, 1984 and 1985, table 19; 1986, 1987, table 20.

Table 2112

ORANGE AND TANGERINE PRODUCTION, 20 LC, 1970–87[a]

(T MET)

	Country	1970	1975	1980	1984	1985	1986[b]	1987[b]
A.	ARGENTINA	1,092	959	918	805‡	850‡	560‡	700‡
B.	BOLIVIA	68	87	109	120†	63†	40	69
C.	BRAZIL	3,343	6,643†	9,327‡	13,902‡	14,649†	13,327	14,978
D.	CHILE[1]	42‡	43	49‡	69	76	73	76
E.	COLOMBIA[1]	..	..	225‡	253‡	260‡	233	252
F.	COSTA RICA[1]	59	68†	75†	78†	80†	81†	82†
G.	CUBA	138	142	328	395	433‡	447	460†
H.	DOMINICAN REP.[1]	60†	68†	71	75†	75†	55†	55†
I.	ECUADOR	197†	303	564	380†	380†	69	80†
J.	EL SALVADOR[2]	41	45†	101†	102†	100†	102	102
K.	GUATEMALA	~	~	~	~	~	~	~
L.	HAITI	6†,b	32†	38†	41†	41†	32†	33†
M.	HONDURAS[1]	48	25†	27†	47†	47†	47†	49†
N.	MEXICO	1,555b	2,478‡	1,810‡	1,730†	2,123†	1,909	2,200†
O.	NICARAGUA[1]	45	50†	52†	55†	55†	55†	56†
P.	PANAMA[1]	42	62	66	34	34	36	36†
Q.	PARAGUAY	225†	154†	272†	283‡	289†	352	374†
R.	PERU	261	241†	170†	177†	169†	147†	147†
S.	URUGUAY	59b	77†	85‡	80	103†	62	66†
T.	VENEZUELA[1]	184	245	433	362	370‡	384‡	392‡
	UNITED STATES	7,761	9,913	11,490	7,012	6,501	6,792	7,019

1. Oranges only.
2. Includes tangerines beginning in 1982.

a. For prior years see previous issues of SALA.
b. Oranges only.

SOURCE: FAO-PY, 1971, table 65; 1976–77 and 1979–81, table 62; 1985, table 70; 1986, 1987, table 71.

Table 2113

POTATO PRODUCTION, 20 LC, 1982–87[a]

(Area = T Ha.; Production = T MET; Yield = kg/Ha.)

	Country	1982			1985			1986			1987		
		Area[1]	Production	Yield[2]	Area[1]	Production	Yield[2]	Area[1]	Production	Yield[2]	Area[1]	Production	Yield[2]
A.	ARGENTINA	102	1,817	17,775	114†	2,000†	17,544	114†	2,100†	18,421	114†	2,147†	18,834
B.	BOLIVIA	159	900	5,648	198	721	3,635	144	697	4,827	125	598	4,784
C.	BRAZIL	183	2,155	11,807	157	1,989	12,641	161	1,834	11,405	177	2,341	13,238
D.	CHILE	77	842	10,871	63	909	14,453	53	792	15,039	58	727	12,599
E.	COLOMBIA	165	2,149	13,008	139	1,910	13,734	156	2,091	13,408	162	2,355	14,575
F.	COSTA RICA	3†	22	7,097	3	39	14,502	3†	40†	14,889	3†	40†	14,107
G.	CUBA	15	258	17,035	15	307	20,621	15†	310†	20,667	15†	310†	20,667
H.	DOMINICAN REP.	1	12	10,632	1	11	13,427	1†	12†	12,000	1	15	11,231
I.	ECUADOR	35	416	11,863	37	423	11,567	33†	512	15,515	38‡	389	10,228
J.	EL SALVADOR	~	6†	19,375	~	7†	18,571	~	7†	19,444	~	2†	9,500
K.	GUATEMALA	6‡	28‡	4,667	9†	42†	4,667	9†	43†	4,778	9†	43†	4,778
L.	HAITI	1†	9†	15,000	1†	10†	16,667	1†	10†	16,667	1†	10†	16,777
M.	HONDURAS	1	8	11,571	1†	11†	12,651	1†	10†	12,500	1†	12†	12,632
N.	MEXICO	68	941	13,842	71†	950†	13,380	71†	950†	13,380	71†	950†	13,380
O.	NICARAGUA	~	2†	4,268	2	23	14,241	1	22	15,270	1†	22†	15,379
P.	PANAMA	2‡	17	11,545	2†	20	10,189	2†	20†	10,000	2†	22†	10,381
Q.	PARAGUAY	1†	9‡	9,000	1	6	6,502	1	6	6,219	1	8	6,833
R.	PERU	217	1,800	8,296	188	1,590	8,451	192	1,687	8,779	212	1,680	7,925
S.	URUGUAY	21	149	7,075	22	163	7,499	16	96†	6,000	15†	126	8,320
T.	VENEZUELA	17	217	12,799	14†	191†	13,643	18†	250†	13,889	15†	195†	13,265
	UNITED STATES	516	16,109	31,248	551	18,466	33,526	492	16,078	32,692	519	17,498	33,271

1. Area harvest.
2. Yield may not equal kg/Ha. due to rounding of area and production data.

a. For prior years see previous issues of SALA.

SOURCE: FAO-PY, 1984 and 1985, table 25; 1986, 1987, table 26.

Table 2114

RICE PADDY PRODUCTION, 20 LC, 1982–87[a]

(Area = T Ha.; Production = T MET; Yield = kg/Ha.)

	Country	1982 Area[1]	1982 Production	1982 Yield[2]	1985 Area[1]	1985 Production	1985 Yield[2]	1986 Area[1]	1986 Production	1986 Yield[2]	1987 Area[1]	1987 Production	1987 Yield[2]
A.	ARGENTINA	114	437	3,849	112	410	3,661	109	405	3,716	119	445	3,739
B.	BOLIVIA	54	87	1,596	120	184	1,540	92	137	1,484	90	130	1,444
C.	BRAZIL	6,025	9,735	1,616	4,760	9,019	1,895	5,590	10,399	1,860	6,015	10,460	1,739
D.	CHILE	37	131	3,549	39	157	4,066	32	127	3,956	37	147	3,945
E.	COLOMBIA	446	2,018	4,526	386	1,798	4,654	333	1,632	4,905	389	1,879	4,833
F.	COSTA RICA	77	146	1,896	71	229	3,229	60	186	3,122	40	133	3,312
G.	CUBA	143	520	3,632	159	3,294	3,294	155[†]	540[†]	3,484	153	466	3,040
H.	DOMINICAN REP.	93	447	4,809	110	494	4,476	97	298	3,055	110	462[‡]	4,204
I.	ECUADOR	132	384	2,918	150	397	2,651	170[†]	393[†]	2,312	140[‡]	417[‡]	2,979
J.	EL SALVADOR	11	35	3,166	17	69	3,988	14	53	3,848	12	42	3,602
K.	GUATEMALA	17	49	2,823	15	38	2,597	14	36	2,550	15[‡]	48[‡]	3,200
L.	HAITI	50[‡]	116[‡]	2,316	35[‡]	165[‡]	4,714	35[‡]	180[†]	5,143	35[†]	180[†]	5,143
M.	HONDURAS	23	38	1,641	15	45	2,972	14	34	2,508	19	49	2,528
N.	MEXICO	156	511	3,270	279	809	2,896	151	523	3,456	181	584	3,227
O.	NICARAGUA	43	176	4,137	41	156	3,813	37	124	3,386	28[†]	104	3,714
P.	PANAMA	106	176	1,662	91	186	2,057	100[‡]	172	1,720	83[‡]	166[‡]	2,000
Q.	PARAGUAY	26	54	2,113	39	96	2,468	31	77[†]	2,484	42	24	586
R.	PERU	169	776	4,578	206	919	4,462	169	745	4,414	235	1,187	5,051
S.	URUGUAY	69	419	6,031	85	423	4,984	85	421	4,965	83[‡]	354[‡]	4,267
T.	VENEZUELA	227	609	2,676	181	472	2,610	124	322	2,590	125	300	2,397
	UNITED STATES	1,320	6,969	5,279	1,009	6,120	6,068	963	6,097	6,330	943	5,793	6,143

1. Area harvested.
2. Yield may not equal kg/Ha. due to rounding of area and production data.

a. For prior years see previous issues of SALA.

SOURCE: FAO-PY, 1984, 1985 and 1986, 1987, table 17.

Table 2115

SUGAR CANE PRODUCTION, 19 LC, 1982–87[a]

(Area = T Ha.; Production = T MET; Yield = kg/Ha.)

	Country	1982 Area[1]	1982 Production	1982 Yield[2]	1985 Area[1]	1985 Production	1985 Yield[2]	1986 Area[1]	1986 Production	1986 Yield[2]	1987 Area[1]	1987 Production	1987 Yield[2]
A.	ARGENTINA	309	15,046	48,771	285	14,300	50,228	300[†]	14,000[‡]	46,667	300[†]	14,000[†]	46,667
B.	BOLIVIA	70	3,103	44,540	78	3,158	40,632	46[†]	1,850[†]	40,217	70	2,730	39,000
C.	BRAZIL	3,084	186,647	60,515	3,900	246,542	63,223	4,055	249,277	61,479	4,323	273,855	63,346
E.	COLOMBIA	274	23,500[†]	85,735	312	25,500	81,836	329	25,000[†]	76,104	340	24,965	73,409
F.	COSTA RICA	51[‡]	2,446	47,965	45	2,950	65,546	40	2,650[†]	66,250	40	3,000	75,000
G.	CUBA	1,327	73,100	55,074	1,346	67,300	49,996	1,350	67,000	49,630	1,500[‡]	65,600[†]	43,733
H.	DOMINCAN REP.	188[‡]	11,805	62,793	175[‡]	8,217	46,954	148[†]	7,300[†]	49,324	170[‡]	8,600[‡]	50,588
I.	ECUADOR	92	5,421	58,757	87	4,995	57,282	87[†]	5,500[†]	63,218	90[†]	5,200[†]	57,778
J.	EL SALVADOR	32	2,372	74,803	39	3,262	84,409	42	3,175	75,598	42	3,179	75,698
K.	GUATEMALA	78[‡]	6,080[‡]	77,949	94[‡]	7,000[†]	74,468	100[‡]	7,000[‡]	66,667	108[‡]	6,900[‡]	63,889
L.	HAITI	80[†]	3,000[‡]	37,500	85[†]	3,150[†]	37,059	85[†]	3,150[†]	37,059	85[†]	3,000[†]	35,294
M.	HONDURAS	95[†]	3,096	32,585	95[†]	3,181	33,480	100[†]	3,200[†]	32,000	42[†]	3,000[†]	71,429
N.	MEXICO	526	34,066	64,766	540[‡]	38,100[‡]	70,556	555[‡]	38,900[‡]	70,090	560[‡]	42,560[‡]	76,000
O.	NICARAGUA	44	2,827	64,053	46	2,831	60,916	46	2,810	61,185	39	2,575	65,676
P.	PANAMA	50	2,094	41,512	35	2,006	57,843	34	1,800[‡]	53,270	31	1,600[‡]	51,948
Q.	PARAGUAY	40	1,500	37,500	35[†]	1,500[†]	42,857	27	1,296	48,000	65	3,188	49,042
R.	PERU	46	6,509	140,481	53	7,329	137,925	50[‡]	6,755	134,206	52[‡]	5,950[‡]	114,423
S.	URUGUAY	10	480	47,241	11	586	55,808	11[‡]	640[‡]	58,182	11[†]	650[†]	61,905
T.	VENEZUELA	81	5,372	66,407	96[‡]	6,051[‡]	63,031	102[‡]	6,535[‡]	64,069	130[‡]	7,000[†]	53,846
	UNITED STATES	300	27,002	89,978	312	25,594	82,138	322	27,053	83,989	335	27,032	80,693

1. Area harvested.
2. Yield may not equal kg/Ha. due to rounding of area and production data.

a. For prior years see previous issues of SALA.

SOURCE: FAO-PY, 1984 and 1985, table 66; 1986, 1987, table 67.

Table 2116

TOBACCO LEAF PRODUCTION, 20 LC, 1982–87[a]

(Area = T Ha.; Production = T MET; Yield = kg/Ha.)

	Country	1982 Area[1]	Production	Yield[2]	1985 Area[1]	Production	Yield[2]	1986 Area[1]	Production	Yield[2]	1987 Area[1]	Production	Yield[2]
A.	ARGENTINA	55	69	1,245	58	61	1,043	50†	66†	1,319	53‡	73‡	1,377
B.	BOLIVIA	2‡	2‡	1,000	1†	1†	1,000	1‡	1‡	909	1†	1†	909
C.	BRAZIL	317	420	1,325	269	411	1,530	280	386	1,385	299	401	1,339
D.	CHILE	2‡	6‡	2,900	3	8	2,795	3	8	2,984	3	9‡	3,205
E.	COLOMBIA	26†	41	1,569	18	28	1,538	19	29	1,549	21	35	1,673
F.	COSTA RICA	1	2	1,392	2	2	1,452	1	2	1,766	1‡	2‡	1,766
G.	CUBA	65	45	696	62	45	717	55†	46†	909	55‡	50‡	909
H.	DOMINICAN REP.	35‡	34	963	20	21	1,029	12	26	2,182	13	27‡	2,158
I.	ECUADOR	2	3	1,890	2	3	1,431	2†	4†	2,139	2‡	4‡	2,141
J.	EL SALVADOR	2	4	1,781	1†	1†	1,820	1†	1†	1,943	1	1	1,874
K.	GUATEMALA	5‡	10‡	1,877	6†	9‡	1,399	6†	7†	1,181	6‡	8‡	1,181
L.	HAITI	1‡	1‡	941	1‡	1‡	1,250	1‡	1‡	1,250	1†	1†	1,251
M.	HONDURAS	10	7	745	10	8	753	7‡	5†	754	5†	4‡	747
N.	MEXICO	39	67	1,709	35†	54†	1,554	48†	76†	1,564	31‡	58‡	1,900
O.	NICARAGUA	2	3	1,776	2	4	1,782	3	5	1,811	2	4	1,875
P.	PANAMA	1	2	1,542	1	1	1,864	1†	1†	1,667	1†	2†	1,667
Q.	PARAGUAY	9	12‡	1,333	16	25	1,579	14	18	1,243	16	25	1,567
R.	PERU	3‡	4‡	1,404	3†	3†	1,240	3†	3†	1,240	3†	3†	1,240
S.	URUGUAY	1‡	1‡	1,649	1†	1†	1,750	1†	1†	1,787	1†	1†	1,750
T.	VENEZUELA	10	16	1,598	8†	14†	1,804	8†	14†	1,808	8‡	15‡	1,876
	UNITED STATES	369	905	2,449	278	686	2,463	242	544	2,249	244	559	2,291

1. Area harvested.
2. Yield may not equal kg/Ha. due to rounding of area and production data.

a. For prior years see previous issues of SALA.

SOURCE: FAO-PY, 1984 and 1985, table 81; 1986, 1987, table 82.

Table 2117

WHEAT PRODUCTION, 13 LC, 1982–87[a]

(Area = T Ha.; Production = T MET; Yield = kg/Ha.)

	Country	1982 Area[1]	Production	Yield[2]	1985 Area[1]	Production	Yield[2]	1986 Area[1]	Production	Yield[2]	1987 Area[1]	Production	Yield[2]
A.	ARGENTINA	7,320	15,000	2,049	5,382	8,700	1,617	4,900	8,900	1,816	4,950‡	10,100‡	2,040
B.	BOLIVIA	96	66	684	93	68	727	106	81	765	110	80	727
C.	BRAZIL	2,828	1,827	646	2,670	4,323	1,619	3,908	5,433	1,390	3,422	5,709	1,668
D.	CHILE	374	650	1,739	506	1,165	2,301	569	1,626	2,856	677	1,874	2,770
E.	COLOMBIA	45	71	1,561	45	76	1,710	46	82	1,768	40	69	1,728
I.	ECUADOR	33	39	1,166	18	18	1,019	20	24	1,196	26‡	20‡	769
K.	GUATEMALA	37	49	1,303	31†	44‡	1,419	32‡	53†	1,656	27‡	46‡	1,704
M.	HONDURAS	1	1	636	1†	1†	682	1†	1†	691	1†	1†	727
N.	MEXICO	1,013	4,468	4,409	1,224	5,207	4,254	1,206	4,772	3,957	1,042	4,409	4,231
Q.	PARAGUAY	60	65	1,083	134	187	1,388	170	253	1,487	180†	270†	1,500
R.	PERU	84	101	1,195	81	92	1,141	98	121	1,235	101	124	1,228
S.	URUGUAY	240	363	1,512	212	246	1,163	188	234	1,247	200‡	350‡	1,750
T.	VENEZUELA	1	~	373	1	~	384	1†	~	500	1‡	1‡	500
	UNITED STATES	31,540	75,251	2,386	26,197	65,992	2,519	24,560	56,792	2,312	22,634	57,295	2,531

1. Area harvested.
2. Yield may not equal kg/Ha. due to rounding of area and production data.

a. For prior years see previous issues of SALA.

SOURCE: FAO-PY, 1984, 1985, and 1986, 1987, table 16.

Table 2118

SWEET POTATO AND YAM PRODUCTION, 17 LC, 1982-87[a]

(Area = T Ha.; Production = T MET; Yield = kg/Ha.)

	Country	1982 Area[1]	1982 Production	1982 Yield[2]	1985 Area[1]	1985 Production	1985 Yield[2]	1986 Area[1]	1986 Production	1986 Yield[2]	1987 Area[1]	1987 Production	1987 Yield[2]
A.	ARGENTINA[3]	32	368	11,536	32	377	11,028	32	149	14,028	32[†]	420[†]	13,075
B.	BOLIVIA[3]	2	9	5,714	2	7	3,813	2[‡]	7[‡]	3,789	2	10	4,000
C.	BRAZIL[4]	103[†]	931[†]	18,075	114[‡]	1,040[‡]	18,322	110	1,000	18,182	111[†]	1,007[†]	18,183
D.	CHILE[3]	1[†]	7[†]	7,000	1[†]	7[†]	7,000	1[†]	7[†]	7,000	1[†]	7[†]	7,000
E.	COLOMBIA[5]	13	96	7,385	13	95	7,550	12	93	7,952	14	122	8,952
G.	CUBA[3]	82[†]	330[†]	4,024	83[†]	330[‡]	4,000	83[‡]	350[‡]	4,217	84[†]	350[†]	4,167
H.	DOMINICAN REP.[4]	5	24	10,826	9	53	19,180	7	40	29,714	8	91[†]	28,236
I.	ECUADOR[3]	1	5	5,441	1	7	4,736	1[‡]	7[‡]	4,828	2[†]	8[†]	5,000
J.	EL SALVADOR[3]	~	~	5,000	~	~	5,000	~	~	5,000	~	~	5,000
L.	HAITI[4]	100[†]	428[†]	8,101	106[†]	485[‡]	8,615	108[‡]	485[‡]	9,432	113[†]	515[†]	8,620
M.	HONDURAS[3]	~	1	3,560	~	2[‡]	3,478	~	2[‡]	3,478	~	2[†]	3,419
N.	MEXICO[3]	3	51	15,969	3[‡]	50[‡]	16,667	3[‡]	50[‡]	16,667	3[†]	50[†]	16,667
P.	PANAMA[5]	2[†]	11	5,728	2[†]	20	10,135	2[‡]	19[‡]	9,500	2[†]	22[†]	10,900
Q.	PARAGUAY[3]	15[†]	119[‡]	7,933	13	102	7,870	11	88	7,850	14	111	7,829
R.	PERU[3]	7	93	13,640	7	100	14,827	14	150	11,126	8	124	15,500
S.	URUGUAY[3]	15[‡]	60[‡]	4,000	15[†]	60[†]	4,000	15[†]	60[†]	4,000	15[†]	60[†]	4,027
T.	VENEZUELA[4]	6	34	8,725	8[‡]	40[†]	10,305	8[‡]	40[‡]	10,256	8[†]	42[†]	10,208
	UNITED STATES[3]	47	673	14,407	43	674	15,815	38	579	15,144	38	549	14,524

1. Area harvested.
2. Yield may not equal kg/Ha. due to rounding of area and production data.
3. Sweet potatoes only.
4. Sweet potatoes and yams.
5. Yams only.

a. For prior years see previous issues of SALA.

SOURCE: FAO-PY, 1984 and 1985, tables 26 and 28; 1986, 1987, tables 27 and 29.

Table 2119

FERTILIZER PRODUCTION,[1] 13 LC, 1970-87[a]

(T MET)

	Country	1970/71	1979	1980	1981	1982	1983	1984	1985	1986/87
A.	ARGENTINA	35	26	31	25	29[‡]	32	28	30	32
B.	BRAZIL	225	1,541	1,967	1,536	1,512	1,569	2,090	2,005	2,248[‡]
D.	CHILE	140	105	112	100	92	98	117	117	112
E.	COLOMBIA	88	102	88[‡]	92[‡]	79[‡]	90	100	81	106
F.	COSTA RICA	12	36[‡]	40[‡]	42[‡]	46[‡]	36[‡]	41[‡]	27[‡]	32[‡]
G.	CUBA	5	139	117	148	100	94	185	195	180
I.	ECUADOR	6[‡]	10	9[‡]	10[‡]	13[‡]	~	~	~	~
J.	EL SALVADOR	10[‡]	17[‡]	~	~	~	~	~	~	~
K.	GUATEMALA	~	4[‡]	17[‡]	16[‡]	23[‡]	17[‡]	19[‡]	20[‡]	20[‡]
N.	MEXICO	580	869	940	1,114	1,320	1,303	1,420	1,573	1,490
R.	PERU	26[‡]	71	78	90	77	30	20	14	35
S.	URUGUAY	27	41	30[‡]	20[‡]	17[‡]	6[‡]	10[‡]	14	29[‡]
T.	VENEZUELA	18	105	168[‡]	179	247[‡]	246[‡]	308[‡]	334	384
	UNITED STATES	15,789	22,508	23,377	19,250	17,983	19,620	22,328	18,195	18,894
	WORLD	72,945	118,727	124,735	119,625	119,939	130,781	139,739	136,186	140,778

1. Includes nitrogenous, phosphate, and potash fertilizers.

a. For 1961-70 data, see SALA, 23-1521; for 1971-79 data, see SALA, 27-2119.

SOURCE: FAO-FY, 1979 and 1981, table 30; 1985, 1986, 1987, table 29.

22
Ranch Production

Table 2200

CATTLE POPULATION, 20 LRC, 1947–87[a]

(T)

	Country	Average 1947/48– 1951/52	Average 1961-65	1975	1980	1982	1984	1985	1986	1987
A.	ARGENTINA	42,320[†]	43,096	59,600[‡]	55,761	52,717	54,594	54,000[‡]	57,485[‡]	55,684[‡]
B.	BOLIVIA	1,450[c]	1,930	2,877	4,000[‡]	4,100[†]	5,985	5,515	5,300	5,380
C.	BRAZIL	51,305	59,770	92,480[‡]	91,000[‡]	93,000[‡]	127,655	128,423	128,918	131,503[‡]
D.	CHILE	2,293	2,850	3,606	3,664	3,800	3,650	3,400	3,500	3,580
E.	COLOMBIA	13,750	16,281	23,888[‡]	23,945	24,499	22,441[†]	23,271	23,593	23,971
F.	COSTA RICA	601	1,074	1,843	2,181	2,276	2,429[†]	2,509[‡]	2,415[‡]	2,360[†]
G.	CUBA	4,333[‡]	5,591	5,450[†]	5,900[†]	6,200[†]	6,100[‡]	5,115	5,020	5,007
H.	DOMINICAN REP.	711	899	1,900	2,153[‡]	1,949	2,020	1,922	2,055	2,058[‡]
I.	ECUADOR	1,467[e]	1,816	2,800	2,916	3,200[†]	3,456	3,578	3,765	3,847[‡]
J.	EL SALVADOR	795	1,158	1,031	1,440	1,055	937	980	1,050	1,024[‡]
K.	GUATEMALA	977[d]	1,216	2,148[‡]	1,653	2,280[‡]	2,224	2,254[‡]	2,284[‡]	2,300[†]
L.	HAITI	582[b]	685	742[†]	1,100[‡]	1,200[‡]	1,350[†]	1,350[†]	1,400[†]	1,474[†]
M.	HONDURAS	884	1,447	1,689[†]	2,262	2,499	2,695[†]	2,770[‡]	2,803[‡]	2,859[‡]
N.	MEXICO	12,980	20,658	27,863	31,094	36,839	30,374	31,489	31,123[‡]	31,156[‡]
O.	NICARAGUA	1,068	1,672	2,500[‡]	2,401[‡]	2,379	2,344	2,369	2,100[‡]	2,100[†]
P.	PANAMA	567	860	1,348	1,525[‡]	1,456	1,452	1,447	1,430	1,490[†]
Q.	PARAGUAY	4,600[‡]	5,348	4,836	5,300[†]	5,152	6,795	6,956	7,151	7,332
R.	PERU	2,830	3,358	4,200[‡]	3,837	4,152	4,031	3,980	3,820	3,850
S.	URUGUAY	7,981	8,630	11,362[†]	10,952	10,959	9,062	9,629	9,961[‡]	10,323[‡]
T.	VENEZUELA	5,768	6,769	9,089	10,607	9,112	11,844[†]	12,083	12,331[‡]	12,654[‡]
	LATIN AMERICA	157,262	185,468	261,252	263,691	267,188	302,942	303,040	307,504	309,952
	UNITED STATES	80,569	103,785	131,826	111,192	115,604	113,700	109,749	105,468	102,000

a. For intervening years see previous issues of SALA.
b. 1950/51.
c. 1949/50.
d. Four-year average.
e. Three-year average.

SOURCE: FAO-PY, 1971, table 107; FAO-PY, 1976–81, table 80; FAO-PY, 1983–85, table 88; 1986, table 89; 1987, table 89.

Table 2201

HORSE POPULATION, 20 LRC, 1947–87[a]

(T)

Country	Average 1947/48– 1951/52	Average 1961-65	1975	1980	1982	1984	1985	1986	1987
A. ARGENTINA	7,265[c]	3,696	3,400[‡]	3,000[‡]	3,000	2,970[†]	3,000[‡]	3,000[‡]	3,000[‡]
B. BOLIVIA	158[d]	197	340[†]	400[†]	410[†]	293	311	311[†]	311[†]
C. BRAZIL	6,942[e]	8,693	5,215	6,300[‡]	5,100[†]	5,442	6,330	6,500[†]	6,800[†]
D. CHILE	523[d]	503	450[‡]	450[‡]	430[†]	480[‡]	490[†]	490[†]	490[†]
E. COLOMBIA	1,208[b]	937	1,435	1,696	1,710[‡]	1,815[†]	1,906[‡]	1,950[†]	1,950[†]
F. COSTA RICA	76[b]	100	112[‡]	113	113[†]	113[†]	113[†]	114[†]	114[†]
G. CUBA	410[d]	488	804	812	820	759	759	740	718
H. DOMINICAN REP.	137	213	201[‡]	204[‡]	204[‡]	204[†]	204[†]	205[†]	205[†]
I. ECUADOR	111[d]	218	285[†]	314	322	331	337	340[†]	345[†]
J. EL SALVADOR	130[d]	73	81[†]	88[‡]	89[†]	90[‡]	92[†]	92[†]	93[†]
K. GUATEMALA	166[b]	159	125[†]	100[†]	100[†]	100[‡]	100[†]	100[†]	100[†]
L. HAITI	253[e]	282	379[†]	410[†]	420[†]	425[‡]	425[†]	425[†]	425[†]
M. HONDURAS	178[b]	262	278[†]	150[†]	152[†]	168[‡]	169[†]	170[†]	170[†]
N. MEXICO	3,181[e]	4,323	6,376	6,300	5,635[†]	6,134	6,135[†]	6,135[†]	6,135[†]
O. NICARAGUA	150[d]	172	164[†]	275[‡]	275[†]	270[‡]	270[†]	270[†]	270[†]
P. PANAMA	138[d]	162	164[†]	165[†]	166[†]	168[‡]	169[†]	170[†]	171[†]
Q. PARAGUAY	302[e]	555	325	330[†]	330[†]	313	314	317	317[†]
R. PERU	496	579	637[‡]	650[‡]	653[‡]	655[‡]	655[†]	655[†]	655[†]
S. URUGUAY	667[c]	473	470[†]	530[‡]	495	469	464	500[†]	500[†]
T. VENEZUELA	344[c]	402	454	478[‡]	481[‡]	491[†]	495[‡]	495[†]	495[†]
LATIN AMERICA	22,835	22,490	21,695	22,765	20,905	21,732	22,738	22,979	23,264
UNITED STATES	7,757	4,579	8,600[†]	9,662[†]	10,155[†]	10,500[‡]	10,580[†]	10,600[†]	10,600[†]

a. For intervening years see previous issues of SALA.
b. Three-year average.
c. 1950/51.
d. Two-year average.
e. Four-year average.

SOURCE: FAO-PY, 1971, table 106; FAO-PY, 1976-81, table 79; FAO-PY, 1983–85, table 87; 1986, table 88; 1987, table 88.

Table 2202

SHEEP POPULATION, 19 LRC, 1947–87[a]

(T)

	Country	Average 1947/48– 1951/52	Average 1961-65	1975	1980	1982	1984	1985	1986	1987
A.	ARGENTINA	52,940[t]	48,023	34,000[‡]	33,000	30,401	33,800[t]	29,441[‡]	29,243[‡]	28,998[‡]
B.	BOLIVIA	7,224[c]	6,136	7,694	8,750[‡]	9,200[‡]	9,287	9,413	9,500[t]	9,500[t]
C.	BRAZIL	14,427	19,996	17,400[‡]	18,000[‡]	18,000	18,447	18,356	18,473[‡]	19,200[‡]
D.	CHILE	5,789	6,356	5,644	6,064	6,000	6,000	5,800	5,980	6,050
E.	COLOMBIA	1,153[d]	1,506	1,921	2,413	2,249	2,689[t]	2,500	2,568	2,652
F.	COSTA RICA	1[t]	1	2[t]	2[t]	3[t]	3[‡]	6[t]	6[t]	6[t]
G.	CUBA	177[t]	229	330[t]	355[t]	365[t]	375[‡]	378[t]	380[t]	382[t]
H.	DOMINICAN REP.	27	38	50[t]	54[t]	55[t]	78[‡]	80[t]	80[t]	84[t]
I.	ECUADOR	1,720[e]	1,699	2,105	2,980	2,391[t]	2,311	2,086[‡]	2,050[t]	2,100[t]
J.	EL SALVADOR	5[f]	3	4[‡]	4[‡]	4[t]	4[‡]	4[t]	5[t]	5[t]
K.	GUATEMALA	735[d]	743	540[‡]	679	500[‡]	660[‡]	670[t]	680[t]	690[t]
L.	HAITI	52[b]	58	79[t]	89[t]	91[t]	92[‡]	92[t]	92[t]	93[t]
M.	HONDURAS	8	8	5[‡]	5[‡]	5[t]	6[‡]	6[‡]	7[‡]	7[‡]
N.	MEXICO	5,041	5,886	7,825	7,318	6,657[t]	6,120	6,373	5,699	5,800[t]
O.	NICARAGUA	1[t]	1	2[‡]	3[‡]	3[t]	3[‡]	3[t]	3[t]	3[t]
Q.	PARAGUAY	207	413	366	430[t]	435[t]	372	378	388	398
R.	PERU	17,515	14,311	15,400	14,473	14,500[t]	12,717	13,800	13,500[‡]	13,500[‡]
S.	URUGUAY	21,935	21,818	15,062[‡]	20,034	20,307[t]	20,738	21,195	23,858	25,560
T.	VENEZUELA	101[b]	88	101	306[‡]	382[‡]	365[t]	422[‡]	422[t]	422[t]
	LATIN AMERICA	46,545	54,166	67,977	73,868	111,498	115,169	111,003	112,934	115,450
	UNITED STATES	31,565	29,144	14,515	12,687	12,966	11,487	10,443	9,983	10,334

a. For intervening years see previous issues of SALA.
b. 1950/51.
c. 1949/50.
d. Four-year average.
e. Three-year average.
f. Two-year average.

SOURCE: FAO-PY, 1971, table 110; FAO-PY, 1976-82, table 81; FAO-PY, 1983–85,
    table 89; 1986, 1987, table 90.

Table 2203

SWINE POPULATION, 20 LRC, 1947–87[a]

(T)

Country	Average 1947/48– 1951/52	Average 1961-65	1975	1980	1982	1984	1985	1986	1987
A. ARGENTINA	3,250	3,476	4,200[‡]	3,800	3,900[‡]	3,800[†]	3,800[‡]	4,000[‡]	4,036[†]
B. BOLIVIA	509[c]	650	1,158	1,450[‡]	1,650[†]	1,136	1,725	1,650	1,690
C. BRAZIL	24,879	26,500	34,192	36,500[‡]	33,500[‡]	32,327	32,248	33,000	32,000[‡]
D. CHILE	710	945	701	1,068	1,150	1,070	1,100	1,130	1,150[‡]
E. COLOMBIA	2,368[d]	1,649	1,877	2,078	2,179	2,312	2,381	2,440	2,511
F. COSTA RICA	111[b]	146	225[‡]	223[‡]	243[‡]	223[†]	220[‡]	222[‡]	238[‡]
G. CUBA	1,315[†]	1,296	1,450[†]	1,950[†]	2,000[†]	2,300[‡]	2,400[†]	2,400[†]	2,400[†]
H. DOMINICAN REP.	739	706	700[‡]	250[‡]	85	1,000	1,850	2,500[†]	2,637[†]
I. ECUADOR	547[c]	1,461	2,543	3,549	3,250	3,792	4,049[‡]	4,181[‡]	4,160[‡]
J. EL SALVADOR	335[†]	392	420[‡]	421	400	379	397	411	398
K. GUATEMALA	408[d]	595	659	792	850[†]	806	834	862	865[†]
L. HAITI	1,137[b]	1,264	1,735[†]	1,100[‡]	600[†]	500[‡]	500[†]	700[†]	700[†]
M. HONDURAS	445	748	511[‡]	534	409	491	558[‡]	563[‡]	567[‡]
N. MEXICO	6,340[c]	9,168	11,466	13,222	18,373	19,393	18,579	18,397	18,662[‡]
O. NICARAGUA	243[c]	423	650[‡]	500[‡]	520[‡]	744	745	750[‡]	749[‡]
P. PANAMA	196[b]	201	166	195[‡]	206	195	208	250	205[†]
Q. PARAGUAY	340[d]	635	975	1,300[†]	1,330[†]	1,109	1,278	1,508	1,690
R. PERU	960	1,813	2,135	2,150	2,050[‡]	2,272	2,150	2,170	2,240
S. URUGUAY	259[a]	414	418[‡]	450[‡]	430[‡]	235	200	195	190
T. VENEZUELA	1,454[b]	1,696	1,795	2,230	2,303	2,699	2,935	3,091[‡]	3,351[‡]
LATIN AMERICA	46,545	54,172	67,977	73,768	75,428	77,757	78,157	80,420	80,439
UNITED STATES	58,895	55,610	54,693	67,353	58,688	56,694	54,073	50,920	53,795

a. For intervening years see previous issues of SALA.
b. 1950/51.
c. Two-year average.
d. Four-year average.

SOURCE: FAO-PY, 1971, table 100; FAO-PY, 1976-81, table 81; FAO-PY, 1983-85, table 89; 1986, 1987, table 90.

Table 2204

COW MILK PRODUCTION,[1] 20 LRC, 1948–87

(T MET)

Country	Average 1948-52	Average 1961-65	1970	1975	1980	1985	1986	1987
A. ARGENTINA	3,758	4,294	4,189	5,650	5,307	5,742	6,118	6,296[‡]
B. BOLIVIA	18[†]	23	25[†]	53	57[‡]	95[†]	95[†]	99[†]
C. BRAZIL	2,581	5,870	7,300[‡]	9,971	10,265[‡]	12,580[†]	11,860[†]	12,350[†]
D. CHILE	683	779	950[‡]	986	1,080	1,012	1,092	1,100[‡]
E. COLOMBIA	1,540[†]	1,843	2,250	2,096	2,419	2,816	3,017	3,142
F. COSTA RICA	138[a]	131	242[‡]	259	318	376	414	410
G. CUBA	180[†]	394	300[†]	612	1,188[†]	1,100[†]	1,150[†]	1,150[†]
H. DOMINICAN REP.	140[†]	186	283	320	431	379	337	350[†]
I. ECUADOR	174[b]	376	530[†]	773	758[‡]	988[‡]	989[‡]	1,000[†]
J. EL SALVADOR	107[b]	156	177[†]	235	291	234	242[†]	250[†]
K. GUATEMALA	78[b]	194	262	310[†]	320[†]	370[†]	370[†]	375[†]
L. HAITI	15[†]	23	20[†]	40[†]	19[†]	22[†]	22[†]	22[†]
M. HONDURAS	99	128	175[‡]	180[†]	205[†]	247	260	295[†]
N. MEXICO	1,539	2,305[a]	3,053	4,980	6,750[‡]	7,173	7,250[†]	7,500[†]
O. NICARAGUA	92[†]	158	200[‡]	246[‡]	165[‡]	125[†]	125[†]	125[†]
P. PANAMA	34[b]	56	73	73	95[†]	98	108	109[†]
Q. PARAGUAY	80[a]	81	92[†]	121	165[†]	182	190[†]	194[†]
R. PERU	229[c]	515	825	814[†]	780	809	829	840[†]
S. URUGUAY	449	764	763	745	838[‡]	922	959	980[†]
T. VENEZUELA	203[a]	548	830	1,224	1,318	1,532	1,580	1,593
LATIN AMERICA	12,137	18,824	22,539	29,688	32,769	36,802	37,007	38,180
UNITED STATES	52,349	56,998	53,268	52,314	58,298	65,166	65,354	64,833

1. Intended to represent the total production for consumption fresh or for conversion into dairy products. The figures generally exclude milk sucked by young animals, but include milk fed to them.

a. Three-year average.
b. Two-year average.
c. Four-year average.

SOURCE: FAO-PY, 1971, table 123; FAO-PY, 1973, table 111; FAO-PY, 1976-81, table 90; FAO-PY, 1983-85, table 98; 1986, 1987, table 99.

Table 2205

MILK YIELD PER THOUSAND MILKING COWS PER ANNUM, 20 LC, 1948–87

(kg)

	Country	Average 1948-52	Average 1961-65	1970	1975	1980	1983	1985	1986	1987
A.	ARGENTINA	1,624[†]	1,836	1,920[†]	1,883	1,698	1,897	1,946	2,081	2,179
B.	BOLIVIA	1,760[b]	1,200	~	1,403	1,295	1,418	1,397	1,397	1,414
C.	BRAZIL	502[†]	746	800[†]	767	752	726	710	700	718
D.	CHILE	2,360[†]	1,787	2,720[†]	1,340	1,470	1,324	1,545	1,606	1,618
E.	COLOMBIA	462	707	1,090[†]	937	985	982	955	973	952
F.	COSTA RICA	~	920	1,175[‡]	1,043	1,077	1,168	1,337	1,424	1,367
G.	CUBA	524[c]	733	840[†]	986	1,398	1,459	1,486	1,513	1,513
H.	DOMINICAN REP.	950	917	~	1,391	1,760	2,009	1,522	1,533	1,556
I.	ECUADOR	1,129[d]	1,301	1,300[†]	1,311	1,217	1,376	1,337	1,311	1,316
J.	EL SALVADOR	795[e]	769	850[‡]	925	960	959	778	781	781
K.	GUATEMALA	980	866	900[‡]	912	913	797	925	925	938
L.	HAITI	382	232	~	357	190	233	238	237	238
M.	HONDURAS	380[a]	480	543[‡]	545	606	652	738	801	886
N.	MEXICO	933[†]	948	1,100[†]	1,360	763	815	1,342	1,330	1,339
O.	NICARAGUA	700[‡]	549	550[‡]	654	825	625	625	625	625
P.	PANAMA	610[†]	872	747[†]	910	1,001	977	1,018	1,022	1,023
Q.	PARAGUAY	180[†]	188	220[†]	201	1,919	1,905	1,897	1,900	1,898
R.	PERU	509[†]	1,019	1,320[†]	1,291	1,068	1,140	1,242	1,256	1,273
S.	URUGUAY	1,332[†]	1,397	1,550[†]	1,702	1,612	1,634	1,739	1,776	1,786
T.	VENEZUELA	400[c]	540	720[†]	1,106	1,097	1,090	1,161	1,284	1,259
	UNITED STATES	2,389	3,519	4,258	4,695	5,393	5,709	5,911	6,030	6,214

a. Four-year average.
b. 1950.
c. 1949.
d. Two-year average.
e. 1952.

SOURCE: FAO-PY, 1971, table 123; FAO-PY, 1973, table 111; FAO-PY, 1976-81, table 90; FAO-PY, 1983-85, table 98; 1986, 1987, table 99.

Table 2206

WOOL OUTPUT, 10 LRC, 1974–87[a]

(MT)

	Country	Code[1]	Average 1974-76	1981	1983	1984	1985	1986	1987
A.	ARGENTINA	I	157,000	150,155	155,000[‡]	153,000[†]	140,000	138,000[‡]	136,000[‡]
		II	85,006	95,845	103,500[†]	102,300	95,000	92,000[‡]	92,000[†]
B.	BOLIVIA	I	7,729	9,060[†]	9,200[†]	9,287[‡]	9,413[†]	9,500[†]	9,500[†]
		II	4,100	4,800[†]	5,000[†]	4,900[‡]	5,000[†]	5,100[†]	5,200[†]
C.	BRAZIL	I	31,486	32,636	30,563	29,768	29,100	31,000[†]	32,000[†]
		II	19,833	19,000[‡]	19,000[‡]	19,000[‡]	19,000[†]	19,600[†]	20,000[†]
D.	CHILE	I	18,530	21,400	21,400	21,200[†]	20,300	21,250	20,000[‡]
		II	9,265	10,700	10,700	10,600[†]	10,150	10,600	10,000[‡]
E.	COLOMBIA	I	1,100	1,570[†]	1,500[†]	1,500[‡]	1,600[†]	1,600[†]	1,600[†]
		II	658	940[†]	900[†]	900[‡]	960[†]	960[†]	960[†]
I.	ECUADOR	I	1,627	3,082[‡]	3,300[†]	3,350[‡]	2,920[†]	2,870[†]	2,940[†]
		II	813	1,540[†]	1,600[†]	1,670[‡]	1,460[†]	1,435[†]	1,470[†]
N.	MEXICO	I	7,367	8,600	6,415	6,291	6,583	4,682	5,300[†]
		II	3,684	4,300[†]	3,200	3,145	3,290	2,340	2,650[†]
Q.	PARAGUAY	I	390	470[†]	490[†]	610	630	621	645[†]
		II	208	250[†]	250[†]	320[‡]	320[†]	320[†]	332[†]
R.	PERU	I	11,465	10,000	11,400	11,000	11,300	11,300	12,000[‡]
		II	5,733	5,000	5,500[‡]	5,500[†]	5,650[‡]	5,650[‡]	6,000[‡]
S.	URUGUAY	I	60,530	74,603	82,000	81,676	81,905	87,178	95,000[‡]
		II	33,664	44,000[‡]	47,000[†]	48,000[†]	53,000[‡]	59,000[‡]	61,500[†]
	LATIN AMERICA	I	297,224	311,576	323,546	319,786	303,751	308,001	314,985
		II	162,964	186,375	198,050	197,724	193,830	197,005	200,112
	UNITED STATES	I	56,201	49,754	45,479	43,304	39,900	39,000[‡]	40,000[‡]
		II	30,725	26,270	24,640	23,170	21,350	21,400[†]	21,950[†]

1. Wool Code: I = greasy; II = clean.

a. For previous years since 1948, see SALA, 25-2206.

SOURCE: FAO-PY, 1983–86, table 103; 1987, table 104.

Table 2207

CHICKEN STOCKS, 20 LC, 1980–87

(M)

	Country	1980	1982	1983	1984	1985	1986	1987
A.	ARGENTINA	39	40 [†]	43	42	42[†]	45[†]	46[†]
B.	BOLIVIA	8.5[†]	9.2[†]	10[†]	6	7	8[†]	8[†]
C.	BRAZIL	447.4	448 [†]	451	463[‡]	481	500[†]	520[†]
D.	CHILE	24 [†]	26 [†]	20[†]	18[†]	19[†]	19[†]	19[†]
E.	COLOMBIA	30 [†]	33	34[†]	35[†]	35[†]	35[†]	36[†]
F.	COSTA RICA	5.5	5.5[†]	6[†]	6[†]	6[†]	6[†]	6[†]
G.	CUBA	24.6	26.2[†]	26	27	26	26	26[†]
H.	DOMINICAN REP.	8.2[†]	8.4[†]	9[†]	14[†]	17[†]	17[†]	17[†]
I.	ECUADOR	22.5	24.9[†]	42[†]	33	41	41[†]	42[†]
J.	EL SALVADOR	5.1	5.5[†]	4	4	5	5	5[†]
K.	GUATEMALA	14 [†]	14.5[†]	15[†]	15[†]	15[†]	15[†]	15[†]
L.	HAITI	4.8[†]	5 [†]	7[‡]	8[†]	8[†]	8[†]	8[†]
M.	HONDURAS	4.8[†]	5.1[†]	5[†]	5[†]	5[†]	5[†]	6[†]
N.	MEXICO	162 [†]	164 [†]	194	203	219	210[†]	210[†]
O.	NICARAGUA	4.7[†]	5 [†]	5[†]	5[†]	5[†]	5[†]	6[†]
P.	PANAMA	4.8	5.3[†]	6	6	6	7	8[†]
Q.	PARAGUAY	13 [†]	13.7[†]	14[†]	13	13	15	15[†]
R.	PERU	37 [†]	39 [†]	40[†]	41	41[†]	43[†]	44[†]
S.	URUGUAY	7.7[†]	8.3[†]	6[†]	6	6	7[†]	6[†]
T.	VENEZUELA	40.1	44 [†]	42[†]	48	51	54	54[†]
	UNITED STATES	400.6	392.1[†]	1,077[‡]	1,080[‡]	1,120[‡]	1,115[‡]	1,200[†]

SOURCE: FAO-PY, 1982, table 80; FAO-PY, 1985, table 90; FAO-PY, 1986, 1987, table 91.

Table 2208

HEN EGG PRODUCTION, 20 LC, 1980–87

(MET)

	Country	1980	1982	1983	1984	1985	1986	1987
A.	ARGENTINA	267,512	300,000[†]	272,250	270,000[‡]	274,000[†]	279,000[†]	285,000[†]
B.	BOLIVIA	24,200	25,000[†]	25,500[†]	26,000[‡]	26,000[†]	26,400[†]	27,500[†]
C.	BRAZIL	782,000[‡]	830,000[†]	789,450[‡]	964,185	1,043,667	1,050,000[†]	1,100,000[†]
D.	CHILE	62,832	91,800[‡]	65,342	73,440	75,480	80,430	91,800
E.	COLOMBIA	187,520	187,000[‡]	158,400	163,125	195,050	208,300	226,000
F.	COSTA RICA	16,960	17,000[†]	17,900[‡]	9,800[‡]	10,840[‡]	13,000[‡]	15,568[‡]
G.	CUBA	104,700	106,300[†]	109,368	115,070	113,564	112,970	111,930
H.	DOMINICAN REP.	29,100[†]	32,364[†]	17,286[‡]	16,750[‡]	20,413[‡]	20,821[‡]	21,000[†]
I.	ECUADOR	50,100[‡]	70,560[‡]	50,000[†]	39,561	43,065	41,300	42,000[†]
J.	EL SALVADOR	35,160[‡]	32,400[‡]	35,300[†]	38,452	33,943	36,600	33,980
K.	GUATEMALA	40,000[†]	40,500[†]	40,050[‡]	40,500[†]	41,200[†]	42,150[†]	42,500[†]
L.	HAITI	2,930[†]	3,100[†]	3,250[†]	3,250[†]	3,250[†]	3,750[†]	3,900[†]
M.	HONDURAS	11,300[†]	12,026[†]	21,090[‡]	21,500[†]	21,200[†]	21,200[†]	21,700[†]
N.	MEXICO	603,900[‡]	640,000[‡]	715,259	740,365	826,400	850,000[†]	860,000[†]
O.	NICARAGUA	29,500[†]	30,000[‡]	31,000[†]	31,000[†]	31,000[†]	31,500[†]	31,500[†]
P.	PANAMA	14,197	15,500[†]	18,292	16,740[‡]	19,000[‡]	19,750[‡]	20,500[†]
Q.	PARAGUAY	25,000	26,000[†]	28,000[†]	30,013	31,005	32,519	33,800[†]
R.	PERU	60,000	65,000	68,000	65,100	77,900	95,100	72,500[†]
S.	URUGUAY	17,935	19,000[†]	2,650[†]	18,310	21,047	21,000	22,100[†]
T.	VENEZUELA	124,150	155,650[‡]	138,177	155,919	150,480[‡]	148,000[‡]	153,945[‡]
	UNITED STATES	4,126,560	4,100,000[†]	4,036,880	4,040,490	4,042,330	4,050,440	4,115,230

SOURCE: FAO-PY, 1982, table 100; FAO-PY, 1985, table 102; FAO-PY, 1986, 1987, table 103.

23

Forestry Production

Table 2300

WORLD RANKING OF ANNUAL LOSS OF TROPICAL FORESTS, 14 LC, 1981–85
(T Acres)

Rank	Country	Acres	Rank	Country	Acres	Rank	Country	Acres
1.	BRAZIL	3,656	21.	BOLIVIA	215	41.	Tanzania	24
2.	COLOMBIA	2,025	22.	Nepal	207	42.	Uganda	24
3.	Indonesia	1,482	23.	Cameroon	198	43.	Belize	22
4.	MEXICO	1,470	24.	COSTA RICA	161	44.	Bangladesh	20
5.	Nigeria	741	25.	Vietnam	161	45.	Ethiopia	20
6.	Ivory Coast	716	26.	Sri Lanka	143	46.	Pakistan	17
7.	PERU	667	27.	Liberia	114	47.	Sierra Leone	15
8.	Malaysia	630	28.	Angola	109	48.	Brunei	12
9.	Thailand	622	29.	Zambia	99	49.	Central African	
10.	PARAGUAY	469	30.	Guinea	89		Republic	12
11.	Zaire	450	31.	PANAMA	89	50.	EL SALVADOR	12
12.	Madagascar	370	32.	ECUADOR	84			
13.	India	363	33.	Cambodia	62			
14.	VENEZUELA	309	34.	Congo	54			
15.	NICARAGUA	299	35.	Ghana	54			
16.	Burma	259	36.	Papua New Guinea	54			
17.	Laos	247	37.	Kenya	47			
18.	Philippines	225	38.	Guinea-Bissau	42			
19.	GUATEMALA	222	39.	Gabon	37			
20.	HONDURAS	222	40.	Mozambique	24			

SOURCE: *Los Angeles Times*, June 14, 1987.

Table 2301

YEARLY RATE OF MAJOR DEFORESTATION
AREAS, 7 LC, 1981–85
(%)

Country	%
Ivory Coast	5.9
PARAGUAY	4.6
Nigeria	4.0
COSTA RICA	3.9
Nepal	3.9
HAITI	3.1
EL SALVADOR	2.9
Gambia	2.8
Benin	2.6
Guinea-Bissau	2.6
NICARAGUA	2.7
HONDURAS	2.4
Thailand	2.4
ECUADOR	2.3
Liberia	2.2

SOURCE: *Los Angeles Times*, June 14, 1987.

Table 2302

ESTIMATED FOREST AREA, NATURAL FORESTS, AND INDUSTRIAL PLANTATIONS
(T Ha. 1980)

				Natural Forest			Forest Plantations			
Subregion	Total Land Area	Total Forest Area	% of Land Area	Productive Coniferous	Share Broadleaf	Annual Deforestation	Total Forest Plantation	Industrial Plantations Coniferous	Industrial Plantations Broadleaf	Annual Planting Area
Latin America	2,014,786	719,735	35.7	15,794	531,147	3,983	5,913.6	2,367.5	1,327.3	297.8[a]
MEXICO	197,255	46,250	23.5	11,720	12,580	530	159.0	37.0	35.0	7.8
Central America	50,862	18,679	36.7	2,512	11,682	382	25.4	15.8	9.6	3.9
Caribbean[1]	56,435	44,511	78.9	277	34,960	21	48.8	26.1	16.0	8.1
BRAZIL	851,196	357,480	42.0	280	300,910	1,360	3,855.0	1,232.0	741.0	158.0
Andean	446,311	206,210	46.2	185	142,975	1,535	372.4	181.8	115.6	26.8
Southern Cone	412,727	46,605	11.3	820	28,040	155	1,453.0	874.8	410.1	93.2

1. Includes Suriname, French Guiana, and Guyana. They account for the large share of forest area in this category.

a. Of which 211.0 are softwoods and 86.8 are hardwoods.

SOURCE: IDB-SPTF, 1983, table IV-5.

Table 2303

TOTAL ROUNDWOOD PRODUCTION,[1,2] 20 LRC, 1970–86
(T Me^3)

Country	1970*	1975	1978	1979	1980	1981	1982	1983	1984	1985	1986
A. ARGENTINA	8,915	9,958	10,258	11,493	10,874	10,461	9,268	11,486	11,314	11,897	12,562
B. BOLIVIA	4,279	1,193	1,321	1,478	1,453	1,369	1,298	1,254	1,282	1,317	1,348
C. BRAZIL	155,568	164,608	188,151[†]	199,040[†]	207,654[†]	211,213[†]	220,061[†]	225,356[†]	230,357[†]	234,085[†]	237,774[†]
D. CHILE	8,269	10,396	12,106	13,876	13,820	13,858	12,747	13,834	14,959	15,678	16,364
E. COLOMBIA	34,295	14,745	15,521	16,089	16,121	16,305	16,319	16,613[†]	16,916[†]	17,224[†]	17,522[†]
F. COSTA RICA	2,362	3,262	3,608	3,685	3,510	3,460	3,262	3,204	3,090	3,055	3,127
G. CUBA	2,064	2,405	2,452	3,348	3,288	3,316	3,371	3,263	3,268	3,278	3,278
H. DOMINICAN REP.	136	453	477	486	900	936	944	957	969	982	982
I. ECUADOR	4,944	5,671	6,110	7,394	7,577	7,628	7,650	7,920	8,234	8,571	8,687
J. EL SALVADOR	2,374	3,564	3,880[†]	4,010[†]	4,137[†]	4,279[†]	4,395[†]	4,494[†]	4,612[†]	4,753[†]	4,899[†]
K. GUATEMALA	8,937	5,780	5,951	5,870	5,956	6,165	6,328	6,467	6,645	6,869	6,983
L. HAITI	4,056[†]	4,676	4,999[†]	5,115[†]	5,235[†]	5,360[†]	5,487[†]	5,624[†]	5,761[†]	5,902[†]	6,056[†]
M. HONDURAS	4,752	4,078[†]	4,714	4,762	4,943	5,033	5,069	4,815	5,078[†]	5,389	5,490
N. MEXICO	10,115	17,155	16,589	17,864	18,508	18,742	19,350	19,736	20,678	21,317	21,228[†]
O. NICARAGUA	2,123	2,868	3,040[†]	3,101[†]	3,168[†]	3,241[†]	3,319[†]	3,404[†]	3,491[†]	3,581[†]	3,674[†]
P. PANAMA	1,366	1,577	1,632	1,632	1,677	2,010	2,047[†]	2,047[†]	2,047[†]	2,047[†]	2,047[†]
Q. PARAGUAY	3,969	4,935	5,654	6,219	6,732	6,762[†]	6,792[†]	6,822[†]	7,506	7,650	8,210
R. PERU	3,326	6,862	7,358	7,635	8,152	7,833	7,769	7,775[†]	7,655	7,729	7,735[†]
S. URUGUAY	1,406	1,750	2,117	2,299	1,564	1,722	2,366	2,357	2,559	2,662	2,668
T. VENEZUELA	6,893	1,123	1,197	1,217	1,237	1,258	1,248[†]	1,265	1,284[†]	1,071	1,174
LATIN AMERICA	169,654	268,026	298,118	317,783	328,032	332,129	340,200	349,796	358,789	366,205	372,914
UNITED STATES	327,945	307,723	394,381	422,134	418,453	419,016	396,896	437,762	452,215	448,488[†]	484,511
WORLD	2,640,080	2,597,645	2,811,326	2,895,545	2,941,956	2,945,040	2,926,418	3,037,720	3,125,822	3,164,378	3,252,353

1. Wood in the rough. Wood in its natural state as felled, or otherwise harvested, with or without bark, round, split, roughly squared or other forms (e.g., roots, stumps, burls, etc.). It may also be impregnated (e.g., telegraph poles) or roughly shaped or pointed. It comprises all wood obtained from removals, i.e., the quantities removed from forests and from trees outside the forest, including wood recovered from natural, felling and logging losses during the period—calendar year or forest year. Commodities included are saw-logs and veneer logs, pitprops, pulpwood, other industrial roundwood, and fuelwood.
2. For coniferous and non-coniferous, see SALA, 23-1800 and 1801.

SOURCE: FAO-YFP, 1981–84, p. 64; 1985, pp. 2–3; 1986, pp. 2–3.

Table 2304

INDUSTRIAL ROUNDWOOD PRODUCTION,[1] 20 LC, 1970–86

(T Me^3)

	Country	1970*	1975	1977	1979	1980	1981	1982	1983	1984	1985	1986
A.	ARGENTINA	3,072	3,628	4,029	4,787	4,070	3,894	4,755	5,883	5,414	5,414	5,414
B.	BOLIVIA	231[‡]	300	229	488	433	323	226	149	149	149	149
C.	BRAZIL	23,823	30,630	37,319[†]	52,026[†]	57,240[†]	57,345[†]	62,691[†]	64,435[†]	65,850[†]	65,961[†]	66,128[†]
D.	CHILE	4,625	5,178	6,022	8,342	8,201	8,154	6,951	7,944	8,979	9,602	10,193
E.	COLOMBIA	2,851	3,002	3,002	3,301	3,054	2,954	2,673	2,673[†]	2,673[†]	2,673[†]	2,673[†]
F.	COSTA RICA	838	1,336	1,492	1,512	1,275	1,158	900	776	601	504	509
G.	CUBA	382[†]	385	474	514	514	514	521	516	521	525	525
H.	DOMINICAN REP.	1	13	4	3	3	10	6	6	6	6	6
I.	ECUADOR	1,506	1,659	1,878	1,868	2,029	2,054	2,052	2,108	2,232	2,692	2,449
J.	EL SALVADOR	79	78	79[†]	91[†]	100[†]	127[†]	120[†]	90[†]	82[†]	83[†]	81[†]
K.	GUATEMALA	530	546[†]	486	231	159	202	194	158	156	195	114
L.	HAITI	239[†]	239[†]	239[†]	239[†]	239[†]	239[†]	239[†]	239[†]	239[†]	239[†]	239[†]
M.	HONDURAS	800	868[†]	1,175	1,064	1,112	1,066	962	566	685[†]	851	808
N.	MEXICO	5,302	6,613	6,995	6,030	6,345	6,253	6,527	6,576	7,177	7,473	7,048[†]
O.	NICARAGUA	445	880	880[†]	880[†]	880[†]	880[†]	880[†]	880[†]	880[†]	880[†]	880[†]
P.	PANAMA	98	117	86	44	339	339[†]	339[†]	339[†]	339[†]	339[†]	339[†]
Q.	PARAGUAY	806	1,155	1,128	1,989	2,412	2,412[†]	2,412[†]	2,412[†]	2,733	2,747	3,240
R.	PERU	1,087	1,475	1,738	1,636	1,988	1,498	1,256	1,256[†]	1,136	1,210	1,210[†]
S.	URUGUAY	148	290	347	427	242	319	222	213	289	257	257
T.	VENEZUELA	558	636	636[†]	636[†]	636[†]	636[†]	636[†]	636[†]	636[†]	405	490
	UNITED STATES	312,653	288,581	320,441	354,707	327,095	317,094	294,974	335,840	350,293	346,566[†]	382,589
	WORLD	1,277,638	1,295,194	1,380,000	1,455,766	1,445,213	1,404,155	1,374,740	1,457,436	1,511,992	1,518,474	1,573,904

1. All wood as defined in "Total Roundwood" with the exception of fuelwood and charcoal.

SOURCE: FAO-YFP, 1981–83, p. 96; 1984, p. 97; 1985, p. 36; 1986, p. 36.

Table 2305

INDUSTRIAL WOOD AS A PERCENTAGE OF TOTAL ROUNDWOOD PRODUCTION,[1] 20 LC, 1970–86

(%)

	Country	1970*	1975	1977	1979	1980	1981	1982	1983	1984	1985	1986
A.	ARGENTINA	34.5	36.4	38.2	41.7	37.4	37.2	51.3	51.2	47.9	45.5	43.1
B.	BOLIVIA	5.4	25.1	19.5	53.3	29.8	23.6	17.4	11.9	11.6	11.3	11.1
C.	BRAZIL	15.3	18.6	21.0	26.1	27.6	27.2	28.5	28.6	28.6	28.2	27.8
D.	CHILE	55.9	49.8	52.8	60.1	59.3	58.8	54.5	57.4	60.0	61.2	62.3
E.	COLOMBIA	8.3	20.4	19.7	20.5	18.9	18.1	16.4	16.1	15.8	15.5	15.3
F.	COSTA RICA	35.5	41.0	42.2	41.0	36.3	33.5	27.6	24.2	19.4	16.5	16.3
G.	CUBA	18.5	16.0	21.8	15.4	15.6	15.5	15.5	15.8	15.9	16.0	16.0
H.	DOMINICAN REP.	.7	2.9	.9	.6	.3	1.1	.6	.6	.6	.6	.6
I.	ECUADOR	30.5	29.3	30.6	25.3	26.8	26.9	26.8	26.6	27.1	31.4	28.2
J.	EL SALVADOR	3.3	2.2	2.1	2.3	2.4	3.0	2.7	2.0	1.8	1.7	1.7
K.	GUATEMALA	5.9	9.4	8.3	3.9	2.7	3.3	3.0	2.4	2.3	2.8	1.6
L.	HAITI	5.9	5.1	4.9	4.7	4.6	4.5	4.4	4.2	4.1	4.0	3.9
M.	HONDURAS	16.8	21.3	25.4	22.3	22.5	21.2	19.0	11.8	13.5	15.8	14.7
N.	MEXICO	52.4	38.5	38.5	33.8	34.3	33.4	33.7	33.3	34.7	35.1	33.2
O.	NICARAGUA	21.0	30.7	29.5	28.4	27.8	27.2	26.5	25.9	25.2	24.6	24.0
P.	PANAMA	7.2	7.4	5.3	2.6	16.9	16.6	16.6	16.6	16.6	16.6	16.6
Q.	PARAGUAY	20.3	23.4	21.8	32.0	35.8	35.7	35.5	35.4	36.4	36.0	39.5
R.	PERU	32.7	21.5	23.4	21.4	24.4	19.1	16.2	16.2	14.8	15.7	15.6
S.	URUGUAY	10.5	16.6	16.8	18.6	15.5	18.5	9.4	9.0	11.3	9.7	9.6
T.	VENEZUELA	8.1	56.6	54.9	52.3	51.4	50.6	51.0	50.3	49.5	37.8	41.7
	UNITED STATES	95.3	93.8	90.9	84.0	78.2	75.7	74.3	76.7	77.5	77.3	79.0
	WORLD	48.4	49.9	50.6	50.3	49.1	47.7	47.0	48.0	48.4	48.0	48.4

1. Industrial roundwood is comprised of all of those woods included in table 2301, above, with the exception of fuelwoods and charcoal. This table thus demonstrates the amount of wood produced for industry rather than fuel. For fuelwood, coal, and bagasse production see Chapter 19, above.

SOURCE: Calculated from tables 2303 and 2304 above.

Table 2306

TOTAL SAWNWOOD AND SLEEPER PRODUCTION,[1,2] 19 LC, 1970–86

($T\ Me^3$)

	Country	1970	1975	1977	1979	1980	1981	1982	1983	1984	1985	1986
A.	ARGENTINA	736	480	859	908	883	1,047	1,192	1,237	1,117	1,117[†]	1,117[†]
B.	BOLIVIA	72	140	109	233	220	172	117	97	97	97	97
C.	BRAZIL	8,035	10,129	12,643	14,070	14,881	15,852	16,470	17,199	17,781	17,781	18,063
D.	CHILE	1,075	1,320	1,267	2,199	2,186	1,735	1,176	1,610	2,001	2,057	2,287
E.	COLOMBIA	1,100	954	934[†]	983	970	1,006	721	721[†]	721[†]	721[†]	721[†]
F.	COSTA RICA	369	612	689	364	524	534	378	306[†]	412	412	412[†]
G.	CUBA	96[†]	105[†]	105[†]	101	112	108	107	104	108	104	104[†]
I.	ECUADOR	704	747	852	830	905	986	980	1,142	1,212	1,215	1,258
J.	EL SALVADOR	20	38	34	37	37	47	45	39	46[†]	43[†]	44[†]
K.	GUATEMALA	204	222	353	138	93	136	130	104	103	131	83
L.	HAITI	13	14[†]	14[†]	14[†]	14[†]	14[†]	14[†]	14[†]	14[†]	14[†]	14[†]
M.	HONDURAS	457	551	628	624	560	560	489	468	427	436	405
N.	MEXICO	1,572	1,986	2,259	2,109	1,991	1,928	1,669	1,827	1,975	2,205	2,141
O.	NICARAGUA	197	402	402[†]	402[†]	402[†]	402[†]	402[†]	222[†]	222[†]	222[†]	222[†]
P.	PANAMA	44	50	33	12[†]	53	53[†]	53[†]	53[†]	53[†]	53[†]	53[†]
Q.	PARAGUAY	214	340	314	524	655	655[†]	655[†]	655[†]	834	758	766
R.	PERU	351	516	476	546	611	653	577	577[†]	479	535	535[†]
S.	URUGUAY	73	105	107	99	99[†]	100	47	16	59	57	57[†]
T.	VENEZUELA	328	349	349[†]	349[†]	349[†]	349[†]	220	210	210[†]	146[‡]	171[‡]
	UNITED STATES	81,854	75,903	92,115	95,982	84,024	75,441	70,307	81,727	88,375	86,800	95,330
	WORLD	415,009	405,042	449,202	460,877	450,431	428,494	422,853	441,274	460,830	465,439	474,668

1. Sawnwood, unplaned, planed, grooved, tongued, etc., sawn lengthwise, or produced by a profile chipping process (e.g., planks, beams, joists, boards, rafters, scantlings, laths, boxboards, "lumber," etc.) and planed wood which may also be finger jointed, tongued or grooved, chamfered, rabbeted, V-jointed, beaded, etc. Wood flooring is excluded. With few exceptions, sawnwood exceeds 5 mm in thickness. Pieces of wood of more or less rectangular section laid transversely on the railway road-bed to support the rails. Sleepers may be sawn or hewn.
2. For coniferous and non-coniferous, see SALA, 23-1802 and 1803.

SOURCE: FAO-YFP, 1982–84, p. 172; 1985, p. 110; 1986, p. 110.

Table 2307

TOTAL WOOD-BASED PANEL PRODUCTION,[1] 17 LC, 1970–86[a]

($T\ Me^3$)

	Country	1970	1975	1977	1979	1980	1981	1982	1983	1984	1985	1986
A.	ARGENTINA	193	331	280	367	414	357	347	390	360[†]	360[†]	447
B.	BOLIVIA	1	2	21	23	28	28	7	5	1	3	3
C.	BRAZIL	819	1,725	2,139	2,236	2,482	2,576	2,398	2,523	2,523[†]	2,523[†]	2,546
D.	CHILE	57	44	74	113	115	142	99	138	183	226	239
E.	COLOMBIA	77	80	112	103	111	106	123	113	113[†]	113[†]	113
F.	COSTA RICA	25	45	73	67	68	57	52	39	46	46	46[†]
G.	CUBA	70	6	6	6	6	6	90	98	135	123	123[†]
I.	ECUADOR	20	39	51	75	87	95	137	169	171	171	171
K.	GUATEMALA	5	21	11	11	9	6	6	6	5	8	8
M.	HONDURAS	6	10	13	14[‡]	11[‡]	11[‡]	5	6	8	7	8
N.	MEXICO	174	253	362	442	604	603	761	696	732	762	844
O.	NICARAGUA	16	10	10[†]	16	14	14[†]	22	14	14[†]	14[†]	14[†]
P.	PANAMA	4	9	14	14[†]	14[†]	14[†]	13	12	12	12	12
Q.	PARAGUAY	15	17	19	43[†]	69[†]	69[†]	69[†]	69[†]	97	88	89
R.	PERU	54	60	64	66	84	78	58	37	42	34	42
S.	URUGUAY	18	15	14	17	16	17	10	12	16	13	13
T.	VENEZUELA	59	81	74	101	136	151	101	129	133[†]	122	493
	UNITED STATES	23,026	25,005	32,464	31,519	26,224	27,300	24,204	29,518	30,904	32,194	34,908
	WORLD	69,591	84,435	101,583	106,368	101,249	100,438	96,251	105,481	108,640	112,206	119,152

1. Includes veneer sheets, plywood, particle board, and fiberboard.

a. For 1962-69 data see SALA, 21-1704.

SOURCE: FAO-YFP, 1981–83, p. 206; 1984, p. 198; 1985, p. 140; 1986, p. 140.

Table 2308

FIBERBOARD PRODUCTION,[1] 8 LC, 1970–86
(T ME^3)

Country	1970	1975	1977	1979	1980	1981	1982	1983	1984	1985	1986
A. ARGENTINA	24	51	52	59	90	86	80	95	80	80†	95
C. BRAZIL	269	504	710†	724‡	780‡	780†	602‡	727‡	727†	727†	750
D. CHILE	20	14	28	44	45	44	44	42	40	45	41
E. COLOMBIA	11	15	13	17	19	17	18	19	19†	19†	19
G. CUBA	~	~	~	~	~	~	44	48	48†	48†	48†
N. MEXICO	21	14	30	26	26	26	26	67	65	65†	65†
S. URUGUAY	4	3	3	3	2	4	3	3	4	4	4
T. VENEZUELA	2	6†	10†	16‡	16‡	16†	4‡	4‡	4†	10†	18
UNITED STATES	5,821	6,236	7,343	7,187	5,098	4,900	4,500	4,790	4,704	5,230	5,330

1. A panel manufacture from fibers of wood or other ligno-cellulosic materials with the primary bond deriving from the felting of the fibers and their inherent adhesive properties. Bonding materials and/or additives may be added. It is usually flat pressed but may be moulded.

SOURCE: FAO-YFP, 1982–83, p. 242; 1984, p. 234; 1985, p. 178; 1986, p. 178.

Table 2309

PARTICLE BOARD PRODUCTION,[1] 14 LC, 1970–86
(T Me^3)

Country	1970	1975	1977	1979	1980	1981	1982	1983	1984	1985	1986
A. ARGENTINA	117	209	176	248	268	217	215	241	230	230†	307
C. BRAZIL	112‡	407	541	550	660	660†	660†	660†	660†	660†	660†
D. CHILE	22	16	32	46	43	72	37	72	114	136	149‡
E. COLOMBIA	9	12†	20‡	30‡	31	42	50	50†	50†	50†	50†
F. COSTA RICA	#	~	24	31	32	23	11	11†	15	15	15†
G. CUBA	4	4†	4†	4†	4†	4†	44	48	85	73	73†
I. ECUADOR	#	~	8	19	26	28	61	80	80	80	80
K. GUATEMALA	4	16†	6	4	3	3	4	4	4	5	5
N. MEXICO	56	125	155	194	316	339	412	335	379	425	467
P. PANAMA	#	2†	2†	2†	~	~	~	~	~	~	~
Q. PARAGUAY	1†	2†	2†	2†	2†	2†	2†	2†	1	1	1
R. PERU	7	8	1	~	~	~	~	~	~	~	~
S. URUGUAY	2	6	6	7	7†	6	4	5	6	5	5†
T. VENEZUELA	24	35	35†	35†	65	66	60	78	78†	78†	78†
UNITED STATES	3,127	4,190	7,140	7,204	6,269	6,100	4,901	6,559	7,775	8,384	9,094
WORLD	19,144	30,713	38,210	41,303	41,339	40,070	37,830	40,575	43,478	45,079	47,705

1. A sheet material manufactured from small pieces of wood or other ligno-cellulosic materials (e.g., chip, flakes, splinters, strands, shreds, shives, etc.) agglomerated by use of an organic binder together with one or more of the following agents: heat, pressure, humidity, a catalyst, etc. (Flaxboard is included. Wood wool and other particle boards, with inorganic binders, are excluded.)

SOURCE: FAO-YFP, 1981–83, p. 234; 1984, p. 226; 1985, p. 170; 1986, p. 170.

Table 2310
PLYWOOD PRODUCTION,[1] 17 LC, 1970–86
(T Me^3)

	Country	1970	1975	1977	1979	1980	1981	1982	1983	1984	1985	1986
A.	ARGENTINA	48	61	50	53	53	50	47	48	45	45†	40
B.	BOLIVIA	1‡	2	3	4	6	6	6	5	1	2	2
C.	BRAZIL	342‡	660	698†	762	826	902	902†	902†	902†	902†	902†
D.	CHILE	13	13	9	16	20	18	10	15	20	36	40‡
E.	COLOMBIA	52	50†	75	52	52	40	48	37	37	37	37†
F.	COSTA RICA	22	40	44	31	31	26	33	23	25	25†	25†
G.	CUBA	2	2†	2	2†	2†	2†	2†	2†	2†	2†	2†
I.	ECUADOR	20	38	40	55	59	65	73	85	85	85	85
K.	GUATEMALA	1	4	4	4	4	3	1	1	~	2	2
M.	HONDURAS	6	10	13	14‡	11‡	11‡	5	6	8	7	8
N.	MEXICO	96	110	171	206	254	304	313	286	286	270	310
O.	NICARAGUA	16	10	10†	16	14	14†	22	14	14†	14†	14†
P.	PANAMA	4	7	12	12†	12†	12†	13	12	12	12†	12†
Q.	PARAGUAY	7	8	3†	4†	4†	4†	4†	4†	3	3	3
R.	PERU	33	49	39	38	49	40	37	22	30	20	23
S.	URUGUAY	12	6	5	7	7†	7	3	4	7	4	4†
T.	VENEZUELA	33	40	29‡	50	55	69	37	47	47†	34‡	397‡
	UNITED STATES	14,078	14,579	17,981	17,128	14,857	16,300	14,803	18,169	18,425	18,580	20,484
	WORLD	33,174	34,288	41,470	42,627	39,386	40,240	38,931	44,123	44,292	45,366	49,160

1. Plywood, veneer plywood, core plywood including veneered wood, blockboard,
laminboard, and battenboard. Other plywood such as cellular board and
composite plywood.

SOURCE: FAO-YFP, 1981–83, 224; 1984, p. 216; 1985, p. 160; 1986, p. 160.

Table 2311
VENEER SHEET PRODUCTION,[1] 11 LC, 1970–86
(T Me^3)

	Country	1970	1975	1977	1979	1980	1981	1982	1983	1984	1985	1986
A.	ARGENTINA	4	10	2	7	3	4	5	6	5	5†	5†
B.	BOLIVIA	#	#	18†	19†	10†	5†	1	~	~	1	1
C.	BRAZIL	96‡	154	190‡	200	216	234	234†	234†	234†	234†	234†
D.	CHILE	2†	2	5	7	7	8	8	9	9	9†	9†
E.	COLOMBIA	5†	4†	4	4	9	7	7	7†	7†	7†	7†
F.	COSTA RICA	3	5	5	5	5†	8	8†	5	6	6	6†
I.	ECUADOR	#	1	3	2	2	2	3	4	6	6	6
K.	GUATEMALA	#	2†	1†	2	2†	1	1	1	1	1	~
N.	MEXICO	1	4†	6	16	8	14	10	8	2	2†	2†
Q.	PARAGUAY	8	8†	14	37†	63†	63†	63†	63†	93	84	85
R.	PERU	14	3†	24	28	35	38	21	15	12	14	19
	WORLD	3,049	3,967	4,099	4,263	4,452	4,545	4,548	4,838	4,911	4,836	4,898

1. Thin sheets of wood of uniform thickness, rotary cut, sliced or sawn, for use in
plywood, laminated construction, furniture, veneer containers, etc. In production
the quantity given excludes veneer sheets used for plywood production within
the country.

SOURCE: FAO-YFP, 1981–83, p. 216; 1984, p. 208; 1985, p. 150; 1986, p. 150.

Table 2312
TOTAL WOOD PULP PRODUCTION,[1] 9 LC, 1970–86[a]
(T MET)

	Country	1970	1975	1977	1979	1980	1981	1982	1983	1984	1985	1986
A.	ARGENTINA	166	259	265	387	309	252	333	545	559	574	610
C.	BRAZIL	811	1,208	1,649	1,992	3,047	2,952	3,279	3,428	3,415	3,653	3,839
D.	CHILE	356	452	599	700	763	743	667	796	839	837	846
E.	COLOMBIA	42	82	110	119	123	126	115	114	114†	140†	149
F.	COSTA RICA	#	#	#	5	5	3	3	2	2	3	3†
N.	MEXICO	319	366	437	461	447	462	482	455	509	578	550
R.	PERU	#	4‡	5‡	5‡	7‡	4‡	1†	1†	1†	1†	1†
S.	URUGUAY	6	15	14	23	24	22	21	23	28	22	28‡
T.	VENEZUELA	#	29	46‡	56‡	63‡	46‡	46‡	60‡	67‡	69	88‡
	UNITED STATES	37,318	36,808	41,618	45,318	46,187	47,200	44,786	47,660	50,398	49,061	51,927
	WORLD	102,118	102,132	112,863	123,288	125,777	125,117	119,571	128,250	135,662	135,431	140,489

1. Wood pulp obtained by grinding or milling into their fibers, coniferous or non-coniferous rounds, quarters, billets, etc. of through refining coniferous or non-coniferous chips. Also called groundwood pulp and refiner pulp. It can be bleached or unbleached. It excludes exploded and defibrated pulp.

a. For 1962-69 data, see SALA, 21-1705.

SOURCE: FAO-YFP, 1981–83, p. 261; 1984, p. 253; 1985, p. 197; 1986, p. 197.

Table 2313
TOTAL PAPER AND PAPERBOARD PRODUCTION,[1] 17 LC, 1970–86
(T MET)

	Country	1970	1975	1977	1979	1980	1981	1982	1983	1984	1985	1986
A.	ARGENTINA	644	650	539	789	713	669	730	879	942	821	954
B.	BOLIVIA	1‡	1	1†	1†	1†	1†	1†	1†	1†	1†	1†
C.	BRAZIL	1,219	1,688	2,236	2,979	3,361	3,102	3,329	3,426	3,768	4,022	4,485
D.	CHILE	234	235	296	276	356	318	306	325	375	371	388
E.	COLOMBIA	220	258	281	325	351	407	366	366	405†	446‡	457
F.	COSTA RICA	5†	7	8	11	12	15	18	13	13	13	13†
G.	CUBA	80	123	70	73†	73†	73†	112	109	122	132	132†
H.	DOMINICAN REP.	8	9†	9†	9†	9†	9†	9†	9†	10	10†	10†
I.	ECUADOR	8	34	34	21	26	31	34	34†	34†	34	34
J.	EL SALVADOR	1†	5	5†	16	16	16	16†	16†	16†	16†	16†
K.	GUATEMALA	14	19	23	29	32	29	12	16	18	14	17
N.	MEXICO	897	1,184	1,463	1,684	1,979	1,893	1,924	2,019	2,239	2,376	2,469
P.	PANAMA	15	9	20†	20†	20†	43	43†	43†	43†	24	26
Q.	PARAGUAY	#	1	1	12	13	13	13†	13†	13†	8	8
R.	PERU	124	142	149	207	205	272	272†	146	138	150‡	152
S.	URUGUAY	40‡	29	35†	52	52	48	39	43	45	44	54‡
T.	VENEZUELA	250	395‡	464‡	512	501	503	482	487	557‡	551	612‡
	UNITED STATES	46,117	45,248‡	53,347‡	57,410‡	56,839‡	57,667‡	54,899‡	58,804	62,366	60,959	64,444

1. Includes printing and writing paper, newsprint, other paper and paperboard products, household and sanitary paper, wrapping and packaging paper, and paperboard.

SOURCE: FAO-YFP, 1981–83, p. 306; 1984, p. 298; 1985, p. 245; 1986, p. 245.

Table 2314

PRINTING AND WRITING PAPER PRODUCTION, 12 LC, 1970-86[a]

(T MET)

	Country	1970	1975	1977	1979	1980	1981	1982	1983	1984	1985	1986
A.	ARGENTINA	123	94	142	236	152	139	156	174	182	161	178
C.	BRAZIL	254	416	577	764	870	876	913	952	1,075	1,146	1,351
D.	CHILE	#	41	44	34	48	52‡	37‡	53	61	63	67
E.	COLOMBIA	44	44	61	66	71	84	70	67	85†	106‡	101
G.	CUBA	20	30	31	31†	31†	31†	37	34	44	59	59†
I.	ECUADOR	#	3	3	4	4	5	5	5†	5†	1	1
K.	GUATEMALA	7	9	12	15	15	15	7	10	11	9	10
N.	MEXICO	122	256	304	360	526	427	390	404	509†	456†	452
P.	PANAMA	#	#	3†	3†	3†	5	5†	5†	5†	~	~
R.	PERU	22	38‡	41‡	41	42†	68†	68†	37	41‡	49‡	49‡
S.	URUGUAY	15‡	11	11†	25	25	23	19	18	25	18	24‡
T.	VENEZUELA	26	56‡	69‡	84‡	84‡	87‡	84	82	113‡	103	106‡
	UNITED STATES	10,046	9,708‡	12,299‡	13,592‡	13,829‡	13,958‡	13,898‡	15,405	16,348	16,468	17,628
	WORLD	27,290	28,192	34,825	49,177	41,205	41,153	41,444	45,192	49,483	50,149	54,424

a. For 1962-69 data, see SALA, 21-1707.

SOURCE: FAO-YFP, 1981–83, p. 323; 1984, p. 315; 1985, p. 262; 1986, p. 263.

Table 2315

NEWSPRINT PRODUCTION, 6 LC, 1970-86[a]

(T MET)

	Country	1970	1975	1977	1979	1980	1981	1982	1983	1984	1985	1986
A.	ARGENTINA	3	#	16	94	97	110	94	168	202	203	226
C.	BRAZIL	103	125	107	109	105	105	107	106	109	208	213
D.	CHILE	124	120	132	134	131	131	124	155	170	172	169
K.	GUATEMALA	#	1	~	~	~	~	~	~	~	~	~
N.	MEXICO	40	29	90	95	116	129	125	157	199	260‡	367
S.	URUGUAY	#	1	#	#	#	#	#	~	~	~	~
	UNITED STATES	3,035	3,348‡	3,512‡	3,685‡	4,238	4,753‡	4,574‡	4,687‡	5,029	4,923	5,108
	WORLD	21,563	20,442	22,308	24,522	25,385	26,497	24,955	25,996	27,803	28,252	29,199

a. For 1962-69 data see SALA, 21-1707.

SOURCE: FAO-YFP, 1981–83, p. 316; 1984, p. 308; 1985, p. 255; 1986, p. 256.

Part VIII

Foreign Trade

Note: This volume contains statistics from numerous sources. Alternative data on many topics are presented. Variations in statistics can be attributed to differences in definition, parameters, coverage, methodology, as well as date gathered, prepared, or adjusted.

24

Selected Commodities
in Foreign Trade

Chapter Outline

Figure 24:1

SHARE OF FOURTEEN MAJOR COMMODITY EXPORTS IN
LATIN AMERICA'S TOTAL EXPORT EARNINGS,[1]
1960–81

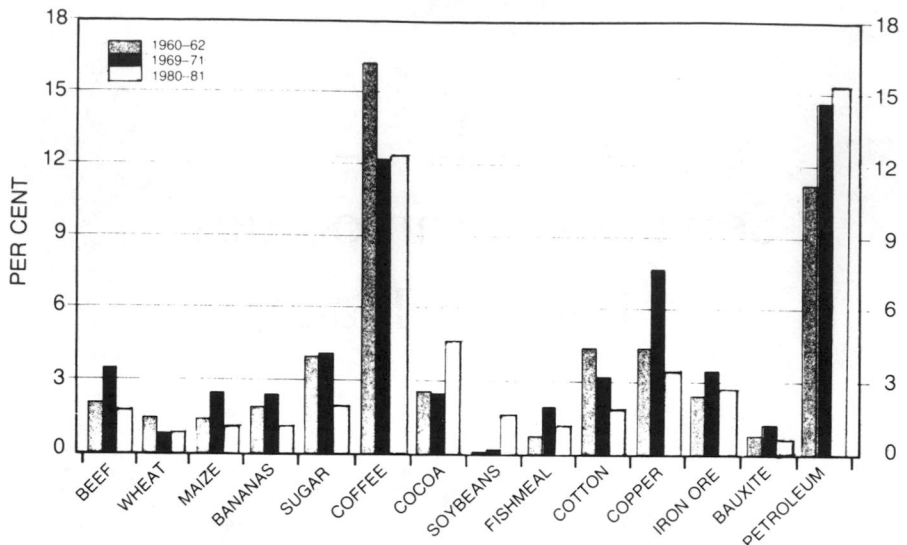

1. Includes Bahamas, Barbados, Guyana, Jamaica, and Trinidad and Tobago.

SOURCE: IDB-SPTF, 1983, p. 13.

Table 2400

PRINCIPAL EXPORT COMMODITIES,[1] 19 LC, 1975

Country and Commodity	Value (M US)	% of Total Exports	Country and Commodity	Value (M US)	% of Total Exports
A. ARGENTINA			M. HONDURAS		
Total Exports	2,961.3	100.0	Total Exports	283.3	100.0
Wheat	300.7	10.2	Bananas	45.3	15.9
Corn	517.8	17.5	Coffee	57.1	20.1
Meat	281.5	9.5	Silver	13.7	4.8
Wool	104.2	3.5	Wood	39.1	13.8
Hides and Skin	71.1	2.4	N. MEXICO		
B. BOLIVIA			Total Exports	2,908.6	100.0
Total Exports	443.2	100.0	Cotton	174.0	5.9
Tin	182.3	41.1	Coffee	184.1	6.3
Tungsten	22.3	5.0	Lead	~	~
Lead	7.4	1.7	Zinc	85.9	2.9
Zinc	39.6	8.9	Sugar	162.1	5.5
Silver	28.5	6.4	Shrimp	118.5	4.0
Antimony	17.1	3.8	Copper	~	~
Crude Petroleum	114.5	25.8	O. NICARAGUA		
C. BRAZIL			Total Exports	376.5	100.0
Total Exports	8,670.0	100.0	Cotton	95.9	25.4
Coffee	855	9.8	Coffee	48.2	12.8
Cotton	98	1.1	Sugar	42.7	11.3
Cacao	220	2.5	Meat	27.0	7.1
Iron Ore	921	10.6	Cotton Seed	~	~
Sugar	974	11.2	P. PANAMA		
D. CHILE[2]			Total Exports	282.5	100.0
Total Exports	2,480.5	100.0	Bananas	59.5	21.0
Copper	1,653.6	66.6	Refined Petroleum	128.6	45.5
Nitrates	496.6	20.0	Shrimp	19.0	6.7
Iron Ore	72.7	2.9	Q. PARAGUAY		
E. COLOMBIA[2]			Total Exports	173.0	100.0
Total Exports	1,508.8	100.0	Timber	27.7	16.0
Coffee	624.8	41.4	Cotton	19.7	11.3
Petroleum	4.5	.2	Quebracho Extract	2.5	1.4
F. COSTA RICA			Hides	1.9	1.0
Total Exports	488.5	100.0	Oilseeds (Vegetable Oils)	10.4	6.0
Bananas	132.8	27.1	Meat	31.6	18.2
Coffee	97.0	19.8	Tobacco	11.8	6.8
H. DOMINICAN REP.			R. PERU[2]		
Total Exports	893.8	100.0	Total Exports	1,499.2	100.0
Sugar	577.2	64.5	Fishmeal	195.8	13.0
Coffee	43.2	4.8	Cotton	93.8	6.2
Cacao	29.0	3.2	Sugar	155.9	10.3
Tobacco	34.5	3.8	Copper	347.9	23.2
Bauxite	16.7	1.8	Silver	165.0	11.0
I. ECUADOR			Iron Ore	60.1	4.0
Total Exports	910.3	100.0	Zinc	160.0	10.6
Bananas	155.6	17.0	Lead	25.8	1.7
Coffee	64.3	7.0	Coffee	34.8	2.3
Cacao	42.3	4.6	S. URUGUAY		
Crude Petroleum	515.9	56.6	Total Exports	383.8	100.0
J. EL SALVADOR			Wool	86.6	22.5
Total Exports	514.7	100.0	Meat	73.4	19.1
Coffee	168.7	32.7	Hides	16.6	4.3
Cotton	76.3	14.8	T. VENEZUELA		
K. GUATEMALA			Total Exports	10,134.4	100.0
Total Exports	646.8	100.0	Petroleum	9,653.9	95.2
Coffee	161.7	25.0	Iron Ore	~	~
Bananas	26.9	4.1	UNITED STATES[2]		
Cotton	74.0	11.4	Total Exports	97,143	100.0
Sugar	115.6	17.8	Food and Live Animals	13,983	14.4
L. HAITI[2]			Crude Metals, Inedibles Except Fuels	10,934	11.3
Total Exports	71.6	100.0	Minerals, Fuel and Related Materials	3,442	3.5
Coffee	23.8	33.2	Chemicals	8,822	9.1
Sisal	3.2	4.4	Machinery and Transport Equipment	38,189	39.3
Sugar	6.4	8.9	Other Manufactured Goods	16,516	17.0
Bauxite	5.9	8.2			

1. Principal exports do not add to 100.0%.
2. 1974.

SOURCE: IMF-IFS, Jan. 1975, Sept. 1976; and U.S. Bureau of the Census, *Statistical Abstract of the United States*, 1974, table 1328. Cf. SALA, 18–2709.

Table 2401

PRINCIPAL EXPORT COMMODITIES,[1] 19 LC, 1980

Country and Commodity	Value (M US)	% of Total Exports	Country and Commodity	Value (M US)	% of Total Exports
A. ARGENTINA			L. HAITI (M Gourdes)		
Total Exports	8,021.4	100.0	Total Exports	972.5	100.0
Wheat	816.1	10.2	Coffee	334.2	34.4
Wool	269.8	3.4	Bauxite	80.5	8.3
Hides and Skin	354.6	4.4	Sugar	24.6	2.5
Meat	935.8	11.7			
Corn	513.3	6.4	H. HONDURAS (M Lempiras)		
			Total Exports	1700.5	100.0
B. BOLIVIA			Bananas	456	26.8
Total Exports	942.2	100.0	Coffee	408.2	24.0
Tin	378.2	40.1	Wood	72.4	4.3
Silver	118.3	12.6	Frozen Beef	121.5	7.1
Antimony	26.4	2.8	Sugar	58.7	3.5
Natural Gas	220.9	23.4			
Zinc	36.7	3.9	N. MEXICO (B Pesos)		
Wolfram	47.4	5.0	Total Exports	357.5	100.0
			Cotton	7.2	2.0
C. BRAZIL			Shrimp	8.0	2.2
Total Exports	20,132	100.0	Petroleum	225.7	63.1
Coffee	2,486	12.3	Coffee	10.2	2.9
Soybeans and Products	2,277	11.3			
Iron Ore	1,564	7.8	O. NICARAGUA (M Córdobas)		
Sugar	942	4.7	Total Exports	4,528.8	100.0
			Cotton	305.6	6.7
D. CHILE			Meat	588.4	13.0
Total Exports	4,671	100.0	Coffee	1,665	36.8
Copper	2,153	46.1			
Iron Ore	158	3.4	P. PANAMA (M Balboas)		
			Total Exports	360.5	100.0
E. COLOMBIA			Bananas	61.6	17.1
Total Exports	3,945	100.0	Refined Petroleum	81.8	22.7
Coffee	2,375.2	60.2	Shrimp	43.7	12.1
Fuel Oil	238.9	6.1	Sugar	65.8	18.3
Cotton	86.1	2.2			
Sugar	160.9	4.1	Q. PARAGUAY (M Guaraníes)		
			Total Exports	39,089	100.0
F. COSTA RICA (M Colones)			Sawn Timber	8,357	21.4
Total Exports	8,585	100.0	Cotton	13,335	34.1
Coffee	2,113	24.6	Soybeans	5,304	13.6
Sugar	348	4.1	Vegetable Oils	2,157	5.5
Beef	606	7.1			
			R. PERU		
H. DOMINICAN REP.			Total Exports	3,898.3	100
Total Exports	961.9	100.0	Copper	751.6	19.3
Sugar	309.9	32.2	Crude Petroleum	628.9	16.1
Coffee	76.8	8.0	Petroleum Products	147.9	3.8
Cocoa Beans and Products	55.8	5.8	Fishmeal	191.8	4.9
Bauxite	18.5	1.9	Iron Ore	94.7	2.4
Dore	259.5	27.0	Silver	312.2	8.0
Ferronickel	101.3	10.5	Zinc	210.3	5.4
			Lead	383.2	9.8
I. ECUADOR					
Total Exports	2,480.8	100.0	S. URUGUAY		
Bananas	237.1	9.6	Total Exports	1,058.6	100.0
Coffee	130.4	5.3	Wool	212.3	20.1
Cocoa Paste	143.2	5.8	Meat	181.8	17.2
Cocoa Butter	34.1	1.4	Hides	40.2	3.8
Crude Petroleum	1,393.9	56.2			
			T. VENEZUELA (M Bolívares)		
J. EL SALVADOR (M Colones)			Total Exports	82,507	100
Total Exports	2,684	100.0	Petroleum	78,328	94.9
Coffee	1,538	57.3			
Cotton	217.9	8.1	UNITED STATES		
			Total Exports (B US)	220.79	100
K. GUATEMALA (M Quetzales)					
Total Exports	1,557.1	100.0			
Coffee	464.9	29.9			
Bananas	82.7	5.3			
Cotton	166.1	10.7			
Sugar	69.3	4.5			
Fresh Meat	29.1	1.9			

1. Principal exports do not add up to 100%.

SOURCE: Percentages calculated from IMF-IFS, March 1987.

Table 2402

PRINCIPAL EXPORT COMMODITIES,[1] 19 LC, 1985

Country and Commodity	Value (M US)	% of Total Exports	Country and Commodity	Value (M US)	% of Total Exports
A. ARGENTINA			L. HAITI (M Gourdes)		
Total Exports	8,396.1	100.0	Total Exports	871	100.0
Wheat	1,133.2	13.5	Bauxite (1982)	74.6	8.6
Wool	269.8	3.2	Coffee	226.4	26.0
Hides and Skin	286.1	3.4	Sugar (1984)	1.9	.2
Meat	370.1	4.4			
Corn	766.1	9.1	M. HONDURAS (M Lempiras)		
			Total Exports	1,491.3	100.0
B. BOLIVIA			Bananas (1984)	464.5	31.1
Total Exports	623.4	100.0	Coffee (1984)	338.2	22.7
Tin	186.7	29.9	Wood (1984)	69.8	4.7
Silver	10.2	1.6	Frozen Beef (1984)	42.4	2.8
Antimony	15.9	2.6	Sugar (1984)	51.3	3.4
Natural Gas	372.6	59.8			
Zinc	29.5	4.7	N. MEXICO (B Pesos)		
Wolfram	10.3	1.7	Total Exports	5,705.1	100.0
			Cotton	23.5	.4
C. BRAZIL			Shrimp	92	1.6
Total Exports	25,639	100.0	Petroleum	3,799	66.6
Coffee	2,369	9.2	Coffee	139.6	2.4
Soybeans and Products	2,540	9.9			
Iron Ore	1,658	6.5	O. NICARAGUA (M Córdobas)		
Sugar	199	0.8	Total Exports	3,945.4	100.0
			Cotton	1,344.8	34.1
D. CHILE			Coffee	1,198.4	30.4
Total Exports	3,823	100.0	Meat	176.9	4.5
Copper	1,761	46.1			
Iron Ore	91	2.4	P. PANAMA (M Balboas)		
			Total Exports	335.35	100.0
E. COLOMBIA			Bananas	78.08	23.3
Total Exports	3,551.6	100.0	Refined Petroleum	19.96	6.0
Coffee	1,784	50.2	Shrimp	59.77	17.0
Fuel Oil	408.8	11.5	Sugar	27.33	8.1
Cotton	58.4	1.6			
Sugar	37	1.0	Q. PARAGUAY (M Guaraníes)		
			Total Exports	96,708	100.0
F. COSTA RICA (M Colones)			Sawn Timber	3,072	3.2
Total Exports	48,526	100.0	Cotton	47,281	48.9
Bananas	10,706	22.1	Soybeans	32,134	33.2
Coffee	15,644	32.2	Vegetable Oils	4,278	4.4
Sugar	478	1.0			
Beef	2,811	5.8	R. PERU		
			Total Exports	2,966.4	100.0
H. DOMINICAN REP.			Fishmeal	116.6	3.9
Total Exports	735.2	100.0	Crude Petroleum	227.3	7.7
Sugar	190.1	25.9	Petroleum Products	418.1	14.1
Coffee	57.6	7.8	Copper	464.2	15.6
Cocoa Beans and Products	64.8	8.8	Silver	139.3	4.7
Tobacco	17.6	2.4	Iron Ore	72.8	2.5
Bauxite	0	0.0	Zinc	268.9	9.1
Dore	113.6	15.5	Lead	200.5	6.8
Ferronickel	120.7	16.4			
			S. URUGUAY		
I. ECUADOR			Total Exports	854.5	100.0
Total Exports	2,904	100.0	Wool	163.8	19.2
Bananas	220	7.6	Meat	117.9	13.8
Coffee	190.8	6.6	Hides	61.3	7.2
Cocoa Paste	2.5	.1			
Cocoa Butter	13.2	.5	T. VENEZUELA (M Bolívares)		
Crude Petroleum	1,824.7	62.8	Total Exports	92,042	100.0
			Petroleum	77,599	84.3
J. EL SALVADOR (M Colones)					
Total Exports	1,690.3	100.0	UNITED STATES		
Coffee	1,131.4	66.9	Total Exports (B US)	213.14	100.0
Cotton	76.9	4.5			
K. GUATEMALA (M Quetzales)					
Total Exports	1,060.1	100.0			
Coffee	450.8	42.5			
Bananas (1984)	56.3	5.0			
Cotton	71.6	6.8			
Sugar	43.8	4.1			
Fresh Meat	9.9	.9			

1. Principal exports do not add up to 100%.

SOURCE: Percentages calculated from IMF-IFS, March 1987.

Table 2403

TWO LEADING EXPORTS AS SHARE OF TOTAL EXPORT VALUE, 20 LC, 1955–88

Country	1955 Exports	% of Total	1965 Exports	% of Total	1970 Exports	% of Total	1975 Exports	% of Total	1980 Exports	% of Total	1985 Exports	% of Total	1988 Exports	% of Total
A. ARGENTINA	Cereals	27.4	Wheat	24.9	Meat	24.7	Wheat	10.2	Meat	11.7	Wheat	13.5	?	?
	Meats	26.3	Meat	22.0	Corn	14.9	Corn	17.5	Wheat	10.2	Corn	9.1	?	?
B. BOLIVIA	Tin	54.9	Tin	67.0	Tin	56.8	Tin	41.1	Tin	40.1	Natural Gas	59.8	Natural Gas	35.8
	Wolframite	13.4	Silver	4.7	Antimony	16.3	Tungsten	5.0	Natural Gas	23.4	Tin	29.9	Tin	12.8
C. BRAZIL	Coffee	60.8	Coffee	43.9	Coffee	34.3	Coffee	9.8	Coffee	12.3	Soybeans and Products	9.9	Soybeans and Products	9.0
	Cacao	5.0	Cotton	6.4	Iron Ore	12.0	Cotton	1.1	Soybeans and Products	11.3	Coffee	9.2	Coffee	5.9
D. CHILE	Metal and Ores	85.6	Copper	70.1	Copper	75.8	Copper	66.6	Copper	46.1	Copper	46.1	Copper	49.3
	Iron	3.8	Iron Ore	11.4	Iron Ore	6.6	Nitrates	20.0	Iron Ore	3.4	Iron Ore	2.4	?	?
E. COLOMBIA	Coffee	76.7	Coffee	64.8	Coffee	56.6	Coffee	41.4	Coffee	60.2	Coffee	50.2	Coffee	33.7
	Petroleum	14.9	Petroleum	13.9	Petroleum	9.3	Petroleum	.2	Fuel Oil	6.1	Fuel Oil	11.5	Fuel Oil	19.2
F. COSTA RICA	Coffee	48.6	Coffee	37.9	Coffee	31.8	Bananas	27.1	Coffee	24.6	Coffee	32.2	Coffee	24.0
	Bananas	38.7	Bananas	24.0	Bananas	29.0	Coffee	19.8	Bananas	20.1	Bananas	22.1	Bananas	18.8
G. CUBA	Sugar	81.2	Sugar	74.4	Sugar	76.9	Sugar	89.0	Sugar	83.0	Sugar	?	Sugar	?
	Tobacco	5.9	Nickel, Cobalt	.4	Nickel, Cobalt	16.5	?	?	?	?	?	?	?	?
H. DOMINICAN REP.	Sugar	58.6	Sugar	55.8	Sugar	51.8	Sugar	64.5	Sugar	32.2	Sugar	25.9	Ferronickel	34.7
	Coffee	15.6	Coffee	15.3	Coffee	13.5	Coffee	4.8	Dore	27	Ferronickel	16.4	Sugar	20.0
I. ECUADOR	Bananas	35.6	Bananas	57.0	Bananas	50.9	Bananas	17.0	Crude Petroleum	56.2	Crude Petroleum	62.8	Crude Petroleum	39.9
	Coffee	30.4	Coffee	14.7	Coffee	23.1	Coffee	7.0	Bananas	9.6	Bananas	7.6	Bananas	13.6
J. EL SALVADOR	Coffee	78.2	Coffee	46.3	Coffee	49.6	Coffee	32.7	Coffee	57.3	Coffee	66.9	?	?
	Cotton	15.6	Cotton	14.2	Cotton	10.1	Cotton	14.8	Cotton	8.1	Cotton	4.5	?	?
K. GUATEMALA	Coffee	79.0	Coffee	49.1	Coffee	34.4	Coffee	25.0	Coffee	29.0	Coffee	42.2	Coffee	?
	Bananas	8.0	Cotton	18.4	Cotton	9.1	Bananas	4.1	Cotton	10.7	Sugar	6.8	Sugar	?
L. HAITI	Coffee	71.9	Coffee	54.8	Coffee	38.1	Coffee	33.2	Coffee	34.4	?	?	Coffee	18.8
	Sisal	13.6	Sisal	7.2	Bauxite	16.4	Sisal	4.4	Bauxite	8.3	Coffee	26.0	?	?
M. HONDURAS	Bananas	61.1	Bananas	49.8	Bananas	40.6	Bananas	15.9	Bananas	26.8	Bananas	35.1	?	?
	Coffee	19.0	Coffee	13.6	Coffee	14.7	Coffee	20.1	Coffee	24.0	Coffee	23.7	?	?
N. MEXICO	Cotton	14.5	Cotton	19.7	Cotton	8.8	Cotton	5.9	Petroleum	63.1	Petroleum	66.6	Petroleum	31.9
	Coffee	13.2	Coffee	7.4	Sugar	7.0	Coffee	6.3	Coffee	2.9	Coffee	2.4	Coffee	2.3
O. NICARAGUA	Coffee	40.0	Cotton	41.3	Cotton	29.4	Cotton	25.4	Coffee	36.8	Cotton	34.1	?	?
	Cotton	30.6	Coffee	15.8	Meat	13.5	Coffee	12.8	Meat	12.9	Coffee	30.4	?	?
P. PANAMA	Bananas	64.0	Bananas	49.8	Bananas	57.4	Bananas	21.0	Refined Petroleum	22.7	Bananas	23.3	Bananas	27.4
	Shrimp	25.8	Refined Petroleum	29.0	Refined Petroleum	18.8	Refined Petroleum	45.5	Sugar	18.3	Shrimp	17.8	Shrimp	18.5
Q. PARAGUAY	Woods	37.2	Meat	28.6	Meat	23.9	Timber	16.0	Cotton	34.1	Cotton	48.9	?	?
	Quebracho Extract	20.4	Timber	21.7	Timber	19.7	Cotton	11.3	Sawn Timber	21.4	Soybeans	33.2	?	?
R. PERU	Cotton	25.1	Fishmeal	24.4	Fishmeal	27.6	Fishmeal	13.0	Copper	19.3	Copper	15.6	Copper	22.5
	Lead	11.9	Copper	23.8	Copper	25.0	Cotton	6.2	Crude Petroleum	16.1	Petroleum Products	14.1	Fishmeal	13.5
S. URUGUAY	Wood	51.0	Wool	45.4	Meat	37.7	Wool	22.5	Wool	20.1	Wool	19.2	Wool	24.8
	Meat	19.7	Meat	24.3	Meat	31.5	Meat	19.1	Meat	17.2	Meat	13.8	Meat	10.8
T. VENEZUELA	Petroleum	91.9	Petroleum	93.6	Petroleum	90.2	Petroleum	95.2	Petroleum	94.9	Petroleum	84.3	Petroleum	84.8
	Iron Ore	4.8	Iron Ore	5.0	Iron Ore	5.7	Iron Ore	?	Crude Petroleum	64.4	Crude Petroleum	48.5	Crude Petroleum	49.2
UNITED STATES	Manufacturing Goods	54.8	Machinery	20.4	Machinery	43.7	Food and Live Animals	14.4	?	?	?	?	?	?
	Semi-Manufactured Goods	15.6	Motor Vehicles	7.2	Other Manufactured Goods	18.7	Crude Metals, Inedible except Fuels	11.3	?	?	?	?	?	?

SOURCE: IMF-IFS, Jan. 1975, Dec. 1969, Aug. 1967, Aug. 1961, Sept. 1958, Mar. 1976, Jan. 1971, and August 1989. Cuban data beginning 1960 are from UCLA; 6 (1962) and 10 (1966), UCLA-Cuba, and Cuba, DGE, AE, 1973, Cf. SALA, 18–2801: SALA, 24–2401.

Table 2404

CONTRIBUTION OF THE TEN MAIN LATIN AMERICAN PRIMARY EXPORT PRODUCTS TO EACH COUNTRY'S TOTAL VALUE OF MERCHANDISE EXPORTS, 19 LR, 1972-87a

(%)

Country	Beef			Maize			Bananas			Sugar			Coffee			Cocoa		
	1972-76	1982-86	1987	1972-76	1982-86	1987	1972-76	1982-86	1987	1972-76	1982-86	1987	1972-76	1982-86	1987	1972-76	1982-86	1987
A. ARGENTINA	9.4	3.2	2.0	13.0	9.4	8.9	#	#	#	#	#	#	#	#	#	#	#	#
B. BOLIVIA	#	#	#	#	#	#	#	#	#	#	#	#	#	#	#	#	#	#
C. BRAZIL	#	#	#	#	#	#	#	#	#	9.1	1.2	.7	16.6	9.3	6.4	#	#	#
D. CHILE	#	#	#	#	#	#	#	#	#	#	#	#	#	#	#	#	#	#
E. COLOMBIA	#	#	#	#	#	#	24.8	21.5	15.4	5.8	1.5	1.2	49.4	52.8	39.8	#	#	#
F. COSTA RICA	7.7	4.8	5.7	#	#	#	#	#	#	#	#	#	25.5	27.5	19.3	#	#	#
H. DOMINICAN REP.	#	#	#	#	#	#	#	#	#	48.3	28.2	17.3	7.3	12.1	12.1	#	#	#
I. ECUADOR	#	#	#	#	#	#	14.3	7.6	14.1	#	#	#	10.5	7.8	12.3	5.6	7.7	8.8
J. EL SALVADOR	#	#	#	#	#	#	#	#	#	8.3	3.8	3.8	41.9	59.1	39.8	#	#	#
K. GUATEMALA	#	#	#	#	#	#	#	#	#	11.1	5.4	6.2	29.8	39.4	60.0	#	#	#
L. HAITI	#	#	#	#	#	#	#	#	#	5.0	2.0	**	32.1	27.9	26.4	#	#	#
M. HONDURAS	6.7	3.1	2.0	#	#	#	26.1	30.8	33.9	#	#	#	18.5	25.5	19.8	#	#	#
N. MEXICO	#	#	#	#	#	#	#	#	#	#	#	#	7.7	2.6	3.2	#	#	#
O. NICARAGUA	9.3	5.7	1.5	#	#	#	#	#	#	7.5	2.7	**	15.9	26.7	17.4	#	#	#
P. PANAMA	7.2	2.9b	#	#	#	#	30.1	22.1	24.0	11.7	8.8	5.1	#	#	#	#	#	#
Q. PARAGUAY	#	#	**	#	#	#	#	#	#	#	#	#	#	#	#	#	#	#
R. PERU	--	#	#	#	#	#	11.4	#	#	#	#	#	#	#	#	#	#	#
S. URUGUAY	29.1	15.2	11.3	#	#	#	#	#	#	#	#	#	#	#	#	#	#	#
T. VENEZUELA	#	#	#	#	#	#	#	#	#	#	#	#	#	#	#	#	#	#
LATIN AMERICA	2.0	.9	1.0	1.5	2.0	1.8	1.3	1.1	1.2	5.4	4.3	4.2	8.7	7.6	5.7	1.1	.5	.5

Country	Soybeans			Cotton			Iron Ore			Copper			Total 10 Products			Total Merchandise Exports
	1972-76	1982-86	1987	1972-76	1982-86	1987	1972-76	1982-86	1987	1972-76	1982-86	1987	1972-76	1982-86	1987	1987
A. ARGENTINA	**	7.1	**	#	#	#	#	#	#	#	#	#	22.4	19.6	11.0	100.0
B. BOLIVIA	#	#	#	#	#	#	#	#	#	#	#	#	#	#	#	100.0
C. BRAZIL	13.1	1.6	1.5	#	#	#	8.3	6.7	6.7	#	#	#	47.1	20.6	16.6	100.0
D. CHILE	#	#	#	#	#	#	5.4	3.1b	**	66.0	40.8	32.1	71.4	43.9	32.1	100.0
E. COLOMBIA	#	#	#	#	#	#	#	#	#	#	#	#	49.4	52.8	39.8	100.0
F. COSTA RICA	#	#	#	#	#	#	#	#	#	#	#	#	63.8	55.3	41.6	100.0
H. DOMINICAN REP.	#	#	#	#	#	#	#	#	#	#	#	#	61.2	48.0	38.2	100.0
I. ECUADOR	#	#	#	#	#	#	#	#	#	#	#	#	35.3	18.5	29.1	100.0
J. EL SALVADOR	#	#	#	10.7	4.1	.6	#	#	#	#	#	#	60.9	67.0	44.2	100.0
K. GUATEMALA	#	#	#	11.3	6.0	14.7	#	#	#	#	#	#	52.2	50.7	80.9	100.0
L. HAITI	#	#	#	#	#	#	#	#	#	#	#	#	37.1	29.9	26.4	100.0
M. HONDURAS	#	#	#	#	#	#	#	#	#	#	#	#	51.3	33.8	35.9	100.0
N. MEXICO	#	#	#	5.6	.6	.6	#	#	#	#	#	#	13.3	3.3	3.8	100.0
O. NICARAGUA	#	#	#	26.8	26.3	17.1	#	#	#	#	#	#	59.5	61.4	36.1	100.0
P. PANAMA	#	#	#	#	#	#	#	#	#	#	#	#	41.8	30.9	29.1	100.0
Q. PARAGUAY	9.8	24.8	23.7	8.7	36.0	30.4	#	#	#	#	#	#	25.7	63.3	54.1	100.0
R. PERU	--	#	#	5.5	1.3	1.2	6.3	2.1	1.5	15.6	13.0	16.4	27.4	16.9	20.0	100.0
S. URUGUAY	#	#	#	#	#	#	#	#	#	#	#	#	29.1	15.2	11.3	100.0
T. VENEZUELA	#	#	#	#	#	#	#	#	#	#	#	#	#	#	#	100.0
LATIN AMERICA	2.9	.8	1.2	2.0	.7	1.0	3.0	2.2	2.3	3.0	1.7	1.8	49.7	21.9	20.6	100.0

a. For previous years after 1971, see SALA, 24-2403.
b. 1982-85 average

SOURCE: IDB-SPTF, 1986, table 64; 1987, table 67; 1988, table F-2.

Table 2405

LATIN AMERICA PARTICIPATION IN TOTAL COMMERCE
OF DEVELOPING COUNTRIES, BY GROUPS OF PRIMARY
COUNTRIES, 1966 and 1983

(%)

Groups of Basic Products	Exports		Imports	
	1966	1983	1966	1983
All Food Types	46.1	51.6	23.8	20.6
Agricultural Value	25.1	16.6	27.3	14.5
Minerals and Metals	40.9	46.6	40.8	17.4
Total Primary Products	40.4	45.1	26.0	19.4
Fuel	30.1	19.6	45.4	34.4
Total of Primary Products Including Fuel	36.8	27.0	31.2	27.4

SOURCE: SELA, chapter 15, January–March 1987, p. 37.

Table 2406

LATIN AMERICA PARTICIPATION IN
WORLD EXPORTS OF SELECTED
BASIC PRODUCTS, 1983

(%)

Product	%
Bananas	79.92
Coffee	61.03
Sugar	58.48
Bauxite	39.15
Soya Oil	33.60
Copper	31.48
Iron Ore	31.48
Cocoa Beans	22.14
Albumine	21.28
Tobacco Leaves	15.92
Hides and Tallow	13.90
Fishery Products	13.03
Cotton	9.71
Wheat and Wheat Powder	8.47
Corn	7.19
Animal Skin	.82

SOURCE: SELA, chapter 15, January–March 1987, p. 37.

Table 2407

AGRICULTURAL AND FOOD TRADE BY CATEGORY, 19 LR, AVERAGE 1984–86[a]
(M US)[1]

Country	Cereals and Preparations		Meat and Preparations		Dairy Products and Eggs		Fruits and Vegetables		Sugar and Honey		Animal and Vegetable Oils	
	Exports	Imports	Exports	Imports	Exports	Imports	Exports	Imports	Exports	Imports	Exports	Imports
A. ARGENTINA	1,970	2	403	9	18	6	357	44	79	1	1,533	6
B. BOLIVIA	1	70	2	1	0	11	2	3	6	0	6	9
C. BRAZIL	36	897	774	112	2	89	1,187	139	500	1	1,064	134
D. CHILE	13	93	4	9	1	13	449	22	2	17	0	47
E. COLOMBIA	13	150	13	11	0	7	156	30	50	3	0	63
F. COSTA RICA	8	32	56	3	1	4	244	9	15	2	0	4
H. DOMINICAN REP.	1	69	13	3	0	16	42	7	220	2	5	40
I. ECUADOR	0	71	0	7	0	4	199	2	11	10	0	33
J. EL SALVADOR	2	41	2	10	0	9	3	15	30	4	6	9
K. GUATEMALA	4	45	34	4	0	13	105	8	69	4	10	14
L. HAITI	0	40	0	6	0	13	3	4	4	4	0	18
M. HONDURAS	3	25	17	5	0	14	274	4	28	1	12	3
N. MEXICO	6	603	184	193	0	159	653	99	66	27	38	637
O. NICARAGUA	1	35	12	5	1	17	16	8	12	0	4	27
P. PANAMA	0	31	2	10	4	15	80	29	28	3	0	13
Q. PARAGUAY	0	7	14	1	0	1	6	0	4	0	89	1
R. PERU	9	199	5	43	0	40	16	12	23	35	1	34
S. URUGUAY	108	18	155	1	23	0	18	9	5	0	5	6
T. VENEZUELA	2	416	8	25	2	104	57	70	0	71	2	201
LATIN AMERICA[2]	2,239	3,003	1,700	584	52	638	3,925	636	1,331	220	2,774	1,338

Table 2407 (Continued)

AGRICULTURAL AND FOOD TRADE BY CATEGORY, 19 LR, AVERAGE 1984-86[a]
(M US)[1]

Country	Fish and Seafood[3] Exports	Fish and Seafood[3] Imports	Other Foods Exports	Other Foods Imports	Subtotal Food[4] Exports	Subtotal Food[4] Imports	Non-Food Products[5] Exports	Non-Food Products[5] Imports	Total Agricultural Trade Exports	Total Agricultural Trade Imports	Total Agricultural Trade Trade Balance
A. ARGENTINA	149	1	3	49	4,494	118	992	123	5,486	241	5,245
B. BOLIVIA	0	1	1	3	13	98	16	5	28	103	-75
C. BRAZIL	176	34	838	5	4,577	1,410	4,931	188	9,508	1,598	7,910
D. CHILE	115	0	0	11	584	211	126	88	710	299	410
E. COLOMBIA	30	14	23	18	325	297	2,319	105	2,643	403	2,241
F. COSTA RICA	17	2	20	7	362	63	324	22	686	85	601
H. DOMINICAN REP.	4	8	77	2	360	145	132	34	492	179	313
I. ECUADOR	184	0	163	5	556	132	277	21	832	153	679
J. EL SALVADOR	18	2	0	2	61	92	455	28	516	121	395
K. GUATEMALA	11	2	70	9	304	98	522	23	827	121	705
L. HAITI	0	7	5	11	13	101	64	16	76	117	-41
M. HONDURAS	33	2	4	2	372	56	233	16	605	72	532
N. MEXICO	468	2	48	16	1,464	1,735	932	253	2,396	1,988	408
O. NICARAGUA	13	0	0	3	59	96	185	12	244	108	136
P. PANAMA	67	5	7	13	189	119	26	26	215	144	70
Q. PARAGUAY	0	0	2	0	115	12	157	30	272	41	231
R. PERU	74	0	23	9	151	372	284	25	435	397	37
S. URUGUAY	47	0	1	3	362	37	140	41	502	78	424
T. VENEZUELA	77	6	20	38	168	931	53	292	220	1,223	-1,003
LATIN AMERICA[2]	1,497	121	1,330	240	14,850	6,782	12,222	1,440	27,072	8,221	18,851

1. FOB Values for Exports and Cif for Imports.
2. The total does not correspond to the sum of country values due to rounding errors.
3. Data for 1984 only.
4. The concept of "food" is that used in the FRO's Production Yearbook, namely "commodities that are considered edible and contain nutrients."
5. "Non-food" consists of those commodities which are included in the agricultural trade statistics of the FRO, but are not considered "food" by the above definition. The main components of the group are coffee, tea, fibers, fishmeal, and forestry products.

a. For previous years see SALA, 27-2407.

SOURCE: IDB-SPTF, 1988, pp. 58-59.

Table 2408

FOOD TRADE BALANCES, 20 L, 1961–75
(M US)

	Exports (FOB)			Imports (CIF)			Balance		
Division	1961	1971	1975	1961	1971	1975	1961	1971	1975
LAFTA	3,284	5,290	10,496	871	1,454	3,835	2,413	3,836	6,661
Andean Pact	650	974	2,102	472	741	1,610	178	233	492
B. BOLIVIA	3	13	73	22	38	57	−19	−25	16
D. CHILE	36	43	120	123	232	455	−32	−189	−335

Continued in SALA, 24-2405.

Table 2409

CEREAL IMPORTS, 20 LC, 1974 AND 1985
(T MET)

	Country	1974	1985
A.	ARGENTINA	#	1
B.	BOLIVIA	209	459
C.	BRAZIL	2,485	4,857
D.	CHILE	1,737	486
E.	COLOMBIA	503	1,021
F.	COSTA RICA	110	146
G.	CUBA	~	~
H.	DOMINICAN REP.	252	492
I.	ECUADOR	152	293
J.	EL SALVADOR	75	224
K.	GUATEMALA	138	164
L.	HAITI	83	227
M.	HONDURAS	52	99
N.	MEXICO	2,881	4,507
O.	NICARAGUA	44	114
P.	PANAMA	63	115
Q.	PARAGUAY	71	83
R.	PERU	637	1,187
S.	URUGUAY	70	31
T.	VENEZUELA	1,270	2,793
	UNITED STATES	460	992

SOURCE: WB-WDR, 1987, table 6.

Table 2410

FISH EXPORT VALUE,[1] 10 LC, 1978–86

				T US					Value as % of Total Market Economy				
Country	1978	1982	1983	1984	1985	1986	1978	1982	1983	1984	1985	1986
A. ARGENTINA	106,014	130,366	85,542	47,391	86,183	129,511[†]	2.8	3.2	~	~	~	~
C. BRAZIL	25,434	73,918	65,715	51,845	37,218[†]	41,946[†]	#	#	~	~	~	~
D. CHILE	6,865	46,428	79,409	83,025	102,597	146,201	#	#	~	~	~	~
E. COLOMBIA	7,128	9,175	4,009	3,036	~	~	#	#	~	~	~	~
G. CUBA	18,099	14,163	17,140	100,205	124,647	71,938[†]	#	#	~	~	~	~
I. ECUADOR	10,707	5,971	7,648	17,898	20,035[†]	23,635[†]	#	#	~	~	~	~
N. MEXICO	26,120	22,256[†]	5,581	11,052[†]	~	~	#	#	~	~	~	~
R. PERU	29,725	10,438	16,389	32,525	5,841[†]	7,766[†]	#	#	~	~	~	~
S. URUGUAY	21,277	92,100	81,946	92,154	101,030	47,312[†]	#	#	~	~	~	~
T. VENEZUELA	~	20,675[†]	21,105	32,847[†]	39,765[†]	39,421[†]	#	#	~	~	~	~
LAIA	233,521	380,794[†]	363,270	360,831	407,818[†]	457,835[†]	6.2	7.4[†]	7.0	6.8	7.1[†]	6.1[†]
CACM	3,726	9,166	7,417[†]	9,832[†]	11,749[†]	20,083[†]	.1	.2	.1[†]	.2[†]	.2[†]	.3[†]
UNITED STATES	366,435	588,078	524,496	519,691	664,102	826,063	9.7	11.4	10.0	9.8	11.5	11.1

1. Fresh, chilled, and frozen.

SOURCE: UN-YITS, 1982, vol. 2, p. 21; 1983, vol. 2, p. 9; 1985, 1986, vol. 2, p. 43.

Table 2411

FISHERY EXPORTS, 11 OAS-L, 1970–80

(% and M US)

Category	1970	%[a]	1975	%[a]	1980	%[a]
Total fishery commodities	R. PERU	65	R. PERU	33	N. MEXICO	30
	N. MEXICO	14	N. MEXICO	25	D. CHILE	19
	D. CHILE	5	C. BRAZIL	7	R. PERU	16
			D. CHILE	6	I. ECUADOR	9
			I. ECUADOR	6	A. ARGENTINA	7
					B. BRAZIL	7
					Rest of OAS-L	12
					$1,942.7	100

Continued in SALA, 24-2407.

Table 2412

MEAT IMPORT VOLUME,[1] 16 L, 1975–87[a]

(T MET)

	Country	1975	1978	1980	1981	1982	1983	1984	1985	1986	1987
A.	ARGENTINA	~	#	20	11	2	2	1.59	1.11	18.85	10.45
B.	BOLIVIA	~	~	~	~	~	~	~	~	~	~
C.	BRAZIL	244	122	70	66	22	23	35.69	54.40	515.22	191.66
D.	CHILE	11	14	11	17	9	3	6.42	7.73	3.82	2.60
E.	COLOMBIA	~	#	#	.5	1	1	1.08	.98	.67	1.17
F.	COSTA RICA	9	3	2	#	#	#	.40	.26	.16	.59
G.	CUBA	~	11	20	22	23	21	18.44	24.94	20.07	20.00[†]
H.	DOMINICAN REP.[3]	14	#	12	11	10	9	2.76	.10	1.11	2.84
J.	EL SALVADOR	3	#	.5	#	#	#	.62	#	.46	.42
K.	GUATEMALA	~	1	#	.6	#	~	.59	.06	.05	.07
M.	HONDURAS	~	#	#	#	#	#	.01	.01	.32	.18
N.	MEXICO[4,3]	147	11	47	94	78	49	79.93	128.61	109.51	103.80
O.	NICARAGUA[3]	3	#	3	3	3	1	.01	#	~	~
P.	PANAMA[2]	1	#	#	1	2	#	.42	1.24	2.41	2.86
R.	PERU	157	4	7	25	31	19	25.32	15.35	74.62	66.00
T.	VENEZUELA[3]	102	75	27	47	40	21	8.00	5.99	.20	21.04

1. Includes meat fresh, chilled, and frozen. Figures refer to "special trade" except where otherwise noted. "Special" imports include goods for domestic consumption and withdrawals from bonded warehouses or free zones for purposes of domestic consumption.
2. Data exclude the free zone of Colón and the Canal Zone.
3. Figures refer to "general trade," i.e., total imports.
4. Imports through free zones are included.

a. For 1934–74, see SALA, 20-2927.

SOURCE: FAO-TY, 1978; 1980, table 10; 1981, table 10; 1982, table 10; 1984, table 10; 1985, table 11; 1986–87, table 11.

Table 2413

MEAT EXPORT VOLUME,[1] 17 LC, 1975–87[a]

(T MET)

	Country	1975	1978	1980	1981	1982	1983	1984	1985	1986	1987
A.	ARGENTINA	79	481	313	342	363	282	179.66	171.69	158.24	142.92
B.	BOLIVIA	2	~	~	~	#	#	.27	~	~	~
C.	BRAZIL	5	110	213	383	428	444	435.79	461.30	340.73	305.42
D.	CHILE	- -	2	5	4	4	2	1.89	3.45	9.38	4.10
E.	COLOMBIA	18	30	12	22	21	14	4.83	3.53	11.18	11.20
F.	COSTA RICA	29	35	26	33	25	14	20.64	27.20	35.74	27.93
H.	DOMINICAN REP.[2]	4	1	1	4	4	3	.48	7.63	13.45	8.41
J.	EL SALVADOR	2	6	2	.6	1	2	1.13	1.07	.44	2.20
K.	GUATEMALA	15	15	11	15	14	12	7.43	5.74	3.37	9.07
L.	HAITI[2]	~	1	.7	2[‡]	2	1	.16	.20	.20	~
M.	HONDURAS	23	23	29	23	16	16	10.26	8.74	10.20	9.14
N.	MEXICO[2]	5	55	19	14	11	9	8.89	5.06	5.59	9.08
O.	NICARAGUA[2]	22	37	21	15	15	14	10.64	6.60	3.74	3.50
P.	PANAMA[4]	1	.3	1	2	4	2	.67	.05	.01	.02
Q.	PARAGUAY	8	4	1	1	1	7	.30	3.14	41.33	18.15
R.	PERU	2[†]	2[‡]	1	1	1	2	.31	12.02	~	~
S.	URUGUAY[2]	79	103	113	167	140	177	106.13	102.61	140.62	62.71
	UNITED STATES[2,3]	370	578	731	800	674	629	617.21	638.01	757.84	889.71
	WORLD	2,394	7,070	8,115	8,889	8,579	8,944	8,779.67	8,983.94	9,824.79	10,023.44

1. Includes meat fresh, chilled or frozen. Figures refer to "special trade" except where otherwise indicated. "Special" exports comprise exports of goods wholly or partly produced or manufactured in the country, together with exports of "nationalized" goods, but not of goods held in bonded warehouses or free zones.
2. Figures refer to "general trade," i.e., total exports including re-exports.
3. The customs area includes the Commonwealth of Puerto Rico.
4. Data exclude the free zone of Colón and the Canal Zone.

a. For 1934–74, see SALA, 20-2926. See SALA, 20-2926 for comparison of Argentina and Australia beef cattle exports.

SOURCE: FAO-TY, 1978; 1980, table 10; 1981, table 10; 1984, table 10; 1985–87, table 11.

Table 2414

MEAT EXPORT VALUE,[1] 15 LC, 1980–86

Country	T US						Value as % of Total Market Economy					
	1980	1982	1983	1984	1985	1986	1980	1982	1983	1984	1985	1986
A. ARGENTINA	519,738	399,299	332,801	167,097	145,863	234,578†	6.4	6.0	4.5	2.6	3.5	~
C. BRAZIL	18,399	188,288	210,318	409,863	213,984†	153,752†	.2	2.6	2.9	6.3	3.4†	2.0†
D. CHILE	36	1,684†	1,666†	5,318	~	~	#	#	#	~	~	~
E. COLOMBIA	26,917	45,386	30,529	10,521	6,128	4,165†	#	#	#	~	~	~
F. COSTA RICA	70,722	53,058	31,237†	39,455†	47,901†	58,039†	#	~	~	~	~	~
H. DOMINICAN REP.	2,883	8,829	6,711	1,968†	11,845†	15,302†	#	#	~	~	~	~
J. EL SALVADOR	4,146	2,600	3,410†	2,669†	3,012†	2,305†	#	#	~	~	~	~
K. GUATEMALA	34,735	7,709†	18,928	15,901†	24,904†	5,535†	#	#	~	~	~	~
L. HAITI	1,463†	1,330†	243†	10	~	~	#	#	~	~	~	~
M. HONDURAS	60,739	33,922	31,339	19,453	13,039†	22,462†	#†	#†	~	~	~	~
N. MEXICO	3,006	2,456†	2,807†	6,958†	7,761†	8,590†	#†	#†	~	~	~	~
O. NICARAGUA	58,551	33,818	32,323†	22,778†	16,368†	2,641†	#	#	~	~	~	~
P. PANAMA	3,148	9,353	4,109	1,462	127	146†	#	#†	~	~	~	~
Q. PARAGUAY	32	2,426†	2,529†	3,579	3,434†	2,696†	#	#†	~	~	~	~
S. URUGUAY	155,777	171,174	218,498	129,995	102,899	98,063†	#	#	~	~	~	~
LAIA	723,905	810,339†	795,158	724,538	480,138†	501,977†	9.0	11.0†	11.1†	11.1	7.6†	6.4†
CACM	228,893	162,762	117,236†	100,256†	105,225†	90,981†	2.8	2.2	1.6†	1.5†	1.7†	1.2†
UNITED STATES	235,436	352,286	371,255	451,119	454,263	605,746	2.9	4.8	5.2	6.9	7.2	7.7

1. Bovine, fresh and frozen.

SOURCE: UN-YITS, 1982, vol. 2, p. 256; 1983, vol. 2, p. 244; 1984–86, vol. 2, p. 278.

Table 2415

MEAT (FRESH) EXPORT VOLUME,
15 LRC, 1960-75
(T MET)

	Country	1960	1965	1970	1975
A.	ARGENTINA	280	349	352	79
B.	BOLIVIA	~	~	~	2

Continued in SALA, 24-2411, with yearly data.

Table 2416

COMPARISON OF ARGENTINA AND AUSTRALIA
BEEF CATTLE EXPORTS, 1938–77
(T MET)

Year	(1) Argentina Exports	(2) Australia Exports	(2/1) Australia % Argentina
1938–43	472.2	110.7	23.4
1955	411.4	224.5	54.6

Continued in SALA, 24-2412.

Table 2417

BANANA EXPORT VOLUME,[1] 14 LC, 1975–87[a]
(T MET)

	Country	1975	1978	1980	1981	1982	1983	1984	1985	1986	1987
B.	BOLIVIA	~	~	#	#	#	~	#	~	~	~
C.	BRAZIL	147	132	67	67	59	89	103.15	105.30	101.17	81.22
E.	COLOMBIA	486	592	692	795	804	787	1,029.82	783.04	987.13	962.00[‡]
F.	COSTA RICA	1,077	1,007	1,027	950	1,011	1,033	1,029.82	856.50	885.23	942.50[‡]
H.	DOMINICAN REP.[2]	26	11	11	28	18	6	5.56	3.24	2.24	1.51
I.	ECUADOR[2]	1,450	1,425	1,437	1,230	1,261	910	907.16	1,075.03	1,365.28	1,401.55
K.	GUATEMALA	260	316	336	370	404	316	320.93	365.83	391.90	380.00[‡]
L.	HAITI[2]	~	#	#	#	#	#	.07	.08	.08	~
M.	HONDURAS	420	760	987	820	914	714	848.32	871.76	771.10	903.50
N.	MEXICO[2]	3	18	16	6[‡]	7	31	32.43	43.83	76.20	88.50[‡]
O.	NICARAGUA[2]	135	123	121	100	147	69	82.94	89.04	78.41	72.30[‡]
P.	PANAMA[3]	558	628	505	573	566	652	655.36	686.22	586.87	675.58
R.	PERU	~	~	#	#	#	#	#	#	#	.1[‡]
T.	VENEZUELA[2]	7	6	6	7[‡]	7[†]	14	26.17	27.99	30.26	15.43
	WORLD	6,641	7,149	6,956	6,929	7,147	6,335	7,016.68	6,822.48	7,315.30	7,520.51

1. Figures refer to "special trade" except where otherwise indicated. For explanation of "Special" exports, see table 2413, n. 1.
2. Figures refer to "general trade," i.e., total exports including re-exports.
3. Data exclude the free zone of Colón and the Canal Zone.

a. For 1934–74, see SALA, 20-2916.

SOURCE: FAO-TY, 1978; 1980; 1981, table 55; 1982, table 55; 1984, table 55; 1985, table 56; 1986, 1987, table 56.

Table 2418

BANANA EXPORT VALUE,[1] 12 LC, 1980–86

Country	T US					Value as % of Total Market Economy				
	1980	1983	1984	1985	1986	1980	1983	1984	1985	1986
C. BRAZIL	11,164	10,676	34,759	20,930[†]	20,692[†]	#	~	~	~	~
D. CHILE	330	581[†]	~	~	~	#	~	~	~	~
E. COLOMBIA	94,141	147,696	197,915	156,165	320,845[†]	7.3	10.4	12.8	8.2	13.7[†]
F. COSTA RICA	214,501	286,177[†]	295,385[†]	280,885[†]	298,969[†]	16.6	20.2[†]	19.1[†]	14.7[†]	12.7[†]
H. DOMINICAN REP.	1,605	887	1,529	968	~	#	~	~	~	~
I. ECUADOR	195,591	145,562	136,460	443,116[†]	417,043[†]	15.1	10.3	8.8	23.2[†]	17.7[†]
K. GUATEMALA	52,418	43,675	63,744[†]	72,973[†]	46,552[†]	4.1	3.1	4.1[†]	3.8[†]	2.0[†]
M. HONDURAS	233,143	199,573	234,595	323,872[†]	285,258[†]	18.0	14.1	15.1	16.9[†]	12.1[†]
N. MEXICO	~	3,667[†]	5,587[†]	8,379[†]	11,159[†]	~	~	~	~	~
O. NICARAGUA	8,386	31,467[†]	33,683[†]	35,177[†]	27,317[†]	#	~	~	~	~
P. PANAMA	61,714	75,492	75,188	46,829	66,990[†]	4.8	5.3	4.9	2.4	2.9[†]
T. VENEZUELA	1,649	2,918	6,051[†]	5,618[†]	7,129[†]	4.7	3.9	~	~	~
LAIA	302,893	310,519	380,783	634,211[†]	776,918[†]	23.4	22.0	24.6	33.1[†]	33.1[†]
CACM	508,448	560,906[†]	627,420[†]	712,907[†]	658,475[†]	39.3[†]	39.6[†]	40.5[†]	37.3[†]	28.0[†]
UNITED STATES	71,505	72,148	70,640	73,273	72,079	5.5	5.1	4.6	3.8	3.1

1. Including fresh and dry plantain.

SOURCE: UN-YITS, 1982, vol 2, p. 292; UN-YITS, 1983, vol. 2, p. 280; UN-YITS, 1984–86,
    vol. 2, p. 314.

Table 2419

BARLEY IMPORT VOLUME,[1] 17 LC, 1975–87[a]
(T MET)

Country	1975	1978	1980	1981	1982	1983	1984	1985	1986	1987
A. ARGENTINA	~	~	#	#	#	~	~	~	~	~
C. BRAZIL	22	32	93	119	102	169	146	178	131	99
D. CHILE	~	~	38	6	#	~	12	6	17	64
E. COLOMBIA	12	108	39	80	98	118	116	107	100	133[‡]
F. COSTA RICA	#	#	17	#	#	#	#	#	~	~
G. CUBA	31	44	57	60[‡]	43	41	43	46	42	39[‡]
H. DOMINICAN REP.	~	~	#	#	#	~	~	~	~	~
I. ECUADOR[3]	10[‡]	28	23	36	26	27	1	18	20	16
J. EL SALVADOR	#	~	#	#	#	#	~	~	~	~
K. GUATEMALA	~	~	#	#	#	~	~	~	~	~
M. HONDURAS	~	~	#	#	#	~	~	~	~	~
N. MEXICO[2,3]	150	88	176	91	20	67	88	38	11	1[‡]
O. NICARAGUA	~	~	#	#	#	#	#	#	~	~
P. PANAMA	#	#	#	#	#	#	.1	.1	.2	6[‡]
R. PERU	33[‡]	21[‡]	36	36	37	19	33	57	60	82[‡]
S. URUGUAY[3]	4	#	7	22	23	31	30	7	30	25[‡]
T. VENEZUELA[3]	#	#	#	#	#	#	#	#	#	1
UNITED STATES	~	~	140	127	198	141	146	105	135	201
WORLD	~	~	14,997	18,599	18,670	17,691	22,987	21,837	23,508	21,280

1. Figures refer to "special trade" except where otherwise indicated. For explanation of
    "Special" imports, see table 2412, n. 1.
2. Imports through free zones included.
3. Figures refer to "general trade," i.e., total imports.

a. For 1934–74, see SALA, 20-2918.

SOURCE: FAO-TY, 1978; 1980; 1981; 1982, table 40; 1984, table 40; 1985, table 41;
    1986, 1987, table 41.

Table 2420

BARLEY EXPORT VOLUME,[1] 4 LC, 1975–87[a]

(T MET)

	Country	1975	1978	1980	1981	1982	1983	1984	1985	1986	1987
A.	ARGENTINA	18	15	43	6	1	31	18	34	.56	12
D.	CHILE	7	#	9	#	8	5	14	#	.43	#
N.	MEXICO[3]	1	- -	#	#	#	#	#	#	#	#
S.	URUGUAY[3]	3	3	22	26	15	23	63	51.81	44.98	20.00[‡]
	UNITED STATES[2,3]	651	649	1,463	2,067	1,375	1,521	1,971	706	1,600.51	3,023.53
	WORLD	12,412	14,596	16,215	19,299	18,472	17,754	23,008	21,899.58	26,059.76	22,172.06

1. Figures refer to "special trade" except where otherwise indicated. See table 2413 n. 1,
   for explanation of "special" exports.
2. The customs area includes the Commonwealth of Puerto Rico.
3. Figures refer to "general trade," i.e., total exports including re-exports.

a. For 1934–74, see SALA, 20-2917.

SOURCE: FAO-TY, 1978; 1980; 1981, table 40; 1982, table 40; 1984, table 40; 1985–87,
   table 41.

Table 2421

BUTTER IMPORT VOLUME,[1] 18 LC, 1975–87[a]

(T MET)

	Country	1975	1979	1980	1981	1982	1983	1984	1985	1986	1987
A.	ARGENTINA	4	3	1	2[‡]	.5[‡]	#	.4	.6	.4	.5
B.	BOLIVIA	~	#	#	#	#	#	.1	.5[‡]	.2[‡]	.3[‡]
C.	BRAZIL	4	1	6	#	#	#	1	3	33	30
D.	CHILE	50	9	7	4	5	2	2	.5	#	.5
E.	COLOMBIA	~	3	3	#	#	1	#	.2	.4	#
F.	COSTA RICA	2	1	1	#	#	~	~	#	~	~
G.	CUBA	~	17	21	20[‡]	15	16	17	17	17	3[‡]
H.	DOMINICAN REP.[3]	#	#	#	#	#	#	2	.1	.2[‡]	.2[†]
J.	EL SALVADOR	1	#	#[‡]	#[†]	#[‡]	#	.2	.1	.1	.1[‡]
K.	GUATEMALA	~	#	#[‡]	#[‡]	#[‡]	#[‡]	.2	.3[‡]	.3[‡]	.3[‡]
L.	HAITI[3]	#	#	#[‡]	#[‡]	#[‡]	·#[‡]	.1	.3[‡]	.2[‡]	.3[‡]
M.	HONDURAS	1	#	#	1[‡]	.8[‡]	#	.1	.1	#	.1[‡]
N.	MEXICO[2,3]	31	19[‡]	25	24	18	17	18	25	17	19
O.	NICARAGUA	~	#	#	1[‡]	.8[‡]	1	1	2	2[‡]	1[‡]
P.	PANAMA[4]	1	2	2	1	1[‡]	1	1	1	1	1[‡]
R.	PERU	110	13	8	7	9	14	12	6	6	9[‡]
S.	URUGUAY	~	#	#	#	#	~	#	#	#	~
T.	VENEZUELA[3]	1	2	2	3[‡]	1	#	#	#	#	~
	UNITED STATES		#	#	1	1	1	1	1	2	4
	WORLD	1,014	1,221	1,380	1,478	1,310	1,283	1,242	1,367	1,308	1,754

1. Figures refer to "special trade" except where otherwise indicated. See table 2412, n.1,
   for explanation of "special" imports.
2. Imports through free zones are included.
3. Figures refer to "general trade," i.e., total imports.
4. Data exclude the free zone of Colón and the Canal Zone.

a. For 1934-76, see SALA, 20-2919.

SOURCE: FAO-TY, 1976; 1978; 1980; 1981, table 30; 1982, table 30; 1984, table 30;
   1985–87, table 31.

Table 2422

CACAO BEAN EXPORT VOLUME,[1] 9 LC, 1975-87[a]

(T MET)

	Country	1975	1978	1979	1980	1981	1982	1983	1984	1985	1986	1987
C.	BRAZIL	177	134	157	124	125	143	153	107	172	135	143
F.	COSTA RICA	5	6	4	2	2[‡]	2	1	1	1	1	1[‡]
H.	DOMINICAN REP.[2]	22	28	26	23	27	39	34	32	31	36	39
I.	ECUADOR[2]	38	16	15	14	24	42	6	47	69	38	44
K.	GUATEMALA	1	3	2[†]	1	#	#	1	1[‡]	1	1	2[‡]
L.	HAITI[2]	1	2[‡]	3	2	3	2	4	2	4	3	3
N.	MEXICO[2]	4	4	2	1	#	3	2	2	2	2	2
P.	PANAMA[3]	~	1	1	1	#	1	#	#	.4	.3	#
T.	VENEZUELA[2]	16	7	7	8	8[‡]	7	9	6	6	5	6
	WORLD	1,169	108	1,017	1,090	1,171	1,251	1,206	1,349	1,393	1,502	1,520

1. Figures refer to "special trade" except where otherwise indicated. See table 2413, n.1, for explanation of "special" imports.
2. Figures refer to "general trade," i.e., total exports including re-exports.
3. Data excluded the free zone of Colón and the Canal Zone.

a. For 1934-74, see SALA, 20-2920.

SOURCE: FAO-TY, 1978; 1980; 1981; table 71; 1982, table 71; 1984, table 71; 1985-87, table 72.

Table 2423

COCOA EXPORT VALUE, 13 LC, 1980-86

	Country	T US					Value as % of Total Market Economy				
		1980	1983	1984	1985	1986	1980	1983	1984	1985	1986
B.	BOLIVIA	1,663[†]	~	443	1,165	~	#[†]	~	~	~	~
C.	BRAZIL	696,586	885,674	1,070,540	512,732[†]	529,899	15.0	18.7	23.4	12.0[†]	12.2[†]
E.	COLOMBIA	4,757	5,825	17,921	15,207	12,965[†]	#	~	~	~	~
F.	COSTA RICA	13,979	3,337[†]	6,519[†]	8,039[†]	7,569[†]	#	~	~	~	~
G.	CUBA	2,677	8,463[†]	22,403[†]	25,948[†]	13,551[†]	#[†]	~	~	~	~
H.	DOMINICAN REP.	53,790	119,638	31,772[†]	12,343[†]	38,427[†]	#	~	~	~	~
I.	ECUADOR	210,188	19,315	115,441	192,332[†]	88,162[†]	4.5	.4	2.5	4.5[†]	2.0[†]
K.	GUATEMALA	3,394	3,869	2,968[†]	1,162[†]	2,152[†]	#	~	~	~	~
L.	HAITI	6,688[†]	2,366[†]	2,957[†]	3,001[†]	2,288[†]	#[†]	~	~	~	~
N.	MEXICO	29,794	~	25,891	~	~	#	~	~	~	~
P.	PANAMA	2,118	4,886	8,763	7,723	744[†]	#	~	~	~	~
R.	PERU	16,742	16,620	24,889	17,581[†]	13,272[†]	#	~	~	~	~
T.	VENEZUELA	28,626	17,480	22,665[†]	16,248[†]	13,282[†]	#	~	~	~	~
	LAIA	988,037	946,384	1,253,224	755,642[†]	659,204[†]	21.1	20.0	27.4	17.7[†]	15.2[†]
	CACM	18,349	10,624[†]	15,356[†]	14,439[†]	14,873[†]	.4	.2[†]	.3[†]	.3[†]	.3[†]
	UNITED STATES	6,547	43,834	53,420	40,915	40,681	#	~	~	~	~

SOURCE: UN-YITS, 1982, vol. 2, p. 40; 1983, vol. 2, p. 28; 1984-86, vol. 2, p. 62.

Table 2424

COFFEE BEAN EXPORT VOLUME,[1] 17 LC, 1975–87
(T MET)

	Country	1975	1979	1980	1981	1982	1983	1984	1985	1986	1987
B.	BOLIVIA	5	7.5	5	5	7	7	3	7	5‡	6‡
C.	BRAZIL	774	562	785	825	888	940	1,032	1,034	478	988
E.	COLOMBIA	489	657	660	544	525	539	599	585	667	677‡
F.	COSTA RICA	75	97	72	106	96	108	113	124	94	136‡
G.	CUBA	8	7	9	6	9†	17	10	12	12‡	15‡
H.	DOMINICAN REP.[2]	32	43	26	32	36	30	35	33	31	30
I.	ECUADOR[2]	64	82	54	56	74	75	71	75	109	112
J.	EL SALVADOR	141	185	147	212‡	141	159	160	148	123	146
K.	GUATEMALA	125	147	125	132‡	141	143	127	173	155	148‡
L.	HAITI	18	14	25	14	15	24	19	18	17	13
M.	HONDURAS	49	66	60	70‡	58	75	69	72	79‡	87‡
N.	MEXICO	142	175	130	122	126	185	174	227	208	223
O.	NICARAGUA[2]	41	55	46	49‡	57	56	42	40	31	39‡
P.	PANAMA[4]	2	3	3	5	4	6	5	5	8	8
Q.	PARAGUAY	6	1	.6	#	#	~	~	#	~	~
R.	PERU	43	70	43	40	40	56	53	60‡	74‡	66‡
T.	VENEZUELA[2]	14	8	2	2	1	2	5	9	19	13
	UNITED STATES[2,3]	55	79	79	70	60	43	63	52	77	60
	WORLD	3,550	3,800	3,717	3,763	3,939	4,039	4,210	4,442	4,034	4,441

1. Figures refer to "special trade" except where otherwise indicated. See table 2413, n.1,
   for explanation of "special" imports.
2. Figures refer to "general trade," i.e., total exports including re-exports.
3. The customs area includes the Commonwealth of Puerto Rico.
4. Data exclude the free zone of Colón and the Canal Zone.

a. For 1934–75, see SALA, 20-2921.

SOURCE: FAO-TY, 1978; 1980; 1981; table 70; 1982, table 70; 1984, table 70; 1985–87,
  table 71.

Table 2425

COFFEE EXPORT VALUE,[1] 16 LC, 1980–86

	Country	T US					Value as % of Total Market Economy				
		1980	1983	1984	1985	1986	1980	1983	1984	1985	1986
B.	BOLIVIA	17,178†	13,066	6,489	13,940	21,673†	#†	~	~	~	~
C.	BRAZIL	2,486,055	2,095,803	5,281,637	3,005,057†	2,675,460†	20.3	22.4	39.3	25.7†	17.7†
E.	COLOMBIA	2,360,804	1,506,187	1,764,504	1,745,521	2,840,377†	19.2	16.1	13.1	14.9	18.8†
F.	COSTA RICA	247,827	174,427	200,814†	246,378†	298,338†	#	~	~	~	~
G.	CUBA	31,388†	337,258	258,663†	238,407†	360,695†	.3†	3.6†	1.9†	2.0†	2.4†
H.	DOMINICAN REP.	77,214	76,200	95,115	90,655	75,849†	#	~	~	~	~
I.	ECUADOR	132,181	153,056	177,267	189,301†	269,875†	#†	~	~	~	~
J.	EL SALVADOR	262,039	389,342†	309,519†	460,741†	559,318†	2.1	4.2†	2.3†	3.9†	3.7†
K.	GUATEMALA	469,305	357,746	344,975†	374,213†	440,035†	3.8	3.8	2.6†	3.2†	2.9†
L.	HAITI	98,592	23,300†	22,294†	21,073†	25,707†	#†	~	~	~	~
M.	HONDURAS	207,458	150,377	165,267	168,567†	326,249†	#	~	~	~	~
N.	MEXICO	437,109	424,273	475,419	346,146†	499,697†	3.6	4.5	3.5	3.0†	3.3†
O.	NICARAGUA	165,670	132,274†	113,023†	91,943†	152,006†	#	~	~	~	~
P.	PANAMA	10,441	15,940	12,987	15,585	10,229†	#	~	~	~	~
R.	PERU	139,760	111,954	129,823	138,299†	263,583†	#	~	~	~	~
T.	VENEZUELA	7,931	3,289	15,590†	17,245†	53,214†	#	~	~	~	~
	LAIA	5,583,342	4,344,869	7,851,781	5,489,458†	6,669,569†	45.4	46.5	58.4	46.9†	44.1†
	CACM	1,352,299	1,204,167†	1,133,598†	1,341,842†	1,775,946†	11.0	12.9†	8.4†	11.5†	11.7†
	UNITED STATES	319,098	161,604	214,851	180,426	320,405	3.0	1.9	~	~	~

1. Including green, roasted, and substitutes.

SOURCE: UN-YITS, 1982, vol. 2, p. 39; 1983, vol. 2, table 071; 1984–86, vol. 2, p. 324.

Table 2426

BRAZIL SHARE OF WORLD COFFEE
EXPORTS, 1953–85

(T 60-kg Bags)

Year	Total	Brazil	% Brazil
1953	34,647	15,562	44.9
1954	29,918	10,918	37.8
1955	33,698	13,696	40.7
1956	38,394	16,804	43.8
1957	36,057	14,319	39.7
1958	36,505	12,894	35.3
1959	42,587	17,723	41.6
1960	42,491	16,819	39.6
1961	43,725	16,971	38.8
1962	46,256	16,377	35.4
1963	48,906	19,514	39.9
1964	46,721	14,948	32.0
1965	44,969	13,497	30.0
1966	49,028	17,031	34.7
1967	50,219	17,331	34.5
1968	53,608	19,035	35.5
1969	54,196	19,613	36.2
1970	52,722	17,085	32.4
1971	53,489	18,399	34.4
1972	57,866	19,215	33.2
1973	62,584	19,817	31.7
1974	54,787	13,280	24.2
1975	57,913	14,604	25.3
1976	58,806	15,602	26.5
1977	47,168	10,083	21.4
1978	56,208	12,551	22.3
1979	62,865	12,010	19.1
1980	59,861	15,269	25.5
1981	60,612	15,697	25.9
1982	64,553	17,208	26.7
1983	66,254	17,846	26.9
1984	68,582	19,505	28.6
1985	70,980	19,153	27.0

SOURCE: *Anuário Estatístico do Café*, 1986, p. 69.

Figure 24:2

BRAZIL SHARE OF WORLD COFFEE EXPORTS, 1953–85

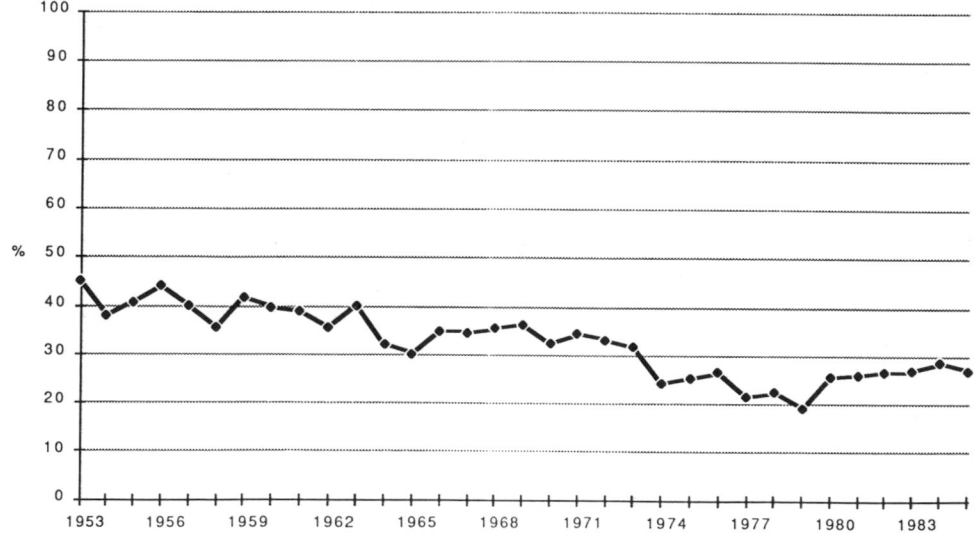

SOURCE: Table 2426, above.

Table 2429

UNITED STATES LEADING SUPPLIERS OF COFFEE
(1986)

Source	Volume (T 60-kg Bags)	%	Value (M US)
E. COLOMBIA	2,629	13.5	656.8
C. BRAZIL	2,200	11.3	501.9
N. MEXICO	2,125	10.9	500.4
K. GUATEMALA	1,658	8.5	363.0
I. ECUADOR	1,371	7.0	257.2
Indonesia	1,346	6.9	217.0
J. EL SALVADOR	1,108	5.7	263.0
Uganda	737	3.8	132.3
Ivory Coast	694	3.6	125.2
R. PERU	675	3.4	148.9
Others	4,940	25.4	1,061.8
Total	19,483	100.0	4,287.5

SOURCE: *Colombia Today*, vol. 22, no. 2, 1987.

Table 2430

MAIZE IMPORT VOLUME,[1] 17 L, 1975–87[a]
(T MET)

Country	1975	1979	1980	1981	1982	1983	1984	1985	1986	1987
B. BOLIVIA	~	#	#	#	#	1	5	.1‡	.3‡	3‡
C. BRAZIL	2	1,526	1,594	902	#	213	254	262	2,424	871
D. CHILE	86	200	357	309	397	144	36	.4	54	136
E. COLOMBIA	18	60	193	80	89	69	10	28	32	44‡
F. COSTA RICA	13	4	61	25	72	51	33	26	21‡	58‡
G. CUBA	~	350	610	580‡	367	402	423	409	449	430‡
H. DOMINICAN REP.[3]	54	102	171	162	172	196	174	149	210‡	375‡
J. EL SALVADOR	27	12	14	11	27	102	87	55‡	26‡	59‡
K. GUATEMALA	68	55	81	52	6	1	#	2‡	74‡	110‡
L. HAITI[3]	:	25‡	5‡	10‡	8‡	8	8‡	30‡	10‡	10‡
M. HONDURAS	44	7	64	23‡	6	14	15	2	13‡	52‡
N. MEXICO[4,3]	2,636	744	3,777	3,065	233	4,687	2,498	1,726	1,703	3,603
O. NICARAGUA[3]	21	2	48	40	25	137	12	34	25	25†
P. PANAMA[2]	6	25	39	26	33	30	14	49	12	33‡
R. PERU	236	101	261	336	498	362	158	291	304	500‡
S. URUGUAY[3]	#	44	10‡	14‡	6	2	5	12	4	44‡
T. VENEZUELA[3]	508	448	1,227	1,008	1,033	1,393	1,323	670	2	#

1. Figures refer to "special trade" except where otherwise noted. See table 2412, n.1, for explanation of "special" imports.
2. Data exclude the free zone of Colón and the Canal Zone.
3. Figures refer to "generate trade," i.e., total imports.
4. Imports through free zones are included.

a. For 1934–74, see SALA, 20-2924.

SOURCE: FAO-TY, 1978; 1980; 1981, table 47; 1982, table 44; 1984, table 41; 1985, table 42; 1986, table 41; 1987, table 42.

Table 2431

MAIZE EXPORT VOLUME,[1] 15 LC, 1975–87[a]

(T MET)

	Country	1975	1979	1980	1981	1982	1983	1984	1985	1986	1987
A.	ARGENTINA	4,001	5,960	3,481	9,163	5,226	6,525	5,518	7,069	7,411	3,963
C.	BRAZIL	1,200	10	6	7	544	766	178	#	#	#
D.	CHILE	~	#	#	#	#	~	85	2	#	#[‡]
E.	COLOMBIA	~	#	#	#	#	~	~	#	#	#
F.	COSTA RICA	~	#	#	#	#	#	#	#	#	#
H.	DOMINICAN REP.[2]	~	#	#	#	#	#	#	#	#	#
I.	ECUADOR[2]	~	#	#	1	15	#	#	#	#	#
J.	EL SALVADOR	~	2	20	10	#	#	#	19	2	#
K.	GUATEMALA	~	#	#	#	#	3	#	5	2[†]	2[†]
M.	HONDURAS	~	#	#	#	6	3	7	21	#	#
N.	MEXICO[2]	4	#	1	#	1	21	5	4	#	#
O.	NICARAGUA[2]	~	3	#	#	#	#	#	#	#	#
Q.	PARAGUAY	6	#	25	2	7	~	12	#	1	#
R.	PERU	7	2	3	2[‡]	1	1	1[‡]	2	1	1[‡]
S.	URUGUAY[2]	~	4	2	6	#	~	~	7	#	#
	WORLD	49,638	76,087	80,280	78,930	69,984	69,046	68,961	69,767	57,632	64,289

1. Figures refer to "special trade" except where otherwise indicated. See table 2413, n. 1,
   for explanation of "special" imports.
2. Figures refer to "general trade," i.e., total exports including re-exports.

a. For 1934–74, see SALA, 20-2923.

SOURCE: FAO-TY, 1978; 1980; 1981, table 41; 1982, table 41; 1984, table 41; 1985,
   table 42; 1986, 1987, table 42.

Table 2432

MILK (DRY) IMPORT VOLUME,[1] 19 L, 1975–87[a]

(T MET)

	Country	1975	1978[b]	1979[b]	1980	1981	1982	1983	1984	1985	1986	1987
A.	ARGENTINA	~	13	18	18	4	#	~	#[‡]	#[‡]	#	3[‡]
B.	BOLIVIA	5	8[‡]	7	8[‡]	7[‡]	4	1	3	6	10[‡]	11[‡]
C.	BRAZIL	14	12	10	62	8	8	19	17	31	214	101
D.	CHILE	9	14	18	16	14	11	15	18	4	#	13
E.	COLOMBIA[6]	4	19[‡]	7	19	36	7	6	3	3	4	4[‡]
F.	COSTA RICA	3	3	2	2	2	2	2	1	#	#	#
G.	CUBA	~	35[‡]	40	39	43	24	33	35	40	37	38[†]
H.	DOMINICAN REP.[2,5]	2	6	7	9	7	3	10	13	10	14[‡]	18[‡]
I.	ECUADOR[5]	3	4	7	7	3	4	4	4	5	2	4[‡]
J.	EL SALVADOR[2]	8	11	11	12	12	8	11	4	4	9	13
K.	GUATEMALA	3	5[‡]	6	8	7	7	9[‡]	18	6	12	13[‡]
L.	HAITI[6,5]	5	5[‡]	2[‡]	4[‡]	2[‡]	5	5[‡]	5	7[‡]	6[‡]	12[‡]
M.	HONDURAS	5	4	5	6	6	4	6	6	7	8	9[‡]
N.	MEXICO[3,5]	38	60	85	185	91	71	108	111	198	171	178
O.	NICARAGUA[5]	1	1	4	2	5[‡]	11	8	11	2	4	6
P.	PANAMA[4]	3	2	2	2	3	3	4	4	4	4	3
Q.	PARAGUAY[6]	#	#	#	.6	1	1[‡]	2	2	1	#	1
R.	PERU	18	18[‡]	16	27	18	27	23	21	28	57	58
T.	VENEZUELA[5]	28	103	73	89	103	103	73	106	75	33	74

1. Figures refer to "special trade" except where otherwise indicated. See table 2412, n. 1,
   for explanation of "special" imports.
2. Includes condensed and powdered milk.
3. Imports through free zones included.
4. Data exclude the free zone of Colón and the Canal Zone.
5. Figures refer to "general trade," i.e., total imports.
6. Includes fresh, condensed, and powdered milk.

a. For 1934–74, see SALA, 20-2928.
b. Powdered milk only.

SOURCE: FAO-TY, 1978; 1980; 1982, table 28; 1984, table 28; 1984, table 29; 1986,
   1987, table 29.

Table 2433

OAT IMPORT VOLUME,[1] 13 L, 1975–87[a]

(T MET)

	Country	1975	1978	1979	1980	1981	1982	1983	1984	1985	1986	1987
B.	BOLIVIA	~	~	~	~	~	.5[‡]	#[‡]	#	#	#	#
C.	BRAZIL	254	33	40	24	18	4	18	11	5	8	16
E.	COLOMBIA	75	9[‡]	13	10	10	11	6	7	11	8	11[‡]
F.	COSTA RICA	1	#	#	#	#	#	.5	#	#	#	#
G.	CUBA	~	27	26	13	10	15	13	11	16	18	15[‡]
H.	DOMINICAN REP.[3]	65	1	2	2	2	1	2	1	2	#	#[‡]
I.	ECUADOR[3]	191	18	22	11	12	25	15	16	15	15	24[‡]
N.	MEXICO[4,3]	1	#	#	.7	21	1	1[‡]	#	#	10	#
O.	NICARAGUA[3]	22	2	3	6	6[†]	2	2	2	1	#	#
P.	PANAMA[2]	4	.9	#	#[‡]	#[‡]	#	#	#	1	#	1
R.	PERU	5	4[‡]	4	#	5	8	6	5	8	7	20
S.	URUGUAY[3]	1	1	19	2	3	7	12	12	9	4	10
T.	VENEZUELA[3]	60	6	4	3	7	4	4	3	6	9	12

1. Figures refer to "special trade" except where otherwise indicated. See table 2412, n. 1, for explanation of "special" imports.
2. Data exclude the free zone of Colón and the Canal Zone.
3. Figures refer to "general trade," i.e., total imports.
4. Imports through free zones included.

a. For 1934–74, see SALA, 20-2930.

SOURCE: FAO-TY, 1978; 1980; 1982, table 43; 1984, table 43; 1985–87, table 44.

Table 2434

OAT EXPORT VOLUME,[1] 4 L, 1975–87[a]

(T MET)

	Country	1975	1979	1980	1981	1982	1983	1984	1985	1986	1987
A.	ARGENTINA	204	83	62	123	54	83	46	100	4	19
D.	CHILE	6	#	2[‡]	1[‡]	1[‡]	1[‡]	1[‡]	3	18	4
N.	MEXICO[2]	1	#	#	#	#	~	~	#	#	#
S.	URUGUAY	2	#	2	1	2[‡]	~	~	1	#	#

1. Figures refer to "special trade" except where otherwise noted. See table 2413, n. 1, for explanation of "special" imports.
2. Figures refer to "general trade," i.e., total exports including re-exports.

a. For 1934–74, see SALA, 20-2929.

SOURCE: FAO-TY, 1978; 1980; 1982, table 43; 1984, table 43; 1985–87, table 44.

Table 2435

RICE IMPORT VOLUME,[1] 20 L, 1975–87[a]

(T MET)

Country	1975	1979	1980	1981	1982	1983	1984	1985	1986	1987
A. ARGENTINA	~	10	3	5[‡]	#	~	#	#	#	#
B. BOLIVIA	2	~	~	~	3	35	8	19	9	2
C. BRAZIL	44	711	239	143	137	315	#	340	1,398	102
D. CHILE	21	9	48	16	21	31	8	3	37	21
E. COLOMBIA	~	14	4	#	#	#	#	#	#	#
F. COSTA RICA	1	#	#	#	1	39	#	#	#	#
G. CUBA	~	161	224	200[‡]	201	207	184	242	189	200[‡]
H. DOMINICAN REP.[3]	50	#	33	65	#	~	~	12	91	55[‡]
I. ECUADOR[3]	20	25	22	10	9[‡]	35	4	14	#	#
J. EL SALVADOR	8	5	5	5	3[‡]	7	12	18[‡]	11[‡]	24[‡]
K. GUATEMALA	6	10	4	4	#	4	2[‡]	#	17	10
L. HAITI[3]	2	17[‡]	23[‡]	24[‡]	25[‡]	15[‡]	5[‡]	7[‡]	17	20[†]
M. HONDURAS	11	5	4	4	3	2	2[‡]	2	5	6[‡]
N. MEXICO[4,3]	~	36	93	74	22	#	170	200	6	#
O. NICARAGUA[3]	~	10	37	22	#	5	18	33	21	25
P. PANAMA[2]	#	#	#	#	#	#	#	#	#	#
Q. PARAGUAY	~	#	#	#	#	~	~	~	~	~
R. PERU	78	202	211	111	59	103[‡]	59	23	193	211[‡]
S. URUGUAY[3]	~	#	#	#	#	#	#	#	#	#
T. VENEZUELA[3]	~	1	#	#	1	#	~	1	#	14

1. Figures refer to "special trade" except where otherwise noted. See table 2412, n. 1, for explanation of "special" imports.
2. Data exclude the free zone of Colón and the Canal Zone.
3. Figures refer to "general trade," i.e., total imports.
4. Imports through free zones included.

a. For 1934–74, see SALA, 20-2931.

SOURCE: FAO-TY, 1978; 1980; 1982, table 39; 1984, table 39; 1985–87, table 40.

Table 2436

SOYBEAN EXPORT VALUE, 11 LC, 1979–86

	T US						Value as % of World Exports					
Country	1979	1980	1983	1984	1985	1986	1979	1980	1983	1984	1985	1986
A. ARGENTINA	702,937	548,418[†]	309,324[†]	401,616[†]	315,709[†]	494,182[†]	10.3	8.6	4.5	9.8[†]	8.8[†]	12.1[†]
B. BOLIVIA	172	~	~	1,856	3,680	5,320[†]	#	~	~	~	~	~
C. BRAZIL	179,506	393,930	1,744,927[†]	1,529,021[†]	1,461,107[†]	1,420,644[†]	31.4[†]	33.3[†]	36.0[†]	37.2[†]	40.6[†]	34.9[†]
E. COLOMBIA	~	98	~	~	~	~	~	#	~	~	~	~
F. COSTA RICA	~	32	~	~	~	~	~	#	~	~	~	~
K. GUATEMALA	29	#	60[†]	~	~	~	#	#	~	~	~	~
M. HONDURAS	7[†]	7[†]	45[†]	~	~	~	#[†]	#[†]	~	~	~	~
N. MEXICO	#	3[†]	4[†]	12	11	~	#	#[†]	~	~	~	~
O. NICARAGUA	46[†]	3	1[†]	49	28	~	#[†]	#	~	~	~	~
Q. PARAGUAY	78,617	42,098	3,640[†]	1,141[†]	5,394[†]	4,102[†]	1.2	.6	4.4[†]	1.7	1.8	~
S. URUGUAY	1,815	1,895	2,137	246[†]	1,247[†]	166[†]	#	#	#[†]	#	~	~
LAIA	963,594	986,444[†]	1,996,338[†]	1,934,206[†]	1,787,316[†]	1,924,572[†]	14.2	14.8	41.2[†]	47.1[†]	49.6[†]	47.3[†]
CACM	76[†]	42[†]	1[†]	12[†]	~	~	#[†]	#[†]	#[†]	0	0	0
UNITED STATES	5,708,063	5,882,911	1,527,074	1,019,337	870,651	1,228,581	41.8	40.4	31.5	24.8	24.2	30.2

SOURCE: UN-YITS, 1982, vol. 2, p. 329; 1983, vol. 2, table 2222; 1984–86, vol. 2, p. 333.

Table 2437

SOYBEAN OIL IMPORT VOLUME,[1] 19 L, 1975–87[a]
(T MET)

Country	1975	1979	1980	1981	1982	1983	1984	1985	1986	1987
A. ARGENTINA	~	#	#	#	#	~	~	~	~	~
B. BOLIVIA	3	4‡	13‡	15	7	8	1	10‡	4‡	5‡
C. BRAZIL	2	77	50	#	22	32	123	114	190	37
D. CHILE	74	53	59	65	75‡	90‡	83	80	42	43
E. COLOMBIA	60	76	79	109	125	104	109	52	60	40‡
F. COSTA RICA	3	2	7	4‡	2‡	#	1	2	2‡	2‡
H. DOMINICAN REP.³	170	19	22	20	39	36	27	34	60‡	52‡
I. ECUADOR³	156	20	30	26	36	65	44‡	35	10	18‡
J. EL SALVADOR	1	2	.6	3	1	2	1	1	2	1
K. GUATEMALA	#	1	#	#	2	3‡	5‡	9	23	9‡
L. HAITI³	53	17	25‡	19‡	16‡	14‡	13‡	22‡	25‡	13‡
M. HONDURAS	1	1	#	.9‡	#	1	1‡	1	1‡	1‡
N. MEXICO⁴,³	18	#	42	5‡	104	#	86	45	40	27
O. NICARAGUA³	1	1	1	.6‡	#	~	3	~	~	~
P. PANAMA²	108	20	32	18	19	21	18	21	25	18‡
Q. PARAGUAY	~	#	#	#	#	~	~	#	#	#
R. PERU	548	14	35	70	64	75	56	37	49	72‡
S. URUGUAY³	#	.9	#‡	#	2	2	#	1	#	#
T. VENEZUELA³	~	36	20	56‡	45	57	111	79	56	86

1. Figures refer to "special trade" except where otherwise indicated. See table 2412, n. 1, for explanation of "special" imports.
2. Data exclude the free zone of Colón and the Canal Zone.
3. Figures refer to "general trade," i.e., total imports.
4. Imports through free zones included.

a. For 1934–74, see SALA, 20-2932.

SOURCE: FAO-TY, 1978; 1980; 1982, table 116; 1984, table 116; 1985, table 116; 1986, 1987, table 117.

Table 2438

SOYBEAN OILCAKE EXPORT VALUE, 8 LC, 1980–86

Country	T US						Value as % of Total Market Economy					
	1980	1982	1983	1984	1985	1986	1980	1982	1983	1984	1985	1986
A. ARGENTINA	60,463†	163,125†	243,578†	643,261	468,551	727,820†	~	3.8	4.2	9.7	10.7	14.2†
B. BOLIVIA	6,888†	2,561†	1,979†	1,856	3,765	5,320†	#	#	~	~	~	~
C. BRAZIL	1,361,920†	1,595,366†	2,661,069†	3,125,320	1,531,888†	1,499,870†	33.3	36.9	46.2	47.2	35.1†	29.3†
I. ECUADOR	467†	430†	~	~	~	~	#	#	~	~	~	~
P. PANAMA	118†	9†	~	~	~	~	#	#	~	~	~	~
Q. PARAGUAY	7,062†	1,832†	3,506	~	13,823†	9,424†	#	#	~	~	~	~
R. PERU	~	11†	~	~	~	~	~	#	~	~	~	~
S. URUGUAY	3,538†	324†	1,239	712	2,066	958†	#	~	~	~	~	~
LAIA	1,439,872	1,763,207	2,411,999	3,771,475	2,020,317†	2,245,577†	35.2	40.8	39.5	57.0	46.2†	43.8†
UNITED STATES	1,654,233	1,411,441	1,527,074	1,052,819	891,164	1,248,020	40.9	32.7	26.5	15.9	20.4	24.3

SOURCE: UN-YITS, 1982, vol. 2, p. 311; 1984, vol. 2, table 08131; 1985, 1986, vol. 2, p. 332.

Table 2439

SUGAR EXPORT VOLUME,[1] 19 L, 1975–87[a]

(T MET)

Country	1975	1979	1980	1981	1982	1983	1984	1985	1986	1987
A. ARGENTINA	197	361	487	726	255	892	416	150	108	82[‡]
B. BOLIVIA	62	125	107	20	44	53	37	6	10[‡]	7[‡]
C. BRAZIL	1,750	1,867	2,626	2,781	2,805	2,572	3,165	2,651	2,535	2,291
D. CHILE	56	18	39	13	#	2	#	#	#	#
E. COLOMBIA	198	241	278	177	314	301	184	292	227	96[‡]
F. COSTA RICA	102	69	72	83	55	54	103	32	76[‡]	84[‡]
G. CUBA	~	7,199[‡]	6,170[‡]	7,071[‡]	7,436	6,747	6,746	6,941	6,405	6,482[‡]
H. DOMINICAN REP.[2]	950	986	794	855	827	918	860	719	456	560
I. ECUADOR[2]	21	69	67	47	#	~	35	19	17	9
J. EL SALVADOR	128	138	37	34	54	92	75	116	100	38
K. GUATEMALA	204	157	199	228	127	267	203	243	286	278[‡]
L. HAITI[2]	25	#	19	#	6	13	15	5[‡]	11[‡]	7[‡]
M. HONDURAS	10	55	78	95	96	106	119	119	95	98
N. MEXICO[2]	178	101	#	#	#	15	~	128	192	510
O. NICARAGUA[2]	89	91	62	89	79	112	90	52	75	49
P. PANAMA[3]	82	135	130	94	107	120	82	84	61	53
Q. PARAGUAY	14	#	6	#	15	15	11	10	11	8[‡]
R. PERU	422	181	54	#	140	10	40	60[‡]	57[‡]	33[‡]
T. VENEZUELA[2]	~	#	#	#	#	#	#	#	#	#

1. Figures refer to "special trade" except where otherwise indicated. See table 2413, n. 1, for explanation of "special" imports.
2. Figures refer to "general" trade.
3. Data exclude the free zone of Colón and the Canal Zone.

a. For 1934–74, see SALA, 20-2933.

SOURCE: FAO-TY, 1978; 1980; 1982, table 66; 1984, table 66; 1985; 1986, table 66; 1987, table 67.

Table 2440

U.S. SUGAR IMPORT QUOTAS, 16 L, 1986–88

	Country	1986–87 Annual Quota		1987–88 Annual Quota	
		%[3]	Short Tons Raw Value[1]	%[3]	Short Tons Raw Value[1]
A.	ARGENTINA	4.3	39,130	4.3	30,100
B.	BOLIVIA	.8	7,500	.8	5,700
C.	BRAZIL	14.5	131,950	14.5	101,500
E.	COLOMBIA	2.4	21,840	2.4	16,800
F.	COSTA RICA[2]	1.5	17,583	1.5	13,110
H.	DOMINICAN REP.	17.6	160,160	17.6	123,200
I.	ECUADOR	1.1	10,010	1.1	7,700
J.	EL SALVADOR[2]	2.6	26,020	2.6	19,766
K.	GUATEMALA	4.8	43,680	4.8	33,600
L.	HAITI	MQ	7,500	MQ	5,700
M.	HONDURAS[2]	1.0	15,917	1.0	11,524
N.	MEXICO	MQ	7,500	MQ	5,700
P.	PANAMA	2.9	26,390	2.9	20,300
Q.	PARAGUAY	MQ	7,500	MQ	5,700
R.	PERU	4.1	37,310	4.1	28,700
S.	URUGUAY	MQ	7,500	MQ	5,700

1. Value of sugar ranging from 94°–98° polarization.
2. Costa Rica, El Salvador, and Honduras each received a portion of Nicaragua's quota.
3. MQ = Minimum quota.

SOURCE: Amerop Sugar Corporation/Westway Trading Company (New Jersey), Newsletter, July, 1987; and June, 1988.

Table 2441

SUGAR EXPORTS TO THE UNITED STATES,[1] 17 LC, 1981–88

(T Tons)

	Country	1981	1984	1985	1986	1987	1988[a]
A.	ARGENTINA	444	221	163	56	39	30
	Barbados	--	7	18	--	8	6
B.	BOLIVIA	8	9	19	7	8	6
C.	BRAZIL	1,099	356	340	225	132	102
E.	COLOMBIA	178	60	181	128	22	17
F.	COSTA RICA	82	92	3	72	18	13
H.	DOMINICAN REP.	761	533	474	317	160	123
I.	ECUADOR	55	19	28	19	10	8
J.	EL SALVADOR	46	68	77	47	26	20
K.	GUATEMALA	224	150	113	133	44	34
L.	HAITI	--	17	--	--	8	6
M.	HONDURAS	95	100	50	32	16	12
	Jamaica	--	33	23	6	10	8
N.	MEXICO	107	--	18	11	8	6
O.	NICARAGUA	80	6	6	--	--	--
P.	PANAMA	104	61	68	37	26	20
Q.	PARAGUAY	16	--	--	12	8	6
R.	PERU	--	108	100	58	37	29
	St. Christopher	--	--	--	12	8	6
	Trinidad and Tobago	--	21	10	13	8	6
S.	URUGUAY	--	8	5	12	8	6
	Total	3,299	1,906	1,702	1,206	607	460

1. Raw value.

a. Quota.

SOURCE: *The Times of the Americas*, Feb. 10, 1987, p. 10.

Table 2442

SUGAR EXPORT VALUE,[1] 16 LC, 1978–86

	Country	T US						Value of % of Total Market Economy						
		1978	1981	1983	1984	1985	1986	1978	1979	1981	1983	1984	1985	1986
A.	ARGENTINA	30,639	260,478	129,708	86,569	24,889	3,194[†]	.5	.5	2.8	1.7	1.2	.4	.1[†]
B.	BOLIVIA	~	11,666[†]	11,666[†]	~	~	~	~	#[†]	#[†]	~	~	~	~
C.	BRAZIL	228,693	665,806	358,960	477,001	44,881[†]	35,173[†]	3.6	3.9	7.1	4.6	6.6	.7[†]	.6[†]
E.	COLOMBIA	19,536	76,881	68,922	37,071	36,857	16,874[†]	.8	.6	.8	.9	~	~	~
F.	COSTA RICA	15,909	42,007	~	9[†]	~	~	#	#	#	~	~	~	~
G.	CUBA	3,854,825	4,159,026	4,859,667	4,618,702	4,804,522	4,777,502	60.0	59.3	44.5	62.6	62.3	74.8	75.4
H.	DOMINICAN REP.	171,540	516,650	262,129	271,886	158,477	1,106[†]	2.7	2.8	5.5	3.4	3.7	2.5	0[†]
I.	ECUADOR	5,453	20,199	~	~	~	~	#	#	#	~	~	~	~
J.	EL SALVADOR	18,915	14,832	3,630[†]	4,063[†]	5,353[†]	3,349[†]	#	#	#	~	~	~	~
K.	GUATEMALA	45,753	84,094					#	#	#	~	~	~	~
M.	HONDURAS	5,501	37,890	27,840	25,672	~	~	#	#	#	~	~	~	~
N.	MEXICO	~	~	~	~	4,258[†]	3,490[†]	~	#	~	~	~	~	~
O.	NICARAGUA	25,549	39,708	2,848[†]	2,602[†]	3[†]	6[†]	#	#	#	~	~	~	~
P.	PANAMA	19,957	52,608	41,308	33,302	27,338	~	#	#	#	~	~	~	~
Q.	PARAGUAY	~	3[†]	2,486[†]	~	~	~	~	~	~	~	~	~	~
R.	PERU	43,641	144[†]	21[†]	18,253	~	~	#	#	#	~	~	~	~
	LAIA	327,973	1,035,034	564,008	634,168	110,887[†]	58,733[†]	5.1	6.4	11.1	7.2	8.5	1.7[†]	.9[†]
	CACM	111,627	218,531	132,604	36,627[†]	13,855[†]	11,869[†]	1.7	1.9	2.3	1.7	.5[†]	.2[†]	.2[†]

1. Raw beet and cane sugar.

SOURCE: UN-YITS, 1982, vol. 2, p. 300; 1983, 1984–86, vol. 2, table 0611.

Table 2443

CUBA SUGAR EXPORTS AS SHARE OF CUBA'S TOTAL EXPORT VALUE,[1] 1900–86

Year	%	Year	%	Year	%
1900	37	1932	77	1964	88
1901	51	1933	73	1965	86
1902	48	1934	74	1966	85
1903	54	1935	80	1967	82
1904	62	1936	82	1968	77
1905	66	1937	80	1969	77
1906	57	1938	79	1970	77
1907	63	1939	79	1971	77
1908	56	1940	75	1972	75
1909	65	1941	79	1973	79
1910	73	1942	79	1974	89
1911	65	1943	80	1975	89
1912	72	1944	75	1976	86
1913	72	1945	72	1977	83
1914	77	1946	74	1978	86
1915	84	1947	89	1979	86
1916	85	1948	90	1980	84
1917	86	1949	88	1981	79
1918	85	1950	89	1982	77
1919	89	1951	88	1983	74
1920	92	1952	86	1984	77
1921	85	1953	83	1985	73
1922	86	1954	80	1986	75
1923	89	1955	80		
1924	88	1956	79		
1925	84	1957	81		
1926	83	1958	81		
1927	85	1959	77		
1928	81	1960	79		
1929	80	1961	85		
1930	71	1962	83		
1931	70	1963	87		

1. Raw Sugar, 96° base.

SOURCE: For most years data are from Cuban Economic Research Project, *A Study on Cuba: The Colonial and Republic Periods; the Socialist Experiment* (Coral Gables: University of Miami Press, 1965), pp. 280, 403, 616; and Cuba, JUCEPLAN, AE, 1973, pp. 193-194. Data for scattered years are from SALA-Cuba, pp. 169 and 174; IBRD (WB), *Report on Cuba* (Baltimore: Johns Hopkins, 1951), p. 801; FAO-TY, 1971, p. 225; K. S. Karol, *Guerrillas in Power: The Course of the Cuban Revolution* (New York: Hill and Wang, 1970), p. 587. Data for 1973-74 are from U.S. Central Intelligence Agency, *Cuba: Foreign Trade,* Intelligence Handbook A(ER) 75-69 (July 1975), tables 1, 4, and 9; and CIA, *Cuban Economy . . . 1968-76*, p. 9. Data for 1975–80 are from Cuba–CEE, AE, 1981, pp. 189, 195; since 1981, FAO-TY, 1985; 1986, UN-YITS, vol. 2, p. 322.

Table 2444

WORLD SUGAR PRODUCTION,[1] 1979/80–1982/83

(Weighted World Average = 100)

Country	Sugar Plant	Index Value
Japan	cane	229
Japan	beet	170
Trinidad	cane	158
Italy	beet	155
Poland	beet	141
Guyana	cane	118
Barbados	cane	113
U.S.	beet	111
U.S. mainland	cane	107
U.K.	beet	102
Jamaica	cane	97
Germany, Fed. Rep.	beet	92
Belize	cane	91
India	cane	90
Thailand	cane	
A. ARGENTINA	cane	79
C. BRAZIL (North/Northeast)	cane	
Philippines	cane	75
Mauritius	cane	
France	beet	73
G. CUBA	cane	71
H. DOMINICAN REP.	cane	69
St. Kitts	cane	66
Australia	cane	62
Fiji	cane	60
C. BRAZIL (Central/South)	cane	57
South Africa	cane	~

1. Average 1979/80–1982/83 exchange rates and base years for data; constant prices; ex-mill costs in terms of raw sugar (96 pol). Costs derived by a synthetic cost engineering approach.

SOURCE: WB Staff Commodity Working Papers, 1987, N18, p. 60.

Table 2445

WHEAT IMPORT VOLUME,[1] 20 L, 1975–87[a]

(T MET)

	Country	1975	1978	1979	1980	1981	1982	1983	1984	1985	1986	1987
A.	ARGENTINA	~	#	#	#	#	#	~	~	~	13	#
B.	BOLIVIA	194	281	371	282	252	300	336	203	394	368	254
C.	BRAZIL	2,106	4,335	3,658	4,759	4,363	4,225	4,182	4,869	4,048	2,250	2,760
D.	CHILE	6,844	926	739	1,069	1,054	1,006	1,177	961	475	156	28
E.	COLOMBIA	302	295	338	641	507‡	535	697	660	618	694	673
F.	COSTA RICA	83	85	88	104	96	101	104	124	109	130	136
G.	CUBA	~	1,124	1,294	1,228	1,244‡	1,268	1,442	1,481	1,387	1,456	1,447‡
H.	DOMINICAN REP.	125	159 .	144	158	198	128	188	125	262	241	253
I.	ECUADOR	210	222	168	200	249	326	281	271	221	243	266
J.	EL SALVADOR	34	68	105	116	106	135	123	148	151	170	100
K.	GUATEMALA	72	65	96	108	108‡	93†	114	130	170	143	164‡
L.	HAITI	82	126‡	149‡	149‡	199‡	167‡	185‡	177	183	170‡	148‡
M.	HONDURAS	52	63	69	71	78	80	68	90	108	105	120‡
N.	MEXICO[2]	864	506	1,148	823	1,028	398	423	345	561	224	435
O.	NICARAGUA	50	56	27	52	37‡	40	69	136	33	83	65
P.	PANAMA[3]	55	57	47	47	62	57	55	63	75	66	76
Q.	PARAGUAY	27	49	65	75	68	38	93	7	82	29	2
R.	PERU	833	732‡	781	800	756	861	805	763	877	1,041	1,080‡
S.	URUGUAY[4]	~	112	92	55	4	#	65	483	#	93	87‡
T.	VENEZUELA	620	506	719	785	890	773	875	978	1,108	952	1,128

1. Wheat and wheat flour in wheat equivalent. Figures refer to "special trade" unless otherwise indicated. See table 2412, n. 1, for explanation of "special" imports.
2. Imports through free zones included.
3. Data exclude the free zone of Colón and the Canal Zone.
4. Figures refer to "general trade," i.e., total exports.

a. For 1934–74, see SALA, 20-2936.

SOURCE: FAO-TY, 1978; 1980; 1982, table 37; 1984, table 37; 1985–87, table 38.

Table 2446

WHEAT EXPORT VOLUME,[1] 5 L, 1975–87[a]
(T MET)

Country	1975	1978	1979	1980	1981	1982	1983	1984	1985	1986	1987
A. ARGENTINA	1,920	1,776	4,364	4,538	3,788	3,837	1,023	7,370	9,716	4,079	4,253
D. CHILE	~	- -	#	#	#	#	~	~	#	#	#
M. HONDURAS	~	#	2	1	1	1	~	~	#	#	#
N. MEXICO[2]	31	17	14	23	23	#	#	#	#	#	#
S. URUGUAY[2]	68	~	#	#	112	147	128	74	#	#	#

1. Includes wheat and wheat flour in wheat equivalent. Figures refer to "special trade" except where otherwise indicated. See table 2413, n. 1, for explanation of "special" exports.
2. Figures refer to "general trade," i.e., total exports including re-exports.

a. For 1934–74, see SALA, 20-2934.

SOURCE: FAO-TY, 1978; 1980, table 347; 1984, table 37; 1985–87, table 38.

Table 2447

WHEAT EXPORT VALUE,[1] 9 LC, 1980–86

Country	T US					Value as % of World Exports				
	1980	1983	1984	1985	1986	1980	1983	1984	1985	1986
A. ARGENTINA	816,137	1,474,040	965,779	1,133,162	321,733[‡]	5.2	9.3	5.7	8.8	2.9[†]
C. BRAZIL	39	602	4,754	~	~	#	~	~	~	~
D. CHILE	#	~	510	355[‡]	862	#	~	~	~	~
G. CUBA	~	54,040[†]	72,139	~	~	~	~	~	~	~
K. GUATEMALA	~	233[†]	~	~	~	~	#	~	~	~
N. MEXICO	1,042[†]	210[†]	3	2	#	#[†]	~	~	~	~
O. NICARAGUA	#	12	11	~	~	#	~	~	~	~
P. PANAMA	827[†]	4,443[†]	~	703[†]	142[†]	~	~	~	~	~
S. URUGUAY	~	19,058	11,114	~	~	~	~	~	~	~
LAIA	817,289	1,493,879	986,076	1,133,517	322,595[†]	5.2	9.4	5.8	8.8	2.9[†]
CACM	#	245	11	~	~	~	#	#[†]	#[†]	#[†]
UNITED STATES	6,374,561	6,239,284	6,476,910	3,603,011	3,005,717	40.3	39.4	40.4	28.0	27.1

1. Unmilled.

SOURCE: UN-YITS, 1982, vol. 2, p. 25; 1983, vol. 2, table 041; 1984, table 041; 1985, 1986, vol. 2, p. 47.

Table 2448

WOOL (CLEAN) EXPORT VOLUME,[1] 5 LC, 1975–87[a]
(T MET)

Country	1975	1978	1979	1980	1981	1982	1983	1984	1985	1986	1987
A. ARGENTINA	27	29	22	27	34[‡]	24	28	27	26	25	26
C. BRAZIL	1	#	#	.4	.6	.4	.7	.4	.2	.1	#
D. CHILE	1	1	#	.2	.06	.7	#	#	.2	.2	.1
R. PERU	1	2[b]	#	.2[‡]	.5[‡]	#	.6	#	#	#	#
S. URUGUAY[2]	6	6	5	6	7	5	9	6	6	17	15
UNITED STATES	~	.4	.4	.4	.3	.9	.4	.5	.9	.4	.7
WORLD	~	278	299	323	346	323	344	360	394	427	482

1. Figures refer to "special trade" unless othewise indicated. See table 2413, n. 1, for explanation of "special" exports.
2. Figures refer to "general trade," i.e., total exports including re-exports.

a. For 1934–74, see SALA, 20-2937.
b. Greasy wool.

SOURCE: FAO-TY, 1978; 1980; 1982, table 114; 1984, table 114; 1985, table 114; 1986, 1987, table 115.

Table 2449

WOOL EXPORT VALUE, 7 LC, 1980–86

	Country	T US					Value as % of World Exports				
		1980	1983	1984	1985	1986	1980	1983	1984	1985	1986
A.	ARGENTINA	247,618	185,572	176,266	156,915	86,024[†]	5.6	4.5	4.6[†]	3.7	2.0[†]
B.	BOLIVIA	609[†]	~	~	~	~	#[†]	~	~	~	~
C.	BRAZIL	69,714	65,060	12,155	10,595	7,465[†]	1.6	1.6	.3	~	~
D.	CHILE	22,811	20,778[†]	21,487	33,102	52,264[†]	#	~	~	~	~
Q.	PARAGUAY	23,158[†]	~	397[†]	450[†]	709[†]	#[†]	~	~	~	~
R.	PERU	30,169	47,040	40,829	35,099	24,347[†]	#	~	~	~	~
S.	URUGUAY	134,031	105,977	170,834	139,851	81,453[†]	3.1	2.6	3.9	3.1	1.9[†]
	LAIA	528,187	425,134[†]	458,804	361,492	252,626[†]	12.0	10.2[†]	10.5	8.0	6.0[†]
	CACM	90	110[†]	66	373[†]	272[†]	#	#[†]	#[†]	#[†]	#[†]
	UNITED STATES	36,976	64,092	55,400	70,040	69,573	.8	1.5	1.3	1.6	1.7

SOURCE: UN-YITS, 1982, vol. 2, p. 69; 1983, 1984–86, vol. 2, table 268.

Table 2450

FOREST PRODUCT EXPORTS, 10 OAS-L, 1970–80
(% and M US)

Category		1970	%[a]		1975	%[a]		1980	%[a]
All Forest Products	C. BRAZIL		51	C. BRAZIL		39	C. BRAZIL		53
	D. CHILE		18	D. CHILE		26	D. CHILE		30
	M. HONDURAS		6	M. HONDURAS		10			
	Q. PARAGUAY		6	Q. PARAGUAY		5			
				B. BOLIVIA		5			

Continued in SALA, 24-2440.

Table 2451

ROUNDWOOD[1] TRADE, 17 LC, 1977–87

(T US)

PART I. VALUE OF IMPORTS

Country	1977	1979	1980	1981	1982	1983	1984	1985	1986	1987
A. ARGENTINA	495	2,457	4,613	2,659	2,216	2,718	2,281	917	882	882
C. BRAZIL	3,911	6,239	6,912	6,485	6,616	6,556	8,125	8,001	7,417	4,708
D. CHILE	#	#	#	#	#	~	~	~	~	~
E. COLOMBIA	#	#	#	#	#	~	~	~	~	~
F. COSTA RICA	726	602	891	577	374	261	261	261[†]	261[†]	#
G. CUBA	200[†]	#	#	#	#	#	3,364	3,228	1,225	5,018
H. DOMINICAN REP.	#	#	9,659	8,478	5,046	6,517	4,630	3,661	5,882	5,882[†]
J. EL SALVADOR	49	60	102	102	#	#	#	#	30	55
K. GUATEMALA	#	149	149	143	320	320	14	22	22	22[†]
L. HAITI	234	234[†]	#	#	#	#	#	#	#	#
M. HONDURAS	#	#	#	#	#	~	~	~	~	~
N. MEXICO	919	8,749	16,116	8,433	3,839	3,839	2,385	2,783	2,783	2,783[†]
O. NICARAGUA	720[†]	1,171	1,171[†]	1,171[†]	65	65[†]	65[†]	65[†]	65[†]	65[†]
P. PANAMA	581	1,055	900[†]	2,269	1,495	359	445	300[†]	1,905	1,905[†]
R. PERU	288	24	411	54	252	252	180	32	32	32[†]
S. URUGUAY	790	1,034	1,070	372	133	62	62[†]	62[†]	62[†]	62[†]
T. VENEZUELA	2,243	2,421	2,329	11,500	15,530	15,507	4,600	1,652	1,652	1,652[†]
UNITED STATES	73,424	79,725	87,900	93,814	89,124	111,870	92,129	76,034	56,716	79,356

PART II. VALUE OF EXPORTS

Country	1977	1979	1980	1981	1982	1983	1984	1985	1986	1987
A. ARGENTINA	43	346	410	302	234	440	625	625[†]	625[†]	625[†]
B. BOLIVIA	925	~	~	~	~	~	~	~	~	~
C. BRAZIL	895	1,951	1,490	1,360	1,370	908	2,039	2,231	1,107	1,085
D. CHILE	4,302	31,235	56,835	17,672	36,891	34,587	29,880	40,371	46,348	81,867
E. COLOMBIA	234[†]	~	~	~	~	~	~	~	~	~
F. COSTA RICA	~	37	17	17[†]	46	26	146	146	146[†]	~
H. DOMINICAN REP.	~	~	~	17	~	~	~	~	~	~
K. GUATEMALA	~	11	11	78	16	32	53	362	290	290[†]
L. HAITI	~	~	~	~	~	~	~	~	~	~
M. HONDURAS	2,678	2,353	4,414	2,774	2,454	632	710	302	352	352[†]
N. MEXICO	145	769	613	746	293	485	196	180	~	~
O. NICARAGUA	322[†]	1,008	1,511	1,511[†]	~	~	~	40	~	~
P. PANAMA	3	~	~	~	~	250	222	17	30	30[†]
Q. PARAGUAY	148	15	23	23	~	~	~	~	~	~
R. PERU	23	~	~	~	~	~	~	~	~	~
T. VENEZUELA	~	~	~	~	~	~	~	~	~	~
UNITED STATES	1,161,676	1,991,549	2,002,106	1,575,329	1,522,411	1,365,904	1,371,513	1,448,478	1,417,960	1,847,856

1. For definitions of roundwood, fuelwood, etc., see SALA, 25-2301.

SOURCE: FAO-YFP, 1982, pp. 68, 72; 1984, pp. 68, 72; 1985, pp. 5, 8; 1986, 1987, pp. 40, 44.

Table 2452

SAWNWOOD AND SLEEPERS TRADE,[1] 18 LC, 1976-87
(T US)

PART I. VALUE OF IMPORTS

	Country	1976	1980	1981	1982	1983	1984	1985	1986	1987
A.	ARGENTINA	24,836	139,409	90,217	51,714	48,850	51,475	27,054	43,834	43,834[†]
C.	BRAZIL	8,782	24,297	17,663	12,871	8,582	10,299	12,840	16,985	12,986
D.	CHILE	#	#	#	#	~	~	~	~	~
E.	COLOMBIA	31[†]	1,365	1,008	390	277	3,109	3,109[†]	220[†]	245[†]
F.	COSTA RICA	254	142	227	226	~	~	~	~	~
G.	CUBA	36,100	88,470	84,475	84,949	70,630	101,759	118,748	133,819	106,297
H.	DOMINICAN REP.	21,500[‡]	21,361	16,388	13,289	10,092	8,932	5,831	5,831[†]	4,100[†]
J.	EL SALVADOR	2,780	680	3,600	800	1,055	1,162	1,040	1,577	3,560
K.	GUATEMALA	487	74	166	25	4	~	~	~	~
L.	HAITI	1,700	1,906	2,200	2,100	2,100	2,100	230	230	230[†]
M.	HONDURAS	#	#	#	#	~	~	~	~	~
N.	MEXICO	20,353	66,547	74,335	38,052	49,936	36,900	39,632	45,632	45,632[†]
O.	NICARAGUA	#	#	#	#	~	~	~	~	~
P.	PANAMA	1,091	1,707	1,204	536	1,079	193	473	1,234	1,234[†]
Q.	PARAGUAY	#	#	#	#	~	~	~	~	~
R.	PERU	1,838	2,827	3,182	2,940	2,940	3,251	2,179	1,161	1,161[†]
S.	URUGUAY	3,358	11,070	9,806	6,212	3,083	3,499	3,499[†]	3,499[†]	3,499[†]
T.	VENEZUELA	32,491	30,656	23,729	24,343	28,480[†]	28,480[†]	8,117	8,117	8,117[†]
	UNITED STATES	1,299,567	1,915,294	1,850,925	1,670,556	2,799,948	2,722,957	2,941,629	2,996,595	3,308,782

PART II. VALUE OF EXPORTS

	Country	1976	1980	1981	1982	1983	1984	1985	1986	1987
A.	ARGENTINA	16	198	471	383	383[†]	907	429	429	~
B.	BOLIVIA	22,000[†]	19,000[†]	9,800[†]	12,150[†]	5,500[†]	5,500[†]	5,500[†]	12,841	18,231
C.	BRAZIL	70,546	211,471	210,404	139,855	178,815	142,981	121,773	119,712	188,921
D.	CHILE	22,680	149,027	95,879	63,524	65,764	74,142	57,508	69,662	114,102
E.	COLOMBIA	3,002	2,597	4,807	536	297	167	167	167[†]	305[†]
F.	COSTA RICA	425	20	505	805	1,113	1,462	1,457	607	~
I.	ECUADOR	8,997	4,078	6,300[†]	5,444	12,044[†]	15,900	8,420	10,397	10,397[†]
J.	EL SALVADOR	#	#	#	#	~	~	~	~	~
K.	GUATEMALA	3,112	3,971	4,448	2,950	1,082	1,374	2,908	3,540	3,540[†]
L.	HAITI	#	#	#	#	~	~	~	~	~
M.	HONDURAS	40,005	20,208[†]	25,106	43,162	34,748	30,370	31,946	27,899	27,899[†]
N.	MEXICO	71	246	359	225	3,725	3,725	982	982	982[†]
O.	NICARAGUA	5,866[†]	539	777	590	1,165	1,165	1,165	1,165	1,165[†]
P.	PANAMA	29[†]	#	#	#	~	~	~	~	~
Q.	PARAGUAY	9,989	52,195	48,836[†]	62,636[†]	49,936[†]	62,400	65,100	57,459	87,198
R.	PERU	1,107	3,032	2,741	2,741	2,741	936	745	413	413[†]
S.	URUGUAY	33	#	#	#	~	~	~	~	~
	UNITED STATES	566,114	1,053,683	925,864	805,025	897,979	834,899	753,780	987,211	1,349,144

1. Cf. SALA, 23-2904 and 2905 for coniferous and nonconiferous sawnwood trade.

SOURCE: FAO-YFP, 1982, pp. 176, 180; 1984, pp. 172, 176; 1985-87, pp. 114, 118.

Table 2453

WOOD PULP TRADE, 15 LC, 1975–87
(T US)

PART I. VALUE OF IMPORTS

Country	1975	1980	1982	1983	1984	1985	1986	1987
A. ARGENTINA	57,713	68,391	73,350	30,886	25,640	15,875	26,330	26,330[†]
C. BRAZIL	44,397	37,755	9,349	5,840	11,236	12,180	17,892	18,485[†]
D. CHILE	1,050	#	#	#	#	#	#	#
E. COLOMBIA	9,921	29,661	26,240	25,410	36,635	30,643	24,099	19,912
F. COSTA RICA	1,401	4,542	2,778	1,203[†]	2,567	439	439	242
G. CUBA	6,800	22,687	16,472	21,643	18,750	20,088	18,804	23,699
H. DOMINICAN REP.	1,000[†]	969[†]	969[†]	969[†]	37	53	53[†]	53[†]
I. ECUADOR	886	5,248	30,745	29,984	10,500	3,563	4,750	4,750[†]
J. EL SALVADOR	375	284	284[†]	3,653	3,653[†]	3,653[†]	3,653[†]	#
K. GUATEMALA	2,112	17,038	868	5,640	4,430	4,286	1,438	1,438[†]
N. MEXICO	56,638	107,000	121,196	80,600	98,100	116,000	127,000	127,000[†]
P. PANAMA	24	642	344	805	636	794	1,194	1,194[†]
R. PERU	14,524	14,469	20,253	13,553	17,312	6,315	16,526	16,526[†]
S. URUGUAY	3,947	5,174	2,787	4,175	3,076	3,076	3,071	3,071[†]
T. VENEZUELA	27,507[†]	54,870[†]	74,698[†]	49,278[†]	75,872[†]	81,822[†]	74,900[†]	100,200[†]
UNITED STATES	1,037,051	1,673,405	1,484,974	1,485,257	1,844,779	1,517,089	1,581,443	2,031,881

PART II. VALUE OF EXPORTS

Country	1975	1980	1982	1983	1984	1985	1986	1987
A. ARGENTINA	~	~	~	11,599	17,573	31,940[†]	26,000[†]	26,000[†]
C. BRAZIL	30,503	364,211	278,504	310,744	396,412	278,043	322,703	297,570[†]
D. CHILE	59,593	197,276	171,800	156,400	200,042	180,811	192,487	262,615
R. PERU	#	#	#	~	~	~	~	~
LATIN AMERICA	90,096	561,487	450,304	478,743	614,027	490,794	541,190	586,185
UNITED STATES	896,516	1,628,666	1,407,655	1,350,732	1,483,491	1,343,466	1,649,892	2,308,669

SOURCE: FAO-YFP, 1982, pp. 264, 267; 1984, pp. 256, 258; 1985–87, pp. 201, 204.

Table 2454

PAPER AND PAPERBOARD TRADE, 20 LC, 1977–87[a]

(T US)

PART I. VALUE OF IMPORTS

	Country	1977	1979	1980	1981	1982	1983	1984	1985	1986	1987
A.	ARGENTINA	100,544	111,167	183,304	162,262	83,392	87,563	50,129	43,190	45,702	45,702[†]
B.	BOLIVIA	8,731	10,200[†]	11,700	12,500[†]	5,800[†]	5,800[†]	4,800[†]	4,300[†]	5,100[†]	5,100[†]
C.	BRAZIL	137,450	157,285	191,085	223,890	259,216	133,181	138,499	109,251	177,955	190,000[†]
D.	CHILE	23,800	43,300	45,100	43,300	24,900	49,300	47,413	41,600	34,436	45,719
E.	COLOMBIA	35,900[‡]	66,977	82,441	118,273	123,952	86,103	106,079	98,700[†]	94,562	90,638
F.	COSTA RICA	35,298	52,164	52,810	75,171	67,763	63,145	65,908	65,189	62,210[†]	60,732
G.	CUBA	22,200[†]	38,608	75,654	64,322[†]	71,013	77,132	97,957	86,103	91,715	94,879
H.	DOMINICAN REP.	20,551[‡]	25,366	38,484	46,489	42,101	40,371	44,312	35,993	37,773	37,773[†]
I.	ECUADOR	55,792	53,554	88,708	89,685	106,934	93,113	109,262	117,884[†]	102,940	102,940[†]
J.	EL SALVADOR	25,288	25,241[†]	26,287	27,450	32,000	27,460	27,460[†]	24,910	17,759	17,759[†]
K.	GUATEMALA	15,262	30,065	74,055	55,309	54,599	54,543	55,302	39,586	42,067	42,067[†]
L.	HAITI	3,076	3,033	2,906	3,523[†]	4,085[†]	4,085[†]	4,085[†]	4,354[†]	4,354[†]	4,354[†]
M.	HONDURAS	33,116	26,749	27,470	31,375	28,412	20,719	20,843[†]	24,876[†]	24,076[†]	24,076[†]
N.	MEXICO	297,909[†]	138,350[†]	398,700	394,000	473,598	227,841	73,100[†]	139,400[†]	134,700[†]	134,700[†]
O.	NICARAGUA	12,927[†]	8,428	12,014	13,014	12,268	11,537	13,137[†]	9,766[†]	10,466[†]	10,466[†]
P.	PANAMA	19,303	24,772	29,911	30,522	29,559	24,090	34,645	52,207	79,977	79,977
Q.	PARAGUAY	5,692	8,611	11,524	8,902	11,971	6,077	7,450	8,566	8,638	10,464
R.	PERU	28,513	8,572	20,120	40,026	50,800[†]	31,400[†]	23,535[†]	28,923[†]	39,390[†]	39,390[†]
S.	URUGUAY	7,044	8,814	14,489	18,753	11,301	6,130	6,520	5,520[†]	4,520[†]	4,520[†]
T.	VENEZUELA	65,393[†]	118,094[†]	116,740[†]	126,416[†]	167,214	140,821	132,800	129,375[†]	124,100[†]	124,100[†]
	UNITED STATES	2,279,547	3,153,597	3,313,973	3,346,918	4,338,482	3,734,478	5,066,782	5,426,956	5,621,240	6,466,418

PART II. VALUE OF EXPORTS

	Country	1977	1979	1980	1981	1982	1983	1984	1985	1986	1987
A.	ARGENTINA	11,399	17,636	11,649	7,690	5,577	4,643	7,498	6,342	4,769	4,769[†]
C.	BRAZIL	20,571	94,048	160,862	224,833	170,431	208,434	345,560	262,587	346,811	312,800[†]
D.	CHILE	38,900	46,028	48,704	45,295	39,323	47,616	58,313	66,300	60,073	73,802
E.	COLOMBIA	541[†]	9,201	10,786	9,904	5,039	8,304	14,953	12,600[†]	12,600[†]	12,600[†]
F.	COSTA RICA	552	3,412	13,217	11,625	12,275	15,145	9,559	10,307	9,675	9,675[†]
J.	EL SALVADOR	1,264	1,364	1,414	2,800	4,000	6,455	6,455	4,404	2,597	2,597[†]
K.	GUATEMALA	8,839	12,695	17,992	18,840	11,991	12,717	8,781	6,765	5,628	5,628[†]
M.	HONDURAS	599	2,375	4,999	4,999	~	~	~	~	~	#
N.	MEXICO	1,033	1,100[†]	2,700[†]	4,000[†]	5,000	5,000[†]	5,000[†]	2,900[†]	2,900[†]	2,900[†]
P.	PANAMA	270	191	635	670	947	538	223	189	965	474
R.	PERU	3,489	3,489	1,427	1,165	509	1,970	1,970	3,013	2,439	2,439[†]
S.	URUGUAY	2,711	6,535	10,381	7,663	4,579	6,646	7,066	7,066[†]	7,066[†]	7,066[†]
T.	VENEZUELA	~	~	~	~	~	~	~	~	~	~
	UNITED STATES	1,121,609	1,340,141	2,016,959	2,013,112	1,714,085	1,719,220	1,813,021	1,559,267	1,898,948	2,218,908

a. For 1962-74 data see SALA, 21-2805.

SOURCE: FAO-YFP, 1982, pp. 314 and 310; 1984, pp. 302, 306; 1985, pp. 249, 253; 1986, 1987, pp. 249, 254.

Table 2455

WOOD-BASED PANEL TRADE,[1] 18 LC, 1975–87[a]

(T US)

PART I. VALUE OF IMPORTS

	Country	1975	1980	1982	1983	1984	1985	1986	1987
A.	ARGENTINA	3,075	15,906	3,612	4,727	3,050	1,019	3,147	3,147
B.	BOLIVIA	#	105	105	#	#	#	#	#
C.	BRAZIL	1,248	19,107	10,696	7,087	6,499	6,113	7,289	6,778
D.	CHILE	#	#	#	~	~	~	~	~
E.	COLOMBIA	#	5,633	7,598	6,598	487	487[†]	487[†]	92
F.	COSTA RICA	924	1,160	245	245	282	129	129	129[†]
G.	CUBA	2,086	17,215	26,271	41,783	34,117	27,041	31,251	39,698
H.	DOMINICAN REP.	713[†]	919	885	885[†]	3,426	3,458	3,458[†]	3,458[†]
I.	ECUADOR	46	#	#	#	#	#	#	#
J.	EL SALVADOR	1,790	2,498	2,441	3,090	3,090	3,090	221	151
K.	GUATEMALA	#	2,616	2,279	2,563	1,517	784	295	295[†]
M.	HONDURAS	222	842	420	#	#	#	#	#
N.	MEXICO	4,304	20,825	4,936	4,936	8,554	9,054	9,054	9,054[†]
O.	NICARAGUA	467	136	35	35	35	35	35	35[†]
P.	PANAMA	740	1,104	1,439	1,119	962	1,283	575	575[†]
R.	PERU	448	2	69	~	~	~	~	~
S.	URUGUAY	1,062	1,423	362	206	206	206	206	206[†]
T.	VENEZUELA	1,972	22,401	36,344	22,237	22,237	11,979	11,979	11,979[†]
	UNITED STATES	333,518	585,526	504,468	852,923	766,153	790,805	852,120	1,098,893

PART II. VALUE OF EXPORTS

	Country	1979	1980	1982	1983	1984	1985	1986	1987
A.	ARGENTINA	932	4,144	4,898	3,335	2,966	2,966	2,966	2,966[†]
B.	BOLIVIA	#	1,450[†]	1,590[†]	423[†]	423[†]	423	422	768
C.	BRAZIL	50,568	124,976	104,942	122,147	140,088	135,981	146,016	162,997
D.	CHILE	54	6,919	9,362	7,741	8,852	9,121	8,600[†]	10,798[†]
E.	COLOMBIA	416	541	2,059	738	1,285	1,285	1,285[†]	1,106
F.	COSTA RICA	1,697	7,647	6,383	6,007	5,392	5,596	4,774	2,686
I.	ECUADOR	450	23,256	23,228	4,125	2,757	3,127	4,945	4,945[†]
K.	GUATEMALA	822	480	161	310	116	#	#	#
M.	HONDURAS	922	1,718	769	#	#	#	#	#
N.	MEXICO	473	7,375	503	9,024	9,024	9,822	9,822	9,822[†]
O.	NICARAGUA	1,412	2,220	1,360	1,404	1,404[†]	1,404[†]	1,404[†]	1,404[†]
Q.	PARAGUAY	1,869[†]	14,233	29,223[†]	20,699	24,836	25,930	9,546	24,669
R.	PERU	373	2,371	3,206[†]	3,206[†]	509	502	503	503[†]
	UNITED STATES	222,018	283,990	251,198	311,246	236,077	227,618	329,677	442,139

1. Includes veneer sheets, plywood, particle board, and fiberboard.

a. For 1962-74 data see SALA, 21-2802.

SOURCE: FAO-YFP, 1982, pp. 214 and 210; 1984, pp. 202, 206; 1985–87, pp. 144, 148.

Table 2456

FUEL[1] AS SHARE OF TOTAL COUNTRY IMPORTS, 20 LC, 1970-80
(% Value)

Year	A. ARGENTINA	B. BOLIVIA	C. BRAZIL
1970	4.7	1.2	12.3
1975	13.2	2.2	26.2
1980	10.3	1.0	50.5[a]

1. Includes coal, petroleum, and natural gas.

a. 1981.

SOURCE: UN-YITS, vol. 1, special table M, 1981.

Table 2457

FUELWOOD AND CHARCOAL TRADE, 7 LC, 1975–87
(T US)

PART I. VALUE OF IMPORTS

	Country	1975	1980	1981	1982	1983	1984	1985	1986	1987
C.	BRAZIL	14	#	#	#	#	#	#	#	#
D.	CHILE	#	#	#	#	~	~	~	~	~
F.	COSTA RICA	184	#	#	#	#	#	#	#	#
J.	EL SALVADOR	#	#	#	#	~	~	~	~	~
N.	MEXICO	118	194	768	236	236[†]	88	136	136[†]	136[†]
S.	URUGUAY	#	#	#	#	~	~	~	~	~
T.	VENEZUELA	26[†]	26[†]	26[†]	26[†]	#	#	#	#	#
	UNITED STATES	1,030	5,967	3,093	1,561	2,089	3,582	3,668	2,950	3,853

PART II. VALUE OF EXPORTS

	Country	1975	1980	1981	1982	1983	1984	1985	1986	1987
C.	BRAZIL	#	1,582	1,010	282	984	#	#	#	#
F.	COSTA RICA	1,088	#	#	#	20	#	#	#	#
N.	MEXICO	158	613	746	293	485	196	180	180[†]	180[†]
	UNITED STATES	4,881	4,566	9,225	5,609	5,609[†]	2,882	2,742	2,515	2,793

SOURCE: FAO-YFP, 1982, pp. 81, 83; 1984, pp. 81, 83; 1985–87, pp. 19, 21.

Table 2458

CRUDE OIL TRADE, 20 L, 1983–87

(T Barrels)

	Country	PART I. VOLUME OF IMPORTS					PART II. VOLUME OF EXPORTS				
		1983	1984	1985	1986	1987‡	1983	1984	1985	1986‡	1987
A.	ARGENTINA	#	#	#	#	#	#	#	3,287	#	#
B.	BOLIVIA	#	#	#	#	#	1,039	310	#	#	#
C.	BRAZIL	266,199	237,707	198,949	219,344	227,872	3,711	#	#	#	#
D.	CHILE	13,839	14,479	15,135	19,093	19,682	#	#	#	#	#
E.	COLOMBIA	13,834	9,801	6,748	#	#	#	#	#	31,310	54,531
F.	COSTA RICA	3,352†	3,250†	3,065	3,000†	2,900	#	#	#	#	#
G.	CUBA	~	~	~	~	~	#	#	#	~	~
H.	DOMINICAN REP.	11,450	13,001	12,485	13,171	14,250	#	#	#	#	#
I.	ECUADOR	#	#	#	#	#	54,432	59,151	66,798	68,068	40,843
J.	EL SALVADOR	4,436	4,419	4,489†	4,100†	5,442	#	#	#	#	#
K.	GUATEMALA	4,376	5,331	4,909	3,753	3,800	2,206	1,128	458	1,783	1,750
L.	HAITI	#	#	#	#	#	#	#	#	#	#
M.	HONDURAS	2,369	3,303	2,389	1,231	1,200	#	#	#	#	#
N.	MEXICO	#	#	#	#	#	561,005	558,004	524,943	470,704	490,925
O.	NICARAGUA	3,769	3,162	3,576	3,963	3,900	#	#	#	#	#
P.	PANAMA	10,370	10,557	7,965	10,100†	10,000	#	#	#	#	#
Q.	PARAGUAY	1,411	1,407	1,463†	1,300†	1,250	#	#	#	#	#
R.	PERU	#	#	#	#	#	8,190	7,240	9,175	4,851	1,200
S.	URUGUAY	8,930	9,074	7,878	9,896	9,800	#	#	#	#	#
T.	VENEZUELA	#	#	#	#	#	359,890	367,555	302,585	346,385	372,665

SOURCE: IDB, 1986, table 67; 1987, table 70 and 71; 1988, tables G-2 and G-3.

Table 2459

REFINED OIL TRADE, 20 L, 1983–87

(T Barrels)

	Country	PART I. VOLUME OF IMPORTS					PART II. VOLUME OF EXPORTS				
		1983	1984	1985	1986	1987‡	1983	1984	1985	1986	1987
A.	ARGENTINA	656	985	423	0	0	14,549	12,228	25,638	6,646	6,700
B.	BOLIVIA	56	50†	50	40	40	155	6	#	#	#
C.	BRAZIL	11,171	4,015	13,140	15,920	18,845	43,620	67,019	61,615	47,917	59,370
D.	CHILE	3,675	3,965	2,444	4,197	1,823	240	215	#	#	198
E.	COLOMBIA	7,435	5,749	9,414	7,741	7,700	15,732	16,862	18,975	20,511	21,864
F.	COSTA RICA	2,883†	2,581†	2,279	2,100	2,100	#	#	305	#	#
G.	CUBA	~	~	~	~	~	~	~	~	~	~
H.	DOMINICAN REP.	4,806	4,693	3,597	5,031	5,200	#	#	#	#	#
I.	ECUADOR	6,913	4,250	4,863	3,510	9,982	4,111	6,244	4,844	6,676	5,709
J.	EL SALVADOR	184	99	101	100†	199	461	575	#	#	#
K.	GUATEMALA	3,571	3,527	3,993	3,851	3,800	#	#	#	#	#
L.	HAITI	1,614†	1,600	1,600	1,500†	1,400	#	#	#	#	#
M.	HONDURAS	2,437	2,124	2,390	3,300	3,200	#	#	#	#	#
N.	MEXICO	6,347	12,111	19,377	21,899	21,000	30,710	40,944	49,413	42,215	23,725
O.	NICARAGUA	477	1,206	1,284	1,207	1,200	5	#	#	#	#
P.	PANAMA	925	1,052	1,057	950†	850	13,560	200	864	#	#
Q.	PARAGUAY	1,667	2,268	2,313	2,200†	2,100	#	#	#	#	#
R.	PERU	2,174	696	223	1,588	1,660	12,885	17,081	18,449	17,240	16,600
S.	URUGUAY	321	332	288	1,098	1,000	223	#	#	230	#
T.	VENEZUELA	#	#	#	#	#	187,245	186,150	197,830	213,525	178,850

SOURCE: IDB-SPTF, 1986, table 67; 1987, table 70, 71; 1988, tables G-2 and G-3.

Table 2460

PETROLEUM AND DERIVATIVES TRADE, 19 L, 1979–87

(M US)

PART I. VALUE OF NET IMPORTS

	Country	1979	1981	1982	1983	1984	1985	1986	1987[‡]
A.	ARGENTINA	941.7	281.4	~	~	~	~	#	#
C.	BRAZIL	6,410.3	9,672.0	8,612.3	6,791.2	5,074.0	4,306.0	2,410.0	3,073.0
D.	CHILE	846.9	983.2	892.0	482.7	495.0	452.1	322.6	370.4
E.	COLOMBIA	420.5	412.2	371.6	239.0	~	#	#	#
F.	COSTA RICA	168.4	180.5	168.0	157.0	151.3	158.9	120.0[†]	125.0
H.	DOMINICAN REP.	314.9	472.3	451.6	461.3	504.7	426.8	264.5	436.0
I.	ECUADOR	**	**	**	**	**	**	**	**
J.	EL SALVADOR	113.3	167.9	134.2	126.6	130.3	133.0	100.0[†]	110.0
K.	GUATEMALA	254.9	344.3	241.5	195.7	240.6	254.5	136.0	145.0
L.	HAITI	45.0	62.0	62.0	60.0[†]	60.0[†]	60.0[†]	32.0[†]	35.0
M.	HONDURAS	112.8	161.1	167.0	163.6	179.4	161.2	102.8	110.0
N.	MEXICO	**	**	**	**	**	**	#	#
O.	NICARAGUA	76.6	187.7	169.3	159.6	141.0	158.7	123.8	130.0
P.	PANAMA	319.4	415.4	399.2	263.3	288.6	236.0	101.0	124.0
Q.	PARAGUAY	123.9	169.3	180.6	145.7	93.5	114.6	84.0[†]	90.0
R.	PERU	**	**	**	**	**	**	#	#
S.	URUGUAY	303.2	493.5	416.0	240.6	260.1	237.0	133.0	134.8
T.	VENEZUELA	**	**	**	**	**	**	**	**

PART II. VALUE OF NET EXPORTS

	Country	1979	1981	1982	1983	1984	1985	1986	1987[‡]
A.	ARGENTINA	**	**	135.5	243.0	275.3	652.2	400.0[†]	200.0
B.	BOLIVIA	44.0	3.3	4.5	34.2	8.5	5.0	3.0[†]	2.0
C.	BRAZIL	**	**	**	**	**	**	**	**
D.	CHILE	**	**	**	**	**	**	**	**
E.	COLOMBIA	**	**	**	**	2.1	0.1	526.0	1,369.7
F.	COSTA RICA	**	**	**	**	**	**	**	**
H.	DOMINICAN REP.	**	**	**	**	**	**	**	**
I.	ECUADOR	989.1	1,710.0	1,508.0	1,605.7	1,823.6	1,728.0	803.0	591.9
J.	EL SALVADOR	**	**	**	**	**	**	**	**
K.	GUATEMALA	**	**	**	**	**	**	**	**
L.	HAITI	**	**	**	**	**	**	**	**
M.	HONDURAS	**	**	**	**	**	**	**	**
N.	MEXICO	3,446.3	13,902.5	16,044.5	15,758.5	15,758.5	14,050.4	5,752.7	8,629.8
O.	NICARAGUA	**	**	**	**	**	**	**	**
P.	PANAMA	**	**	**	**	**	**	**	**
Q.	PARAGUAY	**	**	**	**	**	**	**	**
R.	PERU	645.7	672.2	732.9	477.3	614.2	650.0	208.0	126.0
S.	URUGUAY	**	**	**	**	**	**	**	**
T.	VENEZUELA	13,557.2	19,351.5	15,564.0	13,933.0	14,993.0	13,063.0	7,218.0	9,104.0

SOURCE: IDB-SPTF, 1983, p. 126; 1986, table 69; 1987, table 72; 1988, table G-4.

Table 2461

OPEC[1] CRUDE OIL EXPORTS TO U.S., 1965–87

(T Barrels per Day)

Year	Exports
1965	992
1966	981
1967	740
1968	926
1969	940
1970	935
1971	1,427
1972	1,879
1973	2,406
1974	2,579
1975	2,726
1976	3,635
1977	5,069
1978	5,113
1979	5,102
1980	3,795
1981	2,735
1982	1,441
1983	1,259
1984	1,279
1985	1,187
1986	2,026
1987	1,899

1. The 13 OPEC countries include Ecuador and Venezuela.

SOURCE: *OPEC Annual Statistical Bulletin*, 1985, table 24; 1986, and 1987, table 24.

Figure 24:5

EFFECT OF INTERNATIONAL EVENTS ON OIL PRICES

(US 1985/Barrel[1])

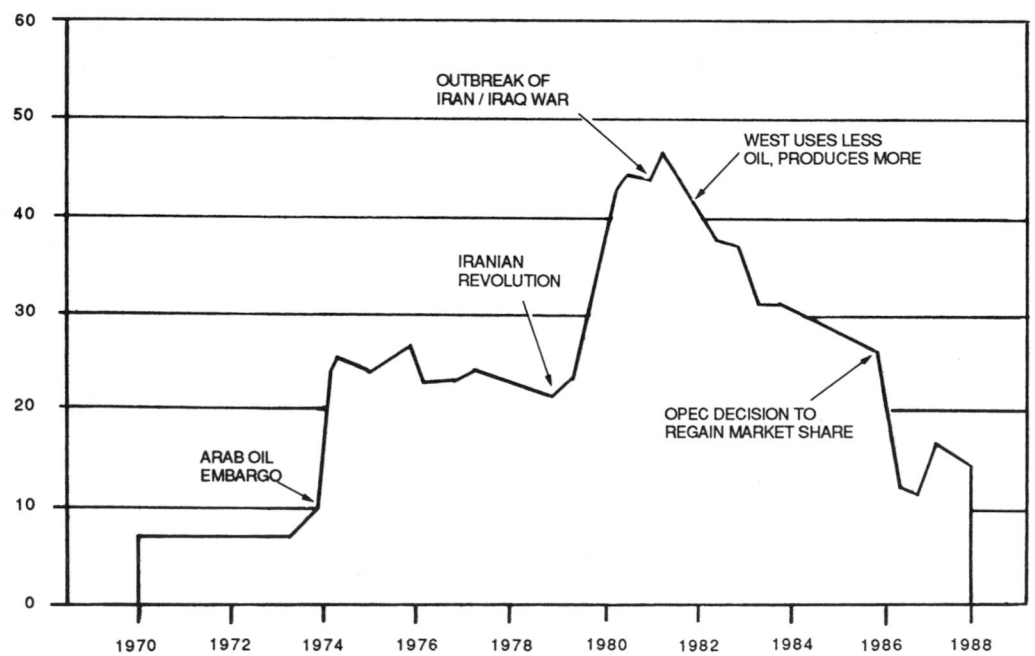

1. Average quarterly cost of crude oil imported by U.S. refiners.

SOURCE: *Los Angeles Times*, Dec. 25, 1988.

Table 2462

OPEC EXPORTS OF REFINED PRODUCTS, 1965–87

(T Barrels/Day)

	Country	1965	1968	1969	1970	1971	1972	1973	1974	1975	1976	1977
	Algeria	14.0	12.1	9.5	11.2	5.8	10.0	35.5	41.6	62.1	40.8	30.5
I.	ECUADOR	~	~	~	.1	.9	1.5	2.0	.9	.3	.9	.9
	Gabon	~	~	10.1	11.3	12.4	12.6	13.3	9.1	6.6	22.0	12.3
	Indonesia	82.9	75.4	92.5	99.3	92.2	125.6	154.9	123.7	100.4	99.1	147.2
	Iran	215.1	209.4	217.5	209.6	194.4	176.8	147.2	163.1	215.1	116.0	118.9
	Iraq	.7	~	4.9	3.1	3.5	.4	7.5	21.3	37.5	39.3	35.7
	Kuwait	223.7	215.0	190.1	251.0	234.2	210.5	205.7	192.5	140.5	336.9	313.3
	Libya	~	~	1.4	.8	~	.4	35.0	27.8	47.2	53.0	91.2
	Nigeria	1.7	1.2	2.5	4.6	8.5	2.5	15.0	3.7	5.3	11.3	13.9
	Qatar	~	~	~	~	~	~	~	~	~	~	~
	Saudi Arabia	179.0	290.7	219.4	347.0	294.2	319.5	331.7	321.5	330.7	390.0	341.4
	United Arab Emirates	~	~	~	~	~	~	~	~	~	~	2.8
T.	VENEZUELA	920.8	913.6	934.8	1,035.0	968.4	932.5	1,026.6	983.6	614.0	761.6	642.9
	Total OPEC	1,637.9	1,717.4	1.682.7	1,973.0	1,814.5	1,792.3	1,974.4	1,888.8	1,559.7	1,870.9	1,751.0

	Country	1978	1979	1980	1981	1982	1983	1984	1985	1986	1987
	Algeria	77.9	69.2	148.1	201.8	404.3	291.6	399.9	362.0	412.9	449.0
I.	ECUADOR	18.1	20.2	24.2	17.3	15.3	11.0	17.6	13.3	18.3	15.6
	Gabon	19.9	14.3	10.5	13.5	13.2	11.1	6.3	4.2	3.0	1.5
	Indonesia	124.0	146.9	162.6	155.8	121.1	130.2	191.9	149.8	159.3	183.0
	Iran	127.5	172.6	155.0	93.5	95.0	97.4	56.7	39.4	10.0	~
	Iraq	33.1	34.1	35.0	53.9	50.0	61.3	61.0	70.0	93.5	130.0
	Kuwait	327.1	423.6	343.4	280.8	370.4	414.3	394.9	492.9	510.9	510.0
	Libya	99.2	84.6	72.5	62.1	78.0	78.7	76.8	90.9	101.9	125.5
	Nigeria	3.8	24.0	74.6	43.4	10.9	16.3	20.0	20.0	8.8	7.1
	Qatar	~	6.7	1.8	13.2	11.6	16.8	23.7	17.4	21.4	25.0
	Saudi Arabia	357.5	375.6	406.8	481.0	537.6	389.2	442.1	574.3	712.3	864.8
	United Arab Emirates	7.9	13.0	19.6	37.7	45.7	60.7	97.7	92.1	111.6	114.0
T.	VENEZUELA	697.5	685.2	564.7	480.1	478.0	507.6	502.3	530.7	566.8	492.3
	Total OPEC	1,893.5	2,070.0	2,018.8	1,934.1	2,231.1	2,046.8	2,290.9	2,457.0	2,730.7	2,917.8

SOURCE: OPEC-SB, 1986; 1988, table 54.

Table 2463

OPEC OIL EXPORTS AS PERCENT OF TOTAL EXPORTS, 2 LC, 1965–87

	Country	1965	1970	1975	1980	1985	1986	1987
	Algeria	77.3	67.5	91.4	91.2	90.4	61.1	73.3
I.	ECUADOR	1.3	.4	53.0	56.2	66.3	45.3	40.6
	Gabon	12.1	31.4	85.1	68.9	84.5	68.9	71.6
	Indonesia	38.3	40.2	74.8	58.7	48.9	37.2	38.4
	Iran	87.2	89.9	97.1	94.2	98.4	88.9	90.2
	Iraq	92.9	92.5	98.5	99.5	97.5	96.0	97.1
	Kuwait	58.7	94.2	91.7	89.1	93.6	88.2	90.0
	Libya	100.0	100.0	88.2	93.3	96.3	95.7	95.8
	Nigeria	25.4	57.5	94.0	96.1	98.2	97.7	85.9
	Qatar	100.0	96.3	97.1	95.0	96.9	90.3	90.3
	Saudi Arabia	99.6	99.7	99.3	99.2	94.4	91.3	90.7
	United Arab Emirates	100.0	95.0	97.8	93.8	79.9	74.1	72.8
T.	VENEZUELA	92.9	90.2	94.6	94.9	84.4	66.8	86.3
	Average OPEC	77.3	85.1	94.3	93.0	86.7	76.5	79.6

SOURCE: OPEC-SB, 1987, table 7.

Table 2464

ECUADOR DESTINATION OF CRUDE OIL EXPORTS, 1981–87
(T Barrels/Day)

	Destination	1981	1982	1983	1984	1985	1986	1987
	North America	49.4	26.3	56.0	65.0	59.4	50.4	29.0
	UNITED STATES	49.4	26.3	56.0	65.0	59.4	50.4	29.0
	Latin America	23.3	33.9	47.6	46.7	38.3	56.6	32.0
C.	BRAZIL	5.0	12.5	~	~	~	~	~
D.	CHILE	2.5	~	2.4	1.0	2.2	8.8	~
E.	COLOMBIA	~	1.0	8.3	.9	2.4	#	~
	Netherlands Antilles	6.6	1.0	3.6	#	#	#	~
P.	PANAMA	1.5	5.9	20.3	16.2	15.0	13.3	~
	Puerto Rico	~	4.9	11.0	26.0	15.2	20.2	~
	Trinidad and Tobago	~	6.2	#	#	#	2.6	~
S.	URUGUAY	7.7	2.4	#	#	#	1.7	~
	Western Europe	~	~	1.0	#	#	#	#
	Asia and Far East	31.1	28.4	21.7	35.4	71.2	66.5	38.0
	Unspecified	1.7	1.5	~	~	~	~	~
	Total	105.5	90.1	126.3	147.1	168.9	173.5	99.0

SOURCE: *OPEC Statistical Bulletin*, 1986, 1987, table 5I.

Table 2465

VENEZUELA DESTINATION OF CRUDE OIL EXPORTS, 1960–87

PART I. OPEC DATA

(T Barrels/Day)

Destination	1981	1982	1983	1984	1985	1986	1987
North America	287.9	290.4	205.0	336.7	365.7	460.7	514.6
Canada	140.3	111.7	46.3	57.4	50.7	35.2	~
UNITED STATES	147.6	178.7	158.7	279.3	314.9	425.5	~
Latin America	637.3	538.6	513.0	444.3	232.4	295.1	339.3
C. BRAZIL	81.9	71.7	55.4	51.4	17.1	9.0	~
D. CHILE	20.7	20.1	20.7	21.9	23.0	19.7	~
Jamaica	13.3	15.9	13.2	7.1	11.7	9.2	~
Netherlands Antilles	277.5	349.6	340.0	264.6	~	.7	~
P. PANAMA	10.1	14.1	9.7	9.6	7.0	3.9	~
Puerto Rico	42.0	1.1	.9	~	3.3	6.4	~
Western Europe	267.5	197.5	237.4	199.9	215.4	186.6	163.6
Belgium	13.5	11.9	16.2	7.1	3.1	6.2	~
France	39.6	22.0	9.8	11.0	11.9	18.7	~
West Germany	16.5	30.7	56.8	57.6	62.1	93.0	~
Italy	76.5	41.0	49.5	34.0	49.5	16.6	~
Netherlands	21.4	15.6	43.0	28.7	25.1	10.2	~
Spain	54.7	39.2	20.0	13.8	23.3	8.1	~
Sweden	12.2	11.5	14.5	15.0	17.8	~	~
United Kingdom	20.7	17.1	18.0	19.5	13.3	14.7	~
Africa	15.1	4.4	2.9	3.0	2.9	1.9	~
Asia and Far East	56.1	26.2	18.4	15.0	9.5	4.4	~
Japan	39.6	20.9	18.4	15.0	9.5	4.4	~
CPEs	2.1	.8	~	~	~	~	~
Unspecified	~	~	~	~	7.0	~	7.2
Total	1,266.0	1,057.9	976.7	998.9	825.9	948.7	1,024.7

SOURCE: *OPEC Statistical Bulletin*, 1988.

PART II. RANDALL DATA

(%)

Year	Western Hemisphere				Eastern Hemisphere				
	North America	Central America	South America	Total	Europe	Asia	Africa	Oceania	Other
1960	54.7	10.9	10.7	76.3	20.1	.4	2.8	.3	.1
1961	53.6	9.6	9.2	72.4	23.5	.7	2.7	.5	.2
1962	52.6	9.7	7.5	69.9	25.8	1.4	2.3	.5	.1
1963	51.5	8.7	9.0	69.2	27.2	1.2	2.0	.3	.1
1964	53.5	9.4	10.0	72.9	23.6	1.4	1.7	.3	.1
1965	54.1	9.9	10.1	74.1	22.6	1.9	1.3	.1	0
1966	54.7	11.2	10.4	76.3	20.0	2.7	.8	.1	.1
1967	54.3	10.8	10.3	75.4	20.6	2.8	1.0	.1	.1
1968	54.5	12.3	11.6	78.4	18.0	2.4	1.1	0	.1
1969	56.2	13.6	10.6	80.4	17.0	1.8	.8	0	0
1970	61.2	14.3	7.6	83.1	15.0	1.1	.7	0	.1
1971	45.3	14.1	27.0	86.5	13.1	.3	0	0	0
1972	47.9	14.4	26.4	88.7	10.8	.3	0	0	0
1973	51.3	13.6	25.4	90.3	9.3	.3	0	0	0
1974	51.6	12.4	26.4	90.5	9.0	.4	0	0	0
1975	46.5	15.3	26.6	88.5	10.9	.3	0	0	0
1976	45.7	13.9	29.0	88.7	10.8	.3	.1	0	0
1977	48.7	14.7	28.2	91.6	7.8	.4	0	0	0
1978	46.0	14.1	28.9	89.0	9.9	.3	0	0	.3
1979	45.3	13	27.3	84.0	14.5	.4	.1	0	.9
1980	34.9	10.3	32.0	77.2	19.0	2.8	0	0	.2
1981	33.0	9.1	32.4	74.5	20.7	3.8	0	0	.4
1982	36.2	7.7	32.4	76.3	19.8	2.3	.5	0	1.1
1983	31.8	8.9	31.9	72.6	23.0	1.9	1.5	0	1.1
1984	44.5	9.6	25.7	86.0	17.6	1.2	.4	0	1.1
1985	58.2	9.4	9.2‡	76.8	19.8	.9	.3	0	2.2

SOURCE: Laura Randall, *The Political Economy of Venezuelan Oil* (New York: Praeger, 1987), p. 186.

Table 2466

U. S. CRUDE OIL PRICE IMPORT COSTS, 2 LC, 1976–88
(U. S. Average/Barrel, FOB Country of Origin)

Year	Mexico	Venezuela[1]	OPEC[2]
1976	~	11.32	~
1977	13.42	12.68	~
1978	13.24	12.45	13.30
1979	20.29	17.37	19.91
1980	31.11	24.78	32.25
1981	33.13	28.86	35.11
1982	28.07	23.77	33.45
1983	25.19	21.48	28.45
1984	26.37	24.16	27.50
1985	25.33	23.64	25.66
1986	11.84	10.92	12.21
1987	16.36	15.08	16.59
1988	10.75	~	~

1. Included in OPEC.
2. Includes Venezuela.

SOURCE: U. S. Energy Information Agency, *Monthly Energy Review*, April 1988, p. 92.

Table 2467

MEXICO UNIFORM COST OF CRUDE OIL EXPORT,[1] 1977–86
(US/Barrel)

Year	Nominal[2]	Real[3]
1977	44.46	158.8
1978	54.00	164.1
1979	80.80	207.7
1980	79.40	161.4
1981	114.63	182.2
1982	196.81	196.8
1983	363.74	180.2
1984	533.00	159.5
1985	979.12	182.0
1986	1,567.46	159.7

1. Excludes reserve for exploration and decline of fields.
2. Pesos.
3. Pesos of 1982.

SOURCE: Francisco Colmenares, *Mexico: Estadísticas Básicas de Producción* [1988], p. 33.

Table 2468

LEAD EXPORT VALUE, 8 LC, 1980–86

	Country	T US						Value as % of Total Market Economy					
		1980	1982	1983	1984	1985	1986	1980	1982	1983	1984	1985	1986
A.	ARGENTINA	3	356	#	~	~	~	#	#[†]	~	~	~	~
B.	BOLIVIA	57[†]	309[†]	90[†]	98	11	71[†]	#	#[†]	~	~	~	~
C.	BRAZIL	898	29	120	77	80[†]	315[†]	#	#	~	~	~	~
E.	COLOMBIA	131	30	4	~	~	~	#	#	~	~	~	~
N.	MEXICO	55,462	22,047	31,370[†]	47,126	22,677[†]	21,753[†]	3.1	2.3	3.6[†]	5.8[†]	3.2[†]	3.4[†]
P.	PANAMA	632	581	148	19	99	4[†]	#	#	~	~	~	~
R.	PERU	58,510	36,786	35,666	17,873	27,107[†]	21,498[†]	3.3	3.8	4.1[†]	2.3[†]	3.9[†]	3.4[†]
T.	VENEZUELA	2	~	~	~	~	~	#	~	~	~	~	~
	LAIA	115,064	65,783	68,848	69,925[†]	49,948[†]	43,682[†]	6.5	6.7	7.9[†]	8.2[†]	7.1[†]	6.9[†]
	CACM	41	108[†]	642[†]	54[†]	60[†]	36[†]	#	#[†]	.1[†]	.1[†]	#[†]	#[†]
	UNITED STATES	164,836	49,102	19,124	15,240	21,045	14,088	9.4	5.0	2.2	1.8	3.0	~

SOURCE: UN-YITS, 1982, vol. 2, p. 159; 1983, vol. 2, p. 147; 1984, vol. 2, p. 178; 1985, 1986, vol. 2, p. 181.

Table 2469

COPPER EXPORT VALUE,[1] 9 LC, 1980–86

	Country	T US					Value as % of Total Market Economy				
		1980	1983	1984	1985	1986	1980	1983	1984	1985	1986
A.	ARGENTINA	411	1,123	890	2,910	7,816[†]	#	~	~	~	~
B.	BOLIVIA	615[†]	56[†]	~	~	~	#[†]	~	~	~	~
C.	BRAZIL	10,606	60,510	124,491	42,720[†]	47,477[†]	#	~	~	~	~
D.	CHILE	2,009,061	2,739,610	2,525,194	2,538,512	2,630,414	15.0	24.3	23.9	23.4	23.7
E.	COLOMBIA	145	~	~	~	~	#	~	~	~	~
K.	GUATEMALA	335	~	~	~	~	#	~	~	~	~
N.	MEXICO	32,831[†]	56,755[†]	66,602	41,921[†]	54,359[†]	#[†]	~	~	~	~
R.	PERU	609,927	350,525[†]	327,213	368,192[†]	366,303[†]	4.7	3.7[†]	~	4.5	~
T.	VENEZUELA	53	1,341[†]	1,102	1,006[†]	2,007[†]	#	~	~	~	~
	LAIA	3,962,032	2,958,528	2,879,791	2,995,389[†]	3,108,464[†]	19.9	26.3	27.2	27.7[†]	28.0[†]
	CACM	344	861[†]	374[†]	96[†]	47[†]	#	#[†]	#[†]	#[†]	#[†]
	UNITED STATES	443,693	392,441	402,969	328,875	259,237	3.3	3.5	3.8	3.0	2.3

1. Except cement copper.

SOURCE: UN-YITS, 1982, vol. 2, p. 156; 1983, vol. 2, p. 144; 1984–86, vol. 2, p. 178.

Table 2470

U. S. IMPORTS OF STEEL MILL PRODUCTS, BY REGION OF ORIGIN
(1988)

Region	%
Asia	32.7
Australia, New Zealand, Africa, Oceania	1.3
Canada	17.9
European Economic Community	28.4
Other European Countries	8.9
Latin America	10.7
Other	.1
Total	100.0

SOURCE: *Los Angeles Times*, Sept. 23, 1988.

Table 2471

TIN EXPORT VALUE, 9 LC, 1980–86

Country	T US					Value as % of Total Market Economy				
	1980	1983	1984	1985	1986	1980	1983	1984	1985	1986
A. ARGENTINA	11	45	12	~	~	~	~	~	~	~
B. BOLIVIA	177,430[†]	164,583[†]	192,906	135,962	56,383[†]	5.7[†]	7.8	8.6	6.3	4.4[†]
C. BRAZIL	63,534	221,867	362,389	229,077[†]	138,386[†]	2.1	9.8	16.1	10.5[†]	10.7[†]
D. CHILE	5,154[†]	8,264[†]	~	~	~	#	~	~	~	~
F. COSTA RICA	~	~	25	8	~	~	~	~	~	~
J. EL SALVADOR	1	~	~	~	~	#	~	~	~	~
K. GUATEMALA	~	~	~	~	~	~	~	~	~	~
N. MEXICO	62[†]	15[†]	272	36[†]	1,495[†]	#	~	~	~	~
R. PERU	269	108	78	24[†]	907[†]	#	~	~	~	~
LAIA	241,306[†]	408,260	568,300	378,095[†]	217,892[†]	7.8[†]	18.0	25.3	17.4[†]	16.8[†]
CACM	103	25[†]	22[†]	7[†]	7[†]	#	#[†]	#[†]	#[†]	#[†]
UNITED STATES	31,120	57,165	48,940	43,190	34,808	1.0	2.5	2.2	2.0	2.7

SOURCE: UN-YITS, 1982, vol. 2, p. 584; 1983, vol. 2, p. 149; 1984–86, vol. 2, p. 183.

Table 2472

ZINC EXPORT VALUE, 7 LC, 1980–86

Country	T US					Value as % of Total Market Economy				
	1980	1983	1984	1985	1986	1980	1983	1984	1985	1986
A. ARGENTINA	185	4	6	6,389[†]	1,609[†]	#	~	~	~	~
C. BRAZIL	106	132	4,877	198[†]	248[†]	#	~	~	~	~
D. CHILE	#	~	~	~	~	#	~	~	~	~
H. DOMINICAN REP.	~	~	~	~	~	~	~	~	~	~
K. GUATEMALA	120	245	52[†]	57[†]	36[†]	#	~	~	~	~
N. MEXICO	10,853	49,154[†]	69,741[†]	44,406[†]	33,359[†]	#	~	~	~	~
R. PERU	32,759	113,814	113,133	74,057[†]	87,640[†]	2.2	4.2[†]	5.2	4.0[†]	5.5[†]
LAIA	141,651	163,170[†]	187,169[†]	126,130[†]	124,245[†]	5.3	9.2[†]	8.6[†]	6.8[†]	7.8[†]
CACM	131	389[†]	201[†]	177[†]	133[†]	#	#[†]	#[†]	#[†]	#[†]
UNITED STATES	14,081	9,212	9,331	13,920	10,726	#	~	~	~	~

SOURCE: UN-YITS, 1982, vol. 2, p. 160; 1983, vol. 2, p. 148; 1984–86, vol. 2, p. 182.

Table 2473

MERCHANDISE TRADE VALUE,[1] 25 ECLA: LR. 1980-87

(M US)

Country	1980 Exports	1980 Imports	1981 Exports	1981 Imports	1983 Exports	1983 Imports	1984 Exports	1984 Imports	1985 Exports	1985 Imports	1986 Exports	1986 Imports	1987‡ Exports	1987‡ Imports
A. ARGENTINA	8,020.0	9,398.3	9,169.1	8,414.5	7,833.6	4,123.1	8,072.0	4,131.8	8,419.2	3,524.2	6,847.8	4,391.2	6,196.0	5,638.0
Bahamas	200.4	801.5	176.9	789.8	224.9	802.5	262.0	868.6	296.8	996.6	293.9	1,018.1	273.1	1,097.4
Barbados	180.8	479.0	162.7	521.4	272.2	564.8	339.7	606.2	300.4	559.1	244.4	522.6	129.0	436.0
B. BOLIVIA	941.8	680.6	913.3	681.8	755.1	473.1	724.5	412.3	623.4	462.8	546.6	596.6	469.9	659.0
C. BRAZIL	20,139.9	22,951.2	23,341.5	22,099.8	21,923.1	15,437.4	27,050.0	13,936.0	25,538.8	13,127.3	22,393.0	14,044.0	26,213.0	15,052.0
D. CHILE	4,705.0	5,469.0	3,835.8	6,512.5	3,827.0	2,818.0	3,650.1	3,356.9	3,804.5	2,953.6	4,198.8	3,099.5	5,223.0	3,994.0
E. COLOMBIA	3,986.6	4,283.3	3,157.8	4,729.6	2,969.7	4,464.0	4,273.3	4,027.3	3,650.1	3,673.5	5,375.5	3,485.5	5,264.8	3,818.1
F. COSTA RICA	1,001.5	1,374.9	1,002.4	1,089.1	853.2	898.9	997.1	996.5	941.3	1,005.1	1,083.3	1,041.5	1,113.6	1,252.5
H. DOMINICAN REP.	962.0	1,519.7	1,188.0	1,451.7	785.2	1,282.2	868.1	1,257.1	738.5	1,285.9	722.1	1,266.2	723.4	1,550.0
I. ECUADOR	2,544.2	2,241.8	2,544.2	2,361.5	2,365.0	1,408.0	2,622.0	1,567.0	2,905.0	1,611.0	2,186.0	1,631.1	2,017.0	2,048.0
J. EL SALVADOR	1,075.3	897.0	798.1	898.4	735.4	830.8	725.9	914.5	679.0	894.9	754.9	872.2	572.7	906.3
K. GUATEMALA	1,518.9	1,471.9	1,282.3	1,544.2	1,090.8	1,056.6	1,131.2	1,183.0	1,065.4	1,077.7	1,047.5	874.4	970.7	1,308.5
Guyana	388.9	386.4	346.4	399.6	193.4	225.8	216.9	201.6	214.0	209.1	238.7	241.1	242.2	198.6
L. HAITI	215.1	318.1	147.2	350.7	185.5	323.9	211.6	355.0	227.5	351.3	197.7	338.0	205.0	300.0
M. HONDURAS	850.3	954.0	783.8	898.6	694.2	760.7	737.0	884.8	805.1	879.2	891.2	874.5	862.5	893.9
Jamaica	962.7	1,038.2	974.0	1,296.7	685.7	1,124.2	702.3	1,037.0	568.6	1,004.2	589.5	837.4	673.5	1,047.7
N. MEXICO	16,070.0	18,902.1	19,891.3	24,050.1	22,329.3	8,564.8	24,185.1	11,288.4	21,667.4	13,217.7	16,027.8	11,451.3	20,656.2	12,222.9
O. NICARAGUA	450.4	802.9	508.2	922.5	428.3	778.1	385.4	799.6	297.6	837.6	244.2	782.0	299.0	837.9
P. PANAMA	2,267.1	2,994.6	2,540.1	3,315.4	1,673.5	2,321.7	1,685.7	2,503.1	1,958.8	2,712.3	2,412.4	2,954.7	2,525.3	3,034.8
Q. PARAGUAY	400.4	675.4	398.6	772.3	326.0	551.4	361.3	649.1	324.4	515.9	573.4	735.8	800.0	934.8
R. PERU	3,899.4	3,065.1	3,248.6	3,804.0	3,018.9	2,723.8	3,148.8	2,141.2	2,977.0	1,808.3	2,508.2	2,511.4	2,559.0	2,903.0
Suriname	514.5	454.1	473.8	507.0	367.3	402.1	374.5	387.4	335.6	336.5	342.6	309.5	291.0	298.0
Trinidad & Tobago	2,541.0	1,764.1	2,607.8	1,733.1	2,272.9	2,315.7	2,110.7	1,704.9	2,110.7	1,354.6	1,363.1	1,209.4	1,399.8	1,160.5
S. URUGUAY	1,058.5	1,668.2	1,229.7	1,592.1	1,156.4	739.7	924.6	732.2	853.6	675.4	1,087.8	791.0	1,189.1	1,079.9
T. VENEZUELA	19,050.5	10,876.9	19,963.2	12,122.9	14,570.5	6,408.7	15,966.6	7,262.2	14,178.2	7,387.6	8,648.6	7,834.4	10,487.0	8,430.0
LATIN AMERICA[2]	93,946.0	95,468.3	100,684.7	102,859.5	91,537.1	61,400.0	101,726.3	63,203.7	95,480.8	62,461.4	80,818.9	63,713.8	91,355.8	71,101.8

1. Exports and imports f.o.b. values.
2. Totals may not add because of rounding.

SOURCE: IDB-SPTF, 1986, p. 419; 1987, p. 451; 1988, tables D-3 and D-4.

Table 2474

GROWTH RATE OF MERCHANDISE IMPORTS, 7 L, 1974–84
(AA–GR of Dollar Value)

	Country	1974–78	1979–80	1981	1982	1983	1984
A.	ARGENTINA	2.0	64.0	−10.5	−45.7	−9.8	1.8
C.	BRAZIL	2.0	29.0	−3.8	−12.2	−20.4	−9.7
D.	CHILE	11.0	38.0	19.9	−47.8	−17.8	19.0
E.	COLOMBIA	14.1	29.0	10.8	13.5	−17.4	−10.8
N.	MEXICO	8.3	54.0	27.2	−40.0	−46.5	33.1
R.	PERU	−4.5	36.0	23.0	−2.1	−26.9	−19.8
T.	VENEZUELA	30.5	−1.6	11.5	12.1	−52.8	12.3

SOURCE: IDB-SPTF, 1985, table I–4.

Table 2475

GROWTH RATE OF MERCHANDISE EXPORTS, 7 L, 1974–84
(AA–GR of Dollar Value)

	Country	1974–78	1979–80	1981	1982	1983	1984
A.	ARGENTINA	13.0	11.9	14.3	−21.9	9.5	11.1
C.	BRAZIL	12.3	26.0	15.7	−13.4	8.5	23.2
D.	CHILE	3.4	38.4	−15.8	−11.8	9.6	−5.0
E.	COLOMBIA	21.0	12.6	−20.8	−.1	−7.6	15.0
N.	MEXICO	20.1	61.0	23.8	6.7	.8	9.7
R.	PERU	6.4	42.2	−17.2	−4.4	−2.8	2.6
T.	VENEZUELA	−5.1	45.0	4.8	−17.3	−10.6	7.7

SOURCE: IDB-SPTF, 1985, table I–7.

Table 2476

STRUCTURE OF TOTAL MERCHANDISE
IMPORTS, 20 LC, 1960–73[a]

		Food and Raw Materials (%)		
	Country	1960	1965	1970	1973
A.	ARGENTINA	26.7	42.2	36.5	~

a. Other categories are fuels and lubricants, machinery and equipment, other manufactured products, and total merchandise imports.

Continued in SALA, 24–2455.

Table 2477

MANUFACTURED GOODS[1] AS SHARE OF
TOTAL VALUE OF COUNTRY TRADE,
20 LC, 1970–80

	Country	Year	Imports CIF	Exports FOB
A.	ARGENTINA	1970	78.2	14.0
		1975	71.6	24.4
		1980	78.9	24.9

Continued in SALA, 24-2456.

Table 2478

CAPITAL GOODS EXPORTS,[1] 16 LR, 1970–82

(M US)

Exporting Country	1970	1971	1972	1973	1974	1975	1976	1977	1978	1979	1980	1981	1982
A. ARGENTINA	55	71	97	205	289	320	311	366	386	393	413	366	469
B. BOLIVIA	0	0	0	0	0	1	0	0	2	5	9	7	5

Continued in SALA, 25-2461.

Table 2479

CAPITAL GOODS IMPORTS AS SHARE OF TOTAL GOODS IMPORTED, 16 LR, 1970–82

(%)

Importing Country	1970	1971	1972	1973	1974	1975	1976	1977	1978	1979	1980	1981	1982
A. ARGENTINA	30.0	31.6	33.2	25.2	17.6	19.1	22.6	33.7	37.5	30.6	33.6	35.0	30.0
B. BOLIVIA	38.5	34.7	34.6	- -	35.8	42.1	45.1	38.7	44.2	38.9	31.0	43.5	37.9

Continued in SALA, 25-2462.

Table 2480

TOTAL MERCHANDISE EXPORTS AS SHARE OF COUNTRY GDP, 1970–82

(%)

Country	1970	1975	1978	1979	1980	1981	1982
LAIA							
A. ARGENTINA	4.2	6.1	12.9	14.7	15.0	18.1	16.0
C. BRAZIL	3.2	6.0	7.4	8.4	10.3	12.1	10.5

Continued in SALA, 24-2457.

Table 2481

COTTON EXPORT VALUE, 11 LC, 1980–86

Country	T US						Value as % of Total Market Economy					
	1980	1982	1983	1984	1985	1986	1980	1982	1983	1984	1985	1986
A. ARGENTINA	126,791	69,432	10,293	66,367	76,611	21,894[†]	1.9	3.0[†]	~	~	~	~
B. BOLIVIA	3,395[†]	2,726[†]	~	~	~	~	#[†]	#[†]	~	~	~	~
C. BRAZIL	17,452	64,593	196,387	95,259	71,425[†]	49,088[†]	.3	1.7	6.6	1.5	1.4[†]	1.2[†]
E. COLOMBIA	82,359	26,707	23,195	49,076	60,507	61,049[†]	#	#	~	~	~	~
J. EL SALVADOR	87,142	45,394	53,617	13,773	27,897[†]	10,542[†]	#	#[†]	~	~	~	~
K. GUATEMALA	172,330	95,686[†]	106,105	66,879[†]	64,513[†]	23,438[†]	2.5	2.0	1.3[†]	~	~	~
M. HONDURAS	13,649	6,629	4,228	13,290	4,534[†]	7,625[†]	#	#[†]	~	~	~	~
N. MEXICO	324,173	183,825	115,698	208,166	77,856[†]	56,570[†]	4.8	3.3	2.1	3.3	1.5[†]	1.4[†]
O. NICARAGUA	30,922	89,095	99,109[†]	126,194[†]	75,557[†]	42,482[†]	#	#	~	~	1.5	~
Q. PARAGUAY	105,833	122,415	79,000	152,896[†]	137,242[†]	54,863[†]	1.6	2.4	1.6	1.6[†]	~	~
R. PERU	62,565	74,691	52,566[†]	14,614[†]	31,793[†]	32,328[†]	#	#	~	~	~	~
LAIA	722,152	541,687	649,384[†]	588,051[†]	456,715[†]	276,628[†]	10.7	9.7[†]	11.6[†]	9.3[†]	8.9[†]	6.9[†]
CACM	305,503	236,805[†]	271,717[†]	218,622[†]	172,588[†]	84,163[†]	4.5	7.2	4.9[†]	3.5[†]	3.4[†]	2.1[†]
UNITED STATES	2,906,646	2,004,918	1,859,514	2,476,094	1,671,177	819,547	43.1	35.8	33.2	39.3	32.6	20.4

a. Datum for 1978: 2.1.

SOURCE: UN-YITS, 1982, vol. 2, p. 64; 1983, vol. 2, p. 52; 1984–86, vol. 2, p. 86.

Table 2482

U.S. COTTON IMPORT QUOTAS, 3 LR,[1] 1986

(% of World Quota)

Country	%
C. BRAZIL	4.3
N. MEXICO	61.2
R. PERU	1.7
LATIN AMERICA	67.2

1. Other Latin American producers are Argentina, Colombia, Ecuador, Haiti, Honduras, and Paraguay. These countries were assigned smaller quotas.

SOURCE: NAFINSA-MV, no. 40, p. 944.

Table 2483

COTTON LINT EXPORT VOLUME,[1] 13 LC, 1975–87

(T MET)

	Country	1975	1979	1980	1981	1982	1983	1934	1985	1986	1987
A.	ARGENTINA	6	62	86	24[‡]	69	8	56	90	5	17[‡]
B.	BOLIVIA	15	10	.6	#	#	#	~	~	~	~
C.	BRAZIL	83	#	9	30	56	180	32	87	37	174
E.	COLOMBIA	86	26	48	52[‡]	18	14	27	49	48	57[‡]
F.	COSTA RICA	~	#	1	#	#	~	~	#	~	~
H.	DOMINICAN REP.[3]	~	#	#	#	#	#	.2	#	.5	#
J.	EL SALVADOR	53	56	53	30	32	37	5	24	6	4
K.	GUATEMALA	107	147	137	110[‡]	66	39	52	51	37	10[‡]
M.	HONDURAS	4	9	9	7[‡]	6	3	5	5	6[‡]	2[‡]
N.	MEXICO[3]	166	212	172	183	126	69	123	77	56	52
O.	NICARAGUA[3]	132	114	20	73[‡]	60	79	82	67	49	37[‡]
Q.	PARAGUAY	17	77	75	91	112	79	89	162	107	86
R.	PERU	46	20	30	32[‡]	53	31	7	25[‡]	22[‡]	9[‡]
	UNITED STATES[2,3]	871	1,527	1,823	1,269	1,392	1,205	1,500	1,095	657	1,195
	WORLD	3,879	4,374	4,815	4,296	4,416	4,307	4,314	4,264	4,647	5,468

1. Figures refer to "special trade" except where otherwise indicated. See table 2413, n. 1, for explanation of "special" exports.
2. The customs area includes the Commonwealth of Puerto Rico.
3. Figures refer to "general trade," i.e., total exports including re-exports.

a. For 1934–75 see SALA, 20-2922.

SOURCE: FAO-TY, 1958; 1980; 1981, table 109; 1982, table 109; 1984, table 109; 1985, 1986, 1987, table 110.

Table 2484

STRUCTURE OF WORLD TRADE IN COMPUTER EQUIPMENT, 1980

(%)

Region and Country	Exports (fob)			Imports (cif)		
	United States	European Community	Japan	United States	European Community	Japan
Developed Countries						
United States	~	4	29	~	45	71
Western Europe	61	82	28	37	51	12
European Community	51	64	23	33	45	11
Japan	8	1	~	17	2	~
Other	17	3	15	39	1	3
Subtotal	86	90	71	93	99	86
COMECON Countries	.3	1	3	.1	.1	Neg.
Developing Countries						
Latin America	8	2	6	2	1	13
Africa	.4	3	.1	~	Neg.	~
Asia/Oceania	4	1	19	5	.2	.1
Middle East	1	4	1	.4	.2	.3
Subtotal	14	9	26	7	1	14
Total World	100	100	100	100	100	100

SOURCE: SELA, "Trade and Foreign Direct Investment in Data Services," August 20, 1985.

Table 2485

COMPUTER IMPORTS, 10 L, 1975–81

(M US)

	Country	1975	1976	1977	1978	1979	1980	1981
A.	ARGENTINA	16	14	37	44	48	172	~
B.	BOLIVIA	.7	1	~	~	~	~	~
C.	BRAZIL	~	~	46	81	86	99	120
D.	CHILE	~	~	11	15	25	40	~
E.	COLOMBIA	~	8	11	10	13	~	~
N.	MEXICO	~	~	38	60	~	~	~
Q.	PARAGUAY	~	~	1	6	~	1	~
R.	PERU	6	7	4	~	~	~	~
S.	URUGUAY	~	2	3	3	4	8	~
T.	VENEZUELA	~	31	28	51	49	60	~

SOURCE: SELA, "Trade and Foreign Direct Investment in Data Services," August 20, 1985.

Table 2486

COMPUTER EXPORTS, 4 L, 1975–81

(M US)

	Country	1975	1976	1977	1978	1979	1980	1981
A.	ARGENTINA	21	17	24	21	25	39	~
C.	BRAZIL	~	39	63	67	79	158	199
N.	MEXICO	~	~	8	5	~	~	~
T.	VENEZUELA	~	9	1	4	~	~	~
	TOTAL	21	65	96	97	104	107	149

SOURCE: SELA, "Trade and Foreign Investment in Data Services," August 20, 1985.

Table 2487

DISTRIBUTION OF COMPUTER SERVICE SALES BY FRENCH FIRMS, 1980

(M Francs and %)

Region	Exports	% of Total Revenues	Sales by Foreign Affiliates	% of Total Revenues	Total Value	Total %
Western Europe	138	23	824	77	962	57
Eastern Europe	79	13	~	~	79	5
Middle East	45	7	16	2	61	4
Africa	182	30	88	8	270	16
North America	77	13	130	12	207	12
Latin America	64	10	5	~	69	4
Other	25	4	7	1	32	2
Total	610	100	1,070	100	1,680	100

SOURCE: SELA, "Trade and Foreign Direct Investment in Data Services," August 20, 1985.

Table 2488

BRAZIL INFORMATION TECHNOLOGY INDUSTRY, DOMESTIC
COMPANIES SUBSECTOR, 1980–86

Category	1980	1983	1986
Number of Companies	29	80	310
Proportion of Total (%)	75	80	90
Sales (M US)	280	687	1,520
Proportion of Total (%)	32	46	51
Amount of Equipment Installed	1,588	7,684	800,000
Proportion of Total (%)	17	91	98
Employment (Direct)	7,264	15,734	40,316
Proportion of Total (%)	40	60	89
R & D Outlays (M US)	30	67	154
Ratio of Sales (%)	8.7	9.8	10.1
R & D Outlays/Employee (US/Employee)	4,130	4,260	3,850
R & D Personnel	1,200	2,045	4,900
Proportion of Total Employment (%)	16.5	13	12.2

SOURCE: IDB-SPTF, 1988, table VII-5.

Table 2489

BRAZIL IMPORTS OF THE INFORMATION
TECHNOLOGY INDUSTRY, 1981–86

(M US)

Category	Domestic Companies 1981	Domestic Companies 1985	Domestic Companies 1986	Transnational Corporations 1981	Transnational Corporations 1985	Transnational Corporations 1986
General Data Processing						
Imports (Value)	81	96	75	223	174	178
Percentage of Sales	21.9	8.9	5.7	33.3	16.8	16.8
Teleprocessing						
Imports (Value)	~	22	40	**	32	54
Percentage of Sales	**	11.5	16.7	**	13.1	20.4

SOURCE: IDB-SPTF, 1988, table VII-8.

25

Structure and Terms
of Trade

Table 2500

ARGENTINA PERCENTAGE VALUE OF TRADE, 1970–86

	Imports by Broad Economic Category								
Category	1970	1975	1980	1981	1982	1983	1984	1985	1986
Total Imports	100.0	100.0	100.0	100.0	100.0	100.0	100.0	100.0	100.0
1. Food and Beverages	5.5	4.4	5.4	4.8	4.3	3.7	4.3	4.5	6.7
Primary	4.2	3.6	3.1	2.6	3.0	2.7	2.9	3.2	5.3
For Industry	2.6	2.1	1.1	1.0	1.7	1.8	1.5	1.9	3.3
For Hshold Consm	1.6	1.5	2.0	1.6	1.3	.9	1.3	1.3	2.0
Processed	1.3	.8	2.3	2.2	1.3	1.0	1.5	1.3	1.4
For Industry	.3	.3	.5	.4	.6	.6	.9	.8	.9
For Hshold Consm	1.0	.5	1.8	1.8	.7	.4	.5	.5	.5
2. Ind. Supplies Nes	53.2	58.3	32.7	30.7	41.5	48.1	48.3	41.8	46.4
Primary	5.0	6.4	2.6	2.7	3.7	4.6	4.9	4.4	5.6
Processed	48.1	51.9	30.1	28.0	37.8	43.4	43.4	37.4	40.8
3. Fuels	4.6	13.1	10.1	10.6	12.4	10.0	10.3	12.0	8.9
Primary	2.8	11.2	8.9	8.4	11.4	9.3	9.2	11.5	8.7
Processed	1.8	1.9	1.2	2.2	1.0	.7	1.1	.5	.1
4. Motor Spirit	0	.2	.7	1.5	.3	0	0	0	0
Other	1.8	1.7	.5	.8	.7	.7	1.0	.5	.1
5. Machinery	25.8	16.7	27.3	29.4	28.9	25.7	23.1	28.0	25.6
Machines Capt. Eqp	21.0	13.3	23.5	25.4	24.2	20.1	17.2	21.6	19.0
Parts Accessories	4.8	3.4	3.8	4.0	4.7	5.7	5.9	6.4	6.6
6. Transport	6.1	4.4	10.6	11.5	6.8	8.4	9.7	9.3	7.7
Passenger Cars	.1	0	2.3	2.6	.5	.1	0	.1	.2
Other	.7	1.3	4.3	4.4	1.6	2.2	2.4	1.9	.7
Parts Accessories	5.3	3.1	4.0	4.5	4.6	6.1	7.3	7.3	6.7
7. Consumer Goods	4.7	3.0	13.8	13.0	6.1	4.0	4.3	4.5	4.8
Durable	1.6	1.3	6.1	5.6	2.2	1.3	1.5	1.5	1.8
Semi-Durable	1.3	.5	5.4	5.2	2.1	1.3	1.2	1.2	1.3
Non-Durable	1.8	1.2	2.3	2.2	1.8	1.5	1.5	1.8	1.7
8. Other	.1	.1	0	.1	.1	0	0	0	0

	Exports by Industrial Origin								
Origin	1970	1975	1980	1981	1982	1983	1984	1985	1986
Total Exports (1 + 2 + 3)	100.0	100.0	100.0	100.0	100.0	100.0	100.0	100.0	100.0
1. Agriculture	39.4	47.1	38.7	45.7	40.1	49.0	47.0	43.3	36.8
2. Mining Quarrying	.3	.4	.4	.3	.3	.3	.3	1.1	.6
3. Manufacturing	60.2	52.6	60.9	54.0	59.6	50.6	52.7	55.5	62.6
31. Food, Bev., Tobac.	43.3	25.8	30.6	24.2	25.3	27.4	28.7	24.9	31.3
32. Textiles	5.5	4.9	8.9	6.9	6.6	5.5	5.7	5.7	8.0
33. Wood, Wood Prod.	#	0	0	0	0	0	0	0	0
34. Paper and Prod.	.9	.9	.9	.6	.6	.5	.6	.7	.8
35. Chemicals	4.0	4.7	8.8	11.6	12.8	9.4	8.8	11.9	7.6
36. Non-Metal Minrl	.1	.2	.4	.3	.5	.2	.2	.2	.3
37. Basic Metal Ind.	1.7	.8	3.5	4.4	5.7	3.5	3.4	5.6	6.3
38. Metal Manufact.	4.5	15.1	7.6	5.5	7.9	4.1	5.3	6.6	8.1
39. Oth. Manf. Ind.	.1	.1	.2	.3	.1	0	0	0	.1

SOURCE: UN-YITS, 1976; 1981; 1983; 1984; 1985; 1986; 1987.

Table 2501

BOLIVIA PERCENTAGE VALUE OF TRADE, 1971–85

Imports by Broad Economic Category

Category	1971	1975	1978	1979	1980	1981	1982	1983	1984
Total Imports	100.0	100.0	100.0	100.0	100.0	100.0	100.0	100.0	100.0
1. Food and Beverages	20.2	16.7	13.1	13.0	18.0	13.7	18.1	19.1	15.5
Primary	3.3	3.2	5.1	5.1	6.7	5.2	9.2	9.9	8.8
For Industry	2.4	2.5	4.2	4.5	5.7	4.3	9.0	9.9	8.2
For Hshold Consm	.9	.6	.9	.6	.9	.9	.2	.1	.6
Processed	17.0	13.5	8.0	7.9	11.3	8.5	8.8	9.1	6.6
For Industry	10.5	8.8	2.9	3.5	3.2	2.6	4.3	5.0	2.2
For Hshold Consm	6.4	4.8	5.2	4.4	8.1	5.9	4.6	4.2	4.4
2. Ind. Supplies Nes.	32.0	28.8	23.4	22.9	27.1	27.7	30.0	32.8	31.2
Primary	.8	.7	.5	.4	.5	.5	.7	1.3	1.7
Processed	31.2	28.1	22.9	22.4	26.6	27.1	29.3	31.6	29.4
3. Fuels	.7	1.7	.9	.7	.3	1.6	1.8	.7	.4
Primary	0	0	0	0	0	0	0	0	0
Processed	.7	1.6	.9	.7	.3	1.6	1.7	.7	.4
Motor Spirit	.5	.6	.5	.3	0	0	0	0	0
Other	.2	1.0	.4	.3	.3	1.6	1.7	.7	.4
4. Machinery	21.7	19.8	31.3	26.7	24.6	25.1	25.6	31.1	23.5
Machines Capt. Eqp	18.5	18.1	29.0	24.2	21.5	22.9	22.8	28.3	21.0
Parts Accessories	3.2	1.7	2.3	2.6	3.1	2.3	2.8	2.7	2.4
5. Transport	13.0	21.7	17.4	19.8	18.5	21.2	14.6	11.2	24.5
Passenger Cars	.6	4.3	3.0	3.7	6.1	7.5	3.1	1.5	10.0
Other	6.4	11.9	9.1	10.6	5.4	6.9	4.8	3.2	7.0
Industrial	6.1	11.3	8.5	10.0	5.2	6.4	4.2	3.1	7.0
Non-Industrial	.2	.6	.7	.5	.3	.5	.6	.1	0
Parts Accessories	6.0	5.5	5.3	5.5	6.9	6.8	6.7	6.6	7.5
6. Consumer Goods	12.2	11.2	12.7	11.5	11.5	10.1	7.9	3.9	3.9
Durable	3.2	4.4	4.4	4.3	3.1	2.5	2.3	.9	.7
Semi-Durable	3.0	2.4	3.0	2.3	2.8	3.1	2.1	.8	1.0
Non Durable	6.0	4.4	5.3	5.0	5.6	4.4	3.5	2.2	2.2
7. Other	.2	.1	1.2	5.4	.2	.6	2.0	1.2	1.0

Exports by Industrial Origin

Origin	1971	1974	1975	1978	1979	1980	1981	1982	1983	1984	1985
Total Exports (1 + 2 + 3)	100.0	100.0	100.0	100.0	100.0	100.0	100.0	100.0	100.0	100.0	100.0
1. Agriculture	5.4	4.5	5.7	6.5	5.2	3.3	2.7	2.9	2.4	1.6	2.7
2. Mining Quarrying	39.3	49.8	48.9	57.4	52.9	58.2	61.2	63.1	70.6	70.0	73.6
3. Manufacturing	55.3	45.7	45.3	36.1	41.9	38.5	36.1	33.9	27.0	28.4	23.7
31. Food, Bev., Tobac.	1.5	3.6	3.5	2.6	4.7	5.6	1.5	2.3	2.3	1.2	1.4
32. Textiles	.3	.1	.2	.3	.6	.4	.6	.7	.3	.1	.1
33. Wood, Wood Prod.	1.4	1.8	1.6	1.7	2.7	3.1	2.1	1.7	.9	.8	.9
34. Paper and Prod.	0	~	0	0	0	0	0	0	0	0	0
35. Chemicals	2.3	2.1	3.2	.3	1.0	2.3	1.2	.7	.6	0	0
36. Non-Metal Minrl	0	.1	0	0	0	0	0	0	0	0	0
37. Basic Metal Ind.	49.5	37.9	36.5	30.4	29.7	25.3	29.0	27.3	22.6	26.2	21.1
38. Metal Manufact.	.3	.1	.1	.6	.9	1.6	1.6	1.1	.3	.2	.2
39. Oth. Manf. Ind.	0	.1	.2	.1	2.3	0	.1	.1	0	0	0

SOURCE: UN-YITS, 1976; 1977; 1978; 1983; 1985; 1986; 1987.

Table 2502
BRAZIL PERCENTAGE VALUE OF TRADE, 1970–87

Imports by Broad Economic Category

Category	1970	1975	1978	1980	1982	1983	1984	1985	1986	1987
Total Imports	100.0	100.0	100.0	100.0	100.0	100.0	100.0	100.0	100.0	100.0
1. Food and Beverages	10.4	5.9	8.7	8.2	8.3	8.0	8.8	8.5	13.1	7.4
Primary	8.3	4.7	7.4	6.7	7.5	6.5	7.4	6.7	8.3	5.5
For Industry	5.2	3.2	4.8	5.1	6.2	5.5	6.2	5.5	3.1	2.9
For Hshold Consm	3.1	1.5	2.6	1.6	1.3	1.0	1.2	1.2	5.1	2.7
Processed	2.1	1.1	1.3	1.5	.8	1.6	1.3	1.9	4.8	1.8
For Industry	.8	.6	.7	.5	.5	.6	1.0	.9	1.0	.6
For Hshold Consm	1.3	.5	.6	1.0	.3	1.0	.3	1.0	3.8	1.2
2. Ind. Supplies Nes.	36.5	33.9	29.4	27.0	18.6	17.2	20.8	22.6	32.1	30.5
Primary	2.0	2.0	3.5	3.4	1.6	2.2	3.0	3.7	6.4	5.0
Processed	34.5	31.9	25.9	23.6	17.0	15.0	17.8	18.9	25.7	25.6
3. Fuels	12.2	25.3	32.5	43.0	53.4	55.8	52.7	47.1	26.5	32.3
Primary	10.6	24.3	31.4	40.7	51.4	54.3	52.1	45.5	25.4	30.7
Processed	1.6	.9	1.1	2.2	2.1	1.5	.6	1.5	1.1	1.6
Motor Spirit	.1	.1	.1	.2	.3	.3	.3	.3	.2	0
Other	1.5	.8	.9	2.0	1.8	1.2	.3	1.3	1.0	1.6
4. Machinery	27.5	27.8	23.3	15.7	14.6	12.0	11.5	14.3	18.4	18.8
Machines Capt. Eqp	23.6	24.0	18.9	11.9	10.7	8.4	7.8	9.6	12.0	12.8
Parts Accessories	3.9	3.8	4.5	3.7	3.9	3.6	3.7	4.7	6.4	6.0
5. Transport	9.0	4.8	3.6	4.5	3.3	5.0	4.7	5.3	7.0	8.1
Passenger Cars	.1	.1	0	0	~	~	~	0	0	0
Other	5.5	1.9	.9	2.0	1.0	2.5	1.8	1.6	1.9	3.1
Industrial	5.4	1.8	.9	1.9	1.0	2.5	1.8	1.6	1.9	3.1
Non-Industrial	#	0	0	0	0	0	0	0	0	0
Parts Accessories	3.5	2.8	2.7	2.6	2.3	2.4	2.8	3.7	5.0	5.0
6. Consumer Goods	3.7	2.3	2.3	1.6	1.7	1.8	1.4	2.0	2.9	2.8
Durable	1.6	1.1	1.0	.6	.5	.4	.4	.8	1.1	.8
Semi-Durable	.9	.5	.4	.3	.3	.4	.3	.4	.6	.6
Non-Durable	1.2	.7	.9	.7	.8	.9	.7	.9	1.2	1.4
7. Other	.6	.1	.2	.1	.1	.2	.2	.1	.1	.2

Exports by Industrial Origin

Origin	1970	1975	1978	1979	1980	1981	1982	1983	1984	1985
Total Exports (1 + 2 + 3)	100.0	100.0	100.0	100.0	100.0	100.0	100.0	100.0	100.0	100.0
1. Agriculture	53.6	28.4	25.8	22.1	19.9	13.5	16.1	17.6	16.1	18.0
2. Mining Quarrying	10.2	13.5	9.5	9.7	9.2	10.0	11.6	8.2	7.2	7.5
3. Manufacturing	36.2	58.1	64.7	68.2	70.9	76.6	72.3	74.1	76.7	74.5
31. Food, Bev., Tobac.	18.1	27.6	27.3	25.2	26.9	28.5	24.1	24.0	23.2	19.5
32. Textiles	2.6	7.6	8.1	8.9	7.1	7.0	6.8	8.0	9.0	8.1
33. Wood, Wood Prod.	3.9	1.6	1.5	1.8	1.9	1.7	1.4	1.4	1.2	1.2
34. Paper and Prod.	.3	.9	1.2	2.1	2.7	2.6	2.4	2.4	2.8	2.2
35. Chemicals	2.1	3.7	3.9	5.1	6.4	9.4	11.3	11.9	14.7	14.6
36. Non-Metal Minrl	.4	.5	.6	.7	.8	.8	.6	.5	.6	.6
37. Basic Metal Ind.	3.8	2.3	4.0	5.6	4.9	4.9	5.5	9.1	10.0	10.5
38. Metal Manufact.	4.0	11.5	16.8	17.6	18.6	19.9	18.8	15.3	14.0	16.7
39. Oth. Manf. Ind.	1.0	2.4	1.2	1.2	1.6	1.8	1.4	1.4	1.2	1.1

SOURCE: UN-YITS, 1977; 1978; 1979; 1980; 1983; 1985; 1986; 1987.

Table 2503

CHILE PERCENTAGE VALUE OF TRADE, 1970–86

Imports by Broad Economic Category

Category	1970	1975	1980	1981	1982	1983	1984	1985	1986
Total Imports	100.0	100.0	100.0	100.0	100.0	100.0	100.0	100.0	100.0
1. Food and Beverages	12.5	16.3	13.1	10.4	13.2	16.6	12.7	7.7	4.3
Primary	8.4	9.8	5.5	5.1	7.1	9.4	7.0	4.5	2.4
For Industry	5.2	8.2	4.0	3.7	5.5	7.9	5.4	3.0	1.3
For Hshold Consm	3.2	1.6	1.5	1.4	1.6	1.5	1.6	1.5	1.1
Processed	4.0	6.5	7.5	5.3	6.2	7.3	5.7	3.2	1.9
For Industry	1.9	5.7	2.9	1.1	1.6	2.8	2.6	2.3	0.9
For Hshold Consm	2.2	.8	4.6	4.2	4.6	4.5	3.1	0.9	1.1
2. Ind. Supplies Nes.	31.1	25.7	22.5	22.6	23.6	29.6	31.1	31.0	34.9
Primary	5.6	4.4	3.2	2.8	3.9	4.1	3.5	3.1	3.2
Processed	25.5	21.3	19.3	19.8	19.7	25.5	27.6	27.9	31.7
3. Fuels	6.0	19.6	18.3	19.4	18.4	21.2	18.3	19.0	14.6
Primary	4.1	19.1	17.0	12.0	9.6	16.0	13.9	17.0	11.6
Processed	1.9	.6	1.3	2.4	8.7	5.2	4.4	2.0	3.0
Motor Spirit	.3	0	.2	1.0	3.2	1.1	.7	.1	.6
Other	1.7	.6	1.0	1.4	5.5	4.1	3.6	1.9	2.4
4. Machinery	27.7	22.6	15.7	16.1	20.4	10.2	20.3	23.5	26.2
Machines Capt. Eqp	23.7	18.7	13.6	14.0	17.7	13.3	17.2	19.7	22.1
Parts Accessories	4.0	3.9	2.1	2.1	2.7	2.9	3.1	3.8	4.2
5. Transport	16.6	11.5	14.9	18.2	10.3	7.1	7.1	8.7	9.9
Passenger Cars	2.5	.8	5.0	7.6	3.3	1.2	.8	1.5	1.1
Other	9.0	7.3	7.3	7.8	4.1	2.7	2.9	3.4	4.7
Industrial	8.9	7.2	7.1	7.5	4.0	2.6	2.8	3.3	4.7
Non-Industrial	#	.1	.2	.2	.1	.1	.1	.0	.0
Parts Accessories	5.1	3.5	2.6	2.8	2.9	3.3	3.4	3.8	4.1
6. Consumer Goods	5.8	3.7	11.9	15.6	14.0	9.2	8.5	7.5	8.5
Durable	1.5	.9	5.3	6.1	3.2	1.9	2.1	1.7	2.5
Semi-Durable	1.7	1.0	4.7	7.1	7.6	4.4	4.0	3.4	3.7
Non-Durable	2.7	1.7	2.0	2.4	3.2	2.9	2.4	2.4	2.3
7. Other	.3	.5	3.6	2.7	.0	.0	2.0	2.6	1.6

Exports by Industrial Origin

Origin	1970	1975	1980	1981	1982	1983	1984	1985	1986
Total Exports (1 + 2 + 3)	100.0	100.0	100.0	100.0	100.0	100.0	100.0	100.0	100.0
1. Agriculture	3.2	5.7	8.7	10.6	12.2	11.3	14.5	16.5	18.7
2. Mining Quarrying	10.0	9.9	11.1	17.0	9.8	8.0	14.7	16.1	14.1
3. Manufacturing	86.8	84.5	80.2	72.4	78.0	80.7	70.9	67.4	67.2
31. Food, Bev., Tobac.	2.2	6.1	8.9	9.3	10.3	11.2	11.6	11.5	12.6
32. Textiles	#	.4	.2	.2	.1	0	.1	.1	.3
33. Wood, Wood Prod.	.7	1.5	3.0	2.5	2.0	2.0	2.3	1.8	2.2
34. Paper and Prod.	2.7	6.0	5.6	6.3	6.1	5.8	7.1	5.9	6.6
35. Chemicals	1.3	4.3	5.4	4.3	10.8	9.7	3.6	3.2	2.6
36. Non-Metal Minrl	#	.3	.2	.1	.1	0	0	0	.1
37. Basic Metal Ind.	78.3	64.2	53.2	46.1	38.6	41.4	36.3	36.8	33.5
38. Metal Manufact.	1.3	1.6	2.8	3.3	9.8	10.4	9.6	7.4	8.3
39. Oth. Manf. Ind.	.1	0	.8	.3	.2	.0	.3	.7	.9

SOURCE: UN-YITS, 1976; 1980; 1983; 1984; 1985; 1986; 1987.

Table 2504

COLOMBIA PERCENTAGE VALUE OF TRADE, 1970–86

Imports by Broad Economic Category

Category	1970	1975	1976	1980	1982	1983	1984	1985	1986
Total Imports	100.0	100.0	100.0	100.0	100.0	100.0	100.0	100.0	100.0
1. Food and Beverages	5.6	8.2	10.8	9.2	8.5	8.9	8.1	7.7	7.1
Primary	3.6	5.2	5.7	5.1	4.4	5.7	5.0	5.1	5.4
For Industry	3.2	4.3	4.6	3.9	3.2	4.4	4.2	4.4	3.4
For Hshold Consm	.5	.9	1.1	1.1	1.2	1.4	.7	.7	.9
Processed	1.9	3.1	5.2	4.2	4.1	3.1	3.1	2.6	2.7
For Industry	.9	1.4	3.0	1.9	2.4	1.7	1.8	1.4	1.4
For Hshold Consm	1.0	1.6	2.2	2.3	1.8	1.4	1.3	1.1	1.4
2. Ind. Supplies Nes.	39.8	45.2	39.2	35.1	34.4	32.7	39.5	44.9	44.1
Primary	3.3	3.1	3.2	2.9	2.5	2.2	2.4	2.9	3.2
Processed	36.5	42.1	36.0	32.2	31.9	30.5	37.1	42.0	40.9
3. Fuels	.4	1.0	2.3	12.1	12.1	12.9	10.4	11.7	3.7
Primary	#	0	1.9	3.2	4.3	7.7	6.3	4.4	0
Processed	.4	1.0	.4	8.9	7.8	5.2	4.1	7.3	3.7
Motor Spirit	#	.7	.1	6.6	4.5	4.3	3.7	6.8	3.3
Other	.4	.2	.3	2.4	3.3	.9	.3	.5	.4
4. Machinery	27.6	23.1	23.6	23.4	24.5	26.2	24.6	19.8	25.4
Machines Capt. Eqp	23.8	19.1	19.9	20.6	21.3	23.0	21.4	16.2	21.1
Parts Accessories	3.8	3.9	3.7	2.8	3.2	3.1	3.2	3.6	4.3
5. Transport	20.0	17.1	16.6	15.0	15.6	14.0	11.7	10.4	13.2
Passenger Cars	3.5	1.4	1.6	3.9	5.1	4.0	3.2	3.2	3.1
Other	8.0	9.5	8.4	5.1	5.1	5.1	3.3	2.3	3.4
Industrial	7.9	9.5	8.3	4.4	4.8	4.9	3.1	2.2	3.3
Non-Industrial	#	.1	.2	.7	.3	.2	.2	.1	.1
Parts Accessories	8.5	6.2	6.6	5.9	5.4	4.9	5.2	4.8	6.6
6. Consumer Goods	6.1	4.8	4.3	4.4	4.2	4.2	3.7	3.2	4.0
Durable	1.2	.8	.9	1.0	.9	.8	.7	.5	.9
Semi-Durable	.8	1.3	1.2	1.1	1.1	1.2	1.2	.9	1.2
Non-Durable	4.1	2.7	2.2	2.3	2.1	2.2	1.8	1.8	1.9
7. Other	.6	.6	3.2	.8	.7	1.2	2.0	2.4	2.5

Exports by Industrial Origin

Origin	1970	1975	1976	1980	1982	1983	1984	1985	1986
Total Exports (1 + 2 + 3)	100.0	100.0	100.0	100.0	100.0	100.0	100.0	100.0	100.0
1. Agriculture	76.6	60.1	67.6	69.1	62.7	60.3	63.5	60.9	67.7
2. Mining Quarrying	8.6	1.1	.9	2.0	1.9	1.7	1.9	4.3	8.7
3. Manufacturing	14.8	38.8	31.6	28.9	35.4	37.9	34.7	34.8	23.6
31. Food, Bev., Tobac.	3.8	11.2	5.6	7.4	5.2	5.5	3.7	3.8	3.4
32. Textiles	2.8	8.1	9.1	7.4	8.9	5.3	4.2	5.0	4.8
33. Wood, Wood Prod.	.6	.4	.7	.3	.4	.3	.2	.3	.2
34. Paper and Prod.	.5	1.1	2.0	1.8	2.4	1.8	2.0	2.1	1.8
35. Chemicals	3.9	11.7	7.5	5.3	10.4	18.0	17.2	16.7	8.2
36. Non-Metal Minrl	1.2	1.8	2.3	1.8	2.0	1.1	1.0	1.0	.8
37. Basic Metal Ind.	.7	.4	.4	.1	.1	1.6	2.2	2.0	1.3
38. Metal Manufact.	1.3	3.6	3.6	3.7	5.1	2.5	1.7	2.1	2.0
39. Oth. Manf. Ind.	.1	.6	.4	1.1	.8	1.8	2.4	1.8	1.1

SOURCE: UN-YITS, 1976; 1981; 1983; 1985; 1986; 1987.

Table 2505

COSTA RICA PERCENTAGE VALUE OF TRADE, 1970–84

Imports by Broad Economic Category

Category	1970	1975	1978	1979	1980	1981	1982	1983	1984
Total Imports	100.0	100.0	100.0	100.0	100.0	100.0	100.0	100.0	100.0
1. Food and Beverages	8.8	8.5	6.2	6.2	7.1	6.7	6.6	~	7.3
Primary	4.8	4.9	2.4	2.5	3.3	3.8	3.7	~	4.1
For Industry	2.6	4.0	1.8	1.8	2.0	2.7	2.2	~	2.6
For Hshold Consm	2.3	.9	.6	.8	1.3	1.1	1.4	~	1.5
Processed	4.0	3.6	3.8	3.7	3.8	2.8	2.9	~	3.2
For Industry	1.3	1.2	.9	.8	1.0	.9	1.1	~	.8
For Hshold Consm	2.7	2.4	2.9	2.9	2.8	2.0	1.8	~	2.4
2. Ind. Supplies Nes.	44.1	43.0	37.0	35.3	38.4	39.6	41.3	~	45.3
Primary	2.6	1.7	1.3	1.5	2.3	1.8	2.9	~	2.6
Processed	41.5	41.3	35.7	33.8	36.1	37.8	38.4	~	42.7
3. Fuels	3.6	10.3	9.3	12.7	14.7	15.9	19.8	~	15.0
Primary	1.8	3.8	3.9	4.5	8.0	10.4	11.2	~	7.7
Processed	1.8	6.5	5.4	8.2	6.7	5.5	8.6	~	7.3
Motor Spirit	.4	1.5	1.2	1.5	1.7	1.1	1.7	~	1.5
Other	.4	5.0	4.2	6.6	4.9	4.4	6.9	~	5.9
4. Machinery	16.8	16.8	17.3	19.2	15.2	16.1	10.7	~	14.3
Machines Capt. Eqp	15.9	15.7	16.3	18.2	14.2	15.2	9.7	~	12.9
Parts Accessories	.9	1.1	1.0	1.0	1.0	.9	1.0	~	1.3
5. Transport	10.9	10.4	12.5	11.2	8.7	6.5	4.4	~	6.5
Passenger Cars	2.2	1.9	2.5	2.4	2.1	1.0	.2	~	.7
Other	3.8	4.0	4.9	4.3	2.1	1.7	1.8	~	1.7
Industrial	3.0	3.8	4.6	4.0	1.7	1.5	1.7	~	1.5
Non-Industrial	.3	.2	.3	.3	.4	.2	.1	~	.2
Parts Accessories	5.4	4.5	5.0	4.5	4.4	3.8	2.4	~	4.1
6. Consumer Goods	15.6	10.4	12.7	11.8	11.7	8.9	7.9	--	11.4
Durable	2.6	1.1	2.4	2.1	1.8	1.4	.8	~	1.4
Semi-Durable	7.0	4.3	5.1	4.6	4.7	3.1	2.5	~	4.0
Non-Durable	6.0	5.0	5.2	5.2	5.2	4.5	4.6	~	6.0
7. Other	.2	.7	5.0	3.6	4.2	6.2	9.3	~	.2

Exports by Industrial Origin

Origin	1970	1975	1978	1979	1980	1981	1982	1983	1984
Total Exports (1 + 2 + 3)	100.0	100.0	100.0	100.0	100.0	100.0	100.0	100.0	100.0
1. Agriculture	63.4	53.3	58.1	58.6	48.1	49.1	58.7	~	59.8
2. Mining Quarrying	0	0	0	0	.1	0	0	~	0
3. Manufacturing	36.6	46.7	41.9	41.4	51.8	50.8	41.3	~	40.2
31. Food, Bev., Tobac.	16.4	20.2	13.1	16.7	16.8	17.6	11.8	~	14.0
32. Textiles	4.4	4.6	3.8	4.5	6.8	5.4	4.6	~	4.5
33. Wood, Wood Prod.	.6	.6	.7	.6	.9	1.0	1.0	~	.8
34. Paper and Prod.	1.1	1.3	.7	1.0	1.9	1.5	1.7	~	1.3
35. Chemicals	6.9	11.2	8.2	8.3	10.2	12.0	10.4	~	9.8
36. Non-Metal Minrl	.1	.1	.3	.9	.9	2.3	1.3	~	1.3
37. Basic Metal Ind.	.7	.9	1.2	1.2	1.7	1.3	.9	~	1.3
38. Metal Manufact.	4.7	5.1	5.2	5.4	6.3	6.2	5.9	~	4.9
39. Oth. Manf. Ind.	1.6	2.8	8.7	2.7	6.4	3.4	3.8	~	2.0

SOURCE: UN-YITS, 1976; 1981; 1983; 1984; 1985; 1986; 1987.

Table 2506

CUBA TOTAL TRADE VALUE, 1950–85, AND PERCENTAGES ACCORDING TO ORIGIN, 1970–87

PART I. HISTORICAL SERIES, 1950–80, SPECIAL TRADE,
IMPORTS CIF, EXPORTS FOB

(M Pesos)

Year	Imports	Exports
1950	515.4	642.0
1951	640.2	766.1
1952	618.2	675.3
1953	489.7	640.3
1954	487.9	539.0
1955	575.1	594.2
1956	649.0	666.2
1957	772.8	807.7
1958	777.0	733.5
1959	673.5	637.4
1960	579.9	618.2
1961	638.7	624.7
1962	759.3	520.7
1963	867.3	543.8
1964	1,018.8	713.8
1965	866.2	690.6
1966	925.5	597.8
1967	999.1	705.0
1968	1,102.3	651.4
1969	1,221.6	666.7
1970	1,311.0	1,049.5
1971	1,386.6	861.2
1972	1,189.8	770.9
1973	1,467.0	1,153.0
1974	2,225.9	2,236.5
1975	3,113.0	2,952.2
1976	3,179.7	2,692.3
1977	3,461.6	2,918.4
1978	3,573.8	3,440.1
1979	3,687.0	3,500.4
1980	4,627.0	3,967.0
1981	5,114.0	4,223.8
1982	5,530.6	4,933.2
1983	6,222.1	5,534.9
1984	7,227.5	5,476.5
1985	8,035.0	5,991.5
1986	7,569.0	5,325.0

PART II. EXPORTS BY INDUSTRIAL ORIGIN

(Percentage of Total Value)[1]

Origin	1970	1975	1976	1977	1978	1979	1980	1981	1982	1983	1985	1986
Total Exports (1 + 2 + 3)	100.0	100.0	100.0	100.0	100.0	100.0	100.0	100.0	100.0	100.0	100.0	100.0
1. Agriculture	5.2	3.5	4.3	4.4	4.4	5.4	4.3	4.7	5.0	4.8	2.8	3.1
2. Mining Quarrying	16.4	4.6	5.9	6.3	4.5	4.4	4.6	7.9	5.9	5.4	5.1	~
3. Manufacturing	78.4	91.9	89.8	89.3	91.1	90.2	91.1	87.4	89.1	89.8	92.1	96.9
31. Food, Bev., Tobac.	78.4	91.9	89.2	86.1	88.9	87.7	85.6	81.9	81.6	78.6	90.9	95.0
32. Textiles	~	0	0	~	~	~	~	~	~	~	.1	.1
33. Wood, Wood Prod.	~	~	~	~	~	~	~	~	~	~	~	~
34. Paper and Prod.	~	~	~	~	~	~	~	~	~	~	~	~
35. Chemicals	~	4.6	5.9	~	0	0	0	4.4	7.1	10.9	.3	.4
36. Non-Metal Minrl	~	~	~	~	~	~	~	.3	.2	~	~	~
37. Basic Metal Ind.	~	~	~	~	~	~	~	.1	.4	.4	.4	.6
38. Metal Manufact.	~	~	~	~	~	~	~	~	~	~	.4	.7
39. Oth. Manf. Ind.	~	~	.6	3.1	2.1	2.5	5.4	1.1	1.2	~	~	~

1. No percentages on imports available in source.

SOURCE: UN-YITS, 1976; 1981; 1983; 1984; 1985; 1986; 1987.

Table 2506 (Continued)

CUBA TOTAL TRADE VALUE, 1950–85, AND PERCENTAGES ACCORDING TO ORIGIN, 1970–87

PART III. CUBA PETROLEUM AND SUGAR REEXPORTS: PRICES, QUANTITIES, AND ESTIMATED PROFITS, 1980–87

	1980	1981	1982	1983	1984	1985	1986	1987
Sugar								
Imports								
Price (US$ per lb)	.287	.170	.084	.085	.052	.041	.060	.066
Cu$/MET[1]	454	302	159	163	103	83	110	146
Total Value (Cu$/M)	~	~	14.1	33.6	101.0	106.4	89.6	138.0
Quantity (T MET)	~	~	88.8	206.0	975.0	1,419.4	812.8	945.0
Reexports (to USSR)								
Price (Cu$/MET)	759	606	658	873	868	986	850	850
Quantity (T MET)	~	~	88.8	206	975.0	1,419.4	812.8	945.0
Profit per MET (Cu$)	~	~	499	710	765	903	740	704
Total Profit (Cu$/M)	~	~	44.3	146.3	745.9	1,281.4	601.5	665.2
Petroleum								
Imports (from USSR)								
Price (Cu$/MET)	83.20	102.70	125.80	147.0	174.2	175	175	175
Total Value (Cu$/M)	878.6	1,139.2	1,468.0	1,824.8	2,169.7	~	~	~
Quantity (T MET)	10,564	11,089	11,668	12,410	12,458	~	~	~
Reexports								
Price (US$ per Barrel)	28.50	32.50	33.48	29.30	27.53	26.50	13.54	17.43
Cu$/MET)	150.00	191.50	210.80	186.60	181.60	180.00	82.40	127.80
Quantity (T MET)	~	790.5	1,243.3	2,666.9	2,666.9	2,926.9	3,016.6	3,000.0
Total Value (Cu$/M)	~	151.4	262.1	497.7	484.4	526.9	248.5	383.4
Profit per Metric Ton (Cu$)	~	88.8	85.0	39.6	7.4	5.0	−92.6	−47.2
Total Profit (Cu$/M)	~	70.2	105.7	105.6	19.7	14.6	−279.3	−141.6
Exchange Rate Used[2]								
Cu$/US$	.717	.804	.859	.869	.90	.92	.83	1.00

1. Conversion factors used: 1 metric ton = 2,204.6 lbs; 1 metric ton of oil = 7.33 barrels.
2. The exchange rate used for currency conversions is the official rate "Contra Certificado de Divisas Indirecto," the rate used for balance of payments and debt accounting purposes. The series indicates devaluation against the U.S. dollar (which was appreciating) from 1980 to 1985, followed by a peso appreciation in 1986. In 1987 there was a major peso devaluation against the U.S. dollar despite the fact that the dollar itself was devalued that year. The fact that, at these official exchange rates, large losses on petroleum reexports were occurring but that trade was being continued only indicates that the exchange rate is seriously overvalued. With a more realistic exchange rate (e.g., US$1 - CU$2) the import price of sugar would be increased and the reexport profits reduced, while the reexport price of petroleum and hence reexport profits would be increased in terms of Cuban pesos.

SOURCE: A.R.M. Ritter, "Cuba's Convertible Currency Debt Problem," CEPAL Review, No. 36, Dec. 1988, p. 138.

Table 2507

DOMINICAN REPUBLIC PERCENTAGE VALUE OF TRADE, 1970–85

Category	Imports by Broad Economic Category								
	1970	1978	1979	1980	1981	1982	1983	1984	1985
Total Imports	100.0	100.0	100.0	100.0	100.0	100.0	100.0	100.0	100.0
1. Food and Beverages	12.7	13.1	13.7	13.5	14.2	12.5	11.7	9.4	9.4
Primary	3.9	6.1	4.8	6.7	7.5	4.5	4.8	2.9	2.6
For Industry	1.4	4.3	2.2	4.0	5.3	2.5	3.1	2.3	1.3
For Hshold Consm	2.5	1.8	2.5	2.7	2.2	2.1	1.7	.6	1.3
Processed	8.8	7.0	8.9	6.8	6.7	7.9	6.9	6.5	6.8
For Industry	.9	3.4	5.2	3.3	3.3	5.6	3.8	3.9	4.1
For Hshold Consm	7.9	3.6	3.7	3.5	3.4	2.4	3.0	2.6	2.7
2. Ind. Supplies Nes.	28.7	32.4	32.2	31.4	26.3	28.4	28.1	28.4	26.2
Primary	2.0	3.8	3.7	3.8	3.5	2.9	3.4	4.0	2.9
Processed	26.7	28.6	28.5	27.6	22.7	25.5	24.6	24.3	23.3
3. Fuels	6.9	22.0	25.9	24.9	32.5	33.7	35.9	40.1	34.8
Primary	2.4	20.8	23.7	23.7	27.5	26.3	26.7	30.4	28.2
Processed	4.5	1.2	2.2	1.2	5.0	7.5	9.1	9.7	6.6
Motor Spirit	2.5	.1	.5	.2	.2	.1	.4	.2	.5
Other	1.9	1.1	1.7	1.0	4.8	7.3	8.7	9.5	6.1
4. Machinery	22.7	14.6	12.9	14.9	13.7	13.1	12.3	10.1	15.3
Machines Capt. Eqp	~	13.2	11.3	13.4	12.5	11.9	10.6	8.5	13.2
Parts Accessories	~	1.3	1.6	1.5	1.2	1.2	1.7	1.6	2.1
5. Transport	13.3	9.5	8.1	8.6	7.6	6.2	5.5	6.9	8.7
Passenger Cars	~	1.9	1.6	1.4	.6	1.0	.4	1.7	2.2
Other	~	3.6	3.1	3.8	3.6	2.0	1.7	2.3	3.2
Industrial	~	3.3	2.7	2.8	2.7	1.3	1.0	1.9	2.6
Non-Industrial	~	.2	.4	1.0	.9	.7	.7	.4	.6
Parts Accessories	~	4.1	3.4	3.4	3.4	3.2	3.5	2.9	3.3
6. Consumer Goods	12.5	8.2	7.0	6.5	5.7	6.1	6.6	5.1	5.5
Durable	.4	1.4	1.2	1.2	.9	.9	1.0	.8	.9
Semi-Durable	4.3	2.3	1.9	1.7	1.4	1.3	1.5	1.2	1.3
Non-Durable	7.9	4.6	3.9	3.6	3.4	3.9	4.1	3.1	3.4
7. Other	3.0	.1	.1	.1	0	0	0	0	0

Origin	Exports by Industrial Origin								
	1970	1978	1979	1980	1981	1982	1983	1984	1985
Total Exports (1 + 2 + 3)	100.0	100.0	100.0	100.0	100.0	100.0	100.0	100.0	100.0
1. Agriculture	32.0	41.3	40.2	26.2	21.7	31.9	28.1	~	~
2. Mining Quarrying	7.3	4.2	3.1	3.0	1.8	1.2	.3	~	~
3. Manufacturing	60.7	54.5	56.7	70.8	76.4	66.9	71.7	~	~
31. Food, Bev., Tobac.	55.6	33.3	30.8	47.1	57.6	50.5	47.6	~	~
32. Textiles	.1	1.4	1.3	1.1	.7	1.2	1.1	~	~
33. Wood, Wood Prod.	0	0	0	0	0	0	0	~	~
34. Paper and Prod.	.1	.1	.1	.1	.1	.1	.1	~	~
35. Chemicals	3.2	5.9	5.4	6.0	4.5	5.7	4.2	~	~
36. Non-Metal Minrl	.1	.1	.3	.7	1.0	1.2	.5	~	~
37. Basic Metal Ind.	.1	12.3	16.5	14.5	11.2	3.9	13.1	~	~
38. Metal Manufact.	.2	1.3	2.4	1.2	1.3	4.3	5.1	~	~
39. Oth. Manf. Ind.	1.4	0	0	.1	0	0	0	~	~

SOURCE: UN-YITS, 1976; 1981; 1983; 1985; 1986; 1987.

Table 2508

ECUADOR PERCENTAGE VALUE OF TRADE, 1972–84

Imports by Broad Economic Category

Category	1972	1975	1976	1977	1978	1980	1981	1982	1983	1984
Total Imports	100.0	100.0	100.0	100.0	100.0	100.0	100.0	100.0	100.0	100.0
1. Food and Beverages	7.8	7.1	6.8	5.4	6.3	7.6	5.6	4.3	9.3	10.1
Primary	3.5	4.2	3.2	2.3	2.5	3.8	3.1	1.6	4.4	5.3
For Industry	3.4	4.0	2.9	2.1	2.1	3.5	2.9	1.4	4.2	5.2
For Hshold Consm	.2	.2	.3	.2	.4	.3	.2	.2	.2	.1
Processed	4.3	2.9	3.6	3.1	3.8	3.8	2.5	2.6	5.0	4.8
For Industry	2.6	1.0	1.7	1.2	1.2	1.1	.7	1.5	2.8	3.4
For Hshold Consm	1.7	1.9	1.9	1.9	2.6	2.6	1.8	1.1	2.2	1.5
2. Ind. Supplies Nes.	33.5	34.7	36.0	35.5	31.9	34.6	27.9	40.2	44.1	46.4
Primary	2.0	1.5	2.0	2.3	1.9	1.2	1.1	1.5	1.8	3.3
Processed	31.5	33.2	34.0	33.2	30.0	33.4	26.7	38.7	42.3	43.1
3. Fuels	6.3	1.9	1.0	.6	.7	1.0	12.9	1.3	1.4	1.3
Primary	1.7	.2	.1	0	0	0	1.3	0	0	0
Processed	4.6	1.6	.9	.6	.7	1.0	11.6	1.3	1.4	1.3
Motor Spirit	.2	0	~	0	0	0	6.4	0	0	0
Other	4.4	1.6	.9	.6	.7	1.0	5.2	1.3	1.4	1.3
4. Machinery	25.3	29.9	30.4	28.9	30.4	28.3	29.4	29.4	26.3	25.6
Machines Capt. Eqp	22.8	27.9	27.9	26.7	28.0	25.9	27.1	26.2	22.7	22.7
Parts Accessories	2.5	2.0	2.4	2.2	2.3	2.4	2.3	3.3	3.6	2.9
5. Transport	15.2	17.1	15.6	20.8	20.0	21.2	17.6	15.8	11.0	11.3
Passenger Cars	1.9	.6	.4	.5	2.9	2.6	1.7	2.2	2.2	1.5
Other	7.3	11.5	10.1	14.6	11.2	11.9	8.5	6.2	3.0	3.4
Industrial	7.3	11.3	9.9	14.5	11.1	11.8	8.5	6.1	2.8	3.4
Non-Industrial	0	?	1	1	.1	0	.1	.1	.1	0
Parts Accessories	5.9	5.1	5.2	5.7	5.9	6.8	7.4	7.3	5.9	6.3
6. Consumer Goods	11.5	8.6	8.5	7.9	8.7	6.4	6.2	8.8	7.5	5.3
Durable	2.9	2.2	2.3	2.2	3.0	1.9	1.4	1.7	1.2	.6
Semi-Durable	1.5	1.8	1.8	1.8	1.8	1.9	1.4	2.2	1.7	1.0
Non-Durable	7.1	4.5	4.4	3.8	3.8	2.5	3.4	4.9	4.6	3.7
7. Other	.3	.7	1.7	1.0	2.1	.8	.3	.1	.4	.1

Exports by Industrial Origin

Origin	1972	1975	1976	1977	1978	1980	1981	1982	1983	1984
Total Exports (1 + 2 + 3)	100.0	100.0	100.0	100.0	100.0	100.0	100.0	100.0	100.0	100.0
1. Agriculture	70.8	29.1	29.6	30.4	33.0	18.8	22.2	25.4	21.4	23.5
2. Mining Quarrying	18.6	60.3	58.9	49.0	40.0	55.5	54.2	64.3	69.7	62.8
3. Manufacturing	10.7	10.6	11.5	20.6	26.9	25.7	23.5	10.4	8.8	13.6
31. Food, Bev., Tobac.	8.0	7.3	8.3	17.1	17.7	14.4	11.8	6.8	3.3	5.7
32. Textiles	.8	1.0	1.1	.6	.6	.6	.6	.4	.2	.2
33. Wood, Wood Prod.	.4	1.0	.9	.9	1.0	1.2	1.6	1.5	.5	.5
34. Paper and Prod.	.2	.1	.1	.1	.1	.1	.1	.1	0	0
35. Chemicals	.8	.4	.4	1.0	6.4	7.9	8.2	.3	4.5	7.1
36. Non-Metal Minrl	0	0	0	0	0	.1	.2	.1	0	0
37. Basic Metal Ind.	0	0	0	0	0	.1	.1	.1	0	0
38. Metal Manufact.	.4	.5	.5	.7	1.0	1.2	1.0	1.0	.2	.1
39. Oth. Manf. Ind.	.1	.2	.1	.1	.1	.1	.1	.1	0	0

SOURCE: UN-YITS, 1977; 1981; 1983; 1984; 1985; 1986; 1987.

Table 2509

EL SALVADOR PERCENTAGE VALUE OF TRADE, 1970–84

Imports by Broad Economic Category

Category	1970	1975	1976	1979	1980	1981	1982	1983	1984
Total Imports	100.0	100.0	100.0	100.0	100.0	100.0	100.0	100.0	100.0
1. Food and Beverages	11.4	9.9	9.6	10.1	15.3	13.7	14.8	~	9.0
Primary	4.9	4.8	4.4	4.2	7.9	6.3	8.3	~	4.6
For Industry	2.4	2.9	2.8	2.1	2.9	1.1	3.6	~	2.9
For Hshold Consm	2.5	1.9	1.6	2.1	5.0	5.1	4.7	~	1.6
Processed	6.5	5.1	5.2	5.9	7.3	7.5	6.5	~	4.4
For Industry	1.2	.6	1.1	.8	1.2	1.6	1.7	~	1.5
For Hshold Consm	5.3	4.5	4.1	5.1	6.1	5.8	4.8	~	2.9
2. Ind. Supplies Nes.	45.0	41.6	40.6	41.1	37.4	38.4	35.0	~	31.1
Primary	1.5	2.2	1.4	2.2	1.7	1.7	1.6	~	2.2
Processed	43.6	39.4	39.2	38.9	35.7	36.6	33.4	~	28.9
3. Fuels	2.2	8.3	7.2	9.3	17.6	20.7	24.4	~	37.7
Primary	1.4	7.7	6.7	8.7	17.0	20.0	23.5	~	36.9
Processed	.8	.6	.5	.6	.6	.7	.9	~	.8
Motor Spirit	.1	.1	.1	.1	.1	.1	.3	~	.3
Other	.6	.5	.5	.5	.5	.6	.6	~	.5
4. Machinery	14.1	19.1	20.1	14.7	9.3	8.2	8.6	~	6.3
Machines Capt. Eqp	13.2	18.2	19.2	13.5	8.5	7.4	7.9	~	5.6
Parts Accessories	.9	.9	.9	1.1	.8	.8	.8	~	.7
5. Transport	9.8	8.0	9.2	9.7	4.5	4.8	3.9	~	5.0
Passenger Cars	3.0	1.2	1.7	1.3	.6	.2	.2	~	.7
Other	3.0	3.9	4.6	5.1	1.6	2.2	1.0	~	1.8
Industrial	3.0	3.7	4.4	4.8	1.4	2.1	.9	~	1.7
Non-Industrial	.1	.1	.2	.3	.2	.1	.1	~	.2
Parts Accessories	3.8	2.9	2.9	3.3	2.4	2.4	2.6	~	2.5
6. Consumer Goods	17.3	13.1	13.1	14.9	15.8	14.2	13.2	~	10.9
Durable	2.4	1.7	1.8	2.3	1.3	1.0	.8	~	.9
Semi-Durable	5.3	4.6	4.7	5.0	5.9	4.7	4.1	~	3.5
Non-Durable	9.6	6.8	6.7	7.7	8.7	8.5	8.2	~	6.6
7. Other	.2	.1	.2	.2	.1	.1	.2	~	.1

Exports by Industrial Origin

Origin	1970	1975	1976	1979	1980	1981	1982	1983	1984
Total Exports (1 + 2 + 3)	100.0	100.0	100.0	100.0	100.0	100.0	100.0	100.0	100.0
1. Agriculture	62.8	50.5	64.5	66.8	53.5	49.4	46.1	~	64.8
2. Mining Quarrying	.2	.3	.3	.1	.4	.3	.5	~	.3
3. Manufacturing	37.0	49.2	35.2	33.1	46.1	50.3	53.3	~	35.0
31. Food, Bev., Tobac.	6.7	19.9	9.3	6.6	5.4	6.6	8.5	~	5.5
32. Textiles	13.8	10.9	10.3	10.4	16.1	16.4	17.5	~	9.2
33. Wood, Wod Prod.	0	0	0	.1	.1	.1	0	~	0
34. Paper and Prod.	1.9	2.9	2.8	3.0	4.8	5.7	6.8	~	4.6
35. Chemicals	7.1	8.4	7.1	6.2	10.1	11.8	10.9	~	9.7
36. Non-Metal Minrl	.2	.2	.2	.8	.9	1.0	1.2	~	.5
37. Basic Metal Ind.	2.0	1.6	1.3	2.0	2.5	2.3	1.7	~	1.9
38. Metal Manufact.	4.6	4.5	3.5	3.4	5.2	5.4	5.6	~	2.8
39. Oth. Manf. Ind.	.5	.8	.7	.6	.9	1.0	1.1	~	.7

SOURCE: UN-YITS, 1976; 1981; 1983; 1984; 1985; 1986; 1987.

Table 2510

GUATEMALA PERCENTAGE VALUE OF TRADE, 1970–84

Imports by Broad Economic Category

Category	1970	1975	1978	1979	1980	1981	1982	1983	1984
Total Imports	100.0	100.0	100.0	100.0	100.0	100.0	100.0	100.0	100.0
1. Food and Beverages	8.7	7.1	5.1	5.4	5.6	4.5	6.5	6.6	5.8
Primary	3.5	3.7	1.7	2.0	2.3	1.9	1.9	2.5	2.1
For Industry	2.9	2.6	1.2	1.6	1.8	1.4	1.5	2.2	1.9
For Hshold Consm	.6	1.0	.5	.4	.5	.5	.4	.3	.2
Processed	5.1	3.4	3.5	3.4	3.3	2.7	4.5	4.2	3.7
For Industry	1.0	.6	.9	.8	.8	.8	1.6	1.7	1.3
For Hshold Consm	4.2	2.8	2.6	2.6	2.5	1.9	3.0	2.5	2.3
2. Ind. Supplies Nes.	46.7	40.9	40.0	40.3	38.5	32.2	40.0	46.3	37.0
Primary	1.7	2.4	2.0	1.9	2.6	1.7	1.2	1.6	1.2
Processed	45.0	38.6	38.0	38.5	35.9	30.4	38.8	44.7	35.8
3. Fuels	1.4	13.7	12.4	10.2	23.8	37.4	18.8	16.4	32.5
Primary	.4	10.1	7.0	1.3	11.4	5.6	10.5	8.1	24.7
Processed	1.1	3.6	5.4	8.9	12.4	31.8	8.3	8.3	7.8
Motor Spirit	.2	1.9	1.8	3.2	5.1	2.3	2.9	2.9	2.8
Other	.9	1.7	3.5	5.7	7.4	29.5	5.3	5.4	5.0
4. Machinery	16.9	16.2	18.1	18.6	12.9	11.4	16.3	11.6	9.4
Machines Cap. Eqp	15.8	15.2	16.8	17.4	11.8	10.5	15.6	10.5	8.6
Parts Accessories	1.1	1.1	1.3	1.2	1.1	.8	.7	1.0	.8
5. Transport	9.9	10.9	11.8	12.4	9.0	5.5	5.7	6.2	5.9
Passenger Cars	2.3	1.6	2.6	3.2	2.1	1.2	1.7	2.3	2.4
Other	3.6	5.5	5.3	5.5	3.9	2.0	1.2	.9	.8
Industrial	3.5	5.4	5.3	5.4	3.8	1.9	1.2	.9	.7
Non-Industrial	.1	0	.1	0	0	.1	0	.1	0
Parts Accessories	4.0	3.9	3.9	3.7	3.1	2.3	2.8	3.0	2.7
6. Consumer Goods	16.2	11.0	12.3	12.7	10.0	8.8	12.7	12.8	9.6
Durable	2.6	2.0	2.9	2.8	2.2	1.7	2.1	2.0	1.6
Semi-Durable	6.8	4.6	5.0	4.8	3.9	3.8	4.9	4.2	3.0
Non-Durable	6.8	4.5	4.4	5.0	4.0	3.3	5.7	6.5	5.0
7. Other	.2	.1	.3	.3	.1	.2	1	0	0

Exports by Industrial Origin

Origin	1970	1975	1978	1979	1980	1981	1982	1983	1984
Total Exports (1 + 2 + 3)	100.0	100.0	100.0	100.0	100.0	100.0	100.0	100.0	100.0
1. Agriculture	55.4	47.6	66.4	65.8	57.6	51.3	59.6	51.3	61.4
2. Mining Quarrying	.3	.7	.3	.4	1.4	2.2	3.3	6.1	2.6
3. Manufacturing	44.3	51.7	33.3	33.8	41.0	46.5	37.1	42.5	36.0
31. Food, Bev., Tobac.	15.2	26.0	11.4	9.4	11.9	16.6	10.1	17.4	12.3
32. Textiles	10.6	7.7	5.6	6.7	7.0	7.0	5.9	5.3	5.9
33. Wood, Wood Prod.	.8	.6	.5	.3	.2	.3	.4	.2	.2
34. Paper and Prod.	1.7	1.6	1.2	1.4	1.5	2.0	1.4	1.3	1.0
35. Chemicals	8.7	8.7	8.4	8.9	10.6	13.6	13.3	13.0	11.8
36. Non-Metal Minrl	2.1	2.7	2.2	1.8	1.6	2.1	1.7	1.7	1.7
37. Basic Metal Ind.	1.3	.8	1.1	2.4	5.3	1.4	1.5	1.3	.8
38. Metal Manufact.	3.5	3.1	2.5	2.6	2.6	3.1	2.5	2.1	2.0
39. Oth. Manf. Ind.	.3	.5	.3	.3	.4	.4	.3	.3	.3

SOURCE: UN-YITS, 1976; 1981; 1983; 1984; 1985; 1986; 1987.

Table 2511

HAITI PERCENTAGE VALUE OF TRADE, 1970–79

Imports by Broad Economic Category

Category	1970	1972	1974	1975	1976	1977	1978	1979
Total Imports	100.0	100.0	100.0	100.0	100.0	100.0	100.0	100.0
1. Food and Beverages	16.5	22.2	19.7	25.1	27.0	23.7	21.9	19.9
Primary	3.0	7.0	6.3	13.1	11.1	9.3	7.8	5.7
For Industry	1.9	5.8	5.2	12.0	10.0	8.0	6.3	4.1
For Hshold Consm	1.2	1.2	1.1	1.1	1.2	1.3	1.5	1.6
Processed	13.4	15.2	13.4	11.9	15.9	14.4	14.1	14.1
For Industry	6.2	6.8	5.2	4.7	6.4	7.8	4.3	5.5
For Hshold Consm	7.2	8.4	8.2	7.3	9.4	6.6	9.8	8.6
2. Ind. Supplies Nes.	32.1	32.0	33.1	29.0	29.5	29.2	30.3	32.3
Primary	2.0	2.2	3.5	4.0	3.3	3.1	3.5	2.4
Processed	30.1	29.9	29.6	25.0	26.3	26.1	26.8	29.9
3. Fuels	5.5	6.0	11.2	9.1	8.2	11.0	11.0	12.9
Primary	~	.2	.3	.3	.2	.2	.2	.2
Processed	~	5.8	10.8	8.8	8.0	10.7	10.7	12.7
Motor Spirit	~	1.5	3.8	2.6	2.2	3.0	3.2	3.8
Other	~	4.3	7.1	6.2	5.8	7.7	7.6	8.9
4. Machinery	12.7	10.0	7.6	10.7	10.1	11.3	7.5	7.6
Machines Capt. Eqp	~	~	7.1	10.2	9.8	10.9	7.2	6.8
Parts Accessories	~	~	.5	.5	.3	.4	.3	.9
5. Transport	10.3	9.2	8.6	9.3	8.0	8.9	12.8	11.9
Passenger Cars	~	2.7	1.6	1.7	1.9	2.1	2.7	5.0
Other	~	.4	3.9	4.3	3.2	3.7	6.6	3.5
Industrial	~	.4	3.9	4.2	3.2	3.6	6.4	3.3
Non-Industrial	~	~	0	.1	.1	.1	.2	.1
Parts Accessories	~	6.1	3.1	3.4	2.8	3.2	3.4	3.4
6. Consumer Goods	20.2	17.0	15.9	12.9	13.6	15.4	16.0	14.8
Durable	2.1	2.0	4.2	3.1	2.7	2.6	2.9	2.5
Semi-Durable	9.7	8.1	5.4	4.6	6.2	8.2	7.9	6.7
Non-Durable	8.4	6.8	6.3	5.2	4.7	4.6	5.2	5.6
7. Other	2.7	3.7	3.9	3.9	3.6	.6	.5	.6

Export by Industrial Origin

Origin	1970	1972	1974	1975	1976	1977	1978	1979
Total Exports (1 + 2 + 3)	100.0	100.0	100.0	100.0	100.0	100.0	100.0	100.0
1. Agriculture	47.0	40.7	43.0	28.2	41.4	49.8	45.2	35.2
2. Mining Quarrying	16.9	16.6	9.6	12.9	15.6	12.1	10.8	12.1
3. Manufacturing	36.1	42.7	47.4	58.9	43.0	38.1	44.0	52.6
31. Food, Bev., Tobac.	10.4	13.7	10.0	19.0	5.3	2.5	4.9	1.5
32. Textiles	8.9	8.3	13.5	14.5	9.2	9.3	6.8	10.6
33. Wood, Wood Prod.	1.7	1.8	1.3	.9	.7	.5	~	~
34. Paper and Prod.	~	~	0	0	0	0	0	.8
35. Chemicals	9.2	9.6	9.2	6.1	7.2	4.7	6.4	5.0
36. Non-Metal Minrl	~	0	0	.1	2.1	2.2	1.8	.5
37. Basic Metal Ind.	~	~	0	~	~	~	~	~
38. Metal Manufact.	2.3	5.9	9.5	14.8	14.2	13.3	15.5	9.2
39. Oth. Manf. Ind.	3.5	3.4	3.8	3.5	4.2	5.6	8.5	25.0

SOURCE: UN-YITS, 1976; 1981; 1983; 1984; 1985; 1986; 1987.

Table 2512

HONDURAS PERCENTAGE VALUE OF TRADE, 1970–85

Imports by Broad Economic Category

Category	1970	1975	1976	1979	1980	1981	1982	1983	1984	1985
Total Imports	100.0	100.0	100.0	100.0	100.0	100.0	100.0	100.0	100.0	100.0
1. Food and Beverages	10.0	10.1	8.8	7.1	7.7	8.7	8.5	8.1	8.7	7.7
Primary	2.4	3.4	2.5	2.1	2.2	2.3	2.7	2.0	2.8	2.4
For Industry	1.7	3.1	2.1	1.7	1.7	1.7	2.3	1.7	2.3	2.1
For Hshold Consm	.7	.3	.4	.4	.6	.7	.4	.3	.5	.2
Processed	7.5	6.6	6.3	5.0	5.4	6.3	5.8	6.1	5.9	5.3
For Industry	1.6	1.4	1.8	.7	1.1	1.5	1.0	1.0	.9	.8
For Hshold Consm	5.9	5.2	4.5	4.3	4.3	4.9	4.8	5.2	5.0	4.5
2. Ind. Supplies Nes.	36.1	34.0	37.3	36.1	33.7	34.7	35.0	38.1	39.8	30.9
Primary	.8	3.1	1.7	1.2	2.4	1.5	1.1	1.6	1.9	.8
Processed	35.4	31.0	35.7	34.9	31.3	33.2	33.9	36.5	37.9	30.0
3. Fuels	6.3	16.7	10.2	12.6	15.6	15.5	21.4	22.0	12.0	25.5
Primary	4.9	15.0	8.8	9.7	11.8	7.3	2.5	12.4	6.3	15.0
Processed	1.4	1.7	1.4	2.9	3.8	8.2	18.9	9.6	5.7	10.5
Motor Spirit	.3	.2	.2	.7	.7	2.1	4.4	2.4	1.2	2.2
Other	1.1	1.5	1.2	2.2	3.0	6.2	14.5	7.2	4.5	8.3
4. Machinery	16.8	17.0	16.5	19.3	18.6	17.1	12.1	12.9	16.4	14.5
Machines Capt. Eqp	16.2	16.3	15.8	18.8	18.0	16.5	11.6	12.3	15.7	13.8
Parts Accessories	.6	.7	.7	.5	.6	.6	.5	.6	.7	.7
5. Transport	12.8	10.6	13.1	12.2	11.1	9.2	8.1	6.4	8.8	8.4
Passenger Cars	2.1	1.0	1.1	1.4	1.3	1.3	1.3	.5	.6	.8
Other	6.3	5.7	7.3	.8	5.9	4.3	3.3	1.8	2.8	2.9
Industrial	6.1	5.5	7.1	.8	5.8	4.1	3.1	1.8	2.7	2.8
Non-Industrial	.2	.1	.2	.1	.2	.2	.2	.1	.1	.1
Parts Accessories	4.4	3.9	4.7	9.9	3.9	3.7	3.5	4.1	5.3	4.7
6. Consumer Goods	17.7	11.3	13.8	12.5	13.2	14.4	14.1	12.1	14.2	12.4
Durable	2.6	2.2	2.7	2.1	2.6	2.7	2.1	1.5	2.5	1.4
Semi-Durable	7.8	3.5	4.4	4.7	4.7	5.1	4.8	3.1	3.8	3.2
Non-Durable	7.3	5.7	6.7	5.8	5.9	6.5	7.2	7.4	7.9	7.8
7. Other	.3	.4	.3	.3	.2	.3	.7	4	1	7

Exports by Industrial Origin

Origin	1970	1975	1976	1979	1980	1981	1982	1983	1984	1985
Total Exports (1 + 2 + 3)	100.0	100.0	100.0	100.0	100.0	100.0	100.0	100.0	100.0	100.0
1. Agriculture	64.0	49.9	62.1	63.5	63.7	63.3	67.8	65.1	71.0	77.1
2. Mining Quarrying	5.2	10.8	8.2	6.2	6.5	5.2	3.9	6.5	5.4	4.4
3. Manufacturing	30.8	39.3	29.7	30.3	29.8	31.5	28.2	28.4	23.6	18.4
31. Food, Bev., Tobac.	9.3	11.5	9.9	13.6	14.3	16.2	13.0	14.0	11.8	9.0
32. Textiles	2.8	2.3	2.5	2.2	2.8	2.7	1.8	1.5	1.3	.6
33. Wood, Wood Prod.	9.6	13.7	10.6	8.4	4.9	5.5	8.3	7.1	6.2	5.6
34. Paper and Prod.	.7	.4	.3	.5	.6	.7	.6	.6	.4	.3
35. Chemicals	7.6	8.4	4.1	3.9	5.1	4.6	3.4	4.0	2.7	1.9
36. Non-Metal Minrl	.1	1.1	.3	0	.1	.4	.1	0	0	0
37. Basic Metal Ind.	.5	.4	.3	.2	.2	.1	.1	0	0	0
38. Metal Manufact.	.2	1.4	1.5	1.4	1.5	1.4	1.0	1.1	1.0	.8
39. Oth. Manf. Ind.	0	.1	.1	1.1	.1	.1	.1	.1	.2	.1

SOURCE: UN-YITS, 1976; 1981; 1983; 1985; 1986; 1987.

Table 2513

MEXICO PERCENTAGE VALUE OF TRADE, 1970–85

Imports by Broad Economic Category

Category	1970	1974	1975	1976	1977	1978	1979	1981	1982	1983	1984	1985
Total Imports	100.0	100.0	100.0	100.0	100.0	100.0	100.0	100.0	100.0	100.0	100.0	100.0
1. Food and Beverages	3.8	12.0	5.9	5.2	8.9	8.2	7.5	11.3	10.5	13.2	12.3	9.7
Primary	1.9	8.0	4.5	3.3	6.6	6.3	5.7	7.6	6.7	9.5	9.6	7.8
For Industry	1.3	7.1	3.2	2.9	5.9	5.7	5.0	5.4	5.1	8.5	8.3	6.2
For Hshold Consm	.6	1.0	1.4	.4	.7	.6	.7	2.2	1.6	1.0	1.3	1.6
Processed	2.0	4.0	1.4	1.9	2.4	1.9	1.8	3.7	3.7	3.7	2.7	1.9
For Industry	.5	1.2	.2	.3	.7	.6	.1	1.7	1.7	2.1	1.2	.3
For Hshold Consm	1.4	2.8	1.2	1.6	1.7	1.4	1.7	2.0	2.1	1.6	1.6	1.6
2. Ind. Supplies Nes.	35.5	38.8	38.8	34.0	37.9	40.0	35.4	33.3	32.1	37.9	36.2	36.5
Primary	8.6	9.0	11.4	6.2	8.2	7.3	6.3	6.2	4.3	10.7	7.6	6.9
Processed	26.8	29.8	27.4	27.8	29.7	32.8	29.1	27.1	27.8	27.2	28.6	29.6
3. Fuels	2.8	6.7	5.0	5.3	2.3	2.7	2.1	1.3	2.7	1.8	3.0	3.8
Primary	1.3	3.5	2.1	1.8	1.5	1.3	.8	.8	1.1	.5	1.7	2.2
Processed	1.5	3.2	2.9	3.4	.8	1.4	1.3	.6	1.6	1.3	1.3	1.6
Motor Spirit	.4	2.0	1.0	1.1	.2	0	0	0	.4	.1	.1	0
Other	1.1	1.2	1.9	2.3	.6	1.4	1.3	.5	1.2	1.2	1.2	1.6
4. Machinery	33.4	23.4	27.0	33.2	29.1	27.1	28.8	31.2	34.8	30.4	31.5	32.6
Machines Capt. Eqp	28.1	20.4	23.6	28.9	24.6	22.7	24.7	27.3	30.3	23.5	22.7	23.8
Parts Accessories	5.3	3.0	3.4	4.3	4.5	4.5	4.1	3.9	4.6	6.9	8.8	8.9
5. Transport	17.6	14.9	19.4	18.1	17.4	17.7	18.6	17.7	14.7	11.7	10.6	10.9
Passenger Cars	4.6	4.2	.1	.1	.1	.1	.1	.7	.6	.1	.1	.2
Other	6.7	6.3	6.6	4.1	5.0	5.0	7.3	6.7	4.6	5.9	3.7	3.1
Industrial	6.7	6.3	6.5	4.1	5.0	5.0	7.3	6.7	4.6	5.9	3.7	3.1
Non-Industrial	0	0	0	0	0	0	0	0	0	0	0	0
Parts Accessories	6.2	4.3	12.7	13.8	12.4	12.6	11.2	10.2	9.5	5.7	6.7	7.6
6. Consumer Goods	6.8	4.1	3.8	4.3	4.2	4.1	4.6	5.1	5.1	4.8	6.4	6.3
Durable	1.5	1.2	1.2	1.2	1.2	1.2	1.4	1.5	1.2	1.7	2.7	2.1
Semi-Durable	3.1	1.3	1.3	1.5	1.4	1.4	1.5	2.1	2.1	2.2	2.5	2.9
Non-Durable	2.2	1.6	1.4	1.7	1.6	1.5	1.6	1.5	1.8	.9	1.1	1.3
7. Other	.1	.2	0	0	0	.1	3.2	.1	.1	.1	.1	.1

Exports by Industrial Origin

Origin	1970	1974	1975	1976	1977	1978	1979	1981	1982	1983	1984	1985
Total Exports (1 + 2 + 3)	100.0	100.0	100.0	100.0	100.0	100.0	100.0	100.0	100.0	100.0	100.0	100.0
1. Agriculture	34.1	27.3	28.9	36.2	33.0	30.1	24.8	9.3	7.8	6.8	7.5	7.1
2. Mining Quarrying	8.7	7.5	20.3	20.7	25.6	31.9	46.8	73.0	78.4	63.5	59.2	57.2
3. Manufacturing	57.2	65.2	50.8	43.1	41.4	38.0	28.4	17.7	13.8	29.7	33.3	35.7
31. Food, Bev., Tobac.	14.2	13.3	9.1	5.7	5.9	6.0	4.3	1.4	1.3	1.2	1.4	1.5
32. Textiles	3.8	8.9	5.5	5.1	4.1	2.8	2.4	.9	.6	1.5	1.8	1.7
33. Wood, Wood Prod.	.6	.7	.6	.8	.9	.8	.6	.2	.2	.4	.3	.3
34. Paper and Prod.	2.1	1.2	1.3	1.3	1.3	1.1	.9	.4	.4	.7	.6	.6
35. Chemicals	11.1	13.9	9.0	8.8	8.0	6.7	6.1	5.4	3.8	6.4	8.5	8.8
36. Non-Metal Minrl	1.4	1.9	2.0	2.3	3.3	2.4	1.5	.6	.6	.9	1.2	1.4
37. Basic Metal Ind.	10.1	12.2	11.2	9.3	8.5	5.9	3.2	4.1	2.5	3.8	2.5	2.7
38. Metal Manufact.	12.7	12.0	11.2	9.1	8.5	11.7	8.8	4.5	4.2	14.1	15.1	17.8
39. Oth. Manf. Ind.	1.3	1.2	.9	.8	.9	.6	.6	.3	.2	.7	.8	.8

SOURCE: UN-YITS, 1976; 1981; 1983; 1984; 1985; 1986; 1987.

Table 2514

NICARAGUA PERCENTAGE VALUE OF TRADE, 1970–84

Imports by Broad Economic Category

Category	1970	1974	1975	1976	1977	1978	1979	1980	1981	1982	1983	1984
Total Imports	100.0	100.0	100.0	100.0	100.0	100.0	100.0	100.0	100.0	100.0	100.0	100.0
1. Food and Beverages	8.2	6.6	7.3	7.3	6.5	8.3	11.9	13.0	15.3	10.3	~	11.2
Primary	3.4	2.9	3.6	3.1	2.6	3.6	3.5	6.0	9.8	4.4	~	5.2
For Industry	2.0	2.0	2.6	2.1	1.5	2.2	1.4	2.1	5.6	3.4	~	4.0
For Hshold Consm	1.4	1.0	1.0	1.0	1.1	1.4	2.1	3.9	4.2	1.0	~	1.2
Processed	4.8	3.7	3.7	4.2	3.9	4.7	8.4	6.9	5.5	5.9	~	6.0
For Industry	.7	.7	.6	.5	.7	.9	1.9	1.9	1.9	1.8	~	1.6
For Hshold Consm	4.1	3.0	3.1	3.7	3.2	3.8	6.6	5.0	3.5	4.2	~	4.4
2. Ind. Supplies Nes.	40.3	44.7	36.7	37.2	35.4	38.7	35.1	37.2	30.6	31.3	~	32.8
Primary	2.2	1.6	1.2	1.8	1.2	1.9	1.5	2.5	1.6	1.4	~	1.1
Processed	38.1	43.2	35.5	35.4	34.1	36.8	33.6	34.7	29.0	29.8	~	31.7
3. Fuels	5.8	10.7	14.2	12.9	13.6	15.1	21.1	19.8	19.9	23.1	~	17.6
Primary	4.0	9.1	12.3	10.7	10.2	9.7	18.2	16.8	17.5	19.5	~	12.1
Processed	1.8	1.5	1.9	2.3	3.4	5.3	2.9	3.0	2.4	3.6	~	5.6
Motor Spirit	.3	.3	.4	.7	.7	1.4	.8	.6	.6	1.0	~	2.7
Other	1.5	1.2	1.5	1.6	2.7	4.0	2.1	2.4	1.9	2.7	~	2.8
4. Machinery	16.3	13.8	17.4	15.4	17.3	13.7	8.8	7.9	13.3	15.2	~	18.8
Machines Capt. Eqp	15.3	13.0	16.5	14.6	16.4	12.8	8.2	7.2	12.5	14.2	~	17.3
Parts Accessories	1.0	.9	.9	.8	.9	.9	.6	.7	.8	1.0	~	1.5
5. Transport	11.4	10.8	10.4	11.4	14.1	11.0	7.2	7.0	9.4	10.2	~	11.3
Passenger Cars	2.4	2.2	2.6	3.4	3.3	2.2	.9	.9	1.1	1.1	~	1.3
Other	4.3	5.0	3.9	4.0	6.5	4.1	2.6	2.8	4.7	4.1	~	4.9
Industrial	4.2	4.8	3.7	3.8	6.3	3.9	2.5	2.7	4.6	4.0	~	4.8
Non-Industrial	.1	.2	.2	.2	.2	.1	.1	.1	.1	0	~	.1
Parts Accessories	4.7	3.7	3.9	4.0	4.3	4.7	3.6	3.3	3.6	5.1	~	5.1
6. Consumer Goods	17.8	13.1	13.5	15.6	12.9	13.0	15.6	15.1	11.3	9.8	~	8.1
Durable	2.1	1.9	1.6	1.7	1.6	1.3	.7	.9	.7	.4	~	.5
Semi-Durable	6.5	5.3	4.9	5.9	4.8	4.4	5.9	6.6	3.1	2.8	~	2.3
Non-Durable	9.2	6.0	7.1	8.0	6.5	7.3	9.0	7.6	7.5	6.6	~	5.3
7 Other	.2	.2	.4	.2	.2	.2	.3	.1	.2	.1	~	.2

Exports by Industrial Origin

Origin	1970	1974	1975	1976	1977	1978	1979	1980	1981	1982	1983	1984
Total Exports (1 + 2 + 3)	100.0	100.0	100.0	100.0	100.0	100.0	100.0	100.0	100.0	100.0	100.0	100.0
1. Agriculture	48.2	57.3	49.6	55.0	62.7	58.9	59.6	58.7	67.1	66.2	~	76.3
2. Mining Quarrying	3.0	2.7	1.5	.9	.8	.4	.1	.1	.1	.1	~	0
3. Manufacturing	48.7	40.0	48.8	44.0	36.5	40.7	40.3	41.3	32.8	33.7	~	23.7
31. Food, Bev., Tobac.	29.7	16.9	28.3	24.2	16.6	21.3	26.5	23.8	20.1	24.0	~	14.5
32. Textiles	6.3	4.8	5.3	4.9	4.9	3.6	2.7	2.5	1.7	1.2	~	2.6
33. Wood, Wood Prod.	2.2	2.1	2.0	2.5	1.8	1.6	1.2	.7	.5	.5	~	.2
34. Paper and Prod.	.3	.4	.1	.2	.2	.2	.1	.1	0	0	~	0
35. Chemicals	6.0	10.3	8.9	8.4	8.7	9.0	6.9	10.6	8.3	6.3	~	4.4
36. Non-Metal Minrl	1.0	1.0	.8	.9	.9	1.0	.7	.7	.2	.1	~	0
37. Basic Metal Ind.	.9	.6	1.0	.7	.8	1.3	.6	1.4	.6	.3	~	1.2
38. Metal Manufact.	2.3	3.1	2.2	2.2	2.4	2.6	1.7	1.5	1.3	1.2	~	.8
39. Oth. Manf. Ind.	.1	.1	.2	.1	.1	0	0	0	0	0	~	0

SOURCE: UN-YITS, 1976; 1981; 1983; 1984; 1985; 1986; 1987.

Table 2515

PANAMA PERCENTAGE VALUE OF TRADE, 1970–85

Imports by Broad Economic Category

Category	1970	1975	1979	1980	1981	1982	1983	1984	1985
Total Imports	100.0	100.0	100.0	100.0	100.0	100.0	100.0	100.0	100.0
1. Food and Beverages	7.9	7.9	8.5	8.6	7.8	8.1	9.2	9.1	10.2
Primary	2.4	2.2	2.2	2.0	2.5	2.3	2.4	2.6	3.0
For Industry	1.0	1.3	.9	.9	1.2	.9	.9	1.2	1.3
For Hshold Consm	1.4	.9	1.3	1.2	1.3	1.4	1.4	1.4	1.7
Processed	5.5	5.7	6.3	6.6	5.4	5.9	6.8	6.5	7.2
For Industry	.7	2.0	2.0	2.0	1.5	1.6	1.9	1.8	2.0
For Hshold Consm	4.8	3.7	4.3	4.6	3.9	4.2	4.9	4.7	5.2
2. Ind. Supplies Nes.	27.8	21.4	26.9	25.4	25.9	24.0	23.8	26.4	26.0
Primary	.7	.7	1.0	1.2	1.0	1.1	.9	.8	1.3
Processed	27.1	20.7	25.9	24.2	24.9	22.9	22.8	25.5	24.7
3. Fuels	18.7	40.3	28.4	30.2	28.0	26.5	27.7	25.9	21.0
Primary	18.0	39.0	27.2	28.6	24.4	25.2	24.8	22.6	19.4
Processed	.7	1.4	1.2	1.5	3.6	1.3	2.8	3.3	1.6
Motor Spirit	0	0	.5	.5	3.0	.9	2.6	3.1	1.2
Other	.7	1.4	.7	1.0	.6	.4	.3	.2	.4
4. Machinery	15.4	12.2	11.3	11.3	13.8	15.9	12.5	11.5	11.1
Machines Capt. Eqp	14.8	11.2	10.1	10.5	12.8	14.6	11.6	10.5	10.0
Parts Accessories	.5	1.1	1.2	.9	1.0	1.3	.9	1.0	1.1
5. Transport	12.1	7.2	9.1	9.7	10.4	11.2	10.7	10.6	12.0
Passenger Cars	3.5	1.4	3.2	3.4	3.4	4.4	4.5	3.8	4.6
Other	4.0	2.7	2.2	2.9	3.3	2.8	2.7	2.3	2.9
Industrial	3.8	2.6	2.0	2.5	3.1	2.7	2.5	2.1	2.7
Non-Industrial	.2	.1	.2	.4	.2	.1	.2	.2	.3
Parts Accessories	4.6	3.1	3.7	3.3	3.7	4.0	3.5	4.5	4.5
6. Consumer Goods	17.8	10.9	15.7	14.7	13.9	14.1	16.0	16.4	17.9
Durable	4.0	2.4	4.2	3.6	3.4	3.6	3.8	3.8	4.4
Semi-Durable	8.7	4.3	6.5	6.3	5.8	5.5	6.2	6.5	7.3
Non-Durable	5.1	4.1	5.1	4.8	4.8	5.0	5.9	6.0	6.2
7. Other	.3	.1	.1	.2	.1	.2	.2	.2	1.9

Exports by Industrial Origin

Origin	1970	1975	1979	1980	1981	1982	1983	1984	1985
Total Exports (1 + 2 + 3)	100.0	100.0	100.0	100.0	100.0	100.0	100.0	100.0	100.0
1. Agriculture	68.6	29.4	44.2	36.4	42.7	45.6	50.8	57.0	56.6
2. Mining Quarrying	0	~	~	0	~	~	~	~	.3
3. Manufacturing	31.3	70.6	55.8	63.6	57.3	54.4	49.2	43.0	43.1
31. Food, Bev., Tobac.	8.2	21.0	19.6	31.0	28.2	18.7	26.3	26.1	21.7
32. Textiles	.2	1.9	5.6	4.2	5.6	7.9	4.6	7.2	6.4
33. Wood, Wood Prod.	0	0	.1	.1	.2	.1	.2	.5	.5
34. Paper and Prod.	.5	.4	1.2	1.6	1.1	1.3	1.1	.9	.8
35. Chemicals	20.4	45.6	26.4	24.7	19.8	24.5	14.8	5.9	11.5
36. Non-Metal Minrl	0	.1	1.1	0	.5	.3	.4	.2	.3
37. Basic Metal Ind.	.5	.4	.8	.6	.4	.4	.7	.4	.6
38. Metal Manufact.	1.4	1.1	.8	1.0	1.0	.7	1.0	1.5	.7
39. Oth. Manf. Ind.	~	.1	.3	.5	.4	.5	.1	.3	.6

SOURCE: UN-YITS, 1976; 1981; 1983; 1984; 1985; 1986; 1987.

Table 2516

PARAGUAY PERCENTAGE VALUE OF TRADE, 1975–86

Imports by Broad Economic Category

Category	1975	1979	1980	1981	1982	1983	1984	1985	1986
Total Imports	100.0	100.0	100.0	100.0	100.0	100.0	100.0	100.0	100.0
1. Food and Beverages	11.9	9.4	8.7	10.5	7.7	7.9	5.6	7.9	8.1
Primary	1.8	2.2	2.1	2.7	1.4	3.6	.6	3.2	1.5
For Industry	1.6	1.9	2.1	2.6	1.3	3.5	.3	3.1	1.5
For Hshold Consm	.2	.3	.1	.1	.1	.1	.3	0	0
Processed	10.1	7.2	6.6	7.8	6.4	4.3	5.0	4.7	6.6
For Industry	1.3	.4	.8	.8	.6	.7	.5	.4	.4
For Hshold Consm	8.8	6.8	5.8	7.0	5.8	3.6	4.5	4.3	6.2
2. Ind. Supplies Nes.	22.2	20.6	10.5	23.6	26.0	27.6	19.1	23.7	22.1
Primary	.9	.8	.8	.9	1.0	1.2	1.0	1.5	.9
Processed	21.3	19.8	19.7	22.7	25.0	26.3	18.1	22.2	21.2
3. Fuels	20.3	24.0	26.7	19.8	26.2	25.9	28.2	27.2	20.7
Primary	16.8	14.2	13.5	15.6	14.4	14.2	11.5	12.4	9.7
Processed	3.5	9.9	13.3	4.3	11.8	11.7	16.7	14.8	11.0
Motor Spirit	1.4	2.6	2.4	.6	2.2	1.4	3.7	3.4	2.4
Other	2.1	7.2	10.8	3.6	9.6	10.3	13.0	11.4	8.6
4. Machinery	20.1	19.1	15.9	21.2	20.8	24.7	20.5	20.6	21.6
Machines Capt. Eqp	18.6	18.0	15.0	20.2	19.6	23.5	19.5	19.3	19.8
Parts Accessories	1.4	1.1	.9	1.0	1.1	1.3	1.0	1.2	1.8
5. Transport	15.9	16.5	19.4	15.1	9.5	7.4	21.1	8.4	7.2
Passenger Cars	2.8	4.0	4.5	4.3	2.8	2.0	3.3	2.7	2.8
Other	9.3	9.3	9.8	7.7	4.4	3.5	16.0	2.6	1.6
Industrial	8.9	8.5	8.9	6.6	3.7	3.1	15.9	2.5	1.3
Non-Industrial	.4	.8	.9	1.1	.7	.3	.1	.1	.3
Parts Accessories	3.8	3.2	5.2	3.1	2.4	1.9	1.8	3.1	2.7
6. Consumer Goods	9.1	10.3	8.5	9.7	9.7	6.4	5.4	12.0	20.2
Durable	1.7	1.7	1.6	3.1	2.4	1.3	1.4	5.3	12.3
Semi-Durable	2.0	1.8	1.6	2.0	2.4	2.0	1.4	3.1	4.2
Non-Durable	5.5	6.8	5.2	4.7	4.9	3.0	2.7	3.6	3.7
7. Other	.5	.1	.3	.1	.1	.2	.2	.2	.1

Exports by Industrial Origin

Origin	1975	1979	1980	1981	1982	1983	1984	1985	1986
Total Exports (1 + 2 + 3)	100.0	100.0	100.0	100.0	100.0	100.0	100.0	100.0	100.0
1. Agriculture	39.6	64.9	65.5	62.1	69.4	68.7	75.5	84.0	59.4
2. Mining Quarrying	0	0	~	~	~	0	0	0	0
3. Manufacturing	60.4	35.1	34.5	37.9	30.6	31.3	24.5	16.0	40.6
31. Food, Bev., Tobac.	35.6	13.7	14.9	14.5	11.8	17.4	12.8	7.7	24.9
32. Textiles	1.2	2.6	1.2	2.2	2.8	3.5	2.3	1.9	4.8
33. Wood, Wood Prod.	15.9	13.8	13.5	14.1	13.3	7.6	6.7	3.2	7.5
34. Paper and Prod.	0	0	~	~	0	0	~	~	~
35. Chemicals	6.1	4.5	4.5	4.1	2.7	2.8	2.7	3.2	3.3
36. Non-Metal Minrl	.4	0	~	~	~	~	0	0	~
37. Basic Metal Ind.	~	0	~	~	0	~	~	~	~
38. Metal Manufact.	0	0	~	~	0	0	0	~	0
39. Oth. Manf. Ind.	1.2	.4	.4	2.9	~	0	0	~	~

SOURCE: UN-YITS, 1976; 1981; 1983; 1984; 1985; 1986; 1987.

Table 2517

URUGUAY PERCENTAGE VALUE OF TRADE, 1970–86

Category	Imports by Broad Economic Category							
	1970	1975	1980	1982	1983	1984	1985	1986
Total Imports	100.0	100.0	100.0	100.0	100.0	100.0	100.0	100.0
1. Food and Beverages	9.0	6.6	6.6	4.7	6.1	7.0	5.8	8.0
Primary	3.8	3.9	4.2	3.2	4.8	5.1	3.8	6.2
For Industry	1.5	1.1	1.4	.9	2.5	2.4	.9	2.7
For Hshold Consm	2.3	2.8	2.9	2.3	2.3	2.8	2.9	3.5
Processed	5.2	2.7	2.4	1.5	1.3	1.9	2.0	1.8
For Industry	3.7	2.3	.6	.3	.3	.4	.4	.4
For Hshold Consm	1.5	.3	1.8	1.2	1.0	1.5	1.7	1.4
2. Ind. Supplies Nes.	40.8	41.4	29.6	25.4	29.4	35.8	37.1	40.3
Primary	8.3	7.1	3.9	3.1	4.1	4.8	4.7	4.4
Processed	32.5	34.3	25.6	22.3	25.3	31.0	32.4	36.0
3. Fuels	14.1	31.0	28.4	38.9	35.9	36.0	33.7	19.3
Primary	~	28.6	25.6	37.8	33.6	33.6	31.6	16.2
Processed	~	2.5	2.8	1.1	2.2	2.4	2.1	3.0
Motor Spirit	~	.2	.2	~	.1	~	0	.3
Other	~	2.3	2.6	1.1	2.1	2.4	2.1	2.8
4. Machinery	12.4	12.0	15.8	13.3	20.4	12.1	12.7	17.0
Machines Capt. Eqp	~	10.4	14.2	12.0	19.0	10.7	11.2	15.2
Parts Accessories	~	1.6	1.6	1.3	1.5	1.4	1.6	1.8
5. Transport	16.4	6.7	14.0	10.9	3.7	4.2	4.7	7.4
Passenger Cars	~	1.7	6.2	3.2	1.3	2.0	2.6	5.0
Other	~	3.2	5.6	6.0	1.2	1.0	.5	.5
Industrial	~	2.9	4.6	5.6	1.1	1.0	.5	.4
Non-Industrial	~	.3	1.0	.4	.1	0	.1	.1
Parts Accessories	~	1.9	2.2	1.7	1.2	1.1	1.5	1.9
6. Consumer Goods	6.5	2.3	5.5	6.8	4.4	4.9	5.9	7.9
Durable	.3	.8	2.5	3.0	1.5	1.5	1.9	3.0
Semi-Durable	2.0	.4	1.6	1.9	1.1	1.4	1.6	2.2
Non-Durable	4.2	1.1	1.4	1.9	1.9	2.1	2.3	2.7
7. Other	.7	0	.2	0	0	0	.1	0

Origin	Exports by Industrial Origin									
	1970	1975	1979	1980	1981	1982	1983	1984	1985	1986
Total Exports (1 + 2 + 3)	100.0	100.0	100.0	100.0	100.0	100.0	100.0	100.0	100.0	100.0
1. Agriculture	22.8	30.6	16.1	21.5	24.6	27.8	22.7	21.2	19.5	18.5
2. Mining Quarrying	1.9	.3	.8	.7	.5	.2	.1	.2	.1	.2
3. Manufacturing	75.3	69.1	83.1	77.8	74.9	72.0	77.2	78.6	80.4	81.2
31. Food, Bev., Tobac.	51.4	29.7	26.9	30.7	35.4	31.0	40.0	29.7	30.7	30.9
32. Textiles	21.1	28.3	39.2	32.3	28.0	29.7	28.7	38.4	37.8	37.3
33. Wood, Wood Prod.	0	0	0	0	0	0	0	0	0	0
34. Paper and Prod.	.1	.6	1.2	1.3	.9	.7	1.1	1.2	1.1	1.2
35. Chemicals	.4	3.4	5.8	4.9	5.9	6.6	3.9	5.2	6.3	7.0
36. Non-Metal Minrl	.5	3.8	3.1	2.6	1.5	1.2	.8	.9	.8	.7
37. Basic Metal Ind.	.1	.5	.8	.7	.4	.4	.4	.7	.6	.6
38. Metal Manufact.	1.3	2.8	5.6	5.0	2.5	1.7	1.6	1.7	2.3	2.8
39. Oth. Manf. Ind.	.3	.1	.4	.4	.2	.6	.6	.8	.7	.7

SOURCE: UN-YITS, 1976; 1981; 1983; 1985; 1986; 1987.

Table 2518

VENEZUELA PERCENTAGE VALUE OF TRADE, 1970–85

Category	Imports by Broad Economic Category							
	1970	1975	1980	1981	1982	1983	1984	1985
Total Imports	100.0	100.0	100.0	100.0	100.0	100.0	100.0	100.0
1. Food and Beverages	9.2	11.4	11.2	14.1	11.7	14.4	12.8	10.9
Primary	5.3	6.3	3.9	5.3	4.0	6.1	4.0	4.2
For Industry	3.8	5.2	2.5	3.4	2.8	4.2	2.9	3.2
For Hshold Consm	1.5	1.0	1.4	1.9	1.2	1.9	1.2	1.0
Processed	3.9	5.2	7.3	8.9	7.7	8.3	8.7	6.7
For Industry	1.3	2.3	2.5	3.3	2.9	4.1	3.5	2.7
For Hshold Consm	2.7	2.9	4.8	5.6	4.9	4.2	5.3	4.0
2. Ind. Supplies	34.3	31.4	33.7	31.5	33.4	36.9	36.6	34.1
Primary	2.7	1.4	4.0	3.0	2.6	5.8	5.6	4.9
Processed	31.6	30.0	29.7	28.5	30.8	31.1	31.0	29.2
3. Fuels	1.3	.5	1.0	.1	.2	2.3	2.4	1.7
Primary	.1	0	.5	0	0	2.0	2.0	1.4
Processed	1.2	.5	.4	.1	.2	.4	.4	.3
Motor Spirit	.3	0	.1	0	0	0	0	0
Other	.9	.5	.4	.1	.2	.3	.4	.2
4. Machinery	28.6	31.8	28.0	26.3	28.7	23.4	22.3	27.9
Machines Capt. Eqp	25.4	28.7	24.5	22.7	24.3	19.6	18.4	23.0
Parts Accessories	3.2	3.1	3.5	3.6	4.3	3.8	3.9	4.9
5. Transport	15.6	16.8	14.3	16.7	14.2	15.1	15.8	14.4
Passenger Cars	5.6	6.5	5.4	6.1	5.3	7.1	6.9	5.5
Other	4.0	5.6	4.2	5.6	3.9	4.0	3.5	3.4
Industrial	3.8	5.4	3.8	5.2	3.6	3.7	3.4	3.3
Non-Industrial	.2	.3	.3	.4	.3	.2	.1	.1
Parts Accessories	5.9	4.7	4.7	5.0	5.0	4.0	5.4	5.4
6. Consumer Goods	10.1	7.7	11.6	11.1	11.5	7.6	9.9	10.7
Durable	3.8	3.3	4.7	4.4	4.2	2.1	2.3	3.1
Semi-Durable	3.7	3.0	5.0	4.9	5.3	2.8	5.1	4.8
Non-Durable	2.6	1.4	1.9	1.8	2.0	2.7	2.5	2.7
7. Other	.9	.3	.2	.1	.2	.2	.2	.4

Origin	Exports by Industrial Origin					
	1970	1975	1980	1981	1982	1983
Total Exports (1 + 2 + 3)	100.0	100.0	100.0	100.0	~	100.0
1. Agriculture	1.4	.7	.3	.4	~	.6
2. Mining Quarrying	68.4	71.0	66.3	80.7	~	58.4
3. Manufacturing	30.2	28.3	33.5	18.9	~	41.1
31. Food, Bev., Tobac.	.2	.3	.1	.1	~	.1
32. Textiles	0	0	0	0	~	0
33. Wood, Wood Prod.	0	0	0	0	~	0
34. Paper and Prod.	0	.1	.1	.1	~	.1
35. Chemicals	28.5	27.5	30.1	14.8	~	37.6
36. Non-Metal Minrl	.1	0	0	0	~	.1
37. Basic Metal Ind.	.7	.1	2.7	3.2	~	3.0
38. Metal Manufact.	.5	.2	.5	.6	~	.3
39. Oth. Manf. Ind.	.1	0	0	0	~	0

SOURCE: UN-YITS, 1976; 1981; 1983; 1984; 1985; 1986; 1987.

Table 2519

UNITED STATES PERCENTAGE VALUE OF TRADE,[1] 1970–87

Category	\multicolumn{11}{c}{Imports by Broad Economic Category}
	1970	1975	1979	1980	1981	1982	1983	1984	1985	1986	1987
Total Imports	100.0	100.0	100.0	100.0	100.0	100.0	100.0	100.0	100.0	100.0	100.0
1. Food and Beverages	15.5	10.2	8.8	7.9	7.3	7.4	7.4	6.8	6.7	6.8	6.2
Primary	8.8	4.9	5.2	4.4	3.9	4.2	4.1	3.5	3.6	3.9	3.5
For Industry	4.0	2.2	2.3	2.0	1.5	1.5	1.4	1.3	1.3	1.5	1.0
For Hshold Consm	4.8	2.7	2.9	2.5	2.4	2.7	2.7	2.3	2.3	2.4	2.5
Processed	6.7	5.3	3.6	3.4	3.4	3.2	3.3	3.2	3.1	2.9	2.7
For Industry	1.3	.9	.6	.4	.4	.3	.4	.4	.4	.3	.3
For Hshold Consm	5.4	4.4	3.0	3.0	3.1	2.9	3.0	2.9	2.7	2.6	2.4
2. Ind. Supplies Nes.	32.5	24.6	22.8	21.0	21.7	20.5	20.8	21.3	20.1	19.5	19.0
Primary	7.0	4.8	3.9	3.7	3.6	3.0	3.0	2.9	2.6	2.6	2.4
Processed	25.5	19.8	18.9	17.2	18.1	17.4	17.8	18.4	17.6	17.0	16.7
3. Fuels	7.6	27.0	29.1	32.7	30.9	26.5	22.2	18.5	15.3	10.3	11.0
Primary	3.9	20.4	24.3	27.9	25.8	21.1	16.4	12.7	10.7	7.2	7.9
Processed	3.6	6.6	4.9	4.8	5.1	5.4	5.8	5.8	4.7	3.1	3.0
Motor Spirit	0	.3	1.0	.9	1.0	1.4	1.6	1.7	1.6	1.1	1.0
Other	3.6	6.2	3.8	3.9	4.1	4.0	4.2	4.2	3.0	2.1	2.0
4. Machinery	8.7	9.2	10.3	10.5	11.2	12.6	14.0	16.2	16.2	17.9	18.9
Machines Capt. Eqp	7.0	7.2	7.8	7.8	8.4	9.1	10.0	11.3	12.1	13.4	13.7
Parts Accessories	1.6	2.0	2.5	2.7	2.8	3.5	4.0	4.8	4.1	4.5	5.2
5. Transport	17.2	14.9	14.6	14.1	14.2	16.1	17.4	18.1	20.6	22.9	22.1
Passenger Cars	9.8	7.8	7.4	7.2	7.0	8.5	9.3	9.2	10.9	12.5	11.8
Other	2.0	1.8	1.9	2.2	2.9	3.0	2.7	2.9	3.3	3.4	3.0
Industrial	1.1	.9	1.4	1.6	2.3	2.5	2.4	2.7	2.9	3.1	2.8
Non-Industrial	.9	.8	.5	.5	.6	.5	.3	.2	.3	.3	.2
Parts Accessories	5.4	5.4	5.3	4.7	4.3	4.6	5.4	6.0	6.5	7.0	7.3
6. Consumer Goods	15.4	11.4	12.7	12.1	12.8	14.7	15.9	17.1	18.5	20.0	20.2
Durable	5.6	4.2	4.7	4.6	4.8	5.3	5.8	6.2	7.0	7.4	6.8
Semi-Durable	8.8	6.5	7.3	6.8	7.1	8.4	9.2	9.8	10.5	11.4	12.0
Non-Durable	.9	.6	.7	.7	.8	1.0	1.0	1.1	1.1	1.3	1.3
7. Other	3.3	2.6	1.6	1.7	1.9	2.3	2.2	2.1	2.4	2.5	2.6

Origin	\multicolumn{11}{c}{Exports by Industrial Origin}
	1970	1975	1979	1980	1981	1982	1983	1984	1985	1986	1987
Total Exports (1 + 2 + 3)	100.0	100.0	100.0	100.0	100.0	100.0	100.0	100.0	100.0	100.0	100.0
1. Agriculture	12.6	17.1	16.3	15.4	15.2	14.1	14.5	14.0	10.8	9.1	8.6
2. Mining Quarrying	4.3	4.7	4.2	4.6	4.5	4.7	3.8	3.5	3.7	3.3	2.6
3. Manufacturing	83.1	78.2	79.6	80.0	80.3	81.3	81.7	82.5	85.5	87.6	88.8
31. Food, Bev., Tobac.	5.9	4.9	5.9	5.5	5.4	5.2	5.5	5.2	4.8	5.4	5.2
32. Textiles	2.3	2.3	2.8	2.7	2.5	2.2	2.0	1.9	1.9	2.1	2.1
33. Wood, Wood Prod.	.8	.8	.9	.9	.8	.7	.8	.7	.6	.8	.9
34. Paper and Prod.	3.4	2.8	2.5	2.8	2.7	2.7	2.8	2.8	2.6	2.9	3.1
35. Chemicals	12.0	10.8	12.9	12.9	12.8	14.2	14.4	14.7	14.5	14.6	14.1
36. Non-Metal Minrl	.9	.7	.8	.8	.8	.8	.8	.8	.7	.7	.7
37. Basic Metal Ind.	5.3	3.6	2.9	4.0	2.7	2.3	2.0	1.8	1.7	1.5	1.6
38. Metal Manufact.	49.7	49.6	48.0	47.1	49.7	50.5	50.8	51.0	54.3	54.9	53.1
39. Oth. Manf. Ind.	2.9	2.6	2.8	3.3	2.7	2.6	2.6	3.6	4.3	4.7	8.0

1. Includes Puerto Rico

SOURCE: UN-YITS, 1977; 1978; 1979; 1980; 1981; 1983; 1985; 1986; 1987.

Table 2520

ARGENTINA ABSOLUTE VALUE OF TRADE, 1970–86

(T US)

Imports

Category	1970	1980	1981	1982	1983	1984	1985	1986
Total Merchandise Trade	1,684,639	10,540,600	9,430,230	5,336,910	4,504,160	4,584,670	3,814,100	4,723,460
Agricultural Products, Total	120,070	682,120	544,520	282,550	249,160	287,170	221,060	415,830
Food and Animals	84,502	506,040	38,527	200,400	149,260	182,180	156,380	303,100
Live Animals	1,409	7,440	5,920	7,690	16,580	2,430	3,000	2,140
Meat and Meat Prep	3	49,550	28,750	4,090	2,220	2,040	1,340	18,530
Dairy Products Eggs	6,207	46,210	30,900	4,200	3,510	6,270	5,410	6,090
Cereals and Prep	651	18,080	12,130	2,180	1,010	2,550	1,950	6,430
Fruits and Vegetables	24,885	185,690	133,370	52,630	28,540	48,930	37,590	64,790
Sugar and Honey	419	14,790	10,140	2,220	1,650	1,280	990	1,590
Coffee, Tea, Cocoa Sp	47,038	164,440	135,000	115,970	89,720	109,060	99,370	192,600
Feeding Stuff	1,040	4,000	3,160	1,620	1,560	2,260	3,150	2,820
Miscellaneous Food	2,850	15,860	25,900	9,810	4,480	7,360	3,590	8,120
Beverages Tobacco	7,113	56,368	46,280	12,410	8,470	5,180	9,800	5,980
Beverages	6,118	44,821	34,260	10,407	6,530	3,970	8,420	5,640
Tobacco	995	11,547	12,030	2,000	1,940	1,210	1,380	340
Crude Materials	26,719	109,330	104,490	60,790	83,210	91,500	50,340	102,100
Hides and Skins	666	3,810	1,640	150	780	1,080	420	1,520
Oilseeds	204	2,370	6,106	950	1,930	2,380	1,030	1,010
Natural Rubber	12,406	38,540	25,690	25,110	38,320	41,130	17,460	28,440
Textile Fibers	11,304	23,980	45,720	13,913	18,880	21,540	9,730	38,960
Crude Mat Nes	2,139	40,630	25,330	20,672	23,300	25,380	21,710	32,170
Animal Vegetable Oil	1,736	10,380	9,160	8,960	8,220	8,300	4,540	4,650
Animal Fats	75	500	350	500	530	360	190	360
Fixed Vegetable Oils	1,298	4,350	4,300	5,420	4,280	6,260	3,350	2,480
Processed Oils	363	5,530	4,510	3,030	3,410	1,680	1,000	1,810
Fish and Fishery Products	~	23,910	25,900	13,910	7,670	9,460	8,080	6,680
Forest Products	~	411,620	336,920	214,280	174,740	132,580	88,060	119,900
Agricultural Requisites	24,289	196,157	129,160	98,170	111,710	140,330	113,060	96,500
Crude Fertilizers	858	584	810	650	300	600	370	2,950
Manuf Fertilizers	5,259	38,539	26,866	29,656	25,990	47,470	45,800	29,950
Pesticides	6,713	43,643	39,500	49,090	67,930	81,600	52,760	59,340
Agriculture Machines	12,459	113,391	61,980	18,770	17,500	10,660	14,130	4,260

Exports

Category	1970	1980	1981	1982	1983	1984	1985	1986
Total Merchandise Trade	1,773,167	8,021,418	9,143,044	7,624,940	7,836,060	8,107,410	8,395,990	6,852,210
Agricultural Products, Total	1,490,606	5,522,120	6,377,530	4,863,690	5,890,160	6,060,430	5,658,540	4,518,650
Food and Animals	1,207,026	3,855,220	4,909,190	3,623,200	4,753,910	3,869,440	3,626,840	3,000,255
Live Animals	22,673	5,697	5,880	6,110	3,330	2,870	4,420	4,404
Meat and Meat Prep	441,313	965,700	930,420	804,910	602,600	413,050	393,830	464,680
Dairy Products Eggs	1,908	21,110	27,070	52,330	48,650	16,410	16,300	23,160
Cereals and Prep	518,523	1,656,781	2,841,610	1,836,380	2,918,580	2,268,020	2,290,480	1,259,840
Fruits and Vegetables	75,683	389,925	341,220	352,570	274,100	250,640	295,040	332,370
Sugar and Honey	17,608	339,357	315,470	91,270	211,620	127,730	59,760	59,320
Coffee, Tea, Cocoa Sp	10,344	38,950	33,400	35,770	43,690	62,980	48,040	33,690
Feeding Stuff	114,016	412,558	396,610	438,080	644,190	723,450	515,110	821,680
Miscellaneous Food	4,958	25,159	17,510	5,780	7,150	4,290	3,870	3,780
Beverages Tobacco	7,128	42,070	42,570	71,180	57,900	54,560	62,770	47,720
Beverages	793	15,210	14,090	12,200	8,380	8,260	6,170	8,040
Tobacco	6,335	26,864	28,480	58,980	49,530	46,310	56,600	39,690
Crude Materials	177,042	1,118,700	1,045,040	742,960	546,160	1,208,700	970,609	805,530
Hides and Skins	62,681	54,060	54,220	13,560	8,620	11,770	12,310	11,980
Oilseeds	282	662,194	639,330	454,250	36,089	948,210	731,490	643,480
Natural Rubber	- -	#	10	#	#	#	#	10
Textile Fibers	113,689	374,880	328,820	260,980	163,740	240,420	222,980	139,440
Crude Mat Nes	390	27,543	22,670	14,170	10,910	8,300	9,320	10,630
Animal Vegetable Oils	99,410	506,123	380,730	426,360	534,180	927,730	992,840	662,850
Animal Fats	21,192	28,894	35,380	14,250	13,220	12,900	9,970	6,940
Fixed Vegetable Oils	73,800	471,885	339,960	408,820	517,190	908,860	976,370	652,190
Processed Oils	4,418	5,344	5,390	3,284	3,770	5,970	6,500	3,730
Fish and Fishery Products	~	143,260	139,350	190,590	168,150	157,730	149,920	183,000
Forest Products	~	16,400	12,460	11,090	20,400	29,570	41,100	34,360
Agricultural Requisites	5,717	20,862	17,480	37,970	3,350	7,980	12,220	14,670
Crude Fertilizers	4	#	130	100	#	#	#	10
Manuf Fertilizers	239	#	620	#	140	160	1,570	670
Pesticides	214	2,457	2,310	1,171	910	2,500	3,090	7,780
Agricultural Machines	5,260	18,405	14,370	36,701	2,300	5,310	7,550	6,210

SOURCE: FAO-TY, 1975, Section IV; 1980, Section IV; 1981, Section IV; 1983, Section IV;
1985, Section IV; 1986, Section IV; 1987, Section IV.

Table 2521

BOLIVIA ABSOLUTE VALUE OF TRADE, 1975–86

(T US)

Category				Imports				
	1975	1980	1981	1982	1983	1984	1985	1986
Total Merchandise Trade	557,900	665,393	898,787	554,135	576,746	488,477	764,945	725,676
Agricultural Products, Total	88,687	121,081	125,119	94,492	126,563	74,580	120,565	90,828
Food and Animals	85,590	105,581	105,703	84,480	108,447	66,218	84,910	86,738
Live Animals	1,900	128	849	222	294	465	#	8
Meat and Meat Prep	75	86	516	317	421	69	1,000	520
Dairy Products Eggs	9,702	18,052	21,812	11,054	8,473	8,293	12,150	13,120
Cereals and Prep	60,020	54,550	52,366	62,085	86,588	46,246	60,485	58,480
Fruits and Vegetables	1,876	4,768	4,020	1,421	2,477	2,541	2,295	5,035
Sugar and Honey	#	807	1,668	364	290	320	400	450
Coffee, Tea, Cocoa Sp	1,555	2,698	3,144	580	386	660	530	825
Feeding Stuff	#	1,030	1,388	805	1,297	1,180	#	#
Miscellaneous Food	10,862	23,462	19,940	7,632	8,600	6,444	8,050	8,300
Beverages Tobacco	2,897	3,632	4,088	1,824	2,937	1,326	450	500
Beverages	#	513	497	244	612	592	#	#
Tobacco	2,897	3,119	3,591	1,588	2,325	734	450	500
Crude Materials	#	2,337	3,853	2,443	2,230	5,490	1,000	1,000
Hides and Skins	#	#	#	#	#	#	#	#
Oilseeds	#	449	1,353	695	954	865	#	#
Natural Rubber	#	296	32	110	13	77	#	#
Textile Fibers	#	778	1,506	553	424	3,711	#	#
Crude Mat Nes	#	814	962	1,085	839	837	1,000[‡]	1,000
Animal Vegetable Oil	200	9,531	11,475	6,055	7,910	3,179	9,110	2,590
Animal Fats	#	107	194	148	193	45	2,000	80
Fixed Vegetable Oils	200	6,817	9,831	4,651	5,269	1,149	7,000	2,400
Processed Oils	#	2,607	1,450	1,256	2,448	1,985	110	110
Fish and Fishery Products	#	4,724	6,321	6,000[‡]	1,133	1,860	1,746	1,800
Forest Products	#	11,805	12,605	5,800	5,800	4,800	4,300	5,100
Agricultural Requisites	16,107	18,376	35,778	9,273	11,941	23,084	20,560	21,504
Crude Fertilizers	#	28	3	776	2	7	#	#
Manuf Fertilizers	3,203	824	4,543	2,515	2,084	4,137	5,360[‡]	2,650
Pesticides	1,200[†]	5,334	7,231	2,099	3,156	6,959	4,500[‡]	3,331
Agriculture Machines	11,704	12,190	24,001	3,883	6,699	11,981	10,700[‡]	15,523

Category				Exports				
	1975	1980	1981	1982	1983	1984	1985	1986
Total Merchandise Trade	444,700	1,036,157	983,424	895,525	817,954	781,508	672,766	629,014
Agricultural Products, Total	67,998	102,229	50,134	58,528	42,903	22,449	28,922	36,307
Food and Animals	49,273	91,860	39,081	49,107	38,778	20,697	25,073	28,564
Live Animals	17,000	9,975	9,975	11,935	5,892	1,696	1,171	2,500
Meat and Meat Prep	#	#	#	587	122	343	#	#
Dairy Products Eggs	#	#	#	#	#	#	#	#
Cereals and Prep	30	505	292	5,139	1,475	1,209	1,607	1,604
Fruits and Vegetables	1,611	3,062	2,860	3,082	2,096	2,510	1,833	3,850
Sugar and Honey	23,553	47,881	5,851	8,860	12,426	6,277	1,637	3,000
Coffee, Tea, Cocoa Sp	7,070	22,503	16,466	15,995	13,480	6,796	15,050	5,600
Feeding Stuff	9	6,485	3,601	3,491	3,278	1,856	3,765	2,000
Miscellaneous Food	#	4	36	18	9	10	10	10
Beverages Tobacco	774	1,072	838	1,492	576	95	241	188
Beverages	724	1,072	838	1,492	576	95	241	188
Tobacco	50	#	#	#	#	#	#	#
Crude Materials	17,951	9,267	8,766	7,424	3,490	1,657	3,581	7,555
Hides and Skins	600	4,118	4,749	2,638	667	645	1,333	1,333
Oilseeds	#	18	27	#	#	#	#	2,000
Natural Rubber	2,012	3,955	3,405	4,146	2,760	750	1,700[‡]	3,900
Textile Fibers	15,339	1,174	585	548	63	262	543	322
Crude Mat Nes	#	2	#	92	#	#	5	#
Animal Vegetable Oils	#	30	1,449	505	59	#	27	#
Animal Fats	#	30	#	#	#	#	#	#
Fixed Vegetable Oils	#	#	1,499	505	59	#	27	#
Processed Oils	#	#	#	#	#	#	#	#
Fish and Fishery Products	~	#	#	#	12	18	#	#
Forest Products	~	20,450	11,310	13,740	5,923	5,923	5,923	5,923
Agricultural Requisites	#	#	#	#	#	#	#	#
Crude Fertilizers	#	#	#	#	#	#	#	#
Manuf Fertilizers	#	#	#	#	#	#	#	#
Pesticides	#	#	#	#	#	#	#	#
Agricultural Machines	#	#	#	#	#	#	#	#

SOURCE: FAO-TY, 1980, Section IV; 1981, Section IV; 1983, Section IV; 1985, Section IV; 1986, Section IV; 1987, Section IV.

Table 2522

BRAZIL ABSOLUTE VALUE OF TRADE, 1970–86

(T US)

Imports

Category	1970	1980	1981	1982	1983	1984	1985	1986
Total Merchandise Trade	2,849,243	24,960,544	24,079,000	21,069,310	16,800,570	15,209,840	14,346,470	15,554,580
Agricultural Products, Total	300,618	2,470,568	2,186,730	1,796,050	1,465,380	1,503,170	1,365,610	2,467,360
Food and Animals	253,999	2,050,629	1,708,290	1,331,080	1,298,550	1,195,960	1,070,320	1,997,330
Live Animals	11,188	33,616	22,060	19,740	17,350	9,620	11,780	15,180
Meat and Meat Prep	895	95,715	76,690	20,710	24,140	29,820	41,010	469,430
Dairy Products Eggs	14,351	90,784	22,100	24,070	28,350	21,600	24,690	283,960
Cereals and Prep	155,130	1,537,363	1,355,880	1,016,310	1,064,960	986,330	864,640	967,410
Fruits and Vegetables	68,974	274,764	212,960	237,470	154,770	143,000	120,450	247,560
Sugar and Honey	168	4,147	4,450	2,670	1,830	920	1,240	3,630
Coffee, Tea, Cocoa Sp	1,675	6,184	6,360	6,262	4,400	2,660	3,290	4,200
Feeding Stuff	1,411	7,213	6,260	2,934	1,890	1,350	1,870	5,390
Miscellaneous Food	207	843	1,540	920	850	660	1,350	1,580
Beverages Tobacco	6,859	19,500	15,180	13,381	13,550	9,910	15,560	30,710
Beverages	6,782	17,801	14,510	12,460	12,440	9,770	15,440	30,300
Tobacco	77	1,699	670	922	1,100	140	120	410
Crude Materials	18,080	295,474	420,150	408,450	99,630	171,780	184,190	309,740
Hides and Skins	1,174	6,511	8,090	4,060	1,840	3,620	4,460	25,270
Oilseeds	65	131,002	279,280	316,860	12,720	43,320	55,540	74,830
Natural Rubber	6,519	97,306	80,122	46,270	43,730	72,310	61,340	73,420
Textile Fibers	4,378	24,487	21,590	12,540	12,470	30,740	36,910	92,450
Crude Mat Nes	5,944	36,168	31,070	28,730	28,880	21,810	25,940	43,770
Animal Vegetable Oil	21,680	104,965	43,104	43,140	53,660	125,520	95,550	129,590
Animal Fats	8,220	42,567	18,234	10,240	13,960	24,130	12,990	37,300
Fixed Vegetable Oils	13,327	61,880	24,650	32,510	39,560	101,280	82,340	92,130
Processed Oils	133	518	221	393	150	110	230	160
Fish and Fishery Products	~	89,650	68,080	77,310	43,160	40,700	47,790	130,530
Forest Products	~	274,220	282,090	298,750	161,250	174,660	148,390	204,540
Agricultural Requisites	185,272	909,995	511,650	345,330	189,000	307,250	285,110	311,770
Crude Fertilizers	8,149	57,830	37,650	16,640	1,980	2,390	3,640	5,380
Manuf Fertilizers	70,637	777,850	436,403	297,260	169,770	297,230	270,840	293,520
Pesticides	18,771	30,991	7,860	7,546	4,950	3,060	5,480	9,180
Agriculture Machines	87,715	43,324	29,741	23,894	12,290	4,570	5,150	3,690

Exports

Category	1970	1980	1981	1982	1983	1984	1985	1986
Total Merchandise Trade	2,738,922	20,132,400	23,293,040	20,175,072	21,899,320	27,005,340	25,639,000	25,594,160
Agricultural Products, Total	1,972,459	9,377,840	9,621,240	8,035,730	8,992,000	1,043,450	9,421,970	7,653,910
Food and Animals	1,589,558	7,769,390	7,780,170	6,721,260	7,298,820	8,489,050	7,172,310	6,615,530
Live Animals	20,320	3,100	2,820	1,700	2,270	2,760	1,360	1,880
Meat and Meat Prep	101,208	540,170	870,910	809,740	832,830	867,240	844,350	678,580
Dairy Products Eggs	435	12,769	23,540	6,180	5,520	2,750	1,980	3,110
Cereals and Prep	88,034	20,243	48,191	75,102	83,470	59,160	16,370	10,270
Fruits and Vegetables	59,868	543,510	871,800	781,830	797,900	1,621,700	1,000,690	925,660
Sugar and Honey	134,492	1,398,202	1,161,430	599,920	571,050	635,530	426,470	467,430
Coffee, Tea, Cocoa Sp	1,107,567	3,592,827	2,486,030	2,637,110	2,998,660	3,673,270	3,555,650	3,131,410
Feeding Stuff	77,541	1,609,672	2,272,490	1,780,740	1,968,990	1,592,940	1,302,630	1,361,110
Miscellaneous Food	93	48,899	42,980	28,960	38,150	33,710	22,820	36,080
Beverages Tobacco	34,440	308,328	385,731	486,440	477,110	475,230	466,350	428,340
Beverages	1,471	13,067	17,070	9,520	5,160	6,660	7,020	15,130
Tobacco	32,969	295,261	368,660	476,930	471,950	468,570	459,330	413,210
Crude Materials	280,597	609,265	575,640	276,250	618,970	609,440	945,290	348,310
Hides and Skins	25,539	470	1,370	8,690	13,100	2,770	1,810	470
Oilseeds	40,758	415,681	436,262	138,131	316,940	464,770	777,300	252,180
Natural Rubber	4,424	91	100	80	10	140	20	20
Textile Fibers	203,009	154,027	101,630	99,450	257,380	104,290	129,080	59,630
Crude Mat Nes	6,867	38,996	36,280	29,900	31,540	37,460	37,090	36,000
Animal Vegetable Oils	67,864	690,852	879,700	551,770	597,090	860,780	838,020	261,740
Animal Fats	22	56	90	64	10	90	120	260
Fixed Vegetable Oils	57,769	670,790	858,680	534,180	581,660	845,150	819,730	238,030
Processed Oils	10,073	20,006	20,930	17,530	15,430	15,550	18,170	23,440
Fish and Fishery Products	~	132,760	155,860	161,600	137,290	179,320	174,280	153,850
Forest Products	~	864,590	944,320	695,380	822,030	1,027,080	800,620	936,350
Agricultural Requisites	2,214	231,863	269,021	203,963	167,360	199,670	179,880	180,320
Crude Fertilizers	108	412	294	194	10	20	~	~
Manuf Fertilizers	11	2,760	4,200	8,581	36,920	13,660	8,350	7,900
Pesticides	376	27,320	31,794	42,710	45,420	59,370	45,280	42,260
Agricultural Machines	1,719	201,371	232,740	152,482	85,000	126,620	126,250	130,160

SOURCE: FAO-TY, 1975, Section IV; 1980, Section IV; 1981, Section IV; 1983, Section IV; 1985, Section IV; 1986, Section IV; 1987, Section IV.

Table 2523

CHILE ABSOLUTE VALUE OF TRADE, 1970–86

(T US)

Imports

Category	1970	1980	1981	1982	1983	1984	1985	1986
Total Merchandise Trade	960,820	5,123,135	6,150,010	3,077,420	2,694,920	3,190,600	2,964,040	2,964,040
Agricultural Products, Total	175,477	812,276	793,607	512,100	530,757	484,233	266,622	197,027
Food and Animals	121,104	668,988	632,980	399,046	404,548	340,880	160,734	112,219
Live Animals	24,747	3,958	6,627	1,303	1,185	1,717	1,383	1,380
Meat and Meat Prep	8,765	18,554	28,925	14,302	4,674	10,290	7,982	4,679
Dairy Products Eggs	6,548	43,087	48,171	29,819	27,973	23,647	5,377	796
Cereals and Prep	37,508	261,580	280,553	216,656	239,195	173,365	72,246	36,441
Fruits and Vegetables	13,435	34,583	43,137	22,171	17,685	14,985	12,528	13,732
Sugar and Honey	4,598	214,691	125,223	49,934	51,255	44,295	2,343	4,321
Coffee, Tea, Cocoa Sp	19,224	63,590	60,011	38,725	38,889	47,426	39,553	34,924
Feeding Stuff	1,695	13,794	17,083	11,898	12,429	13,062	8,030	9,207
Miscellaneous Food	4,584	15,151	23,250	14,238	11,263	12,093	7,172	7,239
Beverages Tobacco	4,197	45,342	54,618	46,139	18,255	9,692	7,648	10,573
Beverages	308	23,374	28,223	13,554	9,927	7,331	5,217	7,516
Tobacco	3,889	21,968	26,395	32,585	8,328	2,361	2,431	3,057
Crude Materials	34,798	49,154	50,164	22,646	41,298	53,705	40,716	48,377
Hides and Skins	3,663	4,077	3,265	60	#	141	101	923
Oilseeds	214	1,420	1,177	857	917	1,023	980	1,656
Natural Rubber	3,441	8,253	7,517	1,199	6,305	8,636	5,861	5,182
Textile Fibers	25,388	26,881	29,344	15,262	25,833	36,148	27,852	33,575
Crude Mat Nes	2,092	8,523	8,861	5,265	8,243	7,757	5,922	7,041
Animal Vegetable Oil	15,378	48,792	55,845	44,269	66,656	79,956	61,644	25,358
Animal Fats	1,512	3,694	3,109	2,108	3,055	4,236	2,193	1,226
Fixed Vegetable Oils	13,428	40,781	48,921	39,438	59,933	71,553	55,034	19,862
Processed Oils	438	4,317	3,815	2,723	3,668	4,167	4,417	4,270
Fish and Fishery Products	~	4,914	5,884	4,529	2,300	1,600	800	200
Forest Products	~	45,100	43,300	24,900	49,300	47,413	41,600	34,436
Agricultural Requisites	40,797	119,504	117,801	36,590	65,800	81,184	100,489	113,904
Crude Fertilizers	1,200†	6	2,803	#	3,875	4,530	939	608
Manuf Fertilizers	20,526	65,778	61,540	19,073	33,922	47,631	49,702	52,907
Pesticides	4,751	20,218	21,193	12,500	25,226	20,000	33,204	37,999
Agriculture Machines	14,320	33,502	32,265	5,017	2,777	9,023	16,644	22,390

Exports

Category	1970	1980	1981	1982	1983	1984	1985	1986
Total Merchandise Trade	1,253,390	4,583,915	3,883,860	3,746,610	3,619,620	3,547,160	3,665,050	4,165,540
Agricultural Products, Total	40,221	391,611	395,609	375,197	357,872	474,949	560,807	740,662
Food and Animals	26,331	316,356	326,707	302,359	292,127	403,412	482,180	648,334
Live Animals	110	2,452	2,434	1,631	1,717	2,293	1,601	2,118
Meat and Meat Prep	- -	7,490	11,289	7,579	4,996	5,640	8,431	15,146
Dairy Products Eggs	- -	2,360	218	65	178	684	1,328	5,059
Cereals and Prep	1,686	21,993	17,093	14,284	9,609	20,259	10,366	9,124
Fruits and Vegetables	24,230	236,590	269,295	264,846	258,032	356,828	445,042	594,151
Sugar and Honey	45	29,362	13,011	1,119	3,171	1,133	2,278	3,006
Coffee, Tea, Cocoa Sp	28	439	247	683	497	478	359	1,291
Feeding Stuff	330	15,539	12,877	11,670	13,908	15,942	12,367	15,321
Miscellaneous Food	- -	131	243	482	19	155	408	2,118
Beverages Tobacco	1,840	20,445	17,125	16,508	14,124	17,308	20,768	20,647
Beverages	1,840	20,414	16,631	13,181	10,851	13,125	13,539	16,641
Tobacco	- -	31	494	3,327	3,273	4,183	7,229	4,006
Crude Materials	11,654	53,287	50,346	55,061	50,435	53,328	56,971	70,885
Hides and Skins	1,026	4,777	3,099	5,985	3,380	3,941	4,236	4,469
Oilseeds	788	159	368	341	194	202	287	334
Natural Rubber	- -	#	#	#	93	#	#	#
Textile Fibers	6,477	22,797	19,799	21,479	16,009	18,003	16,942	25,579
Crude Mat Nes	3,363	25,554	27,080	27,256	30,759	31,182	35,506	40,493
Animal Vegetable Oils	396	1,523	1,431	1,269	1,186	901	888	796
Animal Fats	- -	28	13	#	#	#	#	#
Fixed Vegetable Oils	- -	#	#	#	76	69	43	306
Processed Oils	396	1,495	1,418	1,269	1,110	832	845	490
Fish and Fishery Products	~	322,983	326,554	386,340	419,028	419,373	438,630	516,043
Forest Products	~	458,761	368,597	320,900	312,108	371,229	354,111	369,721
Agricultural Requisites	17,644	57,056	51,106	46,100	53,395	46,577	52,421	56,588
Crude Fertilizers	17,519	37,377	34,380	28,200	29,619	28,291	32,893	35,807
Manuf Fertilizers	- -	17,640	16,256	16,200	22,198	16,486	18,625	18,472
Pesticides	125	1,722	351	1,500	1,378	1,600	859	2,025
Agricultural Machines	- -	317	119	200	200	200	44	284

SOURCE: FAO-TY, 1975, Section IV; 1980, Section IV; 1981, Section IV; 1983, Section IV;
1985, Section IV; 1986, Section IV; 1987, Section IV.

Table 2524

COLOMBIA ABSOLUTE VALUE OF TRADE, 1970–86

(T US)

Imports

Category	1970	1980	1981	1982	1983	1984	1985	1986
Total Merchandise Trade	754,600	4,662,604	5,199,149	5,463,080	4,966,940	4,492,390	4,130,685	3,852,085
Agricultural Products, Total	81,137	534,818	494,054	556,280	541,116	438,911	410,272	342,244
Food and Animals	40,566	334,314	267,991	319,376	344,193	249,610	228,749	201,230
Live Animals	616	6,742	4,229	7,078	8,049	6,412	7,044	3,521
Meat and Meat Prep	230	1,049	2,115	2,847	2,918	2,833	2,247	1,932
Dairy Products Eggs	4,565	36,581	53,991	14,450	14,775	6,940	5,697	6,446
Cereals and Prep	21,055	202,551	121,966	177,865	211,647	164,749	155,996	128,670
Fruits and Vegetables	3,651	55,932	48,851	67,638	68,122	30,956	26,769	35,164
Sugar and Honey	587	5,399	5,594	5,087	3,386	2,982	2,062	2,475
Coffee, Tea, Cocoa Sp	9,366	10,019	10,044	13,418	6,621	7,742	9,395	6,806
Feeding Stuff	255	5,244	6,997	15,842	17,361	17,603	11,451	6,940
Miscellaneous Food	241	10,797	14,204	15,151	11,314	9,393	8,088	9,276
Beverages Tobacco	13,009	49,199	46,335	49,474	42,613	23,541	17,180	17,117
Beverages	4,007	23,456	23,351	24,156	18,651	13,850	9,769	8,606
Tobacco	9,002	25,743	22,984	25,318	23,962	9,691	7,411	8,511
Crude Materials	17,926	62,253	49,044	74,594	74,342	80,402	93,517	68,616
Hides and Skins	43	15	86	294	44	#	66	103
Oilseeds	613	10,360	1,149	20,494	27,386	24,890	35,613	11,230
Natural Rubber	4,256	19,316	19,685	17,664	17,245	20,809	23,255	17,352
Textile Fibers	9,675	20,156	17,616	21,229	13,884	13,820	15,448	13,672
Crude Mat Nes	3,339	12,406	10,508	14,913	15,783	20,883	19,135	26,259
Animal Vegetable Oil	14,636	89,052	130,684	112,836	79,968	85,358	70,826	55,281
Animal Fats	5,369	23,161	21,141	25,720	24,398	27,245	28,128	19,988
Fixed Vegetable Oils	8,650	60,114	107,124	84,566	52,292	53,856	39,175	31,703
Processed Oils	617	5,777	2,419	2,550	2,978	4,257	3,523	3,590
Fish and Fishery Products	~	62,983	84,249	84,183	46,928	76,697	43,746	48,142
Forest Products	~	119,100	169,618	158,180	118,388	146,310	132,939	119,368
Agricultural Requisites	35,573	151,198	153,487	184,346	160,378	158,136	133,848	148,914
Crude Fertilizers	138	2,535	2,752	4,399	2,976	1,967	1,231	1,571
Manuf Fertilizers	20,418	74,798	66,575	88,075	67,738	83,721	86,906	72,913
Pesticides	1,355	19,403	21,406	28,857	30,021	33,249	32,135	49,690
Agriculture Machines	13,662	54,462	62,754	63,015	59,643	39,199	13,576	24,740

Exports

Category	1970	1980	1981	1982	1983	1984	1985	1986
Total Merchandise Trade	735,657	3,945,048	2,956,400	3,094,967	3,080,893	3,483,140	3,551,885	5,107,936
Agricultural Products, Total	597,394	3,045,363	2,102,763	2,154,057	2,001,365	2,310,206	2,268,172	3,588,262
Food and Animals	551,115	2,822,806	1,867,532	1,982,215	1,830,039	2,105,110	2,047,083	3,365,672
Live Animals	36,253	63,247	71,152	98,180	212	604	1,250	812
Meat and Meat Prep	4,734	27,289	53,637	45,662	30,597	10,523	6,326	17,826
Dairy Products Eggs	417	20,448	16,745	10,089	273	#	#	20
Cereals and Prep	1,546	22,836	14,374	5,911	10,012	16,290	18,155	7,046
Fruits and Vegetables	19,927	107,471	142,398	169,355	158,044	205,735	163,860	210,410
Sugar and Honey	15,119	195,990	93,046	64,482	78,877	42,763	43,415	50,939
Coffee, Tea, Cocoa Sp	466,765	2,380,803	1,470,213	1,584,532	1,548,729	1,826,853	1,812,279	307,459
Feeding Stuff	6,252	1,546	1,541	906	552	435	457	910
Miscellaneous Food	102	3,176	4,426	3,098	2,653	1,907	1,341	2,250
Beverages Tobacco	7,217	26,862	21,901	24,656	24,988	24,382	25,556	25,728
Beverages	32	550	960	1,078	1,493	2,139	2,239	2,533
Tobacco	7,185	26,312	20,941	23,578	23,495	22,243	23,317	23,195
Crude Materials	39,038	195,611	213,283	147,147	146,283	180,698	195,533	196,862
Hides and Skins	1,671	#	#	#	#	#	58	58
Oilseeds	1,182	11,317	6,750	5,249	158	238	545	280
Natural Rubber	226	160	5	61	#	#	#	#
Textile Fibers	34,640	82,603	93,857	26,829	23,499	49,224	60,720	45,349
Crude Mat Nes	1,319	101,531	112,671	115,008	122,626	131,236	134,210	151,175
Animal Vegetable Oils	24	84	47	39	55	16	#	#
Animal Fats	- -	#	#	#	#	#	#	#
Fixed Vegetable Oils	- -	26	3	10	#	#	#	#
Processed Oils	24	58	44	29	55	16	#	#
Fish and Fishery Products	~	35,036	33,170	32,712	27,365	29,956	31,695	36,080
Forest Products	~	26,726	15,784	7,634	9,339	16,405	13,952	14,052
Agricultural Requisites	719	32,415	28,038	25,589	28,809	26,717	30,192	28,176
Crude Fertilizers	- -	6	2	53	70	100	#	375
Manuf Fertilizers	6	7,893	2,357	25	2,503	35	5,547	205
Pesticides	424	21,042	21,274	20,948	25,124	25,271	22,117	25,263
Agricultural Machines	289	3,474	4,405	4,563	1,112	1,311	2,528	2,333

SOURCE: FAO-TY, 1975, Section IV; 1980, Section IV; 1981, Section IV; 1983, Section IV; 1985, Section IV; 1986, Section IV; 1987, Section IV.

Table 2525

COSTA RICA ABSOLUTE VALUE OF TRADE, 1970–86

(T US)

Imports

Country	1970	1980	1981	1982	1983	1984	1985	1986
Total Merchandise Trade	316.687	1,523,800	1,208,500	893,125	988,500	1,086,246	1,098,178	1,163,000
Agricultural Products, Total	35,079	143,097	114,697	86,973	106,662	109,592	92,624	80,827
Food and Animals	28,037	108,324	92,036	71,567	90,608	84,537	70,592	59,142
Live Animals	1,885	1,198	476	1,027	3,811	2,605	478	387
Meat and Meat Prep	1,011	7,858	3,259	2,240	3,616	3,784	5,881	3,680
Dairy Products Eggs	1,696	9,672	7,139	2,205	4,984	5,061	3,017	3,050
Cereals and Prep	10,775	45,407	43,052	37,677	50,159	37,922	28,107	27,240
Fruits and Vegetables	6,665	20,316	15,377	13,524	9,266	12,004	10,929	2,485
Sugar and Honey	1,053	3,067	1,770	5,323	1,373	2,345	2,331	3,050
Coffee, Tea, Cocoa Sp	562	3,538	2,608	1,533	2,392	3,365	2,364	2,460
Feeding Stuff	2,612	11,374	15,616	5,630	12,038	12,402	12,415	6,540
Miscellaneous Food	1,677	5,894	2,739	2,408	2,969	5,049	5,070	5,240
Beverages Tobacco	1,644	10,157	7,560	4,776	5,630	6,682	5,901	6,301
Beverages	1,113	9,611	7,371	4,582	5,121	6,370	5,639	6,151
Tobacco	531	546	189	194	509	312	262	150
Crude Materials	2,075	13,096	7,871	6,176	8,172	10,063	7,138	7,806
Hides and Skins	32	1,780	134	710	681	889	#	#
Oilseeds	630	3,244	479	407	433	729	612	500
Natural Rubber	490	2,171	4,319	2,615	2,860	3,060	1,974	2,900
Textile Fibers	419	1,485	860	527	1,198	512	783	406
Crude Mat Nes	504	4,416	2,079	1,917	3,000	4,873	3,769	4,000
Animal Vegetable Oil	3,323	11,520	7,230	4,454	2,252	8,310	8,993	7,578
Animal Fats	63	871	579	391	420	518	546	450
Fixed Vegetable Oils	3,126	10,073	5,619	3,694	1,520	7,376	8,032	6,698
Processed Oils	134	576	1,032	369	312	416	415	430
Fish and Fishery Products	~	4,754	1,829	907	2,931	5,343	5,211	5,270
Forest Products	~	59,545	79,215	71,386	64,854	69,018	66,231	66,831
Agricultural Requisites	17,236	82,679	58,596	55,117	70,126	74,837	61,907	49,175
Crude Fertilizers	9	141	407	139	1,104	2,075	1,683	800
Manuf Fertilizers	7,497	29,724	15,841	15,977	18,249	21,828	18,705	14,824
Pesticides	5,432	35,287	34,954	35,268	42,713	36,508	30,737	19,901
Agricultural Machines	4,298	17,527	7,394	3,733	8,060	14,426	10,782	13,650

Exports

Category	1970	1980	1981	1982	1983	1984	1985	1986
Total Merchandise Trade	231,163	1,001,700	1,008,100	870,416	874,626	951,260	927,515	1,076,600
Agricultural Products, Total	182,315	659,967	666,792	602,885	543,261	682,254	652,549	751,811
Food and Animals	179,984	645,613	656,036	590,122	527,064	663,317	629,710	727,201
Live Animals	101	1,155	2,680	1,777	3,000	249	1,112	2,100
Meat and Meat Prep	18,467	75,547	79,665	56,243	33,488	46,689	55,827	65,100
Dairy Products Eggs	538	363	233	458	1,257	1,556	253	45
Cereals and Prep	1,174	18,910	27,621	8,959	17,438	18,272	1,987	8,224
Fruits and Vegetables	68,943	229,885	241,854	246,664	234,632	271,317	225,058	242,328
Sugar and Honey	10,868	42,701	43,800	17,966	18,803	37,564	6,156	15,282
Coffee, Tea, Cocoa Sp	75,773	265,601	251,572	249,729	214,066	277,418	328,907	384,122
Feeding Stuff	308	1,337	1,611	1,194	951	838	1,880	900
Miscellaneous Food	3,852	10,114	7,500	7,132	3,429	9,414	8,530	9,100
Beverages Tobacco	228	1,058	1,078	1,504	548	659	927	600
Beverages	65	249	402	236	96	138	74	100
Tobacco	163	809	676	1,268	452	521	853	500
Crude Materials	1,874	13,206	9,479	11,078	15,490	17,914	21,789	24,000
Hides and Skins	269	12	#	#	#	2	#	#
Oilseeds	292	1,032	168	581	496	1,061	220	#
Natural Rubber	- -	#	#	#	#	#	#	#
Textile Fibers	403	1,460	14	2	5	18	36	#
Crude Mat Nes	910	10,702	9,297	10,495	14,989[‡]	16,833	21,533	24,000
Animal Vegetable Oil	229	90	199	181	159	364	123	10
Animal Fats	124	#	#	#	#	#	#	#
Fixed Vegetable Oils	92	9	27	181	159	224	80	#
Processed Oils	13	81	172	#	#	140	43	10
Fish and Fishery Products	~	9,247	7,469	6,754	12,276	17,648	28,877	32,260
Forest Products	~	20,901	20,376	19,509	22,311	16,559	16,942	16,942
Agricultural Requisites	3,092	20,931	25,834	21,817	15,667	12,637	12,962	10,655
Crude Fertilizers	- -	#	#	#	#	#	#	#
Manuf Fertilizers	2,410	10,057	15,631	7,864	5,441	5,852	7,854	4,102
Pesticides	581	10,709	10,006	13,749	10,000[†]	6,540	4,911	6,298
Agricultural Machines	101	165	197	204	226	245	197	255

SOURCE: FAO-TY, 1975, Section IV; 1980, Section IV; 1981, Section IV; 1983, Section IV;
1985, Section IV; 1986, Section IV; 1987, Section IV.

Table 2526

CUBA ABSOLUTE VALUE OF TRADE, 1980-86

(T US)

Imports

Category	1980	1981	1982	1983	1984	1985	1986
Total Merchandise Trade	6,349,800	6,443,640	6,609,070	7,435,410	8,159,850	8,726,010	9,173,630
Agricultural Products, Total	1,140,148	1,115,053	1,074,013	1,050,631	1,130,802	1,143,018	1,020,089
Food and Animals	931,942	920,243	915,210	855,039	897,206	912,414	785,966
Live Animals	#	#	#	#	#	#	2,500
Meat and Meat Prep	84,585	96,935	128,659	117,152	119,649	115,181	93,364
Dairy Products Eggs	94,417	82,942	83,811	93,197	90,398	91,420	104,243
Cereals and Prep	501,760	488,498	479,846	425,997	443,862	483,548	347,377
Fruits and Vegetables	93,848	109,752	90,291	78,420	80,682	87,823	72,428
Sugar and Honey	#	#	#	#	#	#	#
Coffee, Tea, Cocoa Sp	28,584	25,851	12,231	2,466	5,420	6,833	11,318
Feeding Stuff	56,397	58,045	61,919	70,234	89,343	58,466	68,520
Miscellaneous Food	72,351	58,222	58,453	67,573	67,852	69,143	86,216
Beverages Tobacco	22,844	14,253	11,617	11,397	8,675	8,436	9,976
Beverages	5,882	9,535	7,002	9,089	8,165	7,599	7,951
Tobacco	16,962	4,718	4,615	2,308	510	837	3,025
Crude Materials	108,699	112,688	89,709	103,568	144,364	137,235	133,062
Hides and Skins	~	~	~	~	~	~	~
Oilseeds	165	459	#	7,054	9,397	7,108	5,738
Natural Rubber	4,871	3,453	1,623	3,761	4,934	2,200‡	2,200
Textile Fibers	62,932	64,963	62,582	61,028	77,235	77,562	72,689
Crude Mat Nes	40,731	43,813	22,504	31,725	52,798	50,365	52,435
Animal Vegetable Oil	76,663	67,867	57,477	80,627	80,557	84,933	91,085
Animal Fats	16,028	15,869	15,340	18,029	16,130	21,292	16,315
Fixed Vegetable Oils	60,635	51,998	42,137	61,849	64,072	63,041	74,020
Processed Oils	#	#	#	749	355	600	750
Fish and Fishery Products	81,357	85,250	35,144	36,372	24,758	54,362	39,780
Forest Products	200,881	180,773	197,270	207,735	253,549	252,747	252,747
Agricultural Requisites	233,974	250,270	271,608	271,321	312,027	291,047	290,100
Crude Fertilizers	1,075	1,032	707	267	1,298	464	1,000
Manuf Fertilizers	112,690	99,351	134,791	141,323	144,990	96,491	101,100
Pesticides	30,463	38,544	23,432	27,848	33,192	68,656	60,000
Agriculture Machines	89,746	111,343	112,578	101,883	132,547	125,436	128,000

Exports

Category	1980	1981	1982	1983	1984	1985	1986
Total Merchandise Trade	5,541,500	5,322,000	5,895,210	6,614,200	6,182,970	6,506,770	6,299,480
Agricultural Products, Total	4,843,859	4,470,328	4,899,097	5,290,112	4,963,277	5,222,792	5,266,470
Food and Animals	4,753,591	4,374,782	4,740,829	5,129,732	4,856,847	5,095,843	5,151,558
Live Animals	343	195	795	499	2,589	650	1,950
Meat and Meat Prep	334	410	192	234	585	682	322
Dairy Products Eggs	116	392	181	966	1,802	#	#
Cereals and Prep	#	#	#	#	#	#	#
Fruits and Vegetables	71,732	114,644	133,377	161,403	150,274	185,438	215,928
Sugar and Honey	4,648,556	4,216,160	4,556,598	4,901,925	4,663,232	4,855,199	4,857,556
Coffee, Tea, Cocoa Sp	32,510	38,261	45,887	56,345	24,082	41,607	56,144
Feeding Stuff	#	#	#	#	#	#	#
Miscellaneous Food	#	4,720	3,799	8,360	14,283	12,267	#
Beverages Tobacco	86,268	90,946	155,509	158,027	103,750	123,511	110,968
Beverages	35,136	20,683	31,469	34,947	39,825	23,669	18,949
Tobacco	51,132	70,263	124,040	123,080	63,925	99,842	92,019
Crude Materials	4,000	4,600	2,759	2,353	2,680	3,436	3,944
Hides and Skins	~	~	~	~	~	~	~
Oilseeds	#	#	#	#	#	#	#
Natural Rubber	#	#	#	#	#	#	#
Textile Fibers	#	1,870	774	#	#	#	#
Crude Mat Nes	4,000‡	2,730	1,985	2,353	2,680	3,438	3,944
Animal Vegetable Oils	#	#	#	#	#	#	#
Animal Fats	#	#	#	#	#	#	#
Fixed Vegetable Oils	#	#	#	#	#	#	#
Processed Oils	#	#	#	#	#	#	#
Fish and Fishery Products	123,813	120,178	146,259	157,523	84,330	117,995	123,080
Forest Products	#	#	#	#	#	#	#
Agricultural Requisites	#	#	#	79	83	#	#
Crude Fertilizers	#	#	#	#	#	#	#
Manuf Fertilizers	#	#	#	79	83	#	#
Pesticides	#	#	#	#	#	#	#
Agricultural Machines	#	#	#	#	#	#	#

SOURCE: FAO-TY, 1980, Section IV; 1981, Section IV; 1983, Section IV; 1985, Section IV; 1986, Section IV; 1987, Section IV.

Table 2527

DOMINICAN REPUBLIC ABSOLUTE VALUE OF TRADE, 1970–86
(T US)

				Imports				
Country	1970	1980	1981	1982	1983	1984	1985	1986
Total Merchandise Trade	278,034	1,498,397	1,450,169	1,255,817	1,279,000	1,257,100	1,247,918	1,432,072
Agricultural Products, Total	35,978	217,082	240,072	183,223	175,211	160,473	166,633	198,981
Food and Animals	25,146	148,909	174,667	104,915	122,102	99,263	105,111	132,327
Live Animals	1,197	2,049	1,518	2,972	3,702	859	1,295	1,091
Meat and Meat Prep	835	17,781	15,038	11,823	7,364	2,151	272	2,060
Dairy Products Eggs	6,926	15,370	13,740	8,618	15,239	12,349	10,814	16,290
Cereals and Prep	6,148	75,157	104,551	52,549	66,000	58,769	65,810	78,598
Fruits and Vegetables	4,579	9,836	5,725	4,805	4,350	3,636	7,903	11,518
Sugar and Honey	343	2,895	3,042	2,401	3,396	1,769	2,639	2,665
Coffee, Tea, Cocoa Sp	526	591	410	645	867	727	733	1,772
Feeding Stuff	2,168	10,714	14,147	12,908	16,585	14,904	12,568	14,643
Miscellaneous Food	2,424	14,516	16,496	8,194	4,599	4,099	3,077	3,690
Beverages Tobacco	2,670	6,366	7,599	5,816	3,594	3,315	2,937	11,592
Beverages	854	2,298	2,428	2,178	1,031	1,628	2,454	3,012
Tobacco	1,816	4,068	5,121	3,638	2,563	1,687	483	8,500
Crude Materials	803	16,283	14,418	9,460	7,894	10,054	10,563	14,760
Hides and Skins	--	1,331	454	#	#	#	#	#
Oilseeds	--	10,327	9,890	5,959	4,544	6,060	6,169	10,193
Natural Rubber	--	129	266	254	317	477	317	160
Textile Fibers	613	1,287	931	678	299	273	359	407
Crude Mat Nes	190[‡]	3,215	2,877	2,569	2,734	3,244	3,718[†]	4,000
Animal Vegetable Oil	7,359	45,518	43,388	63,032	41,621	47,841	48,022	40,382
Animal Fats	1,105	9,988	10,963	14,172	8,068	13,706	11,618	10,500
Fixed Vegetable Oils	6,248	30,290	26,032	46,994	28,218	33,109	35,832	29,310
Processed Oils	6	5,240	6,393	1,866	5,335	1,026	572	572
Fish and Fishery Products	~	24,205	19,027	16,847	15,984	7,901	15,256	15,855
Forest Products	~	71,392	73,145	62,290	58,834	61,337	48,996	54,796
Agricultural Requisites	8,248	71,495	56,621	37,654	34,290	33,775	30,725	35,700
Crude Fertilizers	--	12	1,113	3	43	112	53	50
Manuf Fertilizers	2,300	37,401	25,865	18,780	14,595	14,430	14,481	18,500
Pesticides	1,750[‡]	13,693	16,265	11,042	13,345	11,476	9,938	10,500
Agriculture Machines	4,198	20,389	13,378	7,829	6,307	7,757	6,253	6,650

				Exports				
Category	1970	1980	1981	1982	1983	1984	1985	1986
Total Merchandise Trade	213,957	963,309	1,198,738	791,365	787,710	872,373	753,387	716,896
Agricultural Products, Total	186,876	515,137	785,510	516,858	489,682	566,532	452,846	450,762
Food and Animals	171,598	478,827	713,500	488,367	460,567	517,697	425,891	421,548
Live Animals	--	35	40	43	24	64	61	61
Meat and Meat Prep	3,390	2,886	8,564	8,838	6,718	897	13,883	18,738
Dairy Products Eggs	2	20	#	82	64	#	#	#
Cereals and Prep	214	889	1,510	1,026	675	777	1,238	1,186
Fruits and Vegetables	6,243	26,648	29,303	29,080	31,241	38,955	48,053	59,597
Sugar and Honey	111,248	307,540	538,028	283,587	275,722	302,162	192,763	148,361
Coffee, Tea, Cocoa Sp	48,955	133,485	126,061	156,128	136,818	172,165	160,818	183,705
Feeding Stuff	1,380	1,642	1,876	1,063	1,822	1,402	2,095	1,900
Miscellaneous Food	166	5,682	8,118	8,520	7,483	1,275	6,980	8,000
Beverages Tobacco	14,648	34,374	67,675	24,571	24,524	33,820	23,413	26,102
Beverages	--	275	366	193	384	2,948	867	450
Tobacco	14,648	34,099	67,309	24,378	24,140	30,872	22,546	25,652
Crude Materials	324	1,243	1,655	1,702	2,301	1,854	1,500	2,000
Hides and Skins	35	74	89	89	24	#	#	#
Oilseeds	252	23	45	4	23	2	#	#
Natural Rubber	--	#	#	#	#	#	#	#
Textile Fibers	37	#	#	#	617	352	#	500
Crude Mat Nes	--	1,146	1,521	1,609	1,637	1,500[†]	1,500[†]	1,500
Animal Vegetable Oils	306	693	2,680	2,218	2,290	13,161	2,042	1,112
Animal Fats	--	#	#	#	#	#	#	#
Fixed Vegetable Oils	--	#	1,800	1,517	1,600	12,500	1,575	350
Processed Oils	306	693	880	701	690	661	467	762
Fish and Fishery Products	~	1,098	1,271	1,287	1,443	1,108	3,074[†]	3,180
Forest Products	~	#	17	#	#	#	#	#
Agricultural Requisites	--	19,701	15,750	7,597	1,812	6,147	4,667	4,630
Crude Fertilizers	--	7	#	#	1	#	524	#
Manuf Fertilizers	--	19,638	15,705	7,569	1,790	6,129	4,119	4,600
Pesticides	--	55	36	7	12	10[†]	24	30
Agricultural Machines	--	1	9	21	9	8	#	#

SOURCE: FAO-TY, 1975, Section IV; 1980, Section IV; 1981, Section IV; 1983, Section IV; 1985, Section IV; 1986, Section IV; 1987, Section IV.

Table 2528

ECUADOR ABSOLUTE VALUE OF TRADE, 1970-86
(T US)

Imports

Category	1970	1980	1981	1982	1983	1984	1985	1986
Total Merchandise Trade	238,317	2,253,305	2,439,859	2,168,952	1,487,426	1,616,285	1,766,724	1,810,224
Agricultural Products, Total	19,376	181,864	180,704	174,435	216,249	203,401	156,596	126,645
Food and Animals	9,839	117,178	113,994	105,959	140,505	121,903	100,798	98,828
Live Animals	317	1,859	4,711	4,537	4,908	1,430	10,899	11,336
Meat and Meat Prep	40	81	47	110	28	119	250	440
Dairy Products Eggs	934	8,332	6,131	5,600	5,116	2,730	5,711	3,322
Cereals and Prep	6,503	86,270	87,596	76,923	91,008	81,591	72,073	64,293
Fruits and Vegetables	533	5,220	5,334	5,029	2,115	3,708	2,787	3,648
Sugar and Honey	116	1,713	1,215	3,226	28,771	23,994	5,063	11,630
Coffee, Tea, Cocoa Sp	340	1,247	983	671	547	127	15	36
Feeding Stuff	16	3,232	1,810	1,961	2,972	4,220	#	49
Miscellaneous Food	1,040	9,224	6,167	7,896	5,040	3,934	4,000	4,074
Beverages Tobacco	1,923	21,396	13,438	12,194	7,344	4,646	6,081	7,919
Beverages	364	11,457	7,738	8,258	3,156	1,261	6,081	7,919
Tobacco	1,559	9,939	5,700	3,936	4,188	3,385	#	#
Crude Materials	939	7,621	15,641				14,539	8,900
Hides and Skins	- -	#	#	#	#	#	#	#
Oilseeds	- -	143	6,136	5,069	11,143	10,846	101	125
Natural Rubber	310	4,063	6,714	2,284	2,174	1,601	2,223	3,778
Textile Fibers	461	772	715	831	11,582	19,664	8,015	497
Crude Mat Nes	168	2,643	2,076	5,651	3,845	4,613	4,200[†]	4,500
Animal Vegetable Oil	6,675	35,669	37,631	42,447	39,656	40,128	35,178	10,998
Animal Fats	3,520	10,518	7,604	6,468	7,019	7,616	1,009	3,485
Fixed Vegetable Oils	2,924	24,892	29,937	35,848	32,433	32,308	33,434	7,390
Processed Oils	231	259	90	131	204	204	75	123
Fish and Fishery Products	~	199,968	61	92	40	28	96	5
Forest Products	~	27,334	122,542	137,679	123,097	119,762	121,447	107,690
Agricultural Requisites	10,430	84,126	70,469	91,199	62,193	96,676	125,677	9,170
Crude Fertilizers	- -	865	901	300	6	73	303	34
Manuf Fertilizers	4,092	27,723	16,668	25,604	19,089	30,837	33,702	16,566
Pesticides	2,605	17,966	19,635	25,209	20,906	44,898	40,542	37,580
Agriculture Machines	3,733	35,572	33,265	42,086	22,192	20,868	51,130	37,580

Exports

Category	1970	1980	1981	1982	1983	1984	1985	1986
Total Merchandise Trade	210,300	2,480,804	2,523,838	2,327,487	2,347,751	2,620,419	2,904,746	2,185,849
Agricultural Products, Total	175,760	623,348	530,822	523,368	378,818	511,887	596,182	818,499
Food and Animals	170,998	604,858	504,302	500,652	364,527	497,644	582,228	803,621
Live Animals	2,579	#	#	#	4	28	#	#
Meat and Meat Prep	- -	57	47	631	263	19	#	33
Dairy Products Eggs	- -	#	#	16	#	#	#	#
Cereals and Prep	- -	68	235	5,332	580	645	7	62
Fruits and Vegetables	84,481	199,204	212,829	220,046	154,573	142,802	188,777	271,492
Sugar and Honey	8,739	44,257	21,747	2,479	712	14,792	8,063	8,015
Coffee, Tea, Cocoa Sp	75,112	358,533	268,175	271,154	207,507	338,105	383,788	522,818
Feeding Stuff	87	2,239	791	762	588	1,012	413	1
Miscellaneous Food	- -	500	478	232	300	241	1,180	1,200
Beverages Tobacco	525	1,964	2,065	5,693	1,451	1,480	2,200	3,045
Beverages	5	733	931	985	181	1	8	5
Tobacco	520	1,231	1,134	4,708	1,270	1,479	2,192	3,040
Crude Materials	4,237	12,865	19,842	12,375	11,059	7,936	10,724	10,406
Hides and Skins	155	428	331	26	#	7	283	123
Oilseeds	1,659	545	#	255	345	355	#	53
Natural Rubber	- -	#	#	#	#	12	#	#
Textile Fibers	421	8,442	16,079	8,515	9,046	5,880	8,441	8,230
Crude Mat Nes	2,002	3,450	3,432	3,579	1,668	1,682	2,000	2,000
Animal Vegetable Oils	- -	3,661	4,613	4,648	1,781	4,827	1,030	1,427
Animal Fats	- -	#	#	#	#	#	#	#
Fixed Vegetable Oils	- -	3,661	4,613	4,648	1,781	4,827	1,030	1,427
Processed Oils	- -	#	#	#	#	#	#	#
Fish and Fishery Products	~	199,968	188,821	219,562	219,372	216,067	260,939	383,565
Forest Products	~	27,334	28,487	28,672	16,169	18,657	11,547	15,342
Agricultural Requisites	13	350	252	687	95	11	99	217
Crude Fertilizers	- -	#	#	#	#	#	#	17
Manuf Fertilizers	- -	#	#	#	#	#	#	#
Pesticides	13	209	250[†]	687	90	11	99	200
Agriculture Machines	- -	141	2	#	5	#	#	#

SOURCE: FAO-TY, 1975, Section IV; 1980, Section IV; 1981, Section IV; 1983, Section IV;
1985, Section IV; 1986, Section IV; 1987, Section IV.

Table 2529

EL SALVADOR ABSOLUTE VALUE OF TRADE, 1970–86
(T US)

Imports

Category	1970	1980	1981	1982	1983	1984	1985	1986
Total Merchandise Trade	213,600	1,106,880	985,800	944,839	891,495	1,314,012	961,200	895,356
Agricultural Products, Total	30,837	173,573	179,598	161,825	150,336	171,065	137,356	104,659
Food and Animals	23,833	144,762	144,313	137,614	128,965	128,494	110,399	91,468
Live Animals	1,015	885	681	788	6,916	9,670	3,011	1,419
Meat and Meat Prep	812	7,046	5,239	4,730	4,602	6,950	5,346	5,484
Dairy Products Eggs	4,458	21,938	32,350	17,881	19,821	10,073	8,807	10,639
Cereals and Prep	5,808	43,840	37,529	43,980	45,823	51,864	49,222	40,832
Fruits and Vegetables	6,421	46,473	44,311	41,878	26,967	20,702	14,600	11,872
Sugar and Honey	1,650	4,650	3,733	4,811	3,525	3,757	3,402	3,701
Coffee, Tea, Cocoa Sp	757	4,140	1,952	2,519	1,989	3,600	1,594	663
Feeding Stuff	1,605	7,198	10,088	11,409	10,435	13,060	14,417	5,778
Miscellaneous Food	1,307	8,592	8,430	9,618	8,887	8,818	10,000	11,060
Beverages Tobacco	1,810	4,538	3,655	3,045	2,441	2,784	954	921
Beverages	474	2,075	1,082	1,022	1,132	1,801	195	403
Tobacco	1,336	2,463	2,573	2,023	1,309	983	759	518
Crude Materials	2,049	7,107	9,077	3,607	3,164	5,885	4,229	2,065
Hides and Skins	417	795	1,971	547	1,560	1,351	1,024	287
Oilseeds	255	295	270	282	46	287	1,833	502
Natural Rubber	384	1,868	2,338	1,553	98	1,891	21	36
Textile Fibers	696	1,542	2,932	90	69	1,279	251	40
Crude Mat Nes	297	2,607	1,566	1,135	1,391	1,107	1,100[†]	1,200
Animal Vegetable Oil	3,145	17,166	22,553	17,559	15,766	33,902	21,774	10,205
Animal Fats	2,269	12,022	12,891	11,776	11,732	19,802	16,000[†]	3,527
Fixed Vegetable Oils	850	5,034	8,915	5,460	3,956	13,720	5,763	6,642
Processed Oils	26	110	747	323	78	380	11	36
Fish and Fishery Products	~	3,738	2,417	948	570	1,541	916	1,220
Forest Products	~	29,851	34,677	35,525	35,240	35,347	32,675	19,587
Agricultural Requisites	33,485	42,846	66,717	36,757	41,715	46,579	73,040	38,680
Crude Fertilizers	109	#	#	#	8	18	550	#
Manuf Fertilizers	10,287	27,634	48,089	18,360	26,149	27,788	42,700	17,150
Pesticides	21,248	10,835	15,599	15,811	11,387	13,494	25,600	17,000
Agriculture Machines	1,841	4,377	3,029	2,586	4,171	5,279	4,190	4,530

Exports

Category	1970	1980	1981	1982	1983	1984	1985	1986
Total Merchandise Trade	228,320	1,080,100	791,920	704,040	735,300	615,029	678,800	744,667
Agricultural Products, Total	161,881	832,714	565,751	494,817	528,940	415,418	535,970	561,653
Food and Animals	136,536	734,721	501,473	444,041	465,119	395,995	493,784	548,466
Live Animals	914	1,472	1,545	854	984	740	438	421
Meat and Meat Prep	68	5,063	1,320	2,819	3,571	3,045	1,601	390
Dairy Products Eggs	824	530	212	396	743	184	399	678
Cereals and Prep	2,025	7,667	6,840	2,702	1,967	2,477	3,513	1,079
Fruits and Vegetables	130	6,056	5,003	7,135	2,830	6,780	2,926	2,941
Sugar and Honey	8,008	17,154	19,152	20,963	43,993	20,680	30,943	28,850
Coffee, Tea, Cocoa Sp	120,971	694,709	464,487	406,819	409,692	359,650	453,264	513,017
Feeding Stuff	1,931	804	1,373	1,341	290	1,726	#	190
Miscellaneous Food	1,665	1,266	1,541	1,012	1,049	713	700	900
Beverages Tobacco	204	3,430	2,656	2,233	1,878	2,416	817	866
Beverages	164	1,003	640	498	644	958	#	#
Tobacco	40	2,427	2,016	1,735	1,234	1,458	817	866
Crude Materials	24,360	93,783	61,337	48,415	61,688	16,747	39,133	12,289
Hides and Skins	- -	#	5	#	225	10	#	#
Oilseeds	338	4,063	3,690	992	1,420	5,277	6,823	5,063
Natural Rubber	- -	28	8	#	#	#	#	#
Textile Fibers	23,455	87,143	55,275	45,396	58,390	9,785	30,310	5,226
Crude Mat Nes	567	2,549	2,359	2,027	1,653	1,675	2,000[†]	2,000
Animal Vegetable Oils	781	780	285	128	255	260	2,236	32
Animal Fats	- -	#	#	#	#	#	#	#
Fixed Vegetable Oils	759	714	252	110	207	145	2,183	32
Processed Oils	22	66	33	18	48	115	53	#
Fish and Fishery Products	~	17,319	23,344	22,010	14,484	17,601	14,467	19,080
Forest Products	~	921	2,800	4,000	6,455	6,455	4,404	2,597
Agricultural Requisites	5,188	8,458	4,632	3,446	5,298	4,975	3,372	3,596
Crude Fertilizers	2	#	1	#	#	#	#	#
Manuf Fertilizers	3,211	#	17	100	2	76	#	#
Pesticides	1,920	6,077	4,015	2,924	5,111	4,674	3,107	3,300
Agricultural Machines	55	2,381	599	422	185	225	265	296

SOURCE: FAO-TY, 1975, Section IV; 1980, Section IV; 1981; Section IV; 1983, Section IV;
1985, Section IV; 1986, Section IV; 1987, Section IV.

Table 2530

GUATEMALA ABSOLUTE VALUE OF TRADE, 1970-86

(T US)

Imports								
Category	1970	1980	1981	1982	1983	1984	1985	1986
Total Merchandise Trade	284,274	1,559,085	1,623,612	1,420,370	1,154,340	1,448,334	1,296,736	624,000
Agricultural Products, Total	32,129	146,455	155,594	124,193	116,316	122,805	110,189	127,389
Food and Animals	23,911	119,543	126,980	91,684	84,632	77,551	68,871	80,773
Live Animals	1,769	23,828	28,331	1,293	1,750	2,032	1,192	1,310
Meat and Meat Prep	724	1,980	2,967	2,459	1,664	1,164	918	2,376
Dairy Products Eggs	2,849	13,033	10,023	13,409	7,244	10,316	9,370	15,669
Cereals and Prep	10,123	55,146	54,008	36,382	42,324	36,281	38,589	43,790
Fruits and Vegetables	1,813	11,146	13,322	.14,731	11,779	10,723	4,093	4,536
Sugar and Honey	659	2,132	2,958	3,478	2,732	2,790	1,892	1,859
Coffee, Tea, Cocoa Sp	746	3,149	2,947	2,660	2,771	2,508	2,159	2,204
Feeding Stuff	2,355	7,287	10,146	14,987	12,199	9,480	10,046	8,270
Miscellaneous Food	2,873	1,842	2,278	2,285	2,159	2,257	642	760
Beverages Tobacco	1,817	5,711	4,583	2,808	2,834	7,198	2,310	2,397
Beverages	1,258	3,128	3,136	2,208	2,123	7,085	2,258	2,363
Tobacco	559	2,082	1,447	600	711	113	52	34
Crude Materials	2,322	10,662	7,450	5,409	7,587	10,804	8,736	7,583
Hides and Skins	138	668	487	98	14	10	#	#
Oilseeds	295	2,278	1,789	1,488	538	2,860	563	371
Natural Rubber	567	88	28	14	#	#	24	30
Textile Fibers	727	4,801	2,498	1,934	5,295	5,374	4,964	3,982
Crude Mat Nes	595	2,527	2,648	1,875	1,740	2,560	3,185	3,200
Animal Vegetable Oil	4,079	10,539	16,581	24,292	21,263	27,252	30,272	36,636
Animal Fats	2,672	6,919	9,722	11,473	9,225	10,750	12,656	12,663
Fixed Vegetable Oils	1,328	3,241	5,791	11,392	11,025	15,567	17,332	23,619
Processed Oils	79	379	1,068	1,427	1,013	935	384	384
Fish and Fishery Products	~	2,446	2,301	2,213	1,815[†]	1,820[†]	1,200[†]	750
Forest Products	~	93,932	64,642	58,091	63,070	61,263	44,678	43,822
Agricultural Requisites	13,717	76,253	83,139	44,205	51,944	69,697	62,215	101,070
Crude Fertilizers	- -	47	40	94	3	7	#	#
Manuf Fertilizers	5,000	43,124	50,724	19,662	19,296	32,126	29,000[†]	60,236
Pesticides	3,714	16,506	17,092	16,942	24,856	28,208	26,659	34,154
Agriculture Machines	5,003	16,576	15,283	7,507	7,789	9,356	6,556	6,680

Exports								
Category	1970	1980	1981	1982	1983	1984	1985	1986
Total Merchandise Trade	290,182	1,472,796	1,109,241	1,083,800	1,118,354	1,094,631	991,694	1,062,000
Agricultural Products, Total	203,978	1,032,634	803,437	755,475	765,893	824,476	807,773	882,070
Food and Animals	163,843	769,573	622,602	603,194	652,715	633,523	643,632	763,432
Live Animals	523	17,441	13,728	11,913	6,515	11,074	3,678	5,300
Meat and Meat Prep	14,599	47,693	51,060	41,250	30,837	21,798	25,033	11,180
Dairy Products Eggs	1,162	3,025	3,135	2,122	2,149	2,067	1,124	450
Cereals and Prep	3,064	11,736	7,362	10,439	7,913	6,018	7,707	6,892
Fruits and Vegetables	22,025	100,683	93,591	108,044	106,177	91,634	87,613	105,148
Sugar and Honey	13,146	90,765	107,029	36,023	100,575	74,388	60,000	67,895
Coffee, Tea, Cocoa Sp	103,927	484,265	335,231	385,180	392,332	418,020	451,851	561,117
Feeding Stuff	2,212	4,779	3,257	2,513	1,181	2,836	2,305	850
Miscellaneous Food	3,185	9,186	8,209	5,710	5,036	5,688	4,221	4,600
Beverages Tobacco	3,084	17,887	17,257	20,056	15,375	19,223	14,320	11,700
Beverages	565	504	387	276	654	805	234	264
Tobacco	2,519	17,383	16,870	19,780	14,721	18,418	14,086	11,436
Crude Materials	36,345	244,860	163,484	132,068	97,652	171,397	149,854	106,921
Hides and Skins	107	83	27	44	6	6	#	#
Oilseeds	1,074	11,170	15,431	11,454	9,209	11,810	13,586	5,483
Natural Rubber	- -	#	#	#	#	#	#	#
Textile Fibers	27,215	172,336	111,433	82,107	47,272	72,002	67,996	31,438
Crude Mat Nes	7,949	61,271	36,593	38,463	41,165	87,579	68,272	70,000
Animal Vegetable Oils	706	314	94	157	151	333	67	17
Animal Fats	17	#	#	28	#	#	50	#
Fixed Vegetable Oils	633	222	79	56	1	11	#	#
Processed Oils	56	92	15	73	150	322	17	17
Fish and Fishery Products	~	8,854	7,294	12,843	8,934	11,900	9,307	7,600
Forest Products	~	22,454	23,617	15,118	14,141	10,324	10,035	9,458
Agricultural Requisites	587	28,135	33,417	29,588	21,188	21,000	15,945	9,162
Crude Fertilizers	- -	#	1	2	#	63	#	#
Manuf Fertilizers	- -	4,873	5,175	5,262	4,875	4,445	5,500	4,600
Pesticides	587	23,052	27,992	23,942	15,856	16,354	10,337	4,432
Agricultural Machines	- -	210	249	382	457	138	108	130

SOURCE: FAO-TY, 1975, Section IV; 1980, Section IV; 1981, Section IV; 1983, Section IV;
1985, Section IV; 1986, Section IV; 1987, Section IV.

Table 2531

HAITI ABSOLUTE VALUE OF TRADE, 1980–86

(T US)

Imports

Category	1980	1981	1982	1983	1984	1985	1986
Total Merchandise Trade	354,158	447,960	387,280	411,840	435,420	449,160	367,240
Agricultural Products, Total	120,663	127,927	112,207	112,408	109,070	121,561	115,301
Food and Animals	87,474	91,535	85,987	86,863	77,820	84,864	80,914
Live Animals	189	81	#	220	100	120	80
Meat and Meat Prep	1,430	1,304	1,175	1,383	3,725	5,625	7,990
Dairy Products Eggs	12,847	13,933	14,570	11,790	10,950	15,280	13,300
Cereals and Prep	53,120	54,689	53,445	49,775	42,698	44,783	39,443
Fruits and Vegetables	2,408	2,867	3,222	3,130	3,295	3,177	3,977
Sugar and Honey	11,769	7,703	4,615	11,920	6,620	4,737	5,837
Coffee, Tea, Cocoa Sp	1,052	1,386	1,120	1,155	2,017	1,668	1,473
Feeding Stuff	1,159	1,613	80	110	145	153	153
Miscellaneous Food	3,500	7,959	7,760	7,380	8,270	9,320	8,660
Beverages Tobacco	7,066	6,912	5,610	4,760	6,620	6,574	9,614
Beverages	1,382	2,159	1,990[†]	1,630[†]	2,370[†]	3,414[†]	1,934
Tobacco	5,684	4,753	3,620	3,130	4,250	3,160	7,680
Crude Materials	1,521	1,996	1,420	1,420	1,450	1,459	1,459
Hides and Skins	20	#	#	#	#	#	#
Oilseeds	#	#	#	#	#	#	#
Natural Rubber	10	12	#	#	#	#	#
Textile Fibers	491	790	220	220	250	259	259
Crude Mat Nes	1,000[†]	1,194	1,200[†]	1,200[†]	1,200[†]	1,200[†]	1,200
Animal Vegetable Oil	24,602	27,484	19,190	19,365	23,180	28,664	23,314
Animal Fats	8,125	9,871	8,000	9,500[†]	11,600[†]	9,300[†]	7,500
Fixed Vegetable Oils	16,477	16,844	11,190	9,865	11,580	19,364	15,814
Processed Oils	#	769	#	#	#	#	#
Fish and Fishery Products	4,784	2,050	3,560[†]	3,650[†]	6,580[†]	5,760	5,290
Forest Products	4,812	5,723	6,185	6,185	6,185	4,584	4,584
Agricultural Requisites	3,719	6,842	6,212	5,513	6,130	5,767	5,395
Crude Fertilizers	#	#	#	#	#	#	#
Manuf Fertilizers	1,020	3,292	1,900[†]	900[†]	1,250[†]	920[†]	590
Pesticides	1,283	1,755	2,000[†]	2,200[†]	2,300[†]	2,350[†]	2,250
Agriculture Machines	1,416	1,795[†]	2,312	2,413[†]	2,580[†]	2,497[†]	2,555

Exports

Category	1980	1981	1982	1983	1984	1985	1986
Total Merchandise Trade	225,700	155,100	181,320	188,700	219,380	226,520	193,860
Agricultural Products, Total	112,303	46,450	50,555	70,874	68,290	67,235	69,791
Food and Animals	108,829	44,703	42,204	67,331	64,312	63,299	66,205
Live Animals	#	#	#	#	#	#	#
Meat and Meat Prep	1,802	3,877	2,148	1,708	355	#	#
Dairy Products Eggs	#	#	#	#	#	#	#
Cereals and Prep	#	#	#	#	#	#	#
Fruits and Vegetables	2,108	2,304	2,509	2,408	2,642	2,700	2,700
Sugar and Honey	7,019	615	2,330	4,372	5,204	2,111	5,708
Coffee, Tea, Cocoa Sp	95,400	36,107	38,137	57,216	50,338	55,488	56,997
Feeding Stuff	2,500	1,800	2,080	1,627	5,773	3,000	800
Miscellaneous Food	#	#	#	#	#	#	#
Beverages Tobacco	267	306	187	298	371	381	381
Beverages	267	306	187	298	371	381	381
Tobacco	#	#	#	#	#	#	#
Crude Materials	3,078	1,323	3,164	3,245	3,607	3,555	3,205
Hides and Skins	1,449	771	1,332	2,955	2,671	2,700	2,700
Oilseeds	41	1	10	#	#	#	#
Natural Rubber	#	#	#	#	#	#	#
Textile Fibers	1,508	461	1,722	190	836	755[‡]	405
Crude Mat Nes	80[†]	90[†]	100[†]	100[†]	100[†]	100[†]	100
Animal Vegetable Oils	129	118	#	#	#	#	#
Animal Fats	#	#	#	#	#	#	#
Fixed Vegetable Oils	#	#	#	#	#	#	#
Processed Oils	129	118	#	#	#	#	#
Fish and Fishery Products	612	637	948	697	930	796	770
Forest Products	#	#	#	#	#	#	#
Agricultural Requisites	612	226	#	#	#	#	#
Crude Fertilizers	#	#	#	#	#	#	#
Manuf Fertilizers	#	#	#	#	#	#	#
Pesticides	#	#	#	#	#	#	#
Agricultural Machines	#	#	#	#	#	#	#

SOURCE: FAO-TY, 1980, Section IV; 1981, Section IV; 1983, Section IV; 1985,
Section IV; 1986, Section IV; 1987, Section IV.

Table 2532

HONDURAS ABSOLUTE VALUE OF TRADE, 1970–86

(T US)

				Imports				
Category	1970	1980	1981	1982	1983	1984	1985	1986
Total Merchandise Trade	220,668	1,008,689	945,105	692,118	822,950	813,438	953,450	1,242,600
Agricultural Products, Total	25,740	138,483	121,383	68,667	79,726	91,772	76,696	80,366
Food and Animals	20,728	117,941	98,376	55,884	68,445	75,441	65,295	66,058
Live Animals	485	35,164	22,609	740	600	788	2,563	1,420
Meat and Meat Prep	653	3,430	4,480	1,935	2,851	2,414	1,605	2,815
Dairy Products Eggs	3,315	11,887	13,151	8,540	14,703	14,174	14,107	14,980
Cereals and Prep	8,123	42,631	30,490	22,683	25,522	31,911	22,536	22,382
Fruits and Vegetables	2,652	7,970	9,619	5,616	5,607	6,599	4,407	4,608
Sugar and Honey	744	1,147	1,348	683	476	412	187	7
Coffee, Tea, Cocoa Sp	510	1,863	2,132	1,309	1,578	1,901	1,641	2,079
Feeding Stuff	824	4,909	4,305	5,255	6,326	6,353	7,239	7,234
Miscellaneous Food	3,389	8,940	10,247	9,123	10,782	10,889	11,010	10,515
Beverages Tobacco	1,684	4,406	7,069	4,457	2,509	4,664	1,308	2,698
Beverages	432	3,410	4,636	3,130	1,900	3,206	984	1,175
Tobacco	1,252	996	2,433	1,327	609	1,458	324	1,523
Crude Materials	469	4,502	4,606	2,956	3,830	4,940	4,294	4,757
Hides and Skins	105	7	#	#	#	#	#	#
Oilseeds	36	108	52	234	260	387	333	186
Natural Rubber	- -	105	1,022	174	398	957	1,160	1,270
Textile Fibers	74	1,943	2,217	1,633	1,837	2,092	1,801	2,301
Crude Mat Nes	254	2,339	1,315	915	1,335	1,504	1,000[†]	1,000
Animal Vegetable Oil	2,870	11,634	11,332	5,370	4,942	6,727	5,799	6,853
Animal Fats	1,615	5,001	2,669	2,111	2,236	2,243	2,682	4,500
Fixed Vegetable Oils	1,224	6,245	8,428	3,072	2,563	4,308	3,112	2,348
Processed Oils	31	388	235	187	143	176	5	5
Fish and Fishery Products	~	2,042	1,955	1,271	734	885	872	1,425
Forest Products	~	28,312	31,795	28,832	20,719	20,843	24,876	24,076
Agricultural Requisites	13,206	57,081	66,761	45,657	50,685	51,682	38,743	58,579
Crude Fertilizers	12	148	215	77	7	#	#	#
Manuf Fertilizers	3,329	16,507	21,997	12,602	15,654	19,653	12,361	18,079
Pesticides	3,086	21,321	30,065	26,335	27,088	27,428	23,506	30,807
Agriculture Machines	6,779	19,705	14,484	6,643	7,936	4,601	2,876	9,693

				Exports				
Country	1970	1980	1981	1982	1983	1984	1985	1986
Total Merchandise Trade	169,738	829,414	783,806	676,500	69,850	703,653	835,100	854,500
Agricultural Products, Total	123,766	625,798	572,392	498,111	480,812	527,021	574,594	670,989
Food and Animals	119,115	584,800	532,650	467,526	446,820	486,454	538,058	640,880
Live Animals	565	21,049	24,000	57	562	621	292	20
Meat and Meat Prep	9,719	60,923	47,340	34,560	31,520	19,591	18,251	18,000
Dairy Products Eggs	1	375	531	21	#	116	35	#
Cereals and Prep	1,038	2,318	2,302	2,533	1,684	5,379	6,322	#
Fruits and Vegetables	78,733	255,349	226,001	245,524	227,490	261,273	299,841	280,354
Sugar and Honey	1,675	34,081	56,753	28,261	30,853	29,363	24,404	15,800
Coffee, Tea, Cocoa Sp	26,061	208,678	174,143	155,380	152,745	169,055	188,576	326,156
Feeding Stuff	208	848	499	271	376	43	7	#
Miscellaneous Food	1,115	1,179	1,081	919	1,590	1,013	330	550
Beverages Tobacco	2,599	18,821	20,764	17,701	19,477	15,998	13,598	12,300
Beverages	6	12	52	#	9	57	#	#
Tobacco	2,593	18,809	20,712	17,701	19,468	15,941	13,598	12,300
Crude Materials	1,979	21,768	18,818	12,304	10,134	13,304	13,478	10,563
Hides and Skins	324	1,682	1,420	1,827	2,274	1,291	325	500
Oilseeds	276	2,814	1,360	788	1,152	1,643	3,336	2,063
Natural Rubber	57	82	35	9	#	#	#	#
Textile Fibers	1,232	13,648	12,578	6,630	4,229	7,815	6,817	5,000
Crude Mat Nes	90	3,542	3,425	3,050	2,479	2,555	3,000	3,000
Animal Vegetable Oils	73	409	160	580	4,381	11,265	9,460	7,246
Animal Fats	23	93	#	#	#	#	#	#
Fixed Vegetable Oils	49	309	114	576	4,367	11,265	9,460	7,246
Processed Oils	1	7	46	4	14	#	#	#
Fish and Fishery Products	~	18,700	26,441	28,228	36,143	33,455	27,353	25,531
Forest Products	~	31,339	34,459	46,385	35,380	31,080	32,248	28,251
Agricultural Requisites	52	369	275	89	22	1	2	48
Crude Fertilizers	2	8	4	3	4	#	#	#
Manuf Fertilizers	- -	129	6	#	#	#	#	#
Pesticides	50	232	265	86	18	1	2	48
Agricultural Machines	- -	#	#	#	#	#	#	#

SOURCE: FAO TY, 1975, Section IV; 1980, Section IV; 1981, Section IV; 1983, Section IV;
1985, Section IV; 1986, Section IV; 1987, Section IV.

Table 2533

MEXICO ABSOLUTE VALUE OF TRADE, 1970–86

(T US)

Imports

Category	1970	1980	1981	1982	1983	1984	1985	1986
Total Merchandise Trade	2,319,520	19,516,960	25,053,610	15,067,730	10,797,360	14,457,970	16,151,840	11,432,360
Agricultural Products, Total	216,277	3,140,600	3,508,460	1,911,500	2,196,380	2,522,000	2,370,500	1,671,290
Food and Animals	123,497	2,411,600	2,544,890	1,130,740	1,560,580	1,328,790	1,318,710	861,130
Live Animals	9,144	32,727	68,440	57,880	12,860	59,280	162,980	76,630
Meat and Meat Prep	5,192	45,604	97,830	67,850	32,760	68,790	134,520	88,300
Dairy Products Eggs	18,166	239,057	247,590	181,780	147,250	144,300	172,640	171,040
Cereals and Prep	65,517	1,142,671	1,173,640	406,440	1,138,890	833,140	604,250	271,560
Fruits and Vegetables	10,685	276,760	426,940	147,250	21,540	68,420	143,040	141,600
Sugar and Honey	2,281	568,010	387,760	184,220	130,090	80,410	6,670	5,410
Coffee, Tea, Cocoa Sp	3,030	8,278	21,750	10,460	2,610	8,290	15,280	27,560
Feeding Stuff	1,945	92,400	90,190	42,920	62,240	39,220	45,680	52,360
Miscellaneous Food	7,537	6,083	30,770	31,950	12,350	26,920	33,660	26,650
Beverages Tobacco	4,926	73,388	92,360	55,230	11,760	6,270	9,070	7,440
Beverages	4,100	72,244	92,260	55,190	11,760	6,240	3,100	7,410
Tobacco	826	1,144	100	30	#	30	5,970	30
Crude Materials	76,323	513,094	816,320	597,070	532,600	1,001,600	853,090	603,500
Hides and Skins	18,248	68,100	86,640	80,280	23,840	11,390	124,110	75,580
Oilseeds	18,524	308,514	533,900	376,370	379,050	71,826	530,660	366,930
Natural Rubber	12,847	73,659	75,070	51,020	54,730	61,500	59,510	44,590
Textile Fibers	16,068	37,590	46,350	31,930	15,540	26,140	35,460	26,400
Crude Mat Nes	10,636	50,400‡	74,360	57,480	59,440	84,310	103,360	90,000
Animal Vegetable Oil	11,531	117,357	54,900	128,470	91,440	185,340	189,630	199,220
Animal Fats	3,290	49,938	40,770	41,780	37,500	59,400	52,430	48,000
Fixed Vegetable Oils	5,293	55,448	5,450	77,910	48,400	118,350	127,810	132,640
Processed Oils	2,948	11,971	8,680	8,780	5,550	7,590	9,400	18,590
Fish and Fishery Products	~	35,210	33,870	27,570	4,680	8,790	8,610	8,220
Forest Products	~	609,380	632,460	641,860	367,390	219,130	307,010	319,310
Agricultural Requisites	76,879	390,355	542,300	322,800	242,670	352,200	450,020	427,010
Crude Fertilizers	7,077	73,276	99,860	66,940	11,860	38,300	38,170	29,940
Manuf Fertilizers	5,758	68,147	101,840	106,290	59,610	111,290	120,780	77,070
Pesticides	3,645	19,741	17,933	8,460	10,000	7,660	9,530	10,000
Agriculture Machines	60,399	229,191	322,680	141,110	161,200	194,950	281,530	310,000

Exports

Category	1970	1980	1981	1982	1983	1984	1985	1986
Total Merchandise Trade	1,282,000	15,307,480	19,419,610	21,220,670	2,464,232	2,656,326	2,436,449	16,030,990
Agricultural Products, Total	694,505	1,720,210	1,684,320	1,591,160	1,195,210	1,738,700	1,772,890	2,513,480
Food and Animals	521,228	1,146,704	1,135,980	1,147,700	975,200	1,303,440	1,432,880	2,141,120
Live Animals	79,184	98,350	71,233	127,440	118,080	114,320	143,830	265,360
Meat and Meat Prep	46,109	27,356	14,690	9,360	14,980	15,900	14,290	7,950
Dairy Products Eggs	27	35	280	350	50	130	200	160
Cereals and Prep	5,993	13,640	7,920	7,720	5,700	3,360	13,760	12,720
Fruits and Vegetables	187,148	439,444	632,210	501,970	386,120	592,360	577,740	813,940
Sugar and Honey	103,020	73,793	43,140	44,740	54,810	52,250	51,610	100,450
Coffee, Tea, Cocoa Sp	98,486	491,213	362,390	449,250	384,620	512,740	608,760	915,880
Feeding Stuff	505	1,838	600	1,270	2,720	80	2,270	2,670
Miscellaneous Food	756	1,035	3,520	5,600	8,130	12,300	20,420	22,000
Beverages Tobacco	15,838	126,254	144,720	148,560	63,790	124,850	159,120	206,130
Beverages	4,272	77,444	91,310	94,980	46,620	94,360	130,480	173,480
Tobacco	11,566	48,810	53,410	53,580	17,170	30,490	28,670	32,660
Crude Materials	155,619	442,240	400,750	291,680	154,540	308,310	178,560	163,980
Hides and Skins	16	1,256	140	1,640	370	1,050	280	280
Oilseeds	2,382	57,995	46,380	31,970	18,390	48,970	31,430	36,180
Natural Rubber	3,722	3,251	2,860	1,470	1,070	740	1,110	1,600
Textile Fibers	135,194	329,738	318,870	215,100	106,030	218,590	106,500	83,920
Crude Mat Nes	14,305	50,000‡	32,510	41,510	28,680	38,960	39,250	42,000
Animal Vegetable Oils	1,820	5,014	2,870	3,220	1,680	2,110	2,300	2,240
Animal Fats	- -	468	207	140	40	#	100	10
Fixed Vegetable Oils	- -	442	450	10	90	180	320	280
Processed Oils	1,820	4,104	2,220	3,070	1,550	1,930	1,890	1,950
Fish and Fishery Products	~	580,040	494,480	396,180	436,750	437,370	371,000	423,880
Forest Products	~	10,930	7,080	6,020	18,230	17,950	13,880	13,880
Agricultural Requisites	9,724	27,688	20,930	22,820	38,580	33,070	22,520	31,490
Crude Fertilizers	344	#	1,100	950	610	#	100	#
Manuf Fertilizers	8,051	12,440	4,850	2,430	20,400	18,590	3,260	10,260
Pesticides	938	5,838	2,223	2,360	2,400	2,540	3,100	2,650
Agricultural Machines	391	9,410	12,760	17,080	15,160	11,940	16,070	18,580

SOURCE: FAO-TY, 1975, Section IV; 1980, Section IV; 1981, Section IV; 1983, Section IV;
1985, Section IV; 1986, Section IV; 1987, Section IV.

Table 2534

NICARAGUA ABSOLUTE VALUE OF TRADE, 1970-86

(T US)

Imports

Category	1970	1980	1981	1982	1983	1984	1985	1986
Total Merchandise Trade	198,748	887,211	999,441	775,548	847,470	825,883	891,927	753,600
Agricultural Products, Total	19,996	138,393	176,023	96,311	107,923	123,553	106,156	90,035
Food and Animals	15,870	109,412	149,068	73,001	78,059	83,668	73,947	62,822
Live Animals	737	2,708	4,561	1,464	1,598	2,027	1,782	1,850
Meat and Meat Prep	385	7,630	7,607	910	2,431	4,667	4,121	1,425
Dairy Products Eggs	1,055	6,810	11,547	17,791	11,692	15,612	17,786	11,014
Cereals and Prep	4,817	48,176	77,485	31,990	52,364	44,415	33,233	34,785
Fruits and Vegetables	3,494	32,442	35,887	8,877	3,908	9,127	8,158	4,217
Sugar and Honey	1,009	2,580	5,316	5,464	3,636	1,560	417	357
Coffee, Tea, Cocoa Sp	379	2,234	1,338	508	408	286	441	460
Feeding Stuff	429	453	476	441	301	1,521	953	1,832
Miscellaneous Food	3,565	6,379	4,851	5,556	1,721	4,453	7,056	6,882
Beverages Tobacco	1,304	1,080	799	209	523	527	716	1,400
Beverages	746	550	641	196	389	388	426	400
Tobacco	558	530	158	13	134	139	290	1,000
Crude Materials	1,185	9,470	7,059	7,056	9,924	10,961	5,444	6,795
Hides and Skins	39	#	641	164	#	#	#	#
Oilseeds	391	5,458	2,984	5,555	7,827	8,311	4,063	5,705
Natural Rubber	140	230	273	220	853	553	112	120
Textile Fibers	428	3,023	15	1	179	1,103	469	470
Crude Mat Nes	187	759	3,146	1,116	1,115	994	800	500
Animal Vegetable Oil	1,637	18,431	19,097	16,045	19,367	28,397	26,049	19,018
Animal Fats	1,160	6,127	9,220	6,814	7,555	8,533	10,729	8,000
Fixed Vegetable Oils	381	12,149	9,808	8,999	11,591	19,738	15,320	11,018
Processed Oils	96	155	69	232	221	126	#	#
Fish and Fishery Products	~	1,428	220	1,157	760	64	2	#
Forest Products	~	13,321	10,707	12,368	11,637	13,237	9,866	10,566
Agricultural Requisites	9,139	75,592	72,742	50,622	64,151	71,029	64,476	46,873
Crude Fertilizers	~	1	#	#	#	#	#	#
Manuf Fertilizers	4,112	35,455	24,243	12,003	21,352	22,498	19,117	7,801
Pesticides	2,744	21,458	24,816	15,649	24,766	24,706	27,332	19,452
Agriculture Machines	2,283	18,678	23,683	22,970	18,033	23,825	18,027	19,620

Exports

Category	1970	1980	1981	1982	1983	1984	1985	1986
Total Merchandise Trade	178,623	450,442	499,833	405,793	428,336	386,651	301,509	235,000
Agricultural Products, Total	131,901	343,807	400,101	331,970	339,391	342,910	284,930	217,880
Food and Animals	82,914	301,602	258,769	227,877	212,775	190,655	179,571	164,386
Live Animals	581	30,041	3	#	65	61	#	#
Meat and Meat Prep	26,901	58,800	21,273	33,819	29,594	17,601	12,526	5,648
Dairy Products Eggs	2,356	2	1,877	4,234	#	#	1	1,787
Cereals and Prep	5,218	4,615	8,279	5,103	2,532	2,072	1,294	1,140
Fruits and Vegetables	1,633	9,825	24,501	11,528	20,205	13,570	17,943	15,850
Sugar and Honey	10,367	25,998	54,335	39,267	32,898	23,527	8,356	15,005
Coffee, Tea, Cocoa Sp	32,845	169,716	141,956	128,902	120,191	127,041	136,323	22,160
Feeding Stuff	2,983	2,477	6,489	5,015	7,290	6,766	3,128	2,796
Miscellaneous Food	30	128	56	9	#	17	#	#
Beverages Tobacco	2,442	2,660	5,662	7,035	5,585	5,318	4,781	3,838
Beverages	32	98	139	882	508	309	301	320
Tobacco	2,410	2,562	5,523	6,153	5,077	5,009	4,480	2,518
Crude Materials	42,505	39,537	135,156	96,584	120,972	146,906	100,578	50,656
Hides and Skins	265	586	641	164	94	#	#	#
Oilseeds	3,577	6,957	10,573	6,563	6,528	6,752	5,814	1,476
Natural Rubber	- -	#	#	#	#	#	#	#
Textile Fibers	35,262	30,922	123,639	89,095	113,524	139,939	94,264	48,780
Crude Mat Nes	3,401	1,072	303	762	826	215	500	400
Animal Vegetable Oils	4,040	8	514	474	59	31	#	#
Animal Fats	- -	#	#	#	#	#	#	#
Fixed Vegetable Oils	4,035	8	514	474	59	31	#	#
Processed Oils	5	#	#	#	#	#	#	#
Fish and Fishery Products	~	31,335	18,536	16,482	12,435	12,608	12,889	8,688
Forest Products	~	4,270	3,701	1,950	2,569	2,569	2,609	2,560
Agricultural Requisites	570	1,907	736	440	540	77	100	120
Crude Fertilizers	~	#	#	#	#	#	#	#
Manuf Fertilizers	30	#	6	#	#	#	#	#
Pesticides	540	1,907	730	440	540	77	100	120
Agricultural Machines	- -	#	#	#	#	#	#	#

SOURCE: FAO-TY, 1975, Section IV; 1980, Section IV; 1981, Section IV; 1983, Section IV; 1985, Section IV; 1986, Section IV; 1987, Section IV.

Table 2535

PANAMA ABSOLUTE VALUE OF TRADE, 1970–86

(T US)

					Imports			
Category	1970	1980	1981	1982	1983	1984	1985	1986
Total Merchandise Trade	326,352	1,288,884	1,562,124	1,568,342	1,413,020	1,411,821	1,383,343	1,275,245
Agricultural Products, Total	28,227	120,104	139,526	140,540	144,774	134,123	157,010	146,912
Food and Animals	22,128	91,204	112.634	112.551	116,401	104,432	125,594	114,757
Live Animals	318	146	286	418	347	313	374	699
Meat and Meat Prep	4,106	12,427	12,643	14,456	16,310	10,411	8,109	11,199
Dairy Products Eggs	3,250	16,920	10,345	13,216	13,943	13,257	13,673	14,366
Cereals and Prep	4,863	23,760	37,186	34,865	32,798	28,189	38,920	32,844
Fruits and Vegetables	5,954	21,254	27,960	29,070	27,838	27,313	33,988	28,067
Sugar and Honey	423	2,011	2,215	2,877	2,725	2,802	3,237	2,965
Coffee, Tea, Cocoa Sp	1,109	4,560	5,429	5,792	7,518	8,518	8,488	7,637
Feeding Stuff	1,192	6,683	12,728	8,271	11,171	9,912	12,253	12,259
Miscellaneous Food	809	3,413	3,842	3,586	3,751	3,712	6,552	4,721
Beverages Tobacco	3,116	7,829	9,825	9,828	8,962	9,243	9,375	9,716
Beverages	1,883	5,359	7,308	7,315	6,967	7,676	7,657	8,194
Tobacco	1,233	2,470	2,517	2,513	1,995	1,567	1,718	1,522
Crude Materials	481	2,540	2,435	3,220	3,066	2,965	3,517	4,159
Hides and Skins	- -	22	37	#	47	9	#	#
Oilseeds	111	348	230	499	395	426	333	405
Natural Rubber	- -	595	560	1,010	941	349	622	924
Textile Fibers	121	332	220	282	178	260	512	428
Crude Mat Nes	249	1,243	1,388	1,429	1,505	1,921	2,050	2,402
Animal Vegetable Oil	2,606	18,531	14,632	14,941	16,345	17,483	18,524	18,280
Animal Fats	5	1,273	1,231	948	1,495	1,415	1,056	811
Fixed Vegetable Oils	2,594	17,016	13,225	13,817	14,582	15,856	17,196	17,147
Processed Oils	7	242	176	176	268	212	272	322
Fish and Fishery Products	~	6,313	5,487	6,685	8,041	8,129	7,960	7,385
Forest Products	~	34,264	35,556	33,373	27,452	36,881	54,799	56,716
Agricultural Requisites	12,640	41,004	45,125	41,289	32,717	34,825	35,015	37,759
Crude Fertilizers	1	#	5	1	4	4	428	988
Manuf Fertilizers	2,948	17,715	18,431	10,068	8,163	8,526	10,769	11,063
Pesticides	2,617	14,706	17,534	20,539	18,747	22,532	18,899	20,649
Agriculture Machines	7,074	8,583	9,155	10,681	5,803	3,763	4,919	5,059

					Exports			
Category	1970	1980	1981	1982	1983	1984	1985	1986
Total Merchandise Trade	109,497	353,377	319,420	310,239	303,545	257,610	319,578	345,314
Agricultural Products, Total	71,592	170,938	168,642	137,466	165,758	152,614	149,487	152,271
Food and Animals	70,844	164,803	162,552	131,027	159,149	147,708	143,991	146,821
Live Animals	7	1,382	1,711	2,965	4,109	2,251	1,529	1,144
Meat and Meat Prep	2,448	3,125	5,096	9,372	4,110	1,462	364	26
Dairy Products Eggs	8	7,832	7,618	3,943	3,600	3,502	3,597	3,634
Cereals and Prep	5	115	246	1,428	1,785	146	43	24
Fruits and Vegetables	60,922	65,763	75,337	70,691	81,434	80,888	85,836	80,089
Sugar and Honey	5,689	69,702	55,135	25,588	42,776	37,113	28,614	21,998
Coffee, Tea, Cocoa Sp	1,717	13,024	15,379	15,104	18,883	18,574	20,475	35,350
Feeding Stuff	- -	584	115	206	112	178	76	80
Miscellaneous Food	48	3,276	1,915	1,730	2,340	3,594	3,457	4,476
Beverages Tobacco	20	5,289	5,468	5,042	5,330	4,464	5,174	4,802
Beverages	18	3,886	3,264	2,753	3,214	2,591	2,557	2,503
Tobacco	2	1,403	2,204	2,289	2,116	1,873	2,617	2,299
Crude Materials	728	846	617	1,394	1,279	442	322	648
Hides and Skins	537	396	432	914	919	254	148	83
Oilseeds	- -	#	#	#	#	#	#	#
Natural Rubber	34	#	#	31	#	#	#	#
Textile Fibers	- -	#	#	#	#	#	#	#
Crude Mat Nes	157	450	185	449	860	188	174	565
Animal Vegetable Oils	- -	#	5	3	#	#	#	#
Animal Fats	- -	#	2	3	#	#	#	#
Fixed Vegetable Oils	- -	#	3	#	#	#	#	#
Processed Oils	- -	#	#	#	#	#	#	#
Fish and Fishery Products	~	66,040	57,899	62,031	67,224	60,927	86,093[†]	118,648
Forest Products	~	1,038	1,156	1,234	1,237	1,029	521	521
Agricultural Requisites	- -	1,812	169	149	536	1,384	579	526
Crude Fertilizers	- -	#	#	#	#	#	#	#
Manuf Fertilizers	- -	#	17	7	#	#	#	283
Pesticides	- -	588	152	142	536	1,384	579	243
Agricultural Machines	- -	1,224	#	#	#	#	#	#

SOURCE: FAO-TY, 1975, Section IV; 1980, Section IV; 1981, Section IV; 1983, Section IV;
1985, Section IV; 1986, Section IV; 1987, Section IV.

Table 2536

PARAGUAY ABSOLUTE VALUE OF TRADE, 1980–86

(T US)

				Imports			
Category	1980	1981	1982	1983	1984	1985	1986
Total Merchandise Trade	517,141	506,111	631,421	553,050	631,333	719,224	730,891
Agricultural Products, Total	64,648	84,692	75,138	55,421	46,175	52,479	58,779
Food and Animals	18,983	3,371	24,781	31,193	13,881	19,557	14,668
Live Animals	727	980	885	609	858	2,066	1,116
Meat and Meat Prep	850	619	215	143	121	142	88
Dairy Products Eggs	1,294	1,445	1,434	2,351	2,026	668	629
Cereals and Prep	14,406	18,577	11,581	21,484	5,420	13,320	6,199
Fruits and Vegetables	1,057	2,696	3,718	2,423	1,999	805	423
Sugar and Honey	304	628	1,176	1,185	911	311	3,962
Coffee, Tea, Cocoa Sp	#	540	1,016	435	738	544	592
Feeding Stuff	#	1,173	1,190	718	237	233	411
Miscellaneous Food	345‡	6,713	3,566	1,845	1,572	1,468	1,248
Beverages Tobacco	45,665	46,511	44,039	18,506	29,416	29,649	39,045
Beverages	31,392	35,375	31,222	12,759	20,609	20,288	30,390
Tobacco	14,273	11,136	12,817	5,747	8,807	9,361	8,655
Crude Materials	#	4,116	5,978	5,693	2,828	3,113	4,879
Hides and Skins	#	#	#	#	#	#	#
Oilseeds	#	1,765	3,535	3,665	1,744	2,748	4,276
Natural Rubber	#	#	#	~	~	~	#
Textile Fibers	#	98	72	43	160	6	#
Crude Mat Nes	1,787	2,263	2,371	1,985	924	359	603
Animal Vegetable Oil	#	694	340	29	50	160	187
Animal Fats	#		5	9	7	30	150
Fixed Vegetable Oils	#	547	297	16	34	115	28
Processed Oils	#	147	38	4	9	15	9
Fish and Fishery Products	~	~	~	~	~	~	~
Forest Products	11,524	8,902	11,971	6,077	7,450	8,566	8,638
Agricultural Requisites	25,200	37,161	31,937	29,103	37,874	31,169	22,524
Crude Fertilizers	#	144	213	51	6	#	4
Manuf Fertilizers	2,500†	4,300	5,074	4,402	6,812	8,124	5,961
Pesticides	3,000†	7,613	7,000	7,200	9,516	11,945	8,000
Agriculture Machines	19,700†	25,104	19,650	17,450	21,540	11,100†	8,559

				Exports			
Category	1980	1981	1982	1983	1984	1985	1986
Total Merchandise Trade	310,230	315,000	37,055	342,569	406,871	402,982	300,000
Agricultural Products, Total	229,605	246,732	279,522	241,249	304,576	307,087	209,045
Food and Animals	46,033	25,689	30,907	29,701	28,343	19,579	57,332
Live Animals	#	#	#	26	40	6	521
Meat and Meat Prep	1,054	3	2,075	5,273	4,586	1,437	33,700
Dairy Products Eggs	#	#	#	#	#	#	#
Cereals and Prep	2,493	295	580	18	695	#	100
Fruits and Vegetables	11,247	6,620	9,811	3,746	3,843	1,048	5,273
Sugar and Honey	3,112	101	3,924	5,441	4,186	3,527	3,588
Coffee, Tea, Cocoa Sp	4,233	2,138	475	42	298	179	137
Feeding Stuff	22,394	14,369	12,888	14,178	12,395	11,971	11,746
Miscellaneous Food	1,500†	2,163	1,154	977	2,300	1,411	2,267
Beverages Tobacco	10,197	6,489	5,947	9,941	14,653	5,459	9,882
Beverages	55	31	#	#	#	11	22
Tobacco	10,142	6,458	5,947	9,941	14,653	5,448	9,860
Crude Materials	156,394	192,120	223,863	181,987	243,885	265,645	131,704
Hides and Skins	3,903	6,960	7,203	7,421	7,262	5,371	5,371
Oilseeds	45,272	53,025	92,755	89,649	104,638	117,876	45,555
Natural Rubber	#	#	#	~	~	~	#
Textile Fibers	106,967	132,029	123,831	84,791	131,825	142,187	80,540
Crude Mat Nes	83	106	74	126	160	211	238
Animal Vegetable Oils	16,981	22,434	18,805	19,620	17,695	16,404	10,127
Animal Fats	#	9	#	~	~	~	#
Fixed Vegetable Oils	16,981	22,421	18,805	19,487	17,416	16,227	10,007
Processed Oils	#	4	#	133	279	177	120
Fish and Fishery Products	~	~	~	~	~	~	~
Forest Products	66,451	59,289	91,859	70,635	87,236	91,030	67,005
Agricultural Requisites	#	#	#	#	#	#	#
Crude Fertilizers	#	#	#	#	#	#	#
Manuf Fertilizers	#	#	#	#	#	#	#
Pesticides	#	#	#	#	#	#	#
Agricultural Machines	#	#	#	#	#	#	#

SOURCE: FAO-TY, 1980, Section IV; 1981, Section IV; 1983, Section IV; 1985, Section IV; 1986, Section IV; 1987, Section IV.

Table 2537

PERU ABSOLUTE VALUE OF TRADE, 1970–86

(T US)

Imports

Category	1970	1980	1981	1982	1983	1984	1985	1986
Total Merchandise Trade	621,763	2,573,365	3,159,530	2,940,255	2,234,300	2,140,000‡	2,023,000	2,391,185
Agricultural Products, Total	125,526	524,117	643,969	532,941	555,525	467,232	350,509	572,645
Food and Animals	106,421	466,220	566,880	467,848	481,762	388,401	296,145	503,923
Live Animals	24,201	1,815	2,402	3,812	3,747	2,909	5,184	5,011
Meat and Meat Prep	13,007	12,416	23,566	52,147	22,734	26,709	16,175	86,548
Dairy Products Eggs	11,985	42,089	38,685	62,631	44,526	40,945	33,296	65,902
Cereals and Prep	43,668	325,356	359,673	290,078	395,824	249,318	202,122	241,282
Fruits and Vegetables	7,256	23,596	24,209	24,078	24,754	17,540	12,364	26,923
Sugar and Honey	71	34,894	85,166	2,417	71,318	34,880	1,111	39,375
Coffee, Tea, Cocoa Sp	2,376	6,419	15,035	17,520	4,011	4,752	8,917	7,812
Feeding Stuff	1,617	15,587	13,917	10,349	8,434	7,938	13,281	23,910
Miscellaneous Food	2,240	4,048	4,227	4,816	6,414	3,410	3,695	7,160
Beverages Tobacco	2,410	9,018	8,877	14,720	9,998	7,633	6,849	7,976
Beverages	1,948	5,559	4,975	10,107	7,389	4,190	4,168	5,165
Tobacco	462	3,459	3,902	4,613	2,609	3,443	2,681	2,811
Crude Materials	6,886	19,670	31,569	18,458	17,742	20,480	15,574	33,317
Hides and Skins	1,697	3,008	8,962	1,685	133	345	537	14,041
Oilseeds	788	239	2,881	452	3,599	1,712	4,695	4,333
Natural Rubber	2,001	10,196	8,700	5,298	5,293	8,297	6,327	7,230
Textile Fibers	627	214	87	911	43	2,043	178	296
Crude Mat Nes	1,773	6,013	10,939	10,112	8,674	8,083	3,837	7,417
Animal Vegetable Oil	9,809	29,209	36,643	31,915	46,023	50,718	31,941	27,429
Animal Fats	720	1,730	1,661	1,117	3,243	1,445	1,394	1,797
Fixed Vegetable Oils	8,804	26,694	31,333	28,109	41,930	48,414	28,809	23,368
Processed Oils	285	785	3,649	2,689	850	859	1,738	2,264
Fish and Fishery Products	~	3,742	2,779	741	20,275	8,340	2,230†	170
Forest Products	~	37,829	57,034	74,314	48,145	44,278	37,449	57,109
Agricultural Requisites	16,386	77,020	71,646	70,462	34,669	37,869	37,311	98,016
Crude Fertilizers	111	735	62	14	#	1,216	152	159
Manuf Fertilizers	5,465	26,631	12,722	11,103	7,827	7,624	11,848	32,380
Pesticides	4,258	14,335	16,021	12,344	15,246	12,748	9,488	20,285
Agriculture Machines	6,552	35,319	42,841	47,001	11,596	16,281	15,823	45,192

Exports

Category	1970	1980	1981	1982	1983	1984	1985	1986
Total Merchandise Trade	1,047,858	3,308.990	2,407,711	2,812,830	2,079,780	3,147,000	2,705,000	2,467,000
Agricultural Products, Total	177,463	320,861	223,501	263,547	209,888	240,723	306,306	391,674
Food and Animals	114,797	214,256	142,098	170,691	159,293	200,527	239,089	342,117
Live Animals	247	1,136	1,277	1,007	536	590	415	297
Meat and Meat Prep	- -	2,450	946	1,631	1,950	389	14,280	#
Dairy Products Eggs	- -	1,435	180	50	1,630	#	#	#
Cereals and Prep	140	5,021	2,586	2,054	1,390	737	2,605	1,267
Fruits and Vegetables	2,900	23,635	16,707	22,309	16,378	20,716	21,834	22,808
Sugar and Honey	66,245	15,426	928	18,081	7,342	19,749	25,640	22,910
Coffee, Tea, Cocoa Sp	44,996	162,770	116,501	123,016	129,331	156,313	171,106	293,705
Feeding Stuff	243	1,680	1,503	1,492	282	1,171	51	18
Miscellaneous Food	26	703	1,470	1,051	454	862	3,158	1,112
Beverages Tobacco	285	1,145	1,165	929	514	672	691	759
Beverages	91	849	915	731	149	381	364	584
Tobacco	194	296	250	198	365	291	327	175
Crude Materials	61,387	100,404	78,391	90,207	49,627	35,030	63,891	47,749
Hides and Skins	2,274	201	25	41	92	128	76	65
Oilseeds	- -	52	34	12	8	45	1	4
Natural Rubber	- -	10	19	#	131	102	5	16
Textile Fibers	55,803	93,896	68,775	81,764	39,496	19,672	55,723	40,334
Crude Mat Nes	3,310	6,245	9,538	8,390	9,900	15,083	8,086	7,330
Animal Vegetable Oils	994	5,056	1,847	1,720	454	4,494	2,635	1,049
Animal Fats	- -	#	#	#	#	#	#	#
Fixed Vegetable Oils	- -	#	#	#	#	1,619	1,535	11
Processed Oils	994	5,056	1,847	1,720	454	2,875	1,100	1,038
Fish and Fishery Products	~	321,821	298,822	282,266	163,356	233,167	221,595	258,083
Forest Products	~	6,830	7,133	7,515	8,976	5,415	4,260	3,355
Agricultural Requisites	454	3,980	1,654	1,928	852	1,409	1,062	956
Crude Fertilizers	410	33	388	562	131	354	250	#
Manuf Fertilizers	19	2,720	25	6	#	4	13	21
Pesticides	22	1,043	986	387	680	916	502	600
Agricultural Machines	3	184	255	973	41	135	297	335

SOURCE: FAO-TY, 1975, Section IV; 1980, Section IV; 1981, Section IV; 1982, Section IV;
1985, Section IV; 1986, Section IV; 1987, Section IV.

Table 2538

URUGUAY ABSOLUTE VALUE OF TRADE, 1980–86
(T US)

Imports

Category	1980	1981	1982	1983	1984	1985	1986
Total Merchandise Trade	1,680,350	1,641,117	1,109,976	787,508	775,721	707,762	869,980
Agricultural Products, Total	153,742	134,940	82,582	80,623	93,968	66,738	78,814
Food and Animals	87,495	91,591	47,211	44,877	50,932	33,942	50,366
Live Animals	1,637	1,727	217	179	241	235	339
Meats and Meat Prep	1,171	1,780	563	26	128	1,424	141
Dairy Products Eggs	1,141	1,497	772	190	258	258	367
Cereals and Prep	9,912	14,547	8,325	19,079	19,064	5,591	18,671
Fruits and Vegetables	22,526	24,228	15,086	7,770	11,155	7,756	7,942
Sugar and Honey	8,357	14,188	1,199	427	573	376	261
Coffee, Tea, Cocoa Sp	36,783	28,203	16,843	15,787	18,273	16,811	21,145
Feeding Stuff	4,858	3,449	2,276	531	437	596	641
Miscellaneous Food	1,110	1,972	1,930	888	803	895	859
Beverages Tobacco	19,368	17,614	15,020	7,188	9,738	6,455	6,026
Beverages	9,323	8,764	6,652	3,540	4,789	4,004	4,379
Tobacco	10,045	8,850	8,368	3,648	4,949	2,451	1,647
Crude Materials	35,613	22,919	17,060	22,311	24,929	18,886	19,738
Hides and Skins	7,601	4,175	3,091	3,302	8,684	6,209	7,659
Oilseeds	489	159	94	56	177	422	288
Natural Rubber	7,345	4,505	1,204	2,174	2,357	1,790	2,054
Textile Fibers	13,336	9,365	9,326	13,627	11,750	8,779	7,737
Crude Mat Nes	6,842	4,715	3,345	3,152	1,961	1,686	2,000
Animal Vegetable Oil	11,266	2,816	3,291	6,247	8,369	7,455	2,684
Animal Fats	4,026	150	174	70	841	360	375
Fixed Vegetable Oils	6,951	2,435	2,944	6,067	7,312	6,880	2,047
Processed Oils	289	231	173	110	216	215	262
Fish and Fishery Products	4,842	1,470	1,328	476	756	1,029	850
Forest Products	33,226	33,092	20,795	13,656	13,363	12,363	11,358
Agricultural Requisites	84,000	53,780	33,042	25,243	36,828	38,718	39,726
Crude Fertilizers	6,800	3,057	1,793	1,077	1,722	2,844	1,930
Manuf Fertilizers	27,661	21,778	18,704	13,998	18,349	17,332	16,926
Pesticides	8,088	7,366	7,101	6,508	7,393	7,606	8,800
Agriculture Machines	41,451	21,579	5,444	3,660	9,364	10,936	12,070

Exports

Category	1980	1981	1982	1983	1984	1985	1986
Total Merchandise Trade	1,058,550	1,215,375	1,022,886	1,045,147	924,588	853,614	1,087,830
Agricultural Products, Total	595,123	771,432	635,318	678,121	518,953	489,680	558,418
Food and Animals	337,380	500,283	397,978	476,609	324,447	299,132	338,910
Live Animals	7,905	13,551	14,971	31,028	8,785	1,974	2,448
Meats and Meat Prep	187,477	263,758	208,382	255,516	156,267	127,065	171,105
Dairy Products Eggs	16,701	23,597	15,982	33,228	17,893	22,445	33,477
Cereals and Prep	88,070	166,787	138,932	124,833	113,354	114,912	100,512
Fruits and Vegetables	12,914	11,767	7,038	11,651	13,089	21,569	20,450
Sugar and Honey	2,382	3,097	2,300	8,041	6,007	5,201	4,967
Coffee, Tea, Cocoa Sp	1,972	1,573	395	351	540	258	817
Feeding Stuff	15,345	10,796	8,428	11,675	8,486	5,689	4,604
Miscellaneous Food	4,614	5,357	1,550	286	26	19	530
Beverages Tobacco	1,053	319	443	13	381	495	4,207
Beverages	952	282	366	#	21	231	3,941
Tobacco	101	37	77	13	360	264	266
Crude Materials	238,264	262,998	231,607	193,444	187,658	185,617	207,705
Hides and Skins	3,448	4,235	7,046	6,902	4,664	5,229	3,313
Oilseeds	6,316	6,402	6,136	2,184	2,157	1,415	9,729
Natural Rubber	125	3	262	26	6	#	13
Textile Fibers	221,220	242,653	209,622	175,888	172,569	170,674	186,150
Crude Mat Nes	7,155	9,705	8,541	8,444	8,262	8,299	8,500
Animal Vegetable Oil	18,426	7,832	5,290	8,055	6,467	4,436	7,596
Animal Fats	7,170	2,633	2,253	6,241	3,775	1,919	5,042
Fixed Vegetable Oils	10,722	4,187	2,017	686	1,480	2,192	2,209
Processed Oils	534	1,012	1,020	1,128	1,212	325	345
Fish and Fishery Products	50,898	61,300	47,500	45,694	48,859	54,149	65,150
Forest Products	10,381	7,663	4,579	6,646	7,066	7,066	7,066
Agricultural Requisites	6,483	3,953	4,226	1,118	1,507	2,277	4,179
Crude Fertilizers	#	#	#	#	50	#	#
Manuf Fertilizers	6,122	3,680	3,343	606	1,118	2,027	3,449
Pesticides	41	63	226	263	230	250[†]	700
Agriculture Machines	320	210	657	249	109	#	30

SOURCE: FAO-TY, 1980, Section IV; 1981, Section IV; 1982, Section IV; 1985,
Section IV; 1986, Section IV; 1987, Section IV.

Table 2539

VENEZUELA ABSOLUTE VALUE OF TRADE, 1970-86

(T US)

Imports

Category	1970	1980	1981	1982	1983	1984	1985	1986
Total Merchandise Trade	1,665,031	10,669,150	11,810,900	11,667,000	6,146,400	7,053,970	7,418,100	8,652,200
Agricultural Products, Total	200,829	1,714,550	2,003,720	1,766,080	1,285,500	1,526,560	1,277,380	793,260
Food and Animals	151,369	1,331,100	1,630,500	1,456,580	1,017,770	1,097,510	879,480	519,460
Live Animals	23,510	67,439	74,114	99,710	9,680	16,190	13,920	31,340
Meat and Meat Prep	3,934	52,040	88,433	74,590	46,160	12,450	9,330	500
Dairy Products Eggs	13,079	132,261	212,230	217,130	118,660	158,670	97,430	49,050
Cereals and Prep	70,005	586,025	585,370	445,730	485,720	508,310	462,930	269,650
Fruits and Vegetables	28,303	125,240	179,290	139,220	79,350	94,420	79,780	44,500
Sugar and Honey	418	221,058	301,323	254,270	133,760	113,750	64,170	1,400
Coffee, Tea, Cocoa Sp	1,931	7,705	9,501	9,780	3,620	8,720	6,520	5,160
Feeding Stuff	3,198	103,977	119,053	144,640	125,440	148,880	105,280	101,970
Miscellaneous Food	6,469	35,351	61,201	71,520	15,380	36,130	40,130	15,870
Beverages Tobacco	16,550	152,668	127,730	120,570	61,090	79,660	58,270	64,270
Beverages	16,355	150,713	126,060	117,920	60,210	78,710	57,380	63,470
Tobacco	195	1,955	1,672	2,651	880	950	900	810
Crude Materials	22,233	77,899	85,500	86,850	77,080	127,170	156,910	104,550
Hides and Skins	473	3,013	2,850	3,500	4,250	7,950	15,650	7,090
Oilseeds	8,170	19,735	21,530	18,320	37,730	44,980	75,070	29,740
Natural Rubber	4,869	20,449	19,501	14,280	13,860	14,400	13,530	16,090
Textile Fibers	5,504	3,536	11,931	31,010	7,470	39,340	27,170	13,090
Crude Mat Nes	3,217	31,166	29,690	19,750	13,780	20,490	25,490	38,540
Animal Vegetable Oil	10,677	152,888	159,990	102,080	129,560	222,220	182,720	104,970
Animal Fats	1,570	15,716	11,422	11,220	8,390	15,410	13,380	12,270
Fixed Vegetable Oils	8,501	132,469	145,202	87,330	119,120	202,780	165,110	88,470
Processed Oils	606	4,703	3,370	3,530	2,050	4,030	4,240	4,240
Fish and Fishery Products	~	25,600	29,320	31,060	9,970	5,920	4,200	620
Forest Products	~	227,000	247,180	318,130	256,320	263,990	232,950	220,750
Agricultural Requisites	36,833	223,753	230,630	177,070	64,460	87,500	170,440	271,990
Crude Fertilizers	- -	4,741	2,910	5,100	1,600	2,600	5,340	2,550
Manuf Fertilizers	12,052	117,390	86,100	19,900	2,910	26,060	73,760	86,790
Pesticides	2,236	10,564	13,470	11,464	5,350	9,910	8,980	11,030
Agriculture Machines	22,545	91,058	128,162	140,601	54,600	48,930	82,360	171,620

Exports

Category	1970	1980	1981	1982	1983	1984	1985	1986
Total Merchandise Trade	3,147,702	19,292,832	17,517,960	16,498,000	14,500,900	14,820,210	15,501,610	10,056,650
Agricultural Products, Total	43,337	77,460	77,014	99,660	77,690	100,430	122,440	166,270
Food and Animals	36,531	69,030	60,330	85,310	68,160	84,930	105,030	140,500
Live Animals	19	#	#	690	570	390	440	3,690
Meat and Meat Prep	213	747	642	530	460	1,350	4,880	11,410
Dairy Products Eggs	186	51	120	260	220	720	2,200	2,480
Cereals and Prep	7,600	6,756	264	4,460	1,570	280	910	3,730
Fruits and Vegetables	2,893	21,940	33,920	60,660	43,780	43,940	51,120	41,590
Sugar and Honey	5,690	15	10	10	10	50	20	160
Coffee, Tea, Cocoa Sp	19,607	36,688	24,000	18,170	20,950	3,740	44,730	75,430
Feeding Stuff	238	#	#	#	70	100	30	10
Miscellaneous Food	85	2,834	1,373	540	540	710	720	2,010
Beverages Tobacco	397	6,220	14,691	13,260	8,000	10,560	13,060	20,390
Beverages	50	499	540	334	190	620	590	1,800
Tobacco	347	5,721	14,154	12,922	7,810	9,940	12,470	18,590
Crude Materials	6,409	2,198	2,000	1,080	1,430	4,390	4,330	4,070
Hides and Skins	50	#	#	#	#	#	#	#
Oilseeds	5,850	#	#	#	110	1,740	760	10
Natural Rubber	69	#	10	#	#	#	#	#
Textile Fibers	- -	187	110	#	60	380	480	470
Crude Mat Nes	440	2,005	1,880	1,080	1,260	2,270	3,100	3,580
Animal Vegetable Oils	- -	#	#	10	100	570	20	1,300
Animal Fats	- -	#	#	10	30	20	10	40
Fixed Vegetable Oils	- -	#	#	#	70	540	10	1,260
Processed Oils	- -	#	#	#	#	#	#	#
Fish and Fishery Products	~	4,890	12,430	24,100	55,450	80,400	127,790	188,450
Forest Products	~	#	#	#	#	#	#	#
Agricultural Requisites	- -	30,733	44,793	20,660	39,390	44,380	20,530	21,400
Crude Fertilizers	- -	#	#	1	#	#	#	#
Manuf Fertilizers	- -	26,657	43,351	19,310	37,620	42,660	19,260	19,830
Pesticides	- -	646	700	203	520	420	440	660
Agricultural Machines	- -	3,430	742	1,141	1,250	1,290	830	910

SOURCE: FAO-TY, 1975, Section IV; 1980, Section IV; 1981, Section IV; 1982, Section IV;
1985, Section IV; 1986, Section IV; 1987, Section IV.

Table 2540

UNITED STATES ABSOLUTE VALUE OF TRADE, 1970–86

(T US)

Imports

Category	1970	1980	1981	1982	1983	1984	1985	1986
Total Merchandise Trade	39,963,200	24,119,480	26,098,184	24,395,200	25,804,780	32,572,560	34,527,530	36,865,660
Agricultural Products, Total	6,306,490	1,818,910	1,835,290	1,689,690	1,769,330	2,088,480	2,110,870	2,242,850
Food and Animals	4,537,822	1,289,320	11,262,100	1,140,350	1,190,440	1,427,060	1,460,950	1,594,780
Live Animals	156,674	40,276	33,223	47,292	53,360	62,540	61,500	67,270
Meat and Meat Prep	1,015,480	234,220	199,430	207,530	203,440	203,400	224,200	236,690
Dairy Products Eggs	99,814	31,990	35,743	37,162	40,380	42,430	40,550	41,450
Cereals and Prep	69,612	21,663	24,170	29,690	31,550	42,020	49,580	54,210
Fruits and Vegetables	734,982	203,410	296,220	293,870	303,340	389,870	399,410	420,840
Sugar and Honey	806,463	221,380	240,460	107,894	133,830	161,400	133,500	101,230
Coffee, Tea, Cocoa Sp	1,602,590	516,020	407,500	390,660	389,460	481,020	505,830	619,180
Feeding Stuff	29,093	9,190	11,230	10,993	13,890	15,680	12,750	13,570
Miscellaneous Food	22,673	11,150	14,134	15,260	21,080	28,710	33,630	40,330
Beverages Tobacco	854,992	277,003	313,881	336,400	340,760	365,340	372,670	391,610
Beverages	726,519	224,789	243,254	255,333	268,810	293,860	310,480	323,420
Tobacco	128,473	52,214	70,630	81,070	71,950	71,480	62,190	68,190
Crude Materials	761,759	200,016	212,070	173,080	189,180	226,800	210,580	205,920
Hides and Skins	110,186	23,008	26,890	19,750	18,950	22,960	24,550	20,950
Oilseeds	52,163	5,972	9,890	7,250	9,190	8,780	9,090	6,460
Natural Rubber	240,818	82,099	78,060	53,550	65,530	82,460	65,540	61,620
Textile Fibers	154,504	19,600	25,710	20,210	21,690	27,590	22,780	22,530
Crude Mat Nes	204,088	69,337	71,530	72,320	73,830	85,020	88,620	94,370
Animal Vegetable Oil	152,358	52,570	47,240	39,860	48,950	69,280	66,670	50,540
Animal Fats	4,198	800	470	430	470	790	830	700
Fixed Vegetable Oils	140,510	49,918	44,683	37,694	46,670	66,260	63,930	47,740
Processed Oils	7,650	2,057	2,091	1,740	1,810	2,230	1,910	2,100
Fish and Fishery Products	~	263,316	298,820	317,463	362,140	370,250	405,180	47,870
Forest Products	~	758,210	770,870	808,920	898,660	1,049,640	1,075,620	1,111,110
Agricultural Requisites	466,106	272,656	269,410	229,200	246,360	291,260	282,210	287,900
Crude Fertilizers	8,744	3,669	2,810	2,286	1,960	2,050	2,700	4,850
Manuf Fertilizers	192,202	97,862	110,210	96,300	99,710	114,200	96,700	86,470
Pesticides	10,870	26,624	28,373	26,454	25,120	30,790	39,930	38,090
Agriculture Machines	254,290	144,500	128,012	104,161	119,560	144,220	142,870	158,490

Exports

Category	1970	1980	1981	1982	1983	1984	1985	1986
Total Merchandise Trade	42,593,300	21,659,222	22,888,782	20,715,800	19,596,930	21,205,700	20,692,530	20,637,620
Agricultural Products, Total	7,381,756	4,289,110	4,506,170	3,825,790	3,756,080	3,936,330	3,060,360	2,805,980
Food and Animals	4,226,991	2,722,320	2,959,540	2,325,590	2,349,850	2,394,500	1,848,770	1,641,750
Live Animals	60,115	21,596	27,101	30,794	34,520	30,120	39,460	38,460
Meat and Meat Prep	103,615	129,756	148,502	128,900	119,530	121,280	115,720	142,800
Dairy Products Eggs	137,348	25,559	42,400	41,110	37,500	37,030	38,940	41,330
Cereals and Prep	2,588,402	1,808,333	1,946,262	1,475,360	1,516,740	1,607,730	1,105,760	738,110
Fruits and Vegetables	581,117	302,266	342,072	281,642	252,170	252,660	249,470	277,090
Sugar and Honey	22,677	48,719	69,410	12,441	14,550	15,800	15,720	19,040
Coffee, Tea, Cocoa Sp	31,186	49,903	45,300	41,391	35,020	41,900	35,080	51,030
Feeding Stuff	496,171	284,950	273,080	243,920	279,970	223,460	186,710	258,250
Miscellaneous Food	143,437	51,242	65,430	70,030	59,850	64,510	61,910	75,650
Beverages Tobacco	701,657	269,106	294,031	303,570	283,210	288,070	299,500	296,050
Beverages	22,637	24,619	20,310	19,052	17,400	16,250	19,350	21,170
Tobacco	679,020	244,487	273,730	284,514	265,810	271,820	280,150	274,870
Crude Materials	1,967,353	1,105,810	1,080,190	1,044,610	981,830	1,067,580	771,460	768,710
Hides and Skins	193,660	105,090	103,060	102,740	100,580	137,170	128,920	153,050
Oilseeds	1,263,167	656,060	687,210	683,330	633,990	619,310	414,250	465,960
Natural Rubber	8,903	4,050	3,294	2,623	2,990	4,900	4,850	4,590
Textile Fibers	396,678	294,911	234,470	205,110	192,250	253,340	174,260	88,150
Crude Mat Nes	104,945	45,700	52,150	50,810	52,020	52,860	49,190	56,960
Animal Vegetable Oils	488,678	191,872	172,420	152,023	141,190	186,170	140,620	99,470
Animal Fats	198,731	72,871	70,231	61,290	56,770	64,820	57,670	37,780
Fixed Vegetable Oils	263,274	110,501	95,540	82,224	80,360	115,580	78,870	57,730
Processed Oils	26,673	8,500	6,644	8,510	4,060	5,770	4,070	3,960
Fish and Fishery Products	~	99,335	116,300	106,860	104,790	100,290	116,240	148,100
Forest Products	~	698,997	652,840	570,600	565,070	574,190	533,540	628,620
Agricultural Requisites	999,095	652,231	621,700	471,890	387,450	463,830	369,560	423,290
Crude Fertilizers	91,121	50,853	37,320	29,360	32,730	32,480	26,360	21,170
Manuf Fertilizers	177,659	226,810	173,633	138,840	127,760	181,540	116,790	193,620
Pesticides	102,142	55,454	54,712	60,860	63,130	70,810	60,920	66,410
Agricultural Machines	628,123	319,110	356,040	242,832	163,830	178,990	165,490	142,090

SOURCE: FAO-TY, 1975, Section IV; 1980, Section IV; 1981, Section IV; 1982, Section IV; 1985, Section IV; 1986, Section IV; 1987, Section IV.

Table 2541

IMF IMPORT UNIT VALUE INDEX, 4 LC, 1953–88

(YA, 1980 = 100)

Country	1953	1954	1955	1956	1957	1958	1959	1960	1961	1962	1963	1964	1965	1966	1967	1968
C. BRAZIL	~	~	~	~	~	~	~	~	23.7	23.9	24.5	23.7	24.1	24.6	25.1	25.9
E. COLOMBIA	40.3	40.3	41.1	42.0	45.1	41.0	41.3	40.8	41.3	40.1	39.2	38.8	35.5	36.3	37.4	37.0
J. EL SALVADOR	39.0	28.0	28.0	29.0	29.0	29.0	27.0	28.0	29.0	29.0	31.0	32.0	32.0	40.0	35.0	32.0
O. NICARAGUA	~	~	~	~	~	28.9	28.5	28.9	27.2	27.4	28.2	27.3	28.3	30.9	29.3	31.6
UNITED STATES	22.2	22.6	22.6	22.9	23.3	22.2	21.8	22.1	21.8	21.3	21.4	22.0	22.2	22.8	23.0	23.3

Country	1969	1970	1971	1972	1973	1974	1975	1976	1977	1978	1979	1980	1981	1982	1983	1984	1985
C. BRAZIL	25.4	25.9	26.9	26.5	35.9	52.5	57.1	58.7	61.0	65.2	78.1	100.0	111.1	107.4	101.7	96.6	91.0
E. COLOMBIA	37.6*	38.0	38.6	41.1	48.7	62.6	66.8	69.7	73.8	82.7	91.2	100.0	106.1	108.5	106.1	109.5	103.4
J. EL SALVADOR	32.0	33.0	33.0	35.0	41.0	59.0	65.0	63.0	63.0	70.0	79.0	100.0	111.0	119.0	111.0	~	~
O. NICARAGUA	33.0	34.5	36.1	38.0	42.6	56.1	68.5	67.4	70.9	74.8	80.3	100.0	~	~	~	~	~
UNITED STATES	24.0	25.7	27.0	28.9	34.4	50.9	55.5	57.2	62.0	66.9	80.4	100.0	105.4	103.8	99.5	101.3	98.7

Country	1986	1987	1988
C. BRAZIL	70.7	82.5	~
E. COLOMBIA	96.1	95.6	99.4
J. EL SALVADOR	~	~	
O. NICARAGUA	~	~	
UNITED STATES	95.4	102.3	

SOURCE: IMF-IFS-Y, 1984, line 75d: 1986, line 75d: September 1987, line 75d;
IMF-IFS-Y, 1988, line 75d; IMF-IFS-Y, 1989.

Table 2542

IMF EXPORT UNIT VALUE INDEX, 11 LC, 1953–88

(YA, 1980 = 100)

	Country	1953	1954	1955	1956	1957	1958	1959	1960	1961	1962	1963	1964	1965	1966	1967	1968
B.	BOLIVIA	10.8	10.8	10.8	11.3	10.0	9.6	10.0	10.0	10.8	10.8	11.3	14.6	16.7	15.9	15.0	15.0
C.	BRAZIL	41.6	48.7	38.7	37.1	37.8	34.9	29.5	29.0	30.5	26.6	26.5	31.7	32.0	30.7	30.6	30.2
E.	COLOMBIA	~	~	~	36.8	38.3	29.6	25.2	25.7	25.5	23.2	20.5	24.5	22.9	18.5	22.5	23.0
H.	DOMINICAN REP.	27.1	32.9	27.8	26.7	34.0	29.4	25.4	25.6	26.3	29.7	32.6	34.5	30.6	33.3	33.2	36.0
I.	ECUADOR	12.9	15.6	13.3	13.3	13.3	13.3	12.2	12.9	12.2	15.6	13.3	16.0	16.7	16.7	16.7	17.1
J.	EL SALVADOR	35.0	44.0	39.0	39.0	39.0	32.0	26.0	26.0	25.0	23.0	26.0	29.0	31.0	30.0	28.0	27.0
M.	HONDURAS	27.4	28.5	29.9	30.3	28.1	26.2	23.7	27.8	30.0	31.8	30.4	32.3	31.1	30.9	31.0	30.1
O.	NICARAGUA	44.2	55.7	47.7	50.4	47.3	40.7	34.9	37.5	38.4	39.5	37.6	36.9	38.7	38.9	37.3	37.5
P.	PANAMA	28.0	32.0	31.0	31.0	29.0	27.0	26.0	24.0	23.0	27.0	25.0	26.0	27.0	27.0	28.0	29.0
Q.	PARAGUAY	29.9	39.7	38.8	35.0	34.9	34.0	32.9	26.2	25.9	26.4	30.9	35.8	36.3	37.1	33.7	36.3
R.	PERU	~	~	~	~	~	~	~	20.0	19.0	19.0	20.0	23.0	24.0	28.0	25.0	27.0
	UNITED STATES	29.4	28.9	29.3	30.4	31.4	31.1	31.1	31.3	31.9	31.7	31.7	32.0	33.0	34.0	34.7	35.2

	Country	1969	1970	1971	1972	1973	1974	1975	1976	1977	1978	1979	1980	1981	1982	1983	1984	1985
B.	BOLIVIA	16.3	21.1	17.1	17.8	23.3	40.6	38.8	43.8	54.4	61.5	74.0	100.0	106.9	105.8	107.3	106.9	103.5
C.	BRAZIL	31.1	35.1	33.9	38.3	52.7	66.4	66.4	76.6	93.5	86.0	94.4	100.0	94.1	88.4	83.6	85.3	80.5
E.	COLOMBIA	23.1*	28.5	27.1	30.3	38.2	51.2	50.6	74.1	1089	91.0	89.7	100.0	89.5	88.8	89.0	95.0	88.9
H.	DOMINICAN REP.	39.3	37.6	35.4	39.3	48.0	72.7	114.3	76.5	84.5	76.9	81.1	100.0	128.3	83.0	78.1	90.4	77.2
I.	ECUADOR	15.2	17.1	18.2	15.2	20.9	43.2	39.8	44.8	57.4	52.2	72.9	100.0	91.2	87.4	76.0	75.8	73.4
J.	EL SALVADOR	27.0	32.0	31.0	33.0	41.0	51.0	53.0	77.0	102.0	85.0	97.0	100.0	93.0	88.0	71.0	~	~
M.	HONDURAS	30.0	33.6	32.6	34.2	40.3	47.0	56.2	66.4	91.2	90.7	85.6	100.0	93.3	87.1	87.1	92.3	93.4
O.	NICARAGUA	38.2	39.0	39.4	42.8	47.4	60.7	57.0	74.8	92.6	87.2	71.0	100.0	107.0	91.0	93.0	104.0	246.0
P.	PANAMA	28.0	28.0	28.0	29.0	49.0	69.0	80.0	73.0	66.0	64.0	78.0	100.0	101.5	90.2	98.3	94.9	93.9
Q.	PARAGUAY	37.2	39.9	40.6	44.9	56.3	67.1	71.7	72.7	98.4	90.1	94.0	100.0	109.2	103.8	108.6	117.9	75.0
R.	PERU	30.0	31.0	28.0	30.0	49.0	60.0	41.0	47.0	51.0	50.0	76.0	100.0	80.1	67.5	75.0	66.6	59.7
	UNITED STATES	36.2	38.2	39.4	40.7	47.4	60.5	67.6	69.9	72.4	77.4	88.1	100.0	109.2	110.4	111.6	113.1	112.2

	Country	1986	1987	1988
B.	BOLIVIA	78.6	66.5	65.9
C.	BRAZIL	80.4	80.2	~
E.	COLOMBIA	100.6	77.2	80.9
H.	DOMINICAN REP.	82.4	69.2	96.2
I.	ECUADOR	45.0	50.7	42.7
J.	EL SALVADOR	~	~	~
M.	HONDURAS	92.2	95.2	~
O.	NICARAGUA	392.0	~	~
P.	PANAMA	74.4	81.4	73.8
Q.	PARAGUAY	41.5	75.4	~
R.	PERU	53.9	65.8	76.9
	UNITED STATES	113.3	115.3	123.3

SOURCE: IMF-IFS-Y, 1984, 1986, 1987, 1988, 1989, line 74.

Table 2543

IMF TERMS OF TRADE INDEX,[1] 7 LC, 1960–81

(YA, 1975 = 100)

Year	B. BOLIVIA	H. DOMINICAN REP.	I. ECUADOR	M. HONDURAS	Q. PARAGUAY	R. PERU	T. VENEZUELA	UNITED STATES
1960	52.9	54.9	76.6	145.4	86.2	69.4	33.6	116.3
1961	57.5	56.3	72.0	156.9	85.6	68.5	38.7	120.4
1962	58.0	63.9	92.8	167.0	88.2	71.0	38.8	122.5
1963	59.4	69.2	77.9	157.7	101.8	74.8	37.7	121.2

Continued in SALA, 24-2544.

Table 2544

IMF TERMS OF TRADE INDEX,[1] 4 L, 1955–88

(YA, 1980 = 100)

Year	C. BRAZIL	E. COLOMBIA	J. EL SALVADOR	O. NICARAGUA
1955	~	~	126.2	~
1956	~	87.6	132.4	~
1957	~	84.9	131.4	~
1958	~	72.2	110.7	97.2
1959	~	61.0	95.6	103.5
1960	~	63.0	91.6	85.5
1961	128.7	61.7	86.6	95.2
1962	111.3	58.9	79.0	96.4
1963	108.2	52.3	85.9	109.6
1964	133.8	63.1	92.1	131.1
1965	132.9	64.5	94.7	128.3
1966	124.8	51.0	75.0	120.1
1967	121.9	60.2	81.4	115.0
1968	116.6	62.2	85.3	114.9
1969	122.4	61.4	82.4	115.8[†]
1970	135.5	75.0*	97.6	113.0
1971	126.0	70.2	93.1	109.1
1972	144.5	73.7	93.8	112.6
1973	146.8	78.4	100.0	111.3
1974	126.5	81.8	87.6	108.2
1975	116.3	75.7	81.6	83.2
1976	130.5	106.3	122.6	111.0
1977	153.3	147.6	160.6	130.6
1978	131.9	110.0	120.9	116.6
1979	120.9	98.4	123.1	112.0
1980	100.0	100.0	100.0	100.0
1981	84.7	84.4	83.8	~
1982	82.3	81.9	74.2	~
1983	82.2	83.9	64.4	~
1984	88.3	86.8	~	~
1985	88.4	86.0	~	~
1986	111.5	70.3	~	~
1987	97.2	59.7	~	~
1988	~	81.4	~	~

1. Export unit value divided by import unit value; 100.0 = base; numbers above 100.0 are favorable and those below 100.0 are unfavorable, relative to 1980.

SOURCE: IMF-IFS-Y, 1984; IMF-IFS-S, 1986; IMF-IFS, 1987; IMF-IFS-Y, 1989.

Table 2545

TERMS OF TRADE,[1] 6 L, 1929–38

Export unit value index divided by import unit value index (1929 = 100)

Year	A. ARGENTINA	C. BRAZIL	D. CHILE	E. COLOMBIA	G. CUBA	N. MEXICO
1929	100.0	100.0	100.0	100.0	100.0	100.0
1930	95.9	61.6	95.7	73.6	82.1	77.5
1931	71.4	53.6	67.0	83.6	96.1	59.5
1932	74.5	67.5	55.1	72.9	83.6	59.8
1933	70.4	60.3	60.0	63.6	105.2	61.8
1934	85.7	62.9	57.3	81.4	110.0	66.7
1935	85.7	55.0	61.6	64.3	117.5	77.5
1936	105.1	54.3	70.3	64.3	128.4	64.7
1937	120.4	58.3	76.8	67.1	128.4	61.8
1938	110.2	43.0	54.1	60.0	~	132.4

SOURCE: Angus Maddison, *Two Crises: Latin America and Asia, 1929–38 and 1973–83*
(Paris: Development Centre of the Organisation for Economic Co-operation and
Development, 1985).

Table 2546

ECLA IMPORT UNIT VALUES (FOB), 19 L, 1960–88

(1980 = 100)

	Country	1960	1965	1970	1975	1980	1983	1984	1985	1986	1987	1988[‡]
A.	ARGENTINA	26.5	26.0	29.6	64.0	100.0	91.7	88.2	88.1	89	99	104
B.	BOLIVIA	28.0	30.4	40.2	68.9	100.0	99.4	93.0	89.3	89	87	92
C.	BRAZIL	20.5	23.0	21.8	51.4	100.0	103.9	96.0	94.0	80	95	98
D.	CHILE	21.6	22.4	24.9	57.4	100.0	84.1	86.1	86.5	82	87	92
E.	COLOMBIA	34.1	35.2	33.2	66.3	100.0	94.9	89.3	90.5	92	91	96
F.	COSTA RICA	29.9	29.3	33.4	62.4	100.0	95.2	93.8	92.0	90	94	99
H.	DOMINICAN REP.	30.4	31.8	31.8	61.4	100.0	102.5	101.9	102.0	86	87	90
I.	ECUADOR	45.2	45.2	31.1	65.3	100.0	104.4	99.1	97.9	93	84	84
J.	EL SALVADOR	26.1	28.0	34.1	61.3	100.0	100.3	95.2	93.6	99	106	109
K.	GUATEMALA	24.4	27.7	36.1	58.0	100.0	97.9	95.4	94.6	94	92	96
L.	HAITI	31.2	33.0	33.2	61.4	100.0	103.3	98.3	98.7	95	103	106
M.	HONDURAS	24.7	26.2	29.0	55.7	100.0	98.6	95.6	98.2	107	104	108
N.	MEXICO	29.1	36.6	38.6	67.6	100.0	103.6	107.1	104.1	90	90	94
O.	NICARAGUA	25.2	26.1	31.8	57.6	100.0	97.3	90.6	92.4	87	95	97
P.	PANAMA	24.7	24.8	25.2	55.4	100.0	95.9	96.4	94.8	91	86	91
Q.	PARAGUAY	27.6	28.8	25.7	60.6	100.0	93.5	77.0	74.3	92	71	74
R.	PERU	30.7	36.5	29.7	59.9	100.0	97.5	93.5	89.5	87	84	89
S.	URUGUAY	23.6	27.5	28.6	60.6	100.0	91.9	88.8	86.8	77	83	86
T.	VENEZUELA	29.7	37.7	35.3	65.8	100.0	94.1	92.5	89.6	81	88	92
	LATIN AMERICA[1]	26.1	30.0	29.3	59.1	100.0	~	~	~	86	91	95

1. Includes Barbados, Guyana, Jamaica, Suriname, and Trinidad and Tobago.

SOURCE: ECLA-AE, 1986, table 256; 1988, p. 768.

Table 2547

ECLA EXPORT UNIT VALUES (FOB), 19 L, 1960–88

(1980 = 100)

Country	1960	1965	1970	1975	1980	1981	1982	1983	1984	1985	1986	1987	1988
A. ARGENTINA	30.00	30.80	27.30	62.70	100.00	96.80	82.40	74.60	84.30	72.90	68.10	71.30	81.70
B. BOLIVIA	11.60	21.50	17.10	36.10	100.00	97.80	98.70	96.00	100.50	96.10	84.10	81.00	79.00
C. BRAZIL	32.50	32.90	30.00	61.10	100.00	94.00	87.50	81.20	83.80	78.10	79.00	77.30	85.60
D. CHILE	29.40	33.10	48.10	51.50	100.00	87.20	72.20	71.10	67.20	59.30	61.40	72.20	92.80
E. COLOMBIA	26.30	26.80	28.30	45.40	100.00	88.80	92.10	90.50	93.70	88.30	104.30	84.10	87.50
F. COSTA RICA	31.10	32.90	33.40	54.10	100.00	88.90	84.90	82.30	84.00	83.20	94.90	88.40	94.10
G. DOMINICAN REP.	21.70	25.50	35.90	99.90	100.00	122.50	85.70	79.70	86.20	72.80	78.50	71.50	92.80
H. ECUADOR	17.70	15.40	36.40	42.40	100.00	97.70	91.70	85.00	82.00	79.00	56.00	57.20	51.80
I. EL SALVADOR	32.70	32.50	34.30	55.30	100.00	97.30	99.40	82.50	76.40	73.20	89.20	63.90	70.90
J. GUATEMALA	32.80	33.20	36.40	55.50	100.00	94.20	86.40	83.20	85.50	79.50	95.10	78.00	84.60
K. HAITI	29.10	31.10	34.70	51.60	100.00	73.20	75.40	68.00	81.70	83.90	99.80	110.70	101.20
L. HONDURAS	25.30	31.60	31.20	55.10	100.00	96.00	93.60	92.10	98.60	89.80	103.70	93.70	101.50
N. MEXICO	17.80	19.90	22.90	50.00	100.00	106.80	89.50	78.80	78.50	77.40	56.20	62.30	58.40
O. NICARAGUA	36.00	38.40	35.50	54.20	100.00	94.40	88.10	80.90	94.50	88.80	91.80	95.30	96.70
P. PANAMA	29.10	35.40	40.20	96.10	100.00	101.70	87.60	90.90	94.50	94.10	108.70	104.90	115.50
Q. PARAGUAY	28.50	33.50	33.00	76.90	100.00	107.60	93.30	85.00	107.50	85.40	81.00	99.10	109.00
R. PERU	16.60	20.20	33.20	53.30	100.00	92.00	79.50	91.90	82.50	74.40	70.70	78.80	91.40
S. URUGUAY	34.10	34.70	35.90	52.10	100.00	101.40	92.00	82.20	84.10	78.10	79.30	88.80	97.40
T. VENEZUELA	9.60	8.10	8.10	42.20	100.00	106.20	100.60	91.10	94.70	92.80	45.90	57.90	50.00
LATIN AMERICA	16.70	16.70	19.50	51.80	100.00	99.60	?	?	?	?	?	?	?

SOURCE: ECLA-AE, 1986, table 253; 1989, table 269.

Table 2548

ECLA TOTAL IMPORT, EXPORT, AND TERMS OF TRADE INDEXES FOR LATIN AMERICA,[1]
1930–60[a]
(1970 = 100)

Year	Import Unit Value[2]	Export Unit Value[2]	Terms of Trade[3]
1930	53.6	54.9	102.4
1931	45.1	37.3	82.7

Continued in SALA, 24-2548.

Table 2549

VOLUME OF LATIN AMERICAN EXPORTS, 6 L, 1929–38

	A. ARGENTINA	C. BRAZIL	D. CHILE	E. COLOMBIA	G. CUBA	N. MEXICO
1929 Values ($ M US)	907.6	461.5	282.8	123.5	272.4	284.6
Index (1929 = 100)						
1929	100.0	100.0	100.0	100.0	100.0	100.0
1930	69.3	109.6	65.0	109.8	76.5	81.1
1931	95.3	117.3	60.0	96.1	63.0	82.1
1932	87.4	80.8	28.8	98.0	61.2	58.5
1933	81.9	100.0	41.3	98.0	53.2	62.3
1934	85.8	111.5	66.3	103.9	52.1	84.9
1935	90.6	128.9	67.5	113.7	54.5	86.8
1936	81.9	142.3	67.5	127.5	57.3	95.3
1937	95.6	128.8	95.0	125.5	61.8	112.3
1938	61.4	155.8	88.8	131.4	~	50.0

SOURCE: Angus Maddison, *Two Crises: Latin America and Asia, 1929–38 and 1973–83* (Paris: Development Centre of the Organisation for Economic Co-Operation and Development, 1985).

Table 2550

VOLUME OF LATIN AMERICAN IMPORTS, 6 L, 1929–38

	A. ARGENTINA	C. BRAZIL	D. CHILE	E. COLOMBIA	G. CUBA	N. MEXICO
1929 Values ($ M US)	819.5	421.7	196.8	123.0	216.2	184.2
Index (1929 = 100)						
1929	100.0	100.0	100.0	100.0	100.0	100.0
1930	87.8	59.4	92.0	52.3	76.8	74.1
1931	61.5	39.1	48.0	44.6	51.4	48.1
1932	46.8	36.2	17.0	36.9	40.7	38.9
1933	51.3	50.7	19.0	50.8	35.4	44.4
1934	56.4	55.1	25.0	63.1	49.3	55.6
1935	58.3	62.3	38.0	69.2	60.1	57.4
1936	61.5	63.8	43.0	78.5	61.8	66.7
1937	80.8	78.3	48.0	90.8	69.6	85.2
1938	76.3	72.5	44.0	84.6	~	70.4

SOURCE: Angus Maddison, *Two Crises: Latin America and Asia, 1929–38 and 1973–83* (Paris: Development Centre of the Organisation for Economic Co-Operation and Development, 1985).

Table 2551

VALUE, INDEXES, AND PURCHASING POWER OF FOREIGN TRADE, 19 LR, 1928–76
(Value in Current and 1970 M US; Indexes 1970 = 100)

A. ARGENTINA

Year	Exports				Imports				Indexes	
	Value		Indexes		Value		Indexes		Terms of Trade	Exports Purchasing Power
	Current	1970	Unit Value[1]	Quantum[2]	Current	1970	Value[1]	Quantum[3]		
	A	B	C(A/B)	D	E	F	G	H	I(C/G)	J(D x I)
1928	1,719.0	1,856.4	92.6	104.7	1,364.0	1,833.3	74.4	108.2	124.5	130.4

Continued in SALA, 24-2550.

Table 2552

PURCHASING POWER OF LATIN AMERICAN EXPORTS, 1929–38

	A. ARGENTINA	C. BRAZIL	D. CHILE	E. COLOMBIA	G. CUBA	N. MEXICO
1929 Values ($ M US)	907.6	461.5	282.8	123.5	272.4	284.6
Index (1929 = 100)						
1929	100.0	100.0	100.0	100.0	100.0	100.0
1930	66.9	67.1	62.2	81.7	62.8	63.0
1931	68.5	62.0	40.5	80.3	60.5	49.1
1932	65.3	54.4	15.5	71.8	51.2	35.2
1933	58.1	59.5	25.0	63.4	56.0	38.9
1934	74.2	69.6	37.8	84.5	57.3	56.5
1935	78.2	70.9	41.9	73.2	64.0	67.6
1936	86.3	77.2	47.3	83.1	73.6	62.0
1937	115.3	74.7	73.0	84.5	79.4	69.4
1938	67.7	67.1	48.0	78.9	n.a.	66.7

SOURCE: Angus Maddison, *Two Crises: Latin America and Asia, 1929–38 and 1973–83*
(Paris: Development Centre of the Organisation for Economic Co-Operation and
Development, 1985).

Table 2553

EVOLUTION OF QUANTUM OF EXPORTS AND IMPORTS OF GOODS, 19 L, 1928–50

(1963 = 100)

Year	A. ARGENTINA		B. BOLIVIA		C. BRAZIL		D. CHILE		E. COLOMBIA	
	Exports	Imports	Exports	Imports	Exports	Imports	Exports	Imports	Exports	Imports
1928	126	150	~	~	49	68	75	79	49	76
1929	127	156	29	~	52	69	80	100	51	65
1930	88	137	26	~	57	41	52	92	56	34
1931	121	96	20	~	61	27	48	48	49	29
1932	111	73	23	~	42	25	23	17	50	24
1933	104	80	43	~	52	35	33	19	50	33
1934	109	88	56	~	58	38	53	25	53	41
1935	115	91	50	~	67	43	54	38	58	45
1936	104	96	37	~	74	44	54	43	65	51
1937	121	126	43	46	67	54	76	48	64	59
1938	78	119	33	57	81	50	71	44	67	55
1939	100	100	38	54	83	46	64	56	65	67
1940	85	86	45	53	69	41	70	42	69	47
1941	76	68	49	71	75	41	77	49	53	49
1942	74	56	56	68	57	30	82	41	58	26
1943	76	37	65	73	58	39	75	42	74	31
1944	83	37	65	71	68	48	78	42	48	37
1945	85	41	65	61	74	47	79	45	79	59
1946	88	81	65	68	91	60	72	45	82	73
1947	96	147	82	68	86	86	72	47	79	99
1948	87	164	89	72	90	77	79	62	80	80
1949	56	112	86	79	87	75	71	75	80	64
1950	72	101	04	54	70	85	60	66	70	86

Year	F. COSTA RICA		H. DOMINICAN REP.		I. ECUADOR		J. EL SALVADOR		K. GUATEMALA	
	Exports	Imports	Exports	Imports	Exports	Imports	Exports	Imports	Exports	Imports
1928	~	~	~	~	23	29	28	26	~	~
1929	~	~	~	~	23	29	25	29	~	~
1930	~	~	49	22	24	23	31	16	~	~
1931	~	~	45	18	18	16	30	13	~	~
1932	~	~	52	17	19	12	21	12	~	~
1933	~	~	46	20	17	13	30	14	~	~
1934	~	~	51	19	26	18	25	18	~	~
1935	~	~	59	19	28	23	24	15	~	~
1936	~	~	62	19	25	25	28	15	~	~
1937	51	25	58	20	26	21	37	17	41	32
1938	47	28	64	21	25	23	28	14	43	30
1939	42	36	64	23	25	23	33	16	41	30
1940	35	31	59	18	25	23	15	14	37	24
1941	43	30	67	18	24	19	24	16	37	23
1942	39	20	37	15	27	22	30	15	42	18
1943	42	26	62	16	34	20	33	16	41	19
1944	35	28	94	18	34	27	35	16	41	23
1945	37	31	59	17	29	27	31	18	51	25
1946	36	36	73	24	29	36	27	19	47	33
1947	48	44	71	37	28	42	36	28	56	33
1948	62	34	61	42	29	45	37	29	51	48
1949	58	37	52	30	26	48	42	29	45	52
1950	55	42	57	31	37	46	40	38	44	55

Table 2553 (Continued)

EVOLUTION OF QUANTUM OF EXPORTS AND IMPORTS OF GOODS, 19 L, 1928–50

(1963 = 100)

Year	L. HAITI		M. HONDURAS		N. MEXICO		O. NICARAGUA		P. PANAMA	
	Exports	Imports	Exports	Imports	Exports	Imports	Exports	Imports	Exports	Imports
1928	~	~	~	~	106	47	~	~	~	~
1929	~	~	~	~	106	54	~	~	~	~
1930	45	~	~	~	86	40	~	~	~	~
1931	45	~	~	~	87	26	~	~	~	~
1932	47	~	~	~	62	21	~	~	~	~
1933	70	~	~	~	667	24	~	~	~	~
1934	64	~	~	~	90	30	~	~	~	~
1935	49	~	~	~	92	31	~	~	~	~
1936	70	~	~	~	101	36	~	~	~	~
1937	57	~	53	30	119	46	24	115	33	42
1938	60	~	39	38	53	38	19	15	31	36
1939	66	~	54	30	50	35	20	17	32	41
1940	46	~	52	29	43	33	16	16	31	39
1941	56	~	53	29	47	49	14	22	24	52
1942	47	~	50	18	48	36	14	13	13	46
1943	53	~	25	23	56	43	17	23	13	43
1944	77	~	49	25	46	64	18	16	13	37
1945	72	~	61	30	54	76	15	17	19	43
1946	81	~	64	40	55	102	18	19	28	52
1947	77	~	79	49	56	103	17	24	34	58
1948	73	~	89	52	44	69	32	25	33	41
1949	90	~	84	49	50	60	26	27	32	41
1950	79	115	83	48	57	71	37	31	30	46

Year	Q. PARAGUAY		R. PERU		S. URUGUAY		T. VENEZUELA	
	Exports	Imports	Exports	Imports	Exports	Imports	Exports	Imports
1928	~	~	34	~	~	~	10	41
1929	~	~	37	30	~	~	10	41
1930	~	~	34	22	~	~	12	38
1931	~	~	30	15	~	~	10	21
1932	~	~	26	11	~	~	10	16
1933	~	~	32	12	~	~	10	20
1934	~	~	38	21	~	~	12	17
1935	~	~	40	244	122	80	12	13
1936	~	~	42	25	100	94	13	18
1937	~	~	48	27	112	110	15	26
1938	57	~	39	27	107	106	16	28
1939	60	~	38	25	118	97	16	32
1940	48	~	33	24	111	97	14	29
1941	64	~	37	25	110	101	19	22
1942	65	~	30	19	64	86	12	14
1943	68	~	29	22	118	68	15	13
1944	66	~	30	26	111	69	21	29
1945	95	~	34	26	126	84	27	37
1946	102	~	30	32	121	113	31	52
1947	57	~	29	36	99	143	35	88
1948	63	~	29	33	97	109	41	117
1949	72	~	29	38	106	96	40	115
1950	76	~	35	39	129	118	45	98

SOURCE: Richard Lynn Ground, "The Genesis of Import Substitution in Latin America,"
CEPAL Review, No. 36, Dec. 1988, pp. 184–185.

Table 2554

LATIN AMERICA EVOLUTION OF MERCHANDISE TERMS OF TRADE, 1928–87

Year	Export Price Index	Import Price Index	Merchandise Terms of Trade	Export Quantum	Purchasing Power of Exports	Import Quantum
1928	100.0	100.0	100.0	100.0	100.0	100.0
1929	90.6	96.2	94.2	103.1	97.1	106.4
1930	62.3	93.3	66.8	87.9	58.7	75.8
1931	41.8	79.2	52.8	93.0	49.1	51.9
1932	36.2	65.1	55.6	77.8	43.3	37.9
1933	29.3	56.6	51.8	81.2	42.1	46.3
1934	28.4	48.1	59.9	91.3	53.9	51.9
1935	31.8	48.1	66.1	105.6	69.8	56.1
1936	33.9	48.1	70.5	109.3	77.1	60.3
1937	38.1	52.3	72.8	120.4	87.7	75.7
1938	34.9	50.9	68.6	96.3	66.1	70.1
1939	33.8	49.5	68.3	101.8	69.5	68.7
1940	35.9	53.3	67.4	90.7	61.1	58.9
1941	40.1	57.6	69.6	94.4	69.2	60.3
1942	44.8	67.7	66.2	88.2	58.4	46.3
1943	49.7	73.5	67.6	96.0	64.9	47.7
1944	53.6	73.5	73.0	101.9	74.4	58.9
1945	54.6	79.2	68.9	111.3	76.7	65.9
1946	71.2	92.2	77.2	119.1	81.9	86.9
1947	89.7	115.3	77.8	121.1	89.7	119.1
1948	99.4	123.9	80.2	121.1	94.2	116.3
1949	93.6	123.9	75.5	111.3	84.0	103.7
1950	110.5	118.1	93.6	115.2	107.8	105.1
1951	130.4	141.2	92.4	115.2	106.4	130.3
1952	93.9	144.1	65.2	111.3	72.6	124.7
1953	93.9	134.0	70.1	123.0	86.2	114.9
1954	97.7	136.9	71.4	123.0	87.8	128.9
1955	87.3	139.8	62.4	130.8	81.6	128.9
1956	85.9	139.8	61.4	142.5	87.5	134.5
1957	88.1	141.2	62.4	146.4	91.4	166.6
1958	80.9	139.8	60.0	148.4	89.0	142.9
1959	73.0	135.4	53.9	162.1	87.4	138.7
1960	74.4	138.3	53.8	166.0	89.3	142.9
1961	74.4	141.2	52.7	171.9	90.6	145.7
1962	71.5	144.1	49.6	187.5	93.0	144.3
1963	72.2	144.1	50.1	195.3	97.8	140.1
1964	76.5	149.9	51.1	197.3	100.8	148.5
1965	75.1	152.7	49.2	211.0	103.8	149.9
1966	76.5	152.7	50.1	218.8	109.6	166.9
1967	75.8	154.1	49.2	220.8	108.6	174.0
1968	76.2	152.7	49.9	230.6	115.1	191.0
1969	78.4	155.6	50.4	246.2	124.1	206.6
1970	84.1	159.9	52.6	254.0	133.6	229.2
1971	79.8	164.9	48.3	275.8	133.2	146.7
1972	110.8	178.1	62.1	251.7	158.2	260.2
1973	129.9	204.2	63.6	304.0	193.3	301.4
1974	216.5	293.8	73.6	264.0	194.3	359.0
1975	218.6	325.3	67.2	240.5	161.6	345.2
1976	234.7	331.5	70.8	260.9	184.7	351.8
1977	269.9	358.0	75.4	271.0	204.3	374.9
1978	278.9	392.9	70.9	281.9	199.9	388.5
1979	340.8	458.7	74.2	310.1	230.1	418.2
1980	424.4	553.4	76.7	329.4	352.6	501.2
1981	418.9	581.6	72.0	358.9	258.4	515.6
1982	379.0	544.4	65.9	362.0	238.6	418.3
1983	341.7	522.3	65.3	401.8	262.4	328.9
1984	354.3	501.8	70.6	432.3	305.2	356.0
1985	337.4	493.5	68.3	427.0	291.6	363.4
1986	291.5	469.8	62.1	417.8	259.5	389.0
1987	311.6	487.6	63.6	438.4	278.8	410.8

SOURCE: Richard Lynn Ground, "The Genesis of Import Substitution in Latin America,"
    CEPAL Review, No. 36, Dec. 1988, p. 183.

Table 2555

ECLA MERCHANDISE TERMS OF TRADE INDEX[1] (FOB/CIF),[2] 19 L, 1970–87

(1980 = 100)

	Country	1970	1975	1980	1981	1982	1983	1984	1985	1986	1987
A.	ARGENTINA	90.1	98.3	100.0	96.3	84.9	80.7	96.0	80.0	72.4	70.9
B.	BOLIVIA	43.2	48.1	100.0	90.1	92.8	93.9	105.1	101.0	80.7	77.9
C.	BRAZIL	131.6	117.0	100.0	85.0	79.8	77.7	85.2	82.6	95.0	90.7
D.	CHILE	178.8	86.4	100.0	87.4	75.3	82.1	76.4	71.1	77.2	80.9
E.	COLOMBIA	84.0	68.0	100.0	84.8	86.6	93.1	98.6	90.3	116.3	89.6
F.	COSTA RICA	96.5	85.2	100.0	84.9	82.7	84.3	87.3	84.9	101.9	90.4
H.	DOMINICAN REP.	110.5	159.6	100.0	114.4	80.9	85.1	93.4	79.6	91.1	83.2
I.	ECUADOR	111.7	63.6	100.0	99.6	97.9	80.9	91.8	93.4	69.9	69.2
J.	EL SALVADOR	99.1	89.2	100.0	91.3	93.0	81.5	71.2	67.7	86.6	59.1
K.	GUATEMALA	100.8	93.3	100.0	87.0	81.7	84.0	85.7	80.5	103.9	82.1
L.	HAITI	101.8	82.3	100.0	70.4	72.5	64.5	78.9	81.9	94.2	85.6
M.	HONDURAS	102.0	95.3	100.0	88.6	91.1	91.6	93.5	80.3	98.5	87.0
N.	MEXICO	68.8	77.5	100.0	100.9	92.8	91.4	84.6	86.0	63.9	67.5
O.	NICARAGUA	105.7	92.0	100.0	90.2	79.8	82.0	102.8	94.0	99.4	96.7
P.	PANAMA	154.0	170.1	100.0	94.7	75.3	93.9	96.9	98.4	121.7	115.1
Q.	PARAGUAY	121.3	123.2	100.0	105.6	86.6	88.1	137.5	116.8	116.7	123.9
R.	PERU	108.9	88.4	100.0	88.5	82.7	94.8	91.1	95.6	83.2	86.8
S.	URUGUAY	178.6	117.9	100.0	96.2	91.4	90.3	96.3	87.3	100.4	103.9
T.	VENEZUELA	22.7	63.2	100.0	102.7	94.4	100.9	112.2	103.8	62.5	77.5
	LATIN AMERICA[3]	66.3	87.1	100.0	94.5	~	~	~	~	~	~

1. Export unit value divided by import unit value; 100.0 = base; numbers above 100.0 are favorable and those below 100.0 are unfavorable, relative to 1980.
2. ECLA uses the following procedures to calculate external trade indexes. Sample selection is made bearing in mind: (a) that the products considered were the most important in terms of their value; (b) that the products were homogeneous; (c) that the sample covered a large universe. Laspeyres indexes are used for quantities. Paasche for prices. For imports, indexes are calculated first for nine groupings of the "Foreign Trade Classification by Economic Use or Destination." For the pperiod 1960–69 the year 1963 is used as the base; the data are then linked to the following period using 1970 as the base year; for imports this is done for each group of the "Foreign Trade Classification by Economic Use or Destination"; for exports, the total unit value indexes were linked together since similar groupings are not available.

  Global values of exports and imports are FOB values according to the balance of payments. The values of imports by groupings under the "Foreign Trade Classification" are CIF values and are based on customs declarations.
3. Includes Guyana, Jamaica, Suriname, and Trinidad and Tobago.

SOURCE: ECLA-AE, 1986, table 254; 1987, table 276.

Table 2556

MERCHANDISE IMPORTS, 20 LC, 1965 AND 1987

(AA)

	Country	Food		Fuels		Machinery and Transport Equipment	
		1965	1987	1965	1987	1965	1987
A.	ARGENTINA	6	5	10	11	25	37
B.	BOLIVIA	19	15	1	2	34	45
C.	BRAZIL	20	9	21	27	22	28
D.	CHILE	20	12	6	10	35	39
E.	COLOMBIA	8	8	1	3	45	39
F.	COSTA RICA	9	4	5	10	29	30
G.	CUBA	~	~	~	~	~	~
H.	DOMINICAN REP.	24	13	10	15	23	27
I.	ECUADOR	10	5	9	3	33	52
J.	EL SALVADOR	15	12	5	8	28	20
K.	GUATEMALA	11	6	7	12	29	28
L.	HAITI	25	27	6	11	14	19
M.	HONDURAS	11	5	6	14	26	31
N.	MEXICO	5	11	2	1	50	46
O.	NICARAGUA	12	15	5	11	30	20
P.	PANAMA	11	3	21	8	21	32
Q.	PARAGUAY	24	14	14	8	37	41
R.	PERU	17	13	3	1	41	47
S.	URUGUAY	7	8	17	16	24	30
T.	VENEZUELA	12	14	1	0	44	45
	UNITED STATES	19	8	10	11	14	42

a. Figures are for years other than those specified.

SOURCE: *World Development Report 1987*, table 12; 1989, table 10.

Table 2557

GROWTH OF MERCHANDISE TRADE, 20 LC, 1965–87

(AA)

	Country	Exports		Imports	
		1965–80	1980–87	1965–80	1980–87
A.	ARGENTINA	4.7	–.3	1.8	–9.4
B.	BOLIVIA	2.8	–.8	5.0	–1.6
C.	BRAZIL	9.3	5.6	8.2	–4.2
D.	CHILE	7.9	4.3	2.6	–8.3
E.	COLOMBIA	1.4	7.5	5.3	–4.2
F.	COSTA RICA	7.0	2.6	5.7	–1.5
G.	CUBA	~	~	~	~
H.	DOMINICAN REP.	1.7	–.1	5.5	1.4
I.	ECUADOR	15.1	5.5	6.8	–1.4
J.	EL SALVADOR	2.4	–4.6	2.7	–.7
K.	GUATEMALA	4.8	–1.6	4.6	–4.6
L.	HAITI	7.0	2.0	8.4	–2.5
M.	HONDURAS	3.1	3.1	2.5	–.2
N.	MEXICO	7.6	6.6	5.7	–8.1
O.	NICARAGUA	2.3	–5.2	1.3	.8
P.	PANAMA	~	3.8	~	–3.3
Q.	PARAGUAY	7.9	13.8	4.6	2.2
R.	PERU	2.3	–.8	–.2	–2.5
S.	URUGUAY	4.6	1.4	1.2	–6.5
T.	VENEZUELA	–9.5	–.4	8.7	–7.0
	UNITED STATES	6.4	–.5	5.5	9.7

a. Figures are for years other than those specified.

SOURCE: *World Development Report 1987*, table 10; 1989, table 14.

Table 2558

EVOLUTION OF NOMINAL TARIFFS, 11L, 1925–86

(Percentages)

Country	1925/1927	1932/1937	1945/1950	1960/1965	1967/1970	1972/1977	1978/1981	1982/1986
A. ARGENTINA								
Average	26.0[a]	23.8[b]	12.2[c]	148.8[d]	36.0[e]	93.7[f]	34.4[g]	0–38.0[h]
Consumer Goods	~	22.9–31.4[b]	~	235.0[d]	88.0[e]	100.0[f]	36.5[g]	~
Intermediate Goods	~	1.0–15.0[b]	~	243.0[d]	51.0[e]	95.0[f]	0–30.0[g]	~
Capital Goods	~	18.4[b]	~	156.0[d]	87.0[e]	70.0[f]	36.7[g]	10.0[h]
C. BRAZIL								
Average	~	25.6[i]	14.4[i]	85.0[j]	37.0[j]	55.1[k]	99.0[k]	45.0[l]
Consumer Goods	~	~	~	132.0[j]	67.0[j]	~	~	~
Intermediate Goods	~	~	~	70.0[j]	37.0[j]	~	~	~
Capital Goods	~	~	~	56.0[j]	40.0[j]	~	~	~
D. CHILE								
Average	25.0–30.0[m]	35.0[n]	~	89.0[o]	~	94.0–24.0[p]	10.0[q]	20.0[q]
Consumer goods	~	45.0[n]	62.0[c]	204.0[o]	~	~	10.0	20.0
Intermediate Goods	~	~	3.0[c]	53.0[o]	~	~	10.0	20.0
Capital Goods	~	~	30.0[c]	92.0[o]	~	~	10.0	20.0
E. COLOMBIA								
Average	23.0[r]	25.0[r]	17.0[r]	48.0[r]	13.0[e]	36.0[s]	28.0[s]	~
Consumer Goods	~	~	18.0	53.0	49.0[e]	47.0	43.0	~
Intermediate Goods	~	~	22.0	40.0	11.0[e]	24.0	22.0	~
Capital Goods	~	~	~	~	33.0[e]	28.0	30.0	~
F. COSTA RICA								
Average	~	~	~	~	~	25.8[v]	16.8[v]	~
Consumer Goods	~	~	~	58.1[t]	85.5[u]	28.0	18.3	~
Intermediate Goods	~	~	~	28.3[t]	32.8[u]	17.3	13.0	~
Capital Goods	~	~	~	10.0[t]	11.8[u]	21.0	16.3	~
J. EL SALVADOR								
Average	~	~	~	~	~	47.6[w]	~	~
Consumer Goods	~	~	~	52.2[t]	79.3[u]	32.9[w]	~	~
Intermediate Goods	~	~	~	37.8[t]	38.1[u]	30.4[w]	~	~
Capital Goods	~	~	~	9.8[t]	10.2[u]	10.6[w]	~	~
K. GUATEMALA								
Average	~	~	~	~	~	50.1[w]	29.8[x]	~
Consumer Goods	~	~	~	50.4[t]	79.8[u]	37.0[w]	39.0[x]	~
Intermediate Goods	~	~	~	24.4[t]	28.6[u]	26.3[w]	23.1[x]	~
Capital Goods	~	~	~	6.0[t]	10.3[u]	10.3[w]	23.3[x]	~
M. HONDURAS								
Average	~	~	~	~	~	41.2[w]	21.9	~
Consumer Goods	~	~	~	50.0[t]	91.9[u]	30.3[w]	~	~
Intermediate Goods	~	~	~	31.6[t]	35.7[u]	38.9[w]	~	~
Capital Goods	~	~	~	2.9[t]	9.9[u]	5.7[w]	~	~
N. MEXICO								
Average	18.4[y]	17.0[y]	11.1[y]	20.1[z]	17.7[aa]	28.0[aa]	11.5[aa]	26.5[aa]
Consumer Goods	~	~	~	63.9[z]	~	~	~	~
Intermediate Goods	~	~	~	33.5[z]	~	~	~	~
Capital Goods	~	~	~	10.6[z]	~	~	~	~
O. NICARAGUA								
Average	~	~	~	~	~	54.4[w]	~	~
Consumer Goods	~	~	~	59.6[t]	92.2[u]	42.4[w]	~	~
Intermediate Goods	~	~	~	33.0[t]	56.1[u]	27.7[w]	~	~
Capital Goods	~	~	~	14.0[t]	12.6[u]	10.8[w]	~	~
S. URUGUAY								
Average	~	~	~	~	~	139.0[bb]	~	~
Consumer Goods	~	~	~	~	~	133.0[bb]	~	0–15.0[cc]
Intermediate Goods	~	~	~	~	~	70.0[bb]	~	0–15.0[cc]
Capital Goods	~	~	~	~	~	~	~	0–15.0[cc]

a. Tariff level (1925).
b. 1927. Consumer goods are cotton and wool manufactures; intermediate goods are agricultural inputs, raw materials, oils, etc.
c. Ad valorem tariff. Specific duties not included.
d. 1962 (maximum value).
e. 1969 (nominal protection).
f. 1976. Manufactured goods.
g. 1979. Nominal protection.
h. 1986. Range of tariff rates.
i. 1936 and 1951 respectively (average incidence of customs duties: customs duties divided by the value of imports).
j. 1966 and 1967 respectively (nominal protection).
k. 1977 and 1980 respectively (manufactured goods).
l. 1986 (import duties).
m. Before 1928 (basic tariff).
n. 1932. Consumer goods are luxury goods.
o. 1961 (nominal protection).
p. 94.0 corresponds to 1973 and 24.0 corresponds to 1977.
q. 1979–82 and 1986 respectively.
r. 1927, 1936, 1951 and 1959 respectively. Average of nominal tariff rates for all imports.

s. 1975 and 1979 respectively.
t. 1959 (national tariffs before the Common Market). Average nominal tariff for selected groups of manufactured products.
u. 1967 (Common Market tariffs). Average nominal tariffs for selected groups of manufactured products. Figures used for Nicaragua apply to 1960 and 1968 respectively.
v. 1973 and 1977 respectively (nominal tariff rate. The nominal tariff rate is the nominal tariff divided by imports from outside the CACM.
w. 1972. Ad valorem equivalents of the common external tariff. Intermediate goods are food products.
x. 1981. Nominal tariff rates.
y. 1929, 1937 and 1948, respectively (coefficient of customs duties). The coefficient of customs duties is the quotient, at current values, of customs duties and the total imports.
z. 1960. Nominal tariff protection.
aa. 1970, 1975, 1979 and 1982, respectively. Tariff level (weighted average).
bb. 1976 (average tariff).
cc. 1985–86 (range).

SOURCE: Richard Lynn Ground, "The Genesis of Import Substitution in Latin America," *CEPAL Review*, No. 36, Dec. 1988, pp. 196–197.

26

Direction of Trade and Major Trading Partners

Table 2600

SHARE IN VALUE OF WORLD EXPORTS,[1] 20 LRC AND REGIONAL GROUPINGS, 1950–85

(%)

	Area	1950	1960	1970	1980	1985
	World	100.00	100.00	100.00	100.00	100.00
A.	ARGENTINA	1.92	.84	.56	.40	.46
B.	BOLIVIA	.12	.04	.06	.05	.03
C.	BRAZIL	2.22	.99	.87	1.01	1.40
D.	CHILE	.47	.38	.39	.24	.21
E.	COLOMBIA	.65	.36	.23	.21	.19
F.	COSTA RICA	.09	.07	.07	.05	.05
G.	CUBA	1.10	.48	.33	.20[a]	#
H.	DOMINICAN REP.	.14	.14	.07	.05	.04
I.	ECUADOR	.12	.11	.06	.13	.05
J.	EL SALVADOR	.11	.09	.07	.05	.03
K.	GUATEMALA	.13	.09	.09	.08	.05
L.	HAITI	.06	.02	.01	.01	.01
M.	HONDURAS	.09	.05	.06	.04	.04
N.	MEXICO	.86	.59	.40	.81	1.23
O.	NICARAGUA	.04	.04	.06	.03	.01
P.	PANAMA	.03	.02	.03	.02	.02
Q.	PARAGUAY	.05	.02	.02	.02	.01
R.	PERU	.31	.34	.33	.19	.16
S.	URUGUAY	.42	.10	.07	.05	.05
T.	VENEZUELA	1.91	1.90	1.00	.96	.68
	LATIN AMERICA	10.91	6.70	4.85	4.60	5.43
	ALADI	9.06	5.67	4.02	4.07	4.47
	Andean Group	3.13	2.74	1.70	1.54	1.11
	CACM	.48	.34	.36	.24	.14
	UNITED STATES	16.91	15.91	13.60	10.87	11.84
	JAPAN	1.37	3.16	6.17	6.48	9.84
	WEST GERMANY	3.29	8.90	10.91	9.70	10.22

1. Excluding, through 1970, China and Mongolia and through 1980 North Korea and Vietnam. In 1980 the share for China and Mongolia combined was .93%.

a. Calculated from data in SALA, 23-8500 and Part II of 23-2829.

SOURCE: *CEPAL Review*, Aug. 1982, p. 53; UN-YITS, 1978, I, pp. 23, 27; UN-MB, Oct. 1983, pp. 106, 112, 120; IFS-YB, pp. 121–122.

Figure 26:1

WESTERN HEMISPHERE DECLINING SHARE IN WORLD EXPORTS, 1950-85[a]

(%)

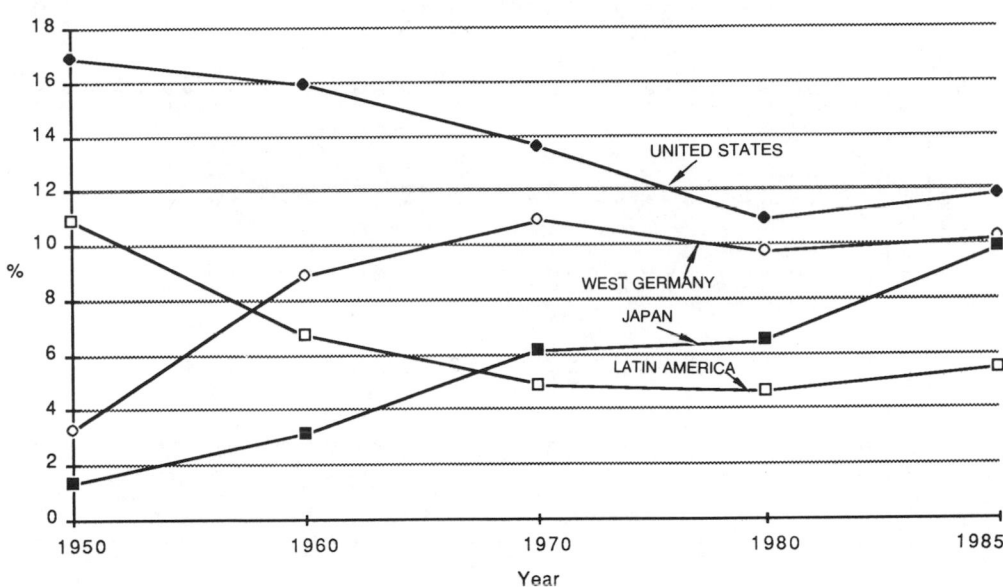

a. Trend line has been smoothed between the 5-year points sampled here.

SOURCE: Table 2600.

Table 2601

IMPORTS AS A PERCENTAGE OF WORLD IMPORTS, 20 LRC, 1950-88[a]

(Value, CIF)

	Country	1950	1955	1960	1965	1970	1975	1980	1985	1988
A.	ARGENTINA	1.66	1.32	1.05	.68	.58	.48	.54	.20	.19
B.	BOLIVIA	.10	.09	.06	.07	.05	.07	.03	.02	.02
C.	BRAZIL	1.87	1.48	1.22	62	.97	1.66	1.28	.75	.56
D.	CHILE	.42	.42	.44	.34	.32	.19	.26	.14	.17
E.	COLOMBIA	.63	.76	.42	.26	.29	.18	.23	.22	.18
F.	COSTA RICA	.08	.10	.09	.10	.11	.09	.08	.05	.05
G.	CUBA	.88	.65	.48	.49	.44	.38	#	#	~
H.	DOMINICAN REP.	.09	.13	.08	.06	.10	.11	.08	.07	.07
I.	ECUADOR	.09	.13	.10	.10	.09	.12	.11	.09	.06
J.	EL SALVADOR	.08	.10	.10	.11	.07	.07	.05	.05	~
K.	GUATEMALA	.12	.12	.10	.13	.10	.09	.08	.06	.06
L.	HAITI	.06	.05	.03	.02	.02	.02	.02	.02	.01
M.	HONDURAS	.08	.08	.06	.07	.07	.05	.05	.04	·
N.	MEXICO	.95	1.00	.99	.89	.84	.81	.99	.74	.70
O.	NICARAGUA	.04	.08	.06	.09	.07	.06	.05	.05	~
P.	PANAMA	.12	.09	.10	.12	.12	.11	.07	.07	.03
Q.	PARAGUAY	.04	.04	.03	.03	.03	.03	.03	.03	.02
R.	PERU	.31	.34	.32	.42	.20	.31	.12	.11	.11
S.	URUGUAY	.34	.26	.18	.09	.08	.07	.86	.07	.04
T.	VENEZUELA	1.02	1.24	1.08	.86	.68	.74	.60	.43	.45
	LATIN AMERICA	8.10	7.83	6.53	5.07	4.77	5.81	5.84	3.92	3.31
	UNITED STATES	16.53	14.10	13.70	13.21	14.44	12.68	13.20 ·	19.12	16.47

a. For yearly data 1948-71, see SALA-SNP, pp. 295-296.

SOURCE: SALA-SNP, pp. 295-296; and IFS, March 1978, except Cuban data (problematic
     since the 1960s because of dollar exchange rate) calculated from Cuba, DGE, AE, 1957, and
     Cuba, JUCEPLAN, AE, 1972 and 1975; IFS-YB, p. 71; 1988, IFS.

Table 2602

MAJOR TRADING PARTNERS, 20 L, 1976-88ª

(%)

Trade with Major Individual Countries

Country	Category	United States								United Kingdom							
		1976	1980	1983	1984	1985	1986	1987	1988	1976	1980	1983	1984	1985	1986	1987	1988
A. ARGENTINA	Export	7.3	8.9	9.9	10.8	12.2	10.3	14.6	15.3	3.1	2.5	~	~	#	.3	1.1	1.1
	Import	17.9	22.6	21.9	18.5	18.2	17.6	16.5	18.8	4.2	3.3	.1	#	#	.1	.1	.4
B. BOLIVIA	Export	34.4	17.3	20.5	20.9	14.1	15.2	16.9	17.2	9.0	7.1	2.6	3.5	9.3	7.9	10.7	3.3
	Import	25.7	18.3	28.2	16.9	21.6	22.7	21.3	21.0	2.6	2.1	3.9	3.6	2.3	4.7	.9	1.5
C. BRAZIL	Export	18.3	17.4	23.2	28.5	26.9	28.2	27.9	25.8	3.8	2.7	3.3	2.6	2.6	2.9	2.9	3.2
	Import	22.6	18.6	15.6	16.6	19.7	22.4	20.7	20.9	2.5	1.9	1.5	2.0	1.9	2.4	2.5	2.7
D. CHILE	Export	10.1	12.1	28.1	26.0	22.7	21.7	22.9	19.7	6.7	6.1	5.4	5.4	6.6	5.2	6.2	5.2
	Import	23.8	27.2	19.9	21.5	21.3	20.5	19.2	19.7	3.1	2.1	2.0	2.3	2.7	2.8	3.2	2.4
E. COLOMBIA	Export	31.2	30.1	28.3	31.5	32.8	29.6	39.8	40.4	2.0	1.8	1.7	2.5	3.0	2.6	2.0	2.0
	Import	42.5	38.5	35.6	34.2	35.3	35.4	35.8	36.7	3.6	2.2	2.2	2.1	2.4	2.6	3.0	2.4
F. COSTA RICA	Export	39.7	33.8	31.8	37.8	39.5	42.8	45.4	44.4	.2	.3	2.6	3.7	2.9	3.9	2.2	1.9
	Import	34.6	34.3	37.8	36.3	34.7	35.8	37.0	39.0	2.8	1.8	1.3	1.3	1.9	1.9	1.6	1.7
G. CUBA¹	Export	~	#	~	~	#	0	0	0	6.1†	5.0†	1.9	1.8	1.0	1.3	2.0	3.4
	Import	#	#	#	.1	#	.1	.1	.2	5.4†	4.6†	4.8	4.5	3.0	3.6	4.1	2.8
H. DOMINICAN REP.	Export	69.6	46.3	67.4	76.7	75.9	77.0	83.0	79.3	1.0	.2	.5	.1	.1	.3	1.0	.7
	Import	47.8	44.8	35.9	34.2	34.7	41.3	53.1	56.3	1.8	1.3	.9	.9	1.1	1.0	1.8	1.0
I. ECUADOR	Export	37.7	28.9	56.6	64.2	53.5	60.9	56.1	45.9	.1	.3	.1	.3	.3	.2	.3	.4
	Import	39.1	38.3	34.0	29.9	33.1	30.2	25.1	33.1	3.7	2.6	3.1	1.8	3.4	2.5	2.2	2.1
J. EL SALVADOR	Export	32.7	39.7	38.6	37.6	48.2	49.3	43.9	39.4	.2	.6	#	.2	.2	.1	.5	.7
	Import	28.6	32.4	32.5	33.3	33.9	40.3	39.3	42.3	2.5	1.3	1.0	1.2	1.2	1.1	1.6	1.3
K. GUATEMALA	Export	35.1	27.7	34.9	33.5	34.0	45.7	46.8	40.2	.4	.4	1.1	.9	.5	.7	1.1	1.6
	Import	36.4	34.5	32.2	32.5	37.4	41.2	40.2	43.0	3.1	2.3	1.1	1.2	1.6	1.8	1.9	2.0
L. HAITI	Export	66.8	69.5	76.1	79.7	87.2	77.6	85.5	89.8	.4	.6	.5	.4	.4	.3	.2	.3
	Import	56.4	57.2	63.3	67.2	67.3	65.4	63.4	62.0	2.3	1.2	1.1	.8	1.0	1.3	1.2	1.6
M. HONDURAS	Export	56.3	49.1	63.4	52.9	48.4	48.9	52.7	49.4	.1	.9	1.3	1.9	1.6	.8	.7	1.9
	Import	43.7	40.4	45.1	40.6	39.0	48.8	54.2	56.8	2.1	2.9	2.2	1.2	1.5	1.8	2.2	1.7
N. MEXICO	Export	60.9	63.2	58.4	58.4	60.4	67.3	69.2	72.9	.8	.5	4.1	4.1	3.1	1.0	1.3	.8
	Import	62.5	65.6	60.5	62.3	66.6	67.1	73.1	74.9	3.1	2.2	1.9	1.8	2.1	1.8	1.6	1.2
O. NICARAGUA	Export	31.1	37.6	22.5	14.1	14.2	.3	.5	.4	.3	.6	.5	.6	.5	.6	.4	.4
	Import	31.5	32.7	18.6	17.1	7.9	.7	.8	1.3	2.5	.8	.5	1.0	1.6	2.6	2.8	2.5
P. PANAMA	Export	48.3	49.3	53.7	60.8	64.1	67.7	67.0	49.5	.1	.1	.3	.1	1.9	.1	0	.2
	Import	32.1	33.8	32.3	31.7	31.5	34.9	34.4	18.7	1.6	1.1	.8	.9	1.0	1.1	1.1	1.2
Q. PARAGUAY	Export	11.9	5.5	8.6	6.3	1.2	4.0	3.9	3.6	6.0	.6	.7	.2	.5	.4	.7	.5
	Import	10.3	9.9	7.3	8.8	7.9	12.7	10.7	10.1	7.6	5.6	5.2	4.2	4.2	5.9	6.6	7.0
R. PERU	Export	24.9	33.0	35.6	39.6	33.9	30.1	27.5	21.7	5.9	4.1	5.3	4.5	4.5	4.7	5.6	5.9
	Import	30.5	38.1	32.8	29.4	28.2	27.2	26.5	29.9	3.4	3.5	1.8	1.8	2.7	2.9	3.0	3.0
S. URUGUAY	Export	10.9	7.8	9.7	14.9	15.2	12.0	14.9	11.3	3.8	3.5	3.9	3.9	4.2	5.3	4.6	4.0
	Import	8.7	9.8	8.3	8.5	8.6	8.5	8.0	7.9	3.7	4.2	2.2	2.1	2.7	2.8	3.1	3.0
T. VENEZUELA	Export	38.4	27.8	31.4	39.9	46.0	44.7	49.3	48.9	2.1	1.2	1.7	1.9	1.7	2.4	1.3	1.2
	Import	44.8	48.2	47.9	50.1	47.5	45.9	44.6	44.0	3.2	2.9	2.2	2.0	3.0	4.1	3.4	3.0

Table 2602 (Continued)

MAJOR TRADING PARTNERS, 20 L, 1976-88ª

(%)

Trade w th Major Individual Countries

Country	Category	Germany 1976	1980	1983	1984	1985	1986	1987	1988	Japan 1976	1980	1983	1984	1985	1986	1987	1988
A. ARGENTINA	Export	5.2	5.1	3.2	3.7	3.4	5.1	6.0	8.8	5.3	2.6	4.8	3.3	4.3	5.7	3.5	4.8
	Import	11.2	9.4	10.5	9.7	10.6	11.1	13.2	10.7	8.2	9.3	6.8	8.2	7.0	7.1	7.6	5.3
B. BOLIVIA	Export	3.4	2.6	2.9	5.6	4.6	5.9	5.9	1.9	3.3	2.7	1.9	1.2	.4	.4	.5	2.6
	Import	7.7	4.3	5.5	4.6	5.3	6.9	7.0	4.6	11.1	7.0	7.3	3.3	8.5	9.8	10.1	3.7
C. BRAZIL	Export	8.9	6.6	5.2	4.7	5.0	4.9	4.7	4.2	6.3	6.1	6.5	5.6	5.5	6.8	6.4	6.7
	Import	8.7	7.0	4.5	4.5	6.5	8.9	9.3	9.5	7.3	4.8	3.7	4.0	4.3	6.3	5.7	6.6
D. CHILE	Export	14.8	12.2	12.6	9.9	9.5	10.4	9.5	11.6	10.7	10.3	9.0	11.1	9.9	9.9	11.0	12.5
	Import	5.7	5.4	6.2	6.2	6.8	8.0	8.3	7.2	11.1	10.4	5.4	8.9	6.1	9.5	9.6	7.7
E. COLOMBIA	Export	16.2	15.7	18.4	16.6	16.2	20.6	11.8	9.8	3.4	4.0	4.4	4.4	4.2	4.9	4.1	4.6
	Import	10.2	6.4	4.9	5.5	6.4	6.5	7.9	7.5	7.7	11.1	11.1	9.6	10.4	8.9	9.1	10.8
F. COSTA RICA	Export	10.5	11.3	12.8	13.3	12.8	14.7	15.1	14.5	1.2	.8	.6	.5	.6	.9	1.1	.7
	Import	5.2	4.8	4.7	5.2	5.3	5.6	5.3	4.3	11.4	11.6	5.3	7.6	9.6	10.6	8.5	6.7
G. CUBA[1]	Export	2.5†	3.9	2.6	1.3	2.1	2.0	2.2	4.9	6.8†	.9	1.9	1.7	2.3	1.7	1.3	2.6
	Import	6.2†	5.5	4.5	4.2	4.1	4.4	4.3	4.6	13.5†	8.0	4.3	4.7	6.3	14.4	10.4	3.6
H. DOMINICAN REP.	Export	.4	.2	.2	.3	.2	.2	.9	.9	.6	.9	1.9	1.7	2.3	1.7	1.3	2.6
	Import	3.5	2.6	3.2	2.7	3.9	3.3	2.0	1.3	6.3	8.0	4.3	4.7	6.3	14.4	10.4	3.6
I. ECUADOR	Export	2.9	1.6	.8	1.2	1.9	3.6	3.3	4.1	1.1	12.2	1.8	.7	2.0	2.6	2.4	2.5
	Import	8.6	7.3	8.7	7.2	9.6	9.5	7.7	6.2	16.5	13.7	9.3	13.7	11.9	13.8	12.7	13.9
J. EL SALVADOR	Export	14.3	19.4	18.9	22.5	21.0	24.1	16.3	23.3	7.9	3.3	4.9	5.5	5.1	3.8	4.3	3.9
	Import	5.9	2.8	4.1	4.4	4.4	4.8	3.4	3.2	9.7	3.7	3.5	4.3	5.2	3.8	6.0	3.6
K. GUATEMALA	Export	10.7	8.3	5.4	2.7	3.5	8.1	6.1	7.4	8.3	2.8	3.4	4.7	3.0	4.2	2.4	2.9
	Import	7.0	5.4	5.0	5.1	5.5	9.4	5.9	5.5	11.1	8.0	4.9	5.1	4.7	6.1	6.6	5.3
L. HAITI	Export	.7	2.6	3.9	3.4	2.7	2.9	1.5	1.6	.6	.2	.4	.3	.5	.5	.8	.6
	Import	3.3	1.8	2.4	1.9	1.9	2.2	3.0	3.8	5.8	5.4	4.3	4.8	6.0	4.6	5.3	5.6
M. HONDURAS	Export	11.7	11.5	5.5	5.8	8.5	6.2	9.0	9.1	3.1	3.7	5.5	7.2	5.5	10.1	6.0	6.3
	Import	4.7	2.1	2.7	3.6	3.0	3.0	2.7	2.6	8.8	8.9	5.9	4.6	5.9	9.5	8.5	8.5
N. MEXICO	Export	2.6	1.7	1.2	.9	1.3	2.3	1.4	1.3	5.1	3.7	6.8	7.5	7.7	6.4	5.5	4.9
	Import	7.0	5.2	4.0	4.1	4.0	5.9	4.1	3.5	5.1	5.3	3.9	4.2	5.4	6.3	7.0	6.4
O. NICARAGUA	Export	9.7	8.6	8.0	6.8	9.7	11.5	11.5	14.4	13.0	2.6	15.1	21.5	17.2	12.9	10.5	12.5
	Import	6.3	2.0	1.8	2.8	2.9	4.4	4.4	3.0	7.9	2.7	1.2	2.0	4.4	2.3	3.1	2.7
P. PANAMA	Export	8.5	5.1	5.7	5.9	5.8	6.2	5.9	10.5	.3	.4	.3	.4	.5	.1	.5	.1
	Import	1.8	1.8	2.3	2.0	2.3	2.4	2.7	1.6	5.6	6.1	7.8	8.3	8.9	8.4	7.4	4.9
Q. PARAGUAY	Export	11.2	12.4	11.8	11.8	13.5	3.3	3.8	3.7	3.5	3.6	1.9	2.4	1.0	.8	.7	2.2
	Import	8.5	6.5	6.8	3.1	5.0	6.0	5.8	6.2	4.7	8.1	4.2	11.8	4.6	5.3	5.8	7.5
R. PERU	Export	7.2	3.9	3.1	4.1	4.5	5.6	4.4	6.6	13.7	10.9	14.4	11.5	10.2	10.6	10.4	12.0
	Import	7.2	6.3	6.7	5.2	8.6	9.1	8.1	8.3	7.7	10.0	6.6	6.3	10.0	9.5	7.4	4.7
S. URUGUAY	Export	12.3	12.9	7.6	8.2	7.7	9.1	10.3	8.3	1.7	.9	1.9	2.2	2.2	1.4	1.5	1.3
	Import	7.6	6.7	6.0	5.9	7.3	7.6	8.1	6.4	1.8	4.1	2.4	1.8	2.3	3.4	3.2	3.0
T. VENEZUELA	Export	1.3	1.1	7.4	5.8	4.3	5.8	5.3	5.5	.4	3.5	3.4	2.7	2.9	3.3	3.0	4.1
	Import	9.7	6.8	4.3	4.6	5.7	7.4	8.6	7.3	8.7	8.1	6.0	5.2	5.7	6.9	6.1	5.3

Table 2602 (Continued)

MAJOR TRADING PARTNERS, 20 L, 1976–88[a]

(%)

		Trade with Major Individual Countries							
		Trade with EEC							
Country	Category	1976	1980	1983	1984	1985	1986	1987	1988
A. ARGENTINA	Export	33.2	27.6	23.9	27.7	24.5	29.0	28.5	30.5
	Import	27.4	25.9	27.2	24.6	28.0	29.1	31.8	27.5
B. BOLIVIA	Export	18.8	21.4	18.1	15.4	20.9	17.7	21.6	18.4
	Import	15.4	12.4	16.9	14.9	14.2	19.9	14.9	12.5
C. BRAZIL	Export	30.7	27.2	28.9	25.2	26.8	26.2	26.5	27.7
	Import	20.0	15.4	12.5	12.6	14.6	22.2	21.9	21.6
D. CHILE	Export	35.7	36.8	34.5	31.1	33.7	34.1	32.7	36.1
	Import	13.8	15.2	17.2	18.0	19.6	21.5	22.7	19.5
E. COLOMBIA	Export	29.9	33.1	39.5	37.5	34.8	39.7	22.8	23.8
	Import	23.0	17.3	16.5	18.2	19.6	22.8	22.2	20.5
F. COSTA RICA	Export	19.0	23.2	24.1	25.9	23.5	28.9	26.4	25.8
	Import	12.2	11.1	12.3	14.2	15.1	27.5	21.2	22.5
G. CUBA[1]	Export	19.1	31.5	31.3	29.9	31.7	29.5	32.0	28.7
	Import	28.3	40.8	30.7	31.9	27.8	27.8	31.0	31.2
H. DOMINICAN REP.	Export	12.0	8.4	11.2	11.1	13.2	13.4	7.2	8.9
	Import	10.3	8.8	11.3	9.2	10.3	11.5	8.3	9.4
I. ECUADOR	Export	8.2	7.6	2.6	3.5	4.6	7.8	7.4	9.2
	Import	18.2	18.2	23.9	18.0	28.1	23.1	20.5	20.8
J. EL SALVADOR	Export	25.2	28.8	23.3	25.8	25.7	28.1	22.3	27.1
	Import	16.2	10.0	11.8	10.2	10.5	11.3	9.9	10.0
K. GUATEMALA	Export	18.3	24.1	16.9	10.8	13.2	16.4	16.8	19.8
	Import	15.5	12.5	11.5	11.8	13.6	19.3	17.9	17.7
L. HAITI	Export	26.8	23.3	16.9	12.7	13.1	17.4	10.3	10.7
	Import	14.3	9.5	11.1	8.7	12.1	11.7	8.7	12.3
M. HONDURAS	Export	19.9	18.0	15.6	17.6	25.0	22.8	23.3	23.9
	Import	12.0	10.5	14.3	14.4	13.9	12.7	13.5	10.5
N. MEXICO	Export	8.6	6.6	17.9	17.8	18.2	12.5	12.0	9.1
	Import	16.3	13.8	15.0	13.1	13.0	14.3	10.7	9.7
O. NICARAGUA	Export	19.7	19.7	23.9	25.7	31.0	43.0	35.8	32.1
	Import	13.0	6.6	12.4	17.6	23.1	35.5	34.5	29.4
P. PANAMA	Export	20.4	12.9	14.4	17.0	16.2	14.3	14.3	21.1
	Import	7.7	6.4	8.7	8.0	8.3	9.0	9.5	10.6
Q. PARAGUAY	Export	40.0	25.3	36.6	40.1	44.9	20.5	34.1	30.6
	Import	20.0	16.1	20.7	15.0	15.9	17.0	21.4	20.0
R. PERU	Export	26.7	16.6	18.5	19.4	22.5	24.9	25.2	29.6
	Import	20.6	21.7	18.5	18.7	23.4	21.1	21.6	21.8
S. URUGUAY	Export	37.5	30.1	20.5	20.7	22.8	25.9	28.6	26.2
	Import	18.3	17.9	15.1	17.4	19.3	19.8	21.0	20.9
T. VENEZUELA	Export	8.7	12.6	19.4	16.0	20.2	15.7	11.6	11.1
	Import	24.8	20.6	22.2	23.0	23.1	26.9	27.3	26.6

1. Cuban % trade total here excludes Cuba's trade with socialist countries.

a. For prior years from 1915, see SALA, SNP, table XV-3.

SOURCE: Calculated from IMF-DOT-Y, 1982, 1986, 1987, 1988, and 1989.

Table 2603

LAFTA, CACM, AND ECLA:L INTRAZONAL IMPORTS AS SHARE OF EACH COUNTRY'S TOTAL IMPORTS, 25 ECLA:L, 1960–87[a]

(%)

	Country	1960	1970	1980	1981	1982	1983	1985	1986	1987
A.	ARGENTINA	13.6	21.1	19.3	19.5	29.2	26.9	31.7	27.3	24.8
B.	BOLIVIA	12.5	20.4	50.3	44.0	48.0	50.1	49.1	85.8	70.4
C.	BRAZIL	13.7	10.8	11.6	14.0	15.4	13.4	11.1	11.5	10.3
D.	CHILE	17.1	19.4	26.9	24.5	26.8	27.9	27.6	24.1	25.0
E.	COLOMBIA	1.9	8.6	15.7	19.5	20.9	19.5	20.2	14.5	16.6
I.	ECUADOR	6.2	9.8	14.3	12.8	14.5	16.8	20.7	17.6	20.2
N.	MEXICO	.2	2.8	3.8	4.6	3.3	2.2	3.3	2.4[†]	1.5
Q.	PARAGUAY	28.9	37.7	59.7	62.3	64.6	61.4	55.1	53.2	46.8
R.	PERU	7.9	15.0	15.2	15.1	16.7	14.5	24.4	26.5	25.6
S.	URUGUAY	26.9	35.2	37.6	46.6	45.4	38.1	38.3	58.3	57.0
T.	VENEZUELA	1.9	3.7	9.0	11.5	10.8	10.3	9.7	9.6	11.8
	Total LAFTA	8.9	11.0	13.1	13.9	14.7	14.2	13.2	13.9	13.3
F.	COSTA RICA	6.3	30.5	33.1	36.8	38.9	30.6	28.8	25.0	25.9[†]
J.	EL SALVADOR	15.1	32.0	45.4	48.0	47.1	41.1	37.7	24.3	32.3[†]
K.	GUATEMALA	10.3	33.1	34.7	32.4	35.3	42.4	31.9	22.5	30.8[†]
M.	HONDURAS	8.8	32.4	29.4	28.8	34.8	31.7	32.7	20.0[†]	20.5[†]
Q.	NICARAGUA	9.0	32.9	56.4	57.9	46.8	45.5	32.7	21.8[†]	21.0[†]
	Total CACM	10.3	32.1	38.4	39.3	40.1	38.3	32.7	23.0	26.9
	Barbados	6.7	28.0	21.1	23.2	23.6	18.7	26.2	21.2	19.5
	Guyana	12.5	17.0	31.5	35.5	49.2	47.8	53.2	23.4[†]	17.5[†]
	Jamaica	3.2	9.3	10.4	27.9	25.7	20.9	24.2	16.4	11.3[†]
	Trinidad and Tobago	32.4	28.8	5.5	6.8	8.1	11.2	11.2	9.0	11.6
	Bahamas	5.4	6.7	4.9	3.0	3.4	3.8	4.3	3.0[†]	7.9[†]
L.	HAITI	~	2.4	8.5	10.4	7.6	8.6	6.4	4.0[†]	4.0[†]
P.	PANAMA	8.1	13.2	8.2	10.0	8.6	12.3	8.1	6.6	9.9[†]
H.	DOMINICAN REP.	~	5.4	6.0	28.2	29.8	33.6	31.4	19.9[†]	23.0[†]
	Suriname	.7	3.1	36.2	36.2	30.3	27.5	27.3	22.2	28.7[†]
	Total Region	9.4	12.9	13.7	14.9	15.6	15.8	14.3	13.5	13.9

a. For 1975, see SALA-27, table 2603.

SOURCE: ECLA-AE, 1988, p. 151.

Table 2604

CACM INTRAREGIONAL TRADE, 5 LR, 1984–88

(M US)

Year	Importing Countries	Exporting Countries				
		COSTA RICA	EL SALVADOR	GUATEMALA	HONDURAS	NICARAGUA
F. COSTA RICA						
1984	114.9	**	30.8	59.4	8.3	16.3
1985	92.7	**	30.1	46.4	7.2	8.9
1986	106.3	**	33.8	61.3	5.9	5.3
1987	115.2	**	36.7	64.3	5.1	9.0
1988†	118.7	**	33.1	68.8	4.8	11.9
J. EL SALVADOR						
1984	251.4	44.8	**	186.8	16.9	2.9
1985	216.8	54.1	**	149.6	10.6	2.4
1986	157.1	37.8	**	108.7	9.2	1.4
1987	181.4	38.9	**	128.0	10.3	4.2
1988†	201.4	45.6	**	142.1	10.2	3.4
K. GUATEMALA						
1984	186.6	62.8	94.7	**	14.2	14.9
1985	99.5	37.2	49.4	**	5.1	7.7
1986	102.5	35.7	53.2	**	5.7	7.8
1987	132.1	43.5	73.6	**	11.5	3.5
1988†	153.0	54.0	85.2	**	12.0	1.6
L. HONDURAS						
1984	99.0	44.6	8.9	41.3	**	4.2
1985	75.2	33.1	7.3	32.8	**	2.0
1986	58.2	24.3	8.0	24.6	**	1.2
1987	57.9	22.1	9.4	25.5	**	.8
1988†	52.4	10.4	11.1	29.2	**	1.7
O. NICARAGUA						
1984	74.5	19.3	11.6	29.2	14.4	**
1985	56.7	15.1	9.1	25.5	7.0	**
1986	38.2	9.6	10.5	15.6	2.5	**
1987	38.0	15.0	8.7	13.1	1.2	**
1988†	36.8	14.8	8.1	13.4	1.5	**
Central America						
1984	726.3	171.4	146.0	316.7	53.8	38.4
1985	540.8	139.6	95.9	254.4	30.0	21.0
1986	462.1	107.4	105.5	210.2	23.4	15.6
1987	524.5	119.5	128.5	231.0	28.1	17.4
1988†	563.3	124.9	137.6	253.5	28.6	18.6

SOURCE: IDB-ESPLA, 1989, table V-3.

Table 2605

CACM TRADE WITH 18 ECR COUNTRIES,[1] 1970–80

(%)

Country	1970	1971	1972	1973	1974	1975	1976	1977	1978	1979	1980	Average 1970–1980
Exports	1.2	1.4	1.6	1.8	2.2	1.7	1.1	1.0	1.1	1.0	1.0[a]	1.2[b]
F. COSTA RICA	.2	.3	.2	.2	.4	.3	.3	1.0	1.8	1.8	1.5	1.0
J. EL SALVADOR	.1	.1	.1	.1	.1	.2	.3	.2	.3	.2	~	.2[c]
Imports	.8	1.1	.6	1.0	1.0	1.0	2.9	3.5	2.8	5.2	4.5[a]	2.9[b]
F. COSTA RICA	.7	.8	.7	.9	1.1	1.3	2.5	6.1	2.2	8.8	2.0	3.3
J. EL SALVADOR	.5	.3	.4	.1	.2	.3	.3	.2	.2	.2	~	.2[c]

Continued in SALA, 24–2611.

Table 2606

LAIA INTRAREGIONAL TRADE, 11 LR, 1984–88
(M US)

Importing Countries	Total LAIA	A. ARGENTINA	B. BOLIVIA	C. BRAZIL	D. CHILE	E. COLOMBIA	I. ECUADOR	N. MEXICO	Q. PARAGUAY	R. PERU	S. URUGUAY	T. VENEZUELA
A. ARGENTINA												
1984	1,673.7	**	382.3	853.0	116.6	58.6	15.4	75.5	40.5	31.9	96.4	3.3
1985	1.196.8	**	375.9	548.1	84.5	36.7	8.7	23.6	15.6	32.5	70.2	1.1
1986	1,576.0	**	340.7	681.3	160.5	67.3	23.0	119.4	35.0	48.6	94.3	5.9
1987	1,711.7	**	259.9	831.8	174.9	41.9	18.0	169.4	53.6	37.8	113.2	11.3
1988	1,775.1	**	227.5	985.0	180.2	51.0	6.5	139.1	28.7	20.5	102.9	33.8
B. BOLIVIA												
1984	270.3	88.2	**	140.0	14.6	1.2	.2	.7	0	24.1	1.4	.1
1985	269.6	69.2	**	170.6	14.2	.7	.1	.1	.3	13.2	1.0	.3
1986	306.6	60.4	**	203.6	30.4	1.3	.2	.7	.1	8.8	.9	.4
1987	485.4	90.7	**	224.3	44.5	1.4	.3	1.4	.5	9.4	.8	112.0
1988	326.4	86.7	**	186.4	42.7	2.5	.2	2.9	.2	2.0	1.5	1.2
C. BRAZIL												
1984	2,040.0	478.2	8.1	**	227.6	14.2	1.6	589.9	53.2	43.2	132.5	491.6
1985	1,513.5	496.2	3.4	**	209.7	6.0	2.5	279.7	60.0	52.3	151.9	251.7
1986	1,742.5	697.9	26.0	**	294.0	8.1	33.5	176.6	91.6	61.9	295.3	57.7
1987	1,606.1	539.3	19.5	**	348.2	18.5	17.9	164.1	62.2	96.7	204.1	135.6
1988	1,553.2	573.1	13.9	**	339.8	15.7	10.9	110.1	88.1	70.4	204.4	126.8
D. CHILE												
1984	803.3	149.9	5.0	280.4	**	15.8	27.0	21.3	16.8	49.8	11.8	225.5
1985	736.6	110.9	5.6	236.7	**	20.9	43.5	9.7	13.1	51.7	4.6	239.7
1986	691.8	136.7	19.9	246.0	**	32.3	52.9	26.9	13.6	46.3	7.2	110.0
1987	867.1	145.9	16.6	354.8	**	99.6	33.5	45.2	21.2	26.9	8.8	114.5
1988	1,193.8	259.4	12.1	521.2	**	50.6	58.7	49.2	23.4	42.0	11.7	165.6
E. COLOMBIA												
1984	826.3	60.6	4.6	170.9	43.0	**	44.6	94.1	0	83.3	4.4	320.9
1985	769.8	132.7	4.1	102.3	44.8	**	65.0	111.3	.9	76.7	7.4	224.5
1986	521.9	61.0	1.9	106.4	40.5	**	30.0	109.8	.2	45.3	5.2	121.6
1987	613.5	61.2	4.1	140.9	51.0	**	35.3	136.9	1.0	37.1	8.1	138.0
1988	889.0	74.0	13.6	236.4	62.5	**	43.5	213.2	.6	61.9	5.5	177.8
I. ECUADOR												
1984	305.1	15.6	.1	140.9	27.8	44.3	**	43.3	.2	28.8	2.0	2.0
1985	342.1	14.5	.1	119.0	34.5	56.3	**	45.7	0	68.5	1.4	2.1
1986	311.8	11.1	.1	133.4	28.1	58.9	**	58.2	0	11.9	1.0	9.0
1987	324.4	14.4	2.3	103.1	32.6	65.2	**	70.0	0	12.1	1.1	23.5
1988	341.8	22.3	.1	120.8	35.1	53.3	**	50.7	0	25.2	.6	15.5
N. MEXICO												
1984	499.5	171.5	.1	285.1	8.9	9.6	1.1	**	.1	15.7	5.2	2.1
1985	568.0	255.5	.2	221.8	51.1	6.4	1.8	**	.2	10.1	8.0	12.9
1986	354.1	158.3	0	156.3	9.7	10.9	3.0	**	.4	3.7	6.7	5.1
1987	288.7	37.3	.1	171.3	2.8	8.3	7.6	**	.4	43.1	10.0	7.8
1988	512.3	136.8	3.0	270.5	10.1	9.5	19.7	**	.2	39.7	15.6	7.2
Q. PARAGUAY												
1984	440.6	94.4	0	331.1	4.5	0	0	.3	**	0	10.0	.1
1985	386.4	72.2	0	301.2	5.8	.1	.1	.2	**	0	6.9	.1
1986	369.3	67.4	.4	290.8	5.4	.1	.1	.5	**	.1	4.6	0
1987	367.0	60.9	.7	288.7	8.9	.2	.1	.8	**	.4	6.3	.1
1988	441.8	80.0	.1	341.0	12.1	.2	.1	.9	**	.1	6.7	.4
R. PERU												
1984	394.0	127.9	9.6	124.2	45.0	20.9	6.3	21.8	1.3	**	6.7	30.3
1985	391.0	161.9	12.6	91.6	45.6	31.9	5.9	11.0	.6	**	2.2	27.5
1986	605.0	189.1	22.3	156.8	65.9	70.9	9.9	33.4	3.8	**	10.8	42.2
1987	744.4	139.1	24.0	208.5	85.8	118.1	51.0	50.9	7.2	**	4.3	55.4
1988	763.0	165.9	2.5	185.5	71.4	80.3	129.0	55.3	10.6	**	4.1	58.4
S. URUGUAY												
1984	283.3	82.9	0	135.7	8.7	.1	.1	44.9	6.8	2.5	**	1.6
1985	284.8	98.9	0	139.8	12.3	.3	.1	23.5	6.4	2.4	**	1.1
1986	415.0	129.1	.4	202.8	11.0	.4	3.9	54.0	6.3	1.9	**	5.2
1987	551.1	168.4	.1	267.7	15.4	.6	.1	83.7	11.3	3.1	**	.7
1988	607.1	186.4	.2	311.8	21.5	1.0	.1	77.7	3.8	2.9	**	1.8
T. VENEZUELA												
1984	738.1	113.9	1.4	364.7	40.1	89.9	3.1	59.8	7.8	49.5	8.0	**
1985	603.9	72.8	0	294.9	33.6	129.0	2.6	25.7	.1	41.3	3.9	**
1986	691.3	44.8	0	348.0	40.6	150.2	2.8	55.1	.1	45.4	4.2	**
1987	880.4	56.8	.3	374.1	71.2	220.2	10.2	85.1	.3	60.2	2.1	**
1988	1,202.3	125.2	.4	501.8	107.0	253.0	4.5	83.9	.2	125.1	1.1	**
LAIA												
1984	8,274.2	1,383.1	411.2	2,826.1	536.9	254.7	99.5	951.5	126.7	338.7	268.5	1,077.3
1985	7,062.6	1,485.0	402.0	2,226.0	536.0	288.2	130.3	530.5	97.2	355.6	250.7	761.1
1986	7,585.4	1,555.7	411.7	2,525.4	686.1	400.4	159.3	634.7	151.1	278.3	425.7	357.1
1987	8,439.8	1,313.9	327.6	2,965.2	835.3	573.9	174.0	807.5	158.1	332.7	352.6	598.9
1988	9,605.7	1,709.8	273.6	3,669.4	882.6	517.0	273.1	791.9	156.0	396.4	347.9	588.0

SOURCE: IDB-ESPLA, 1989, table V-1.

Table 2607

ANDEAN GROUP INTRAREGIONAL TRADE, 6 LR, 1984–88

(M US)

Importing Countries	Andean Group	Exporting Countries				
		B. BOLIVIA	E. COLOMBIA	I. ECUADOR	R. PERU	T. VENEZUELA
B. BOLIVIA						
1984	25.5	**	1.2	.2	24.1	.1
1985	14.2	**	.7	.1	13.2	.3
1986	10.6	**	1.3	.2	8.8	.4
1987	123.2	**	1.4	.3	9.4	112.0
1988	5.9	**	2.5	.2	2.0	1.2
E. COLOMBIA						
1984	453.4	4.6	**	44.6	83.3	320.9
1985	370.4	4.1	**	65.0	76.7	224.5
1986	198.7	1.9	**	30.0	45.3	121.6
1987	214.5	4.1	**	35.3	37.1	138.0
1988	296.7	13.6	**	43.5	61.9	177.8
I. ECUADOR						
1984	75.2	.1	44.3	**	28.8	2.0
1985	127.1	.1	56.3	**	68.5	2.1
1986	79.9	.1	58.9	**	11.9	9.0
1987	103.2	2.3	65.2	**	12.1	23.5
1988	94.1	.1	53.3	**	25.2	15.5
R. PERU						
1984	67.0	9.6	20.9	6.3	**	30.3
1985	77.9	12.6	31.9	5.9	**	27.5
1986	145.3	22.3	70.9	9.9	**	42.2
1987	248.5	24.0	118.1	51.0	**	55.4
1988	270.2	2.5	80.3	129.0	**	58.4
T. VENEZUELA						
1984	143.8	1.4	89.9	3.1	49.5	**
1985	172.8	0	129.0	2.6	41.3	**
1986	198.5	0	150.2	2.8	45.4	**
1987	290.8	.3	220.2	10.2	60.2	**
1988	383.0	.4	253.0	4.5	125.1	**
Andean Group						
1984	765.0	15.6	156.3	54.2	185.6	353.2
1985	762.5	16.8	217.9	73.6	199.7	254.4
1986	633.1	24.2	281.4	42.9	111.4	173.2
1987	980.2	30.7	405.0	96.8	118.8	329.0
1988	1,050.0	16.6	389.2	117.1	214.2	252.9

SOURCE: IDB-ESPLA, 1989, table V-2.

Table 2608

ORIGIN OF ANDEAN GROUP IMPORTS, 1961–77

(%)

Origin	1961-63	1975-77
United States	49.0	39.0
European Economic Community	29.0	25.5
Canada	3.0	3.5
Japan	4.0	9.5
Latin America		
(including Andean Group)	6.5	12.5
Rest of World	8.5	10.0
Total	100.0	100.0

SOURCE: *Colombia Today* 15:9 (1980).

Table 2609

INTRAREGIONAL EXPORTS AS A PERCENTAGE OF TOTAL EXPORTS, 25 LR, 1960–87

(%)

	Country	1960	1970	1975	1980	1981	1982	1983	1984	1985	1986	1987
A.	ARGENTINA	15.8	21.0	25.9	23.6	19.3	20.3	14.0	18.2	18.6	23.8	21.5
B.	BOLIVIA	12.3	8.9	35.9	36.7	42.5	51.8	55.0	57.0	60.1	54.5	57.8
C.	BRAZIL	7.1	11.6	15.5	18.1	19.1	15.0	10.3	11.3	9.6	14.4	13.2
D.	CHILE	7.7	12.2	23.7	23.5	21.6	19.3	11.9	15.0	14.4	17.2	17.4
E.	COLOMBIA	3.2	9.6	20.7	16.6	22.7	20.8	11.1	10.3	11.9	10.7	15.7
I.	ECUADOR	7.8	10.0	33.6	20.2	17.9	22.2	18.3	9.9	8.0	9.6	7.9[†]
N.	MEXICO	2.9	9.5	13.0	5.8	9.7	8.4	7.6	6.1	5.3	5.9[†]	7.7
Q.	PARAGUAY	33.0	38.2	35.6	45.3	50.2	50.8	40.2	37.9	27.4	57.2	30.7[†]
R.	PERU	9.8	6.5	16.9	21.2	12.7	11.2	8.8	9.8	14.1	14.5	17.6
S.	URUGUAY	2.5	12.6	29.3	37.3	26.7	30.8	23.3	26.4	28.0	39.1	30.4
T.	VENEZUELA	11.2	12.5	12.3	9.8	14.5	15.2	14.0	12.6	12.5	9.5	11.3
	Total LAFTA	9.3	12.5	17.4	15.4	16.4	15.0	11.6	11.3	10.9	13.5	13.3
F.	COSTA RICA	5.2	23.8	29.0	34.3	33.2	28.0	29.0	26.0	22.8	17.1	13.5[†]
J.	EL SALVADOR	10.8	31.7	30.0	28.5	27.2	26.3	25.3	23.1	17.1	14.0	18.4[†]
K.	GUATEMALA	5.2	36.7	29.9	32.6	41.3	37.6	34.4	30.6	29.0	22.1	14.5[†]
M.	HONDURAS	18.0	17.0	22.0	13.5	17.2	13.6	12.5	10.2	10.8	5.5[†]	5.3[†]
O.	NICARAGUA	4.5	27.4	25.7	10.3	16.1	17.4	10.1	11.5	8.6	8.0[†]	10.3[†]
	Total CACM	8.4	28.4	28.0	26.4	29.4	26.9	25.0	22.4	20.0	13.6	12.4
	Barbados	5.4	6.6	12.5	17.3	22.8	22.6	18.5	17.2	18.1	7.2	11.1
	Guyana	14.1	1.7	15.3	14.1	27.7	21.8	23.4	13.8	10.1	5.2[†]	4.2[†]
	Jamaica	2.0	4.1	5.6	7.6	9.9	14.6	14.4	9.1	9.1	7.6	7.6[†]
	Trinidad and Tobago	5.9	9.9	11.1	15.0	16.8	18.9	14.3	13.0	11.7	9.3	13.4
	Bahamas	1.8	3.9	4.1	2.0	2.3	2.1	2.6	2.6	1.5	2.7[†]	3.1[†]
L.	HAITI	~	1.6	1.2	1.8	1.1	1.2	3.3	3.1	1.0	2.4[†]	2.7[†]
P.	PANAMA	.5	4.2	6.6	19.2	16.0	16.0	13.1	13.3	14.0	11.7	8.1[†]
H.	DOMINICAN REP.	.2	.9	1.0	10.4	8.4	5.8	3.2	5.3	2.7	1.3[†]	1.3[†]
	Suriname	1.6	.7	#	2.9	2.6	14.1	14.0	6.5	10.6	14.9	11.7[†]
	Total Region	8.8	12.8	16.0	15.4	16.5	15.3	11.8	11.6	11.1	13.0	12.8

SOURCE. ECLA-AE, 1986, p. 187; 1988, p. 150.

Table 2610

VALUE OF IMPORTS FROM COUNTRIES WITH CENTRALLY PLANNED ECONOMIES, 9 L, 1980–87[a]

(M US)

		Imports										
		Total[1]	Asia[2]	Europe[3] & USSR	China[2]	Bulgaria	Czechoslovakia	German Dem. Rep.[4]	Hungary[5]	Poland	Romania	USSR
Developing	1980	8,271	612	7,659	600	183	397	483	331	717	219	5,329
Market	1983	9,725	1,543	8,183	1,495	274	331	526	330	158	234	6,327
Economies,	1984	9,452	1,065	8,387	1,012	382	420	500	348	323	165	6,248
America	1985	10,986	1,986	9,000	1,944	338	421	345	269	286	254	7,086
	1986	10,431	1,643	8,788	1,632	295	473	1,017	259	281	~	6,165
	1987	11,260	1,248	10,013	1,237	~	~	~	237	325	~	7,299
A. ARGENTINA	1980	2,132	196	1,935	189	7	44	~	7	80	7	1,791
	1983	2,512	651	1,861	651	37	29	~	11	28	6	1,751
	1984	1,689	86	1,603	86	23	95	~	8	100	14	1,363
	1985	2,060	334	1,726	329	66	55	~	14	91	29	1,470
	1986	910	350	559	348	59	78	~	25	66	~	273
	1987	~	~	~	330	~	~	~	11	24	~	659
B. BOLIVIA	1980	51	0	51	0	0	18	~	2	0	0	31
	1983	25	0	25	0	0	6	~	1	0	0	18
	1984	21	0	21	0	0	17	~	1	0	0	3
	1985	13	0	13	0	0	11	~	0	1	0	1
	1986	7	~	6	1	0	6	~	0	0	~	0
	1987	~	~	~	0	~	~	~	0	0	~	0
C. BRAZIL	1980	1,468	74	1,394	72	19	164	~	212	509	100	390
	1983	1,652	275	1,377	272	44	107	~	233	77	120	796
	1984	1,548	423	1,125	423	131	73	~	250	159	52	460
	1985	1,892	985	908	984	39	65	~	136	136	76	454
	1986	1,387	~	678	709	23	35	~	113	170	~	336
	1987	~	~	~	450	~	62	~	123	211	~	398
E. COLOMBIA	1980	112	5	107	5	0	15	~	5	57	11	18
	1983	56	5	51	5	0	8	~	7	1	15	18
	1984	52	5	47	1	0	14	~	12	1	2	18
	1985	60	0	60	0	0	21	~	7	2	5	25
	1986	69	2	67	2	0	43	~	10	12	~	0
	1987	~	~	~	3	~	~	~	9	10	~	4
G. CUBA	1980	3,519	130	3,389	127	132	103	~	26	50	31	3,048
	1983	4,271	~	4,069	202	194	123	~	12	32	80	3,628
	1984	4,924	~	4,798	126	229	159	~	18	27	89	4,275
	1985	5,612	~	5,506	107	228	173	~	22	10	126	4,947
	1986	5,881	~	5,797	84	206	167	~	17	8	~	5,398
	1987	~	~	~	77	~	215	~	21	31	~	6,051
I. ECUADOR	1980	46	0	46	0	0	6	~	39	1	0	0
	1983	12	1	10	1	0	5	~	6	0	0	0
	1984	20	9	11	9	0	6	~	5	0	0	0
	1985	34	~	30	5	0	5	~	25	0	0	0
	1986	28	~	26	2	0	8	~	18	0	~	0
	1987	~	~	~	7	~	~	~	8	0	~	0
N. MEXICO	1980	51	~	51	~	17	12	~	3	9	7	3
	1983	130	82	48	38	0	11	~	21	2	2	12
	1984	152	110	42	68	0	9	~	6	10	0	18
	1985	171	105	66	75	0	26	~	8	7	5	19
	1986	189	~	90	99	0	64	~	9	6	~	11
	1987	~	~	~	74	~	~	~	1	30	~	44
R. PERU	1980	107	20	87	20	7	10	~	28	3	23	16
	1983	135	94	40	94	0	8	~	7	0	4	22
	1984	125	60	64	58	0	1	~	7	3	1	53
	1985	241	~	164	77	5	7	~	11	0	11	130
	1986	226	~	143	83	6	16	~	15	0	~	107
	1987	~	~	~	84	~	~	~	20	0	~	83
S. URUGUAY	1980	54	1	54	1	0	12	~	3	5	0	33
	1983	112	21	92	21	0	12	~	6	2	0	71
	1984	116	36	80	36	0	16	~	5	1	0	58
	1985	101	36	65	36	0	17	~	7	2	0	39
	1986	116	64	52	64	0	13	~	9	2	~	29
	1987	~	~	~	53	~	~	~	11	4	~	37

1. Figures for total imports of the centrally planned economies include unadjusted data for Albania, China, DPR Korea, Mongolia and Vietnam derived from the statistics of their trade partners.
2. Unofficial figures derived from the statistics of the trade partners of these countries which are not adjusted for freight and insurance, time lag, or other similar factors.
3. For Albania and beginning in 1975 for German Democratic Republic, trade data included in the totals of CPE Europe and USSR are unadjusted values as reported by trade partners or estimates based on other indicators.

4. Beginning in 1975 official data not available by country of origin and destination. Figures given are unadjusted data as reported by trade partners of German Democratic Republic.
5. Imports, CIF.

a. For 1960, see SALA, 22-2847. For years prior to 1983, see SALA, 25-2610.

SOURCE: UN-YITS, 1987, Special Table K.

Table 2611

VALUE OF EXPORTS FROM COUNTRIES WITH CENTRALLY PLANNED ECONOMIES, 9 L, 1980–87[a]

(M US)

				Exports								
		Total[1]	Asia[2]	Europe[3] & USSR	China[2]	Bulgaria	Czechoslovakia	German Dem. Rep.[4]	Hungary[5]	Poland	Romania	USSR
Developing	1980	5,511	494	5,017	478	192	248	372	92	315	118	3,679
Market	1983	7,030	562	6,468	531	261	269	456	147	284	210	4,841
Economies,	1984	7,339	573	6,767	548	323	304	540	154	261	164	5,020
America	1985	7,448	649	6,799	624	238	293	568	132	239	207	5,123
	1986	8,314	464	7,850	454	252	374	571	136	309	~	5,966
	1987	8,659	502	8,157	490	~	~	~	119	196	~	6,492
A. ARGENTINA	1980	136	32	104	32	6	19	~	10	14	8	47
	1983	87	4	83	4	5	11	~	3	15	15	35
	1984	94	4	90	4	6	7	~	7	22	16	32
	1985	121	3	118	3	12	4	~	4	16	7	75
	1986	171	10	161	10	3	39	~	15	21	~	76
	1987	~	~	~	10	~	~	~	15	16	~	64
B. BOLIVIA	1980	21	5	16	4	0	7	~	0	0	0	8
	1983	6	3	3	1	0	2	~	0	1	0	1
	1984	7	1	5	1	0	4	~	0	0	0	1
	1985	4	~	3	1	0	3	~	0	1	0	0
	1986	4	~	3	1	0	2	~	0	0	~	0
	1987	~	~	~	4	~	~	~	0	1	~	0
C. BRAZIL	1980	449	263	185	263	0	23	~	9	80	38	34
	1983	778	362	416	362	34	16	~	53	134	36	144
	1984	805	384	421	384	101	11	~	42	136	14	117
	1985	803	429	374	429	0	26	~	29	162	73	85
	1986	683	255	428	255	0	37	~	43	254	~	43
	1987	~	~	~	243	~	20	~	31	130	~	72
E. COLOMBIA	1980	43	1	42	0	0	7	~	1	15	5	14
	1983	100	2	98	1	0	5	~	1	72	14	5
	1984	72	1	71	1	0	5	~	3	52	7	5
	1985	31	1	31	1	0	5	·	4	6	9	6
	1986	21	3	18	3	0	3	~	4	2	~	0
	1987	~	~	~	6	~	~	~	4	2	~	6
G. CUBA	1980	4,110	93	4,018	93	181	123	~	46	83	60	3,525
	1983	5,347	~	5,249	97	223	195	~	64	53	140	4,574
	1984	5,377	~	5,283	94	216	216	~	76	39	113	4,623
	1985	5,360	~	5,242	118	225	189	~	77	35	84	4,632
	1986	6,050	~	5,954	95	250	211	~	52	27	~	5,415
	1987	~	~	~	80	~	268	~	48	38	~	5,901
I. ECUADOR	1980	10	1	10	1	0	6	~	0	3	0	0
	1983	11	3	8	3	0	4	~	3	1	0	1
	1984	15	4	11	4	0	4	~	6	1	0	0
	1985	17	~	15	3	0	9	~	3	1	0	1
	1986	16	~	11	5	0	3	~	7	1	~	0
	1987	~	~	~	3	~	~	~	2	1	~	0
N. MEXICO	1980	63	~	63	~	3	22	~	8	8	3	18
	1983	34	6	28	6	0	13	~	6	0	4	4
	1984	41	15	26	10	0	13	~	3	0	8	2
	1985	58	27	31	21	0	13	~	6	1	6	5
	1986	29	~	19	11	0	10	~	1	1	~	6
	1987	~	~	~	9	~	~	~	3	2	~	10
R. PERU	1980	41	1	40	0	2	8	~	6	19	1	5
	1983	19	5	15	4	0	5	~	3	0	0	6
	1984	45	6	39	6	0	5	~	4	0	0	31
	1985	21	~	18	3	0	3	~	1	0	0	14
	1986	42	13	30	13	0	7	~	4	0	~	13
	1987	~	~	~	29	~	~	~	5	0	~	94
S. URUGUAY	1980	27	3	24	3	0	12	~	2	7	0	4
	1983	12	0	12	0	0	0	~	9	0	0	2
	1984	29	0	29	0	0	0	~	0	0	0	28
	1985	44	1	43	1	0	0	~	2	0	0	40
	1986	13	1	12	1	0	1	~	2	1	~	6
	1987	~	~	~	2	~	~	~	1	1	~	3

1. Figures for total imports of the centrally planned economies include unadjusted data for Albania, China, DPR Korea, Mongolia and Vietnam derived from the statistics of their trade partners.
2. Unofficial figures derived from the statistics of the trade partners of these countries which are not adjusted for freight and insurance, time lag, or other similar factors.
3. For Albania and beginning in 1975 for German Democratic Republic, trade data included in the totals of CPE Europe and USSR are unadjusted values as reported by trade partners or estimates based on other indicators.

4. Beginning in 1975 official data not available by country of origin and destination. Figures given are unadjusted data as reported by trade partners of German Democratic Republic.
5. Imports, CIF.
a. For 1960, see SALA, 22-2848. For years prior to 1983, see SALA, 25-2611.

SOURCE: UN-YITS, 1987, Special Table K.

Table 2612

ARGENTINA ABSOLUTE VALUE OF GOODS TRADED WITH SELECTED REGIONS AND COUNTRIES,[1] 1982–88 (M US)[2]

Category	Exports							Imports						
	1982	1983	1984	1985	1986	1987	1988	1982	1983	1984	1985	1986	1987	1988
IFS World Total	7,624.9	7,836.1	8,107.4	8,396.1	6,852.2	6,360.2	~	5,336.9	4,504.2	4,584.7	3,814.2	4,724.1	5,817.8	~
DOTS World Total	7,622.6	7,835.7	8,107.3	8,396.1	6,851.9	6,360.1	9,307.2	5,341.0	4,504.0	4,584.6	3,814.2	4,724.0	5,818.9	6,193.6
Industrial Countries	3,263.3	3,097.5	3,466.9	3,525.1	3,138.9	3,109.3	4,926.8	3,356.1	2,833.3	2,664.8	2,304.3	2,833.2	3,576.9	3,604.9
United States	1,022.1	773.2	876.9	1,027.9	705.6	930.6	1,425.7	1,177.1	986.6	847.4	694.4	833.2	957.3	1,161.4
Canada	40.1	32.1	49.0	58.8	53.8	76.5	99.0	55.5	54.1	66.9	35.2	49.5	56.8	47.6
Australia	3.7	8.8	10.5	28.9	30.5	38.9	48.3	53.9	48.2	62.2	51.1	58.1	53.9	75.5
Japan	283.1	376.6	271.2	360.9	391.1	223.9	450.8	429.6	307.3	375.9	265.5	336.7	441.5	327.7
New Zealand	.5	1.7	1.9	3.4	10.2	9.0	10.4	1.0	2.0	.7	.6	.6	3.3	2.8
Austria	8.1	4.6	2.7	4.0	2.3	3.4	16.5	29.6	33.5	26.8	29.6	14.4	18.9	34.4
Belgium-Luxembourg	68.6	123.3	207.2	148.8	190.5	161.7	236.5	75.1	75.7	100.0	72.4	149.0	191.7	81.2
Denmark	86.2	66.0	35.2	20.7	8.4	12.2	107.4	27.3	22.3	22.1	10.8	12.7	14.3	18.5
Finland	10.0	6.1	5.9	4.8	3.9	5.1	41.2	24.3	15.5	14.1	14.9	19.6	17.9	18.6
France	141.5	133.5	132.1	122.3	102.9	128.3	288.4	196.8	197.3	204.1	207.9	236.7	236.3	293.7
Germany	335.9	248.7	297.6	289.2	352.8	382.9	818.9	478.7	474.5	442.5	404.0	523.4	765.6	663.3
Iceland	.1	.1		.1		.7	.4							
Ireland	4.0	1.2	1.3	1.5	2.2	.7	10.1	7.7	4.2	5.6	3.8	5.4	6.7	5.1
Italy	288.9	340.3	377.2	300.7	285.5	232.1	408.1	230.7	230.4	190.5	233.9	239.5	371.5	380.9
Netherlands	604.0	734.9	892.5	856.4	735.8	617.9	473.6	97.1	63.5	65.8	63.1	97.1	122.6	67.5
Norway	9.2	6.4	34.0	28.3	30.0	9.7	32.0	11.9	6.0	3.1	8.1	5.1	3.8	19.0
Spain	224.2	198.3	232.7	230.9	170.6	154.9	243.8	181.9	153.0	89.8	67.9	102.9	121.4	146.9
Sweden	23.3	15.7	21.1	17.3	20.2	18.9	46.7	76.8	49.2	54.4	36.0	51.1	73.1	95.6
Switzerland	36.3	26.0	18.0	20.3	23.9	30.8	62.7	132.7	106.7	92.6	103.4	92.2	113.0	139.6
United Kingdom	73.7	~		.2	18.7	71.8	106.6	68.5	3.4	.4	1.8	6.0	7.3	25.7
Developing Countries	2,671.9	2,904.8	3,083.2	3,248.6	3,167.4	2,323.3	3,267.3	1,927.5	1,621.1	1,867.1	1,448.8	1,823.6	2,131.9	2,456.5
Africa	272.7	321.7	296.5	260.4	209.7	92.9	135.9	32.3	29.2	18.2	14.9	33.1	73.2	81.5
Algeria	136.6	55.3	75.2	28.0	84.5	21.6	23.8	~	~	~	~	~	18.1	19.0
Angola	16.0	17.3	20.6	36.2	9.4	4.0	4.8	~	~	~	~	~	~	~
Benin	.9	~	~	5.2	1.1	.5	.6	~	~	~	~	~	~	~
Botswana	~	~	~	~	2.0	~	~	~	~	~	~	~	~	~
Burkina Faso	~	.1	~	~	~	~	~	~	~	~	~	~	~	~
Cameroon	7.9	3.3	.2	.8	2.5	.7	.9	.1	.2	.1	~	1.3	.1	.1
Cape Verde	~	2.6	2.5	2.2	.6	.2	.3	~	~	~	~	~	~	~
Central African Rep.	~	~	~	~	9.4	~	~	~	~	~	~	~	~	~
Congo	3.8	3.3	.7	.5	1.3	.8	.9	.7	.8	1.4	.3	.3	2.3	2.4
Côte d'Ivoire	2.8	.7	.1	6.5	.1	.5	.6	~	.2	~	~	.3	.2	.2
Equatorial Guinea	~	~	~	~	.3	~	~	~	~	~	~	~	~	~
Ethiopia	.1	4.4	.1	.8	~	~	~	~	~	~	~	~	~	~
Gabon	4.5	3.7	2.4	3.1	3.2	4.4	4.9	~	~	~	.3	.3	~	~
Ghana	~	1.7	.8	~	.7	~	~	~	~	~	~	~	~	.1
Guinea	~	~	~	8.7	.1	~	.1	~	~	~	~	~	~	~
Kenya	2.2	2.9	1.1	.1	.1	.1	.1	.1	~	~	~	~	~	~
Liberia	~	.2	~	~	.2	.1	.1	~	4.6	~	~	~	.1	.1
Madagascar	3.7	~	~	~	.2	~	~	~	~	~	~	~	~	~
Malawi	~	~	.4	~	.1	~	~	~	~	~	~	~	~	~
Mauritania	~	~	.7	~	.8	.2	2.5	.1	~	~	~	~	~	~
Mauritius	14.5	10.6	13.1	22.7	7.7	2.2	9.3	~	~	~	~	~	~	2.5
Morocco	~	1.3	4.9	.9	~	.6	~	14.5	10.6	13.1	22.7	7.7	2.2	9.3
Mozambique	.1	~	~	~	~	~	~	~	1.3	4.9	.9	~	.6	~
Niger	22.5	20.7	6.4	33.7	6.6	2.6	2.8	.1	~	~	~	~	~	~
Nigeria	~	~	~	~	.4	.1	.1	22.5	20.7	6.4	33.7	6.6	2.6	2.8
Reunion	8.2	6.4	2.6	1.0	~	3.2	3.8	~	~	~	~	~	.1	.1
Senegal	.1	~	.7	~	~	~	~	8.2	6.4	2.6	1.0	.4	3.2	3.8
Somalia	19.2	172.0	122.7	77.4	46.5	38.0	45.6	~	~	~	~	~	~	~
South Africa								31.1	23.5	16.5	14.4	31.1	48.8	58.6
Sudan	.1	.1	.4	~	.7	.4	.5	~	~	~	~	~	~	.1

Table 2612 (Continued)

ARGENTINA ABSOLUTE VALUE OF GOODS TRADED WITH SELECTED REGIONS AND COUNTRIES,[1] 1982–88 (M US)[2]

Category	Exports							Imports						
	1982	1983	1984	1985	1986	1987	1988	1982	1983	1984	1985	1986	1987	1988
Developing Countries (Continued)														
Africa (Continued)														
Tanzania	1.9	?	.7	1.4	2.3	1.8	2.2	?	?	?	?	?	?	?
Togo	.3	.1	.1	5.4	.1	.3	.3	?	?	?	?	?	?	?
Tunisia	4.5	6.8	27.9	20.1	23.7	7.1	27.4	?	?	?	?	?	3.5	?
Uganda	?	?	.2	?	?	.2	.3	?	?	?	?	?	?	?
Zaire	22.9	8.2	4.1	5.5	5.1	3.6	4.3	?	?	?	?	?	?	?
Zambia	?	?	?	.2	.2	?	?	?	?	?	?	?	?	?
Zimbabwe	?	?	8.3	?	?	?	?	.3	?	.1	.1	.1	?	.9
Asia	300.8	801.7	408.5	542.5	473.4	459.4	881.2	93.4	76.0	96.5	55.2	104.5	144.0	187.0
Bangladesh	2.1	.1	2.4	8.0	5.7	3.8	11.3	.1	.2	.2	?	?	2.6	.8
Brunei	.1	.5	.1	?	?	?	?	?	?	?	?	?	?	?
China, People's Rep.	136.6	498.6	74.9	311.0	252.1	265.6	376.9	10.3	4.7	6.1	4.3	9.6	12.8	7.0
Guam	.1	.1	.1	?	?	?	.3	?	?	?	?	?	?	?
Hong Kong	3.3	.3	.4	8.2	8.0	23.8	70.9	17.7	1.9	1.7	.2	4.2	1.9	5.6
India	11.5	37.9	163.7	55.4	38.5	39.9	47.8	1.4	2.1	1.3	1.2	1.4	2.0	2.4
Indonesia	12.5	15.5	9.6	27.0	15.8	22.0	46.3	?	.1	?	?	.1	?	.2
Korea	15.1	49.1	26.6	19.5	62.1	37.3	70.7	14.6	8.9	20.7	11.1	28.9	45.4	76.4
Macao	?	?	?	?	.1	?	.1	?	.3	.7	?	.7	.3	.1
Malaysia	15.2	69.9	14.7	28.1	25.4	11.2	75.6	1.5	.3	.1	.1	1.0	1.4	22.2
Pakistan	6.3	10.2	9.0	17.1	17.9	5.3	2.9	.7	.7	.4	.1	1.1	.5	.5
Philippines	.7	9.1	38.6	.9	2.8	3.3	1.6	.5	.2	.1	.7	.6	.5	.2
Singapore	76.4	36.1	16.3	9.0	8.5	13.2	55.5	26.6	41.9	49.5	23.4	35.0	46.4	55.5
Sri Lanka	.1	19.7	4.3	25.2	.1	.7	.2	1.0	.5	.3	.7	1.4	1.0	1.7
Thailand	2.3	10.9	21.0	8.7	12.3	14.9	43.8	?	.5	?	?	.1	.1	.3
Vanuatu	?	?	.1	?	1.0	?	?	?	?	?	?	?	?	?
Asia not specified	?	?	?	?	?	?	.1	?	?	?	?	?	?	?
Taiwan Province of China	18.4	43.9	26.8	24.6	23.5	18.4	70.4	19.0	13.9	15.3	12.6	20.5	29.2	14.3
Europe	99.3	77.0	250.9	311.4	377.0	95.7	229.7	34.7	36.0	69.5	42.3	42.4	87.7	81.1
Cyprus	4.9	8.7	4.9	.1	8.4	1.5	3.8	?	.9	3.6	?	?	?	?
Gibraltar	?	?	?	?	.1	.1	.1	?	?	?	?	?	?	?
Greece	22.6	8.2	11.3	14.4	21.9	14.7	17.6	.4	.1	2.9	.1	.1	10.2	12.2
Hungary	11.1	6.6	3.7	11.1	17.2	6.2	7.7	7.1	2.6	4.5	5.7	2.7	3.0	4.9
Malta	7.3	5.7	3.1	3.6	7.9	3.4	6.1	?	1.0	?	?	?	?	?
Poland	21.8	17.5	121.5	98.2	100.7	18.5	22.3	12.4	19.3	25.5	22.6	24.9	16.3	19.6
Portugal	28.6	23.6	59.2	73.9	96.1	37.7	131.5	3.3	2.8	2.2	2.9	2.8	5.6	5.4
Romania	.4	4.3	24.5	16.7	56.9	8.2	9.9	10.0	7.6	29.4	9.6	6.6	31.0	37.2
Turkey	.5	1.6	3.2	76.7	43.7	3.0	4.3	.1	?	?	?	.4	?	1.0
Yugoslavia	2.0	.7	19.7	15.9	24.1	2.4	26.0	1.5	1.8	1.4	1.3	4.9	18.9	.8
Europe not specified	?	?	?	?	.1	?	?	?	?	?	?	?	?	?
Middle East	442.5	601.2	626.6	564.0	468.3	299.6	326.8	164.3	10.7	10.4	14.8	11.7	39.7	41.1
Bahrain	.1	.1	.1	.4	.2	.2	?	?	?	?	?	?	.1	.1
Egypt	108.6	88.6	67.2	143.7	90.8	38.2	45.9	?	?	?	.2	?	.1	.1
Iran, I.R. of	134.4	396.4	430.2	313.9	256.3	191.8	211.0	?	?	?	?	?	?	?
Iraq	115.5	9.5	2.8	.4	2.0	.3	.3	?	?	?	?	?	?	?
Israel	40.8	51.1	38.4	31.1	30.7	39.5	35.4	10.7	10.5	9.7	10.1	11.7	13.0	14.6
Jordan	8.7	3.9	6.4	12.7	3.4	3.3	8.4	?	?	?	?	?	?	?
Kuwait	2.0	1.7	1.4	1.3	1.0	1.0	.1	?	?	?	?	?	?	?
Lebanon	4.3	5.9	35.3	39.9	19.2	6.7	8.1	?	.1	?	?	?	?	?
Libya	.6	.3	7.8	.3	15.3	2.6	2.8	?	?	?	?	?	?	?
Oman	?	2.8	2.5	?	?	.1	.1	?	?	?	?	?	?	?
Qatar	.3	.2	.1	?	?	?	?	?	?	?	?	4.6	?	?
Saudi Arabia	23.0	33.9	15.8	12.7	12.3	8.4	9.2	153.5	?	.7	?	?	25.0	26.3
Syrian Arab Rep.	4.0	4.8	16.7	4.3	36.5	6.7	4.7	.1	.2	?	?	?	?	?
United Arab Emirates	.1	2.0	1.9	3.3	.5	1.1	?	?	?	?	?	?	1.6	?
Yemen, P.D. Rep.	?	.1	?	?	?	?	?	?	?	?	?	?	?	?

Table 2612 (Continued)

ARGENTINA ABSOLUTE VALUE OF GOODS TRADED WITH SELECTED REGIONS AND COUNTRIES,[1] 1982–88 (M US)[2]

Category	Exports 1982	1983	1984	1985	1986	1987	1988	Imports 1982	1983	1984	1985	1986	1987	1988
Developing Countries (Continued)														
Western Hemisphere	1,556.8	1,103.3	1,500.7	1,570.3	1,639.0	1,375.8	1,693.7	1,602.9	1,469.1	1,672.5	1,321.6	1,631.9	1,787.2	2,065.9
Antigua and Barbuda	.1	.1	.1	.1	.1	.4	.4	~	~	~	~	~	~	~
Bahamas, The	.8	.7	.3	.6	.7	.8	1.0	.4	.3	1.0	.9	1.2	.2	.3
Barbados	.9	1.9	.8	1.7	1.4	1.3	1.3	~	~	~	~	~	~	~
Belize	.1	.1	~	~	~	.1	.1	~	~	~	~	~	~	~
Bermuda	.2	~	.1	~	~	~	~	~	~	~	~	~	~	~
B. BOLIVIA	113.9	56.4	88.2	69.3	60.5	90.7	108.8	395.7	394.5	391.7	382.9	352.8	304.8	365.7
C. BRAZIL	567.5	358.4	478.2	496.3	698.1	539.4	671.8	687.9	666.4	831.2	611.6	691.3	819.3	1,072.6
D. CHILE	164.2	188.9	149.9	111.1	136.8	146.0	253.3	146.6	116.1	118.5	85.4	148.5	152.4	184.9
E. COLOMBIA	69.6	59.5	60.6	132.7	61.0	61.2	87.1	25.9	24.3	24.5	23.2	69.4	30.1	51.4
F. COSTA RICA	1.6	1.9	7.8	3.5	3.1	3.4	4.6	.3	.2	.1	2.4	10.6	4.3	1.1
Dominica	~	~	~	~	~	.1	.2	~	~	~	~	~	~	~
H. DOMINICAN REP.	1.0	10.9	31.9	9.9	11.4	3.5	4.2	~	~	~	~	~	~	~
I. ECUADOR	19.8	13.4	15.6	14.6	11.2	14.4	15.9	35.7	12.1	8.8	11.5	28.2	22.0	7.2
J. EL SALVADOR	9.4	2.6	1.7	3.6	2.1	3.3	4.0	.1	.4	1.7	.3	.1	~	.1
Grenada	.1	~	.5	.1	.1	.2	~	~	.3	.1	.1	~	1.3	1.6
K. GUATEMALA	1.8	1.8	2.0	2.6	1.7	5.3	6.3	1.2	~	~	~	~	.1	.1
Guyana	~	~	~	~	4.0	~	~	~	~	~	~	~	.5	.7
L. HAITI	.3	20.9	11.5	6.4	1.9	.4	.5	~	~	~	~	~	~	~
M. HONDURAS	4.3	.3	1.4	6.9	3.4	2.6	3.2	.1	~	~	~	.2	.1	.1
Jamaica	.2	.6	.7	.3	1.1	2.9	3.5	21.7	~	~	~	~	~	~
Leeward Islands	~	~	~	~	~	.1	.1	~	~	~	~	~	~	~
N. MEXICO	111.8	33.4	171.6	255.5	158.3	37.3	41.0	61.9	69.3	78.5	59.8	100.1	153.0	160.7
Montserrat	~	.1	~	~	~	~	~	~	~	~	~	~	~	~
Netherlands Antilles	3.7	6.8	21.8	8.8	3.9	5.4	6.5	10.4	.9	3.2	2.0	~	18.4	22.0
O. NICARAGUA	2.2	17.3	21.1	26.4	18.5	11.4	13.7	~	~	~	~	~	~	~
P. PANAMA	5.4	7.1	10.3	8.8	20.9	14.3	17.5	25.6	18.8	24.8	17.2	22.8	21.7	2.7
Q. PARAGUAY	145.9	87.3	94.4	72.2	67.4	60.9	58.7	49.3	38.6	50.4	20.1	47.4	70.2	36.9
R. PERU	109.8	94.6	127.9	162.0	189.1	139.1	152.4	21.3	31.4	35.0	36.5	60.1	46.2	19.0
St. Kitts & Nevis	.1	.1	.1	.3	.1	.2	.3	~	~	~	~	~	~	~
St. Lucia	.1	.1	.1	.2	.1	.8	.9	~	~	~	~	~	~	~
St. Vincent	.1	.2	.1	.2	1.1	1.4	1.7	~	~	~	~	~	~	~
Suriname	~	~	~	.1	~	~	~	8.6	~	~	~	~	~	~
Trinidad and Tobago	9.3	2.8	4.9	4.2	7.0	3.9	9.4	~	.6	~	~	~	~	~
S. URUGUAY	115.5	76.8	82.9	99.0	129.3	168.4	162.7	89.9	89.0	98.1	65.9	93.0	114.0	110.0
T. VENEZUELA	97.4	58.4	114.0	72.8	44.8	56.8	62.5	20.5	6.0	4.9	1.6	6.0	12.6	13.2
Western Hem. not specified	~	~	~	.2	~	.1	.1	~	~	~	~	~	~	~
U.S.S.R. and Other Nonmembers	1,687.4	1,833.4	1,557.3	1,622.3	545.7	927.5	1,113.1	57.4	49.6	52.7	61.2	67.3	110.1	132.1
Albania	.4	~	~	~	1.5	~	~	~	~	~	~	~	~	~
Bulgaria	3.6	31.2	24.6	51.7	45.3	46.7	56.0	5.4	6.9	7.6	5.0	3.1	3.7	4.4
G. CUBA	47.9	128.4	233.7	283.4	181.8	133.7	160.4	~	.1	.6	.3	1.2	.9	1.1
Czechoslovakia	30.1	31.0	93.7	58.0	94.7	83.1	99.7	14.9	8.5	4.4	5.2	1.8	1.6	1.9
Eastern Germany	19.0	6.6	17.5	16.4	11.3	21.8	26.2	3.8	2.7	4.5	8.8	2.0	13.5	16.2
Mongolia	~	.2	~	.1	.1	.1	.1	~	~	~	~	~	~	~
North Korea	~	~	~	~	.2	1.4	1.7	~	~	~	~	~	~	~
U.S.S.R.	1,586.4	1,635.9	1,187.8	1,212.7	208.8	640.8	768.9	33.3	31.5	35.6	41.9	59.2	90.5	108.6
Memorandum Items														
EEC	1,878.2	1,878.1	2,246.1	2,058.8	1,985.4	1,814.8	2,842.3	1,367.5	1,227.1	1,126.1	1,068.6	1,375.5	1,853.2	1,700.3
Oil Exporting Countries	544.9	596.6	667.7	493.6	439.1	308.2	359.8	174.0	6.1	5.6	6.1	6.1	57.5	58.9
Non-Oil Developing Countries	2,127.0	2,308.2	2,415.4	2,755.0	2,728.3	2,015.2	2,907.4	1,753.5	1,614.9	1,861.5	1,442.6	1,817.5	2,074.4	2,397.7

Table 2612 (Continued)

ARGENTINA ABSOLUTE VALUE OF GOODS TRADED WITH SELECTED REGIONS AND COUNTRIES,[1] 1982-88
(M US)[2]

Category	Exports							Imports						
	1982	1983	1984	1985	1986	1987	1988	1982	1983	1984	1985	1986	1987	1988
% Distribution														
Industrial Countries	42.8	39.5	42.8	42.0	45.8	48.9	52.9	62.8	62.9	58.1	60.4	60.0	61.5	58.2
Developing Countries	35.1	37.1	38.0	38.7	46.2	36.5	35.1	36.1	36.0	40.7	38.0	38.6	36.6	39.7
Africa	3.6	4.1	3.7	3.1	3.1	1.5	1.5	.6	.6	.4	.4	.7	1.3	1.3
Asia	3.9	10.2	5.0	6.5	6.9	7.2	6.5	1.7	1.7	2.1	1.4	2.2	2.5	3.0
Europe	1.3	1.0	3.1	3.7	5.5	1.5	2.5	.6	.8	1.5	1.1	.9	1.5	1.3
Middle East	5.8	7.7	7.7	6.7	6.8	4.7	3.5	3.1	.2	.2	.4	.2	.7	.7
Western Hemisphere	20.4	14.1	18.5	18.7	23.9	21.6	18.2	30.0	32.6	36.5	34.6	34.5	30.7	33.4
U.S.S.R. and Other Nonmembers, etc.	22.1	23.4	19.2	19.3	8.0	14.6	12.0	1.1	1.1	1.1	1.6	1.4	1.9	2.1
Annual PC														
World	-16.6	2.8	3.5	3.6	-18.4	-7.2	46.3	-43.4	-15.7	1.8	-16.8	23.9	23.2	6.4
Industrial Countries	-3.7	-5.1	11.9	1.7	-11.0	-.9	58.5	-48.5	-15.6	-5.9	-13.5	23.0	26.2	.8
Developing Countries	.8	8.7	6.1	5.4	-2.5	-26.6	40.6	-32.0	-15.9	15.2	-22.4	25.9	16.9	15.2
Africa	59.8	18.0	-7.8	-12.2	-19.5	-55.7	46.3	-73.6	-9.4	-37.6	-18.3	122.1	121.5	11.3
Asia	12.6	166.6	-49.1	32.8	-12.7	-3.0	91.8	-72.0	-18.6	26.9	-42.8	89.3	37.9	29.8
Europe	-33.4	-22.4	225.9	24.1	21.1	-74.6	140.0	-59.7	3.8	93.1	-39.1	.3	106.6	-7.5
Middle East	67.2	35.9	4.2	-10.0	-17.0	-36.0	9.1	-46.2	-93.5	-2.3	41.9	-20.7	238.5	3.4
Western Hemisphere	-13.5	-29.1	36.0	4.6	4.4	-16.1	23.1	-19.4	-8.3	13.8	-21.0	23.5	9.5	15.6
U.S.S.R. anc Other Nonmembers, etc.	-45.6	8.7	-15.1	4.2	-66.4	70.0	20.0	-29.2	-13.5	6.2	16.1	10.0	63.7	20.0

1. DOT data may differ between countries and from IFS data because of the time it takes for an export to become an import, etc.
2. Data may be calculated from partner's reported data or estimated on basis of less than 12 months.

SOURCE: IMF-DOT-Y, 1989.

Table 2613

BOLIVIA ABSOLUTE VALUE OF GOODS TRADED WITH SELECTED REGIONS AND COUNTRIES,[1] 1982-88
(M US)[2]

Category	Exports							Imports						
	1982	1983	1984	1985	1986	1987	1988	1982	1983	1984	1985	1986	1987	1988
IFS World Total	827.7	755.2	724.5	623.4	563.8	565.8	601.1	577.5	589.1	491.6	551.9	716.2	776.0	604.2
DOTS World Total	898.5	786.7	781.5	672.5	640.3	569.8	643.5	496.3	530.7	409.0	683.3	666.6	757.5	775.5
Industrial Countries	425.9	335.7	350.7	248.8	220.7	229.5	267.6	296.8	295.6	186.9	350.5	368.1	378.0	308.9
United States	260.5	160.9	145.7	94.8	97.1	96.1	110.4	143.8	149.5	86.4	140.6	151.1	161.0	163.0
Canada	.1	?	.1	.1	.1	.1	18.3	5.8	4.0	3.2	5.3	4.7	8.5	5.0
Australia	?	?	?	?	?	?	.1	?	.1	?	?	?	?	?
Japan	16.5	15.1	8.4	2.9	2.6	2.9	16.7	54.4	39.0	24.1	66.2	65.3	76.4	28.9
Austria	?	.2	?	?	?	.4	3.7	?	1.3	.7	?	1.0	2.3	.6
Belgium-Luxembourg	18.4	31.6	31.5	13.9	10.9	17.7	21.0	3.7	2.8	3.8	9.9	16.4	9.3	2.4
Denmark	?	?	?	.1	1.2	.8	.2	?	3.4	.9	2.3	15.1	2.8	5.7
Finland	?	?	?	?	?	?	.2	?	.6	.1	?	?	?	.5
France	14.8	14.5	5.6	7.6	5.6	5.2	36.4	6.4	21.1	7.4	10.8	6.2	13.1	5.2
Germany	24.1	22.5	25.7	31.2	37.9	33.4	12.4	36.3	29.2	28.3	52.1	45.9	53.0	35.7
Ireland	?	?	?	?	?	?	?	?	.2	.4	?	?	?	1.2
Italy	.9	.6	.5	.7	1.5	1.8	19.2	8.5	3.9	3.6	4.3	5.5	7.5	24.3
Netherlands	36.3	46.7	74.1	21.6	.7	.2	3.6	6.3	5.7	6.3	10.6	5.8	15.6	5.3
Norway	?	.1	.1	?	?	?	.1	?	.1	.1	?	?	?	.1
Spain	4.7	6.1	2.9	2.6	4.7	2.8	3.4	?	2.2	4.0	7.7	6.6	5.1	5.1
Sweden	.6	.1	.2	?	?	?	.1	5.9	7.2	3.2	5.9	8.7	10.6	9.4
Switzerland	18.6	16.6	14.5	10.6	7.5	7.0	.6	5.9	4.5	3.8	4.7	4.8	6.1	4.5
United Kingdom	30.4	20.6	41.5	62.7	50.9	61.0	21.4	19.8	20.8	10.7	30.2	31.0	6.8	11.8
Developing Countries	470.0	435.8	415.2	405.8	414.2	339.5	374.9	179.4	228.3	208.2	324.8	278.0	373.6	459.4
Africa	.8	?	?	?	?	.8	?	?	3.5	.5	?	?	?	?
Algeria	?	?	?	?	?	?	?	?	.1	?	?	?	?	?
Morocco	.8	?	?	?	?	.8	?	?	?	?	?	?	?	?
Nigeria	.8	?	?	?	?	?	?	?	?	?	?	?	?	?
South Africa	?	?	?	?	?	?	?	?	3.3	.5	?	?	?	?
Asia*	?	?	?	?	.7	4.0	12.9	8.1	3.6	6.1	4.7	6.8	18.3	14.7
China, People's Rep.	?	?	?	?	?	?	?	?	.7	.4	?	1.2	4.3	3.7
Hong Kong	?	?	?	?	.1	.8	?	?	.2	.2	?	?	?	.3
India	?	?	?	?	?	?	?	?	.2	.1	?	?	?	?
Indonesia	?	?	?	?	?	?	.1	?	?	?	?	?	?	.2
Korea	?	1.2	.9	?	.2	?	12.3	?	?	3.1	3.1	3.4	7.1	7.6
Malaysia	?	?	?	?	.4	4.0	?	?	.1	.2	?	?	?	.3
Sri Lanka	?	?	?	?	?	?	2.4	?	?	?	?	?	?	.2
Asia not specified	?	?	?	?	?	?	?	8.1	?	?	?	?	?	?
*of which														
Taiwan Province of China	?	?	?	?	?	?	.4	?	.1	.5	?	?	?	?
Europe	5.4	3.0	2.7	1.1	.2	5.1	9.4	8.4	1.0	5.0	1.7	2.2	6.9	2.3
Faeroe Islands	?	?	?	?	?	?	?	?	.1	.1	?	1.9	3.0	3.9
Hungary	?	?	?	?	?	?	?	?	.1	.1	?	?	?	?
Poland	?	?	?	1.1	?	?	?	?	.7	3.9	?	1.9	3.0	3.6
Portugal	?	?	1.1	?	?	?	.9	?	.2	.1	?	?	?	.1
Romania	5.4	3.0	2.7	?	?	5.0	6.0	?	.1	.8	3.1	?	?	?
Turkey	?	?	?	?	?	?	.1	?	?	.1	?	?	?	?
Yugoslavia	?	?	?	?	.2	4.0	2.4	8.4	?	?	?	?	?	.2
Europe not specified	?	?	?	?	?	?	?	8.1	?	.2	?	?	?	?
Middle East	?	?	?	?	.5	.4	.3	?	.2	.9	2.1	2.2	1.0	.4
Egypt	?	?	?	?	.5	.4	.3	?	.1	.9	2.1	1.9	1.0	.4
Israel	?	?	?	?	.4	?	?	?	.1	?	?	?	?	?
Qatar	?	?	?	?	.1	.2	.3	?	?	?	?	?	?	?
Saudi Arabia	?	?	?	?	?	?	?	?	?	?	?	?	?	?
United Arab Emirates	?	?	?	?	?	.1	?	?	?	?	?	?	?	?

Table 2613 (Continued)

BOLIVIA ABSOLUTE VALUE OF GOODS TRADED WITH SELECTED REGIONS AND COUNTRIES,[1] 1982-88
(M US)[2]

Category	Exports 1982	1983	1984	1985	1986	1987	1988	Imports 1982	1983	1984	1985	1986	1987	1988
Developing Countries (Continued)														
Western Hemisphere	463.8	432.7	412.4	404.7	413.0	329.3	352.4	162.9	220.0	195.7	318.0	267.4	351.2	440.4
A. ARGENTINA	399.7	362.6	382.3	375.9	340.7	259.9	311.9	72.4	75.6	63.4	117.4	75.6	107.0	128.5
B. BRAZIL	18.2	39.4	8.1	4.5	26.0	19.5	10.6	50.5	73.9	89.3	134.5	124.4	155.8	215.9
D. CHILE	11.1	6.8	5.0	5.6	19.9	16.6	10.8	14.8	16.2	14.1	23.8	34.3	46.3	48.0
E. COLOMBIA	5.8	3.8	4.6	4.1	1.9	4.1	4.9	1.8	1.6	1.5	1.6	1.2	1.9	2.3
F. COSTA RICA	~	~	~	~	~	~	.1	~	.8	.1	~	~	~	~
H. DOMINICAN REP.	~	~	~	~	~	~	.1	~	~	~	~	~	~	~
I. ECUADOR	1.0	5.0	.1	~	.1	2.3	.1	.6	.3	.1	~	~	~	.2
N. MEXICO	.2	~	.1	.2	~	~	.1	.8	32.5	~	2.1	4.3	7.9	8.3
P. PANAMA	~	.1	1.2	1.5	1.2	1.7	2.0	~	2.7	2.8	9.6	11.4	17.5	20.9
Q. PARAGUAY	5.0	~	~	~	.4	.7	~	5.0	~	.7	1.9	.3	.8	~
R. PERU	23.1	14.8	9.6	12.6	22.3	24.0	11.3	13.6	13.5	21.8	25.4	14.9	11.8	13.7
S. URUGUAY	.3	.2	~	~	.4	.1	.3	1.0	2.4	1.3	1.8	.9	1.1	1.4
T. VENEZUELA	4.3	.2	1.4	~	~	.3	.3	.1	.5	.4	~	~	1.2	1.2
Western Hem. not specified	~	~	~	~	~	~	~	1.3	~	~	~	~	~	~
U.S.S.R. and Other Nonmembers														
G. CUBA	2.6	14.2	15.7	17.9	5.4	.8	.9	7.5	6.9	13.8	8.0	20.4	6.0	7.2
Czechoslovakia	.3	5.3	13.8	15.0	2.4	.8	.9	~	.1	.1	.1	9.9	1.7	2.0
Eastern Germany	~	~	~	~	~	~	~	~	2.9	1.9	6.7	1.7	.9	1.0
U.S.S.R.	2.3	8.9	1.9	2.9	3.0	~	~	7.5	3.9	11.8	1.2	8.8	3.4	4.1
U.S.S.R., etc. not specified	~	~	~	~	~	~	~	~	~	~	~	~	~	~
Country or area not specified	~	1.1	~	~	~	~	~	12.6	~	~	~	~	~	~
Memorandum Items														
EEC	129.6	142.7	181.7	140.5	113.4	123.1	118.5	81.0	89.5	65.5	127.9	132.5	113.1	96.8
Oil Exporting Countries	5.2	.2	1.4	~	~	.6	.5	.1	.7	.5	~	~	1.2	1.4
Non-Oil Developing Countries	464.9	435.5	413.8	405.8	414.2	338.9	374.4	179.3	227.6	207.8	324.8	278.0	372.4	458.0
% Distribution														
Industrial Countries	47.4	42.7	44.9	37.0	34.5	40.3	41.6	53.8	55.7	45.7	51.3	55.2	49.9	39.8
Developing Countries	52.3	55.4	53.1	60.3	64.7	59.6	68.3	33.1	43.0	50.9	47.5	41.7	49.3	59.2
Africa	.1	~	~	~	~	.1	~	~	.7	.1	~	~	.1	~
Asia	~	.4	.3	.2	.1	.7	2.0	1.6	.7	1.5	.7	1.0	2.4	1.9
Europe	.6	~	~	~	~	.9	1.5	1.7	.2	1.2	.3	.3	.4	.5
Middle East	~	~	~	~	.1	.1	~	~	~	.2	.3	~	.1	.1
Western Hemisphere	51.6	55.0	52.8	60.2	64.5	57.8	64.8	32.8	41.5	47.8	46.5	40.1	46.4	56.8
U.S.S.R. and Other Nonmembers, etc.	.3	1.8	2.0	2.7	.9	.1	.1	1.5	1.3	3.4	1.2	3.1	.8	.9
Annual PC														
World	-9.7	-12.4	-.7	-13.9	-4.8	-11.0	12.9	-45.9	6.9	-22.9	67.1	-2.5	13.6	2.4
Industrial Countries	-18.0	-21.2	4.5	-29.0	-11.3	4.0	16.6	-44.2	-.4	-36.8	87.5	5.0	2.7	-18.3
Developing Countries	6.4	-7.3	-4.7	-2.3	2.1	-18.0	10.4	-49.4	27.2	-8.8	56.0	-14.4	34.4	23.0
Africa	~	-99.9	~	-83.3	~	~	~	~	~	-84.2	~	~	~	~
Asia	-100.0	~	-15.4	-54.5	~	507.5	222.5	-71.9	-55.0	68.4	-23.1	44.4	169.5	-19.8
Europe	-8.0	-44.4	-10.5	-59.1	-85.4	-16.4	85.1	-66.1	-87.8	382.5	127.9	~	59.2	30.6
Middle East	~	-62.5	33.3	~	~	~	-31.0	~	~	494.9	127.9	-7.9	-46.9	-57.4
Western Hemisphere	9.5	-6.7	-4.7	-1.9	2.0	-20.3	7.0	-45.9	35.0	-11.0	62.5	-15.9	31.3	25.4
U.S.S.R. and Other Nonmembers, etc.	-91.7	442.8	10.5	14.1	-69.6	-85.5	20.1	-42.1	-8.5	100.9	-42.5	156.7	-70.8	20.0

1. DOT data may differ between countries and from IFS data because of the time it takes for an export to become an import, etc.
2. Data may be calculated from partner's reported data or estimated on basis of less than 12 months.

SOURCE: IMF-DOT-Y, 1989.

Table 2614

BRAZIL ABSOLUTE VALUE OF GOODS TRADED WITH SELECTED REGIONS AND COUNTRIES,[1] 1982-88 (M US)[2]

PART I. BRAZIL INDICATORS OF TRADE WITH THE WORLD, 1982-88

Category	Exports							Imports						
	1982	1983	1984	1985	1986	1987	1988	1982	1983	1984	1985	1986	1987	1988
IFS World Total	20,175	21,899	27,005	25,639	22,349	26,225	33,783	21,069	16,801	15,210	14,332	15,557	16,581	16,047
DOTS World Total	20,168	21,853	27,007	25,635	22,405	26,223	33,785	21,069	16,803	15,210	14,335	15,557	16,583	16,048
Industrial Countries	12,048	13,639	17,107	16,327	14,812	17,041	21,759	8,122	6,440	6,038	6,471	9,100	9,257	9,205
United States	4,131	5,061	7,710	6,956	6,315	7,327	8,717	3,164	2,627	2,526	2,825	3,488	3,428	3,347
Canada	231	311	408	428	437	562	874	516	556	582	448	486	467	473
Australia	137	136	201	163	148	157	250	20	52	64	75	72	114	102
Japan	1,313	1,428	1,515	1,398	1,515	1,676	2,274	973	618	609	613	979	939	1,058
New Zealand	17	24	26	22	13	16	23	?	?	?	?	38	15	3
Austria	58	96	92	131	112	76	83	20	21	8	12	32	23	25
Belgium-Luxembourg	401	504	638	577	484	611	921	155	81	85	82	113	142	141
Denmark	91	104	123	120	109	94	82	21	20	17	18	45	38	27
Finland	64	75	87	61	62	67	62	46	49	28	31	45	65	65
France	863	884	836	800	720	678	850	597	489	397	326	619	653	614
Germany	1,182	1,130	1,256	1,309	1,101	1,229	1,424	934	758	682	933	1,390	1,546	1,529
Iceland	2	1	3	2	4	4	3	1	3	2	1	3	2	1
Ireland	40	30	34	20	16	20	28	8	8	10	11	56	19	16
Italy	984	978	1,115	1,150	911	1,270	1,378	518	229	216	201	380	362	313
Netherlands	1,132	1,259	1,361	1,558	1,303	1,608	2,585	149	172	156	178	275	310	265
Norway	92	88	104	93	90	77	67	64	34	47	46	94	71	67
Spain	368	526	495	533	448	444	749	102	76	45	61	94	120	98
Sweden	171	176	233	198	193	138	144	286	156	72	102	149	173	208
Switzerland	97	108	161	175	187	231	181	278	237	190	235	365	363	421
United Kingdom	672	721	708	632	647	756	1,065	270	253	304	273	375	408	431
Developing Countries	7,058	6,921	8,747	8,215	6,883	8,098	10,147	12,588	10,056	8,868	7,680	6,279	7,094	6,676
Africa	1,218	1,061	1,706	1,763	777	931	875	881	597	1,374	1,835	764	594	721
Algeria	125	150	239	136	131	118	97	185	163	130	207	107	114	92
Angola	85	47	90	129	93	206	179	105	228	135	158	126	110	230
Benin	17	13	25	22	15	2	4	?	?	?	?	?	?	?
Burkina Faso		?	?	?	5	?	1	?	?	?	?	?	?	?
Burundi		?	?	?	?	?	1	?	?	?	?	?	?	?
Cameroon	4	4	6	6	9	13	11	?	?	?	?	?	?	12
Cape Verde	?	3	3	7	2	3	4	?	?	?	?	?	?	?
Central African Rep.	?	?	?	?	?	?	1	?	?	?	?	?	?	?
Comoros	?	?	?	?	2	1	?	?	?	?	?	?	?	?
Congo	65	10	8	9	3	1	2	?	?	?	?	1	?	10
Côte d'Ivoire	60	6	13	13	16	15	24	1	1	?	2	3	?	?
Ethiopia	2	7	1	1	1	2	3	?	?	?	?	?	?	?
Gabon	5	2	8	1	1	?	12	226	42	21	21	23	?	84
Gambia, The	?	?	?	?	1	1	2	?	?	?	?	?	?	?
Ghana	16	19	11	6	2	9	4	1	?	?	?	?	1	?
Guinea	31	20	35	36	12	3	6	?	?	?	?	?	?	?
Guinea-Bissau	1	?	?	?	?	?	?	?	?	?	?	?	?	?
Kenya	3	4	6	5	11	13	8	?	?	?	?	?	?	?
Liberia	62	80	37	124	42	75	16	?	?	?	?	1	1	1
Madagascar	2	2	2	2	1	1	1	?	?	?	?	?	?	?
Malawi	?	?	?	?	?	?	1	?	?	?	?	?	?	?
Mali	?	?	?	?	?	?	1	?	?	?	?	?	?	?
Mauritania	4	2	1	?	2	3	8	?	?	?	?	?	?	?
Mauritius	4	3	1	1	2	3	4	?	?	?	?	?	4	?
Morocco	56	52	53	31	26	62	60	2	3	12	1	26	63	49
Mozambique	99	87	20	4	6	3	9	14	11	?	?	?	?	?
Niger	1	?	?	2	1	?	1	?	?	?	?	?	?	?
Nigeria	244	194	654	915	248	217	141	237	87	1,019	1,422	399	223	141
Reunion	?	?	?	?	1	3	4	?	?	?	?	?	?	?
Rwanda	?	?	?	?	?	1	2	?	?	?	?	?	?	?

Table 2614 (Continued)

BRAZIL ABSOLUTE VALUE OF GOODS TRADED WITH SELECTED REGIONS AND COUNTRIES,[1] 1982–88
(M US)[2]

Category	Exports							Imports						
	1982	1983	1984	1985	1986	1987	1988	1982	1983	1984	1985	1986	1987	1988
Developing Countries (Continued)														
Africa (Continued)														
Senegal	7	2	85	44	1	4	6	?	?	?	?	?	?	?
Seychelles	?	1	?	?	?	?	?	?	?	?	?	?	?	?
Sierra Leone	1	1	1	1	?	1	2	?	?	?	?	?	?	?
Somalia	?	1	3	1	4	2	3	?	?	?	?	?	?	?
South Africa	103	138	131	53	48	90	178	85	25	51	22	60	71	87
Sudan	8	3	4	8	2	3	2	?	?	?	?	?	?	?
Tanzania	7	13	3	2	1	2	2	?	?	?	?	?	?	?
Togo	7	5	3	1	2	1	3	?	?	?	?	?	?	?
Tunisia	35	28	28	21	13	10	19	?	31	?	1	3	1	?
Uganda	?	1	1	?	?	1	3	?	?	?	?	?	?	?
Zaire	147	148	126	154	70	59	31	15	3	3	1	11	5	14
Zambia	13	15	1	2	2	?	?	10	3	2	2	1	?	?
Zimbabwe	7	2	106	24	?	2	11	?	?	?	?	?	?	?
Africa not specified	?	?	?	?	?	?	?	?	?	?	?	?	?	1
Asia	929	1,338	1,625	1,777	1,462	1,649	2,765	469	761	604	693	707	600	364
Afghanistan	1	?	?	6	13	6	1	?	?	4	1	17	21	25
Bangladesh	?	5	9	6	13	6	13	?	?	?	?	?	?	?
China, People's Rep.	86	272	453	818	518	362	718	366	596	434	502	395	387	95
Fiji	2	2	?	?	?	?	?	?	?	?	?	?	?	?
Hong Kong	83	106	137	123	85	184	349	9	19	9	16	27	26	32
India	180	281	404	333	208	218	133	4	1	1	2	3	3	11
Indonesia	87	59	56	62	74	80	96	4	4	2	4	8	?	2
Korea	110	163	159	125	142	240	314	5	34	97	40	19	18	24
Malaysia	19	26	43	35	39	58	110	5	26	?	9	27	40	50
Myanmar	?	?	?	?	?	?	?	2	?	?	?	5	?	?
Pakistan	35	48	84	29	47	28	64	5	27	?	19	45	8	1
Papua New Guinea	5	1	1	?	?	?	1	?	?	?	?	?	?	?
Philippines	100	91	37	34	73	91	134	?	5	3	2	1	2	1
Singapore	72	63	72	55	54	91	173	39	26	44	45	51	62	91
Sri Lanka	1	2	8	7	6	8	6	?	2	2	1	?	1	?
Thailand	52	64	64	55	41	68	196	?	26	2	33	68	6	?
Taiwan Province of China	94	152	96	92	162	216	405	15	18	8	20	42	26	31
Europe	598	743	852	720	729	902	932	211	289	206	222	391	304	270
Cyprus	35	40	10	8	11	21	25	?	?	?	?	?	?	?
Gibraltar	?	1	?	?	3	3	6	?	?	?	?	?	?	?
Greece	61	79	85	61	77	105	92	11	14	10	19	28	21	18
Hungary	138	215	222	124	104	105	115	?	?	?	?	?	?	?
Malta	11	5	8	9	8	6	7	?	?	?	?	?	?	?
Poland	168	125	211	161	224	293	306	127	216	161	155	200	171	184
Portugal	68	106	162	136	65	126	171	25	17	13	17	102	32	30
Romania	57	85	56	76	55	55	26	44	41	18	27	51	36	17
Turkey	23	46	57	90	110	138	146	2	1	2	3	4	38	8
Yugoslavia	38	40	41	55	74	51	39	1	?	3	2	5	4	12
Middle East	1,172	1,509	1,453	1,473	1,142	1,354	1,502	7,337	5,930	4,281	3,145	2,327	3,528	3,221
Bahrain	3	3	6	7	9	6	10	?	?	?	?	4	1	2
Egypt	154	157	258	243	155	104	183	52	421	185	108	83	371	213
Iran, I.R. of	210	347	298	212	181	221	294	2,735	2,249	2,203	1,973	1,132	1,639	1,358
Iraq	318	412	350	630	372	305	298	26	8	21	?	?	34	34
Israel	55	35	67	37	36	28	47	?	?	?	29	32	?	?
Jordan	44	32	35	25	10	47	78	229	295	3	10	13	40	88
Kuwait	24	28	39	34	37	30	52	?	?	246	?	?	156	?
Lebanon	25	31	21	14	25	37	43	?	?	?	?	2	?	?
Libya	11	17	9	13	16	24	40	350	84	?	?	?	?	7

Table 2614 (Continued)

BRAZIL ABSOLUTE VALUE OF GOODS TRADED WITH SELECTED REGIONS AND COUNTRIES,[1] 1982–88 (M US)[2]

Category	Exports							Imports						
	1982	1983	1984	1985	1986	1987	1988	1982	1983	1984	1985	1986	1987	1988
Developing Countries (Continued)														
Middle East (Continued)														
Oman	2	5	8	11	19	12	20	~	~	~	~	~	119	123
Qatar	19	13	14	16	20	17	48	339	272	145	~	~	107	131
Saudi Arabia	267	377	261	168	214	481	315	3,196	2,396	1,478	1,025	1,059	982	1,090
Syrian Arab Rep.	20	22	40	26	16	12	14	~	~	~	~	1	~	~
United Arab Emirates	16	25	41	35	28	29	60	411	206	~	~	~	79	174
Yemen Arab Rep.	3	6	6	3	4	~	~	~	~	~	~	~	~	~
Western Hemisphere	3,140	2,271	3,110	2,482	2,774	3,262	4,074	3,660	2,479	2,403	1,786	2,090	2,068	2,100
A. ARGENTINA	650	661	853	548	682	832	975	594	374	539	493	776	612	739
Antigua and Barbuda	~	1	~	~	1	1	2	~	~	~	~	~	~	~
Bahamas, The	30	30	3	8	6	4	3	28	35	37	9	9	4	2
Barbados	5	6	5	5	5	7	7	~	~	~	~	~	~	2
Belize	~	3	~	~	1	~	1	~	~	~	~	~	~	~
Bermuda	~	~	2	3	~	~	1	3	1	8	2	4	7	3
B. BOLIVIA	80	108	141	171	204	224	196	30	20	16	10	14	15	12
D. CHILE	289	208	281	238	247	355	541	330	177	240	228	299	377	367
E. COLOMBIA	272	146	171	103	108	143	226	4	2	6	5	8	20	11
F. COSTA RICA	10	13	19	18	28	36	42	~	~	~	~	3	1	~
Dominica	~	1	7	~	~	~	~	~	~	~	~	~	~	~
H. DOMINICAN REP.	17	22	21	27	30	35	45	~	~	~	~	~	~	~
I. ECUADOR	65	69	141	119	134	103	131	254	72	2	6	21	20	12
J. EL SALVADOR	2	4	4	5	5	7	12	~	~	2	~	~	~	~
Grenada	1	~	1	1	~	~	1	~	~	~	~	~	~	~
Guadeloupe	1	1	~	1	1	2	7	~	~	~	~	~	~	~
K. GUATEMALA	10	6	14	12	15	30	41	~	~	~	1	~	1	~
Guiana, Grench	1	1	1	1	1	2	4	~	~	~	1	~	~	~
Guyana	5	2	6	7	2	3	2	~	~	2	1	~	~	~
L. HAITI	4	4	6	7	4	5	14	~	~	~	~	~	~	~
M. HONDURAS	5	11	30	12	27	16	22	2	9	16	3	21	22	26
Jamaica	18	12	8	6	13	17	26	2	~	~	~	15	~	~
Leeward Islands	~	~	~	~	~	1	1	~	~	~	~	~	~	~
Martinique	~	~	~	1	1	3	6	~	~	~	~	~	~	~
N. MEXICO	324	168	285	222	156	171	274	845	761	681	414	170	240	125
Netherlands Antilles	14	13	40	12	10	13	28	77	56	23	10	27	54	50
O. NICARAGUA	5	11	14	7	6	11	15	~	~	~	~	~	~	~
P. PANAMA	36	40	44	60	41	41	36	36	23	19	32	56	53	59
Q. PARAGUAY	324	234	333	302	291	288	341	170	33	41	76	153	67	118
R. PERU	222	75	124	92	157	216	193	75	60	51	59	76	120	89
St. Kitts & Nevis	~	~	~	7	3	5	6	~	~	~	~	~	~	~
St. Lucia	~	~	~	~	~	~	1	~	~	~	~	~	~	~
St. Vincent	~	~	~	~	~	1	1	~	~	~	~	~	~	~
Suriname	15	15	26	15	8	20	17	~	~	~	4	~	~	~
Trinidad and Tobago	30	31	29	32	28	28	30	6	2	10	6	1	7	~
S. URUGUAY	138	104	136	140	203	268	321	156	134	125	142	305	249	316
T. VENEZUELA	470	270	365	295	349	374	503	1,048	719	587	278	108	172	157
Western Hem. not specified	94	~	~	5	8	2	4	~	~	~	3	~	~	~
U.S.S.R. and Other Nonmembers	801	1,021	870	671	483	895	620	359	308	304	184	179	231	167
Albania	1	1	1	1	1	~	~	~	4	3	3	14	3	~
Bulgaria	21	56	179	48	26	137	120	10	~	~	~	4	4	~
G. CUBA	~	~	~	~	1	3	23	~	~	~	~	4	~	~
Czechoslovakia	83	127	82	53	47	105	76	19	16	12	5	19	27	38
Eastern Germany	187	164	206	114	142	271	166	116	98	121	102	90	110	97
North Korea	~	3	~	1	1	~	1	~	~	~	~	~	~	~
U.S.S.R.	509	671	402	456	266	379	233	213	190	168	75	53	87	32

Table 2614 (Continued)

BRAZIL ABSOLUTE VALUE OF GOODS TRADED WITH SELECTED REGIONS AND COUNTRIES,[1] 1980–87
(M US)[2]

PART II. BRAZIL INDICATORS OF TRADE WITH THE UNITED STATES, 1964–84

| | % of Total Foreign Trade | | | | | |
| | | Imports | | AA-GR | | Bilateral Trade Balance |
Year	Exports	Total	Excluded Crude Oil	Exports	Imports	
1964	33.2	26.2	39.4	−10.7	−6.7	99.4
1965	32.6	17.7	34.3	9.7	−24.9	238.6
1966	33.4	30.0	44.5	11.8	85.7	58.5
1967	33.1	−30.9	38.4	−5.8	−2.4	37.2
1968	33.3	32.6	35.7	14.5	20.0	14.3
1969	26.4	26.5	33.2	−2.7	.1	−3.5
1970	24.7	30.1	35.3	10.9	34.3	−147.7
1971	26.2	32.9	31.9	12.4	15.9	−194.9
1972	23.3	30.4	42.0	22.5	26.9	−280.6
1973	18.1	29.3	32.6	20.5	50.1	−696.0
1974	21.9	38.7	30.5	54.8	69.3	−1,341.5
1975	15.4	35.2	32.5	−23.0	.2	−1,748.9
1976	18.2	28.0	31.8	37.8	−8.0	−996.3
1977	17.7	19.8	28.5	16.6	−15.4	−252.7
1978	22.7	22.8	30.0	33.5	20.3	−19.6
1979	19.3	21.3	27.4	2.5	12.1	−298.7
1980	17.4	20.4	30.2	19.3	26.6	−691.4
1981	17.7	15.0	30.5	17.1	−14.6	607.8
1982	20.0	14.2	28.9	−1.9	−18.3	1,173.0
1983	23.1	15.6	31.7	25.5	−15.8	2,654.3
1984 first quarter	30.4	14.3	29.5	64.1[a]	−18.0[a]	1,253.3

a. As compared to first quarter of 1983.

SOURCE: ECLA-EIC, 1985, p. 80.

Table 2614 (Continued)

BRAZIL ABSOLUTE VALUE OF GOODS TRADED WITH SELECTED REGIONS AND COUNTRIES,[1] 1982–88 (M US)[2]

Category	Exports 1982	1983	1984	1985	1986	1987	1988	Imports 1982	1983	1984	1985	1986	1987	1988
Country or area not specified	~	~	~	159	71	16	998	~	~	~	~	~	~	~
Special categories	261	273	283	264	156	173	261	~	~	~	~	~	~	~
Memorandum Items														
EEC	5,862	6,320	6,815	6,896	5,881	6,941	9,345	2,779	2,104	1,924	2,100	3,450	3,631	3,464
Oil Exporting Countries	1,795	1,896	2,334	2,526	1,688	1,909	1,963	8,825	6,891	5,995	5,017	2,898	3,964	3,575
Non-Oil Developing Countries	5,263	5,026	6,413	5,689	5,195	6,189	8,184	3,763	3,164	2,873	2,664	3,380	3,131	3,101
% Distribution														
Industrial Countries	59.7	62.4	63.3	63.7	66.1	65.0	64.4	38.6	38.3	39.7	45.1	58.5	55.8	57.4
Developing Countries	35.0	31.7	32.4	32.0	30.7	30.9	30.0	59.7	59.8	58.3	53.6	40.4	42.8	41.6
Africa	6.0	4.9	6.3	6.9	3.5	3.5	2.6	4.2	3.6	9.0	12.8	4.9	3.6	4.5
Asia	4.6	6.1	6.0	6.9	6.5	6.3	8.2	2.2	4.5	4.0	4.8	4.5	3.6	2.3
Europe	3.0	3.4	3.2	2.8	3.3	3.4	2.8	1.0	1.7	1.4	1.6	2.5	1.8	1.7
Middle East	5.8	6.9	5.4	5.7	5.1	5.2	4.4	35.0	35.3	28.1	21.9	15.0	21.3	20.1
Western Hemisphere	15.6	10.4	11.5	9.7	12.4	12.4	12.1	17.4	14.8	15.8	12.5	13.4	12.5	13.1
U.S.S.R. and Other Nonmembers	4.0	4.7	3.2	2.6	2.2	3.4	1.8	1.7	1.8	2.0	1.3	1.1	1.4	1.0
Annual PC														
World	-13.5	8.4	23.6	-5.1	-12.6	17.0	28.8	-12.5	-20.2	-9.5	-5.8	8.5	6.6	-3.2
Industrial Countries	-3.7	13.2	25.4	-4.6	-9.3	15.0	27.7	-19.2	-20.7	-6.2	7.2	40.6	1.7	-.6
Developing Countries	-26.2	-1.9	26.4	-6.1	-16.2	17.7	25.3	-9.3	-20.1	-11.8	-13.4	-18.2	13.0	-5.9
Africa	-29.4	-12.9	60.8	3.3	-55.9	19.8	-6.0	-48.5	-32.3	130.2	33.6	-58.4	-22.3	21.4
Asia	-12.2	44.0	21.5	9.4	-17.7	12.8	67.7	-46.1	62.1	-20.5	14.7	2.0	-15.1	-39.4
Europe	-42.2	24.2	14.8	-15.5	1.2	23.8	3.3	2.1	37.1	-29.0	8.2	75.8	-22.4	-11.0
Middle East	-5.8	28.7	-3.7	1.4	-22.5	18.6	10.9	-2.8	-19.5	-27.8	-26.5	-26.0	51.6	-8.7
Western Hemisphere	-30.1	-27.7	37.0	-20.2	11.7	17.6	24.9	4.4	-32.3	-3.0	-25.7	17.0	-1.0	1.5
U.S.S.R. and Other Nonmembers	-11.1	27.5	-14.7	-22.9	-28.0	85.3	-30.7	156.0	-14.3	-1.2	-39.6	-2.8	29.6	-27.8

1. DOT data may differ between countries and from IFS data because of the time it takes for an export to become an import, etc.
2. Data may be calculated from partner's reported data or estimated on basis of less than 12 months.

SOURCE: IMF-DOT-Y, 1989.

Table 2615

CHILE ABSOLUTE VALUE OF GOODS TRADED WITH SELECTED REGIONS AND COUNTRIES,[1] 1982–88 (M US)[2]

Category	Exports							Imports						
	1982	1983	1984	1985	1986	1987	1988	1982	1983	1984	1985	1986	1987	1988
IFS World Total	3,709.5	3,835.5	3,657.2	3,822.9	4,222.4	5,090.9	7,045.7	3,528.5	2,754.0	3,190.6	2,742.5	2,914.2	3,793.4	4,730.8
DOTS World Total	3,709.5	3,850.0	3,658.0	3,893.4	4,225.5	5,101.6	7,051.3	3,536.1	2,967.7	3,480.5	3,079.3	3,131.6	4,023.7	5,074.1
Industrial Countries	2,590.1	2,868.7	2,545.4	2,665.6	2,853.0	3,449.6	4,930.9	2,015.5	1,486.5	1,817.6	1,575.7	1,764.2	2,242.0	2,651.7
United States	800.7	1,083.3	951.2	877.3	915.2	1,140.5	1,393.2	916.1	703.5	747.8	654.6	641.5	773.1	1,002.1
Canada	33.6	60.4	31.1	75.9	58.4	71.1	48.2	55.5	60.9	66.5	59.2	54.3	66.4	110.7
Japan	440.0	348.1	407.7	384.9	420.1	561.3	831.3	229.6	161.2	312.7	188.5	296.4	387.2	391.8
Belgium-Luxembourg	100.0	95.3	67.1	89.1	77.9	58.6	107.3	36.7	24.8	44.6	32.0	45.7	41.3	39.2
Denmark	.5	.5	1.0	1.2	1.2	1.2	2.3	27.3	11.3	10.9	12.2	12.6	19.1	23.1
France	151.7	176.7	163.4	142.4	153.1	178.6	353.7	124.6	82.9	97.6	78.6	94.1	129.3	149.6
Germany	426.3	484.8	365.5	370.6	441.2	483.4	817.9	214.3	185.2	215.7	209.0	250.1	335.1	365.1
Ireland	2.5	.8	.4	.9	13.6	9.1	~	6.6	2.6	2.8	2.6	3.4	9.1	7.7
Italy	174.8	169.8	160.9	196.0	215.8	273.8	420.7	73.1	51.3	66.1	50.3	64.0	95.8	120.3
Netherlands	106.0	106.2	92.2	141.3	153.6	164.2	247.4	36.0	26.9	28.2	24.8	30.1	33.9	38.5
Spain	85.5	72.2	75.8	73.5	122.2	146.8	178.4	149.8	64.3	81.1	105.5	82.2	116.6	117.9
Sweden	40.3	46.6	24.6	51.1	53.5	52.3	55.7	26.1	24.0	33.1	41.1	47.6	51.3	77.5
Switzerland	41.4	14.7	8.4	5.2	7.4	55.5	89.2	43.7	26.9	30.9	33.0	53.7	55.5	84.9
United Kingdom	186.8	209.3	196.1	256.2	219.8	317.8	365.6	76.1	60.7	79.6	84.3	88.5	128.3	123.3
Developing Countries	1,043.0	869.1	1,029.9	1,142.6	1,302.8	1,561.9	1,975.5	1,091.7	1,213.9	1,360.6	1,156.0	1,134.0	1,525.6	2,224.0
Africa	20.7	31.3	40.4	34.8	32.5	39.0	39.9	20.4	102.1	164.7	101.1	86.8	132.3	198.2
Gabon	~			~	~			~	~	113.3	27.1	~	~	33.3
Nigeria	~							~	~	25.0	50.5	49.5	75.0	100.8
South Africa	20.7	31.3	40.4	27.1	29.3	31.0	25.4	~	~	25.7	22.2	34.6	40.4	43.3
Africa not specified				7.7	3.2	8.0	14.5	20.4	102.1	.7	1.3	2.7	16.9	20.8
Asia	178.0	207.9	270.5	367.6	324.3	403.5	638.9	191.5	105.2	150.7	112.5	167.9	302.8	524.0
China, People's Rep.	61.9	93.7	125.3	145.8	100.2	78.7	99.1	21.7	9.9	12.4	24.0	21.0	57.1	55.0
Hong Kong	7.5	3.4	8.5	9.6	13.3	14.0	46.4	27.3	13.7	19.8	11.3	15.7	24.4	26.5
Korea	52.1	56.6	64.9	88.4	91.8	109.0	146.1	51.2	23.3	40.7	24.2	48.0	82.2	107.5
Asia not specified	37.5	23.3	27.1	85.2	57.6	72.2	102.0	43.9	31.6	40.5	29.5	45.3	84.5	268.0
Taiwan Province of China	19.0	30.9	44.7	38.6	61.4	129.6	245.3	47.4	26.7	37.3	23.5	37.9	54.6	67.0
Europe	52.3	74.4	70.5	80.2	136.2	156.2	258.5	38.8	30.1	37.9	45.2	61.7	75.6	87.9
Greece	15.1	12.9	14.8	22.0	29.0	23.4	26.0				.1	.2	1.4	1.1
Portugal	6.3	8.6	12.9	11.9	13.9	21.0	29.4			2.5	2.8	3.2	3.1	3.6
Romania	~		7.5	6.8	10.9			~					~	~
Turkey	~	~	~	~	~	51.3	44.2							
Yugoslavia	15.1	19.3	15.3	12.9	33.2	14.2	61.2							
Europe not specified	15.8	33.6	20.0	26.6	49.2	46.3	97.7	38.8	30.1	35.3	42.3	58.3	71.1	83.2
Middle East	72.1	90.5	98.5	94.1	89.4	96.8	111.2	11.6	87.9	29.3	80.0	38.1	42.6	33.7
Egypt	7.8	2.9	13.3	9.1	10.8	13.6	8.0				76.8	34.1	20.7	16.5
Iran, I.R. of		12.5						5.5						
Kuwait	6.6	7.7	15.1	14.7	9.2	13.4	13.4							
Qatar														
Saudi Arabia	28.4	30.5	30.5	39.9	44.6	41.7	53.0	6.1	15.1	26.1	.1	~		
United Arab Emirates	18.9	27.0	23.0	16.6	14.0	14.0	20.9		30.7					
Middle East not specified	10.4	9.9	16.6	13.8	10.8	14.1	15.9		40.1	3.2	3.1	4.0	21.9	17.2
Western Hemisphere	719.9	465.0	550.0	565.9	720.4	866.4	925.0	829.4	888.6	978.0	817.2	779.5	972.3	1,380.2
A. ARGENTINA	151.3	119.4	116.7	84.5	160.6	174.9	168.1	151.9	200.6	160.9	105.9	122.5	159.0	278.6
B. BOLIVIA	11.2	11.0	14.7	14.3	30.5	44.5	43.6	9.0	8.7	6.6	4.5	5.0	8.4	11.9
C. BRAZIL	308.2	164.3	227.5	211.3	292.9	348.2	341.7	258.4	190.2	296.4	248.9	247.6	380.0	554.9
E. COLOMBIA	46.3	42.3	43.0	54.8	40.5	51.0	67.8	11.2	12.8	21.5	21.9	38.3	99.6	126.5
F. COSTA RICA	~	5.1	4.8	5.7	7.3	6.4	10.2							
H. DOMINICAN REP.	4.7					8.4	14.8							
I. ECUADOR	51.3	33.8	27.8	33.6	28.1	32.6	35.4	32.3	40.4	46.0	48.1	58.8	37.2	55.5
N. MEXICO	22.3	1.0	8.9	51.0	9.7	2.8	24.0	11.0	16.9	21.8	14.7	20.1	44.0	69.0

Table 2615 (Continued)

CHILE ABSOLUTE VALUE OF GOODS TRADED WITH SELECTED REGIONS AND COUNTRIES,[1] 1982-88 (M US)[2]

Category	Exports							Imports						
	1982	1983	1984	1985	1986	1987	1988	1982	1983	1984	1985	1986	1987	1988
Developing Countries (Continued)														
Western Hemisphere (Continued)														
Netherlands Antilles	~	~	~	~	~	~	~	~	120.2	74.8	29.1	41.9	16.5	10.3
P. PANAMA	6.8	3.8	5.3	5.5	6.5	~	~	21.1	3.2	1.0	2.4	4.3	2.5	1.6
Q. PARAGUAY	7.5	2.4	4.5	5.8	5.4	8.9	12.4	14.0	22.4	36.5	27.0	29.4	42.7	50.5
R. PERU	49.0	39.4	44.9	45.6	65.9	85.8	63.0	33.4	37.2	49.2	41.1	56.3	27.9	33.0
S. URUGUAY	13.1	6.2	8.7	12.3	11.0	15.4	20.7	21.2	8.0	9.3	4.1	6.2	7.6	11.4
T. VENEZUELA	43.4	29.7	40.2	33.7	40.6	71.2	105.0	260.4	224.8	251.8	267.7	148.2	143.7	165.0
Western Hem. not specified	4.8	6.6	3.0	7.8	21.4	16.3	28.3	5.0	3.2	2.2	1.8	.9	3.2	12.0
U.S.S.R. and Other Nonmembers	20.1	53.9	32.6	43.6	30.8	44.2	77.1	7.2	4.2	6.6	5.6	8.3	14.0	33.0
Eastern Germany	19.5	48.7	32.5	39.9	24.4	32.8	64.8	~	~	~	~	~	~	~
U.S.S.R., etc. not specified	.6	5.2	.1	3.7	6.4	11.4	12.3	7.2	4.2	6.6	5.6	8.3	14.0	33.0
Country or area not specified	56.3	58.3	50.1	41.6	38.9	45.9	49.8	421.7	263.1	295.7	202.9	225.1	230.0	145.2
Special categories	~	~	~	~	~	~	~	~	~	~	139.1	~	~	~
Memorandum Items														
EEC	1,249.2	1,328.5	1,150.1	1,305.1	1,441.3	1,668.8	2,548.7	744.5	510.0	629.2	602.2	674.1	913.0	989.4
Oil Exporting Countries	97.3	107.4	108.8	104.9	108.4	140.3	192.3	272.0	310.7	302.9	318.3	197.7	218.7	265.8
Non-Oil Developing Countries	945.7	761.7	921.1	1,037.7	1,194.4	1,421.6	1,781.2	819.7	903.2	1,057.7	837.7	936.3	1,306.9	1,958.2
% Distribution														
Industrial Countries	69.8	74.5	69.6	68.5	67.5	67.6	70.3	57.0	50.1	52.2	51.2	56.3	55.7	52.3
Developing Countries	28.1	22.6	28.2	29.3	30.8	30.6	27.9	30.9	40.9	39.1	37.5	36.2	37.9	43.8
Africa	.6	.8	1.1	.9	.8	.8	.6	.6	3.4	4.7	3.3	2.8	3.3	3.9
Asia	4.8	5.4	7.4	9.4	7.7	7.9	9.0	5.4	3.5	4.3	3.7	5.4	7.5	10.3
Europe	1.4	1.9	1.9	2.1	3.2	3.1	3.7	1.1	1.0	1.1	1.5	2.0	1.9	1.7
Middle East	1.9	2.4	2.7	2.4	2.1	1.9	1.6	.3	3.0	.8	2.6	1.2	1.1	.7
Western Hemisphere	19.4	12.1	15.0	14.5	17.0	17.0	13.1	23.5	29.9	28.1	26.5	24.9	24.2	27.2
U.S.S.R. and Other Nonmembers	.5	1.4	.9	1.1	.7	.9	1.1	.2	.1	.2	.2	.3	.3	.7
Annual PC														
World	-6.1	3.8	-5.0	6.4	8.5	20.7	38.4	-44.4	-16.1	17.3	-11.5	1.7	28.5	26.1
Industrial Countries	2.4	10.8	-11.3	4.7	7.0	20.9	43.8	-47.8	-26.2	22.3	-13.3	12.0	27.1	18.3
Developing Countries	-21.2	-16.7	18.5	10.9	14.0	19.9	26.4	-50.9	11.2	12.1	-15.0	-1.9	34.5	45.8
Africa	-62.6	51.2	29.1	-13.9	-6.6	20.0	2.3	-88.5	400.5	61.3	-38.6	-14.1	52.4	49.8
Asia	-12.3	16.8	30.1	35.9	-11.8	24.4	58.3	-21.3	-45.1	43.3	-25.3	49.2	80.3	73.1
Europe	-34.8	42.3	-5.2	13.8	69.8	14.7	65.5	-19.2	-22.4	25.9	19.3	36.5	22.5	16.3
Middle East	-39.8	25.5	8.8	-4.5	-5.0	8.3	14.9	-90.7	657.8	-66.7	173.0	-52.4	11.8	-20.9
Western Hemisphere	-16.8	-35.4	18.3	2.9	27.3	20.3	6.8	-49.1	7.1	10.1	-16.4	-4.6	24.7	42.0
U.S.S.R. and Other Nonmembers	-13.7	168.2	-39.5	33.7	-29.4	43.5	74.4	-4.0	-41.7	57.1	-15.2	48.2	68.7	135.7

1. DOT data may differ between countries and from IFS data because of the time it takes for an export to become an import, etc.

2. Data may be calculated from partner's reported data or estimated on basis of less than 12 months.

SOURCE: IMF-DOT-Y, 1989.

Table 2616

COLOMBIA ABSOLUTE VALUE OF GOODS TRADED WITH SELECTED REGIONS AND COUNTRIES,1 1982-88 (M US)2

Category	Exports							Imports						
	1982	1983	1984	1985	1986	1987	1988	1982	1983	1984	1985	1986	1987	1988
IFS World Total	3,095.0	3,080.9	3,461.6	3,551.6	5,101.6	4,642.2	5,037.0	5,477.7	4,968.1	4,497.5	4,140.9	3,861.5	4,321.9	5,001.8
DOTS World Total	3,095.0	3,080.8	3,482.8	3,551.8	5,107.9	5,024.4	4,889.8	5,477.7	4,968.1	4,492.4	4,130.7	3,930.6	4,227.3	5,030.2
Industrial Countries	2,244.7	2,411.4	2,821.5	2,801.9	4,248.2	3,605.5	3,929.9	3,855.7	3,514.5	3,217.2	3,007.6	2,929.0	3,234.5	3,883.1
United States	722.7	872.1	1,097.5	1,165.9	1,531.1	1,998.0	1,975.4	1,895.6	1,768.6	1,535.5	1,456.6	1,389.5	1,514.7	1,848.1
Canada	34.0	26.8	56.9	40.0	73.1	67.5	72.6	90.2	176.2	232.3	159.0	116.3	174.6	218.4
Australia	1.2	3.9	1.6	1.9	2.8	2.2	4.5	1.2	.7	.9	.3	7.8	7.3	12.7
Japan	127.6	136.8	153.5	149.9	249.4	203.7	272.0	608.0	551.6	431.2	428.6	349.6	386.2	545.0
New Zealand	.1	—	.2	.1	—	.3	.4	.2	.5	.4	1.5	2.7	.9	.2
Austria	3.8	6.3	5.0	9.8	32.6	20.9	12.6	12.0	16.1	11.9	10.9	15.3	11.0	13.7
Belgium-Luxembourg	42.4	67.1	103.8	63.4	111.9	72.4	65.5	43.0	29.8	34.6	29.0	29.4	35.6	53.7
Denmark	27.7	19.3	20.1	33.9	107.5	94.3	80.7	28.2	16.4	26.6	15.1	10.5	10.0	10.3
Finland	59.6	49.1	62.9	67.8	108.8	50.5	65.5	27.1	24.0	21.5	24.0	18.9	19.9	18.6
France	56.0	71.4	73.2	75.1	131.3	112.6	132.1	145.7	161.1	188.3	136.3	154.7	166.0	184.0
Germany	560.8	566.6	577.7	574.4	1,051.2	592.3	576.0	317.6	241.0	245.3	265.9	256.0	334.5	378.1
Iceland	.2	.3	.4	.5	.4	.3	.3	.2	.2	.3	.4	—	.4	.3
Ireland	3.8	6.9	19.2	9.0	13.1	12.5	26.2	2.4	4.6	5.3	6.9	2.8	2.9	4.5
Italy	181.8	169.2	135.9	98.2	73.8	68.3	84.5	124.4	98.7	91.3	68.6	98.7	72.9	94.0
Netherlands	174.4	168.2	204.8	190.1	265.8	—	230.4	39.7	32.8	40.9	62.3	71.3	75.5	59.6
Norway	24.9	25.1	37.6	33.7	53.4	25.7	32.7	3.0	3.1	2.2	2.2	2.6	12.0	12.5
Spain	76.3	82.1	82.5	78.4	124.6	80.8	86.1	141.4	129.1	90.6	127.6	167.1	114.6	125.5
Sweden	88.1	75.2	90.9	85.5	152.9	83.1	88.6	75.9	72.3	83.7	41.1	50.6	56.8	63.1
Switzerland	13.3	11.2	12.2	18.3	31.2	19.9	27.6	83.5	80.6	81.9	72.3	81.5	111.3	122.6
United Kingdom	46.2	53.7	85.7	106.2	133.5	100.1	96.3	116.2	107.3	92.5	98.9	103.4	127.6	118.3
Developing Countries	787.1	532.0	591.5	651.7	687.0	984.4	881.5	1,571.0	1,409.1	1,235.4	1,071.7	938.8	927.9	1,101.9
Africa	25.2	28.6	53.4	65.5	10.7	23.0	53.3	10.5	9.2	5.0	2.5	2.2	3.8	1.1
Algeria	19.3	20.4	49.3	60.5	—	11.1	28.6	—	—	—	—	—	—	—
Benin	—	—	—	—	—	—	.2	—	—	—	—	—	—	—
Cameroon	—	.1	—	—	—	.2	.2	—	—	—	—	—	—	—
Côte d'Ivoire	—	—	.2	—	—	.1	—	—	.1	.1	.1	.2	.3	—
Ghana	—	—	—	—	—	—	.1	—	—	—	—	—	—	—
Guinee-Bissau	—	—	—	—	—	—	.2	—	—	—	—	—	—	.2
Kenya	—	.1	.1	—	.6	.2	—	—	—	—	—	—	—	—
Liberia	—	.5	—	—	—	.2	—	—	—	.1	—	—	—	—
Madagascar	—	—	—	.1	—	—	—	—	—	—	—	—	.1	—
Mali	—	—	.1	—	—	—	—	—	—	—	—	—	—	—
Mauritania	—	—	—	—	—	—	—	—	—	—	—	—	—	—
Morocco	2.4	4.9	2.8	4.5	7.3	10.4	17.1	.3	—	—	—	.2	.1	17.1
Nigeria	1.9	.3	—	—	2.1	.3	—	.9	1.7	2.1	.9	—	.1	—
Senega	—	.3	.4	—	—	—	—	—	.1	.1	—	—	—	—
Seychelles	—	—	—	—	—	—	—	—	—	—	—	—	—	—
South Africa	.5	.4	.5	.2	.4	.5	6.6	10.2	9.0	4.9	2.3	1.7	2.8	1.0
Sudan	.1	.1	—	.1	—	—	.1	.4	.5	—	—	—	—	.1
Tunisia	.9	1.7	.3	—	2.2	—	.4	.1	—	—	—	—	—	.4
Zaire	.2	—	—	—	—	—	—	.6	—	—	—	.1	—	—
Asia	15.2	20.2	19.9	31.6	16.9	20.7	50.5	46.0	31.6	32.0	25.5	27.9	38.4	223.8
Bangladesh	6.7	—	1.1	—	2.1	2.5	21.5	—	—	—	.1	—	—	—
China, People's Rep.	1.9	—	—	—	2.1	2.5	1.6	.9	1.7	2.1	.9	3.4	5.1	1.6
French Polynesia	—	.3	—	—	.1	.3	—	—	.1	.1	.9	.1	—	—
Hong Kong	1.1	.2	.4	2.2	2.2	8.4	17.3	—	2.8	2.1	1.2	1.4	2.1	163.2
India	—	2.2	—	15.1	—	—	—	4.8	2.8	2.1	1.2	1.4	2.1	1.0
Indonesia	.5	.1	—	.3	—	—	.1	.4	.5	.9	1.2	.6	.4	1.0
Korea	4.8	14.8	14.3	13.6	11.8	6.4	7.1	10.6	5.0	6.8	2.8	3.7	8.2	22.6
Malaysia	.3	—	—	.1	—	—	.1	1.6	.8	.6	.4	.5	.5	2.5
Nauru	—	—	—	—	—	—	—	—	—	—	—	—	—	.1

Table 2616 (Continued)

COLOMBIA ABSOLUTE VALUE OF GOODS TRADED WITH SELECTED REGIONS AND COUNTRIES,[1] 1982–88
(M US)[2]

Category	Exports 1982	1983	1984	1985	1986	1987	1988	Imports 1982	1983	1984	1985	1986	1987	1988
Developing Countries (Continued)														
Asia (Continued)														
Pakistan	?	?	?	?	?	?	?	.2	.2	.2	.2	.2	.1	.2
Papua New Guinea	?	?	?	?	?	?	?	.1	.1	.4	.2	.3	.3	.4
Philippines	.3	2.7	?	?	?	.1	?	.9	?	?	?	?	?	.1
Singapore	.1	.1	.1	.1	.3	.8	1.9	12.2	11.9	14.3	16.0	10.0	11.0	14.4
Sri Lanka	?	?	.1	?	?	?	?	.4	.1	.3	?	.1	?	.2
Thailand	1.1	.1	.2	.2	.1	?	1.1	.4	.1	.3	?	.1	.1	?
Vanuatu	?	?	?	?	?	?	.4	?	?	?	?	?	?	?
Viet Nam	?	?	3.7	?	?	.4	?	?	?	?	?	?	?	.5
Asia not specified	?	?	?	?	.3	?	?	?	?	?	?	?	?	?
Taiwan Province of China	1.0	?	.1	?	.3	2.1	.9	13.8	8.5	4.3	2.4	7.7	10.5	17.0
Europe	73.3	45.7	45.3	43.8	68.8	58.2	87.0	38.0	101.9	52.1	28.5	28.9	29.5	26.4
Gibraltar	?	?	?	?	?	.1	?	.1	?	?	?	?	.1	?
Greece	.9	1.9	.3	4.7	11.4	4.1	4.3	?	.1	?	?	?	.1	?
Hungary	7.5	17.7	37.8	27.8	9.1	13.1	22.9	1.2	1.1	3.2	5.0	5.7	4.0	2.7
Malta	?	?	?	?	?	.1	?	?	?	?	?	?	?	?
Poland	35.7	1.7	1.5	1.6	35.4	16.7	35.1	14.0	74.8	29.8	6.1	3.7	2.4	1.9
Portugal	1.3	3.2	2.1	2.5	4.1	7.9	17.1	.9	.4	.6	.3	.5	.5	1.5
Romania	27.5	20.9	3.0	5.9	.6	2.2	2.1	13.6	14.8	11.8	8.6	8.0	9.7	8.6
Turkey	.4	.3	.6	.3	.2	5.9	5.4	.4	1.6	1.1	.2	.4	1.7	.6
Yugoslavia	?	?	?	1.0	8.0	8.2	.1	8.2	9.1	5.6	8.1	10.5	11.1	11.0
Europe not specified	?	?	?	?	?	?	?	.1	.1	.1	.1	?	?	?
Middle East	2.4	4.8	3.1	11.9	9.5	12.8	51.2	6.5	5.4	10.5	12.6	19.1	40.1	19.0
Bahrain	?	?	.1	.2	?	?	?	?	?	?	?	?	?	?
Egypt	.2	?	?	?	?	.1	.4	?	?	?	?	?	?	?
Israel	1.2	.8	2.6	10.0	8.5	9.7	45.5	6.5	5.3	10.4	12.5	19.0	39.9	18.9
Jordan	.1	?	?	?	?	?	.1	?	?	?	?	?	?	?
Kuwait	?	.5	.2	.4	.2	.1	.1	?	?	?	?	?	?	?
Lebanon	.2	.8	?	.3	.4	.1	?	?	?	?	?	?	?	?
Libya	.3	?	?	.5	?	?	?	?	?	?	?	?	?	?
Qatar	?	?	?	.1	?	?	?	?	?	?	?	?	?	?
Saudi Arabia	.4	2.6	.1	.3	.3	2.8	4.9	?	?	?	?	?	?	?
Syrian Arab Rep.	?	?	?	?	.3	?	.2	?	?	?	?	?	?	?
United Arab Emirates	?	.1	.2	.1	.1	.1	.1	?	?	?	?	?	?	.1
Western Hemisphere	671.2	432.8	469.8	498.8	581.1	869.8	639.6	1,470.1	1,261.1	1,135.8	1,002.7	860.6	816.1	831.7
A. ARGENTINA	36.4	43.0	58.7	36.7	67.3	41.9	41.9	73.3	49.9	45.6	106.2	85.2	58.2	72.7
Antigua and Barbuda	?	?	?	?	.2	.7	.2	?	?	?	?	?	?	3.4
Bahamas, The	7.6	.4	9.2	36.0	23.9	11.8	.4	1.0	9.9	1.2	.1	.1	?	?
Barbados	1.2	.8	.4	.6	.2	.7	.3	?	.2	?	.1	.1	.3	.3
Belize	.4	?	?	?	?	.3	.1	?	?	?	?	?	?	.1
Bermuda	?	?	?	?	?	?	.2	.5	?	?	?	?	.3	?
B. BOLIVIA	.9	1.6	1.3	.7	1.3	1.5	1.7	6.8	3.4	7.5	1.7	7.7	6.6	8.6
C. BRAZIL	3.7	5.4	14.3	6.0	8.1	18.5	9.5	286.3	166.7	178.8	129.2	139.2	150.5	166.8
D. CHILE	11.7	11.1	16.0	20.9	32.3	99.6	120.1	68.0	56.7	48.8	52.7	51.5	55.7	66.4
F. COSTA RICA	3.9	5.0	7.3	8.2	8.9	16.3	17.1	2.8	1.6	1.3	.9	1.5	1.1	3.4
Dominica	?	?	?	?	.1	?	?	.5	?	?	?	?	?	?
H. DOMINICAN REP.	4.5	5.1	5.6	19.8	9.8	19.0	14.3	3.9	1.3	.4	1.7	7.7	6.6	1.6
I. ECUADOR	51.9	42.7	47.3	56.3	58.9	65.3	32.4	90.2	160.1	68.9	81.4	47.0	37.8	49.2
J. EL SALVADOR	1.1	7.6	5.8	10.4	5.1	3.7	3.9	.5	4.1	5.5	5.1	4.1	3.4	3.4
Grenada	?	?	.2	.4	.4	.5	.1	.5	.1	.3	1.9	1.9	1.9	.1
Guadeloupe	.7	.7	.6	.3	.4	.2	.3	.1	?	?	?	?	?	?
K. GUATEMALA	3.3	3.7	4.7	5.2	3.8	7.1	6.0	.3	.1	.5	1.3	2.1	2.1	2.4
Guiana, French	.1	.1	.2	?	?	.1	.2	?	?	?	?	?	?	?
Guyana	.6	.4	.8	?	.2	1.2	.2	?	?	?	?	?	?	?
L. HAITI	.5	.8	?	1.9	1.8	4.1	2.3	?	?	?	?	?	?	.1

Table 2616 (Continued)

COLOMBIA ABSOLUTE VALUE OF GOODS TRADED WITH SELECTED REGIONS AND COUNTRIES,[1] 1982–88
(M US)[2]

Category	Exports							Imports						
	1982	1983	1984	1985	1986	1987	1988	1982	1983	1984	1985	1986	1987	1988
Developing Countries (Continued)														
Western Hemisphere (Continued)														
M. HONDURAS	3.2	4.5	4.8	5.3	5.7	10.1	7.8	1.1	1.4	.7	1.2	1.3	2.3	1.9
Jamaica	.6	1.3	.4	.5	4.5	1.5	1.9	1.3	.1	.3	1.2	.5	—	.4
Leeward Islands	.1	—	.4	.1	.1	—	3.7	—	—	—	.1	—	.1	—
Martinique	.1	.1	.1	—	.1	.2	.5	—	—	—	—	—	—	—
N. MEXICO	17.2	20.8	9.7	6.4	11.0	8.3	15.7	80.9	99.2	111.8	149.3	118.4	148.6	168.7
Netherlands Antilles	24.8	65.4	107.1	73.2	30.7	77.4	37.6	146.8	161.2	89.1	34.1	27.7	17.7	2.6
O. NICARAGUA	2.7	4.9	13.7	3.6	2.8	2.0	4.5	.3	.1	—	—	—	—	—
P. PANAMA	67.9	52.1	31.7	36.8	73.7	127.3	69.6	175.1	80.3	84.0	71.8	85.0	132.1	78.7
Q. PARAGUAY	.4	.2	.1	.1	.1	.2	—	1.8	1.1	1.5	1.7	79.1	.9	.7
R. PERU	34.0	19.6	23.3	31.9	70.9	118.1	73.0	151.5	62.6	92.9	108.4	79.1	66.1	68.8
St. Kitts & Nevis	—	—	—	—	.1	.1	.1	—	—	—	—	—	.1	—
St. Lucia	.9	.4	.7	.5	1.1	1.0	.9	—	—	—	—	—	—	—
St. Vincent	.8	.4	.4	.4	.8	.5	.6	—	—	—	—	—	—	—
Suriname	2.1	2.9	2.8	3.1	3.7	1.1	1.0	.1	2.5	.6	—	—	.2	—
Trinidad and Tobago	20.4	13.1	5.4	3.1	2.3	8.8	8.3	10.3	.5	.6	.2	.1	.2	1.0
S. URUGUAY	.8	.4	.1	.3	.5	.6	.7	2.6	4.4	8.7	9.7	10.0	10.5	4.9
T. VENEZUELA	366.1	117.9	96.6	129.0	150.2	220.2	162.7	354.6	393.6	387.4	238.5	118.6	120.5	130.1
Western Hem. not specified	.5	.3	.2	1.0	.3	.3	.2	.1	—	—	5.2	.1	.2	—
U.S.S.R. and Other Nonmembers	62.4	71.4	33.7	53.7	133.9	287.8	78.0	45.0	39.5	28.4	26.3	47.1	35.3	31.1
Albania	—	—	—	—	1.0	—	—	—	.6	.3	.1	1.9	.3	—
Bulgaria	—	4.5	.1	2.5	7.8	6.5	16.4	.2	.6	.3	—	—	.3	.4
G. CUBA	4.5	1.6	1.9	4.6	2.2	.9	5.9	.6	5.8	.2	3.8	3.3	.6	.5
Czechoslovakia	6.9	12.8	10.5	13.3	45.7	21.1	33.0	3.3	7.2	6.2	4.7	6.4	3.8	4.7
Eastern Germany	33.9	31.0	1.2	12.0	76.1	254.7	16.1	27.2	18.2	16.2	13.4	24.9	22.0	18.0
North Korea	—	—	.2	—	.3	.3	—	.5	1.5	.4	.1	.5	.9	.3
U.S.S.R.	17.1	21.6	20.0	21.2	1.2	4.6	6.5	7.4	6.2	5.1	4.1	10.1	7.8	7.2
Country or area not specified	.7	66.0	36.1	44.6	38.8	146.5	.5	.7	.6	2.3	6.0	3.9	28.6	1.1
Special categories	.1	—	—	—	—	.2	—	5.2	4.3	9.1	19.1	12.0	1.1	13.0
Memorandum Items														
EEC	1,171.6	1,209.7	1,305.2	1,235.8	2,028.1	1,145.3	1,399.3	959.6	821.0	816.0	810.9	894.5	940.1	1,029.5
Oil Exporting Countries	388.1	141.5	146.4	191.2	150.8	234.5	96.5	354.9	393.6	387.4	238.5	118.7	120.7	130.5
Non-Oil Developing Countries	399.1	390.6	445.2	460.4	536.2	749.9	685.0	1,216.1	1,015.5	848.0	833.2	820.1	807.2	971.4
% Distribution														
Industrial Countries	72.5	78.3	81.0	78.9	83.2	71.8	80.4	70.4	70.7	71.6	72.8	74.5	76.5	77.2
Developing Countries	25.4	17.3	17.0	18.3	13.4	19.6	18.0	28.7	28.4	27.5	25.9	23.9	21.9	21.9
Africa	.5	.9	.9	1.8	.3	.5	1.1	.2	.2	.7	.1	.1	.1	4.4
Asia	2.4	.7	.6	.9	.3	.4	1.0	.8	.6	.6	.6	.7	.9	.5
Europe	.1	1.5	1.3	1.2	1.3	1.2	1.8	.7	2.1	1.2	.7	.7	.7	.4
Middle East	—	.2	.1	.3	.2	—	1.0	.1	.1	.2	.3	.5	.9	—
Western Hemisphere	21.7	14.0	13.5	14.0	11.4	17.3	13.1	26.8	25.4	25.3	24.3	21.9	19.3	16.5
U.S.S.R. and Other Nonmembers	2.0	2.3	1.0	1.5	2.6	5.7	1.6	.8	.8	.6	.6	1.2	.8	.6

Table 2616 (Continued)

COLOMBIA ABSOLUTE VALUE OF GOODS TRADED WITH SELECTED REGIONS AND COUNTRIES,[1] 1982-88

(M US)[2]

Category	Exports							Imports						
	1982	1983	1984	1985	1986	1987	1988	1982	1983	1984	1985	1986	1987	1988
Annual PC														
World	4.7	-.5	13.0	2.0	43.8	-1.6	-2.7	5.4	-9.3	-9.6	-8.1	-4.8	7.5	19.0
Industrial Countries	8.2	7.4	17.0	-.7	51.6	-15.1	9.0	4.9	-8.8	-8.5	-6.5	-2.6	10.4	20.1
Developing Countries	-4.8	-32.4	11.2	10.2	5.4	43.3	-10.5	7.1	-10.3	-12.3	-13.3	-12.4	-1.2	18.8
Africa	-17.2	13.5	86.6	22.8	-83.7	115.3	132.0	5.3	-11.8	-45.8	-49.4	-12.3	72.5	-71.3
Asia	86.4	33.2	-1.5	58.8	-46.6	22.7	143.7	-9.1	-31.3	1.5	-20.5	9.5	37.8	482.6
Europe	-7.1	-37.6	-.7	-3.3	57.0	-15.5	49.5	-3.8	168.5	-48.9	-45.4	1.7	1.9	-10.5
Middle East	-68.2	102.1	-34.2	279.3	-20.1	34.3	300.2	-18.7	-17.8	95.3	20.1	52.1	110.0	-52.5
Western Hemisphere	-4.4	-35.5	8.6	6.2	16.5	49.7	-26.5	8.1	-14.2	-9.9	-11.7	-14.2	-5.2	1.9
U.S.S.R. and Other Nonmembers	13.8	14.5	-52.9	59.4	149.5	115.0	-72.9	-17.0	-12.4	-28.1	-7.5	79.2	-25.1	-11.8

1. DOT data may differ between countries and from IFS data because of the time it takes for an export to become an import, etc.
2. Data may be calculated from partner's reported data or estimated on basis of less than 12 months.

SOURCE: IMF-DOT-Y, 1989.

Table 2617

COSTA RICA ABSOLUTE VALUE OF GOODS TRADED WITH SELECTED REGIONS AND COUNTRIES, [1] 1982–88

(M US)[2]

Category	Exports							Imports						
	1982	1983	1984	1985	1986	1987	1988	1982	1983	1984	1985	1986	1987	1988
IFS World Total	870.4	872.6	1,006.4	976.0	1,120.5	1,158.3	1,319.8	889.0	987.8	1,093.7	1,098.2	1,147.5	1,382.5	1,409.3
DOTS World Total	871.4	860.9	985.6	923.7	1,091.4	1,114.1	1,226.6	893.3	989.7	1,091.2	1,096.7	1,144.6	1,384.5	1,409.3
Industrial Countries	570.4	525.5	675.8	643.9	861.1	860.3	918.1	502.7	581.5	673.5	692.2	758.4	886.1	878.8
United States	291.8	273.8	372.1	364.8	467.1	506.1	545.2	318.2	374.3	395.8	380.2	409.6	512.8	549.1
Canada	7.0	6.5	5.5	10.9	14.4	18.8	21.2	14.2	18.6	21.8	18.5	22.4	28.1	23.2
Australia	.6	.8	.5	3.4	.9	.6	.5	.4	.1	.2	.3	.7	.4	.2
Japan	6.1	4.9	4.8	5.2	10.3	11.9	8.7	37.2	52.8	82.4	105.2	121.0	117.0	94.4
New Zealand	—	.2	.2	.3	.2	.2	.3	—	—	—	—	—	—	.1
Austria	.1	—	.1	—	—	—	—	1.3	2.7	2.9	4.4	3.0	3.4	2.9
Belgium-Luxembourg	11.0	9.6	10.5	11.1	13.7	10.9	11.3	4.8	4.7	5.8	9.5	9.4	8.8	11.5
Denmark	.4	.2	.6	—	.8	.3	1.1	1.8	1.4	1.8	2.3	2.2	3.5	3.0
Finland	19.3	19.7	19.4	21.8	24.9	24.1	14.9	1.3	1.3	1.2	2.2	2.0	2.0	2.1
France	11.5	11.1	11.5	11.6	17.5	14.7	16.4	11.6	9.8	21.2	16.0	21.6	12.4	19.3
Germany	124.5	110.6	131.5	117.9	160.7	168.0	178.0	35.1	46.7	56.7	58.3	64.4	73.8	60.3
Iceland	.3	.3	.7	.4	.3	.5	.1	.1	—	—	—	—	—	.2
Ireland	.6	.8	.7	.3	.7	.3	.4	3.3	6.8	3.3	3.8	3.4	4.3	3.2
Italy	32.9	27.3	33.9	19.8	36.6	33.2	44.3	13.3	17.1	20.3	20.2	22.1	26.7	25.3
Netherlands	24.9	21.0	22.2	19.3	28.7	30.5	36.5	4.1	6.1	10.5	9.7	13.3	22.1	17.5
Norway	3.6	4.0	5.1	4.6	6.1	1.3	1.5	.4	.3	.9	.7	.4	1.1	1.1
Spain	5.4	4.4	8.6	9.4	13.1	6.2	1.9	17.1	16.0	21.2	25.7	17.5	23.7	17.7
Sweden	8.8	6.8	10.0	12.0	17.4	6.1	9.2	9.6	2.8	3.8	5.4	10.2	9.6	9.0
Switzerland	1.8	1.6	1.3	4.0	5.6	1.9	3.5	5.3	7.4	9.6	9.4	13.0	14.2	14.7
United Kingdom	19.8	22.0	36.7	27.1	42.4	24.8	23.0	23.8	12.6	14.2	20.4	22.2	22.1	24.0
Developing Countries	277.3	295.8	289.8	256.4	216.2	219.7	285.9	388.8	406.4	413.2	399.8	380.5	488.6	520.0
Africa	3.5	5.5	2.2	2.7	.8	1.6	3.6	.1	.1	—	—	.1	.2	—
Botswana	—	.4	.1	—	—	—	—	—	—	—	—	—	—	—
Djibouti	—	.1	—	—	—	—	—	—	—	—	—	—	—	—
Lesotho	1.6	.7	.3	.6	.3	.6	1.0	—	—	—	—	—	—	—
Morocco	.4	.6	.2	—	.1	.1	1.2	—	—	—	—	—	—	—
Mozambique	—	—	—	.2	—	—	—	—	—	—	—	—	—	—
South Africa	.1	1.8	1.1	.4	.4	.9	1.3	—	—	—	—	—	.1	—
Sudan	—	1.9	.2	—	—	—	—	—	—	—	—	—	—	—
Tanzania	—	—	—	—	—	—	—	—	—	—	—	—	—	—
Tunisia	1.4	—	—	.1	—	—	—	—	—	—	—	—	—	—
Zimbabwe	—	—	.2	.9	—	—	—	—	—	—	—	—	—	—
				.5	.1									
Asia	3.7	4.4	2.7	2.7	4.1	8.6	23.9	25.6	20.1	29.8	34.1	48.4	74.1	70.6
Afghanistan	.1	—	.1	.2	.2	—	—	.1	.2	.3	.2	.1	.2	.2
China, People's Rep.	—	.4	.3	.3	.1	.1	3.0	1.2	2.5	3.7	5.4	5.8	10.3	12.7
Hong Kong	.3	—	—	.6	—	—	—	—	—	—	—	—	—	—
India	1.0	—	.1	.1	.1	.1	.4	.1	.3	.1	.1	.3	.3	.4
Indonesia	.1	.1	—	.2	—	—	—	.4	.3	—	—	.3	—	.3
Kiribati, Rep. of	—	.1	.4	.3	.5	5.0	11.1	5.3	5.6	7.3	7.1	13.5	26.9	22.6
Korea	—	1.4	—	—	.5	—	—	—	—	—	.1	—	—	—
Macao	—	—	—	—	—	—	—	—	—	—	—	—	—	—
Malaysia	.1	.1	—	—	.2	.2	.9	—	.1	—	.1	1.1	.3	.2
Pakistan	—	.2	—	—	.1	.1	.3	—	—	—	.1	—	—	—
Philippines	.2	.3	.4	.1	.1	.4	.3	—	.3	.3	.9	.2	.2	.2
Singapore	.3	.3	.1	.1	.1	—	2.4	12.8	.3	.3	.9	.2	.5	.5
Sri Lanka	.7	.6	1.0	.9	.7	1.0	1.4	—	.2	.1	.1	—	.1	.1
Thailand	—	—	—	—	—	—	—	—	—	—	—	—	—	3.3
Asia not specified	—	—	—	—	—	—	—	—	—	—	—	.1	—	—
Taiwan Province of China	.8	1.1	.4	.5	2.0	1.7	4.5	5.5	10.9	18.0	19.6	26.8	35.1	30.2

Table 2617 (Continued)

COSTA RICA ABSOLUTE VALUE OF GOODS TRADED WITH SELECTED REGIONS AND COUNTRIES,[1] 1982–88

(M US)[2]

Category	Exports 1982	1983	1984	1985	1986	1987	1988	Imports 1982	1983	1984	1985	1986	1987	1988
Developing Countries (Continued)														
Europe														
Cyprus	3.3	5.8	11.8	23.9	13.6	16.8	30.1	.8	.8	1.6	1.3	1.8	8.0	2.7
Gibraltar	?	.1	.1	?	?	?	?	?	?	?	?	?	?	?
Hungary	.6	.6	4.1	8.5	?	.3	4.2	.1	.2	.2	.1	.3	.1	.6
Poland	.4	2.9	6.4	14.5	12.4	3.7	20.3	.1	.1	.5	.3	.3	.5	.3
Portugal	?	?	?	.6	1.1	5.3	4.0	.3	.3	.4	.4	.5	.4	.6
Romania	2.5	1.7	.9	.2	?	?	?	?	?	?	.1	?	.1	.2
Turkey	.2	.1	.1	?	?	7.5	1.4	.2	?	.3	?	.2	1.6	?
Yugoslavia	?	?	?	?	.1	7.5	.1	.3	.3	.3	.3	.4	3.7	.9
Europe not specified	.1	.1	.1	?	?	?	?	.1	?	.1	?	?	1.6	?
Middle East														
Bahrain	11.9	16.6	10.5	12.6	5.6	8.2	15.8	.6	2.6	1.5	2.5	3.1	3.6	5.1
Egypt	1.0	.1	.2	.1	.4	.3	.2	?	?	?	?	?	?	.2
Iran, I.R. of	?	?	?	?	?	.2	?	?	?	?	?	?	?	?
Israel	1.1	4.1	2.6	5.2	1.8	2.5	6.1	.6	2.6	1.5	2.2	2.7	3.5	4.9
Jordan	.6	2.5	2.5	1.8	.1	.6	.9	?	?	?	?	?	?	?
Kuwait	.7	2.8	1.4	1.6	.7	1.1	1.7	?	?	?	?	?	?	?
Lebanon	3.0	.8	.1	.4	.2	.4	1.2	?	?	?	?	?	?	?
Oman	.7	1.9	2.3	1.7	1.7	2.6	5.1	?	?	?	?	?	?	?
Qatar	.1	.1	.1	.1	.1	.1	.2	?	?	?	?	?	?	?
Saudi Arabia	4.3	4.1	1.0	1.0	.6	.4	.5	?	?	?	?	.4	.2	.2
Syrian Arab Rep.	.4	?	.1	.5	?	?	?	?	?	?	?	?	?	?
Yemen, P.D. Rep.	?	?	.4	?	?	?	?	?	?	?	?	?	?	?
Western Hemisphere	255.0	263.6	262.6	214.5	192.0	184.4	212.5	361.7	382.8	380.3	361.9	327.1	402.7	441.5
A. ARGENTINA	.1	.2	.1	2.1	10.6	3.1	1.1	1.9	2.5	2.5	6.9	3.3	3.6	5.0
Antigua and Barbuda	?	?	?	?	?	?	.1	?	?	?	?	?	?	?
Bahamas, The	.3	.2	.1	.1	.1	.1	.4	?	.2	.2	?	.1	.2	.1
Barbados	.5	.4	.3	.2	.4	.3	.5	?	.1	.2	?	?	?	?
Belize	.8	.4	.4	.3	.5	.8	1.4	?	?	?	.1	?	.3	?
Bermuda	.2	.2	.9	.1	?	.8	.5	.4	?	?	?	.4	.3	.1
B. BOLIVIA	?	.2	.2	.1	2.4	.5	1.0	?	?	?	?	?	.3	.1
C. BRAZIL	2.4	.6	.2	.1	.1	.2	1.4	12.2	14.1	20.2	23.9	33.9	33.7	56.1
D. CHILE	3.4	1.9	1.7	1.8	2.0	1.5	.7	1.3	3.1	1.0	3.6	10.1	5.9	9.4
E. COLOMBIA	2.3	2.7	2.3	2.6	5.8	4.7	4.5	4.2	5.5	8.6	7.2	10.0	16.6	24.2
Dominica	?	?	?	.1	.1	.3	.2	?	?	?	?	?	?	.1
H. DOMINICAN REP.	1.6	.4	1.4	2.6	1.9	1.8	4.6	1.4	3.9	.9	.1	?	.5	.1
I. ECUADOR	33.1	41.6	44.6	46.3	28.9	36.3	1.7	.8	.4	1.5	15.6	13.1	9.4	5.2
J. EL SALVADOR	.1	.2	.5	.1	.4	.1	45.3	22.7	29.7	30.8	30.1	33.8	37.0	36.0
Grenada	.1	.2	.5	.1	.4	.1	.2	?	?	?	?	?	?	.2
Guadeloupe	?	?	?	?	?	?	?	?	?	?	?	?	?	?
K. GUATEMALA	64.3	88.5	75.9	39.2	37.2	43.6	58.3	56.2	59.4	59.4	46.4	61.3	64.6	65.0
Guyana	.1	.3	?	?	?	1.5	1.6	?	.9	.9	.6	.3	.1	.1
L. HAITI	1.2	1.4	.4	.6	1.0	1.5	1.6	?	?	?	?	?	?	?
M. HONDURAS	23.2	27.2	44.8	30.8	22.7	17.5	15.2	11.9	11.0	8.3	7.2	5.9	6.2	2.4
Jamaica	1.2	.9	.5	1.2	4.7	3.4	3.0	?	3.8	.6	.6	.1	.5	.9
Martinique	?	.3	.3	.8	.9	.3	.3	?	?	?	?	?	?	?
N. MEXICO	13.5	.1	13.5	7.7	5.7	1.6	2.9	80.3	81.6	76.4	32.0	55.5	74.3	84.5
Netherlands Antilles	7.2	11.0	4.7	2.1	2.4	1.4	1.9	20.7	46.6	24.1	16.7	4.3	.1	.1
O. NICARAGUA	46.6	40.9	27.9	27.2	11.6	11.9	15.9	21.6	20.2	16.3	8.9	5.3	9.0	11.2
P. PANAMA	41.4	37.1	37.2	39.7	44.0	47.7	40.3	13.8	20.7	25.6	20.5	22.0	27.4	26.5
Q. PARAGUAY	?	.1	?	?	?	.1	?	.1	.1	.1	.3	.1	1.0	.2
R. PERU	1.4	1.0	.4	.2	2.8	1.0	.9	3.0	3.7	8.0	14.0	6.0	5.0	7.2
St. Kitts & Nevis	.3	.2	.1	?	?	.1	.1	?	?	?	?	?	?	?
St. Lucia	.3	.3	?	.3	.7	.5	1.0	?	?	?	?	?	?	?
St. Vincent	?	?	?	?	?	?	?	?	?	?	?	?	?	?

Table 2617 (Continued)

COSTA RICA ABSOLUTE VALUE OF GOODS TRADED WITH SELECTED REGIONS AND COUNTRIES,[1] 1982–88
(M US)[2]

Category	Exports 1982	1983	1984	1985	1986	1987	1988	Imports 1982	1983	1984	1985	1986	1987	1988
Developing Countries (Continued)														
Western Hemisphere (Continued)														
Suriname	.4	.3	.2	.9	.5	~	~	~	~	~	~	~	10.7	~
Trinidad and Tobago	1.6	.9	1.5	1.3	.7	.3	.5	2.2	3.0	1.2	1.5	1.5	1.5	4.4
S. URUGUAY										.1	.1		.1	.3
T. VENEZUELA	5.6	3.0	1.8	5.7	3.3	2.0	6.1	107.3	72.4	93.5	123.7	58.2	89.1	102.1
Western Hem. not specified	1.4	.9	.6	.5	.6	.7	.9		.2		1.8	1.8	4.1	~
U.S.S.R. and Other Nonmembers	23.6	39.5	20.0	22.6	2.5	23.2	19.9	1.7	1.9	3.0	2.3	2.7	4.3	4.2
Albania	7.3	3.5	.4	~	~	~	~	~	~	~	~	~	~	~
Bulgaria	1.6	1.5	.2	.3	.4	.1	.1	~	~	~	~	~	.1	.2
G. CUBA	~	~	~	~	~	~	.3	~	~	~	~	~	~	.2
Czechoslovakia	7.4	8.9	12.1	18.5	1.4	6.9	9.0	1.1	1.3	1.5	1.4	1.4	1.7	1.7
Eastern Germany	5.7	.7	.4	3.8	.6	8.3	.5	.1	.2	~	.2	.1	.1	.1
North Korea	.4	.3	.1	~	~	.5	.6	~	~	1.2	.1	.5	.1	.4
U.S.S.R.	1.3	24.7	6.9	~	~	7.5	9.5	.5	.4	.2	.6	.7	2.3	1.8
Country or area not specified	~	~	~	~	~	~	~	1.4	~	1.4	.7	~	2.1	1.9
Special categories	~	~	~	.8	11.7	10.9	2.7	.1	~	1.4	1.6	3.0	3.4	4.5
Memorandum Items														
EEC	231.1	207.1	256.1	217.1	315.3	294.2	317.0	115.1	121.4	155.3	166.1	176.6	197.9	182.5
Oil Exporting Countries	11.4	11.9	6.5	10.2	6.5	6.2	13.5	107.7	72.7	93.6	123.9	59.0	89.3	102.6
Non-Oil Developing Countries	265.9	283.9	283.3	246.1	209.7	213.5	272.4	281.1	333.7	319.7	275.9	321.6	399.3	417.4
% Distribution														
Industrial Countries	65.5	61.0	68.6	69.7	78.9	77.2	74.8	56.3	58.8	61.7	63.1	66.3	64.0	62.4
Developing Countries	31.8	34.4	29.4	27.8	19.8	19.7	23.3	43.5	41.1	37.9	36.5	33.2	35.3	36.9
Africa	.4	.6	.2	.3	.1	~	.3	~	~	~	~	~	~	~
Asia	.4	.5	.3	.3	.4	.8	1.9	2.9	2.0	2.7	3.1	4.2	5.4	5.0
Europe	.4	.7	1.2	2.6	1.2	1.5	2.5	.1	.1	.2	.1	.2	.6	.2
Middle East	1.4	1.1	1.1	1.4	.5	.7	1.3	.1	.3	.1	.2	.3	.3	.4
Western Hemisphere	29.3	30.6	26.6	23.2	17.6	16.6	17.3	40.5	38.7	34.8	33.0	28.6	29.1	31.3
U.S.S.R. and Other Nonmembers	2.7	4.6	2.0	2.5	.2	2.1	1.6	.2	.2	.3	.2	.2	.3	.3
Annual PC														
World	-13.6	-1.2	14.5	-6.3	18.2	2.1	10.1	4.4	10.8	10.3	.5	4.4	21.0	1.8
Industrial Countries	-5.3	-7.9	28.6	-4.7	33.7	-.1	6.7	-31.7	15.7	15.8	2.8	9.6	16.8	-.8
Developing Countries	-27.6	6.7	-2.1	-11.5	-15.7	1.6	30.2	-17.3	4.5	1.7	-3.2	-4.8	28.4	6.4
Africa	139.3	57.5	-60.4	22.4	-68.7	96.3	117.3	-48.9	-60.6	-13.0	-19.1	136.8	67.8	-75.5
Asia	-2.7	20.2	-38.7	1.5	49.1	112.3	176.3	15.7	-21.5	48.2	14.5	42.1	53.1	-4.7
Europe	-62.9	76.4	103.6	102.5	-43.1	23.2	79.7	-40.3	-8.5	113.9	-24.0	44.9	338.9	-66.4
Middle East	32.7	39.3	-36.6	19.8	-55.2	45.2	94.0	-48.9	365.7	-42.8	69.8	22.3	17.4	41.5
Western Hemisphere	-29.1	3.4	-.4	-18.3	-10.5	-4.0	15.2	-18.8	5.9	-.7	-4.8	-9.6	23.1	9.6
U.S.S.R. and Other Nonmembers	1.5	67.0	-49.3	13.1	-89.1	842.4	-14.3	-41.9	9.7	59.3	-22.8	14.3	60.5	-2.9

1. DOT data may differ between countries and from IFS data because of the time it takes for an export to become an import, etc.
2. Data may be calculated from partner's reported data or estimated on basis of less than 12 months.

SOURCE: IMF-DOT-Y, 1989.

Table 2618
CUBA ABSOLUTE VALUE OF GOODS TRADED WITH SELECTED REGIONS AND COUNTRIES,[1] 1982–88 (M US)[2]

PART I. NON-COMMUNIST TRADE

Category	Exports							Imports						
	1982	1983	1984	1985	1986	1987	1988	1982	1983	1984	1985	1986	1987	1988
DOTS World Total	1,288.7	1,045.1	851.7	861.1	878.9	967.7	1,345.7	1,760.1	1,812.4	2,444.3	2,989.2	2,658.4	1,790.1	2,151.8
Industrial Countries	521.4	462.1	390.5	417.7	446.3	468.6	581.5	1,022.2	985.5	1,327.3	1,494.3	1,456.6	985.9	1,073.5
United States	1.5	~	~	~	~	~	~	1.0	.7	1.1	1.1	1.5	1.4	3.7
Canada	77.1	45.3	49.5	31.9	50.2	37.3	68.3	289.8	323.9	287.1	270.6	287.9	225.5	199.3
Australia	.5	.6	1.2	1.5	.3	.4	.8	.5	1.6	9.3	5.3	5.7	2.5	1.1
Japan	103.5	83.8	71.0	84.7	120.2	106.6	125.4	138.6	115.2	274.7	333.6	326.0	127.0	128.5
New Zealand	4.2	~	10.9	~	~	~	~	5.2	~	5.2	20.8	19.0	~	~
Austria	3.5	1.9	2.2	2.0	1.9	3.1	2.6	7.1	9.3	13.7	18.1	23.8	10.8	5.4
Belgium–Luxembourg	8.9	12.0	5.9	1.8	3.0	3.2	2.6	17.0	15.4	13.5	29.7	25.2	10.4	25.1
Denmark	.5	1.2	3.4	1.9	1.1	.5	1.5	6.7	6.2	8.2	10.0	9.8	8.3	12.5
Finland	24.0	13.3	4.4	13.7	9.4	10.8	3.2	3.0	2.6	4.0	3.0	4.3	2.6	15.5
France	50.5	51.6	30.7	36.2	50.3	73.7	58.2	62.1	111.3	113.6	115.6	59.2	59.9	82.7
Germany	29.0	26.9	10.8	18.4	17.3	21.1	65.5	71.0	70.8	87.0	115.7	116.6	76.5	99.5
Ireland	.3	.2	.1	.7	.6	~	~	27.9	28.5	27.2	~	~	~	~
Italy	39.5	33.6	42.2	34.7	49.8	45.6	49.7	42.3	32.6	79.7	69.3	74.0	70.3	102.6
Netherlands	43.0	81.9	56.0	57.0	37.9	43.5	69.1	65.6	43.5	43.7	32.6	32.9	42.7	55.1
Norway	.1	.1	~	1.2	3.7	~	~	1.4	1.1	1.1	.9	.9	.8	.5
Spain	100.0	85.0	79.6	112.5	79.4	90.2	74.4	120.7	98.1	196.3	320.0	320.8	212.0	231.0
Sweden	.5	.2	2.0	5.8	2.6	5.5	5.2	22.4	18.6	43.1	32.9	29.7	17.8	20.5
Switzerland	6.4	5.1	5.4	5.5	7.3	7.9	8.5	19.4	29.6	24.4	30.9	24.1	43.0	29.5
United Kingdom	28.5	19.6	15.4	8.5	11.4	19.1	46.0	125.7	76.6	94.7	83.5	95.3	74.2	61.0
Developing Countries	767.3	583.0	461.2	443.4	432.6	499.1	764.3	737.9	326.9	117.0	494.9	201.8	304.2	1,078.4
Africa	87.1	72.3	38.4	8.2	11.2	9.0	9.4	6.2	9.3	5.7	4.3	8.4	9.3	.9
Algeria	82.5	67.6	32.9	~	~	~	~	.2	1.0	~	~	~	~	~
Angola	.1	.1	.1	.1	.1	~	.1	~	~	~	~	~	~	~
Burundi	~	~	~	~	~	~	~	~	~	~	~	~	~	~
Cameroon	~	~	~	~	~	~	.2	~	~	~	~	~	~	~
Cape Verde	1.9	.3	~	.3	.3	.4	.5	~	~	.4	.1	.1	.1	~
Comoros	.1	~	.1	.1	.1	.2	.2	~	~	~	~	~	~	~
Congo	~	.3	.5	.3	.2	.3	.3	~	~	~	.1	~	~	~
Ethiopia	.6	.6	.2	.8	.9	1.0	1.3	~	~	~	~	~	~	.1
Guinea-Bissau	.6	.6	.7	.7	.7	.9	1.1	~	~	~	~	~	~	.1
Mauritania	~	~	~	~	~	~	~	~	1.6	~	.3	~	~	~
Morocco	~	~	~	~	~	~	~	4.1	1.6	~	~	~	~	~
Reunion	.9	~	~	.5	.7	.8	.9	1.9	~	~	~	~	~	~
Senegal	.9	~	~	.5	.7	.8	.9	~	~	~	~	~	~	~
Seychelles	~	~	~	~	~	~	~	~	~	~	~	~	~	~
Tunisia	~	3.2	4.0	5.3	8.1	5.2	4.8	~	6.7	5.2	4.0	8.4	9.2	.8
Asia	270.0	198.0	136.7	108.5	88.8	84.6	289.5	140.0	120.5	118.3	147.1	107.0	98.1	206.0
Bangladesh	.3	.4	.1	.2	.1	.3	.3	~	~	.9	~	~	~	~
China, People's Rep.	243.7	182.7	121.1	97.8	76.5	70.2	266.3	128.7	106.8	104.2	128.5	105.4	87.4	171.2
Hong Kong	3.1	3.1	3.4	3.5	3.7	4.4	5.3	1.0	.1	.2	.2	.1	.8	.9
India	9.2	~	~	~	~	4.5	2.9	.5	.5	.6	.6	.6	.8	.9
Indonesia	13.5	7.2	10.8	4.3	8.2	2.9	10.7	.2	.6	.6	.7	.1	.1	~
Malaysia	.2	.2	1.3	.8	.2	.2	.3	~	~	~	.1	.1	.1	~
Philippines	~	~	~	~	~	~	.3	~	~	~	~	~	~	~
Singapore	.2	.2	1.3	.8	.2	.2	.3	2.6	3.0	1.8	1.8	.8	1.4	3.1
Sri Lanka	~	4.4	~	1.9	~	2.0	3.9	~	~	~	1.2	~	~	~
Thailand	~	~	~	~	~	~	~	7.0	9.4	10.0	14.2	~	8.3	30.7
Europe	164.9	111.9	145.3	182.4	188.5	233.7	276.4	317.0	266.4	256.2	305.6	249.7	254.9	306.1
Cyprus	.1	.7	.5	.6	.1	.1	.3	4.3	~	~	~	~	~	~
Greece	.1	.1	.1	.3	5.0	8.3	10.0	4.3	~	~	~	~	.1	.1
Hungary	54.1	11.2	16.4	20.4	15.9	18.8	17.1	77.9	69.8	83.7	83.7	57.5	53.1	58.4
Malta	.5	~	~	~	~	~	~	~	~	~	~	~	~	~

Table 2618 (Continued)

CUBA ABSOLUTE VALUE OF GOODS TRADED WITH SELECTED REGIONS AND COUNTRIES,[1] 1982–88
(M US)[2]

PART I. NON-COMMUNIST TRADE (Continued)

Category	Exports							Imports						
	1982	1983	1984	1985	1986	1987	1988	1982	1983	1984	1985	1986	1987	1988
Developing Countries (Continued)														
Europe (Continued)														
Poland	32.8	31.6	27.4	28.8	30.2	36.3	43.6	58.1	58.7	42.6	44.7	47.0	56.4	67.6
Portugal	39.9	5.8	8.5	3.7	3.4	3.9	8.8	4.2	4.3	5.4	7.7	6.5	1.3	1.0
Romania	37.5	62.5	89.1	125.6	131.9	158.3	189.9	165.1	133.4	124.3	92.5	97.1	116.5	139.8
Turkey	~	~	3.2	1.5	2.1	4.3	4.4	.3	.2	.2	.3	~	1.0	1.2
Yugoslavia	.1	~	~	1.5	2.1	3.7	2.3	7.1	~	~	76.8	41.6	26.7	38.2
Middle East														
Egypt	141.5	128.5	67.3	71.0	69.4	83.1	90.3	5.5	5.5	6.0	6.7	6.7	8.0	9.6
Jordan	51.1	31.5	12.6	26.3	35.6	42.7	51.2	~	~	~	.4	~	~	~
Lebanon	~	~	~	.1	~	.2	.1	5.5	5.5	6.0	6.3	6.7	8.0	9.6
Libya	31.1	29.5	26.6	23.9	19.1	21.0	23.1	~	~	~	~	~	~	~
Saudi Arabia	3.8	9.0	2.5	1.5	1.1	.6	.7	~	~	~	~	~	~	~
Syrian Arab Rep.	55.4	57.1	24.0	17.6	10.0	14.3	10.0	~	~	~	~	~	~	~
United Arab Emirates	.1	.1	.2	~	~	~	~	~	~	~	~	~	~	~
Yemen Arab Rep.	.2	1.4	1.5	1.6	1.7	2.0	2.4	~	~	~	~	~	~	~
Yemen, P.D. Rep.	~	~	~	~	2.0	2.4	2.8	~	~	~	~	~	~	~
Western Hemisphere	103.7	72.4	73.5	73.3	74.7	88.8	98.7	269.2	425.2	730.8	1,031.1	830.1	434.0	555.8
A. ARGENTINA	~	.1	.6	.3	1.1	.9	1.0	52.7	141.2	257.1	311.7	200.0	147.0	176.4
Bahamas, The	.2	.2	.1	.2	.2	.2	.3	~	~	~	~	~	~	~
Barbados	2.6	1.4	.4	.1	.2	.2	.3	.1	~	~	5.8	6.1	7.3	8.8
Bermuda	.1	.2	~	~	~	~	~	~	~	~	~	~	~	.1
B. BOLIVIA	~	.1	.1	~	~	~	~	~	~	~	~	~	~	~
C. BRAZIL	~	~	~	~	3.2	3.3	~	~	~	~	~	1.5	3.3	25.5
E. COLOMBIA	.5	5.3	.2	3.5	3.0	.6	.5	4.9	1.8	2.1	5.1	2.4	1.0	6.5
F. COSTA RICA	~	~	~	~	~	.1	.2	~	~	~	~	~	~	.3
H. DOMINICAN REP.	34.4	~	~	~	~	~	~	34.4	.2	~	~	~	~	~
Grenada	2.3	.3	.4	.4	.4	.5	.6	~	~	~	~	~	~	~
Guadeloupe	~	~	~	~	~	~	~	~	~	~	~	~	~	~
Guiana, French	.4	~	~	.2	~	~	~	~	~	~	~	~	~	~
Guyana	1.1	~	1.7	2.5	2.6	3.1	3.7	~	~	2.4	1.6	1.7	2.0	2.4
Jamaica	2.4	~	~	~	~	~	~	~	~	.2	.3	.3	.2	.2
Martinique	~	~	~	~	~	~	~	~	.1	.1	~	.1	.1	~
N. MEXICO	58.7	23.2	12.3	2.3	2.1	2.3	2.5	28.8	38.9	89.2	76.7	48.6	55.9	58.7
Netherlands Antilles	1.7	4.5	14.4	15.1	15.9	19.1	22.9	122.7	148.3	151.9	159.5	167.5	201.0	241.2
O. NICARAGUA	27.8	27.8	30.6	32.1	33.7	40.5	48.6	1.4	1.4	1.5	1.6	1.7	2.0	2.5
P. PANAMA	.1	.3	.1	.2	.4	.2	.2	.5	.8	1.8	1.3	1.0	1.4	3.2
R. PERU	~	5.7	10.0	.1	7.5	2.4	.9	~	~	~	~	2.2	3.6	14.6
St. Vincent	.3	.3	.3	.3	.4	.4	.5	~	~	~	~	~	~	~
Suriname	1.4	1.9	~	~	~	~	~	~	.2	.2	~	~	~	~
Trinidad and Tobago	.2	.2	.1	~	~	.2	~	~	~	~	~	~	4.7	9.9
S. URUGUAY	~	~	~	~	.1	.2	.1	~	~	~	~	1.2	4.4	5.5
T. VENEZUELA	4.0	1.0	2.0	16.0	4.0	15.0	16.5	22.0	92.4	224.4	467.5	396.0	~	~
Memorandum Items														
EEC	340.2	317.8	252.6	275.7	259.1	309.2	386.1	547.4	487.2	669.2	784.3	740.2	555.7	670.5
Oil Exporting Countries	130.6	107.2	64.1	41.4	24.2	41.1	43.2	22.3	93.4	224.4	467.5	396.0	~	~
Non-Oil Developing Countries	636.7	475.8	397.1	402.0	408.4	458.0	721.1	715.7	733.5	892.6	1,027.4	805.8	804.2	1,078.4

Table 2618 (Continued)

CUBA ABSOLUTE VALUE OF GOODS TRADED WITH SELECTED REGIONS AND COUNTRIES, [1] 1982–88 (M US)[2]

PART I. NON-COMMUNIST TRADE (Continued)

	Exports							Imports						
Category	1982	1983	1984	1985	1986	1987	1988	1982	1983	1984	1985	1986	1987	1988
Annual PC														
World	-13.2	-18.9	-18.5	1.1	2.1	10.1	39.1	-21.4	3.0	34.9	22.3	-11.1	-32.7	20.2
Industrial Countries	-13.8	-11.4	-15.5	7.0	6.9	5.0	24.1	-33.2	-3.6	34.7	12.6	-2.5	-32.3	8.9
Developing Countries	-12.9	-24.0	-20.9	-3.9	-2.4	15.4	53.1	4.1	12.1	35.1	33.8	-19.6	-33.1	34.1
Africa	-40.4	-17.1	-46.8	-78.7	36.6	-19.7	4.2	128.3	49.6	-39.2	-23.5	94.7	10.1	-90.6
Asia	25.9	-26.7	-30.9	-20.6	-18.2	-4.8	242.3	40.1	-13.9	-1.9	24.4	-27.3	-8.4	110.1
Europe	-27.1	-32.2	29.9	25.6	3.3	24.0	18.3	15.9	-16.0	-3.8	19.3	-18.3	2.1	20.1
Middle East	-4.2	-9.2	-47.6	5.5	-2.3	19.8	8.6	-4.2	-.9	10.0	11.1	-.7	20.0	20.3
Western Hemisphere	-28.9	-30.2	1.5	-.2	1.9	18.8	11.2	-17.6	57.9	71.9	41.1	-19.5	-47.7	28.1

1. DOT data may differ between countries and from IFS data because of the time it takes for an export to become an import, etc.
2. Data may be calculated from partner's reported data or estimated on basis of less than 12 months.

SOURCE: IMF-DOT-Y, 1989.

Table 2618 (Continued)

CUBA ABSOLUTE VALUE OF GOODS TRADED WITH SELECTED REGIONS AND COUNTRIES, [1] 1982–88

PART II. ALL TRADE, 1970–85

(M Pesos)

Catetory	1970	1973	1974	1975	1976	1977	1978	1979‡	1980	1981‡	1982	1983	1984	1985‡
Exports	1,050	1,153	2,237	2,962	2,962	2,912	3,440	3,500	3,967	4,259	4,940	5,535	5,462	5,983
USSR	529	477	811	1,661	1,638	2,066	2,496	2,370	2,253	2,455	3,297	3,882	3,938	4,468
Rest of Socialist Countries	248	268	472	341	452	378	420	514	534	823	882	883	953	842
Rest of World	273	408	954	949	602	468	524	616	1,180	981	761	770	571	673
Imports	1,311	1,463	2,226	3,113	3,180	3,433	3,574	3,687	4,627	5,081	5,537	6,222	7,207	7,905
USSR	691	811	1,025	1,250	1,490	1,858	2,328	2,524	2,904	3,223	3,756	4,245	4,776	5,310
Rest of Socialist Countries	226	224	328	437	374	467	521	534	709	877	1,153	1,169	1,282	1,330
Rest of World	394	428	873	1,456	1,316	1,108	725	629	1,014	981	628	808	1,149	1,265
Balance	-261	-310	11	-161	-488	-521	-134	-187	-660	-822	-597	-687	-1,745	-1,922
USSR	-162	-334	-214	412	148	208	168	-154	-651	-768	-459	-363	-838	-841
Rest of Socialist Countries	22	44	144	-66	78	-89	-101	-20	-175	-54	-271	-286	-329	-488
Rest of World	-121	-20	81	-507	-714	-640	-201	-13	166	~	133	-38	-578	-593

SOURCE: ECLA-S, 1981, p. 691; 1983, p. 255; 1985, p. 236.

Table 2618 (Continued)
CUBA ABSOLUTE VALUE OF GOODS TRADED WITH SELECTED REGIONS AND COUNTRIES,[1] 1982-88 (M US)[2]

PART III. TRADE WITH WORLD REGIONS, 1959-73

	1959-68[a]		1969		1970		1971		1972[‡]		1973[‡]	
	Export	Import	Export	Import	Export	Import	Export	Import	Export	Import	Export	Import
Absolute Total (M pesos)	630	843	667	1,222	1,049	1,312	861	1,388	771	1,190	1,151	1,391
Percentage Total	100	100	100	100	100	100	100	100	100	100	100	100
Socialist Eastern Europe	50	57	54	66	65	63	54	63	45	70	56	65
Other Eastern Europe	5	4	7	4	4	3	5	2	6	2	4	3
European Common Market	4	7	6	10	3	13	3	11	4	6	6	13
European Free Trade Area	4	4	4	8	3	7	3	7	4	6	2	1
Asia	16	12	24	9	22	10	25	12	28	11	24	13
Middle East	3	1	2	1	1	--	3	1	5	--	2	--
Africa	3	1	2	1	1	1	3	--	2	--	2	--
Americas	15	14	1	1	1	2	4	3	5	4	3	5

a. Yearly average.

SOURCE: Cuba: JUCEPLAN, AE, 1973, pp. 188-191.

PART IV. TRADE WITH LATIN AMERICAN COUNTRIES, 1959-73 (%)

	D. CHILE		N. MEXICO		R. PERU		OTHER	
Year	Exports	Imports	Exports	Imports	Exports	Imports	Exports	Imports
1959-68[a]	#	#	#	#	#	#	.1	.2
1969	#	#	#	#	#	#	#	#
1970	#	#	#	#	#	#	#	#
1971	.2	.1	#	#	#	#	#	#
1972	.4	.1	#	.1	#	.1	#	#
1973	.2	.1	#	.1	#	#	#	#

a. Yearly average.

SOURCE: Cuba, JUCEPLAN, AE, 1973. pp. 1980-191.

Table 2619

CUBA'S MOST IMPORTANT TRADING PARTNERS, 1900–86
(% Value)

PART I. UNITED STATES, 1900–62

Year	Exports from Cuba	Imports to Cuba
1900	71	43
1905	87	45
1910	86	53
1915	83	64
1919	77	76
1925	75	63
1929	77	59
1937	81	69
1942	90[a]	84[b]
1945	79	79
1950	59	79
1955	67	74
1959	73	73
1960	69	39
1961	6	2
1962	1	2

PART II. SOVIET UNION, 1960–86

Year	Exports from Cuba	Imports to Cuba
1960	17	14
1961	48	45
1962	42	54
1963	30	53
1964	39	40
1965	47	50
1966	46	56
1967	52	58
1968	45	61
1969	35	55
1970	50	53
1971	35	53
1972	29	60
1973	41	56
1974	36	46
1975	56	40
1976	61	47
1977	71	54
1978	73[c]	65
1979	68	68[c]
1980	57	62
1981	57	63
1982	66	67
1983	70	68
1984	72	66
1985	74	67
1986	73	70

a. Highest U.S. figure.
b. Second highest U.S. figure; highest import figure, 87%, came in 1942.
c. Highest Soviet figure.

SOURCE: For U.S. trade, SALA-SNP, p. 248, revised with data in Schroeder, pp. 432–433,
and William M. Leogrande, *Cuban Dependency* (Buffalo, N.Y.: Special Studies Series,
Council on International Studies, 1978), p. 17. For Soviet data, Leogrande, *Cuban
Dependency*, p. 18; SALA-Cuba, p. 168; ECLA-S, 1980, 1981, 1984, and 1986.

Table 2620

CROSS REFERENCES TO CUBA DATA IN SALA 20

Volume and Table Number	Table Title
20-2772	Cuba Total Exports and Exports to Europe, 1959–75
20-2773	Cuba Exports to EEC, 1959–75
20-2774	Cuba Exports to EFTA, 1959–75
20-2775	Cuba Exports to Rest of Western Europe, 1959–75
20-2776	Cuba Exports to Eastern Europe, 1959–75
20-2777	Cuba Exports to Asia, 1959–75
20-2778	Cuba Exports to Africa, 1959–75
20-2779	Cuba Exports to the Americas and North America, 1959–75
20-2780	Cuba Exports to Latin America and Oceania, 1959–75
20-2781	Cuba Total Imports and Imports from Europe, 1959–75
20-2782	Cuba Imports from EEC, 1959–75
20-2783	Cuba Imports from EFTA, 1959–75
20-2784	Cuba Imports from Rest of Western Europe, 1959–75
20-2785	Cuba Imports from Eastern Europe, 1959–75
20-2786	Cuba Imports from Asia, 1959–75
20-2787	Cuba Imports from Africa, 1959–75
20-2788	Cuba Imports from the Americas and North America, 1959–75
20-2789	Cuba Imports from Latin America and Oceania, 1959–75

Table 2621

DOMINICAN REPUBLIC ABSOLUTE VALUE OF GOODS TRADED WITH SELECTED REGIONS AND COUNTRIES,[1] 1982–88

(M US)[2]

Category	Exports							Imports						
	1982	1983	1984	1985	1986	1987	1988	1982	1983	1984	1985	1986	1987	1988
IFS World Total	767.7	785.2	868.1	735.2	717.6	711.3	890.1	1,255.8	1,279.0	1,257.1	1,293.0	1,245.8	1,591.5	1,608.0
DOTS World Total	809.0	803.6	874.9	743.4	731.0	1,332.4	1,696.7	1,250.1	1,277.7	1,257.0	1,286.5	1,367.4	2,150.0	2,418.1
Industrial Countries	623.4	711.1	799.9	683.8	687.5	1,258.6	1,601.3	728.4	704.7	639.0	716.1	964.7	1,620.6	1,756.6
United States	437.2	541.4	670.9	560.7	562.7	1,106.2	1,344.7	486.1	458.6	429.5	471.4	564.6	1,142.3	1,361.8
Canada	10.0	16.9	15.4	17.7	14.1	22.1	29.3	32.5	29.7	19.2	18.2	24.4	41.9	48.6
Australia	~	~	~	~	~	.2	.1	.1	.1	.1	.1	1.8	.1	.8
Japan	6.1	15.0	15.2	13.2	12.2	17.0	44.9	64.3	55.0	58.6	78.4	197.2	222.6	88.1
New Zealand	~	~	~	~	~	~	~	.6	5.7	7.1	9.2	8.2	11.6	12.6
Austria	~	~	~	~	~	.5	.1	.6	.4	.4	.4	.5	3.7	2.6
Belgium-Luxembourg	24.2	19.5	11.7	20.0	16.8	30.1	38.8	9.8	10.8	7.5	9.3	12.3	11.5	10.1
Denmark	.2	2.7	.7	.1	.4	.4	.9	2.8	1.0	.9	.9	1.1	3.3	5.5
Finland	~	~	~	~	~	11.4	27.5	.8	.9	.5	.5	.5	1.5	.9
France	3.5	1.5	.5	2.1	.5	12.7	14.2	13.8	13.8	9.4	8.6	15.1	27.3	24.6
Germany	1.3	1.3	2.9	1.2	1.5	11.9	15.1	28.1	40.4	33.4	48.7	45.2	43.3	32.2
Iceland	~	~	~	~	~	~	~	~	~	.7	~	.3	~	~
Ireland	~	~	~	~	~	~	.1	.2	.1	~	.3	1.1	1.6	1.8
Italy	2.4	2.1	2.4	3.9	5.1	~	14.4	10.5	11.3	9.8	13.1	28.5	~	75.5
Netherlands	20.6	36.6	62.1	53.0	58.5	2.1	2.4	8.7	10.3	14.8	11.9	12.7	14.9	15.4
Norway	2.0	~	~	~	~	~	.2	2.4	3.3	2.8	5.5	4.6	2.3	4.7
Spain	13.1	21.9	15.2	10.9	12.8	25.1	48.2	46.5	43.9	28.0	21.4	26.0	34.8	33.8
Sweden	1.0	~	2.0	~		4.1	7.3	1.8	2.4	1.7	1.5	1.6	6.1	3.9
Switzerland	100.5	48.1	.3	.2	.6	2.0	1.5	4.3	4.4	3.0	3.2	4.8	12.2	10.0
United Kingdom	1.3	4.1	.7	.7	2.1	12.9	11.8	14.3	12.7	11.7	13.5	14.3	39.6	23.7
Developing Countries	85.9	50.9	61.3	34.5	26.9	53.9	71.5	521.6	572.8	617.8	569.6	397.8	523.6	654.6
Africa	17.4	13.0	7.1	1.1	~	10.5	10.7	2.6	.3	.5	3.1	3.0	3.6	4.4
Algeria	3.0	~	~	~	~	~	~	~	~	~	~	~	~	~
Botswana	~	~	~	~	~	~	~	~	~	~	.1	~	~	~
Cameroon	~	~	~	~	~	~	.1	~	~	~	~	~	~	~
Morocco	9.9	7.1	7.1	1.1	~	9.9	10.4	~	~	~	~	~	~	~
Senegal	4.2	4.7	~	~	~	~	~	~	~	~	~	~	~	~
South Africa	~	~	~	~	~	~	~	2.5	.2	.5	2.8	3.0	3.6	4.4
Tunisia	.3	~	~	~	~	.5	.2	~	~	~	~	~	~	~
Africa not specified	~	1.1	~	~	~	~	~	.1	~	~	.2	~	~	~
Asia	~	7.5	.8	1.0	.2	.5	.7	21.9	26.1	24.2	29.2	30.3	105.6	115.8
Brunei	~	~	~	~	~	~	~	~	.1	~	~	~	~	~
China, People's Rep.	~	~	~	~	~	~	~	~	.1	.1	.1	.4	~	~
Hong Kong	~	~	~	.1	~	.1	.2	2.1	3.1	2.2	2.1	2.8	30.3	21.9
India	~	~	~	~	~	~	~	.1	~	.2	.7	.2	.3	.3
Indonesia	~	~	~	~	~	~	~	~	.1	.1	.1	.1	~	~
Korea	~	~	~	.3	.2	.1	.1	4.6	4.0	5.0	8.7	6.5	8.1	41.5
Macao	~	~	~	~	~	~	~	~	.2	.1	~	~	.1	~
Malaysia	~	~	~	~	~	~	~	~	~	~	~	~	.1	.2
Myanmar	~	~	~	.3	~	~	~	~	~	~	~	~	~	~
Pakistan	~	~	~	~	~	~	~	~	~	~	.1	.1	.1	~
Philippines	~	6.0	.1	~	~	.1	~	.1	.3	.1	1.7	~	~	~
Singapore	~	~	~	~	~	~	~	.3	.4	.4	.4	.4	1.4	2.0
Thailand	~	~	~	~	~	~	~	.1	~	~	~	.8	4.1	1.5
Asia not specified	~	~	~	.3	~	~	~	.1	~	~	~	.3	.3	.4
Taiwan Province of China	~	1.5	.7	~	~	.2	.3	14.5	17.8	16.0	15.3	18.7	60.7	48.0

Table 2621 (Continued)

DOMINICAN REPUBLIC ABSOLUTE VALUE OF GOODS TRADED WITH SELECTED REGIONS AND COUNTRIES,[1] 1982–88 (M US)[2]

Category	Exports							Imports						
	1982	1983	1984	1985	1986	1987	1988	1982	1983	1984	1985	1986	1987	1988
Developing Countries (Continued)														
Europe														
Greece	13.3	.2	1.2	1.7	.5	.8	4.8	.5	.4	1.0	1.6	.8	1.3	6.9
Hungary	~	~	~	~	~	~	~	~	~	.4	.4	.1	~	~
Malta	~	~	~	~	~	~	~	.1	~	~	~	.1	~	~
Portugal	13.3	.2	.7	.1	.5	.7	4.7	.3	.3	.5	.6	.4	1.2	5.6
Turkey	~	~	.6	~	~	~	~	~	~	.1	.1	~	~	.2
Yugoslavia	~	~	~	~	~	~	~	.2	~	.1	.1	~	~	~
Europe not specified	~	~	~	1.6	~	~	~	~	~	~	~	~	~	1.0
Middle East														
Iraq	~	~	~	~	~	~	~	.3	.7	2.4	1.2	1.3	2.1	3.6
Israel	~	~	~	~	~	.1	.1	.1	~	~	~	.1	.1	.2
Jordan	~	~	~	~	~	.1	~	.2	.7	.7	.9	1.2	2.0	3.4
Libya	~	~	~	~	~	~	~	~	~	1.0	~	~	~	~
Saudi Arabia	~	~	~	~	~	~	~	~	~	.7	.2	~	~	.1
Western Hemisphere	55.2	30.3	52.1	30.8	26.2	42.1	55.4	496.3	545.4	589.8	534.6	362.4	411.0	524.0
A. ARGENTINA	~	.1	.2	.1	~	.2	.1	1.0	6.2	20.3	16.4	6.0	3.5	4.2
Antigua and Barbuda	~	~	.2	.1	.6	~	.8	~	~	~	~	~	~	~
Bahamas, The	.3	~	.2	.8	.4	.7	.9	~	~	~	~	~	~	.8
Barbados	1.2	.1	.1	.2	.4	.8	~	~	~	.1	~	~	.1	.9
Belize	~	~	~	.1	~	~	~	~	~	~	~	~	.1	~
Bermuda	~	~	~	~	~	~	~	.8	.2	.6	.8	~	~	~
B. BOLIVIA	~	~	~	~	~	~	.1	~	.1	.2	~	~	~	.1
C. BRAZIL	2.4	2.8	.5	.4	.3	.2	~	15.0	20.1	21.5	22.6	23.5	34.6	44.8
D. CHILE	3.0	4.2	.3	.1	.3	1.0	5.9	4.5	5.2	4.3	5.3	4.1	8.4	14.8
E. COLOMBIA	.7	.2	.4	.3	~	.4	.1	3.9	5.1	4.4	15.0	7.4	18.9	62.4
F. COSTA RICA	.1	~	~	.1	~	~	~	1.9	2.6	2.1	2.2	2.9	4.7	31.0
Dominica	~	.2	.4	.3	~	~	~	~	.1	.2	~	~	~	~
I. ECUADOR	.1	~	4.1	.1	~	.1	.1	~	~	~	.1	.1	~	~
J. EL SALVADOR	.2	.1	.4	.1	~	.1	.1	1.6	1.9	1.0	1.4	1.8	2.2	2.6
Grenada	.9	.6	1.0	1.3	~	.8	1.0	~	~	~	.1	~	~	~
Guadeloupe	.1	.6	.2	.2	.1	~	~	~	~	~	.1	~	~	~
K. GUATEMALA	~	.1	.2	.1	.1	.1	.1	7.3	5.7	3.7	5.2	5.6	6.8	8.1
Guyana	~	~	.1	.1	1.6	1.9	2.3	~	~	~	~	.1	.1	.1
L. HAITI	5.1	5.6	6.4	5.6	5.4	6.5	7.8	2.4	10.8	10.6	5.9	2.0	2.4	2.9
M. HONDURAS	.5	1.8	1.1	.7	1.1	1.3	1.5	2.5	1.7	.5	.4	2.3	2.8	3.3
Jamaica	1.3	2.1	4.2	.6	.8	1.1	1.3	1.7	3.2	2.8	1.5	1.5	.9	1.0
Leeward Islands	.1	~	.1	.1	~	~	~	.4	~	~	~	~	~	~
Martinique	~	.1	.1	.3	~	~	~	~	~	~	~	~	~	~
N. MEXICO	.2	1.7	2.5	1.7	2.1	2.5	3.1	170.7	151.8	147.7	101.8	113.0	129.9	136.4
Montserrat	~	~	~	~	~	~	~	~	~	~	~	~	~	~
Netherlands Antilles	2.7	1.8	~	~	~	~	~	48.3	45.6	23.2	6.7	2.9	3.5	4.2
O. NICARAGUA	.8	.6	.1	.8	1.2	.2	~	~	~	.3	~	.1	~	~
P. PANAMA	.6	~	.1	.8	1.2	.2	1.5	11.4	13.4	11.7	13.4	24.5	.2	.5
Q. PARAGUAY	~	~	~	.2	~	~	~	~	~	~	.1	.9	~	~
R. PERU	.5	~	.3	.2	~	.4	~	.1	.2	.3	.8	.3	.4	.6
St. Kitts & Nevis	1.8	.6	.4	.2	~	~	~	.1	~	~	~	~	~	~
St. Lucia	1.4	.6	.4	.2	~	~	~	~	~	~	~	~	~	~
St. Vincent	~	~	.7	.3	~	~	~	~	~	~	~	~	~	~
Suriname	.8	.6	~	~	.2	~	~	.6	.7	1.5	.5	.1	~	~
Trinidad and Tobago	.8	.6	.7	1.2	.2	11.7	14.0	1.0	1.6	.6	1.3	2.7	6.8	11.4
S. URUGUAY	2.4	2.0	10.0	7.0	2.2	1.4	1.2	.1	~	~	1.3	.3	.3	1.5
T. VENEZUELA	28.2	3.8	17.7	1.8	1.1	.8	.9	221.0	268.9	332.7	332.3	159.4	183.3	192.5
Western Hem. not specified	.5	1.3	.1	5.8	8.9	10.7	12.8	~	~	~	.7	.8	.9	1.1

Table 2621 (Continued)

DOMINICAN REPUBLIC ABSOLUTE VALUE OF GOODS TRADED WITH SELECTED REGIONS AND COUNTRIES,[1] 1982–88
(M US)[2]

Category	Exports							Imports						
	1982	1983	1984	1985	1986	1987	1988	1982	1983	1984	1985	1986	1987	1988
U.S.S.R. and Other Nonmembers	99.8	41.6	13.7	22.1	6.0	7.2	8.6	.2	.1	.2	.5	4.6	5.5	6.6
G. CUBA	31.2	~	~	~	~	~	~	~	~	~	~	~	~	~
Czechoslovakia	~	~	~	~	~	~	~	~	.1	~	.1	~	.2	.2
Eastern Germany	~	~	2.5	~	.4	.4	.5	.1	.1	.1	.3	3.7	4.4	5.3
North Korea	~	~	~	.1	~	~	~	~	~	~	.1	.7	.9	1.0
U.S.S.R.	68.5	41.6	11.3	21.9	5.6	6.8	8.1	~	~	~	~	~	~	.1
Country or area not specified	~	~	~	3.0	10.6	12.7	15.3	~	~	~	.3	.2	.3	.3
Memorandum Items														
EEC	79.9	89.9	96.7	92.0	98.3	95.9	50.5	135.2	144.4	116.2	128.7	156.8	177.5	228.2
Oil Exporting Countries	31.2	3.8	17.7	1.8	1.1	.8	.9	221.1	268.9	334.5	332.6	159.7	183.5	192.6
Non-Oil Developing Countries	54.7	47.2	43.6	32.7	25.9	53.1	70.7	300.5	303.9	283.3	237.0	238.2	340.1	461.9
% Distribution														
Industrial Countries	77.1	88.5	91.4	92.0	94.0	94.5	94.4	58.3	55.2	50.8	55.7	70.6	75.4	72.6
Developing Countries	10.6	6.3	7.0	4.6	3.7	4.0	4.2	41.7	44.8	49.1	44.3	29.1	24.4	27.1
Africa	2.2	1.6	.8	.1	~	.8	.6	.2	~	~	.2	.2	.2	.2
Asia	~	.9	.1	.1	~	~	~	1.7	2.0	1.9	2.3	2.2	4.9	4.8
Europe	1.6	~	~	.2	.1	.1	.3	~	~	~	~	.1	.1	.3
Middle East	~	~	~	~	~	~	~	~	.1	.2	.1	.1	~	.1
Western Hemisphere	6.8	3.8	6.0	4.1	3.6	3.2	3.3	39.7	42.7	46.9	41.6	26.5	19.1	21.7
U.S.S.R. and Other Nonmembers	12.3	5.2	1.6	3.0	.8	.5	.5	~	~	~	~	.3	.3	.3
Annual PC														
World	-31.5	-.7	8.9	-15.0	-1.7	82.3	27.3	-11.6	2.2	-1.6	2.3	6.3	57.2	12.5
Industrial Countries	-39.8	14.1	12.5	-14.5	.5	83.1	27.2	-16.4	-3.3	-9.3	12.1	34.7	68.0	8.4
Developing Countries	-34.7	-40.7	20.3	-43.7	-22.0	100.3	32.7	-3.8	9.8	7.9	-7.8	-30.2	31.6	25.0
Africa	-2.8	-25.6	-45.2	-84.5	~	~	2.1	50.0	-89.8	75.9	560.8	-1.2	20.1	20.0
Asia	-71.4	~	88.8	15.5	-80.4	178.9	24.5	-10.4	19.2	-7.0	20.5	3.8	248.7	9.7
Europe	~	-98.6	572.2	36.4	-67.3	38.9	534.7	-15.5	-25.0	140.0	61.1	-48.9	58.4	436.2
Middle East	~	~	~	~	~	~	~	-3.7	182.1	230.4	-50.2	12.3	61.6	65.7
Western Hemisphere	-51.3	-45.1	72.1	-40.9	-14.9	60.6	31.6	~	9.9	8.1	-9.4	-32.2	13.4	27.5
U.S.S.R. and Other Nonmembers	608.6	-58.3	-67.0	60.7	-72.8	20.0	20.0	-87.7	-15.8	18.8	210.5	757.6	20.0	20.1

1. DOT data may differ between countries and from IFS data because of the time it takes for an export to become an import, etc.
2. Data may be calculated from partner's reported data or estimated on basis of less than 12 months.

SOURCE: IMF-DOT-Y, 1989.

Table 2622

ECUADOR ABSOLUTE VALUE OF GOODS TRADED WITH SELECTED REGIONS AND COUNTRIES,[1] 1982–88

(M US)[2]

Category	Exports 1982	1983	1984	1985	1986	1987	1988	Imports 1982	1983	1984	1985	1986	1987	1988
IFS World Total	2,327.4	2,347.7	2,620.4	2,904.7	2,171.5	2,021.3	2,192.0	2,168.9	1,487.4	1,616.3	1,766.6	1,810.0	2,251.5	1,713.7
DOTS World Total	2,139.9	2,227.5	2,580.1	2,905.6	2,171.1	1,998.6	2,192.9	1,988.2	1,465.2	1,767.3	1,857.2	1,811.3	2,229.0	1,713.5
Industrial Countries	1,149.1	1,379.1	1,775.1	1,860.1	1,562.0	1,331.3	1,276.2	1,564.6	1,088.6	1,235.1	1,349.0	1,345.6	1,416.1	1,251.2
United States	1,025.3	1,259.9	1,657.2	1,659.3	1,321.8	1,121.2	1,006.2	741.2	498.2	528.0	566.6	547.9	558.8	567.6
Canada	4.0	13.7	3.3	3.9	4.9	4.8	2.3	53.1	39.9	29.2	47.1	31.6	33.2	32.2
Australia	2.4	2.1	1.8	2.1	2.4	4.0	2.3	10.2	2.5	11.9	7.9	10.7	1.0	9.6
Japan	16.9	39.9	16.9	59.4	57.1	47.1	54.1	245.3	136.4	242.3	245.0	250.4	282.4	238.4
New Zealand	6.6	4.5	3.9	3.9	5.9	6.3	8.0	.1	5.1	13.8	5.6	5.3	2.0	.2
Austria	.2	.3	.3	.1	~	.1	1.4	5.5	9.2	7.4	11.3	8.6	10.0	6.7
Belgium-Luxembourg	21.0	15.1	7.5	8.8	8.6	10.0	15.7	10.3	8.0	20.0	13.4	12.2	13.6	13.5
Denmark	.1	.1	.1	.1	.1	.2	.4	19.0	2.7	9.8	5.2	5.7	4.8	4.3
Finland	2.5	1.6	2.0	3.1	3.4	3.6	2.9	1.6	4.9	3.2	1.2	1.6	1.3	.9
France	6.4	2.5	2.8	7.1	6.3	6.1	9.4	28.5	31.8	29.2	22.0	30.4	41.4	37.8
Germany	24.0	17.3	31.2	54.3	77.7	66.8	90.8	158.8	127.4	127.4	195.2	172.1	172.3	106.6
Ireland	4.4	3.2	3.2	5.9	4.7	4.1	.3	2.2	2.5	1.8	4.1	3.0	3.0	2.5
Italy	13.7	6.4	9.0	12.8	18.3	15.1	29.2	70.7	73.5	39.3	45.3	57.0	80.6	64.2
Netherlands	15.4	6.4	18.6	28.8	27.6	20.0	21.1	22.9	13.9	17.4	20.5	29.7	26.0	18.6
Norway	.1	~	~	~	.1	~	~	8.8	1.3	14.4	7.6	6.0	3.8	1.0
Spain	3.7	3.1	8.7	4.0	17.5	15.2	23.1	49.9	41.4	36.6	50.0	61.6	65.3	67.8
Sweden	.1	~	.1	.2	~	.2	.1	24.5	11.7	37.7	12.0	22.2	16.5	8.6
Switzerland	.1	~	.4	.5	.3	~	.1	52.1	32.2	34.2	39.8	44.6	51.3	35.3
United Kingdom	2.4	3.0	8.1	6.1	5.4	6.6	9.0	60.1	45.9	31.7	49.2	45.0	48.8	35.3
Developing Countries	974.2	838.6	796.5	1,032.8	599.7	656.3	903.5	409.8	357.5	522.5	496.5	458.5	787.1	448.2
Africa	21.8	4.0	1.3	11.1	9.6	3.3	9.7	16.0	8.6	6.5	18.1	31.1	42.8	16.6
South Africa	.9	1.9	.6	.2	.2	.3	.3	15.6	6.9	6.3	18.1	13.7	16.7	16.0
Africa not specified	20.9	2.2	.7	10.9	9.4	3.3	9.4	.5	1.6	.1	~	17.4	26.1	.7
Asia	412.3	343.3	453.7	678.4	312.6	199.6	284.3	72.3	48.0	53.9	64.3	64.3	104.2	64.2
China, People's Rep.	~	~	~	1.3	.6	2.5	~	.7	.1	~	.3	.1	.1	.6
Indonesia	~	~	~	~	.2	1.2	1.9	2.1	2.3	.3	1.4	1.7	3.3	2.0
Malaysia	.3	~	~	~	~	~	~	1.8	2.2	3.4	.5	~	~	1.6
Singapore	~	~	~	~	~	58.7	.3	~	~	~	~	~	1.4	.8
Asia not specified	400.4	250.5	384.5	547.6	275.0	92.9	234.5	24.1	17.4	26.2	26.5	27.4	62.7	26.8
Taiwan Province of China	11.6	92.8	69.1	129.5	36.8	44.2	47.6	43.7	25.9	23.9	35.6	35.1	36.7	32.4
Europe	15.2	13.2	14.4	39.6	27.3	17.7	15.5	11.4	12.4	20.4	16.0	22.1	19.5	41.3
Greece	.1	~	~	.6	~	~	.1	2.9	~	~	~	~	~	~
Hungary	7.7	2.9	8.8	29.1	20.4	10.3	8.6	.9	4.0	6.9	5.9	7.0	1.8	5.8
Poland	~	5.4	1.3	.3	.2	.8	1.8	2.5	.7	1.8	2.0	2.1	.8	1.2
Portugal	.9	.8	.6	.3	2.4	3.9	3.7	1.9	2.4	4.3	2.6	2.5	2.3	5.1
Romania	1.2	.1	.8	4.8	.4	~	~	~	3.6	2.6	1.6	1.5	.5	.5
Yugoslavia	5.2	3.7	2.7	2.6	3.7	2.6	1.3	3.1	1.6	3.1	2.9	8.8	2.9	1.1
Europe not specified	.1	.2	.2	1.9	.2	.1	.1	.1	~	1.8	1.0	.3	11.2	27.5
Middle East	~	.2	~	.6	~	~	~	2.4	2.2	11.0	1.7	~	~	~
Libya	~	.2	~	.6	~	~	~	2.4	2.2	11.0	1.7	~	~	~
Western Hemisphere	524.9	477.9	327.2	303.3	250.2	435.7	594.0	307.7	286.5	430.8	396.4	341.0	620.7	326.1
A. ARGENTINA	25.3	8.6	5.0	8.7	21.2	18.0	6.5	24.4	15.9	20.3	37.4	14.5	13.8	17.5
B. BOLIVIA	.2	.1	.2	.1	.2	.3	.2	1.3	~	.1	.1	.3	.2	.1
C. BRAZIL	155.8	2.7	1.6	2.5	23.2	17.9	10.9	77.9	73.6	224.9	121.3	110.0	117.3	109.8
D. CHILE	29.2	37.0	27.1	45.6	47.1	33.7	58.7	34.8	42.7	33.9	30.0	37.2	38.1	33.4
E. COLOMBIA	91.9	133.6	44.5	65.2	29.7	35.6	43.5	47.4	49.6	42.0	51.6	45.8	43.3	34.8
F. COSTA RICA	.4	.5	1.1	.6	6.8	1.0	7.7	4.3	1.9	3.2	6.7	4.4	6.7	4.7
J. EL SALVADOR	.6	~	.3	.6	.9	.1	5.1	~	~	8.5	.1	~	.1	.1
K. GUATEMALA	.3	~	.4	.1	.2	.4	1.0	9.5	25.8	11.3	2.8	4.0	7.2	10.5
M. HONDURAS	.1	~	.1	.6	.1	.2	.2	~	1.3	~	~	2.5	.7	~

Table 2622 (Continued)

ECUADOR ABSOLUTE VALUE OF GOODS TRADED WITH SELECTED REGIONS AND COUNTRIES,[1] 1982–88
(M US)[2]

Category	Exports							Imports						
	1982	1983	1984	1985	1986	1987	1988	1982	1983	1984	1985	1986	1987	1988
Developing Countries (Continued)														
Western Hemisphere (Continued)														
N. MEXICO	2.4	.3	1.2	1.8	9.2	7.7	9.3	21.4	16.9	27.0	28.4	58.9	92.0	56.8
O. NICARAGUA	~	~	~	.4	.1	.2	~	~	.1	~	.3	.3	~	1.3
P. PANAMA	70.1	216.9	165.5	136.1	58.6	53.2	34.8	16.5	6.1	3.7	6.6	7.7	19.0	10.1
Q. PARAGUAY	.1	.1	.1	.1	.1	.1	.1	~	.1	.4	.4	~	~	.1
R. PERU	11.3	4.5	6.3	5.9	9.8	51.3	129.0	36.0	29.1	30.1	74.4	36.5	24.1	21.8
S. URUGUAY	32.4	.3	.1	.2	3.8	37.9	.1	.6	1.0	1.6	.7	.7	1.0	.5
T. VENEZUELA	54.3	2.0	3.1	2.6	2.8	37.9	4.5	15.3	6.5	2.7	1.1	8.6	219.4	21.5
Western Hem. not specified	50.7	71.4	70.7	32.4	36.5	177.7	272.4	18.3	15.8	21.1	35.0	9.5	37.8	3.2
U.S.S.R. and Other Nonmembers	16.3	9.7	8.4	12.6	9.3	11.0	13.3	13.8	19.0	8.1	11.0	7.0	8.6	9.4
Bulgaria	2.1	.4	.8	~	~	.5	~	1.1	.3	.8	.2	~	~	.1
Czechoslovakia	6.3	3.4	3.3	2.7	2.0	4.1	2.5	6.4	5.8	6.5	6.2	4.1	6.1	5.0
Eastern Germany	.9	~	.1	3.8	7.3	1.8	6.7	.3	9.9	.7	.2	.2	.7	2.3
U.S.S.R.	7.0	5.9	4.3	6.1	~	4.6	4.0	6.1	3.0	.4	4.4	2.6	1.6	2.0
Country or area not specified	.3	.1	~	.1	.1	.1	~	~	~	~	.8	.2	17.2	4.8
Special categories	~	~	~	~	~	~	~	~	~	1.7	~	~	~	~
Memorandum Items														
EEC	92.0	57.9	89.9	128.5	168.4	147.9	202.6	427.1	349.5	317.4	407.4	419.2	457.9	355.7
Oil Exporting Countries	54.3	2.2	3.2	3.2	3.0	39.1	6.5	19.8	11.0	14.1	4.2	10.3	222.7	23.5
Non-Oil Developing Countries	919.9	836.4	793.4	1,029.7	596.7	617.1	837.0	390.0	346.5	508.4	492.3	448.2	564.5	424.6
% Distribution														
Industrial Countries	53.7	61.9	68.8	64.0	71.9	66.6	58.2	78.7	74.3	69.9	72.6	74.3	63.5	73.0
Developing Countries	45.5	37.6	30.9	35.5	27.6	32.8	41.2	20.5	24.4	29.6	26.7	25.3	35.3	26.2
Africa	1.0	.2	.1	.4	.4	.2	.4	.3	.6	.4	1.0	1.7	1.9	1.0
Asia	19.3	15.4	17.6	23.3	14.4	10.0	13.0	3.6	3.3	3.0	3.5	3.6	4.7	3.7
Europe	.7	.6	.6	1.4	1.3	.9	.7	.1	.8	1.2	.9	1.2	.9	2.4
Middle East	~	~	~	~	~	~	~	.1	.2	.6	.1	~	~	~
Western Hemisphere	24.5	21.5	12.7	10.4	11.5	21.8	27.1	16.5	19.6	24.4	21.3	18.8	27.8	19.0
U.S.S.R. and Other Nonmembers	.8	.4	.3	.4	.4	.5	.6	.7	1.3	.5	.6	.4	.4	.5
Annual PC														
World	-15.8	4.1	15.8	12.6	-25.3	-7.9	9.7	-11.5	-26.3	20.6	5.1	-2.5	23.1	-23.1
Industrial Countries	-18.7	20.0	28.7	4.8	-16.0	-14.8	-4.1	-8.2	-30.4	13.5	9.2	-.2	5.2	-11.6
Developing Countries	-12.5	-13.9	-5.0	29.7	-41.9	9.4	37.7	-26.7	-12.7	46.1	-5.0	-7.6	71.7	-43.1
Africa	~	-81.5	-67.5	745.8	-13.7	-65.7	194.8	-40.9	-46.7	-24.4	180.0	72.1	37.4	-61.1
Asia	-18.8	-16.7	32.1	49.5	-53.9	-36.2	42.5	-65.3	-33.6	12.3	19.4	38.3	62.0	-38.4
Europe	-43.3	-13.5	9.1	175.7	-30.9	-35.2	-12.7	-46.6	8.2	65.0	-21.6	38.3	-12.0	112.2
Middle East	~	~	-80.0	~	~	~	~	-48.6	-7.1	394.6	-84.8	~	~	~
Western Hemisphere	-9.1	-9.0	-31.5	-7.3	-17.5	74.1	36.3	1.9	-6.9	50.4	-8.0	-14.0	82.1	-47.5
U.S.S.R. and Other Nonmembers	17.6	-40.4	-13.7	50.5	-26.1	17.2	21.0	-62.2	37.9	-57.4	35.3	-36.5	22.6	9.7

1. DOT data may differ between countries and from IFS data because of the time it takes for an export to become an import, etc.
2. Data may be calculated from partner's reported data or estimated on basis of less than 12 months.

SOURCE: IMF-DOT-Y, 1989.

Table 2623

EL SALVADOR ABSOLUTE VALUE OF GOODS TRADED WITH SELECTED REGIONS AND COUNTRIES,[1] 1982–88 (M US)[2]

Category	Exports							Imports						
	1982	1983	1984	1985	1986	1987	1988	1982	1983	1984	1985	1986	1987	1988
IFS World Total	699.4	735.3	717.3	679.0	756.5	590.9	~	856.8	891.5	977.4	961.4	923.1	994.1	~
DOTS World Total	699.5	741.3	717.5	679.0	734.7	621.5	688.9	856.7	891.5	977.4	961.4	911.9	1,090.8	1,257.2
Industrial Countries	505.9	506.8	506.5	552.2	618.6	487.7	535.5	398.2	452.7	488.6	499.3	523.7	639.8	748.5
United States	248.1	286.1	269.7	327.4	362.5	272.8	271.4	233.1	289.6	325.2	325.8	367.3	428.9	531.3
Canada	10.8	13.1	11.6	14.9	20.3	32.5	32.3	13.5	13.5	11.4	9.3	6.4	13.0	20.5
Australia	.1	~	~	~	~	~	~	.7	.1	.1	~	.1	.1	.5
Japan	23.4	36.6	39.7	34.4	27.7	26.6	26.8	26.8	31.3	41.9	49.6	34.3	65.8	45.3
New Zealand	~	~	~	~	~	~	.1	~	.4	~	~	~	5.3	2.4
Austria	~	~	.6	~	~	10.3	6.6	1.2	1.0	.9	1.0	.9	2.0	.9
Belgium-Luxembourg	.9	2.1	4.6	11.4	12.9	.6	1.3	9.1	16.4	7.6	5.9	9.0	4.3	7.1
Denmark	.4	~	~	~	~	.5	.3	1.8	1.2	1.7	1.2	.8	3.8	2.2
Finland	~	.1	~	.2	.1	.5	1.3	.2	2.1	.8	3.5	.1	1.0	1.8
France	.5	6.6	.6	1.5	.3	6.8	7.2	19.5	9.1	3.7	4.9	5.3	7.1	14.9
Germany	204.9	139.9	161.2	142.4	177.3	101.0	160.2	39.8	36.3	43.1	42.0	43.7	37.3	40.1
Ireland	~	~	~	~	~	~	~	.7	1.2	.1	.1	1.4	.5	1.7
Italy	7.7	2.9	.5	1.3	.3	2.4	2.0	6.9	4.8	6.9	6.3	8.0	17.8	16.3
Netherlands	2.3	2.3	.6	.9	1.7	6.1	8.0	19.4	17.8	15.1	15.4	13.2	11.4	14.0
Norway	~	~	~	~	~	~	1.2	.1	.2	.1	1.9	3.0	2.5	3.6
Spain	5.2	16.7	15.2	15.1	12.8	18.1	3.0	6.6	8.7	9.4	12.5	9.3	7.8	12.3
Sweden	.7	.1	~	1.0	1.5	1.8	6.7	10.7	3.9	5.5	4.2	4.5	4.2	5.2
Switzerland	.7	.3	.6	.1	.1	4.7	2.0	2.8	6.1	3.8	4.1	5.9	9.6	12.5
United Kingdom	.9	.3	1.6	1.6	1.1	2.8	4.8	5.3	9.2	11.4	11.4	10.4	17.3	16.1
Developing Countries	188.5	218.5	182.7	118.6	106.5	122.3	139.9	452.8	434.6	477.3	448.5	335.1	387.3	432.3
Africa	~	.1	1.4	~	~	~	~	.2	.3	.3	.2	.1	.2	.2
Morocco	~	~	~	~	~	~	~	.1	.1	~	~	~	~	~
South Africa	~	.1	1.4	~	~	~	~	.1	.3	.3	.2	.1	.2	.2
Asia	2.6	20.0	.5	2.2	.5	.9	1.0	7.4	12.0	11.7	15.6	10.7	34.2	35.0
China, People's Rep.	~	~	.2	~	~	~	.2	1.2	.9	1.7	2.6	3.7	5.2	2.8
Hong Kong	1.5	2.1	.2	.1	.3	.3	.5	~	~	~	~	.1	2.1	2.4
India	~	~	~	~	~	~	~	~	~	~	~	~	.1	.2
Korea	~	5.3	~	~	~	~	.3	~	3.1	~	~	~	11.7	14.1
Pakistan	~	~	~	~	~	~	~	~	~	~	~	~	.1	.1
Philippines	~	~	~	~	~	~	~	~	~	~	.2	~	~	~
Singapore	~	.2	.2	.2	~	~	~	.4	1.1	1.9	3.3	.2	~	2.1
Sri Lanka	.4	.2	.2	.1	.1	~	~	~	.2	~	~	.2	.1	~
Taiwan Province of China	1.1	~	.2	1.9	.1	.7	~	.1	~	~	~	.1	~	.4
Europe	1.1	12.4	2.2	~	2.9	3.4	5.0	5.8	6.6	8.0	9.6	6.7	14.8	12.9
Greece	~	8.9	2.2	.6	2.9	3.4	.2	.3	.8	.9	1.3	1.9	1.0	1.2
Poland	~	7.0	1.3	.4	2.4	2.9	3.5	~	~	~	~	~	.1	.1
Portugal	1.1	1.8	.9	~	.4	.3	~	.3	.8	.9	1.3	1.9	.8	~
Turkey	~	~	~	~	~	~	~	~	~	~	~	~	.1	.7
Yugoslavia	~	~	~	~	~	~	1.2	~	~	~	~	~	.1	.4
Middle East	~	~	~	~	~	~	~	~	~	~	~	~	.3	.6
Israel	~	~	~	~	~	~	~	~	~	~	~	~	.3	.6
Western Hemisphere	184.9	189.6	178.6	116.4	103.2	118.0	134.0	444.8	421.5	464.4	431.4	322.4	351.7	395.3
A. ARGENTINA	~	.7	1.5	.6	~	.1	.1	6.0	1.5	2.9	2.3	3.0	3.7	4.4
Barbados	.6	.6	.7	.4	.3	.6	.7	~	~	.1	.1	~	.1	~
Belize	~	~	~	~	~	~	~	.1	~	~	~	~	~	~
C. BRAZIL	.1	~	~	~	~	~	~	2.4	3.2	3.9	5.9	6.7	7.5	13.4
D. CHILE	~	~	.1	~	~	~	~	.1	.5	.3	.2	2.4	~	~
E. COLOMBIA	~	~	~	3.4	~	~	.2	1.6	4.5	4.5	8.1	9.6	4.0	4.3
F. COSTA RICA	21.5	22.1	27.0	24.7	26.9	33.6	32.7	35.9	42.6	46.7	54.1	38.9	40.0	35.0

Table 2623 (Continued)

EL SALVADOR ABSOLUTE VALUE OF GOODS TRADED WITH SELECTED REGIONS AND COUNTRIES,[1] 1982-88
(M US)[2]

Category	Exports								Imports						
	1982	1983	1984	1985	1986	1987	1988	1982	1983	1984	1985	1986	1987	1988
Developing Countries (Continued)														
Western Hemisphere (Continued)														
H. DOMINICAN REP.	1.3	1.8	1.5	1.3	2.2	2.6	3.2	~	.1	.1	~	.1	.1	.1
I. ECUADOR	~	~	~	~	~	.1	~	.3	.1	~	.1	.2	.5	5.6
K. GUATEMALA	131.6	123.1	117.3	61.4	49.3	59.1	71.0	209.9	172.3	187.5	149.6	112.0	134.4	161.2
L. HAITI	.1	.1	.1	~	~	~	~	.3	~	~	.3	.4	.4	.5
M. HONDURAS	3.8	7.9	7.9	6.4	7.8	9.4	11.2	8.2	15.2	16.7	10.6	9.5	11.4	13.7
Jamaica	~	~	~	~	~	~	~	~	~	~	~	~	1.0	1.2
N. MEXICO	.1	~	~	~	.2	.2	.2	70.6	82.3	97.4	89.5	63.1	72.6	76.2
Netherlands Antilles	.2	1.9	12.1	.1	.1	.1	.1	1.0	1.0	1.6	1.7	~	~	~
O. NICARAGUA	17.3	15.0	5.1	3.2	5.4	6.5	7.7	6.8	3.5	3.2	2.4	1.4	1.7	2.0
P. PANAMA	8.2	15.9	5.3	14.8	11.0	5.3	6.0	23.9	23.7	31.4	30.6	14.1	2.8	2.8
R. PERU	~	~	~	~	~	.1	~	1.4	1.2	2.1	2.9	1.8	3.6	3.4
Suriname	~	.6	~	~	~	.1	.4	~	~	~	~	~	~	~
Trinidad and Tobago	~	~	~	~	~	.1	~	.2	.2	.1	~	~	~	~
S. URUGUAY	~	~	.1	~	~	~	~	~	~	~	~	~	~	~
T. VENEZUELA	~	~	~	~	~	~	~	76.1	69.6	66.0	72.7	59.0	67.9	71.3
U.S.S.R. and Other Nonmembers	~	.7	~	~	~	~	~	.5	.2	.7	.3	.2	.3	.3
Czechoslovakia	~	.7	~	~	~	~	~	.5	.2	.6	.3	.2	.3	.3
Country or area not specified	5.0	15.2	28.3	8.2	9.6	11.5	13.8	5.3	3.9	10.8	13.3	52.9	63.4	76.1
Memorandum Items														
EEC	223.9	172.4	185.2	174.2	206.8	138.8	187.0	109.6	105.5	99.8	101.0	103.1	108.3	125.4
Oil Exporting Countries	~	~	.1	~	~	~	~	76.1	69.6	66.0	72.7	59.0	67.9	71.3
Non-Oil Developing Countries	188.5	218.5	182.6	118.6	106.5	122.3	139.9	376.7	365.0	411.4	375.8	276.1	319.4	361.0
% Distribution														
Industrial Countries	72.3	68.4	70.6	81.3	84.2	78.5	77.7	46.5	50.8	50.0	51.9	57.4	58.7	59.5
Developing Countries	27.0	29.5	25.5	17.5	14.5	19.7	20.3	52.8	48.8	48.8	46.7	36.7	35.5	34.4
Africa	.4	~	.2	~	~	~	.1	~	~	~	~	~	~	~
Asia	.2	2.7	.1	.3	.1	.1	.7	.9	1.3	1.2	1.6	1.2	3.1	2.8
Europe	~	1.2	.3	~	.4	.5	~	~	.1	.1	.1	.2	.1	.1
Western Hemisphere	26.4	25.6	24.9	17.1	14.0	19.0	19.4	51.9	47.3	47.5	44.9	35.4	32.2	31.4
U.S.S.R. and Other Nonmembers	~	.1	~	~	~	~	~	.1	~	.1	~	~	~	~
Annual PC														
World	-12.2	6.0	-3.2	-5.4	8.2	-15.4	10.9	-12.7	4.1	9.6	-1.6	-5.2	19.6	15.3
Industrial Countries	34.3	.2	-.1	9.0	12.0	-21.2	9.7	-13.5	13.7	7.9	2.2	4.9	22.2	17.0
Developing Countries	-21.7	15.9	-16.4	-35.1	-10.2	14.8	4.4	2.0	-4.0	9.8	-6.0	-25.3	15.6	11.6
Africa	~	~	~	~	~	~	~	-43.2	72.9	.3	-33.7	-40.7	26.6	14.2
Asia	-80.1	682.4	-97.5	337.6	-78.5	92.6	8.9	-23.8	61.1	-2.4	34.0	-31.6	219.6	2.5
Europe	-79.6	695.0	-74.9	~	~	19.0	46.3	-68.9	147.8	14.5	40.4	49.1	-49.5	27.0
Middle East	~	~	~	~	~	~	~	~	~	~	~	~	~	66.7
Western Hemisphere	-16.9	2.5	-5.8	-34.8	-11.4	14.4	3.6	2.9	-5.2	10.2	-7.1	-25.3	9.1	12.4
U.S.S.R. and Other Nonmembers	~	~	~	~	~	~	~	19.3	-48.7	183.2	-50.8	-33.2	19.8	19.9

1. DOT data may differ between countries and from IFS data because of the time it takes for an export to become an import, etc.
2. Data may be calculated from partner's reported data or estimated on basis of less than 12 months.

SOURCE: IMF-DOT-Y, 1989.

Table 2624

GUATEMALA ABSOLUTE VALUE OF GOODS TRADED WITH SELECTED REGIONS AND COUNTRIES,[1] 1982–88
(M US)[2]

Category	Exports							Imports						
	1982	1983	1984	1985	1986	1987	1988	1982	1983	1984	1985	1986	1987	1988
IFS World Total	1,153.2	1,189.5	1,136.5	1,054.2	1,103.4	1,084.1	~	1,388.0	1,126.1	1,278.6	1,174.9	959.5	1,479.4	1,557.0
DOTS World Total	1,119.8	1,158.9	1,094.6	991.4	572.0	1,053.5	1,080.3	1,388.0	1,135.0	1,448.3	1,296.7	1,156.5	1,314.1	1,511.6
Industrial Countries	588.5	668.5	662.7	573.6	402.0	788.2	761.1	799.1	594.9	691.9	676.3	814.2	904.5	1,041.8
United States	306.0	405.1	419.2	359.3	261.5	492.6	433.9	432.3	365.3	402.4	404.0	477.0	528.3	649.9
Canada	4.8	5.2	11.3	9.0	4.3	24.9	30.6	18.8	18.5	17.2	10.2	12.6	16.8	16.6
Australia	.1	~	~	.2	.2	.4	1.3	.2	1.2	.1	.1	.2	.1	.2
Japan	55.5	39.4	49.0	36.4	24.3	25.0	31.1	72.7	55.7	67.7	56.2	70.2	86.8	79.8
New Zealand	.1	.1	~	.1	~	.3	.1	.8	.3	1.3	1.4	1.6	2.2	2.3
Austria	.6	1.6	1.1	1.0	.4	9.2	6.1	2.6	2.1	4.0	4.4	3.8	5.6	2.1
Belgium-Luxembourg	10.1	10.2	12.1	6.6	4.9	6.3	5.2	8.8	5.7	5.8	6.6	7.0	9.1	7.8
Denmark	.9	.6	.4	.4	.1	1.8	3.8	3.3	3.2	3.3	1.8	2.4	6.6	4.2
Finland	15.2	14.5	15.2	12.3	7.2	20.1	16.1	2.6	.2	.4	2.3	.6	2.8	1.2
France	8.4	37.9	~	5.7	3.5	14.9	17.8	19.2	16.8	17.6	24.9	17.8	27.3	36.2
Germany	78.2	62.4	64.5	64.9	46.1	64.4	80.0	77.1	56.6	73.0	81.3	108.6	77.0	83.4
Iceland	~	~	.1	.4	~	.3	.3	~	~	~	~	.1	~	~
Ireland	.1	~	~	~	~	.8	.7	6.5	4.6	8.6	4.1	8.2	2.7	2.8
Italy	41.1	34.6	36.1	44.5	17.0	46.3	53.7	18.0	11.6	10.4	9.0	15.1	50.5	60.2
Netherlands	38.5	31.3	30.8	20.1	16.1	23.2	28.3	13.9	5.7	19.5	13.8	18.0	15.1	24.7
Norway	3.3	1.1	1.9	1.9	1.6	2.9	1.2	3.8	2.0	2.8	.4	4.4	4.5	2.2
Spain	4.3	4.0	6.1	1.6	1.0	4.9	4.7	75.9	13.1	16.5	16.1	25.2	21.0	17.0
Sweden	1.5	4.4	1.4	4.0	7.4	10.2	10.9	5.0	3.1	4.0	3.9	7.2	6.6	6.6
Switzerland	1.4	3.0	2.0	1.5	2.4	28.6	17.9	20.6	16.5	18.2	15.9	14.1	16.0	14.4
United Kingdom	18.6	12.9	11.5	3.5	4.1	11.2	17.3	17.0	12.7	18.9	19.9	20.4	25.5	30.2
Developing Countries	510.9	467.5	431.8	402.4	167.0	261.7	314.9	574.9	535.9	754.4	618.6	336.1	402.3	461.0
Africa	3.3	4.1	.5	2.9	1.0	.8	1.0	.9	.2	.4	1.2	1.6	1.9	2.8
Gabon	~	~	~	~	~	~	~	~	~	~	~	.1	.1	.1
Kenya	~	~	~	~	.7	.8	1.0	~	~	~	~	~	~	~
Lesotho	~	~	~	~	~	~	~	~	~	~	~	~	~	.1
Mauritius	~	~	~	~	~	~	~	~	~	~	~	~	~	.1
Morocco	.5	2.1	~	.3	.3	~	~	~	~	~	~	~	~	~
South Africa	1.4	.4	.4	.7	~	~	~	.9	.1	.4	1.1	1.5	1.8	2.1
Sudan	~	~	.1	~	~	~	~	~	~	~	~	~	~	~
Tunisia	~	~	~	~	~	~	~	~	~	~	~	~	~	~
Zimbabwe	~	~	~	1.9	.5	~	~	~	~	~	~	~	~	~
Africa not specified	1.4	1.6	~	~	.1	~	~	~	~	~	~	~	~	.4
Asia	34.9	12.2	21.0	12.0	6.6	11.1	34.1	21.9	20.7	33.9	28.7	49.0	73.9	91.3
Bangladesh	15.1	.6	2.4	~	2.7	.2	.5	~	~	.3	.7	.2	~	~
China, People's Rep.	.4	.2	.2	.4	.1	.2	12.2	.7	1.6	1.8	2.1	1.0	3.8	5.2
Hong Kong	.2	.3	.7	~	.1	.1	1.1	3.3	2.5	2.8	2.7	3.6	12.5	19.7
India	.8	.2	.2	~	~	.1	.1	.1	.1	.2	.4	.6	.7	.8
Indonesia	1.2	.6	3.6	1.7	.5	3.2	2.1	~	~	.1	~	~	~	~
Korea	~	~	~	1.0	~	1.0	3.0	3.3	3.6	9.4	5.7	14.0	29.1	32.1
Malaysia	~	.2	.2	~	.5	~	~	~	~	.1	~	.2	~	~
Pakistan	.1	.2	~	1.0	~	.9	2.1	~	.1	~	~	.1	.3	.1
Philippines	.6	.1	.3	.1	~	~	~	~	~	~	.1	.2	~	.1
Singapore	~	~	.1	~	~	~	~	.9	.7	.6	.6	.4	~	.1
Sri Lanka	.3	~	.1	1.9	~	3.4	3.4	.2	.4	.6	.2	.2	.4	.7
Thailand	~	~	.4	~	.1	~	.8	~	~	.4	.2	~	.1	.3
Asia not specified	9.8	9.4	~	~	~	~	~	2.2	1.3	~	~	~	~	~
Taiwan Province of China	6.4	.3	12.9	6.8	2.5	2.3	8.8	11.1	10.3	17.6	15.9	28.5	26.8	32.3
Europe	3.9	2.9	4.4	50.2	5.5	7.3	7.5	3.0	.8	4.9	7.3	10.6	11.3	13.9
Cyprus	~	.9	.3	1.7	.8	.1	1.5	~	~	~	~	~	~	~
Greece	~	~	~	~	~	.2	.3	~	~	.2	.2	.1	~	~
Hungary	~	1.6	1.6	21.1	~	~	~	~	~	~	.2	.5	~	~

Table 2624 (Continued)

GUATEMALA ABSOLUTE VALUE OF GOODS TRADED WITH SELECTED REGIONS AND COUNTRIES,[1] 1982-88

(M US)[2]

Category	Exports							Imports						
	1982	1983	1984	1985	1986	1987	1988	1982	1983	1984	1985	1986	1987	1988
Developing Countries (Continued)														
Europe (Continued)														
Malta	?	?	?	.8	.1	.3	.1	?	?	?	?	?	.2	.3
Poland	?	?	?	19.8	.6	.7	.9	?	?	.2	.1	1.0	1.0	1.1
Portugal	2.8	1.8	2.3	4.4	1.2	2.8	2.0	2.8	.7	1.1	.8	8.0	9.6	11.5
Romania	?	?	?	1.9	2.7	2.3	1.6	?	?	3.3	6.0	?	.1	.2
Turkey	.6	.1	.2	.1	?	.9	1.1	?	?	.1	?	.7	.3	.8
Yugoslavia	?	?	?	.4	?	?	?	.1	.1	.1	?	.1	.1	.1
Europe not specified	.5	.1	?	?	?	?	?	?	?	?	?	?	?	?
Middle East	46.3	34.8	69.7	82.7	26.6	50.6	53.2	.6	.5	.8	2.3	5.4	1.4	3.4
Bahrain	1.2	.1	2.5	1.4	?	?	?	?	?	?	?	?	?	?
Egypt	.1	.1	?	.4	.1	.1	.1	?	?	?	?	?	?	?
Israel	.6	?	2.0	19.5	.6	?	.3	.6	.4	.8	2.2	4.8	1.4	3.4
Jordan	?	?	22.2	24.1	7.5	2.8	.4	?	?	?	?	?	?	?
Kuwait	?	?	20.1	6.6	2.6	2.9	3.2	?	?	?	?	?	?	?
Lebanon	?	?	1.7	1.0	.3	.4	.5	?	?	?	?	?	?	?
Oman	?	?	3.4	4.2	.1	?	?	?	?	?	?	?	?	?
Qatar	?	?	.6	.2	.1	.3	.3	?	?	?	?	.6	?	?
Saudi Arabia	15.9	14.7	17.0	24.4	14.2	44.1	48.5	?	?	?	.1	?	?	?
Syrian Arab Rep.	?	?	.1	.9	.1	?	?	?	?	?	?	?	?	?
United Arab Emirates	?	?	?	?	1.0	?	?	?	?	?	?	?	?	?
Middle East not specified	29.1	19.9	?	?	?	?	?	?	?	?	?	?	?	?
Western Hemisphere	422.5	413.6	336.1	254.7	127.4	191.9	219.2	548.5	513.7	714.4	579.1	269.6	313.8	349.6
A. AFGENTINA	1.1	.5	?	?	.1	.1	.1	3.9	2.6	3.7	3.4	3.2	5.8	7.0
Antigua and Barbuda	?	?	?	?	.1	.1	.2	?	?	?	?	.1	.1	.2
Bahamas, The	?	?	.1	.1	.1	.2	.6	?	?	?	?	.1	.1	.2
Barbados	?	?	.1	.3	.1	.6	.6	?	?	?	.1	.4	.3	.3
Belize	1.4	1.3	.8	.5	.4	1.7	2.0	?	?	?	.1	?	.3	?
B. BOLIVIA	.1	?	?	?	?	?	?	12.6	6.6	14.8	18.1	19.9	33.4	44.7
C. BRAZIL	.2	6.8	?	?	?	.5	?	2.1	2.2	1.2	2.6	8.9	?	?
D. CHILE	.4	.2	.3	1.5	.7	1.9	2.1	2.0	4.6	4.4	5.2	5.9	7.8	6.6
E. COLOMBIA	4.8	52.4	52.5	43.2	28.8	58.7	59.1	58.0	82.0	62.8	37.2	41.9	48.0	45.8
F. COSTA RICA	51.6	5.6	4.1	4.4	3.3	4.0	4.8	.2	.2	.1	.3	1.1	1.3	1.6
H. DOMINICAN REP.	7.2	16.9	7.2	3.9	3.3	6.5	9.5	1.3	.2	.3	1.3	1.4	.4	1.1
I. ECUADOR	5.0	?	?	?	?	?	?	?	?	?	?	?	?	?
J. EL SALVADOR	190.3	163.4	173.7	120.8	54.6	65.5	78.7	117.5	103.8	94.7	49.4	59.4	71.3	85.5
Grenada	?	?	?	.2	?	?	?	?	?	?	?	?	?	?
Guadeloupe	?	?	?	.2	?	?	?	?	?	.2	?	.1	.1	.1
L. HAITI	.3	.2	.5	.3	.3	.1	.1	.1	?	?	?	.1	.1	?
M. HONDURAS	50.6	54.3	31.8	27.6	11.8	14.2	17.0	28.3	26.9	14.2	5.1	6.1	7.4	8.8
Jamaica	.5	2.8	1.0	5.0	1.5	3.1	3.7	.9	3.2	2.9	1.2	1.6	1.6	1.9
Martinique	?	?	.1	.1	?	?	?	?	?	?	?	?	?	?
N. MEXICO	35.1	14.8	10.8	11.2	3.3	3.6	4.0	102.2	89.0	185.3	195.8	66.3	76.3	80.1
Netherlands Antilles	.4	13.4	.1	.8	.3	.4	.4	98.2	68.6	94.7	57.6	6.0	7.2	8.7
O. NICARAGUA	44.9	50.8	27.2	13.5	7.1	8.5	10.3	14.3	12.4	14.9	7.7	11.4	13.7	16.4
P. PANAMA	21.9	16.2	18.7	18.3	9.8	15.1	17.1	4.4	5.5	4.2	9.8	6.5	5.1	4.1
R. PERU	.1	13.7	5.6	?	?	1.8	.2	.5	1.3	.8	.1	.9	.8	.6
St. Lucia	?	?	?	.8	?	.1	.1	?	?	?	?	?	?	?
St. Perre-Miquelon	?	?	?	?	?	.3	.1	?	?	?	?	.3	.3	.4
Suriname	?	?	.1	.3	.1	.3	.4	?	?	?	?	.3	.3	.4
Trinidad and Tobago	.2	.1	.8	1.4	1.5	2.8	6.3	18.3	2.4	6.8	2.8	.7	1.4	2.5
S. URUGUAY	?	.1	.5	.3	.1	.2	?	.1	.1	?	?	.2	?	?
T. VENEZUELA	6.3	?	?	?	.1	2.0	2.2	82.4	102.2	208.3	181.5	27.4	31.5	33.1
Western Hem. not specified	?	?	?	?	.2	.2	.2	?	?	?	?	?	?	?

Table 2624 (Continued)

GUATEMALA ABSOLUTE VALUE OF GOODS TRADED WITH SELECTED REGIONS AND COUNTRIES,[1] 1982-88
(M US)[2]

Category	Exports							Imports						
	1982	1983	1984	1985	1986	1987	1988	1982	1983	1984	1985	1986	1987	1988
U.S.S.R. and Other Nonmembers														
Bulgaria	19.1	19.9	.2	15.4	3.0	3.6	4.3	8.4	3.5	2.1	1.9	6.0	7.2	8.7
Czechoslovakia	8.4	~	~	1.0	.6	.7	.8	1.3	.7	.6	.6	4.2	5.0	6.0
Eastern Germany	~	1.0	~	5.9	~	~	~	~	~	1.1	1.0	.4	.5	.6
North Korea	~	~	~	7.6	~	~	~	~	~	~	~	1.2	1.5	1.8
U.S.S.R.	~	~	.2	~	.5	.6	.7	~	~	.3	.3	.1	.1	.2
U.S.S.R., etc. not specified	10.7	18.9	~	.9	1.9	2.3	2.8	7.0	2.8	~	~	~	~	~
Country or area not specified	1.3	3.0	~	~	~	~	~	5.6	.6	~	~	~	~	~
Special categories	~	~	~	~	~	~	~	~	~	~	~	.1	.1	.1
Memorandum Items														
EEC	203.0	196.7	163.8	151.8	93.9	176.9	213.8	242.7	130.7	174.7	178.4	223.6	235.7	267.6
Oil Exporting Countries	23.0	15.0	41.9	35.6	18.2	52.5	56.4	82.5	102.2	208.4	181.6	28.0	31.5	33.1
Non-Oil Developing Countries	487.8	452.5	389.9	366.8	148.8	209.3	258.6	492.4	433.7	546.0	437.0	308.1	370.8	427.9
% Distribution														
Industrial Countries	52.6	57.7	60.5	57.9	70.3	74.8	70.5	57.6	52.4	47.8	52.2	70.4	68.8	68.9
Developing Countries	45.6	40.3	39.4	40.6	29.2	24.8	29.2	41.4	47.2	52.1	47.7	29.1	30.6	30.5
Africa	.3	.4	~	.3	.2	.1	.1	.1	~	~	.1	.1	.1	.2
Asia	3.1	1.1	1.9	1.2	1.2	1.1	3.2	1.6	1.8	2.3	2.2	4.2	5.6	6.0
Europe	.4	.2	.4	5.1	1.0	.7	.7	.2	.1	.3	.6	.9	.9	.9
Middle East	4.1	3.0	6.4	8.3	4.6	4.8	4.9	~	~	.1	.2	.5	.1	.2
Western Hemisphere	37.7	35.7	30.7	25.7	22.3	18.2	20.3	39.5	45.3	49.3	44.7	23.3	23.9	23.1
U.S.S.R. and Other Nonmembers	1.7	1.7	~	1.6	.5	.3	.4	.6	.3	.1	.1	.5	.5	.6
Annual PC														
World	-8.7	3.5	-5.5	-9.4	-42.3	84.2	2.5	-17.1	-18.2	27.6	-10.5	-10.8	13.6	15.0
Industrial Countries	3.8	13.6	-.9	-13.4	-29.9	96.0	-3.4	-21.2	-25.6	16.3	-2.3	20.4	11.1	15.2
Developing Countries	-21.6	-8.5	-7.6	-6.8	-58.5	56.7	20.3	-9.5	-6.8	40.8	-18.0	-45.7	19.7	14.6
Africa	-38.6	25.5	-87.2	452.6	-65.4	-19.7	20.0	179.2	-78.8	104.9	212.6	38.3	18.2	45.0
Asia	-60.2	-65.1	72.6	-42.9	-45.1	68.5	206.6	-27.9	-5.5	63.7	-15.3	70.6	50.9	23.6
Europe	-76.6	-26.8	54.0	~	-89.1	33.7	2.3	-29.6	-72.7	498.9	47.0	45.5	6.8	22.9
Middle East	39.9	-24.9	100.4	18.6	-67.8	90.5	5.1	1.2	-12.1	58.6	177.7	135.2	-73.5	138.0
Western Hemisphere	-17.0	-2.1	-18.7	-24.2	-50.0	50.6	14.2	-8.5	-6.3	39.1	-18.9	-53.5	16.4	11.4
U.S.S.R. and Other Nonmembers	278.6	4.1	-99.1	~	-80.7	20.0	20.0	100.7	-58.0	-41.4	-9.5	223.3	20.0	20.0

1. DOT data may differ between countries and from IFS data because of the time it takes for an export to become an import, etc.
2. Data may be calculated from partner's reported data or estimated on basis of less than 12 months.

SOURCE: IMF-DOT-Y, 1989.

Table 2625

HAITI ABSOLUTE VALUE OF GOODS TRADED WITH SELECTED REGIONS AND COUNTRIES,[1] 1982–88
(M US)[2]

Category	Exports 1982	1983	1984	1985	1986	1987	1988	Imports 1982	1983	1984	1985	1986	1987	1988
IFS World Total	162.68	153.80	178.62	174.24	186.10	220.14	200.20	387.28	440.52	449.54	441.56	354.76	374.36	344.26
DOTS World Total	376.10	420.01	448.80	449.28	457.38	436.28	428.38	545.79	632.60	685.38	699.92	651.01	796.35	849.10
Industrial Countries	367.95	403.95	433.69	440.28	448.32	430.21	420.59	445.27	521.62	577.17	588.74	555.01	674.63	701.57
United States	296.00	319.73	358.64	369.00	355.09	372.82	363.09	328.46	402.49	461.23	435.49	426.03	504.79	526.57
Canada	6.97	8.72	12.95	7.01	8.83	6.52	5.54	20.96	13.61	16.15	20.83	16.57	20.80	16.89
Australia	.49	.42	.59	.46	.31	.20	.22	.01	.01	.71	.27	.06	.01	~
Japan	2.77	1.89	1.54	2.41	2.36	3.30	2.64	28.04	27.49	32.73	41.26	30.14	42.12	47.36
New Zealand	.01	.02	.02	~	.01	~	?	.88	.87	.41	1.22	.39	1.19	.29
Austria	.14	.14	.56	.32	?	.07	.24	.96	.64	1.46	1.00	?	.39	.34
Belgium-Luxembourg	8.99	8.56	8.50	10.00	10.44	5.89	8.41	3.88	3.64	3.27	3.30	3.53	7.35	5.02
Denmark	.81	1.48	.77	.67	1.82	.37	.32	.77	.87	1.21	.86	1.58	1.46	1.20
Finland	.97	1.13	.80	.70	.25	.06	.14	.25	.25	.27	.27	.33	3.40	.11
France	18.15	20.47	14.84	14.96	24.24	13.02	12.64	15.34	25.79	18.60	27.06	26.97	28.81	24.94
Germany	12.02	16.41	15.38	12.10	13.45	6.35	6.68	12.52	15.09	12.77	13.14	14.19	23.81	32.16
Ireland	.58	.02	.09	.07	.03	?	.03	.25	.67	.42	.48	.27	.67	.25
Italy	11.33	17.63	12.62	16.47	20.83	15.79	14.32	7.53	8.26	6.58	15.20	5.09	5.30	7.35
Netherlands	1.49	3.61	1.91	2.86	3.91	2.42	1.78	10.00	8.39	9.99	12.88	12.79	14.92	16.03
Norway	.04	.08	.09	.06	.17	.14	~	2.38	1.50	1.54	2.14	2.04	2.17	2.04
Spain	.99	.73	1.24	.48	3.49	.25	.44	1.08	1.02	1.28	2.21	3.04	3.48	3.76
Sweden	.11	.13	.05	.08	.26	.38	.45	1.63	1.42	.52	.79	.66	1.02	.54
Switzerland	1.96	.49	1.43	.85	1.63	1.68	2.28	3.14	2.66	2.37	3.06	3.03	3.36	3.51
United Kingdom	4.14	2.28	1.67	1.80	1.21	.91	1.37	7.22	6.97	5.65	7.29	8.31	9.58	13.23
Developing Countries	7.86	15.77	14.79	8.66	8.70	5.65	7.28	95.71	110.17	107.32	110.24	95.01	20.54	46.11
Africa	?	.03	.06	.02	.01	.01	.01	.22	.96	.05	?	.62	?	.01
Cameroon	?	.01	.01	.01	?	?	?	?	?	?	?	?	?	?
Congo	?	?	.03	?	?	?	.01	?	?	?	?	?	?	?
Gabon	?	.17	.01	.05	.07	.05	.08	.01	?	?	?	?	?	?
Mauritius	?	?	?	?	?	?	?	?	?	.05	?	?	?	.01
Senegal	?	.02	?	?	.01	?	?	?	.95	?	?	?	?	?
South Africa	?	?	?	?	?	?	.01	?	.01	?	?	?	?	?
Tunisia	?	?	?	?	?	.01	.01	.21	?	?	?	?	?	?
Zimbabwe	?	?	?	?	?	?	?	?	?	?	?	.62	?	?
Asia	.43	.24	.34	.13	.40	.22	.23	15.30	17.93	21.13	29.00	33.73	44.28	47.81
Bangladesh	?	?	?	?	?	?	?	.05	.14	.26	.33	.15	.05	.10
China, People's Rep.	.09	.17	.06	.05	.07	.05	.01	3.90	4.24	3.77	4.46	4.90	7.97	10.80
Hong Kong	?	?	?	?	?	?	.08	.09	.09	.10	.10	.11	.13	.15
India	?	.01	?	?	.01	?	?	4.24	4.93	5.41	9.06	7.86	12.30	14.93
Korea	?	?	?	?	?	?	?	.03	.01	.01	?	.05	.01	.04
Macao	?	?	?	?	.01	.01	.01	?	?	?	?	?	?	?
Pakistan	?	?	?	?	?	?	?	?	?	?	?	?	?	?
Papua New Guinea	.03	?	?	?	.01	.01	.01	?	.01	?	?	?	.01	.14
Philippines	?	?	?	?	?	?	?	?	?	?	?	?	?	?
Sri Lanka	?	?	?	?	?	?	?	?	1.56	.15	.03	.02	.06	.34
Thailand	?	.06	.07	.07	.07	.09	.10	?	?	?	?	.23	?	?
Asia not specified	.06	.06	.07	.07	.07	.09	.10	?	?	?	?	?	?	?
Taiwan Province of China	.25	?	.22	.01	.24	.07	.02	7.50	6.96	11.43	15.02	20.42	23.46	21.11
Europe	1.83	.04	.06	.06	.03	.02	?	.31	.19	.16	.19	.13	.68	.90
Cyprus	.66	.01	.04	.05	.02	?	?	.05	?	.01	.01	.06	.01	.06
Greece	?	?	?	?	?	?	?	.02	?	.01	.10	.06	.01	.01
Malta	1.15	.03	?	?	.01	?	?	?	?	?	?	?	?	?
Portugal	?	?	.01	.01	.01	.02	.10	.12	.19	.15	.08	.06	.66	.47
Turkey	.02	.03	?	?	?	.02	.02	?	?	?	?	?	?	?
Yugoslavia	?	?	?	?	?	?	?	.18	?	?	?	?	?	.36

Table 2625 (Continued)

HAITI ABSOLUTE VALUE OF GOODS TRADED WITH SELECTED REGIONS AND COUNTRIES,[1] 1982–88
(M US)[2]

Category	Exports							Imports						
	1982	1983	1984	1985	1986	1987	1988	1982	1983	1984	1985	1986	1987	1988
Developing Countries (Continued)														
Middle East	~	~	~	.08	~	~	~	.11	.33	.77	.22	.11	.22	.99
Israel	~	~	~	~	~	~	~	.11	.33	.77	.22	.11	.22	.99
Saudi Arabia	~	~	~	.08	~	~	~	~	~	~	~	~	~	~
Western Hemisphere	5.60	15.46	14.34	8.38	8.26	5.40	7.04	83.28	90.77	85.21	80.83	60.43	75.36	96.41
A. ARGENTINA	.02	.01	.02	.01	~	~	.03	.31	22.98	12.65	7.03	2.06	.45	.54
Antigua and Barbuda	~	.02	.02	.02	.02	.03	.03	~	~	~	~	~	~	~
Bahamas, The	.22	.22	.83	.52	.54	.65	.78	.21	.21	.49	.44	.47	.56	.67
Barbados	.14	.56	.10	.22	.05	.16	.82	.40	.42	.25	.32	.44	.49	1.02
Belize	~	~	~	~	~	~	~	~	~	~	~	.02	.06	.07
B. BOLIVIA	~	.01	~	~	~	~	~	~	~	~	~	~	~	~
C. BRAZIL	.01	.01	.02	.01	.02	.01	.06	4.68	4.26	6.18	7.44	4.13	5.59	15.29
E. COLOMBIA	.01	~	~	~	.01	.01	.12	.59	.83	.84	2.04	1.99	4.49	2.56
F. COSTA RICA	~	.83	.78	.58	.30	.12	.06	1.37	1.49	.44	.61	1.07	1.62	1.37
Dominica	~	~	.04	.04	.04	.05	~	~	~	~	~	~	~	~
H. DOMINICAN REP.	2.42	10.84	10.59	5.94	2.02	2.42	2.91	5.62	6.18	7.08	6.19	5.93	7.11	8.53
J. EL SALVADOR	.24	~	.35	.28	.34	.41	.49	.06	.07	.15	.05	.04	.05	.06
Guadeloupe	.45	.32	.18	.37	.38	.46	.55	~	~	~	~	~	~	~
K. GUATEMALA	.10	.07	.01	~	.05	.06	.07	.35	.17	.58	.34	.11	.13	.15
Guiana, French	.02	~	.02	~	~	~	~	.08	.12	.09	.08	.04	.05	.06
Guyana	.06	.05	.02	~	~	~	~	~	.01	.03	~	~	~	~
Jamaica	.19	.22	.31	.03	.12	.23	.27	.96	.94	.97	1.29	1.17	1.26	1.51
Martinique	.03	.10	.21	.22	.23	.27	.33	.10	1.01	.23	.24	.25	.30	.36
N. MEXICO	.09	.01	~	.03	.01	~	.01	.21	.58	.76	1.24	.48	.55	.58
Netherlands Antilles	~	~	.01	~	~	~	~	41.31	33.85	34.87	36.61	38.44	46.13	55.35
P. PANAMA	.01	.01	~	.03	.01	~	~	.03	.02	.13	.04	.01	.03	.78
R. PERU	~	~	~	~	~	~	~	.37	.12	.15	.19	.10	.16	.44
Suriname	.01	~	~	~	~	~	~	~	.09	.03	~	~	~	~
Trinidad and Tobago	.52	.15	.80	.05	.04	.07	.04	26.63	17.43	16.01	2.39	3.70	5.91	6.47
S. URUGUAY	~	~	~	~	~	~	~	~	~	~	~	~	~	~
T. VENEZUELA	1.00	2.00	~	~	4.00	.33	.36	~	~	3.30	14.30	~	~	.08
Western Hem. not specified	.08	.08	.08	.09	.09	.11	.13	~	~	~	~	~	~	~
U.S.S.R. and Other Nonmembers	.15	.15	.17	.18	.19	.22	.27	.81	.81	.89	.94	.98	1.18	1.42
Czechoslovakia	.15	.15	.17	.18	.19	.22	.27	.81	.81	.89	.94	.98	1.18	1.42
Country or area not specified	.14	.14	.16	.17	.17	.21	.25	~	~	~	~	~	~	~
Memorandum Items														
EEC	59.16	71.23	57.06	59.46	79.44	45.05	45.98	58.71	70.88	59.93	82.60	75.89	96.05	104.42
Oil Exporting Countries	1.00	2.00	~	.08	4.00	.33	.36	~	~	3.30	14.30	~	~	~
Non-Oil Developing Countries	6.86	13.77	14.79	8.58	4.70	5.32	6.92	99.71	110.17	104.02	95.94	95.01	120.54	146.11
% Distribution														
Industrial Countries	97.8	96.2	96.6	98.0	98.0	98.6	98.2	81.6	82.5	84.2	84.1	85.3	84.7	82.6
Developing Countries	2.1	3.8	3.3	1.9	1.9	1.3	1.7	18.3	17.4	15.7	15.8	14.6	15.1	17.2
Africa	.1	.1	.1	~	.1	.1	.1	~	.2	~	.1	.1	.1	.1
Asia	.5	~	~	~	~	~	~	2.9	2.8	3.1	4.1	5.2	5.6	5.6
Europe	~	~	~	~	~	~	~	.1	.1	.1	~	~	~	.1
Middle East	~	~	~	~	~	~	~	~	.1	.1	~	~	.1	.1
Western Hemisphere	1.5	3.7	3.2	1.9	1.8	1.2	1.6	15.3	14.3	12.4	11.5	9.3	9.5	11.4
U.S.S.R. and Other Nonmembers	~	~	~	~	~	.1	.1	.1	.1	.1	.1	.2	.1	.2

Table 2625 (Continued)

HAITI ABSOLUTE VALUE OF GOODS TRADED WITH SELECTED REGIONS AND COUNTRIES,[1] 1982–88
(M US)[2]

Category	Exports							Imports						
	1982	1983	1984	1985	1986	1987	1988	1982	1983	1984	1985	1986	1987	1988
Annual PC														
World	145.7	11.7	6.9	.1	1.8	–4.6	–1.8	45.3	15.9	8.3	2.1	–7.0	22.3	6.6
Industrial Countries	146.7	9.8	7.4	1.5	1.8	–4.0	–2.2	52.4	17.1	10.6	2.0	–5.7	21.6	4.0
Developing Countries	114.9	100.7	–6.2	–41.5	.5	–35.1	28.9	20.7	10.5	–2.6	2.7	–13.8	26.9	21.2
Africa	~	~	120.0	–60.0	–68.2	14.3	12.5	–66.7	342.1	–95.0	–97.9	~	–99.4	25.0
Asia	35.9	–44.2	41.8	–61.9	208.5	–45.0	2.7	52.4	13.5	17.8	37.3	16.3	31.3	8.0
Europe	~	–97.9	50.0	–3.5	–43.6	–25.8	~	–60.8	–38.8	–15.4	18.2	–32.4	433.9	32.2
Middle East	~	~	~	~	~	~	~	~	200.0	133.3	–71.4	–50.0	100.0	350.0
Western Hemisphere	116.4	176.4	–7.3	–41.6	–1.3	–34.7	30.5	17.7	9.0	–6.1	–5.1	–25.2	24.7	27.9
U.S.S.R. and Other Nonmembers	–4.9	~	9.7	4.7	5.1	19.9	20.2	–5.0	~	10.0	5.1	5.0	20.0	20.0

1. DOT data may differ between countries and from IFS data because of the time it takes for an export to become an import, etc.
2. Data may be calculated from partner's reported data or estimated on basis of less than 12 months.

SOURCE: IMF-DOT-Y, 1989.

Table 2626

HONDURAS ABSOLUTE VALUE OF GOODS TRADED WITH SELECTED REGIONS AND COUNTRIES,[1] 1982–88
(M US)[2]

Category	Exports							Imports						
	1982	1983	1984	1985	1986	1987	1988	1982	1983	1984	1985	1986	1987	1988
IFS World Total	659.50	671.80	725.35	780.05	854.20	768.55	~	700.50	802.60	893.40	888.10	875.05	897.07	~
DOTS World Total	667.76	660.06	766.38	787.38	905.74	974.48	948.94	692.11	819.99	937.48	826.54	818.40	848.41	926.04
Industrial Countries	560.89	535.51	662.91	700.90	802.35	870.18	827.30	416.87	475.38	566.39	534.70	607.18	675.47	742.10
United States	351.32	363.67	409.09	393.18	443.09	513.45	469.09	273.50	295.95	354.09	338.69	399.63	459.47	526.24
Canada	1.34	2.74	23.58	15.31	14.89	12.79	21.44	8.93	9.90	26.39	11.52	10.65	11.17	17.30
Australia	~	~	.46	.12	.13	~	.24	.03	.01	.03	.02	.02	.03	~
Japan	38.49	39.67	55.57	45.09	91.34	58.29	60.04	45.20	36.70	40.33	51.54	77.91	72.11	78.53
New Zealand	~	~	.05	.11	~	~	.93	~	~	.46	.37	.42	1.15	.75
Austria	~	~	6.28	8.47	12.23	12.01	4.43	1.13	1.89	1.98	3.38	1.85	1.48	.55
Belgium-Luxembourg	38.73	26.07	10.76	17.27	11.86	12.67	15.15	5.73	7.35	7.18	4.40	5.09	5.46	4.77
Denmark	.13	~	1.70	1.97	1.93	3.54	3.43	1.61	2.88	2.12	2.80	2.97	3.69	2.87
Finland	.66	.32	4.23	3.89	3.42	5.51	5.71	.27	.12	1.01	.31	.55	.32	2.52
France	5.64	3.33	9.04	9.59	15.81	12.15	11.29	6.61	22.60	14.63	19.19	22.27	21.98	13.03
Germany	58.51	35.11	44.71	69.17	56.24	88.10	86.58	22.63	27.92	31.71	25.75	24.59	23.32	24.38
Iceland	~	~	.13	1.29	.46	.55	.50	.01	~	~	.19	~	.01	~
Ireland	.02	~	.05	.23	1.48	1.53	3.63	.58	2.34	3.49	3.37	4.93	2.93	.53
Italy	14.67	14.45	20.54	55.88	66.71	59.42	43.84	13.51	14.60	16.67	13.54	8.18	7.42	12.43
Netherlands	17.34	14.76	11.87	15.35	15.88	16.28	15.47	9.33	17.69	13.35	17.98	11.11	17.88	13.30
Norway	2.58	2.84	3.67	2.68	2.89	4.87	3.12	.08	.25	.59	.37	.51	.44	.85
Spain	21.63	17.80	20.29	19.73	28.05	22.95	30.19	4.85	5.45	25.25	16.76	9.45	11.97	8.77
Sweden	3.48	4.73	11.00	10.18	6.83	18.23	18.83	4.11	2.31	2.27	2.36	2.73	2.02	1.23
Switzerland	.94	.95	15.09	18.46	21.97	20.89	19.83	4.76	12.24	13.97	9.10	9.42	13.70	18.53
United Kingdom	5.43	9.08	14.79	12.92	7.13	6.95	13.56	14.03	15.19	10.86	13.07	14.90	18.92	15.53
Developing Countries	106.39	115.71	93.75	76.27	92.67	91.43	106.20	272.82	335.76	361.35	281.62	200.49	160.06	168.48
Africa	.03	3.08	5.40	4.72	4.22	5.09	6.11	.53	.58	.96	2.46	.12	.12	.57
Cameroon	~	~	~	~	~	~	~	~	~	~	~	.02	~	~
Cape Verde	~	~	.13	.42	.44	.52	.63	~	~	~	~	~	~	~
Gabon	~	~	.01	~	~	~	~	~	~	~	~	~	~	~
Mauritius	~	~	.01	~	~	.04	~	~	~	~	.03	.02	.01	~
Morocco	~	~	~	~	~	~	~	.03	~	~	~	~	~	~
Somalia	.03	~	~	.14	.01	.01	.01	~	~	~	~	~	~	~
South Africa	~	~	.51	.22	.01	.01	.01	~	.58	.94	2.39	.08	.10	.12
Tunisia	~	~	1.36	.38	.03	.03	.08	.49	~	~	.04	~	~	.45
Zambia	~	~	~	~	~	~	~	~	~	.02	~	~	~	~
Africa not specified	~	3.08	3.39	3.55	3.73	4.48	5.37	~	~	~	~	~	~	~
Asia	5.53	.06	.71	.84	8.24	4.21	11.85	15.25	7.84	22.84	25.37	26.32	31.79	40.74
Bangladesh	1.65	~	~	~	~	~	~	~	~	~	~	.04	.30	.08
China, People's Rep.	.07	~	.13	.42	.14	.02	.17	2.83	1.64	2.50	2.28	2.68	3.24	3.31
Hong Kong	~	~	.01	.12	~	.09	.63	1.78	1.55	3.77	4.03	3.53	4.19	8.12
India	~	~	~	~	~	.04	~	.35	.17	.19	.20	.21	.25	.30
Indonesia	~	~	~	~	.07	.02	~	.03	~	~	~	~	.04	.03
Korea	.03	~	.03	.38	4.42	2.77	10.73	3.21	4.39	5.03	8.72	8.46	11.54	16.20
Macao	~	~	~	~	.01	.04	~	~	~	~	.03	~	~	~
Malaysia	~	~	~	~	~	~	~	1.19	.08	.04	.05	.21	.08	.06
Pakistan	1.19	~	.28	~	.03	~	~	.08	~	.05	.03	.09	.04	.13
Philippines	.08	~	~	.02	~	~	~	~	~	~	~	~	~	~
Singapore	.01	~	~	~	~	~	.02	.14	~	~	~	~	~	~
Sri Lanka	~	~	~	~	~	~	~	.10	~	.17	.16	.06	.04	.04
Thailand	~	~	.01	~	.34	.01	.04	~	~	.04	.02	.16	.08	.21
Asia not specified	~	.06	.07	.07	.07	.09	.10	~	.01	.01	.01	.01	.01	.01
Taiwan Province of China	3.79	~	.20	.25	3.15	1.18	.17	5.54	~	11.05	9.85	10.88	11.99	12.26

Table 2626 (Continued)

HONDURAS ABSOLUTE VALUE OF GOODS TRADED WITH SELECTED REGIONS AND COUNTRIES,[1] 1982–88
(M US)[2]

Category	Exports							Imports						
	1982	1983	1984	1985	1986	1987	1988	1982	1983	1984	1985	1986	1987	1988
Developing Countries (Continued)														
Europe														
Cyprus	.72	7.39	2.05	1.03	12.41	7.57	10.55	.54	1.47	.61	3.78	.86	4.82	1.72
Faeroe Islands	~	~	~	.06	.06	.07	.09	.03	~	~	~	~	~	~
Gibralter	~	~	~	.23	.17	.70	.84	.01	~	.20	.01	.13	.45	.54
Greece	.22	1.95	.06	~	.16	.28	4.58	.18	.15	~	~	~	~	.33
Hungary	~	~	~	~	~	~	~	.02	~	~	~	~	~	~
Malta	~	~	~	~	~	~	.89	~	~	~	~	~	~	~
Poland	.34	4.31	~	~	~	~	~	.02	~	~	~	~	~	~
Portuga	.15	.05	1.98	.59	1.16	2.84	2.40	.22	.94	.41	3.74	.67	.60	.74
Romania	~	~	.01	.11	.03	.20	.04	.02	.36	~	.02	.06	.10	.02
Turkey	~	1.09	~	.05	10.84	3.47	1.71	.04	~	~	~	~	~	.08
Yugoslavia	~	~	~	~	~	~	~	.02	.02	~	~	~	3.66	~
Europe not specified	.05	1.54	~	~	~	~	~	.01	~	~	~	~	~	~
Middle East	1.43	17.63	5.24	3.42	5.24	5.14	6.15	.26	.59	.33	.66	2.31	5.61	1.54
Egypt	.65	1.24	.64	~	~	~	~	~	~	~	~	~	~	~
Israel	.24	5.05	.36	.27	~	~	~	.26	.59	.33	.66	2.31	5.61	1.54
Jordan	.02	~	~	~	~	.12	.45	~	~	~	~	~	~	~
Kuwait	~	~	~	~	~	~	~	~	~	~	~	~	~	~
Lebanon	.31	1.20	1.32	1.39	1.46	1.75	2.10	~	~	~	~	~	~	~
Oman	~	~	1.16	.12	~	.04	.04	~	~	~	~	~	~	~
Qatar	~	~	~	~	~	~	~	~	~	~	~	~	~	~
Saudi Arabia	.16	8.08	1.75	1.64	3.78	3.24	3.56	~	~	~	~	~	~	~
Syrian Arab Rep.	~	.53	~	~	~	~	~	~	~	~	~	~	~	~
United Arab Emirates	.05	1.54	~	~	~	~	.04	~	~	~	~	~	~	~
Western Hemisphere	98.69	87.55	80.35	66.26	62.56	69.42	71.55	256.24	325.28	336.62	249.35	170.88	117.72	123.91
A. ARGENTINA	.04	.53	.58	.61	.18	.10	.12	1.04	1.25	1.55	7.60	3.75	2.91	3.49
Antigua and Barbuda	.71	~	~	~	.64	.77	.92	~	~	.22	.11	.12	.14	.17
Bahamas, The	.98	1.86	3.13	3.10	4.31	4.15	4.31	.03	~	.08	.45	.18	.13	.15
Barbados	2.37	.59	1.11	1.08	2.68	1.11	1.33	.06	~	.15	.14	.18	.13	.15
Belize	.04	.09	.02	.07	.09	.14	.01	~	~	~	~	~	~	~
C. BRAZIL	.01	~	~	~	~	~	~	8.44	10.12	32.94	12.88	29.24	17.49	23.85
D. CHILE	~	~	~	~	~	~	~	.05	.09	.15	.14	.18	.13	.01
E. COLOMBIA	1.33	1.22	.61	1.08	1.16	2.08	1.74	2.90	5.37	5.24	5.83	6.30	11.12	8.58
F. COSTA RICA	10.65	9.61	7.56	6.55	5.39	5.63	2.21	26.09	34.23	49.23	33.90	25.02	19.30	13.00
Dominica	.10	~	~	~	.01	.01	.01	.01	~	~	~	~	~	~
H. DOMINICAN REP.	2.27	.34	.46	.42	2.32	2.79	3.34	.48	.69	1.20	.77	1.18	1.41	1.69
I. ECUADOR	.13	~	~	~	2.29	.60	.02	.13	.81	.09	.63	.06	.22	.18
J. EL SALVADOR	10.47	13.84	15.17	9.63	8.65	10.37	12.45	3.84	8.25	8.65	7.06	8.59	10.31	12.37
Guadeloupe	2.68	2.45	2.70	2.83	2.97	3.57	4.28	~	~	~	~	~	~	~
K. GUATEMALA	26.38	28.23	12.88	4.68	5.58	6.69	8.03	48.04	58.72	35.02	30.38	13.02	15.62	18.74
Guyana	.10	~	~	.01	.01	.01	.01	~	~	~	~	~	~	~
Jamaica	1.45	.04	.18	.76	1.45	1.34	1.61	.45	.62	3.25	1.86	.07	.09	.11
Martinique	1.12	.73	1.18	1.24	1.30	1.56	1.87	~	~	~	~	~	~	~
N. MEXICO	4.77	.07	.16	5.77	3.13	3.45	3.79	15.18	35.05	51.01	31.09	24.44	28.11	29.52
Montserrat	.19	~	~	~	~	~	~	~	~	~	~	~	~	~
Netherlands Antilles	.33	~	~	~	~	~	~	6.81	8.46	1.81	1.90	2.00	2.40	2.88
O. NICARAGUA	8.26	9.66	10.63	11.16	11.72	14.06	16.87	8.88	3.55	3.91	4.10	4.31	5.17	6.20
P. PANAMA	1.79	1.49	1.17	1.94	2.13	2.69	2.85	18.38	37.80	2.19	2.28	2.41	2.37	2.24
R. PERU	.03	.27	.30	.31	.33	.39	.47	.12	.58	~	.79	.40	.17	.31
St. Lucia	.35	~	~	~	~	~	~	.01	~	~	~	~	~	~
St. Pierre-Miquelon	~	~	~	~	~	~	~	.01	~	~	~	~	~	~
St. Vincent	.35	.43	.48	.50	.53	.63	.76	~	~	~	~	~	~	~
Suriname	1.69	1.63	.49	~	~	~	~	~	~	~	~	~	~	~
Trinidad and Tobago	13.98	14.28	21.47	14.45	5.63	5.01	1.99	101.74	36.15	31.16	.87	.28	.75	.43
S. URUGUAY	.06	~	~	~	~	2.21	.03	.04	~	.02	.01	.02	.03	.01
T. VENEZUELA	6.02	.12	~	.08	.09	.10	2.43	13.43	83.56	108.90	106.70	49.50	~	~
Western Hem. not specified	.13	.07	.08	~	~	~	.12	.23	~	~	~	~	~	~

Table 2626 (Continued)

HONDURAS ABSOLUTE VALUE OF GOODS TRADED WITH SELECTED REGIONS AND COUNTRIES,[1] 1982–88 (M US)[2]

Category	Exports							Imports						
	1982	1983	1984	1985	1986	1987	1988	1982	1983	1984	1985	1986	1987	1988
U.S.S.R. and Other Nonmembers	.41	4.54	4.99	5.24	5.50	6.60	7.92	2.08	1.15	1.27	1.33	1.40	1.68	2.01
Albania	~	1.67	1.83	1.92	2.02	2.42	2.91	~	~	~	~	~	~	~
Czechoslovakia	.04	2.87	3.16	3.32	3.48	4.18	5.02	.88	.51	.56	.58	.61	.73	.88
Eastern Germany	.37	~	~	~	~	~	~	.27	.36	.39	.41	.43	.52	.62
North Korea	~	~	~	~	~	~	~	.09	~	~	~	~	~	~
U.S.S.R.	~	~	~	~	~	~	~	.84	.29	.32	.34	.35	.42	.51
Country or area not specified	.07	4.30	4.73	4.97	5.22	6.26	7.52	.34	7.70	8.47	8.89	9.34	11.21	13.45
Memorandum Items														
EEC	162.25	120.64	135.80	202.94	206.41	227.12	226.38	79.08	116.96	125.88	120.61	104.30	114.63	96.89
Oil Exporting Countries	6.25	9.73	2.91	1.76	3.86	5.50	6.04	13.46	83.56	108.90	106.70	49.50	.04	.03
Non-Oil Developing Countries	100.14	105.98	90.84	74.51	88.81	85.93	100.17	259.36	252.20	252.45	174.92	150.99	160.01	168.45
% Distribution														
Industrial Countries	84.0	81.1	86.5	89.0	88.6	89.3	87.2	60.2	58.0	60.4	64.7	74.2	79.6	80.1
Developing Countries	15.9	17.5	12.2	9.7	10.2	9.4	11.2	39.4	40.9	38.5	34.1	24.5	18.9	18.2
Africa	~	.5	.7	.6	.5	.5	.6	.1	.1	.1	.3	~	~	.1
Asia	.8	~	.1	.1	.9	.4	1.2	2.2	1.0	2.4	3.1	3.2	3.7	4.4
Europe	.1	1.1	.3	.1	1.4	.8	1.1	.1	.2	.1	.5	.1	.6	.2
Middle East	.2	2.7	.7	.4	.6	.5	.6	~	.1	~	.1	.3	.7	.2
Western Hemisphere	14.8	13.3	10.5	8.4	6.9	7.1	7.5	37.0	39.7	35.9	30.2	20.9	13.9	13.4
U.S.S.R. and Other Nonmembers	.1	.7	.7	.7	.6	.7	.8	.3	.1	.1	.2	.2	.2	.2
Annual PC														
World	-8.3	-1.2	16.1	2.7	15.0	7.6	-2.6	-26.8	18.5	14.3	-11.8	-1.0	3.7	9.2
Industrial Countries	-8.4	-4.5	23.8	5.7	14.5	8.5	-4.9	-32.0	14.0	19.1	-5.6	13.6	11.2	9.9
Developing Countries	-8.2	8.8	-19.0	-18.6	21.5	-1.3	16.2	-17.2	23.1	7.6	-22.1	-28.8	-20.2	5.3
Africa	-90.3	~	75.5	-12.6	-10.6	20.7	20.0	290.4	10.4	64.3	157.0	-95.0	-4.1	385.5
Asia	-30.0	-98.9	~	17.5	881.5	-48.9	181.8	-13.5	-48.6	191.2	11.1	3.7	20.8	28.2
Europe	-75.5	925.4	-72.3	-49.6	~	-39.0	39.4	-70.6	173.8	-58.6	519.0	-77.2	459.8	-64.4
Middle East	-49.5	~	-70.3	-34.8	53.3	-1.9	19.6	-35.3	122.0	-43.7	100.0	250.0	142.9	-72.5
Western Hemisphere	-3.2	-11.3	-8.2	-17.5	-5.6	11.0	3.1	-17.2	26.9	3.5	-25.9	-31.5	-31.1	5.3
U.S.S.R. and Other Nonmembers	~	~	10.0	5.0	5.0	20.0	20.0	-23.7	-44.7	10.0	5.1	5.0	20.0	20.0

1. DOT data may differ between countries and from IFS data because of the time it takes for an export to become an import, etc.
2. Data may be calculated from partner's reported data or estimated on basis of less than 12 months.

SOURCE: IMF-DOT-Y, 1989.

Table 2627

MEXICO ABSOLUTE VALUE OF GOODS TRADED WITH SELECTED REGIONS AND COUNTRIES,[1] 1982–88 (M US)[2]

Category	Exports 1982	1983	1984	1985	1986	1987	1988	Imports 1982	1983	1984	1985	1986	1987	1988
IFS World Total	21,214	21,819	24,407	22,108	16,237	20,887	20,768	14,504	7,619	11,257	13,443	11,459	12,159	18,711
DOTS World Total	21,209	22,313	24,382	22,105	16,588	26,972	29,373	13,687	8,200	10,327	13,441	12,319	19,950	27,546
Industrial Countries	17,682	19,080	20,950	19,484	14,675	24,404	26,530	12,058	6,897	8,871	12,099	11,456	18,904	26,064
United States	11,129	13,034	14,130	13,341	11,163	18,654	21,404	8,188	4,958	6,440	8,954	8,272	14,583	20,644
Canada	584	467	495	393	302	886	366	291	206	207	235	227	398	398
Australia	13	7	10	15	18	39	53	19	6	39	75	25	30	48
Japan	1,450	1,512	1,868	1,709	1,065	1,495	1,446	777	320	457	723	771	1,402	1,772
New Zealand	2	2	4	6	9	16	22	32	15	33	38	25	23	68
Austria	54	102	85	38	37	64	39	31	6	9	11	22	15	18
Belgium-Luxembourg	67	58	82	62	85	204	173	74	42	75	88	92	119	141
Denmark	2	8	5	6	9	12	13	40	15	11	16	15	17	40
Finland	11	6	2	6	2	13	12	22	16	10	19	13	20	20
France	931	832	928	816	382	612	544	318	327	230	275	240	353	540
Germany	240	270	231	293	389	368	392	831	331	440	536	723	827	963
Ireland	…	…	1	…	…	6	13	19	5	22	41	25	42	48
Italy	418	149	305	301	101	122	132	393	152	204	210	186	179	249
Netherlands	18	40	35	89	74	175	105	94	55	54	77	75	82	109
Norway	…	3	7	3	8	35	27	8	13	30	18	16	7	19
Spain	1,815	1,617	1,703	1,700	791	1,306	1,005	336	152	179	214	190	176	235
Sweden	14	10	8	3	8	14	16	161	50	96	137	165	141	189
Switzerland	22	48	33	25	56	24	35	173	74	144	148	157	164	223
United Kingdom	913	916	1,020	678	174	361	234	253	155	191	284	217	327	341
Developing Countries	3,220	2,744	2,593	2,136	1,586	2,192	2,349	961	395	619	903	662	825	1,238
Africa	16	57	51	81	29	78	108	40	20	42	78	55	135	78
Algeria	2	15	32	17	5	1	…	…	…	…	…	…	…	…
Cameroon	…	…	…	…	…	1	1	…	…	…	…	…	3	3
Congo	…	…	…	…	…	…	…	1	…	…	8	7	10	15
Côte d'Ivoire	…	…	…	…	1	1	…	1	…	…	…	…	…	…
Liberia	7	4	3	1	1	1	3	5	7	18	13	10	11	12
Mauritius	…	…	…	48	3	3	3	…	…	…	…	…	…	…
Morocco	3	15	4	5	5	46	58	25	9	18	21	24	95	30
Mozambique	…	…	…	…	…	…	…	1	…	…	…	…	…	…
Nigeria	1	10	4	7	…	2	3	…	…	…	…	…	…	…
South Africa	…	1	…	7	1	2	…	1	…	…	…	…	…	…
Tunisia	…	…	…	…	…	7	24	1	…	…	1	…	…	…
Zaire	…	…	…	…	…	…	1	…	…	…	…	…	1	1
Zimbabwe	1	…	…	1	3	1	18	3	2	5	35	14	15	17
Africa not specified	2	11	7	3	15	17	…	…	…	…	…	…	…	…
Asia	418	327	314	289	299	550	768	240	102	100	154	169	326	657
Bangladesh	…	…	…	…	…	…	3	…	…	…	…	…	…	…
China, People's Rep.	87	54	92	83	109	67	149	59	10	22	62	42	9	14
Hong Kong	5	18	21	14	12	56	74	66	4	5	12	14	33	85
India	3	7	10	17	18	21	22	21	4	5	7	5	6	6
Indonesia	3	1	1	2	1	9	20	18	17	10	10	13	11	18
Korea	207	136	156	102	92	165	199	23	19	14	11	30	133	280
Macao	…	…	…	…	…	…	…	…	…	…	…	…	…	1
Malaysia	3	4	2	1	1	7	9	5	3	3	5	12	7	12
Nauru	…	…	…	…	…	…	…	…	15	…	…	…	…	1
Pakistan	1	…	1	1	1	3	6	1	…	…	…	17	…	…
Philippines	81	74	3	4	3	6	6	4	18	2	1	1	1	3
Singapore	1	2	3	5	4	15	43	13	9	17	21	8	21	37
Sri Lanka	…	…	…	18	…	1	…	8	2	4	9	6	8	12
Thailand	4	1	3	17	27	61	51	…	…	13	9	1	3	11
Asia not specified	22	29	25	25	21	24	25	22	…	5	7	10	11	12
Taiwan Province of China	…	…	…	…	11	116	61	…	…	…	…	9	81	166

Table 2627 (Continued)

MEXICO ABSOLUTE VALUE OF GOODS TRADED WITH SELECTED REGIONS AND COUNTRIES,[1] 1982-88

(M US)[2]

Category	Exports 1982	1983	1984	1985	1986	1987	1988	Imports 1982	1983	1984	1985	1986	1987	1988
Developing Countries (Continued)														
Europe														
Greece	167	153	171	129	120	135	125	22	10	18	31	57	34	35
Hungary	1	1	4	2	2	1	1	1	~	4	3	1	~	~
Poland	10	40	7	10	1	1	3	4	3	4	4	3	3	4
Portugal	3	9	22	24	9	10	10	6	~	1	9	1	1	1
Romania	109	101	129	83	69	76	75	3	~	~	2	2	4	4
Turkey	28	2	6	8	10	11	12	4	3	5	6	14	15	16
Yugoslavia	12	~	3	3	15	12	9	~	1	3	6	35	7	6
Middle East														
Egypt	762	543	505	439	131	16	18	23	3	12	9	16	14	13
Iran, I.R. of	2	1	1	1	2	2	3	~	~	~	~	~	~	~
Iraq	10	4	6	~	~	~	~	~	~	~	1	1	2	2
Israel	738	531	486	432	125	4	4	11	2	6	8	13	9	8
Jordan	~	~	~	~	~	1	~	~	~	~	~	~	1	~
Kuwait	2	~	~	~	1	1	2	~	~	~	~	~	~	~
Lebanon	~	3	3	~	~	~	~	~	~	~	~	~	~	~
Libya	~	1	1	3	1	4	5	1	~	~	~	~	~	~
Saudi Arabia	6	3	2	3	~	4	5	8	~	6	1	2	2	2
Middle East not specified	4	4	4	2	3	3	3	3	~	~	1	2	2	2
Western Hemisphere	1,858	1,665	1,552	1,199	1,007	1,413	1,330	635	261	446	630	365	315	454
A. ARGENTINA	50	37	45	37	111	139	146	122	32	155	269	139	37	41
Bahamas, The	14	9	24	3	37	43	45	3	1	2	4	3	3	4
Barbados	~	1	~	~	~	2	1	~	~	~	~	~	~	~
Belize	5	6	6	5	9	11	12	~	~	3	~	2	10	10
Bermuda	1	1	1	~	1	7	8	~	~	~	1	1	~	~
B. BOLIVIA	1	~	1	~	1	7	8	~	~	3	4	1	~	3
C. BRAZIL	715	640	562	298	150	219	113	315	125	209	204	142	171	274
D. CHILE	11	17	16	16	26	40	52	25	4	13	52	10	3	24
E. COLOMBIA	48	69	69	121	90	135	153	12	8	8	6	10	8	16
F. COSTA RICA	72	68	60	21	52	67	77	13	8	13	8	1	1	3
Dominica	~	~	~	~	~	~	1	1	~	~	~	~	~	~
H. DOMINICAN REP.	166	150	163	132	94	108	113	~	3	~	~	~	~	~
I. ECUADOR	22	25	39	48	56	84	52	3	~	1	2	7	8	19
J. EL SALVADOR	69	89	77	89	47	82	86	5	~	9	~	1	1	~
K. GUATEMALA	107	69	103	101	51	59	62	35	12	9	16	9	10	11
Guyana	~	3	3	1	~	~	1	1	1	2	2	1	1	~
L. HAITI	10	22	46	28	22	25	27	~	3	~	6	3	3	4
M. HONDURAS	77	51	13	47	10	51	54	~	~	~	~	~	~	~
Jamaica	2	15	11	15	5	5	6	6	3	6	6	3	3	3
Netherlands Antilles	141	154	69	30	9	10	11	10	8	6	20	14	3	2
O. NICARAGUA	150	134	151	119	99	101	55	56	54	8	1	~	~	~
P. PANAMA	~	~	~	~	1	~	~	3	~	1	11	2	39	20
Q. PARAGUAY	~	~	~	~	~	4	~	5	2	6	1	2	5	2
R. PERU	26	17	14	13	27	40	33	6	3	6	11	8	10	18
Trinidad and Tobago	1	6	~	1	~	4	7	~	1	~	~	~	~	~
S. URUGUAY	80	49	43	24	64	78	56	6	3	5	6	8	10	18
T. VENEZUELA	88	32	35	39	44	99	148	9	1	1	13	7	~	~
Western Hem. not specified	2	4	3	9	2	2	2	3	3	3	5	1	2	2
U.S.S.R. and Other Nonmembers	51	109	126	92	66	76	80	90	33	29	26	20	22	25
G. CUBA	26	35	81	70	44	51	53	59	23	12	2	2	2	2
Czechoslovakia	15	30	19	11	14	16	17	14	6	10	14	10	11	12
Eastern Germany	2	38	12	3	~	~	~	6	1	3	3	3	3	3
U.S.S.R.	8	6	14	8	7	8	9	11	3	4	7	6	6	7

Table 2627 (Continued)

MEXICO ABSOLUTE VALUE OF GOODS TRADED WITH SELECTED REGIONS AND COUNTRIES,[1] 1982-88
(M US)[2]

Category	Exports							Imports						
	1982	1983	1984	1985	1986	1987	1988	1982	1983	1984	1985	1986	1987	1988
Country or area not specified	4	380	376	131	12	14	15	15	462	323	413	181	199	219
Special categories	252	~	338	263	249	287	301	563	414	485	~	~	~	~
Memorandum Items														
EEC	4,518	3,992	4,442	4,030	2,076	3,242	2,686	2,361	1,234	1,411	1,744	1,767	2,127	2,669
Oil Exporting Countries	112	65	82	69	53	114	178	36	18	18	24	21	13	21
Non-Oil Developing Countries	3,108	2,679	2,511	2,067	1,533	2,078	2,170	925	377	601	879	640	812	1,217
% Distribution														
Industrial Countries	83.4	85.5	85.9	88.1	88.5	90.5	90.7	88.1	84.1	85.9	90.0	93.0	94.8	94.6
Developing Countries	15.2	12.3	10.6	9.7	9.6	8.1	8.0	7.0	4.8	6.0	6.7	5.4	4.1	4.5
Africa	.1	.3	.2	.4	.2	.3	.4	.3	.2	.4	.6	.4	.7	.3
Asia	2.0	1.5	1.3	1.3	1.8	2.0	2.6	1.8	1.2	1.0	1.1	1.4	1.6	2.4
Europe	.8	.7	.7	.6	.7	.5	.4	.2	.1	.2	.2	.5	.2	.1
Middle East	3.6	2.4	2.1	2.0	.8	.1	.1	.2	~	.1	.1	.1	.1	~
Western Hemisphere	8.8	7.5	6.4	5.4	6.1	5.2	4.5	4.6	3.2	4.3	4.7	3.0	1.6	1.6
U.S.S.R. and Other Nonmembers	.2	.5	.5	.4	.4	.3	.3	.7	.4	.3	.2	.2	.1	.1
Annual PC														
World	9.4	5.2	9.3	-9.3	-25.0	62.6	8.9	-37.6	-40.1	25.9	30.2	-8.3	61.9	38.1
Industrial Countries	9.3	7.9	9.8	-7.0	-24.7	66.3	9.1	-37.3	-42.8	28.6	36.4	-5.3	65.0	37.9
Developing Countries	1.5	-14.8	-5.5	-17.6	-25.8	38.2	7.1	-35.8	-58.9	56.8	45.9	-26.7	24.6	50.1
Africa	-60.3	258.2	-10.2	58.5	-64.3	172.1	38.3	-33.3	-51.4	113.5	86.3	-29.4	145.9	-42.1
Asia	-6.7	-21.7	-4.0	-8.0	3.6	84.1	39.5	-19.0	-57.6	-1.7	54.2	9.6	92.9	101.4
Europe	64.0	-8.0	11.7	-24.4	-7.3	12.8	-7.7	-54.7	-56.6	92.4	70.3	80.8	-39.4	2.9
Middle East	12.3	-28.8	-7.0	-13.1	-70.2	-88.2	16.8	48.0	-87.7	338.7	-23.5	70.2	-13.0	-7.8
Western Hemisphere	-2.5	-10.4	-6.8	-22.8	-16.0	40.2	-5.9	-40.3	-58.9	71.0	41.2	-42.1	-13.7	44.3
U.S.S.R. and Other Nonmembers	37.4	111.3	15.8	-27.3	-27.9	14.8	4.9	-46.5	-63.4	-13.2	-7.9	-22.4	9.8	9.7

1. DOT data may differ between countries and from IFS data because of the time it takes for an export to become an import, etc.
2. Data may be calculated from partner's reported data or estimated on basis of less than 12 months.

SOURCE: IMF-DOT-Y, 1989.

Table 2628

NICARAGUA ABSOLUTE VALUE OF GOODS TRADED WITH SELECTED REGIONS AND COUNTRIES,[1] 1982-88
(M US)[2]

Category	Exports							Imports						
	1982	1983	1984	1985	1986	1987	1988	1982	1983	1984	1985	1986	1987	1988
IFS World Total	405.55	428.80	385.66	301.50	247.17	299.90	~	775.55	825.60	848.40	964.30	856.80	922.60	~
DOTS World Total	370.19	429.11	427.78	300.51	300.93	253.32	311.41	774.88	747.32	665.09	544.24	465.62	493.91	540.40
Industrial Countries	249.65	304.51	323.15	227.57	228.60	164.84	204.60	320.72	288.45	318.58	265.47	236.06	231.83	240.41
United States	82.34	98.64	62.55	45.09	.82	1.27	1.09	147.56	145.09	122.65	46.20	3.19	3.74	6.93
Canada	1.57	22.84	35.41	18.88	24.59	21.61	51.68	12.59	14.19	19.82	14.91	17.83	6.99	19.45
Australia	.16	.39	.51	.18	.18	.03	.24	.32	.03	~	.10	.05	2.85	.03
Japan	42.60	66.01	95.33	54.38	38.75	26.63	38.99	18.51	9.62	14.28	25.92	10.49	15.34	14.73
New Zealand	~	.07	.05	~	~	~	.02	~	.89	2.32	~	.02	~	.03
Austria	~	5.31	6.19	3.48	16.75	10.96	5.24	1.05	6.79	7.49	4.05	3.70	3.22	.83
Belgium-Luxembourg	6.71	2.67	3.81	4.55	12.96	13.03	5.00	3.03	2.25	2.82	1.10	6.85	2.07	2.77
Denmark	1.53	.13	.72	1.56	2.78	2.58	2.05	1.56	.70	1.49	2.19	9.14	6.91	5.55
Finland	1.90	.45	3.30	1.04	2.39	2.27	3.88	.05	1.34	3.07	3.98	5.29	12.49	10.68
France	19.25	25.80	36.20	20.15	25.07	19.16	13.25	32.43	30.69	34.08	39.35	48.45	40.01	18.68
Germany	52.46	34.90	30.18	30.87	34.45	29.04	44.98	28.85	13.70	19.91	17.18	20.65	21.67	16.08
Iceland	~	.01	.01	~	~	~	.01	~	~	~	~	~	~	~
Ireland	~	.15	.41	.39	.24	.47	.69	8.25	1.45	2.36	2.92	1.23	3.26	.42
Italy	8.42	14.00	10.53	7.69	11.39	3.84	3.74	20.86	13.25	15.07	17.02	23.17	42.45	33.81
Netherlands	16.27	9.08	8.29	9.40	18.53	10.94	10.52	10.26	8.77	8.95	9.10	12.86	15.77	35.54
Norway	.03	.24	.02	.16	.38	.47	1.08	.03	.21	1.78	2.61	2.95	3.30	3.85
Spain	13.79	15.15	20.52	21.49	21.51	10.14	13.71	21.99	21.08	33.80	36.72	30.75	23.55	32.09
Sweden	.03	.23	.32	.17	.43	1.08	.84	1.57	5.64	9.27	11.37	8.02	4.27	11.98
Switzerland	2.61	6.18	6.22	6.55	15.64	10.26	6.46	7.51	8.81	12.41	21.47	19.55	9.98	13.63
United Kingdom	~	2.26	2.58	1.55	1.74	1.08	1.12	4.31	3.96	7.02	9.26	11.89	13.95	13.33
Developing Countries	88.64	92.70	69.55	36.10	33.65	42.06	51.11	357.51	362.23	40.20	67.14	12.35	21.43	131.21
Africa	~	30.43	15.43	~	.04	.01	.01	1.82	.02	~	~	.09	~	~
Algeria	~	30.41	15.43	~	~	~	~							
Rwanda	~	~	~	~	~	~	~	~	~	~	~	~	~	~
Senegal	~	~	~	~	.02	~	.01	~	~	~	~	~	~	~
South Africa	~	~	~	~	~	~	~	1.82	.02	~	~	~	~	~
Tunisia	~	~	~	~	.02	~	.01	~	~	~	~	~	~	~
Zimbabwe	~	.01	~	~	~	~	~	~	~	~	~	.09	~	~
Asia	19.81	15.49	9.36	12.61	8.37	9.81	6.73	4.43	6.30	8.76	11.78	6.34	5.25	8.43
Bangladesh	~	~	~	~	~	~	~	~	~	~	~	~	~	.14
China, People's Rep.	19.52	8.43	~	~	~	~	~	~	~	~	~	~	~	~
Hong Kong	.04	~	~	~	.02	.75	.63	.20	.06	.04	1.30	1.27	.13	.11
India	~	~	~	~	~	.01	.01	.53	.07	.33	.35	.37	.44	.53
Indonesia	.12	.09	.73	.52	.24	.08	.09	.30	.30	~	~	~	.02	~
Korea	~	~	.47	.12	1.02	.89	.19	3.24	1.83	4.42	2.52	.47	2.17	3.88
Pakistan	~	.84	.01	.08	2.00	.19	~	~	~	~	.02	.07	.62	.80
Philippines	.10	~	~	~	.07	~	~	~	~	~	~	~	~	~
Singapore	~	~	~	~	~	~	~	.15	.07	.07	.04	~	~	~
Sri Lanka	~	~	~	2.34	1.99	.41	4.93	~	~	2.26	~	~	~	~
Thailand	.04	~	~	.17	.17	.41	~	~	~	~	~	~	~	~
Taiwan Province of China	~	6.12	8.15	9.38	3.04	7.91	5.91	4.43	3.98	1.63	7.54	4.16	1.88	2.97
Europe	.45	.64	.77	1.53	.93	1.42	5.76	.41	.52	.82	3.26	3.97	1.17	1.21
Cyprus	~	~	.01	~	~	.01	.01	~	~	~	~	~	.01	~
Faeroe Islands	~	~	~	~	~	.60	.72	~	~	~	~	~	~	~
Gibralter	.41	.41	.45	.48	.50	~	.01	~	.20	.81	~	.05	.43	.52
Greece	~	.03	.02	.34	.19	.08	.09	.16	~	~	~	~	~	~
Hungary	~	~	~	~	.07	~	~	~	~	~	~	~	~	~
Malta	.04	.19	.28	.37	.17	.41	4.93	.15	.29	~	.01	.36	.13	.09
Portugal	~	~	~	~	.01	~	~	.02	.03	~	~	~	.02	.06
Romania	~	~	~	~	~	.02	.01	~	~	~	~	~	~	~
Turkey	~	~	~	.35	~	.33	~	.09	~	~	3.25	3.56	.57	.54
Yugloslavia														

Table 2628 (Continued)

NICARAGUA ABSOLUTE VALUE OF GOODS TRADED WITH SELECTED REGIONS AND COUNTRIES,[1] 1982–88
(M US)[2]

Category	Exports							Imports						
	1982	1983	1984	1985	1986	1987	1988	1982	1983	1984	1985	1986	1987	1988
Developing Countries (Continued)														
Middle East	.40	~	~	.01	.01	.06	.11	1.18	1.43	1.10	.11	.22	4.26	3.81
Egypt	~	~	~	.01	.01	.01	.01	~	~	~	~	~	.01	.01
Israel	~	~	~	~	~	~	~	1.18	1.43	1.10	.11	.22	.77	1.98
Jordan	~	~	~	~	~	.05	.09	~	~	~	~	~	3.49	1.83
Saudi Arabia	.40	~	~	~	~	~	~	~	~	~	~	~	~	~
Western Hemisphere	67.99	46.15	43.98	21.95	24.31	30.76	38.51	349.68	353.96	229.52	152.00	101.73	110.75	117.77
A. ARGENTINA	~	~	~	~	~	~	~	3.42	18.97	23.22	29.07	20.39	12.56	15.07
Belize	~	~	~	~	~	~	~	~	.01	~	~	~	.01	.02
C. BRAZIL	~	~	~	~	~	~	~	7.81	11.62	15.95	7.29	6.21	11.67	16.43
D. CHILE	~	~	~	~	~	~	~	1.33	~	~	~	~	~	~
E. COLOMBIA	.19	.12	.01	.02	~	~	~	1.58	5.40	15.08	3.97	3.08	2.20	4.94
F. COSTA RICA	24.85	18.32	14.85	8.11	4.82	8.18	10.23	46.06	44.94	30.66	29.95	12.81	13.03	13.65
H. DOMINICAN REP.	~	.32	.01	~	.08	.09	.11	~	~	~	~	~	~	~
I. ECUADOR	~	.07	~	~	.30	~	1.14	~	~	.01	.45	.05	.17	~
J. EL SALVADOR	5.49	3.20	2.93	2.18	1.29	1.54	1.85	18.02	16.45	5.65	3.57	5.92	7.10	8.52
K. GUATEMALA	14.29	11.25	13.56	6.97	10.37	12.44	14.93	44.50	55.87	29.91	14.87	7.84	9.40	11.28
M. HONDURAS	7.45	3.23	3.55	3.73	3.92	4.70	5.64	8.37	10.63	11.69	12.28	12.89	15.47	18.56
Jamaica	~	~	~	~	.03	.03	.03	~	~	~	~	~	~	~
N. MEXICO	14.18	8.40	6.11	.08	2.91	3.20	3.51	154.93	169.40	75.48	33.36	9.73	11.19	11.75
Netherlands Antilles	~	~	~	~	~	~	~	6.38	15.18	8.25	8.66	9.10	10.92	13.10
P. PANAMA	1.44	1.25	.70	.86	.60	.48	.60	12.26	.95	1.27	1.28	2.26	2.13	1.26
R. PERU	~	~	~	~	~	.07	.44	1.57	2.32	6.83	1.73	3.42	8.85	2.75
Suriname	~	~	2.26	~	~	~	~	~	~	~	~	.34	~	~
Trinidad and Tobago	~	~	.01	~	~	.03	.02	~	.01	~	.03	~	6.06	.44
S. URUGUAY	~	~	~	~	~	~	~	~	~	~	~	~	~	~
T. VENEZUELA	.10	~	~	~	~	~	~	40.46	2.20	5.50	5.50	7.70	~	~
U.S.S.R. and Other Nonmembers	24.01	24.01	26.41	27.73	29.11	34.93	41.92	88.36	88.86	97.74	102.63	107.76	129.32	155.18
Bulgaria	4.38	4.38	4.82	5.06	5.31	6.38	7.65	6.27	6.27	6.89	7.24	7.60	9.12	10.94
G. CUBA	1.27	1.27	1.40	1.47	1.54	1.85	2.22	30.58	30.58	33.64	35.32	37.09	44.50	53.41
Czechoslovakia	5.42	5.42	5.96	6.25	6.57	7.88	9.46	1.47	1.47	1.62	1.70	1.79	2.14	2.57
Eastern Germany	4.77	4.77	5.25	5.51	5.78	6.94	8.33	11.63	11.63	12.79	13.43	14.11	16.93	20.31
North Korea	~	~	~	~	~	~	~	.12	.12	.13	.14	.15	.18	.21
U.S.S.R.	8.17	8.17	8.99	9.44	9.91	11.89	14.27	38.79	38.79	42.67	44.80	47.04	56.45	67.74
Country or area not specified	8.17	7.89	8.68	9.12	9.57	11.49	13.78	7.79	7.79	8.57	9.00	9.45	11.34	13.60
Memorandum Items														
EEC	121.07	104.35	113.55	98.37	129.02	90.76	100.08	131.68	96.33	126.32	134.85	165.39	170.20	158.89
Oil Exporting Countries	.62	30.50	16.16	.52	.24	.08	.01	40.46	2.20	5.50	5.50	7.70	.02	~
Non-Oil Developing Countries	88.03	62.20	53.39	35.58	33.41	41.98	51.10	317.06	360.03	234.70	161.64	104.65	121.41	131.21
% Distribution														
Industrial Countries	67.4	71.0	75.5	75.7	76.0	65.1	65.7	41.4	38.6	47.9	48.8	50.7	46.9	44.5
Developing Countries	23.9	21.6	16.3	12.0	11.2	16.6	16.4	46.1	48.5	36.1	30.7	24.1	24.6	24.3
Africa	~	7.1	~	~	~	~	~	.2	.8	1.3	2.2	1.4	1.1	1.6
Asia	5.4	3.6	3.6	4.2	2.8	3.9	2.2	.6	.1	.1	.6	.9	.2	.2
Europe	.1	.1	2.2	.5	.3	.6	1.8	.1	.1	.2	~	~	~	~
Middle East	.1	~	.2	~	~	~	~	.2	.2	~	~	~	.9	.7
Western Hemisphere	18.4	10.8	10.3	7.3	8.1	12.1	12.4	45.1	47.4	34.5	27.9	21.8	22.4	21.8
U.S.S.R. and Other Nonmembers	6.5	5.6	6.2	9.2	9.7	13.8	13.5	11.5	11.9	14.7	18.9	23.1	26.2	28.7

Table 2628 (Continued)

NICARAGUA ABSOLUTE VALUE OF GOODS TRADED WITH SELECTED REGIONS AND COUNTRIES,[1] 1982–88 (M US)[2]

Category	Exports							Imports						
	1982	1983	1984	1985	1986	1987	1988	1982	1983	1984	1985	1986	1987	1988
Annual PC														
World	-22.2	15.9	-.3	-29.8	.1	-15.8	22.9	-22.1	-3.6	-11.0	-18.2	-14.4	6.1	9.4
Industrial Countries	-18.6	22.0	6.1	-29.6	.5	-27.9	24.1	-29.7	-10.1	10.4	-16.7	-11.1	-1.8	3.7
Developing Countries	-27.9	4.6	-25.0	-48.1	-6.8	25.0	21.5	-28.4	1.3	-33.7	-30.4	-32.8	8.1	8.1
Africa	~	~	-49.3	~	~	-87.8	20.0	~	-98.8	~	~	~	~	~
Asia	-41.8	-21.8	-39.6	34.6	-33.6	17.3	-31.4	-4.2	42.5	38.9	34.5	-46.2	-17.1	60.4
Europe	-58.3	42.3	20.3	99.2	-39.3	52.7	305.4	-29.9	27.0	58.3	297.6	21.9	-70.6	3.3
Middle East	-58.6	~	~	133.3	42.9	500.0	75.0	~	21.1	-23.1	-90.0	100.0	~	-10.4
Western Hemisphere	-21.7	-32.1	-4.7	-50.1	10.7	26.5	25.2	-29.2	1.2	-35.2	-33.8	-33.1	8.9	6.3
U.S.S.R. and Other Nonmembers	-16.3	~	10.0	5.0	5.0	20.0	20.0	166.0	~	10.0	5.0	5.0	20.0	20.0

1. DOT data may differ between countries and from IFS data because of the time it takes for an export to become an import, etc.
2. Data may be calculated from partner's reported data or estimated on basis of less than 12 months.

SOURCE: IMF-DOT-Y, 1989.

Table 2629

PANAMA ABSOLUTE VALUE OF GOODS TRADED WITH SELECTED REGIONS AND COUNTRIES,[1] 1982-88

(M US)[2]

Category	Exports 1982	1983	1984	1985	1986	1987	1988	Imports 1982	1983	1984	1985	1986	1987	1988
IFS World Total	374.8	321.1	276.0	335.3	349.6	356.7	279.8	1,569.3	1,411.9	1,423.1	1,391.8	1,229.2	1,306.2	751.0
DOTS World Total	308.1	299.3	251.5	300.6	331.7	336.6	286.9	1,569.3	1,411.9	1,423.0	1,391.4	1,284.7	1,306.2	3,150.8
Industrial Countries	189.3	214.0	201.9	248.1	280.7	286.9	212.5	841.7	724.4	739.5	744.6	738.3	702.8	1,239.1
United States	127.9	160.8	152.9	192.6	224.6	225.4	142.1	549.0	456.4	450.5	438.0	448.3	448.8	588.5
Canada	13.2	2.7	.6	1.1	1.3	4.8	5.0	13.6	13.7	15.1	15.2	12.2	13.2	25.2
Australia	…	…	…	.1	.3	…	…	1.1	.1	.8	1.7	1.9	.1	.3
Japan	.3	.9	1.0	.2	.1	1.8	.2	119.5	110.2	117.9	123.5	108.3	96.1	155.1
New Zealand	…	…	…	…	…	…	…	2.2	2.7	5.5	6.7	6.6	4.7	4.3
Austria	…	…	…	…	.3	.6	…	1.8	1.4	1.2	1.8	1.9	2.0	1.7
Belgium-Luxembourg	13.4	15.4	13.4	13.9	13.6	13.8	10.3	5.7	8.6	10.8	5.3	4.5	6.9	10.5
Denmark	…	…	…	…	…	…	.2	4.2	5.9	3.9	3.1	4.6	5.4	6.4
Finland	…	…	…	…	…	…	1.0	.9	1.1	1.1	.4	1.1	.8	.7
France	.6	.6	.3	.5	1.4	1.5	1.6	24.5	16.6	15.6	14.5	15.8	10.3	54.8
Germany	18.2	17.1	14.8	17.5	20.5	19.8	30.2	28.7	32.0	29.2	31.4	31.0	34.7	51.8
Iceland	…	…	…	…	…	…	…	.5	.2	.1	…	…	…	…
Ireland	…	…	…	…	…	…	…	1.3	2.2	2.5	2.9	3.0	3.7	3.0
Italy	8.2	8.1	10.8	6.7	7.6	8.3	12.2	17.1	23.7	14.7	15.2	12.0	14.7	87.7
Netherlands	1.2	.8	.8	4.1	2.5	.9	1.0	10.9	7.1	8.4	9.2	9.4	15.0	17.2
Norway	3.0	1.1	1.2	1.5	2.6	1.1	…	5.5	2.0	1.4	1.3	3.0	.8	51.8
Spain	.1	.2	3.0	.2	1.1	3.1	3.0	13.3	13.6	14.7	18.4	20.2	16.7	61.6
Sweden	2.6	5.1	3.5	4.1	4.5	5.5	5.1	17.3	9.2	8.8	8.4	4.4	5.9	5.1
Switzerland	.1	.3	…	…	.4	.1	…	5.3	5.5	24.7	33.8	37.6	7.7	76.2
United Kingdom	.5	.9	.3	5.7	…	…	.5	13.3	12.0	12.6	13.6	14.2	14.9	37.1
Developing Countries	60.7	48.4	48.0	51.2	49.7	48.5	64.1	573.4	524.5	661.4	634.4	533.0	591.8	1,898.4
Africa	2.0	.2	.2	…	…	…	…	2.4	1.1	.2	.3	.2	.5	4.0
Algeria	…	…	…	…	…	…	…	…	…	…	…	…	…	.1
Morocco	…	…	…	…	…	…	…	2.1	.4	…	…	…	…	2.3
Nigeria	…	…	…	…	…	…	…	.3	.6	.2	.2	.2	…	…
South Africa	…	…	…	…	…	…	…	…	…	…	…	…	.4	.5
Tunisia	…	…	…	…	…	…	…	…	…	…	.1	…	…	1.2
Africa not specified	2.0	.2	.2	…	…	…	…	…	…	…	…	…	…	…
Asia	.2	.2	.3	.1	.2	.2	2.1	46.4	40.8	47.0	49.9	63.0	76.4	1,361.8
China, People's Rep.	.2	.2	…	…	…	…	…	2.2	2.1	1.3	1.2	1.8	1.2	33.0
Hong Kong	…	.1	.3	.1	.1	.1	.6	10.7	9.6	10.5	11.2	12.0	13.4	263.8
India	…	…	…	…	…	…	…	.1	.3	.1	.4	.5	.5	.5
Indonesia	…	…	…	…	…	…	…	.1	…	…	…	.1	.3	2.6
Korea	…	…	…	…	…	…	1.0	12.5	9.4	10.9	11.8	16.0	24.1	552.3
Macao	…	…	…	…	…	…	…	.4	.4	…	…	…	…	1.0
Malaysia	…	…	…	…	…	…	…	.2	.4	.1	.1	.2	.4	9.3
Pakistan	…	…	…	…	…	…	…	.2	…	.1	.2	.8	.1	.3
Philippines	…	…	…	…	…	…	…	.3	.3	.8	.3	.4	.4	31.1
Singapore	…	…	.1	…	…	…	.2	.7	.6	.2	.4	.3	.4	176.1
Sri Lanka	…	…	…	…	…	…	…	.1	.1	.1	.1	.1	…	…
Thailand	…	…	…	…	…	…	…	.4	.1	.1	.1	.1	.3	65.5
Western Samoa	…	…	…	…	…	…	.2	.3	…	…	…	…	…	…
Asia not specified	…	…	…	…	…	…	…	…	…	…	…	…	…	…
Taiwan Province of China	…	…	…	.5	…	.1	…	18.3	17.9	23.0	24.3	30.7	32.9	226.2
Europe	…	…	…	.5	.7	.7	4.0	1.7	3.5	1.9	2.4	1.8	3.0	25.3
Gibralter	…	…	…	…	…	…	…	…	…	…	…	…	…	.1
Greece	…	…	…	…	…	…	…	…	…	…	…	…	…	.1
Hungary	…	…	…	…	…	…	.2	.1	.9	.5	…	…	…	.7
Poland	…	…	…	…	…	…	…	.2	.8	.2	.2	.1	.6	2.8
Portugal	…	…	…	…	…	.6	1.4	1.1	1.5	1.0	1.2	1.1	1.9	.1
Romania	…	…	…	…	…	…	.3	.1	.1	…	.1	.1	…	.1
Turkey	…	…	…	…	…	…	…	.1	…	…	…	…	…	21.4
Yugoslavia	…	…	…	…	…	…	…	.1	…	…	.3	.2	.1	…

Table 2629 (Continued)

PANAMA ABSOLUTE VALUE OF GOODS TRADED WITH SELECTED REGIONS AND COUNTRIES,[1] 1982–88
(M US)[2]

Category	Exports							Imports						
	1982	1983	1984	1985	1986	1987	1988	1982	1983	1984	1985	1986	1987	1988
Developing Countries (Continued)														
Middle East	3.0	3.6	9.5	4.1	2.2	4.1	2.6	.9	.5	.5	1.9	1.8	19.9	22.0
Egypt	.3	.2	.1	.4	.2	?	.3	?	?	?	?	.2	?	?
Israel	.2	.2	.1	.4	.2	?	1.1	.9	.4	.5	1.4	1.4	.5	2.0
Jordan	?	?	?	?	?	?	?	?	?	.1	.1	?	?	?
Kuwait	?	?	?	?	?	1.3	.6	?	?	?	?	?	?	?
Saudi Arabia	2.3	3.4	3.7	3.7	2.0	2.4	.6	?	?	?	.3	.3	19.3	20.0
United Arab Emirates	?	?	5.7	?	?	.3	?	?	?	?	.1	?	?	?
Yemen Arab Rep.	.2	?	?	?	?	?	?	?	?	?	?	?	?	?
Western Hemisphere	55.4	44.6	38.0	46.5	46.7	43.4	55.4	522.0	478.6	611.9	579.9	466.1	492.0	485.3
A. ARGENTINA	?	?	?	6.6	?	?	?	1.7	2.3	5.2	3.8	8.7	9.3	12.8
Bahamas, The	.1	?	?	?	?	?	?	?	?	?	?	?	?	?
Belize	?	?	?	?	.1	.1	.1	.1	?	?	?	.1	?	?
B. BOLIVIA	?	.2	?	.1	.4	.3	.1	?	?	?	?	?	?	?
C. BRAZIL	.3	.2	.2	.1	.2	.1	.1	20.7	20.1	22.2	28.7	24.5	26.9	3.9
D. CHILE	3.7	4.1	1.0	1.1	1.6	1.1	1.3	5.5	3.7	3.6	4.7	5.4	6.9	1.0
E. COLOMBIA	10.1	15.2	20.6	17.6	17.5	19.4	20.6	9.7	8.4	12.4	12.6	14.3	21.6	63.8
F. COSTA RICA	.7	.9	.2	.9	.1	.2	.5	39.5	36.1	35.0	34.6	41.8	39.6	24.0
H. DOMINICAN REP.	?	?	?	?	?	?	.3	.7	.3	.2	.2	.3	.2	.3
I. ECUADOR	2.3	.9	.7	2.1	3.0	1.6	2.4	86.7	110.5	83.1	81.4	45.8	26.2	21.2
J. EL SALVADOR	3.4	4.8	2.4	2.9	3.9	2.6	2.9	5.7	5.8	5.3	5.7	5.3	5.9	6.6
Guadeloupe	?	?	?	?	.2	?	?	?	?	.1	?	?	?	.1
K. GUATEMALA	2.5	2.2	3.0	3.3	2.6	4.6	3.8	17.9	15.9	17.4	17.0	14.9	16.6	18.8
Guiana, French	.4	.6	?	?	.2	?	?	?	?	?	?	?	?	?
Guyana	?	?	.2	?	?	?	.7	.1	?	.1	?	?	?	?
L. HAITI	?	?	?	?	?	?	?	?	?	?	?	?	?	?
M. HONDURAS	9.1	1.8	2.0	2.1	2.2	2.2	2.0	2.3	1.8	1.3	2.1	2.3	3.0	3.1
Jamaica	.1	.1	.1	.3	.1	?	.1	.2	1.1	.7	.1	1.2	.4	.8
Leeward Islands	.5	?	.1	?	?	?	.1	?	?	?	?	?	?	?
N. MEXICO	.9	4.3	2.7	2.6	2.9	2.3	1.7	146.1	127.1	129.0	110.2	66.7	110.7	110.2
Netherlands Antilles	4.9	.9	1.2	1.2	2.1	1.9	2.4	9.7	13.1	31.1	10.2	9.8	5.3	6.5
O. NICARAGUA	2.5	?	?	?	?	?	4.4	2.1	1.4	.8	1.0	.7	.5	.7
Q. PARAGUAY	?	?	?	?	?	?	?	?	.1	.1	.1	?	.1	?
R. PERU	.9	4.5	.4	1.2	1.3	2.8	5.8	4.5	5.3	7.0	7.0	5.6	9.5	1.1
St. Pierre-Miquelon	.2	.2	.2	.2	?	.2	.5	.4	.4	.2	.2	?	.2	.3
Suriname	?	.2	.2	.2	.1	.2	.2	?	?	?	?	?	?	?
Trinidad and Tobago	.1	2.8	?	.2	?	.1	.1	9.0	3.5	8.2	6.4	3.4	2.7	1.6
S. URUGUAY	?	?	?	?	?	?	?	.1	?	.1	.1	2.1	.1	.5
T. VENEZUELA	12.5	1.1	1.1	2.5	3.3	1.1	1.2	157.7	121.4	103.7	88.3	44.5	52.4	41.6
Windward Islands	?	?	?	?	?	?	?	1.6	?	?	?	?	?	?
Western Hem. not specified	?	?	1.8	1.8	4.8	2.3	4.1	?	.1	145.1	165.7	168.7	154.1	166.2
U.S.S.R. and Other Nonmembers	.5	1.3	1.7	1.3	1.3	1.2	6.4	1.3	1.3	1.0	2.1	2.6	1.5	1.6
Bulgaria	?	?	?	?	?	?	.3	?	?	?	?	?	?	?
G. CUBA	.5	.8	1.7	1.2	.9	1.2	2.9	.1	.3	.1	.2	.4	.2	.1
Czechoslovakia	?	.3	?	.2	.3	?	.4	.7	.9	.7	1.6	2.1	1.2	1.4
Eastern Germany	?	?	?	.1	.1	?	2.7	?	?	.1	.3	.1	.1	?
U.S.S.R.	?	.3	?	?	?	?	?	.4	?	?	?	?	?	?
Country or area not specified	?	?	?	?	?	?	?	.1	.1	?	?	?	.1	.1
Special categories	57.7	35.6	?	?	?	?	3.8	152.9	161.7	21.1	10.1	10.8	10.0	11.6
Memorandum Items														
EEC	42.3	43.1	42.7	48.6	47.4	48.3	60.4	125.1	123.4	113.6	114.9	116.1	124.5	333.0
Oil Exporting Countries	14.9	4.5	10.5	6.2	5.4	5.2	2.4	159.9	121.9	103.7	88.8	44.8	72.1	64.2
Non-Oil Developing Countries	45.8	43.9	37.5	45.0	44.3	43.3	61.7	413.5	402.5	557.7	545.7	488.1	519.7	1,834.2

Table 2629 (Continued)

PANAMA ABSOLUTE VALUE OF GOODS TRADED WITH SELECTED REGIONS AND COUNTRIES,[1] 1982–88 (M US)[2]

Exports

Category	1982	1983	1984	1985	1986	1987	1988
% Distribution							
Industrial Countries	61.4	71.5	80.3	82.5	84.6	85.2	74.1
Developing Countries	19.7	16.2	19.1	17.0	15.0	14.4	22.4
Africa	.7	~	.1	~	~	~	~
Asia	.1	.1	.1	.2	.2	.1	.7
Europe	~	.2	~	.2	.2	.2	1.4
Middle East	1.0	1.2	3.8	1.4	.7	1.2	.9
Western Hemisphere	18.0	14.9	15.1	15.5	14.1	12.9	19.3
U.S.S.R. and Other Nonmembers	.1	.4	.7	.4	.4	.4	2.2
Annual PC							
World	-2.7	-2.8	-16.0	19.5	10.3	1.5	-14.8
Industrial Countries	-17.0	13.1	-5.7	22.9	13.2	2.2	-25.9
Developing Countries	-13.5	-20.3	-.8	6.8	-3.1	-2.5	32.4
Africa	960.7	-99.7	~	-99.5	75.6	32.5	29.0
Asia	-38.3	-11.6	59.2	-71.7	22.5	9.7	933.0
Europe	~	~	~	~	~	~	459.6
Middle East	7.8	18.4	164.3	-57.0	-45.7	84.5	-36.8
Western Hemisphere	.3	-19.5	-14.8	22.5	.2	-6.9	27.6
U.S.S.R. and Other Nonmembers	-41.5	193.2	24.0	-22.1	.4	-5.0	4'6.7

Imports

Category	1982	1983	1984	1985	1986	1987	1988
% Distribution							
Industrial Countries	53.6	51.3	52.0	53.5	57.5	53.8	39.3
Developing Countries	36.5	37.1	46.5	45.6	41.5	45.3	60.3
Africa	.2	.1	~	~	~	~	.1
Asia	3.0	2.9	3.3	3.6	4.9	5.9	43.2
Europe	.1	.2	~	.2	.1	.2	.8
Middle East	.1	~	~	.1	.1	1.5	.7
Western Hemisphere	33.3	33.9	43.0	41.7	36.3	37.7	15.4
U.S.S.R. and Other Nonmembers	.1	.1	.1	.2	.2	.1	~
Annual PC							
World	1.9	-10.0	.8	-2.2	-7.7	1.7	141.2
Industrial Countries	7.0	-13.9	2.1	.7	-.9	-4.8	76.3
Developing Countries	-5.9	-8.5	26.1	-4.1	-16.0	11.0	220.8
Africa	~	-55.3	-83.2	57.9	-40.2	186.9	729.0
Asia	-3.0	-12.1	15.1	6.4	26.2	21.2	~
Europe	-16.5	110.4	-46.4	27.0	-24.1	65.2	750.3
Middle East	-99.2	-48.5	9.9	260.3	-3.8	993.1	10.8
Western Hemisphere	18.5	-8.3	27.8	-5.2	-19.6	5.6	-1.4
U.S.S.R. and Other Nonmembers	-61.5	5.6	-26.7	118.3	21.9	-41.0	2.3

1. DOT data may differ between countries and from IFS data because of the time it takes for an export to become an import, etc.
2. Data may be calculated from partner's reported data or estimated on basis of less than 12 months.

SOURCE: IMF-DOT-Y, 1989.

Table 2630

PARAGUAY ABSOLUTE VALUE OF GOODS TRADED WITH SELECTED REGIONS AND COUNTRIES,[1] 1982–88
(M US)[2]

Category	Exports							Imports						
	1982	1983	1984	1985	1986	1987	1988	1982	1983	1984	1985	1986	1987	1988
IFS World Total	329.78	269.18	334.52	303.91	233.53	353.38	509.85	581.47	478.26	513.07	442.27	508.81	517.48	494.75
DOTS World Total	329.80	269.18	334.47	303.90	232.48	353.38	528.45	581.51	478.27	514.35	442.97	550.01	517.49	494.75
Industrial Countries	136.20	138.15	156.07	163.84	70.33	161.15	231.36	200.70	162.72	199.48	137.30	202.40	203.21	194.21
United States	9.10	23.27	17.73	3.83	9.36	13.91	18.88	52.30	34.81	45.16	35.00	69.83	55.25	49.79
Canada	?	.47	.20	.15	.21	?	?	.40	.42	9.87	.71	.70	?	?
Japan	25.50	5.24	7.90	3.17	1.90	2.61	11.86	32.00	20.17	60.74	20.20	29.22	30.01	36.86
Austria	?	.05	.03	.09	.10	?	?	1.10	1.00	.44	1.47	.85	?	?
Belgium–Luxembourg	6.10	6.61	9.75	18.59	5.79	11.40	24.41	2.10	1.78	1.15	1.27	1.23	4.33	3.46
Denmark	.30	.14	?	.01	.02	?	?	1.00	.50	.26	.71	.39	?	?
Finland	?	?	?	?	.02	?	?	.10	.04	.02	.01	.03	?	?
France	7.20	4.91	8.07	23.79	1.92	6.36	6.78	10.60	16.95	25.97	6.97	12.82	6.82	10.28
Germany	40.90	31.86	39.56	41.00	7.77	13.48	19.42	37.30	32.32	16.06	21.97	32.98	30.17	30.82
Ireland	.40	.01	.02	.01	?	?	?	?	.02	.02	.02	.07	?	?
Italy	5.70	3.11	6.01	3.60	4.29	12.06	25.37	6.60	4.89	3.17	3.54	6.68	25.96	8.64
Netherlands	16.00	38.59	41.26	38.39	22.52	63.59	67.97	9.90	1.71	6.67	2.31	2.12	1.86	2.91
Norway	?	?	.03	?	?	?	?	.10	.10	.02	.12	.05	?	?
Spain	6.90	2.81	12.11	9.64	1.77	11.10	15.13	6.10	16.08	2.50	16.00	4.63	7.61	8.06
Sweden	?	?	?	?	.14	?	?	2.20	2.26	.88	1.73	2.25	1.53	2.02
Switzerland	14.20	19.18	12.76	20.02	13.61	24.14	38.91	4.90	4.94	5.10	6.79	6.13	5.69	6.54
United Kingdom	3.90	1.91	.65	1.57	.93	2.52	2.62	34.00	24.73	21.46	18.48	32.42	33.98	34.84
Developing Countries	193.60	131.02	177.95	139.65	162.15	127.07	155.14	379.80	314.54	314.41	304.79	306.42	260.71	252.04
Africa	9.30	6.17	12.26	2.34	2.70	?	?	76.50	67.65	49.65	43.63	34.93	38.04	37.07
Algeria	.90	.74	?	?	.70	?	?	75.60	65.56	48.45	41.33	33.56	38.04	37.07
Côte d'Ivoire	.20	?	?	?	?	?	?	?	?	?	?	?	?	?
Madagascar	.20	?	?	?	?	?	?	?	?	?	?	?	?	?
Mali	.10	?	?	?	?	?	?	?	?	?	?	?	?	?
Morocco	.40	?	?	?	?	?	?	?	?	?	?	?	?	?
Nigeria	.80	?	?	?	?	?	?	?	?	?	?	?	?	?
Senegal	.30	?	?	?	?	?	?	?	?	?	?	?	?	?
South Africa	6.20	4.40	11.04	1.54	1.39	?	?	.90	2.09	1.20	2.30	1.37	?	?
Tunisia	.20	?	1.21	.79	.61	?	?	?	?	?	?	?	?	?
Africa not specified	?	1.03	?	?	?	?	?	?	?	?	?	?	?	?
Asia	6.80	2.17	7.40	6.22	.74	?	?	8.00	4.62	2.00	9.38	26.25	?	?
Hong Kong	.80	.96	.30	?	?	?	?	.80	1.25	.22	2.97	7.40	?	?
India	?	?	.02	?	?	?	?	.40	.21	.05	.05	.07	?	?
Indonesia	1.70	?	?	?	?	?	?	?	?	?	?	?	?	?
Korea	1.50	.37	.61	2.71	.59	?	?	1.60	.39	.68	.79	1.29	?	?
Malaysia	.50	?	?	?	?	?	?	?	?	?	?	?	?	?
Myanmar	.20	?	?	?	?	?	?	?	?	?	?	?	?	?
Philippines	.10	?	?	?	?	?	?	?	?	?	?	?	?	?
Singapore	1.20	?	?	?	?	?	?	?	?	?	?	?	?	?
Asia not specified	?	.40	5.31	2.14	.11	?	?	?	.19	.05	.20	.16	?	?
Taiwan Province of China	.80	.44	1.16	1.37	.04	?	?	5.20	2.58	1.00	5.36	17.33	?	?
Europe	9.40	8.69	16.66	15.60	2.64	?	?	1.30	.12	.17	.03	.06	?	?
Greece	?	.67	4.79	3.47	?	?	?	?	.04	.01	?	?	?	?
Hungary	?	?	?	?	?	?	?	.20	?	?	?	?	?	?
Poland	.20	?	?	?	?	?	?	.60	?	?	?	?	?	?
Portugal	8.90	8.02	11.82	12.13	2.63	?	?	.40	.06	.15	.03	.04	?	?
Romania	.40	?	?	?	?	?	?	.10	.02	.02	?	?	?	?
Turkey	.10	?	?	?	?	?	?	?	?	?	?	?	?	?
Yugoslavia	.50	?	.04	?	?	?	?	?	?	?	?	.01	?	?
Europe not specified	?	?	?	?	.01	?	?	?	?	?	?	?	?	?

Table 2630 (Continued)

PARAGUAY ABSOLUTE VALUE OF GOODS TRADED WITH SELECTED REGIONS AND COUNTRIES,[1] 1982–88 (M US)[2]

Category	Exports							Imports						
	1982	1983	1984	1985	1986	1987	1988	1982	1983	1984	1985	1986	1987	1988
Developing Countries (Continued)														
Middle East	.60	1.00	1.14	2.67	.14	?	?	.40	.33	.15	1.17	.38	?	?
Iraq	.10	?	?	?	?	?	?	?	?	?	?	?	?	?
Israel	.50	?	?	?	?	?	?	.40	?	?	?	?	?	?
Middle East not specified	?	1.00	1.14	2.67	.14	?	?	?	.33	.15	1.17	.38	?	?
Western Hemisphere	167.50	113.00	140.51	112.83	155.94	127.07	155.14	293.60	241.82	262.43	250.59	244.80	222.68	214.96
A. ARGENTINA	59.20	32.14	40.53	15.69	35.17	53.57	33.59	113.20	90.36	80.96	74.88	69.54	46.10	58.68
B. BOLIVIA	.40	.36	.01	.26	.08	?	?	.20	.11	.07	.09	.04	?	?
C. BRAZIL	83.40	56.62	53.22	60.08	92.13	62.24	17.12	154.30	136.21	167.89	159.87	160.84	169.00	150.59
D. CHILE	6.90	8.87	16.75	13.12	13.61	?	?	7.30	2.72	3.61	4.31	4.41	?	?
E. COLOMBIA	.20	.01	?	.89	.24	?	?	.40	.06	.04	.02	.05	?	?
I. ECUADOR	?	.02	.17	.01	?	?	?	.10	.06	.01	.10	.04	?	?
Jamaica	?	?	?	?	?	?	?	2.80	?	?	?	?	?	?
N. MEXICO	.90	.14	.06	.21	.36	?	?	.70	.29	.17	.42	.47	?	?
Netherlands Antilles	?	?	?	?	?	?	?	3.30	2.49	1.29	.79	?	?	?
P. PANAMA	2.60	2.32	1.34	.65	3.82	?	?	2.40	.11	.11	.06	.14	?	?
R. PERU	.20	?	?	?	?	?	?	.20	?	?	?	?	?	?
Trinidad and Tobago	?	?	?	?	?	?	?	.40	?	?	?	?	?	?
S. URUGUAY	4.40	4.70	6.80	6.43	6.40	11.27	4.43	8.20	7.67	4.77	5.79	4.43	7.57	5.69
T. VENEZUELA	9.30	2.91	7.75	.17	.11	?	?	.10	.09	.18	.09	.09	?	?
Western Hem. not specified	?	4.92	13.88	15.34	4.03	?	?	?	1.65	3.33	4.17	4.75	?	?
U.S.S.R. and Other Nonmembers	?	?	.44	.41	?	?	?	.00	1.01	.40	.88	.48	?	?
Bulgaria	?	?	?	?	?	?	?	.10	?	?	?	?	?	?
Czechoslovakia	.10	?	?	?	?	?	?	?	?	?	?	?	?	?
U.S.S.R., etc. not specified	.90	?	.44	.41	?	?	?	.90	1.01	.40	.88	.48	?	?
Country or area not specified	.01	?	?	?	?	65.15	141.95	?	?	.06	?	40.70	53.56	48.51
Memorandum Items														
EEC	96.30	98.63	134.04	152.19	47.63	120.50	161.70	108.00	99.08	77.40	71.29	93.38	110.73	99.00
Oil Exporting Countries	12.80	3.64	7.76	.17	.81	?	?	75.70	65.65	48.63	41.42	33.65	38.04	37.07
Non-Oil Developing Countries	180.80	127.38	170.20	139.48	161.34	127.07	155.14	304.10	248.89	265.78	263.37	272.77	222.68	214.96
% Distribution														
Industrial Countries	41.3	51.3	46.7	53.9	30.3	45.6	43.8	34.5	34.0	38.8	31.0	36.8	39.3	39.3
Developing Countries	58.7	48.7	53.2	46.0	69.7	36.0	29.4	65.3	65.8	61.1	68.8	55.7	50.4	50.9
Africa	2.8	2.3	3.7	.8	1.2	?	?	13.2	14.1	9.7	9.8	6.4	7.4	7.5
Asia	2.1	.8	2.2	2.0	.3	?	?	1.4	1.0	.4	2.1	4.8	?	?
Europe	2.9	3.2	5.0	5.1	1.1	?	?	.2	?	?	.3	.1	?	?
Middle East	.2	.4	.3	.9	.1	?	?	.1	.1	?	.1	.1	?	?
Western Hemisphere	50.8	42.0	42.0	37.1	67.1	36.0	29.4	50.5	50.6	51.0	56.6	44.5	43.0	43.4
U.S.S.R. and Other Nonmembers	?	?	.1	.1	.1	?	?	.2	.2	.1	.2	.1	?	?
Annual PC														
World	11.0	-18.4	24.3	-9.1	-23.5	52.0	49.5	14.8	-17.8	7.5	-13.9	24.2	-5.9	-4.4
Industrial Countries	12.7	1.4	13.0	5.0	-57.1	129.1	43.6	1.9	-18.9	22.6	-31.2	47.4	.4	-4.4
Developing Countries	10.4	-32.3	35.8	-21.5	16.1	-21.6	22.1	23.0	-17.2	?	-3.1	.5	-14.9	-3.3
Africa	67.5	-33.7	98.7	-80.9	15.7	?	?	172.4	-11.6	-26.6	-12.1	-19.9	8.9	-2.5
Asia	9.3	-68.1	241.6	-16.0	-88.2	?	?	-8.9	-42.2	-56.7	368.7	179.8	?	?
Europe	-35.3	-7.6	91.7	-6.4	-83.1	?	?	-40.8	-90.9	46.9	-83.8	103.2	?	?
Middle East	?	66.3	13.8	135.0	-94.9	?	?	-86.0	-17.7	-54.1	673.5	-67.5	?	?
Western Hemisphere	12.3	-32.5	24.3	-19.7	38.2	-18.5	22.1	13.1	-17.6	8.5	-4.5	-2.3	-9.0	-3.5
U.S.S.R. and Other Nonmembers	?	?	?	-7.7	?	?	?	27.6	1.0	-60.5	120.0	-44.9	?	?

1. DOT data may differ between countries and from IFS data because of the time it takes for an export to become an import, etc.
2. Data may be calculated from partner's reported data or estimated on basis of less than 12 months.

SOURCE: IMF-DOT-Y, 1989.

Table 2631

PERU ABSOLUTE VALUE OF GOODS TRADED WITH SELECTED REGIONS AND COUNTRIES,[1] 1982–88 (M US)[2]

Exports

Category	1982	1983	1984	1985	1986	1987	1988
IFS World Total	3,721.0	2,722.0	3,147.1	2,978.5	2,530.6	2,660.8	2,694.9
DOTS World Total	2,919.1	2,577.4	3,086.4	2,980.6	2,504.5	2,605.0	2,688.8
Industrial Countries	2,099.4	2,044.8	2,225.4	2,093.4	1,707.5	1,753.9	1,822.1
United States	1,045.7	972.3	1,141.8	1,009.3	754.2	716.0	583.5
Canada	24.4	57.4	54.5	19.1	18.2	46.5	39.9
Australia	1.8	1.8	6.0	2.9	2.1	2.0	5.0
Japan	432.7	410.7	319.8	303.5	266.1	272.0	323.5
New Zealand	.3	.2	.1	.1	.1	.1	.1
Austria	1.2	.4	~	44.8	5.6	5.2	7.4
Belgium–Luxembourg	95.1	89.5	130.6	136.3	108.5	128.1	122.6
Denmark	4.8	4.9	5.9	3.8	5.1	8.3	9.7
Finland	3.4	10.2	2.5	6.6	1.4	.4	.5
France	52.7	35.5	58.6	41.7	26.6	42.0	43.7
Germany	84.7	79.6	118.4	134.8	140.8	115.7	177.7
Iceland	~	.1	~	.1	.1	.6	1.4
Ireland	.1	.2	~	1.5	.8	.6	1.4
Italy	91.9	82.6	96.5	79.5	81.1	106.1	119.4
Netherlands	89.6	106.6	75.3	107.1	99.9	76.6	103.8
Norway	2.0	1.0	3.0	.9	3.6	1.1	.9
Spain	14.2	18.0	20.8	11.4	23.3	21.4	39.1
Sweden	13.2	15.6	27.1	20.5	19.1	28.6	39.7
Switzerland	5.3	6.1	12.0	36.3	33.6	38.7	45.7
United Kingdom	136.4	152.2	152.4	133.4	117.2	144.6	158.4
Developing Countries	717.1	426.6	519.3	695.0	655.1	726.9	775.2
Africa	66.4	13.9	~	16.3	18.5	20.4	17.4
Algeria	.4	~	~	~	9.0	17.5	12.8
Benin	59.1						
Burkina Faso							
Burundi		.1					
Cameroon		.4					
Central African Rep.		.2		3.0			
Congo	.4						.1
Côte d'Ivoire							
Ethiopia	.1	.1				.2	
Liberia	.1	.1		12.3	6.7	.2	
Malawi	.1					.2	
Mauritius	.1	.3		.2	.8	.9	1.2
Morocco	.2	1.7	.3			.2	.5
Nigeria		.1					
Senegal		.1					
South Africa	5.5	10.8		.4	1.2	1.6	2.2
Tanzania		.2		.3			
Tunisia	.4	.1		.3		.1	.3
Zaire							
Zambia							
Asia	118.3	108.4	117.9	168.4	178.5	181.4	266.0
Bangladesh		.3		.7	1.4	.7	.8
Brunei						.1	
China, People's Rep.	19.4	19.4	.3	55.5	63.4	60.0	134.1
Fiji		.1					
Hong Kong	4.3	2.5	12.5	7.2	9.0	10.4	30.4
India	12.4	3.2	.7	7.9	12.3	4.9	5.6
Indonesia	3.6	3.3		1.8	4.4	5.1	.5
Korea	55.2	29.2	2.2	63.9	43.0	47.9	51.0

Imports

Category	1982	1983	1984	1985	1986	1987	1988
IFS World Total	3,473.3	2,540.8	1,843.3	1,686.1	2,424.0	2,968.6	2,567.0
DOTS World Total	3,001.3	2,034.9	1,492.3	1,423.8	1,740.9	3,068.0	2,109.1
Industrial Countries	2,313.9	1,597.1	1,070.3	991.7	1,207.0	2,002.0	1,395.8
United States	1,118.7	773.0	468.8	401.3	473.2	813.9	629.9
Canada	65.0	64.7	53.9	28.3	51.2	85.6	44.3
Australia	9.7	5.1	7.7	7.1	9.3	14.7	19.9
Japan	367.4	207.8	136.5	142.7	165.5	228.2	98.6
New Zealand	50.1	23.0	13.5	12.2	33.1	41.7	27.2
Austria	18.5	5.9	3.5	6.8	8.1	15.6	11.6
Belgium–Luxembourg	25.0	20.2	25.6	26.4	22.8	62.8	51.1
Denmark	7.9	3.3	2.3	~	5.5	8.7	15.1
Finland	6.5	5.7	3.7	5.7	6.0	5.1	3.9
France	60.7	98.8	33.3	48.0	39.7	63.0	44.1
Germany	198.2	138.9	111.4	122.4	159.2	247.1	175.6
Iceland							
Ireland	3.1	1.5	2.5	5.2	9.8	11.4	6.4
Italy	77.6	45.4	33.3	28.1	50.2	66.6	42.4
Netherlands	34.8	29.3	16.2	23.4	27.6	54.9	23.0
Norway	3.3	8.1	2.1	1.1	2.1	2.4	1.6
Spain	121.4	64.4	63.1	39.6		55.9	37.7
Sweden	40.2	33.4	34.7	28.4	23.9	40.7	30.4
Switzerland	41.7	26.4	25.2	25.9	68.5	91.6	69.4
United Kingdom	64.0	42.4	33.1	39.0	51.0	92.2	63.4
Developing Countries	678.1	428.7	393.6	429.8	517.5	813.3	701.3
Africa	18.6	11.7	1.2	8.7	.2	7.0	7.0
Algeria				.1			
Benin							
Burkina Faso							
Burundi			.9				
Cameroon							
Central African Rep.							
Congo							
Côte d'Ivoire					.1		
Ethiopia							
Liberia		.3				.4	
Malawi			.2				
Mauritius							
Morocco						.1	1.2
Nigeria			.9	.2		.2	.5
Senegal							
South Africa	18.5	11.4		8.6		6.5	5.8
Tanzania							
Tunisia							
Zaire							
Zambia					.1		
Asia	71.0	33.4	32.2	52.4	47.5	66.5	40.0
Bangladesh			1.4				.2
Brunei	.1						
China, People's Rep.	1.4	1.1	4.3	1.1	6.7	19.6	2.4
Fiji							
Hong Kong	12.7	4.6	3.0	2.3	3.1	6.6	2.3
India	2.4	.7	.5	.4	.7	1.1	.6
Indonesia							
Korea	8.6	11.0	2.8	4.7	9.3	10.9	7.5

Table 2631 (Continued)

PERU ABSOLUTE VALUE OF GOODS TRADED WITH SELECTED REGIONS AND COUNTRIES,[1] 1982–88
(M US)[2]

Category	Exports							Imports						
	1982	1983	1984	1985	1986	1987	1988	1982	1983	1984	1985	1986	1987	1988
Developing Countries (Continued)														
Asia (Continued)														
Malaysia	2.6	.4	~	.2	~	~	~	.1	.2	.2	~	.4	.1	.1
New Caledonia	.9	.5	~	.7	~	1.6	~	~	~	~	.2	.2	.2	.2
Pakistan	.8	.1	~	~	.9	~	3.4	.3	~	.1	.1	.2	.2	.1
Papua New Guinea	4.4	.7	.1	4.1	7.5	6.1	6.1	1.5	.1	1.5	.3	.5	~	~
Philippines	2.8	1.1	~	.4	.2	.8	.8	4.6	.9	8.5	5.3	5.5	8.8	12.9
Singapore	.1	.1	~	.1	.2	.1	.7	.5	.1	~	.7	8.0	.7	.5
Sri Lanka	2.3	~	~	~	~	~	~	~	~	~	~	~	~	~
Thailand	.1	~	~	~	~	~	~	~	~	~	~	~	~	~
Viet Nam	.1	~	~	~	~	~	~	~	~	~	~	~	~	~
Western Samoa														
Asia not specified														
Taiwan Province of China	28.7	47.8	102.1	26.0	36.2	43.9	32.6	38.6	14.7	9.8	37.3	13.0	18.3	13.5
Europe	76.2	35.4	33.7	79.3	66.2	70.9	86.7	4.5	9.5	5.1	3.2	7.4	12.4	9.5
Cyprus	5.9	3.0	.5	10.0	8.5	.1	.4	2.2	2.6	.1	.2	.8	.3	.1
Greece	4.4	2.5	3.5	11.0	8.3	1.7	4.2	1.2	.9	2.5	~	1.8	3.8	.2
Hungary	~	~	~	.2	~	10.9	18.0	~	~	~	1.2	.7	.1	2.7
Malta	3.9	7.5	2.1	9.9	3.6	5.4	2.8	1.2	3.7	.2	~	.3	.1	.1
Poland	8.8	8.3	9.7	11.3	11.7	12.3	16.8	2.1	1.5	1.2	1.2	1.6	1.3	1.4
Portugal	15.8	~	1.3	7.8	2.3	2.9	~	7.0	.1	.1	.1	1.1	4.6	4.7
Romania	~	~	~	4.4	.4	~	.1	.4	.4	.7	.2	.8	1.8	.2
Turkey	37.3	14.2	16.6	24.7	31.4	37.5	44.1	.4	.3	.4	.3	.3	.3	.2
Yugoslavia	~	~	~	~	~	~	.3	~	~	~	~	~	~	~
Europe not specified														
Middle East	7.9	1.6	~	10.1	29.5	33.8	15.3	1.0	.9	2.3	1.3	1.1	9.4	20.8
Egypt	.6	.6	~	~	~	.8	~	~	~	~	~	~	~	~
Iran, I.R. of	5.9	~	~	4.9	24.6	29.0	11.7	~	~	~	~	~	~	~
Iraq	~	~	~	~	~	~	~	~	~	~	.1	.1	~	~
Israel	.3	.1	~	4.4	4.2	2.1	1.9	.8	.8	1.5	1.3	.9	6.6	20.8
Jordan	.2	~	~	.1	~	.2	.2	~	~	~	~	~	~	~
Kuwait	~	.1	~	.1	~	~	.1	~	~	~	~	.1	~	~
Lebanon	~	~	~	~	~	.6	.1	~	~	~	~	~	~	~
Libya	~	~	~	~	~	.6	.4	.1	~	.8	~	~	2.8	~
Saudi Arabia	.3	.5	~	.2	.3	.4	.4	~	~	~	~	~	~	~
Syrian Arab Rep.	.5	.2	~	.5	.4	.9	.3	~	~	~	~	~	~	~
United Arab Emirates	~	.1	~	.1	.1	.4	.5	~	~	~	~	~	~	~
Western Hemisphere	448.3	267.4	367.7	420.9	362.4	420.4	389.9	573.0	373.2	352.8	364.1	461.4	717.9	624.1
A. ARGENTINA	22.2	29.9	34.1	35.9	57.2	38.0	17.3	110.3	105.4	128.8	144.6	133.1	125.4	152.4
Bahamas, The	.2	~	7.0	6.0	~	.1	.1	.1	~	.4	.1	.4	6.4	.3
Barbados	.1	~	~	.2	.2	.2	.3	~	~	~	.1	~	~	~
Belize	~	~	~	~	~	~	~	~	~	~	~	~	~	~
Bermuda	.1	~	~	~	.1	.4	.6	~	~	~	~	~	~	.1
B. BOLIVIA	22.5	13.5	30.0	13.1	10.6	11.2	12.5	21.2	16.1	3.1	10.0	5.3	31.2	11.3
C. BRAZIL	63.7	51.8	45.5	53.5	73.8	110.6	82.0	240.0	90.6	91.8	84.8	116.6	179.6	146.3
D. CHILE	34.0	39.4	50.8	49.9	49.0	31.8	39.8	43.8	35.8	27.0	47.0	46.7	88.0	65.6
E. COLOMBIA	123.9	44.0	75.4	75.5	66.0	61.7	84.2	29.7	20.2	20.2	24.2	57.9	88.6	56.8
F. COSTA RICA	1.8	3.6	~	15.5	5.2	4.9	5.5	1.1	1.5	.5	.2	3.3	.9	.5
Dominica	~	~	~	.5	.1	.4	.6	~	.1	~	~	~	~	~
H. DOMINICAN REP.	.2	~	~	~	~	~	~	~	~	~	~	~	~	~
I. ECUADOR	42.7	28.4	29.9	74.9	28.7	23.3	28.0	29.5	5.6	2.7	6.8	5.1	20.6	51.2
J. EL SALVADOR	1.4	1.0	~	3.1	2.2	3.2	3.1	~	~	~	~	~	~	~
Guadeloupe	.1	~	~	~	~	~	~	~	~	~	~	~	~	~
K. GUATEMALA	.1	.5	~	~	.2	.7	.6	.1	17.7	4.7	~	.3	1.8	.2
Guiana, French	.3	~	~	~	~	~	~	~	~	.6	~	~	~	~
Guyana	.1	.1	~	~	~	~	~	~	.5	~	.2	~	~	.1

Table 2631 (Continued)

PERU ABSOLUTE VALUE OF GOODS TRADED WITH SELECTED REGIONS AND COUNTRIES,[1] 1982–88 (M US)[2]

Category	Exports							Imports						
	1982	1983	1984	1985	1986	1987	1988	1982	1983	1984	1985	1986	1987	1988
Developing Countries (Continued)														
Western Hemisphere (Continued)														
L. HAITI	.3	.1	.1	.2	.1	.1	.4	?	?	?	?	?	?	?
M. HONDURAS	.1	.5	?	.7	.4	.2	.3	?	.1	?	?	?	?	?
Jamaica	?	?	?	.2	?	?	.1	?	.1	?	?	?	?	.1
N. MEXICO	13.3	14.0	19.1	11.0	3.4	38.5	20.0	26.6	22.9	18.4	4.2	23.7	39.7	33.1
Netherlands Antilles	5.6	.1	?	?	?	?	?	10.2	14.8	9.4	1.4	.1	.1	?
O. NICARAGUA	1.2	2.1	6.2	1.6	3.1	8.0	2.5	.1	?	?	?	?	?	.4
P. PANAMA	63.1	9.5	16.5	35.3	14.5	22.0	7.6	20.7	11.3	10.2	9.9	10.8	68.5	39.3
Q. PARAGUAY	.1	?	?	?	.1	.3	.1	1.4	3.6	2.3	2.2	9.6	9.1	9.4
Trinidad and Tobago	.1	?	?	?	?	.1	.1	1.2	?	?	.4	.1	?	.1
S. URUGUAY	1.3	2.0	2.6	2.4	2.1	3.1	2.7	18.0	6.4	7.5	1.8	9.2	10.5	17.2
T. VENEZUELA	50.0	27.1	50.5	41.6	45.7	61.8	82.3	19.0	20.7	25.1	26.0	39.0	47.4	39.7
U.S.S.R. and Other Nonmembers	23.8	30.1	8.5	161.5	125.9	103.4	62.2	9.2	9.1	24.1	2.2	15.4	31.6	10.3
Albania	?	?	?	1.1	.2	?	?	?	?	?	?	.1	.3	.2
Bulgaria	14.7	6.4	8.5	15.2	6.0	9.3	8.9	.3	5.7	10.0	.1	7.5	2.4	.9
G. CUBA	?	?	?	?	2.0	3.2	13.3	5.8	2.6	3.5	1.3	2.5	4.6	4.1
Czechoslovakia	?	4.1	?	3.2	14.3	18.0	5.0	?	.2	9.7	.5	2.6	.9	.3
Eastern Germany	5.8	1.6	?	.1	.1	2.4	7.6	?	.2	?	.1	.1	.9	1.0
North Korea	.8	.9	?	4.6	3.8	1.9	1.0	?	?	?	.1	?	9.8	?
U.S.S.R.	8.2	17.1	?	137.3	99.6	68.6	27.4	3.0	.4	.8	.2	2.6	13.6	3.9
Country or area not specified	78.8	75.9	333.3	30.7	16.1	20.9	29.3	?	?	4.3	.2	1.0	221.0	1.8
Memorandum Items														
EEC	584.3	580.3	668.7	670.7	623.5	657.3	796.6	597.1	448.2	322.1	333.6	368.2	664.2	460.5
Oil Exporting Countries	60.4	32.7	50.5	48.7	84.0	115.2	109.0	19.1	20.7	25.9	26.1	39.2	50.2	40.8
Non-Oil Developing Countries	656.7	394.0	468.8	646.3	571.1	611.7	666.3	659.0	408.0	367.7	403.7	478.3	763.1	660.5
% Distribution														
Industrial Countries	71.9	79.3	72.1	70.2	68.2	67.3	67.8	77.1	78.5	71.7	69.7	69.3	65.3	66.2
Developing Countries	24.6	16.6	16.8	23.3	26.2	27.9	28.8	22.6	21.1	26.4	30.2	29.7	26.5	33.2
Africa	2.3	.5	?	.5	.7	.8	.6	.6	.6	.1	.6	?	.2	.3
Asia	4.1	4.2	3.8	5.7	7.1	7.0	9.9	2.4	1.6	2.2	3.7	2.7	2.2	1.9
Europe	2.6	1.4	1.1	2.7	2.6	2.7	3.2	.5	.5	.3	.2	.4	.4	.5
Middle East	.3	.1	?	.3	1.2	1.3	.6	?	?	.2	.1	.1	.3	1.0
Western Hemisphere	15.4	10.4	11.9	14.1	14.5	16.1	14.5	19.1	18.3	23.6	25.6	26.5	23.4	29.6
U.S.S.R. and Other Nonmembers	.8	1.2	.3	5.4	5.0	4.0	2.3	.3	.4	1.6	.2	.9	1.0	.5
Annual PC														
World	-10.1	-11.7	19.7	-3.4	-16.0	4.0	3.2	-12.6	-32.2	-26.7	-4.6	22.3	76.2	-31.3
Industrial Countries	-3.0	-2.6	8.8	-5.9	-18.4	2.7	3.9	1.0	-31.0	-33.0	-7.3	21.7	65.9	-30.3
Developing Countries	2.8	-40.5	21.7	33.8	-5.7	11.0	6.7	13.3	-36.8	-8.2	9.2	20.4	57.2	-13.8
Africa	148.9	-79.1	-99.9	?	13.3	10.7	-15.1	-9.1	-37.1	-89.7	622.6	-97.9	?	-1.2
Asia	-25.0	-8.3	8.7	42.9	6.0	1.6	46.6	-.1	-52.9	-3.6	62.8	-9.4	40.1	-40.0
Europe	3.8	-53.6	-4.7	135.4	-16.5	7.1	22.3	4.5	-34.3	-46.3	-37.7	131.4	68.3	-23.0
Middle East	-66.8	-79.7	?	?	193.2	14.5	-54.9	109.8	-6.5	151.0	-43.8	-13.5	749.2	120.4
Western Hemisphere	7.8	-40.4	37.5	14.5	-13.9	16.0	-7.2	16.3	-34.9	-5.5	3.2	26.7	55.6	-13.1
U.S.S.R. and Other Nonmembers	-67.9	26.5	-71.7	?	-22.1	-17.9	-39.9	6.3	-1.2	164.7	-91.0	606.7	106.1	-67.4

1. DOT data may differ between countries and from IFS data because of the time it takes for an export to become an import, etc.
2. Data may be calculated from partner's reported data or estimated on basis of less than 12 months.

SOURCE: IMF-DOT-Y, 1989.

Ch. 26, Direction of Trade and Major Trading Partners 741

Table 2632

URUGUAY ABSOLUTE VALUE OF GOODS TRADED WITH SELECTED REGIONS AND COUNTRIES,[1] 1982–88
(M US)[2]

Category	Exports							Imports						
	1982	1983	1984	1985	1986	1987	1988	1982	1983	1984	1985	1986	1987	1988
IFS World Total	1,022.9	1,045.1	933.8	909.0	1,087.8	1,189.2	1,404.5	1,110.0	787.5	776.7	707.7	870.0	1,141.9	1,157.2
DOTS World Total	1,032.3	1,063.2	937.8	858.5	1,088.0	1,189.1	1,388.5	1,110.0	624.2	774.3	707.7	869.9	1,141.9	1,176.9
Industrial Countries	375.6	378.4	374.7	354.8	451.1	581.9	559.5	335.3	185.9	246.0	216.3	322.1	426.6	431.5
United States	76.7	103.5	127.1	129.6	130.8	177.0	156.3	35.0	52.1	66.0	53.8	74.2	91.2	93.3
Canada	7.3	25.9	11.9	6.8	6.7	9.7	11.2	10.2	2.6	6.3	4.2	7.5	15.7	5.7
Australia	.6	.9	3.0	2.8	2.5	9.3	3.7	5.3	4.4	3.2	2.0	3.8	3.5	.7
Japan	18.1	20.0	25.6	19.0	15.5	17.4	18.0	30.5	14.9	14.3	15.8	29.5	36.4	34.9
New Zealand	~	.2	.1	~	~	.1	.1	.1	.1	3.0	.1	.3	2.0	.5
Austria	6.8	3.2	2.6	.6	.9	2.3	2.5	3.8	2.5	2.3	2.4	2.9	7.4	3.7
Belgium-Luxembourg	15.5	11.6	6.6	5.1	5.9	7.0	6.2	4.1	3.1	4.1	3.9	4.5	5.9	5.1
Denmark	.7	.5	.3	.3	.8	1.5	1.1	2.8	1.4	1.5	2.1	2.8	4.6	6.2
Finland	4.5	4.5	6.9	4.2	4.8	7.4	~	.4	.1	.4	1.0	1.9	2.8	2.6
France	23.4	17.8	14.6	14.2	26.5	34.4	40.5	26.6	15.0	14.8	12.1	23.9	38.3	52.1
Germany	91.8	80.4	79.3	66.1	99.0	121.9	114.8	77.0	37.4	45.9	49.4	66.2	92.6	75.4
Ireland	~	~	~	~	~	.7	.7	.6	.7	.6	.4	.8	.8	.7
Italy	38.3	20.7	19.6	22.2	36.5	59.9	52.9	21.8	9.6	30.4	15.4	21.6	24.8	29.5
Netherlands	29.6	30.4	22.7	27.4	32.9	32.6	59.5	9.0	7.3	8.4	6.9	13.4	14.6	15.3
Norway	.2	.3	.4	.2	.5	.1	2.0	.6	.5	.1	1.3	.5	1.4	.3
Spain	11.0	6.9	9.1	13.3	16.1	22.8	20.4	13.2	5.7	12.6	10.5	15.0	22.9	24.9
Sweden	2.3	1.5	1.3	1.0	2.5	6.6	4.0	4.2	3.8	1.8	4.5	10.0	6.5	44.7
Switzerland	12.1	8.2	6.1	6.3	11.5	15.7	9.6	12.8	10.9	14.1	13.0	19.3	20.4	9.6
United Kingdom	36.7	41.9	37.7	35.6	57.6	54.5	55.9	27.1	13.8	16.1	17.4	24.0	35.0	35.8
Developing Countries	560.2	599.5	482.4	438.1	590.9	544.5	716.8	719.8	426.0	498.6	447.2	537.7	706.4	717.5
Africa	30.8	23.0	19.9	9.1	10.1	10.2	13.7	136.3	108.5	117.4	74.4	23.5	61.5	20.4
Algeria	.3	.3	.6	~	~	1.4	.8	~	~	~	~	~	~	~
Angola	~	.5	3.3	~	3.8	~	~	~	~	~	~	~	~	~
Benin	~	~	~	~	~	1.9	~	~	~	~	~	~	~	~
Cameroon	.6	1.0	1.2	1.4	1.4	1.1	~	~	~	~	~	.1	~	~
Congo	~	.4	.9	~	.3	~	.6	~	~	~	~	~	~	~
Côte d'Ivoire	1.0	.5	~	.4	~	.4	.3	~	~	~	~	~	~	~
Ethiopia	~	~	~	~	~	.2	~	~	~	~	~	~	~	~
Gabon	.3	.1	.2	.2	~	~	1.9	~	~	.1	.1	~	~	~
Ghana	~	2.2	~	.2	1.2	.7	~	~	~	~	~	~	~	~
Liberia	~	~	.4	.8	~	~	~	~	~	~	~	~	~	~
Morocco	2.0	.6	.3	~	.2	.2	~	.2	~	.1	~	.8	1.3	.2
Mozambique	~	~	~	.1	~	~	~	~	~	~	~	~	~	~
Nigeria	14.7	10.8	3.1	.2	~	.2	~	127.8	103.1	114.0	69.6	16.3	52.4	14.5
Senegal	.6	~	~	~	3.8	1.9	~	.6	.7	1.1	.6	.8	1.1	~
Sierra Leone	~	~	~	~	~	~	6.7	~	~	~	~	~	~	~
South Africa	7.8	5.3	8.8	5.5	2.6	3.0	2.7	2.9	4.1	1.6	2.6	4.2	2.8	1.9
Sudan	~	~	~	~	~	~	~	~	~	.1	~	.8	.8	~
Togo	~	~	.1	~	~	~	~	.5	.2	.2	1.1	.8	1.3	2.1
Tunisia	4.2	.1	.2	.3	.6	1.2	.6	3.9	.5	.3	.3	.4	1.7	1.6
Zaire	~	~	.2	~	~	~	~	~	.2	.3	.2	.1	.1	.1
Zimbabwe	~	1.1	~	~	~	~	.1	.3	.3	~	~	~	~	~
Asia	29.4	37.5	76.3	76.1	103.0	92.2	182.3	22.5	9.9	12.0	11.0	21.3	34.8	40.0
Bangladesh	9.0	12.2	38.4	43.1	60.6	44.7	135.9	1.6	1.7	2.3	1.3	1.9	2.5	1.6
China, People's Rep.	5.8	5.6	6.4	9.4	13.9	16.7	21.8	2.4	.6	.5	.5	.8	1.7	2.1
Hong Kong	.4	.1	.2	~	.2	~	.5	4.0	.9	1.3	2.1	4.6	7.7	9.3
India	.1	1.3	~	~	~	~	~	1.8	1.4	.3	.2	.8	.9	1.2
Indonesia	1.0	5.0	6.4	3.6	2.6	5.9	7.5	~	.3	.1	.1	~	.1	~
Korea	~	~	~	~	~	~	~	2.1	.5	.8	.8	2.1	5.6	8.2
Macao	~	.2	.2	.3	.6	.3	.1	~	.2	.2	.3	~	.1	.1
Malaysia	.2	.2	~	.6	1.4	~	~	1.6	1.6	2.5	1.2	1.3	2.6	2.9

Table 2632 (Continued)

URUGUAY ABSOLUTE VALUE OF GOODS TRADED WITH SELECTED REGIONS AND COUNTRIES,[1] 1982-88
(M US)[2]

Category	Exports							Imports						
	1982	1983	1984	1985	1986	1987	1988	1982	1983	1984	1985	1986	1987	1988
Developing Countries (Continued)														
Asia (Continued)														
Pakistan	?	?	?	?	?	?	?	?	?	?	?	?	?	.1
Philippines	.3	.4	.1	.8	1.0	.8	.7	.1	.2	?	?	.3	.3	.1
Singapore	.2	.3	1.9	2.2	3.2	2.1	2.4	.2	.7	1.2	1.3	3.1	3.2	3.4
Sri Lanka	?	?	?	?	?	?	?	2.2	.7	.5	.5	.6	.5	.6
Thailand	?	?	?	?	.5	?	.5	.7	.3	?	?	?	?	.1
Asia not specified	?	?	?	1.1	2.3	6.0	2.8	?	?	?	?	?	?	?
Taiwan Province of China	12.4	12.5	22.7	15.3	17.8	15.7	10.0	5.9	1.6	2.5	2.9	5.6	9.7	10.1
Europe	32.6	20.9	23.0	20.6	20.4	21.5	25.9	6.1	2.0	1.2	1.6	6.5	4.7	10.1
Cyprus	.5	.3	.1	.1	.1	.2	.4	?	.2	?	?	?	?	?
Greece	6.3	2.4	3.8	3.1	?	?	3.5	.1	.2	.1	?	?	?	.5
Hungary	6.7	3.9	4.9	7.5	6.3	9.6	7.5	1.1	.4	.4	.9	3.2	1.6	2.2
Malta	.4	.5	.6	.7	.6	.3	.3	?	?	?	?	?	?	?
Poland	1.8	3.9	.8	1.9	3.3	4.2	4.4	.8	.3	.3	.4	.5	2.0	1.4
Portugal	7.3	5.2	9.5	6.8	6.4	5.3	8.2	.4	.2	.2	?	.3	.5	.3
Romania	?	.1	.5	?	.1	?	?	1.1	.1	.2	?	2.3	?	4.9
Turkey	1.5	1.2	?	.1	.1	.7	.9	.1	?	.1	?	.2	.4	.4
Yugoslavia	8.1	3.4	2.9	.5	3.6	1.1	.7	.1	?	?	.1	.1	.2	.3
Europe not specified	?	?	?	?	?	?	?	2.5	.8	?	?	?	?	.1
Middle East	149.2	266.4	117.5	93.5	30.8	59.7	114.3	90.8	29.4	79.7	104.4	46.1	45.9	43.2
Egypt	46.6	83.5	18.0	?	?	.4	12.0	89.2	29.2	78.8	103.4	17.7	18.0	14.3
Iran, I.R. of	55.0	119.8	49.2	61.6	7.8	26.8	24.0	?	?	?	?	?	?	?
Iraq	.2	8.1	?	?	?	2.1	32.0	?	?	?	?	?	?	?
Israel	12.7	21.0	19.4	14.2	13.7	20.8	25.6	1.7	.3	.9	1.0	4.3	3.4	1.5
Jordan	11.3	2.4	.8	.6	.3	1.3	.9	?	?	?	?	?	?	?
Kuwait	8.4	2.4	3.1	2.2	.4	1.0	1.7	?	?	?	?	?	?	?
Lebanon	3.6	.3	.1	?	?	?	.1	?	?	?	?	?	?	?
Libya	?	.2	1.9	?	?	?	7.6	?	?	?	?	?	?	?
Qatar	?	1.7	?	?	?	?	?	?	?	?	?	?	?	?
Saudi Arabia	11.2	26.4	24.2	14.3	8.4	6.1	10.3	?	?	?	?	?	?	4.1
United Arab Emirates	.1	.5	1.7	.6	.1	.3	.1	?	?	?	?	?	4.8	11.5
Yemen, P.D. Rep.	?	?	?	?	?	1.0	?	?	?	?	?	24.1	19.7	11.7
Western Hemisphere	318.2	251.7	245.7	238.9	426.6	360.8	380.7	464.1	276.3	288.3	255.8	440.4	559.5	603.7
A. ARGENTINA	109.1	91.1	88.3	63.1	88.7	113.2	100.0	86.0	62.3	87.4	86.4	123.8	156.7	179.0
Bahamas, The	.2	.1	.2	.1	.2	.3	.2	?	.1	.1	.1	.1	.1	.1
Barbados	.2	.2	.3	.1	.5	.1	.6	?	?	?	?	?	?	?
Bermuda	?	?	?	?	.1	?	?	?	?	?	?	?	?	?
B. BOLIVIA	1.0	1.8	1.4	1.0	.9	.8	1.2	.1	.1	?	.2	?	?	.3
C. BRAZIL	145.8	121.3	114.8	143.4	296.3	204.1	229.1	140.6	69.9	127.1	125.8	212.2	279.1	307.0
D. CHILE	21.8	9.3	10.5	4.0	6.7	7.9	10.4	9.0	5.7	6.1	9.1	13.4	17.0	22.9
E. COLOMBIA	3.0	3.6	3.9	6.8	4.4	4.9	4.5	.5	.3	.1	.4	.4	.6	.6
F. COSTA RICA	?	?	?	?	?	.1	.3	?	?	?	?	.1	?	?
Dominica	?	?	?	?	?	?	?	?	?	?	?	?	?	?
H. DOMINICAN REP.	?	.2	.1	?	?	?	?	.4	.4	.2	?	?	?	.2
I. ECUADOR	1.2	.9	1.3	1.4	1.0	.3	1.5	34.4	?	.1	.1	4.3	.1	.1
L. HAITI	?	?	?	?	?	.7	.5	?	?	?	?	?	?	?
M. HONDURAS	?	?	?	?	?	?	.1	.1	?	?	?	?	?	?
Jamaica	.1	?	?	.1	?	?	.5	.9	?	?	?	?	?	?
N. MEXICO	3.9	3.3	4.8	6.8	7.1	10.1	18.2	83.3	66.1	47.3	15.5	64.2	86.1	61.7
Netherlands Antilles	?	.5	?	.3	.2	.8	.7	6.0	4.7	2.1	4.2	?	?	4.6
P. PANAMA	3.2	?	.3	.3	3.2	?	?	2.3	3.4	1.6	1.6	2.3	3.9	3.6
Q. PARAGUAY	9.9	8.2	7.4	6.1	4.6	6.8	7.5	5.7	7.0	11.4	8.2	11.9	11.0	14.0
R. PERU	16.6	5.0	6.3	1.8	10.0	8.1	3.8	1.0	2.0	2.7	2.4	2.2	3.9	4.1
Trinidad and Tobago	?	.2	.3	?	?	?	?	2.6	1.1	.5	?	?	?	2.6
T. VENEZUELA	2.1	2.4	5.5	3.7	2.5	2.3	1.4	91.1	53.1	1.7	1.7	5.4	.9	2.9
Western Hem. not specified	?	3.7	?	.1	?	?	.1	.1	?	?	?	?	?	?

Table 2632 (Continued)

URUGUAY ABSOLUTE VALUE OF GOODS TRADED WITH SELECTED REGIONS AND COUNTRIES,[1] 1982–88 (M US)[2]

Category	Exports							Imports						
	1982	1983	1984	1985	1986	1987	1988	1982	1983	1984	1985	1986	1987	1988
U.S.S.R. and Other Nonmembers	92.5	73.6	67.6	59.9	40.5	59.1	109.7	4.7	12.3	29.7	43.5	9.7	8.4	27.8
Bulgaria	.1	.4	.5	.4	.5	~	1.3	1.2	.3	~	~	.2	~	.1
G. CUBA	~	~	~	~	1.1	4.0	5.0	~	~	~	~	.2	.2	.2
Czechoslovakia	6.4	8.2	17.8	12.3	10.9	8.9	16.3	1.2	.3	.6	.4	1.4	2.3	3.4
Eastern Germany	7.4	3.1	3.6	4.5	4.7	5.4	6.1	.6	9.3	.7	1.2	.9	2.4	3.6
North Korea	~	~	~	~	.9	.1	.4	~	~	~	~	.1	.2	~
U.S.S.R.	78.6	61.9	45.7	42.7	23.3	40.0	80.7	1.7	2.4	28.4	41.8	7.2	3.3	20.5
Country or area not specified	.7	11.7	12.9	5.8	5.5	3.7	2.5	.2	~	.1	.7	.4	.5	.2
Special categories	3.2	~	~	~	~	~	~	~	~	~	~	~	~	~
Memorandum Items														
EEC	260.5	217.8	203.1	194.0	281.8	340.6	363.7	182.9	94.4	134.6	118.2	172.4	239.9	245.8
Oil Exporting Countries	92.1	174.0	89.2	82.7	19.3	40.0	78.0	308.1	185.7	194.4	174.8	63.5	95.9	59.1
Non-Oil Developing Countries	468.2	425.4	393.2	355.4	571.6	504.5	638.8	411.6	240.4	304.2	272.4	474.2	610.5	658.4
% Distribution														
Industrial Countries	36.4	35.6	40.0	41.3	41.5	48.9	40.3	34.7	29.8	31.8	30.6	37.0	37.4	36.7
Developing Countries	54.3	56.4	51.4	51.0	54.3	45.8	51.6	64.8	68.2	64.4	63.2	61.8	61.9	61.0
Africa	3.0	2.2	2.1	1.1	.9	.9	1.0	12.3	17.4	15.2	10.5	2.7	5.4	1.7
Asia	2.8	3.5	8.1	8.9	9.5	7.8	13.1	2.0	1.6	1.5	1.6	2.4	3.0	3.4
Europe	3.2	2.0	2.4	2.4	1.9	1.8	1.9	.5	.3	.2	.2	.8	.4	.9
Middle East	14.5	25.1	12.5	10.9	2.8	5.0	8.2	8.2	4.7	10.3	14.8	5.3	4.0	3.7
Western Hemisphere	30.8	23.7	26.2	27.8	39.2	30.3	27.4	41.8	44.3	37.2	36.1	50.6	49.0	51.3
U.S.S.R. and Other Nonmembers	9.0	6.9	7.2	7.0	3.7	5.0	7.9	.4	2.0	3.8	6.1	1.1	.7	2.4
Annual PC														
World	-12.7	3.0	-11.8	-8.4	26.7	9.3	16.8	-31.8	-43.8	24.0	-8.6	22.9	31.3	3.1
Industrial Countries	-23.0	.7	-1.0	-5.3	27.2	29.0	-3.9	-33.8	-51.7	32.3	-12.0	48.9	32.4	1.2
Developing Countries	-8.5	7.0	-19.5	-9.2	34.9	-7.9	31.7	-30.5	-40.8	17.0	-10.3	20.2	31.4	1.6
Africa	-60.1	-25.2	-13.5	-54.3	11.1	.7	34.7	-38.8	-20.4	8.2	-36.6	-68.5	162.2	-66.8
Asia	3.5	27.6	103.6	-.3	35.4	-10.5	97.6	-44.6	-56.1	21.2	-8.1	93.4	63.4	15.0
Europe	-13.3	-36.1	10.0	-10.3	-1.0	5.4	20.5	-36.9	-67.8	-36.8	26.1	319.8	-28.0	114.5
Middle East	-2.9	78.6	-55.9	-20.5	-67.1	94.0	91.3	356.3	-67.6	170.6	31.1	-55.9	-.3	-5.8
Western Hemisphere	1.0	-20.9	-2.4	-2.8	78.6	-15.4	5.5	-37.5	-40.5	4.4	-11.3	72.2	27.1	7.9
U.S.S.R. and Other Nonmembers	11.9	-20.5	-8.1	-11.4	-32.4	46.0	85.7	-49.6	161.9	142.4	46.2	-77.7	-13.9	233.0

1. DOT data may differ between countries and from IFS data because of the time it takes for an export to become an import, etc.
2. Data may be calculated from partner's reported data or estimated on basis of less than 12 months.

SOURCE: IMF-DOT-Y, 1989.

Table 2633

VENEZUELA ABSOLUTE VALUE OF GOODS TRADED WITH SELECTED REGIONS AND COUNTRIES,[1] 1982–88 (M US)[2]

Category	Exports							Imports						
	1982	1983	1984	1985	1986	1987	1988	1982	1983	1984	1985	1986	1987	1988
IFS World Total	16,499	15,048	13,458	12,272	10,049	8,402	9,629	11,661	7,847	6,842	7,367	8,591	7,876	11,407
DOTS World Total	16,957	14,755	16,094	14,189	8,412	10,843	10,365	11,650	5,786	7,007	7,304	7,635	8,711	10,472
Industrial Countries	10,523	10,470	10,696	10,871	5,739	7,545	7,128	9,789	4,777	5,757	6,076	6,513	7,390	8,779
United States	4,712	4,588	6,772	6,526	3,764	5,347	5,071	5,332	2,673	3,395	3,469	3,503	3,889	4,611
Canada	1,440	557	730	716	272	454	371	458	291	267	281	194	232	310
Australia	759	1,696	236	153	1	1	2	33	3	9	5	8	11	15
Japan	563	394	376	415	279	327	422	1,190	328	337	416	529	529	555
New Zealand	~	~	~	6	~	6	1	48	34	28	33	15	56	75
Austria	~	~	4	20	19	1	2	17	12	12	27	41	32	56
Belgium-Luxembourg	148	218	118	98	69	97	124	146	64	92	88	117	141	103
Denmark	6	21	~	40	~	1	1	34	38	50	46	34	36	73
Finland	3	5	6	~	~	3	7	14	34	25	28	26	35	32
France	256	196	182	166	134	93	93	392	240	238	256	331	309	460
Germany	391	595	573	606	487	580	567	600	313	373	414	562	750	762
Ireland	~	~	~	~	~	~	~	23	11	16	7	8	28	39
Italy	980	843	669	742	147	200	121	549	221	300	312	356	434	596
Netherlands	417	801	442	720	237	82	62	211	129	165	155	132	144	154
Norway	6	2	20	43	30	28	20	14	5	10	21	16	35	29
Spain	383	173	138	224	41	63	50	307	150	152	183	193	228	274
Sweden	221	140	114	154	55	121	82	63	46	44	40	39	70	130
Switzerland	2	1	~	~	1	6	9	98	58	73	75	97	136	188
United Kingdom	236	240	316	242	203	136	124	260	127	171	220	312	296	317
Developing Countries	3,944	3,432	3,271	2,855	1,816	2,312	2,203	1,756	927	1,187	1,179	1,083	1,290	1,660
Africa	5	156	26	10	7	1	~	5	3	2	50	34	45	55
Algeria	~	5	20	10	7	1	~	~	~	~	~	1	~	~
Morocco	~	~	~	~	~	1	~	1	~	~	2	2	6	5
South Africa	57	~	~	~	~	~	~	~	~	~	30	26	~	~
Tunisia	~	~	~	~	~	~	~	1	~	1	~	~	6	7
Africa not specified	5	151	6	~	~	~	~	4	3	2	18	5	39	43
Asia	155	34	34	192	98	105	105	251	75	110	154	150	162	227
China, People's Rep.	~	3	3	114	45	32	15	49	11	13	14	3	17	20
Hong Kong	~	3	9	11	5	15	16	52	15	13	28	25	17	48
India	~	~	~	14	6	7	7	1	1	1	1	1	1	2
Indonesia	~	~	~	~	~	~	1	11	7	10	6	5	9	1
Korea	50	4	1	20	2	3	6	45	14	37	27	33	36	65
Malaysia	~	~	~	~	2	2	1	4	~	~	~	~	~	3
Pakistan	4	2	~	~	~	2	5	1	~	~	~	~	2	~
Philippines	~	~	~	~	~	1	~	7	3	~	5	5	~	~
Singapore	23	~	6	~	~	1	6	7	~	5	4	3	6	13
Thailand	2	12	10	18	12	14	4	13	~	4	~	6	~	1
Asia not specified	1	~	~	~	25	29	30	~	3	4	~	6	6	6
Taiwan Province of China	18	13	4	15	3	2	13	67	23	27	74	69	84	68
Europe	141	70	108	32	23	23	31	39	6	16	36	41	51	82
Cyprus	33	~	~	~	~	~	~	6	~	1	~	1	1	2
Greece	~	~	~	5	1	~	~	6	~	1	1	1	1	2
Hungary	~	~	~	~	~	~	~	2	~	1	1	1	2	4
Poland	~	~	1	2	4	5	5	3	~	3	~	7	3	9
Portugal	103	67	99	18	3	3	6	20	5	7	7	24	8	35
Romania	~	~	3	~	12	14	15	3	~	1	16	6	32	3
Turkey	4	3	5	3	2	32	4	2	~	2	7	2	2	2
Yugoslavia	1	~	~	4	1	2	1	3	~	1	5	2	2	27

Table 2633 (Continued)

VENEZUELA ABSOLUTE VALUE OF GOODS TRADED WITH SELECTED REGIONS AND COUNTRIES,[1] 1982-88
(M US)[2]

Category	Exports							Imports						
	1982	1983	1984	1985	1986	1987	1988	1982	1983	1984	1985	1986	1987	1988
Developing Countries (Continued)														
Middle East														
Egypt	15	81	12	18	2	5	5	5	7	6	3	—	35	50
Iran, I.R. of	14	2	3	—	—	3	5	2	—	—	—	—	—	—
Israel	—	66	—	—	2	—	—	3	6	—	3	—	32	45
Jordan	1	—	2	—	—	1	—	—	—	—	—	—	—	—
Kuwait	—	5	7	—	—	—	—	—	—	—	—	—	—	—
Lebanon	—	—	—	—	—	—	—	—	—	—	—	—	—	—
Libya	—	—	—	18	—	1	1	—	—	6	—	—	1	2
Saudi Arabia	—	8	—	—	—	—	1	—	—	—	—	—	1	2
Syrian Arab Rep.	—	—	—	—	—	—	—	—	—	—	—	—	—	—
Western Hemisphere	3,628	3,091	3,091	2,603	1,686	2,179	2,062	1,456	836	1,053	936	858	996	1,246
A. ARGENTINA	14	4	3	1	8	12	12	133	60	126	84	42	72	79
Barbados	26	20	20	31	21	17	18	—	—	1	—	—	—	—
B. BOLIVIA	—	—	—	—	—	—	1	5	1	1	—	—	—	—
C. BRAZIL	900	553	510	252	69	157	142	469	345	366	310	344	372	503
D. CHILE	241	209	226	240	116	131	150	51	36	41	34	40	75	105
E. COLOMBIA	301	323	321	225	105	110	118	239	91	113	111	80	106	117
F. COSTA RICA	104	63	92	122	51	81	93	3	3	2	5	6	2	5
Dominica	—	—	—	—	—	—	—	—	—	—	—	1	1	1
H. DOMINICAN REP.	239	287	324	277	135	155	163	46	4	29	4	2	1	1
I. ECUADOR	36	6	2	2	5	199	20	56	4	3	2	2	8	4
J. EL SALVADOR	78	70	73	79	56	64	68	—	—	—	1	—	2	2
K. GUATEMALA	78	97	93	74	41	47	50	10	—	5	1	1	2	2
L. HAITI	—	—	3	13	—	—	1	1	2	—	—	4	—	—
M. HONDURAS	26	67	99	97	45	52	54	6	8	1	—	—	2	2
Jamaica	206	144	93	146	63	45	47	9	—	—	—	—	—	3
N. MEXICO	22	1	2	13	6	9	14	79	56	57	55	60	99	148
O. NICARAGUA	39	2	5	5	7	8	8	—	—	—	—	—	—	—
P. PANAMA	179	121	120	118	43	48	7	191	43	84	106	91	98	107
Q. PARAGUAY	—	—	—	—	—	—	—	12	1	23	7	—	6	—
R. PERU	20	21	20	27	31	47	40	50	29	45	47	54	64	82
Suriname	—	—	2	3	2	7	7	33	21	22	27	21	3	3
Trinidad and Tobago	8	82	87	52	34	15	24	12	21	9	8	14	16	10
S. URUGUAY	88	11	2	1	—	1	3	4	3	8	4	3	3	1
Western Hem. not specified	1,023	1,010	994	825	848	975	1,024	47	127	118	131	93	67	74
U.S.S.R. and Other Nonmembers	27	98	205	442	363	417	438	19	9	13	24	15	30	33
Bulgaria	—	—	1	28	9	4	6	—	1	1	—	—	—	2
G. CUBA	20	84	204	425	360	414	435	4	1	2	16	4	15	16
Czechoslovakia	—	—	—	14	3	3	4	3	8	10	7	10	11	12
Eastern Germany	6	8	—	3	—	3	—	—	—	—	—	—	—	—
U.S.S.R.	1	6	1	—	—	—	—	1	—	—	1	1	2	3
Country or area not specified	2,463	755	1,922	21	494	568	597	86	73	50	25	24	—	—
Memorandum Items														
EEC	2,953	3,154	2,537	2,861	1,322	1,256	1,149	2,548	1,298	1,565	1,688	2,053	2,375	2,788
Oil Exporting Countries	—	71	31	28	9	4	6	11	8	16	6	6	12	5
Non-Oil Developing Countries	3,944	3,361	3,240	2,827	1,807	2,309	2,197	1,745	919	1,171	1,173	1,077	1,279	1,655
% Distribution														
Industrial Countries	62.1	71.0	66.5	76.6	68.2	69.6	68.8	84.0	82.6	82.2	83.2	85.3	84.8	83.8
Developing Countries	23.3	23.3	20.3	20.1	21.6	21.3	21.3	15.1	16.0	16.9	16.1	14.2	14.8	15.9
Africa	—	1.1	.2	.1	.1	—	—	—	.1	—	.7	.4	.5	.5
Asia	.9	.2	.2	1.4	1.2	1.0	1.0	2.2	1.3	1.6	2.1	2.0	1.9	2.2
Europe	.8	.5	.7	.2	.3	.2	.3	.3	.1	.2	.5	.5	.6	.8
Middle East	.1	.5	.1	.1	—	—	.1	—	.1	.1	—	—	.4	.5
Western Hemisphere	21.4	20.9	19.2	18.3	20.0	20.1	19.9	12.5	14.4	15.0	12.8	11.2	11.4	11.9
U.S.S.R. and Other Nonmembers	.2	.7	1.3	3.1	4.3	3.8	4.2	.2	.2	.2	.3	.2	.3	.3

Table 2633 (Continued)

VENEZUELA ABSOLUTE VALUE OF GOODS TRADED WITH SELECTED REGIONS AND COUNTRIES,[1] 1982-88

(M US)[2]

Category	Exports							Imports						
	1982	1983	1984	1985	1986	1987	1988	1982	1983	1984	1985	1986	1987	1988
Annual PC														
World	-15.2	-13.0	9.1	-11.8	-40.7	28.9	-4.4	-3.7	-50.3	21.1	4.2	4.5	14.1	20.2
Industrial Countries	-9.6	-.5	2.2	1.6	-47.2	31.5	-5.5	-6.0	-51.2	20.5	5.5	7.2	13.5	18.8
Developing Countries	-50.7	-13.0	-4.7	-12.7	-36.4	27.3	-4.7	5.8	-47.2	28.0	-.7	-8.1	19.1	28.7
Africa	-97.1	~	-83.3	-61.5	-30.0	-90.0	-71.4	-95.5	-40.0	-33.3	~	-32.0	33.7	20.2
Asia	-42.3	-78.1	~	464.7	-49.0	7.2	-.4	3.3	-70.1	46.7	40.0	-2.6	8.1	40.1
Europe	-39.2	-50.4	54.3	-70.4	-28.1	-1.3	36.1	-21.0	-84.6	166.7	125.0	13.9	25.1	59.9
Middle	~	440.0	-85.2	50.0	-88.9	125.0	20.0	-21.4	40.0	-14.3	-50.0	~	~	42.0
Western Hemisphere	-50.5	-14.8	~	-15.8	-35.2	29.3	-5.4	16.5	-42.6	26.0	-11.1	-8.3	16.1	25.1
U.S.S.R. and Other Nonmembers	-71.9	263.0	109.2	115.6	-17.9	15.0	5.0	-14.3	-52.6	44.4	84.6	-37.5	103.0	9.9

1. DOT data may differ between countries and from IFS data because of the time it takes for an export to become an import, etc.
2. Data may be calculated from partner's reported data or estimated on basis of less than 12 months.

SOURCE: IMF-DOT-Y, 1989.

Table 2634

UNITED STATES VALUE OF GOODS TRADED WITH EACH LATIN AMERICAN COUNTRY, 19 LC, 1982–88
(M US)

Category	Exports 1982	1983	1984	1985	1986	1987	1988	Imports 1982	1983	1984	1985	1986	1987	1988
Western Hemisphere	33,591	25,717	29,682	31,020	31,071	34,995	43,803	39,602	43,581	50,065	49,096	44,112	49,094	53,705
A. ARGENTINA	1,294	965	900	721	943	1,090	1,056	1,222	939	1,042	1,167	939	1,176	1,568
B. BOLIVIA	99	102	106	120	112	140	148	113	172	160	101	127	113	121
C. BRAZIL	3,423	2,557	2,640	3,140	3,885	4,040	4,289	4,643	5,381	8,273	8,147	7,340	8,433	9,977
D. CHILE	925	729	805	682	824	796	1,065	729	1,053	871	858	935	1,105	1,326
E. COLOMBIA	1,903	1,514	1,450	1,468	1,319	1,412	1,758	883	1,058	1,253	1,456	2,039	2,414	2,349
G. COSTA RICA	330	382	423	422	483	582	696	421	453	544	570	720	750	861
H. DOMINICAN REP.	664	632	646	742	921	1,142	1,362	669	855	1,068	1,031	1,139	1,217	1,479
I. ECUADOR	828	597	655	591	601	621	684	1,227	1,520	1,804	1,975	1,603	1,390	1,370
J. EL SALVADOR	292	365	426	446	518	390	483	333	362	406	413	401	300	299
K. GUATEMALA	390	316	377	405	400	480	591	365	404	479	448	647	542	477
L. HAITI	299	366	419	396	387	459	479	326	352	395	406	391	410	399
M. HONDURAS	275	299	322	308	363	418	478	426	435	450	433	487	565	516
N. MEXICO	11,817	9,082	11,992	13,635	12,392	14,582	20,643	15,770	17,019	18,267	19,392	17,558	20,520	23,545
O. NICARAGUA	119	132	112	42	3	3	6	98	109	69	50	1		1
P. PANAMA	845	748	757	675	712	742	633	289	378	365	467	412	402	297
Q. PARAGUAY	78	37	64	99	171	183	194	41	34	44	25	31	24	40
R. PERU	1,117	900	751	496	693	814	798	1,150	1,204	1,402	1,152	858	815	701
S. URUGUAY	190	86	80	64	100	92	100	265	390	576	571	486	369	289
T. VENEZUELA	5,206	2,811	3,377	3,399	3,141	3,585	4,611	4,957	5,173	6,820	6,830	5,446	5,881	5,578
IFS World Total	216,442	205,639	223,976	218,815	227,307	254,484	321,600	254,884	269,878	346,364	352,463	382,295	424,442	459,570
DOTS World Total	212,274	200,528	217,889	213,146	217,292	252,884	320,385	254,882	269,880	341,170	361,620	387,075	424,068	459,910
Industrial Countries	117,195	117,617	130,421	129,647	137,422	161,002	198,882	143,682	154,443	204,037	227,729	249,893	260,908	281,325

SOURCE: IMF-DOT-Y, 1989.

Part IX

Financial Flows

Note: This volume contains statistics from numerous sources. Alternative data on many topics are presented. Variations in statistics can be attributed to differences in definition, parameters, coverage, methodology as well as date gathered, prepared, or adjusted.

27

Balance of Payments
and International Liquidity

SDR DEFINED

SDRs were initially expressed in terms of a fixed amount of gold that was equivalent to the gold content of the U.S. dollar. After the value of the dollar was severed from gold and allowed to float in exchange markets, the value of the SDR had to be redefined. Thus, since June 1974 the value of the SDR in terms of the U.S. dollar is determined by the sum of the dollar value of sixteen currencies, based on market exchange rates. The weight given to each of these currencies is based on the country's participation in world trade, subject to some modifications.[1] The new approach to the valuation of SDRs created a relatively stable measure of value in a time when the values of independent currencies were fluctuating widely in the foreign exchange market. As a result, many participants in the international financial markets who were looking for some stability in the value of international financial transactions began to use the SDR as a unit of account.

1. Effective July 1, 1978, the value of the SDR is the sum of the dollar value of the following number of units in each of the sixteen currencies:

U.S. dollar	.40	Belgian franc	1.60
German mark	.32	Saudi Arabian riyal	.13
Japanese yen	21.00	Swedish krona	.11
French franc	.42	Iranian rial	1.70
Pound sterling	.05	Australian dollar	.017
Italian lira	52.00	Spanish peseta	1.50
Netherlands guilder	.14	Norwegian krone	.10
Canadian dollar	.07	Austrian schilling	.28

SOURCE: Rita Rodríguez and Eugene Carter, *International Financial Management* (Englewood Cliffs, N.J.: Prentice-Hall, 1978), p. 85.

Table 2700

GUIDE TO BALANCE OF PAYMENTS ANALYSIS

(IMF Focuses on Reserves; ECLA Focuses on the Balance of Current and Capital Accounts)

A. Current Account[1,7]
Merchandise: exports f.o.b.
Merchandise: imports f.o.b.
    Trade Balance
Other goods, services, and income:
    credit

Other goods, services, and income:
    debit

      Total goods, services and income
Private unrequited transfers[2,a]
      Total, excl. official unrequited transfers
Official unrequited transfers[2,b]

B. Direct Investment and Other Long-Term[3] Capital
Direct investment

Portfolio investment
Other long-term capital
    Resident official sector

    Deposit money banks

    Other sectors

      Total, Groups A plus B

C. Other Short-Term Capital[3]

Resident official sector

Deposit money banks

Other sectors

D. Net Errors and Omissions

    Total, Groups A through D

E. Counterpart Items
Monetization/demonetization of gold
Allocation/cancellation of SDRs
Valuation changes in reserves

    Total, Groups A through E

F. Exceptional Financing

    Total, Groups A through F

G. Liabilities Constituting Foreign[5] Authorities' Reserves

    Total, Groups A through G

H. Total Change in Reserves[4,6]
Monetary gold
SDRs
Reserve position in the Fund
Foreign exchange assets
Other claims
Use of Fund credit

---

1. ECLA inclusions are as follows (cf. table 2725):
   A. Goods, Services and Income
      Merchandise
      Shipment
      Other Transportation
        Passenger Services
        Port Services, etc.
      Travel
      Investment Income
        Direct Investment Income
          Reinvested Earnings
          Distributed Earnings
        Other
          Resident Official, Including Interofficial
          Foreign Official, Excluding Interofficial
          Private
      Other Goods, Services, and Income
        Official
          Interofficial
          Other, Resident Official
          Other, Foreign Official
        Private
          Labor Income, nie
          Property Income, nie
          Other
   B. Private Unrequited Transfers
      Migrants' Transfers
      Workers' Remittances
      Other
2. Required = payment for goods or services.
3. ECLA inclusions are as follows:
   A. Official Unrequited Transfers
      Interofficial
      Other, Resident Official
      Other, Foreign Official
   B. Capital Other Than Reserves
      Long-Term Capital
      Direct Investment
      Other Private Loans
      General Government Securities and Assets
      Short-Term Capital
      Deposit Money Banks
      Other Private
      Reserve Banks
   C. Net Errors and Omissions

   D. Exceptional Financing
   E. Counterpart Items
     Monetization/Demonetization of Gold
     Allocation of SDRs
4. Reserves (and related items) bring categories I and II into zero balance and include:
   A. Use of IMF Credit
   B. Other Liabilities
   C. Monetary Gold
   D. SDRs
   E. Reserve Position in IMF
   F. Foreign Exchange and Other Claims

According to Høst (cited in Source, below, pp. 50-51), "reserves and related items, as now defined, have always been considered to be the hard core of financing below the line of the balance of payments surpluses and deficits, as representing the response of monetary authorities at home or abroad to surplus or deficit situations. It was invariably so considered when the concept of compensatory official financing was used in the early days of the Fund's activities. For many years, a similar concept was used in the United States in its publication of balance of payments statistics as one measure of surplus or deficit, the so-called official settlements balance. Such a balance ceased to be published in the United States in 1976. For several reasons, reserves and related items have become less adequate for the assessment of the balance of payments. First, a build-up of reserves by the monetary authorities of a number of countries in a reserve center or other financial centers may not, in an environment of general floating of exchange rates, reflect surpluses or deficits in the countries holding the reserves. It may be the response to interest differentials between financial markets or confidence factors, inducing countries to adjust the currency composition of their foreign exchange portfolios. Moreover, after the sharp rise in the price of oil which began in 1973, part of the foreign assets held by the monetary authorities of some of the major oil exporting countries must be regarded to be in the nature of investments rather than balances held for the financing of balance of payments deficits. For all these reasons, it has become increasingly difficult to assess the surplus or deficit in the balance of payments calling for adjustment. But these difficulties do not apply to the great majority of developing countries."

5. Liabilities Constituting Foreign Authorities' Reserves.
6. Cf. ECLA's concept of compensatory financing in table 2725ff., the last three items of which equal change in reserves.
7. Because the Basic Balance (current account + official unrequited transfers) is not separately available prior to 1967 for most countries, IFS-Y standard format for all years precludes presentation for Basic Balance for any years.

a. One definition considers this item to belong to capital account.
b. ECLA's definition considers this item to belong to capital account.

SOURCE: Data are from IMF-IFS-Y, 1979. Analysis is also adapted from Poul Høst-Madsen, *Macroeconomic Accounts: An Overview*, Pamphlet Series No. 29 (Washington, D.C.: IMF, 1979), pp. 39, 49-51. Cf. table 2725ff.

Table 2701

IMF DATA ON BALANCE OF PAYMENTS, 19 LC, 1983–87
(M SDR)

A. ARGENTINA

Category	1983	1984	1985	1986	1987
A. Current Account, excl. Group F	−2,282	−2,480	−946	−2,435	−3,307
Merchandise: exports f.o.b.	7,328	7,875	8,292	5,840	4,915
Meat	552	380	365	395	~
Other	6,776	7,495	7,927	5,445	~
Merchandise: imports f.o.b.	−3,857	−4,031	−3,469	−3,743	−4,137
Trade balance	3,471	3,845	4,823	2,097	778
Other goods, services, and income: credit	1,805	1,762	1,907	1,697	1,562
Other goods, services, and income: debit	−7,573	−8,089	−7,676	−6,230	−5,641
Total goods, services, and income	−2,297	−2,482	−946	−2,436	−3,301
Private unrequited transfers	15	2	#	2	−6
Total, excl. official unrequited transfers	−2,282	−2,480	−946	−2,435	−3,307
Official unrequited transfers	#	#	#	#	#
B. Direct Investment and Other Long-Term					
Capital, excl. Groups F through H	−579	−1,210	−135	−143	−241
Direct investment	170	262	897	491	−13
Portfolio investment	612	361	−622	−473	−445
Other long-term capital					
Resident official sector	−1,350	880	1,265	181	−151
Loans received by general government	−805	1,744	1,555	423	−144
Loans received by Central Bank	−534	−520	#	#	#
Other liabilities	#	#	#	#	#
Assets	−11	−343	−290	−242	−7
Deposit money banks	36	−31	−1	−3	−39
Other sectors	−46	−2,681	−1,674	−339	408
Loans received	119	2,611	1,400	233	462
Other	−165	−171	−183	−106	−54
Total, Groups A plus B	−2,861	−3,690	−1,082	−2,578	−3,548
C. Other Short-Term Capital, excl. Groups F					
through H	−1,551	1,290	946	495	−195
Resident official sector	−435	154	290	227	111
Deposit money banks	298	−510	639	−18	12
Other sectors	−1,415	1,646	17	286	−318
D. Net Errors and Omissions	−414	−51	−517	264	144
Total, Groups A through D	−4,826	−2,452	−652	−1,818	−3,599
E. Counterpart Items	119	−115	−235	−148	−238
Monetization/demonetization of gold	#	#	#	#	#
Allocation/cancellation of SDRs	#	#	#	#	#
Valuation changes in reserves	119	−115	−235	−148	−238
Total, Groups A through E	−4,708	−2,567	−887	−1,967	−3,836
F. Exceptional Financing	2,654	2,395	1,832	1,078	2,185
Bonds issued to cancel external obligations	459	375	110	149	376
Rescheduled debt	#	#	1,741	880	441
Long-term loans received by Central Bank	1,676	501	2,977	1,040	927
Short-term loans received by Central Bank	216	609	−604	#	27
Payments arrears	304	910	−2,393	−991	415
Total, Groups A through F	−2,054	−172	944	−888	−1,651
G. Liabilities Constituting Foreign Authorities'					
Reserves	−141	196	−217	−5	93
Total, Groups A through G	−2,194	25	728	−893	−1,558
H. Total Change in Reserves	2,194	−25	−728	893	1,558
Monetary gold	#	#	#	#	#
SDRs	#	#	1	#	#
Reserve position in the Fund	91	#	#	#	#
Foreign exchange assets	983	−24	−1,713	758	1,082
Other claims	#	#	#	#	#
Use of Fund credit	1,121	#	985	136	475
Conversion rates: australes per SDR	.0113	.0693	.6110	1.1063	2.7727

Table 2701 (Continued)

IMF DATA ON BALANCE OF PAYMENTS, 19 LC, 1983-87
(M SDR)

B. BOLIVIA

Category	1983	1984	1985	1986	1987
A. Current Account, excl. Group F	−129.9	−170.6	−278.1	−327.5	−377.2
Merchandise: exports f.o.b.	706.4	706.8	614.0	465.0	363.5
Crude petroleum and gas	381.2	374.7	367.0	283.1	198.1
Metals	270.3	306.1	207.4	98.1	67.7
Other	54.8	26.0	39.6	83.8	97.8
Merchandise: imports f.o.b.	−464.0	−402.2	−455.8	−508.5	−508.9
Trade balance	242.4	304.6	158.2	−43.5	−145.4
Other goods, services, and income: credit	134.6	120.5	112.3	118.2	110.6
Other goods, services, and income: debit	−605.5	−681.4	−626.9	−487.5	−442.4
Total: goods, services, and income	−228.5	−256.3	−356.4	−412.7	−477.2
Private unrequited transfers	37.6	21.3	19.4	15.8	15.6
Total, excl. official unrequited transfers	−190.9	−235.0	−337.0	−397.0	−461.5
Official unrequited transfers	61.0	64.4	58.9	69.5	84.3
B. Direct Investment and Other Long-Term Capital, excl. Groups F through H	−202.2	−143.8	−231.3	−138.4	−53.2
Direct investment	6.5	6.8	9.8	8.5	17.0
Portfolio investment	−1.7	−.9	−.9	#	#
Other long-term capital					
Resident official sector	−123.9	−108.3	−196.5	−137.1	−75.0
Deposit money banks	−13.6	−11.6	−8.5	−9.9	4.8
Other sectors	−69.5	−29.9	−35.3	#	#
Total, Groups A plus B	−332.1	−314.4	−509.4	−465.9	−430.4
C. Other Short-Term Capital, excl. Groups F through H	−106.2	199.9	−2.2	91.6	6.0
Resident official sector	1.4	2.7	1.3	−2.7	1.0
Deposit money banks	−15.6	13.3	−26.3	−12.0	5.4
Other sectors	−92.0	183.9	22.8	106.4	−.4
D. Net Errors and Omissions	67.4	−11.7	187.1	118.7	7.5
Total, Groups A through D	−370.8	−126.2	−324.5	−255.6	−416.9
E. Counterpart Items	9.6	18.7	−20.0	−31.1	−47.3
Monetization/demonetization of gold	.8	.9	−.1	#	#
Allocation/cancellation of SDRs	#	#	#	#	#
Valuation changes in reserves	8.7	17.8	−19.9	−31.1	−47.3
Total, Groups A through E	−361.3	−107.6	−344.4	−286.7	−464.2
F. Exceptional Financing	625.3	276.0	347.3	399.2	341.7
Grants from Subsidy Account	.8	.7	.5	.2	.1
Debt cancellation	#	#	#	#	2.4
Rescheduled debt	471.7	#	#	#	47.5
Other long-term loans received	#	#	#	85.2	19.3
Short-term loans received by Central Bank	−15.0	−6.3	17.2	−20.0	#
Overdrafts with foreign banks	11.3	16.1	−23.7	#	#
Deferred payments					
Resident official sector	58.7	−157.8	#	#	#
Deposit money banks	15.0	−26.5	#	#	#
Other sectors	51.3	−94.9	#	#	#
Payments arrears					
Resident official sector	19.7	518.3	321.3	333.8	244.5
Deposit money banks	1.1	17.1	5.8	#	#
Other sectors	10.7	9.4	26.2	#	27.8
Total, Groups A through F	264.0	168.4	2.8	112.6	−122.6
G. Liabilities Constituting Foreign Authorities' Reserves	−215.5	−36.8	−61.8	−50.5	31.6
Total, Groups A through G	48.5	131.7	−58.9	62.1	−90.9
H. Total Change in Reserves	−48.5	−131.7	58.9	−62.1	90.9
Monetary gold	−.8	−.9	.1	#	#
SDRs	−.1	.1	#	−2.0	2.0
Reserve position in the Fund	#	#	#	#	#
Foreign exchange assets	−11.1	−104.3	79.7	−42.6	102.9
Other claims	−43.5	−6.2	−2.7	−107.1	5.2
Use of Fund credit	7.2	−20.3	−18.2	89.6	−19.1
Conversion rates: pesos per SDR	245	2,340	~	~	~
Conversion rates: bolivianos per SDR	#	#	.425	2.255	2.657

Table 2701 (Continued)

IMF DATA ON BALANCE OF PAYMENTS, 19 LC, 1983–87
(M SDR)

C. BRAZIL

Category	1983	1984	1985	1986
A. Current Account, excl. Group F	–6,360	52	–333	–3,742
Merchandise: exports f.o.b.	20,508	26,390	25,153	19,137
Coffee	1,962	2,500	2,340	1,727
Iron ore	1,415	1,567	1,627	1,380
Other	17,131	22,322	21,186	16,029
Merchandise: imports f.o.b.	–14,441	–13,596	–12,929	–11,943
Trade balance	6,068	12,794	12,224	7,194
Other goods, services, and income: credit	2,288	3,131	3,633	2,482
Other goods, services, and income: debit	–14,816	–16,039	–16,342	–13,492
Investment income	–10,954	–12,426	–12,611	–10,051
Other	–3,862	–3,614	–3,731	–3,441
Total: goods, services, and income	–6,461	–115	–485	–3,816
Private unrequited transfers	99	157	138	82
Total, excl. official unrequited transfers	–6,362	42	–348	–3,734
Official unrequited transfers	2	10	15	–8
B. Direct Investment and Other Long-Term Capital, excl. Groups F through H	–1,281	–2,759	–6,496	–7,928
Direct investment	1,285	1,517	1,262	284
Portfolio investment	–270	–265	–231	–366
Other long-term capital				
Resident official sector	–86	–1,256	–2,562	–1,185
Loans received by general government	2,184	6,425	3,527	–172
Loans received by Central Bank	–2,368	–7,827	–5,911	–971
Other	98	145	–178	–42
Deposit money banks	–1,419	–1,378	–2,590	–3,140
Other sectors	–791	–1,377	–2,375	–3,521
Total, Groups A plus B	–7,642	–2,707	–6,828	–11,670
C. Other Short-Term Capital, excl. Groups F through H	–1,076	–3,110	–1,526	412
Resident official sector	–78	–280	–18	–19
Deposit money banks	–663	958	–547	160
Other sectors	–335	–3,788	–960	272
D. Net Errors and Omissions	–577	396	–488	–452
Total, Groups A through D	–9,294	–5,421	–8,842	–11,710
E. Counterpart Items	655	815	–987	–974
Monetization/demonetization of gold	521	328	257	116
Allocation/cancellation of SDRs	#	#	#	#
Valuation changes in reserves	134	487	–1,244	–1,089
Total, Groups A through E	–8,639	–4,606	–9,829	–12,684
F. Exceptional Financing	8,756	10,208	8,763	8,665
Project I deposits	3,902	6,184	#	#
Rescheduled debt				
Project II	4,167	4,755	6,511	7,559
Paris Club	678	1,298	2,253	1,105
Short-term loans	–2,183	201	#	#
Payments arrears	2,192	–2,231	#	#
Total, Groups A through F	116	5,601	–1,066	–4,019
G. Liabilities Constituting Foreign Authorities' Reserves	–1,213	491	–436	331
Total, Groups A through G	–1,097	6,093	–1,502	–3,688
H. Total Changes in Reserves	1,097	–6,093	1,502	3,688
Monetary gold	–147	–328	–551	175
SDRs	#	–1	#	1
Reserve position in the Fund	260	#	#	#
Foreign exchange assets	–764	–7,368	1,993	4,020
Other claims	–279	–140	124	18
Use of Fund credit	2,027	1,744	–64	–526
Conversion rates: cruzados per SDR	.617	1.894	6.296	16.021

Table 2701 (Continued)

IMF DATA ON BALANCE OF PAYMENTS, 19 LC, 1983–87
(M SDR)

D. CHILE

Category	1983	1984	1985	1986	1987
A. Current Account, excl. Group F	−1,045	−2,010	−1,308	−969	−627
Merchandise: exports f.o.b.	3,584	3,561	3,747	3,579	4,040
Copper	1,754	1,565	1,762	1,498	1,728
Other	1,830	1,996	1,985	2,082	2,312
Merchandise: imports f.o.b.	−2,661	−3,275	−2,909	−2,642	−3,089
Trade balance	922	286	837	938	951
Other goods, services, and income: credit	935	1,136	852	980	978
Other goods, services, and income: debit	−2,993	−3,528	−3,057	−2,959	−2,646
Investment income	−1,824	−2,281	−2,069	−1,803	−1,455
Other	−1,169	−1,247	−988	−1,156	−1,190
Total: goods, services, and income	−1,136	−2,106	−1,368	−1,041	−717
Private unrequited transfers	51	40	46	34	43
Total, excl. official unrequited transfers	−1,085	−2,066	−1,322	−1,007	−674
Official unrequited transfers	40	57	14	38	46
B. Direct Investment and Other Long-Term Capital, excl. Groups F through H	−1,187	−576	−1,627	−1,764	−708
Direct investment	123	65	61	49	75
Portfolio investment	#	#	49	223	639
Other long-term capital					
Resident official sector	−40	128	73	−170	−144
Loans received by general government	3	151	174	9	52
Loans received by Central Bank	−9	−23	−101	−180	−196
Other	−34	#	#	#	#
Deposit money banks	−748	−479	−1,060	−1,210	−1,091
Other sectors	−522	−290	−750	−655	−187
Total, Groups A plus B	−2,232	−2,585	−2,935	−2,733	−1,336
C. Other Short-Term Capital, excl. Groups F through H	−1,840	575	368	265	−122
Resident official sector	−13	#	#	#	#
Deposit money banks	−1,253	244	35	111	116
Other sectors	−574	331	333	154	−238
D. Net Errors and Omissions	75	97	3	76	−35
Total, Groups A through D	−3,997	−1,914	−2,564	−2,392	−1,493
E. Counterpart Items	107	212	−253	−361	−201
Monetization/demonetization of gold	22	60	2	8	5
Allocation/cancellation of SDRs	#	#	#	#	#
Valuation changes in reserves	85	151	−255	−369	−207
Total, Groups A through E	−3,889	−1,702	−2,817	−2,753	−1,695
F. Exceptional Financing	3,502	1,931	2,473	2,199	1,539
Rescheduled debt					
Resident official sector	#	579	293	202	316
Deposit money banks	#	1,998	992	1,069	593
Other sectors	#	704	515	655	283
Other long-term financing	1,216	761	826	550	173
Short-term borrowing by Central Bank	94	176	−153	−277	174
Deferred payments					
Resident official sector	208	−217	#	#	#
Deposit money banks	1,548	−1,615	#	#	#
Other sectors	437	−456	#	#	#
Total, Groups A through F	−387	229	−344	−554	−156
G. Liabilities Constituting Foreign Authorities' Reserves	11	72	−4	−21	60
Total, Groups A through G	−376	301	−347	−575	−96
H. Total Change in REserves	376	−301	347	575	96
Monetary gold	43	−60	−2	−8	−5
SDRs	12	−7	11	#	−29
Reserve position in the Fund	71	#	#	#	#
Foreign exchange assets	−324	−450	142	485	186
Other claims	#	#	#	#	#
Use of Fund credit	573	216	196	98	−56
Conversion rates: Chilean pesos per SDR	84.28	101.12	163.55	226.44	283.88

Table 2701 (Continued)

IMF DATA ON BALANCE OF PAYMENTS, 19 LC, 1983–87
(M SDR)

E. COLOMBIA

Category	1983	1984	1985	1986	1987
A. Current Account, excl. Group F	−2,809	−1,367	−1,782	326	197
Merchandise: exports f.o.b.	2,778	4,169	3,595	4,544	4,408
Coffee	1,350	1,692	1,676	2,547	1,230
Petroleum products	406	434	403	528	1,033
Other	1,022	2,043	1,516	1,470	2,145
Merchandise: imports f.o.b.	−4,176	−3,929	−3,618	−2,906	−2,996
Trade balance	−1,398	240	−23	1,638	1,412
Other goods, services, and income: credit	1,060	1,029	951	1,094	1,086
Transportation	365	385	364	333	334
Other	695	644	587	760	752
Other goods, services, and income: debit	−2,625	−2,928	−3,164	−3,075	−3,075
Transportation	−598	−581	−565	−509	−478
Investment income	−1,362	−1,591	−1,662	−1,613	−1,693
Other	−665	−755	−937	−953	−904
Total: goods, services, and income	−2,963	−1,659	−2,236	−343	−577
Private unrequited transfers	136	282	448	676	774
Total, excl. official unrequited transfers	−2,827	−1,377	−1,788	333	197
Official unrequited transfers	18	10	6	−7	#
B. Direct Investment and Other Long-Term					
Capital, excl. Groups F through H	1,429	1,778	2,314	2,103	193
Direct investment	481	547	1,001	547	270
Portfolio investment	−2	−3	−1	26	37
Other long-term capital					
Resident official sector	95	346	293	401	−163
Loans received by general government	98	359	279	321	−174
Loans received by Bank of the Republic	−3	−13	21	82	11
Other	#	#	−6	−2	#
Deposit money banks	#	#	#	#	#
Other sectors	855	887	1,021	1,129	49
Government-owned enterprises	787	841	831	967	94
Private enterprises	68	46	190	161	−45
Total, Groups A plus B	−1,380	411	533	2,429	391
C. Other Short-Term Capital, excl. Groups F					
through H	−93	−860	−111	−1,112	−141
Resident official sector	79	18	14	49	2
Deposit money banks	60	−183	3	−1,118	−97
Other sectors	−231	−695	−128	−43	−46
D. Net Errors and Omissions	−255	82	−269	−208	71
Total, Groups A through D	−1,727	−368	153	1,109	321
E. Counterpart Items	235	−667	−42	−145	−746
Monetization/demonetization of gold	166	−635	167	55	−398
Allocation/cancellation of SDRs	#	#	#	#	#
Valuation changes in reserves	69	−32	−209	−199	−348
Total, Groups A through E	−1,492	−1,035	111	964	−425
F. Exceptional Financing	#	#	#	#	#
Total, Groups A through F	−1,492	−1,035	111	964	−425
G. Liabilities Constituting Foreign Authorities'					
Reserves	5	4	−1	−3	−10
Total, Groups A through G	−1,487	−1,031	110	961	−435
H. Total Change in Reserves	1,487	1,031	−110	−961	435
Monetary gold	−166	635	−167	−55	398
SDRs	−26	189	#	−114	#
Reserve position in the Fund	−87	262	#	#	#
Foreign exchange assets	1,798	−27	−61	−638	29
Other claims	−32	−29	118	−155	9
Use of Fund credit	#	#	#	#	#
Conversion rates: Colombian pesos per SDR	84.30	103.34	144.49	227.90	313.71

Table 2701 (Continued)

IMF DATA ON BALANCE OF PAYMENTS, 19 LC, 1983–87
(M SDR)

F. COSTA RICA

Category	1983	1984	1985	1986	1987
A. Current Account, excl. Group F	−296.5	−250.0	−287.4	−139.1	−280.5
Merchandise: exports f.o.b.	798.1	972.8	927.1	923.7	863.0
Bananas	225.1	244.1	205.6	184.7	185.9
Coffee	215.3	260.7	312.0	333.4	260.0
Other	357.8	467.9	409.5	405.6	417.1
Merchandise: imports f.o.b.	−840.9	−972.2	−989.9	−893.1	−965.6
Trade balance	−42.8	.5	−62.8	30.7	−102.6
Other goods, services, and income: credit	299.3	308.2	326.6	303.3	291.0
Other goods, services, and income: debit	−587.0	−598.7	−604.0	−533.9	−528.4
Total: goods, services, and income	−330.5	−289.9	−340.2	−199.9	−340.0
Private unrequited transfers	21.4	31.1	42.0	31.9	28.2
Total, excl. official unrequited transfers	−309.1	−258.8	−298.2	−168.1	−311.8
Official unrequited transfers	12.5	8.8	10.8	29.0	31.3
B. Direct Investment and Other Long-Term					
Capital, excl. Groups F through H	−61.8	−180.1	−128.8	−215.6	−332.5
Direct investment	51.7	50.7	64.2	48.9	58.0
Portfolio investment	−2.5	−.2	−12.5	−2.1	#
Other long-term capital					
Resident official sector	−62.4	−120.8	−130.5	−201.8	−329.2
Loans received by general government	17.6	27.1	−1.9	35.2	−18.4
Loans received by Central Bank	−73.7	−123.9	−91.5	−192.0	−309.2
Other	−6.3	−24.1	−37.1	−45.0	−1.7
Deposit money banks	−14.2	−26.2	−16.1	−12.0	−6.2
Other sectors	−34.5	−83.6	−34.0	−48.5	−55.1
Loans received by government-owned					
enterprises	−3.6	−52.7	−18.7	−37.3	−49.3
Loans received by private enterprises	−30.9	−30.8	−15.3	−11.3	−5.8
Total, Groups A plus B	−358.4	−430.1	−416.3	−354.6	−613.0
C. Other Short-Term Capital, excl. Groups F					
through H	−56.2	−93.2	−99.2	−43.4	−32.6
Resident official sector	.5	3.6	−29.6	7.8	#
Deposit money banks	−32.1	10.5	#	2.1	6.2
Other sectors	−24.6	−107.3	−69.5	−53.4	−38.8
D. Net Errors and Omissions	63.8	108.2	156.1	74.7	121.7
Total, Groups A through D	−350.8	−415.1	−359.3	−323.3	−523.9
E. Counterpart Items	29.6	14.9	−58.7	−37.9	−3.0
Monetization/demonetization of gold	7.0	−12.9	11.3	3.4	−3.0
Allocation/cancellation of SDRs	#	#	#	#	#
Valuation changes in reserves	22.6	27.8	−70.0	−41.3	#
Total, Groups A through E	−321.2	−400.2	−418.0	−361.2	−526.9
F. Exceptional Financing	417.5	414.6	484.0	391.0	558.9
Grants from AID	30.6	99.9	165.4	68.1	92.0
IBRD structural adjustment loans	#	#	37.1	34.0	#
Long-term borrowing by Central Bank	1,174.6	243.2	427.4	134.2	37.7
Short-term borrowing by Central Bank	−12.3	−84.1	−4.5	2.9	6.1
Payments arrears					
Resident official sector	−460.1	125.9	−105.7	116.1	361.0
Deposit money banks	−58.4	1.6	−2.3	.6	4.8
Other sectors	−256.8	28.1	−33.4	35.1	57.2
Rescheduling of government-owned enterprises'					
arrears	#	#	#	#	#
Total, Groups A through F	96.3	14.4	66.0	29.8	32.0
G. Liabilities Constituting Foreign Authorities'					
Reserves	−23.5	−48.5	−53.4	1.3	−4.4
Total, Groups A through G	72.8	−34.0	12.6	31.2	27.6
H. Total Change in Reserves	−72.8	34.0	−12.6	−31.2	−27.6
Monetary gold	−1.2	12.9	−11.3	−3.4	3.0
SDRs	−2.8	2.7	.1	#	#
Reserve position in the Fund	#	#	#	#	#
Foreign exchange assets	−178.0	25.0	−8.9	17.3	28.1
Other claims	10.1	17.7	−5.1	−14.4	−11.0
Use of Fund credit	99.1	−24.3	12.7	−30.7	−47.7
Conversion rates: Costa Rican colones per SDR	43.930	45.646	51.227	65.681	81.174

Table 2701 (Continued)

IMF DATA ON BALANCE OF PAYMENTS, 19 LC, 1983–87
(M SDR)

H. DOMINICAN REP.

Category	1983	1984	1985	1986
A. Current Account, excl. Group F	−390.9	−159.4	−106.0	−101.5
Merchandise: exports f.o.b.	734.5	846.9	727.3	615.5
Sugar	279.6	312.2	205.0	146.4
Other	454.9	534.7	522.4	469.2
Merchandise: imports f.o.b.	−1,196.4	−1,226.4	−1,266.5	−1,079.3
Trade balance	−461.9	−379.5	−539.1	−463.8
Other goods, services, and income: credit	433.6	494.9	596.7	600.1
Other goods, services, and income: debit	−563.7	−533.4	−514.5	−468.8
Investment income	−284.4	−241.2	−244.2	−227.3
Other	−279.3	−292.2	−270.4	−241.5
Total: goods, services, and income	−592.0	−417.9	−456.9	−332.5
Private unrequited transfers	182.4	200.0	238.3	206.3
Total, excl. official unrequited transfers	−409.6	−217.9	−218.5	−126.2
Official unrequited transfers	18.7	58.5	112.6	24.7
B. Direct Investment and Other Long-Term Capital, excl. Groups F through H	58.6	286.9	182.7	230.1
Direct investment	45.1	66.8	35.7	42.6
Portfolio investment	#	#	#	#
Other long-term capital				
Resident official sector	75.4	231.5	158.9	187.5
Deposit money banks	8.5	−2.3	~	~
Other sectors	−70.4	−9.1	−11.8	~
Total, Groups A plus B	−332.4	127.5	76.7	128.6
C. Other Short-Term Capital, excl. Groups F through H	−125.7	−68.3	−108.3	−6.6
Resident official sector	−9.4	−118.2	#	~
Deposit money banks	−219.4	−21.1	−108.3	−6.6
Other sectors	103.1	71.0	~	~
D. Net Errors and Omissions	12.2	28.9	155.0	−8.7
Total, Groups A through D	−445.8	88.1	123.4	113.4
E. Counterpart Items	−8.5	−14.1	−34.7	−30.2
Monetization/demonetization of gold	−13.7	−21.6	.1	~
Allocation/cancellation of SDRs	#	#	#	#
Valuation changes in reserves	5.2	7.5	−34.8	−30.2
Total, Groups A through E	−454.3	74.0	88.7	83.1
F. Exceptional Financing	337.8	−1.1	−48.3	−21.7
Long-term borrowing by Central Bank	38.4	~	~	~
Rescheduled debt of the resident official sector	425.0	~	~	~
Short-term borrowing by Central Bank	−28.3	−29.3	−8.2	~
Payments arrears	−97.3	28.2	−40.1	−21.7
Deposits received for balance of payments support	#	#	#	#
Total, Groups A through F	−116.6	73.0	40.4	61.4
G. Liabilities Constituting Foreign Authorities' Reserves	−19.6	7.6	−31.4	−41.8
Total, Groups A through G	−136.1	80.6	9.0	19.6
H. Total Change in Reserves	136.1	−80.6	−9.0	−19.6
Monetary gold	11.7	21.6	−.1	~
SDRs	.3	−.2	−28.4	28.8
Reserve position in the Fund	−7.4	7.4	#	#
Foreign exchange assets	−39.6	−102.2	−22.6	−26.8
Other claims	#	2.3	−2.7	#
Use of Fund credit	171.1	−9.5	44.7	−21.6
Conversion rates: Dominican pesos per SDR	1.0690	1.0250	3.1604	3.4073

Table 2701 (Continued)

IMF DATA ON BALANCE OF PAYMENTS, 19 LC, 1983–87
(M SDR)

I. ECUADOR

Category	1983	1984	1985	1986	1987
A. Current Account, excl. Group F	–3.7	–144.4	146.4	–522.5	–918.7
Merchandise: exports f.o.b.	2,196.4	2,558.0	2,861.1	1,863.3	1,562.9
Bananas	143.1	132.7	216.7	224.2	206.5
Coffee	139.4	170.7	188.1	254.9	148.5
Crude petroleum	1,533.2	1,638.0	1,797.4	777.4	571.5
Other	380.7	616.6	658.9	606.9	636.5
Merchandise: imports f.o.b.	–1,329.3	–1,528.8	–1,586.7	–1,390.3	1,588.5
Trade balance	867.2	1,029.3	1,274.4	473.1	–25.5
Other goods, services, and income: credit	318.1	341.5	411.7	367.4	343.4
Other goods, services, and income: debit	–1,211.4	–1,534.6	–1,618.6	–1,401.3	–1,294.6
Shipment	–104.8	–147.3	–116.2	–106.5	–108.3
Investment income	–732.5	–935.6	–950.8	–780.8	–722.3
Other	–374.2	–451.7	–551.5	–514.0	–464.0
Total: goods, services, and income	–26.2	–163.9	67.6	–560.9	–976.7
Private unrequited transfers	~	~	~	~	~
Total, excl. official unrequited transfers	–26.2	–163.9	67.6	–560.9	–976.7
Official unrequited transfers	22.5	19.5	78.8	38.4	58.0
B. Direct Investment and Other Long-Term					
Capital, excl. Groups F through H	–1,075.8	–825.4	–679.6	–229.3	123.7
Direct investment	46.8	48.8	61.1	59.7	58.0
Portfolio investment	#	#	#	#	#
Other long-term capital					
Resident official sector	–240.4	–317.1	–643.1	–243.8	66.5
Loans received	–228.3	–310.2	–636.2	–230.1	71.9
Other	–12.2	–6.8	–6.9	–13.6	–5.4
Deposit money banks	–6.5	–8.8	#	#	#
Other sectors	–875.6	–548.3	–97.5	–45.2	–.8
Total, Groups A plus B	–1,079.5	–969.7	–533.2	–751.8	–795.0
C. Other Short-Term Capital, excl. Groups F					
through H	–1,027.1	–260.5	–282.7	–75.9	17.0
Resident official sector	–555.7	–22.4	105.4	–75.9	17.0
Deposit money banks	6.5	15.6	–62.0	~	~
Other sectors	–478.0	–253.7	–326.0	~	~
D. Net Errors and Omissions	–173.3	–72.8	77.6	–152.3	–22.8
Total, Groups A through D	–2,279.9	–1,303.1	–738.3	–979.9	–800.7
E. Counterpart Items	33.6	47.3	–68.3	–51.3	–53.4
Monetization/demonetization of gold	#	#	#	#	#
Allocation/cancellation of SDRs	#	#	#	#	#
Valuation changes in reserves	33.6	47.3	–68.3	–51.3	–53.4
Total, Groups A through E	–2,246.3	–1,255.8	–806.6	–1,031.2	–854.1
F. Exceptional Financing	2,313.4	1,294.6	867.7	873.7	723.9
Debt rescheduling					
Resident official sector	1,956.0	1,176.6	1,127.7	875.4	709.9
Other sectors	#	#	18.7	12.8	13.9
Long-term loans received from commercial banks	403.2	#	~	#	#
Payments arrears	–45.8	118.0	–278.7	–14.5	#
Total, Groups A through F	67.1	38.8	61.1	–157.5	–130.2
G. Liabilities Constituting Foreign Authorities'					
Reserves	69.2	–70.2	–105.4	–40.1	–.8
Total, Groups A through G	136.3	–31.4	–44.3	–197.6	–131.0
H. Total Change in Reserves	–136.3	31.4	44.3	197.6	131.0
Monetary gold	#	#	#	#	#
SDRs	–.1	–.4	–25.7	–19.6	45.1
Reserve position in the Fund	–11.4	11.4	#	#	#
Foreign exchange assets	–328.3	–19.0	–4.6	146.8	135.3
Other claims	#	#	–9.8	#	3.1
Use of Fund credit	203.5	39.4	84.4	70.4	–52.5
Conversion rates: sucres per SDR	47.16	64.10	70.62	144.04	220.42

Table 2701 (Continued)

IMF DATA ON BALANCE OF PAYMENTS, 19 LC, 1983–87
(M SDR)

J. EL SALVADOR

Category	1983	1984	1985
A. Current Account, excl. Group F	−34.6	−52.2	−28.2
Merchandise: exports f.o.b.	688.0	708.2	668.7
Coffee	376.3	438.8	444.5
Cotton	51.9	8.9	30.3
Other	259.8	260.5	193.9
Merchandise: imports f.o.b.	−777.3	−892.2	−881.4
Trade balance	−89.3	−184.0	−212.7
Other goods, services, and income: credit	161.7	222.7	268.3
Other goods, services, and income: debit	−360.9	−391.1	−422.2
Total: goods, services, and income	−288.5	−352.3	−366.7
Private unrequited transfers	91.1	115.1	127.4
Total, excl. official unrequited transfers	−197.5	−237.2	−239.2
Official unrequited transfers	162.9	185.0	211.0
B. Direct Investment and Other Long-Term			
Capital, excl. Groups F through H	198.0	33.1	97.9
Direct investment	26.3	12.1	12.2
Portfolio investment	.1	#	#
Other long-term capital			
Resident official sector	166.7	30.8	86.8
Loans received by general government	151.0	91.5	100.0
Loans received by Central Reserve Bank	17.1	−58.6	−5.6
Other	−1.5	−2.1	−7.6
Deposit money banks	−.8	−.5	−.3
Other sectors	5.8	−9.3	−.8
Loans received	5.8	−9.3	−.8
Other	#	#	#
Total, Groups A plus B	163.4	−19.2	69.7
C. Other Short-Term Capital, excl. Groups F			
through H	−111.4	−14.5	−71.5
Resident official sector	−23.9	−32.4	−15.9
Deposit money banks	−30.5	−7.0	−47.4
Other sectors	−57.0	24.9	−8.3
D. Net Errors and Omissions	−38.7	−50.6	22.4
Total, Groups A through D	13.3	−84.3	20.5
E. Counterpart Items	15.1	14.8	−5.6
Monetization/demonetization of gold	#	#	#
Allocation/cancellation of SDRs	#	#	#
Valuation changes in reserves	15.1	14.8	−5.6
Total, Groups A through E	28.4	−69.5	14.9
F. Exceptional Financing	14.0	77.7	~
Long-term loans received by the Central Reserve			
Bank	98.2	48.7	~
Short-term borrowing by the Central Reserve Bank	−84.2	29.0	~
Total, Groups A through F	42.5	8.2	14.9
G. Liabilities Constituting Foreign Authorities'			
Reserves	−5.2	13.3	6.1
Total, Groups A through G	37.3	21.5	21.0
H. Total Change in Reserves	−37.3	−21.5	−21.0
Monetary gold	1.9	#	#
SDRs	1.6	.1	#
Reserve position in the Fund	#	#	#
Foreign exchange assets	−56.2	−16.2	5.6
Other claims	#	#	#
Use of Fund credit	15.5	−5.4	−26.6
Conversion rates: Salvadoran colones per SDR	2.6725	2.5625	2.5384

Table 2701 (Continued)

IMF DATA ON BALANCE OF PAYMENTS, 19 LC, 1983–87
(M SDR)

K. GUATEMALA

Category	1983	1984	1985	1986	1987
A. Current Account, excl. Group F	−211.7	−372.4	−236.8	−9.7	−360.2
Merchandise: exports f.o.b.	1,020.4	1,103.6	1,049.3	892.9	760.2
Coffee	289.0	352.5	444.8	430.0	276.1
Other	731.4	751.1	604.5	462.9	484.1
Merchandise: imports f.o.b.	−988.4	−1,154.1	−1,061.4	−745.3	−1,053.2
Trade balance	32.1	−50.5	−12.2	147.5	−292.9
Other goods, services, and income: credit	105.8	126.7	127.9	134.7	146.3
Other goods, services, and income: debit	−378.1	−476.6	−372.1	−355.6	−361.9
Shipment and other transportation	−92.5	−109.4	−105.8	−78.1	−97.3
Investment income	−133.6	−229.3	−189.0	−206.2	−155.6
Other	−152.0	−137.9	−77.2	−71.3	−109.0
Total: goods, services, and income	−240.2	−400.5	−256.3	−73.4	−508.5
Private unrequited transfers	27.8	27.4	18.7	42.6	78.0
Total, excl. official unrequited transfers	−212.4	−373.1	−237.6	−30.8	−430.5
Official unrequited transfers	.8	.7	.8	21.1	70.3
B. Direct Investment and Other Long-Term Capital, excl. Groups F through H	25.3	−47.5	−65.5	−253.7	−111.8
Direct investment	42.0	37.1	59.9	57.5	117.5
Portfolio investment	−.1	−9.2	−25.7	−9.8	−12.6
Other long-term capital					
Resident official sector	−11.2	−29.0	−100.1	−334.3	−224.3
Loans received by general government	86.8	41.3	66.1	19.7	−12.2
Loans received by Bank of Guatemala	−98.0	−73.4	−144.6	−318.0	−212.1
Other	#	3.1	−21.6	−36.0	#
Deposit money banks	#	#	#	#	#
Other sectors	−5.4	−46.5	.3	32.9	7.5
Loans received	−6.7	−46.8	1.1	−3.1	7.5
Other	1.2	.3	−.7	36.0	#
Total, Groups A plus B	−186.4	−419.9	−302.4	−263.5	−471.9
C. Other Short-Term Capital, excl. Groups F through H	113.7	−61.2	−73.3	−32.8	255.0
Resident official sector	34.3	−88.5	−179.0	−63.8	24.1
Deposit money banks	66.9	9.2	−63.8	9.0	30.0
Other sectors	12.5	18.1	169.6	22.2	200.9
D. Net Errors and Omissions	−34.9	14.1	43.4	57.4	−32.7
Total, Groups A through D	−107.6	−467.0	−332.2	−238.8	−249.6
E. Counterpart Items	13.3	21.6	−38.7	−42.2	−51.2
Monetization/demonetization of gold	#	#	#	#	#
Allocation/cancellation of SDRs	#	#	#	#	#
Valuation changes in reserves	13.3	21.6	−38.7	−42.2	−51.2
Total, Groups A through E	−94.2	−445.4	−370.9	−281.0	−300.8
F. Exceptional Financing	116.7	487.0	428.9	329.6	206.8
Bonds issued to cancel external obligations	73.5	66.3	166.9	24.2	#
Long-term borrowing by Bank of Guatemala	167.4	179.1	139.2	265.7	217.6
Short-term borrowing by Bank of Guatemala	−50.7	4.0	56.3	−43.9	−10.8
Payments arrears					
Resident official sector	#	#	21.5	35.9	#
Other sectors	−73.5	237.6	45.0	47.6	#
Total, Groups A through F	22.5	41.6	58.0	48.6	−94.0
G. Liabilities Constituting Foreign Authorities' Reserves	39.3	−5.9	3.8	3.3	.7
Total, Groups A through G	61.8	35.6	61.8	51.9	−93.3
H. Total Change in Reserves	−61.8	−35.6	−61.8	−51.9	93.3
Monetary gold	#	#	#	#	#
SDRs	−.5	−1.5	2.0	#	−1.2
Reserve position in the Fund	−7.9	7.9	#	#	#
Foreign exchange assets	−90.6	−85.5	3.8	−22.1	94.3
Other claims	−1.1	24.3	−19.8	18.2	15.7
Use of Fund credit	38.3	19.1	−47.8	−48.0	−15.5
Conversion rates: quetzales per SDR	1.0690	1.0250	1.0153	2.2220	3.2336

Table 2701 (Continued)

IMF DATA ON BALANCE OF PAYMENTS, 19 LC, 1983–87
(M SDR)

L. HAITI

Category	1983	1984	1985	1986	1987
A. Current Account, excl. Group F	−132.2	−120.5	−95.1	−39.4	−24.8
Merchandise: exports f.o.b.	173.5	206.4	224.1	167.1	157.5
Bauxite	#	#	#	#	#
Coffee	47.6	44.0	48.8	47.9	27.8
Other	125.9	162.3	175.3	119.2	129.7
Merchandise: imports f.o.b.	−329.2	−346.3	−346.4	−265.6	−244.3
Trade balance	−155.8	−139.9	−122.3	−98.5	−86.8
Other goods, services, and income: credit	100.4	104.8	119.9	92.7	91.7
Other goods, services, and income: debit	−179.5	−203.6	−238.4	−166.6	−174.9
Shipment and other transportation	−82.5	−94.1	−114.4	−66.5	−74.2
Distributed earnings on direct investment	−11.1	−5.8	−6.7	−4.4	−5.5
Other	−86.0	−103.8	−117.4	−95.6	−95.1
Total: goods, services, and income	−234.9	−238.7	−240.9	−172.4	−169.9
Private unrequited transfers	43.1	43.3	48.8	45.6	44.7
Total, excl. official unrequited transfers	−191.7	−195.5	−192.1	−126.8	−125.3
Official unrequited transfers	59.5	75.0	97.0	87.4	100.5
B. Direct Investment and Other Long-Term					
Capital, excl. Groups F through H	55.4	58.4	21.1	15.6	28.3
Direct investment	7.8	4.3	4.9	4.2	3.7
Portfolio investment	#	#	#	#	#
Other long-term capital					
Resident official sector	28.5	51.4	9.7	−3.8	12.4
Deposit money banks	#	#	#	#	#
Other sectors	19.0	2.7	6.5	15.2	12.2
Total, Groups A plus B	−76.9	−62.1	−74.1	−23.8	3.6
C. Other Short-Term Capital, excl. Groups F					
through H	2.1	4.4	−7.4	−5.6	−3.8
Resident official sector	.4	9.6	7.2	5.0	3.7
Deposit money banks	1.7	−5.2	−14.6	−10.6	−7.6
Other sectors	#	#	#	#	#
D. Net Errors and Omissions	95.5	78.7	55.5	−1.1	−20.1
Total, Groups A through D	20.7	21.1	−26.0	−30.5	−20.4
E. Counterpart Items	#	#	#	#	#
Monetization/demonetization of gold	#	#	#	#	#
Counterpart to allocation/cancellation	#	#	#	#	#
Valuation changes in reserves	#	#	#	#	#
Total, Groups A through E	20.7	21.1	−26.0	−30.5	−20.4
F. Exceptional Financing	.1	.8	9.9	15.3	1.0
Arrears	.1	.8	9.9	15.3	1.0
Subsidy Account grants	#	#	#	#	#
Trust Fund loans	#	#	#	#	#
Total, Groups A through F	20.8	21.9	−16.1	−15.2	−19.4
G. Liabilities Constituting Foreign Authorities'					
Reserves	#	#	#	#	#
Total, Groups A through G	20.8	21.9	−16.1	−15.2	−19.4
H. Total Change in Reserves	−20.8	−21.9	16.1	15.2	19.4
Monetary gold	#	#	#	1.1	#
SDRs	−3.0	3.1	.1	#	−.7
Reserve position in the Fund	#	#	#	#	#
Foreign exchange assets	6.1	−4.0	6.8	−2.3	9.9
Other claims	#	#	#	#	#
Use of Fund credit	−24.0	−21.0	9.3	16.4	10.1
Conversion rates: gourdes per SDR	5.3771	5.1988	4.9759	5.7087	6.2968

Table 2701 (Continued)

IMF DATA ON BALANCE OF PAYMENTS, 19 LC, 1983–87
(M SDR)

M. HONDURAS

Category	1983	1984	1985	1986	1987
A. Current Account, excl. Group F	−205.1	−308.7	−201.0	−89.6	−141.7
Merchandise: exports f.o.b.	653.6	719.0	777.7	759.7	667.1
Bananas	190.0	225.4	269.4	218.9	250.8
Coffee	141.4	165.0	182.4	274.5	161.1
Wood	37.8	34.0	33.6	27.5	28.1
Other	284.3	294.7	292.3	238.8	227.1
Merchandise: imports f.o.b.	−707.4	−863.2	−865.9	−745.0	−691.3
Trade balance	−53.9	−144.2	−88.2	14.7	−24.2
Other goods, services, and income: credit	108.8	123.1	126.7	111.6	101.2
Other goods, services, and income: debit	−301.6	−365.7	−382.9	−350.8	−331.9
Total: goods, services, and income	−246.7	−386.8	−344.5	−224.5	−254.9
Private unrequited transfers	9.1	10.0	12.2	11.1	12.4
Total, excl. official unrequited transfers	−237.6	−376.7	−332.2	−213.5	−242.5
Official unrequited transfers	32.6	68.0	131.2	123.9	100.8
B. Direct Investment and Other Long-Term Capital, excl. Groups F through H	121.5	241.2	205.0	57.2	18.3
Direct investment	19.6	20.0	27.1	25.6	27.8
Portfolio investment	.1	−1.8	1.2	−.8	.5
Other long-term capital					
Resident official sector	32.2	81.0	62.8	37.9	42.7
Loans received by general government	43.0	61.1	43.3	45.5	9.0
Loans received by Central Bank	−2.7	22.3	64.3	26.5	44.6
Other	−8.1	−2.4	−44.7	−34.1	−10.9
Deposit money banks	−2.7	−4.1	7.2	−.5	−1.9
Other sectors	72.2	146.2	106.7	−4.9	−50.8
Total, Groups A plus B	−83.6	−67.5	3.9	−32.4	−123.4
C. Other Short-Term Capital, excl. Groups F through H	−19.4	16.4	−11.2	14.7	36.0
Resident official sector	−31.6	7.1	15.1	15.2	4.3
Deposit money banks	7.2	−6.1	5.3	−.2	22.9
Other sectors	5.0	15.4	−31.6	−.3	8.8
D. Net Errors and Omissions	12.2	−8.1	−55.1	8.4	42.1
Total, Groups A through D	−90.8	−59.3	−62.4	−9.2	−45.4
E. Counterpart Items	7.0	14.8	1.3	12.1	−43.3
Monetization/demonetization of gold	#	#	#	#	#
Allocation/cancellation of SDRs	#	#	#	#	#
Valuation changes in reserves	7.0	14.8	1.3	12.1	−43.3
Total, Groups A through E	−83.8	−44.4	−61.1	2.8	−88.7
F. Exceptional Financing	50.5	44.8	45.1	34.6	105.6
Loans from CAMSF	#	#	#	#	#
Loans from VIF	17.0	13.9	12.1	3.8	1.7
Trust Fund Loans	#	#	#	#	#
Payments arrears	33.5	30.9	33.1	30.9	103.9
Total, Groups A through F	−33.4	.3	−16.0	37.4	16.9
G. Liabilities Constituting Foreign Authorities' Reserves	−3.9	24.8	#	#	#
Total, Groups A through G	−37.2	25.2	−16.0	37.4	16.9
H. Total Change in Reserves	37.2	−25.2	16.0	−37.4	−16.9
Monetary gold	#	#	#	#	#
SDRs	−.5	2.0	.2	#	#
Reserve position in the Fund	−4.2	4.2	#	#	#
Foreign exchange assets	−2.1	−28.4	34.3	5.3	16.4
Other claims	−1.9	−1.4	−1.7	−1.4	−1.0
Use of Fund credit	45.9	−1.6	−16.7	−41.4	−32.4
Conversion rates: lempiras per SDR	2.1380	2.0500	2.0307	2.3463	2.5861

Table 2701 (Continued)

IMF DATA ON BALANCE OF PAYMENTS, 19 LC, 1983–87
(M SDR)

N. MEXICO

Category	1983	1984	1985	1986	1987
A. Current Account, excl. Group F	5,064	4,078	1,175	−1,443	3,019
Merchandise: exports f.o.b.	20,888	23,595	21,340	13,662	15,969
Merchandise: imports f.o.b.	−8,012	−11,013	−13,018	−9,761	−9,434
Trade balance	12,876	12,581	8,322	3,901	6,535
Other goods, services, and income: credit	5,899	8,073	7,975	6,531	7,035
Travel	2,551	3,200	2,882	2,551	2,705
Other	3,348	4,873	5,093	3,980	4,330
Other goods, services, and income: debit	−13,994	−16,978	−16,101	−12,271	−11,067
Travel	−1,484	−2,123	−2,231	−1,851	−1,822
Investment income	−9,893	−11,938	−10,690	−7,931	−7,146
Other	−2,617	−2,917	−3,181	−2,488	−2,099
Total: goods, services, and income	4,781	3,677	196	−1,839	2,503
Private unrequited transfers	114	224	306	222	226
Total, excl. official unrequited transfers	4,896	3,901	502	−1,617	2,729
Official unrequited transfers	168	177	673	174	290
B. Direct Investment and Other Long-Term Capital, excl. Groups F through H	−224	−330	−1,319	345	3,022
Direct investment	427	381	494	1,290	2,497
Portfolio investment	−584	−739	−995	−693	−27
Other long-term capital					
Resident official sector	6,600	5,781	10,133	−222	3,106
Deposit money banks	1,351	451	70	431	77
Other sectors	−8,019	−6,204	−11,022	−462	−2,631
Total, Groups A plus B	4,840	3,748	−144	−1,098	6,041
C. Other Short-Term Capital, excl. Groups F through H	−7,859	−3,473	−1,773	622	−2,384
Resident official sector	#	#	#	#	#
Deposit money banks	−548	328	−18	59	−245
Other sectors	−7,311	−3,801	−1,755	563	−2,140
D. Net Errors and Omissions	−981	−974	−1,813	334	730
Total, Groups A through D	−4,000	−698	−3,729	−142	4,387
E. Counterpart Items	221	490	−527	−223	−562
Monetization/demonetization of gold	112	63	71	39	57
Allocation/cancellation of SDRs	#	#	#	#	#
Valuation changes in reserves	109	427	−597	−262	−619
Total, Groups A through E	−3,779	−208	−4,256	−365	3,825
F. Exceptional Financing	7,032	2,780	1,008	~	~
Rescheduled debt	2,349	~	~	~	~
Other loans for balance of payments support	4,683	2,780	1,008	~	~
Total, Groups A through F	3,254	2,571	−3,248	−365	3,825
G. Liabilities Constituting Foreign Authorities' Reserves	−1,141	#	#	#	#
Total, Groups A through G	2,113	2,571	−3,248	−365	3,825
H. Total Change in Reserves	−2,113	−2,571	3,248	365	−3,825
Monetary gold	−134	−94	#	−82	6
SDRs	−17	19	3	−7	−491
Reserve position in the Fund	−91	91	#	#	#
Foreign exchange assets	−2,874	−3,791	2,949	−162	−3,660
Other claims	#	#	#	#	#
Use of Fund credit	1,003	1,204	296	616	320
Conversion rates: Mexican pesos per SDR	128.4	172.0	260.8	717.7	1,782.1

Table 2701 (Continued)

IMF DATA ON BALANCE OF PAYMENTS, 19 LC, 1983–87

(M SDR)

O. NICARAGUA

Category	1983	1984	1985	1986
A. Current Account, excl. Group F	−523.6	−623.7	−748.0	−590.7
Merchandise: exports f.o.b.	401.1	376.3	296.9	210.7
Coffee	143.8	119.4	119.1	93.4
Cotton	102.4	130.5	89.6	38.5
Other	154.9	126.3	88.2	78.8
Merchandise: imports f.o.b.	−127.9	−780.1	−788.1	−619.3
Trade balance	−326.8	−403.8	−491.2	−408.6
Other goods, services, and income: credit	45.6	48.5	50.4	40.6
Other goods, services, and income: debit	−316.6	−355.9	−389.9	−320.4
Total: goods, services, and income	597.8	−711.2	−830.6	−688.4
Private unrequited transfers	3.4	2.0	15.8	7.4
Total, excl. official unrequited transfers	−594.4	−709.3	−814.8	−681.0
Official unrequited transfers	70.8	85.6	66.9	90.3
B. Direct Investment and Other Long-Term Capital, excl. Groups F through H	23.2	143.3	418.6	217.2
Direct investment	7.3	1.8	#	#
Portfolio investment	#	#	#	#
Other long-term capital				
Resident official sector	.2	149.3	445.4	226.1
Deposit money banks	22.0	12.3	−10.9	7.8
Other sectors	−6.4	−20.1	−15.9	−16.7
Total, Groups A plus B	−500.5	−480.4	−329.4	−373.5
C. Other Short-Term Capital, excl. Groups F through H	21.2	104.0	−284.3	18.0
Resident official sector	43.5	111.2	42.8	−16.3
Deposit money banks	−3.6	−29.4	−17.8	14.3
Other sectors	−18.7	22.1	−309.3	19.9
D. Net Errors and Omissions	−81.7	10.0	136.0	−186.7
Total, Groups A through D	−561.0	−366.4	−477.7	−542.2
E. Counterpart Items	8.6	21.5	−44.6	−33.0
Monetization/demonetization of gold	~	~	~	~
Allocation/cancellation of SDRs	#	#	#	#
Valuation changes in reserves	8.6	21.5	−44.6	−33.0
Total, Groups A through E	−552.4	−344.8	−522.3	−575.2
F. Exceptional Financing	694.6	663.0	488.7	439.4
Long-term loans received	#	~	~	~
Short-term loans received	21.2	−17.0	−3.4	−16.6
Overdrafts with foreign banks	#	143.0	103.5	−147.8
Rescheduled debt				
Resident official sector	577.9	312.3	334.6	293.2
Deposit money banks	3.1	7.1	16.1	#
Other sectors	13.6	6.8	8.6	5.0
Payments arrears				
Resident official sector	62.4	202.7	14.2	286.7
Deposit money banks	9.4	−2.7	13.1	4.7
Other sectors	6.9	10.7	2.1	14.2
Total, Groups A through F	142.2	318.2	−33.6	−135.8
G. Liabilities Constituting Foreign Authorities' Reserves	−116.7	−55.8	7.7	−62.5
Total, Groups A through G	25.5	262.4	−25.9	−198.3
H. Total Change in Reserves	−25.5	−262.4	25.9	198.3
Monetary gold	−17.3	−13.9	−4.6	46.2
SDRs	.9	#	#	#
Reserve position in the Fund	#	#	#	#
Foreign exchange assets	−20.0	−268.2	36.4	159.1
Other claims	15.1	23.9	3.2	−7.0
Use of Fund credit	−4.3	−4.3	−9.0	#
Conversion rates: córdobas per SDR	.0107	.0103	.0269	.0780

Table 2701 (Continued)

IMF DATA ON BALANCE OF PAYMENTS, 19 LC, 1983-87
(M SDR)

Q. PARAGUAY

Category	1983	1984	1985	1986	1987
A. Current Account, excl. Group F	−231.9	−309.7	−222.1	−305.9	−103.2
Merchandise: exports f.o.b.	305.0	352.5	319.5	488.8	735.9
Cotton	73.8	128.0	139.7	68.8	77.8
Soybeans	70.8	96.9	99.0	37.4	95.0
Other	160.3	127.6	80.9	382.6	563.1
Merchandise: imports f.o.b.	−515.8	−633.3	−508.1	−627.2	−811.1
Trade balance	−210.9	−280.8	−188.6	−138.4	−75.2
Other goods, services, and income: credit	218.9	492.4	841.3	247.1	293.6
Other goods, services, and income: debit	−245.7	−530.3	−882.2	−424.0	−342.5
Total: goods, services, and income	−237.7	−318.7	−229.5	−315.3	−124.0
Private unrequited transfers	1.3	2.0	1.8	.6	1.5
Total, excl. official unrequited transfers	−236.4	−316.7	−227.7	−314.7	−122.5
Official unrequited transfers	4.5	7.0	5.6	8.8	19.3
B. Direct Investment and Other Long-Term					
Capital, excl. Groups F through H	270.5	214.0	119.5	180.7	15.7
Direct investment	4.6	5.1	.7	26.9	10.7
Portfolio investment	3.1	#	8.2	#	#
Other long-term capital					
Resident official sector	129.7	123.8	107.2	116.8	−14.6
Deposit money banks	6.7	31.0	14.7	5.3	12.8
Other sectors	126.4	54.1	−11.2	31.8	6.9
Trade credits received	−2.1	−18.4	−7.0	−2.6	−3.2
Other loans received	128.4	72.6	−4.2	34.4	10.1
Total, Groups A plus B	38.6	−95.6	−102.6	−125.2	−87.5
C. Other Short-Term Capital, excl. Groups F					
through H	.7	63.2	−58.8	−18.8	119.9
Resident official sector	23.9	93.3	−53.1	−47.6	15.5
Deposit money banks	13.9	−5.2	13.7	−18.0	−12.3
Other sectors	−37.1	−24.9	−19.4	46.9	116.6
D. Net Errors and Omissions	−86.4	17.2	47.9	18.2	7.3
Total, Groups A through D	−47.0	−15.2	−113.5	−125.8	39.7
E. Counterpart Items	31.8	39.4	−57.6	−40.2	−44.8
Monetization/demonetization of gold	#	#	#	#	#
Allocation/cancellation of SDRs	#	#	#	#	#
Valuation changes in reserves	31.8	39.4	−57.6	−40.2	−44.8
Total, Groups A through E	−15.1	24.2	−171.1	−166.1	−5.1
F. Exceptional Financing	#	#	#	#	#
Total, Groups A through F	−15.1	24.2	−171.1	−166.1	−5.1
G. Liabilities Constituting Foreign Authorities'					
Reserves	−2.5	1.8	6.1	16.5	−10.7
Total, Groups A through G	−17.7	26.0	−165.0	−149.6	−15.8
H. Total Change in Reserves	17.7	−26.0	165.0	149.6	15.8
Monetary gold	#	#	#	#	#
SDRs	−6.7	−4.6	−3.8	−3.3	−2.7
Reserve position in the Fund	−4.7	#	.7	6.7	5.3
Foreign exchange assets	31.6	−25.4	167.1	146.2	13.2
Other claims	−2.5	4.0	1.0	#	#
Use of Fund credit	#	#	#	#	#
Conversion rates: guaraníes per SDR	134.69	206.03	311.37	397.90	711.39

Table 2701 (Continued)

IMF DATA ON BALANCE OF PAYMENTS, 19 LC, 1983–87

(M SDR)

P. PANAMA

Category	1983	1984	1985	1986	1987
A. Current Account, excl. Group F	388.8	212.9	296.8	387.6	264.1
Merchandise: exports f.o.b.	1,567.4	1,644.6	1,952.6	2,047.5	1,939.9
By enterprises in Colón Free Zone	1,250.9	1,361.5	1,626.7	1,745.7	1,668.9
By others					
Bananas	70.2	72.8	76.9	59.6	~
Petroleum	34.0	5.2	19.7	~	~
Other	212.3	205.1	229.3	242.2	~
Merchandise: imports f.o.b.	−2,171.0	−2,447.9	−2,688.7	−2,546.6	−2,347.1
By enterprises in Colón Free Zone	−1,061.1	−1,301.4	−1,561.9	−1,699.5	−1,576.9
By others	−1,109.9	−1,146.5	−1,126.7	−847.1	−770.2
Trade balance	−603.6	−803.3	−736.0	−499.1	−407.2
Other goods, services, and income: credit	5,241.3	4,733.5	4,267.5	3,216.8	2,630.6
Other goods, services, and income: debit	−4,290.4	−3,826.8	−3,341.7	−2,413.5	−2,020.7
Total: goods, services, and income	347.3	103.4	189.8	304.2	202.8
Private unrequited transfers	−56.2	−30.8	−30.3	−27.5	−25.6
Total, excl. official unrequited transfers	291.1	72.6	159.5	276.7	177.2
Official unrequited transfers	97.7	140.3	137.4	110.9	87.0
B. Direct Investment and Other Long-Term					
Capital, excl. Groups F through H	347.9	233.2	−282.8	25.7	~
Direct investment	67.0	9.3	58.3	−61.4	~
Portfolio investment	58.6	57.8	−180.4	43.0	~
Other long-term capital					
Resident official sector	113.6	79.7	30.3	105.5	~
Deposit money banks	191.0	112.1	−158.9	−91.5	~
Other sectors	−82.2	−25.7	−32.1	30.1	~
Loans received by public enterprises	60.4	69.3	19.1	31.6	~
Loans received by private enterprises	−144.7	−82.7	−49.2	1.9	~
Other	2.1	−12.2	−2.0	−3.4	~
Total, Groups A plus B	730.7	446.0	14.0	413.3	264.1
C. Other Short-Term Capital, excl. Groups F					
through H	−257.2	−182.5	137.4	36.1	~
Resident official sector	.3	1.9	−5.3	2.4	~
Deposit money banks	−139.2	−81.3	−135.4	−6.7	~
Other sectors	−118.3	−103.1	278.1	40.4	~
D. Net Errors and Omissions	−528.0	−364.6	−263.6	−397.7	−290.8
Total, Groups A through D	−48.5	−101.1	−112.1	51.6	−26.7
E. Counterpart Items	8.8	11.7	−25.5	−7.0	−12.8
Monetization/demonetization of gold	#	#	#	#	#
Allocation/cancellation of SDRs	#	#	#	#	#
Valuation changes in reserves	8.8	11.7	−25.5	−7.0	−12.8
Total, Groups A through E	−39.7	−89.4	−137.6	44.7	−39.5
F. Exceptional Financing	37.6	19.5	#	#	~
IBRD Structural adjustment loans	37.6	19.5	#	#	~
Total, Groups A through F	−2.1	−69.9	−137.6	44.7	−39.5
G. Liabilities Constituting Foreign Authorities'					
Reserves	#	#	#	#	~
Total, Groups A through G	−2.1	−69.9	−137.6	44.7	−39.5
H. Total Change in Reserves	2.1	69.9	137.6	−44.7	39.5
Monetary gold	#	#	#	#	#
SDRs	3.4	.4	−11.7	10.3	1.4
Reserve position in the Fund	−8.7	8.7	#	#	#
Foreign exchange assets	−100.6	−31.6	142.5	−60.2	82.8
Other claims	#	#	#	#	#
Use of Fund credit	108.0	92.5	6.8	5.3	−44.7
Conversion rates: balboas per SDR	1.0690	1.0250	1.0153	1.1732	1.2931

Table 2701 (Continued)

IMF DATA ON BALANCE OF PAYMENTS, 19 LC, 1983–87
(M SDR)

R. PERU

Category	1983	1984	1985	1986	1987
A. Current Account, excl. Group F	–820	–220	122	–908	–1,152
Merchandise: exports f.o.b.	2,824	3,072	2,932	2,156	2,015
Copper	415	430	468	383	397
Petroleum and petroleum products	509	604	635	198	212
Other	1,900	2,038	1,828	1,575	1,405
Merchandise: imports f.o.b.	–2,548	–2,089	–1,781	–2,201	–2,370
Trade balance	275	983	1,150	–45	–355
Other goods, services, and income: credit	775	809	932	792	817
Other goods, services, and income: debit	–2,072	–2,163	–2,090	–1,782	–1,716
Investment income	–1,169	–1,293	–1,120	–779	–641
Other	–904	–870	–971	–1,003	–1,075
Total: goods, services, and income	–1,022	–372	–8	–1,035	–1,254
Private unrequited transfers	~	~	~	~	~
Total, excl. official unrequited transfers	–1,022	–372	–8	–1,035	–1,254
Official unrequited transfers	203	152	130	127	102
B. Direct Investment and Other Long-Term					
Capital, excl. Groups F through H	202	–605	–815	–1,018	–948
Direct investment	35	–86	–1	17	20
Portfolio investment	#	#	#	#	#
Other long-term capital					
Resident official sector	247	–408	–692	–976	–925
Deposit money banks	#	#	#	#	#
Other sectors	–80	–111	–122	–59	–43
Total, Groups A plus B	–617	–824	–693	–1,926	–2,100
C. Other Short-Term Capital, excl. Groups F					
through H	–495	–154	–341	41	87
Resident official sector	199	50	–33	–21	–1
Deposit money banks	51	–7	20	10	#
Other sectors	–745	–196	–328	51	88
D. Net Errors and Omissions	119	–539	–298	37	–183
Total, Groups A through D	–993	–1,517	–1,332	–1,848	–2,196
E. Counterpart Items	77	116	–191	–182	–157
Monetization/demonetization of gold	#	#	#	#	#
Allocation/cancellation of SDRs	#	#	#	#	#
Valuation changes in reserves	77	116	–191	–182	–157
Total, Groups A through E	–917	–1,402	–1,524	–2,030	–2,353
F. Exceptional Financing	963	1,765	1,490	1,602	1,603
Grants from Subsidy Account	3	2	2	1	#
Long-term financing received by					
Government (debt rescheduling)	960	478	206	#	#
Payments arrears					
Resident official sector	#	1,284	1,282	1,541	1,479
Other sectors	#	#	#	60	124
Total, Groups A through F	46	363	–34	–428	–750
G. Liabilities Constituting Foreign Authorities'					
Reserves	#	#	#	#	#
Total, Groups A through G	46	363	–34	–428	–750
H. Total Change in Reserves	–46	–363	34	428	750
Monetary gold	#	#	#	#	#
SDRs	29	–22	23	#	#
Reserve position in the Fund	#	#	#	#	#
Foreign exchange assets	–111	–336	–23	494	750
Other claims	–42	–27	83	–23	~
Use of Fund credit	78	22	–49	–43	#
Conversion rates: intis per SDR	1.741	3.554	11.143	16.363	21.770

Table 2701 (Continued)

IMF DATA ON BALANCE OF PAYMENTS, 19 LC, 1983–87

(M SDR)

S. URUGUAY

Category	1983	1984	1985	1986	1987
A. Current Account, excl. Group F	−55.9	−125.9	−118.3	77.7	−96.2
Merchandise: exports f.o.b.	1,081.8	902.0	840.7	927.2	919.6
Hides	70.5	89.4	60.4	63.7	64.9
Meat	231.4	142.3	116.1	155.1	100.0
Wood	157.7	160.5	161.3	171.8	186.8
Manufactures: leather	59.6	53.6	51.8	62.9	88.9
Manufactures: wool	91.7	114.3	96.2	97.9	110.3
Other	470.8	341.9	354.9	375.9	368.8
Merchandise: imports f.o.b.	−692.0	−714.3	−665.2	−674.2	−835.1
Trade balance	389.8	187.7	175.5	253.0	84.5
Other goods, services, and income: credit	297.0	441.0	469.4	430.0	361.6
Other goods, services, and income: debit	−753.0	−764.4	−773.8	−626.9	−548.5
Total: goods, services, and income	−66.2	−135.7	−128.9	56.2	−102.4
Private unrequited transfers	#	#	#	#	#
Total, excl. official unrequited transfers	−66.2	−135.7	−128.9	56.2	−102.4
Official unrequited transfers	10.3	9.8	10.6	21.6	6.2
B. Direct Investment and Other Long-Term Capital, excl. Groups F through H	602.0	29.5	58.3	117.0	30.9
Direct investment	5.2	3.3	−7.8	−3.8	3.8
Portfolio investment	−14.6	6.6	94.5	73.6	10.1
Other long-term capital					
Resident official sector	308.0	45.0	−22.5	37.7	7.0
Deposit money banks	34.4	−1.1	−4.9	−.6	4.3
Other sectors	268.8	−24.4	−1.1	10.1	5.6
Total, Groups A plus B	546.0	−96.5	−60.0	194.8	−65.3
C. Other Short-Term Capital, excl. Groups F through H	−336.0	155.1	−134.0	−128.0	152.1
Resident official sector	37.9	47.0	123.0	4.7	131.4
Deposit money banks	−62.3	65.8	−145.9	−58.7	−10.6
Other sectors	−311.6	42.3	−111.2	−74.0	31.3
D. Net Errors and Omissions	−276.1	−140.6	257.7	178.4	−53.5
Total, Groups A through D	−66.1	−81.9	63.7	245.2	33.3
E. Counterpart Items	−41.5	17.2	−5.6	−28.8	−54.2
Monetization/demonetization of gold	−48.6	7.4	5.6	.7	2.0
Allocation/cancellation of SDRs	#	#	#	#	#
Valuation changes in reserves	7.2	9.8	−11.2	−29.5	−56.2
Total, Groups A through E	−107.6	−64.8	58.1	216.4	−20.9
F. Exceptional Financing	#	#	#	#	30.9
IBRD structural adjustment loans	#	#	#	#	30.9
Total, Groups A through F	−107.6	−64.8	58.1	216.4	10.0
G. Liabilities Constituting Foreign Authorities' Reserves	.3	−1.2	−.3	−.2	3.2
Total, Groups A through G	−107.3	−65.9	57.8	216.2	13.2
H. Total Change in Reserves	107.3	65.9	−57.8	−216.2	−13.2
Monetary gold	48.6	−7.4	−5.6	−.7	−2.0
SDRs	−1.9	−1.5	−8.2	3.6	−38.4
Reserve position in the Fund	−9.5	9.5	#	#	#
Foreign exchange assets	−80.7	53.7	−13.2	−238.7	58.5
Other claims	10.8	11.7	−122.5	15.0	15.2
Use of Fund credit	140.0	#	91.8	4.5	−46.5
Conversion rates: new pesos per SDR	36.92	57.53	102.99	178.31	293.09

Table 2701 (Continued)

IMF DATA ON BALANCE OF PAYMENTS, 19 LC, 1983–87
(M SDR)

T. VENEZUELA

Category	1983	1984	1985	1986	1987
A. Current Account, excl. Group F	4,141	5,286	3,039	−1,714	−245
Merchandise: exports f.o.b.	13,630	15,577	13,964	7,372	8,110
Oil	12,609	14,433	12,668	6,153	7,041
Other	1,022	1,144	1,296	1,220	1,070
Merchandise: imports f.o.b.	−5,995	−7,085	−7,276	−6,678	−6,519
Trade balance	7,635	8,493	6,687	694	1,591
Other goods, services, and income: credit	2,591	2,946	2,682	2,174	1,811
Other goods, services, and income: debit	−5,888	−6,019	−6,204	−4,502	−3,605
Total: goods, services, and income	4,339	5,419	3,165	−1,635	−203
Private unrequited transfers	−175	−105	−100	−61	−26
Total, excl. official unrequited transfers	4,164	5,314	3,065	−1,696	−230
Official unrequited transfers	−22	−28	−26	−18	−15
B. Direct Investment and Other Long-Term					
Capital, excl. Groups F through H	266	−1,283	−689	−1,182	−1,067
Direct investment	80	41	104	14	46
Portfolio investment	188	−125	~	~	~
Other long-term capital					
Resident official sector	308	−937	−801	−1,014	−379
Deposit money banks	#	#	#	#	#
Other sectors	−311	−262	7	−182	−735
Assets of Venezuelan Investment Fund	−116	−22	−45	38	−19
Other	−195	−240	52	−219	−716
Total, Groups A plus B	4,407	4,003	2,350	−2,896	−1,312
C. Other Short-Term Capital, excl. Groups F					
through H	−3,848	−2,772	−746	−270	617
Resident official sector	−16	23	23	58	−14
Deposit money banks	−324	−622	79	−35	~
Other sectors	−3,509	−2,173	−847	−293	631
D. Net Errors and Omissions	−251	316	−297	−186	172
Total, Groups A through D	308	1,547	1,308	−3,353	−868
E. Counterpart Items	320	731	−1,369	−1,062	−534
Monetization/demonetization of gold	#	#	#	#	#
Allocation/cancellation of SDRs	#	#	#	#	#
Valuation changes in reserves	320	731	−1,369	−1,062	−534
Total, Groups A through E	628	2,278	−61	−4,414	−1,402
F. Exceptional Financing	~	~	~	~	~
Total, Groups A through F	628	2,278	−61	−4,414	−1,402
G. Liabilities Constituting Foreign Authorities'					
Reserves	#	#	#	#	#
Total, Groups A through G	628	2,278	−61	−4,414	−1,402
H. Total Change in Reserves	−628	−2,278	61	4,414	1,402
Monetary gold	#	#	#	#	#
SDRs	62	−45	−69	−47	−36
Reserve position in the Fund	−195	50	82	89	183
Foreign exchange assets	−1,202	−1,785	−265	4,026	914
Other claims	707	−497	313	347	340
Use of Fund credit	#	#	#	#	#
Conversion rates: bolívares per SDR	4.594	7.193	7.615	9.483	18.750

Table 2701 (Continued)

IMF DATA ON BALANCE OF PAYMENTS, 19 LC, 1983–87
(M SDR)

UNITED STATES[1]

Category	1983	1984	1985	1986	1987
A. Current Account, excl. Group F	−43.71	−104.98	−114.71	−118.05	−119.26
Merchandise: exports f.o.b.	188.84	214.64	212.98	190.96	192.75
Merchandise: imports f.o.b.	−251.88	−324.54	−332.69	−313.97	−316.67
Trade balance	−63.05	−109.90	−119.71	−123.01	−123.92
Other goods, services, and income: credit	123.68	136.80	140.56	128.90	135.29
Reinvested earnings	6.66	8.07	17.91	16.98	27.41
Other investment income	65.67	75.75	68.77	59.95	52.58
Other	51.36	52.98	53.88	51.97	55.31
Other goods, services, and income: debit	−95.44	−119.93	−120.55	−110.92	−120.31
Reinvested earnings	−.09	−2.82	1.17	1.87	−2.07
Other investment income	−48.97	−63.04	−63.36	−59.04	−62.44
Other	−46.38	−54.07	−58.36	−53.75	−55.80
Total: goods, services, and income	−34.81	−93.03	−99.71	−105.04	−108.93
Private unrequited transfers	−.93	−1.40	−1.89	−1.18	−.94
Total, excl. official unrequited transfers	−35.74	−94.43	−101.60	−106.21	−109.88
Official unrequited transfers	−7.97	−10.55	−13.11	−11.84	−9.38
Grants (excluding Military)	−5.91	−8.40	−10.98	−10.01	−7.68
Other	−2.06	−2.16	−2.13	−1.83	−1.70
B. Direct Investment and Other Long-Term Capital, excl. Groups F through H	−1.73	38.21	72.19	61.39	22.77
Direct investment	10.79	21.91	2.19	4.62	−1.70
In United States	11.20	24.73	18.88	28.71	32.45
Abroad	−.41	−2.82	−16.69	−24.08	−34.16
Portfolio investment	4.38	28.56	62.42	61.26	25.25
Other long-term capital					
Resident official sector	−4.36	−4.15	−1.14	−.48	−1.41
Disbursements on loans extended	−7.64	−7.58	−5.84	−6.06	−3.74
Repayments on loans extended	4.29	3.98	4.23	4.81	5.53
Other	−1.01	−.56	.48	.77	−3.20
Deposit money banks	−12.54	−8.11	8.72	−4.02	.63
Other sectors	~	~	~	~	~
Total, Groups A plus B	−45.44	−66.77	−42.53	−56.67	−96.49
C. Other Short-Term Capital, excl. Groups F through H	31.20	40.78	29.61	14.41	39.08
Resident official sector	5.24	1.39	−1.37	−.31	−1.36
Deposit money banks	27.65	26.47	24.11	22.80	35.62
Other sectors	−1.69	12.92	6.88	−8.07	4.81
D. Net Errors and Omissions	10.40	26.42	18.74	13.59	13.70
Total, Groups A through D	−3.84	.43	5.82	−28.66	−43.70
E. Counterpart Items	−.43	−.59	1.24	1.46	.97
Monetization/demonetization of gold	−.26	−.23	−.04	−.20	.12
Allocation/cancellation of SDRs	#	#	#	#	#
Valuation changes in reserves	−.17	−.36	1.28	1.66	.85
Total, Groups A through E	−4.27	−.16	7.06	−27.20	−42.73
F. Exceptional Financing	#	#	#	#	#
Security issues in foreign currencies	#	#	#	#	#
Total, Groups A through F	−4.27	−.16	7.06	−27.20	−42.73
G. Liabilities Constituting Foreign Authorities' Reserves	4.96	2.64	−2.21	28.39	36.71
Total, Groups A through G	.68	2.48	4.85	1.19	−6.03
H. Total Change in Reserves	−.68	−2.48	−4.85	−1.19	6.03
Monetary gold	.25	.23	.05	.21	−.12
SDRs	−.04	−.95	−.88	−.22	−.39
Reserve position in the Fund	−4.14	−.97	.90	1.29	1.59
Foreign exchange assets	3.25	−.78	−4.91	−2.46	4.94
Other claims	#	#	#	#	#
Use of Fund credit	#	#	#	#	#
Conversion rates: U.S. dollars per SDR	1.0690	1.0250	1.0153	1.1732	1.2931

1. Billions of SDRs.

a. For an alternative series, 1953–81 data, see SALA, 23-2720; for data for previous years, see SALA, 24-2710 through 2720.

SOURCE: IMF-BPS-Y, vol. 36, no. 1, 1985; vol. 37, no. 1, 1986; vol. 38, no. 1, 1987; vol. 39, part 1, 1988.

Table 2702

IMF DATA ON VALUE OF MERCHANDISE IMPORTS,[1] 19 LC, 1955–88

(M US)

Year	A. ARGENTINA	B. BOLIVIA	C. BRAZIL	D. CHILE	E. COLOMBIA	F. COSTA RICA	H. DOMINICAN REP.	I. ECUADOR	J. EL SALVADOR	K. GUATEMALA
1955	-1,038	-77.6	-1,099	-327	~	-77.7	-100.2	-94.7	-91.9	-98.1
1956	-988	-79.1	-1,046	-332	-614	-81.6	-110.0	-95.9	-105.0	-126.9
1957	-1,160	-85.9	-1,285	-383	-451	-92.0	-117.5	-98.5	-115.2	-136.1
1958	-1,091	-74.1	-1,179	-363	-384	-88.9	-134.4	-102.2	-108.3	-138.1
1959	-879	-62.4	-1,210	-361	-402	-93.5	-111.5	-96.1	-99.7	124.3
1960	-1,106	-68.2	-1,293	-474	-496	-98.9	-90.3	-109.8	-122.6	-124.8
1961	-1,200	-74.7	-1,292	-532	-531	-96.0	-72.1	-108.7	-109.0	-120.6
1962	-1,200	-92.5	-1,304	-512	-537	-102.4	-132.3	-112.1	-124.9	-122.9
1963	-868	-98.1	-1,294	-490	-497	-112.7	-164.6	-118.7	-152.2	-150.4
1964	-953	-106.7	-1,086	-529	-582	-125.8	-202.4	-140.0	-191.8	-180.5
1965	-1,062	-126.6	-941	-530	-430	-160.9	-120.7	-151.8	-185.7	-206.1
1966	-995	-138.8	-1,303	-661	-639	-162.1	-166.9	-160.3	-201.0	-201.8
1967	-970	-151.8	-1,441	-651	-464	-173.7	-174.7	-195.7	-204.9	-226.5
1968	-1,035	-161.5	-1,855	-726	-615	-193.7	-196.8	-231.6	-198.2	-237.6
1969	-1,395	-173.4	-1,993	-786	-648	-221.5	-217.2	-218.7	-193.0	-240.9
1970	-1,499	-132.2	-2,507	-867	-802	-286.8	-278.0	-249.6	-194.7	-266.6
1971	-1,653	-144.3	-3,256	-927	-903	-317.2	-390.7	-306.8	-226.0	-290.0
1972	-1,685	-153.2	-4,193	-1,012	-850	-337.1	-337.7	-284.1	-249.7	-294.8
1973	-1,978	-193.2	-6,154	-1,329	-983	-412.1	-421.9	-397.5	-339.8	-391.4
1974	-3,216	-324.1	-12,562	-1,901	-1,511	-648.9	-673.0	-875.2	-522.2	-631.5
1975	-3,510	-469.9	-12,042	-1,520	-1,415	-627.2	-772.7	-1,006.3	-550.7	-672.4
1976	-2,765	-512.3	-12,347	-1,473	-1,654	-695.4	-763.6	-1,047.9	-681.0	-950.7
1977	-3,799	-579.0	-12,023	-2,151	-1,970	-925.1	-849.3	-1,360.5	-861.0	-1,087.0
1978	-3,488	-723.9	-13,631	-2,886	-2,552	-1,049.4	-862.4	-1,704.0	-951.1	-1,283.8
1979	-6,028	-815.0	-17,961	-4,190	-2,978	-1,257.2	-1,137.5	-2,096.8	-954.7	-1,401.7
1980	-9,394	-680.1	-22,955	-5,469	-4,283	-1,375.2	-1,519.7	-2,241.8	-897.0	-1,472.6
1981	-8,431	-680.1	-22,091	-6,513	-4,730	-1,090.6	-1,451.7	-2,361.5	-898.4	-1,540.0
1982	-4,859	-496.0	-19,395	-3,643	-5,358	-804.9	-1,257.3	-2,187.0	-799.8	-1,284.3
1983	-4,119	-496.0	-15,429	-2,845	-4,464	-894.3	-1,279.0	-1,421.0	-832.2	-1,056.0
1984	-4,118	-412.3	-13,916	-3,357	-4,027	-992.9	-1,257.1	-1,567.0	-914.5	-1,182.2
1985	-3,518	-462.8	-13,168	-2,954	-3,673	-1,001.0	-1,285.9	-1,611.0	-895.0	-1,076.7
1986	-4,406	-596.5	-14,044	-3,099	-3,490	-1,045.2	-1,351.7	-1,631.0	-902.3	-875.7
1987	-5,392	-646.3	~	~	~	-1,248.0	-1,550.0	-2,054.0	~	-1,333.2
1988	~	-485.1	-15,052	-3,994	-3,793	~	~	-1,614.0	~	~

Table 2702 (Continued)

IMF DATA ON VALUE OF MERCHANDISE IMPORTS,[1] 19 LC, 1955–88

(M US)

Year	L. HAITI	M. HONDURAS	N. MEXICO	O. NICARAGUA	P. PANAMA	Q. PARAGUAY	R. PERU	S. URUGUAY	T. VENEZUELA	UNITED STATES[2]
1955	~	-55.3	-840	~	-98	-33.9	~	~	~	-11.52
1956	~	-57.7	-1,108	-57.6	-107	-37.1	-341	~	-1,170	-12.78
1957	~	-68.6	-1,102	-68.4	-122	-39.2	-397	~	-1,775	-13.29
1958	~	-65.7	-1,090	-65.3	-94	-44.3	-331	~	-1,512	-12.95
1959	~	-61.6	-964	-52.7	-97	-36.5	-273	-151.7	-1,520	-15.31
1960	~	-64.1	-1,132	-56.4	-109	-43.9	-327	-187.9	-1,145	-14.76
1961	~	-65.2	-1,086	-58.7	-124	-47.9	-408	-182.8	-1,055	-14.54
1962	~	-72.8	-1,097	-78.7	-145	-41.1	-468	-207.6	-1,161	-16.26
1963	-39.1	-88.3	-1,186	-91.0	-164	-41.4	-509	-151.6	-1,037	-17.05
1964	-37.1	-94.7	-1,424	-109.8	-168	-45.1	-511	-168.6	-1,192	-18.70
1965	-42.6	-113.2	-1,498	-133.9	-192	-56.7	-653	-123.1	-1,354	-21.51
1966	-43.7	-138.0	-1,581	-151.8	-218	-63.3	-803	-132.2	-1,316	-25.49
1967	-40.3	-152.0	-1,760	-172.2	-232	-65.7	-810	-146.4	-1,366	-26.87
1968	-38.7	-169.4	-1,892	-166.5	-246	-73.5	-673	-135.9	-1,510	-32.99
1969	-42.1	-169.7	-1,983	-159.3	-285	-81.2	-659	-170.0	-1,554	-35.81
1970	-47.8	-203.4	-2,236	-178.6	-331	-76.6	-699	-203.1	-1,713	-39.86
1971	-53.2	-178.0	-2,158	-190.2	-364	-82.9	-730	-203.0	-1,896	-45.58
1972	-57.3	-176.5	-2,610	-205.5	-409	-78.7	-812	-178.7	-2,222	-55.80
1973	-66.5	-243.4	-3,656	-327.5	-458	-127.3	-1,097	-248.6	-2,626	-70.50
1974	-96.5	-387.5	-5,791	-541.8	-761	-198.3	-1,909	-433.6	-3,876	-103.82
1975	-122.1	-372.4	-6,278	-482.1	-823	-227.3	-2,389	-494.0	-5,462	-98.18
1976	-164.2	-432.5	-5,771	-485.0	-783	-236.4	-2,099	-536.6	-7,337	-124.23
1977	-199.9	-550.1	-5,625	-704.2	-790	-360.1	-2,164	-686.7	-10,194	-151.91
1978	-207.4	-654.5	-7,992	-553.3	-862	-432.0	-1,601	-709.8	-11,234	-176.03
1979	-220.1	-783.5	-12,131	-388.9	-1,086	-577.1	-1,951	-1,166.2	-10,004	-212.03
1980	-319.0	-954.1	-18,896	-802.9	-2,995	-675.3	-3,062	-1,668.2	-10,877	-249.77
1981	-360.1	-898.6	-24,037	-922.4	-3,316	-772.4	-3,802	-1,592.1	-12,123	-265.08
1982	-301.9	-680.7	-14,435	-723.5	-3,045	-711.3	-3,721	-1,038.4	-13,584	-247.65
1983	-325.9	-756.3	-8,550	-778.1	-2,321	-551.4	-2,722	-739.7	-6,409	-268.89
1984	-337.9	-884.8	-11,255	-799.6	-2,509	-649.1	-2,140	-732.2	-7,260	-332.41
1985	-344.7	-879.2	-13,212	-800.2	-2,731	-515.9	-1,806	-675.4	-7,530	-338.09
1986	-303.2	-874.1	-11,432	-726.5	-2,921	-735.8	-2,596	-791.0	-7,862	-368.52
1987	-311.2	-893.9	-12,222	~	-3,116	-1,048.8	-3,182	-1,079.9	-8,832	-409.85
1988	-283.9	~	-18,905	~	-2,515	-1,029.5	-2,750	~	~	-446.43

1. FOB.
2. Data in billions.

SOURCE: IMF-IFS-Y, 1981 and 1985; IMF-IFS, June 1987; IMF-IFS-Y, 1988, line 77abd; IMF-IFS, Aug. 1989, line 77abd.

Table 2703

VALUE OF MERCHANDISE EXPORTS,[1] 19 LC, 1955-88
(M US)

Year	A. ARGENTINA	B. BOLIVIA	C. BRAZIL	D. CHILE	E. COLOMBIA	F. COSTA RICA	H. DOMINICAN REP.	I. ECUADOR	J. EL SALVADOR	K. GUATEMALA
1955	929	81.0	1,419	487	~	80.7	115.0	114.9	106.5	106.3
1956	944	84.6	1,483	489	654	64.7	121.8	117.8	123.0	122.5
1957	974	76.9	1,392	402	590	82.7	161.5	137.1	127.1	115.9
1958	994	51.3	1,244	364	527	93.1	126.4	136.9	118.0	107.9
1959	1,009	61.6	1,282	451	514	76.0	131.8	144.2	111.8	103.7
1960	1,079	54.4	1,270	480	480	87.0	157.4	146.3	102.6	115.9
1961	964	63.8	1,405	444	462	83.3	138.9	132.0	118.8	114.0
1962	1,216	63.6	1,215	484	462	92.7	169.6	149.1	138.9	119.0
1963	1,365	71.9	1,406	493	474	94.9	174.3	150.9	150.2	153.4
1964	1,410	100.1	1,430	592	623	114.4	179.4	161.9	175.5	174.3
1965	1,493	115.1	1,596	692	581	111.7	125.5	181.0	190.0	192.1
1966	1,593	130.9	1,741	860	526	135.7	136.7	187.3	189.5	231.9
1967	1,464	153.2	1,654	883	552	143.3	156.2	198.9	207.9	203.9
1968	1,368	155.5	1,881	908	605	170.0	163.5	210.7	211.7	233.5
1969	1,612	177.8	2,311	1,172	672	189.6	183.4	193.4	202.1	262.5
1970	1,773	190.4	2,739	1,113	788	231.0	214.0	234.9	236.1	297.1
1971	1,740	181.6	2,891	1,000	754	225.3	240.7	238.0	243.9	286.9
1972	1,941	201.3	3,941	851	979	278.8	347.6	323.2	301.7	335.9
1973	3,266	260.8	6,093	1,316	1,263	344.8	442.1	584.7	358.4	442.0
1974	3,930	556.5	7,814	2,152	1,495	440.2	636.8	1,225.4	464.5	582.3
1975	2,961	444.7	8,492	1,590	1,683	493.1	893.8	1,012.8	533.0	640.9
1976	3,918	563.0	9,961	2,116	2,202	592.4	716.4	1,307.2	744.6	760.4
1977	5,651	634.3	11,923	2,186	2,660	827.8	780.5	1,400.8	973.5	1,160.2
1978	6,401	627.3	12,473	2,460	3,155	863.9	675.5	1,529.2	801.6	1,092.4
1979	7,810	761.8	15,244	3,835	3,441	942.1	868.6	2,150.5	1,132.3	1,221.4
1980	8,021	941.9	20,132	4,705	3,986	1,000.9	961.9	2,544.2	1,075.3	1,519.8
1981	9,143	909.1	23,276	3,836	3,158	1,002.6	1,188.0	2,544.2	798.0	1,291.3
1982	7,623	827.7	20,173	3,706	3,114	869.0	767.7	2,327.0	699.6	1,170.4
1983	7,835	755.1	21,898	3,831	2,970	852.5	785.2	2,348.0	758.0	1,091.7
1984	8,100	724.5	27,002	3,650	4,273	997.5	868.1	2,622.0	725.9	1,132.2
1985	8,396	623.4	25,634	3,804	3,650	939.1	738.5	2,905.0	679.0	1,059.7
1986	6,852	545.5	22,392	4,199	5,331	1,084.8	722.1	2,186.0	777.9	1,043.8
1987	6,360	518.7	26,210	5,224	5,661	1,107.0	711.2	2,021.0	~	977.9
1988	~	542.5	~	~	~	~	~	2,203.0	~	~

Table 2703 (Continued)
VALUE OF MERCHANDISE EXPORTS,[1] 19 LC, 1955–88
(M US)

Year	L. HAITI	M. HONDURAS	N. MEXICO	O. NICARAGUA	P. PANAMA	Q. PARAGUAY	R. PERU	S. URUGUAY	T. VENEZUELA	UNITED STATES[2]
1955	~	53.7	861	~	76	38.7	~	~	~	14.26
1956	~	72.9	844	65.5	73	36.8	-321	~	2,221	17.35
1957	~	64.8	740	70.6	70	36.9	332	~	2,764	19.39
1958	~	69.5	752	70.4	40	33.4	292	~	2,508	16.26
1959	~	68.5	744	75.0	43	35.4	323	108.3	2,326	16.30
1960	~	63.1	778	63.9	39	36.5	445	129.4	2,384	19.65
1961	~	73.0	826	69.9	41	43.1	510	174.7	2,453	20.11
1962	~	81.5	930	90.4	60	40.4	556	153.5	2,544	20.78
1963	43.2	84.4	985	106.6	73	39.5	555	166.2	2,464	22.27
1964	37.9	95.1	1,054	125.5	82	46.2	685	183.6	2,480	25.50
1965	37.8	128.2	1,146	149.2	93	60.8	685	196.3	2,482	26.46
1966	34.8	144.4	1,244	142.5	103	53.6	789	190.3	2,404	29.31
1967	32.3	155.9	1,152	147.9	109	50.4	742	159.8	2,495	30.67
1968	36.3	181.0	1,258	162.3	118	50.0	850	179.3	2,468	33.63
1969	36.7	170.9	1,454	158.7	133	55.2	881	199.2	2,409	36.41
1970	39.1	178.2	1,348	178.6	130	65.3	1,034	224.1	2,602	42.45
1971	45.3	194.6	1,409	187.3	138	66.5	890	196.8	3,103	43.31
1972	39.2	212.1	1,717	249.4	146	85.6	945	281.6	3,152	49.38
1973	49.6	266.6	2,141	278.4	162	128.0	1,112	327.6	4,721	71.41
1974	62.8	300.3	2,999	381.0	251	173.2	1,506	281.4	11,085	98.31
1975	71.2	309.7	3,007	374.9	331	188.0	1,291	384.9	8,853	107.09
1976	99.7	411.7	3,475	541.8	269	202.1	1,360	565.0	9,253	114.74
1977	137.6	529.9	4,604	636.2	289	327.1	1,726	611.5	9,556	120.81
1978	149.9	626.2	6,246	646.0	304	356.1	1,941	686.1	9,084	142.05
1979	138.0	756.5	9,301	615.9	356	384.5	3,491	788.1	14,159	184.47
1980	215.8	850.3	16,066	450.4	2,267	400.3	3,898	1,058.5	19,051	224.27
1981	151.1	783.8	19,838	508.2	2,540	398.5	3,249	1,229.7	19,963	237.01
1982	177.1	676.5	21,230	406.0	2,411	396.2	3,293	1,256.4	16,332	211.20
1983	186.6	698.7	22,312	428.4	1,676	326.0	3,015	1,156.4	14,571	201.81
1984	214.6	737.0	24,196	385.7	1,686	361.3	3,147	924.6	15,841	219.90
1985	223.0	789.6	21,663	301.5	1,974	324.4	2,978	853.6	14,660	215.94
1986	190.8	891.3	16,031	247.2	2,386	573.4	2,531	1,087.8	9,122	223.98
1987	210.1	862.6	20,655	~	2,521	951.6	2,661	1,189.1	10,567	249.57
1988	156.1	~	20,657	~	2,338	1,098.1	2,694	~	~	320.14

1. FOB.
2. Data in billions.

SOURCE: IMF-IFS-Y, 1981 and 1985; IMF-IFS, June 1987; IMF-IFS-Y, 1988, line 77ad; IMF-IFS, Aug. 1988, line 77aad.

Table 2704

TRADE BALANCES, 19 LC, 1955–88
(M US)

Year	A. ARGENTINA	B. BOLIVIA	C. BRAZIL	D. CHILE	E. COLOMBIA	F. COSTA RICA	H. DOMINICAN REP.	I. ECUADOR	J. EL SALVADOR	K. GUATEMALA
1955	-109	3.4	320	160	~	3.0	14.8	20.2	14.6	8.2
1956	-54	5.5	437	157	40	-16.9	11.8	21.9	18.0	-4.4
1957	-186	-9.0	107	19	139	-9.3	44.0	38.6	11.9	-20.2
1958	-97	-22.8	65	1	143	4.2	-8.0	34.7	9.7	-30.2
1959	130	-.8	72	90	112	-17.5	20.3	48.1	12.1	-20.6
1960	-27	-13.8	-23	6	-16	-11.9	67.1	36.5	-20.0	-8.9
1961	-328	-10.9	113	-88	-69	-12.7	66.8	23.3	9.8	-6.6
1962	16	-28.9	-89	-28	-75	-9.7	37.3	37.0	14.0	-3.9
1963	497	-26.2	112	3	-23	-17.8	9.7	32.2	-2.0	3.0
1964	457	-6.6	344	63	41	-11.4	-23.0	21.9	-16.3	-6.2
1965	431	-11.5	655	162	151	-49.2	4.8	29.2	4.3	-14.0
1966	598	-7.9	438	199	-113	-26.4	-30.2	27.0	-11.5	30.1
1967	494	1.4	213	232	88	-30.4	-18.5	3.2	3.0	-22.6
1968	333	-6.0	26	182	-10	-23.7	-33.3	-20.9	13.5	-4.1
1969	217	4.4	318	386	24	-31.9	-33.8	-25.3	9.1	21.6
1970	274	55.2	232	246	-14	-55.8	-64.0	-14.7	41.4	30.5
1971	87	37.3	-365	73	-148	-92.0	-69.0	-68.8	18.0	-3.1
1972	256	48.1	-252	-161	129	-58.3	9.9	39.1	52.0	41.1
1973	1,289	67.6	-61	-13	280	-67.4	20.2	187.3	18.6	50.7
1974	714	232.4	-4,748	250	-17	-208.8	-36.2	350.2	-57.7	49.2
1975	-549	-25.1	-3,550	70	268	-134.2	121.1	6.6	-17.7	-31.4
1976	1,153	50.7	-2,386	643	548	-103.0	-47.2	259.3	63.7	-190.3
1977	1,852	55.3	-100	35	690	-97.3	-68.8	40.3	112.5	73.2
1978	2,913	-96.6	-1,158	-426	603	-185.5	-186.9	-174.8	-149.4	-191.4
1979	1,782	-53.2	-2,717	-355	464	-315.1	-268.9	53.7	177.6	-180.3
1980	-1,373	261.8	2,833	-764	-297	-374.3	-557.8	302.4	178.4	47.2
1981	712	229.0	1,185	-2,677	-1,572	-88.0	-263.7	182.7	-100.3	-248.7
1982	2,764	331.7	778	63	-2,244	64.1	-489.6	140.0	-100.2	-113.9
1983	3,716	259.1	6,469	986	-1,494	-41.8	-493.8	927.0	-74.3	35.7
1984	3,982	312.2	13,086	293	246	4.6	-398.0	1,055.0	-188.6	-50.0
1985	4,878	160.6	12,466	850	-23	-61.9	-547.4	1,294.0	-216.0	-17.0
1986	2,446	-51.0	8,348	1,100	1,922	39.6	-629.6	555.0	-124.4	168.1
1987	968	-127.6	11,158	1,230	1,868	-141.0	-838.8	-33.0	~	-355.3
1988	~	57.4	~	~	~	~	~	589.0	~	~

Table 2704 (Continued)

TRADE BALANCES, 19 LC, 1955–88

(M US)

Year	L. HAITI	M. HONDURAS	N. MEXICO	O. NICARAGUA	P. PANAMA	Q. PARAGUAY	R. PERU	S. URUGUAY	T. VENEZUELA	UNITED STATES[1]
1955	-17.1	-1.6	21	~	-21	4.8	~	~	~	2.75
1956	-6.1	15.2	-174	7.9	-34	-.3	-20	~	1,051	4.57
1957	-13.3	-3.8	-362	2.2	-52	-2.3	-65	~	989	6.10
1958	-5.4	3.8	-338	5.1	-54	-10.9	-39	~	996	3.31
1959	-9.5	6.9	-220	22.3	-54	-1.1	50	-43.4	806	.99
1960	-5.3	-1.0	-354	7.5	-70	-7.4	118	-58.5	1,239	4.89
1961	-21.4	7.8	-260	11.2	-82	-4.8	102	-8.1	1,398	5.57
1962	-7.1	8.7	-167	11.7	-85	-.7	88	-54.1	1,383	4.52
1963	4.1	-3.9	-201	15.6	-91	-1.9	46	14.6	1,427	5.22
1964	.8	.4	-370	15.7	-86	1.1	174	15.0	1,288	6.80
1965	-4.8	15.0	-325	15.3	-100	4.1	32	73.2	1,128	4.95
1966	-8.9	6.4	-337	-9.3	-114	-9.7	-14	58.1	1,088	3.82
1967	-8.0	3.9	-608	-24.3	-123	-15.3	-68	13.4	1,129	3.80
1968	-2.4	11.6	-634	-4.2	-129	-23.5	177	43.4	958	.64
1969	-5.4	1.2	-529	-.6	-153	-26.0	222	29.2	855	.60
1970	-8.7	-25.2	-888	#	-201	-11.3	335	21.0	889	2.59
1971	-9.7	16.5	-749	-2.9	-226	-16.4	159	-6.2	1,207	-2.27
1972	-18.0	35.6	-894	43.9	-263	6.8	133	102.9	930	-6.42
1973	-16.9	23.1	-1,515	-49.1	-296	.7	15	79.0	2,095	.91
1974	-33.7	-87.2	-2,791	-160.8	-510	-25.1	-403	-52.2	7,209	-5.51
1975	-50.9	-62.7	-3,272	-107.2	-492	-39.3	-1,099	-109.2	3,391	8.91
1976	-64.5	-20.8	-2,295	56.8	-514	-34.3	-740	28.4	1,916	-9.49
1977	-62.3	-20.3	-1,021	-68.0	-502	-33.0	-438	-75.2	-638	-31.10
1978	-57.5	-28.4	-1,745	92.7	-558	-75.9	340	-23.7	-2,150	-33.98
1979	-82.1	-26.9	-2,830	227.0	-730	-192.6	1,540	-378.1	4,155	-27.56
1980	-103.2	-103.8	-2,830	-352.5	-727	-275.0	837	-609.7	8,174	-25.50
1981	-209.0	-114.8	-4,099	414.2	-775	-373.9	-553	-362.4	7,840	-27.98
1982	-124.8	-4.2	6,795	-317.5	-634	-315.1	-428	218.0	2,748	-36.45
1983	-139.3	-57.6	13,762	-349.3	-645	-225.4	293	416.7	8,162	-67.08
1984	-123.3	-147.8	12,941	-413.9	-823	-287.8	1,007	192.4	8,581	-112.51
1985	-121.7	-89.6	8,451	-498.7	-757	-191.5	1,172	178.2	7,130	-122.15
1986	-112.5	17.2	4,599	-479.3	-535	-162.4	-65	296.8	1,260	-144.54
1987	-101.1	-31.3	8,433	~	-596	-97.2	-521	109.2	1,735	-160.28
1988	-127.8	~	1,752	~	-177	68.6	-56	~	~	-126.29

1. Data in billions.

SOURCE: IMF-IFS-Y, 1982 and 1985; IMF-IFS, June 1987; IMF-IFS-Y, 1988; IMF-IFS,
    Aug. 1989, line 77acd.

Table 2705

REAL TRADE BALANCES, 19 L, 1951–88

(M US of 1980)

	Country	1951	1952	1953	1954	1955	1956	1957	1958	1959	1960	1961	1962
A.	ARGENTINA[1]	~	~	1,353.7	557.1	–372.0	–176.5	–592.4	–311.9	418.0	–86.3	–1,028.2	50.5
B.	BOLIVIA	115.2	–7.5	–25.2	2.4	11.6	18.0	–28.7	–73.3	–2.6	–44.1	–34.2	–91.2
C.	BRAZIL	225.6	–969.5	1,438.8	519.0	1,092.2	1,428.1	340.8	209.0	231.5	–73.5	354.2	–280.8
D.	CHILE	235.7	444.1	119.1	373.7	546.1	513.1	60.5	3.22	289.4	19.2	–275.9	–88.3
E.	COLOMBIA	~	~	~	~	~	130.7	442.7	459.8	360.1	–51.1	–216.3	–236.6
F.	COSTA RICA	44.4	444.4	49.3	51.2	10.2	–55.2	–29.6	13.5	–56.3	–38.0	–39.8	–30.6
H.	DOMINICAN REP.	143.4	724.1	62.2	130.1	50.6	38.6	140.1	–25.7	65.3	214.4	209.4	117.7
I.	ECUADOR	62.3	540.7	103.7	86.9	68.9	71.6	122.9	111.6	154.7	116.6	73.0	116.7
J.	EL SALVADOR	55.9	528.1	65.3	61.9	49.8	58.8	37.9	31.2	38.9	–63.9	30.7	44.2
K.	GUATEMALA	12.1	549.8	71.4	65.7	28.0	–14.4	–64.3	–97.1	–66.2	–28.4	–20.7	–12.3
L.	HAITI	19.2	8.8	–22.8	27.7	–58.4	–19.9	–42.4	–17.4	–30.6	–16.9	–67.1	–22.4
M.	HONDURAS	67.7	418.0	52.0	14.2	–5.4	49.7	–12.1	12.2	22.2	–3.2	24.5	27.4
N.	MEXICO	~	~	–57.5	–31.8	71.7	–568.6	–1,152.9	–1,086.8	–707.4	–1,131.0	–815.1	–526.8
O.	NICARAGUA	~	~	~	~	~	25.8	7.0	16.4	71.7	24.0	35.1	36.9
P.	PANAMA	~	~	~	~	–71.7	–111.1	–165.6	–173.6	–173.6	–223.6	–257.1	–268.1
Q.	PARAGUAY	38.4	218.6	–18.7	1.4	16.4	–1.0	–7.3	–35.1	–3.5	–23.6	–15.1	–2.2
R.	PERU	~	~	~	~	~	–65.4	–207.0	–125.4	160.8	377.0	319.8	277.6
S.	URUGUAY	~	~	~	~	~	~	~	~	–139.6	–186.9	–25.4	–170.7
T.	VENEZUELA	~	~	~	~	~	3,434.6	3,149.7	3,202.6	2,591.6	3,958.4	4,382.5	4,362.8
	UNITED STATES[2]	~	~	4.4	8.5	9.4	14.9	19.4	10.6	3.2	15.6	17.4	14.3

	Country	1963	1964	1965	1966	1967	1968	1969	1970	1971	1972	1973	1974
A.	ARGENTINA[1]	1,667.8	1,428.3	1,306.1	1,758.8	1,423.6	946.0	599.5	717.3	220.8	629.0	2,719.4	1,180.2
B.	BOLIVIA	–82.3	–20.6	–34.9	–23.2	4.0	–17.1	12.2	144.5	94.7	118.2	142.6	384.1
C.	BRAZIL	353.3	1,075.0	1,984.9	1,288.2	613.8	73.9	878.5	607.3	–926.4	–619.2	–128.7	–7,847.9
D.	CHILE	9.46	196.9	490.9	585.3	668.6	517.1	1,066.3	644.0	185.3	–395.6	–27.4	413.2
E.	COLOMBIA	–72.6	128.1	457.6	–332.4	253.6	–28.4	66.3	–36.7	–375.6	317.0	590.7	–28.1
F.	COSTA RICA	–56.2	–35.6	–149.1	–77.7	–87.6	–67.3	–88.1	–146.1	–233.5	–143.2	–142.2	–345.1
H.	DOMINICAN REP.	30.6	–71.9	14.6	–88.8	–53.3	–94.6	–93.4	–167.5	–175.1	24.3	42.6	–59.8
I.	ECUADOR	101.6	68.4	88.4	79.4	9.22	–59.4	–69.9	–38.4	–174.6	96.1	395.1	578.8
J.	EL SALVADOR	–6.3	–50.9	13.0	–33.8	8.65	38.4	25.1	108.4	45.7	127.8	39.2	–95.4
K.	GUATEMALA	9.5	–19.4	–42.4	88.5	–65.1	–11.7	59.7	79.8	–7.9	101.0	107.0	81.3
L.	HAITI	12.9	2.5	–14.6	–26.2	–23.1	–6.8	–14.9	–22.8	–24.6	–44.2	–35.7	–55.7
M.	HONDURAS	–12.3	1.3	45.5	18.8	11.2	33.0	3.3	–66.0	41.9	87.4	48.7	–144.1
N.	MEXICO	–634.1	–1,156.3	–984.9	–991.2	–1,752.2	–1,801.1	–1,461.3	–2,324.6	–1,901.0	–2,196.6	–3,196.2	–4,613.2
O.	NICARAGUA	49.2	49.1	46.4	–27.4	–70.0	–11.9	–1.7	0	–7.36	107.9	–103.6	–265.8
P.	PANAMA	–287.1	–268.8	–303.0	–335.3	–354.5	–366.4	–422.7	–526.2	–573.6	–646.2	–624.5	–843.0
Q.	PARAGUAY	–6.0	3.4	12.4	–28.5	–44.1	–66.8	–71.8	–29.6	–41.6	16.7	1.5	–41.4
R.	PERU	145.1	543.8	97.0	–41.2	–196.0	502.8	613.3	877.0	404.0	326.8	31.6	–666.1
S.	URUGUAY	46.1	46.9	221.8	170.9	38.6	123.3	80.7	55.0	–15.7	252.8	166.7	–86.3
T.	VENEZUELA	4,501.6	4,025.0	3,418.2	3,200.0	3,253.6	2,721.6	2,361.9	2,327.2	3,063.5	2,285.0	4,420.0	11,915.7
	UNITED STATES[2]	16.4	21.3	15.0	11.2	11.0	1.8	1.7	6.8	–5.8	–15.8	1.9	–9.1

Table 2705 (Continued)

REAL TRADE BALANCES, 19 L, 1951–88
(M US of 1980)

Country	1975	1976	1977	1978	1979	1980	1981	1982	1983	1984	1985	1986	1987	1988
A. ARGENTINA[1]	-812.1	1,649.5	2,558.0	3,763.6	2,022.7	-1,373.0	652.0	2,503.6	3,329.7	3,520.8	4,347.6	2,158.9	839.5	?
B. BOLIVIA	-37.1	72.5	76.4	-124.8	-60.4	261.8	209.7	300.45	332.2	276.0	143.1	-45.0	-110.7	-46.6
C. BRAZIL	-5,251.5	-3,413.5	-138.1	1,496.1	3,084.0	2,833.0	1,085.2	704.7	5,796.6	11,570.3	11,110.5	7,368.0	9,677.4	?
D. CHILE	103.6	919.9	48.3	-550.4	-403.0	-764.0	-2,451.5	57.1	883.5	259.1	757.6	970.9	1,066.8	?
E. COLOMBIA	396.5	784.0	953.0	779.1	526.7	-297.0	-1,439.6	2,032.6	-1,338.7	217.5	-20.5	1,696.4	1,620.1	?
F. COSTA RICA	-199.0	-147.4	-134.4	-239.7	-357.7	-374.3	-80.6	58.1	-37.5	4.1	-55.2	35.0	-122.3	?
H. DOMINICAN REP.	179.1	-67.5	-95.0	-241.4	-305.2	-557.8	-241.4	-443.4	442.4	-351.9	-343.9	-555.7	-727.5	?
I. ECUADOR	9.8	371.0	55.7	-225.8	60.9	302.4	167.3	126.8	830.6	932.8	1,153.3	489.8	-28.6	477.7
J. EL SALVADOR	-26.2	91.1	155.4	-193.0	201.6	178.4	-91.9	-90.8	-66.6	-166.8	-192.5	-109.8	?	?
K. GUATEMALA	-46.5	-272.3	101.1	-247.3	-204.7	47.2	-227.8	-103.2	32.0	-44.2	-15.2	148.4	-308.2	?
L. HAITI	-75.3	-92.3	-86.1	-74.3	-93.2	-103.2	-191.4	-113.0	-124.8	-109.0	-108.5	-99.3	87.7	-103.6
M. HONDURAS	-92.8	-29.8	-28.0	-36.7	-30.5	-103.8	-105.1	-3.8	-51.6	-130.7	-79.9	15.2	-27.1	?
N. MEXICO	-4,840.2	-3,283.3	-1,410.2	-2,254.5	-3,212.3	-2,830.0	-3,753.7	6,154.9	12,331.5	11,442.1	7,532.1	4,059.1	7,314.0	1,420.9
O. NICARAGUA	-158.6	81.3	-93.9	119.8	257.7	-352.5	379.3	-287.6	-313.0	-366.0	-444.5	-423.0	?	?
P. PANAMA	-727.8	-735.3	-693.4	-720.9	-828.6	-727.0	-709.7	-574.3	-578.0	-727.7	-674.7	-472.2	-516.9	-143.6
Q. PARAGUAY	-58.1	-49.1	-45.6	-98.1	218.6	-275.0	-342.4	285.4	-202.0	-254.4	-170.7	-143.3	-84.3	55.6
R. PERU	-1,625.7	-1,058.7	-605.0	-439.3	1,748.0	837.0	-506.4	-387.7	262.5	890.4	1,044.6	-57.4	-451.9	-45.4
S. URUGUAY	-161.5	40.6	-103.9	-30.6	-429.2	-609.7	-331.9	197.4	373.3	170.1	158.8	261.9	94.7	?
T. VENEZUELA	5,016.3	2,741.1	-881.2	-2,777.8	4,716.2	8,174.0	7,179.4	2,489.1	7,313.6	7,587.1	6,354.7	1,112.1	1,504.8	?
UNITED STATES[2]	13.2	-13.6	-43.0	-43.9	-31.3	-25.5	-25.6	-33.0	-60.1	-99.5	-108.9	-127.6	-139.0	-102.4

1. Nominal data in source deflated here using U.S. export price index (table 3231).
2. B US of 1980.

SOURCE: IMF-IFS-Y, 1987 and 1988; IMF-IFS, Aug. 1989, line 77acd.

Table 2706

PHYSICAL HOLDINGS OF GOLD, 18 LC, 1950-88[a]

(M Ounces, YE)

Country	1950	1951	1952	1953	1954	1955	1956	1957	1958	1959	1960	1961	1962	1963	1964	1965	1966	1967	1968	1969	1970
A. ARGENTINA	2.36	5.57	8.19	10.61	10.61	10.61	6.40	3.59	1.70	1.60	2.96	5.42	1.73	2.22	2.03	1.88	2.39	2.39	3.11	3.85	3.99
B. BOLIVIA	.65	.65	.59	.63	.14	#	.03	.02	.03	.03	.03	.03	.09	.06	.13	.19	.21	.27	.31	.33	.36
C. BRAZIL	9.09	9.11	9.14	9.17	9.20	9.23	9.26	9.26	9.29	9.33	8.20	8.14	7.87	8.15	2.61	1.80	1.30	1.30	1.29	1.29	1.29
D. CHILE	1.15	1.36	1.19	1.20	1.21	1.27	1.31	1.15	1.15	1.19	1.29	1.37	1.22	1.23	1.23	1.25	1.29	1.29	1.32	1.35	1.33
E. COLOMBIA	2.11	1.37	2.14	2.46	2.43	2.46	1.63	1.77	2.06	2.03	2.23	2.51	1.63	1.77	1.66	1.00	.71	.89	.89	.74	.49
F. COSTA RICA	.06	.06	.06	.06	.06	.06	.06	.06	.06	.06	.06	.06	.06	.06	.06	.06	.06	.06	.06	.06	.06
H. DOMINICAN REP.	.11	.35	.35	.35	.35	.35	.33	.33	.33	.30	.30	.09	.09	.09	.09	.09	.09	.09	.09	.09	.09
I. ECUADOR	.54	.64	.65	.65	.65	.65	.62	.62	.62	.58	.57	.55	.55	.53	.32	.32	.31	.49	.75	.63	.55
J. EL SALVADOR	.66	.73	.84	.83	.82	.81	.80	.90	.90	.87	.86	.51	.51	.51	.51	.52	.51	.51	.51	.49	.49
K. GUATEMALA	.78	.78	.78	.78	.78	.78	.78	.78	.78	.67	.67	.67	.67	.66	.66	.62	.57	.57	.57	.57	.50
L. HAITI	.07	.07	.07	.06	.06	.06	.06	.02	.02	.02	.02	.02	.02	.02	.02	.02	#	#	#	#	#
M. HONDURAS	#	#	#	#	#	#	#	#	#	#	#	#	#	#	#	#	#	#	#	#	#
N. MEXICO	5.94	5.94	4.11	4.51	1.77	4.06	4.77	5.14	4.09	4.06	3.89	3.20	2.69	3.97	4.83	4.51	3.11	4.74	4.71	4.83	5.03
O. NICARAGUA	.03	.08	.08	.08	.08	.08	.04	.04	.04	.01	.01	.01	.02	.01	.01	.01	.03	.02	.02	.01	.02
Q. PARAGUAY	.01	.01	.01	.01	.01	.01	.01	#	#	#	#	#	#	#	#	#	#	#	#	#	#
R. PERU	.89	1.31	1.31	1.04	1.00	1.00	1.00	.79	.55	.80	1.21	1.35	1.35	1.64	1.93	1.92	1.85	.58	.57	.71	1.13
S. URUGUAY	6.74	6.31	5.91	6.49	6.49	6.16	5.33	5.13	5.13	5.13	5.13	5.13	5.13	4.90	4.90	4.43	4.19	3.99	3.81	4.71	4.61
T. VENEZUELA	10.66	10.66	10.66	10.66	11.51	11.54	17.29	20.57	20.57	18.71	11.46	11.46	11.46	11.46	11.46	11.46	11.46	11.46	11.51	11.51	10.97
UNITED STATES	652.00	653.51	664.34	631.17	622.66	621.51	630.23	653.06	588.06	557.34	508.69	484.20	458.77	445.60	442.03	401.86	378.14	344.71	311.20	338.83	316.34

Country	1971	1972	1973	1974	1975	1976	1977	1978	1979	1980	1981	1982	1983	1984	1985	1986	1987	1988
A. ARGENTINA	2.56	3.99	4.00	4.00	4.00	4.00	4.18	4.28	4.37	4.37	4.37	4.37	4.37	4.37	4.37	4.37	4.37	4.37
B. BOLIVIA	.38	.41	.41	.41	.41	.41	.60	.64	.68	.76	.83	.89	.91	.91	.89	.89	.89	.89
C. BRAZIL	1.32	1.33	1.33	1.33	1.33	1.52	1.52	1.61	1.70	1.88	2.20	.15	.54	1.47	3.10	2.43	2.43	2.73
D. CHILE	1.35	1.36	1.38	1.44	1.30	1.34	1.36	1.39	1.52	1.70	1.70	1.71	1.53	1.53	1.53	1.53	1.53	1.53
E. COLOMBIA	.40	.43	.43	.43	1.13	1.41	1.73	1.96	2.32	2.79	3.37	3.82	4.22	1.37	1.84	2.01	.68	1.10
F. COSTA RICA	.06	.06	.06	.06	.06	.06	.07	.08	.09	.09	.03	.05	.09	.02	.06	.07	.06	.02
H. DOMINICAN REP.	.09	.09	.09	.09	.09	.09	.10	.10	.11	.13	.14	.08	.08	.02	.02	.02	.02	.02
I. ECUADOR	.53	.36	.39	.39	.39	.39	.40	.41	.41	.41	.41	.41	.41	.41	.41	.41	.41	.41
J. EL SALVADOR	.49	.49	.49	.49	.49	.49	.50	.50	.51	.52	.52	.52	.47	.47	.47	.47	.47	.47
K. GUATEMALA	.50	.49	.49	.49	.49	.49	.51	.51	.52	.52	.52	.52	.52	.52	.52	.52	.52	.52
L. HAITI	~	~	~	#	#	#	.01	.01	.01	.02	.02	.02	.02	.02	.02	.02	.02	.02
M. HONDURAS	#	#	1.00	1.00	1.00	1.00	1.00	1.00	1.16	1.40	1.40	1.40	1.40	1.40	1.95	2.14	1.50	1.71
N. MEXICO	5.26	4.94	4.63	3.66	3.66	1.60	1.76	1.89	1.98	2.06	2.26	2.07	2.31	2.42	2.36	2.57	2.54	2.55
O. NICARAGUA	.02	.01	.02	.02	.02	.02	.03	.03	.02	.02	.02	.02	.12	~	~	~	~	~
Q. PARAGUAY	#	#	#	#	#	#	.01	.01	.04	.04	.04	.04	.04	.04	.04	.04	.04	.04
R. PERU	1.13	1.09	1.00	1.00	1.00	1.00	1.00	1.00	1.40	1.40	1.40	1.40	1.40	1.40	1.95	2.14	1.50	1.71
S. URUGUAY	4.23	3.54	3.54	3.54	3.54	3.54	3.58	3.64	3.31*	3.42	3.39	2.86	2.60	2.62	2.62	2.61	2.61	2.61
T. VENEZUELA	11.17	11.17	11.17	11.18	11.18	11.32	11.32	11.39	11.46	11.46	11.46	11.46	11.46	11.46	11.46	11.46	11.46	11.46
UNITED STATES	291.60	275.97	275.97	274.71	274.68	277.55	277.55	276.41	264.60	264.32	264.11	264.03	263.39	262.79	262.65	262.04	262.38	261.87

a. Cf. table 2725.

SOURCE: IMF-IFS-Y, 1980, pp. 40—43; 1986, pp. 60-63; 1987, pp. 64-67; 1988, pp. 66-67; IMF-IFS, Aug. 1989, line 1ad.

Table 2707

WEEKS OF IMPORTS AVAILABLE IN TERMS OF TOTAL RESERVES (EXCLUDING GOLD), 19 L, 1950–86

	Country	1950	1955	1959	1960	1961	1962	1963	1964	1965	1966	1967	1968	1969	1970	1971
A.	ARGENTINA	24.0	3.8	11.5	17.6	7.0	2.1	10.2	4.0	7.4	6.1	30.5	28.9	13.3	16.3	5.4
B.	BOLIVIA	5.6	4.0	4.9	4.2	4.3	.5	4.2	9.0	11.6	12.7	9.8	9.7	9.5	10.7	12.2
C.	BRAZIL	16.6	6.7	1.5	2.1	6.6	2.1	2.4	6.3	20.0	13.2	4.8	5.2	14.0	20.8	23.8
D.	CHILE	3.1	5.7	10.9	6.5	2.3	3.3	3.2	3.9	8.1	8.8	5.9	11.3	17.0	18.9	9.0
E.	COLOMBIA	5.6	3.9	18.1	9.2	4.9	2.7	2.6	4.1	7.0	4.0	5.4	11.5	14.8	11.7	10.5
F.	COSTA RICA	3.3	11.1	6.3	5.3	2.0	4.8	5.7	6.2	5.2	4.4	4.4	4.5	5.7	2.3	4.0
H.	DOMINICAN REP.	17.3	11.6	11.9	8.0	3.9	5.8	11.0	9.0	25.6	11.6	7.8	7.6	7.8	5.0	7.7
I.	ECUADOR	20.8	5.5	12.2	9.4	9.3	13.0	13.3	13.9	10.9	15.0	12.6	6.3	9.2	10.5	5.7
J.	EL SALVADOR	19.8	6.2	3.8	1.3	3.2	3.5	9.1	9.7	10.0	9.2	8.6	10.7	11.6	11.1	9.7
K.	GUATEMALA	8.3	14.1	9.0	13.1	13.4	9.7	10.2	9.4	10.5	10.2	9.5	9.5	11.2	11.1	12.8
L.	HAITI	7.6	9.6	4.5	5.5	4.7	3.1	3.5	2.6	2.2	3.0	2.7	3.5	4.7	4.1	8.9
M.	HONDURAS	12.4	14.6	9.2	9.6	8.8	8.6	6.7	10.0	9.9	9.5	7.9	8.8	8.7	4.7	5.9
N.	MEXICO	8.3	17.6	16.3	13.4	13.7	15.1	17.2	14.6	12.7	14.7	12.5	13.1	12.3	12.0	17.4
O.	NICARAGUA	1.7	8.7	9.0	8.3	9.6	9.3	14.8	14.7	18.5	16.4	8.0	13.4	12.8	12.7	14.4
P.	PANANA	3.2	4.0	2.0	3.2	1.9	1.6	2.1	1.5	1.4	1.3	1.4	2.2	2.5	2.3	2.8
Q.	PARAGUAY	4.6	7.7	6.1	1.2	3.1	2.7	4.2	7.0	9.6	10.1	8.9	8.7	6.5	12.0	13.1
R.	PERU	7.0	4.0	5.5	4.6	7.0	6.7	7.3	8.3	7.7	5.7	6.8	7.5	12.3	24.8	26.3
S.	URUGUAY	18.6	.5	2.0	2.1	2.8	5.2	4.2	3.9	8.2	9.5	6.8	11.1	5.1	3.1	4.6
T.	VENEZUELA	.4	6.1	2.3	9.1	7.8	7.3	14.6	18.2	15.6	14.4	16.9	16.2	16.0	17.7	27.4

	Country	1972	1973	1974	1975	1976	1977	1978	1979	1980	1981	1982	1983	1984	1985	1986	1987
A.	ARGENTINA	8.6	26.8	16.4	3.8	24.8	39.4	67.4	72.9	33.1	18.0	24.4	13.5	14.1	42.6	37.3	15.1
B.	BOLIVIA	12.4	12.4	25.0	12.6	13.2	18.6	11.5	9.5	8.1	5.3	14.0	14.1	26.6	18.8	15.5	6.5
C.	BRAZIL	44.9	47.3	19.1	15.2	24.6	28.2	40.9	23.5	12.0	14.3	9.7	13.5	39.3	38.5	26.9	16.3
D.	CHILE	5.3	5.8	1.1	2.2	12.8	9.8	18.9	23.9	31.7	26.3	26.7	38.4	37.5	46.5	42.0	31.6
E.	COLOMBIA	18.7	25.3	14.0	16.5	33.5	44.8	43.4	61.8	53.9	47.4	36.7	19.9	15.8	20.0	36.3	33.8
F.	COSTA RICA	5.7	5.5	3.0	3.7	6.4	9.7	8.6	4.4	4.9	5.7	13.2	16.4	19.3	24.0	23.6	~
H.	DOMINICAN REP.	7.4	9.0	5.6	6.6	7.3	9.6	8.1	10.2	6.4	7.0	4.6	6.1	9.1	11.9	~	8.5
I.	ECUADOR	19.8	27.5	24.4	13.3	25.9	27.3	22.0	23.5	23.4	14.6	8.0	22.9	18.5	23.2	18.5	13.9
J.	EL SALVADOR	11.9	5.7	7.2	9.3	13.1	11.8	13.6	7.1	4.2	3.8	6.6	9.3	8.8	9.7	~	~
K.	GUATEMALA	18.7	23.1	13.5	20.1	30.4	33.0	30.0	24.1	14.5	4.7	4.2	9.6	11.2	13.3	30.4	12.3
L.	HAITI	13.5	10.7	8.2	4.3	7.0	8.3	8.6	10.5	2.2	2.7	~	~	.8	.4	~	~
M.	HONDURAS	9.5	8.3	6.1	12.5	15.0	16.1	13.7	13.2	7.5	5.4	7.9	7.2	7.0	6.2	6.8	~
N.	MEXICO	18.7	15.8	10.6	10.9	10.2	14.6	12.7	8.9	7.9	8.8	2.9	25.4	32.1	18.2	18.7	45.8
O.	NICARAGUA	19.1	18.5	9.7	12.2	14.3	10.1	4.4	21.2	3.8	5.8	11.5	11.8	~	~	~	~
P.	PANAMA	5.1	4.3	2.5	2.0	4.8	4.3	8.3	5.2	4.2	4.0	3.3	7.6	7.9	3.7	4.6	~
Q.	PARAGUAY	19.8	24.2	22.8	29.1	37.2	45.2	60.9	60.8	64.4	69.9	57.2	64.8	59.1	56.7	40.3	~
R.	PERU	28.9	26.9	31.4	8.7	7.4	9.7	10.3	43.4	41.2	14.6	16.8	23.3	38.3	47.0	26.3	16.3
S.	URUGUAY	17.0	18.4	8.6	5.5	15.6	23.0	24.2	13.9	11.9	13.6	5.4	13.7	9.0	12.8	30.5	23.1
T.	VENEZUELA	28.0	35.9	75.0	72.8	55.1	36.8	26.7	35.7	29.0	32.4	26.4	45.6	60.9	64.7	35.1	36.0

SOURCE: IMF-IFS-Y, 1987, pp. 48–49; and 1988, pp. 50–51.

Table 2708

ARGENTINA TOTAL REAL SDR RESERVES, MINUS GOLD,[1] 1950–87

(M US of 1980)

Year	Nominal Value	Real Value	Year	Nominal Value	Real Value
1950	445	1,718.1	1969	403	1,113.3
1951	253	851.9	1970	533	1,395.3
1952	133	450.8	1971	177	449.2
1953	160	544.2	1972	289	710.1
1954	152	526.0	1973	952	2,008.4
1955	85	290.1	1974	935	1,545.5
1956	158	516.3	1975	246	363.9
1957	160	509.6	1976	1,244	1,779.7
1958	38	122.2	1977	2,596	3,595.6
1959	220	707.4	1978	3,812	4,925.1
1960	422	1,348.2	1979	7,127	8,089.7
1961	196	614.4	1980	5,268	5,268.0
1962	54	170.3	1981	2,808	2,571.4
1963	192	605.7	1982	2,272	2,058.0
1964	82	256.3	1983	1,120	1,003.6
1965	170	515.2	1984	1,268	1,121.1
1966	132	388.2	1985	2,980	2,656.0
1967	643	1,853.0	1986	2,222	1,961.2
1968	651	1,849.4	1987	1,140	988.7

1. Nominal data in source deflated here using U.S. export price index (table 3231).

SOURCE: IMF-IFS-Y, 1987 and 1988; IMF-IFS,, Aug. 1989, p. 47.

Figure 27:20

ARGENTINA TOTAL REAL SDR RESERVES, MINUS GOLD, 1950–87

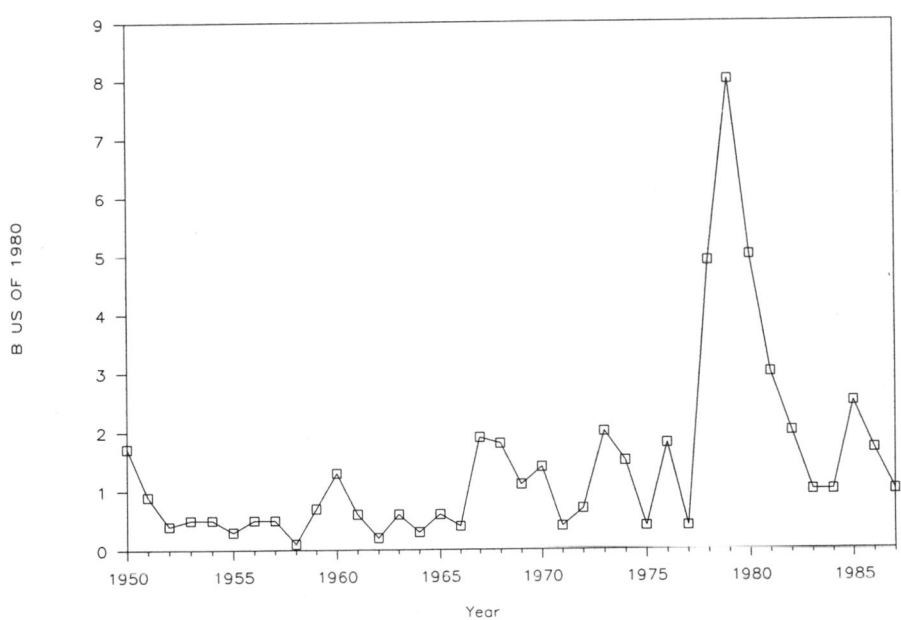

SOURCE: Table 2708.

Table 2709

BOLIVIA TOTAL REAL SDR RESERVES, MINUS GOLD,[1] 1950–87

(M US of 1980)

Year	Nominal Value	Real Value	Year	Nominal Value	Real Value
1950	6	23.17	1969	30	82.87
1951	12	40.40	1970	33	86.39
1952	8	27.12	1971	37	93.91
1953	3	10.20	1972	41	100.74
1954	6	20.76	1973	46	97.05
1955	6	20.48	1974	144	238.02
1956	3	9.80	1975	119	176.04
1957	6	19.11	1976	130	185.98
1958	2	6.43	1977	174	241.00
1959	6	19.29	1978	130	167.96
1960	6	19.17	1979	135	153.23
1961	6	18.81	1980	83	83.00
1962	1	3.15	1981	86	78.75
1963	8	25.24	1982	141	127.72
1964	18	56.25	1983	153	137.10
1965	30	90.91	1984	257	227.23
1966	34	100.00	1985	182	162.21
1967	29	83.57	1986	134	118.27
1968	29	82.39	1987	69	59.84

1. Nominal data in source deflated here using U.S. export price index (table 3231).

SOURCE: IMF-IFS-Y, 1987 and 1988; IMF-IFS, Aug. 1989, p. 47.

Figure 27:21

BOLIVIA TOTAL REAL SDR RESERVES, MINUS GOLD, 1950–87

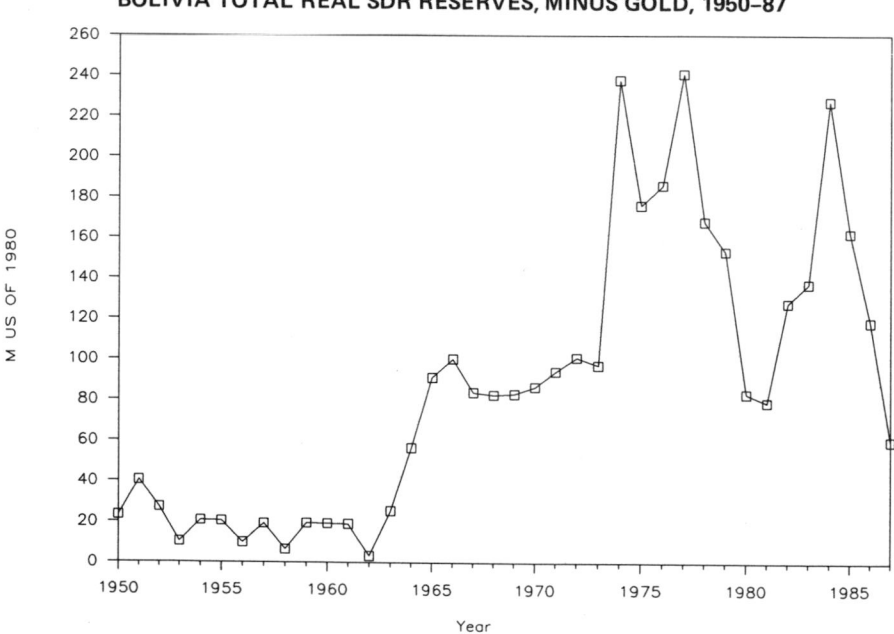

SOURCE: Table 2709.

Table 2710

BRAZIL TOTAL REAL SDR RESERVES, MINUS GOLD,[1] 1950–87

(M US of 1980)

Year	Nominal Value	Real Value	Year	Nominal Value	Real Value
1950	348	1,343.6	1969	611	1,687.8
1951	198	666.7	1970	1,142	2,989.5
1952	209	708.5	1971	1,563	3,967.0
1953	284	966.0	1972	3,806	9,351.4
1954	161	557.1	1973	5,272	11,122.4
1955	168	573.4	1974	4,260	7,041.3
1956	287	937.9	1975	3,400	5,029.6
1957	152	484.1	1976	5,584	7,988.6
1958	140	450.2	1977	5,921	8,200.8
1959	40	128.6	1978	9,078	11,728.7
1960	58	185.3	1979	6,806	7,725.3
1961	185	579.9	1980	4,524	4,524.0
1962	60	189.3	1981	5,673	5,195.1
1963	69	217.7	1982	3,560	3,225.5
1964	154	481.3	1983	4,160	3,727.6
1965	421	1,275.8	1984	11,740	10,380.2
1966	380	1,117.6	1985	9,654	8,604.3
1967	154	443.8	1986	4,744	4,187.1
1968	212	602.3	1987	4,440	3,850.8

1. Nominal data in source deflated here using U.S. export price index (table 3231).

SOURCE: IMF-IFS-Y, 1987 and 1988; IMF-IFS, Aug. 1989, p. 47.

Figure 27:22

BRAZIL TOTAL REAL SDR RESERVES, MINUS GOLD, 1950–87

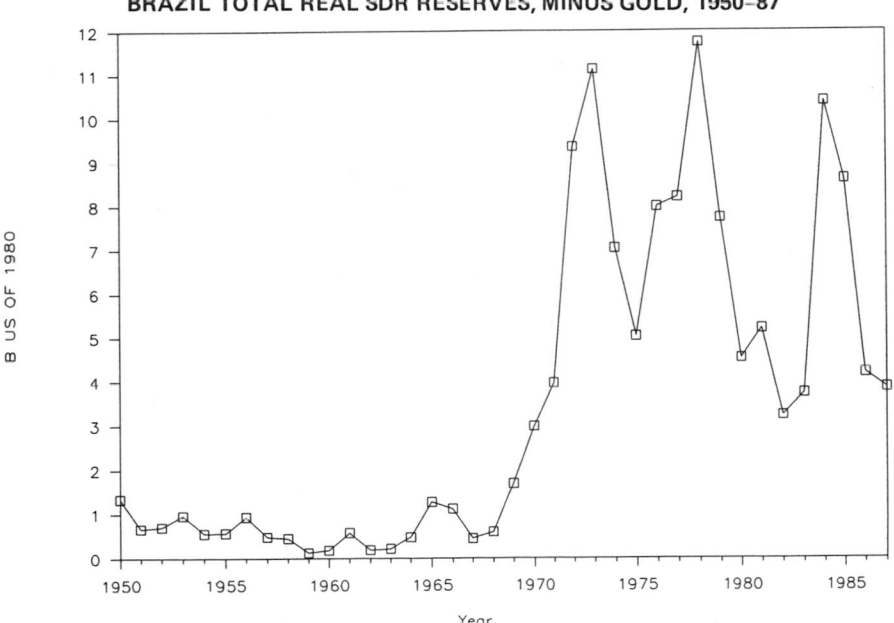

SOURCE: Table 2710.

Table 2711

CHILE TOTAL REAL SDR RESERVES, MINUS GOLD,[1] 1950–87

(M US of 1980)

Year	Nominal Value	Real Value	Year	Nominal Value	Real Value
1950	15	57.9	1969	296	817.7
1951	15	50.5	1970	342	895.3
1952	33	111.9	1971	157	398.5
1953	26	88.4	1972	89	218.7
1954	13	45.0	1973	101	213.1
1955	42	143.3	1974	34	56.2
1956	38	124.2	1975	48	71.0
1957	11	35.0	1976	349	499.3
1958	23	74.0	1977	351	486.1
1959	86	276.5	1978	837	1,081.4
1960	66	210.9	1979	1,471	1,669.7
1961	26	81.5	1980	2,449	2,449.0
1962	36	113.6	1981	2,761	2,528.4
1963	34	107.3	1982	1,645	1,490.0
1964	46	143.8	1983	1,945	1,742.8
1965	94	284.8	1984	2,349	2,076.9
1966	127	373.5	1985	2,230	1,987.5
1967	81	233.4	1986	1,922	1,696.4
1968	162	460.2	1987	1,765	1,530.8

1. Nominal data in source deflated here using U.S. export price index (table 3231).

SOURCE: IMF-IFS-Y, 1987 and 1988; IMF-IFS, Aug. 1989, p. 47.

Figure 27:23

CHILE TOTAL REAL SDR RESERVES, MINUS GOLD, 1950–87

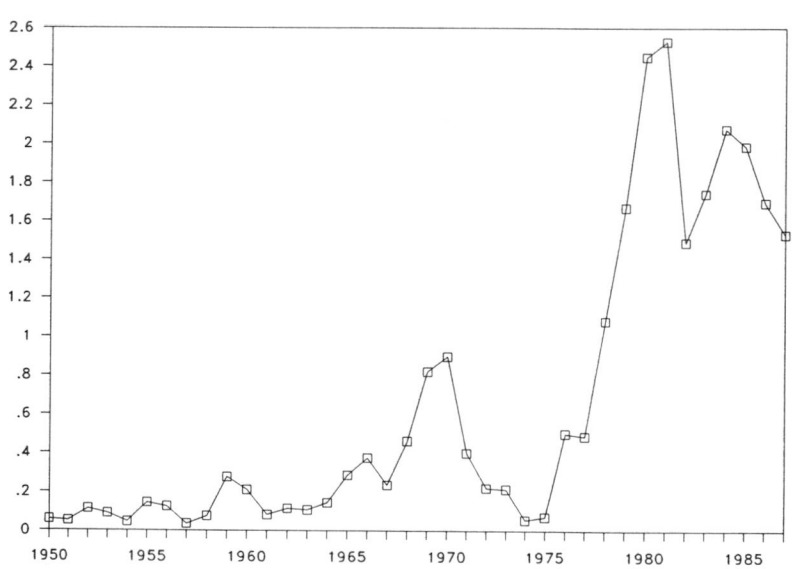

SOURCE: Table 2711.

Table 2712

COLOMBIA TOTAL REAL SDR RESERVES, MINUS GOLD,[1] 1950-87

(M US of 1980)

Year	Nominal Value	Real Value	Year	Nominal Value	Real Value
1950	40	154.4	1969	195	538.7
1951	90	303.0	1970	189	494.8
1952	92	311.9	1971	188	477.2
1953	117	398.0	1972	309	759.2
1954	172	595.2	1973	516	1,088.6
1955	50	170.6	1974	431	712.4
1956	74	241.8	1975	475	702.7
1957	83	264.3	1976	1,101	1,575.1
1958	89	286.2	1977	1,747	2,419.7
1959	145	466.2	1978	2,366	3,056.8
1960	92	293.9	1979	3,844	4,363.2
1961	52	163.0	1980	4,831	4,831.0
1962	28	88.3	1981	4,741	4,341.6
1963	25	78.9	1982	3,500	3,170.3
1964	46	143.8	1983	1,816	1,526.3
1965	61	184.8	1984	1,392	1,230.8
1966	52	152.9	1985	1,452	1,294.1
1967	52	149.9	1986	2,204	1,945.3
1968	142	403.4	1987	2,175	1,886.4

1. Nominal data in source deflated here using U.S. export price index (table 3231).

SOURCE: IMF-IFS-Y, 1987 and 1988; IMF-IFS, Aug. 1989, p. 47.

Figure 27:24

COLOMBIA TOTAL REAL SDR RESERVES, MINUS GOLD, 1950-87

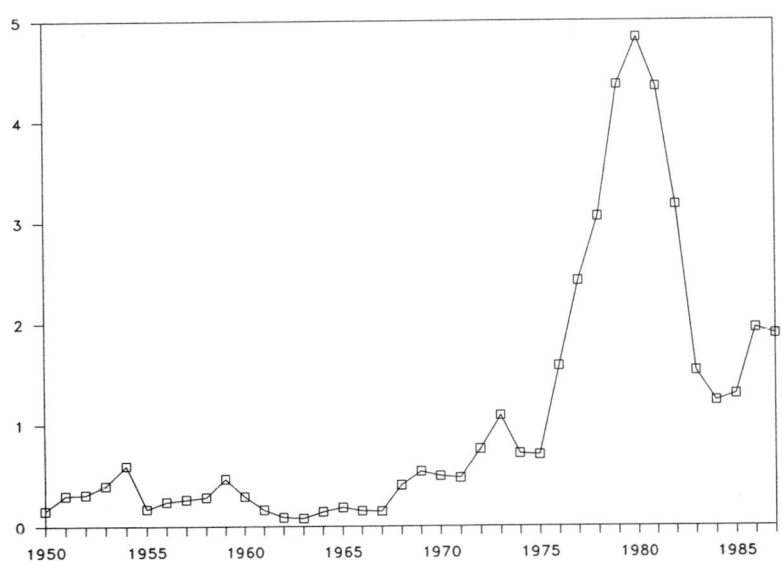

SOURCE: Table 2712.

Table 2713

COSTA RICA TOTAL REAL SDR RESERVES, MINUS GOLD,[1] 1950–87

(M US of 1980)

Year	Nominal Value	Real Value	Year	Nominal Value	Real Value
1950	3	11.58	1969	27	74.59
1951	7	23.57	1970	14	36.65
1952	14	47.46	1971	25	63.45
1953	17	57.82	1972	37	90.91
1954	15	51.90	1973	40	84.39
1955	19	64.85	1974	34	56.20
1956	11	35.95	1975	42	62.13
1957	11	35.03	1976	82	117.31
1958	19	61.09	1977	157	216.85
1959	12	38.59	1978	149	192.51
1960	11	35.14	1979	90	102.16
1961	4	12.54	1980	114	114.00
1962	11	34.70	1981	113	103.48
1963	14	44.16	1982	205	185.69
1964	17	53.13	1983	297	266.13
1965	18	54.55	1984	413	365.16
1966	15	44.12	1985	461	410.87
1967	16	46.11	1986	428	377.76
1968	18	51.14	1987	345	299.22

1. Nominal data in source deflated here using U.S. export price index (table 3231).

SOURCE: IMF-IFS-Y, 1987 and 1988; IMF-IFS, Aug. 1989, p. 47.

Figure 27:25

COSTA RICA TOTAL REAL SDR RESERVES, MINUS GOLD, 1950–87

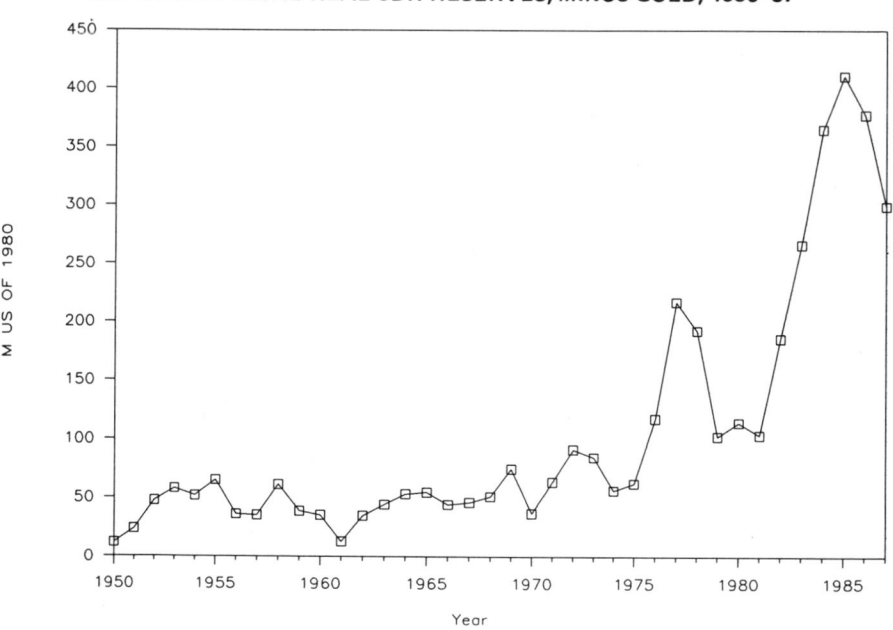

SOURCE: Table 2713.

Table 2714

DOMINICAN REPUBLIC TOTAL REAL SDR RESERVES, MINUS GOLD,[1] 1950–87
(M US of 1980)

Year	Nominal Value	Real Value	Year	Nominal Value	Real Value
1950	17	65.64	1969	37	102.21
1951	19	63.97	1970	29	75.92
1952	21	71.19	1971	49	124.37
1953	17	57.82	1972	51	125.31
1954	25	86.51	1973	70	147.68
1955	25	85.32	1974	71	117.36
1956	28	91.50	1975	96	142.01
1957	37	117.83	1976	106	151.65
1958	36	115.76	1977	148	204.42
1959	31	99.68	1978	118	152.45
1960	15	47.92	1979	181	205.45
1961	6	18.81	1980	158	158.00
1962	17	53.63	1981	193	176.74
1963	39	123.03	1982	117	105.98
1964	38	118.75	1983	164	146.95
1965	48	145.45	1984	259	229.00
1966	41	120.59	1985	310	276.29
1967	29	83.57	1986	308	271.84
1968	33	93.75	1987	128	111.01

1. Nominal data in source deflated here using U.S. export price index (table 3231).

SOURCE: IMF-IFS-Y, 1987 and 1988; IMF-IFS, Aug. 1987, p. 47.

Figure 27:26

DOMINICAN REPUBLIC TOTAL REAL SDR RESERVES, MINUS GOLD, 1950–87

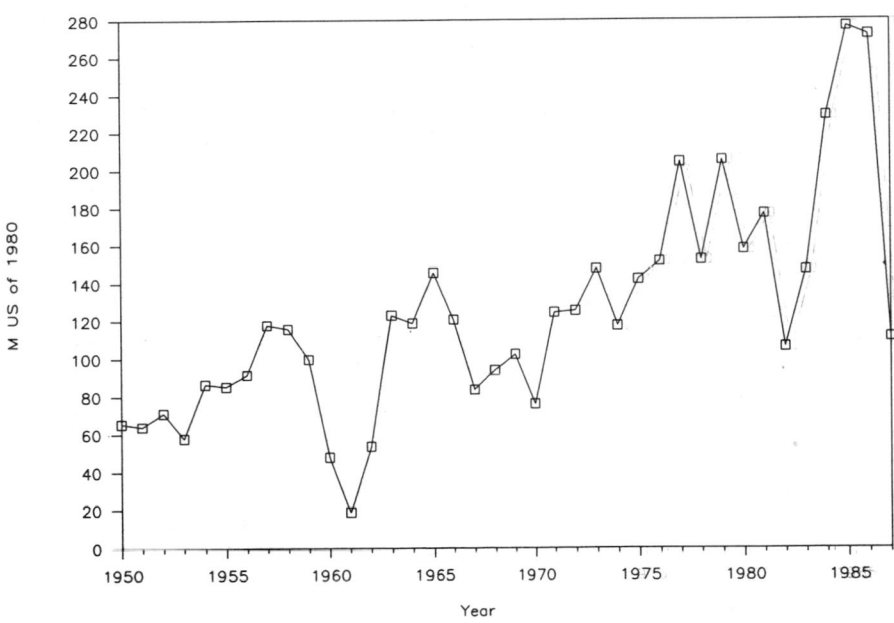

SOURCE: Table 2714.

Table 2715

ECUADOR TOTAL REAL SDR RESERVES, MINUS GOLD,[1] 1950–87

(M US of 1980)

Year	Nominal Value	Real Value	Year	Nominal Value	Real Value
1950	20	77.22	1969	43	118.78
1951	10	33.67	1970	55	143.98
1952	22	74.58	1971	34	86.29
1953	17	57.82	1972	112	275.18
1954	17	58.82	1973	174	367.09
1955	12	40.96	1974	260	429.75
1956	13	42.48	1975	216	319.53
1957	17	54.14	1976	411	587.98
1958	16	51.45	1977	513	708.56
1959	23	73.95	1978	488	630.49
1960	21	67.09	1979	548	622.02
1961	19	59.56	1980	794	794.00
1962	24	75.71	1981	543	497.25
1963	33	104.10	1982	276	250.00
1964	40	125.00	1983	616	551.97
1965	35	106.06	1984	624	551.72
1966	50	147.06	1985	654	582.89
1967	52	149.86	1986	527	465.14
1968	31	88.07	1987	346	300.09

1. Nominal data in source deflated here using U.S. export price index (table 3231).

SOURCE: IMF-IFS-Y, 1987 and 1988; IMF-IFS, Aug. 1989, p. 47.

Figure 27:27

ECUADOR TOTAL REAL SDR RESERVES, MINUS GOLD, 1950–87

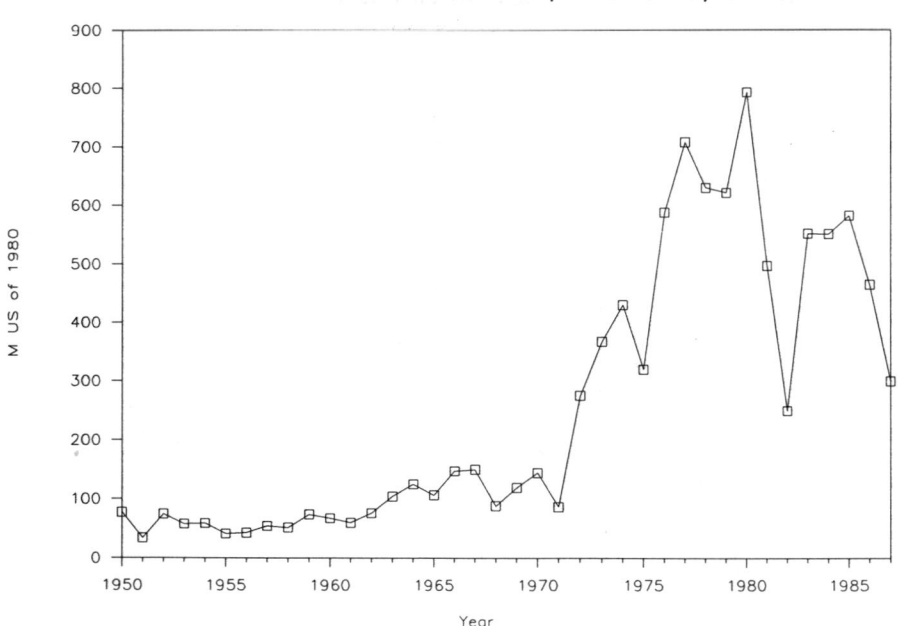

SOURCE: Table 2715.

Table 2716

EL SALVADOR TOTAL REAL SDR RESERVES, MINUS GOLD,[1] 1950–87

(M US of 1980)

Year	Nominal Value	Real Value	Year	Nominal Value	Real Value
1950	19	73.36	1969	47	129.83
1951	17	57.24	1970	45	117.80
1952	15	50.85	1971	43	109.14
1953	15	51.02	1972	59	144.96
1954	16	55.36	1973	34	71.73
1955	11	37.54	1974	63	104.13
1956	11	35.95	1975	91	134.62
1957	10	31.85	1976	160	228.90
1958	8	25.72	1977	174	240.33
1959	7	22.51	1978	206	266.15
1960	3	9.58	1979	108	122.59
1961	7	21.94	1980	61	61.00
1962	9	28.39	1981	62	56.78
1963	27	85.17	1982	98	88.77
1964	36	112.50	1983	153	137.10
1965	38	115.15	1984	169	149.43
1966	39	114.71	1985	164	146.17
1967	37	106.63	1986	139	122.68
1968	44	125.00	1987	131	113.62

1. Nominal data in source deflated here using U.S. export price index (table 3231).

SOURCE: IMF-IFS-Y, 1987 and 1988; IMF-IFS, Aug. 1989, p. 47.

Figure 27:28

EL SALVADOR TOTAL REAL SDR RESERVES, MINUS GOLD, 1950–87

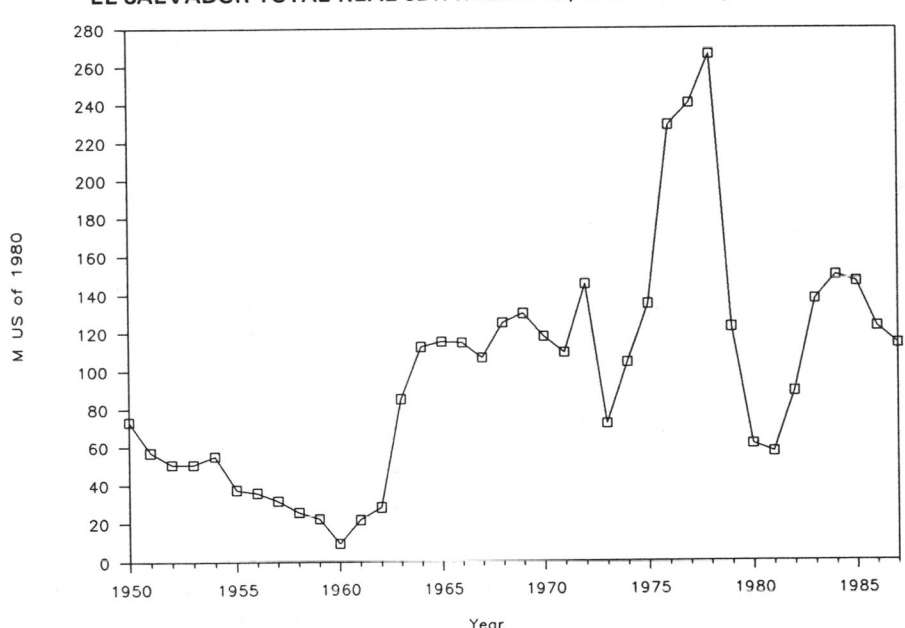

SOURCE: Table 2716.

Table 2717

GUATEMALA TOTAL REAL SDR RESERVES, MINUS GOLD,[1] 1950–87

(M US of 1980)

Year	Nominal Value	Real Value	Year	Nominal Value	Real Value
1950	11	42.5	1969	47	129.8
1951	14	47.1	1970	45	117.8
1952	17	57.6	1971	69	175.1
1953	15	51.0	1972	107	262.9
1954	16	55.4	1973	159	335.4
1955	11	37.5	1974	148	244.6
1956	11	35.9	1975	242	358.0
1957	10	31.8	1976	423	605.2
1958	8	25.7	1977	551	761.0
1959	7	22.5	1978	569	735.1
1960	3	9.6	1979	529	600.5
1961	7	21.9	1980	349	349.0
1962	9	28.4	1981	129	118.1
1963	27	85.2	1982	102	92.4
1964	36	112.5	1983	201	180.1
1965	38	115.2	1984	280	247.6
1966	39	114.7	1985	274	244.2
1967	37	106.6	1986	296	261.3
1968	44	125.0	1987	203	176.1

1. Nominal data in source deflated here using U.S. export price index (table 3231).

SOURCE: IMF-IFS-Y, 1987 and 1988; IMF-IFS, Aug. 1989, p. 47.

Figure 27:29

GUATEMALA TOTAL REAL SDR RESERVES, MINUS GOLD, 1950–87

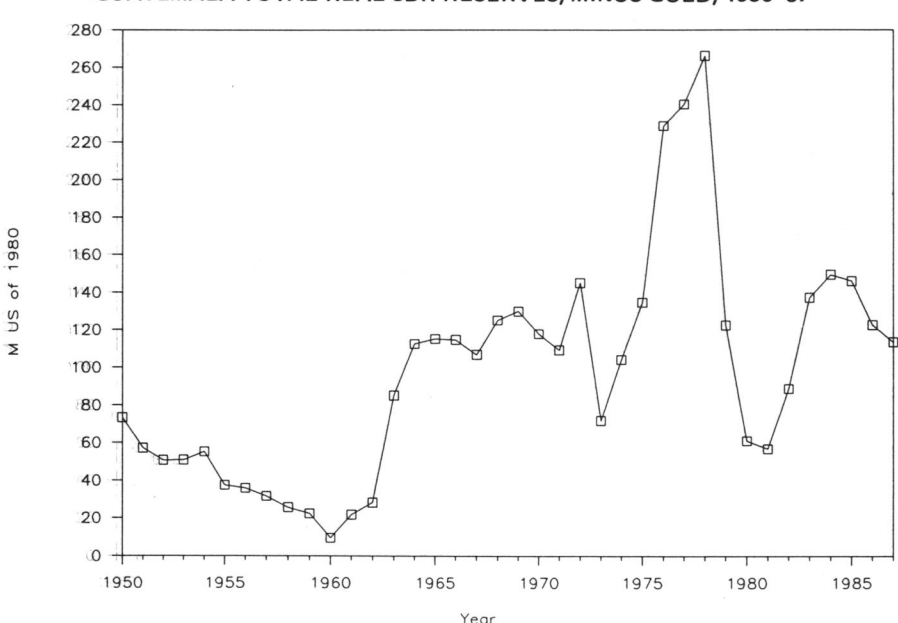

SOURCE: Table 2717.

Table 2718

HAITI TOTAL REAL SDR RESERVES, MINUS GOLD,[1] 1950–87

(M US of 1980)

Year	Nominal Value	Real Value	Year	Nominal Value	Real Value
1950	5	19.3	1969	4	11.0
1951	9	30.3	1970	4	10.5
1952	10	33.9	1971	10	25.4
1953	5	17.0	1972	16	39.3
1954	10	34.6	1973	14	29.5
1955	7	23.9	1974	16	26.4
1956	6	19.6	1975	11	16.3
1957	6	19.1	1976	24	34.3
1958		.0	1977	28	38.7
1959	3	9.6	1978	30	38.8
1960	4	12.8	1979	42	47.7
1961	3	9.4	1980	13	13.0
1962	2	6.3	1981	21	19.2
1963	3	9.5	1982	4	3.6
1964	2	6.3	1983	9	8.1
1965	1	3.0	1984	13	11.5
1966	2	5.9	1985	6	5.3
1967	2	5.8	1986	13	11.5
1968	3	8.5	1987	12	10.4

1. Nominal data in source deflated here using U.S. export price index (table 3231).

SOURCE: IMF-IFS-Y, 1987 and 1988; IMF-IFS, Aug. 1989, p. 47.

Figure 27:30

HAITI TOTAL REAL SDR RESERVES, MINUS GOLD, 1950–87

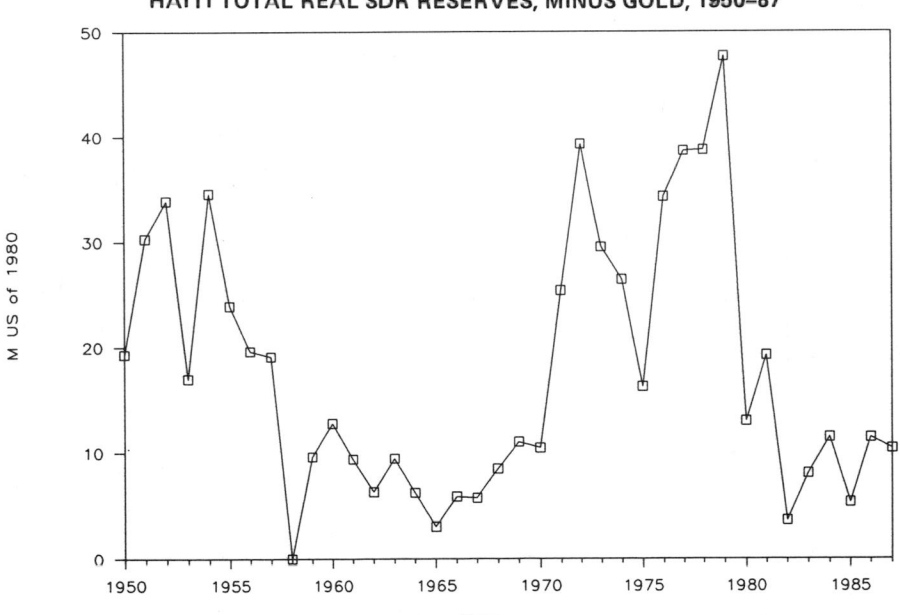

SOURCE: Table 2718.

Table 2719

HONDURAS TOTAL REAL SDR RESERVES, MINUS GOLD,[1] 1950–87

(M US of 1980)

Year	Nominal Value	Real Value	Year	Nominal Value	Real Value
1950	11	42.5	1969	31	85.6
1951	20	67.3	1970	20	52.4
1952	22	74.6	1971	20	50.8
1953	23	78.2	1972	32	78.6
1954	24	83.0	1973	35	73.8
1955	20	68.3	1974	36	59.5
1956	18	58.8	1975	83	122.8
1957	16	51.0	1976	113	161.7
1958	10	32.2	1977	148	204.4
1959	12	38.6	1978	142	183.5
1960	13	41.5	1979	159	180.5
1961	12	37.6	1980	117	117.0
1962	13	41.0	1981	87	79.7
1963	12	37.9	1982	102	92.4
1964	20	62.5	1983	109	97.7
1965	23	69.7	1984	131	115.8
1966	27	79.4	1985	96	85.6
1967	25	72.0	1986	91	80.3
1968	31	88.1	1987	75	65.0

1. Nominal data in source deflated here using U.S. export price index (table 3231).

SOURCE: IMF-IFS-Y, 1987 and 1988; IMF-IFS, Aug. 1989, p. 47.

Figure 27:31

HONDURAS TOTAL REAL SDR RESERVES, MINUS GOLD, 1950–87

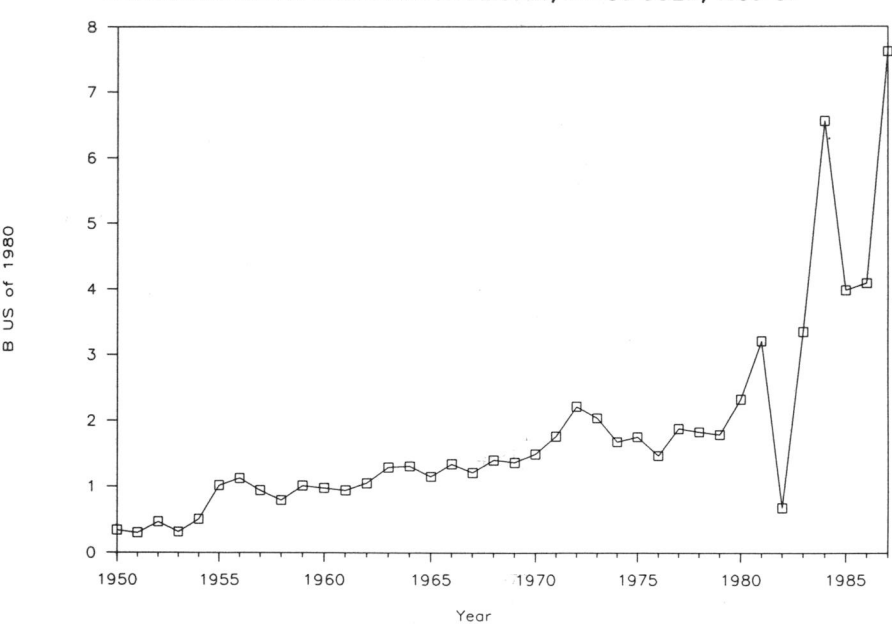

SOURCE: Table 2719.

Table 2720

MEXICO TOTAL REAL SDR RESERVES, MINUS GOLD,[1] 1950–87

(M US of 1980)

Year	Nominal Value	Real Value	Year	Nominal Value	Real Value
1950	89	343.6	1969	493	1,361.9
1951	89	299.7	1970	568	1,486.9
1952	138	467.8	1971	693	1,758.9
1953	92	312.9	1972	899	2,208.8
1954	147	508.7	1973	962	2,029.5
1955	299	1,020.5	1974	1,011	1,671.1
1956	345	1,127.5	1975	1,182	1,748.5
1957	296	942.7	1976	1,023	1,463.5
1958	248	797.4	1977	1,357	1,874.3
1959	316	1,016.1	1978	1,414	1,826.9
1960	306	977.6	1979	1,573	1,785.5
1961	301	943.6	1980	2,321	2,321.0
1962	333	1,050.5	1981	3,500	3,205.1
1963	409	1,290.2	1982	756	684.8
1964	418	1,306.3	1983	3,737	3,348.6
1965	380	1,151.5	1984	7,419	6,559.7
1966	455	1,338.2	1985	4,467	3,981.3
1967	420	1,210.4	1986	4,635	4,090.9
1968	492	1,397.7	1987	8,786	7,620.1

1. Nominal data in source deflated here using U.S. export price index (table 3231).

SOURCE: IMF-IFS-Y, 1987 and 1988; IMF-IFS, Aug. 1989, p. 47.

Figure 27:32

MEXICO TOTAL REAL SDR RESERVES, MINUS GOLD, 1950–87

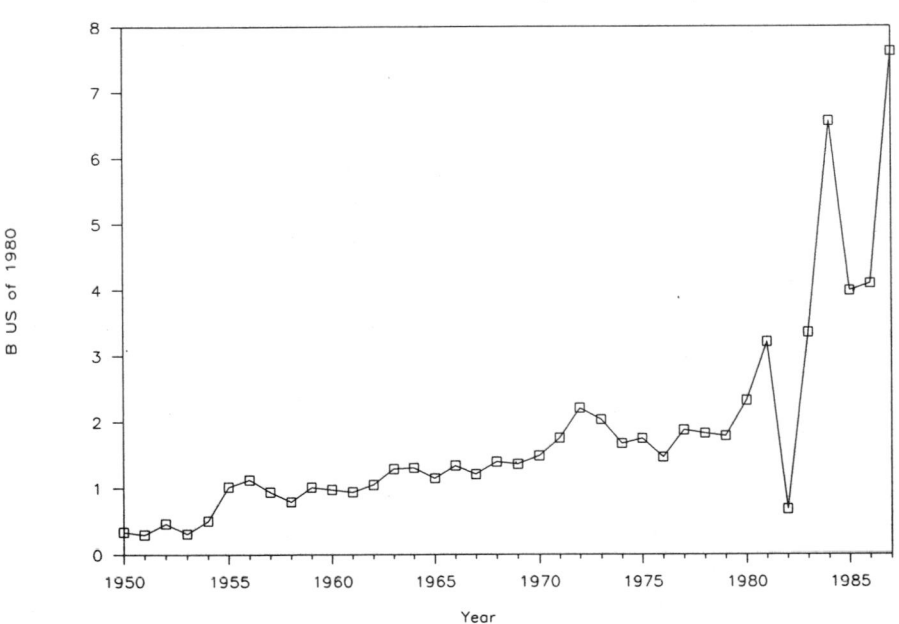

SOURCE: Table 2720.

Table 2721

NICARAGUA TOTAL REAL SDR RESERVES, MINUS GOLD,[1] 1950–83

(M US of 1980)

Year	Nominal Value	Real Value	Year	Nominal Value	Real Value
1950	1	3.86	1967	31	89.34
1951	6	20.20	1968	48	136.36
1952	13	44.07	1969	44	121.55
1953	14	47.62	1970	49	128.27
1954	11	38.06	1971	54	137.06
1955	12	40.96	1972	74	181.82
1956	6	19.61	1973	96	202.53
1957	10	31.85	1974	85	140.50
1958	6	19.29	1975	104	153.85
1959	12	38.59	1976	126	180.26
1960	11	35.14	1977	122	168.51
1961	13	40.75	1978	39	50.39
1962	17	53.63	1979	111	125.99
1963	32	100.95	1980	51	51.00
1964	39	121.88	1981	96	87.91
1965	57	172.73	1982	155	140.40
1966	57	167.65	1983	167	149.64

1. Nominal data in source deflated here using U.S. export price index (table 3231).

SOURCE: IMF-IFS-Y, 1987 and 1988; IMF-IFS, Aug. 1989, p. 47.

Figure 27:33

NICARAGUA TOTAL REAL SDR RESERVES, MINUS GOLD, 1950–87

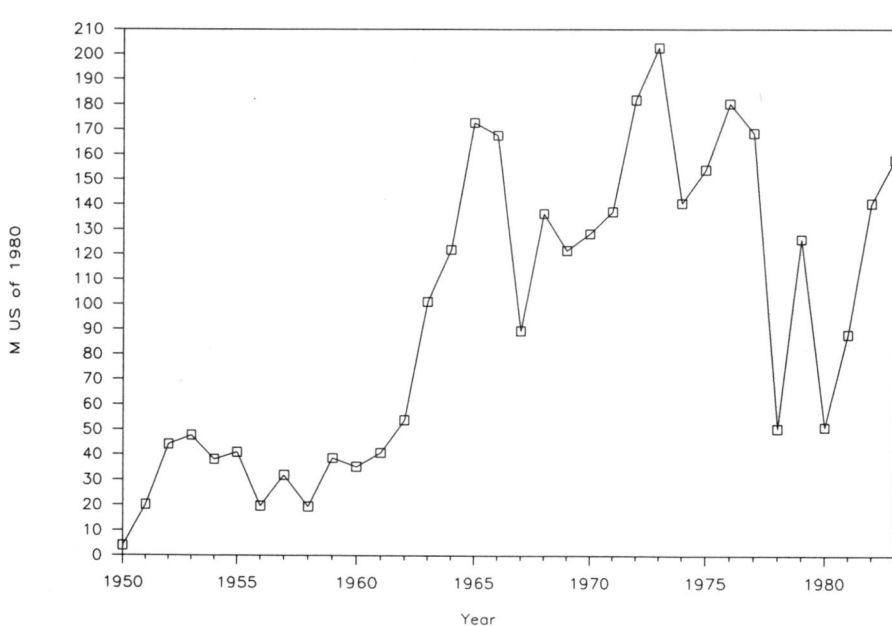

SOURCE: Table 2721.

Table 2722

PANAMA TOTAL REAL SDR RESERVES, MINUS GOLD,[1] 1950–87

(M US of 1980)

Year	Nominal Value	Real Value	Year	Nominal Value	Real Value
1950	4	15.44	1969	14	38.67
1951	2	6.73	1970	16	41.88
1952	3	10.17	1971	19	48.22
1953	5	17.01	1972	40	98.28
1954	7	24.22	1973	35	73.84
1955	6	20.48	1974	32	52.89
1956	8	26.14	1975	30	44.38
1957	4	12.74	1976	68	97.28
1958	9	28.94	1977	58	80.11
1959	4	12.86	1978	116	149.87
1960	7	22.36	1979	90	102.16
1961	5	15.67	1980	92	92.00
1962	5	15.77	1981	103	94.32
1963	7	22.08	1982	92	83.33
1964	5	15.63	1983	197	176.52
1965	6	18.18	1984	220	194.52
1966	6	17.65	1985	89	79.32
1967	7	20.17	1986	139	123.56
1968	11	31.25	1987	55	47.7

1. Nominal data in source deflated here using U.S. export price index (table 3231).

SOURCE: IMF-IFS-Y, 1987 and 1988; IMF-IFS, Aug. 1989, p. 47.

Figure 27:34

PANAMA TOTAL REAL SDR RESERVES, MINUS GOLD, 1950–87

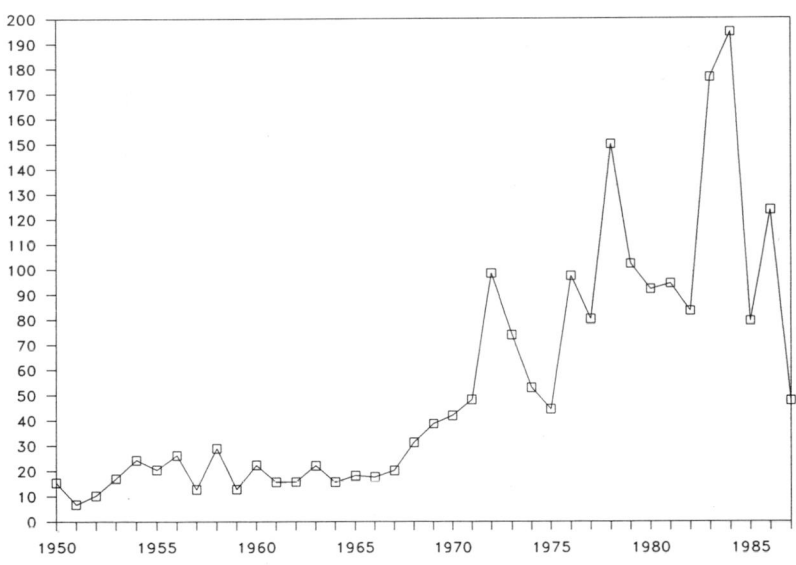

SOURCE: Table 2722.

Table 2723

PARAGUAY TOTAL REAL SDR RESERVES, MINUS GOLD,[1] 1950–87

(M US of 1980)

Year	Nominal Value	Real Value	Year	Nominal Value	Real Value
1950	2	7.72	1969	10	27.62
1951	13	43.77	1970	18	47.12
1952	7	23.73	1971	19	48.22
1953	6	20.41	1972	29	71.25
1954	5	17.30	1973	47	99.16
1955	6	20.48	1974	71	117.36
1956	8	26.14	1975	98	144.97
1957	5	15.92	1976	136	194.56
1958	7	22.51	1977	221	305.25
1959	4	12.86	1978	344	444.44
1960	1	3.19	1979	462	524.40
1961	2	6.27	1980	597	597.00
1962	2	6.31	1981	692	633.70
1963	3	9.46	1982	670	606.88
1964	5	15.63	1983	650	582.44
1965	10	30.30	1984	680	601.24
1966	11	32.35	1985	486	433.16
1967	12	34.58	1986	365	322.15
1968	12	34.09	1987	350	303.56

1. Nominal data in source deflated here using U.S. export price index (table 3231).

SOURCE: IMF-IFS-Y, 1987 and 1988; IMF-IFS, Aug. 1989, p. 47.

Figure 27:35

PARAGUAY TOTAL REAL SDR RESERVES, MINUS GOLD, 1950–87

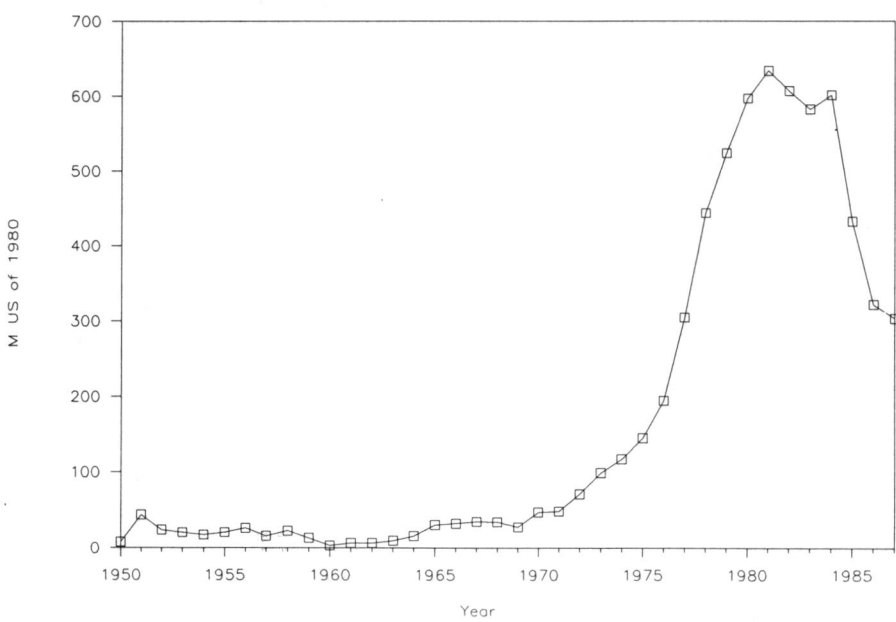

SOURCE: Table 2723.

Table 2724

PERU TOTAL REAL SDR RESERVES, MINUS GOLD,[1] 1950–87

(M US of 1980)

Year	Nominal Value	Real Value	Year	Nominal Value	Real Value
1950	26	100.4	1969	142	392.3
1951	18	60.6	1970	296	774.9
1952	16	54.2	1971	351	890.9
1953	19	64.6	1972	408	1,002.5
1954	27	93.4	1973	436	919.8
1955	23	78.5	1974	756	1,249.6
1956	38	124.2	1975	363	537.0
1957	12	38.2	1976	249	356.2
1958	12	38.6	1977	294	406.1
1959	31	99.7	1978	299	386.3
1960	34	108.6	1979	1,154	1,309.9
1961	63	197.5	1980	1,552	1,552.0
1962	69	217.7	1981	1,031	944.1
1963	78	246.1	1982	1,223	1,107.8
1964	93	290.6	1983	1,304	1,168.5
1965	107	324.2	1984	1,663	1,470.4
1966	90	264.7	1985	1,677	1,494.7
1967	106	305.5	1986	1,150	1,015.0
1968	91	258.5	1987	455	394.6

1. Nominal data in source deflated here using U.S. export price index (table 3231).

SOURCE: IMF-IFS-Y, 1987 and 1988; IMF-IFS, Aug. 1989, p. 47.

Figure 27:36

PERU TOTAL REAL SDR RESERVES, MINUS GOLD, 1950–87

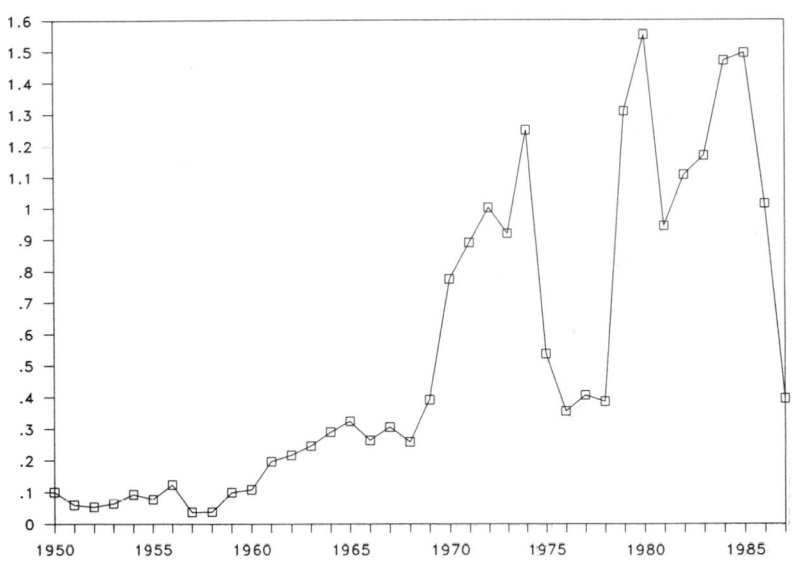

SOURCE: Table 2724.

Table 2725

URUGUAY TOTAL REAL SDR RESERVES, MINUS GOLD,[1] 1950–87

(M US of 1980)

Year	Nominal Value	Real Value	Year	Nominal Value	Real Value
1950	76	293.4	1969	19	52.5
1951	46	154.9	1970	14	36.6
1952	113	383.1	1971	19	48.2
1953	141	479.6	1972	64	157.2
1954	106	366.8	1973	83	175.1
1955	2	6.8	1974	66	109.1
1956	9	29.4	1975	50	74.0
1957	2	6.4	1976	152	217.5
1958	8	25.7	1977	265	366.0
1959	7	22.5	1978	271	350.1
1960	9	28.8	1979	245	278.1
1961	11	34.5	1980	301	301.0
1962	23	72.6	1981	369	337.9
1963	14	44.2	1982	105	95.1
1964	15	46.9	1983	198	177.4
1965	24	72.7	1984	137	121.1
1966	30	88.2	1985	159	141.7
1967	22	63.4	1986	394	347.7
1968	34	96.6	1987	374	324.4

1. Nominal data in source deflated here using U.S. export price index (table 3231).

SOURCE: IMF-IFS-Y, 1987 and 1988; IMF-IFS, Aug. 1989, p. 47.

Figure 27:37

URUGUAY TOTAL REAL SDR RESERVES, MINUS GOLD, 1950–87

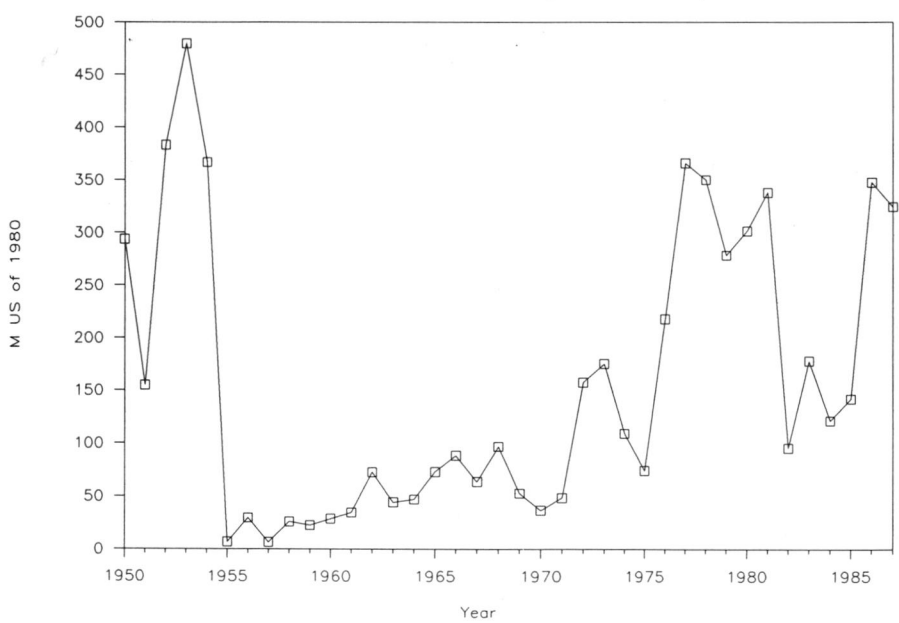

SOURCE: Table 2725.

Table 2726

VENEZUELA TOTAL REAL SDR RESERVES, MINUS GOLD,[1] 1950–87
(M US of 1980)

Year	Nominal Value	Real Value	Year	Nominal Value	Real Value
1950	5	19.3	1969	530	1,464.1
1951	4	13.5	1970	637	1,667.5
1952	70	237.3	1971	1,010	2,563.5
1953	111	377.6	1972	1,204	2,958.2
1954	79	273.4	1973	1,609	3,394.5
1955	130	443.7	1974	4,928	8,145.5
1956	347	1,134.0	1975	7,178	10,618.3
1957	739	2,353.5	1976	6,992	10,002.9
1958	342	1,099.7	1977	6,368	8,795.6
1959	69	221.9	1978	4,632	5,984.5
1960	208	664.5	1979	5,557	6,307.6
1961	179	561.1	1980	5,178	5,178.0
1962	182	574.1	1981	7,014	6,423.1
1963	344	1,085.2	1982	5,964	5,402.2
1964	431	1,346.9	1983	7,300	6,541.2
1965	418	1,266.7	1984	9,081	8,015.0
1966	376	1,105.9	1985	9,332	8,317.3
1967	471	1,357.3	1986	5,263	4,678.2
1968	519	1,474.4	1987	4,203	3,645.3

1. Nominal data in source deflated here using U.S. export price index (table 3231).

SOURCE: IMF-IFS-Y, 1987 and 1988; IMF-IFS, Aug. 1989, p. 47.

Figure 27:38

VENEZUELA TOTAL REAL SDR RESERVES, MINUS GOLD, 1950–87

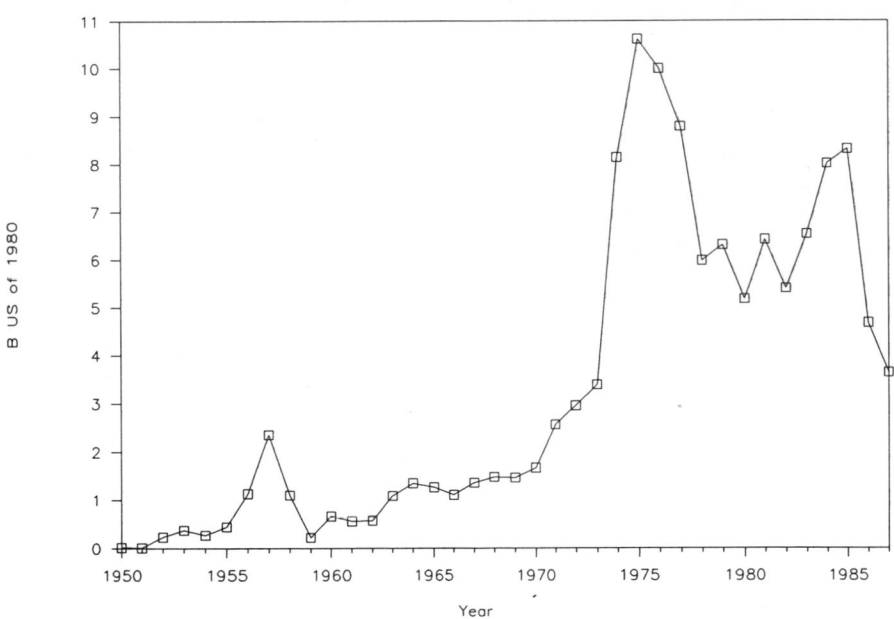

SOURCE: Table 2726.

Table 2727

UNITED STATES TOTAL REAL SDR RESERVES, MINUS GOLD,[1] 1950–87

(M US of 1980)

Year	Nominal Value	Real Value	Year	Nominal Value	Real Value
1950	1,446	5,583.0	1969	5,105	14,102.2
1951	1,426	4,801.3	1970	3,415	8,939.8
1952	1,462	4,955.9	1971	1,942	4,928.9
1953	1,367	4,649.7	1972	2,453	6,027.0
1954	1,185	4,100.3	1973	2,260	4,767.9
1955	1,044	3,563.1	1974	3,456	5,712.4
1956	1,608	5,254.9	1975	3,952	5,846.2
1957	1,975	6,289.8	1976	6,153	8,802.6
1958	1,958	6,295.8	1977	6,250	8,632.6
1959	1,998	6,424.4	1978	5,357	6,921.2
1960	1,555	4,968.1	1979	5,909	6,707.2
1961	1,806	5,661.4	1980	12,228	12,228.0
1962	1,163	3,668.8	1981	16,258	14,888.3
1963	1,247	3,933.8	1982	20,677	18,729.2
1964	1,201	3,753.1	1983	21,612	19,365.6
1965	1,385	4,197.0	1984	24,319	21,502.2
1966	1,647	4,844.1	1985	29,220	26,042.8
1967	2,765	7,968.3	1986	30,619	27,024.7
1968	4,818	13,687.5	1987	24,474	21,226.4

1. Nominal data in source deflated here using U.S. export price index (table 3231).

SOURCE: IMF-IFS-Y, 1987 and 1988; IMF-IFS, Aug. 1989, p. 45.

Figure 27:39

UNITED STATES TOTAL REAL SDR RESERVES, MINUS GOLD, 1950–87

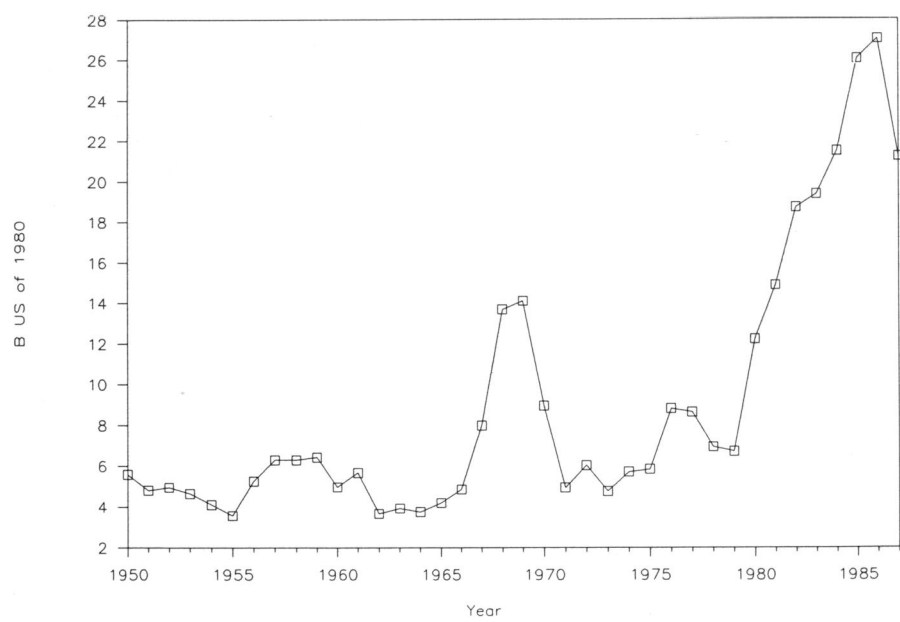

SOURCE: Table 2727.

Table 2728

TOTAL CHANGE IN DOLLAR RESERVES, 19 LC, 1951–88

(M US)

Year	A. ARGENTINA	B. BOLIVIA	C. BRAZIL	D. CHILE	E. COLOMBIA	F. COSTA RICA	H. DOMINICAN REP.	I. ECUADOR	J. EL SALVADOR	K. GUATEMALA
1951	25	-5.5	137	-2	~	-4.7	-10.3	5.0	-1.6	-2.3
1952	49	4.0	-32	-19	~	-6.2	-2.5	-11.5	-1.0	-3.2
1953	-86	6.9	63	10	~	.2	4.0	2.9	.2	.1
1954	-30	12.1	38	15	~	-7.3	-7.6	2.3	-.8	2.5
1955	68	3.3	-15	-21	~	-3.9	-1.4	5.8	5.5	-15.5
1956	38	9.9	-148	3	8	7.8	-2.3	.2	2.6	-15.7
1957	175	-3.8	173	51	-7	#	-8.2	-2.4	-5.0	-3.9
1958	154	1.5	49	-1	-9	-7.8	.7	-1.2	2.0	26.0
1959	-178	-6.7	8	-73	-70	6.2	5.7	-5.9	4.7	5.1
1960	-258	3.9	24	4	41	1.2	21.1	2.8	10.4	-10.0
1961	232	-1.9	-101	92	69	10.9	16.8	12.7	5.0	-1.1
1962	297	4.7	114	-18	61	-10.0	-11.7	-7.1	-7.0	9.9
1963	-141	-5.1	39	42	47	6.4	-26.6	-11.7	-15.9	-12.0
1964	74	-16.5	-33	-2	-30	-4.0	9.3	-4.8	-10.9	-4.5
1965	-127	-14.0	-219	-50	-16	4.4	6.8	11.7	-5.2	-8.8
1966	-26	-4.6	14	-49	17	3.2	13.5	-10.1	14.5	12.8
1967	-541	3.3	193	30	28	-4.8	7.9	-8.8	2.1	4.8
1968	-33	3.5	-70	-73	-69	-10.4	-10.6	1.6	-4.2	-2.8
1969	222	.5	-399	-157	-55	-17.4	1.1	4.5	-4.6	-12.3
1970	-135	-5.5	-530	-99	-36	11.6	-.4	-7.7	-6.4	14.6
1971	390	-6.5	-55.6	213	7	-13.0	-18.9	10.7	3.9	-13.4
1972	14	-4.1	-2,437	116	-180	-19.5	-10.1	-74.3	-19.0	-42.9
1973	-814	2.5	-2,227	-16	-207	-16.5	-33.4	-99.5	13.1	-77.3
1974	-127	-127.2	1,144	16	85	33.0	-2.8	-108.2	-14.4	-6.3
1975	1,071	33.5	1,235	271	-97	16.6	-25.3	65.3	-30.4	-102.5
1976	-921	-47.1	-2,508	-333	-633	-64.1	14.4	-224.0	-84.5	-219.4
1977	-1,828	-75.8	-712	-156	-668	-109.5	-50.3	-146.3	-41.0	-182.9
1978	-2,297	81.8	-4,638	-724	-669	-25.6	41.3	-13.0	-56.9	-10.4
1979	-4,381	-25.4	2,860	-1,128	-1,615	113.6	-7.8	-86.5	125.2	18.3
1980	2,749	137.0	3,321	-1,402	-1,231	-98.9	-44.4	-291.0	71.4	252.5
1981	3,437	-21.7	-750	-77	-218	66.6	-54.1	380.6	42.7	300.8
1982	758	-33.4	4,904	1,373	722	-137.1	160.4	328.2	27.0	33.0
1983	2,427	-47.0	1,277	499	1,753	-61.0	145.7	-127.2	-38.9	-56.4
1984	-16	-121.5	-5,933	-196	1,166	57.3	-82.7	58.3	-18.4	-20.9
1985	-817	35.8	926	173	-285	-50.8	-13.6	4.4	-16.5	-97.0
1986	984	-99.1	3,942	527	-1,354	-78.3	-28.9	200.9	-32.4	-101.8
1987	2,213	80.5	-1,029	-26	106	-11.4	173.3	160.3	~	62.1
1988	~	~	~	~	~	~	~	~	~	~

Table 2728 (Continued)

TOTAL CHANGE IN DOLLAR RESERVES, 19 LC, 1951–88

(M US)

Year	L. HAITI	M. HONDURAS	N. MEXICO	O. NICARAGUA	P. PANAMA	Q. PARAGUAY	R. PERU	S. URUGUAY	T. VENEZUELA	UNITED STATES[1,2]
1951	-1.6	-9.7	~	~	~	-6.2	~	~	~	~
1952	-2.8	-2.1	~	~	~	1.9	~	~	~	~
1953	5.8	-.6	32	~	~	1.5	~	~	~	1.26
1954	-4.5	-1.2	40	~	~	5.8	~	~	~	.48
1955	2.7	4.1	-231	~	#	2.3	~	~	~	.18
1956	1.2	2.0	-72	7.3	-2	-21	-15	~	-417	-.87
1957	3.2	4.1	36	-2.4	4	4.0	33	~	-505	-1.16
1958	2.9	4.3	80	1.9	-4	-.3	3	~	395	2.29
1959	1.6	-.8	-62	-4.6	5	1.6	-32	2.6	338	1.04
1960	-2.2	-.4	16	.1	-3	2.7	-17	-5.9	115	2.14
1961	-2.8	1.8	29	.1	3	-3.4	-34	-5.9	29	.61
1962	4.1	.2	-14	-3.9	#	-.1	-6	6.4	-2	1.53
1963	2.5	-.1	-120	-8.5	-3	-1.5	-19	17.0	-163	.38
1964	.3	-4.7	-42	-6.2	2	-2.3	-25	-.6	-86	.17
1965	.9	-6.2	61	-18.2	-1	-5.5	-15	8.0	-11	1.22
1966	1.2	5.0	-2	-2.6	#	-.4	17	1.2	67	.57
1967	2.0	-.4	-27	19.4	-1	-.7	30	8.2	-95	.05
1968	-3.1	-6.5	-94	-4.0	-2	.1	18	15.7	-50	-.88
1969	-1.2	.6	53	4.7	3	2.0	-31	-28.4	-11	-1.26
1970	-3.8	9.7	-75	-11.3	4	-7.3	-187	16.7	-87	2.48
1971	-10.7	-2.6	-197	-8.1	3	-3.4	-90	-.4	-469	2.18
1972	-9.8	-13.3	-223	-27.5	-22	-10.4	-30	-3.1	-208	#
1973	3.5	-6.9	-168	-67.8	2	-25.7	-94	-23.8	-637	-.06
1974	11.4	17.4	-43	35.2	11	-30.1	-413	40.9	-4,480	-1.46
1975	8.5	-54.1	-112	-41.3	16	-27.9	499	57.0	-2,669	-.20
1976	-11.1	-38.0	682	-2.9	15	-42.4	312	-73.8	-2,377	-2.52
1977	-12.1	-66.2	-384	-9.3	10	-112.4	-59	-174.3	-847	-.56
1978	-14.3	-9.9	-455	82.8	-78	-179.5	-5	-152.0	977	1.06
1979	-11.4	-25.0	-396	-35.0	21	-165.1	-1,066	-123.1	-4,234	2.76
1980	26.3	73.0	-1,027	196.6	-17	-152.9	-609	-113.6	-3,823	-7.64
1981	56.7	69.0	-1,122	-62.4	68	-43.1	575	-20.1	12	-3.21
1982	-38.4	52.8	3,542	-36.6	9	64.8	65	505.1	8,215	-3.86
1983	-22.4	39.4	-2,183	-19.0	3	56.1	-2	111.0	-88	.45
1984	-22.7	-26.8	-2,355	-247.6	69	18.1	-296	63.6	-1,482	-.97
1985	16.0	18.6	2,972	-18.7	158	100.8	-110	-42.2	-1,255	-8.21
1986	17.3	-42.5	232	193.9	-30	119.7	373	-249.7	3,781	-5.11
1987	24.4	-26.2	-5,684	~	85	50.3	952	-33.6	721	2.58
1988	~	~	~	~	~	~	~	~	~	-1.83

1. Cf. SALA, 25-2701 to 2720.
2. Data in billions.

SOURCE: IMF-IFS-Y, 1981, line 79 kd,d; 1986, line 79 cd; 1988, line 79 cd; IMF-IFS, May 1989, line 79 cd.

Table 2729

ECLA BALANCE OF PAYMENTS, 19 L, 1983–87
(M US)

Category	A. ARGENTINA 1983	1984	1985	1986	1987[‡]	B. BOLIVIA 1983	1984	1985	1986	1987[‡]	C. BRAZIL 1983	1984	1985	1986	1987[‡]
Balance on current account	-2,436	-2,495	-963	-2,861	-4,350	-204	-241	-342	-466	-597	-6,842	33	-353	-4,381	-1,456
Trade balance	3,469	3,648	4,765	1,957	550	120	155	14	-174	-316	4,079	11,345	10,735	6,337	8,777
Exports of goods and services	9,291	9,607	10,063	8,435	7,800	858	818	720	667	592	23,619	28,939	27,617	24,348	28,100
Goods FOB	7,838	8,101	8,419	6,851	6,200	755	724	623	546	470	21,906	27,001	25,539	22,451	26,156
Real services[1]	1,454	1,506	1,644	1,584	1,600	103	93	96	121	122	1,712	1,937	2,077	1,897	1,944
Transport and insurance	755	833	893	746	675	35	35	38	48	40	1,119	1,309	1,515	1,272	1,320
Travel	453	440	523	561	620	42	32	30	35	38	40	64	66	84	102
Imports of goods and services	5,822	5,959	5,298	6,478	7,250	738	663	706	840	908	19,540	17,594	16,882	18,011	19,322
Goods FOB	4,120	4,119	3,524	4,391	5,230	496	412	463	597	658	15,434	13,915	13,127	14,011	15,050
Real services[1]	1,700	1,841	1,774	2,087	2,020	242	251	244	244	250	4,106	3,678	3,724	3,999	4,274
Transport and insurance	737	898	708	745	890	149	136	149	164	180	2,025	2,070	1,873	1,718	2,139
Travel	507	600	679	894	800	20	30	30	27	30	431	218	440	570	287
Factor services	-5,922	-6,144	-5,728	-4,818	-4,900	-365	-418	-375	-311	-301	-11,025	-11,473	-11,228	-10,814	-10,346
Profits	424	-439	-427	-485	-550	-59	-36	-53	-40	-47	-1,453	-1,267	-1,605	-1,680	-1,534
Interest received	440	265	253	358	200	39	28	16	15	18	707	1,245	1,521	962	526
Interest paid	-5,425	-5,537	-5,149	-4,297	-4,150	-342	-408	-337	-281	-265	-10,267	-11,449	-11,124	-10,072	-9,308
Others	-514	-433	-404	-393	-400	-2	-2	-2	-4	-7	-13	-2	-20	-25	-31
Unrequited private transfer payments	16	2	#	1	#	40	22	20	19	20	106	161	140	96	113
Balance on capital account	-13	2,660	1,940	1,987	2,750	246	357	301	597	530	4,943	5,342	-170	1,197	3,588
Unrequited official transfer payments	#	#	#	#	#	66	67	60	82	109	2	10	15	-9	-43
Long-term capital	1,715	-322	4,396	1,976	20	288	-147	-235	-62	…	7,997	9,773	2,302	865	-1,010
Direct investment	183	267	968	575	…	7	7	10	10	22	1,372	1,557	1,281	333	1,078
Portfolio investment	1,140	759	-504	-381	…	-2	-1	-1	#	#	-286	-272	-235	-429	-429
Other long-term capital	393	-1,349	3,932	1,782	…	283	-154	-244	-72	…	6,911	8,489	1,255	961	-1,659
Official sector[2]	376	1,440	5,433	2,130	…	372	-111	-200	-61	…	9,279	11,283	6,296	8,775	7,949
Loans disbursed	2,497	2,332	6,538	3,131	…	578	143	100	330	…	13,329	20,561	15,160	13,292	11,039
Amortization payments	-2,110	-541	-948	-287	…	-202	-247	-294	-378	…	-4,153	-9,427	-8,683	-4,467	-3,027
Commercial banks[2]	38	-33	#	-1	…	-15	-12	1	-12	…	-1,520	-1,404	-2,630	-3,684	-2,183
Loans disbursed	264	8	16	15	…	7	6	9	2	…	1,136	1,230	327	76	746
Amortization payments	-227	-40	-16	-16	…	-22	-18	-9	-14	…	-2,656	-2,631	-2,957	-3,760	-2,929
Other sectors[2]	-22	-2,756	-1,501	-347	…	-74	-31	-36	#	…	-848	-1,390	-2,411	-4,131	-7,425
Loans disbursed	2,447	279	544	761	…	21	11	8	#	…	2,527	2,079	2,126	1,129	2,094
Amortization payments	-2,295	-2,862	-2,057	-1,038	…	-95	-42	-44	#	…	-3,358	-4,128	-5,133	-5,773	-9,152
Short-term capital (net)	-1,289	3,037	-2,142	-294	…	-181	449	287	416	…	-2,464	-4,844	-1,991	872	5,444
Official sector	-91	1,896	-2,810	-660	…	-149	345	258	306	…	-1,390	-1,942	-461	365	5,026
Commercial banks	311	-523	651	29	…	1	4	-21	-14	…	-710	1,001	-555	188	441
Other sectors	-1,509	1,664	17	337	…	-32	101	50	125	…	-364	-3,903	-975	319	-23
Errors and omissions	-440	-55	-315	305	…	72	-12	188	162	…	-592	404	-495	-530	-807
Global balance[3]	-2,450	165	978	-874	-1,600	42	116	-42	132	-67	-1,899	5,375	-523	-3,184	2,132
Total variation in reserves (minus sign indicates an increase)	2,379	-17	-2,113	1,600	1,100	-25	-148	44	-68	43	1,214	-6,102	1,893	-3,934	2,132
Monetary gold	#	#	#	#	…	-1	-1	#	-2	…	-156	-336	-559	205	-13
Special Drawing Rights	#	-1	1	#	…	#	#	#	#	…	#	#	#	1	#
IMF reserve position	100	#	#	#	…	#	#	#	#	…	287	-1	#	#	#
Foreign exchange assets	1,105	57	-2,029	555	…	19	-116	57	-40	…	-714	-7,173	1,901	3,824	90
Other assets	#	#	#	616	…	-47	-6	-1	-141	…	-297	-141	126	21	#
Use made of IMF credit	1,174	-73	1,211	429	…	3	-25	-12	115	…	2,094	1,549	426	-118	-525

Table 2729 (Continued)

ECLA BALANCE OF PAYMENTS, 19 L, 1983–87

(M US)

Category	D. CHILE					E. COLOMBIA					F. COSTA RICA				
	1983	1984	1985	1986	1987[‡]	1983	1984	1985	1986	1987[‡]	1983	1984	1985	1986	1987[‡]
Balance on current account	-1,160	-2,118	-1,342	1,135	-871	-3,022	-1,411	-1,815	413	-52	-330	-265	-303	-193	-341
Trade balance	578	-102	547	750	816	-1,970	-149	-617	1,397	861	-16	24	-56	51	-131
Exports of goods and services	4,628	4,493	4,468	5,030	6,306	3,784	5,167	4,476	6,343	6,372	1,133	1,275	1,223	1,395	1,459
Goods FOB	3,831	3,650	3,804	4,199	5,224	2,970	4,273	3,650	5,375	5,325	853	997	941	1,084	1,114
Real services[1]	796	843	664	831	1,082	815	894	825	968	1,045	280	278	282	310	345
Transport and insurance	292	307	301	359	433	390	395	370	469	495	59	60	50	54	60
Travel	98	129	116	145	187	235	245	192	232	232	133	121	123	139	150
Imports of goods and services	4,049	4,595	3,921	4,280	5,490	5,754	5,316	5,093	4,946	5,510	1,149	1,252	1,279	1,343	1,590
Goods FOB	2,845	3,357	2,954	3,099	3,994	4,464	4,027	3,674	3,485	3,907	898	997	1,005	1,048	1,253
Real services[1]	1,204	1,238	967	1,181	1,496	1,290	1,288	1,419	1,461	1,603	250	255	274	295	337
Transport and insurance	537	615	513	591	679	639	596	574	626	634	133	134	144	150	172
Travel	243	327	269	319	351	315	329	313	355	354	52	55	58	67	82
Factor services	-1,793	-2,057	-1,936	-1,925	-1,742	-1,197	-1,552	-1,653	-1,748	-1,901	-337	-321	-290	-282	-253
Profits	-136	-176	-155	-168	-213	-437	-441	-380	-526	-536	7	-8	-22	-14	-43
Interest received	189	316	197	221	178	272	108	91	133	174	34	33	44	41	27
Interest paid	-1,801	-2,158	-1,943	-1,940	-1,664	-1,011	-1,177	-1,293	-1,269	-1,427	-374	-340	-304	-300	-227
Others	-45	-39	-35	-38	-43	-21	-42	-71	-87	-112	-4	-7	-8	-8	-10
Unrequited private transfer payments	55	41	47	40	55	145	289	455	764	988	23	32	43	37	43
Balance on capital account	644	2,209	1,240	883	917	1,181	1,038	1,970	946	-70	377	209	375	274	337
Unrequited official transfer payments	43	58	14	44	61	19	10	6	11	13	46	111	179	114	146
Long-term capital	31	3,553	1,014	836	?	1,528	1,821	2,349	2,372	238	1,190	65	341	-59	-435
Direct investment	131	67	62	57	?	514	561	1,016	673	238	55	52	65	57	83
Portfolio investment	#	#	50	262	?	-2	-3	-1	39	238	-3	#	-13	-2	#
Other long-term capital	-100	3,486	902	?	?	1,016	1,264	1,334	1,660	238	1,137	13	288	-114	-518
Official sector[2]	1,257	1,504	1,210	?	?	102	355	297	472	238	1,189	126	339	-43	-496
Loans received	1,432	1,640	1,431	?	?	290	645	633	899	238	1,362	384	594	-279	?
Amortization payments	-139	-136	-221	?	?	-188	-290	-329	-427	238	-180	-231	-255	-309	?
Commercial banks[2]	-800	1,557	-69	-126	?	#	#	#	#	238	-15	-27	-16	-14	-14
Loans received	135	2,138	1,072	1,297	?	#	#	#	#	238	1	1	#	#	?
Amortization payments	-952	-589	-1,198	-1,439	?	#	#	#	#	238	-16	#	-16	-14	?
Other sectors[2]	-558	425	-239	?	?	914	909	1,037	1,188	238	-37	-27	-35	-57	-8
Loans received	367	1,206	794	?	?	1,360	1,419	1,539	2,006	238	64	-86	67	69	?
Amortization payments	-925	-781	-1,033	?	?	-446	-510	-502	-818	238	-101	41	-102	-125	?
Short-term capital (net)	489	-1,501	215	52	?	-93	-878	-114	-1,267	-437	-927	-127	-303	132	458
Official sector	320	32	-159	-350	?	90	22	13	54	?	-530	-72	-196	150	521
Commercial banks	316	-1,405	36	130	?	64	-188	3	-267	?	-97	-3	-2	3	#
Other sectors	-148	-128	338	272	?	-247	-712	-130	-1,054	129	-301	12	-104	-21	-63
Errors and omissions	80	99	-3	-49	-60	-273	84	-273	-171	129	68	-81	158	87	168
Global balance[3]	-516	91	-102	-252	46	-1,841	-373	154	1,359	-122	47	-56	72	81	-4
Total variation in reserves (minus sign indicates an increase)	652	-263	196	113	?	1,748	1,039	-162	-1,427	28	-64	84	-72	-61	4
Monetary gold	46	27	22	-49	?	-177	651	-170	-63	?	-1	14	-11	-4	?
Special Drawing Rights	14	-6	11	-1	?	-19	198	#	-139	?	-3	3	#	#	?
IMF reserve position	78	#	#	#	?	-81	274	#	#	?	#	#	#	#	?
Foreign exchange assets	-87	-458	-145	21	?	2,060	-54	-112	-962	?	-170	82	-88	-24	?
Other assets	#	#	#	#	?	-34	-30	120	-263	?	11	21	-5	-17	?
Use made of IMF credit	600	175	307	242	?	#	#	#	#	?	99	-36	32	-16	?

Table 2729 (Continued)
ECLA BALANCE OF PAYMENTS, 19 L, 1983-87
(M US)

Category	H. DOMINICAN REPUBLIC 1983	1984	1985	1986	1987‡	I. ECUADOR 1983	1984	1985	1986	1987‡	J. EL SALVADOR 1983	1984	1985	1986	1987‡
Balance on current account	-438	-223	-222	-148	-400	-28	-268	69	-658	-1,261	-211	-243	-243	-80	-209
Trade balance	-336	-187	-238	-140	-354	821	755	1,119	352	-216	-187	-260	-279	-127	-280
Exports of goods and services	1,242	1,370	1,323	1,409	1,556	2,643	2,895	3,294	2,589	2,442	873	894	906	1,025	913
Goods FOB	785	868	758	722	711	2,348	2,622	2,905	2,186	2,017	735	726	679	755	573
Real services [1]	457	501	584	687	845	295	273	389	403	425	138	168	227	270	340
Transport and insurance	27	29	35	34	36	112	95	177	186	176	30	44	58	60	67
Travel	320	371	451	506	568	120	120	133	133	167	24	30	43	35	47
Imports of goods and services	1,578	1,557	1,560	1,550	1,910	1,822	2,140	2,175	2,237	2,658	1,061	1,153	1,184	1,152	1,193
Goods FOB	1,279	1,257	1,286	1,266	1,550	1,421	1,567	1,611	1,631	2,048	831	915	895	876	907
Real services [1]	299	300	275	283	360	401	573	564	606	610	230	239	289	276	286
Transport and insurance	150	127	121	120	175	182	296	257	272	319	81	86	89	82	91
Travel	88	89	83	90	95	152	155	196	210	170	74	74	89	71	72
Factor services	-297	-241	-226	-250	-306	-849	-1,023	-1,050	-1,010	-1,045	-121	-101	-94	-127	-127
Profits	#	#	#	#	-89	-60	-70	-126	-139	-130	-36	-40	-32	-40	-40
Interest received	7	6	22	17	12	45	77	29	28	19	13	17	16	15	15
Interest paid	-304	-247	-248	-267	-229	-723	-889	-839	-777	-801	-107	-110	-101	-127	-122
Others	#	#	#	#	#	-111	-14	-114	-122	-133	10	32	23	25	20
Unrequited private transfer payments	195	205	242	242	260	#	#	#	#	#	97	118	129	174	198
Balance on capital account	301	320	267	208	182	138	187	-44	486	1,181	235	250	270	155	260
Unrequited official transfer payments	20	60	114	29	95	24	20	80	45	75	174	190	214	219	347
Long-term capital	558	294	186	270	69	1,372	358	474	773	75	317	74	99	-10	-67
Direct investment	48	68	36	50	89	50	50	62	70	75	28	12	12	#	#
Portfolio investment	#	#	#	#	#	#	#	#	#	?	#	#	#	#	#
Other long-term capital	510	226	149	220	-20	1,322	308	412	703	?	289	62	87	-10	-67
Official sector [2]	576	237	161	220	-20	2,265	879	492	741	?	283	72	88	64	30
Loans received	698	305	203	220	154	2,641	1,531	1,731	2,004	?	421	257	250	114	26
Amortization payments	-122	-68	-41	#	-174	-363	-643	-1,232	-1,247	?	-137	-183	-154	-50	-56
Commercial banks [2]	9	-2	#	#	#	-7	-9	#	#	?	-1	-1	#	1	#
Loans received	11	#	#	#	#	-1	1	#	#	?	-1	#	#	1	#
Amortization payments	-2	-2	#	#	#	-1	-1	#	#	?	#	-10	-1	#	#
Other sectors [2]	-75	-9	-12	#	#	-936	-562	-80	-38	?	6	9	-1	-75	-97
Loans received	16	20	7	#	#	150	78	22	18	?	28	-18	17	141	101
Amortization payments	-92	-30	-19	#	#	-1,085	-639	-102	-56	?	-22	28	-18	-216	-198
Short-term capital (net)	-289	-63	-192	-82	18	-1,073	-200	-677	-153	?	-215	10	-67	30	-4
Official sector	-165	-114	-81	-75	18	-520	-95	-63	-136	?	-121	-7	-10	?	?
Commercial banks	-235	-22	-110	-8	#	7	34	#	#	?	-33	26	-48	?	?
Other sectors	110	73	#	#	#	-560	-139	-614	-17	?	-61	-8	-8	?	?
Errors and omissions	13	30	158	-9	#	-185	9	79	-179	?	-41	-42	23	-84	-16
Global balance [3]	-136	97	45	59	-218	110	-81	24	-172	-80	24	7	27	75	51
Total variation in reserves (minus sign indicates an increase)	147	-84	-14	-29	146	-127	58	5	201	80	-39	-19	-30	-75	-51
Monetary gold	13	22	#	#	?	#	#	#	#	?	2	#	#	?	?
Special Drawing Rights	#	#	31	32	?	#	#	-28	-27	?	2	#	#	?	?
IMF reserve position	-8	8	#	#	?	-12	12	#	#	?	–	#	#	?	?
Foreign exchange assets	-34	-91	55	-68	195	-328	21	-78	101	?	-53	-6	-14	?	?
Other assets	#	2	-3	#	?	#	#	-10	#	?	–	#	#	?	?
Use made of IMF credit	176	-25	75	7	-49	213	25	121	127	?	11	-13	17	?	?

Table 2729 (Continued)

ECLA BALANCE OF PAYMENTS, 19 L, 1983-87
(M US)

Category	K. GUATEMALA 1983	1984	1985	1986	1987‡	L. HAITI 1983	1984	1985	1986	1987‡	M. HONDURAS 1983	1984	1985	1986	1987‡
Balance on current account	-225	-382	-241	-36	-366	-205	-203	-194	-168	-178	-254	-372	-322	-271	-313
Trade balance	-142	-201	-92	126	-369	-237	-230	-223	-204	-214	-111	-204	-144	-73	-107
Exports of goods and services	1,172	1,228	1,165	1,170	1,121	288	319	337	292	314	801	856	919	1,019	984
Goods FOB	1,092	1,131	1,065	1,048	964	186	215	223	191	198	699	746	805	901	863
Real services[1]	80	97	100	122	157	103	104	114	101	116	102	110	114	118	121
Transport and insurance	18	10	7	8	10	7	8	8	7	8	44	51	54	54	54
Travel	7	11	13	29	48	85	85	93	82	90	22	23	24	26	27
Imports of goods and services	1,314	1,429	1,257	1,044	1,490	525	549	560	497	528	912	1,060	1,063	1,092	1,091
Goods FOB	1,056	1,183	1,078	874	1,232	352	360	348	326	311	756	880	879	902	894
Real services[1]	257	246	180	169	258	173	189	212	170	217	156	181	184	190	197
Transport and insurance	99	112	107	92	122	88	98	114	76	93	78	87	88	90	103
Travel	89	61	24	15	32	39	40	43	36	42	21	25	27	30	35
Factor services	-113	-209	-168	-212	-188	-14	-18	-20	-15	-20	-152	-178	-190	-211	-222
Profits	-39	-83	-21	-38	-40	-8	-2	5	5	-6	-33	-57	-58	-67	-70
Interest received	27	30	28	32	30	1	#	#	#	#	12	14	13	11	10
Interest paid	-102	-152	-171	-202	-173	-7	-17	-25	-20	-14	-131	-135	-145	-155	-162
Labour and property	—	-4	-5	-5	-5	#	#	#	#	#	#	10	#	13	#
Unrequited private transfer payments	30	28	19	50	191	46	45	49	52	56	10	10	12	13	16
Balance on capital account	276	397	343	147	292	227	182	123	148	214	207	382	333	300	355
Unrequited official transfer payments	1	1	1	25	~	64	78	97	100	127	35	70	111	116	130
Long-term capital	283	203	244	42	176	59	61	21	17	60	148	269	255	99	36
Direct investment	45	38	61	67	73	8	4	5	5	5	21	21	28	30	~
Portfolio investment	77	59	143	17	~	#	#	#	#	#	#	-2	1	-1	~
Other long-term capital	161	106	40	-42	~	51	56	16	12	55	127	250	227	70	~
Official sector[2]	167	154	40	-80	86	30	53	10	-5	34	53	91	103	63	~
Disbursements	310	277	277	429	275	36	63	36	34	~	104	128	171	152	~
Amortization payments	-143	-126	-215	-467	-189	-5	-9	-16	-27	~	-43	-34	-56	-74	~
Commercial banks[2]	#	#	#	#	~	#	#	#	#	#	-3	-4	-7	-1	~
Disbursements	#	#	#	#	~	#	#	#	#	#	3	2	13	9	~
Amortization payments	#	#	#	#	~	#	#	#	#	#	-6	-6	-6	-11	~
Other sectors[2]	-6	-48	14	39	~	20	3	6	17	21	77	163	116	9	~
Disbursements	11	6	-13	6	~	27	20	14	21	~	177	263	202	99	~
Amortization payments	-18	-54	54	-10	~	-7	-18	-8	-3	~	-100	-100	-86	-90	~
Short-term capital (net)	29	179	-99	-80	91	2	6	5	7	27	11	74	19	41	27
Official sector	24	-93	-65	11	~	1	11	17	23	~	-2	64	46	39	~
Commercial banks	71	9	218	82	~	2	-5	-12	-16	~	8	-6	5	#	~
Other sectors	-67	262	44	67	~	#	#	#	#	~	5	16	-32	2	~
Errors and omissions	-37	14	44	67	25	102	38	-2	24	#	13	-30	-53	44	#
Global balance[3]	51	14	102	110	-74	22	-21	-71	-20	36	-47	11	11	28	42
Total variation in reserves (minus sign indicates an increase)	-64	-30	-81	-85	74	32	5	5	~	-36	39	~	~	-43	-42
Monetary gold	#	#	#	#	~	#	#	#	-1	~	#	#	#	#	~
Special Drawing Rights	-1	-1	2	#	~	-1	1	#	#	~	#	#	#	#	~
IMF reserve position	-8	8	#	#	~	#	#	#	#	~	-4	2	#	-6	~
Foreign exchange assets	-89	-72	-28	-61	~	10	-5	~	-1	~	3	4	~	-2	~
Other assets	#	25	-20	21	~	#	#	#	#	~	-2	-1	-2	-35	~
Use made of IMF credit	35	10	-35	-46	~	22	9	~	~	~	43	-11	-2	~	~

Table 2729 (Continued)

ECLA BALANCE OF PAYMENTS, 19 L, 1983–87

(M US)

Category	N. MEXICO					O. NICARAGUA					P. PANAMA				
	1983	1984	1985	1986	1987‡	1983	1984	1985	1986	1987‡	1983	1984	1985	1986	1987‡
Balance on current account	5,242	4,059	510	1,495	3,626	-638	-753	-827	-799	-710	311	-45	162	325	245
Trade balance	14,493	14,016	9,259	5,733	10,399	-430	-503	-587	-563	-480	255	35	156	262	303
Exports of goods and services	27,188	30,157	27,639	22,012	27,510	471	422	351	294	331	2,951	2,932	3,308	3,674	3,754
Goods FOB	22,320	24,196	21,667	16,028	20,656	429	385	301	247	281	1,676	1,686	1,983	2,402	2,525
Real services [1]	4,867	5,961	5,971	5,984	6,854	42	37	50	47	50	1,276	1,247	1,326	1,271	1,229
Transport and insurance	471	570	579	567	662	14	10	15	13	15	717	676	707	665	653
Travel	2,727	3,284	2,926	2,989	3,498	13	8	14	13	12	172	189	208	205	188
Imports of goods and services	12,695	16,142	18,380	16,279	17,111	901	925	938	857	811	2,696	2,897	3,152	3,411	3,451
Goods FOB	8,553	11,256	13,218	11,451	12,223	778	800	800	727	691	2,321	2,503	2,730	2,988	3,035
Real services [1]	4,141	4,887	5,162	4,828	4,888	123	125	138	130	120	375	394	422	424	416
Transport and insurance	1,279	1,387	1,394	1,309	1,335	55	58	91	86	80	203	223	219	234	209
Travel	1,582	2,168	2,265	2,108	2,362	15	6	11	10	9	71	67	65	73	87
Factor services	-9,373	-10,186	-9,060	-7,518	-7,195	-211	-253	-257	-245	-240	116	-25	36	95	-25
Profits	-383	-458	-627	-626	-1,047	-1	#	-5	1	#	-81	-121	-115	-56	-62
Interest received	1,281	2,073	1,827	1,427	1,857	7	5	2	1	1	4,326	3,592	3,007	2,502	2,173
Interest paid	-10,190	-11,775	-10,227	-8,393	-8,116	-213	-257	-253	-246	-241	-4,119	-3,487	-2,847	-2,341	-2,123
Work and ownership	-81	-26	-32	75	111	-3	#	#	#	#	-10	-10	-9	-11	-13
Unrequited private transfer payments	121	230	311	290	422	4	2	16	9	10	-60	-54	-31	-32	-33
Balance on capital account	-3,207	-1,902	-3,272	1,485	2,300	656	1,000	846	605	533	-323	-39	-276	-264	-336
Unrequited official transfer payments	180	180	683	199	246	76	88	68	106	122	104	144	140	130	112
Long-term capital	7,302	2,504	-316	104	4,356	719	552	790	605	771	412	302	-287	30	52
Direct investment:	462	389	502	895	3,248	8	2	#	#	771	72	103	59	-72	-6
Portfolio investment	-625	-757	-1,010	-541	…	#	#	#	#	771	63	13	-183	50	-49
Other long-term capital	7,464	2,872	193	-250	4,997	712	550	790	605	771	278	186	-163	52	107
Official sector [2]	14,606	2,826	11,313	-259	…	727	563	792	609	771	162	102	31	124	39
Loans received	15,545	2,827	11,564	386	6,690	1,037	727	956	941	771	232	287	60	155	…
Amortization payments	-938	-1	-260	-646	-1,693	-298	-158	-164	-332	771	-70	-180	-30	-29	…
Commercial banks [2]	1,431	459	71	561	…	24	29	5	9	771	204	115	-161	-107	95
Loans received	2,382	1,461	1,785	2,529	…	34	38	22	15	771	221	115	-161	-107	…
Amortization payments	-951	-1,003	-1,714	-1,969	…	-11	-9	-17	-6	771	-17	#	#	#	…
Other sectors [2]	-8,573	-414	11,191	-551	…	-39	-41	-7	-14	771	-88	-31	-33	35	-27
Loans received	1,417	913	1,012	963	…	31	14	10	8	771	143	160	87	118	…
Amortization payments	-9,872	-1,354	-12,250	-1,492	…	-70	-55	-17	-21	771	-233	-175	-117	-78	…
Short-term capital	-9,608	-3,579	-1,800	-1,435	-3,157	-97	230	-149	113	147	-275	-232	140	42	167
Official sector	-1,216	#	#	-63	…	-70	307	167	51	5	--	2	-5	3	2
Commercial banks	-576	342	-18	1,498	…	16	-34	-5	22	4	-149	-83	-137	-8	252
Other sectors	-7,817	-3,921	-1,782	-256	855	-43	-43	-312	40	138	-126	-151	282	47	-87
Net errors and omissions	-1,074	-1,006	-1,841	#	…	-42	130	138	-219	-285	-565	-253	-268	-467	-667
Global balance [3]	2,034	2,157	-2,763	-9	5,926	18	247	19	-194	-77	-12	-84	-114	61	-91
Total variation in reserves (minus sign indicates an increase)	-2,046	-2,146	-2,961	202	-6,924	-72	-148	19	196	77	3	70	157	-30	88
Monetary gold	-6	122	-23	-124	…	#	#	-5	54	#	#	#	#	#	…
Special Drawing Rights	-17	20	3	-9	…	1	#	#	#	…	4	#	-13	12	…
IMF reserve position	-95	95	#	#	…	#	#	#	#	…	-9	9	#	--	…
Foreign exchange assets	-2,967	-3,488	2,377	-755	…	-86	-170	30	150	…	-100	-19	131	-84	…
Other assets	#	#	#	#	855	19	26	3	-8	…	#	#	#	#	…
Use made of IMF credit	1,039	1,104	604	1,091	…	-5	-5	-9	#	…	109	79	39	43	…

Table 2729 (Continued)

ECLA BALANCE OF PAYMENTS, 19 L, 1983–87
(M US)

Q. PARAGUAY

Category	1983	1984	1985	1986	1987‡
Balance on current account	-253	-262	-167	-369	-361
Trade balance	-245	-272	-158	-296	-287
Exports of goods and services	464	696	805	792	1,055
Goods FOB	326	538	620	573	800
Real services[1]	138	158	185	218	255
Transport and insurance	2	2	8	3	4
Travel	49	96	105	148	150
Imports of goods and services	709	968	963	1,087	1,341
Goods FOB	551	740	727	736	935
Real services[1]	157	228	236	351	407
Transport and insurance	75	113	104	146	198
Travel	44	44	47	48	48
Factor services	-9	7	-11	-74	-75
Profits	-39	-26	-20	-55	-42
Interest received	63	70	79	58	60
Interest paid	-66	-61	-80	-91	-118
Others	33	24	9	14	25
Unrequited private transfer payments	1	2	2	1	1
Balance on capital account	200	248	39	241	370
Unrequited official transfer payments	5	7	6	10	11
Long-term capital	289	219	121	212	?
Direct investment	5	5	1	32	?
Portfolio investment	3	#	8	#	?
Other long-term capital	281	214	112	181	?
Official sector[2]	139	127	109	137	?
Loans disbursed	162	150	137	185	?
Amortization payments	-23	-23	-28	-48	?
Commercial banks[2]	7	32	15	6	?
Loans disbursed	10	40	20	14	?
Amortization payments	-3	-9	-5	-8	?
Other sectors[2]	135	55	-11	37	?
Loans disbursed	168	109	59	102	?
Amortization payments	-33	-53	-71	-64	?
Short-term capital (net)	-2	67	-62	15	50
Official sector	23	97	-56	-19	?
Commercial banks	15	-5	14	-21	?
Other sectors	-40	-26	-20	55	?
Errors and omissions	-92	-45	-27	4	19
Global balance[3]	-53	-14	-128	-128	9
Total variation in reserves (minus sign indicates an increase)	56	17	135	85	-53
Monetary gold	-6	#	-2	-2	?
Special Drawing Rights	-6	-3	-8	-9	?
IMF reserve position	-3	2	-3	4	?
Foreign exchange assets	68	13	145	92	?
Other assets	-3	4	1	#	?
Use made of IMF credit	#	#	#	#	?

R. PERU

Category	1983	1984	1985	1986	1987‡
Balance on current account	-1,091	-379	-19	-1,113	-1,627
Trade balance	39	787	995	-307	-858
Exports of goods and services	3,728	3,818	3,790	3,304	3,600
Goods FOB	3,017	3,147	2,977	2,508	2,605
Real services[1]	711	671	813	795	995
Transport and insurance	262	206	257	250	260
Travel	209	208	300	300	350
Imports of goods and services	3,689	3,031	2,795	3,611	4,458
Goods FOB	2,723	2,141	1,808	2,512	3,068
Real services[1]	966	891	986	1,099	1,390
Transport and insurance	447	378	293	340	415
Travel	191	182	266	323	390
Factor services	-1,132	-1,166	-1,014	-805	-769
Profits	-137	-54	-74	-43	-42
Interest received	115	156	133	94	61
Interest paid	-1,110	-1,268	-1,073	-855	-788
Others	#	#	#	#	#
Unrequited private transfer payments	1	2	2	1	1
Balance on capital account	1,058	628	179	825	821
Unrequited official transfer payments	220	158	134	96	132
Long-term capital	1,237	-118	-617	-1,212	?
Direct investment	38	-89	-1	20	25
Portfolio investment	#	#	#	#	#
Other long-term capital	1,199	-29	-616	-1,232	925
Official sector[2]	1,284	84	-492	-1,163	925
Loans disbursed	2,555	1,525	902	473	925
Amortization payments	-1,292	-1,441	-1,336	-1,456	925
Commercial banks[2]	#	#	#	#	925
Loans disbursed	#	#	#	#	925
Amortization payments	#	#	#	#	925
Other sectors[2]	-85	-114	-124	-69	925
Loans disbursed	131	100	44	35	925
Amortization payments	-217	-213	-168	-104	925
Short-term capital (net)	-520	1,022	954	1,994	-104
Official sector	290	1,207	1,267	1,870	-104
Commercial banks	-22	40	20	12	-104
Other sectors	-788	-225	-333	113	-104
Errors and omissions	122	-431	-292	-55	-104
Global balance[3]	-34	249	159	-289	-806
Total variation in reserves (minus sign indicates an increase)	-10	-317	-83	397	?
Monetary gold	#	#	#	#	?
Special Drawing Rights	32	-22	23	#	?
IMF reserve position	#	12	#	#	?
Foreign exchange assets	48	-246	216	397	?
Other assets	-43	-27	84	-27	?
Use made of IMF credit	48	-22	26	27	?

S. URUGUAY

Category	1983	1984	1985	1986	1987‡
Balance on current account	-71	-139	-119	66	-132
Trade balance	217	222	233	344	149
Exports of goods and services	1,411	1,289	1,251	1,500	1,554
Goods FOB	1,156	925	854	1,088	1,189
Real services[1]	255	365	397	412	365
Transport and insurance	71	69	68	71	73
Travel	90	210	235	258	208
Imports of goods and services	1,194	1,067	1,018	1,156	1,405
Goods FOB	740	732	675	791	1,080
Real services[1]	455	335	342	365	325
Transport and insurance	85	80	77	99	102
Travel	259	154	162	150	129
Factor services	-288	-362	-352	-278	-281
Profits	#	#	#	#	#
Interest received	63	87	76	93	103
Interest paid	-350	-449	-428	-371	-384
Others	#	#	#	#	#
Unrequited private transfer payments	#	#	#	#	#
Balance on capital account	#	54	183	187	255
Unrequited official transfer payments	11	10	11	25	8
Long-term capital	643	30	59	137	?
Direct investment	6	3	-8	-5	?
Portfolio investment	#	#	#	#	?
Other long-term capital	653	20	-29	55	?
Official sector[2]	329	46	-23	44	?
Loans disbursed	531	90	21	74	?
Amortization payments	-198	-43	-44	-30	?
Commercial banks[2]	37	-1	-5	-1	?
Loans disbursed	43	#	#	#	?
Amortization payments	-9	-1	-1	-1	?
Other sectors[2]	287	-25	-1	12	?
Loans disbursed	346	62	30	39	?
Amortization payments	-58	-87	-31	-27	?
Short-term capital (net)	-359	158	-136	-150	?
Official sector	41	47	125	5	?
Commercial banks	-67	67	-148	-69	?
Other sectors	-333	43	113	-87	?
Errors and omissions	-295	-144	250	175	-130
Global balance[3]	-70	-85	64	253	123
Total variation in reserves (minus sign indicates an increase)	71	105	-43	-245	-41
Monetary gold	52	-8	-6	-1	-3
Special Drawing Rights	-2	-1	-10	3	-56
IMF reserve position	-10	10	#	#	#
Foreign exchange assets	-122	106	-30	-310	2
Other assets	12	12	-124	18	18
Use made of IMF credit	142	-15	128	45	-2

Table 2729 (Continued)

ECLA BALANCE OF PAYMENTS, 19 L, 1983–87

(M US)

Category	1983	1984	1985	1986	1987[‡]
Balance on current account	4,451	5,447	3,112	−1,990	−1,103
Trade balance	6,745	6,910	5,397	−374	399
Exports of goods and services	15,825	16,806	15,004	9,527	11,279
Goods FOB	14,570	15,967	14,178	8,649	10,567
Real services[1]	1,254	838	825	879	712
Transport and insurance	673	438	282	278	386
Travel	310	358	416	443	309
Imports of goods and services	9,080	9,896	9,607	9,902	10,880
Goods FOB	6,409	7,262	7,388	7,834	8,832
Real services[1]	2,671	2,634	2,219	2,066	2,048
Transport and insurance	930	1,154	1,066	919	1,170
Travel	1,073	1,063	597	543	358
Factor services	−2,107	−1,354	−2,182	−1,544	−1,374
Profits	−188	−155	−157	−109	−111
Interest received	1,500	2,173	1,890	1,672	1,411
Interest paid	−3,425	−3,370	−3,922	−3,107	−2,674
Others	6	−2	8	#	#
Unrequited private transfer payments	−187	−108	−102	−72	−128
Balance on capital account	−4,116	−3,858	−1,402	−1,969	225
Unrequited official transfer payments	−24	−29	−26	−21	−22
Long-term capital	239	−1,022	−692	−1,387	−1,481
Direct investment	86	42	106	16	21
Portfolio Investment					
Other long-term capital	−47	−936	−798	−1,403	−1,502
Official sector[2]	332	−929	−805	−1,190	−700
Loans disbursed	1,259	398	#	#	658
Amortization payments	−827	−1,322	−784	−1,147	−1,358
Commercial banks[2]	#	#	#	#	#
Loans disbursed	#	#	#	#	#
Amortization payments	#	#	#	#	#
Other sectors[2]	−379	−9	7	−214	−802
Loans disbursed	505	28	53	48	23
Amortization payments	−702	−269	#	−305	−825
Short-term capital (net)	−4,338	−3,886	−756	−510	1,414
Official sector	−17	24	23	68	131
Commercial banks	−827	−408	80	−194	#
Other sectors	−3,493	−3,501	−860	−385	1,283
Errors and omissions	7	1,077	63	−50	314
Global balance[3]	336	1,589	1,710	−3,958	−878
Total variation in reserves					
(minus sign indicates an increase)	−283	−1,818	−1,747	2,908	934
Monetary gold	#	#	#	#	#
Special Drawing Rights	87	−22	−121	−113	−148
IMF reserve position	−166	106	−6	16	131
Foreign exchange assets	−960	−1,392	−1,199	2,712	881
Other assets	756	−509	−421	293	270
Use made of IMF credit	#	#	#	#	#

1. Real services also include other official and private transactions, but exclude factor services.
2. In addition to loans received and amortization payments on these, this entry includes net loans granted and other assets and liabilities.
3. The global balance is the sum of the balance on the capital and current accounts. The difference between the total variation in reserves with the opposite sign and the global balance represents the value of counterpart items: monetization of gold, allocation of Special Drawing Rights and variations due to revaluation.

SOURCE: For total current account data, 1950–77, see SALA, 24-2748; 24-2749; 24-2450; and 24-2751. ECLA-S, 1982, vol. 1, p. 444; 1983, vol. 1, p. 454; 1985, vol. 1; 1986, vol. 1; 1987.

28
International Assistance

Table 2800

ASSISTANCE FROM INTERNATIONAL ORGANIZATIONS,[1] 20 LRC, 1949-88
(M US)

U.S. Fiscal Year[6]

Country/Organization	1949-52	1953-61	1962-78	1979	1980	1981	1982	1983	1984	1985	1986	1987	1988	Total
A. ARGENTINA														
Total	0	42.1	2,739.7	388.7	485.9	479.4	533.4	593.9	210.8	563.5	864.4	1,437.9	770.6	8,903.6
IBRD	0	31.0	963.2	96.0	237.0	68.0	400.0	100.0	0	180.0	544.5	965.0	626.5	4,183.6
IFC	0	5.2	83.5	6.0	15.0	65.0	10.0	.5	42.7	63.4	156.4	87.7	74.1	607.9
IDB	0	0	1,653.7	280.7	232.2	346.4	119.2	490.5	167.6	319.1	162.1	382.3	70.0	4,046.0
UNDP	0	5.0	36.8	6.0	1.7	#	4.2	2.9	.5	1.0	1.4	2.9	#	62.5
Other U.N.	0	.9	2.5	0	0	0	0	0	0	0	0	#	#	3.6
B. BOLIVIA														
Total	#	15.4	788.0	149.7	99.3	8.2	99.9	211.3	130.6	2.6	72.4	224.4	248.5	1,983.0
IBRD	0	0	249.3	0	50.0	0	0	0	0	0	0	#	0	296.0
IFC	0	0	3.6	0	0	5.7	0	0	0	0	0	1.2	10.0	20.5
IDA	0	0	69.3	10.5	25.0	0	0	0	0	0	70.0	75.4	112.0	362.2
IDB	0	10.0	431.5	136.6	22.6	0	97.0	211.1	126.8	0	0	143.7	126.5	1,241.9
UNDP	#	4.7	27.9	2.6	1.5	1.0	2.9	.2	.8	2.6	2.4	4.1	#	50.6
Other U.N.	0	.7	6.4	0	.2	1.5	0	0	3.0	0	0	#	#	11.8
C. BRAZIL														
Total	117.6	178.8	6,903	963.3	1,102.8	1,551.1	1,222.8	1,807.0	2,192.8	2,010.3	2,051.7	1,766.9	2,005.7	23,615.3
IBRD	117.5	149.5	3,666.7	674.0	695.0	844.0	722.1	1,457.5	1,604.3	1,523.0	1,620.0	1,261.5	1,359.5	15,665.4
IFC	0	9.9	389.1	65.1	74.0	229.2	206.6	77.5	61.2	44.6	107.1	125.3	284.4	1,638.6
IDB	0	11.2	2,767.8	221.3	329.9	477.3	284.6	269.5	524.6	442.5	323.5	366.2	361.8	6,186.8
UNDP	.1	7.2	64.5	2.5	2.6	.6	8.2	2.0	.2	.2	1.1	10.8	#	99.7
Other U.N.	0	1.0	14.7	.4	1.3	0	1.3	.5	2.7	0	0	3.1	#	24.8
D. CHILE														
Total	1.0	135.3	881.4	35.0	43.8	260.1	192.4	573.7	355.8	545.2	713.0	790.6	329.1	5,182.1
IBRD	.9	95.1	247.5	0	38.0	78.0	0	128.0	0	287.0	456.0	366.5	250.0	1,960.3
IFC	0	5.8	15.4	0	0	0	10.2	44.5	0	73.7	0	60.0	22.6	225.3
IDA	0	19.0	#	0	0	0	0	0	0	0	0	0	0	19.0
IDB	0	5.7	568.0	35.0	0	180.9	182.0	400.5	352.2	182.8	256.8	361.8	56.1	2,901.6
UNDP	.1	9.0	43.7	#	5.8	.9	.2	.7	3.6	1.5	.2	2.3	.4	67.6
Other U.N.	0	.7	6.8	0	0	.3	0	0	0	.2	0	#	#	8.3
E. COLOMBIA														
Total	30.1	191.5	2,708.6	523.8	727.4	830.7	512.3	222.4	1,043.8	1,210.1	827.2	369.3	980.7	10,143.4
IBRD	30.0	170.6	1,710.1	311.5	518.0	550.0	291.3	78.4	464.1	707.5	700.3	180.3	465.0	6,169.6
IFC	0	2.2	49.2	0	.3	34.8	14.6	28.8	6.8	23.0	8.9	13.4	51.2	226.5
IDA	0	0	19.5	0	0	0	0	0	0	0	0	0	0	19.5
IDB	0	10.8	876.1	206.0	201.0	244.6	206.1	106.2	570.4	478.1	115.8	173.6	459.8	3,628.2
UNDP	.1	6.9	41.1	4.9	1.0	1.3	.3	3.2	2.5	1.5	2.2	2.0	#	66.9
Other U.N.	0	1.0	12.6	1.4	7.1	0	0	5.8	0	0	0	#	4.7	32.7
F. COSTA RICA														
Total	#	18.8	642.5	36.4	105.6	120.4	29.8	124.4	35.8	155.4	105.3	98.8	158.9	1,620.1
IBRD	0	17.3	271.8	34.0	30.0	29.0	0	25.2	0	83.5	0	26.0	#	515.9
IFC	0	0	3.1	2.1	0	0	0	1.5	0	0	0	1.8	#	8.5
IDA	0	0	4.6	0	0	0	0	0	0	0	0	0	#	4.6
IDB	0	0	351.6	0	74.5	91.3	29.2	97.2	35.8	71.6	105.0	68.9	158.9	1,072.9
UNDP	#	1.1	8.8	.1	1.0	.1	.6	.4	#	.1	.3	2.1	#	14.7
Other U.N.	0	.4	2.6	0	.1	0	0	.1	0	.2	0	#	#	3.5

Table 2800 (Continued)

ASSISTANCE FROM INTERNATIONAL ORGANIZATIONS,[1] 20 LRC, 1949–88

(M US)

U.S. Fiscal Year[6]

Country/Organization	1949–52	1953–61	1962–78	1979	1980	1981	1982	1983	1984	1985	1986	1987	1988	Total
G. CUBA														
Total	#	1.7	26.5	3.0	1.6	#	7.7	1.3	1.0	.3	2.2	5.4	#	50.8
UNDP	#	1.5	22.9	3.0	1.3	#	7.7	1.1	1.0	.3	2.2	5.2	#	46.4
Other U.N.	0	.2	3.6	0	.3	0	0	.2	0	0	0	.2	#	4.4
H. DOMINICAN REP.														
Total	0	.6	352.6	176.1	210.5	119.9	91.2	168.4	119.2	193.3	189.2	142.7	106.6	1,365.8
IBRD	0	0	64.0	52.0	120.0	24.0	25.4	7.1	3.8	5.8	35.8	#	105.0	442.9
IFC	0	0	13.4	0	2.0	.4	0	10.5	0	0	7.6	#	.1	33.8
IDA	0	0	22.0	0	0	0	0	0	0	0	0	#	#	22.0
IDB	0	0	232.4	120.5	87.5	95.0	61.9	150.0	113.7	187.0	145.5	141.4	#	830.4
UNDP	0	.4	17.0	1.8	1.0	0	3.9	.8	1.4	.5	.3	1.3	#	28.1
Other U.N.	0	.2	3.8	1.8	0	0	0	0	0	0	0	#	1.5	8.6
I. ECUADOR														
Total	.1	52.5	718.8	182.1	270.7	94.6	444.0	209.1	117.8	287.8	473.7	465.5	364.6	3,625.3
IBRD	0	45.0	205.5	58.0	106.0	20.0	228.7	40.6	0	8.0	253.5	159.0	160.0	1,283.1
IFC	0	0	22.4	4.3	1.3	10.8	9.3	.1	.1	0	0	21.6	#	69.8
IDA	0	0	36.9	0	0	0	0	0	0	0	0	0	#	36.5
IDB	0	0	419.6	113.2	161.0	63.5	202.5	167.3	117.7	279.0	217.8	283.6	204.6	2,175.3
UNDP	.1	6.3	28.3	6.1	.6	.3	3.5	.4	#	.8	.6	1.3	#	48.4
Other U.N.	0	1.2	6.1	.5	1.8	0	.3	.9	0	0	1.8	#	#	12.2
J. EL SALVADOR														
Total	12.6	24.7	443.4	60.0	48.9	40.5	112.8	53.3	115.2	23.1	1.7	24.2	232.6	1,191.9
IBRD	12.5	22.2	157.2	23.5	0	0	0	0	0	0	0	0	65.0	280.1
IFC	0	.1	.8	.8	0	0	0	0	0	0	0	#	#	1.0
IDA	0	0	25.6	0	0	0	0	0	0	0	0	#	#	25.6
IDB	0	.2	242.7	29.5	48.5	40.4	112.4	52.9	114.0	21.0	0	23.0	166.0	849.6
UNDP	.1	1.8	12.9	5.6	.4	.1	.4	.4	.9	1.2	1.7	1.2	1.6	26.8
Other U.N.	0	.4	4.2	1.4	0	0	0	0	.3	.9	0	#	#	8.8
K. GUATEMALA														
Total	#	21.6	595.6	2.2	86.9	26.5	45.9	102.4	135.8	237.4	81.5	136.1	39.6	1,655.0
IBRD	0	18.2	242.3	0	17.0	0	0	18.5	50.0	44.6	81.0	23.0	29.0	523.6
IFC	0	.2	18.0	0	0	0	0	0	0	0	0	0	#	18.2
IDB	0	.1	315.7	.3	66.0	25.5	42.5	83.3	84.5	191.0	0	109.6	10.6	1,072.6
UNDP	#	2.3	12.8	1.9	2.8	1.0	.9	.6	1.3	1.8	.5	2.2	#	28.1
Other U.N.	0	.8	6.8	0	1.1	0	2.5	0	0	0	0	1.3	#	12.5
L. HAITI														
Total	.1	8.4	225.7	61.1	9.8	33.9	47.2	89.5	38.1	45.7	15.9	127.7	3.7	681.5
IBRD	0	2.6	0	0	0	0	0	0	0	0	0	0	#	2.6
IFC	0	0	0	0	0	3.2	0	0	0	0	0	.2	#	3.4
IDA	0	0	93.5	16.5	0	21.2	18.0	56.0	19.1	32.1	0	63.0	#	319.4
IDB	0	2.9	109.7	38.3	4.1	9.1	17.6	32.6	17.4	11.9	12.8	56.0	#	287.1
UNDP	.1	2.4	16.3	6.3	3.7	.4	6.5	.9	1.6	1.7	3.1	8.5	#	51.6
Other U.N.	0	.5	6.2	0	2.0	0	6.1	0	0	0	0	#	3.7	17.4

Table 2800 (Continued)

ASSISTANCE FROM INTERNATIONAL ORGANIZATIONS,[1] 20 LRC, 1949–88
(M US)

U.S. Fiscal Year[6]

Country/Organization	1949–52	1953–61	1962–78	1979	1980	1981	1982	1983	1984	1985	1986	1987	1988	Total
M. HONDURAS														
Total	#	32.5	504.5	.177.0	224.0	35.5	37.0	89.6	154.3	16.5	128.8	101.4	2.0	1,553.6
IBRD	0	19.9	167.9	65.0	128.0	28.0	30.0	45.0	19.6	6.9	37.4	4.4	#	552.0
IFC	0	0	10.4	0	0	0	0	0	0	0	.6	#	2.0	13.0
IDA	0	8.4	49.2	0	25.0	0	0	0	0	0	0	#	#	82.6
IDB	0	2.2	259.9	106.3	71.0	7.5	0	42.2	134.1	8.4	90.6	93.4	#	866.2
UNDP	#	1.7	13.2	4.2	#	0	7.0	2.4	0	1.2	.2	2.4	#	32.3
Other U.N.	0	.3	3.9	1.5	0	0	0	0	.6	0	0	1.2	#	7.5
N. MEXICO														
Total	80.4	153.7	4,945.4	963.4	971.7	1,439.4	804.5	1,373.2	883.3	674.9	1,525.7	1,840.9	2,275.9	18,310.7
IBRD	80.3	145.8	3,013.8	552.0	300.0	1,081.0	657.3	887.9	598.0	598.0	904.0	1,678.0	2,030.0	12,408.4
IFC	0	1.4	99.0	125.6	275.3	61.2	10.5	179.2	25.2	0	39.0	59.7	82.5	957.8
IDB	0	0	1,777.7	280.2	396.2	295.5	134.1	306.0	281.0	74.3	580.6	100.0	163.4	4,864.2
UNDP	.1	4.3	40.4	5.0	.2	.2	2.6	.1	.8	.1	2.1	3.2	#	59.1
Other U.N.	0	2.2	14.5	.6	0	1.5	0	0	0	2.5	0	#	#	21.2
O. NICARAGUA														
Total	5.2	33.7	410.7	39.0	55.3	117.9	51.3	31.3	.8	.3	2.3	.7	#	745.9
IBRD	5.2	30.2	126.0	0	20.0	33.7	16.0	0	0	0	0	#	#	231.1
IFC	0	0	9.5	0	0	0	0	0	0	0	0	#	#	9.5
IDA	0	0	23.0	0	32.0	5.0	0	0	0	0	0	#	#	60.0
IDB	0	2.0	236.0	36.8	0	75.0	34.4	30.7	0	0	0	.7	#	412.8
UNDP	#	1.0	11.9	1.7	3.3	3.5	.9	.6	.5	.3	1.2	#	#	25.7
Other U.N.	0	.5	3.7	.5	0	.7	0	0	.3	0	1.1	#	#	6.8
P. PANAMA														
Total	#	15.4	505.1	68.2	149.9	74.5	126.9	137.7	82.6	137.4	39.7	202.5	21.7	1,620.7
IBRD	0	14.0	209.7	34.0	58.0	45.5	24.4	85.0	74.2	51.0	0	100.0	#	695.8
IFC	0	0	5.3	3.0	0	5.0	0	0	0	37.5	23.2	#	5.0	74.0
IDB	0	0	267.8	29.0	91.4	28.5	99.0	52.0	8.4	48.7	16.2	102.1	16.7	818.9
UNDP	#	1.0	18.9	1.7	.5	.5	3.5	.6	0	.1	.3	.4	#	27.5
Other U.N.	0	.4	3.4	.5	0	0	0	.1	0	.1	0	#	#	4.5
Q. PARAGUAY														
Total	4.6	6.7	450.2	97.2	76.6	88.8	176.4	114.7	45.4	40.3	1.2	12.6	67.8	1,149.7
IBRD	4.5	0	124.9	64.0	36.0	58.8	99.4	40.0	30.0	0	0	#	#	457.6
IFC	0	0	5.4	0	0	1.2	10.4	0	.3	.8	0	#	#	18.0
IDA	0	0	45.5	0	0	0	0	0	0	0	0	#	#	45.5
IDB	0	3.2	253.5	31.2	39.4	27.5	64.9	72.9	14.1	37.5	0	12.1	67.8	591.4
UNDP	.1	2.8	16.3	1.4	1.2	1.3	1.0	1.8	1.0	1.0	1.2	.5	#	29.7
Other U.N.	0	.7	4.6	.6	0	0	.7	0	0	0	0	#	#	7.5
R. PERU														
Total	2.5	93.9	997.1	191.2	247.5	461.6	443.3	454.1	317.6	73.3	26.4	79.5	#	3,302.4
IBRD	2.4	79.6	470.5	123.8	111.0	148.0	286.7	302.2	122.5	31.0	13.5	#	#	1,690.9
IFC	0	4.4	19.3	2.5	3.2	8.5	18.2	8.0	9.2	16.8	10.0	#	#	100.1
IDB	0	3.9	461.9	60.2	132.5	305.0	130.0	142.3	184.8	24.3	0	70.0	#	1,430.0
UNDP	.1	5.2	36.6	2.7	.8	.1	5.4	1.6	1.1	1.2	1.8	3.6	#	59.9
Other U.N.	0	.8	8.8	2.0	0	0	3.0	0	0	0	1.1	5.9	#	21.5

Table 2800 (Continued)

ASSISTANCE FROM INTERNATIONAL ORGANIZATIONS,[1] 20 LRC, 1949-88

(M US)

Country/Organization	1949-52	1953-61	1962-78	1979	1980	1981	1982	1983	1984	1985	1986	1987	1988	Total
									U.S Fiscal Year[6]					
S. URUGUAY														
Total	33.0	39.4	375.6	70.3	168.5	108.1	51.3	49.1	167.8	74.5	66.8	261.0	100.8	1,429.8
IBRD	33.0	38.0	145.9	26.5	98.0	30.0	40.0	45.0	0	64.0	45.2	105.4	22.3	679.1
IFC	0	0	3.8	6.4	10.7	0	0	2.8	0	8.9	3.0	#	12.0	47.5
IDB	0	0	209.1	35.7	57.5	78.0	10.0	0	167.8	0	18.0	154.1	66.5	674.5
UNDP	0	1.2	16.2	1.7	2.3	.1	1.3	1.3	0	1.6	.6	1.5	#	27.8
Other U.N.	0	.2	.6	0	0	0	0	0	0	0	0	#	#	.9
T. VENEZUELA														
Total	#	15.2	710.3	6.2	1.8	.1	2.0	.4	64.8	514.3	140.2	38.1	299.8	1,700.9
IBRD	0	0	378.0	0	0	0	0	0	0	0	0	#	#	348.0
IFC	0	3.2	22.2	0	0	0	0	0	0	0	0	37.6	74.8	137.7
IDB	0	9.2	283.5	2.3	0	0	0	0	64.3	514.0	138.0	#	225.0	1,174.2
UNDP	#	2.6	24.6	3.9	1.8	.1	2.0	.4	.5	.3	2.2	.5	#	38.9
Other U.N.	0	.2	2.0	0	0	0	0	0	0	0	0	#	#	2.1
LATIN AMERICA REGIONAL[3]														
Total	.1	32.8	350.7	225.7	1.3	56.3	30.0	4.1	1.0	31.5	.8	11.5	.8	899.9
IFC	0	0	10.0	0	0	0	0	0	0	0	0	#	#	10.0
IDB	0	0	130.4	210.2	0	50.3	24.0	0	0	29.6	0	#	#	599.0
UNDP	.1	18.2	99.9[a]	14.6	.6	4.7	6.0	2.6	1.0	1.9	0	11.5	#	161.2
Other U.N.	0	11.1	29.8	.9	.7	1.3	0	1.5	0	0	.8	#	.8	45.2
EEC	0	3.5	80.6	0	0	0	0	0	0	0	0	#	#	84.5
LATIN AMERICA (TOTAL)														
Total	287.5	1,119.7	27,194.0	4,617.6	5,214.9	6,123.1	5,326.3	6,605.5	6,445.1	7,285.9	7,499.6	8,387.5	8,124.2	93,814.2
IBRD	286.3	880.1	12,808.0	2,232.8	2,595.0	3,119.0	2,962.9	3,396.6	3,003.4	3,654.3	4,701.2	4,994.6	5,152.0	49,585.2
IFC	0	32.6	787.2	218.2	381.7	422.2	301.1	363.3	146.3	546.3	366.5	409.7	618.5	4,532.3
IDA	0	27.4	412.6	32.0	89.0	34.2	25.0	63.0	24.1	45.9	70.0	157.4	112.0	1,092.2
IDB	0	61.3	12,229.3	2,030.0	2,090.6	2,507.9	1,946.6	2,755.6	3,238.1	3,005.0	2,282.9	2,716.6	2,205.3	36,887.0
UNDP	1.2	89.7	672.3	84.0	40.9	24.0	78.0	52.7	21.2	25.5	36.4	75.0	#	1,181.4
Other U.N.	0	25.1	156.2	12.6	15.2	5.8	12.7	9.3	10.0	4.9	5.0	12.4	15.1	281.9
EEC	0	3.5	128.4	8.0	2.5	10.0	0	15.0	2.0	4.0	37.6	21.5	21.3	254.2
WORLD REGIONAL[4]														
Total	835.4	5,071.1	80,526.5	14,401.0	16,856.8	18,468.3	18,873.5	20,804.3	23,317.8	22,633.5	24,113.9	26,895.0	28,778.7	300,659.0
IBRD	830.8	4,252.8	39,101.8	6,989.0	7,644.2	8,808.9	10,329.6	11,136.3	11,949.2	11,358.3	13,328.8	14,388.2	14,762.0	154,398.5
IFC	0	41.8	1,959.5	425.4	680.6	810.7	611.8	844.5	695.6	937.2	1,156.2	919.9	1,270.1	10,281.4
IDA	0	99.3	13,983.9	2,961.5	3,829.5	3,482.1	2,636.5	3,340.7	3,575.0	3,028.1	3,114.6	3,543.5	4,458.7	47,947.9
IDB	0	61.3	12,229.3	2,030.0	2,090.6	2,507.9	1,946.6	2,735.6	3,238.1	3,005.0	2,282.9	2,716.6	2,205.3	36,887.0
ADB	0	0	4,749.4	985.8	1,433.4	1,453.0	1,651.2	1,656.1	2,116.5	2,009.3	1,942.2	2,309.6	3,083.9	23,408.6
AFDB[5]	0	0	923.3	170.9	247.7	250.0	428.3	238.5	910.3	1,110.0	1,273.4	1,881.4	2,588.8	10,012.4
UNDP	4.6	329.4	3,185.4	471.9	335.4	337.5	537.7	333.0	300.9	261.8	347.0	623.4	#	7,029.5
Other U.N.	0	98.2	1,470.6	186.3	164.5	355.8	206.4	109.4	105.0	303.1	84.5	130.6	221.0	3,460.8
ECC	0	188.3	2,923.6	180.2	430.9	462.4	435.4	410.2	427.2	620.7	584.3	381.8	188.9	7,232.9

Table 2800 (Continued)

ASSISTANCE FROM INTERNATIONAL ORGANIZATIONS,[1] 20 LRC, 1949–88

(M US)

1. The data represent assistance from all sources available to the various organizations, including contributions, subscriptions, bond issues, etc. The data do not represent the United States contributions to these organizations. Data are based on United States fiscal years except for "UNDP" and "Other U.N." programs. These are calendar year figures, shown in the fiscal year in which the calendar year ends. As of FY 1982 UNDP data are based on United States fiscal years. Recipient countries have been grouped by region.

WORLD BANK GROUP

International Bank for Reconstruction and Development (IBRD): Data cover loan authorizations of the IBRD made either to governments, government enterprises, or to private firms with government guarantee. No adjustments are made for subsequent sales of loans. Cancellations are deducted from loans authorized in the year originally authorized. Fiscal year activity from FY 1978 onward contains only new loan authorizations.

International Development Association (IDA): Data cover value of agreements with governments for development credits. Cancellations are deducted from credits authorized in the year originally authorized. Fiscal year activity from FY 1978 onward contains only new loan authorizations.

International Finance Corporation (IFC): Data cover the commitments made by the IFC to invest in private enterprises in the various countries. Cancellations are deducted from commitments in the year originally committed.

Starting in FY 1974 reductions are reflected in the cumulative total with no adjustments in annual amounts. Fiscal year activity for FY 1980 onward contains only new loan authorizations; increases in loans authorized in prior years appear only in cumulative data.

OTHER INTERNATIONAL ORGANIZATIONS

Asian Development Bank (ADB): Data cover loan authorizations of the Asian Development Bank which made its first loan in 1968.

African Development Bank (AFDB): Data cover loan authorizations of the African Development Bank which made its first loans in U.S. FY 1968; and the African Development Fund with its first loans in U.S. FY 1974.

Inter-American Development Bank (IDB): Data cover loan authorizations of the IDB made either to governments, government enterprises or to private firms from Ordinary Capital and from the Fund for Special Operations. Cancellations are deducted from authorizations in the year originally authorized. Data exclude original loans from the Social Progress Trust Fund administered by the Bank for the United States; they include, however, any loans purchased from the Bank with SPTF reflows.

United Nations Development Program: Data are shown combining the Special Fund (UNDP-SF) and Technical Assistance (UNDP-TA). Each was previously a separate program—the Special Fund and the Expanded Program of Technical Assistance (EPTA), respectively. These were combined to form the United Nations Development

Programme (UNDP). The Special Fund data cover allocations primarily for costs of preinvestment surveys. In FY 1973 the data represent the value of large-scale and small-scale projects approved and budgeted in the previous calendar year. Starting in FY 1974 the data are project approvals from the UNDP Compendium of Approved Projects.

Other United Nations Programs: Data cover allocations for approved projects and for administrative and operational services financed from government contributions and other sources by the United Nations Childrens' Fund (UNICEF). The data also include the Regular and other programs of technical assistance by U.N. specialized agencies (UNTA). Data for the specialized agencies are not available from FY 1969 onward.

European Economic Community (EEC): Data include obligations from the European Development Funds and from the European Investment Bank (EIB) for developing countries.

2. Transitional quarter.
3. Latin America Regional

AID and Predecessor Agencies. — Excludes Alliance for Progress funds obligated for nonregional programs in FY 1963–71.

Food for Peace (PL 480), Title II—Total Grants, Voluntary Relief Agencies. — Includes programs for French Guiana, Guadeloupe, and Martinique.

Other Economic Assistance, Other. — Represents primarily technical assistance grants for various countries and administrative funds under the Social Progress Trust Fund; Inter-American Foundation, $38.3 million.

Other U.S. Loans, All Other. — Represents OPIC direct loan.

4. World Regional

A.I.D. and Predecessor Agencies, Grants. — Excludes reimbursements by the Department of Defense for grants to Vietnam.

Other Economic Assistance, Contributions to International Financial Institutions (IFI). — Data excludes callable capital.

Other U.S. Loans, All Other. — Represents short-term credits by the Department of Agriculture under the Commodity Credit Corporation Charter Act unless otherwise identified on individual country pages.

5. Data exclude African Development Bank from FY 1979 onward.
6. From 1946 to 1948 Latin America received no assistance with the exception of Chile, which received 16 million dollars in IBRD loans compared to World IBRD total of 512.8 million dollars.

a. Includes $825,000 approved in FY 1965 for Paraguay, transferred to Latin America Regional in FY 1971.

SOURCE: USAID-OLG, July 1, 1945–September 30, 1986, pp. 195, 203–212; July 1, 1945–September 30, 1987, pp. 195, 203–212; July 1, 1945–September 30, 1988, pp. 195, 203–212.

Table 2801

AVERAGE FINANCING TERMS OF LOANS TO LATIN AMERICA AUTHORIZED BY THE U.S. GOVERNMENT AND MULTILATERAL INSTITUTIONS, 1961–86

(%)

Agency	1961–65	1966–70	1971	1973	1974	1976	1979	1980	1982	1985	1986
Average interest rate	3.63	4.73	5.53	5.71	5.90	6.90	6.71	~	~	~	~
AID	1.55	2.43	2.78	2.76	2.75	2.75	2.64	~	~	~	~
IDB	3.68	4.38	4.57	5.17	5.54	5.29	5.80	5.82	7.73	8.84	~

Continued in SALA, 27-2831.

Table 2802

IDB TECHNICAL COOPERATION GRANTS, 19 L, 1984–88

(T US)

	Country	1984	1985	1986	1987	1988
A.	ARGENTINA	94.0	93.0	156.6	3,170.0	119.6
B.	BOLIVIA	956.5	47.5	855.5	2,825.6	1,937.1
C.	BRAZIL	595.6	154.5	6,531.4	84.8	4,007.3
D.	CHILE	51.8	115.6	144.2	18.2	39.4
E.	COLOMBIA	143.8	749.2	41.5	174.3	1,029.3
F.	COSTA RICA	2,048.1	175.5	168.4	1,024.1	1,454.3
H.	DOMINICAN REP.	2,854.6	1,556.1	862.8	735.0	2,056.2
I.	ECUADOR	619.9	1,816.2	109.7	492.6	1,103.9
J.	EL SALVADOR	771.8	332.8	1,575.8	7,590.4	1,900.0
K.	GUATEMALA	942.0	1,478.4	526.0	442.1	3,042.0
L.	HAITI	3,356.5	2,721.9	30.3	58.0	226.1
M.	HONDURAS	2,489.4	1,385.5	288.5	737.3	1,376.3
N.	MEXICO	21.7	160.6	27.2	39.4	254.4
O.	NICARAGUA	58.8	55.0	16.3	103.5	200.0
P.	PANAMA	67.4	2,297.7	1,550.7	1,222.9	~
Q.	PARAGUAY	3,117.5	242.3	373.2	240.0	1,055.4
R.	PERU	1,134.4	634.7	123.5	38.7	250.0
S.	URUGUAY	1,195.8	197.0	871.0	95.0	1,252.0
T.	VENEZUELA	271.7	103.3	27.3	389.2	231.9

a. Technical cooperation is extended on a grant basis, or on a contingent recovery basis. Contingent repayment cooperation, which represents a small amount of the total, is subject to repayment only if, as a result of the cooperation, a loan is made subsequently by the bank or another external financial institution for the execution of a project or program.

SOURCE: WB-AR, 1988, pp. 48 and 11.

Table 2803

IDB SMALL PROJECTS FINANCING, 19 L, 1984–88

(T US)

Country	1984	1985	1986	1987	1988
A. ARGENTINA	500.0	#	500.0	#	300.0
B. BOLIVIA	#	#	800.0	1,500.0	500.0
C. BRAZIL	500.0	#	#	#	500.0
D. CHILE	#	#	#	#	#
E. COLOMBIA	1,700.0	350.0	#	#	1,000.0
F. COSTA RICA	1,500.0	#	#	500.0	1,000.0
H. DOMINICAN REP.	501.1	875.0	500.0	#	500.0
I. ECUADOR	500.0	500.0	#	1,500.0	#
J. EL SALVADOR	#	385.0	#	1,000.0	
K. GUATEMALA	300.0	300.0	#	1,000.0	700.0
L. HAITI	#	340.0	#	#	250.0
M. HONDURAS	300.0	500.0	1,500.0	500.0	500.0
N. MEXICO	500.0	1,100.0	500.0	#	700.0
O. NICARAGUA	#	#	#	#	#
P. PANAMA	#	1,500.0	500.0	250.0	#
Q. PARAGUAY	500.0	#	#	750.0	#
R. PERU	#	600.0	#	#	265.0
S. URUGUAY	500.0	450.0	#	500.0	#
T. VENEZUELA	#	#	#	500.0	1,000.0

a. Small project financing was extended for up to 40 years, with grace periods of up to
10 years. A commission of 1% was charged on the financing, which need not be
guaranteed.

SOURCE: WB-AR, 1988.

Table 2804

IBRD AND IDA DISBURSEMENTS FOR GOODS, WORKS, AND SERVICES PROCURED ON BEHALF OF BORROWING COUNTRIES, 11 L, 1988

(M US)

Borrowing Countries	A. Local Procurement	B. Foreign Procurement	C. Total Amount	C/Total IBRD and IDA World Disbursements
A. ARGENTINA	147.8	36.8	184.6	1.2
B. BOLIVIA	17.5	8.6	26.1	.2
C. BRAZIL	926.8	224.6	1,151.5	7.5
D. CHILE	141.4	47.9	189.3	1.2
E. COLOMBIA	160.4	44.9	205.3	1.3
I. ECUADOR	47.9	11.0	58.9	.4
N. MEXICO	526.4	52.8	579.1	3.8
P. PANAMA	5.8	47.3	53.0	.3
Q. PARAGUAY	10.8	10.8	21.6	.1
R. PERU	11.2	15.7	26.9	.2
S. URUGUAY	18.9	10.0	28.9	.2

SOURCE: WB-AR, 1988, p. 57.

Table 2805

INTERNATIONAL AID[1] TO NICARAGUA[2]

(M US, 1979–82)

Donor	Pledged				Received			
	Cash	Kind	Total	% of Total	Cash	Kind	Total	% of Total
United Nations System	5.98	29.47	35.45	10.48	5.82	10.07	15.89	6.04
Latin America	6.55	56.78	63.33	18.73	6.55	56.78	63.33	24.06

Continued in SALA, 27-2833.

Table 2806

NICARAGUA LOANS AND LINES OF CREDIT OBTAINED,[1] 1979–83

(M US)

Source	1979	1980	1981	1982	1983	Total	%
Multilateral Organizations	213.0	170.9	86.2	93.6	34.4	598.1	25.5
Bilateral Agreements	58.7	356.7	600.9	448.1	282.0	1,746.1	74.2
Western Europe	14.6	63.2	60.2	38.7	86.7	263.4	11.2
North America	0	72.6	0	0	0	72.6	3.1
Latin America	44.1	118.9	336.0	203.4	75.5	777.9	32.2
Africa and Asia	0	0	103.0	3.0	59.8	165.8	7.1
Eastern Europe and USSR	0	102.0	101.7	203.0	60.0	466.7	19.9
Total (Multi- and bilateral)	271.7	527.6	687.1	541.7	316.4	2,344.5	100

1. Preliminary figures.

SOURCE: Rubén Berríos, "Relations between Nicaragua and the Socialist Countries," in
Augusto Varas, ed., *Soviet–Latin American Relations in the 1980s* (Boulder, Colo.:
Westview Press, 1987), p. 156.

Table 2807

NICARAGUA LOANS AND LINES OF CREDIT CONTRACTED[1]

(M US, 1979–84)

Source[2]	Amount	%
Multilateral Organizations	632.2	25.3
CABEI (Central American Bank for Economic Integration)	125.9	
World Bank	106.1	

Continued in SALA, 27-2835.

Table 2808

REAL SOVIET ECONOMIC AND MILITARY AID TO LESS DEVELOPED COUNTRIES, 1954–85

(M US of 1980)

Year	Total		Economic		Military	
	Appropriated	Drawn	Appropriated	Drawn	Appropriated	Drawn
1954–75	119,821	71,055	85,560	41,682	34,260	29,374
1974	10,826	4,835	1,347	1,157	9,479	3,678
1975	7,626	3,743	2,914	740	4,712	3,003
1976	10,329	5,107	1,545	658	8,784	4,449
1977	13,923	7,390	601	739	13,322	6,651
1978	7,364	8,521	3,876	672	3,488	7,849
1979	14,342	10,165	4,313	698	10,028	9,467
1980	17,465	9,075	2,605	950	14,860	8,125
1981	6,758	8,329	774	842	5,984	7,486
1982	10,861	9,058	933	1,214	9,928	7,844
1983	5,125	8,185	2,854	1,470	2,272	6,716
1984	10,287	7,675	2,193	1,304	8,095	6,370
1985	4,029	6,181	2,130	1,252	1,898	4,929

SOURCE: Charles N. Grimes, "Soviet Economic Relations with Latin America," SALA,
27-3425.

Table 2809

REAL SOVIET ECONOMIC AND MILITARY AID
TO LESS DEVELOPED COUNTRIES, 1954–85

(%)

Year	Military as % Total Appropriated	Economic as % Total Appropriated	Economic as % Total Drawn	Military as % Total Drawn
1954–75	28.59	71.41	58.66	41.34
1974	87.56	12.44	23.93	76.07
1975	61.78	38.22	19.76	80.24
1976	85.04	14.96	12.89	87.11
1977	95.68	4.32	10.00	90.00
1978	47.37	52.63	7.88	92.12
1979	69.92	30.08	6.87	93.13
1980	85.08	14.92	10.47	89.53
1981	88.55	11.45	10.12	89.88
1982	91.41	8.59	13.40	86.60
1983	44.32	55.68	17.95	82.05
1984	78.69	21.31	16.99	83.01
1985	47.12	52.88	20.26	79.74

SOURCE: Charles N. Grimes, "Soviet Economic Relations with Latin America," SALA, 27–3426.

Table 2810

SOVIET ECONOMIC AID AGREEMENTS, BY REGION, 1955–85

(M US of 1980)

Region	1955–64	1965–74	1975–79	1980	1981	1982	1983	1984	1985
North Africa	796	750	3,150	315	~	#	248	#	315
Sub-Saharan Africa	1,561	950	446	310	114	630	278	509	191
Middle East	4,618	6,300	5,187	~	50	3	1,462	1,189	~
South Asia	4,586	5,888	1,578	1,195	92	81	771	210	1,423
East Asia	478	275	#	~	~	~	~	~	~
Latin America	95	1,488	453	250	156	159	163	286	187
Total	12,118	15,638	10,815	2,070	408	874	2,924	2,194	2,116
Latin America (30-year Total)	3,237								

SOURCE: Andrej Korbonski and Francis Fukuyama, *The Soviet Union and the Third World: The Last Three Decades* (Ithaca: Cornell University Press, 1987), p. 79.

Table 2811

SOVIET ECONOMIC AID AGREEMENTS, BY REGION, 1955–85

(%)

Region	1955–64	1965–74	1975–79	1980–85
North Africa	7	5	29	8
Sub-Saharan Africa	13	6	4	19
Middle East	38	40	48	26
South Asia	38	38	15	35
East Asia	4	2	#	#
Latin America	1	10	4	11

SOURCE: Table 2810.

Table 2812

AUTHORIZED U.S. ASSISTANCE FOR GRANTS AND LOANS,[1] 19 L, 1970–88[a]

(M US)

Country	Fiscal Year	Total[2] Loans and Grants[3] (A+C)	"Other" Loans		Economic and Military Loans and Grants			Some Economic and Military Subtotals			I. Total Loans[12] (A+H)
			A. Total[4]	B. Ex-Im Subtotal[5]	C. Total[6] (D+E)	D. Military[7]	E. Economics[8]	F. AID[9]	G. Food[10]	H. Loans[11]	
A. ARGENTINA	1970	23.9	22.3	22.3	1.6	.6	1.0	1.0	#	#	22.3
	1975	94.9	64.7	64.7	30.2	30.1	.1	#	#	30.0	94.7
	1978	27.4	27.4	27.4	#	#	#	#	#	#	27.4
	1979	32.8	32.7	32.7	.1	#	.1	#	#	.1	32.8
	1980	81.0	81.0	81.0	#	#	#	#	#	#	81.0
	1981	82.6	82.6	82.6	#	#	#	#	#	#	82.6
	1982	551.1	551.0	551.0	.1	#	.1	#	#	#	551.0
	1983	#	#	#	#	#	#	#	#	#	#
	1984	.1	0	0	.1	0	.1	0	0	0	0
	1985	0	0	0	0	0	0	0	0	0	0
	1986	0	0	0	#	0	#	0	0	0	0
	1987	2.4	0	0	2.4	0	2.4	0	0	2.4	2.4
	1988	0	0	12.8	.1	.1	0	0	0	0	12.8
B. BOLIVIA	1970	9.5	#	#	9.5	1.5	8.0	3.0	3.6	#	#
	1975	33.2	#	#	33.2	7.4	25.8	20.1	5.1	21.2	21.2
	1978	71.5	17.5	5.5	54.0	.8	53.2	34.3	16.5	39.1	56.6
	1979	57.9	#	#	57.9	6.7	51.2	28.9	19.0	38.0	38.0
	1980	30.4	#	#	30.4	.3	30.1	4.5	24.8	17.3	17.3
	1981	12.8	#	#	12.8	#	12.8	2.3	9.5	.2	.2
	1982	19.7	#	#	19.7	#	19.7	2.1	16.4	10.0	10.0
	1983	63.0	#	#	63.0	#	63.0	11.4	49.2	40.4	40.4
	1984	78.1	0	0	78.1	.1	78.0	52.3	22.1	49.5	49.5
	1985	54.0	0	0	54.0	3.4	50.6	18.4	29.5	24.0	24.0
	1986	79.0	2.9	0	76.1	1.5	74.6	38.4	32.2	28.3	31.2
	1987	79.2	0	0	79.2	1.2	78.0	28.7	36.6	23.9	23.9
	1988	92.0	4.0	0	92.0	29.4	91.6	37.5	34.8	20.0	24.0
C. BRAZIL	1970	218.0	63.2	63.2	154.8	.8	154.0	88.0	62.4	95.0	158.2
	1975	337.2	257.1	256.5	80.1	65.4	14.7	3.1	0.4	60.0	317.1
	1978	106.8	104.7	104.7	2.1	#	2.1	#	.1	#	104.7
	1979	262.0	259.9	212.6	2.1	#	2.1	#	.6	#	259.9
	1980	101.7	99.3	68.8	2.4	#	2.4	#	1.4	#	99.3
	1981	117.0	115.9	115.9	1.1	#	1.1	#	.6	#	115.9
	1982	91.7	91.0	91.0	.7	#	.7	#	.3	.1	91.1
	1983	30.7	30.3	29.3	.4	#	.4	#	.1	#	30.3
	1984	28.5@	28.5	28.5	#	0	#	0	#	0	28.5
	1985	38.2	37.4	37.4	.8	0	.8	0	0	0	37.4
	1986	125.1	124.4	124.4	.7	0	.7	0	0	0	124.4
	1987	124.0	118.6	0	5.4	0	5.4	0	2.1	0	118.6
	1988	16.9	13.9	10.7	3.0	.1	2.8	0	.1	0	13.9
D. CHILE	1970	27.1	#	#	27.1	.8	26.3	18.0	7.2	15.0	15.0
	1975	128.6	32.4	23.0	96.2	.7	95.5	31.3	62.4	88.2	120.6
	1978	53.1	46.0	#	7.1	#	7.1	.2	5.6	#	46.0
	1979	13.6	#	#	13.6	#	13.6	.3	9.0	#	#
	1980	10.2	#	#	10.2	#	10.2	.1	5.0	#	#
	1981	12.1	#	#	12.1	#	12.1	#	7.7	.1	.1
	1982	6.7	#	#	6.7	#	6.7	#	2.3	#	#
	1983	2.8	#	#	2.8	#	2.8	#	1.0	#	#
	1984	1.7	0	0	1.7	0	1.7	0	0	0	0
	1985	2.6	1.3	1.3	1.3	0	1.3	0	0	0	1.3
	1986	2.2	1.1	0	1.1	0	1.1	0	0	0	1.1
	1987	1.1	0	0	1.1	0	1.1	0	0	0	0
	1988	1.4	1.4	1.7	1.4	0	1.4	0	0	0	1.7
E. COLOMBIA	1970	151.8	13.3	13.3	138.5	7.4	131.1	75.8	53.5	84.1	97.4
	1975	32.7	3.5	3.5	29.2	.7	28.5	14.0	11.5	12.2	15.7
	1978	89.5	30.0	30.0	59.5	52.2	7.3	#	2.6	51.0	81.0
	1979	64.5	42.5	42.5	22.0	13.0	9.0	.3	1.6	12.5	55.0
	1980	47.5	24.1	24.1	23.4	.3	23.1	.3	4.6	#	24.1
	1981	51.1	45.1	45.1	6.0	.3	5.7	#	#	#	45.1
	1982	553.5	540.3	540.3	13.5	10.5	3.0	#	#	10.0	550.3
	1983	4.6	3.8	3.8	4.6	.7	3.9	#	#	#	#
	1984	37.5	4.0	4.0	33.5	25.3	8.2	0	0	0	4.0
	1985	142.1	130.0	130.0	12.1	.8	11.3	0	0	0	130.0
	1986	15.8	0	0	15.8	4.3	11.5	0	0	0	0
	1987	17.1	0	0	17.1	5.1	12.0	0	0	0	0
	1988	44.5	30.3	30.3	14.2	4.0	10.2	0	.1	0	30.3

Table 2812 (Continued)

AUTHORIZED U.S. ASSISTANCE FOR GRANTS AND LOANS,[1] 19 L, 1970–88[a]

(M US)

Country	Fiscal Year	Total[2] Loans and Grants[3] (A+C)	"Other" Loans A. Total[4]	B. Ex-Im Subtotal[5]	Economic and Military Loans and Grants C. Total[6] (D+E)	D. Military[7]	E. Economics[8]	Some Economic and Military Subtotals F. AID[9]	G. Food[10]	H. Loans[11]	I. Total Loans[12] (A+H)
F. COSTA RICA	1970	20.9	.2	.2	20.7	#	20.7	19.5	.5	17.5	17.7
	1975	9.0	5.3	3.8	3.7	#	3.7	.7	1.0	#	5.3
	1978	13.2	4.1	4.0	9.1	#	9.1	6.9	.8	5.5	9.6
	1979	22.7	4.8	2.7	17.9	#	17.9	16.4	#	15.1	19.9
	1980	22.4	6.4	6.0	16.0	#	16.0	13.6	.4	12.0	18.4
	1981	20.4	5.1	5.1	15.3	#	15.3	11.5	1.8	10.0	15.1
	1982	56.8	3.0	#	53.8	#	51.7	31.5	19.1	42.7	45.7
	1983	218.7	#	#	218.7	4.6	214.1	184.2	28.2	166.2	166.2
	1984	181.1	2.1	0	179.0	9.1	169.9	145.5	22.5	69.9	72.0
	1985	232.1	.9	0	231.2	11.2	220.0	195.5	21.6	32.1	33.0
	1986	167.0	1.6	0	165.4	2.6	162.8	139.2	20.3	26.3	27.9
	1987	187.1	4.1	0	183.0	1.7	181.3	160.8	17.3	31.9	36.0
	1988	120.6	0	0	120.6	.2	120.4	101.3	15.1	15.0	15.0
H. DOMINICAN REP.	1970	21.9	#	#	21.9	2.1	19.8	5.2	14.0	9.6	9.6
	1975	20.6	7.3	7.3	13.3	1.6	11.7	5.6	5.5	5.3	12.6
	1978	7.0	.2	.2	6.8	.7	6.1	1.3	3.9	#	.2
	1979	75.4	26.0	.7	49.4	1.0	48.4	26.4	20.7	39.2	65.2
	1980	70.1	10.8	3.7	59.3	3.5	55.8	34.6	19.7	36.9	47.7
	1981	43.1	1.2	1.2	41.9	3.4	38.5	17.4	18.6	32.0	33.2
	1982	87.9	#	#	87.9	5.5	82.4	60.0	19.3	76.5	76.5
	1983	69.7	#	#	69.7	6.6	63.1	34.6	25.3	57.4	57.4
	1984	104.6	0	0	104.6	6.4	98.2	64.4	31.3	85.3	85.3
	1985	179.8	.5	0	179.3	8.7	170.6	125.5	42.4	54.4	54.9
	1986	107.8	1.5	0	106.3	4.5	101.8	67.1	31.8	41.2	42.7
	1987	44.4	3.4	0	41.0	3.4	37.6	20.0	14.9	16.3	19.7
	1988	60.0	4.6	0	60.0	1.3	58.7	32.5	23.3	20.0	24.6
I. ECUADOR	1970	31.2	3.0	3.0	28.2	2.4	25.8	23.2	1.6	19.4	22.4
	1975	14.4	6.0	6.0	8.4	.4	8.0	2.1	3.4	#	6.0
	1978	19.9	3.7	.5	16.2	10.7	5.5	.8	2.4	10.0	13.7
	1979	33.1	26.4	26.4	6.7	.4	6.3	.5	2.7	#	26.4
	1980	16.3	1.2	#	15.1	3.3	11.8	8.3	.9	9.0	10.2
	1981	25.5	2.7	#	22.8	4.3	18.5	12.5	2.3	13.6	6.7
	1982	27.9	#	#	27.9	5.0	22.9	17.3	2.4	16.6	16.6
	1983	31.2	#	#	31.2	4.6	26.6	21.5	1.8	6.7	6.7
	1984	37.1	1.5	0	35.6	6.7	28.9	22.6	2.7	14.0	15.5
	1985	58.6	0	0	58.6	6.7	51.9	33.2	14.9	21.3	21.3
	1986	64.9	0	0	64.9	4.5	60.4	49.8	6.5	15.4	15.4
	1987	52.0	1.9	0	50.1	4.5	45.6	37.2	4.0	1.1	3.0
	1988	21.6	0	0	21.6	.7	20.9	14.5	1.6	0	0
J. EL SALVADOR	1970	13.2	#	#	13.2	.6	12.6	10.3	1.8	7.8	7.8
	1975	10.0	.6	.6	9.4	5.5	3.9	1.3	1.6	3.0	3.6
	1978	10.9	#	#	10.9	#	10.9	8.0	1.7	5.7	57
	1979	11.5	.1	.1	11.4	#	11.4	6.9	2.9	4.2	4.3
	1980	64.3	.1	.1	64.2	5.9	58.3	52.3	5.5	46.1	47.2
	1981	149.5	#	#	149.5	35.5	114.0	78.3	35.3	90.0	90.0
	1982	264.2	#	#	264.2	82.0	182.2	154.6	27.6	80.3	80.3
	1983	326.9	#	#	326.9	81.3	245.6	198.8	46.8	133.1	133.1
	1984	412.5	0	0	412.5	196.6	215.9	161.4	54.5	81.2	81.2
	1985	570.2	0	0	570.2	136.3	433.9	376.1	57.8	70.0	70.0
	1986	444.4	0	0	444.4	121.8	322.6	268.2	54.4	52.0	52.0
	1987	574.4	0	0	574.4	111.5	462.9	414.5	48.4	42.0	42.0
	1988	395.6	0	0	395.6	81.5	314.1	265.7	48.4	35.5	35.5
K. GUATEMALA	1970	33.6	#	#	33.6	1.4	32.2	29.1	2.5	25.1	25.1
	1975	17.8	.8	.8	17.0	2.9	14.1	9.4	3.4	9.3	10.1
	1978	10.6	#	#	10.6	#	10.6	4.5	4.6	#	#
	1979	24.7	#	#	24.7	#	24.7	17.4	5.3	14.6	14.6
	1980	13.8	.8	#	13.0	#	13.0	7.8	3.3	5.0	5.8
	1981	19.0	#	#	19.0	#	19.0	9.1	7.5	5.6	5.6
	1982	15.5	#	#	15.5	#	15.5	8.2	5.6	3.0	3.0
	1983	29.7	#	#	19.7	#	29.7	22.3	5.4	17.5	17.5
	1984	20.3	0	0	20.3	0	20.3	4.5	13.2	6.7	6.7
	1985	107.4	.2	0	107.4	.5	106.9	75.7	28.2	59.7	59.9
	1986	122.1	0	0	122.1	5.4	116.7	89.8	24.0	47.9	47.9
	1987	193.5	.2	0	193.3	5.5	187.8	153.5	31.2	32.9	33.1
	1988	141.6	0	0	141.6	9.4	132.2	109.5	18.6	23.1	23.1

Table 2812 (Continued)

AUTHORIZED U.S. ASSISTANCE FOR GRANTS AND LOANS,[1] 19 L, 1970–88[a]

(M US)

Country	Fiscal Year	Total[2] Loans and Grants[3] (A+C)	"Other" Loans A. Total[4]	B. Ex-Im Subtotal[5]	Economic and Military Loans and Grants C. Total[6] (D+E)	D. Military[7]	E. Economics[8]	Some Economic and Military Subtotals F. AID[9]	G. Food[10]	H. Loans[11]	I. Total Loans[12] (A+H)
L. HAITI	1970	3.8	.1	.1	3.7	#	3.7	1.6	2.1	#	.1
	1975	9.3	#	#	9.3	#	9.3	3.6	5.6	2.3	2.3
	1978	29.4	1.2	#	28.2	.7	27.5	8.9	18.5	11.0	12.2
	1979	25.5	.3	#	25.2	.4	24.8	9.1	15.4	8.8	9.1
	1980	27.2	#	#	27.2	.1	27.1	11.1	15.8	8.6	8.6
	1981	35.8	.8	#	35.0	.4	34.6	9.2	24.5	8.9	9.7
	1982	35.6	.8	#	34.8	.5	34.3	12.0	22.2	13.3	14.1
	1983	48.2	1.3	#	46.9	.7	46.2	27.3	18.5	11.3	12.6
	1984	47.5	0	0	47.5	1.0	46.5	25.7	19.8	11.0	11.0
	1985	56.7	.4	0	56.3	.7	55.6	30.7	23.2	15.0	15.4
	1986	80.1	.5	0	79.6	1.9	77.7	46.9	29.2	15.0	15.5
	1987	102.4	0	0	102.4	1.3	101.1	74.9	23.5	10.5	10.5
	1988	40.2	0	0	40.2	.2	40.0	31.2	7.9	0	0
M. HONDURAS	1970	8.6	1.0	1.0	7.6	.4	7.2	5.5	.9	2.7	3.7
	1975	41.1	1.3	1.3	39.8	4.2	35.6	25.4	9.0	27.3	28.6
	1978	20.8	.5	.5	20.3	3.2	17.1	13.0	2.4	12.5	13.0
	1979	32.3	.8	.8	31.5	2.3	29.1	22.0	4.8	20.0	20.8
	1980	66.8	13.7	12.5	57.0	3.9	53.1	45.8	5.2	44.1	156.1
	1981	37.3	.9	.9	45.3	8.9	36.4	25.7	8.2	32.2	33.1
	1982	112.6	.6	.3	112.0	31.3	80.7	67.9	10.1	80.5	81.1
	1983	154.3	#	#	154.3	48.3	106.0	87.3	15.5	54.0	54.0
	1984	172.6	.2	0	172.4	77.4	95.0	71.0	20.2	38.3	38.6
	1985	298.4	2.0	0	296.4	67.4	229.0	204.6	19.4	34.8	36.8
	1986	198.1	.4	0	197.7	61.1	136.6	111.8	19.6	30.6	31.0
	1987	259.0	0	0	259.0	61.2	197.8	174.5	18.1	28.1	28.1
	1988	198.1	0	0	198.1	41.2	156.9	129.9	20.4	25.0	25.0
N. MEXICO	1070	36.6	35.5	35.5	1.1	.1	1.0	1.0	#	#	35.5
	1975	196.0	195.7	195.7	.3	.1	.2	#	#	#	195.7
	1978	629.1	608.5	608.5	20.6	.1	20.5	#	#	#	608.5
	1979	170.9	157.2	157.2	13.7	.2	13.5	#	#	#	157.2
	1980	188.3	180.8	180.8	7.5	.1	7.4	#	#	#	180.8
	1981	662.5	652.6	652.6	9.9	.1	9.8	#	#	#	652.6
	1982	302.2	293.4	293.4	8.8	.1	8.7	#	#	#	293.4
	1983	96.5	88.2	37.2	8.3	.1	8.2	#	#	#	88.2
	1984	88.0	79.4	66.5	8.6	.2	8.4	0	0	0	79.4
	1985	21.4	10.1	10.1	11.3	.2	11.1	0	1.2	0	10.1
	1986	12.1	0	0	12.1	.2	11.9	0	.3	0	0
	1987	22.9	5.1	5.1	17.8	.3	17.5	0	2.2	0	5.1
	1988	103.5	85.0	0	18.5	.2	18.3	0	3.2	0	85.0
O. NICARAGUA	1970	4.4	.1	#	4.3	1.2	3.1	2.3	.4	#	4.4
	1975	46.8	.3	#	46.5	4.3	42.2	40.1	1.4	42.0	42.3
	1978	14.6	.2	.2	14.4	.4	14.0	12.5	.1	10.5	10.7
	1979	18.5	#	#	18.5	#	18.5	9.7	7.0	2.6	2.6
	1980	38.7	#	#	38.7	#	38.7	19.4	18.0	30.0	30.0
	1981	59.9	#	#	59.9	#	59.9	58.4	1.2	48.0	48.0
	1982	6.3	#	#	6.3	#	6.3	5.8	.4	#	#
	1983	#	#	#	#	#	#	#	#	#	#
	1984	.1	0	0	.1	0	.1	0	0	0	0
	1985	0	0	0	0	0	0	0	0	0	0
	1986	0	0	0	0	0	0	0	0	0	0
	1987	0	0	0	0	0	0	0	0	0	0
	1988	.4	0	0	.4	0	.4	0	0	0	0
P. PANAMA	1970	17.0	2.5	2.5	14.5	1.0	13.5	11.8	1.0	8.5	11.0
	1975	51.9	30.1	30.1	21.8	.6	21.2	8.3	.9	6.7	36.8
	1978	23.6	#	#	23.6	.5	23.1	21.3	1.3	20.0	20.0
	1979	26.3	3.7	3.6	22.6	1.4	21.2	19.9	1.1	17.0	20.7
	1980	2.3	#	#	2.3	.3	2.0	1.0	1.0	#	#
	1981	11.0	#	#	11.0	.4	10.6	8.7	1.9	6.4	6.4
	1982	18.4	#	#	18.4	5.4	13.0	11.7	1.3	13.1	13.1
	1983	12.9	#	#	12.9	5.5	7.4	6.3	1.1	8.8	8.8
	1984	25.7	.2	0	25.5	13.5	12.0	10.7	1.3	5.0	5.2
	1985	85.1	0	0	85.1	10.6	74.5	74.3	.1	7.9	7.9
	1986	41.9	.3	.3	41.6	8.2	33.4	33.3	.1	7.5	7.8
	1987	15.6	0	0	15.6	3.5	12.1	12.1	#	0	0
	1988	1.2	0	0	1.2	0	0	1.2	0	0	0

Table 2812 (Continued)

AUTHORIZED U.S. ASSISTANCE FOR GRANTS AND LOANS,[1] 19 L, 1970–88[a]

(M US)

Country	Fiscal Year	Total[2] Loans and Grants[3] (A+C)	"Other" Loans A. Total[4]	B. Ex-Im Subtotal[5]	Economic and Military Loans and Grants C. Total[6] (D+E)	D. Military[7]	E. Economics[8]	Some Economic and Military Subtotals F. AID[9]	G. Food[10]	H. Loans[11]	I. Total Loans[12] (A+H)
Q. PARAGUAY	1970	9.3	#	#	9.3	1.2	8.1	7.1	.5	4.6	4.6
	1975	9.6	#	#	9.6	1.6	8.0	6.7	.4	5.2	5.2
	1978	4.1	#	#	4.1	.6	3.5	1.8	.3	#	#
	1979	10.3	#	#	10.3	#	10.3	7.1	.3	5.0	5.0
	1980	3.6	#	#	3.6	#	3.6	1.3	.4	#	#
	1981	6.2	#	#	6.2	#	6.2	2.0	.7	#	#
	1982	67.7	63.9	63.9	3.8	#	3.8	#	.1	#	63.9
	1983	4.4	1.1	#	3.3	.1	3.2	#	#	#	1.1
	1984	2.8	0	0	2.8	.1	2.7	.2	0	0	0
	1985	3.6	0	0	3.6	.1	3.5	1.0	0	0	0
	1986	3.4	0	0	3.4	.1	3.3	1.1	.3	0	0
	1987	3.2	0	0	3.2	.1	3.1	1.0	0	0	0
	1988	4.2	0	0	4.2	.1	4.1	.8	0	0	0
R. PERU	1970	17.5	#	#	17.5	.6	16.9	11.3	4.2	#	#
	1975	68.8	31.3	16.3	37.5	21.4	16.1	8.9	6.4	27.5	58.8
	1978	138.5	74.9	.7	63.6	8.9	54.7	22.0	31.9	52.0	126.9
	1979	139.0	62.8	#	76.2	5.5	70.7	34.1	35.3	53.8	116.6
	1980	102.9	46.3	6.2	56.6	3.3	53.3	18.7	33.0	36.0	82.3
	1981	100.5	16.0	13.1	84.5	4.3	80.2	34.5	42.5	51.0	67.0
	1982	59.6	#	#	59.6	5.0	54.6	35.8	16.2	48.7	48.7
	1983	124.4	26.3	26.3	98.1	4.6	93.5	35.5	55.9	52.5	78.8
	1984	175.6	.3	0	175.3	10.7	164.6	118.9	42.9	119.0	119.3
	1985	89.1	1.3	0	87.8	8.7	79.1	37.9	38.8	25.5	26.8
	1986	59.0	0	0	59.0	.6	58.4	25.9	28.8	20.0	20.0
	1987	65.6	1.8	0	63.8	.1	63.7	21.3	33.7	24.1	25.9
	1988	71.1	0	0	71.1	.4	70.7	28.0	35.0	21.7	21.7
S. URUGUAY	1970	22.9	#	#	22.9	3.5	19.4	16.9	2.4	17.4	17.4
	1975	22.2	#	#	22.2	9.2	12.9	12.8	#	19.3	19.3
	1978	.2	#	#	2	#	.2	#	#	#	#
	1979	.2	#	#	.2	#	.2	#	#	#	#
	1980	#	#	#	#	#	#	#	#	#	#
	1981	15.0	14.9	14.9	.1	#	.1	#	#	#	14.9
	1982	.8	#	#	.8	#	.8	#	#	#	#
	1983	1.1	#	#	1.1	.1	1.0	#	#	#	#
	1984	.7	0	0	.7	.1	.6	0	0	0	0
	1985	.1	0	0	.1	.1	#	0	0	0	0
	1986	14.5	0	0	14.5	.1	14.4	0	0	0	0
	1987	12.9	0	0	12.9	.7	12.2	12.2	0	0	0
	1988	.1	0	0	.1	.1	0	0	0	0	0
T. VENEZUELA	1970	17.0	13.5	13.5	3.5	.8	2.7	1.1	#	#	13.5
	1975	16.4	14.1	14.1	2.3	.7	1.6	#	#	#	14.1
	1978	22.4	22.3	22.3	.1	.1	#	#	#	#	22.3
	1979	18.5	18.5	18.5	#	#	#	#	#	#	18.5
	1980	160.2	160.2	160.2	#	#	#	#	#	#	160.2
	1981	59.6	59.5	59.5	.1	#	.1	#	#	#	59.5
	1982	26.2	26.0	26.0	.2	#	.2	#	#	#	26.0
	1983	12.2	12.0	12.0	.2	.1	.1	#	#	#	12.0
	1984	.4	0	0	.4	#	.4	0	0	0	0
	1985	.9	0	0	.9	.1	.8	0	0	0	0
	1986	.2	0	0	.2	.1	.1	0	0	0	0
	1987	.2	0	0	.2	.2	#	0	0	0	0
	1988	.1	0	0	.1	.1	#	0	0	0	0

Table 2812 (Continued)

AUTHORIZED U.S. ASSISTANCE FOR GRANTS AND LOANS,[1] 19 L, 1970–88[a]

(M US)

1. The definition of "assistance" is highly debatable and often full of irony as in the case of funding by the Export-Import (Ex-Im) Bank: The U.S. government formerly classified Ex-Im Bank loans as offering "assistance" when interest rates were relatively high in relation to other U.S. aid; since the 1970s when the government accepted criticism of its classification of Ex-Im Bank and took its funding out of figures on "assistance," however, other aid (including U.S. AID) rates and private rates have not compared so favorably and Ex-Im loans perhaps should be classified as offering assistance — indeed, U.S. business firms have complained that Ex-Im Bank loans offer more favorable terms to foreigners than to U.S. companies. Although it can be argued that Ex-Im Bank loans are tied to purchase of U.S. goods and services, it should be remembered that in the end Ex-Im Bank loans must compete in the international finance market or lose borrowers. (Cf. SALA-SNP, part III, for a discussion of supranational policy problems.) Ex-Im loans here are classified as part of U.S. assistance.
2. Total includes U.S. obligations (i.e., authorizations to expend in contrast to actual expenditures) for assistance administered by (a) the U.S. Agency for International Development (AID or USAID); (b) Peace Corps; (c) other U.S. agencies; and assistance administered through (d) Food for Peace Programs; (e) Social Progress Trust Funds of the Inter-American Development Bank; other selected U.S. programs (e.g., Inter-American Highway) — may include some disbursements; (f) military programs; as well as actual loans held by (h) the U.S. Ex-Im Bank. Does not include AID administrative overhead costs in the host country. Excludes regional obligations to more than one country. Excludes payments made through international agencies (e.g., IDB, IBRD) over which the U.S. has no direct control.
3. The data may reflect subsequent yearly retrospective revisions made by USAID.
4. Includes short-term credits by U.S. Department of Agriculture.
5. Before 1973 Ex-Im Bank deobligated sums (except for repayments) for years when originally authorized as it canceled, decreased, terminated, or sold loans to non-U.S. government purchasers. Includes (since 1969 only) loans of less than 5 years maturity. Excludes loans for military assistance (which are included under the military category.)
6. In source, this total is labeled "Total Economic and Military Grants and Loans," but actually economic obligations include funds for social purposes (such as education) as well as administrative functions (such as "Supporting Assistance" to maintain political stability for security objectives).
7. Military data included Ex-Im Bank military loans (but not guarantees) and also represent grant and loan actual assistance prior to FY 1962. Exclude AID obligations for Supporting Assistance (see notes 3 and 9). Excludes excess stock deliveries included in SALA-SNP, XVII-5.

8. Includes AID programs and Food for Peace.
9. AID was established November 4, 1961. Its predecessor agencies were, successively: Economic Cooperation Administration (April 3, 1948 — October 31, 1951); Mutual Security Agency (November 1, 1951 — July 31, 1953); Foreign Operations Administration (August 1, 1953 — June 30, 1955); International Cooperation Administration (July 1, 1955 — November 3, 1961); and the Development Loan Fund (August 14, 1957 — November 3, 1961); see AID/Washington, *U.S. Economic Assistance Programs Administered by the Agency for International Development and Predecessor Agencies*, April 3, 1948 — June 30, 1967. AID data include grant and loan Supporting Assistance for military infrastructure; and includes "402" Mutual Security Aid Program obligations for U.S. agricultural exports.
10. Food for Peace involves (a) sales on credit terms (for dollars and/or local currency) and (b) donations (for emergency relief or for volunteer relief agencies such as CARE) of surplus U.S. agricultural commodities. Former are valued at export market price; latter are valued at cost through FY 1969, subsequently at market value, plus ocean freight. (Donations to volunteer relief agencies do not, however, include ocean freight.) This subtotal does not include any funds generated by such activity as interest on local currency deposits.
11. Included in col. C.
12. Loans include "capitalized interest" (interest for prior years which is due but not paid) added during the year it becomes an accrued liability. Data exclude the export guarantees and insurance which are included in SALA-SNP, XVII-9. Refunding of loans generally is excluded.

a. For prior years, see SALA-SNP, XVII-1. Data here are revised to include deobligations; for data on announced assistance from 1946 to 1988, in deflated and per capita terms, see Christof Anders Weber, "Announced U.S. Assistance to Latin America, 1946–88: Who Gets It? How Much? And When?," SALA, 28, Chapter 35.

SOURCE: Adapted from USAID-OLG, July 1, 1945–June 30, 1975; July 1, 1945–September 30, 1983; July 1, 1945–September 30, 1986; July 1, 1945–September 30, 1987; July 1, 1945–September 30, 1988.

Table 2813

YEARLY U.S. PROJECTED ASSISTANCE TO
LATIN AMERICA, 1946–88
(M US)

Fiscal Year	Total Grants and Loans[1]	Loans' Share
1946	104.7	91.7
1947	108.3	86.8
1948	55.9	17.1
1949	70.7	44.5
1950	196.9	169.2
1951	219.1	201.7
1952	103.0	78.7
1953	439.9	388.8
1954	95.0	17.9
1955	357.1	246.2
1956	368.6	217.1
1957	672.4	485.9
1958	398.9	238.6
1959	623.5	488.5
1960	306.1	174.5
1961	923.2	681.3
1962	1,036.0	695.4
1963	984.1	649.9
1964	1,164.2	836.9
1965	961.6	669.6
1966	1,090.6	761.0
1967	1,102.5	886.7
1968	1,080.0	890.2
1969	644.2	493.0
1970	685.1	461.5
1971	647.5	490.0
1972	1,007.3	823.2
1973	896,0	751.8
1974	1,216.2	1,079.1
1975	1,160.3	1,010.0
1976	959.1	809.7
TQ[2]	181.1	136.8
1977	537.0	383.6
1978	1,292.6	1,158.5
1979	1,039.7	866.6
1980	1,051.6	875.8
1981	1,520.9	1,297.4
1982	2,304.4	1,955.4
1983	1,235.1	710.9
1984	1,414.9	663.0
1985	1,766.5	322.4
1986	1,537.6	416.9
1987	1,757.0	348.3
1988	1,625.7	312.3

1. Excludes amounts and sums allocated to more than one country
   (e.g., Regional Programs in Central America — ROCAP).
2. Transitional quarter to new fiscal-year basis.

SOURCE: SALA-SNP, p. 360, and calculated since 1970 from
table 2812, first and last columns, above.

Table 2814

A.I.D. COMMITMENTS TO INDIVIDUAL LATIN AMERICAN COUNTRIES, 20 L, 1949–88

(M US, Descending Order)

	Country	Amount	%
1.	EL SALVADOR	2,078.7	16.8
2.	BRAZIL	1,429.6	11.5
3.	COSTA RICA	1,130.9	9.1
4.	HONDURAS	1,120.9	9.1
5.	COLOMBIA	917.8	7.4
6.	DOMINICAN REP.	821.6	6.6
7.	BOLIVIA	765.8	6.2
8.	GUATEMALA	754.3	6.1
9.	PERU	674.1	5.4
10.	CHILE	662.4	5.4
11.	PANAMA	414.5	3.3
12.	HAITI	406.1	3.3
13.	ECUADOR	401.5	3.2
14.	NICARAGUA	283.4	2.3
15.	ARGENTINA	134.5	1.1
16.	PARAGUAY	124.3	1.0
17.	URUGUAY	105.6	.9
18.	MEXICO	77.8	.6
19.	VENEZUELA	71.7	.6
20.	CUBA	2.8	.02
	LATIN AMERICA	12,378.3	100.0

SOURCE: Calculated from table 2812, above.

Table 2815

PER CAPITA A.I.D. COMMITMENTS TO INDIVIDUAL LATIN AMERICA COUNTRIES, 20 L, 1949–88

(M US, Descending Order)

	Country	Amount
1.	COSTA RICA	~
2.	EL SALVADOR	633.36
3.	HONDURAS	431.44
4.	PANAMA	298.20
5.	DOMINICAN REP.	207.63
6.	BOLIVIA	170.74
7.	NICARAGUA	155.54
8.	GUATEMALA	148.33
9.	HAITI	96.66
10.	CHILE	74.37
11.	ECUADOR	68.90
12.	PARAGUAY	53.80
13.	PERU	52.05
14.	COLOMBIA	46.56
15.	URUGUAY	17.33
16.	BRAZIL	16.08
17.	VENEZUELA	7.03
18.	ARGENTINA	5.83
19.	MEXICO	1.59
20.	CUBA	~

SOURCE: Calculated from table 2814, above, using average population.

Table 2816

GROSS PROJECTED A.I.D. ASSISTANCE DURING FOUR PERIODS, 20 L, 1949-88

(M US, Descending Order)

Mutual Security Years, 1949-58		Peak Years of Alliance for Progress, 1959-66		Years of U.S. Congressional Disillusionment, 1967-74		Years of Latin America's Rising Foreign Debt, 1975-88	
1. BOLIVIA	92.4	1. BRAZIL	842.8	1. COLOMBIA	647.3	1. EL SALVADOR	1,990.6
2. GUATEMALA	54.5	2. CHILE	499.2	2. BRAZIL	586.9	2. HONDURAS	847.
3. CHILE	24.2	3. COLOMBIA	316.3	3. DOMINICAN REP.	146.3	3. COSTA RICA[1]	775.6
4. BRAZIL	23.4	4. BOLIVIA	222.8	4. BOLIVIA	145.4	4. GUATEMALA	558.7
5. PERU	18.4	5. DOMINICAN REP.	202.2	5. PANAMA	127.6	5. DOMINICAN REP.	506.4
6. HAITI	16.6	6. ARGENTINA	141.0	6. CHILE	126.3	6. PERU	452.5
7. HONDURAS	16.1	7. PERU	116.1	7. GUATEMALA	98.2	7. BOLIVIA	338.4
8. ECUADOR	14.7[a]	8. ECUADOR	107.5	8. PERU	92.2	8. HAITI	332.0
9. PARAGUAY	14.7[a]	9. MEXICO	70.9	9. NICARAGUA	87.3	9. PANAMA	249.2
10. PANAMA	10.1	10. PANAMA	70.8	10. HONDURAS	68.4	10. EDUCADOR	220.3
11. COSTA RICA	8.7	11. VENEZUELA	64.2	11. COSTA RICA	59.7	11. NICARAGUA	165.0
12. COLOMBIA	8.1	12. NICARAGUA	56.3	12. ECUADOR	59.6	12. CHILE	53.7
13. MEXICO	6.4	13. GUATEMALA	53.7	13. EL SALVADOR	47.9	13. COLOMBIA	36.6
14. EL SALVADOR	5.5	14. COSTA RICA	47.0[a]	14. PARAGUAY	43.0	14. PARAGUAY	30.2
15. NICARAGUA	4.9	15. EL SALVADOR	47.0[a]	15. URUGUAY	42.1	15. URUGUAY	26.3
16. CUBA	2.6	16. HAITI	42.5	16. HAITI	28.6	16. BRAZIL	4.5
17. URUGUAY	1.9	17. HONDURAS	41.4	17. VENEZUELA	6.8	17. ARGENTINA[a]	#
18. DOMINICAN REP.	1.7	18. PARAGUAY	40.7	18. ARGENTINA	5.3	18. CUBA[a]	~
19. VENEZUELA	1.0	19. URUGUAY	27.9	19. MEXICO	1.6	19. MEXICO[a]	#
20. ARGENTINA	.2	20. CUBA	.7	20. CUBA	0	20. VENEZUELA[a]	#

1. Does not include 1988 data.

a. Tie ranking.

SOURCE: Phillip Paul Boucher, "U.S. Foreign Aid to Latin America: Hypotheses and Patterns in Historical Statistics, 1934-1974," Ph.D. dissertation, University of California, Los Angeles, 1979, p. 98; 1975-86, calculated from table 2812, above.

Table 2817

PER CAPITA GROSS PROJECTED A.I.D. ASSISTANCE DURING FOUR PERIODS, 20 L, 1949-88

(M US, Descending Order)

Mutual Security Years, 1949-58		Peak Years of Alliance for Progress, 1959-66		Years of U.S. Congressional Disillusionment, 1967-74		Years of Latin America's Rising Foreign Debt, 1975-88	
1. BOLIVIA	28.90	1. PANAMA	64.40	1. PANAMA	85.10	1. EL SALVADOR	30.3
2. GUATEMALA	17.60	2. CHILE	61.60	2. NICARAGUA	45.90	2. COSTA RICA[1]	28.5
3. PANAMA	11.20	3. DOMINICAN REP.	61.30	3. DOMINICAN REP.	35.70	3. HONDURAS	15.5
4. HONDURAS	10.10	4. BOLIVIA	54.30	4. COSTA RICA	33.20	4. PANAMA	8.9
5. PARAGUAY	9.80	5. NICARAGUA	37.50	5. BOLIVIA	31.60	5. DOMINICAN REP.	6.10
6. COSTA RICA	8.70	6. COSTA RICA	33.60	6. COLOMBIA	31.00	6. NICARAGUA	~
7. HAITI	4.60	7. ECUADOR	22.90	7. HONDURAS	26.30	7. GUATEMALA	5.4
8. ECUADOR[a]	4.10	8. PARAGUAY	21.40	8. PARAGUAY	18.70	8. HAITI	4.10
9. NICARAGUA[a]	4.10	9. HONDURAS	20.70	9. GUATEMALA	18.50	9. BOLIVIA	3.35
10. CHILE	3.70	10. COLOMBIA	18.90	10. URUGUAY	15.60	10. ECUADOR	1.84
11. EL SALVADOR	2.60	11. EL SALVADOR	17.40	11. EL SALVADOR	13.70	11. PERU	1.78
12. PERU	2.10	12. GUATEMALA	13.10	12. CHILE	13.30	12. PARAGUAY	.65
13. URUGUAY	.83	13. HAITI	11.90	13. ECUADOR	9.80	13. URUGUAY	.63
14. DOMINICAN REP.	.68	14. BRAZIL	11.20	14. PERU	6.80	14. CHILE	.33
15. COLOMBIA	.65	15. PERU	10.80	15. HAITI	6.70	15. COLOMBIA	.09
16. CUBA	.43	16. URUGUAY	10.70	16. BRAZIL	6.30	16. ARGENTINA[a]	#
17. BRAZIL	.40	17. VENEZUELA	8.00	17. VENEZUELA	.65	17. BRAZIL[a]	#
18. MEXICO	.23	18. ARGENTINA	6.70	18. ARGENTINA	.22	18. CUBA[a]	~
19. VENEZUELA	.17	19. MEXICO	1.80	19. MEXICO	.03	19. MEXICO[a]	#
20. ARGENTINA	.01	20. CUBA	.09	20. CUBA	#	20. VENEZUELA[a]	#

1. Does not include 1988 data.

a. Tie ranking.

SOURCE: Calculated by SALA table 2837, above. Population statistics are from SALA, 25-Ch. 6; IMF-IFS, June 1987, and UN-MB, August 1987; IMF-IFS, June 1988. Calculated from population 1975-88.

Table 2818

A.I.D. ACTUAL DISBURSEMENT FOR LOANS AND GRANTS, 19 L, 1979–85

(T US)

	Country	1979	1980	1981	1982	1983	1984	1985
A.	ARGENTINA	2	~	~	~	~	~	~
B.	BOLIVIA	26,524	21,162	16,397	11,289	8,851	9,926	24,604
C.	BRAZIL	6,762	92	327	95	563	87	132
D.	CHILE	9,144	3,098	588	4	~	~	~
E.	COLOMBIA	11,425	8,061	1,063	220	95	297	242
F.	COSTA RICA	7,067	4,873	4,026	24,729	109,948	146,337	224,234
H.	DOMINICAN REP.	11,992	17,621	19,517	23,113	54,754	50,139	110,038
I.	ECUADOR	705	1,752	2,492	3,306	6,953	14,871	22,205
J.	EL SALVADOR	3,787	12,692	89,869	134,987	148,728	151,412	247,645
K.	GUATEMALA	5,756	7,442	11,922	13,544	26,631	13,735	17,829
L.	HAITI	10,277	11,397	15,423	16,298	17,296	19,608	25,097
M.	HONDURAS	15,599	16,445	22,093	62,153	45,075	102,625	132,353
N.	MEXICO	85	107	131	117	192	300	405
O.	NICARAGUA	11,228	31,882	53,873	6,945	4,315	1,145	336
P.	PANAMA	12,503	14,399	13,441	19,039	14,902	15,982	67,775
Q.	PARAGUAY	4,920	1,711	2,656	2,094	2,301	1,447	2,250
R.	PERU	14,843	20,782	22,860	20,440	21,581	63,904	82,952
S.	URUGUAY	2,281	4,042	2,835	91	~	~	~
T.	VENEZUELA	72	66	34	30	··	··	~
	TOTAL	154,973	177,626	279,547	338,495	462,184	591,815	958,098

SOURCE: Unpublished data provided by A.I.D. W-211.

Table 2819

A.I.D. STATUS OF LOAN AGREEMENTS, 20 L, 1958–86

(T US)

	Country	Agreement Amount	Amount Utilized	Principal Repayments	Balance Outstanding	Interest Collection
A.	ARGENTINA	130,467.61	130,467.61	81,320.92	35,185.25	27,982.68
B.	BOLIVIA	391,793.92	337,648.67	57,221.66	261,787.11	64,614.38
C.	BRAZIL	1,428,366.86	1,428,344.18	225,810.83	1,005,671.77	309,862.05
D.	CHILE	633,837.29	633,837.29	260,963.06	354,549.60	167,898.44
E.	COLOMBIA	880,492.49	880,492.49	252,130.15	600,662.37	254,489.39
F.	COSTA RICA	365,158.14	321,381.83	17,276.26	303,808.69	26,654.91
G.	CUBA	~	~	~	~	~
H.	DOMINICAN REP.	412,044.34	357,035.17	68,116.93	288,918.24	56,954.82
I.	ECUADOR	176,478.51	142,928.25	54,335.72	88,166.82	30,392.39
J.	EL SALVADOR	306,642.91	272,632.98	20,161.86	252,471.11	27,863.03
K.	GUATEMALA	233,661.91	176,182.59	28,006.27	148,176.32	27,391.87
L.	HAITI	21,475.20	21,217.25	2,781.44	18,199.00	5,900.50
M.	HONDURAS	344,388.13	272,869.14	22,132.71	250,736.43	32,312.88
N.	MEXICO	83,996.55	83,996.55	59,108.91	24,887.63	29,649.34
O.	NICARAGUA	218,072.95	218,072.95	12,520.20	205,552.75	21,470.36
P.	PANAMA	252,688.73	223,193.55	46,112.01	177,081.54	46,094.42
Q.	PARAGUAY	70,370.35	69,766.82	30,341.77	36,920.35	20,292.99
R.	PERU	442,925.84	392,931.77	77,916.32	308,339.96	53,398.64
S.	URUGUAY	76,202.98	76,202.98	19,448.06	42,405.55	18,466.21
T.	VENEZUELA	55,000.00	55,000.00	55,000.00	#	11,087.56

SOURCE: *Status of Loan Agreements* (Office of Financial Management, Agency for International Development, September 1986).

Table 2820

EX-IM BANK ACTUAL LOANS, 20 L, 1973–81[a]

(T US)

	Country	FY 1973	1974	1975	1976	1977	1978	1979	1980	1981
A.	ARGENTINA	32,212	5,945	29,142	36,098	19,636	21,000	19,893	11,767	33,552
B.	BOLIVIA	#	#	#	4,261	107	6,215	8,188	#	96

Continued in SALA, 24-2844.

Table 2821

EX-IM BANK AUTHORIZATIONS BY COUNTRY
(October 1, 1980 – September 30, 1989)
(T US)

Country	1980–81	1981–82	1983–84	1984–85	1985–86	1986–87	1987–88	1988–89[a]
A. ARGENTINA								
Direct Loans	81,460	500,000	#	#	#	#	#	#
Off Loans	1,154	#	#	#	#	#	#	#
Financial and Other Guar	#	16,150	#	#	#	#	#	#
Bank, Preship, and CNG Guar	13,532	7,820	#	#	#	#	#	#
M/T Insurance Policies	25,590	13,328	#	#	#	2,587	3,706	29
Total Authorizations	121,736	587,298	#	#	#	2,707	20,493	11,681
S/T Insurance Shipments	168,850	72,214	1,473	328	161	3,643	56,692	51,254
Total Auth and Shipments	290,585	659,512	#	328	161	6,349	77,185	62,935
B. BOLIVIA								
M/T Insurance Policies	231	#	#	#	#	#	#	#
Total Authorizations	231	#	#	#	#	#	#	#
S/T Insurance Shipments	9,278	1,535	–50	#	#	#	#	#
Total Auth and Shipments	9,509	1,535	–50	#	#	#	#	#
C. BRAZIL								
Direct Loans	141,445	109,083	28,538	37,400	124,355	#	#	#
Off Loans	7,255					#	#	#
Financial and Other Guar	110,702	16,698	18,556	135,260	14,821	#	#	#
Off Guars and Colps	6,380	#	#	#	#	#	#	#
Bank, Preship, and CNG Guar	19,184	21,796	25,196	134,865	67,322	#	#	#
M/T Insurance Policies	10,693	35,115	30,778	35,965	40,933	#	510	70,960
Total Authorizations	295,659	182,692	103,067	343,490	247,431	275,000	11,165	226,771
S/T Insurance Shipments	148,275	164,240	385,388	292,084	196,840	319,372	282,350	181,272
Total Auth and Shipments	443,934	346,932	488,455	635,574	444,271	594,372	293,515	408,044
D. CHILE								
Direct Loans	#	#	#	1,275	#	#	#	#
Financial and Other Guar	#	#	11,454	14,988	40,000	#	#	#
Bank, Preship, and CNG Guar	19,804	10,099	6,255	8,330	8,907	#	#	#
M/T Insurance Policies	9,712	7,285	6,557	7,859	11,599	#	859	24,344
Total Authorizations	29,156	17,584	24,465	32,453	60,506	23,603	7,146	29,167
S/T Insurance Shipments	13,744	60,383	28,593	67,271	54,474	58,548	73,463	46,980
Total Auth and Shipments	43,260	77,967	52,859	99,724	114,980	82,150	80,609	76,147
E. COLOMBIA								
Direct Loans	45,116	540,264	4,015	130,000	#	#	#	#
Financial and Other Guar	8,164	67,500	535	182,360	#	#	#	#
Bank, Preship, and CNG Guar	7,733	4,731	55,559	55,225	48,186	#	#	#
M/T Insurance Policies	19,305	19,106	33,131	3,453	13,183	3,277	#	#
Total Authorizations	80,318	631,601	93,240	371,038	61,369	13,125	38,568	29,129
S/T Insurance Shipments	60,548	77,166	45,734	58,445	61,840	57,690	74,014	50,101
Total Auth and Shipments	140,866	708,767	138,974	429,483	123,209	70,815	112,582	79,230
F. COSTA RICA								
Off Loans	942	#	#	#	#	#	#	#
Financial and Other Guar	1,277	#	#	#	#	#	#	#
Off Guars and Colps	942	#	#	#	#	#	#	#
Bank, Preship, and CNG Guar	897	#	#	#	#	#	#	#
M/T Insurance Policies	4,623	442	#	#	#	#	#	#
Total Authorizations	12,833	442	#	#	#	#	#	#
S/T Insurance Shipments	51,968	13,437	10,338	19,451	44,862	62,629	66,303	38,175
Total Auth and Shipments	64,801	13,879	10,338	19,451	44,862	62,629	66,303	38,175
H. DOMINICAN REP.								
Off Loans	1,155	#	#	#	#	#	#	#
Financial and Other Guar	8,955	#	#	#	#	#	#	#
Bank, Preship, and CNG Guar	6,336	#	#	#	#	#	#	#
M/T Insurance Policies	3,557	319	#	145	#	#	#	#
Total Authorizations	20,003	319	#	145	#	#	#	#
S/T Insurance Shipments	20,949	26,428	7,016	7,909	159	14,638	21,438	16,381
Total Auth and Shipments	40,952	26,747	7,016	8,054	159	14,638	21,438	16,381
I. ECUADOR								
Financial and Other Guar	7,225	#	14,100	#	#	#	#	#
Bank, Preship, and CNG Guar	24,718	11,540	2,180	5,625	18,103	#	#	#
M/T Insurance Policies	39,882	17,404	1,297	#	23,376	9,400	14,553	#
Total Authorizations	71,825	28,943	17,577	5,625	41,480	30,358	17,550	#
S/T Insurance Shipments	78,897	77,831	25,164	31,419	47,315	36,107	23,821	2,084
Total Auth and Shipments	150,722	106,775	42,741	37,044	88,795	66,465	41,370	2,084

Table 2821 (Continued)

EX-IM BANK AUTHORIZATIONS BY COUNTRY
(October 1, 1980 – September 30, 1989)
(T US)

Country	1980–81	1981–82	1983–84	1984–85	1985–86	1986–87	1987–88	1988–89[a]
J. EL SALVADOR								
Bank, Preship, and CNG Guar	#	#	102	5,683	6,706	#	#	#
Financial and Other Guar	#	#	#	#	#	#	3,070	129
M/T Insurance Policies	12	−230	7,650	#	452	#	#	#
Total Authorizations	12	−230	7,752	5,683	7,158	2,644	3,070	129
S/T Insurance Shipments	11,617	6,223	6,309	12,621	62,007	95,159	200,694	154,490
Total Auth and Shipments	11,628	5,993	14,061	18,304	69,165	97,803	203,763	154,619
K. GUATEMALA								
Financial and Other Guar	540	#	#	#	#	#	#	#
Bank, Preship, and CNG Guar	1,778	1,775	1,523	3,877	826	#	#	#
M/T Insurance Policies	4,463	3,158	#	11,422	#	#	#	#
Total Authorizations	6,781	4,913	1,523	15,300	826	#	#	#
S/T Insurance Shipments	66,143	44,254	7,055	3,464	34,584	36,581	108,165	85,691
Total Auth and Shipments	72,925	49,167	8,578	18,764	35,410	36,581	108,165	85,691
L. HAITI								
S/T Insurance Shipments	271	1,031	525	836	168	40	2	15
Total Auth and Shipments	271	1,031	525	836	168	40	2	15
M. HONDURAS								
Off Loans	888							
Off Guars and Colps	891	#	#	#	#	#	#	#
Bank, Preship, and CNG Guar	7,011	18,320	327	#	#	#	#	#
Financial and Other Guar	#	#	#	#	#	#	1,029	−637
M/T Insurance Policies	5,171	1,797		#	#	570	119	#
Total Authorizations	13,962	20,117	327	#	#	570	1,148	−637
S/T Insurance Shipments	38,848	26,337	11,806	20,192	19,253	36,707	10,778	4,084
Total Auth and Shipments	52,810	46,454	12,132	20,192	19,253	36,277	11,926	3,447
N. MEXICO								
Direct Loans	654,519	293,448	66,517	10,141	#	#	38,742	#
Intermediary Loans	#	#	#	#	#	#	38,742	33,237
Financial and Other Guar	3,520		54,867	89,031	39,525	#	67,504	48,757
Bank, Preship, and CNG Guar	145,728	95,631	11,021	23,748	92,527	#	#	#
M/T Insurance Policies	144,764	80,503	100,203	82,999	17,482	189,659	81,967	234,530
Total Authorizations	948,530	469,581	232,609	205,919	149,534	335,191	188,213	316,525
S/T Insurance Shipments	858,140	906,192	302,277	478,512	587,868	361,372	468,805	425,866
Total Auth and Shipments	1,780,670	1,375,773	534,885	684,431	737,402	696,563	657,018	742,391
O. NICARAGUA								
M/T Insurance Policies	12	#	#	#	#	#	#	#
Total Authorizations	12	#	#	#	#	#	#	#
S/T Insurance Shipments	−58	4,669	#	#	#	#	#	#
Total Auth and Shipments	−46	4,669	#	#	#	#	#	#
P. PANAMA								
Financial and Other Guar	32,461	#	#	#	#	#	#	#
Bank, Preship, and CNG Guar	2,466	7,054	1,018	383	425	#	#	#
M/T Insurance Policies	2,775	4,096	9,791	395	541	588	#	#
Total Authorizations	37,702	11,149	10,809	778	966	588	#	#
S/T Insurance Shipments	64,753	56,238	21,335	15,849	13,305	17,785	8,840	348
Total Auth and Shipments	102,455	67,338	32,144	16,626	14,271	18,374	8,840	348
Q. PARAGUAY								
Bank, Preship, and CNG Guar	1,048	2,591	36	1,466	#	#	#	3,532
M/T Insurance Policies	2,302	1,666	1,443	2,550	#	#	#	#
Total Authorizations	3,350	4,258	1,479	4,016	#	#	#	3,532
S/T Insurance Shipments	17,886	9,393	483	509	237	233	1,456	1,948
Total Auth and Shipments	21,236	13,650	1,962	4,525	237	233	1,456	5,480
R. PERU								
Direct Loans	8,503	63,890	#	#	#	#	#	#
Off Loans	4,613							
Financial and Other Guar	720	7,568	#	#	#	#	#	#
Off Guars and Colps	3,620	#	#	#	#	#	#	#
Bank, Preship, and CNG Guar	44,543	63,156	16,676	#	#	#	#	#
M/T Insurance Policies	10,344	11,237	1,452	#	#	#	#	#
Total Authorizations	72,343	145,850	18,127	#	#	#	#	#
S/T Insurance Shipments	60,182	51,866	16,034	27,823	2,623	394	13	#
Total Auth and Shipments	132,525	197,715	34,161	27,823	2,623	394	13	#

Table 2821 (Continued)

EX-IM BANK AUTHORIZATIONS BY COUNTRY
(October 1, 1980 – September 30, 1989)

(T US)

Country	1980–81	1981–82	1983–84	1984–85	1985–86	1986–87	1987–88	1988–89[a]
S. URUGUAY								
Direct Loans	14,850	#	#	#	#	#	#	#
Bank, Preship, and CNG Guar	4,244	1,383	4,526	638	#	#	734	#
M/T Insurance Policies	3,078	1,458	850	#	85	#	#	#
Total Authorizations	22,171	2,841	5,376	638	85	#	734	#
S/T Insurance Shipments	23,967	20,525	6,629	5,093	2,771	3,417	4,816	3,932
Total Auth and Shipments	46,138	23,366	12,005	5,730	2,856	3,417	5,551	3,932
V. VENEZUELA								
Direct Loans	59,516	26,000	#	#	#	#	#	#
Off Loans	637	#	#	#	#	#	#	#
Financial and Other Guar	#	#	177,497	#	#	#	42,824	210,306
Bank, Preship, and CNG Guar	51,741	43,102	2,261	#	#	#	#	#
M/T Insurance Policies	69,714	82,974	14,373	272	53	5,449	2,649	#
Total Authorizations	181,607	152,076	194,131	272	53	67,224	83,189	210,306
S/T Insurance Shipments	460,078	392,378	34,378	16,467	7,407	218,253	446,119	299,986
Total Auth and Shipments	641,685	594,454	228,509	16,739	7,460	285,477	529,308	510,291
LATIN AMERICA								
Direct Loans	1,052,875	1,637,244	142,372	195,066	126,305	10,493	55,393	1,938
Intermediary Loans	#	#	#	#	#	#	38,742	35,787
Off Loans	16,644	#	#	#	#	#	#	#
Financial and Other Guar	185,738	119,057	277,062	421,640	113,801	#	197,494	492,952
Off Guars and Colps	11,833	#	#	#	#	#	#	#
Bank, Preship, and CNG Guar	366,207	313,475	145,388	247,232	256,776	#	#	#
M/T Insurance Policies	359,770	286,892	212,450	154,853	108,550	220,801	108,719	329,864
Total Authorizations	1,993,067	2,356,668	777,274	1,018,791	605,432	799,538	400,348	860,542
S/T Insurance Shipments	2,280,860	2,188,518	1,029,127	1,143,839	1,206,861	1,437,155	2,015,548	1,449,966
Total Auth and Shipments	4,273,927	4,545,186	1,806,400	2,162,630	1,812,293	2,236,692	2,415,895	2,310,508

a. October 1, 1988–July 31, 1989.

SOURCE: Data provided by Joe Sorbera, Reports Division, Export-Import Bank.

Table 2822

U.S. PEACE CORPS WORLDWIDE BUDGET, 1961–89

Fiscal Year	Budget Request Dollars (T US)	Appropriated Dollars (T US)	Volunteers (N)
1961	~	~	124
1962	40,000	30,000	2,816
1963	63,750	59,000	6,646
1964	108,000	95,964	10,078
1965	115,000	104,100	13,248
1966	125,200	114,000	15,556
1967	110,500	110,000	14,968
1968	124,400	107,500	13,823
1969	112,800	102,000	12,131
1970	109,800	98,000	9,513
1971	98,800	90,000	7,066
1972	71,200	72,500	6,894
1973	88,027	81,000	7,341
1974	77,000	77,000	8,044
1975	82,256	77,687	7,015
1976	80,826	81,266	5,958
1977	67,155	80,000	5,752
1978	74,800	86,234	7,072
1979	95,135	99,179	6,328
1980	105,404	105,795	5,994
1981	118,800	118,531	5,445
1982	121,900	105,000	5,380
1983	97,500	105,000	5,483
1984	108,500	117,000	5,699
1985	115,000	128,600	6,264
1986	124,400	130,000[a]	5,162
1987	126,200	130,760	4,771
1988	130,682	146,200	4,800[†]
1989	150,000	~	5,200[†]

a. Includes $5,590 sequestered under the Balanced Budget and Emergency Deficit Control Act of 1985.

SOURCE: *The Times of the Americas* (Washington, D.C.), July 9, 1986, p. 14; *Peace Corps Congressional Presentation*, 1989, p. 10.

Table 2823

U.S. PEACE CORPS VOLUNTEERS AND TRAINEES, BY SKILL, WORLDWIDE, 1962–85

Year	Natural Resources N	%	Skilled Trades N	%	Professional Skills[1] N	%	Education N	%	Liberal Arts N	%
1962	310	11	113	4	394	14	394	14	1,605	57
1963	399	6	199	3	997	15	1,130	17	3,921	59
1964	403	4	202	2	1,512	15	1,814	18	6,148	61
1965	530	4	397	3	2,650	20	4,372	33	5,299	40
1966	467	3	311	2	2,333	15	3,733	24	8,712	56
1967	299	2	150	1	1,796	12	3,892	26	8,831	59
1968	691	5	138	1	1,935	14	4,147	30	6,912	50
1969	728	6	121	1	1,698	14	3,882	32	5,702	47
1970	856	9	285	3	1,807	19	2,854	30	3,711	39
1971	777	11	353	5	1,272	18	2,120	30	2,544	36
1972	758	11	345	5	1,448	21	1,999	29	2,344	34
1973	881	12	441	6	1,468	20	2,055	28	2,496	34
1974	965	12	321	4	1,770	22	2,494	31	2,494	31
1975	1,052	15	421	6	1,403	20	2,034	29	2,105	30
1976	894	15	238	4	1,370	23	2,086	35	1,370	23
1977	920	16	230	4	1,438	25	1,898	33	1,266	22
1978	1,202	17	283	4	1,839	26	2,263	32	1,485	21
1979	1,266	20	316	5	1,709	27	1,898	30	1,139	18
1980	1,319	22	360	6	1,738	29	1,618	27	959	16
1981	1,143	21	382	7	1,742	32	1,416	26	762	14
1982	968	18	377	7	1,883	35	1,453	27	699	13
1983	987	18	329	6	1,919	35	1,480	27	768	14
1984	969	17	285	5	1,881	33	1,709	30	855	15
1985	1,002	16	313	5	2,130	34	1,879	30	940	15

1. Professional Skills include business, engineering, health, and social work.

SOURCE: Gerard T. Rice, *Peace Corps In the 80's* (Washington, D.C.: Peace Corps, Office of Public Affairs, December 1985), p. 33.

Table 2824

U.S. PEACE CORPS VOLUNTEERS, BY SKILL CLASSIFICATION, 9 L

(N, 1980)

	Country	Health	Nutrition	Food	Water	Knowledge/ Skills	Economic Development	Housing	Energy Conservation	Community Services	Total
	Belize	9	0	8	0	27	7	0	0	7	58
C.	BRAZIL	5	0	0	0	17	0	0	2	0	24

Continued in SALA, 25–2854.

Table 2825

U.S. PEACE CORPS SERVICE IN LATIN AMERICA, 17 L

(1986)

	Country	Entered	Departed
B.	BOLIVIA	1962	1971
C.	BRAZIL	1962	1981
D.	CHILE	1961	1982
E.	COLOMBIA	1961	1981
F.	COSTA RICA	1963	**
H.	DOMINICAN REP.	1962	**
I.	ECUADOR	1962	**
J.	EL SALVADOR	1962	1980
K.	GUATEMALA	1963	**
L.	HAITI	1983	**
M.	HONDURAS	1963	**
O.	NICARAGUA	1968	1979
P.	PANAMA	1963	1971
Q.	PARAGUAY	1967	**
R.	PERU	1962	1975
S.	URUGUAY	1963	1974
T.	VENEZUELA	1962	1977

SOURCE: Select Committee on Hunger, U.S. House of Representatives, *The Peace Corps: 25 Years of Alleviating Hunger* (Washington, D.C.: U.S. Government Printing Office, March 1986), Chart 2.

Table 2826

U.S. PEACE CORPS BUDGETS, TRAINEES, VOLUNTEERS, AND
FULL-TIME EQUIVALENTS (FTEs), 8 L, 1984–89[a]

Country	Fiscal Year	Budget Funds (T US)	Trainees	Volunteer Years	FTE Level
F. COSTA RICA	1984	1,826	65	119	11.1
	1985	3,464	190	134	14.0
	1986	3,806	190	230	16.0
	1987	2,950	105	169	16.0
	1988	3,235	125	164	15.9
	1989	3,411	130	188	16.0
H. DOMINICAN REP.	1984	2,316	68	127	10.7
	1985	2,408	70	101	10.0
	1986	2,103	65	90	10.0
	1987	2,357	66	138	10.6
	1988	2,343	85	122	11.4
	1989	2,358	100	120	12.0
I. ECUADOR	1984	3,401	151	249	16.8
	1985	3,115	98	191	16.0
	1986	2,417	68	164	14.0
	1987	3,212	121	150	14.8
	1988	3,563	110	195	16.5
	1989	3,668	125	196	17.0
K. GUATEMALA	1984	2,605	117	129	12.0
	1985	3,525	120	156	13.0
	1986	3,584	120	168	13.0
	1987	3,076	140	188	14.2
	1988	4,057	157	222	15.0
	1989	3,865	130	240	15.0
L. HAITI	1984	428	15	0	2.3
	1985	812	20	24	4.0
	1986	771	20	31	4.0
	1987	998	15	42	6.9
	1988	1,189	75	28	7.0
	1989	1,534	60	60	7.0
M. HONDURAS	1984	3,788	149	216	16.1
	1985	5,171	202	225	19.0
	1986	5,809	200	360	21.0
	1987	5,169	134	281	21.0
	1988	5,615	229	244	21.0
	1989	5,694	175	303	21.0
P. PANAMA	1984	~	~	~	~
	1985	~	~	~	~
	1986	800	36	10	3.0
	1987	~	~	~	~
	1988	~	~	~	~
	1989	~	~	~	~
Q. PARAGUAY	1984	2,088	74	137	12.0
	1985	2,236	60	136	12.0
	1986	1,725	41	94	10.0
	1987	1,958	85	92	12.0
	1988	2,378	98	123	12.0
	1989	2,475	100	143	12.0

a. For 1975–81, see SALA, 25-2852.

SOURCE: *Peace Corps Congressional Presentation*, 1986, p. 46; 1989, p. 59.

Figure 28:1

PEACE CORPS OFFICES, 3 LC

(September 1985)

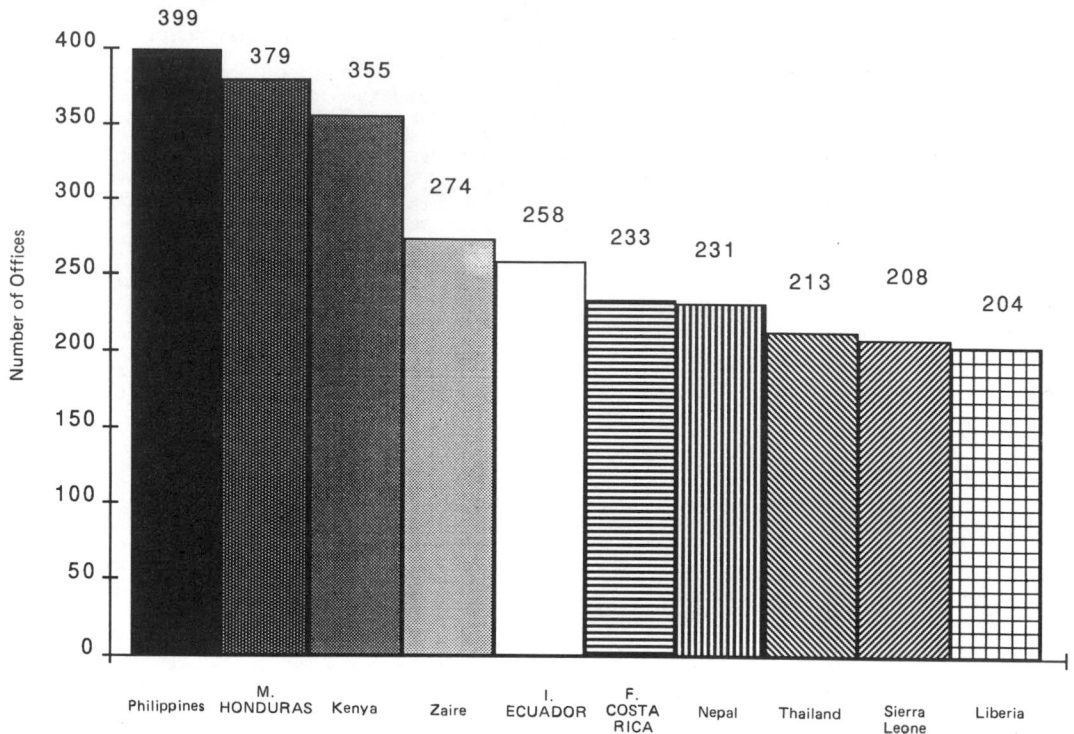

SOURCE: Gerard T. Rice, *Peace Corps in the 80s* (Washington, D.C.: Peace Corps, Office of
Public Affairs, December 1985), p. 37.

Table 2827

INTER-AMERICAN FOUNDATION GRANTS,
BY PROGRAM AREA,[1] 1986–87
(%)

Program Area	1971–87	1986	1987
Agriculture and Rural Development	43	48	46
Education and Training	18	13	22
Community Services	15	18	15
Urban Enterprises	12	15	12
Learning and Dissemination	9	5	4
Cultural Expression	3	1	1
Total (M US)	250.1	19.0	19.6

1. Includes grants and supplements.

SOURCE: *Inter-American Foundation Annual Report*, 1986, p. 8; 1987, p. 13.

Table 2828

INTER-AMERICAN FOUNDATION[1] FUND ACCOUNT FOR LATIN AMERICA
AND THE CARIBBEAN, 1971–87
(T US)

	Budget Sources					Expenditures				
Fiscal Year	Appropriations	%	Social Progress Trust Fund	%	Total Allocated	Grants and Other Programs[2]	%	Administrative Costs	%	Total Budget
1971	~	~	~	~	..	..	..	376	100	376
1972	2,794	100	~	~	2,794	2,794	71	1,125	29	3,919
1973	2,998	100	~	~	2,998	2,998	67	1,482	33	4,480
1974	7,210	57	5,494	43	12,704	12,704	89	1,604	11	14,308
1975	4,524	33	9,126	67	13,650	13,650	88	1,889	12	15,539
1976	5,257	42	7,335	58	12,592	12,592	83	2,552	17	15,144
1977	4,240	28	11,004	72	15,244	15,244	88	2,181	12	17,425
1978	3,905	32	8,280	68	12,185	12,185	85	2,219	15	14,404
1979	10,543	61	6,815	39	17,358	17,358	88	2,488	12	19,846
1980	8,945	39	14,017	61	22,962	22,962	89	2,943	11	25,905
1981	11,691	52	10,896	48	22,587	22,587	87	3,330	13	25,917
1982	11,952	53	10,458	47	22,410	22,410	86	3,631	14	26,041
1983	9,657	51	9,256	49	18,913	18,913	83	3,894	17	22,807
1984	9,041	47	10,180	53	19,221	19,221	82	4,095	18	23,316
1985	8,974	36	15,735	64	24,709	24,709	85	4,465	15	29,174
1986	~	~	~	~	~	22,000	82	4,700	18	26,700
1987	~	~	~	~	~	22,300	83	4,400	17	26,700
Total	~	~	~	~	~	264,627	84	47,374	21	312,001

1. The Foundations's funds come from Congressional appropriations and from the Social Progress Trust Fund. The Fund, which is administered by the Inter-American Development Bank, holds repayments from loans made under the Alliance for Progress by the U.S. government to Latin American and Caribbean countries.
2. Other program activities have included such items as evaluations, fellowships, in-country technical assistance, and publications. Approximately 9 million dollars has been utilized for this purpose during fiscal years 1972–85.

SOURCE: 1971–85, *The Times of the Americas* (Washington, D.C.), Oct. 15, 1986, Part B, p. 8; 1986–87, *Inter-American Foundation Annual Report*, 1987, p. 13.

Table 2829

INTER-AMERICAN FOUNDATION GRANTS,
19 L, 1972–87

(T US)

	Country	1985	1986	1987	1972–87
A.	ARGENTINA	922	1,391	2,420	12,809
B.	BOLIVIA	1,646	1,166	863	15,437
C.	BRAZIL	1,594	1,979	1,941	14,852
D.	CHILE	1,251	1,137	1,094	31,886
E.	COLOMBIA	2,169	1,666	937	22,918
F.	COSTA RICA	2,038	1,224	610	8,583
H.	DOMINICAN REP.	367	968	567	10,454
I.	ECUADOR	634	1,004	1,269	8,577
J.	EL SALVADOR	12	323	805	4,739
K.	GUATEMALA	1,009	560	1,116	7,338
L.	HAITI	838	850	1,697	6,998
M.	HONDURAS	545	657	558	8,017
N.	MEXICO	1,130	771	947	17,002
O.	NICARAGUA	730	6	0	6,721
P.	PANAMA	656	929	876	7,642
Q.	PARAGUAY	721	154	640	10,754
R.	PERU	2,126	1,613	1,012	21,304
S.	URUGUAY	435	815	504	10,832
T.	VENEZUELA	768	582	656	3,010
	TOTAL	19,591	18,817	19,553	250,106

SOURCE: Adapted from *The Times of the Americas* (Washington, D.C.), Oct. 15, 1986,
Part B, p. 8; *Inter-American Foundation Annual Report*, p. 63, 1986; *Inter-American
Foundation Annual Report*, pp. 62–63.

Table 2830

CONGRESSIONAL APPROPRIATIONS
TO INTER-AMERICAN FOUNDATION

(FY, M US)

Year	Amount
1970–1978	50.0
1979	10.0
1980	12.6
1981	15.8
1982	12.0
1983	14.0
1984	13.0
1985	12.0
1986	11.5
1987	11.8
1988	13.0

SOURCE: *Inter-American Foundation Annual Report*, 1986, p. 61;
1987, p. 61.

Table 2831

INTER-AMERICAN DEVELOPMENT BANK LOANS, YEARLY LENDING, 19 L, 1974–88
(M US)

Country	1974	1975	1977	1978	1979	1980	1981
A. ARGENTINA	89.1	201.0	317.8	57.1	280.5	359.2	292.4
B. BOLIVIA	46.2	54.1	83.3	180.7	12.2	42.6	97.0
C. BRAZIL	187.0	269.5	361.5	283.2	365.5	424.4	383.1
D. CHILE	97.3	70.7	24.5	54.0	~	19.9	161.0
E. COLOMBIA	#	75.8	112.7	199.0	151.0	194.6	180.6
F. COSTA RICA	53.8	41.6	79.6	90.0	35.9	132.9	35.2
H. DOMINICAN REP.	36.7	35.5	#	66.3	195.5	80.5	71.8
I. ECUADOR	55.5	43.7	73.1	94.3	210.0	84.5	168.5
J. EL SALVADOR	33.4	43.0	109.4	13.2	47.8	63.4	52.4
K. GUATEMALA	19.4	120.6	60.5	#	15.0	76.5	112.5
L. HAITI	#	41.1	15.7	43.5	4.1	10.1	8.7
M. HONDURAS	35.6	28.7	32.0	114.0	15.8	67.6	7.5
N. MEXICO	186.4	167.3	256.9	238.2	266.4	284.0	279.0
O. NICARAGUA	10.5	16.5	20.0	32.0	81.5	70.6	8.0
P. PANAMA	14.5	42.2	122.0	19.0	27.6	77.7	90.2
Q. PARAGUAY	49.0	3.2	13.8	60.5	32.4	27.4	32.5
R. PERU	65.5	16.0	21.0	29.5	148.6	177.6	226.7
S. URUGUAY	21.4	35.4	29.7	#	35.5	57.5	78.0
T. VENEZUELA	#	#	#	#	#	#	#

Country	1982	1983	1984	1985	1986	1987	1988
A. ARGENTINA	402.4	80.1	458.8	108.9	516.3	13.1	291.4
B. BOLIVIA	201.0	58.9	78.0	~	20.9	89.7	121.2
C. BRAZIL	372.2	441.0	393.7	395.3	428.8	369.9	7.1
D. CHILE	302.5	548.0	293.3	522.5	359.8	~	136.7
E. COLOMBIA	191.2	405.9	405.0	413.3	87.0	546.6	200.0
F. COSTA RICA	67.4	41.8	92.6	6.0	179.9	112.8	61.1
H. DOMINICAN REP.	155.4	96.2	205.5	146.2	140.0	.4	2.7
I. ECUADOR	101.4	83.3	306.4	274.4	272.7	263.5	~
J. EL SALVADOR	128.4	25.0	110.2	26.2	25.2	169.3	7.2
K. GUATEMALA	46.0	167.9	13.9	192.0	65.8	43.8	10.6
L. HAITI	33.4	18.8	.4	27.4	56.5	~	~
M. HONDURAS	49.0	130.2	42.0	69.8	122.9	1.5	58.4
N. MEXICO	323.2	286.2	229.8	401.5	327.9	164.1	204.0
O. NICARAGUA	35.1	30.5	~	~	~	~	~
P. PANAMA	37.3	112.0	8.4	52.8	98.4	16.7	~
Q. PARAGUAY	98.3	48.6	37.5	~	~	32.1	47.8
R. PERU	180.1	264.9	195.8	14.5	19.2	85.9	18.0
S. URUGUAY	10.0	50.0	119.8	21.6	73.2	153.2	~
T. VENEZUELA	#	30.0	448.3	238.0	~	225.0	50.0

SOURCE: *IMF Survey*, April 17, 1978, p. 115; IDB-AR, 1980; 1982, p. 41; and 1985,
p. 47, 1986, p. 47; 1987, p. 51; 1988, p. 47.

Table 2832

INTER-AMERICAN DEVELOPMENT BANK LOAN DISTRIBUTION BY SECTOR, 1961–86

(M US)

Sector	1986	%	1961–86	%
Productive Sectors				
Agriculture and Fishing	636.0	20.9	7,483.1	21.1
Mining and Industry	102.0	3.4	5,639.4	15.9
Tourism	156.0	5.2	511.0	1.4
Physical Infrastructure				
Energy	750.7	24.7	9,777.2	27.6
Transportation, Communication	362.9	11.9	4,544.7	12.8
Social Infrastructure				
Public Health and Welfare	468.6	15.5	3,175.9	9.0
Education, Science, Technology	179.2	5.9	1,584.0	4.5
Urban Development	288.8	9.5	1,443.1	4.1
Other				
Export Financing	68.4	2.2	713.1	2.0
Preinvestment	7.2	.2	407.8	1.2
Other	17.2	.6	158.5	.4
Total	3,037.0	100	35,437.7	100

SOURCE: Mexico-BNCE-CE, June 1987, p. 465.

Table 2833

RESOURCES OF IDB'S SOCIAL PROGRESS TRUST FUND

(M US)

Year	Amount
1974–1976	31.0
1977–1979	48.0
1980–1982	48.0
1983–1985	48.0
1986–1988	48.6

SOURCE: *Inter-American Foundation Annual Report*, 1986, p. 61.

Table 2834

U.S. VOTING POWER IN MULTILATERAL AGENCIES

(%)

	United States	Central America
IMF	20.0	.8
IBRD	20.8	.6
IDA	21.4	1.2
IFC	28.4	.6
IDB	34.6	3.1

SOURCE: Tom Berry et al., *Dollars and Dictators* (Albuquerque, N.M.: The Resource Center, 1982), p. 55.

Table 2835

INTERNATIONAL FOOD AID IN CEREALS, 20 L
(T MET)

	Country	1974/75	1984/85	1985/86	1986/87
A.	ARGENTINA	~	~	~	~
B.	BOLIVIA	22	111	293	219
C.	BRAZIL	31	10	6	7
D.	CHILE	323	10	10	18
E.	COLOMBIA	28	4	6	0
F.	COSTA RICA	1	164	119	54
G.	CUBA	~	~	~	~
H.	DOMINICAN REP.	16	107	125	117
I.	ECUADOR	13	18	5	~
J.	EL SALVADOR	4	194	278	227
K.	GUATEMALA	9	23	53	~
L.	HAITI	25	101	133	89
M.	HONDURAS	31	118	135	137
N.	MEXICO	~	6	11	4
O.	NICARAGUA	3	43	41	35
P.	PANAMA	3	1	0	1
Q.	PARAGUAY	10	4	4	~
R.	PERU	37	216	180	237
S.	URUGUAY	6	~	0	0
T.	VENEZUELA	- -	- -	- -	- -

SOURCE: WB-WDR, 1987, table 6; 1988, table 7.

Table 2836

PERU MAJOR SOURCES OF FOREIGN AID, 1978–87
(M US)

Source	Amount	Implementation	Terms	Objectives
Pan American Health Organization	1.100	1978–84	Grant	Maternal and child health care
World Bank	33.500	1983–88	Loan	Primary Health care expansion
Interamerican Development Bank	.675	1982–84	Grant	Health care training
US Agency for International Development	5.800 1.350	1979–85	Loan Grant	Primary health care expansion
US Agency for International Development	4.000 6.900	1981–86	Loan Grant	Primary health care expansion and family planning
US Agency for International Development	10.000 1.000	1980–87	Loan Grant	Potable water and basic sanitation for villages
German Technical Assistance Program	4.000 1.400	1980–85	Loan Grant	Primary health care expansion and hospital renovation
Subtotal	57.300 12.325		Loan Grant	
Total	69.625			

SOURCE: Dieter K. Zschock, ed., *Health Care in Peru: Resources and Policy* (Boulder, Colo.: Westview Press, 1986), p. 227.

29

Debt

Editor's Note: Since the "debt crisis" began in 1982, international agencies have sought to monitor more closely figures reported by national governments, which prior to 1982 tried to understate and/or conceal the full extent of the indebtedness. With each year since 1982, retrospective data have been improved and each subsequent revision for any year gives even higher totals. For discussion and a case study of ECLA successive revisions of data between 1978 and 1984, see "Views of Latin America's Reality," SALA, 25, pp. ix–xvii. See also Figure 29:1 in this chapter. For the report by an international working group on external debt statistics of the World Bank, IMF, Bank for International Settlements, and OECD, see *External Debt: Definitions, Statistical Coverage, and Methodology* (Paris, 1988). Because of varying definitions and parameters, data on the debt depend upon the agency making the calculation and the year of calculation.

Table 2900

TOTAL PUBLIC AND PRIVATE EXTERNAL DEBT, 19 L
(1987)

	Country	B US
A.	ARGENTINA	54.5
B.	BOLIVIA	4.4
C.	BRAZIL	116.9
D.	CHILE	20.5
E.	COLOMBIA	15.7
F.	COSTA RICA	3.8
H.	DOMINICAN REP.	3.7
I.	ECUADOR	9.6
J.	EL SALVADOR	2.2
K.	GUATEMALA	2.7
L.	HAITI[1]	.7
M.	HONDURAS	3.1
N.	MEXICO	105.6
O.	NICARAGUA	6.2
P.	PANAMA	4.9
Q.	PARAGUAY	2.0
R.	PERU	15.3
S.	URUGUAY	5.6
T.	VENEZUELA	32.2

1. Public debt.

SOURCE: *The Times of the Americas* (Washington, D.C.), Nov. 2-16, 1988, p. 35.

Table 2901

TOTAL EXTERNAL DEBT, 19 L, 1970, 1987

	Country	Long-Term (M US)				Use of IMF Credit (M US)		Short-Term Debt (M US)		Total External Debt (M US)	
		Public and Publicly Guaranteed		Private Nonguaranteed							
		1970	1987	1970	1987	1970	1987	1970	1987	1970	1987
A.	ARGENTINA	1,880	47,451	3,291	2,858	0	3,854	~	2,651	~	56,813
B.	BOLIVIA	480	4,599	11	200	6	141	~	608	~	5,548
C.	BRAZIL	3,421	91,653	1,706	14,434	0	3,977	~	13,868	~	123,932
D.	CHILE	2,067	15,536	501	2,466	2	1,465	~	1,772	~	21,239
E.	COLOMBIA	1,297	13,828	283	1,524	55	0	~	1,654	~	17,006
F.	COSTA RICA	134	3,629	112	290	0	132	~	676	~	4,727
H.	DOMINICAN REP.	212	2,938	141	133	7	284	~	341	~	3,695
I.	ECUADOR	193	9,026	49	30	14	490	~	891	~	10,437
J.	EL SALVADOR	88	1,597	88	70	7	6	~	89	~	1,762
K.	GUATEMALA	106	2,345	14	116	0	59	~	305	~	2,825
L.	HAITI	40	674	0	0	2	52	~	79	~	804
M.	HONDURAS	90	2,681	19	115	0	68	~	439	~	3,303
N.	MEXICO	3,196	82,771	2,770	14,148	0	5,163	~	5,800	~	107,882
O.	NICARAGUA	147	6,150	0	0	8	0	~	1,141	~	7,291
P.	PANAMA	194	3,722	0	0	0	346	~	1,256	~	5,324
Q.	PARAGUAY	112	2,218	~	28	0	0	~	201	~	2,447
R.	PERU	856	12,485	1,799	1,433	10	845	~	3,295	~	18,058
S.	URUGUAY	269	3,048	29	144	18	392	~	651	~	4,235
T.	VENEZUELA	728	25,245	236	7,504	0	0	~	3,770	~	36,519

SOURCE: World Development Report, 1989, table 21, pp. 204-205.

Table 2902

TOTAL EXTERNAL PUBLIC AND PRIVATE DEBT AND DEBT SERVICE RATIOS, 19 L, 1970, 1987

| | | Total Long-Term Debt Disbursed and Outstanding | | | | Total Interest Payments On Long-Term Debt M US | | Total Long-Term Debt % | | | |
| | | M US | | % of GNP | | | | GNP | | Exports of Goods and Services | |
	Country	1970	1987	1970	1987	1970	1987	1970	1987	1970	1987
A.	ARGENTINA	5,171	50,309	23.8	65.5	338	3,775	5.1	5.8	51.7	52.0
B.	BOLIVIA	491	4,799	49.3	115.6	7	62	2.6	3.3	12.6	22.1
C.	BRAZIL	5,128	106,087	12.2	33.7	224	5,834	1.6	3.0	21.8	33.2
D.	CHILE	2,568	18,002	32.1	103.6	104	1,420	3.9	9.9	24.5	26.4
E.	COLOMBIA	1,580	15,352	22.5	45.3	59	1,177	2.8	7.6	19.0	36.3
F.	COSTA RICA	246	3,919	25.3	95.9	14	139	5.7	5.3	19.9	14.3
H.	DOMINICAN REP.	353	3,071	26.1	66.3	13	106	2.9	4.1	15.2	~
I.	ECUADOR	242	9,056	14.8	93.2	10	279	2.2	5.4	14.0	21.9
J.	EL SALVADOR	176	1,667	17.3	36.0	9	76	3.1	4.2	12.0	21.0
K.	GUATEMALA	120	2,461	6.5	35.8	7	153	1.6	4.4	8.2	25.8
L.	HAITI	40	674	10.2	30.2	0	9	1.0	1.0	59.4	7.0
M.	HONDURAS	109	2,796	15.6	73.6	4	92	1.4	6.8	5.0	26.1
N.	MEXICO	5,966	96,919	16.2	69.6	283	7,091	3.5	8.2	44.3	38.4
O.	NICARAGUA	147	6,150	19.5	207.8	7	12	3.0	1.2	10.5	~
P.	PANAMA	194	3,722	19.5	72.6	7	226	3.1	7.5	7.7	6.5
Q.	PARAGUAY	~	2,246	~	49.5	~	96	~	5.0	~	21.7
R.	PERU	2,655	13,918	37.3	31.2	162	203	7.0	1.0	40.0	12.9
S.	URUGUAY	298	3,192	12.5	44.2	17	273	2.9	5.9	23.6	25.7
T.	VENEZUELA	964	32,749	7.6	67.8	53	2,518	.9	8.5	4.3	32.4

SOURCE: World Development Report, 1989, table 23, pp. 208-209.

Table 2903

COMPOSITION OF DEBT OUTSTANDING, 12 L, 1970–87

(% of Total Long-Term Debt)

| | | Debt from Official Sources | | | Debt from Private Sources | | | Debt at Floating Rate | | |
	Country	1970–72	1980–82	1987	1970–72	1980–82	1987	1973–75	1980–82	1987
A.	ARGENTINA	12.6	9.0	14.2	87.4	91.0	85.8	6.6	29.2	79.3
B.	BOLIVIA	58.2	50.3	73.3	41.8	49.7	26.7	7.4	28.0	27.9
C.	BRAZIL	30.7	12.6	24.1	69.3	88.3	76.2	26.1	46.1	58.3
D.	CHILE	47.0	11.0	22.0	53.0	89.0	78.0	8.3	23.4	68.2
E.	COLOMBIA	68.2	46.1	53.8	31.8	53.9	46.2	5.4	33.7	36.8
F.	COSTA RICA	39.8	36.8	51.0	60.2	63.2	49.0	15.6	42.4	49.8
I.	ECUADOR	51.8	30.6	34.9	48.2	69.4	65.1	8.2	36.5	68.6
K.	GUATEMALA	47.5	71.0	66.0	52.5	29.0	34.0	3.5	5.6	29.4
N.	MEXICO	19.5	10.9	16.4	80.5	89.1	83.6	32.0	61.7	67.6
R.	PERU	15.5	39.3	46.0	84.5	60.7	54.0	16.1	23.0	29.9
S.	URUGUAY	44.2	21.1	20.3	55.8	78.9	79.7	10.1	28.5	65.0
T.	VENEZUELA	29.9	3.0	3.4	70.1	97.0	96.6	17.1	60.3	68.7

SOURCE: World Development Report, 1989, table A12.

Figure 29:1

THREE ECLA VIEWS OF LATIN AMERICA'S TOTAL DISBURSED FOREIGN DEBT, 1978–84

(B US YE)

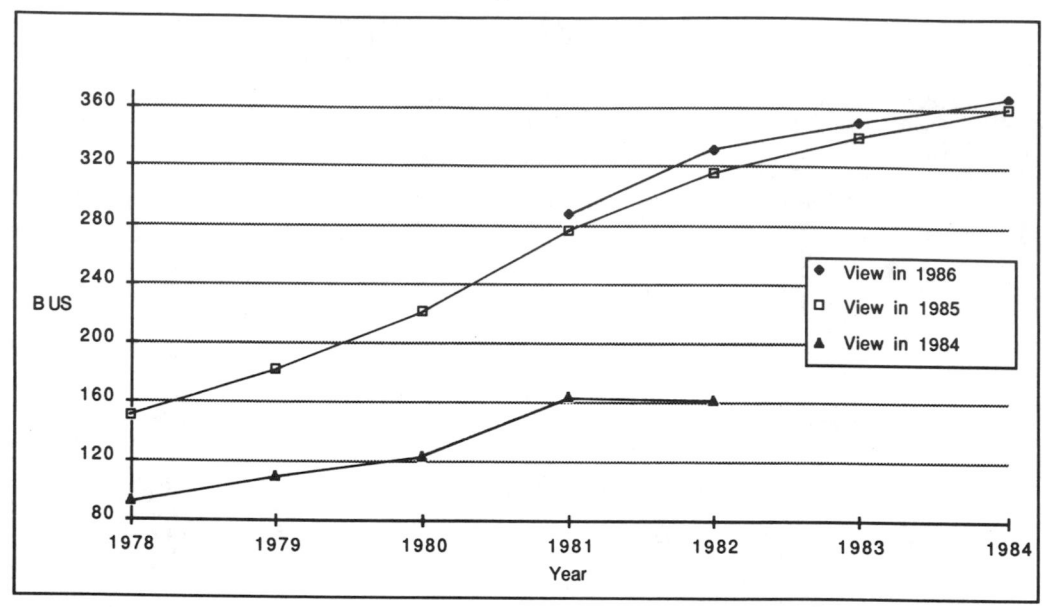

SOURCE: SALA, 25, p. xii.

Table 2904

ECLA DATA ON DISBURSED PORTION OF THE EXTERNAL DEBT,[1] 19 L, 1979–88[‡]

Grouping and Country	Balance at Year End (M US)						Annual Growth Rates				
	1983	1984	1985	1986	1987	1988[‡]	1979–1981	1982–1983	1984–1986	1987	1988[‡]
Latin America	352,183	369,848	376,667	389,336	410,505	401,360	23.3	11.0	3.4	5.4	−2.2
Petroleum Exporters	152,626	156,589	156,406	158,873	164,158	159,230	25.5	9.5	1.3	3.1	−3.0
B. BOLIVIA	3,265	3,272	3,287	3,636	4,215	3,930	15.8	7.7	3.7	15.9	−6.8
I. ECUADOR	6,908	7,198	7,772	8,624	9,900	10,500	25.5	8.5	7.7	14.8	6.1
N. MEXICO	93,800	96,700	97,800	100,500	102,350	96,700	30.8	12.0	2.3	1.8	−5.5
R. PERU	12,445	13,338	13,721	14,477	15,441	16,200	1.0	14.0	5.2	6.7	4.9
T. VENEZUELA[2]	36,208	36,081	33,826	31,636	32,252	31,900	27.5	4.1	−4.4	1.9	−1.1
Non-Petroleum Exporters	199,557	213,259	220,261	230,463	246,347	242,130	21.7	12.1	4.9	6.9	−1.7
A. ARGENTINA	45,069	46,903	48,312	51,400	54,700	56,800	42.1	12.8	4.5	6.4	3.8
C. BRAZIL	98,175[a]	105,275[a]	106,731[a]	111,045	121,264	114,600	14.4	10.8	4.2	9.2	−5.5
D. CHILE	18,037	19,659	20,403	20,716	20,551	19,100	30.7	7.6	4.7	−.8	−7.1
E. COLOMBIA	11,458	12,350	14,063	14,987	15,651	15,900	28.0	16.1	9.3	4.4	1.6
F. COSTA RICA	3,532	3,752	3,742	3,791	3,914	4,100	13.3	14.7	2.4	3.2	4.8
H. DOMINICAN REP.	3,313	3,536	3,690	3,525	3,680	3,840	24.4	14.0	2.1	4.4	4.3
J. EL SALVADOR	1,890	1,949	1,980	1,928	1,876	1,850	19.1	8.4	.7	−2.7	−1.4
K. GUATEMALA	2,149	2,505	2,695	2,668	2,718	2,840	19.3	24.8	7.5	1.9	4.5
L. HAITI[3]	551	607	600	697	741	800	21.1	22.3	8.2	6.3	8.0
M. HONDURAS	2,162	2,392	2,794	3,018	3,101	3,230	17.8	17.0	11.8	2.8	4.2
O. NICARAGUA[3]	3,788	4,362	4,936	5,760	6,270	6,700	27.4	21.5	15.0	8.9	6.9
P. PANAMA[4]	3,392	3,644	3,642	3,835	3,950	4,170	7.5	20.6	4.2	3.0	5.6
Q. PARAGUAY	1,469	1,654	1,773	1,855	2,043	2,150	12.4	24.4	8.1	10.1	5.2
S. URUGUAY	4,572	4,671	4,900	5,238	5,888	6,050	36.1	22.0	4.6	12.4	2.8

1. Includes debt with IMF.
2. Total debt according to official information and international financial organizations.
3. Public sector debt.
4. Total debt according to information from the World Bank.

a. Total debt according to information from the World Bank.

SOURCE: ECLA-AE, 1988, pp. 778–779.

Table 2905

ECLA DATA ON DISBURSED FOREIGN DEBT,[1] 19 LR, 1978–87

(B US YE)

Grouping and Country	1978	1980	1981	1982	1983	1984	1985	1986	1987[†]
Petroleum Exporters	64,390	96,894	126,691	143,201	152,626	156,589	156,406	158,873	164,168
B. BOLIVIA	1,762	2,340	2,824	2,889	3,265	3,272	3,287	3,636	4,215
I. ECUADOR	2,975	4,652	5,868	6,186	6,908	7,198	7,772	8,624	9,900
N. MEXICO	33,946	50,700	74,900	87,600	93,800	96,800	97,800	101,500	102,350
R. PERU	9,324	9,594	9,688	11,465	12,445	13,338	13,721	14,477	15,441
T. VENEZUELA	16,383	29,608	33,411	35,061	36,208	36,081	33,826	31,636	32,252
Non-Petroleum Exporters	86,503	133,464	158,841	186,140	199,577	213,259	220,261	230,463	242,130
A. ARGENTINA	12,496	27,162	35,671	43,634	45,069	46,903	48,312	51,400	54,700
C. BRAZIL	52,285	70,025	79,978[b]	91,576[b]	98,175[b]	105,275[b]	106,731[b]	111,045	121,264
D. CHILE	6,664	11,207	15,591	17,159	18,037	19,659	20,403	20,716	20,551
E. COLOMBIA	4,247	6,300	8,042	10,269	11,408	12,350	14,063	14,987	15,651
F. COSTA RICA	1,870	3,183	3,360	3,188	3,532	3,752	3,742	3,791	3,914
H. DOMINICAN REP.	1,309	2,059	2,886	2,966	3,313	3,536	3,690	3,525	3,680
J. EL SALVADOR	986	1,176	1,608	1,710	1,890	1,949	1,980	1,928	1,876
K. GUATEMALA	821	972	1,385	1,841	2,149	2,505	2,695	2,668	2,718
L. HAITI[a]	210	290	372	410	551	607	600	697	741
M. HONDURAS	971	1,510	1,508	1,986	2,162	2,392	2,794	3,018	3,101
O. NICARAGUA[a]	961	1,825	2,566	3,139	3,789	4,362	4,936	5,760	6,270
P. PANAMA[a]	1,774	~	~	2,820	3,392	3,644	3,642	3,835	3,950
Q. PARAGUAY	669	861	949	1,204	1,469	1,654	1,773	1,855	2,043
S. URUGUAY	1,240	2,138	3,112	4,238	4,572	4,670	4,900	5,258	5,888
LATIN AMERICA	150,893	230,358	285,532	329,341	352,183	369,848	376,677	389,336	410,505

1. Comparability varies between countries and over time. Data for any country may or
   may not include short-term debts (less than 90 days or one year) and/or debts non-
   guaranteed by government. Debt of the private commercial banks is generally excluded,
   except for Mexico after the 1982 nationalization of the private banking system.

a. Public debt.
b. Including the total medium-term and long-term debt plus the short-term debt with
   financial institutions reporting to the Bank for International Settlements.

SOURCE: ECLA-SP, 1985, p. 32; 1986, p. 21; 1988, pp. 500–501.

Table 2906

ECLA DATA ON RELATIONSHIP BETWEEN TOTAL PUBLIC AND PRIVATE INTEREST PAYMENTS AND THE EXPORTATION OF GOODS AND SERVICES,[1] 20 LC, 1977–85

(%)

Country	1977	1978	1979	1980	1981	1982	1983	1984	1985[‡]
Non-Petroleum Exporters									
A. ARGENTINA	7.6	9.6	12.8	22.0	35.5	53.6	58.4	58.7	54.5
C. BRAZIL	18.9	24.5	31.5	34.1	40.4	57.1	43.5	38.7	43.5
D. CHILE	13.7	17.0	16.5	19.3	38.8	49.5	39.4	50.0	46.5
E. COLOMBIA	7.4	7.7	10.1	11.8	21.8	25.8	26.5	23.6	23.0
F. COSTA RICA	7.1	9.9	12.8	18.0	28.0	36.1	32.8	30.7	28.0
G. CUBA	~	~	~	~	~	~	~	~	~
H. DOMINICAN REP.	8.8	14.0	14.4	14.7	20.2	22.6	24.5	19.7	18.5
J. EL SALVADOR	2.9	5.1	5.3	5.9	7.9	11.9	12.3	13.2	14.0
K. GUATEMALA	2.4	3.6	3.1	5.3	7.5	7.8	8.7	8.9	11.5
L. HAITI	2.3	2.8	3.3	2.0	2.5	2.2	2.4	5.3	5.0
M. HONDURAS	7.2	8.2	8.6	10.6	14.5	22.4	16.4	17.1	17.0
O. NICARAGUA	7.0	9.3	9.7	17.8	22.2	32.2	14.3	11.7	17.0
P. PANAMA	~	~	~	~	~	~	~	~	~
Q. PARAGUAY	6.7	8.5	10.7	14.3	16.4	15.6	16.4	14.3	13.0
S. URUGUAY	9.8	10.4	9.0	11.0	12.9	22.4	24.8	33.8	35.5
TOTAL	11.9	15.1	18.8	23.1	32.7	45.2	39.4	38.7	40.0
Petroleum Exporters									
B. BOLIVIA	9.9	13.7	18.1	24.5	32.1	43.5	44.4	63.1	60.0
I. ECUADOR	4.8	10.3	13.6	18.2	24.3	30.1	27.4	27.8	24.5
N. MEXICO	25.4	24.0	24.8	23.3	29.0	46.0	39.3	40.2	37.0
R. PERU	17.9	21.2	14.7	16.0	24.1	25.1	29.8	34.0	34.5
T. VENEZUELA	4.0	7.2	6.9	8.1	12.7	21.0	21.6	17.5	22.5
TOTAL	13.0	16.0	15.7	16.6	22.6	35.1	32.4	32.2	32.0
LATIN AMERICA	12.4	15.5	17.4	19.9	27.6	40.5	35.9	35.7	36.0

1. Interest payments include short-term debt interest.

SOURCE: Mexico, NAFINSA-MV, January 1984, No. 4, p. 89; and February 1985, No. 5, pp. 134–135.

Table 2907

U.S. DATA ON COMPOSITION OF DEBT OUTSTANDING, 12 L, 1970–86

(% of Total Long-Term Debt)

Total = 100

Country	Official			Private			% at Floating Exchange Rates		
	1970–72	1980–82	1986	1970–72	1980–82	1986	1973–75	1980–82	1986
A. ARGENTINA	9.5	6.7	11.4	65.5	68.3	88.6	4.9	21.9	74.4
B. BOLIVIA	43.7	38.6	57.6	31.3	36.4	42.4	5.5	19.8	20.4
C. BRAZIL	23.0	9.4	20.6	52.0	65.6	79.4	17.8	34.1	58.4
D. CHILE	35.3	8.2	16.4	39.7	66.8	83.6	5.9	17.8	69.7
E. COLOMBIA	51.2	34.5	49.4	23.8	40.5	50.6	4.0	25.3	38.1
F. COSTA RICA	29.8	27.4	43.5	45.2	47.6	56.5	11.1	32.2	53.3
I. ECUADOR	38.8	22.9	28.9	36.2	52.1	71.1	6.0	27.4	71.6
K. GUATEMALA	35.6	53.2	63.4	39.4	21.8	36.6	0	4.2	29.6
N. MEXICO	14.6	8.1	12.6	60.4	66.9	66.0	22.4	46.5	66.0
R. PERU	11.7	30.1	39.8	63.3	44.9	60.2	11.2	17.2	32.3
S. URUGUAY	33.1	15.8	17.8	41.9	59.2	82.2	7.5	21.4	68.0
T. VENEZUELA	22.4	1.8	.4	52.6	73.2	99.6	13.1	45.5	70.0

SOURCE: USBG-FRB, December 1988, table A.12.

Table 2908

ECLA DATA ON RATIO OF TOTAL DISBURSED EXTERNAL DEBT
TO EXPORTS OF GOODS AND SERVICES, 18 L, 1980–88
(%)

Country	1980	1981	1982	1983	1984	1985	1986	1987	1988[‡]
Oil Exporting Countries	187	220	279	304	288	306	412	361	343
B. BOLIVIA	262	348	317	380	400	457	545	706	595
I. ECUADOR	162	202	231	261	249	236	333	404	388
N. MEXICO	216	259	335	345	321	354	460	372	339
R. PERU	207	239	281	334	349	362	430	429	442
T. VENEZUELA	148	160	200	229	216	217	313	286	290
Non-Oil-Exporting Countries	236	273	386	405	377	399	434	417	337
A. ARGENTINA	275	329	475	485	488	481	610	673	541
C. BRAZIL	321	313	417	416	364	385	457	430	321
D. CHILE	188	311	370	390	437	457	404	326	236
H. DOMINICAN REP.	171	183	260	267	258	279	249	237	220
E. COLOMBIA	128	199	232	303	239	314	233	227	218
F. COSTA RICA	184	229	286	312	294	306	272	271	260
J. EL SALVADOR	97	174	208	216	218	219	188	205	185
K. GUATEMALA	61	96	144	183	204	232	229	239	225
L. HAITI	87	155	152	191	190	178	239	239	276
M. HONDURAS	147	180	259	270	283	309	299	316	290
O. NICARAGUA	369	464	702	804	1,013	1,405	1,958	1,894	2,068
Q. PARAGUAY	152	171	195	317	214	163	234	158	324
S. URUGUAY	141	183	276	324	362	391	349	379	354
LATIN AMERICA	212	247	331	354	333	354	424	393	339

SOURCE: ECLA-AE, 1988, p. 782.

Table 2909

ECLA DATA ON RATIO OF TOTAL INTEREST EARNED TO EXPORTS
OF GOODS AND SERVICES, 18 L, 1980–88
(%)

Country	1980	1981	1982	1983	1984	1985	1986	1987	1988[‡]
Oil Exporting Countries	16.8	22.5	35.6	31.4	33.8	32.1	34.8	28.0	28.3
B. BOLIVIA	25.0	34.6	43.4	39.8	49.8	46.8	42.1	43.9	34.8
I. ECUADOR	18.3	22.8	30.3	27.4	30.7	25.5	30.0	32.8	33.3
N. MEXICO	23.3	29.0	47.3	37.5	39.1	36.9	38.2	29.8	29.1
R. PERU	18.4	24.1	25.1	29.8	33.2	27.9	26.2	21.9	21.8
T. VENEZUELA	8.1	12.7	21.0	21.6	24.1	25.3	31.1	23.7	26.4
Non-Oil-Exporting Countries	23.9	33.8	46.8	40.9	39.0	38.4	36.6	31.0	27.9
A. ARGENTINA	22.0	35.5	53.6	58.4	57.6	51.1	50.9	51.0	40.4
C. BRAZIL	34.1	40.4	57.1	43.5	39.6	40.0	41.4	33.1	29.7
D. CHILE	19.3	38.8	49.5	38.9	48.0	43.5	37.9	26.4	22.6
H. DOMINICAN REP.	19.9	19.1	22.7	24.5	18.1	18.7	18.9	14.7	13.2
E. COLOMBIA	11.8	21.9	25.9	26.7	22.8	28.9	20.5	20.7	20.8
F. COSTA RICA	18.0	28.0	36.1	33.0	26.6	24.9	21.8	21.2	19.7
J. EL SALVADOR	5.9	7.8	11.9	12.2	12.3	11.1	12.3	13.4	10.0
K. GUATEMALA	5.3	7.6	7.8	8.7	12.3	14.9	17.4	13.6	13.0
L. HAITI	2.1	2.7	2.4	2.4	5.2	5.4	5.2	6.3	6.9
M. HONDURAS	10.6	14.4	22.4	16.4	15.9	16.1	15.4	16.5	14.3
O. NICARAGUA	24.3	37.4	41.8	44.8	56.1	72.0	83.6	81.8	103.0
Q. PARAGUAY	13.4	14.8	13.5	14.3	10.1	8.3	18.5	9.8	11.6
S. URUGUAY	11.0	12.9	22.4	24.8	34.8	34.2	24.7	24.7	23.4
LATIN AMERICA	20.4	28.0	41.0	36.2	36.4	35.4	35.8	29.7	28.0

SOURCE: ECLA-AE, 1988.

Table 2910

TERMS OF EXTERNAL PUBLIC BORROWING, 19 L, 1970, 1987

Country	Commitments (M US)		Average Interest Rate (%)		Average Maturity (Years)		Average Grace Period (Years)		Public Loans with Variable Interest Rates as % of Public Debt	
	1970	1987	1970	1987	1970	1987	1970	1987	1970	1987
A. ARGENTINA	494	3,322	7.3	8.2	12	12	3	5	0	84.1
B. BOLIVIA	24	301	1.9	6.7	48	26	4	6	0	29.1
C. BRAZIL	1,439	2,107	6.8	8.3	14	14	3	4	11.8	67.5
D. CHILE	361	1,011	6.8	7.9	12	14	4	4	0	79.1
E. COLOMBIA	363	700	6.0	8.4	21	11	5	3	0	40.9
F. COSTA RICA	58	102	5.6	6.7	28	20	6	5	7.5	53.8
H. DOMINICAN REP.	20	172	2.4	7.3	28	19	5	4	0	25.8
I. ECUADOR	78	1,045	6.2	7.3	20	17	4	4	0	68.9
J. EL SALVADOR	12	221	4.7	5.1	23	26	6	7	0	5.7
K. GUATEMALA	50	189	3.7	4.7	26	27	6	7	10.3	30.9
L. HAITI	5	182	4.8	1.4	10	37	1	9	0	1.3
M. HONDURAS	23	265	4.1	5.5	30	23	7	6	0	18.2
N. MEXICO	858	11,069	7.9	7.7	12	14	3	5	5.7	79.1
O. NICARAGUA	23	350	7.1	4.1	18	17	4	4	0	22.1
P. PANAMA	111	189	6.1	7.2	15	15	4	4	0	59.1
Q. PARAGUAY	14	150	5.7	5.9	25	21	6	5	0	13.7
R. PERU	125	317	7.4	6.6	14	16	4	4	0	33.3
S. URUGUAY	71	354	7.9	8.4	12	14	3	4	.7	68.1
T. VENEZUELA	198	260	7.8	8.3	8	17	2	3	2.6	89.1

SOURCE: World Development Report, 1989, table 25, pp. 212-213.

Table 2911

IDB DATA ON EXTERNAL PUBLIC SECTOR DEBT OUTSTANDING,[1] 19 L, 1960–87

(M US YE)[2]

Country	1960	1970	1975	1976	1977	1978	1979	1980	1981	1982	1983	1984	1985	1986	1987
A. ARGENTINA	1,275	2,456.3	5,249	6,519.5	7,530.1	8,946.1	10,765.9	12,317.8	14,395.2	19,536.4	27,406.4	28,935.5	38,547.1	41,224.0	50,077.4
B. BOLIVIA	179	553.3	1,288.7	1,666.9	2,074.8	2,554.2	2,970.1	3,177.2	3,540.4	3,574.1	4,287.6	4,419.2	4,418.7	4,970.3	5,617.6
C. BRAZIL	2,407	4,894.3	17,897	23,430	29,018	39,096.9	46,317.8	51,351.6	57,902.7	64,969.9	72,698.0	81,429.8	80,043.5	90,594.6	98,498.4
D. CHILE	562	2,536.3	4,390.3	4,289.9	4,643.7	5,615.7	5,537.3	5,137.1	5,006.0	5,887.1	7,800.0	11,602.2	14,610.2	16,114.2	17,396.3
E. COLOMBIA	377	1,878.8	3,037.0	3,381.2	3,716.2	4,362.7	5,331.6	6,549.7	7,817.7	9,762.2	10,604.2	12,429.3	15,059.4	16,790.6	18,204.4
F. COSTA RICA	55	229.1	731.6	1,008.1	1,292.0	1,553.6	1,929.7	2,505.3	2,957.4	3,233.4	3,946.5	3,870.6	4,293.4	4,304.7	4,104.2
H. DOMINICAN REP.	6	276.3	707.7	831.5	924.3	1,065.0	1,490.1	1,851.3	2,075.7	2,279.9	2,896.0	3,000.8	3,396.8	3,370.2	3,443.8
I. ECUADOR	95	334.8	744.8	1,039.1	1,757.2	2,890.4	3,474.2	4,339.6	5,229.1	5,053.8	6,898.4	7,640.0	8,457.3	9,541.9	10,822.0
J. EL SALVADOR	33	126.1	382.7	450.5	450.6	641.9	719.7	929.4	1,098.3	1,450.0	1,675.7	1,764.7	1,821.9	1,767.0	1,948.1
K. GUATEMALA	51	175.7	267.8	542.0	634.3	743.2	818.9	1,049.9	1,400.3	1,558.9	1,850.3	2,466.7	2,834.8	2,902.7	3,057.0
L. HAITI	38	45.2	106.4	192.6	222.0	278.0	367.4	411.3	496.3	545.2	628.2	669.4	706.4	769.3	956.8
M. HONDURAS	23	143.8	452.3	593.2	812.8	967.7	1,256.7	1,722.8	1,984.5	2,102.1	2,402.4	2,418.4	2,742.2	3,035.3	3,405.1
N. MEXICO	1,151	3,751.0	13,682.2	18,150.6	24,995.6	30,896.4	35,857.0	38,751.6	48,421.5	57,919.7	73,301.7	76,595.2	79,211.3	85,077.1	96,929.4
O. NICARAGUA	41	208.7	801.6	956.9	1,102.9	1,132.6	1,389.2	2,110.1	2,605.4	3,146.5	4,067.0	4,835.8	5,108.3	5,437.3	6,229.3
P. PANAMA	59	290.5	1,124.1	1,435.5	1,832.9	2,374.6	2,573.1	2,865.3	3,199.6	3,564.9	3,968.1	3,638.1	3,765.6	3,921.8	4,001.2
Q. PARAGUAY	22	158.7	429.5	462.8	545.1	749.3	1,156.4	1,200.3	1,529.5	1,906.4	2,006.9	2,018.3	2,344.8	2,511.0	2,911.0
R. PERU	265	1,092.4	4,002.2	5,559.3	6,458.7	6,770.6	8,037.1	8,502.0	8,601.4	10,083.5	11,547.9	11,958.1	13,023.3	13,967.2	15,115.2
S. URUGUAY	132	355.8	1,034.3	1,152.6	1,204.7	1,249.2	1,415.6	1,645.5	1,930.8	2,257.3	3,065.6	3,251.1	3,286.7	3,402.1	3,660.4
T. VENEZUELA	363	924.1	1,393.3	3,204.0	4,780.7	7,192.9	10,036.7	11,076.8	11,770.0	13,191.1	14,572.0	18,674.4	17,380.7	25,882.4	25,935.7

1. Includes the undisbursed portion. Does not necessarily include external debt of decentralized agencies. For total public and private sector loans, see table 2808, below.

2. Excludes loans under one year. Debts under 90 days normally have been considered to involve only "cash flow" management, but in recent years such loans have been simply "rolled over" to disguise what are in effect loans for an unspecified term. Excludes private sector debt and "purchase" and "repurchase" transactions with IMF.

SOURCE: IDB-SFTF, 1985, p. 424; 1986, p. 430; 1988, p. 583; 1989, table E-4, p. 506.

Table 2912

IDB DATA ON EXTERNAL PUBLIC SECTOR DEBT SERVICE AS SHARE OF EXPORTS OF GOODS[1] AND SERVICES, 19 L, 1960-85

(%)[2]

Country	1960	1966	1970	1973	1975	1976	1977	1978	1979	1980	1981	1982	1983	1985
A. ARGENTINA	20.5	25.5	21.8	17.9	22.4	18.8	15.7	28.2	16.1	19.9	18.2	24.5	24.0	41.8
B. BOLIVIA	27.6	4.9	11.0	15.5	14.6	16.2	21.5	49.8	30.3	26.2	27.0	28.2	30.5	29.1
C. BRAZIL	38.7	30.6	12.6	13.9	17.5	19.3	21.5	31.9	38.5	36.1	31.9	42.1	28.7	26.5
D. CHILE	14.2	10.5	19.2	10.9	28.7	31.5	33.4	40.9	27.1	23.5	27.2	18.8	18.3	26.2
E. COLOMBIA	13.9	16.4	11.9	13.4	11.5	9.9	9.1	10.0	14.5	11.2	13.4	17.5	21.3	29.2
F. COSTA RICA	4.8	12.3	10.0	10.3	10.6	9.5	9.0	23.4	23.0	16.7	15.3	12.5	50.6	36.6
H. DOMINICAN REP.	~	12.5	4.7	5.6	5.0	6.5	7.5	10.8	21.6	12.8	10.6	18.7	22.7	16.1
I. ECUADOR	7.1	6.4	9.3	7.5	4.5	5.8	7.3	12.1	30.0	14.4	17.8	30.8	32.5	28.8
J. EL SALVADOR	2.6	2.9	3.5	5.3	9.1	4.4	6.3	3.0	2.4	3.5	3.5	4.6	6.4	16.3
K. GUATEMALA	1.5	5.7	7.4	3.6	1.7	1.5	1.3	2.2	2.7	3.7	3.3	6.6	11.7	21.3
L. HAITI	3.6	~	7.5	7.7	7.5	7.1	6.9	5.6	3.6	4.5	6.6	5.1	5.0	5.8
M. HONDURAS	2.8	1.9	3.0	3.7	4.9	6.4	7.2	8.7	12.9	10.2	12.7	18.8	14.9	17.6
N. MEXICO	15.5	20.9	24.2	24.3	25.5	31.6	44.3	56.7	65.6	33.2	28.2	29.5	35.9	37.0
O. NICARAGUA	3.8	5.2	11.2	22.0	12.5	12.3	14.1	13.7	8.1	14.6	~	~	18.3	~
P. PANAMA	1.6	2.8	7.6	16.9	18.5	12.3	17.9	60.1	34.6	33.5	11.5	13.8	6.8	6.9
Q. PARAGUAY	6.8	7.8	11.2	10.7	10.5	8.1	6.7	7.6	9.7	12.8	9.8	10.3	14.9	12.9
R. PERU	10.5	9.8	11.7	29.7	26.1	26.1	30.7	31.5	22.7	32.7	44.9	36.7	19.6	7.9
S. URUGUAY	5.8	12.5	21.7	22.9	41.4	29.6	30.3	46.8	10.4	12.3	9.5	13.4	19.8	30.6
T. VENEZUELA	4.4	2.7	3.0	6.1	5.8	4.2	8.1	7.7	10.3	14.8	12.4	15.6	15.0	12.8

1. Service = amortization plus interest. Exports of merchandise (f.o.b.). Does not necessarily include external debt service of decentralized agencies.
2. Excludes loans under one year. Debts under 90 days normally have been considered to involve only "cash flow" management, but in recent years such loans have been simply "rolled over" to disguise what are in effect loans for an unspecified term.

SOURCE: IDB-SPTF, 1982, p. 393; and for 1981-83 data, WB-WDR, 1983-85, table 16; 1987, table 19.

Table 2913

IDB DATA ON DISBURSED PORTION OF THE EXTERNAL PUBLIC SECTOR DEBT OUTSTANDING,[1] 19 L, 1960–87
(M US)[2]

	Country	1960	1970	1975	1976	1977	1978	1979	1980	1981	1982	1983	1984	1985	1986	1987
A.	ARGENTINA	987	1,879.6	3,120.7	4,428.6	5,032.9	6,746.1	8,599.9	10,180.6	10,570.2	15,886.1	25,444.9	26,699.6	35,706.4	38,773.8	47,451.4
B.	BOLIVIA	168	480.2	824.3	1,065.6	1,429.4	1,718.5	1,907.8	2,228.2	2,765.2	2,861.1	3,279.3	3,385.6	3,484.3	4,064.0	4,598.7
C.	BRAZIL	2,202	3,421.2	13,923.1	17,637.9	22,082.8	30,394.3	35,920.9	40,434.1	45,260.4	50,797.4	59,123.5	69,936.5	73,671.3	84,349.3	91,652.5
D.	CHILE	456	2,067.2	3,733.4	3,593.0	3,665.0	4,357.0	4,811.2	4,705.3	4,487.0	5,243.3	6,765.1	10,722.9	12,903.7	14,603.8	15,536.2
E.	COLOMBIA	312	1,296.5	2,377.3	2,476.4	2,696.4	2,811.7	3,384.0	4,088.5	5,076.3	5,990.4	6,874.5	7,732.3	9,570.1	12,185.0	13,828.1
F.	COSTA RICA	44	134.2	420.9	541.9	736.7	946.6	1,300.7	',691.7	2,192.4	2,378.1	3,128.5	3,159.7	3,505.1	3,579.7	3,628.6
H.	DOMINICAN REP.	6	212.0	449.0	574.9	652	735.7	867.6	',219.7	1,400.3	1,665.5	2,192.4	2,343.9	2,631.6	2,758.0	2,938.0
I.	ECUADOR	71	193.1	434.0	590.0	1,110.5	2,217.0	2,602.2	3,300.3	4,349.3	4,042.3	5,494.8	6,553.0	7,160.5	8,193.3	9,025.9
J.	EL SALVADOR	23	87.6	382.7	450.5	450.6	330.2	407.8	523.7	723.8	972.1	1,339.5	1,408.8	1,478.1	1 496.8	1 597.4
K.	GUATEMALA	26	106.4	267.8	542.0	634.3	304.0	426.8	548.8	806.5	1,144.1	1,386.1	1,947.3	2,136.3	2,263.7	2,345.0
L.	HAITI	37	39.9	100.4	182.6	222.0	184.8	226.7	266.6	361.8	415.6	447.8	491.1	534.0	585.1	673.6
M.	HONDURAS	11	90.3	452.3	593.2	812.8	594.6	760.2	996.8	1,257.2	1,430.5	1,648.9	1,793.4	2,163.0	2,398.6	2,681.2
N.	MEXICO	827	3,195.7	13,682.2	18,150.6	24,995.6	25,532.6	29,068.0	33,987.3	43,114.4	51,642.2	66,857.3	69,811.9	72,710.9	75,990.6	82,771.0
O.	NICARAGUA	22	146.8	801.6	956.9	1,102.9	941.6	1,084.8	1,661.5	2,076.6	2,487.5	3,383.1	4,088.3	4,483.9	5,227.7	6,149.8
P.	PANAMA	32	193.9	1,124.1	1,435.5	1,832.9	1,875.1	2,071.8	2,270.8	2,429.6	2,917.2	3,145.3	3,185.1	3,339.6	3,572.4	3,721.7
Q.	PARAGUAY	20	112.1	429.5	462.8	545.1	445.4	523.8	633.2	709.1	940.0	1,144.5	1,252.7	1,536.6	1,832.0	2,217.8
R.	PERU	162	856.0	4,002.2	5,559.3	6,458.7	5,398.6	5,932.5	6,167.3	6,011.9	6,955.7	8,327.7	9,314.6	10,350.8	11,278.0	12,485.4
S.	URUGUAY	115	268.8	1,034.3	1,152.6	1,204.7	793.8	932.5	1,126.8	1 348.2	1,700.2	2,510.3	2,527.8	2,695.0	2,886 3	3 047.7
T.	VENEZUELA	252	727.9	1,393.3	3,204.0	4,780.7	6,701.4	9,602.8	1C,774.1	11 545.0	12,342.0	13,962.4	18,353.6	17,097.8	25,199.8	25,244.4

1. Included in table 2911, above.
2. Excludes loans under one year. Debts under 90 days normally have been considered to involve only "cash flow" management, but in recent years such loans have been simply "rolled over" to disguise what are in effect loans for an unspecified term. Excludes private sector debt and "purchase" and "repurchase" transactions with IMF.

SOURCE: IDB-SPTF, 1985, p. 425; 1986, p. 431; 1988, p. 584; 1989, p. 512.

Table 2914

IDB DATA ON SERVICE PAYMENTS ON THE EXTERNAL PUBLIC SECTOR DEBT,[1] 19 L, 1960–87 (M US)[2]

Country	1960	1966	1970	1975	1977	1978	1979	1980	1981	1982	1983	1984	1985	1986	1987
A. ARGENTINA	254	455	464.4	788.9	1,039.9	2,115.8	1,463.6	1,986.9	2,152.5	2,322.0	2,441.7	2,559.5	4,259.2	4,699.8	3,894.0
B. BOLIVIA	16	7	23.2	75.9	159.1	361.0	271.8	290.2	281.0	287.5	287.4	307.1	249.4	161.3	136.7
C. BRAZIL	554	573	390.4	1,781.3	2,872.7	4,484.6	6,529.1	8,050.3	9,090.8	10,155.8	7,022.4	7,537.8	7,839.1	8,639.4	7,655.8
D. CHILE	78	103	244.2	501.8	886.2	1,224.4	1,259.6	1,374.6	1,660.1	1,022.0	872.8	1,237.8	1,230.0	1,527.8	1,366.4
E. COLOMBIA	82	109	119.2	238.7	315.6	389.8	637.8	528.7	670.3	874.5	912.6	1,085.2	1,412.4	1,847.9	2,371.6
F. COSTA RICA	5	20	27.7	64.2	87.0	238.3	255.3	204.8	199.4	133.4	605.0	328.0	447.7	383.7	182.1
H. DOMINICAN REP.	~	20	11.5	51.2	72.1	87.6	246.2	153.8	229.1	256.1	221.1	159.0	201.7	271.9	162.3
I. ECUADOR	11	13	22.3	49.1	115.9	207.0	947.7	559.2	922.5	1,134.4	535.5	983.3	896.4	854.6	493.8
J. EL SALVADOR	3	6	9.5	54.1	69.4	29.9	33.4	41.7	47.6	68.1	153.6	193.7	196.0	183.1	179.9
K. GUATEMALA	2	10	26.1	14.1	17.2	26.1	37.3	44.8	60.2	102.4	145.9	193.4	256.1	282.1	291.6
L. HAITI	2	~	3.8	7.6	18.8	18.5	12.3	20.5	20.8	15.2	14.0	17.7	20.7	18.7	22.2
M. HONDURAS	2	3	5.6	16.9	42.0	59.2	105.4	97.7	115.8	147.8	121.0	125.6	163.1	186.2	228.7
N. MEXICO	210	456	691.2	1,582.0	3,540.8	6,302.8	10,032.5	7,900.6	8,550.8	9,424.9	11,442.1	11,289.7	10,632.9	8,808.7	8,971.7
O. NICARAGUA	3	9	22.9	54.9	98.2	97.7	52.4	82.2	160.6	162.9	82.4	63.8	46.8	32.3	34.1
P. PANAMA	2	7	30.5	72.3	161.4	564.9	387.8	466.3	494.2	618.4	480.1	537.0	409.6	470.0	383.1
Q. PARAGUAY	3	5	10.4	21.8	26.6	35.6	52.9	80.3	70.9	80.8	84.6	115.3	155.0	203.5	222.6
R. PERU	52	89	143.6	440.3	653.4	753.9	928.0	1,501.1	1,893.4	1,521.1	761.2	630.9	699.1	490.0	448.4
S. URUGUAY	10	31	63.2	228.4	245.0	427.2	125.5	197.4	184.9	226.4	304.0	409.8	404.0	336.5	404.0
T. VENEZUELA	111	67	82.2	539.4	827.2	749.5	1,531.1	2,949.4	2,653.3	3,255.7	2,690.6	2,770.8	2,372.9	3,214.2	2,869.3

1. Service = amortization plus interest on the debt. Does not necessarily include service payments on external debt by decentralized agencies.
2. Excludes loans under one year. Debts under 90 days normally have been considered to involve only "cash flow" management, but in recent years such loans have been simply "rolled over" to disguise what are in effect loans for an unspecified term.

SOURCE: IDB-SPTF, 1985, p. 429; 1986, p. 435; 1988, p. 588; 1989, table E-9, p. 511.

Table 2915

IDB DATA ON AMORTIZATION PAYMENTS ON THE EXTERNAL PUBLIC SECTOR DEBT, 19 L,[1] 1970-87
(M US)[2]

Country	1970	1975	1976	1977	1978	1979	1980	1981	1982	1983	1984	1985	1986	1987
A. ARGENTINA	343.5	522.5	604.1	721.9	1,613.3	895.3	1,145.8	1,092.8	1,010.2	963.9	482.7	835.6	1,509.3	506.6
B. BOLIVIA	16.9	51.4	70.7	100.1	274.7	149.7	126.3	110.1	106.4	104.6	117.3	151.0	106.4	74.3
C. BRAZIL	255.9	925.2	1,086.3	1,680.0	2,635.8	3,604.0	3,857.5	3,938.1	4,200.0	2,026.3	2,388.1	2,178.4	2,590.1	2,942.1
D. CHILE	165.2	345.1	546.4	684.8	933.7	904.0	891.2	1,175.6	474.2	321.5	311.9	233.1	286.0	186.0
E. COLOMBIA	75.2	123.9	144.6	175.9	220.4	408.0	249.8	261.6	303.8	392.7	539.9	646.6	968.6	1,263.9
F. COSTA RICA	20.6	40.9	40.3	51.2	173.3	171.9	75.2	83.6	55.5	104.3	105.8	125.6	188.2	60.9
H. DOMINICAN REP.	7.3	32.1	38.7	47.3	47.5	190.6	61.6	109.1	148.1	114.7	59.1	72.6	98.9	68.1
I. ECUADOR	15.6	32.0	55.5	71.3	109.5	739.8	271.5	481.2	544.7	164.5	191.0	178.0	208.8	222.5
J. EL SALVADOR	5.9	47.2	22.2	54.0	12.3	12.7	17.2	17.7	32.3	93.1	122.0	128.4	116.2	105.7
K. GUATEMALA	19.9	7.5	9.2	8.0	10.4	14.8	15.2	22.5	43.7	70.7	109.3	149.4	136.3	146.6
L. HAITI	3.6	6.4	8.7	15.0	14.1	8.6	15.3	15.1	8.6	7.8	11.3	13.5	11.2	13.6
M. HONDURAS	3.4	6.7	13.8	20.1	28.1	59.6	38.9	37.3	51.4	38.9	47.3	69.5	79.1	142.4
N. MEXICO	475.0	753.4	1,144.3	2,230.6	4,404.9	7,138.6	4,010.1	3,717.8	3,241.3	4,836.9	3,897.3	3,105.7	2,571.6	3,249.3
O. NICARAGUA	16.2	19.4	34.0	46.6	47.3	15.5	44.4	70.0	53.8	45.0	29.6	18.8	11.1	22.1
P. PANAMA	23.7	31.1	44.7	88.2	442.9	190.1	214.6	213.2	280.9	188.6	232.7	107.1	148.4	157.7
Q. PARAGUAY	7.0	14.2	11.8	16.1	20.0	30.9	45.0	38.9	39.6	39.2	57.5	75.6	114.7	128.2
R. PERU	100.2	253.8	256.1	404.9	435.9	490.5	956.0	1,364.4	972.6	360.4	261.0	360.7	280.4	250.4
S. URUGUAY	47.2	182.2	148.5	187.2	366.0	54.8	93.0	60.8	70.6	93.9	126.2	124.3	87.7	134.1
T. VENEZUELA	42.0	435.9	285.1	604.6	356.2	889.7	1,735.0	1,399.3	1,611.1	950.6	1,254.7	945.6	1,469.1	1,209.2

1. Included in table 2914, above.

2. Excludes loans under one year. Debts under 90 days normally have been considered to involve only "cash flow" management, but in recent years such loans have been simply "rolled over" to disguise what are in effect loans for an unspecified term.

SOURCE: IDB-SPTF, 1986, p. 434; 1988, p. 587; 1989, table E-8, p. 510.

Table 2916

IDB DATA ON INTEREST PAYMENTS ON THE EXTERNAL PUBLIC SECTOR DEBT,[1] 19 L, 1960–87

(M US)[2]

Country	1960	1970	1975	1976	1977	1978	1979	1980	1981	1982	1983	1984	1985	1986	1987
A. ARGENTINA	50	121	264	265	318	502.5	568.3	841.1	1,059.7	1,311.8	1,477.8	2,076.8	3,423.6	3,190.5	3,387.4
B. BOLIVIA	3	7	24	38	59	86.3	122.1	163.9	170.9	181.1	182.8	189.8	98.4	54.9	62.4
C. BRAZIL	134	135	856	961	1,193	1,848.8	2,925.1	4,192.8	5,152.7	5,955.8	4,996.1	5,149.7	5,660.7	6,049.3	4,713.7
D. CHILE	14	78	157	209	201	290.7	355.6	483.4	484.5	547.8	551.3	925.9	996.9	1,241.8	1,180.4
E. COLOMBIA	14	44	115	125	140	169.4	229.8	278.9	408.7	570.7	519.9	545.3	765.8	879.3	1,107.7
F. COSTA RICA	1	7	23	27	36	65.0	83.4	129.6	115.8	77.9	500.7	222.2	322.1	195.5	121.2
H. DOMINICAN REP.	~	4	19	20	25	40.1	55.6	92.2	120.0	108.0	106.4	99.9	129.1	173.0	94.2
I. ECUADOR	2	7	17	25	45	97.5	207.9	287.7	441.3	589.7	371.0	792.3	718.4	645.8	271.3
J. EL SALVADOR	1	4	7	14	15	17.6	20.7	24.5	29.9	35.8	60.5	71.7	67.6	66.9	74.2
K. GUATEMALA	1	6	7	8	9	15.7	22.5	29.6	37.7	58.7	75.2	84.1	106.7	145.8	145.0
L. HAITI	#	#	1	1	4	4.4	3.7	5.2	5.7	6.6	6.2	6.4	7.2	7.5	8.6
M. HONDURAS	1	3	10	16	22	31.1	45.8	58.8	78.5	96.4	82.1	78.3	93.6	107.1	86.3
N. MEXICO	29	216	829	1,082	1,310	1,897.9	2,893.9	3,890.5	4,833.0	6,183.6	6,605.2	7,392.4	7,527.2	6,237.1	5,722.4
O. NICARAGUA	1	7	36	41	52	50.4	36.9	37.8	90.6	109.1	37.4	34.2	28.0	21.2	12.0
P. PANAMA	1	7	41	56	73	122.0	197.7	251.7	281.0	337.5	291.5	304.3	302.5	321.6	225.4
Q. PARAGUAY	1	3	8	8	11	15.6	22.0	35.3	32.0	41.2	45.4	57.8	79.4	88.8	94.4
R. PERU	7	43	187	199	248	318.0	437.5	545.1	529.0	548.5	400.8	369.9	338.4	209.6	198.0
S. URUGUAY	4	16	46	57	58	61.2	70.7	104.4	124.1	155.8	210.1	283.6	279.7	248.8	269.9
T. VENEZUELA	18	40	103	122	223	393.3	641.4	1,214.4	1,254.0	1,644.6	1,740.0	1,516.1	1,427.3	1,745.1	1,660.1

1. Included in table 2915, above.

2. Does not necessarily include external debts of decentralized agencies. Includes also financial institutions other than banks. Excludes debts under one year. Debts under 90 days normally have been considered to involve only "cash flow" management, but in recent years such loans have been simply "rolled over" to disguise what are in effect loans for an unspecified term.

SOURCE: IDB-SPTF, 1985, p. 427; 1986, p. 433; 1988, p. 586; 1989, table E-7, p. 509.

Table 2917

IDB DATA ON STRUCTURE OF THE LATIN AMERICAN EXTERNAL
PUBLIC SECTOR DEBT,[1] BY TYPE OF CREDITOR, 1961–87
(%)[2]

Year	Private					Official			Disbursed Portion	Undisbursed Portion
	Suppliers	Banks[3]	Bond Issues	Nationa-lization	Total Private	Multi-lateral	Bilateral	Total Debt		
1961	25.0	14.2	8.1	.9	48.2	15.3	36.5	51.8	74.6	25.4
1962	31.6	11.5	8.0	.7	51.8	15.8	32.4	48.2	79.1	20.9
1963	29.0	11.2	7.7	.5	48.4	18.5	33.1	51.6	75.2	24.8
1964	25.6	13.1	7.2	.8	46.7	19.8	33.5	53.3	76.3	23.7
1965	20.2	12.0	7.5	1.0	40.7	22.5	36.8	59.3	76.8	23.2
1966	19.5	10.5	7.7	1.6	39.3	23.4	37.3	60.7	75.5	24.5
1967	17.2	11.1	6.1	4.4	38.8	22.1	39.1	61.2	74.2	25.8
1968	17.4	12.0	6.7	3.4	39.5	22.8	37.7	60.5	73.2	26.8
1969	16.7	18.3	6.6	2.1	43.7	24.0	32.3	56.3	75.0	25.0
1970	17.1	19.7	5.9	2.3	45.0	24.0	31.0	55.0	76.0	24.0
1971	16.8	22.6	5.6	2.1	47.1	24.3	28.6	52.9	74.0	26.0
1972	15.2	26.2	5.4	1.7	48.5	24.1	27.4	51.5	74.3	25.7
1973	13.0	32.7	4.7	1.4	51.8	22.4	25.8	48.2	74.1	25.9
1974	12.0	38.0	4.1	2.0	56.2	19.7	24.1	43.8	75.1	24.9
1975	10.8	42.9	3.8	1.4	58.9	19.9	21.2	41.1	76.0	24.0
1976	9.1	46.3	3.7	2.2	61.3	18.6	20.1	38.7	76.0	24.0
1977	8.1	50.2	5.8	1.3	65.5	17.2	17.4	34.5	76.1	23.9
1978	7.2	52.7	6.9	.9	67.7	16.3	15.9	32.3	77.9	22.1
1979	6.9	56.0	6.3	.6	69.8	16.5	13.7	30.2	77.8	22.2
1980	6.2	56.6	6.0	.3	69.1	17.0	13.9	30.9	80.4	19.6
1981	5.7	57.6	5.9	.2	69.4	17.2	13.4	30.6	80.4	19.6
1982	4.9	57.6	7.4	.1	69.9	17.3	12.8	30.1	81.0	19.0
1983	4.1	61.7	6.3	.1	72.2	15.7	12.1	27.8	84.6	15.4
1984	3.2	64.0	5.8	.1	73.2	14.7	12.1	26.8	86.7	13.3
1985	3.0	62.5	5.4	.1	70.9	16.3	12.7	29.1	88.6	11.4
1986	2.9	61.4	5.0	0	69.3	17.7	13.0	30.7	89.7	10.3
1987	2.7	60.5	3.5	0	66.8	18.9	14.3	33.2	80.0	11.0

1. Including the undisbursed portion at year end. Does not necessarily include external debts of decentralized agencies.
2. Excludes debts under one year. Debts under 90 days normally have been considered to involve only "cash flow" management, but in recent years such loans have been simply "rolled over" to disguise what are in effect loans for an unspecified term.
3. Includes also financial institutions other than banks.

SOURCE: IDB-SPTF, 1985, p. 426; 1986, p. 432; 1988, p. 585; 1989, table E-6.

Table 2918

WORLD BANK (INTERNATIONAL BANK FOR RECONSTRUCTION
AND DEVELOPMENT) ACTUAL LOANS, 20 LR, FY 1949–76
(M US)[1]

A. ARGENTINA

1949	1950	1951	1952	1953	1954	1955	1956	1957	1958	1959	1960	1961
#	#	#	#	#	#	#	#	#	#	#	#	#

1962	1963	1964	1965	1966	1967	1968	1969	1970	1971	1972	1973	1974	1975	1975
5.9	47.5	36.0	17.1	5.2	4.2	7.0	28.5	44.0	31.6	44.9	54.2	50.2	41.4	13.3

Continued in SALA, 22-3108.

Table 2919

IMF FINANCIAL TARGETS ESTABLISHED IN AGREEMENTS WITH 13 LC

(AA–GR)

| Country | Date of Agreement | Ultimate Targets | | | Intermediate Targets | | | Money[4] | | Operational Targets | | Policy Instruments | | | | |
| | | Net External Assets | Inflation | | Ex-post Real Exchange Rate (1980 + 100) | | | | | | | Public-Sector Deficit (as Percentage of GDP[6]) | | | Net Domestic Credit to Public Sector | |
			1	2	1981	1982	1983‡	M_1	M_2	Monetary Base	Public External Indebtedness[5]	1982	1983	1984	Nominal	Real[7]
						Stand-by Arrangements										
A. ARGENTINA	24 Jan. 1983	−29	−23	−16	143	189	191	170	44	119	8.3	14.0	8.0	5.0	209	−4
Barbadoes	1 Oct. 1982	~	~	~	95	88	85	~	~	~	~	6.6	~	1.8	~	~
D. CHILE	10 Jan. 1983	−23	100	−29	99	125	138	−14	−18	−18	9.4	4.0	2.3	~	10	−10

Continued in SALA, 26-2811.

Table 2920

IMF FINANCING AGREEMENTS, 13 LC

(In Force at End of 1983)

| Country | Date of Agreement | Duration (Months) | Conditioned Financing | | Non-Conditioned Financing[1] | | Total Financing In Relation to Deficit on Current Account[3] | | | Amount Drawn in Relation to Financing[2] | | |
| | | | Millions of SDRs | In Relation to IMF Quota[2] | Millions of SDRs | In Relation to IMF Quota[2] | 1981 | 1982 | 1983 | On Date of Agreement | | To Date |
										Conditioned	Total	Total
					Stand-by Arrangements							
A. ARGENTINA	24 Jan. 1983	15	500	187	520	65	40	72	91	20	41	55
Barbados	1 Oct. 1982	20	32	125	13	51	12	31	~	30	64·	91
F. COSTA RICA	20 Dec. 1982	12	92	150	16	26	31	58	29	#	#	77

Continued in SALA, 26-2812.

Table 2921

IMF DEFINITIONS FOR FUND ACCOUNT DATA

Members of the Fund may draw on its financial resources to meet their balance of payments needs through a **reserve tranche** and four additional **credit tranches**. When a member borrows from ("draws on") the Fund, it uses its own currency to *purchase* the currencies of other members or SDRs held by the Fund's General Account. Thus, a drawing results in an increase in the Fund's holdings of a member's currency and in a corresponding decrease in the General Account's holdings of the currencies of other members or of SDRs. As a result, the composition of the Fund's resources changes without affecting the total. Drawings under reserve tranche policies do not cause Fund holdings of a member's currency to exceed its quota; they are unconditional and are referred to as reserve tranche drawings. Drawings in each of four credit tranches are available in amounts equal to 25 percent of a member's quota. The conditionality imposed by the Fund for these drawings is progressively more rigorous after the first tranche. Most credit tranche drawings are made under **stand-by** arrangements, which assure a member that it will be able to draw on the Fund's resources up to a specified amount without a further review of its position and policies. A member is required to repurchase drawings under regular tranche policies in three to five years, or earlier, if its balance of payments position improves.

The Fund's special facilities permit additional use of Fund resources under particular circumstances. The **compensatory financing facility** enables members to draw on the Fund up to 100 percent of quota when they experience payments difficulties as a result of temporary shortfalls in export receipts—or up to 100 percent of quota when they experience payments difficulties as a result of excess cereal import costs—and their payments difficulties are largely beyond their control, as long as total drawings under the facility do not exceed 125 percent of quota. The **buffer stock financing facility** may be used by members in balance of payments difficulty to draw up to 50 percent of quota to finance contributions to international buffer stock arrangements. The **extended facility** assists members suffering from serious balance of payments difficulties resulting from structural imbalances in production, trade, and prices, or having economies characterized by slow growth and inherently weak payments positions, when the Fund is satisfied that its resources are required for longer periods and in larger amounts relative to quota than are available under the regular tranche policies.

Under the Fund's **enlarged access policy**, which replaced the **supplementary financing facility**, the Fund provides supplementary financing in conjunction with the use of the Fund's ordinary resources to all members facing serious payments imbalances that are large in relation to their quotas. It is used only in support of economic programs under stand-by arrangements reaching into the upper credit tranches or under extended arrangements. Such drawings are subject to Fund conditionality, phasing, and performance criteria. The period of such arrangements normally exceeds one year and may extend up to three years in certain cases.

IMF Fund Account Data Abbreviations

Amt. Appr.	Amount Approved	Imp.	Import
Comp. Financ. Pur	Compensatory Financing Facility Purchases	Oil Fac.	Oil Facility
		Ord.	Ordinary
Dist.	Distribution	Outstand. Sh-Term Fund Borrow	Outstanding Short-Term Fund Borrowing
EAR	Enlarged Access to the Fund's Resources	Pur.	Purchases
Exp.	Expected	Repurch.	Repurchases
Extend.	Extended	SFF	Supplement Financing Facility
GAB	Guaranteed Arrangements to Borrow	St-By	Stand-by

Table 2922

IMF FUND ACCOUNTS, 19 L, 1985-88

Category[1]	A. ARGENTINA				B. BOLIVIA				C. BRAZIL				D. CHILE			
	1985	1986	1987	1988	1985	1986	1987	1988	1985	1986	1987	1988	1985	1986	1987	1988
General Department																
Millions of SDRs End of Period																
Quota	1,113.0	1,113.0	1,113	1,113	90.7	90.7	90.7	90.7	1,461.0	1,461.0	1,461	1,461	440.5	440.5	440.5	440.5
St-By Arrangements Amount Drawn	710	#	451	#	#	32.7	#	#	#	#	#	365	#	#	#	#
St-By Arrangements Undrawn Balance	710	#	662	#	#	17.3	#	#	#	#	#	731	#	#	#	#
Reserve Position in the Fund	#	#	#	#	#	#	#	#	#	#	#	#	#	#	#	#
Use of Fund Credit	2,105	2,241	2,716	2,733	46.7	136.3	117.2	139.7	4,205	3,680	2,803	2,477	990.6	1,088.3	1,032	982.6
Comp. Financ. Purch. Exp. Shortfalls	795	600	859	924	17.9	75.3	66.3	75.3	1,213	789	244	62	365.6	255.0	107.5	61.8
Fund Holdings of Currency: Amount	3,218	3,354	3,829	3,846	137.4	208.9	189.8	198.7	5,667	5,141	4,264	3,938	1,431.1	1,528.8	1,472.9	1,423.1
Percent of Quota	289	301	344	346	151.5	230.3	209.2	219.1	388	352	292	270	324.9	347	344.4	323.1
Millions of SDRs During Period																
Total Purchases[2]	984.5	473	969.8	398.7	#	96.8	#	45.3	#	#	#	365.3	195.6	250	225	150
Reserve Tranche	~	~	~	~	~	~	~	~	~	~	~	~	~	~	~	~
Gold Distributions	~	~	~	~	~	~	~	~	~	~	~	~	~	~	~	~
Total Repurchases	#	337.3	494.4	381.9	18.2	25.3	19.2	36.3	64.5	525.5	877.0	691.4	#	152.4	280.9	199.8
Repurchases of Purchases	#	337.3	494.4	381.9	18.2	25.3	19.2	36.3	64.5	525.5	877.0	691.4	#	152.4	280.9	199.8
SDR Holdings																
Millions of SDRs End of Period																
Net Cumulative Allocations	#	#	#	#	#	2.0	#	#	1	#	#	#	.3	.2	28.8	32.9
Percent of Allocations	#	#	#	#	#	7.6	#	.1	#	#	#	.1	.2	.1	23.6	27.0

Category[1]	E. COLOMBIA				F. COSTA RICA				H. DOMINICAN REP.				I. ECUADOR			
	1985	1986	1987	1988	1985	1986	1987	1988	1985	1986	1987	1988	1985	1986	1987	1988
General Department																
Millions of SDRs End of Period																
Quota	394	394	394	394	84.1	84.1	84.1	84.1	112.1	112.1	112.1	112.1	150.7	150.7	150.7	150.7
St-By Arrangements: Amount Drawn	#	#	#	#	34.0	#	#	#	61.4	#	#	#	84.4	15.1	#	15.1
St-By Arrangements: Undrawn Balance	#	#	#	#	20.0	#	50	40	17.1	#	#	#	21.1	60.3	#	60.3
Reserve Position in the Fund	#	#	#	#	#	#	#	#	#	#	#	#	#	#	#	#
Use of Fund Credit	#	#	#	#	171.6	141	93.3	53	270.4	248.8	200	161.8	327.3	397.7	345.2	300.7
Comp. Financ. Purch. Exp. Shortfalls	#	#	#	#	26.1	16.3	7	#	85.2	51.2	20.8	15.5	85.4	125.1	82.4	82.4
Fund Holdings of Currency: Amount	394	394	394	394	255.8	225.1	177.4	137.2	382.5	360.9	312	273.9	478	548.4	495.9	451.4
Percent of Quota	100	100	100	100	304.1	267.6	210.9	163.1	341.2	322	278.3	244.3	317.2	363.9	329.1	
Millions of SDRs During Period																
Total Purchases[2]	#	#	#	#	34	#	#	#	76.9	17.1	#	#	84.4	75.9	37.7	57.8
Reserve Tranche	~	~	~	~	~	~	~	~	~	~	~	~	~	~	~	~
Gold Distributions	~	~	~	~	~	~	~	~	~	~	~	~	~	~	~	~
Total Repurchases	#	#	#	#	21.4	30.7	47.7	40.2	32.2	38.7	49.0	38.2	21.4	5.5	90.2	102.2
Repurchases of Purchases	#	#	#	#	21.4	30.7	47.7	40.2	32.2	38.7	49.0	38.2	21.4	5.5	90.2	102.2
SDR Holdings																
Millions of SDRs End of Period																
Net Cumulative Allocations	#	114	114	114	.02	.01	.01	.01	28.8	#	#	#	26.2	45.7	.7	1
Percent of Allocations	#	100	100	100	.08	.04	.04	.04	91.1	#	#	.1	79.5	138.9	2	3

Table 2922 (Continued)

IMF FUND ACCOUNTS, 19 L, 1985–88

Top block

Category[1]	J. EL SALVADOR 1985	1986	1987	1988	K. GUATEMALA 1985	1986	1987	1988	L. HAITI 1985	1986	1987	1988	M. HONDURAS 1985	1986	1987	1988
General Department									*Millions of SDRs End of Period*							
Quota	89	89	89	89	108	108	108	108	44.1	44.1	44.1	44.1	67.8	67.8	67.8	67.8
St-By Arrangements Amount Drawn	#	#	#	#	#	#	#	23.2	#	#	#	#	#	#	#	#
St-By Arrangements Undrawn Balance	#	#	#	#	#	#	#	30.8	#	#	#	#	#	#	#	#
Reserve Position in the Fund	#	#	#	#	#	#	#	#	.1	.1	.1	.1	#	#	#	#
Use of Fund Credit	80.9	35.1	3.9	#	105.2	57.2	41.7	65.4	74.4	63.5	45.4	31.2	121.7	80.3	47.9	23.64
Comp. Financ. Purch. Exp. Shortfalls	40.3	12.1	#	#	38.3	#	#	21.6	10.6	#	#	#	37.7	14.5	2.9	~
Fund Holdings of Currency: Amount	169.9	124.1	92.9	89	213.2	165.2	149.7	173.4	118.4	98.7	80.6	66.5	189.5	148.1	115.7	91.44
Percent of Quota	190.9	139.4	104.4	100	197.4	153.0	138.6	160.6	268.6	223.8	182.7	150.7	279.5	218.4	170.7	134.87
									Millions of SDRs During Period							
Total Purchases[2]	#	#	#	#	#	#	#	44.8	#	#	#	#	#	#	#	#
Reserve Tranche	~	~	~	~	~	~	~	~	~	~	~	~	~	~	~	~
Gold Distributions																
Total Repurchases	26.6	45.8	31.2	3.9	47.8	48	15.5	21.0	11.8	19.7	18.1	14.1	16.7	41.4	32.4	24.3
Repurchases of Purchases	26.6	45.8	31.2	3.9	47.8	48	15.5	21.0	11.8	19.7	18.1	14.1	16.7	41.4	32.4	24.3
SDR Holdings									*Millions of SDRs End of Period*							
Net Cumulative Allocations	#	#	#	#	#	#	1.2	.1	#	5.4	#	#	.01	#	#	#
Percent of Allocations	.2	#	.1	#	#	#	4.3	.4	.1	39.3	#	#		#	#	#

Bottom block

Category[1]	N. MEXICO 1985	1986	1987	1988	O. NICARAGUA 1985	1986	1987	1988	P. PANAMA 1985	1986	1987	1988	Q. PARAGUAY 1985	1986	1987	1988
General Department									*Millions of SDRs End of Period*							
Quota	1,166	1,166	1,166	1,166	68.2	68.2	68.2	68.2	102.2	102.2	102.2	102.2	48.4	48.4	48.4	48.4
St-By Arrangements: Amount Drawn	#	450	1,050	#	#	#	#	#	35	79	#	#	#	#	#	#
St-By Arrangements: Undrawn Balance	#	950	350	#	#	#	#	#	55	11	#	#	#	#	#	#
Reserve Position in the Fund	#	#	#	#	.01	#	#	#	#	#	#	#	#	#	#	#
Use of Fund Credit	2,703	3,319	3,639	3,570	#	#	#	#	283.4	288.6	243.9	243.8	31.6	24.9	19.6	15
Comp. Financ. Purch. Exp. Shortfalls	#	#	#	#	#	#	#	#	55.9	44.2	22.1	22	~	~	~	~
Fund Holdings of Currency: Amount	3,869	4,485	4,805	4,736	68.2	68.2	68.2	68.2	385.6	390.8	346.1	34.6	16.8	23.6	28.8	33.4
Percent of Quota	332	385	412	406	100	100	100	100	377.3	382.4	338.7	338.6	34.8	48.7	59.6	69.1
									Millions of SDRs During Period							
Total Purchases[2]	295.8	741.4	600.0	350	#	#	#	#	35	44	11.0	#	#	#	#	#
Reserve Tranche	~	~	~	~	~	~	~	~	~	~	~	~	~	~	~	~
Gold Distributions																
Total Repurchases	#	125.4	280.1	419	#	#	#	#	28.3	38.7	55.7	#	#	#	.1	.1
Repurchases of Purchases	#	125.4	280.1	419	#	#	#	#	28.3	38.7	55.7	#	#	#	.1	.1
SDR Holdings									*Millions of SDRs End of Period*							
Net Cumulative Allocations	#	7	498	293	#	#	.01	#	#	1.4	#	#	38.8	42.1	44.8	47.4
Percent of Allocations	#	2	172	101	#	#	.05	#	#	5.5	#	#	283.2	307.2	326.9	345.8

Table 2922 (Continued)

IMF FUND ACCOUNTS, 19 L, 1985–88

Category[1]	R. PERU 1985	1986	1987	1988	S. URUGUAY 1985	1986	1987	1988	T. VENEZUELA 1985	1986	1987	1988
General Department												
Millions of SDRs End of Period												
Quota	330.9	330.9	330.9	330.9	164	164	164	164	1,372	1,372	1,372	1,372
St-By Arrangements: Amount Drawn	#	#	#	#	35	88	#	#	#	#	#	#
St-By Arrangements: Undrawn Balance	#	#	#	#	88	35	#	#	#	#	#	#
Reserve Position in the Fund	#	#	#	#	#	#	#	#	745	656	473	30
Use of Fund Credit	639.0	595.5	595.4	595.4	319	323	277	230	~	~	~	~
Comp. Financ. Purch. Exp. Shortfalls	274.6	238.6	238.5	238.5	105	83	66	66				
Fund Holdings of Currency: Amount	969.9	926.4	926.4	926.4	482	487	440	393	892	891	990	1,372
Percent of Quota	293.1	280	280	279.9	294	297	269	240	65	65	72	100
Millions of SDRs During Period												
Total Purchases[2]	#	#	#	#	101.2	52.7	35.1	#	~	~	~	253.9
Reserve Tranche	~	~	~	~	~	~	~	~	~	~	~	~
Gold Distributions	~	~	~	~	~	~	~	~	~	~	~	~
Total Repurchases	49.3	43.5	.1	#	9.5	48.2	81.5	47	~	~	~	~
Repurchases of Purchases	49.3	43.5	.1	#	9.5	48.2	81.5	47	~	~	~	~
SDR Holdings												
Millions of SDRs End of Period												
Net Cumulative Allocations	#	#	#	#	13	10	48	22	451	498	534	56
Percent of Allocations	#	#	#	#	27	19	96	44	142	157	168	18

1. For definitions of terms, see table 2919. For SDR exchange rate, see tables 3202 and 3203.
2. Equals "all drawing."

a. For data from years 1947–74, see SALA, 23,3100 through 3118.

SOURCE: IMF-IFS-Y, 1985, 1986, 1987, 1988, 1989.

Table 2923

LATIN AMERICAN EXPOSURE OF U.S. BANKS BY PERCENT
OF EQUITY AND OUTSTANDING LOANS
(1986)

Bank	Equity		Outstanding Loans	
	Rank	Percent	Rank	Amount (M US)
Mfrs. Hanover	1	199	3	7,505
Bank America	2	188	2	7,623
Irving Bank	3	146	11	1,541
Chase Manhattan	4	143	4	7,020
Chemical New York	5	142	6	4,445
Bankers Trust N.Y.	6	118	7	3,222
Citicorp	7	114	1	10,400
Marine Midland Bks	8	107	12	1,474
First Chicago	9	102	8	2,410
J. P. Morgan & Co.	10	89	5	4,614
Continental Illinois	11	88	9	1,816
Wells Fargo	12	69	10	1,638
Republicbank	13	64	17	786
Republic New York	14	61	18	699
Bank of Boston	15	60	15	1,065
Mellon Bank	16	54	16	998
First Interstate	17	51	14	1,414
Security Pacific	18	49	13	1,424
Bank of New York	19	47	19	504
First Bank System	20	30	20	426
PNC Financial	21	29	21	410
Bank of New England	22	23	22	274
NBD Bancorp	23	20	23	232
MCORP	24	16	25	194
NCNB Corp	25	15	24	204
Sun Trust Banks	26	8	26	129
First Union	27	4	27	72

SOURCE: *Barrons*, May 25, 1987, p. 11.

Table 2924

EXPOSURE OF U.S. BANK HOLDING COMPANIES, 4 L
(B US, Sept. 30, 1983)[a]

Country	Citicorp	Bank America	Chase Manhattan	Manufacturers Hanover	J. P. Morgan	Chemical N.Y.	First Interstate	Continental Illinois	Security Pacific	Bankers Trust
A. ARGENTINA	1.1	.3	.8	1.3	.7	.4	.8	.4[a]	.2[†]	.2[†]
C. BRAZIL	4.7	2.5	2.6	2.1	1.8	1.3	.5	.5[a]	.5	.7

Continued in SALA, 24-2845.

Table 2925

U.S. CLAIMS ON UNAFFILIATED FOREIGNERS[1] AS REPORTED BY NONBANKING BUSINESS ENTERPRISES TO THE FEDERAL RESERVE, 3 L, 1980–88

(M US)

| | | | | | Financial Claims | | | | | |
	Country	1980	1981	1982	1983	1984	1985	1986	1987[a]	1988[a]
C.	BRAZIL	96	30	62	53	100	78	86	63	47
N.	MEXICO	208	313	274	293	215	180	174	172	151
T.	VENEZUELA	137	148	139	134	125	48	21	19	22

| | | | | | Commercial Claims | | | | | |
	Country	1980	1981	1982	1983	1984	1985	1986	1987[a]	1988[a]
C.	BRAZIL	861	668	258	493	214	206	234	226	295
N.	MEXICO	1,102	1,022	775	884	583	510	412	368	460
T.	VENEZUELA	410	424	351	272	206	157	237	296	226

1. The term "foreigners" covers all institutions and individuals domiciled outside the United States (including U.S. citizens domiciled abroad), and the foreign branches, subsidiaries, and offices of U.S. banks and business concerns; the central governments, central banks, and other official institutions of foreign countries, wherever located; and international and regional organizations, wherever located. The term "foreigners" also includes persons in the United States when it is known by reporting institutions that they are acting on behalf of foreigners. (See the *Annual Statistical Digest*, 1970–1979, of the Board of Governors of the Federal Reserve System, pp. 580–582, for an outline of revisions in international statistics.)

a. As of December of corresponding year.

SOURCE: USBG-FRB, June 1985, September 1986, August 1987, December 1988, table 3.23; August 1989, table 3.23.

Table 2926

U.S. CLAIMS ON FOREIGN COUNTRIES HELD BY U.S. OFFICES AND FOREIGN BRANCHES OF U.S. — CHARTERED BANKS,[1] 9 L, 1979–89

(B US)

	Country	1979	1980	1981	1982	1983	1984	1985	1986	1987	1988	1989[b]
A.	ARGENTINA	5.0	7.9	9.4	8.9	9.5	6.3	6.6	9.5	9.4	8.9	8.4
C.	BRAZIL	15.2	16.2	19.1	22.9	23.1	18.6	17.4	25.2[a]	24.7	22.5	22.8
D.	CHILE	2.5	3.7	5.8	6.3	6.4	5.1	4.9	7.1	6.9	5.7	5.6
E.	COLOMBIA	2.2	2.6	2.6	3.1	3.2	2.5	2.3	2.1	2.0	2.0	1.9
I.	ECUADOR	1.7	2.1	2.2	2.2	2.2	1.7	1.7	2.2	1.9	1.7	1.7
M.	MEXICO[2]	12.0	15.9	21.6	24.5	26.1	18.2	15.5	23.8[a]	23.7[a]	19.0	18.3
P.	PANAMA[2]	4.3	5.4	7.7	7.5	5.8	3.1	2.6	5.1	3.7	2.6	2.3
R.	PERU	1.5	1.8	2.0	2.6	2.4	1.9	1.5	1.4[a]	1.1	.8	.7
T.	VENEZUELA	8.7	9.1	9.9	10.5	9.9	6.5	6.3	8.6	8.1[a]	7.9	8.0

1. The banking offices covered by these data are the U.S. offices and foreign branches of U.S.-owned banks and of U.S. subsidiaries of foreign-owned banks. Offices *not* covered include (1) U.S. agencies and branches of foreign banks, and (2) foreign subsidiaries of U.S. banks. To minimize duplication, the data are adjusted to exclude the claims on foreign branches held by a U.S. office or another foreign branch of the same banking institution.
2. Includes Canal Zone, beginning December 1979.

a. Preliminary data as of December of corresponding year.
b. Data as of March of corresponding year.

SOURCE: USBG-FRB, September 1984, September 1986, August 1987, December 1988, table 3.21; August 1989, table 3.21.

Table 2927

U.S. BANKS' OWN CLAIMS ON FOREIGNERS AS REPORTED
TO THE FEDERAL RESERVE, 12 L, 1981–89
(M US, YE)

	Country	1981[a]	1982	1983	1984	1985	1986	1987	1988[b]	1989[c]
A.	ARGENTINA	7,527	10,974	11,749	11,050	11,462	12,091	11,996	11,804	11,681
C.	BRAZIL	16,926	23,271	24,667	26,315	25,283	25,716	25,897	25,735	25,990
D.	CHILE	3,690	5,513	6,072	6,839	6,603	6,558	6,308	5,401	5,234
E.	COLOMBIA	2,018	3,211	3,745	3,499	3,249	2,821	2,740	2,938	2,655
G.	CUBA	3	3	0	0	0	0	1	1	2
I.	ECUADOR	1,531	2,062	2,307	2,420	2,390	2,439	2,286	2,075	2,029
K.	GUATEMALA	124	124	129	158	194	140	144	198	210
N.	MEXICO	22,439	29,552	34,802	34,885	31,799	30,698	29,532	24,636	24,122
P.	PANAMA	6,794	10,210	7,848	7,707	6,645	5,436	4,744	2,506	2,431
R.	PERU	1,218	2,357	2,536	2,384	1,947	1,661	1,329	1,012	947
S.	URUGUAY	157	686	977	1,088	960	940	963	910	876
T.	VENEZUELA	7,069	10,643	11,287	11,017	10,871	11,108	10,843	10,732	10,680

a. Liabilities and claims of banks in the United States were increased, beginning in
   December 1981, by the shift from foreign branches to international banking facilities
   in the United States of liabilities to, and claims on, foreign residents.
b. Preliminary data as of December of corresponding year.
c. Preliminary data as of August of corresponding year.

SOURCE: USBG-FRB, June 1985, September 1986, August 1987, December 1988,
   table 3.18; August 1989, table 3.18.

Table 2928

U.S. LIABILITIES DUE TO FOREIGNERS AS REPORTED
TO THE FEDERAL RESERVE, 12 L, 1981–89
(M US)

	Country	1981[a]	1982	1983	1984	1985	1986	1987	1988	1989[c]
A.	ARGENTINA	2,445	3,578	4,038	4,394	6,032	4,757	5,006	7,749	6,280
C.	BRAZIL	1,568	2,014	3,168	5,275	5,373	4,325	4,005[b]	5,268	5,554
D.	CHILE	664	1,626	1,842	2,001	2,049	2,054	2,210	2,917	2,931
E.	COLOMBIA	2,993	2,594	1,689	2,514	3,104	4,285	4,204[b]	4,317	4,175
G.	CUBA	9	9	8	10	11	7	12	10	10
I.	ECUADOR	434	455	1,047	1,092	1,239	1,236	1,082	1,356	1,376
K.	GUATEMALA	479	670	788	896	1,071	1,123	1,082	1,186	1,272
N.	MEXICO	7,235	8,377	10,392	12,303	14,060	13,745	14,480	15,093	14,269
P.	PANAMA	4,857	4,805	5,924	6,951	7,514	6,886	7,414	4,206	4,347
R.	PERU	694	1,147	1,166	1,266	1,167	1,163	1,275	1,626	1,763
S.	URUGUAY	367	759	1,244	1,394	1,552	1,537	1,582[b]	1,895	2,255
T.	VENEZUELA	4,245	8,417	8,632	10,545	11,922	10,171	9,048	9,095	9,553

a. Liabilities and claims of banks in the United States were increased, beginning in
   December 1981, by the shift from foreign branches to international banking facilities
   in the United States of liabilities to, and claims on, foreign residents.
b. Preliminary data as of December of corresponding year.
c. Preliminary data as of August of corresponding year.

SOURCE: USBG-FRB, June 1985, September 1986, August 1987, December 1988,
   table 3.17; August 1989, table 3.17.

Table 2929

LATIN AMERICAN LOAN VALUES ON THE SECONDARY MARKET, 11 L, 1984–89

(Real % of Nominal Value)

Month and Year

	Country	12/84	12/85	6/86	12/86	6/87	7/87	8/87	9/87	10/87	11/87	12/87	1/88	2/88	3/88	4/88
A.	ARGENTINA	66.00	66.00	65.75	64.00	52.00	46.50	46.00	38.00	36.00	38.00	36.00	32.00	30.00	29.00	29.00
B.	BOLIVIA	25.00	8.50	7.75	9.00	12.00	12.00	12.00	10.00	10.00	10.00	10.00	11.00	11.00	11.00	11.00
C.	BRAZIL	85.00	78.00	75.00	74.00	60.00	53.00	47.00	39.00	42.00	46.00	46.00	46.00	46.00	46.00	50.00
D.	CHILE	65.00	68.00	68.50	68.50	68.50	67.00	62.00	55.00	52.00	57.00	59.00	62.00	61.00	61.00	59.00
E.	COLOMBIA	85.00	85.00	83.00	84.00	83.00	83.00	80.00	78.00	74.00	68.00	63.00	65.00	65.00	65.00	65.00
F.	COSTA RICA[1]	0	0	36.00	36.00	35.00	35.00	32.00	27.00	25.00	25.00	15.00	15.00	15.00	15.00	15.00
I.	ECUADOR	72.00	72.00	64.00	65.00	49.00	45.00	38.00	31.00	33.00	34.00	34.00	36.00	34.00	32.00	27.00
N.	MEXICO	83.00	70.00	58.00	56.00	56.00	53.00	50.00	48.00	51.00	53.00	50.00	51.00	48.00	48.00	51.00
P.	PANAMA	80.00	78.00	70.00	67.00	65.00	60.00	55.00	45.00	45.00	40.00	35.00	35.00	27.00	25.00	20.00
R.	PERU[1]	0	0	22.00	21.00	13.00	13.00	8.00	8.00	8.00	8.00	8.00	8.00	8.00	8.00	8.00
T.	VENEZUELA	57.00	82.00	76.00	73.50	71.00	66.00	64.00	50.00	50.00	56.00	42.00				

	Country	5/88	6/88	7/88	8/88	9/88	10/88	11/88	12/88	1/89	2/89	3/89	4/89	5/89	6/89	7/89
A.	ARGENTINA	28.00	24.50	27.00	22.50	23.00	21.00	20.00	22.00	18.50	18.00	16.75	16.00	13.25	14.38	17.75
B.	BOLIVIA	11.00	11.00	11.00	11.00	11.00	11.00	11.00	11.00	11.00	11.00	11.00	11.00	11.00	11.00	11.00
C.	BRAZIL	54.00	51.75	51.50	46.50	46.50	44.25	40.25	40.00	34.00	28.50	34.50	35.50	32.25	31.25	33.88
D.	CHILE	60.50	60.75	60.75	60.00	60.00	58.00	55.00	58.00	60.00	57.00	59.00	59.00	60.00	63.88	64.75
E.	COLOMBIA	65.00	66.00	67.00	66.50	66.00	62.00	58.50	58.00	57.00	55.00	55.00	57.50	57.50	58.50	63.00
F.	COSTA RICA[1]	14.00	12.50	12.50	12.00	12.00	12.00	12.00	12.00	12.50	11.00	13.00	13.00	13.00	15.00	15.00
I.	ECUADOR	26.50	26.00	26.00	21.00	16.00	14.00	14.00	14.00	13.00	12.50	12.50	12.50	13.00	13.50	18.00
N.	MEXICO	53.00	51.50	50.50	46.50	46.50	46.25	43.00	43.00	38.00	33.50	40.50	41.50	39.00	40.75	43.75
P.	PANAMA	20.00	23.50	24.00	22.00	20.00	20.00	20.00	20.00	14.00	14.00	13.00	12.00	10.00	10.00	10.00
R.	PERU[1]	8.00	8.00	8.00	6.00	5.00	5.00	5.00	5.00	5.00	5.00	5.00	5.00	5.00	5.00	5.00
T.	VENEZUELA	55.00	55.00	55.00	50.00	48.50	44.50	40.50	40.50	36.00	27.50	34.00	37.50	36.50	37.50	40.13

1. Price "0" is used so calculation will not be distorted.

SOURCE: Supplied by Merrill Lynch Internationa, August 12, 1987; December 20, 1988; August 1989.

Table 2930

CHILE REAL DEBT, 1960–85
(M US of 1983)

Year	(A) Debt (as of Dec. 31)	(B) Reserves (as of Dec. 31)	(C) Net Position (as of Dec. 31) (A – B)	(D) Interest Payments
1960	746	73	673	19
1961	1,010	–5	1,015	28
1962	1,255	15	1,240	36
1963	1,469	–24	1,493	42

Continued in SALA, 25-2837.

Table 2931

CUBA TOTAL DISBURSED DEBT IN CONVERTIBLE CURRENCY AND
INDICATORS OF DEBT BURDEN, 1969–87

Year	Total Debt					Debt Services[a]	
	Current Pesos[b] M	Current M US	Annual Change in Current Pesos (%)	Total Debt/C (Current Pesos)	Total Debt as % of GSP	Interest Only (%)	Interest and Principal (%)
1969	291.0	291		34.3	~	~	~
		1,632	1969 to 1975	142.9	2.1		
1975	1,338.0		29.0%			~	~
			1975 to 1978				
1978	2,883.8	3,845	29.2%	297.7	17.5	19.2	57.7
1979	5,267.3	4,476	13.3	335.0	19.2	19.4	45.3
1980	3,226.8	4,545	–1.2	332.9	18.3	17.7	28.7
1981	3,169.6	4,064	–1.8	325.0	14.3	19.3	35.9
1982	2,668.7	3,140	–16.5	271.0	11.6	21.0	64.7
1983	2,789.7	3,207	4.5	280.5	11.5	20.1	~
1984	2,988.8	3,321	7.1	297.6	11.5	16.5	~
1985	3,621.0	3,936	21.2	356.7	13.5	17.4	41.8
1986	3,870.4	4,663	6.9	379.4	14.1	21.7	67.8
1987 (Sept.)	5,555.1	5,555	43.5	536.7	21.0	~	~

a. "Debt service" is defined as interest and interest plus principal as a percentage of total exports of goods and services in the convertible currency area.

b. The total debt figures in current Cuban pesos are translated into current U.S. dollars using the official exchange rates from table 7 in Source.

SOURCE: A.R.M. Ritter, "Cuba's Convertible Currency Debt Problem," *CEPAL Review* No. 36, December 1988, p. 120.

Table 2932

CUBA FOREIGN DEBT IN CONVERTIBLE CURRENCY, 1979–87
(M NC)

Year	1979	1980	1981	1982	1983	1984	1985	1986	1987[a]
Total Disbursed Debt	3,267.3	3,226.8	3,169.6	2,668.7	2,789.7	2,988.8	3,621.0	3,870.4	5,555.1
Official Bilateral	1,279.9	1,353.6	1,293.7	1,275.8	1,332.5	1,578.7	1,820.4	1,627.8	2,464.8
Intergovernmental Loans	236.4	278.7	221.4	198.7	191.7	174.3	135.9	112.8	145.7
Credits for Development Assistance	21.4	28.3	27.2	28.2	27.4	27.1	32.2	41.2	60.0
Export Credits with Government Guarantee	1,022.1	1,046.4	1,045.1	1,048.9	1,113.3	1,377.3	1,652.3	1,473.9	2,259.1
Official Multilateral	~	7.9	15.2	18.2	25.0	17.2	21.5	18.0	22.3
Suppliers' Credits	33.2	27.0	33.4	46.8	96.7	228.5	433.2	861.7	1,184.7
Financial Institutions	1,952.6	1,837.1	1,826.4	1,327.3	1,334.9	1,164.2	1,345.7	1,362.8	1,883.1
Bank Loans and Deposits	1,927.7	1,800.8	1,787.2	1,277.0	1,284.5	1,076.5	1,237.9	1,199.2	1,643.0
Medium and Long-Term	658.6	562.9	505.3	416.8	495.2	453.6	495.5	457.0	615.0
Short-Term Deposits	1,269.1	1,237.9	1,281.9	860.2	789.3	622.9	742.4	742.2	1,028.0
Credits for Current Imports	24.9	36.3	39.2	50.3	50.4	87.7	107.8	163.6	240.1
Other Credits	1.6	1.2	.9	.7	.7	.2	.2	1	.2

a. Sept. 30.

SOURCE: A.R.M. Ritter, "Cuba's Convertible Currency Debt Problem," *CEPAL Review*,
No. 36, Dec. 1988, p. 124.

Table 2933

MEXICO AMORTIZATION CALENDAR WITH COMMERCIAL BANKS AFTER DEBT RESTRUCTURING
(M US)

Year	Before	After
1986	1,208	258
1987	513	0
1988	1,016	0
1989	3,000	572
1990	3,499	1,897
1991	4,291	1,897
1992	4,803	1,897
1993	5,293	1,897
1994	5,492	1,606
1995	5,582	1,026
1996	5,811	2,623
1997	6,091	1,872
1998	6,118	2,666
1999	~	3,182
2000	~	3,672
2001	~	4,652
2002	~	5,609
2003	~	5,839
2004	~	6,120
2005	~	3,072
2006	~	3,072

SOURCE: *Mexico Today*, April 1987.

Table 2934

MEXICO RESULTS OF NEGOTIATIONS
WITH PRIVATE BANKS

(M US)

1. Restructured Debt, 1985–90	43,700
2. Previous Credits, 1983–84	8,500
3. New Credits	6,000
4. Credit to Ensure Growth[1]	500
5. Credit to Ensure Investment[1]	1,200
6. Private Debt (FIORCA)	9,700
7. Inter-Banking Lines of Credit	6,000
Total	75,650

1. Contingencies.

SOURCE: *Mexico Today*, April 1987.

Table 2935

MEXICO NEW FINANCING, 1987

(M US)

New Credit	12,000
Official Sources	6,000
IMF	1,700
Multilateral	2,500
Bilateral	1,800
Commercial Banks	6,000
Facility 1	5,000
Facility	1,000
Credit Contingencies	2,420
Oil	720
Facility 3	500
Facility 4	1,200
Total	14,420

SOURCE: *Mexico Today*, April 1987.

Table 2936

THREE VIEWS OF THE CUMULATIVE FOREIGN LOANS DISBURSED TO
MEXICO'S PUBLIC SECTOR,[1] 1970–82

(YE)

Year	M US[3]		1981 = 100.0	M US of 1981
	(A) Nominal Debt One Year or Longer	(B) Nominal Debt 90 Days or Longer[2]	(C) U.S. Export Price Index	(D) Real Debt 90 Days or Longer[2] (B/C)
1970	3,245	4,262	35.2	12,108
1971	3,523	4,546	36.3	12,523
1972	3,962	5,064	37.3	13,576

Continued in SALA, 25-2838.

Table 2937

MEXICO PUBLIC AND PRIVATE DEBT, 1985–87

(M US)

	1985 December	1986 December	1987 March	1987 June	1987 September	1987 December
Public Sector	72,081	75,351	76,546	79,294	78,965	81,407
Commercial Banks	57,915	58,787	59,185	61,536	61,288	62,498
Restructured	43,978	43,924	44,150	43,460	43,119	42,982
Non-Restructured	13,937	14,863	15,035	18,076	18,169	19,516
Pemex Acceptances	3,315	3,321	3,351	3,353	3,356	3,399
Other[1]	10,622	11,542	11,684	14,723	14,813	16,117
Other Creditors	14,166	16,564	17,361	17,758	17,677	18,909
World Bank and IDB	5,945	7,411	7,674	7,829	7,629	8,125
Bilateral	4,314	5,619	6,377	6,857	7,037	7,989
Private Placements	655	681	666	581	537	544
Suppliers	167	132	124	123	112	109
Bonds	3,085	2,721	2,520	2,368	2,362	2,142
Currency Composition of Total Public Sector Debt						
Austrian Schillings	22	29	31	31	32	39
Belgian Francs	152	241	282	321	327	395
Canadian Dollars	132	603	595	596	649	635
Deutsche Marks	1,416	1,994	2,155	2,343	2,366	2,727
Dutch Guilders	162	219	239	290	253	335
ECUs	0	512	587	679	721	788
French Francs	412	630	727	961	988	1,283
Italian Lire	101	180	227	327	358	428
Japanese Yen	2,001	3,247	4,016	4,863	4,797	6,229
Pounds Sterling	921	1,147	1,323	1,465	1,556	1,786
Swiss Francs	640	864	779	827	819	899
U.S. Dollars	64,670	65,561	65,459	66,476	65,969	65,722
Other	1,452	124	126	115	130	141
Mexican Banks	4,824	5,551	5,186	4,986	5,139	5,837
Commercial Banks[2]	3,913	4,972	4,585	4,142	4,193	5,276
Other Creditors[3]	911	579	601	844	946	560
Private Sector[4]	16,719	16,061	16,061	15,881[a]	15,881[a]	15,090
Commercial Banks	13,724	13,401	13,401	13,930	13,930	13,301
FICORCA	9,530	9,367	9,367	8,893	8,893	5,342
Reportos (Back-to-Backs)	956	718	718	618	618	322
Other	3,238	3,316	3,316	4,419	4,419	7,637
Other Creditors	2,995	2,660	2,660	1,951	1,951	1,789
FICORCA	1,551	1,165	1,165	767	767	651[b]
Bilateral Sources	916	955	955	766	766	766
Other	528	540	540	418	418	372
IMF (Banco de México)	2,943	4,028	4,179	4,611	4,777	5,119
Total External Debt (A+B+C+D)[5]	96,567	100,991	101,972	104,772	104,762	107,453

1. Includes direct and syndicated, short-term and new money of 1983, 1984, and 1987.
2. Outstanding debt of Commercial banks; excludes CCC and US $3142.0 million of Mexican banks' share in syndicated credits.
3. CCC.
4. As registered (excludes unregistered debt, mainly short-term credits granted by national credit institutions).
5. Line items for short-term external debt and long-term external debt (based on original maturity) will be shown when applicable.

a. Most recent available data of private sector foreign debt registry.
b. Includes US$615 million of foreign debt registered in FICORCA Systems 2 and 4.

SOURCE: Mexico, Secretaría de Hacienda y Crédito Público, *Mexico: Economic and Financial Statistics, Data Book* (February 29, 1988), p. 18.

Figure 29:2

MEXICO FOREIGN PUBLIC DEBT AMORTIZATION CONVERSION
OF OLD DEBT, 1988–2008
(B US)

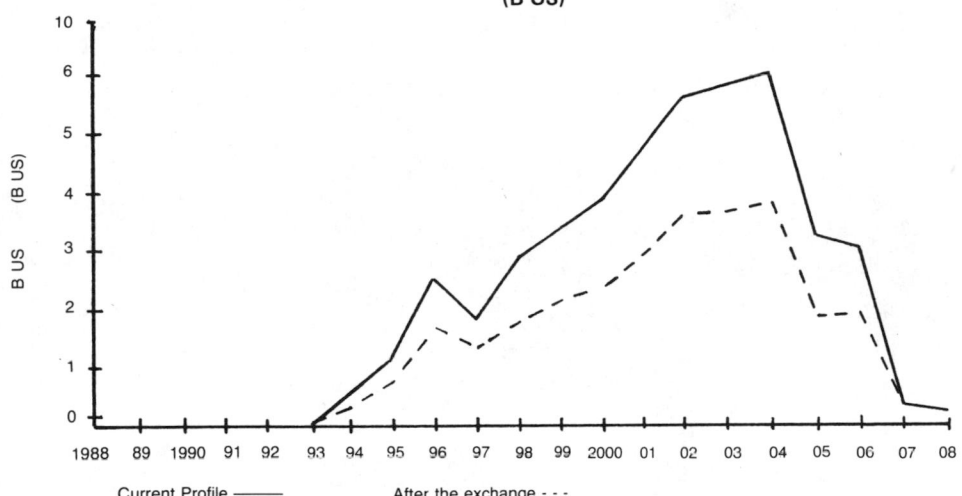

Current Profile ——   After the exchange - - -

SOURCE: *Mexico Today*, February 1988, p. 11.

30

Investments and
Corporate Business Activity

DEFINITIONS OF TERMS

Direct Foreign Investment includes all business enterprises in which U.S. investors have a controlling interest or an important voice in management (usually a 25 percent minimum of voting stock); and this investment excludes miscellaneous holdings of those stocks and bonds issued by foreign corporations or governments which ordinarily are termed "portfolio investments." *See* U.S. Department of Commerce, Office of Business Economics, *Direct Private Foreign Investment of the United States*: Census of 1950, pp. 4, 27, 36–42.

Table 3000

U.S. DIRECT FOREIGN INVESTMENT IN LATIN AMERICA, 19 LRC, 1950–87
(Cumulative M US in Book Value)

Country	Year	Total[2]	Mining	Petroleum	Manufacturing[3]	Transport, Communications, and Public Utilities	Trade	Other Industries
A. ARGENTINA	1950	356	~a	~b	161	77	35	16
	1951	360	~a	~a	167	~a	41	~
	1952	382	~a	~a	192	~a	47	~
	1953	391	~a	~a	193	~a	49	~
	1954	405	~a	~a	208	~a	47	~
	1955	418	~a	~a	218	~a	42	~
	1956	429	~a	~a	233	~a	40	~
	1957	333	~a	~a	164	~a	22	~
	1958	330	~a	~a	154	~a	19	~
	1959	366	~a	~a	160	~a	16	~
	1960	473	~a	~a	214	~a	21	~
	1961	560	~a	~a	307	22	29	~
	1962	799	~a	~a	413	23	34	~
	1963	829	~a	~a	454	24	38	~
	1964	882	~a	~a	500	25	40	~
	1965	992	~a	187	618	25	47	327
	1966	758	~a	121	510	9	23	~
	1967	803	~a	125	536	9	31	~
	1968	870	~a	120	589	10	~	50
	1969	973	~a	115	659	8	~	60
	1970	1,022	28	137	669	6	~a	~
	1971	1,089	39	148	712	5	~a	~
	1972	1,128	~a	~a	749	~a	~a	~
	1973	1,144	44	141	768	~a	~a	~
	1974	1,138	50	147	737	11	70	68
	1975	1,154	~	142	764	8	87	60
	1976	1,366	53	174	898	~a	105	~a
	1977	1,490	55	223	921	~	132	~
	1978	1,658	53	259	983	~	157	~
	1979	1,850	~	305	1,184	289	136	~
	1980	2,494	~	395	1,584	409	216	~
	1981	2,735	69	483	1,570	308	202	107
	1982	2,979	71	629	1,718	~e	168	93
	1983	2,702	~	500	1,555	~d	167	105
	1984	2,746	~	443	1,568	~d	174	122
	1985	2,713	~	471	1,505	174	135	112
	1986	2,986	~	473	1,749	255	158	101
	1987	2,854	~	398	1,616	~d	169	68
B. BOLIVIA	1950	11	6	~	~b	2	2	~b
C. BRAZIL	1950	644	2	112	285	138	73	35
	1951	784	2	131	387	142	88	34
	1952	977	1	167	507	151	112	37
	1953	970	3	197	477	149	106	39
	1954	992	4	165	527	150	114	33
	1955	1,052	4	179	560	156	121	32
	1956	1,143	9	188	612	171	129	35
	1957	835	10	130	378	182	116	19
	1958	795	6	93	398	186	91	20
	1959	828	5	84	432	192	93	21
	1960	953	10	76	515	200	130	23
	1961	1,006	14	92	548	198	129	25
	1962	1,084	26	79	616	191	136	35
	1963	1,132	30	60	664	193	148	38
	1964	997	40	53	668	41	153	41
	1965	1,074	51	57	723	37	162	45
	1966	882	28	70	574	~	92	~
	1967	961	28	76	627	22	88	31
	1968	1,122	27	79	757	17	92	43
	1969	1,290	26	95	899	15	86	52
	1970	1,526	30	114	1,075	15	119	54
	1971	1,745	26	141	1,225	14	150	70
	1972	2,180	45	164	1,561	15	175	80
	1973	2,885	31	198	2,046	16	212	103
	1974	3,760	94	244	2,578	18	363	183
	1975	4,579	130	288	3,106	22	406	269
	1976	5,416	140	336	3,673	26	496	31
	1977	5,930	~	364	3,937	26	495	~

Table 3000 (Continued)

U.S. DIRECT FOREIGN INVESTMENT IN LATIN AMERICA, 19 LRC, 1950–87
(Cumulative M US in Book Value)

	Country	Year	Total[2]	Mining	Petroleum	Manufacturing[3]	Transport, Communications, and Public Utilities	Trade	Other Industries
C.	BRAZIL	1978	7,170	268	424	4,684	25	552	521
	(Continued)	1979	7,186	110	301	4,902	548	506	194
		1980	7,703	141	365	5,145	679	571	206
		1981	8,253	152	422	5,420	590	581	216
		1982	9,031	138	448	5,958	633	625	223
		1983	9,060	~	358	6,451	734	394	212
		1984	9,377	~	302	6,764	899	410	178
		1985	8,889	~	206	6,888	1,026	375	99
		1986	9,135	~	151	7,095	1,187	452	112
		1987	9,955	~	273	7,730	1,228	397	108
D.	CHILE	1950	540	351	~b	29	~b	15	3
		1951	582	382	~a	33	~a	14	~
		1952	626	423	~a	33	~a	11	~
		1953	660	452	~a	34	~a	9	~
		1954	635	418	~a	35	~a	10	~
		1955	643	421	~a	37	~a	11	~
		1956	682	454	~a	39	~a	12	~
		1957	666	483	~a	22	~a	9	~
		1958	687	498	~a	21	~a	8	~
		1959	729	526	~a	21	~a	10	~
		1960	738	517	~a	22	~a	12	~
		1961	735	504	~a	27	171	14	~
		1962	755	504	~a	29	187	14	~
		1963	768	503	~a	27	201	15	~
		1964	769	~a	~a	30	214	20	~
		1965	829	509	~a	39	~a	24	257
		1966	765	430	~a	47	~a	19	~
		1967	820	~	~a	56	~d	21	
		1968	916	566	~a	57	~a	21	12
		1969	817	443	~a	57	~a	20	16
		1970	758	490	~a	57	135	24	20
		1971	739	486	~a	48	133	23	19
		1972	642	~	~a	50	131	25	17
		1973	643	~	~a	47	131	28	16
		1974	287	25	~	44	129	27	23
		1975	174	12	~	49	4	28	~
		1976	179	5	~	49	6	34	~
		1977	193	~	~	56	7	39	~
		1978	230	~	~	71	10	51	26
		1979	260	5	70	~	~	49	~
		1980	536	209	91	~	~	64	~
		1981	834	~	98	112	~	80	~
		1982	854	~d	79	60	~	71	~d
		1983	108	~	59	-289	~d	64	151
		1984	46	~	44	-276	~d	49	136
		1985	85	~	49	-281	~d	42	123
		1986	193	~	48	-277	~d	37	125
		1987	224	~	~	-221	~d	21	49
E.	COLOMBIA	1950	193	~a	112	25	29	9	~
		1951	221	~	131	27	31	11	~
		1952	261	~a	152	37	31	19	~
		1953	271	~a	159	41	28	22	~
		1954	310	~a	166	51	31	36	~
		1955	336	~a	178	58	33	42	~
		1956	371	~a	193	68	39	44	~
		1957	396	~a	245	61	24	34	~
		1958	383	~a	225	68	26	35	~
		1959	401	~a	225	77	28	41	~
		1960	424	~a	233	92	28	46	~
		1961	425	~a	230	95	29	49	~
		1962	455	~a	257	100	27	52	~
		1963	465	~a	246	120	27	52	~
		1964	508	~a	255	148	30	53	~
		1965	526	~a	269	160	29	49	20
		1966	459	~a	86	193	~	27	15
		1967	482	~a	105	200	~	29	17
		1968	520	~a	130	212	~	25	~
		1969	574	~a	147	240	27	29	~

Table 3000 (Continued)

U.S. DIRECT FOREIGN INVESTMENT IN LATIN AMERICA, 19 LRC, 1950–87
(Cumulative M US in Book Value)

Country	Year	Total[2]	Mining	Petroleum	Manufacturing[3]	Transport, Communications, and Public Utilities	Trade	Other Industries
E. COLOMBIA (Continued)	1970	584	12	137	250	26	37	~
	1971	650	~a	146	302	25	35	~
	1972	635	~a	129	299	26	37	~
	1973	608	~a	76	326	~a	45	14
	1974	617	18	58	366	14	54	~
	1975	848	17	62	381	13	64	16
	1976	654	11	56	388	~	64	~
	1977	696	9	72	432	~	66	~
	1978	769	9	85	490	~	69	~
	1979	842	~	198	492	~	95	~
	1980	1,012	~	265	548	~	97	~
	1981	1,174	~	318	574	~	98	~
	1982	1,655	~d	569	651	~d	105	~d
	1983	2,123	~	1,010	637	~d	91	~d
	1984	2,267	~	1,075	694	~d	83	~d
	1985	2,142	~	1,005	661	~d	51	~d
	1986	2,049	~	965	677	~d	42	~d
	1987	2,037	~	1,013	585	~d	65	~d
F. COSTA RICA	1950	60	~	4	~	11	1	~b
	1955‡	61	~	6	~	11	~b	~b
G. CUBA	1950	642	~b	20	54	271	21	269c
	1955	736	~b	~b	55	312	30	298
	1960‡	956	~a	147	111	313	44	341
H. DOMINICAN REP.	1950	106	~	~b	9	11	1	81
	1955‡	134	6	~b	13	5	~b	103
	1960	105	~b	~b	~b	~b	~b	~
I. ECUADOR	1950	14	~	~b	1	5	2	4
	1955‡	25	~	~b	~b	6	2	8
	1982	405	#	225	133	5	37	-9
	1983	442	~	~d	117	9	27	~d
	1984	371	~	192	126	10	26	11
	1985	361	~	~d	140	12	~	~d
	1986	536	~	319	152	13	28	12
	1987	497	~	237	157	~d	33	~d
J. EL SALVADOR	1950	19	~b	2	~b	17	1	~b
K. GUATEMALA	1950	106	~b	4	~b	72	3	~b
	1955‡	103	~b	6	~b	73	~b	~b
	1960	131‡	~a	26‡	~a	66‡	5‡	34‡
L. HAITI	1950	13	~	~b	~b	2	~b	8
	1955‡	18	~	~b	~b	3	~b	9
M. HONDURAS	1950	62	~a	~a	~a	9	~b	~a
	1955‡	101	~a	~a	~a	12	~b	~a
	1960	100‡	~a	~a	~a	23‡	1‡	76‡
N. MEXICO	1950	414	121	13	133	107	30	11
	1951	468	126	9	194	87	41	11
	1952	481	128	10	205	89	38	11
	1953	497	138	11	207	89	39	11
	1954	503	135	13	208	88	44	16
	1955	577	143	15	262	87	54	16
	1956	667	158	22	309	88	72	19
	1957	739	139	31	335	134	68	32
	1958	745	139	32	326	120	84	34
	1959	758	137	30	353	118	84	36
	1960	795	130	32	391	119	85	39
	1961	830	129	54	418	29	97	104
	1962	867	121	73	442	26	97	107
	1963	907	116	65	502	25	93	105
	1964	1,034	128	56	606	27	111	106
	1965	1,182	104	48	756	27	138	110
	1966	1,329	95	29	927	20	136	39
	1967	1,426	~a	26	1,016	18	151	~a
	1968	1,566	97	25	1,147	19	165	59
	1969	1,756	117	15	1,277	20	179	94
	1970	1,912	127	10	1,380	23	207	122
	1971	1,980	103	7	1,492	26	224	82
	1972	2,161	98	10	1,631	26	263	82
	1973	2,379	85	10	1,800	31	305	88

Table 3000 (Continued)

U.S. DIRECT FOREIGN INVESTMENT IN LATIN AMERICA, 19 LRC, 1950–87
(Cumulative M US in Book Value)

Country	Year	Total[2]	Mining	Petroleum	Manufacturing[3]	Transport, Communications, and Public Utilities	Trade	Other Industries
N. MEXICO (Continued)	1974	2,854	83	18	2,173	34	400	550
	1975	3,200	80	22	2,443	35	476	87
	1976	2,984	88	17	2,223	47	453	105
	1977	3,230	98	26	2,391	~	502	~
	1978	3,712	97	41	2,752	~	563	~
	1979	4,490	76	145	3,451	508	537	~
	1980	5,989	95	150	4,489	750	727	~
	1981	6,962	77	189	5,140	846	878	~
	1982	5,584	~e	193	4,166	726	626	~e
	1983	4,381	~	75	3,446	430	352	327
	1984	4,568	~	76	3,632	461	410	261
	1985	5,070	~	52	4,073	774	522	257
	1986	4,826	~	42	3,926	841	456	~d
	1987	4,997	~	65	3,959	1,018	277	~d
O. NICARAGUA	1950	9	~b	~b	~b	1	1	~
P. PANAMA	1950	58	- -	6	2	18	11	23
	1951	67	- -	6	2	17	14	28
	1952	69	- -	6	3	18	12	30
	1953	86	- -	7	4	18	14	43
	1954	100	- -	9	4	20	18	49
	1955	109	.	10	5	21	15	57
	1956	157	1	1	8	24	30	94
	1957	201	5	13	3	19	70	91
	1958	268	8	25	6	20	94	115
	1959	327	16	29	8	21	118	135
	1960	405	17	56	9	22	145	156
	1961	486	17	62	10	25	195	177
	1962	537	19	81	5	25	224	183
	1963	616	19	94	12	26	273	193
	1964	663	19	107	23	29	281	205
	1965	724	19	130	24	36	293	221
	1966	847	- -	70	18	52	235	151
	1967	872	- -	~a	~a	54	240	155
	1968	971	- -	47	48	60	250	178
	1969	1,055	- -	27	49	62	259	184
	1970	1,190	- -	39	64	60	274	211
	1971	1,380	- -	33	77	63	301	225
	1972	1,352	- -	25	88	51	318	230
	1973	1,549	1	~a	89	42	375	~a
	1974	1,604	-1	55	115	43	456	324
	1975	1,907	1	125	122	39	542	359
	1976	1,957	1	94	139	45	572	381
	1977	2,249	1	106	158	24	654	386
	1978	2,385	1	68	180	26	707	406
	1979	2,874	5	289	214	#	542	242
	1980	3,171	- -	503	262	#	601	~
	1981	3,671	- -	601	302	#	672	377
	1982	4,404	~e	776	327	#	655	~d
	1983	4,837	~	1,101	189	#	704	90
	1984	4,467	~	548	~d	#	701	~d
	1985	4,004	~	514	245	0	639	33
	1986	4,352	~	498	253	0	784	48
	1987	4,780	~	648	278	0	27	~d
R. PERU	1950	145	55	~b	16	~b	13	1
	1951	199	107	~a	21	~a	18	~
	1952	233	129	~a	17	~a	24	~
	1953	274	150	~a	16	~a	29	~
	1954	278	150	~a	18	~a	31	~
	1955	292	154	~a	23	~a	36	~
	1956	332	178	~a	25	~a	38	~
	1957	383	196	86	29	14	42	16
	1958	409	218	86	29	19	38	18
	1959	428	242	79	31	19	36	20
	1960	496	307	79	35	19	42	20
	1961	486	292	71	36	20	45	23
	1962	503	298	66	46	20	48	26
	1963	498	290	56	64	21	41	27
	1964	514	291	60	65	27	46	31
	1965	515	262	60	79	21	54	38

Table 3000 (Continued)

U.S. DIRECT FOREIGN INVESTMENT IN LATIN AMERICA, 19 LRC, 1950–87
(Cumulative M US in Book Value)

Country	Year	Total[2]	Mining	Petroleum	Manufacturing[3]	Transport, Communications, and Public Utilities	Trade	Other Industries
R. PERU (Continued)	1966	651	360	~[a]	128	~[a]	52	24
	1967	712	416	57	140	~[a]	45	24
	1968	749	440	62	146	~[a]	~[a]	26
	1969	771	~[a]	66	154	−2	37	26
	1970	744	~[a]	67	156	−1	35	24
	1971	729	~[a]	74	156	−1	33	29
	1972	769	442	97	155	−3	32	36
	1973	859	466	149	161	−2	42	32
	1974	900	412	239	155	−2	54	74
	1975	1,221	700	246	166	−1	62	37
	1976	1,367	~	~	168	−1	64	43
	1977	1,397	807	316	159	−1	62	46
	1978	1,429	~[a]	~[a]	158	−1	57	47
	1979	1,537	~[a]	~[a]	~[a]	~[a]	52	24
	1980	1,665	~[a]	~[a]	~[a]	~[a]	64	19
	1981	1,928	~	~	106	10	76	~
	1982	2,262	~[d]	~[d]	106	30	76	23
	1983	2,042	~	1,213	127	~[d]	61	~[d]
	1984	1,903	~	1,083	111	~[d]	68	~[d]
	1985	1,652	~	906	55	0	64	~[d]
	1986	1,118	~	422	47	0	64	~[d]
	1987	1,102	~	367	63	0	78	~[d]
S. URUGUAY	1950	55	~	3	33	2	4	13
	1955[‡]	74	~	4	36	2	10	22
	1960	47	~[a]	~[a]	20	~[a]	4	23
T. VENEZUELA	1950	993	~[b]	857	24	10	24	20
	1951	968	~[a]	811	29	11	30	~
	1952	1,134	~[a]	907	36	12	34	~
	1953	1,237	~[a]	939	41	13	38	~
	1954	1,271	~[a]	939	51	14	45	~
	1955	1,311	~[a]	965	67	15	57	~
	1956	1,676	~[a]	1,278	86	23	83	~
	1957	2,465	~[a]	1,934	124	24	113	~
	1958	2,658	~[a]	2,071	151	27	129	~
	1959	2,690	~[a]	2,046	161	29	166	~
	1960	2,569	~[a]	1,995	180	32	165	~
	1961	3,007	~[a]	2,368	195	34	185	~
	1962	2,816	~[a]	2,197	193	35	175	~
	1963	2,808	~[a]	2,166	202	36	185	~
	1964	2,780	~[a]	2,133	220	18	199	~
	1965	2,705	~[a]	2,024	246	19	223	192
	1966	2,136	~[a]	1,544	281	18	115	~
	1967	2,081	~[a]	1,481	288	18	131	~
	1968	2,158	~[a]	1,480	347	~[a]	~[a]	23
	1969	2,196	79	1,474	378	~[a]	~[a]	22
	1970	2,241	78	1,440	416	~[a]	~[a]	33
	1971	2,199	~[a]	1,327	461	~[a]	~[a]	31
	1972	2,172	~[a]	1,225	487	28	~[a]	37
	1973	2,051	~[a]	~[a]	517	30	214	70
	1974	1,804	21	659	620	31	244	94
	1975	1,872	~	687	668	32	268	~
	1976	1,571	−21	230	747	~	289	~
	1977	1,896	~	325	932	25	325	~
	1978	2,015	~	290	1,059	26	321	~
	1979	1,797	- -	57	940	22	319	~
	1980	1,908	- -	40	1,032	~	361	~
	1981	2,175	- -	126	1,156	−50	406	~
	1982	2,371	~[e]	~[d]	1,278	−39	445	~[e]
	1983	1,711	~	245	949	−16	180	81
	1984	1,762	~	265	950	−46	163	55
	1985	1,588	~	75	814	−98	253	144
	1986	1,843	~	243	928	101	212	154
	1987	2,124	~	534	1,061	114	134	109
LATIN AMERICA	1977	18,882	1,197	1,873	8,409	~	2,411	~[b]
	1978	21,467	1,248	2,148	10,961	~	2,644	~[b]
	1979	22,553	979	2,657	12,048	~	2,385	2,193
	1980	25,964	1,097	3,033	14,044	~	2,806	2,897

Table 3000 (Continued)

U.S. DIRECT FOREIGN INVESTMENT IN LATIN AMERICA, 19 LRC, 1950–87
(Cumulative M US in Book Value)

Country	Year	Total[2]	Mining	Petroleum	Manufacturing[3]	Transport, Communications, and Public Utilities	Trade	Other Industries
LATIN AMERICA	1981	38,883	1,916	4,499	15,762	~	3,933	3,978
(Continued)	1982	33,039	2,295	6,465	15,625	~	3,799	2,113
	1983	24,133	~	7,359	13,995	1,558	2,774	2,523
	1984	25,229	~	6,320	14,566	1,631	2,841	2,595
	1985	27,901	~	5,035	14,760	1,909	2,836	2,323
	1986	34,970	~	5,227	15,193	2,464	2,923	2,162
	1987	42,337	~	5,771	15,902	2,051	2,942	2,959
WORLD	1977	149,848	~	~	~	~	~	149,848
	1978	167,804	~	~	~	~	~	167,804
	1979	186,760	~	~	~	~	~	186,760
	1980	215,578	~	~	~	~	~	215,578
	1981	227,342	~	~	~	~	~	227,342
	1982	221,343	~	~	~	~	~	221,343
	1983	207,203	~	57,574	82,907	10,512	21,278	13,312
	1984	212,994	~	59,089	85,253	10,701	21,790	13,165
	1985	229,748	~	58,030	95,104	11,780	22,710	13,061
	1986	259,890	~	61,151	107,241	14,258	25,246	12,795
	1987	308,793	~	66,381	126,640	17,708	31,330	13,179

1. The table is updated only insofar as U.S. Department of Commerce data permit. Since post-1950 data for several republics (e.g., El Salvador, Nicaragua) have been included only under the general category of "Other Countries" in Latin America, latest data available for some countries are for 1950.
2. Subtotals do not necessarily add to total; finance and insurance excluded here.
3. Includes food products, chemicals and allied products, primary and fabricated metals, machinery, transportation equipment and other manufacturing.

a. Included in "Other."
b. Included in "Total."
c. Includes $262.7 million in agriculture.
d. Suppressed to avoid disclosure of data of individual companies.
e. Less than $500,000 (±).

SOURCE: U.S. Department of Commerce, *Selected Data on U.S. Direct Investment Abroad, 1966–78*; USDC-SCB, 61:8 (Aug. 1981), pp. 31–32; 62:8 (Aug. 1982), pp. 21–22; Aug. 1985, table 10; Aug. 1987; Aug. 1988, table 13.

Table 3001

DIRECT INVESTMENT FLOW,[1] 19 L, 1975–83[a]
(M US; Minus = Debit)

Country	1975	1976	1977	1978	1979	1980	1981	1982	1983
A. ARGENTINA	#	#	83	273	265	788	944	257	183
B. BOLIVIA	53.4	−8.1	−1.2	11.5	18.0	41.5	59.9	36.9	42.1

Continued in SALA, 24-2900.

Table 3002

RATES OF RETURN ON U.S. DIRECT FOREIGN INVESTMENT
(%)

Region	1980	1981	1982	1983	1984	1985
Developed Countries	16.5	11.7	8.0	9.0	9.0	16.2
Petroleum	26.5	20.3	12.9	14.8	16.8	16.2
Manufacturing	12.4	8.1	5.9	7.5	6.3	17.8
Other	15.7	10.9	7.4	7.1	7.2	14.1
Latin America	18.8	15.8	7.6	2.4	5.4	10.0
Petroleum	23.0	23.0	17.1	9.7	.2	8.3
Manufacturing	15.8	11.5	1.6	-1.4	6.6	10.1
Other	20.0	17.4	10.4	3.3	10.3	11.0
Other Developing Countries	41.3	40.9	29.9	22.5	23.8	18.6
Petroleum	79.7	65.3	42.6	26.1	28.5	21.2
Manufacturing	18.3	18.2	12.8	18.4	20.1	17.6
Other	24.2	25.9	22.9	19.7	18.7	15.2

SOURCE: *Transnational Corporations in World Development* (New York: United Nations Commission on Transnationals, 1987), p. 82.

Table 3003

DEVELOPING REGIONS DIRECT FOREIGN INVESTMENT INFLOWS AS A PROPORTION OF DOMESTIC CAPITAL FORMATION, TOTAL FOREIGN CAPITAL INFLOWS, AND DEBT SERVICE, 1975–79 AND 1980–85
(As a Percentage of)

Region	Gross Fixed Capital Formation		Total Long-Term Capital Inflow		Interest Payments on Foreign Debt 1980–85	Total Debt Servicing 1980–85
	1975–79	1980–84	1975–79	1980–85		
Developing Regions	3.0	3.1	14.5	17.2	30.1	18.1
Africa	3.8	3.9	13.0	19.4	29.2	14.0
South and South-East Asia	1.4	2.0	17.2	19.3	38.1	20.8
Latin America and the Caribbean	3.7	3.8	18.0	18.8	15.7	10.2
Western Asia	1.6	.5	2.0	1.3	~	~
Southern Europe	12.6	10.4	4.2	8.2	2.5	1.2

SOURCE: *Transnational Corporations in World Development* (New York: United Nations Commission on Transnationals, 1987), p. 182.

Table 3004

INDICATORS OF THE RELATIVE IMPORTANCE OF DIRECT FOREIGN INVESTMENT AND DEBT STOCKS, 9 LRC, 1975 AND 1985

(%)

	1975			1985			
	FDI	Debt	Debts as Percentage of Exports	FDI	Debt	Debt as Percentage of Exports	Bank Debt to Total Debt
Region/Country	As Percentage of GDP			As Percentage of GDP			
Developing Countries	6.3	14.0	109.6	8.7	44.7	182.3	55.4
Africa	15.0	18.9	72.4	12.6	63.2	174.8	36.3
Algeria	~	29.8	84.9	~	122.9	122.0	51.2
Egypt	.5	36.1	177.0	20.3	110.3	320.0	31.4
Ivory Coast	12.6	25.9	66.7	19.1	128.4	203.0	46.3
Morocco	2.3	19.5	69.2	6.0	119.0	335.7	37.6
Nigeria	20.9	3.2	12.1	5.4	26.3	152.0	48.6
Asia	4.7	16.4	102.7	5.9	30.4	137.7	49.1
Indonesia	3.2	14.7	148.6	6.4	43.3	105.1	43.2
Korea, Republic of	2.8	30.6	103.3	1.9	58.1	148.2	70.2
Malaysia	24.7	19.7	40.9	28.6	59.8	105.1	66.3
Philippines	3.1	17.7	84.8	6.1	80.7	324.7	54.8
Thailand	3.4	9.2	45.0	5.9	50.5	187.4	53.4
Latin America and the Caribbean	8.9	19.3	150.1	13.6	62.2	310.7	69.9
A. ARGENTINA	5.9	16.9	183.3	12.9	73.6	466.3	69.1
C. BRAZIL	5.6	19.1	237.0	13.9	56.0	358.9	73.1
D. CHILE	5.7	59.7	244.4	14.0	134.4	447.9	67.5
E. COLOMBIA	7.4	20.9	122.7	11.8	38.1	247.2	49.6
I. ECUADOR	11.6	16.5	63.6	8.3	69.3	263.6	67.1
N. MEXICO	5.5	17.7	243.8	8.9	54.9	324.3	78.2
R. PERU	11.0	32.9	300.0	15.4	90.2	400.0	49.7
S. URUGUAY	~	18.6	116.7	~	111.9	376.9	46.9
T. VENEZUELA	13.7	5.4	14.9	15.0	75.6	221.9	82.1
Europe	2.1	14.1	79.5	3.2	33.6	88.2	48.1
Turkey	1.6	9.3	100.0	.8	58.4	217.6	43.9
Yugoslavia	.5	18.8	72.5	.3	43.5	128.7	54.4

SOURCE: *Transnational Corporation in World Development* (New York: United Nations Commission on Transnationals, 1987), p. 129.

Table 3005

SELECTED DEVELOPED MARKET ECONOMIES SECTORAL DISTRIBUTION OF OUTWARD STOCK OF DIRECT FOREIGN INVESMENT, 1975 AND 1985

(%)

Country	Extractive		Manufacturing		Services[1]		Other[2]	
	1975	1985	1975	1985	1975	1985	1975	1985
Canada[3]								
Total	21.1	22.9	50.5	46.2	28.4	30.9	~	~
Developing Countries	21.2	46.4	18.2	20.4	60.6	33.2	~	~
Developed Market Economies	21.1	18.6	60.3	50.9	18.6	30.4	~	~
Germany, Federal Republic of[4]								
Total	4.1	3.8	48.3	43.0	41.9	48.3	5.7	4.9
Developing Countries	12.6	9.9	64.1	57.7	23.4	32.4	~	~
Developed Market Economies	2.1	3.0	47.7	43.0	50.2	54.1	~	~
Japan[5]								
Total	28.1	15.5	32.4	29.2	36.2	51.8	3.4	3.5
Developing Countries	31.9	21.9	43.8	32.7	19.1	41.5	5.1	3.9
Developed Market Economies	23.6	9.2	19.1	25.7	56.0	62.0	1.3	3.1
Netherlands[6]								
Total	46.5	55.4	38.6	22.2	14.7	22.1	.3	.3
Developing Countries	34.1	41.9	38.7	23.3	25.9	34.8	1.2	--
Developed Market Economies	48.9	57.9	38.5	22.0	12.5	19.8	.1	.3
United Kingdom[7]								
Total	11.1	33.3	59.5	31.8	29.4	34.8	~	~
Developing Countries	18.2	31.9	48.2	24.7	33.6	43.4	~	~
Developed Market Economies	8.9	33.6	63.0	33.4	28.1	32.9	~	~
United States								
Total	26.4	23.1	45.0	37.9	24.3	33.7	4.3	5.2
Developing Countries	20.0	27.6	44.9	31.7	24.5	34.5	10.5	6.4
Developed Market Economies	26.4	19.9	48.4	41.1	22.2	34.4	3.0	4.5

1. Breakdown by region and sector is available for a narrower definition of services for the United States and the Federal Republic of Germany than is used elsewhere in the study. However, the trend is the same for both definitions. For Canada, the Federal Republic of Germany, and the United Kingdom, agriculture, forestry, and fishing are included in services.
2. Other: for United States, agriculture, forestry and fishing, construction, mining (1985), transportation, communication and public utilities (1985), retail trade; for the Federal Republic of Germany, loans from dependent holding companies to other foreign associated enterprises; for the Netherlands and Japan, agriculture, forestry and fisheries; for Japan, establishment of branches and purchase of real estate.
3. Canadian data are for 1975 and 1983.
4. Data for the Federal Republic of Germany are for 1976 and 1985.
5. Japanese stock data based on cumulative flows rather than on the historical book values as is the case in other countries.
6. Data for the Netherlands are for 1975 and 1984. The extractive sector is defined as mining, oil and chemicals.
7. Data for the United Kingdom are for 1974 and 1984. For 1974, oil companies, banks and insurance companies are excluded.

SOURCE: *Transnational Corporations in World Development* (New York: United Nations Commission on Transnationals, 1988), p. 92.

Table 3006

DISTRIBUTION OF DIRECT FOREIGN INVESTMENT INFLOWS BY REGION, 1975–85

(%)

Region	1975	1980	1981	1982	1983	1984	1985	Annual Averages 1975–80	Annual Averages 1981–85
Developed Market Economies	70.6	80.5	73.6	69.8	76.8	78.5	76.7	76.6	75.2
United States	12.1	32.4	44.7	31.1	27.0	51.7	38.9	24.6	39.2
Western Europe	47.0	41.0	29.7	32.9	37.0	19.8	33.7	43.3	30.4
Japan	.9	.6	.4	.9	.9	~	1.2	.3	.6
Other	10.2	6.7	1.2	4.5	11.6	6.7	2.8	8.4	4.5
Developing Countries	29.3	19.3	26.4	30.2	23.2	21.3	23.3	23.4	24.8
Africa	2.3	.4	3.2	3.8	3.6	3.1	3.4	2.5	3.3
Latin America and the Caribbean	15.3	11.9	13.6	14.4	7.7	7.0	9.1	12.5	10.5
Western Asia	3.3	.6	~	.7	.7	1.2	1.0	1.9	.8
Other Asia and Oceania	7.4	6.1	9.3	10.8	10.7	9.6	9.1	6.2	9.9
Southern Europe	.9	.2	.4	.2	.2	.4	.4	.3	.4
World[1]	100	100	100	100	100	100	100	100	100
B US	21.5	52.2	56.8	44.5	44.1	49.0	49.3	32.1	48.7

1. Excluding the centrally planned economics of Europe.

SOURCE: *Transnational Corporations in World Development* (New York: United Nations
Commission on Transnationals, 1988), p. 87.

Table 3007

INWARD STOCKS OF DIRECT FOREIGN INVESTMENT, BY MAJOR HOST REGION, 1975–85

(B US)

Region	1975 Value	1975 Percentage of Total	1975 Percentage of GDP	1983 Value	1983 Percentage of Total	1983 Percentage of GDP	1985 Value	1985 Percentage of Total	1985 Percentage of GDP
Developed Market Economies	185.3	75.1	4.5	401.0	75.6	5.1	478.2	75.0	5.5
Western Europe	100.6	40.8	5.8	159.6	30.1	5.6	184.3	28.9	6.6
United States	27.7	11.2	1.8	137.1	25.9	4.2	184.6	29.0	4.7
Other[1]	57.0	23.1	7.0	104.3	19.7	6.0	109.2	17.1	5.7
Japan	1.5	.6	.3	5.0	.9	.4	6.1	1.0	.5
Developing Countries and Territories	61.5	24.9	6.4	138.4	24.4	7.4	159.0	25.0	8.5
Africa[2]	16.5	6.7	15.7	19.6	3.7	9.4	22.3	3.5	10.8
Asia[3]	13.0	5.3	3.2	40.1	5.8	4.9	49.6	7.8	5.7
Latin America and the Caribbean[4]	29.7	12.0	8.9	73.2	13.8	11.9	80.5	12.6	13.6
Other[5]	2.3	.9	2.1	5.4	1.0	2.4	6.6	1.0	3.4
Total[6]	246.8	100.0	4.9	539.4	100.0	5.5	637.2	100.0	6.1

1. Australia, Canada, Japan, New Zealand, South Africa.
2. Botswana, Cameroon, Central Africa Republic, Congo, Egypt, Gabon, Ghana, Ivory
   Coast, Kenya, Liberia, Libyan Arab Jamahiriya, Malawi, Mauritius, Morocco, Nigeria,
   Senegal, Seychelles, Sierra Leone, Togo, United Republic of Tanzania, Zaire, Zambia,
   Zimbabwe.
3. Bangledesh, China, Hong Kong, India, Indonesia, Malaysia, Pakiston, Philippines,
   Republic of Korea, Singapore, Sri Lanka, Taiwan Province, Thailand.
4. Argentina, Barbados, Brazil, Chile, Colombia, Dominican Republic, Ecudaor, Guyana,
   Jamaica, Mexico, Panama, Paraguay, Peru, Trinidad and Tobago, Uruguay, Venezuela.
5. Fiji, Papua New Guinea, Saudi Arabia, Turkey, Yugoslavia.
6. Excluding the centrally planned economies of Europe, for which no precise data are
   available.

SOURCE: *Transnational Corporation in World Development* (New York: United Nations
Commission on Transnationals, 1988), p. 25.

Table 3008

U.S. DIRECT FOREIGN INVESTMENT, 1977–87

(M US)

PART I. LATIN AMERICA

Year	Direct Investment Position	Net Capital Outflows (Minus = Inflows)	Equity and Intercompany Account Outflows (Minus = Inflows)	Reinvested Earnings of Incorporated Affiliates	Income	Fees and Royalties
1977	27,514	3,949	2,526	1,423	3,712	299
1978	31,770	4,014	2,096	1,918	4,779	372
1979	35,220	3,362	438	2,924	6,520	422
1980	38,761	2,833	−533	3,366	6,968	581
1981	38,864	−37	−197	3,497	6,143	671
1982	28,161	−5,138	−6,500	2,137	3,494	590
1983	24,133	−3,692	−3,066	1,712	1,034	514
1984	25,229	324	−2,230	2,554	1,327	151
1985	28,261	3,838	−1,182	1,599	2,338	119
1986	34,790	7,360	~	1,933	3,403	178
1987	42,337	7,166	~	3,507	3,870	182

PART II. WORLD

Year	Direct Investment Position	Net Capital Outflows (Minus = Inflows)	Equity and Intercompany Account Outflows (Minus = Inflows)	Reinvested Earnings of Incorporated Affiliates	Income	Fees and Royalties
1977	145,990	11,893	5,497	6,396	19,673	3,883
1978	162,727	16,056	4,713	11,343	25,458	4,705
1979	187,858	25,222	6,258	18,964	38,183	4,980
1980	215,375	19,222	2,205	17,017	37,146	5,780
1981	228,348	9,680	−3,803	13,483	32,446	5,813
1982	207,752	−2,369	−4,756	6,375	21,380	5,572
1983	207,203	373	−4,209	9,090	20,449	6,275
1984	212,994	3,858	−5,268	9,126	21,509	3,923
1985	229,748	17,267	−1,912	18,357	33,202	4,224
1986	259,362	27,811	~	19,709	38,417	5,427
1987	308,793	44,455	~	35,669	52,308	6,917

SOURCE: USDC-SCB, 59:8 (Aug. 1979); 60:8 (Aug. 1980); 61:8 (Aug. 1981); 62:8
(Aug. 1982); 64:8 (Aug. 1984); 66:8 (Aug. 1986); 67:8 (Aug. 1987); 68:8
(Aug. 1988).

Table 3009

PORTFOLIO INVESTMENT FLOW,[1] 19L, 1976–87

(M SDR)

	Country	1976	1978	1979	1980	1981	1982	1983	1984	1985	1986	1987
A.	ARGENTINA	−57	81	173	118	957	2.67	612	361	−622	−473	−445
B.	BOLIVIA	#	#	#	−2.7	−.8	−13.6	−1.7	−.9	−.9	#	#
C.	BRAZIL	#	#	510	272	−1	−3	−270	−265	−231	−366	~
D.	CHILE	−5	#	39	#	#	#	#	#	49	223	639
E.	COLOMBIA	−1	−2	−26	−2	−2	−6	−2	−3	−1	26	37
F.	COSTA RICA	#	16.7	#	94.2	−2.1	−1.8	−2.5	−.2	−12.5	−2.1	#
H.	DOMINICAN REP.	#	#	#	#	#	#	#	#	#	#	#
I.	ECUADOR	4.9	#	#	#	#	#	#	#	#	#	#
J.	EL SALVADOR	15.4	3.2	−4.4	−.8	#	−.9	.1	#	#	~	~
K.	GUATEMALA	.1	9.4	4.2	3.0	.3	.5	−.1	−9.2	−25.7	−9.8	−12.6
L.	HAITI	#	#	#	#	#	#	#	#	#	#	#
M.	HONDURAS	#	−.4	−.1	#	−.2	−.2	.1	−1.8	1.2	−.8	.5
N.	MEXICO	373	603	−306	−57	845	844	−584	−739	−995	−693	−27
O.	NICARAGUA	#	#	#	#	#	#	#	#	#	#	#
P.	PANAMA	.1	56.2	−186	−680.3	172.2	318.6	58.6	57.8	−180.4	43	~
Q.	PARAGUAY	#	#	#	#	5.0	−6.8	3.1	#	8.2	#	#
R.	PERU	#	#	#	#	#	#	#	#	#	#	#
S.	URUGUAY	28.2	−6.9	−24.1	−5.2	2.6	−6.2	−14.6	6.6	94.5	73.6	10.1
T.	VENEZUELA	626	99	−1,014	1,007	70	1,433	188	−125	~	~	~
	U.S. Dollars per SDR	1.1545	1.2520	1.2920	1.3015	1.1792	1.1040	1.0690	1.0250	1.0153	1.1732	1.2931

1. Portfolio Investments are miscellaneous holdings of stocks and bonds issued by foreign
governments or corporations which do not usually exceed 25 percent of voting stock.
Holdings of more than 25 percent of voting stock are usually considered Direct Foreign
Investment (see Direct Investment, tables 3000–3006, above). For definitions, see
SALA-SNP, p. 252.

SOURCE: IMF-BPS-Y, 1984; IMF-BPS, Nov. 1984; IMF-BPS, Jan. 1984; IMF-BPS-Y, 1986;
IMF-BPS-Y, 1988.

Table 3010

CAPITAL EXPENDITURES BY U.S. MAJORITY-OWNED FOREIGN AFFILIATES,[1] 9 LR, 1981-89

(M US)

Country	Year	All Industries	Mining	Petroleum	Manufacturing Total	Food and Kindred Products	Chemicals and Allied Products	Primary and Fabricated Metals	Machinery, Except Electrical	Electric and Electronic Equipment	Transportation Equipment	Other Manufacturing	Trade	Wholesale	Finance[2]	Services[2]	Other Industries
A. ARGENTINA	1981[a]	635	5	130	434	57	80	~c	142	4	~c	~c	57	?	#	?	9
	1982[b]	412	4	124	246	35	60	4	54	3	~c	~c	30	?	#	?	7
	1983[b]	425	4	124	263	61	42	7	~c	8	66	~c	25	?	#	?	9
	1984[d]	458	2	132	287	46	63	5	77	7	49	40	20	?	#	?	17
	1985	333	2	73	216	42	51	5	75	1	13	29	37	?	#	?	6
	1986	263	5	61	149	39	51	3	21	1	10	24	37	?	#	?	10
	1987[e]	260	?	74	140	45	41	~c	~c	2	~c	12	?	21	8	2	15
	1988[e]	296	?	105	156	61	23	~c	~c	2	~c	19	?	13	5	4	12
	1989[e]	330	?	101	199	78	32	4	~c	~c	3	22	?	12	5	3	10
C. BRAZIL	1981[a]	1,640	2	86	1,325	108	247	88	250	60	385	188	175	?	~c	?	~c
	1982[b]	1,747	1	100	1,434	100	244	251	258	48	335	199	157	?	25	?	30
	1983[b]	1,962	~c	~c	1,656	119	292	~c	262	78	308	~c	165	?	9	?	27
	1984[d]	1,506	~c	125	1,136	62	170	~c	246	50	159	~c	187	?	10	?	~c
	1985	1,387	14	96	1,030	60	171	174	197	44	218	167	212	?	10	?	24
	1986	1,527	4	103	1,182	66	221	101	226	54	314	200	202	?	11	?	24
	1987[e]	1,495	?	99	1,220	79	199	94	224	160	248	216	?	110	12	35	19
	1988[e]	1,700	?	124	1,350	84	253	95	250	146	288	293	?	172	17	19	17
	1989[e]	2,068	?	157	1,657	82	351	97	336	136	230	426	?	~c	~c	22	40
D. CHILE	1981[a]	287	~c	34	12	1	5	2	#	#	#	4	43	?	~c	?	~c
	1982[b]	142	65	27	13	2	3	3	#	1	#	5	21	?	~c	?	~c
	1983[b]	107	49	16	13	3	4	1	#	1	#	4	15	?	#	?	14
	1984[d]	144	78	17	19	1	2	~c	#	1	#	~c	25	?	#	?	5
	1985	104	~c	13	11	2	2	3	#	1	#	3	31	?	2	?	~c
	1986	139	75	17	12	3	3	3	#	1	#	3	31	?	#	?	3
	1987[e]	86	?	1	36	1	#	#	0	1	#	2	?	19	4	1	27
	1988[e]	168	?	?	51	1	3	#	0	1	~c	3	?	37	~c	~c	27
	1989[e]	398	~c	~c	~c	2	3	~c	0	~c	#	~c	?	21	~c	2	~c
E. COLOMBIA	1981[a]	345	3	235	61	10	32	3	~c	1	5	~c	40	?	1	?	6
	1982[b]	529	2	430	64	13	31	~c	#	2	~c	9	28	?	1	?	5
	1983[b]	602	1	492	73	21	28	3	#	1	~c	~c	25	?	~c	?	5
	1984[a]	376	1	254	90	24	43	3	#	4	~c	~c	25	?	1	?	5
	1985	795	~c	510	41	10	16	1	#	1	1	12	13	10	2	?	~c
	1986	694	~c	438	63	12	23	2	#	2	1	22	20	10	1	?	~c
	1987[e]	317	?	182	46	10	24	3	#	1	3	6	?	?	~c	10	69
	1988[e]	352	?	229	70	13	24	2	#	1	3	27	?	?	~c	7	~c
	1989[e]	365	?	200	107	16	23	1	#	1	~c	~c	~c	?	?	7	~c

Table 3010 (Continued)

CAPITAL EXPENDITURES BY U.S. MAJORITY-OWNED FOREIGN AFFILIATES,[1] 9 LR, 1981-89
(M US)

Country	Year	All Industries	Mining	Petroleum	Manufacturing Total	Food and Kindred Products	Chemicals and Allied Products	Primary and Fabricated Metals	Machinery, Except Electrical	Electric and Electronic Equipment	Transportation Equipment	Other Manufacturing	Trade	Wholesale	Finance[2]	Services	Other Industries
I. ECUADOR	1981a	62	#	25	21	3	5	1	#	2	#	9	17	ℓ	#	ℓ	#
	1982b	46	#	22	14	3	5	1	#	2	#	3	10	ℓ	#	ℓ	#
	1983b	48	#	29	11	2	3	1	#	2	#	3	8	ℓ	#	ℓ	#
	1984d	57	#	36	14	2	8	#	#	1	#	3	4	ℓ	2	ℓ	1
	1985	44	#	22	13	2	5	1	#	1	#	4	8	ℓ	1	ℓ	#
	1986	65	#	46	9	2	3	#	#	2	#	2	9	ℓ	1	ℓ	#
	1987e	38	ℓ	25	5	1	1	0	0	2	#	1	ℓ	4	#	1	2
	1988e	51	ℓ	38	5	#	2	0	0	1	#	1	ℓ	3	#	2	3
	1989e	26	ℓ	15	5	#	2	0	0	2	#	1	ℓ	3	#	2	2
N. MEXICO	1981a	1,198	3	12	913	123	100	50	24	103	379	135	212	ℓ	3	ℓ	55
	1982b	933	2	10	745	56	91	33	20	73	328	144	140	ℓ	2	ℓ	34
	1983b	775	1	4	619	78	92	21	14	67	243	104	112	ℓ	1	ℓ	39
	1984d	690	#	3	544	52	100	18	7	68	248	51	120	ℓ	#	ℓ	23
	1985	788	#	3	623	41	89	16	23	36	335	84	145	ℓ	1	ℓ	16
	1986	949	#	3	786	60	91	13	34	38	478	72	145	ℓ	1	ℓ	13
	1987e	507	ℓ	2	435	38	73	14	17	55	175	63	ℓ	28	1	33	9
	1988e	622	ℓ	2	521	53	68	19	24	52	226	79	ℓ	46	3	35	15
	1989e	819	ℓ	2	694	66	93	12	27	59	335	102	ℓ	56	3	44	20
P. PANAMA	1981a	74	#	3	5	2	2	#	#	#	#	1	7	ℓ	22	ℓ	37
	1982b	43	#	2	4	2	2	#	#	#	#	#	4	ℓ	18	ℓ	15
	1983b	32	#	2	5	2	2	#	#	#	#	1	6	ℓ	15	ℓ	4
	1984d	36	#	6	3	1	1	#	#	#	#	1	10	ℓ	3	ℓ	14
	1985	20	#	3	2	1	1	#	#	#	#	1	7	ℓ	2	ℓ	5
	1986	23	#	5	3	1	2	#	#	#	#	1	8	ℓ	3	ℓ	4
	1987e	34	ℓ	11	3	1	1	#	0	0	0	1	ℓ	7	2	2	10
	1988e	26	ℓ	10	3	1	1	#	0	0	0	1	ℓ	6	#	#	7
	1989e	29	ℓ	10	4	2	1	#	0	0	0	1	ℓ	8	#	#	6
R. PERU	1981a	455	ℓ[c]	345	9	2	2	3	#	1	#	2	ℓ[c]	ℓ	ℓ[c]	ℓ	ℓ[c]
	1982b	419	32	340	15	2	7	2	#	1	#	4	30	ℓ	ℓ[c]	ℓ	ℓ[c]
	1983b	361	11	#	11	4	3	1	#	1	#	2	ℓ[c]	ℓ	2	ℓ	2
	1984d	260	ℓ[c]	191	10	2	2	2	#	1	#	3	25	ℓ	#	ℓ	ℓ[c]
	1985	108	8	75	4	#	1	#	#	#	#	2	20	ℓ	1	ℓ	1
	1986	174	ℓ[c]	128	6	1	1	#	#	#	#	3	19	9	2	ℓ	ℓ[c]
	1987e	69	ℓ	50	9	1	5	1	0	0	0	1	ℓ	9	0	#	#
	1988e	106	ℓ	ℓ[c]	13	2	9	1	0	#	0	1	ℓ	13	0	#	ℓ[c]
	1989e	93	ℓ	ℓ[c]	ℓ[c]	3	7	ℓ[c]	0	1	0	2	ℓ	ℓ[c]	0	1	ℓ[c]

Table 3010 (Continued)

CAPITAL EXPENDITURES BY U.S. MAJORITY-OWNED FOREIGN AFFILIATES,[1] 9 LR, 1981–89 (M US)

Country	Year	All Industries	Mining	Petroleum	Manufacturing									Trade	Wholesale	Finance[2]	Services	Other Industries
					Total	Food and Kindred Products	Chemicals and Allied Products	Primary and Fabricated Metals	Machinery, Except Electrical	Electric and Electronic Equipment	Transportation Equipment	Other Manufacturing					
T. VENEZUELA	1981a	377	#	66	197	42	58	7	~c	9	~c	28	93	?	1	?	20
	1982b	420	#	60	225	41	55	4	7	4	~c	~c	118	?	#	?	17
	1983b	380	#	37	188	57	50	5	~c	5	~c	18	145	?	#	?	10
	1984d	247	#	24	170	58	37	4	6	2	~c	~c	42	?	#	?	12
	1985	176	#	27	114	38	25	1	2	1	8	39	39	?	#	?	5
	1986	159	#	17	101	27	14	1	1	4	12	41	33	?	1	?	~c
	1987e	149	?	8	114	45	~c	3	~c	9	~c	31	?	8	#	15	4
	1988e	166	?	22	112	31	20	3	~c	11	~c	32	?	14	#	~c	~c
	1989e	171	?	9	128	27	28	~c	~c	13	~c	42	?	16	#	14	5
LATIN AMERICA	1981a	5,072	13	936	3,077	348	531	154	416	180	669	367	644	?	27	?	127
	1982b	4,691	106	1,115	1,760	154	498	298	339	134	663	364	538	?	46	?	108
	1983b	4,692	66	704	2,839	347	516	39	276	163	617	132	501	?	27	?	105
	1984d	4,176	171	956	2,359	269	445	289	337	149	498	372	477	?	38	?	176
	1985	4,125	308	995	2,117	218	371	215	298	92	575	349	519	?	21	?	164
	1986	4,463	287	1,052	2,380	231	432	133	282	106	816	379	524	?	23	?	197
	1987e	3,251	?	562	2,060	236	382	149	272	231	447	343	?	232	43	163	191
	1988e	3,823	?	728	2,356	268	439	168	321	217	476	470	?	335	84	124	193
	1989e	4,848	?	727	3,055	293	574	286	415	226	586	674	?	330	82	212	442

1. Capital expenditure estimates are for majority-owned nonbank foreign affiliates of nonbank U.S. parents. (An affiliate is majority owned when the combined ownership of all U.S. parents exceeds 50%.) Capital expenditures are those that are made to acquire, add to, or improve property, plant, and equipment, and that are charged to capital accounts. They are on a gross basis; sales and other dispositions of fixed assets are not netted against them. Capital expenditures are in current dollars; they are not adjusted for price changes in host countries or for changes in the value of foreign currencies because the data needed for these adjustments are unavailable.
2. Excludes banking, insurance, and real estate for 1981–86; for 1987–89 excludes only banking.

a. Based on survey taken in June 1982.
b. Based on survey taken in December 1982.
c. Data suppressed (by source) to avoid disclosure of individual companies.
d. Based on survey taken in December 1983.
e. Based on survey taken in December 1988.

SOURCE: USDC-SCB, 63:3 (March 1983); 64:3 (March 1984); 65:3 (March 1985); 67:3 (March 1987); 68:3 (March 1988); 69:3 (March 1989).

Table 3011

GROSS PRODUCT OF U.S. MAJORITY-OWNED FOREIGN AFFILIATES,[1] 9 LR
(M US, 1977)

Country	All Industries	Mining	Petroleum	Manufacturing Total	Trade	Finance	Other Industries
A. ARGENTINA	1,449	~2	306	945	143	3	~2
B. BRAZIL	6,485	12	736	5,169	311	26	231

Continued in SALA, 24-2909.

Table 3012

GROSS PRODUCT OF U.S. MAJORITY-OWNED FOREIGN AFFILIATES IN LATIN AMERICA[1]
(M US)

Category	1977
All Industries	16,036
Mining	579
Metal Mining	569
Iron	3
Copper, Lead, Zinc, Gold, and Silver	250
Bauxite, Other Ores, and Services	317
Coal and Other Nonmetallic Minerals	10
Petroleum	3,072
Oil and Gas Extraction	1,194
Crude Petroleum (No Refining) and Gas	1,033
Oil and Gas Field Services	161

Continued in SALA, 24–2910.

Table 3013

SHARES OF JAPANESE AFFILITATES IN DEVELOPING COUNTRIES EXPORTS OF MANUFACTURES, 1974 AND 1983
(%)

Region	Year	Total Manufacturing	Foods	Chemicals	Metals	Machinery Non-Electrical	Electrical	Transport Equipment	Other Manufacturing
Developing Countries	1974	2.8	1.0	2.0	.7	2.7	12.7	4.6	3.3
	1983	3.4	.7	3.4	3.2	2.0	9.9	4.0	2.9
Developing Asia	1974	4.9	2.6	4.5	2.1	4.3	14.4	8.5	4.0
	1983	4.2	1.5	5.3	1.8	2.1	10.4	6.0	3.1
Latin America	1974	.8	.3	2.1	.2	~	.6	1.6	2.2
	1983	1.9	.2	1.3	5.2	1.7	.5	1.1	3.7

SOURCE: *Transnational Corporations in World Development* (New York: United Nations Commission on Transnationals, 1988), p. 164.

Table 3014

DEVELOPING COUNTRIES AND TERRITORIES SHARES IN WORLD EXPORTS OF MANUFACTURES OF UNITED STATES GOODS, 1966, 1977, AND 1983

(%)

Region	Year	Total Manufacturing	Foods	Chemicals	Metals	Machinery Non-Electrical	Machinery Electrical	Transport Equipment	Other Manufacturing
All Developing	1966	.44	1.51	.72	.36	.18	I	.04	.27
Countries/Territories	1977	.77	.88	.60	.48	.43	3.72	.33	.37
	1983	I.00	.72	.82	.23	1.08	4.55	.57	.39
Latin America	1966	.28	1.18	.60	.03	.06	I	.04	.14
	1977	.33	.61	.38	.30	.25	.54	.31	.17
	1983	.40	.57	.58	.15	.52	.54	.45	.23
Asian Newly	1966	.09	.03	~	~	.10	I	~	~
Industrializing	1977	.29	.02	.12	~	.15	2.42	~	~
Countries/Territories	1983	.38	.01	.06	.01	.05	2.43	.10	.08

SOURCE: *Transnational Corporations in World Development* (New York: United Nations Commission on Transnationals, 1988), p. 161.

Table 3015

INDICATORS OF THE IMPORTANCE OF FOREIGN AFFILITATES' PRODUCTION AND EXPORTS ON DEVELOPING COUNTRIES AND TERRITORIES

(%)

Region/Country/Territory	Employment	Production	Exports
Africa			
Sierra Leone	13.0 (1981)	~	~
Zaire	30.4 (1974)	~	~
Zimbabwe	~	70.0 (1982)	~
Asia and Oceania			
Fiji	29.0 (1977)	31.8 (1980)	~
Hong Kong	9.8 (1984)	13.9 (1981)	16.5 (1984)
India	13.0 (1977)	7.0 (1979)	~
Korea, Republic of	9.5 (1978)	19.3 (1978)	24.6 (1978)
Malaysia	19.7 (1975)	44.0 (1978)	34.6 (1980)
Philippines	8.6 (1976)	~	51.5 (1983)
Singapore	54.6 (1982)	62.9 (1982)	89.7 (1983)
Taiwan Province	16.7 (1981)	~	25.6 (1981)
Latin America			
A. ARGENTINA	18.9 (1981)	29.4 (1983)	26.6 (1983)
C. BRAZIL	23.0 (1977)	32.0 (1977)	32.3 (1980)
D. CHILE	~	28.0 (1979)	21.7 (1979)
E. COLOMBIA	~	29.0 (1983)	16.9 (1980)
F. COSTA RICA	~	~	70.1 (1980)
N. MEXICO	21.0 (1970)	27.0 (1972)	42.4 (1977)
R. PERU	13.5 (1975)	25.2 (1974)	8.0 (1978)
Trinidad and Tobago	44.0 (1977)	~	~
S. URUGUAY	~	11.5 (1978)	12.6 (1978)
T. VENEZUELA	~	35.9 (1975)	~

SOURCE: *Transnational Corporations in World Development* (New York: United Nations Commission on Transnationals, 1988), p. 159.

Table 3016

STOCK OF JAPANESE DIRECT FOREIGN INVESTMENT IN LATIN AMERICA IN THE MANUFACTURING, RESOURCE DEVELOPMENT, AND COMMERCE AND SERVICES SECTORS, 1977–84

(M US)

Sector	1977	1978	1979	1980	1981	1982	1983	1984	Growth Rates 1980–84 (%)
Manufacturing									
Foodstuffs	97	115	120	134	150	154	161	187	8.7
Textiles	297	324	339	351	361	372	390	406	3.7
Lumber and Pulp	165	170	188	188	188	1,889	190	197	1.2
Chemicals	431	467	481	501	507	521	547	557	2.7
Iron and Steel/Nonferrous Metals	368	416	667	735	825	1,037	1,297	1,469	18.9
Machinery	206	220	225	249	276	296	334	347	8.7
Electric/Electronic	163	183	195	212	251	273	291	300	9.1
Transport Machinery	243	280	292	333	378	488	610	667	19.0
Other	51	66	75	79	97	103	104	106	7.6
Manufacturing Total	2,024	2,244	2,583	2,781	3,034	3,435	3,924	4,236	11.1
Resource Development									
Agriculture/Forestry	96	118	124	133	150	163	168	171	6.5
Fisheries	30	47	59	64	79	83	85	86	7.7
Mining	604	638	1,176	1,188	1,223	1,404	1,421	1,421	4.6
Resource Development Total	730	803	1,359	1,385	1,451	1,650	1,674	1,678	4.9
Commerce and Services									
Construction	72	82	134	136	141	142	158	165	5.0
Commerce	256	321	386	437	537	651	698	957	21.6
Finance/Insurance	282	291	294	296	433	470	569	781	27.4
Others	378	610	799	1,084	1,692	2,447	3,648	5,139	47.6
Commerce and Services Total	988	1,304	1,613	1,953	2,803	3,710	5,073	7,042	37.8
Other									
Real Estate	~	17	19	23	23	23	23	23	.0
Branches	6	8	8	24	33	35	36	41	14.3
Grand Total	3,757	4,373	5,580	6,168	7,349	9,227	10,730	13,020	20.5

SOURCE: *The Third Symposium on Financial and Business Cooperation between Latin America and Japan: Final Report* (Tokyo, Japan: IDB, October 14 and 15, 1985).

Table 3017

JAPAN DIRECT FOREIGN INVESTMENT IN LATIN AMERICA, 13 L, 1965–84

(%)

	Country	1965	1973	1977	1984
A.	ARGENTINA	4.1	2.7	.8	1.4
B.	BOLIVIA	.5	.3	.4	.2
C.	BRAZIL	76.7	58.6	54.7	36.9
D.	CHILE	3.2	7.4	2.7	1.3
E.	COLOMBIA	0	.2	.3	.1
F.	COSTA RICA	0	.4	.3	.4
J.	EL SALVADOR	2.3	1.1	.5	.3
M.	HONDURAS	0	.5	.4	.1
N.	MEXICO	3.2	8.0	5.2	10.9
P.	PANAMA	0	5.0	3.4	30.2
Q.	PARAGUAY	1.4	.6	.5	.3
R.	PERU	7.8	8.5	13.8	6.3
T.	VENEZUELA	.5	.5	1.6	1.1

SOURCE: *The Third Symposium on Financial and Business Cooperation between Latin America and Japan: Final Report* (Tokyo, Japan: IDB, October 14 and 15, 1985).

Figure 30:1

JAPAN DIRECT FOREIGN INVESTMENT IN LATIN AMERICA, 4 L, 1965

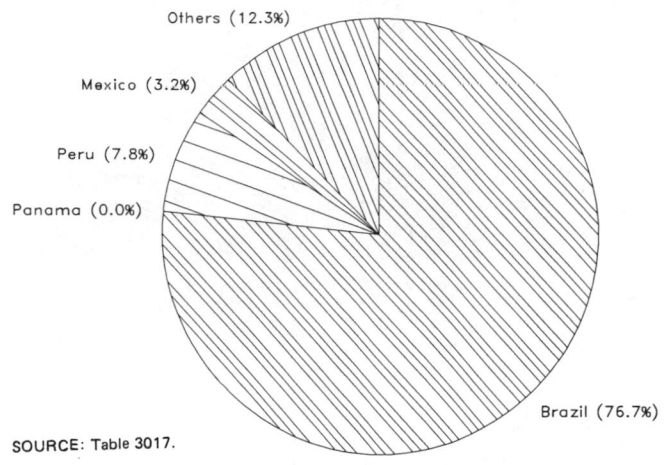

Others (12.3%)

Mexico (3.2%)

Peru (7.8%)

Panama (0.0%)

Brazil (76.7%)

SOURCE: Table 3017.

Figure 30:2

JAPAN DIRECT FOREIGN INVESTMENT IN LATIN AMERICA, 4 L, 1973

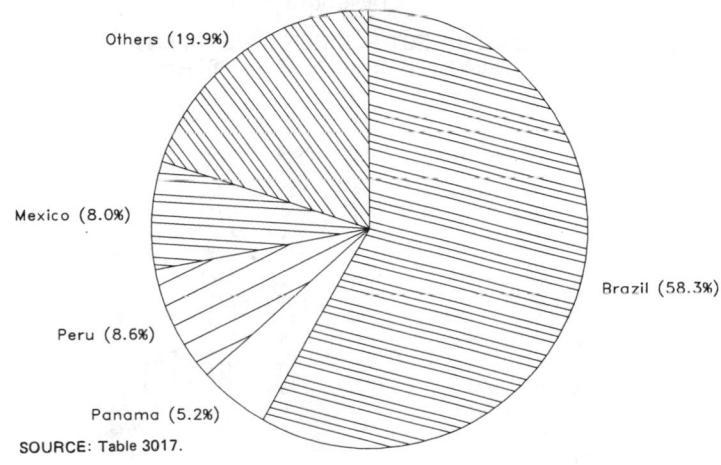

Others (19.9%)

Mexico (8.0%)

Brazil (58.3%)

Peru (8.6%)

Panama (5.2%)

SOURCE: Table 3017.

Figure 30:3

JAPAN DIRECT FOREIGN INVESTMENT IN LATIN AMERICA, 4 L, 1977

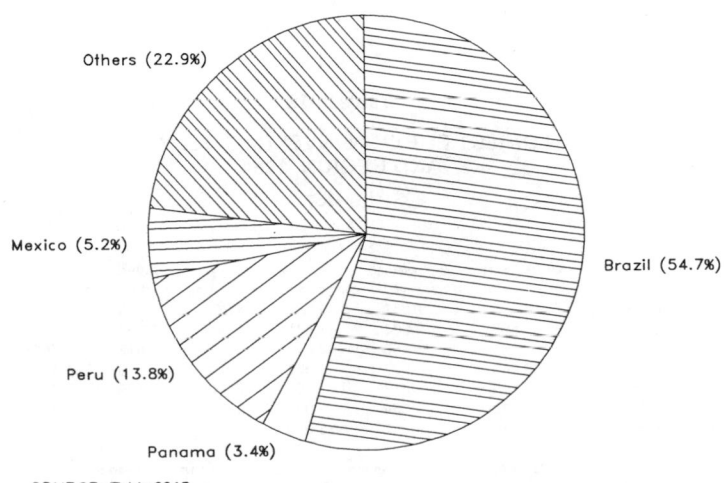

Others (22.9%)

Mexico (5.2%)

Brazil (54.7%)

Peru (13.8%)

Panama (3.4%)

SOURCE: Table 3017.

Figure 30:4

JAPAN DIRECT FOREIGN INVESTMENT IN LATIN AMERICA, 4 L, 1984

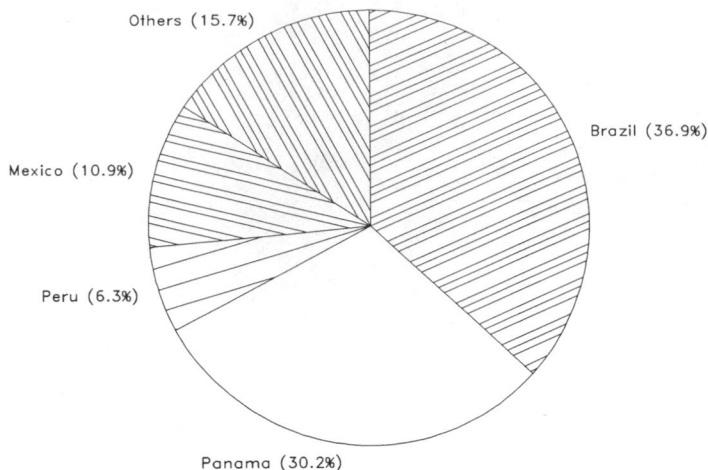

SOURCE: Table 3017.

Table 3018

**JAPAN DIRECT FOREIGN INVESTMENT
IN LATIN AMERICA, 13 L, 1965–84**

(M US)

	Country	1965	1973	1977	1984
A.	ARGENTINA	9	27	28	151
B.	BOLIVIA	1	3	14	17
C.	BRAZIL	168	579	1,805	4,274
D.	CHILE	7	73	89	179
E.	COLOMBIA	0	2	10	16
F.	COSTA RICA	0	4	11	41
J.	EL SALVADOR	5	11	18	32
M.	HONDURAS	~	5	12	20
N.	MEXICO	7	79	171	1,220
P.	PANAMA	0	49	112	4,916
Q.	PARAGUAY	3	6	16	34
R.	PERU	17	84	457	685
T.	VENEZUELA	1	5	53	130
	Total	218	927	2,796	11,715

SOURCE: *The Third Symposium on Financial and Business
Cooperation between Latin America and Japan: Final Report*
(Tokyo, Japan: IDB, October 14 and 15, 1985).

Table 3019

**JAPAN DIRECT FOREIGN INVESTMENT, BY SECTOR
AND REGION, 1984**

(M US)

Sector	United States	Asia	Latin America	Europe	Others	Total
Industry	6,483	7,057	4,236	1,765	2,508	22,049
Mining	896	5,883	1,421	862	1,096	11,158
Transport	44	168	3,530	6	912	4,660
Trade	6,645	922	957	2,076	528	11,128
Finance	2,729	613	781	2,742	189	7,054
Other	4,672	3,384	2,095	1,621	3,610	15,382
Total	21,469	18,027	13,020	9,072	9,843	71,431

SOURCE: *The Third Symposium on Financial and Business Cooperation between
Latin American and Japan: Final Report* (Tokyo, Japan: IDB, October 14 and 15,
1985).

Figure 30:5

JAPAN DIRECT FOREIGN INVESTMENT, BY REGION, 1965

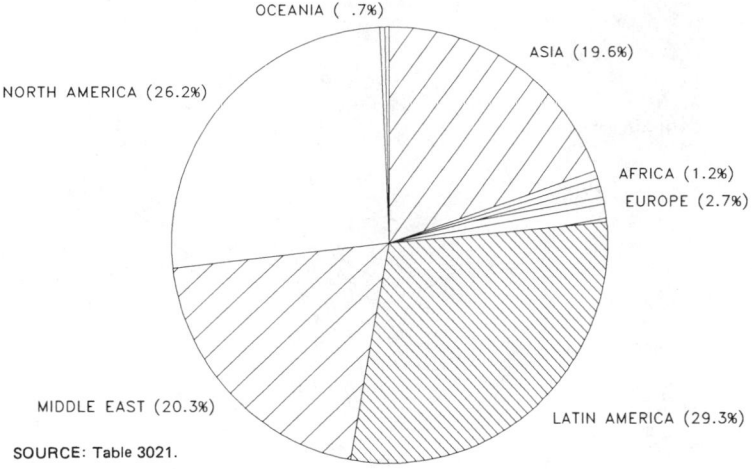

SOURCE: Table 3021.

Figure 30:6

JAPAN DIRECT FOREIGN INVESTMENT, BY REGION, 1973

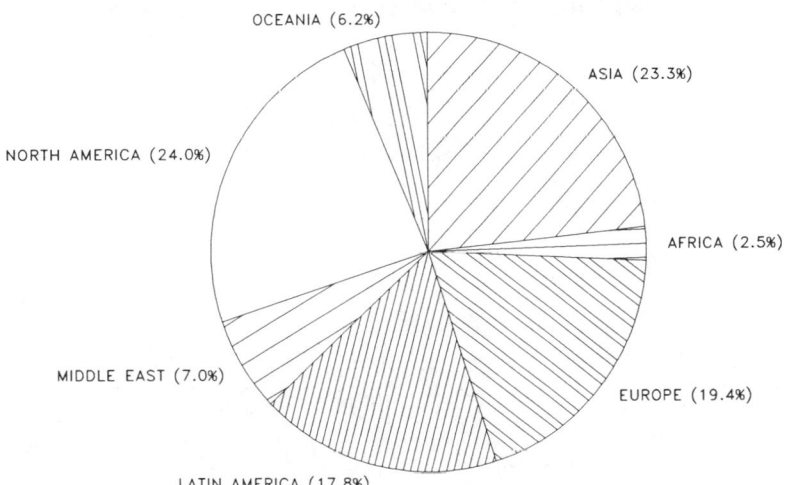

SOURCE: Table 3021.

Table 3020

**JAPAN DIRECT FOREIGN INVESTMENT
IN ANDEAN GROUP COUNTRIES,
5 LC, 1984**

(M US)

	Country	1984	%
B.	BOLIVIA	~	~
E.	COLOMBIA	13	0
I.	ECUADOR	~	~
R.	PERU	685	5.3
T.	VENEZUELA	130	1
	LATIN AMERICA	13,020	100

SOURCE: *The Third Symposium on Financial and Business
Cooperation between Latin America and Japan: Final Report*
(Tokyo, Japan: IDB, October 14 and 15, 1985).

Figure 30:7

JAPAN DIRECT FOREIGN INVESTMENT, BY REGION, 1977

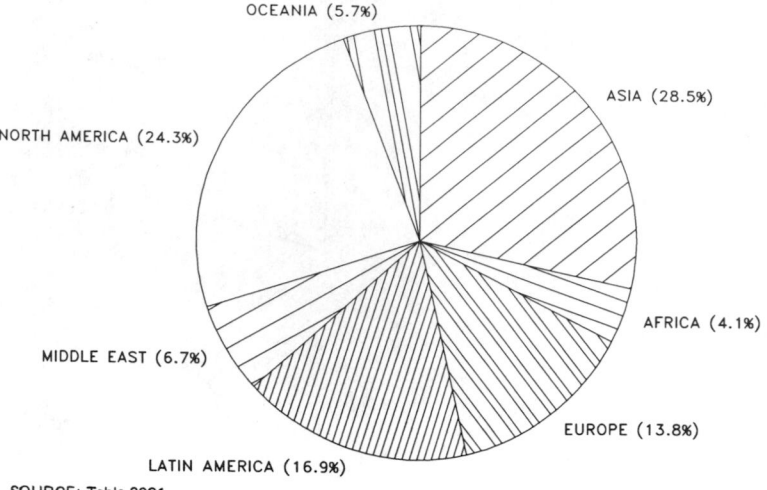

SOURCE: Table 3021.

Figure 30:8

JAPAN DIRECT FOREIGN INVESTMENT, BY REGION, 1984

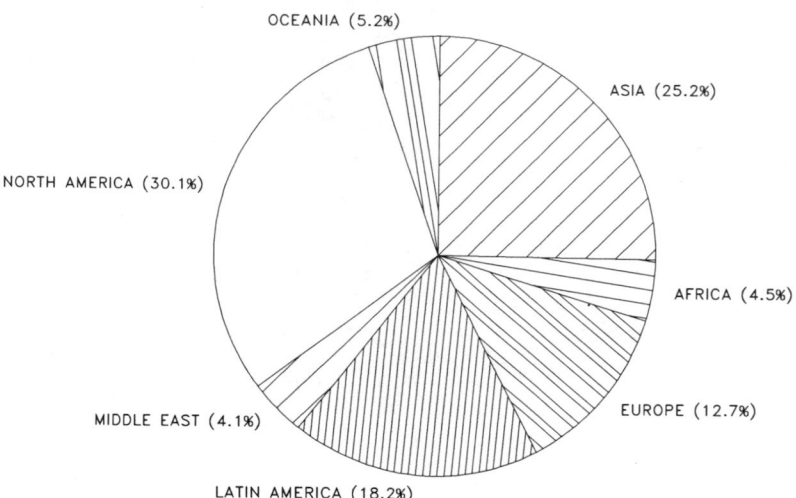

SOURCE: Table 3021.

Table 3021

**JAPAN WORLDWIDE, DIRECT FOREIGN INVESTMENT,
BY REGION, 1965–84**

(%)

Region	1965	1973	1977	1984
Asia	19.8	23.3	28.5	25.2
Africa	1.2	2.5	4.1	4.5
Europe	2.7	19.4	13.8	12.7
Latin America	29.6	17.8	16.9	18.2
Middle East	20.5	7.0	6.7	4.1
North America	26.4	24.0	24.3	30.1
Oceania	.7	6.2	5.7	5.2

SOURCE: *The Third Symposium on Financial and Business Cooperation between Latin
America and Japan: Final Report* (Tokyo, Japan: IDB, October 14 and 15, 1985).

Table 3022

WORLD EXPROPRIATION ACTS, 1960–85

Year	Number of Acts	Percentage of Total	Number of Countries Expropriating
1960	6	1.0	5
1961	8	1.4	5
1962	8	1.4	5
1963	11	1.9	7
1964	22	3.8	10
1965	14	2.4	11
1966	5	.9	3
1967	25	4.4	8
1968	13	2.3	8
1969	24	4.2	14
1970	48	8.4	18
1971	51	8.9	20
1972	56	9.8	30
1973	30	5.2	20
1974	68	11.8	29
1975	83	14.5	28
1976	40	7.0	14
1977	15	2.6	13
1978	15	2.6	8
1979	17	2.9	13
1980	5	.9	5
1981	4	.7	2
1982	1	.2	1
1983	3	.5	3
1984	1	.2	1
1985	1	.2	1
Total	574[a]	100.0[b]	

a. The dates are missing for four acts.
b. Error due go rounding.

SOURCE: *Transnational Corporations in World Development* (New York: United Nations Commission on Transnationals, 1988), p. 315.

Table 3023

TIME PATTERN OF WORLD EXPROPRIATIONS, 1960–85

Period	Number of Acts	Percentage of Total	Average Number of Acts/Year
1960–64	55	9.6	11.0
1965–69	81	14.1	16.2
1970–75	336	58.5	56.0
1976–79	87	15.2	21.8
1980–85	15	2.6	2.5
1960–85	574	100.0	22.1

SOURCE: *Transnational Corporations in World Development* (New York: United Nations Commission on Transnationals, 1987), p. 315.

Table 3024

LATIN AMERICAN COMPONENTS OF *SOUTH* MAGAZINE'S TOP-RATED COMPANIES OF THE DEVELOPING WORLD[1, 2, 5]

(M US OF 1985–86)

1987 Ranking	1986 Ranking	Company	Headquarters	Sales[3]	Net Profit	Net Assets	Nature of Business
1	4	Petróleos de Venezuela	Venezuela	14,808	~	40,143	Oil
3	1	Petróleos Mexicanos (PEMEX)	Mexico	14,341	~	36,837	Oil
5	8	Petrobras	Brazil	9,465	1056.1	12,859	Oil
13	24	Yacimientos Petrolíferos Fiscales	Argentina	4,903	679.8	9,235	Oil
25	25	Petrobras Distribuidora	Brazil	2,426	20.6	387	Petroleum Distribution
35	30	Comisión Federal de Electricidad[4]	Mexico	1,870	~	16,238	Electricity
36	70	Pão de Açucar	Brazil	1,821	24.3	~	Supermarkets
39	24	Conasupo[4]	Mexico	1,661	~	3,591	Food
42	37	CEPE	Ecuador	1,550	~	~	Oil
44		Telebras	Brazil	1,521	367.7	7,250	Telecommunication
46	39	Codelco	Chile	1,433	150.4	3,758	Copper Mining
48	35	Empresa Colombiano de Petróleos	Colombia	1,349	150.1	2,071	Oil
54	59	Empresa, Nacional de Petróleo	Chile	1,145	1.0	992	Petroleum Products
64	78	Petróleos del Perú	Peru	966	30.3	968	Oil
65	50	Federación Nacional de Cafeteros	Colombia	957	474.0	1,372	Coffee Exports
67	87	Gas del Estado	Argentina	920	10.3	3,446	Gas
72	313	Mendes Junior	Brazil	866	77.3	989	Construction and Engineering
74	68	Copersucar	Brazil	855	~	~	Sugar and Alcohol
76	~	Org Diego Cisneros	Venezuela	833	~	~	Food
77	81	Vale do Rio Doce	Brazil	826	340.9	2,647	Iron Mining

1. Companies owned, controlled, and managed by Third World nationals or governments.
2. Data are supplied by companies and supplemented by press reports and business publications.
3. Sales/turnover figures converted into U.S. dollars at the prevailing year-end rates. Turnover rates for the utility companies are devalued because of a lack of trading.
4. 1984–85.
5. Selected by SALA from *South's* list of the 600 top-rated companies of the developing world.

SOURCE: *South*, April 1987.

Table 3025

CORPORATE BUSINESS ACTIVITY,[1] 18 L

(1982, except asterisk indicates 1983)

A. ARGENTINA

Sales Rank	Company	Type of Business	M US Sales/ Turnover 1982	1982 Profit or Loss	1982 Employees	M US 1982 Net Assets	Transnational Parent
1	YPF – Yacimentos Petroliferos Fiscales	Petroleum	2,420.7*	7,577.1	31,353	5,357.0	**
2	ENTEL – Emip Nac de Telecomunicaciones	Communications	809.0	–507.3	45,441	10,108.0	**
3	Massalin-Particulares	Tobacco	787.0	29.6	1,800	357.7	Phil mon US

Continued in SALA, 24–2911.

Table 3026

RANKING OF CORPORATE BUSINESS ACTIVITY, 9 L

(1986)

A. ARGENTINA

Ranking	Previous Year	Company	Type of Business	Sales/Turnover	Net Profit/(Loss)	Net Assets	Employees	Foreign Ownership
1	(1)	Yacimientos Petrolíferos Fiscales	Petroleum	4,903	(679.8)	9,235	32,216	
2	(2)	Esso	Petroleum	935	31.7	~	~	Exxon, U.S.
3	(4)	Gas del Estado	Gas	920	(10.3)	3,446	9,723	

Continued in SALA, 27-2926.

Table 3027

DIRECT EMPLOYMENT ABROAD BY WEST GERMAN, JAPANESE, AND U.S. TRANSNATIONAL CORPORATIONS (TNC), BY REGION, 1980 AND 1985

(T US)

Country of Origin of TNC	Developed Market Economies					Developing Market Economies					Total
	Total	Europe	Japan	North America	Other	Total	Africa	Latin America and the Caribbean	Western Asia	Other Asia	
Federal Republic of Germany											
1980	1,180	711	21	393	55	562	56	371	20	115	1,743
1985	1,255	759	25	407	64	526	54	345	15	112	1,785
Japan											
1980	144	34	~	84	26	572	27	128	12	405	716
1985	269	73	~	157	39	657	24	131	14	488	926
United States											
1977–82[a]	4,715	2,939	346	989	442	2,161	138	1,349	146	528	6,918
1984	4,343	2,694	315	897	437	2,014	107	1,216	138	552	6,389

a. Average

SOURCE: *Transnational Corporations in World Development* (New York: United Nations Commission on Transnationals, 1988), p. 217.

Table 3028

INVESTMENT PER WORKER,[1] 19 LR, 1960–87

	Country	1960	1970	1980	1981	1982	1983	1984	1985	1986	1987
A.	ARGENTINA	55.6	76.8	100.0	75.7	60.1	53.1	46.9	36.9	43.1	49.5
B.	BOLIVIA	60.5	108.4	100.0	111.9	63.8	62.6	54.3	70.3	40.8	46.3
C.	BRAZIL	33.4	56.4	100.0	84.2	75.8	56.8	55.5	63.1	76.3	76.0
D.	CHILE	47.4	97.0	100.0	119.2	40.4	32.5	55.8	50.9	56.7	69.7
E.	COLOMBIA	63.8	78.4	100.0	110.3	113.2	107.9	98.9	87.0	89.1	94.3
F.	COSTA RICA	39.2	60.0	100.0	60.6	43.9	56.9	61.4	64.3	71.4	66.1
H.	DOMINICAN REP.	20.5	52.5	100.0	86.2	77.4	76.6	68.5	69.1	68.6	83.0
I.	ECUADOR	33.2	48.2	100.0	84.0	91.9	61.3	58.7	60.5	59.4	58.8
J.	EL SALVADOR	97.7	93.7	100.0	93.2	81.2	72.1	72.0	65.9	77.6	73.7
K.	GUATEMALA	50.4	74.9	100.0	112.0	88.0	71.0	73.1	57.1	55.0	63.4
L.	HAITI	26.2	35.9	100.0	98.7	90.2	93.1	95.5	104.3	93.6	90.1
M.	HONDURAS	39.1	72.6	100.0	80.7	46.4	54.2	73.7	70.4	63.0	60.0
N.	MEXICO	36.8	67.2	100.0	111.2	81.6	57.7	59.3	64.4	49.6	50.3
O.	NICARAGUA	75.8	130.5	100.0	147.2	116.9	122.3	118.8	113.8	108.2	98.5
P.	PANAMA	33.9	88.1	100.0	109.4	98.8	76.1	65.8	68.3	74.7	67.0
Q.	PARAGUAY	14.0	26.6	100.0	113.6	91.6	72.8	71.7	70.3	70.8	70.4
R.	PERU	54.9	59.5	100.0	117.1	105.7	63.8	55.9	46.1	57.2	56.8
S.	URUGUAY	48.5	43.3	100.0	90.5	73.5	46.2	46.6	37.7	37.2	46.3
T.	VENEZUELA	67.8	102.3	100.0	96.8	105.6	49.8	59.3	58.1	60.1	59.2
	LATIN AMERICA[2]	43.1	67.3	100.0	95.8	80.4	58.9	58.7	60.4	62.0	63.3

1. Gross domestic investment divided by labor force, 1980 = 100 (index calculated in constant 1986 U.S. dollars).
2. Includes Barbados, Guyana, Jamaica, Suriname, and Trinidad and Tobago.

SOURCE: IDB, *Monthly News*, October 1988.

Part X

National Accounts, Government Policy and Finance, and Prices

General notes:

Expenditures may be projected or disbursed terms; deficits may not include amortization of the debt and may exclude "off-budget" spending; for example, for United States in 1981 such spending reached $21.0 billion more than the registered deficit of $72.6 billion shown in SALA, 23-2421. (With regard to "off-budget" spending, see *U.S. News and World Report*, Oct. 4, 1982, p. 77.)

Central government expenditures may include subsidies for decentralized agencies.

Note: This volume contains statistics from numerous sources. Alternative data on many topics are presented. Variations in statistics can be attributed to differences in definition, parameters, coverage, methodology, as well as date gathered, prepared, or adjusted.

31

Government Plans, Revenue and Expenditure, and Money Supply

Table 3100

CURRENT DEVELOPMENT PLANS, 17 L

PART I. GOALS

Country	AAGR		Duration[3]	Scope[1]	Yearly % Planned Growth Rate									Yearly % Planned Investment[2]			
	Population	Domestic Demand for Food			GDP	Total Employment	Agricultural Production		Fertilizer Consumption	Export Earnings			Share of Public Investment in Total Investment	Share of Agriculture in		Land and Water Development in Total Investment	External Resources in Total Plan Outlay
							Total	Cereals		Total	Agricultural	Of GDP		Total Investment	Public Investment		
A. ARGENTINA	1.3	2.0	1974-77	PS	7.5	2.8	6.5	~	~	19.6	~	9.8[a]	42.0	~	~	~	~
B. BOLIVIA	2.5	5.0	1976-80	C/AS	7.7[b]	2.9	7.4	6.8	9.2	~	17.9	28.0[c]	70.0	9.6	10.1	~	31.0

PART II. ACHIEVEMENTS (AAGR)

Country	Year	Total GDP		GDP/C		Total Manufacturing[1]	
		Goal	Result	Goal	Result	Goal	Result
A. ARGENTINA	1970-75	7.0	3.2	5.5	1.8	8.6	4.5
C. BRAZIL	1972-74	9.0	9.3	6.0	6.6	11.0	10.2

Continued in SALA, 24-3000.

Table 3101

CENTRAL GOVERNMENT EXPENDITURES, LENDING PAYMENTS, AND DEFICITS, 20 LC

(%)

	Country	Year	Code[1]	(1) Total Expenditure and Lending Repayment (2 + 5)	(2) Total Expenditure (3 + 4)	(3) Current Expenditure	(4) Capital Expenditure	(5) Lending Minus Repayment
A.	ARGENTINA	1986	~	100.00	93.30	85.77	7.53	6.70
B.	BOLIVIA	1984	E	100.00	99.77	97.88	1.88	.23
C.	BRAZIL	1985	D	100.00	67.29	66.89	2.57	32.71
D.	CHILE	1986	A	100.00	101.78	90.46	11.32	−1.78
E.	COLOMBIA	1983	C	100.00	100.143	82.42	23.45	−.13
F.	COSTA RICA	1986	A	100.00	99.28	81.85	18.84	.72
G.	CUBA	~	~	100.00	~	~	~	~
H.	DOMINICAN REP.	1985	A	100.00	98.98	73.74	25.22	1.02
I.	ECUADOR	~	~	100.00	~	~	~	~
J.	EL SALVADOR	1987	~	100.00	97.53	86.38	7.39	2.47
K.	GUATEMALA	1983	B	100.00	98.11	74.51	25.23	1.89
L.	HAITI	1982	~	100.00	100.00	89.32	10.68	~
M.	HONDURAS	1976	A	100.00	99.47	63.47	36.00	.53
N.	MEXICO	1988	C	100.00	99.26‡	87.73‡	11.52‡	.74‡
O.	NICARAGUA	1986	B	100.00	100.0	91.85	8.15	~
P.	PANAMA	1986	A	100.00	101.28	94.36	6.93	−1.28
Q.	PARAGUAY	1986	A	100.00	96.69	87.04	9.65	3.31
R.	PERU	1981	~	100.00	100.00	75.54	24.46	~
S.	URUGUAY	1986	~	100.00	98.34	93.74	4.60	1.66
T.	VENEZUELA	1986	~	100.00	88.68	67.05	22.44	11.32
	UNITED STATES	1987	E	100.00	99.68	95.45	4.00	.32

1. Letters A–G indicate percent of General Government tax revenue accounted by Central
Government, where data are available, as follows: A, 95 and over; B, 90–94.9;
C, 80–89.9; D, 70–79.9; E, 60–69.9; F, 50–59.9; G, 20–49.9.

SOURCE: IMF-GFSY, 1986, pp. 36–37; 1987, pp. 36–37; 1988, pp. 37–39.

Table 3102

CENTRAL GOVERNMENT CURRENT SAVINGS, 19 L, 1970–88

(% of GDP)

	Country	1970	1980	1982	1983	1984	1985	1986	1987	1988‡
A.	ARGENTINA[1]	1.2	2.3	1.0	−6.0	−4.5	−3.2	.9	−2.8	.4
B.	BOLIVIA	−.5	−3.9	−4.9	−6.3	−33.6	4.5	−.1	−4.4	−.7
C.	BRAZIL	2.7	3.5	3.4	5.2	2.6	.9	~	8.3	11.4
D.	CHILE[2]	6.1	6.4	−2.0	−.2	1.5	2.8	5.0	8.3	11.4
E.	COLOMBIA	3.0	.7	.6	−.8	−1.7	.3	1.3	1.9	1.3
F.	COSTA RICA	2.0	−3.3	.5	.3	.3	.9	.5	.4	.1
H.	DOMINICAN REP.	4.3	2.6	−.7	.4	1.5	1.5	2.9	6.1	7.7
I.	ECUADOR[2]	#	.9	−1.8	0	0	5.0	.6	1.4	1.5
J.	EL SALVADOR	.3	−.7	−2.7	−2.5	−2.0	.1	1.4	−.3	0
K.	GUATEMALA	.9	.9	.2	.2	−1.1	.2	0	−.3	0
L.	HAITI[2]	.5	−.8	−.3	−8.9	−9.0	−6.9	−4.1	−5.1	−4.4
M.	HONDURAS	1.6	.5	−1.7	−3.1	−1.6	−2.2	−2.3	−2.4	−2.3
N.	MEXICO	2.2	1.7	−3.8	−4.3	−4.2	−4.0	−9.3	−10.9	~
O.	NICARAGUA	1.8	−3.9	−6.3	−7.3	−8.4	−15.8	−9.4	−6.9	−17.0
P.	PANAMA	.9	.7	−1.3	−2.7	−1.1	.5	.2	.9	−2.9
Q.	PARAGUAY	1.9	2.4	.6	−.9	.4	.9	1.2	1.7	1.9
R.	PERU	2.8	2.0	.2	−4.1	−.9	.4	−.8	−3.4	−.7
S.	URUGUAY	#	2.0	−4.7	−1.6	−3.3	−.1	.1	.5	~
T.	VENEZUELA	4.5	7.3	8.2	5.3	7.7	7.1	6.1	5.4	4.2

1. National Administration.
2. General Government.

SOURCE: IDB-SPTF, 1985 and 1986, table 21; 1988, table C-3, pp. 552; 1989, table C-3,
p. 475.

Table 3103

CENTRAL GOVERNMENT OVERALL SURPLUS OR DEFICIT, 19 L, 1970–88

(% of GDP)

Country	1970	1980	1982	1983	1984	1985	1986	1987	1988[‡]
A. ARGENTINA[1]	−1.4	−2.6	−3.7	−14.1	−7.2	−4.5	−3.1	−7.2	−1.7
B. BOLIVIA	−.8	−4.9	−6.4	−6.7	−34.2	−6.3	−.6	−5.1	−4.7
C. BRAZIL	−.4	−2.3	.1	−4.6	−5.8	−11.7	~	~	~
D. CHILE[2]	−2.0	3.5	−2.3	−3.6	−2.9	−1.9	−.5	2.5	3.9
E. COLOMBIA	−1.0	−2.0	−3.8	−3.5	−4.3	−2.7	−1.3	−.5	−1.4
F. COSTA RICA	.1	−8.0	−3.0	−3.6	−3.0	−2.0	−3.3	−2.0	−2.1
H. DOMINICAN REP.	−1.6	−3.1	−3.0	−2.7	−.9	−1.4	.6	−2.0	−1.5
I. ECUADOR[2]	−2.8	−1.4	−4.5	−2.5	−.8	2.8	−1.7	−2.3	−.8
J. EL SALVADOR	−1.6	−6.7	−7.7	−3.4	−2.6	−2.7	−1.4	−1.3	−1.5
K. GUATEMALA	−1.3	−4.7	−4.7	−3.3	−3.8	−1.8	−1.5	−1.3	−1.4
L. HAITI[2]	−.7	−5.6	−6.5	−3.8	−7.6	−3.7	−2.3	−1.5	~
M. HONDURAS	−3.1	−7.8	−9.7	−9.8	−9.5	−7.4	−6.1	−6.0	−6.1
N. MEXICO	−1.7	−2.8	−9.8	8.1	−7.5	−7.7	−13.0	−14.2	~
O. NICARAGUA	−1.2	−11.6	−12.0	30.0	−22.5	21.3	−14.5	−13.7	−23.6
P. PANAMA	−4.8	−5.9	−6.6	−5.2	−7.7	−3.5	−4.6	−4.2	−4.3
Q. PARAGUAY	−.1	−.2	−.6	2.6	−2.9	−1.5	.5	−.1	.7
R. PERU	−1.4	−2.4	−3.9	−7.2	4.1	−2.0	−3.8	−5.7	−2.3
S. URUGUAY	−1.3	.1	−7.2	3.7	−5.0	−1.9	−1.4	−1.3	~
T. VENEZUELA	−1.2	−6.0	−1.3	−.6	2.8	2.	−.4	−1.6	−2.9

1. National Administration
2. General Government.

SOURCE: IDB-SPTF, 1985 and 1986, table 22; 1988, table C-4, p. 552; 1989, table C-4, p. 475.

Table 3104

CENTRAL GOVERNMENT NET DOMESTIC BORROWING, 19 L, 1970–88

(% of GDP)

Country	1970	1980	1982	1983	1984	1985	1986	1987	1988
A. ARGENTINA[1]	1.1	1.9	6.2	16.4	7.8	3.9	2.7	~	~
B. BOLIVIA	.9	6.9	5.8	17.5	33.5	6.1	1.5	1.6	1.2
C. BRAZIL	.4	~	−.1	~	~	~	~	~	~
D. CHILE[2]	2.0	−2.7	2.6	3.6	2.2	−.6	−2.7	−2.7	−6.3
E. COLOMBIA	−.1	.9	3.2	3.7	3.7	1.7	−.2	.8	.1
F. COSTA RICA	−.7	6.1	2.0	3.1	1.6	−.5	2.0	1.4	1.9
H. DOMINICAN REP.	.7	1.4	2.3	1.7	.2	0	0	.1	.8
I. ECUADOR[2]	2.8	.9	2.1	2.9	1.3	−1.6	~	1.6	1.5
J. EL SALVADOR	1.3	5.3	5.0	.6	.8	0	0	.1	.6
K. GUATEMALA	−.1	3.0	3.6	2.8	2.9	1.4	0	.8	1.2
L. HAITI[2]	.3	2.9	2.7	1.5	4.5	1.9	1.3	.6	1.6
M. HONDURAS	.8	2.8	3.0	4.8	2.8	2.9	3.1	3.3	3.4
N. MEXICO	1.4	2.3	7.8	5.3	5.9	7.5	~	~	~
O. NICARAGUA	.1	3.4	9.2	24.9	11.3	9.1	13.0	13.5	22.3
P. PANAMA	.7	−.8	−.6	3.3	2.4	1.8	2.2	2.9	.3
Q. PARAGUAY	−.1	−.2	.6	1.9	1.9	.8	−.7	1.5	−.9
R. PERU	.8	1.8	.9	3.3	.8	−.5	2.3	4.8	1.4
S. URUGUAY	1.2	−.1	7.4	4.2	5.6	3.2	1.4	1.2	~
T. VENEZUELA	.5	−1.0	.1	2.1	−.2	.3	3.3	−.3	1.5

1. National Administration.
2. General Government.

SOURCE: IDB-SPTF, 1985 and 1986, table 23; 1988, table C-5, p. 553; 1989, table C-5, p. 476.

Table 3105

CENTRAL GOVERNMENT NET FOREIGN BORROWING, 19 L, 1979–88
(% of GDP)

	Country	1970	1980	1982	1983	1984	1985	1986	1987	1988[‡]
A.	ARGENTINA[1]	.3	.7	-2.5	-2.3	-.6	.5	.3	~	~
B.	BOLIVIA	#	-.1	-.6	-.1	-.1	.2	-.9	~	~
C.	BRAZIL	0	~	0	~	~	~	~	~	~
D.	CHILE[2]	0	-.8	-.3	0	.8	2.6	3.2	1.9	2.2
E.	COLOMBIA	1.1	1.1	.6	-.2	.7	1.0	1.5	-.3	1.3
F.	COSTA RICA	.6	1.8	1.0	.6	1.3	2.4	1.4	.6	.2
H.	DOMINICAN REP.	1.0	1.6	.7	.5	.9	1.7	.8	.7	.7
I.	ECUADOR[2]	#	.5	2.4	-.4	-.5	-.3	~	.7	-.7
J.	EL SALVADOR	.3	1.4	2.7	8.3	1.8	1.9	1.4	1.2	.9
K.	GUATEMALA	1.3	1.4	1.1	.9	.2	.7	.6	.5	.7
L.	HAITI[2]	.4	2.6	3.8	1.8	1.7	.3	2.0	1.4	.9
M.	HONDURAS	2.4	5.0	6.7	5.0	6.7	4.5	3.1	2.0	~
N.	MEXICO	.3	.5	2.0	2.8	1.6	.2	~	~	~
O.	NICARAGUA	1.1	5.0	2.8	6.4	4.1	8.3	1.1	.2	1.2
P.	PANAMA	3.6	6.6	7.2	3.0	3.6	1.9	1.8	.4	0
Q.	PARAGUAY	.4	.5	~	.7	1.4	.8	.1	.6	.4
R.	PERU	.6	.6	3.1	3.9	3.2	2.5	1.4	.4	1.0
S.	URUGUAY	.2	.1	-.2	-.2	-.3	-.4	-.2	.1	~
T.	VENEZUELA	.6	2.9	1.2	.1	0	0	0	.3	-.1

1. National Administration.
2. General Government.

SOURCE: IDB-SPTF, 1985 and 1986, table 24; 1988, table C-6, p. 553; 1989, table C-6, p. 476.

Table 3106

CENTRAL GOVERNMENT INTEREST PAYMENTS, 19 L, 1970–88
(% of Total Expenditures)

	Country	1970	1980	1982	1983	1984	1985	1986	1987	1988[‡]
A.	ARGENTINA[1]	3.2	.3	1.2	.4	5.9	19.2	12.8	9.9	4.2
B.	BOLIVIA	5.3	7.1	11.0	7.1	4.7	~	5.7	~	~
C.	BRAZIL	4.5	7.2	2.5	13.7	24.0	28.7	~	~	~
D.	CHILE[2]	2.5	2.7	1.4	3.5	3.9	5.8	4.9	6.2	7.9
E.	COLOMBIA	4.7	0	6.0	6.9	7.8	8.6	9.1	11.8	11.2
F.	COSTA RICA	10.9	10.5	11.8	14.3	13.1	12.9	12.9	15.3	15.5
H.	DOMINICAN REP.	.5	7.3	6.2	5.8	3.7	2.9	.9	.4	1.0
I.	ECUADOR[2]	12.3	9.4	18.5	~	~	22.6	18.0	13.4	13.2
J.	EL SALVADOR	1.2	2.4	9.0	9.5	7.4	7.0	7.6	6.7	6.8
K.	GUATEMALA	4.2	4.0	6.5	7.6	8.0	7.2	12.2	~	~
L.	HAITI[2]	4.1	2.5	3.3	3.8	5.8	5.7	6.4	6.4	~
M.	HONDURAS	3.3	4.7	6.1	8.9	8.5	9.5	11.5	13.2	13.5
N.	MEXICO	9.4	9.5	20.9	35.3	35.8	36.7	46.7	56.5	~
O.	NICARAGUA	2.6	7.0	12.8	5.7	3.0	4.3	2.6	.8	.1
P.	PANAMA	5.3	21.4	26.9	23.6	26.7	28.1	29.6	26.7	15.6
Q.	PARAGUAY	2.8	3.3	3.2	3.1	4.2	5.1	7.2	9.7	9.9
R.	PERU	5.2	18.4	18.3	23.2	23.5	25.2	14.9	12.1	17.1
S.	URUGUAY	3.1	2.2	4.2	6.1	9.5	11.5	10.4	8.9	~
T.	VENEZUELA	1.6	4.6	7.5	8.5	11.7	11.1	11.4	15.3	12.6

1. National Administration.
2. General Government.

SOURCE: IDB-SPTF, 1985 and 1986, table 35; 1988, table C-17, p. 559; 1989, table C-17, p. 482.

Table 3107

CENTRAL GOVERNMENT CURRENT REVENUES, 19 L, 1970–88

(% of GDP)

	Country	1970	1980	1982	1983	1984	1985	1986	1987	1988[‡]
A.	ARGENTINA[1]	7.8	12.7	11.3	5.9	5.7	10.5	15.1	12.0	3.9
B.	BOLIVIA	8.7	9.1	7.3	2.6	3.0	9.1	12.1	17.2	17.9
C.	BRAZIL	9.1	22.3	9.1	25.5	22.9	25.6	~	~	~
D.	CHILE[2]	35.7	32.9	36.0	30.3	31.6	31.2	32.5	33.4	34.4
E.	COLOMBIA	9.0	8.4	7.6	7.8	8.0	9.0	9.8	10.7	10.3
F.	COSTA RICA	12.9	12.8	14.4	16.6	16.6	16.2	15.4	15.7	15.2
H.	DOMINICAN REP.	16.1	14.3	9.5	10.5	11.1	11.7	12.2	12.8	14.5
I.	ECUADOR	10.6	12.8	11.0	10.7	12.3	17.1	13.3	13.1	13.1
J.	EL SALVADOR	10.9	11.4	12.3	12.4	13.2	13.4	14.4	11.9	10.7
K.	GUATEMALA	8.7	9.5	8.4	8.2	7.0	7.7	8.9	9.4	10.2
L.	HAITI[2]	13.6	9.3	11.6	11.6	11.5	13.1	11.7	13.2	13.1
M.	HONDURAS	12.3	14.9	13.8	13.3	15.1	15.6	15.5	16.4	16.2
N.	MEXICO	9.1	15.3	16.3	17.8	16.9	16.7	16.0	16.9	~
O.	NICARAGUA	10.7	21.3	25.1	30.9	34.9	32.1	32.0	27.7	19.9
P.	PANAMA	15.7	19.9	20.2	20.3	19.9	20.4	20.3	20.5	11.0
Q.	PARAGUAY	11.7	9.2	9.3	8.0	8.0	7.9	7.8	8.1	7.7
R.	PERU	16.1	17.1	17.5	11.5	13.1	14.0	12.2	8.8	9.0
S.	URUGUAY	13.8	16.2	15.2	16.3	13.8	15.4	15.0	15.4	~
T.	VENEZUELA	18.3	20.9	26.9	21.0	24.2	23.1	20.6	21.0	18.1

1. National Administration.
2. General Government.

SOURCE: IDB-SPTF, 1985 and 1986, table 19; 1988, table C-1, p. 551; 1989, table C-1, p. 474.

Table 3108

CENTRAL GOVERNMENT TAX REVENUES, 19 L, 1970–88

(% of Current Revenue)[1]

	Country	1970	1980	1982	1983	1984	1985	1986	1987	1988[‡]
A.	ARGENTINA[2]	88.1	75.1	78.5	91.6	95.6	85.6	70.8	85.7	98.3
B.	BOLIVIA	92.9	92.5	67.4	90.5	91.8	~	72.2	~	~
C.	BRAZIL	90.6	81.5	73.9	73.2	67.4	62.7	~	~	~
D.	CHILE[3]	77.1	73.1	52.5	64.0	64.7	64.2	62.0	62.2	57.7
E.	COLOMBIA	96.4	97.7	97.4	97.0	95.0	95.2	92.7	89.7	89.9
F.	COSTA RICA	95.6	96.6	97.8	97.3	91.3	92.7	88.5	92.1	93.0
H.	DOMINICAN REP.	89.7	77.4	88.4	88.1	92.9	95.1	95.3	83.4	84.5
I.	ECUADOR[3]	94.0	95.7	95.3	99.3	95.9	98.0	96.5	58.1	55.7
J.	EL SALVADOR	93.8	97.5	86.2	85.5	87.7	86.4	90.6	91.4	91.8
K.	GUATEMALA	90.0	92.7	85.8	82.8	78.8	78.6	79.0	86.2	86.2
L.	HAITI[3]	60.1	92.7	88.9	88.8	84.7	87.7	95.1	95.8	96.7
M.	HONDURAS	89.7	91.7	92.6	88.7	90.2	90.3	84.5	84.5	84.0
N.	MEXICO	90.3	94.9	93.0	94.2	95.4	94.9	81.0	76.4	~
O.	NICARAGUA	85.3	88.9	83.2	87.5	89.3	87.0	87.5	91.1	92.2
P.	PANAMA	80.5	76.0	74.6	74.1	69.9	68.8	72.3	72.6	73.4
Q.	PARAGUAY	89.1	89.3	86.8	78.7	82.2	85.6	85.8	86.5	86.3
R.	PERU	86.2	92.3	90.5	89.9	83.4	88.6	91.4	94.2	95.4
S.	URUGUAY	91.6	92.0	86.6	86.0	90.3	93.6	97.8	~	~
T.	VENEZUELA	63.6	83.9	78.7	85.7	86.3	84.4	82.5	82.0	80.7

1. Current Revenue: Includes all non-repayable receipts raised by the central government in the form of tax and non-tax, revenue, both excludes social security contributions and the sale of fixed government capital assets. Current revenue excludes the proceeds from central government borrowings and from the issuance of government bonds and the sale of other financial assets. In Haiti donations are included under current revenue and classified as a form of non-tax revenue.
2. National Administration.
3. General Government.

SOURCE: IDB-SPTF, 1985 and 1986, table 25; 1988, table C-7, p. 554; 1989, table C-7, p. 477.

Table 3109

CENTRAL GOVERNMENT DIRECT TAXES, 19 L, 1970–88

(% of Current Revenue)[1]

	Country	1970	1980	1982	1983	1984	1985	1986	1987	1988[‡]
A.	ARGENTINA[2]	33.8	21.8	10.4	4.8	2.7	11.2	12.9	18.8	20.5
B.	BOLIVIA	17.1	13.0	27.1	22.0	7.9	~	49.6	~	~
C.	BRAZIL	24.1	45.5	29.3	43.8	45.1	~	~	~	~
D.	CHILE[3]	~	18.7	15.8	16.8	11.2	10.6	10.0	11.7	19.0
E.	COLOMBIA	48.3	35.8	34.5	41.3	38.6	35.4	33.3	33.3	32.1
F.	COSTA RICA	23.7	22.5	22.9	24.1	19.5	17.6	17.0	15.9	17.4
H.	DOMINICAN REP.	22.4	20.0	29.9	24.8	23.9	22.4	21.3	19.5	23.2
I.	ECUADOR[3]	15.8	45.4	56.1	57.6	56.1	66.4	51.8	11.2	9.1
J.	EL SALVADOR	22.2	30.8	26.6	24.4	22.2	20.1	18.5	25.8	26.7
K.	GUATEMALA	15.0	13.5	14.7	18.1	12.8	14.6	13.2	16.5	21.6
L.	HAITI[3]	10.5	14.5	22.0	16.3	14.7	13.5	12.7	~	~
M.	HONDURAS	25.0	31.1	26.7	24.6	24.8	22.9	22.6	24.2	25.3
N.	MEXICO	39.7	36.9	31.1	23.4	25.0	24.5	26.6	23.2	~
O.	NICARAGUA	20.9	26.6	20.5	20.1	20.2	19.6	22.3	22.9	18.6
P.	PANAMA	38.8	34.0	36.6	37.2	35.4	36.2	36.9	37.0	38.5
Q.	PARAGUAY	15.4	21.9	30.1	22.5	27.4	28.5	27.5	26.8	26.5
R.	PERU	33.8	35.5	26.5	24.1	23.5	18.7	29.3	27.1	28.5
S.	URUGUAY	13.8	19.8	14.7	18.3	14.0	17.1	21.1	~	~
T.	VENEZUELA	48.3	71.9	66.6	59.6	62.3	61.5	46.9	47.6	57.2

1. For definition of current revenue, see table 3002.
2. National Administration.
3. General Government.

SOURCE: IDB-SPTF, 1985 and 1986, table 26; 1988, table C-8, p. 554; 1989, table C-8,
    p. 477.

Table 3110

CENTRAL GOVERNMENT INCOME TAXES, 19 L, 1970–88

(% of Current Revenue)[1]

	Country	1970	1980	1982	1983	1984	1985	1986	1987	1988[‡]
A.	ARGENTINA[2]	17.7	18.6	7.7	3.6	2.0	6.9	7.8	12.5	13.0
B.	BOLIVIA	15.0	12.9	27.1	21.8	7.9	~	42.6	~	~
C.	BRAZIL	24.1	18.3	29.3	19.2	21.8	~	~	~	~
D.	CHILE[3]	19.4	18.4	23.6	16.8	11.2	~	~	11.7	19.0
E.	COLOMBIA	45.4	35.7	33.6	41.2	38.6	35.4	33.3	33.3	32.1
F.	COSTA RICA	18.2	19.0	22.8	22.0	17.5	15.7	15.0	14.1	14.8
H.	DOMINICAN REP.	19.1	19.2	24.2	22.0	21.6	20.7	19.7	16.3	18.5
I.	ECUADOR[3]	15.8	44.6	55.3	55.7	53.5	65.0	50.7	11.2	9.1
J.	EL SALVADOR	14.2	23.2	20.3	18.7	17.4	15.5	15.2	20.4	20.6
K.	GUATEMALA	11.3	12.7	13.9	17.3	11.8	12.5	12.1	~	~
L.	HAITI[3]	7.0	12.9	16.5	13.5	13.1	12.3	11.4	9.9	~
M.	HONDURAS	23.9	30.3	25.8	23.7	23.9	22.1	21.2	22.6	24.3
N.	MEXICO	38.2	36.1	28.9	22.8	24.4	23.9	23.2	20.7	~
O.	NICARAGUA	9.4	10.4	10.9	14.7	15.4	15.8	18.4	20.4	17.4
P.	PANAMA	34.0	29.0	31.3	34.2	31.0	31.7	32.5	32.7	32.6
Q.	PARAGUAY	9.0	17.3	19.3	14.8	12.0	14.3	14.5	13.3	15.8
R.	PERU	29.8	29.2	14.8	17.4	14.9	12.4	22.1	19.9	21.1
S.	URUGUAY	8.1	14.9	7.1	11.8	9.4	11.7	15.3	~	~
T.	VENEZUELA	47.9	71.8	66.4	59.3	62.0	61.2	46.6	47.0	56.2

1. For definition of current revenue see table 3002.
2. National Administration.
3. General Government.

SOURCE: IDB-SPTF, 1985 and 1986, table 27; 1988, table C-9, p. 555; 1989, table C-9, p. 478.

Table 3111

CENTRAL GOVERNMENT PROPERTY TAXES, 18 L, 1970–88

(% of Current Revenue)[1]

Country	1970	1980	1982	1983	1984	1985	1986	1987	1988[‡]
A. ARGENTINA[2]	15.5	3.2	2.7	1.3	.7	4.3	5.1	6.4	7.6
B. BOLIVIA	2.1	.1	.5	.1	#	~	1.5	~	~
C. BRAZIL	#	.1	#	#	#	~	~	~	~
D. CHILE[3]	4.1	.3	.8	#	#	~	~	~	~
E. COLOMBIA	1.6	0	.3	.1	#	#	#	~	~
F. COSTA RICA	.6	1.1	.9	.7	.6	.4	.5	.6	.8
H. DOMINICAN REP.	3.3	.7	3.2	2.7	2.3	1.8	1.6	3.2	1.7
I. ECUADOR[3]	0	.8	.5	2.0	2.6	1.3	1.1	0	0
J. EL SALVADOR	6.4	5.9	4.7	4.0	3.2	2.8	2.0	4.0	4.1
K. GUATEMALA	3.1	.7	.8	.7	.9	2.0	1.1	~	~
L. HAITI[3]	3.6	1.5	1.7	1.3	1.4	1.3	1.3	~	~
M. HONDURAS	1.1	.8	1.0	.9	.8	.8	.7	.8	~
N. MEXICO	~	~	~	~	~	~	~	~	~
O. NICARAGUA	9.4	7.5	4.6	2.8	3.1	2.2	2.1	1.4	.8
P. PANAMA	4.3	5.0	3.9	4.1	4.4	4.5	4.4	4.2	5.9
Q. PARAGUAY	6.3	4.6	12.0	7.7	5.9	4.8	4.5	5.3	10.7
R. PERU	4.0	3.2	3.9	3.6	2.9	2.4	4.6	4.2	5.1
S. URUGUAY	5.7	4.9	5.8	6.5	4.5	5.4	5.8	~	~
T. VENEZUELA	.4	.2	.2	.3	.3	.4	.3	.2	~

1. For definition of current revenue see table 3002.
2. National Administration.
3. General Government.

SOURCE: IDB-SPTF, 1985 and 1986, table 28; 1988, table C-9, p. 555; 1989, table C-10, p. 478.

Table 3112

CENTRAL GOVERNMENT PRODUCTION AND SALES TAX, 19 L, 1970–88

(% of Current Revenue)[1]

Country	1970	1980	1982	1983	1984	1985	1986	1987	1988[‡]
A. ARGENTINA[2]	32.8	39.3	44.2	12.3	10.3	29.5	30.1	37.2	38.9
B. BOLIVIA	34.5	40.1	16.2	33.2	51.9	~	1.7	~	~
C. BRAZIL	59.0	30.5	32.7	25.3	18.0	~	~	~	~
D. CHILE[3]	43.4	49.3	3.5	24.6	23.5	23.2	37.6	35.9	30.5
E. COLOMBIA	8.6	23.1	40.4	24.7	25.6	27.8	27.2	26.7	27.8
F. COSTA RICA	40.7	44.7	31.4	36.6	40.9	41.5	38.1	43.8	48.1
H. DOMINICAN REP.	20.2	21.5	33.8	32.7	36.0	36.0	39.1	24.7	21.1
I. ECUADOR[3]	16.5	17.4	20.3	20.1	17.7	13.7	24.0	28.1	27.1
J. EL SALVADOR	25.6	28.5	33.2	16.3	16.3	15.2	11.1	13.8	13.9
K. GUATEMALA	43.3	10.7	51.2	15.2	32.3	24.9	25.4	~	~
L. HAITI[3]	10.9	10.2	20.2	26.7	27.7	34.5	35.8	~	~
M. HONDURAS	36.0	24.0	30.8	29.2	29.9	29.9	28.2	27.7	28.9
N. MEXICO	27.5	21.7	24.5	30.5	32.2	31.4	37.0	33.8	~
O. NICARAGUA	36.3	46.8	44.8	45.9	50.7	56.9	54.5	59.8	57.1
P. PANAMA	14.2	19.8	23.3	16.0	10.6	9.3	9.9	11.3	14.5
Q. PARAGUAY	27.1	16.2	22.9	18.8	7.3	8.6	9.7	10.4	45.9
R. PERU	31.2	37.2	47.1	51.7	47.3	55.4	47.6	52.7	51.2
S. URUGUAY	40.3	58.4	53.0	51.3	58.2	59.6	59.9	~	~
T. VENEZUELA	6.1	4.0	4.9	6.0	4.4	5.6	9.1	7.7	8.6

1. For definition of current revenue see table 3002.
2. National Administration.
3. General Government.

SOURCE: IDB-SPTF, 1985 and 1986, table 30; 1988, table C-12, p. 556; 1989, table C-12, p. 479.

Table 3113

CENTRAL GOVERNMENT INTERNATIONAL TRADE TAXES, 19 L, 1970–88

(% of Current Revenue) [1]

	Country	1970	1980	1982	1983	1984	1985	1986	1987	1988[‡]
A.	ARGENTINA[2]	20.9	11.2	16.0	37.6	32.5	26.2	15.2	15.1	31.9
B.	BOLIVIA	67.5	29.3	53.1	20.5	27.6	~	~	~	~
C.	BRAZIL	7.1	5.5	5.1	4.1	4.3	~	~	~	~
D.	CHILE[3]	27.0	4.2	3.1	18.0	23.5	25.3	7.7	8.6	7.9
E.	COLOMBIA	27.3	26.6	21.8	17.6	16.9	18.8	20.6	21.2	21.4
F.	COSTA RICA	29.8	29.3	38.1	36.6	30.9	33.6	33.3	32.4	27.5
H.	DOMINICAN REP.	45.1	31.1	24.7	26.8	29.2	33.5	32.4	36.6	40.2
I.	ECUADOR[3]	56.6	30.8	19.0	21.1	21.4	17.3	20.7	18.7	17.4
J.	EL SALVADOR	40.5	37.0	25.2	22.2	24.2	27.8	41.1	25.5	24.7
K.	GUATEMALA	28.0	36.5	17.1	19.7	20.0	10.2	26.8	~	~
L.	HAITI[3]	36.3	59.4	38.7	36.6	29.5	24.3	23.7	17.6	14.7
M.	HONDURAS	28.6	36.6	35.3	34.8	35.4	37.5	34.3	33.4	29.8
N.	MEXICO	18.2	33.5	21.5	39.5	37.2	38.3	15.9	18.0	~
O.	NICARAGUA	28.1	13.5	17.2	6.9	6.4	5.1	8.0	6.6	12.4
P.	PANAMA	23.5	12.9	12.3	13.0	13.3	13.0	14.8	13.6	9.0
Q.	PARAGUAY	34.2	33.2	15.2	17.4	11.6	12.0	12.9	16.1	10.7
R.	PERU	21.3	27.6	21.4	21.7	19.5	22.1	21.1	21.7	23.0
S.	URUGUAY	20.3	12.8	13.1	15.6	17.4	16.4	16.4	14.7	~
T.	VENEZUELA	7.8	8.0	6.7	20.1	19.6	17.2	26.5	26.7	15.0

1. For definition of current revenue see table 3002.
2. National Administration.
3. General Government.

SOURCE: IDB-SPTF, 1985 and 1986, table 31; 1988, table C-13, p. 557; 1989, table C-13,
   p. 480.

Table 3114

CENTRAL GOVERNMENT TOTAL EXPENDITURE, 19 L, 1970–88

(% of GDP)

	Country	1970	1980	1982	1983	1984	1985	1986	1987	1988[‡]
A.	ARGENTINA[1]	9.2	15.3	15.0	20.0	12.8	15.0	18.1	19.3	5.6
B.	BOLIVIA	9.5	14.1	13.5	9.3	37.2	15.4	12.9	~	~
C.	BRAZIL	9.5	25.2	9.0	30.8	29.2	37.7	~	~	~
D.	CHILE[2]	40.8	31.1	39.7	34.2	34.6	33.4	33.3	31.1	30.7
E.	COLOMBIA	10.0	10.3	11.9	11.3	12.3	11.6	11.1	11.1	11.7
F.	COSTA RICA	12.8	20.8	16.0	20.1	19.6	18.2	18.8	17.7	17.3
H.	DOMINICAN REP.	17.7	17.5	12.5	13.2	12.1	13.4	12.9	15.1	16.0
I.	ECUADOR[2]	13.4	14.2	15.5	13.2	13.1	14.3	15.0	15.4	13.9
J.	EL SALVADOR	12.8	18.6	20.0	21.2	19.1	17.1	17.4	15.5	13.8
K.	GUATEMALA	9.9	14.2	13.1	11.5	10.9	9.6	10.8	11.9	12.7
L.	HAITI[2]	14.3	14.9	16.6	23.3	22.9	22.1	17.5	20.5	~
M.	HONDURAS	15.4	22.7	23.5	23.6	26.5	24.6	23.3	23.8	23.4
N.	MEXICO	10.8	18.1	26.2	25.9	24.4	24.3	29.0	31.1	~
O.	NICARAGUA	11.9	33.3	36.4	63.6	59.3	54.9	48.0	41.9	43.9
P.	PANAMA	20.5	25.8	26.8	25.5	27.7	24.1	24.9	24.8	15.4
Q.	PARAGUAY	11.8	9.5	10.8	10.6	10.9	9.5	7.3	8.2	7.0
R.	PERU	17.5	19.5	21.6	18.7	17.3	16.1	16.0	14.4	11.4
S.	URUGUAY	15.1	16.1	23.9	19.9	18.8	17.3	16.4	16.7	~
T.	VENEZUELA	19.4	26.9	28.1	21.6	21.4	21.2	21.0	22.6	21.0

1. National Administration.
2. General Government.

SOURCE: IDB-SPTF, 1985 and 1986, table 20; 1988, table C-2, p. 551; 1989, table C-2,
   p. 474.

Table 3115

TOTAL EXPENDITURE[1] AND DEFICIT OF CENTRAL GOVERNMENTS, 19 L, 1975-87

(M NC)

Country	Code[2]	1975	1980	1981	1982	1983	1984	1985	1986	1987
A. ARGENTINA[3]	I	212	25.0	59.7	18.3	122.5	594.0	7,578	11,000	~
	II	−155	7.9	25.9	−9.2	−82.3	−300.0	2,867	2,300	~
B. BOLIVIA	I	6,395	21,521	24,347	3,276	1,862	8.2	2,087.4	1,423.6	1,309.5
	II	706	−9,728	−10,461	−1,378	−6,696	−7.7	−1,881.7	−582.6	−282.7
C. BRAZIL[3]	I	95.4	1,798.9	3,310.1	~	~	~	~	~	~
	II	#	2.0	3.0	~	~	~	~	~	~
D. CHILE[3]	I	7.4	226.4	291.5	323.4	400.3	501.3	782	906	1,078
	II	.5	13.0	25.4	−22.7	−52.0	−59.0	−140	−69	−6
E. COLOMBIA[3]	I	39,351	163.2	214.9	291.2	344.7	464.6	575.4	750.8	975.7
	II	−909	−11.4	−58.3	−101.4	−106.0	−161.9	−134.3	−90.0	−56.9
F. COSTA RICA	I	2,942	8,279	9,911	16,294	27,656	34,867	37,600	46,300	50,100
	II	−681	−3,297	−2,457	−3,346	−6,599	−7,586.0	−7,900	−8,300	−5,600
H. DOMINICAN REP.	I	653	1,053	1,068	988	1,142	1,246	1,845	2,252	3,012
	II	−17	−184	−160	−243	−237	−97	−218	−95	−161
I. ECUADOR	I	11,755	46,156	53,395	66,536	80,462	116,964	179,326	216,500	278,600
	II	609	8,589	−20,098	−21,647	−11,786	−17,091	11,742	−29,600	−47,800
J. EL SALVADOR	I	600	1,514	~	~	2,761	2,723	2,609	3,782	3,989
	II	−22	−484	~	~	−1,499	−1,177	−696	−895	−1,261
K. GUATEMALA	I	395	1,256	1,740	1,258	1,097	1,132.0	1,188	1,706	1,941
	II	−43	−509	−633	−528	−356	466.0	−321	−300	−310
L. HAITI	I	495	1,202	1,325	1,303	1,871	1,990.0	2,013.0	1,962	2,004
	II	−270	−511	−664	−540	−918	−914	−734	−622	−716
M. HONDURAS	I	438	1,243	1,906	2,365	1,583	1,935	2,084	2,140	2,274
	II	−155	−485	−672	−1,030	−805	−985	−1,020	−988	−985
N. MEXICO[3]	I	156	1,061	1,318	2,658	4,597	7,177	11,632	22,781	59,954
	II	−54	−381	−383	−1,126	−1,418	−2,136	−3,581	−10,230	−27,377
O. NICARAGUA	I	2,106	6,364	8,412	11,109	20,083	26,898	64,222	217,800	1,083,200
	II	−783	−1,838	−3,030	−3,863	−9,870	−11,148	−26,916	−76,700	−366,900
P. PANAMA	I	420	1,065	1,217	1,625	1,370	1,493	1,366	1,764	1,902
	II	−123	−370	−427	−777	−464	−577	−359	−723	−808
Q. PARAGUAY[3]	I	18,609	52,976	69,977	87.0	80.7	96.1	132.2	132.2	186.8
	II	−714	−1,385	−8,215	−12.5	−35.8	−10.5	−21.4	−10.7	−16.5
R. PERU	I	131.4	1,370	2,276	3,051	6,083	12,563	32,307	58,033	108,302
	II	−43.5	−351	−753	−558	−2,351	2,917	−4,072	−12,702	−41,878
S. URUGUAY	I	1,349	13,081	18,817	27,503	33,159	55,500	91,425.0	161,200	293,000
	II	−363	75	−117	−11,210	−7,411	−15,676	−14,638.0	−11,300	−22,000
T. VENEZUELA[3]	I	32.3	72.9	94.0	180.2	78.2	89.6	99.5	103.3	151.4
	II	8,553	−10,172	1,307	−6.5	−6.4	9.6	8.3	−1.9	−.8

1. Current plus capital expenditures.
2. I = Total expenditure;
   II = Deficit (positive number indicates surplus), i.e., current income less total
   expenditure.
3. BNC (for Paraguay after 1981).

a. Excluding treasury certificates issued and redeemed in the same year, since their introduction in 1978.

SOURCE: ECLA-S, 1978, 1979, 1980, 1981, 1984, 1985, 1986, 1987.

Table 3116

FUNCTIONAL ANALYSIS OF CENTRAL GOVERNMENT EXPENDITURE, 20 LC (%)[1]

Country	Year	General Public Services	Defense	Education	Health	Social Security and Welfare	Housing and Community Amenities	Recreational, Cultural, and Religious	Fuel and Energy	Agriculture, Forestry, Fishing, and Hunting	Mining, Manufacturing, and Construction	Transportation and Communication	Other Economic
A. ARGENTINA	1986	8.00	5.95	6.03	1.89	32.30	.41	.72	6.51	.94	1.57	7.78	1.34
B. BOLIVIA	1984	~	5.40	12.23	1.48	5.21	.20	.10	.07	.53	.15	3.89	~
C. BRAZIL	1985	12.09	3.06	2.96	6.42	23.37	.32	.16	.16	4.17	1.25	3.54	2.09
D. CHILE	1986	12.53‡	10.74‡	12.53‡	5.99‡	38.01‡	4.54‡	.74‡	.02‡	1.78‡	.26‡	4.46	2.68‡
E. COLOMBIA	1983	18.90	7.79	20.86	4.40	18.40	4.67	.60	5.31	1.76	.26	12.53	6.40
F. COSTA RICA	1986	9.86	2.19	16.22	19.34	19.23	7.45	3.27	.09	3.60	#	7.97	.61
G. CUBA	~	~	~	~	~	~	~	~	~	~	~	~	~
H. DOMINICAN REP.	1985	11.57	8.05	12.84	8.99	7.04	5.95	1.66	7.42	19.64	.94	8.86	6.63
I. ECUADOR	~	~	~	~	~	~	~	~	~	~	~	~	~
J. EL SALVADOR	1987	16.81	26.84	17.08	7.38	~	1.65	1.09	.03	3.69	.29	7.52	2.30
K. GUATEMALA	1983	~	~	~	~	~	~	~	~	~	~	~	~
L. HAITI	1982	14.49	9.86	7.33	7.39	5.39	.17	~	~	4.71	~	.51	~
M. HONDURAS	1976	27.72	10.49	20.69	14.69	4.73	2.57	.93	#	3.10	.66	12.35	2.65
N. MEXICO	1988	1.45‡	1.38‡	7.43‡	1.10‡	8.29‡	1.00‡	.26‡	1.48‡	2.64‡	2.48‡	2.70‡	2.15‡
O. NICARAGUA	~	~	~	~	~	~	~	~	~	~	~	~	~
P. PANAMA	1986	24.09	~	15.91	15.47	10.05	4.00	.60	.26	3.12	.24	3.07	1.36
Q. PARAGUAY	1986	23.36	12.15	12.23	3.05	29.61	2.68	.16	#	1.82	.42	3.84	3.98
R. PERU	1981	10.44	13.81	11.34	5.30	.15	.92	1.26	.17	4.07	1.29	~	.52
S. URUGUAY	1986	10.98	10.25	7.12	4.77	49.43	.05	.95	1.78	1.37	.38	5.86	7.00
T. VENEZUELA	1986	7.07	5.80	19.56	10.02	6.91	4.76	.89	~	3.02	1.51	5.48	~
UNITED STATES	1987	6.05	25.59	1.69	12.16	28.36	2.94	.26	.53	2.91	.05	2.66	1.51

1. Total expenditure = 100 percent. Owing to adjustment items and unallocated transactions, components may not add to totals.
2. Includes other unspecified categories, as well as Agriculture, Roads, and Transportation.

SOURCE: IMF-GFSY, 1988, pp. 40–41.

Table 3117

DEFENSE AND SOCIAL EXPENDITURES,[1] 20 L, 1972-87

Country	Total Expenditure (% of GNP)						Central Government Expenditure[2] Per Capita (US 1975)																					
							Defense[3]					Education[4]					Health[5]											
	1972	1981	1983	1985	1986	1987	1972	1981	1983	1985	1986	1972	1981	1983	1985	1986	1972	1981	1983	1985	1986
A. ARGENTINA	16.5	23.6	22.3	18.0	25.8	~	8.8	11.4	9.1	8.8	5.2	8.8	7.3	7.6	9.5	6.0	2.9	1.4	1.4	1.8	1.3
B. BOLIVIA	9.2	12.7	11.3	39.9	32.0	~	16.2	22.7	10.8	5.4	5.8	30.6	24.4	26.9	12.2	11.6	8.6	7.2	3.1	1.5	1.4
C. BRAZIL	16.6	19.5	21.4	21.1	26.4	26.1	8.3	3.4	4.1	4.0	3.1	6.8	3.8	3.7	3.7	3.0	6.4	7.4	7.3	7.6	6.4
D. CHILE	42.3	31.0	34.8	35.5	33.6	31.9	6.1	12.0	12.0	11.5	10.7	14.3	14.4	13.7	13.2	12.5	8.2	6.4	6.0	6.1	6.0
E. COLOMBIA	13.0	~	~	~	~	14.7	~	~	~	~	~	~	~	~	~	~	~	~	~	~	~
F. COSTA RICA	18.9	23.7	26.4	24.5	29.3	28.3	2.8	2.6	3.0	3.0	2.2	28.3	23.7	19.4	19.4	16.2	3.8	29.7	22.5	22.5	19.3
G. CUBA	~	~	~	~	~	~	~	~	~	~	~	~	~	~	~	~	~	~	~	~	~
H. DOMINICAN REP.	18.5	44.9	15.6	14.2	15.3	15.3	~	8.9	8.7	8.4	8.1	~	13.9	15.3	15.1	12.8	~	9.7	10.5	10.3	9.0
I. ECUADOR	13.4	17.1	14.3	14.5	15.7	16.3[a]	6.6	11.8	10.6	11.3	11.8	27.5	30.1	26.0	27.7	24.5	4.5	7.9	7.5	8.3	7.3
J. EL SALVADOR	12.8	18.5	17.4	19.8	12.9	12.4	~	16.8	15.8	20.3	28.7	21.4	17.9	16.6	14.5	17.5	10.9	8.4	8.4	5.9	7.5
K. GUATEMALA	9.9	16.2	13.1	~	~	~	11.0	~	10.6	~	~	19.4	~	26.0	~	~	9.5	~	7.5	~	~
L. HAITI	14.5	19.4	17.6	18.8	~	~	~	~	~	8.4	~	~	~	~	6.0	~	~	~	~	5.7	~
M. HONDURAS	15.4	~	~	~	~	~	12.4	~	~	~	~	22.3	~	~	~	~	10.2	~	~	~	~
N. MEXICO	12.1	20.8	27.9	24.9	27.3	22.7	4.2	2.5	2.0	~	2.5	16.6	18.2	11.0	12.4	11.5	5.1	1.9	1.2	1.5	1.4
O. NICARAGUA	15.5	30.2	~	~	56.4	58.0	12.3	11.0	~	27.7	~	16.6	11.6	11.0	~	~	4.0	14.6	13.1	~	~
P. PANAMA	27.6	36.1	40.4	~	32.5	34.6	~	~	~	~	~	~	12.8	11.0	~	16.0	~	13.2	~	~	15.8
Q. PARAGUAY	13.1	10.7	11.7	10.8	7.9	7.9	13.8	13.2	12.5	10.2	12.1	12.0	11.0	12.0	10.7	12.2	3.5	4.5	3.7	5.8	3.1
R. PERU	17.1	20.2	18.6	12.9	14.1	14.7[a]	14.8	13.8	27.6	~	~	22.7	11.3	18.5	~	~	6.2	5.3	6.2	~	~
S. URUGUAY	25.0	24.4	25.9	24.8	24.7	23.9	5.6	12.9	12.7	10.8	10.2	9.5	7.7	6.5	6.4	7.1	1.6	3.8	3.4	4.1	4.8
T. VENEZUELA	21.3	28.9	27.4	25.6	26.6	22.0	10.3	3.9	5.2	6.1	4.9	18.3	18.3	19.1	17.7	19.8	11.7	7.3	8.6	7.6	8.1

1. Both current and capital (development) expenditures are included. The inadequate statistical coverage of state, provincial, and local governments and the nonavailability of data for these lower levels of government have dictated the use of only central government data. This may seriously understate or distort the statistical portrayal of the allocation of resources for various purposes, especially in large countries where lower levels of government have considerable autonomy and are responsible for many social services. Great caution should therefore be exercised in using the data for cross-economy comparisons.

2. Central Government Expenditure comprises the expenditure by all government offices, departments, establishments, and other bodies that are agencies or instruments of the central authority of a country. It does not necessarily comprise all public expenditure.

3. Defense Expenditure comprises all expenditure, whether by defense or other departments, for the maintenance of military forces, including the purchase of military supplies and equipment, construction, recruiting, and training. Also falling in this category is expenditure for strengthening the public services to meet wartime emergencies, for training civil defense personnel, and for foreign military aid and contributions to military organizations and alliances.

4. Education Expenditure comprises public expenditure for the provision, management, inspection, and support of preprimary, primary, and secondary schools; of universities and colleges; and of vocational, technical, and other training institutions by central governments. Also included is expenditure on the general administration and regulation of the education system; on research into its objectives, organization, administration, and methods; and on such subsidiary services as transportation and medical and dental services in schools.

5. Health Expenditure covers public expenditure on hospitals, medical and dental centers, and clinics with a major medical component; on national health and medical insurance schemes; and on family planning and preventive care. Also included is expenditure on the general administration and regulation of relevant government departments, hospitals and clinics, health and sanitation, and national health and medical insurance schemes.

a. Refers to budgetary data.

SOURCE: WB-WDR, 1983, 1986, table 22; 1987, table 23; 1988, table 23; 1989, table 11.

Table 3118

ARGENTINA CENTRAL GOVERNMENT REVENUE, EXPENDITURE, AND FINANCING THE DEFICIT, 1975–86

(B NC)

Category	1975	1977	1978	1979	1980	1981	1982	1983	1984	1985	1986
1. Current Income	57	1,388	3.5	9.5	17.1	33.9	9.1	40.2	294.2	4,711	8,700
Tax Revenue	47	1,196	2.8	6.8	15.3	29.3	8.2	35.8	276.3	4,134	8,000
Non-Tax Revenue	9	192	.8	2.7	1.9	4.5	.9	4.4	17.9	577	700[a]
2. Current Expenditure	182	1,422	3.9	10.3	22.1	48.6	16.4	84.2	444.3	4,259	8,700
Wages and Salaries	47	490	1.5	3.9	9.2	17.7	3.9	17.5	113.9	~	1,700
Non-Personal Goods and Services	~	167	.5	1.1	2.4	5.5	1.3	5.5	19.0	211	500
Interest	11	97	.2	.4	.1	.4	5.7	13.2	107.6	984	1,300
Transfers	114	660	1.6	4.8	10.2	24.3	5.6	46.1	197.5	2,067	5,000
Other Current Expenditure	10	8	~	.1	.2	.7	.6	2.9	6.3	79	200
3. Current Savings[1]	-125	-34	-.4	-.8	-4.9	-14.7	-7.3	-44.0	-150.1	453	~
4. Capital Expenditure	189	463	.6	1.6	2.9	11.1	1.9	38.3	149.7	3,320	2,300
Real Investment	7	184	.4	1.0	1.6	4.8	.8	2.2	6.8	33	100
Loans (Net of Repayments)	23	279	.2	.6	1.3	6.3	1.2	36.1	142.8	3,287	2,200
5. Total Expenditure[2]	212	1,885	4.5	11.9	25.0	59.7	18.3	122.5	594.0	7,578	11,000
6. Fiscal Deficit[3]	-155	-497	1.0	2.3	7.8	25.9	-9.2	-82.3	-299.8	2,867	2,300
7. Financing Deficit											
Central Bank	119	312	~	~	9.8	27.8	7.1	104.0	268.1	1,034	~
Unified Official Account Fund	20	231	.4	1.0	1.6	1.6	.6	3.2	22.4	42	600
Issue of Securities[4]	27	471	1.7	4.3	2.7	16.1	5.4	5.5	67.0	842	900
Bond of Amortization Payments	-11	-561	-1.0	-2.9	-1.5	-2.4	-2.1	-2.0	-56.6	-749	-700
Other	#	44	.1	-.1	-.5	-2.3	-.3	-28.2	-1.0	1,746	2,200[b]

1. Current Income minus Current Expenditure.
2. Current Expenditure plus Capital Expenditure.
3. For 1975 and 1976 the National Treasury calculated the deficit by considering Amortization of the Public Debt as expenditure and Issues of Securities as income.
4. Less debt amortization payments (1975 and 1976).

a. Includes finance from economic emergency (non obligatory).
b. Includes the external finance from the National Government net deposits from the Government and BCRA in foreign currency.

SOURCE: ECLA-S, 1978–80, 1984, 1985, and 1986, p. 108.

Table 3119

BOLIVIA CENTRAL GOVERNMENT REVENUE, EXPENDITURE, AND FINANCING THE DEFICIT, 1975–87

(M NC)

Category	1975	1977	1978	1979	1980	1984	1985	1986	1987[‡]
1. Current Income	5,689	7,641	8,540	8,384	11,793	.6	205.8	841.0	1,026.9
Inland Revenue	1,724	2,748	3,165	3,621	4,460	.2	22.1	174.2	274.7
Custom Revenue	1,550	1,694	1,960	2,064	2,563	.1	22.7	98.6	146.0
Additional Export Tax	622	535	470	807	127	~	6.0	1.5	5.4
Mining Royalties	478	1,258	1,545	1,333	1,771	.1	122.0	313.2	505.5
Petroleum and Gas Royalties	819	918	919	80	1,852	.1	33.0	253.6	95.3
Other Income	496	488	481	480	1,020	.1			
2. Current Expenditure	6,395	10,954	11,542	15,035	21,521	8.2	2,087.4	1,423.6	1,309.5
Personal Services	2,686	3,795	4,704	5,948	9,706	1.7	144.8	360.1	516.5
Non-personal Services	~	~	513	587	946	.1	19.6	49.9	67.0
Materials and Supplies	744	931	684	692	1,512	.2	179.3	114.8	122.7
Fixed and Financial Assets	230	293	256	317	1,345	.1	20.0	52.1	43.4
Public Debt	845	925	1,165	1,831	3,817	.5	452.7	145.6	164.3
Transfers and Contributions	1,789	3,153	3,211	3,424	2,552	4.5	567.5	244.3	164.3
Other Expenditure	300	1,857	1,009	2,236	1,642	1.1	703.6	456.8	251.2
3. Deficit	-706	-3,113	-3,002	-6,651	-9,728	-7.7	-1,881.7	-582.6	-282.7

SOURCE: ECLA-S, 1978–81, 1984, 1985, 1986, 1987, p. 138.

Table 3120

BRAZIL CENTRAL GOVERNMENT REVENUE, EXPENDITURE,
AND FINANCING THE DEFICIT, 1975-87[a]

(B NC)

Category	1975	1977	1978	1979	1980	1981[‡]	1984[b]	1985[b]	1986[b]	1987[b]
1. Current income	76.8	242.9	349.2	509.8	1,219.4	2,262.0	33.8	134.5	394.0	1,202.4
Tax Income	~	211.0	309.6	445.1	958.2	1,837.2	29.5	110.1	288.4	782.0
Other Income	~	~	~	~	~	~	~	24.4	52.0	341.6

a. For other categories, see SALA, 24-3020.
b. In MNC.

SOURCE: ECLA-S, 1978, 1979, 1980, 1981, 1986, and 1987, p. 172.

Table 3121

CHILE CENTRAL GOVERNMENT REVENUE; EXPENDITURE,
AND FINANCING THE DEFICIT, 1975-87

Category	1975	1979	1980	1981	1982	1983	1984	1985	1986	1987[‡]
A. INCOME AND EXPENDITURE IN NATIONAL CURRENCY										
(Billions of current pesos of each year)										
1. Current Income	7.9	157.1	239.4	319.9	300.7	348.3	442.3	642	837	1,084
Direct Taxes	2.4	45.3	65.6	81.1	80.1	70.0	86.5	108	131	152
Indirect Taxes	5.1	104.3	154.1	203.7	190.7	260.3	339.6	500	641	834
Non-tax Revenue	.4	7.5	19.7	35.1	29.9	18.6	16.2	34	65	98
2. Total Expenditure	7.4	151.2	226.4	291.5	323.4	400.3	501.3	782	906	1,078
Servicing of Public Debt	~	7.8	15.8	2.9	4.2	13.0	34.6	110	84	101
Other Expenditure	7.4	143.4	210.6	288.7	319.2	387.3	466.7	672	822	977
3. Deficit (1-2)	.5	5.9	13.0	28.4	-22.7	-52.0	-59.0	-140	-69	-6
4. Deficit/Total (Percentage)	6.1	3.9	5.8	9.7	-7.0	-13.0	-11.8	-17.9	-7.6	-.5
B. INCOME AND EXPENDITURE IN FOREIGN CURRENCY										
(Millions of dollars at current prices)										
1. Current Income	219	864	1,007	523	439	548	413	368	409	622
Copper	177	840	976	449	402	518	361	349	389	513
Other	42	24	31	74	37	30	52	19	20	109
2. Total Expenditure	556	679	1,178	1,550	564	648	668	608	599	683
Service of Public Debt	388	524	958[a]	1,270[b]	410	462	122	143	115	79
Other Expenditure	168	156	220	280	154	18	546	465	484	604
3. Deficit (1-2)	-337	184	-171	-1,037	-125	-100	-255	-240	-190	-61
4. Deficit/Total Expenditure (Percentage)	-60.6	27.1	-14.5	-66.9	-22.2	-15.4	-38.2	-39.5	-31.7	-8.9
C. CONSOLIDATED INCOME AND EXPENDITURE										
(Millions of dollars at 1976 prices)[e]										
1. Current Income	2,360	3,104	3,579	3,842	3,239	3,025	3,235	4,359	4,748	5,563
Copper	193	509	519	219	192	244	166	349	389	513
Direct Taxes	674	752	842	915	809	559	598	676	683	698
Indirect Taxes	1,388	1,717	1,963	2,291	1,926	2,070	2,337	3,113	3,238	3,808
Non-tax Revenue	105	126	255	417	312	152	134	221	348	544
2. Total Expenditure	2,607	2,896	3,504	4,025	3,528	3,485	3,753	5,471	5,295	5,596
Servicing of Public Debt	447	446	710[c]	652[d]	238	321	407	830	549	539
Other Expenditure	2,160	2,450	2,797	3,373	3,290	3,164	3,346	4,641	4,746	5,057
3. Deficit (1-2)	-247	208	75	-183	-289	-460	-518	-1,112	-547	-33

a. Includes advance payments of US $422 million.
b. Includes advance payments of US $867 million.
c. Includes advance payments of US $346 million at 1976 prices.
d. Includes advance payments of US $423 million at 1976 prices.
e. For 1985 and later millions of dollars at current prices.

SOURCE: ECLA-S, 1984, 1987, p. 302.

Table 3122

COLOMBIA CENTRAL GOVERNMENT REVENUE, EXPENDITURE, AND FINANCING THE DEFICIT, 1975–87

(B NC)

Category	1975	1978	1979	1980	1981	1982	1983	1984	1985	1986	1987[‡]
1. Current Income	38.4	84.1	114.6	151.8	156.6	189.8	238.7	302.7	441.1	646.4	918.8
Tax Revenue	37.4	82.0	112.6	148.8	152.8	184.8	231.6	291.2	424.5	607.3	824.2
Income and Complementary Taxes	18.0	30.4	37.3	47.1	53.0	65.2	97.8	118.2	157.9	218.1	307.0
Sales Taxes	7.7	17.5	23.0	30.5	40.3	49.6	58.7	.4	3.3	~	~
Customs Duties and Surcharges	5.4	13.4	16.6	24.8	29.4	36.6	37.8	79.1	124.0	~	~
Profits on Exchange Operations	3.6	10.9	23.8	30.1	~	~	~	48.3	84.0	~	~
Gasoline Taxes	1.7	5.8	8.0	11.3	18.1	20.1	24.7	3.6	5.6	~	~
Other	.8	4.0	4.3	4.9	4.8	6.7	.4	.4	~	~	~
Non-tax Revenue	.9	2.1	2.0	3.0	3.8	5.0	7.1	10.7	16.1	39.1	80.4
2. Current Expenditure	26.1	57.1	82.6	121.3	153.8	211.0	262.9	362.2	425.1	570.5	763.3
3. Current Savings	12.2	26.9	31.9	30.6	2.8	−21.2	−24.2	−60.1	16.0	90.3	155.5
4. Investment	13.1	21.0	26.0	42.0	61.1	80.2	81.8	102.4	150.3	180.3	212.4
5. Total Expenditure	39.3	78.2	108.6	163.3	214.9	291.2	344.7	464.6	575.4	750.8	975.7
6. Fiscal Deficit (or surplus)	−.9	5.9	6.0	−11.4	−58.3	−101.4	−106.0	−161.9	−134.3	−90.0	−56.9
7. Financing of Deficit											
External Credit	−.5	−2.2	5.2	16.5	19.5	14.9	9.4	25.8	48.5	101.8	−17.5
Domestic Credit	1.3	−3.7	−11.2	−5.9	38.8	80.5	125.9	114.4	114.3	−11.8	74.4

SOURCE: ECLA-S, 1978–81, 1984, 1985, 1986, 1987, p. 205.

Table 3123

COSTA RICA CENTRAL GOVERNMENT REVENUE, EXPENDITURE, AND FINANCING THE DEFICIT,[1] 1975–87

(M NC)

Category	1975	1977	1979	1980	1981	1982	1983	1984	1985[b]	1986[a,b]	1987[b,‡]
1. Current Income	2,261	3,487	4,239	4,982	7,454	12,948	21,057	27,281	29,700	38,000	44,500
Tax Revenue	2,090	3,281	4,126	4,692	6,933	12,281	19,870	24,426	26,800	33,700	41,400
Direct	447	781	1,066	1,080	1,555	3,014	4,860	4,895	5,200	5,900	7,500
Indirect	1,643	1,501	3,060	3,612	2,255	3,573	6,264	11,200	12,100	14,700	20,500
On Foreign Trade	678	999	~	~	3,123	5,694	6,746	8,300	9,500	13,100	13,414
Non-tax Revenue	171	206	103	290	521	667	1,187	−2,855	23,045	~	~
2. Current Expenditure	2,210	3,372	5,152	6,349	7,938	13,108	21,514	25,999	29,600	36,900	43,400
Wages and Salaries	1,384	2,006	~	~	3,483	5,131	7,524	9,100	10,700	13,700	15,600
Other Current Expenditures	326	1,366	~	~	4,455	7,977	13,990	16,900	18,900	23,200	27,700
3. Current Saving (1–2)	51	−115	−913	−1,367	−484	−160	−457	1,282	100	1,100	1,100
4. Capital Expenditure	732	1,282	1,477	1,930	1,973	3,186	6,142	8,932	8,100	9,400	6,700
Real Investment	370	696	~	~	1,201	1,444	2,843	4,252	3,200	2,800	2,500
Debt Amortization Payments	210	299	~	~	420	−807	1,164	2,839	2,500	2,000	1,800
Other Capital Expenditures	152	287	~	~	352	935	2,135	1,841	2,400	6,600	4,300
5. Total Expenditures (2+4)	2,942	4,654	6,629	8,279	9,911	16,294	27,656	34,931	37,600	46,300	50,100
6. Fiscal Deficit (1–5)	−681	−1,167	−2,390	−3,297	−2,457	−3,346	6,559	−7,650	−7,900	−8,300	−5,600
7. Financing of Deficit											
Domestic Financing	452	857	1,725	2,838	1,551	1,967	4,731	5,165	4,000	13,500	~
Central Bank	24	81	~	~	4,696	−1,533	−836	−400	−2,100	−1,000	~
Issue of Securities	161	548	~	~	1,532	1,935	4,032	4,100	3,200	8,600	~
Other	268	228	~	~	−4,677	1,565	1,535	1,400	2,900	6,000	~
External Financing	229	310	665	459	906	1,379	1,868	2,485	3,900	3,300	~

1. Includes extra budgetary operations.

a. Includes indirect tax revenue.
b. Rounded to the nearest hundred.

SOURCE: ECLA-S, 1978–80, 1984, 1985, 1986, 1987, p. 230.

Table 3124

DOMINICAN REPUBLIC CENTRAL GOVERNMENT REVENUE, EXPENDITURE,
AND FINANCING THE DEFICIT, 1975–87

(M NC)

Category	1975	1978	1979	1980	1981	1982	1983	1984	1985	1986	1987[‡]
1. Current Income	636	578	674	869	908	745	905	1,149	1,627	2,133	2,851
Tax Revenue	592	552	623	696	735	661	782	1,099	1,527	2,013	2,521
Direct	142	129	151	220	225	223	224	274	365	454	593
Indirect	95	144	166	189	238	253	296	414	586	834	738
On Foreign Trade	332	251	276	287	272	185	243	336	545	691	1,143
Others	22	28	30	~	~	~	19	25	31	34	48
Non-tax Revenue	45	26	51	173	173	84	123	100	100	120	329
Extraordinary Income	21	~	~	~	~	~	~	~	~	~	~
2. Total Expenditure	653	675	1,005	1,053	1,068	988	1,142	1,246	1,845	2,252	3,012
Current Expenditure	353	443	644	729	776	792	878	1,002	1,400	1,622	1,471
Capital Expenditure	300	232	356	324	292	196	264	244	445	630	1,541
Real Investment	249	155	97	128	121	98	117	78	131	234	888
Amortization of the Debt	8	17	25	~	~	~	~	~	~	~	~
Capital Transfers	43	53	166	193	160	83	118	116	240	348	530
Other Expenditures	~	7	68	3	11	15		50	74	48	123
3. Fiscal Deficit (–) or Surplus	–17	–97	–331	–184	–160	–243	–237	–97	–218	–95	–161

SOURCE: ECLA-S, 1978–80, 1984, 1985, 1986, 1987, p. 622.

Table 3125

ECUADOR CENTRAL GOVERNMENT REVENUE, EXPENDITURE,
AND FINANCING THE DEFICIT, 1975–87

(M NC)

Category	1975	1978	1979	1980	1981	1982	1983	1984	1985	1986[‡]	1987[a,‡]
1. Total Income[1]	12,364	13,057	23,080	37,631	39,297	45,996	68,676	99,873	191,068	197,287	230.8
Current Income	12,364	19,660	23,722	38,512	40,510	47,787	60,852	99,925	190,596	191,984	235.4
Traditional	~	17,501	19,372	23,915	25,379	25,741	31,864	51,052	71,842	~	~
Tax Revenue	10,826	16,748	18,445	22,445	23,744	23,454	30,521	48,111	70,830	117,377	150.7
Direct	3,333	2,954	3,419	4,179	6,137	6,007	7,154	9,428	13,978	20,593	26.7
Indirect	2,376	5,541	6,527	8,616	8,098	9,037	12,740	21,262	30,839	54,674	73.4
On Foreign Trade	5,184	8,253	8,499	9,650	9,509	8,410	10,633	17,421	26,013	36,109	42.3
Other Income	1,815	753	927	1,470	1,635	2,287	1,381	2,942	4,095	5,913	8.3
From Petroleum	2,490	2,159	4,350	14,229	15,131	21,627	28,950	46,804	113,975	73,612	80 6
2. Total Expenditure	11,755	26,155	28,189	47,557	59,395	64,579	80,462	116,964	179,326	216,500	278.6
3. Deficit (1-2)	609	–7,098	–5,109	9,926	–20,098	18,583	–11,786	–17,091	11,742	–29,600	–47.8
4. Financing	~	6,394	3,890	5,733	16,838	18,583	13,832	6,785	–10,777	~	~
Indebtedness	–237	6,541	4,260	5,956	8,301	17,587	14,189	9,472	10,078	~	~
Foreign	–235	1,179	~	1,553	7,658	9,988	–2,250	–4,058	–4,446	~	~
Domestic	2	5,362	4,260	4,403	643	7,599	16,439	13,530	–5,632	~	~
Cash Balances[2]	–1,176	–147	–370	–284	–1,220	280	–358	–2,687	–699	~	~
Difference (3-4)[3]	~	704	1,219	4,193	3,260	~	~	~	~	~	~

1. Net total income taxes paid with savings certificates and agrarian reform bonds have
been deducted.
2. Use or net accumulation of funds during the financial year, according to whether the
balance is positive or negative.
3. Balance of payments deferred until the next year (positive sign) and of payments made
to cover expenditure of the previous year (negative sign).

a. B NC.

SOURCE: ECLA-S, 1978–80, 1984, 1985, 1986, 1987, p. 329.

Table 3126

EL SALVADOR CENTRAL GOVERNMENT REVENUE, EXPENDITURE, AND FINANCING THE DEFICIT, 1975–87

(M NC)

Category	1975	1978	1979	1980	1981	1982	1983	1984	1985	1986	1987[‡]
1. Current Income	578	1,027	1,215	1,040	1,107	1,110	1,262	1,545	1,913	2,887	2,728
Tax Revenue (a + b)	541	972	1,162	989	990	952	1,080	1,351	1,660	2,581	2,476
a. Direct	154	286	277	312	297	294	306	341	385	525	669
b. Indirect	~	686	885	677	693	658	774	1,010	1,275	2,056	1,807
c. On Foreign Trade	205	401	571	375	322	279	279	373	533	1,168	692
d. Non-tax Revenue	37	55	53	51	117	158	182	194	253	306	252
2. Current Expenditure	445	783	862	1,077	1,233	1,347	1,507	1,770	1,909	2,568	2,801
Wages and Salaries	229	411	475	618	657	~	789	1,005	1,182	1,457	1,748
Other Current Expenditure[2]	217	372	387	459	576	~	718	765	727	1,111	1,053
3. Current Savings (1-2)	133	244	353	–37	–126	–237	–245	–224	4	319	–73
4. Capital Expenditure	154	375	444	584	507	472	1,254	719	700	1,214	1,188
Real Investment	62	219	274	438	381	298	395	346	370	485	525
Debt Amortization Payments	20	33	29	21	60	77	607	267	152	342	338
Other Capital Expenditure	73	123	141	125	66	97	252	106	178	387	325
5. Total Expenditure (2+4)	600	1,158	1,306	1,514	1,740	1,820	2,761	2,723	2,609	3,782	3,989
6. Fiscal Deficit (–) or Surplus (1–5)	–22	–131	–91	–484	–633	–710	–1,499	–943	–696	–895	–1,261
7. Financing of Deficit											
Domestic Financing[1]	–62	72	33	393	375	448	97	296	224	125	354
Central Bank	~	8	–8	143	176	~	–147	147	215	–302	85
Issue of Securities	~	22	100	300	299	333	~	41	45	115	56
Other	~	42	–59	–50	–100	115	194	136	–36	312	213
External Financing	83	59	58	91	258	262	1,452	853	472	770	907

1. Includes financing provided by the Central Reserve Bank of El Salvador, sale of securities, changes in treasury position, use of balances remaining from previous financial years, etc. (1975–76).
2. Includes goods and services, interest, transfers, and others.

SOURCE: ECLA-S, 1978–80, 1984, 1985, 1986, and 1987, p. 351.

Table 3127

GUATEMALA CENTRAL GOVERNMENT REVENUE, EXPENDITURE, AND FINANCING THE DEFICIT, 1975–87

(M NC)

Category	1975	1978	1979	1980	1981	1982	1983	1984	1985	1986	1987[‡]
1. Current Income	330	661	668	747	741	730	741	666	867	1,406	1,631
Tax Revenue (a + b)	301	621	621	678	652	626	573	498	679	1,111	1,414
a. Direct	63	102	97	100	110	108	134	86	126	186	272
b. Indirect	135	519	524	578	542	518	439	412	553	925	1,142
c. On Foreign Trade	91	264	241	259	171	125	106	107	88	349	421
2. Current Expenditure	269	476	540	678	759	710	721	767	838	1,407	1,640
Wages and Salaries	~	~	~	~	~	~	367	385	429	583	~
Other Current Expenditure	~	~	~	~	~	~	354[a]	381[a]	410[a]	824[a]	~
3. Saving on Current Account (1-2)	61	185	128	69	–18	20	20	–101	29	–1	–9
4. Capital Expenditure	126	323	382	578	724	548	376	365	350	299	301
Real Investment[2]	85	216	310	438	621	432	316	263	231	299	301
Debt Amortization Payments	31	64	72	140	103	116	60	102	119	~	~
Other Capital Expenditure	~	43	~	~	~	~	~	~	~	~	~
5. Total Expenditure (2+4)	395	799	922	1,256	1,483	1,258	1,097	1,132	1,188	1,706	1,941
6. Fiscal Deficit (1–5)	–43	–138	–254	–509	–742	–528	–356	–466	–321	–300	–310
7. Financing of Deficit											
Domestic Financing[1]	52	37	122	391	634	416	256	413	222	209	235
External Financing	19	101	132	118	108	112	100	53	99	91	75

1. Includes the floating debt (1975, 1976).
2. Includes other capital expenditure prior to 1986.

a. Includes goods and services, interest, transfers, and others.

SOURCE: ECLA-S, 1978–80, 1984, 1985, 1986, and 1987, p. 375.

Table 3128

HAITI CENTRAL GOVERNMENT REVENUE, EXPENDITURE, AND FINANCING THE DEFICIT,[1] 1975–87

(M NC)

Category	1975	1978	1979	1980	1981	1982	1983	1984	1985	1986	1987[‡]
1. Current Income	225	541	606	691	661	763	953	1,076	1,279	1,340	1,288
Tax Revenue	185	428	494	629	645	710	846	914	1,124	1,275	1,234
Direct and Indirect	73	210	250	268	366	457	482	584	798	810	786
On Foreign Trade	112	218	244	361	279	253	349	313	306	311	226
2. Current Expenditure	204	325	407	540	797	817	1,649	1,776	1,804	1,780	1,783
Wages and Salaries	123	180	208	293	355	402	391	448	494	522	656
Other Current Expenditure	~	145	199	247	319	337	172	249	281	1,258[a]	1,128[a]
3. Saving on Current Account (1-2)	21	216	199	151	-136	-54	-696	-700	-525	-440	-496
4. Capital Expenditure	291	586	641	662	528	486	222	214	209	182	221
Real Investment	~	569	626	642	365	173	105	~	~	~	~
Debt Amortization Payments	~	17	15	20	163	313	406	~	~	~	~
5. Total Expenditure (2+4)	495	911	1,048	1,202	1,325	1,303	1,871	1,990	2,013	1,962	2,004
6. Fiscal Deficit (1-5)	-270	-370	-442	-511	-664	-540	-918	-914	-734	-622	-716
7. Financing of Deficit											
External Financing	153	~	330	340	434	124	151	159	34	91	111
Grants[2]	95	~	209	183	325	346	347	~	~	386	561
Loans	58	~	121	157	106	172	151	~	~	~	~
Domestic Financing	117	~	112	171	290	70	126	413	184	145	44

1. For 1975 and 1976, fiscal years October to September.
2. Excludes food imports from the U.S. on concessional terms under that country's law on agricutural surpluses (P. L. 480, Title I), and donations by non-governmental organizations.

a. Includes non-budgetary expenditure.

SOURCE: ECLA-S, 1978–81, 1984, 1985, 1986, 1987, p. 396.

Table 3129

HONDURAS CENTRAL GOVERNMENT REVENUE, EXPENDITURE, AND FINANCING THE DEFICIT, 1975–87

(M NC)

Category	1975	1978	1979	1980	1981	1982	1983	1984	1985	1986	1987[‡]
1. Current Income	283	541	632	758	741	770	778	950	1064	1,152	1,289
Tax Revenue	252	503	574	697	695	715	723	888	997	1,087	1,226
Direct	78	128	153	236	186	206	197	242	249	258	308
Indirect	174	375	421	461	509	509	526	646	748	829	917
2. Current Expenditure	254	471	527	727	791	865	977	1,057	1,205	1,326	1,482
Wages and Salaries	160	258	299	353	468	~	515	551	621	702	720
Other Current Expenditure[1]	94	213	278	374	323	~	462	506	584	624	762
3. Current Saving (1-2)	29	70	105	31	-50	-95	-199	-107	-141	-174	-193
4. Capital Expenditure	184	371	385	516	473	729	606	878	879	814	792
Real Investment	76	172	152	193	133	178	155	158	163	155	171
Debt Amortization Payments	37	70	88	93	114	144	202	312	384	451	450
Other Capital Expenditure	71	129	145	231	226	407	249	408	332	208	171
5. Total Expenditure (2+4)	438	842	912	1,243	1,265	1,594	1,583	1,935	2,089	2,140	2,274
6. Fiscal Deficit (1-5)	-155	-301	-280	-485	-525	-824	-805	-985	-1,020	-988	-985
7. Financing											
Domestic	60	117	123	219	248	422	444	427	511	603	663
External	95	184	157	266	276	402	361	558	509	440	322

1. From years 1983 to 1987, other current expenditures include goods and services, interest, and transfers.

SOURCE: ECLA-S, 1978–80, 1984, 1985, 1986, 1987, p. 423.

Table 3130

MEXICO CENTRAL GOVERNMENT REVENUE, EXPENDITURE,
AND FINANCING THE DEFICIT, 1975–87

(B NC)

Category	1975	1978	1979	1980	1981	1982	1983	1984	1985	1986	1987[‡]
1. Current Income	102	302	412	680	935	1,532	3,181	4,975	7,990	12,551	32,577
Tax Revenue (a + b + c)	95	289	395	651	647	967	1,828	3,036	4,837	8,859	20,503
a. Direct	49	134	173	247	339	464	727	1,204	1,923	3,335	7,556
b. Indirect	37	120	158	220	241	418	1,015	1,695	2,608	4,852	11,468
c. On Foreign Trade	9	35	64	184	67	85	86	137	306	672	1,479
Non-tax Revenue	7	13	17	29	54	107	183	231	413	756	1,911
2. Current Expenditure	92	286	382	579	937	2,182	3,916	6,226	9,840	20,076	53,655
Wages and Salaries	34	93	120	159	225	~	580	999	1,549	2,495	5,939
Other Current Expenditure	58	193	262	420	712	~	744	1,335	1,932	17,586[a]	13,775[a]
3. Saving on Current Account (1–2)	10	16	30	101	−2	−650	−735	−1,251	−1,850	−7,525	−21,078
4. Capital Expenditure[1]	63	190	351	482	381	476	680	951	1,792	2,705	6,299
Real Investment	37	57	86	169	90	145	139	263	451	797	1,841
Debt Amortization Payments[1]	10	108	232	258	244	253	441	540	1,077	1,790	4,201
Other Capital Expenditure	16	133	265	313	47	77	100	148	265	118	257
5. Total Expenditure[1] (2+4)	156	476	733	1,061	1,318	2,658	4,597	7,177	11,632	22,781	59,954
6. Fiscal Deficit[1] (1–5)	−54	−174	−321	−381	−383	−1,126	−1,415	−2,202	−3,642	−10,230	−27,377
7. Financing of Fiscal Deficit											
Domestic Financing[1]	37	148	296	332	376	~	~	~	~	~	~
External Financing	17	26	25	49	24	~	~	~	~	~	~

1. Excluding treasury certificates issued and redeemed in the same year, since their
   introduction in 1978.

a. Includes interest, transfers and other current expenditure.

SOURCE: ECLA-S, 1978–81, 1984, 1985, 1986, and 1987, p. 457.

Table 3131

NICARAGUA CENTRAL GOVERNMENT REVENUE, EXPENDITURE,
AND FINANCING THE DEFICIT, 1975–87

Category	M NC					B NC					
	1975	1978	1979	1980	1981	1982	1983	1984	1985	1986	1987[‡]
1. Current Income	1,323	1,621	1,892	4,526	5,382	7.2	10.2	15.8	37.3	141.0	716.4
Tax Revenue	1,151	1,449	1,487	3,991	4,576	5.8	8.5	13.8	32.0	120.0	636.2
Direct	265	363	309	934	1,199	1.3	1.8	3.2	7.5	31.2	150.7
Indirect	535	702	763	1,840	3,377	4.5	6.7	10.6	24.5	89.4	485.5
From Taxes on External Trade	352	384	415	1,217	806	~	~	~	~	~	~
Non-tax Revenue	172	~	~	~	~	1.5	1.7	1.9	5.2	21.0	80.1
2. Current Expenditure	1,121	1,875	2,587	5,008	6,986	9.1	12.7	19.2	52.0	187.6	971.8
Wages and Salaries	444	702	903	1,562	1,904	~	2.8	4.0	11.0	37.5	167.5
Other Current Expenditure	677	1,173	1,684	3,446	4,082	~	~	~	~	150.1[a]	804.3[a]
3. Saving on Current Account (1–2)	202	−254	−695	−482	−1,604	−1.8	−2.5	−3.5	−14.	−46.5	−255.4
4. Capital Expenditure	985	1,412	395	1,356	1,426	2.0	7.4	7.7	12.2	30.2	111.4
Real Investment	291	921	314	972	882	1.1	2.2	3.6	8.6	18.1	82.8
Amortization of Debt	144	384	81	170	274	.3	.4	.5	1.0	1.8	3.4
Other Capital Expenditure	550	107	~	214	270	.6	4.8	3.6	2.5	10.3	25.2
5. Total Expenditure (2+4)	2,106	3,287	2,982	6,364	8,412	11.1	20.0	26.9	64.2	217.8	1,083.2
6. Fiscal Deficit (−) or Surplus (1–5)	−783	−1,666	−1,090	−1,838	−3,030	−3.9	−9.9	−11.1	−26.9	−76.7	−366.9
7. Financing of Deficit											
Domestic	49	920	996	450	2,096	1.5	8.2	9.2	25.5	69.0	346.2
External	734	746	94	1,388	934	2.3	1.7	1.9	1.4	7.7	20.7

a. Includes goods and services, transfers, and interest.

SOURCE: ECLA-S, 1978–80, 1984, 1985, 1986, 1987, p. 489.

Table 3132

PANAMA CENTRAL GOVERNMENT REVENUE, EXPENDITURE, AND FINANCING THE DEFICIT, 1975–87

(M NC)

Category	1975	1979	1980	1981	1982	1983	1984	1985	1986	1987[‡]
1. Current Income	297	490	695	790	848	906	916	1,006	1,041	1,094
Tax Revenue	227	406	507	582	615	662	635	689	753	790
Direct	114	193	255	315	332	367	321	363	385	402
Indirect	113	213	252	267	238	295	313	326	368	388
On Foreign Trade	58	80	91	99	106	115	121	130	154	148
Non-tax Revenue	~	~	~	208	233	245	281	318	288	304
2. Current Expenditure	283	612	766	771	930	929	955	985	1,182	1,196
Wages and Salaries	170	264	297	298	319	356	351	424	432	437
Other Current Expenditure[1]	113	348	469	473	611	573	604	562	639	745
3. Current Saving (1-2)	14	-122	-71	-19	-82	-23	-39	21	-141	-102
4. Capital Expenditure	134	321	299	446	695	441	538	381	582	706
Fixed Investment, Financial Investment, and Transfers	111	53	52	66	112	102	~	~	105	72
Other Capital Expenditure	~	210	162	271	384	138	~	~	~	~
Amortization of the Debt[2]	23	58	85	111	199	201	256	187	477	634
5. Total Expenditure (2+4)	420	933	1,065	109	199	1,370	1,493	1,366	1,764	1,902
6. Fiscal Deficit (1-5)	-123	-443	-370	1,217	1,625	464	-577	-359	-723	-808
7. Financing of Deficit	~	138	179	-427	-777	-464	158	191	203	218
Domestic	8	52	71	82	42	107	121	89	111	153
External	115	305	191	248	300	133	166	95	92	65

1. Includes operation and administration costs, interest, and debt costs.
2. Usually financed through renewable loans except 1987.

SOURCE: ECLA-S, 1978–81, 1984, 1985, 1986, 1987, p. 529.

Table 3133

PARAGUAY CENTRAL GOVERNMENT REVENUE, EXPENDITURE, AND FINANCING THE DEFICIT, 1975–87

(M NC)

Category	1975	1978	1979	1980	1981	1982	1983	1984	1985	1986	1987[‡]
1. Current Income	17,394	34,333	43,629	51,592	59,107	68,200	65,600	85,200	110,200	143,300	202,400
Tax Revenue	15,877	30,334	38,810	46,137	52,351	60,900	53,100	71,800	94,400	121,300	174,600
Direct Taxes	~	~	8,449	11,323	14,235	20,500	18,800	21,000	22,600	29,000	44,600
On Personal Income	~	~	~	~	~	~	~	~	~	~	~
On Corporative Earnings	~	~	6,846	9,395	11,735	13,200	10,700	11,000	15,800	20,000	34,800
On Real Estate	~	~	1,603	1,928	2,500	7,300	8,100	10,000	13,800	~	~
Indirect Taxes	~	~	30,367	34,814	38,116	31,700	34,300	50,800	71,800	92,100	89,200
On External Trade	~	~	15,786	17,213	17,325	12,500	9,800	12,300	14,000	22,000	32,600
Imports	~	~	14,645	15,945	16,623	8,900	7,400	8,900	11,000	21,600	30,800
Exports	~	~	1,141	1,268	1,202	400	300	700	~	900	1,800
On Domestic Trade	~	~	6,945	8,280	8,691	18,300	15,100	25,900	34,600	69,600	56,600
Others	~	~	7,636	9,321	11,600	8,800	8,600	11,800	16,200	29,000	40,800
Non-tax Income	2,017	3,999	4,819	5,455	6,756	7,300	12,500	13,500	15,900	22,000	27,800
2. Current Expenditure	14,412	21,616	27,193	38,064	52,998	65,100	74,400	78,300	97,600	119,800	164,700
Consumption	~	16,306	20,105	28,278	40,191	38,700	43,500	44,800	60,300	65,900	95,200
Wages and Salaries	6,126	~	12,205	15,938	22,474	28,300	32,900	33,500	40,800	47,100	63,800
Goods and Non-Personal Services	~	~	5,344	7,324	9,803	10,400	10,600	11,300	14,400	18,800	31,400
Others	8,286	~	2,556	5,016	7,914	4,200	5,600	6,200	7,700	14,000	~
Interest Payments	~	~	1,345	1,766	2,147	2,500	2,700	4,900	6,700	9,700	19,900
Transfers	~	5,310	5,743	7,792	10,653	19,700	22,600	22,400	25,900	28,700	35,800
Subsidies	~	~	63	83	92	~	~	~	~	~	~
Transfers to the Private Sector	~	~	3,289	4,725	3,941	15,400	17,400	17,800	20,800	21,300	26,200
Transfers to the Public Sector	~	~	2,151	2,915	3,941	4,300	5,100	4,600	4,900	7,500	9,600
Other	~	~	241	298	357	420	560	6,200	7,700	14,000	13,800
3. Saving	3,482	12,717	16,436	13,527	6,117	3,100	–8,800	6,900	12,700	22,300	37,700
4. Capital Expenditure	4,198	9,160	13,434	14,912	25,974	21,900	28,000	17,700	34,700	14,000	22,100
Capital Formation	~	~	11,379	10,694	14,743	14,500	17,800	10,200	29,700	10,800	21,000
Financial Investment	3,471	7,887	257	2,533	9,075	~	~	~	~	~	~
Transfers to the Public	~	~	1,799	1,672	2,153	6,900	10,100	7,500	1,300	100	300
Other Capital Expenditure	727	~	~	~	~	500	1,100	~	~	3,100	800
5. Total Expenditure	18,609	30,776	40,628	52,976	78,964	87,000	80,700	96,100	132,200	132,200	186,800
6. Global Balance	–714	3,557	3,024	–1,385	–19,857	–12,500	–35,800	–10,500	–21,400	–10,700	–16,500
7. Financing	~	~	–3,024	–1,385	19,857	12,500	35,800	10,500	21,400	–10,700	–16,500
Domestic (net)	–649	–263	–4,980	1,153	17,646	5,800	19,000	–8,600	10,700	–13,200	–7,500
Indebtedness	~	~	1,052	–1,813	2,644	~	~	~	~	~	~
Direct Loans	~	~	1,350	–1,011	2,801	~	~	~	~	~	~
Central Bank	91	270	585	236	379	3,200	17,100	7,300	7,700	6,500	9,700
Suppliers	~	~	435	230	3,417	~	~	~	~	~	~
Other	–774	–125	330	–1,477	–995	~	–2,300	9,800	17,300	–1,200	15,800
Bonds	–217	–407	–298	–802	–157	~	~	~	~	~	~
Sale	~	~	~	~	~	~	~	~	~	~	~
Amortization	~	~	–298	–802	–157	~	2,900 ·	–4,300	–5,400	–10,600	~
Cash Variation	~	~	6,032	660	15,002	~	~	~	~	~	~
(minus sign indicates increase)											
External (net)	1,363	1,968	1,956	2,538	2,211	6,600	16,800	19,000	10,700	2,500	2,800
Loans	~	~	1,923	2,515	2,167	~	~	~	~	~	~
Disbursements	~	~	4,226	4,066	4,639	9,200	19,700	23,300	16,100	12,500	21,900
Amortization	~	~	–2,303	–1,551	–2,472	–2,600	–2,900	–4,300	–5,400	–8,400	–19,100
Variations in Reserves	~	5,262	~	~	~	~	4,000	–22,800	–14,300	–29,800	–33,000
Donations	~	~	33	23	45	~	~	~	~	~	~

a. Amounts actually registered (preliminary figures).

SOURCE: ECLA-S, 1978–80, 1984, 1985, 1986, 1987, p. 558.

Table 3134

PERU CENTRAL GOVERNMENT REVENUE, EXPENDITURE, AND FINANCING THE DEFICIT, 1982–87

(M NC)

Category	1982	1983	1984	1985	1986	1987[‡]
1. Current Income	2,485	3,732	9,554	27,963	45,191	66,424
Tax Revenue	2,249	3,361	7,957	24,762	40,800	61,948
Income Tax	480	649	1,422	3,459	9,853	13,126
Property Tax	96	135	281	666	2,064	2,759
Tax on External Trade	942	1,257	1,860	6,168	9,410	14,308
Production and Consumer Taxes	822	1,488	4,518	15,479	21,236	34,670
Other Tax Revenue	83	118	536	1,106	1,185	1,925
Less Credit Documents[1]	−174	−286	−660	−2,116	−2,948	−4,840
Non-tax Revenue[2]	192	330	1,597	3,201	4,391	4,476
Other Resources and Transfers	44	41	~	~	~	~
2. Capital Income	8	~	92	272	140	~
3. Total Expenditure	3,051	6,083	12,563	32,307	58,033	108,302
Current Expenditure	2,456	5,065	10,203	27,255	46,927	91,238
Remunerations	545	1,009	2,928	7,412	14,750	29,955
Goods and Services	69	153	579	1,741	3,409	4,987
Transfers	230	563	1,683	3,460	9,353	21,463
Interest	557	1,411	2,957	8,140	8,723	13,131
Domestic Debt	259	492	724	2,255	2,018	6,473
External Debt	298	919	2,233	5,885	6,705	6,658
Defense and Interior	1,055	1,929	2,056	6,502	10,692	21,702
Capital Expenditure	595	1,018	2,360	5,052	11,106	17,064
Gross Capital Formation	440	599	2,075	4,579	8,487	10,351
Transfers	144	407	279	443	2,525	4,963
Others	11	12	6	30	94	1,750
Deficit (1–3)	−558	−2,351	−2,917	−4,072	−12,702	−41,878
4. Current Savings	~	~	−649	708	−2,564	−24,814

1. Mainly tax reimbursements for non-traditional exports, tax capitalization, and tax payment promissory notes.
2. Mainly property income, fines, and deductions from pensions.

SOURCE: ECLA-S, 1984, 1985, 1986, 1987, p. 597.

Table 3135

URUGUAY CENTRAL GOVERNMENT REVENUE, EXPENDITURE, AND FINANCING THE DEFICIT, 1975–87

(M NC)

Category	1975	1978	1979	1980	1981	1982	1983	1984	1985[‡]	1986[†]	1987[‡]
1. Current Income	989	4,350	8,424	14,955	21,260	19,552	29,486	39,797	76,787	149,900	271,000
Internal Taxes	929	3,256	5,704	10,695	14,804	13,487	18,214	28,187	58,402	110,200	210,000
On Production, Consumption and Transactions	~	3,067	5,221	9,287	13,514	12,758	16,753	27,259	54,179	98,700	~
Value Added	~	1,526	2,751	5,676	8,515	7,970	9,718	15,942	30.218	55,700	~
Fuels	~	582	973	1,661	2,117	1,997	3,609	5,908	12,125	19,600	~
Tobacco	~	297	459	912	1,251	1,535	2,046	2,672	4,897	7,800	~
Other	~	662	1,038	1,038	1,631	1,256	1,380	2,737	6,937	15,600	~
On Income	~	569	1,038	2,363	2,427	2,028	3,147	2,942	4,764	8,800	~
On Wealth	~	211	282	725	1,094	1,293	2,074	1,935	4,369	8,600	~
Other	57	59	81	116	116	134	113	169	538	4,100	~
Less: Documents Received	~	−527	−717	−1,475	−2,235	2,414	−2,964	−4,021	−5,448	−10,000	~
Adjustments[1]	~	−122	−198	−320	−111	−311	−909	−97	~	~	~
Taxes on Foreign Trade	~	550	1,597	2,753	3,199	2,669	4,582	5,917	10,227	24,300	40,000
Other Income	~	544	1,123	1,507	3,257	3,396	6,690	5,693	8,158	15,400	21,000
2. Current Expenditure	1,204	4,042	7,260	1,381	18,817	27,503	33,159	50,560	83,612	146,800	262,000
Wages and Salaries[3]	871[a]	1,948	3,282	5,980	8,800	~	~	31,420	53,837	93,200	~
Purchase of Goods and Services	~	765	1,397	2,466	3,766	3,526	4,112	6,944	11,185	25,400	~
Other Current Expenditure[2]	333	664	1,104	846	978	1,594	2,289	6,911	7,787	11,300	~
3. Saving on Current Account (1–2)	−218	308	1,163	1,874	2,443	−7,951	−3,673	−10,300	−6,825	3,100	9,000
4. Investments	145	708	1,040	1,799	2,559	3,258	3,738	4,913	7,813	14,400	31,000
5. Total Expenditure (2+4)	1,349	4,750	8,301	14,880	21,377	30,761	36,897	55,473	91,425	161,200	293,000
6. Fiscal Deficit or Surplus (1–5)	−363	−401	124	75	−117	−11,210	7,411	−15,676	−14,638	−11,300	−22,000
7. Financing											
Net Credit Central Bank	95	159	206	−168	396	8,915	5,765	7,470	1,405	−11,300	−13,000
Issue of Securities (Net)	263	151	−287	−220	54	1,680	1,557	9,413	16,053	20,600	~
Other		−90	123	−9	374	−238	815	532	−271	4,100	~

1. Discrepancy between treasury information and tax office information.
2. Including transfer payments, interest payments on the public debt and affected income (1978–80).
3. Includes contributions and assistance to social security.

a. Wages and salaries and contributions and assistance to Social Security combined.

SOURCE: ECLA-S, 1978–80, 1984, 1985, 1986, 1987, p. 658.

Table 3136

VENEZUELA CENTRAL GOVERNMENT REVENUE, EXPENDITURE, AND FINANCING THE DEFICIT, 1982–87[a]

(B NC)

Category	1982	1983	1984	1985	1986	1987[‡]
1. Current Income	78.2	71.8	99.2	107.9	101.5	150.6
Petroleum Revenue	47.0	40.5	60.6	62.1	42.9	66.4
Income Tax[1]	39.1	34.1	51.5	53.3	32.5	47.7
Income Tax on Petroleum Products	1.1	1.5	1.5	~	~	~
Royalties	6.7	6.5	9.1	8.8	10.4	18.7
Other Tax Revenue	21.5	26.0	32.2	34.3	46.6	69.4
Direct	13.0	8.7	10.3	12.8	15.1	23.3
Customs	5.2	2.5	2.8	4.0	5.0	9.8
Indirect Domestic	3.1	17.3	21.9	21.6	31.4	46.2
Exchange Profits	~	10.1	14.3	11.1	16.7	24.7
2. Current Expenditure	54.4	55.7	69.9	74.7	72.2	113.7
Remunerations	19.2	19.3	20.3	22.3	24.2	36.6
Financial Subsidies	3.1	1.2	1.6	1.1	.8	
Interest Payments	8.4	6.3	10.3	10.8	12.7	24.6
On External Debt	7.0	3.9	7.1	7.3	7.1	16.9
On Domestic Debt	1.4	2.4	3.2	3.5	5.6	7.6
Other Current Expenditure	23.8	5.8	6.5	5.0	5.0	7.1
3. Current Savings (1–2)	23.8	16.1	29.3	33.1	29.2	36.9
4. Capital Expenditure	27.4	22.5	19.7	24.8	31.1	37.7
Real Investment	6.1	6.7	4.2	3.9	9.5	13.4
Other Capital Expenditure	21.3	15.8	15.4	20.8	21.6	24.3
5. Total Expenditure (2+4)	81.9	78.2	89.6	99.5	103.3	151.4
6. Fiscal Deficit (1–5)	-3.6	-6.4	9.6	8.3	-1.9	-.8
7. Financing of the Deficit	3.6	6.4	-9.6	-8.3	1.9	.8
Use of Domestic Surplus	5.5	6.7	-5.6	-4.0	9.5	7.6
Central Bank	~	7.0	~	~	~	17.6[b]
Sale of Securities	.4	1.3	3.6	4.1	14.3	15.1
Amortization	-.9	-2.3	-10.3	-13.8	-7.5	-11.0
Other Forms of Financing[2]	6.0	-1.8	-3.2	3.1	4.5	-4.2
External Financing	-1.9	-.4	-4.0	-4.4	-7.6	-6.8
Disbursements	3.4	6.8	2.2	.7	~	.4
Amortization	-5.3	7.2	-6.2	-5.1	-7.6	-7.2

1. Includes technology tax.
2. Includes agriculture debt, administrative debt, and variation of the amortization fund.

a. For 1975–81, see SALA, 24-3036.
b. Includes 10 million bolívares from sale of Folocam.

SOURCE: ECLA-S, 1986, 1987, p. 690.

Table 3137

UNITED STATES CENTRAL GOVERNMENT REVENUE, EXPENDITURE, AND FINANCING THE DEFICIT, 1970–88

(B NC)

Category	1970	1975	1977	1978	1979	1980	1981	1982	1983	1984	1985	1986	1987	1988[‡]
Deficit (–) or Surplus	-11.38	-53.93	-52.23*	-58.74	-35.95	-76.18	-78.74	-125.69	-202.52	-178.26	-212.11	-212.60	-150.00	-149.5
Revenue	190.49	292.70	371.52*	416.73	488.76	546.08	63.86	659.92	653.44	718.53	791.68	823.20	912.10	966.3
Expenditure and Lending	201.87	346.63	423.75*	475.67	524.71	622.26	718.60	785.61	855.96	896.79	1,003.79	1,035.80	1,062.20	1,115.9
Expenditure	201.00	333.12	414.28*	457.73	506.26	596.64	687.61	764.89	842.60	881.92	977.29	1,032.50	1,066.10	1,109.5
Lending Minus														
Repayments	.87	13.51	9.47*	17.94	18.45	25.62	30.99	20.72	13.36	14.87	26.50	3.30	2.10	6.4
Financing														
Net Borrowing	11.86	53.09	55.83*	61.99	39.82	76.61	84.80	138.76	215.59	174.08	200.54	233.10	148.6	~
Use of Cash Balances	-1.52	.84	-3.60*	-3.05	-3.87	-.43	-6.06	-13.07	-13.07	4.18	11.57	-20.40	-1.0	~

SOURCE: IMF-IFS-Y, 1986, lines 80–87; IMF-IFS-S, June 1987, lines 80–87; November 1988, p. 545, IMF-IFS, August 1989.

Table 3138

ARGENTINA MONEY SUPPLY, 1976–88[a]
(M NC[1] YE)

Year	A, Money[2] (M_1)	B, Quasi-Money[3]	C, Total[4] (M_2)
1976	.11	.05	.16
1977	.23	.29	.52
1978	.59	.87	1.46
1979	1.40	2.95	4.35
1980	2.75	5.47	8.22
1981	4.67	12.82	17.49
1982	16.23	29.70	45.93
1983	74.96	155.20	230.20
1984	451.20	1,186.80	1,637.50
1985	3,029.70	5,400.90	8,430.60
1986	5,600.00	12,156.00	17,756.00
1987	12,580.00	35,840.00	48,420.00
1988	~	~	~

1. Australes.
2. Sum of currency outside banks and private sector deposits.
3. Time, savings, and foreign currency deposits by residents.
4. Calculated by adding columns A and B.

a. For previous years, see SALA, 24-3038.

SOURCE: IMF-IFS-Y, 1987, 1988, 1989.

Table 3139

BOLIVIA MONEY SUPPLY, 1952–88
(NC YE)

Year	A. Money[1] (M_1)	B. Quasi-Money[2]	C. Total[3] (M_2)
1952	9	1	10
1953	16	1	17
1954	27	1	28
1955	56	3	59
1956	197	6	203
1957	291	10	301
1958	301	9	310
1959	386	15	401
1960	419	16	435
1961	496	17	513
1962	556	29	585
1963	665	37	702
1964	803	50	853
1965	943	52	995
1966	1,153	100	1,253
1967	1,192	151	1,343
1968	1,287	226	1,513
1969	1,361	306	1,667
1970	1,532	381	1,913
1971	1,766	493	2,259
1972	2,210	634	2,844
1973	2,969	807	3,776
1974	4,257	1,192	5,449
1975	4,759	1,956	6,715
1976	6,497	3,405	9,902
1977	7,855	4,960	12,815
1978	8,831	5,650	14,481
1979	10,304	6,328	16,632
1980	14,694	8,430	23,124
1981	17,587	11,831	29,418
1982	57,827	39,375	97,202
1983	177,500	87,600	265,100
1984[a]	3,370	684	4,053
1985[a]	207*	88*	296
1986	363	448	811
1987	502	681	1,183
1988	661	1,020	1,681

1. Sum of currency outside of banks and private sector demand deposits, source line 34.
2. Time, savings, and foreign currency deposits by residents, source line 35.
3. Calculated by adding columns A and B.

a. Thousands of Bolivianos for 1984 and millions for 1985.

SOURCE: IMF-IFS-Y, 1982, 1987, 1988, 1989.

Table 3140

BRAZIL MONEY SUPPLY,[1] 1948–87
(M NC YE)

PART I. 1948–59

Year	A. Money[2] (M_1)	B. Quasi-Money[3]	C. Total[4] (M_2)
1948	49	16	65
1949	58	18	76
1950	78	19	97
1951	91	20	111
1952	104	21	125
1953	124	22	146
1954	151	25	176
1955	178	24	202
1956	217	25	242
1957	211	29	240
1958	353	33	386
1959	501	39	540

SOURCE: IMF-IFS-S, 1965–66.

PART II. 1960–87

Year	A. Money[1] (M_1)	B. Quasi-Money[2]	C. Total[3] (M_2)
1960	.7	.1	.8
1961	1.0	.1	1.1
1962	1.7	.1	1.8
1963	2.8	.1	2.9
1964	5.1	.2	5.3
1965	9.1	.3	9.4
1966	10.0	.9	10.9
1967	15.0	1.7	16.7
1968	21.3	2.7	24.0
1969	27.4	4.4	31.8
1970	34.7	6.0	40.7
1971	42.0*	3.3*	45.3
1972	59.0	6.1	65.1
1973	87.0	7.1	94.1
1974	116.8	8.1	124.9
1975	168.5	12.0	180.5
1976	231.1	19.1	250.2
1977	318.5	44.2	362.7
1978	434.0*	94.2	529.0*
1979	759.0	154.6	913.0
1980	1,288.0	184.4	1,472.0
1981	2,353.0	509.0	2,862.0
1982	3,963.0	1,335.0	5,297.0
1983	7,735.0	4,769.0	12,504.0
1984	23,090.0	21,905.0	44,995.0
1985	100,363.0	97,013.0	197,376.0
1986	~	~	~
1987	~	~	~

1. Differences between Parts I and II reflect a change in unit of account and not a discontinuity in the series.
2. Sum of currency outside of banks and private sector demand deposits.
3. Time, savings, and foreign currency deposits by residents.
4. Calculated by adding columns A and B.

SOURCE: IMF-IFS-Y, 1986, 1987, 1988, 1989.

Table 3141

CHILE MONEY SUPPLY, 1955–88
(M NC YE)

PART I. 1955–64 (M NC)

Year	A. Money[1] (M_1)	B. Quasi-Money[2]	C. Total[3] (M_2)
1955	93	16	109
1956	130	25	155
1957	165	38	203
1958	222	54	276
1959	294	162	456
1960	384	211	595
1961	432	266	698
1962	557	389	946
1963	747	459	1,206
1964	1,129	720	1,849

SOURCE: IMF-IFS-S, 1965–66.

PART II. 1965–88 (B NC)

Year	A. Money[1] (M_1)	B. Quasi-Money[2]	C. Total[3] (M_2)
1965	.002	.001	.003
1966	.003	.002	.005
1967	.003	.002	.005
1968	.005	.003	.008
1969	.006	.005	.011
1970	.010	.007	.017
1971	.021	.011	.032
1972	.1	.03	.13
1973	.22	.22	.44
1974	.84	1.19	2.03
1975	2.98	4.52	7.50
1976	8.80	11.17	19.97
1977	18.32	27.62	45.94
1978	30.58	57.092	87.67
1979	50.31	96.59	146.90
1980	78.87	152.15	231.02
1981	74.12	237.11	311.23
1982	81.12	311.33	392.40
1983	102.72	308.99	411.71
1984	116.2	441.0	557.20
1985	~	~	717.7
1986	~	~	~
1987	~	~	~
1988	~	~	~

1. Sum of currency outside banks and private sector demand deposits.
2. Time, savings, and foreign currency deposits by residents.
3. Calculated by adding columns A and B.

SOURCE: IMF-IFS-Y, 1985, 1987, 1988, 1989.

Table 3142

COLOMBIA MONEY SUPPLY, 1952–88

(B NC YE)

Year	A. Money[1] (M_1)	B. Quasi-Money[2]	C. Total[3] (M_2)
1952	1.32	.20	1.52
1953	1.55	.21	1.76
1954	1.84	.38	2.22
1955	1.91	.50	2.41
1956	2.38	.84	3.22
1957	2.70	.65	3.35
1958	3.26	.64	3.90
1959	3.63	.77	4.40
1960	3.99	.76	4.75
1961	4.96	.92	5.88
1962	5.93	1.55	7.48
1963	6.69	1.51	8.20
1964	8.25	1.45	9.70
1965	9.64	2.19	11.83
1966	11.24	1.81	13.05
1967	13.68	2.10	15.78
1968	15.86	2.22	18.08
1969	19.40	2.70	22.10
1970	22.40	3.38	25.78
1971	25.06	4.13	29.19
1972	31.85	5.86	37.71
1973	41.65	9.25	50.90
1974	49.07	14.64	63.71
1975	58.92	19.58	78.50
1976	79.38	25.76	105.14
1977	103.50	37.19	140.69
1978	132.93*	47.08*	180.01*
1979	165.89	55.10	220.99
1980	212.40	108.08	321.20
1981	256.37	178.36	434.73
1982	321.40	204.25	525.65
1983	396.74	262.49	659.23
1984	492.39	324.45	816.84
1985	545.26	436.84	982.10
1986	~	~	~
1987	1,019.57	795.72	1,815.29
1988	1,282.04	916.39	2,198.42

1. Sum of currency outside of banks and private sector demand deposits, source line 34.
2. Time, savings, and foreign currency deposits by residents, source line 35.
3. Calculated by adding columns A and B.

SOURCE: IMF-IFS-Y, 1982, 1987, 1988, 1989.

Table 3143

COSTA RICA MONEY SUPPLY, 1952–88

(M NC YE)

Year	A. Money[1] (M_1)	B. Quasi-Money[2]	C. Total[3] (M_2)
1952	265	38	303
1953	291	45	336
1954	325	49	374
1955	340	61	401
1956	342	71	413
1957	370	83	453
1958	399	103	502
1959	427*	120*	547
1960	433	128	561
1961	422	124	546
1962	480	137	617
1963	535	148	683
1964	568	166	734
1965	598	185	783
1966	622	186	808
1967	832	248	1,080
1968	849*	219	1,068
1969	959	236	1,195
1970	1,006	270	1,276
1971	1,317	494	1,811
1972	1,501	665	2,166
1973	1,874	767	2,641
1974	2,146	1,300	3,446
1975	2,771	2,133	4,904
1976	3,408	3,182	6,590
1977	4,504	4,160	8,664
1978	5,625	5,442	11,067
1979	6,226	8,642	14,868
1980	7,271	9,965	17,236
1981	10,832	21,439	32,271
1982	18,448	22,545	40,993
1983	25,619	30,524	56,143
1984	30,132	35,632	65,764
1985	32,439	43,563	76,002
1986	42,487	49,671	92,158
1987	42,611	64,535	107,146
1988	~	~	~

1. Sum of currency outside of banks and private sector demand deposits, source line 34.
2. Time, savings, and foreign currency deposits by residents, source line 35.
3. Calculated by adding columns A and B.

SOURCE: IMF-IFS-Y, 1982, 1987, 1988, 1989.

Table 3144

DOMINICAN REPUBLIC MONEY SUPPLY, 1952–88
(M NC YE)

Year	A. Money[1] (M_1)	B. Quasi- Money[2]	C. Total[3] (M_2)
1952	62.1	13.1	75.2
1953	60.2	12.2	72.4
1954	68.6	26.2	94.8
1955	76.5	32.7	109.2
1956	76.9	37.4	114.3
1957	87.4	43.1	130.5
1958	107.2	36.8	144.0
1959	91.9	36.7	128.6
1960	101.9	27.2	129.1
1961	104.4	22.0	126.4
1962	114.0	26.0	140.0
1963	130.2	27.3	157.5
1964	116.6	30.8	147.4
1965	135.0	60.8	195.8
1966	116.1	49.3	165.4
1967	120.2	53.2	173.4
1968	139.1	72.2	211.3
1969	149.3	93.7	243.0
1970	171.7	118.1	289.8
1971	188.1	144.9	333.0
1972	222.5	188.2	410.7
1973	260.1	244.8	504.9
1974	364.2	361.3	725.5
1975	379.7	467.5	847.2
1976	390.4	484.6	875.0
1977	460.0	545.4	1,005.4
1978	458.0	533.1	991.1
1979	598.4	556.3	1,154.7
1980	579.6	594.9	1,174.5
1981	660.5	677.0	1,337.5
1982	731.5	803.9	1,535.4
1983	781.4	895.1	1,676.5
1984	1,159.5	1,010.4	2,169.9
1985	1,355.2	1,235.3	2,590.5
1986	1,988.7	2,296.7	4,285.4
1987	2,609.4	2,324.4	4,933.8
1988	~	2,107.0	~

1. Sum of currency outside of banks and private sector demand deposits, source line 34.
2. Time, savings, and foreign currency deposits by residents, source line 35.
3. Calculated by adding columns A and B.

SOURCE: IMF-IFS-Y, 1982, 1987, 1988, 1989.

Table 3145

ECUADOR MONEY SUPPLY, 1952–88
(M NC YE)

Year	A. Money[1] (M_1)	B. Quasi- Money[2]	C. Total[3] (M_2)
1952	1,051	182	1,233
1953	1,088	230	1,318
1954	1,273	270	1,543
1955	1,193	352	1,545
1956	1,358	388	1,746
1957	1,412	469	1,881
1958	1,400	391	1,791
1959	1,577	440	2,017
1960	1,732	469	2,201
1961	1,778	598	2,376
1962	2,000	678	2,678
1963	2,241	609	2,850
1964	2,626	569	3,195
1965	2,670	616	3,286
1966	3,016	831	3,847
1967	3,439	1,021	4,460
1968	4,172	1,391	5,563
1969	4,751	1,547	6,298
1970	5,989	1,746	7,735
1971	6,719	2,175	8,894
1972	8,376	2,595	10,971
1973	11,299	3,132	14,431
1974	16,866	4,167	21,033
1975	18,343	4,741	23,084
1976	22,809	6,006	28,815
1977	29,876	6,087	35,963
1978	32,920	6,820	39,740
1979	41,952	10,227	52,179
1980	53,584	12,590	66,174
1981	61,807	13,896	75,703
1982	73,130	20,499	93,629
1983	95,145	22,868	118,013
1984	129,058	40,223	169,281
1985	158,118	63,787	221,905
1986	191,061	84,797	275,858
1987	265,737	137,710	403,447
1988	396,500	249,000	645,500

1. Sum of currency outside of banks and private sector demand deposits, source line 34.
2. Time, savings, and foreign currency deposits by residents, source line 35.
3. Calculated by adding columns A and B.

SOURCE: IMF-IFS-Y, 1982, 1987, 1988, 1989.

Table 3146

EL SALVADOR MONEY SUPPLY, 1952–88

(M NC YE)

Year	A. Money[1] (M_1)	B. Quasi-Money[2]	C. Total[3] (M_2)
1952	163.7	10.3	174.0
1953	171.8	10.9	182.7
1954	190.4	15.6	206.0
1955	187.4	19.8	207.2
1956	215.0	26.1	241.1
1957	215.2	37.2	252.4
1958	202.3	55.0	257.3
1959	205.7	75.6	281.3
1960	193.0	83.0	276.0
1961	184.2	100.3	284.5
1962	183.4	122.8	306.2
1963	220.9	154.0	374.9
1964	233.5	189.6	423.1
1965	234.2	204.3	438.5
1966	247.0	231.6	478.6
1967	252.7	236.2	488.9
1968	264.7	244.8	509.5
1969	288.1	273.8	561.9
1970	295.3	300.2	595.5
1971	315.4	342.8	658.2
1972	389.6	417.5	807.1
1973	466.0	491.6	957.6
1974	556.6	559.7	1,116.3
1975	648.1	704.6	1,352.7
1976	916.7	853.7	1,770.4
1977	988.3	1,015.3	2,003.6
1978	1,086.9	1,154.4	2,241.3
1979	1,320.9	1,124.8	2,445.7
1980	1,428.6	1,134.7	2,563.3
1981	1,437.2	1,397.0	2,834.2
1982	1,716.6*	1,599.5*	3,316.1*
1983	1,657.0	1,979.0	3,637.0
1984	1,961.0	2,405.0	4,366.0
1985	2,488.0	3,068.0	5,556.0
1986	3,047.0	4,147.0	7,194.0
1987	3,147.0	4,609.0	7,756.0
1988	3,425.0	5,223.0	8,648.0

1. Sum of currency outside of banks and private sector demand deposits, source line 34.
2. Time, savings, and foreign currency deposits by residents, source line 35.
3. Calculated by adding columns A and B.

SOURCE: IMF-IFS-Y, 1982, 1987, 1988, 1989.

Table 3147

GUATEMALA MONEY SUPPLY, 1952–88

(M NC YE)

Year	A. Money[1] (M_1)	B. Quasi-Money[2]	C. Total[3] (M_2)
1952	63.6	7.0	70.6
1953	76.1	7.2	83.3
1954	77.6	6.7	84.3
1955	86.7	8.6	95.3
1956	103.9	14.6	118.5
1957	116.3	19.0	135.3
1958	106.8	22.7	129.5
1959	108.8	26.4	135.2
1960	105.5	31.3	136.8
1961	106.7	36.4	143.1
1962	108.7	42.5	151.2
1963	121.4	48.4	169.8
1964	129.3	64.8	194.1
1965	135.6	73.8	209.4
1966	143.0	91.5	234.5
1967	148.3	114.5	262.8
1968	151.1	126.2	277.3
1969	160.9	148.3	309.2
1970	172.8	170.9	343.7
1971	178.9	204.4	383.3
1972	214.4	262.5	476.9
1973	264.3	315.5	579.8
1974	305.4	362.9	668.3
1975	353.6	454.9	808.5
1976	493.8	558.0	1,051.8
1977	594.1	655.0	1,249.1
1978	664.0	759.6	1,423.6
1979	734.9	802.3	1,537.2
1980	752.8	939.6	1,692.4
1981	777.8	1,128.9	1,906.7
1982	786.6	1,404.1	2,190.7
1983	833.8	1,321.3	2,155.1
1984	869.4	1,529.7	2,399.1
1985	1,346.5	1,846.4	3,192.9
1986	1,608.4	2,266.7	3,875.1
1987	1,765.6	2,402.2	4,167.8
1988	2,019.0	2,976.0	4,995.0

1. Sum of currency outside of banks and private sector demand deposits, source line 34.
2. Time, savings, and foreign currency deposits by residents, source line 35.
3. Calculated by adding columns A and B.

SOURCE: IMF-IFS-Y, 1982 , 1987, 1988, 1989.

Table 3148

HAITI MONEY SUPPLY, 1952–87

(M NC YE)

Year	A. Money[1] (M_1)	B. Quasi- Money[2]	C. Total[3] (M_2)
1952	98.3	21.2	119.5
1953	94.4	21.3	115.7
1954	116.8	27.8	144.6
1955	117.8	29.4	147.2
1956	126.9	34.8	161.7
1957	121.4	34.3	155.7
1958	102.6	32.0	134.6
1959	104.4	32.1	136.5
1960	104.3	34.1	138.4
1961	118.0	37.6	155.6
1962	122.5	37.8	160.3
1963	130.7	38.8	169.5
1964	132.5	38.7	171.2
1965	133.4	37.9	171.2
1966	123.2	38.1	161.4
1967	142.2	36.5	178.7
1968	160.0	40.8	200.8
1969	175.6	48.8	224.4
1970	190.6	58.0	248.6
1971	214.6	75.4	290.0
1972	271.2	110.3	381.6
1973	332.8	154.5	487.3
1974	342.4	241.3	583.7
1975	402.6	332.2	734.8
1976	549.6	465.6	1,015.2
1977	629.1	587.8	1,216.8
1978	717.8	713.7	1,431.5
1979	1,107.8	764.9	1,872.7
1980	945.4	992.9	1,938.3
1981	1,174.6	1,022.9	2,197.5
1982	1,164.3	1,102.9	2,267.2
1983	1,174.7	1,172.9	2,347.6
1984	1,400.1	1,268.6	2,668.7
1985	~	~	~
1986	~	~	~
1987	2,097.9	1,595.7	3,793.6

1. Sum of currency outside of banks and private sector demand deposits, source line 34.
2. Time, savings, and foreign currency deposits by residents, source line 34.
3. Calculated by adding columns A and B.

SOURCE: IMF-IFS-Y, 1982 , 1987, 1988, 1989.

Table 3149

HONDURAS MONEY SUPPLY, 1952–88

(M NC YE)

Year	A. Money[1] (M_1)	B. Quasi- Money[2]	C. Total[3] (M_2)
1952	52.5	7.4	59.9
1953	59.4	8.8	68.2
1954	68.6	10.3	78.9
1955	60.6	11.5	72.1
1956	67.2	15.8	83.0
1957	64.3	12.6	76.9
1958	63.0	11.7	74.7
1959	65.9	14.7	80.6
1960	64.3	20.7	85.0
1961	65.7	23.7	89.4
1962	72.7	29.5	102.2
1963	79.1	34.7	113.8
1964	89.8	39.4	129.2
1965	104.6	46.5	151.1
1966	106.9	58.6	165.5
1967	114.3	68.7	183.0
1968	127.4	85.8	213.2
1969	148.1	104.2	252.3
1970	158.9	129.5	288.4
1971	169.4	151.7	321.1
1972	192.9	172.8	365.7
1973	238.4	206.6	445.0
1974	242.4	217.8	460.2
1975	262.7	244.5	507.2
1976	361.0	311.0	672.0
1977	411.3	384.5	795.8
1978	480.4	482.0	962.4
1979	545.6	494.8	1,040.4
1980	610.3	517.4	1,127.7
1981	637.4	588.9	1,226.3
1982	716.9	761.2	1,478.1
1983	814.9	918.5	1,733.4
1984	846.0	1,065.4	1,911.4
1985	855.6	1,016.6	1,872.2
1986	953.2	1,096.8	2,050.0
1987	1,119.1	1,377.4	2,496.5
1988	1,252.6	1,616.6	2,869.2

1. Sum of currency outside of banks and private sector demand deposits, source line 34.
2. Time, savings, and foreign currency deposits by residents, source line 35.
3. Calculated by adding columns A and B.

SOURCE: IMF-IFS-Y, 1982, 1987, 1988, 1989.

Table 3150

MEXICO MONEY SUPPLY, INFLATION, AND GDP, 1952–88

	(A)	(B)	(C)	(D)	(E)	(F)
		B NC YE		M_2 Index	Price Index[4]	Real M_2 Index (D/E)
Year	Money[1] (M_1)	Quasi-Money[2]	Total[3] (M_2)			
				(1980 = 100.0)		
1952	7.3	1.9	9.2	6.3	~	~
1953	8.0	2.1	10.1	7.1	~	~
1954	9.0	3.0	12.0	8.7	39.1	22.1
1955	10.8	3.4	14.2	9.4	~	~
1956	12.0	3.7	15.7	11.0	~	~
1957	12.8	4.7	17.5	11.8	~	~
1958	13.7	5.5	19.2	12.6	45.0	28.0
1959	15.9	5.3	21.2	14.2	47.4	29.9
1960	17.4	5.4	22.8	15.0	47.6	31.4
1961	18.0	6.0	24.0	16.5	48.5	34.1
1962	20.9	6.6	27.5	19.7	48.8	40.3
1963	24.3	8.1	32.4	22.8	50.9	44.9
1964	28.6	9.2	37.8	24.4	51.8	47.2
1965	30.2	10.4	40.6	27.6	52.4	52.6
1966	33.9	11.8	45.7	29.1	54.1	53.8
1967	37.0	13.1	50.1	34.6	55.0	63.0
1968	42.3	14.8	57.1	40.2	56.5	71.1
1969	48.6	16.9	65.5	44.1	59.7	73.9
1970	53.8	18.2	72.0	47.2	62.1	76.1
1971	57.9	19.6	77.5	55.1	63.8	86.4
1972	68.2	22.9	91.1	70.1	73.8	94.9
1973	83.5	31.6	115.1	84.3	90.3	93.3
1974	100.8	38.4	139.2	100.0	100.0	100.0
1975	122.4	41.7	164.1	147.2	122.1	120.6
1976	158.0	85.0	243.0	318.9	172.4	185.0
1977	208.2[a],*	317.0[a]	525.2	424.4	199.7	212.5
1978	270.2	429.0	699.2	576.4	236.2	244.0
1979	360.9	588.0	948.9	787.4	294.1	267.7
1980	477.2	820.0	1,297.2	1,173.2	365.9	320.7
1981	635.0	1,298.0	1,933.0	1,854.3	571.2	324.7
1982	1,031.0*	2,024.0*	3,055.0*	3,001.6	1,184.4	253.4
1983	1,447.0	3,498.0	4,945.0	5,057.5	2,017.6	250.7
1984	2,315.0	6,017.0	8,332.0	7,244.9	3,098.2	233.8
1985	3,462.0	8,474.0	11,936.0	12,922.8	5,683.5	227.4
1986	5,790.0	15,509.0	21.299.0	31,959.1	~	~
1987	12,627.0	40,029.0	52,656.0	~	~	~
1988	20,774.0	22,149.0	42,923.0	~	~	~

1. Sum of currency outside of banks and private sector demand deposits, source line 34.
2. Time, savings, and foreign currency deposits in Mexico by residents, source line 35.
   According to data calculated from Banco de México, *Indicadores Económicos*, August
   1982, p. 6, foreign currency in checking accounts, liquid savings, and in time deposits
   made up the following % of M_4 (or IMF's M_2): 1968, 5.1%; 1969, 4.3%; 1970, 3.8%;
   1971, 2.9%; 1972, 2.2%; 1973, 3.2%; 1974, 2.5%; 1975, 3.1%; 1976, 10.6%; 1977,
   14.0%; 1978, 12.5%; 1979, 14.8%; 1980, 18.1%; Mar. 1982, 25.0%. Cf. Leroy O.
   Laney, "Currency Substitution: The Mexican Case." *Voice* (Federal Reserve Bank of
   Dallas), January 1981, pp. 1-10.
3. Calculated by adding columns A and B.
4. Bank of Mexico Wholesale Price Index (210 national and import goods), period
   average, source line 63.

a. Expanded coverage which approximates the Bank of Mexico's concept of M_4.

Method: A,B: 1952-74, IFS-Y, 1982; IMF-IFS-Y, 1987, lines 34 and 35.
       C: Calculated (A + B).
       D: Calculated from column C.
       E: See source A, B, line 63.
       F: Calculated (D/E).

SOURCE: SALA 22-2; updated here according to data given in "Method," above.

Figure 31:1

MEXICO MONEY SUPPLY (*M*$_2$) AND INFLATION INDEXES, 1952–82

(1975 = 100)

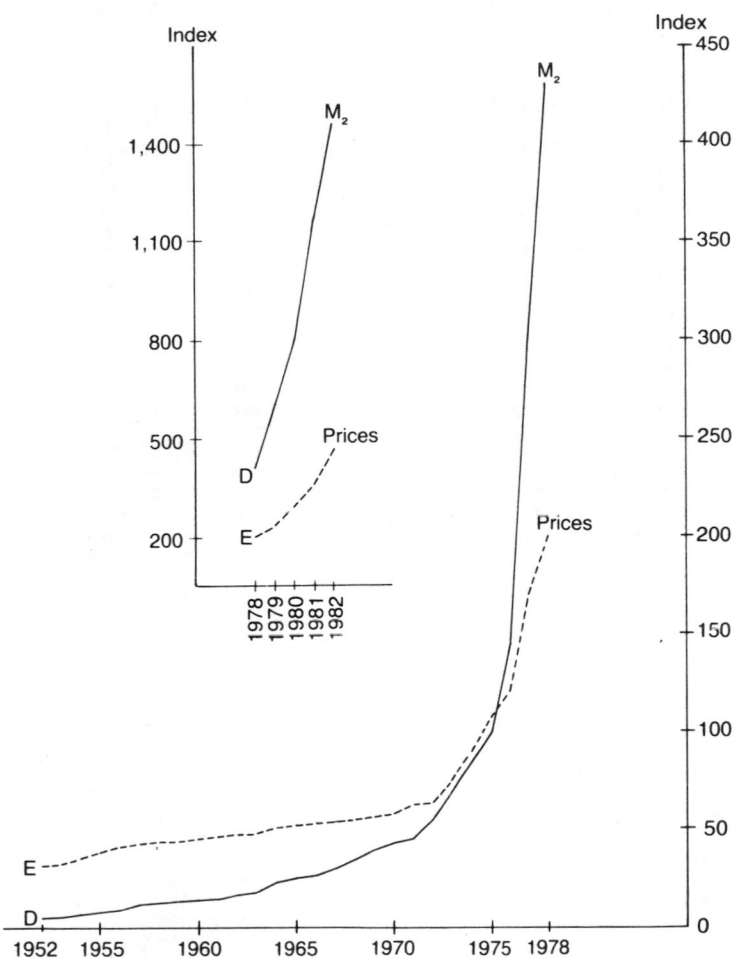

Trajectories D and E are keyed to
columns D and E in table 3050

SOURCE: SALA, 22, p. xi.

Table 3151

NICARAGUA MONEY SUPPLY, 1952–88

(M NC YE)

Year	A. Money[1] (M_1)	B. Quasi-Money[2]	C. Total[3] (M_2)
1952	180.2	2.0	182.2
1953	230.2	9.2	239.4
1954	264.4	7.5	271.9
1955	272.5	18.1	290.6
1956	267.0	18.1	285.1
1957	259.6	19.4	279.0
1958	251.6	22.9	274.5
1959	253.2	28.8	282.0
1960	264.0	33.1	297.1
1961	272.7	32.0	304.7
1962	352.9	31.5	384.4
1963	397.4	51.3	448.7
1964	460.3	84.9	545.2
1965	537.3	135.2	672.5
1966	565.1	185.8	750.9
1967	540.7	219.3	760.0
1968	484.8	197.2	682.0
1969	513.1	207.9	721.0
1970	578.2	250.5	828.7
1971	618.9	330.3	949.2
1972	748.7	477.3	1,226.0
1973	1,146.4	587.9	1,734.3
1974	1,313.3	703.0	2,016.3
1975	1,255.8	774.0	2,029.8
1976	1,615.5	1,083.7	2,699.2
1977	1,699.2	1,156.2	2,855.4
1978	1,579.3	1,072.9	2,652.2
1979	2,654.1	772.6	3,426.7
1980	4,102.4	1,644.2	5,746.6
1981	5,206.3	2,720.4	7,926.7
1982	6,545.8	3,349.3	9,895.1
1983	10,937.0	4,252.9	15,189.9
1984	~	~	~
1985	~	~	~
1986	~	~	~
1987	~	~	~
1988	~	~	~

1. Sum of currency outside of banks and private sector demand deposits, source line 34.
2. Time, savings, and foreign currency deposits by residents, source line 35.
3. Calculated by adding columns A and B.

SOURCE: IMF-IFS-Y, 1982, 1986, and 1987; IMF-IFS, August 1989.

Table 3152

PANAMA MONEY SUPPLY, 1952–88

(M NC YE)

Year	A. Money[1] (M_1)	B. Quasi-Money[2]	C. Total[3] (M_2)
1952	26.6	17.7	44.3
1953	30.2	18.4	48.6
1954	32.6	18.5	41.1
1955	32.7	19.8	52.5
1956	34.2	22.1	56.3
1957	38.0	23.4	61.4
1958	39.9	25.3	65.2
1959	41.6	27.1	68.7
1960	42.1	28.2	70.3
1961	43.9	31.4	75.3
1962	48.8	38.1	86.9
1963	59.7	51.0	110.7
1964	50.8	54.1	104.9
1965	55.5	69.2	124.7
1966	61.9	87.0	148.9
1967	70.3	110.4	180.7
1968	80.9	125.6	206.5
1969	84.8	111.7*	196.5*
1970	100.5	155.8	256.3
1971	105.4	196.8	302.2
1972	153.6	239.3	392.9
1973	161.1	283.4	444.5
1974	196.3	333.9	530.2
1975	173.1	374.7	547.8
1976	190.0	388.0	578.0
1977	213.2	459.3	672.5
1978	246.0	586.7	832.7
1979	301.3	742.2	1,043.5
1980	335.3	980.4	1,315.7
1981	359.7	1,201.1	1,560.8
1982	379.3	1,369.8	1,749.1
1983	372.6	1,375.6	1,748.2
1984	381.0	1,481.9	1,862.9
1985	409.5	1,543.0	1,952.5
1986	~	~	~
1987	~	~	~
1988	~	~	~

1. Sum of currency outside of banks and private sector demand deposits, source line 34.
2. Time, savings, and foreign currency deposits by residents, source line 35.
3. Calculated by adding columns A and B.

SOURCE: IMF-IFS-Y, 1982, 1986, and 1987; IMF-IFS, August, 1989.

Table 3153

PARAGUAY MONEY SUPPLY, 1952–88

(M NC YE)

Year	A. Money[1] (M_1)	B. Quasi- Money[2]	C. Total[3] (M_2)
1952	582	50	632
1953	861	82	943
1954	1,070	102	1,172
1955	2,384	376	2,545
1956	1,941	95	2,036
1957	1,997	180	2,177
1958	2,384	376	2,760
1959	2,609	265	2,874
1960	2,674	357	3,031
1961	3,391	542	3,933
1962	3,311	825	4,136
1963	3,685	1,244	4,929
1964	4,473	1,761	6,234
1965	4,913	2,365	7,279
1966	5,034	2,822	7,856
1967	6,691*	3,648*	10,339*
1968	5,786	4,324	10,111
1969	6,557	5,300	11,857
1970	7,308	6,200	13,508
1971	7,848	7,394	15,242
1972	9,421	9,420	18,840
1973	12,494	11,808	24,302
1974	15,120	14,260	29,380
1975	17,829	19,258	37,087
1976	21,590	24,159	45,749
1977	28,574	31,576	60,150
1978	39,812	38,682	78,494
1979	49,537	47,952	97,489
1980	62,364	68,893	131,257
1981	62,432	94,355	156,787
1982	60,200	105,487	165,687
1983	75,587	117,838	193,425
1984	97,807	128,131	225,938
1985	125,202	147,735	272,937
1986	158,674	188,977	347,651
1987	243,667	225,663	469,330
1988	328,488	234,737	563,225

1. Sum of currency outside of banks and private sector demand deposits, source line 34.
2. Time, savings, and foreign currency deposits by residents, source line 35.
3. Calculated by adding columns A and B.

SOURCE: IMF-IFS-Y, 1982, 1986, 1987, 1988, 1989.

Table 3154

PERU MONEY SUPPLY, 1952–88

(M NC YE)

Year	A. Money[1] (M_1)	B. Quasi- Money[2]	C. Total[3] (M_2)
1952	2.7	1.6	4.3
1953	3.1	1.8	4.9
1954	3.4	2.0	5.4
1955	3.6	2.5	6.1
1956	4.2	3.0	7.2
1957	4.4	3.5	7.9
1958	4.7	3.8	8.5
1959	6.0	4.0	10.0
1960	7.1	4.7	11.8
1961	8.3	5.5	13.8
1962	8.9	6.6	15.5
1963	10.3	7.7	18.0
1964	13.0	9.6	22.6
1965	15.6	12.3	27.9
1966	17.8	13.7	31.5
1967	20.1	14.1	34.2
1968	22.2	14.4	36.6
1969	26.3	14.5	40.8
1970	40.8	14.1	54.9
1971	45.0	15.5	60.5
1972	57.9	16.8	74.7
1973	72.5	19.1	91.6
1974	102.6	21.2	123.8
1975	120.0	23.3	143.3
1976	151.0	26.9	177.9
1977	182.4	39.8	222.2
1978	265.3	91.9	357.2
1979	451.7	234.5	686.2
1980	712.6	546.1	1,258.7
1981	1,044.8	1,077.3	2,122.1
1982	1,408.4	2,191.2	3,599.6
1983	2,763.2	4,560.2	7,323.4
1984	5,967.0	11,038.0	17,006.0
1985	23,002.0	20,765.0	43,767.0
1986	42,713.0	24,117.0	66,830.0
1987	~	~	~
1988	~	~	~

1. Sum of currency outside of banks and private sector demand deposits, source line 34.
2. Time, savings, and foreign currency deposits by residents, source line 35.
3. Calculated by adding columns A and B.

SOURCE: IMF-IFS-Y, 1982, 1986, 1987, 1988, 1989.

Table 3155

URUGUAY MONEY SUPPLY, 1952–88

(B NC YE)

Year	A. Money[1] (M_1)	B. Quasi- Money[2]	C. Total[3] (M_2)
1952	~	~	~
1953	~	~	~
1954	~	~	~
1955	~	~	~
1956	~	~	~
1957	~	~	~
1958	~	~	~
1959	~	~	~
1960	~	#	#
1961	#	#	#
1962	#	#	.01
1963	#	#	.01
1964	.01	.01	.02
1965	.01	.01	.02
1966	.01	.01*	.02*
1967	.03	.02	.05
1968	.05	.02	.07
1969	.08	.03	.11
1970	.09	.04	.13
1971	.14	.06	.20
1972	.20	.12	.32
1973	.36	.18	.54
1974	.59	.34	.92
1975	.83*	.78*	1.61*
1976	1.38	1.85	3.23
1977	1.94	3.9	5.83
1978	3.59	7.53	11.11
1979	6.16	14.44	20.60
1980	9.08	26.51	35.59
1981	9.84	43.45	53.29
1982	13.70*	58.77*	72.47*
1983	14.93	66.93	81.86
1984	22.16	110.76	132.88
1985	45.99	213.80	259.79
1986	84.16	394.26	478.42
1987	135.16	567.97	703.13
1988	~	110.47	~

1. Sum of currency outside of banks and private sector demand deposits, souce line 34.
2. Time savings, and foreign currency deposits by residents, source line 35.
3. Calculated by adding columns A and B.

SOURCE: IMF-IFS-Y, 1982, 1986, 1987, and 1988; IMF-IFS, August 1989.

Table 3156

VENEZUELA MONEY SUPPLY, 1952–88

(M NC YE)

Year	A. Money[1] (M_1)	B. Quasi- Money[2]	C. Total[3] (M_2)
1952	1,909	273	2,182
1953	2,085	372	2,457
1954	2,169	494	2,663
1955	2,414	669	3,083
1956	2,756	922	3,678
1957	3,649	1,501	5,150
1958	4,017	1,860	5,877
1959	3,823	2,083	5,906
1960	3,574	1,691	5,265
1961	3,684	1,643	5,327
1962	3,604	1,806	5,410
1963	3,623	2,501	6,124
1964	4,399	3,022	7,421
1965	4,489	3,096	7,585
1966	4,620	2,928	7,548
1967	5,237	3,397	8,634
1968	5,699	3,771	9,470
1969	6,186	4,299	10,485
1970	6.732	4,718	11,450
1971	7,868	5,526	13,394
1972	9,467	6,981	16,448
1973	11,318	8,438	19,757
1974	16,006	9,980	25,987
1975	23,312	15,416	38,728
1976	27,105	21,567	48,671
1977	34,027	27,482	61,509
1978	38,987	31,848	70,835
1979	42,460	32,657	75,117
1980	50,209	38,432	88,642
1981	54,954	48,231	103,185
1982	58,015	57,979	115,994
1983	70,049	69,994	140,043
1984	86,693	76,787	163,481
1985	93,707	88,603	182,310
1986	98,479‡	119,418‡	217,897‡
1987	133,779	154,325	288,104
1988	166,076	190,348	356,424

1. Sum of currency outside of banks and private sector demand deposits, source line 34.
2. Time, savings, and foreign currency deposits by residents, source line 35.
3. Calculated by adding columns A and B.

SOURCE: IMF-IFS-Y, 1982, 1986, 1987, 1988, 1989.

Table 3157

MONEY SUPPLY[1] CHANGES, 19 LC, 1958-88

(PC Calculated from Indexes)

Country	1958	1959	1960	1961	1962	1963	1964	1965	1966	1967	1968	1969	1970	1971	1972	1973
A. ARGENTINA	~	~	~	~	~	~	~	~	~	~	~	~	~	~	~	72.3
B. BOLIVIA	~	22.2	13.4	18.1	14.6	15.6	23.1	22.7	19.9	5.2	7.3	9.6	9.0	10.9	20.8	35.0
C. BRAZIL	~	27.1	38.5	44.3	53.3	58.2	86.1	83.7	38.6	34.6	42.0	32.3	29.2	31.1	32.5	42.0
D. CHILE	~	~	~	156.7	~	~	~	~	~	~	~	~	52.9	99.3	100.9	264.4
E. COLOMBIA	16.7	16.2	6.6	16.3	19.8	17.1	24.1	14.3	16.0	22.2	19.3	21.1	19.8	10.3	19.3	28.3
F. COSTA RICA	7.0	7.2*	2.1	-6.3	13.0	12.3	11.0	4.5	2.6	19.6	16.9	.8	4.9	30.9	19.5	23.0
H. DOMINICAN REP.	16.4	5.8	-7.7	12.9	-1.7	9.3	8.1	-2.5	-1.4	-2.3	9.1	8.8	14.4	7.4	15.5	17.0
I. ECUADOR	3.7	8.3	10.6	6.0	5.9	12.0	26.3	-.9	8.4	15.5	17.5	11.7	22.6	20.5	16.6	31.3
J. EL SALVADOR	-6.5	-5.7	1.7	-7.7	2.4	7.8	5.5	2.0	2.9	3.8	.4	5.7	7.6	3.6	13.4	19.0
K. GUATEMALA	2.5	-4.7	-2.5	-1.7	.9	13.4	16.2	3.6	9.3	-3.5	6.9	1.1	6.4	-1.2	12.3	23.8
L. HAITI	-3.1	-14.4	10.3	6.4	4.2	5.6	3.8	-3.0	~	3.8	11.3	10.7	10.3	18.0	17.3	22.9
M. HONDURAS	-2.0	4.6	-2.4	2.2	10.7	8.7	14.5	13.9	6.9	-2.1	14.3	12.9	13.6	3.7	6.4	21.8
N. MEXICO	6.6	13.1	12.1	6.0	8.3	14.0	19.8	9.0	8.4	10.1	12.3	12.6	11.3	8.1	13.5	22.8
O. NICARAGUA	3.3	-6.4	1.9	4.8	21.3	21.2	11.3	17.4	6.8	-.7	-3.6	-1.7	6.6	4.6	17.8	51.4
P. PANAMA	2.8	13.2	-.4	3.2	7.0	19.1	-9.7	9.3	11.5	8.9	11.2	7.7	13.7	9.5	27.2	21.8
Q. PARAGUAY	12.3	14.7	3.0	18.6	12.6	2.9	17.8	16.0	-.9	5.6	4.1	-7.2	6.3	14.8	14.1	33.0
R. PERU	3.6	6.9	19.3	13.0	7.4	8.6	36.5	25.3	14.6	8.5	16.9	12.0	42.5	27.2	19.6	26.9
S. URUGUAY	~	~	~	~	~	~	~	~	68.6	49.0	87.0	69.4	31.4	32.1	49.3	63.5
T. VENEZUELA	18.0	7.5	-16.5	7.0	-1.5	5.0	12.7	12.2	2.3	4.8	2.8	8.2	9.9	11.8	18.3	21.9
UNITED STATES	1.6	2.1	~	2.2	2.4	3.2	3.8	4.2	4.6	4.0	7.0	5.9	3.8	6.8	7.2	7.2

Country	1974	1975	1976	1977	1978	1979	1980	1981	1982	1983	1984	1985	1986	1987	1988
A. ARGENTINA	83.5	90.5	310.8	144.2	145.6	131.4	115.9	53.9	195.7	287.8	522.6	650.2	143.8	98.2	106.0
B. BOLIVIA	42.8	22.6	18.9	31.9	13.5	13.8	38.4	15.1	120.6	198.9	790.9	7,834.1	315.7	53.9	~
C. BRAZIL	36.5	35.7	42.4	37.0	40.9	52.2	76.0	65.1	82.0	95.0	141.1	274.6	~	~	~
D. CHILE	315.5	239.5	216.1	156.7	81.2	60.0	62.6	23.4	-5.5	28.3	18.9	~	~	~	~
E. COLOMBIA	28.6	9.7	30.2	36.2	35.4	25.2	24.8	24.6	23.1	19.7	21.4	22.7	26.1	12.7	~
F. COSTA RICA	42.7	68.0	83.7	31.4	21.9	10.4	9.6	38.8	70.4	45.3	26.2	8.6	~	~	~
H. DOMINICAN REP.	26.1	26.9	-2.5	9.5	12.7	9.5	15.9	2.3	15.9	9.0	30.8	24.5	42.4	40.3	~
I. ECUADOR	43.4	23.0	9.2	43.2	13.9	20.1	25.7	21.7	21.6	22.3	27.2	27.8	23.2	25.3	50.9
J. EL SALVADOR	27.0	14.7	25.4	33.1	-1.2	12.0	25.2	-2.7	7.4	-1.0	5.1	26.0	23.5	18.0	5.1
K. GUATEMALA	25.1	7.1	33.9	28.6	12.2	11.0	5.7	1.0	6.6	.1	5.0	24.8	38.2	13.4	10.2
L. HAITI	15.1	-.5	37.2	21.3	17.5	12.8	13.2	24.9	2.1	4.3	13.5	14.7	-5.0	14.4	13.4
M. HONDURAS	11.3	.3	27.5	26.7	11.4	17.6	7.3	8.5	3.0	13.4	13.6	.9	8.6	14.4	~
N. MEXICO	19.2	21.5	22.3	26.6	37.2	31.4	31.1	36.8	43.5	44.1	53.2	53.7	51.3	106.5	106.0
O. NICARAGUA	25.6	-12.4	21.4	15.6	-2.2	18.5	105.3	21.7	19.9	73.0	~	3.0	~	~	~
P. PANAMA	11.2	9.6	13.1	10.1	13.5	16.1	16.8	8.7	7.0	.7	3.7	23.2	25.4	46.8	~
Q. PARAGUAY	21.4	16.6	20.6	36.6	34.1	32.2	20.4	13.7	-5.5	8.4	37.3	23.2	~	~	42.6
R. PERU	31.3	28.8	21.6	21.6	34.3	59.5	71.1	43.4	33.7	75.4	97.3	204.2	175.6	78.7	~
S. URUGUAY	80.0	50.1	64.2	46.5	56.5	99.5	34.9	33.9	-.8	27.7	24.0	71.8	94.9	20.3	~
T. VENEZUELA	31.1	47.3	27.0	25.0	18.9	7.4	14.1	11.4	9.9	11.6	26.8	14.1	7.2	20.3	26.8
UNITED STATES	5.0	4.6	5.7	7.6	8.2	8.0	6.3	7.1	6.6	11.1	7.0	9.2	13.4	10.5	4.3

1. "Money" equals M_1 (the sum of currency outside banks and private sector demand deposits).

SOURCE: IMF-IFS-Y, 1986 and 1987, pp. 88-91; 1988, pp. 91-93; 1989, pp. 72-75.

Table 3158

INCOME VELOCITY OF MONEY,[1] 18 L, 1951-82

(1980 = 100)

Country	1951	1952	1953	1954	1955	1956	1957	1958	1959	1960	1961	1962
A. ARGENTINA	~	~	~	~	~	~	~	~	~	~	~	~
B. BOLIVIA	~	137.7	236.1	274.1	317.4	165.6	120.4	122.9	115.6	118.3	108.9	103.9

Country	1963	1964	1965	1966	1967	1968	1969	1970	1971	1972	1973	1974
A. ARGENTINA	44.4	43.6	46.6	45.1	42.8	37.7	37.6	36.6	50.7	61.2	55.6	40.2
B. BOLIVIA	96.8	88.6	80.3	74.1	79.6	84.2	83.2	85.5	84.4	89.0	99.5	115.9

Country	1975	1976	1977	1978	1979	1980	1981	1982
A. ARGENTINA	63.3	80.3	90.9	91.8	106.6	100.0	125.7	~
B. BOLIVIA	107.3	103.5	90.7	93.7	99.1	100.0	~	~

1. Money equals the sum of currency outside banks and private sector demand deposits.
   Income velocity is defined here as "money" divided by GDP.

Continued in SALA, 24-3058.

Table 3159

INCOME VELOCITY OF MONEY PLUS QUASI-MONEY,[1] 19 LC, 1951-88

(1980 = 100)

Country	1951	1952	1953	1954	1955	1956	1957	1958	1959	1960	1961	1962
A. ARGENTINA	~	~	~	~	~	~	~	~	~	~	~	~
B. BOLIVIA	~	192.1	343.8	417.9	478.9	254.0	184.0	189.6	178.2	181.5	168.2	159.3
C. BRAZIL	~	~	~	~	~	~	~	41.0	46.1	46.2	47.2	50.4
D. CHILE	~	~	~	~	~	~	~	~	~	~	~	~
E. COLOMBIA	~	~	~	~	11.7	~	~	~	11.0	11.7	11.4	10.6
F. COSTA RICA	240.6	221.6	221.2	214.2	218.2	218.1	216.5	207.0	193.3*	199.9	213.6	208.0
H. DOMINICAN REP.	141.4	128.6	132.8	105.5	94.7	101.2	100.0	99.9	88.8	106.9	95.7	125.4
I. ECUADOR	165.3	153.5	152.1	145.2	154.0	138.9	137.7	137.2	134.1	133.1	130.8	127.7
J. EL SALVADOR	183.7	159.0	161.1	154.3	150.5	148.8	144.9	137.1	136.2	125.4	131.7	134.4
K. GUATEMALA	219.6	211.9	192.4	202.0	185.2	165.1	150.7*	148.6	160.4	160.0	159.6	162.0
L. HAITI	~	~	~	~	239.7	232.6	239.6	246.6	255.1	232.8	217.3	217.7
M. HONDURAS	189.6	178.4	169.9	139.0	159.8	144.4	156.7	182.4	171.7	166.7	168.5	160.7
N. MEXICO	123.3	122.7	110.4	106.5	110.9	116.0	115.2	113.6	110.8	117.7	117.5	117.2
O. NICARAGUA	~	~	~	~	~	~	~	~	~	184.1	189.4	174.6
P. PANAMA	~	~	~	~	231.1	224.5	227.0	219.4	208.2	211.0	225.3	221.1
Q. PARAGUAY	~	131.9	161.4	166.8	161.5	153.6	187.9	187.0	181.5	202.4	192.8	186.5
R. PERU	104.0	94.9	90.2	94.9	93.0	88.4	89.3	93.1	102.1	102.0	120.3	104.4
S. URUGUAY	~	~	~	~	~	~	~	~	~	~	~	~
T. VENEZUELA	257.9	235.0	221.2	226.0	214.5	205.8	172.1	144.5	132.5	158.0	162.9	178.2
UNITED STATES	74.3	74.1	76.3	73.5	92.4	77.2	79.1	89.8	94.4	94.5	91.6	91.4

Country	1963	1964	1965	1966	1967	1968	1969	1970	1971	1972	1973	1974
A. ARGENTINA	107.3	103.2	108.4	106.7	102.4	90.1	87.5	82.9	288.1	126.3	104.2	82.3
B. BOLIVIA	146.4	133.8	121.4	148.0	135.7	121.7	106.7	95.2	82.8	134.1	151.1	143.3
C. BRAZIL	67.8*	70.5	62.7	64.9	64.0	63.5	63.6	59.5	60.2	59.2	56.5	61.8*
D. CHILE	~	~	~	~	~	313.7	129.3	118.8	97.1	85.2	98.9	147.8
E. COLOMBIA	11.6	11.6	11.4	12.0	11.1	10.8	10.3	10.3	10.9	11.1	11.1	11.4
F. COSTA RICA	200.5	190.8	194.4	205.9	187.1	176.1	212.2	229.6	178.5	156.8	30.4	28.8
H. DOMINICAN REP.	131.1	131.4	110.3	118.2	119.5	106.5	107.1	98.5	98.1	98.2	91.9	85.3
I. ECUADOR	123.7	121.4	128.9*	125.1	119.9	107.4	104.8	101.4	95.8	95.7	98.1	104.3
J. EL SALVADOR	125.4	123.8	125.1	124.2	123.2	127.0	124.7	122.5	120.2	110.9	106.9	103.4
K. GUATEMALA	159.0	136.1	128.4	118.7	117.0	114.9	112.9	112.2	111.1	99.4	97.2	100.9
L. HAITI	219.8	235.0	263.5	273.2	265.0	241.7	229.7	215.1	196.1	163.9	173.4	124.6
M. HONDURAS	151.3	147.4	144.0	139.3	143.5	131.9	118.2	107.4	104.1	102.3	95.7	95.9
N. MEXICO	107.9	109.4	106.5	109.8	106.9	105.8	103.3	111.1	114.2	115.9	115.3	119.4
O. NICARAGUA	158.4	158.7	141.1	132.0	137.2	144.3	150.5	159.2	149.2	122.0	107.2	121.4
P. PANAMA	202.5	217.0	205.0	188.6	178.4	166.7	168.7	150.2	133.1	123.5	109.9	113.8
Q. PARAGUAY	181.2	158.3	141.9	140.6	131.9	126.9	132.0	127.8	120.1	118.1	115.8	127.6
R. PERU	99.2	93.9	89.1	91.1	97.2	104.0	108.3	98.9	91.2	86.7	85.2	84.1
S. URUGUAY	~	~	96.1*	130.2	142.6	166.7	140.2	127.7	114.6	125.3	160.4	160.2
T. VENEZUELA	176.3	169.4	161.8	161.1	161.4	161.2*	152.6	153.3	151.7	134.4	132.9	160.2
UNITED STATES	89.0	88.3	88.7	91.3	90.3	91.2	92.8	94.1	91.0	88.9	90.6	92.6

Table 3159 (Continued)

INCOME VELOCITY OF MONEY PLUS QUASI-MONEY,[1] 19 LC, 1951-88

(1980 = 100)

Country		1975	1977	1978	1979	1980	1981	1982	1983	1984	1985	1986	1987	1988
A.	ARGENTINA	147.4	146.7	117.3	114.5	100.0	101.1	112.7	134.3	156.2	160.2	132.7	~	~
B.	BOLIVIA	137.1	102.8	99.2	99.9	100.0	102.9	119.6	158.5	317.9	502.4	184.5	~	~
C.	BRAZIL	64.8	78.9	76.5	80.4	100.0	116.7	113.8	132.7	133.2	119.1	~	~	~
D.	CHILE	143.1	147.6	125.3	112.4	100.0	75.4	57.7	70.3	67.9	~	~	~	~
E.	COLOMBIA	12.9	12.8	91.6	97.2	100.0	86.9	83.2	86.0	86.9	89.3	~	96.1	~
F.	COSTA RICA	21.7	42.1	115.2	101.9	100.0	90.7	108.1	96.1	103.9	106.4	112.0	108.7	~
H.	DOMINICAN REP.	79.0	88.4	83.6	95.0	100.0	107.0	97.9	94.2	95.9	110.2	83.1	73.2	~
I.	ECUADOR	99.7	100.5	103.4	103.5	100.0	100.4	96.8	108.5	117.1	117.2	113.2	~	~
J.	EL SALVADOR	100.5	98.9	103.3	104.1	100.0	92.1	84.6	87.5	88.3	84.5	88.7	90.4	~
K.	GUATEMALA	99.6	95.7	92.9	94.6	100.0	98.9	84.9	84.4	82.7	85.2	91.2	~	~
L.	HAITI	131.9	106.4	90.5	83.8	100.0	85.7	83.3	85.7	87.2	~	~	~	~
M.	HONDURAS	99.7	92.8	90.2	89.0	100.0	101.5	95.3	82.0	75.4	79.7	81.3	~	~
N.	MEXICO	125.3	104.5	98.5	97.3	100.0	94.7	92.8	105.8	103.3	112.0	–	~	~
O.	NICARAGUA	132.2	118.6	123.6	120.3	100.0	81.4	79.3	59.7	~	~	~	~	~
P.	PANAMA	117.5	111.2	108.7	99.6	100.0	88.4	84.9	~	~	~	~	~	~
Q.	PARAGUAY	118.5	98.0	92.4	97.2	100.0	101.6	93.3	93.2	102.3	112.2	125.3	120.8	133.3
R.	PERU	82.1	107.4	118.6	122.9	100.0	104.7	101.3	99.4	104.0	103.0	~	~	~
S.	URUGUAY	166.3	123.8	109.0	100.6	100.0	81.0	65.1	63.6	66.9	65.2	64.1	~	~
T.	VENEZUELA	116.5	88.6	81.8	91.9	100.0	98.6	83.4	73.8	72.6	68.6	65.0	~	70.5
	UNITED STATES	92.2	90.0	93.8	97.3	100.0	105.5	102.8	95.2	96.5	93.6	91.4	91.3	93.3

1. "Money" equals the sum of currency outside banks and private sector demand
deposits. "Quasi-Money" is time, savings, and foreign currency deposits by residents.
"Income Velocity" is here defined as "money" plus "quasi-money" divided by "GDP"
and then converted to index format. Data "are designed to exhibit variability in the
income velocity of money, and not International differences in the ratio of income to
money. The ratio is therefore expressed in index number form, rather than in amounts
of national currency income per unit of domestic currency" (IMF-IFS-S, no. 5, 1983,
p. viii).

SOURCE: IMF-IFS-S, no. 5, 1983, pp. 54–57; IMF-IFS-Y, 1986, 1987, 1988, pp. 100–103;
1989, pp. 104–105.

Table 3160

MONEY MULTIPLIERS, 12 LC, 1978-82

Country		Monetary Multiplier (M_1)				Monetary Multiplier (M_2)			
		Average	Minimum	Maximum	Coefficient of Variation	Average	Minimum	Maximum	Coefficient of Variation
A.	ARGENTINA	1.26	.74	3.75	62.26	2.47	1.01	3.90	39.44
	Barbados	1.50	1.32	1.74	7.69	4.69	4.21	5.64	9.68
C.	BRAZIL	1.85	1.73	2.00	3.54	2.26	2.10	2.51	4.81
D.	CHILE	.85	.60	1.32	20.99	3.10	1.76	6.40	48.42
F.	COSTA RICA	1.42	1.01	1.85	15.51	3.28	3.01	3.65	6.06
H.	DOMINICAN REP.	1.00	.92	1.14	2.07	2.13	1.88	2.52	6.97
	Dominica	1.64	1.02	2.65	31.84	5.28	2.83	8.63	35.95
I.	ECUADOR	1.61	1.42	1.92	12.35	2.02	1.64	2.46	11.91
	Grenada	1.28	1.11	1.49	8.35	3.13	2.66	3.91	10.91
K.	GUATEMALA	1.06	.94	1.15	4.89	2.47	2.06	2.92	12.22
L.	HAITI	.97	.66	1.53	22.31	1.82	1.32	2.48	17.25
	Jamaica	1.68	1.30	2.02	11.81	4.33	3.35	6.40	19.93
M.	HONDURAS	1.52	1.45	1.83	9.54	3.19	2.73	4.03	10.30
N.	MEXICO	.64	.47	.72	13.88	1.75	1.60	1.90	4.42
R.	PERU	.92	.67	1.12	16.90	1.55	1.39	1.75	6.51
S.	URUGUAY	1.02	.77	1.32	12.64	4.56	2.30	6.76	29.76

SOURCE: Richard Lynn Ground, "Orthodox Adjustment Programmes in Latin America:
A Critical Look at the Policies of the International Monetary Fund," *Cepal Review*
(Santiago, 1984).

32

Exchange Rates

Table 3200

IMF SDR YEAR-END EXCHANGE RATES,[1] 19 LC, 1970–88

(NC per SDR)[2]

Country	1970	1971	1972	1973	1974	1975	1976	1977	1978
A. ARGENTINA	.004	.0005	.0005	.0006	.0006	.00001*	.00003	.00007	.00013
B. BOLIVIA	11.88	12.90	21.71	24.13	24.49	23.41	23.24	24.29	26.06
C. BRAZIL	4.95	.01*	.01	.01	.01	.01	.01	.02	.03
D. CHILE	.01	.02	.03	.43	2.29	9.95	20.24	33.96	44.23
E. COLOMBIA	19.09	22.70	24.74	29.91	35.05	38.59	42.20	46.11	53.41
F. COSTA RICA	6.64	7.20	7.20	8.02	10.49	10.03	9.96	10.41	11.17
H. DOMINICAN REP.	1.00	1.09	1.09	1.21	1.22	1.17	1.16	1.21	1.30
I. ECUADOR	25.00	27.14	27.14	30.16	30.61	29.27	29.05	20.37	32.57
J. EL SALVADOR	2.50	2.71	2.71	3.02	3.06	2.93	2.90	3.04	3.26
K. GUATEMALA	1.00	1.09	1.09	1.21	1.22	1.17	1.16	1.21	1.30
L. HAITI	5.00	5.43	5.43	6.03	6.12	5.85	5.81	6.07	6.51
M. HONDURAS	2.00	2.17	2.17	2.41	2.45	2.34	2.32	2.43	2.61
N. MEXICO	12.50	13.57	13.57	15.08	15.30	14.63	23.18	27.62	29.61
O. NICARAGUA	7.03	7.63	7.63	8.48	8.60	8.23	8.16	8.54	9.15
P. PANAMA	1.00	1.09	1.09	1.21	1.22	1.17	1.16	1.21	1.30
Q. PARAGUAY	126.00	136.80	136.80	152.00	154.27	147.50	146.39	153.05	164.15
R. PERU	.04*	.04	.04	.05	.05	.05	.08	.16	.26
S. URUGUAY	.25	.40	.80	1.13	2.03	3.20	4.65	6.57	9.19
T. VENEZUELA	4.45	4.72	4.72	5.17	5.25	5.02	4.99	5.21	5.59
UNITED STATES	1.00	1.09	1.09	1.21	1.22	1.17	1.16	1.21	1.30

Country	1979	1980	1981	1982	1983	1984	1985	1986	1987	1988
A. ARGENTINA	.00021	.00025	.00084	.00536	.02435	.17520	.87929	1.53755	5.3200	17.9920
B. BOLIVIA	32.29	31.26	28.53	216.21	523.48	8,821.89	1.8585	2.3522	3.1352	3.3239
C. BRAZIL	.06	.08	.15	.28	1.03	3.12	11.52	18.27	102.50	1.02986
D. CHILE	51.38	49.74	45.39	81.00	91.64	125.71	201.96	250.42	337.84	332.62
E. COLOMBIA	57.96	64.94	68.76	77.54	92.94	111.64	189.15	267.88	374.10	451.97
F. COSTA RICA	11.290	10.930	42.007	44.400	45.438	46.805	58,985	72.015	98.24	106.983
H. DOMINICAN REP.	1.3173	1.2754	1.1640	1.1031	1.0470	.9802	3.2294	3.7633	7.0366	8.6259
I. ECUADOR	32.933	31.885	29.049	36.568	56.640	65.846	105.174	179.197	314.233	582.03
J. EL SALVADOR	3.2933	3.1885	2.9099	2.7578	2.6174	2.4505	2.7461	6.1160	7.0933	6.7285
K. GUATEMALA	1.3173	1.2754	1.1640	1.1031	1.0470	.9802	1.0984	3.0580	3.5467	3.6041
L. HAITI	6.5867	6.3770	5.8198	5.5156	5.2347	4.9011	5.4921	6.1160	7.0933	6.7285
M. HONDURAS	2.6347	2.5508	2.3279	2.2062	2.0939	1.9604	2.1968	2.4464	2.8373	2.6914
N. MEXICO	30.04	29.66	30.53	106.43	150.55	188.75	408.28	1,129.62	3,134.81	3,069.5
O. NICARAGUA	13.239	12.818	11.698	11.086	10.522	9.851	30.756	85.623	99.306	~
P. PANAMA	1.3173	1.2754	1.1640	1.1031	1.0470	.9802	1.0984	1.2232	1.4187	1.3457
Q. PARAGUAY	165.98	160.70	146.66	138.99	131.92	235.25	351.49	672.75	780.26	740.14
R. PERU	.33	.44	.59	1.09	2.38	5.88	15.32	17.06	46.82	672.85
S. URUGUAY	11.150	12.786	13.495	37.230	45.281	73.271	137.302	221.397	398.643	606.91
T. VENEZUELA	5.6546	5.4747	4.9963	4.7351	4.5019	7.3516	8.2382	17.7363	20.5706	19.5127
UNITED STATES	1.31733	1.27541	1.16396	1.10311	1.04695	.98021	1.09842	1.22319	1.41866	1.34510

1. Special Drawing Right (SDR) values are based on a market basket of currencies.
2. Line aa, Market Rate.

SOURCE: IMF-IFS-Y, 1986; IMF-1FS, June 1987; IMF-IFS-Y, 1988; IMF-IFS, July 1989.

Table 3201

IMF SDR AVERAGE EXCHANGE RATES,[1] 19 LC, 1970–87
(NC per SDR)[2]

Country	1970	1971	1972	1973	1974	1975	1976	1977	1978
A. ARGENTINA	.0004	.0005	.0009	.0011	.0011	.0044	.00002*	.00005	.00010
B. BOLIVIA	11.88	11.92	14.43	23.84	24.05	24.28	23.09	23.35	25.04
C. BRAZIL	~	.01*	.01	.01	.01	.01	.01	.02	.02
D. CHILE	.01	.01	.02	.13	1.00	5.96	15.07	25.14	39.63
E. COLOMBIA	18.44	19.99	23.74	28.18	31.35	37.55	40.06	42.94	48.95
F. COSTA RICA	6.63	6.65	7.20	7.92	9.54	10.41	9.89	10.01	10.73
H. DOMINICAN REP.	1.0000	1.0030	1.0857	1.1921	1.2026	1.2142	1.1545	1.1675	1.2520
I. ECUADOR	20.917	25.074	27.143	29.803	30.066	30.354	28.863	29.188	31.300
J. EL SALVADOR	2.5000	2.5075	2.7143	2.9803	3.0066	3.0354	2.8863	2.9188	3.1300
K. GUATEMALA	1.0000	1.0030	1.0857	1.1921	1.2026	1.2142	1.1545	1.1675	1.2520
L. HAITI	5.0000	5.0149	5.4286	5.9607	6.0132	6.0708	5.7726	5.8376	6.2600
M. HONDURAS	2.0000	2.0060	2.1714	2.3843	2.4053	2.4283	2.3090	2.3350	2.5040
N. MEXICO	12.500	12.537	13.571	14.902	15.033	15.177	17.809	26.354	28.505
O. NICARAGUA	7.000	7.021	7.600	8.345	8.434	8.531	8.112	8.203	8.797
P. PANAMA	1.0000	1.0030	1.0857	1.1921	1.2026	1.2142	1.1545	1.1675	1.2520
Q. PARAGUAY	126.00	126.38	136.80	150.21	151.53	152.98	145.47	147.11	157.75
R. PERU	.04*	.04	.04	.05	.05	.05	.06	.10	.20
S. URUGUAY	.250	.256	.582	1.032	1.439	2.737	3.851	5.462	7.582
T. VENEZUELA	4.5000	4.4600	4.7771	5.1315	5.1533	5.2026	4.9528	5.0116	5.3742
UNITED STATES	1.00000	1.00298	1.08571	1.19213	1.20264	1.21415	1.15452	1.16752	1.25200

Country	1979	1980	1981	1982	1983	1984	1985	1986	1987
A. ARGENTINA	.00017	.00024	.00052	.00286	.01126	.06934	.61104	1.10634	2.77273
B. BOLIVIA	26.81	31.90	28.90	70.79	245.63	2,232.24	.4487	2.2548	2.6571
C. BRAZIL	.03	.07	.11	.20	.62	1.89	6.30	16.02	50.73
D. CHILE	48.12	50.76	45.99	56.20	84.28	101.123	163.55	226.440	283.881
E. COLOMBIA	54.98	61.54	64.25	70.77	84.30	103.34	144.49	227.902	313.708
F. COSTA RICA	11.07	11.15	25.66	41.30	43.93	45.646	51.227	65.681	81.174
H. DOMINICAN REP.	1.2920	1.3015	1.1792	1.1040	1.0690	1.0250	3.1604	3.4073	4.9715
I. ECUADOR	32.300	32.538	29.479	33.149	47.159	64.100	70.623	144.041	220.419
J. EL SALVADOR	3.2300	3.2538	2.9479	2.7600	2.6725	2.5625	2.5384	5.6924	6.4654
K. GUATEMALA	1.2920	1.3015	1.1792	1.1040	1.0690	1.0250	1.0153	2.1994	3.2327
L. HAITI	6.4600	6.5077	5.8958	5.5201	5.3450	3.1251	5.0767	5.8659	6.4654
M. HONDURAS	2.5840	2.6031	2.3583	2.2080	2.1380	2.0500	2.0307	2.3463	2.5861
N. MEXICO	29.464	29.871	28.907	62.268	128.380	172.025	260.812	717.713	1,782.09
O. NICARAGUA	11.958	13.080	11.851	11.095	10.743	10.301	26.911	78.016	90.515
P. PANAMA	1.2920	1.3015	1.1792	1.1040	1.0690	1.0250	1.0153	1.1732	1.2931
Q. PARAGUAY	162.79	163.99	148.57	139.11	134.69	206.03	311.37	397.90	711.19
R. PERU	.29	.38	.50	.77	1.74	3.55	11.14	16.36	21.77
S. URUGUAY	10.156	11.843	12.759	15.356	36.923	57.525	102.987	178.314	293.095
T. VENEZUELA	5.5459	5.5868	5.0615	4.7390	4.5940	7.1930	7.6150	9.4831	18.7495
UNITED STATES	1.29200	1.30153	1.17916	1.10401	1.06900	1.02501	1.01534	1.17317	1.29307

1. Special Drawing Right (SDR) values are based on a market basket of currencies.
2. Line rb, Market Rate.

SOURCE: IMF-IFS-Y, 1986; IMF-IFS-Y, 1987; IMF-IFS-Y, 1988.

Table 3202

IMF DOLLAR VALUE OF SDR, 1969–88
(YE and YA)

Year	US Dollar/SDR Rate (YE)	US Dollar/SDR Rate (YA)[1]	SDR/US Dollar Rate (YE)	SDR/US Dollar Rate (YA)[1]
1969	1.00000	1.00000	1.00000	1.00000
1970	1.00000	1.00000	1.00000	1.00000
1971	1.08571	1.00298	.92105	.99702
1972	1.08571	1.98571	.92105	.92105
1973	1.20635	1.19213	.82895	.83883
1974	1.22435	1.20264	.81676	.83150
1975	1.17066	1.21415	.85422	.82362
1976	1.16183	1.15452	.86071	.86616
1977	1.21471	1.16752	.82324	.85652
1978	1.30279	1.25200	.76758	.79872
1979	1.31733	1.29200	.75911	.77399
1980	1.27541	1.30153	.78406	.76833
1981	1.16396	1.17916	.85914	.84806
1982	1.10311	1.10401	.90653	.90579
1983	1.04695	1.06900	.95515	.93545
1984	.98021	1.02501	1.02019	.97560
1985	1.09842	1.01534	.91040	.98489
1986	1.22319	1.17317	.81753	.85239
1987	1.41866	1.29307	.70489	.77335
1988	1.34570	1.34392	.74311	.74409

1. Geometric average.
2. Prior to 1970 one dollar equals one SDR (Special Drawing Right).

SOURCE: IMF-IFS-Y, 1986; IMF-IFS, June 1987; IMF-IFS-Y, 1988; IMF-IFS, July 1989.

Table 3203

IMF DOLLAR YEAR-END EXCHANGE RATES,[1] 20 L, 1948-88[a]

(NC per US)

Year	A. ARGENTINA	B. BOLIVIA	C. BRAZIL	D. CHILE	E. COLOMBIA	F. COSTA RICA	G.[3] CUBA	H. DOMINICAN REP.	I. ECUADOR	J. EL SALVADOR	K. GUATEMALA
1948	.0481	.042	.019	.0066	1.960	6.200	1.00	1.00	13.500	2.500	1.00
1949	.0902	.042	.019	.0099	1.960	6.200	1.00	1.00	13.500	2.500	1.00
1950	.1402	.060	.019	.0073	1.960	5.920	1.00	1.00	15.000	2.500	1.00
1951	.1446	.060	.019	.0093	2.510	5.635	1.00	1.00	15.000	2.500	1.00
1952	.1398	.060	.057	.0013	2.510	5.635	1.00	1.00	15.000	2.500	1.00
1953	.1398	.190	.074	.0011	2.510	5.635	1.00	1.00	15.000	2.500	1.00
1954	.1398	.190	.067	.0011	2.510	5.635	1.00	1.00	15.000	2.500	1.00
1955	.3610	.190	.066	.0065	2.510	5.635	1.00	1.00	15.000	2.500	1.00
1956	.3745	7.760	.091	.0069	5.425	5.635	1.00	1.00	15.000	2.500	1.00
1957	.3745	8.565	.141	.0099	6.400	5.635	1.00	1.00	15.000	2.500	1.00
1958	.7000	11.935	.184	.0105	6.400	5.635	1.00	1.00	15.000	2.500	1.00
1959	.8325	11.880	.195	.0105	6.700	5.635	1.00	1.00	15.000	2.500	1.00
1960	.8270	11.880	.307	.0105	6.700	5.635	1.00	1.00	15.000	2.500	1.00
1961	.8302	11.880	.475	.0105	9.000	5.635	1.00	1.00	15.000	2.500	1.00
1962	1.341	11.880	.620	.0024	9.000	6.635	1.00	1.00	18.000	2.500	1.00
1963	1.325	11.880	1.850	.0030	9.000	6.635	1.00	1.00	18.000	2.500	1.00
1964	1.509	11.880	2.220	.0033	13.500	6.635	1.00	1.00	18.000	2.500	1.00
1965	1.885	11.880	2.220	.004	15.760	6.635	1.00	1.00	18.000	2.500	1.00
1966	2.473	11.880	2.715	.044	16.880	6.635	1.00	1.00	18.000	2.500	1.00
1967	3.500	11.880	3.830	.0058	17.850	6.635	1.00	1.00	18.000	2.500	1.00
1968	3.500	11.880	4.350	.008	19.090	6.635	1.00	1.00	18.000	2.500	1.00
1969	4.00	11.880	4.950	.0010	20.910	6.635	1.00	1.00	18.000	2.500	1.00
1970	5.00	11.880	5.635	.0122	22.790	6.635	1.00	1.00	18.000	2.500	1.00
1971	5.00	11.880	6.215	.0158	24.790	6.635	.92	1.00	25.000	2.500	1.00
1972	5.00	20.000	6.220	.025	28.630	6.635	.92	1.00	25.000	2.500	1.00
1973	5.00	20.000	6.220	.360	32.960	6.650	.83	1.00	25.000	2.500	1.00
1974	5.00	20.000	7.435	1.870	36.320	8.570	.83	1.00	25.000	2.500	1.00
1975	60.9	20.000	9.070	8.500	37.960	8.570	.83	1.00	25.000	2.500	1.00
1976	274.5	20.000	12.345	17.420	41.000	8.570	.83	1.00	25.000	2.500	1.00
1977	597.5	20.000	16.050	27.960	44.000	8.570	.83	1.00	25.000	2.500	1.00
1978	.100	20.000	20.920	33.950	50.920	8.570	.740	1.00	25.000	2.500	1.00
1979	.162	20.000	42.530	39.000	59.000	8.570	.720	1.00	25.000	2.500	1.00
1980	.199	24.510	65.500	39.000	70.290	8.570	.710	1.00	25.000	2.500	1.00
1981	.725	24.510	127.80	39.000	88.770	36.090	.830	1.00	25.000	2.500	1.00
1982	4.855	196.000	252.67	73.430	113.890	40.250	.850	1.00	33.150	2.500	1.00
1983	23.261	500.000	.98*	87.530	172.200	43.400	.870	1.00	54.100	2.500	1.00
1984	178.735	9.000	3.18	128.240	219.000	47.750	.900	1.00	67.175	2.500	1.00
1985	.8005*	1.6920	10.49	183.860	263.700	53.700	.910	2.9400	95.750	2.500	1.00
1986	1.2570	1.9230	14.89	204.730	335.86	58.875	.793	3.0766	146.500	5.000	2.50
1987	3.7500	2.2100	72.25	238.140	263.700	69.250	.773	4.9600	221.500	5.000	2.50
1988	13.3700	2.4700	.76530*	247.20	335.86	79.500	.776[b]	6.4100	432.51	5.000	2.71

Table 3203 (Continued)

IMF DOLLAR YEAR-END EXCHANGE RATES,[1] 20 L, 1948-88[a]
(NC per US)

Year	L. HAITI	M. HONDURAS	N. MEXICO	O. NICARAGUA	P. PANAMA	Q. PARAGUAY	R. PERU[2]	S. URUGUAY[2]	T. VENEZUELA[2]
1948	5.00	2.00	4.855	5.145	1.00	3.12	16.10	.0019	3.220
1949	5.00	2.00	8.650	5.145	1.00	3.12	14.81	.0019	3.220
1950	5.00	2.00	8.650	6.826	1.00	3.12	14.95	.0019	3.220
1951	5.00	2.00	8.650	6.826	1.00	6.00	15.28	.0019	3.220
1952	5.00	2.00	8.650	6.826	1.00	15.00	15.60	.0019	3.220
1953	5.00	2.00	8.650	6.826	1.00	15.00	19.89	.0019	3.220
1954	5.00	2.00	12.500	6.826	1.00	21.00	19.00	.0021	3.220
1955	5.00	2.00	12.500	6.826	1.00	21.00	19.00	.0021	3.220
1956	5.00	2.00	12.500	6.826	1.00	10.00	19.00	.0021	3.220
1957	5.00	2.00	12.500	7.026	1.00	111.30	19.00	.0021	3.220
1958	5.00	2.00	12.500	7.026	1.00	111.30	19.00	.0021	3.220
1959	5.00	2.00	12.500	7.026	1.00	122.00	24.49	.0110	3.220
1960	5.00	2.00	12.500	7.026	1.00	126.00	27.70	.0200	3.220
1961	5.00	2.00	12.500	7.026	1.00	126.00	26.76	.0110	3.220
1962	5.00	2.00	12.500	7.026	1.00	126.00	26.81	.0164	3.220
1963	5.00	2.00	12.500	7.026	1.00	126.00	26.82	.0187	3.220
1964	5.00	2.00	12.500	7.026	1.00	126.00	26.82	.0600	4.450
1965	5.00	2.00	12.500	7.026	1.00	126.00	26.82	.0762	4.450
1966	5.00	2.00	12.500	7.026	1.00	126.00	26.82	.2000	4.450
1967	5.00	2.00	12.500	7.026	1.00	126.00	26.82	.2500	4.450
1968	5.00	2.00	12.500	7.026	1.00	126.00	38.70	.2500	4.450
1969	5.00	2.00	12.500	7.026	1.00	126.00	38.70	.2500	4.450
1970	5.00	2.00	12.500	7.026	1.00	126.00	38.70	.2500	4.450
1971	5.00	2.00	12.500	7.026	1.00	126.00	38.70	.3700	4.350
1972	5.00	2.00	12.500	7.026	1.00	126.00	38.70	.7320	4.350
1973	5.00	2.00	12.500	7.026	1.00	126.00	38.70	.9370	4.285
1974	5.00	2.00	12.500	7.026	1.00	126.00	38.70	1.6560	4.285
1975	5.00	2.00	12.500	7.026	1.00	126.00	38.70	2.7300	4.285
1976	5.00	2.00	19.950	7.026	1.00	126.00	45.00	4.0000	4.293
1977	5.00	2.00	22.736	7.026	1.00	126.00	69.37	5.4100	4.293
1978	5.00	2.00	22.724	7.026	1.00	126.00	130.38	7.0540	4.293
1979	5.00	2.00	22.803	10.050	1.00	126.00	196.18	8.4640	4.293
1980	5.00	2.00	23.256	10.050	1.00	126.00	250.12	10.0250	4.293
1981	5.00	2.00	26.229	10.050	1.00	126.00	.342*	11.5940	4.293
1982	5.00	2.00	96.480	10.050	1.00	126.00	.507	33.7500	4.293
1983	5.00	2.00	143.930	10.050	1.00	126.00	.990	43.250	4.293
1984	5.00	2.00	192.560	10.050	1.00	126.00	2.271	74.750	4.300
1985	5.00	2.00	371.700	28.000	1.00	240.00	5.696	125.000	7.500
1986	5.00	2.00	923.500	70.000	1.00	320.00	13.945	181.000	7.500
1987	5.00	2.00	2,209.700	70.000	1.00	550.00	33.000	281.000	14.500
1988	5.00	2.00	2,281.0	~	1.00	550.00	500.00	451.00	14.500

1. Line ae, Market Rate/Par Rate (or Central Rate).
2. For multiple exchange rates, see SALA, 17, ch. 24.
3. Beginning 1971, data reflect noncommercial rates applied to tourism and to remittances from outside the ruble area available at the U.N. Statistical Office.

a. For previous years after 1937, see SALA, 17, ch. 24.
b. Fourth quarter.

SOURCE: IMF-IFS-S, no. 1, 1981; IMF-IFS-Y, 1986, and IMF-AFS, June 1987; Cuba data from UN-MB, various monthly, 1969-89; IMF-IFS, October 1988; IMF-IFS, July 1989.

Table 3204

IMF DOLLAR AVERAGE EXCHANGE RATES,[1] 19 L, 1965–88[a]

(NC per US)

	Country	1965	1970	1972	1973	1974	1975	1976	1977	1978	1979
A.	ARGENTINA	1.7	3.8	8.2	9.4	8.9	36.6	.00001*	.00004	.00008	.00013
B.	BOLIVIA	11.88	11.88	13.29	20.00	20.00	20.00	20.00	20.00	20.00	20.39
C.	BRAZIL	1.90	4.59	.01	.01	.01	.01	.01	.01	.02	.03
D.	CHILE	.003	.012	.020	.111	.832	4.911	13.054	21.529	31.656	37.246
E.	COLOMBIA	10.475	18.443	21.886	23.637	26.064	30.929	34.694	36.775	39.095	42.550
F.	COSTA RICA	6.625	6.625	6.635	6.647	7.930	8.570	8.570	8.570	8.570	8.570
H.	DOMINICAN REP.	1.00	1.00	1.00	1.00	1.00	1.00	1.00	1.00	1.00	1.00
I.	ECUADOR	18.000	20.917	25.000	25.000	25.000	25.000	25.000	25.000	25.000	25.000
J.	EL SALVADOR	2.50	2.50	2.50	2.50	2.50	2.50	2.50	2.50	2.50	2.50
K.	GUATEMALA	1.00	1.00	1.00	1.00	1.00	1.00	1.00	1.00	1.00	1.00
L.	HAITI	5.00	5.00	5.00	5.00	5.00	5.00	5.00	5.00	5.00	5.00
M.	HONDURAS	2.00	2.00	2.00	2.00	2.00	2.00	2.00	2.00	2.00	2.00
N.	MEXICO	12.500	12.500	12.500	12.500	12.500	12.500	15.426	22.573	22.767	22.805
O.	NICARAGUA	7.000	7.000	7.000	7.000	7.013	7.026	7.026	7.026	7.026	9.255
P.	PANAMA	1.00	1.00	1.00	1.00	1.00	1.00	1.00	1.00	1.00	1.00
Q.	PARAGUAY	126.00	126.00	126.00	126.00	126.00	126.00	126.00	126.00	126.00	126.00
R.	PERU	.03*	.04	.04	.04	.04	.04	.06	.08	.16	.225
S.	URUGUAY	.0523	.2500	.5630	.8746	1.2155	2.2991	3.3950*	4.678	6.060	7.861
T.	VENEZUELA	4.4997	4.4983	4.4000	4.3045	4.2845	4.2850	4.2899	4.2925	4.2925	4.2925

	Country	1980	1981	1982	1983	1984	1985	1986	1987	1988
A.	ARGENTINA	.00018	.00044	.00259	.01053	.06765	.60181	.94303	2.1443	8.7526
B.	BOLIVIA	24.51	24.51	64.12	229.78	2,177.78	.4419*	1.9220	2.0549	2.3502
C.	BRAZIL	.05	.09	.18	.58	1.85	6.20	13.654	39.2290	.26238*
D.	CHILE	39.000	39.000	50.909	78.842	98.656	161.081	193.020	219.5400	245.05
E.	COLOMBIA	47.280	54.491	64.085	78.854	100.817	142.311	194.260	242.6100	299.17
F.	COSTA RICA	8.570	21.763	37.580	41.094	44.533	50.453	55.986	62.7760	75.085
H.	DOMINICAN REP.	1.00	1.00	1.00	1.00	1.00	3.1126	2.9043	3.8448	6.1396
I.	ECUADOR	25.000	25.000	30.026	44.115	62.536	69.556	122.779	170.4620	301.61
J.	EL SALVADOR	2.50	2.50	2.50	2.50	2.50	2.50	5.000	5.0000	5.000
K.	GUATEMALA	1.00	1.00	1.00	1.00	1.00	1.00	1.8750	2.5000	2.6196
L.	HAITI	5.00	5.00	5.00	5.00	5.00	5.00	5.00	5.00	5.00
M.	HONDURAS	2.00	2.00	2.00	2.00	2.00	2.00	2.00	2.00	2.00
N.	MEXICO	22.951	24.515	56.402	120.094	167.828	256.872	611.770	1,405.8	2,273.1
O.	NICARAGUA	10.050	10.050	10.050	10.050	10.050	26.504	66.500	70.000	~
P.	PANAMA	1.00	1.00	1.00	1.00	1.00	1.00	1.00	1.00	1.00
Q.	PARAGUAY	126.00	126.00	126.00	126.00	201.00	306.67	339.17	550.00	55.00
R.	PERU	.29	.42	.70	1.63	3.47	10.97	13.95	16.84	128.83
S.	URUGUAY	9.099	10.820	13.909	34.540	56.122	101.431	151.993	226.670	359.44
T.	VENEZUELA	4.2925	4.2925	4.2925	4.2975	7.0175	7.500	8.083	14.500	14.500

1. Line rf, Implicit Rate/Market Rate.

a. For previous years after 1937, see SALA, 17, ch. 24, and SALA, 22-2501. Rounding by source makes data for Argentina and Chile problematic for all but the last few years.

SOURCE: IMF-IFS-Y, 1986; IMF-IFS, June 1987; IMF-IFS, October 1988; IMF-IFS, July 1989.

Table 3205

EXCHANGE RATE HISTORY,[1] 13 L, 1937-74

(U per US; 1937-74 = A; 1948-74 = YE)

A. ARGENTINA

Year	Free	Official	Selling (P)	Selling (B)	Selling (A)	Selling (F)	Selling (C)	Buying (S)	Buying (P)	Buying (B)
1937[a]	3.41	*	3.23	3.23	*	3.33	*	*	3.03	3.03
1938	4.38	*	3.21	36.31	*	3.92	*	*	3.07	3.07
1939	4.40[g]	*	3.83[g]	3.83[g]	*	4.33	*	*	3.27	3.27
1940	*	*	3.73	4.23	*	4.37	*	*	3.36	3.26
1941	*	*	3.73	4.23	4.94	4.24	*	*	4.22	3.36
1942	*	*	3.73	4.23	4.94	4.23	*	*	4.22	3.36
1943	*	*	3.73	4.23	4.94	4.06	*	*	4.04	3.36
1944	*	*	3.73	4.23	4.94	4.02	*	*	3.98	3.36
1945	*	*	3.73	4.23	4.94	4.04	*	*	3.98	3.36
1946	*	*	3.73	4.23	4.94	4.09	*	*	3.98	3.36
1947	*	*	3.73	4.23	4.94	4.08	4.80	*	3.98	3.36
1948[b]	4.81	3.36	3.73	4.23	4.94	4.45	9.25	5.00[h]	3.98	3.36
1949[c]	9.02	3.36	5.37[i]	6.09	10.26	9.02	15.80	7.20[i]	5.73[i]	3.36
1950[d]	14.02	5.00	5.00[j]	5.00	*[k]	14.03	19.50	7.50[j]	7.50[j]	5.00[i]
1951	14.46	5.00	*	*	*	14.46	27.60	7.50	7.50	5.00
1952	13.98	5.00	*	*	*	13.98	23.20	7.50	7.50	5.00
1953	13.98	5.00	*	*	*	*	20.85	7.50	7.50	5.00
1954	13.98	5.00	*	*	*	*	*	*	*	*
1955	36.10	18.00	*	*	*	*	*	*	*	*
1956	37.45	18.00	*	*	*	*	*	*	*	*
1957	37.00	18.00	*	*	*	*	*	*	*	*
1958	70.00	18.00	*	*	*	*	*	*	*	*
1959[e]	*	83.25[l]	*	*	*	*	*	*	*	*
1960	*	82.70	*	*	*	*	*	*	*	*
1961	*	83.02	*	*	*	*	*	*	*	*
1962	*	134.10	*	*	*	*	*	*	*	*
1963	*	132.50	*	*	*	*	*	*	*	*
1964	*	150.90	*	*	*	*	*	*	*	*
1965	*	188.50	*	*	*	*	*	*	*	*
1966	*	247.30	*	*	*	*	*	*	*	*
1967	*	350.00	*	*	*	*	*	*	*	*
1968	*	350.00	*	*	*	*	*	*	*	*
1969	*	4.00[m]	*	*	*	*	*	*	*	*
1970	*	5.00	*	*	*	*	*	*	*	*
1971[f]	8.25[n]	5.00	*	*	*	*	*	*	*	*
1972	9.98	5.00	*	*	*	*	*	*	*	*
1973	9.98	5.00	*	*	*	*	*	*	*	*
1974	9.98[o]	5.00[o]	*	*	*	*	*	*	*	*

1. Code: A, auction; B, basic; C, curb; F, free; P, preferential; S, special

a. Selling rate: subdivided into preferential, basic auction free, and curb (1937-49);
    buying rate: special, preferential, basic.

b. 1948-72: two categories listed — free and official.

c. October 3, 1949: Argentina readjusted her multiple currency structure, the degree of
    adjustments varying widely depending upon the particular transactions and
    commodities to which applied.

d. On August 29, 1950, the number of effective rates was reduced from 9 to 3. The
    preferential import rates of 3.73 and 5.37 pesos per U.S. dollar and the basic export
    rate of 3.35 pesos were consolidated into a single rate of 5.00 per U.S. dollar.
    (Source: IFS, September 1950-country notes.)

e. A new exchange system was made effective January 12, 1959, when the previous
    official and free market were replaced by a single market for all transactions with a
    fluctuating exchange rate.

f. On September 20, 1971, a dual exchange rate system was introduced consisting of an
    official market with a fixed rate of 5.00 pesos per U.S. dollar and a financial market
    in which the rate is allowed to fluctuate.

g. January/August. Rates quoted for 1940 were established in August 1939. On August
    1939 free market discontinued and a system of multiple official rates was established.

h. Beginning June 23.

i. Beginning October 3.

j. Beginning August 29.

k. Auction abolished August 28.

l. Beginning January 12, 1959.

m. A new peso equal to 100 old pesos was introduced on January 1, 1970.

n. On September 20, 1971, a dual exchange rate system was introduced, consisting of an
    official market with a fixed rate of 5.00 pesos per U.S. dollar and a financial market
    in which the rate is allowed to fluctuate.

o. August 1974.

Continued in SALA, 17-2401 through 2413.

Table 3206

LATIN AMERICA OFFICIAL, COMMERCIAL, FINANCIAL, PARALLEL, PREFERENTIAL, AND FREE MARKET EXCHANGE RATES, 20 L, 1988

(NC per US)

	Country	Currency	Rate	1988 Average	Current[1]
A.	ARGENTINA	Austral	Official	5.8	650.0
B.	BOLIVIA	Boliviano	Official	2.4	2.6
			Parallel	2.4	2.6
C.	BRAZIL	New Cruzado	Official	.2	1.8
			Parallel	.3	3.5
D.	CHILE	Peso	Official	245.2	271.8
			Parallel	282.0	290.0
E.	COLOMBIA	Peso	Official	297.0	389.0
			Parallel	297.6	390.0
F.	COSTA RICA	Colón	Official	75.1	78.3
			Parallel	78.0	85.0
G.	CUBA	Peso	Official	.8	.8
			Parallel	5.8	6.0
H.	DOMINICAN REP.	Peso	Free	5.6	6.4
I.	ECUADOR	Sucre	Commercial	287.9	518.0
			Free	453.5	545.0
J.	EL SALVADOR	Colón	Commercial	5.0	5.0
			Parallel	5.4	5.9
K.	GUATEMALA	Quetzal	Official	2.7	2.7
			Parallel	2.7	2.7
L.	HAITI	Gourde	Official	5.0	5.0
M.	HONDURAS	Lempiral	Official	2.0	2.0
			Parallel	2.7	3.3
N.	MEXICO	Peso	Official	2,248.9	2,436.2
			Free	2,285.6	2,504.9
O.	NICARAGUA	Nuevo Córdoba	Commercial	200.0	20,900.0
			Parallel	9,600.0	22,000.0
P.	PANAMA	Balboa	Official	1.0	1.0
Q.	PARAGUAY	Guaraní	Free	921.9	1,178.9
R.	PERU	Inti	Official	160.3	2,065.26
			Parallel	265.0	2,972.3
S.	URUGUAY	Peso	Official	353.5	594.0
T.	VENEZUELA	Bolívar	Free	14.5	37.2

1. Current data to October 7, 1989.

SOURCE: Adapted from *Latin America Weekly Report*, WR-86-13, March 28, 1986; WR-86-24, June 26, 1986; WR-86-37, Sept. 25, 1986; WR-86-50, Dec. 25, 1986; WR-89-28, July 20, 1989.

Table 3207

PARALLEL OR BLACK MARKET EXCHANGE RATES OF U.S. DOLLARS, 16 L, 1948–87
(NC per US, YE)

Year	A. ARGENTINA	B. BOLIVIA	C. BRAZIL	D. CHILE	E. COLOMBIA	F. COSTA RICA	G. CUBA	H. DOMINICAN REP.
1948	9.25	91.00	26.55	65.55	?	7.00	?	?
1949	15.80	116.00	30.75	99.10	?	8.80	?	?
1950	16.50	130.00	32.00	72.50	?	8.75	?	?
1951	27.00	210.00	29.75	94.00	?	7.50	?	?
1952	23.15	275.00	37.25	135.50	3.05	6.66	?	?
1953	20.10	950.00	56.50	218.00	3.03	6.66	?	?
1954	26.70	1,820.00	78.00	315.00	3.46	6.65	?	?
1955	36.00	4,050.00	68.50	680.00	4.13	6.70	?	?
1956	36.55	8,000.00	67.50	601.00	6.30	6.65	?	?
1957	37.20	8,500.00	91.50	785.00	8.22	6.90	?	?
1958	70.50	11,940.00	139.50	1,120.00	7.00	6.90	?	?
1959	83.20	12,100.00	202.00	1,056.00	7.24	6.92	1.65	?
1960	82.65	11,990.00	204.00	1.06	9.05	7.40	5.25	?
1961	82.53	11,990.00	405.00	1.20	11.22	8.00	5.50	?
1962	134.00	13.00	808.00	2.41	10.00	7.85	22.50	?
1963	132.50	13.00	1,220.00	3.11	12.85	7.80	25.00	?
1964	192.00	13.00	1,850.00	4.50	18.35	8.00	23.00	1.32
1965	248.00	12.55	2,200.00	6.10	19.75	7.85	22.00	1.25
1966	269.00	14.00	2,210.00	6.55	18.25	7.75	22.00	1.25
1967	350.00	14.25	3.45	10.00	18.00	8.65	8.00	1.20
1968	350.00	13.55	4.05	10.25	19.40	8.35	5.00	1.22
1969	352.00	17.00	4.85	14.85	24.50	7.50	6.00	1.23
1970	4.38*	20.00	5.15	28.00	23.30	6.70	7.00	1.23
1971	10.10	19.75	6.35	74.70	25.50	11.00	9.70	1.23
1972	11.60	23.00	6.85	340.00	27.00	11.50	9.90	1.22
1973	11.00	21.00	6.80	790.00	29.80	9.10	9.75	1.21
1974	23.15	21.00	8.15	2,010.00	34.50	10.00	9.25	1.25
1975	136.00	21.00	13.55	8.90*	37.70	9.30	8.60	1.28
1976	280.00	21.20	15.55	19.00	38.20	9.95	10.40	1.34
1977	605.00	21.00	20.10	28.30	41.30	8.90	11.74	1.37
1978	1,011.00	23.00	26.50	34.80	44.75	9.00	13.60	1.42
1979	1,620.00	25.00	46.00	41.00	51.50	9.80	13.00	1.30
1980	1,999.00	30.50	66.80	41.30	59.25	14.50	18.00	1.37
1981	10,700.00	38.50	158.00	43.00	70.50	50.00	22.00	1.35
1982	63,500.00	350.00	435.00	95.00	107.00	68.00	19.00	1.70
1983	25.90*	2,000.00	1,350.00	103.00	137.00	49.00	18.50	1.85
1984	179.00	24,100.00	3,775.00	140.00	187.75	58.00	22.00	3.13
1985	1.12*	1,600,000.00	15,625.00	225.00	243.90	66.50	25.00	3.35
1986	2.10	2,130,000.00	31.50*	232.60	249.00	76.90	29.00	3.22
1987[a]	2.63	2.17*	37.04	238.00		76.90	32.50	3.23

Table 3207 (Continued)

PARALLEL OR BLACK MARKET EXCHANGE RATES OF U.S. DOLLARS, 16 L, 1948–87

(NC per US, YE)

Year	I. ECUADOR	J. EL SALVADOR	N. MEXICO	O. NICARAGUA	Q. PARAGUAY	R. PERU	S. URUGUAY	T. VENEZUELA
1948	18.00	?	7.10	6.55	?	15.20	2.38	?
1949	18.35	?	8.72	7.05	?	16.25	3.10	?
1950	18.60	?	8.65	7.65	?	15.10	2.07	?
1951	17.75	?	8.64	7.15	31.50	15.60	2.38	?
1952	17.50	?	8.61	7.32	49.50	15.65	2.73	?
1953	17.40	?	8.60	7.75	58.75	19.75	3.06	?
1954	17.55	?	12.51	7.20	68.50	19.00	3.22	?
1955	17.40	?	12.50	7.55	68.25	19.50	3.62	?
1956	19.25	?	12.50	7.50	112.00	18.96	3.76	?
1957	16.64	?	12.49	7.65	110.20	19.10	4.59	?
1958	16.65	?	12.49	7.55	112.60	25.10	10.70	?
1959	17.41	?	12.49	7.85	128.00	27.71	11.10	?
1960	17.75	?	12.49	9.00	126.00	26.75	11.02	4.65
1961	23.25	3.25	12.49	9.10	126.50	27.35	10.97	4.65
1962	22.20	3.10	12.49	9.10	140.00	27.00	11.30	4.52
1963	19.00	3.10	12.48	8.65	153.00	27.80	17.25	4.53
1964	19.25	2.60	12.49	8.64	157.00	28.00	24.00	4.49
1965	18.75	2.70	12.49	8.00	142.00	27.65	69.00	4.54
1966	22.25	2.85	12.49	8.35	140.00	27.40	77.00	4.51
1967	20.40	2.94	12.49	8.25	136.00	40.50	200.00	4.51
1968	22.35	2.92	12.49	8.35	142.50	44.70	251.00	4.51
1969	21.95	2.94	12.49	8.33	146.00	46.00	255.00	4.50
1970	28.50	2.94	12.49	8.34	152.00	58.00	290.00	4.50
1971	27.80	2.94	12.50	8.34	156.00	70.00	640.00	4.41
1972	27.70	2.94	12.50	8.50	170.00	70.00	940.00	4.40
1973	25.00	2.94	12.50	8.33	150.00	72.00	925.00	4.30
1974	25.15	2.94	12.50	8.33	141.00	59.00	2,470.00	4.30
1975	26.20	3.00	12.50	8.40	142.00	70.00	290.00	4.30
1976	27.80	3.22	21.00	8.40	136.00	90.50	410.00	4.30
1977	26.00	3.30	23.00	8.60	133.00	145.00	5.32*	4.30
1978	26.90	3.00	23.00	12.00	145.00	213.00	7.04	4.30
1979	27.10	3.90	23.00	20.00	137.00	252.00	8.40	4.30
1980	28.25	5.00	24.00	19.15	135.00	341.00	9.96	4.30
1981	32.20	4.60	27.25	30.40	172.00	503.00	11.20	4.30
1982	65.00	5.10	160.00	37.00	291.00	989.00	33.00	4.65
1983	88.50	4.95	173.00	95.00	350.00	2,350.00	43.25	13.00
1984	128.25	5.00	232.00	447.00	447.00	5,885.00	76.95	13.35
1985	141.50	14.30	465.00	1,535.00	1,000.00	21,000.00	140.00	18.00
1986	161.50	9.10	980.00	5,100.00	885.00	22.75*	200.00	25.00
1987[a]	166.60	9.15	1,205.00	5,000.00	880.00	22.75	212.75	24.40

a. March.

SOURCE: *Pick's Currency Yearbook*, and since 1984 *World Currency Yearbook*, various years.

Table 3208

CENTRAL AMERICA OFFICIAL, FINANCIAL, AND BLACK MARKET EXCHANGE RATES, 7 L, 1985–87
(NC per US)

PART I. FIRST QUARTER 1985

Country	Official	Financial or Tourist	Parallel, or Black Market
K. GUATEMALA (quetzal)	1.00	1.50-1.79	1.65
Belize (dollar)	2.00	~	~
J. EL SALVADOR (colón)	2.50	3.75	4.15-5.00
M. HONDURAS (lempira)	2.00	~	2.75
O. NICARAGUA (córdoba)	10.00	28.50	500-600
F. COSTA RICA (colón)	20.00	47.95	53
P. PANAMA (balboa)	1.00	~	~

PART II. SECOND QUARTER 1985

	Official	Parallel or Financial[1]	Free or Black Market[2]
K. GUATEMALA (quetzal)	1.00	2.00-2.85	2.90
Belize (dollar)	2.00	~	~
J. EL SALVADOR (colón)	2.50	3.75	4.65-4.90
M. HONDURAS (Lempira)	2.00	~	2.75
O. NICARAGUA (córdoba)	10.00	48.00-60.00	500-600
F. COSTA RICA (colón)	20.00	49.50	53
P. PANAMA (balboa)	1.00	~	~

PART III. THIRD QUARTER 1986

K. GUATEMALA (quetzal)	1.00-2.50	2.90-2.98	2.97
Belize (dollar)	2.00	~	~
J. EL SALVADOR (colón)	5.00	~	5.40-5.45
M. HONDURAS (Lempira)	2.00	~	2.30-2.35
O. NICARAGUA (córdoba)	28.00[a]	1,200	2,000
F. COSTA RICA (colón)	20.00[b]	56.30	57.50
P. PANAMA (balboa)	1.00	~	~

PART IV. SECOND QUARTER 1987

Belize (dollar)	2.00	~	~
F. COSTA RICA (colón)	20.00	60.50	63.50
J. EL SALVADOR (colón)	5.00	~	5.30
K. GUATEMALA (quetzal)	2.50	2.67	2.66
M. HONDURAS (lempira)	2.00	~	2.30
O. NICARAGUA (córdoba)	70.00	4,500	7,000
P. PANAMA (balboa)	1.00	~	~

1. An alternative, officially authorized, exchange rate for certain specified transactions. In some countries (such as Guatemala) it fluctuates; in others (such as Nicaragua) it is fixed.
2. Estimated, since in some countries (Honduras, Costa Rica) this market is clandestine, or (as in Nicaragua) the rate fluctuates widely.

a. For oil imports.
b. For students.

SOURCE: *Central America Report* (Guatemala City), first quarter 1985, second quarter 1985, third quarter 1986, and second quarter 1987.

Table 3209

ANNUAL VALUE OF THE U.S. DOLLAR IN BOLIVIAN PESOS, 1937–85

Year	Official Value — Average	Official Value — End of Year if Varies from Average	Parallel Market — End of Year
1937	17		
1938	30		
1939	32		
1940	39		
1941	46		
1942	46		
1943	42		
1944	42		
1945	42		
1946	42		
1947	42		
1948	42		91
1949	42		116
1950	60		130
1951	60		210
1952	60		275
1953	190		950
1954	190		1,820
1955	190		4,050
1956	7,760		8,000
1957	8,330	8,565	8,500
1958	9,698	11,935	11,940
1959	11,880		12,100
1960	11,880		11,990
1961	11,880		11,990
1962	11,880		11,990
1963	11.9[a]		13.0[a]
1964	11.9		13.0
1965	11.9		12.6
1966	11.9		14.0
1967	11.9		14.3
1968	11.9		13.6
1969	11.9		17.0
1970	11.9		20.0
1971	11.9		19.8
1972	13.3	20	23
1973	20.0		21
1974	20.0		21
1975	20.0		21
1976	20.0		21
1977	20.0		21
1978	20.0		23
1979	20.4	25	25
1980	24.5		
1981	24.5		
1982	64	196	290
1983	230	500	1,200[b]
1984	2,314	9,000	23,381[c]
1985	455,083	1,589,000	1,715,000[d]

a. Conversion: 1,000 to 1.
b. Average = 695.
c. Average = 8,191.
d. Average = 829,833.

SOURCE: James W. Wilkie, "Bolivia: Ironies in the National Revolutionary Process, 1952-1986," SALA, 25, ch. 35.

Table 3210

MONTHLY VALUE OF THE U.S. DOLLAR IN BOLIVIAN PESOS, 1984–86

Year	Month	A. Official Value	B. Parallel Market
1982	Nov.	200	250
	Dec.	200	290
1983	Jan.	200	390
	Feb.	200	500
	March	200	500
	April	200	420
	May	200	380
	June	200	390
	July	200	600
	Aug.	200	780
	Sept.	200	785
	Oct.	200	1,050
	Nov.	500	1,350
	Dec.	500	1,200
1984	Jan.	500	1,900
	Feb.	500	2,100
	March	500	2,780
	April	2,000	3,560
	May	2,000	3,480
	June	2,000	3,330
	July	2,000	3,500
	Aug.	5,000[a]	7,190
	Sept.	5,000[a]	13,515
	Oct.	5,000[a]	15,160
	Nov.	9,000	18,394
	Dec.	9,000	23,381
1985	Jan.	9,000	68,000
	Feb.	50,000	132,000
	March	50,000	126,000
	April	50,000	162,000
	May	75,000	250,000
	June	75,000	470,000
	July	75,000	847,000
	Aug.	75,000	1,149,000
	Sept.	1,081,000	1,065,000
	Oct.	1,107,000	1,118,000
	Nov.	1,225,000	1,333,000
	Dec.	1,589,000	1,715,000
1986	Jan.	2,040,000	2,279,000
	Feb.	1,840,000	1,890,000
	Oct.	1,921,000	1,935,000

a. Rate for essential imports = 2,000.

SOURCE: James W. Wilkie, "Bolivia: Ironies in the National Revolutionary Process, 1952-1986," SALA, 25, ch. 35.

Table 3211

EXCHANGE RATE AGREEMENTS, 19 L
(As of March 31, 1987)

Currency Pegged to U.S. Dollar	Exchange Rate Adjusted According to a Set of Indicators[1]	Other Managed Floating	Independently Floating
J. EL SALVADOR	C. BRAZIL	A. ARGENTINA	B. BOLIVIA
K. GUATEMALA	D. CHILE	F. COSTA RICA	H. DOMINICAN REP.
L. HAITI	E. COLOMBIA	I. ECUADOR	S. URUGUAY
M. HONDURAS			UNITED STATES
O. NICARAGUA		N. MEXICO	
P. PANAMA		R. PERU	
Q. PARAGUAY			
T. VENEZUELA			

1. Includes exchange arrangements under which the exchange rate is adjusted at relatively frequent intervals, on the basis of indicators determined by the respective member countries.

SOURCE: IMF-IFS, June 1987.

Table 3212

IMF U.S. DOLLAR EFFECTIVE EXCHANGE RATE INDEX (MERM),[1] 1970–88

(1980 = 100, YA)

Year	Index	Year	Index
1970	128.6	1980	100.0
1971	125.4	1981	112.7
1972	116.4	1982	125.9
1973	106.8	1983	133.2
1974	109.5	1984	143.7
1975	106.7	1985	150.2
1976	112.2	1986	122.5
1977	111.7	1987	108.0
1978	102.1	1988	101.7
1979	99.9		

1. Combines the exchange rates here between U.S. currency and other major currencies with weights derived from IMF's Multilateral Exchange Rate Model (MERM).

SOURCE: IMF-IFS-Y, 1985, line amx; and IMF-IFS, June 1987, line amx; and IMF-IFS, July 1988, line amx; July 1989, line amx.

Table 3213

ARGENTINA EVOLUTION OF REAL EXCHANGE RATES, 1970–87

		(1980 = 100)	
		Indexes of Effective Real Exchange Rate[1]	
Year and Quarter	Nominal Exchange Rate (Australes per Dollar)	Exports	Imports
1970–79	.00003	143.7	148.3
1980	.0002	100.0	100.0
1981	.0005[a]	134.4	143.1
1982	.002[a]	166.3	169.6
1983	.01	157.9	166.6
1984	.07	150.2	168.4
1985	.60	171.8	190.8
1986	.94	189.6	190.3
1987	2.14	216.0	212.8
1985			
I	.25	162.3	186.4
II	.56	164.5	195.4
III	.80	178.5	196.6
IV	.80	181.8	184.7
1986			
I	.80	188.4	190.2
II	.85	188.1	189.2
III	.97	188.7	189.1
IV	1.15	193,0	192,6
1987			
I	1.41	210.4	208.4
II	1.61	214.4	211.9
III	2.15	210.4	207.3
IV	3.42	229.1	224.0

1. These indexes were obtained by multiplying the weightings of exports or imports by the real exchange rate indexes. The products are added together to give the effective real exchange rate indexes.

a. The second half of 1981 and 1982, for which the figure used is the 50/50 average of the commercial rate and the financial rate.

SOURCE: ECLA-S, 1987, vol. 1, p. 101.

Table 3214

BOLIVIA EVOLUTION OF REAL EXCHANGE RATES
AND PRICE INDEXES, 1975–87

| Year and Quarter | Nominal Exchange Rates in Pesos per Dollar | | 1980 = 100 | |
	Official Exchange Rate[1] for Buyers	Parallel Market Exchange Rate[2] for Buyers	Indexes of Effective Real Exchange Rate[3]	
			Exports	Imports
1975–79	.000018		104.1	110.1
1980	.000025		100.0	100.0
1981	.000025		67.7	78.7
1982	.0001[a]	.0002	105.2	130.6
1983	.0002	.0007	65.5	77.5
1984	.002	.008	45.5	53.6
1985	.45	.68	54.2	66.6
1986	1.92	1.96	90.3	113.0
1987	2.06	2.08	89.4	114.4
1985				
I	.03	.10	41.0	50.2
II	.06	.28	31.2	37.2
III	.40	.98	46.3	56.7
IV	1.28	1.37	98.3	122.1
1986				
I	1.95	2.04	98.4	124.1
II	1.91	1.95	89.6	111.8
III	1.91	1.93	86.9	108.4
IV	1.92	1.94	86.2	107.8
1987				
I	1.95	1.96	86.3	108.2
II	2.04	2.06	88.7	113.7
III	2.09	2.10	91.2	115.3
IV	2.15	2.18	92.4	120.4

1. Exchange rates used in the banking system for converting foreign currency into domestic currency.
2. Quarterly average exchange rate.
3. These indexes were obtained by multiplying the weightings of exports or imports by the real exchange rate indexes. The products are added together to give the effective real exchange rate indexes.

a. During the period March–Oct. 1982, use was made of an exchange rate obtained from the average of the official rate weighted 40 percent and of the open market rate weighted 60 percent.

SOURCE: ECLA-S, 1987, vol. 1, p. 133.

Figure 32:1

BOLIVIA OFFICIAL AND FREE EXCHANGE RATES, 1982–84

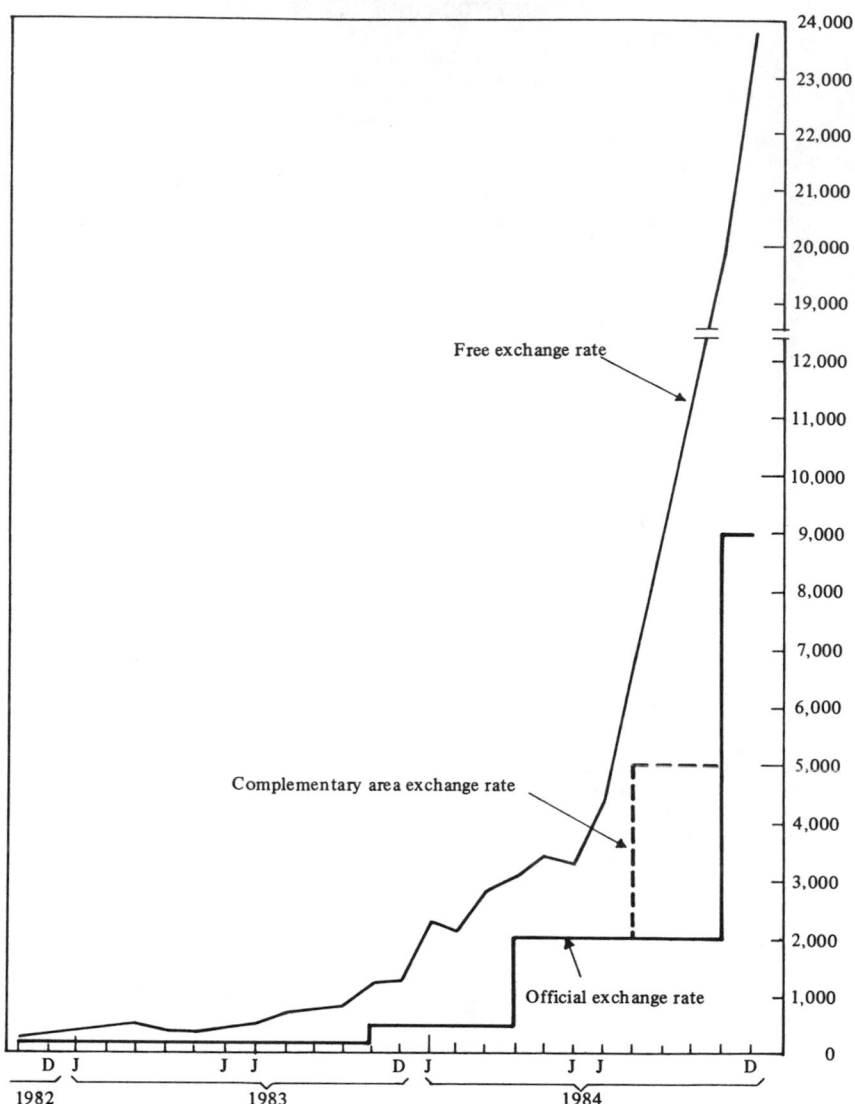

SOURCE: ECLA-S, 1984, vol. 1, p. 110.

Table 3215

BRAZIL EVOLUTION OF REAL EXCHANGE RATES, 1970–87

1980 = 100

| | | Indexes of Effective Exchange Rate[1] | | |
| | | | Imports | |
Year and Quarter	Nominal Exchange Rate (Cruzados per Dollar)	Exports	(1)	(2)[a]
1970–79	.01	78.5	65.9	80.1
1980	.05	100.0	100.0	100.0
1981	.09	83.3	89.4	86.3
1982	.18	80.9	85.7	82.7
1983	.58	96.4	96.5	98.6
1984	1.85	90.4	90.2	93.6
1985	6.20	91.9	91.0	95.5
1986	13.65	93.0	72.4	91.8
1987	39.23	96.1	72.9	92.3
1985				
I	3.76	84.8	86.4	89.6
II	5.23	94.5	94.7	99.3
III	6.80	95.3	93.7	98.4
IV	9.01	93.1	89.3	94.8
1986				
I	12.73	89.2	75.1	89.2
II	13.84	94.4	71.8	93.5
III	13.84	95.2	71.5	93.5
IV	14.21	93.1	71.0	90.8
1987				
I	18.23	95.2	71.3	90.7
II	31.32	94.4	71.9	90.5
III	47.31	98.8	75.8	95.7
IV	60.06	96.0	72.4	92.2

1. These indexes were obtained by multiplying the weightings of exports or imports by the real exchange rate indexes. The products were added together to give the effective real exchange rate indexes.

a. Excludes Saudi Arabia, Iraq, and Nigeria.

SOURCE: ECLA-S, 1987, vol. 1, p. 162.

Table 3216

CHILE EVOLUTION OF REAL EXCHANGE RATES, 1970–87

	Nominal Exchange Rate[1]		1980 = 100			
			Indexes of Effective Real Exchange Rate			
	Official		Exports		Imports	
Year and Quarter	Principal	Parallel	(1)[a]	(2)[b]	(1)[a]	(2)[b]
1970–79	11		128.2	98.1	123.7	94.8
1980	39		100.0	100.0	100.0	100.0
1981	39		90.1	82.9	92.9	85.5
1982	51	- -	107.2	95.5	112.3	100.0
1983	79	92	113.8	112.9	117.7	116.8
1984	99	113	114.2	116.6	118.6	121.1
1985	161	180	132.1	144.9	138.1	151.4
1986	193	206	146.4	165.5	145.6	164.5
1987	220	231	151.8	173.8	144.8	165.8
1985						
I	136	139	120.1	128.6	127.8	136.8
II	152	172	125.6	136.6	132.2	143.8
III	176	200	137.5	153.5	143.1	159.7
IV	181	210	145.1	160.7	149.4	165.4
1986						
I	187	202	150.7	164.5	152.2	166.1
II	189	199	147.3	162.2	146.8	161.6
III	195	207	143.5	167.4	141.7	165.3
IV	202	216	144.0	167.8	141.5	165.0
1987						
I	206	217	154.3	169.9	146.2	161.0
II	214	227	152.6	172.9	145.3	164.7
III	225	235	146.2	172.6	140.6	166.1
IV	233	246	154.3	179.9	147.0	171.5

1. Pesos per dollar.

a. These indexes were obtained by multiplying the weightings of exports or imports by the real exchange rate indexes. The products are added together to give the effective real rate indexes. The wholesale price index for domestic products was used.

b. A procedure similar to that described in Note a was employed, except that the calculations were based on the following price indexes: 1975–78, corrected consumer price index of R. Cortázar and J. Marshall; 1979–85, consumer price index of the National Statistical Institute (INT).

SOURCE: ECLA-S, 1987, vol. 1 p. 294.

Table 3217

COLOMBIA EVOLUTION OF REAL
EXCHANGE RATES, 1970–87

Year and Quarter	Nominal Exchange Rate (Pesos per Dollar)	1980 = 100	
		Indexes of Effective Real Exchange Rate[1]	
		Exports	Imports
1970–79	29.40	111.8	113.9
1980	47.28	100.0	100.0
1981	54.49	92.2	97.4
1982	64.08	85.9	91.2
1983	78.85	85.4	90.5
1984	100.82	90.4	97.2
1985	142.30	102.6	110.4
1986	194.26	127.8	131.8
1987	242.61	139.8	140.2
1985			
I	118.86	89.5	98.2
II	135.43	96.6	104.5
III	150.28	105.8	113.2
IV	164.68	118.4	125.6
1986			
I	176.88	122.3	128.1
II	188.44	124.5	129.4
III	199.40	130.1	134.0
IV	212.50	135.2	135.8
1987			
I	224.96	134.6	134.2
II	237.33	138.5	138.9
III	249.25	140.4	141.4
IV	258.89	145.8	146.4

1. These indexes were obtained by multiplying the weightings of exports or imports by the real exchange rate indexes. The products were added together to give the effective real exchange rate indexes.

SOURCE: ECLA-S, 1987, vol. 1, p. 197.

Table 3218

COSTA RICA EVOLUTION OF REAL EXCHANGE RATES, 1970–87

Year and Quarter	Nominal Exchange Rate[1] (Colones per Dollar)	1980 = 100 Indexes of Effective Real Exchange Rate[2]	
		Exports	Imports
1970–79	7.74	106.7	104.5
1980	9.23	100.0	100.0
1981	20.58	145.0	150.4
1982	38.93	129.1	130.4
1983	42.20	114.3	113.4
1984	44.54	113.8	113.1
1985	50.45	121.5	120.3
1986	56.00	121.4	118.0
1987	62.78	129.0	121.6
1985			
I	48.30	114.0	114.8
II	49.49	118.0	118.2
III	51.27	123.7	121.4
IV	52.75	130.3	126.9
1986			
I	54.00	126.8	123.5
II	55.29	122.0	119.1
III	56.62	117.4	114.8
IV	58.03	119.3	114.7
1987			
I	59.40	123.7	114.5
II	61.34	127.7	119.9
III	63.40	129.0	122.7
IV	66.97	135.4	129.1

1. These indexes were obtained by multiplying the weightings of exports or imports by the real exchange rate indexes. The products are added together to give the effective real exchange rate indexes. In calculating these indexes for Costa Rica, the wholesale price index was used.

SOURCE: ECLA-S, 1987, vol. 1, p. 224.

Table 3219

CUBA EVOLUTION OF REAL EXCHANGE RATE INDEXES, 1980–86

Year and Quarter	Cuban Pesos per:				
	US Dollar	Pound Sterling	Swiss Franc	Deutsch Mark	Japanese[1] Yen
1980	.7113	1.6432	.4294	.3968	.3113
1981	.7814	1.6071	.4001	.3510	.3572
1982	.8333	1.4686	.4139	.3443	.3372
1983	.8598	1.3167	.4128	.3411	.3609
1984	.8861	1.1999	.3820	.3141	.3755
1985	.9174	1.1777	.3731	.3096	.3829
1986	.8664	1.2100	.4587	.3802	.4901

1. 100 Yen.

SOURCE: ECLA-S, 1986, vol. 1, p. 256.

Table 3220

DOMINICAN REPUBLIC EVOLUTION OF
REAL EXCHANGE RATES, 1970–87

Year and Quarter	Nominal Exchange Rate (Pesos per Dollar)	1980 = 100	
		Indexes of Effective Real Exchange Rate[1]	
		Exports	Imports
1970–79	1.18	96.0	98.1
1980	1.26	100.0	100.0
1981	1.28	99.9	93.7
1982	1.46	106.6	86.5
1983	1.60	112.2	88.1
1984	2.74	153.5	123.8
1985	3.12	126.8	106.3
1986	2.91	108.5	88.7
1987	3.84	129.3	104.3
1985			
I	3.27	141.7	118.8
II	3.17	129.9	110.1
III	3.00	119.0	99.2
IV	3.00	116.6	97.2
1986			
I	2.87	108.1	89.5
II	2.84	108.2	88.7
III	2.86	107.5	87.6
IV	3.05	109.9	88.8
1987			
I	3.17	113.5	88.9
II	3.59	124.6	99.6
III	3.89	129.5	105.3
IV	4.73	149.6	123.3

1. These indexes were obtained by multiplying the weightings of exports or imports by the real exchange rate indexes. The products are added together to give the effective rate indexes.

SOURCE: ECLA-S, 1987, vol. 1, p. 619.

Table 3221

ECUADOR EVOLUTION OF REAL EXCHANGE RATES, 1970–87

| Year and Quarter | Nominal Exchange Rates (Sucres per Dollar) | | | 1980 = 100 | |
| | | | | Indexes of Effective Real Exchange Rate[1] | |
	Official	Free[2]	Free	Exports	Imports
1970–79	25	~	~	116.7	110.8
1980	25	27	28	100.0	100.0
1981	25	28	31	93.2	90.4
1982	30	34	50	97.7	92.3
1983	44	83	84	97.1	90.0
1984	63	93	96	132.3	120.7
1985	71	97	116	127.2	116.0
1986	96	123	151	129.3	129.4
1987	96	171	219	143.2	149.8
1985					
I	67	97	122	136.7	122.2
II	67	97	115	128.5	115.5
III	67	97	109	123.0	112.6
IV	83	97	124	120.7	113.8
1986					
I	96	106	140	122.0	119.0
II	96	110	164	118.9	118.2
III	96	131	158	135.1	137.2
IV	96	147	145	141.1	143.2
1987					
I	96	147	149	133.9	138.3
II	96	155	178	133.3	139.3
III	96	173	299	143.4	148.0
IV	96	209	249	162.2	173.6

1. These indexes were obtained by multiplying the weightings of exports or imports by the real exchange rate indexes. The products are added together to give the effective rate indexes.
2. Central Bank of Ecuador.

SOURCE: ECLA-S, 1987, vol. 1, p. 324.

Table 3222

GUATEMALA EVOLUTION OF REAL
EXCHANGE RATES, 1970–87

Year and Quarter	Nominal Exchange Rate (Quetzales per Dollar)		1980 = 100 Indexes of Effective Real Exchange Rate[1]	
	Official	Banking Rate	Exports	Imports
1970–79	1		98.9	98.0
1980	1		100.0	100.0
1981	1		93.7	94.4
1982	1		96.3	93.8
1983	1		96.6	91.9
1984	1		97.0	91.7
1985	1	2.76	87.2	81.4
1986	1.88	2.87	107.9	101.7
1987	2.50	2.70	143.1	130.7
1985				
I	1	1.60	93.9	89.0
II	1	2.61	91.4	86.2
III	1	3.53	83.2	77.0
IV	1	3.33	80.2	73.4
1986				
I	1	2.90	63.4	61.0
II	1.50	2.96	87.2	82.9
III	2.50	2.95	140.2	132.0
IV	2.50	2.68	140.8	131.0
1987				
I	2.50	2.78	141.4	128.0
II	2.50	2.72	143.5	130.7
III	2.50	2.72	142.8	131.3
IV	2.50	2.59	144.5	132.7

1. These indexes were obtained by multiplying the weightings of exports or imports by the real exchange rate indexes. The products are added together to give the effective rate indexes.

SOURCE: ECLA-S, 1987, vol. 1, p. 372.

Table 3223

HONDURAS EVOLUTION OF REAL
EXCHANGE RATES, 1970–87

Year and Quarter	Nominal Exchange Rate (Lempiras per Dollar)	1980 = 100	
		Indexes of Effective Real Exchange Rate[1]	
		Exports	Imports
1970–79	2	93.5	92.9
1980	2	100.0	100.0
1981	2	95.5	95.6
1982	2	87.7	86.6
1983	2	81.7	81.4
1984	2	79.0	79.7
1985	2	76.9	78.5
1986	2	76.4	78.2
1987	2	78.8	80.1
1985			
I	2	76.5	78.2
II	2	77.0	78.8
III	2	76.1	77.8
IV	2	77.8	79.3
1986			
I	2	78.1	79.7
II	2	76.1	77.3
III	2	75.6	77.9
IV	2	75.8	77.7
1987			
I	2	77.5	78.9
II	2	78.8	80.2
III	2	78.5	80.1
IV	2	80.2	81.3

1. These indexes were obtained by multiplying the weightings of exports or imports by the real exchange rate indexes. The products were added together to give the effective rate indexes.

SOURCE: ECLA-S, 1987, vol. 1, p. 416.

Table 3224

MEXICO EVOLUTION OF REAL EXCHANGE RATES, 1970–87

| Year and Quarter | Official Exchange Rate (Pesos per Dollar) | | Indexes of Effective Real Exchange Rate[1] 1980 = 100 | | | |
| | Free | Controlled | Exports | | Imports | |
			(1)[a]	(2)[b]	(1)[a]	(2)[b]
1970–79	16		109.4		108.0	~
1980	23		100.0		100.0	
1981	25		90.5		91.1	
1982	56		133.2		135.0	
1983	150	120	169.8	135.7	173.9	138.9
1984	185	168	124.3	112.6	127.4	115.4
1985	310	257	133.1	111.2	136.0	113.7
1986	637	612	153.4	146.4	154.1	147.1
1987	1,406	1,378	155.2	153.3	154.6	152.7
1985						
I	218	201	109.8	101.1	112.9	103.9
II	236	219	107.5	99.6	110.2	102.0
III	336	275	142.5	116.5	145.5	118.9
IV	451	334	172.4	127.6	175.3	129.8
1986						
I	463	424	147.3	134.8	148.8	136.2
II	554	522	151.7	143.1	152.5	143.8
III	687	666	155.8	151.0	156.0	151.3
IV	847	836	158.6	156.6	159.2	157.1
1987						
I	1,018	1,026	162.2	163.5	162.4	163.7
II	1,230	1,242	155.6	157.1	155.3	156.8
III	1,452	1,461	144.4	145.3	144.0	144.9
IV	1,923	1,785	158.4	147.1	156.8	145.5

1. These indexes were obtained by multiplying the weightings of exports or imports by the real exchange rate indexes. The products are added together to give the effective real exchange rate indexes.

a. Based on the free rate.
b. Based on the controlled rate.

SOURCE: ECLA-S, 1987, vol. 1, p. 446.

Table 3225

OFFICIAL AND REAL MEXICAN PESO VALUES COMPARED TO MEXICO'S REAL TRADE DEFICITS, 1952-82

	(A)	(B)	(C)	(D)	(E)	(F)	(G)	(H)
						Mexico YE		
Year	Official Peso Exchange Rate for Dollars (YA)	Mexico's Wholesale Price Index YA; 1963=100.0	U.S. Wholesale Price Index	Peso 1963 Parity Exchange Rate[1] 12.5 in Col. A Times (B/C)	Peso's Value Index (D/A)[2] 1963=100.0	Merchandise Trade Balance FOB M US	Trade Index 1963 Equals -100.0	Real Merchandise Balance Index[3] 1963 Equals -100 (G/C)
1952	8.650	65.6	93.9	8.7	100.6	~	~	~
1953	8.650	64.3	92.6	8.7	100.6	-169	-84.1	-90.8
1954	12.500	70.5	92.8	9.5	76.0	-92	-45.8	-49.4
1955	12.500	80.1	93.0	10.8	86.4	21	10.5	11.3
1956	12.500	83.8	96.1	10.9	87.2	-174	-86.6	-90.1
1957	12.500	87.5	98.7	11.1	88.8	-362	-180.1	-182.5
1958	12.500	91.4	100.2	11.4	91.2	-338	-168.2	-167.9
1959	12.500	92.4	100.4	11.5	92.0	-220	-109.5	-109.1
1960	12.500	96.9	100.6	12.0	96.0	-354	-176.1	-175.0
1961	12.500	97.7	100.2	12.2	97.6	-260	-129.4	-129.1
1962	12.500	99.6	100.4	12.4	99.2	-167	-83.1	-82.8
1963	12.500	100.0	100.0	12.5	100.0	-201	-100.0	-100.0
1964	12.500	104.3	100.2	13.0	104.0	-370	-184.1	-183.7
1965	12.500	106.4	102.2	13.0	104.0	-352	-175.1	-171.3
1966	12.500	107.6	105.7	12.7	101.6	-337	-167.7	-158.7
1967	12.500	110.7	105.9	13.1	104.8	-608	-302.5	-285.6
1968	12.500	112.9	108.5	13.0	104.0	-634	-315.4	-290.7
1969	12.500	115.8	112.8	12.8	102.4	-529	-263.2	-233.2
1970	12.500	122.5	116.9	13.1	104.8	-888	-441.8	-377.9
1971	12.500	127.3	120.8	13.2	105.6	-749	-372.6	-308.4
1972	12.500	130.7	126.1	13.0	104.0	-894	-444.8	-352.7
1973	12.500	151.4	142.6	13.3	106.4	-1,515	-753.7	-528.5
1974	12.500	185.5	169.4	13.7	109.6	-2,791	-1,388.6	-819.7
1975	12.500	204.9	185.2	13.8	138.0	-3,271	-1,627.4	-878.7
1976	15,426	250.6	193.7	16.2	105.0	-2,296	-1,142.3	-589.7
1977	22.573	353.7	205.6	21.5	95.2	-1,021	-508.0	-247.0
1978	22.767	409.4	221.7	23.1	101.5	-1,746	-868.7	-391.8
1979	22.805	484.4	249.4	24.3	106.6	-2,830	-1,408.0	-564.6
1980	22.951	603.1	284.4	26.5	115.5	-2,310	-1,149.3	-404.1
1981	24.515	752.0	310.2	30.3	123.6	-3,329	-1,656.2	-533.9
1982[a]	46.758	1,010.2	316.1[c]	39.9	85.3	116[b]	57.8[b]	33.9[b]

1. The year 1963 was selected for parity comparison because of the following characteristics: low increase of .4% in Mexican wholesale price index (column B); relatively low deficit of $201 million real dollars in merchandise trade balance (column F); and healthy real GDP gain of 8.0% (see SALA, 22-3).
2. More than 100.0 equals peso "overvaluation" which discourages exports from Mexico and foreign tourism to Mexico; it encourages imports to Mexico, Mexican tourism abroad, and a Mexican shift from pesos into "cheap" dollars. Also in terms of 1963 value, the greater the undervaluation of the peso the greater the chances to reduce Mexico's trade deficit, to increase Mexico's money balance from tourism, and to encourage investment in pesos rather than dollars. Undervalued pesos allow foreigners to buy more goods and services in Mexico than do overvalued pesos.
3. In no years did value of exports equal that of imports (theoretically zero on the index scale). The real merchandise trade deficit of $201 million equals -100.0 on the index scale.

a. May.
b. January—April.
c. January—April = 170.5 U.S. wholesale price index.

Method:
A: 1952-74, IFS-Y, 1982; 1975-82, IFS, Aug. 1982, line *rf*.
B: Bank of Mexico 210-item wholesale price index calculated (base converted) from source A, line 63.
C: Calculated from source A, line 63.
D: Calculated (datum for 1963 in column A times B/C).
E: Calculated (A/D), according to ECLA methodology in ECLA-S2, 1980, p. 394.
F: 1952-74, IFS-Y, 1982, line 77*ad*; 1975-81, IFS, Aug. 1982, calculated from lines 77*aad* and 77*abd*; 1982 calculated from CE, Aug. 1982, p. 904.
G: Calculated from column F.
H: Calculated (G/C).

SOURCE: James W. Wilkie, "Mexico's 'New' Financial Crisis of 1982 in Historical Perspective," SALA, 22, Preface.

Table 3226

NICARAGUA EVOLUTION OF REAL EXCHANGE RATES, 1980–86

Year and Month	Exchange Rate (Córdobas per Dollar)	
	Official	Parallel
1980	10.00	17.68
1981	10.00	25.96
1982	10.00	28.50
1983	10.00	28.50
1984	10.00	~
1985	26.50	651.88
January	10.00	~
February	28.00	~
March	28.00	~
April	28.00	~
May	28.00	640.00
June	28.00	350.00
July	28.00	670.00
August	28.00	675.00
September	28.00	700.00
October	28.00	700.00
November	28.00	730.00
December	28.00	750.00
1986	66.50	1,337.50
January	28.00	750.00
February	70.00	950.00
March	70.00	950.00
April	70.00	950.00
May	70.00	950.00
June	70.00	1,300.00
July	70.00	1,300.00
August	70.00	1,300.00
September	70.00	1,800.00
October	70.00	1,800.00
November	70.00	1,800.00
December	70.00	2,200.00

SOURCE: ECLA-S, 1986, vol. 1, p. 505.

Table 3227

PANAMA EVOLUTION OF REAL EXCHANGE RATES, 1970–85

	Exchange Rate		Panama Wholesale Price Index (3)	US Wholesale Price Index (4)	Index of Adjusted Real Exchange Rate (2)/$\frac{(3)}{(4)}$ (5)	Parity Exchange Rate (3)/(4) (6)
Year	(Balboas per Dollar) (1)	Index (2)				
1970	1,000	100.0	100.0	100.0	100.0	1.00
1980	1,000	100.0	300.7	243.6	81.0	1.23
1981	1,000	100.0	330.9	265.8	80.3	1.24
1982	1,000	100.0	358.2	271.2	75.7	1.32
1983	1,000	100.0	366.7	274.6	74.9	1.34
1984	1,000	100.0	370.4	281.1	75.9	1.32
1985	1,000	100.0	393.4	292.1[‡]	74.3	1.35

1970 = 100

SOURCE: ECLA-S, 1985, vol. 1, p. 497.

Table 3228

PARAGUAY EVOLUTION OF REAL EXCHANGE RATES, 1970–87

	Exchange Rate (Guaraníes per Dollar)			1980 = 100 Indexes of Effective Real Exchange Rate			
	Official			Official[1]		Parallel[2]	
Year and Quarter	Exports	Imports	Parallel	Exports	Imports	Exports	Imports
1970–79	126	126	139	110.6	106.4	109.3	113.2
1980	126	126	135	100.0	100.0	100.0	100.0
1981	126	126	153	86.5	89.9	98.0	101.9
1982	142	137	205	90.6	88.8	122.1	124.1
1983	158	146	312	76.3	70.4	140.7	140.5
1984	222	245	381	83.4	93.5	133.6	135.7
1985	312	387	595	92.6	115.1	164.3	166.4
1986	388	474	695	92.8	104.5	155.7	143.2
1987	605	624	802	143.9	131.8	177.9	158.0
1985							
I	288	304	414	85.0	92.8	114.0	117.9
II	320	344	546	99.5	109.6	158.4	162.4
III	320	443	740	94.9	132.5	204.7	206.6
IV	320	444	678	91.1	125.4	180.1	178.7
1986							
I	332	472	787	81.0	109.5	179.3	170.3
II	327	528	729	78.8	117.0	163.9	150.7
III	435	443	658	102.7	94.6	145.0	131.1
IV	459	454	608	108.7	96.7	134.4	120.8
1987							
I	565	569	716	139.6	124.7	165.2	146.5
II	567	595	783	142.9	133.8	184.2	164.3
III	619	628	819	144.4	130.5	178.4	158.9
IV	669	705	886	148.6	138.2	183.6	162.1

1. These indexes were obtained by multiplying the weightings of exports or imports by the real exchange rate indexes. The products are added together to give the effective real exchange rate indexes.
2. These indexes correspond to a weighted average of the real exchange rate indexes for Paraguay with respect to Argentina, Brazil, the United States, Japan, Italy, France, and the Federal Republic of Germany, calculated on the basis of their relative shares in non-registered trade flows with this country. In calculating these indexes, the parallel exchange rate was used.

SOURCE: ECLA-S, 1987, vol. 1, p. 547.

Table 3229

PERU EVOLUTION OF REAL EXCHANGE RATES, 1970–87

	Nominal Exchange Rate (Intis per Dollar)		1980 = 100			
			Indexes of Effective Real Exchange Rate[1]			
Year and Quarter			Exports		Imports	
	Exports	Imports	(1)[a]	(2)[b]	(1)[a]	(2)[b]
1970–79		.08	84.8	79.2	84.7	79.1
1980		.29	100.0	100.0	100.0	100.0
1981		.42	85.5	85.8	83.8	84.1
1982		.70	89.2	85.6	87.1	83.5
1983		1.63	92.9	94.0	89.9	90.9
1984		3.47	89.3	95.2	96.8	92.5
1985		10.97	102.6	113.3	99.4	109.7
1986		14.58	90.5	92.2	87.9	89.4
1987[c]	21.77	20.31	91.7	78.9	83.7	72.2
1985						
I		7.00	100.4	108.9	97.7	105.9
II		9.70	102.7	112.6	99.4	109.0
III		13.26	104.0	117.2	100.5	113.2
IV		13.94	103.3	114.3	100.0	110.7
1986						
I		14.20	98.5	105.2	95.8	102.2
II		14.23	92.0	94.1	88.9	91.0
III		14.54	87.5	87.2	84.8	84.4
IV		15.38	84.0	82.1	81.9	80.1
1987[c]						
I	16.99	16.94	86.0	80.0	83.6	77.7
II	18.68	18.18	85.6	76.4	80.9	72.2
III	22.02	19.84	89.4	74.4	78.1	65.0
IV	29.34	26.48	105.7	84.7	92.1	73.8

1. These indexes were obtained by multiplying the weightings of exports or imports by the real exchange rate indexes. The products are added together to give the effective real exchange rate indexes.

a. Based on national price index.

b. Based on consumer index.

c. For 1987, two sets of exchange rates are used, one for exports and one for imports. Each was used to calculate its respective index.

SOURCE: ECLA-S, 1987, vol. 1, p. 589.

Table 3230

URUGUAY EVOLUTION OF REAL
EXCHANGE RATES, 1970–86

		1980 = 100		
		Indexes of Effective Real Exchange Rate[1]		
			Imports	
Year and Quarter	Nominal Exchange Rate	Exports	(1)[a]	(2)[b]
1970–79	2.75	120.4	103.3	121.7
1980	9.10	100.0	100.0	100.0
1981	10.82	96.5	95.5	95.8
1982	13.91	106.8	101.6	103.6
1983	34.54	146.2	131.9	136.8
1984	56.12	136.1	121.6	127.1
1985	101.42	135.8	118.4	125.2
1986	151.97	133.1	~	120.3
1984				
I	47.82	145.4	130.0	135.8
II	53.27	141.8	126.8	132.6
III	56.66	127.7	114.0	119.3
IV	66.73	129.3	115.4	120.8
1985				
I	84.65	140.5	124.2	130.7
II	94.17	129.5	112.6	118.8
III	106.34	133.5	115.7	122.4
IV	120.53	139.7	121.1	128.8
1986				
I	131.69	139.1	~	126.2
II	145.05	137.4	~	124.3
III	158.27	130.6	~	118.1
IV	172.85	125.4	~	112.4

1. These indexes were obtained by multiplying the weightings of exports or imports by the real exchange rate indexes. The products are added together to give the effective real exchange rate.

a. Includes principal oil exporting countries.
b. Excludes principal oil exporting countries.

SOURCE: ECLA-S, 1986, vol. 1, p. 692.

Table 3231

VENEZUELA EVOLUTION OF REAL EXCHANGE RATES
AND PRICE INDEXES, 1970–87

	Nominal Exchange Rate (Bolívares per Dollar)			1980 = 100 Indexes of Effective Real Exchange Rate[1]	
Year and Quarter	Commercial	Free	Average[2]	Exports	Imports
1970–79	4.29	4.29	4.29	114.8	109.5
1980	4.29	4.29	4.29	100.0	100.0
1981	4.29	4.29	4.29	91.2	91.3
1982	4.29	4.29	4.29	84.8	84.2
1983	5.05	5.72	10.59	92.5	91.6
1984	6.46	7.38	13.51	101.4	100.8
1985	7.05	7.50	13.97	91.9	91.3
1986	8.79	7.82	20.26	107.3	107.0
1987[‡]	14.02	14.50	27.86	134.3	133.6
1985					
I	6.93	7.50	13.28	92.7	92.1
II	6.99	7.50	13.36	91.2	90.7
III	7.11	7.50	14.39	91.9	91.2
IV	7.17	7.50	14.85	91.7	91.3
1986					
I	8.11	7.50	18.41	102.4	102.2
II	8.20	7.50	18.98	101.4	101.1
III	8.45	7.50	20.00	103.6	103.5
IV	10.48	8.78	23.65	121.6	121.1
1987					
I	13.21	14.50	23.07	144.3	143.3
II	14.13	14.50	27.03	139.1	143.3
III	14.38	14.50	30.70	128.2	127.5
IV	14.37	14.50	30.62	125.5	125.3

1. These indexes were obtained by multiplying the weightings of exports or imports by the real exchange rate indexes. The products are added together to give the effective real exchange rate indexes.
2. Central Bank of Venezuela.

SOURCE: ECLA-S, 1987, vol. 1, p. 682.

33

Price Changes, Commodity Prices, and Interest Rates

Table 3300

GUIDE TO TABLES 3201–3223: CONSUMER PRICE CHANGES
(Calculations by Waldo W. Wilkie)

Alternative PC series are presented for each country to illustrate that there is no single measure of price change. The reader must look at the series to interpret trends.

Differences amounting to several percent between alternative series may be due only to rounding in the original data (e.g., between a figure ending in .4 that rounds downward and a figure ending in .5 that rounds upward).

Differences in series may also be due, however, to one or more of the following factors:

1. number of items included in the series
2. weights attached to each item
3. calculations based upon different base years
4. coverage geographically of capital city in contrast to major urban areas, all urban areas, or national scope
5. consumer prices keyed to varying definition of "consumer" as involving:
   a. all households
   b. wage earner households
   c. wage and salary earner households
   d. low income earners
   e. low and middle income earners
   f. middle income earners
   g. "average" working class family with a specified number of dependents
   h. government employees

According to IMF-IFS-S, No. 2, 1981, pp. ii-iii:

The increasing interdependence of national economies, and the increased transmission of inflation between them, has brought with it a need for global measures of price change in order to enable analysts to quantify the magnitude of global inflation and to examine its diffusion and dispersion around the world. The three most commonly used indicators of global price change are consumer prices, GDP deflators, and wholesale prices. GDP deflators have particular relevance in this context since they reflect, in concept, the aggregate price change of all goods and services produced in the domestic economy. As such they have been viewed as broader measures of price change than consumer price indexes, which cover only items of private consumption expenditure. The GDP deflator has several deficiencies, however, as a measure of global inflation. Although its sectoral coverage is wider than that of consumer or wholesale price indexes, the techniques used to obtain constant price data for components of the national accounts other than private consumption expenditure are less than satisfactory in most countries. . . .

[Therefore, the IMF emphasizes] consumer prices. There is a fair degree of similarity in concepts and methodologies between countries for these series. Country coverage is also more comprehensive than that for GDP deflators and wholesale prices.

[In summary,] it should be emphasized [that price] measures are only approximate indicators of overall price trends. In order to summarize into one aggregate measure the large number of transactions whose price movements they purport to reflect, a number of judgements must be made. Depending on the assumptions made concerning such aspects of methodology as the choice of base year, weights, formulae, sample selection, and specification of prices, different results, although perhaps equally appropriate depending on the context in which the measures are to be used, can ensue. In this sense, price index numbers cannot be rigorously defined independent of the methods used in their construction.

Table 3301

ARGENTINA COMPARATIVE PC OF PRICES,[1] 1980–88
(YA)

PART II.[a]

| | Consumer[2] | | | | | GDP Deflator | |
| | A. | B. | C. | D. | E. | F. | G. |
Year	Economía Argentina (1930–40)	Díaz Alejandro (1936–66)	Martin (1941–73)	IMF (1953–88)	UN-SY[3] (1973–88)	IMF[4] (1961–87)	Díaz Alejandro (1936–65)
1980				100.8	100.8	.1	
1981				104.5	104.5	.1	
1982				164.8*	164.8	.4	
1983				343.8	343.8	1.7	
1984				626.7*	626.7	12.7	
1985				672.1	672.1	100.0	
1986				90.1	91.0	178.0	
1987				131.3	131.3	~	
1988				342.7	342.9	~	

1. See table 3300.
2. Buenos Aires.
3. Greater Buenos Aires since 1981.
4. 1985 = 100.

a. For 1914–1979, see SALA, 24-3201.

SOURCE: Calculations were made from the following:
A. *Revista de Economía Argentina* 36 (1937), pp. 268-269, and 40 (1941), p. 105.
B. Carlos F. Díaz Alejandro, *Essays on the Economic History of the Argentine Republic* (New Haven: Yale University Press, 1970), p. 528.
C. J. L Martin, SALA, 18-1411.
D. IMF-IFS-Y, 1983, pp. 70; IMF-IFS-Y, 1984, pp. 102-103; IMF-IFS-Y, 1986; IMF-IFS-Y, 1988; IMF-IFS, August 1989.
E. UN-MB, Dec., 1984, p. 220; UN-SY, 1981, p.169, UN-MB, Nov. 1986, p. 212; UN-MB, Dec. 1988; UN-MB, July 1989, p. 172.
F. IMF-IFS-S, No. 2, 1981, pp. 10-11; IMF-IFS-S, No. 8, 1984, pp. 76-77; IMF-IFS-Y, 1986; IMF-IFS-Y, 1987; IMF-IFS-Y, 1988.

Table 3302

BOLIVIA COMPARATIVE PC OF PRICES,[1] 1980–88[a]
(YA)

Year	Consumer[2]				GDP Deflator
	A. Wilkie (1932-66)	B. Martin (1941-75)	C. IMF (1953-88)	D. UN-SY (1973-88)	E. IMF[3] (1957-87)
1980			47.2*	47.2	#
1981			28.6	32.2	#
1982			133.3	123.5	#
1983			269.0	275.6	.1
1984			1,281.4	1,281.2	.8
1985			11,749.6	11,749.6	100.0
1986			276.3	276.3	392.4
1987			14.6	15.6	~
1988			16.0	16.0	~

1. See table 3300.
2. La Paz.
3. 1985 = 100.

a. For 1932–79, see SALA, 24-3202.

SOURCE: Calculations were made from the following:
  A. James W. Wilkie, *The Bolivian Revolution and U.S. Aid Since 1952* (Los
     Angeles: UCLA Latin American Center Publications, 1969), p. 4.
  B. J. L. Martin, SALA, 18-1412.
  C. IMF-IFS-Y, 1983, pp. 70; IMF-IFS-Y, 1984, pp. 102-103; IMF-IFS-Y, 1986;
     IMF-IFS-Y, 1988, IMF-IFS, August 1989.
  D. UN-MB, Dec. 1984, p. 220; UN-SY, 1981, p. 169, UN-MB, Nov. 1986, p. 212;
     UN-MB, Dec. 1988; UN-MD, July 1989, p. 172.
  E. IMF-IFS-S, No. 2, 1981, pp. 10-11; IMF-IFS, No. 8, 1984, pp. 76-77; IMF-IFS-Y,
     1986; IMF-IFS-Y, 1987; IMF-IFS-Y, 1988.

Table 3303

BRAZIL COMPARATIVE PC OF PRICES,[1] 1980–88
(YA)

PART II.[a]

Year	Consumer[2]					GDP Deflator
	A. Simonson (1930-39)	B. Martin (1941-75)	C. IMF (1958-88)	D. ILO (1930-45)	E. UN-SY (1937-88)	F. IMF[3] (1964-87)
1980			82.8		78.0	1.0
1981			105.6		95.6	2.0
1982			97.8		89.3	4.0
1983			142.1		135.8	9.6
1984			197.0		172.5	30.2
1985			226.9		201.5	100.0
1986			145.2		130.0	243.8
1987			229.7		221.0	754.1
1988			695.3		586.3[b]	5,917.0

1. See table 3300.
2. Rio de Janeiro.
3. 1985 = 100.

a. For 1913–79, see SALA, 24-3203.
b. São Paulo.

SOURCE: Calculations were made from the following:
  A. Mario Henrique Simonson, "Brazilian Inflation: Postwar Experience and Outcome
     of the 1964 Reforms," *Economic Development Issues: Latin America* (New York:
     Committee for Economic Development, 1967), p. 269.
  B. J. L. Martin, SALA, 18-1413.
  C. IMF-IFS-Y, 1983, p. 70; IMF-IFS-Y, 1984, pp. 102-103; IMF-IFS-Y, 1986;
     IMF-IFS-Y, 1988; IMF-IFS, August 1989.
  D. ILO-YLS, 1945/1946, p. 194.
  E. UN-MB, Dec. 1984, p. 220; UN-SY, 1981, p. 169; UN-MB, Nov. 1986, p. 212;
     UN-MB, Dec. 1988; UN-MD, July 1989, p. 172.
  F. IMF-IFS-S, No. 8, 1984, pp. 76-77; IMF-IFS-Y, 1986; IMF-IFS-Y, 1987;
     IMF-IFS-Y, 1988.

Table 3304

CHILE COMPARATIVE PC OF PRICES,[1] 1980–88

(YA)

PART II.[a]

| Year | Consumer[2] | | | | | GDP Deflator |
	A. Latorre[3] (1929–57)	B. UN-SY (1931–88[b])	C. Martin (1941–75)	D. IMF (1964–88)	E. Chile (1930–40)	F. IMF[4] (1962–87)
1980		35.1		35.1		40.9
1981		19.7		19.7		45.9
1982		9.9		9.9		52.0
1983		27.3		27.3		65.9
1984		19.8		19.9		75.3
1985		30.4		30.7		100.0
1986		19.5		19.5		119.2
1987		19.8		19.9		~
1988		14.7		14.7*		~

1. See table 3300.
2. Santiago.
3. Food only.
4. 1985 = 100.

a. For 1899-1979, see SALA, 24-3204.
b. Selected periods only.

SOURCE: Calculations were made from the following:
   A. Adolfo Latorre Subercaseaux, "Relación Entre el Circulante y los Precios en Chile," Memoria para Optar al Título de Ingeniero Comercial, Universidad Católica de Chile, 1958.
   B. UN-SY, 1949-50, p. 401; UN-MB, Dec. 1984, p. 220; UN-SY, 1981, p. 170; UN-MB, Nov. 1986, p. 212; UN-MB, Dec. 1988; UN-MB, July 1989, p. 172.
   C. J. L. Martin, SALA, 18-1414.
   D. IMF-IFS-Y, 1984, pp. 102-103; IMF-IFS-Y, 1986; IMF-IFS-Y, 1988; IMF-IFS, August 1989.
   E. Chile, DGE, *Estadística Chilena*, Sept. 1933, Jan. 1936, Jan.-Feb., 1940, Aug. 1941.
   F. IMF-IFS-S, No. 8, 1984, pp. 76-77; IMF-IFS-Y, 1986, IMF-IFS-Y, 1987; IMF-IFS-Y, 1988.

Table 3305

COLOMBIA COMPARATIVE PC OF PRICES,[1] 1980–88[a]

(YA)

Year	Consumer[2]					GDP Deflator
	A. Urrutia (1929-48)	B. IMF (1938-54)	C. Martin (1941-75)	D. IMF (1953-88)	E. UN-SY[3] (1973-88)	F. IMF[4] (1951-87)
1980				26.5	28.0	35.5
1981				27.5	29.4	43.6
1982				24.5	24.0	54.4
1983				19.8	19.5	65.5
1984				16.1	16.2	80.1
1985				24.0	25.2	100.0
1986				18.9	17.9	129.2
1987				23.3	22.2	158.6
1988				28.1*		~

1. See table 3300.
2. Bogotá.
3. Low income group.
4. 1985 = 100.

a. For 1929–79, see SALA, 24-3205.

SOURCE: Calculations were made from the following:
  A. Miguel Urrutia Montoya and Mario Arrubla, eds., *Compendio de Estadísticas Históricas de Colombia* (Bogotá, D.E.: Universidad Nacional de Colombia, 1970), pp. 81-82.
  B. IMF-IFS, July 1950 and Jan. 1956.
  C. J. L. Martin, SALA, 18-1415.
  D. IMF-IFS-Y, 1983, p. 70; IMF-IFS-Y, 1984, pp. 102-103; IMF-IFS-Y, 1986; IMF-IFS-Y, 1988; IMF-IFS, August 1989.
  E. UN-MB, Dec. 1984, p. 220; UN-SY, 1981, p. 170; UN-MB, Nov. 1986, p. 212; UN-MB, Dec. 1988.
  F. IMF-IFS-S, No. 2, 1981, pp. 10-11; IMF-IFS-S, No. 8, 1984, pp. 76-77; IMF-IFS-Y, 1986; IMF-IFS-Y, 1987; IMF-IFS-Y, 1988.

Table 3306

COSTA RICA COMPARATIVE PC OF PRICES,[1] 1980–88[a]

(YA)

Year	Consumer[2]				GDP Deflator
	A. Banco-Central (1937-68)	B. Martin (1941-75)	C. IMF (1953-88)	D. UN-SY[3] (1973-88)	E. IMF[4] (1961-87)
1980			18.1	18.2	21.2
1981			37.1	37.0	29.9
1982			90.1	90.0	55.1
1983			32.6	32.7	69.5
1984			12.0	11.9	83.0
1985			15.1	14.5	100.0
1986			11.8	12.4	118.1
1987			16.8	16.7	129.4
1988			20.8	30.2	157.2

1. See table 3300.
2. San José.
3. Greater San José.
4. 1985 = 100.

a. For 1937–79, see SALA, 24-3206.

SOURCE: Calculations were made from the following:
  A. Costa Rica, Banco Central, data provided to SALA.
  B. J. L. Martin, SALA, 18-1416.
  C. IMF-IFS-Y, 1983, p. 70; IMF-IFS-Y, 1984, pp. 102-103; IMF-IFS-Y, 1986; IMF-IFS-Y, 1988; IMF-IFS, August 1989.
  D. UN-MB, Dec. 1984, p. 220; UN-SY, 1981, p. 70; UN-MB, Nov. 1986, p. 212; UN-MB, Dec. 1988; UN-MB, July 1989, p. 172.
  E. IMF-IFS-S, No. 2, 1981, pp. 10-11; IMF-IFS-S, No. 8, 1984, pp. 76-77; IMF-IFS-Y, 1986; IMF-IFS-Y, 1987; IMF-IFS-Y, 1988.

Table 3307

CUBA PRICES,[1] 1938–88

Year	A. DGE (1938-62)[a]	B. Havana Related to New York City[2]
1938	-.5	
1939	-5.8	
1940	-1.8	
1941	8.6	
1942	32.5	
1943	13.9	
1944	14.0	
1945	13.0	
1946	9.5	
1947	16.9	
1948	9.1	
1949	-13.2	
1950	-2.7	
1951	10.5	
1952	.3	
1953	-2.4	
1954	-5.5	
1955	-2.3	
1956	-.7	
1957	6.5	
1958	3.1	
1959	~	
1960	~	
1961	~	
1962	5.8[b]	
1963		~
1964		~
1965		~
1966		~
1967		~
1968		~
1969		-3.1[f]
1970		~
1971		~
1972		~
1973		~
1974		2.3[g]
1975		-5.6[h]
1976		0[i]
1977		0[j]
1978		-1.2[k]
1979		13.3
1980		~
1981		~
1982		10.3[d]
1983		-11.5[a]
1984		~
1985		~
1986		~
1987		~
1988		~

1. See table 3300.
2. Cost of living for U.N. officials converted to PC.

a. Havana food prices.
b. May 1961 to May 1962.
c. June 1978 to April 1979.
d. December 1981 to March 1982.
e. March 1982 to July 1983.
f. October 1968 to December 1969.
g. March 1973 to April 1974.
h. April 1974 to May 1975.
i. May 1975 to May 1976.
j. May 1976 to May 1977.
k. May 1977 to June 1978.

SOURCE: Calculations were made from the following:
    A. Cuba, DGE, AE, 1957, pp. 409-410, and for 1962, Dudley Seers, ed., *Cuba: The Economic and Social Revolution* (Chapel Hill: University of North Carolina Press, 1964), p. 33.
    B. SALA, 20-2520 and SALA, 24-3222; UN-MB, Nov. 1986, p. 212; UN-MB, Dec. 1988; UN-MB, July 1989, p. 172.

Table 3308

DOMINICAN REPUBLIC COMPARATIVE PC OF PRICES,[1] 1980–88[a]

(YA)

| Year | Consumer[2] | | | GDP Deflator |
	A. UN-SY[3] (1942-88)	B. Martin (1942-75)	C. IMF (1953-88)	D. IMF[4] (1951-87)
1980	~		16.8	51.6
1981	7.5		7.5	54.4
1982	7.6		7.6	58.7
1983	7.0		4.8	60.3
1984	24.3		27.0	72.0
1985	37.0		37.5	100.0
1986	9.9		9.7	122.4
1987	28.8		16.0	140.6
1988	~		~	201.3

1. See table 3300.
2. Santo Domingo.
3. Including direct taxes, 1981–82.
4. 1985 = 100.

a. For 1942–79, see SALA, 24-3208.

SOURCE: Calculations were made from the following:
   A. UN-SY, 1949-50, p. 41; for 1950–54 data, see UN-SY, 1955, p. 446; UN-MB, Dec. 1984, p. 220; UN-SY, 1981, p. 170. Selected periods only. UN-MB, Nov. 1986, p. 212; UN-MB, Dec. 1988; UN-MB, July 1989, p. 172.
   B. J.L. Martin, SALA, 18-1417.
   C. IMF IFS-Y, 1983, p. 70; IMF-IFS-Y, 1984, pp. 102-103; IMF-IFS-Y, 1986; IMF-IFS-Y, 1988; IMF-IFS, August 1989.
   D. IMF-IFS-S, No. 2, 1981, pp. 10-11; IMF-IFS-S, No. 8, 1984, pp. 76-77; IMF-IFS-Y, 1986; IMF-IFS-Y, 1987; IMF-IFS-Y, 1988.

Table 3309

ECUADOR COMPARATIVE PC OF PRICES,[1] 1980–88[a]

(YA)

| Year | Consumer[2] | | | | | GDP Deflator |
	A. Rodríguez[2] (1930-42)	B. Banco Central[2] (1940-51)	C. Martin (1951-75)	D. IMF (1953-88)	E. UN-SY[3] (1973-88)	F. IMF[4] (1951-87)
1980				13.0*	12.8	29.4
1981				13.0*	12.0	33.6
1982				16.3	16.3	39.6
1983				48.4	48.4	54.9
1984				31.1	31.2	76.4
1985				28.0	28.0	100.0
1986				23.0	23.1	120.7
1987				29.5	29.7	166.6
1988				58.3	58.2	~

1. See table 3300.
2. Quito.
3. Quito.
4. 1985 = 100.

a. For 1922–79, see SALA, 24-3209.

SOURCE: Calculations were made from the following:
   A. Linda A. Rodríguez, *The Search for Public Policy: Regional Politics and Government Finances in Ecuador*, 1830–1940 (Berkeley and Los Angeles: University of California Press, 1985).
   B. Ecuador, Banco Central, *Boletín*, July-Aug. 1952, p. 142.
   C. J. L. Martin, SALA, 18-1418.
   D. IMF-IFS-Y, 1983, p. 70; IMF IFS-Y, 1984, pp. 102-103; IMF-IFS-Y, 1986; IMF-IFS-Y, 1988; IMF-IFS, August 1989.
   E. UN-MB, Dec. 1984, p. 220; UN-SY, 1981, p. 170; UN-MB, Nov. 1986, p. 212; UN-MB, Dec. 1988; UN-MB, July 1989, p. 172.
   F. IMF-IFS-S, No. 2, 1981, pp. 10-11; IMF-IFS-S, No. 8, 1984, pp. 76-77; IMF-IFS-Y, 1986; IMF-IFS-Y, 1987; IMF-IFS-Y, 1988.

Table 3310

EL SALVADOR COMPARATIVE PC OF PRICES,[1] 1980–88[a]
(YA)

| Year | Consumer[2] | | | GDP Deflator |
	A. UN-SY[3] (1938-88)	B. Martin (1941-75)	C. IMF (1953-88)	D. IMF (1952-87)
1980	17.0		17.4	56.6
1981	14.7		14.8	59.9
1982	11.7		11.7	65.8
1983	13.2		13.3	73.9
1984	11.7		11.5	83.0
1985	22.2		22.3	100.0
1986	31.8		31.9	137.0
1987	25.3		24.9	157.2
1988	19.7		19.7	~

1. See table 3300.
2. San Salvador.
3. Urban areas since 1983. Selected periods.

a. For 1938–79, see SALA, 24-3210.

SOURCE: Calculations were made from the following:
  A. UN-SY, 1955, p. 446; UN-MB, Dec. 1984, p. 220; UN-SY, 1981, p. 170; UN-MB,
     Nov. 1986, p. 212; UN-MB, Dec. 1988; UN-MB, July 1989, p. 172.
  B. J. L. Martin, SALA, 18-1419.
  C. IMF-IFS-Y, 1983, p. 70; IMF-IFS-Y, 1984, pp. 102-103; IMF-IFS-Y, 1986;
     IMF-IFS-Y, 1988; IMF-IFS, August 1989.
  D. IMF-IFS-S, No. 2, 1981, pp. 10-11; IMF-IFS-S, No. 8, 1984, pp. 76-77; IMF-IFS-Y,
     1986; IMF-IFS-Y, 1987; IMF-IFS-Y, 1988.

Table 3311

GUATEMALA COMPARATIVE PC OF PRICES,[1] 1980–88[a]
(YA)

| Year | Consumer[2] | | | | GDP Deflator |
	A. Adler, et al. (1939-49)[b]	B. Martin (1941-75)	C. IMF (1953-88)	D. UN-SY[3] (1973-88)	E. IMF[4] (1951-87)
1980			10.8	10.7	66.6
1981			11.4	11.4	72.3
1982			.3	#	77.2
1983			4.5	-12.0[c]	80.9
1984			3.4	1.8[d]	84.2
1985			18.7	18.6	100.0
1986			36.9	37.3	141.2
1987			12.3	12.3	~
1988			10.9	10.8	~

1. See table 3300.
2. Guatemala City.
3. Urban areas since 1975 (prior to 1975, Guatemala City only).
4. 1985 = 100.

a. For 1939-79, see SALA, 24-3211.
b. Wholesale prices spliced to consumer price index beginning in 1946.
c. Marked break in series.
d. Base 1984 = 100 (beginning 1983).

SOURCE: Calculations were made from the following:
  A. John H. Adler et al., *Las Finanzas Públicas y el Desarrollo de Guatemala*
     (México, D.F.: Fondo de Cultura Económica, 1952), p. 256.
  B. J. L. Martin, SALA, 18-1420.
  C. IMF-IFS-Y, 1983, p. 70; IMF-IFS-Y, 1984, pp. 102-103; IMF-IFS-Y, 1986;
     IMF-IFS-Y, 1988; IMF-IFS, August 1989.
  D. UN-MB, Dec. 1984, p. 222; UN-SY, 1981, p. 171; UN-MB, Nov. 1986, p. 212;
     UN-MB, Dec. 1988; UN-MB, July 1989, p. 172.
  E. IMF-IFS-S, No. 2, 1981, pp. 10-11; IMF-IFS-S, No. 8, 1984, pp. 76-77; IMF-IFS-Y,
     1986; IMF-IFS-Y, 1987; IMF-IFS-Y, 1988.

Table 3312

HAITI COMPARATIVE PC OF PRICES,[1] 1980–88[a]

(YA)

Year	Consumer[2]		GDP Deflator
	A. IMF (1949-88)	B. UN-SY (1973-88)	C. IMF[3] (1956-87)
1980	17.8*	17.9	68.0
1981	10.9*	11.0	72.0
1982	7.4	7.2	74.9
1983	10.2	10.3	81.5
1984	6.4	6.3	90.6
1985	10.6	10.7	100.0
1986	3.3	3.2	111.0
1987	−11.5	−11.3	97.1
1988	.4	~	~

1. See table 3300.
2. Port-au-Prince.
3. 1985 = 100.

a. For 1949–79, see SALA, 24-3212.

SOURCE: Calculations were made from the following.
- A.   IMF-IFS-Y, 1972, p. 144; for 1954: IMF-IFS-Y, 1983, p. 70; since 1955: IMF-IFS-Y, 1984, pp. 102-103; IMF-IFS-Y, 1986; IMF-IFS-Y, 1988; IMF-IFS, August 1989.
- B.   UN-MB, Dec. 1984, p. 222; UN-SY, 1981, p. 171; UN-MB, Nov. 1986, p. 214; UN-MB, Dec. 1988; UN-MB, July 1989, p. 174.
- C.   IMF-IFS-S, No. 2, 1981, pp. 10-11; IMF-IFS-S, No. 8, 1984, pp. 76-77; IMF-IFS-Y, 1986; IMF-IFS-Y, 1987; IMF-IFS-Y, 1988.

Table 3313

HONDURAS COMPARATIVE PC OF PRICES,[1] 1980–88[a]

(YA)

Year	Consumer[2]				GDP Deflator
	A. Banco Central (1930-53)[b]	B. Martin (1949-75)	C. IMF (1953-88)	D. UN-SY[3] (1973-88)	E. IMF[4] (1951-87)
1980			18.1	18.6	76.8
1981			9.4	9.4	82.6
1982			9.0	9.4	87.4
1983			8.3	8.9	91.7
1984			4.7	4.8	95.6
1985			3.4	1.8	100.0
1986			4.4	3.6	105.2
1987			3.6	2.7	106.3
1988			4.5	~	~

1. See table 3300.
2. Tegucigalpa.
3. Honduras.
4. 1985 = 100.

a. For 1926–79, see SALA, 24-3213.
b. San Pedro Sula.
c. Marks break in the comparability of data. Data after "b" do not form a consistent series with those for earlier years.

SOURCE: Calculations were made from the following:
- A.   Honduras, Banco Central, *Boletín*, 4: (1954), p. 38.
- B.   J. L. Martin, SALA, 18-1421.
- C.   IMF-IFS-Y, 1983, p. 70; IMF-IFS-Y, 1986; IMF-IFS-Y, 1988; IMF-IFS, August 1989.
- D.   UN-MB, Dec. 1984, p. 222; UN-SY, 1981, p. 171; UN-MB, Nov. 1986, p. 214; UN-MB, Dec. 1988; UN-MB, July 1989, p. 174.
- E.   IMF-IFS-S, No. 2, 1981, pp. 10-11; IMF-IFS-S, No. 8, 1984, pp. 76-77; IMF-IFS-Y, 1986; IMF-IFS-Y, 1987; IMF-IFS-Y, 1988.

Table 3314

MEXICO COMPARATIVE PC OF PRICES,[1] 1980-88[a]

(YA)

Year	Consumer[2]				GDP Deflator
	A. DGE (1930-75)	B. Martin (1935-75)	C. IMF (1953-88)[b]	D. UN-SY (1973-88)	E. IMF[3] (1949-87)
1980			26.4	26.3	10.2
1981			27.9	28.0	13.0
1982			58.9	58.9	20.9
1983			101.8	101.9	40.2
1984			65.5	65.5	63.9
1985			57.7	57.7	100.0
1986			86.2	86.0	174.0
1987			131.8	131.9	~
1988			114.2	114.2	~

1. See table 3300.
2. Mexico City.
3. 1985 = 100.

a. For 1901-79, see SALA, 24-3214.
b. Bank of Mexico Series.

SOURCE: Calculations were made from the following:
A.   James W. Wilkie, *The Mexican Revolution: Federal Expenditure and Social Change Since 1910* (Berkeley: University of California Press, 1967), p. 23 (and sources cited there); and since 1964 Mexico, DGE, *Compendio Estadístico*, 1970, p. 296.
B.   J. L. Martin, SALA 18-1422.
C.   IMF-IFS-Y, 1983, p. 70; IMF-IFS-Y, 1984, pp. 102-103; IMF-IFS-Y, 1986; IMF-IFS-Y, 1988.
D.   UN-MB, Dec. 1984, p. 222; UN-SY, 1981, p. 173; UN-MB, Nov. 1986, p. 216; UN-MB, Dec. 1988; UN-MB, July 1989, p. 174.
E.   IMF-IFS-S, No. 2, 1981, pp. 10-11; IMF-IFS-S, No. 8, 1984, pp. 76-77; IMF-IFS-Y, 1986; IMF-IFS-Y, 1987; IMF-IFS-Y, 1988.

Table 3315

NICARAGUA COMPARATIVE PC OF PRICES,[1] 1980-88[a]

(YA)

Year	Consumer[2]					GDP Deflator
	A. UN-SY Food Prices (1938-49)	B. Martin (1941-71)	C. IMF (1956-88)	D. DeFranco and Chamorro (1969-77)	E. UN-SY[3] (1974-88)	F. IMF[4] (1961-87)
1980			35.3*		35.1	18.6
1981			23.9		~	20.8
1982			24.8		~	24.3
1983			31.1		~	26.9
1984			35.4		~	37.4
1985			219.5		~	100.0
1986			681.4		~	379.9
1987			911.4		~	2,048.0
1988			~		~	~

1. See table 3300.
2. Managua.
3. Metropolitan area.
4. 1985 = 100.

a. For 1938-79, see SALA, 24-3215.

SOURCE: Calculations were made from the following:
A.   UN-SY, 1949-50, p. 401.
B.   J. L. Martin, SALA, 18-1423.
C.   IMF-IFS-Y, 1972, pp. 156-157; IMF-IFS-Y, 1983, p. 71; IMF-IFS-Y, 1984, p. 103; IMF-IFS-Y, 1986; IMF-IFS-Y, 1988; IMF-IFS, August 1989.
D.   Mario A. De Franco and Carlos F. Chamorro, "Nicaragua: Crecimiento Industrial y Desempleo," in D. Camacho et al., *El Fracaso Social de la Integración Centroamericana* (San José, Costa Rica: Editorial Universitaria Centroamericano, 1979), cited in John A. Booth, *The End and the Beginning: The Nicaraguan Revolution* (Boulder, Colorado: Westview Press, 1982), p. 79.
E.   UN-SY, 1981, p. 173; UN-SY, 1982, p. 174; UN-MB, Dec. 1988; UN-MB, July 1989, p. 174.
F.   IMF-IFS-S, No. 2, 1981, p. 10; IMF-IFS-S, No. 8, 1984, pp. 76-77; IMF-IFS-Y, 1986; IMF-IFS-Y, 1987; IMF-IFS-Y, 1988.

Table 3316

PANAMA COMPARATIVE PC OF PRICES,[1] 1980–88[a]

(YA)

| Year | Consumer[2] | | | GDP Deflator |
	A. Martin (1941-75)	B. IMF (1953-88)	C. UN-SY (1973-88)	D. IMF[3] (1952-87)
1980		13.8	13.9	83.5
1981		7.3	7.3	87.4
1982		4.3	4.2	91.4
1983		2.1	2.1	93.1
1984		1.6	1.6	97.6
1985		1.0	1.0	100.0
1986		−.1	0	101.6
1987		1.0	.1	102.5
1988		.3	.3	~

1. See table 3300.
2. Panama City.
3. 1985 = 100.

a. For 1941–79, see SALA, 24-3216.

SOURCE: Calculations were made from the following:
    A. J. L. Martin, SALA, 18-1424.
    B. IMF-IFS-Y, 1983, p. 70; IMF-IFS-Y, 1984, pp. 102-103; IMF-IFS-Y, 1986;
       IMF-IFS-Y, 1988; IMF-IFS, August 1989.
    C. UN-MB, Dec. 1984, p. 224; UN-SY, 1981, p. 174; UN-MB, Nov. 1986, p. 216;
       UN-MB, Dec. 1988; UN-MB, July 1989, p. 174.
    D. IMF-IFS-S, No. 2, 1981, p. 10; IMF-IFS-S, No. 8, 1984, pp. 76-77; IMF-IFS-Y,
       1986; IMF-IFS-Y, 1987; IMF-IFS-Y, 1988.

Table 3317

PARAGUAY COMPARATIVE PC OF PRICES,[1] 1980–88[a]

(YA)

| Year | Consumer[2] | | | GDP Deflator |
	A. UN-SY (1939-88)	B. Martin (1941-75)	C. IMF (1953-88)	D. IMF[3] (1951-87)
1980	22.5		22.4	45.0
1981	13.0		14.0	52.3
1982	5.1		6.8	55.0
1983	~		13.4	62.9
1984	~		20.3	79.8
1985	~		25.2	100.0
1986	31.7		31.7	131.5
1987	21.8		21.8	171.5
1988	~		22.7	222.3

1. See table 3300.
2. Asunción.
3. 1985 = 100.

a. For 1939–79, see SALA, 24-3217.

SOURCE: Calculations were made from the following:
    A. UN-SY, 1949-50, p. 402; UN-MB, Dec. 1984, p. 224; UN-SY, 1981, p. 174;
       UN-SY, 1986, p. 177; UN-MB, July 1989, p. 174.
    B. J. L. Martin, SALA, 18-1425.
    C. IMF-IFS-Y, 1983, p. 70; IMF-IFS-Y, 1984, pp. 102-103; IMF-IFS-Y, 1986;
       IMF-IFS-Y, 1988; IMF-IFS, August 1989.
    D. IMF-IFS-S, No. 2, 1981, p. 10; IMF-IFS-S, No. 8, 1984, pp. 76-77; IMF-IFS-Y,
       1986; IMF-IFS-Y, 1987; IMF-IFS-Y, 1988.

Table 3318

PERU COMPARATIVE PC OF PRICES,[1] 1980–88[a]

(YA)

Year	A. Peru (1930–41)	B. UN-SY[3,4] (1931–88)	C. Martin (1941–75)	D. IMF (1938–88)	E. League (1929–38)	GDP Deflator F. IMF[5] (1961–87)
			Consumer[2]			
1980		~*		59.2		3.1
1981		75.4		75.4		5.1
1982		64.5		64.4		8.4
1983		111.2		111.2		17.7
1984		110.2		110.2		38.5
1985		163.3		163.4		100.0
1986		77.6		77.9		~
1987		86.1		85.8		~
1988		666.9		~		~

1. See table 3300.
2. Lima.
3. Lima and Callao, 1973–80.
4. Metropolitan area, 1981–83.
5. 1985 = 100.

a. For 1914–79, see SALA, 24-3218.

SOURCE: Calculations were made from the following:
  A. Peru, Dirección Nacional de Estadística, *Extracto Estadístico*, 1927, p. 103; English version, 1931-33, p. 53, 1941, p. 384.
  B. UN-SY, 1949-50, p. 402; UN-MB, Dec. 1984, p. 224; UN-SY, 1981, p. 174; UN-MB, Nov. 1986, p. 216; UN-MB, Dec. 1988; UN-MB, July 1989, p. 174.
  C. J. L. Martin, SALA, 18-1426.
  D. IMF-IFS-Y, 1983, p. 70; for 1938-52: IMF-IFS, June 1948 and Nov. 1950; IMF-IFS-Y, 1971; IMF-IFS-Y, 1984, pp. 102-103; IMF-IFS-Y, 1986; IMF-IFS-Y, 1988; IMF-IFS, August 1989.
  E. League of Nations, *Monthly Bulletin of Statistics*, Jan. 1939, p. 32.
  F. IMF-IFS-S, No. 2, 1981, p. 10; IMF-IFS-S, No. 8, 1984, pp. 76-77; IMF-IFS-Y, 1986; IMF-IFS-Y, 1987; IMF-IFS-Y, 1988.

Table 3319

URUGUAY COMPARATIVE PC OF PRICES,[1] 1980–88[a]

(YA)

Year	A. Instituto de Economía (1930-54)	B. UN-SY (1931-88)	C. Martin (1941-75)	D. IMF (1953-88)	GDP Deflator E. IMF[3] (1961-87)
			Consumer[2]		
1980		63.5		63.5	15.0
1981		34.0		34.0	19.5
1982		19.0		19.0	22.7
1983		49.2		49.2	34.6
1984		55.3		55.3	55.9
1985		72.2[b]		72.2	100.0
1986		76.4		76.4	172.8
1987		63.5		63.6	291.7
1988		62.2		62.2	472.5

1. See table 3300.
2. Montevideo.
3. 1985 = 100.

a. For 1930–79, see SALA, 24-3219.
b. Marks a break in comparability of data. Hence data after "a" do not form a consistent series with those for earlier years.

SOURCE: Calculations were made from the following:
  A. Uruguay, Instituto de Economía, *Estadísticas Básicas* (Montevideo: Universidad de Uruguay, 1969), p. 93.
  B. UN-SY, 1949-50, p. 402; and since 1950: UN-SY, 1955, p. 448; UN-MB, Dec. 1984, p. 226; UN-SY, 1981, p. 176; UN-MB, Nov. 1986, p. 216; UN-MB, Dec. 1988; UN-MB, July 1989, p. 178.
  C. J. L. Martin, SALA, 18-1427.
  D. IMF-IFS-Y, 1983, p. 70; IMF-IFS-Y, 1984, pp. 102-103; IMF-IFS-Y, 1986; IMF-IFS-Y, 1988; IMF-IFS, August 1989.
  E. IMF-IFS-S, No. 2, 1981, p. 10; IMF-IFS-S, No. 8, 1984, pp. 76-77; IMF-IFS-Y, 1986; IMF-IFS-Y, 1987; IMF-IFS-Y, 1988.

Table 3320

VENEZUELA COMPARATIVE PC OF PRICES,[1] 1980–88[a]

(YA)

| | Consumer[2] | | | | GDP Deflator |
| | A. DGE (1929-48) | B. Martin (1941-75) | C. IMF (1953-88) | D. UN-SY[3] (1973-88) | E. IMF[4] (1951-87) |
Year					
1980			21.5	23.4	51.8
1981			16.2	16.0	58.3
1982			9.6	9.6	59.1
1983			6.3	6.4	62.5
1984			12.2[b]	12.2	89.3
1985			11.4	11.9	100.0
1986			11.5	11.6	99.5
1987			28.1	28.2	140.7
1988			29.5	~	168.0

1. See table 3300.
2. Caracas.
3. Metropolitan area.
4. 1985 = 100.

a. For 1929–79, see SALA, 24-3220.
b. Marks a break in comparability of data. Hence data after "b" do not form a consistent series with those for earlier years.

SOURCE: Calculations were made from the following:
   A.   Venezuela, DGE, *Boletín de Estadística*, July 1949, p. 18.
   B.   J. L. Martin, SALA, 18-1428.
   C.   IMF-IFS-Y, 1983, p. 68; IMF-IFS-Y, 1986; IMF-IFS-Y, 1988; IMF-IFS, August 1989.
   D.   UN-MB, Dec. 1984, p. 226; UN-SY, 1981, p. 176; UN-MB, Nov. 1986, p. 216; UN-MB, Dec. 1988; UN-MB, July 1989, p. 178.
   E.   IMF-IFS-S, No. 2, 1981, p. 8; IMF-IFS-S, No. 8, 1984, pp. 74-75; IMF-IFS-Y, 1986; IMF-IFS-Y, 1987; IMF-IFS-Y, 1988.

Table 3321

UNITED STATES COMPARATIVE PC OF PRICES,[1] 1980–88[a]

(YA)

| | Consumer[2] | | | | GDP Deflator |
| | A. USBC (1930–69) | B. Martin (1941–75) | C. IMF (1953–88) | D. UN-SY (1973–88) | E. IMF[3] (1949–87) |
Year					
1980			13.5	13.4	77.3
1981			10.4	10.4	84.7
1982			6.2	6.1	90.1
1983			3.2	3.2	93.6
1984			4.3	4.3	97.3
1985			3.6	3.5	100.0
1986			1.9	2.8	102.7
1987			3.7	5.9	106.1
1988			3.9	4.1	109.7

1. See table 3300.
2. National Index.
3. 1985 = 100.

a. For 1901–79, see SALA, 24-3221.

SOURCE: Calculations were made from the following:
   A.   USBC-HS, 1975, vol. I, series E135.
   B.   J. L. Martin, SALA 18-1429.
   C.   IMF-IFS-Y, 1983, p. 68; IMF-IFS-Y, 1984, pp. 100-101; IMF-IFS-Y, 1986, p. 111; IMF-IFS-Y, 1988; IMF-IFS, August 1989.
   D.   UN-MB, Dec. 1984, p. 226; UN-SY, 1981, p. 176; UN-MB, Nov. 1986, p. 218; UN-MB, Dec. 1988; UN-MB, July 1989, p. 178.
   E.   IMF-IFS-S, No. 2, 1981, p. 8; IMF-IFS-S, No. 8, 1984, pp. 74-75; IMF-IFS-Y, 1986, p. 165; IMF-IFS-Y, 1987; IMF-IFS-Y, 1988.

Table 3322

SUMMARY OF IMF PC OF CONSUMER PRICE INDEX, 19 LC, 1970–88

(YA)

	Country	1970	1971	1972	1973	1974	1975	1976	1977	1978	1979	1980	1981	1982	1983	1984	1985	1986	1987	1988
	Antigua and Barbuda	~	~	~	~	~	~	~	13.8	6.1	16.3	19.0	11.5	4.2	2.3	3.9	1.0	~	~	~
A.	ARGENTINA	13.6	34.8	58.4	61.2	23.5*	182.3	443.2	176.1	175.5	159.5	100.8	104.5	164.8*	343.8	626.7*	672.1	90.1	131.3	342.7
	Bahamas, The	6.2	4.8	6.8	5.5	13.3	10.2	4.2	3.2	6.1	9.1	12.1	11.1	6.0	4.1	3.9	4.6	5.4	5.7	4.2
	Barbados	7.8	12.4	7.0	16.9	38.9	20.3	5.0	8.3	9.5	13.2*	14.5	14.6	10.3	5.3	4.6	3.9	1.3	3.3	4.8
	Belize	~	~	~	~	~	~	~	~	~	~	~	11.2	6.8	5.0	3.7	3.7	1.0	2.3	~
B.	BOLIVIA	3.8	3.7	6.5	31.5	62.8	8.0	4.5	8.1	10.4	19.7	47.2*	28.6	133.3	269.0	1,281.4	11,749.6	276.3	14.6	16.0
C.	BRAZIL	22.3	20.2	16.5	12.7	27.6	29.0*	42.0	43.7	38.7	52.7	82.8	105.6*	97.8	142.1	197.0	226.9	145.2	229.7	695.3
D.	CHILE	33.0	19.2	77.3	353.6	504.7	374.7*	211.8	91.9	40.1	33.4	35.1	19.7	9.9	27.3	19.9	30.7	19.5	19.9	14.7*
E.	COLOMBIA	6.8	9.0*	13.4	20.8	24.3	22.9	20.2	33.1	17.8	24.7	26.5	27.5	24.5	19.8	16.1	24.0	18.9	23.3	28.1*
F.	COSTA RICA	4.7	3.1	4.6	15.2	30.1	17.4*	3.5	4.2	6.0	9.2	18.1	37.1	90.1	32.6	12.0	15.1	11.8	16.8	20.8
	Dominica	12.4	3.6	3.7	12.1	36.3	18.3	10.9	9.5	7.8	19.9	30.6	13.3	4.5	4.0	2.2	2.1	3.0	4.8	~
H.	DOMINICAN REP.	3.8	4.3	7.8	15.1	14.5	13.2	7.8	12.8	3.5*	9.2	16.8	7.5	7.6	4.8	27.0	37.5	9.7	16.0	~
I.	ECUADOR	5.1	8.4	7.9	13.0*	23.3	15.4	10.7	13.0	11.7	10.3	13.0*	16.4*	16.3	48.4	31.2	28.0	23.0	29.5	58.3
J.	EL SALVADOR	2.8	.4	1.6	6.4	16.9	19.2	7.0	11.8	13.2	14.6	17.4	14.8	11.7	13.3	11.5	22.3	31.9	24.9	19.7
	Grenada	~	-.5	.5	~	~	~	~	18.5	18.1	21.5	21.2	18.8	7.8	6.1	5.6	2.5	.5	-.9	~
K.	GUATEMALA	2.4	~	.5	13.8	16.5	13.2*	10.7*	12.3	8.3	11.3	10.8	11.4	.3	4.5	3.4	18.7	36.9	12.3	10.9
	Guyana	3.4*	1.0	5.0	7.5	17.5	7.8	9.0	8.3	15.2	17.8	14.1	24.7	20.2	13.3	25.2	15.0	7.9	28.7	39.9
L.	HAITI	1.3	9.5	3.2	22.7	15.0	16.8	7.0	6.5	-2.7	13.1	17.8*	10.9*	7.4	10.2	6.4	10.6	3.3	-11.5	.4
M.	HONDURAS	2.9	2.2	3.6	5.2	12.8	8.4	4.9	8.4	5.7*	12.1	18.1	9.4	9.0	8.3	4.7	3.4	4.4	2.5	4.5
	Jamaica	7.7*	5.3	5.4	17.7	27.2	17.4	9.8	11.2	34.9	29.1	27.3	12.7	6.5	11.6	27.8	25.7	15.1	6.7	8.2
N.	MEXICO	5.2	5.3	5.0	12.0	23.8	15.2	15.8	29.0	17.5	18.2	26.4	27.9	58.9	101.8	65.5	57.7	86.2	131.8	114.2
	Netherlands Antilles	3.6*	2.1	4.1	8.1	19.4	15.6	5.2	5.5	8.2	11.4	14.6	12.2	6.1	2.8	2.1	.5	~	3.8	2.6
O.	NICARAGUA	~	~	~	27.0	13.3	7.5	2.8	11.4	4.6	48.2	35.3	23.9	24.8	31.1	35.4	219.5	681.4	911.9	~
P.	PANAMA	3.1	2.0	5.3	6.9	16.8	5.5*	4.0	4.5	4.2	7.9	13.8	7.3	4.3	2.1	1.6	1.0	-.1	1.0	.3
Q.	PARAGUAY	-.7	4.8	9.5	12.5	25.2	6.8	4.6	9.3	10.6	28.3	22.4	14.0	6.8	13.4	20.3	25.2	31.7	21.8	22.7
R.	PERU	5.0	6.8	7.2	9.5	16.9	23.6	33.5	38.1	57.8	66.7*	59.2	75.4	64.4	111.2	110.2	163.4	77.9	85.8	~
	St. Lucia	13.4	8.4	7.9	13.4	34.2	17.8	9.7	8.9	10.9	9.4	19.5	15.1	4.6	1.5	1.2	1.3	2.3	~	~
	St. Vincent	~	~	~	~	~	6.8	11.3	10.2	8.4	15.6	17.2*	12.7*	7.2	5.5	2.7	2.1	~	~	~
	Suriname	2.6	.2	3.3	13.0	16.9	8.4	10.1	9.7	8.8*	14.9	14.1*	8.7	7.3	4.4	3.7	~	~	~	~
	Trinidad and Tobago	2.5	3.5	9.3	14.8	22.0	17.0	10.6	11.8	10.2	14.7	17.5	14.3	11.5	16.7*	13.3	7.6	7.7	10.8	7.7
S.	URUGUAY	17.0	24.0	76.5	97.0*	77.2	81.4	50.6	58.2	44.5	66.8	63.5	34.0	19.0	49.2	55.3	72.2*	76.4	63.6	62.2
T.	VENEZUELA	2.5	3.2	2.8	4.1	8.3	10.3	7.6	7.8	7.1	12.4	21.5	16.2	9.6	6.3	12.2*	11.4	11.5	28.1	29.5
	Western Hemisphere	12.3	14.8	20.0	28.5	28.0	37.3	51.0	44.0	37.8	50.5	54.8	59.8	73.4	118.5	146.1	161.5	82.0	118.5	82.3

SOURCE: IMF: IMF-IFS-Y, 1987; IMF-IFS-Y, 1988; IMF-IFS, August 1989.

Table 3323

RETAIL PRICE INDEX RELATING TO LIVING EXPENDITURES OF U.N. OFFICIALS IN LATIN AMERICAN CAPITALS, 20 L, 1966-88

(New York City = 100, December of Each Year)

	Country	1966	1973	1974	1975[l]	1976[l]	1977	1978	1979	1980	1981	1982	1983	1984	1985	1986	1987	1988
A.	ARGENTINA	~	78[a]	84[i]	46[h]	47	78	143	143	216	110	81	80	73	73	87	90	67
B.	BOLIVIA	81	73[b]	83[e]	82	85	95	93[e]	109	103	104	62[i]	83	89	43	83	67	65
C.	BRAZIL	108	93	100[i]	101	102[a]	100	104[i]	78	94	84	84	64	61	46	60	70	64
D.	CHILE	76	36[i]	68[i]	75	77	93	97	111	116	132	92	85	73	53	54	63	65
E.	COLOMBIA	63	64[g]	67[i]	67	66[h]	79	84	96	96[i]	107	102[h]	90	66	56	53	63	81
F.	COSTA RICA	84	79[a]	91	95[e]	95[j]	93	86	99	105	49	52	70[i]	70	69	70	75	69
G.	CUBA	~	87[b]	89[c]	84[k]	84[k]	84[k]	83[da]	94[c]	~	87[a]	78[ba]	69	~	67[a]	83[a]	86	84[a]
H.	DOMINICAN REP.	~	94[g]	95[i]	100[g]	98	97	90[g]	88[g]	97	91[e]	95[d]	95[e]	102	57	57	65	64
I.	ECUADOR	~	83[j]	82[j]	80	79	73	86	85	87[i]	80	60[j]	59	51	54	61	66	64
J.	EL SALVADOR	~	83	89[e]	87[g]	87	86	96[f]	99	104[e]	98	87[f]	70[g]	70	61	70	73	80
K.	GUATEMALA	91	77[d]	86[i]	88	88[j]	94	101	100[i]	100[i]	99	86[j]	86[b]	95	58	70	81	82
L.	HAITI	~	86[g]	94[k]	92[d]	90[d]	94[g]	99[g]	98	92[d]	97[c]	104[c]	104	75	71	73	83	92
M.	HONDURAS	~	88[k]	87[f]	90[e]	88	91	89[i]	94[g]	99	93	86[h]	87[i]	87	87	89	82	82
N.	MEXICO	95	89[g]	90[i]	92	90[a]	71	79	86	95	100	71	61	54	39	43	57	66
O.	NICARAGUA	~	88[k]	93[c]	91	95	98	91	87[c]	~	111[f]	1.0[h]	65	65	85	59	78	67
P.	PANAMA	~	86[g]	88[g]	88[g]	88	88	90[g]	90[g]	95[h]	98	73[i]	90[i]	97	101	84	80	84
Q.	PARAGUAY	~	71[g]	75[h]	80[h]	79	84	88[f]	104	110[f]	116[i]	101[h]	104[h]	46	41	49	57	51
R.	PERU	94	82[e]	84[g]	90	93[g]	84	72	80	100	104	101	91	67	54	80	91	68
S.	URUGUAY	66	70[d]	69[i]	72	73	83	81[i]	102[i]	115	123	100	70	55	56	63	69	77
T.	VENEZUELA	103	91	88[g]	87[h]	87	92	123[h]	141[i]	142	141[g]	145[h]	71	68	47	35	47	59

a. Calculated on the basis of the cost of government or subsidized housing which is normally lower than prevailing rentals.
b. March.
c. April.
d. June.
e. July.
f. August.
g. September.
h. October.
i. November.
j. Prior to devaluation of the peso.
k. May.
l. November unless noted otherwise.

SOURCE: UN-MB, various monthly since 1966.

Table 3324
IMF WHOLESALE PRICE INDEX,[1] 13 LC, 1970-88
(YA, 1980 = 100)

Country	1970	1973	1974	1975	1976	1977	1978	1979	1981	1982	1983	1984	1985	1986	1987	1988
A. ARGENTINA[2]	.05	.18	.21	.62	3.73	9.30	22.87	57.00	209.58	746.60	3,440.5	23,175	176,798	289,949	645,313	3,309,659
C. BRAZIL[3]	4.05	6.73	8.69	11.06	15.85	22.58	31.07	48.43	208.18	402	1,075	3,617	11,900	28,583	87,766	699,720
BRAZIL[2]	4.11	6.79	8.78	11.23	15.75	22.15	30.76	47.80	213.04	412	1,088	3,625	11,718	28,092	87,714	698,041
D. CHILE[2]	.007	.086	.965	5.616	18.032	33.549	47.963	71.654	109.085	116.927	107.2	211.5	303.3	363.3	433.2	458.9
CHILE[4]	.008	.091	.932*	5.464	17.817	32.545	47.234	71.447	110.120	117.187	166.2	204.9	287.6	355.0	430.8	453.5
E. COLOMBIA[2]	11.95	20.16	27.42	34.39	42.27	53.56	62.99	80.52	124.06	155.92	189.8	224.5	280.5	342.3	427.4	548.1
F. COSTA RICA[5]	24.5	31.9	44.7	54.3	59.3	63.8	69.6	80.8	165.3	344.2	434.3	467.6	516.2	562.7	622.4	733.5
I. ECUADOR[6]	~	~	50.1	57.1	66.6	72.1	84.2	93.2	109.6	128.1	147.1	181.0	228.3	279.2	386.2	672.8
J. EL SALVADOR[7]	32.6	39.6	49.6	50.5	68.0	100.2	80.3	86.4	110.0	119.4	127.5	134.9	153.6	~	~	~
EL SALVADOR[8]	33.7	42.1	55.0	58.9	65.5	73.2	76.7	84.5	112.4	122.0	131.7	141.0	166.2	~	~	~
K. GUATEMALA[9]	37.8	43.8	53.8	60.4	66.8	75.5	78.2	86.2	111.7	105.3	106.2	112.2	138.3	197.7	~	~
GUATEMALA[10]	37.8	43.6	53.0	59.9	66.1	75.8	78.6	86.4	111.9	104.4	105.3	110.9	137.5	200.4	~	~
N. MEXICO[11]	20.32	25.11	30.75	33.97	41.55	58.64	67.89	80.31	124.44	194.20	402.7	686.0	1,053.4	1,932.4	4,675.9	733.5
P. PANAMA[12]	33.3	42.0	54.8	62.4	67.3	72.2	76.0	86.7	110.0	119.1	114.6	115.8	115.3	96.9	98.3	91.5
Q. PARAGUAY[13]	21.5	39.7	52.0	59.9	60.3	65.1	73.5	92.8	112.2	116.1	141.6	181.6	224.2	~	364.0	462.5
S. URUGUAY[14]	.77	3.78	6.74	11.63	17.51	26.32	39.10	70.54	123.44	139.36	241.77	428.85	757.24	1,265.9	2,066	3,256.1
T. VENEZUELA[15]	39.6	45.3	52.8	60.1	64.4	71.0	76.3	83.3	113.84	123.03	131.62	154.6	182.8	211.5	303.3	371.3
VENEZUELA[16]	37.5	42.2	49.4	56.4	61.0	68.5	73.7	81.3	115.1	124.9	134.3	157.5	188.9	225.5	291.5	365.1
UNITED STATES	41.1	50.1	59.6	65.0	68.1	72.2	77.9	87.6	109.1	111.3	112.7	115.4	114.9	111.52	114.5	119.0

1. For data covering period 1952-70 see SALA, 23-2623.
2. Home and import goods.
3. Wholesale prices.
4. Home goods.
5. Wholesale prices in San José. Home and import goods.
6. Index compiled by the Central University of Ecuador.
7. Index of wholesale prices based on a sample of 91 commodities, including coffee.
8. Index of wholesale prices based on a sample of 91 commodities, excluding coffee.
9. Wholesale prices in Guatemala City; compiled by the Dirección General de Estadística from a sample of 65 commodities.
10. Home and export goods series. Refers to national products in K.1. Guatemala.
11. Covers 210 home and import goods in Mexico City.
12. Index for the entire country, covering the agricultural, industrial and import sectors.
13. Data as reported directly by the Central Bank to the IMF; covers Asunción only.
14. Covers home and export goods in agriculture and manufacturing.
15. Covers home and import goods for domestic consumption.
16. Covers home goods for domestic consumption.

SOURCE: IMF-IFS-S, 1983; IMF-IFS, June 1984, line 63; IMF-IFS-Y, 1986; IMF-IFS-Y, 1986, line 63; IMF-IFS-Y, 1988, line 63; IMF-IFS-Y, 1989, line 63.

Table 3325

PC OF WHOLESALE PRICE INDEX, 13 LR, 1970-88

(YA)

Country	1970	1971	1972	1973	1974	1975	1976	1977	1978	1979	1980	1981	1982	1983	1984	1985	1986	1987	1988
A. ARGENTINA	14.0	39.0	76.7	50.4	19.9	192.5	499.1	149.5	146.0	149.3	75.4	109.6	256.2	360.9*	573.4	662.9	63.9	122.9	412.6
C. BRAZIL	22.0*	20.0	18.6	16.8	29.2	27.2*	43.3	42.5	37.6	55.9	106.4	108.2*	93.2	167.4	236.3	229.0	140.2	207.1	697.2
D. CHILE	36.8	17.7	70.3	510.7	1,021.3*	481.9	221.1	86.1	43.0	49.4	39.6	9.1	7.2	45.5	24.3	43.4	19.8	19.2	5.9
E. COLOMBIA	7.6*	11.5	18.3	28.0	36.0	25.4	22.9	26.7	17.6	27.8	24.2	24.1	25.7	21.7	18.3	24.9	22.0	24.9	28.3
F. COSTA RICA	6.5	6.4	5.5	16.3	39.8	21.6	9.3	7.5	7.8*	16.1	23.7	65.3	108.2	26.2	7.7	10.4	9.0	10.6	17.9
I. ECUADOR	~	~	~	~	~	14.0	16.7	8.2	16.7	10.7	7.3	9.6	16.9	14.9	23.1	26.1	22.3	31.6	74.2
J. EL SALVADOR	8.7	-5.4	5.9	21.1	25.3	1.8	34.7	47.3	-19.8*	7.6	15.8	10.0	8.5	6.8	5.9	13.8	~	~	~
K. GUATEMALA	2.4	2.1	-.7	14.3	22.8	12.3	10.5	13.0	3.6	10.3	16.0	11.7	-5.8	.9	5.6	23.3	42.9	~	~
N. MEXICO	6.0	3.7	2.8	15.7	22.5	10.5	22.3	41.2	15.8*	18.3	24.5	24.4	56.1	107.4	70.3	53.6	83.4	135.6	107.8
P. PANAMA	3.1	5.4	8.5	10.5	30.2	14.0	7.8	7.2	5.4	14.0	15.3	10.0	8.3*	-3.8	1.1	-.4	-16.0	1.4	-6.8
Q. PARAGUAY	-4.0	12.9	18.5*	38.0	30.5	15.2	1.1	8.0	12.8	26.3	7.8	12.2	3.5	22.0	28.3	23.4	~	11.9	27.1
S. URUGUAY	13.7	20.3	84.9	121.0	78.6	72.4	50.6	50.3	48.6	80.4	41.8	23.4	12.9	73.5	77.4	76.6	67.2	63.2	57.4
T. VENEZUELA	1.6	3.5	3.4	6.7	16.7	13.7	7.2	10.3	7.4	9.3	20.0	13.8	8.1	7.0	17.5	18.2	15.7	44.8	19.3
Western Hemisphere	13.5	15.9	24.2	34.6	32.1	38.8	60.1	47.7	35.7	52.2	56.9	61.0	84.6	134.9	160.8	161.6	76.2	126.1	222.9

SOURCE: IMF-IFS-Y, 1987; IMF-IFS-Y, 1988; IMF-IFS-Y, 1989.

Table 3326

U.N. WHOLESALE PRICE INDEX, 15 LC, 1971–81

(YA, 1970 = 100)

Country	Index	1971	1972	1973	1974	1975	1976	1977	1978	1979	1980	1981
A. ARGENTINA	General	140	247	370	455	1,301	7,770	19,412	47,729	119,082	209,098	437,826
	Finished goods[2]	136	280	354	441	1,379	8,117	19,860	49,190	122,360	220,324	465,074
	Domestic goods	140	247	369	440	1,270	7,408	18,678	47,086	120,457	213,880	~
	Imported goods	123	247	402	550	1,967	15,549	35,175	61,877	119,561	208,383	536,904
	Farm products	148	289	412	455	1,109	6,906	18,318	44,541	111,110	181,761	351,049
	Textiles	133	234	363	468	1,294	6,698	17,045	43,060	107,895	190,666	~

Continued in SALA, 23-2624.

Table 3327

ECLA IMPORT AND EXPORT PRICE CHANGES, 19 LR, 1976–80

(%)

	Imports						Exports				
Category	1976	1877	1978	1979	1880		1976	1977	1978	1979	1980
Oil-Exporting Countries	6.3	8.5	8.6	8.9	12.8		5.0	5.8	-6.3	35.3	35.6

Continued in SALA, 23-2630.

Table 3328

COMMODITY PRICES, 1970–88[a]

(YA)

Commodity	Code[1]	1970	1975	1980	1981	1982	1983	1984	1985	1986	1987	1988
Aluminum (US cents/pound)												
Canada (United Kingdom)	w	27.86	39.39	80.51	57.28	44.98	65.25	56.77	47.21	52.15	70.99	115.51
Bananas (US cents/pound)												
Latin America (US Ports)	w	7.53	11.15	17.01	18.20	16.99	19.46	16.76	17.25	17.93	17.09	20.21
Bauxite (US $/metric ton)												
Guyana (Baltimore)	w	42.39	105.31	212.45	216.34	203.35	179.54	164.95	164.28	164.85	164.76	~
Beef (US cents/pound)												
All Origins (US Ports)	w	59.16	60.20	125.19	112.12	108.39	110.67	103.11	97.67	94.98	108.18	114.17
Argentina (frozen)	u	33.14	38.87	93.12	76.87	64.07	66.59	57.78	~	110.11	158.03	~
Argentina (corned)	u	39.30	74.83	144.27	135.20	99.99	91.33	82.46	82.23	92.79	113.95	~
Butter (US cents/pound)												
New Zealand	w	28.61	50.46	73.80	78.79	79.05	110.06	75.55	57.15	56.89	63.64	70.13
Cacao (US cents/pound)												
Brazil	u	29.42	56.59	107.06	87.50	68.29	83.10	105.32	94.97	92.04	83.96	72.68
Coal (US $/short ton)												
US (Pennsylvania mines)	w	16.60	44.86	46.18	61.03	68.21	65.83	65.81	~	~	~	~
Coconut Oil (US cents/pound)												
Philippines	w	12.80	17.00	28.06	23.27	19.75	24.15	44.83	24.18	12.10	16.74	23.34
Coffee (US cents/pound)												
All Coffee (New York)	w	50.53	72.48	150.71	115.82	125.62	127.94	141.24	133.47	170.28	107.32	115.11
Brazil (New York)	w	55.80	82.58	208.79	186.44	143.68	142.75	149.65	148.93	231.19	106.37	121.84
Brazil	u	44.26	49.57	143.75	83.34	94.88	101.16	112.72	103.97	173.30	89.98	107.24
Colombia (New York)	w	56.66	81.71	178.83	128.09	139.71	131.69	144.25	145.56	192.74	112.29	135.10
Colombia	u	54.22	62.38	161.70	121.77	134.62	120.13	133.35	134.87	202.33	113.13	140.56
El Salvador	u	49.37	54.39	151.41	123.77	128.87	105.64	~	~	~	~	
Uganda (New York)	w	41.44	61.05	147.15	102.91	111.04	124.12	138.18	121.24	148.24	102.34	95.11
Copper (US cents/pound)												
Canada	u	62.84	57.30	99.76	81.96	71.73	72.53	54.66	62.24	63.69	138.59	~
Copra (US $/metric ton)												
Philippines	u	179.91	226.41	390.45	310.53	276.66	275.78	~	~	140.60	248.30	~
Cotton (US cents/pound)												
United States (10 markets)	w	25.10	45.10	81.30	72.02	60.03	68.42	68.15	58.68	52.72	63.45	57.35
Mexico	u	26.26	51.14	83.36	74.82	64.57	77.90	80.30	61.74	52.85	76.13	~
Fishmeal (US $/metric ton)												
Peru	u	155.72	202.46	453.00	505.84	~	~	~	~	~	~	~
Gold (US $/fine ounce)												
United Kingdom (London)	w	35.94	159.25	607.87	459.75	375.80	422.47	360.36	317.18	367.68	444.50	437.15
Groundnuts (US $/metric ton)												
Nigeria (London)	w	228.17	432.97	485.57	622.72	383.20	349.44	349.76	349.85	963.86	933.02	~
Groundnut Cake (US $/metric ton)												
All Origins (Europe)	w	115.06	157.76	271.41	269.26	208.33	229.00	187.50	146.25	166.00	154.17	~
Groundnut Oil (US $/metric ton)												
West Africa (Europe)	w	378.54	778.17	858.75	1,042.75	585.17	710.92	1,016.67	905.25	569.42	499.75	590.5
Hides (US cents/pound)												
United States (Chicago)	w	12.90	23.28	45.92	41.72	38.56	45.13	58.87	51.18	63.76	79.84	87.65
Australia	u	24.79	43.92	84.65	60.76	57.72	48.73	51.94	47.08	58.09	86.35	105.67
Iron Ore (US $/metric ton)												
Brazil (North Sea Ports)	w	15.22	22.81	27.25	24.62	26.21	23.97	23.11	22.66	21.89	22.23	23.12
Jute (US $/metric ton)												
Bangladesh (Chita-Chaina)	w	269.60	370.98	313.65	278.38	283.22	298.39	569.80	698.57	326.03	325.36	370.00
Lamb (US cents/pound)												
New Zealand	u	24.33	39.80	72.28	74.90	64.97	62.37	56.75	53.86	51.84	60.76	~
Lead (US cents/pound)												
United States (New York)	w	15.70	21.60	43.50	37.46	26.69	22.53	27.00	19.63	20.30	35.92	36.57
Linseed Oil (US cents/pound)												
United States (Minneapolis)	w	11.00	41.00	30.80	37.17	33.13	31.95	36.36	37.62	~	~	~
Logs (US $/cubic meter)												
Philippines (Tokyo)	w	43.17	67.51	192.95	144.44	143.08	136.43	149.59	132.32	~	~	~
Maize (US $/bushel)												
United States (US Gulf Pts)	w	1.48	3.04	3.19	3.32	2.75	3.45	3.45	2.85	2.23	1.92	2.72
Manganese (US $/long ton)												
India (US Ports)	w	55.33	140.00	155.25	167.80	164.12	151.82	143.21	141.01	140.83	127.50	~
Newsprint (US $/short ton)												
United States (New York)	w	150.50	256.70	388.53	428.47	440.71	422.41	450.71	463.41	453.82	493.22	522.43
Nickel (US cents/pound)												
Canada (Canadian Ports)	w	127.63	207.33	295.68	270.03	219.43	211.95	215.56	222.22	176.39	221.00	~
Palm Kernels (US $/metric ton)												
Nigeria (Europe)	w	167.55	206.75	344.50	317.33	264.83	365.33	524.75	284.67	141.42	181.42	~
Palm Oil (US $/metric ton)												
Malaysia	u	214.82	473.33	529.53	490.91	416.81	437.54	650.55	493.83	269.97	337.94	415.87

Table 3328 (Continued)

COMMODITY PRICES, 1970–88[a]

(YA)

Commodity	Code[1]	1970	1975	1980	1981	1982	1983	1984	1985	1986	1987	1988
Pepper, Black (US cents/pound)												
Malaysia (New York)	w	57.30	90.95	90.43	71.84	70.43	76.63	103.34	173.20	219.16	~	~
Petroleum (US $/Barrel)												
Libya (Es Sidra)	w	2.58	11.59	35.87	39.83	35.49	30.89	30.15	29.66	14.60	18.52	~
Saudi Arabia (Ras Tanura)	w	1.30	10.72	28.67	32.50	33.47	29.31	28.47	~	~	~	~
Venezuela (Tia Juana)	w	1.73	10.89	27.60	32.03	32.03	28.05	27.03	26.44	11.60	16.65	~
Phosphate Rock (US $/metric ton)												
Morocco (Casablanca)	w	11.00	68.00	46.71	49.50	42.38	36.92	38.25	33.92	34.37	31.95	34.75
Potash (US $/metric ton)												
Canada (Vancouver)	w	31.50	81.33	115.71	113.67	83.25	75.50	83.71	83.96	68.79	68.21	81.54
Plywood (US cents/sheet)												
Philippines (Tokyo)	w	103.06	121.83	273.84	245.46	234.35	229.87	227.03	210.91	274.15	398.72	358.84
Pulp (US $/metric ton)												
Canada	u	154.16	373.04	470.23	481.36	435.46	368.08	440.34	354.24	~	~	~
Rice (US $/metric ton)												
United States (New Orleans)	w	189.60	418.87	496.04	565.48	366.70	378.46	379.74	382.50	342.83	323.53	429.90
Rubber (US cents/pound)												
All Origins (New York)	w	21.10	29.90	73.50	57.00	45.28	56.17	49.58	41.79	41.20	44.11	48.83
Sawnwood (US $/cubic meter)												
Malaysia (French Ports)	w	93.23	166.44	369.66	314.14	302.11	304.28	306.77	276.26	266.18	275.44	306.44
Shrimp (US $/pound)												
United States (N. York Gulf)	w	1.24	2.67	4.60	4.41	6.21	6.00	5.24	4.76	5.85	5.18	5.64
Silver (US cents/troy ounce)												
United States (New York)	w	177.10	441.90	2,057.80	1,052.1	794.9	1,144.1	814.1	614.2	546.9	700.9	653.5
Sisal (US $/metric ton)												
Tanzania	u	115.25	413.24	540.61	587.94	476.13	495.81	371.06	562.43	404.98	~	~
Sorghum (US $/metric ton)												
United States (U.S. Gulf Ports)	w	51.80	111.87	128.86	126.54	108.35	128.42	118.19	102.97	82.41	72.82	98.46
Soybeans (US $/metric ton)												
United States (Rotterdam)	w	116.92	221.67	296.25	288.42	244.50	281.67	282.08	224.42	208.42	215.75	303.50
Soybean Meal (US $/metric ton)												
United States (Rotterdam)	w	102.58	155.00	258.58	252.67	218.00	237.83	197.17	157.17	184.75	203.25	267.50
Soybean Oil (US $/metric ton)												
All Origins (Dutch Ports)	w	286.33	563.33	598.25	506.92	447.33	526.92	725.17	576.00	342.41	334.25	461.17
Sugar (US cents/pound)												
US Import Price (NY)	w	7.50	22.47	30.03	19.73	19.92	22.04	21.74	20.35	20.96	21.84	22.12
EEC Import Price	w	5.09	15.44	22.09	18.93	18.12	17.57	16.04	15.99	18.61	20.95	23.81
Caribbean (New York)	w	3.76	20.56	28.67	16.89	8.41	8.47	5.20	4.05	6.05	6.76	10.19
Brazil	u	5.10	29.18	21.79	16.92	9.42	9.46	9.17	6.66	7.09	6.80	8.42
Dominican Republic	u	6.15	26.77	16.41	27.47	14.45	13.02	~	~	~	~	~
Australia	u	4.97	19.95	21.07	19.16	9.99	10.32	7.82	5.84	7.97	7.49	9.57
Philippines	u	6.62	27.03	16.22	20.65	15.09	13.44	12.70	14.94	17.59	16.63	19.01
Superphosphate (US $/metric ton)												
United States (US Gulf Ports)	w	42.50	205.00	178.04	160.87	140.04	134.04	131.25	121.38	121.17	138.25	158.38
Tea (US cents/pound)												
Average Auction (London)	w	49.55	69.70	101.06	91.59	87.62	105.44	156.79	89.98	87.48	77.45	81.18
Tin (US cents/pound)												
All Origins (New York)	w	174.40	340.10	774.60	644.92	583.33	601.42	573.04	534.49	~	~	~
Bolivia	u	174.41	312.55	760.36	633.80	574.63	586.48	554.40	539.32	257.59	309.97	320.51
Tobacco (US cents/pound)												
United States (All Markets)	w	80.61	103.78	142.59	160.86	182.72	185.52	185.60	184.33	163.60	156.96	162.59
Urea (US $/metric ton)												
Any Origin (Europe)	w	48.25	197.67	221.88	217.33	159.54	124.46	171.29	136.33	107.00	117.13	155.00
Wheat (US $/bushel)												
Australia	u	1.42	4.57	4.91	5.07	4.41	4.67	3.89	3.50	3.14	2.43	3.19
United States (US Gulf Pts)	w	1.49	4.06	4.70	4.76	4.36	4.28	4.15	3.70	3.13	3.07	3.95
Argentina	u	1.48	4.65	4.94	5.51	4.54	3.90	3.63	3.13	2.67	2.28	~
Wool (US cents/kilogram)												
New Zealand (greasy wool)	u	66.14	131.82	275.58	243.55	212.98	197.79	208.83	201.29	214.33	299.18	~
Zinc (US cents/pound)												
United States (New York)	w	15.90	38.90	38.10	45.67	40.01	42.82	49.95	43.22	40.50	44.08	57.76
Canada	u	11.93	36.18	34.51	39.19	36.09	36.30	44.71	37.37	33.05	36.24	~
Peru	u	6.41	16.73	21.91	25.25	24.22	~	~	~	~	~	~

1. Code: w = wholesale price.
        u = unit price (reported value data divided by reported volume data).

a. For data 1949–70 see SALA, 21-2526.

SOURCE: IMF-IFS-Y, 1979; IMF-IFS-Y, 1980; IMF-IFS-Y, 1981; IMF-IFS-Y, 1982; IMF-IFS, May 1985, pp. 74-77; IMF-IFS-Y, 1986, pp. 169–171; IMF-IFS-Y, 1986, pp. 174–177; IMF-IFS-Y, 1988, pp. 180–183; IMF-IFS, August 1989, pp. 82–85.

Table 3229

REAL "MANUFACTURES PURCHASING POWER INDEX" OF PRIMARY COMMODITIES EXPORTED BY DEVELOPING COUNTRIES, 1948–85

(1977–79 = 100)

Year	Petroleum	33 Commodities[1] (Excluding Energy) (100.0)[a]	Agriculture Total (71.8)	Food Total (58.1)	Beverages (26.4)	Cereals (7.5)	Fats and Oils (8.6)	Other (15.6)	Non-Food (13.6)	Timber (4.8)	Metals and Minerals (23.4)
1948	47	109	116	110	58	162	162	145	139	54	100
1949	40	109	114	110	68	169	126	145	128	60	107
1950	41	146	158	142	99	183	153	190	227	72	125
1951	36	153	163	138	95	172	157	184	269	91	135
1952	34	130	128	115	86	164	125	135	179	65	150
1953	37	122	120	115	90	168	130	123	152	61	139
1954	40	132	134	132	131	160	124	125	143	86	136
1955	39	130	125	114	102	139	113	123	172	68	156
1956	38	128	122	115	104	136	112	126	152	63	159
1957	37	125	124	120	93	127	110	166	145	60	139
1958	34	109	107	101	83	126	102	120	131	56	127
1959	31	108	106	95	74	121	111	108	151	67	125
1960	29	107	104	92	71	114	104	111	155	72	125
1961	28	100	95	84	66	120	106	96	131	73	120
1962	26	98	94	85	62	130	98	97	128	79	115
1963	26	117	121	121	62	130	105	223	121	78	115
1964	24	115	111	109	70	129	106	167	120	65	138
1965	24	107	92	86	66	125	117	84	117	75	158
1966	23	106	89	83	62	136	110	76	114	76	164
1967	23	98	87	82	60	143	103	79	107	80	136
1968	23	100	88	82	60	140	100	80	112	83	140
1969	22	103	92	86	59	132	94	105	114	76	146
1970	20	102	91	89	64	113	104	109	100	76	143
1971	25	92	86	83	53	103	99	116	96	73	117
1972	26	94	92	92	54	101	89	155	91	67	107
1973	32	122	120	119	59	178	157	170	124	100	135
1974	108	157	164	175	56	212	150	374	114	99	149
1975	95	112	113	119	48	149	89	241	89	67	116
1976	100	109	110	110	90	119	94	149	111	89	111
1977	100	112	116	119	138	100	106	105	102	91	104
1978	87	93	94	93	89	104	97	93	97	80	92
1979	111	97	93	91	81	96	98	103	102	124	104
1980	166	113	113	115	66	105	82	219	106	137	106
1981	186	91	89	89	54	112	79	141	92	102	93
1982	186	77	73	70	58	84	66	86	83	106	85
1983	165	82	78	74	59	91	79	89	95	99	88
1984	164	81	78	75	70	88	96	65	90	113	85
1985	159	73	67	64	62	80	73	54	81	109	84

1. The commodities included in each group are: beverages—coffee, cocoa, tea; cereals—maize, rice, wheat, grain sorghum; fats and oils—palm oil, coconut oil, groundnut oil, soybeans, copra, groundnut meal, soybean meal; other foods—sugar, beef, bananas, oranges; non-foods—cotton, jute, rubber, tobacco; timber—logs; metals and minerals copper, tin, nickel, bauxite, aluminum, iron ore, manganese ore, lead, zinc, phosphate rock.

a. Weighted by 1977–1979 developing countries export values.

SOURCE: WB, *Commodity Trade and Price Trends* (Baltimore: The Johns Hopkins University Press, 1986), p. 40.

Table 3330

WESTERN HEMISPHERE EXPORT PRICE INDEX, 12 LC, 1950–88

(1980 = 100)

	Country	1950	1955	1959	1960	1961	1962	1963	1964	1965	1966	1967	1968	1969	1970	1971	1972
B.	BOLIVIA	9.6	10.8	10.0	10.0	10.8	10.8	11.3	14.6	16.7	15.8	15.0	15.0	16.3	21.1	17.1	17.8
C.	BRAZIL	36.2	38.7	29.6*	29.0	30.5*	26.6	26.5	31.7	32.0	30.7	30.6	30.2	31.1	35.1	33.9	38.3
E.	COLOMBIA	~	~	25.2	25.7	25.5	23.4	20.5	24.5	22.9	18.5	22.5	23.0	23.1	28.5*	27.1	30.3
H.	DOMINICAN REP.	27.2	27.8	25.4	25.6	26.3	29.7	32.6	34.5	30.6	33.3	33.2	36.0	39.3	37.6	35.4	39.3
I.	ECUADOR	~	13.3	12.2	12.9	12.2	15.6	13.3	16.0	16.7	16.7	16.7	17.1	15.2	17.1	18.2	15.2
J.	EL SALVADOR	35.2	38.5	26.1	26.1	25.1	22.9	26.3	29.1	30.6	30.0	28.1	27.2	26.6	32.1	30.9	33.3
	Grenada	~	~	~	~	~	~	~	~	~	~	~	28.9	31.8	29.7	26.9	25.0
	Guyana	~	~	~	~	19.0	19.3	23.8	22.5	20.2	20.7	20.4	20.5	21.7	24.7	26.5	29.8
M.	HONDURAS	24.7	29.9	23.7	27.8	30.0	31.8	30.4	32.3	31.1	30.9	31.0	30.1	30.0	33.6	32.6	34.2
O.	NICARAGUA	33.8	47.7	34.9	37.5	38.4	39.5	37.6	36.9	38.7	38.9	37.3	37.5	38.2	39.0	39.4	42.8
P.	PANAMA	26.7	30.9	26.3	23.5	23.1	27.3	24.8	26.3	27.0	27.5	27.7	29.5	27.6	27.6	27.6	29.5
Q.	PARAGUAY	31.8	38.8	29.5	24.7	25.9	26.4	30.9	35.8	36.3	37.1	33.7	36.3	37.2	39.9	40.6	44.9
R.	PERU	~	~	~	20.0	18.7	18.9	20.4	23.4	23.9	28.4	25.2	26.6	30.2	31.3	28.4	29.9
	Suriname	~	~	~	~	~	~	~	~	26.7	26.4	26.4	27.0	28.1	30.0	30.6	31.3
	Trinidad and Tobago	~	~	~	~	~	~	~	~	~	9.9	10.2	9.6	9.7	9.8	11.1	11.6
T.	VENEZUELA	~	5.3	5.4	5.6	6.5	6.5	6.5	6.7	6.7	6.7	6.7	6.7	6.6	6.7	8.4	9.0
	Western Hemisphere	~	17.5	15.5	15.9	17.0	16.4	16.4	18.1	18.0	17.9	17.9	18.0	18.4	19.8	20.8	22.6

	Country	1973	1974	1975	1976	1977	1978	1979	1980	1981	1982	1983	1984	1985	1986	1987	1988
B.	BOLIVIA	23.3	40.6	38.8	43.8	54.4	61.5	74.9	100.0	97.1	92.3	94.5	93.0	88.6	64.7	58.3	56.3
C.	BRAZIL	52.7	66.4	66.4	76.6	93.5	86.0	94.4	100.0	94.1	88.4	83.6	85.3	80.5	80.4	~	~
E.	COLOMBIA	38.2	51.2	50.6	74.1	108.9	91.0	89.7	100.0	89.5	88.8	89.0	95.1	88.9	100.6	77.3	80.9
H.	DOMINICAN REP.	48.0	72.6	114.3	76.4	84.5	76.9	81.1	100.0	132.1	88.1	79.8	91.5	76.9	86.5	69.0	95.7
I.	ECUADOR	19.3	41.7	38.5	42.4	49.1	45.1	72.9	100.2	91.9	99.2	83.7	80.2	83.3	51.3	56.0	48.9
J.	EL SALVADOR	41.3	51.4	52.6	77.1	101.5	85.0	96.9	100.0	93.0	88.1	71.3	~	~	~	~	~
	Grenada	42.6	66.7	83.9	62.7	64.2	83.1	99.9	100.0	87.6	78.0	79.6	70.7	87.0	129.5	153.0	~
	Guyana	30.8	59.8	79.0	66.0	74.1	68.9	75.2	100.0	93.3	87.4	80.1	~	~	~	~	~
M.	HONDURAS	40.3	47.0	57.8	66.4	90.1	86.0	84.9	100.0	94.1	90.1	91.6	96.1	97.4	95.5	~	~
O.	NICARAGUA	47.4	60.7	57.0	74.8	92.6	87.2	89.9	100.0	~	~	..	~	~	~	~	~
P.	PANAMA	49.2	69.3	80.4	72.7	65.6	63.7	77.7	100.0	104.9	84.4	92.3	91.3	86.1	~	~	67.7
Q.	PARAGUAY	56.3	67.1	71.7	72.7	98.4	90.1	94.0	100.0	112.7	121.6	104.9	114.6	76.8	~	~	~
R.	PERU	49.4	59.6	41.2	46.8	50.9	50.2	76.5	100.0	83.0	71.7	75.9	68.3	62.2	51.9	62.5	80.2
	Suriname	31.2	42.3	57.0	61.9	68.8	74.5	81.9	100.0	109.0	105.7	95.4	89.2	68.8	67.1	~	92.4
	Trinidad and Tobago	14.9	38.0	41.6	42.8	47.4	47.3	62.6	100.0	110.3	105.6	104.8	104.1	96.5	60.9	~	~
T.	VENEZUELA	13.3	37.4	40.0	41.6	45.5	45.3	60.9	100.0	116.0	115.6	101.6	~	~	~	~	~
	Western Hemisphere	31.5	52.0	53.2	58.7	69.4	65.7	78.1	100.0	101.9	98.3	90.6	91.2	84.9	79.0	~	~

SOURCE: IMF-IFS-Y, 1987; IMF-IFS-Y, 1988; IMF-IFS-Y, 1989.

Table 3331

U.S. EXPORT PRICE INDEX,[1] 1880–1988

Year	1970 = 100	1980 = 100	Year	1970 = 100	1980 = 100
1880	37.5	14.3	1935	36.0	13.8
1881	38.3	14.6	1936	36.8	14.1
1882	39.5	15.1	1937	39.1	14.9
1883	37.4	14.3	1938	36.2	13.8
1884	36.0	13.8	1939	35.4	13.5
1885	33.6	12.8	1940	37.9	14.5
1886	31.6	12.1	1941	40.8	15.6
1887	31.5	12.0	1942	49.5	18.9
1888	33.1	12.6	1943	54.6	20.9
1889	31.7	12.1	1944	62.5	23.9
1890	31.4	12.0	1945	62.3	23.8
1891	32.4	12.4	1946	59.0	22.5
1892	30.2	11.5	1947	70.4	26.9
1893	29.6	11.3	1948	74.8	28.6
1894	26.0	9.9	1949	69.6	26.6
1895	26.5	10.1	1950	67.8	25.9
1896	26.2	10.0	1951	77.7	29.7
1897	25.5	9.7	1952	77.3	29.5
1898	25.2	9.6	1953	77.0	29.4
1899	26.7	10.2	1954	75.7	28.9
1900	30.0	11.5	1955	76.7	29.3
1901	29.3	11.2	1956	80.0	30.6
1902	30.0	11.5	1957	82.2	31.4
1903	32.0	12.2	1958	81.4	31.1
1904	32.1	12.3	1959	81.4	31.1
1905	31.0	11.8	1960	81.9	31.3
1906	36.5	13.9	1961	83.5	31.9
1907	35.1	13.4	1962	83.0	31.7
1908	33.2	12.7	1963	83.0	31.7
1909	34.8	13.3	1964	83.8	32.0
1910	37.7	14.4	1965	86.4	33.0
1911	34.5	13.2	1966	89.0	34.0
1912	35.2	13.4	1967	90.8	34.7
1913	36.9	14.1	1968	92.1	35.2
1914	36.1	13.8	1969	94.8	36.2
1915	38.8	14.8	1970	100.0	38.2
1916	50.0	19.1	1971	103.1	39.4
1917	65.3	24.9	1972	106.5	40.7
1918	76.1	29.1	1973	124.1	47.4
1919	80.0	30.6	1974	158.4	60.5
1920	86.6	33.1	1975	177.0	67.6
1921	56.5	21.6	1976	183.0	69.9
1922	52.4	20.0	1977	189.5	72.4
1923	59.8	22.8	1978	202.6	77.4
1924	55.1	21.0	1979	230.6	88.1
1925	51.8	19.8	1980	261.8	100.0
1926	55.1	21.0	1981	285.9	109.2
1927	48.1	18.4	1982	289.0	110.4
1928	48.9	18.7	1983	292.1	111.6
1929	48.5	18.5	1984	296.1	113.1
1930	43.3	16.5	1985	293.7	112.2
1931	33.3	12.7	1986	294.5	113.3
1932	28.8	11.0	1987	301.8	115.3
1933	30.0	11.5	1988	301.6	123.3
1934	35.3	13.5			

1. The U.S. export price index constructed here has been used to deflate the commodity
   prices in tables 3229 through 3241.

SOURCE: *Historical Statistics of the United States*, various years; IMF-IFS-4, 1987;
IMF-IFS-Y, 1988; IMF-IFS, August 1989, line 74.

Figure 33:1

U.S. EXPORT PRICE INDEX, 1880–1987

PART I. 1880–1930

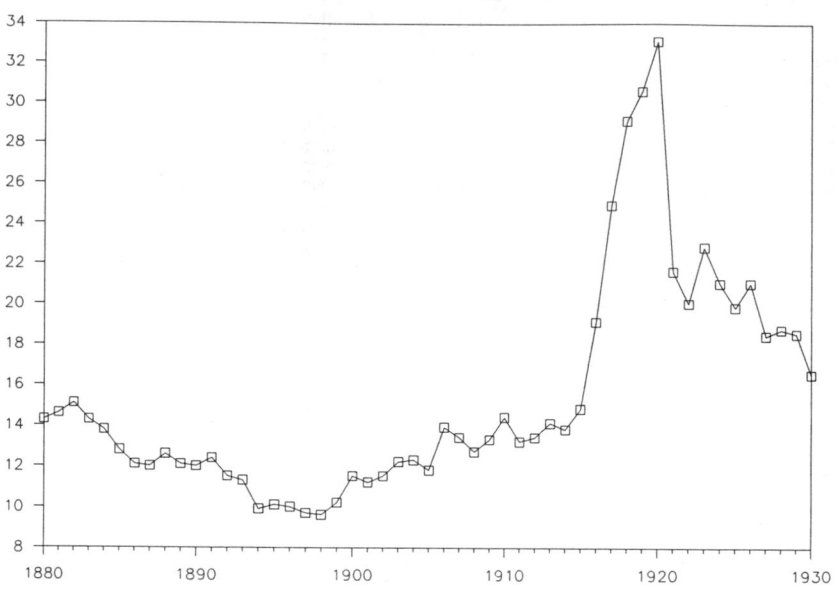

PART II. 1931–1987

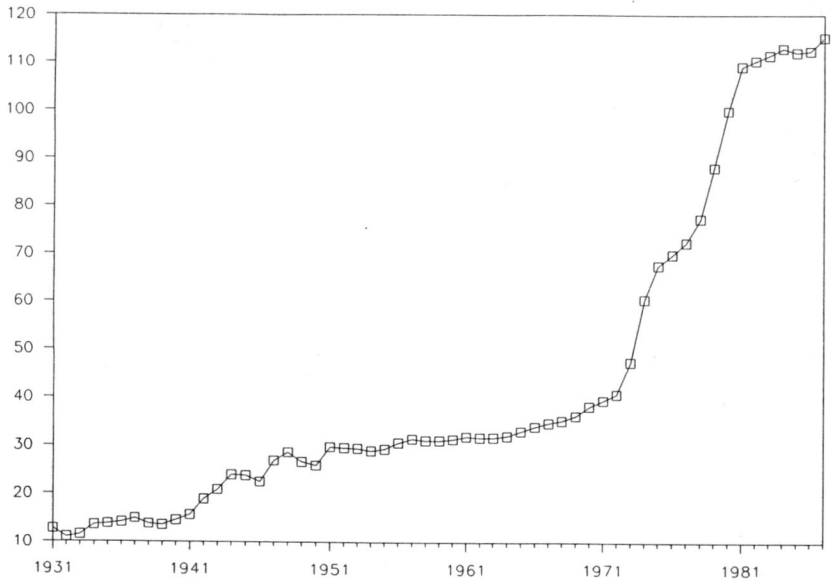

SOURCE: SALA, 27-3231.

Table 3332

BANANAS, REAL PRICE,[1] 1951–88

(US Cents of 1970/lb)

Year	Real Price	Year	Real Price
1951	9.40	1971	6.17
1952	9.57	1972	6.88
1953	9.61	1973	6.02
1954	10.04	1974	5.27
1955	9.78	1975	6.30
1956	9.50	1976	6.41
1957	9.73	1977	6.53
1958	9.09	1978	6.42
1959	11.43	1979	6.41
1960	11.17	1980	6.50
1961	10.63	1981	6.37
1962	10.17	1982	5.88
1963	9.75	1983	6.66
1964	9.26	1984	5.66
1965	8.39	1985	5.87
1966	7.85	1986	6.09
1967	7.87	1987	5.66
1968	7.52	1988	6.70
1969	7.64		
1970	7.53		

1. Nominal data in source deflated here using U.S. export price index (table 3231).

SOURCE: IMF-IFS-Y, various years.

Figure 33:2

BANANAS, REAL PRICE, 1951–87

(US Cents of 1970/lb)

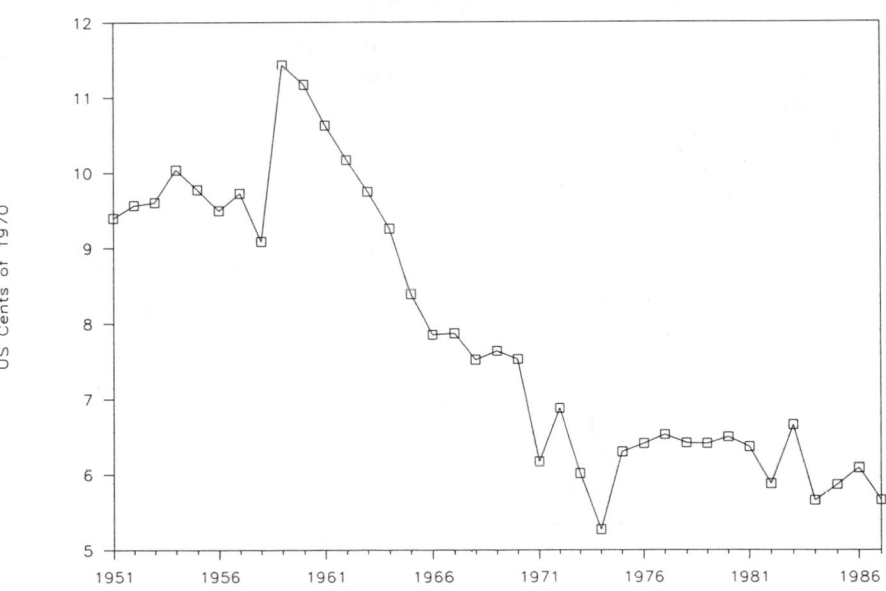

SOURCE: SALA, 27-3232.

Table 3333

BAUXITE (GUYANIAN), REAL PRICE,[1] 1965–88
(US of 1970/MET)

Year	Real Price
1965	37.27
1966	40.73
1967	46.26
1968	46.74
1969	44.72
1970	42.39
1971	48.04
1972	50.05
1973	48.90
1974	45.40
1975	59.50
1976	64.09
1977	71.15
1978	68.32
1979	66.18
1980	81.15
1981	75.67
1982	72.09
1983	61.47
1984	55.71
1985	55.93
1986	55.97
1987	54.63
1988	~

1. Nominal data in source deflated here using the U.S.
   export price index (table 3231).

SOURCE: IMF-IFS-Y, various years.

Figure 33:3

BAUXITE (GUYANIAN), REAL PRICE, 1965–87
(US of 1970/MET)

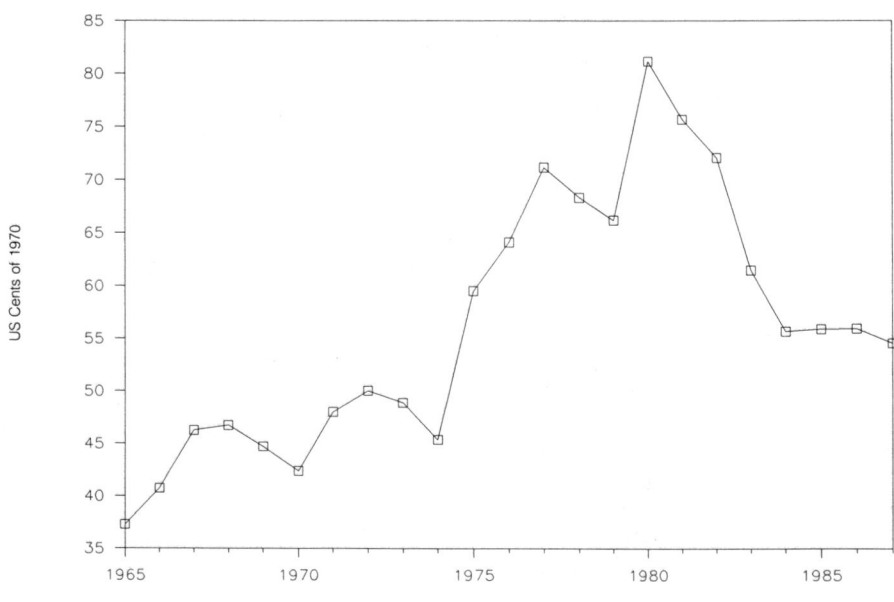

SOURCE: SALA, 27-3233.

Table 3334

BEEF (ARGENTINE FROZEN), REAL PRICE,[1] 1950–88

(US Cents of 1970/lb)

Year	Real Price	Year	Real Price
1950	14.07	1970	33.14
1951	18.21	1971	38.95
1952	16.56	1972	48.68
1953	20.70	1973	57.34
1954	20.67	1974	53.01
1955	25.24	1975	21.96
1956	19.15	1976	22.56
1957	18.14	1977	27.89
1958	21.56	1978	25.93
1959	23.81	1979	37.69
1960	24.76	1980	35.57
1961	21.74	1981	26.89
1962	19.65	1982	22.17
1963	20.81	1983	22.80
1964	27.92	1984	19.51
1965	32.84	1985	19.20
1966	28.94	1986	37.38
1967	23.63	1987	52.36
1968	30.42	1988	~
1969	26.91		

1. Nominal data in source deflated here using U.S. export price index (table 3231).

SOURCE: IMF-IFS-Y, various years.

Figure 33:4

BEEF (ARGENTINE FROZEN), REAL PRICE, 1950–86

(US Cents of 1970/lb)

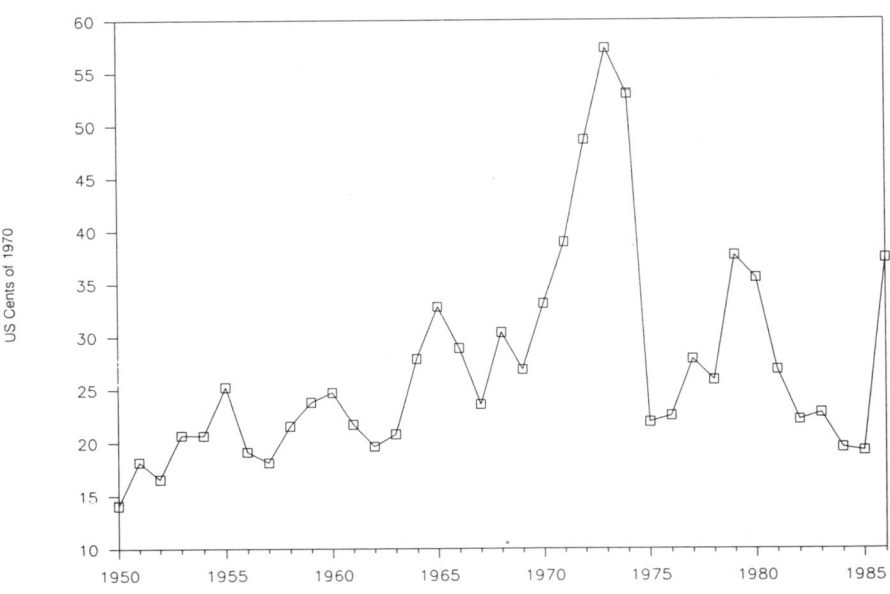

SOURCE: SALA, 27-3234.

Table 3335

CACAO, REAL PRICE,[1] 1913–88

(US Cents of 1970/lb)

Year	Real Price	Year	Real Price
1913	11.65	1953	40.77
1914	9.07	1954	67.17
1915	21.62	1955	44.09
1916	15.64	1956	30.29
1917	8.33	1957	35.06
1918	7.93	1958	48.17
1919	10.87	1959	41.63
1920	8.08	1960	30.54
1921	20.17	1961	23.95
1922	33.77	1962	23.93
1923	37.63	1963	27.87
1924	36.51	1964	25.23
1925	35.14	1965	15.81
1926	38.37	1966	22.98
1927	75.11	1967	25.85
1928	60.94	1968	29.95
1929	49.99	1969	42.22
1930	36.69	1970	29.42
1931	34.20	1971	22.79
1932	32.05	1972	24.64
1933	30.77	1973	39.09
1934	29.55	1974	46.31
1935	28.22	1975	31.97
1936	40.19	1976	42.09
1937	41.45	1977	96.85
1938	31.46	1978	75.78
1939	29.49	1979	61.03
1940	28.79	1980	40.89
1941	35.07	1981	30.61
1942	37.69	1982	23.63
1943	33.29	1983	28.45
1944	29.85	1984	35.57
1945	27.22	1985	32.34
1946	52.59	1986	31.25
1947	96.75	1987	27.81
1948	128.65	1988	24.10
1949	64.41		
1950	142.43		
1951	42.15		
1952	41.84		

1. Nominal data in source deflated here using U.S. export price index (table 3231).

SOURCE: IMF-IFS-Y, various years.

Figure 33:5

CACAO, REAL PRICE, 1913–87
(US Cents of 1970/lb)

PART I. 1913–50

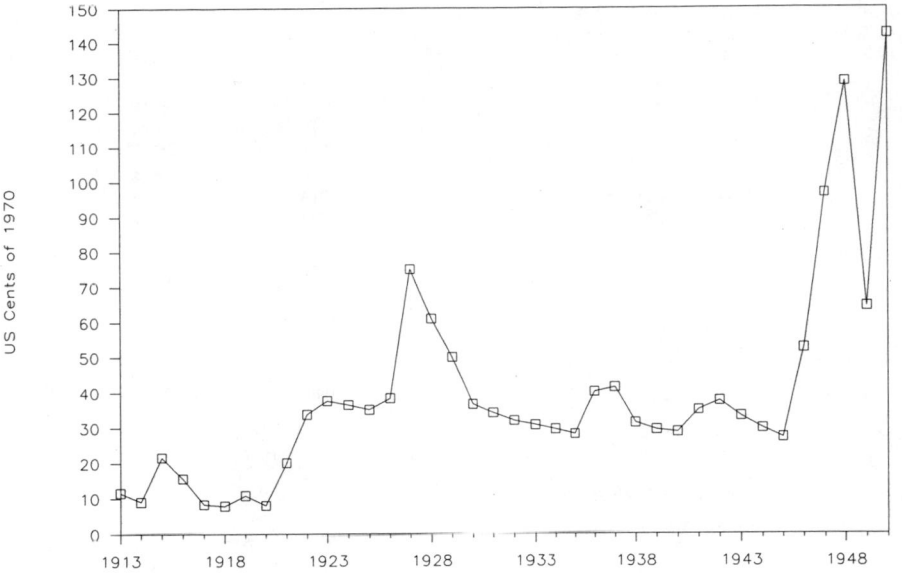

PART II. 1951–87

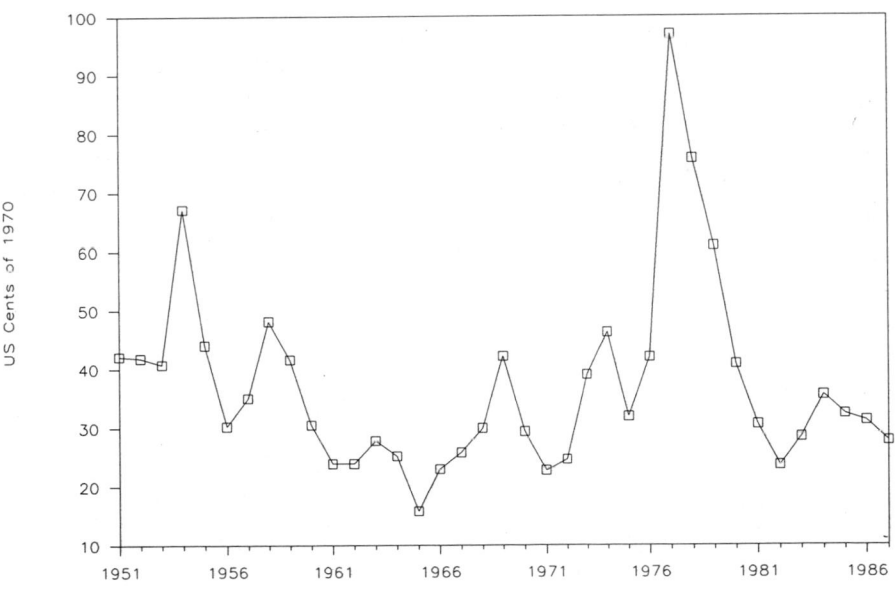

SOURCE: SALA, 27-3235.

Table 3336

COFFEE (BRAZILIAN), REAL PRICE,[1] 1950–88
(US Cents of 1980/lb)

Year	Real Price	Year	Real Price
1950	170.31	1970	141.94
1951	164.78	1971	116.75
1952	169.32	1972	122.46
1953	179.83	1973	140.95
1954	194.71	1974	113.06
1955	158.98	1975	92.28
1956	151.41	1976	168.08
1957	142.17	1977	299.30
1958	129.71	1978	215.58
1959	102.19	1979	156.04
1960	135.11	1980	161.70
1961	129.12	1981	111.51
1962	120.66	1982	121.94
1963	117.79	1983	113.02
1964	145.25	1984	117.90
1965	139.42	1985	120.20
1966	135.53	1986	179.85
1967	115.27	1987	92.25
1968	114.60	1988	86.97
1969	110.86		

1. Nominal data in source deflated here using U.S. export price index (table 3231).

SOURCE: IMF-IFS-Y, various years.

Figure 33:6

COFFEE (BRAZILIAN), REAL PRICE, 1950–87
(US Cents of 1980/lb)

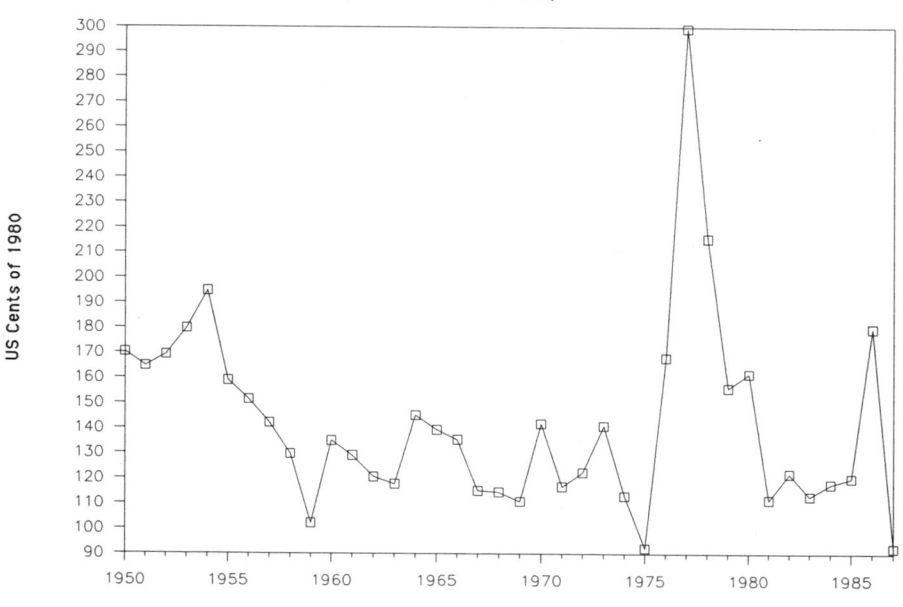

SOURCE: SALA, 27-3236.

Table 3337

COPPER, REAL PRICE,[1] 1950–88

(US Cents of 1980/lb)

Year	Real Price	Year	Real Price
1950	82.01	1970	150.97
1951	81.48	1971	130.53
1952	82.03	1972	124.37
1953	97.96	1973	124.20
1954	102.73	1974	126.69
1955	127.95	1975	93.99
1956	136.67	1976	98.47
1957	94.20	1977	90.90
1958	82.83	1978	84.64
1959	100.26	1979	104.73
1960	102.40	1980	101.40
1961	93.79	1981	76.94
1962	96.53	1982	66.04
1963	96.53	1983	69.77
1964	99.75	1984	59.13
1965	106.12	1985	58.71
1966	106.41	1986	57.47
1967	110.12	1987	70.39
1968	118.89	1988	95.64
1969	131.16		

1. Nominal data in source deflated here using U.S. export price index (table 3231).

SOURCE: IMF-IFS-Y, various years.

Figure 33:7

COPPER, REAL PRICE, 1950–87

(US Cents of 1980/lb)

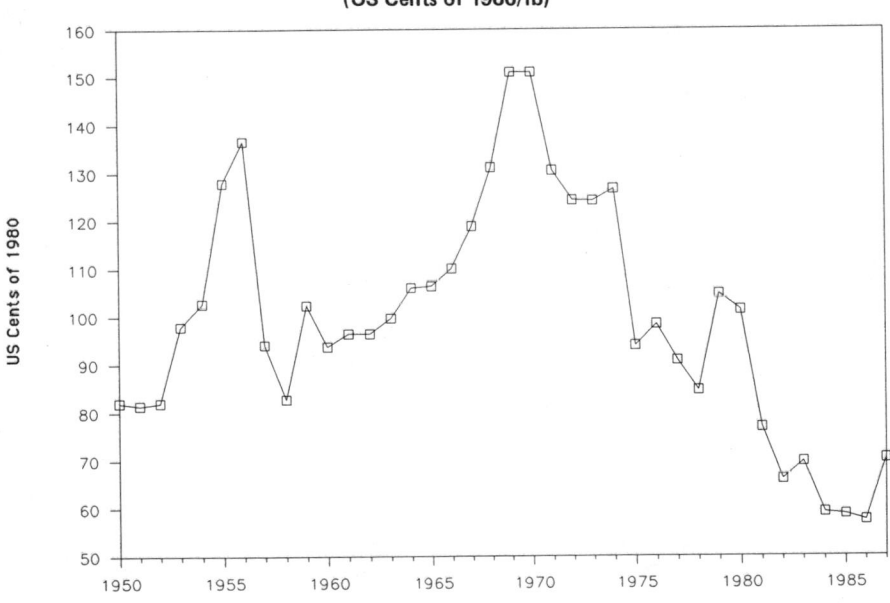

SOURCE: SALA, 27-3237.

Table 3338

COTTON (MEXICAN), REAL PRICE,[1] 1950–88

(US Cents of 1980/lb)

Year	Real Price	Year	Real Price
1950	14.94	1970	6.87
1951	13.01	1971	8.32
1952	12.46	1972	8.08
1953	10.00	1973	8.89
1954	11.61	1974	8.19
1955	10.10	1975	7.57
1956	9.24	1976	12.87
1957	8.67	1977	8.76
1958	8.14	1978	9.03
1959	7.16	1979	8.43
1960	7.24	1980	8.34
1961	7.45	1981	6.85
1962	7.35	1982	5.85
1963	7.56	1983	6.98
1964	7.54	1984	7.10
1965	7.13	1985	5.50
1966	6.89	1986	4.70
1967	6.94	1987	6.60
1968	6.95	1988	~
1969	6.63		

1. Nominal data in source deflated here using U.S. export price index (table 3231).

SOURCE: IMF-IFS-Y, various years.

Figure 33:8

COTTON (MEXICAN), REAL PRICE, 1950–87

(US Cents of 1980/lb)

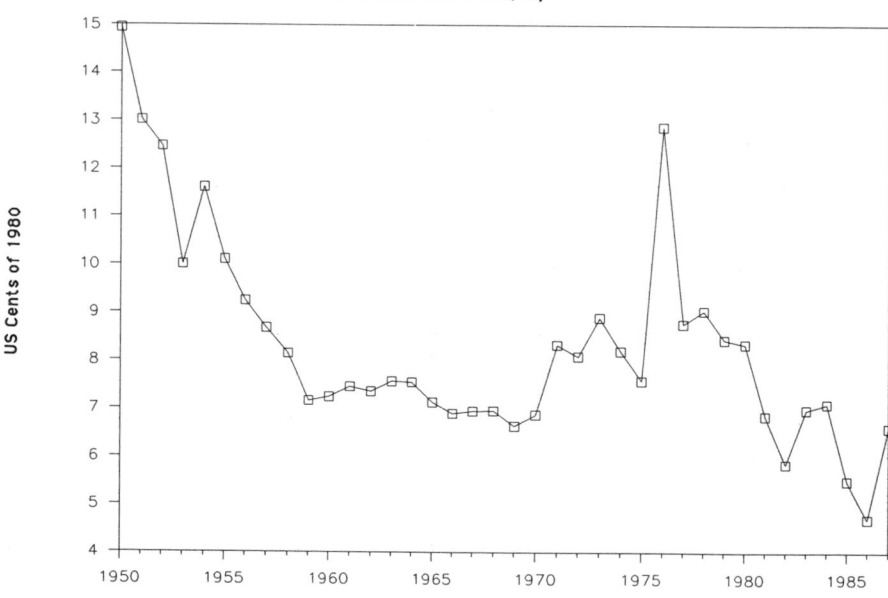

SOURCE: SALA, 27-3238.

Table 3339

IRON ORE (BRAZILIAN), REAL PRICE,[1] 1950–88
(US of 1970/MET)

Year	Real Price	Year	Real Price
1950	18.29	1970	15.22
1951	26.55	1971	13.06
1952	28.85	1972	12.01
1953	26.04	1973	13.80
1954	22.59	1974	11.99
1955	23.73	1975	12.89
1956	26.70	1976	12.14
1957	27.31	1977	11.39
1958	26.39	1978	9.57
1959	20.98	1979	10.16
1960	20.85	1980	10.41
1961	21.31	1981	8.61
1962	20.18	1982	9.07
1963	18.90	1983	8.21
1964	18.72	1984	7.80
1965	18.16	1985	7.72
1966	17.13	1986	7.43
1967	14.87	1987	7.36
1968	13.71	1988	7.67
1969	12.32		

1. Nominal data in source deflated here using U.S. export price index (table 3231).

SOURCE: IMF-IFS-Y, various years.

Figure 33:9

IRON ORE (BRAZILIAN), REAL PRICE, 1950–87
(US of 1970/MET)

SOURCE: SALA, 27-3239.

Table 3340

PETROLEUM (VENEZUELAN), REAL PRICE,[1] 1950–88
(US of 1980/Barrel)

Year	Real Price	Year	Real Price
1950	5.48	1970	4.53
1951	4.78	1971	5.61
1952	4.44	1972	5.82
1953	4.32	1973	7.51
1954	4.33	1974	16.93
1955	4.23	1975	16.11
1956	3.99	1976	16.14
1957	3.50	1977	17.15
1958	3.70	1978	16.05
1959	4.18	1979	19.04
1960	4.35	1980	27.60
1961	5.42	1981	29.33
1962	5.46	1982	29.01
1963	5.46	1983	25.13
1964	5.41	1984	23.90
1965	5.24	1985	23.57
1966	5.09	1986	10.00
1967	4.99	1987	14.44
1968	4.91	1988	10.26
1969	4.78		

1. Nominal data in source deflated here using U.S. export price index (table 3231).

SOURCE: IMF-IFS-Y, various years.

Figure 33:10

PETROLEUM (VENEZUELAN), REAL PRICE, 1950–86
(US of 1980/Barrel)

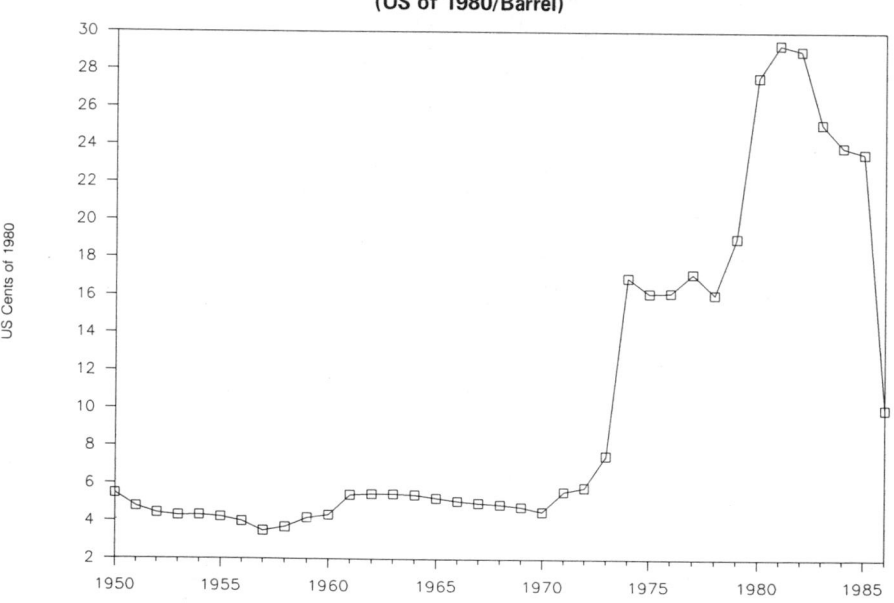

SOURCE: SALA, 27-3240.

Table 3341

SOYBEANS, REAL PRICE,[1] 1958–88

(US of 1970/MET)

Year	Real Price	Year	Real Price
1958	116.71	1974	174.82
1959	115.48	1975	125.24
1960	112.33	1976	126.32
1961	132.93	1977	147.85
1962	120.48	1978	132.44
1963	132.53	1979	129.12
1964	131.26	1980	113.16
1965	135.32	1981	100.88
1966	141.85	1982	84.60
1967	123.99	1983	96.43
1968	115.01	1984	95.27
1969	108.65	1985	76.41
1970	116.92	1986	70.77
1971	121.80	1987	71.49
1972	131.46	1988	100.63
1973	233.95		

1. Nominal data in source deflated here using U.S. export price index (table 3231).

SOURCE: IMF-IFS-Y, various years.

Figure 33:11

SOYBEANS, REAL PRICE, 1958–87

(US of 1970/MET)

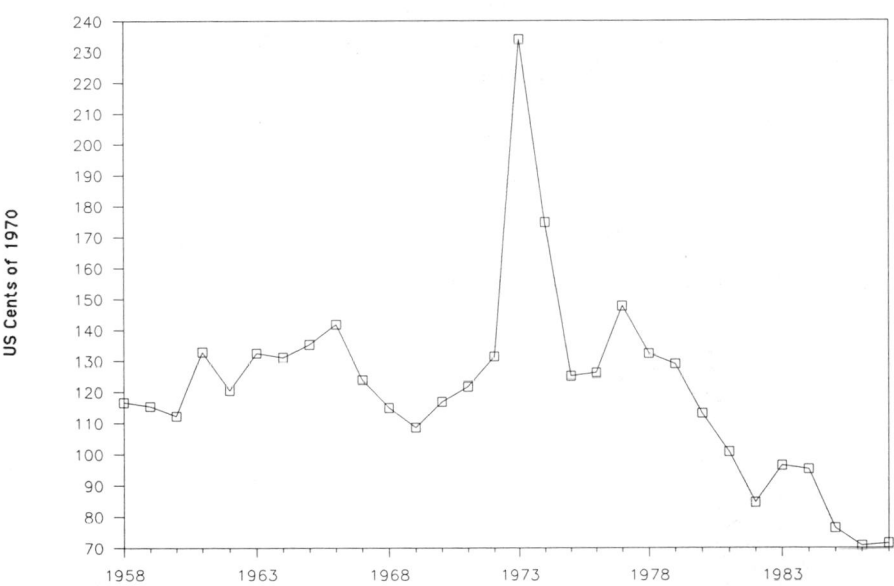

SOURCE: SALA, 27-3241.

Table 3342

SUGAR (BRAZILIAN), REAL PRICE,[1] 1951–88
(US Cents of 1980/lb)

Year	Real Price	Year	Real Price
1951	14.78	1971	13.96
1952	9.42	1972	17.74
1953	13.47	1973	18.90
1954	12.01	1974	41.95
1955	12.39	1975	43.17
1956	12.68	1976	16.48
1957	15.64	1977	11.38
1958	11.03	1978	9.95
1959	10.13	1979	9.98
1960	10.89	1980	21.79
1961	11.91	1981	15.49
1962	12.68	1982	8.53
1963	19.78	1983	8.48
1964	18.53	1984	8.11
1965	10.27	1985	5.94
1966	10.71	1986	6.30
1967	10.49	1987	5.89
1968	12.76	1988	6.83
1969	13.12		
1970	13.35		

1. Nominal data in source deflated here using U.S. export price index (table 3231).

SOURCE: IMF-IFS-Y, various years.

Figure 33:12

SUGAR (BRAZILIAN), REAL PRICE, 1951–87
(US Cents of 1980/lb)

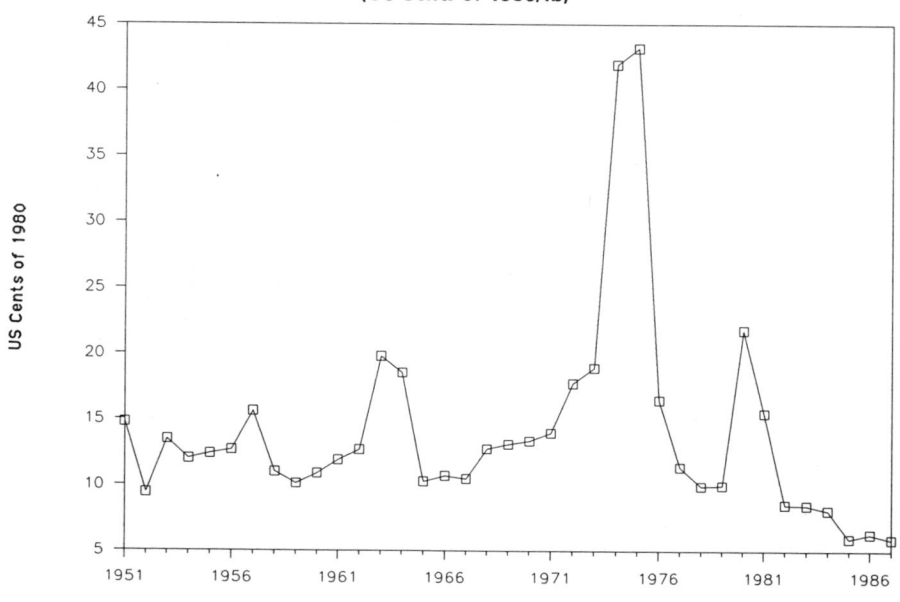

SOURCE: SALA, 27-3242.

Table 3343

TIN (BOLIVIAN), REAL PRICE,[1] 1950–88

(US Cents of 1970/lb)

Year	Real Price	Year	Real Price
1950	133.24	1970	174.41
1951	161.90	1971	153.76
1952	153.04	1972	159.28
1953	120.78	1973	167.40
1954	122.85	1974	228.08
1955	119.43	1975	176.58
1956	123.41	1976	187.92
1957	112.17	1977	250.73
1958	112.53	1978	279.82
1959	121.25	1979	291.57
1960	120.40	1980	290.44
1961	131.84	1981	221.69
1962	135.22	1982	198.83
1963	135.53	1983	200.78
1964	179.45	1984	187.23
1965	201.63	1985	183.63
1966	181.18	1986	87.00
1967	165.63	1987	102.79
1968	154.97	1988	106.27
1969	163.66		

1. Nominal data in source deflated here using U.S. export price index (table 3231).

SOURCE: IMF-IFS-Y, various years.

Figure 33:13

TIN (BOLIVIAN), REAL PRICE, 1950–87

(US Cents of 1970/lb)

SOURCE: SALA, 27-3243.

Table 3344

WHEAT (ARGENTINE), REAL PRICE,[1] 1950–88

(US of 1980/Bushel)

Year	Real Price	Year	Real Price
1950	6.25	1970	3.87
1951	6.53	1971	4.11
1952	6.81	1972	4.45
1953	6.97	1973	5.59
1954	4.98	1974	8.69
1955	6.31	1975	6.88
1956	5.46	1976	5.32
1957	5.16	1977	3.60
1958	5.21	1978	4.15
1959	4.92	1979	4.37
1960	4.98	1980	4.94
1961	5.27	1981	5.05
1962	5.24	1982	4.11
1963	5.46	1983	3.49
1964	5.56	1984	3.21
1965	4.61	1985	2.79
1966	4.41	1986	2.38
1967	4.64	1987	1.98
1968	4.43	1988	~
1969	4.45		

1. Nominal data in source deflated here using U.S. export price index (table 3231).

SOURCE: IMF-IFS-Y, various years.

Figure 33:14

WHEAT (ARGENTINE), REAL PRICE, 1950–86

(US of 1980/Bushel)

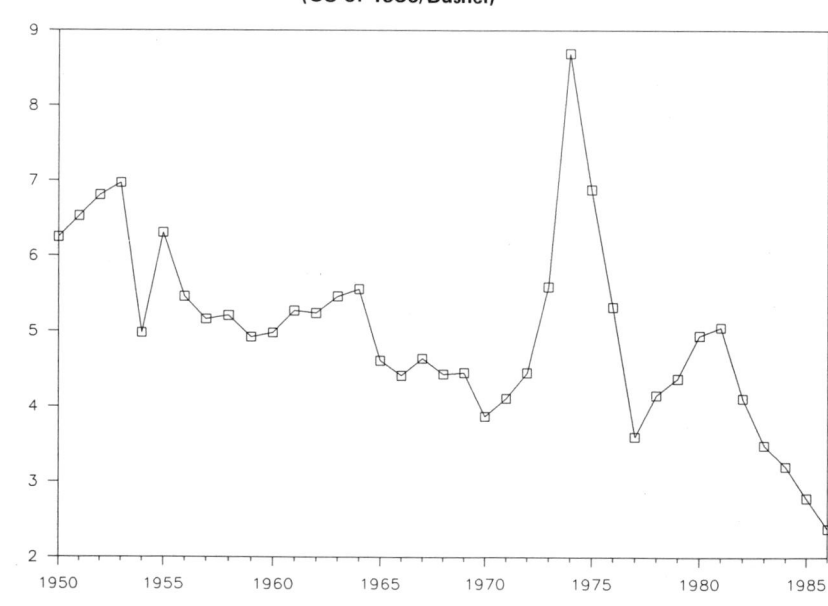

SOURCE: SALA, 27-3244.

Table 3345

WOOL (AUSTRALIAN), REAL PRICE,[1] 1958–88
(US Cents of 1970/kg)

Year	Real Price	Year	Real Price
1958	149.88	1974	159.10
1959	167.78	1975	103.06
1960	164.11	1976	108.19
1961	166.80	1977	119.79
1962	147.34	1978	115.96
1963	171.94	1979	110.36
1964	179.73	1980	115.48
1965	145.81	1981	114.81
1966	153.12	1982	105.91
1967	134.36	1983	92.26
1968	126.60	1984	95.18
1969	139.11	1985	88.01
1970	98.13	1986	80.74
1971	77.28	1987	113.84
1972	110.61	1988	188.11
1973	246.00		

1. Nominal data in source deflated here using U.S. export price index (table 3231).

SOURCE: IMF-IFS-Y, various years.

Figure 33:15

WOOL (AUSTRALIAN), REAL PRICE, 1958–87
(US Cents of 1970/kg)

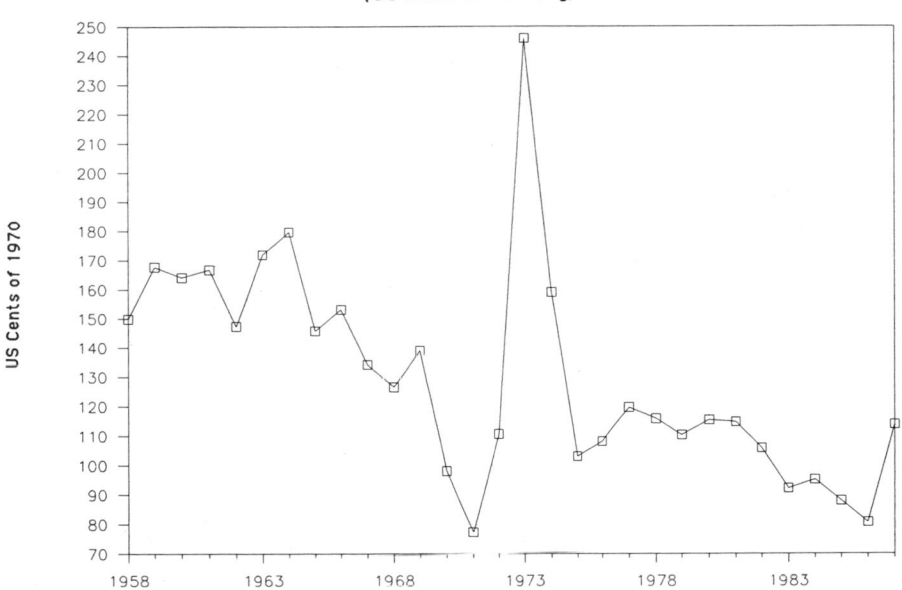

SOURCE: SALA, 27-3245.

Table 3346

MEXICAN BANK INTEREST PAID ON DEPOSITS, 1975–87

(AA)

Month	1975	1976	1977	1978	1979	1980	1981	1982	1983	1984	1985	1986	1987
January	#	11.86	12.05	14.33	15.98	17.90	25.46	32.34	50.29	55.95	47.17	68.55	95.89
February	#	11.83	12.00	14.47	15.97	18.39	25.98	33.43	54.24	55.16	47.33	70.30	96.20
March	#	11.78	11.99	14.62	15.98	19.20	26.59	33.67	56.16	53.11	49.36	71.79	96.26
April	#	11.79	12.03	14.87	15.99	19.83	26.91	34.39	57.21	51.10	51.93	73.48	95.79
May	#	11.78	11.93	15.02	16.02	20.39	27.22	36.26	58.14	50.12	53.76	75.02	94.79
June	#	11.76	12.59	15.16	16.04	20.47	27.66	39.59	58.63	50.38	54.92	76.97	93.76
July	#	11.74	13.25	15.26	16.08	20.53	28.42	43.23	58.73	50.69	57.00	81.36	92.91
August	11.91	11.74	13.52	15.29	16.10	20.82	29.50	46.42	58.23	50.93	59.06	84.40	92.15
September	11.91	11.74	13.57	15.38	16.51	21.51	30.45	47.88	57.78	50.60	60.98	87.72	91.02
October	11.91	11.96	13.64	15.49	16.69	22.42	31.22	45.99	57.14	49.34	62.29	91.48	90.30
November	11.92	12.03	13.93	15.81	17.37	22.77	31.77	45.51	56.82	48.31	63.39	94.19	~
December	11.97	12.12	14.04	15.88	17.52	24.25	31.81	46.12	56.44	47.54	65.66	95.33	~

SOURCE: NAFINSA-MV, April 20, 1987, and October 26, 1987.

Table 3347

PRIME RATE OF INTEREST CHARGED BY U.S. BANKS, 1960–89

PART I. % PER YEAR

Year	%
1960	4.82
1965	4.54
1970	7.91
1971	5.72
1972	5.25
1973	8.03
1974	10.81
1975	7.86
1976	6.84
1977	6.83
1978	9.06
1979	12.67
1980	15.27
1981	18.87
1982	14.86
1983	10.79
1984	12.04
1985	9.93
1986	8.33
1987	8.22
1988	9.32

PART II. % PER MONTH

Month	1982	1983	1984	1985	1986	1987	1988	1989
January	15.75	11.16	11.00	10.61	9.50	7.50	8.75	10.50
February	16.66	10.98	11.00	10.50	9.50	7.50	8.51	10.93
March	16.50	10.50	11.21	10.50	9.10	7.50	8.50	11.50
April	16.50	10.50	11.93	10.31	8.83	7.75	8.50	11.50
May	16.50	10.50	12.39	9.78	8.50	8.14	8.84	11.50
June	16.50	10.50	12.60	9.50	8.50	8.25	9.00	11.07
July	16.26	10.50	13.00	9.50	8.16	8.25	9.29	~
August	14.39	10.89	13.00	9.50	7.90	8.25	9.84	~
September	13.50	11.00	12.97	9.50	7.50	8.70	10.00	~
October	12.52	11.00	12.58	9.50	7.50	9.07	10.00	~
November	11.85	11.00	11.77	9.50	7.50	8.78	10.05	~
December	11.50	11.00	11.06	9.50	7.50	8.75	10.50	~

SOURCE: 1960: USBC-SA, 1978, table 890; USBC-SA, 1981, table 873; USBC-SA, 1983, table 852; since 1982: USDC-SCB, May 1984, March 1985, USDC-SCB, September 1986, July 1987; USDC-SCB, August 1988; USDC-SCB, July 1989, p. S-14.

Table 3348

INTEREST ON U. S. COMMERCIAL PAPER, 1900–88
(4 to 6 month paper, YA)

Year	%	Year	%
1900	5.71	1948	1.44
1901	5.40	1949	1.49
1902	5.81	1950	1.45
1903	6.16	1951	2.16
1904	5.14	1952	2.33
1905	5.18	1953	2.52
1906	6.25	1954	1.58
1907	6.66	1955	2.18
1908	5.00	1956	3.31
1909	4.67	1957	3.81
1910	5.72	1958	2.46
1911	4.75	1959	3.97
1912	5.41	1960	3.85
1913	6.20	1961	2.97
1914	5.47	1962	3.26
1915	4.01	1963	3.55
1916	3.84	1964	3.97
1917	5.07	1965	4.38
1918	6.02	1966	5.55
1919	5.37	1967	5.10
1920	7.50	1968	5.90
1921	6.62	1969	7.83
1922	4.52	1970	7.72
1923	5.07	1971	5.11
1924	3.98	1972	4.69
1925	4.02	1973	8.15
1926	4.34	1974	9.87
1927	4.11	1975	6.33
1928	4.85	1976	5.35
1929	5.85	1977	5.60
1930	3.59	1978	7.99
1931	2.64	1979	10.91[a]
1932	2.73	1980	12.29[a]
1933	1.73	1981	14.76[a]
1934	1.02	1982	11.89[a]
1935	.75	1983	8.89
1936	.75	1984	10.16
1937	.94	1985	8.01
1938	.81	1986	6.39
1939	.59	1987	6.85
1940	.56	1988	7.68
1941	.53		
1942	.66		
1943	.69		
1944	.73		
1945	.75		
1946	.81		
1947	1.03		

a. Daily average.

SOURCE: 1900–54: USBC-HS, 1975, series X-445; 1954–78: USBG-FRB, Sept. 1984; since 1979, data are for 6 month paper: USDC-SCB, May 1979–85, USDC-SCB, May 1986, p. S-14, August 1987, p. S-14; August 1988, p. S-14; July 1989, p. S-14.

Table 3349

U.S. FEDERAL FUNDS[1] INTEREST RATE, 1955–88
(YA % Per Annum)

Year	%
1955	1.78
1956	2.73
1957	3.11
1958	1.58
1959	3.30
1960	3.22
1961	1.96
1962	2.68
1963	3.18
1964	3.50
1965	4.07
1966	5.12
1967	4.22
1968	5.67
1969	8.21
1970	7.18
1971	4.66
1972	4.43
1973	8.73
1974	10.50
1975	5.82
1976	5.05
1977	5.54
1978	7.93
1979	11.20
1980	13.36
1981	16.38
1982	12.26
1983	9.09
1984	10.23
1985	8.10
1986	6.81
1987	6.66
1988	6.71

1. Short-term borrowings between financial institutions.

SOURCE: IMF-IFS, July 1987, line 60 b; IMF-IFS-Y, 1988; IMF-IFS, August 1989, line 60 b.

Table 3350

COMMERCIAL DISCOUNT INTEREST RATE, 10 LC, 1983–87

	Country	1983	1984	1985	1986	1987
	Bahamas	9.0	9.0	8.5	7.5	7.5
	Barbados	16.0	16.0	13.0	8.0	~
B.	BOLIVIA	61.0	149.0	~	~	~
C.	BRAZIL	156.6	215.3	~	50.7	391.5
E.	COLOMBIA	27.0	27.0	27.0	~	~
F.	COSTA RICA	30.0	28.0	28.0	27.5	31.4
I.	ECUADOR	9.0	11.0	~	~	~
K.	GUATEMALA	9.0	9.0	9.0	9.0	9.0
M.	HONDURAS	24.0	24.0	24.0	24.0	24.0
R.	PERU	60.0	60.0	~	~	~
	Trinidad and Tobago	7.5	7.5	7.5	6.0	~
S.	URUGUAY	112.7	~	~	~	~
T.	VENEZUELA	~	15.9	12.9	12.8	12.5

SOURCE: OAS-SB, July–Dec., 1986, pp. 82–83; July–Dec., 1987, pp. 80–81.

34

Gross Product

DEFINITION OF TERMS
I. Market-Country System

National accounting results in a statistical statement of the gross value of goods and services produced by a country's economy in a given period of time, usually one year. Included are primary production (agriculture, forestry, fishing, and mining), whether or not it enters the exchange economy, and all other goods and services produced and exchanged. Nonprimary production performed by producers outside their own trade and consumed by themselves is omitted.

Gross value of output can be calculated either by factor cost or market price:

Gross value of output by *market price* (or purchasers' values) equals market value of output before depreciation provisions for fixed capital consumption.

Gross value of output by *factor cost* equals market value of output less indirect payments (such as excise and sales taxes, depreciation, government subsidies, transfer payments).

Gross domestic product (GDP) and **gross national product (GNP)** differ mainly in treatment of *factor income earned abroad*. Factor income earned abroad (or factor payment abroad) is foreign investment income (rent, interest, dividends, branch profits, undistributed earnings of subsidiaries) and income from working in other countries.

GDP (gross domestic product) equals total value of output accruing *within* a country. Thus, it includes factor income generated by foreign investors or suppliers in the country but excludes factor income invested or supplied abroad by normal residents of the country.

GNP (gross national product) equals total value of output accruing *to* a country. Thus, it excludes factor income earned by foreign investors or suppliers in the country but includes factor income earned in other countries by normal residents of the country.

II. Non-Market-Country System
(Cf. table 3407)

GSP	(Gross Social Product)
GMP	(Gross Material Product)

Table 3400

GENERAL SOURCES AND METHODS FOR COMPARATIVE PC OF REAL GDP SERIES PRESENTED IN TABLES 3401 THROUGH 3422[a,b]

Series	Source[1]
ECLA Factor	At factor cost in 1970 prices: through 1976 from ECLA-SHCAL, pp. 74-195 and 25-88, then also from ECLA-S, 1981, 1980 (table 3 for each country), 1979, 1978, 1977. and for 1976–84 ECLA-SY, 1985, p. 231. Data for table 3301 are calculated from 1970 dollars at purchasing power exchange rate for each country. ECLA-SY, 1985. Cf "ECLA Market" series below.
IMF	In 1975 prices: through 1957 from IMF-IFS-Y, 1982; after 1957 from IMF-IFS-Y, 1986. IMF data are, in general, from UN sources at market prices. Revised with data in 1980 prices (calculated from indexes) in IMF-IFS-Y, 1986, IMF-IFS-Y, 1987.
OECD	Index 1968 = 100 for 1960-70, 1978 = 100 for 1971, and 1980 = 100 for 1972-83; data through 1959 from *National Accounts of Less Developed Areas, 1950-1966,* July 1968, p. 20; after 1960 data are from *Latest Information on National Accounts of Developing Countries, 1960–83,* Nov. 1983, p. 17 and Dec. 1985, No. 17, p. 19. Data are in market prices.
SALA	In 1970 dollars at official exchange rates, based upon USAID data synthesized in SALA-SNP, pp. 393-394 and also data given in SALA, 18-2200. Data are, in general, at market prices. For comparison of USAID estimated at three different times, see SALA-SNP, pp. 395-396.
ECLA Market	At market prices in 1970 dollars (compared to factor cost terms in "ECLA Factor" given above). Data are from ECLA-S, 1980, ECLA-N, Jan. 1983, and Mexico-NAFINSA-MV, March 11, 1985; 1981-85 data from ECLA-SP, 1986, p. 24. ECLA-SP, 1986. Cf. "ECLA Factor" series above.
IDB	In 1984 dollars at market prices. Data from IDB-SPTF, 1986, table II-4; IDB-SPTF, 1987, table 11-6, 1988, table 11-5; 1989, table 11-3.

1. PC calculations by Waldo W. Wilkie.

a. For Cuba sources, see table 3407; for other Mexico sources, see table 3414; for U.S. sources, see table 3422.

b. For definition of GDP and GNP, see title page to this chapter and tables 3440 through 3460; on GSP and GMP, see table 3407. About GNP (and GDP), the World Bank's *World Development Report*, 1982, includes the following cautions (p. 20): "Gross national product (GNP) measures economic activity—not welfare. But as a measure of aggregate economic output and expenditure, GNP data are often ambiguous or deficient. Ambiguity exists, for example, because public services such as administration and defense are treated as final rather than as intermediate services, and purchases of consumer durables other than residences are regarded as consumption rather than investment. Moreover, GNP does not make allowance for the varying amounts of capital, including mineral and other natural resources, used up during production. These are notoriously difficult to estimate. Gaps exist in basic data, most notably for subsistence production in developing countries and for illegal activities in most countries. Measurement problems also arise because of lack of consistency among countries in calculating changes in real output over time; this is particularly true between the market economies and the centrally planned economies. Moreover, major problems arise in intercountry comparisons of levels of GNP converted to a common currency by using exchange rates.

   Welfare could not be fully measured even if it were possible to collect perfect GNP data for each country, based on Standard National Accounting definitions, and make international comparisons. . . . GNP does not measure items that are important to welfare in most societies, such as the distribution of income and wealth, employment status, job security, and opportunities for advancement, availability of health and education services, unpaid services, the quality of the environment, and climatic differences. . . . [Thus economists settle] for partial measures such as GNP—which at least covers most of the goods and services available to meet important consumption needs. GNP data, however, need to be complemented by other indicators, particularly those which relate more directly to the 'quality of life'."

Ch. 34, Gross Product 1017

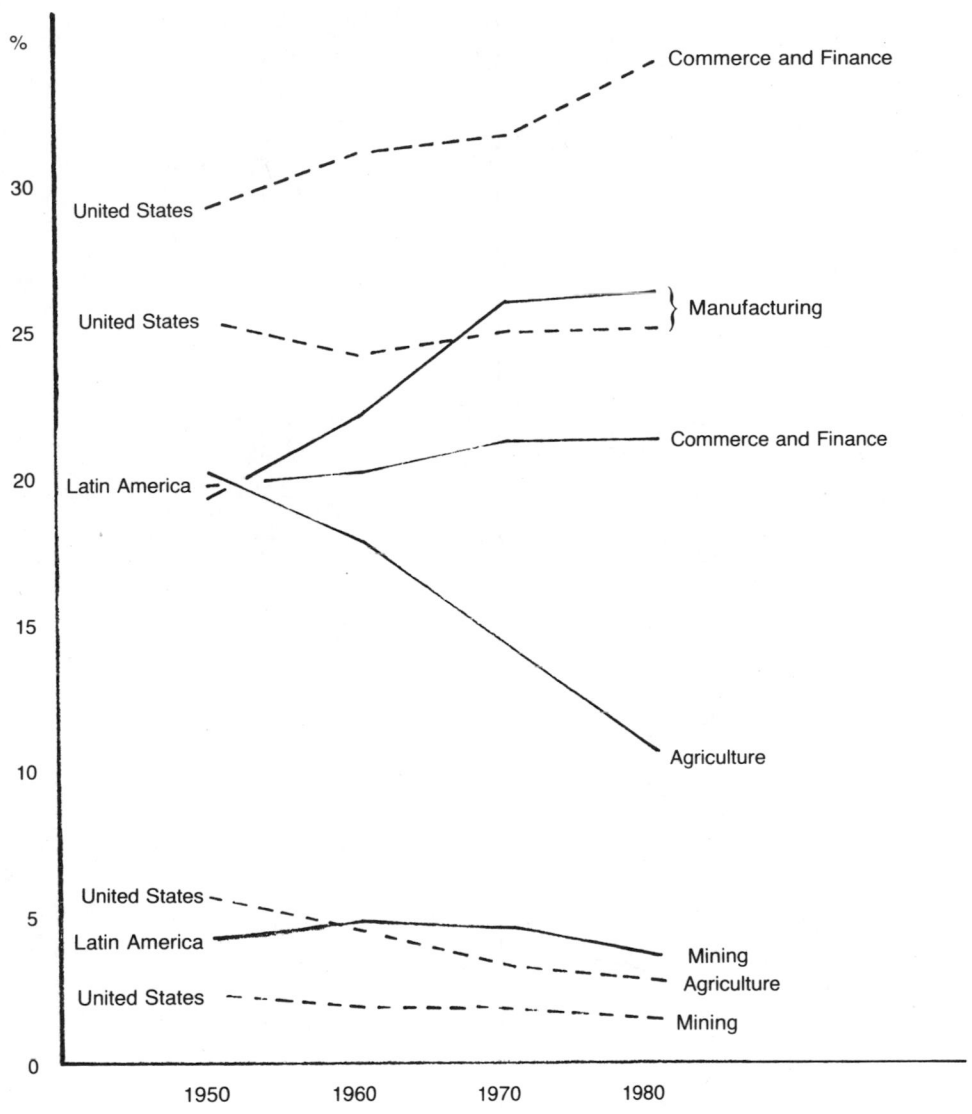

Figure 34:1

GDP SHARES OF IMPORTANT ACTIVITIES FOR TOTAL
LATIN AMERICA AND THE UNITED STATES,
TEN-YEAR INTERVALS, 1950–80

(%)

SOURCE: SALA, 23-2324; SALA, 23-2325; SALA, 23-2326; SALA, 23-2330.

Figure 34:2

PC OF GDP FOR TOTAL LATIN AMERICA AND GNP
FOR THE UNITED STATES, 1940–82

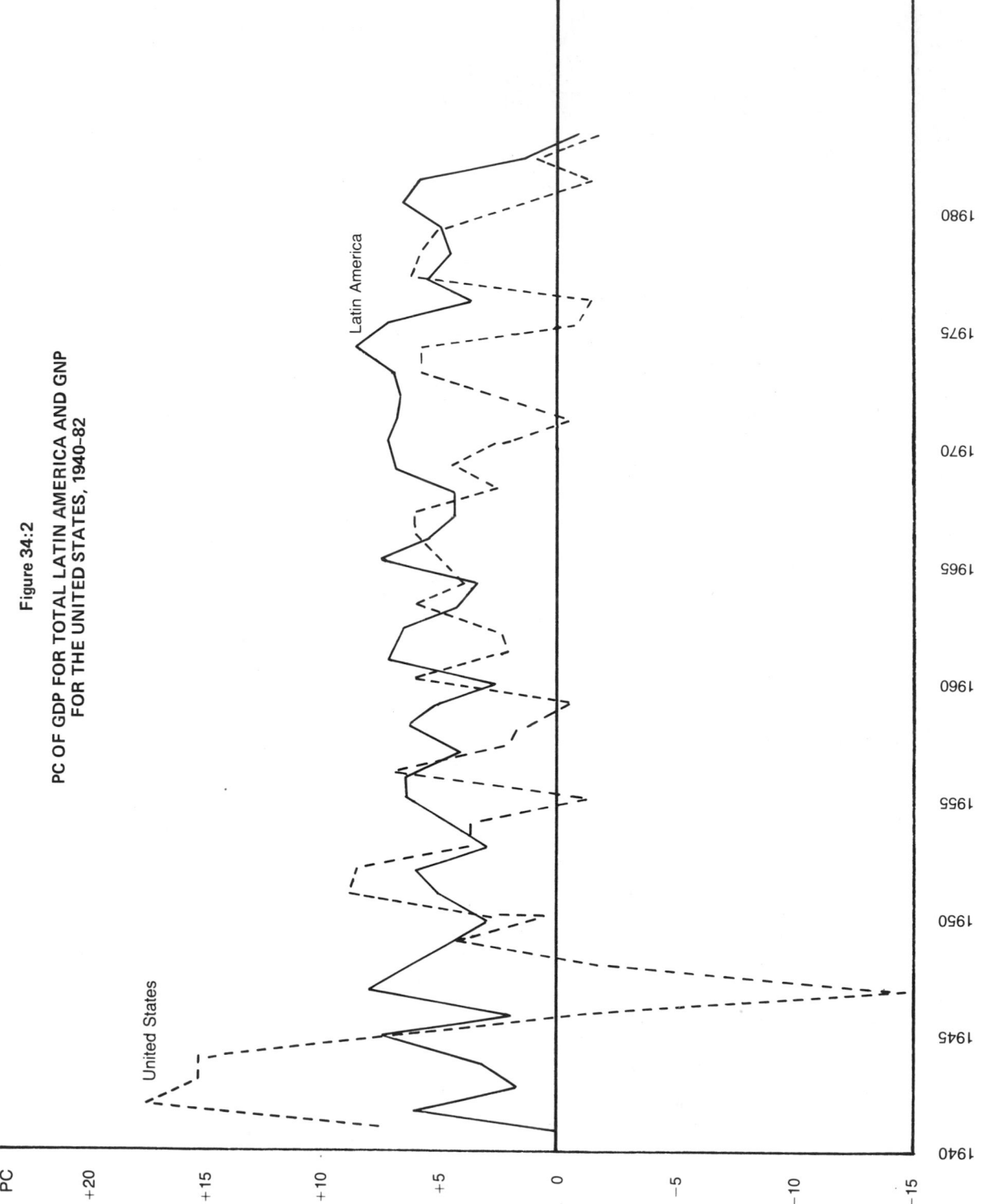

SOURCE:

Latin America: SALA, 23-2331, "ECLA Factor" series through 1974, then "ECLA
Market" series; series overlap 1975-79 has an average difference in PC of .4%.

United States: SALA, 23-2322, USDC-SCB series.

Table 3401

ARGENTINA COMPARATIVE PC OF REAL GDP, 1901–88

I. 1901-39 II. 1940-88

Year	ECLA Factor (1901-39)	Year	ECLA Factor (1940–87)	IMF (1953–87)	OECD (1951–87)	SALA (1951–74)	ECLA Market (1975–87)	IDB (1981-88)
		1940	–2.0					
1901	8.5	1941	4.9					
1902	–2.1	1942	4.6					
1903	4.3	1943	.7					
1904	10.6	1944	9.7					
1905	13.2	1945	–4.8					
1906	5.0	1946	8.3					
1907	2.2	1947	13.7					
1908	9.8	1948	1.2					
1909	5.0	1949	–4.6					
1910	7.2	1950	1.6					
1911	1.8	1951	3.9		4.1	3.4		
1912	8.2	1952	–5.1		–6.4	–6.7		
1913	1.1	1953	5.4	6.9	7.1	6.8		
1914	–10.4	1954	4.1	5.0	3.8	3.2		
1915	.5	1955	7.1	12.5	6.9	7.4		
1916	–2.9	1956	2.8	–5.3	1.6	1.2		
1917	7.2	1957	5.1	–3.3	5.5	4.4		
1918	1.4	1958	6.1	8.0	7.2	6.7		
1919	3.7	1959	–6.4	–10.0	–5.8	–6.1		
1920	7.3	1960	7.8	11.1	7.9	8.5		
1921	2.6	1961	7.1	10.0	7.1	6.8		
1922	8.0	1962	–1.6	#	–1.6	–1.5		
1923	11.0	1963	–2.4	–3.7*	–2.4	–2.4		
1924	7.8	1964	10.3	–2.3	10.3	10.4		
1925	–.4	1965	9.1	11.6	9.2	9.3		
1926	4.8	1966	.6	10.1	.6	.4		
1927	7.1	1967	2.7	.8	2.6	2.5		
1928	6.2	1968	4.3	3.3	4.3	4.5		
1929	4.6	1969	8.6	4.9	8.5	7.9		
1930	–14.1	1970	5.4	2.6*	5.4	4.4		
1931	–6.9	1971	4.8	3.4	4.7	3.0		
1932	–3.3	1972	3.1	2.2	3.8	4.8		
1933	4.7	1973	6.1	3.2	3.4	5.6		
1934	7.9	1974	6.1	5.2	5.7	6.1		
1935	4.4	1975	–.9	#	–.4		–.9	
1936	1.2	1976	–1.7	#	–.5		–.2	
1937	8.1	1977	4.9	5.9	6.4		6.0	
1938	1.3	1978	–3.9	–2.8	–3.4		–3.9	
1939	3.6	1979	6.7	6.7	6.7		7.1	
		1980	.7	1.8	.7		3.7	
		1981	–7.1	–6.7	–6.2		–6.7	–6.8
		1982	–5.3	–5.0	–4.8		–6.3	–4.6
		1983	2.4	2.9	4.0		3.0	2.8
		1984	2.4	2.5	2.9		2.2	2.6
		1985	–4.6	–4.4	–5.7		–4.4	–4.5
		1986	5.8	5.4	7.0		5.5	5.5
		1987	1.6	~	.9		1.6	2.0
		1988	~	~	~		~	–1.1‡

SOURCE AND METHODS: See table 3400.

Table 3402

BOLIVIA COMPARATIVE PC OF REAL GDP, 1946–88

Year	ECLA Factor (1946–87)	IMF (1953–87)	OECD (1951–87)	SALA (1951–74)	ECLA Market (1975–87)	IDB (1981-88)
1946	1.8					
1947	1.7					
1948	2.1					
1949	2.1					
1950	2.1					
1951	7.0		6.4	6.9		
1952	3.0		2.5	1.6		
1953	-9.5	-9.5	-11.4	-10.9		
1954	2.1	2.1	.7	0		
1955	5.3	5.3	7.0	7.1		
1956	-5.9	-5.9	-4.8	-5.0		
1957	-3.3	-3.3	-3.5	-3.4		
1958	2.4	2.4	2.9*	3.9		
1959	-.3	-.3	-.3	-1.3		
1960	4.3	8.6	4.3	6.3		
1961	2.1	1.3	2.1	2.1		
1962	5.6	2.4	5.6	5.8		
1963	6.4	6.8	6.4	6.0		
1964	4.8	4.0	4.8	4.5		
1965	4.9	4.9	6.9	6.9		
1966	7.2	7.2	7.0	6.9		
1967	6.3	6.3	6.3	4.1		
1968	8.5	8.5*	7.2	8.3		
1969	4.5	4.6	4.8	4.4		
1970	5.2	7.8	-.5	5.8		
1971	4.9	4.9	4.9	6.9		
1972	5.9	5.8	5.8	6.6		
1973	6.9	6.7	6.7	6.1		
1974	6.1	5.1	5.1	5.0		
1975	5.3	6.6	6.6		5.1	
1976	6.8	6.1	6.1		6.8	
1977	4.0	4.2	4.2		3.4	
1978	3.1	3.4	3.4		3.1	
1979	1.8	.2	1.8		1.8	
1980	.6	-1.4	.6		1.2	
1981	.4	1.0	-1.1		.3	.3
1982	-4.3	-4.4	-9.1		-2.8	-2.8
1983	-6.5	-6.6	-7.6*		-6.6	-6.6
1984	-.3	-.3	-.9		-.9	-.3
1985	-.1	-.2	-1.7		-1.7	-.2
1986	-2.9	-2.4	-2.9		-3.5	-2.9
1987	2.5	2.1	2.1		2.4	2.0
1988	~	~	~		~	2.8‡

SOURCE AND METHODS: See table 3400.

Table 3403

BRAZIL COMPARATIVE PC OF REAL GDP, 1921–88

I. 1921-39			II. 1940-88					
Year	ECLA Factor (1921-39)	Year	ECLA Factor (1940-87)	IMF (1966-88)	OECD (1951-87)	SALA (1952-74)	ECLA Market (1975-87)	IDB (1981-88)
		1940	1.0					
1921	.2	1941	4.9					
1922	5.0	1942	-2.8					
1923	5.8	1943	5.8					
1924	.2	1944	4.6					
1925	4.2	1945	.9					
1926	.2	1946	7.8					
1927	5.3	1947	2.4					
1928	8.2	1948	7.4					
1929	.7	1949	6.6					
1930	-3.4	1950	6.5					
1931	-.6	1951	5.9		5.1	5.9		
1932	1.1	1952	8.7		5.7	8.9		
1933	5.6	1953	2.5		3.2	2.4		
1934	6.8	1954	10.1		7.6	10.2		
1935	2.8	1955	6.9		6.8	6.8		
1936	9.1	1956	3.2		1.9	3.2		
1937	2.6	1957	8.1		6.9	8.1		
1938	4.1	1958	7.7		6.6	7.7		
1939	2.8	1959	3.0		7.3	5.6		
		1960	12.5		9.7	9.7		
		1961	10.3		10.3	10.3		
		1962	5.2		5.2	5.3		
		1963	1.6		1.5	1.6		
		1964	2.9	2.6	2.9	2.8		
		1965	2.7	23.1	2.7	2.9		
		1966	3.8	3.5	3.8	5.1		
		1967	4.9	5.4	4.9	4.8		
		1968	11.2	10.8	11.2	9.4		
		1969	9.9	9.8	9.9	9.0		
		1970	8.8	2.6	8.9	9.5		
		1971	13.3	12.2	12.0*	11.0		
		1972	11.7	10.9	11.1	11.7		
		1973	13.9	13.5	13.6	11.3		
		1974	9.8	9.7	9.7	10.9		
		1975	5.7	4.2	5.4		5.7	
		1976	9.0	9.8	9.7		9.0	
		1977	4.7	4.6	5.7		4.7	
		1978	6.0	4.8	5.0		6.0	
		1979	6.4	7.2	6.4		6.4	
		1980	7.2	9.1	7.2		6.8	
		1981	-3.4	-3.3	-1.6		-2.0	-3.3
		1982	.9	.9	.9		1.4	.9
		1983	-2.3	-2.5	-3.2		-2.7	-2.5
		1984	5.7	5.7	5.7		4.8	5.7
		1985	8.3	8.3	8.4		8.2	8.3
		1986	8.0	8.2	8.0		8.0	7.6
		1987	2.9	3.5	2.9		2.9	3.6
		1988	~	-.2	~		~	-.3‡

SOURCE AND METHODS: See table 3400.

Table 3404

CHILE COMPARATIVE PC OF REAL GDP, 1946–88

Year	ECLA Factor (1940–87)	IMF (1953–87)	OECD (1951–87)	SALA (1951–74)	ECLA Market (1974–87)	IDB (1981-88)
1940	5.0					
1941	.1					
1942	5.5					
1943	4.2					
1944	1.4					
1945	9.1					
1946	6.2					
1947	-6.7					
1948	11.5					
1949	-.5					
1950	4.8					
1951	5.2		4.4	4.4		
1952	3.4		5.7	5.9		
1953	7.1	5.1	5.2	5.8		
1954	.7	.5	.3	.4		
1955	2.7	#	-.1	-1.0		
1956	.7	.5	.6	.2		
1957	2.7	10.5	10.5	11.8		
1958	4.8	3.9	2.7	3.9		
1959	6.9	-.6	-.5	-1.1		
1960	5.1	5.7	7.0	6.7		
1961	6.1	6.1	6.1*	6.2		
1962	4.6	4.5	4.6	4.7		
1963	5.1	4.9	5.1	4.9		
1964	4.3	4.7	4.3	4.0		
1965	5.1	5.0	5.1	4.6		
1966	7.0	6.9	7.0	6.1		
1967	2.4	2.5	2.4	1.9		
1968	3.0	2.9	3.0	3.0		
1969	3.5	3.3	3.5	3.2		
1970	3.6	1.4*	2.1	9.2[a]		
1971	7.7	9.0	9.0	9.0		
1972	-.1	-1.2	-1.2	1.8		
1973	-3.6	-5.6	-5.6	-3.6		
1974	5.7	1.0	1.0	3.7	5.7	
1975	-11.3	-12.9	-12.9		-12.9	
1976	4.1	3.5	3.5		3.5	
1977	8.6	9.9	9.9		9.9	
1978	7.8	8.2	8.2		8.2	
1979	8.3	8.3	8.3		8.3	
1980	7.8	7.8	7.8		8.0	
1981	5.2	5.5	5.7		5.2	5.5
1982	-13.0	-14.1	-14.3		-13.1	-14.1
1983	-.5	-.7	-.8		-.5	-.7
1984	6.1	6.3	6.3		6.0	6.3
1985	2.5	2.4	2.4		2.4	2.4
1986	5.4	5.7	5.7		5.0	5.7
1987	5.5	5.4	5.7		5.4	5.7
1988	~	~	~		~	7.4[‡]

a. USAID calculations in 1973 dollars show PC of 4.5%. Cf. SALA-SNP, p. 416.

SOURCE AND METHODS: See table 3400.

Table 3405

COLOMBIA COMPARATIVE PC OF REAL GDP, 1926–88

I. 1926–39			II. 1940–88					
Year	ECLA Factor (1926–39)	Year	ECLA Factor (1940–87)	IMF (1953–87)	OECD (1951–87)	SALA (1951–74)	ECLA Market (1975–87)	IDB (1981-88)
		1940	2.2					
1926	9.5	1941	1.7					
1927	9.0	1942	.2					
1928	7.3	1943	.4					
1929	3.6	1944	6.8					
1930	-.9	1945	4.7					
1931	-1.6	1946	9.1					
1932	6.6	1947	3.9					
1933	5.6	1948	3.1					
1934	-2.1	1949	5.5					
1935	11.2	1950	1.8					
1936	5.3	1951	3.1		3.1	3.4		
1937	1.6	1952	6.3		6.4	6.7		
1938	6.5	1953	5.8	6.1	6.0	6.0		
1939	6.1	1954	6.6	6.9	7.0	7.2		
		1955	4.0	3.9	3.9	4.0		
		1956	4.1	4.1	4.0	3.9		
		1957	2.4	2.2	2.2	1.5		
		1958	2.5	2.5	2.5	2.3		
		1959	7.1	7.2	6.9	7.8		
		1960	4.1	4.3	4.3	4.4		
		1961	5.0	5.1	5.1	4.8		
		1962	5.4	5.4	5.4	5.0		
		1963	3.2	3.3	3.3	3.5		
		1964	6.1	6.2	6.2	5.7		
		1965	3.5	3.6	3.6	3.6		
		1966	5.2	5.4	5.4	5.3		
		1967	4.2	4.2	4.2	4.1		
		1968	6.3	6.1	6.1	5.8		
		1969	6.3	6.3	6.4	6.0		
		1970	6.6	9.3	6.7	6.9		
		1971	5.8	6.0	6.0	6.0		
		1972	7.9	7.7	7.7	6.6		
		1973	7.6	6.7	6.7	8.0		
		1974	6.5	5.7	5.7	6.6		
		1975	4.3	2.3	2.3		3.8	
		1976	4.2	4.7	4.7		4.6	
		1977	4.7	4.2	4.1		4.9	
		1978	8.8	8.5	8.5		8.9	
		1979	4.3	5.4	5.4		5.1	
		1980	5.5	4.1	4.1		4.7	
		1981	2.3	2.3	2.3		2.3	2.3
		1982	1.1	.9	.9		1.0	.9
		1983	1.9	1.6	1.6		1.9	1.6
		1984	3.8	3.4	3.4		3.6	3.4
		1985	3.8	3.1	3.1		2.6	3.1
		1986	5.9	5.1	5.1		5.0	5.1
		1987	5.5	5.4	5.4		5.4	5.3
		1988	~	~	~		~	3.7[‡]

SOURCE AND METHODS: See table 3400.

Table 3406

COSTA RICA COMPARATIVE PC OF REAL GDP, 1946-88

Year	ECLA Factor (1946–87)	IMF (1961–88)	OECD (1954–87)	SALA (1951–74)	ECLA Market (1975–87)	IDB (1981-87)
1946	7.9					
1947	19.0					
1948	5.7					
1949	4.0					
1950	4.1					
1951	2.7			3.6		
1952	12.1			12.6		
1953	15.2			11.5		
1954	.8		4.6	5.3		
1955	11.6		4.5	4.8		
1956	-2.8		1.4	2.3		
1957	8.5		9.2	6.9		
1958	12.4		6.7	6.4		
1959	3.7		3.1	3.9		
1960	8.7		6.1*	3.1		
1961	4.2	-.8	-1.0	2.0		
1962	6.1	8.1	8.1	6.2		
1963	8.6	4.8	4.8	6.4		
1964	4.9	4.1	4.1	-.9		
1965	9.1	9.8	9.8	9.6		
1966	7.8	7.9	7.9	6.6		
1967	6.1	5.7	5.7	8.6		
1968	7.7	8.5	8.5	9.2		
1969	6.7	5.5	5.5	9.5		
1970	6.6	7.5	7.5	5.4		
1971	6.6	6.8	6.8	4.0		
1972	8.2	8.2	8.2	6.7		
1973	7.7	7.7	7.7	7.2		
1974	5.5	5.5	5.5	4.2		
1975	2.1	2.1	2.1		2.1	
1976	5.5	5.5	5.5		5.5	
1977	8.9	8.9	8.9		8.9	
1978	6.3	6.3	6.3		6.3	
1979	4.9	4.9	4.9		4.9	
1980	.8	.8	.8		2.8	
1981	-2.3	-2.3	-2.3		-2.4	-2.3
1982	-7.2	-7.3	-7.3		-7.3	-7.3
1983	2.7	2.9	2.9		2.7	2.9
1984	7.9	8.0	8.0		7.9	8.0
1985	.9	.7	.7		.9	.7
1986	5.3	5.4	5.4		3.0	5.4
1987	3.8	3.9	3.9		4.5	3.4‡
1988	~	2.9	~		~	~

SOURCE AND METHODS: See table 3400.

Table 3407

CUBA COMPARATIVE PC OF
REAL PRODUCT, 1947–87
(Cf. table 3400)

PART I. GMP AND GSP[1] DEFINED

(From SALA-Cuba, p. 204)

Category	Example[1] for 1962
(a) Personal Consumption	2,491.1
(b) Collective Consumption	417.1
(c) Gross Capital Formation	607.6
(d) Increase in Stock[2]	277.1
(e) Net Exports	–94.7
(I) Gross Material Product (a + b + c + d + e)	3,698.2
(f) Consumption of Fixed Capital	188.7
(II) Net Material Product (I) – (f)	3,509.5
(III) Expenditures on Non-material Services	2,384.2
(IV) Gross Social Product (I + III)	6,082.4

1. Data refer to the total expenditures (in millions of 1965 pesos) on Gross Social Product (GSP). GSP includes expenditures on Gross Material Product (GMP) which is defined as the total net value of goods and "productive" services (including agriculture, industry, construction, transportation, communication, commerce, and turn-over taxes) produced in the course of the year. In contrast, non-material services cover those economic activities classified as "non-productive" (including public administration, education, health, defense, personal and professional services, and similar activities). Readers should note that calculations of GSP and GMP do not correspond to standard GNP systems. Differences in national accounting practices prevent comparability without adjustment as in the SALA series given in Part II, below, where GNP was computed in source by adding to Cuba's GMP the value added in non-productive services. Cf. CEPAL, *Cuentas Nacionales y Producto Material en América Latina* (Santiago, 1982).

2. Data for "Increase in Stock" not available in original sources and have been approximated by subtracting the sum of available items from GMP.

Table 3407 (Continued)

CUBA COMPARATIVE PC OF REAL PRODUCT, 1947–87

PART II. SERIES, 1947–87

Year	CERP[1] GNP[2] (1947–58)	SALA[3] GNP (1951–75)[a]	Mesa-Lago[4] GMP (1963–80)	ECLA[5] GMP[6] (1971–87)	ECLA[7] GSP (1963–85)	Cuba-CEE[8] GSP (1977–81)
1947	12.1					
1948	–7.5					
1949	–.3					
1950	15.9					
1951	.5	0				
1952	4.3	5.9				
1953	–10.6	–12.0				
1954	1.7	–.1				
1955	2.1	1.0				
1956	9.5	5.1				
1957	6.0	10.7				
1958	–3.9	–3.5				
1959		~				
1960		~				
1961		~				
1962		~				
1963		0	1.0		–1.1	
1964		9.8	9.0		7.3	
1965		2.0	1.5		4.9	
1966		–3.9	–3.7		–.9	
1967		–2.0	2.4		7.5	
1968		6.2	6.7		1.7	
1969		–8.7	–4.0		–1.3	
1970		6.4	.6		15.5	
1971		–3.0	14.6	4.2	6.9	
1972		1.0	25.1	9.7	15.8	
1973		6.1	11.3	13.1	15.1	
1974		1.9	10.5	7.8	12.7	
1975		3.8	19.8	12.3	3.7	
1976			–.1	4.4	1.2	
1977			4.1	1.8	2.6	3.9
1978			9.4	7.7	11.8	4.2
1979			4.3	4.2	2.8	3.8
1980			3.0	2.2	–1.2	4.1
1981				16.0	16.0	14.8
1982				3.9	3.8	
1983				4.9	4.9	
1984				7.2	7.3	
1985				4.6	4.8[‡]	
1986				1.2		
1987				–3.6[‡]		

1. CERP: *Cuban Economic Research Project: A Study on Cuba* (Coral Gables: University of Miami Press, 1965), p. 605, given in Schroeder, p. 570.
2. Deflated here with U.S. export price index given in SALA, 22-2625.
3. Calculated from index numbers in SALA, 19-200, 201. After 1969, Cuban data converted to GNP by CIA source wherein GMP adjusted to include "non-productive" services such as education and health (see Part I, above).
4. Carmelo Mesa-Lago, *The Economy of Socialist Cuba: A Two-Decade Appraisal* (Albuquerque: University of New Mexico Press, 1982), p. 34.
5. ECLA-S, 1978–81 and 1984, pp. 296 and 215 respectively; ECLA-S, 1986, p. 15. Cf. table 3347.
6. According to ECLA-S, e.g. 1979, p. 183, all data are in constant prices because for Cuba "current" and "constant" prices are equivalent in the case of material product (at producer prices). See also ECLA-S, 1981, p. 303, note 6, for discussion of frozen prices through 1980.
7. ECLA-AE, 1980, pp. 264–265; and for 1979–84 data at 1981 constant prices, ECLA-SY, 1985, pp. 312–313.
8. Cuba-CEE, AE, 1981, p. 67.

a. For 1950s, calculated from index based at 1950; for 1962–75, index based at 1970.

Table 3407 (Continued)

CUBA COMPARATIVE PC OF REAL PRODUCT, 1947–87

PART III. PEREZ–LOPEZ ESTIMATED OUTPUT INDICATORS, 1965–82

(1970 = 100)

Year	Industry	Agriculture	Material Product	GSP	GDP
1965	80	74	76	76	73
1966	83	70	78	80	77
1967	91	79	92	89	86
1968	90	79	85	81	81
1969	91	82	84	79	80
1970	82	96	80	76	77
1971	83	86	78	83	83
1972	88	85	87	88	87
1973	96	90	95	95	95
1974	100	100	100	100	100
1975	108	105	106	104	105
1976	107	111	105	106	108
1977	108	119	111	111	113
1978	115	124	112	114	120
1979	116	127	116	118	123
1980	113	129	111	116	120
1981	120	142	118	122	130
1982	120	141	119	124	133

PART IV. AA–GR FOR SELECTED INDICATORS OF ECONIMIC ACTIVITY[1]

(%)

Indicator	AA–GR			
	1966–70	1971–75	1976–80	1981–82
Industry				
Official	6.5	11.1	3.9	11.2
Brundenius	5.7	8.6	2.9	~
Estimated[2]	.5	5.7	.9	3.1
Agriculture				
Official	2.0	2.4	7.6	4.8
Brundenius	2.5	.2	4.4	~
Estimated	5.3	1.8	4.2	4.5
Material product				
Official	4.8	10.9	4.0	9.4
Brundenius	3.3	8.9	4.0	~
Estimated	1.0	5.8	.9	3.5
GSP				
Official	4.4	10.9	4.7	9.5
Estimated	0	6.5	2.2	3.4
GDP				
Official	~	12.3	7.0	~
Brundenius	.8	7.7	5.7	~
Estimated	1.1	6.4	2.7	5.3

1. Jorge F. Pérez–López, *Measuring Cuban Economic Performance* (Austin: University of Texas Press, 1987), pp. iii, 120.
2. Estimates are by Pérez–López; see note 1 above.

Table 3408

DOMINICAN REPUBLIC COMPARATIVE PC
OF REAL GDP, 1946–87

Year	ECLA Factor (1946–87)	IMF (1953–87)	OECD (1951–87)	SALA (1951–74)	ECLA Market (1975–87)	IDB (1981-87)
1946	-7.3					
1947	10.2					
1948	10.5					
1949	12.5					
1950	17.9					
1951	11.8		11.8	9.1		
1952	8.1		8.1	11.8		
1953	-1.3	-1.3	-1.3	.8		
1954	5.7	5.8	5.8	5.9		
1955	6.2	6.2	6.2	6.3		
1956	10.0	10.0	9.9	11.2		
1957	6.3	6.3	6.4	5.2		
1958	5.3	5.3	5.3	6.3		
1959	.6	.7	.6	.1		
1960	4.9	1.3	4.9	6.6		
1961	-2.3	-2.2	-2.2	-3.9		
1962	17.0	17.0	17.0	17.3		
1963	6.5	7.5	6.5	8.5		
1964	6.7	4.1	6.7	3.8		
1965	-12.4	-10.9	-12.4	-10.4		
1966	13.4	13.1	13.4	12.2		
1967	3.4	3.4	3.4	3.4		
1968	.2	.5	.2	1.0		
1969	10.9	12.2	11.0	12.0		
1970	10.6	8.5	10.6	11.1		
1971	10.6	10.9	10.9	11.0		
1972	10.4	10.4	10.4	11.7		
1973	12.9	12.9	12.9	8.9		
1974	5.5	6.0	6.0	8.2		
1975	2.1	5.2	5.2		5.2	
1976	5.5	6.7	6.7		6.7	
1977	8.9	5.0	5.0		5.0	
1978	5.7	2.1	2.1		2.2	
1979	4.5	4.5	4.5		4.8	
1980	6.1	6.1	6.1		5.3	
1981	4.0	4.1	4.1		4.0	4.1
1982	1.3	1.6	1.6		1.4	1.7
1983	5.1	4.9	4.6		4.4	3.9
1984	1.8	1.0	.3		.5	.5
1985	-3.9	-3.6	-2.6		-2.0	-4.2
1986	2.5	3.2	3.2		3.1	2.6
1987	7.6	8.1	8.1		8.0	8.0[‡]

SOURCE AND METHODS: See table 3400.

Table 3409

ECUADOR COMPARATIVE PC OF REAL GDP, 1940–87

Year	ECLA Factor (1940–87)	IMF (1953–87)	OECD (1951–87)	SALA (1951–74)	ECLA Market (1974–87)	IDB (1981–87)
1940	6.6					
1941	.5					
1942	4.2					
1943	12.7					
1944	1.3					
1945	.4					
1946	11.9					
1947	11.1					
1948	13.7					
1949	1.8					
1950	8.7					
1951	1.1		2.7	3.4		
1952	12.3		10.4	8.6		
1953	2.1	8.6	3.3	3.6		
1954	8.1	8.1	8.1	8.7		
1955	2.6	2.6	2.6	2.5		
1956	3.7	3.7	3.6	3.0		
1957	4.5	5.1	5.3	5.4		
1958	2.9	2.3	2.3	3.0		
1959	5.4	5.2	5.1	4.6		
1960	6.5	6.6	4.5*	6.8		
1961	2.5	1.5	1.7	1.4		
1962	5.3	4.5	4.5	4.9		
1963	2.6	3.9	3.8	4.8		
1964	7.0	7.8	7.8	7.2		
1965	9.6	12.5	3.2	3.0		
1966	2.6	2.4	8.0	4.6		
1967	5.3	6.9	8.0	6.1		
1968	5.5	4.0	4.5	5.9		
1969	5.5	2.3	4.2	2.7		
1970	7.0	6.5	4.8	8.8		
1971	6.8	6.3	5.0	2.0		
1972	8.0	14.4	7.0*	8.4		
1973	17.9	25.3	25.4	13.0		
1974	4.0	6.4	6.4	4.8	9.0	
1975	7.5	5.6	5.6		6.8	
1976	8.1	9.2	9.3		9.3	
1977	6.4	6.5	6.5		7.5	
1978	6.6	6.6	6.5		5.4	
1979	5.3	5.3	5.1		5.1	
1980	4.9	4.9	4.8		5.1	
1981	3.8	3.9	4.3		3.8	3.9
1982	1.2	1.2	1.4		1.1	1.2
1983	-1.2	-2.8	-2.7		-1.2	-2.8
1984	4.8	4.2	4.2		4.5	4.2
1985	4.9	4.5	4.3		4.3	4.5
1986	3.4	3.1	5.1		1.5	2.8
1987	-7.0	-5.5	5.3		-8.7	-3.5[‡]

SOURCE AND METHODS: See table 3400.

Table 3410

EL SALVADOR COMPARATIVE PC
OF REAL GDP, 1946–87

Year	ECLA Factor (1946–87)	IMF (1953–87)	OECD (1951–87)	SALA (1951–74)	ECLA Market (1975–87)	IDB (1981–87)
1946	1.6					
1947	25.8					
1948	27.4					
1949	–9.2					
1950	2.9					
1951	2.0		–3.6	5.0		
1952	7.5		8.0	7.3		
1953	3.1	2.6	11.5*	4.4		
1954	1.2	3.1	3.6*	2.1		
1955	5.1	4.3	3.6	4.1		
1956	7.9	6.0	4.6	4.0		
1957	5.3	5.6	5.0	5.7		
1958	2.2	1.0	1.0	0		
1959	4.5	4.5	1.9	1.8		
1960	4.1	4.0	4.1	3.0		
1961	3.5	3.5	3.5	3.4		
1962	12.0	12.0	12.0	11.6		
1963	4.3	4.3	4.3	4.3		
1964	9.3	9.3	9.3	9.4		
1965	5.4	5.4	5.4	5.1		
1966	7.2	7.2	7.2	7.3		
1967	5.4	5.4	5.4	5.4		
1968	3.2	3.2	3.2	3.3		
1969	3.5	3.5	3.5	3.4		
1970	3.0	3.0	3.0	3.6		
1971	4.6	4.8	4.8	4.0		
1972	5.7	5.5	5.5	5.8		
1973	5.1	5.1	5.1	5.4		
1974	6.4	6.4	6.4	5.2		
1975	5.6	5.6	5.6		5.6	
1976	4.0	4.0	4.0		4.0	
1977	5.0	6.1	6.1		5.9	
1978	4.4	6.4	6.4		4.4	
1979	–1.7	–1.7	–1.7		–1.5	
1980	–8.7	–8.7	–8.7		–5.3	
1981	–8.4	–8.3	–9.0		–8.4	–8.3
1982	–5.6	–5.6	–6.3		–5.7	–5.6
1983	.6	.8	.8		.6	.8
1984	2.3	2.3	2.3		1.4	2.3
1985	1.8	2.0	2.0		1.4	2.0
1986	.5	.6	.6		–.5	.6
1987	2.7	2.7	2.8		2.7	2.6[‡]

SOURCE AND METHODS: See table 3400.

Table 3411

GUATEMALA COMPARATIVE PC
OF REAL GDP, 1946–87

Year	ECLA Factor (1946–87)	IMF (1953–87)	OECD (1951–87)	SALA (1951–74)	ECLA Market (1975–87)	IDB (1981–87)
1946	7.9					
1947	12.7					
1948	–.8					
1949	–7.9					
1950	.3					
1951	1.4		1.5	1.8		
1952	2.1		2.1	2.1		
1953	3.7	3.6	3.6	2.8		
1954	1.9	1.9	1.9	1.8		
1955	2.5	2.5	2.4	2.8		
1956	9.1	9.1	9.1	9.4		
1957	5.6	5.6	5.7	5.5		
1958	4.7	4.7	4.2	4.6		
1959	4.9	4.9	4.9	4.8		
1960	2.4	2.4	2.4	2.4		
1961	4.3	4.3	4.3	4.2		
1962	3.5	3.5	3.5	3.6		
1963	9.5	9.5	9.5	9.5		
1964	4.6	4.6	4.6	4.5		
1965	4.4	4.4	4.4	4.4		
1966	5.5	5.5	5.5	4.6		
1967	4.1	4.1	4.1	4.0		
1968	8.8	8.8	8.8	8.5		
1969	4.7	4.7	4.7	3.8		
1970	5.7	5.7	5.7	6.8		
1971	5.6	5.6	5.6	5.0		
1972	7.3	7.3	7.3*	8.1		
1973	6.8	6.8	7.3	8.1		
1974	6.4	6.4	6.1	6.6		
1975	1.9	1.9	1.9		1.9	
1976	7.4	7.4	7.4		7.4	
1977	7.8	7.8	7.8		7.8	
1978	5.5	5.0	5.0		5.0	
1979	4.7	4.7	4.7		4.7	
1980	3.8	3.7	3.7		4.2	
1981	1.0	.7	.9		1.0	.7
1982	3.3	–3.5	–3.4		–3.4	–3.5
1983	–2.7	–2.6	–2.0*		–2.7	–2.5
1984	.1	.5	.6		#	.5
1985	–1.0	–.6	–1.1		–.9	–1.0
1986	.3	#	0		#	.4
1987	2.5	~	2.9		3.1	2.5‡

SOURCE AND METHODS: See table 3400.

Table 3412

HAITI COMPARATIVE PC OF REAL GDP, 1946–87

Year	ECLA Factor (1946–87)	IMF (1953–87)	OECD (1951–87)[a]	SALA (1951–74)[b]	ECLA Market (1975–87)	IDB (1981–87)
1946	.9					
1947	1.7					
1948	1.0					
1949	1.1					
1950	1.6					
1951	1.5		1.4	1.3		
1952	5.7		5.7	5.4		
1953	-3.2	-3.2	-3.3	-2.4		
1954	8.2	8.1	8.1	6.2		
1955	-4.0	-4.0	-4.0	-2.3		
1956	8.7	8.7	8.8	7.5		
1957	-5.9	-5.9	-6.1	-4.7		
1958	7.9	7.9	8.0	7.3		
1959	-4.7	-4.7	-4.8	-4.4		
1960	6.5	2.6	7.3	3.4*		
1961	-4.1	-2.4	-3.0	-2.5		
1962	9.6	8.3	7.9	8.2		
1963	-6.5	-2.9	-1.9	-2.1		
1964	-2.3	-1.6	-1.6	-1.1		
1965	1.1	2.1	2.1	1.1		
1966	-.6	.1	-.6	0		
1967	-2.0	-2.1	-2.1	-1.1		
1968	3.9	3.2	3.1	4.3		
1969	3.3	3.8	3.9	4.4		
1970	4.7	.7	.6	2.0		
1971	6.5	6.5	6.5	9.0		
1972	3.6	.9	-1.9	7.4		
1973	4.5	4.8	7.8	3.3		
1974	4.3	5.8	5.8	4.2		
1975	2.2	1.1	1.1		2.2	
1976	5.3	8.4	8.4		5.3	
1977	1.3	.5	.5		1.3	
1978	3.9	4.9	4.8		4.4	
1979	7.3	7.6	7.6		4.7	
1980	7.7	7.3	7.2		7.5	
1981	-2.7	-2.9	-2.7		-2.7	-2.7
1982	-3.4	-3.4	-4.0		-3.5	-3.5
1983	.7	.8	.9*		.6	.8
1984	.5	.3	.3		.4	.3
1985	.5	.2	.3		3.5	.3
1986	.6	.6	.6		-1.5	.6
1987	-.5	-.6	-.6		-.6	-.6[‡]

a. Data are at factor cost through 1959.
b. Through 1959 from UN-YNAS, 1970, III, p. 34.

SOURCE AND METHODS: See table 3400.

Table 3413

HONDURAS COMPARATIVE PC OF REAL GDP, 1926–88

	I. 1926–39			II. 1940–88					
Year	ECLA Factor (1926–39)	Year	ECLA Factor (1940–87)	IMF (1953–88)	OECD (1951–87)	SALA (1951–74)	ECLA Market (1975–87)	IDB (1981–87)
		1940	6.9					
1926	.9	1941	-.3					
1927	9.8	1942	-8.6					
1928	12.5	1943	.2					
1929	-1.0	1944	15.2					
1930	6.5	1945	9.4					
1931	2.2	1946	7.6					
1932	-10.4	1947	6.4					
1933	-6.2	1948	2.1					
1934	-3.1	1949	1.4					
1935	-4.4	1950	3.2					
1936	1.8	1951	5.4		4.6	7.2		
1937	-4.4	1952	3.8		3.0	6.1		
1938	5.8	1953	7.8	6.1	6.0	6.4		
1939	2.8	1954	-5.7	-6.1	-5.1	.9		
		1955	2.6	5.9	2.7	3.0		
		1956	8.1	4.4	9.2	3.8		
		1957	4.6	4.2	6.4	11.1		
		1958	3.2	5.5	2.5	1.3		
		1959	2.5	2.3	4.5	5.2		
		1960	6.2	2.3	1.7	5.4		
		1961	2.6	2.0	2.8	.7		
		1962	5.8	6.2	6.1	3.5		
		1963	3.7	3.5	3.3	3.0		
		1964	5.2	5.7	6.0	1.2		
		1965	8.6	8.7	10.3	7.8		
		1966	5.8	5.4	5.9	8.3		
		1967	5.6	5.4	4.6	4.4		
		1968	5.9	6.3	7.3	8.9		
		1969	.8	.8	.3	2.9		
		1970	2.6	6.2	6.6*	5.3		
		1971	3.8	2.3	5.4*	4.0		
		1972	4.2	6.2	3.1*	3.8		
		1973	4.2	4.7	3.7*	5.5		
		1974	-.6	-.1	-.1	2.6		
		1975	-1.9	-2.6	-3.0		-1.7	
		1976	6.1	10.6	8.0		8.4	
		1977	5.8	1.0	11.5		8.7	
		1978	7.9	17.5	7.4		7.0	
		1979	6.1	6.3	6.8		6.6	
		1980	3.3	1.3	2.7		4.7	
		1981	1.1	1.5	1.2		1.0	1.0
		1982	-1.6	-2.0	-1.8		-1.6	-2.6
		1983	.5	-.2	-.7		-.6	-1.1
		1984	3.2	2.8	2.8		3.1	2.8
		1985	1.5	3.2	3.2		1.4	3.2
		1986	2.5	2.7	2.7		2.0	2.7
		1987	4.2	4.2	4.2		4.2	4.2‡
		1988	~	.3	~		~	~

SOURCE AND METHODS: See table 3400.

Table 3414

MEXICO COMPARATIVE PC OF REAL GDP, 1896–1987a

PART I. 1896–1939

Year	ECLA Factor (1922–39)	Bank of Mexico[1] (1896–1939)
1896		3.1
1897		6.7
1898		5.8
1899		-4.8
1900		.8
1901		8.6
1902		-7.1
1903		11.2
1904		1.8
1905		10.4
1906		-1.1
1907		5.9
1908		-.2
1909		2.9
1910		.9
1911		?
1912		?
1913		?
1914		?
1915		?
1916		?
1917		?
1918		?
1919		?
1920		?
1921		7.7
1922	2.3	2.3
1923	3.4	3.4
1924	-1.6	-1.6
1925	6.2	6.2
1926	7.7	6.0
1927	-2.3	-4.4
1928	1.8	.6
1929	-3.3	-3.9
1930	-6.8	-6.3
1931	3.7	3.3
1932	-16.2	-14.9
1933	10.7	11.3
1934	6.6	6.8

PART II. 1940–87

Year	ECLA Factor (1940–87)	IMF (1953–87)	OECD (1951–87)	Bank of Mexico[2] (1940–80)	Bank of Mexico New System of National Accounts[3] (1971–84)	SALA (1951–74)	ECLA Market (1975–87)	IDB (1981–87)
1940	-.3			1.4				
1941	14.8			9.7				
1942	5.6			5.6				
1943	3.6			3.7				
1944	7.6			8.2				
1945	6.3			3.1				
1946	7.3			6.6				
1947	3.7			3.4				
1948	3.6			4.1				
1949	7.6			5.5				
1950	9.4	9.9		9.9				
1951	7.5	?	7.8	7.7		9.1		
1952	3.0	?	3.9	4.0		3.3		
1953	5.4	.3	.2	.3		4.6		
1954	5.4	10.0	10.5	10.0		5.4		
1955	7.9	8.6	8.8	8.5		7.5		
1956	5.3	6.8	6.6	6.9		5.3		
1957	7.5	7.5	7.7	7.6		7.5		
1958	4.6	5.4	5.4	5.4		4.2		
1959	4.3	3.0	2.9	3.0		3.9		
1960	7.5	8.1	8.1	8.1		7.6		
1961	4.9	4.9	4.9	4.9		4.9		
1962	4.7	4.7	4.7	4.7		4.5		
1963	8.0	8.0	8.0	8.0		8.0		
1964	11.7	11.7	11.7	11.7		11.6		
1965	6.5	6.5	6.5	6.5		6.3		
1966	6.9	6.9	6.9	6.9		6.8		
1967	6.3	6.3	6.3	6.3		6.1		
1968	8.1	8.1	8.1	8.1		8.0		
1969	6.3	6.3	6.3	6.3		6.4		
1970	6.9	6.9*	6.9*	6.9	6.9	6.8		
1971	3.4	4.2	3.4*	4.2	4.2	6.0		
1972	7.3	8.5	7.3*	8.5	8.5	4.7		
1973	7.6	8.4	7.6*	8.4	8.4	8.1		
1974	5.9	6.1	6.1	6.1	6.1	5.1		
1975	4.1	5.6	5.6	5.6	5.6		5.6	
1976	2.1	4.2	4.2	4.2	4.2		4.2	
1977	3.3	3.4	3.4	3.4	3.4		3.4	
1978	7.0	8.3	8.3	8.2	8.2		8.1	
1979	9.2	9.2	9.2	9.2	9.2		9.2	

Table 3414 (Continued)

MEXICO COMPARATIVE PC OF REAL GDP, 1896–1987[a]

PART I. 1896-1939

Year	ECLA Factor (1922–39)	Bank of Mexico[1] (1896–1939)
1935	5.1	7.4
1936	10.4	8.0
1937	3.4	3.3
1938	1.8	1.6
1939	5.3	5.4

PART II. 1940-87

Year	ECLA Factor (1940–87)	IMF (1953–87)	OECD (1951–87)	Bank of Mexico[2] (1940–80)	Bank of Mexico New System of National Accounts[3] (1971–84)	SALA (1951–74)	ECLA Market (1975–87)	IDB (1981–87)
1980	8.4	8.3	8.3	8.3	8.3		8.8	
1981	8.4	7.9	7.9	7.9	7.9		8.3	7.9
1982	-.5	-.6	-.6	-.5	-.5		#	-.5
1983	-5.1	-5.3	-4.6	-5.3	-5.3		-5.2	-5.3
1984	3.6	3.7	3.7	3.7	3.5		3.5	3.6
1985	2.5	2.8	2.8	2.8			2.7	2.6
1986	-3.8	-3.7	-3.7	-3.8			-4.0	-4.0
1987	1.4	~	1.1	~			1.4	1.4

1. Leopoldo Solís, *La Realidad Económica Mexicana: Retrovisión y Perspectivas*, rev. ed. (México, D.F.: Siglo XXI, 1981), p. 79.
2. SALA-SEM, "Introduction."
3. Data are in 1970 prices from NAFINSA-EMC, 1981, p. 51; Banco Nacional de México, *Informe*, 1982, pp. 30 and 50; and Banco Nacional de México, *Review of the Economic Situation of Mexico*, Aug. 1985, vol. 61, p. 10.

a. SALA recommends that the Bank of Mexico series be used which is essentially the same as IMF.

SOURCE AND METHODS: See table 3400.

Table 3415

NICARAGUA COMPARATIVE PC
OF REAL GDP, 1946–87

Year	ECLA Factor (1946–87)	IMF (1953–87)	OECD (1951–87)	SALA (1951–74)[a]	ECLA Market (1975–87)	IDB (1981–87)
1946	8.6					
1947	.3					
1948	8.7					
1949	−1.8					
1950	16.6					
1951	6.8		6.8	6.8		
1952	16.9		16.9	14.5		
1953	2.4	2.4	2.4	1.5		
1954	9.3	9.3	9.4	12.5		
1955	6.7	6.8	6.7	3.5		
1956	−.1	−.1	−.1	1.8		
1957	8.4	8.5	8.5	9.5		
1958	.3	.3	.3	−.5		
1959	1.5	1.5	1.5	1.9		
1960	1.4	3.6	1.4	1.6		
1961	7.5	7.5	7.5*	7.3		
1962	10.9	10.9	10.9	10.2		
1963	10.9	10.9	10.9	6.7		
1964	11.7	11.7	11.7	11.2		
1965	9.5	9.5	9.5	9.9		
1966	3.3	3.3	3.3	3.0		
1967	7.0	7.0	7.0	6.7		
1968	1.3	1.4	1.3	.3		
1969	6.7	6.2	6.2	5.0		
1970	1.0	1.3	2.0	4.5		
1971	4.9	4.9	3.9	5.0		
1972	3.2	3.2*	4.2	4.8		
1973	5.1	6.4	4.3	1.8		
1974	12.7	14.2	13.0	9.4		
1975	2.2	−.2	1.4		2.2	
1976	5.0	5.2	5.8		5.0	
1977	6.3	8.4	6.6		6.3	
1978	−7.2	−7.8	−6.5		−7.2	
1979	−26.5	−26.4	−25.9		−25.5	
1980	10.0	4.5	10.0		−10.0	
1981	5.4	5.4	8.6		5.4	5.4
1982	−.8	−.8	−1.3		−.8	−.8
1983	4.5	4.6	−4.0		4.4	4.6
1984	−1.4	−1.6	−3.9		−1.4	−1.6
1985	−4.0	−4.1	6.2		−2.6	−4.1
1986	−.6	−.6	.3		#	−.6
1987	1.8	1.7	4.5		1.7	1.7‡

a. Calculated from SALA, 19-2200.

SOURCE AND METHODS: See table 3400.

Table 3416

PANAMA COMPARATIVE PC
OF REAL GDP, 1946–87

Year	ECLA Factor (1946–87)	IMF (1953–87)	OECD (1951–87)	SALA (1951–74)	ECLA Market (1975–87)	IDB (1981–87)
1946	1.6					
1947	4.2					
1948	-5.9					
1949	2.3					
1950	.5					
1951	-.9		-.8	-.7		
1952	5.4		5.4	5.7		
1953	6.1	6.1	6.0	6.4		
1954	3.6	3.6	3.6	1.9		
1955	5.8	5.8	5.8	5.9		
1956	5.2	5.2	5.2	5.2		
1957	10.5	10.5	10.5	10.8		
1958	.8	.8	.8	1.8		
1959	6.4	6.4	6.3	7.6		
1960	6.0	6.0	6.0	7.3		
1961	10.8	10.8	10.8	11.7		
1962	8.4	8.2	8.2	8.8		
1963	9.4	8.5	8.5	8.8		
1964	4.3	4.4	4.4	5.2		
1965	8.8	9.2	9.2	7.4		
1966	7.4	7.6	7.6	7.7		
1967	8.4	8.6	8.6	7.7		
1968	7.3	7.0	7.0	6.9		
1969	7.8	8.4	8.4	8.9		
1970	6.0	4.1	6.9*	7.2		
1971	8.1	9.6	9.6	8.0		
1972	5.3	4.6	4.6	6.5		
1973	6.1	5.4	5.4*	6.1		
1974	.8	2.4	2.4	4.1		
1975	.6	1.7	1.7		.6	
1976	-1.1	1.7	1.6		-.3	
1977	3.3	1.1	1.1		4.6	
1978	3.8	9.8	9.8		6.5	
1979	4.5	4.5	4.5		7.0	
1980	15.1	15.1	15.2		9.7	
1981	4.0	4.2	4.2		4.0	4.2
1982	5.0	5.5	5.5		4.9	5.5
1983	#	.4	.4		-.1	.4
1984	-.4	-.4	-.4		-.4	-.4
1985	4.1	4.7	4.7		3.3	4.7
1986	3.1	2.9	3.4		3.0	2.9
1987	2.7	2.9	2.4		2.2	2.9‡

SOURCE AND METHODS: See table 3400.

Table 3417

PARAGUAY COMPARATIVE PC
OF REAL GDP, 1939–88

Year	ECLA Factor (1939–87)	IMF (1953–88)	OECD (1951–87)	SALA (1951–74)	ECLA Market (1976–87)	IDB (1981–87)
1939	17.5					
1940	–15.1					
1941	13.3					
1942	5.9					
1943	2.1					
1944	2.1					
1945	–3.5					
1946	9.8					
1947	–13.0					
1948	1.1					
1949	16.8					
1950	–1.6					
1951	1.9		–.4	1.1		
1952	–1.7		3.1	–1.0		
1953	2.8	5.2	1.3	5.3		
1954	1.7	2.6	3.8	2.7		
1955	4.6	6.3	7.1	6.2		
1956	4.2	2.4	–1.2	2.5		
1957	4.6	6.0	7.0	10.8		
1958	5.6	6.6	5.3	1.9		
1959	.4	–1.1	–.3	–1.1		
1960	.2	–.4	–.5*	–.5		
1961	4.8	6.0	5.9	5.9		
1962	7.0	5.9	5.5	5.9		
1963	2.7	2.0	2.7	1.7		
1964	4.3	4.3	4.4	4.0		
1965	5.7	5.7	5.7	6.8		
1966	1.1	1.1	1.2	1.3		
1967	6.3	6.3	6.3	5.9		
1968	3.6	3.7	3.5	4.8		
1969	3.9	3.8	3.9	4.0		
1970	6.2	3.8	6.2*	5.7		
1971	4.4	5.4	5.4	5.0		
1972	5.1	6.5	6.5	4.8		
1973	7.8	7.2	7.2	7.2		
1974	8.3	8.2	8.2	8.5		
1975	5.0	6.3	6.3			
1976	7.5	7.0	7.0		7.0	
1977	11.8	12.8	12.8		12.8	
1978	10.3	10.8	10.8		10.9	
1979	11.4	10.7	10.7		10.7	
1980	11.4	11.4	11.4		11.4	
1981	8.7	8.5	8.4		8.7	8.7
1982	–.6	–.8	–2.0*		–.7	–1.0
1983	–2.9	–3.0	–3.7*		–3.0	–3.0
1984	3.3	3.1	3.1		3.3	3.1
1985	4.1	4.0	4.0		4.0	4.0
1986	–.3	#	#		1.0	#
1987	4.6	4.3	4.3		4.5	4.3‡
1988	~	5.8	~		~	~

SOURCE AND METHODS: See table 3400.

Table 3418

PERU COMPARATIVE PC
OF REAL GDP, 1946–87

Year	ECLA Factor (1946–87)	IMF (1953–87)[a]	OECD (1951–87)[b]	SALA (1951–74)	ECLA Market (1975–87)	IDB (1981–87)
1946	4.0					
1947	3.0					
1948	3.4					
1949	7.1					
1950	5.0					
1951	11.3		10.5	10.2		
1952	2.7		2.8	3.0		
1953	2.2	2.5	2.2	2.0		
1954	9.6	8.8	9.6	9.8		
1955	4.9	7.0	4.9	5.0		
1956	5.0	2.6	4.6	4.4		
1957	1.0	1.1	1.1	1.1		
1958	3.2	3.3	3.3	3.3		
1959	4.4	5.4	3.6	3.5		
1960	9.0	9.4	11.4	9.2		
1961	8.2	8.8	7.0	8,0[c]		
1962	8.8	10.3	8.2	9.3[c]		
1963	3.9	4.2	4.1	3.8		
1964	6.8	6.9	7.3	6.9		
1965	4.8	5.1	5.2	4.8		
1966	5.7	7.0	6.4	5.8		
1967	1.8	3.5	3.4	1.6		
1968	.6	#	-.3	.7		
1969	4.4	4.1	3.9	2.4		
1970	9.1	7.3	5.4	9.1		
1971	5.1	5.1	5.0	6.5[c]		
1972	5.8	5.8	1.7	6.1[c]		
1973	6.2	6.2	4.3	6.2		
1974	6.9	6.9	7.5	5.8		
1975	3.3	2.4	4.6		4.5	
1976	3.0	3.3	2.0		2.0	
1977	-1.2	-.3	-.1		-.1	
1978	-.5	-1.7	-.5		-.5	
1979	4.1	4.3	4.1		4.1	
1980	3.8	2.9	3.8		4.0	
1981	4.4	3.0	3.9		4.0	3.1
1982	-.4	.9	.4		.1	.9
1983	-11.7	-12.0	-11.9*		-11.9	-12.0
1984	4.8	4.8	4.7		3.8	4.1
1985	2.5	1.6	2.5		1.6	1.9
1986	9.0	~	9.5		8.8	8.5
1987	6.6	~	6.9		6.5	6.7[‡]

a. 1970 prices through 1960.
b. GNP through 1959.
c. Corrects SALA, 18-2200; recalculated from USAID source, in 1973 dollars.

SOURCE AND METHODS: See table 3400.

Table 3419

URUGUAY COMPARATIVE PC OF REAL GDP, 1936–88

Year	ECLA Factor (1936–87)	IMF (1956–88)	OECD (1951–87)	SALA (1951–74)	ECLA Market (1975–87)	Kravis et al.[1] (1951–77)	IDB (1981–87)
1936	3.6						
1937	8.7						
1938	-4.9						
1939	-.8						
1940	-2.2						
1941	5.9						
1942	-9.1						
1943	1.5						
1944	12.9						
1945	2.3						
1946	11.1						
1947	6.7						
1948	2.6						
1949	3.7						
1950	3.1						
1951	-8.2		8.2	8.2		12.9	
1952	-.4		-.3	-.5		-3.5	
1953	6.5		6.4	6.5		4.6	
1954	5.7		5.8	5.7		5.5	
1955	1.6		1.5*	1.8		1.6	
1956	1.7	1.8	1.8	1.8		-.5	
1957	1.0	1.2	1.0	.9		13.5	
1958	-3.5	-3.5	-3.6	-3.6		-5.7	
1959	-2.8	-3.0	-2.8	-2.8		3.6	
1960	3.5	3.7	1.1	3.6		2.5	
1961	2.9	3.0	2.8	2.8		-.1	
1962	-2.3	-2.3	-2.3	-2.3		-2.9	
1963	.5	.6	.5	-1.1		-.5	
1964	2.0	1.8	2.0	2.8		1.6	
1965	1.2	1.2	1.2	1.0		-1.7	
1966	3.4	3.4	3.4	3.2		3.5	
1967	-4.1	-3.9	-4.1	-5.5		-5.8	
1968	1.6	1.1	1.6	1.3		.3	
1969	6.1	6.3	6.1	6.2		5.0	
1970	4.7	6.5	4.7*	5.9		4.1	
1971	-1.0	.1	.1	-1.0		-1.1	
1972	-3.3	-1.6	-1.6	-3.0		-2.1	
1973	.8	.4	.40			1.1	
1974	3.1	3.1	3.1	1.0		3.8	
1975	4.4	5.9	5.9		4.8	.2	
1976	2.6	4.0	4.0		4.2	3.0	
1977	3.4	1.2	1.2		1.8	1.9	
1978	3.9	5.3	5.3		6.2		
1979	6.2	6.2	6.2		9.6		
1980	6.1	6.0	6.0		5.8		
1981	1.5	1.9	1.9		1.4		1.9
1982	-10.0	-9.4	-9.7		-10.1		-9.4
1983	-6.0	-5.9	-4.7		-6.0		-5.9
1984	-1.2	-1.5	-1.5		-1.3		-1.5
1985	.2	.3	.3		.2		.3
1986	7.1	6.6	6.6		7.0		6.6
1987	5.4	4.9	4.8		5.3		4.9‡
1988	~	.5	~		~		~

1. Irving B. Kravis, Alan Heston, and Robert Summers, *World Product and Income: International Comparisons of Real Gross Product* (Baltimore: Published for the World Bank by the Johns Hopkins University Press, 1982), pp. 330–336. Kravis et al. give the results of the International Comparison Project (ICP), supervised by the UN Statistical Office with funding from a consortium organized by the World Bank, which developed international dollars comparable from country to country by applying a common set of prices (representative of the world price structure) to the quantities of the commodities and services entering into each country's final expenditure on GDP. The results theoretically overcome the problem of using nominal exchange rates, as does the "ECLA Factor approach." Data are calculated from 1975 dollars at market prices.

SOURCE AND METHODS: See table 3400.

Table 3420

VENEZUELA COMPARATIVE PC
OF REAL GDP, 1937–88

Year	ECLA Factor (1937–87)	IMF (1953–88)	OECD (1951–87)	SALA (1951–74)	ECLA Market (1975–87)	IDB (1981–87)
1937	7.3					
1938	3.2					
1939	4.3					
1940	2.8					
1941	7.9					
1942	−4.6					
1943	5.6					
1944	11.3					
1945	9.7					
1946	17.6					
1947	16.4					
1948	12.7					
1949	4.8					
1950	2.4					
1951	11.7		11.6	12.0		
1952	7.3		7.2	7.6		
1953	6.2	6.2	6.2	7.5		
1954	9.6	9.7	9.5	10.1		
1955	8.9	8.9	8.9	7.8		
1956	10.6	10.6	10.5	8.0		
1957	11.6	3.6	11.6	10.3		
1958	1.3	1.3	1.3	7.1		
1959	7.9	8.0	7.9	8.9		
1960	1.4	4.0	4.0*	3.3		
1961	5.0	4.9	5.0	4.5		
1962	9.1	9.1	9.1	8.3		
1963	6.9	7.0	6.9	7.1		
1964	9.7	9.6	9.7	12.9		
1965	5.9	6.0	5.9	5.7		
1966	2.3	2.5	2.3	2.7		
1967	4.0	3.8	4.0	4.6		
1968	5.3	4.9	5.3	5.2		
1969	4.5	4.5	4.5	3.9		
1970	7.1	8.8	8.8	6.2		
1971	3.3	3.0	3.0	0		
1972	3.0	2.7	2.7	5.0		
1973	6.7	6.3	6.3	4.8		
1974	5.8	6.1	6.1	7.3		
1975	5.2	6.1	6.1		5.9	
1976	7.8	8.8	8.8		8.4	
1977	7.6	6.7	6.7		6.8	
1978	4.8	2.1	2.1		3.2	
1979	1.3	1.3	1.3		.9	
1980	−2.0	−2.0	−2.0		−3.4	
1981	−.9	−.3	−.3		−1.0	−.3
1982	−1.2	.7	.7		−1.3	.7
1983	−5.5	−5.6	−4.8		−5.6	−5.6
1984	−1.0	−1.4	−1.4		−1.5	−1.2
1985	1.3	.3	.3		1.3	1.3
1986	6.9	5.2	5.2		6.8	6.8
1987	3.0	2.9	1.7		3.0	1.7‡
1988	~	4.1	~		~	~

SOURCE AND METHODS: See table 3400.

Table 3421

LATIN AMERICA COMPARATIVE PC OF REAL GDP, 1940–87

Year	ECLA Factor[1] (1940–87)	IMF (1953–87)[2]	OECD[3] (1951–87)	SALA[4] (1951–74)	ECLA[5] Market (1975–87)	IDB (1981–87)
1940	.2					
1941	6.2					
1942	1.8					
1943	3.1					
1944	7.3					
1945	1.7					
1946	7.8					
1947	6.3					
1948	4.7					
1949	2.7					
1950	4.9					
1951	5.9		5.4	6.2		
1952	3.0		2.3	2.5		
1953	4.5	2.4	3.6	4.6		
1954	6.2	5.2	6.4	5.9		
1955	6.3	4.5	6.3	2.5		
1956	4.1	.7	3.8	3.3		
1957	6.1	2.6	6.4	6.3		
1958	4.9	5.7	4.9	4.5		
1959	2.6	1.7	2.2	1.9		
1960	7.0	6.3	7.4	6.0		
1961	6.6	5.6	6.6	6.6		
1962	4.2	3.6	4.3	4.0		
1963	3.4	3.2	3.2	3.2		
1964	7.5	4.4	6.9	7.6		
1965	5.4	12.0	5.1	5.4		
1966	4.4	6.2	4.4	4.5		
1967	4.3	4.0	4.4	4.1		
1968	6.9	6.9	6.9	6.3		
1969	7.1	6.8	7.1	6.7		
1970	6.9	4.5	6.6	7.0		
1971	6.7	6.5	5.9	7.0		
1972	6.9	6.8	6.1	6.5		
1973	8.5	7.7	8.0	7.9		
1974	7.1	7.0	6.1	7.3		
1975	3.2	3.6	3.3		3.7	
1976	4.6	5.5	5.6		5.5	
1977	4.6	4.5	5.1		4.8	
1978	4.7	4.2	4.4		5.0	
1979	6.4	7.5	6.1		6.5	
1980	5.7	5.7	5.2		6.1	
1981	.5	−.1	1.5		.5	.5
1982	−1.2	−1.5	−1.1		−1.4	−.8
1983	−2.5	−2.3	−2.7		−2.4	−2.9
1984	3.7	3.5	3.4		3.8	3.6
1985	3.6	2.5	3.0		3.7	3.4
1986	3.8	3.7	2.4		3.9	3.9
1987	2.6	~	2.3		2.6	2.6[‡]

1. Excludes Cuba and through 1944 excludes Bolivia, Costa Rica, Dominican Republic, El Salvador, Guatemala, Haiti, Nicaragua, Panama, and Peru, but the ten countries included generated 88.7% of GDP for the region in 1945.
2. Excludes Cuba and Venezuela. Includes Dominica since 1977, Guyana since 1978, Jamaica since 1961, St. Lucia since 1976, Suriname since 1974. (Reported as Western Hemisphere in Source.)
3. Includes Jamaica, Trinidad and Tobago and five other unspecified countries; includes Netherlands Antilles and Guyana for 1956–59; includes more than ten small republics of the Caribbean through 1959.
4. Excludes Cuba and Haiti.
5. Excludes Cuba, from 1981.

SOURCE AND METHODS: See table 3400.

Figure 34:3

LATIN AMERICA COMPARATIVE PC OF REAL GDP, 1940–88

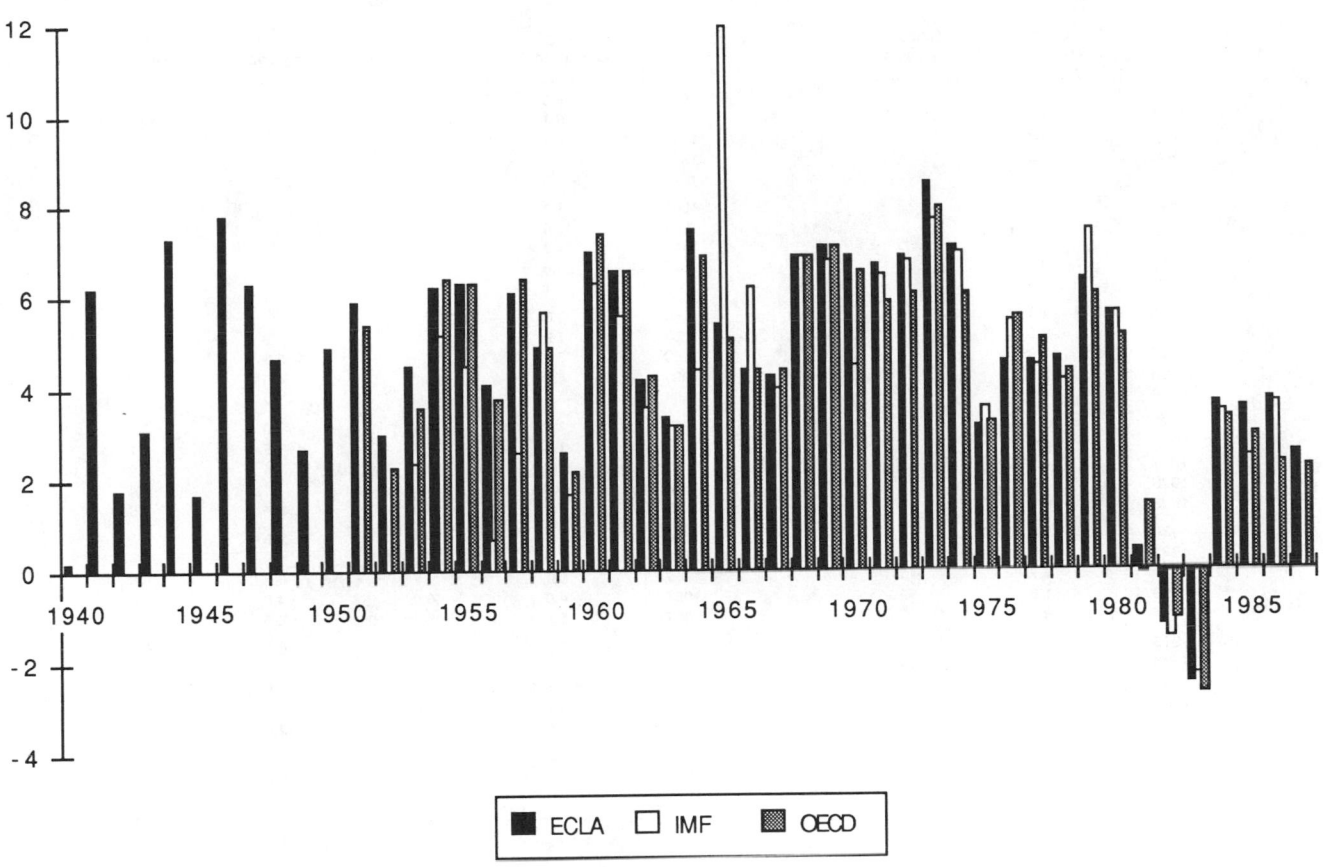

ECLA   IMF   OECD

SOURCE: Table 3421.

Table 3422

UNITED STATES COMPARATIVE
PC OF REAL GNP, 1910–88[a]

PART I. 1910–39

Year	USBC[1] (1910–39)	USDC-SCB[2] (1930–39)
1910	2.8	
1911	2.6	
1912	5.7	
1913	.9	
1914	−4.3	
1915	−.8	
1916	7.9	
1917	.7	
1918	12.3	
1919	−3.5	
1920	−4.3	
1921	−8.6	
1922	15.8	
1923	12.1	
1924	−.2	
1925	8.4	
1926	5.9	
1927	.0	
1928	.6	
1929	6.7	
1930	−9.8	−9.5
1931	−7.6	−7.8
1932	−14.7	−13.8
1933	−1.8	−2.2
1934	9.1	7.6
1935	9.9	8.7
1936	13.9	13.7
1937	5.3	5.0
1938	−5.0	−4.4
1939	8.6	7.8

PART II. 1940–88

Year	USBC[1] (1940–70)	IMF[3] (1953–88)	SALA[4] (1951–74)	USDC-SCB[2] (1940–88)
1940	8.5			7.6
1941	16.1			16.3
1942	12.9			15.3
1943	13.2			15.6
1944	7.2			7.1
1945	−1.7			−1.5
1946	−11.9			−14.7
1947	−.9			−1.7
1948	4.5			4.1
1949	.1			.5
1950	9.6			8.7
1951	7.9		7.9	8.3
1952	3.1		3.1	3.7
1953	4.5	3.8	4.5	3.8
1954	−1.3	−1.2	−1.4	−1.2
1955	7.6	6.7	7.6	6.7
1956	1.9	2.1	1.9	2.1
1957	1.4	1.8	1.4	1.8
1958	−1.1	−.3	−1.1	−.4
1959	6.4	6.0	6.4	6.0
1960	2.5	2.1	2.5	2.2
1961	2.0	2.6	1.9	2.6
1962	6.6	5.7	6.5	5.8
1963	4.0	4.0	4.0	4.0
1964	5.5	5.2	5.5	5.3
1965	6.3	6.0	6.3	6.0
1966	6.5	6.1	6.5	6.0
1967	2.6	2.7	2.6	2.7
1968	4.7	4.6	4.7	4.6
1969	2.6	2.8	2.6	2.8
1970	−.6	−.5	−.7	−.2
1971		3.2	3.0	3.4
1972		5.3	6.8	5.7
1973		4.4	5.5	5.8
1974		−1.7	−1.7	−.6
1975		−1.9		−1.1
1976		6.0		6.1
1977		5.5		5.9
1978		4.9		5.0
1979		1.5		2.8
1980		−1.8		−.3
1981		2.2		2.0
1982		−1.9		−1.9
1983		5.0		3.7
1984		8.5		6.8
1985		2.8		3.4
1986		2.7		2.7
1987		3.1		3.7
1988		3.7		4.4

1. USBC-HS, Series F-31, in 1958 dollars.
2. USDC-SCB, *The National Income and Product Accounts of the United States, 1929–1976* (Washington, D.C., 1981), revised since 1976 with USDC-SCB, July 1982, April 1985, October 1986, and August 1988. All data calculated in 1972 dollars except for 1985, 1986, 1987, and 1988 in 1982 constant dollars.
3. IMF-IFS-Y, 1984 through 1988.
4. SALA, 18-2200.

a. At market prices.

SOURCE AND METHODS: See table 3400.

Table 3423

GDP LEVELS AND GROWTH, 6 L, 1929–83

	A. ARGENTINA	C. BRAZIL	D. CHILE	E. COLOMBIA	G. CUBA	N. MEXICO
1929 Levels, million 1929 $ at US Relative Prices	4,806	2,690	1,077	729	890	1,385
1929	100.0	100.0	100.0	100.0	100.0	100.0
1930	95.9	97.9	95.9	99.1	94.2	93.2
1931	89.2	94.7	76.9	97.6	79.1	96.6
1932	86.2	98.8	73.5	104.0	63.5	81.0
1933	90.3	107.6	83.5	109.9	68.7	89.7
1934	97.4	117.5	94.7	107.6	80.7	95.6
1935	101.7	120.9	98.4	119.6	94.4	100.5
1936	103.0	135.5	101.6	126.0	110.0	110.9
1937	111.3	141.7	109.4	127.9	126.4	114.7
1938	112.6	148.1	109.4	136.3	98.1	116.8
1950	159.6	268.3	172.5	212.1	193.0	239.1
1973	374.6	1,354.4	393.9	676.8	313.1	969.1
1973 Levels, million 1973 $ at US Relative Prices	62,074	124,564	14,750	16,949	9,685	46,858
1973	100.0	100.0	100.0	100.0	100.0	100.0
1974	105.7	109.7	101.0	105.7	88.7	106.1
1975	105.3	115.7	87.9	108.2	85.0	112.1
1976	104.8	126.9	91.0	113.3	86.1	116.8
1977	111.5	134.2	100.0	118.0	87.3	120.8
1978	107.7	140.9	108.2	128.0	88.4	130.8
1979	115.5	149.9	117.2	134.9	88.5	142.8
1980	115.8	160.7	126.3	140.4	88.6	154.7
1981	108.6	158.2	133.3	143.6	92.1	167.0
1982	102.8	159.7	114.5	145.0	94.4	166.0
1983	105.7	154.6	113.7	146.1	99.1	157.3

SOURCE: Angus Maddison, *Two Crises: Latin America and Asia, 1929–38 and 1973–83*
(Paris: Development Centre of the Organisation for Economic Co-Operation and
Development, 1985).

Table 3424

GDP IN CONSTANT DOLLARS OF 1970, 19 LR, 1940–85
(ECLA Factor Series)[1]

PART I. PURCHASING POWER EQUIVALENCES OF LATIN
AMERICAN CURRENCY IN RELATION
TO THE DOLLAR IN 1970

	Country	1 Dollar U.S. Currency Equals:
A.	ARGENTINA	2.95 pesos argentinos
B.	BOLIVIA	9.03 pesos bolivianos
C.	BRAZIL	4.14 novos cruzeiros
D.	CHILE	.01 pesos chilenos
E.	COLOMBIA	10.68 pesos colombianos
F.	COSTA RICA	5.09 colones costarricenses
H.	DOMINICAN REP.	.87 pesos dominicanos
I.	ECUADOR	14.00 sucres
J.	EL SALVADOR	1.70 colones salvadoreños
K.	GUATEMALA	.81 quetzales
L.	HAITI	3.99 gourdes
M.	HONDURAS	1.75 lempiras
N.	MEXICO	8.88 pesos mexicanos
O.	NICARAGUA	6.41 córdobas
P.	PANAMA	.76 balboas
Q.	PARAGUAY	85.41 guaraníes
R.	PERU	30.72 soles
S.	URUGUAY	.20 pesos uruguayos
T.	VENEZUELA	3.96 bolívares

1. Owing to timing of revisions, the implicit PC since 1970 here
   may not agree with explicit PC for ECLA factor series in tables
   3301 through 3321 above.

SOURCE: ECLA-SHCAL, p. 8.

Table 3424 (Continued)

GDP IN CONSTANT DOLLARS OF 1970, 19 LR, 1940–85
(ECLA Factor Series)[1]

PART II. SERIES, 1940–85 (M US)[1]

Year	A. ARGENTINA	B. BOLIVIA	C. BRAZIL	D. CHILE	E. COLOMBIA	F. COSTA RICA	H. DOMINICAN REPUBLIC	I. ECUADOR	J. EL SALVADOR	K. GUATEMALA
1940	10,048	?	8,024	2,495	3,013	?	?	424	?	?
1941	10,538	?	8,421	2,498	3,063	?	?	426	?	?
1942	11,028	?	8,183	2,636	3,070	?	?	444	?	?
1943	11,108	?	8,660	2,746	3,082	?	?	500	?	?
1944	12,189	?	9,057	2,785	3,090	?	?	507	?	?

Continued in SALA 26, 33-24.

Table 3425

STRUCTURE AND GROWTH OF GDP, BY SECTOR, 1960–88
(%)

Sector	Structure								Growth Rates								
	Average			Annual						Cumulative			Annual					
	1960–69	1970–79	1980–88	1983	1984	1985	1986	1987	1988‡	1961–70	1971–80	1981–88	1983	1984	1985	1986	1987	1988‡
Primary Sector	20.9	15.9	15.4	15.3	15.7	15.8	15.1	15.3	15.5	7.3	7.0	3.1	-.3	8.6	5.4	.6	6.8	3.5
Agriculture	15.1	11.7	11.2	11.3	11.5	11.6	10.9	11.3	11.4	3.4	3.5	1.9	.6	3.3	4.9	-2.5	7.0	1.3
Mining	5.8	4.2	4.2	4.1	4.2	4.2	4.2	4.0	4.1	3.9	3.5	1.2	-2.6	5.3	.5	3.1	-.2	2.2
Secondary Sector	27.9	30.8	29.7	28.6	29.0	29.3	30.0	29.8	29.2	21.9	22.8	3.5	-5.5	9.2	15.0	19.9	7.2	1.4
Manufacturing	21.4	23.3	22.3	21.5	22.1	22.2	22.8	22.6	22.1	6.7	6.4	.5	-4.2	5.1	4.3	6.3	2.3	-1.5
Construction	5.6	6.1	5.4	5.2	4.9	5.0	5.1	5.0	4.8	4.8	7.1	-1.6	-14.1	-3.6	4.1	6.4	1.0	-2.5
Electricity, Gas, Water	.9	1.4	2.0	1.9	2.0	2.1	2.1	2.2	2.3	10.4	9.3	4.6	5.4	7.7	6.6	7.2	3.9	5.4
Tertiary Sector	50.1	53.0	51.5	53.9	52.5	52.1	51.3	51.3	51.5	28.8	29.9	7.6	-1.8	22.6	14.1	11.2	13.3	7.4
Finance	11.6	13.4	12.4	12.2	12.4	12.6	12.8	12.8	13.0	6.5	5.5	2.4	.6	3.3	4.9	5.2	3.5	2.1
Commerce	18.3	18.1	17.4	17.3	17.4	17.2	16.9	16.9	16.8	5.7	5.8	.4	-5.3	2.6	2.4	3.1	2.2	-.2
Transport and Communications	5.1	5.6	6.6	6.4	6.6	6.6	6.7	6.8	6.9	5.7	7.7	2.1	-1.6	4.0	3.6	5.1	4.8	2.7
Public Administration	6.0	6.1	6.6	6.8	6.9	6.7	6.5	6.5	6.5	5.0	5.4	1.5	1.9	3.0	1.2	.8	1.6	1.6
Other Services	9.1	9.8	8.5	11.3	9.2	9.0	8.4	8.3	8.3	5.9	5.5	1.2	-1.0	9.7	2.0	-3.0	1.2	1.2
Gross Domestic Product	100.0	100.0	100.0	100.0	100.0	100.0	100.0	100.0	100.0	5.6	5.9	1.0	-2.7	3.4	3.5	3.9	3.0	.6

SOURCE: IDB-SPTF, 1988, table 11-6; 1989, table 11-4.

Table 3426

AGRICULTURAL SECTOR: VALUE ADDED, DISTRIBUTION, AND GROWTH, 19 LR, 1961-88

(%)

| | Proportion of GDP | | | | | | | | | Growth Rates | | | | | | | | |
| | Average | | | Annual | | | | | | Cumulative | | | Annual | | | | | |
Country	1960-69	1970-79	1980-88	1983	1984	1985	1986	1987	1988‡	1961-70	1971-80	1981-88	1983	1984	1985	1986	1987	1988‡
A. ARGENTINA	12.9	11.8	13.1	13.5	13.7	14.1	12.9	13.1	13.9	2.4	2.1	2.5	1.9	3.1	-1.7	-3.2	3.6	5.2
B. BOLIVIA	20.5	18.0	21.1	18.0	22.2	24.3	23.8	23.3	22.7	2.8	4.4	1.5	-16.4	22.9	9.1	-4.7	-.1	-.1
C. BRAZIL	17.5	11.3	10.8	10.9	11.3	11.4	9.8	10.8	10.8	3.0	4.7	3.1	1.8	3.0	10.1	-7.9	14.0	-.4
D. CHILE	9.4	8.6	9.2	9.2	9.3	9.6	9.9	9.6	9.4	1.9	2.2	3.8	-2.5	7.5	5.6	8.8	3.2	5.5
E. COLOMBIA	27.2	23.6	22.0	22.5	22.2	21.9	21.3	21.5	21.3	3.7	4.4	2.5	2.8	1.8	1.6	3.3	6.1	3.0
F. COSTA RICA	24.5	20.9	19.3	20.1	20.5	19.2	19.1	18.8	19.1	5.1	2.6	2.8	4.0	10.1	-5.5	4.8	4.0	5.3
H. DOMINICAN REP.	26.7	18.7	16.5	17.0	17.1	16.9	16.3	15.5	15.1	1.5	3.4	1.2	3.1	0	-3.5	-.5	2.9	-1.7
I. ECUADOR	27.0	18.0	15.2	13.2	14.0	14.7	15.7	17.8	17.1	3.3	3.0	4.3	-13.9	10.6	10.0	9.9	7.5	3.8
J. EL SALVADOR	28.0	24.2	24.9	25.3	25.6	24.8	23.9	23.7	22.7	3.9	3.0	-2.2	-3.2	3.3	-1.1	-3.1	2.1	-3.8
K. GUATEMALA	28.8	27.1	25.4	25.3	25.6	25.9	25.6	25.7	25.6	4.4	4.7	.5	-1.7	1.6	.4	-.8	3.6	3.0
L. HAITI	44.6	39.0	32.2	31.0	32.0	32.1	32.5	32.7	32.5	.8	1.5	-.5	-3.7	3.4	.6	2.4	.3	-1.0
M. HONDURAS	33.3	27.9	25.3	25.6	25.2	25.2	25.0	25.6	25.3	5.5	3.0	2.3	-.7	1.2	2.9	2.4	6.7	2.5
N. MEXICO	13.3	9.7	8.3	8.4	8.4	8.5	8.6	8.6	8.4	3.9	3.4	1.2	2.0	2.7	3.8	-2.7	1.8	-1.6
O. NICARAGUA	25.2	24.4	23.8	25.3	24.3	24.1	22.2	21.7	23.6	6.7	0	-.7	5.8	-5.3	-4.8	-8.8	-3.2	-.2
P. PANAMA	16.9	12.9	10.1	9.9	10.1	10.2	9.6	10.1	11.2	5.4	1.5	1.6	3.1	1.7	5.0	-2.2	7.8	-8.4
Q. PARAGUAY	34.2	29.0	26.1	26.0	26.7	26.9	25.2	25.9	27.2	3.0	6.7	3.7	-2.4	5.9	4.6	-6.1	7.0	11.3
R. PERU	16.1	12.9	11.7	11.4	12.2	12.4	11.8	11.5	13.3	4.3	-.6	4.0	-10.8	11.8	3.7	6.2	5.0	5.7
S. URUGUAY	11.6	10.6	10.5	11.2	10.6	11.1	10.8	10.4	10.4	3.0	.6	.6	2.1	-6.8	4.5	4.3	2.6	.5
T. VENEZUELA	5.3	4.8	5.3	5.1	5.3	5.6	5.7	5.8	5.8	5.6	3.0	3.4	.4	.8	8.3	8.3	4.1	4.3
LATIN AMERICA[1]	15.2	11.7	11.2	11.3	11.5	11.6	10.9	11.3	11.4	3.4	3.5	1.9	.6	3.3	4.9	-2.5	7.0	1.3

1. Includes Bahamas, Barbados, Guyana, Jamaica, Suriname, and Trinidad and Tobago.

SOURCE: IDB-SPTF, 1988, table IV-1; 1989, table IV-1.

Table 3427

MANUFACTURING SECTOR: VALUE ADDED, DISTRIBUTION, AND GROWTH, 19 LR, 1961-88
(%)

| | Proportion of GDP | | | | | | | | | Growth Rates | | | | | | | | |
| | Average | | | Annual | | | | | | Cumulative | | | Annual | | | | | |
Country	1960-69	1970-79	1980-88	1983	1984	1985	1986	1987	1988‡	1961-70	1971-80	1981-88	1983	1984	1985	1986	1987	1988‡
A. ARGENTINA	23.0	24.1	20.7	21.2	21.3	20.0	21.4	20.8	20.1	5.2	1.6	-1.7	-10.8	3.8	-10.3	12.9	-.6	-4.9
B. BOLIVIA	11.3	13.4	11.7	12.5	10.8	9.8	10.3	10.4	10.8	6.4	6.2	-4.8	-4.6	-14.0	-9.3	2.1	3.3	6.5
C. BRAZIL	26.5	28.8	26.7	25.1	26.3	26.3	27.2	26.5	25.7	6.8	9.0	.6	-6.1	6.1	8.3	11.3	1.0	-3.4
D. CHILE	24.2	23.8	20.6	20.0	20.7	20.4	20.8	20.8	21.1	5.3	1.1	1.8	3.1	9.8	1.2	8.0	5.5	8.7
E. COLOMBIA	20.9	22.8	21.2	20.7	21.2	21.2	21.2	21.2	20.9	5.7	6.0	2.4	1.1	6.0	3.0	5.9	5.0	2.3
F. COSTA RICA	16.2	20.8	21.9	21.2	21.6	21.9	22.3	22.3	22.3	8.8	7.4	2.2	1.8	10.4	2.0	7.3	5.5	4.0
H. DOMINICAN REP.	14.9	18.6	17.5	17.6	17.2	16.4	17.0	17.6	16.8	7.4	6.8	1.4	.7	-2.4	-7.1	7.0	11.6	-3.4
I. ECUADOR	12.6	16.1	18.0	19.3	18.2	17.5	16.6	17.6	16.4	5.0	12.8	.8	-1.4	-1.8	.2	-1.7	.3	.7
J. EL SALVADOR	17.0	18.7	17.4	17.1	16.9	17.2	17.5	17.6	17.9	8.1	3.0	-.6	2.0	1.3	3.7	2.5	3.0	2.4
K. GUATEMALA	14.4	15.9	15.9	15.9	15.9	15.8	15.9	15.7	15.5	7.6	6.2	-.7	-1.9	.5	-.8	.7	1.7	2.5
L. HAITI	14.0	15.1	16.4	17.6	16.5	16.0	15.9	15.3	15.2	.5	8.4	-2.8	5.5	-5.9	-2.9	.4	-3.9	.8
M. HONDURAS	10.6	13.3	13.2	13.1	13.8	13.1	13.1	13.6	13.7	7.1	6.5	2.6	5.3	8.4	-2.2	2.7	8.4	4.9
N. MEXICO	19.3	21.7	21.2	20.4	20.7	21.3	20.9	21.2	21.4	9.2	7.1	.6	-7.8	5.0	6.0	-5.7	2.6	2.2
O. NICARAGUA	19.0	21.8	25.3	25.5	26.0	25.9	26.7	26.4	21.1	10.0	2.4	-3.2	5.6	.4	-4.7	2.1	-1.6	-26.4
P. PANAMA	11.6	11.7	9.2	9.2	9.2	8.9	8.8	8.9	8.0	10.8	3.6	-3.1	-1.8	-.5	2.0	2.2	3.4	-25.4
Q. PARAGUAY	17.0	17.6	16.5	16.2	16.4	16.6	16.4	16.2	16.1	6.6	8.3	1.6	-4.2	4.5	5.0	-1.4	3.5	5.3
R. PERU	25.3	24.8	22.9	21.5	21.6	22.1	23.2	24.5	23.0	5.3	3.3	.5	-16.9	5.5	4.9	16.8	13.7	-14.3
S. URUGUAY	19.8	20.1	18.3	17.0	17.8	17.4	18.2	19.3	18.5	1.2	3.3	-1.2	-7.0	2.8	-1.6	12.1	12.4	-3.7
T. VENEZUELA	14.9	15.9	18.7	18.1	19.1	19.8	19.9	19.8	19.8	7.5	5.2	2.9	-1.7	4.6	4.8	7.1	2.5	4.4
LATIN AMERICA[1]	21.4	23.3	22.3	21.5	22.1	22.2	22.8	22.6	22.1	6.7	6.4	.5	-4.2	5.1	4.3	6.3	2.3	-1.5

1. Includes Bahamas, Barbados, Guyana, Jamaica, Suriname, and Trinidad and Tobago.

SOURCE: IDB-SPTF, 1988, table IV-5; 1989, table IV-5.

Table 3428

SHARES OF AGRICULTURAL GDP IN TOTAL GDP, 19 LR, 1950-75
(%)

| | Agricultural GDP/Total GDP | | | | Agricultural GDP PI/Nonagricultural GDP PI | | | |
Country	1950-52	1959-61	1969-71	1973-75	1950-52	1959-61	1969-71	1973-75
A. ARGENTINA	16.5	15.5	12.8	12.0	60.4	73.6	75.1	76.9

Continued in SALA, 24-3328.

Table 3429

AGRICULTURE[1] SHARE IN GDP, 19 LR, 1920-87[a]
(%)[b]

Year	A. ARGENTINA	B. BOLIVIA	C. BRAZIL	D. CHILE	E. COLOMBIA	F. COSTA RICA	H. DOMINICAN REPUBLIC	I. ECUADOR	J. EL SALVADOR	K. GUATEMALA	L. HAITI	UNITED STATES
1920	30.0	~	22.8	~	~	~	~	~	~	~	~	~
1930	22.6	~	23.5	~	52.4	~	~	~	~	~	~	~
1940	23.2	~	21.4	13.0	44.7	~	~	38.3	~	~	~	~
1950	16.2	25.4	16.8	11.6	37.7	38.4	34.5	42.1	40.9	35.5	52.2	5.5
1960	14.9	24.5	13.4	9.8	32.7	29.4	33.9	39.0	36.0	33.4	49.2	4.4
1970	12.9	19.7	10.0	7.9	28.6	25.0	25.8	29.7	30.6	30.1	50.8	3.2
1980	12.9	17.1	7.3	7.7	25.4	18.3	18.6	21.1	28.0	28.0	42.0	2.7
1981‡	13.7	18.4	8.1	6.9	25.6	19.8	18.3	15.3	29.9	27.7	42.0	~
1982‡	15.2	21.7	7.8	8.3	23.9	21.5	20.5	15.8	27.5	28.0	43.5	~
1983‡	15.2	17.4	8.4	8.2	24.0	21.5	19.2	13.8	29.5	27.8	34.2	~
1984‡	15.4	19.0	9.5	7.4	23.5	21.2	19.0	14.9	29.5	27.6	33.3	~
1985‡	10.9	19.6	14.3	8.3	18.5	19.8	20.4	11.5	26.6	25.1	33.2	~
1986‡	10.3	19.8	9.7	7.7	17.7	19.0	19.4	12.6	26.4	27.9	33.9	~
1987‡	10.2	23.2	10.6	8.4	18.0	17.8	18.7	15.0	26.2	27.7	34.1	~

Year	M. HONDURAS	N. MEXICO	O. NICARAGUA	P. PANAMA	Q. PARAGUAY	R. PERU	S. URUGUAY	T. VENEZUELA	LATIN AMERICA[2]
1920	~	~	~	~	~	~	~	~	~
1930	55.2	18.7	~	~	49.2	~	~	~	~
1940	50.5	19.7	36.6	~	40.8	~	16.3	19.2	25.1
1950	44.8	19.4	29.5	32.6	39.2	25.5	13.5	9.2	19.7
1960	32.8	16.2	27.0	26.1	34.3	24.4	11.0	7.9	17.1
1970	32.5	12.7	26.8	20.0	30.0	20.3	12.9	7.6	13.8
1980	27.0	9.4	28.0	17.0	29.5	13.3	9.8	7.0	11.2ᶜ
1981‡	27.5	9.1	28.0	16.3	29.2	12.8	10.1	7.0	~
1982‡	28.1	9.1	28.2	10.0	28.7	13.2	10.7	6.8	~
1983‡	28.6	10.0	26.4	10.4	29.5	13.2	11.1	6.6	~
1984‡	29.0	9.9	24.6	10.0	31.4	14.1	12.1	7.7	~
1985‡	27.5	8.7	22.9	9.1	29.5	10.1	12.3	6.9	~
1986‡	25.9	9.0	22.7	8.9	30.2	11.5	11.8	7.0	~
1987‡	26.0	8.6	~	9.3	~	11.4	11.6	7.0	~

1. Includes hunting, fishing, and forestry.
2. For coverage, see table 3321, note 1.

a. For yearly data since 1900, see SALA, 20-2205ff. and 22-2305ff.
b. Calculations based upon constant dollars, factor cost.
c. For 1979 from ECLA-AE, 1980, p. 119.

SOURCE: Latin American data calculated from ECLA-SHCAL, pp. 74ff.; and for 1960-85 from ECLA-S, 1980-87, table 3, by country. U.S. data calculated from USDC sources given in SALA, 25-3322, note 2.

Table 3430

MINING AND QUARRYING SHARE IN GDP, 19 LR, 1920-87[a] (%)[b]

Year	A. ARGENTINA	B. BOLIVIA	C. BRAZIL	D. CHILE	E. COLOMBIA	F. COSTA RICA[1]	H. DOMINICAN REPUBLIC	I. ECUADOR	J. EL SALVADOR	K. GUATEMALA
1920	.3	?	.6	?	?	?	?	?	?	?
1930	.3	?	.4	?	3.0	?	?	?	?	?
1940	.9	?	.5	19.4	3.0	?	?	2.2	1.0	.2
1950	.7	19.8	.4	12.4	2.4	?	.3	1.2	.2	.2
1960	1.3	12.3	.5	11.1	2.7	?	1.9	1.4	.2	.2
1970	2.2	8.0	.8	11.7	2.1	?	1.7	1.2	.1	.1
1980	2.5	5.5	.9	12.2	1.1	?	4.9	4.7	.1	.4
1981‡	2.6	5.2	.9	10.7	1.2	?	5.0	5.0	.1	.4
1982‡	2.7	5.2	1.0	13.9	1.0	?	3.5	5.2	.2	.4
1983‡	2.8	5.8	.9	13.6	1.1	?	4.4	?	.2	.3
1984‡	2.7	5.1	1.0	13.4	1.3	?	4.7	?	.2	.4
1985‡	2.7	12.6	1.1	10.3	4.1	?	5.3	8.3	.1	.3
1986‡	2.5	10.5	.9	9.9	4.6	?	4.6	26.9	.1	.4
1987‡	2.4	11.4	.9	9.4	6.2	?	5.3	16.9	.2	.4

Year	L. HAITI	M. HONDURAS	N. MEXICO	O. NICARAGUA	P. PANAMA	Q. PARAGUAY	R. PERU	S. URUGUAY[1]	T. VENEZUELA	LATIN AMERICA[2]	UNITED STATES
1920	?	?	?	?	?	?	?	?	?	?	?
1930	?	2.0	8.5	?	?	?	?	?	?	?	?
1940	?	3.1	6.0	?	?	?	?	?	?	?	?
1950	3.3	2.3	4.1	1.5	.2	?	7.2	?	20.3	4.3	2.1
1960	5.0	1.9	2.4	1.2	.3	.2	11.2	?	27.3	4.0	1.8
1970	1.7	2.3	4.1	.7	.3	.1	7.2	?	27.5	4.6	1.8
1980	.9	1.8	3.1	.2	.3	.7	8.1	?	22.6	4.3	1.5
1981‡	.5	1.8	3.4	.2	.3	.7	7.3	?	8.8	3.5c	?
1982‡	1.0	2.1	3.7	.1	.2	.7	8.0	?	8.8	?	?
1983‡	?	2.1	3.8	.2	.3	.6	8.4	?	.7	?	?
1984‡	#	2.2	3.7	.1	.2	.6	8.2	?	.6	?	?
1985‡	.1	2.2	7.9	.4	.1	.4	11.9	?	.4	?	?
1986‡	.1	2.7	7.6	.5	.1	.5	13.2	?	.7	?	?
1987‡	.1	2.2	3.8	.5	.1	.5	11.9	?	.9	?	?

1. Included in table 3331.
2. For coverage, see table 3321, note 1.

a. For yearly data since 1900, see SALA, 20-2205ff. and 22-2305ff.
b. Calculations based upon constant dollars, factor cost.
c. Includes petroleum refining.

SOURCE: See table 3429.

Table 3431

MANUFACTURING SHARE IN GDP, 19 LR, 1920-87[a]
(%)[b]

Year	A. ARGENTINA	B. BOLIVIA	C. BRAZIL	D. CHILE	E. COLOMBIA	F. COSTA RICA[1]	H. DOMINICAN REPUBLIC	I. ECUADOR	J. EL SALVADOR	K. GUATEMALA
1920	17.4	~	12.1	~	~	~	~	~	~	~
1930	20.5	~	12.0	~	5.5	~	~	~	~	~
1940	22.7	~	15.0	11.8	~	~	8.3	16.0	~	~
1950	23.7	12.2	21.2	23.1	14.5	11.5	12.4	16.0	12.9	11.1
1960	26.5	11.6	26.3	24.8	16.7	12.5	14.6	15.7	13.9	11.9
1970	28.0	14.5	28.4	27.2	17.5	15.1	16.7	16.8	17.6	14.6
1980	25.3	15.4	30.2	24.2	18.3	18.1	16.6	20.1	16.3	15.6
1981‡	22.1	15.4	29.0	21.8	17.6	18.4	16.3	23.0	15.2	15.3
1982‡	22.4	14.0	28.6	20.2	16.9	17.7	16.8	22.5	15.5	14.6
1983‡	24.1	14.2	26.1	20.8	15.8	16.5	16.5	~	16.1	14.5
1984‡	24.8	12.6	26.1	21.7	16.7	17.6	15.8	26.7	16.1	14.7
1985‡	23.5	9.8	26.4	20.1	22.5	18.7	14.2		14.9	16.7
1986‡	25.0	10.0	28.5	20.6	22.3	19.4	14.3	8.1	14.8	16.9
1987‡	24.4	10.6	28.0	20.7	22.0	19.3	14.6	8.5	15.0	16.7

Year	L. HAITI	M. HONDURAS	N. MEXICO	O. NICARAGUA	P. PANAMA	Q. PARAGUAY	R. PERU	S. URUGUAY[1]	T. VENEZUELA	LATIN AMERICA[2]	UNITED STATES
1920	~	~	~	~	~	~	~	~	~	~	~
1930	~	4.7	13.8	~	~	~	~	~	~	~	~
1940	~	6.8	16.9	~	~	16.0	~	17.3	13.6	16.6	~
1950	8.1	9.1	18.8	10.8	8.2	15.9	14.2	20.3	11.2	18.7	24.7
1960	8.9	15.3	19.3	13.0	11.8	15.1	17.1	24.3	14.0	21.3	23.5
1970	9.8	13.8	23.4	19.2	15.8	17.3	21.1	23.1	11.2	25.1	24.2
1980	12.5	16.4	23.8	20.6	12.0	15.8	21.2	23.9	14.1	25.4c	24.3
1981‡	13.2	16.4	24.0	19.3	11.4	16.1	20.2	23.5	14.8	~	~
1982‡	12.1	14.4	23.5	18.5	9.7	15.7	19.6	21.5	14.5	~	~
1983‡	18.1	15.5	22.9	21.2	9.6	15.5	18.2	18.8	14.8	~	~
1984‡	17.4	13.9	23.4	21.7	9.3	15.1	17.8	20.8	18.7	~	~
1985‡	16.1	15.3	22.6	25.4	8.7	15.5	26.1	26.4	19.3	~	~
1986‡	14.5	14.3	22.2	26.4	8.6	15.3	20.2	26.6	19.0	~	~
1987‡	14.1	15.7	21.1	26.3	8.8	15.1	20.9	27.9	18.7	~	~

1. Includes mining and quarrying.
2. For coverage, see table 3321, note 1.

a. For yearly data since 1900, see SALA, 20-2205ff. and 22-2305ff.
b. Calculations based upon constant dollars, factor cost.
c. For 1979 from ECLA-S, 1980, p. 119.

SOURCE: See table 3429.

Table 3432

CONSTRUCTION SHARE IN GDP, 19 LR, 1920-87[a]
(%)[b]

Year	A. ARGENTINA	B. BOLIVIA	C. BRAZIL	D. CHILE	E. COLOMBIA	F. COSTA RICA	H. DOMINICAN REPUBLIC	I. ECUADOR	J. EL SALVADOR	K. GUATEMALA
1920	1.5	?	?	?	?	?	?	?	?	?
1930	5.5	?	?	?	3.0	?	?	?	?	?
1940	3.7	?	7.5	4.2	4.5	?	?	1.3	?	?
1950	5.3	1.6	9.2	4.4	4.0	4.7	3.8	1.3	2.4	4.2
1960	4.8	3.8	8.3	4.4	4.7	5.0	3.0	2.6	3.3	2.7
1970	6.4	4.4	5.8	4.2	5.5	4.7	5.5	4.4	3.0	2.2
1980	7.6	4.3	6.9	3.3	3.5	6.9	7.7	5.7	4.6	4.0
1981‡	7.8	3.9	6.7	4.5	3.9	5.4	7.4	3.4	3.3	4.4
1982‡	6.1	1.8	6.6	3.9	4.4	4.2	6.9	3.3	3.3	4.2
1983‡	4.7	1.8	5.1	3.9	4.5	4.0	7.6	2.8	3.8	4.1
1984‡	3.6	3.4	5.0	3.9	4.5	4.7	7.8	2.9	3.5	2.9
1985‡	4.1	3.3	4.0	5.6	5.0	4.2	6.4	6.2	3.4	2.7
1986‡	3.9	3.4	5.9	5.3	5.2	4.2	7.4	5.8	3.2	2.6
1987‡	4.1	2.8	5.5	5.6	5.5	4.4	9.8	6.5	3.5	2.7

Year	L. HAITI	M. HONDURAS	N. MEXICO	O. NICARAGUA	P. PANAMA	Q. PARAGUAY	R. PERU	S. URUGUAY	T. VENEZUELA	LATIN AMERICA[1]	UNITED STATES
1920	?	?	?	?	?	?	?	?	?	?	?
1930	?	3.5	?	?	?	?	?	?	?	?	?
1940	?	4.5	3.2	?	?	1.3	?	3.8	3.5	4.4	?
1950	?	5.4	4.1	1.2	4.2	1.3	6.7	5.0	6.5	5.6	5.5
1960	?	4.5	4.8	2.2	5.7	2.3	5.3	5.4	5.4	5.5	6.3
1970	2.3	4.8	5.5	3.5	6.3	3.0	3.2	3.9	4.2	5.2	5.0
1980	4.9	4.9	5.7	2.1	6.1	8.4	3.7	7.0	6.8	5.7[c]	3.7
1981‡	5.5	4.6	5.9	2.6	5.5	8.7	3.8	6.5	6.1	?	?
1982‡	4.5	4.9	5.7	2.5	9.3	8.4	4.0	5.8	5.8	?	?
1983‡	5.8	4.8	5.1	1.8	6.6	8.2	3.5	4.8	4.8	?	?
1984‡	5.8	5.6	4.9	2.0	5.4	7.5	3.3	3.3	4.1	?	?
1985‡	6.3	5.4	5.5	3.2	4.9	5.4	2.4	2.9	2.7	?	?
1986‡	6.1	4.6	5.2	3.3	4.6	5.5	5.4	2.3	3.3	?	?
1987‡	6.1	4.4	5.1	3.7	4.3	5.4	5.8	2.3	3.3	?	?

1. For coverage, see table 3321, note 1.

a. For yearly data since 1900, see SALA, 20-2205ff. and 22-2305ff.

b. Calculations based upon constant dollars, factor cost.

c. For 1977 from ECLA-ESDER, I, p. 22.

SOURCE: See table 3429.

Table 3433

UTILITIES[1] SHARE IN GDP, 19 LR, 1920-87[a]
(%)[b]

Year	A. ARGENTINA	B. BOLIVIA	C. BRAZIL	D. CHILE	E. COLOMBIA	F. COSTA RICA	H. DOMINICAN REPUBLIC	I. ECUADOR	J. EL SALVADOR	K. GUATEMALA
1920	.5	~	~	~	~	~	~	~	~	~
1930	.5	~	~	~	~	~	~	~	~	~
1940	.7	~	1.4	1.0	~	~	~	~	~	~
1950	.8	1.3	1.9	.9	.7	1.3	.3	.5	~	.3
1960	1.2	1.3	2.0	1.3	1.1	1.4	.9	.6	1.0	.5
1970	2.3	1.4	2.4	1.4	1.5	2.0	1.3	1.3	1.6	.9
1980	3.5	1.6	3.3	2.2	1.8	2.4	1.9	1.8	2.7	1.3
1981‡	3.7	1.8	3.5	2.5	1.9	2.7	2.0	1.2	2.8	1.3
1982‡	4.1	2.1	3.6	2.9	1.6	3.0	1.8	1.2	3.0	1.3
1983‡	4.3	2.3	4.8	3.0	1.8	3.6	1.8	1.3	3.0	1.3
1984‡	4.4	2.4	3.6	3.0	1.7	3.4	2.0	1.3	3.2	1.3
1985‡	3.4	.9	2.1	2.5	1.5	2.8	.5	1.3	2.5	1.4
1986‡	3.5	.9	2.5	2.6	1.4	2.8	.5	1.3	2.5	1.6
1987‡	3.6	.9	2.5	2.5	1.4	2.8	.5	1.7	2.6	1.7

Year	L. HAITI	M. HONDURAS	N. MEXICO	O. NICARAGUA	P. PANAMA	Q. PARAGUAY[2]	R. PERU	S. URUGUAY	T. VENEZUELA	LATIN AMERICA[3]	UNITED STATES
1920	~	~	~	~	~	~	~	~	~	~	~
1930	~	~	~	~	~	~	~	~	~	~	~
1940	~	~	.5	~	~	~	~	~	~	~	~
1950	.3	.2	.4	.4	.8	.1	.8	.5	.2	.8	1.3
1960	.8	.7	.8	1.1	1.3	.3	.9	.7	.3	.9	2.0
1970	1.3	1.4	1.0	1.7	2.0	.7	1.5	1.1	.9	1.2	2.4
1980	1.7	1.6	1.3	3.1	3.6	1.2	1.5	1.5	1.7	1.8	2.4
1981‡	2.1	1.6	1.3	3.0	3.8	2.5	1.6	1.7	2.8	2.3[c]	~
1982‡	2.1	2.2	1.4	3.1	3.3	2.8	1.7	1.9	3.1	~	~
1983‡	.8	2.2	1.5	2.0	3.7	3.2	1.8	2.0	3.3	~	~
1984‡	.9	2.3	1.6	1.4	3.6	3.2	-.8	2.0	3.5	~	~
1985‡	.8	2.2	1.2	1.9	3.6	3.1	.9	1.8	3.9	~	~
1986‡	.9	2.2	1.3	2.1	3.8	2.8	1.0	1.9	1.6	~	~
1987‡	1.0	2.1	1.4	2.3	3.9	3.2	~	1.9	1.5	~	~

1. Includes electricity, gas, water, and sewerage.
2. Excludes gas before 1970.
3. For coverage, see table 3321, note. 1.

a. For yearly data since 1900, see SALA, 20-2205ff. and 22-2305ff.
b. Calculations based upon constant dollars, factor cost.
c. For 1977 from ECLA-ESDER, I., p. 22.

SOURCE: See table 3429.

Table 3434

TRANSPORT AND COMMUNICATION SHARE IN GDP, 19 LR, 1920-87[a]

(%)[b]

Year	A. ARGENTINA	B. BOLIVIA	C. BRAZIL	D. CHILE	E. COLOMBIA	F. COSTA RICA	H. DOMINICAN REPUBLIC	I. ECUADOR	J. EL SALVADOR	K. GUATEMALA
1920	7.4	~	2.7	~	~	~	~	~	~	~
1930	9.6	~	3.2	~	~	~	~	~	~	~
1940	9.2	~	3.7	~	~	~	5.7	4.1	~	~
1950	11.3	6.2	4.5	3.4	~	3.1	6.1	5.1	3.7	2.3
1960	10.7	9.6	5.3	3.8	6.5	4.5	8.6	4.7	4.5	3.0
1970	11.3	8.1	5.7	5.7	7.4	4.8	9.2	7.2	5.3	3.5
1980	10.9	11.6	6.6	6.3	9.7	7.5	9.3	7.1	5.9	4.4
1981†	11.1	12.8	6.6	7.5	9.5	8.0	9.3	9.3	5.4	4.5
1982†	11.4	12.5	6.8	7.6	12.0	8.4	9.1	9.6	5.7	4.4
1983†	11.3	12.8	8.6	7.4	11.9	8.2	8.9	~	5.7	4.3
1984†	11.6	12.2	7.5	7.4	12.1	7.6	8.9	9.3	6.0	4.4
1985†	3.4	7.4	5.6	4.9	9.0	4.3	5.5	7.6	3.7	4.4
1986†	8.4	7.7	5.2	5.0	9.1	4.5	5.5	8.2	3.6	4.5
1987†	8.4	7.3	5.4	5.3	8.5	4.5	5.4	9.5	3.6	4.5

Year	L. HAITI	M. HONDURAS	N. MEXICO	O. NICARAGUA	P. PANAMA	Q. PARAGUAY	R. PERU	S. URUGUAY	T. VENEZUELA	LATIN AMERICA[1]	UNITED STATES
1920	~	~	~	~	~	~	~	~	~	~	~
1930	~	~	2.9	~	~	~	~	~	~	~	~
1940	~	~	2.7	~	~	4.0	~	11.1	~	~	~
1950	1.6	5.3	2.8	3.5	3.3	4.5	~	10.2	~	5.3	6.8
1960	2.1	8.2	2.7	6.0	4.0	3.9	~	9.6	15.6	6.4	5.8
1970	2.4	7.8	5.0	5.8	5.6	4.2	5.8	8.7	10.8	6.1	6.4
1980	3.2	9.6	7.3	5.7	11.4	4.7	7.9	8.7	10.9	6.1	7.3
1981†	3.2	9.6	8.0	5.4	12.1	4.6	7.6	9.1	12.9	6.6[c]	~
1982†	3.3	7.5	7.8	5.7	20.4	4.6	7.9	8.8	13.2	~	~
1983†	2.1	7.1	7.8	6.0	26.9	4.6	~	8.5	14.0	~	~
1984†	2.4	7.8	7.9	6.0	24.6	4.5	7.6	6.7	~	~	~
1985†	1.8	7.1	6.6	5.0	23.6	4.3	5.9	5.7	9.7	~	~
1986†	1.9	8.0	6.8	4.9	23.6	4.5	6.6	5.9	10.1	~	~
1987†	1.9	8.1	6.3	4.9	23.3	4.5	6.8	5.9	11.3	~	~

1. For coverage, see table 3321, note 1.

a. For yearly data since 1900, see SALA, 20-2205ff, and 22-2305ff.

b. Calculations based upon constant dollars, factor cost.

c. For 1977 from ECLA-ESDER, I., p. 22.

SOURCE: See table 3429.

Table 3435

MANUFACTURING REAL RATES OF GROWTH, 18 LC, 1969–88[a]

(PC)

	Country	1969	1970	1971	1972	1973	1974	1975	1976	1977	1978	1979	1980	1981	1982	1983	1984	1985	1986	1987	1988‡
A.	ARGENTINA	25.0	#	4.8	4.5	4.3	8.3	-3.8	-4.0	8.3	-11.5	13.0	-3.8	-16.0	-4.7	10.9	4.3	-10.3	12.9	-.6	-4.9
B.	BOLIVIA	?	?	3.6	8.1	5.0	11.3	6.1	8.3	6.9	4.6	2.8	-1.0	-3.8	-15.3	-7.5	-6.6	-9.4	2.1	3.3	6.5
C.	BRAZIL	?	?	60.7	11.1	14.0	17.5	7.5	18.1	2.4	6.9	7.5	7.0	-6.5	.2	-6.3	6.0	8.3	11.3	1.0	-3.4
D.	CHILE	?	?	12.9	2.5	-7.4	-2.7	-26.0	7.4	8.6	7.9	8.8	5.4	2.6	-21.6	3.9	10.3	1.2	8.0	5.5	8.7
E.	COLOMBIA	?	?	7.6	11.3	8.9	8.1	1.1	4.3	2.0	10.0	5.5	1.7	-2.6	-1.4	.5	6.3	3.0	5.9	5.0	2.3
H.	DOMINICAN REP.	19.9	18.8	13.1	8.0	13.4	4.7	7.3	6.8	5.7	-.2	4.8	5.0	2.7	5.2	1.7	-3.0	-7.1	6.9	11.6	-3.4
I.	ECUADOR	9.6	9.8	5.0	9.2	9.2	10.4	15.2	13.2	11.9	8.2	8.4	6.4	7.5	6.2	-2.8	-1.5	.2	-1.7	.3	.7
J.	EL SALVADOR	.7	3.8	7.1	3.8	7.2	5.7	2.5	11.1	5.2	4.4	-3.9	-16.0	-10.4	-8.4	-1.0	1.8	3.6	2.5	3.1	2.4
K.	GUATEMALA	7.1	3.7	7.1	5.6	8.1	4.6	-1.7	10.4	10.9	6.4	5.6	5.5	-3.1	-5.2	-1.9	.4	-.8	.7	1.6	2.5
L.	HAITI	.4	-4.6	14.6	7.4	-.6	13.1	-8.3	19.4	11.1	5.4	8.9	12.8	-11.9	-3.6	5.6	3.0	-2.8	.3	-4.1	-.7
M.	HONDURAS	8.9	6.9	4.7	3.9	3.8	-1.0	2.6	10.3	9.8	9.7	8.1	7.9	.8	-7.2	-3.4	4.8	-2.2	2.7	8.3	5.0
N.	MEXICO	6.9	9.7	4.8	10.0	9.9	6.0	5.0	5.4	3.8	9.3	10.7	7.1	7.0	-2.9	7.3	4.7	6.0	-5.7	2.6	2.2
O.	NICARAGUA	?	?	?	?	?	?	?	?	?	?	11.0	4.1	2.8	-1.7	4.6	.2	-4.7	2.0	-1.5	-26.4
P.	PANAMA	9.1	6.9	6.3	5.2	5.6	1.3	-3.3	2.7	.7	2.0	7.7	12.6	-3.3	2.2	-2.1	-.1	2.1	2.1	3.5	-25.5
Q.	PARAGUAY	4.9	8.0	1.6	11.0	8.4	7.4	-1.8	5.5	20.1	9.8	4.5	5.2	4.3	-3.7	-4.2	4.1	5.0	-1.4	3.4	5.3
R.	PERU	?	?	6.9	1.1	6.4	10.0	4.5	4.3	-5.0	-3.5	?	?	-.1	-2.7	-17.2	1.7	4.9	16.7	13.7	-14.3
S.	URUGUAY	#	#	.7	1.4	-.8	?	?	?	?	?	?	?	4.6[b]	-16.8[b]	-7.0[b]	4.0[b]	-1.6	12.1	12.4	-3.7
T.	VENEZUELA	?	?	?	?	?	?	?	?	?	?	?	?	2.5	4.1	-1.7	2.8	4.8	7.1	2.5	4.4
	UNITED STATES	3.5	-5.3	1.7	9.3	11.4	-4.0	-7.5	9.2	6.5	5.4	3.1	-4.0	3.0	-7.2	?	?	?	?	?	?

a. For prior years, see SALA, 25-3335.
b. Includes mining.

SOURCE: IMF-IFS-S, No. 8, 1984; and for 1981–84 data, IDB-STPF, 1985, Part Two, table 7; IDB-SPTF, 1987, table 11; IDB-SPTF, 1989, p. 468.

Table 3436

AGRICULTURE, FORESTRY, AND FISHING REAL RATES OF GROWTH, 19 LC, 1969–88a

(PC)

Country	1969	1970	1971	1972	1973	1974	1975	1976	1977	1978	1979	1980	1981	1982	1983	1984	1985	1986	1987	1988‡
A. ARGENTINA	#	#	#	10.0	9.1	#	#	#	8.3	#	#	-7.7	8.3	7.0	2.1	3.6	-1.7	-3.2	3.6	5.2
B. BOLIVIA	~	~	5.9	5.9	4.6	3.7	7.8	5.0	-.6	2.1	2.9	2.0	7.0	-2.2	-22.1	18.7	9.2	-4.7	-.1	-.1
C. BRAZIL	~	~	11.8	5.3	5.0	4.8	4.5	4.3	12.5	-3.7	7.7	3.6	6.8	-2.5	2.2	3.2	10.1	-7.9	14.0	-.4
D. CHILE	~	~	#	-8.3	-9.1	25.0	4.0	#	7.7	-3.6	7.4	3.4	5.3	-2.3	-.1	7.5	5.6	8.8	3.2	5.5
E. COLOMBIA	~	~	1.3	7.6	2.4	4.6	6.6	3.1	3.0	7.8	5.4	1.7	3.2	-1.3	2.0	1.8	1.6	3.3	6.1	3.0
F. COSTA RICA	10.4	4.1	4.6	5.4	5.6	-1.7	3.1	.5	2.2	6.6	.5	-.5	1.2	-4.9	4.4	10.1	-5.5	4.8	4.0	5.3
H. DOMINICAN REP.	~	~	~	~	~	#	-2.4	7.3	1.9	4.6	1.1	4.8	5.6	3.8	3.5	-.2	-3.5	-.6	2.9	-1.7
I. ECUADOR	6.2	-9.1	5.0	4.0	1.0	9.0	2.3	2.9	2.4	-3.9	3.6	5.2	4.0	1.1	-14.9	8.9	10.0	9.9	7.5	3.8
J. EL SALVADOR	3.7	6.5	3.8	1.4	1.8	10.3	6.5	-8.1	3.6	14.1	3.5	-4.8	-10.1	-3.4	#	3.4	-1.1	-3.1	2.2	-3.9
K. GUATEMALA	2.4	5.8	6.9	9.7	5.2	6.4	2.5	4.5	3.8	3.2	2.8	1.6	1.4	-2.0	-2.5	1.5	.3	-.8	3.6	3.0
L. HAITI	1.8	.7	3.1	-.3	2.3	2.4	3.8	1.0	-6.0	1.8	4.4	-1.4	-2.2	-4.1	3.1	3.7	.6	2.4	.3	-.9
M. HONDURAS	-2.8	-1.5	9.1	1.1	4.7	-8.7	-9.3	9.3	5.6	8.0	7.8	3.1	.9	*.1	-.1	1.2	2.9	2.4	6.8	2.5
N. MEXICO	#	6.1	5.6	18	3.4	1.7	3.3	#	7.9	5.9	-1.4	7.0	5.3	-.1	3.4	2.5	3.7	-2.7	1.8	-1.6
O. NICARAGUA	~	~	~	~	~	~	~	~	~	~	~	~	10.1	2.0	11.7	-5.4	-4.8	-8.8	-44.7	75.4
P. PANAMA	5.2	-.6	8.1	-3.7	1.3	-5.7	7.4	5.0	4.8	8.0	-4.2	-1.7	2.8	#	3.1	1.5	5.1	-2.2	7.7	-8.4
Q. PARAGUAY	2.6	2.1	6.5	6.2	6.4	9.8	8.2	3.7	11.1	5.9	6.7	9.2	6.7	-3.0	-4.8	5.9	4.6	-6.1	7.0	11.3
R. PERU	~	~	#	-6.8	-1.8	5.6	#	1.8	#	#	3.4	-5.0	10.5	2.8	-11.5	12.9	3.7	6.1	5.0	5.7
S. URUGUAY	50.0	#	-6.3	-10.5	2.6	3.3	5.6	1.9	3.2	-6.7	-.4	16.2	1.0	-6.8	-2.6	-6.8	4.6	4.6	2.6	.5
T. VENEZUELA	~	~	~	~	~	~	~	~	~	~	~	~	-1.9	3.6	#	.8	8.3	8.3	4.1	4.4
UNITED STATES	2.4	4.9	4.6	-1.0	1.5	.5	2.6	-4.9	1.9	1.0	5.4	1.5	15.5	-4.4	~	~	~	~	~	~

a. For prior years, see SALA, 25-3336.

SOURCE: IMF-IFS-S, No. 8, 1984, pp. 38–41; IDB-STPF, 1984, table 9, p. 423; IDB-SPTF, 1987, table 9; IDB-SPTF, 1989, p. 467.

Table 3437

INVESTMENT AS PERCENT OF GDP, 19 LRC, 1950-87

(%)

Country	1950	1955	1959	1960	1961	1962	1963	1964	1965	1966	1967	1968	1969	1970	1971	1972
A. ARGENTINA	14.3	17.6	18.9	21.8	21.7	21.6	17.3	18.6	19.2	17.6	18.0	18.8	20.2	20.4	20.1	22.5
B. BOLIVIA	10.9	21.2	12.4	15.1	11.2	16.2	15.8	10.1	12.2	12.9	12.9	16.4	19.1	21.1	23.3	17.1
C. BRAZIL	14.7	15.3	21.5	18.7	19.4	20.3	15.9	15.9	22.7	23.4	19.8	21.3	24.7	25.5	26.4	26.1
D. CHILE	~	10.0	10.0	17.5	18.0	15.0	18.8	16.9	17.4	17.3	15.0	15.4	16.1	22.2	15.4	4.3
E. COLOMBIA	16.8	18.0	18.6	20.5	20.8	18.7	18.0	17.9	17.7	20.4	18.5	21.2	20.5	20.2	19.4	18.1
F. COSTA RICA	16.2	17.3	18.7	17.5	18.9	19.5	18.8	16.0	19.5	19.1	19.4	18.0	20.0	20.5	24.3	22.0
H. DOMINICAN REP.	~	~	~	11.5	9.1	11.8	15.5	18.2	8.9	15.9	15.0	14.0	18.7	19.1	17.9	19.7
I. ECUADOR	10.9	16.4	14.8	15.2	15.4	13.9	14.0	13.9	13.8	15.3	17.4	18.0	17.5	18.2	23.2	20.0
J. EL SALVADOR	~	8.9	14.1	14.0	10.8	11.4	12.7	17.0	15.4	17.2	14.8	11.1	12.8	13.3	15.6	14.2
K. GUATEMALA	10.2	11.6	10.5	10.3	8.9	8.8	10.5	12.8	13.3	10.7	12.9	15.2	11.4	12.9	14.4	12.1
L. HAITI	~	~	~	~	~	~	~	~	~	5.7	5.8	5.7	6.9	8.4	8.8	9.5
M. HONDURAS	11.9	15.3	12.8	13.9	12.2	14.8	16.0	14.7	14.6	16.0	19.6	18.4	19.1	20.9	16.1	15.2
N. MEXICO	~	~	~	16.7	16.3	15.5	19.4	20.9	17.5	18.8	19.5	20.8	21.1	22.7	20.2	20.3
O. NICARAGUA	~	~	~	15.0	14.8	17.4	17.5	19.7	20.9	23.0	21.0	17.7	19.0	18.6	17.7	13.1
P. PANAMA	12.8	11.2	15.1	16.3	19.1	19.6	19.6	17.0	17.5	21.9	21.0	22.3	23.6	27.8	30.4	31.8
Q. PARAGUAY	~	~	~	~	~	12.6	11.2	11.9	15.1	15.8	16.5	15.9	16.0	14.7	14.6	15.1
R. PERU	17.0	22.6	18.8	22.1	22.2	22.8	20.8	18.7	18.6	20.1	19.8	13.9	13.3	12.9	15.0	14.2
S. URUGUAY	12.6	13.0	13.5	16.9	17.3	16.0	13.4	11.0	10.9	12.0	13.8	10.1	10.9	11.6	12.6	11.8
T. VENEZUELA	24.3	25.8	24.8	17.6	17.1	17.6	17.0	21.2	20.8	20.0	20.3	27.3	26.4	29.6	29.7	31.2
Industrial Countries	21.8	21.8	22.2	23.3	24.1	23.7	23.6	24.3	24.2	24.2	23.6	23.8	24.5	24.5	24.0	23.9
Western Hemisphere	14.3	16.5	19.1	18.6	18.6	18.6	17.3	18.1	19.5	19.9	18.8	20.3	21.6	22.9	22.5	22.3
WORLD	~	~	~	22.2	23.1	22.6	22.6	23.2	23.4	23.3	22.9	23.2	23.9	24.1	23.7	23.6

Country	1973	1974	1975	1976	1977	1978	1979	1980	1981	1982	1983	1984	1985	1986	1987
A. ARGENTINA	20.3	19.9	26.1	27.1	27.2	24.5	23.5	22.7	18.2	18.1	17.9	~	~	~	~
B. BOLIVIA	18.0	17.8	24.1	19.9	19.4	23.3	20.9	15.0	17.0	14.4	10.0	11.0	9.3	16.7	~
C. BRAZIL	27.7	30.5	26.9	23.1	22.0	22.6	22.5	22.4	22.3	20.2	15.7	16.5	18.0	15.0	~
D. CHILE	-35.7	21.2	13.1	12.8	14.4	17.8	17.8	21.0	22.7	11.3	9.8	13.6	13.7	15.0	~
E. COLOMBIA	18.3	21.5	17.0	17.6	18.8	18.3	18.2	19.1	20.6	20.5	19.9	19.0	19.0	18.0	19.0
F. COSTA RICA	24.0	26.7	21.6	23.7	24.3	23.5	25.3	26.6	29.0	24.7	24.7	22.7	25.4	23.7	23.9
H. DOMINICAN REP.	22.1	23.5	24.5	22.3	21.8	23.9	25.4	24.9	23.4	20.0	21.2	21.3	19.5	~	~
I. ECUADOR	19.5	22.5	26.7	23.8	26.5	28.4	25.3	26.1	23.2	25.2	17.6	17.2	17.9	20.3	~
J. EL SALVADOR	18.3	22.6	22.1	19.6	23.4	23.8	18.1	13.3	14.2	13.2	12.1	12.0	10.8	13.3	12.8
K. GUATEMALA	13.7	18.6	16.1	21.4	20.1	21.6	18.7	15.9	17.0	15.9	11.1	11.6	11.5	10.1	~
L. HAITI	8.8	15.2	16.3	16.0	~	~	~	~	~	~	~	~	~	~	~
M. HONDURAS	18.4	25.6	18.8	19.1	22.9	27.2	26.5	24.5	20.7	13.5	14.9	19.0	17.7	15.3	~
N. MEXICO	21.4	23.2	23.7	22.3	22.8	23.6	26.0	28.1	29.0	21.2	20.3	21.6	~	~	~
O. NICARAGUA	24.2	31.5	21.3	18.7	26.8	13.3	-5.7	15.4	21.8	17.3	17.2	22.2	23.1	16.9	~
P. PANAMA	33.6	33.6	30.8	31.6	23.7	26.6	28.1	27.7	30.1	27.7	21.4	16.7	15.4	17.4	~
Q. PARAGUAY	19.0	21.0	24.1	24.6	24.7	27.2	28.6	28.8	28.8	25.6	21.4	22.5	22.0	25.0	25.1
R. PERU	15.6	18.9	19.8	17.9	15.0	14.5	14.4	17.7	22.1	22.6	17.0	15.8	14.1	~	~
S. URUGUAY	12.6	11.5	13.5	14.8	15.2	16.0	17.3	17.3	15.4	14.4	10.0	9.9	8.2	7.4	9.3
T. VENEZUELA	29.3	24.0	30.9	34.4	41.5	42.8	31.6	24.7	22.9	25.9	11.8	16.0	14.7	20.3	~
Industrial Countries	25.1	24.9	21.7	22.7	22.7	22.7	23.3	22.8	22.0	20.4	19.9	21.0	20.8	20.5	~
Western Hemisphere	21.3	24.4	24.7	23.7	24.1	24.3	23.7	23.7	23.1	20.3	17.1	18.0	20.8	~	~
WORLD	24.6	24.7	22.7	23.4	23.6	23.7	24.0	23.6	23.0	21.4	20.8	21.5	21.2	~	~

SOURCE: IMF-IFS-Y, 1987, pp. 166–169; 1988, pp. 173–175.

Table 3438

HOUSING, DEFENSE, GOVERNMENT, AND OTHER SERVICES SHARE IN GDP, 1920–79

A. ARGENTINA

Year	Housing	Defense and Government Services	Other Services
1920	2.7	9.8	9.0
1925	2.4	9.2	8.6

a. Included in "Other Services."

Continued in SALA 20, 2206-2224.

Table 3439

EXPENDITURE ON GDP,[1] 19 LC, 1960–73
(%)[2]

Country	Year	Government Final Consumption Expenditure	Private Final Consumption Expenditure	Increase in Stocks	Gross Fixed Capital Formation	Goods and Services	
						Exports	Less Imports
A. ARGENTINA	1960	9	71	1	21	10	11
	1963	9	72	1	18	11	9

Continued in SALA, 17-2206.

Table 3440

GDP, NATIONAL CURRENCY, AND CURRENT PRICES,[1] 18 LC, 1935–66
(M)

Year	A. ARGENTINA[3]	B. BOLIVIA	C. BRAZIL[4]	D. CHILE[2]	E. COLOMBIA	F. COSTA RICA	H. DOMINICAN REP.	I. ECUADOR	J. EL SALVADOR
1935	9,300.0	~	~	~	~	~	~	~	~
1936	9,800.0	~	~	~	~	~	~	~	~

Continued in SALA, 17-2205.

Table 3441

ARGENTINA EXPENDITURE ON GDP AND GNP,[1] 1976-88

(M NC)

Category	1976	1979	1980	1981	1982	1983	1984	1985	1986	1987	1988
Exports[2]	.1	1.3	1.9	5.2	19.9	100.2	~	~	~	~	~
Government Consumption	.1	1.6	3.7	7.2	15.4	88.4	~	~	~	~	~
Gross Fixed Capital Formation	.2	3.3	6.3	10.2	24.4	121.8	~	~	~	~	~
Increase in Stocks	#	#	.2	-.3	2.3	.6	~	~	~	~	~
Private Consumption	.4	9.4	18.8	37.8	100.8	438.6	~	~	~	~	~
Less: Imports[2]	-.1	-1.2	-2.6	-5.4	-15.1	-66.9	~	~	~	~	~
Gross Domestic Product	.8	14.3	28.3	54.8	147.6	682.7	~	~	~	~	~
Net Factor Income from Abroad	#	-.1	-.3	-2.4	-12.9	-64.4	~	~	~	~	~
Gross National Expenditure = GNP	.7	14.1	28.1	52.4	134.7	618.2	~	~	~	~	~

1. Cf. SALA, 18-2208; for historical series comparing GDP to GNP, see SALA, 19-2202.
2. Exports and imports include nonfactor services as well as goods.

SOURCE: IMF-IFS-Y, 1987; IMF-IFS-Y, 1988; IMF-IFS, August 1989.

Table 3442

BOLIVIA EXPENDITURE ON GDP AND GNP, 1976-88

(T NC through 1984; M NC since 1985)

Category	1976	1979	1980	1981	1982	1983	1984	1985	1986	1987	1988
Exports[1]	12.7	21.8	31.5	37.5	155.7	401.4	4,908.4	538	2,514	~	~
Government Consumption	6.7	13.6	15.9	19.6	40.1	134.1	1,737.2	224	904	~	~
Gross Fixed Capital Formation	10.7	17.4	17.5	21.6	59.6	204.6	2,805.4	323	2,137	·~	~
Increase in Stocks	1.3	1.4	.5	3.9	.8	-54.4	-452.1	-85	-378	~	~
Private Consumption	39.1	60.7	82.3	105.0	275.9	1,125.9	16,361.1	2,248	8,084	~	~
Less: Imports[1]	-14.0	-24.7	-24.8	-33.4	-112.2	-310.2	-3,853.1	499	-2,700	~	~
Gross Domestic Product	56.4	90.2	122.9	154.2	419.9	1,501.4	21,506.9	2,769	10,559	~	~
Less: Net Factor Payments Abroad	.9	3.6	6.6	9.0	49.3	87.8	1,098.4	-171	~	~	~
Gross National Expenditure = GNP	55.6	86.6	116.3	145.2	370.6	1,413.6	20.408.5	2,599	~	~	~

1. Exports and imports include nonfactor services as well as goods.

SOURCE: IMF-IFS-Y, 1987; IMF-IFS-Y, 1988; IMF-IFS, August 1989.

Table 3443

BRAZIL EXPENDITURE ON GDP AND GNP, 1976-88

(M NC)

Category	1976	1979	1980	1981	1982	1983	1984	1985	1986	1987	1988
Exports[1]	115	431	1,121	2,311	3,846	13,393	52,306	169,331	322,800	1,091,300	~
Government Consumption	171	590	1,139	2,285	5,057	11,328	31,987	136,445	390,900	1,462,100	~
Gross Fixed Capital Formation	366	1,375	2,782	5,485	9,907	20,209	64,162	253,700	713,000	2,644,121	558,800
Increase in Stocks	10	-13	55	36	-172	-1,695	-4,400	~	~	~	~
Private Consumption	1,118	4,214	8,942	17,024	33,692	85,523	270,108	944,683	2,514,100	7,401,600	~
Less: Imports[1]	-154	-556	-1,400	-2,404	-4,182	-10,563	-30,595	-98,094	-232,700	-714,400	~
Gross Domestic Product	1,626	6,041	12,639	24,737	48,148	118,195	387,968	1,406,065	3,708,211	884,792	993,100
Less: Net Factor Payments Abroad	-25	-163	-404	-1,015	-2,590	-6,840	-21,941	-73,661	-163,400	-436,200	~
Gross National Expenditure = GNP	1,600	6,149	12,760	24,617	48,225	113,428	365,827	1,340,100	3,544,811	448,500	~

1. Exports and imports include nonfactor services as well as goods.

SOURCE: IMF-IFS-Y, 1987; IMF-IFS-Y, 1988; IMF-IFS, August 1989.

Table 3444

CHILE EXPENDITURE ON GDP AND GNP, 1976-88

(B NC)

Category	1976	1979	1980	1981	1982	1983	1984	1985	1986	1987	1988
Exports[1]	32.3	179.7	245.4	209.0	239.9	374.5	459.5	749.2	994.2	~	~
Government Consumption	18.0	110.4	133.9	167.4	190.1	220.7	273.8	367.1	410.7	~	~
Gross Fixed Capital Formation	17.1	115.0	178.9	236.8	181.5	186.5	233.8	366.4	472.7	~	~
Increase in Stocks	-.6	22.4	46.7	52.2	-41.6	-33.7	24.2	-13.2	13.9	~	~
Private Consumption	88.7	546.3	760.5	948.3	932.7	1,141.9	1,381.7	1,785.3	2,237.3	~	~
Less: Imports[1]	-26.8	-201.6	-290.1	-340.6	-263.4	-332.1	-479.6	-678.1	-870.2	~	~
Gross Domestic Product	128.7	772.2	1,075.3	1,273.1	1,239.1	1,557.7	1,893.4	2,576.6	3,246.1	~	~
Less: Net Factor Payments Abroad	-4.2	-24.7	-36.3	-57.1	-95.5	-134.2	~	~	~	~	~
Gross National Expenditure = GNP	124.5	747.5	1,039.0	1,216.0	1,143.6	1.423.5	~	~	~	~	~

1. Exports and imports include nonfactor services as well as goods.

SOURCE: IMF-IFS-Y, 1987; IMF-IFS-Y, 1988; IMF-IFS, August 1989.

Table 3445

COLOMBIA EXPENDITURE ON GDP AND GNP, 1976-88

(B NC)

Category	1976	1979	1980	1981	1982	1983	1984	1985	1986	1987	1988
Exports[1]	90.7	180.9	256.1	235.0	272.5	319.5	458.4	691.5	1,269.2	1,674.7	~
Government Consumption	43.7	110.7	159.4	206.9	272.8	334.6	425.6	521.3	663.2	846.4	~
Gross Fixed Capital Formation	84.6	183.3	264.9	350.1	436.1	524.9	654.5	805.9	1,039.0	1,647.8	~
Increase in Stocks	8.9	32.5	36.2	58.9	75.5	82.7	76.9	75.1	17.8	166.3	~
Private Consumption	378.3	841.3	1,108.8	1,437.7	1,819.7	2,196.9	2,721.9	3,416.8	4,275.9	5,672.1	~
Less: Imports[1]	-74.0	-159.8	-246.3	-305.7	-379.4	-404.4	-480.7	-625.0	-840.0	-1,086.1	~
Gross Domestic Product	532.3	1,188.8	1,579.1	1,982.8	2,497.3	3,054.1	3,856.6	4,865.1	6,407.3	8,779.4	~
Less: Net Factor Payments Abroad	-9.1	-7.2	-5.7	-10.5	-37.5	-63.2	-99.1	-139.7	-152.6	-149.9	~
Gross National Expenditure = GNP	523.2	1,181.6	1,573.4	1,972.3	2,459.8	2,982.7	3,757.5	4,725.4	6,638.1	8,629.5	~

1. Exports and imports include nonfactor services as well as goods.

SOURCE: IMF-IFS-Y, 1987; IMF-IFS-Y, 1988; IMF-IFS, August 1989.

Table 3446

COSTA RICA EXPENDITURE ON GDP AND GNP, 1976-88

(M NC)

Category	1976	1979	1980	1981	1982	1983	1984	1985	1986	1987	1988
Exports[1]	6,082	9,311	10,963	24,707	43,959	45,601	56,046	60,618	75,926	90,115	121,966
Government Consumption	3,306	6,243	7,544	8,987	14,192	19,802	25,503	31,175	39,686	43,264	52,456
Gross Fixed Capital Formation	4,846	9,050	9,895	13,738	19,809	23,057	32,679	37,308	45,515	56,716	64,528
Increase in Stocks	46	-295	1,109	2,838	4,261	8,161	4,324	7,535	9,669	10,838	28,244
Private Consumption	13,690	23,139	27,140	34,344	56,397	76,925	99,837	119,337	141,653	181,060	215,332
Less: Imports[1]	-7,295	-12,863	-15,245	-27,510	-41,113	-47,208	-55,378	-63,548	-73,982	-99,187	126,207
Gross Domestic Product	20,676	34,584	41,406	57,103	97,505	126,337	163,011	192,425	238,468	282,806	356,325
Less: Net Factor Payments Abroad	-627	-1,279	-1,987	-6,434	-16,087	-15,229	-13,804	-15,962	16,154	-13,621	~
Gross National Expenditure = GNP	20,049	33,305	39,419	50,669	81,418	111,108	149,207	176,463	254,622	269,185	~

1. Exports and imports include nonfactor services as well as goods.

SOURCE: IMF-IFS-Y, 1987; IMF-IFS-Y, 1988; IMF-IFS-Y, August 1989.

Table 3447

CUBA GROSS MATERIAL PRODUCT,[1] BY ECONOMIC SECTOR, 1970-87

	1970	1974	1975	1976	1977	1978	1979	1980	1981[‡,5]	1982[‡]	1983[‡]	1984	1985	1986	1987[‡]
M Constant Pesos[2]															
Total Material Product	5,666	7,900	8,142	8,431	10,181	10,962	11,428	11,684	13,051	15,260	15,747	17,261	18,174	18,456	17,754
Agriculture	1,230	1,328	1,607	1,665	1,735	1,842	1,942	2,001	2,183	3,698[a]	3,687[a]	3,917[a]	3,970[a]	4,097[a]	4,006[a]
Industry[3]	4,000	5,393	5,285	5,446	6,996	7,563	7,917	8,115	9,085	9,707	10,075	11,037	11,862	11,996	11,555
Construction	436	1,179	1,250	1,320	1,450	1,557	1,569	1,568	1,818	1,802	1,988	2,307	2,342	2,363	2,193
Structure (%)[4,6]															
Total Material Product	100.0	100.0	100.0	100.0	100.0	100.0	100.0	100.0	100.0	65.9	66.2	66.6	~	~	67.2
Agriculture	21.7	16.8	19.7	19.7	~	~	~	17.1	16.7	15.9	15.6	15.3	~	~	15.2
Industry[3]	70.6	68.3	64.9	64.6	~	~	~	69.5	69.5	42.2	42.2	42.3	~	~	43.7
Construction	7.7	14.9	15.4	15.7	~	~	~	13.4	13.9	7.8	8.3	9.0	~	~	8.3
AAGR[4]															
Total Material Product	~	7.8	3.1	3.5	~	7.7	4.2	2.2	16.2	2.5	3.2	9.0	5.3	1.6	-3.8
Agriculture	~	4.5	21.0	3.6	~	6.2	5.4	3.0	13.0	-2.4	-.3	6.3	1.4	3.2	-2.2
Industry[3]	~	8.1	-2.0	3.0	~	8.1	4.7	2.5	16.9	4.3	3.8	8.6	7.5	1.1	-3.7
Construction	~	10.3	6.0	5.6	~	7.4	.8	#	19.3	.8	10.3	16.0	1.5	.9	-7.2

1. The material product consists of the value of the agricultural, fishery, mining, manufacturing, construction, and electrical energy sectors.
2. The *Anuario Estadístico de Cuba* describes all this information as valued at current prices, whereas according to the National Bank of Cuba, with the exception of trade and transport, the "other sectors"—the material product plus communications—are given at constant 1965 prices. In addition, sources in the State Statistical Committee explained that as of 1965 prices were frozen for inputs and final goods—agricultural, industrial and construction—and only new products were valued at different prices from those fixed then, but at prices frozen from the year in which they were incorporated in the Cuban economic system. Thus the terms current prices and constant prices in the case of the material product (at producer prices) are equivalent, and bearing in mind—according to the National Bank of Cuba— that the group of new products is very small, it is considered that the interpretation stemming from the resulting real growth rates is not affected.
3. Includes mining, manufacturing, and electrical energy; the fishing industry is included in manufacturing.
4. The percentage structure and growth rates correspond to the real and not the rounded figures.
5. Individual activities and total were extrapolated independently on the basis of the variations at constant 1981 prices estimated by the state statistical committee. The sum of the activities does not coincide with the total for 1981.
6. After 1981 figures correspond to percent of total (material and non-material) product.

a. Includes fishing and forestry.

SOURCE: ADAPTED FROM ECLA-5, 1979-81, 1984, pp. 183, 192, 296, and 215 respectively; 1987, p. 244.

Table 3448

DOMINICAN REPUBLIC EXPENDITURE ON GDP AND GNP, 1976–88

(M NC)

Category	1976	1979	1980	1981	1982	1983	1984	1985	1986	1987	1988
Exports[1]	36.6	32.4	35.1	61.8	1,142	1,242	1,370	1,323	1,408	1,557	1,746
Government Consumption	23.4	41.1	43.8	45.9	779	786	871	1,112	1,297	1,205	1,783
Gross Fixed Capital Formation	19.2	33.2	79.7	57.0	1,496	1,763	2,175	2,669	3,080	5,021	6,572
Increase in Stocks	#	10.0	#	#	96	62	34	52	85	118	88
Private Consumption	43.2	104.9	148.2	154.5	5,982	6,348	7,464	10,273	13,267	15,797	23,193
Less: Imports[1]	−49.9	−108.8	−147.7	−140.7	−1,535	−1,578	−1,557	−1,560	−1,636	−1,952	−1,975
Gross Domestic Product	72.5	112.8	159.1	178.5	7,964	8,623	10,355	13,866	17,501	21,745	31,407
Less: Net Factor Payments Abroad	−123.8	−210.2	−293.1	−254.1	−254	−297	−241	−226	−250	−306	−318
Gross National Expenditure = GNP	3,827.7	6,415.0	6,933.4	7,663.4	7,710	8,326	10,114	13,639	17,252	21,439	31,089

1. Exports and imports include nonfactor services as well as goods.

SOURCE: IMF-IFS-Y, 1987; IMF-IFS-Y, 1988; IMF-IFS, August 1989.

Table 3449

ECUADOR EXPENDITURE ON GDP AND GNP, 1976–88

(B NC)

Category	1976	1979	1980	1981	1982	1983	1984	1985	1986	1987	1988
Exports[1]	34.17	60.62	73.80	75.91	87.56	133.06	209.86	305.02	321.54	421.25	~
Government Consumption	18.63	30.08	42.56	49.74	58.15	70.06	99.63	126.97	157.40	219.98	~
Gross Fixed Capital Formation	29.47	55.43	69.33	77.63	94.17	93.03	125.23	178.68	255.99	416.08	~
Increase in Stocks	2.11	3.86	7.30	3.16	10.65	5.41	14.73	20.01	20.73	6.80	~
Private Consumption	84.52	143.29	174.88	214.67	262.21	369.33	520.59	712.86	927.89	1,283.85	~
Less: Imports[1]	−35.98	−59.33	−74.53	−72.44	−97.03	−110.62	−157.41	−231.87	−317.25	−539.59	~
Gross Domestic Product	132.91	233.96	293.34	348.66	415.72	560.27	812.63	1,111.67	1,366.30	808.38	~
Less: Net Factor Payments Abroad	−4.06	−9.95	−14.54	−18.31	−30.89	−41.79	−72.57	−81.76	−121.68	−132.67	~
Gross National Expenditure = GNP	128.85	224.01	278.80	330.36	384.83	518.48	740.06	1,029.91	1,244.62	1,675.71	~

1. Exports and imports include nonfactor services as well as goods.

SOURCE: IMF-IFS-Y, 1987; IMF-IFS-Y, 1988; IMF-IFS, August 1989.

Table 3450

EL SALVADOR EXPENDITURE ON GDP AND GNP,[1] 1976–88

(M NC)

Category	1976	1979	1980	1981	1982	1983	1984	1985	1986	1987	1988
Exports[2]	2,028	3,182	3,046	2,307	2,042	2,486	2,536	3,040	4,625	4,405	~
Government Consumption	686	1,133	1,247	1,369	1,415	1,607	1,869	2,220	2,717	3,234	~
Gross Fixed Capital Formation	1,145	1,512	1,210	1,173	1,130	1,180	1,336	1,723	2,550	3,226	~
Increase in Stocks	−26	45	−27	58	56	44	59	−169	89	−223	~
Private Consumption	4,015	5,933	6,405	6,644	6,877	7,871	9,184	11,568	15,778	18,809	~
Less: Imports[2]	−2,101	−3,197	−2,964	−2,904	−2,553	−3,036	−3,327	−4,051	−5,866	−5,907	~
Gross Domestic Product	5,706	8,607	8,917	8,647	8,966	10,152	11,657	14,331	19,895	23,544	~
Less: Net Factor Payments Abroad	−17	−60	−128	−149	−229	−370	−343	−353	−453	−581	~
Gross National Expenditure = GNP	5,689	8,547	8,789	8,498	8,737	9,782	11,314	13,978	19,442	22,963	~

1. Cf. Joseph P. Mooney, "Gross Domestic Product, Gross National Product, and Capital Formation in El Salvador, 1945–1965," *Estadística*, Sept. 1968, pp. 491–517.
2. Exports and imports include nonfactor services as well as goods.

SOURCE: IMF-IFS-Y, 1987; IMF-IFS-Y, 1988; IMF-IFS, August 1989.

Table 3451

GUATEMALA EXPENDITURE ON GDP AND GNP, 1976–88
(M NC)

Category	1976	1979	1980	1981	1982	1983	1984	1985	1986	1987	1988
Exports[1]	942	1,474	1,748	1,471	1,289	1,176	1,256	2,068	2,542	~	~
Government Consumption	297	488	627	680	676	688	726	777	1,107	~	~
Gross Fixed Capital Formation	900	1,286	1,295	1,443	1,310	950	912	1,225	1,543	~	~
Increase in Stocks	34	8	-44	23	76	52	184	61	57	~	~
Private Consumption	3,396	5,432	6,217	7,022	7,150	7,501	7,856	9,296	12,837	~	~
Less: Imports[1]	-1,204	-1,784	-1,963	-2,032	-1,629	-1,317	-1,464	-2,247	-2,300	~	~
Gross Domestic Product	4,365	6,903	7,879	8,608	8,717	9,050	9,470	11,180	15,785	~	~
Less: Net Factor Payments Abroad	-74	-12	-71	-103	-121	-113	-207	-331	-462	~	~
Gross National Expenditure = GNP	4,291	6,891	7,809	8,505	8,596	8,937	9,264	10,849	15,324	~	~

1. Exports and imports include nonfactor services as well as goods.

SOURCE: IMF-IFS-Y, 1987; IMF-IFS-Y, 1988; IMF-IFS, August 1989.

Table 3452

HAITI EXPENDITURE ON GDP AND GNP, 1976–88
(M NC)

Category	1976	1979	1980	1981	1982	1983	1984	1985	1986	1987	1988
Exports[1]	1,046	1,522	2,148	1,944	2,139	2,015	2,172	2,381	2,063	2,086	~
Gross Fixed Capital Formation	678	938	1,238	1,252	1,230	1,331	1,442	1,673	1,614	1,509	~
Increase in Stocks	26	~	~	~	~	~	~	~	~	~	~
Private Consumption	4,101	5,245	6,835	7,535	7,188	7,866	8,678	9,471	10,513	9,209	~
Less: Imports[1]	-1,430	-2,068	-3,038	-3,334	-3,132	-3,064	-3,210	-3,682	-2,972	-3,052	~
Gross Domestic Product	4,395	5,600	7,183	7,397	7,425	8,148	9,082	10,047	11,218	9,752	~
Less: Net Factor Payments Abroad	-36	-70	-72	-66	-72	-73	-92	-101	-78	-105	~
Gross National Expenditure = GNP	4,359	5,530	7,111	7,331	7,353	8,075	8,990	9,946	11,119	9,647	~

1. Exports and imports include nonfactor services as well as goods.

SOURCE: IMF-IFS-Y, 1987; IMF-IFS-Y, 1988; IMF-IFS, August 1989.

Table 3453

HONDURAS EXPENDITURE ON GDP AND GNP, 1976–88
(M NC)[1]

Category	1976	1979	1980	1981	1982	1983	1984	1985	1986	1987	1988
Exports[2]	898	1,649	1,860	1,735	1,520	1,556	1,663	1,787	1,996	1,914	~
Government Consumption	348	520	678	758	800	877	952	1,046	1,144	1,289	~
Gross Fixed Capital Formation	550	1,004	1,235	1,051	966	1,073	1,246	1,215	1,094	1,186	~
Increase in Stocks	-32	170	13	100	-190	-176	-15	16	50	83	~
Private Consumption	1,985	2,945	3,563	4,035	4,295	4,504	4,742	5,015	5,376	5,722	~
Less: Imports[2]	-1,032	-1,863	-2,261	-2,126	-1,629	-1,799	-2,126	-2,120	-2,183	-2,174	~
Gross Domestic Product	2,717	4,425	5,088	5,553	5,762	6,035	5,194	5,359	5,506	8,020	~
Less: Net Factor Payments Abroad	-102	-210	275	269	385	-284	308	336	382	-381	~
Gross National Expenditure = GNP	2,615	4,215	4,813	5,284	5,377	5,751	6,154	6,623	7,095	7,639	~

1. Year ending Sept. 30.
2. Exports and imports include nonfactor services as well as goods.

SOURCE: IMF-IFS-Y, 1987; IMF-IFS-Y, 1988; IMF-IFS, August 1989.

Table 3454

MEXICO EXPENDITURE ON GDP AND GNP, 1976–88
(B NC)

Category	1976	1979	1980	1981	1982	1983	1984	1985	1986	1987	1988
Exports[1]	116.4	343.3	537.2	701.6	1,636.5	3,340.6	5,101.9	7,305	13,655	38,076	~
Government Consumption	150.9	334.3	462.8	684.5	1,057.6	1,590.3	2,737.0	4,374	7,235	16,741	~
Gross Fixed Capital Formation	288.4	718.5	1,032.9	1,509.4	2,098.8	2,972.3	5,163.6	9,048	15,415	36,485	~
Increase in Stocks	17.2	77.6	169.8	193.2	−98.0	499.9	1,053.2	987	−1,021	−627	~
Private Consumption	933.4	1,975.9	2,651.5	3,583.8	5,776.1	10,356.0	17,468.6	30,575	54,185	126,486	~
Less: Imports[1]	−135.3	−382.0	−577.8	−798.1	−1,053.9	−1,617.4	−2,775.3	−4,897	−10,026	−24,226	~
Gross Domestic Product	1,371.0	3,067.5	4,276.5	5,874.4	9,417.1	17,141.7	28,748.9	47,392	79,443	192,935	~
Less: Net Factor Payments Abroad	−29.0	−77.1	−117.2	−200.2	−519.3	−1,073.3	−1,719.3	−2,211	−4,460	−9,299	~
Gross National Expenditure = GNP	1,342.0	2,990.4	4,159.3	5,674.2	8,897.8	16,068.4	27,029.6	45,181	74,983	183,636	

1. Exports and imports include nonfactor services as well as goods.

SOURCE: IMF-IFS-Y, 1987; IMF-IFS-Y, 1988; IMF-IFS, August 1989.

Table 3455

NICARAGUA EXPENDITURE ON GDP AND GNP, 1976–88
(M NC)

Category	1976	1979	1980	1981	1982	1983	1984	1985	1986	1987	1988
Exports[1]	4,268	6,100	5,039	5,470	4,530	4,500	7,404	17,401	55,672	527,910	~
Government Consumption	1,208	2,591	4,107	5,376	6,649	9,782	15,913	41,245	154,039	589,130	~
Gross Fixed Capital Formation	2,613	967	2,882	5,055	4,497	5,384	8,737	23,920	60,346	187,850	~
Increase in Stocks	−252	−1,800	482	567	653	787	1,273	2,782	13,293	71,420	~
Private Consumption	8,876	10,739	18,381	19,534	21,204	23,607	24,965	55,616	243,194	1,387,850	~
Less: Imports[1]	−4,119	−4,083	−8,999	−10,229	−7,837	−8,277	−13,262	−25,188	−9,772	−37,465	~
Gross Domestic Product	12,594	14,514	21,892	25,773	29,696	35,783	45,030	115,404	435,742	2,389,500	~
Less: Net Factor Payments Abroad	−491	−801	−922	−1,016	−1,380	−671	~	~	~	~	~
Gross National Expenditure = GNP	12,103	13,713	20,970	24,757	28,316	35,112	~	~	~	~	~

1. Exports and imports include nonfactor services as well as goods.

SOURCE: IMF-IFS-Y, 1987; IMF-IFS-Y, 1988; IMF-IFS, August 1989.

Table 3456

PANAMA EXPENDITURE ON GDP AND GNP, 1976–88
(M NC)

Category	1976	1979	1980	1981	1982	1983	1984	1985	1986	1987	1988
Exports[1]	837.8	1,124.8	1,567.1	1,632.0	1,689.6	1,709.5	1,622.1	1,740.4	1,738.6	1,741.8	~
Government Consumption	386.1	567.2	680.5	812.9	962.6	941.5	1,001.3	1,037.8	1,123.7	1,231.2	~
Gross Fixed Capital Formation	608.6	661.2	866.4	1,079.6	1,185.4	917.8	779.9	736.5	895.1	939.3	~
Increase in Stocks	10.2	124.5	120.5	87.6	−.8	16.3	−18.9	−26.3	−37.5	.5	~
Private Consumption	1,088.8	1,693.8	2,009.5	2,107.4	2,311.5	2,480.0	2,878.0	3,091.4	2,933.8	3,053.2	~
Less: Imports[1]	−975.2	−1,371.3	−1,685.2	−1,841.5	−1,869.4	−1,691.4	−1,696.9	−1,698.3	−1,565.9	−1,648.6	~
Gross Domestic Product	1,956.3	2,800.2	3,558.8	3,878.0	4,278.9	4,373.7	4,565.5	4,881.5	5,121.2	5,317.4	~
Less: Net Factor Payments Abroad	−55.5	−102.8	−110.0	−78.6	−138.9	2.2	−123.6	−47.0	46.0	−76.0	~
Gross National Expenditure = GNP	1,900.8	2,697.4	3,448.8	3,799.4	4,140.0	4,375.9	4,441.9	4,834.5	5,167.2	5,241.4	~

1. Exports and imports include nonfactor services as well as goods.

SOURCE: IMF-IFS-Y, 1987; IMF-IFS-Y, 1988; IMF-IFS, August 1989.

Table 3457

PARAGUAY EXPENDITURE ON GDP AND GNP, 1976–88

(B NC)

Category	1976	1979	1980	1981	1982	1983	1984	1985	1986	1987	1988
Exports[1]	31.38	69.13	77.60	79.11	89.46	70.05	194.36	286.60	300.98	704.7	1,052.1
Government Consumption	13.41	24.71	34.73	48.63	52.27	58.02	69.28	90.21	121.40	176.6	221.9
Gross Fixed Capital Formation	48.75	116.14	152.65	194.22	176.87	164.51	226.79	259.24	350.50	591.42	749.0
Increase in Stocks	3.97	6.83	8.55	10.06	12.05	10.72	14.30	18.50	23.68	34.40	46.2
Private Consumption	155.17	306.50	399.40	504.07	552.02	642.20	835.15	1,066.04	1,410.92	1,882.61	2,649.9
Less: Imports[1]	–38.62	–92.80	–112.37	–127.40	–145.63	–127.39	–269.43	–326.70	–373.68	–896.12	–1,321.1
Gross Domestic Product	214.07	430.51	560.46	708.69	737.04	818.11	1,070.44	1,393.89	1,833.80	2,493.3	3,432.9
Less: Net Factor Payments Abroad	–1.09	1.29	5.26	8.76	8.26	5.00	–2.32	6.54	10.76	–50.06	–92.8
Gross National Expenditure = GNP	212.98	431.81	565.72	717.45	745.30	823.10	1,068.12	1,386.99	1,823.04	2,154.44	3,340.1

1. Exports and imports include nonfactor services as well as goods.

SOURCE: IMF-IFS-Y, 1987; IMF-IFS-Y, 1988; IMF-IFS, August 1989.

Table 3458

PERU EXPENDITURE ON GDP AND GNP, 1976–88

(B NC)

Category	1976	1979	1980	1981	1982	1983	1984	1985	1986	1987	1988
Exports[1]	96	942	1,335	1,697	2,862	6,141	13,312	40,545	~	~	~
Government Consumption	101	301	628	1,096	1,939	3,559	6,720	17,841	~	~	~
Gross Fixed Capital Formation	128	441	847	1,734	3,083	4,781	9,630	22,668	~	~	~
Increase in Stocks	9	7	33	152	118	–308	–189	–362	~	~	~
Private Consumption	570	1,982	3,273	5,917	9,561	10,210	40,555	107,010	~	~	~
Less: Imports[1]	–139	–553	–1,145	–2,076	–3,382	–6,076	–10,602	–29,725	~	~	~
Gross Domestic Product	765	3,119	4,972	8,520	14,183	26,313	59,865	157,977	~	~	~
Less: Net Factor Payments Abroad	–12	–142	–142	–245	–406	–979	–1,751	–4,918	~	~	~
Gross National Expenditure = GNP	753	2,977	4,830	8,275	13,778	25,334	58,114	153,059	~	~	~

1. Exports and imports include nonfactor services as well as goods.

SOURCE: IMF-IFS-Y, 1987; IMF-IFS-Y, 1988; IMF-IFS, August 1989.

Table 3459

URUGUAY EXPENDITURE ON GDP AND GNP, 1976–88

(M NC)

Category	1976	1979	1980	1981	1982	1983	1984	1985	1986	1987	1988[a]
Exports[1]	2,350	9,400	13,861	17,987	18,072	44,700	72,065	122,080	227,097	350,449	631.79
Government Consumption	1,755	6,789	11,482	17,336	20,100	25,653	36,851	69,084	129,582	216,929	370.11
Gross Fixed Capital Formation	1,952	9,312	15,422	19,205	19,382	20,329	27,331	38,304	69,279	144,559	272.62
Increase in Stocks	–81	663	572	–403	–827	–1,902	1,784	1,467	2,885	13,674	8.11
Private Consumption	9,107	43,441	70,479	91,147	94,076	137,826	216,282	392,451	691,858	1,290,795	2,091.88
Less: Imports[1]	–2,445	–11,980	–19,612	–22,819	–22,107	–41,600	–59,954	–103,228	–175,664	–315,847	–519.18
Gross Domestic Product	12,638	57,625	92,204	122,453	128,696	185,006	294,359	520,158	945,037	1,700,559	2,855.32
Less: Net Factor Payments Abroad	–244	–454	–864	–797	–2,729	–9,895	–20,210	–35,592	–41,616	–63,399	–110.00
Gross National Expenditure = GNP	12,783	57,171	91,340	121,656	125,967	175,111	274,149	484,566	903,421	1,637,160	2,745.32

1. Exports and imports include nonfactor services as well as goods.

a. B NC.

SOURCE: IMF-IFS-Y, 1987; IMF—IFS-Y, 1988; IMF-IFS, August 1989.

Table 3460

VENEZUELA EXPENDITURE ON GDP AND GNP, 1976–88

(B NC)

Category	1976	1979	1980	1981	1982	1983	1984	1985	1986	1987	1988
Exports[1]	41.06	64.03	85.46	89.62	75.20	74.07	105.15	101.60	97.75	160.20	~
Government Consumption	19.78	27.76	35.12	42.64	42.59	41.34	44.65	48.73	53.77	72.30	~
Gross Fixed Capital Formation	42.77	65.55	64.15	69.78	70.16	55.35	47.75	57.47	77.55	135.60	~
Increase in Stocks	3.73	.10	−1.35	−4.37	5.17	−21.20	8.14	−2.89	4.50	39.00	~
Private Consumption	66.94	110.33	135.38	160.53	182.24	183.44	208.73	232.18	271.88	466.80	~
Less: Imports[1]	−39.18	−60.03	−64.55	−72.99	−84.09	−42.50	−65.96	−65.06	−101.58	−154.50	~
Gross Domestic Product	135.10	207.74	254.20	285.21	291.27	290.49	348.45	372.03	403.86	719.40	895.40
Less: Net Factor Payments Abroad	.18	−.76	1.20	2.26	−6.60	−9.86	−6.71	−14.77	−15.84	−19.50	~
Gross National Expenditure = GNP	135.29	206.98	255.40	287.47	284.67	280.63	339.01	357.26	388.02	699.90	~

1. Exports and imports include nonfactor services as well as goods.

SOURCE: IMF-IFS-Y, 1987; IMF-IFS-Y, 1988; IMF-IFS, August 1989.

Table 3461

UNITED STATES EXPENDITURE ON GDP AND GNP, 1976–88

(B US)

Category	1976	1979	1980	1981	1982	1983	1984	1985	1986	1987	1988
Exports[1]	146.2	223.1	272.6	292.3	270.3	263.8	282.1	278.6	284.0	333.2	407.9
Government Consumption and Investment	357.0	467.8	530.3	588.1	641.7	675.0	733.4	815.4	864.2	922.8	964.9
Of Which Gross Fixed Capital Formation	49.0	60.5	71.5	73.1	77.2	64.4	73.3	97.1	101.1	98.7	93.1
Private Gross Fixed Capital Formation	261.7	441.9	445.3	491.5	471.8	509.4	598.0	650.0	677.0	671.6	718.1
Increase in Stocks	16.0	13.0	−8.3	24.0	−24.5	−7.1	64.1	11.1	6.7	46.1	48.4
Private Consumption	1,129.4	1,566.7	1,732.6	1,915.1	2,050.7	2,234.5	2,428.2	2,600.5	2,762.5	2,967.9	3,227.6
Less: Imports[1]	−148.5	−248.2	−288.1	−310.5	−295.2	−319.8	−388.3	−398.6	−425.4	−480.2	−527.4
Gross Domestic Product	1,761.7	2,464.4	2,684.4	3,000.5	3,114.9	3,355.9	3,717.5	3,957.0	4,168.9	4,461.2	4,839.4
Net Factor Income from Abroad	21.1	43.8	47.6	52.1	51.2	49.9	47.5	41.2	37.2	27.4	24.9
Gross National Expenditure = GNP	1,782.8	2,508.2	2,732.0	3,052.6	3,166.0	3,405.7	3,765.0	3,998.1	4,206.1	4,488.6	4,864.3

1. Exports and imports include nonfactor services as well as goods.

SOURCE: IMF-IFS-Y, 1987; IMF-IFS-Y, 1988; IMF-IFS, August 1989.

Table 3462

PROVINCIAL LEVEL GDP AND GDP/C IN MEXICO, 1970 AND 1980

PART I. 1970							PART II. 1980				
State (or Territory)	GDP M Pesos	%	Population T	%	GDP/C	Index (Total = 100.0)	State (or Territory)	GDP M Pesos	%	GDP/C	Index (Total = 100.0)
Aguascalientes	2,061.0	.5	338.1	.7	6,095.8	69.4	Aguascalientes	25,991	.61	51,629	81.3
Baja California	11,735.6	2.8	870.4	1.8	13,483.0	153.6	Baja California	95,860	2.24	78,225	123.3

Continued in SALA, 24-3361.

Table 3463

GDP AND PER CAPITA GDP AT MARKET PRICES,[1] 19 LRC, 1960–88

PART I. GDP

(M 1986 Dollars)

	Country	1960	1970	1980	1985	1986	1987	1988[‡]
A.	ARGENTINA	49,775	74,690	96,145	86,009	90,705	92,540	91,493
	Bahamas	955	1,836	2,233	2,424	2,487	2,596	2,648
	Barbados	462	844	994	963	1,012	1,038	1,075
B.	BOLIVIA	2,175	3,536	5,473	4,913	4,772	4,869	5,006
C.	BRAZIL	73,544	131,466	300,851	318,190	342,311	354,664	353,688
D.	CHILE	14,046	21,252	27,284	26,758	28,273	29,895	32,095
E.	COLOMBIA	14,399	24,060	41,138	45,973	48,651	51,239	53,155
F.	COSTA RICA	1,774	3,159	5,469	5,546	5,853	6,170	6,404
H.	DOMINICAN REP.	2,660	4,364	8,530	9,209	9,500	10,274	10,363
I.	ECUADOR	3,402	5,472	12,840	14,273	14,734	13,958	15,070
J.	EL SALVADOR	2,139	3,703	5,089	4,631	4,660	4,786	4,808
K.	GUATEMALA	4,358	7,447	12,906	12,196	12,214	12,596	13,042
	Guyana	573	811	921	768	770	775	752
L.	HAITI	1,215	1,316	2,092	1,988	2,008	2,003	1,998
M.	HONDURAS	1,199	2,053	3,494	3,681	3,794	3,955	4,107
	Jamaica	2,623	4,419	4,080	4,094	4,172	4,380	4,472
N.	MEXICO	54,182	106,721	202,226	222,600	214,083	217,260	219,649
O.	NICARAGUA	1,575	3,070	3,179	3,281	3,248	3,225	2,967
P.	PANAMA	1,397	3,000	5,128	5,900	6,098	6,245	5,176
Q.	PARAGUAY	1,381	2,189	5,074	5,678	5,679	5,925	6,290
R.	PERU	12,250	20,503	29,686	29,214	32,524	35,055	31,942
	Suriname	530	869	1,310	1,293	1,308	1,202	1,228
	Trinidad and Tobago	3,244	5,060	8,668	7,417	7,175	6,641	6,375
S.	URUGUAY	5,968	6,959	9,368	8,049	8,652	9,164	9,209
T.	VENEZUELA	29,102	52,396	78,497	74,422	79,500	81,904	85,223
	LATIN AMERICA	284,927	491,193	872,674	899,470	934,184	962,369	968,237

Table 3463 (Continued)

GDP AND PER CAPITA GDP AT MARKET PRICES,[1] 19 LRC, 1960–88

PART II. PER CAPITA GDP

(1988 Dollars)

	Country	1960	1970	1980	1988[‡]
A.	ARGENTINA	2,384	3,075	3,359	2,862
	Bahamas	8,448	10,737	10,631	11,317
	Barbados	2,000	3,530	3,994	4,233
B.	BOLIVIA	634	818	983	724
C.	BRAZIL	1,013	1,372	2,481	2,449
D.	CHILE	1,845	2,236	2,448	2,518
E.	COLOMBIA	927	1,157	1,595	1,739
F.	COSTA RICA	1,435	1,825	2,394	2,235
H.	DOMINICAN REP.	823	987	1,497	1,509
I.	ECUADOR	771	904	1,581	1,477
J.	EL SALVADOR	832	1,032	1,125	955
K.	GUATEMALA	1,100	1,420	1,866	1,502
	Guyana	1,008	1,111	1,215	995
L.	HAITI	331	292	386	319
M.	HONDURAS	619	782	954	851
	Jamaica	1,610	2,364	1,880	1,843
N.	MEXICO	1,425	2,022	2,872	2,588
O.	NICARAGUA	1,055	1,495	1,147	819
P.	PANAMA	1,264	2,017	2,622	2,229
Q.	PARAGUAY	779	931	1,612	1,557
R.	PERU	1,233	1,554	1,716	1,503
	Suriname	887	2,337	3,722	3,420
	Trinidad and Tobago	3,848	4,927	8,116	5,510
S.	URUGUAY	2,352	2,478	3,221	2,989
T.	VENEZUELA	3,879	4,941	5,225	4,544
	LATIN AMERICA	1,374	1,802	2,512	2,336

1. In view of the fact that national series in constant prices have different base years from country to country, their conversion into dollars of a given year—in this instance 1988—was accomplished by multiplying each constant price series by the rate of variation in the implicit deflator of the U.S. gross national product between the year of the constant price series and the year 1984. Each conversion factor is expressed by:

$$\frac{\sum_{k=b-1}^{b+1} GDP_k \, ER_k}{\sum_{k=b-1}^{b+1} GDP_k} \cdot \frac{USD_{1988}}{USD_b}$$

Where "b" represents the base year chosen by the country for the presentation of its constant price national account figures; GDP is the current value of a country's gross domestic product; ER is the reciprocal of the implicit market exchange rate (rf) factor published in the *International Financial Statistics* of the International Monetary Fund; and USD is the U.S. gross national product implicit deflator published in the *Survey of Current Business*.

SOURCE: IDB-SPTF, 1989, p. 463.

Table 3464

GROWTH OF GDP AND PER CAPITA GDP, 19 LR, 1960-88

(%)

Country	Regional Proportion			Growth of GDP AA-GR			Annual Variation								GDP per Capita AA-GR		Annual			
	1960-69	1970-79	1981-88	1961-70	1971-80	1981-84	1981	1982	1983	1984	1985	1986	1987	1988‡	1961-80	1981-85	1985	1986	1987	1988‡
A. ARGENTINA	16.2	13.0	10.0	4.1	2.6	-1.6	-6.8	-4.6	2.8	2.6	-4.5	5.5	2.0	-1.1	1.7	-3.6	-6.0	4.1	.7	-2.4
B. BOLIVIA	.7	.7	.6	5.0	4.5	-2.6	.3	-2.8	-6.6	-.3	-.2	2.6	4.4	2.0	2.2	-4.7	-2.8	.7	-.7	0
C. BRAZIL	25.7	31.5	34.9	6.0	8.6	-.6	-3.3	.9	-2.5	5.7	8.3	7.6	3.6	-.3	4.6	-1.1	.7	5.3	1.4	-2.3
D. CHILE	4.8	3.4	3.1	4.2	2.5	-1.1	5.5	-14.1	-.7	6.3	2.4	5.7	5.7	7.4	1.4	-2.0	.7	3.9	4.0	5.6
E. COLOMBIA	5.0	4.8	5.1	5.3	5.5	2.0	2.3	.9	1.6	3.4	3.1	5.8	5.3	3.7	2.8	.1	.9	3.6	3.1	1.6
F. COSTA RICA	.6	.6	.6	5.9	5.6	.2	-2.3	-7.3	2.9	8.0	.7	5.5	5.4	3.8	2.6	-2.6	-2.2	2.7	2.6	1.1
H. DOMINICAN REP.	.9	1.0	1.0	5.1	6.9	2.6	4.1	1.7	3.9	.5	-2.6	3.2	8.2	.9	3.0	-.8	-6.4	.8	5.7	-1.3
I. ECUADOR	1.2	1.4	1.5	4.9	8.9	1.6	3.9	1.2	-2.8	4.2	4.4	3.2	-5.3	8.0	3.7	-.8	1.6	.4	-7.9	5.0
J. EL SALVADOR	.8	.7	.5	5.6	3.2	-2.8	-8.3	-5.6	.8	2.3	2.0	.6	2.7	.5	1.5	-2.9	.7	-1.0	.9	-1.5
K. GUATEMALA	1.5	1.5	1.4	5.5	5.7	-1.3	.7	-3.5	-2.5	.5	-.6	.1	3.1	3.5	2.7	-3.9	-3.7	-2.7	.2	.6
L. HAITI	.3	.2	.2	.8	4.7	-1.3	-2.7	-3.5	.8	.3	.3	1.0	-.2	-.2	.8	-2.8	-1.6	-.9	-2.1	-2.1
M. HONDURAS	.4	.4	.4	5.5	5.5	.5	1.0	-2.6	1.1	2.8	3.2	3.1	4.2	3.8	2.2	-2.5	-.3	-.3	.9	.6
N. MEXICO	20.4	21.8	24.0	7.0	6.6	1.8	7.9	-.5	-5.3	3.6	2.6	-3.8	1.5	1.1	3.6	-.5	.2	-6.0	-.8	-1.1
O. NICARAGUA	.6	.6	.4	6.9	.3	1.9	5.4	-.8	4.6	-1.6	-4.1	-1.0	-.7	-8.0	.4	-2.7	-7.3	-4.3	-4.0	-11.1
P. PANAMA	.6	.6	.6	7.9	5.5	2.4	4.2	5.5	.4	-.4	4.7	3.4	2.4	-17.1	3.7	.6	2.5	1.2	.3	-18.8
Q. PARAGUAY	.5	.5	.6	4.7	8.8	1.9	8.7	-1.0	-3.0	3.1	4.0	0	4.3	6.2	3.7	-.9	.8	-3.0	1.3	3.1
R. PERU	4.4	3.8	3.4	5.3	3.8	-1.0	3.1	.9	-12.0	4.8	2.4	11.3	7.8	-8.9	1.7	-2.9	-.1	8.5	5.1	-11.1
S. URUGUAY	1.7	1.2	1.0	1.5	3.0	-3.8	1.9	-9.4	-5.9	-1.5	.3	7.5	5.9	.5	1.6	-3.7	-.4	6.7	5.1	.3
T. VENEZUELA	10.7	10.1	8.7	6.1	4.1	-1.6	-.3	.7	-5.6	-1.2	1.3	6.8	3.0	4.1	1.5	-3.8	-1.4	4.0	.3	1.4
LATIN AMERICA¹	100.0	100.0	100.0	5.6	5.9	-.1	.5	-.8	-2.9	3.6	3.5	3.9	3.0	.6	3.1	-1.6	1.1	1.6	.8	-1.5

1. Includes Bahamas, Barbados, Guyana, Jamaica, Surinama, and Trinidad and Tobago.

SOURCE: IDB-SPTF, 1989, p. 10.

Table 3465

TOTAL CONSUMPTION, 19 LR, 1960–88

(M 1986 Dollars)

	Country	1960	1970	1980	1985	1986	1987	1988[‡]
A.	ARGENTINA	41,114	58,680	79,996	70,592	76,209	77,045	72,440
B.	BOLIVIA	1,558	2,505	4,370	4,185	4,148	4,213	4,244
C.	BRAZIL	63,816	107,510	237,487	246,572	269,474	277,883	270,851
D.	CHILE	13,142	18,957	22,597	21,334	22,147	22,993	25,056
E.	COLOMBIA	11,331	19,709	34,354	38,084	39,225	40,832	42,906
F.	COSTA RICA	1,584	2,692	4,259	4,132	4,332	4,517	4,623
H.	DOMINICAN REP.	2,128	3,848	7,271	7,667	7,878	7,969	7,658
I.	ECUADOR	3,000	4,964	10,724	11,438	11,499	11,704	11,365
J.	EL SALVADOR	1,905	3,334	4,514	4,243	4,263	4,293	4,322
K.	GUATEMALA	3,939	6,335	10,558	10,370	10,496	10,890	11,289
L.	HAITI	1,016	1,215	2,018	1,844	1,879	1,894	1,945
M.	HONDURAS	1,005	1,631	2,772	2,868	3,015	3,171	3,276
N.	MEXICO	43,152	82,325	151,893	164,693	162,232	161,932	164,587
O.	NICARAGUA	1,355	2,532	3,251	3,048	2,972	2,998	2,773
P.	PANAMA	1,178	2,265	3,634	4,555	4,528	4,642	3,846
Q.	PARAGUAY	1,128	1,902	3,820	4,662	4,814	4,913	5,178
R.	PERU	8,507	16,349	21,200	21,372	24,017	26,290	24,583
S.	URUGUAY	5,757	6,734	8,202	6,795	7,451	8,126	8,033
T.	VENEZUELA	10,614	15,519	59,211	52,982	54,686	53,556	60,625
	LATIN AMERICA[1]	222,513	367,241	684,180	693,698	727,618	741,478	740,935

1. Includes Bahamas, Barbados, Guyana, Jamaica, Suriname, and Trinidad and Tobago.

SOURCE: IDB-SPTF, 1989, p. 465.

Table 3466

GROSS DOMESTIC INVESTMENT, 19 LR, 1960–88

(M 1986 Dollars)

	Country	1960	1970	1980	1985	1986	1987	1988[‡]
A.	ARGENTINA	9,955	15,837	22,764	8,899	10,378	12,175	13,543
B.	BOLIVIA	331	708	804	647	386	527	486
C.	BRAZIL	12,367	28,198	70,115	49,316	60,993	62,091	62,415
D.	CHILE	2,055	4,964	6,517	3,726	4,252	5,347	5,802
E.	COLOMBIA	2,468	4,941	8,087	8,882	8,375	8,933	9,626
F.	COSTA RICA	299	640	1,561	1,152	1,508	1,775	1,597
H.	DOMINICAN REP.	263	835	2,159	1,904	2,024	2,822	3,012
I.	ECUADOR	671	1,265	3,411	2,435	2,488	2,497	2,292
J.	EL SALVADOR	330	446	638	490	595	585	633
K.	GUATEMALA	470	893	1,476	981	983	1,291	1,293
L.	HAITI	77	120	365	422	386	379	373
M.	HONDURAS	195	464	872	748	629	664	616
N.	MEXICO	10,056	24,033	54,921	36,958	31,583	32,294	37,554
O.	NICARAGUA	229	522	533	733	724	713	719
P.	PANAMA	239	835	1,209	951	1,033	1,070	887
Q.	PARAGUAY	113	271	1,441	1,175	1,219	1,301	1,447
R.	PERU	2,724	3,590	8,392	4,711	7,194	8,188	6,827
S.	URUGUAY	765	737	1,739	679	708	877	898
T.	VENEZUELA	5,432	10,847	17,051	12,416	13,474	17,009	15,753
	LATIN AMERICA[1]	50,820	102,838	207,976	142,417	151,136	162,566	167,878

1. Includes Bahamas, Barbados, Guyana, Jamaica, Suriname, and Trinidad and Tobago.

SOURCE: IDB-SPTF, 1989, p. 465.

Table 3467

GROSS CAPITAL FORMATION AS A PERCENTAGE OF GDP, 18 L, 1962–83

(% of GDP at Market Prices)

Country	1962	1965	1970	1975	1976	1977	1978	1979	1980	1981	1982	1983
A. ARGENTINA	21.31	19.20	20.40	26.57	27.18	27.24	23.91	22.62	22.78	18.20	17.53	~
B. BOLIVIA	16.44	16.96	17.07	24.44	21.17	20.80	20.00	17.62	13.06	12.20	8.49	~

Continued in SALA, 24-3366.

Table 3468

ESTIMATES OF NATIONAL INCOME,[1] 18 LRC, 1960–80

	Total (M US)							Per Capita (US)						
Country	1960	1970	1975	1977	1978	1979	1980	1960	1970	1975	1977	1978	1979	1980
A. ARGENTINA	12,129	23,366	35,227	~	~	~	~	588	984	1388	~	~	~	~
B. BOLIVIA	339	970	2,334	~	~	~	~	102	226	477	~	~	~	~

Continued in SALA, 24-3367.

Table 3469

ESTIMATES OF NATIONAL DISPOSABLE INCOME,[1] 15 LRC, 1960–80

	Total (M US)							Per Capita (US)						
Country	1960	1970	1975	1977	1978	1979	1980	1960	1970	1975	1977	1978	1979	1980
B. BOLIVIA	346	962	2,311	~	~	~	~	104	224	472	~	~	~	~
D. CHILE	1,752	7,242	4,388	~	~	~	~	231	773	425	~	~	~	~

Continued in SALA, 24-3368.

Table 3470

GROSS PRODUCT PER CAPITA BY ICP AND *ATLAS* [1] METHODS, 16 LC, 1980–85
(United States = 100)

Economy	1980 ICP	1980 Atlas	1984 ICP	1984 Atlas	1985 ICP	1985 Atlas
A. ARGENTINA	33.5	17.1	27.9	14.0	25.9	13.0
Austria	75.4	86.6	74.6	58.9	75.5	55.8
Belgium	82.4	103.9	78.5	55.5	78.3	51.5
B. BOLIVIA	14.2	4.4	10.0	3.2	9.5	2.9
Botswana	13.9	8.0	17.8	6.0	18.7	5.1
C. BRAZIL	29.3	17.2	25.3	11.1	26.4	10.0
Cameroon	7.9	6.5	9.4	5.2	9.8	4.9
Canada	101.5	90.3	98.4	85.6	99.8	83.4
D. CHILE	31.9	20.6	26.9	11.0	26.6	8.8
E. COLOMBIA	24.8	11.0	23.4	9.1	23.3	8.0
F. COSTA RICA	27.7	17.3	23.5	7.7	22.8	7.9
Côte d'Ivoire	12.0	9.5	8.7	4.1	8.7	3.8
Denmark	85.9	108.4	87.5	72.1	88.3	68.5
H. DOMINICAN REP.	17.3	9.2	16.0	6.2	15.2	4.9
I. ECUADOR	22.6	11.8	20.2	7.4	20.0	7.1
J. EL SALVADOR	12.4	6.3	9.9	4.6	9.8	4.3
Ethiopia	2.4	.9	2.2	.7	2.0	.7
Finland	75.5	91.2	77.3	69.5	78.5	66.3
France	85.4	105.4	82.0	63.1	81.3	58.2
Germany, Fed. Rep.	89.1	114.1	86.6	71.8	87.4	66.7
Greece	44.5	36.9	41.9	24.3	42.0	21.6
K. GUATEMALA	20.3	9.7	16.3	7.7	15.4	7.6
M. HONDURAS	10.6	5.5	8.8	4.5	8.7	4.5
Hong Kong	62.4	47.0	72.3	41.0	70.9	37.9
Hungary	40.4	16.7	41.8	13.3	41.0	11.8
India	5.0	2.1	5.3	1.7	5.4	1.5
Indonesia	9.6	4.4	9.7	3.6	9.6	3.2
Ireland	47.9	46.7	47.7	32.0	46.8	29.5
Israel	59.4	40.9	55.8	32.8	55.1	30.0
Italy	68.0	60.3	64.5	41.4	64.7	39.8
Japan	73.4	77.9	79.0	68.5	81.1	69.1
Kenya	5.6	3.5	4.9	2.0	4.8	1.8
Korea, Rep. of	22.5	13.6	27.3	13.8	27.9	13.3
Luxembourg	92.8	131.9	86.6	84.9	87.4	81.6
Madagascar	5.0	3.2	3.8	1.7	3.7	1.5
Malawi	3.7	1.6	3.1	1.2	3.0	1.0
Mali	3.0	1.7	2.4	.9	2.3	.9
Morocco	10.5	8.1	9.8	4.3	9.8	3.7
Netherlands	81.4	102.5	75.5	61.4	75.5	56.0
Nigeria	7.8	8.8	5.3	4.8	5.2	4.6
Norway	99.0	117.1	100.4	89.9	101.5	84.7
Pakistan	9.6	2.7	10.0	2.4	10.3	2.3
P. PANAMA	27.9	14.6	26.4	12.7	26.4	12.3
Q. PARAGUAY	18.6	12.6	16.6	7.0	16.5	5.7
R. PERU	21.9	9.6	17.9	6.6	17.5	5.9
Philippines	15.2	6.3	13.2	4.2	12.1	3.7
Poland	37.7	- -	33.4	13.6	33.2	12.9
Portugal	33.4	20.8	31.4	12.7	31.7	12.0
Senegal	6.0	4.3	5.7	2.4	5.6	2.3
Spain	55.5	48.2	52.4	28.6	52.2	26.6
Sri Lanka	10.7	2.3	11.7	2.3	11.7	2.3
Tanzania	3.1	2.4	2.6	1.9	2.5	1.6
Tunisia	17.4	11.8	17.4	8.2	17.6	7.4
United Kingdom	72.1	81.3	71.2	55.3	72.3	51.2
United States	100.0	100.0	100.0	100.0	100.0	100.0
S. URUGUAY	37.2	29.6	28.9	12.4	28.4	10.1
T. VENEZUELA	47.4	33.6	37.2	22.4	35.7	19.0
Yugoslavia	35.3	27.9	33.3	14.6	32.7	12.6
Zambia	6.4	5.5	5.3	3.1	5.2	2.4
Zimbabwe	7.8	6.4	7.5	4.9	7.7	4.0
UNITED STATES (US)	11,450	11,650	15,330	15,540	16,160	16,400

1. *Atlas* refers to the World Bank method of calculating GNP per capita.

a. ICP values for 1980 are actual Phase IV results; for other years they are extrapolated from
the 1980 values. *Atlas* estimates are based on the current *Atlas* method applied to current
data and are GNP per capita. ICP values relate to GDP per capita.

SOURCE: WB-WDR, 1987, page 270.

Table 3471

REAL GDP FORECAST, 6 L, 1985–92
(PC)

Country	1985	1986	1987	1988	1989	1990	1991	1992
A. ARGENTINA	-3.5	5.5	1.5	2.8	2.6	1.6	2.4	3.1
C. BRAZIL	8.3	7.1	-2.5	2.7	4.8	3.1	5.1	4.9
D. CHILE	1.8	5.7	4.7	3.9	4.8	2.5	3.0	3.4
E. COLOMBIA	2.4	4.5	4.0	4.2	3.9	2.6	5.2	4.1
N. MEXICO	2.8	-3.7	2.6	3.7	.9	3.2	4.2	4.8
T. VENEZUELA	.3	3.1	2.5	2.6	1.9	1.8	2.7	2.3

SOURCE: Wharton Econometric Forecasting Associates, "World Economic Outlook,"
April 1987.

Table 3472

MEXICO ALTERNATIVE GDP FORECAST, 1983–92
(PC)

	1983	1984	1985	1986	1987	1988	1989	Azteca Plan[1] 1990	1991	1992
Alternative 1	-5.3	3.7	2.8	-3.7	2.2	3.6	.9	3.2	4.0	4.5
Alternative 2	-5.3	3.7	2.8	-3.7	1.4	2.9	-4.7	2.1	3.0	3.5
Alternative 3	-5.3	3.7	2.8	-3.7	.9	2.3	-2.5	2.2	3.1	3.7

1. Azteca Plan applies only to Alternative 1.

SOURCE: *CIEMEX-WEFA: Mexican Economic Outlook*, May 1987, tables 5.1, 12.1, 12.3.

Table 3473

LATIN AMERICA ECONOMIC AND INDUSTRIAL EXPANSION
AND RETROCESSION, 19 LR, 1950–83

		Gross National Income				Industrial Retrocession[1]	
		Total		Industrial		Industrial Product	Industrialization Degree
	Country	1950–80	1980–83	1950–80	1980–83		
A.	ARGENTINA	3.2	-3.2	3.8	-4.5	1971	1960
B.	BOLIVIA	3.4	-5.5	4.4	-6.2	1975	1978
C.	BRAZIL	7.1	-2.0	8.4	-4.5	1978	1968
D.	CHILE	3.6	-3.4	3.1	-6.1	1967	Before 1950
E.	COLOMBIA	5.1	1.2	6.0	-1.0	1980	1961
F.	COSTA RICA	6.5	-3.8	7.8	-7.1	1976	1973
H.	DOMINICAN REP.	5.9	3.2	6.9	3.3	1983	1970
I.	ECUADOR	6.2	.8	6.9	1.3	1981	1982
J.	EL SALVADOR	4.5	-5.4	5.4	-8.7	1969	1961
K.	GUATEMALA	5.0	-1.7	6.1	-3.7	1979	1968
L.	HAITI	2.2	#	3.5	2.9	1981	1983
M.	HONDURAS	4.4	-.5	7.3	#	1980	1981
N.	MEXICO	6.6	1.0	7.4	-1.0	1980	1970
O.	NICARAGUA	4.4	3.0	6.8	.3	1974	1977
P.	PANAMA	5.1	3.4	7.6	.1	1980	1961
Q.	PARAGUAY	5.2	1.5	5.5	.5	1980	1967
R.	PERU	4.6	-2.8	5.5	-6.1	1973	Before 1960
S.	URUGUAY	2.2	-4.8	2.8	-10.0	1971	1950
T.	VENEZUELA	5.9	-.4	7.2	-.6	1981	1980
	LATIN AMERICA	5.6	-.9	6.5	-3.1	1979	1966

1. Year in which the 1983 figure had been reached.

SOURCE: *Problemas de la Industria Latinoamericana en la Face Crítica*
(Santiago: Cepal, 1986).

Table 3474

LATIN AMERICA ECONOMIC EXPANSION AND INDUSTRIALIZATION, 19 LR, 1950–83

| | | | Industrialization in the Long Run | | | | Recent Deindustrialization | | | |
| | | | Product Growth | | Degree of Industrialization (%) | | | Product Growth | | Degree of Industrialization (%) |
	Country	Period	Total	Industrial	1950	Final Year	Period	Total	Industrial	1983
A.	ARGENTINA	1950–74	3.6	4.9	23.1	31.2	1974–83	.0	-1.9	26.2
B.	BOLIVIA	1950–80	3.5	4.4	12.6	16.3	1980–83	-5.5	-6.2	15.9
C.	BRAZIL	1950–73	7.2	8.8	19.7	27.6	1973–83	4.3	3.4	25.3
D.	CHILE	1950–72	4.1	5.2	21.5	27.5	1972–83	.7	-2.0	20.4
E.	COLOMBIA	1950–73	5.2	6.9	16.1	23.6	1973–83	3.8	1.8	19.4
F.	COSTA RICA	1950–78	6.8	8.4	13.7	21.2	1978–83	-1.2	-3.7	18.7
H.	DOMINICAN REP.	1950–71	5.6	7.2	13.9	18.9	1971–83	5.7	5.4	18.3
I.	ECUADOR	1950–82	6.0	6.8	17.6	22.5	1982–83	-3.5	-5.6	22.0
J.	EL SALVADOR	1950–76	5.2	6.7	13.7	19.9	1976–83	-2.2	-5.4	15.8
K.	GUATEMALA	1950–80	4.9	6.1	12.0	16.7	1980–82	-1.3	-3.7	15.9
L.	HAITI	1950–83	2.0	3.5	7.9	12.5	#	#	#	12.5
M.	HONDURAS	1950–81	4.3	7.1	6.7	15.3	1981–82	-1.0	-1.5	15.2
N.	MEXICO	1950–79	6.5	7.5	19.4	25.2	1979–83	2.8	1.0	23.5
O.	NICARAGUA	1950–80	4.4	6.7	11.5	22.5	1980–83	3.0	.3	20.8
P.	PANAMA	1950–69	6.4	10.0	6.7	12.7	1969–83	5.0	2.9	9.6
Q.	PARAGUAY	1950–73	3.9	4.6	14.7	17.0	1973–83	7.1	6.1	15.4
R.	PERU	1950–76	5.0	6.3	18.7	25.5	1976–83	-.2	-2.5	21.7
S.	URUGUAY	1950–79	2.1	2.8	21.9	26.8	1979–83	-2.3	-7.0	21.9
T.	VENEZUELA	1950–80	5.9	7.2	12.1	17.4	1980–83	-.4	-.6	17.3
	LATIN AMERICA	1950–73	5.6	6.9	19.2	25.2	1973–83	3.5	2.6	23.2

SOURCE: *Problemas de la Industrial Latinoamericana en la Face Crítica*
(Santiago: Cepal, 1986).

Table 3475

MEXICO GROSS FORMATION OF CAPITAL BY TYPES OF ASSETS
(B Pesos, at 1970 Consumer Prices)

Year	Total	Gross Formation of Fixed Capital	Construction	Machinery and Equipment	Change in Stock
1960	56.1	38.6	23.2	15.4	17.5
1961	54.6	39.0	32.1	15.9	15.6
1962	54.3	39.8	24.6	15.2	14.5
1963	61.1	45.1	28.1	17.0	16.0
1964	74.7	54.9	32.7	22.2	19.8
1965	75.8	57.1	32.4	24.7	18.7
1966	80.1	62.6	36.8	25.8	17.5
1967	89.1	69.9	41.4	28.5	19.2
1968	94.9	76.7	44.4	32.3	18.2
1969	97.1	82.0	48.5	33.5	15.1
1970	101.0	88.7	50.8	37.9	12.3
1971	96.0	87.1	49.9	37.2	8.9
1972	106.1	97.8	55.8	42.0	8.3
1973	122.3	112.2	63.1	49.1	10.1
1974	143.6	121.1	66.7	54.4	22.5
1975	150.9	132.3	71.7	60.6	18.6
1976	147.4	132.9	74.6	58.3	14.5
1977	146.9	124.0	72.6	51.4	22.9
1978	164.5	142.8	82.2	60.6	21.7
1979	193.4	171.7	92.9	78.8	21.7
1980	236.0	197.4	104.6	92.8	38.6
1981	272.8	226.4	116.4	110.0	46.4
1982	194.5	190.3	110.5	79.8	4.2
1983	146.0	137.2	88.5	48.7	8.8
1984	157.1	144.8	91.5	53.3	12.3
1985	178.3	154.0	94.8	59.2	24.3

SOURCE: NAFINSA-MV, April 20, 1987.

Table 3476

GROSS DOMESTIC PRODUCT,[1] 5 L, 1920–84

Year	F. COSTA RICA	J. EL SALVADOR	K. GUATEMALA	M. HONDURAS	O. NICARAGUA
1920	283.8	165.4	228.6	218.7	170.0
1921	271.4	162.9	241.9	214.9	176.4
1922	295.6	168.4	219.6	224.6	159.1
1923	267.1	172.7	233.0	214.8	170.2
1924	298.6	180.4	243.4	195.9	177.7
1925	291.1	164.0	232.5	228.1	196.2
1926	315.0	189.5	227.2	222.4	168.0
1927	285.9	164.1	236.0	241.4	168.7
1928	294.5	187.0	232.6	265.2	213.8
1929	276.6	184.5	252.0	257.3	235.4
1930	284.3	185.3	255.4	268.2	190.0
1931	275.2	163.7	231.6	268.4	175.3
1932	248.3	145.9	197.2	235.6	157.8
1933	290.2	163.4	194.0	216.6	195.7
1934	251.1	166.6	216.0	207.7	175.3
1935	267.1	180.9	244.7	194.7	173.2
1936	279.7	174.6	329.5	194.5	134.1
1937	314.9	188.7	315.3	182.5	141.6
1938	328.1	173.3	317.9	189.6	144.6
1939	326.6	183.5	351.1	191.3	172.9
1940	308.2	196.9	392.0	199.2	184.5
1941	339.6	190.4	403.7	195.2	199.5
1942	295.1	203.1	400.1	174.0	187.6
1943	290.1	218.8	262.2	172.9	201.1
1944	255.1	204.1	249.0	194.4	194.7
1945	282.3	193.3	247.5	209.3	191.3
1946	307.6	194.2	286.2	220.0	201.2
1947	356.0	241.5	282.3	228.8	195.7
1948	366.2	302.6	284.1	228.5	208.5
1949	371.1	270.3	301.7	225.0	198.7
1950	372.0	275.2	314.8	225.6	225.0
1951	368.0	274.7	310.4	231.4	233.8
1952	372.2	284.8	307.3	230.9	266.0
1953	415.3	297.6	309.3	242.6	265.3
1954	401.9	292.4	304.1	221.9	282.7
1955	430.9	298.8	301.2	223.5	291.8
1956	402.9	313.5	318.9	233.1	282.3
1957	421.5	421.4	327.3	235.5	299.1
1958	457.3	319.9	331.2	235.1	291.0
1959	458.1	324.5	337.2	233.3	286.7
1960	474.1	329.4	335.5	240.1	282.4
1961	474.8	332.8	339.3	237.2	295.2
1962	485.2	355.6	341.8	243.1	316.5
1963	511.7	358.7	362.8	244.7	341.8
1964	517.9	378.2	369.0	247.7	372.0
1965	545.9	383.5	376.4	261.4	397.4
1966	569.3	396.1	389.2	267.3	400.7
1967	585.2	403.1	388.0	273.0	416.1
1968	614.7	400.9	409.8	279.4	414.4
1969	632.4	403.7	413.8	272.5	429.6
1970	658.6	406.1	416.7	279.5	424.3
1971	674.7	411.7	427.8	287.1	424.4
1972	718.1	420.8	446.0	290.3	420.5
1973	761.7	427.1	463.0	297.3	434.1
1974	782.8	438.6	467.3	285.9	479.0
1975	778.9	443.3	456.4	267.1	460.6
1976	801.5	451.9	478.9	275.3	469.4
1977	851.8	469.0	498.7	290.9	493.3
1978	883.8	486.6	507.6	301.5	441.2
1979	906.1	468.5	515.7	310.7	310.4
1980	892.4	399.9	519.5	308.2	314.2
1981	853.0	357.8	507.6	301.2	318.2
1982	773.8	328.9	475.6	285.9	303.0
1983	775.2	312.3	450.0	274.9	302.6
1984	805.6	307.8	440.1	273.3	283.6

1. 1970 prices, net factor cost. Calculated at purchasing-power parity exchange rates.

SOURCE: Victor Bulmer–Thomas, *The Political Economy of Central America Since 1920* (Cambridge: Cambridge University Press, 1987).

Part XI

Development of Data

35

Announced U.S. Assistance to Latin America, 1946−88: Who Gets It? How Much? And When?

CHRISTOF ANDERS WEBER

James W. Wilkie, Enrique C. Ochoa, and David E. Lorey, eds., *Statistical Abstract of Latin America*, vol. 28 (Los Angeles: UCLA Latin American Center Publications, University of California, 1990).

U.S. authorizations for assistance to Latin America are used for purposes of political propaganda in the recipient countries. Further, such figures add to perceptions in the United States about which countries are benefiting from U.S. policy. It is therefore important to understand that the data involved are announced authorizations. My purpose here is to present as consistently as possible the data needed by policy analysts to better understand U.S. foreign assistance programs. The data presented here allow observers to analyze patterns implicit in the time-series statistics.

This project builds upon earlier work by James Wilkie. In 1974 Wilkie wrote:[1]

> What is [U.S.] assistance? . . . . The following arguments (among others) might be used *against* categories included: Military funds do not really involve assistance because they only have assisted in repression of the population. Peace Corps assistance has done more to assist U.S. citizens in learning about Latin America than to assist in the development of Latin America. Food for Peace has not only stunted the development of Latin American agriculture but lulled recipient nations into an easy solution for feeding a rapidly expanding population, thus making it possible for governments to avoid implementation of controversial but necessary birth-control programs. Since Export–Import Bank loans are granted for the purchase of U.S. produced goods, Latin

Americans pay higher prices than might be obtainable elsewhere, U.S. exporters effectively receiving the assistance in the form of a subsidy. And AID funds, like Social Progress Trust Funds, result in a heavy debt burden for Latin America.

> While there is some degree of truth in all of these statements, the following counter arguments are persuasive: Since military items and food will be imported anyway, low or subsidized prices provided by the United States free scarce funds for national development. Export–Import Bank loans have been made at such relatively low interest rates (generally five to six per cent) that the Bank is under fire from U.S. business leaders who note that it charges half the current U.S. rate of interest to finance competition for U.S. concerns. Not only had AID funds involved grants as well as loans, but also the grants exceeded loans until 1962. Interest rate charged on loans by AID is generally much less than one third of the interest rate prevailing in Latin American countries, the AID rate averaging 2.3 per cent yearly between 1961 and 1970. Social Progress Trust Fund loans were administered through the Inter-American Development Bank as part of multilateral instead of bilateral assistance at the same low rates of interest. And no doubt the Peace Corps has planted, at relatively low cost, some seeds of local initiative. In any case, should the reader not agree with any of these categories, they may be deducted from the full data given . . . .

Although U.S. interest rates have increased since the 1970s, they are usually lower than market rates and they offer funds otherwise not available.

Further, U.S. assistance is fungible. The matter of fungibility of U.S. assistance has been addressed by Phillip Boucher, who argues that, whether or not U.S. assistance is tied to specific expenditures, it frees otherwise scarce Latin American government funds for discretionary use by officials.[2]

To help readers understand the data series presented here, I define the categories of assistance and discuss the

CHRISTOF ANDERS WEBER is studying international relations and Latin American Studies at UCLA. He has been a member of the SALA research staff for three years, and plans to pursue graduate studies in international relations with a focus on Latin America and the Pacific Rim.

AUTHOR'S NOTE: The author would like to acknowledge the research contribution of Tim Mullane, who compiled data on this topic several years ago. While Mullane's format for presentation of the data has been adapted for use here, the data developed here were gathered and analyzed by Weber.

[1] James W. Wilkie, *Statistics and National Policy* [SNP] (Los Angeles: UCLA Latin American Center, 1974), pp. 147–148. Further, Wilkie has developed several case studies of U.S. assistance to Latin America. See his *The Bolivian Revolution and U.S. Aid since 1952* (Los Angeles: UCLA Latin American Center, 1969), and "U.S. Foreign Policy and Economic Assistance in Bolivia, 1948–1976," in SALA, 22, Chapter 38.

[2] See Phillip Boucher, "U.S. Foreign Aid to Latin America: Hypotheses and Patterns in Historical Statistics," Ph.D. dissertation, University of California, Los Angeles, 1979.

methods by which the U.S. government has recorded nominal data. (These methods have varied over time.) One can only see how each of the twenty Latin American nations has fared in relation to the others by deflating the nominal data in relation to the changing value of the dollar (using the Export Price Index) and in relation to the growing population of each nation. The deflated data can then be expressed in terms of the total quantity given yearly to each nation or in terms of the quantity given per capita to each nation.

With regard to the nominal figures on U.S. authorizations for Latin America (and the world), we are fortunate to have the yearly volume *Overseas Loans and Grants and Assistance from International Organizations: Obligations and Loan Authorizations* (USAID-OLG), published at the behest of the U.S. Congress by the U.S. Agency for International Development (USAID). Although these annual volumes are extremely useful in that they give much detail, they are not consistent over time. For example, USAID counted U.S. Export-Import Bank loans in U.S. assistance totals until the 1970s when critics charged that such loans do not constitute assistance; subsequently USAID has published the data apart from the total for U.S. assistance. Here, to remedy this inconsistency, I include Export-Import Bank loans as U.S. assistance, just as I also include U.S. funds directed to Latin America through the Social Progress Trust Fund of the Inter-American Development Bank. (I do not include assistance allocated by international accounts or agencies over which the United States does not have immediate control, e.g., the Inter-American Development Bank itself, the International Monetary Fund [IMF], or the World Bank.) Time has shown criticism of development bank loans to be erroneous—their funds are fungible and do provide new funds that allow governments to spend their budgets in ways otherwise not possible.

With further regard to USAID-OLG, it is important to note that—except for Export-Import figures—the nominal data have been published in gross obligations since the 1972 edition (with publication date of 1973). Data for previous years were published in net terms, which fluctuated with revision as assistance was reduced or changed from the original authorization. In order to know how much assistance has been promised at different times, the data used here are from each volume since 1959.

Data for years prior to 1960 were taken from *U.S. External Assistance, Obligations and Other Commitments, July 1, 1945 through June 30, 1959*, the earliest source used in compiling the data, first published by the International Cooperation Administration and later continued by the AID. It is therefore possible that the data for years prior to 1959 may not be in gross terms, that is, what was actually promised, but rather in net terms, that is, what was actually given.

A similar problem occurred with the data for 1963 and 1964. I was unable to locate copies of USAID-OLG for these fiscal years. Because the title for USAID-OLG includes the years covered in each annual publication (e.g., July 1, 1945 through September 30, 1985), most libraries have discarded earlier published USAID-OLG upon receiving the next annual publication, not knowing that they were throwing away data that would otherwise be unavailable.

The Agency for International Development refused to provide the USAID-OLG for 1963 and 1964. According to a senior official at USAID, it is not necessary to study the unrevised numbers, and no numbers are completely correct except for those most recently published in USAID-OLG or its companion volume USAID-OLG *Series of Yearly Data* (personal communication). Consequently, the data used in Tables 3500 through 3530 for 1963 and 1964 were taken from the next available publication, USAID-OLG, 1965. It is hoped that little or no revision of the data had occurred up to that time.

As can be seen from this official's lack of understanding that the announced authorizations of assistance to Latin American countries are of value, one can begin to understand why a data series such as that presented here could be vital to policy analysts seeking to study the assistance programs. Although data are published annually for the period of this study, no series of gross authorizations (announced) has been constructed.

Although military assistance data are available for years 1952 through 1959 in *U.S. Foreign Assistance 1960*, they are not included in the tables below because, according to *U.S. External Assistance 1959* (the predecessor to *U.S. Foreign Assistance* and later to the USAID-OLG), this information was classified. Because the purpose of this essay is to present the quantities which Latin American nations were first promised, inclusion of these data would not be consistent with the purpose of this study.

Readers need to know how much the U.S. government has actually disbursed, not just obligated, annually to the countries of Latin America. Presenting this information would require a separate research project more complex than the one at hand. The United States government does not publish data on disbursements. Unfortunately, much of U.S. planning for assistance to Latin America may be wasted precisely because plans not based on reality cannot be carried out effectively, as Wilkie has shown for Bolivia.[3] The U.S. Congress should require USAID to gather data on disbursements in the same way that it gathers data on obligations and authorizations. We know that there may be no direct correlation between projected and actual expenditures. Wilkie proves just this in the case of outlays by the Bolivian and Mexican governments as does Gruening for Chile.[4]

---

[3] Wilkie, *Bolivian Revolution*, passim.

[4] Wilkie, *Bolivian Revolution*; and James W. Wilkie, *The Mexican Revolution: Federal Expenditure and Social Change Since 1910*, 2d ed. (Berkeley and Los Angeles: University of California Press, 1970). On budgets, see also James W. Wilkie, ed., *Money and Politics in Latin America* (Los Angeles: UCLA Latin American Center Publications, 1977), pp. xi–xix, for an introduction to the literature; and Wilkie, SNP, Chapter VI. For Gruening on Chile, see Wilkie, SNP, Chapter XX.

For another analysis of U.S. disbursements to Latin America, readers may consult Wilkie's *Statistics and National Policy* (1974, Chapter XVII). Wilkie was able to work with officials in Washington, D.C., to synthesize data from the many agencies involved, but he was not able to continue development of his series because subsequent budgetary "savings" eliminated the positions of U.S. budget officers whose job it was to know how their respective agencies disburse funds.

Regarding development of data on disbursements or actual expenditures, Wilkie has written that few officials in the U.S. government

> recognize the value of comparing projected and actual amounts. Indeed, each agency wishes only to be responsible for its own programs perhaps because, in a situation where competition for funds is forceful, if the flow of international assistance funds were understood according to function, some agencies might suffer reduced budgets— presumably if each agency leaves others alone, all will benefit. Although one might have expected the U.S. Department of State to lead the way in gathering full data, such has not been the case; for example, the External Research arm of the State Department has been confined by bureaucratic protocol to investigating non-U.S. affairs. And since the internal orientation of State involves assessing the activity of the Department itself, the arena of assessing the interaction of U.S. assistance with the policy of recipient countries falls between the lines of bureaucratic table of organization charts. Policy, then is evaluated on the basis of projected rather than actual expenditures.[5]

Further, it is Wilkie's view that only with the data on U.S. obligations—as developed here in terms deflated for inflation and population—is it possible for policy makers to determine a fair allocation in relation to each country's need through time.

Readers should note eight parameters of this study.

1. The series date only from 1946 because no earlier information is available. They conclude in 1988, the last year for which data are available at the time of writing. The information for 1989 is available but was not used because USAID informed its subscribers that 1989 USAID-OLG contained errors. (It will be reprinted to correct the errors.)

2. Although only figures for total assistance are graphed (Figures 35:1 through 35:68), I present here the nominal data for four subcategories of economic assistance. The first subcategory is labeled "USAID" and Predecessors. The USAID was created in 1961 by combining the International Cooperation Administration with various other smaller agencies. The second subcategory, labeled "FFP" (Food for Peace, at times called Food for Freedom), gives data for monies and goods promised under Public Law 480. The third subcategory, labeled "EXP/ IMP", includes loans given by the Export-Import Bank to help Latin American countries cover their trade deficits, allowing them to continue to purchase goods from the United States. Although some may not regard this as true assistance, it frees funds that can then be used for either military or economic purposes. The fourth, and final, subcategory of economic assistance, labeled "Other," includes money given by the Social Progress Trust Fund and other organizations. The Military category includes monies given as MAP Grants, Credit Financing, Excess Stock, and other programs. The total assistance is the sum of economic and military assistance. This is presented in both nominal and deflated terms.

3. Subtotals for grants and loans are not presented here separately as in USAID-OLG, because in some cases loans have been converted to grants. For such totals, consult USAID-OLG.

4. The concept of "obligations" does not make a distinction between assistance given in the form of cash or in the form of commodities. Commodities donated or sold to Latin American countries constitute "virtual assistance" and—in theory—are valued at market prices by the U.S. government; however— in fact—commodity values are affected by politics. During the height of the Cold War, military commodities may have been overvalued in order to please the U.S. Congress, which was concerned about the "rising tide of world communism." With the waning of guerrilla movements in Latin America at the end of the 1970s, military commodities seem to have been grossly undervalued in order to avoid limitations by the U.S. Congress on U.S. military assistance. No compensation for problems of valuation can be made here; the reader is advised to bear in mind that no data are perfect.

5. This study includes only U.S. assistance allocated to individual countries. It does not include assistance to regions such as Central America. (The reader can note that Central American countries generally receive a higher per capita assistance than do Mexico or South American nations; see Tables 3500 and 3527.)

6. Capitalized interest on loans (interest due for previous years) is added by the U.S. government to totals in the year that it becomes an accrued liability. Such interest should not be confused with new assistance.

[5] Wilkie, SNP, p. 147.

7. Deflation of nominal data is developed here through the use of population data and the U.S. Export Price Index (EPI). The latter is more appropriate than the price indexes for U.S. wholesale or consumer goods, which are based on internal U.S. costs. In order to yield standard dollars of 1970, the EPI is keyed to 1970 = 100.

8. The population used as a divisor for calculating per capita U.S. assistance is taken from the series for each of the twenty Latin American countries (see SALA 27, Tables 601–621). Yearly data on total U.S. assistance in dollars of 1970 are divided by the population for each country.

What then can be learned from the following tables and figures? The first set of tables and figures, which present U.S. assistance to Latin America, illustrate several trends. Yearly total assistance and per capita total assistance were greatest during the 1960s when the Alliance for Progress was in full force (Figures 35:1 and 35:2 and Tables 3524 through 3527). Countries can be compared both in terms of the total and per capita assistance that has been authorized to them over the 43 years covered by this study (see Tables 3500 through 3504 and Figures 35:3 and 35:4). For information for each country by year, see either the set of tables and figures presented for each country or summary tables 3524 through 3530.

Although Central American countries receive less than Mexico or South American countries in terms of the total assistance, they in fact receive more money per capita than do most other Latin American countries. Of the top six recipient nations in terms of total assistance, only one is among the top six recipients in terms of per capita assistance. Who then is receiving the most assistance from the United States? A table including data and calculations is presented for each of the twenty Latin American nations (e.g., Argentina: Table 3504 and Figures 35:9, 35:10, and 35:11). The three figures presented for each country show (i) total assistance (military plus economic), (ii) per capita total assistance, and (iii) the relationship to the average Latin American per capita total assistance. The third figure readily demonstrates whether a particular nation receives more or less than the per capita average for all Latin American nations.

Following the individual country tables and figures (Tables 3504 through 3523 and Figures 35:9 through 35:68), deflated data are presented in summary form for total assistance (Table 3524), economic assistance (Table 3525), and military assistance (Table 3526). Next, tables are presented on per capita assistance (Table 3527), demonstrating how each country compares to the average Latin American per capita and total assistance (Tables 3528 and 3529), and each country's annual percentage of total assistance to Latin America (Table 3530).

It is the author's hope that the data and figures presented here help analysts study U.S. assistance to Latin America. Studies are vital to politicians and economists who determine what quantities of assistance should be given to each country. President George Bush has moved to pump 500 million dollars into Panama and 300 million dollars into Nicaragua, quantities which are disproportionate in per capita terms to amounts received by more populous Latin American nations. This study has shown several ways to present data to permit clearer understanding of where U.S. assistance is focused.

There is a need to analyze not only data on actual disbursements to Latin American nations, but also a need to study the announced assistance. Analyzing what is actually promised to Latin America, in terms of assistance packages, along with what is actually given, will provide analysts with a much better understanding of the U.S. assistance scenario. Knowing who gets assistance, when they get it, and how much they actually receive will allow the assistance program to become more effective.

DATA SOURCES

U.S. Overseas Loans and Grants and Assistance from International Organizations Obligations and Loan Authorizations:

July 1, 1945 – June 30, 1965
July 1, 1945 – June 30, 1966
July 1, 1945 – June 30, 1967
July 1, 1945 – June 30, 1968
July 1, 1945 – June 30, 1969
July 1, 1945 – June 30, 1970
July 1, 1945 – June 30, 1971
July 1, 1945 – June 30, 1972
July 1, 1945 – June 30, 1973
July 1, 1945 – June 30, 1974
July 1, 1945 – June 30, 1975
July 1, 1945 – September 30, 1976
July 1, 1945 – September 30, 1977
July 1, 1945 – September 30, 1978
July 1, 1945 – September 30, 1979
July 1, 1945 – September 30, 1980
July 1, 1945 – September 30, 1981
July 1, 1945 – September 30, 1982

July 1, 1945 – September 30, 1983
July 1, 1945 – September 30, 1984
July 1, 1945 – September 30, 1985
July 1, 1945 – September 30, 1986
July 1, 1945 – September 30. 1987
July 1, 1945 – September 30, 1988

Office of Planning and Budgeting, Bureau for Program and Policy Coordination, Agency for International Development.

U.S. Foreign Assistance and Assistance from International Organizations Obligations and Loan Authorizations:

July 1, 1945 – June 30, 1960
July 1, 1945 – June 30, 1961
July 1, 1945 – June 30, 1962

Agency for International Development, Statistics and Reports Division.

U.S. External Assistance Obligations and Other Commitments July 1, 1945 – June 30, 1959, International Cooperation Administration, Office of Statistics and Reports.

Table 3500

AVERAGE YEARLY PER CAPITA ANNOUNCED TOTAL U.S. ASSISTANCE, 20 L,[1] 1946–88

(US)

PART I. ALPHABETICAL

A.	ARGENTINA	1.90
B.	BOLIVIA	5.94
C.	BRAZIL	1.91
D.	CHILE	6.86
E.	COLOMBIA	2.90
F.	COSTA RICA	8.73
G.	CUBA	.54
H.	DOMINICAN REP.	5.77
I.	ECUADOR	2.60
J.	EL SALVADOR	6.86
K.	GUATEMALA	3.53
L.	HAITI	2.14
M.	HONDURAS	5.33
N.	MEXICO	1.57
O.	NICARAGUA	4.92
P.	PANAMA	10.19
Q.	PARAGUAY	2.78
R.	PERU	3.25
S.	URUGUAY	2.43
T.	VENEZUELA	2.48
	Latin America Per Capita Average	2.54

PART II. RANK ORDER

1.	PANAMA	10.19
2.	COSTA RICA	8.73
3.	CHILE	6.86
4.	EL SALVADOR	6.86
5.	BOLIVIA	5.94
6.	DOMINICAN REP.	5.77
7.	HONDURAS	5.33
8.	NICARAGUA	4.92
9.	GUATEMALA	3.53
10.	PERU	3.25
11.	COLOMBIA	2.90
12.	PARAGUAY	2.78
13.	ECUADOR	2.60
	Latin America Per Capita Average	2.54
14.	VENEZUELA	2.48
15.	URUGUAY	2.43
16.	HAITI	2.14
17.	BRAZIL	1.91
18.	ARGENTINA	1.90
19.	MEXICO	1.57
20.	CUBA	.54

1. Deflated using Export Price Index (Table 3331) in 1970 U.S. dollars.

SOURCE: Table 3527.

Table 3501

CUMULATIVE ANNOUNCED TOTAL U.S. ASSISTANCE, 20 LR,[1] 1946–88

(M US)

PART I. ALPHABETICAL

A.	ARGENTINA	1,781.3
B.	BOLIVIA	1,121.9
C.	BRAZIL	6,403.2
D.	CHILE	2,431.2
E.	COLOMBIA	2,388.9
F.	COSTA RICA	709.5
G.	CUBA	53.8
H.	DOMINICAN REP.	1,045.7
I.	ECUADOR	614.9
J.	EL SALVADOR	1,312.3
K.	GUATEMALA	779.0
L.	HAITI	407.3
M.	HONDURAS	777.2
N.	MEXICO	3,107.9
O.	NICARAGUA	373.5
P.	PANAMA	604.8
Q.	PARAGUAY	254.1
R.	PERU	1,739.8
S.	URUGUAY	278.7
T.	VENEZUELA	971.0
	Total Latin America	27,155.9
	Latin America Average	1,429.3

PART II. RANK ORDER

1.	BRAZIL	6,403.2
2.	MEXICO	3,107.9
3.	CHILE	2,431.2
4.	COLOMBIA	2,388.9
5.	ARGENTINA	1,781.3
6.	PERU	1,739.8
	Latin America Average	1,429.3
7.	EL SALVADOR	1,312.3
8.	BOLIVIA	1,121.9
9.	DOMINICAN REP.	1,045.7
10.	VENEZUELA	971.0
11.	GUATEMALA	779.0
12.	HONDURAS	777.2
13.	COSTA RICA	709.5
14.	ECUADOR	614.9
15.	PANAMA	604.8
16.	HAITI	407.3
17.	NICARAGUA	373.5
18.	URUGUAY	278.7
19.	PARAGUAY	254.1
20.	CUBA	53.8

1. Deflated using Export Price Index (Table 3331) in 1970 U.S. dollars.

SOURCE: Table 3524.

Table 3502	Table 3503
CUMULATIVE ANNOUNCED U.S. ECONOMIC ASSISTANCE, 20 LR,[1] 1946–88	CUMULATIVE ANNOUNCED U.S. MILITARY ASSISTANCE, 20 LR,[1] 1946–88
(M US)	(M US)

PART I. ALPHABETICAL (Table 3502)

A.	ARGENTINA	1,560.2
B.	BOLIVIA	1,064.2
C.	BRAZIL	5,974.9
D.	CHILE	2,264.1
E.	COLOMBIA	2,211.3
F.	COSTA RICA	693.9
G.	CUBA	53.0
H.	DOMINICAN REP.	1,001.3
I.	ECUADOR	538.9
J.	EL SALVADOR	1,011.2
K.	GUATEMALA	739.9
L.	HAITI	398.2
M.	HONDURAS	624.4
N.	MEXICO	3,088.2
O.	NICARAGUA	351.0
P.	PANAMA	579.5
Q.	PARAGUAY	235.8
R.	PERU	1,569.1
S.	URUGUAY	225.8
T.	VENEZUELA	816.4
	Latin America	25,001.1
	Latin America Average	1,300.0

PART I. ALPHABETICAL (Table 3503)

A.	ARGENTINA	221.1
B.	BOLIVIA	57.7
C.	BRAZIL	428.3
D.	CHILE	167.0
E.	COLOMBIA	177.5
F.	COSTA RICA	15.6
G.	CUBA	.9
H.	DOMINICAN REP.	44.4
I.	ECUADOR	76.0
J.	EL SALVADOR	301.1
K.	GUATEMALA	39.1
L.	HAITI	9.1
M.	HONDURAS	152.8
N.	MEXICO	19.7
O.	NICARAGUA	22.5
P.	PANAMA	25.4
Q.	PARAGUAY	18.4
R.	PERU	170.7
S.	URUGUAY	53.0
T.	VENEZUELA	154.6
	Total Latin America	2,154.8
	Latin America Average	112.8

PART II. RANK ORDER (Table 3502)

1.	BRAZIL	5,974.9
2.	MEXICO	3,088.2
3.	CHILE	2,264.1
4.	COLOMBIA	2,211.3
5.	PERU	1,569.1
6.	ARGENTINA	1,560.2
	Latin America Average	1,300.0
7.	BOLIVIA	1,064.2
8.	EL SALVADOR	1,011.2
9.	DOMINICAN REP.	1,001.3
10.	VENEZUELA	816.4
11.	GUATEMALA	739.9
12.	COSTA RICA	693.9
13.	HONDURAS	624.4
14.	PANAMA	579.5
15.	ECUADOR	538.9
16.	HAITI	398.2
17.	NICARAGUA	351.0
18.	PARAGUAY	235.8
19.	URUGUAY	225.8
20.	CUBA	53.0

PART II. RANK ORDER (Table 3503)

1.	BRAZIL	428.3
2.	EL SALVADOR	301.1
3.	ARGENTINA	221.1
4.	COLOMBIA	177.5
5.	PERU	170.7
6.	CHILE	167.0
7.	VENEZUELA	154.6
8.	HONDURAS	152.8
	Latin America Average	112.8
9.	ECUADOR	76.0
10.	BOLIVIA	57.7
11.	URUGUAY	53.0
12.	DOMINICAN REP.	44.4
13.	GUATEMALA	39.1
14.	PANAMA	25.4
15.	NICARAGUA	22.5
16.	MEXICO	19.7
17.	PARAGUAY	18.4
18.	COSTA RICA	15.6
19.	HAITI	9.1
20.	CUBA	.9

1. Deflated using Export Price Index (Table 3331) in 1970 U.S. dollars.

SOURCE: Table 3525.

1. Deflated using Export Price Index (Table 3331) in 1970 U.S. dollars.

SOURCE: Table 3526.

Figure 35:1

LATIN AMERICA: YEARLY ANNOUNCED TOTAL
U.S. ASSISTANCE,[1] 1946–88

(M US)

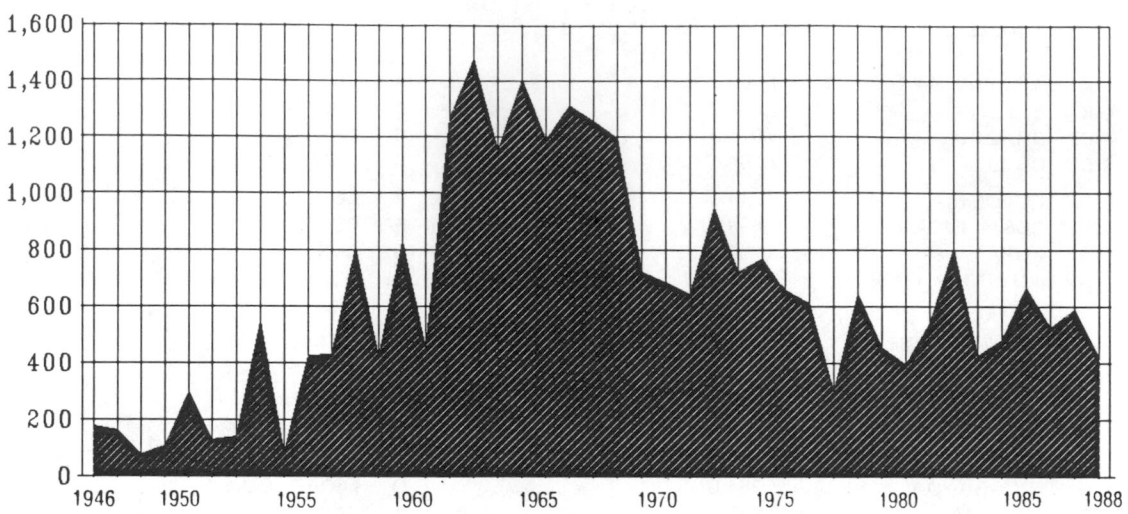

1. Deflated using Export Price Index in 1970 U.S. dollars.

SOURCE: Table 3524.

Figure 35:2

LATIN AMERICA: YEARLY PER CAPITA ANNOUNCED TOTAL
U.S. ASSISTANCE,[1] 1946–88

(US)

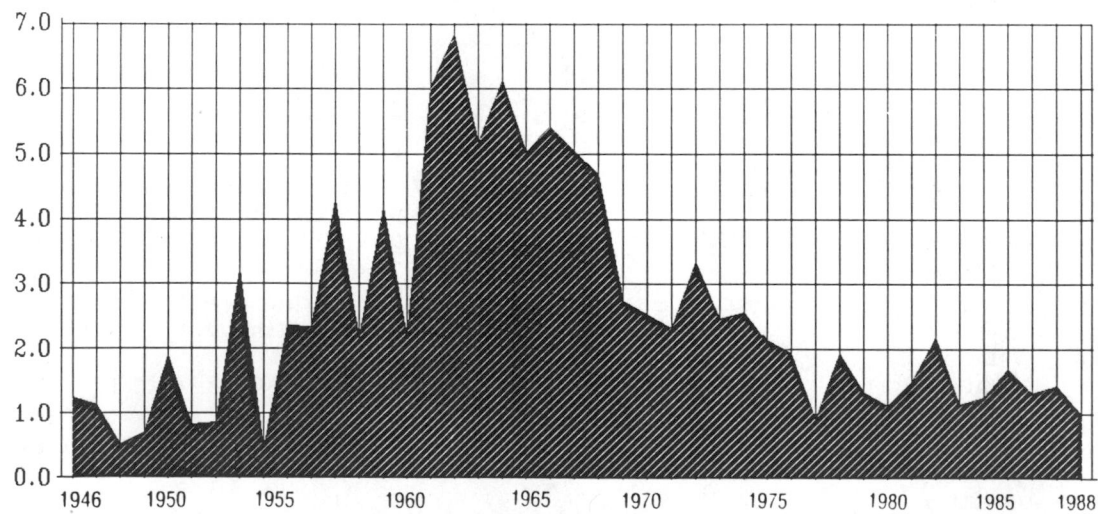

1. Deflated using Export Price Index in 1970 U.S. dollars.

SOURCE: Table 3527.

Figure 35:3

AVERAGE YEARLY ANNOUNCED TOTAL U.S. ASSISTANCE, 20 L,[1] 1946–88

(M US)

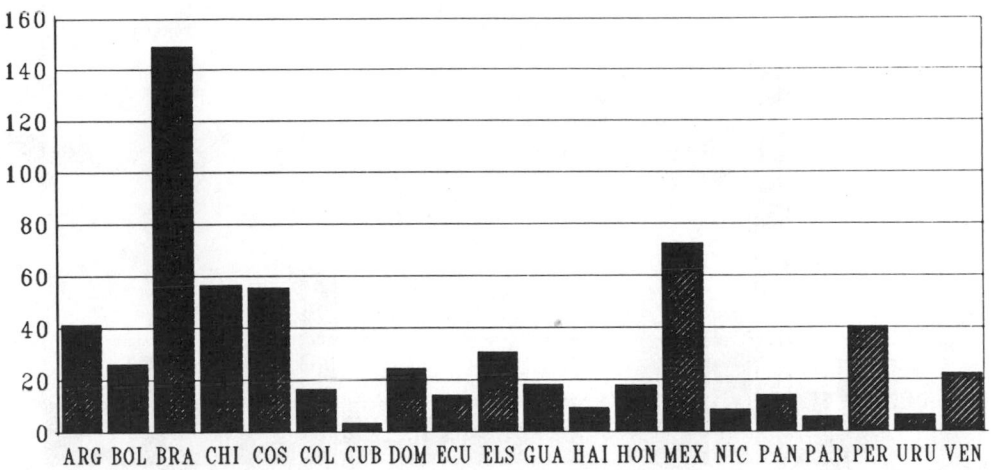

1. Deflated using Export Price Index in 1970 U.S. dollars.

SOURCE: Calculated from Table 3524.

Figure 35:4

AVERAGE YEARLY PER CAPITA ANNOUNCED TOTAL U.S. ASSISTANCE, 20 L,[1] 1946–88

(US)

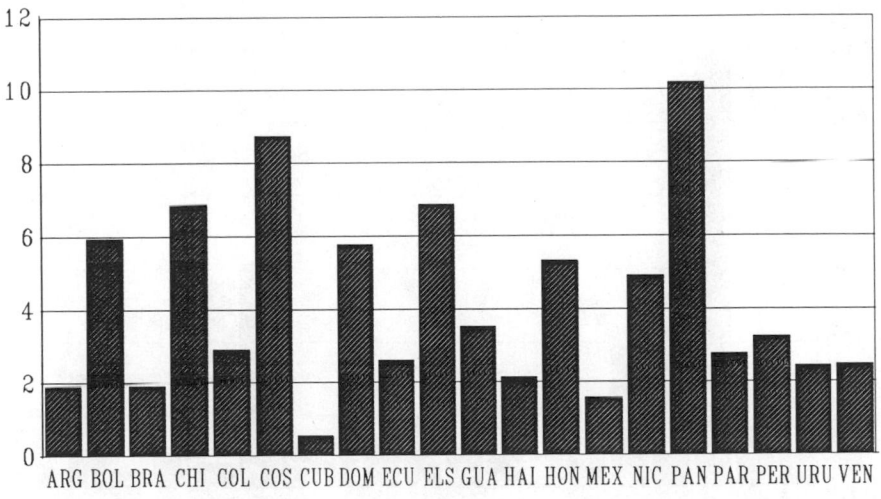

1. Deflated using Export Price Index in 1970 U.S. dollars.

SOURCE: Table 3500.

Figure 35:5

CUMULATIVE ANNOUNCED TOTAL U.S. ASSISTANCE, 20 L,[1] 1946–88

(M US)

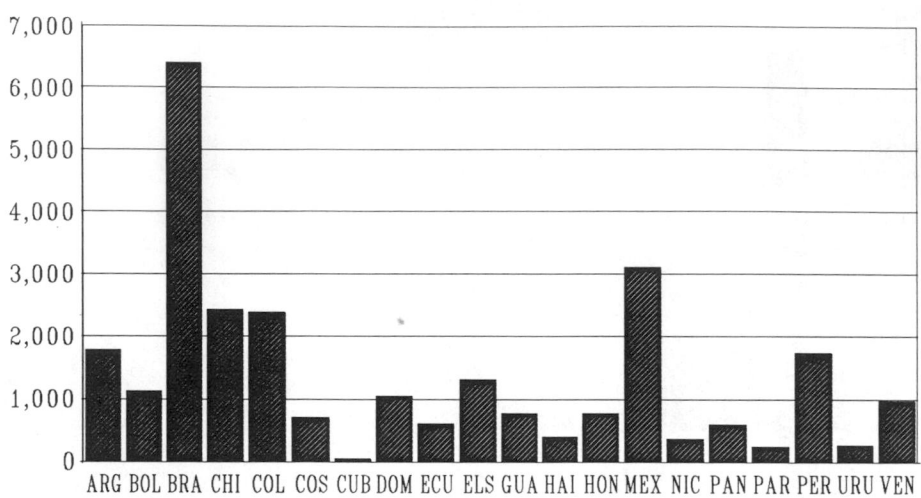

1. Deflated using Export Price Index in 1970 U.S. dollars.

SOURCE: Table 3501.

Figure 35:6

CUMULATIVE ANNOUNCED U.S. ECONOMIC ASSISTANCE, 20 L,[1] 1946–88

(M US)

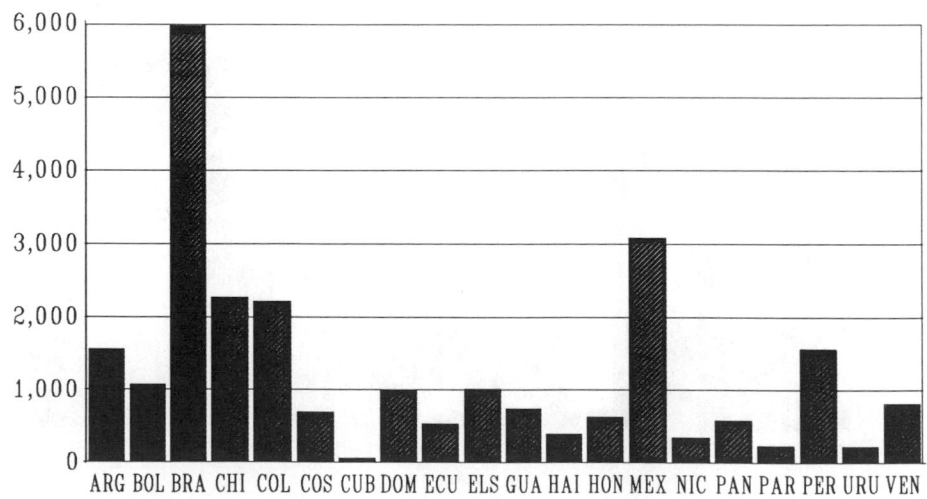

1. Deflated using Export Price Index in 1970 U.S. dollars.

SOURCE: Table 3502.

Figure 35:7

CUMULATIVE ANNOUNCED U.S. MILITARY ASSISTANCE, 20 L,[1] 1946−88
(M US)

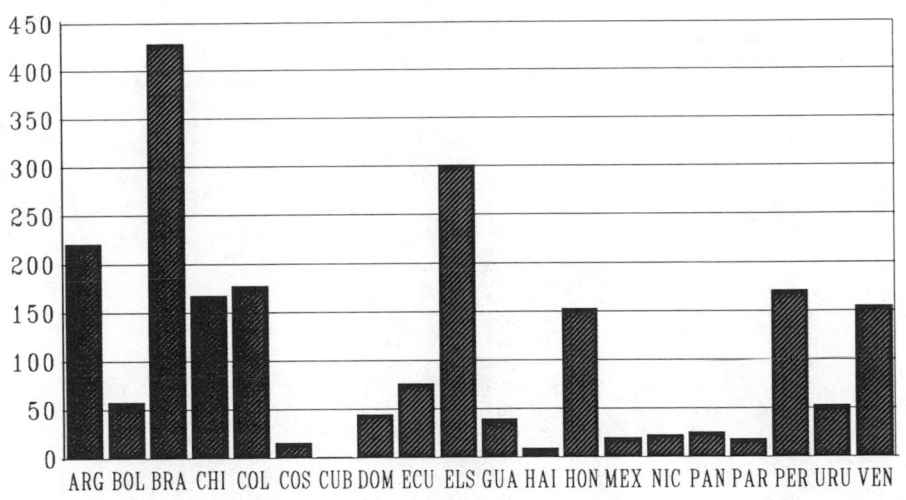

1. Deflated using Export Price Index in 1970 U.S. dollars.

SOURCE: Table 3503.

Figure 35:8

PERCENTAGE OF ANNOUNCED TOTAL U.S. ASSISTANCE TO LATIN AMERICA, 20 L, 1946−88
(%)

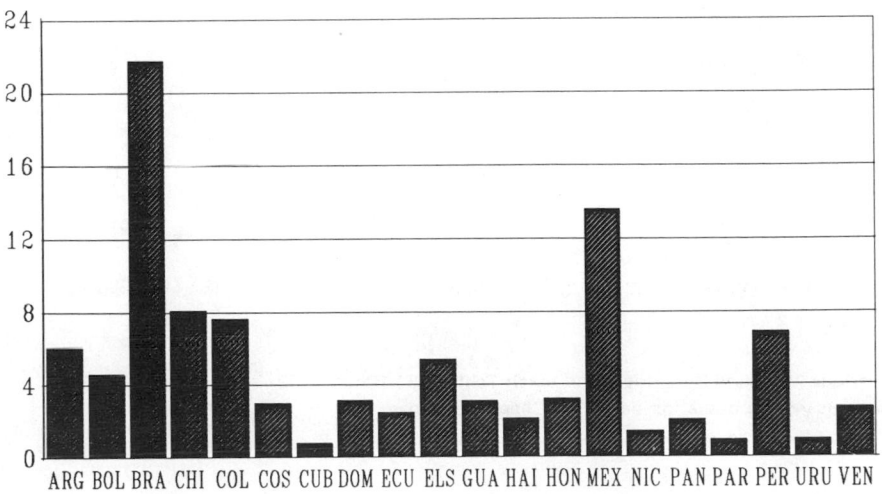

SOURCE: Table 3530.

Table 3504

ARGENTINA: ANNOUNCED AUTHORIZED U.S. ASSISTANCE, NOMINAL AND DEFLATED,[1] 1946–88

		Economic Assistance Nominal (M US)				Economic Total (M US)		Military Total (M US)		Total (M US)		Economic + Military Per Capita (US)
Year	A. Population (M)	B. USAID	C. FFP	D. EXP/IMP	E. Other	F. Nominal (B+C+D+E)	G. Deflated (F/EPI = 100)	H. Nominal	I. Deflated (H/EPI = 100)	J. Nominal (F+H)	K. Deflated (G+I)	L. Deflated (K/A)
1946	15.65	0	0	0	0	0	0	0	0	0	0	0
1947	15.93	0	0	.2	0	.2	.3	0	0	.2	.3	.02
1948	16.27	0	0	0	0	0	0	0	0	0	0	0
1949	16.66	0	0	0	0	0	0	0	0	0	0	0
1950	17.07	0	0	96.5	0	96.5	142.3	0	0	96.5	142.3	8.34
1951	17.48	0	0	5.0	0	5.0	6.4	0	0	5.0	6.4	.37
1952	17.70	0	0	0	0	0	0	0	0	0	0	0
1953	17.96	0	0	0	0	0	0	0	0	0	0	0
1954	18.24	0	0	0	0	0	0	0	0	0	0	0
1955	18.53	0	2.3	60.0	0	62.3	81.2	0	0	62.3	81.2	4.38
1956	18.80	.1	16.0	0	0	16.1	20.1	0	0	16.1	20.1	1.07
1957	19.10	0	0	100.0	0	100.0	121.7	0	0	100.0	121.7	6.37
1958	19.38	.1	0	0	0	.1	.1	0	0	.1	.1	.01
1959	19.66	25.2	16.5	129.2	0	170.9	210.0	0	0	170.9	210.0	10.68
1960	19.92	.8	0	0	0	.8	1.0	.1	.1	.9	1.1	.06
1961	20.24	6.9	0	62.0	0	68.9	82.5	10.7	12.8	79.6	95.3	4.71
1962	20.54	21.9	0	51.9	5.0	78.8	94.9	31.8	38.3	110.6	133.3	6.49
1963	20.85	99.3	0	3.6	30.0	132.9	160.1	1.6	1.9	134.5	162.0	7.77
1964	21.17	9.5	0	1.4	0	10.9	13.0	2.0	2.4	12.9	15.4	.73
1965	22.18	(16.3)	0	22.7	3.5	9.9	11.5	6.3	7.3	16.2	18.7	.85
1966	22.49	(6.3)	0	29.1	5.0	27.8	31.2	6.4	7.2	34.2	38.4	1.71
1967	22.80	1.3	0	1.2	0	2.5	2.8	10.3	11.3	12.8	14.1	.62
1968	23.11	(8.9)	0	41.0	0	32.1	34.9	13.7	14.9	45.8	49.7	2.15
1969	23.43	.9	0	58.4	0	59.3	62.6	17.7	18.7	77.0	81.2	3.47
1970	23.75	.9	0	22.4	0	23.3	23.3	10.6	10.6	33.9	33.9	1.43
1971	24.07	.5	0	38.7	0	39.2	38.0	16.5	16.0	55.7	54.0	2.24
1972	24.39	0	0	44.7	0	44.7	42.0	20.3	19.1	65.0	61.0	2.50
1973	24.82	0	0	30.1	0	30.1	24.3	12.1	9.8	42.2	34.0	1.37
1974	25.22	0	0	41.2	0	41.2	26.0	23.0	14.5	64.2	40.5	1.61
1975	26.05	0	0	64.7	.1	64.8	36.6	30.1	17.0	94.9	53.6	2.06
1976	26.48	0	0	5.2	0	5.2	2.8	34.4	18.8	39.6	21.6	.82
1977	26.91	0	0	15.5	.1	15.6	8.2	.7	.4	16.3	8.6	.32
1978	27.35	0	0	27.4	0	27.4	13.5	0	0	27.4	13.5	.49
1979	27.79	0	0	32.7	.1	32.8	14.2	0	0	32.8	14.2	.51
1980	28.24	0	0	79.2	0	79.2	30.3	0	0	79.2	30.3	1.07
1981	28.69	0	0	82.6	0	82.6	28.9	0	0	82.6	28.9	1.01
1982	29.16	0	0	551.0	.1	551.1	190.7	0	0	551.1	190.7	6.54
1983	29.63	0	0	0	0	0	0	0	0	0	0	0
1984	30.10	0	0	0	.1	.1	0	0	0	.1	0	0
1985	30.56	0	0	0	0	0	0	0	0	0	0	0
1986	31.03	0	0	0	0	0	0	0	0	0	0	0
1987	31.50	0	0	0	2.4	2.4	.8	0	0	2.4	.8	.03
1988	31.96	0	0	12.8	0	12.8	4.0	.1	0	12.9	4.0	.12
Total		135.9	34.8	1,710.4	46.4	1,927.5	1,560.2	248.4	221.1	2,175.9	1,781.3	1.9[a]

1. Deflated using Export Price Index (Table 3331) in 1970 U.S. dollars.

a. Per capita average, 1946–88.

SOURCE: USAID–OLG, various years (see Data Sources in text); Table 3331 (Chapter 33, above); IMF-IFS-SY, various years; population data from Chapter 6, above.

Figure 35:9

ARGENTINA: YEARLY ANNOUNCED TOTAL U.S. ASSISTANCE,[1] 1946–88

(M US)

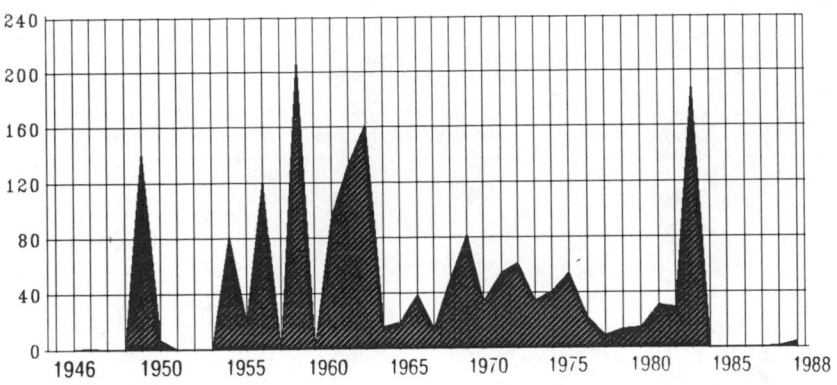

SOURCE: Table 3504.

Figure 35:10

ARGENTINA: YEARLY PER CAPITA ANNOUNCED TOTAL U.S. ASSISTANCE,[1] 1946–88

(US)

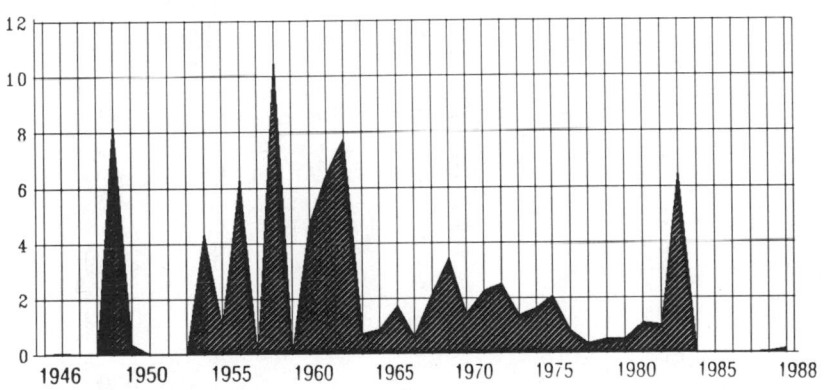

SOURCE: Table 3504.

Figure 35:11

ARGENTINA: PER CAPITA ASSISTANCE COMPARED TO AVERAGE YEARLY LATIN AMERICA PER CAPITA ASSISTANCE,[1] 1946–88

(US)

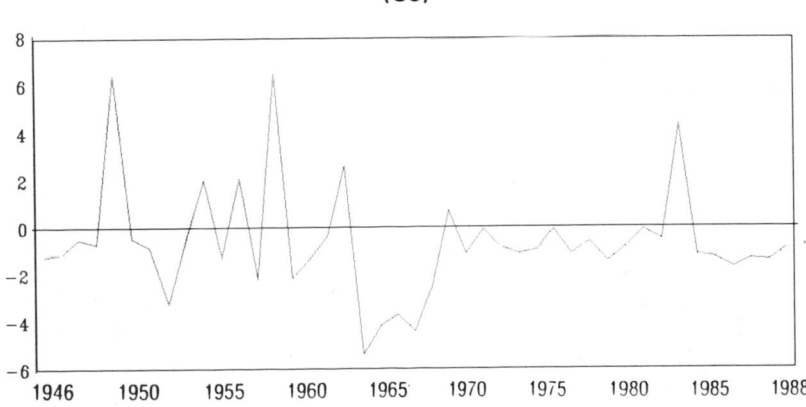

SOURCE: Table 3529.

Table 3505

BOLIVIA: ANNOUNCED AUTHORIZED U.S. ASSISTANCE, NOMINAL AND DEFLATED,[1] 1946–88

| Year | A. Population (M) | Economic Assistance Nominal (M US) | | | | Economic Total (M US) | | Military Total (M US) | | Economic + Military Total (M US) | | Per Capita (US) |
		B. USAID	C. FFP	D. EXP/IMP	E. Other	F. Nominal (B+C+D+E)	G. Deflated (F/EPI = 100)	H. Nominal	I. Deflated (H/EPI = 100)	J. Nominal (F+H)	K. Deflated (G+I)	L. Deflated (K/A)
1946	2.88	0	0	0	.4	.4	.7	0	0	.4	.7	.24
1947	2.92	0	0	3.0	.4	3.4	4.8	0	0	3.4	4.8	1.65
1948	2.95	0	0	0	.4	.4	.5	0	0	.4	.5	.18
1949	2.96	0	0	.3	.4	.7	1.0	0	0	.7	1.0	.34
1950	3.01	0	0	16.0	.5	16.5	24.3	0	0	16.5	24.3	8.09
1951	3.07	0	0	0	.5	.5	.6	0	0	.5	.6	:21
1952	3.13	1.5	0	.2	0	1.7	2.2	0	0	1.7	2.2	.70
1953	3.19	1.3	0	0	0	1.3	1.7	0	0	1.3	1.7	.53
1954	3.26	7.5	.3	0	8.0	15.8	20.9	0	0	15.8	20.9	6.40
1955	3.34	11.0	16.0	4.7	0	31.7	41.3	0	0	31.7	41.3	12.37
1956	3.42	25.4	2.7	0	0	28.1	35.1	0	0	28.1	35.1	10.27
1957	3.50	23.3	4.0	0	0	27.3	33.2	0	0	27.3	33.2	9.49
1958	3.59	22.4	0	0	0	22.4	27.5	0	0	22.4	27.5	7.67
1959	3.70	24.5	.4	0	0	24.9	30.6	0	0	24.9	30.6	8.27
1960	3.82	14.8	.2	0	0	15.0	18.3	0	0	15.0	18.3	4.79
1961	3.92	24.1	2.9	0	3.8	30.8	36.9	.4	.5	31.2	37.4	9.53
1962	4.02	31.8	4.6	0	.9	37.3	44.9	2.2	2.7	39.5	47.6	11.84
1963	4.12	35.5	21.0	0	11.2	67.7	81.6	2.4	2.9	70.1	84.5	20.50
1964	4.23	58.4	14.6	0	3.3	76.3	91.1	3.2	3.8	79.5	94.9	22.43
1965	4.33	2.4	4.6	0	5.5	12.5	14.5	1.9	2.2	14.4	16.7	3.85
1966	4.45	27.5	6.2	0	2.6	36.3	40.8	2.4	2.7	38.7	43.5	9.77
1967	4.48	14.3	1.5	10.1	2.2	28.1	30.9	2.9	3.2	31.0	34.1	7.62
1968	4.51	7.8	10.6	0	1.7	20.1	21.8	3.5	3.8	23.6	25.6	5.68
1969	4.55	8.0	15.4	8.3	1.5	33.2	35.0	1.6	1.7	34.8	36.7	8.07
1970	4.58	.6	3.2	0	1.4	5.2	5.2	1.2	1.2	6.4	6.4	1.40
1971	4.62	3.7	6.8	0	1.0	11.5	11.2	1.8	1.7	13.3	12.9	2.79
1972	4.64	55.6	4.4	0	0	60.0	56.3	4.8	4.5	64.8	60.8	13.11
1973	4.67	17.0	10.3	0	0	27.3	22.0	4.1	3.3	31.4	25.3	5.42
1974	4.75	38.4	8.3	0	.3	47.0	29.7	7.4	4.7	54.4	34.3	7.23
1975	4.89	20.1	5.1	0	.6	25.8	14.6	7.4	4.2	33.2	18.8	3.84
1976	5.03	24.2	7.4	5.0	1.9	38.5	21.0	13.6	7.4	52.1	28.5	5.66
1977	5.16	35.8	6.7	15.7	12.1	70.3	37.1	3.1	1.6	73.4	38.7	7.51
1978	5.30	34.3	16.5	5.5	14.4	70.7	34.9	.8	.4	71.5	35.3	6.66
1979	5.45	28.9	19.0	0	3.3	51.2	22.2	6.7	2.9	57.9	25.1	4.61
1980	5.60	4.5	24.8	0	.8	30.1	11.5	.3	.1	30.4	11.6	2.07
1981	5.76	2.3	9.5	0	1.0	12.8	4.5	0	0	12.8	4.5	.78
1982	5.92	2.1	16.4	0	1.2	19.7	6.8	0	0	19.7	6.8	1.15
1983	6.08	11.4	49.2	0	2.4	63.0	21.6	0	0	63.0	21.6	3.55
1984	6.25	52.3	22.1	0	3.6	78.0	26.3	.1	0	78.1	26.4	4.22
1985	6.43	18.4	29.5	0	2.7	50.6	17.2	3.4	1.2	54.0	18.4	2.86
1986	6.55	38.4	32.2	0	6.9	77.5	26.3	1.5	.5	79.0	26.8	4.10
1987	6.80	28.7	36.6	0	12.7	78.0	25.8	1.2	.4	79.2	26.2	3.86
1988	6.99		37.5	34.8	23.3	95.6	29.6	.4	.1	96.0	29.7	4.25
Total		758.2	450.5	103.6	132.9	1,445.2	1,064.2	78.3	57.7	1,523.5	1,121.9	5.94[a]

1. Deflated using Export Price Index (Table 3331) in 1970 U.S. dollars.

a. Per capita average, 1946–88.

SOURCE: USAID-OLG, various years (see Data Sources in text); Table 3331 (Chapter 33, above); IMF-IFS-SY, various years; population data from Chapter 6, above.

Figure 35:12

BOLIVIA: YEARLY ANNOUNCED TOTAL U.S. ASSISTANCE,[1] 1946–88

(M US)

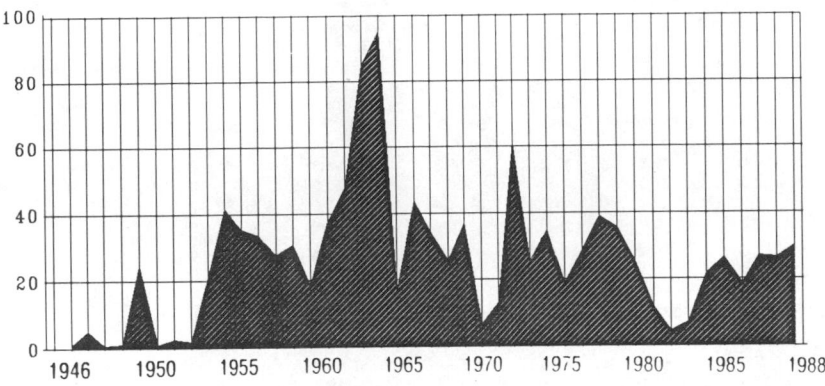

SOURCE: Table 3505.

Figure 35:13

BOLIVIA: YEARLY PER CAPITA ANNOUNCED TOTAL U.S. ASSISTANCE,[1] 1946–88

(US)

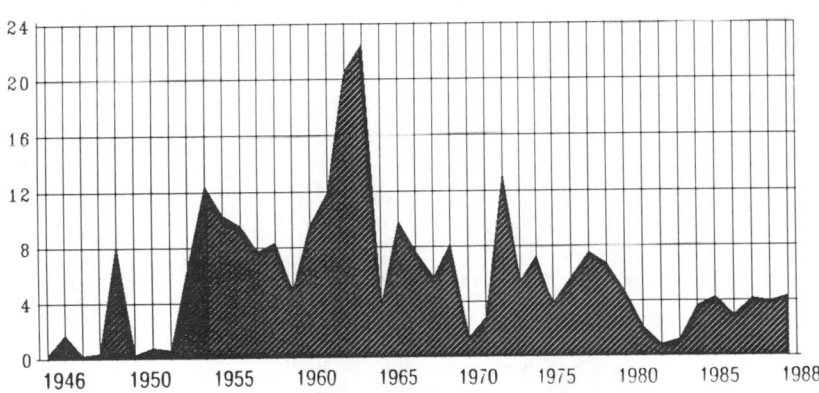

SOURCE: Table 3505.

Figure 35:14

BOLIVIA: PER CAPITA ASSISTANCE COMPARED TO AVERAGE YEARLY LATIN AMERICA PER CAPITA ASSISTANCE,[1] 1946–88

(US)

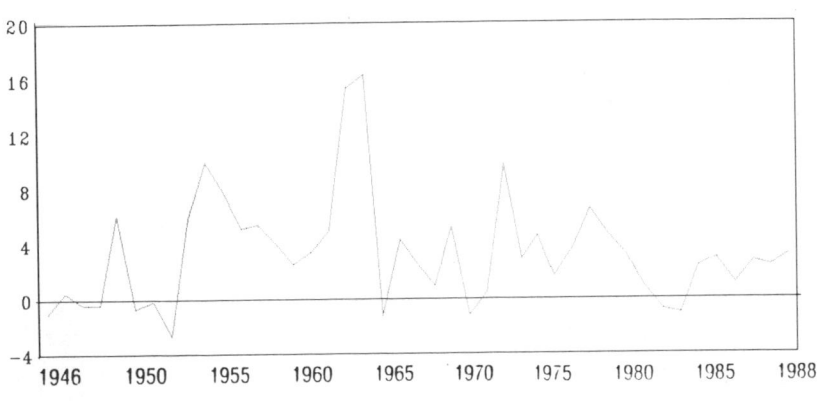

SOURCE: Table 3529.

Table 3506

BRAZIL: ANNOUNCED AUTHORIZED U.S. ASSISTANCE, NOMINAL AND DEFLATED,[1] 1946–88

Year	A. Population (M)	Economic Assistance Nominal (M US)				Economic Total (M US)		Military Total (M US)		Economic + Military Total (M US)		Per Capita (US)
		B. USAID	C. FFP	D. EXP/IMP	E. Other	F. Nominal (B+C+D+E)	G. Deflated (F/EPI = 100)	H. Nominal	I. Deflated (H/EPI = 100)	J. Nominal (F+H)	K. Deflated (G+I)	L. Deflated (K/A)
1946	46.97	0	0	39.6	17.2	56.8	96.3	0	0	56.8	96.3	2.05
1947	48.16	0	0	21.8	1.3	23.1	32.8	0	0	23.1	32.8	.68
1948	49.42	0	0	0	1.4	1.4	1.9	0	0	1.4	1.9	.04
1949	50.76	0	0	9.6	.8	10.4	14.9	0	0	10.4	14.9	.29
1950	52.18	0	0	14.4	.8	15.2	22.4	0	0	15.2	22.4	.43
1951	53.68	0	0	26.1	1.2	27.3	35.1	0	0	27.3	35.1	.65
1952	55.10	2.6	0	56.7	0	59.3	76.7	0	0	59.3	76.7	1.39
1953	56.74	3.2	0	370.6	15.0	388.8	504.9	0	0	388.8	504.9	8.90
1954	58.44	2.5	0	1.9	.1	4.5	5.9	0	0	4.5	5.9	.10
1955	60.18	3.0	2.5	46.6	.3	52.4	68.3	0	0	52.4	68.3	1.14
1956	61.98	3.6	35.6	55.1	.5	94.8	118.5	0	0	94.8	118.5	1.91
1957	63.83	4.5	119.8	195.0	6.6	325.9	396.5	6.9	8.4	332.8	404.9	6.34
1958	65.74	4.0	3.6	18.7	0	26.3	32.3	0	0	26.3	32.3	.49
1959	67.70	5.8	2.9	123.6	.5	132.8	163.1	12.4	15.2	145.2	178.4	2.63
1960	69.72	7.2	1.8	6.9	0	15.9	19.4	26.4	32.2	42.3	51.6	.74
1961	71.94	7.5	92.0	204.9	0	304.4	364.6	23.9	28.6	328.3	393.2	5.47
1962	74.17	84.5	70.1	0	47.9	202.5	244.0	42.1	50.7	244.6	294.7	3.97
1963	76.53	86.3	50.9	0	7.4	144.6	174.2	10.0	12.0	154.6	186.3	2.43
1964	78.73	178.6	197.2	0	6.5	382.3	456.2	16.6	19.8	398.9	476.0	6.05
1965	81.01	230.7	23.6	6.0	11.3	271.6	314.4	14.3	16.6	285.9	330.9	4.08
1966	82.93	241.7	118.5	17.2	6.2	383.6	431.0	22.6	25.4	406.2	456.4	5.50
1967	85.24	212.6	22.0	31.3	3.5	269.4	296.7	16.9	18.6	286.3	315.3	3.70
1968	87.62	187.7	87.5	50.8	3.9	329.9	358.2	26.8	29.1	356.7	387.3	4.42
1969	90.07	−11.7	10.3	29.1	3.5	31.2	32.9	19.0	20.0	50.2	53.0	.59
1970	92.52	61.2	68.6	65.6	3.0	198.4	198.4	13.0	13.0	211.4	211.4	2.28
1971	95.17	79.4	40.6	74.0	2.9	196.9	191.0	10.3	10.0	207.2	201.0	2.11
1972	97.85	12.1	5.7	299.8	4.7	322.3	302.6	20.8	19.5	343.1	322.2	3.29
1973	99.92	40.6	9.6	142.3	7.0	199.5	160.8	17.7	14.3	217.2	175.0	1.75
1974	102.40	5.0	6.2	325.7	7.0	343.9	217.1	52.7	33.3	396.6	250.4	2.45
1975	104.94	3.1	8.4	256.5	3.8	271.8	153.6	65.4	36.9	337.2	190.5	1.82
1976	107.54	.9	2.2	116.9	3.4	123.4	67.4	44.7	24.4	168.1	91.9	.85
1977	110.21	.5	1.3	47.3	2.5	51.6	27.2	.1	.1	51.7	27.3	.25
1978	112.94	0	.1	104.7	2.0	106.8	52.7	0	0	106.8	52.7	.47
1979	115.74	0	.6	212.6	48.8	262.0	113.6	0	0	262.0	113.6	.98
1980	121.27	0	1.4	57.7	31.5	90.6	34.6	0	0	90.6	34.6	.29
1981	124.02	0	.6	115.9	.5	117.0	40.9	0	0	117.0	40.9	.33
1982	126.81	0	.3	91.0	.4	91.7	31.7	0	0	91.7	31.7	.25
1983	129.66	0	.1	29.3	1.3	30.7	10.5	0	0	30.7	10.5	.08
1984	132.58	0	0	28.5	0	28.5	9.6	0	0	28.5	9.6	.07
1985	135.56	0	0	37.4	.8	38.2	13.0	0	0	38.2	13.0	.10
1986	138.49	0	0	124.4	.7	125.1	42.5	0	0	125.1	42.5	.31
1987	141.45	0	2.1	0	121.9	124.0	41.1	0	0	124.0	41.1	.29
1988	144.43	0	.1	10.7	6.0	16.8	5.2	.1	0	16.9	5.2	.04
Total		1,457.1	986.2	3,466.2	384.1	6,293.6	5,974.9	462.7	428.3	6,756.3	6,403.2	1.91[a]

1. Deflated using Export Price Index (Table 3331) in 1970 U.S. dollars.

a. Per capita average, 1946–88.

SOURCE: USAID-OLG, various years (see Data Sources in text); Table 3331 (Chapter 33, above); IMF-IFS-SY, various years; population data from Chapter 6, above.

Figure 35:15

BRAZIL: YEARLY ANNOUNCED TOTAL U.S. ASSISTANCE,[1] 1946–88

(M US)

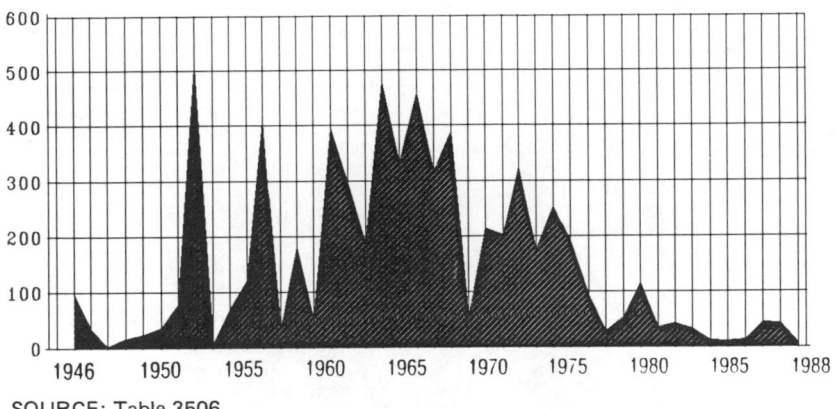

SOURCE: Table 3506.

Figure 35:16

BRAZIL: YEARLY PER CAPITA ANNOUNCED TOTAL U.S. ASSISTANCE,[1] 1946–88

(US)

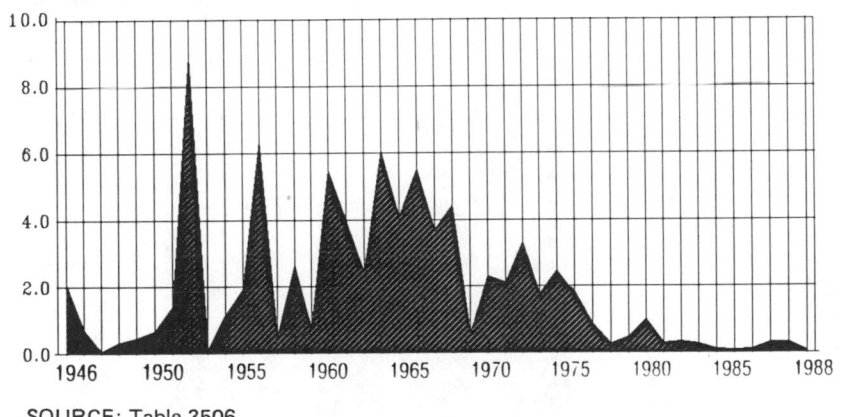

SOURCE: Table 3506.

Figure 35:17

BRAZIL: PER CAPITA ASSISTANCE COMPARED TO AVERAGE YEARLY
LATIN AMERICA PER CAPITA ASSISTANCE,[1] 1946–88

(US)

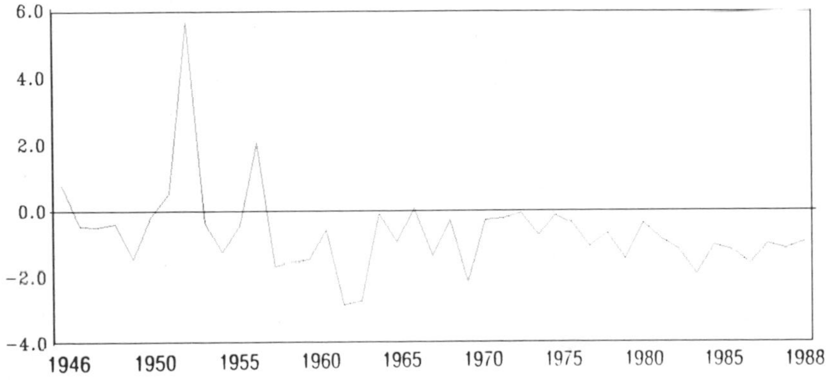

SOURCE: Table 3529.

Table 3507

CHILE: ANNOUNCED AUTHORIZED U.S. ASSISTANCE, NOMINAL AND DEFLATED,[1] 1946–88

Year	A. Population (M)	Economic Assistance Nominal (M US)				Economic Total (M US)		Military Total (M US)		Total (M US)		Economic + Military Per Capita (US)
		B. USAID	C. FFP	D. EXP/IMP	E. Other	F. Nominal (B+C+D+E)	G. Deflated (F/EPI = 100)	H. Nominal	I. Deflated (H/EPI = 100)	J. Nominal (F+H)	K. Deflated (G+I)	L. Deflated (K/A)
1946	5.64	0	0	31.7	1.4	33.1	56.1	0	0	33.1	56.1	9.95
1947	5.75	0	0	10.4	1.7	12.1	17.2	0	0	12.1	17.2	2.99
1948	5.85	0	0	0	.9	.9	1.2	0	0	.9	1.2	.21
1949	5.96	0	0	21.4	.4	21.8	31.3	0	0	21.8	31.3	5.26
1950	6.07	0	0	27.9	.3	28.2	41.6	0	0	28.2	41.6	6.85
1951	6.21	0	0	1.8	.4	2.2	2.8	0	0	2.2	2.8	.46
1952	6.30	1.1	0	11.2	0	12.3	15.9	0	0	12.3	15.9	2.53
1953	6.46	1.3	0	0	0	1.3	1.7	0	0	1.3	1.7	.26
1954	6.62	1.4	0	0	0	1.4	1.8	0	0	1.4	1.8	.28
1955	6.79	2.1	4.1	0	0	6.2	8.1	0	0	6.2	8.1	1.19
1956	6.96	2.2	27.2	0	0	29.4	36.8	0	0	29.4	36.8	5.28
1957	7.14	3.3	1.1	43.9	0	48.3	58.8	0	0	48.3	58.8	8.23
1958	7.32	2.8	15.0	25.0	0	42.8	52.6	0	0	42.8	52.6	7.18
1959	7.49	3.2	11.6	29.0	0	43.8	53.8	5.9	7.2	49.7	61.1	8.15
1960	7.58	18.4	8.7	16.9	.5	44.5	54.3	2.7	3.3	47.2	57.6	7.60
1961	7.76	31.2	30.4	77.0	.1	138.7	166.1	9.0	10.8	147.7	176.9	22.79
1962	7.95	142.4	23.8	46.4	19.7	232.3	279.9	12.3	14.8	244.6	294.7	37.07
1963	8.14	40.4	26.5	15.5	5.8	88.2	106.3	25.1	30.2	113.3	136.5	16.77
1964	8.33	78.5	30.5	16.5	6.0	131.5	156.9	9.7	11.6	141.2	168.5	20.23
1965	8.51	99.0	12.9	8.2	8.5	128.6	148.8	8.0	9.3	136.6	158.1	18.58
1966	8.68	85.6	17.8	.1	4.2	107.7	121.0	8.5	9.6	116.2	130.6	15.04
1967	8.85	12.0	8.0	262.2	2.4	284.6	313.4	5.4	5.9	290.0	319.4	36.09
1968	9.03	53.9	36.9	14.5	2.0	107.3	116.5	7.6	8.3	114.9	124.8	13.82
1969	9.20	34.6	35.0	37.3	.9	107.8	113.7	4.6	4.9	112.4	118.6	12.89
1970	9.37	17.2	7.6	3.3	1.1	29.2	29.2	12.8	12.8	42.0	42.0	4.48
1971	9.53	1.5	6.3	0	0	7.8	7.6	5.8	5.6	13.6	13.2	1.38
1972	9.70	1.0	5.9	1.6	.5	9.0	8.5	10.9	10.2	19.9	18.7	1.93
1973	9.86	.8	2.5	3.1	.5	6.9	5.6	15.0	12.1	21.9	17.6	1.79
1974	10.03	5.3	3.2	57.0	42.4	107.9	68.1	15.9	10.0	123.8	78.2	7.79
1975	10.20	31.3	62.4	23.0	11.2	127.9	72.3	.7	.4	128.6	72.7	7.12
1976	10.37	21.2	61.1	1.8	10.6	94.7	51.7	0	0	94.7	51.7	4.99
1977	10.55	.6	31.5	0	1.1	33.2	17.5	0	0	33.2	17.5	1.66
1978	10.73	.2	5.6	0	47.3	53.1	26.2	0	0	53.1	26.2	2.44
1979	10.92	.3	9.0	0	4.3	13.6	5.9	0	0	13.6	5.9	.54
1980	11.10	.1	5.0	0	5.1	10.2	3.9	0	0	10.2	3.9	.35
1981	11.29	0	7.7	0	4.4	12.1	4.2	0	0	12.1	4.2	.37
1982	11.49	0	2.3	0	4.4	6.7	2.3	0	0	6.7	2.3	.20
1983	11.68	0	1.0	0	1.8	2.8	1.0	0	0	2.8	1.0	.08
1984	11.88	0	0	0	1.7	1.7	.6	0	0	1.7	.6	.05
1985	12.07	0	0	1.3	1.3	2.6	.9	0	0	2.6	.9	.07
1986	12.33	0	0	0	2.2	2.2	.7	0	0	2.2	.7	.06
1987	12.54	0	0	0	1.1	1.1	.4	0	0	1.1	.4	.03
1988	12.75	.4	0	1.7	1.0	3.1	1.0	0	0	3.1	1.0	.08
Total		693.3	500.6	789.7	197.2	2,180.8	2,264.1	159.9	167.0	2,340.7	2,431.2	6.86[a]

1. Deflated using Export Price Index (Table 3331) in 1970 U.S. dollars.

a. Per capita average, 1946–88.

SOURCE: USAID–OLG, various years (see Data Sources in text); Table 3331 (Chapter 33, above); IMF-IFS-SY, various years; population data from Chapter 6, above.

Figure 35:18

CHILE: YEARLY ANNOUNCED TOTAL U.S. ASSISTANCE,[1] 1946–88

(M US)

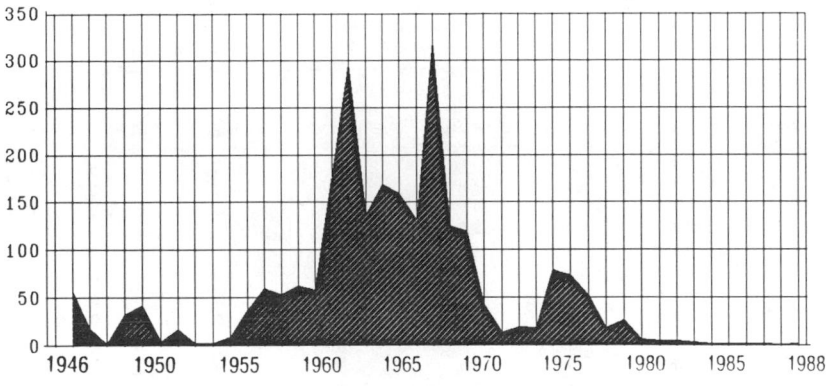

SOURCE: Table 3507.

Figure 35:19

CHILE: YEARLY PER CAPITA ANNOUNCED TOTAL U.S. ASSISTANCE,[1] 1946–88

(US)

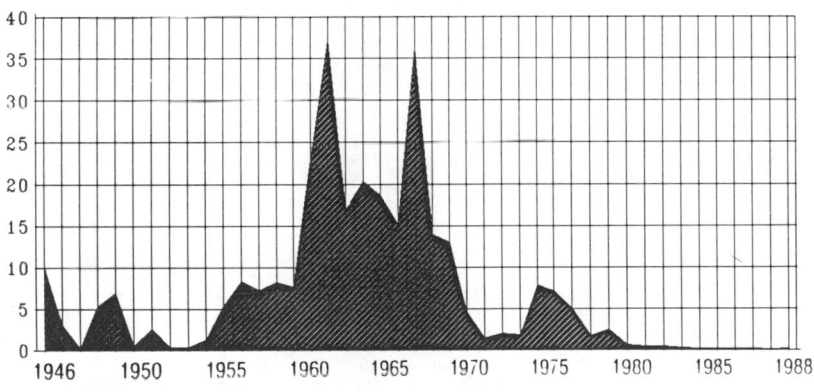

SOURCE: Table 3507.

Figure 35:20

CHILE: PER CAPITA ASSISTANCE COMPARED TO AVERAGE YEARLY
LATIN AMERICA PER CAPITA ASSISTANCE,[1] 1946–88

(US)

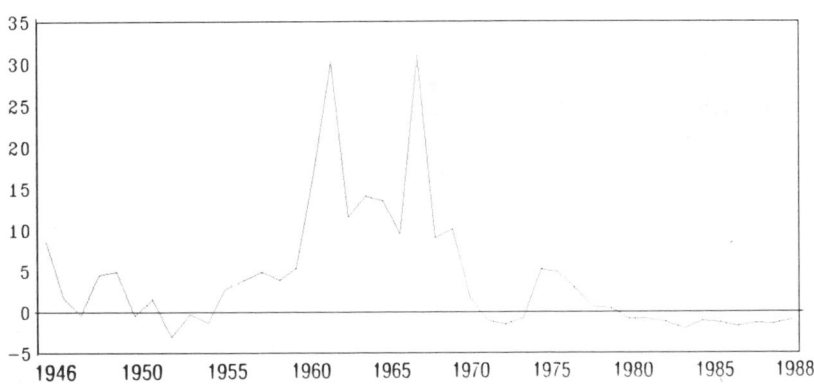

SOURCE: Table 3529.

Table 3508

COLOMBIA: ANNOUNCED AUTHORIZED U.S. ASSISTANCE, NOMINAL AND DEFLATED,[1] 1946–88

Year	A. Population (M)	Economic Assistance Nominal (M US)				Economic Total (M US)		Military Total (M US)		Economic + Military		
		B. USAID	C. FFP	D. EXP/IMP	E. Other	F. Nominal (B+C+D+E)	G. Deflated (F/EPI = 100)	H. Nominal	I. Deflated (H/EPI = 100)	J. Nominal (F+H)	K. Deflated (G+I)	L. Deflated (K/A)
1946	10.53	0	0	0	.5	.5	.8	0	0	.5	.8	.08
1947	10.80	0	0	0	1.1	1.1	1.6	0	0	1.1	1.6	.14
1948	10.85	0	0	11.0	.2	11.2	15.0	0	0	11.2	15.0	1.38
1949	11.09	0	0	3.6	.2	3.8	5.5	0	0	3.8	5.5	.49
1950	11.33	0	0	2.2	.3	2.5	3.7	0	0	2.5	3.7	.33
1951	11.62	0	0	2.1	.3	2.4	3.1	0	0	2.4	3.1	.27
1952	11.81	.7	0	2.6	0	3.3	4.3	0	0	3.3	4.3	.36
1953	12.07	1.0	0	4.5	0	5.5	7.1	0	0	5.5	7.1	.59
1954	12.34	1.2	.2	0	0	1.4	1.8	0	0	1.4	1.8	.15
1955	12.97	1.4	3.1	.6	0	5.1	6.6	0	0	5.1	6.6	.51
1956	13.59	1.3	10.0	.2	0	11.5	14.4	0	0	11.5	14.4	1.06
1957	14.03	1.2	15.1	0	0	16.3	19.8	0	0	16.3	19.8	1.41
1958	14.48	1.3	10.5	83.7	0	95.5	117.3	0	0	95.5	117.3	8.10
1959	14.94	1.7	4.0	0	0	5.7	7.0	2.6	3.2	8.3	10.2	.68
1960	15.42	1.9	26.2	25.5	0	53.6	65.4	2.7	3.3	56.3	68.7	4.46
1961	15.91	28.2	4.9	56.6	.2	89.9	107.7	11.2	13.4	101.1	121.1	7.61
1962	16.42	37.9	13.8	0	24.1	75.8	91.3	6.0	7.2	81.8	98.6	6.00
1963	16.94	93.4	18.4	3.4	12.2	127.4	153.5	8.4	10.1	135.8	163.6	9.66
1964	17.48	74.2	13.5	23.2	13.4	124.3	148.3	6.6	7.9	130.9	156.2	8.94
1965	18.04	3.6	11.4	6.8	14.0	35.8	41.4	5.7	6.6	41.5	48.0	2.66
1966	18.47	75.4	20.5	3.4	5.2	104.5	117.4	8.3	9.3	112.8	126.7	6.86
1967	18.96	104.3	15.2	20.4	3.6	143.5	158.0	7.9	8.7	151.4	166.7	8.79
1968	19.46	76.2	22.5	5.9	3.0	107.6	116.8	12.2	13.2	119.8	130.1	6.68
1969	19.98	99.1	7.5	19.8	2.2	128.6	135.7	6.7	7.1	135.3	142.7	7.14
1970	20.53	74.1	38.2	13.4	1.5	127.2	127.2	3.9	3.9	131.1	131.1	6.39
1971	21.09	84.0	12.1	6.5	1.6	104.2	101.1	5.9	5.7	110.1	106.8	5.06
1972	21.67	92.6	21.0	18.7	2.4	134.7	126.5	8.6	8.1	143.3	134.6	6.21
1973	22.34	76.9	17.6	.3	2.1	96.9	78.1	10.6	8.5	107.5	86.6	3.88
1974	22.98	40.1	10.1	19.3	3.3	72.8	46.0	.6	.4	73.4	46.3	2.02
1975	23.64	14.0	11.5	3.5	3.0	32.0	18.1	.7	.4	32.7	18.5	.78
1976	24.33	20.6	13.7	6.2	7.6	48.1	26.3	20.8	11.4	68.9	37.7	1.55
1977	25.05	1.4	5.3	0	2.4	9.1	4.8	.7	.4	9.8	5.2	.21
1978	25.64	0	2.6	30.0	4.7	37.3	18.4	52.2	25.8	89.5	44.2	1.72
1979	26.36	.3	1.6	42.5	7.1	51.5	22.3	13.0	5.6	64.5	28.0	1.06
1980	27.09	.3	4.6	23.6	18.3	46.8	17.9	.3	.1	47.1	18.0	.66
1981	26.73	0	0	45.1	5.7	50.8	17.8	.3	.1	51.1	17.9	.67
1982	27.19	0	0	540.3	3.0	543.3	188.0	10.5	3.6	553.8	191.6	7.05
1983	27.52	0	0	3.8	3.9	7.7	2.6	.7	.2	8.4	2.9	.10
1984	28.22	0	0	4.0	8.2	12.2	4.1	25.3	8.5	37.5	12.7	.45
1985	28.62	0	0	130.0	11.3	141.3	48.1	.8	.3	142.1	48.4	1.69
1986	29.19	0	0	0	11.5	11.5	3.9	4.3	1.5	15.8	5.4	.18
1987	29.73	0	0	0	12.0	12.0	4.0	5.1	1.7	17.1	5.7	.19
1988	30.24	0	.1	30.3	10.2	40.6	12.6	4.0	1.2	44.6	13.8	.46
Total		1,008.3	335.2	1,193.0	200.3	2,736.8	2,211.3	246.6	177.5	2,983.4	2,388.9	2.90[a]

1. Deflated using Export Price Index (Table 3331) in 1970 U.S. dollars.

a. Per capita average, 1946–88.

SOURCE: USAID–OLG, various years (see Data Sources in text); Table 3331 (Chapter 33, above); IMF-IFS-SY, various years; population data from Chapter 6, above.

Figure 35:21

COLOMBIA: YEARLY ANNOUNCED TOTAL U.S. ASSISTANCE,[1] 1946–88

(M US)

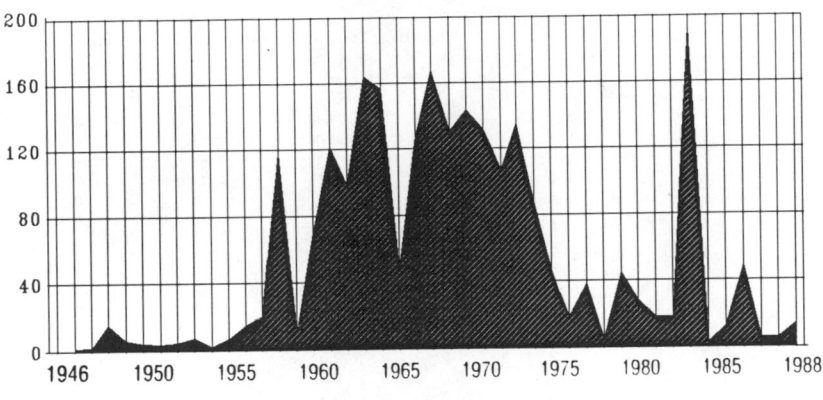

SOURCE: Table 3508.

Figure 35:22

COLOMBIA: YEARLY PER CAPITA ANNOUNCED TOTAL U.S. ASSISTANCE,[1] 1946–88

(US)

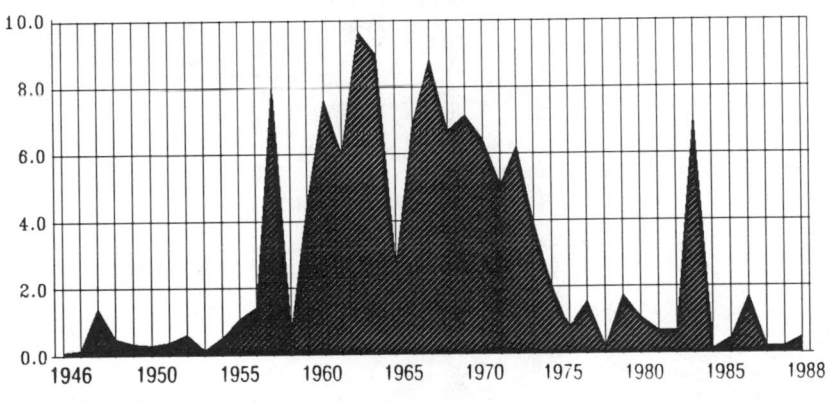

SOURCE: Table 3508.

Figure 35:23

COLOMBIA: PER CAPITA ASSISTANCE COMPARED TO AVERAGE YEARLY LATIN AMERICA PER CAPITA ASSISTANCE,[1] 1946–88

(US)

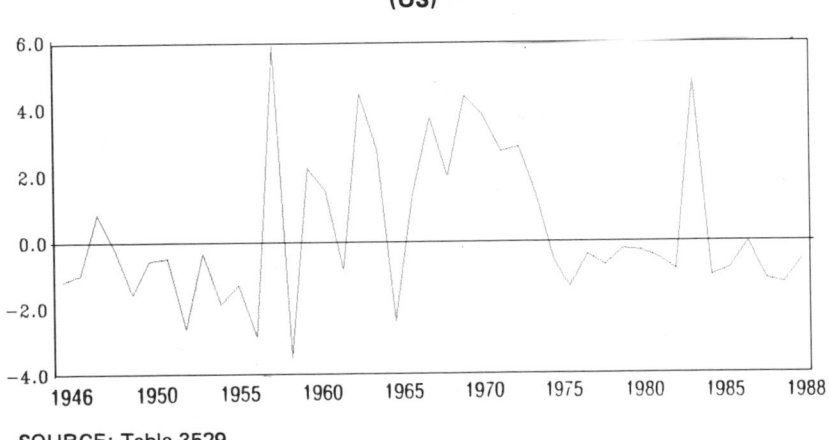

SOURCE: Table 3529.

Table 3509

COSTA RICA: ANNOUNCED AUTHORIZED U.S. ASSISTANCE, NOMINAL AND DEFLATED,[1] 1946–88

Year	A. Population (M)	Economic Assistance Nominal (M US)				Economic Total (M US)		Military Total (M US)		Economic + Military Total (M US)		Per Capita (US)
		B. USAID	C. FFP	D. EXP/IMP	E. Other	F. Nominal (B+C+D+E)	G. Deflated (F/EPI = 100)	H. Nominal	I. Deflated (H/EPI = 100)	J. Nominal (F+H)	K. Deflated (G+I)	L. Deflated (K/A)
1946	.71	0	0	0	2.0	2.0	3.4	0	0	2.0	3.4	4.77
1947	.73	0	0	0	.4	.4	.6	0	0	.4	.6	.78
1948	.75	0	0	0	.2	.2	.3	0	0	.2	.3	.36
1949	.77	0	0	0	.1	.1	.1	0	0	.1	.1	.19
1950	.80	0	0	0	.4	.4	.6	0	0	.4	.6	.74
1951	.83	0	0	0	.7	.7	.9	0	0	.7	.9	1.09
1952	.92	1.3	0	0	.9	2.2	2.8	0	0	2.2	2.8	3.09
1953	.95	.8	0	0	1.7	2.5	3.2	0	0	2.5	3.2	3.42
1954	.99	.7	0	0	1.2	1.9	2.5	0	0	1.9	2.5	2.54
1955	1.07	.9	0	3.3	1.1	5.3	6.9	0	0	5.3	6.9	6.46
1956	1.07	.9	.3	9.5	10.0	20.7	25.9	0	0	20.7	25.9	24.18
1957	1.11	3.0	.4	.2	7.7	11.3	13.7	0	0	11.3	13.7	12.38
1958	1.15	1.1	.3	0	1.3	2.7	3.3	0	0	2.7	3.3	2.88
1959	1.19	1.4	.1	5.0	1.7	8.2	10.1	0	0	8.2	10.1	8.47
1960	1.25	1.3	0	3.0	6.2	10.5	12.8	0	0	10.5	12.8	10.26
1961	1.30	10.0	0	0	.1	10.1	12.1	.1	.1	10.2	12.2	9.40
1962	1.35	1.9	0	4.5	3.9	10.3	12.4	.1	.1	10.4	12.5	9.28
1963	1.39	12.8	1.1	0	.3	14.2	17.1	.6	.7	14.8	17.8	12.83
1964	1.44	9.9	2.0	0	4.7	16.6	19.8	.5	.6	17.1	20.4	14.17
1965	1.49	8.1	1.7	0	5.7	15.5	17.9	.2	.2	15.7	18.2	12.20
1966	1.54	1.6	.9	10.2	1.1	13.8	15.5	.1	.1	13.9	15.6	10.14
1967	1.59	6.2	1.2	0	.8	8.2	9.0	.1	.1	8.3	9.1	5.75
1968	1.63	4.1	.7	0	5.8	10.6	11.5	.1	.1	10.7	11.6	7.13
1969	1.69	13.7	1.1	0	3.3	18.1	19.1	0	0	18.1	19.1	11.30
1970	1.73	17.4	.5	.5	.2	18.6	18.6	0	0	18.6	18.6	10.75
1971	1.80	6.4	.8	.5	.7	8.4	8.1	.1	.1	8.5	8.2	4.58
1972	1.84	1.7	1.1	.1	1.0	3.9	3.7	0	0	3.9	3.7	1.99
1973	1.87	1.3	.8	.9	.5	3.5	2.8	0	0	3.5	2.8	1.51
1974	1.92	8.9	.5	3.5	1.2	14.1	8.9	0	0	14.1	8.9	4.64
1975	1.96	.7	1.0	3.8	3.5	9.0	5.1	0	0	9.0	5.1	2.59
1976	2.01	6.9	1.6	1.2	2.5	12.2	6.7	0	0	12.2	6.7	3.32
1977	2.07	6.4	3.9	.1	1.4	11.8	6.2	5.0	2.6	16.8	8.9	4.28
1978	2.12	6.9	.8	4.0	1.5	13.2	6.5	0	0	13.2	6.5	3.07
1979	2.17	16.4	0	2.7	3.6	22.7	9.8	0	0	22.7	9.8	4.54
1980	2.25	13.6	.4	6.0	2.4	22.4	8.6	0	0	22.4	8.6	3.80
1981	2.27	11.5	1.8	5.1	2.0	20.4	7.1	0	0	20.4	7.1	3.14
1982	2.32	31.5	19.1	0	4.1	54.7	18.9	2.1	.7	56.8	19.7	8.47
1983	2.38	184.2	28.2	0	1.7	214.1	73.3	4.6	1.6	218.7	74.9	31.46
1984	2.42	145.5	22.5	0	4.0	172.0	58.1	9.1	3.1	181.1	61.2	25.27
1985	2.49	195.5	21.6	0	3.8	220.9	75.2	11.2	3.8	232.1	79.0	31.74
1986	2.67	139.2	20.3	0	4.9	164.4	55.8	2.6	.9	167.0	56.7	21.24
1987	2.78	160.8	17.3	0	7.3	185.4	61.4	1.7	.6	187.1	62.0	22.30
1988	2.85	101.3	15.1	0	4.0	120.4	37.3	.2	.1	120.6	37.3	13.09
Total		1,135.8	167.1	64.1	111.6	1,478.6	693.9	38.4	15.6	1,517.0	709.5	8.73[a]

1. Deflated using Export Price Index (Table 3331) in 1970 U.S. dollars.

a. Per capita average, 1946–88.

SOURCE: USAID–OLG, various years (see Data Sources in text); Table 3331 (Chapter 33, above); IMF-IFS-SY, various years; population data from Chapter 6, above.

Figure 35:24

COSTA RICA: YEARLY ANNOUNCED TOTAL U.S. ASSISTANCE,[1] 1946–88

(M US)

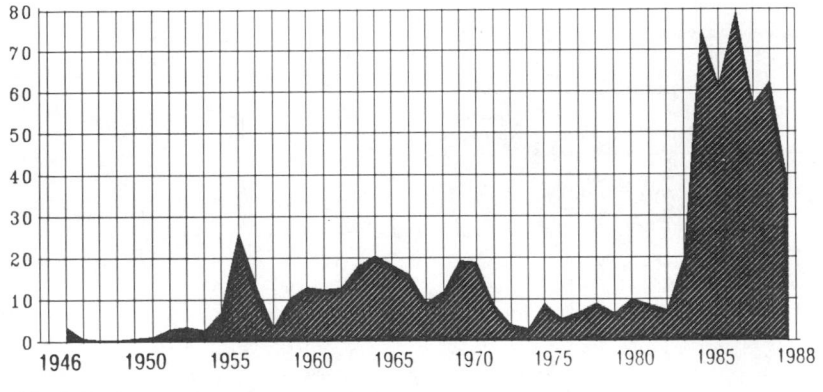

SOURCE: Table 3509.

Figure 35:25

COSTA RICA: YEARLY PER CAPITA ANNOUNCED TOTAL U.S. ASSISTANCE,[1] 1946–88

(US)

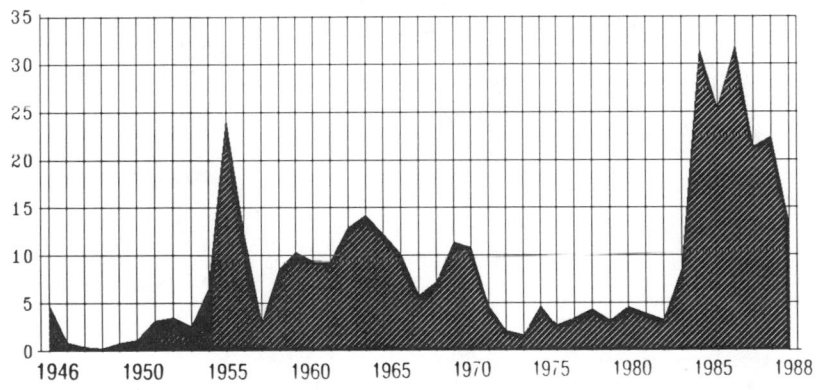

SOURCE: Table 3509.

Figure 35:26

COSTA RICA: PER CAPITA ASSISTANCE COMPARED TO AVERAGE YEARLY LATIN AMERICA PER CAPITA ASSISTANCE,[1] 1946–88

(US)

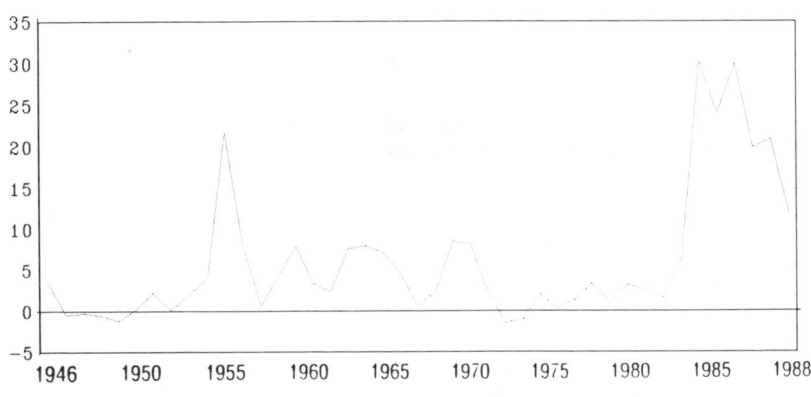

SOURCE: Table 3529.

Table 3510

CUBA: ANNOUNCED AUTHORIZED U.S. ASSISTANCE, NOMINAL AND DEFLATED,[1] 1946–88[a]

Year	A. Population (M)	Economic Assistance Nominal (M US)				Economic Total (M US)		Military Total (M US)		Economic + Military Total (M US)		Per Capita (US)
		B. USAID	C. FFP	D. EXP/IMP	E. Other	F. Nominal (B+C+D+E)	G. Deflated (F/EPI = 100)	H. Nominal	I. Deflated (H/EPI = 100)	J. Nominal (F+H)	K. Deflated (G+I)	L. Deflated (K/A)
1946	5.04	0	0	0	.1	.1	.2	0	0	.1	.2	.03
1947	5.15	0	0	0	.1	.1	.1	0	0	.1	.1	.03
1948	5.27	0	0	0	.1	.1	.1	0	0	.1	.1	.03
1949	5.39	0	0	0	0	0	0	0	0	0	0	0
1950	5.51	0	0	0	0	0	0	0	0	0	0	0
1951	5.62	0	0	12.0	.1	12.1	15.6	0	0	12.1	15.6	2.77
1952	5.73	.1	0	0	0	.1	.1	0	0	.1	.1	.02
1953	6.04	.2	0	0	0	.2	.3	0	0	.2	.3	.04
1954	6.16	.2	0	8.0	0	8.2	10.8	0	0	8.2	10.8	1.76
1955	6.28	.5	0	0	0	.5	.7	0	0	.5	.7	.10
1956	6.41	.5	0	1.2	0	1.7	2.1	0	0	1.7	2.1	.33
1957	6.54	.6	0	0	0	.6	.7	0	0	.6	.7	.11
1958	6.76	.5	0	16.3	0	16.8	20.6	0	0	16.8	20.6	3.05
1959	6.90	.4	0	0	0	.4	.5	.4	.5	.8	1.0	.14
1960	7.03	.3	.6	0	0	.9	1.1	.2	.2	1.1	1.3	.19
1961	7.13	0	0	0	0	0	0	.1	.1	.1	.1	.02
1962												
1963												
1964												
1965												
1966												
1967												
1968												
1969												
1970												
1971												
1972												
1973												
1974												
1975												
1976												
1977												
1978												
1979												
1980												
1981												
1982												
1983												
1984												
1985												
1986												
1987												
1988												
Total		3.3	.6	37.5	.4	41.8	53.0	.7	.9	42.5	53.8	

1. Deflated using Export Price Index (Table 3331) in 1970 U.S. dollars.

a. U.S. assistance to Cuba was terminated in 1961.

b. Per capita average, 1946–88.

SOURCE: USAID-OLG, various years (see Data Sources in text); Table 3331 (Chapter 33, above); IMF-IFS-SY, various years; population data from Chapter 6, above.

Figure 35:27

CUBA: YEARLY ANNOUNCED TOTAL U.S. ASSISTANCE,[1] 1946–88

(M US)

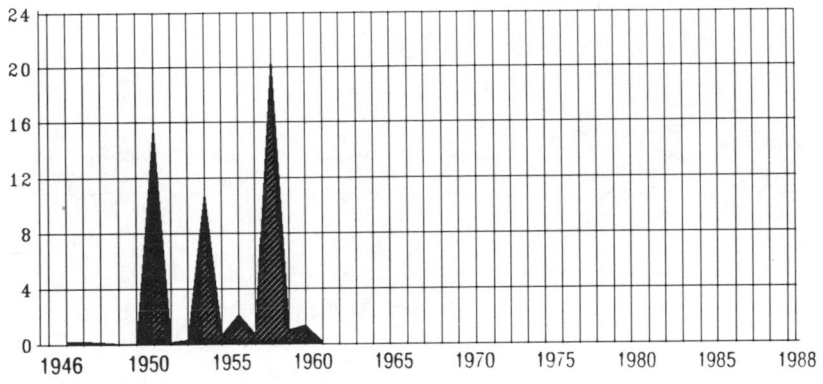

SOURCE: Table 3510.

Figure 35:28

CUBA: YEARLY PER CAPITA ANNOUNCED TOTAL U.S. ASSISTANCE,[1] 1946–88

(US)

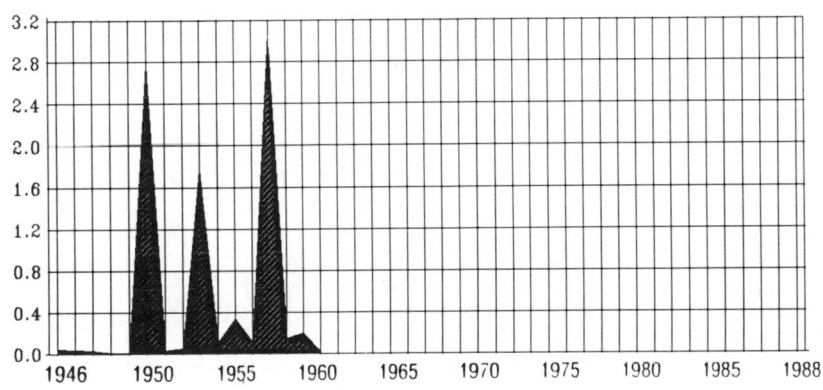

SOURCE: Table 3510.

Figure 35:29

CUBA: PER CAPITA ASSISTANCE COMPARED TO AVERAGE YEARLY
LATIN AMERICA PER CAPITA ASSISTANCE,[1] 1946–88

(US)

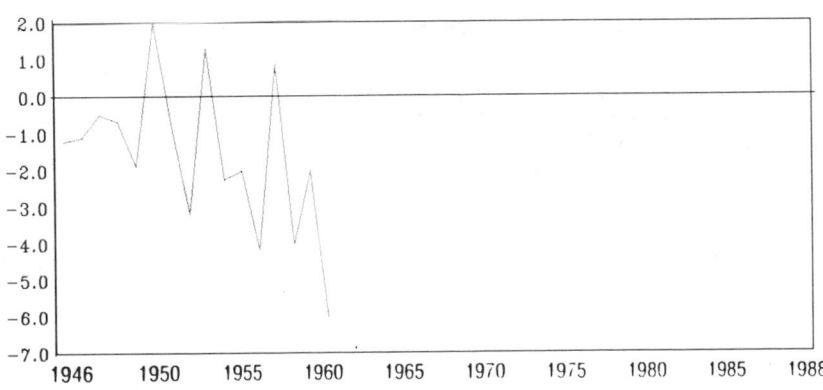

SOURCE: Table 3529.

Table 3511

DOMINICAN REPUBLIC: ANNOUNCED AUTHORIZED U.S. ASSISTANCE, NOMINAL AND DEFLATED,[1] 1946–88

| | | Economic Assistance Nominal (M US) | | | | Economic Total (M US) | | Military Total (M US) | | Economic + Military | | |
| | | | | | | | | | | Total (M US) | | Per Capita (US) |
Year	A. Population (M)	B. USAID	C. FFP	D. EXP/IMP	E. Other	F. Nominal (B+C+D+E)	G. Deflated (F/EPI = 100)	H. Nominal	I. Deflated (H/EPI = 100)	J. Nominal (F+H)	K. Deflated (G+I)	L. Deflated (K/A)
1946	2.03	0	0	0	.2	.2	.3	0	0	.2	.3	.17
1947	2.08	0	0	0	.2	.2	.3	0	0	.2	.3	.14
1948	2.13	0	0	0	.1	.1	.1	0	0	.1	.1	.06
1949	2.19	0	0	0	0	0	0	0	0	0	0	0
1950	2.24	0	0	0	0	0	0	0	0	0	0	0
1951	2.31	0	0	0	.1	.1	.1	0	0	.1	.1	.06
1952	2.29	.2	0	0	0	.2	.3	0	0	.2	.3	.11
1953	2.37	.3	0	0	0	.3	.4	0	0	.3	.4	.16
1954	2.45	.2	0	0	0	.2	.3	0	0	.2	.3	.11
1955	2.54	.3	0	0	0	.3	.4	0	0	.3	.4	.15
1956	2.63	.3	0	0	0	.3	.4	0	0	.3	.4	.14
1957	2.73	.2	0	0	0	.2	.2	0	0	.2	.2	.09
1958	2.83	.2	0	0	0	.2	.2	0	0	.2	.2	.09
1959	2.93	.2	0	0	0	.2	.2	.8	1.0	1.0	1.2	.42
1960	3.04	.3	0	0	0	.3	.4	.2	.2	.5	.6	.20
1961	3.12	.1	0	0	0	.1	.1	0	0	.1	.1	.04
1962	3.21	26.0	.8	9.6	.2	36.6	44.1	.2	.2	36.8	44.3	13.81
1963	3.31	29.6	14.2	0	7.8	51.6	62.2	1.9	2.3	53.5	64.5	19.47
1964	3.41	−.7	13.2	0	1.2	13.7	16.3	2.5	3.0	16.2	19.3	5.67
1965	3.51	52.9	16.4	12.7	4.9	86.9	100.6	1.2	1.4	88.1	102.0	29.05
1966	3.62	93.8	10.2	8.1	.9	113.0	127.0	1.7	1.9	114.7	128.9	35.60
1967	3.72	53.2	4.2	0	.8	58.2	64.1	3.4	3.7	61.6	67.8	18.24
1968	3.83	43.2	20.2	6.3	1.0	70.7	76.8	2.3	2.5	73.0	79.3	20.69
1969	3.95	11.3	16.2	4.3	−.9	30.9	32.6	2.2	2.3	33.1	34.9	8.84
1970	4.06	4.6	15.0	0	.5	20.1	20.1	2.1	2.1	22.2	22.2	5.47
1971	4.18	13.5	14.3	0	.5	28.3	27.4	1.4	1.4	29.7	28.8	6.89
1972	4.30	6.9	19.0	0	3.9	29.8	28.0	1.9	1.8	31.7	29.8	6.92
1973	4.43	1.0	14.2	8.8	6.2	30.2	24.3	2.1	1.7	32.3	26.0	5.88
1974	4.56	12.6	4.2	30.7	4.4	51.9	32.8	.8	.5	52.7	33.3	7.30
1975	4.70	5.6	5.5	7.3	.6	19.0	10.7	1.6	.9	20.6	11.6	2.48
1976	4.89	16.1	12.4	24.1	20.7	73.3	40.1	1.9	1.0	75.2	41.1	8.40
1977	5.03	.9	11.9	.5	1.1	14.4	7.6	1.5	.8	15.9	8.4	1.67
1978	5.17	1.3	3.9	.2	.9	6.3	3.1	.7	.3	7.0	3.5	.67
1979	5.30	26.4	20.7	.7	26.6	74.4	32.3	1.0	.4	75.4	32.7	6.17
1980	5.44	34.6	19.7	3.3	8.6	66.2	25.3	3.5	1.3	69.7	26.6	4.89
1981	5.58	17.4	18.6	1.2	2.5	39.7	13.9	3.4	1.2	43.1	15.1	2.70
1982	5.74	60.0	19.3	0	3.1	82.4	28.5	5.5	1.9	87.9	30.4	5.30
1983	5.96	34.6	25.3	0	3.2	63.1	21.6	6.6	2.3	69.7	23.9	4.00
1984	6.10	64.4	31.3	0	2.5	98.2	33.2	6.4	2.2	104.6	35.3	5.79
1985	6.24	125.5	42.4	0	3.2	171.1	58.3	8.7	3.0	179.8	61.2	9.81
1986	6.42	67.1	31.8	0	4.4	103.3	35.1	4.5	1.5	107.8	36.6	5.70
1987	6.72	20.0	14.9	0	6.1	41.0	13.6	3.4	1.1	44.4	14.7	2.19
1988	6.87	32.5	23.3	0	2.9	58.7	18.2	1.3	.4	60.0	18.6	2.70
Total		856.6	443.1	117.8	118.4	1,535.9	1,001.3	74.7	44.4	1,610.6	1,045.7	5.77[a]

1. Deflated using Export Price Index (Table 3331) in 1970 U.S. dollars.

a. Per capita average, 1946–88.

SOURCE: USAID–OLG, various years (see Data Sources in text); Table 3331 (Chapter 33, above); IMF-IFS-SY, various years; population data from Chapter 6, above.

Figure 35:30

DOMINICAN REPUBLIC: YEARLY ANNOUNCED TOTAL U.S. ASSISTANCE,[1] 1946–88

(M US)

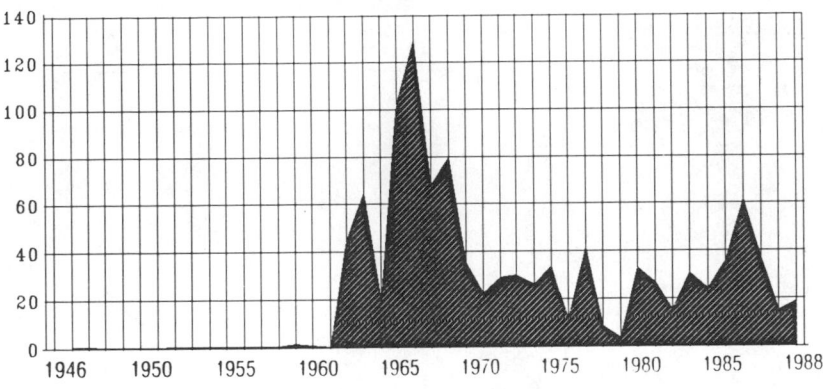

SOURCE: Table 3511.

Figure 35:31

DOMINICAN REPUBLIC: YEARLY PER CAPITA ANNOUNCED TOTAL U.S. ASSISTANCE,[1] 1946–88

(US)

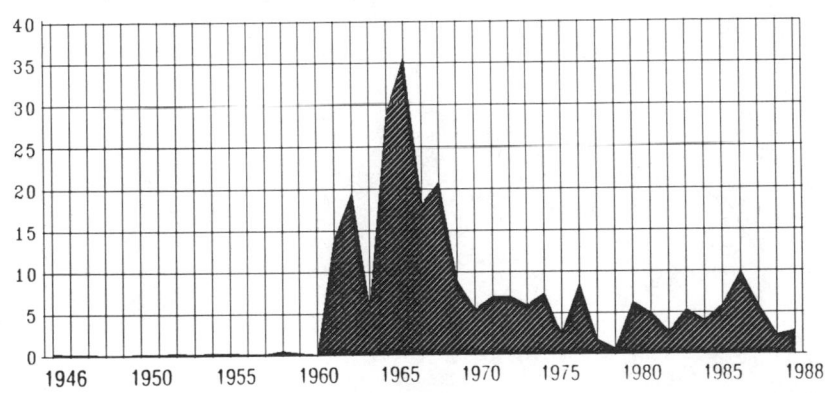

SOURCE: Table 3511.

Figure 35:32

DOMINICAN REPUBLIC: PER CAPITA ASSISTANCE COMPARED TO AVERAGE YEARLY LATIN AMERICA PER CAPITA ASSISTANCE,[1] 1946–88

(US)

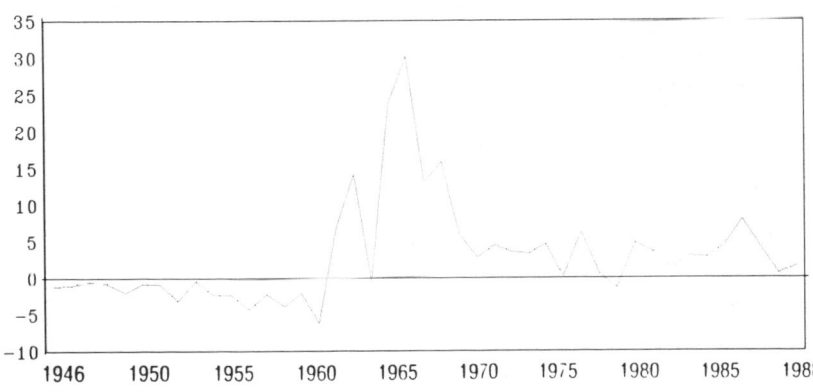

SOURCE: Table 3529.

Table 3512

ECUADOR: ANNOUNCED AUTHORIZED U.S. ASSISTANCE, NOMINAL AND DEFLATED,[1] 1946–88

Year	A. Population (M)	Economic Assistance Nominal (M US)				Economic Total (M US)		Military Total (M US)		Economic + Military		
		B. USAID	C. FFP	D. EXP/IMP	E. Other	F. Nominal (B+C+D+E)	G. Deflated (F/EPI = 100)	H. Nominal	I. Deflated (H/EPI = 100)	J. Nominal (F+H)	K. Deflated (G+I)	L. Deflated (K/A)
1946	2.85	0	0	0	.6	.6	1.0	0	0	.6	1.0	.36
1947	2.94	0	0	0	.7	.7	1.0	0	0	.7	1.0	.34
1948	3.02	0	0	2.7	.6	3.3	4.4	0	0	3.3	4.4	1.46
1949	3.10	0	0	.3	.5	.8	1.1	0	0	.8	1.1	.37
1950	3.20	0	0	7.1	.6	7.7	11.4	0	0	7.7	11.4	3.55
1951	3.25	0	0	0	.7	.7	.9	0	0	.7	.9	.28
1952	3.43	1.4	0	1.0	0	2.4	3.1	0	0	2.4	3.1	.91
1953	3.53	1.0	0	0	0	1.0	1.3	0	0	1.0	1.3	.37
1954	3.64	1.3	0	5.9	0	7.2	9.5	0	0	7.2	9.5	2.61
1955	3.75	1.4	.2	2.7	0	4.3	5.6	0	0	4.3	5.6	1.50
1956	3.87	1.7	2.7	.9	0	5.3	6.6	0	0	5.3	6.6	1.71
1957	3.98	3.8	3.4	.5	0	7.7	9.4	0	0	7.7	9.4	2.35
1958	4.11	4.1	1.4	0	0	5.5	6.8	0	0	5.5	6.8	1.64
1959	4.23	6.6	.8	1.1	0	8.5	10.4	2.8	3.4	11.3	13.9	3.28
1960	4.36	7.9	.3	.9	0	9.1	11.1	2.5	3.1	11.6	14.2	3.25
1961	4.50	9.6	3.3	.4	0	13.3	15.9	5.5	6.6	18.8	22.5	5.00
1962	4.65	19.9	2.2	0	14.4	36.5	44.0	2.3	2.8	38.8	46.7	10.05
1963	4.78	18.1	6.1	1.3	11.5	37.0	44.6	3.7	4.5	40.7	49.0	10.26
1964	4.93	19.2	4.4	0	3.7	27.3	32.6	3.1	3.7	30.4	36.3	7.36
1965	5.07	11.1	6.9	8.0	2.4	28.4	32.9	2.3	2.7	30.7	35.5	7.01
1966	5.27	15.1	1.8	6.3	5.6	28.8	32.4	3.9	4.4	32.7	36.7	6.97
1967	5.40	.4	3.0	0	1.5	4.9	5.4	3.1	3.4	8.0	8.8	1.63
1968	5.55	3.2	1.4	7.5	1.5	13.6	14.8	2.8	3.0	16.4	17.8	3.21
1969	5.77	5.7	6.3	0	1.0	13.0	13.7	2.6	2.7	15.6	16.5	2.85
1970	5.96	23.0	1.7	3.0	1.0	28.7	28.7	2.0	2.0	30.7	30.7	5.15
1971	6.17	15.3	6.6	2.0	.8	24.7	24.0	.4	.4	25.1	24.3	3.95
1972	6.38	4.9	3.2	1.1	3.3	12.5	11.7	0	0	12.5	11.7	1.84
1973	6.60	4.6	11.1	.1	2.0	17.8	14.3	0	0	17.8	14.3	2.17
1974	6.83	2.5	3.3	3.3	1.8	10.9	6.9	0	0	10.9	6.9	1.01
1975	7.03	2.1	3.4	6.0	2.5	14.0	7.9	.4	.2	14.4	8.1	1.16
1976	7.24	0	2.2	2.2	3.2	7.6	4.2	10.5	5.7	18.1	9.9	1.37
1977	7.45	0	1.3	0	3.6	4.9	2.6	15.4	8.1	20.3	10.7	1.44
1978	7.67	.8	2.4	.5	5.5	9.2	4.5	10.7	5.3	19.9	9.8	1.28
1979	7.89	.5	2.7	26.4	3.1	32.7	14.2	.4	.2	33.1	14.4	1.82
1980	8.12	8.3	.9	0	3.9	13.1	5.0	3.3	1.3	16.4	6.3	.77
1981	8.36	12.5	2.3	0	6.4	21.2	7.4	4.3	1.5	25.5	8.9	1.07
1982	8.61	17.3	2.4	0	3.2	22.9	7.9	5.0	1.7	27.9	9.7	1.12
1983	8.86	21.5	1.8	0	3.3	26.6	9.1	4.6	1.6	31.2	10.7	1.21
1984	9.11	22.6	2.7	0	5.1	30.4	10.3	6.7	2.3	37.1	12.5	1.38
1985	9.38	33.2	14.9	0	3.8	51.9	17.7	6.7	2.3	58.6	20.0	2.13
1986	9.65	49.8	6.5	0	4.1	60.4	20.5	4.5	1.5	64.9	22.0	2.28
1987	9.92	37.2	4.0	0	6.3	47.5	15.7	4.5	1.5	52.0	17.2	1.74
1988	10.20	14.5	1.6	0	4.8	20.9	6.5	.7	.2	21.6	6.7	.66
Total		402.1	119.2	91.2	113.0	725.5	538.9	114.7	76.0	840.2	614.9	2.60[a]

1. Deflated using Export Price Index (Table 3331) in 1970 U.S. dollars.

a. Per capita average, 1946–88.

SOURCE: USAID-OLG, various years (see Data Sources in text); Table 3331 (Chapter 33, above); IMF-IFS-SY, various years; population data from Chapter 6, above.

Figure 35:33

ECUADOR: YEARLY ANNOUNCED TOTAL U.S. ASSISTANCE,[1] 1946–88

(M US)

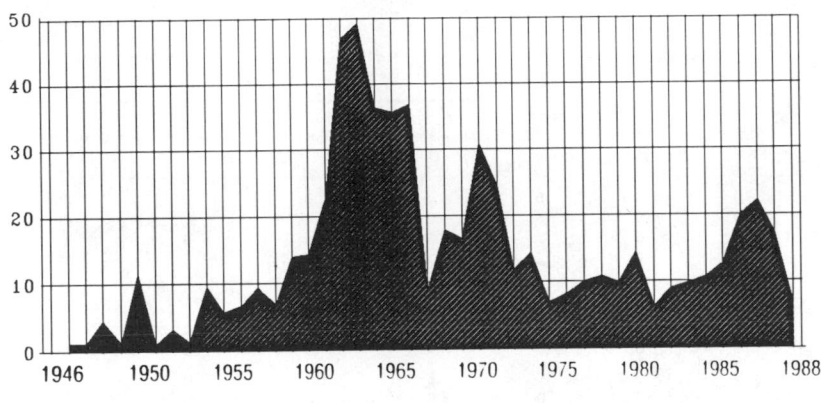

SOURCE: Table 3512.

Figure 35:34

ECUADOR: YEARLY PER CAPITA ANNOUNCED TOTAL U.S. ASSISTANCE,[1] 1946–88

(US)

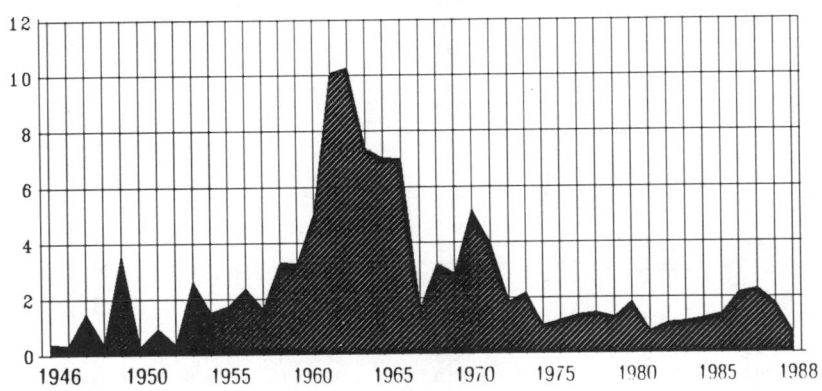

SOURCE: Table 3512.

Figure 35:35

ECUADOR: PER CAPITA ASSISTANCE COMPARED TO AVERAGE YEARLY
LATIN AMERICA PER CAPITA ASSISTANCE,[1] 1946–88

(US)

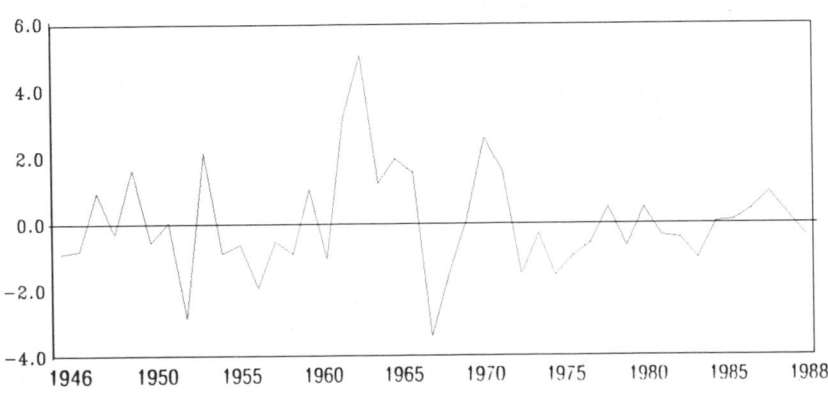

SOURCE: Table 3529.

Table 3513

EL SALVADOR: ANNOUNCED AUTHORIZED U.S. ASSISTANCE, NOMINAL AND DEFLATED,[1] 1946-88

Year	A. Population (M)	Economic Assistance Nominal (M US)				Economic Total (M US)		Military Total (M US)		Economic + Military Total (M US)		Per Capita (US)
		B. USAID	C. FFP	D. EXP/IMP	E. Other	F. Nominal (B+C+D+E)	G. Deflated (F/EPI = 100)	H. Nominal	I. Deflated (H/EPI = 100)	J. Nominal (F+H)	K. Deflated (G+I)	L. Deflated (K/A)
1946	1.76	0	0	0	.5	.5	.8	0	0	.5	.8	.48
1947	1.78	0	0	0	.3	.3	.4	0	0	.3	.4	.24
1948	1.81	0	0	0	.3	.3	.4	0	0	.3	.4	.22
1949	1.84	0	0	0	.2	.2	.3	0	0	.2	.3	.16
1950	1.86	0	0	0	.3	.3	.4	0	0	.3	.4	.24
1951	1.90	0	0	0	.2	.2	.3	0	0	.2	.3	.14
1952	1.97	.5	0	0	0	.5	.6	0	0	.5	.6	.33
1953	2.02	.7	0	0	0	.7	.9	0	0	.7	.9	.45
1954	2.08	.5	0	0	.1	.6	.8	0	0	.6	.8	.38
1955	2.14	.8	0	0	0	.8	1.0	0	0	.8	1.0	.49
1956	2.20	.9	.2	0	0	1.1	1.4	0	0	1.1	1.4	.63
1957	2.26	1.1	.6	0	0	1.7	2.1	0	0	1.7	2.1	.92
1958	2.32	1.0	.1	0	0	1.1	1.4	0	0	1.1	1.4	.58
1959	2.39	1.0	.1	0	0	1.1	1.4	0	0	1.1	1.4	.57
1960	2.45	1.0	0	0	0	1.0	1.2	0	0	1.0	1.2	.50
1961	2.51	2.9	.1	3.7	0	6.7	8.0	.2	.2	6.9	8.3	3.29
1962	2.63	3.1	2.3	6.0	11.8	23.2	28.0	.6	.7	23.8	28.7	10.90
1963	2.72	19.3	2.6	0	.3	22.2	26.7	1.0	1.2	23.2	28.0	10.28
1964	2.87	10.9	3.5	0	.4	14.8	17.7	.9	1.1	15.7	18.7	6.53
1965	2.93	5.5	1.9	0	10.9	18.3	21.2	.8	.9	19.1	22.1	7.54
1966	3.04	3.3	2.6	2.5	.9	9.3	10.4	.7	.8	10.0	11.2	3.70
1967	3.15	.9	1.9	0	.4	3.2	3.5	.6	.7	3.8	4.2	1.33
1968	3.27	8.1	.7	0	.5	9.3	10.1	.6	.7	9.9	10.7	3.29
1969	3.36	10.4	1.8	1.0	.5	13.7	14.5	.3	.3	14.0	14.8	4.40
1970	3.44	10.2	2.0	0	.5	12.7	12.7	.2	.2	12.9	12.9	3.75
1971	3.55	2.5	1.7	1.0	.5	5.7	5.5	.4	.4	6.1	5.9	1.67
1972	3.67	12.5	3.4	0	.7	16.6	15.6	1.8	1.7	18.4	17.3	4.71
1973	3.77	2.0	1.1	1.0	.4	4.5	3.6	.4	.3	4.9	3.9	1.05
1974	3.89	7.8	1.3	.4	1.1	10.6	6.7	1.1	.7	11.7	7.4	1.90
1975	3.99	1.3	1.6	.6	1.0	4.5	2.5	5.5	3.1	10.0	5.6	1.42
1976	4.12	1.8	3.4	6.6	2.1	13.9	7.6	1.1	.6	15.0	8.2	1.99
1977	4.26	0	2.7	0	2.9	5.6	3.0	.6	.3	6.2	3.3	.77
1978	4.35	8.0	1.7	0	1.2	10.9	5.4	0	0	10.9	5.4	1.24
1979	4.44	6.9	2.9	.1	1.6	11.5	5.0	0	0	11.5	5.0	1.12
1980	4.75	52.3	5.5	0	.6	58.4	22.3	5.9	2.3	64.3	24.6	5.17
1981	4.87	78.3	35.3	0	.4	114.0	39.9	35.5	12.4	149.5	52.3	10.74
1982	5.00	154.6	27.6	0	0	182.2	63.0	82.0	28.4	264.2	91.4	18.28
1983	5.23	198.8	46.8	0	0	245.6	84.1	81.3	27.8	326.9	111.9	21.40
1984	4.78	161.4	54.5	0	0	215.9	72.9	196.6	66.4	412.5	139.3	29.14
1985	4.82	376.1	57.8	0	0	433.9	147.7	136.3	46.4	570.2	194.1	40.28
1986	4.91	268.2	54.4	0	0	322.6	109.5	121.8	41.4	444.4	150.9	30.73
1987	5.01	414.5	48.4	0	0	462.9	153.4	111.5	36.9	574.4	190.3	37.99
1988	5.11	265.7	48.4	0	0	314.1	97.2	81.5	25.2	395.6	122.4	23.95
Total		2,094.8	418.9	22.9	40.6	2,577.2	1,011.2	869.2	301.1	3,446.4	1,312.3	6.86[a]

1. Deflated using Export Price Index (Table 3331) in 1970 U.S. dollars.

a. Per capita average, 1946-88.

SOURCE: USAID-OLG, various years (see Data Sources in text); Table 3331 (Chapter 33, above); IMF-IFS-SY, various years; population data from Chapter 6, above.

Figure 35:36

EL SALVADOR: YEARLY ANNOUNCED TOTAL U.S. ASSISTANCE,[1] 1946–88

(M US)

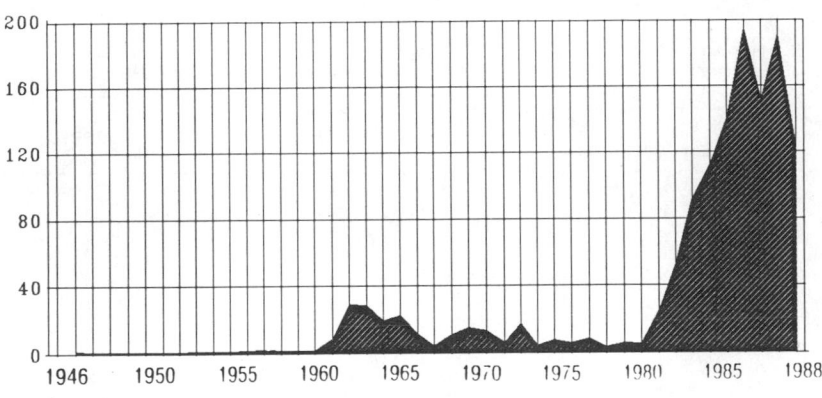

SOURCE: Table 3513.

Figure 35:37

EL SALVADOR: YEARLY PER CAPITA ANNOUNCED TOTAL U.S. ASSISTANCE,[1] 1946–88

(US)

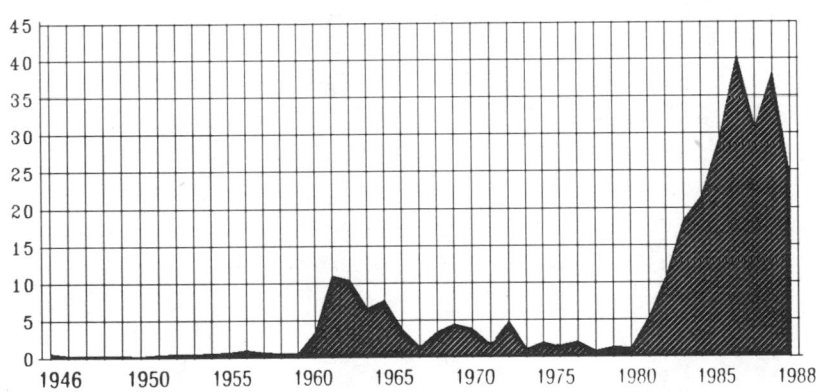

SOURCE: Table 3513.

Figure 35:38

EL SALVADOR: PER CAPITA ASSISTANCE COMPARED TO AVERAGE YEARLY
LATIN AMERICA PER CAPITA ASSISTANCE,[1] 1946–88

(US)

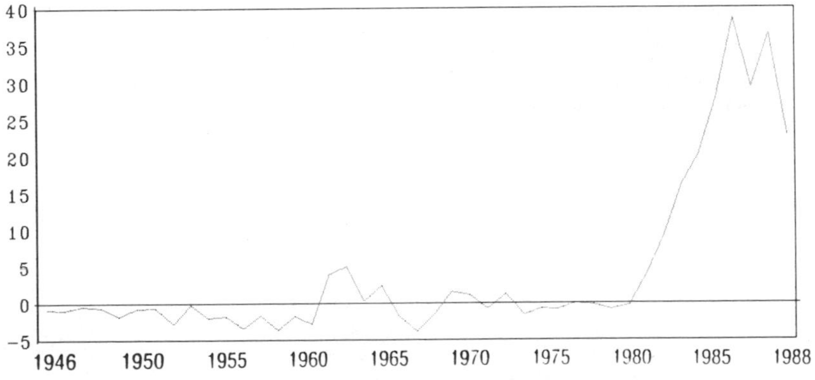

SOURCE: Table 3529.

Table 3514

GUATEMALA: ANNOUNCED AUTHORIZED U.S. ASSISTANCE, NOMINAL AND DEFLATED,[1] 1946–88

Year	A. Population (M)	Economic Assistance Nominal (M US)				Economic Total (M US)		Military Total (M US)		Economic + Military Total (M US)		Per Capita (US)
		B. USAID	C. FFP	D. EXP/IMP	E. Other	F. Nominal (B+C+D+E)	G. Deflated (F/EPI = 100)	H. Nominal	I. Deflated (H/EPI = 100)	J. Nominal (F+H)	K. Deflated (G+I)	L. Deflated (K/A)
1946	2.50	0	0	0	.8	.8	1.4	0	0	.8	1.4	.54
1947	2.57	0	0	0	1.0	1.0	1.4	0	0	1.0	1.4	.55
1948	2.64	0	0	0	1.7	1.7	2.3	0	0	1.7	2.3	.86
1949	2.72	0	0	0	2.9	2.9	4.2	0	0	2.9	4.2	1.53
1950	2.81	0	0	0	1.7	1.7	2.5	0	0	1.7	2.5	.89
1951	2.89	0	0	0	.7	.7	.9	0	0	.7	.9	.31
1952	2.98	.2	0	0	.9	1.1	1.4	0	0	1.1	1.4	.48
1953	3.07	.2	0	0	0	.2	.3	0	0	.2	.3	.08
1954	3.18	.2	0	0	0	.2	.3	0	0	.2	.3	.08
1955	3.29	5.6	3.0	0	1.5	10.1	13.2	0	0	10.1	13.2	4.00
1956	3.39	18.2	.5	1.2	14.5	34.4	43.0	0	0	34.4	43.0	12.68
1957	3.49	17.5	.3	0	1.3	19.1	23.2	0	0	19.1	23.2	6.66
1958	3.61	12.6	.2	0	4.7	17.5	21.5	0	0	17.5	21.5	5.96
1959	3.72	8.0	.3	0	3.5	11.8	14.5	.1	.1	11.9	14.6	3.93
1960	3.83	5.9	.3	5.0	.7	11.9	14.5	.2	.2	12.1	14.8	3.86
1961	3.95	21.0	.4	10.5	0	31.9	38.2	.4	.5	32.3	38.7	9.79
1962	4.06	4.2	.7	0	4.4	9.3	11.2	1.3	1.6	10.6	12.8	3.15
1963	4.19	3.1	1.0	0	9.0	13.1	15.8	2.6	3.1	15.7	18.9	4.51
1964	4.31	5.6	3.0	4.6	.5	13.7	16.3	1.4	1.7	15.1	18.0	4.18
1965	4.41	7.0	1.1	0	4.8	12.9	14.9	1.5	1.7	14.4	16.7	3.78
1966	4.50	−1.1	.9	0	4.0	3.8	4.3	1.2	1.3	5.0	5.6	1.25
1967	4.70	11.1	1.9	6.5	.7	20.2	22.2	1.4	1.5	21.6	23.8	5.06
1968	4.84	10.9	3.0	0	3.4	17.3	18.8	2.3	2.5	19.6	21.3	4.40
1969	5.02	5.8	2.4	70.0	.7	78.9	83.2	1.1	1.2	80.0	84.4	16.81
1970	5.27	28.7	2.6	0	.6	31.9	31.9	2.0	2.0	33.9	33.9	6.43
1971	5.42	14.2	2.0	2.9	.5	19.6	19.0	6.6	6.4	26.2	25.4	4.69
1972	5.58	12.5	3.4	0	.7	16.6	15.6	1.8	1.7	18.4	17.3	3.10
1973	5.74	9.5	1.7	13.5	1.3	26.0	21.0	3.5	2.8	29.5	23.8	4.14
1974	6.05	2.5	1.2	.6	1.9	6.2	3.9	1.4	.9	7.6	4.8	.79
1975	6.24	9.4	3.4	.8	1.3	14.9	8.4	2.9	1.6	17.8	10.1	1.61
1976	6.43	32.7	12.8	.2	3.4	49.1	26.8	2.2	1.2	51.3	28.0	4.36
1977	6.63	14.3	4.5	6.2	2.0	27.0	14.2	.5	.3	27.5	14.5	2.19
1978	6.84	4.5	4.6	0	1.5	10.6	5.2	0	0	10.6	5.2	.76
1979	7.05	17.4	5.3	0	2.0	24.7	10.7	0	0	24.7	10.7	1.52
1980	7.26	7.8	3.3	0	2.7	13.8	5.3	0	0	13.8	5.3	.73
1981	7.48	9.1	7.5	0	2.4	19.0	6.6	0	0	19.0	6.6	.89
1982	7.70	8.2	5.6	0	1.7	15.5	5.4	0	0	15.5	5.4	.70
1983	7.46	22.3	5.4	0	2.0	29.7	10.2	0	0	29.7	10.2	1.36
1984	7.60	4.5	13.2	0	2.6	20.3	6.9	0	0	20.3	6.9	.90
1985	7.96	75.7	28.2	0	3.2	107.1	36.5	.5	.2	107.6	36.6	4.60
1986	8.19	89.8	24.0	0	2.9	116.7	39.6	5.4	1.8	122.1	41.5	5.06
1987	8.44	153.5	31.2	0	3.3	188.0	62.3	5.5	1.8	193.5	64.1	7.60
1988	8.68	109.5	18.6	0	4.1	132.2	40.9	9.4	2.9	141.6	43.8	5.05
Total		762.1	197.5	122.0	103.5	1,185.1	739.9	55.2	39.1	1,240.3	779.0	3.53[a]

1. Deflated using Export Price Index (Table 3331) in 1970 U.S. dollars.

a. Per capita average, 1946–88.

SOURCE: USAID–OLG, various years (see Data Sources in text); Table 3331 (Chapter 33, above); IMF-IFS-SY, various years; population data from Chapter 6, above.

Figure 35:39

GUATEMALA: YEARLY ANNOUNCED TOTAL U.S. ASSISTANCE,[1] 1946–88

(M US)

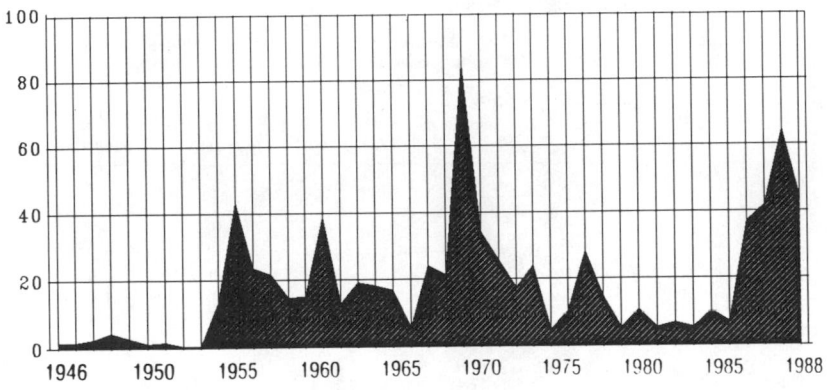

SOURCE: Table 3514.

Figure 35:40

GUATEMALA: YEARLY PER CAPITA ANNOUNCED TOTAL U.S. ASSISTANCE,[1] 1946–88

(US)

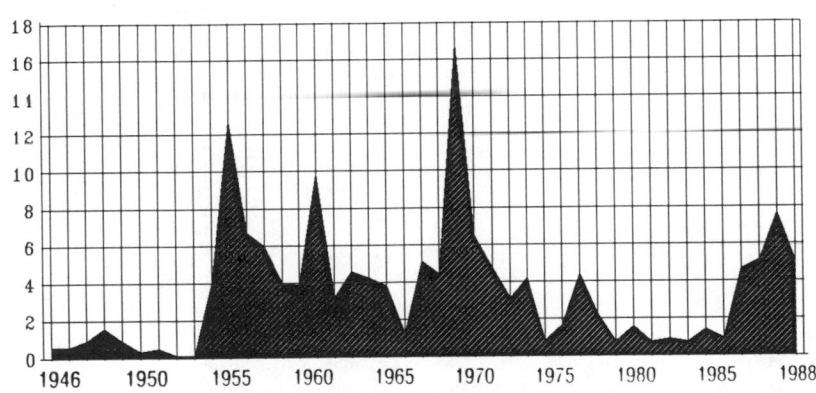

SOURCE: Table 3514.

Figure 35:41

GUATEMALA: PER CAPITA ASSISTANCE COMPARED TO AVERAGE YEARLY LATIN AMERICA PER CAPITA ASSISTANCE,[1] 1946–88

(US)

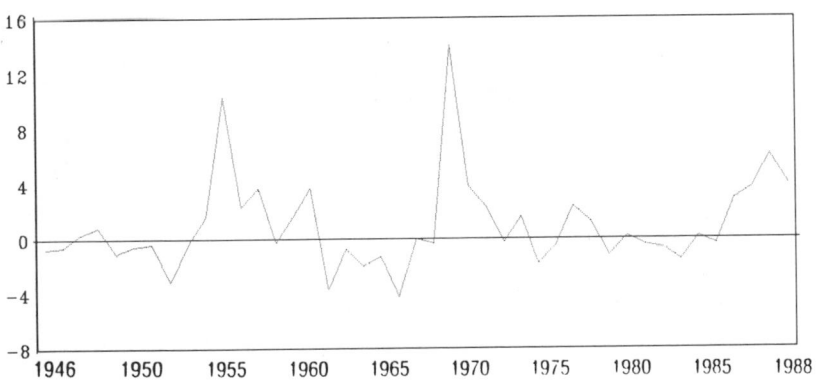

SOURCE: Table 3529.

Table 3515

HAITI: ANNOUNCED AUTHORIZED U.S. ASSISTANCE, NOMINAL AND DEFLATED,[1] 1946–88

Year	A. Population (M)	Economic Assistance Nominal (M US)				Economic Total (M US)		Military Total (M US)		Economic + Military Total (M US)		Per Capita (US)
		B. USAID	C. FFP	D. EXP/IMP	E. Other	F. Nominal (B+C+D+E)	G. Deflated (F/EPI = 100)	H. Nominal	I. Deflated (H/EPI = 100)	J. Nominal (F+H)	K. Deflated (G+I)	L. Deflated (K/A)
1946	3.14	0	0	0	.3	.3	.5	0	0	.3	.5	.16
1947	3.20	0	0	0	.3	.3	.4	0	0	.3	.4	.13
1948	3.26	0	0	0	.8	.8	1.1	0	0	.8	1.1	.33
1949	3.32	0	0	4.0	.4	4.4	6.3	0	0	4.4	6.3	1.90
1950	3.39	0	0	0	.5	.5	.7	0	0	.5	.7	.22
1951	3.44	0	0	10.0	.6	10.6	13.6	0	0	10.6	13.6	3.97
1952	3.51	.7	0	0	.1	.8	1.0	0	0	.8	1.0	.29
1953	3.58	.6	0	0	0	.6	.8	0	0	.6	.8	.22
1954	3.65	1.0	0	0	0	1.0	1.3	0	0	1.0	1.3	.36
1955	3.72	2.3	3.1	7.0	0	12.4	16.2	0	0	12.4	16.2	4.35
1956	3.80	6.4	.6	6.0	0	13.0	16.3	0	0	13.0	16.3	4.28
1957	3.75	2.1	1.1	0	0	3.2	3.9	0	0	3.2	3.9	1.04
1958	3.70	3.5	.5	0	0	4.0	4.9	0	0	4.0	4.9	1.33
1959	3.67	11.4	1.3	0	0	12.7	15.6	0	0	12.7	15.6	4.25
1960	3.62	11.0	1.1	0	0	12.1	14.8	3.4	4.2	15.5	18.9	5.23
1961	3.68	10.7	1.1	0	0	11.8	14.1	.6	.7	12.4	14.9	4.04
1962	3.74	6.8	.7	0	0	7.5	9.0	.5	.6	8.0	9.6	2.58
1963	3.79	.2	.9	0	0	1.1	1.3	.2	.2	1.3	1.6	.41
1964	3.85	−1.4	2.2	0	0	.8	1.0	0	0	.8	1.0	.25
1965	3.91	1.4	.7	0	0	2.1	2.4	0	0	2.1	2.4	.62
1966	3.97	2.4	.7	3.0	0	6.1	6.9	0	0	6.1	6.9	1.73
1967	4.03	1.8	.7	0	0	2.5	2.8	0	0	2.5	2.8	.68
1968	4.10	2.1	1.6	0	0	3.7	4.0	0	0	3.7	4.0	.98
1969	4.16	1.9	1.3	0	0	3.2	3.4	0	0	3.2	3.4	.81
1970	4.24	1.5	2.3	.1	0	3.9	3.9	0	0	3.9	3.9	.92
1971	4.31	2.8	1.5	0	0	4.3	4.2	0	0	4.3	4.2	.97
1972	4.37	3.2	1.7	0	.4	5.3	5.0	0	0	5.3	5.0	1.14
1973	4.44	6.3	1.2	0	0	7.5	6.0	0	0	7.5	6.0	1.36
1974	4.51	8.7	2.0	0	.7	11.4	7.2	0	0	11.4	7.2	1.60
1975	4.58	3.6	5.6	0	.1	9.3	5.3	0	0	9.3	5.3	1.15
1976	4.67	20.3	14.8	0	.5	35.6	19.5	.1	.1	35.7	19.5	4.18
1977	4.75	21.1	19.3	0	.3	40.7	21.5	.6	.3	41.3	21.8	4.59
1978	4.83	8.9	18.5	0	1.3	28.7	14.2	.7	.3	29.4	14.5	3.00
1979	4.92	9.1	15.4	0	.6	25.1	10.9	.4	.2	25.5	11.1	2.25
1980	5.01	11.1	15.8	0	.2	27.1	10.4	.1	0	27.2	10.4	2.07
1981	5.10	9.2	24.5	0	1.7	35.4	12.4	.9	.3	36.3	12.7	2.49
1982	5.05	12.0	22.2	0	.9	35.1	12.1	.5	.2	35.6	12.3	2.44
1983	5.12	27.3	18.5	0	1.7	47.5	16.3	.7	.2	48.2	16.5	3.22
1984	5.18	25.7	19.8	0	1.0	46.5	15.7	1.0	.3	47.5	16.0	3.10
1985	5.27	30.7	23.2	0	2.1	56.0	19.1	.7	.2	56.7	19.3	3.66
1986	5.36	46.9	29.2	0	2.1	78.2	26.6	1.9	.6	80.1	27.2	5.07
1987	5.44	74.9	23.5	0	2.7	101.1	33.5	1.3	.4	102.4	33.9	6.24
1988	5.52	31.2	7.9	0	.9	40.0	12.4	.2	.1	40.2	12.4	2.25
Total		419.4	284.5	30.1	20.2	754.2	398.2	13.8	9.1	768.0	407.3	2.14[a]

1. Deflated using Export Price Index (Table 3331) in 1970 U.S. dollars.

a. Per capita average, 1946–88.

SOURCE: USAID–OLG, various years (see Data Sources in text); Table 3331 (Chapter 33, above); IMF-IFS-SY, various years; population data from Chapter 6, above.

Figure 35:42

HAITI: YEARLY ANNOUNCED TOTAL U.S. ASSISTANCE,[1] 1946–88

(M US)

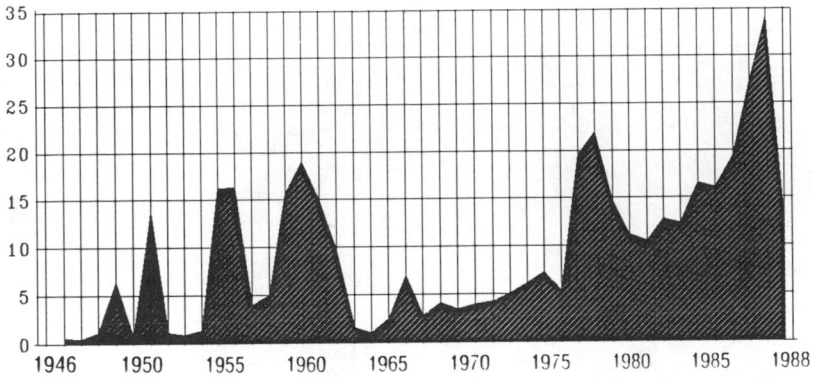

SOURCE: Table 3515.

Figure 35:43

HAITI: YEARLY PER CAPITA ANNOUNCED TOTAL U.S. ASSISTANCE,[1] 1946–88

(US)

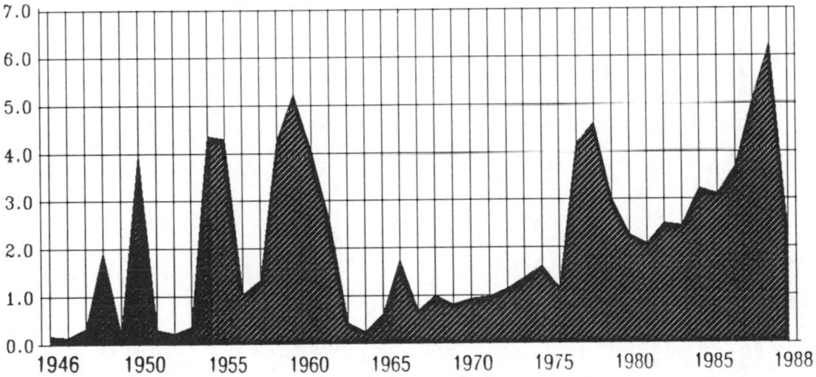

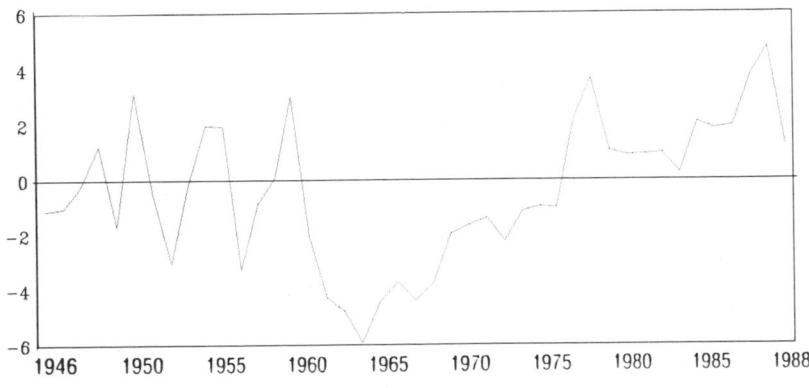

SOURCE: Table 3515.

Figure 35:44

HAITI: PER CAPITA ASSISTANCE COMPARED TO AVERAGE YEARLY
LATIN AMERICA PER CAPITA ASSISTANCE,[1] 1946–88

(US)

SOURCE: Table 3529.

Table 3516

HONDURAS: ANNOUNCED AUTHORIZED U.S. ASSISTANCE, NOMINAL AND DEFLATED,[1] 1946–88

		Economic Assistance Nominal (M US)				Economic Total (M US)		Military Total (M US)		Economic + Military		
										Total (M US)		Per Capita (US)
Year	A. Population (M)	B. USAID	C. FFP	D. EXP/IMP	E. Other	F. Nominal (B+C+D+E)	G. Deflated (F/EPI = 100)	H. Nominal	I. Deflated (H/EPI = 100)	J. Nominal (F+H)	K. Deflated (G+I)	L. Deflated (K/A)
1946	1.29	0	0	0	.3	.3	.5	0	0	.3	.5	.39
1947	1.32	0	0	0	.6	.6	.9	0	0	.6	.9	.65
1948	1.35	0	0	0	.3	.3	.4	0	0	.3	.4	.30
1949	1.39	0	0	0	.2	.2	.3	0	0	.2	.3	.21
1950	1.43	0	0	0	.1	.1	.1	0	0	.1	.1	.10
1951	1.47	0	0	0	.2	.2	.3	0	0	.2	.3	.18
1952	1.53	.7	.1	0	0	.8	1.0	0	0	.8	1.0	.68
1953	1.57	.7	0	0	0	.7	.9	0	0	.7	.9	.58
1954	1.62	1.1	0	0	0	1.1	1.5	0	0	1.1	1.5	.90
1955	1.65	1.2	.8	0	0	2.0	2.6	0	0	2.0	2.6	1.58
1956	1.68	1.2	.1	0	1.4	2.7	3.4	0	0	2.7	3.4	2.01
1957	1.71	4.3	.7	1.6	1.6	8.2	10.0	0	0	8.2	10.0	5.83
1958	1.75	6.9	.5	1.1	.4	8.9	10.9	0	0	8.9	10.9	6.25
1959	1.80	1.9	.2	.8	1.6	4.5	5.5	.1	.1	4.6	5.7	3.14
1960	1.85	4.1	.2	0	-.4	3.9	4.8	.1	.1	4.0	4.9	2.64
1961	1.91	5.2	.3	0	0	5.5	6.6	.3	.4	5.8	6.9	3.64
1962	1.97	2.9	.2	0	0	3.1	3.7	1.5	1.8	4.6	5.5	2.81
1963	2.04	6.5	.3	0	5.8	12.6	15.2	0	0	12.6	15.2	7.44
1964	2.11	6.7	.7	0	2.4	9.8	11.7	.4	.5	10.2	12.2	5.77
1965	2.18	2.2	.4	.4	1.2	4.2	4.9	.7	.8	4.9	5.7	2.60
1966	2.26	11.9	1.0	0	1.0	13.9	15.6	.7	.8	14.6	16.4	7.26
1967	2.28	8.9	.6	0	.6	10.1	11.1	1.0	1.1	11.1	12.2	5.36
1968	2.31	12.8	.4	0	.7	13.9	15.1	1.0	1.1	14.9	16.2	7.00
1969	2.45	2.5	.8	0	.8	4.1	4.3	.6	.6	4.7	5.0	2.02
1970	2.64	5.2	1.0	2.0	.8	9.0	9.0	.3	.3	9.3	9.3	3.52
1971	2.72	5.2	1.1	.6	.8	7.7	7.5	.6	.6	8.3	8.1	2.96
1972	2.81	3.6	1.2	1.6	1.0	7.4	6.9	.5	.5	7.9	7.4	2.64
1973	2.90	5.6	.9	7.3	.7	14.5	11.7	.5	.4	15.0	12.1	4.17
1974	2.99	24.6	1.2	3.2	1.2	30.2	19.1	.6	.4	30.8	19.4	6.50
1975	3.04	25.4	9.0	1.3	1.2	36.9	20.8	4.2	2.4	41.1	23.2	7.64
1976	3.20	16.7	6.2	4.0	1.5	28.4	15.5	3.5	1.9	31.9	17.4	5.45
1977	3.32	7.8	2.8	0	2.2	12.8	6.8	3.1	1.6	15.9	8.4	2.53
1978	3.44	13.0	2.4	.5	1.7	17.6	8.7	3.2	1.6	20.8	10.3	2.98
1979	3.56	22.0	4.8	.8	2.4	30.0	13.0	2.3	1.0	32.3	14.0	3.93
1980	3.69	45.8	5.2	11.9	3.3	66.2	25.3	3.9	1.5	70.1	26.8	7.26
1981	3.83	25.7	8.2	.9	2.5	37.3	13.0	8.9	3.1	46.2	16.2	4.22
1982	3.96	67.9	10.1	.3	3.0	81.3	28.1	31.3	10.8	112.6	39.0	9.84
1983	4.09	87.3	15.5	0	3.2	106.0	36.3	48.3	16.5	154.3	52.8	12.92
1984	4.23	71.0	20.2	0	4.0	95.2	32.2	77.4	26.1	172.6	58.3	13.78
1985	4.37	204.6	19.4	0	7.0	231.0	78.7	67.4	22.9	298.4	101.6	23.25
1986	4.51	111.8	19.6	0	5.6	137.0	46.5	61.1	20.7	198.1	67.3	14.91
1987	4.66	174.5	18.1	0	5.2	197.8	65.5	61.2	20.3	259.0	85.8	18.42
1988	4.80	129.9	20.4	0	6.6	156.9	48.5	41.2	12.7	198.1	61.3	12.77
Total		1,129.3	174.6	38.3	72.7	1,414.9	624.4	425.9	152.8	1,840.8	777.2	5.33[a]

1. Deflated using Export Price Index (Table 3331) in 1970 U.S. dollars.

a. Per capita average, 1946–88.

SOURCE: USAID–OLG, various years (see Data Sources in text); Table 3331 (Chapter 33, above); IMF-IFS-SY, various years; population data from Chapter 6, above.

Figure 35:45

HONDURAS: YEARLY ANNOUNCED TOTAL U.S. ASSISTANCE,[1] 1946–88

(M US)

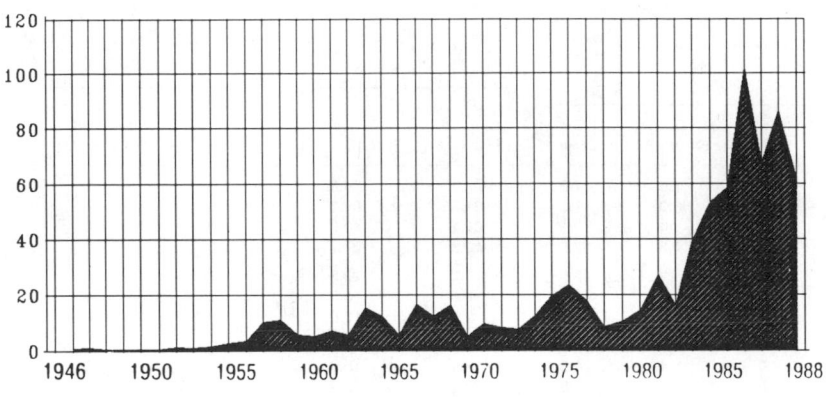

SOURCE: Table 3516.

Figure 35:46

HONDURAS: YEARLY PER CAPITA ANNOUNCED TOTAL U.S. ASSISTANCE,[1] 1946–88

(US)

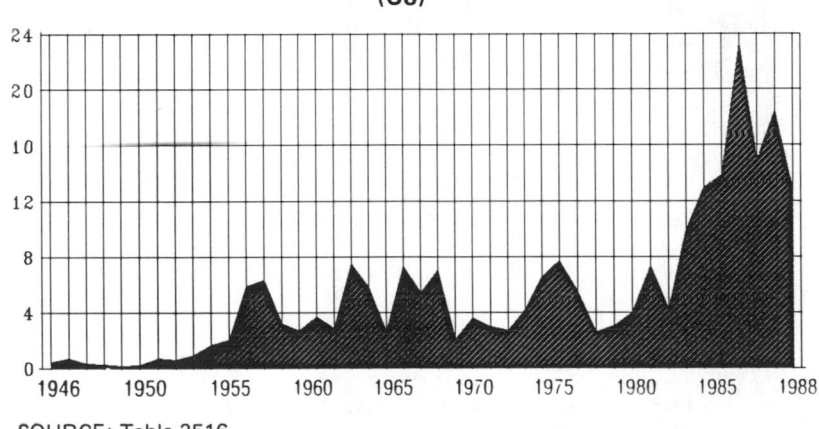

SOURCE: Table 3516.

Figure 35:47

HONDURAS: PER CAPITA ASSISTANCE COMPARED TO AVERAGE YEARLY LATIN AMERICA PER CAPITA ASSISTANCE,[1] 1946–88

(US)

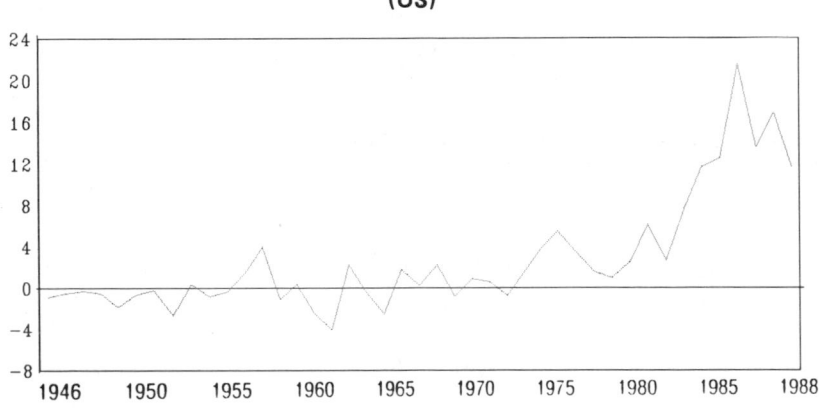

SOURCE: Table 3529.

Table 3517

MEXICO: ANNOUNCED AUTHORIZED U.S. ASSISTANCE, NOMINAL AND DEFLATED,[1] 1946–88

| Year | A. Population (M) | Economic Assistance Nominal (M US) | | | | Economic Total (M US) | | Military Total (M US) | | Economic + Military Total (M US) | | Per Capita (US) |
		B. USAID	C. FFP	D. EXP/IMP	E. Other	F. Nominal (B+C+D+E)	G. Deflated (F/EPI = 100)	H. Nominal	I. Deflated (H/EPI = 100)	J. Nominal (F+H)	K. Deflated (G+I)	L. Deflated (K/A)
1946	22.78	0	0	1.5	1.2	2.7	4.6	0	0	2.7	4.6	.20
1947	23.44	0	0	50.0	11.3	61.3	87.1	0	0	61.3	87.1	3.71
1948	24.13	0	0	0	30.1	30.1	40.2	0	0	30.1	40.2	1.67
1949	24.83	0	0	1.5	17.8	19.3	27.7	0	0	19.3	27.7	1.12
1950	25.79	0	0	.2	20.0	20.2	29.8	0	0	20.2	29.8	1.16
1951	25.59	0	0	0	8.2	8.2	10.6	0	0	8.2	10.6	.41
1952	27.85	.7	0	4.0	4.6	9.3	12.0	0	0	9.3	12.0	.43
1953	28.70	.7	0	5.4	.9	7.0	9.1	0	0	7.0	9.1	.32
1954	29.61	1.4	0	1.4	4.8	7.6	10.0	0	0	7.6	10.0	.34
1955	30.56	1.4	0	0	.8	2.2	2.9	0	0	2.2	2.9	.09
1956	31.56	.7	.4	51.5	0	52.6	65.8	0	0	52.6	65.8	2.08
1957	32.61	.9	.6	24.8	0	26.3	32.0	0	0	26.3	32.0	.98
1958	33.76	.6	11.7	48.0	0	60.3	74.1	0	0	60.3	74.1	2.19
1959	34.86	.7	1.1	109.0	0	110.8	136.1	.5	.6	111.3	136.7	3.92
1960	36.05	.7	1.3	46.3	0	48.3	59.0	2.7	3.3	51.0	62.3	1.73
1961	37.22	1.2	3.2	27.8	0	32.2	38.6	.4	.5	32.6	39.0	1.05
1962	38.54	20.6	5.2	105.3	10.6	141.7	170.7	.7	.8	142.4	171.6	4.45
1963	39.87	.2	15.4	23.2	8.0	46.8	56.4	1.5	1.8	48.3	58.2	1.46
1964	41.25	22.4	18.0	52.0	12.1	104.5	124.7	3.3	3.9	107.8	128.6	3.12
1965	42.69	24.9	7.2	163.2	4.8	200.1	231.6	.8	.9	200.9	232.5	5.45
1966	44.14	.2	.1	127.9	0	128.2	144.0	.2	.2	128.4	144.3	3.27
1967	45.67	.3	0	101.2	0	101.5	111.8	.2	.2	101.7	112.0	2.45
1968	47.27	.1	0	87.3	0	87.4	94.9	.1	.1	87.5	95.0	2.01
1969	48.93	.2	0	17.5	0	17.7	18.7	.1	.1	17.8	18.8	.38
1970	50.69	1.0	0	40.4	−.5	40.9	40.9	.1	.1	41.0	41.0	.81
1971	52.45	0	0	41.2	−.1	41.1	39.9	4.5	4.4	45.6	44.2	.84
1972	54.27	0	0	51.6	.5	52.1	48.9	2.0	1.9	54.1	50.8	.94
1973	56.16	0	0	143.0	0	143.0	115.2	0	0	143.0	115.2	2.05
1974	58.12	0	0	162.9	.4	163.3	103.1	0	0	163.3	103.1	1.77
1975	60.15	0	0	195.7	.1	195.8	110.6	.1	.1	195.9	110.7	1.84
1976	62.33	0	0	180.2	.6	180.8	98.8	.1	.1	180.9	98.9	1.59
1977	64.59	0	0	60.9	1.1	62.0	32.7	.1	.1	62.1	32.8	.51
1978	65.43	0	0	608.5	20.5	629.0	310.5	.1	0	629.1	310.5	4.75
1979	67.42	0	0	157.2	13.5	170.7	74.0	.2	.1	170.9	74.1	1.10
1980	69.35	0	0	180.2	7.4	187.6	71.7	.1	0	187.7	71.7	1.03
1981	71.19	0	0	652.6	9.8	662.4	231.7	.1	0	662.5	231.7	3.26
1982	73.01	0	0	293.4	8.7	302.1	104.5	.1	0	302.2	104.6	1.43
1983	75.10	0	0	37.2	59.2	96.4	33.0	.1	0	96.5	33.0	.44
1984	76.79	0	0	66.5	21.3	87.8	29.7	.2	.1	88.0	29.7	.39
1985	78.52	0	1.2	10.1	9.9	21.2	7.2	.2	.1	21.4	7.3	.09
1986	79.56	0	.3	0	11.6	11.9	4.0	.2	.1	12.1	4.1	.05
1987	81.16	0	2.2	5.1	15.3	22.6	7.5	.3	.1	22.9	7.6	.09
1988	82.73	0	3.2	0	100.1	103.3	32.0	.2	.1	103.5	32.0	.39
Total		78.9	71.1	3,935.7	414.6	4,500.3	3,088.2	19.2	19.7	4,519.5	3,107.9	1.57[a]

1. Deflated using Export Price Index (Table 3331) in 1970 U.S. dollars.

a. Per capita average, 1946–88.

SOURCE: USAID-OLG, various years (see Data Sources in text); Table 3331 (Chapter 33, above); IMF-IFS-SY, various years; population data from Chapter 6, above.

Figure 35:48

MEXICO: YEARLY ANNOUNCED TOTAL U.S. ASSISTANCE,[1] 1946–88

(M US)

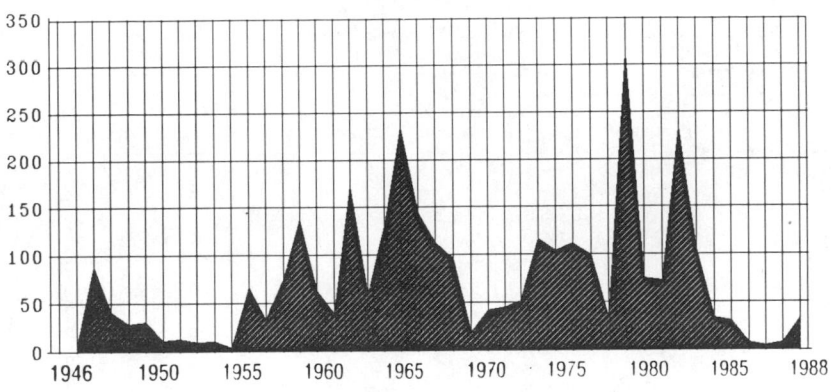

SOURCE: Table 3517.

Figure 35:49

MEXICO: YEARLY PER CAPITA ANNOUNCED TOTAL U.S. ASSISTANCE,[1] 1946–88

(US)

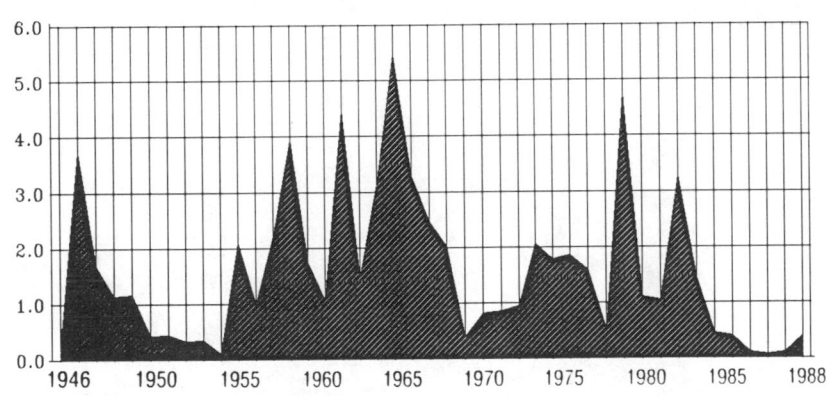

SOURCE: Table 3517.

Figure 35:50

MEXICO: PER CAPITA ASSISTANCE COMPARED TO AVERAGE YEARLY LATIN AMERICA PER CAPITA ASSISTANCE,[1] 1946–88

(US)

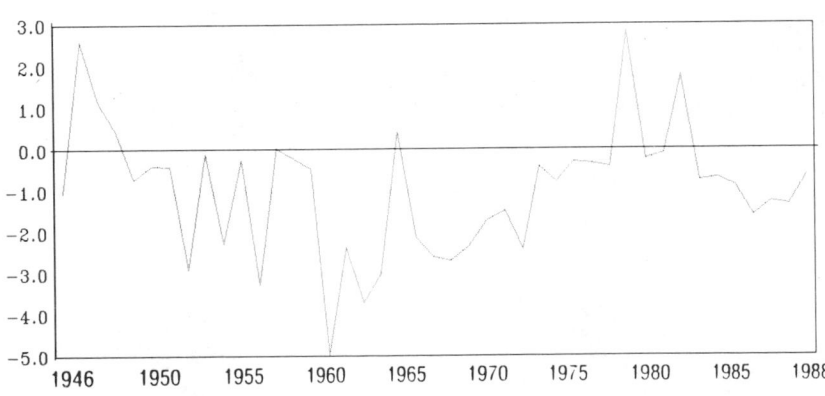

SOURCE: Table 3529.

Table 3518

NICARAGUA: ANNOUNCED AUTHORIZED U.S. ASSISTANCE, NOMINAL AND DEFLATED,[1] 1946–88

| Year | A. Population (M) | Economic Assistance Nominal (M US) | | | | Economic Total (M US) | | Military Total (M US) | | Economic + Military | | |
		B. USAID	C. FFP	D. EXP/IMP	E. Other	F. Nominal (B+C+D+E)	G. Deflated (F/EPI = 100)	H. Nominal	I. Deflated (H/EPI = 100)	J. Nominal (F+H)	K. Deflated (G+I)	L. Deflated (K/A)
1946	.95	0	0	0	1.7	1.7	2.9	0	0	1.7	2.9	3.03
1947	.98	0	0	0	1.7	1.7	2.4	0	0	1.7	2.4	2.46
1948	1.00	0	0	0	.5	.5	.7	0	0	.5	.7	.67
1949	1.03	0	0	0	.4	.4	.6	0	0	.4	.6	.56
1950	1.06	0	0	0	.4	.4	.6	0	0	.4	.6	.56
1951	1.09	0	0	.6	.7	1.3	1.7	0	0	1.3	1.7	1.53
1952	1.12	.6	0	0	.2	.8	1.0	0	0	.8	1.0	.92
1953	1.15	.6	0	0	.3	.9	1.2	0	0	.9	1.2	1.02
1954	1.18	.5	0	0	.7	1.2	1.6	0	0	1.2	1.6	1.34
1955	1.22	.9	0	0	2.7	3.6	4.7	0	0	3.6	4.7	3.85
1956	1.26	.8	0	0	1.8	2.6	3.3	0	0	2.6	3.3	2.58
1957	1.29	.7	0	2.0	3.5	6.2	7.5	0	0	6.2	7.5	5.85
1958	1.33	.8	0	0	2.7	3.5	4.3	0	0	3.5	4.3	3.23
1959	1.37	1.7	0	.5	2.1	4.3	5.3	.1	.1	4.4	5.4	3.95
1960	1.41	3.3	0	9.0	0	12.3	15.0	.2	.2	12.5	15.3	10.82
1961	1.45	8.3	.2	2.0	1.4	11.9	14.3	.6	.7	12.5	15.0	10.32
1962	1.50	3.5	.7	0	9.5	13.7	16.5	1.0	1.2	14.7	17.7	11.81
1963	1.54	3.4	1.4	0	2.6	7.4	8.9	1.6	1.9	9.0	10.8	7.04
1964	1.58	3.9	1.9	1.2	0	7.0	8.4	1.2	1.4	8.2	9.8	6.19
1965	1.62	16.2	.9	0	6.1	23.2	26.9	1.2	1.4	24.4	28.2	17.43
1966	1.66	16.0	1.2	2.8	.3	20.3	22.8	1.0	1.1	21.3	23.9	14.42
1967	1.70	11.3	.8	0	0	12.1	13.3	1.0	1.1	13.1	14.4	8.49
1968	1.74	22.1	.2	4.9	−.1	27.1	29.4	1.3	1.4	28.4	30.8	17.72
1969	1.79	1.7	.4	0	.2	2.3	2.4	.7	.7	3.0	3.2	1.77
1970	1.83	2.3	.4	0	.4	3.1	3.1	1.1	1.1	4.2	4.2	2.30
1971	1.89	12.5	.3	2.1	.4	15.3	14.8	.9	.9	16.2	15.7	8.31
1972	1.95	2.5	1.7	.1	.5	4.8	4.5	.8	.8	5.6	5.3	2.70
1973	2.01	22.5	3.0	0	1.8	27.3	22.0	1.5	1.2	28.8	23.2	11.55
1974	2.08	12.4	2.4	3.4	2.4	20.6	13.0	1.3	.8	21.9	13.8	6.65
1975	2.16	40.1	1.4	0	1.0	42.5	24.0	4.3	2.4	46.8	26.4	12.24
1976	2.24	1.4	.4	3.4	1.5	6.7	3.7	3.1	1.7	9.8	5.4	2.39
1977	2.32	17.7	1.0	12.4	1.5	32.6	17.2	3.8	2.0	36.4	19.2	8.28
1978	2.41	12.5	.1	.2	1.4	14.2	7.0	.4	.2	14.6	7.2	2.99
1979	2.54	9.7	7.0	0	1.8	18.5	8.0	0	0	18.5	8.0	3.16
1980	2.73	19.4	18.0	0	1.3	38.7	14.8	0	0	38.7	14.8	5.41
1981	2.86	58.4	1.2	0	.3	59.9	21.0	0	0	59.9	21.0	7.33
1982	2.96	5.8	.4	0	.1	6.3	2.2	0	0	6.3	2.2	.74
1983	3.06	0	0	0	0	0	0	0	0	0	0	0
1984	3.14	0	0	0	.1	.1	0	0	0	.1	0	.01
1985	3.27	0	0	0	0	0	0	0	0	0	0	0
1986	3.38	0	0	0	0	0	0	0	0	0	0	0
1987	3.50	0	0	0	0	0	0	0	0	0	0	0
1988	3.63	0	0	0	.4	.4	.1	0	0	.4	.1	.03
Total		313.5	45.0	44.6	54.3	457.4	351.0	27.1	22.5	484.5	373.5	4.92[a]

1. Deflated using Export Price Index (Table 3331) in 1970 U.S. dollars.

a. Per capita average, 1946–88.

SOURCE: USAID–OLG, various years (see Data Sources in text); Table 3331 (Chapter 33, above); IMF-IFS-SY, various years; population data from Chapter 6, above.

Figure 35:51

NICARAGUA: YEARLY ANNOUNCED TOTAL U.S. ASSISTANCE,[1] 1946–88

(M US)

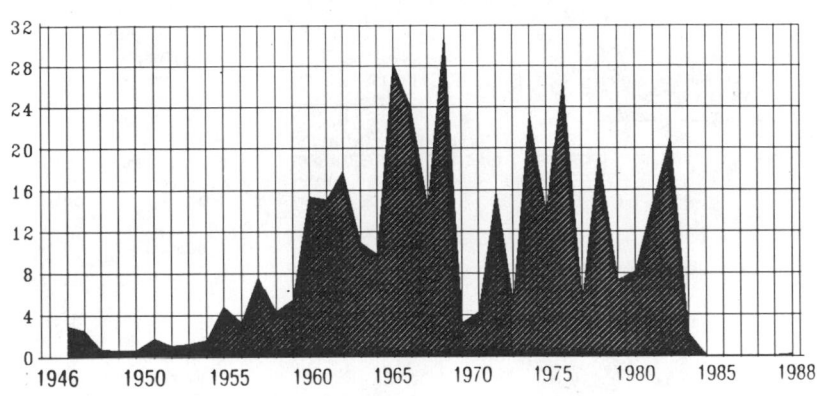

SOURCE: Table 3518.

Figure 35:52

NICARAGUA: YEARLY PER CAPITA ANNOUNCED TOTAL U.S. ASSISTANCE,[1] 1946–88

(US)

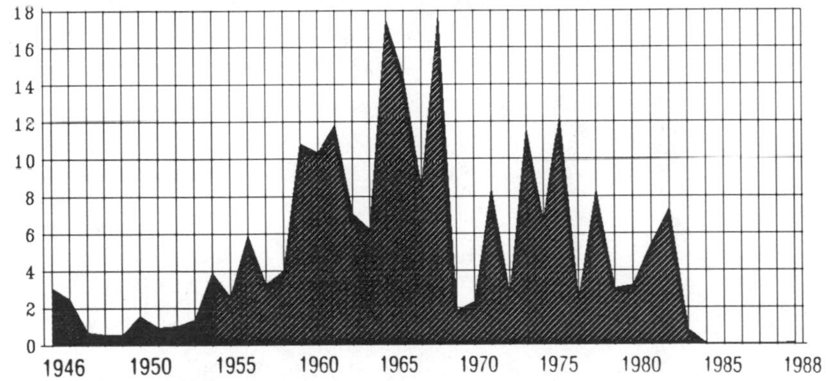

SOURCE: Table 3518.

Figure 35:53

NICARAGUA: PER CAPITA ASSISTANCE COMPARED TO AVERAGE YEARLY LATIN AMERICA PER CAPITA ASSISTANCE,[1] 1946–88

(US)

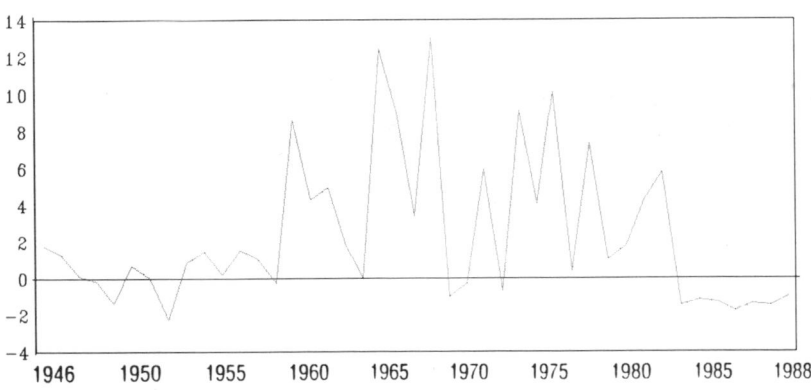

SOURCE: Table 3529.

Table 3519

PANAMA: ANNOUNCED AUTHORIZED U.S. ASSISTANCE, NOMINAL AND DEFLATED,[1] 1946–88

Year	A. Population (M)	Economic Assistance Nominal (M US) B. USAID	C. FFP	D. EXP/IMP	E. Other	Economic Total (M US) F. Nominal (B+C+D+E)	G. Deflated (F/EPI = 100)	Military Total (M US) H. Nominal	I. Deflated (H/EPI = 100)	Economic + Military Total (M US) J. Nominal (F+H)	K. Deflated (G+I)	Per Capita (US) L. Deflated (K/A)
1946	.72	0	0	0	.2	.2	.3	0	0	.2	.3	.47
1947	.74	0	0	0	.2	.2	.3	0	0	.2	.3	.38
1948	.76	0	0	0	.2	.2	.3	0	0	.2	.3	.35
1949	.78	0	0	2.0	.3	2.3	3.3	0	0	2.3	3.3	4.24
1950	.80	0	0	0	.2	.2	.3	0	0	.2	.3	.37
1951	.82	0	0	.5	.4	.9	1.2	0	0	.9	1.2	1.41
1952	.84	1.3	0	1.5	.2	3.0	3.9	0	0	3.0	3.9	4.62
1953	.87	.8	0	0	.7	1.5	1.9	0	0	1.5	1.9	2.24
1954	.89	1.1	.1	0	.4	1.6	2.1	0	0	1.6	2.1	2.37
1955	.92	1.4	.4	0	1.1	2.9	3.8	0	0	2.9	3.8	4.11
1956	.95	1.1	1.2	0	7.5	9.8	12.3	0	0	9.8	12.3	12.89
1957	.97	3.0	1.6	12.8	9.2	26.6	32.4	0	0	26.6	32.4	33.36
1958	1.00	1.4	1.4	0	2.7	5.5	6.8	0	0	5.5	6.8	6.76
1959	1.03	1.5	.5	0	0	2.0	2.5	0	0	2.0	2.5	2.39
1960	1.06	1.6	.1	.3	0	2.0	2.4	0	0	2.0	2.4	2.30
1961	1.09	15.7	.4	0	.1	16.2	19.4	.1	.1	16.3	19.5	17.91
1962	1.13	12.4	.4	2.0	10.4	25.2	30.4	.3	.4	25.5	30.7	27.19
1963	1.17	8.1	.7	0	.4	9.2	11.1	.7	.8	9.9	11.9	10.19
1964	1.20	8.9	.8	7.4	7.7	24.8	29.6	.1	.1	24.9	29.7	24.76
1965	1.24	10.9	.5	3.5	8.7	23.6	27.3	.2	.2	23.8	27.5	22.21
1966	1.27	11.7	.5	0	1.1	13.3	14.9	.4	.4	13.7	15.4	12.12
1967	1.31	33.9	.6	0	.7	35.2	38.8	.5	.6	35.7	39.3	30.01
1968	1.35	18.8	.3	.5	.9	20.5	22.3	.3	.3	20.8	22.6	16.73
1969	1.39	15.8	.6	0	.8	17.2	18.1	.4	.4	17.6	18.6	13.36
1970	1.43	7.3	1.0	2.5	.7	11.5	11.5	.4	.4	11.9	11.9	8.32
1971	1.48	11.1	.6	2.7	.5	14.9	14.5	.5	.5	15.4	14.9	10.09
1972	1.52	22.8	1.2	30.1	9.8	63.9	60.0	.5	.5	64.4	60.5	39.78
1973	1.57	7.1	.5	45.6	7.9	61.1	49.2	.6	.5	61.7	49.7	31.67
1974	1.62	10.8	.7	2.8	16.4	30.7	19.4	.6	.4	31.3	19.8	12.20
1975	1.68	8.3	.9	30.1	12.0	51.3	29.0	.6	.3	51.9	29.3	17.45
1976	1.72	26.7	1.2	8.9	4.9	41.7	22.8	1.4	.8	43.1	23.6	13.69
1977	1.77	13.7	2.2	0	.4	16.3	8.6	3.1	1.6	19.4	10.2	5.78
1978	1.81	21.3	1.3	0	.5	23.1	11.4	.5	.2	23.6	11.6	6.44
1979	1.85	19.9	1.1	3.6	.3	24.9	10.8	1.4	.6	26.3	11.4	6.16
1980	1.90	1.0	1.0	0	0	2.0	.8	.3	.1	2.3	.9	.46
1981	1.94	8.7	1.9	0	0	10.6	3.7	.4	.1	11.0	3.8	1.98
1982	2.04	11.7	1.3	0	0	13.0	4.5	5.4	1.9	18.4	6.4	3.12
1983	2.09	6.3	1.1	0	0	7.4	2.5	5.5	1.9	12.9	4.4	2.11
1984	2.13	10.7	1.3	0	.2	12.2	4.1	13.5	4.6	25.7	8.7	4.07
1985	2.18	74.3	.1	0	.1	74.5	25.4	10.6	3.6	85.1	29.0	13.29
1986	2.23	33.3	.1	0	.3	33.7	11.4	8.2	2.8	41.9	14.2	6.38
1987	2.27	12.1	0	0	0	12.1	4.0	3.5	1.2	15.6	5.2	2.28
1988	2.32	1.2	0	0	0	1.2	.4	0	0	1.2	.4	.16
Total		457.7	27.6	156.8	108.1	750.2	579.5	60.0	25.4	810.2	604.8	10.19[a]

1. Deflated using Export Price Index (Table 3331) in 1970 U.S. dollars.

a. Per capita average, 1946–88.

SOURCE: USAID-OLG, various years (see Data Sources in text); Table 3331 (Chapter 33, above); IMF-IFS-SY, various years; population data from Chapter 6, above.

Figure 35:54

PANAMA: YEARLY ANNOUNCED TOTAL U.S. ASSISTANCE,[1] 1946–88

(M US)

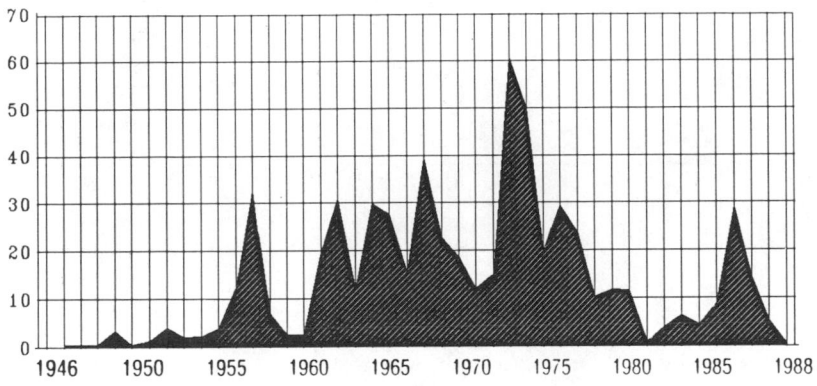

SOURCE: Table 3520.

Figure 35:55

PANAMA: YEARLY PER CAPITA ANNOUNCED TOTAL U.S. ASSISTANCE,[1] 1946–88

(US)

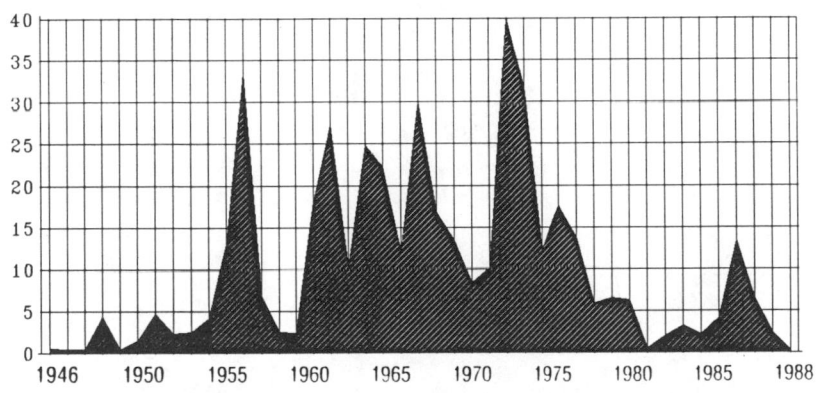

SOURCE: Table 3519.

Figure 35:56

PANAMA: PER CAPITA ASSISTANCE COMPARED TO AVERAGE YEARLY LATIN AMERICA PER CAPITA ASSISTANCE,[1] 1946–88

(US)

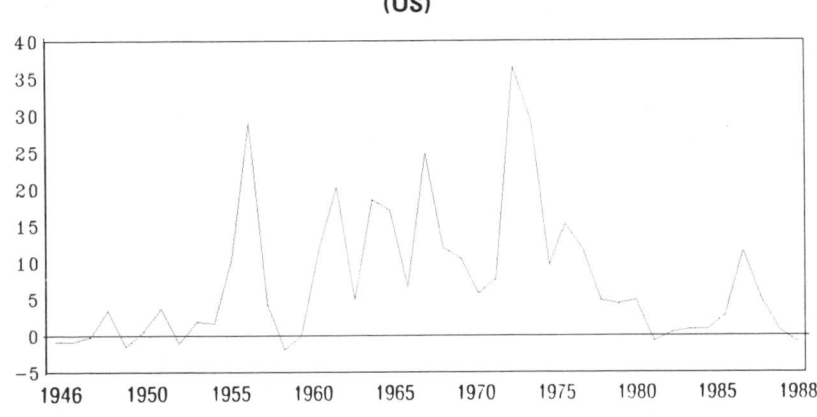

SOURCE: Table 3529.

Table 3520

PARAGUAY: ANNOUNCED AUTHORIZED U.S. ASSISTANCE, NOMINAL AND DEFLATED,[1] 1946–88

Year	A. Population (M)	Economic Assistance Nominal (M US)				Economic Total (M US)		Military Total (M US)		Economic + Military Total (M US)		Per Capita (US)
		B. USAID	C. FFP	D. EXP/IMP	E. Other	F. Nominal (B+C+D+E)	G. Deflated (F/EPI = 100)	H. Nominal	I. Deflated (H/EPI = 100)	J. Nominal (F+H)	K. Deflated (G+I)	L. Deflated (K/A)
1946	1.28	0	0	0	.4	.4	.7	0	0	.4	.7	.53
1947	1.31	0	0	0	.4	.4	.6	0	0	.4	.6	.43
1948	1.34	0	0	0	.4	.4	.5	0	0	.4	.5	.40
1949	1.37	0	0	0	.4	.4	.6	0	0	.4	.6	.42
1950	1.40	0	0	0	.5	.5	.7	0	0	.5	.7	.53
1951	1.43	0	0	0	.7	.7	.9	0	0	.7	.9	.63
1952	1.46	1.6	0	0	0	1.6	2.1	0	0	1.6	2.1	1.42
1953	1.50	.8	0	0	0	.8	1.0	0	0	.8	1.0	.69
1954	1.53	1.2	0	0	0	1.2	1.6	0	0	1.2	1.6	1.04
1955	1.57	1.8	.2	7.7	0	9.7	12.6	0	0	9.7	12.6	8.06
1956	1.61	1.8	2.3	0	0	4.1	5.1	0	0	4.1	5.1	3.18
1957	1.68	2.5	.2	.1	0	2.8	3.4	0	0	2.8	3.4	2.03
1958	1.68	5.0	.2	1.3	0	6.5	8.0	0	0	6.5	8.0	4.75
1959	1.71	5.3	.3	0	0	5.6	6.9	0	0	5.6	6.9	4.02
1960	1.75	2.4	.5	1.3	0	4.2	5.1	.1	.1	4.3	5.3	3.00
1961	1.80	9.7	1.1	0	0	10.8	12.9	.2	.2	11.0	13.2	7.32
1962	1.85	1.1	6.9	0	0	8.0	9.6	.2	.2	8.2	9.9	5.34
1963	1.91	3.0	3.4	0	2.9	9.3	11.2	1.3	1.6	10.6	12.8	6.69
1964	1.97	5.3	3.0	0	0	8.3	9.9	1.2	1.4	9.5	11.3	5.75
1965	2.03	2.3	2.5	0	4.9	9.7	11.2	1.5	1.7	11.2	13.0	6.39
1966	2.07	11.6	3.4	0	0	15.0	16.9	1.0	1.1	16.0	18.0	8.68
1967	2.13	3.9	.6	0	.3	4.8	5.3	1.1	1.2	5.9	6.5	3.05
1968	2.18	2.4	3.1	0	.4	5.9	6.4	1.8	2.0	7.7	8.4	3.84
1969	2.24	9.5	3.6	3.1	.5	16.7	17.6	1.0	1.1	17.7	18.7	8.34
1970	2.30	7.1	.6	0	.5	8.2	8.2	.8	.8	9.0	9.0	3.91
1971	2.36	6.9	5.4	0	.4	12.7	12.3	1.0	1.0	13.7	13.3	5.63
1972	2.43	2.8	1.7	0	.4	4.9	4.6	.8	.8	5.7	5.4	2.20
1973	2.50	6.0	.9	0	.4	7.3	5.9	.8	.6	8.1	6.5	2.61
1974	2.57	4.4	.3	0	1.2	5.9	3.7	1.5	.9	7.4	4.7	1.82
1975	2.69	6.7	.4	0	.9	8.0	4.5	1.6	.9	9.6	5.4	2.02
1976	2.78	5.5	.1	0	1.2	6.8	3.7	3.3	1.8	10.1	5.5	1.99
1977	2.87	1.7	.2	0	1.3	3.2	1.7	.7	.4	3.9	2.1	.72
1978	2.97	1.8	.3	0	1.4	3.5	1.7	.6	.3	4.1	2.0	.68
1979	3.07	7.1	.3	0	2.9	10.3	4.5	0	0	10.3	4.5	1.45
1980	3.17	1.3	.4	0	2.0	3.7	1.4	0	0	3.7	1.4	.45
1981	3.27	2.0	.7	0	3.5	6.2	2.2	0	0	6.2	2.2	.66
1982	3.37	0	.1	63.9	3.7	67.7	23.4	0	0	67.7	23.4	6.95
1983	3.47	0	0	0	4.3	4.3	1.5	.1	0	4.4	1.5	.43
1984	3.28	.2	0	0	2.5	2.7	.9	.1	0	2.8	.9	.29
1985	3.68	1.0	0	0	2.5	3.5	1.2	.1	0	3.6	1.2	.33
1986	3.81	1.1	.3	0	1.9	3.3	1.1	.1	0	3.4	1.2	.30
1987	3.92	1.0	0	0	2.1	3.1	1.0	.1	0	3.2	1.1	.27
1988	4.04	.8	0	0	3.3	4.1	1.3	.1	0	4.2	1.3	.32
Total		128.6	43.0	77.4	48.2	297.2	235.8	21.1	18.4	318.3	254.1	2.78[a]

1. Deflated using Export Price Index (Table 3331) in 1970 U.S. dollars.

a. Per capita average, 1946–88.

SOURCE: USAID-OLG, various years (see Data Sources in text); Table 3331 (Chapter 33, above); IMF-IFS-SY, various years; population data from Chapter 6, above.

Figure 35:57

PARAGUAY: YEARLY ANNOUNCED TOTAL U.S. ASSISTANCE,[1] 1946–88

(M US)

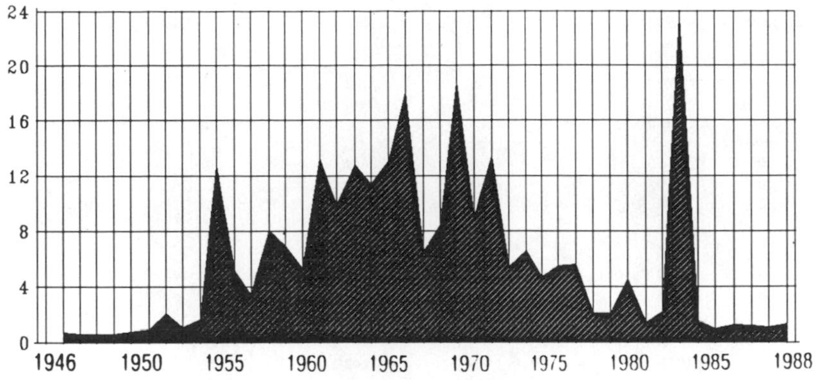

SOURCE: Table 3520.

Figure 35:58

PARAGUAY: YEARLY PER CAPITA ANNOUNCED TOTAL U.S. ASSISTANCE,[1] 1946–88

(US)

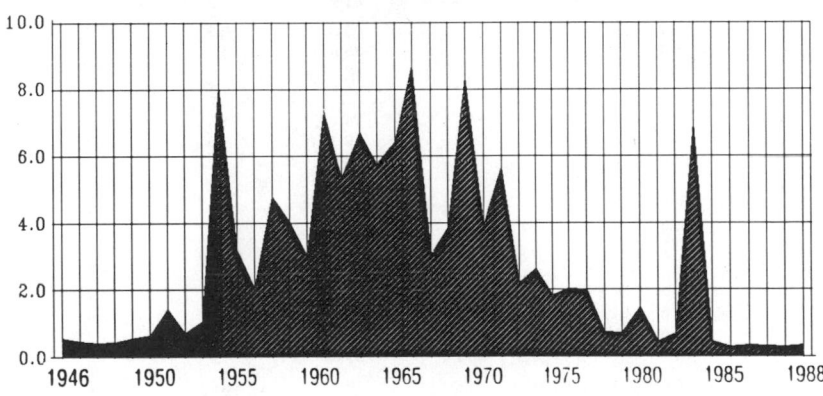

SOURCE: Table 3520.

Figure 35:59

PARAGUAY: PER CAPITA ASSISTANCE COMPARED TO AVERAGE YEARLY LATIN AMERICA PER CAPITA ASSISTANCE,[1] 1946–88

(US)

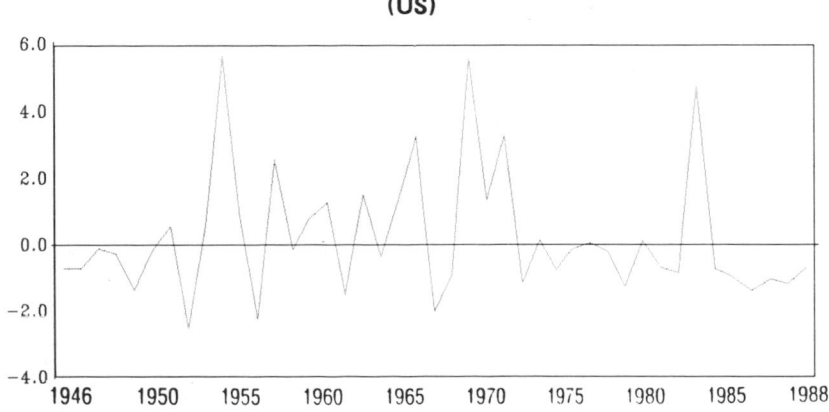

SOURCE: Table 3529.

Table 3521

PERU: ANNOUNCED AUTHORIZED U.S. ASSISTANCE, NOMINAL AND DEFLATED,[1] 1946–88

		Economic Assistance Nominal (M US)				Economic Total (M US)		Military Total (M US)		Economic + Military Total (M US)		Per Capita (US)
Year	A. Population (M)	B. USAID	C. FFP	D. EXP/IMP	E. Other	F. Nominal (B+C+D+E)	G. Deflated (F/EPI = 100)	H. Nominal	I. Deflated (H/EPI = 100)	J. Nominal (F+H)	K. Deflated (G+I)	L. Deflated (K/A)
1946	7.42	0	0	0	.6	.6	1.0	0	0	.6	1.0	.14
1947	7.55	0	0	0	5.6	5.6	8.0	0	0	5.6	8.0	1.05
1948	7.68	0	0	0	1.3	1.3	1.7	0	0	1.3	1.7	.23
1949	7.82	0	0	0	.9	.9	1.3	0	0	.9	1.3	.17
1950	7.97	0	0	0	.9	.9	1.3	0	0	.9	1.3	.17
1951	8.12	0	0	20.8	1.3	22.1	28.4	0	0	22.1	28.4	3.50
1952	8.27	1.8	0	.6	0	2.4	3.1	0	0	2.4	3.1	.38
1953	8.43	1.7	0	0	0	1.7	2.2	0	0	1.7	2.2	.26
1954	8.60	2.4	.2	0	0	2.6	3.4	0	0	2.6	3.4	.40
1955	8.79	2.4	6.3	101.2	0	109.9	143.3	0	0	109.9	143.3	16.30
1956	9.00	2.8	8.7	0	0	11.5	14.4	0	0	11.5	14.4	1.60
1957	9.23	4.6	11.5	.1	0	16.2	19.7	0	0	16.2	19.7	2.14
1958	9.48	2.7	6.2	11.6	0	20.5	25.2	0	0	20.5	25.2	2.66
1959	9.75	2.8	1.0	54.9	0	58.7	72.1	4.4	5.4	63.1	77.5	7.95
1960	10.02	7.3	9.9	8.1	0	25.3	30.9	3.5	4.3	28.8	35.2	3.51
1961	10.32	29.2	3.4	26.5	0	59.1	70.8	14.4	17.2	73.5	88.0	8.53
1962	10.63	26.6	9.0	17.1	25.5	78.2	94.2	13.7	16.5	91.9	110.7	10.42
1963	10.96	-3.0	6.6	10.7	4.1	18.4	22.2	8.1	9.8	26.5	31.9	2.91
1964	11.30	28.6	15.1	28.2	6.4	78.3	93.4	10.5	12.5	88.8	106.0	9.38
1965	11.65	6.3	6.5	14.2	9.2	36.2	41.9	8.2	9.5	44.4	51.4	4.41
1966	12.01	18.3	8.2	3.7	13.2	43.4	48.8	9.8	11.0	53.2	59.8	4.98
1967	12.31	22.0	2.4	5.7	2.2	32.3	35.6	6.7	7.4	39.0	43.0	3.49
1968	12.67	3.9	7.0	4.7	1.6	17.2	18.7	9.9	10.7	27.1	29.4	2.32
1969	13.05	3.6	7.8	16.0	1.3	28.7	30.3	2.9	3.1	31.6	33.3	2.55
1970	13.45	8.2	4.6	0	1.3	14.1	14.1	1.9	1.9	16.0	16.0	1.19
1971	13.59	6.9	6.9	4.3	1.4	19.5	18.9	.6	.6	20.1	19.5	1.43
1972	13.95	31.7	11.1	0	32.5	75.3	70.7	1.0	.9	76.3	71.6	5.14
1973	14.35	3.8	4.2	0	71.0	79.0	63.7	.8	.6	79.8	64.3	4.48
1974	15.16	12.1	3.7	55.3	7.4	78.5	49.6	15.9	10.0	94.4	59.6	3.93
1975	15.47	8.9	6.4	16.3	15.8	47.4	26.8	21.4	12.1	68.8	38.9	2.51
1976	15.57	13.6	9.7	38.3	54.8	116.4	63.6	21.1	11.5	137.5	75.1	4.83
1977	15.99	17.4	5.3	2.2	74.3	99.2	52.3	10.9	5.8	110.1	58.1	3.63
1978	16.41	22.0	31.9	.7	75.0	129.6	64.0	8.9	4.4	138.5	68.4	4.17
1979	16.85	34.1	35.3	0	64.1	133.5	57.9	5.5	2.4	139.0	60.3	3.58
1980	17.30	18.7	33.0	0	41.7	93.4	35.7	3.3	1.3	96.7	36.9	2.14
1981	17.75	34.5	42.5	13.1	6.1	96.2	33.6	4.3	1.5	100.5	35.2	1.98
1982	18.23	35.8	16.2	0	2.6	54.6	18.9	5.0	1.7	59.6	20.6	1.13
1983	18.71	35.5	55.9	26.3	2.1	119.8	41.0	4.6	1.6	124.4	42.6	2.28
1984	19.20	118.9	42.9	0	3.1	164.9	55.7	10.7	3.6	175.6	59.3	3.09
1985	19.70	37.9	38.8	0	3.7	80.4	27.4	8.7	3.0	89.1	30.3	1.54
1986	20.21	25.9	28.8	0	3.7	58.4	19.8	.6	.2	59.0	20.0	.99
1987	20.73	21.3	33.7	0	10.5	65.5	21.7	.1	0	65.6	21.7	1.05
1988	21.26	28.0	35.0	0	7.7	70.7	21.9	.4	.1	71.1	22.0	1.03
Total		679.2	555.7	480.6	552.9	2,268.4	1,569.1	217.8	170.7	2,486.2	1,739.8	3.25[a]

1. Deflated using Export Price Index (Table 3331) in 1970 U.S. dollars.

a. Per capita average, 1946–88.

SOURCE: USAID–OLG, various years (see Data Sources in text); Table 3331 (Chapter 33, above); IMF-IFS-SY, various years; population data from Chapter 6, above.

Figure 35:60

PERU: YEARLY ANNOUNCED TOTAL U.S. ASSISTANCE,[1] 1946–88

(M US)

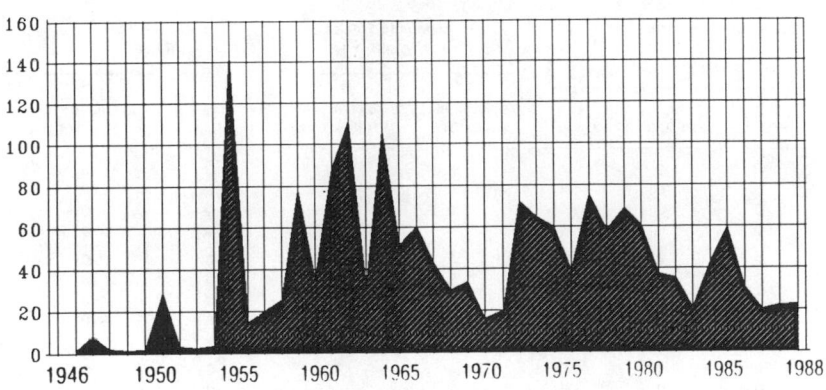

SOURCE: Table 3521.

Figure 35:61

PERU: YEARLY PER CAPITA ANNOUNCED TOTAL U.S. ASSISTANCE,[1] 1946–88

(US)

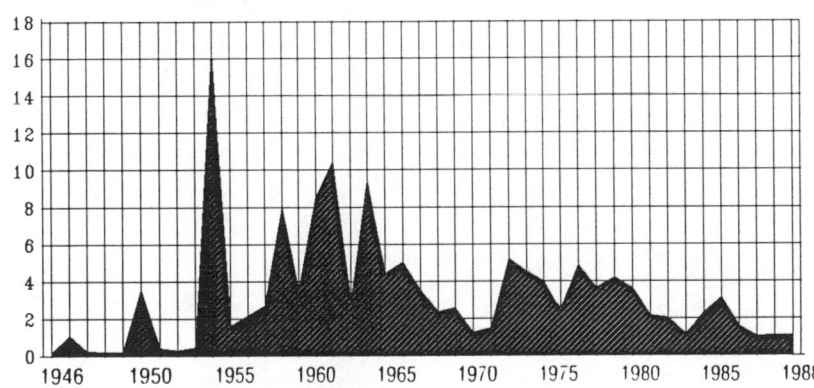

SOURCE: Table 3521.

Figure 35:62

PERU: PER CAPITA ASSISTANCE COMPARED TO AVERAGE YEARLY
LATIN AMERICA PER CAPITA ASSISTANCE,[1] 1946–88

(US)

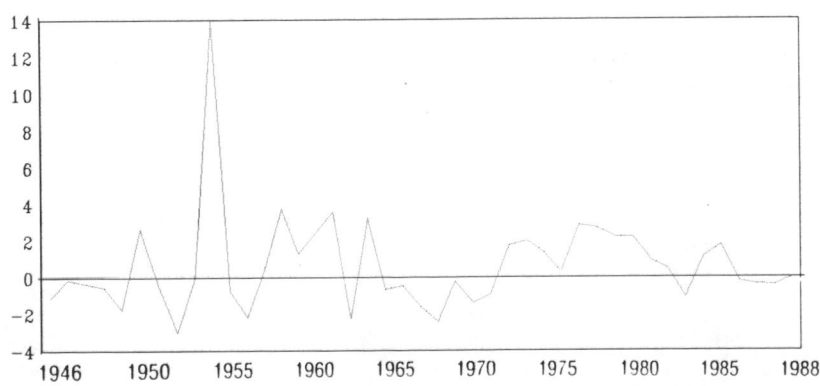

SOURCE: Table 3529.

Table 3522

URUGUAY: ANNOUNCED AUTHORIZED U.S. ASSISTANCE, NOMINAL AND DEFLATED,[1] 1946–88

Year	A. Population (M)	Economic Assistance Nominal (M US)				Economic Total (M US)		Military Total (M US)		Economic + Military Total (M US)		Per Capita (US)
		B. USAID	C. FFP	D. EXP/IMP	E. Other	F. Nominal (B+C+D+E)	G. Deflated (F/EPI = 100)	H. Nominal	I. Deflated (H/EPI = 100)	J. Nominal (F+H)	K. Deflated (G+I)	L. Deflated (K/A)
1946	2.10	0	0	0	.6	.6	1.0	0	0	.6	1.0	.48
1947	2.12	0	0	0	.1	.1	.1	0	0	.1	.1	.07
1948	2.14	0	0	0	2.0	2.0	2.7	0	0	2.0	2.7	1.25
1949	2.17	0	0	0	.1	.1	.1	0	0	.1	.1	.07
1950	2.20	0	0	0	.1	.1	.1	0	0	.1	.1	.07
1951	2.22	0	0	2.6	.2	2.8	3.6	0	0	2.8	3.6	1.62
1952	2.26	.4	0	0	0	.4	.5	0	0	.4	.5	.23
1953	2.70	.2	0	0	0	.2	.3	0	0	.2	.3	.10
1954	3.33	.2	0	0	0	.2	.3	0	0	.2	.3	.08
1955	3.36	.4	0	0	0	.4	.5	0	0	.4	.5	.16
1956	2.40	.2	0	0	0	.2	.3	0	0	.2	.3	.10
1957	2.43	.3	0	0	0	.3	.4	0	0	.3	.4	.15
1958	2.46	.2	0	0	0	.2	.2	0	0	.2	.2	.10
1959	2.50	9.0	6.3	0	0	15.3	18.8	4.4	5.4	19.7	24.2	9.68
1960	2.54	.1	23.3	0	0	23.4	28.6	1.4	1.7	24.8	30.3	11.92
1961	2.58	.1	2.7	0	0	2.8	3.4	2.9	3.5	5.7	6.8	2.65
1962	2.61	.3	1.8	2.1	2.5	6.7	8.1	3.4	4.1	10.1	12.2	4.66
1963	2.65	7.9	.6	5.0	8.6	22.1	26.6	2.2	2.7	24.3	29.3	11.05
1964	2.68	6.2	1.0	0	.2	7.4	8.8	1.8	2.1	9.2	11.0	4.10
1965	2.71	−1.5	.7	0	.3	−.5	−.6	2.4	2.8	1.9	2.2	.81
1966	2.75	5.8	.5	0	.4	6.7	7.5	2.5	2.8	9.2	10.3	3.76
1967	2.69	2.4	.6	0	.2	3.2	3.5	1.6	1.8	4.8	5.3	1.97
1968	2.70	13.2	23.9	0	.2	37.3	40.5	2.0	2.2	39.3	42.7	15.80
1969	2.71	1.3	.3	2.0	.1	3.7	3.9	1.7	1.8	5.4	5.7	2.10
1970	2.73	16.8	2.4	0	1	19.3	19.3	1.9	1.9	21.2	21.2	7.77
1971	2.74	4.9	.4	1.1	−.1	6.3	6.1	5.2	5.0	11.5	11.2	4.07
1972	2.75	1.4	8.6	0	.1	10.1	9.5	4.2	3.9	14.3	13.4	4.88
1973	2.76	1.2	7.0	0	.9	9.1	7.3	1.5	1.2	10.6	8.5	3.09
1974	2.77	.9	0	.8	0	1.7	1.1	3.9	2.5	5.6	3.5	1.28
1975	2.83	12.8	0	0	.1	12.9	7.3	9.2	5.2	22.1	12.5	4.41
1976	2.85	.7	0	0	0	.7	.4	3.7	2.0	4.4	2.4	.84
1977	2.86	.6	0	0	0	.6	3	0	0	.6	.3	.11
1978	2.88	0	0	0	.2	.2	.1	0	0	.2	.1	.03
1979	2.89	0	0	0	.2	.2	.1	0	0	.2	.1	.03
1980	2.91	0	0	0	0	0	0	0	0	0	0	0
1981	2.93	0	0	14.9	.1	15.0	5.2	0	0	15.0	5.2	1.79
1982	2.95	0	0	0	.8	.8	.3	0	0	.8	.3	.09
1983	2.97	0	0	0	1.0	1.0	.3	.1	0	1.1	.4	.13
1984	2.99	0	0	0	.6	.6	.2	.1	0	.7	.2	.08
1985	3.01	0	0	0	0	0	0	.1	0	.1	0	.01
1986	2.98	14.4	0	0	0	14.4	4.9	.1	0	14.5	4.9	1.65
1987	3.04	12.2	0	0	0	12.2	4.0	.7	.2	12.9	4.3	1.41
1988	3.06	0	0	0	0	0	0	.1	0	.1	0	.01
Total		112.6	80.1	28.5	19.6	240.8	225.8	57.1	53.0	297.9	278.7	2.43[a]

1. Deflated using Export Price Index (Table 3331) in 1970 U.S. dollars.

a. Per capita average, 1946–88.

SOURCE: USAID-OLG, various years (see Data Sources in text); Table 3331 (Chapter 33, above); IMF-IFS-SY, various years; population data from Chapter 6, above.

Figure 35:63

URUGUAY: YEARLY ANNOUNCED TOTAL U.S. ASSISTANCE,[1] 1946–88

(M US)

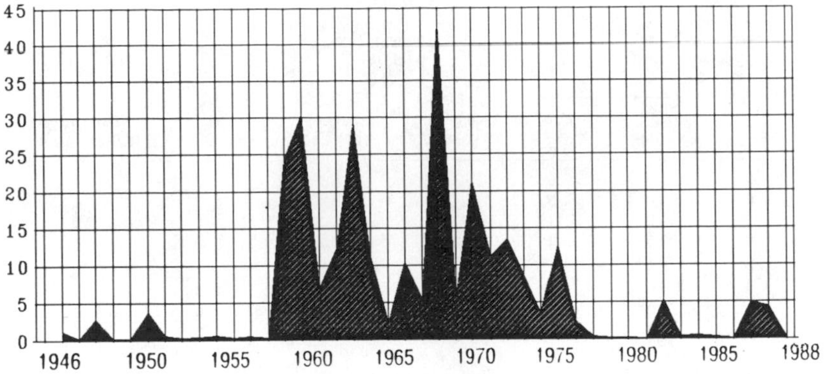

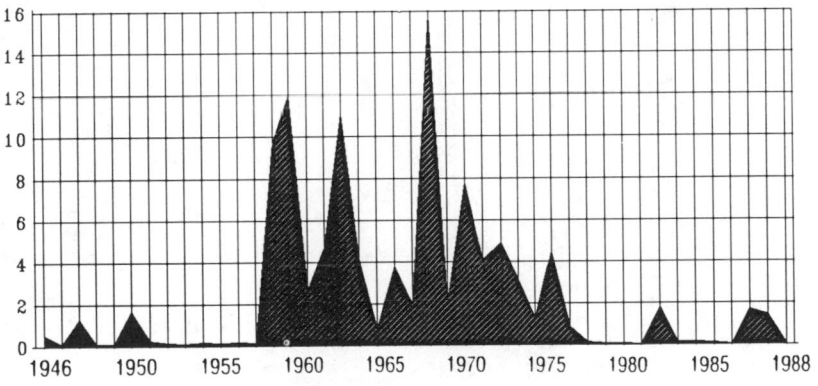

SOURCE: Table 3522.

Figure 35:64

URUGUAY: YEARLY PER CAPITA ANNOUNCED TOTAL U.S. ASSISTANCE,[1] 1946–88

(US)

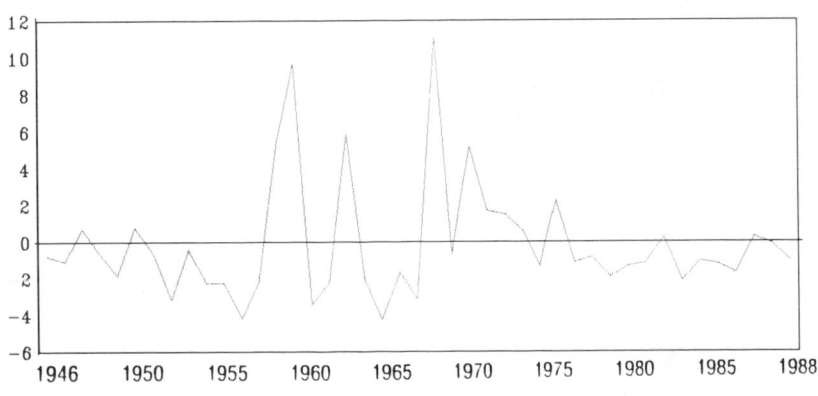

SOURCE: Table 3522.

Figure 35:65

URUGUAY: PER CAPITA ASSISTANCE COMPARED TO AVERAGE YEARLY LATIN AMERICA PER CAPITA ASSISTANCE,[1] 1946–88

(US)

SOURCE: Table 3529.

Table 3523

VENEZUELA: ANNOUNCED AUTHORIZED U.S. ASSISTANCE, NOMINAL AND DEFLATED,[1] 1946–88

Year	A. Population (M)	Economic Assistance Nominal (M US)				Economic Total (M US)		Military Total (M US)		Economic + Military Total (M US)		Per Capita (US)
		B. USAID	C. FFP	D. EXP/IMP	E. Other	F. Nominal (B+C+D+E)	G. Deflated (F/EPI = 100)	H. Nominal	I. Deflated (H/EPI = 100)	J. Nominal (F+H)	K. Deflated (G+I)	L. Deflated (K/A)
1946	4.39	0	0	0	.6	.6	1.0	0	0	.6	1.0	.23
1947	4.55	0	0	0	.3	.3	.4	0	0	.3	.4	.09
1948	4.69	0	0	0	.1	.1	.1	0	0	.1	.1	.03
1949	4.83	0	0	2.0	.2	2.2	3.2	0	0	2.2	3.2	.65
1950	4.97	0	0	4.8	.1	4.9	7.2	0	0	4.9	7.2	1.45
1951	5.14	0	0	0	.2	.2	.3	0	0	.2	.3	.05
1952	5.39	.1	0	3.0	0	3.1	4.0	0	0	3.1	4.0	.74
1953	5.62	.1	0	0	0	.1	.1	0	0	.1	.1	.02
1954	5.58	.1	0	0	0	.1	.1	0	0	.1	.1	.02
1955	6.09	.2	0	0	0	.2	.3	0	0	.2	.3	.04
1956	6.33	.2	0	0	0	.2	.3	0	0	.2	.3	.04
1957	6.57	.1	0	3.5	0	3.6	4.4	0	0	3.6	4.4	.67
1958	6.83	.2	0	0	0	.2	.2	0	0	.2	.2	.04
1959	7.09	.1	0	.6	0	.7	.9	13.3	16.3	14.0	17.2	2.43
1960	7.35	.1	0	16.3	0	16.4	20.0	8.3	10.1	24.7	30.2	4.10
1961	7.61	15.2	0	104.4	0	119.6	143.2	9.6	11.5	129.2	154.7	20.33
1962	7.86	11.1	11.9	0	42.6	65.6	79.0	10.4	12.5	76.0	91.6	11.65
1963	8.12	33.1	1.2	.4	11.8	46.5	56.0	7.7	9.3	54.2	65.3	8.04
1964	8.40	1.6	10.3	31.5	2.0	45.4	54.2	10.0	11.9	55.4	66.1	7.87
1965	8.71	1.6	4.2	12.5	22.2	40.5	46.9	6.6	7.6	47.1	54.5	6.26
1966	9.03	1.4	3.9	0	3.6	8.9	10.0	8.8	9.9	17.7	19.9	2.20
1967	9.31	1.1	2.3	30.7	2.4	36.5	40.2	10.7	11.8	47.2	52.0	5.58
1968	9.62	1.2	1.7	65.3	2.0	70.2	76.2	9.4	10.2	79.6	86.4	8.98
1969	9.94	.9	.6	1.4	1.6	4.5	4.7	3.1	3.3	7.6	8.0	.81
1970	10.28	1.1	0	16.0	1.6	18.7	18.7	2.7	2.7	21.4	21.4	2.08
1971	10.61	1.0	0	18.7	1.5	21.2	20.6	8.4	8.1	29.6	28.7	2.71
1972	10.94	.8	4.7	36.9	1.4	43.8	41.1	9.7	9.1	53.5	50.2	4.59
1973	11.28	.4	0	15.4	1.3	17.1	13.8	10.3	8.3	27.4	22.1	1.96
1974	11.63	.3	0	24.5	2.3	27.1	17.1	8.4	5.3	35.5	22.4	1.93
1975	12.67	0	0	14.1	1.6	15.7	8.9	.7	.4	16.4	9.3	.73
1976	13.12	0	0	51.9	.7	52.6	28.7	10.7	5.8	63.3	34.6	2.64
1977	13.59	0	0	0	.1	.1	.1	.1	.1	.2	.1	.01
1978	14.07	0	0	22.3	0	22.3	11.0	.1	0	22.4	11.1	.79
1979	14.55	0	0	18.5	0	18.5	8.0	0	0	18.5	8.0	.55
1980	15.02	0	0	159.4	0	159.4	60.9	0	0	159.4	60.9	4.05
1981	15.48	0	0	59.5	.1	59.6	20.8	.1	0	59.7	20.9	1.35
1982	15.94	0	0	26.0	.2	26.2	9.1	0	0	26.2	9.1	.57
1983	16.39	0	0	12.0	.1	12.1	4.1	.1	0	12.2	4.2	.25
1984	16.85	0	0	0	.4	.4	.1	0	0	.4	.1	.01
1985	17.32	0	0	0	.8	.8	.3	.1	0	.9	.3	.02
1986	17.79	0	0	0	.1	.1	0	.1	0	.2	.1	0
1987	18.27	0	0	0	0	0	0	.2	.1	.2	.1	0
1988	18.75	0	0	0	0	0	0	.1	0	.1	0	0
Total		72.0	40.8	751.6	101.9	966.3	816.4	149.7	154.6	1,116.0	971.0	2.48[a]

1. Deflated using Export Price Index (Table 3331) in 1970 U.S. dollars.

a. Per capita average, 1946–88.

SOURCE: USAID–OLG, various years (see Data Sources in text); Table 3331 (Chapter 33, above); IMF-IFS-SY, various years; population data from Chapter 6, above.

Figure 35:66

VENEZUELA: YEARLY ANNOUNCED TOTAL U.S. ASSISTANCE,[1] 1946–88

(M US)

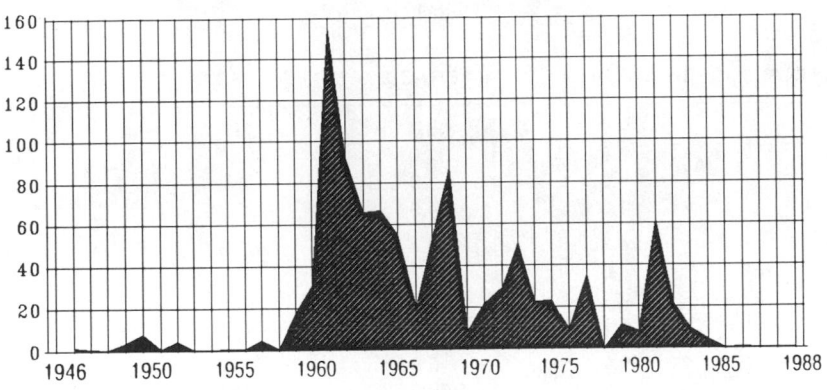

SOURCE: Table 3523.

Figure 35:67

VENEZUELA: YEARLY PER CAPITA ANNOUNCED TOTAL U.S. ASSISTANCE,[1] 1946–88

(US)

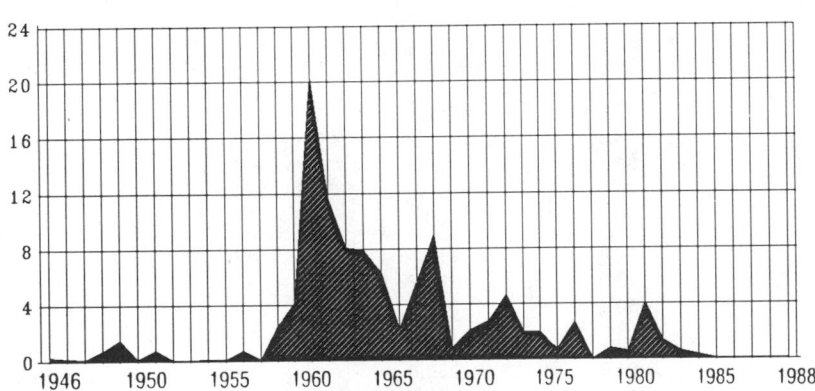

SOURCE: Table 3523.

Figure 35:68

VENEZUELA: PER CAPITA ASSISTANCE COMPARED TO AVERAGE YEARLY LATIN AMERICA PER CAPITA ASSISTANCE,[1] 1946–88

(US)

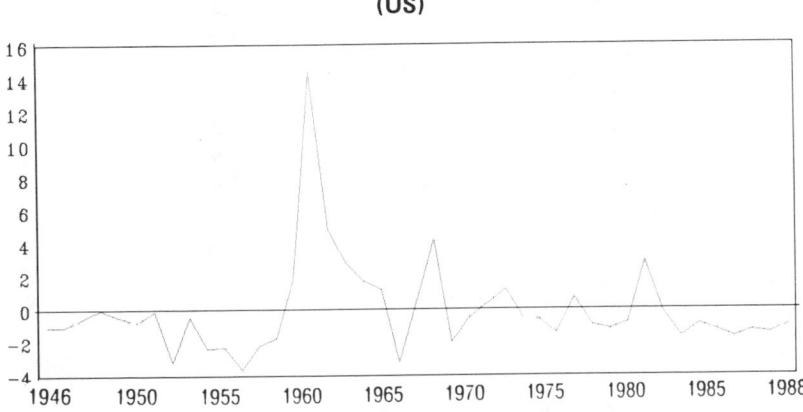

SOURCE: Table 3529.

Table 3524

YEARLY ANNOUNCED TOTAL U.S. ASSISTANCE,
TOTALS AND AVERAGES, 20 LR,[1] 1946-88

(M US)

Year	A. ARGENTINA	B. BOLIVIA	C. BRAZIL	D. CHILE	E. COLOMBIA	F. COSTA RICA
1946	0	.7	96.3	56.1	.8	3.4
1947	.3	4.8	32.8	17.2	1.6	.6
1948	0	.5	1.9	1.2	15.0	.3
1949	0	1.0	14.9	31.3	5.5	.1
1950	142.3	24.3	22.4	41.6	3.7	.6
1951	6.4	.6	35.1	2.8	3.1	.9
1952	0	2.2	76.7	15.9	4.3	2.8
1953	0	1.7	504.9	1.7	7.1	3.2
1954	0	20.9	5.9	1.8	1.8	2.5
1955	81.2	41.3	68.3	8.1	6.6	6.9
1956	20.1	35.1	118.5	36.8	14.4	25.9
1957	121.7	33.2	404.9	58.8	19.8	13.7
1958	.1	27.5	32.3	52.6	117.3	3.3
1959	210.0	30.6	178.4	61.1	10.2	10.1
1960	1.1	18.3	51.6	57.6	68.7	12.8
1961	95.3	37.4	393.2	176.9	121.1	12.2
1962	133.3	47.6	294.7	294.7	98.6	12.5
1963	162.0	84.5	186.3	136.5	163.6	17.8
1964	15.4	94.9	476.0	168.5	156.2	20.4
1965	18.7	16.7	330.9	158.1	48.0	18.2
1966	38.4	43.5	456.4	130.6	126.7	15.6
1967	14.1	34.1	315.3	319.4	166.7	9.1
1968	49.7	25.6	387.3	124.8	130.1	11.6
1969	81.2	36.7	53.0	118.6	142.7	19.1
1970	33.9	6.4	211.4	42.0	131.1	18.6
1971	54.0	12.9	201.0	13.2	106.8	8.2
1972	61.0	60.8	322.2	18.7	134.6	3.7
1973	34.0	25.3	175.0	17.6	86.6	2.8
1974	40.5	34.3	250.4	78.2	46.3	8.9
1975	53.6	18.8	190.5	72.7	18.5	5.1
1976	21.6	28.5	91.9	51.7	37.7	6.7
1977	8.6	38.7	27.3	17.5	5.2	8.9
1978	13.5	35.3	52.7	26.2	44.2	6.5
1979	14.2	25.1	113.6	5.9	28.0	9.8
1980	30.3	11.6	34.6	3.9	18.0	8.6
1981	28.9	4.5	40.9	4.2	17.9	7.1
1982	190.7	6.8	31.7	2.3	191.6	19.7
1983	0	21.6	10.5	1.0	2.9	74.9
1984	0	26.4	9.6	.6	12.7	61.2
1985	0	18.4	13.0	.9	48.4	79.0
1986	0	26.8	42.5	.7	5.4	56.7
1987	.8	26.2	41.1	.4	5.7	62.0
1988	4.0	29.7	5.2	1.0	13.8	37.3
Total	1,781.3	1,121.9	6,403.2	2,431.2	2,388.9	709.5

Table 3524 (Continued)

YEARLY ANNOUNCED TOTAL U.S. ASSISTANCE, TOTALS AND AVERAGES, 20 LR,[1] 1946–88

(M US)

Year	G. CUBA	H. DOMINICAN REP.	I. ECUADOR	J. EL SALVADOR	K. GUATEMALA	L. HAITI
1946	.2	.3	1.0	.8	1.4	.5
1947	.1	.3	1.0	.4	1.4	.4
1948	.1	.1	4.4	.4	2.3	1.1
1949	0	0	1.1	.3	4.2	6.3
1950	0	0	11.4	.4	2.5	.7
1951	15.6	.1	.9	.3	.9	13.6
1952	.1	.3	3.1	.6	1.4	1.0
1953	.3	.4	1.3	.9	.3	.8
1954	10.8	.3	9.5	.8	.3	1.3
1955	.7	.4	5.6	1.0	13.2	16.2
1956	2.1	.4	6.6	1.4	43.0	16.3
1957	.7	.2	9.4	2.1	23.2	3.9
1958	20.6	.2	6.8	1.4	21.5	4.9
1959	1.0	1.2	13.9	1.4	14.6	15.6
1960	1.3	.6	14.2	1.2	14.8	18.9
1961	.1	.1	22.5	8.3	38.7	14.9
1962		44.3	46.7	28.7	12.8	9.6
1963		64.5	49.0	28.0	18.9	1.6
1964		19.3	36.3	18.7	18.0	1.0
1965		102.0	35.5	22.1	16.7	2.4
1966		128.9	36.7	11.2	5.6	6.9
1967		67.8	8.8	4.2	23.8	2.8
1968		79.3	17.8	10.7	21.3	4.0
1969		34.9	16.5	14.8	84.4	3.4
1970		22.2	30.7	12.9	33.9	3.9
1971		28.8	24.3	5.9	25.4	4.2
1972		29.8	11.7	17.3	17.3	5.0
1973		26.0	14.3	3.9	23.8	6.0
1974		33.3	6.9	7.4	4.8	7.2
1975		11.6	8.1	5.6	10.1	5.3
1976		41.1	9.9	8.2	28.0	19.5
1977		8.4	10.7	3.3	14.5	21.8
1978		3.5	9.8	5.4	5.2	14.5
1979		32.7	14.4	5.0	10.7	11.1
1980		26.6	6.3	24.6	5.3	10.4
1981		15.1	8.9	52.3	6.6	12.7
1982		30.4	9.7	91.4	5.4	12.3
1983		23.9	10.7	111.9	10.2	16.5
1984		35.3	12.5	139.3	6.9	16.0
1985		61.2	20.0	194.1	36.6	19.3
1986		36.6	22.0	150.9	41.5	27.2
1987		14.7	17.2	190.3	64.1	33.9
1988		18.6	6.7	122.4	43.8	12.4
Total	53.8	1,045.7	614.9	1,312.3	779.0	407.3

Table 3524 (Continued)

YEARLY ANNOUNCED TOTAL U.S. ASSISTANCE, TOTALS AND AVERAGES, 20 LR,[1] 1946–88

(M US)

Year	M. HONDURAS	N. MEXICO	O. NICARAGUA	P. PANAMA	Q. PARAGUAY	R. PERU
1946	.5	4.6	2.9	.3	.7	1.0
1947	.9	87.1	2.4	.3	.6	8.0
1948	.4	40.2	.7	.3	.5	1.7
1949	.3	27.7	.6	3.3	.6	1.3
1950	.1	29.8	.6	.3	.7	1.3
1951	.3	10.6	1.7	1.2	.9	28.4
1952	1.0	12.0	1.0	3.9	2.1	3.1
1953	.9	9.1	1.2	1.9	1.0	2.2
1954	1.5	10.0	1.6	2.1	1.6	3.4
1955	2.6	2.9	4.7	3.8	12.6	143.3
1956	3.4	65.8	3.3	12.3	5.1	14.4
1957	10.0	32.0	7.5	32.4	3.4	19.7
1958	10.9	74.1	4.3	6.8	8.0	25.2
1959	5.7	136.7	5.4	2.5	6.9	77.5
1960	4.9	62.3	15.3	2.4	5.3	35.2
1961	6.9	39.0	15.0	19.5	13.2	88.0
1962	5.5	171.6	17.7	30.7	9.9	110.7
1963	15.2	58.2	10.8	11.9	12.8	31.9
1964	12.2	128.6	9.8	29.7	11.3	106.0
1965	5.7	232.5	28.2	27.5	13.0	51.4
1966	16.4	144.3	23.9	15.4	18.0	59.8
1967	12.2	112.0	14.4	39.3	6.5	43.0
1968	16.2	95.0	30.8	22.6	8.4	29.4
1969	5.0	18.8	3.2	18.6	18.7	33.3
1970	9.3	41.0	4.2	11.9	9.0	16.0
1971	8.1	44.2	15.7	14.9	13.3	19.5
1972	7.4	50.8	5.3	60.5	5.4	71.6
1973	12.1	115.2	23.2	49.7	6.5	64.3
1974	19.4	103.1	13.8	19.8	4.7	59.6
1975	23.2	110.7	26.4	29.3	5.4	38.9
1976	17.4	98.9	5.4	23.6	5.5	75.1
1977	8.4	32.8	19.2	10.2	2.1	58.1
1978	10.3	310.5	7.2	11.6	2.0	68.4
1979	14.0	74.1	8.0	11.4	4.5	60.3
1980	26.8	71.7	14.8	.9	1.4	36.9
1981	16.2	231.7	21.0	3.8	2.2	35.2
1982	39.0	104.6	2.2	6.4	23.4	20.6
1983	52.8	33.0	0	4.4	1.5	42.6
1984	58.3	29.7	0	8.7	.9	59.3
1985	101.6	7.3	0	29.0	1.2	30.3
1986	67.3	4.1	0	14.2	1.2	20.0
1987	85.8	7.6	0	5.2	1.1	21.7
1988	61.3	32.0	.1	.4	1.3	22.0
Total	777.2	3,107.9	373.5	604.8	254.1	1,739.8

Table 3524 (Continued)

YEARLY ANNOUNCED TOTAL U.S. ASSISTANCE, TOTALS AND AVERAGES, 20 LR,[1] 1946–88

(M US)

Year	S. URUGUAY	T. VENEZUELA	LATIN AMERICA	LATIN AMERICA Average
1946	1.0	1.0	173.6	8.7
1947	.1	.4	160.7	8.0
1948	2.7	.1	73.9	3.7
1949	.1	3.2	101.9	5.1
1950	.1	7.2	290.3	14.5
1951	3.6	.3	127.3	6.4
1952	.5	4.0	136.2	6.8
1953	.3	.1	539.4	27.0
1954	.3	.1	76.6	3.8
1955	.5	.3	420.2	21.0
1956	.3	.3	425.1	21.3
1957	.4	4.4	801.3	40.1
1958	.2	.2	418.3	20.9
1959	24.2	17.2	824.0	41.2
1960	30.3	30.2	447.0	22.4
1961	6.8	154.7	1,263.8	63.2
1962	12.2	91.6	1,473.4	77.5
1963	29.3	65.3	1,148.1	60.4
1964	11.0	66.1	1,399.4	73.7
1965	2.2	54.5	1,184.4	62.3
1966	10.3	19.9	1,308.5	68.9
1967	5.3	52.0	1,250.9	65.8
1968	42.7	86.4	1,193.7	62.8
1969	5.7	8.0	716.4	37.7
1970	21.2	21.4	681.0	35.8
1971	11.2	28.7	640.3	33.7
1972	13.4	50.2	946.6	49.8
1973	8.5	22.1	717.2	37.7
1974	3.5	22.4	764.5	40.2
1975	12.5	9.3	655.5	34.5
1976	2.4	34.6	607.6	32.0
1977	.3	.1	296.0	15.6
1978	.1	11.1	638.0	33.6
1979	.1	8.0	450.9	23.7
1980	0	60.9	393.4	20.7
1981	5.2	20.9	535.3	28.2
1982	.3	9.1	797.5	42.0
1983	.4	4.2	422.8	22.3
1984	.2	.1	477.8	25.1
1985	0	.3	660.7	34.8
1986	4.9	.1	522.1	27.5
1987	4.3	.1	582.2	30.6
1988	0	0	412.1	21.7
Total	278.7	971.0	27,155.9	1,429.3

1. Deflated using Export Price Index (Table 3331) in 1970 U.S. dollars.

SOURCE: Country Tables 3504–3523.

Table 3525

YEARLY ANNOUNCED TOTAL ECONOMIC ASSISTANCE, TOTALS AND AVERAGES, 20 LR,[1] 1946-88

(M US)

Year	A. ARGENTINA	B. BOLIVIA	C. BRAZIL	D. CHILE	E. COLOMBIA	F. COSTA RICA
1946	0	.7	96.3	56.1	.8	3.4
1947	.3	4.8	32.8	17.2	1.6	.6
1948	0	.5	1.9	1.2	15.0	.3
1949	0	1.0	14.9	31.3	5.5	.1
1950	142.3	24.3	22.4	41.6	3.7	.6
1951	6.4	.6	35.1	2.8	3.1	.9
1952	0	2.2	76.7	15.9	4.3	2.8
1953	0	1.7	504.9	1.7	7.1	3.2
1954	0	20.9	5.9	1.8	1.8	2.5
1955	81.2	41.3	68.3	8.1	6.6	6.9
1956	20.1	35.1	118.5	36.8	14.4	25.9
1957	121.7	33.2	396.5	58.8	19.8	13.7
1958	.1	27.5	32.3	52.6	117.3	3.3
1959	210.0	30.6	163.1	53.8	7.0	10.1
1960	1.0	18.3	19.4	54.3	65.4	12.8
1961	82.5	36.9	364.6	166.1	107.7	12.1
1962	94.9	44.9	244.0	279.9	91.3	12.4
1963	160.1	81.6	174.2	106.3	153.5	17.1
1964	13.0	91.1	456.2	156.9	148.3	19.8
1965	11.5	14.5	314.4	148.8	41.4	17.9
1966	31.2	40.8	431.0	121.0	117.4	15.5
1967	2.8	30.9	296.7	313.4	158.0	9.0
1968	34.9	21.8	358.3	116.5	116.8	11.5
1969	62.6	35.0	32.9	113.7	135.7	19.1
1970	23.3	5.2	198.4	29.2	127.2	18.6
1971	38.0	11.2	191.0	7.6	101.1	8.1
1972	42.0	56.3	302.6	8.5	126.5	3.7
1973	24.3	22.0	160.8	5.6	78.1	2.8
1974	26.0	29.7	217.1	68.1	46.0	8.9
1975	36.6	14.6	153.6	72.3	18.1	5.1
1976	2.8	21.0	67.4	51.7	26.3	6.7
1977	8.2	37.1	27.2	17.5	4.8	6.2
1978	13.5	34.9	52.7	26.2	18.4	6.5
1979	14.2	22.2	113.6	5.9	22.3	9.8
1980	30.3	11.5	34.6	3.9	17.9	8.6
1981	28.9	4.5	40.9	4.2	17.8	7.1
1982	190.7	6.8	31.7	2.3	188.0	18.9
1983	0	21.6	10.5	1.0	2.6	73.3
1984	0	26.3	9.6	.6	4.1	58.1
1985	0	17.2	13.0	.9	48.1	75.2
1986	0	26.3	42.5	.7	3.9	55.8
1987	.8	25.8	41.1	.4	4.0	61.4
1988	4.0	29.6	5.2	1.0	12.6	37.3
Total	1,560.2	1,064.2	5,974.9	2,264.1	2,211.3	693.9

Table 3525 (Continued)

YEARLY ANNOUNCED TOTAL ECONOMIC ASSISTANCE, TOTALS AND AVERAGES, 20 LR,[1] 1946–88

(M US)

Year	G. CUBA	H. DOMINICAN REP.	I. ECUADOR	J. EL SALVADOR	K. GUATEMALA	L. HAITI
1946	.2	.3	1.0	.8	1.4	.5
1947	.1	.3	1.0	.4	1.4	.4
1948	.1	.1	4.4	.4	2.3	1.1
1949	0	0	1.1	.3	4.2	6.3
1950	0	0	11.4	.4	2.5	.7
1951	15.6	.1	.9	.3	.9	13.6
1952	.1	.3	3.1	.6	1.4	1.0
1953	.3	.4	1.3	.9	.3	.8
1954	10.8	.3	9.5	.8	.3	1.3
1955	.7	.4	5.6	1.0	13.2	16.2
1956	2.1	.4	6.6	1.4	43.0	16.3
1957	.7	.2	9.4	2.1	23.2	3.9
1958	20.6	.2	6.8	1.4	21.5	4.9
1959	.5	.2	10.4	1.4	14.5	15.6
1960	1.1	.4	11.1	1.2	14.5	14.8
1961	0	.1	15.9	8.0	38.2	14.1
1962		44.1	44.0	28.0	11.2	9.0
1963		62.2	44.6	26.7	15.8	1.3
1964		16.3	32.6	17.7	16.3	1.0
1965		100.6	32.9	21.2	14.9	2.4
1966		127.0	32.4	10.4	4.3	6.9
1967		64.1	5.4	3.5	22.2	2.8
1968		76.8	14.8	10.1	18.8	4.0
1969		32.6	13.7	14.5	83.2	3.4
1970		20.1	28.7	12.7	31.9	3.9
1971		27.4	24.0	5.5	19.0	4.2
1972		28.0	11.7	15.6	15.6	5.0
1973		24.3	14.3	3.6	21.0	6.0
1974		32.8	6.9	6.7	3.9	7.2
1975		10.7	7.9	2.5	8.4	5.3
1976		40.1	4.2	7.6	26.8	19.5
1977		7.6	2.6	3.0	14.2	21.5
1978		3.1	4.5	5.4	5.2	14.2
1979		32.3	14.2	5.0	10.7	10.9
1980		25.3	5.0	22.3	5.3	10.4
1981		13.9	7.4	39.9	6.6	12.4
1982		28.5	7.9	63.0	5.4	12.1
1983		21.6	9.1	84.1	10.2	16.3
1984		33.2	10.3	72.9	6.9	15.7
1985		58.3	17.7	147.7	36.5	19.1
1986		35.1	20.5	109.5	39.6	26.6
1987		13.6	15.7	153.4	62.3	33.5
1988		18.2	6.5	97.2	40.9	12.4
Total	53.0	1,001.3	538.9	1,011.2	739.9	398.2

Table 3525 (Continued)

YEARLY ANNOUNCED TOTAL ECONOMIC ASSISTANCE, TOTALS AND AVERAGES, 20 LR,[1] 1946–88

(M US)

Year	M. HONDURAS	N. MEXICO	O. NICARAGUA	P. PANAMA	Q. PARAGUAY	R. PERU
1946	.5	4.6	2.9	.3	.7	1.0
1947	.9	87.1	2.4	.3	.6	8.0
1948	.4	40.2	.7	.3	.5	1.7
1949	.3	27.7	.6	3.3	.6	1.3
1950	.1	29.8	.6	.3	.7	1.3
1951	.3	10.6	1.7	1.2	.9	28.4
1952	1.0	12.0	1.0	3.9	2.1	3.1
1953	.9	9.1	1.2	1.9	1.0	2.2
1954	1.5	10.0	1.6	2.1	1.6	3.4
1955	2.6	2.9	4.7	3.8	12.6	143.3
1956	3.4	65.8	3.3	12.3	5.1	14.4
1957	10.0	32.0	7.5	32.4	3.4	19.7
1958	10.9	74.1	4.3	6.8	8.0	25.2
1959	5.5	136.1	5.3	2.5	6.9	72.1
1960	4.8	59.0	15.0	2.4	5.1	30.9
1961	6.6	38.6	14.3	19.4	12.9	70.8
1962	3.7	170.7	16.5	30.4	9.6	94.2
1963	15.2	56.4	8.9	11.1	11.2	22.2
1964	11.7	124.7	8.4	29.6	9.9	93.4
1965	4.9	231.6	26.9	27.3	11.2	41.9
1966	15.6	144.0	22.8	14.9	16.9	48.8
1967	11.1	111.8	13.3	38.8	5.3	35.6
1968	15.1	94.9	29.4	22.3	6.4	18.7
1969	4.3	18.7	2.4	18.1	17.6	30.3
1970	9.0	40.9	3.1	11.5	8.2	14.1
1971	7.5	39.9	14.8	14.5	12.3	18.9
1972	6.9	48.9	4.5	60.0	4.6	70.7
1973	11.7	115.2	22.0	49.2	5.9	63.7
1974	19.1	103.1	13.0	19.4	3.7	49.6
1975	20.8	110.6	24.0	29.0	4.5	26.8
1976	15.5	98.8	3.7	22.8	3.7	63.6
1977	6.8	32.7	17.2	8.6	1.7	52.3
1978	8.7	310.5	7.0	11.4	1.7	64.0
1979	13.0	74.0	8.0	10.8	4.5	57.9
1980	25.3	71.7	14.8	.8	1.4	35.7
1981	13.0	231.7	21.0	3.7	2.2	33.6
1982	28.1	104.5	2.2	4.5	23.4	18.9
1983	36.3	33.0	0	2.5	1.5	41.0
1984	32.2	29.7	0	4.1	.9	55.7
1985	78.7	7.2	0	25.4	1.2	27.4
1986	46.5	4.0	0	11.4	1.1	19.8
1987	65.5	7.5	0	4.0	1.0	21.7
1988	48.5	32.0	.1	.4	1.3	21.9
Total	624.4	3,088.2	351.0	579.5	235.8	1,569.1

Table 3525 (Continued)

YEARLY ANNOUNCED TOTAL ECONOMIC ASSISTANCE, TOTALS AND AVERAGES, 20 LR,[1] 1946–88

(M US)

Year	S. URUGUAY	T. VENEZUELA	LATIN AMERICA	LATIN AMERICA Average
1946	1.0	1.0	173.6	8.7
1947	.1	.4	160.7	8.0
1948	2.7	.1	73.9	3.7
1949	.1	3.2	101.9	5.1
1950	.1	7.2	290.3	14.5
1951	3.6	.3	127.3	6.4
1952	.5	4.0	136.2	6.8
1953	.3	.1	539.4	27.0
1954	.3	.1	76.6	3.8
1955	.5	.3	420.2	21.0
1956	.3	.3	425.1	21.3
1957	.4	4.4	792.9	39.6
1958	.2	.2	418.3	20.9
1959	18.8	.9	765.3	38.3
1960	28.6	20.0	380.2	19.0
1961	3.4	143.2	1,155.3	57.8
1962	8.1	79.0	1,316.0	69.3
1963	26.6	56.0	1,051.0	55.3
1964	8.8	54.2	1,309.9	68.9
1965	−.6	46.9	1,110.5	58.4
1966	7.5	10.0	1,218.4	64.1
1967	3.5	40.2	1,168.5	61.5
1968	40.5	76.2	1,087.6	57.2
1969	3.9	4.7	646.4	34.0
1970	19.3	18.7	624.0	32.8
1971	6.1	20.6	571.6	30.1
1972	9.5	41.1	861.7	45.4
1973	7.3	13.8	651.6	34.3
1974	1.1	17.1	679.2	35.7
1975	7.3	8.9	566.9	29.8
1976	.4	28.7	511.3	26.9
1977	.3	.1	269.7	14.2
1978	.1	11.0	599.1	31.5
1979	.1	8.0	437.5	23.0
1980	0	60.9	385.4	20.3
1981	5.2	20.8	514.9	27.1
1982	.3	9.1	746.5	39.3
1983	.3	4.1	369.0	19.4
1984	.2	.1	360.6	19.0
1985	0	.3	573.7	30.2
1986	4.9	0	448.5	23.6
1987	4.0	0	515.8	27.1
1988	0	0	368.8	19.4
Total	225.8	816.4	25,001.1	1,300.0

1. Deflated using Export Price Index (Table 3331) in 1970 U.S. dollars.

SOURCE: Country Tables 3504–3523.

Table 3526

YEARLY ANNOUNCED TOTAL MILITARY ASSISTANCE, TOTALS AND AVERAGES, 20 LR,[1] 1946–88

(M US)

Year	A. ARGENTINA	B. BOLIVIA	C. BRAZIL	D. CHILE	E. COLOMBIA	F. COSTA RICA
1946	0	0	0	0	0	0
1947	0	0	0	0	0	0
1948	0	0	0	0	0	0
1949	0	0	0	0	0	0
1950	0	0	0	0	0	0
1951	0	0	0	0	0	0
1952	0	0	0	0	0	0
1953	0	0	0	0	0	0
1954	0	0	0	0	0	0
1955	0	0	0	0	0	0
1956	0	0	0	0	0	0
1957	0	0	8.4	0	0	0
1958	0	0	0	0	0	0
1959	0	0	15.2	7.2	3.2	0
1960	.1	0	32.2	3.3	3.3	0
1961	12.8	.5	28.6	10.8	13.4	.1
1962	38.3	2.7	50.7	14.8	7.2	.1
1963	1.9	2.9	12.0	30.2	10.1	.7
1964	2.4	3.8	19.8	11.6	7.9	.6
1965	7.3	2.2	16.6	9.3	6.6	.2
1966	7.2	2.7	25.4	9.6	9.3	.1
1967	11.3	3.2	18.6	5.9	8.7	.1
1968	14.9	3.8	29.1	8.3	13.2	.1
1969	18.7	1.7	20.0	4.9	7.1	0
1970	10.6	1.2	13.0	12.8	3.9	0
1971	16.0	1.7	10.0	5.6	5.7	.1
1972	19.1	4.5	19.5	10.2	8.1	0
1973	9.8	3.3	14.3	12.1	8.5	0
1974	14.5	4.7	33.3	10.0	.4	0
1975	17.0	4.2	36.9	.4	.4	0
1976	18.8	7.4	24.4	0	11.4	0
1977	.4	1.6	.1	0	.4	2.6
1978	0	.4	0	0	25.8	0
1979	0	2.9	0	0	5.6	0
1980	0	.1	0	0	.1	0
1981	0	0	0	0	.1	0
1982	0	0	0	0	3.6	.7
1983	0	0	0	0	.2	1.6
1984	0	0	0	0	8.5	3.1
1985	0	1.2	0	0	.3	3.8
1986	0	.5	0	0	1.5	.9
1987	0	.4	0	0	1.7	.6
1988	0	.1	0	0	1.2	.1
Total	221.1	57.7	428.3	167.0	177.5	15.6

Table 3526 (Continued)

YEARLY ANNOUNCED TOTAL MILITARY ASSISTANCE, TOTALS AND AVERAGES, 20 LR,[1] 1946–88

(M US)

Year	G. CUBA	H. DOMINICAN REP.	I. ECUADOR	J. EL SALVADOR	K. GUATEMALA	L. HAITI
1946	0	0	0	0	0	0
1947	0	0	0	0	0	0
1948	0	0	0	0	0	0
1949	0	0	0	0	0	0
1950	0	0	0	0	0	0
1951	0	0	0	0	0	0
1952	0	0	0	0	0	0
1953	0	0	0	0	0	0
1954	0	0	0	0	0	0
1955	0	0	0	0	0	0
1956	0	0	0	0	0	0
1957	0	0	0	0	0	0
1958	0	0	0	0	0	0
1959	.5	1.0	3.4	0	.1	0
1960	.2	.2	3.1	0	.2	4.2
1961	.1	0	6.6	.2	.5	.7
1962		.2	2.8	.7	1.6	.6
1963		2.3	4.5	1.2	3.1	.2
1964		3.0	3.7	1.1	1.7	0
1965		1.4	2.7	.9	1.7	0
1966		1.9	4.4	.8	1.3	0
1967		3.7	3.4	.7	1.5	0
1968		2.5	3.0	.7	2.5	0
1969		2.3	2.7	.3	1.2	0
1970		2.1	2.0	.2	2.0	0
1971		1.4	.4	.4	6.4	0
1972		1.8	0	1.7	1.7	0
1973		1.7	0	.3	2.8	0
1974		.5	0	.7	.9	0
1975		.9	.2	3.1	1.6	0
1976		1.0	5.7	.6	1.2	.1
1977		.8	8.1	.3	.3	.3
1978		.3	5.3	0	0	.3
1979		.4	.2	0	0	.2
1980		1.3	1.3	2.3	0	0
1981		1.2	1.5	12.4	0	.3
1982		1.9	1.7	28.4	0	.2
1983		2.3	1.6	27.8	0	.2
1984		2.2	2.3	66.4	0	.3
1985		3.0	2.3	46.4	.2	.2
1986		1.5	1.5	41.4	1.8	.6
1987		1.1	1.5	36.9	1.8	.4
1988		.4	.2	25.2	2.9	.1
Total	.9	44.4	76.0	301.1	39.1	9.1

Table 3526 (Continued)

YEARLY ANNOUNCED TOTAL MILITARY ASSISTANCE,
TOTALS AND AVERAGES, 20 LR,[1] 1946–88

(M US)

Year	M. HONDURAS	N. MEXICO	O. NICARAGUA	P. PANAMA	Q. PARAGUAY	R. PERU
1946	0	0	0	0	0	0
1947	0	0	0	0	0	0
1948	0	0	0	0	0	0
1949	0	0	0	0	0	0
1950	0	0	0	0	0	0
1951	0	0	0	0	0	0
1952	0	0	0	0	0	0
1953	0	0	0	0	0	0
1954	0	0	0	0	0	0
1955	0	0	0	0	0	0
1956	0	0	0	0	0	0
1957	0	0	0	0	0	0
1958	0	0	0	0	0	0
1959	.1	.6	.1	0	0	5.4
1960	.1	3.3	.2	0	.1	4.3
1961	.4	.5	.7	.1	.2	17.2
1962	1.8	.8	1.2	.4	.2	16.5
1963	0	1.8	1.9	.8	1.6	9.8
1964	.5	3.9	1.4	.1	1.4	12.5
1965	.8	.9	1.4	.2	1.7	9.5
1966	.8	.2	1.1	.4	1.1	11.0
1967	1.1	.2	1.1	.6	1.2	7.4
1968	1.1	.1	1.4	.3	2.0	10.7
1969	.6	.1	.7	.4	1.1	3.1
1970	.3	.1	1.1	.4	.8	1.9
1971	.6	4.4	.9	.5	1.0	.6
1972	.5	1.9	.8	.5	.8	.9
1973	.4	0	1.2	.5	.6	.6
1974	.4	0	.8	.4	.9	10.0
1975	2.4	.1	2.4	.3	.9	12.1
1976	1.9	.1	1.7	.8	1.8	11.5
1977	1.6	.1	2.0	1.6	.4	5.8
1978	1.6	0	.2	.2	.3	4.4
1979	1.0	.1	0	.6	0	2.4
1980	1.5	0	0	.1	0	1.3
1981	3.1	0	0	.1	0	1.5
1982	10.8	0	0	1.9	0	1.7
1983	16.5	0	0	1.9	0	1.6
1984	26.1	.1	0	4.6	0	3.6
1985	22.9	.1	0	3.6	0	3.0
1986	20.7	.1	0	2.8	0	.2
1987	20.3	.1	0	1.2	0	0
1988	12.7	.1	0	0	0	.1
Total	152.8	19.7	22.5	25.4	18.4	170.7

Table 3526 (Continued)

YEARLY ANNOUNCED TOTAL MILITARY ASSISTANCE, TOTALS AND AVERAGES, 20 LR,[1] 1946–88

(M US)

Year	S. URUGUAY	T. VENEZUELA	LATIN AMERICA	LATIN AMERICA Average
1946	0	0	0	0
1947	0	0	0	0
1948	0	0	0	0
1949	0	0	0	0
1950	0	0	0	0
1951	0	0	0	0
1952	0	0	0	0
1953	0	0	0	0
1954	0	0	0	0
1955	0	0	0	0
1956	0	0	0	0
1957	0	0	8.4	.4
1958	0	0	0	0
1959	5.4	16.3	58.7	2.9
1960	1.7	10.1	66.8	3.3
1961	3.5	11.5	108.5	5.4
1962	4.1	12.5	157.3	8.3
1963	2.7	9.3	97.1	5.1
1964	2.1	11.9	89.5	4.7
1965	2.8	7.6	73.8	3.9
1966	2.8	9.9	90.1	4.7
1967	1.8	11.8	82.4	4.3
1968	2.2	10.2	106.1	5.6
1969	1.8	3.3	69.9	3.7
1970	1.9	2.7	57.0	3.0
1971	5.0	8.1	68.8	3.6
1972	3.9	9.1	84.9	4.5
1973	1.2	8.3	65.7	3.5
1974	2.5	5.3	85.3	4.5
1975	5.2	.4	88.6	4.7
1976	2.0	5.8	96.3	5.1
1977	0	.1	26.4	1.4
1978	0	0	38.9	2.0
1979	0	0	13.4	.7
1980	0	0	8.0	.4
1981	0	0	20.4	1.1
1982	0	0	51.0	2.7
1983	0	0	53.9	2.8
1984	0	0	117.3	6.2
1985	0	0	87.0	4.6
1986	0	0	73.7	3.9
1987	.2	.1	66.4	3.5
1988	0	0	43.3	2.3
Total	53.0	154.6	2,154.8	112.8

1. Deflated using Export Price Index (Table 3331) in 1970 U.S. dollars.

SOURCE: Country Tables 3504–3523.

Table 3527

YEARLY PER CAPITA ANNOUNCED TOTAL ASSISTANCE, TOTALS AND AVERAGES, 20 LR,[1] 1946–88

(US)

Year	A. ARGENTINA	B. BOLIVIA	C. BRAZIL	D. CHILE	E. COLOMBIA	F. COSTA RICA
1946	0	.24	2.05	9.95	.08	4.77
1947	.02	1.65	.68	2.99	.14	.78
1948	0	.18	.04	.21	1.38	.36
1949	0	.34	.29	5.26	.49	.19
1950	8.34	8.09	.43	6.85	.33	.74
1951	.37	.21	.65	.46	.27	1.09
1952	0	.70	1.39	2.53	.36	3.09
1953	0	.53	8.90	.26	.59	3.42
1954	0	6.40	.10	.28	.15	2.54
1955	4.38	12.37	1.14	1.19	.51	6.46
1956	1.07	10.27	1.91	5.28	1.06	24.18
1957	6.37	9.49	6.34	8.23	1.41	12.38
1958	.01	7.67	.49	7.18	8.10	2.88
1959	10.68	8.27	2.63	8.15	.68	8.47
1960	.06	4.79	.74	7.60	4.46	10.26
1961	4.71	9.53	5.47	22.79	7.61	9.40
1962	6.49	11.84	3.97	37.07	6.00	9.28
1963	7.77	20.50	2.43	16.77	9.66	12.83
1964	0.73	22.43	6.05	20.23	8.94	14.17
1965	.85	3.85	4.08	18.58	2.66	12.20
1966	1.71	9.77	5.50	15.04	6.86	10.14
1967	.62	7.62	3.70	36.09	8.79	5.75
1968	2.15	5.68	4.42	13.82	6.68	7.13
1969	3.47	8.07	.59	12.89	7.14	11.30
1970	1.43	1.40	2.28	4.48	6.39	10.75
1971	2.24	2.79	2.11	1.38	5.06	4.58
1972	2.50	13.11	3.29	1.93	6.21	1.99
1973	1.37	5.42	1.75	1.79	3.88	1.51
1974	1.61	7.23	2.45	7.79	2.02	4.64
1975	2.06	3.84	1.82	7.12	.78	2.59
1976	.82	5.66	.85	4.99	1.55	3.32
1977	.32	7.51	.25	1.66	.21	4.28
1978	.49	6.66	.47	2.44	1.72	3.07
1979	.51	4.61	.98	.54	1.06	4.54
1980	1.07	2.07	.29	.35	.66	3.80
1981	1.01	.78	.33	.37	.67	3.14
1982	6.54	1.15	.25	.20	7.05	8.47
1983	0	3.55	.08	.08	.10	31.46
1984	0	4.22	.07	.05	.45	25.27
1985	0	2.86	.10	.07	1.69	31.74
1986	0	4.10	.31	.06	.18	21.24
1987	.03	3.86	.29	.03	.19	22.30
1988	.12	4.25	.04	.08	.46	13.09
Yearly Average	1.90	5.94	1.91	6.86	2.90	8.73

Table 3527 (Continued)

YEARLY PER CAPITA ANNOUNCED TOTAL ASSISTANCE, TOTALS AND AVERAGES, 20 LR,[1] 1946—88

(US)

Year	G. CUBA	H. DOMINICAN REP.	I. ECUADOR	J. EL SALVADOR	K. GUATEMALA	L. HAITI
1946	.03	.17	.36	.48	.54	.16
1947	.03	.14	.34	.24	.55	.13
1948	.03	.06	1.46	.22	.86	.33
1949	0	0	.37	.16	1.53	1.90
1950	0	0	3.55	.24	.89	.22
1951	2.77	.06	.28	.14	.31	3.97
1952	.02	.11	.91	.33	.48	.29
1953	.04	.16	.37	.45	.08	.22
1954	1.76	.11	2.61	.38	.08	.36
1955	.10	.15	1.50	.49	4.00	4.35
1956	.33	.14	1.71	.63	12.68	4.28
1957	.11	.09	2.35	.92	6.66	1.04
1958	3.05	.09	1.64	.58	5.96	1.33
1959	.14	.42	3.28	.57	3.93	4.25
1960	.19	.20	3.25	.50	3.86	5.23
1961	.02	.04	5.00	3.29	9.79	4.04
1962		13.81	10.05	10.90	3.15	2.58
1963		19.47	10.26	10.28	4.51	.41
1964		5.67	7.36	6.53	4.18	.25
1965		29.05	7.01	7.54	3.78	.62
1966		35.60	6.97	3.70	1.25	1.73
1967		18.24	1.63	1.33	5.06	.68
1968		20.69	3.21	3.29	4.40	.98
1969		8.84	2.85	4.40	16.81	.81
1970		5.47	5.15	3.75	6.43	.92
1971		6.89	3.95	1.67	4.69	.97
1972		6.92	1.84	4.71	3.10	1.14
1973		5.88	2.17	1.05	4.14	1.36
1974		7.30	1.01	1.90	.79	1.60
1975		2.48	1.16	1.42	1.61	1.15
1976		8.40	1.37	1.99	4.36	4.18
1977		1.67	1.44	.77	2.19	4.59
1978		.67	1.28	1.24	.76	3.00
1979		6.17	1.82	1.12	1.52	2.25
1980		4.89	.77	5.17	.73	2.07
1981		2.70	1.07	10.74	.89	2.49
1982		5.30	1.12	18.28	.70	2.44
1983		4.00	1.21	21.40	1.36	3.22
1984		5.79	1.38	29.14	.90	3.10
1985		9.81	2.13	40.28	4.60	3.66
1986		5.70	2.28	30.73	5.06	5.07
1987		2.19	1.74	37.99	7.60	6.24
1988		2.70	.66	23.95	5.05	2.25
Yearly Average	.54	5.77	2.60	6.86	3.53	2.14

Table 3527 (Continued)

YEARLY PER CAPITA ANNOUNCED TOTAL ASSISTANCE, TOTALS AND AVERAGES, 20 LR,[1] 1946–88

(US)

Year	M. HONDURAS	N. MEXICO	O. NICARAGUA	P. PANAMA	Q. PARAGUAY	R. PERU
1946	.39	.20	3.03	.47	.53	.14
1947	.65	3.71	2.46	.38	.43	1.05
1948	.30	1.67	.67	.35	.40	.23
1949	.21	1.12	.56	4.24	.42	.17
1950	.10	1.16	.56	.37	.53	.17
1951	.18	.41	1.53	1.41	.63	3.50
1952	.68	.43	.92	4.62	1.42	.38
1953	.58	.32	1.02	2.24	.69	.26
1954	.90	.34	1.34	2.37	1.04	.40
1955	1.58	.09	3.85	4.11	8.06	16.30
1956	2.01	2.08	2.58	12.89	3.18	1.60
1957	5.83	.98	5.85	33.36	2.03	2.14
1958	6.25	2.19	3.23	6.76	4.75	2.66
1959	3.14	3.92	3.95	2.39	4.02	7.95
1960	2.64	1.73	10.82	2.30	3.00	3.51
1961	3.64	1.05	10.32	17.91	7.32	8.53
1962	2.81	4.45	11.81	27.19	5.34	10.42
1963	7.44	1.46	7.04	10.19	6.69	2.91
1964	5.77	3.12	6.19	24.76	5.75	9.38
1965	2.60	5.45	17.43	22.21	6.39	4.41
1966	7.26	3.27	14.42	12.12	8.68	4.98
1967	5.36	2.45	8.49	30.01	3.05	3.49
1968	7.00	2.01	17.72	16.73	3.84	2.32
1969	2.02	.38	1.77	13.36	8.34	2.55
1970	3.52	.81	2.30	8.32	3.91	1.19
1971	2.96	.84	8.31	10.09	5.63	1.43
1972	2.64	.94	2.70	39.78	2.20	5.14
1973	4.17	2.05	11.55	31.67	2.61	4.48
1974	6.50	1.77	6.65	12.20	1.82	3.93
1975	7.64	1.84	12.24	17.45	2.02	2.51
1976	5.45	1.59	2.39	13.69	1.99	4.83
1977	2.53	.51	8.28	5.78	.72	3.63
1978	2.98	4.75	2.99	6.44	.68	4.17
1979	3.93	1.10	3.16	6.16	1.45	3.58
1980	7.26	1.03	5.41	.46	.45	2.14
1981	4.22	3.26	7.33	1.98	.66	1.98
1982	9.84	1.43	.74	3.12	6.95	1.13
1983	12.92	.44	0	2.11	.43	2.28
1984	13.78	.39	.01	4.07	.29	3.09
1985	23.25	.09	0	13.29	.33	1.54
1986	14.91	.05	0	6.38	.30	.99
1987	18.42	.09	0	2.28	.30	1.05
1988	12.77	.39	.03	.16	.27	1.03
Yearly Average	5.33	1.57	4.92	10.19	2.78	3.25

Table 3527 (Continued)

YEARLY PER CAPITA ANNOUNCED TOTAL ASSISTANCE, TOTALS AND AVERAGES, 20 LR,[1] 1946–88

(US)

Year	S. URUGUAY	T. VENEZUELA	LATIN AMERICA Average
1946	.48	.23	1.23
1947	.07	.09	1.12
1948	1.25	.03	.50
1949	.07	.65	.67
1950	.07	1.45	1.87
1951	1.62	.05	.80
1952	.23	.74	.83
1953	.10	.02	3.20
1954	.08	.02	.44
1955	.16	.04	2.35
1956	.10	.04	2.32
1957	.15	.67	4.26
1958	.10	.04	2.16
1959	9.68	2.43	4.15
1960	11.92	4.10	2.19
1961	2.65	20.33	6.02
1962	4.66	11.65	6.82
1963	11.05	8.04	5.16
1964	4.10	7.87	6.11
1965	.81	6.26	5.02
1966	3.76	2.20	5.40
1967	1.97	5.58	5.03
1968	15.80	8.98	4.68
1969	2.10	.81	2.73
1970	7.77	2.08	2.53
1971	4.07	2.71	2.32
1972	4.88	4.59	3.33
1973	3.09	1.96	2.46
1974	1.28	1.93	2.55
1975	4.41	.73	2.13
1976	.84	2.64	1.92
1977	.11	.01	.91
1978	.03	.79	1.92
1979	.03	.55	1.32
1980	0	4.05	1.12
1981	1.79	1.35	1.49
1982	.09	.57	2.17
1983	.13	.25	1.13
1984	.08	.01	1.25
1985	.01	.02	1.69
1986	1.65	0	1.31
1987	1.41	0	1.43
1988	.01	0	.99
Yearly Average	2.43	2.48	2.54

1. Deflated using Export Price Index (Table 3331) in 1970 U.S. dollars.

SOURCE: Country Tables 3504–3523.

Table 3528

RELATIONSHIP BETWEEN LATIN AMERICAN AVERAGE ANNOUNCED TOTAL
ASSISTANCE AND AVERAGE YEARLY ANNOUNCED ASSISTANCE,
20 L,[1] 1946–88

(M US)

Year	A. ARGENTINA	B. BOLIVIA	C. BRAZIL	D. CHILE	E. COLOMBIA
1946	−8.7	−8.0	87.6	47.4	−7.8
1947	−7.7	−3.2	24.8	9.2	−6.5
1948	−3.7	−3.2	−1.8	−2.5	11.3
1949	−5.1	−4.1	9.8	26.2	.4
1950	127.8	9.8	7.9	27.1	−10.8
1951	.1	−5.7	28.8	−3.5	−3.3
1952	−6.8	−4.6	69.9	9.1	−2.5
1953	−27.0	−25.3	478.0	−25.3	−19.8
1954	−3.8	17.0	2.1	−2.0	−2.0
1955	60.2	20.3	47.3	−12.9	−14.4
1956	−1.1	13.9	97.2	15.5	−6.9
1957	81.6	−6.9	364.8	18.7	−20.2
1958	−20.8	6.6	11.4	31.7	96.4
1959	168.8	−10.6	137.2	19.9	−31.0
1960	−21.3	−4.0	29.3	35.3	46.4
1961	32.1	−25.8	330.0	113.7	57.9
1962	55.7	−30.0	217.2	217.2	21.0
1963	101.6	24.0	125.8	76.1	103.2
1964	−58.3	21.2	402.4	94.8	82.6
1965	−43.6	−45.7	268.6	95.8	−14.3
1966	−30.4	−25.4	387.5	61.7	57.9
1967	−51.7	−31.7	249.5	253.5	100.9
1968	−13.1	−37.2	324.5	61.9	67.2
1969	43.5	−1.0	15.3	80.9	105.0
1970	−1.9	−29.4	175.6	6.2	95.3
1971	20.3	−20.8	167.3	−20.5	73.1
1972	11.2	11.0	272.3	−31.1	84.7
1973	−3.7	−12.4	137.3	−20.1	48.9
1974	.3	−5.9	210.1	37.9	6.1
1975	19.1	−15.7	156.0	38.2	−16.0
1976	−10.3	−3.5	59.9	19.8	5.7
1977	−7.0	23.2	11.7	1.9	−10.4
1978	−20.1	1.7	19.1	−7.4	10.6
1979	−9.5	1.4	89.9	−17.8	4.2
1980	9.5	−9.1	13.9	−16.8	−2.7
1981	.7	−23.7	12.8	−23.9	−10.3
1982	148.7	−35.2	−10.2	−39.7	149.7
1983	−22.3	−.7	−11.7	−21.3	−19.4
1984	−25.1	1.2	−15.5	−24.6	−12.5
1985	−34.8	−16.4	−21.8	−33.9	13.6
1986	−27.5	−.7	15.0	−26.7	−22.1
1987	−29.8	−4.4	10.4	−30.3	−25.0
1988	−17.7	8.0	−16.5	−20.7	−7.9
Average	8.6	−6.8	116.1	23.7	22.7

Table 3528 (Continued)

RELATIONSHIP BETWEEN LATIN AMERICAN AVERAGE ANNOUNCED TOTAL ASSISTANCE AND AVERAGE YEARLY ANNOUNCED ASSISTANCE, 20 L,[1] 1946–88

(M US)

Year	F. COSTA RICA	G. CUBA	H. DOMINICAN REP.	I. ECUADOR	J. EL SALVADOR
1946	−5.3	−8.5	−8.3	−7.7	−7.8
1947	−7.5	−7.9	−7.7	−7.0	−7.6
1948	−3.4	−3.6	−3.6	.7	−3.3
1949	−4.9	−5.1	−5.1	−3.9	−4.8
1950	−13.9	−14.5	−14.5	−3.2	−14.1
1951	−5.5	9.2	−6.2	−5.5	−6.1
1952	−4.0	−6.7	−6.6	−3.7	−6.2
1953	−23.7	−26.7	−26.6	−25.7	−26.1
1954	−1.3	7.0	−3.6	5.7	−3.0
1955	−14.1	−20.4	−20.6	−15.4	−20.0
1956	4.6	−19.1	−20.9	−14.6	−19.9
1957	−26.3	−39.3	−39.8	−30.7	−38.0
1958	−17.6	−.3	−20.7	−14.2	−19.6
1959	−31.1	−40.2	−40.0	−27.3	−39.8
1960	−9.5	−21.0	−21.7	−8.2	−21.1
1961	−51.0	−63.1	−63.1	−40.7	−54.9
1962	−65.0	−77.5	−33.2	−30.8	−48.9
1963	−42.6	−60.4	4.0	−11.4	−32.5
1964	−53.2	−73.7	−54.3	−37.4	−54.9
1965	−44.2	−62.3	39.6	−26.8	−40.2
1966	−53.3	−68.9	60.0	−32.1	−57.6
1967	−56.7	−65.8	2.0	−57.0	−61.7
1968	−51.2	−62.8	16.4	−45.0	−52.1
1969	−18.6	−37.7	−2.8	−21.2	−22.9
1970	−17.2	−35.8	−13.6	−5.1	−22.9
1971	−25.5	−33.7	−4.9	−9.4	−27.8
1972	−46.2	−49.8	−20.1	−38.1	−32.5
1973	−34.9	−37.7	−11.7	−23.4	−33.8
1974	−31.3	−40.2	−7.0	−33.4	−32.9
1975	−29.4	−34.5	−22.9	−26.4	−28.9
1976	−25.3	−32.0	9.1	−22.1	−23.8
1977	−6.7	−15.6	−7.2	−4.9	−12.3
1978	−27.1	−33.6	−30.1	−23.8	−28.2
1979	−13.9	−23.7	9.0	−9.4	−18.7
1980	−12.1	−20.7	5.9	−14.4	3.9
1981	−21.0	−28.2	−13.1	−19.3	24.1
1982	−22.3	−42.0	−11.6	−32.3	49.4
1983	52.6	−22.3	1.6	−11.6	89.7
1984	36.0	−25.1	10.2	−12.6	114.2
1985	44.3	−34.8	26.4	−14.8	159.4
1986	29.2	−27.5	9.1	−5.4	123.4
1987	31.4	−30.6	−15.9	−13.4	159.7
1988	15.6	−21.7	−3.1	−15.0	100.7
Average	−16.4	−31.6	−8.5	−18.6	−2.3

Table 3528 (Continued)

RELATIONSHIP BETWEEN LATIN AMERICAN AVERAGE ANNOUNCED TOTAL ASSISTANCE AND AVERAGE YEARLY ANNOUNCED ASSISTANCE, 20 L,[1] 1946–88

(M US)

Year	K. GUATEMALA	L. HAITI	M. HONDURAS	N. MEXICO	O. NICARAGUA
1946	-7.3	-8.2	-8.2	-4.1	-5.8
1947	-6.6	-7.6	-7.2	79.0	-5.6
1948	-1.4	-2.6	-3.3	36.5	-3.0
1949	-.9	1.2	-4.8	22.6	-4.5
1950	-12.0	-13.8	-14.4	15.3	-13.9
1951	-5.5	7.3	-6.1	4.2	-4.7
1952	-5.4	-5.8	-5.8	5.2	-5.8
1953	-26.7	-26.2	-26.1	-17.9	-25.8
1954	-3.6	-2.5	-2.4	6.2	-2.2
1955	-7.8	-4.8	-18.4	-18.1	-16.3
1956	21.7	-5.0	-17.9	44.5	-18.0
1957	-16.8	-36.2	-30.1	-8.1	-32.5
1958	.6	-16.0	-10.0	53.2	-16.6
1959	-26.6	-25.6	-35.5	95.5	-35.8
1960	-7.6	-3.4	-17.5	39.9	-7.1
1961	-24.5	-48.3	-56.2	-24.1	-48.2
1962	-64.8	-67.9	-72.0	94.0	-59.8
1963	-41.5	-58.9	-45.2	-2.2	-49.6
1964	-55.6	-72.7	-61.5	55.0	-63.9
1965	-45.7	-59.9	-56.7	170.2	-34.1
1966	-63.3	-62.0	-52.5	75.4	-44.9
1967	-42.0	-63.1	-53.6	46.2	-51.4
1968	-41.5	-58.8	-46.6	32.2	-32.0
1969	46.7	-34.3	-32.7	-18.9	-34.5
1970	-1.9	-31.9	-26.5	5.2	-31.6
1971	-8.3	-29.5	-25.7	10.5	-18.0
1972	-32.5	-44.8	-42.4	1.0	-44.6
1973	-14.0	-31.7	-25.7	77.5	-14.5
1974	-35.4	-33.0	-20.8	62.9	-26.4
1975	-24.4	-29.2	-11.3	76.2	-8.1
1976	-3.9	-12.5	-14.5	66.9	-26.6
1977	-1.1	6.2	-7.2	17.2	3.6
1978	-28.3	-19.1	-23.3	276.9	-26.4
1979	-13.0	-12.7	-9.7	50.4	-15.7
1980	-15.4	-10.3	6.1	51.0	-5.9
1981	-21.5	-15.5	-12.0	203.6	-7.2
1982	-36.6	-29.7	-3.0	62.6	-39.8
1983	-12.1	-5.8	30.6	10.8	-22.3
1984	-18.3	-9.1	33.1	4.6	-25.1
1985	1.9	-15.5	66.8	-27.5	-34.8
1986	14.0	-.3	39.8	-23.4	-27.5
1987	33.5	3.3	55.2	-23.1	-30.6
1988	22.1	-9.2	39.6	10.3	-21.6
Average	-14.7	-23.4	-14.8	39.4	-24.2

Table 3528 (Continued)

RELATIONSHIP BETWEEN LATIN AMERICAN AVERAGE ANNOUNCED TOTAL ASSISTANCE AND AVERAGE YEARLY ANNOUNCED ASSISTANCE, 20 L,[1] 1946–88

(M US)

Year	P. PANAMA	Q. PARAGUAY	R. PERU	S. URUGUAY	T. VENEZUELA
1946	–8.3	–8.0	–7.7	–7.7	–7.7
1947	–7.7	–7.5	–.1	–7.9	–7.6
1948	–3.4	–3.2	–2.0	–1.0	–3.6
1949	–1.8	–4.5	–3.8	–4.9	–1.9
1950	–14.2	–13.8	–13.2	–14.4	–7.3
1951	–5.2	–5.5	22.1	–2.8	–6.1
1952	–2.9	–4.7	–3.7	–6.3	–2.8
1953	–25.0	–25.9	–24.8	–26.7	–26.8
1954	–1.7	–2.2	–.4	–3.6	–3.7
1955	–17.2	–8.4	122.3	–20.5	–20.7
1956	–9.0	–16.1	–6.9	–21.0	–21.0
1957	–7.7	–36.7	–20.4	–39.7	–35.7
1958	–14.2	–12.9	4.3	–20.7	–20.7
1959	–38.7	–34.3	36.3	–17.0	–24.0
1960	–19.9	–17.1	12.8	7.9	7.8
1961	–43.7	–50.0	24.8	–56.4	91.5
1962	–46.8	–67.7	33.2	–65.4	–14.0
1963	–48.5	–47.7	–28.5	–31.1	4.9
1964	–43.9	–62.3	32.3	–62.7	–7.5
1965	–34.8	–49.4	–10.9	–60.1	–7.8
1966	–53.5	–50.9	–9.1	–58.5	–49.0
1967	–26.5	–59.3	–22.9	–60.5	–13.9
1968	–40.2	–54.5	–33.4	–20.2	23.6
1969	–19.1	–19.0	–4.4	–32.0	–29.7
1970	–23.9	–26.8	–19.8	–14.6	–14.4
1971	–18.8	–20.4	–14.2	–22.5	–5.0
1972	10.7	–44.5	21.8	–36.4	.4
1973	12.0	–31.2	26.6	–29.2	–15.7
1974	–20.5	–35.6	19.4	–36.7	–17.8
1975	–5.2	–29.1	4.4	–22.0	–25.2
1976	–8.4	–26.5	43.2	–29.6	2.6
1977	–5.3	–13.5	42.5	–15.3	–15.5
1978	–21.9	–31.6	34.8	–33.5	–22.5
1979	–12.3	–19.3	36.5	–23.6	–15.7
1980	–19.8	–19.3	16.2	–20.7	40.2
1981	–24.3	–26.0	7.0	–22.9	–7.3
1982	–35.6	–18.5	–21.3	–41.7	–32.9
1983	–17.8	–20.7	20.3	–21.9	–18.1
1984	–16.5	–24.2	34.2	–24.9	–25.0
1985	–5.8	–33.5	–4.4	–34.7	–34.5
1986	–13.3	–26.3	–7.4	–22.6	–27.4
1987	–25.5	–29.6	–8.9	–26.4	–30.6
1988	–21.3	–20.4	.3	–21.7	–21.7
Average	–18.8	–26.9	7.6	–26.4	–10.3

1. Deflated using Export Price Index (Table 3331) in 1970 U.S. dollars.

SOURCE: Calculated from Table 3524.

Table 3529

RELATIONSHIP BETWEEN LATIN AMERICAN PER CAPITA ANNOUNCED TOTAL ASSISTANCE AND PER CAPITA ASSISTANCE, 20 L,[1] 1946-88

(US)

Year	A. ARGENTINA	B. BOLIVIA	C. BRAZIL	D. CHILE	E. COLOMBIA
1946	-1.23	-.99	.82	8.72	-1.15
1947	-1.10	.53	-44	1.87	-.98
1948	-.50	-.32	-.46	-.29	.88
1949	-.67	-.33	-.38	4.59	-.18
1950	6.47	6.22	-1.44	4.98	-1.54
1951	-.43	-.59	-.15	-.34	-.53
1952	-.83	-.13	.56	1.70	-.47
1953	-3.20	-2.67	5.70	-2.94	-2.61
1954	-.44	5.96	-.34	-.16	-.29
1955	2.03	10.02	-1.21	-1.16	-1.84
1956	-1.25	7.95	-.41	2.96	-1.26
1957	2.11	5.23	2.08	3.97	-2.85
1958	-2.15	5.51	-1.67	5.02	5.94
1959	6.53	4.12	-1.52	4.00	-3.47
1960	-2.13	2.60	-1.45	5.41	2.27
1961	-1.31	3.51	-.55	16.77	1.59
1962	-.33	5.02	-2.85	30.25	-.82
1963	2.61	15.34	-2.73	11.61	4.50
1964	-5.38	16.32	-.06	14.12	2.83
1965	-4.17	-1.17	-.94	13.56	-2.36
1966	-3.69	4.37	.10	9.64	1.46
1967	-4.41	2.59	-1.33	31.06	3.76
1968	-2.53	1.00	-.26	9.14	2.00
1969	.74	5.34	-2.14	10.16	4.41
1970	-1.10	-1.13	-.25	1.95	3.86
1971	-.08	.47	-.21	-.94	2.74
1972	-.83	9.78	-.04	-1.40	2.88
1973	-1.09	2.96	-.71	-.67	1.42
1974	-.94	4.68	-.10	5.24	-.53
1975	-.07	1.71	-.31	4.99	-1.35
1976	-1.10	3.74	-1.07	3.07	-.37
1977	-.59	6.60	-.66	.75	-.70
1978	-1.43	4.74	-1.45	.52	-.20
1979	-.81	3.29	-.34	-.78	-.26
1980	-.05	.95	-.83	-.77	-.46
1981	-.48	-.71	-1.16	-1.12	-.82
1982	4.37	-1.02	-1.92	-1.97	4.88
1983	-1.13	2.42	-1.05	-1.05	-1.03
1984	-1.25	2.97	-1.18	-1.20	-.80
1985	-1.69	1.17	-1.59	-1.62	0
1986	-1.31	2.79	-1.00	-1.25	-1.13
1987	-1.40	2.43	-1.14	-1.40	-1.24
1988	-.87	3.26	-.95	-.91	-.53
Average	-.62	3.33	-.61	4.23	.36

Table 3529 (Continued)

RELATIONSHIP BETWEEN LATIN AMERICAN PER CAPITA ANNOUNCED TOTAL ASSISTANCE AND PER CAPITA ASSISTANCE, 20 L,[1] 1946–88

(US)

Year	F. COSTA RICA	G. CUBA	H. DOMINICAN REP.	I. ECUADOR	J. EL SALVADOR
1946	3.54	−1.20	−1.06	−.87	−.75
1947	−.34	−1.09	−.98	−.78	−.88
1948	−.14	−.47	−.44	.96	−.28
1949	−.48	−.67	−.67	−.30	−.51
1950	−1.13	−1.87	−1.87	1.68	−1.63
1951	.29	1.97	−.74	−.52	−.66
1952	2.26	−.81	−.72	.08	−.50
1953	.22	−3.16	−3.04	−2.83	−2.75
1954	2.10	1.32	−.33	2.17	−.06
1955	4.11	−2.25	−2.20	−.85	−1.86
1956	21.86	−1.99	−2.18	−.61	−1.70
1957	8.12	−4.15	−4.17	−1.91	−3.34
1958	.72	.89	−2.07	−.52	−1.58
1959	4.32	−4.01	−3.73	−.87	−3.58
1960	8.07	−2.00	−1.99	1.06	−1.69
1961	3.38	−6.00	−5.98	−1.02	−2.73
1962	2.46	−6.82	6.99	3.23	4.08
1963	7.67	−5.16	14.31	5.10	5.12
1964	8.06	−6.11	−.44	1.25	.42
1965	7.18	−5.02	24.03	1.99	2.52
1966	4.74	−5.40	30.20	1.57	−1.70
1967	.72	−5.03	13.21	−3.40	−3.70
1968	2.45	−4.68	16.01	−1.47	−1.39
1969	8.57	−2.73	6.11	.12	1.67
1970	8.22	−2.53	2.94	2.62	1.22
1971	2.26	−2.32	4.57	1.63	−.65
1972	−1.34	−3.33	3.59	−1.49	1.38
1973	−.95	−2.46	3.42	−.29	−1.41
1974	2.09	−2.55	4.75	−1.54	−.65
1975	.46	−2.13	.35	−.97	−.71
1976	1.40	−1.92	6.48	−.55	.07
1977	3.37	−.91	.76	.53	−.14
1978	1.15	−1.92	−1.25	−.64	−.68
1979	3.22	−1.32	4.85	.50	−.20
1980	2.68	−1.12	3.77	−.35	4.05
1981	1.65	−1.49	1.21	−.42	9.25
1982	6.30	−2.17	3.13	−1.05	16.11
1983	30.33	−1.13	2.87	.08	20.27
1984	24.02	−1.25	4.54	.13	27.89
1985	30.05	−1.69	3.12	.44	38.59
1986	19.93	−1.31	4.39	.97	29.42
1987	20.87	−1.43	.76	.31	36.56
1988	12.10	−.99	1.71	−33	22.96
Average	6.06	−2.28	3.16	.06	4.22

Table 3529 (Continued)

RELATIONSHIP BETWEEN LATIN AMERICAN PER CAPITA ANNOUNCED TOTAL ASSISTANCE AND PER CAPITA ASSISTANCE, 20 L,[1] 1946–88

(US)

Year	K. GUATEMALA	L. HAITI	M. HONDURAS	N. MEXICO	O. NICARAGUA
1946	−.69	−1.07	−.84	−1.03	1.80
1947	−.57	−.99	−.47	2.59	1.34
1948	.36	−.17	−.20	1.17	.17
1949	.86	1.23	−.46	.45	−.11
1950	−.98	−1.65	−1.77	−.71	−1.31
1951	−.49	3.17	−.62	−.39	.73
1952	−.35	−.54	−.15	−.40	.09
1953	−3.12	−2.98	−2.62	−2.88	−2.18
1954	−.36	−.08	.46	−.10	.90
1955	1.65	2.00	−.77	−2.26	1.50
1956	10.36	1.96	−.31	−.24	.26
1957	2.40	−3.22	1.57	−3.28	1.59
1958	3.80	−.83	4.09	.03	1.07
1959	−.22	.10	−1.01	−.23	−.20
1960	1.67	3.04	.45	−.46	8.63
1961	3.77	−1.98	−2.38	−4.97	4.30
1962	−3.67	−4.24	−4.01	−2.37	4.99
1963	−.65	−4.75	2.28	−3.70	1.88
1964	−1.93	−5.86	−.34	−2.99	.08
1965	−1.24	−4.40	−2.42	.43	12.41
1966	−4.15	−3.67	1.86	−2.13	9.02
1967	.03	−4.35	.33	−2.58	3.46
1968	−.28	−3.70	2.32	−2.67	13.04
1969	14.08	−1.92	−.71	−2.35	−.96
1970	3.90	−1.61	.99	−1.72	−.23
1971	2.37	−1.35	.64	−1.48	5.99
1972	−.23	−2.19	−.69	−2.39	−.63
1973	1.68	−1.10	1.71	−.41	9.09
1974	−1.76	−.95	3.95	−.78	4.10
1975	−52	−.98	5.51	−.29	10.11
1976	2.44	2.26	3.53	−.33	.47
1977	1.28	3.68	1.62	−.40	7.37
1978	−1.16	1.08	1.06	2.83	1.07
1979	.20	.93	2.61	−.22	1.84
1980	−.39	.95	6.14	−.09	4.29
1981	−.60	1.00	2.73	1.77	5.84
1982	−1.47	.27	7.67	−.74	−1.43
1983	.23	2.09	11.79	−.69	−1.13
1984	−.35	1.85	12.53	−.86	−1.24
1985	2.91	1.97	21.56	−1.60	−1.69
1986	3.75	3.76	13.60	−1.26	−1.31
1987	6.17	4.81	16.99	−1.34	−1.43
1988	4.06	1.26	11.78	−.60	−.96
Average	.97	−.39	2.73	−.95	2.33

Table 3529 (Continued)

RELATIONSHIP BETWEEN LATIN AMERICAN PER CAPITA ANNOUNCED
TOTAL ASSISTANCE AND PER CAPITA ASSISTANCE, 20 L,[1] 1946–88

(US)

Year	P. PANAMA	Q. PARAGUAY	R. PERU	S. URUGUAY	T. VENEZUELA
1946	−.76	−.70	−1.09	−.75	−1.00
1947	−.74	−.69	−.07	−1.05	−1.03
1948	−.15	−.10	−.27	.75	−.47
1949	3.57	−.25	−.50	−.60	−.02
1950	−1.50	−1.34	−1.70	−1.80	−.42
1951	.61	−.17	2.70	.82	−.75
1952	3.79	.59	−.45	−.60	−.09
1953	−.96	−2.51	−2.94	−3.10	−3.18
1954	1.93	.60	−.04	−.36	−.42
1955	1.76	5.71	13.95	−2.19	−2.31
1956	10.57	.86	−.72	−2.22	−2.28
1957	29.10	−2.23	−2.12	−4.11	−3.59
1958	4.60	2.59	.50	−2.06	−2.12
1959	−1.76	−.13	3.80	5.53	−1.72
1960	.11	.81	1.32	9.73	1.91
1961	11.89	1.30	2.51	−3.37	14.31
1962	20.37	−1.48	3.60	−2.16	4.83
1963	5.03	1.53	−2.25	5.89	2.88
1964	18.65	−.36	3.27	−2.01	1.76
1965	17.19	1.37	−.61	−4.21	1.24
1966	6.72	3.28	−.42	−1.64	−3.20
1967	24.98	−1.98	−1.54	−3.06	.55
1968	12.05	−.84	−2.36	11.12	4.30
1969	10.63	5.61	−.18	−.63	−1.92
1970	5.79	1.38	−1.34	5.24	−.45
1971	7.77	3.31	−.89	1.75	.39
1972	36.45	−1.13	1.81	1.55	1.26
1973	29.21	.15	2.02	.63	−.50
1974	9.65	−.73	1.38	−1.27	−.62
1975	15.32	−.11	.38	2.28	−1.40
1976	11.77	.07	2.91	−1.08	.72
1977	4.87	−.19	2.72	−.80	−.90
1978	4.52	−1.24	2.25	−1.89	−1.13
1979	4.84	.13	2.26	−1.29	−.77
1980	−.66	−.67	1.02	−1.12	2.93
1981	.49	−.83	.49	.30	−.14
1982	.95	4.78	−1.04	−2.08	−1.60
1983	.98	−.70	1.15	−1.00	−.88
1984	2.82	−.96	1.84	−1.17	−1.24
1985	11.60	−1.36	−.15	−1.68	−1.67
1986	5.07	−1.01	−.32	.34	−1.31
1987	.85	−1.16	−.38	−.02	−1.43
1988	−.83	−.67	.04	−.98	−.99
Average	7.48	.24	.69	−.10	−.06

1. Deflated using Export Price Index (Table 3331) in 1970 U.S. dollars.

SOURCE: Calculated from Table 3527.

Table 3530

PERCENTAGE OF ANNOUNCED TOTAL U.S. ASSISTANCE
TO LATIN AMERICA, 20 L, 1946–88

(%)

Year	A. ARGENTINA	B. BOLIVIA	C. BRAZIL	D. CHILE	E. COLOMBIA
1946	0	.39	55.47	32.32	.49
1947	.18	3.01	20.42	10.70	.97
1948	0	.72	2.53	1.63	20.25
1949	0	.99	14.67	30.75	5.36
1950	49.02	8.38	7.72	14.33	1.27
1951	5.03	.51	27.60	2.22	2.43
1952	0	1.61	56.32	11.68	3.13
1953	0	.31	93.62	.31	1.32
1954	0	27.24	7.76	2.41	2.41
1955	19.33	9.84	16.26	1.92	1.58
1956	4.73	8.26	27.87	8.64	3.38
1957	15.18	4.14	50.52	7.33	2.47
1958	.03	6.58	7.72	12.57	28.05
1959	25.48	3.71	21.65	7.41	1.24
1960	.25	4.10	11.55	12.89	15.38
1961	7.54	2.96	31.11	14.00	9.58
1962	9.04	3.23	20.00	20.00	6.69
1963	14.11	7.36	16.22	11.89	14.25
1964	1.10	6.78	34.02	12.04	11.16
1965	1.58	1.41	27.94	13.35	4.06
1966	2.94	3.32	34.88	9.98	9.69
1967	1.13	2.73	25.21	25.53	13.33
1968	4.17	2.15	32.44	10.45	10.90
1969	11.34	5.12	7.39	16.55	19.92
1970	4.98	.94	31.04	6.17	19.25
1971	8.44	2.01	31.38	2.06	16.68
1972	6.45	6.43	34.03	1.97	14.22
1973	4.74	3.53	24.40	2.46	12.08
1974	5.30	4.49	32.75	10.22	6.06
1975	8.18	2.86	29.06	11.08	2.82
1976	3.56	4.69	15.12	8.52	6.20
1977	2.91	13.08	9.22	5.92	1.75
1978	2.12	5.53	8.26	4.11	6.92
1979	3.15	5.57	25.20	1.31	6.20
1980	7.69	2.95	8.80	.99	4.57
1981	5.40	.84	7.65	.79	3.34
1982	23.91	.85	3.98	.29	24.03
1983	0	5.10	2.49	.23	.68
1984	.01	5.52	2.01	.12	2.65
1985	0	2.78	1.97	.13	7.32
1986	0	5.14	8.14	.14	1.03
1987	.14	4.51	7.06	.06	.97
1988	.97	7.21	1.27	.23	3.35
Average Percentage	6.05	4.63	21.74	8.09	7.66

Table 3530 (Continued)

PERCENTAGE OF ANNOUNCED TOTAL U.S. ASSISTANCE
TO LATIN AMERICA, 20 L, 1946–88
(%)

Year	F. COSTA RICA	G. CUBA	H. DOMINICAN REP.	I. ECUADOR	J. EL SALVADOR
1946	1.95	.10	.20	.59	.49
1947	.35	.09	.18	.62	.27
1948	.36	.18	.18	5.97	.54
1949	.14	0	0	1.13	.28
1950	.20	0	0	3.91	.15
1951	.71	12.23	.10	.71	.20
1952	2.09	.09	.19	2.28	.47
1953	.60	.05	.07	.24	.17
1954	3.28	14.14	.34	12.41	1.03
1955	1.64	.16	.09	1.33	.25
1956	6.09	.50	.09	1.56	.32
1957	1.72	.09	.03	1.17	.26
1958	.79	4.93	.06	1.62	.32
1959	1.22	.12	.15	1.68	.16
1960	2.87	.30	.14	3.17	.27
1961	.97	.01	.01	1.78	.65
1962	.85	0	3.01	3.17	1.95
1963	1.55	0	5.61	4.27	2.43
1964	1.46	0	1.38	2.59	1.34
1965	1.53	0	8.61	3.00	1.87
1966	1.19	0	9.85	2.81	.86
1967	.79	0	5.42	.70	.33
1968	.97	0	6.64	1.49	.90
1969	2.67	0	4.87	2.30	2.06
1970	2.73	0	3.26	4.51	1.89
1971	1.29	0	4.50	3.80	.92
1972	.39	0	3.14	1.24	1.83
1973	.39	0	3.63	2.00	.55
1974	1.16	0	4.35	.90	.97
1975	.78	0	1.78	1.24	.86
1976	1.10	0	6.76	1.63	1.35
1977	2.99	0	2.83	3.62	1.11
1978	1.02	0	.54	1.54	.84
1979	2.18	0	7.25	3.18	1.11
1980	2.17	0	6.77	1.59	6.24
1981	1.33	0	2.82	1.67	9.77
1982	2.46	0	3.81	1.21	11.46
1983	17.71	0	5.64	2.53	26.47
1984	12.80	0	7.39	2.62	29.15
1985	11.96	0	9.27	3.02	29.38
1986	10.86	0	7.01	4.22	28.90
1987	10.65	0	2.53	2.96	32.69
1988	9.06	0	4.51	1.62	29.70
Average Percentage	3.00	.77	3.14	2.46	5.41

Table 3530 (Continued)

PERCENTAGE OF ANNOUNCED TOTAL U.S. ASSISTANCE
TO LATIN AMERICA, 20 L, 1946–88

(%)

Year	K. GUATEMALA	L. HAITI	M. HONDURAS	N. MEXICO	O. NICARAGUA
1946	.78	.29	.29	2.64	1.66
1947	.88	.27	.53	54.20	1.50
1948	3.07	1.45	.54	54.43	.90
1949	4.09	6.21	.28	27.22	.56
1950	.86	.25	.05	10.26	.20
1951	.71	10.72	.20	8.29	1.31
1952	1.04	.76	.76	8.83	.76
1953	.05	.14	.17	1.69	.22
1954	.34	1.72	1.90	13.10	2.07
1955	3.13	3.85	.62	.68	1.12
1956	10.11	3.82	.79	15.47	.76
1957	2.90	.49	1.24	3.99	.94
1958	5.14	1.17	2.61	17.71	1.03
1959	1.77	1.89	.69	16.59	.66
1960	3.31	4.23	1.09	13.93	3.41
1961	3.06	1.18	.55	3.09	1.18
1962	.87	.65	.38	11.64	1.20
1963	1.65	.14	1.32	5.07	.94
1964	1.29	.07	.87	9.19	.70
1965	1.41	.21	.48	19.63	2.38
1966	.43	.52	1.25	11.03	1.83
1967	1.90	.22	.98	8.95	1.15
1968	1.78	.34	1.36	7.96	2.58
1969	11.78	.47	.69	2.62	.44
1970	4.98	.57	1.37	6.02	.62
1971	3.97	.65	1.26	6.91	2.45
1972	1.83	.53	.78	5.37	.56
1973	3.31	.84	1.69	16.07	3.24
1974	.63	.94	2.54	13.48	1.81
1975	1.53	.80	3.54	16.88	4.03
1976	4.61	3.21	2.87	16.27	.88
1977	4.90	7.36	2.83	11.07	6.49
1978	.82	2.27	1.61	48.67	1.13
1979	2.38	2.45	3.11	16.44	1.78
1980	1.34	2.64	6.81	18.23	3.76
1981	1.24	2.37	3.02	43.29	3.91
1982	.67	1.54	4.89	13.11	.27
1983	2.40	3.90	12.49	7.81	0
1984	1.43	3.36	12.20	6.22	.01
1985	5.54	2.92	15.38	1.10	0
1986	7.94	5.21	12.88	.79	0
1987	11.01	5.83	14.74	1.30	0
1988	10.63	3.02	14.87	7.77	.03
Average Percentage	3.11	2.13	3.22	13.61	1.41

Table 3530 (Continued)

PERCENTAGE OF ANNOUNCED TOTAL U.S. ASSISTANCE
TO LATIN AMERICA, 20 L, 1946–88

(%)

Year	P. PANAMA	Q. PARAGUAY	R. PERU	S. URUGUAY	T. VENEZUELA
1946	.20	.39	.59	.59	.59
1947	.18	.35	4.95	.09	.27
1948	.36	.72	2.35	3.62	.18
1949	3.24	.56	1.27	.14	3.10
1950	.10	.25	.46	.05	2.49
1951	.91	.71	22.35	2.83	.20
1952	2.85	1.52	2.28	.38	2.94
1953	.36	.19	.41	.05	.02
1954	2.76	2.07	4.48	.34	.17
1955	.90	3.01	34.10	.12	.06
1956	2.88	1.21	3.38	.06	.06
1957	4.04	.43	2.46	.05	.55
1958	1.62	1.91	6.02	.06	.06
1959	.30	.83	9.41	2.94	2.09
1960	.55	1.17	7.87	6.77	6.75
1961	1.54	1.04	6.96	.54	12.24
1962	2.09	.67	7.51	.83	6.21
1963	1.04	1.11	2.78	2.55	5.69
1964	2.12	.81	7.57	.78	4.72
1965	2.33	1.09	4.34	.19	4.60
1966	1.18	1.37	4.57	.79	1.52
1967	3.14	.52	3.43	.42	4.16
1968	1.89	.70	2.46	3.57	7.24
1969	2.59	2.61	4.65	.80	1.12
1970	1.75	1.32	2.35	3.11	3.14
1971	2.33	2.08	3.04	1.74	4.48
1972	6.39	.57	7.57	1.42	5.31
1973	6.93	.91	8.97	1.19	3.08
1974	2.58	.61	7.80	.46	2.93
1975	4.47	.83	5.93	1.90	1.41
1976	3.88	.91	12.37	.40	5.69
1977	3.46	.70	19.63	.11	.04
1978	1.83	.32	10.71	.02	1.73
1979	2.53	.99	13.37	.02	1.78
1980	.22	.36	9.39	0	15.48
1981	.72	.41	6.57	.98	3.90
1982	.80	2.94	2.59	.03	1.14
1983	1.04	.36	10.07	.09	.99
1984	1.82	.20	12.41	.05	.03
1985	4.39	.19	4.59	.01	.05
1986	2.73	.22	3.84	.94	.01
1987	.89	.18	3.73	.73	.01
1988	.09	.32	5.34	.01	.01
Average Percentage	2.05	.92	6.90	.97	2.75

SOURCE: Calculated from Table 3524.

36

U.S.—Latin American Senior-Level Exchanges, 1953—88

JOHN L. MARTIN

James W. Wilkie, Enrique C. Ochoa, and David E. Lorey, eds., *Statistical Abstract of Latin America*, vol. 28 (Los Angeles: UCLA Latin American Center Publications, 1990).

One important aspect of the web of societal interactions between the United States and its hemispheric neighbors to the south which influences foreign policy is the personal relationships established among key policymakers as a result of their face-to-face meetings. A historical look at the frequency and regional or country-specific emphasis of meetings among heads of government and other senior officials offers a glimpse at the framework upon which policies have been shaped.

Data are presented in this study in two ways. Table 3600 shows the number of visits by U.S. VIPs (Very Important Person(s)) to Latin America by presidential period since 1953. Table 3601 gives the data yearly for visits and length of stay by name of the senior Latin American and U.S. officials.[1]

Table 3600 shows that since 1953 there have been only four years—one in each decade (1957, 1964, 1975, and 1987)—in which no U.S. VIP visitor traveled to Latin America or the Caribbean. The average number of trips over the 32-year period, including those four years, is over two visits per year. The average number of countries in the region visited each year during that same period is nearly five.

As President Bush charts the course of U.S. policy toward Latin America and the Caribbean, his views are bound to be influenced by his six trips to the region as President Reagan's vice president. He visited Mexico, major South American countries (e.g., Brazil and Argentina), and key smaller countries such as Panama, Guatemala, and Honduras. In addition, he has had the opportunity to meet with many other regional leaders when they visited the United States.

During the Reagan administration, U.S. policy toward Latin America was marked by pitched controversy, particularly with regard to Central America. It also was marked by the first use of U.S. military power in the region—in Grenada—since the 1965 peacekeeping operation in the Dominican Republic. However, a focus on VIP exchanges during this period documents that senior-level U.S. relations with our hemispheric partners during this eight-year period were extremely close. In fact, a high-water mark was reached in VIP visits in both directions during this period. President Reagan, Vice President Bush, and Secretaries of State Haig and Shultz made 33 trips visiting 20 southern neighbors.[2] During the same years, Regan and Bush met in the United States over 60 times with presidents and prime ministers from Latin America and the Caribbean. The pattern of these meetings reveals areas of key concern: El Salvador's President Duarte, eight visits; Jamaican President Seaga, seven visits; Suazo and Azcona of Honduras, five visits, etc.

This high point in senior-level foreign policy leadership contacts is significantly above the comparable level for the next most active administration: the Kennedy/Johnson/Humphrey/Rusk years. During the Alliance for Progress era, from 1961 to 1968, those four officials made a combined total of 17 visits to 14 southern neighbors. They received 21 official visits from hemispheric leaders during the same period, with none visiting more than twice.

At the low end of the scale for hemispheric VIP visits are the Nixon/Ford administrations. During that eight-year span, the respective number of high-level visits to neighbors to the sough was 13, and the number of countries visited was 14. The Nixon/Ford White House received 15 visits from regional heads of state.

The number of visits, shown in Table 3600, is one measure of the amount of time spent in high-level personal diplomacy. It does not, however, distinguish between a largely ceremonial one-day trip and a longer regional tour, data for which are given in Table 3601. A look at the number of days spent by the top U.S. officials in visits to Latin America shows that the Eisenhower administration comes out on top with 106 days of travel to Latin America and the Caribbean. That total received a big boost from two visits to the region totaling 45 days by then Vice President Nixon.

JOHN MARTIN graduated from Lewis and Clark College in Portland, Oregon, with a degree in political science. He served in Mexico, Nicaragua, and Paraguay as well as in the Inter-American Affairs Bureau of the U.S. Department of State during his career in the U.S. Foreign Service. Currently, he is an evaluation specialist with Aguirre International working on that firm's process evaluation of the Agency for International Development's Caribbean and Latin American Scholarship Program. He studied in the UCLA Latin American Area Studies program 1975–76 and authored the first study of Latin America's Real Industrial Wage Index, which was published in the *Statistical Abstract of Latin America*, vol. 18 (1977), and later editions.

[1] Most travel by the president and secretary of state is recorded in the Department of State *Bulletin*. This information was checked and supplemented by reference to *Facts on File*, which was the primary source for vice-presidential travel.

[2] In this study, when a president was accompanied by his vice president and/or secretary of state it is treated as only one trip.

In second position is the Reagan administration with 91 days. The Kennedy/Johnson record (70 days) comes in third. The Carter administration accounted for ten VIP visits in four years totaling 36 days, which, on the average, put it ahead of the 50 days logged during eight years of the Nixon/Ford era.

The senior-level investment in travel time to hemispheric trouble spots is noteworthy for its absence. Cuba is an example. During the seven years prior to the Castro takeover in 1959, there was only one visit (Nixon in 1955), and none by the secretary of state. Nicaragua, prior to the Sandinista takeover in 1979, had not been visited by any top official of the Carter administration, nor had any other country of Central America received a VIP visit.

The lack of Carter administration senior-level visitors to Nicaragua is understandable, in that the United States had major policy disagreements with the Somoza regime on human rights and democratization. Other examples of countries receiving similar treatment are prominent. Since their respective revolutions, Cuba and Nicaragua have had no high-level U.S. visits, with the exception of the brief 1984 visit of Secretary Shultz to Nicaragua designed to establish that the United States was not entirely closed-minded to hemispheric efforts to bring Nicaragua into the democratic fold. States on the right wing of the ideological spectrum, like Nicaragua before the 1979 revolutionary government took power, also are isolated in the frequency of high-level visitors. Chile, for example, has been visited only once since the 1973 coup which brought General Pinochet to power. Paraguay last received a U.S. VIP visit in 1958, four years after General Stroessner took power. Stroessner was shunned not only by the United States but also by other democratic leaders. Paraguay's isolation appears to be ending with the ouster of Stroessner by General Rodríguez and the May 1, 1989, election, as was indicated by the presence of the presidents of Argentina, Brazil, and Uruguay at Rodríguez's subsequent inauguration.

Needless to say, the record of meetings between the president, vice president, and secretary of state with their hemispheric counterparts reflects only the highly visible tip of the iceberg. Hidden from view is the rich fabric of more frequent and also important contacts that range from respective diplomatic staffs stationed abroad in permanent representation of their countries to congressional and other VIP travel. Not included in this recent history of U.S.–Latin American VIP visitor exchanges are the array of contacts that go on among cabinet, subcabinet, and lower policy-making levels in Washington, at the U.N. General Assembly, at regional conferences, and so on. Also not included is a record of the receptions of lesser luminaries than heads of of government at the White House or in the Department of State that occur on a daily basis.

Two examples of the type of important high-level contacts that fall outside of the scope of this study are VIP travels in the late 1950s. Not reflected in the record of Latin American VIP visitors to the United States is the 1959 visit by Fidel Castro. He was visiting unofficially in response to private invitations, and was officially received only by the undersecretary of state. Similarly, not reflected among the visits of U.S. leaders to Latin America was the 1958 visit to Latin America by Dr. Milton Eisenhower. He was, in effect, engaged in a fact-finding trip for his brother, and his report undoubtedly influenced the views of the Eisenhower administration, but he was traveling as a private citizen.

The year 1953 was selected as the beginning point of this study of U.S.–Latin American VIP travel, because earlier data for travel of Latin American VIPs to the United States and senior U.S. visitors to Latin America, with the exception of the president, are not comprehensively available. Additionally, the 1953–88 period covers most of the post–World War II era, when the global foreign engagement which characterizes present-day U.S. Policy was first accepted.

For reference purposes, the data on earlier presidential travel, compiled by the State Department's Historical Office, are presented below. The 1906 visit to Panama by President Theodore Roosevelt was the first foreign travel by a sitting U.S. president. It is interesting to note how the nature of international travel significantly changed with the advent of air transportation. President Roosevelt was the last U.S. president who visited Latin America by sea. Five of his eight visits to the region were casual stops while vacationing or while en route elsewhere.

President	Country	Dates	Comment
		1906	
T. Roosevelt	Panama	11/14–17	Inspection Canal construction
		1909	
Taft	Panama	1/29–2/7	President-elect, Canal inspection
	Mexico	10/16	
		1920	
Harding	Panama	11/24	President-elect, informal visit
		1928	
Coolidge	Cuba	1/15–17	6th International Conference of American States
Hoover	Honduras	11/26	President-elect, goodwill tour
	El Salvador	11/26	
	Nicaragua	11/27	
	Costa Rica	11/28	
	Ecuador	12/1	
	Peru	12/5	
	Chile	12/10–11	
	Argentina	12/13–15	

President	Country	Dates	Comment
Hoover (Continued)	Uruguay	12/16–18	
	Brazil	12/21–23	
		1934	
Roosevelt	Haiti	7/5	Vacation
	Colombia	7/10	
	Panama	7/11–12	
		1935	
	Panama	10/16	Informal
		1936	
	Brazil	11/27	
	Argentina	11/30–12/2	Inter-American Peace Conference
	Uruguay	12/3	
		1938	
	Panama	8/4–5	Vacation
		1940	
	Panama	2/27	Vacation
		1941	
	Argentina	August	At sea with Churchill

President	Country	Dates	Comment
		1943	
Roosevelt (Continued)	Brazil	1/12–13	Stop on way to and from Casablanca Conference
		1/28–29	
	Mexico	4/29	
		1947	
Truman	Mexico	3/3–6	
	Brazil	9/1–7	

The principal sources used in this survey were the Department of State *Bulletin*, *Facts on File*, unofficial records of the State Department Protocol Office, and the Department of State's historical series *Foreign Relations of the United States*. Data compiled on presidential travel were checked with, and found to coincide with, a study prepared earlier by the State Department's Office of the Historian and published in the September 1981 issue of the *Bulletin*. In a few instances missing dates were discovered in biographies or in microfiche copies of the *New York Times*. The Protocol Office record goes back only to 1969, and none of the other sources systematically record visits of hemispheric heads of state, so some omissions may exist in this compilation.

(Table 3600 on following page)

Table 3600

U.S. VIP VISITORS TO LATIN AMERICA, BY U.S. PRESIDENTIAL PERIOD, 1953–88

PART I. EISENHOWER ADMINISTRATION[1]

Country	1953	1954	1955	1956	1957	1958	1959	1960
A. ARGENTINA						RN		DE/CH
Bahamas								
Barbados								
B. BOLIVIA						RN		
C. BRAZIL				RN		JD		DE/CH
D. CHILE							CH	DE/CH
E. COLOMBIA				JD		RN		
F. COSTA RICA			RN					
G. CUBA			RN					
H. DOMINICAN REP.			RN					
I. ECUADOR				JD		RN		
J. EL SALVADOR			RN					
Grenada								
K. GUATEMALA			RN					
L. HAITI			RN					
M. HONDURAS			RN					
Jamaica								
N. MEXICO	DE		RN			JD	DE	CH
O. NICARAGUA			RN					
P. PANAMA			RN	DE/JD				
Q. PARAGUAY						RN		
R. PERU				JD		RN		
St. Lucia								
Suriname								
Trinidad and Tobago						RN		
S. URUGUAY						RN		DE/CH
T. VENEZUELA		JD				RN		

1. DE – Dwight Eisenhower
   RN – Richard Nixon
   CH – Christian Herter
   JD – John Dulles

Table 3600 (Continued)

U.S. VIP VISITORS TO LATIN AMERICA, BY U.S. PRESIDENTIAL PERIOD, 1953–88

PART II. KENNEDY AND JOHNSON ADMINISTRATIONS[1]

Country	1961	1962	1963	1964	1965	1966	1967	1968
A. ARGENTINA					DR		DR	
Bahamas		JK						
Barbados								
B. BOLIVIA								
C. BRAZIL					DR			
D. CHILE								
E. COLOMBIA	JK							
F. COSTA RICA			JK/DR					LJ/DR
G. CUBA								
H. DOMINICAN REP.			LJ			HH		
I. ECUADOR								LJ/DR
J. EL SALVADOR								LJ/DR
Grenada								
K. GUATEMALA								LJ/DR
L. HAITI								
M. HONDURAS								LJ/DR
Jamaica								
N. MEXICO		JK/LJ/ DR				LJ-2/ DR-3	LJ/DR	HH
O. NICARAGUA								LJ/DR
P. PANAMA								
Q. PARAGUAY								
R. PERU								
St. Lucia								
Suriname							LJ/DR	
Trinidad and Tobago								
S. URUGUAY		DR			DR		LJ/DR	
T. VENEZUELA	JK				DR			

1. JK – John Kennedy
   LH – Lyndon Johnson
   HH – Hubert Humphrey
   DR – Dean Rusk

Table 3600 (Continued)

U.S. VIP VISITORS TO LATIN AMERICA, BY U.S. PRESIDENTIAL PERIOD, 1953–88

PART III. NIXON AND FORD ADMINISTRATIONS[1]

Country	1969	1970	1971	1972	1973	1974	1975	1976
A. ARGENTINA					WR			
Bahamas								
Barbados								
B. BOLIVIA								HK
C. BRAZIL					WR			HK
D. CHILE								HK
E. COLOMBIA					WR			HK
F. COSTA RICA			WR					HK
G. CUBA								
H. DOMINICAN REP.								HK
I. ECUADOR								
J. EL SALVADOR								
Grenada								
K. GUATEMALA								HK
L. HAITI								
M. HONDURAS								
Jamaica					WR			
N. MEXICO	RN/WR	RN/WR-2		GF	WR	GF/HK-2		HK-2
O. NICARAGUA					WR			
P. PANAMA						HK		
Q. PARAGUAY								
R. PERU					WR			HK
St. Lucia								
Suriname								
Trinidad and Tobago								
S. URUGUAY								
T. VENEZUELA					WR			HK

1. RN – Richard Nixon
   GF – Gerald Ford
   HK – Henry Kissinger
   WR – William Rogers

Table 3600 (Continued)

U.S. VIP VISITORS TO LATIN AMERICA, BY U.S. PRESIDENTIAL PERIOD, 1953–88

PART IV. CARTER ADMINISTRATION[1]

	Country	1977	1978	1979	1980
A.	ARGENTINA				
	Bahamas				
	Barbados				
B.	BOLIVIA			CV	
C.	BRAZIL		JC/CV	WM	
D.	CHILE				
E.	COLOMBIA				
F.	COSTA RICA				
G.	CUBA				
H.	DOMINICAN REP.				
I.	ECUADOR			CV	
J.	EL SALVADOR				
	Grenada	CV			
K.	GUATEMALA				
L.	HAITI				
M.	HONDURAS				
	Jamaica				
N.	MEXICO		EM/CV	JC/CV	EM
O.	NICARAGUA				
P.	PANAMA		JC/CV	WM	
Q.	PARAGUAY				
R.	PERU				
	St. Lucia				
	Suriname				
	Trinidad and Tobago	CV			
S.	URUGUAY				
T.	VENEZUELA		JC/CV	WM	

1. JC – Jimmy Carter
   WM – Walter Mondale
   EM – Edmund Muskie
   CV – Cyrus Vance

Table 3600 (Continued)

U.S. VIP VISITORS TO LATIN AMERICA, BY U.S. PRESIDENTIAL PERIOD, 1953–88

PART V. REAGAN ADMINISTRATION[1]

Country	1981	1982	1983	1984	1985	1986	1987	1988
A. ARGENTINA		AH	GB					GS
Bahamas	AH							
Barbados		RR/AH		GS				
B. BOLIVIA								GS
C. BRAZIL	GB	RR/GS		GS	GB			GS
D. CHILE								
E. COLOMBIA	GB	RR/GB/GS						
F. COSTA RICA		RR/GS						GS-2
G. CUBA								
H. DOMINICAN REP.	GB							
I. ECUADOR				GB				GS
J. EL SALVADOR			GB	GS-3		GS		GS-3
Grenada				GS	GB	RR/GS		
K. GUATEMALA						GB		GS-2
L. HAITI								
M. HONDURAS		RR/GS			GB	GB		GS-2
Jamaica		RR/AH	GB					
N. MEXICO	RR-2/GB AH-2	RR/GS	RR/GS-2	GS	GS	RR/GS		RR/GS-2
O. NICARAGUA				GS				
P. PANAMA			GB	GS				
Q. PARAGUAY								
R. PERU								
St. Lucia	AH							
Suriname								
Trinidad and Tobago								
S. URUGUAY								GS
T. VENEZUELA				GS				

1. RR – Ronald Reagan
   GB – George Bush
   GS – George Shultz
   AH – Alexander Haig

SOURCE: For travel by president and secretary of state, see Department of State *Bulletin* (especially September 1981 issue) and *Facts on File*; the latter was also the primary source for vice-presidential travel. See also Department of State, *Foreign Relations of the United States*.

Table 3601

LATIN AMERICAN AND U.S. VIP VISITS, BY YEAR
AND DURATION, 1953–88

1953

President Eisenhower: 1 trip, 1 country, 1 day

    October 19   Mexico (Nuevo Guerrero)[1]

Latin American VIP Visitors: 3

    March 6, WH Office Visit: Gen. Trujillo (Dominican Republic)[2]
    September 28–Oct. 1, Official Visit: President Remón (Panama)[3]
    October 19, Working Visit (Falcon Dam): Pres. Ruiz (Mexico)

1954

Secretary Dulles: 1 trip, 1 country, 13 days

    March 1–13   Venezuela

Latin American VIP Visitors: none

1955

Vice President Nixon: 1 trip, 10 countries, 26 days

February 7–10	Cuba
February 10–13	Mexico
February 13–16	Guatemala
February 16–18	El Salvador
February 18–20	Honduras
February 20–22	Nicaragua
February 22–24	Costa Rica
February 24–27	Panama
March 2–4	Dominican Republic
March 4–6	Haiti

Latin American VIP Visitors: 3

    January 26–February 9, State Visit: Pres. Magloire (Haiti)
    October 31–November 3, State Visit: Pres. Castillo (Guatemala)
    December 5–17, Official Visit: Pres. Battle (Uruguay)

1956

President Eisenhower: 1 trip, 1 country, 4 days

    July 20–23   Panama

Vice President Nixon: 1 trip, 1 country, 7 days

    January 29–February 4   Brazil

Secretary Dulles: 1 trip, 4 countries, 9 days

July 20–24	Panama
July 24–25	Colombia
July 25–26	Ecuador
July 26–28	Peru

Latin American VIP Visitors: 2

    January 5–11, Working Visit: Pres.–elect Kubitschek (Brazil)
    March 26–28, Tripartite (with Canada): Pres. Ruiz (Mexico), White Sulphur Springs, W.V.

1957

U.S. VIP Travel to Latin America: none

Latin American VIP Visitors: 1

    October 14, WH Office Visit: P.M. Cisneros (Peru)

Table 3601 (Continued)

LATIN AMERICAN AND U.S. VIP VISITS, BY YEAR AND DURATION, 1953–88

1958

Vice President Nixon: 1 trip, 8 countries, 19 days

April 27	Trinidad and Tobago
April 27–29	Uruguay
April 29–30	Paraguay
April 30–May 3	Argentina
May 3–8	Bolivia
May 8–9	Peru
May 9–11	Ecuador
May 11–13	Colombia
May 13–15	Venezuela

Secretary Dulles: 2 trips, 2 countries, 9 days

August 4–6	Brazil
November 30–December 5	Mexico

Latin American VIP Visitors: none

1959

President Eisenhower: 1 trip, 1 country, 2 days

February 19–20	Mexico (Acapulco)

Secretary Herter: 1 trip, 1 country, 10 days

August 11–20	Chile

Latin American VIP Visitors: none

1960

President Eisenhower: 2 trips, 5 countries, 10 days

February 23–26	Brazil
February 26–29	Argentina
February 29–March 2	Chile
March 2–3	Uruguay
October 24	Mexico (Ciudad Acuña)

Secretary Herter: 2 trips, 5 countries, 10 days

February 23–26	Brazil
February 26–29	Argentina
February 29–March 2	Chile
March 2–3	Uruguay
September 16	Mexico

Latin American VIP Visitors: 2

April 5–7, Official Visit:	Pres. Lleras (Colombia)
October 24, Informal Visit:	Pres. López (Mexico)

1961

President Kennedy: 1 trip, 2 countries, 2 days

December 16–17	Venezuela
December 17	Colombia

Latin American VIP Visitors: none

Table 3601 (Continued)

LATIN AMERICAN AND U.S. VIP VISITS, BY YEAR
AND DURATION, 1953–88

1962

President Kennedy: 2 trips, 2 countries, 7 days

June 29–July 1	Mexico
December 18–21	Bahamas (then U.K.)

Vice President Johnson: 1 trip, 1 country, 3 days

June 29–July 1	Mexico

Secretary Rusk: 2 trips, 2 countries, 14 days

January 22–February 1	Uruguay (Punta del Este)
June 29–July 1	Mexico

Latin American VIP Visitors: 3

April 3–4, Official Visit:	Pres. Goulart (Brazil)
June 23, WH Office Visit:	Pres.–elect Valencia (Colombia)
December 11–12, State Visit:	Pres. Alessandri (Chile)

1963

President Kennedy: 1 trip, 1 country, 3 days

March 18–20	Costa Rica

Vice President Johnson: 1 trip, 1 country, 1 day

February 27	Dominican Republic

Secretary Rusk: 1 trip, 1 country, 3 days

March 18–20	Costa Rica

Latin American VIP Visitors: 4

January 10, WH Office Visit:	Pres.–elect Bosch (Dominican Republic)
February 19–21, Official Visit:	Pres. Betancourt (Venezuela)
October 22–24, Official Visit:	Pres. Paz (Bolivia)
November 24–25, JFK Funeral:	P.M. Bustamante (Jamaica)

1964

U.S. VIP Visitors to Latin America: none

Latin American VIP Visitors: 3

February 21–22, Working Visit:	Pres. López (Mexico)
June 30–July 2, Official Visit:	Pres. Orlich (Costa Rica)
November 12, LBJ Ranch Visit:	Pres.–elect Díaz (Mexico)

1965

Secretary Rusk: 1 trip, 4 countries, 13 days

November 13–14	Venezuela
November 14–15	Argentina
November 15–16	Uruguay
November 16–25	Brazil (OAS)

Latin American VIP Visitors: none

Table 3601 (Continued)

LATIN AMERICAN AND U.S. VIP VISITS, BY YEAR
AND DURATION, 1953–88

1966

President Johnson: 2 trips, 1 country, 3 days

April 14–15	Mexico
December 4	Mexico (Ciudad Acuña)

Vice President Humphrey: 1 trip, 1 country, 1 day

July 1	Dominican Republic

Secretary Rusk: 3 trips, 1 country, 5 days

April 14–15	Mexico
September 30–October 1	Mexico
December 4	Mexico (Ciudad Acuña)

Latin American VIP Visitors: 1

July 21–31, Informal Visit:	P.M. Burnham (Guyana)

1967

President Johnson: 2 trips, 3 countries, 5 days

April 11–14	Uruguay (Punta del Este)
April 14	Suriname
October 28	Mexico

Secretary Rusk: 3 trips, 4 countries, 19 days

February 13–21	Argentina (OAS)
April 6–14	Uruguay (Punta del Este)
April 14	Suriname
October 28	Mexico

Latin American VIP Visitors: 4

January 25–28, Informal Visit:	Pres.-elect da Costa (Brazil)
April 6, Informal Visit:	Pres.-elect Somoza (Nicaragua)
October 13, State Visit:	P.M. Shearer (Jamaica)
October 26–28, State Visit:	Pres. Díaz (Mexico)

1968

President Johnson: 1 trip, 5 countries, 3 days

July 6–8	El Salvador
July 8	Nicaragua
July 8	Costa Rica
July 8	Honduras
July 8	Guatemala

Vice President Humphrey: 1 trip, 1 country, 2 days

March 31–April 1	Mexico

Secretary Rusk: 1 trip, 5 countries, 3 days

July 6–8	El Salvador
July 8	Nicaragua
July 8	Costa Rica
July 8	Honduras
July 8	Guatemala

Table 3601 (Continued)

LATIN AMERICAN AND U.S. VIP VISITS, BY YEAR
AND DURATION, 1953–88

1968 (Continued)

Latin American VIP Visitors: 6

March 20–21, Official Visit:	Pres. Stroessner (Paraguay)
June 4–5, State Visit:	Pres. Trejos (Costa Rica)
June 7, Informal Visit:	P.M. Shearer (Jamaica)
July 5–6, LBJ Ranch Visit:	Pres. Barrientos (Bolivia)
July 26, Informal Visit:	P.M. Burnham (Guyana)
December 13, Official Visit:	P.M. Barrow (Barbados)

1969

President Nixon: 1 trip, 1 country, 1 day

September 8	Mexico (Ciudad Acuña)

Secretary Rogers: 1 trip, 1 country, 1 day

September 8	Mexico (Ciudad Acuña)

Latin American VIP Visitors: 2

June 12–14, State Visit:	Pres. Lleras (Colombia)
September 12–14, Official Visit:	President Díaz (Mexico)

1970

President Nixon: 1 trip, 1 country, 2 days

August 20–21	Mexico (Puerto Vallarta)

Secretary Rogers: 2 trips, 1 country, 3 days

August 20–21	Mexico (Puerto Vallarta)
December 1	Mexico

Latin American VIP Visitors: 6

June 2–5, State Visit:	Pres. Caldera (Venezuela)
September 3, State Dinner (Calif.):	Pres. Díaz (Mexico)
October 24, Dinner NYC:	Pres. Somoza (Nicaragua)
	Pres. Lakas (Panama)
	Pres. Figueres (Costa Rica)
	P.M. Shearer (Jamaica)

1971

Secretary Rogers: 1 trip, 1 country, 1 day

April 15	Costa Rica (OAS)

Latin American VIP Visitors: 3

June 2, WH Office Call:	Pres. Somoza (Nicaragua)
September 3, Official Visit:	President Díaz (Mexico)
December 6–9, State Visit:	Medici (Brazil)

1972

U.S. VIP Visitors to Latin America: none

Latin American VIP Visitors: 1

June 15–17, State Visit:	Pres. Echeverría (Mexico)

Table 3601 (Continued)

LATIN AMERICAN AND U.S. VIP VISITS, BY YEAR
AND DURATION, 1953–88

1973

Secretary Rogers: 1 trip, 9 countries, 18 days

May 12–14	Mexico
May 14	Nicaragua
May 14–15	Venezuela
May 15–17	Peru
May 17–19	Colombia
May 19–23	Brazil
May 23–26	Argentina
May 26–28	Jamaica

Latin American VIP Visitors: none

1974

President Ford: 1 trip, 1 country, 1 day

October 21	Mexico (Magdelena de Kino)

Secretary Kissinger: 3 trips, 2 countries, 6 days

February 7	Panama
February 20–23	Mexico
October 21	Mexico (Magdelena de Kino)

Latin American VIP Visitors: 1

October 21, Official Visit (Nogales):	Pres. Echeverría (Mexico)

1975

U.S. VIP Visitors to Latin America: none

Latin American VIP Visitors: 2

February 21, WH Office Call:	P.M. Williams (Trinidad and Tobago)
September 23–27, Office Working Visit:	Pres. López (Colombia)

1976

Secretary Kissinger: 3 trips, 10 countries, 21 days

February 16–18	Venezuela
February 18–19	Peru
February 19–23	Brazil
February 23	Colombia
February 23–24	Costa Rica
February 24	Guatemala
June 6–7	Dominican Republic
June 7	Bolivia
June 7–10	Chile (OASGA)
June 10–13	Mexico
November 29–December 2	Mexico

Latin American VIP Visitors: none

1977

Secretary Vance: 1 trip, 2 countries, 4 days

June 14–16	Grenada (OAS)
June 16–17	Trinidad and Tobago

Latin American VIP Visitors: 19

February 13–17, State Visit:	Pres. López Portillo (Mexico)
June 28–29, State Visit:	Pres. Pérez (Venezuela)

Table 3601 (Continued)

LATIN AMERICAN AND U.S. VIP VISITS, BY YEAR
AND DURATION, 1953–88

1977 (Continued)

Latin American VIP Visitors (Continued)

September 6–9, Panama Canal Treaty Signing Ceremony:

September 5, WH Office Visit:	General Torrijos (Panama)
September 6, WH Office Visit:	Pres. Morález Bermúdez (Peru)
	Pres. Stroessner (Paraguay)
	Pres. López (Colombia)
	Pres. Pinochet (Chile)
September 7, WH Office Visit:	Pres. Pérez (Venezuela)
	P.M. Gairy (Grenada)
	Pres. Laugerud (Guatemala)
	P.M. Pindling (Bahamas)
September 8, WH Office Visit:	Pres. Poveda (Ecuador)
	Pres. Banzer (Bolivia)
	Pres. Balaguer (Dominican Republic)
	Pres. Romero (El Salvador)
	Pres. Melgar (Honduras)
September 9, WH Office Visit:	Gen. Videla (Argentina)
	Pres. Méndez (Uruguay)
	Pres. Oduber (Costa Rica)
October 14, Official Working Visit:	Gen. Torrijos (Panama)
December 16, Official Working Visit:	P.M. Manley (Jamaica)

1978

President Carter: 2 trips, 3 countries, 6 days

March 28–29	Venezuela
March 29–31	Brazil
June 16–17	Panama

Vice President Mondale: 1 trip, 1 country, 3 days

January 20–22	Mexico

Secretary Vance: 3 trips, 4 countries, 9 days

March 28–29	Venezuela
March 29–31	Brazil
May 3–5	Mexico
June 16–17	Panama

Latin American VIP Visitors: none

1979

President Carter: 1 trip, 1 country, 3 days

February 14–16	Mexico

Vice President Mondale: 2 trips, 3 countries, 7 days

March 21–23	Brazil
March 23–24	Venezuela
September 30–October 2	Panama

Secretary Vance: 3 trips, 3 countries, 11 days

February 14–16	Mexico
August 9–12	Ecuador
October 20–23	Bolivia (OASGA)

Table 3601 (Continued)

LATIN AMERICAN AND U.S. VIP VISITS, BY YEAR
AND DURATION, 1953–88

1979 (Continued)

Latin American VIP Visitors: 5

April 9, WH Office Call:	Pres. Royo (Panama)
May 10, WH Office Call:	Pres. Royo (Panama)
September 24, WH Office Call:	Junta Members Ortega, Robelo, Ramírez (Nicaragua)
September 28–29, Official Working Visit:	Pres. López (Mexico)

1980

Secretary Muskie: 1 trip, 1 country, 2 days

November 29–30	Mexico

Latin American VIP Visitors: 3

March 2, WH Office Call:	Pres. Paz (Honduras)
April 28 WH Office Call:	P.M. Adams (Barbados)
December 1, WH Office Call:	Pres. Carazo (Costa Rica)

1981

President Reagan: 2 trips, 1 country, 5 days

January 5 (elect)	Mexico (Ciudad Juárez)
October 21–24	Mexico (Cancún)

Vice President Bush: 2 trips, 4 countries, 9 days

September 16–17	Mexico
October 11–14	Dominican Republic
October 14–16	Colombia
October 16–17	Brazil

Secretary Haig: 5 trips, 3 countries, 11 days

July 11–12	Bahamas
August 1–2	Mexico
October 22–23	Mexico (Cancún)
November 23–24	Mexico
December 2–4	St. Lucia (Castries)

Latin American VIP Visitors: 5

January 27–29, Official Working Visit:	P.M. Seaga (Jamaica)
March 17, WH Office Call:	Pres.–des. Viola (Argentina)
June 7–9, Official Working Visit:	Pres. López (Mexico)
September 17, Mtg. Grand Rapids, MI:	Pres. López (Mexico)
September 21, WH Office Call:	Pres. Duarte (El Salvador)
September 30, WH Office Call:	Pres. Duarte (El Salvador)
November 16–19, State Visit:	Pres. Herrera (Venezuela)

1982

President Reagan: 3 trips, 7 countries, 11 days

April 7–8	Jamaica
April 8–11	Barbados
October 8	Mexico (Tijuana)
November 30–December 3	Brazil
December 3	Colombia
December 3–4	Costa Rica
December 4	Honduras

Table 3601 (Continued)

**LATIN AMERICAN AND U.S. VIP VISITS, BY YEAR
AND DURATION, 1953–88**

1982 (Continued)

Vice President Bush: 1 trip, 1 country, 3 days

August 6–8	Colombia

Secretary Haig (to June): 1 trip, 3 countries, 9 days

April 7–8	Jamaica
April 8–10	Barbados
April 10–11 & 16–19	Argentina

Secretary Schultz (from June): 2 trips, 5 countries, 6 days

October 8	Mexico (Tijuana)
November 30–December 3	Brazil
December 3	Colombia
December 3–4	Costa Rica
December 4	Honduras

Latin American VIP Visitors: 6

February 15, WH Office Call:	Pres.–elect Jorge (Dominican Republic)
May 11–13, State Visit:	Pres. Figueiredo (Brazil)
June 21–24, Official Working Visit:	Pres. Monge (Costa Rica)
July 13–15, Official Working Visit:	Pres. Suazo (Honduras)
October 1, WH Office Call:	PRes. de la Espriella (Panama)
October 8, Mtg. Coronado, CA:	Pres.–elect de la Madrid (Mexico)

1983

President Reagan: 1 trip, 1 day, 1 country

August 14	Mexico (La Paz)

Vice President Bush: 2 trips, 4 countries, 5 days

October 17–18	Jamaica
December 9–11	Argentina
December 11	Panama
December 11	El Salvador

Secretary Shultz: 2 trips, 1 country, 4 days

April 17–19	Mexico
August 14	Mexico (La Paz)

Latin American VIP Visitors: 6

February 22, WH Office Call:	P.M. Seaga (Jamaica)
April 7–9, Official Working Visit:	Pres. Hurtado (Ecuador)
May 11–14, Official Working Visit:	P.M. Price (Belize)
June 16–18, Office Working Visit:	Pres. Magaña (El Salvador)
October 25, WH Office Call:	P.M. Charles (Dominica)
October 27, WH Office Call:	P.M. Compton (St. Lucia)
November 6, WH Office Call:	P.M. Seaga (Jamaica)

1984

Vice President Bush: 1 trip, 1 country, 1 day

August 10	Ecuador

Secretary Shultz: 3 trips, 8 countries, 13 days

January 31	El Salvador
February 1–3	Venezuela
February 3–7	Brazil
February 7	Grenada
February 7–8	Barbados

Table 3601 (Continued)

LATIN AMERICAN AND U.S. VIP VISITS, BY YEAR AND DURATION, 1953–88

1984 (Continued)

Latin American VIP Visitors (Continued)

June 1	El Salvador
June 1	Nicaragua
October 10	El Salvador
October 10–11	Panama
October 11–12	Mexico

Latin American VIP Visitors: 12

February 3, WH Office Call:	P.M. Charles (Dominica)
April 9–14, State Visit:	Pres. Jorge (Dominican Republic)
April 13, V.P. Office Visit:	P.M. Seaga (Jamaica)
May 14–17, State Visit:	Pres. de la Madrid (Mexico)
May 21, WH Office Call:	Pres.–elect Duarte (El Salvador)
June 26, WH Office Call:	Pres.–elect Febres (Ecuador)
July 19, Meeting Charleston, SC:	P.M. Charles (Dominica), P.M. Seaga (Jamaica), P.M. Simmons (St. Kitts), P.M. Compton (St. Lucia)
July 23, WH Office Call:	Pres. Duarte (El Salvador)
July 27, WH Office Call:	Pres.–elect Barletta (Panama)
September 27, WH Office Call:	Pres. Belaúnde (Peru)
September 29, V.P. Office Call:	P.M. Charles (Dominica)
December 3–8, State Visit:	Pres. Lusinchi (Venezuela)

1985

Vice President Bush: 1 trip, 3 countries, 3 days

March 14	Grenada
March 14–16	Brazil
March 16	Honduras

Secretary Shultz: 1 trip, 1 country, 2 days

July 25–26	Mexico

Latin American VIP Visitors: 11

February 1, V.P. Office Call:	P.M. Seaga (Jamaica)
February 2, WH Office Call:	Pres.–elect Neves (Brazil)
March 17–25, Off. Working Visit:	Pres. Alfonsín (Argentina)
April 2–4, Official Working Visit:	Pres. Betancur (Colombia)
April 15, WH Office Call:	Pres. Monge (Costa Rica)
May 16, WH Office Call:	Pres. Duarte (El Salvador)
May 20–22, Official Working Visit:	Pres. Suazo (Honduras)
October 22, WH Office Call:	P.M. Blaize (Grenada)
October 31, WH Office Call:	Pres. Duarte (El Salvador)

1986

President Reagan: 2 trips, 2 countries, 2 days

January 3	Mexico (Mexicali)
February 20	Grenada

Vice President Bush: 2 trips, 2 countries, 2 days

January 14	Guatemala
January 27	Honduras

Secretary Shultz: 3 trips, 3 countries, 3 days

January 3	Mexico (Mexicali)
February 20	Grenada
October 16	El Salvador

Table 3601 (Continued)

LATIN AMERICAN AND U.S. VIP VISITS, BY YEAR AND DURATION, 1953–88

1986 (Continued)

Latin American VIP Visitors: 10

January 12–16, State Visit:	Pres. Febres (Ecuador)
January 17, V.P. Office Call:	Pres.–elect Azcona (Honduras)
May 26–29, Official Working Visit:	Pres. Azcona (Honduras)
June 16–20, State Visit:	Pres. Sanguinetti (Uruguay)
June 20, V.P. Office Call:	P.M. Seaga (Jamaica)
August 12–14, Off. Visit:	Pres. De la Madrid (Mexico)
September 14, V.P. Office Call:	P.M. Esquivel (Belize)
September 9–13, State Visit:	Pres. Sarney (Brazil)
November 17, WH Office Call:	Pres. Alfonsín (Argentina)
November 21, WH Office Call:	Pres. Namphy (Haiti)
December 3–6, Off. Working Visit:	Pres. Arias (Costa Rica)

1987

U.S. VIP Travel to Latin America: none

Latin American VIP Visitors: 5

May 12–15, Official Working Visit:	Pres. Cerezo (Guatemala)
June 17, WH Office Call:	Pres. Arias (Costa Rica)
September 21, WH Office Call:	Pres. Arias (Costa Rica)
October 13–18, State Visit:	Pres. Duarte (El Salvador)
October 19, WH Office Call:	Pres. Azcona (Honduras)
November 17, WH Office Call:	Pres. Alfonsín (Argentina)

1988

President Reagan: 1 trip, 1 country, 1 day

February 13	Mexico (Mazatlán)

Secretary Shultz: 5 trips, 12 countries, 17 days

February 13	Mexico (Mazatlán)
June 29–30	Guatemala
June 30	El Salvador
June 30–July 1	Honduras
July 1	Costa Rica
August 1	Guatemala
August 2–4	Argentina
August 4	Uruguay
August 4–8	Brazil
August 8–9	Bolivia
August 9	Honduras
August 9	El Salvador
August 9–10	Costa Rica
August 10	Ecuador
November 14–15	El Salvador (OAS)
December 1–2	Mexico

Latin American VIP Visitors: 7

March 25, Office Working Visit:	Pres. Balaguer (Dominican Republic)
April 14, V.P. Office Call:	Pres. Arias (Costa Rica)
June 7, WH Office Call:	Pres. Duarte (El Salvador)
August 10, WH Office Call:	Pres. Duarte (El Salvador)
September 13, WH Office Call:	Pres. Hoyte (Guyana)
October 3, WH Office Call:	P.M. Seaga (Jamaica)
December 2, V.P. Office Call:	Pres. Alfonsin (Argentina)
December 14, WH Office Call:	Pres.–elect Pérez (Venezuela)

1. Visits that took place outside of the capital city are annotated as to where they took place.

2. Data are shown only for those visits during which Latin American VIPs met with the U.S. President or Vice President. Visits at the invitation of the United States are designated either State or Official visits. Other visits, at the initiative of the Latin American VIP, usually reflect whether they included a meeting with the President (WH Office Call/Visit) or the Vice President (V.P. Office Call/Visit). Where the term "Informal Visit" or "Working Visit" appears, although it is not clear with whom the visitor met, it may be presumed to be the U.S. President.

3. The dates listed for State and Official Visits are limited to the period the visiting VIP is a guest of the United States and is usually in the Washington, D.C., area meeting with senior Executive and Legislative branch officials. In a few instances the State or Official Visit takes place outside of the capital and is so stated. The dates do not reflect additional periods when the visiting VIP may be elsewhere in the United States.

SOURCE: For travel by president and secretary of state, see Department of State *Bulletin* (especially September 1981 issue) and *Facts on File*; the latter was also the primary source for vice-presidential travel. See also Department of State, *Foreign Relations of the United States*.

37

Monterrey, Mexico, during the Porfiriato and the Revolution: Population and Migration Trends in Regional Evolution

DAVID E. LOREY

James W. Wilkie, Enrique C. Ochoa, and David E. Lorey, eds., *Statistical Abstract of Latin America*, vol. 28 (Los Angeles: UCLA Latin American Center Publications, 1990).

During the Porfiriato and the early phases of the Mexican Revolution, the northern city of Monterrey grew into one of Mexico's most important industrial and financial centers. Over the same period, and principally because of its growing economic might, Monterrey also became a regional political power second in importance only to Mexico City. In these two capacities, as economic engine and political force, Monterrey put a distinctive stamp on Mexico's evolution from the late nineteenth century to the present. The patterns most closely associated with Mexico's modern economic growth appeared first in Monterrey after 1890. By 1940 the economic importance of the city, and the political clout of its elite families, gave it a central place in the economic and political history of twentieth-century Mexico.

Given the importance of Monterrey, on both regional and national levels, it is surprising that historians have neglected to examine closely the evolution of the city's society and economy over the last two centuries. The few studies of Monterrey that have appeared present narrative accounts of the city's political history or focus on Monterrey's elite clans and their clashes with the national government in faraway Mexico City. A few accounts emphasize the region's key industries, income distribution, and social mobility, but generally have short-term focuses. The history of the changing socioeconomic reality underlying the long-term development of this industrial metropolis remains largely uncharted.

This essay takes a first step in exploring the intertwined economic and social history of the regional power of Monterrey by sketching long-term trends in population growth in the city, treating not only the central city but also its satellite urban areas. The study develops estimates of the rate of population growth due to migration from other regions of Mexico to Monterrey. Rates of migration and population growth are placed in the context of historical cycles and trends in industrial growth and employment opportunities in the state of Nuevo León and in Monterrey.[1]

Past Regional Approaches to Mexican History

The approach here represents a new avenue for understanding the history of Mexico's regions, and for turning regional history to the task of illuminating national-level structures and trends. The focus on an urban area and its socioeconomic evolution over the long term from the early nineteenth century to the present opens new territory in the historiography of late nineteenth and early twentieth century Mexico.

While the framework of the regional approach is here expanded to consider urban change, the aims of this study are similar to those of historians of Mexico's regional variations. An examination of the evolution of a particular Mexican region sheds light on broad social and economic aspects of national development.

Historians of Mexico's regions have generally focused on socioeconomic patterns of rural areas to illuminate the regional variations of national trends. Rural emphasis has long characterized historical study of individual Mexican states.[2] Rural estates (haciendas) and elite families have most often served as the principal avenues of approach to regional topics, providing detailed portraits of rural social and occupational structures and the relationship between family and

DAVID E. LOREY is Coordinator of the Program on Mexico in the UCLA Latin American Center. He wrote his doctoral dissertation at UCLA on the social economy of the university in Mexico since 1929. He has taught at UCLA and Pomona College in the United States and at the Universidad de las Américas in Mexico. Lorey is editor of *United States–Mexico Border Statistics since 1900*.

[1] This essay is the first result of an ongoing research project on Mexico's urban regional powers, coordinated through the UCLA Program on Mexico. Monterrey and Guadalajara have been selected for study of the century from roughly 1880 to 1980. I would like to thank Martín Valadez, a member of the research team, for research and bibliographical assistance.

[2] See Thomas Benjamin's *A Rich Land, A Poor People: Politics and Society in Modern Chiapas* (Albuquerque: University of New Mexico Press, 1989); Stuart F. Voss, *On the Periphery of Nineteenth-Century Mexico: Sonora and Sinaloa, 1810–1877* (Tucson: University of Arizona, 1982); Allen Wells, *Yucatán's Gilded Age: Haciendas, Henequen, and International Harvester, 1860–1915* (Albuquerque: University of New Mexico Press, 1985); Romana Falcón, *El Agrarismo en Veracruz: La Etapa Radical (1928–1935)* (México, D.F.: n.p., 1977); and Heather Fowler Salamini, *Agrarian Radicalism in Veracruz, 1920–38* (Lincoln: University of Nebraska Press, 1977). Ramón Eduardo Ruiz, *Yankee Capitalists and the People of Sonora* (Tucson: University of Arizona Press, 1987).

business enterprises.[3] While a few studies of provincial towns have appeared, they point up the essentially rural foundations of isolated population centers in the Mexican countryside.[4] The rural bias of Mexican regional history has been facilitated, if not determined, by the preservation in good condition of state, hacienda, and family records in scattered archives in Mexico and the United States.

Portraits of Mexican regional society have not only emerged from direct approaches, however. Many engaging histories of rural caudillos and peasant leaders, for example, have revealed the history of regions.[5] Topical histories and thematic treatments have likewise shed a great deal of light on regional evolution through the centuries.[6] Conversely, regional concentrations have sometimes been adopted primarily to uncover national trends or events; the historical process most written about from the regional perspective is, of course, the Mexican Revolution of 1910, with its important regional beginnings and dynamic.[7] Studies of this sort help to explain not only regional events but also the relationship between regional and national evolution.[8]

Mexico's urban centers have not received the same attention from regional historians as the rural periphery.[9] As might be imagined, studies of Mexico's urban history during the national period have been devoted almost exclusively to Mexico City, the national capital and the traditional

[3] See Jan Bazant, *Cinco Haciendas Mexicanas: Tres Siglos de Vida Rural en San Luis Potosí (1600–1900)* (México, D.F.: El Colegio de México, 1975); David A. Brading, *Haciendas and Ranchos in the Mexican Bajío: León, 1700–1860* (Cambridge: Cambridge University Press, 1978); Mark Wasserman, "Oligarchy and Foreign Enterprise in Porfirian Chihuahua, Mexico, 1876–1911" (Ph.D. diss., University of Chicago, 1975); David Walker, *Kinship, Business and Politics: The Martínez del Río Family in Mexico, 1823–1867* (Austin: University of Texas Press, 1986); and Charles A. Harris, *A Mexican Family Empire: The Latifundia of the Sánchez Navarro Family, 1767–1867* (Austin: University of Texas Press, 1985).

[4] See Carlos B. Gil, *Life in Provincial Mexico: National and Regional History Seen from Mascota, Jalisco, 1867–1972* (Los Angeles: UCLA Latin American Center Publications, 1983); Frans J. Schryer, *The Rancheros of Pisaflores* (Toronto: University of Toronto Press, 1980); Luis González, *Pueblo en Vilo* (México, D.F.: El Colegio de México, 1968); and Paul Friedrich, *Agrarian Revolt in a Mexican Village* (Chicago: University of Chicago Press, 1970, 1977).

[5] See John Womack, *Zapata and the Mexican Revolution* (New York: Vintage Books, 1968); David Brading, *Caudillo and Peasant in the Mexican Revolution* (Cambridge: Cambridge University Press, 1980); William H. Beezley, *Insurgent Governor: Abraham González and the Mexican Revolution in Chihuahua* (Lincoln: University of Nebraska Press, 1973); Héctor Aguilar Camín, *La Frontera Nómada: Sonora y la Revolución Mexicana* (México, D.F.: Siglo XXI, 1986); Friedrich Katz, "Villa: Reform Governor of Chihuahua," in George Wolfskill and Douglas W. Richmond, eds., *Essays on the Mexican Revolution: Revisionist Reviews of the Leaders* (Cambridge: Cambridge University Press, 1980), pp. 17–58; and David G. LaFrance, *Madero y la Revolución Mexicana en Puebla* (Puebla: UAP, n.d.).

[6] Studies of the regional dynamics of Mexico's textile industry are examples of this phenomenon: see particularly Bernardo García Díaz, *Un Pueblo Fabril del Porfiriato: Santa Rosa, Veracruz* (México, D.F.: n.p., 1982); Richard J. Salvucci, *Textiles and Capitalism in Mexico: An Economic History of the Obrajes, 1539–1840* (Princeton: Princeton University Press, 1987); and Dawn Keremitsis, *La Industria Textil Mexicana en el Siglo XIX* (México, D.F.: SEP, 1973). In a similar vein, also see Harry E. Cross's "The Mining Economy of Zacatecas, Mexico, in the Nineteenth Century," (Ph.D. diss., Columbia University, 1965). On the broader issue of rural riot and rebellion, see Friedrich Katz, ed., *Riot, Rebellion, and Revolution: Rural Social Conflict in Mexico* (Princeton: Princeton University Press, 1988).

[7] Brian Hamnett uses regional social change to examine the roots of insurgency and political struggle during the decade of the Wars for Independence in his *Roots of Insurgency: Mexican Regions, 1750–1824* (Cambridge and London: Cambridge University Press, 1986). For another approach to the entire nineteenth century, see John Tutino, *From Insurrection to Revolution in Mexico: Social Bases of Agrarian Violence, 1750–1940* (Princeton: Princeton University Press, 1986). On the Reform period, see Charles Berry's *The Reform in Oaxaca, 1856–76* (Lincoln: University of Nebraska Press, 1981). Many regional studies of the Mexican Revolution's early period have appeared: see Raymond Th. Buve, "Peasant Movements. Caudillos, and Land Reform during the Revolution (1910–1917) in Tlaxcala, Mexico," *Boletín de Estudios Latinoamericanos y del Caribe*, no. 16 (June, 1975), pp. 3–15; Ian Jacobs, *Ranchero Revolt: The Mexican Revolution in Guerrero* (Austin: University of Texas Press, 1983); Gilbert Joseph, *Revolution from Without: Yucatán, Mexico, and the United States, 1880–1924* (Cambridge: Cambridge University Press, 1982); Linda B. Hall and Don M. Coerver, *Revolution on the Border: The United States and Mexico, 1910–1920* (Albuquerque: University of New Mexico Press, 1989); and Mark Wasserman, "Social Origins of the 1910 Revolution in Chihuahua," *Latin American Research Review* 15 (1980), 15–28. Ramón Eduardo Ruiz's *The Great Rebellion: Mexico, 1905–1924* (New York: Norton, 1980) also has a strong regional flavor.

[8] See Thomas Benjamin and William McNellie's important edited volume *Other Mexicos: Essays on Regional Mexican History, 1876–1911* (Albuquerque: University of New Mexico Press, 1984). This book has a parallel in James Lockhart and Ida Altman, eds., *Provinces of Early Mexico: Variants of Spanish American Regional Evolution* (Los Angeles: UCLA Latin American Center Publications, 1976), but there is no counterpart for twentieth-century Mexico.

[9] There are some exceptions in the colonial historiography. See John C. Super, *La Vida en Querétaro durante la Colonia, 1531–1810* (México, D.F.: Fondo de Cultura Económica, 1983); David Brading, *Miners and Merchants in Bourbon Mexico, 1763–1810* (Cambridge: Cambridge University Press, 1971); and Eric Van Young, *Hacienda and Market in Eighteenth-Century Mexico: The Rural Economy of the Guadalajara Region, 1675–1830* (Berkeley and Los Angeles: University of California Press, 1981). The last volume deals extensively with the urban as well as the rural aspects of the regional economy. A similarly broad treatment of both urban and rural aspects of regional dynamics is found in William B. Taylor, *Landlord and Peasant in Colonial Oaxaca* (Stanford: Stanford University Press, 1972).

focus of Mexican history.[10] This bias has made some sense, of course, as Mexico City has dominated national life, and particularly national political events, from colonial times to the present. The recent publication of Kendall's *La Capital: A Biography of Mexico City* (1988) has even given Mexico City's history a popular treatment.[11]

The major exception to the general neglect of important regional urban entities is the group of relatively recent works which focus on the cities of the U.S.–Mexican border. Oscar Martínez's *Border Boomtown* (1975) led the way by using statistics on long-term population dynamics to tell the story of Ciudad Juárez–El Paso and to paint its history of boom and bust. More recently, Ted Proffitt has followed with his history of Tijuana and its changing social and economic structure on what he terms the "symbiotic frontier" (1988).[12]

Mexico's three most important, nonborder urban powers—Monterrey, Guadalajara, and Puebla—have received strikingly little attention from historians. We know little of their long-term evolution from very different beginnings to important locations of industry and population in the twentieth century. Demographic shifts and migrant flows, as well as the economic changes that shaped them, have long been ignored. At the social level, the detailed typologies of occupations that have been developed by historians for rural society have not been carried out for urban centers.[13] In sum, new research is needed on crucial aspects of the historical development of these cities: demographic shifts, patterns of urbanization, rural-urban migration, and changing occupations. The experiences of regional powers such as these are central to understanding the national historical experience.

Of Mexico's three regional powers, Monterrey has probably received the least serious scholarly attention. Non-narrative studies of Monterrey have tended to focus narrowly on the city's famous Garza-Sada clan and particularly on the conflicts between this industrial elite and the Mexican state in the late 1930s (during the presidency of Lázaro Cárdenas) and in the early 1970s (during the administration of President Luis Echeverría).[14] Economic focuses have produced works that outline the development of the city's most important industries and industrial groups.[15] A few studies of social themes such as income distribution and social mobility have emphasized short-term and relatively recent changes.[16]

Monterrey offers a fascinating economic and social history that merits attention on its own account and calls for in-depth research of both economic and social trends. The history of the city during its phase of rapid expansion provides a useful avenue into the study of Mexican development in the late nineteenth and early twentieth centuries. It was in Monterrey that Mexico's modern industrial growth began, with its characteristic traits and peculiarities. And it was in Monterrey that many of the social impacts of the Mexican push to industrialize were first noticed.

This brief study discusses two of the most basic aspects of Monterrey's development during the last one hundred and fifty years: population growth and migration. Like many of the regional studies mentioned above, the regional case of Monterrey and its historical development is used here to provide insight into national structures and trends. The study examines population and migration factors for clues to the impact of rapid industrialization on Mexican society. While population data are developed for the period from 1753 to 1980, the principal periods of analysis here are the two great waves of Mexico's industrialization, from roughly 1890 to 1940 and from about 1940 to 1960.[17]

A Capsule History of Monterrey, 1596–1940

The modern city of Monterrey began inauspiciously with almost three hundred years of sluggish growth on the outermost fringes of Mexican society and economy. After its founding in 1596, the town languished in a region of

[10] See, for example, Fernando Benítez, *La Ciudad de México* (México, D.F.: Salvat, 1981); and Gustavo Garza, *El Proceso de Industrialización en la Ciudad de México, 1821–1970* (México, D.F.: El Colegio de México, 1985). Mexico City has also received its share of studies of more specific issues: see Silvia Marina Arrom, *The Women of Mexico City, 1790–1857* (Stanford: Stanford University Press, 1985); Enrique Contreras Suárez, *Estratificación y Movilidad Social en la Ciudad de México* (México, D.F.: UNAM, 1978); and Wayne Cornelius, *Politics and the Migrant Poor in Mexico City* (Stanford: Stanford University Press, 1975).

[11] New York: Random House. The title of the book is actually somewhat misleading; in fact, the book is a general survey of Mexican history, but its narrow focus on political chronology means that the focus is limited to the capital city.

[12] Oscar Martínez, *Border Boomtown: Ciudad Juárez since 1848* (Austin: University of Texas Press, 1975, 1978); and Thurber Proffitt, "The Symbiotic Frontier: The Emergence of Tijuana since 1769," (Ph.D. diss., University of California, Los Angeles, 1988).

[13] There are some important exceptions for colonial Mexico. See, for example, John Kizca, *Colonial Entrepreneurs: Family and Business in Bourbon Mexico City* (Austin: University of Texas Press, 1983).

[14] The best narrative account is probably Andrés Montemayor Hernández, *Historia de Monterrey* (Monterrey: Asociación de Editores y Libreros de Monterrey, A.C., 1971). See Alex Saragoza, *The Monterrey Elite and the Mexican State, 1880–1940* (Austin: University of Texas Press, 1988); and Nora Hamilton, *The Limits of State Autonomy: Post-Revolutionary Mexico* (Princeton: Princeton University Press, 1982).

[15] See, for example, Menno Vellinga, *Desigualdad, Poder, y Cambio Social en Monterrey* (México, D.F.: Siglo XXI, 1988).

[16] Jorge Balán, Harley L. Browning, and Elizabeth Jelin, *Men in a Developing Society: Geographic and Social Mobility in Monterrey, Mexico* (Austin: University of Texas Press, 1973); and Jesús Puente Leyva, *Distribución del Ingreso en un Area Urbana: El Caso de Monterrey* (México, D.F.: Siglo XXI, 1969).

[17] For an in-depth study of this first phase, see Stephen Haber's *Industry and Underdevelopment: The Industrialization of Mexico, 1890–1940* (Stanford: Stanford University Press, 1989).

nomadic Indians, far removed from the web of the central-Mexican economy, a distant backwater of colonial society. Persistent drought, disease, and Indian attack characterized the early period.[18]

But Monterrey's apparently unpromising location would prove a boon in later years. Although abundant mineral wealth did not present itself, the city was founded on one of the few reliable sources of water in the arid northeastern region, the Santa Catarina River. Even more fortuitous, the city is located at the northern end of the Sierra Madre Oriental, and thus sits astride the main overland route between the Gulf coast and Mexico's interior. Monterrey also straddled the overland route from Central Mexico to the far northern provinces. The protection offered by its presidio helped to make Monterrey an important regional trading center. The proximity of the city to the United States after the mid-nineteenth century would also prove to be a major stimulus to the city's commercial growth and eventual industrial success.

By the late eighteenth century, Monterrey had become a bustling, if still small, town, thriving on livestock raising and trade between the Gulf of Mexico and the inland mining regions of Zacatecas, Durango, Coahuila, and Chihuahua. It had also become by this time a key regional distribution center for foreign-made goods. Although providing an important logistical link among mining centers, Central Mexico, and the Gulf area, Monterrey developed independently from other areas of Mexico. This independence, primarily the result of geographical isolation, meant that the disruption of the colonial economy brought by the decade of the Independence wars did not have the same impact on Monterrey's population or economy that it had in other, more central, regions.

The early nineteenth century saw Monterrey's further growth and development based on trade and limited agriculture and livestock raising. Commerce in Monterrey was much stimulated by trade with colonists in Texas, and with the establishment of the Lone Star Republic in 1836 Monterrey's commercial position improved further. *Regiomontanos* began to import finished goods from the United States for resale in the interior of Mexico. The port of Tampico, founded in 1823, became the major sea connection for Monterrey and further strengthened Monterrey's trading position. Monterrey's trade also improved during the war between Mexico and the United States at mid-century, as shipping through Veracruz and Mexico City was restricted. Profiting from war would become a major theme in the development of the city with the U.S. Civil War and French Intervention of the early 1860s.

The period from the mid-nineteenth century to the end of the U.S. Civil War coincides with a prolonged period of development in Monterrey, securely founded on increasing trade and political stability. Growing trade resulted from the indictment of southern U.S. cotton shipments by Union forces and from political stability from the governor of Nuevo León and caudillo of northeast Mexico from 1855 to 1865, Santiago Vidaurri. Shrewdly, Vidaurri established his most important political alliances with Monterrey's merchants, thereby assuring continued growth and stability for the region. Vidaurri made the region a "free zone," a zone of unrestricted import of North American goods and supported the creation of a legal free zone in the neighboring state of Tamaulipas in 1858.[19]

With the end of the Civil War and the lucrative contraband trade in cotton and other goods, the economy of Monterrey faltered and then entered a slow decline for over two decades. The depressed national economy, and particularly the depressed mining sector following the French Intervention, and the conservative-liberal conflicts slowed the development of the regiomontano economy significantly. The political stability of the Vidaurri era ended with Vidaurri's death in 1865, and merchants almost immediately experienced increased difficulties due to banditry and transportation bottlenecks. The extension of the border free zone in 1870 benefited the Monterrey economy little, as the central government stepped up its customs patrols to curtail the smuggling that had become the lifeblood of Monterrey merchants.

Cotton, so important to Monterrey's prosperity during the U.S. Civil War era, would again come to the rescue of Monterrey's faltering economy after 1880. Cotton was becoming increasingly important in the Laguna, a region along the border of the states of Durango and Coahuila, as irrigation and railways transformed Mexico's cotton production and transportation system. The cotton boom in the Laguna led to the resurgence of Monterrey's economy based on trade of Mexican cotton to the United States and to the Gulf ports.

Strategic rail connections, finally completed in 1890 and 1891, also stimulated Monterrey's dormant trade-based economy. The railways carried the cotton produced in the Laguna to market by way of Monterrey. Further, the railways made it possible for Monterrey to extend its economic influence into neighboring states. And at the same time that Chihuahua, Coahuila, San Luis Potosí, and Zacatecas came within Monterrey's grasp, the key Gulf coast port of Tampico became connected by rail to Monterrey. All of these changes in the northeastern transportation network had the effect of placing Monterrey in the position it had enjoyed early on: the main hub linking Mexico's most dynamic economic regions with the United States and the world.

---

[18] The following historical sketch is drawn from numerous sources, the most important of which are the following: Saragoza, *The Monterrey Elite*, and Isidro Vizcaya Canales, *Los Orígenes de la Industrialización de Monterrey: Una Historia Económica y Social desde la Caída del Segundo Emperio hasta el Fin de la Revolución (1867–1920)* (Monterrey: ITESM, 1969).

---

[19] The free zone allowed Mexicans to buy U.S. goods tax free for local use but not for resale to other parts of Mexico.

Although it was during the 1890s that Monterrey's first famous industries began operations, Monterrey had seen some early industrial development. The dimmest beginnings of industrial production can be traced to the "import-substituting" production by Monterrey merchants throughout its history. Because of its geographical isolation, Monterrey had always relied on local production to meet demand for such basic consumer goods as cloth, mescal, food products, and other domestic necessities. These activities increased during the depression after 1870. Various government encouragements to industry, particularly tax exemptions for the first years of operation, were passed into law during the 1870s and 1880s. Textile factories were the first true industries to be located in Monterrey: the textile mill La Fama was established in 1854, El Porvenir in 1872, and La Leona in 1874. Textile manufacturing was followed in importance by various food processing industries. In 1872 Monterrey could boast the following industries: 159 sugar mills, 32 soap factories, 20 wheat mills, 15 mescal and aguardiente factories, 3 tanneries, 3 cotton-deseeding plants, and 1 gunpowder factory.[20]

During the boom brought by cotton and the railroad after 1890 modern industries sprung to life in Monterrey. Brought by the national economic recovery in the late 1880s, new and larger markets, led by mining, commercial agriculture, and cotton, made large-scale manufacturing profitable. Monterrey's commercial tradition, as well as the lack of local investment opportunities in agriculture and mining, inclined Monterrey's merchant families toward investment in industrial ventures. Demand was high for manufactured goods from the United States, particularly for mining supplies, but such foreign-made goods were expensive. The merchants of Monterrey were able to finance industrial plants to produce products that could undersell, or at least compete with, U.S. products. The protectionist McKinley Tariff of 1890, although bemoaned by many Mexicans involved in mining (Mexico's most important exports to the United States were mineral products), gave an additional boost to Monterrey's industrialists, for it pressed them to build up mineral-smelting capacity within Mexico. U.S. capitalists such as the Guggenheims were also quick to seize the opportunity for profits in Mexican industrial ventures, investing heavily in Mexican smelting plants.

The year 1890 marks the founding of the first significant regiomontano industries and industrial groups. In that year, the first of the "new" industries were established in Monterrey: foundries and other mineral refining plants, cigar factories, and breweries. In the three years between 1890 and 1892, fourteen new industrial operations, most of them metallurgical plants, opened their gates. These factories had a combined capitalization of 1,500,000 pesos, a

tremendous sum for the day, and could employ 800 workers at maximum output.[21]

During the next two decades, the large industries that would come to characterize Monterrey's twentieth-century industrialization were born. The Cervecería Cuauhtémoc began operations in 1890, the Fundidora de Fierro y Acero in 1900, and the Vidrera Monterrey in 1909. This burst of new manufacturing activity was accompanied by a surge of optimism among investors and public men about Monterrey and its industrial future. The new industrial ventures were backed by an impressive financial establishment that developed in Monterrey in the 1890s, led by the Banco de Nuevo León and the Banco Mercantil de Monterrey.

The industrial activity of Monterrey during its first florescence at the very end of the nineteenth century was already complex. The production of consumer goods was concentrated in four basic areas: food, clothing, hygiene, and construction materials. Preserved meats, bread, flour, oil, butter, beer, soft drinks, ice, chocolate, candies, finished and unfinished textiles, hats, shoes, leather goods, matches, candles, soap, cosmetics, cigarettes, beds and mattresses, books, and home furniture were all produced in Monterrey for primarily local consumption. A second level of industry produced intermediate products for use by the growing number of industries, such products as nails, wire, lead pipe, packaging materials, bottles, iron tools, bricks, and glycerine. Finally, a third, a smaller, group of manufacturing plants produced heavy intermediate and producer goods. The most important component of this third group was the elaboration of metal products, basic metal refining, and steel production, as well as limited production of machinery for agriculture and mining and cement for the construction industry.[22]

The period of industrial development begun in the 1890s was accompanied by a lengthy period of political stability. Between 1889 and 1909, Nuevo León was governed by Bernardo Reyes. Like his predecessor, Santiago Vidaurri, Reyes made alliances with Monterrey's merchants and developing industrialists and supported the expansion of their interests. Under Reyes's administration, laws were passed in 1889 and 1890 to protect industry and grant tax exemptions to new industrial ventures. The construction industry was given a great boost at the same time by tax exemption provisions for two years.

The industrial boom of the 1890–1910 period had a multiplier effect on the entire urban and regional economy of Monterrey. Monterrey's role as northern Mexico's leading trading power was reasserted and its position as the most important center of modern industry in Mexico was estab-

[20] Vizcaya Canales, Los Orígenes, p. 31.

[21] Ibid., p. 70.

[22] See Mario Cerutti, "División Capitalista de la Producción, Industrias, y Mercado Interior. Un Estudio Regional: Monterrey (1890–1910)," in Mario Cerutti, ed., El Siglo XIX en México: Cinco Procesos Regionales: Morelos, Monterrey, Yucatán, Jalisco, y Puebla (México, D.F.: Claves Latinoamericanas, 1985), pp. 75–76.

lished. The prosperity and importance of Monterrey were recognized with President Porfirio Díaz's well-publicized visit to the city in 1898.

Monterrey's first great era of economic boom based on industrialization faded to bust after 1907. The financial crisis in the United States in that year and the resulting slump in investment and purchases, as well as growing unemployment and harvest failure in many parts of Mexico, put the brakes on Monterrey's rapid development. The explosion of the Mexican Revolution in 1910 ended the first great cycle of Monterrey's industrial growth and development as a regional power.

Although the Revolution did not destroy Monterrey's industrial plant, as has been suggested by some scholars, it did have a significant dampening effect on industrial investment and production. Little of the social change wrought by the Revolution in its earliest phase was noticeable in the area of Monterrey: the small number of independent agricultural villages and large haciendas, along with the weight of industrial activity, tended to impede insurrection forces in the northeast.[23] Although the Revolution had little effect in Monterrey between 1900 and 1912, after the establishment in the city of Venustiano Carranza's Constitutionalist headquarters in 1914, Monterrey moved into the eye of the revolutionary storm. Not until the end of the violent first phase of the Revolution in 1920 was Monterrey able to return to normalcy.

As the nation struggled back to its feet in the 1920s, Monterrey grappled with the problems of manufacturing and conducting business in general, in the wake of the violent phase of the Revolution. Political instability and the increasing mobilization of the working class worked together to undermine investors' confidence in manufacturing. It is possible that the period was characterized by capital flight as demand fell, output declined, profits disappeared, and new investment slowed.[24] During the Depression of the 1930s the Mexican economy began forming the bases of growth for its takeoff after 1940. Ironically, heavy industry did better than industry oriented toward consumer goods during the Depression in Mexico. Monterrey's industries benefited from continuing high demand for steel, cement, and other goods for government-funded infrastructure.[25]

By the mid-1930s, Monterrey's economy was entering the period of expansion that would culminate in Mexico's economic revolution after 1940. Political stability had returned under President Lázaro Cárdenas (1934–40) and Cárdenas's "social revolution," with its heavy emphasis on infrastructure expenditures, encouraged investment and

industrial expansion in Monterrey. The Cárdenas presidency, the rhetoric of which may have seemed threatening to some capitalists, was in fact a model of the close state-industry bonds that became dominant in the period of rapid industrialization between 1940 and 1960.

To sum up this brief historical sketch of Monterrey's development during the first phase of Mexican industrialization, we can say that Monterrey grew after 1890 into Mexico's most important regional power by means of rapid industrialization based to a large extent on locally accumulated commercial capital. Monterrey's merchant families capitalized on numerous geographic and temporal advantages, as well as generous incentives and political stability provided by state and national governments, to invest in manufacturing. The strong tradition of independent action that characterized the inhabitants of the isolated town left its mark in the quick response of Monterrey merchants to opportunities for investment in manufacturing.

Long-Term Demographic Change in Monterrey

We turn now from the narrative account of Monterrey's evolution from an isolated frontier town into one of Mexico's key regional economic powers to consider time-series data on the long-term cycles and trends in the city's social development. In the following sections, historical data on Monterrey's population growth and migration to the city are developed and analyzed.

The early population of Monterrey is difficult to judge accurately because most population estimates were made by travelers in the far-northern region and casual visitors to the city, whose estimates were generally based on impressions and heresay. Population estimates up to about 1900 do not include accurate estimates for Monterrey's industrial suburbs, which were already growing by the last quarter of the nineteenth century.

By the middle of the eighteenth century, the Monterrey urban area had a population of at least 3,000 (see Tables 3700 and 3701 and Figure 37:1). By the early years of the nineteenth century, the city's population had doubled to about 6,000. Growth during the second half of the eighteenth century took place at an average annual rate of 1.8 percent.[26]

In the nineteenth century, population estimates for the Monterrey region were made more frequently. Soon after Independence, Monterrey's population had doubled over its 1803 figure to more than 12,000 inhabitants, growing at an increased average rate of 4.4 percent per year. The population of Monterrey reached an early high of about 16,000 in 1837. By mid-century, Monterrey's population had apparently

[23] Alan Knight, "Peasant and Caudillo in Revolutionary Mexico, 1900–1917," in Brading, ed., *Caudillo and Peasant in the Mexican Revolution*, p. 26.

[24] Haber, *Industry and Underdevelopment*, pp. 149, 150.

[25] See Enrique Cárdenas, *La Industrialización Mexicana durante la Gran Depresión* (México, D.F.: El Colegio de México, 1987).

[26] AAPC or average annual percent change figures are used throughout. See note on calculating annual rates of change in James W. Wilkie and David Lorey, eds., *SALA* 25 (1987), p. xxx.

Table 3700

MONTERREY MUNICIPIO POPULATION ESTIMATES, 1753–1895

Year	Population	Alternate Data		Source
1753	3,334			Vizcaya Canales
1803	6,412			Vizcaya Canales
1824	12,282[a]			Vizcaya Canales
1837	16,377			Vizcaya Canales
1846	15,000			EHM
1852	13,534			EHM
1857	13,534			EHM
1862	14,534	13,500	16,435	EHM
1869	14,000			EHM
early–1870s	25,000			Vizcaya Canales
1872	33,811[b]			Vizcaya Canales
1881	40,000			EHM
1882	42,000			Boyer and Davies[c]
1883	41,842[d]			Vizcaya Canales
1890	41,700			EHM
1891	40,785			Vizcaya Canales
1895	45,695[e]	56,855[f]		

a. Vizcaya Canales notes that this figure refers to the entire Monterrey region, including suburbs.
b. Datum for municipio; central city figure: 28,000.
c. Richard E. Boyer and Keith A. Davies, *Urbanization in Nineteenth-Century Latin America: Statistics and Sources* (Los Angeles: UCLA Latin American Center, 1973).
d. Datum for municipio; central city figure: 35,356.
e. EHM.
f. Woodrow Borah et al., *Ensayos sobre el Desarrollo Urbano de México* (México, D.F.: SEP, 1974), p. 158.

Table 3701

MONTERREY POPULATION ESTIMATES AND GROWTH RATES, 1753–1895

PART I. ALL YEARS

Year	Population	PC	AAPC[1]
1753	3,334	~	~
1803	6,412	92.3	1.8
1824	12,282	91.5	4.4
1837	16,377	33.3	2.6
1846	15,000	–8.4	–.9
1852	13,534	–9.8	–1.6
1857	13,534	0	0
1862	14,534	7.4	1.5
1869	14,000	–3.7	–.5
1870	25,000	78.6	78.6
1872	33,811	35.2	17.6
1881	40,000	18.3	2.0
1883	41,842	4.6	2.3
1890	41,700	–.3	0
1891	40,785	–2.2	–2.2
1895	45,695	12.0	3.0

PART II. ROUGH DECADES

Year	Population	PC	AAPC
1753	3,334	~	~
1803	6,412	92.3	1.8
1824	12,282	91.5	4.4
1837	16,377	33.3	2.6
1846	15,000	–8.4	–.9
1852	13,534	–9.8	–1.6
1862	14,534	7.4	.7
1870	25,000	72.0	9.0
1881	40,000	60.0	5.5
1890	41,700	4.3	.5

1. Growth rate is measured by average annual percent change (AAPC).

SOURCE: Table 3700.

leveled off and through the early 1860s fluctuated around a figure of about 14,000.

Between the early 1860s and the early 1870s, the population of Monterrey experienced one of its first major growth spurts. From 1862 to 1870, the population grew at an average annual rate of 9 percent and from 1870 to 1881 at a slightly lower average rate of 5.5 percent per year. The population remained stable throughout the 1880s. A second nineteenth-century growth spurt came at the very end of the century, between 1890 and 1900, when the population grew from roughly 42,000 to almost 73,000, an average annual rate of 7.5 percent.

Comparison of Monterrey's early growth with that in the state of Nuevo León and in Mexico as a whole (Tables 3701, 3702, and 3703) shows that Monterrey grew much faster than either the surrounding state or the republic during the late nineteenth century. In the second part of Tables 3701, 3702, and 3703, population data have been reorganized into rough decades for estimation of decennial growth rates and average annual percent change over time. Compar-

able years and the most reliable data were abstracted from the longer series in the first part of the tables.[27]

By the beginning of the twentieth century, population data on Monterrey and its satellite suburbs had begun to be collected in an organized fashion by the Mexican census. The greater reliability and comparability of these census data make possible close analysis of long-term population change in the region. Data on the four central industrial suburbs of Monterrey—Garza García, Guadalupe, San Nicolás de los Garza, and Santa Catarina—have generally been left out of

[27] The rough decades will also be used below to gauge the rate of immigration to Monterrey.

Figure 37:1

MONTERREY ESTIMATED POPULATION, 1753-1895

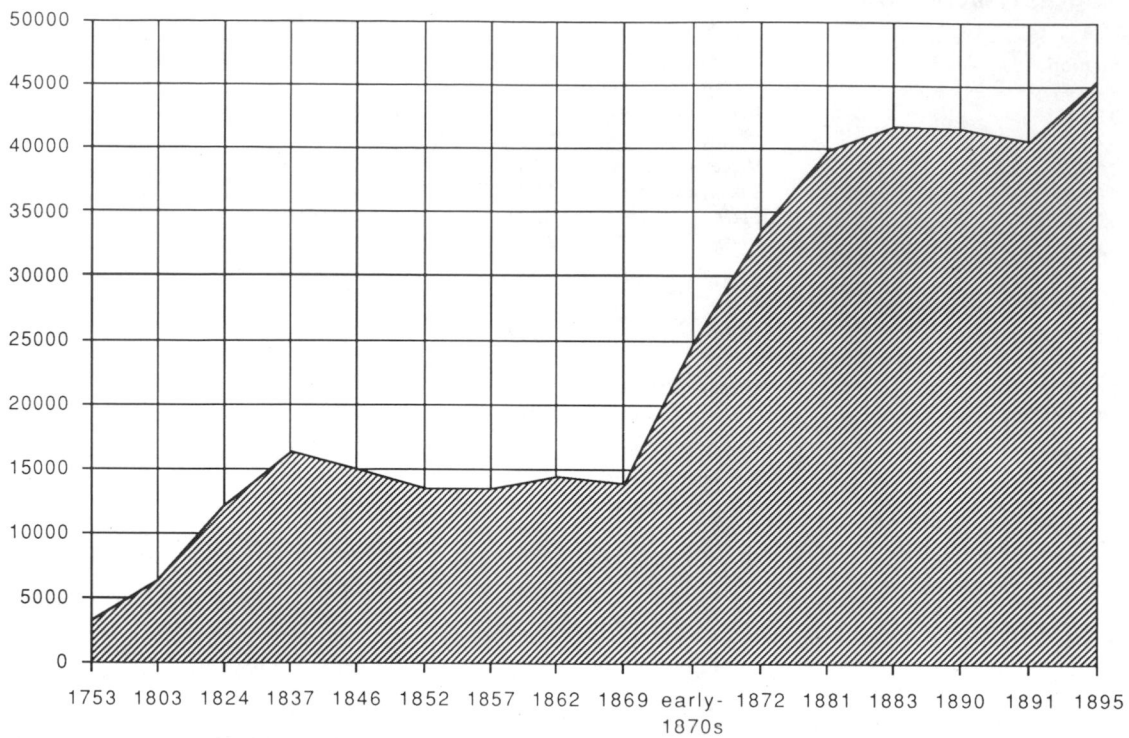

SOURCE: Table 3700.

analysis of Monterrey's history in the twentieth century. One prominent statistical source includes data for these four *municipios*, but only for the years between 1940 and 1970, and the totals for the four suburbs are simply added to the figure for Monterrey, leaving an aggregate number that is difficult to use.[28] Monterrey's four most important industrial suburbs must be considered separately in analysis, as they can be expected to show most clearly the drawing power of Monterrey's developing economy. The suburbs were important from the earliest phases of Monterrey's industrial growth; the first textile mills, for example, were established in such suburbs: La Fama in Santa Catarina and La Leona in Garza García.

In the approach adopted here, city and municipio figures are considered individually and then combined for different estimates of the total population of the urban area of Monterrey. Organized in this manner the data allow for calculations of long-term growth patterns. The rates of

growth for cities, municipios, and total urban areas are gauged using data on both cities and municipios.

The relationship between the population of Monterrey's central city area and of its suburban satellites is presented in Tables 3704-3707 and in Figures 37:2 and 37:3. The data on cities (Figure 37:2) and municipios (Figure 37:3) reveal the rapid growth of the city and the particularly quick pace of growth in the larger metropolitan area composed of the four suburbs. Whereas up until 1940 the larger metropolitan area was only slightly larger than the central city, by 1980 it was almost twice as large. Growth of the entire metropolitan area was extremely rapid between 1960 and 1980.

The decennial growth rates of central Monterrey and its metropolitan area from 1900 to 1980 are compared in Figure 37:4 (see also Tables 3708 and 3709). The data show two key historical changes in the development of Monterrey: (1) the fastest growth of the Monterrey metropolitan area as a whole occurred between 1940 and 1960; (2) the largest difference in the growth rates of the central city and the larger metropolitan area was experienced between 1960 and 1980, and particularly in the decade from 1970 to 1980.

The growth rates of Monterrey's industrial-worker suburbs and the central city have followed different paths. Up until 1940, the central city and surrounding metropolitan area (including the suburbs of Garza García, Guadalupe, San Nicolás, and Santa Catarina) grew at similar rates, but there-

---

[28] See, for example, *Estadísticas Históricas de México* (EHM), vol. 1, p. 28. A municipio is comparable to a U.S. county. Another secondary work is Mary Catherine Megee, *Monterrey, Mexico: Internal Patterns and External Relations*, Department of Geography Research Paper no. 59 (Chicago: University of Chicago, 1958). Megee includes partial data for 1895-1950 and estimates for 1958.

Table 3702

NUEVO LEON POPULATION ESTIMATES AND GROWTH RATES, 1826–95

PART I. ALL YEARS

Year	Population	PC	AAPC
1826	83,093	~	~
1839	101,188	21.8	1.7
1851	137,070	35.5	3.0
1856	145,779	6.4	1.3
1869	173,203	18.8	1.4
1870	174,000	.5	.5
1873	178,872	2.8	.9
1881	210,826	17.9	2.2
1883	210,826	0	0
1891	271,987	29.0	3.6
1895	309,252	13.7	3.4

PART II. ROUGH DECADES

Year	Population	PC	AAPC
1826	83,093	~	~
1830	95,022	14.4	3.6
1839	101,188	6.5	.7
1851	137,070	35.5	3.0
1856	145,779	6.4	1.3
1870	174,000	19.4	1.4
1881	210,826	21.2	1.9
1891	271,987	29.0	2.9

SOURCE: EHM.

Table 3703

MEXICO POPULATION ESTIMATES, 1790–1895

PART I. ALL YEARS

Year	Population	PC	AAPC
1790	4,636,074	~	~
1803	5,764,731	24.3	1.9
1838	7,004,140	21.5	.6
1846	7,000,000	–.1	0
1852	7,661,919	9.5	1.6
1858	8,604,000	12.3	2.0
1862	8,396,524	–2.4	–.6
1869	8,812,850	5.0	.7
1872	9,141,661	3.7	1.2
1882	10,001,884	9.4	.9
1885	10,879,398	8.8	2.9
1893	11,994,347	10.2	1.3
1895	12,632,427	14.9	7.4

PART II. ROUGH DECADES

Year	Population	PC	AAPC
1790	4,636,074	~	~
1803	5,764,731	24.3	1.9
1838	7,004,140	21.5	.6
1852	7,661,919	9.4	.7
1858	8,604,000	12.3	2.0
1869	8,912,850	2.4	.2
1882	10,001,884	13.5	1.0
1893	11,994,347	19.9	1.8

SOURCE: EHM.

after, the rates for the two subgroups within the metropolitan area diverged markedly. Whereas between 1960 and 1970 the central city and central municipio grew at roughly the 1930–40 rate, the population of Metropolitan Area 2 (municipios) grew at about twice that rate. In the ten years from 1970 to 1980, the gap in growth rates was even larger: while the central city grew at the lowest rate since 1900–10, Metropolitan Area 1 (cities) grew at its highest rate ever. The growth rates of Vellinga's Metropolitan Area (Table 3710), which I term Metropolitan Area 3 here, and of the urban population of the state of Nuevo León (Tables 3709 and 3711) are compared in Figure 37:5.[29] These data reveal the same basic trends seen in the data displayed in Figure 37:4, although Metropolitan Area 3 shows a lower growth rate after 1960.

Clearly, the industrial suburbs of Monterrey have experienced major immigrant inflow over time. In the late nineteenth century, two spurts in population propelled the

growth of the city during its development into the key commercial and industrial hub of northern Mexico. In the period of rapid industrialization between 1940 and 1960, the central city and the industrial suburbs grew at their most rapid historical rate. The fact that they grew at similar rates during this period suggests a balanced development of metropolitan Monterrey. Between 1970 and 1980, the growth of the suburbs far outpaced the development of the central city. This pattern reveals the slow growth of the densely settled central zone and the rapid growth of shantytowns built on the edges of the central city by new arrivals. Recent growth has put an increasing strain on public services such as water supply, drainage, transportation, and health care.

Migration

The population data developed above provide an avenue for exploring the long-term dynamics of net migration to Monterrey. We can compare the rates of growth of the Monterrey area with those for Mexico as a whole to estimate the number of immigrants to Monterrey by decade.

[29] Vellinga's Metro Area (termed Metropolitan Area 3 in the present study) includes the suburbs of Apodaca and General Escobedo. It is not clear whether Vellinga's data refer to cities or municipios.

Table 3704

MONTERREY POPULATION,[1] 1900–80

Year	Monterrey City	Monterrey Municipio
1900	62,266	72,963
1910	78,528	86,294
1921	88,479	98,305
1930	132,577	137,388
1940	186,092	190,074
1950	333,422	339,282
1960	596,939	601,085
1970	858,107	858,107
1980	1,084,722	1,090,009

1. City population data are for the central city area; municipio data are for the large municipio which takes the name of the central city. A Mexican municipio is comparable to a U.S. county.

SOURCE: Derived from Mexican decennial census in consultation with the following secondary works: David E. Lorey, ed., *United States–Mexico Border Statistics since 1900* (Los Angeles: UCLA Latin American Center Publications, 1990); EHM; Frédéric Mauro, "Le Développement économique de Monterrey (1890–1960)," *Caravelle*, no. 2 (1964), 35–126; and Luis Unikel, *El Desarrollo Urbano de México: Diagnóstico e Implicaciones Futuras* (México, D.F.: COLMEX, 1976).

The historical population growth of central Monterrey, of Nuevo León, and of Mexico from the eighteenth century to 1980, organized into rough decades for the nineteenth century and decades for the years after 1930, is presented in Tables 3712, 3713, and 3714. Nineteenth-century data for Monterrey are spliced with data on Metropolitan Area 1 for this series, because those data provide the closest fit and constitute a compromise between the low figure of the central city and the high figure of Metropolitan Area 3.

We are forced by lack of reliable data on births and deaths in nineteenth-century Mexico to rely on the national growth rate for comparison with the share of growth of Monterrey due to natural increase. Unlike Argentina and Brazil, Mexico received only a small trickle of European and African migrants during the nineteenth and twentieth centuries. Table 3716 shows that international migrants have historically made up a negligible portion of the Mexican population. Moreover, in the nineteenth century immigration to Mexico appears to have been roughly offset by emigration to the United States. Thus the national growth rate closely reflects the rate of natural increase.

For the twentieth century, the data on the natural increase of Mexico's population are more reliable but are of limited utility in calculating decennial rates of migration to Monterrey. The central problem is that data on births and deaths for 1930 and 1940, for example, tell us little about change in the rate of increase in the 1930–40 decade. Data on long-term rates of natural increase confirm that Monter-

rey has historically experienced births and deaths at about the national average rate. Table 3715 compares the rates of natural population increase of Mexico as a whole and Monterrey from 1900 to 1980. This comparison suggests that little distortion will be introduced into our calculations if we take the national average of population increase as the rate of natural increase in both Mexico and Monterrey for the nineteenth and twentieth centuries.

While international migration did not have a major impact on Mexican society in the nineteenth and twentieth centuries, large internal redistributions of population have taken place in the national period. Table 3717 shows that recent immigrants to the state of Nuevo León, for example, have constituted an important part of regional society in the twentieth century. Between 1940 and 1970, almost one out of every ten persons in Nuevo León responding to the census had arrived in the state during the previous decade.

What are the quantitative dimensions of historical migration to Monterrey? More generally, what has been the role of migration in the development of the city? Table 3718 compares the rates of growth of Monterrey and Mexico and shows the resulting share of population increase in Monterrey that can be safely attributed to immigration to the city. Figure 37:6 graphs this comparison. Over time, the percentage of population change attributable to immigration has declined from a high of 98 percent in the cotton-boom period from 1862 to 1870 to a low of 23 percent between 1960 and 1970. The average is high, at 60.8 percent for the 120 years from 1862 to 1980.

The comparison of growth rates makes it possible to estimate the number of migrants to Monterrey for the period spanning 1862 to 1980. Table 3719 uses the calculations of Table 3718 to estimate in rough thousands the number of immigrants to Monterrey from 1862–79 to 1970–80. The data show that while the percentage of population growth due to migration to Monterrey has fallen over time, the absolute number of migrants has increased dramatically (Figure 37:7). From between 8,000 and 14,000 up until the beginning of the Revolution, the migrant tide swelled to roughly 30,000 between 1921 and 1940 and then jumped to 100,000 in the first decade of Mexico's industrial revolution, 1940 to 1950. The number of migrants continued to climb through 1960, declined in the 1960–70 decade, and rose to an all-time high of more than 400,000 migrants between 1970 and 1980.

These patterns in the historical migrant flow to Monterrey can be fit, with some modifications, to the narrative account of Monterrey's evolution presented in capsule form above. In general, the pattern of migration has conformed to Monterrey's changing needs for skilled and unskilled labor as Mexico industrialized beginning in the Porfiriato. The development of manufacturing in Monterrey occurred in two great swings, one stretching from the end of the nineteenth century up until the beginning of the Revolution in 1910, the other picking up steam between the mid-1930s and 1950.

Figure 37:2

POPULATION OF MONTERREY CENTRAL AND SUBURBAN CITIES, 1900–80

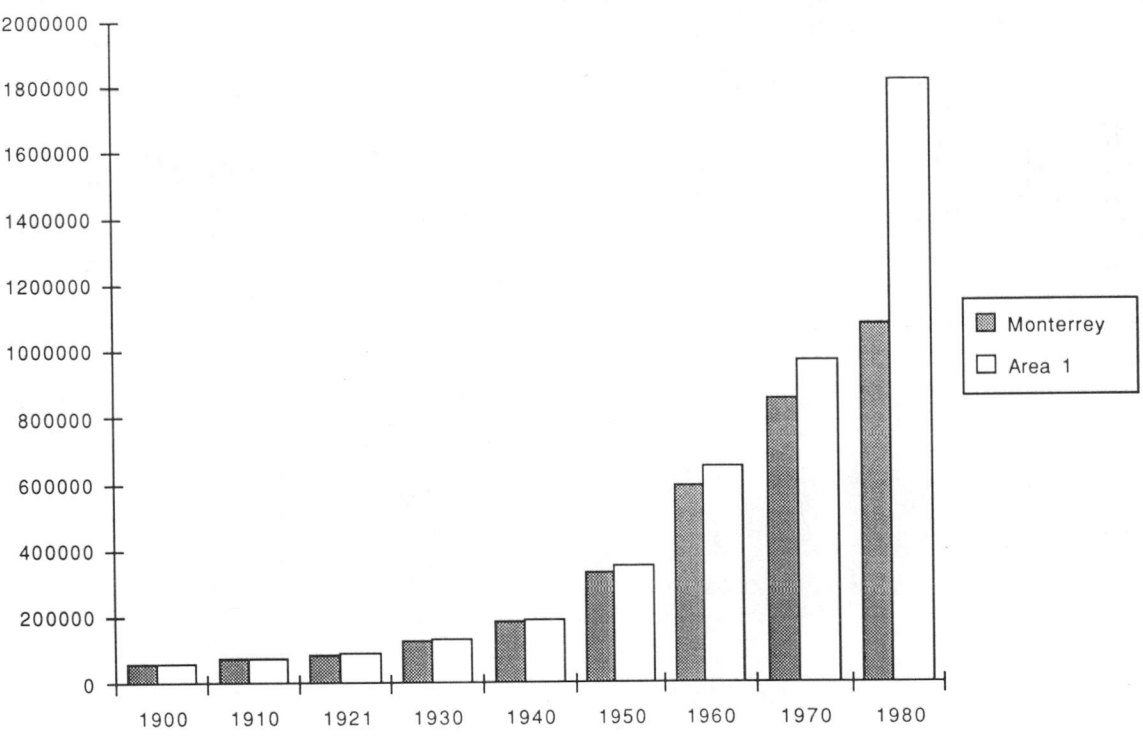

SOURCE: Tables 3704 and 3707.

Table 3705

MONTERREY INDUSTRIAL SUBURB POPULATION, CITIES, 1921–80

Year	Garza García	San Nicolás de los Garza	Guadalupe	Santa Catarina	Total Industrial Suburb Cities
1921	788	1,368	1,044	1,095	4,295
1930	1,015	2,049	1,625	1,128	5,817
1940	1,665	3,038	2,371	1,067	8,141
1950	2,659	6,665	10,394	2,450	22,168
1960	7,525	15,437	27,020	4,608	54,590
1970	20,934	28,803	51,899	14,116	115,752
1980	81,967	280,688	370,515	~	733,170

SOURCE: See Table 3704.

Figure 37:3

POPULATION OF MONTERREY CENTRAL AND SUBURBAN MUNICIPIOS, 1900–80

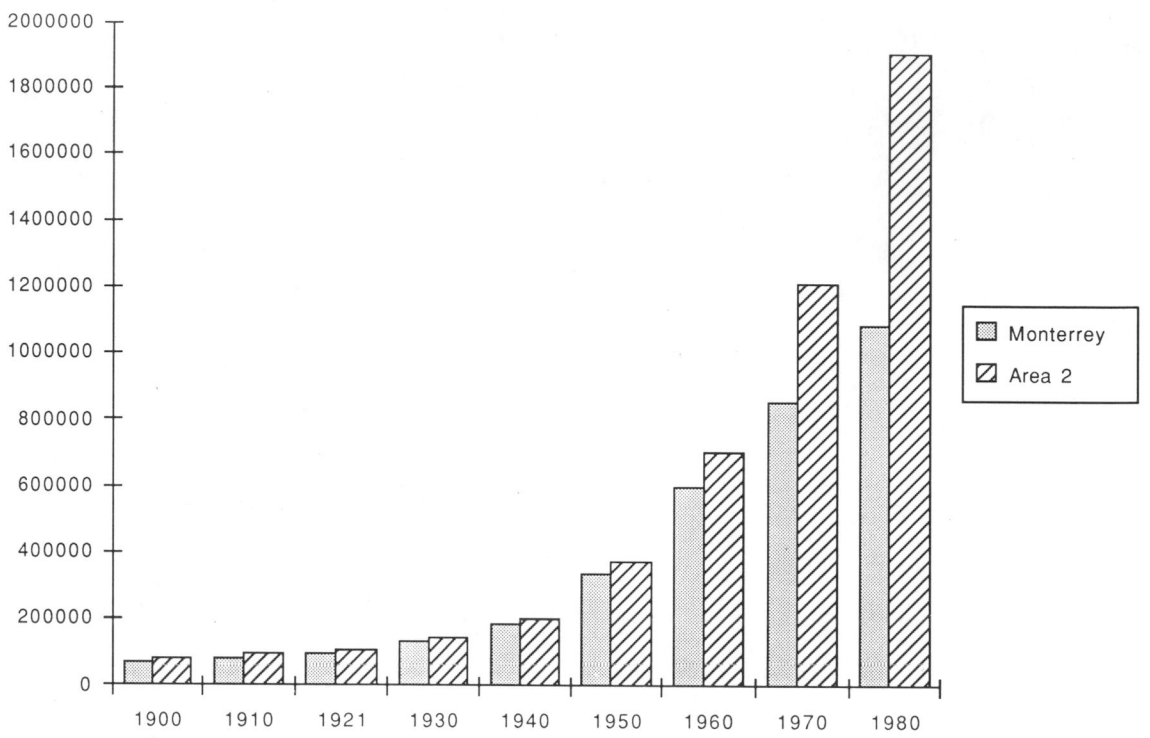

SOURCE: Tables 3704 and 3707.

Table 3706

MONTERREY INDUSTRIAL SUBURB POPULATION, MUNICIPIOS, 1900–80

Year	Garza García	San Nicolás de los Garza	Guadalupe	Santa Catarina	Total Industrial Suburb Cities
1900	1,957	2,414	3,202	4,383	11,956
1910	1,750	2,644	3,516	4,158	12,068
1921	1,838	1,918	2,586	3,410	9,752
1930	2,082	2,937	3,174	3,799	11,992
1940	2,780	4,149	4,391	4,758	16,078
1950	5,228	10,543	12,610	7,377	35,758
1960	14,943	41,243	38,233	12,895	107,314
1970	45,983	113,074	159,930	36,385	355,372
1980	81,974	280,696	370,908	89,488	823,066

SOURCE: See Table 3704.

Table 3707

TOTAL MONTERREY METROPOLITAN AREA POPULATION, 1900–80

Year	Total Metropolitan Area 1[a]	Total Metropolitan Area 2[b]
1900	65,000†	84,919
1910	82,000†	98,362
1921	92,774	108,057
1930	138,394	149,380
1940	194,233	206,152
1950	355,590	375,040
1960	651,529	708,399
1970	973,859	1,213,479
1980	1,817,892	1,913,075

a. Cities.
b. Municipios.

SOURCE: See Table 3704.

Table 3708

CENTRAL MONTERREY POPULATION AND GROWTH RATES, 1900–80

Year	Monterrey City	PC	AAPC
1900	62,266	~	~
1910	78,528	26.1	2.6
1921	88,479	12.7	1.2
1930	132,577	49.8	5.5
1940	186,092	40.4	4.0
1950	333,422	79.2	7.9
1960	596,939	79.0	7.9
1970	858,107	43.8	4.4
1980	1,084,722	26.4	2.6

Year	Monterrey Municipio	PC	AAPC
1900	72,963	~	~
1910	86,294	18.3	1.8
1921	98.305	13.9	1.3
1930	137,388	39.8	4.4
1940	190,074	38.3	3.8
1950	339,282	78.5	7.8
1960	601,085	77.2	7.7
1970	858,107	42.8	4.3
1980	1,090,009	27.0	2.7

SOURCE: Calculated from Table 3704.

Figure 37:4

GROWTH RATE OF MONTERREY AND SUBURBS (CITIES AND MUNICIPIOS), 1900–80

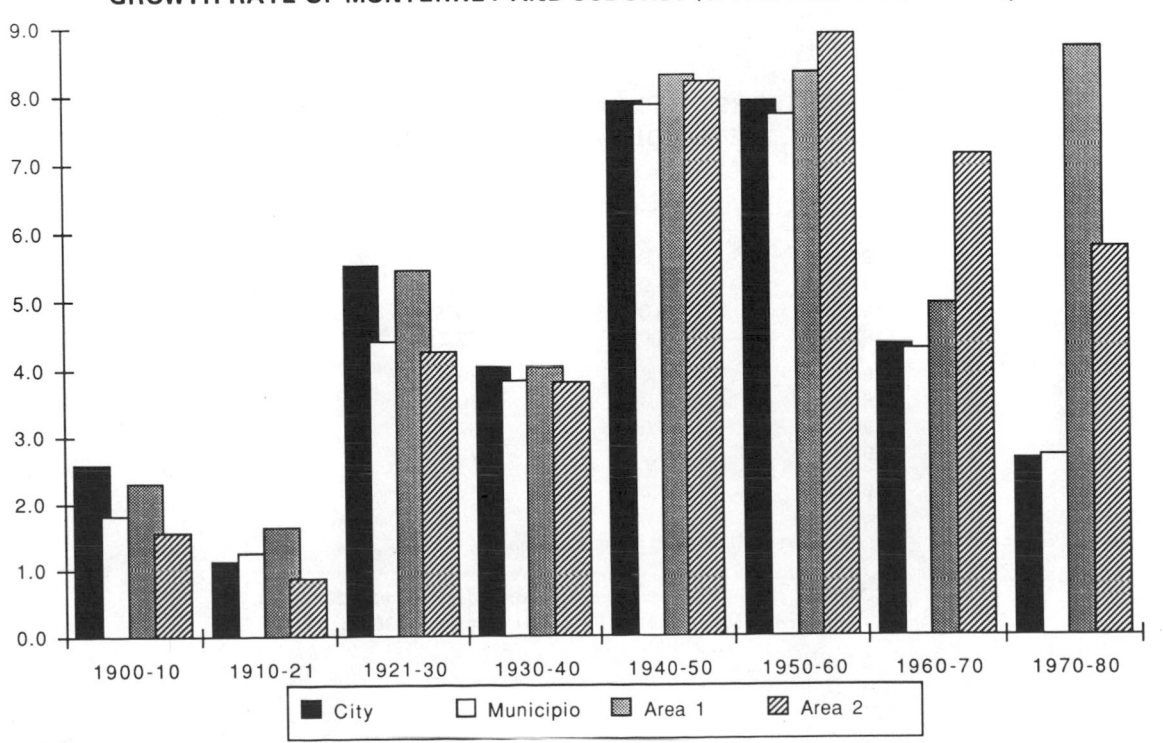

SOURCE: Tables 3708 and 3709.

Table 3709

MONTERREY DECENNIAL AND AVERAGE ANNUAL GROWTH RATES, 1900–80

Year	Total Metropolitan Area 1	Decennial Growth Rate	AAPC	Total Metropolitan Area 2	Decennial Growth Rate	AAPC
1900	65,000[†]	~	~	84,919	~	~
1910	82,000[†]	26.2	2.6	98,362	15.8	1.6
1921	92,774	18.1	1.6	108,057	9.9	.9
1930	138,394	49.2	5.5	149,380	38.2	4.2
1940	194,233	40.3	4.0	206,152	38.0	3.8
1950	355,590	83.1	8.3	375,040	81.9	8.2
1960	651,529	83.2	8.3	708,399	88.9	8.9
1970	973,859	49.5	4.9	1,213,479	71.3	7.1
1980	1,817,892	86.7	8.7	1,913,075	57.7	5.8

Year	Population Nuevo León	Decennial Growth Rate	AAPC	Nueva León Urban[a]	Decennial Growth Rate	AAPC
1900	327,937	~	~	110,205	~	~
1910	365,150	11.3	1.1	123,648	12.2	1.2
1921	336,412	-7.9	-.7	126,856	2.6	.2
1930	417,491	24.1	2.7	172,175	35.7	4.0
1940	541,147	29.6	3.0	237,725	38.1	3.8
1950	740,191	36.8	3.7	413,911	74.1	7.4
1960	1,078,848	45.8	4.6	759,061	83.4	8.3
1970	1,694,689	57.1	5.7	1,296,843	70.8	7.1
1980	2,513,044	48.3	4.8	2,197,288	69.4	6.9

a. As defined by census.

SOURCE: Calculated from Table 3707.

Table 3710

MONTERREY POPULATION AND GROWTH RATES,
METROPOLITAN AREA 3,[a] 1900–80

Year	Population	PC	AAPC
1900	90,000	~	~
1910	104,000	15.6	1.6
1921	113,000	8.7	.8
1930	155,000	37.2	4.1
1940	212,000	36.8	3.7
1950	382,000	80.2	8.0
1960	716,000	87.4	8.7
1970	1,243,000	73.6	7.4
1980	1,946,000	56.6	5.7

a. Includes Apodaca and General Escobedo.

SOURCE: Menno Vellinga, *Desigualdad, Poder, y Cambio Social en Monterrey* (México, D.F.: Siglo XXI Editores, 1988), p. 41.

Table 3711

NUEVO LEON URBAN POPULATION, 1900–80

Year	Population Nuevo León	Nuevo León Urban	% Urban	% Monterrey Metro Area 1	% Monterrey Metro Area 2
1900	327,937	110,205	33.6	19.8	25.9
1910	365,150	123,648	33.9	22.5	26.9
1921	336,412	126,856	37.7	27.6	32.1
1930	417,491	172,175	41.2	33.1	35.8
1940	541,147	237,725	43.9	35.9	38.1
1950	740,191	413,911	55.9	48.0	50.7
1960	1,078,848	759,061	70.4	60.4	65.7
1970	1,694,689	1,296,843	76.5	57.5	71.6
1980	2,513,044	2,197,288	87.4	72.3	76.1

SOURCE: Calculated from EHM and Table 3707.

Figure 37:5

GROWTH OF NUEVO LEON URBAN POPULATION AND MONTERREY METROPOLITAN AREA 3, 1900–80

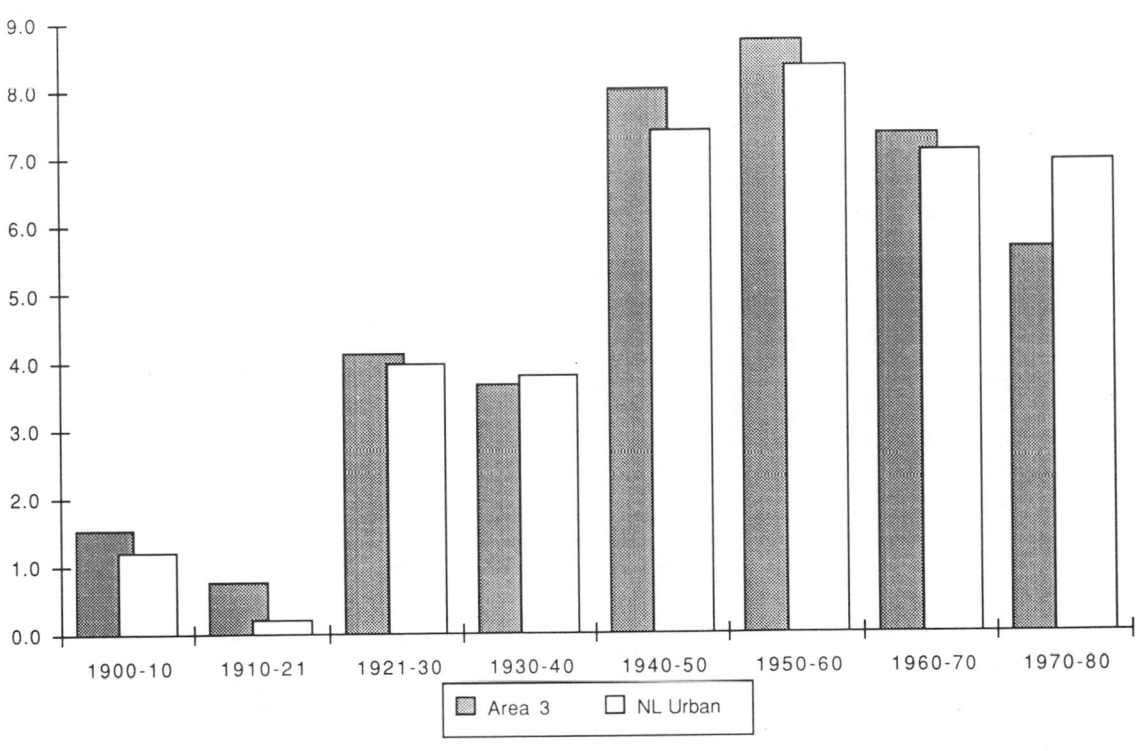

SOURCE: Tables 3710 and 3711.

Table 3712

MONTERREY POPULATION AND GROWTH RATES, 1753–1980

Year	Population	PC	AAPC
1753	3,334	~	~
1803	6,412	92.3	1.8
1824	12,282	91.5	4.4
1837	16,377	33.3	2.6
1846	15,000	−8.4	−.9
1852	13,534	−9.8	−1.6
1862	14,534	7.4	.7
1870	25,000	72.0	9.0
1881	40,000	60.0	5.5
1890	41,700	4.3	.5
1900	63,800	53.0	5.3
1910	78,528	23.1	2.3
1921	92,774	18.1	1.6
1930	138,394	49.2	5.5
1940	194,233	40.3	4.0
1950	355,590	83.1	8.3
1960	651,529	83.2	8.3
1970	973,859	49.5	4.9
1980	1,817,892	86.7	8.7

SOURCE: Calculated from Tables 3701 and 3707.

Table 3713

NUEVO LEON POPULATION AND GROWTH RATES, 1804–1980

Year	Population	PC	AAPC
1804	43,739	~	~
1826	83,093	90.0	4.1
1830	95,022	14.4	.7
1839	101,188	6.5	.7
1851	137,070	35.5	3.0
1856	145,779	6.4	1.3
1870	174,000	19.4	1.4
1881	210,826	21.2	1.9
1891	271,987	29.0	2.9
1900	327,937	20.6	2.3
1910	365,150	11.3	1.1
1921	336,412	−7.9	−.7
1930	417,491	24.1	2.7
1940	541,147	29.6	3.0
1950	740,191	36.8	3.7
1960	1,078,848	45.8	4.6
1970	1,694,689	57.1	5.7
1980	2,513,044	48.3	4.8

SOURCE: Calculated from EHM.

Table 3714

MEXICO POPULATION AND GROWTH RATES, 1790–1980

Year	Population	PC	AAPC
1790	4,636,074	~	~
1803	5,764,731	24.3	1.9
1838	7,004,140	21.5	.6
1852	7,661,919	9.4	.7
1858	8,604,000	12.3	2.0
1869	8,812,850	2.4	.2
1882	10,001,884	13.5	1.0
1893	11,994,347	19.9	1.8
1900	13,607,272	13.4	1.9
1910	15,160,369	11.4	1.1
1921	14,334,780	−5.4	−.5
1930	16,552,722	15.5	1.7
1940	19,653,552	18.7	1.9
1950	25,791,017	31.2	3.1
1960	34,923,129	35.4	3.5
1970	48,225,238	38.1	3.8
1980	69,392,835	43.9	4.4

SOURCE: Calculated from Table 3703.

Table 3715

MEXICO AND MONTERREY RATES OF NATURAL POPULATION INCREASE, 1900–80

PART I. MEXICO

Year	A. Births (PTI)	B. Deaths (PTI)	A−B	% Growth Rate
1900	34.0	32.7	1.3	.13
1922	31.4	25.3	6.1	.61
1930	49.5	26.7	22.8	2.28
1940	44.3	22.8	21.5	2.15
1950	45.6	16.1	29.5	2.95
1960	46.1	11.5	34.6	3.46
1970	44.2	10.1	34.1	3.41
1980	35.0	6.3	28.7	2.87

PART II. MONTERREY

Year	A. Births (PTI)	B. Deaths (PTI)	A−B	% Growth Rate
1900	39.4	24.9	14.5	1.5
1907	40.1	28.4	11.7	1.2
1922	35.4	24.0	11.4	1.1
1930	38.9	20.2	18.7	1.9
1940	44.9	17.4	27.5	2.8
1950	43.7	11.6	32.1	3.2
1960	47.2	8.4	38.8	3.9
1970	43.4	7.3	36.1	3.6
1980	~	~	~	~

SOURCE: Calculated from EHM.

Figure 37:6

MONTERREY AND MEXICO COMPARATIVE GROWTH RATES, 1852–1980

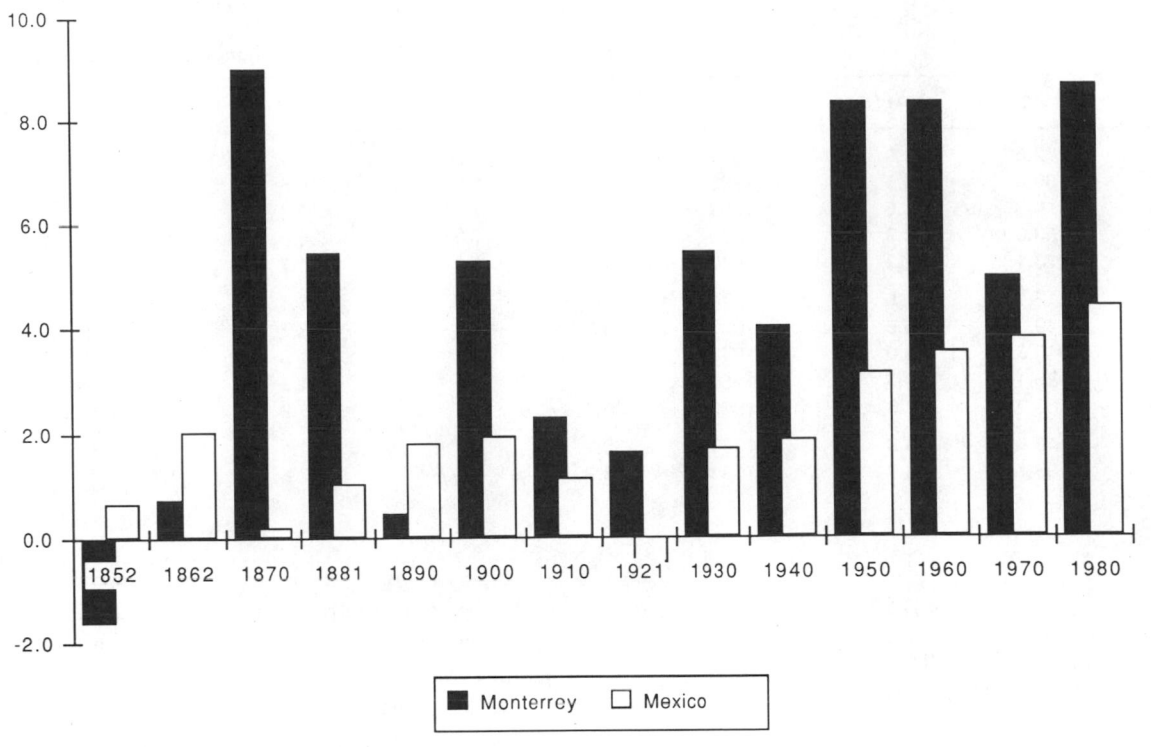

SOURCE: Tables 3712 and 3714.

<table>
<tr><td colspan="3">Table 3716</td></tr>
</table>

Table 3716

FOREIGNERS IN MEXICO, 1900–80

Year	Foreigners	% of Total Population
1900	57,644	.4
1910	117,119	.8
1920	100,862	.7
1930	159,844	1.0
1940	67,548	.3
1950	106,315	.4
1960	223,468	.6
1970	191,184	.4
1980	268,900	.4

SOURCE: Calculated from EHM.

Table 3717

INTERCENSAL MIGRATION TO NUEVO LEON, 1930–70

Year	Migrants	Total Population	Migrants as % of Total Population
1930–40	32,991	541,147	6.1
1940–50	21,979	740,191	3.0
1950–60	64,376	1,078,848	6.0
1960–70	150,600	1,694,689	8.9

SOURCE: Calculated from EHM.

Table 3718

ESTIMATED PERCENTAGE OF POPULATION GROWTH DUE TO MIGRATION, 1862–1980

Monterrey			Mexico			PC Due to Migration to Monterrey		% of AAPC Due to Migration
Year	PC	AAPC	Year	PC	AAPC	PC	AAPC	
1862–1870	72.0	9.0	1869	2.4	.2	69.6	8.8	98
1870–1881	60.0	5.5	1882	13.5	1.0	46.5	4.4	81
1881–1890	4.3	.5	1893	19.9	1.8	−15.7	−1.3	~
1890–1900	53.0	5.3	1900	13.4	1.9	39.6	3.4	64
1900–1910	23.1	2.3	1910	11.4	1.1	11.7	1.2	51
1910–1921	18.1	1.6	1921	−5.4	−.5	23.6	2.1	~
1921–1930	49.2	5.5	1930	15.5	1.7	33.7	3.7	69
1930–1940	40.3	4.0	1940	18.7	1.9	21.6	2.2	54
1940–1950	83.1	8.3	1950	31.2	3.1	51.8	5.2	62
1950–1960	83.2	8.3	1960	35.4	3.5	47.8	4.8	57
1960–1970	49.5	4.9	1970	38.1	3.8	11.4	1.1	23
1970–1980	86.7	8.7	1980	43.9	4.4	42.8	4.3	49

SOURCE: Calculated from Tables 3712 and 3714.

Table 3719

ESTIMATED IMMIGRANTS TO MONTERREY, 1862–1980

Year	Population Increase	% Due to Migration	Immigrants (T)
1862–1870	10,466	98	10
1870–1881	15,000	81	12
1881–1890	1,700	~	~
1890–1900	22,100	64	14
1900–1910	14,728	51	8
1910–1921	14,246	~	~
1921–1930	45,620	69	31
1930–1940	55,839	54	30
1940–1950	161,357	62	100
1950–1960	295,939	57	169
1960–1970	322,330	23	74
1970–1980	844,033	49	414

SOURCE: Calculated from Tables 3712 and 3718.

As economic activity, and particularly industrialization, accelerated in Mexico, the demand for labor in the Monterrey area grew apace. Higher wages resulted from a shortage of permanent, skilled and semi-skilled labor. Migrants were attracted to the higher wages and left their homes in neighboring states to go to Monterrey, frequently changing occupations in the process. The city's mineral-smelting and refining industries particularly demanded large numbers of skilled and semiskilled laborers. The pressure exerted by U.S. demand for labor and the level of wages in the United States forced employers in Monterrey to raise their wages and thus helped to attract migrants to the Mexican north.

Employers in Monterrey began early to offer nonmonetary wages such as basic healthcare and housing to maintain the migrant flow.

Already in 1895, 38 percent of Monterrey's inhabitants had been born in other states.[30] The large influx of labor to Monterrey during the late Porfiriato was also characteristic of other northern states such as Coahuila and Durango, where some of the highest wages in Mexico were offered to recent immigrants.[31] The railways provided a crucial link in enabling the migrant population to arrive at the factory gate in Monterrey from neighboring states. Migration to the region picked up dramatically after 1890, when major connections between Monterrey and the rest of the country were completed.

Trends apparent in the late nineteenth century carried over into the period of rapid industrialization after 1940. A significant migrant flow in the 1920s and 1930s, crucial years in the formation of the economic infrastructure on which Mexican industrialization after 1940 would be based, became a flood in the 1940s, 1950s, and 1960s. After a decline in the 1970s, the flow swelled again in the 1970s to reach its highest mark ever during the early years of the Mexican oil boom. These data will have to be compared with similar data, not yet available, from the years of Mexico's economic crisis after 1982. Did the flow to Monterrey de-

[30] Vizcaya Canales, Los Orígenes, p. 78.
[31] See William K. Meyers, "La Comarca Lagunera: Work, Protest, and Popular Mobilization in North Central Mexico," in Thomas Benjamin and William McNellie, eds., Other Mexicos: Essays on Regional Mexican History, 1876–1911 (Albuquerque: University of New Mexico Press, 1984), pp. 243–274.

Figure 37:7

ESTIMATED MIGRANTS TO MONTERREY, 1862–1980

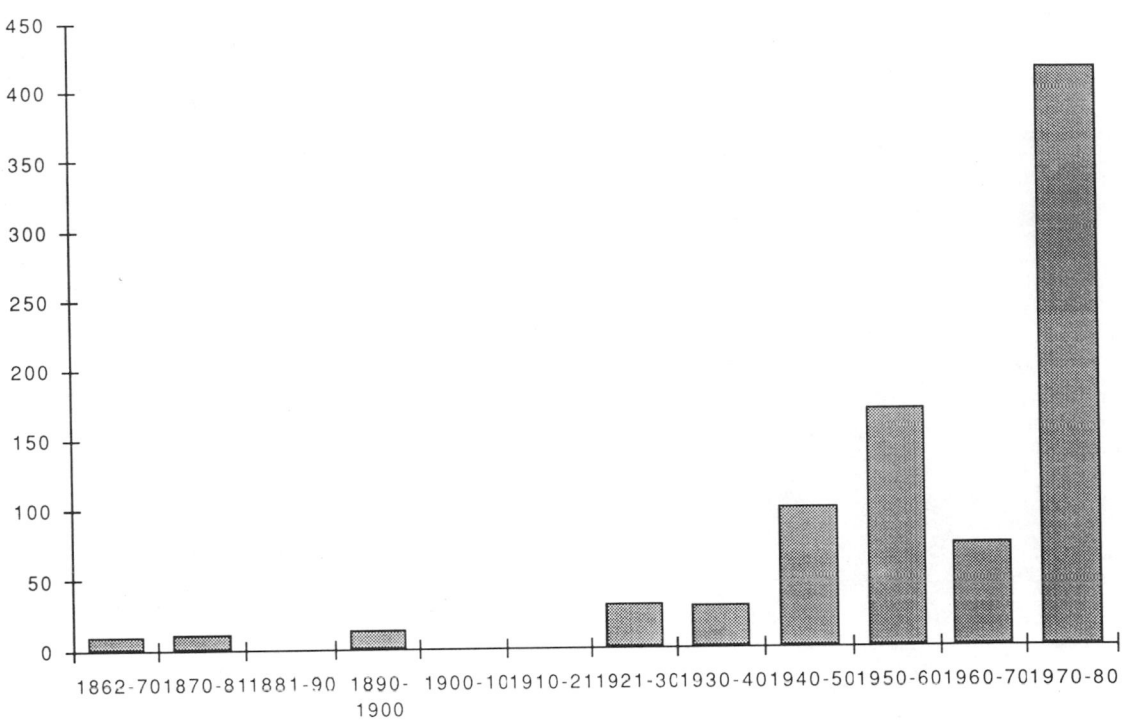

SOURCE: Table 3719.

cline in this period? Has migration experienced a resurgence with the economic restructuring plans of presidential administrations after the mid-1980s?

Conclusions and Implications for Further Research

Basic data sets on population and migration in the Monterrey area presented here reveal several interrelated historical developments. From roughly the middle of the nineteenth century to 1980, the population of Monterrey expanded at a rapid rate in several distinct periods—the 1880s, the 1920s and 1930s, the boom period of Mexico's economic revolution between 1940 and 1960, and the decade of the 1970s. In general these periods reflect the evolution of Monterrey into Mexico's most important regional power outside of Mexico City. Migration to Monterrey has coincided with the pattern of development of the city, particularly responding to changing demands for skilled and semiskilled laborers over time.

The findings presented here indicate several important lacunae in our knowledge of the industrial cities in Mexico from the end of the nineteenth century to the end of the twentieth. The most intriguing perhaps is the question of changing occupations in cities like Monterrey as industrialization proceeded. Data on occupations in Monterrey and Nuevo León present a major challenge to the analyst of population and migration trends in the region. Clearly, important change has occurred. We need to quantify such changes more exactly to know how the process of industrialization shaped occupational structure in the metropolitan area of Monterrey after 1880. In general, we need to know more about the relationship between historical economic development and social life in Mexico's most important regional urban centers.

38

The People Speak:
A Database and Sample Analysis of
Latin American Public Opinion Polls,
1947–86

LOUISE HARRIS BERLIN

James W. Wilkie, Enrique C. Ochoa, and David E. Lorey, eds., *Statistical Abstract of Latin America*, vol. 28 (Los Angeles: UCLA Latin American Center Publications, 1990).

Through surveys and "man on the street" interviews, social scientists and commercial poll takers have long sought to achieve what to many seems impossible: the quantification, or "objectification," of inherently subjective attitudes, feelings, and opinions. In Latin America, due in large part to its relationship with the United States, the search for the "collective consciousness" has been undertaken with varying degrees of fervor over the past four decades.

This essay provides an introduction to survey-taking activity which occurred in twenty Latin American countries between 1947 and 1986. Despite limitations, which are discussed below, the study sheds light on a particular period in recent Latin American history when, it seemed, man actually took an interest in what the people had to say.

My research on the availability of Latin American public opinion polls located in the United States has produced good news and bad news. The good news is that such surveys do exist, and in relative abundance. The bad news is that they do not exist in a form conducive to data manipulation.

Consequently I decided to create a database from which I could assemble time-series data by country, year, type of survey, and so on. At the same time, I surmised that it would not be that much more difficult to create a database that scholars and other interested parties could use to access information on Latin American surveys to help them in their own work. I called my project the Latin American Public Opinion (LAPO) database. What followed was a painful education in the creation of a workable database. Design and data input proved to be difficult and time-consuming, while the analysis of the data turned out to be the simplest part.

Raw Material

Most of the Latin American public opinion surveys for the years 1947 to 1986 which are available in the United States can be found in a relatively few number of repositories. The main archives for such material are the Roper Center at the University of Connecticut, the Inter-University Consortium for Political and Social Research (ICPSR) at the University of Michigan, and the Data and Program Library Service

LOUISE HARRIS BERLIN holds a master's degree in history from UCLA, and a master's degree in broadcasting from San Francisco State University. She currently owns her own writing and consulting firm in Santa Clarita, California.

(DPLS) at the University of Wisconsin. Entries for the database were taken primarily from catalogs provided by those institutions. In addition there are U.S. government agencies, foreign archives, and a host of smaller repositories whose Latin American holdings are minimal, but worth including. Appendix One contains a list of the repositories included in this study.

Indispensable to the compilation of the database was a 1985 study titled "Locations of Publicly-Available Mico-data Sets from Studies in Developing Nations," by Gerald Hursh-Cesar. Working under the auspices of the Foreign Opinion Research Advisory (FORA), Hursch-Cesar compiled a directory of surveys funded by the U.S. government for all Third World nations, including Latin America. His work provided an excellent cross-reference as well as information on surveys located in lesser-known archives. It also discusses in detail such topics as the relative merits of actual data sets and how one goes about obtaining them—areas this project does not attempt to cover.

Another valuable source of information was Joseph Robert Hanc's "Inventory of Quantitative Data Files Relating to Non-Western Nations" (1982). Like Hursh-Cesar, Hanc provided an extremely useful cross-reference as well as perspective on the "Big Picture" related to Latin American data sets.

The first limitation of this study is that the database does not include all available public opinion surveys taken during the study period. The reader's only condolence is that the LAPO database can be easily updated should additional surveys come to light.

Creation of the Database

Appendix Two contains a detailed list of the characteristics which made up each record for the LAPO database. Each record contains 12 fields which offer the following information:

1. Country	7. Decade
2. Year	8. Survey Organization
3. Sample Size	9. Repository
4. Notes	10. Survey Type
5. Title	11. Sample Type
6. Reference Number	12. Data Format

Except for country, year, decade, and repository, each of the fields proved difficult at times to complete. The result, in some instances, has limited the usefulness of the database; for that reason each difficult field and how it was dealt with is discussed in detail below.

Sample Size.—This information was not listed for every survey; when not listed, the option "N/A" for "not available" was recorded. The lack of such information would not be critical except to: (1) those wishing to know such things as precisely how many large- versus small-sample surveys were taken, and (2) those who put credence only in those surveys that adequately represent the total survey population. For the latter group, it must be reported that nearly half of the surveys were taken using relatively small samples (44 percent had either 300 or fewer respondents or an unknown sample size). Does this mean that the opinions gathered did not necessarily reflect the true consciousness of the group in question? Statistically, probably yes. One may assume, however, that more than one economic or public policy decision was influenced by the result of the surveys, regardless of their statistical veracity.

Notes.—This field was filled in at my discretion, most often to highlight multinational studies, cross-references, subjects covered in "omnibus" surveys, etc. The field would have no bearing on an analysis of the data (other than to flesh out the subject matter), but would be useful to a researcher trying to narrow down the selection of records.

Title.—Not every survey had a descriptive title. In fact, many were called simply "Omnibus." In those instances I tried to fill in additional information in the "notes" section.

Reference Number.—This field proved difficult to handle consistently because different sources (e.g., Hanc and Roper) used different reference numbers for the same survey, and some sources (e.g., Roper) did not seem to assign numbers to every survey. When recording Roper and smaller archive material, I used Hanc's identification system because it contains enough clues to find an individual survey, assuming one knows the repository (which is listed separately in the database). For example, the tag "CHUSIAWS3" stands for "Chile–U.S. Information Agency–World Survey 3." A researcher would be able to take that number to the Roper Center and be reasonably sure that someone at the archive would know which study it referred to. Other archives, such as DPLS and ICPSR, were more straightforward; therefore, their identification numbers consist of the letters of the archive and a specific number (e.g. "ICPSR 7054"). The database was constructed to elimate duplicates, which is important in terms of aggregating and analyzing the data.

Survey Organization.—I could not always determine from the description the sponsor of the research—whether it was an organization or an individual. If it was an organization, the affiliation was often unclear. For example, in many instances, although the surveying organization was from the host country, the survey itself was more than likely underwritten by U.S. interests (this was deduced from the content

of many of the surveys). It would be interesting in a future study to clarify the organization in order to show the extent of U.S. influence on Latin American survey activity during the period in question. As the data stand now, however, I would not consider them accurate enough for aggregate analysis.

Survey Type.—This information was based on information contained either in the title or a description of the survey. As shown in Appendix Two, there are several categories to choose from; the "fine lines" (e.g., social versus cultural; social versus sociopolitical) were created in an attempt to be as accurate as possible. Nonetheless it was impossible at times to be entirely objective, especially when the questions in a given survey covered several topics. Finally, where there was neither a title nor a description, the designation "N/A" was used. Overall, 56, or 8.9 percent, fell into that category. It is the reader's prerogative to accept or reject my choice of survey type designations.

Sample Type.—This was another difficult category, simply because survey respondents invariably fell into multiple categories. In some cases one characteristic of the sample population stood out, such as women and youth, but these were the exception rather than the rule. Usually, when there were two strong characteristics (e.g., "adults in Rio"), I chose the more specific of the two. In the case of "adults in Rio," I chose "urban" because it narrowed down the population more than would have been the case with the label "adults." Here again, subjectivity played a role and it is up to the reader to accept or reject the data's validity on that basis.

Data Form.—This information was not always available, which makes aggregate analysis unreliable. Furthermore, the status of much of the data has changed over the years. For that reason, those using the database to obtain specific surveys should contact the repository once they have determined which surveys they are interested in viewing. The archive will then be able to tell them not only its present format but its availability.

Other Limitations.—A few other problems presented themselves during the course of this project. One is the question of series surveys, i.e., those that were conducted over a number of years. In those cases, I treated the final year as the year of the survey, and noted that it was a series under the "notes" section. Unfortunately, there is no way to pull out series surveys only; one must read all the notes sections to find them. Cross-national surveys were another anomaly. In those cases, each country received its own entry and a different identification number. Again, the "notes" section was used to identify it as cross-national, and the only way to determine that would be by reading all "notes" sections.

Despite the many problems encountered in creating the LAPO database, on the whole it contains accurate information about the most commonly archived data sets concerning Latin American public opinion surveys for the years

1947–86. From the aggregate figures in the next section emerges a clear picture of the kinds of surveys taken, when they were taken, and where.

General Analysis of the Data

Appendix Three contains an abbreviated version of the LAPO database in column format, displaying the categories of country, year, survey type, and repository in chronological order. Although 631 entries were recorded, three of them were nineteenth-century studies and one was listed for 1910. For the purposes of this analysis they were excluded, leaving a total number of 627.

By Nation

An analysis of surveys by nation shows that the larger countries—Brazil, Argentina, and Mexico— garnered the largest share of activity (62 percent). Chile, Venezuela, Colombia, and Uruguay claim fewer, but still significant, numbers, while the surveys collected for the Andean countries (Bolivia, Peru, Ecuador) and Central America are far fewer in number. Twenty-three of the surveys were broad enough to be classified under "Latin America." More than just surveys, the latter often represent aggregate time-series data collected for each country. Table 3800 and Figure 38:1 show the surveys taken, by country, including percentage of the total database.

Table 3800

LATIN AMERICAN PUBLIC OPINION SURVEYS, 20 LR

	Country/Group	Surveys (N)	% of Total
A.	ARGENTINA	89	14.2
B.	BOLIVIA	2	.3
C.	BRAZIL	258	41.1
D.	CHILE	44	7.0
E.	COLOMBIA	21	3.3
F.	COSTA RICA	12	1.9
G.	CUBA	10	1.6
H.	DOMINICAN REP.	5	.8
I.	ECUADOR	9	1.4
J.	EL SALVADOR	10	1.6
K.	GUATEMALA	5	.8
L.	HAITI	6	1.0
M.	HONDURAS	4	.6
N.	MEXICO	42	6.7
O.	NICARAGUA	1	.2
P.	PANAMA	9	1.4
Q.	PARAGUAY	3	.5
R.	PERU	12	1.9
S.	URUGUAY	32	5.1
T.	VENEZUELA	30	4.8
	LATIN AMERICA	23	3.7
	TOTAL	627	99.9
	Andean Countries	23	3.6
	Central America	43	6.9

Figure 38:1

LATIN AMERICAN PUBLIC OPINION SURVEYS, BY COUNTRY AND REGION, 1947–86

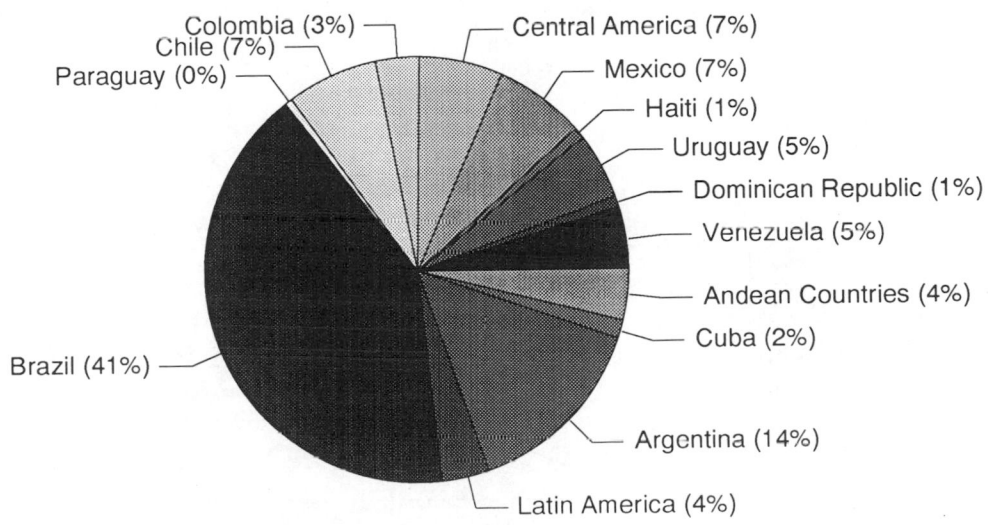

By Decade

A breakdown by decade shows that four studies were filed for the 1940s; 40 for the 1950s; 374 for the 1960s; 187 for the 1970s; and 22 for the 1980s, illustrated in percentage form in Table 3801 and Figure 38:2.

The 1960s were the "Golden Age" of public opinion surveys; since poll-taking had existed for many years prior to the sixties, one must assume that its use flourished not because it was a novel way of collecting data, but because the information itself was deemed important enough to collect by an increasing number of interested parties.

By Survey Type

A look at the types of surveys on file reveals something about the surge of survey-taking in the 1960s and 1970s. Out of 627 studies on file, 150 were political; 98 were socio-political; 69 were social; 64 were cultural; 60 were socio-economic; 47 were economic; and 46 were health-related. A total of 13 fell into the categories of scientific, agricultural, environmental, and religious. Twenty-four were Omnibus and 56 were unable to be categorized. Table 3802 and Figure 38:3 show the breakdown by percentage, and Appendix Four shows the breakdown of survey type by decade for each country.

By Repository

As mentioned above, one can find a majority of the archived Latin American public opinion surveys on file in three repositories: the Roper Center, the ICPSR, and the DPLS. These sources constitute 86.2 percent of the total (Table 3803 and Figure 38:4). Those wishing to find out more about a particular archive may do so by writing to the institution (see Appendix One for the addresses).

Sample National Data Analysis: Mexico

To illustrate the LAPO database in more detail I have included the complete records which pertain to Mexico.

Table 3801

LATIN AMERICAN PUBLIC OPINION SURVEYS, BY DECADE

Decade	Studies (N)	% of Total
1940s	4	.6
1950s	40	6.4
1960s	374	59.6
1970s	187	29.8
1980s	22	3.5
Total	627	99.9

Figure 38:2

LATIN AMERICAN PUBLIC OPINION SURVEYS, BY DECADE

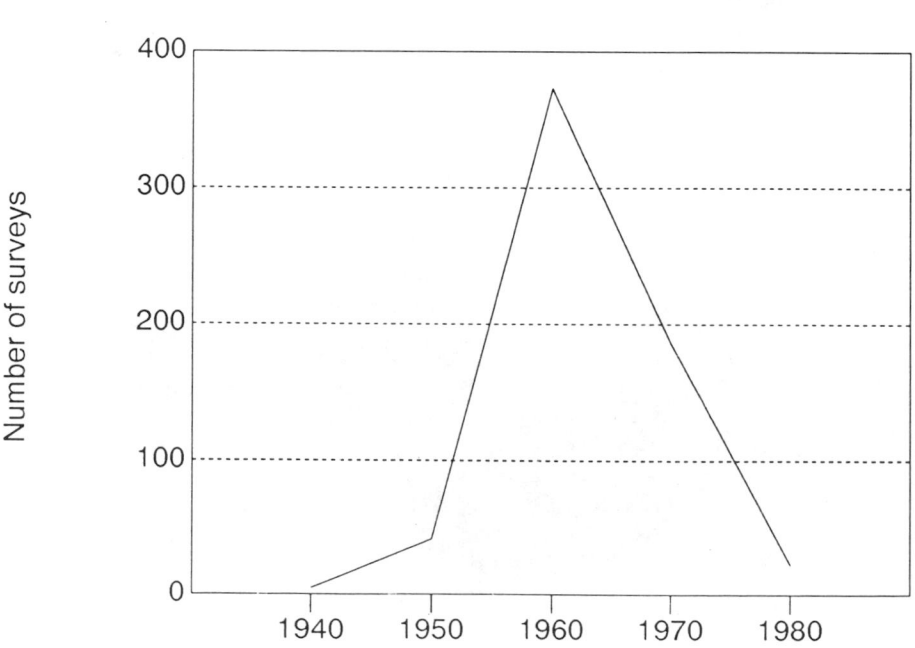

Table 3802

LATIN AMERICAN PUBLIC OPINION SURVEYS, BY TYPE

Survey Type	Studies (N)	% of Total
Political	150	23.9
Sociopolitical	98	15.6
Social	69	11.0
Cultural	64	10.2
Socioeconomic	60	9.6
N/A	56	8.9
Economic	47	7.5
Health	46	7.3
Omnibus	24	3.8
Other	13	2.1
Total	627	99.9

Table 3805

MEXICAN PUBLIC OPINION SURVEYS, BY TYPE

Survey Type	Surveys (N)	% of Total
Agricultural	2	4.7
Cultural	2	4.7
Economic	7	16.3
Health	3	7.0
Political	17	39.5
Social	4	9.3
Socioeconomic	4	9.3
Sociopolitical	3	7.0
N/A	1	2.3
Total	43	100.1

Table 3806

MEXICAN PUBLIC OPINION SURVEYS, BY ARCHIVE

Archive	Surveys (N)	% of Total
DAEDAC	1	2.3
DPLS	7	10.0
Host Country	1	2.3
ICPSR	5	11.6
PSDL–IN	1	2.3
ROPER	21	48.8
USNA	3	7.0
Other	1	2.3
N/A	3	7.0
Total	43	99.9

Table 3803

LATIN AMERICAN PUBLIC OPINION SURVEYS, BY ARCHIVE

Archive	Surveys (N)	% of Total
Roper	424	67.6
DPLS	68	10.8
ICPSR	49	7.8
All Others	86	13.7
Total	627	99.9

Table 3804

MEXICAN PUBLIC OPINION SURVEYS, BY DECADE

Decade	Surveys (N)	% of Total
1910	1	2.3
1920	*	**
1930	*	**
1940	*	**
1950	8	18.6
1960	20	46.5
1970	11	25.6
1980	3	7.0
Total	43	100.0

Those records, 43 in all, are contained in Appendix Five; they include a study dating back to 1917. Tables 3804, 3805, and 3806 include information on chronology, survey type, and archive, respectively.

It is apparent from the data that most of the surveys currently archived were undertaken during the 1960s and 1970s, and that nearly half were politically oriented in whole or in part.

Avenues for Further Study

Creating the LAPO database was no small undertaking, and I hope that with some modifications (such as transferring the data from the working software program, Cornerstone, to Lotus 1-2-3[1]) it will become a useful tool for those

---

[1] Lotus 1-2-3 is a trademark of the Lotus Development Corporation.

Figure 38:3

LATIN AMERICAN PUBLIC OPINION SURVEYS, BY TYPE

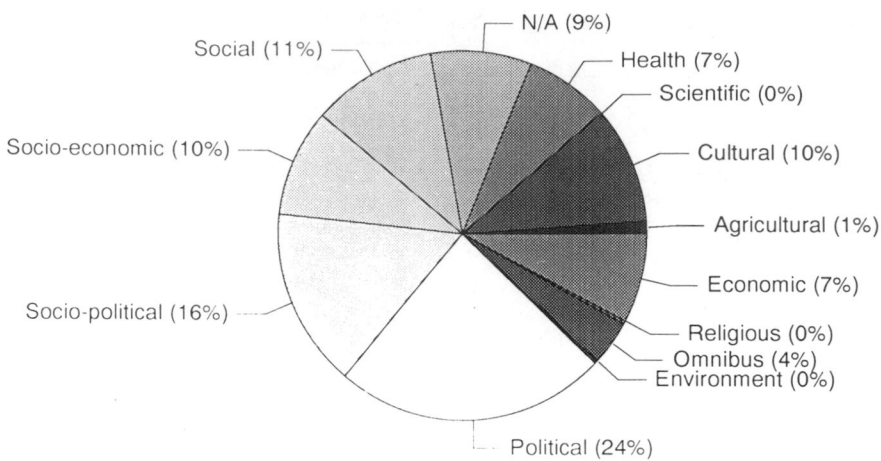

Figure 38:4

LATIN AMERICAN PUBLIC OPINION SURVEYS, BY ARCHIVE

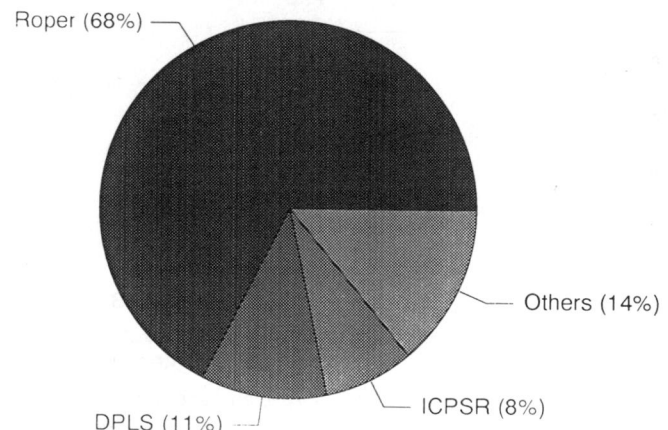

interested in researching specific public opinion surveys. Currently, a complete copy of the LAPO database is housed in disc and printed form at the UCLA Latin American Center.

In aggregate form, the data suggest an intense period in recent Latin American History when social scientists and politicians sought answers to relevant questions of the day outside of hallowed halls and smokey back rooms. Whether motivated by idealism, Cold War paranoia, or some combination thereof, the sponsors of such surveys seemed acutely interested in what the "man on the street" was thinking. It would be worthwhile, I think, to delve more deeply into the sponsorship of the surveys. For example, what percentage were directly or indirectly conducted by the U.S. government? Were the sponsors sincere in seeking public opinion or did they harbor ulterior motives? To what extent were public policy decisions influenced by the survey results? What motivated academicians and other nonpolitical organizations? Why did the survey-taking dry up? As in any field of inquiry, a small inroad often leads to more questions than answers.

APPENDIX ONE

ACRONYMS AND ADDRESSES OF ARCHIVES
USED IN THE DATABASE

BASS
Archives Belges en Science Sociales
Place Montesquieu, a boite 18
B-1348 Louvain-la-neuve (Belgium)
Université Catholique de Louvain

BSL-Cin
Behavioral Sciences Laboratory
University of Cincinnati
Mail Location #132
Cincinnati, Ohio 45221

CCSDA-York
Canadian Social Science Archive
Institute for Behavioral Research
York University
4700 Keele Street
Downsview, Ontario
Canada M3J2R6

DAEDAC
Drug Abuse Epidemiology Data Center
Institute of Behavioral Research
Texas Christian University
Fort Worth, Texas 76129

DPLS
Data and Program Library Service
Data and Computation Center
4452 Social Science Building
University of Wisconsin
Madison, Wisconsin 53706

ICPSR
Inter-University Consortium for
    Political and Social Research
Member Services
P.O. Box 1248
Ann Arbor, Michigan 48106

MULHALL
Project MULHALL
c/o Department of Economics BEB-400
University of Texas
Austin, Texas 78712

PrinU
Princeton University Computer Center
87 Prospect Avenue
Princeton, New Jersey 08540

PSDL-IN
Political Science Data Library
Department of Political Science
Woodburn Hall 214 A
Indiana University
Bloomington, Indiana 47405

Roper
The Roper Center
Office of Archival Development and
    User Service
The University of Connecticut
Box U-164R
Storrs, Connecticut 06268

SSDA-Carl
Social Science Data Archive
Carleton University
Department of Sociology and
    Anthropology
Room A 711, Loeb Building
Ottawa, Canada K1S 5B6

SSRC-UK
Social Science Research Council
Survey Archive
University of Essex, Wivenhoe Park
Colchester, Essex C04 3SQ
United Kingdom

Stein
Steinmetzarchief
Herengracht 410
1017 RR Amsterdam
Netherlands

USNA
Reference Service
Machine Readable Archives Division
    (NNR)
National Archives and Records Division
Washington, D.C. 20408

SOURCE: "Inventory of Quantitative Data Files Relating to Non-Western Nations," by Joseph Robert Hanc (University of Chicago, Civilizations Course Materials Project, 1982).

APPENDIX TWO

DATABASE FIELDS AND CHOICE OF ATTRIBUTES

COUNTRY:

Argentina	Haiti
Bolivia	Mexico
Brazil	Panama
Chile	Paraguay
Colombia	Peru
Costa Rica	Uruguay
Cuba	Venezuela
Dominican Republic	Latin America
Ecuador	Central America
El Salvador	South America
Guatemala	

YEAR: 1700–1988

SAMPLE SIZE: Any number

NOTES: When appropriate

TITLE: Per study

REFERENCE NUMBER: Per study; no duplicates

DECADE: Derived from year

SURVEY ORGANIZATION:
Individual – Academica
Academic Organization
U.S. Government
Host Country
Commercial
U.S. Contractor
Other
N/A

REPOSITORY:

BASS	Other
BSL-Cin	PrinU
CCSDA-York	PSDL-IN
CCSDA-York	Roper

REPOSITORY (Continued):

DAEDAC	SSSA-Carl
DPLS	SSRC-UK
Host Country	Stein
ICPSR	USNA
Individuals	N/A
Mulhall	

SURVEY TYPE:

Agricultural	Political
Cultural	Religious
Economic	Social
Environment	Socio-economic
Health	Socio-political
Omnibus	Scientific
N/A	

SAMPLE TYPE:

Adults	N/A
Children/Youth/Students	Other
Clergy	Professionals
Elite	Regional
Labor	Rural
Male Adults	Teachers
Management/White Collar	University Students
Military	Urban
Mixed Groups	Various
National	Women

DATA FORMAT:
Card
Magnetic Tape
Disk
Manual
Other
N/A

APPENDIX THREE

PUBLIC OPINION SURVEYS, 20 L, 1947–86

Country	Year	Survey Type	Repository
Cuba	1820	Economic	DPLS
Brazil	1830	Economic	DPLS
Brazil	1852	Economic	DPLS
Mexico	1917	Political	DPLS
Argentina	1947	Political	DPLS
Venezuela	1947	N/A	Roper
Argentina	1947	Political	DPLS
Argentina	1947	Political	DPLS
Cuba	1950	Socio-economic	Roper
Latin America	1950	Economic	MULHALL
Argentina	1955	Political	DPLS
Brazil	1955	Political	Roper
Chile	1955	Socio-economic	Roper
Cuba	1955	Political	Roper
Brazil	1955	Political	Roper
Colombia	1955	Political	Roper
Venezuela	1955	Political	Roper
Mexico	1955	Political	Roper
Venezuela	1955	Political	Roper
Argentina	1955	Political	DPLS
Chile	1956	N/A	DPLS
Brazil	1956	N/A	Roper
Chile	1956	Socio-economic	Roper
Chile	1956	N/A	Roper
Cuba	1956	Socio-economic	Roper
Chile	1956	Social	Roper
Mexico	1956	Political	Roper
Uruguay	1956	Political	Roper
Chile	1956	Economic	PSDL–IN
Guatemala	1957	Political	Roper
Venezuela	1957	Economic	Roper
Chile	1958	Political	ICPSR
Chile	1958	Political	DPLS
Chile	1958	Political	Roper
Chile	1958	Socio-political	Roper
Cuba	1958	Economic	Roper
Mexico	1958	Economic	Roper
Mexico	1958	Socio-economic	Roper
Mexico	1958	Political	Roper
Venezuela	1958	Cultural	Roper
Venezuela	1958	Political	Roper
Uruguay	1958	Political	Roper
Mexico	1959	Political	ICPSR
Mexico	1959	Political	ICPSR
Brazil	1959	Socio-economic	DPLS
Brazil	1959	N/A	Roper
Mexico	1959	Socio-political	Roper
Venezuela	1959	Political	Roper
Argentina	1960	Social	ICPSR

APPENDIX THREE (Continued)

PUBLIC OPINION SURVEYS, 20 L, 1947–86

Country	Year	Survey Type	Repository
Brazil	1960	Social	ICPSR
Brazil	1960	Socio-economic	ICPSR
Brazil	1960	Socio-economic	ICPSR
Brazil	1960	Socio-political	ICPSR
Cuba	1960	Political	ICPSR
Cuba	1960	Social	ICPSR
Mexico	1960	Socio-political	ICPSR
Argentina	1960	Socio-economic	DPLS
Brazil	1960	Socio-economic	DPLS
Brazil	1960	N/A	DPLS
Cuba	1960	N/A	DPLS
Dominican Republic	1960	N/A	DPLS
Mexico	1960	Socio-economic	DPLS
El Salvador	1960	Socio-economic	DPLS
Costa Rica	1960	Socio-economic	DPLS
Brazil	1960	Political	Roper
Chile	1960	Economic	Roper
Costa Rica	1960	Social	Roper
El Salvador	1960	Social	DPLS
Cuba	1960	Socio-political	Roper
Mexico	1960	Socio-economic	Roper
Latin America	1960	Socio-political	PSDL-IN
Mexico	1960	Social	OTHER
Brazil	1960	Social	DPLS
Brazil	1961	Cultural	ICPSR
Chile	1961	Socio-economic	ICPSR
Argentina	1961	Scientific	DPLS
Brazil	1961	N/A	DPLS
Chile	1961	Socio-economic	DPLS
Latin America	1961	Socio-economic	DPLS
Argentina	1961	Political	Roper
Brazil	1961	Health	Roper
Brazil	1961	Political	Roper
Brazil	1961	Political	Roper
Mexico	1961	Political	Roper
Colombia	1961	Political	Roper
Mexico	1961	Health	Roper
Mexico	1961	Political	Roper
Peru	1961	Cultural	Roper
Peru	1961	Cultural	Roper
Peru	1961	Cultural	Roper
Venezuela	1961	Political	Roper
Uruguay	1961	Political	Roper
Uruguay	1961	Political	Roper
Brazil	1961	Social	BASS
Brazil	1962	Socio-economic	ICPSR
Chile	1962	Socio-economic	ICPSR
Panama	1962	Socio-political	ICPSR
Colombia	1962	Political	ICPSR

APPENDIX THREE (Continued)

PUBLIC OPINION SURVEYS, 20 L, 1947–86

Country	Year	Survey Type	Repository
Dominican Republic	1962	Socio-political	ICPSR
Brazil	1962	Social	DPLS
Chile	1962	N/A	HOST COUNTRY
Panama	1962	N/A	DPLS
Argentina	1962	Socio-economic	Roper
Brazil	1962	Political	Roper
Chile	1962	Political	Roper
Colombia	1962	Political	Roper
Bolivia	1962	Political	Roper
Brazil	1962	Political	Roper
Dominican Republic	1962	Political	Roper
Ecuador	1962	Political	Roper
El Salvador	1962	Socio-economic	Roper
El Salvador	1962	Socio-economic	Roper
Panama	1962	Political	Roper
Venezuela	1962	Political	Roper
Chile	1962	N/A	BASS
Brazil	1962	Social	DPLS
Argentina	1963	Political	ICPSR
Argentina	1963	Political	ICPSR
Argentina	1963	Political	ICPSR
Brazil	1963	Cultural	ICPSR
Chile	1963	Agricultural	ICPSR
Chile	1963	Social	ICPSR
Mexico	1963	Social	ICPSR
Argentina	1963	Economic	HOST COUNTRY
Mexico	1963	Cultural	DPLS
Argentina	1963	Health	Roper
Argentina	1963	Political	Roper
Argentina	1963	Cultural	Roper
Argentina	1963	Health	Roper
Brazil	1963	Cultural	Roper
Brazil	1963	Social	Roper
Brazil	1963	Socio-political	Roper
Brazil	1963	Socio-political	Roper
Brazil	1963	Political	Roper
Brazil	1963	Political	Roper
Chile	1963	Political	Roper
Chile	1963	Agricultural	Roper
Argentina	1963	N/A	Roper
Argentina	1963	Political	Roper
Mexico	1963	Political	Roper
Chile	1963	Political	Roper
Venezuela	1963	Political	Roper
Venezuela	1963	Political	Roper
Chile	1964	Political	ICPSR
Chile	1964	Socio-economic	ICPSR
Brazil	1964	Socio-political	ICPSR
Brazil	1964	Socio-political	ICPSR

APPENDIX THREE (Continued)

PUBLIC OPINION SURVEYS, 20 L, 1947–86

Country	Year	Survey Type	Repository
Panama	1964	Political	ICPSR
Venezuela	1964	Religious	ICPSR
Colombia	1964	Political	ICPSR
Brazil	1964	Economic	HOST COUNTRY
Chile	1964	Socio-economic	DPLS
Colombia	1964	Cultural	DPLS
Costa Rica	1964	Health	DPLS
Costa Rica	1964	Economic	DPLS
Argentina	1964	Health	Roper
Argentina	1964	Political	Roper
Brazil	1964	Health	Roper
Brazil	1964	Political	Roper
Chile	1964	Political	Roper
Chile	1964	Political	Roper
Chile	1964	Social	Roper
Chile	1964	Social	Roper
Chile	1964	Social	Roper
Chile	1964	Social	Roper
Chile	1964	Socio-economic	Roper
Chile	1964	Political	Roper
Chile	1964	Political	Roper
Chile	1964	N/A	Roper
Costa Rica	1964	Cultural	Roper
Mexico	1964	Political	Roper
Mexico	1964	Political	Roper
Colombia	1964	Health	Roper
Chile	1964	Political	Roper
Venezuela	1964	Political	Roper
Mexico	1964	Socio-economic	Roper
Venezuela	1964	Health	Roper
Venezuela	1964	Political	Roper
Chile	1964	Political	Roper
Panama	1964	Health	Roper
Venezuela	1964	Socio-economic	Roper
Uruguay	1964	Political	Roper
Costa Rica	1964	Economic	DPLS
Argentina	1965	Socio-economic	ICPSR
Argentina	1965	Political	ICPSR
Latin America	1965	Socio-political	ICPSR
Latin America	1965	Omnibus	DPLS
Latin America	1965	Health	DPLS
Argentina	1965	Political	Roper
Argentina	1965	Political	Roper
Brazil	1965	Political	Roper
Brazil	1965	Socio-economic	Roper
Brazil	1965	Socio-political	Roper
Ecuador	1965	Health	Roper
Argentina	1965	Political	Roper
Mexico	1965	Political	Roper

APPENDIX THREE (Continued)

PUBLIC OPINION SURVEYS, 20 L, 1947–86

Country	Year	Survey Type	Repository
Mexico	1965	Economic	Roper
Mexico	1965	Economic	Roper
Venezuela	1965	Political	Roper
Guatemala	1965	Cultural	Roper
Costa Rica	1965	Cultural	Roper
Uruguay	1965	Socio-political	Roper
Uruguay	1965	Political	Roper
Uruguay	1965	Political	Roper
Uruguay	1965	Political	Roper
Uruguay	1965	Political	Roper
Uruguay	1965	Political	Roper
Argentina	1965	Economic	CSSDA–York
Latin America	1965	Political	BSL–Cin
Latin America	1965	N/A	STEIN
Latin America	1965	Economic	SSDA–CARL
Latin America	1965	N/A	DPLS
Latin America	1965	Socio-political	BSL–Cin
Latin America	1965	Social	SSDA–CARL
Latin America	1965	Economic	PrinU
Latin America	1965	Social	DPLS
Costa Rica	1965	Health	DPLS
Brazil	1966	Political	ICPSR
Uruguay	1966	Political	ICPSR
Paraguay	1966	Political	ICPSR
Argentina	1966	Social	DPLS
Brazil	1966	Economic	DPLS
Colombia	1966	Agricultural	DPLS
Mexico	1966	Agricultural	DPLS
Uruguay	1966	Political	DPLS
Argentina	1966	N/A	Roper
Argentina	1966	N/A	Roper
Argentina	1966	N/A	Roper
Argentina	1966	N/A	Roper
Argentina	1966	N/A	Roper
Argentina	1966	N/A	Roper
Argentina	1966	N/A	Roper
Argentina	1966	N/A	Roper
Argentina	1966	N/A	Roper
Argentina	1966	N/A	Roper
Argentina	1966	N/A	Roper
Argentina	1966	N/A	Roper
Argentina	1966	N/A	Roper
Argentina	1966	N/A	Roper
Argentina	1966	N/A	Roper
Argentina	1966	Cultural	Roper
Brazil	1966	Social	Roper
Costa Rica	1966	Socio-political	Roper
Uruguay	1966	Political	Roper

APPENDIX THREE (Continued)

PUBLIC OPINION SURVEYS, 20 L, 1947–86

Country	Year	Survey Type	Repository
Uruguay	1966	Political	Roper
Uruguay	1966	Political	Roper
Uruguay	1966	N/A	Roper
Uruguay	1966	Political	Roper
Uruguay	1966	Political	Roper
Uruguay	1966	Political	Roper
Uruguay	1966	Political	Roper
Colombia	1966	Agricultural	DPLS
Uruguay	1966	Political	DPLS
Brazil	1966	Social	DPLS
Peru	1966	N/A	LSDB
Latin America	1967	Political	ICPSR
Latin America	1967	Political	ICPSR
Argentina	1967	Religious	Roper
Argentina	1967	N/A	Roper
Argentina	1967	N/A	Roper
Argentina	1967	N/A	Roper
Argentina	1967	N/A	Roper
Argentina	1967	N/A	Roper
Argentina	1967	N/A	Roper
Argentina	1967	N/A	Roper
Argentina	1967	N/A	Roper
Argentina	1967	N/A	Roper
Argentina	1967	Political	Roper
Brazil	1967	Economic	Roper
Brazil	1967	Omnibus	Roper
Brazil	1967	Omnibus	Roper
Brazil	1967	Omnibus	Roper
Brazil	1967	Omnibus	Roper
Brazil	1967	Socio-political	Roper
Brazil	1967	Socio-political	Roper
Brazil	1967	Political	Roper
Brazil	1967	Socio-political	Roper
Brazil	1967	Economic	Roper
Venezuela	1967	Political	Roper
Uruguay	1967	Political	Roper
Uruguay	1967	Socio-political	Roper
Uruguay	1967	Socio-political	Roper
Uruguay	1967	Socio-political	Roper
Uruguay	1967	Socio-political	Roper
Uruguay	1967	Socio-political	Roper
Uruguay	1967	N/A	Roper
Latin America	1967	Socio-political	PSDL–IN
Brazil	1967	Economic	PSDL–IN
Colombia	1967	Economic	PSDL–IN
Mexico	1967	Economic	PSDL–IN
Peru	1967	Economic	PSDL–IN
Venezuela	1967	Economic	PSDL–IN

APPENDIX THREE (Continued)

PUBLIC OPINION SURVEYS, 20 L, 1947–86

Country	Year	Survey Type	Repository
Brazil	1968	Social	DPLS
Brazil	1968	Cultural	DPLS
Peru	1968	Cultural	DPLS
Argentina	1968	N/A	Roper
Brazil	1968	Political	Roper
Brazil	1968	Political	Roper
Brazil	1968	Political	Roper
Brazil	1968	Political	Roper
Brazil	1968	Political	Roper
Brazil	1968	Political	Roper
Brazil	1968	Political	Roper
Brazil	1968	Political	Roper
Brazil	1968	Political	Roper
Brazil	1968	Health	Roper
Brazil	1968	Health	Roper
Brazil	1968	Health	Roper
Brazil	1968	Political	Roper
Brazil	1968	Cultural	Roper
Brazil	1968	Social	Roper
Brazil	1968	Political	Roper
Brazil	1968	Political	Roper
Brazil	1968	Social	Roper
Brazil	1968	Social	Roper
Brazil	1968	Socio-political	Roper
Brazil	1968	Political	Roper
Brazil	1968	Political	Roper
Brazil	1968	Socio-political	Roper
Brazil	1968	Omnibus	Roper
Brazil	1968	Political	Roper
Brazil	1968	Socio-political	Roper
Brazil	1968	Omnibus	Roper
Brazil	1968	Omnibus	Roper
Brazil	1968	Socio-political	Roper
Brazil	1968	Socio-political	Roper
Brazil	1968	Socio-political	Roper
Brazil	1968	Socio-political	Roper
Brazil	1968	Socio-political	Roper
Brazil	1968	Socio-political	Roper
Brazil	1968	Socio-political	Roper
Brazil	1968	Socio-political	Roper
Brazil	1968	Socio-political	Roper
Brazil	1968	Religious	Roper
Brazil	1968	Cultural	Roper
Brazil	1968	Social	Roper
Brazil	1968	Social	Roper
Brazil	1968	Social	Roper
Brazil	1968	Social	Roper
Brazil	1968	Economic	Roper
Brazil	1968	Socio-political	Roper

APPENDIX THREE (Continued)

PUBLIC OPINION SURVEYS, 20 L, 1947–86

Country	Year	Survey Type	Repository
Brazil	1968	Socio-political	Roper
Brazil	1968	Socio-political	Roper
Brazil	1968	Socio-economic	Roper
Brazil	1968	Political	Roper
Chile	1968	Socio-economic	Roper
Chile	1968	Socio-economic	Roper
Colombia	1968	Political	Roper
Cuba	1968	Political	Roper
El Salvador	1968	Socio-political	Roper
El Salvador	1968	Social	Roper
Mexico	1968	Cultural	Roper
Mexico	1968	Political	Roper
Venezuela	1968	Political	Roper
Argentina	1968	Socio-political	PSDL–IN
Brazil	1968	Social	DPLS
Argentina	1968	Social	DPLS
Brazil	1968	Social	DPLS
Peru	1968	Cultural	DPLS
Brazil	1968	Socio-political	Roper
Brazil	1968	Socio-political	Roper
Argentina	1969	Omnibus	Roper
Argentina	1969	Socio-economic	Roper
Argentina	1969	Economic	Roper
Argentina	1969	Economic	Roper
Brazil	1969	Socio-political	Roper
Brazil	1969	Socio-political	Roper
Brazil	1969	Socio-political	Roper
Brazil	1969	Socio-political	Roper
Brazil	1969	Socio-political	Roper
Brazil	1969	Socio-economic	Roper
Brazil	1969	Socio-political	Roper
Brazil	1969	Socio-political	Roper
Brazil	1969	Socio-political	Roper
Brazil	1969	Socio-political	Roper
Brazil	1969	Socio-political	Roper
Brazil	1969	Socio-political	Roper
Brazil	1969	Socio-political	Roper
Brazil	1969	Socio-economic	Roper
Brazil	1969	Socio-political	Roper
Brazil	1969	Socio-political	Roper
Brazil	1969	Economic	Roper
Brazil	1969	Socio-political	Roper
Brazil	1969	Socio-political	Roper
Brazil	1969	Socio-political	Roper
Brazil	1969	Socio-political	Roper
Brazil	1969	Socio-political	Roper
Brazil	1969	Socio-political	Roper
Brazil	1969	Socio-political	Roper

APPENDIX THREE (Continued)

PUBLIC OPINION SURVEYS, 20 L, 1947–86

Country	Year	Survey Type	Repository
Brazil	1969	Socio-political	Roper
Brazil	1969	Socio-political	Roper
Brazil	1969	Socio-economic	Roper
Brazil	1969	Socio-political	Roper
Brazil	1969	Political	Roper
Brazil	1969	Socio-political	Roper
Brazil	1969	Socio-political	Roper
Brazil	1969	Socio-political	Roper
Brazil	1969	Cultural	Roper
Brazil	1969	Political	Roper
Brazil	1969	Cultural	Roper
Brazil	1969	Socio-political	Roper
Brazil	1969	Socio-political	Roper
Brazil	1969	Social	Roper
Brazil	1969	Socio-political	Roper
Brazil	1969	Socio-political	Roper
Brazil	1969	Social	Roper
Brazil	1969	Socio-political	Roper
Brazil	1969	Socio-political	Roper
Brazil	1969	Socio-political	Roper
Brazil	1969	Social	Roper
Brazil	1969	Social	Roper
Brazil	1969	Cultural	Roper
Colombia	1969	Political	Roper
Colombia	1969	Political	Roper
Colombia	1969	Political	Roper
Dominican Republic	1969	Economic	BASS
Brazil	1969	Socio-political	Roper
Brazil	1969	Socio-political	Roper
Brazil	1969	Socio-political	Roper
Brazil	1970	Omnibus	DPLS
Brazil	1970	Omnibus	DPLS
Brazil	1970	Omnibus	DPLS
Brazil	1970	Omnibus	DPLS
Brazil	1970	Omnibus	DPLS
Chile	1970	N/A	HOST COUNTRY
Chile	1970	Omnibus	HOST COUNTRY
Argentina	1970	Economic	Roper
Argentina	1970	Economic	Roper
Argentina	1970	Cultural	Roper
Brazil	1970	Social	Roper
Brazil	1970	Social	Roper
Brazil	1970	Political	Roper
Brazil	1970	Political	Roper
Brazil	1970	Cultural	Roper
Brazil	1970	Cultural	Roper
Brazil	1970	Socio-political	Roper
Brazil	1970	Social	Roper
Brazil	1970	Social	Roper

APPENDIX THREE (Continued)

PUBLIC OPINION SURVEYS, 20 L, 1947–86

Country	Year	Survey Type	Repository
Brazil	1970	Socio-political	Roper
Brazil	1970	Cultural	Roper
Brazil	1970	Socio-political	Roper
Brazil	1970	Socio-economic	Roper
Brazil	1970	Socio-political	Roper
Brazil	1970	Social	Roper
Brazil	1970	Socio-economic	Roper
Brazil	1970	Socio-economic	Roper
Brazil	1970	Social	Roper
Brazil	1970	Economic	Roper
Brazil	1970	Social	Roper
Brazil	1970	Social	Roper
Brazil	1970	Cultural	Roper
Brazil	1970	Cultural	Roper
Brazil	1970	Cultural	Roper
Brazil	1970	Cultural	Roper
Brazil	1970	Cultural	Roper
Brazil	1970	Cultural	Roper
Brazil	1970	Social	Roper
Brazil	1970	Political	Roper
Brazil	1970	Socio-economic	Roper
Brazil	1970	Economic	Roper
Brazil	1970	Social	Roper
Brazil	1970	Socio-political	Roper
Brazil	1970	Cultural	Roper
Brazil	1970	Cultural	Roper
Brazil	1970	Social	Roper
Brazil	1970	Cultural	Roper
Brazil	1970	Socio-economic	Roper
Brazil	1970	Socio-political	Roper
Argentina	1970	Political	Roper
Venezuela	1970	Cultural	Roper
Uruguay	1970	Cultural	Roper
Peru	1970	Social	STEIN
Argentina	1970	N/A	Roper
Haiti	1971	Health	OTHER
Mexico	1971	Political	DPLS
Latin America	1971	Socio-economic	DPLS
Argentina	1971	Economic	Roper
Argentina	1971	Political	Roper
Argentina	1971	Socio-economic	Roper
Argentina	1971	Omnibus	Roper
Argentina	1971	Political	Roper
Argentina	1971	Political	Roper
Argentina	1971	Socio-economic	Roper
Argentina	1971	N/A	Roper
Argentina	1971	N/A	Roper
Argentina	1971	N/A	Roper
Argentina	1971	N/A	Roper

APPENDIX THREE (Continued)

PUBLIC OPINION SURVEYS, 20 L, 1947–86

Country	Year	Survey Type	Repository
Argentina	1971	Omnibus	Roper
Brazil	1971	Economic	Roper
Brazil	1971	Socio-economic	Roper
Brazil	1971	Cultural	Roper
Brazil	1971	Political	Roper
Brazil	1971	Cultural	Roper
Brazil	1971	Cultural	Roper
Brazil	1971	Cultural	Roper
Brazil	1971	Cultural	Roper
Brazil	1971	Socio-economic	Roper
Brazil	1971	Socio-economic	Roper
Brazil	1971	Social	Roper
Brazil	1971	Cultural	Roper
Brazil	1971	Health	Roper
Brazil	1971	Cultural	Roper
Brazil	1971	Social	Roper
Brazil	1971	Cultural	Roper
Brazil	1971	Cultural	Roper
Brazil	1971	Cultural	Roper
Ecuador	1971	N/A	Roper
Ecuador	1971	Socio-political	Roper
Ecuador	1971	Socio-economic	Roper
Mexico	1971	Political	Roper
Venezuela	1971	Political	Roper
Venezuela	1971	Socio-political	Roper
Venezuela	1971	Political	Roper
Colombia	1971	Economic	USNA
Mexico	1971	Political	DPLS
Latin America	1971	Socio-political	SSDA–CARL
Latin America	1971	Socio-economic	ICPSR
Argentina	1972	Socio-economic	ICPSR
Argentina	1972	Socio-political	Roper
Argentina	1972	Cultural	Roper
Brazil	1972	Cultural	Roper
Brazil	1972	Social	Roper
Argentina	1972	Omnibus	Roper
Argentina	1972	Omnibus	Roper
Brazil	1972	Socio-economic	Roper
Brazil	1972	Cultural	Roper
Brazil	1972	Social	Roper
Brazil	1972	Cultural	Roper
Brazil	1972	Cultural	Roper
Brazil	1972	Social	Roper
Brazil	1972	Cultural	Roper
Brazil	1972	Economic	Roper
Brazil	1972	Cultural	Roper
Brazil	1972	Cultural	Roper
Brazil	1972	Social	Roper
Brazil	1972	Social	Roper

APPENDIX THREE (Continued)

PUBLIC OPINION SURVEYS, 20 L, 1947–86

Country	Year	Survey Type	Repository
Brazil	1972	Social	Roper
Brazil	1972	Social	Roper
Brazil	1972	Cultural	Roper
Brazil	1972	Socio-economic	Roper
Brazil	1972	Socio-economic	Roper
Brazil	1972	Political	Roper
Brazil	1972	Cultural	Roper
Brazil	1972	Cultural	Roper
Brazil	1972	Social	Roper
Guatemala	1972	Political	Roper
Mexico	1972	Political	Roper
Venezuela	1972	Political	Roper
Venezuela	1972	Political	Roper
Mexico	1972	N/A	USNA
Brazil	1973	Political	ICPSR
Brazil	1973	Omnibus	DPLS
Brazil	1973	Omnibus	DPLS
Mexico	1973	Agricultural	DPLS
Brazil	1973	Socio-political	Roper
Brazil	1973	Social	Roper
Brazil	1973	Political	Roper
Uruguay	1973	Socio-political	Roper
Mexico	1973	Social	DAEDAC
Costa Rica	1973	Social	SSRC–UK
Latin America	1973	Cultural	USNA
Argentina	1974	Socio-economic	HOST COUNTRY
Peru	1974	Socio-economic	HOST COUNTRY
Peru	1974	Socio-economic	HOST COUNTRY
Brazil	1974	Cultural	Roper
Colombia	1974	Economic	USNA
Peru	1975	Economic	ICPSR
Colombia	1975	Economic	ICPSR
Ecuador	1975	Economic	ICPSR
Brazil	1975	Economic	DPLS
Dominican Republic	1975	Health	HOST COUNTRY
El Salvador	1975	Health	OTHER
Argentina	1975	Cultural	Roper
Chile	1975	Cultural	Roper
Chile	1975	Cultural	Roper
Brazil	1975	Socio-economic	DPLS
Venezuela	1975	Social	USNA
Brazil	1976	Economic	DPLS
Colombia	1976	Health	HOST COUNTRY
Costa Rica	1976	Health	HOST COUNTRY
Guatemala	1976	Health	OTHER
Panama	1976	Health	HOST COUNTRY
Mexico	1976	Economic	USNA
Nicaragua	1976	Social	DAEDAC
Cuba	1976	Political	SSRC–UK

APPENDIX THREE (Continued)

PUBLIC OPINION SURVEYS, 20 L, 1947–86

Country	Year	Survey Type	Repository
Mexico	1976	Social	USNA
Venezuela	1976	Social	USNA
Bolivia	1977	Agricultural	OTHER
Ecuador	1977	Socio-economic	HOST COUNTRY
Haiti	1977	Health	HOST COUNTRY
Mexico	1977	Health	HOST COUNTRY
Mexico	1977	Economic	N/A
Paraguay	1977	Health	N/A
Venezuela	1977	Health	HOST COUNTRY
Colombia	1977	Economic	USNA
Ecuador	1977	Social	USNA
Brazil	1978	Omnibus	DPLS
Colombia	1978	Economic	HOST COUNTRY
Costa Rica	1978	Health	OTHER
El Salvador	1978	Health	OTHER
El Salvador	1978	Socio-economic	OTHER
Guatemala	1978	Health	OTHER
Peru	1978	Health	HOST COUNTRY
Uruguay	1978	Agricultural	HOST COUNTRY
Colombia	1979	Omnibus	OTHER
Paraguay	1979	Health	HOST COUNTRY
Brazil	1980	Health	OTHER
Brazil	1980	Omnibus	DPLS
Honduras	1980	Environment	N/A
Mexico	1980	Economic	N/A
Panama	1980	Health	N/A
Panama	1980	Health	N/A
Haiti	1981	Health	N/A
Haiti	1981	Health	N/A
Latin America	1982	Socio-political	ICPSR
Haiti	1982	Health	N/A
Haiti	1982	Health	N/A
Venezuela	1982	Socio-political	DPLS
Latin America	1983	Socio-economic	ICPSR
Chile	1983	Health	OTHER
Ecuador	1983	N/A	OTHER
El Salvador	1983	Health	OTHER
Honduras	1983	Health	N/A
Honduras	1983	Health	N/A
Honduras	1983	N/A	N/A
Mexico	1983	Health	N/A
Panama	1983	Health	N/A
Mexico	1986	Socio-political	ICPSR

APPENDIX FOUR

SURVEY TYPES BY DECADE FOR INDIVIDUAL LATIN AMERICAN COUNTRIES
AND AGGREGATE STUDIES

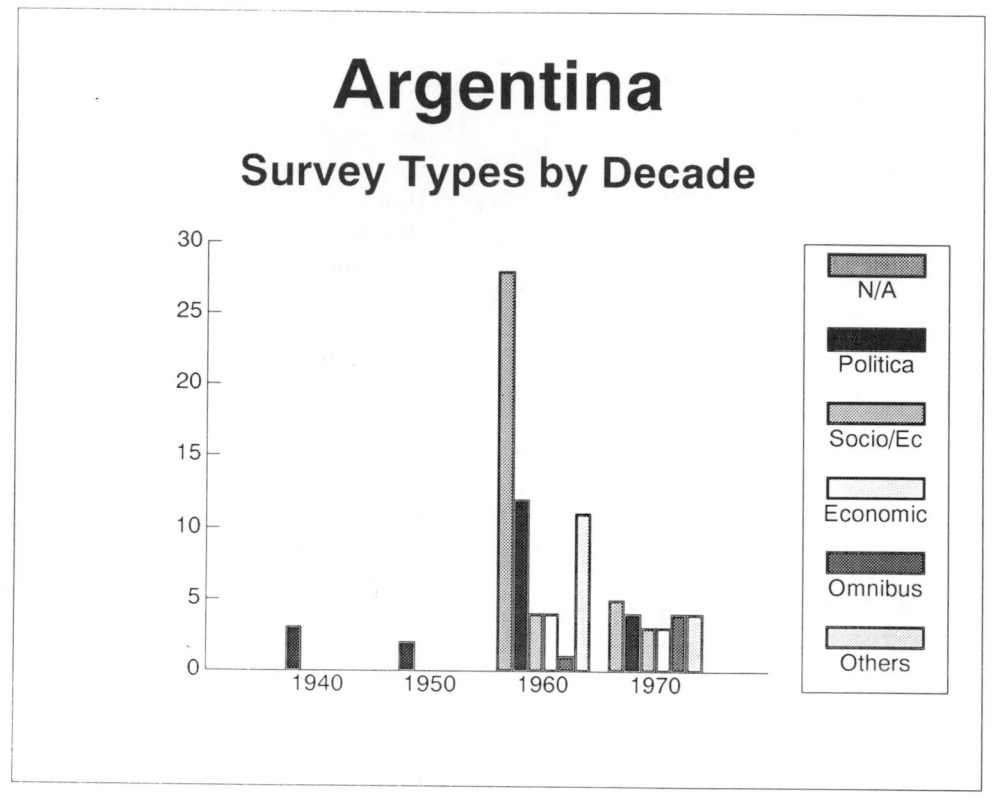

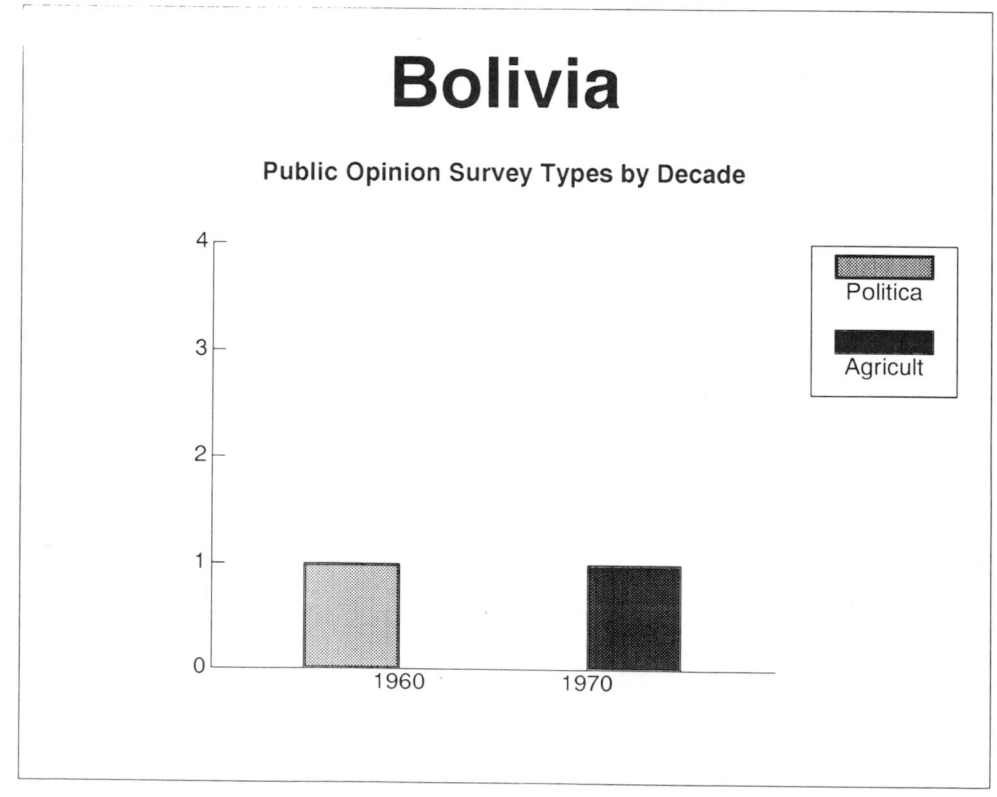

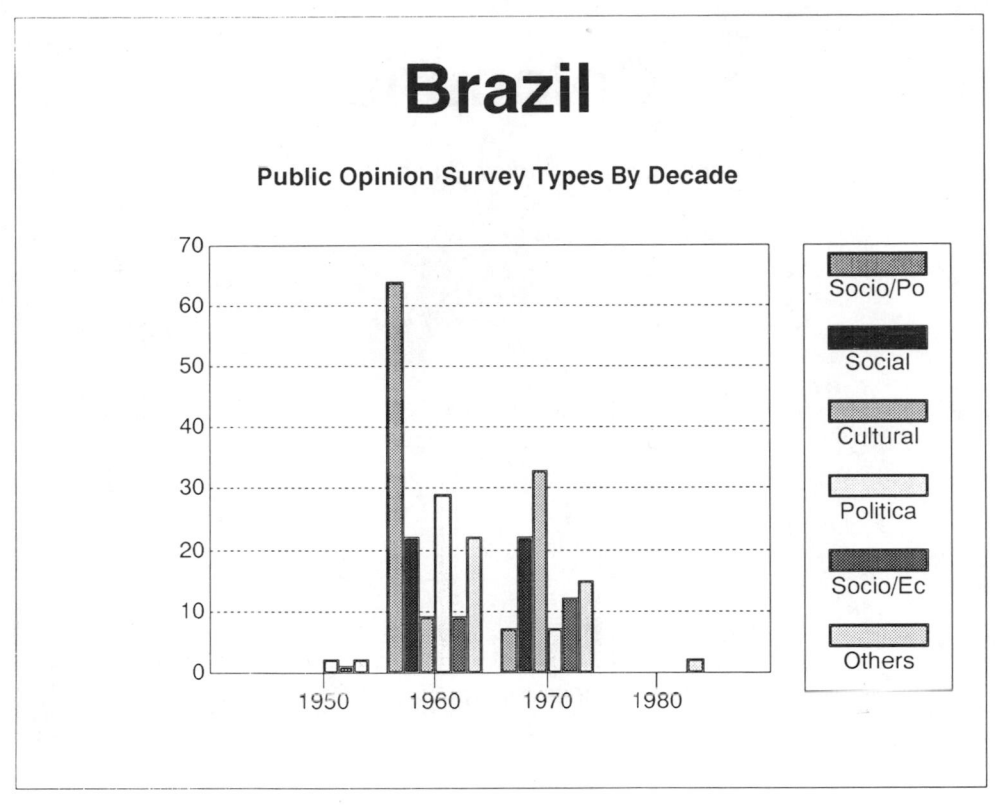

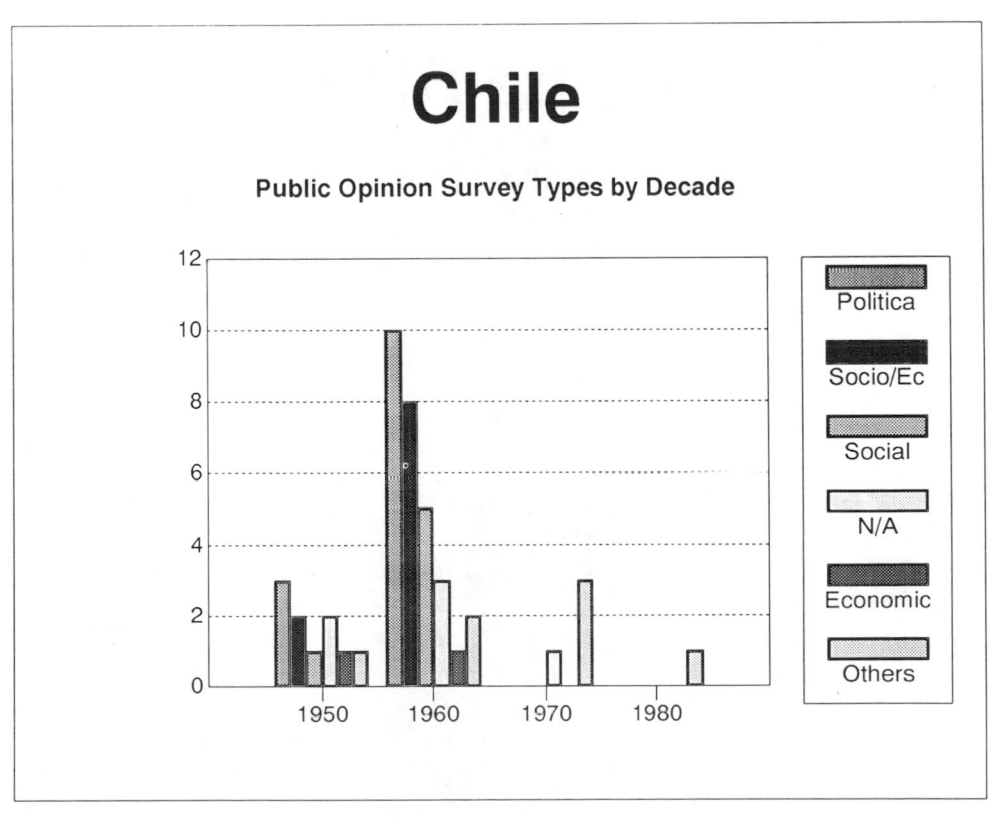

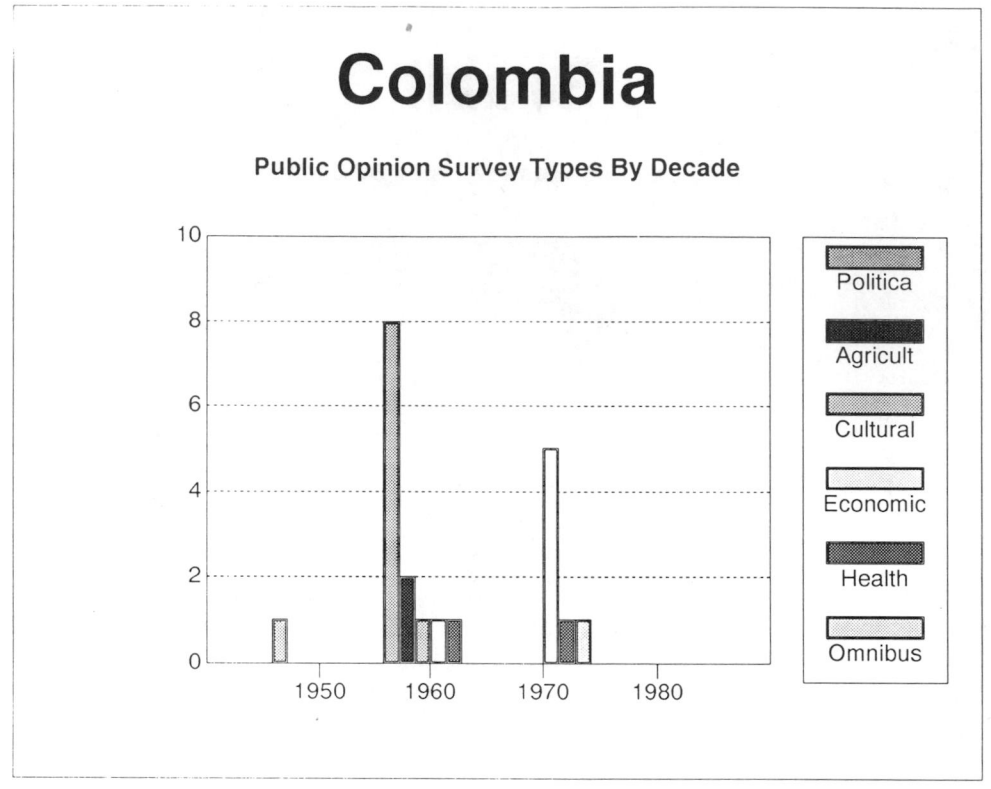

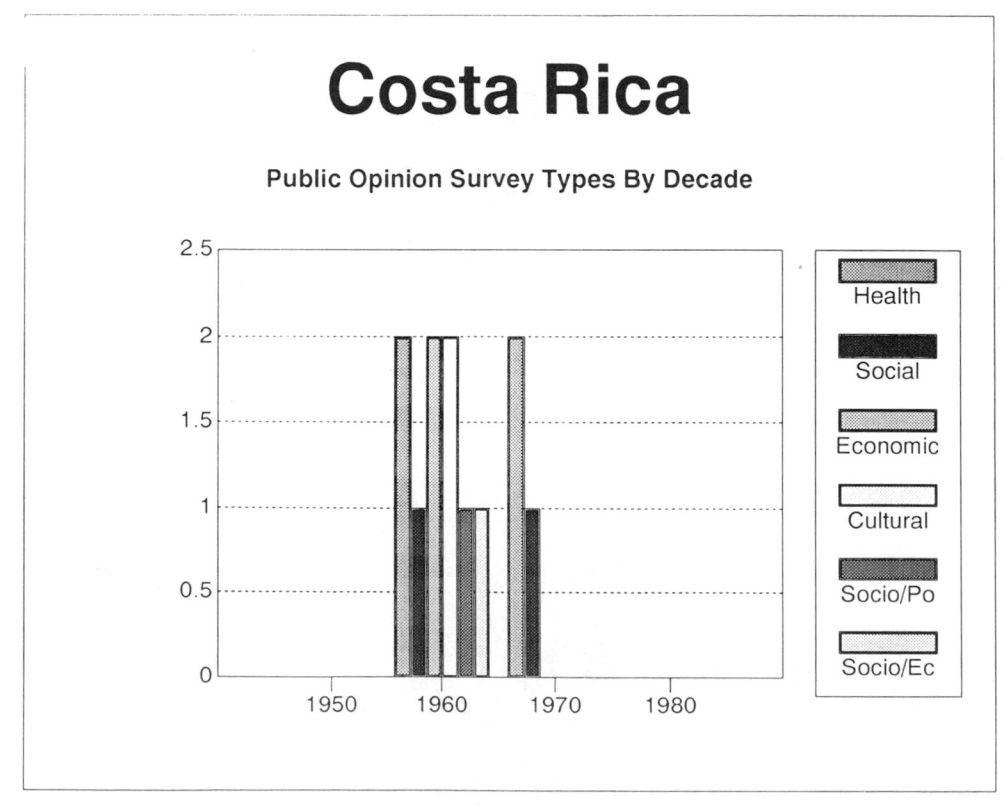

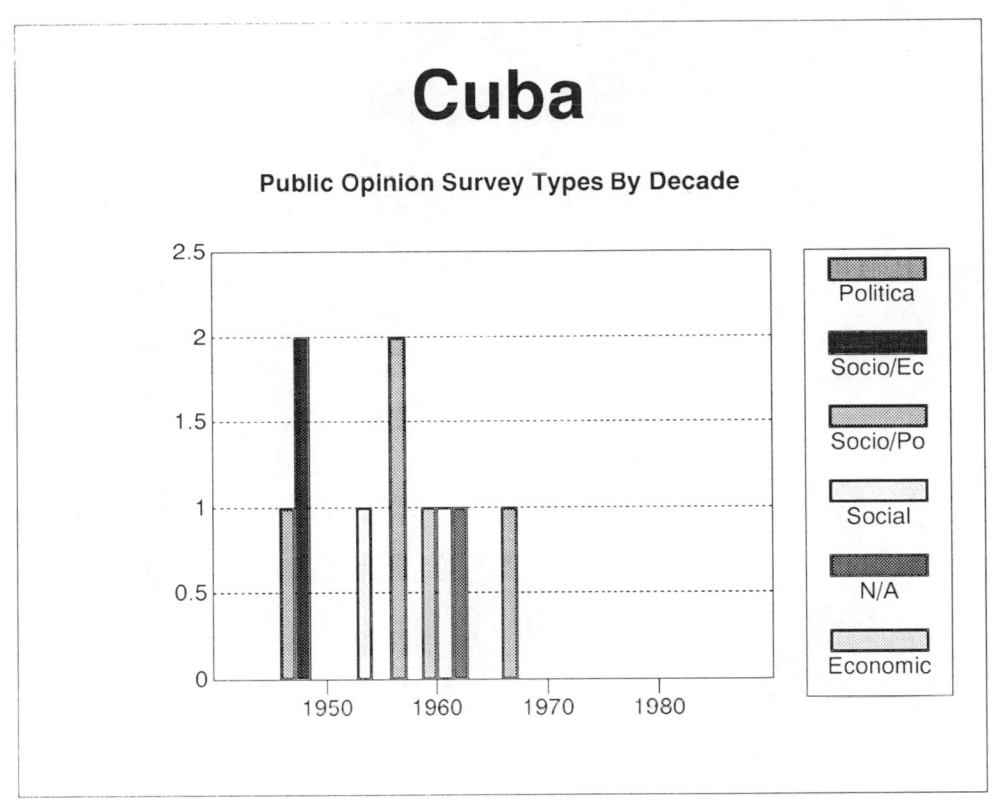

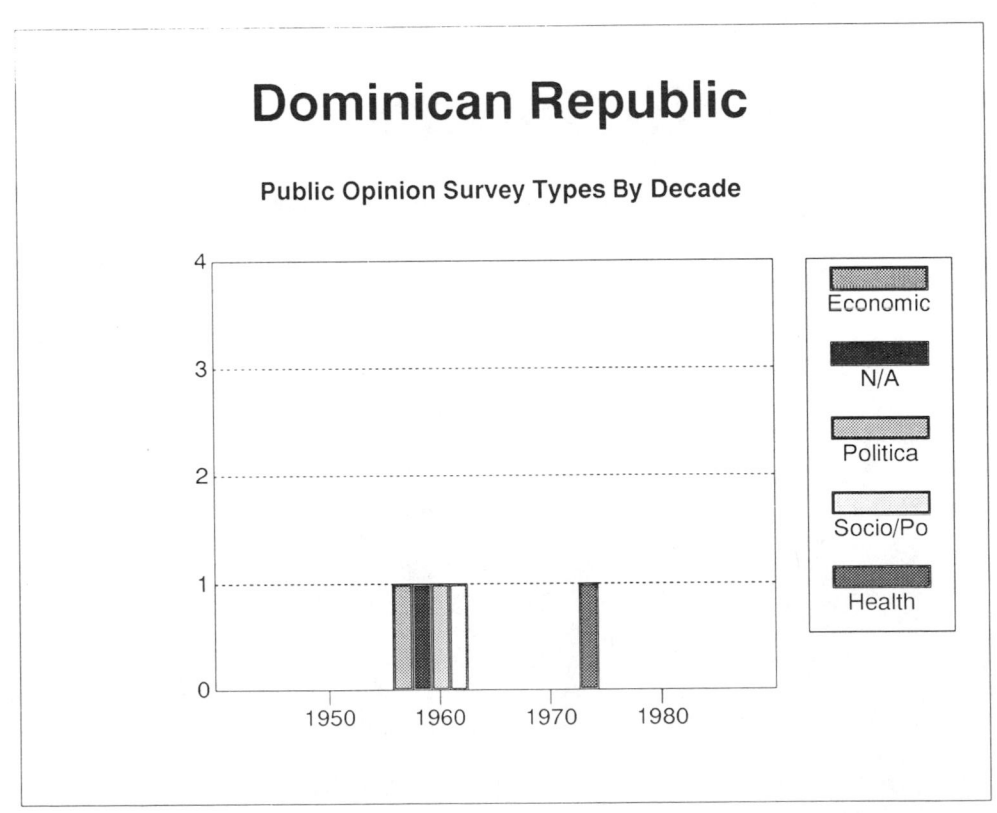

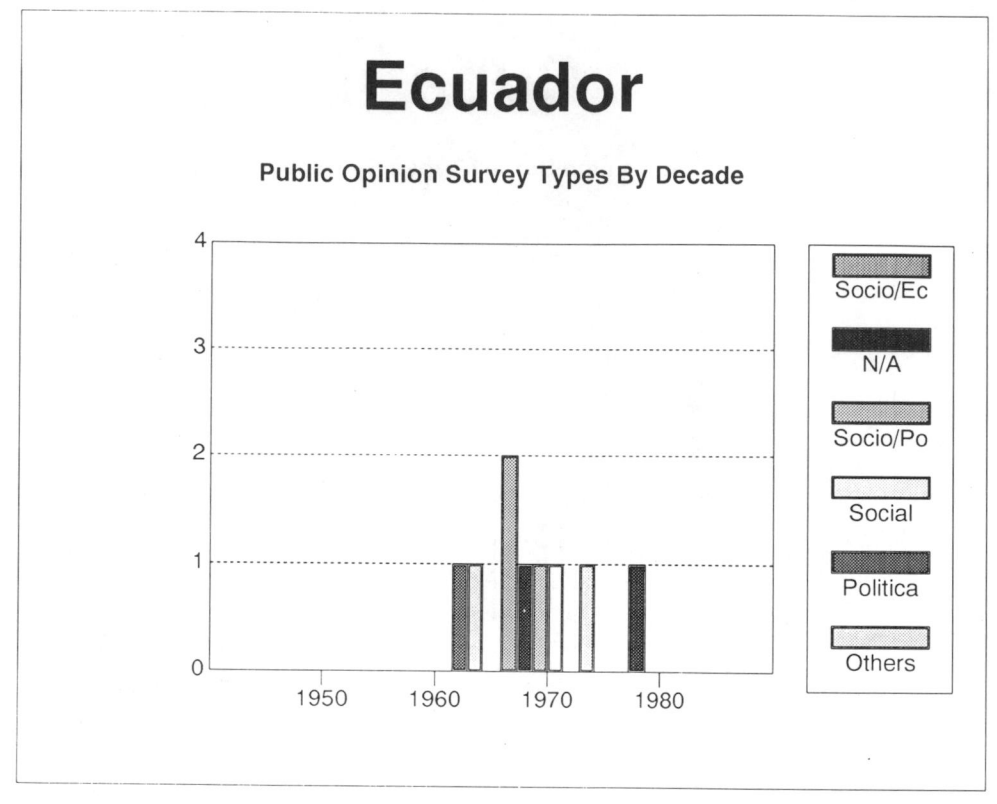

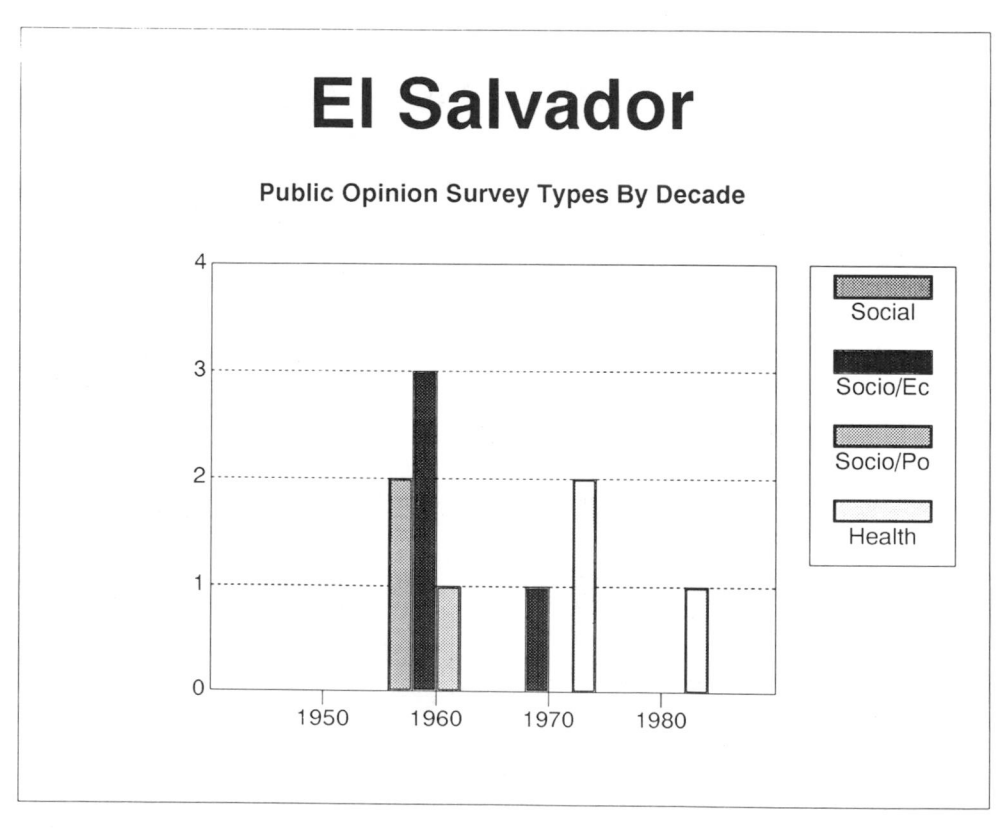

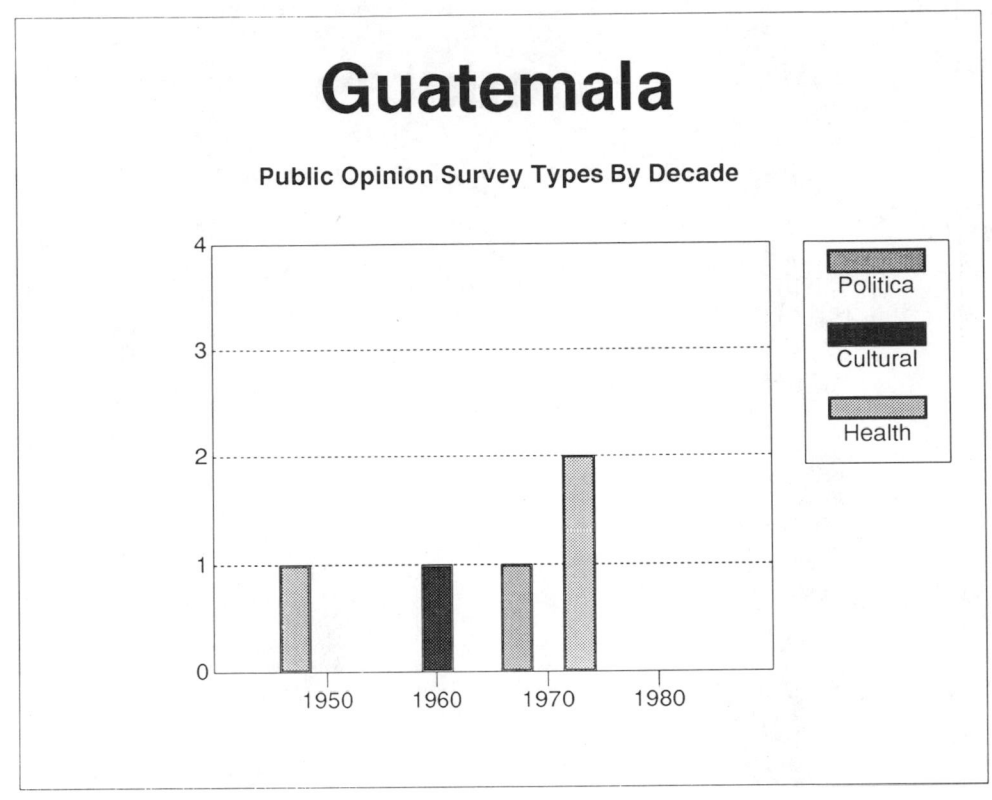

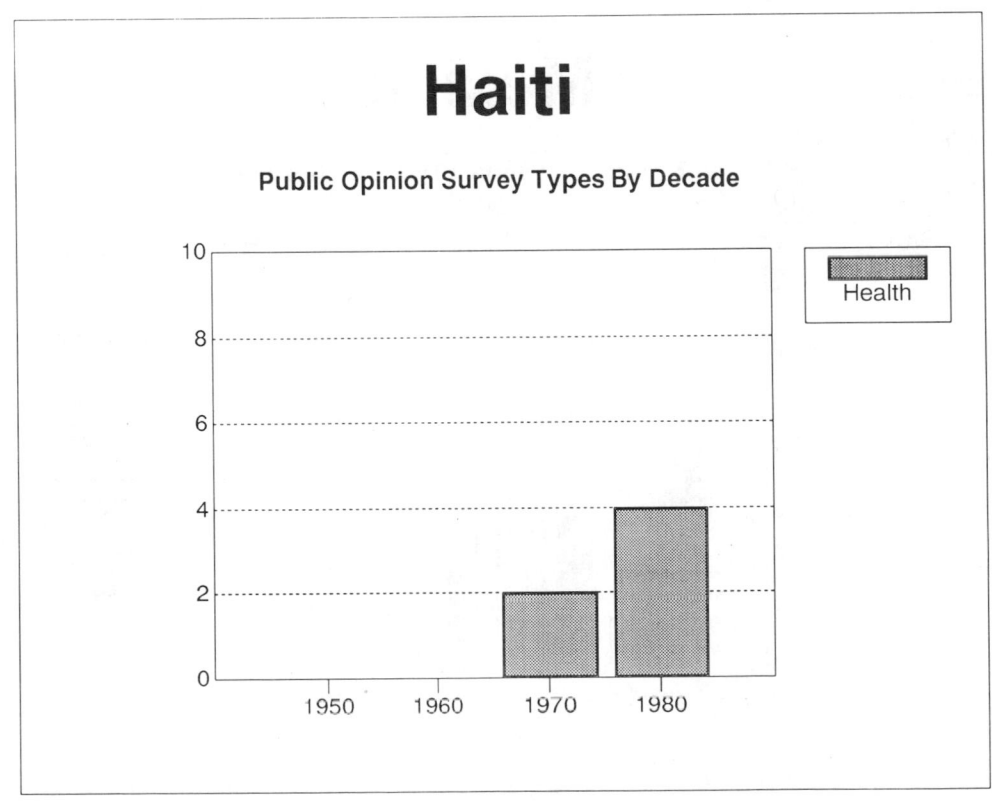

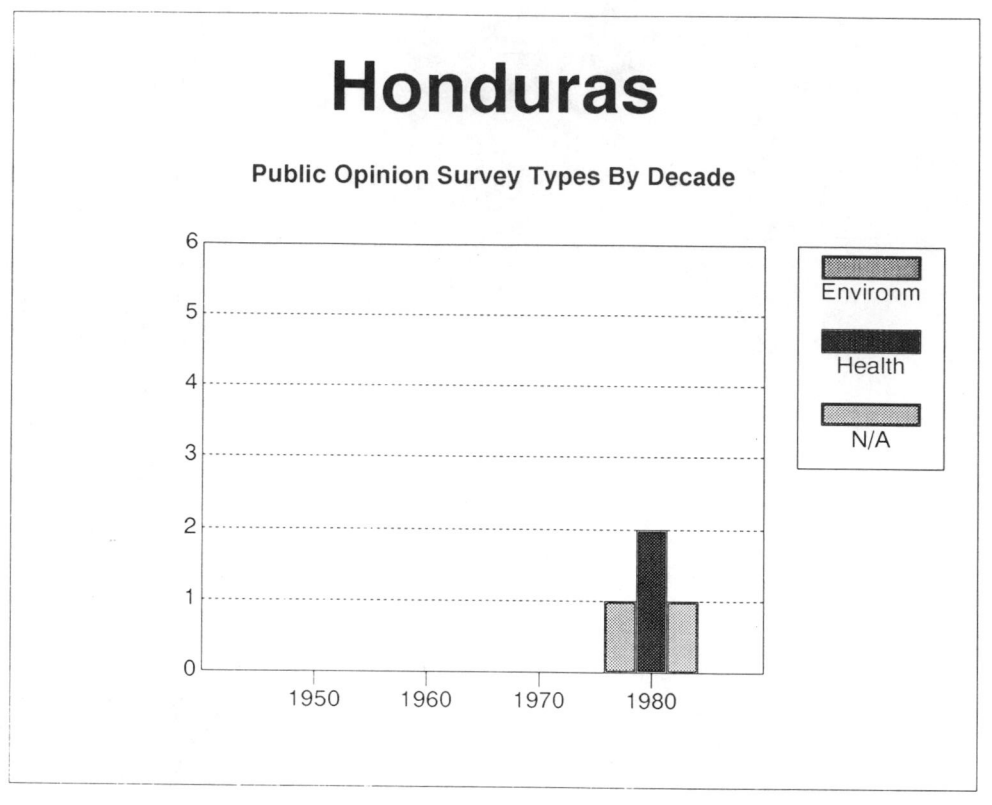

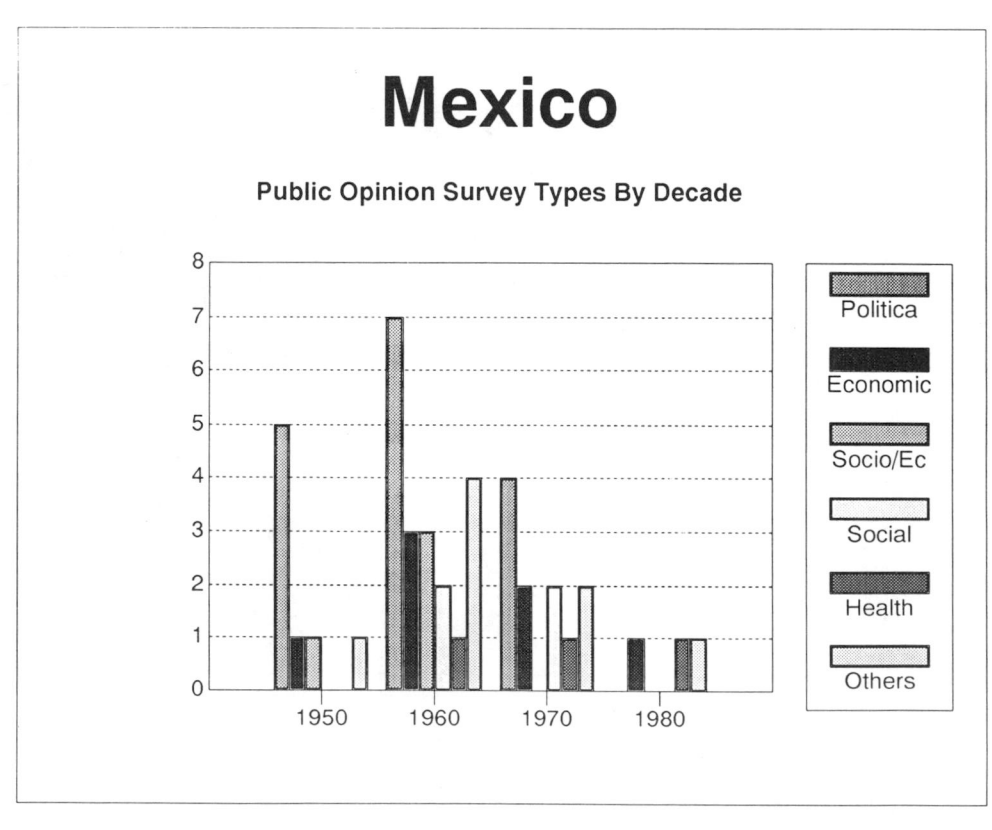

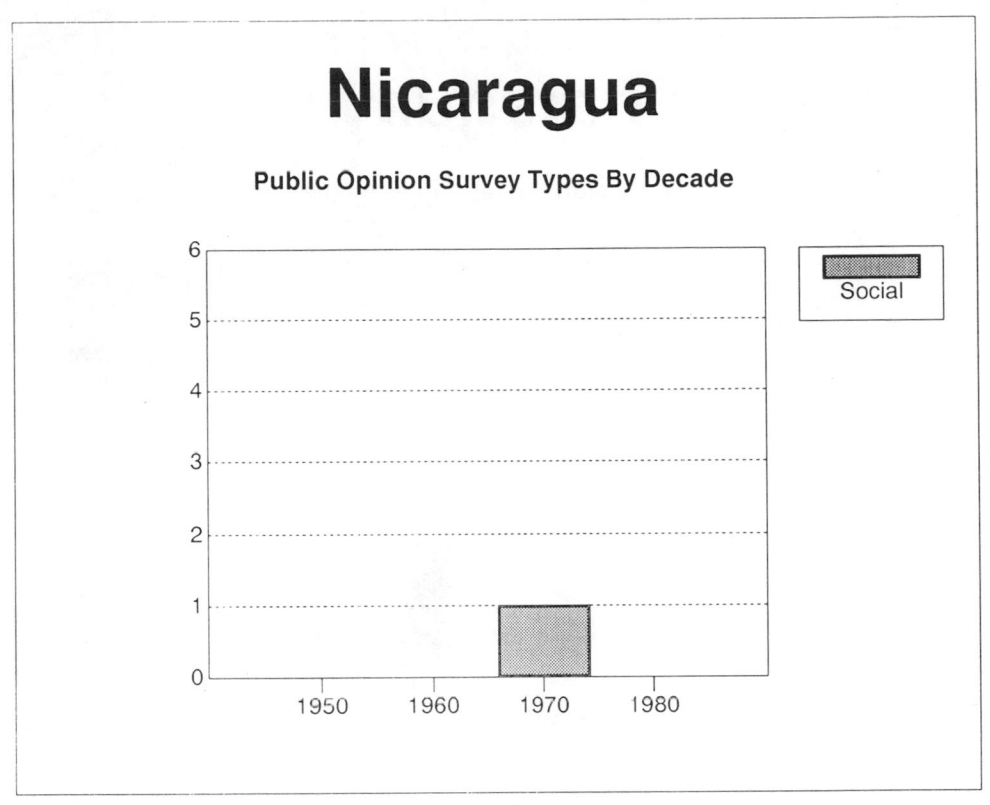

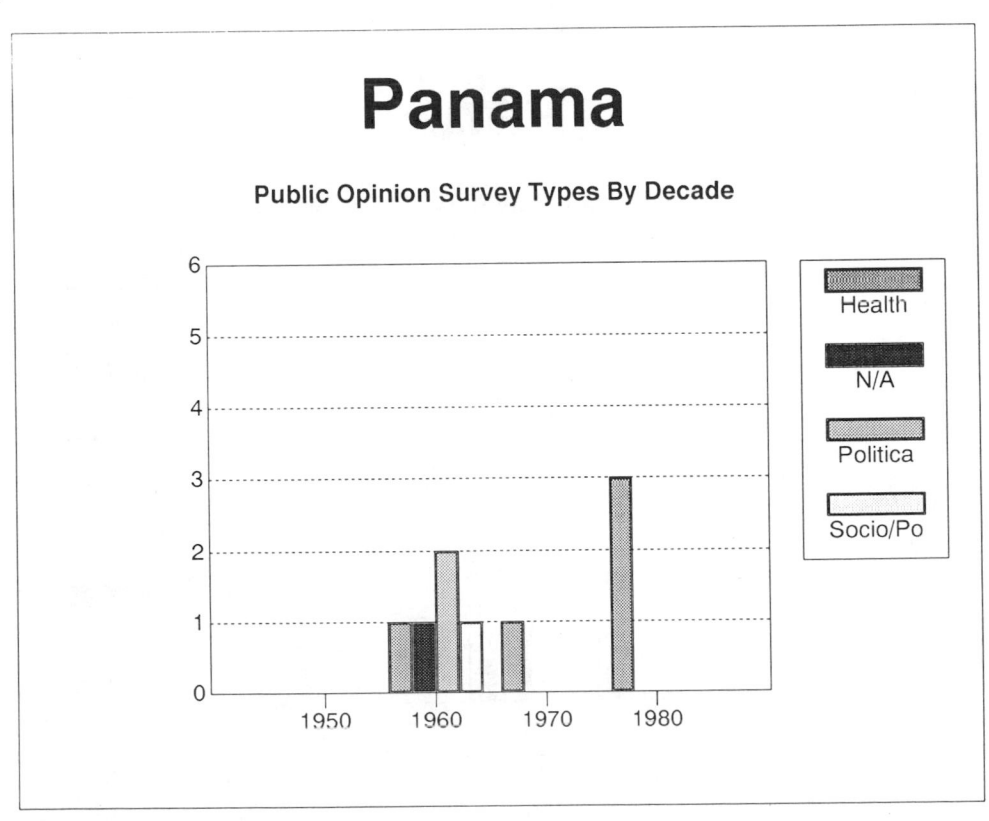

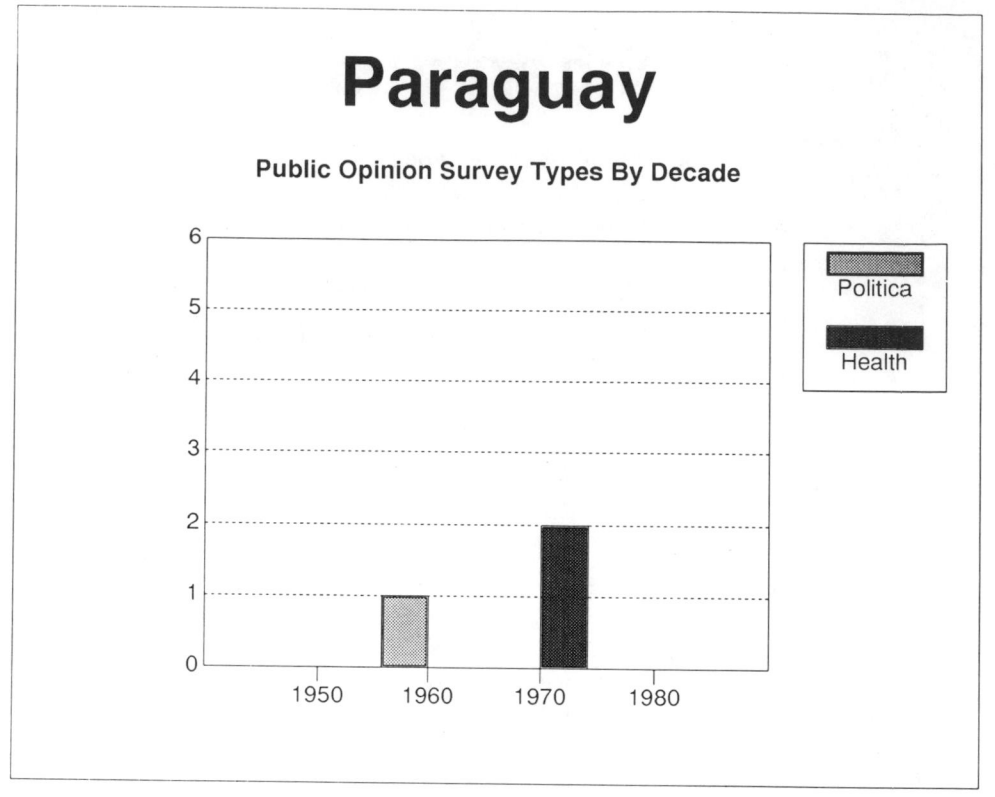

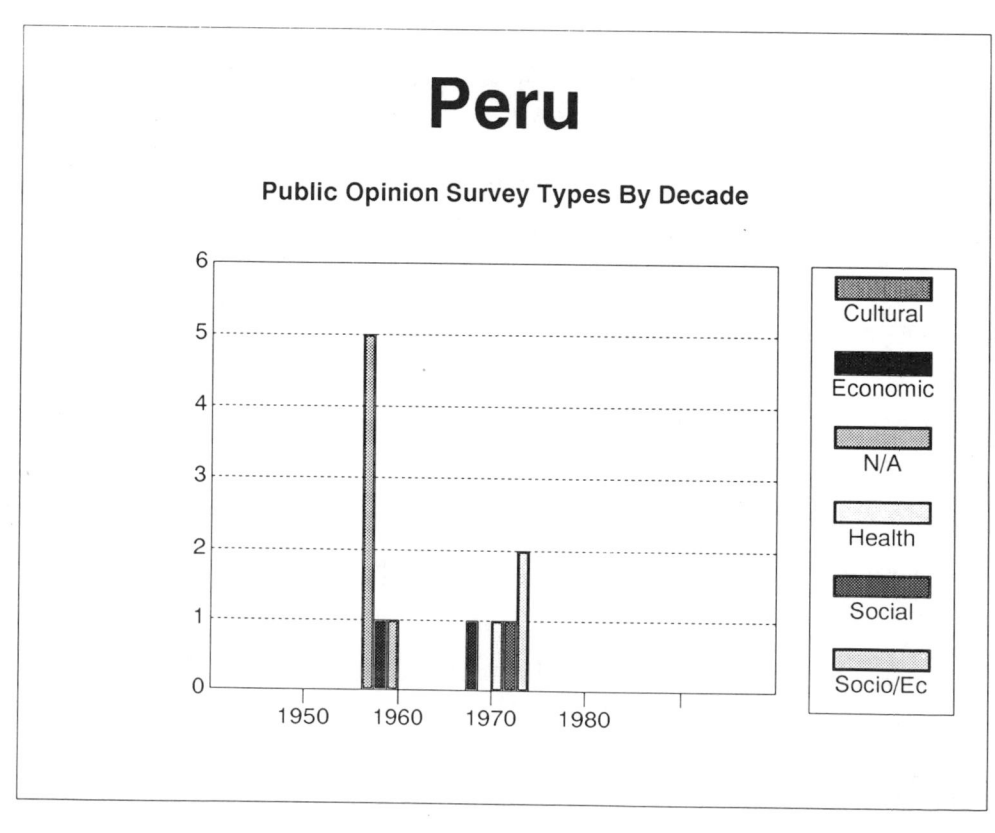

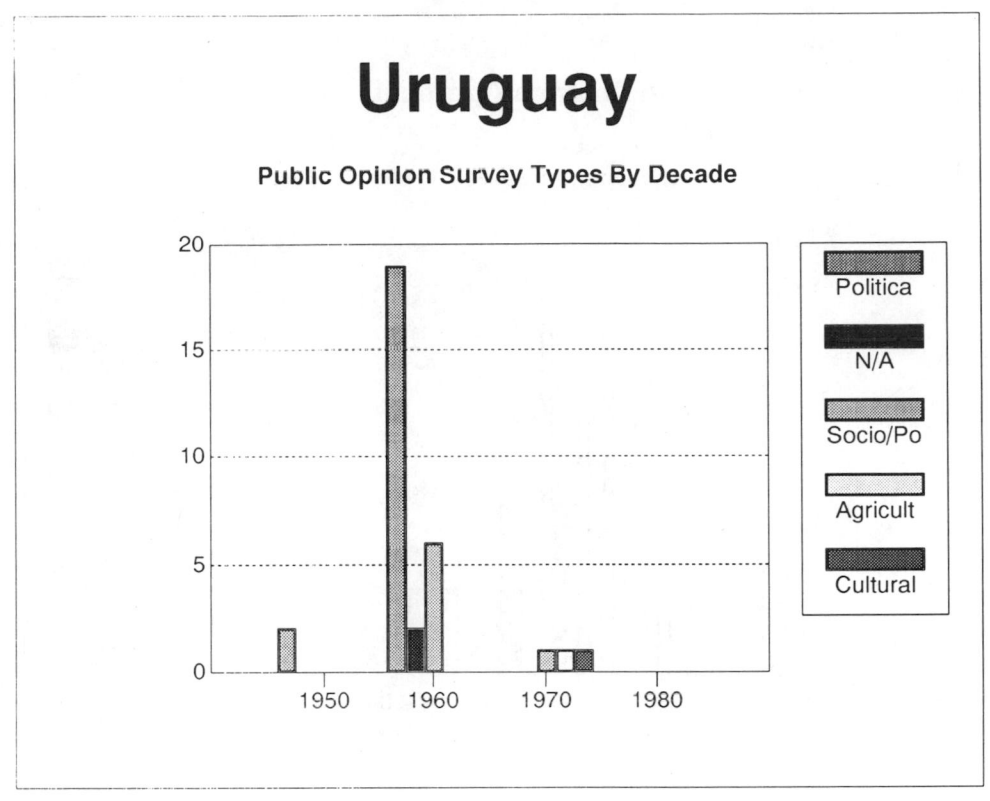

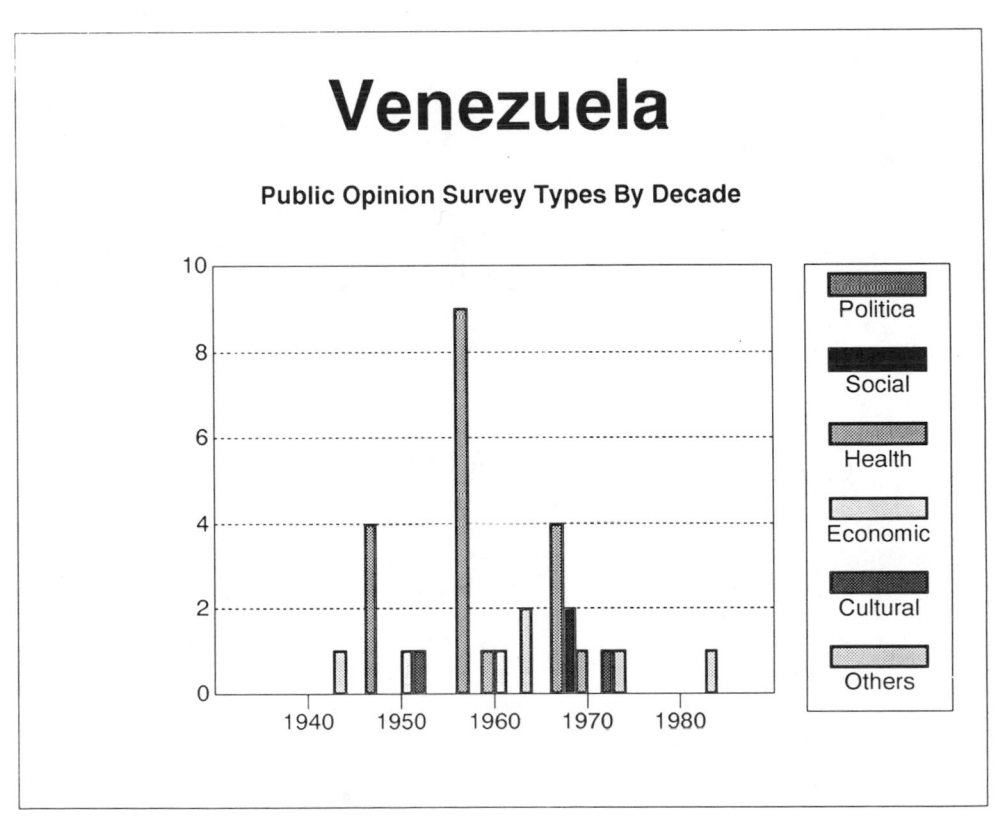

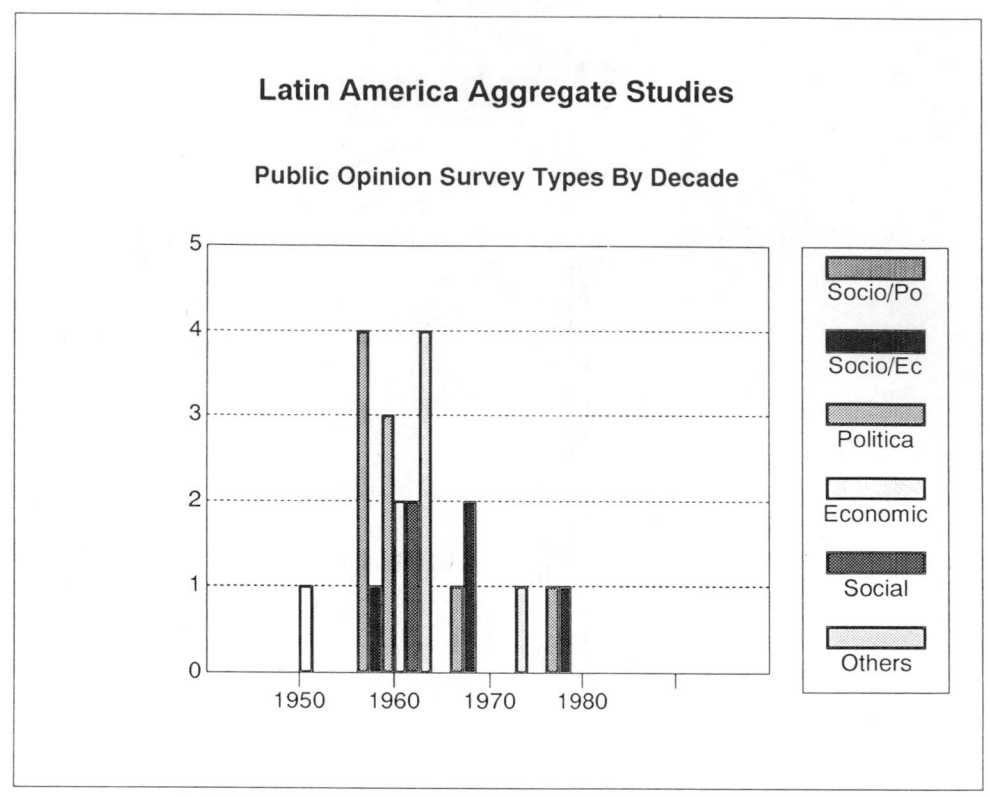

Latin America Aggregate Studies

Public Opinion Survey Types By Decade

APPENDIX FIVE

SAMPLE DATABASE:
MEXICAN PUBLIC OPINION SURVEYS,
1917–86

Country: Mexico
Year: 1917
Sample size: N/A
Notes: Historical data
Title: Mexican Constitutional Congress, 1916–17: Roll Call Records and
       Member Characteristics
Reference number: MA501001MEX1916-1
Decade: 1910
Survey Organization: N/A
Repository: DPLS
Survey Type: Political
Sample Type: Other
Data Format: N/A

Country: Mexico
Year: 1955
Sample size: 1,918
Notes: Adults surveyed in 27 cities
Title: Barometer Study on Public Opinion, Mexico, 1955
Reference number: MX55USIALA3
Decade: 1950
Survey Organization: U.S. Government
Repository: Roper
Survey Type: Political
Sample Sype: Urban
Data Format: N/A

Country: Mexico
Year: 1956
Sample size: 973
Notes: Same survey used in Chile; adults surveyed in 19 cities of 10,000 or
       more inhabitants
Title: Radio Listening and Various International Issues, Mexico, 1956
Reference number: MX56USIALA6
Decade: 1950
Survey Organization: U.S. Government
Repository: Roper
Survey Type: Political
Sample Type: Urban
Data Format: N/A

APPENDIX FIVE (Continued)

SAMPLE DATABASE:
MEXICAN PUBLIC OPINION SURVEYS,
1917–86

Country: Mexico
Year: 1958
Sample size: N/A
Notes: Same survey taken in Cuba
Title: Advertising Survey, Mexico, 1958
Reference number: MX58INRA299
Decade: 1950
Survey Organization: U.S. Contractor
Repository: Roper
Survey Type: Economic
Sample Type: Adults
Data Format: N/A

Country: Mexico
Year: 1958
Sample size: 320
Notes: Same questionnaire used in Cuba
Title: Advertising Survey, Mexico, 1958
Reference number: MXINRA299
Decade: 1950
Survey Organization: Commercial
Repository: Roper
Survey Type: Socio-econimic
Sample Type: Adults
Data Format: MAGNETIC TAPE

Country: Mexico
Year: 1958
Sample size: 250
Notes: Same survey taken in Peru, Uruguay and Venezuela
Title: Latin American Reactions to Nixon's Visit, Mexico City, 1958
Reference number: MX58INRA301
Decade: 1950
Survey Organization: Commercial
Repository: Roper
Survey Type: Political
Sample Type: Adults
Data Format: N/A

APPENDIX FIVE (Continued)

SAMPLE DATABASE:
MEXICAN PUBLIC OPINION SURVEYS,
1917–86

Country: Mexico
Year: 1959
Sample size: 830
Notes:
Title: University Students' Values, Vocations, and Political Orientations:
    Mexico, 1962
Reference number: ICPSR 7059
Decade: 1950
Survey Organization: Individual Academic
Repository: ICPSR
Survey Type: Political
Sample Type: University Students
Data Format: MAGNETIC TAPE

Country: Mexico
Year: 1959
Sample size: 1008
Notes: Cross-national survey; other countries are not in Latin America
Title: Civic Culture Study 1959–1960
Reference number: ICPSR 7201
Decade: 1950
Survey Organization: Individual Academic
Repository: ICPSR
Survey Type: Political
Sample Type: National
Data Format: MAGNETIC TAPE

Country: Mexico
Year: 1959
Sample size: 1,295
Notes: Survey taken in urban centers of more than 10,000 inhabitants
Title: Five Nation Study, Mexico, 1959
Reference number: MX59ALMOND–VERBA
Decade: 1950
Survey Organization: Individual Academic
Repository: Roper
Survey Type: Socio-political
Sample Type: Adults
Data Format: MAGNETIC TAPE

APPENDIX FIVE (Continued)

SAMPLE DATABASE:
MEXICAN PUBLIC OPINION SURVEYS,
1917–86

Country: Mexico
Year: 1960
Sample size: N/A
Notes: Decennial survey from 1910–1960; includes socio-economic and
        political subject matter
Title: Comparative Socio-Economic, Public Policy, and Political Data,
        1900–1960
Reference number: ICPSR 0034
Decade: 1960
Survey Organization: Individual Academic
Repository: ICPSR
Survey Type: Socio-political
Sample Type: National
Data Format: MAGNETIC TAPE

Country: Mexico
Year: 1960
Sample size: N/A
Notes: Time Series Data 1950 and 1960
Title: Characteristics of Municipios: Data from the 1950 and 1960 Censuses
        of Mexico
Reference number: DPLS-AC-501-001-MEX
Decade: 1960
Survey Organization: Host Country
Repository: DPLS
Survey Type: Socio-economic
Sample Type: National
Data Format: N/A

Country: Mexico
Year: 1960
Sample size: 80
Notes:
Title: Life Insurance Study, Mexico, 1960
Reference number: MX60INRAINSURANCE
Decade: 1960
Survey Organization: Commercial
Repository: Roper
Survey Type: Socio-economic
Sample Type: N/A
Data Format: N/A

APPENDIX FIVE (Continued)

SAMPLE DATABASE:
MEXICAN PUBLIC OPINION SURVEYS,
1917–86

Country: Mexico
Year: 1960
Sample size: N/A
Notes: AES Listed on Hanc reference, but acronym not explained
Title: International Citizenship Survey, Mexico, 1960
Reference number: AES0030B
Decade: 1960
Survey Organization: N/A
Repository: OTHER
Survey Type: Social
Sample Type: N/A
Data Format: N/A

Country: Mexico
Year: 1961
Sample size: 1,479
Notes: Same survey used in Argentina, Brazil, Peru, Uruguay and Venezuela; adults surveyed in 3 cities of 10,000 or more inhabitants in northern, coastal and central agricultural areas of Mexico
Title: Survey on International Affairs, Mexico, 1961
Reference number: MX61USIALA8
Decade: 1960
Survey Organization: U.S. Government
Repository: Roper
Survey Type: Political
Sample Type: Adults
Data Format: MAGNETIC TAPE

Country: Mexico
Year: 1961
Sample size: 400
Notes:
Title: Care and Feeding of Babies, Mexico, 1961
Reference number: MX61INRABABIES
Decade: 1960
Survey Organization: Commercial
Repository: Roper
Survey Type: Health
Sample Type: N/A
Data Format: N/A

APPENDIX FIVE (Continued)

**SAMPLE DATABASE:
MEXICAN PUBLIC OPINION SURVEYS,
1917–86**

Country: Mexico
Year: 1961
Sample size: 1,511
Notes: Adults surveyed in cities of 10,000 or more inhabitants
Title: Barometer Study of Mexican Public Opinion, 1961
Reference number: MX61USIALA9
Decade: 1960
Survey Organization: U.S. Government
Repository: Roper
Survey Type: Political
Sample Type: Urban
Data Format: N/A

Country: Mexico
Year: 1963
Sample size: 740
Notes: Contains rural and urban respondents
Title: Career Values in Mexico, 1963
Reference number: ICPSR 7058
Decade: 1960
Survey Organization: Individual Academic
Repository: ICPSR
Survey Type: Social
Sample Type: Mixed groups
Data Format: MAGNETIC TAPE

Country: Mexico
Year: 1963
Sample size: N/A
Notes:
Title: Career Values in Mexico, 1963
Reference number: DPLS-SB-502-002-MEX
Decade: 1960
Survey Organization: N/A
Repository: DPLS
Survey Type: Cultural
Sample Type: National
Data Format: N/A

APPENDIX FIVE (Continued)

SAMPLE DATABASE:
MEXICAN PUBLIC OPINION SURVEYS,
1917–86

Country: Mexico
Year: 1963
Sample size: 389
Notes: Same survey used in Argentina, Brazil and Venezuela
Title: Mexican Public Opinion on Selected Political Issues, Mexico City, 1963
Reference number: MX63USIAWS1
Decade: 1960
Survey Organization: U.S. Government
Repository: Roper
Survey Type: Political
Sample Type: Urban
Data Format: N/A

Country: Mexico
Year: 1964
Sample size: 506
Notes: Same questionnaire used in Argentina, Brazil and Venezuela
Title: Public Opinion on Various Political Issues, Mexico City, 1964
Reference number: MXUSIA64WS2
Decade: 1960
Survey Organization: U.S. Government
Repository: Roper
Survey Type: Political
Sample Type: Adults
Data Format: MAGNETIC TAPE

Country: Mexico
Year: 1964
Sample size: 2,359
Notes: Same survey used in Chile, Peru and Venezuela
Title: University Students' Attitudes, Mexico, 1964
Reference number: MXINRA64UNIV
Decade: 1960
Survey Organization: Commercial
Repository: Roper
Survey Type: Political
Sample Type: University Students
Data Format: MAGNETIC TAPE

APPENDIX FIVE (Continued)

SAMPLE DATABASE:
MEXICAN PUBLIC OPINION SURVEYS,
1917–86

Country: Mexico
Year: 1964
Sample size: 4,582
Notes:
Title: Baby Food Survey, Phase II, Mexico, 1964
Reference number: MX64INRABABYFOOD2
Decade: 1960
Survey Organization: Commercial
Repository: Roper
Survey Type: Socio-economic
Sample Type: N/A
Data Format: N/A

Country: Mexico
Year: 1965
Sample size: 492
Notes: Same questionnaire used in Argentina, Brazil, Chile and Venezuela
Title: International Relations, Mexico City, 1965
Reference number: MX65USIAWS3
Decade: 1960
Survey Organization: U.S. Government
Repository: Roper
Survey Type: Political
Sample Type: Adults
Data Format: MAGNETIC TAPE

Country: Mexico
Year: 1965
Sample size: N/A
Notes:
Title: Market for Snacks, Mexico, 1965
Reference number: MX65INRASNACKS
Decade: 1960
Survey Organization: Commercial
Repository: Roper
Survey Type: Economic
Sample Type: Management/white collar
Data Format: N/A

APPENDIX FIVE (Continued)

SAMPLE DATABASE:
MEXICAN PUBLIC OPINION SURVEYS,
1917–86

Country: Mexico
Year: 1965
Sample size: 500
Notes:
Title: Air Travel Survey, Mexico, 1965
Reference number: MX65INRAAIRTRAVEL
Decade: 1960
Survey Organization: Commercial
Repository: Roper
Survey Type: Economic
Sample Type: N/A
Data Format: N/A

Country: Mexico
Year: 1966
Sample size: N/A
Notes:
Title: Innovative Corn Farming Practices, Zinacantan, Province of Chiapas,
        Mexico, 1966
Reference number: DPLS-CA-501-008-MEX
Decade: 1960
Survey Organization: N/A
Repository: DPLS
Survey Type: Agricultural
Sample Type: Regional
Data Format: N/A

Country: Mexico
Year: 1967
Sample size: N/A
Notes: Time Series Data
Title: Sunshine Data: Economic Data for Mexico, 1950–67
Reference number: PSDL-IN-IUO30072
Decade: 1960
Survey Organization: N/A
Repository: PSDL-IN
Survey Type: Economic
Sample Type: N/A
Data Format: N/A

APPENDIX FIVE (Continued)

SAMPLE DATABASE:
MEXICAN PUBLIC OPINION SURVEYS,
1917–86

Country: Mexico
Year: 1968
Sample size: 507
Notes:
Title: Book Reading Habits in Three Principal Cities, Mexico, 1968
Reference number: MX68USIAREADINGHABIT
Decade: 1960
Survey Organization: U.S. Government
Repository: Roper
Survey Type: Cultural
Sample Type: Elite
Data Format: N/A

Country: Mexico
Year: 1968
Sample size: 1,011
Notes: Adults surveyed in 10 specified elite occupations in cities of 10,000
        or more inhabitants in 24 of 29 Mexican states; same survey used in
        Brazil and Colombia
Title: Voice of America Study, Mexico, 1968
Reference number: MX68USIAVOA
Decade: 1960
Survey Organization: U.S. Government
Repository: Roper
Survey Type: Political
Sample Type: Elite
Data Format: N/A

Country: Mexico
Year: 1971
Sample size: N/A
Notes: Time series data 1900–1971
Title: Mexican Political Elites, 1900–1971
Reference number: DPLS-HA-501-001-MEX
Decade: 1970
Survey Organization: N/A
Repository: DPLS
Survey Type: Political
Sample Type: Women
Data Format: N/A

APPENDIX FIVE (Continued)

SAMPLE DATABASE:
MEXICAN PUBLIC OPINION SURVEYS,
1917–86

Country: Mexico
Year: 1971
Sample size: 3,414
Notes: Same survey used in Argentina, Brazil, Colombia, Ecuador and
        Venezuela
Title: Latin American Image Study, Mexico, 1971
Reference number: MX71USIAIMAGE
Decade: 1970
Survey Organization: U.S. Government
Repository: Roper
Survey Type: Political
Sample Type: N/A
Data Format: N/A

Country: Mexico
Year: 1971
Sample size: N/A
Notes: Time Series Data
Title: Mexican Political Elites, 1900–71
Reference number: HA501001MEXDPLS19001
Decade: 1970
Survey Organization: N/A
Repository: DPLS
Survey Type: Political
Sample Type: N/A
Data Format: N/A

Country: Mexico
Year: 1972
Sample size: 208
Notes: Mail survey; same survey used in Argentina, Colombia, Peru and
        Venezuela
Title: VOA Listening Habits and Program Preferences in 5 Latin American
        Countries, Mexico, 1972
Reference number: MX72USIAVOA
Decade: 1970
Survey Organization: U.S. Government
Repository: Roper
Survey Type: Political
Sample Type: Adults
Data Format: N/A

APPENDIX FIVE (Continued)

SAMPLE DATABASE:
MEXICAN PUBLIC OPINION SURVEYS,
1917–86

Country: Mexico
Year: 1972
Sample size: N/A
Notes: Also surveyed in Colombia
Title: Broadcasting Audience Survey, Colombia, Mexico, 1972
Reference number: USNA-3-306-80-14-C
Decade: 1970
Survey Organization: N/A
Repository: USNA
Survey Type: N/A
Sample Type: N/A
Data Format: N/A

Country: Mexico
Year: 1973
Sample size: N/A
Notes:
Title: Adaptive Strategies of Farmers, Temascalcingo, Province of Mexico,
    Mexico, 1973
Reference number: DPLS-CA-501-007-MEX
Decade: 1970
Survey Organization: N/A
Repository: DPLS
Survey Type: Agricultural
Sample Type: Regional
Data Format: N/A

Country: Mexico
Year: 1973
Sample size: N/A
Notes:
Title: Study of the Incidents and Correlates of Student Drug Use, Monterray,
    Mexico, 1973
Reference number: DAEDAC-19
Decade: 1970
Survey Organization: N/A
Repository: DAEDAC
Survey Type: Social
Sample Type: N/A
Data Format: N/A

APPENDIX FIVE (Continued)

**SAMPLE DATABASE:
MEXICAN PUBLIC OPINION SURVEYS,
1917–86**

Country: Mexico
Year: 1976
Sample size: N/A
Notes:
Title: International Economic Issues – Investment, Mexico, 1976
Reference number: MX3-306-80-14-F
Decade: 1970
Survey Organization: N/A
Repository: USNA
Survey Type: Economic
Sample Type: N/A
Data Format: N/A

Country: Mexico
Year: 1976
Sample size: N/A
Notes: Survey also undertaken in 1974
Title: Broadcasting Audience Survey, Mexico, 1974, 1976
Reference number: USNA33068014(A)MEX
Decade: 1970
Survey Organization: N/A
Repository: USNA
Survey Type: Social
Sample Type: N/A
Data Format: N/A

Country: Mexico
Year: 1977
Sample size: N/A
Notes:
Title: World Fertility Survey: Mexico
Reference number: M5236020029
Decade: 1970
Survey Organization: Host Country
Repository: HOST COUNTRY
Survey Type: Health
Sample Type: National
Data Format: N/A

APPENDIX FIVE (Continued)

SAMPLE DATABASE:
MEXICAN PUBLIC OPINION SURVEYS,
1917–86

Country: Mexico
Year: 1977
Sample size: N/A
Notes:
Title: San Pable Autopan: Operations Research
Reference number: 523005
Decade: 1970
Survey Organization: U.S. Contractor
Repository: N/A
Survey Type: Economic
Sample Type: Women
Data Format: N/A

Country: Mexico
Year: 1980
Sample size: N/A
Notes:
Title: New Strategies–Operations Research: Baseline and Follow-Up Surveys
Reference number: 523003
Decade: 1980
Survey Organization: U.S. Contractor
Repository: N/A
Survey Type: Economic
Sample Type: Women
Data Format: N/A

Country: Mexico
Year: 1983
Sample size: N/A
Notes:
Title: Comparison of Contraceptive Distribution Systems
Reference number: 523004
Decade: 1980
Survey Organization: U.S. Contractor
Repository: N/A
Survey Type: Health
Sample Type: Women
Data Format: N/A

APPENDIX FIVE (Continued)

SAMPLE DATABASE:
MEXICAN PUBLIC OPINION SURVEYS,
1917–86

Country: Mexico
Year: 1986
Sample size: 1875
Notes:
Title: New York Times Mexico Survey, 1986
Reference number: ICPSR 8666
Decade: 1980
Survey Organization: Commercial
Repository: ICPSR
Survey Type: Socio-political
Sample Type: National
Data Format: CARD

INDEX

NAFINSA-MV	*Mercado de Valores*
OAS	Organization of American States (WDC)
OAS-A	*Latin America's Development and the Alliance for Progress* (1973)
OAS-DB	*Datos Básicos de Población*
OASL	OAS's definition of L (*see* SALA, 24-1000)
OAS-SB	*Statistical Bulletin*
PAHO	Pan American Health Organization (WDC)
PAHO-F	*Facts on Health Progress*
PAHO-HC	*Health Conditions in the Americas*
PC	Population Council (NYC)
PC-PFP	*Population and Family Planning*
PC-RPFP	*Report on Population/Family Planning*
SA	*South American Handbook*
SALA	*Statistical Abstract of Latin America*
SALA, 23:1	Volume 23, figure 1 (sample reference)
SALA, 23-100	Volume 23, table 100 (sample reference)
SALA-Cuba	Supplement 1: *Cuba 1968*
SALA LAPUA	Supplement 8: *Latin American Population and Urbanization Analysis*
SALA-MB	Supplement 9: *Statistical Abstract of the United States—Mexico Borderlands*
SALA-MLR	Supplement 5: *Measuring Land Reform*
SALA-SEM	Supplement 10: *Society and Economy in Mexico*
SALA-SNP	Supplement 3: *Statistics and National Policy*
SALA-TNG	Supplement forthcoming: *The Narrowing Gap*
Schroeder	Susan Schroeder, *Cuba: A Handbook of Historical Statistics* (Boston: G. K. Hall, 1982)
SELA	Sistema Económico para Latinoamérica
SIPRI-Y	Stockholm International Peace Research Institute, *Yearbook*
SY	Statistical Yearbook
UN	United Nations (NYC)
UN-CSS	*Compendium of Social Statistics*
UN-DY	*Demographic Yearbook*
UN-MB	*Monthly Bulletin of Statistics*
UN-SP	*Statistical Papers*
UN-SP-A	*Series A, Population and Vital Statistics*
UN-SP-J	*Series J, World Energy Supplies*
UN-SP:T	*Series T, Direction of International Trade*
UN-SY	*Statistical Yearbook*
UN-YCS	*Yearbook of Construction Statistics*
UN-YIS	*Yearbook of Industrial Statistics*
UN-YITS	*Yearbook of International Trade Statistics*
UN-YNAS	*Yearbook of National Account Statistics*
UN-YWES	*Yearbook of World Energy Statistics*
UNESCO	UN Educational and Scientific Organization (NYC)
UNESCO-SY	*Statistical Yearbook*
U.S.	United States (WDC)
USAID	U.S. Agency for International Development
USAID-OLG	*U.S. Overseas Loans and Grants and Assistance from International Organizations*
USBC	U.S. Bureau of the Census
USBC-HS	*Historical Statistics of the United States*
USBC-SA	*Statistical Abstract of the United States*
USBG	U.S. Board of Governors, Federal Reserve System
USBG-FRB	*Federal Reserve Bulletin*
USBOM	U.S. Bureau of the Mines
USBOM-MCP	*Mineral Commodity Profiles*
USBOM-MIS	*Mineral Industry Surveys*
USBOM-MY	*Minerals Yearbook*
USCIA	U.S. Central Intelligence Agency
USDA	U.S. Department of Agriculture
USDA-AT	*Agricultural Trade of the Western Hemisphere*
USDA-ERS	Economic Research Service
USDA-FAT	*Foreign Agricultural Trade*
USDC-SCB	U.S. Dept. of Commerce, *Survey of Current Business*
USDOD	U.S. Department of Defense
USDOD-FMSA	*Foreign Military Sales Assistance*
USEX-IM	U.S. Export-Import Bank
USINS	U.S. Immigration and Naturalization Service
USINS-AR	*Annual Report*
USINS-SY	*Statistical Yearbook*
USNCC	U.S. National Climatic Center
USNCC-MCDW	*Monthly Climatic Data of the World*
WA	*World Almanac*
WB	World Bank (formerly IBRD)
WB-AR	*Annual Report*
WB-EDC	*Energy in Developing Countries*
WB-WDR	*World Development Report*
WB-WT	*World Bank Tables*, published by Johns Hopkins University Press, 1976, 1980
WCE	*World Christian Encyclopedia*
WHO	World Health Organization
WHO-WHSA	*World Health Statistics Annual*
Wilkie	*See* SALA
WTO	World Tourism Organization (Madrid)
WTO-WTS	*World Tourism Statistics*
YC	Yearbook Compendium